THE
PULPIT COMMENTARY

THE
PULPIT COMMENTARY

Edited by

H. D. M. Spence

and

Joseph S. Exell

Volume 5
I & II KINGS

Wm. B. Eerdmans Publishing Company, Grand Rapids, Michigan

THE PULPIT COMMENTARY

Edited by

H. D. M. Spence *and* Joseph S. Exell

This large-type edition republished
from new plates by

WM. B. EERDMANS PUBLISHING COMPANY
Grand Rapids, Michigan

ISBN 0-8028-8062

Reprinted, September 1980

PHOTOLITHOPRINTED BY EERDMANS PRINTING COMPANY
GRAND RAPIDS, MICHIGAN, UNITED STATES OF AMERICA

I KINGS

EXPOSITION AND HOMILETICS BY

J. HAMMOND

HOMILIES BY VARIOUS AUTHORS

E. DE PRESSENSE   A. ROWLAND

J. WAITE   J. A. MACDONALD

J. URQUHART

THE

BOOKS OF THE KINGS

——❖——

INTRODUCTION

I. Unity of the Work

THE Books now known to us as the First and Second Books of the Kings, like 1 and 2 Samuel, were originally and are really but one work, by one writer or compiler, and it is only for convenience of reference and because of long established usage that we here treat them as two. In all Hebrew MSS. down to the time of Jerome certainly, and probably down to A.D. 1518, when the Hebrew text was first printed by D. Bomberg at Venice, the division into two books was unknown. It was first made in the Greek version by the Septuagint translators, who followed a prevailing custom of the Alexandrine Greeks of dividing ancient works for facility of reference. The division thus introduced was perpetuated in the Latin version of Jerome, who took care, however, while following the LXX. usage, to notice the essential unity of the work;* and the authority of the Septuagint in the Eastern, and of the Vulgate in the Western Church, has ensured the continuance of this bipartite arrangement in all later time.

That the two books, however, are really one is proved by the strongest internal evidence. Not only is there no break between them—the separation at 1 Kings xxii. 53 being so purely arbitrary and artificial that it is actually made haphazard in the middle both of the reign of Ahaziah and of the ministry of Elijah—but the unity of purpose is conspicuous throughout. Together they afford us a continuous and complete history of the kings and kingdoms of the chosen people. And the language of the two books points conclusively

---

* "Quartus *Melachim, i.e.,* Regum, qui iii. et iv. Regum volumine continetur" (Prolog. Galeat.) Similarly *Origen* in *Euseb.* "Eccles. Hist." vi. 25 : Βασιλειῶν τρίτη, τετάρτη ἐν ἑνὶ Οὐαμμέλεχ Δαβὶδ, ὅπέρ ἐστι βασιλεία Δαβίδ.

to a single writer. While there are no indications of the manner of speech of a later period, no contradictions or confusions such as would arise from different writers, there are many phrases and formulæ, tricks of expression, and turns of thought, which show the same hand and mind throughout the entire work, and effectually exclude the idea of a divided authorship.

While, however, it is indisputable that we have in these two portions of Holy Scripture the production of a single writer, we have no sufficient warrant for concluding as some (Eichhorn, Jahn, *al.*) have done, that the division between them and the Books of Samuel is equally artificial, and that they are parts of a much greater work (called by Ewald "the Great Book of the Kings")—a work which comprised along with them Judges, Ruth, and 1 and 2 Samuel. The arguments in support of this view are stated at considerable length by Lord Arthur Hervey in Smith's "Dictionary of the Bible" (vol. ii. p. 21), but to my thinking they are entirely inconclusive, and have been effectually disposed of by, among others, Bähr,[*] Keil,[†] and Rawlinson, [‡] each of whom cites a number of peculiarities not only of diction, but of manner, arrangement, materials, &c.,[§] which clearly distinguish the Books of Kings from those which precede them in the sacred Canon.

II. Title.

The name KINGS (מלכים) requires but little notice. Whether these scriptures bore this name from the first or not—and it is hardly likely that they did, the probability being that the Book was originally cited, like those of the Pentateuch, &c., by its initial words, והמלך דוד, and was only called "Kings" from its contents (like the Book of "Samuel") at a later period—this one word aptly describes the character and subject-matter of this composition and sufficiently distinguishes it from the rest of its class. It is simply a history of the kings of Israel and Judah, in the order of their reigns. The LXX. Title, Βασιλειῶν. γ. δ. (*i.e.* "*Kingdoms*"), expresses the same idea, [||] for in Eastern despotisms, and especially under the Hebrew theocracy, the history of the *kingdom* was practically that of its *kings*.

---

* "Die Könige," Einleitung, § 3.

† "The Books of the Kings." English Translation. Introduction, pp. 9, 10. Compare his "Introduction to the Old Testament," vol. i. pp. 254—260.

‡ "Speaker's Commentary," vol. ii. p. 468.

§ For example. The chronology of the Kings is precise and detailed, whilst that of 1 and 2 Samuel is extremely vague and general ; the Kings abound in references to the Mosaic law, which are nowhere found in Samuel ; the author of the former constantly refers to his authorities, the writer of the latter never.

|| Jerome, in his "Prologus Galeatus," questions the fitness of this title, but with insufficient reason. The books contain the history of *two kingdoms*, though of but one nation.

III. Contents and Purpose.

It must bo romomborod, howovor, that tho history of tho kings of the chosen people will necessarily have a different character and a different design from the chronicles of all other reigns and dynasties ; it will, in fact, be such history as a pious Jew would naturally write. Such a one, even without the guidance of Inspiration, would inevitably view all the events in the history both of his own and of neighbouring nations, not so much in their secular or purely historical as in their religious aspect. His firm belief in a particular Providence superintending the affairs of men, and re-quiting them according to their deserts by *temporal* rewards and punishments, would alone give a stamp and colour to his narrative very different from that of the profane historian. But when we remember that the historians of Israel were in every case *prophets;* that is, that they were the advocates and spokesmen * of the Most High, we may be quite sure that history in their hands will have a " purpose," and that they will write with a distinctly religious aim. Such was assuredly the case with the author of the KINGS. His is an ecclesiastical or theocratic rather than a civil history. Indeed, as Bähr well observes, "Hebrew antiquity does not know the secular. historian." † The different kings, consequently, are pourtrayed not so much in their relations to their subjects, or to other nations, as to the Invisible Ruler of Israel, whose representatives they were, whose religion they were charged to uphold, and of whose holy law they were the executors. It is this consideration accounts, as Rawlinson remarks, for the great length at which certain reigns are recorded as compared with others. It is this again, and not any " prophetico-didactic tendency," or any idea of advancing the prophetic order, accounts for the prominence given to the ministries of Elijah and Elisha, and to the interpositions of various prophets at different crises of the nation's life (see 1 Kings i. 45 ; xi. 29—40 ; xiii. 12, 21—24 ; xiv. 5—16 ; xxii. 8 ; 2 Kings xix. 20 ; xx. 16 ; xxii. 14, &c.) It explains too the constant references to the Pentateuch, and to the previous history of the race (1 Kings ii. 3 ; iii. 14 ; vi. 11, 12 ; viii. 56, &c. ; 2 Kings x. 31 ;

---

* The προ-φήτης is properly one who *speaks for* another, as advocate or interpreter. It is a mistake to explain the word of prediction or *foretelling*. The προ has no reference to time. Apollo is called Διὸς προφήτης—" the *interpreter* of Jove " (Aesch. Eumen. 19). And Plato calls poets Μουσῶν προφῆται (Phaedr. 262 D). It is true that the term נָבִיא conveys primarily the idea of *inspiration*, or possession (נָבָא, *ebullivit*, Gesenius, Thesaurus, ii. 838 ; cf. μάντις from μαίνομαι), but this word also, at an early period, had the meaning of " spokesman," as in Exod. vii. 1, " Aaron thy brother shall be thy *prophet*." The " prophets" of the New Testament (1 Cor. xi. 4, 5 ; xiv. *passim*), it is well known, were *preachers* rather than predicters, and the term " prophesying " was formerly used in our own language of *expounding*.

† In the American translation of Lange's " Bibelwerk" unfortunately rendered, " The secular historian does not know Hebrew antiquity."

xiv. 6 ; xvii. 13, 15, 37 ; xviii. 4—6, &c.), and the constant comparison of the successive monarchs with the king " after God's own heart " (1 Kings xi. 4, 33 ; xiv. 8 ; xv. 3, 11, &c.), and their judgment by the standard of the Mosaic law (1 Kings iii. 14 ; vi. 11, 12 ; viii. 56, &c.) The object of the historian clearly was, not to chronicle the naked facts of Jewish history, but to show how the rise, the glories, the decline and the fall of the Hebrew kingdoms were respectively the results of the piety and faithfulness or of the irreligion and idolatry of the different kings and their subjects. Writing during the captivity, he would teach his countrymen how all the miseries which had come upon them, miseries which had culminated in the destruction of their temple, the overthrow of their monarchy, and their own transportation from the land of their forefathers, were the judgments of God upon their sins and the fruits of the national apostasy, He would trace, too, the fulfilment, through successive generations, of the great promise of 2 Sam. vii. 12—16, the charter of the house of David, on which promise indeed the history is a continuous and striking commentary. True to his mission as the Divine ambassador, he would teach them everywhere to see the finger of God in their nation's history, and by the record of incontrovertible facts, and especially by showing the fulfilment of the promises and threatenings of the Law, he would preach a return to the faith and morals of a purer age, and would urge " his contemporaries, living in exile with him, to cling faithfully to the covenant made by God through Moses, and to honour steadfastly the one true God." *

The two Books embrace a period of four and a half centuries ; viz. from the accession of Solomon in B.c. 1015 to the close of the captivity of Jehoiachin in B.c. 562.

IV. Date.

The date of the composition of the Kings can be fixed, with much greater facility and certainty than that of many portions of Scripture, from the contents of the Books themselves. It must lie somewhere between B.c. 561 and B.c. 538 ; that is to say, it must have been in the latter part of the Babylonian captivity. It cannot have been *before* B.c. 561, for that is the year of the accession of Evil-Merodach, whose kindly treatment of Jehoiachin, "in the year that he began to reign," is the last event mentioned in the history. Assuming that this is not an addition by a later hand, which we have no reason to think is the case,† we have thus one limit—a *maximum* of antiquity—fixed with certainty. And it cannot have been *after* B.c. 538, the date of the return under Zerubbabel, as it is quite inconceivable that the historian should have omitted to notice an event of such profound importance, and one too which had such a direct bearing on

* Thenius.   † See Keil, Introduction to Kings, p. 9.

the purpose for which the history was penned—which was partly, as we have already remarked, to trace the fulfilment of 2 Sam. vii. 12—16, in the fortunes of David's house—had that event occurred at the time when he wrote. We may safely assign this year, consequently, as the *minimum* date for the composition of the work.

And with this conclusion, that the Books of Kings were written during the captivity, the style and diction of the Books themselves agree. "The language of Kings belongs unmistakably to the period of the captivity" (Rawlinson, "Speaker's Commentary," pp. 469, 470). * Lord A. Hervey, indeed, contends that "the general character of the language is that of the time *before* the Babylonish captivity"—elsewhere he mentions "the age of Jeremiah"—but even if we allow this, it does not in the least invalidate the conclusion that the work was given to the world between B.C. 460 and B.C. 440, and probably about B.C. 460.

V. The Authorship

is a question of much greater difficulty. † It was long held, and it is still maintained by many scholars, that the Kings are the work of the prophet Jeremiah. And in support of this view may be alleged—1. Jewish tradition. The Talmud (Baba Bathra, f. 15. 1) unhesitatingly ascribes the work to him. *Jeremias scripsit librum suum et librum regum et threnos.* 2. The last chapter of 2 Kings agrees, except in some few particulars, with Jer. lii. The spelling in the latter is more archaic and the facts recorded in vers. 28—30 differ from those of 2 Kings xxv. 22—26, but the general agreement is very striking. It is alleged, accordingly, and not without reason, that the two narratives must have had a common origin, and more, that the final page of Jeremiah's history of the Kings, with a few alterations and additions made by a later hand, was appended to his collection of prophecies, as forming a fitting conclusion to those writings. And certainly this arrangement, though it does not prove Jeremiah's authorship of the Kings, does afford evidence of a very ancient *belief* that he was the writer. 3. There is in many cases a marked resemblance between the language of Kings and that of Jeremiah. Hävernick, perhaps the most powerful and energetic advocate of this view, has furnished a striking list of phrases and expressions common to both. ‡ And so marked are the correspondences between them that even Bahr, who summarily rejects this hypothesis, is constrained to allow that "the mode of

---

* Rawlinson gives, *loc. cit.*, an interesting list of the words and phrases which substantiate this assertion. And see Dict. Bib. vol. ii. p. 26.

† "As regards the authorship of these Books, but little difficulty presents itself" (Lord A. Hervey, who ascribes them to Jeremiah). But Bähr, Keil, *al.* reject this idea with equal positiveness.

‡ Einleitung, vol. ii. pp. 171 sqq. This list is accessible to the English reader in the "Speaker's Commentary," ii. p. 471.

thinking and expression resembles that of Jeremiah," and he accounts for the similarity by the conjecture that our author had before him the writings of the prophet or was, perhaps, his pupil,* while Stähelin is driven to the conclusion that the writer was an imitator of Jeremiah. But the resemblance is not confined to words and phrases : there is in both writings the same *tone*, the same air of despondency and hopelessness, † while many of the facts and narratives again are more or less common to the history and the prophecy. ‡ 4. Another consideration which is equally striking is the omission of all mention of the prophet Jeremiah in the Books of Kings—an omission easily accounted for if he was the author of those Books, but difficult to explain on any other supposition. Modesty would very naturally lead the historian to omit all mention of the share he himself had taken in the transactions of his time, especially as it was recorded at length elsewhere. But the part Jeremiah sustained in the closing scenes of the history of the kingdom of Judah was one of so much importance that it is hard to conceive any impartial, not to say pious or theocratic historian, completely ignoring both his name and his work.§

But a string of arguments, equally numerous and equally influential, can be adduced *against* the authorship of Jeremiah, prominent among which are the following : 1. That if Jeremiah did compile these histories, he must have been at the time about eighty-six or eighty-seven years of age. Bähr regards this one consideration as conclusive. He, like Keil and others, points out that Jeremiah's ministry began in the thirteenth year of the reign of Josiah (Jer. i. 2), when, it is urged, he must have been at least twenty years of age. But the Book of KINGS, as we have just seen, cannot have been penned earlier than B.C. 562 ; that is to say, at least sixty-six years afterwards. In reply to this, however, it may fairly be remarked (1) that it is quite possible that Jeremiah's entrance upon the prophetic office took place *before* he was twenty years old. He calls himself a child (נַעַר Jer. i. 6), and though the word is not always to be taken literally, or as furnishing any definite chronological datum,‖ yet the tradition that he was but a boy of fourteen is not wholly irrational or incredible. (2) It is quite within the bounds of possibility that the work may have been written by an octogenarian. We have had conspicuous instances amongst our own contemporaries of men far advanced in years retaining all their mental vigour

---

* This latter supposition is also the view of Thenius. Bleek suggests Baruch.

† Compare 2 Kings xvii. 14 with Jer. vii. 26 ; 1 Kings ix. 8 with Jer. xxii. 8 ; and 2 Kings xxi. 12 with Jer. xix. 3. These parallels are the more striking since they disclose at the same time a similarity of tone and of language.

‡ For a list of these, see " Dictionary of the Bible," vol. ii. pp. 28—30.

§ It is true Jeremiah is only mentioned twice by the Chronicler, but this is easily accounted for by the brevity and incompleteness of his work.

‖ Nägelsbach, " Jeremias," in Lange's " Bibelwerk," p. 2.

and engaging in arduous literary labours. And (3) it does not absolutely follow, because the last paragraph of the Kings carries us down to B.C. 562 that that is also the date of the composition or compilation of the rest. It is quite obvious that the bulk of the work might have been written by Jeremiah some years before, and that these concluding sentences might have been added by him in extreme old age. There is much greater force, however, in a second objection, viz., that the KINGS must have been written or completed in Babylon, whilst Jeremiah spent the concluding years of his life and died in Egypt. For, though it is not absolutely certain, it is extremely probable that the work *was* finished and published in Babylon. There is not much weight perhaps in Bahr's remark that it cannot have been composed for the handful of fugitives who accompanied Jeremiah to Egypt, but must have been designed for the kernel of the people in captivity, for the prophet may have composed the work in Tahpenes, and have at the same time hoped, perhaps even provided, for its transmission to Babylon. But it cannot be denied that while the writer was evidently familiar with what transpired in the court of Evil-Merodach, and was acquainted with details which could hardly have been known to a resident in Egypt, there is an absence of all reference to the latter country and the fortunes of the remnant there. The last chapter of the work, that is to say, points to Babylon as the place where it was written. So also, *primâ facie*, does the expression of 1 Kings iv. 24, " beyond the river " (Auth. Vers. " on this side the river "). The " region beyond the river " can only mean that *west* of the Euphrates, and therefore the natural conclusion is that the writer must have dwelt *east* of the Euphrates, i.e., in Babylon. It is alleged, however, that this expression, which is also found in Ezra and Nehemiah, had come at this time to have a meaning different from its strict geographical signification, and was used by Jews, wherever they might happen to reside, of the provinces of the Babylonian Empire (including Palestine), west of the Great River, just as a Roman, even after residing in the country, might speak of *Gallia Transalpina*, and it cannot be denied that the expression is used indifferently of either side of the Jordan, and therefore presumably it may designate either side of the Euphrates.* But it is to be observed—1. that in the majority of instances where the expression is used of the Euphrates (Ezra vi. 6 ; vii. 21, 25 ; Neh. ii. 7), it is found in the lips of persons residing in Babylonia or Media; 2. that in other instances (Ezra iv. 10, 11, 16) it is used in letters of state by Persian officers, who would naturally adapt their language to the usages of the Persian court and of their own country, even when resident abroad, and lastly, that in the one instance (Ezra viii. 36) where the words are employed

* See note on ch. iv. 24.

of Jews resident in Palestine, it is by a Jew who had just returned from Persia. While therefore it is perhaps impossible to arrive at any positive conclusion from the use of this formula, it is difficult to resist the impression that on the whole it suggests that the Book was written in Babylon, and therefore *not* by Jeremiah. 3. A third consideration alleged by Keil in his earlier edition,* viz., that the variations of style and diction between 2 Kings xxv. and Jer. lii. are such as to negative the supposition of their having proceeded from the same pen, or rather such as to compel the belief that "this section has been extracted by the author or editor in the two cases from a common or more copious source," is too precarious to require much notice, the more so, as (1) these variations, when carefully examined, prove to be inconsiderable, and (2) even if the distinct authorship of these two portions, or their having been copied from a common authority, were established, it would by no means necessarily follow that Jeremiah had not copied them, or had had no share in the rest of the work.

It would seem, therefore, that the arguments for and against Jeremiah's authorship of the KINGS are so evenly balanced that it is impossible to speak positively one way or the other. Professor Rawlinson has stated the conclusion to which an impartial survey conducts us with great fairness and caution. "Though Jeremiah's authorship appears, all things considered, to be highly probable, we must admit that it has not been proved, and is, therefore, to some extent, uncertain."†

VI. SOURCES OF THE WORK.

The Books of Kings being obviously and necessarily, from their historical character, to a very large extent, a compilation from other sources, the question now presents itself, What and of what sort were the records from which this narrative was constructed?

What they were the writer himself informs us. He mentions three " *books* " from which his information must have been largely derived—" *the book of the acts of Solomon* " (1 Kings xi. 41) ; " *the book of the Chronicles of* (*lit.* of the words [*or* events] of the days to) *the kings of Judah* " (1 Kings xiv. 29 ; xv. 7, 22 ; xxii. 45 ; 2 Kings *passim*) ; and " *the book of the Chronicles* (" the words of the days ") *of the kings of Israel*" (1 Kings xiv. 19 ; xv. 31, &c.) That he made abundant use of these authorities is evident from the fact that he refers to them more than thirty times ; that he constantly quoted from them *verbatim* is clear from the fact that passages agreeing almost *verbatim* with those of the Kings are found in the Books of Chronicles, and also from

---

* Professor Rawlinson appears to have only had the edition of 1846 before him. But the KINGS of Keil and Delitzsch's Commentary is practically a new work, and differs very materially from its predecessor.

† " Speaker's Commentary," ii. 472.

the use of expressions which manifestly belong, not to our author, but to some document which he cites.* It is consequently more than " a reasonable supposition that " this " history was, in part at least, derived from the works in question."† And there is a strong presumption that these were his only authorities, with the exception perhaps of a narrative of the ministry of the prophets Elijah and Elisha, for though he refers to them so constantly, he never once refers to any other. What, however, was the *precise character* of these writings is a matter of considerable uncertainty. We are warranted in the belief, from the way in which they are cited, that they were three separate and independent works, and that they contained fuller and more extended accounts of the reigns of the several kings than any which we now possess, for the invariable formula in which they are referred to is this, " And the *rest of the acts* of . . . . are they not written in the Book of the Chronicles," &c. It hardly follows, however, as Bähr thinks, that this formula implies that the works, at the time our history was written, were "in general circulation," or " in the hands of many,' for our author surely might reasonably refer to them, even if they were not generally known or readily accessible. But the great question in dispute is this : Were " the books of the words of the days to the kings," as their name at first sight seems to imply, state papers ; *i.e.*, public archives prepared by appointed officers, or were they private memoirs of the different prophets. The former opinion has the support of many great names.‡ It is alleged in its favour that there was, at any rate in the kingdom of Judah, a state functionary, " the recorder," whose business it was to chronicle events and prepare memoirs of the different reigns, a " court historian," as he has been called ; § that such memoirs were certainly prepared in the kingdom of Persia by an authorized officer, and were afterwards preserved as state annals,‖ and, lastly, that such public documents appear to be sufficiently indicated by the very name they bear, " The book of the chronicles to the kings." There is no question, however, despite these allegations, that the second view is the correct one, and that the " Chronicles " were the compilations, not of state officials, but of various members of the schools of the prophets. For, to begin with, the name by which these writings are known,

---

* The expression "*unto this day*," in the great majority of cases, cannot refer to the date of authorship—the time of the captivity—but belongs to a period when the southern kingdom was still in existence, and the temple was still standing. See 1 Kings viii. 8 ; ix. 13 ; x. 12 ; 2 Kings ii. 22 ; x. 27 ; xiv. 7 ; xvi. 6 ; xx. 17, &c.

† Rawlinson.

‡ Among others, Berthold, Hävernick, Movers, and Ewald.

§ Ewald, "History of Israel," iii. p. 270. Ewald, however, does not identify this officer with the *Mazkir* or Remembrancer (see p. 267) as many writers do. See, *e.g.*, Dict. Bible, Art. " King."

‖ A similar institution is said to exist in modern Persia. Vide Malcolm's " History of Persia," ch. xxiii.

and which has been thought to imply a civil origin, really means no more than this, "*the Book of the history of the times of the Kings*," &c., as Keil interprets it, and by no means indicates any official archives. And, in the second place, we have no evidence in support of the view that the *recorder* or any other officer was charged with the preparation of the history of his time. The word מַזְכִּיר properly means "*remembrancer*," and he was no doubt so called, not "because he kept the memory of events alive," * but because he *reminded* the king of the state affairs which required his attention. It is generally admitted † that he was "more than an annalist," but is not so well understood that in no case in which he figures in the history is he in any way connected with the public records, but always appears as the king's advisor or chancellor (cf. 2 Kings xviii. 18, 37; 2 Chron. xxxiv. 8). Moreover, there are almost insuperable difficulties in the way of believing that the "books of the Chronicles" can have been compiled by this remembrancer. For example, (1) there is no trace of the existence of any such functionary in the kingdom of *Israel*; (2) David is said to have instituted the office of "court and state scribe," but we find that David's history was recorded, not in any state annals prepared by this functionary, but in "the book of *Samuel the seer*, and in the book of *Nathan the prophet*, and in the book of *Gad the seer*" (1 Chron. xxix. 29). Now, surely, if any such officer charged with such a duty had existed, the record of David's life would have been composed by him, and not by unofficial and irresponsible persons. But (3) the state archives of the two kingdoms, including the memoirs—if such there were—of the different kings, can hardly have escaped the sack of Samaria and the burning of Jerusalem. It has been conjectured, indeed, that the Assyrian and Babylonian monarchs preserved the records of conquered nations in their respective capitals, and permitted such of the exiles as had acquired their favour to have access to them,‡ but this, as Bähr observes, is obviously a supposition "as unfounded as it is arbitrary," and is beset with difficulties. Seeing that not only the royal palace, but also "all the great houses were burned" (2 Kings xxv. 9), the conclusion is almost inevitable that all the *public* records must have perished. And such records—in the kingdom of Israel, at least — had also had to run the gauntlet of intestine warfare and dissension. A dynasty cannot be changed nine times, and each time be destroyed, root and branch, without the greatest danger to the archives of sharing the same fate. That amid all the changes and chances of the two kingdoms, changes which culminated in the transportation of the two entire nations to distant lands, the state annals had been preserved and were accessible to a historian of the time of

---

* Dict. Bib., Art. "King."
† See Dict. Bib., Art. "Recorder."
‡ Stähelin, Einleitung, s. 129, cited by Bähr.

the captivity, seems almost incredible. But our author manifestly refers to the " Books of the Chronicles," &c., as still existent in his time, and, if not generally circulated, yet guarded and accessible somewhere. But a still more conclusive argument against the " state paper" origin of our histories is found in their contents. Their tone and language absolutely forbid the supposition that they were based on the records of any court historiographer. They are to a very large extent histories of the sins, idolatries, and enormities of the respective sovereigns whose reigns they describe. " The history of the reign of each of the nineteen kings of Israel begins with the formula, ' He did that which was evil in the sight of the Lord.' The same formula occurs again with respect to twelve out of the twenty kings of Judah. . . . Even of the greatest and most glorious king, Solomon, it is related at length how deeply he fell. ' The sin of Jeroboam who made Israel to sin ' is represented as the source of all the evils of the kingdom: the conspiracies and murders of a Baasha, a Shallum, a Menahem ; the shameful acts of an Ahab, a Jezebel, and a Manasseh are recorded without any indulgence." * And these are the deeds and the reigns with respect to which we are referred for fuller information " to the Books of the Chronicles." For that these " Chronicles " contained accounts of the impieties and abominations of the various kings is clear from 2 Chron. xxxvi. 8, where we read (of Jehoiakim), " His abominations which he did and that which was found in him, behold they are written in the book of the kings of Israel and Judah." Now, it is altogether out of the question that any court scribe can have described his late master's reign in such terms as these ; indeed no one could or would have used such language, but men who lived at a later period, and those, courageous and high-minded prophets, who were perfectly independent of the court and regardless of its favours. And, lastly, the constant change of dynasty on the throne of Israel is fatal to the supposition. We have already mentioned those changes as endangering the preservation of the state papers, but they are equally an argument against the memoirs of the different royal houses having been written by the " recorder," for the object of each successive dynasty would be, not to preserve a faithful record of the reigns of its predecessor, but to stamp them with infamy, or consign them to oblivion.

We find, therefore, that the prevailing opinion as to the character of the " books of the words of the days " is encompassed with difficulties. But these vanish at once, if we see in these records the compilations of the schools of the prophets. We have incontrovertible evidence that prophets *did* act as historians. Samuel, Nathan, Gad, Iddo, Ahijah, Shemaiah, Jehu the son of Hanani, Isaiah the son of Amoz, are all mentioned by

---

* Bähr (Einleitung, p. 12), whom I have largely followed in this note.

name as the compilers of memoirs. We know, too, that for portions of this very history we must be indebted to members, probably unknown members, of the prophetic order. The histories of Elijah and Elisha never formed part of the " books of the Chronicles," and they contain matters which, in the nature of things, can only have been contributed by these prophets themselves, or by their scholars or servants. The history of Elisha, especially, has several marks of a separate origin. It is distinguished by a number of peculiarities—" provincialisms" they have been called—which betray a different hand, while the narratives are such as can only have proceeded, originally, from an eye-witness. But perhaps it is hardly necessary to mention these particulars, as it is " universally allowed that prophets generally were the historians of the Israelitish people."* It was almost as essential a part of their office to trace the hand of God in the past history of the Hebrew race as to predict future visitations, or to promise deliverances. They were preachers of righteousness, spokesmen for God, interpreters of his just laws and dealings, and to be this they only needed to be faithful and impartial historians. It is not without significance, in this connexion, that the historical books of the Old Testament were known to the Jewish fathers by the name נְבִיאִים " and are distinguished from the books strictly prophetical only in this, that the adjective ראשונים *priores*, is applied to them, and to the latter אחרונים *posteriores*." †

But we have evidence of the most positive and conclusive kind, evidence almost amounting to demonstration, that the three authorities to which our historian so repeatedly refers, were in their original form the works of different prophets, and not of the public annalist. For we find that where the author of KINGS, after transcribing a string of passages, which agree almost word for word with a series in the Books of Chronicles,‡ and which must therefore have been derived from a common source, refers to " the book of the *acts of Solomon* (1 Kings xi. 41), the chronicler indicates as the documents upon which he has drawn, " the book of *Nathan the prophet*, and the *prophecy of Ahijah* the Shilonite, and the visions of *Iddo the seer*. The conclusion, therefore, is irresistible (2 Chron. ix. 29), that the " book of the words of the days to Solomon," if not identical with the writings of the three prophets who were the historians of that reign, was nevertheless based on those writings, and to a large extent composed of extracts from

---

* Bähr, who cites Knobel, " Der Prophet. der Hebr." i. 58 sqq. Josephus (Contra Apion. i. 8) expressly says, " The prophets, who were after Moses, wrote down what was done in their time in thirteen books."

† Bähr.

‡ Compare 1 Kings viii. 12 – 50 with 2 Chron. vi. 1—40; 1 Kings viii. 64—ix. 9 with 2 Chron. vii. 7—22; 1 Kings x. 1—28, with 2 Chron. ix. 1—28, &c.

them. It is possible, and indeed probable, that in the one "book of the Chronicles," the memoirs of the three historians had been condensed, arranged, and harmonized; but it hardly admits of doubt that the latter were the originals of the former. And the same remarks apply, *mutatis mutandis*, to the "book of the Chronicles of the kings of Judah." The history of Rehoboam in 1 Kings xii. 1—19 is identical with the account of that monarch in 2 Chron. x. 1—4; the words of 1 Kings xii. 20—24 are the same that are found in 2 Chron. xi. 1—4; while 2 Chron. xii. 13 is practically a repetition of 1 Kings xiv. 21. But the authority to which our author refers is the "book of the chronicles of the kings of Judah," whereas that mentioned by the Chronicler is "the book of *Shemaiah the prophet,* and of *Iddo the seer."* Now it is clear that these parallel passages are derived from the same source, and that source must be the book or books of these two prophets.*

Nor does it invalidate this contention that the Chronicler, in addition to the prophetic writings just named, also cites occasionally the "book of the kings of Israel and Judah" (2 Chron. xvi. 11; xxv. 26; xxvii. 7; xxviii. 26; xxxii. 32; xxxv. 27, &c.); in one place apparently called "the book of the kings of Israel" (2 Chron. xx. 34), together with a "*Midrash* of the book of the Kings" (2 Chron. xxiv. 27). For we have no evidence whatsoever that any of these authorities were of a public and civil character. On the contrary, we have ground for believing that they were composed of the memoirs of the prophets. It is not quite clear what the Midrash just referred to was, but the two works first cited were probably identical with "the Books of the Chronicles" so often mentioned by our historian. And in one case (2 Chron. xx. 34), we have distinct mention of a prophetic book or writing—that of Jehu, the son of Hanani—which was embodied in the book of the kings of Israel.†

We can hardly be mistaken, therefore, in concluding from these data that the prime "sources of this work" were really the prophetic memoirs mentioned by the Chronicler (1 Chron. xxvii. 24; xxix. 29; 2 Chron. ix. 29; xii. 15; xiii. 22; xx. 34; xxiv. 27; xxvi. 22; xxxii. 32; xxxiii. 18) which, together, perhaps, with other writings, the authors of which are unknown to us, furnish the materials for the "Books of the Words of the Days," &c.

The relation of the KINGS to the Books of the CHRONICLES will be more appropriately discussed in the Introduction to that volume.

---

* The fact that the Chronicler alleges his authority, and that a different one from the authority given by the KINGS, forbids the assumption that the agreement is the result of copying on the part of the former from the latter.

† הֶעֱלָה, literally *was made to ascend upon, i.e.,* was introduced or incorporated into the history of the kings of Israel.

VII. Credibility.

But the question may possibly arise, Are these writings, whatever their origin, to be accepted as authentic, sober history ?

It is a question, happily, which may be dismissed with few words, for their veracity has never been seriously doubted. If we except the miraculous portions of the history—to which the only serious objection is that they are miraculous, and therefore in the nature of things must be mythical—there is absolutely no reason for challenging the veracity and honesty of the narrative. Not only has it throughout the air of sober history; not only is it accepted as such—including the supernatural portions—by our Lord and His apostles (Matt. vi. 29; xi. 14; Luke iv. 25–27; ix. 8, 54; Mark i. 6; Acts vii. 47, 48; Rom. xi. 3, 4; Heb. xi. 35; James v. 17, 18; Rev. ii. 20; xi. 9), but it is everywhere confirmed by the monuments of antiquity and the records of profane historians, whensoever it and they happen to have points of contact. The reign of Solomon, for example, his friendly relations with Hiram, his Temple, and his wisdom are mentioned by the Tyrian historians, from whom Dius and Menander of Ephesus derived their information (Jos., Contra Apion. i. sectt. 17, 18). The proficiency of the Zidonians in the mechanical arts and their knowledge of the sea is attested both by Homer and Herodotus.* The invasion of Judah by Shishak in the reign of Reho-boam, and the conquest of many of the cities of Palestine, is proved by the inscription of Karnak.† The name and the importance of Omri are pro-claimed by the inscriptions of Assyria, which also tell of the defeat of " Ahab of *Jezreel* " by the Assyrian armies, of the defeat of Azariah, and the conquest of Samaria and Damascus by Tiglath Pileser.‡ And, to pass by later matters and points of less moment, the recently discovered Moabite stone bears its silent but most striking witness to the conquest of Moab by Omri, and its oppression by him, and by his son and successor, for forty years,§ and to the successful rebellion of Moab against Israel,‖ and also mentions by name Mesha, Omri, Chemosh, and Jehovah. In the face of such remarkable and minute corroborations of the statements of our historian, and in the absence of any well-founded instances of misstatement on his part, and, indeed, of any solid grounds for impeaching his historical accuracy, it would be the very wantonness of criticism to deny the credibility and truthfulness of these records.

VIII. Chronology.

There is one particular, however, in which our text, as it now stands, is open to some suspicion, and that is the matter of *dates*. Some of these, it

---

* See note on ch. v. 6. † See note on ch. xiv. 25.
‡ See notes on 2 Kings xvi. 7—16.
§ See note on 2 Kings i. 1, and iii. 4, 5.
‖ See note on 2 Kings iii. 3.

would appear, have been accidentally altered in the course of transcription —a result which need cause us no surprise, if we remember that anciently numbers were represented by letters, and that the Assyrian, or square characters, in which the Scriptures of the Old Testament have been handed down to us, are extremely liable to be confounded. The reader will see at a glance that the difference between ב and כ (which represent respectively *two* and *twenty*), between ד and ר (*four* and *two hundred*), between ח and ת (*eight* and *four hundred*), is extremely slight. But other dates would appear to have been altered, or inserted—probably from the margin—by some reviser of the text. We have nothing more than what we find elsewhere in Scripture, and even in the text of the New Testament—the marginal gloss finding its way, almost unconsciously, into the body of the work.* It will be sufficient to mention here as instances of such imperfect or erroneous chronologies, 1 Kings vi. 1; xiv. 21; xvi. 23; 2 Kings i. 17 (cf. iii. 1); xiii. 10 (cf. xiii. 1); xv. 1 (cf. xiv. 23); xvii. 1 (cf. xv. 30, 33). But this fact, though it has occasioned no little difficulty to the commentator, in no way detracts, it need hardly be said, from the value of our history. And it does this less because those corrections or interpolations are as a rule sufficiently conspicuous, and because, as has been justly remarked, "the chief difficulties of the chronology and almost all the actual contradictions disappear, if we subtract from the work those portions which are generally parenthetic."†

IX. Literature.

Amongst the works available for the exposition and illustration of the text, and to which reference is most frequently made in this Commentary, are the following :—

1. *Commentar über der Bücher der Könige.* Von Dr. Karl Fried. Kiel. Moskau, 1846.

2. *Biblischer Commentar über die prophetischen-Geschichts-bücher des A. T. Dritter Band: Die Bücher der Könige.* Leipzig, 1874. By the same author. Both these works are accessible to the English reader in translations published by Messrs. Clark of Edinburgh (1857 and 1877). I have thought it well to refer to both volumes, as though the latter, no doubt, represents Keil's matured judgment, still the former occasionally contains valuable materials not included in the latter work.

3. *Die Bücher der Könige.* Von Dr. Karl C. W. F. Bähr. Bielefeld, 1873. This is one of the most valuable volumes of Lange's *Theologisch Homiletisches Bibelwerk.* It has been translated, under the editorship of Dr. Philip Schaff, by Dr. Harwood, of New Haven, Conn. (Edinb., Clark) ; and as the translation, especially in its "Textual and Grammatical" section, contains additional and occasionally useful matter, I have referred both to it and to the original.

4. *Symbolik des Mosaischen Cultus.* By the same author. Heidelberg, 1837. For all that concerns the Temple and its ritual, this work is indispensable, and though occasionally somewhat fanciful, is a monument of Bähr's profound and varied learning.

---

* Scrivener, "Introduction to New Testament Criticism," pp. 12, 13.
† Rawlinson, "Speaker's Commentary," p. 476.

5. *Die Bücher der Könige.* Von Otto Thenius. Leipzig, 1849. This work, I regret to say, I only know indirectly. But some proofs of its suggestiveness, and some of its destructive tendencies, will be found in the Exposition.

6. *Holy Bible with Commentary.* ("Speaker's Commentary.") *The Books of Kings,* by the Rev. Canon Rawlinson. London, 1872. This, though perhaps somewhat meagre in its textual criticism and exegesis, is especially rich, as might be expected from the well-known learning of its author, in historical references. I have also occasionally cited his "Historical Illustrations of the Old Testament" (S. P. C. K.), and his "Bampton Lectures."

7. *The History of Israel.* By Heinrich Ewald. English Translation. London, 1878. Vols. III. and IV.

8. *Syntax of the Hebrew Language.* By the same author. London, 1879. The citations from this latter work are distinguished from those from the "History of Israel" by the sectional number and letter, thus : 280 *b.*

9. *The Holy Bible.* Vol. III. By Bishop Wordsworth. Oxford, 1877. The great feature of this commentary, it is hardly necessary to say, in addition to the patristic learning which it reveals, and the piety which breathes through it, is the moral and spiritual teaching which the author never fails to draw from the text. There is perhaps a tendency to over-spiritualize, and I have been unable to follow the writer in many of his mystical interpretations.

10. *Lectures on the Jewish Church.* Vol. II. By Dean Stanley. London, 1865. Though differing repeatedly and very widely from his conclusions, I am very sensible of the great charm of picturesqueness and the graphic power which marks everything that this highly gifted author touches.

11. *Sinai and Palestine.* By the same. Fifth Edition. London, 1858.

12. *Biblical Researches in the Holy Land.* By the Rev. Dr. Robinson. 3 vols. London, 1856.

13. *Handbook for Travellers in Syria and Palestine.* By the Rev. J. L. Porter. London, Murray, 1858.

14. *The Land and the Book.* By the Rev. Dr. Thomson. 2 vols. London, 1859.

15. *Tent-work in Palestine.* By Lieut. Conder, R.E. This is by far the most readable and valuable work which the recent Exploration of Palestine has produced. New Edition. London, 1880.

16. *Handbook to the Bible.* By F. R. Conder and C. R. Conder, R.E. London, 1879. This is cited as "Conder, Handbook." "Conder" alone always refers to the "Tent-work."

17. *Narrative of a Journey through Syria and Palestine.* By Lieut. C. W. M. Van de Velde. 2 vols. Edinburgh and London, 1854.

18. *Contemplations on the Historical Passages of the Old Testament.* By Bishop Hall. 3 vols. S. P. C. K.

19. *Manners and Customs of the Ancient Egyptians.* By Sir J. Gardner Wilkinson. New Edition. London, 1880.

20. *Elias der Thisbiter.* Von F. W. Krummacher. Elberfeld, 1835.

21. *Gesenii Thesaurus Philologicus Criticus Linguae Hebraeae Veteris Testamenti.* Lipsiae, 1835.

22. *Gesenius's Hebrew Grammar.* Fourteenth Edition, enlarged and improved by E. Roediger. London, 1846.

THE FIRST
BOOK OF THE KINGS

———✦✦———

EXPOSITION.

CHAPTER I.

THE REVOLT OF ADONIJAH AND THE ACCESSION OF SOLOMON. — The first chapter of this book is occupied with the accession of Solomon and with the circumstances which preceded, marked, and followed that event. The author, or compiler, evidently considered that his work properly began with the reign of Israel's third king, and David's illness and death are only introduced into the narrative because they necessitated a hasty and premature coronation of Solomon, and exercised an important influence on the beginning of his reign (ch. ii). In the natural order of events, Solomon would not have succeeded until his father's death, but Adonijah's attempt to possess himself of the kingdom required the immediate elevation of Solomon to the throne, and this attempt having been suggested by David's extreme feebleness, the author is compelled to begin his history with an account of David's decay and death. In the opening verses, consequently, he introduces us into the chamber of sickness. His materials for this part of the history were no doubt derived from the "Book of Nathan the prophet" (1 Chron. xxix. 20; 2 Chron. ix. 29). The date of these events is B.C. 1015.

Ver. 1.—**Now** [Heb. *and*, but "now" more nearly expresses the import of the original, for ‍ has here little or no connect-ing force. It is commonly found at the beginning of a book (as in Exod., Levit., Josh., Judges, 2 Sam., Ruth, &c.), and that where there is no connection whatever with any earlier writing (as in Esther, Ezek., Jonah, &c.) It can hardly imply, therefore, "that the historian regards his work as a *continuation* of a preceding history" (Rawlinson), nor is there any need to suppose that it "has been taken from a writing containing the earlier history of David." Keil] **King** [Heb. *the* king. The frequent use of this title, "*King* David," "*King* Solomon," "*King* Asa," &c., is characteristic of our author. The expression is not unknown in 2 Sam., but it occurs so rarely as to constitute a distinction (not a link, as Wordsworth) between that book and the Kings.] **David was old** [yet 2 Sam. v. 4, 5, shows that he cannot have been more than seventy. (He was thirty at his accession; his reign at Hebron lasted seven years and a half; at Jerusalem thirty-three years.) Rawlinson says, "the Jews at this time were not long lived." Certainly, the Jewish *kings* were not. Only David, Solomon, and Manasses exceeded threescore] **and stricken** [Heb. *gone, i.e.*, advanced] **in years.** [A common expression, only found with בָּא as in Gen. xviii. 11; xxiv. 1; Josh. xiii. 1, &c.] **And they covered him with clothes** [lit. *coverings*. בֶּגֶד is used of *any* covering, whether of the person (Gen. xxxix. 12; 1 Kings xxii. 10), or the bed (1 Sam. xix. 13), or even a table (Num. iv. 6). Indeed, the outer garment was used, at least by the poor, for a covering at night (Exod. xxii. 27). The context (ver. 47) shows that *bedclothes* are intended here] but he gat no heat. [A common experience of the aged. David's early hardships and later sorrows and anxieties appear to have aged him prematurely. Possibly he was also afflicted with disease.]

Ver. 2.—Wherefore [Heb. *and*] his servants [according to Josephus (Antiq. vii. 14, 3), his physicians] said unto him, Let there be sought [lit. as marg., "*let them seek*"] for my lord the king [the singular pronoun is used as representing the servant who was spokesman for the rest] a young virgin [marg., "*a damsel, a virgin.*" She must be young, to impart heat, and a virgin, as befitted a king. Though she was recommended as a nurse, they would naturally suppose she might be taken as a concubine] and let her stand before the king [*i.e.*, as servant (ver. 4). Cf. ch. xii. 6, 8; Gen. xli. 46; Dan. i. 5; Deut. i. 38 (with Josh. i. 1) 1 Kings x. 8. In the East, servants still stand and wait their masters' pleasure. Cf. 2 Kings v. 25], and let her cherish him [So also the LXX., καὶ ἔσται αὐτὸν θάλπουσα. But Gesenius, *al.* "be a companion to him"] and let her lie in thy [or "his," LXX. αυτοῦ, Vulg. *suo*] bosom [the expression is generally, but not invariably (see 1 Kings iii. 20; Ruth iv. 16) used *de complexu venereo*] that my lord the king may get heat. [This close embrace of youth was an obvious way of imparting animal heat to age ("Calor a corpore juvenili ac sano maxime prodest senibus." Grotius), and was the more favoured because other and internal remedies were not then known. It is recognized by Galen, and is said to have been prescribed by a Jewish physician to the Emperor Frederick Barbarossa (Bähr). It is stated by Roberts that it is still largely followed in the East.]

Ver. 3.—So [Heb. *and*] they sought (cf. Esth. ii. 2), for a fair [this word points to the same conclusion as "virgin" in ver. 2] damsel throughout all the coasts [*i.e.*, borders (*costa*=rib, side). An old writer speaks of the "*coasts* and quarters of heaven"] of Israel, and found Abishag [="Father of error." Names compounded with *Ab*, "father," were and are very common in the East. We have, *e.g.*, *Ab*-salom in ver. 6, and *Abi*-athar in ver. 7] a [Heb. *the*] Shunammite [Shunem, a town of Issachar (Josh. xix. 18), now called Sôlam, "a flourishing village encompassed by gardens" (Porter), and "in the midst of the finest cornfields in the world" (Grove), lies on the lower slope of "Little Hermon," and has before it the wide plain of Esdraelon. Another Shunammite appears in the sacred history (2 Kings iv. 8)] and brought her to the king.

Ver. 4.—And the damsel was very fair [lit., *fair to exceeding*] and cherished [see on ver. 2] the king, and ministered to him; but the king knew her not. [This is mentioned to explain the history of chap. ii. 13–25. Had it been otherwise, Adonijah could never have presumed to seek her in marriage, and Bathsheba would never have promised her help in his suit. Such an incestuous alliance would not only have been contrary to the law (Levit. xvii. 8), but abhorrent to all true Israelites (cf. 1 Cor. v. 1). In this fact, which the court knew, and which the nation at large did not know—*they* could only suppose that such a "search" for one so exceeding "fair" meant the increase of the seraglio—Adonijah found his *point d'appui* for a second attempt on the throne. The older expositors and some of the modern, notably Wordsworth, assume that Abishag was David's wife, in the sense of being legally married to him. (Corn. à Lap. discusses the question at considerable length, and with needless pruriency.) But this idea finds no support in Scripture, which represents her as simply an attendant. It is idle to remark, consequently, that "the Jewish law allowed polygamy" (Rawlinson).

Ver. 5.—Then Adonijah [="Jehovah is my Lord." The fourth son of David, and now apparently the eldest surviving. It seems probable that Chileab, or Daniel (1 Chron. iii. 1), David's second son, died in infancy. For Amnon's death, see 2 Sam. xiii. 29; for Absalom's, *ibid.* xviii. 14. He must now have been between thirty-three and forty years of age (having been born in Hebron)] the son of Haggith [="Festive" (Gesen.) "the dancer" (Stanley)] exalted himself, saying [to himself and his confederates], I will be king. [It is not difficult to trace this resolve to its sources. They were (1) his seniority (ch. ii. 22). It is true there was no "right of primogeniture" in the Hebrew monarchy. "The God-King had reserved to Himself the choice of the earthly king" (Keil). David himself was not the eldest, but the youngest brother. At the same time primogeniture, *ceteris paribus*, would have, and as a matter of fact had, considerable weight. The firstborn had the birthright; can we doubt he would expect the crown, and think it hard if he were passed over? (see 2 Chron. xxi. 3). (2) His personal attractions. Adonijah would think that his beauty and stature (Josephus mentions the latter) marked him out, as similar gifts had done Saul (1 Sam. ix. 2), for the throne. (3) He was encouraged in his pretensions, if indeed they were not suggested to him, by others, by Joab, for example (see on ver. 7). (4) Possibly love for the beautiful Shunammite and the desire to gain possession of her 'may have strengthened his resolves. It is noteworthy that he and his beauty are mentioned just after her and hers]: **and he prepared** [Heb. *made*] **him chariots and horsemen** [rather *horses*, as in 1 Sam. viii. 11 ; 1 Kings v. 6, Heb. The former passage almost settles the meaning here. Keil *assumes* that a mounted escort is meant], **and fifty men to run before him** [as Absalom before him (2 Sam. xv. 1). Adonijah seems in every way to have imitated Absalom. Josephus says he resembled him in disposition. Chariots, horses, and outrunners are mentioned (1 Sam. viii. 11) as the very first of the king's insignia. Horses were such natural and familiar tokens of royal state (not being employed in agriculture or for travelling), that the Hebrew kings were warned (Deut. xvii. 16) against multiplying them. Outrunners again, such as the Roman emperors had (called by them *cursores*), and such as we find at the present day in Egypt, *foot*-men who precede the chariot at full speed, and by their shrill cries clear the way, are admirably calculated to impress the public mind. According to Morier, "runners before the king's horse in Persia are indispensable to the royal state." Adonijah hoped by this display of regal pomp to win the suffrages of the people.]

Ver. 6.—**And his father had not displeased** [or *pained, afflicted*. The LXX. has ἀπεκώλυσεν] **him at any time** [Heb. *from his days, i.e.*, all his days, LXX. οὐδέποτε, Vulg. *a diebus ejus. Sein Lebtage* (Bähr). Some (Seb. Schmidt, *e.g.*) would understand "since the days of his ambition and display"] **in saying, Why hast thou done so? and he also** [*i.e.*, he also, as well as Absalom, mentioned presently; or, possibly, he as well as Abishag just mentioned. Bähr's rendering, "Und dazu war er sehr schön," &c. "And *moreover he*" was, &c. will not stand] **was a very goodly man** [cf. 2 Sam. xiv. 25. This accounted in part not only for his ambition, but also for his following]; **and his mother** [the two last words are not in the original, which simply has "*and she bare*," יָלְדָה. There is no need, with Thenius, to read, יָלַד *genuit*, or with others, הוֹלִיד. We have a similar ellipsis in Num. xxvi. 59. The meaning is quite clear, viz., that Haggith bare Adonijah to David next after Maachah bore him Absalom. This fact is mentioned to show that he was the eldest surviving son; and it shows therefore that seniority counted for something (cf. ch. ii. 25)] **bare him after Absalom.**

Ver. 7.—**And he conferred** [Heb. "*his words were*" (2 Sam. iii. 17, Heb.)] **with Joab** [Joab's share in this conspiracy, despite his hitherto unwavering fidelity to David, is easily accounted for. He must have known that he was under David's displeasure, and he must have feared, too, that he would be an object of dislike and distrust to a successor trained, as Solomon had been, under David's and Nathan's immediate influence. He could hardly be unconscious that under a new reign his position—unless he took measures to assure it—would be a precarious one. He resolved, therefore, to secure himself by helping Adonijah to his throne. It is also highly probable that Adonijah's ambitious character was much more to his liking than that of the pious and pacific Solomon. Adonijah's physical qualities, again, would no doubt commend him to this rough soldier, who may also have sympathised with him as the eldest son. And there may have been other circumstances (such, *e.g.*, as close personal friendship), of which we know nothing] **the son of Zeruiah, and with Abiathar** [in 2 Sam. viii. 17, we read that "Ahimelech son of Abiathar" was priest. Similarly, 1 Chron. xxiv. 6. An obvious transposition] **the priest.** ["Abiathar's defection is still more surprising" than Joab's (Rawlinson). It is certainly remarkable, when we consider the close ties which subsisted between Abiathar and David, ties which were cemented by the blood of eighty-five persons (1 Sam. xxii. 18), and strengthened by the many afflictions which they had shared in common (*ibid.* ver. 23 to ch. xxviii.; 2 Sam. xv. 24—30), that he should have joined in a plot to defeat David's cherished hopes and plans—plans, too, which he must surely have known, had the sanction of religion (1 Chron. xxviii. 5), and there must have been some powerful motive to account for this. May we not find one in jealousy of Zadok, who had for some time been associated with him in the priesthood, who is generally mentioned first (2 Sam. viii. 17; xv. 29, 35, 36; xx. 25), as if he were the more important and influential, and whose advancement, after the prophecy of 1 Sam. ii. 33—36, Abiathar could not contemplate without suspicion and dread. Is it not highly probable that among the "words" Adonijah had with him was a promise to restore the priesthood to his family exclusively, as the reward of his allegiance]: **and they following Adonijah helped him** (lit., as marg., "helped after Adonijah." It is a pregnant construction, "they aided having followed the side of Adonijah" (Gesenius).

Ver. 8.—**But Zadok the priest** [2 Sam. viii. 17. It is generally said to be difficult to explain "how Zadok and Abiathar came both to be 'priests at this time." Raw-linson, who adds that "the best expla-nation is that Abiathar was the real high priest," officiating in Zion, while Zadok acted as chief priest at the tabernacle at Gibeon. (Bähr, by a strange oversight, assigns to Zadok the care of the ark on Mount Zion, whereas 1 Chron. xvi. 39, distinctly connects his ministry with the tabernacle of witness at Gibeon.) But the precedence (see on ver. 7) generally assigned to Zadok is hardly consistent with the idea that Abiathar was "the real high priest." The fact is that a duality of high priests, associated, apparently, on pretty equal terms, was not unknown in Jewish history. The cases of Eleazer and Ithamar, Hophni and Phinehas, Annas and Caiaphas, will occur to all. 2 Kings xxv. 18, speaks of "the chief priest" and "the second priest;" 2 Chron. xxxi. 10, of the "chief priest of the house of Zadok.' And a dual priest-hood would be the more necessary in David's days, because of the two sanctu-aries, Zion and Gibeon. We find, however, from 1 Chron. xv. 11, that Zadok was already priest at the time of the bringing up of the ark. And the true explanation, no doubt, is that Zadok had succeeded some member of his family, in all probability Jehoiada, called in 1 Chron. xii. 27, "the leader of Aaron " (Heb.), who had certainly been high priest in the time of Saul (1 Chron. xxvii. 5), and who would hardly be degraded when, with 3700 followers, he joined David at Hebron. On his decease, or cession of office, Zadok, who had joined at the same time with a large contingent, was associated with Abiathar in the priest's office. This dual arrangement, consequently, was the result of David's having taken over a high priest from Saul, together with the kingdom, when he had Abiathar as priest already,] **and Benaiah the son of Jehoiada**, [*i.e.*, Jehoiada the high priest (1 Chron. xxvii. 5). Benaiah was consequently a Levite, and of the family of Aaron; set, however, by David, because of his prowess (2 Sam. xxiii. 20, 21; 1 Chron. xi. 22) over the body-guard (2 Sam. viii. 18; 1 Chron. xviii. 17). Probably he was a near relative of Zadok.], **and Nathan the prophet** [a Jewish tradi-tion makes Nathan the eighth son of Jesse. He comes before us 2 Sam. vii. 2, 3, 17; xii. 1—12, 25] **and Shimei** [by Ewald iden-tified with Shammah (1 Sam. xvi. 9), or Shimeah, David's brother (2 Sam. xiii. 3; xxi. 21). Others suppose him to be the Shimei of 1 Kings iv. 18. But see note on chap. ii. 8. Josephus calls Shimei (not Rei, as Bähr states) ὁ Δαυίδου φίλος], **and Rei** [this name occurs here only. Ewald would identify him with Raddai (1 Chron.

ii. 14), another brother of David, but on very slender grounds], **and the mighty men** [or heroes. Gesen. "chiefs." Not the 600 men who formed David's band in his wan-derings (1 Sam. xxv. 13; xxvii. 2) (Rawlin-son), but the 30 (or 37) to whom this name of *Gibborim* is expressly given, 2 Sam. xxiii. 8; 1 Chron. xi. 15, 25; xxix. 24. Comp. 2 Kings x. 25, Heb.] **which belonged to David** [same expression as in 2 Sam. xxiii. 8] **were not with Adonijah.**

Ver. 9.—**And Adonijah slew** [or sacrificed, LXX. ἐθυσίασεν. It was a sacrificial feast, like Absalom's, 2 Sam. xv. 12 (where see Speaker's note). Religious festivity, *i.e.*, was the apparent object of their assembling: religion was invoked, not merely to cloke their designs, but to cement them together] **sheep and oxen and fat cattle by** [Heb. *with ;* same expression, 2 Sam. xx. 8] **the stone of Zoheleth,** [*i.e.*, "the serpent"(Gesen.) "No satisfactory explanation has been given of this name" (Rawlinson). See Smith's "Dict. Bible" *sub voc.*, where the various interpretations are given. The stone, which served as "a natural altar for the sacrificial feast," the spring, which afforded "water for the necessary ablutions," and the situa-tion with respect to the adjoining city recommended this place as a rendezvous] **which is by En-Rogel** [Josh. xv. 7; xviii. 16; 2 Sam. xvii. 17. Perhaps " the spring of the spy." The Chald., Arab., and Syr. render "the spring, of the fuller "—the Orientals wash clothes, &c., by *treading* (rogel) them. Josephus says it was without the city, in the royal garden (ἐν βασιλικῷ παρα-δείσῳ). The authorities are divided between the "Fountain of the virgin" (Ain um ed-Deraj), and the "Well of Job" (Bîr Eyub.) See the arguments in Bonar's "Land of Promise," App. 5; Thomson's "Land and Book," vol. ii. p. 528; and Mr. Grove's Art. in Smith's "Dict. Bib." Porter ("Hand-book of Palestine") identifies En-Rogel with Bîr Eyub without remark. There is much to be said on either side. The pool of Siloam ("Bib. Museum") has nothing in its favour] **and called all his brethren the king's sons** [including, it would seem, even the elder sons of David and Bathsheba, who would bring up the number to fifteen (1 Chron. iii. 5). They too, if living, would naturally resent the preference of the youngest brother], **and all the men of Judah, the king's servants** ["all the Judeans who were serving at court, as being members of his own tribe" (Keil). The fierce jealousy between Ephraim and Judah would almost compel the king to surround himself with soldiers and attend-ants of the latter tribe. Some of the invited guests, no doubt, like Absalom's two hundred, "went in their simplicity and knew not anything " (2 Sam. xv. 11).

Ver. 10. But Nathan the prophet, and Benaiah, and the mighty men, and Solomon his brother, he called not. [It is clear from this verse that Adonijah perfectly understood that he had in Solomon a rival. The intentions and promises (ver. 13) of his father can hardly have been unknown to him. The name "Jedidiah," too, bestowed upon Solomon by Nathan (2 Sam. xii. 25), taken in connexion with the prophecy of Nathan (*ibid.* vii. 12; cf. 1 Chron. xxii. 9, 10), must have proved to him that Solomon was marked out for David's successor. He seems to have been well aware also who were Solomon's supporters. To some of them he may have made indirect overtures.

The historian having recorded Adonijah's preparations for a *coup d'état*, now relates the manner in which the plot was frustrated. The prophet, who had been the guardian and preceptor of Solomon's youth, and who knew the Divine will respecting the succession (1 Chron. xxii. 9, 10), takes prompt and energetic measures to defeat the conspiracy.

Ver. 11.—Wherefore Nathan spake unto Bathsheba the mother of Solomon [the person after Solomon most directly concerned and also best fitted to approach the king] **saying, Hast thou not heard that Adonijah the son of Haggith** [possibly there is a touch of worldly wisdom here, as Rawlinson suggests, " Haggith, thy rival." We may be sure David's harem was not without its fierce jealousies. But (see ver. 5, and ch. ii. 13) the patronymic is so common in Heb. that we cannot safely found an argument upon it. See on chap. ii. 5] **doth reign** [Heb. *did reign*. LXX. ἐβασίλευσεν, aor. = " succeeded." " Schon so gut wie König geworden ist." Bähr and Keil] **and David our Lord knoweth it not.**

Ver. 12.—Now therefore come, let me give [Heb. *counsel*] **thee counsel, that thou mayest save** [Heb. *and save, i.e.,* by acting upon it] **thine own life, and the life of thy son Solomon.** The custom of Eastern kings—to secure their thrones by a massacre of their rivals—has received many illustrations, notably among the Ottomans, and is receiving one in Burmah at the present moment (May, 1879). We have Scripture instances in Judges ix. 5; 1 Kings xv. 29; 2 Kings x. 7, 14; xi. 1 (cf. 1 Sam. xxiv. 21). To put a royal *mother* to death, along with her offspring, though perhaps unusual, was not unknown. Rawlinson cites the instances of Cleopatra, widow of Philip of Macedon, who was murdered with her infant son

Caranus by Olympias; and Roxana, widow of Alexander the Great, who, with her son, was put to death by Cassander. Nathan does not say this will be, but may be, Bathsheba's fate.

Ver. 13.—Go and get thee in [Heb. *come*] **unto king David, and say unto him, Didst not thou, my lord, O king, swear unto thine handmaid** [this oath of David's to Bathsheba (see vers. 17, 30) is not elsewhere recorded, but it was evidently well known to Nathan, and probably, therefore, to others also] **saying, Assuredly** [Heb. *that,* כִּי, *recitantis*] **Solomon thy son shall reign after me, and he** [emphatic] **shall sit upon my throne ? why therefore doth Adonijah reign ?**

Ver. 14.—Behold, while thou yet talkest there [the original is more graphic, "thou art yet talking . . . and I"] **with the king, I also will come after thee and confirm** [marg., " fill up," cf. πληρώσω, LXX. Still an idiom of the East. Roberts (quoted in the "Biblical Museum") cites many illustrations. The meaning is, not to add to, amplify, but to corroborate. See ch. ii. 27; viii. 15, 24) **thy words.**

Ver. 15.—And Bathsheba went in unto the king into the chamber [lit., inner chamber, θάλαμος, *cubiculum penetrale*, Buxtorf. Same word 2 Sam. iv. 7; xiii. 10] **and the king was very old** [the repetition (see ver. 1) is not idle or unmeaning. Here the word refers to feebleness rather than age. It is mentioned to explain David's confinement to his chamber] **and Abishag the Shunammite ministered unto the king.** [This is introduced to show the king's helplessness. It does not prove that " there was a disinterested witness present" (Rawlinson), for she may have withdrawn, as Bathsheba did presently (ver. 23), and Nathan (ver. 32). It is a graphic touch, painted probably from the life, and by the hand of Nathan, from whom this narrative is derived.

Ver. 16.—And Bathsheba bowed, and did obeisance [cf. 2 Sam. xiv. 4. But we are hardly justified in seeing here " more than the ordinary Eastern salutation " (Rawlinson). The Jewish court seems to have been very ceremonious and stately (1 Sam. xxiv. 8; 2 Sam. xix. 24). The king was the representative of Heaven]. **And the king said, What wouldest thou** [marg., What to thee ? Not necessarily, What thy supplication ? (as Rawlinson). It rather means generally, " What thy business ? " *Quid tibi,* not *quid petis.*

Ver. 17.—And she said unto him, My Lord, thou swarest by the Lord thy God unto thine handmaid, *saying,* **Assuredly Solomon thy son shall reign after me, and he shall sit upon my throne.**

Ver. 18. — And now, behold, Adonijah

reigneth; and now my Lord the king, thou knowest *it* not.

Ver. 19.—**And he hath slain oxen and fat cattle and sheep in abundance, and hath called all the sons of the king, and Abiathar the priest, and Joab the captain of the host; but Solomon thy servant hath he not called.** [Said, not to " show that Solomon had reason to fear the worst if Adonijah should succeed" (Keil), but to prove that there was a plot. It showed the cloven foot.]

Ver. 20.—**And thou** [instead of וְאַתָּה, the Chald., Syr., and Vulg., with many MSS. read וְעַתָּה "and now;" but this looks like an emendation, and " *proclivi lectioni præstat ardua.*" Similarly, the second "now" in ver. 18 appears as "thou" in 200 MSS. These variations are of very little consequence, but the received text, in both cases, is somewhat the more spirited] **my lord, O king** [the repetition (see vers. 18, 21, 24, 27) illustrates the profound deference and court paid to the Hebrew monarch (see on ver. 16), especially when we remember that these are the words of a wife], **the eyes of all Israel are upon thee** (cf. ch. ii. 15) **that thou shouldest tell them who shall sit on the throne of my lord the king after him.** This shows that there was no "right of primogeniture." The kings of the East have always designated their successor amongst their sons. "Alyattes designated Crœsus; Cyrus designated Cambyses, and Darius designated Xerxes" (Rawlinson). "The Shah of Persia, at the beginning of this century, had sixty sons, all brought up by their mothers, with the hope of succeeding" (Morier, quoted by Stanley). And the kings of Israel claimed and exercised a similar right (2 Chron. xi. 22; xxi. 3).

Ver. 21.—**Otherwise** [there is no corresponding word in the Heb.] **it shall come to pass, when my lord the king shall sleep** [strictly, "lie down:" see on ch. ii. 10] **with his fathers** [this phrase, so common in the books of Kings and Chronicles, only occurs "once in the Pentateuch (Deut. xxxi. 16) and once in the historical books before Kings" (Rawlinson). It was evidently the product of an age when the nation was settled, and men had their family sepulchres] **that I and my son Solomon shall be counted** [Heb. *be*] **offenders** [Heb. as marg., *sinners*. The primary meaning of חָטָא is "to miss the mark." Like ἁμαρτάνειν, it came to be used of all *err*-ing and transgression. Bathsheba and Solomon would be obnoxious to Adonijah, as representing a rival cause; possibly also as guilty of high treason (Clericus, Bähr, *al.*)

Ver. 22.—**And lo, while she yet talked with the king, Nathan the prophet also came in.** [Heb. *came, i.e.*, to the palace. "*Came in*" almost implies that he entered the room, which he did not till summoned (ver. 23). Observe, Nathan's words convey no *suggestio falsi*. He does not deny a previous interview with Bathsheba, nor does he confess it. If there is an appearance of artifice, there was no intention to deceive. And the artifice, such as it was, was not only harmless, but for the public good.

Ver. 22.—**And they told the king, saying, Behold Nathan the prophet** [we are scarcely justified in seeing in this " solemn announcement of his approach" an "indication of the consideration in which he was held" (Stanley). It is difficult to see how otherwise he could be announced. It is clear that he was constantly spoken of as "the prophet" (vers. 10, 22, 34, 38, &c. Cf. 2 Sam. vii. 2; xii. 25]. **And when he was come in before** [Heb. *and he came before* —three words instead of six] **the king, he bowed himself before the king with his face to the ground** [see on vers. 16, 20; and cf. ver. 31, where we have a similar expression. "In the Assyrian sculptures, ambassadors are represented with their faces actually touching the earth before the feet of the monarch" (Rawlinson). This profound reverence on the part of Nathan is the more remarkable, when we remember how he had once denounced David to his face (2 Sam. xii. 7)].

Ver. 24.—**And Nathan said, My Lord, O king, hast thou said** [the Heb. has no question, but a strong affirmation: " *thou hast* said," *i.e.*, "thou must have said (Du hast wohl gesagt." Bähr). Nathan puts it thus forcibly, in order to draw from the king a disclaimer], **Adonijah shall reign after me, and he shall sit upon my throne?** [Same words as in vers. 13, 17, and possibly designedly so. The coincidence conveys the meaning, " Thou hast *sworn* Solomon shall reign," &c. "Thou hast *said*, Adonijah shall reign," &c.]

Ver. 25.—**For** [proof that the king must have decreed that Adonijah should succeed him. There appears to be an undertone of reproof in these words. Nathan assumes that Adonijah cannot have done all this without David's knowledge and sanction, because "his father had not displeased him at any time" (ver. 6). This uprising was the result of David's over-indulgence and want of firmness] **he is gone down this day, and hath slain** [see on ver. 9] **oxen and fat cattle and sheep in abundance, and hath called all the king's sons, and the captains of the host** [Joab was *the* captain (ver. 19). The plural shows that other high officers had followed his lead. "Under the captains of the host (ver. 25), the servants of the king (ver. 10) are included" (Bähr). Bähr's accidental miscitation (ver. 10 for ver. 9) has apparently led his American translator (p. 24) to the serious mistake of identifying these "captains of the host" with "the mighty men" (Gibborim) of ver. 10, who, it is distinctly said, "were *not* with Adonijah] **and Abiathar the priest, and behold, they eat and drink before him** [*convivia apta conjurationibus.* Grotius] **and say, God save king Adonijah.** [Heb. "let *the* king (not "king," as marg.) Adonijah live," or better, "live the king," &c. (comp. the *vivat rex,* and the *vives* and *vivas* of later days.) This was the customary acclamation wherewith the Jews greeted their kings (cf. ver. 39; 1 Sam. x. 24; 2 Sam. xvi. 16; 2 Kings xi. 12; 2 Chron. xxiii. 11).

Ver. 26.—**But me, even me** [Heb. *I*] **thy servant** [to Nathan this omission was most significant. He seems to say that he had not been called because he had been concerned in the appointment of a successor 2 Sam. vii. 13] **and Zadok the priest, and Benaiah the son of Jehoiada, and thy servant Solomon** [Bähr thinks that "we have in the order of these names a climax, in which Solomon, as the highest personage, is named last"] **hath he not called.**

Ver. 27.—**Is this thing done** [□אֹ=*an,* or perhaps, *num,* "Is it then the case that," &c.] **by** [lit., from with] **my lord the king** [*i.e.,* with his privity and by his appointment], **and thou hast not shewed it unto thy servant** [Heb. "made thy servant know." Nathan submits that he has a strong claim (2 Sam. xii. 25) to be informed, should there be any change in the king's plans], **who should sit upon the throne of my lord the king after him?** [Same expression as in ver. 20. The repetition was well calculated to impress upon the king the importance of nominating a successor at once.

Ver. 28.—**Then king David** [see on ver. 1] **answered and said, Call me Bathsheba** [she evidently left the chamber when Nathan entered it. "This was done, not to avoid the appearance of a mutual arrangement (Cler., Then. *al.*), but for reasons of propriety, inasmuch as in audiences granted by the king to his wife or one of his counsellors, no third person ought to be present unless the king required his assistance." Keil.] **And she came into the king's presence, and stood before the king.** [Here, as in numberless other instances, our translators have disregarded literalness in favour of euphony. The Hebrew has here an exact repetition, "came before the king, and stood before the king." The Authorized

Version rendering was adopted as the more spirited and rhythmical.

Ver. 29.—**And the king sware** [see on ver. 51] **and said, As the Lord liveth** [or "by the life of Jehovah." Cf. "by the life of Pharaoh" (Gen. xlii. 15). This was the common form of oath. See, *e.g.,* ch. ii. 24; Judges viii. 19; Ruth iii. 13; 1 Sam. xiv. 39; xix. 6; xx. 21; xxix. 6; and especially Jer. iv. 2; v. 2; Hos. iv. 15. It is characteristic of David to introduce into the formula some such clause as the following], **that hath redeemed my soul** [*i.e.,* life] **out of all distress.** Same expression as in 2 Sam. iv. 9. Similar expressions are found in Psa. xxv. 22, and xxxiv. 22. The repeated deliverance out of straits and danger—"out of the hand of all his enemies, and out of the hand of Saul"—was one of the most remarkable features of David's life, and it is no wonder that he repeatedly commemorates it, converting every adjuration into an act of thanksgiving. Similarly, Jacob (Gen. xlviii. 16.)

Ver. 30.—**Even as I sware unto thee by the Lord God of Israel, saying, Assuredly** [Heb. כִּי *tkat,* often prefixed to the *oratio directa;* not lending any emphasis (=*immo*), as Keil says the first and third כִּי of this verse do, but in English simply redundant. See on vers. 13, 17] **Solomon thy son shall reign after me, and he shall sit upon my throne** [same words as in vers. 13, 17, 24. These close repetitions are the habit of the East] **in my stead, even so** [Heb. *that so*] **will I** [certainly [not in Heb.] **do this day.**

Ver. 31.—**Then Bathsheba bowed with her face to the earth, and did reverence to the king** [see on vers. 16, 23], **and said, Let my lord king David live for ever.** [This hyperbolical expression is here only used of a Hebrew monarch. It was constantly addressed to the Babylonian and Persian kings. See Dan. ii. 4; iii. 9; v. 10; vi. 21; Nehem. ii. 3.

Ver. 32.—**And king David said** [this prompt and vigorous action shows that David's force of character and mental power were unimpaired], **Call me Zadok the priest, and Nathan the prophet, and Benaiah the son of Jehoiada.** ["the order of the names marks the position of the persons with respect to the matter in hand." Rawlinson]. **And they came before the king.**

Ver. 33.—**The king also said** [Heb. "And the king said," which is everyway preferable. The "also" is somewhat confusing], **Take with you the servants** [*i.e.,* the Cherethites and Pelethites, ver. 38] **of your lord,** [Heb. *lords;* probably a *pluralis majestatis* (cf Gen. xxxix. 2; xlii. 30; 2 Kings ii. 3, 5, 16), suggested to David by the *usus loquendi* of the court. This expression seems at first a strange periphrasis for "my servants." But David naturally adopts the language those around him were always using. See ver. 43 ; also 2 Sam. xi. 11, and xx. 6. Note : The latter passage, which refers to the *king*, has the plur. ; the former, referring to Joab, the sing.] **and cause Solomon my son to ride upon mine own mule**, [lit., " the she-mule " (the most prized in the East. Cf. Judges v. 10, Heb.) "which is mine." This was not merely a mark of honour (cf. Gen. xli. 43 ; Esth. vi. 8, 9), but a public and very significant indication of David's will respecting his successor. The populace would perceive at once who was destined to sit in David's seat. " The Rabbins tell us that it was death to ride on the king's mule without his permission " (Rawlinson). פִּרְדָּה, the fem. form is only found here and in vers. 38, 44. The mule would seem to have been a recent importation into Palestine—we never read of them before the time of David—and the Israelites were forbidden to breed them (Levit. xix. 19). Their use, consequently, was naturally restricted to royal or distinguished personages (2 Sam. xiii. 29). Wordsworth sees in the word a proof that David had not disobeyed God by multiplying *horses* to himself], **and bring him down to Gihon**. [Not Gibeon, which Thenius most arbitrarily would substitute for the received text. Where was Gihon ? The popular belief (accepted by Bähr and Keil, as well as by some geographers) is that it was in the valley of the Son of Hinnom, a part of which still bears the name of Gihon, *i.e.*, to the west of Jerusalem, and not far from the Jaffa gate. By many indeed the present *Birket-es-Sultan* is identified with the Lower Pool of Gihon. But others (Ferguson, Rawlinson, &c.) see in it the ancient name of the Tyropæon. Scripture does not speak of it as a *spring*, though the "source of the waters of Gihon " is mentioned 2 Chron. xxxii. 30, Heb. The text shows that it was *below* the city (" bring him *down* upon Gihon," ver. 33. Cf. also ver. 40). 2 Chron. xxxiii. 14, speaks of " Gihon in the valley," where it is very noticeable that the word used is *Nachal* (*i.e.* Wâdy, watercourse). But this " is the word always employed for the valley of the Kedron, east of Jerusalem, the so-called valley of Jehoshaphat ; *ge* (ravine or glen) being as constantly employed for the valley of Hinnom, south and west of the town " (Grove, " Dict. Bible," art. Gihon). It is also to be noticed that the text last cited mentions Gihon in connection with *Ophel*, which lies south-east of Jerusalem. The Chald., Arab., and Syr. are probably right, therefore, in identifying Gihon here with *Siloam*

(which lies at the foot of Ophel), in favour of which it may further be said that it would be admirably suited for David's purpose—of a counter demonstration—and that whether En-Rogel is to be found at the Well of the Virgin or the Well of Job. Siloam is at no great distance from either, and quite within earshot, whereas the traditional Gihon is altogether out of the way. It must be borne in mind that this procession to and from Gihon was ordained, not because there was any special reason for anointing Solomon there—for it was not a holy place—but purely as a demonstration to the populace, and to checkmate the conspirators. It was probably a public place, and would accommodate a large concourse (Poole).

Ver. 34.—**And let Zadok the priest and Nathan the prophet** [Bähr sees in the fact that Nathan was associated with Zadok in the anointing, " the high significance David attributed to the prophetic office in Israel." But the prophets constantly performed this ceremony. Samuel anointed both Saul and David ; Elisha anointed Jehu (2 Kings ix. 1), and was commissioned to anoint Hazael (1 Kings xix. 15, 16)] **anoint him** [the king, being a sacred personage, was set apart to the office, like the priest and prophet, by anointing. Saul was probably anointed twice (1 Sam. x. 1 ; xi. 15. Cf. xii. 3). David was anointed thrice (1 Sam. xvi. 13 ; 2 Sam. ii. 4 ; v. 3. Solomon was anointed twice (ver. 39 ; 1 Chron. xxix. 22). The Rabbins have always held that subsequent kings were not anointed, where the succession was regular. But this opinion must be taken *quantum valet*. It is true that we only *read* of the anointing of Jehu (2 Kings ix. 6), Joash (*ibid.* xi. 12), and Jehoahaz (*ibid.* xxiii. 30), and that in these three cases the accession was irregular. But it is obvious that other kings may have been anointed as well, though the fact is not recorded. There would be no reason for recording it in ordinary cases It seems hardly likely, too, that any king would readily dispense with an ordinance which would so much strengthen his title] **there king over Israel : and blow ye with the trumpet** [the sound of the trumpet would almost seem to have been a necessary accompaniment of coronations, or the proclamation of a new king. See 2 Sam. xv. 10 ; 2 Kings ix. 13 ; xi. 14], **and say, God save king Solomon.** [See on ver. 25.]

Ver. 35.—**Then ye shall come up** (after him [not in the LXX. Cod. Vat.] **that he may** [Heb. *and he shall*] **come and sit upon my throne** [in every possible way his accession was to be proclaimed and confirmed], **for he shall be king in my stead** [David *i.e.*, virtually abdicates in Solomon's favour. Cf. vers. 46, 51, 53; 1 Chron. xxix. 23, 26], **and I have appointed him** [he and him are emphasised in the original] **to be ruler over Israel and over Judah.** It is possible, as Bähr thinks, that Israel and Judah were severally mentioned because David had once been king over Judah only, and because Israel had gone over to the side of Absalom. It is more probable, however, that "Israel and Judah" was even then the current designation of the two component parts of the realm (see 2 Sam. ii. 9, 10; xix. 11, 41, &c.). Besides, we can hardly suppose that the historian has in every case, though he probably has in this, preserved the exact words of the speaker; and it need cause us no surprise had he put into David's mouth the phraseology of a later age. In the nature of things he can only give us the *substance* of conversations such as these.

Ver. 36.—**And Benaiah the son of Johoiada** [probably he spoke, not because the execution of the order depended upon him (Bähr); for both Zadok and Nathan had a much more important part to perform, but as a blunt soldier who was accustomed to speak his mind] **answered the king and said, Amen: the Lord God** [lit., " Jehovah, he God," &c.] **of my lord the king say so too.**

Ver. 37.—**As the Lord hath been with my lord the king** [cf. 1 Sam. xx. 13. " This phrase expresses a very high degree of the Divine favour" (Rawlinson). See Gen. xxvi. 3, 4; xxviii. 15; xxxix. 2, 21; Exod. iii. 12; Josh. i. 5; 1 Chron. xxii. 11, &c.], **even so be he with Solomon, and make his throne greater than the throne of my lord king David.** [This was said from a full and honest heart, not to flatter David's vanity (Thenius). It is thoroughly characteristic of the man so far as we know him. And the prayer was fulfilled (ch. iii. 11, 12).]

Ver. 38.—**So Zadok the priest, and Nathan the prophet, and Benaiah the son of Jehoiada, and the Cherethites, and the Pelethites** [these were the royal body-guard —Σωματοφύλακες Josephus calls them—who were commanded by Benaiah (2 Sam. viii. 18; xv. 18; xx. 23; xxiii. 23). But while their functions are pretty well understood, great difference of opinion exists as to the origin or meaning of the words. By some they are supposed to be *Gentile* names. A tribe of Cherethites is mentioned 1 Sam. xxx. 14. (Cf. Ezek. xxv. 16; Zeph. ii. 5), and in close connexion with the Philistines (ver. 16). Hence Cherethite has been thought to be another name for Philistine; and as the LXX. and Syr. render the word "Cretans," it has been conjectured that the Philistines had their origin from Crete.

They did come from Caphtor, and that is probably Crete (see Gen. x. 14; Jer. xlvii. 4; Amos ix. 7; Deut. ii. 23). פְּלֵיתִי again, is not unlike פְּלִשְׁתִּי. In favour of this view is the fact that David certainly *had* a body-guard of foreign mercenaries (2 Sam. xv. 18, where the "Gittites" are connected with the Cherethites). Nor does it make against it that "two designations" would thus "be employed side by side for one and the same people"—as if we should speak of Britons and Englishmen (Bähr). For the names look like a *paronomasia*—of which the Jews were very fond—and a trick of this kind would at once account for the tautology. [Since writing this, I find the same idea has already occurred to Ewald.] But the other view, adopted by Gesenius, is that the names are names of office and function. Cherethite he would derive from כָּרַת, cut, slay; and by Cherethites he would understand "executioners," which the royal body-guard were in ancient despotisms (Gen. xxxix. 1, Heb.; Dan. ii. 14, &c. See on ch. 11. 25). In the Pelethites (פֶּלֶת, swiftness) he would see the public couriers (ἄγγαροι) of Eastern monarchies (see Herod. viii. 98 and 2 Chron. xxx. 6). We see the guard discharging the function first named in 2 Kings x. 25; xi. 4, 8; and the latter in 1 Kings xiv. 27 (marg.)] **went down** [i.e., from the palace on Mount Zion] **and caused Solomon to ride upon King David's mule, and brought him to** [עַל: cf. ii. 26] **Gihon** [Chald., Syr., Arab., *Shiloha*].

Ver. 39.—**And Zadok the priest took an horn of oil** [Heb. *the* oil. The "holy anointing oil," Exod. xxx. 25, 31, compounded as directed in vers. 23—25, was evidently part of the furniture of the tabernacle (Exod. xxxi. 11; xxxix. 38). Eleazer was charged with its preservation (Num. iv. 16), and the Rabbins say it lasted till the captivity] **out of the tabernacle** [the tabernacle on Mount Zion, containing the ark (2 Sam. vi. 17; 1 Chron. xv. 1) must be meant here. There was not time to have gone to the tabernacle at Gihon (Stanley), which was three hours distance from Jerusalem (Keil). Though Abiathar had charge of this sanctuary, yet Zadok would readily gain access to it, especially in the king's name] **and anointed Solomon. And they blew the trumpet** [cf. 2 Sam. xv. 10; 2 Kings ix. 13; xi. 14]; **and all the people said, God save king Solomon.** [Notice the exact fulfilment of the threefold charge of ver. 34 and its result. Solomon was confirmed in his office by the suffrages of the people.]

Ver. 40.—**And all the people came up after**

him [same expression as ver. 35. The procession, the sound of the trumpets, &c., had collected a large crowd, which followed Solomon on his return], **and the people piped** [Heb. *were piping*] **with pipes** [pipes or flutes were used on occasions of rejoicing (Isa. v. 12 ; xxx. 29. Cf. 1 Sam. x. 5), and also of mourning (Jer. xlviii. 36 ; Matt. ix. 23). It is true that a very slight change (מְחַלְּלִים בַּחֲלָלִים) instead of מְחֹלְלִים בְּחִילִים will give the meaning, "dancing with dances," which Ewald prefers, on the ground that "*all* the people" could not have produced their pipes at a moment's notice. But the objection loses its force when it is observed (Rawlinson) that the text implies that only *some* of the people piped. "*All* the people came up . . . and *the people*," &c. Besides, even if it were not so, some allowance is surely to be made for Eastern hyperbole. And the received text is to be preferred on other grounds. The LXX., however, has ἐχόρευον ἐν χοροῖς, **and rejoiced with great joy** [Heb. "were rejoicing a great joy"], **and the earth rent** [this is certainly a strangly hyperbolical expression. For בָּקַע strictly means to cleave asunder, tear open (see, *e.g.*, Num. xvi. 31; Amos i. 13; 2 Chron. xxv. 12). And Thenius suggests a slight emendation of the text, viz., וַתִּתְקַע (*i.e.*, "resounded") for וַתִּבָּקַע which would obviate this difficulty. He points out that while the LXX. Cod. Vat. has ἐρράγη, some versions have ἤχησεν, and the Vulg. *insonuit*. But perhaps it is safer to keep to the *lectio ardua*] **with the sound of them** [Heb. "with their voices"].

Ver. 41.—**And Adonijah and all the guests that were with him heard it** [it is probable they "were listening with some anxiety to hear if anything would occur." Rawlinson] **as they had made an end** [Heb. "and they had finished"] **of eating, And when Joab heard the sound of the trumpet** [the original almost implies that Joab's practised ear was the first to catch the note of the trumpet. He seems to have been the first to suspect its significance], **he said, Wherefore is this noise of the city being in an uproar?** [More exactly, "in commotion." הוֹמָה, an onomatopoetic word, like our English "hum." We speak of the "hum of the city," "the buzz of business," &c.]

Ver. 42.—**And while he yet spake, behold, Jonathan the son of Abiathar the priest** [Cf. 2 Sam. xv. 36 ; xvii. 17. His experience had marked him out for the post of watchman] **came** [That he had not arrived before shows how prompt, and even hurried, had been the measures taken by

Solomon's party] **and Adonijah said unto him** [Heb. and LXX. omit "unto him"] **Come in** [Heb. *come*. See on ver. 22. "Come *in*" suggests the idea of a house or tent, whereas the feast was *al fresco*]; **for thou art a valiant man** [it is Adonijah (not Joab, as Bähr—of course by an oversight—says) who speaks thus. Perhaps "able," "honest," or "worthy man" (cf. ver. 52 ; same word in Heb. ; also Prov. xii. 4) would be nearer the mark. "Valiant" is clearly out of place] **and bringest good tidings.** [A similar expression 2 Sam. xviii. 27. It was evidently a familiar saying. The idea, "a good man will bring good news" corresponds with that of the proverb of 1 Sam. xxiv. 13. Adonijah's misgivings reveal themselves in these words. He fears the worst, but strives to put on a cheerful face and to encourage his guests.]

Ver. 43.—**And Jonathan answered and said to Adonijah, Verily** [Rather, "nay but," "on the contrary" (*immo vero*). See Gen. xvii. 19, Heb., "Nay, but Sarah thy wife," &c., and Gesen., Thesaurus, *sub voce* אֲבָל. This particle has not "always an objecting force" (Rawlinson)—see Gen. xlii. 21, and especially 2 Sam. xiv. 5 ; 2 Kings iv. 14 —but only in the later Hebrew, *e.g.*, 2 Chron. xix. 3; xxxiii. 17] **our Lord king David hath made Solomon king.**

Ver. 44.—**And the king hath sent with Zadok the priest, and Nathan the prophet, and Benaiah the son of Jehoiada, and the Cherethites, and the Pelethites** [see on ver. 38], **and they have caused him to ride upon the king's mule.**

Ver. 45.—**And Zadok the priest and Nathan the prophet have anointed him king in Gihon: and they are come up from thence rejoicing, so that the city** [קִרְיָה same word as in ver. 41. Elsewhere almost exclusively found in poetry] **rang again** [rather, "is in commotion." Same expression in ver. 41 and Ruth i. 19, where it is translated, "the city was *moved*"). **This is the noise** [Heb. *voice*] **that ye have heard.**

Ver. 46.—**And also** [the same two words are found at the beginning of vers. 47, 48. They accord well with the breathless and excited state of the speaker, and suggest how each successive detail told on the hearers] **Solomon sitteth** [rather, "sate, took his seat," ἐκάθισε (LXX.) aorist. See ver. 35] **on the throne of the kingdom** [rather, "the royal throne." So Gesen. All David's directions were now fulfilled].

Ver. 47.—**And moreover** [וְגַם as before] **the king's servants** [see on ver. 33] **came to bless our lord king David** [Jonathan here refers in all probability to the words of Benaiah, vers. 36, 37. He does not know the exact particulars, and ascribes to the "servants" the words of their commander. Of course it is possible that "the bodyguard took up the words of Jehoiada (Benaiah ?) their captain and repeated them with some slight alteration." Rawlinson] **saying, God** [so the Keri. The Cethib has "thy God"] **make the name of Solomon better than thy name and make his throne greater than thy throne** [This prayer was fulfilled (chap. iii. 12 ; iv. 21–24]. **And the king bowed himself** [in worship. Cf. Gen. xlvii. 31] **upon the bed.**

Ver. 48.—**And also thus saith the king, Blessed be the Lord God of Israel, which hath given one to sit on my throne this day, mine eyes even seeing it.** [These last words are added because it is quite an exceptional thing for a king to see his successor on the throne.]

Ver. 49.—**And all the guests** [Heb. *called*, LXX. κλητοί] **that were with** [Heb. *to*] **Adonijah were afraid** [Heb. *trembled*] **and rose up** [LXX. omits] **and went every man his way.** [This fear and flight betray a consciousness of guilt. They cannot have believed in the right of primogeniture.]

Ver. 50.—**And Adonijah feared because of Solomon and he arose and went and caught hold of the horns of the altar.** [Cf. chap. ii. 28. Probably the altar of Mount Zion, chap. iii. 15 ; 2 Sam. vi. 17. Though it is impossible to say positively whether this or the altar at Gibeon (chap. iii. 4) or that recently erected on the threshing floor of Araunah (2 Sam. xxiv. 25) is meant. For the " horns," see Exod. xxvii. 2; xxxviii. 2 ; and compare xxx. 2. They were of shittim (*i.e.*, acacia) wood overlaid with brass, and served a double purpose. Victims were bound to them (Psa. cxviii. 27), and blood was put upon them, Exod. xxix. 12. As to the altar as a place of sanctuary, see on chap. ii. 28. Evidently *a* right of sanctuary existed amongst both Jews and Gentiles at the time of the Exodus, and probably from time immemorial. It is referred to in Exod. xxi. 14, but it was much circumscribed by the appointment of the cities of refuge (Num. xxxv. 10 sqq.) By "laying hold of the horns the offender thereby placed himself under the protection of the saving and helping grace of God" (Bähr, "Symbolik," i. 474)

Ver. 51.—**And it was told Solomon, saying, Behold Adonijah feareth King Solomon, for lo, he hath caught hold on the horns of the altar, saying, let king Solomon** [this repetition of the title is striking. Both courtiers and criminals hasten to give the young king his new honours. In Adonijah's mouth it is also a virtual abdication of his claim to the throne and a direct acknowledgment of the new monarch. But see on vers. 1 and 35.] **swear unto me to-day** [Cf. 2 Sam. xix. 23. This is one of many passages which show how lightly the Jews esteemed promises in comparison with oaths. The sentiment possibly took its rise in the oaths sworn by the Divine Being (Gen. xxii. 16 ; xxiv. 7 ; Exod. xvii. 16, &c.), though it is possible, on the other hand, that these asseverations were made in deference to the popular sentiment. Be that as it may, the oath held a much more conspicuous and important place in the Jewish than the Christian economy. See Gen. xxi. 23 ; xxxi. 23 ; Num. xiv. 2 ; xxx. 2 ; Judges xv. 12; xxi. 1 ; 1 Sam. xiv. 28 ; Jer. v. 2, and, to omit other passages, 1 Kings i. 13 ; ii. 8, 23, 42. Even our Lord, who rebuked the habit (Matt. v. 34—37; xxiii. 16—22) respected the adjuration of Caiaphas, and St. Paul frequently appeals to God (Acts xxvi. 29 ; 2 Cor. i. 23 ; xi. 31 ; Phil. i. 8.) The Christian religion, as it has gradually begotten a reverence for *truth*, has made the simple word into a bond] **that he will not slay his servant** [Cf. "I will be King," ver. 5.] **with the sword** [the usual form of capital punishment, ch. ii. 8, 25, 31, 46. Adonijah indirectly confesses that he had merited death].

Ver. 51.—**And Solomon said** [*i.e.*, he refused to swear], **If he will shew himself a worthy man** [בֶּן־חַיִל, cf. אִישׁ־חַיִל, ver. 42], **there shall not an hair of him fall to the earth** [*i.e.*, not a single hair shall be injured. Same expression 1 Sam. xiv. 45 ; 2 Sam. xiv. 11; Acts xxvii. 34. It was evidently a familiar saying] **but if wickedness shall be found in him,** [*i.e.*, if he shall commit any fresh crime] **he shall die** [Heb. וָמֵת, "then he shall die," emphatic.]

Ver. 53.—**So King Solomon sent and they brought him down** [The altar was elevated : probably a slope, not steps (Exod. xx. 26) led to it] **from** [Heb. *from upon*. He was still clinging to it] **the altar. And he came and bowed himself to king Solomon** [*i.e.*, made obeisance to him as king. Cf. vers. 16, 23, 31] **and Solomon said unto him, Go to thine house.** This was not a sentence of banishment from court, but merely a dismissal to a private life, involving a tacit admonition to live quietly and be thankful that his life was spared him. "*Vade in domum tuam, ibi quiesce et res tuas age, nec te publicis regni mei negotiis immisceas*" (Corn. à Lapide).

HOMILETICS.

Ver. 1.—*The chamber of sickness.* This opening chapter of 1 Kings introduces us into the privacy of a sick room. Stretched upon a couch, covered with many folds of rich Eastern drapery, we see a feeble, decrepit, attenuated man. At his side stands a fair young girl, assiduously ministering to his wants. From time to time the door opens, and prophet, priest, and warrior enter to receive his instructions; for happily the mind is not a wreck like the body. Its vigour is hardly abated, though the bodily strength is well-nigh exhausted. He has but reached the appointed threescore years and ten, and yet—such have been the hardships of his life—the vital force is spent. They cover him with clothes, but he gets no heat. The flame of life is slowly but surely expiring. But we see at once that this is no ordinary room; that this is no common patient. The gorgeous apparel, the purple and fine linen, the "attendance of ministers, the standing of servants," proclaim it a king's court. And the insignia, the pomp, the profound homage proclaim that this sick man is a king. Yes, it is David, second king of Israel, but second to none in goodness and true greatness, who lies here. His chequered life, so full of romance, of chivalry, of piety, is drawing near its close. But the hour of death is preceded by a period of feebleness and decay. For sickness is no respecter of persons. It, too, like death, "thunders at the palace gates of kings and the dwellings of the poor." There is no release in that war,

> "Sceptre and crown must tumble down,
> And in the dust be equal made
> With the poor common scythe and spade."

The sickness of David, then, may fittingly suggest some thoughts as to sickness in general. What, let us ask, is its purpose, what its uses? Why is it that, as a rule, a period of gradual decay precedes death? For it is worthy of remark that man alone, of all the animals, dies of disease. Among all the myriad forms of life, that is, he alone dies gradually. The lower animals, as a rule, prey upon each other. Beasts, birds, fishes, insects, all die a violent death. No sooner is one of them attacked by sickness, or enfeebled by old age, than it is dispatched and devoured by its fellows. It is thus the balance of the species is preserved. But in the case of men, sudden death is the exception. For them there remains, as a rule, a discipline of pain prior to dissolution. It is well to ask why this is. The general answer is, of course, obvious. It is because of that other life, that future reckoning which awaits men after death. Let us consider, however, in what ways sickness and pain are a preparation for the life and the judgment to come.

I. SICKNESS IS GOD'S NOTICE TO QUIT. We should think it hard to be ejected from our home and turned into the street without due notice. We want a little time to make preparations. Especially is this the case when we are leaving our earthly tabernacle—leaving not a *home*, but a *world*. Now God has given us abundant and repeated notice in the various accidents and occurrences of life. Too often, however, both the lessons of Providence and the warnings of the preacher are unheeded. So the Lover of souls will give men a final warning, and one that they cannot mistake, cannot well disregard. They shall *feel* it in their own persons. Sickness shall bid them set their house in order and prepare to meet their God. A German fable tells us that once upon a time Death promised a young man that he would not summon him until he had first sent several messengers to apprize him of his coming. So the youth took his fill of pleasure, and wasted health and strength in riotous living. Presently, a fever laid him low. But as no messenger had appeared, he had no apprehensions; and when he recovered, he returned forthwith to his former sins. He then fell a prey to other maladies, but, remembering his covenant with Death, made light of them. "I am not going to die," he cried; "the first messenger has not yet come." But one day some one tapped him on the shoulder. He turned, and saw Death standing at his elbow. "Follow me."

said the King of Terrors; "the hour of thy departure is come." "How is this?" exclaimed the youth; "thou art false to thy word! Thou didst promise to send me messengers, and I have seen none." "Silence!" sternly answered the Destroyer. "I have sent thee messenger after messenger. What was the fever? What was the apoplexy? What was each sickness that befel thee? Each was my herald; each was my messenger." Yes, the first use of sickness is to remind men of death. And how much they need that reminder we may learn from the case of David. He had long been familiar with death. He was no stranger to "th' imminent deadly breach," had known many "hairbreadth 'scapes," and often there had been "but a step between his soul and death." Nay, he had once seen the Destroyer himself, seen him standing with his drawn sword ready to smite. And yet the man who had faced death, who had long carried his life in his hand, receives a final warning ere its close. That sickness, perhaps, first brought home to him his mortality, first cried to him, "Thus saith the LORD GOD, Remove the diadem and take off the crown" (Ezek. xxi. 26). But

II. SICKNESS IS GOD'S WAY OF WEANING MEN FROM THE WORLD. It is natural to cling to life; but it is necessary we should be made willing to leave it. The wrench is felt the less when some of the ties which bind us to earth have been sundered: when life loses its attractions. It is the office of pain and sickness to make life valueless, to make men anxious to depart. How often it happens that men who at the beginning of illness will not hear of death are presently found praying for their release. Such are the "uses of adversity." An old writer compares affliction to the bitter unguent which nursing mothers who would wean their offspring sometimes put upon their breast. A few weeks on the couch of pain, and we soon cry out that life is not worth the living.

III. SICKNESS IS GOD'S DISCIPLINE FOR PARADISE. True it is that all "earthly care is a heavenly discipline." All the ills that flesh is heir to are designed to be the instruments of our perfection. Like the Captain of our salvation, we are "made perfect through sufferings." For us, as for Him, "the cross is the ladder to heaven." Those are two suggestive words, which only differ by one letter—παθήματα, μαθήματα, "afflictions, instructions." But while all affliction is a school, the last illness should be the finishing school. At the last assay the furnace must be heated more than it has been wont to be. "I have learnt more," said Mr. Cecil, "within these curtains in six weeks than I have learnt in all my life before." The chamber of sickness is an enforced Retreat. There, ears "that the preacher could not school" are compelled to listen. There, "lips say 'God be pitiful' which ne'er said 'God be praised.'" There, many have learnt for the first time to know themselves. And how necessary is this last discipline David's sick-chamber may teach us; for he had already had his share of troubles. His life had been largely spent in the school of adversity. "In journeyings often, in peril of robbers," &c. (2 Cor. xi. 25, 26), these words aptly describe his early career. And even since he ascended the throne, how often has the sword gone through his soul. Amnon, Absalom, Tamar, Abner, Amasa, what tragedies are connected with these names. Few men have experienced such a long and bitter discipline as he; and it would seem, too, to have accomplished its work. If we may judge by some of his later Psalms, full of contrition, of humility, of devout breathings after God, that sweet and sanctified soul had "learned obedience by the things which he suffered." But he is not spared the final chastening. The sweet singer of Israel, the man after God's own heart, must go awhile into the gloom and the silence of the sick-room, there to be made fully "meet for the inheritance of the saints in light." Men often pray to be spared a long sickness, often commiserate those who experience one. But we have learned that it has its uses. We see that it is a last chance given to men: a last solemn warning, a final chastening to prepare them for the beatific vision. The Neapolitans call one of the wards of their hospital L'Antecamera della Morte—the ante-chamber of death. It is thus that we should regard every "chamber of sickness."

Ver. 5 sqq. with ch. ii. 13 sqq.—*Adonijah's history and its lessons.*
I. HE WAS A SPOILT CHILD.—"His father had not displeased him at any time."

(ch. i. 7). There is no greater unkindness and injustice to a child than over-indulgence. The child is the father of the man. The boy who has all his own way will certainly want it in after life, and will not get it, to his own disappointment and the unhappiness of all around him. He that loveth his son chasteneth him betimes. David was probably so engrossed with pnblic cares and duties that his first care, after God—his family—was neglected. How unwise are those parents who devolve the care of their children at the most critical and impressionable time of life on domestics, who are often ill-suited or unequal to the charge. One of the first duties a child demands of its parents is that it should be corrected and conquered. The will must be broken in youth. The sapling may be bent, not so the trunk. David's unwise indulgence, his sparing the rod, prepared a rod for his own and Adonijah's back. It was the sin of Eli that " his sons made themselves vile and he restrained them not." And one sin of David was that he, had not checked and " displeased " this wilful son.

II. HE WAS ENDOWED BY NATURE WITH A DANGEROUS PROPERTY. " He also was a very goodly man." Gifts of form and feature, much as all admire them, and much as some covet them, are frequently a snare to their possessor. Perhaps, upon the whole, personal beauty has oftener proved a curse than a blessing. " For the most part," says Lord Bacon, " it maketh a dissolute youth." Oftener still it spoils the character. The conceit of the Platonists, that a beautiful body loves to have a beautiful soul to inhabit it, is unhappily not borne out by facts. " A pretty woman," it has been said, and it is often true, " adores herself " (Eugénie de Guérin). The natural tendency of this possession is to engender pride, selfishness, conceit, ambition. A striking exterior has often cost its possessor dear. It did both Absalom and Adonijah no good. It is worthy of notice that it was David's " goodly " sons conspired against him, and it was his " fair " daughter Tamar was dishonoured. Adonijah's face was an important factor in his history : it contributed to his ruin. It favoured, perhaps it suggested, his pretensions to the throne. He thought, no doubt, " the first in beauty should be first in might." Had he been blessed with an insignificant appearance he would probably have saved his head. As it was, courted and admired, he thought the fairest woman of her time was alone a fit match for him ; and pride whispered that a man of such a presence was marked out for a king, and so urged him to his ruin. Let us teach our children to covet only " the beauty of the soul."

III. HE WAS CURSED WITH AN INORDINATE AMBITION. " I will be king." " Cursed," for it has cursed and blighted many lives. Like the ignis fatuus, it has lured men to their destruction. It has been well called " a deadly tyrant, an inexorable master." " Ambition," says the most eloquent of divines, " is the most troublesome and vexatious passion that can afflict the sons of men. It is full of distractions, it teems with stratagems, and is swelled with expectations as with a tympany. . . . It is an infinite labour to make a man's self miserable ; he makes his days full of sorrow to acquire a three years' reign." What a striking illustration of these words does Adonijah's history supply. If he could but have been content to fill the second place he might have lived honoured, happy, and useful. But ambition soured and then cut short his life. How much of the misery of the world is caused by despising " that state of life unto which it has pleased God to call us " and stretching out after another for which we are not fitted. Adonijah's history teaches this lesson—Solomon may have partly drawn it from his life and death—" Pride goeth before destruction," &c.

IV. HE STOOPED TO UNWORTHY MEANS TO ATTAIN HIS OBJECT. " Chariots," " horses, fifty men to run before him." It is much like the Roman device, " Panem et circenses." History repeats itself. But these things were almost innocent compared with the measures he took when these failed. The smooth intrigue of a marriage, the employment of the king's mother as his tool, the plausible words, the semblance of resignation to the Divine will—and all this to overthrow a brother who had generously spared his life. And all this was the outcome of ambition—ambition which makes men trample on the living and the dead. Alas ! we never know to what base courses we may be reduced if we once embark in immoral enterprises.

Adonijah's "I will be king" led to conspiracy, rebellion, intrigue, ingratitude; to defiance of a father, of a brother, of God.

V. HE WAS NOT WITHOUT WARNING, BUT IT WAS IN VAIN. The failure of his first conspiracy, the abject terror which followed, the flight to the sanctuary, the terrified clinging to the horns of the altar, the piteous entreaty for life—these things should have been remembered, should have "changed his hand and checked his pride." Still more, his brother's magnanimity, "there shall not an hair of him fall to the earth;" or, if not that, his message, "If wickedness be found in him he shall die." All are of no avail. The passion for empire, like the passion for play, is almost incurable. Adonijah was playing for a throne: he staked honour, safety, piety—and lost. He played again—and this time a drawn sword was suspended over his head—he staked his life, and lost it.

VI. HE WAS SUDDENLY CUT OFF, AND THAT WITHOUT REMEDY. And this was the end of the spoiled child, of the "curled darling;" this the end of his pomp and circumstance, of his flattery and intrigue, of his steadfast resistance of the will of heaven—that the sword of the headsman smote him that he died. Instead of the throne, the tomb; instead of the sceptre, the sword. Chariots and horses, visions of empire, visions of love—one fell thrust of the steel put an end to all that. Died Adonijah as a fool dieth, ingloriously, ignobly. "When we are dead, all the world sees who was the fool." Adonijah's death was the fitting and natural conclusion of his life. He has sowed to the wind: what wonder if he reaps to the whirlwind.

Ver. 5.—*Adonijah and the Lord's Anointed.* The conspiracy of Adonijah and its issue may suggest some lessons as to the kingdom of Christ and those who oppose His reign. For consider—

I. SOLOMON IS A TYPE OF OUR BLESSED LORD. This is universally allowed. The true "son of David" is the Son of God. He is the Divine Wisdom, the true Anointed One, the eternal King of Israel. Solomon "the peaceful" prefigured the great "Prince of Peace."

II. THE KINGDOM OF SOLOMON FORESHADOWED CHRIST'S REIGN. This is taught "by most certain warrants of Holy Scripture" (see *e.g.*, Luke i. 32, 33, and cf. 2 Sam. vii. 11, 12; Ps. lxxii. 11, sqq.; Isa. ix. 7; xvi. 5; Jer. xxiii. 5).

III. THE OPPOSITION TO SOLOMON'S RULE PREFIGURED THE RESISTANCE OF THE POWERS OF THIS WORLD TO CHRIST. The second Psalm, the primary reference of which is to Solomon, has its absolute fulfilment in our Lord (Acts iv. 25-27). Note here (1) As against Solomon were leagued princes, priest, and general, so against the Christ were gathered tetrarch, priests, and proconsul. (2) As the aid of religion was invoked against Solomon by Adonijah and Abiathar (note on ver. 9), so it was invoked against our blessed LORD by Annas and Caiaphas (St. Matt. xxvi. 65; St. John xix. 7). In both cases, religion was used as a cloke. Now observe—

IV. THE COURSE OF ADONIJAH'S CONSPIRACY FORESHADOWS (1) THE BRIEF SUCCESS, AND (2) THE SUDDEN OVERTHROW, OF THE POWERS OF EVIL. (1) *The brief success.* As for a time everything seemed to favour the conspirators—David's indecision, Adonijah's following, &c.—so now the powers of this world seem to have their own way. The silence of God, a corrupt priesthood, physical force, the chariots and horses of the world, the pomp and glitter of wealth—all seem to promise success. The cause of Christ, like that of Solomon, seems to be desperate. But (2) *The sudden overthrow.* In the very hour of apparent success, amid cries of "God save King Adonijah," the trumpet blast proclaimed the destruction of their hopes, and the trembling and terrified guests hurriedly dispersed to their homes. So, at the trump of the archangel, if not before, the "gates of hell" shall be overcome and the enemies of our Lord shall be put to confusion, and flee to the mountains and hills to cover them (St. Luke xxiii. 30). Meanwhile the Church and her ministers, like Bathsheba and Nathan, must cry to the Eternal Father, "Lord, how long" (Rev. vi. 10)?

V. THE DURATION OF THE CONSPIRACY PREFIGURES (1) THE BRIEF REJECTION AND (2) THE ETERNAL REIGN OF CHRIST. The conspiracy lasted at the longest a few weeks; the peaceful reign of Solomon extended over forty years. The conspiracy against Christ has lasted over 1800 years—for "we see not yet all things put under him"—but what is this compared with eternity, and "He shall reign *for ever and ever*" (Rev. xi. 15 ; cf. Dan. vi. 26).

VI. THE END OF THE CONSPIRATORS FORESHADOWS (1) THE JUDGMENT AND (2) THE DOOM OF THE ENEMIES OF CHRIST. (1) *The judgment.* No sooner was Solomon anointed king than he sate in judgment upon Adonijah (ver. 52), and no long time afterwards upon Joab and Abiathar. (2) *The doom.* He condemned Abiathar to banishment (ch. ii. 26), and appointed Adonijah and Joab to be slain. Even so our Lord will presently sit upon the judgment throne and will in like manner banish ("Depart, ye cursed") and deliver to death ("These mine enemies, which would not that I should reign over them, bring hither and *slay* them before me") the opposers of His glorious reign.

Ver. 11 sqq.—*The Jewish prophet : an example to the Christian pastor.* The dealings of Nathan with David may suggest some thoughts as to (1) the office, and (2) the duties of the Christian minister. For observe—

THE CHRISTIAN MINISTER OCCUPIES IN THE NEW DISPENSATION A POSITION SOME-WHAT ANALOGOUS TO THAT OF THE PROPHET IN THE OLD. Prophecy, that is to say, is *one* of his functions. For *prophecy* does not, strictly and properly, mean *prediction* (or foretelling), but *preaching* (or forthtelling). The *prophétés* was the spokesman or interpreter of God. (See Introduction, note.) The "prophesyings" of the New Testament (1 Cor. xi. xiv) were preachings or expositions ; and in this sense the word is used by Lord Bacon, and others. So the prophet was, and the preacher is, an ambassador for God, an expounder of his laws, a herald of his kingdom. The former, therefore, may well serve as a pattern to the latter. Now the dealings of the prophet Nathan with King David were of two kinds: 1. *He admonished him in health ;* 2. *He counselled him in sickness.* Hence let us learn that we owe doctrine, reproof, correction, instruction in righteousness ; in other words, "both public and private monitions and exhortations, as well to the sick as to the *whole* within our cures." (See "The Ordering of Priests," Book of Common Prayer.) The latter are liable to be overlooked. But the prophet further suggests to us (1) *what are the ministrations or admonitions the pastor owes to his flock, and* (2) *what is the spirit in which he should offer them.* He teaches the former by his dealings with David in health, and the latter by his dealings with David in sickness.

I. Under the first head, observe that, 1. *He boldly denounced David's sin* (2 Sam. xii. 7) at the risk, perhaps, of his life, and fearlessly threatened him with shame (ver. 11) and sword (ver. 10). 2. *He proclaimed forgiveness on David's repentance* (ver. 13). 3. *He ministered comfort in David's sorrow* (ver. 25). 4. *He encouraged and advised David in his undertakings* (2 Sam. vii. 3—17. Behold here, the principal duties of the pastoral office—to rebuke sin, to pronounce absolution, to comfort the sorrowing, to guide the conscience. And note: in all these functions, Nathan merely echoed the word the Lord had given him. We must take care not to "go beyond the word of the Lord, to do more or less."

II. Under the second category, we find that, 1. *He was faithful to his God.* He had been employed by God to declare Solomon the heir to the throne. He would have been unfaithful had he permitted another to usurp the crown. 2. *He was faithful and deferential to his king.* As keeper of the king's conscience, as trusted adviser and counsellor, he owed it to the king to apprize him of Adonijah's plot. It is a sacred duty to speak, and he speaks—speaks with the profound reverence which even the Lord's prophet owes to the Lord's anointed (ver. 23). (A great churchman confessed that he had not served his God as faithfully as he had served his king. Nathan was true to both.) 3. *He was disinterested.* He asks no favours for himself. It is for the Hebrew commonwealth, for the Jewish Church, that he acts and speaks. He does not abuse his position to extort gifts from a dying man. (Compare Savonarola dictating the terms of absolution to Lorenzo de' Medici.) 4. *He was discreet.* "Wise as serpent, but harmless as dove." He approaches Bathsheba (ver. 11), excites her alarm (ver. 12), uses her as the most likely agent to prevail with the king, instructs her (ver. 13), follows her (ver. 22). "The policy of Nathan was of use as well as his prophecy" (Bp. Hall). Thus the prophet teaches the pastor to use all fidelity, to show true loyalty and courtesy, to act purely and unselfishly, to use the means God has put within his reach with consideration and discretion.

The Benedictus of the Old Testament, and the Benedictus of the New (Ver. 48; Luke i. 68).

On two memorable occasions this doxology has been found on the lips of the saints. No doubt the formula, "Blessed be the Lord God of Israel," was a favourite one with the people of Israel; no doubt the words were often used (cf. Ps. xli. 13; lxxii. 18). But there are two occasions of pre-eminent interest and importance when this thanksgiving broke from joyful lips. Let us consider them. 1. It was used (as we see) by the aged King David on the day that he saw his son Solomon (Peace) *a* forerunner of the Messiah, seated on the throne of Israel. 2. It was used by the aged priest Zacharias on the day that he saw his son John (Grace), *the* forerunner of Messiah, brought into the commonwealth of Israel. It is just possible, but hardly probable, that the words, as used by the latter (under the guidance of the Holy Ghost, Luke i. 67) had a reference to their use by the former. But it may be instructive, nevertheless, to compare these two ascriptions of praise, for they are more or less characteristic, the one of the old dispensation, the other of the new. Let us observe,

I. Their points of contact. II. Their points of contrast.

I. They are alike in three particulars. 1. *Each Benedictus was in some sort the "Nunc Dimittis" of an aged saint.* Each proceeded from a man "old and stricken in years" (1 Kings i. 1; Luke i. 7); each from a man of fervent piety (1 Kings xi. 4; Luke i. 6); each was suggested by the speaker's son rising up to take his place, and to carry on his and God's work. 2. *Each Benedictus was connected with a son of David.* The first was a grateful acknowledgment of the anointing of *a* Son of David to be King; the second was in thankful anticipation of the coming of *the* Son of David to be Prophet, Priest, and King. Note: all the praises of Scripture connect themselves directly or indirectly with Christ. 3. *Each Benedictus was elicited by God's gracious fulfilment of His promise.* The first commemorated the realization of the promise of a successor made through the prophet Nathan (2 Sam. vii. 12); the second, the (proximate) fulfilment of the promises of a Saviour, made by "all the holy prophets since the world began" (Luke i. 70), and of which the promise of 2 Sam. vii., was a foretaste and pledge. Note: in all ages the faithfulness of God has elicited the thankfulness of his people.

II. But let us now consider their points of contrast. These are four in number, and show how the thanksgiving of David was for temporal, and that of Zacharias for spiritual benefits. 1. The Benedictus of David celebrated the ascent of the throne of Israel by his Son; that of Zacharias, the leaving of the throne of Heaven by the Son of God. Solomon was beginning his glory: Jesus had laid His aside. Solomon was going to be ministered unto: Jesus to minister to others. 2. The Benedictus of David commemorated the gift of a son to rule His people: that of Zacharias, the gift of a Saviour to redeem the world (vers. 68, 77, 79). 3. The Benedictus of David proclaimed that the succession to the throne was preserved in his house: that of Zacharias, that through the "house of David" a "horn of salvation" was raised up for men. The aged king, doubtless, thought that in Solomon God had "made the horn of David to bud" (Ps. cxxxii. 17); but Zacharias celebrated the true fulfilment of that promise—its blossoming into salvation. 4. The Benedictus of David celebrated the reign of a son who should be a man of peace (1 Chron. xxii. 9): that of Zacharias, the coming of one who should guide men's "feet into the way of peace" (ver. 79). We said each Benedictus was a sort of *Nunc Dimittis.* That last sentence of David's—"Mine eyes also seeing it"—carry our thoughts to another of the Evangelical Hymns, the *Nunc Dimittis* of Simeon —"Mine eyes have seen Thy salvation." Zacharias was not a greater poet than David. And David, as well as he, spake by the Holy Ghost (2 Sam. xxiii. 2). Yet how much grander, and every way nobler, is the Benedictus of the latter than that of the former; of the New Testament than the Old. It is because the theme is so much higher, and the benefits are so much greater, because "a greater than Solomon is here."

The two triumphal entries.—Twice in the history of Jerusalem has a Son of David ridden through her streets, sitting on ass or mule, amid the shouts and praises of the people. Let us compare the two occasions. They will furnish a further proof and illustration of the typical character of Solomon; a further proof that a "greater than Solomon is here." Observe—

I. THE TRIUMPHAL RIDE THROUGH THE CITY WAS IN EACH CASE AFTER AN ANOINTING.—Solomon had been anointed by prophet and priest: JESUS, the Divine Solomon, by God himself. Solomon's anointing was with holy oil out of the tabernacle (ver. 39); that of Jesus with the Holy Ghost (Luke iv. 18; Acts iv. 27; x. 38). Solomon was anointed to be king: Jesus to be King, and Priest, and Prophet.

II. EACH RODE THROUGH THE CITY AS KING (vers. 34, 35).—"God save King Solomon," cried the populace. "Blessed is the king that cometh in the name of the Lord" (Luke xix. 38). In each case the words were true, "Behold thy King cometh" (Matt. xxi. 5; John xii. 15). And

III. EACH RODE AS THE SON OF DAVID (1 Kings i. 43; Matt. xxi. 9).—Did the populace remember the triumphal progress of Solomon, one thousand years before, through those same streets, as they cried, "Hosanna to the *Son of David*" (Matt. xxi. 9—15).

IV. EACH RODE AMID THE ACCLAMATIONS OF THE PEOPLE.—Each, that is to say, was acknowledged as king by popular acclaim. In each case, a curious Oriental hyperbole expresses the enthusiastic rejoicing and the deafening cries of the throng. "The earth rent" (1 Kings i. 40). "The stones would immediately cry out" (Luke xix. 40; cf. Matt. xxi. 10). But here the resemblance ends. Henceforward how great and striking is the contrast.

I. ALL THE GREAT PEOPLE SURROUNDED SOLOMON: OUR LORD WAS PRECEDED AND FOLLOWED BY THE POOR. The dignitaries of the realm, both in church and state, prophet and priest, soldier and civilian, all assembled to do Solomon honour. But our Lord had none of these to do Him reverence. "Master, rebuke Thy disciples" (Luke xix. 39). The pomp and grandeur were all on the side of Solomon.

II. SOLOMON WENT TO SIT ON HIS THRONE: JESUS TO SUFFER AND REIGN ON THE CROSS. The former rode to ease and glory and pomp and unparalleled magnificence; the latter to shame and spitting, to denial and death. But, *crux scala caeli*.

III. SOLOMON RODE TO GLORY: JESUS TO BRING OTHERS TO GLORY. The triumphal entry of Solomon was an ordinary thing. Such royal progresses have often been before and since. But never has the world seen such an entry as that of our Redeemer. He might have reigned as a king, but He chose to suffer as a felon: He might have lived for self, He chose to die for others. Shall we deny Him our hosannas? Shall not earth and heaven ring with His praises?

HOMILIES BY VARIOUS AUTHORS.

Ver. 5.—*The sin of ambition.* Ambition is not always wrong. It is a common inspiration; and when the desire for distinction is associated with fitness for it, the call to effort and advance is from God. But for such ambition the world would stagnate. When the schoolboy is working for a prize, when the writer or speaker resolves to be amongst the foremost men of his age, when the man of business presses on towards the front ranks in the commercial world, we see what should be applauded and not condemned, so long as lawful objects are sought by lawful means. Let us, in all our pursuits, remember God's laws for exaltation. Men are to go higher, when they have fulfilled the duties of the lower sphere. They are to rise on performances, and not on discontent. Hence, if ambition be conscientious, it will prompt to the minutely faithful performance of trivial duties. With a tireless hand crooked things will be made straight, and rough places plain, before the glory is revealed. If, however, ambition be not ruled by righteousness, or modified by love, if it is regardless of the rights of others and of the will of God, then it is a sin; the sin which was the herald of disobedience and death, the source of the tyranny and bloodshed which have desolated the world. It was this sin of which Adonijah was guilty when he "exalted himself, saying, I will be king!" Let us see wherein the sinfulness of his sin lay.

I. THIS AMBITION PROMPTED ADONIJAH TO AN INFRINGEMENT OF THE DIVINE ORDINANCE. It has been said that his act was natural, though foolishly precipitate; for, according to the usual law of primogeniture, he had a right to expect the throne. But the law of primogeniture was never the law of the kingdom of Israel, which in spirit was a theocracy throughout. The invisible King distinctly reserved to himself the right of appointment (Deut. xvii. 14, 15). True, seniority was a tacit indication of the Divine will, but this was always overruled by any special revelation of God's choice. He who had chosen David from amongst his brothers, chose Solomon, and there was fitness in the choice; not only because as a man of peace he was qualified to build the Temple (1 Chron. xxii. 8, 9), but also because his succession was a pledge to his parents, and to all the people, that after the death of their first child the sin of David and Bathsheba was buried in oblivion (comp. Psa. li. 2, 7, 9, with Isa. xliii. 25, &c.). This Divine choice was publicly known. Nathan sided with Solomon not as "the leader of a court cabal," but as the prophet of the Lord; and Adonijah himself was well aware of the election of his brother (ch. ii. 15). When Adonijah said "I will be king," he deliberately set up his will against God's. A deep significance underlies God's choice of men. He elects according to fitness and fits according to election, so that there is ultimate harmony between circumstances and character. The two sons of Zebedee were taught this. They had as much seeming right to the place of honour which they sought as had Adonijah to the throne. They belonged to "the twelve," were personally beloved of their Lord, and their mother was related to the Virgin Mary, and was of those who ministered to Jesus. But Jesus said, "to sit on my right hand and on my left is not mine to give, but it shall be given to those for whom it is *prepared* of my Father." In other words, honours would be given by law and not by favour; not from arbitrary impulse, but from a knowledge of what was right and fitting. Draw lessons of contentment from the assurance that our lot is appointed by God. Show the necessity for our own sakes of submissiveness in prayer, lest God should give us our request and send leanness into our soul.

II. THIS AMBITION WAS A CRAVING FOR OUTWARD HONOUR, AND NOT FOR INWARD WORTH. "*He prepared him chariots and horsemen and fifty men to run before him.*" His ambition was to have these for their own sakes, not to increase his influence for good. Nor was he the last man who cared for glitter and show. The candidate for a competitive examination, who seeks only for honours, and cares nothing for the learning and studious habits which may be acquired, will never be a true student. So with the professional man who works for money only, &c. Honours thus won are unsatisfying and transient. Their worth is fitly represented in the ceremonies observed at the coronation of a Pope. The M. C. holds in one hand a lighted taper, and in the other a reed surmounted by a piece of flax. The flax is ignited and flashes up into light, but in a few moments the flame dies out and the thin ashes fall at the Pontiff's feet, while a sonorous voice chants the words, "Pater sanctus, sic transit gloria mundi." The pagans understood to some extent the lesson we seek to enforce. Their temple of honour had only one entrance, and that was through the temple of virtue. Over the gates of the kingdom of Christ these words are written, "He that humbleth himself shall be exalted, and he that exalteth himself shall be abased." In the day when spiritual realities shall be revealed there shall be not the glorification, but the "*manifestation* of the sons of God," and in the outcome of character inwrought by God's Spirit true and lasting glory shall be found.

III. THIS AMBITION ASSERTED ITSELF WITH A COMPLETE DISREGARD FOR THE RIGHTS OF OTHERS.—David still reigned; Solomon was his appointed successor; but Adonijah trampled their rights beneath his feet as he mounted the throne. Selfishness is the chief of those elements in ambition which constitute its sinfulness.

Hence we may test ambition, by asking ourselves how we regard our competitors. If a man envies others ; if, without compunction, he will crush another to the wall that he may pass him by ; if he refuses to help another in sore straits, who is within his reach, on the ground that every man is for himself ; then his ambition is a sin. This is more clearly revealed by our Lord than by the old dispensation.   He has taught us not only to love our neighbours, but our competitors, and even our foes. He has urged us to " bear one another's burdens," to deny ourselves, and take up our cross to follow Him.   The Christian Church has a sacrifice for its basis, and a cross for its banner.

IV. THIS AMBITION WAS NURTURED IN DEFIANCE OF SIGNIFICANT WARNING. Adonijah repeated his brother's offence.   (Comp. 2 Sam. xv.)   He knew how that bright young life had closed in darkness, when Absalom died helpless and unpitied by the hand of Joab.   He had often seen his father sitting looking at himself with a far-off look in his eyes, as if he still were saying, "O, Absalom, would God I had died for thee, O Absalom, my son, my son !"   Yet the same sin which had been so signally punished he resolved to commit.   History is crowded with illustrations of the fact that men who have lived as Adonijah did have found their honours unsatisfying, and have died in disappointment and despair.   Alexander, who conquered the world, died, after setting fire to a city, in a scene of awful debauchery. Hannibal, who at one time could fill three bushels with the gold rings of fallen knights, died by poison, administered by his own hand, unwept in a foreign land. Cæsar, who conquered eight hundred cities, fell stabbed to the heart by his friends, in the place of his noblest triumph.   Napoleon, the conqueror of Europe, died a heart-broken captive.   It has been writ large, in letters of blood, so that he who runs may read, " the expectation of the wicked shall be cut off !"

Conclusion.—Will you, with the nobler possibilities set before you in the gospel, whom angel voices are calling to higher things, whose conscience is whispering of duty and love, to whom Christ, the suffering Saviour, the King of Glory, says, " Follow Me !" will you, like Adonijah, turn to the ways of self-indulgence and vainglory, to prove as he did that " the wages of sin is death."—A. R.

Ver. 6.—*Moral ruin in a religious home.*   It is a notorious fact that the sons of devout men sometimes prove a curse to their parents, and bring dishonour on the cause of God.   When sin entered the world, it caused the earth, on which flowers had aforetime blossomed, to bring forth thorns and briars. This is a picture of a sad truth, known in the first home, and in many another since.   Eve rejoiced over the fair child she had "gotten from the Lord," and did not suspect that passions were sleeping within him which would nerve his arm to strike the fatal blow which slew his brother and destroyed his mother's peace.   Such sorrow has been experienced in subsequent history.   Isaac's heart was rent by the deceit of Jacob and the self-will of Esau.   Jacob found his own sin repeated against himself, for he who had deceived his father when he was old and blind, suffered an agony of grief for years, because he was falsely told by his sons that Joseph was dead. Probably few have had more domestic sorrow than David.   He experienced, in its bitterest form, the grief of a parent who has wished that before his son had brought such dishonour on the home, he had been, in the innocence of his childhood, laid to rest beneath the daisies.   Of David's sons, Amnon, the eldest, after committing a hideous sin, had been assassinated by the order of Absalom, his brother.   Absalom himself had rebelled against his father, and had been killed by Joab, as he hung helpless in the oak.   Chileab (or Daniel) was dead.   And now of the fourth son, the eldest surviving, Adonijah, this sad story is told.   Adonijah's sin seems so unnatural at first sight that we must try and discover the sources whence so bitter and desolating a stream flowed.   We shall find them in THREE ADVERSE INFLUENCES AROUND HIM AT HOME, which are hinted at in our text.

I. ADONIJAH INHERITED A CONSTITUTIONAL TENDENCY _ AMBITION AND SELF-CONCEIT.   His association with Absalom is not without significance.   The two brothers were alike in their sin and in the tendencies which led to it.   These were inherited.

(1) *The law that "like produces like,"* which is proved to demonstration in the breeding of lower animals (illustrations from horses bred for speed or endurance, dogs for fleetness or scent, pigeons for swiftness or beauty, &c.), asserts itself in man. Not only are *physical* qualities inherited, so that we recognise a "family likeness" between children of the same parents; but *mental* qualities are inherited too ; statesmanship, heroism, or artistic gift, reappearing in the same family for generations. *Moral tendencies* are transmitted too ; and Scripture exemplifies it. If Isaac is so luxurious that he must have his savoury dish, we do not so much wonder that Esau, his son. sells his birthright for a mess of pottage. If Rebekah, like Laban her brother, is greedy and cunning, her son Jacob inherits her tendency, and must live a life of suffering, and present many an agonising prayer before he is set free from his besetting sin. So is it still. The drunkard gives to his offspring a craving for drink, which is a disease. In more senses than one, "The evil that men do lives after them." Surely, then, when not only future happiness, but the destiny of children depends on the choice of a life partner, there should be regard paid not merely to physical beauty, or mental endowment, or social position, but, above all these, to moral and spiritual worth.

(2) *It is argued that this law of moral heritage affects personal responsibility;* that it is hardly fair to condemn a man for a sin to which he is naturally prone. But "shall not the Judge of all the earth do right?" Whatever your parentage, you are not "committed to do these abominations." If the *disposition* be evil, it need never become the *habit* of life. It is something you may yield to, but it is something you may resist; for "He is faithful who will not suffer you to be tempted above what you are able to bear." Rather should any tendencies to evil be recognised as God's voice calling attention to the weak places of character, that there we may keep most eager watch and ward. And because we are weak, He has sent His Son to bring deliverance to the captives, that through Him we may be inspired with hope, and fitted with strength, and rejoice in the liberty wherewith Christ makes His people free.

II. ADONIJAH WAS MISLED BY ADULATION. "*He was also a very goodly man.*" Physically, as well as morally, he was a repetition of Absalom. His parents were guilty of partiality. David loved him the more because (like the lost boy) Adonijah was so fair, so noble in mien, so princely in stature. Courtiers and soldiers (who looked, as they did in Saul's time, for a noble-looking king) flattered him. Joab and Abiathar joined the adulators. Intoxicated with vanity, Adonijah set up a royal court, as Absalom had done (see ver. 5). Every position in life has its own temptations. The ill-favoured child who is the butt at school and the scapegoat at home is tempted to bitterness and revenge. His character is likely to be unsightly, as a plant would be, which grows in a damp, dark vault. There can be little beauty if there is no sunshine. On the other hand, if the gift of physical beauty attracts attention and wins admiration, or if conversational power be brilliant, &c., it is a source of peril. Many a one has thus been befooled into sin and misery, or entrapped into an unhappy marriage, and by lifelong sadness paid the penalty of folly, or venturing too far, prompted by ambition, has fallen, like Icarus when his waxen wings melted in the sunshine. When that time of disappointment and disenchantment comes, happy is it when such an one, like the prodigal, comes to himself, and says, "I will arise, and go to my father!"

III. ADONIJAH WAS UNDISCIPLINED AT HOME. "*His father had not displeased him at any time in saying, Why hast thou done so?*" This refers not only to the special act of rebellion, but to the tendencies and habits leading up to it, which David had not checked, for fear of vexing the high-spirited lad. The weak indulgence of children (such as that which Eli exhibited) is the cause of untold misery. Not many parents blazon abroad the story of their domestic grief. Loyal hands draw down the veil over the discord at home, and that agony of prayer which is heard by "the Father who seeth in secret." You do not see the girl who mars the beauty of her early womanhood by a flippant disregard of her parents, and whose own pleasure seems to be the only law of her life. You do not see the child whose hasty passion and uncontrolled temper are the dread of the household ; who, by his ebullitions of rage, gets what he wishes, till authority is disregarded and trodden underfoot. You do not see the son who thinks it manly to be callous to a mother's anxiety and a father's counsels, who likes to forget home associations, and is sinking in haunts of evil, where you may weep over him as a wreck. But, though you see them not, they exist. Far otherwise, in some of these sad experiences, it might have been. Suppose there had been firm resolution instead of habitual indulgence; suppose that authority had been asserted and used in days before these evil habits were formed; suppose that, instead of leaving the future to chance, counsels and prayers had moulded character during moulding-time—might there not have been joy where now there is grief? Heavy are our responsibilities as parents. Yet splendid are our possibilities! These children who may prove our curses may, with God's blessing on our fidelity, grow up to be wise, pure-hearted, courageous men of God, who will sweeten the atmosphere of the home, and purge this nation of its sins, and make the name of "the King of saints" honoured and praised throughout the world! "Train them up in the nurture and admonition of the Lord."—A. R.

Vers. 39–41.—*The dethronement of the false by the enthronement of the true.* When Bathsheba and Nathan brought David news of Adonijah's revolt, and told him that Joab and Abiathar were at the coronation feast at En-rogel, it is noteworthy that the king made no direct attack on the conspirators. He merely commanded that Solomon should be seated on the royal mule, that he should ride in state to Gihon, and that there Zadok should anoint him king, and proclaim by the sound of trumpet that he was appointed ruler. It was this which paralysed the traitorous assembly. The sound of the trumpet was to their scheme what the blast of the rams' horns was to the walls of Jericho, when they fell in irreparable ruin. David's method was the wisest, the surest; for it not only removed a present evil, but provided a future good. The lesson is obvious, and is susceptible of wide application; that the false is most surely dethroned by the enthronement of the true. The strong man armed keeps his goods in peace, until a stronger than he shall come. (See Luke xi. 21, 22.) Suggest: applications of this principle.

I. Vain thoughts are to be expelled by the incoming of what is wise and good. The Psalmist hated "vain thoughts," because he loved God's law (Psa. cxix. 113). When the heart is empty, swept, and garnished, there is room for worse evils to come (Matt. xii. 44). The full mind and heart are safe. Apply to the conquest of wandering thoughts in worship, of vanity in children, &c.

II. Self-will is to be conquered by a nobler and stronger will. We are early taught this. Every child carries out his own wishes without regard to others, till he recognizes that the parent's will is authoritative. Sooner or later there is a struggle, and only when it is decided in one way is there rest. Similarly we have to learn to subordinate our thoughts to God's revelation, our wishes to His will, and this lesson is more painfully learnt as the years pass by and the habit of self-rule grows stronger.

III. Unworthy affections are to be overcome by a worthy love. When love is set on the unworthy, force is useless, argument is vain. But if the love is diverted to a nobler object, it naturally disentangles its tendrils from the unworthy. In the highest sphere it may be said of love to our Lord, "that love shall all vain love expel."

IV. Error is to be subdued by truth. The hatred of artizans to machinery when first introduced was not conquered by dragoons, nor by prisons, but by the discovery on their part of the mistake they had ignorantly made. So with all errors. We shall not destroy heathenism by the abuse of the idols, but by the presentation of Christ.

V. Care is to be extirpated by prayer. In many hearts care is enthroned. To many a one our Lord might say, "Thou art careful and troubled about many things." We cannot reason away our anxieties, nor force them from our minds, but we can have the rest our children have, who never trouble about the morrow, because they trust in us. It would be vain to say, "Be careful for nothing," unless the apostle could add the alternative, "*but* in everything, by prayer and supplication, with thanksgiving, make your requests known unto God; and the peace of God which passeth all understanding shall keep your hearts and minds."

VI. EVILS REIGNING IN SOCIETY ARE TO BE OVERTHROWN BY WHAT IS NOBLER THAN THEY.—Apply this broadly, *e.g.*, wholesome literature must defeat pernicious. Low amusements, intoxicating drinks, &c., will pass away when there is the establishment of nobler substitutes for these.

The whole subject is summed up in Christ—the true King of humanity, the incarnation of all that is worthy of being loved and enthroned. Draw the analogy between Solomon the anointed king, as he rides on the mule into Jerusalem amid the acclamations of the people, and the entry of our Lord into Jerusalem as described Matt. xxi. If worldliness, or selfishness, or ambition, or lust has been reigning in your heart, the usurped will be dethroned when you welcome Christ as King and say, " O Lord our God, other lords besides thee have had dominion over us, but now we acknowledge Thee to be our Lord, to the glory of God the Father."

> Descend to Thy Jerusalem, O Lord,
> Her faithful children cry with one accord;
> Come, ride in triumph on; behold, we lay
> Our guilty lusts and proud wills in Thy way.
>
> Thy road is ready, Lord; Thy paths, made straight,
> In longing expectation seem to wait
> The consecration of Thy beauteous feet,
> And, hark, hosannas loud Thy footsteps greet.—A. R.

EXPOSITION.

CHAPTER II. 1—11.

THE LAST WORDS AND DEATH OF DAVID. —The death of David, and of course the charge which preceded it, did not follow immediately (as the casual reader might be tempted to suppose) on the events related in chap. i. We find from 1 Chron. xxiii.— xxix. 23, that the aged king recovered sufficient strength to leave his sick room, to gather round him the princes of Israel (1 Chron. xxiii. 2), to make a number of fresh arrangements respecting the priests and Levites and the services of the sanctuary, and even to "stand up upon his feet" (1 Chron. xxviii. 2) and address a large assembly respecting the erection and adornment of the Temple. And once more, in strains which are among the noblest and sweetest which the sweet singer of Israel ever penned, he "blessed the Lord before all the congregation" (ch. xxix. 10. sqq.); he also instituted festal sacrifices on a scale of great magnificence, and witnessed a second and probably more formal and public consecration of his son to the kingly office (vers. 21, 22; cf. 1 Sam. xi. 15; 2 Sam. v. 3). But the recovery cannot have been otherwise than transient—it was

but the sudden brightening of the flame before it dies out in the socket—and we see him in this second chapter, once more in the ante-chamber of death. Now, he has already given his parting charge to the princes of the realm, and has publicly exhorted Solomon to discharge his duties faithfully (2 Chron. xxviii. 9, 10); but as he feels the end approaching, he summons him to his side to impart to him his last and private instructions, and addresses him thus:

Ver. 1.—**I go the way** [lit., I am walking (same word as in ver. 3) in the way] **of all the earth** [*i.e.*, of all the sons of earth, all mankind (cf. 1 Sam. 17, 46; 1 Kings x., 24; Psa. lxvi. 4, &c.) The path to Sheol, the path which all his forefathers, and untold millions more, have trod, he is treading it now. The words sound like a reminiscence of Josh. xxiii. 24. Perhaps, too, the thought of Joshua suggested to his mind the next words]: **but be thou strong, and be a man.** [Similar, though not identical, words were four times addressed to Joshua (Josh. i. 6, 7, 9, 18), and David may well have thought that his son, in entering upon his difficult duties, was not at all unlike Joshua when he succeeded Moses in the leadership of Israel, and that he needed similar encouragement. It is not necessary to suppose, as Canon Rawlinson does (" Speaker's Com.," vol. ii. p. 489), that in the words, " show thyself a man," we have a reference· to Solomon's *youth;* for words precisely similar were addressed to each other by the Philistines at Aphek (1 Sam. iv. 9). The age of Solomon at his accession is very doubtful. David said, " Solomon my son is young and tender " (1 Chron. xxii. 5; xxix. 1) ; and Solomon says of himself, " I am a little child " נַעַר קָטֹן (1 Kings iii. 7). Josephus, probably reflecting the tradition of his time, fixes his age at fourteen ; Eupolemus at twelve. I incline to think that the words " young and tender" almost forbid the favourite opinion that he was about twenty.]

Ver. 3.—**And keep the charge** [lit., " watch the watch " (*custodies custodiam Jehovae*), or, " serve the service." Bähr paraphrases, " be a true watcher in the service of Jehovah." The words are constantly employed to denote a strict performance of the service of the tabernacle or of the duties of the priests and Levites (Lev. viii. 35; xviii. 30; Numb. i. 53; iii. 7, 8, 25, 28, 32, 38 ; xxxi. 30 ; 1 Chron. xxiii. 32, &c. ; also Gen. xxvi. 5). " The reference," says Rawlinson, " is to the charge given to all the kings in Deut. xvii. 18—20." But there is no necessity for restricting it to that one injunction. What the charge is is explained presently] **of the Lord thy God to walk in His ways, to keep** [same word] **His statutes, and His commandments, and His judgments, and His testimonies** [it is impossible to draw any clear and sharp distinction between these four words, as the older expositors do. " The phrase is derived from the Pentateuch " (Wordsworth). The force of the accumulation of practically synonymous terms is to represent the law in its entirety (*"Die Totalität des Gesetzes,"* Keil) ; cf. Deut. v. 31, viii. 11, and especially Psa. cxix.], **that thou mayest prosper.** [The marginal rendering, " do wisely," is preferred by some (Keil, *e.g.*) ; but the translation of the text has the authority of Gesenius and others on its side, and gives a better meaning. " The context evidently requires 'prosper' here, as in Josh. i. 7 " (Rawlinson). " That thou mayest . . . *do wisely* " is a very lame and impotent conclusion to ver. 3. We have here an evident reminiscence of Josh. i. 7 ; possibly also of Deut. xxix. 9. David was unquestionably well versed in the Scriptures of that age, of which every king was commanded to make a copy.

Ver. 4.—**That the Lord may continue** [rather, " establish " (*ut confirmet*), as it is rendered in 2 Sam. vii. 25, where this same

word of promise is spoken of. Cf. 1 Kings viii. 26] **His word which He spake concerning me** [by the mouth of Nathan, 2 Sam. vii. 12—17 (cf. Psa. lxxxix. 4) ; or David may refer to some subsequent promise made to him directly. In the promise of 2 Sam. vii. there is no mention of any stipulations, *"If thy children," &c.* But both here and in Psa. cxxxii. 12, and in 1 Kings viii. 25, special prominence is given to the *condition* (*dum se bene gesserint*), which no doubt was understood, if not expressed, when the promise was first made], **saying, If thy children take heed to** [lit., " keep," same word as in vers. 2, 3] **their way, to walk before me in truth with all their heart and with all their soul there shall not fail thee** [lit., " be cut off to thee," as marg. (cf. 1 Sam ii. 29; Josh. ix. 23). This word does not occur in the original promise made through Nathan. But it *does* occur in subsequent versions of the promise, 1 Kings viii. 25, ix. 5, as well as here—a strong presumption that the promise must have been repeated to David in another shape], **said he, a man on the throne of Israel.**

But this thought—that the permanence of his dynasty depended on the faithful observance of the law as it is written in the book of Moses (*i.e.*, in all its details), seems to have reminded the dying man that he himself had not always kept the statutes he was urging his successor to keep. It had been his duty as king, as the power ordained of God, to visit all violations of the law of God with their appropriate penalties ; and this duty, in some instances at least, had been neglected. For the law of Moses, reaffirming the primæval law which formed part of the so-called " precepts of Noah " (Gen. 6)—that ix. blood must be expiated by blood—enjoined, with singular emphasis and distinctness, the death of the murderer (Numb. xxxv. 16, 17, 18, 19, 30—33 ; Exod. xxi. 14). It declared that so long as murder remained unpunished, the whole land was defiled and under a curse (Numb. xxxv. 33). And it gave the king no power to pardon, no discretion in the matter. Until the red stain of blood was washed out " by the blood of him that shed it " the Divine Justice was not satisfied, and a famine or pestilence or sword might smite the land. Now, David knew all this : he could not fail to know it, for he had seen his country, a few years before, visited by a famine because of the unavenged blood of the Gibeonites (2 Sam. xxi. 1). And yet, one notorious and infamous murderer had *not* been put to death. The assassin of Abner and of Amasa still polluted the earth, still occupied a distinguished position, and defied punishment. But if the law of Moses was to be kept, then, whatever it might cost, and however painful it might be (Deut. xix. 13), he must die; and David, for the welfare of his kingdom, the stability of his throne, and above all, the honour of God, must require his death. No doubt it had often burdened his mind, especially during these last days of feebleness, the thought that punishment had been so long delayed; and therefore, as he sees the end approaching, he feels that he must enjoin upon his successor the fulfilment of that duty which he had been too "weak" to discharge (2 Sam. iii. 39). Hence he proceeds,

Ver. 5.—"**Moreover, thou knowest also what Joab, the son of Zeruiah** [there is no "emphasis on these words: he who was mine own sister's son," as Wordsworth, see on i. 11], **did to me and** [this last word has no place in the original, and should be left out, as it is misleading. It makes David demand the death of Joab partly because of the *private injuries* he had suffered at his hands, and partly because of his two brutal murders mentioned presently. But this is just what David did not do; for he is careful to *exclude* all mention of his private wrongs. It is true, he says, "what Job did *to me*," but that is because "the sovereign is smitten in the subject" (Bp. Hall), and because the first of these murders had caused David to be suspected of complicity, while each had deprived him of an able officer. And the words that follow] **what he did to the two captains of the hosts of Israel** [these words are clearly explicative of the "what he did to me." Only thus can we explain the absence of the "*and*"] **unto Abner the son of Ner** [2 Sam. iii. 27. This was one of those foul murders to which the law expressly denied any right of sanctuary, for it was "with guile" (Exod. xxi. 14). Joab "took Abner aside in the gate to speak with him peaceably, and smote him there in the abdomen"], **and unto Amasa the son of Jether** [or Ithra. In 2 Sam. xxvii. 24, Ithra is called "an Israelite," an obvious mistake for "Ishmaelite," as indeed it stands in 1 Chron. ii. 17. Amasa's mother, Abigail, was sister of David and Zeruiah; Amasa, consequently, was Joab's first

cousin. This murder was even fouler than that of Abner. Here there were ties of blood; they were companions in arms, and there was no pretence of a *vendetta*], **whom he slew and shed** [lit., "put," a somewhat strange expression. It almost looks as if עָלָיו, "upon him," had dropped out. The meaning "make," which Keil assigns to שִׂים is not borne out by his references, Deut. xiv. 1; Exod. x. 2. "Showed," "displayed," is nearer the original], **the blood of war in peace** [the meaning is obvious. Blood might lawfully be shed in time of war, in fair fight; and Joab might have slain the two captains in battle without guilt. But he slew them when they were at peace with him and unprepared, by treachery], **and put the blood of war** [the LXX. has αἷμα ἀθῷον, "innocent blood"] **upon his girdle that was about his loins, and in his shoes that were on his feet** [we are not to suppose that the girdle and sandal are mentioned as "*die Zeichen des Kriegerstandes*" (Bähr), *i.e.*, military insignia; nor yet that the idea is "*from* the girdle *to* the sandal" (Ewald), *i.e.*, copiously. These are usual (hardly "principal," as Keil) articles of Eastern dress, of the civilian's as well as of the soldier's, and these two are mentioned because, no doubt, the horrible details of the two murders, and especially of the last (see 2 Sam. xx. 8), had been reported to David. He had been told at the time how the blood of Amasa had spurted on to the girdle of Joab, and streamed down into his sandals, and these details, which no doubt made a deep impression upon his mind, are recited here to show how dastardly and treacherous was the deed, and how thoroughly Joab was stained with innocent blood, blood which cried to heaven for vengeance (Gen. iv. 10)].

Ver. 6.—**Do therefore according to thy wisdom** [cf. Prov. xx. 26. It needed great discretion in exacting the punishment of death in the case of one who was so powerful, who had such influence with the army and the people, whose crimes had been passed over for so long a time, to whom David was so much indebted—Joab had partly won and had twice preserved for him his crown—and to whom he was allied by ties of blood. To act precipitately or unwisely might provoke a revolution], **and let not his hoar head** [see on ver. 9. Joab, though David's nephew, could not have been much his junior, and David was now seventy] **go down to the grave in peace.** [He must die a violent, not a natural death, as Corn. à Lap. This expression, no doubt, looks vindictive, but that is solely because we forget the character of the Old Testament dispensation (as one of *temporal* rewards and punishments. See the "Expositor," vol. iii. p. 114), the position of David as king (as the authorized dispenser of punishments, and as responsible to God for dispensing them without fear or favour), and the principles of the Mosaic code (as a *lex talionis*, demanding blood for blood, and requiring the magistrates and people to purge themselves of the guilt of blood by demanding "the blood of him that shed it"). Let these considerations be borne in mind, and there is absolutely no warrant for charging David with malevolence. Wordsworth lays stress on the fact that Joab had not repented of his crimes. But we need have recourse to no such suppositions. The Jewish law afforded no place of repentance to the murderer. No amount of contrition would cleanse the land of blood. The *temporal* penalty must be paid. In the case of David himself, it was only commuted by special revelation (2 Sam xii. 10, 13, 14), not remitted.

Ver. 7.—**And to the sons of Barzillai** [the "Beni-Barzillai" would include son, or sons, and all other descendants. It is highly probable, though it is not expressly stated, that Chimham was the son of Barzillai (2 Sam. xix. 37). Rawlinson says, "Who the other sons were is not known." It would be more correct to say that we do not know whether there were any other sons. The family was still existing *temp.* Ezra (Ezra ii. 61), where, it is worth noticing, we read of the *daughters* of Barzillai (cf. Nehem. vii. 63). In Jeremiah xli. 17, we read of the "habitation (גֵּרוּת, caravanserai, khan) of Chemoham," where the Keri has Chimham. It has been argued from the mention of this name, and the fact that their khan was near Bethlehem, that David or Solomon gave the family land there], **and let them be of those that eat at thy table** [*i.e.*, of those who have their sustenance from the royal table, not necessarily at it (Keil) ; cf. Dan. i. 5 ; 2 Kings xxv. 29. Presence *at* the table is expressed by עַל שֻׁלְחָן (2 Sam. ix. 11, 12). It was esteemed an essential part of royal munificence throughout the East that the king should feed a large number of retainers and dependants. Cf. the account of Solomon's daily provision in 1 Kings iv. 22, 23 ; also 2 Sam. xix. 28; Judges i. 7] ; **for so** [*i.e.*, in like manner, with *food*] ; **they came to me** [lit., "*came near*." The Hebrew קָרַב often includes, as here, the idea of succour. Cf. Ps. lxix. 19 ; Lam. iii. 57. Barzillai certainly came (2 Sam. xvii. 27), and probably **Chimham**, but the Speaker's Commentary is mistaken when it says that "Chimham is mentioned as present." He was present at the return of David (2 Sam. xix. 31, 38, but not necessarily before] **when I fled because of** [lit., "from the face of"] **Absalom thy brother.**

The mention of Absalom, and those terrible days of revolt and anarchy, when he was constrained to flee for his life, seems to have reminded the dying king of one of the bitterest ingredients of that bitter cup of shame and suffering—the cruel curses of Shimei. He remembers that the sin of Shimei, which was nothing else than treason and blasphemy, has so far escaped punishment. In a moment of generous enthusiasm, he had included Shimei in the general amnesty which he proclaimed on his return (2 Sam. xix. 23). He had thought, no doubt, at the time only of the offence against himself; he had forgotten his sacred and representative character as "the Lord's anointed;" or if he had remembered it (ver. 21) the emotions of that memorable day had obscured or perverted his sense of justice and duty. But he has since realized—and the thought weighs upon his conscience in the chamber of death—that he then pardoned what he had no power to pardon, viz., a sin to which the Mosaic law attached the penalty of death. For blasphemy, as for murder, there was no expiation short of the death of the blasphemer (Lev. xxiv. 14—16 ; cf. 1 Kings xxi. 10, 13) ; and blasphemy, like murder, though not perhaps to the same extent, involved those who heard it in its guilt, until they had discharged themselves of their sin upon the head of the guilty (Lev. xiv. 14 ; cf. Lev. v. 1). But Shimei, so far from having suffered the penalty of the law, had been twice protected against it ; twice preserved alive, in defiance of law, by the supreme magistrate, the executor of law. And David, who has been charging his son to keep the law, now realizes that he himself has been a law-breaker. He has kept his oath, sworn to his own or his people's hurt, and he will keep it to the end. But Solomon is under no such obligation. *He* can demand the long arrears of justice, none the less due because of the time that has elapsed and the royal *laches* ("*nullum tempus occurrit regi*") ; he can deal with the blasphemer as the law directs, and this David now charges him to do.

Ver. 8.—**And, behold, thou hast with thee** [Bähr understands by עִמָּךְ, "near thee," (*in deiner Nähe*) because Bahurim was near Jerusalem. Keil gathers from this word that Shimei "was living at that time in Jerusalem," and refers to ver. 36, which, if anything, implies that he was not. But it is worth suggesting whether Shimei may not be the Shimei to whom reference is made in ch. i. 8. (Dean Stanley notices this as a possibility, but alleges nothing in support of it: "Jewish Church," vol. ii. p. 171, note.) We there find Shimei and Rei mentioned as firm adherents of Solomon at the time of Adonijah's rising, and in these words, they "were not *with Adonijah*." Surely it is not an unfair presumption—if there is nothing to rebut it—that the Shimei subsequently mentioned as "*with*" Solomon is the same person. But it has been objected (*e.g.*, by Kitto) that the false part that Shimei played at the time of Absalom's revolt would have for ever prevented his being recognized and mentioned as one of Solomon's supporters. I very much doubt it The great influence which Shimei possessed must be taken into account. Nothing shows that influence more clearly than the fact that on the day of David's restoration, despite the part he had taken, and the possible disgrace and danger that awaited him, he could still command the attendance of one thousand men of Benjamin (2 Sam. xix. 17). Probably the secret of his influence lay in the fact that he was "of the family of the house of Saul," and possibly, owing to the insignificance of Saul's descendants, was the mainstay and chief representative of that house. And if so, there is nothing at all surprising in the mention of the fact that he was "not with Adonijah," and was subsequently "with" Solomon. It may have been a matter of great consequence at that critical time, which side Shimei—and the thousand or more Benjamites at his back—espoused. And if he *did* then declare for Solomon, it could hardly fail to procure him some amount of favour and consideration. He would thenceforward rank amongst the friends of the young king, and the words "thou hast with thee" would accurately describe his position] **Shimei, the son of Gera** [another Shimei, the son of Elah, is mentioned (1 Kings iv. 11) as Solomon's officer *in Benjamin*. Gera must not be thought of as the "father" of Shimei, except in the sense of ancestor. He was removed from him by many generations, being the son of Bela

and the grandson of Benjamin (Gen. xlvi. 21; cf. 1 Chron. vii. 6). Ehud, three hundred years earlier, is also described as "a son of Gera," Judg. iii. 15] , **a Benjamite** [lit., *the* Benjamite, meaning that Gera, not Shimei, was the Benjamite. He was well known as the son of Benjamin's firstborn (1 Chron. viii. 1), and the head of a house in Benjamin. Professor Gardiner (American translation of Lange, textual note, p. 29), following the LXX. and Vulg., insists that, בֶּן־הַיְמִינִי (with the article) can only mean "son of the Jaminite, *i.e.*, of the descendants of Jamin, a son of Simeon." But this is directly contrary to what we read 2 Sam. xvi., viz., that Shimei was of "a family of the house of Saul," *i.e.*, a Benjamite. And to this the grammar agrees. Judges iii. 15 is an exact parallel, and compare בֵּית־הַשִּׁמְשִׁי, 1 Sam. vi. 14, 18, and בֵּית־הַלַּחְמִי, 1 Sam. xvi. 1, 18; xvii. 58] **of Bahurim** [the name means "*The young men.*" It was some six miles distant from Jerusalem, in Benjamin, and on (or off, as Josephus, Ant. vii. 9, 7, implies) the main road to Jericho and the Jordan valley. It may have lain in one of the wâdies branching out from the ravine which runs continuously alongside the steep descent to Jericho. The event narrated in 2 Sam. iii. 16 as happening at Bahurim may well have served to inflame Shimei's hatred. In spite of his rancorous hostility, however, we gather from 2 Sam. xvii. 18, that David had some faithful adherents there], **which** [lit., "and he"] **cursed me with a grievous** [acc. to Gesenius, *al.*, "strong," *i.e.*, sweeping; Keil, vehement; Thenius, "*heillos*," flagitious. LXX., κατάραν ὀδυνηρὰν. Vulg., *maledictio pessima*] **curse in the day when I went to Mahanaim** [2 Sam. xvi. 5] ; **but he came down to meet me at Jordan** [lit., *the* Jordan, *i.e.*, the descender, so called from the rapidity of the stream (it has a fall of 1400 feet in about 100 miles) or from the steep descents which lead to it. The word always has the defin. art.], **and I sware to him by the Lord, saying, I will not put thee to death with the sword** [2 Sam. xix. 23].

Ver. 9.—**Now therefore** [lit., "*and now.*" Possibly the "now" is a note of time in apposition to the "day" of ver. 8, or rather the time of David's oath. "I then unadvisedly sware unto him, but now the law must have its course." Probably it is merely inferential,—*quae cum ita sint*] **hold him not guiltless** [rather, *thou shalt not leave him unpunished* (Vatablus, Gesen., Bähr, *al.*); cf. Exod. xx. 7 ; Jer. xxx. 11]; **for thou art a wise man** [φρόνιμος rather than σοφός (LXX.) Gesen. renders here, "endued with ability to judge." David clearly desires that wisdom and justice, not malice or passion, should be Solomon's guide], **and knowest what thou oughtest to** [lit., *shalt* or *shouldest*] **do to him ; but** [Heb. *and*] **his hoar head** [mentioned, not maliciously, but with the idea that punishment, which had been long delayed, must overtake him nevertheless. The age of Joab and Shimei would make the Divine Nemesis the more conspicuous. Men would "see that there was a God that judgeth in the earth"] **bring thou down to the grave with blood.** The Auth. Version here needlessly alters the *order* of the original, which should be followed wherever it can be (and it generally can) without sacrifice of idiom and elegance. In this case the alteration, by the slight prominence it gives to "hoar head" and to "blood," gives a factitious harshness to the sentence. The Hebrew stands thus : "And thou shalt bring down his hoar head with blood to Sheol." This order of the words also exhibits somewhat more clearly the sequence of thought, which is this: "Thou art wise, therefore thou knowest what by law thou shouldest do. What thou shalt do is, thou shalt bring down," &c. It is clear from these words that if David was actuated by malice, by a "passionate desire to punish those who had wronged him" (Plumptre, Dict. Bib., art. "Solomon"), or by "fierce and profound vindictiveness" (Stanley, "Jewish Church," vol. ii. p. 135), he was profoundly unconscious of it. If it was "a dark legacy of hate" (*ibid.*) he was bequeathing to Solomon, then he stands before us in these last hours either as an unctuous hypocrite, or as infatuated and inconsistent to the last degree. That the man who, in his opening words (ver. 3), enjoined upon his son, in the most emphatic manner, a strict and literal obedience to the law of Heaven, should in these subsequent words, delivered almost in the same breath, require him to satiate a long-cherished and cruel revenge upon Joab and Shimei (the latter of whom he had twice delivered from death), is an instance of self-contradiction which is almost, if not quite, without parallel. But as I have showed elsewhere, at some length, it is a superficial and entirely erroneous view of David's last words, which supposes them to have been inspired by malice or cruelty. His absorbing idea was clearly this, that he had not "kept the charge of the Lord ; " that he, the chief magistrate, the "revenger to execute wrath," by sparing Joab and Shimei, the murderer and the blasphemer, both of whose lives were forfeited to justice, had failed in his duty, had weakened the sanctions of law, and compromised the honour of the Most High. He is too old and too weak to execute the sentence of the law now, but for the safety of his people, for the security of his throne, it must be done, and therefore Solomon, who was under no obligation to spare the criminals his father had spared, must be required to do it. Of the Jewish king it might be said with a special propriety, "*Rex est lex loquens*," and seldom has the voice of law spoken with greater dignity and fidelity than by David in this dying charge. To say, as Harwood does, (Lange, American Trans., p. 32) that "nothing but sophistry can justify his [David's] charge to Solomon, not to let the unfortunate man [Shimei] die in peace," merely shows how imperfectly the writer has entered into the spirit of the theocratic law, that law under which David lived, and by which alone he could be governed and govern others.

Ver. 10.—**So** [Heb. *and*] **David slept** [Heb. *lay down*]. The idea of שָׁכַב is not that of *sleep* so much as of the recumbent posture of the dead. It points to the grave rather than to Sheol (Gesen.), though the latter idea is not excluded. Wordsworth (after à Lapide) finds here "an assertion of the doctrine of the existence of the soul after death, and of the resurrection of the body," but it is not in the text] **with his fathers** (cf. the Latin expression *abiit ad plures*, and the Greek ἐς πλεόνων ἱκέσθαι], **and was buried in the city of David** [*i.e.* the hill of Zion, which he had fortified, His citadel became his sepulchre, and thenceforward bore his name. Intramural interment was permitted only to prophets and kings. Jerusalem is completely undermined by caves and caverns, and Zion is no exception to the rule. One of these, possibly enlarged, probably became the burying-place of the kings. It was known, not only in Nehemiah's day (Nehem. iii. 15, 16), but down to the age of the apostles (Acts ii. 29). Probably owing to a misunderstanding of St. Peter's words, "his sepulchre is *with us*," &c., the *Coenaculum* is now shown as David's tomb. Josephus says Solomon placed a vast quantity of treasure with the body, three thousand talents of which were taken out by Hyrcanus (Ant. xiii. 8. 4). He has also a curious story of an attempted plunder of the tomb by Herod (Ant. xvi. 7. 1)

Ver. 11.—**And the days that David reigned over Israel were forty years : seven years reigned he in Hebron, and thirty and three years reigned he in Jerusalem** [as elsewhere (1 Chron. xxix. 27), the historian has disregarded the fraction of a year in giving the length of David's reign. He reigned at Hebron, according to 2 Sam. v. 5, "seven years and six months."

HOMILETICS.

Vers. 1—11.—*A Jewish deathbed.* A brilliant poet and essayist once summoned his stepson, the young Earl of Warwick, to his bedside, and with perfect dignity and composure bade him mark "how a Christian man can die." In this section, one far greater, and yet in one sense far less, than Addison,—greater as a poet, as a statesman, as a patriot; less, inasmuch as "he that is least in the kingdom of heaven is greater than he,"—beckons us to the chamber of death, and bids us witness the departure of a pious Jew—of a typical Hebrew of the Hebrews. In one sense, David is the greatest figure in the Old Testament. He alone, of all that are born of women, has been called a "man after God's own heart." And more : If Solomon is of all Old Testament characters the most secular, certainly David is by far the most *spiritual.* Proof : His songs are still chanted in church as well as synagogue, and Christian souls find no fitter expression for their devout longings and aspirations than in the language of his exquisite Psalms. Let us hear his last recorded words. The last utterances of great men are allowed to have a special interest. They have often been intensely characteristic. Let us listen to "the last words of David." Let us carefully notice (1) *What he does say,* and no less carefully (2) *What he does not say.*

I. WHAT HE DOES SAY. 1. *He says he is not afraid to meet death.* His conduct, his demeanour says this. See how calmly he looks it in the face. "I go the way," &c. He hardly knows what death means; knows but little of the life beyond; his hopes and fears are bounded by the pale and shadowy realm of Sheol, but he can trust the living God, and he thinks—he believes—"*they cannot cease to live whom God does not cease to love.*" And so he goes into the gloom and the shadows with the trust of a child that holds the father's hand ; he approaches the grave

> " As one who wraps the drapery of his couch
> About him, and lies down to pleasant dreams."

We have a far nobler creed—a livelier hope than his. Jesus Christ has "brought life and immortality to light." We have heard of the rest of Paradise ; of the resurrection ; of the beatific vision. Shall we then dread to die ? Shall we be put to shame by a Jew ? The Mohammedan calls death the "terminator of delights and the separator of companions." Socrates said, "Whether it is best to live or die, the gods only know." Shall we act as if we had no better belief ? Surely our beneficent religion, and its gospel of immortality, should make us brave to die. 2. *He bids us be mindful of our mortality.* There are Christians who will not think, will not speak of death. Not so David. He saw the end approaching, and he faced it. It is well we should have from time to time, as we constantly have in daily life, in the dispensations of God's providence, a *memento mori.* Pagan and Moslem monarchs have had their heralds daily and publicly remind them of their frailty. The ancient Egyptians would bring a mummy to their feasts. The Kaffirs ever keep the boards for their coffins in their houses. With their dismal and often hopeless creeds, they yet remember death. Shall we, who know that death is but the gate of life, ostrich-like, shut our eyes to it, and all "think all men to be mortal but ourselves ?" 3. *He teaches us in death to think of duty ;* to remember those who will come after us—our friends, enemies, church, and country. He leaves a son "young and tender." He is concerned for his piety, for his prosperity ; and through him, for the piety and prosperity of the nation. He knows that the words of the dying have weight. He will not depart without a solemn dying charge. It is the last best gift he can bestow. The Christian must not die selfishly. Even in pain and feebleness, he must care for others. If he can, he ought to charge his children and connexions ; to warn them, to bless them. Should *he* be less jealous for their present and eternal welfare, or less concerned for the honour and glory of God, than was this dying Jew ? 4. *He reminds us that men die as they have lived.* David has kept the law, "save in the matter of Uriah," &c. His death is of a piece with his life—

it is the natural outcome, the good fruit from a good tree. During life, he has been
very zealous for the Lord God of Israel. The ruling passion displays itself in death.
The great desire of the man who has kept the law is that his son may keep it.   To
die well, one must live well.   The last struggle works no change in the character.
Deathbed repentance is generally delusive.   They deceive *themselves*, who,

> " Dying, put on the weeds of Dominic,
> Or as Franciscans think to pass disguised."

5. *He warns us to set our house in order,* to pay our debts and square our
accounts before we die.   David, we read, " prepared abundantly (for the temple)
before his death."   He has made royal provision for the house that should be built.
But he remembers at last that three debts of his are still undischarged ; a debt of
gratitude to the sons of Barzillai, a debt of retribution to Joab, and another to
Shimei.   " Due punishment of malefactors is the debt of authority " (Bp. Hall).   He
will not, like some, " go on sinning in his grave ; " he will have these debts discharged.   He cannot depart in peace while they burden his conscience.   And we,
too, go where " there is neither work, nor device, nor knowledge," where wrongs
cannot be redressed, where accounts cannot be settled.   Have we any crime uncon-
fessed, or injury unrepaired, any enemy unforgiven ?   " What thou doest, do
quickly."   But let us now consider—
    II. WHAT DAVID DOES NOT SAY.   The silence of Scripture is often golden, is some-
times as instructive as its voices.   Here is a case in point.   The most spiritual of Old
Testament saints—the man after God's own heart—is dying, and he knows it.   He
gives his son his parting counsels, and what are they ?   They are all of this world.
Observe—1. *There is no mention of a future life* ; no " hope full of immortality,"
no talk of reunion, but rather a sad *" vale, vale in aeternum vale."*   The most
remarkable feature in David's last words is, that there is not one word about another
life.   The Christian could not die thus.   Even " half-inspired heathens" have
expressed a livelier hope—witness Cicero's " O præclarum diem cum ad illud divi-
num animorum concilium coetumque proficiscar "—and how immeasurably higher
than this, again, is St. Paul's desire to depart and be with Christ!   " I go the way
of all the earth "—it is like the sound of the clods upon the coffin, without the
faintest whisper of a " *Resurgam.*"   What a contrast between this and the apostle's
exultant cry, " Death is swallowed up in victory ! "   And the very humblest Christian could hardly depart as David did, with absolutely no reference to the realm of
the future.   There would assuredly be some comforting word about the many mansions, the rest for the weary, the gates of pearl, the streets of fine gold.   Of all this
David said nothing, neither in life nor death, because he knew nothing.   He had
hopes, anticipations, convictions almost, as some of the Psalms show, but he had
not what the Christian has, the " full assurance of faith," the " sure and certain
hope of a resurrection to eternal life."   In this respect how much greater was
Addison, how much more " full of all blessed conditions" his death.   In this
respect, every Christian deathbed has a glory and a consecration and a triumph
which we miss in the death chamber of the sweet Psalmist of Israel, the most
saintly and spiritual of all the Jews.   As Coleridge,

> " Is that a deathbed where the Christian lies?
> Yes, but not his ; 'tis death itself there dies."

2. *There is no idea of a future recompense.*   Hence, partly, his urgent demand
for the punishment of Joab and Shimei.   He does not know of a " judgment *to
come ;* " of any distribution of rewards and punishments after death.   He has been
taught that the righteous and the wicked alike are to be " recompensed *in the
earth,*" and therefore Joab and Shimei, albeit old and greyheaded, must not die in
peace.   If they do, justice, he thinks, will be robbed of its due.   How different the
conception of the Christian !   He views with calmness the miscarriage of justice ;
he sees the wicked in great prosperity ; he " bears the whips and scorns of time,"
" suffers the stings and arrows of outrageous fortune," knowing that this world is

not all; that " God is patient because he is *eternal*," and that " the crooked shall
be made straight, and the rough places plain," at the judgment-seat of Christ.
3. *There was no hope of a kingdom and a crown.* David's idea was that he was
leaving a kingdom ; St. Paul's that he was going to one. "Remove the diadem and
take off the crown"—this was the message of death to the Hebrew kings. And to
us death brings a crown (Rev. ii. 10, iii. 11; 2 Tim. iv. 8; James i. 12, &c.), a
throne (Rev. iii. 21), a sceptre (Rev. ii. 27), a kingdom (Dan. vii. 18 ; Luke xxii. 29 ;
Heb. xii. 28, &c.) To the Jew death was practically the end of life and of glory ;
to the Christian it is the beginning of both.

Vers. 1—11.—*Eikon Basiliké*. The king, the close of whose chequered and
romantic career is narrated in this section, was the pattern king of the Hebrew
people, and is in many respects a model for all kings. The portrait drawn here
and in the Psalms is a veritable *Eikon Basiliké*, both truer and worthier of regard
than that " Portraiture of his sacred Majesty," so famous and so influential in the
history of our own country. We see him gathered to his fathers. Let us honestly
frame his *eulogium*.

I. HE WAS ONE OF NATURE'S KINGS. The first king of Israel seems to have been
chosen because of his physical, the second because of his moral, qualifications. His
was a kingly soul. " Kind hearts are more than coronets "—yes, and more than
crowns. Few nobler and greater men have ever lived. Witness his magnanimity,
his chivalry, his loyalty, his bravery, his tenderness, his forgiveness of wrongs. See
the records of 1 Sam. xvi, 12, 21 ; xvii, 32—37, 50; xviii. 14—16; xxii. 23; xxiv.
5, 22; xxv. 16 ; xxvi. 9—25 ; 2 Sam, i. 11—15 ; ii. 5, 6 ; iii. 31—39 ; iv. 9—12 ; ix. 1 ;
xvi. 10, 12 ; xviii. 33 ; xix. 22. Such a man, had he lived and died among the
sheepfolds, would have been "king of men for all that."

II. HE WAS ONE OF HEAVEN'S KINGS. "The powers that be are ordained of God."
All legitimate monarchs reign *de jure divino*. But not all equally so. He was
expressly chosen of God (1 Sam. xvi. 1 ; Psa. lxxxix. 20), was taken from the sheepfolds and from perilous watches against the lion and the bear to be the viceroy of
Heaven. And he proved himself a king after God's own heart. He is the standard
with which subsequent monarchs are compared, and by which they are judged.
(2 Kings xi. 4, 33 ; xv. 3—5, 11 ; 2 Kings xiv. 3, &c.)

III. HE WAS FAITHFUL TO THE KING OF KINGS. "He did that which was right
in the eyes of the Lord, and turned not aside from anything that he commanded
him all the days of his life, save only," &c. (1 Kings xv. 5). " His heart was perfect
with the Lord his God " (1 Kings xi. 4). He kept God's commandments and
statutes (ver. 34). He was qualified to govern by having learnt to obey. He required nothing from his subjects which he did not himself render to his sovereign
Lord.

IV. HE FAITHFULLY EXECUTED THE JUDGMENTS OF A KING. The powers that be
are appointed " to execute wrath on him that doeth evil." The Church at her altar
prays " that they may truly and indifferently minister justice, to the punishment of
wickedness and vice." "A wise king scattereth the wicked and bringeth the wheel
over them." "The execution of justice on the guilty is essential even to the exercise
of mercy to those whose safety depends on the maintenance of the law " (Wordsworth). David was never more kingly than when he " cut off all wicked doers
from the city of the LORD " (Psa. ci. 8).

V. HE WAS A KING TO THE LAST. " David did never so wisely and carefully
marshal the affairs of God as when he was fixed to the bed of his age and death "
(Bp. Hall). It is the king speaks in this dying charge. It was because he was
king, and as such owed obedience to the King of kings, and owed protection and
the vindication of law to his subjects, that he could not pardon Joab and Shimei.
A private person can forgive private wrongs ; a king may not forgive public injuries,
for he may not give away what is not his to give. It is true the son of David
prayed for the forgiveness of his murderers. It is true that *we* are to forgive those
who have wronged us. But we are not to defeat the ends of justice, and bid the
malefactor go free. Nor will the Son of David forgive conscious and inveterate

rebellion. He it is, the fount of all mercy, who will say, "Those mine enemies, who would not that I should reign over them, bring hither, and slay them before me" (Luke xix. 27).

VI. HE SOUGHT AND FOUND MERCY FROM THE KING OF KINGS. He was not perfect, not sinless. "Save only in the matter of Uriah the Hittite." It is not the "fierce light that beats upon a throne" discloses David's imperfections; it is his own confessions. In Psalm li. he has himself recorded his sin and his profound penitence; in Psalm xxxii. he tells us of his pardon. The king of Israel tells us how the King of Heaven forgives. And here most of all, perhaps, is he a pattern for all kings, for all men, to the end of time. This *Eikon Basiliké* has many goodly and noble features, but the fairest lineament of all is the story of his sin and its forgiveness (2 Sam. xii. 1–13).

HOMILIES BY VARIOUS AUTHORS.

Vers. 1—11.—Holy Scripture gives us many a touching and pathetic description of the death of the father of a family, showing how it at once sanctions and sanctifies natural affection. The farewells of David remind us of those of Jacob. Death sometimes seems to fill the men of God of the old covenant with the spirit of prophecy, as if the summit of the earthly life was illuminated with a purer radiance falling upon it from a higher sphere. Death is indeed to all the messenger of God to reveal to us great truths; it is a great prophet.

I. Death shows to us WHERE ENDS THE WAY OF ALL THE EARTH (1 Kings ii. 2). Pascal says, "However brilliant the tragedy may have been, the end is always death. From every grave which is dug comes a voice crying, *Memento mori.*"

II. DEATH TEACHES US TO LOOK AT OUR PAST EXISTENCE AS A WHOLE, as from a height we look down on the plain below. It brings out the great object of life, the essential truth too often drowned in the busy hum of the world. David thinks no more at this hour of the glory or of the pleasures of life. Its one great end stands out more clearly before him—to walk in the ways of the Lord, to keep His statutes and His commandments. This is wisdom and prudence.

III. DEATH REMINDS THE SERVANTS OF GOD THAT THEIR WORK DOES NOT PERISH WITH THEM; that none of them, not even the greatest, is an indispensable instrument of the work; that they are only links in the chain. Thus the torch which is to enlighten the world is passed from hand to hand.

IV. THE INHERITANCE OF A HOLY WORK TO BE CARRIED ON is the best of those blessings which, according to God's promise, are to rest upon His people to the third and fourth generations (Exod. xx. 6). A great responsibility rests upon a Christian family, and their education ought to be conducted with a view to it. This succession in piety, in living and acting faith, is more important and more real than the succession by means of official ordination.

V. Every servant of God, in his death, may say with Jesus Christ, "IT IS EXPEDIENT FOR YOU THAT I GO AWAY;" "YE SHALL DO GREATER THINGS THAN THESE." It is well to know, when our work is done, that it will be carried on by another. With Solomon, the Jewish theocracy received a new development, such as it had never known in the time of David. It is well for us to die, even for the sake of the work of God, which we are called to accomplish up to a certain point, but no further.

VI. How much BETTER STILL IS IT FOR US TO DIE, when we look at it in the light of eternity. "David slept with his fathers (ver. 10), but only like them to be carried home to God, to rest in Abraham's bosom" (Luke xvi. 22). For ourselves, we may say with St. Paul, "To depart, and be with Christ is far better" (Phil. i. 18).—E. DE P.

Ver. 2.—"*Show thyself a man.*" The religion of God is the religion of man. True religion is the perfecting of our humanity.

I. MAN WAS MADE IN THE IMAGE OF GOD. This is His essential characteristic.

The more He reflects this image, the more truly manly He is. The religion of the Bible restores His manhood.

II. THERE IS NO FACULTY IN MAN WHICH DOES NOT FIND ITS COMPLEMENT AND ITS DEVELOPMENT IN GOD. His reason finds in God alone the truth which it seeks. His heart only finds an object adequate to its power of loving in the God who is Love. His conscience has for its ideal and its law the Divine holiness. "*Be ye perfect, even as your Father which is in heaven is perfect*" (Matt. v. 48). His will derives its power alone from God. 1. The Son of God was the Son of man, and realized the true idea of humanity in His holy life. 2. The religion of God honours and exalts man, even as falsehood and error degrade and debase him. 3. The Divine morality is in profound harmony with true human morality, that law which is written in the natural conscience. The petty religiousness which says, "Touch not, taste not, handle not" (Col. ii. 21), and creates all sorts of artificial duties, is not in accordance with true piety, the one great commandment of which —love to God and man—approves itself at once to the gospel and to the conscience. 4. *Be a man* means, finally, Do thy duty like a man. Be one of the violent who take the kingdom by force. Let us be careful not to effeminate our Christianity by a soft sentimentalism. Let us learn from the Son of God to be truly men "after God's own heart."—E. DE P.

Vers. 1—4.—*A royal father's last words.* David's eventful life is drawing to a close. He has proved himself to be "a man after God's own heart." Not a *perfect* man, for he had grievous defects. But, in the main, he recognized the grandeur of his position as "the Lord's anointed." He lived by the inspiration of a Divine purpose. He "served his own generation by the will of God" (Acts xiii. 36). His very faults bore witness to the native force of his character. The height of the precipice measures the depth that frowns beneath it. Great natures are most capable of great temptations, great sorrows, and great sins. But now great David dies, and the sovereignty of Israel must pass into other hands.

I. THE CALMNESS OF A GOOD MAN IN THE FACE OF DEATH. "I go the way of all the earth." There is a tone of quiet composure and satisfaction in these words—remarkable feature of the way in which most of the Old Testament saints confronted death. More than mere Oriental courage, mere passive submission to the inevitable,—faith in the Unseen and Eternal—fortitude of a soul that has found a nobler inheritance than earth supplies—peaceful self-surrender into the hands of the Living God. Yet not like the clear and certain vision of *Christian* faith. Compare this, "I go the way," &c., with St. Paul's "I have fought a good fight," &c. (2 Tim. iv. 7, 8). He who has a living hold on Christ can say, not merely "I go the way of all the earth," but "I go my way to the eternal home of the redeemed." "Absent from the body; present with the Lord." Composure in the face of death very much a matter of natural temperament—dependent on physical conditions—to be distinguished from the higher triumph of faith. Men of faith sometimes in "bondage through fear of death." Live much with Christ, and when the fatal hour comes the sting and the terror shall be taken away.

II. THE CARE OF A GODLY FATHER FOR THE WELL-BEING OF HIS SON. Often in the life of David we see, through the garb of his kingly character, the throbbing of the true fatherly heart. The spirit of fatherhood here takes the form of wise and solemn counsel befitting the time. Fine touch of nature in this. The true father desires that his sons should be nobler, better, happier than himself. He lives over again in their life, and would have them to avoid the errors and evils into which he has fallen. David's yearning for Solomon is at once intensified and hallowed by the remembrance of his own wrong-doing. "Be strong and shew thyself a man." Solomon's youth, gentle disposition, heavy responsibilities, alike demanded such counsel. Supreme lesson of life for the young—the path of obedience to the Divine law is that of safety and prosperity. The wisdom and strength God gives will enable the "little child" in the noblest sense to "play the man." Each generation on a vantage ground as compared with those that went before it—children "heirs of all the ages." Best legacy the fathers leave them—

the great principles of truth and righteousness, as illustrated by their own living history.   Chart of the ocean of life in the children's hands; rocks and shoals and hidden currents traced by the care and toil and suffering of those who sailed before them.   Let them use it wisely if they would have a safe and prosperous voyage.

III. THE STEADFASTNESS OF GOD'S PURPOSE AMID ALL THE CHANGES OF HUMAN HISTORY.   David dies in the faith that "the Lord will continue His word."   The " everlasting covenant ordered in all things and sure " is not fluctuating and perishable as the things and beings of earth.   Steadfast order of the heavenly bodies and of the seasons a symbol of the sure covenant (Jer. xxxiii. 20).   The frailty of man often serves to deepen our impression of the eternity of God.   Human life a tale soon told, but "the counsel of the Lord standeth fast," &c.   This is our security for the triumph of the cause of truth and righteousness in the world,   " All flesh is grass," &c. (1 Peter i. 24).   Man dies, but God lives; and the hope that stays itself upon His word can never be put to shame.

IV. THE CONDITIONAL NATURE OF DIVINE PROMISES.   " If thy children take heed," &c.   All Divine promises are thus conditional.   Faith and practical submission needed to place us in the line of their fulfilment.   God "continues His word" to those who continue in His ways.   The promises are " Yea and amen" in Christ. Be " in Him " if you would realize them.—W.

Vers. 2, 3.—*A charge from a dying king.*   The utterances of dying men naturally have weight.   Those who stand on the border line between time and eternity have less temptation to disguise the truth, and are more likely than others to see things in their true relations.   When those who speak to us thence are men who have long loved us, and who have ever proved worthy of our love, we must be callous indeed if their words are powerless.   Exemplify by the mention of any whose whole future destiny turned upon the wish and the counsel of a dying father or friend.   David's counsel to Solomon had this double value.   He spoke as a dying man, and as a wise and loving father.   Happy would it have been for the son had this counsel always been the law of his life.   1. *The anxiety of David for the moral and spiritual welfare of his son.*   Some parents deem their duty done if they see their sons and daughters fairly " settled in life," without much consideration for character.   David cared first for character, and next for circumstances. He believed that if the heart were right with God, things would of themselves go right with men.   2. *The willingness of Solomon to receive such counsels.*   How different was his spirit from that of Adonijah (1 Kings i. 5).   Though young, high-spirited, of princely rank, and already anointed king, he bows to listen to his aged father.   Lessons of reverence for age, and respect to parents, to be drawn from this. In his charge to Solomon, David inculcates—

I. THE IMPORTANCE OF COMPLETE OBEDIENCE TO GOD.   He had seen the terrible effects of partial obedience in Saul, his own predecessor. (Illustrate from Saul's life.) 1. *This implies the recognition of God as King.*   He is King of kings, and Lord of lords, and even princely Solomon was to remember that he had a Master in heaven.   This would be not only for his own good, but for the welfare of his kingdom.   The tyrannies, the exactions, the cruelties of an ordinary Eastern despot would be impossible to one who habitually acknowledged that he was responsible to God, and that wrongs which no human court could avenge would receive just retribution from "the Judge of all the earth."   The wishes of his dying father might somewhat restrain him, but these could not have the abiding power of the law of the ever-living and ever-present God.   What safety belongs to him who, like Joseph, says in the hour of temptation, " How can I do this great wickedness, and sin against *God?*"   That thought may be ours in the darkness as well as in the light, amid strangers as well as in the precincts of home.   To the lad setting out from his father's house, to the man undertaking new responsibilities, the message comes, " Keep the charge of the Lord thy God, to walk in His ways."   2. *This involves thoroughness in obedience.*   David uses no vain repetitions when he speaks of " statutes, commandments, judgments, and testimonies."   The *whole* law, not a part of it only, was to be remembered.   We are all tempted to partial obedience.

It is easy, natural, profitable to obey some commands. Disobedience will bring disease, or shame, or loss of reputation, and, fearing such penalties, some refrain from transgression. But there are other laws of God, obedience to which brings dishonour rather than glory, impoverishment and not advantage; and these also are to be obeyed if we would "walk before God in truth, with all our heart." Again there are some precepts which seem of trifling value, and we are tempted to say we need not be too precise. But we forget that God's laws, even the least of them, are terribly precise. Science is proving this in every department of nature. The tide, for example, will not stop short a foot in space, nor a moment in time, to save the life of the helpless man penned in between the rocks. And are moral laws less inexorable? Besides, the crucial test of obedience is found in relation to *little* things. If your child obeys your important command, because he sees its importance, you are glad; but you are much more pleased when he does something you told him to do, merely because you wished it, for this is a higher proof of genuine obedience than that.

II. The NECESSITY OF PERSONAL RESOLUTION. "Be thou strong, therefore, and show thyself a man." This sounds like an echo of God's own words to Joshua (i. 7). The occasions too were similar. Joshua was entering on his leadership, and Solomon was on the steps of his throne. David would evoke the manly resolution of his son. There was the more necessity for this, because his honoured and heroic father could no longer stand beside him. One of God's reasons for taking away our parents by death is to develope and strengthen our character. When the saplings grow under the shelter of the parent tree, they are weakly; but when the giant of the forest falls, and the winds of heaven begin to buffet those which have had its protection, their strength becomes greater, and their roots strike deeper. "Show thyself a man," says David to Solomon. Some suppose they show their manhood by aping the airs of the elders (smoking, swearing, &c.) But in David's sense, to show yourself a man is to prove yourself wise, valorous, virtuous, and above all, loyal of heart to God. This exhortation then implies the manifestation of moral courage and strength. These are required in order to the obedience we have described, for such obedience implies struggle. 1. *There is conflict with self.* We have to check the uprising of passion, to fight against the pride which would make us refuse to submit to the revelation, and to the righteousness of God, &c. 2. *There is resistance to the evil influences of others.* When Solomon was misled by his wives, and began to worship their gods, he was forgetting the command, "Be strong and show thyself a man." Point out the necessity for moral courage, and for the renewal of strength, by waiting on God, to those surrounded by evil associates. 3. *There is antagonism to popular customs.* In school, in business, in national policy, in church routine, it is easier to float with the stream than to contend against it. He must needs "be strong, and show himself a man," who would say, "We must obey God rather than man!" Show where Solomon found this strength, and where he lost it. Give examples of both from sacred history. *E.g.*, the disciples were cowards when Christ was away, but they became heroes when the promise was fulfilled at Pentecost: "They were endued with power from on high."

III. The ASSURANCE OF RESULTING BLESSEDNESS. "That thou mayest prosper," &c. As an historical fact, this promise was fulfilled. The kingdom of Solomon prospered as long as he was faithful to the God of his father. His apostasy sowed the seeds of its decay. God's promises are contingent, not absolute. They have attached to them implied conditions. This, which was shown in material blessings under the covenant of the old economy, is abidingly true. It is not that man merits the blessings of God by his obedience, but that he unfits himself to receive them by disobedience. This is yet more clearly seen under the light of the new dispensation. God gives a man that which he is fit for, on earth and in heaven. In and through Jesus Christ He has broadened our views of recompense. Beyond death the fulfilment of this promise extends, and he who is faithful with the few things shall be at last a ruler over many. In a spirit of humble obedience and prayerful dependence, let us seek to keep the charge and win the blessedness revealed in these dying words of the sweet Singer of Israel.—A. R.

ADONIJAH'S INTRIGUE

EXPOSITION.

CHAPTER II. 12—25.

Ver. 12.—**And Solomon sate on the throne of David his father, and his kingdom** [*i.e.*, dominion, sway] **was established greatly.** [Cf. 2 Chron. i. 1, 2. This verse serves as a kind of heading or introduction to the rest of the chapter. It was principally by the removal of rivals and disaffected persons that his sway was established.

Ver. 13.—**And Adonijah, the son of Haggith, came to Bathsheba, the mother of Solomon.** [The LXX. adds καὶ προσεκύνησεν αὐτῷ, but the words are probably inserted from ver. 19. The historian now relates the plot of Adonijah and its defeat. Foiled in his purpose to mount the throne by direct means, Adonijah and his advisers have recourse to intrigue and subtlety. By the aid of Abishag, he hopes to accomplish what his chariots and horsemen (ch. i. 5) had failed to effect. And he first addresses himself to the queen mother (*"Aggreditur mulierem, ut regnandi ignaram ita amoribus facilem."* Grotius). The position of the queen dowager in the Hebrew kingdom was an influential one; not unlike that of the Validé sultana amongst the Ottomans. Hence the constant mention of each king's mother (1 Kings xiv. 31; xv. 10, where notice ver. 13; 2 Kings xi. 1; xii. 1; xiv. 2; xv. 2, &c.; hence, too, the part which such a queen mother as Athaliah found it possible to take. This pre-eminence was a natural result of the polygamy of Eastern sovereigns (and the consequent intrigues of the harem), coupled with the high estimation in which the mother was held in the East.] **And she said, Comest thou peaceably.** [Heb. *Is it peace thy coming?* Bathsheba was evidently surprised by his visit. Owing to the part he had taken against her son, there would naturally have been but few dealings, if not positive alienation, between them. Her first thought, consequently, is, " What can this coming mean?" The prominence of the idea of *peace* in all Eastern salutations has often been noticed. Cf. 1 Sam. xvi. 4; 2 Kings ix. 22; iv. 26; v. 21; Luke x. 5; John xx. 19—21, &c.] **And he said, Peaceably** [Heb. *peace.*]

Ver. 14.—**He said moreover** [Heb. *And he said*] **I have somewhat to say unto thee** [lit., " a word to me (cf. *est mihi*) for thee." This expression throws some light on the New Testament phrase, τί ἐμοὶ καὶ σοί, John ii. 4, &c.] **And she said, Say on.**

Ver. 15.—**And he said, Thou knowest that** the kingdom was mine [*schon so gut wie mein* (Bähr). Adonijah evidently made much of the right of primogeniture (cf. ver. 22), which was not unrecognized amongst the Jews. There is possibly in these words, too, a hint at the part Bathsheba had taken in defeating his claims] **and that all Israel set their faces** [*i.e.*, eyes] **upon me that I should reign** [Heb. *upon* me *all Israel set*, &c. The "*me*" is emphatic by its position. So is the "*mine*" just before used. Several commentators remark that Adonijah's words were not strictly true. But we hardly expect to find truth on such an occasion. Adonijah was adroit and diplomatic, and puts the case as it best serves his purpose. In order to propitiate Bathsheba, he exaggerates his loss and disappointment, just as in the next words, in order to put her off her guard, he plays the saint and obtrudes his piety and resignation]: **howbeit** [lit., *and*] **the kingdom is turned about and is become my brother's, for it was his from the Lord.** [This verse shows pretty clearly that Adonijah had not renounced his pretensions to the throne. Despite the pitiful failure of his first conspiracy, and notwithstanding Solomon's generous condonation of his treason, he cannot forget that he was, and is, the eldest surviving son, and had been very near the throne. And as to the kingdom being his brother's by Divine appointment, he cannot have been ignorant of that long ago (2 Sam. xii. 25), yet he conspired all the same. And it is not difficult to read here between the lines, that he has not relinquished his hopes, and does not acquiesce in Solomon's supremacy.]

Ver. 16.—**And now I ask one petition of thee** [Heb. *request one request*] **deny me not** [marg., " turn not away my face." Better, Turn not *back*, *i.e.*, repulse not. Rawlinson paraphrases, " Make me not to hide my face through shame at being refused; " but this is not the idea of the original, which means, Reject me not; send me not away. In the Heb. " face " often stands for "person," for eyes (ver. 15), looks, mien]. **And she said unto him, Say on.**

Ver. 17.—**And he said, Speak, I pray thee, unto Solomon the king; for he will not say thee nay,** [will not repulse thee. Same words as ver. 16. There is a spice of flattery in these words. He now exaggerates her influence with the king] **that he may give me Abishag the Shunammite to wife.** [We are hardly justified in concluding, as some commentators have done, that love had nothing to do with this request. It is not improbable, on the contrary, that a passion for the beautiful Shunamnite, perhaps the fairest woman of her time, may have first given a powerful impulse to Adonijah's ambition (see on ch. i. 5). At the same time, he must have had ulterior motives (see on ver. 22).

Ver. 18. — **And Bathsheba said, Well** [there is no reason why the strict rendering "good," should not be preserved here. The A.V. follows the LXX. καλῶς. Similarly Luther, *wohl;* but Bähr, *gut*], **I will speak for thee** [LXX. περὶ σοῦ] **unto the king.**

Ver. 19.—**Bathsheba therefore** [lit., *And Bathsheba*] **went unto king** [Heb. *the king*] **Solomon, to speak unto him for Adonijah. And the king rose up to meet her, and bowed himself unto her,** [the LXX. reads, "and kissed" her (καὶ κατεφίλησεν αὐτὴν). There is not necessarily a pregnant construction, as Keil insists : "rose up and went down to meet her." We get here a glimpse of the stateliness of Solomon's court] **and sat down on his throne, and caused a seat** [lit., *throne*, same word] **to be set** [most probably the servants of Solomon placed the seat for the queen mother, as the LXX. (ἐτέθη θρόνος) and most translators. The reception was clearly a public one, if the interview was private. But the original is simply, " and he set," &c., suggesting that Solomon *may* have done it, as a mark of respect, with his own hands. He " received his mother as בְּיָרָה " (ch. xv. 13). Bähr] **for the mother of the king, and she sat on his right hand.** [The place of honour. Cf. Psa. cx. 1 ; Matt. xx. 21; xxv. 33; Acts vii. 56 ; Rom. viii. 34; Heb. i. 3 ; viii. 1, &c. It was also the place of honour amongst Arabians (Keil), Greeks, and Romans, as the very names εὐώνυμος—an euphemism for ἀριστερός—and *sinistra*, show.

Ver. 20.—**Then she said, I desire one small petition of thee.** [So it seemed, no doubt, to her, in her inexperience and ignorance of Adonijah's real motives. She thought she held the threads of a love story in her hands, and that it would be a small thing for Solomon to make these handsome lovers happy]: **I pray thee, say me not nay. And the king said unto her, Ask on, my mother: for I will not say thee nay.** [The readiness of the king to grant *whatever* she asked proves that the reasons which induced him to deny her request must have been weighty ; *i.e.*, Adonijah's suit cannot have been devoid of political consequence.

Ver. 21.—**And she said, Let Abishag the Shunammite be given to Adonijah thy brother to wife.** [For the construction (אֵת with a nominative, or, as some think, יֻתַּן used impersonally — *man gebe*), cf. Gen.

xxvii. 42 ; Exod. x. 8 ; and especially Num. xxxii. 5 ; and see Gesen., Lex. *s. v.* אֵת, and Ewald, Syntax, 295 *b*.]

Ver. 22.—**And king Solomon answered and said unto his mother, And why dost thou ask Abishag the Shunammite for Adonijah ?** [Professor Plumptre (Dict. Bib., art. " Solomon ") says this " narrative is not a little perplexing." He then specially remarks on the strangeness of Bathsheba's interceding for Adonijah, and also on Solomon's " flashing into fiercest wrath " at her request. He explains the facts, however, by " Mr. Grove's ingenious theory identifying Abishag with the Shulamite (Cant. vi. 13), the heroine of the Song of Songs." It is " the passionate love of Solomon for ' the fairest among women ' that has made Bathsheba, " hitherto supreme, to fear a rival influence, and to join in any scheme for its removal." The king's vehement abruptness is in like manner accounted for. He sees in the request at once an attempt to deprive him of the woman he loves and a plot to keep him still in the tutelage of childhood. Of the ingenuity of this theory no one can doubt, nor yet that it may *possibly* represent the actual facts. But it is not necessary, nor does it help much to the explanation of the narrative. Bathsheba's intervention may easily be accounted for by (1) her desire to conciliate her son's most formidable rival ; (2) her feminine interest in a love match ; and (3) her pride, which could not but be flattered, on being assured that her influence with the king was so great. Nor is it any more difficult to assign a reason for Solomon's sudden outburst of anger. This request is evidence to him of a fresh plot against his throne, a plot so skilfully laid that its abettors have been able to deceive his own mother, and have made her a tool for its advancement. Surely this is quite enough to account for Solomon's indignation. And the theory of a love story has this disadvantage, that the young king completely ignores it in what follows, all his concern being about the kingdom, and not one word being said about the woman ; and again—and this is almost fatal—his mention of Joab and Abiathar, and his subsequent dealings with them, prove conclusively that he suspected a conspiracy against his crown, not a scheme, in which these latter could have had no interest, and therefore no part, to rob him of a mistress] **ask for him the kingdom also** [Heb. *and ask for him* =and (you will next) ask for him ; or, Aye, ask for him, &c. It was quite natural that Solomon should see in Adonijah's suit for Abishag an indirect, but none the less real or dangerous, attempt to compass his own downfall. For it was one of the customs of

Oriental monarchies that the harem of a sovereign descended to his successor. Thus the impostor Smerdis took possession of the harem of Cambyses (Herod. iii. 68), while Darius in turn had some of the wives of Smerdis (iii. 88). And what is much more to the point, a similar custom obtained amougst the Jews. David, for example, succeeded to the wives, along with the kingdom, of Saul (2 Sam. xii. 8). And we see from the case of Abner and Rizpah (Ibid. iii. 8), and still more from that of Absalom (ch. xvi. 22), that to "take possession of the harem was the most decided act of sovereignty" (Lord A. Hervey, Speak. Com. on 2 Sam. xvi. 21). Now all these instances were of too recent a date, and had attracted far too much attention at the time, to have made it possible for them to have escaped either Solomon's or Adonijah's observation. They manifest "such a close connection in public opinion between the title to the crown and the possession of the deceased monarch's wives, that to have granted Adonijah's request would have been the strongest encouragement to his pretensions" (Rawlinson in loco). It may be said that Abishag had not really been the concubine of David (ch. i. 4), which is true, and which explains what would otherwise have been the astonishing impiety of Adonijah (Lev. xviii. 8, xx. 11; cf. 1 Cor. v. 1), and the wonderful complaisance of Bathsheba. There is no warrant for charging Adonijah (as is done by à Lapide, Wordsworth, al.) with defying the Divine law and seeking an incestuous alliance, for the historian is careful to represent Abishag as David's attendant, and not as his wife. But it is hardly probable that the nation at large knew this. People generally could only suppose that this fair young girl, chosen out of all the thousands of Israel because of her beauty, had become to all intents and purposes one of the royal seraglio. It is almost a certainty, therefore, that Adonijah's request concealed a plot for using Abishag as a stepping-stone to the throne, and Solomon certainly is not to be blamed if he interpreted it by the light of contemporaneous history, and by the usages of his time and country. He knew that his brother had made one deliberate effort to supplant him, and therefore he could only conclude that this was a second, though veiled, attempt to deprive him of his kingdom]; **even for him, and for Abiathar the priest, and for Joab the son of Zeruiah.** [The LXX. and other translators appear to have had a slightly different text before them. The LXX. renders, καὶ αὐτῷ 'Αβιάθαρ καὶ αὐτῷ 'Ιωαβ, κ. τ. λ; the Vulgate, "et habet Abiathar," &c. The Chald. paraphrases, "nonne in

consilio fuerunt ille et Abiathar," &c. Keil well remarks that "the repetition of לֹ answers entirely to the emotional character of the words." We can hardly believe, however, that in these conversations we have the ipsissima verba of the speakers If so, how were they preserved and handed down to the author? Even a "court scribe" would hardly catch every turn of expression. And possibly this interview with Bathsheba was private. It would almost seem, from the immediate mention of Joab and Abiathar, as if Solomon had received some prior intimation of this second conspiracy. Possibly his romarkable penetration had divined that mischief was brewing from the bearing of the three, who no doubt would be narrowly watched. Or he may have heard of frequent meetings on their part. Anyhow, Adonijah's suit is to him conclusive proof of a plot].

Ver. 23.—**Then king Solomon sware by the Lord, saying, God do so to me, and more also** [a common form of adjuration (Ruth i. 17; 1 Sam. xiv. 44; xx. 13; 2 Sam. iii. 9; xix. 13, &c.) = Gott soll mich fort und fort strafen. Bähr], **if** [or "that." כִּי constantly follows formulæ of swearing, as in all the passages just cited. Cf. the use of ὅτι in New Testament. The order of the next words in the Hebrew is noticeable] **against his life spake Adonijah this word.** [בְּנַפְשׁוֹ, "at the peril or cost of his life." Cf. 2 Sam. xxiii. 17; Josh. xxiii. 11.]

Ver. 24.—**Now therefore** [Heb. and now], **as the Lord liveth, which hath established me, and set me** [a ' has here crept into the text; obviously owing to the fact that this same letter both precedes and follows] **on the throne of David my father, and who hath made me an house** [Keil and Wordsworth understand by this expression, "hath given me issue." "Solomon," says Keil, "had already one son, viz., Rehoboam, about a year old (comp. xi. 42 with xiv. 21, and 2 Chron. xii. 13)." But some doubt seems to attach to the "forty and one years" mentioned as the age of Rehoboam at his accession. Bähr says Solomon's "marriage did not occur till afterwards (iii. 1). And we find from 1 Kings xi. 38; 2 Sam. vii. 11, 27, that to 'make,' or 'build an house,' means to found a lasting dynasty"], **as he promised** [Heb. spake, i.e., at 2 Sam. vii. 11—13], **Adonijah shall be put to death this day.**

Ver. 25.—**And King Solomon sent by the hand** [i.e., the instrumentality; not necessarily eigenhändig, as Thenius. Cf. Exod. iv. 13; 1 Sam. xvi. 20, Heb.; 1 Kings xii. 15; xiv. 18; Jer. xxxvii. 2 ("which he spake by the hand of Jeremiah"), &c. The same expression is found in ver. 46 of this chapter] **of Benaiah** [in the East the captain of the king's body-guard has always been the "chief of the executioners," the title given to Potiphar, Gen. xxxvii. 36, Heb.; in 2 Kings xxv. 8 to Nebuzar-Adan; and in Dan. ii. 14 to Arioch "the captain of the king's guard, which was gone forth *to slay* the wise men, &c.] **and he fell upon him so that he died.** [Solomon has been accused of "a cold-blooded vengeance" and of "that jealous cruelty so common in Oriental despots," in ordering the execution of his brother. But unjustly. It is to be remembered that on the occasion of Adonijah's first rebellion the young monarch had displayed the greatest magnanimity towards him. He might then have justly decreed against him the death which no doubt the conspirators had designed against him (1 Kings i. 12.) Adonijah, by fleeing to the altar, showed that he had good grounds for fearing the avenging sword. He was clearly conscious that he had merited the death of the traitor. But Solomon spared him, during good behaviour. He warned him that "if wickedness were found in him" he should die (1 Kings i. 52.) His first treason, consequently, was not to be lost sight of, in case he were guilty of a fresh offence. And now that he is found conspiring again; now that he abuses the royal clemency, and seeks by chicanery and intrigue to snatch his brother's crown, the sentence of death takes effect. This renewed attempt, after failure and forgiveness, must have convinced the king that Adonijah's pretensions would be a standing menace to the peace and prosperity of his empire, and therefore he owed it to himself, to his subjects, and above all to God, who had entrusted him with the crown, to put this restless and dangerous plotter out of the way. To pass over a second offence would be a virtual encouragement of sedition, for it would show that the king was weak and might be trifled with. Adonijah therefore must die, not only in expiation of his treason, but as an example to the subjects of Solomon, that the disaffected, including all Adonijah's partizans, might be awed into obedience.

HOMILETICS.

Vers. 22—25.—*The Brothers.* It may be instructive if, after the manner of ancient writers, we draw out a comparison between the two brothers whose history is recorded in part in this section, and who here appear as rivals. Their careers were very different. The one reigned with almost unparalleled magnificence for forty years; the other fell in the very May-morn of his life by the sword of the executioner. What were the causes which produced such different results? Let us consider some few of them.

I. ADONIJAH WAS ENDUED WITH BEAUTY, SOLOMON WITH WISDOM. The first had goodliness; the second goodness. Men admired Adonijah; the Lord loved Solomon (2 Sam. xii. 24). To the elder brother the Allwise Providence allotted the gifts of face and form—exterior advantages; to the latter He gave "wisdom and understanding exceeding much, and largeness of heart"—the quiet, unobtrusive adornment of the spirit. Wisdom is better than rubies; yes, and better than beauties.

II. ADONIJAH WAS AMBITIOUS; SOLOMON WAS PIOUS. The first loved self, and sought his own advancement. The second "loved the LORD" (1 Kings iii. 3). The first, by his own showing, resisted and defied the will of Heaven (1 Kings ii. 15); the latter "walked in the statutes of David his father." Adonijah desired riches, honours, the life of his enemies; Solomon asked for none of these things, but for an understanding heart (chap. iii. 9, 11). Their lives consequently were regulated on totally different principles. The first acted as if he were master (chap. i. 5); the second remembered he was but a servant (ver. 9). And Adonijah lost everything, even his life, while Solomon gained everything—the wisdom for which he asked; the "richest honour" for which he did *not* ask. Verily "godliness is profitable *unto all things*" (1 Tim. iv. 8).

III. ADONIJAH SOUGHT TO FORCE EVENTS; SOLOMON WAITED PATIENTLY FOR THE LORD. Adonijah would not wait till his father was dead; he would snatch the sceptre from the old man's feeble grasp; he would be king at any cost, and *at once*. It is worth noticing that Solomon on the other hand took no part in the measures which placed him on the throne. "He that believeth shall not make haste." The one sought to frustrate the designs of Providence, the other "committed himself to him that judgeth righteously." And *he* was crowned and Adonijah was executed.

IV. ADONIJAH REBELLED AGAINST HIS FATHER; SOLOMON REVERENCED HIS MOTHER. Treatment of parents is a test of character. To honour father and mother is "the first commandment with promise." Adonijah repaid his father's indulgence with treason against his throne; Solomon, when seated on his throne, had a throne set for his mother. If he were king, his mother should be queen. He received her with the profoundest respect, though she was his subject; for he "counted her uncrowned womanhood to be the royal thing." The fortunes of these two brothers were not more diverse than their characters, as revealed by their treatment of their elders. And their histories accorded with their principles; their lives and deaths illustrated the commandment.

V. GOD CHOSE SOLOMON AND REFUSED ADONIJAH. As in the case of Esau and Jacob, as in the case of Manasseh and Ephraim, the younger is preferred to the elder. And yet the elder was apparently the popular favourite. "Man looketh on the outward appearance, but the LORD looketh on the heart." It is the case of David and his brethren over again. In all these cases "the Lord hath set apart *him that is godly* for himself." The meek, pacific Solomon, the rejected of Joab and Abiathar, is the accepted of Jehovah. And the brilliant and beautiful Adonijah, his advantages, his influence, his efforts, all these avail him nothing, for "the proud"—and we may add, the selfish, the disobedient—"the LORD knoweth afar off." (Psa. cxxxviii. 6), while "the wicked and him that loveth violence his soul hateth" (Psa. xi. 5).

EXPOSITION.

CHAPTER II. 26—35.

THE DEPOSITION OF ABIATHAR AND THE DEATH OF JOAB.

Ver. 26.—And unto Abiathar the priest [see note on 1 Kings i. 8. The historian now relates the end of Adonijah's confederates] said the king, get thee to Anathoth [The Heb. is extremely curt and authoritative, corresponding well with the anger and determination of the speaker. Anathoth, the home of Abiathar, was also the residence of another high priest, Hilkiah (Jer. i. 1). It was in Benjamin, a priests' city, and had suburbs (Jos. xxi. 13, 17, 18). It has been identified by Robinson with Anâta, a village 1¼ hrs. N.N.E. of Jerus. The name (= Answers) according to Gesenius, means, "*answers to prayer,*" but according to the Talmud, "*echoes* "], unto [עֵל is here almost the equivalent of אֶל. Cf. 2 Sam. xv. 4, 20, Heb. &c.] thine own fields [the patrimony of his family] for thou art worthy of death; [Heb. *a man of death;* LXX. ἀνὴρ θανάτου, i.e., ἔνοχος θανάτου, Matt. xxvi. 66.] but I will not at this time [Heb. *in this day*] put thee to death [*i.e.*, the sentence of death was deferred during good behaviour. It is hardly correct to say that Abiathar was "spared for a time, but only for a time" (Stanley). More correctly Corn. à Lapide: "*Misit eum in patriam ut ibi vitam, quam ei condonabat, quiete traduceret.*" For aught we know, he died in peace [because thou barest the ark of the Lord God before David my father [Thenius, quite needlessly would read for "ark," "ephod" (1 Sam.

xxiii. 6). Zadok and Abiathar had borne the ark (not of course in person, but *per alios*, viz., the Levites Uriel, Joel, &c.: 1 Chron. xv. 11), when David brought it up to Jerusalem, and also during his flight from Absalom (2 Sam. xv. 24—29). Abiathar had thus been associated both with David's joys and sorrows] and because thou hast been afflicted in all wherein my father was afflicted. [See 1 Sam. xxii. 17—23 ; 2 Sam. xv. 24, &c.]

Ver. 27.—So Solomon thrust out Abiathar from being priest unto the Lord, that he might fulfil [Heb. *to fulfil.* "An addition of the narrator, not the intention of Solomon. It is the ἵνα πληρωθῇ of the New Testament." Bähr] the word of the Lord, which he spake concerning the house of Eli in Shiloh [1 Sam. ii. 31—35. Abiathar was the last descendant of the house of Ithamar. With his deposition the high priesthood reverted to the house of Eleazar, and so another "word of the Lord" had its fulfilment (Num. xxv. 15).]

No one can justly accuse Solomon of unnecessary severity or of cruelty in his treatment of Abiathar. On the occasion of his first conspiracy, Abiathar seems to have escaped even censure. And yet that conspiracy, had it succeeded, would almost certainly have involved Solomon's death (ch. i. 12). He is now found plotting again, for the action of Solomon proves that there had been a second plot. Oriental usages would have justified his death. He is simply warned and banished.

Ver. 28.—Then tidings [Heb. *And the re-*

port, &c. Not necessarily of Abiathar's deposition, but certainly of Adonijah's death] **came to Joab, for Joab had turned after** [same expression as in Exod. xxiii. 2 ; Judges ix. 3] **Adonijah, though** [lit., and] **he turned not after Absalom.** [The LXX. (Cod. Vat.), Vulg., and all ancient versions except the Chald., here read *Solomon*, which Ewald and Thenius adopt. This reading is perhaps too summarily dismissed by most commentators, as involving a statement which would be self-evident and superfluous. But it is not so. The meaning would then be that Joab had inclined to Adonijah, and had not, subsequently, gone over to the side of Solomon — information which is much less obvious than that he had not " gone after Absalom." The Arabic version may thus be nearest the truth, which reads, " Neither did he love Solomon." Somewhat similarly Josephus.] **And Joab fled unto the tabernacle of the Lord, and caught hold of the horns of the altar.** [As Adonijah had done before him (ch. i. 50). His flight is almost certain evidence of his guilt. (" Joab vero seipsum prodidit." Münster.) Why should he flee, if conscious of innocence ? Solomon had acted generously before, and Joab would not be aware of David's dying instructions. His two assassinations had remained so long unpunished that he would hardly expect to be called to an account for them now. We have here, therefore, another indication of a second conspiracy, and it is an old belief (Theodoret, *al.*) that Joab had suggested to Adonijah the plan of marriage with Abishag. Some have asked why Joab should flee to the altar when his crimes deprived him of the right of the sanctuary. But a drowning man grasps at a straw. It is probable that he never thought of his murders, but only of his treason. According to the Rabbis, death at the altar ensured him burial amongst his fathers (Münster). But, if this were so, it would hardly enter into his calculations.

Ver. 29.—**And it was told king Solomon that Joab was fled unto the tabernacle of the Lord ; and, behold, he is by the altar.** [The LXX. here inserts, " *And Solomon the king sent to Joab, saying, What has happened thee, that thou art fled to the altar ? And Joab said, Because I feared before thee, and I fled to the Lord.*" This is only a gloss, but it is an instructive one. It shows that the author regarded Joab's flight as betraying a guilty conscience] **Then Solomon sent Benaiah, the son of Jehoiada, saying, Go, fall upon him.** [The LXX. adds, " *and bury him.*"]

Ver. 30.—**And Benaiah came to the tabernacle of the Lord, and said unto him** [Benaiah evidently " hesitated to stain the

altar with blood." It was only the sanctity of the altar which made it an asylum. There was strictly no "*right* of sanctuary"], **Thus saith the king, Come forth.** [Probably Solomon had directed that Joab should, if possible, be induced to leave the altar. Every Jew would dread its profanation by strife and bloodshed.] **And he said, Nay ; but I will die here.** [Heb. " *here will I die.*" Joab may possibly have thought that Solomon would hardly venture to put him to death there, and that so he might somehow escape with his life. But it is more probable that he counted on death, and that a feeling of superstition, or of defiance, had decided him to meet his doom there. It should be borne in mind that gross superstition not uncommonly accompanies irreligion and brutality ; and it is quite conceivable that Joab hoped for some indefinable benefit from the shadow of the altar, much as the poor Polish Jew expects from burial in Jerusalem. Or his motive *may* have been defiance, thinking he would " render Solomon odious to the people, as a profaner of the Holy Place" (M. Henry). It can hardly have been to put off for ever so short a time the execution, as Bishop Hall imagines.]

Ver. 31.—**And the king said unto him, Do as he hath said, and fall upon him** [the law decreed (Exod. xxi. 14) that, if a man had slain his neighbour with guile, he should be *taken from* the altar to die. Possibly the desperate character of Joab made literal compliance with this command well-nigh impossible. The attempt to drag him from his place of refuge might have led to a bloody encounter. And the king evidently felt that Joab's crimes justified exceptional measures], **and bury him** [why this injunction ? Possibly because the *spirit* of Deut. xxi. 23 seemed to Solomon to require it. Both Bähr and Keil think it was that Joab's services to the kingdom might be requited with an honourable sepulture. Was it not rather that the corpse might be removed with all possible haste from the sanctuary, which it defiled, and hidden from view, as one accursed of God, in the earth ? So Bishop Hall : " He sends Benaiah to take away the offender both from God and men, from the altar and the world "]; **that thou mayest take away** [LXX. " to-day," σήμερον] **the innocent blood** [for the construction cf. 1 Sam. xxv. 31 ; Neh. ii. 12 ; and Ewald, 287*d*. Innocent blood, *i.e.*, blood not shed in war, or forfeited to justice, rested upon the community, or the authorities responsible for its punishment (Num. xxxv. 33 ; Deut. xix. 10, 13 ; xxi. 9. Cf. Gen. iv. 10) until satisfaction was made. See on ver. 5], **which Joab shed, from me, and from the house of my father.** [Heb.

"from *upon* me." Solomon evidently believed that the guilt of blood was upon him and his house so long as Abner's and Amasa's blood remained unavenged ("The blood that is not required from the murderer will be required from the magistrate." Henry), and that he and his seed might have to answer for it, as Saul's seed had done (2 Sam. xxi. 1, 9). This is one of the many considerations which show that both David and Solomon were actuated not by "cold-blooded vengeance" or "long-cherished resentment" (Stanley), but by a sense of duty. In fact, Jewish law imperatively demanded the death of Joab, and to spare him was to violate all law, and to imperil the throne and the people. "Only a superficial observer," says Ewald, "can here reproach Solomon with needless severity."]

Ver. 32.—**And the Lord shall return** [LXX. ἐπέστρεψε, returns, or returned] **his blood** [LXX. τὸ αἷμα τῆς ἀδικίας αὐτοῦ, *i.e.*, the blood he had shed. Cf. vers. 33, 44] **upon his own head, who fell upon** [same word as in vers. 29, 31. So that it was strictly a *re-taliation*. The *lex talionis* was carried out to the letter] **two men more righteous and better than he, and slew them with the sword, my father David not knowing.** [Heb. "*and my father David knew not*," *i.e.*, was not privy thereto. Solomon thinks of the unjust suspicions which these crimes cast upon his father.]

Ver. 33.—**Their blood shall therefore return upon the head of Joab, and upon the head of his seed** [according to Exod. xx. 5; xxxiv. 7; Lev. xx. 5; xxvi. 39. There is an obvious reference to David's curse 2 Sam. iii. 29, which thoroughly agreed with the spirit of the Old Testament in comprehending the children in its sweep. And it is to be noticed that the sins of the fathers are still, by the operation of natural laws, and by the constitution and laws of society, visited upon the children, to the third and fourth generation] **for ever : but upon** [Heb. *to*] **David, and upon his seed, and upon his house, and upon his throne, shall there be** [or "*be*," optative ; LXX.

γένοιτο] **peace** [*i.e.*, prosperity] **for ever from the Lord.** [So persuaded is Solomon *that he is fulfilling a religious duty* in decreeing the execution of Joab ; so little thought has he of malice, revenge, or any baser motive, that he counts on the Divine blessing in perpetuity for the deed.]

Ver. 34.—**So Benaiah, the son of Jehoiada, went up** [not because the altar "stood higher up Mount Zion than Solomon's house" (Keil), but because Gibeon, where the tabernacle and brazen altar then were, stood higher than Jerusalem. It is remarkable that retribution thus overtook Joab on the very scene of his last murder, for it was "at the great stone which is in Gibeon" (2 Sam. xx. 8), that he slew Amasa. Cf. 2 Kings ix. 26 : "I will requite thee in this plat, saith the Lord"], **and fell upon him, and slew him : and he was buried in his own house** [possibly in the courtyard : hardly in the garden. The same is recorded of Samuel (1 Sam. xxv. 1). It was evidently an exceptional occurrence. Remembering the estimation in which the Jew held the corpse and the grave (Num. xix. 11, 16, 22 ; cf. Matt. xxiii. 27), it must have been a singular honour to make of the house a mausoleum. No doubt it was designed to be such in Joab's case. Whatever his crimes, his services had deserved well of his country. Possibly his friends were led to pay him this special honour as a kind of counterpoise to the ignominy of his death] **in the wilderness** [*i.e.*, of Judah. Joab's mother was of Bethlehem, which was on the border of the desert. The "wilderness of Tekoah" (2 Chron. xx. 20), according to Jerome, was visible from Bethlehem, being but six Roman miles distant.

Ver. 35.—**And the king put Benaiah the son of Jehoiada in his room over the host : and Zadok the priest did the king put in the room of Abiathar.** [It is hardly likely that Joab would be retained in command of the army after the conspiracy of chap. i., nor is this implied in this verse, the meaning of which is that Benaiah took the place of Joab, and that Zadok henceforward was sole high priest.]

HOMILETICS.

Vers. 26, 27.—*The Degraded High Priest.* We may find in this section a sermon on *Cæsarism.* The relations of the world-power to the Church; the province of the State and the prerogatives of the clergy; what are the proper limits of the temporal power and what is the exclusive domain of the spiritual; these have been vexed questions for many centuries. They are prominent topics at the present day. We may perhaps find in this history a few principles to guide us. For we learn

I. THAT PRIESTS HAD BETTER NOT MEDDLE WITH POLITICS. No one can deny their abstract right to do so. They are men, if they are clergymen, and "*nihil humani*," &c. As citizens, they may have convictions. Having convictions, they may surely give effect to them. No one can deny again that they have often interfered to good purpose. Witness the case of Jehoiada. It may sometimes be a duty to interfere. But all the same, their plane is not the plane of politics. Their πολίτευμα is the Church. And what is lawful, is not always expedient. Their meddling has often cost not only them, but the Church, dear. Well had it been for Abiathar; well for the Wolseys, Richelieus, and many more, had they never given up "to party what was meant for mankind." There are questions—imperial questions of right and wrong—where the clergy must speak out; there are other questions—party questions—where, for their own and their flocks' sake, they had better hold their peace.

II. THAT PRIESTS ARE MEN OF LIKE PASSIONS WITH OTHER MEN. Abiathar apparently was not free from that "last infirmity of noble minds." It was probably jealousy of Zadok impelled him to conspire against Solomon, and to join hands with the murderer Joab against the prophet Nathan. Neither the holy anointing oil nor the discharge of the priest's office destroys the *phronema sarkos* (see Art. IX.) It is worthy of note that the first high priest was guilty of idolatry, envy, and murmurings; that the sons of Eli committed abominable crimes; and that the high priests Annas and Caiaphas condemned the Lord of Glory. Every high priest needed to "make atonement for *his own sins*" (Lev. xvi. 6, 11). Abiathar, the minister of God, was a traitor against God and His anointed. Having the frailties, temptations, and passions of other men, priests often commit sins, sometimes commit crimes.

III. THAT PRIESTS MAY BE PUNISHED FOR THEIR CRIMES BY THE SECULAR POWER. For centuries the Latin Church contended with our forefathers for the exemption of ecclesiastics from the authority of civil tribunals. But the Jewish priests enjoyed no such exemption. Abiathar was threatened by Solomon with death, and was thrust out of his office. Our Great High Priest respected the tribunal of Pontius Pilate. And His apostle answered for himself before Felix and Festus, and before great Cæsar himself. (Cf. Art. xxxvii. of the "Articles of Religion.") But

IV. PRIESTS ARE TO BE TREATED WITH THE REVERENCE DUE TO THEIR OFFICE. "Because thou barest the ark of the LORD GOD." Criminous c'ergy are not to be so punished as to bring their sacred calling into contempt (not, *e.g.*, to be set to sweep the streets, as General Butler forced one of the American bishops to do in New Orleans). If the man is entitled to no consideration, the office is. He wears the livery of the Great King. The vessel is "earthen," but the treasure "heavenly" (2 Cor. iv. 7). "As men are to God's ministers, they will find Him to them."

V. PRIESTS MAY BE DEGRADED FROM THEIR POSITION, BUT CANNOT BE DEPRIVED OF THEIR PRIESTHOOD. They did not derive their authority from the civil power. It did not give, and it cannot take away. David did not make Abiathar priest, and Solomon could not unmake him. We find from chapter iv. 4 that he was still called "priest." He that is "called of God, as was Aaron," can only be recalled of God. When Solomon "thrust out Abiathar," he "deprived him of his dignity, but did not strip him of his priesthood" (Theodoret). The state may fine, imprison, banish, put to death Christ's ambassadors according to their deserts, but it may not alter their message, tamper with their creeds, confer their orders, or prescribe their ordinances. "To Cæsar the things which are Cæsar's, and unto God the things that are God's."

VI. IN REMOVING THE UNWORTHY PRIEST THE CIVIL POWER IS FULFILLING THE WILL OF THE LORD. The "sure word of prophecy"—indeed a double prophecy—had its fulfilment when Solomon banished Abiathar. The secular power thereby accomplished the good pleasure of God declared four hundred years before (Num. xxv. 13). And the magistrate who, in the exercise of the authority conferred on him by God for the punishment of evil doers, degrades the criminous priest, silences him, visits him with appropriate pains and penalties, is doing God service; is fulfilling the will of God, who would have evil ministers above all others brought to justice and chastised; the more influential their example, the more need of conspicuous and exemplary punishment.

Vers. 26—35.—*The Death of Joab.* "Know ye not that there is a prince and a great man fallen this day in Israel"—so might men say as they heard, so may we say as we read, the history of Joab's death. After David, he was by far the greatest man—the ablest general, the bravest soldier, the most capable statesman—of that age. He was "the Marlborough, the Belisarius of the Jewish empire." He had fought David's battles, won his conquests, captured his citadel, and twice preserved for him his crown. It is a sad and tragic ending of such a brilliant career. The idol of the army, the man who was first in the deadly breach (2 Chron. xi. 6), the ever victorious hero, dies miserably, by the thrust of an old comrade. For him the sanctuary of God has no protection. Though he clings to the horns of the altar, it avails him nothing. No, the blood of the white-headed warrior, winner of a hundred well-fought fields, streams round the consecrated structure and stains the place of the Divine Presence. What are the lessons, let us ask, of such a death? And, first—

I. WHY IS HE HERE? It is (1) *because his conscience has made him a coward.* He who never turned his back on the foe, has fled before a breath, a mere rumour. He has not been attacked, not even threatened; but the secret is out, the conspiracy is discovered, his head is forfeited. He betrays his guilt by his flight. Time was when he would have faced almost any danger, when he would have died rather than fled. But then he had a support and stay, in the consciousness of rectitude, which he has not now. Now, his own heart denounces him.

> "None have accused thee; 'tis thy conscience cries."

The man whose conscience is burdened with crime has an enemy, a traitor, within the camp. But why has he fled to the *sanctuary;* why chosen the tabernacle of God for his refuge? For Joab has not loved the habitation of God's house. The tabernacle of the Lord could not be "amiable" to that guilty heart. *His* choice would be "the congregation of evildoers." A stranger to the tabernacle and its services, why is he here? It is (2) *because men often betake themselves in adversity to the religion they despised in prosperity.* Yes, Joab's is no solitary case. It is too common. Witness the so-called deathbed repentances; witness the cries and prayers which go up in the hour of peril from lips which never prayed before. Men who have neglected God and contemned the ordinances of religion in health often turn to Him and to them in sickness. "It is the fashion of our foolish presumption to look for protection where we have not cared to yield obedience." *But* (3) *the altar of God is for sacrifice, not for sanctuary.* The purpose of the altar, its *raison d'être,* was that sacrifices, *i.e.,* that worship, might be offered thereon. It was an accident, so to speak, that made of it a sanctuary; the accident of its sacredness. Because it was ordained of God, fashioned after a Divine pattern and employed in the Divine service, it was naturally and rightly regarded as holy, as a structure not to be profaned, and hence the manslayer fled thither for protection. But this use of the altar was quite beside its original intention. It was made for *worship,* for the service of God, not for the defence of man. Joab disregarded its proper use; he used it for his own convenience. And have we not seen something like this in our own days? Religion is ordained for man to live by. Its primary purpose is the glory of God. It exists that man may offer "spiritual sacrifices, acceptable to God;" that man may be himself "a living sacrifice." But there are those who would use it only as a sanctuary, as a place to flee to when they can sin no longer. They want the benefits of religion without its obligations; they pervert it from its proper and holy, to a purely selfish purpose; they want it for *death* and it was meant for *life.* They act, *i.e.,* much as Joab did, and it is to be feared their last end will not be unlike his. The altar they have slighted will not shelter them in the day of evil.

II. But let us now ask, secondly, WHY IS HE PUT TO DEATH HERE? The altar was never meant to be stained with *human* blood. If it was not for sanctuary, still less was it for slaughter. And it has sheltered many; why may it afford *him* no asylum? It is (1) *Because he has come to it too late.* Had he come before, and come as a worshipper, he would not have needed to come now as a fugitive. Had he even come, after his great crimes, as a sincere penitent, he might, perchance, have found forgiveness. David was delivered from blood-guiltiness, and why not Joab?

But he only comes to the altar because he is driven to it; because he can do nothing else. Yes, " it is too late to cry for mercy when it is the time of justice." Those who put off repentance till they can sin no longer find that such feigned repentance profits them nothing. There is a time when " the door is shut." 2. *Because " he shall have judgment without mercy that showed no mercy."* Joab's murders could not have been more treacherous, more cruel. " The blood of war in peace." " Took him aside in the gate to speak with him peaceably " (2 Sam. iii. 27, marg.). " Took Amasa by the beard with the right hand to kiss him" (ib. xx. 9). There is a *lex talionis* which governs the dealings of God with transgressors. The cruel murderer shall be cruelly murdered. The assassin shall be executed at the altar. He that " showed no pity " shall receive none. 3. *Because God pays sure, even if he pays slowly.* It was thirty-four years—an entire generation—since Abner's blood first cried from the ground. Eight years had elapsed since Amasa's death. And Joab, meanwhile, had maintained his position. Still " over all the host of Israel," still second only to the king. If ever he or others had dreamed of punishment, they must by this time have given up all fear, or all hope. David had died and Joab still lived. Joab had conspired once and yet he was spared. Is there, men would ask, a retributive Justice? is there a " God that judgeth the earth " ? Yes, though Joab has " hoar hairs," though he has all but gone down to the grave in peace, his sin has found him out. And the blood which reddens those gray hairs, the blood which crimsons the sanctuary, proves that there is a Nemesis for crime : that if Justice has a halting foot, she nevertheless overtakes the fleetest offender ; that " if 'the mills of God grind slowly, yet they grind exceedingly small." 4. *Because " without shedding of blood there is no remission."* Only the blood of Joab could expiate the bloodshed he had wrought. Nothing else could cleanse the land. For innocent blood guilty blood ; this was the law. How different is the gospel. The blood of Christ speaketh better things than the blood of Abel, ay, than the blood of Joab. The blood of Joab made an atonement for the land. There the guilty died because of the innocent. The blood of JESUS made an atonement for the world. Here the innocent dies because of the guilty. The blood of Joab tells of vengeance, of retribution, of death. The blood of JESUS speaks of mercy, of restitution, of life and love and peace. Yes, the death of Joab may surely speak to us, but it speaks to little purpose, unless it tells us of " the precious blood of Christ."

EXPOSITION.

CHAPTER II. 36—46.

THE END OF SHIMEI.—This fresh intrigue of Adonijah's warns the king that he must be on his guard and keep a watch over suspected persons. Prominent among these, from his antecedents and connexions, would be Shimei.

Ver. 36.—**And the king sent and called for Shimei** [probably from Bahurim. But see on ver. 8] **and said unto him, Build thee** [Not necessarily as "a guarantee for his residence there" (Wordsworth). Jewish law would make a purchase difficult. Lev. xxv. 23. Cf. 1 Kings xxi. 3] **an house in Jerusalem and dwell there** [where he would be under *surveillance* and where his sinister influence with the men of Benjamin would be neutralized] **and go not forth thence any whither** [or, " hither and thither." *Weder dahin noch dorthin.* Bähr.]

Ver. 37.—**For it shall be, on the day thou goest out and passest over the brook** [lit., watercourse, wâdy. The Kidron is quite dry, except during and for a short time after the winter rains] **Kidron** [The Kidron is mentioned specially because that was the direction which, it might be presumed, Shimei would take, his old home being at Bahurim], **thou shalt know for certain that thou shalt surely die** [The Hebrew is, if possible, still more striking and emphatic, " To know thou shalt know that to die thou shalt die." Shimei could not say that he had not been plainly warned]: **thy blood shall be upon thine own head.** [Cf. Lev. xx. 9, and especially Joshua ii. 19 ; also ver. 31 of this chapter.

Ver. 38.—**And Shimei said to the king, The saying** [or thing, matter, רָבָד, like λόγος ῥῆμα, in Greek (cf. *Sache*, in Germ., from *sagen*) means (1) word and (2) deed] **is good** [Shimei cannot complain of the condition, remembering what he had done (2 Sam. xv. 5-7) and that Solomon was not bound by his father's oath (2 Sam. xix. 23)]:

as my lord the king hath said, so will thy servant do. And Shimei dwelt [in obedience to this behest] in Jerusalem many days.

Ver. 39.—And it came to pass at the end of three years that two of the servants of Shimei ran away [it has been thought by some that their flight was preconcerted with their master. But the narrative does not favour this supposition] to Achish, son of Maachah, king of Gath. [This may well have been the "Achish, son of Maoch" (1 Sam. xxi. 11; xxvii. 2), to whom David fled fifty years before. Longer reigns than this are not unknown to history. Or it may have been his grandson]. And they told Shimei, saying, Behold, thy servants be in Gath.

Ver. 40.—And Shimei arose and saddled his ass [not necessarily himself. *Qui facit per alium, facit per se.* Matthew Henry thinks Shimei did it himself for the sake of secrecy. Many expositors also think that he went by night. The text rather suggests the idea that both the going and the return were perfectly open and undisguised] and went to Gath. [It is impossible to avoid the question, What can have led to this infatuated disregard of his oath and life? Now his perversity may of course have been judicial—*quos Deus vult perdere, prius dementat*—but as to the means which led to this issue, it is enough if we may believe he had been *dared* to it either by his servants or others. The fierce Benjamite would naturally be galled to the quick by the thought that his slaves could thus openly set him at defiance; he may have heard from those who came from Gath that they were exulting over him; and he may have resolved at all hazards to teach them a lesson. He cannot have *forgotten* either Solomon's explicit warning or his own solemn oath (ver. 42); he must have gone to Gath with his eyes open, and nothing but a great provocation, such as mockery and defiance, will account for his going.] And Shimei went and brought his servants from Gath.

Ver. 41.—And it was told Solomon that Shimei had gone from Jerusalem to Gath and was come again. [He, no doubt, persuaded himself that his immediate *return*, especially when taken in connexion with the object of his journey, would excuse him to the king. He would perhaps argue that a magnanimous sovereign like Solomon could never deal hardly with one who thus placed his life in his hands. He can hardly have built his hopes on his not having crossed the *Kidron*, for he must have perfectly understood that he was to go "*no whither*."

Ver. 42.—And the king sent and called for Shimei, and said unto him, Did I not make thee swear by the Lord [it thus comes out quite incidentally that Solomon had bound Shimei by an oath. The LXX. embodies this information as a direct statement in the text of ver. 37, καὶ ὥρκισεν αὐτὸν ὁ βασιλεὺς ἐν τῇ ἡμέρᾳ ἐκείνῃ, but it is obviously a gloss] and protested unto thee, saying, Know for a certain, on the day that thou goest out and walkest abroad any whither, that thou shalt surely die? and thou saidst unto me, The word that I have heard is good. [The LXX. (Vat.) omits "And thou saidst," &c. This last sentence has been punctuated thus: "Good is the word. I have heard." Probably אֲשֶׁר, "which," is to be understood.

Ver. 43.—Why then hast thou not kept the oath of the Lord and the commandment that I have charged [Heb. *commanded*] thee with. ["Shimei ought to have been warned against trifling with Solomon's forbearance by the punishment already inflicted on Adonijah and Joab." Wordsworth.]

Ver. 44.—The king said, moreover [Heb. *And the king said*] Thou knowest all the wickedness which thine heart is privy to [Heb. *knoweth*] that thou didst to David my father [Solomon brings a threefold charge against Shimei. He has violated a solemn oath, "by the life of Jehovah," and so has "profaned the name of his God" (Lev. xix. 12). He has broken his parole and set at naught the king's commandment. He has defied and blasphemed the Lord's anointed. He must die] therefore the Lord shall return ["hath returned," or "returns." LXX. ἀνταπέδωκε, aor. The king regards himself as merely the instrument and dispenser of the Divine Justice. According to him, it is God, not spite, demands and has brought about Shimei's execution] thy wickedness upon thine own head [Every Jew, taught to expect that "every transgression and disobedience" would receive its "just recompense of reward" in this life present would see in Shimei's almost unaccountable infatuation the finger of God. To them he would seem delivered up to destruction.

Ver. 45.—And king Solomon shall be blessed, and the throne of David shall be established before the Lord for ever. [It is inconceivable that Solomon could have spoken thus if he had been conscious either of sharp practice, or spite, or cruelty. The words are those of one who is sure that he is doing God service.]

Ver. 46.—So the king commanded Benaiah, the son of Jehoiada, which went out and fell upon him that he died. [The execution of Shimei has, perhaps, on the whole given more offence than that of Joab or even Adonijah. He, at any rate, was not "a murderer whom vengeance suffereth not to live," nor had he taken any part in recent conspiracies. On the contrary, he seems to have lived quietly enough under the eye of the king. And it consequently has the appearance of cruelty and malevolence that Solomon should "press the letter of a compact against him," especially when, by returning to Jerusalem, he placed his life at Solomon's mercy. But it is not difficult to offer a complete justification of Solomon's action in this matter. In the first place, it is to be remembered that cruelty had no part in his character. In his long reign of forty years there are absolutely no evidences of a brutal and tyrannical disposition. There is a strong presumption, consequently, that he was not actuated by cruelty on this occasion, a presumption which finds support in the consideration that Solomon was much too sagacious to prejudice himself in popular estimation at the commencement of his reign by proceedings which would have the least suspicion of vindictiveness. And (2) with this probability the facts of the case entirely agree. Shimei's life, as we have seen, was forfeited to Jewish law. As he had so long been spared, however, the king gave him a gracious respite. The conditions imposed were not onerous. Shimei had but to keep his parole and he would live; to break it and he would assuredly die. He *did* break it; not without provocation, it may be, but he broke it, and broke too his solemn oath. It may be said it was hard he should lose his slaves, but better, surely, lose them than his life. Besides, there

were other ways of recovering them; or, if he must pursue them in person, his proper course was evidently to ask the king's permission. That he did not do so is in itself a suspicious circumstance, and Solomon might reasonably think that the flight of the slaves was but a feint, and that Shimei's visit to a foreign court had really a political object. But, be that as it may, the king had protested unto him that if he went any whither, he should most certainly die. When he went, when he despised the royal command and disregarded his sacred oath, how was it possible for Solomon to break his word? To do so would have been inevitably to compromise himself with his subjects, and to forfeit their reverence and trust. Besides, there was a duty he owed to his dead father, and above all, one which he owed to the living God. He had now the opportunity for which his father bade him wait, of putting into force the provisions of the Mosaic law, of requiring the death of the blasphemer, of showing his subjects that the law could not be defied with impunity, that though vengeance was not executed speedily against evil works, still retribution was certain in the long run, and so of teaching them a much needed lesson of obedience and respect of authority. Every consideration, therefore, of justice, morality, filial piety, and religion warranted him in putting Shimei to death. Every imputation of weakness, irresolution, disregard of his plighted word, compromise of his royal dignity, and indifference to religion might justly have been levelled against him, had he interfered between Shimei and the sword of Justice.

HOMILETICS.

Vers. 44—46.—*The End of the Transgressor.* Such was the end of Shimei— violent, sanguinary, shameful. Old man as he is, he may not die in peace: his hoar hairs must be crimsoned with his blood. What does this teach? what its message to Christian men? It is twofold. It speaks (1) OF THE SIN, (2) OF THE RETRIBUTION.

I. It teaches (1) *The sin of treason.* He had offered insult and defiance to his lawful king. Rebellion against constituted authority can only be justified by intolerable tyranny and outrage. He who

> "dares to wield
> The regicidal steel"

must answer to Him by whom kings govern. We are to "honour the king," to "be subject to the higher powers." "They that resist shall receive to themselves damnation," as did this rebel Benjamite. 2. *The sin of blasphemy.* "A grievous curse." Aimed at the king, it reached the King of kings. It was not only destructive of authority; not only an affront offered to the majesty of law; it was an indirect blow at the Majesty of Heaven. Men cannot "speak evil of dignities" without sin. Those who "curse God" will "die" (Job ii. 9). How little do men make of blasphemy! But Shimei had to pay for it with his life. 3. *The sin of perjury.* It was this in the strict sense of the word. He *broke through* his oath. Though he said, "the Lord liveth," he swore falsely. He thus profaned the awful incommunicable name, and incurred the Divine curse (Zech. v. 4). Perjuries are plentiful in our days, our police courts being witness. (Some kiss the thumb, and not the book.) "The Lord will not hold him guiltless," &c. 4. *The sin of disobedience.* The king had adjured him, had "protested," had said "know for certain," &c.; and even if the Kidron were mentioned arbitrarily, still it served to test his obedience. The prohibition, therefore, could not have been plainer. He disregarded it, and died. "Fool," does any one say? Stay! The great King has said, "The soul that sinneth, it shall die." He has solemnly testified what will be the doom of disobedience, and yet how often have *we* crossed our Kidron—the bound of His law—have gone after our own lusts and pleasures, and it is only because He is God and not man, only because

"the heart of the Eternal
Is most wonderfully kind,"

that we have not died. 5. *The sin and folly of presumption.* Whatever may have led Shimei to go after his slaves, it was certainly presumption brought him back. He would hardly have returned had he not counted on forgiveness. No doubt he had persuaded himself either that Solomon would never know, or that, if he did, he would be magnanimous. "Allowance will be made for me," he had said; "my return will disarm suspicion and ensure clemency." But the sword of Benaiah soon undeceived him. And such will be the end—death, shame, everlasting contempt—of those who presume on the mercy of God. How many say, "God is so good, He will never be hard upon us," &c. But is God *true?* Can He deny Himself? Even Solomon could not go back from his word; and can the Holy One? Alas, if despair has slain its thousands, presumption has slain its ten thousands. It is a significant fact that since the invention of the safety lamp there have been more accidents in mines than there were before.

II. As to the RETRIBUTION, we are reminded, 1. *That curses commonly come home to roost.* The "grievous curse" of Shimei did not hurt David. But it was his own destruction. The poisoned arrow missed its mark, but it recoiled on the archer. The engineer is hoist by his own petard. A curse rests on those who curse the king (cf. Eccles. x. 20). 2. *That respite does not mean release.* When David "sware" to him, Shimei thought himself safe. Surely the bitterness of death was past. He would die in his nest. We often mistake God's forbearance for forgetfulness. He is long-suffering, and men ask, "Where is the promise of His coming?" Because "He does not settle His accounts once a week" (Goethe) the heart of the sons of men is fully set in them to do evil. But the day of retribution comes as a thief, as the flood, as the sword, as the snare. 3. *That if we die, it is our own fault.* Shimei had his life in his own hands. It rested with him alone whether he lived or died. He should live, if he would but live at Jerusalem. But he chose death. Men cause their own destruction. God has no pleasure in their death. "Thou hast *destroyed thyself.*" 4. *That warnings are commonly lost on the wicked.* "How could Shimei be so infatuated?" we ask. What, have we not seen his infatuation paralleled? Have we never seen repeated warnings repeatedly neglected? Yes, souls, sins, warnings, results, are the same in all ages. 5. *That when God reckons, He reckons for all.* The sword avenged the sin of eight years before. And in the Great Assize, everything—both cup of cold water and idle word—will receive its just recompense of reward.

HOMILIES BY VARIOUS AUTHORS.

Vers. 41—46.—*Retributions.* This is one example of the way in which Solomon carried out David's dying command, as given in verses 5—9. Shimei's violation of his promise in reference to not leaving Jerusalem, though the immediate occasion, was thus not the real reason of his punishment. He had been all along a doomed man. A great deal in David's command in reference to these men that we cannot regard with complacency; so far as there was anything of personal vindictiveness in it, our moral sense condemns it. Would it not have been more magnanimous if with his dying breath he had freely forgiven these old offenders? Solomon's conduct, however, wears a different aspect. A father's word would be to him an imperious authority; to vindicate a father's honour the instinctive impulse of filial affection; to avenge the innocent blood a sacred obligation. Moreover, these men deserved their fate. Joab had been a traitor and murderer; Abiathar had abused the sanctity of his priestly office by helping the cause of the usurper; Shimei had "cursed the Lord's anointed." This incident suggests—

I. THE ETERNAL LAW THAT WRONG-DOING MUST BE FOLLOWED BY ITS DUE RECOMPENSE. Recognise the Divine element in this act of human retribution. There is a Nemesis that tracks the steps of the transgressor, and sooner or later overtakes him; not a natural law merely, but an intelligent Divine will and power. The superstition of the Melitans had a deep and solemn truth in it (Acts xxviii. 4). Striking correspondence often between the sin and the penalty. Men suffer in forms resembling the injury they inflict. "Whoso sheddeth man's blood," &c. "All they that take the sword," &c. The weapon used wrongfully recoils upon the head of him who wielded it. "Curses, like birds, come home to roost." In the teaching of Christ and His apostles, however, the law of retribution appears, not in its old bare, crude form, but in a more vital and spiritual form. New Testament idea—sin bears within itself the germ of its own punishment. The penalty is a development rather than an arbitrary infliction. "Sin, when it is finished, bringeth forth death." Sin may be divinely forgiven, and yet go on to produce in this world all sorts of bitter fruits. "May one be pardoned and retain the offence?" No; but the pardoned man may retain in himself the evil effects of what he has done, and see, with infinite remorse, the evil effects in others. The sin, as a "finished" fact, takes its place in the general procession of cause and effect, independently of God's mercy to the transgressor. On the other hand, the worst retribution is in the moral nature of the sinner himself.

> "There is no future pang
> Can deal that justice on the self-condemn'd
> He deals on his own soul." (*Manfred.*)
>
> (*E.g.*, SHAKESPEARE'S *Macbeth*; MILTON'S *Satan*.)

No escape from this retribution but in "the cross." "The blood of Jesus Christ his Son," &c. It will not wipe out *all* the effects of transgression, but it will arrest the eternal penalty, and perfectly cleanse the fountain from which the evil springs.

II. THE NOBLENESS OF A TRUTHFUL AND FEARLESS DISCHARGE OF DUTY. Solomon's deed a homage to the sense of duty. Magnanimity blended with severity. He spares Abiathar, but has no mercy on Joab and Shimei. Note the reasons of this distinction. As a "man of peace" he had no love for this retributive work. It might involve him in trouble. But he shrinks not from doing the thing he conceives to be right. Men often constrained by force of circumstances, or persuasion of a Divine voice within them, to do what they have no natural inclination for doing. Essence of all moral nobleness to make duty rather than inclination or policy the law of one's life. In men of highest nature conscience is the ruling power. However it may appear, that Life is the most blessed which is the most perfect homage to the law of right.

II. THE SUPERIORITY OF CHRISTIAN ETHICS ABOVE THE MORAL STANDARD OF OLDEN TIMES. In following the chronicles of these old Hebrew kings we feel that we are moving in a moral region of somewhat dim light and low level. It must needs be so if there is a real law of development in Scripture and the dispensations of God. We may recognise the working of Divine principles of truth and righteousness amid the confusions of the time, and yet feel that we have in the law of Christ a far higher rule of conduct. We admit what is good in David and Solomon, but HE is our model who, on the cross of sacrifice, prayed, "Father, forgive them, for they know not what they do."—W.

EXPOSITION.

CHAPTER III. 1—15.

THE BEGINNING OF SOLOMON'S REIGN.—
In the preceding chapter we have seen
the establishment of Solomon's rule (ver.
46) by the removal of internal foes, *i.e.*,
of disaffected and rebellious subjects. In
this we see him strengthening his position
by an external alliance, by a marriage with
an Egyptian princess. This event, however,
is related here, not because the historian
had this connexion of ideas in his mind, but
probably because the marriage came next in
order of time.

Ver. 1.—**And Solomon made affinity** [Not
" alliance " (as some have supposed) but
relationship. Lit., *made himself son-in-law*]
with Pharaoh king of Egypt [which of
the Pharaohs this was, it is impossible to
say with certainty. As, however, Shishak
(ch. xi. 40 ; xiv. 25) is undoubtedly the
Sheshonk who succeeded to the throne of
Egypt in the 26th year of Solomon (Poole),
and who was the first king of the 22nd
dynasty of Manetho, we may safely identify
this Pharaoh with " a late king of the 21st
(or Janite) dynasty." It has been assumed
(Bunsen, Ewald, Brugsch, *al.*) that it was
Psusennes II., the last king of that house,
on the supposition that he reigned 35 years,
(as stated by Eusebius), but according to
Africanus, his reign was limited to 14 years.
It is wiser to say, therefore, with Mr. Poole
(Dict. Bib., " Pharaoh ") that this Pharaoh
" cannot yet be identified on Manetho's
list." It is also impossible to decide whether
the alliance was first sought by Solomon
with a view to win over a powerful and
dangerous neighbour (Thenius), to whose
inroads his northern border was exposed,
and especially to counteract the influence (ch.
xi. 21) of Hadad (Plumptre), or whether the
marriage was proposed by Pharaoh because
the 21st dynasty "had then become very
weak" (Rawlinson) and its head desired
" friendly relations with the kingdom of
Israel, which had grown into a power to
be dreaded " (Keil). But we may reasonably
suppose that the alliance " must have been
to most Israelites a very startling one "
(Plumptre.) Egypt (Rahab, Psa. lxxxix.
10 ; Isa. li. 9) was to every Israelite a
name both of triumph and dread. The
Pharaohs were their ancestral foes], **and
took Pharaoh's daughter** [A marriage such
as this was not without precedent (Gen. xli.
45 ; Exod. ii. 21 ; Num. xii. 1 ; Matt. i. 5 ;

Ruth iv. 13), nor was it condemned by the
Law, which only forbade intermarriage with
the nations of Canaan (Exod. xxxiv. 16 ;
Deut. vii. 3), and sanctioned the union of
an Israelite with a captive taken in war
(Deut. xxi. 13 ; cf. xx. 14). " At the same
time, it was only when the foreign wives
renounced idolatry . . . that such marriages
were in accordance with the spirit of the
law " (Keil). As Solomon at this period of
his life faithfully observed the law, as he is
never blamed for this marriage, and as there
is no trace whatever of the introduction of
Egyptian rites into Israel, it is a fair presumption that the Egyptian princess conformed to the religion of her adopted
country], **and brought her into the city of
David** [2 Chron. viii. 11 speaks of her
dwelling in " the *house* of David," *i.e.*, it
would seem, the palace which David had
occupied] **until he had made an end** [this
hardly shows that he had begun to build,
as Keil infers. He did not begin building
the Temple until the fourth (1 Kings vi. 1), nor
his own house until the eleventh year (*ib.*
vii. 1) after his accession, and the marriage,
though not at the very commencement of
his reign, can hardly have been delayed to
the eleventh year, and may have taken place
before the death of Shimei] **of building his
own house** [cf. ch. vii. 7] **and the house of
the Lord** [cf. ch. vi. ; vii. 51] **and the wall of
Jerusalem round about.** [Probably, he
both strengthened and extended the city
walls, as Josephus (Ant. viii. 6. 1) affirms.
Acc. to the LXX. addition to ch. xii., it was
on this task that Jeroboam was employed
(ch. xi. 27 ; cf. ix. 15). David had fortified
a part of the city (2 Sam. v. 9).

Ver. 2.—**Only** [The word perhaps signifies
" that there was one exception to the flourishing condition of things which the writer
has been describing" (Rawlinson), though
the people are nowhere blamed for sacrificing on the high places, and Solomon's sacrifice at " the great high place " was full of
blessing. The idea rather is that just as he
was obliged to bring his Egyptian wife into
the city of David, because his palace was
not yet finished, so the people were compelled to sacrifice on the high places, because the temple was not yet built (Keil),
and " the place " where God would put His
name had only just been chosen (1 Chron.
xxii. 1)] **the people sacrificed** [Heb. *were
sacrificing*, *i.e.*, habitually, constantly] **in
high places** [All nations have chosen hill tops
for acts of worship, perhaps as being nearer
heaven. " Even Abraham built an altar to
the Lord on a mountain near Bethel (Gen.

xii. 7, 8; cf. xxii. 2, 9; xxxi. 54)." And the use of high places for this purpose was not *distinctly* condemned in the Law. It is true the Hebrews were commanded to have but one place of sacrifice (Lev. xvii. 9; Deut. xii. 5, 11, 13, 26, 27; cf. Jos. xxii, 29), and this no doubt was, if not an indirect prohibition, a discouragement of such sanctuaries. It has been held, however, that this command was purely prospective, and it is certainly remarkable that even when the Israelites were settled in the promised land, and the tabernacle was set up (Josh. xviii. 1), altars were constantly built and sacrifices offered on high places, and sometimes, as in the case of Gideon (Judg. vi. 26), and Manoah (*ib.* xiii. 19, 20), by express Divine command. Later on we find Samuel (1 Sam. vii. 9, 10; xi. 15; xvi. 5), Saul (xiii. 9; xiv. 35), David (1 Chron. xxi. 26), Solomon and Elijah (1 Kings xviii. 30), offering sacrifices in various places, which they could not have done had it seemed to them that this was condemned beforehand by the Law. It is highly probable, therefore, that though the contemporaries of Joshua took a different view (as Josh. xxii. 15—31 proves), the men of a later age excused themselves on the ground stated in the text, that "there was no house built unto the name of the Lord." It has been held by some that " had they not sacrificed and burnt incense on high places, they could not have sacrificed or burnt incense at all " (Bp. Horsley); but this seems to overlook the fact that there was one place provided for sacrifices—the door of the tabernacle—and that for some reason or other they sacrificed elsewhere. And the reason, no doubt, was the one assigned by the historian. It should be added that this term " high place " (בָּמָה) came to be used of *all* places of worship, not only on heights, but even those in valleys (2 Kings xvii. 9; Jer. vii. 31; xxxii. 35). The Bamah sometimes consisted of an altar only, but as a rule, there was a shrine or sanctuary erected hard by (ch. xiii. 32; 2 Kings xvii. 29; xxiii. 19), the *Beth-Bamah*, for which the word *Bamah* is sometimes loosely employed (ch. xi. 7; xiv. 23; 2 Kings xxi. 3)], **because there was no house built unto the name of the Lord until those days.**

Ver. 3.—**And Solomon loved the Lord** [thus keeping the first and great commandment, the " Shema Israel " (Deut. vi. 5; cf. xxx. 16; Matt. xxii. 37; Luke x, 27], **walking in the statutes of David his father** [*i.e.*, those which David had kept (verses 6, 14) and commanded him to keep (ch. ii. 4)] : **only he sacrificed and burnt incense in high places.** [These words clearly show that the worship of the high places, although condoned, and

indeed accepted, by God (ver. 5) was not strictly lawful and right. It was an ignorance that God winked at. The historian, remembering what the worship of the high places became, notices this as an imperfection of Solomon's early reign, though he does not say that such worship was sinful.

Ver. 4.—**And the king went to Gibeon** [Josh. ix. 3; x. 2; xviii. 25; xxi. 17; 2 Sam. xxi. 1. Now known as *El-Jib*, a commanding eminence (as the name implies) some six miles north of Jerusalem. Strictly, it consists of *two* heights, on one of which, it is conjectured, the town stood, while the other was the high place. Solomon was accompanied to Gibeon by " all the congregation," including the captains, judges, governors, &c. (2 Chron. i. 2, 3] **to sacrifice there** [This religious service was designed to inaugurate his reign (2 Chron. i. 13), after the precedent of 1 Sam. xi. 15; cf. 2 Sam. vi. 2. His object was also to supplicate the Divine blessing on his undertakings. If his visit served at the same time as a farewell, or " honourable funeral to the tabernacle " (Wordsw.) this was an accident] ; **for that was the great high place** [being the place of the tabernacle and brazen altar. In 1 Sam. xxi. 6 we find the tabernacle at Nob, though without the ark (1 Sam. iv. 2). After the massacre of the priests it lost the ephod (1 Sam. xxii. 20; xxiii. 6). It could hardly remain in a spot stained by so much blood ; but how or when it found its way to Gibeon, we do not know. See 1 Chron. xvi. 37, 39; 2 Chron. i. 3-6] : **a thousand burnt offerings** [such numbers were not infrequent at festivals. See on ch. viii. 62, and cf. 2 Chron. xxix. 33, 34. Rawlinson reminds us that " Xerxes offered 1000 oxen at Troy" (Herod. vii. 43).] **did Solomon offer** [not, of course, personally, as some (Ewald. *e.g.*) have supposed. He is said to have " offered " them, because he (together with the congregation, perhaps) provided them. The immense number alone shows that he cannot have offered in person. The festival probably lasted for seven or eight days, but even then a thousand victims can hardly have been offered whole (עֹלָה) unless the altar was greatly enlarged, or additional temporary altars were erected. This latter supposition is not negatived by the next words. See on ch. viii. 63, 64.] **upon that altar.**

Ver. 5.—**In Gibeon the Lord appeared unto Solomon in a dream** [cf. Num. xii. 6. A vision is not necessarily implied (as in Gen. xxviii. 12; cf. xv. 12), though he may have seen some angelic form (*angelus Dei nomine ei apparuit loquens.* Grotius)— of course, only in his dream. Cf. Matt. i. 20; ii. 12. Probably " appeared " is the equivalent of " revealed Himself." Bähr] by night; and God said, Ask what I shall give thee [cf. Matt. vii. 7. This was the answer to the sacrifices. The night was probably that which followed the last day on which they were offered (ver. 15).]

Ver. 6.—And Solomon said, Thou hast shewed unto [Heb. *wrought with*] thy servant David my father great mercy [marg., *favour*] according as he walked before thee in truth, and in righteousness, and in uprightness of heart with thee [cf. 2 Kings xx. 3, where Hezekiah uses much the same language of himself. Also ch. xi. 4], and thou hast kept for him this great kindness [Heb. *favour ;* same word as above. David himself had regarded this as a singular mercy (ch. i. 48)], that thou hast given him a son to sit [Heb. *sitting*] upon his throne, as it is this day. [Same expression Deut. vi. 24 ; viii. 18 ; 1 Sam. xxii. 8. ; Ezra ix. 7.]

Ver. 7.— And now, O Lord my God, thou hast made thy servant king instead of David my father ; and I am but [Heb. *and I . . .*] a little child : [These words are generally understood as indicating Solomon's humility rather than his age. No doubt, there is some exaggeration in the expression, which manifestly is not to be taken *au pied de la lettre ;* at the same time it is questionable whether such words would be used of himself by a young man of twenty, which Solomon is commonly supposed to have been. See on ch. ii. 2, and xii. 8] I know not how to go out or come in. [The same phrase is found in the Pentateuch, Deut. xxviii. 6 ; xxxi. 2. Also in 1 Sam. xviii. 13 ; 2 Sam. iii. 25 ; Ps. cxxi. 8. It is the formula for expressing behaviour, conduct, the outward life of man.]

Ver. 8.—And thy servant is in the midst of thy people which thou hast chosen [see Deut. vii. 6], a great people, that cannot be numbered nor counted for multitude. [The promises of Gen. xiii. 16 ; xv. 5, lived in the thoughts and language of the Jews, and were doubtless the original of this expression. Cf. also Num. xxiii. 10.]

Ver. 9.— Give therefore thy servant an understanding [Heb. *hearing.* Cf. ver. 11 (Heb. " to *hear* judgment.") The idea is not docility, as the Vulg. (*cor docile*), but discrimination, penetration. Cf. 2 Sam. xiv. 17 (Heb.) ; Phil. i. 9, 10 (marg.)] heart [*i.e.*, a judicial mind. The " hearing heart " was desired, not that it might " give heed to the law" (Keil), but to qualify him] to judge thy people [The Hebrew king, like most ancient monarchs, was supreme judge as well as governor (" prince and *judge*," Exod. ii. 14 ; and cf. Exod. xviii. 16). The Jews desired a king that he might *judge* them (1 Sam. viii. 5). Their rulers so far had

been purely "Judges" (שֹׁפְטִים ; compare the Carthaginian name, *suffetes*.) When they desired one who should lead their armies, they still put his judicial functions in the first place (*loc. cit.* ver. 20). And what were the duties of a king in this respect, Absalom's words (2 Sam. xv. 4) show. In vers. 16—28 we see Solomon sitting as Chief Justice], that I may discern between good and bad [*i.e.*, right and wrong, true and false ; cf. Heb. v. 14) : for who is able to judge this thy so great [Heb. *heavy, i.e.*, numerous ; compare *graves greges*] a people. [The number of the Israelites at this period is referred to in ch. iv. 20.]

Ver. 10.—And the speech [Heb. *thing ;* same word as below] pleased the Lord, that Solomon had asked this thing. [Though in a dream the judgment and will were not suspended. Our dreams accord with our waking thoughts. This would have been Solomon's choice at any time.]

Ver. 11.—And God said unto him, Because thou hast asked this thing, and hast not asked for thyself long life [Heb. *many days*]; neither hast asked riches for thyself, nor hast asked the life [*i.e.*, destruction in battle] of thine enemies [not so much personal enemies, like Hadad and Rezon, (Rawlinson) as military foes. The meaning is explained by the corresponding word, "honour" (כָּבוֹד *glory*) in ver. 13]; but hast asked [The word is repeated, according to Hebrew usage, now for the sixth time] for thyself understanding to discern [Heb. *hear* ; see on ver. 9] judgment ,

Ver. 12.—Behold, I have done according to thy words [*i.e.*, granted thy prayer, as the next words show] : lo [Heb. *behold*] I have given thee a wise and an understanding heart, so that there was none like thee before thee, neither after thee shall any arise like unto thee. [Cf. 1 Chron. xxix. 25 ; 2 Chron. ix. 22. But there is no need to restrict the reference to kings and princes.]

Ver. 13.—And I have also given thee that which thou hast not asked, both riches and honour [Heb. *glory*]; so that there shall not be any among the kings like unto thee all thy days.

Ver. 14.—And if thou wilt walk in my ways, to keep my statutes and my commandments, as thy father David did walk [ver. 6 ; xv. 4. This is the Divine confirmation of David's words to his son (ch. ii. 3, 4) and of the son's description of his father's piety (ver. 6 *supra*)], then I will lengthen thy days [Solomon's days were not of an unusual length, as he can hardly have been more than sixty (if so much), although called זָקֵן (ch. xi. 4) at the time of his decease. But he had not fulfilled the condition (ch. xi. 9—12).

Ver. 15.—And Solomon awoke; and, behold, it was a dream [That is to say, this passed while Solomon *slept ;* but it was more than a dream. The same words are used of Pharaoh (Gen. xli. 7) when God showed him what He was about to do (vers. 25, 28, cf. ch. xl. 8), and this was such a dream as Pharaoh's and as Joseph's (Matt. i. 20 ; ii. 19). It was a dream, *i.e.,* in which a Divine revelation was made to him. Wordsw. refers to Solomon's words, " I sleep, but *my heart waketh* " (Cant. v. 2), and "He giveth to his beloved (Jedidiah) in sleep " (Ps. cxxvii. 2)]. And he came to Jerusalem, and stood before

the ark of the covenant [the other sanctuary of that period (2 Sam. vi. 17 ; 1 Chron. xvi. 37—40)] and offered up burnt offerings [probably in continuation of the sacrifices of Gibeon, ver. 4], and offered peace offerings [in testimony of his thankfulness for the signal favour recently vouchsafed to him] and made a feast [lit., a *drinking.* After the example of David, 1 Chron. xvi. 3. Cf. 1 Kings viii. 65. It was not exclusively a *symposium.* The flesh of the animals offered in sacrifice was eaten by the worshippers and their guests (Lev. vii. 15, 31 ; 1 Sam. ii. 16 ; 1 Cor. viii. 13). This was " a sacrificial meal of the שְׁלָמִים " (Keil). See on ch. viii. 63] to all his servants.

HOMILETICS.

Ver. 3.—*The Grace and Place of Love.* "And Solomon loved the Lord, walking in all the statutes of David his father, only . . . . he sacrificed," &c.

Of how many men, as well as of the wisest of men, may some such words be used. Of some few it may perhaps be averred that they have loved the Lord " with a perfect heart," of fewer still, if any, that they have loved Him with all the heart, and all the mind, and all the soul, and all the strength. But in the case of most, a qualifying clause must be added, an "*only.*" Along with sincere piety, with devout love to Him who first loved us, how often are there found imperfections, infirmities, sins. Sometimes, *e.g.,* the loved is tinged with superstition, as in the case of St. Theresa, Lacordaire, and many Romanists ; sometimes, as in the case of Calvin and many Protestants, it is marked by harshness and intolerance ; sometimes, as in the case of Schleiermacher and Bunsen, it is infected with rationalism. The love, that is to say, is not without alloy ; it is not the pure refined gold. In some of the blessed saints we find narrowness and bigotry, in others fanaticism ; in others, again, Pharisaism and presumption. Now all these "love the Lord . . . . only . . . ." But observe. Solomon was loved of God ; blessed, enriched, and prospered of God, despite this " only ;" notwithstanding, *i.e.,* that his sacrifice and service were marked by imperfection. Hence learn—

I. THAT GOD LOVES THOSE WHO LOVE HIM, DESPITE THEIR IMPERFECTIONS. Of course God loves men who do *not* love Him. "God commendeth His love towards us in that while we were yet sinners," &c. We often say to children, "God doesn't love you when you are naughty," but this is vicious theology. If this were so, there had been no hope for our world. But He is good to the unthankful and evil. Yes, the love must *begin* with God. "We love Him because He *first* loved us." And the love that bore with our sins, in the days of our impenitence, now bears also with our infirmities and ignorances. Neither superstition nor narrowness nor fanaticism "nor any other creature can separate us from the love of God," &c.

II. THAT GOD FORGIVES THOSE WHO LOVE HIM, NOTWITHSTANDING THEIR INFIRMITIES. It is not meant here that our love can make any atonement or reparation for our sins. We know of no merits or mediation but His. "Your sins are forgiven you for *His name's sake.*" But where there is love, there is forgiveness (Luke vii. 47). Why, love involves penitence and faith, and ensures obedience. (Observe the next words, "Walking in all the statutes," &c.) Thus, the three conditions of forgiveness are all comprehended in love.

III. THAT GOD WILL RECEIVE THOSE WHO LOVE HIM, DESPITE THEIR IGNORANCES. The gate of heaven is never shut against love, and only love will open it.

> " O merchant, at heaven's gate, for heavenly ware
> Love is the only coin that passes there."

It must be so, for " love is heaven, and heaven is love."

IV. THAT WE OUGHT TO LOVE THOSE WHO LOVE GOD, DESPITE THEIR IGNORANCES, INFIRMITIES, AND IMPERFECTIONS. If the Eternal Love overlooks our "*only*," surely we ought to overlook the "*only*" of others. We may regret their views, we may think them unsound in the faith, we may lament their superstition, their lack of "sweetness and light," their vulgarity, or fanaticism, but if God loves them, and receives them notwithstanding, what right have we to do otherwise? If they love our Lord, then they are entitled to our love. "Grace be unto all them that *love* our Lord Jesus Christ in sincerity." We find, consequently, in the religion both of the Old Testament and of the New—

V. THAT LOVE IS EVERYTHING. It is 1. *The fulfilling of the law* (Rom. xiii. 8. 10; Matt. xxii. 37—40). We cannot break the law if we love. "*Habe caritatem et fac quicquid vis*," said St. Augustine. 2. *The stamp and seal royal of the Christian.* "He that loveth, is born of God." "By this shall all men know that ye are my disciples, if ye have love," &c. It has been said, "*Pectus est quod theologum facit.*" It is equally true that the heart makes the *Christian*. 3. *The glory of the man.* It was the greatest glory of Solomon. The highest praise recorded of him is, not that "he was wiser than all men" (ch. iv. 31), nor yet that he "exceeded all the kings of the earth for riches and wisdom" (ch. x. 33), but that he loved the Lord. "The best thing that can be said of a man is that he loves God." Solomon in all his glory is not greater than the poorest of the saints. 4. *The one thing needful.* The one thing God demands is the *heart*. (Adelaide Procter's beautiful poem, "*Give me thy heart*," affords a fine illustration here.) It is the mainspring of the man. The life depends on the heart. In the reign of Queen Elizabeth, when the Roman Catholics were commanded to attend Church under pains and penalties, some of their leaders applied to the Pope for guidance. "Let the Catholics of England," was the astute reply, "give me their hearts, and the Queen may do what she likes with the rest."

Vers. 5—15.—*God's Gifts and Solomon's Choice.* "And God said, Ask what I shall give thee," &c. "Happy Solomon!" we exclaim, as we read these words. He had all that *earth* could give already—youth, wealth, prosperity, glory, greatness. He stood already on the topmost pinnacle of human felicity. And now *Heaven* offers him his choice of blessings; now the treasure-house of the infinite God is opened, and he is bidden to take what he will. Behold the favourite of Heaven! It is indeed true "there was none like thee before thee, neither after thee shall any arise like unto thee" (ver. 12). But stay! Solomon's is not an exceptional case. If we have not his temporal advantages, we may share his spiritual blessings. For to us—to all, that is, who, like Solomon, "love the Lord" —does the same voice speak, saying, "Ask what I shall give thee." Yes; He who spake to this new-crowned king in the night visions hath in these last days spoken unto us by His Son, saying, "Ask, and it shall be given you." Let us consider—

I. LIKE SOLOMON, WE ARE COMMANDED TO ASK. It is not that we are *permitted* so to do: it is made a positive duty. If we do not ask, we sin. "Ask," "seek," "knock"—these are the injunctions of our Lord and Master. Asking is an essential part of our religion. "Prayer is the Christian's vital breath."

II. LIKE SOLOMON, WE HAVE BUT TO ASK, AND GOD WILL GIVE. Solomon was *not* a favourite of Heaven. God has no favourites—that would argue imperfection in the Deity. "*Every one* that asketh receiveth," &c. "*Whosoever* shall call on the name of the Lord," &c. "If *any of you* lack wisdom, let him ask of God, . . . and it shall be given him." If we have not wisdom, blessing, pardon, peace, it is all for want of asking. God is "more ready to hear than we to pray." And observe here: we are commanded to ask, and God is sure to give, because He loves to give; it is His nature and property to give. Not only (as has been beautifully said) is "the greatest Being in the world the greatest giver," but it is an essential part of His perfections to give. We often *say* "It is more blessed to give than to receive," but God *acts* on this principle. It is the nature of man to take. The first lesson the child learns is to grasp. Covetousness, the desire to have, is a part of our being. It is a part of His being to desire to impart. He abhors a vacuum.

III. LIKE AHAZ, MANY SAY, "I WILL NOT ASK." They will not believe in the wonderful charity of God. To some it seems too good to be true. But many have no room for God's gifts. Their heart is full already. "No room for *Him* in the inn."

IV. LIKE SOLOMON, LET US ASK THE BEST GIFTS. That is an instructive fable which tells how Hercules, on attaining manhood, went out into solitude, and sitting down there, deliberated long and anxiously with himself which of the two ways before him it were better to take—the way of pleasure, or the way of virtue. Such a crisis, involving such a choice, happens in every life. Solomon must now make his choice, and it really lies between pleasure and duty, between temporal and eternal blessings. He may choose glory, wealth, renown—in a word, earthly pleasure and prosperity—or he may choose character, wisdom, goodness; in other words, heavenly and abiding treasure. We know which he chose. So each one of us has to choose in turn between the showy and the solid, between the higher and the lower, between God and Mammon.

" Once to every man and nation, comes the moment to decide
    In the strife of Truth with Falsehood, for the good or evil side.

*   *   *   *   *   *   *   *

Then it is the brave man chooses, while the coward stands aside,
    Doubting in his abject spirit, till his Lord is crucified."

V. IF, LIKE SOLOMON, WE CHOOSE THE BEST GIFTS, THE OTHER AND INFERIOR BLESSINGS ARE THROWN IN WITH THEM. Consider : God gave Solomon wisdom because he asked for it, and at the same time gave him wealth because he did not ask for it. His choice of the higher showed he was fit to be entrusted with the lower. The gifts men covet most, viz., " riches and honour," are of so little account with God that He adds them as a make-weight. Just as when we buy a jewel the case is thrown in as part of the purchase, so those who choose the better part receive at the same time all that is necessary for them. " Seek ye *first* the kingdom of God and his righteousness, and *all these things shall be added unto* you." And here again observe, that not only is it God's nature to give, but to give " exceeding abundantly, above all that we ask or think." He is " wont to do more than either we desire or deserve." Thus the disciples asked for a form of prayer (Luke xi. 1). Our blessed Lord gave them their desire, and gave at the same time what they never dreamed of asking for—some precious directions as to the spirit of prayer, as to perseverance in prayer, &c. (*ib.* vers. 5—13). The same idea is embodied in a stanza of Wordsworth's—

" I knelt before Thy gracious throne,
    And asked for peace with suppliant knee ;
And peace was given ; *not peace alone,*
    But love and joy and ecstasy."

It was in the night visions that God spoke to Solomon. It is in no dream, no vision, but in His own written word, He says to us, " Ask what I shall give *thee.*" Which shall we imitate, Solomon or Ahaz ? Shall we have all or none ? But it may be said, Solomon's wisdom did him no great service after all. His prayer did not keep him from falling. But why was this ? It was just because he ceased to care for wisdom and piety, and ceased to ask for it. Learn, then, in conclusion—

VI. IF, LIKE SOLOMON, WE CEASE TO COVET THE BEST GIFTS, AND CARE ONLY FOR THE LOWER, WE SHALL CERTAINLY LOSE THE FORMER, AND MAY POSSIBLY LOSE BOTH. So that Solomon's prayer may teach us this last lesson, that " men ought always to pray, and not to faint." Yes, it seems, as we think of the beginning and then of the end of this puissant prince—it seems as if his father's last words must have been prophetic—"If thou seek him, he will be found of thee; but if thou forsake him, he will cast thee off for ever " (1 Chron. xxviii. 9) ; and Solomon's fall solemnly echoes and emphasizes the words which follow—O that he had laid them to heart !—" *Take heed now*" (ver. 10).

HOMILIES BY VARIOUS AUTHORS.

Vers. 3—16; iv. 2—34.—*The prayer of Solomon and its fulfilment.* "Ask what I shall give thee."

THE PRAYER OF SOLOMON IS THE TYPE OF TRUE PRAYER. We learn from it (1) The power of prayer; (2) The condition on which it is granted; (3) Its result.

I. THE POWER. "Prayer," said Adolphe Monod, "sets in motion the whole power of God." The words of God to Solomon show us this Almighty power, placing itself, as it were, at the disposition of human weakness. When the Son of God came to earth, taking upon Himself our frail humanity, that He might perfectly sympathize with all its woes, He spoke in the same way to the poor blind Bartimæus: "What wilt thou that I should do unto thee?" (Mark x. 51). Before going back to heaven He addressed the same language to His disciples: "*Whatsoever ye shall ask the Father in my name*, He will give it you" (John xvi. 23). Let us then ask all that we need with holy boldness, for it is God Himself who bids us do so. Like the father of the prodigal son, He always comes to meet us. Our hopes and desires can never be so large as His promises. We truly honour Him when we make His love the measure of our trust.

II. THE CONDITIONS ON WHICH OUR PRAYERS ARE GRANTED ARE: (*a*) Full trust in this infinite love, and grateful remembrance of favours received: "Thou hast showed unto David my father great mercy . . . . and hast given him a son to sit on his throne" (ver. 6). (*b*) The consciousness of our own helplessness and weakness: "*I am but as a little child, and know not how to go out or come in*" (ver. 7). (*c*) The precedence given to spiritual over temporal gifts: "*Give thy servant an understanding heart*" (ver. 9). Prayer is not intended to bring to us at once all material prosperity. Such an answer to prayer might be often injurious, hardening the heart, and depriving us of the salutary discipline of trial. If the thing we sought beyond all else was material prosperity, we should be mere mercenaries. We are always heard, but not always in the way we desire, so far as our earthly life is concerned. But when we ask of God a new and understanding heart, we are asking that which He is pledged to grant, for it is written: "If any man lack wisdom, let him ask of God, who giveth to all men liberally and upbraideth not."

III. THE RESULT OF THE PRAYER OF SOLOMON was not only the spiritual grace he sought, but also the prosperity and glory of his reign. "I have also given thee that which thou hast not asked" (ver. 13). There is a general application both to individuals and nations of the words of Christ: "Seek first the kingdom of God and His righteousness, and all other things shall be added unto you" (Matt. vi. 33), with the exception of afflictions, which may be necessary as discipline, and on the condition that we walk in the ways of the Lord (ver. 14), for the mercy of God, free as it is, is still bound up with His holiness, and cannot suffer the violation of His laws.—E. DE P.

Vers. 5—16.—*A wise prayer.* Gibeon, the scene of this incident, was one of the "high places" of the land. Worship in high places had been forbidden. Law against it not rigidly enforced until the place was chosen "where the Lord would cause his name to dwell." That Solomon's act in sacrificing at Gibeon was not condemned is proved by his being favoured with this direct Divine communication. Every scene of real worship may become the scene of special Divine manifestation. "The Lord appeared unto Solomon in a dream of the night." Whatever our theory of these dreams of the olden times, it was evidently an articulate and intelligible Divine communication that Solomon had, and his spirit was intensely active. His choice of wisdom rather than riches, &c., was an act of judgment, a decision of the will, and therefore indicative of moral character. The whole spirit of his prayer most honourable to him. The prayer is, in a sense, answered before it is presented. Every holy yearning of the pious soul contains within itself the pledge of its own fulfilment.

I. THE NATURE OF TRUE WISDOM. A power of moral discernment. "An understanding heart to judge," &c. This was the virtue of Solomon's prayer—it craved a *moral* rather than more circumstantial, or even intellectual, endowment. He had the wisdom of the man of science, the "minute philosopher" (see chap. iv. 33). But higher wisdom was wanted for higher work—for guiding and governing the people—and this is what he prayed for. Little trace in Solomon of the pure, fervent spirit of devotion that glowed in his father David. The yearning of David's heart was not so much for wisdom as for holiness. But Solomon has a lofty ideal of kingly rule before him, and this is how he seeks to realize it.

1. Wisdom is a *practical* quality ; not merely theoretical ; consists less in true ideas than in the ability to embody them in a real and living form; not knowledge or insight, but power to turn what is known and understood to highest account. In common affairs of life—in matters of business, science, art—how many clever theoretical men are there whose cleverness never takes a tangible, practical form ! You can point to nothing that they have ever *done* as a worthy expression of their native capacity. Only in a qualified sense are such men " wise." How much more in the higher sphere of moral and religious life. Here also a science and an art, the ideal and the practical. Wisdom is the combination of the two. It is thought and it is life—the science of spiritual truth and reality married to the divine art of living under the influence of what is real and true.

2. *Wisdom deals with those eternal principles that underlie the surface appearances of life.* The judgment of Solomon in the dispute between the two women about the child (verse 16 to end) is suggestive here. Its peculiarity is, that instead of trusting to appearances to decide the doubt, he leaves the decision to the deep instinct of the mother's nature, *i.e.*, his wisdom is seen in calling to its aid a principle profounder and less fallible than itself. Apply this to the higher conduct of life. We want something more reliable than our own observation or reason as a guide. " The fear of the Lord is the beginning of wisdom." Lay hold on God. Walk by faith. Let there be a divine element in your life :

> " There is more wisdom in a whisper'd prayer
> Than in the ancient lore of all the schools."

How great the wisdom of him whose whole daily life is a heaven-ascending prayer !

II. THE DIVINE ORIGIN OF WISDOM. " Ask what I shall give thee." God is the infinite Fount of Wisdom, and He " gives" from His exhaustless fulness. " The Father of Lights." What a world of wonders is the book of Nature ! What creative thought, constructive skill, wise adaptation are here ! A world of profounder wonders is the Book of Truth. " O the depth of the riches," &c. But this is *revelation ;* we have to think of *impartation.* God will *give* wisdom. " Ask what I shall give thee." " If any man lack wisdom let him ask of God," &c. All true light that guides man in any right path is His gift. Most of all those right thoughts, high aspirations, holy energies, which are the very life of men. Man can only *disclose* his mental riches. The philosopher cannot " give" the rustic wisdom, nor the father or teacher the child. God sheds the light of His Spirit into the soul. " If ye being evil," &c.

III. THE ABUNDANT REWARD OF WISDOM. " And I have also given thee," &c. (ver. 13). God's beneficence exceeds the expectations of His children. " Able to do exceeding abundantly," &c. (Eph. iii. 20). " Seek ye first the kingdom of God," &c. (Matt. vi. 33). -W.

Ver. 5.—SERMON FOR CHILDREN. *Waiting for God's voice.* Little children are sometimes intended to do great things. God has a special place for everyone to fill. Sometimes the child who is least thought of in the home or in the class is to have the noblest destiny. Two brothers once lived in the same tent. One was brave and manly, a great hunter, and a popular, generous man, but his younger and feebler brother, Jacob, became greater than he. In Jesse's family at Bethlehem there were young men, tall, comely, and heroic, yet their shepherd brother, whom they despised, was chosen to be their king. Now in David's own family God made His choice ; and overlooking the beautiful Absalom, and the ambitious Adonijah, he selected Solomon, their youngest and gentlest brother, to be king over one of the richest kingdoms in the world, and to rule His own people in the time of their greatest prosperity. It may be that some lads here, who are little thought of, may become the leaders of a nation to a nobler life, the teachers of their age, to whom the world will gladly listen. But whatever sphere you have to fill, you will only be ready to fill it well when you begin, as Solomon began his reign, by listening to the voice of God. This was the most interesting part of Solomon's life. He was now at his best. Ascending his father's throne, he was conscious of his responsibility, and asked God to give him wisdom (James i. 5, 6). In youth our future is generally decided. If we go wrong then, it is not easy to be set right. An injury done to a living thing during its growing time is irreparable. The man who was crippled when he was a child, the tree blasted when it was a sapling, cannot by any subsequent care be made straight and whole. Solomon, however, started well— going up to the ancient tabernacle in Gibeon, to offer sacrifice to the Lord.

Let us see *what preparation Solomon had for the dream* spoken of here. Many a child says, " I wish God would come to me, and tell me I might ask for whatever I liked. I often say my prayers, but God does not seem real to me. I never see Him or hear Him." You will not see Him as did Solomon, nor hear Him as did Samuel. But you may feel Him in your thoughts—in the prompting to do right, or to speak the truth when doing this may get you into trouble ; and in the relief and rest you know after telling God about the sorrow you have. [Quote part of Faber's hymn : " Dear Jesus, ever at my side." Tell some story of a child who has found help, relief, and rest in prayer. This will bring the old story of Solomon near to the experience of children.]

Three things prepared Solomon for listening to God.

I. SOLOMON HAD COME FROM WORSHIP. Describe the old tabernacle, now pitched on the top of the hill at Gibeon ; the coming of the procession of nobles, soldiers, priests, &c., to the sacred festival; the offering of the thousand victims ; the song of praise, the united prayers, &c. This worship prepared the young king for his dream. Children go to Sunday schools who are seldom found in God's house. Trace the lads and girls leaving the senior classes to spend their Sundays in pleasure and sin—their forced merriment, their aching hearts. Trying to forget God, they are not prepared to see Him as Solomon did. Contrast with this the day spent in *worship*. The children whose hearts are uplifted by songs of praise, who have been hearing of the love of God in Christ, who have been reminded of those who knew the Lord, are prepared to say, as Samuel said, " Speak, Lord, for thy servant heareth ! "

II. SOLOMON WAS ALONE WITH GOD. The crowd had dispersed. The shouts, and songs, and music were silent. The stars shone down on the camp, and in his own royal tent the young king had retired to rest. As he slept he dreamed, and a happy night followed a holy day. Dreams were often used by God in olden days. Give examples. These were overruled, but they were natural. A dream is the product of familiar thoughts. Boys don't dream of protoplasm, of which they know nothing, but of cricket, lessons, companions, &c. The elements of a dream are in the mind before sleep ; *e.g.*, the Midianitish soldier dreamt of a barley cake, which was his ordinary food ; the Egyptian butler, of Pharaoh's cup ; the baker, of his white baskets of bakemeats, &c. So Solomon had been thinking about his kingdom— the greatness of his father, the overruling providence of God ; he had been filled with a desire to rule wisely, had been fired with devotion during the day, and all these things re-appeared in his dream. If you have never had such dream, you have had quiet times when you were ill, or before going to rest, when God seemed real to you. Recall the first time when the old form of prayer had a new meaning, when God seemed close, and loving, and gracious. An example from child life may be readily found.

III. SOLOMON WAS LISTENING TO GOD, who said, " Ask what I shall give thee." Sometimes children wish that the fairies, of whom they read, actually existed ; that one, with her fair form and beautiful wand, would come and say, " Ask what I shall give thee." Many, like Cinderella, would exchange drudgery for glitter.

God does not do this. If He did, many of us would ignorantly ask for foolish things. We do not know what we shall be doing or wanting even to-morrow. If you were going abroad and did not know for what country you were destined, nor even whether it was hot or cold, civilized or uncivilized, it would not be wise to provide things on the chance they might be useful. You might get weapons of defence for a country where they would not be wanted, and have to wear in the tropics clothing only suited to the polar seas. It would not be really kind for your father to say, " Now go into that shop, and get whatever you like." You would say, " No, thank you ; as you know where I am going, and I don't, I would rather trust you ; though if *you* think it would be good, I should like this, or that." So we are taught to pray to our Heavenly Father. Give examples. Sometimes God does give us what we foolishly choose, as the father did to the prodigal, and then sorrow teaches us the folly of our self-will. The freedom to ask anything can only be given safely to those who are like Solomon. He had just given himself up to God as a living sacrifice, and had asked God to accept him and use him for His service ; for it was this which he expressed by his offering of a thousand burnt sacrifices. (Romans xii. 1.) If you can say in your heart, " Lord, I want to become like Jesus Christ, and always to be obedient to Thy will ; I long to be earnest and humble, and pure, and loving, and to live altogether for Thee ; " then He says, of all that will keep you toward that, " Ask and ye shall receive, and your joy shall be full."

Show the necessity of prayer to children ; point out their special temptations to neglect it ; and close by the story of Esther going into the king's presence with trembling, only to see the golden sceptre extended, and to hear the gracious encouragement, " What is thy petition, and what is thy request? and it shall be done unto thee !" " When thou saidst, ' Seek ye my face,' my heart said unto Thee, ' Thy face, Lord, will I seek.' "—A. R.

Vers. 6, 7.—*The reverent prayer of a royal petitioner.* Solomon had a more peaceful reign and greater outward glory than David. Yet much is said in Scripture about the father, and little about the son. This revelation of God's truth about men and things is less concerned with splendid surroundings than with secret struggles. Few, if any, are made great by splendour. Hence a few verses suffice to tell of Solomon's ships and palaces, and gold and ivory ; but many chapters are devoted to accounts of David's temptations, deliverances, and prayers. We have God's estimate of Solomon's magnificence in the memorable words of Christ, " Consider the lilies of the field how they grow ; they toil not, neither do they spin ; and yet I say unto you, that even Solomon, in all his glory, was not arrayed like one of these." From these words we infer that human greatness does not claim God's regard, but that He cares for lilies as well as for kings ; so that from none of us, however lowly our lot, is the privilege of prayer, granted to Solomon, withheld.

The prayer before us was characterized by the following excellences :—

I. GRATITUDE. (Ver. 6.) Solomon thanked God for what his father had been. David was far from being a sinless man, but his son loyally veiled his faults, and praised God for what he had been to himself and others. What reasons for gratitude many have in this respect. Loving care during the feebleness of infancy ; provision for education, &c., often the result of habitual self-denial ; protection of the home not only from physical, but from moral evils, in the shape of bad literature, companions, &c. These are the ordinary blessings from parenthood, but often there are more than these, *e.g.*, the moral heritage of wholesome tendencies ; the good name, to be chosen rather than great riches ; the repression of evil, and encouragement of good habits of thought and action ; the counsels and warnings to the inexperienced ; the Christian truth revealed in the holy life, proclaimed by the loving lips. Few blessings are greater than these ; but few are less thankfully recognized. Gratitude should reveal itself in tender consideration, in graceful courtesies, in prompt obedience, &c., in the home, and should express itself in praise to the Giver of all good gifts. [This is but an example of subjects for gratitude : others may be suggested.]

II. SOLEMNITY. The young king seemed overwhelmed with a sense of responsibility. He was about to succeed a father renowned as a warrior, as a statesman, as a poet, as a ruler of men. He was about to rule a numerous and prosperous people, who had been specially declared to be the Lord's, so that he would be henceforth the representative of Jehovah. He foresaw that there would be snares not easy to avoid, difficulties hard to surmount; and therefore he dared not go forward without the prayer, "O God of my father, stand by me." Contrast this with the light spirit in which life-work is often undertaken. Describe a father about to vacate his plan in business, or in the Church, whose honour has been unstained, who has been a king amongst men, and urge on any who are about to succeed to such an inheritance the responsibility incurred, that they may feel " who is sufficient for these things ? " To go on to unknown temptations, to unattempted duties, in a flippant, godless spirit, is to show the foolhardiness of the captain who, in strange waters, wrecks his vessel on the hidden shoal, because he scorns to employ a pilot.

III. HOPEFULNESS. In ver. 4 he tacitly refers to what God had done for his father, as an example and pledge of what God could do for him. He implies that the promise, like the throne, came by inheritance. This was the teaching of the patriarchal dispensation. It was not withdrawn by Christ, who came " not to destroy, but to fulfil." Hence, in the first sermon preached after the baptism of the Church by the Holy Spirit, Peter refers to, and endorses for this dispensation, the declaration of Joel, " The promise is unto you, and to your *children.*" Show how the privileges of Christian parentage keep pace with its responsibilities. What God had been to David was a sign to Solomon, his son, of what God would do for him; and therefore he prayed with eager hope.

IV. HUMILITY. " I am but a little child." Solomon had enough to make him proud. He was immensely rich, was flattered by courtiers, was obeyed by a disciplined army, was strikingly handsome (Psalm xlv.), and was at an age (twenty years old) when no one thinks least of himself. But he recognized that *God* made him what he was (" Thou hast made Thy servant king "), and that, so far as wisdom and ability were concerned, he was " but a little child." Such has been the spirit of all truly great men, *e.g.,* Moses, when called in Midian (Exod. iii. 11); Isaiah, when he saw the Lord in the temple (Isa. vi.) ; Jeremiah, when invested with prophetic office (Jer. i.) This humility should characterize all who approach God. Refer to the Pharisee and publican (Luke xviii. 10—14) ; also to declaration that except we become as little children we cannot enter the kingdom. Contrast Solomon with his brothers, Absalom and Adonijah. He was content to wait God's time, and so was prepared for the place prepared for him. The chrysalis waits—is kept back—in its inactive stage, till both the wings are ready for the sunshine, and the sunshine ready for the wings. Humbly let us wait for the higher spheres of earth and the highest spheres of heaven.—A. R.

Vers. 9—13. *The wisdom of Solomon's choice.* Solomon was never more kingly than when he made this choice. Subsequently he became enervated by prosperity, corrupted by heathen associations, &c., but now he ruled as a king over himself. The bright promise of life is often gradually overcast, till it ends in the gloom of a hopeless night. Examples from Scripture, *e.g.,* Saul the King, Esau. It is well to know the kind of choice that "pleased the Lord." In Solomon's there was *true wisdom,* for it had these elements—

I. THE CHOICE WAS FOR THE GOOD OF OTHERS RATHER THAN FOR THE ADVANTAGE OF HIMSELF. It was not like asking for knowledge and wisdom that he might himself be admired as a sage. This followed, but this he did not seek. He wished to rule God's people well for *their* good, and asked that he might do what was just in judgment, what was equitable in law. Such equity establishes any rule on a sure foundation. Our hold on India is chiefly due to the righteousness of our magistrates, and the trustworthiness of men like the Lawrences, Lord Mayo, &c. Natives would not hesitate to bring an action in one of our English law courts against an Englishman, so certain are they of even-handed justice. This Solomon sought, and the peace and prosperity of his kingdom (ch. iv. 25) arose from the fact that God gave it him. To ask God to make us wise and capable for the sake of others, is a prayer consonant with His will. Unselfishness is commended and exalted under the new dispensation as it never was under the old. Christ Himself came not to be ministered unto, but to minister, and to give His life " a ransom for many." The prayer of selfishness, greed, avarice, can never be put up in Christ's name.

II. THE CHOICE WAS MADE OF INWARD WORTH AND NOT OF OUTWARD SHOW. He did not ask for himself riches and honour. What will make us noble is always more readily given by God than what will make us wealthy. A wise father would rather that his son should be truthful than that he should win popularity among his schoolfellows by anything surreptitious and deceitful.   So our heavenly Father cares little that we should make money, or win applause ; but He cares much that we should be wise, and true, and loving ; and these graces He will in no wise withhold from those who seek. Sometimes He answers our prayers for these inward blessings in modes we resent. The illness that throws us back upon Him, the failure that proves a man's life does not consist in the abundance of things that he possesseth, &c., may work *in* us the peaceable fruits of righteousness. The Lord Jesus, who was at once the King of Glory and the village carpenter, showed us this; and in the inward gladness His disciples experienced amid their outward woes, we have confirmation of it. Show how, in New Testament history, and in the lives of the saints, the words which begin the Sermon on the Mount have been fulfilled. Blessedness of the highest kind comes to the poor in spirit, to them that mourn, to the meek, to them which do hunger and thirst after righteousness, to the merciful, to the pure in heart, to the peacemakers, and even to those who are persecuted for righteousness' sake.

III. THE CHOICE MADE OF THE HIGHER BROUGHT WITH IT THE LOWER BLESSINGS. (Vers. 11—13.) Because Solomon asked wisdom God gave him that, but added to it wealth and honour. If we ask grace to fulfil our mission, and rightly do our life-work, our heavenly Father will see that we do not want for life's necessities. "Seek ye first the kingdom of God, and his righteousness, and all these things shall be added unto you." The teaching of Christ (Matt. vi. 24—34) goes to show that a man who is chiefly concerned to please God need have no anxiety or care about lower things. If God feeds the birds, He will feed you ; if He clothes the lilies, He will clothe you ; if He gives the life, He will give the "meat" that is less than life. Ask God for the higher blessings: pardon, righteousness, reverence, wisdom, &c., and He will give you not only those, but all things necessary for us, and all the riches and honours that are good for us.

Solomon's wisdom was great, but there has come into the world one greater than Solomon, more worthy far of our adoration and love. As the child in Nazareth, Jesus grew in wisdom, and in stature, and in favour with God and man. His wisdom was purer, deeper, truer than Solomon's, because it was united with purity of life, with victory over sin, and with sacrifice of self. He is the true Shelômôh, " the Prince of Peace;" the true Jedidiah, " the well beloved of the Father;" and to Him now let us humbly bow the knee, as to One worthy to be exalted both as Prince and Saviour. A. R.

EXPOSITION.

CHAPTER III. 16—28.

IN this section we see how remarkably the gracious promise of Gibeon (ver. 12) was fulfilled. The " understanding to discern judgment " has been richly bestowed. And this, no doubt, is the reason why the story is related here. Ἐπιδεῖξαί τὴν τοῦ βασιλέως ἐβουλήθη σοφίαν (Theodoret). It is just possible, as Thenius maintains, that the narrative was handed down to a succeeding age by tradition, and was not incorporated into any of the documents from which our historian compiled his narrative ; but this argues nothing against its authenticity or its inspiration. It is, as Bähr observes, a thoroughly Oriental story.

Ver. 16.—**Then came there two women that were harlots** [The Jewish writers here, as in the case of Rahab (Josh. ii. 1), would understand " hostess," " inn-keeper " (פונדקיתא, not פונדקן, as Bähr, which=· πανδοκεῖον, " inn "). In support of which it is alleged that prostitutes never have children, or if they have are not solicitous about them. The meaning " hostess," however (as if from זון, to feed), is not to be entertained for a moment, but we may readily admit that these children, though born out of wedlock, were not necessarily the offspring of professed harlots, though the fact that their mothers dwelt together and alone (ver. 17) is certainly suspicious ; and see Gesen. s. v. זָנָה. Grotius, from Deut. xxiii. 17, concludes that they must have been foreigners. But it is equally probable that the law was constantly violated] **unto the king** [as supreme judge] **and stood before him.**

Ver. 17.—**And the one woman said, O my lord, I and this woman dwell in one house ; and I was delivered of a child with her in the house.**

Ver. 18.—**And it came to pass the third day after that I was delivered, that this woman was delivered also : and we were together ; there was no stranger with us in the house, save we two in the house.** [Emphasis is laid on this fact, as showing the possibility of the fraud and the impossibility of producing proof. Hebrew women have always required but little assistance in child-bearing. That which is written in Exodus i. 19 is true to this day.

Ver. 19.—**And this woman's child died in the night ; because she overlaid it.**

Ver. 20.—**And she arose at midnight** [rather, in the middle, i.e., dead of the night. The sleeper could not know it was midnight], **and took my son from beside me, while thine handmaid slept, and laid it in her bosom, and laid her dead child in my bosom.**

Ver. 21.—**And when I rose in the morning** [while it was still dusk] **to give my child suck, behold it was dead : but when I had considered it in the morning** [i.e., in broad daylight ; Vulg. clara luce] **behold** [this second " behold " marks a second discovery] **it was not my son which I did bear.**

Ver. 22.—**And the other woman said, Nay, but the living is my son and the dead is thy son. And this said, No, but the dead is thy son and the living is my son.** [It is somewhat difficult to account for the pertinacious claim to the child, preferred even before the king by the pretended mother. The most probable explanation is, that having taken the child in the first

instance on the spur of the moment, in order to avoid the reproach of having killed her offspring by her clumsiness and neglect, she found it difficult to draw back from her false position—which indeed she could not do without owning herself both child-stealer and liar—and so she put on a bold face and maintained the imposture even before the monarch himself. That she did not really care for the child is evident from ver. 26.] **Thus they spake** [Heb. " And they spake," i.e., affirmed and contradicted] **before the king.**

Ver. 23.—**Then** [promptly, without hesitation] **said the king, The one saith** [Heb. " this is saying," i.e., keeps saying] **This is my son that liveth, and thy son is the dead ; and the other saith, Nay, but thy son is the dead and my son is the living.**

Ver. 24.—**And the king said, Bring me a sword. And they brought a** [Heb. the ; the sword, i.e., of the executioner, or the sword for which he asked] **sword before the king.**

Ver. 25.—**And the king said, Divide the living child in two, and give half to the one and half to the other** [Heb. one].

Ver. 26.—**Then spake the woman whose the living child was unto the king, for her bowels** [thought by most of the ancients to be the seat of the affections, probably because of the sensations which strong emotions excite there. Cf. τὰ σπλάγχνα in the New Testament (2 Cor. vi. 12 ; Phil. ii. 1 ; Philem. 7, 20, &c.] **yearned** [Heb. glowed. We speak of " glowing with pity," &c.] **upon her son, and she said, O my lord, give her the living child, and in no wise slay it. But the other** [Heb. this] **said** [Heb. saying] **Let it be neither mine nor thine, but divide it.** [The Hebrew is strikingly concise, " divide." We have here by far the greatest difficulty in the story. When the pretender, who has clamoured for the child, is at last offered it by its mother, she refuses the gift and heartlessly urges that it shall be cut in two. We can only account for her strange conduct on the supposition that· she caught eagerly at any way of escape from the dilemma in which she had placed herself, and thought, no doubt, that to accept his decision would be to flatter and please the king. (See Homiletics.)

Ver. 27.—**Then the king answered and said** [He simply echoes the exact words of the mother. This is clear from the fact that the word יָלוּד=natus, "the one born," here and in ver. 26 rendered " child," is a very unusual one], **Give her the living child, and in no wise slay it** [The LXX., which reads " Give the child to her who said, Give it to her," &c., obscures the evidently designed repetition] she is the mother thereof [Heb. *she, his mother*].

Ver. 28.—**And all Israel heard of the judgment which the king had judged, and they feared the king** [*i.e.*, were impressed and awed by his almost supernatural penetration. Bähr refers to Luke iv. 36 ; viii. 25], **for they saw that the wisdom of God** [for which he asked (ver. 9) and which God gave (ver. 12] **was in him** [Heb. *within him*] **to do judgment.** [Most of the commentators cite from Grotius, the familiar story found in Diodorus Siculus, of Ariopharnes, king of Thrace. Three youths claimed before this king each to be the son, and therefore successor, of a deceased king of the Cimmerians. He decided that that one was the real son who refused to cast a javelin at his father's corpse.]

HOMILETICS.

Ver. 28. — *Solomon's Judgment a Foreshadowing of the Judgment to come.* Again we see in Solomon a type of the true " Son of David." The arraignment of the two harlots is an adumbration of the " great assize." This striking scene— the young king sitting on his throne, probably in a void place at the gate of the city, in the bright clear Eastern morning ; around him his guards, counsellors, and ministers of state (ch. xii. 6) ; before him the two harlots and the helpless child— carries our thoughts to a day of storm and cloud, a day of darkness and dread, when the " Son of Man shall sit upon the throne of His glory," with " the holy angels " around Him and " all nations " before Him (St. Matt. xxv. 31). Let us see in this first judgment, then, an outline of the last. Observe :

I. THE JUDGE. It is (1) *the Son of David.* We do not read of David's judgments. This a duty which he was apparently remiss in discharging (2 Sam. xv.) He devolved the duty of judging and punishing upon his son (1 Kings ii. 1—10). Even so, the " Eternal Father judgeth no man, but hath committed all judgment to the Son." Because He is the Son of David, *i.e.*, the Son of Man, our Lord will judge the sons of men. The Judge is, therefore, one who knows us, one who feels for us. It is (2) the wisest of men. " He was wiser than all men " (ch. iv. 31). The wisdom of God was in him to do judgment (ch. iii. 28). But the Judge of men and angels not only *has*, but *is* the Wisdom of God (Prov. ix. ; 1 Cor. i. 24). The Supreme, the Essential Wisdom will sit upon the great white throne. His judgments, therefore, must be " just and true." Now consider

II. THE JUDGED. They were (1) *of two classes.* There was the innocent babe and the impure women. And of the latter one was true, the other false ; one right, the other wrong. There will be two classes, and only two, in the judgment to come : sheep and goats, wheat and tares, good fish and bad, the righteous and the sinner. (2) *Both were harlots.* " Whoremongers and adulterers GOD will judge." Men cannot, or do not. Our pleasant vices are often undetected ; or, if known, are not reprobated. But see 1 Cor. v. 11 ; vi. 9—19 ; Gal. v. 19—21.

III. THE JUDGMENT. Thereby (1) *a sin was brought to light.* No eye saw that midnight theft. They two were alone. But the deed is now dragged to the light of day. And the Lord " will bring to light the hidden things of darkness." What was " whispered in the ear in closets shall be proclaimed upon the housetops." (2) *A wrong was redressed.* The pretended mother probably held the child when they came before the king. The true mother carried it in her arms when they left the judgment-seat. Restitution, *i.e.*, was enforced. And the judgment-seat of Christ shall accomplish the restitution of all things. There every wrong shall have its remedy. Now the " foundations of the earth are out of course." Might stands for right. Possession is nine points of the law. But in that day " *suum cuique.*" It is related of one of the Wesleys that on paying an account which was a gross imposition, he wrote upon the bill, " To be re-adjusted in that day." (3) *Character was revealed.* The true mother and the pretended alike proclaim themselves. A word from each decides the question, and reveals their inmost thoughts. So shall it be at the end of the world. " Out of thine own mouth will I judge thee." " By thy words thou shalt be justified, and by thy words thou shalt be condemned." The Son of Man shall "make manifest the counsels of the heart."

IV. THE REWARD AND PUNISHMENT. To the one the tribunal brought justification, joy, peace. To the other, condemnation, shame, contempt. But notice especially (1) *the difference it made in their emotions and* (2) *the difference in their reputations.* (1) The joy of the mother who had received her child again may be better imagined than described. The same may be said of the vexation, confusion, remorse, of the pretender when her villainy was made manifest. And in these emotions we may see a faint image of the unspeakable joy of the saved: of the weeping and gnashing of teeth of the lost. (2) The true mother would have the sympathy of bystanders, the congratulations of her friends, &c.; the other would be pointed at with scorn and reproach. Here, too, we have a picture, albeit an imperfect one, of the issues of the day of judgment. To the saint, the "Come ye blessed" of the Judge will lead to "pleasures for evermore;" to the sinner, "Depart ye cursed" will be the beginning of "shame and everlasting contempt."

Ver. 26.—"*Let it be neither mine nor thine, but divide it.*" "The Word of God is quick and powerful, and sharper than any two-edged sword .... and is a discerner of the thoughts and intents of the heart." The judgment of Solomon is a striking commentary on this passage; indeed, it is possible that the writer had this incident in his mind when he penned these words. For assuredly the word of Solomon, "*Divide,*" &c., was sharper than the sword they had just brought him * in wounding the mother's heart (Cf. Luke ii. 35); while not more surely would the king's sword, had it not been stayed, have pierced to the "*dividing asunder of the joints and marrow*" of the child, than did the king's word distinguish between the true and the false, revealing both the tenderness and yearning love of the real mother, and also the thoughts and intents and workings of heart of the pretender. It is probably, in part at least, because of their *revelation of character* that they are recorded here. Let us now, therefore, consider the character and motives of the pseudo-mother, as disclosed to us in her words and conduct.

And first, let us ask, what can have led to this cruel and unnatural speech? Here is a woman who has recently become a mother, and who claims to be the mother of the child, having no pity on a helpless babe. At one moment, she strenuously contends before the king for its possession, and at the next she connives at, and indeed clamours for, its murder. She has surreptitiously taken it from one who would have guarded and cherished it; she loudly protests that it is hers; she is so anxious to have it that she will plead for it before the royal tribunal, and yet, when it is gravely proposed to cut the hapless child in two, she is loud in her approval of the plan. How can we account for such strange inconsistency?

The usual explanation is that she was impelled to do and say what she did by spite, by jealousy. And, without doubt, there *was* an element of spite in her conduct. If *she* was to be denied the child, she was resolved that none else should have it. She would never submit to the humiliation of leaving the judgment-seat with the character of an impostor, while that other one carried off the babe in her arms in triumph. But while the feeling of "dog in the manger" explains much, it does not explain all. It does not account, for example, for her having cumbered herself with the care of the child in the first instance; and it hardly explains her proceeding to the extremity of judicial murder.

Nor even if we combine with spite the desire to flatter the youthful king, do we find a sufficient explanation of her inconsistency. No doubt she thought it would be a compliment to her prince readily to acquiesce in his proposal. It is not the first time or the last that men have readily assented to wrong-doing because a crowned head suggested it. We see in her cry, "Divide it," a cringing, fawning desire to ingratiate herself into Solomon's favour, or if not that, at least to play the courtier; but we do not see in this desire alone a sufficient explanation of this

---

* "A blow with a word strikes deeper than a blow with a sword."—WHICHCOTE.

clamour for the life of a puling and innocent babe. No, if we are to get at the very root of her strange and shameful conduct, we must first ask another question, viz., What led her to *steal* this child from its mother's arms and to claim it for her own? What induced her when she woke in the night and found her own child dead, to creep in the darkness to her companion's couch and take a changeling for her son. For this was surely a strange thing to do. We could more readily understand her rejoicing in the death of her own child of shame than this eager desire to burden herself with a bastard that she had not borne.

Now, it is quite possible that there were special circumstances connected with this case, which, if we knew them, would offer a complete and certain explanation of her conduct. For example, to pass by other possibilities, hers may have been such a case as Tamar's (Gen. xxxviii.) But as we do not and cannot know what these peculiar circumstances were, if there were any, we can only collect her motives, as best we may, from the record of facts which we possess.

It is clear, then, that she was *not* actuated by love for the child. It is unlikely that a woman such as she was could have love for a child such as this was; while it is inconceivable that if she really loved it, she would have consented to and counselled its death. Nor can it have been the pride and joy of having a man-child to call her son (1 John xvi. 21). For the child was not hers, and no one knew this better than herself. No doubt the Jewish mother had special reasons for desiring offspring and for cherishing her children, but this was the child of a stranger.

What then *were* her motives? Were they not these? First, the fear of reproach, and secondly, jealousy of her more fortunate companion. Fear of reproach; for no woman, in any age of the world, or under any circumstances, can fail to be morti-fied and humbled and ashamed at having occasioned, by her maladroitness, the death of her child. She knew what the tongues of the neighbours would say: she could see them, perhaps, even mocking her as a murderess. For they could not know that the death was accidental and some of them, she feared, might *think*, if they did not *say*, that there had been foul play on her part. These thoughts, as they rushed through her mind in the black and dark night, would be accentuated and made well-nigh intolerable by the thought that her companion had been more careful or more fortunate. What may have passed between these two women we cannot say. For aught we know, each may have boasted of her child, or the one may have disparaged the child of the other. There must almost have been some-thing of the kind—and it may have been something extremely simple—to account for this act of child-stealing.

It is quite possible, of course, that this woman, had she been interrogated after the fraud was detected, would have found it difficult to say what led her to play this false part. For we may rest assured she did not argue about it, did not stop to parley with herself or to weigh the consequences. She acted on a blind, hasty, unreasoning impulse. But all the same it is not difficult for us to see that these must have been among the springs of her conduct. And when the fatal move was once made, the rest of her sin is easily explained. There was then nothing for her to do but to brazen it out. It was impossible for her to stop, without proclaiming herself both liar and thief. As she had lied to her companion, so she must lie to the neighbours, and as she had lied to the neighbours, so she must lie even before the king. There was no help for it. *Vestigia nulla retrorsum!* She must go on to the bitter end.

But it is easy to see how terribly trying and painful her position would at last become. The constant fear of detection, or the fear lest she should betray herself, must have made it almost insupportable. Any moment something might ooze out which would reveal the deceit and cover her with infamy. Bitterly must she have regretted that she had ever embarked on this course of fraud; eagerly must she have cast about for any chance of escape.

And so when the king proposed to cut the Gordian knot; when he proposed, that is, to extricate her from the toils which she had woven round herself, is there any wonder that she caught eagerly at the first chance that offered, and that without a moment's reflection as to the morality of the remedy, and without the least perception of the snare that was spread for her. All she thought was that it promised an honourable retreat from ground which was every moment becoming more insecure; that it opened to her, in her despair and dread of detection, a door of escape. It is this accounts for the cry, "Divide it." The murder would cover her multitude of lies, the blood of the innocent would efface the traces of her guilt.

The lessons taught by this history must be very briefly indicated. Among them are these:

1. *Impurity almost inevitably leads to deceit.* The root of all the mischief here was the unchastity. The sin against the body makes other sins comparatively easy. "It is only the first step that costs." And what a step is that!

2. *Moral cowardice may lead to murder.* The fear which prompted the hasty resolve to possess herself of the living child, led this miserable woman to stealing, lying, persistent falseness, and to murder, in thought and will. *Facilis descensus Averni,* &c.

3. *Falsehood leads to falsehood.* The proverb says, "If we tell one lie we must tell twenty more to bury it." "One lie must be thatched with another or it will soon rain through."

> "O what a tangled web we weave
> When once we venture to deceive."

4. *Jealousy dries up the milk of human kindness.* It is "cruel as the grave."

> "Fiercer than famine, war, or spotted pestilence;
> Baneful as death, and horrible as hell."

It led this woman to act like a fiend; to desire the butchery of an innocent babe.

5. *Sin overreaches itself.* The pretender was caught in her own toils. She had no sooner said, "Divide it," than she saw she was undone. She proclaimed her own falseness. "Out of thine own mouth will I judge thee."

6. *When the sinner is most secure, then sudden destruction comes upon him.* This woman had never breathed freely till Solomon said, "Divide it." That seemed such a certain deliverance that she echoed the cry. Now she began to feel safe. The next moment she was disgraced, condemned, ruined. Cf. Matt. xxiv. 50; xxv. 44; 1 Thess. v. 3, &c.

EXPOSITION.

CHAPTER IV. 1—19.

SOLOMON'S STATE AND COURT OFFICIALS.— The account of Solomon's marriage and entry upon his religious and judicious functions is appropriately followed by a description of his court, of the great functionaries of the realm, of his royal state and magnificence, and, lastly, of his varied and unprecedented wisdom. It must not be supposed, however, from the occurrence of the lists in this particular place, that they necessarily represent the appointments of the early part of Solomon's reign. The mention of two of the married daughters of the king (vers. 11, 15) has been generally thought to prove that the record belongs to a much later period, and it certainly affords a powerful presumption in favour of a later date. Too much stress, however, must not be laid on this consideration, as the girls of the East marry early, and these may well have been given to officers much their seniors, who had long been in office, and who had merited this distinction (cf. Josh. xv. 16; 1 Sam. xvii. 25; xviii. 17) by the important services they had rendered to the State. Ewald sees in these lists unmistakeable evidence of compilation from the public archives. But see Introduction, sect. vi. If the historians of Israel were the prophets, nothing is more natural than that they should record such details of the Augustan age of their race.

Ver. 1.—**So King Solomon was king over all Israel.** [All later kings ruled but a part of the land of Israel, as also did David at first.]

Ver. 2.—**And these were the princes** [*i.e.,*

ministers, officers. Cf. 2 Sam. viii. 15–18, and xx. 23–26] **which he had, Azariah the son** [i.e., descendant, probably grandson. See on 1 Chron. vi. 10] **of Zadok the priest.** [We are here confronted by two questions of considerable difficulty. First, to whom does the *title* "priest" here belong, to Azariah or to Zadok? Second, what are we to understand by the *term*, a spiritual, or a more or less secular person—ἱερεύς or βουλευτής? As to 1, the Vulgate (*sacerdotis*) and apparently the Authorized Version, with the Rabbins, Luther, and many later expounders, connect the title with Zadok (who is mentioned as priest in ver. 4), and understand that Azariah, the son of the high priest Zadok, was, together with the sons of Shisha, one of the scribes (ver. 3). It is true that this view obviates some difficulties, but against it are these considerations. (1) The accents. (2) The Chaldee and LXX. (ὁ ἱερεύς Cod. Alex.; Cod. Vat. omits the words) Versions. (3) Hebrew usage, according to which the patronymic is regarded as almost parenthetical. (4) The fact that in every other case in this list the title is predicate nominative (vers. 3—6). (5) The position of Azariah's name, first in the list—a position which would hardly be assigned to a scribe. (6) The absence of any copula (וֹ), which, it is submitted, would be required if Azariah *and* the sons of Shisha alike were scribes. The question is one of some nicety, but the balance of evidence is distinctly in favour of connecting the title with Azariah, i.e., "Azariah son of Zadok was the priest." This brings us to 2. What are we to understand by "the priest"—הכהן? It is urged by Keil, Bähr, *al.* that this cannot mean "priest" in the ordinary sense of the word, still less "high priest," for the following reasons: (1) Because the high priests of Solomon are mentioned presently, viz., Abiathar and Zadok, and the Jews never had *three* high priests. (2) Because the Azariah who was high priest under Solomon—for the words of 1 Chron. vi. 10, "He it is that executed the priest's office," &c., must belong to the Azariah of ver. 9, and have got accidentally misplaced—was the son of Ahimaaz, not of Zadok. (3) Because no grandson of Zadok could then be old enough to sustain the office of high priest. (4) Because in one passage (2 Sam. viii. 18, compared with 1 Chron. xviii. 17) כהנים is used of privy councillors and of the sons of David, who cannot have been sacrificing priests. Keil consequently would understand that Azariah was "administrator of the kingdom, or prime minister." Similarly Bähr. But in favour of the ordinary meaning of the word are these powerful

considerations: (1) All the versions translate the word by "priest," i.e., they understand by the term a spiritual person. (2) Whatever may be the case with כהן, הכהן, "*the* priest" (*par excellence*) can only be understood of the *high* priest (ch. i. 8, 38; Exod. xxix. 30; Lev. xxi. 21; 2 Kings xi. 9, 15; xxii. 4, 8, 10, 12, 14. Comp. 2 Chron. xxvi. 17). (3) It is extremely doubtful whether כהן is ever used except in the sense of ἱερεύς. Rawlinson, who says it sometimes indicates "a civil officer, with perhaps a semi-priestly character," refers to Gesenius *sub hac voce*, who, however, distinctly affirms that the word only means priest, and accounts for the application of the term to the sons of David (2 Sam. viii. 18) on the supposition that the Jews had priests who were not of the tribe of Levi. The question is discussed with great learning by Professor Plumptre (Dict. Bib., art. "Priest"), who suggests that "David and his sons may have been admitted, not to distinctively priestly functions, such as burning incense (Numb. xvi. 40; 2 Chron. xxvi. 18), but to an honorary, titular priesthood. To wear the ephod in processions (2 Sam. vi. 14) at the time when this was the special badge of the order (1 Sam. xxii. 18), to join the priests and Levites in their songs and dances, might have been conceded, with no deviation from the Law, to the members of the royal house." There is one difficulty however in the way of accepting this ingenious and otherwise sufficient explanation, namely, that it seems hardly likely that the title of priest would be freely accorded by Hebrew writers to men who were expressly *excluded* from all "distinctively priestly functions," especially after the use of the same word in the preceding verse (17) to designate the high priest. And I venture to suggest that the discharge by David's sons of the semi-priestly functions just referred to occasioned so much remark as to lead to the application of the term "priest" to them in a special conventional sense; in fact, that it became a sort of *soubriquet*, which rather implied that they were *not* priests than that they were. (Notice the *order* of 2 Sam. viii. 18, Heb.) And observe (4), if we are to understand by "*the* priest*" in ver. 2, "prime minister;" by "*priests*" in ver. 4, "high priests," and by "*priest*" in ver 5, "principal officer," language has no certain meaning. (5) The mention of Azariah as "the priest" in the same list with Zadok and Abiathar is easily accounted for. We know that Abiathar was deposed at the beginning of Solomon's reign (ch. ii. 27), and Zadok must then have been an old man. Their names consequently are recorded (ver. 4) because they were high priests for a brief period of the reign, but Azariah is mentioned first as "*the* priest" because he was high priest during most of the time. (6) "Azariah the *son* of Zadok" is quite compatible with the fact that Azariah was really the son of Ahimaaz. בֶּן is constantly used in the sense of "descendant," and especially "grandson." (Gen. xxix. 5: xxxi. 28, 55: and see on ch. ii. 8, "the son of Gera.") Zadok is no doubt mentioned as better known than Ahimaaz, and probably because Azariah succeeded him directly in the office. (7) The age of Azariah must be uncertain, and Solomon's reign was a long one. (8) The position of his name—first—accords well with the idea that he was high priest, which I conclude that he was. It is worthy of remark that in the lists of David the military officers of the kingdom occupy the first place; in those of Solomon, the civil and religious dignitaries. "The princes of Solomon are, with one exception (ver. 4) ministers of peace."— Wordsworth.

Ver. 3.—**Elihoreph and Ahiah, the sons of Shisha** [probably the same person who is mentioned in 2 Sam. xx. 25 as *Sheva;* in 2 Sam. viii. 17, as *Seraiah ;* and in 1 Chron. xviii. 16, as *Shavsha*, David's scribe. The office thus descended from father to sons. The variations in this name are instructive. Compare Kishi and Kushaiah, Abijah and Abijam, Michaiah and Maachah, Absalom and Abishalom, &c. Names written *ex ore dictantis* are sure to differ. See below on ver. 12], **scribes** [the scribes, סֹפְרִים, were Secretaries of State : they wrote letters and proclamations, drew up edicts, and apparently kept the accounts (2 Kings xii. 10). Their position in the list indicates their importance]; **Jehoshaphat the son of Ahilud, the recorder.** [He held the same office under David, and is mentioned in all three lists (2 Sam. viii. 17; xx. 25 ; 1 Chron. xviii. 15). The recorder or "remembrancer" (marg.) was, perhaps, "chancellor" (Keil), or keeper of the king's conscience, rather than, as is generally supposed, chronicler of public events, and keeper of the archives. See Introduction, sect. vi.]

Ver. 4.—**And Benaiah the son of Jehoiada** [see on ch. i. 32] **was** [the A. V. supplies *was* and *were* quite needlessly in this and succeeding verses. This is simply a list of Solomon's princes and of the offices they discharged] **over the host** [cf. ii. 35] : **and Zadok and Abiathar were the priests** [the mention of Abiathar's name after his deposition (ch. ii. 27, 35) has occasioned much remark, and has even led to the belief that he was subsequently pardoned and restored

to office (Clericus). Theodoret remarks quite truly, τὴν ἀρχὴν ἀφείλατο, οὐ τῆς ἱερωσύνης ἐγύμνωσεν, and similarly Grotius. But a simpler explanation is that his name is put down here because he *had* been high priest, though for a brief period only, under Solomon. See above on ver. 2.]

Ver. 5.—**And Azariah the son of Nathan** [Azariah was clearly not an uncommon name (ver. 2, and cf. 1 Chron. ii. 39; v. 36—40 Heb.; A. V. vi. 9—14), especially in the high priest's family. Keil and Bähr pronounce somewhat positively that this Nathan is not the prophet of that name, but Nathan the son of David (2 Sam. v. 14; Luke iii. 31). It is quite impossible to decide with certainty which is meant, if either, though Zech. xii. 12 undoubtedly favours the supposition that the latter is here intended] **was over the officers** [the twelve prefects mentioned in vers. 7 sqq.] : **and Zabud the son of Nathan was principal officer** [Heb. *priest*, Vulg. *sacerdos*. Singularly, as before, the LXX. (Vat.) omits the word. The expression can hardly mean "the son of Nathan the priest," but it may either signify that "Zabud ben Nathan, a priest, was king's friend," or that (as in the A. V.) he was a priest *and* king's friend. But the former is every way preferable. I find it easier to believe that the true import of 2 Sam. viii. 18—the passage which is cited (sometimes along with *ib.* xx. 26, where the LXX., however, has ἱερεύς) to prove that there were secular "priests"—is not yet understood, than to hold (with Gesenius, Ewald, &c.), that there were sacrificing priests who were not of the sons of Aaron (cf. 2 Chron. xxvi. 18), or that the word כֹּהֵן, the meaning of which was thoroughly fixed and understood, can have been familiarly applied, except in the strictly conventional way already indicated, to lay persons], **and** [omit] **the king's friend.** ["This appears to have been now a recognized office (2 Sam. xv. 37; xvi. 16 ; 1 Chron. xxvii. 33)," Rawlinson.]

Ver. 6.—**And Ahishar was over the household** [steward and manager of the palace. We meet this office here for the first time, an evidence of the growing size and magnificence of the court (cf. 1 Kings xviii. 3 ; 2 Kings xviii. 18 ; Isa. xxii. 15). That such an officer was needed, the fact mentioned below (on ver. 23) as to the enormous size of the royal household will prove]: **and Adoniram** [see on ch. xii. 18] **the son of Abda was over the tribute.** [Marg. "levy," *i.e.*, the forced labour (ch. v. 13, 14). See on ch. xii. 3.]

Ver. 7.—**And Solomon had twelve officers** [lit., persons "*placed*" or "*set* over" others, *i.e.*, superintendents. The term is used of Doeg (1 Sam. xxii. 9). They were twelve, not because of the twelve tribes, but the twelve months] **over all Israel, which provided victuals for** [Heb. *nourished*] **the king and his household: each man his month in a year made provision** [lit., *a month in the year it was* (*i.e.*, devolved) *upon each to nourish*. It has been thought by some that these superintendents were also governors of provinces (ἡγεμόνες καὶ σταρηγοί, Jos. Ant. viii. 2, 3), as well as purveyors. But of this nothing is said in the text. Their principal function was to collect the royal dues or taxes which were evidently paid, as they still are in the East, in kind].

Ver. 8.—**And these are their names** [the order is not geographical, nor do the districts correspond, except roughly, with the territories of the tribes. The order is probably that of the months for which they were severally responsible, and the districts were marked out according to the capabilities of the country]: **The son of Hur** [Heb. as marg., *Ben Hur*. Of the twelve prefects, five are only known by their patronymics, for it is hardly likely that these are proper names, like Ben-hanan and Ben-zoheth (1 Chron. iv. 20). No satisfactory explanation of this curious circumstance has hitherto been given. The most probable is that in the document from which this list was compiled, the part of the page containing the missing names had been accidentally destroyed], **in mount Ephraim.** [See on ch. xii. 25. This district, which practically coincided with the territory of Ephraim, was one of the most fertile in Palestine. Hence, possibly, it stands first.]

Ver. 9.—**The son of Dekar** [*Ben-Dekar*], **in Makaz** [unknown otherwise], **and in Shaalbim** [Josh. xix. 42; Judg. i. 35] **and Beth-shemesh** [called Irshemesh, Josh. xix. 41. Now *'Ain Shemes*], **and Elon-beth-hanan.** [Elon, Josh. xix. 43. Probably Beth-hanan is a different place, the " and " (ו) having accidentally dropped out of the text. The LXX. (ἕως Βηθανὰν) favours this view. It has been identified by Robinson with Beit Hunûn. This second district embraces Dan.]

Ver. 10.—**The son of Hesed** [*Ben-Hesed*], **in Aruboth** (Heb. Arubboth, unknown]; **to him pertained Sochoh** [there were two cities of this name, one in the mountain (Josh. xv. 48), and one in the "valley" (the *Shefelah*, Josh. xv. 33, 35), and both in the tribe of Judah, from which, therefore, this third district was taken], **and all the land of Hepher.** [Josh. xii. 17. Ewald holds that this place was in Manasseh, and that "it is impossible in the twelve districts to find any portion of . . . . Judah." But see above.]

Ver. 11.—**The son of Abinadab** [*Ben Abinadab*. Possibly the Abinadab of 1 Sam. xvi. 8; xvii. 13. If so, this officer, who married Solomon's daughter, was also his cousin], **in** [Heb. omits] **all the region** [נפת, height; the term is only used in connection with Dor] **of Dor** [Josh. xi. 2; xii. 23; xvii. 11. Dor, now represented by the miserable village of Tantura, lies on the strand of the Mediterranean, north of Cæsarea. A " spur of Mount Carmel, steep and partially wooded, runs parallel to the coast-line, at the distance of about a mile and a half " (Porter). This is the " height of Dor." Thenius supposes this fourth district embraced the plain of Sharon. Josephus (viii. 2. 3.) limits this prefecture to the sea coast, which may well include Sharon. Indeed, without it, this district would have been destitute of cornlands] **which had Taphath, the daughter of Solomon, to wife.** [" It has always been a practice amongst Oriental potentates to attach to themselves the more important of their officers by giving them for wives princesses of the royal house. . . . The practice of polygamy has generally enabled them to carry out this system to a very wide extent " (Rawlinson).

Ver. 12.—**Baana, the son of Ahilud** [cf. ver. 3. Probably the recorder's brother], **to him pertained** [the original, true to its character as a list, omits these words, simply giving the name of the officer and then the towns of his district or province] **Taanach and Megiddo** [similarly associated, Josh. xii. 21; Judg. v. 19; i. 27. These towns, which became famous in later Jewish history (2 Kings xxiii. 29; 2 Chron. xxxv. 22), lay at the foot of the E. spurs of Carmel, on the margin of the plain of Esdraelon. See Conder's " Tent Work in Palestine," p. 67] **and all Bethshean** [Josh. xvii. 11, 16; Judg. i. 27. Otherwise Bethshan (1 Sam. xxxi. 10, 12; 2 Sam. xxi. 12), now *Beisân*. The LXX. here translate the word ὁ οἶκος Σάν; elsewhere they write βαιθσὰν or βαιθσάμ, and in Judges i. 27 explain ἥ ἐστι Σκυθῶν πόλις, hence its later name Scythopolis. Rawlinson, by an oversight, interprets the name to mean " house of the sun," which is the translation of Bethshemesh. Bethshan prob. means " house of rest." " The site of the town is on the brow of the descent by which the great plain of Esdraelon drops down to the level of the Ghor." The present writer was much struck (in 1861) by its situation. See Conder, pp. 233, 234. The text shows that it gave its name to the adjoining district], **which is by Zartanah** [probably the Zaretan of Josh. iii. 16 and the Zarthan (same word in the Heb.) of 1 Kings vi. 46, which place is called Zeredathah in 2 Chron. iv. 17, and is probably the Zererath of Judg. vii. 22. (The variations in spelling are again to be noticed). Here Solomon cast the Temple vessels. By some it is identified with Kurn Sartabeh (but see Quart. Stat. of Pal. Explor. Fund, July, 1874, and Conder, pp. 233, 234), a few miles below Bethshan. It is noticeable (in connexion with Josh. iii.16) that at this point the Jordan valley narrows (Keil). It occupies high ground and commands an extensive view (Robinson)] **beneath** [or *below*] **Jezreel** [Wordsworth remarks that "Jezreel, now Zerin, is a lofty site." But the idea of "beneath" is not that of depression, but of geographical position = the district south-east of Jezreel] **from** [LXX. *and from*) **Bethshean to Abelmeholah** [lit. *meadow of the dance.* It lay ten miles south of Bethshean. It is mentioned in connexion with Zererath (Zaretan) in Judg. vii. 22, but is best known as the home of Elisha (1 Kings xix. 16)] **even unto the place that is beyond** [Heb. *unto the other side of*] **Jokneam.** [Properly, *Jokmeam.* Identified by the Survey (Conder, p. 68) with *Tell Keimûn.* A Levitical town (1 Chron. vi. 68) probably the same as Kibzaim (cf. Josh. xxi. 22). This district coincided practically with the tribe of Manasseh. It embraced a part (see ver. 17) of the fertile plain of Esdraelon and of the Jordan valley.]

Ver. 13.—**The son of Geber** [possibly son of the Geber mentioned in ver. 19] **in Ramoth-gilead** [two districts east of the Jordan are now enumerated. And first, the territory of Gad. Ramoth-gilead was a Levitical city (Deut. iv. 43 ; Josh. xxi. 38). Its selection as a city of refuge (Josh. xx. 8), and as the seat of Bengeber's prefecture, together with the constant wars waged for its possession (1 Kings xxii. 3 ; 2 Kings viii. 28 ; ix. 14) show that it was a position of great strength and importance] ; **to him pertained the towns of Jair** [the *Havoth Jair* are strictly the *lives* (*i.e.*, villages, because men *live* there) of Jair. So Gesenius, who cites *Eisleben* and similar names] **the son Manasseh** [it is doubtful whether the judge of that name (Judg. x. 3) or Jair, the son of Segub (called a "son of Manasseh" in Numb. xxxii. 41, because his grandmother was a daughter of the great Machir, though his father belonged to Judah, 1 Chron. ii. 21), is intended. Probably it is the latter. (They can hardly be one and the same person, though they are often identified, as, *e.g.*, in the Speaker's Comm. on Judg. x. 3. But they belong to different periods.) Curiously enough, the Havoth Jair are mentioned in connexion with each (see Numb. xxxii. 41 ; Deut. iii. 4, 5, 14 ; Josh. xiii. 30 ; 1 Chron. ii. 22 ; Judg. x. 4), but in every case except the last the reference is to the son of Segub. As the judge was probably one of his de-

scendants, it is not surprising that the judge's sons should possess some of the villages of Jair], **which are in Gilead ; to him also pertained the region** [חֶבֶל, lit., *measuring cord,* came to signify the region measured] **of Argob** [elsewhere "*the* Argob," *i.e.*, the stony. This is the region subsequently known as Trachonitis, now called the Lejah. It is distinguished here and in Josh. xiii. 30, and 1 Chron. ii. 22 from the Gileadite district just mentioned, with which it is sometimes confounded. Both seem to have been conquered by Jair, but the towns of the former bore the name of *Havoth Jair* and these of *Bashan Havoth Jair.* Cf. Deut. iii. 4, 5, 14 with Numb. xxxii. 41. The latter consisted of threescore cities, with walls, gates, and bars. This remarkable district, twenty-two miles in length by fourteen in breadth, is "wholly composed of black basalt, which appears to have issued from innumerable pores in the earth in a liquid state. . . . Before cooling, its surface was violently agitated, and it was afterwards shattered and rent by convulsions. . . . Strange as it may seem, this ungainly and forbidding region is thickly studded with deserted cities and villages" (Porter, "Giant Cities of Bashan," also in Kitto's Cycl. iii. p. 1032 ; Dict. Bib. i. 104)] **which is in Bashan, threescore great cities with walls and brazen bars.** [These words are a reminiscence of Deut. iii. 4, 5.]

Ver. 14.—**Ahinadab the son of Iddo** [probably the seer of that name, 2 Chron. ix. 29] **had Mahanaim** [Heb. *to Mahanaim,* as marg. That is, went, or was appointed, to Mahanaim. Rawlinson understands that his district was "from the places last mentioned to Mahanaim," but for this the *usus loquendi* of the writer would lead us to expect עַד. For Mahanaim, see Gen. xxxii. 2 ; Joshua xiii. 26].

Ver. 15.—**Ahimaaz** [probably the son of Zadok, 2 Sam. xv. 27 ; xvii. 17] **was in Naphtali ; he also** [like Ben-Abinadab, ver. 11] **took Basmath the daughter of Solomon to wife.**

Ver. 16.—**Banaah** [or Baana, the second prefect of that name (ver. 12). The names are identical in the Hebrew. In 2 Sam. iv. 2 the name is Baanah] **the son of Hushai** [the Archite, David's friend. Cf. 2 Sam. xv. 32] **was in Asher and Aloth.** [No town or district of this name is known. Probably the word should be Bealoth, as in the LXX., Syr., and Vulg. Our translators have taken the initial בְּ for a prefix, but it is almost certainly part of the name. There was a Baaloth in Judah (Josh. xv. 24) and a Baaloth in Dan (ibid. xix. 44), but neither of these can be meant here.]

Ver. 17.—**Jehoshaphat the son of Paruah,**

in Issachar. [He had consequently the plain of Esdraelon, with the exception mentioned above, ver. 12.]

Ver. 18.—**Shimei the son of Elah** [by some identified with the Shimei of chapter i. 8. But see note there], **in Benjamin.** [It is noteworthy that Shimei was a Benjamite name, 2 Sam. xvi. 5, 11.]

Ver. 19.—**Geber the son of Uri was in the country of Gilead** [i.e., he presided over the parts not already assigned to Bengeber (perhaps his son) and Ahinadab. Gilead is often used (see Deut. xxxiv. 1; Judg. xx. 1) to designate *all* the country east of the Jordan. And so apparently here, for] **the country of Sihon king of the Amorites, and of Og king of Bashan**] embraced the whole trans-Jordanic region, Deut. iii. 8; Num. xxi. 24—35: cf. Psa. cxxxv. 11; cxxxvi. 19, 20]; **and he was the only officer which was in the land.** [This cannot mean " the only officer in Gilead," notwithstanding the great extent of territory—the usual interpretation—for that would contradict vers. 13, 14. Nor can it mean the only officer in his *district*, or *portion*, of Gilead, for that is self-evident, and the remark would apply equally to all the other prefects. And we are hardly

justified in translating נְצִיב אֶחָד "he was the first (*i.e.*, superior), officer" (set over those mentioned above, vers. 13, 14), as Schulze. אֶחָד *is* used as an ordinal number, but it is only in connexion with days and years (Gesen. s. v.) Some, following the LXX. (εἰς ἐν γῇ Ἰούδα) would detach Judah from ver. 20, where it must be allowed it occurs with a suspicious abruptness, and where the absence of the copula, so usual in the Hebrew, suggests a corruption of the text, and would connect it with this verse, which would then yield the sense, " and he was," (or " there was ") " one officer which purveyed in the land of Judah." It is to be observed, however, that though no mention has as yet been made of Judah in any of the districts, yet the prefecture of Ben Hesed (ver. 10) appears to have extended over this tribe, and the remark consequently seems superfluous. (Can it be the object of the writer to show that the royal tribe was not favoured or exempted from contributing its share?) On the whole, the difficulty would seem still to await a solution. We can hardly, in the teeth of ver. 7, suppose with Ewald, *al.* that a *thirteenth* officer is here intended.

HOMILETICS.

Vers. 2 sqq.—*The Servants of Solomon.* " These were the princes which he had." " All Scripture is . . . . . profitable for instruction," &c. A bare list of names may teach some lessons. We shall find in this list, first, some proofs of Solomon's wisdom, and secondly, some principles to guide our own conduct. First, however, let us remember that to select faithful and efficient servants is one of the most difficult tasks of rulers. The welfare of the whole State depends very largely on the choice. (Cf. Ps. ci. 5—7.) Now observe that here—

I. THE FIRST PLACE IS FILLED BY GOD'S PRIEST (ver. 2). The minister of religion takes precedence of the ministers of state. The universal tendency is to put man first and God second. Solomon—if this list preserves the order of his arrangements —put God first, in the person of His high priest. Under the theocracy the king was a sort of *summus episcopus.* It was meet that next to the anointed Prince should stand the anointed Pontiff.

II. PRIORITY IS GIVEN TO THE OFFICERS OF PEACE (vers. 3, 4). Scribes come before warriors. In David's day it was otherwise. But there has been an advance, and here is the proof of it. War is essentially barbarous. Among savage tribes warfare is chronic. As men become wiser and more civilized, the appeal to brute force is less frequent. Wiser, for war means unwisdom somewhere. More civilized, for the history of civilization tells how the wager of battle, which is now confined to nations, was once employed by tribes, provinces, and private persons. So that, in this particular, the wise son was greater than the pious father. For this reason Solomon may build the temple which his father's blood-red hand may not touch. For this reason the son, not the father, is the favourite type of the Prince of Peace. One of the world's greatest generals (Napoleon) said there were but two great powers, the sword and the pen, and that, in the long run, the former was sure to be overcome by the latter. Solomon would seem to have been of the same opinion. The " scribes " and the " recorder " precede the " captain of the host."

III. MANY PLACES ARE FILLED BY THE FUNCTIONARIES OF HIS FATHER (vers. 3, 4, 6, and cf. ver. 16). An Eastern autocrat generally appoints his associates of the harem (ch. xii. 10), his personal favourites, to positions of trust. Solomon showed his wisdom in retaining the faithful servants of his predecessor (compare the folly of Rehoboam, ch. xii. 8), and his example thus confirms his precept (Prov. xxvii. 10), " Thine own friend and *thy father's friend* forsake not."

IV. SOME PLACES ARE FILLED BY HIS OWN SONS-IN-LAW (vers. 11, 15). This does not argue nepotism, or favouritism as the hand of the king's daughter was often bestowed as the reward of distinguished services (1 Sam. xvii. 25 ; xviii. 17, 27). It may have been the due recognition of fidelity and ability. In any case the alliances would strengthen Solomon's throne.

> " The friends thou hast, and their adoption, tried,
> Grapple them to thy heart with hooks of steel."

Alien princes would, no doubt, have been proud to espouse Solomon's daughters, but he preferred to marry them to faithful subjects. Blood is thicker than water.

V. ALL PLACES OF TRUST WERE FILLED BY PERSONS OF PIETY. The number of priests' or prophets' sons employed by Solomon is very remarkable (vers. 4, 5, 14, and possibly 15). He knew that those who were taught in the law of the Lord would best keep and best enforce the law of the realm. Those who " fear God " are those who " honour the king " (1 Peter ii. 17). Witness Joseph, Obadiah, Daniel, and the three Hebrew children. Even irreligious masters know the value of God-fearing servants. God blesses the house of Potiphar for the sake of its pious steward. Piety involves probity and excludes peculation and malfeasance.

VI. EVERY OFFICER HAD HIS PLACE AND KEPT IT. There were definite duties, definite districts. The prefectures were so many parishes. Each was responsible for his own and for that only. Order is Heaven's first law. The prosperity of Solomon's reign may have been largely due to his system and method. There is a hierarchy and a due order in heaven. The angels would almost seem to have their districts (Deut. xxxii. 8, LXX.) The great King gives " to every man according to his work " (Mark xiii. 34).

Vers. 7—19.—*The Twelve Prefects and the Twelve Apostles.* "And Solomon had twelve officers over all Israel." Considering how closely he foreshadows our blessed Lord, the twelve officers of Solomon can hardly fail to remind us of the twelve Apostles of the Lamb. It may be instructive to compare their dignities, functions, &c. Observe—

I. THEIR RESPECTIVE POSITIONS. *The officers of Solomon were princes* (ver. 2); *the officers of Jesus were peasants and fishermen.* Ability, energy, &c., dictated Solomon's choice ; humility, dependence, weakness, our Blessed Lord's (Matt. xviii. 3, 4 ; xxiii. 11 ; and cf. xi. 11). " Not many mighty, not many noble are called," &c. (1 Cor. i. 26). " Unlearned and ignorant men " (Acts iv. 13).

II. THEIR RESPECTIVE REPUTATIONS. *The officers of Solomon were reverenced and feared ; the apostles of our Lord were despised and defamed.* Each of the twelve prefects was, no doubt, a little potentate. The court of Abinadab in Mahanaim, or Shimei in Benjamin, would be a copy in miniature of that of the king in Jerusalem. And we know what the Eastern tax-gatherer is like, what despotic powers he wields, &c. Witness the Pashas and Valis of Turkey. How different were the twelve apostles. The contrast could not well be greater. " Hated of all men," esteemed " the filth and offscouring of all things ; " " a spectacle unto the world, and to angels, and to men " (1 Cor. iv. 9–13). What the life of an apostle was like we may learn from 2 Cor. xi. 24—29. " Behold, they which are gorgeously apparelled and live delicately are in king's courts " (1 Luke vii. 25). " Behold, we have forsaken all and followed thee " (Matt. xix. 27).

III. THEIR RESPECTIVE JURISDICTIONS. *The twelve officers presided over tribes ; the twelve apostles ministered to continents.* The whole of Palestine is about the size of Wales, and this strip of territory was divided into twelve parts. Compare with this the apostolic commission, " Go ye into *all the world,*" &c. " Ye shall be witnesses unto me . . . . unto the uttermost part of the earth." Judaism was a tribal religion; the faith of Christ is for humanity.

IV. THEIR RESPECTIVE FUNCTIONS. 1. *The twelve officers were receivers-general; the twelve apostles were general givers.* The first took from the people to give to the king: the latter received from their King to bestow on the people. To the former, the subjects of Solomon brought taxes or tribute; the latter have obtained blessings and gifts from their Lord for men. (Cf. Acts i. 8; ii. 18; viii. 18; 1 Tim. iv. 14; 2 Tim. i. 6, &c.) "It is more blessed to give," &c. 2. *The officers nourished the king* (ver. 27, Heb.) *and his armies: the apostles fed the Church.* (Cf. Acts xx. 28.) The 14,000 dependants of the court, the 4000 charioteers, the 12,000 horsemen, all were maintained by the twelve purveyors. Through the apostles, the Lord fed, now 4000, now 7000, and through them, their doctrine and their successors, He still feeds, with word and sacrament, the millions of the Church.

So far the comparison is largely in favour of the prefects. As regards this world's gifts and dignities, they bear away the palm. In their lifetime they received their good things and the apostles evil things. But an old authority—it is the *dictum* of Solon to Crœsus (Herod. i. 30—33)—warns us to pronounce on no man's fortune or happiness until we have seen the end. And the real end is not in this world. Let us therefore consider (1) *What is the verdict of posterity?* and (2) *What will be the issue of futurity* as to these two classes? Here we observe—

I. THE NAMES OF SOME OF THE PREFECTS ARE FORGOTTEN; THE NAMES OF THE APOSTLES ARE IN EVERLASTING REMEMBRANCE. The fame of Solomon's twelve was shortlived. Several of them are now known to us only by their patronymics. Those much dreaded satraps, before whom subjects trembled, their very names are in some cases lost in oblivion. But the apostolic college, every member is still famed, reverenced, loved throughout the whole round world. Their names are heard, Sunday by Sunday, in the Holy Gospel (cf. Matt. xxvi. 13). Better still, their "names are written in heaven" (Luke x. 20; cf. Phil. iv. 3). As to

II. THE TWELVE APOSTLES WILL JUDGE THE TWELVE PREFECTS. In their time, the latter sate on twelve thrones, each in his capital city, ruling the twelve tribes of Israel. But their glory, like that of the Roman general's pageant, "*lacked continuance.*" In the midst of their brief authority

> "Comes the blind Fury with the abhorrèd shears
> And slits the thin-spun life."

The dominion of the apostles is in the future. It belongs to the "regeneration." "When the Son of Man"—the true Son of David—"shall sit on the throne of his glory," then shall they "sit on twelve thrones, judging the twelve tribes," &c. (Matt. xix. 28). The despised fishermen shall judge the high and mighty officers —yes, and magnificent Solomon himself. Even now, it may be, their glory is in part begun.

> "Lo, the twelve, majestic princes
> In the court of Jesus sit,
> Calmly watching all the conflict
> Raging still beneath their feet."

Shall we follow the officers of Solomon, or the twelve apostles of the Lamb? Shall we, that is, desire earthly advancement, high position, contemporary fame, or shall we count all as dross that we may "win Christ and be found in Him" (Phil. iii. 8—11). "What shall it profit a man, if he gain," &c. We cannot all be ἡγεμόνες καὶ στρατηγοί, still less can we all wed kings' daughters. But we may all sit with Christ upon His throne (Rev. iii. 21); may all receive the crown of life (Rev. ii. 10); may all be "called unto the marriage supper of the Lamb" (Rev. xix. 7—9).

EXPOSITION.

CHAPTER IV. 20—34.

SOLOMON'S RULE, STATE, AND WISDOM.—
The remainder of this chapter, which describes to us the extent and character of
Solomon's sway (vv. 20, 21, 24, 25), the pomp
and provision of his household (vv. 22, 23,
26—28), and his profound and varied wisdom
(vv. 29—34), has every appearance of a compilation from different sources. It scarcely
has the order and coherence which we should
find in the narrative of a single writer.

Ver. 20.—**Judah and Israel were many, as
the sand which is by the sea in multitude**
[a reminiscence of Gen. xiii. 16; xxii. 17;
xxxii. 12 (cf. ch. iii. 8). In the reign of
Solomon these promises had their fulfil-
ment], **eating and drinking, and making
merry.** [Cf. 1 Sam. xxx. 16. The Hebrew
here begins a new chapter. The LXX. omits
vers. 20, 21, 25, 26, and places vers. 27, 28,
"and those officers," &c., after the list of
prefects, ver. 19.]

Ver. 21.—**And Solomon reigned** [Heb. *was
reigning*] **over all kingdoms** [Heb. *the*
kingdoms. That is, as suzerain, as is explained presently. So that Psa. lxxii. 10,
11 had its fulfilment] **from the river** [*i.e.*,
the Euphrates, *the* river of that region: so
called Gen. xxxi. 21; Exod. xxiii. 31; 2
Sam. x. 16. In Gen. xv. 18 it is called "the
great river, the river Euphrates." Similarly
Josh. i. 4] **unto** [not in the Hebrew. It is
found in the parallel passage, 2 Chron. ix.
26, and perhaps we may safely supply it
here. Its omission may have been occasioned
by the recurrence of the same word (עַד) presently. Some would render, "reigned . . .
over the land," &c., supplying בְּ in thought
from above. But "unto" seems to be required after "from." Cf. ver. 24] **the land
of the Philistines** [this, *i.e.*, the Mediterranean shore, was the western border of his
realm], **and unto the border of Egypt** [this
was his southern boundary. We have here
a reference to Gen. xv. 18, the promise
which now first received its fulfilment]:
they brought presents [*i.e.*, tribute. Similar
expressions, 2 Sam. viii. 2; 2 Kings xvii.
3, 4, and especially Psa. lxxii. 10. What the
presents were we are told ch. x. 25, where,
however, see note], **and served Solomon all
the days of his life.**

The daily consumption of the royal household is now related to show the grandeur
and luxury of the court. And it agreed well
with the greatness of the kingdom. The
lavish provision of Oriental palaces was
evidently a subject of wonder and of boasting to the ancients, as the inscriptions and
monuments show.

Ver. 22.—**And Solomon's provision** [marg.
bread, but לֶחֶם, strictly signifies any kind
of food] **for one day was thirty measures**
[Heb. *cors*. The כֹּר was both a liquid and
a dry measure (ch. v. 11) and was the equivalent to the homer (Ezek. xlv. 14), but its
precise capacity is doubtful. According to
Josephus, it contained eighty-six gallons;
according to the Rabbins, forty-four] **of fine
flour and threescore measures of meal.**
[Thenius calculates that this amount of
flour would yield 28,000 lbs. of bread, which
(allowing 2 lbs. to each person) would give
14,000 as the number of Solomon's retainers. This computation, however, could
have but little value did not his calculations, based on the consumption of flesh,
mentioned presently (allowing 1½ lbs. per
head), lead to the same result.

Ver. 23.—**Ten fat** [Heb. *fatted, i.e.*, for
table] **oxen, and twenty fat oxen out of the
pastures, and an hundred sheep, beside
harts and roebucks** [or gazelles] **and
fallowdeer** [*Roebucks*. The name *Yahmûr* is
still current in Palestine in this sense (Conder, p. 91)], **and fatted fowl.** [This word
(בַּרְבֻּרִים) occurs nowhere else. The meaning
most in favour is *geese*.]

Ver. 24.—**For** [the connexion seems to
be: Solomon could well support such lavish
expenditure, because] **he had dominion over
all the region on this side** [בְּעֵבֶר strictly
means, *on the other side, beyond* (עָבַר,
transiit). But here it must obviously
mean on the *west* side, for Solomon's rule
did not extend east of the Euphrates. The
use of this word in this sense (Josh. v. 1;
ix. 1; xii. 7; 1 Chron. xxvi. 30; Ezra
viii. 36; Neh. ii. 7) is generally accounted
for on the supposition that the writers were
living in Babylon in the time of the captivity; but this appears to be by no means certain. (See, *e.g.*, Ezra iv. 10, 11.) The truth
seems to be, not that "the expression belonged to the time of the captivity, but was
retained after the return and without regard
to its geographical signification, just, for
instance, like the expression, *Gallia Transalpina*" (Bähr), but that from the first it
was employed, now of one side, now of the
other, of the Jordan; of the west in Gen.

l. 10, 11; Josh. ix. 1, &c.; of the east in Num. xxii. 1; xxxii. 32; "and even in the same chapter is used first of one and then of the other Deut. iii. 8, 20, 25" (Spk. Comm. on Deut. i. 1), and that it was subsequently applied, with similar variations of meaning, to the Euphrates. See Introduction, sect. v.] **from Tiphsah** [cf. 2 Kings xv. 16, apparently the town on the west bank of the Euphrates, known to the Greeks as Thapsacus. It derived its name from the fact that the river at that point was fordable פֶּסַח = pass over; תִּפְסָה = crossing. A bridge of boats was maintained here by the Persians. It was here that the river was forded by Cyrus and the Ten Thousand, and was crossed by the armies of Darius Codomannus and Alexander] **to Azzah** [i.e., Gaza, now called *Guzzeh*, the southernmost city of Philistia, ten miles from the Mediterranean, and the last town in Palestine on the Egyptian frontier. Cf. ver. 21], **over all the kings on this side the river** [" Petty kings were numerous at this time in all the countries dependent upon Judæa" (Rawlinson). Cf. 1 Sam. vi. 16; 2 Sam. viii. 3–10; 1 Kings xx. 1. The "kings on this side the river" were those of Syria (2 Sam. viii. 6. Cf. x. 19) conquered by David, and of Philistia, 2 Sam. viii. 1]: **and he had peace on all sides** [Heb. *from all his servants*] **round about him** [in fulfilment of 1 Chron. xxii. 9. The objection of Thenius that this statement contradicts that of ch. xi. 23, sqq., is hardly deserving of serious notice. The reign of Solomon, on the whole, was undoubtedly a peaceful one.

Ver. 25.—**And Judah and Israel** [here we have the copula, the absence of which in ver. 20 suggests a corruption or confusion of the text] **dwelt safely** [Heb. *confidently*. Cf. Judges viii. 11; 1 Sam. xii. 11], **every man under his vine and under his fig tree.** [A proverbial expression (see 2 Kings xviii. 31, where it is used by Rabshakeh; Micah iv. 4; Zech. iii. 10) to denote rest and the undisturbed enjoyment of the fruits of the earth, not necessarily, as Keil, "the most costly products of the land." In invasions, raids, &c., it is still the custom of the East to cut and carry off all the crops, and fruits. Wordsworth notices that the vine often "clustered on the walls of houses (Psa. cxxviii. 3), or around and over the courtyards"], **from Dan even to Beersheba** [i.e., from the extreme northern to the extreme southern (not eastern, as the American translator of Bähr) boundary, Judg. xx. 1; 1 Sam. iii. 20; 2 Sam. iii. 10].

Ver. 26.—**And Solomon had forty thousand stalls of horses** [40,000 is certainly a clerical error, probably for 4000 (i.e.,

אַרְבָּעִים for אַרְבָּעָה). For (1) in the parallel passage in Chronicles the number is stated as 4000. (2) 4000 agrees, and 40,000 does not, with the other numbers here given. The chariots, e.g., numbered 1400; the horsemen 12,000. Now for 1400 chariots the proper allowance of horses would be about 4000. We see from the monuments that it was customary to yoke two horses (seldom three) to a chariot; but a third or supernumerary horse was provided to meet emergencies or accidents. 4000 horses would hence be a liberal provision for Solomon's chariots, and it would also agree well with the number of his cavalry. 12,000 cavalry and 40,000 chariot horses are out of all proportion. As to stalls, it seems clear that in ancient, as in modern times, each horse had a separate crib (Vegetius in Bochart, quoted by Keil). Gesenius, however, understands by אֻרְוֹת, not *stalls*, but *teams*, or *pairs*] **for his chariots** [or *chariotry :* the word is singular and collective] **and twelve hundred horsemen** [rather, *horses, i.e.,* riding or cavalry, as distinguished from chariot-horses above. See note on ch. i. 5. It has been supposed that this warlike provision is mentioned to account for the peace ("*si vis pacem, para bellum*") of Solomon's reign, and was designed to overawe the tributary kings. But it is more probable that the idea of the historian was, partly to exhibit the pomp and circumstance of Israel's greatest king, and partly to record a contravention of the law (Deut. xvii. 16), which was one of the precursors of his fall].

Ver. 27.—**And those** [rather, *these, i.e.,* the officers mentioned vv. 7–19] **officers provided victual for** [Heb. *nourished*] **king Solomon and for all that came unto king Solomon's table** [we can hardly see here (with Keil) "a further proof of the blessings of peace." The words were probably suggested by the mental wonder how the cavalry, &c., could be maintained, and so the author states that this great number of horses and horsemen depended on the twelve purveyors for their food] **every man in his month; they lacked nothing** [rather, *suffered nothing to be lacking*. So Gesen.; and the context seems to require it].

Ver. 28.—**Barley also** [the food of horses at the present day in the East, where oats are not grown. (Cf. Hom. Il. v. 196)] **and straw for the horses and dromedaries** [marg. *mules or swift beasts*. Coursers, or fleet horses of superior breed are intended. רֶכֶשׁ = Germ. *Renner*. These coursers were for the use of the king's messengers or posts. See Esther viii. 10, 14] **brought they unto the place where the officers were** [" officers " is not in the Hebrew. The LXX. and Vulg. supply "king" (the verb is singular, "*was*"). But the true meaning is to be gathered from chap. x. 26. There we learn that the horses were distributed in different towns throughout the land. To these different depôts, therefore, the purveyors must forward the provender, "unto the place where *it* should be" (יִהְיֶה), not, as Rawlinson, "where the horses were."] **every man according to his charge.**

Ver. 29.—**And God gave Solomon** [in fulfilment of the promise of chap. iii. 12] **wisdom and understanding** (חָכְמָה, *wisdom*, *knowledge;* תְּבוּנָה, *discernment, penetration.* The historian, after describing the prosperity of the realm, proceeds to speak of the personal endowments of its head] **and largeness of heart exceeding much** [the Easterns speak of the heart where we should talk of head or intellect (chap. iii. 9, 12; x. 24. Cf. Matt. xv. 19; Ephes. i. 18 (Greek); Heb. iv. 12). The "large heart" is the *ingenium capax*, as Thenius. These different words indicate the variety and scope of his talents, in agreement with ver. 33] **as the sand that is on the sea shore.** [Same expression in Gen. xxii. 17; xxxii. 12; xli. 49; Josh. xi. 4; Judg. vii. 12, &c.]

Ver. 30.—**And Solomon's wisdom excelled** [or exceeded; same word as in ver. 29] **the wisdom of all the children of the east country** [By the *Beni-Kedem* we are hardly to understand (with Rawlinson) a distinct tribe on the banks of the Euphrates. It is true that the land of the Beni-Kedem is identified with Haran or Mesopotamia (Gen. xxix. 1), and the mountains of Kedem (Num. xxiii. 7) are evidently those of Aram. It is also true that "the children of the East" are apparently distinguished from the Amalekites and Midianites (Judg. vi. 3, 33; vii. 12; viii. 10). It is probable, nevertheless, that the name is here employed to designate all the Arabian tribes east and south-east of Palestine—Sabæans, Idumeans, Temanites, Chaldeans. What their wisdom was like, we may see in the Book of Job. Cf. Jer. xlix. 7; Obad. 8] **and all the wisdom of Egypt.** [The learning of Egypt was of great repute in the Old World. It differed very considerably from the wisdom of Kedem, being scientific rather than gnomic (Isa. xix. 11, 12; xxxi. 2, 3; Acts vii. 22) and including geometry, astronomy, magic, and medicine. See Jos., Ant. viii. 2.5; Herod. ii. 109. 160. Wilkinson, "Ancient Egyptians" vol. ii. pp. 316—465.

Ver. 31.—**For** (Heb. *and*) **he was wiser than all men** [Keil adds "of his time," but we have no right to restrict the words to his contemporaries (see note on chap. iii. 12).

It is very doubtful whether the names mentioned presently are those of contemporaries] **than Ethan the Ezrahite, and Heman, and Chalcol, and Darda** [It is impossible to say whether these are the same persons as the Ethan and Heman and Chalcol and Dara of 1 Chron. ii. 6, or the Ethan and Heman who were David's singers. The resemblance is certainly remarkable. Not only are the names practically the same (*Dara* may well be a clerical error: many MSS., together with the Syr. and Arab., read *Darda*), but they occur in the same order. Our first impression, consequently, is that the two lists represent the same persons, and if so, these four sages were the "sons" of Zerah, the son of Judah (Gen. xxxviii. 30). But against this it is urged that Ethan is here called the Ezrahite, as are both Ethan and Heman in the titles of Psalms lxxxix. and lxxxviii. respectively. The resemblance, however, of Ezrahite (אֶזְרָחִי) to Zerahite (זַרְחִי) is so close as to suggest identity rather than difference. There is, perhaps, more weight in the objection that Chalcol and Darda are here distinctly said to be "the sons of Mahol," though here again it has been observed that Mahol (מָחוֹל) means *pipe* or *dance*, and the "sons of Mahol," consequently, may merely be a synonym, agreeably to Eastern idiom (Eccles. xii. 4, with which cf. 2 Sam. xix. 35), for "musicians." We may therefore allow that the four names may be those of sons (*i.e.*, descendants) of Zerah. But the question now presents itself: Are Ethan and Heman to be identified with the well-known precentors of David? Against their identity are these facts: 1. That Ethan the singer (1 Chron. vi. 31) is described as the son of Kishi (1 Chron. vi. 44), elsewhere called Kushaiah (*ib.* xv. 17), and of the family of Merari; as a Levite that is, instead of a descendant of Judah, and that Heman, who is called the singer, or musician (*ib.* vi. 33), and the "king's seer" ib. xxv. 5) is said to be a son of Joel, a grandson of the prophet Samuel, and one of the Kohathite Levites (*ib.* xv. 17). The first impression in this case, therefore, is that they *must* be distinct. But it should be remembered (1) that the sons—in the strict sense—of Zerah are nowhere else named for their wisdom, whereas the royal singer and seer probably owed their appointments to their genius, and (2) that though Levites, they may have been incorporated (possibly like Jair, through marriage—see note on ver. 13 above, and cf. Ezra ii. 61) into the tribe of Judah. "The Levite in Judg. xvii. 7 is spoken of as belonging to the family of Judah, because he dwelt in Bethlehem of Judah, and Elkanah the Levite is called an

Ephraimite in 1 Sam. i. 1, because in his civil capacity he was incorporated into the tribe of Ephraim " (Keil). It must be admitted, however, that the *natural* interpretation of 1 Chron. ii. 6 is that the " sons " of Zerah there mentioned were his immediate and actual descendants, and not Levites who long centuries afterwards were somehow incorporated into his family. But the question is one of so much nicety that it is hardly possible to come to a positive conclusion] and his fame [Heb. *name*] was in all [Heb. all *the*] nations round about. [Cf. x. 24, &c.]

Ver. 32.—And he spake three thousand proverbs : and his songs were a thousand and five. [Of the former, less than one-third are preserved in the Book of Proverbs (see i. 1 ; xxv. 1) ; the rest are lost to us. The Book of Ecclesiastes, even if the composition of Solomon, can hardly be described as proverbs. Of his songs *all* have perished, except the Canticles, and possibly Psalms lxxii., cxxvii. (see the titles), and, according to some, cxxviii.

Ver. 33.—And he spake of [*i.e.*, discoursed, treated, not necessarily wrote] trees [In his proverbs and songs he exceeded the children of the East. But his knowledge was not only speculative, but scientific. In his acquaintance with natural history he outshone the Egyptians, ver. 20], from the cedar tree that is in Lebanon [A favourite illustration. The Jews had a profound admiration for all trees, and of these they justly regarded the cedar as king. Cf. Judg. ix. 15 ; Ps. lxxx. 10 ; civ. 16 ; Cant. v. 15 ; Ezek. xxxi. 3] unto the hyssop that springeth out of the wall [His knowledge, *i.e.*, embraced the least productions of nature as well as the greatest. The common hyssop (Exod. xii. 22 ; Lev. xiv. 4) can hardly be intended here, as that often attains a considerable height (two feet), but a miniature variety or moss-like hyssop in appearance, probably *Orthotrichum saxatile*]: he spake also of beasts, and of fowl, and of creeping things, and of fishes. [" The usual Biblical division of the animal kingdom " (Rawlinson). The arrangement is hardly according to manner of motion (Bähr). If anything, it is according to elements—earth, sky, sea. Both Jewish and Mohammedan writers abound in exaggerated or purely fabulous accounts of Solomon's attainments and gifts. We may see the beginning of these in Jos., Ant. viii. 2. 5.

Ver. 34.—And there came of all people [Heb. *the peoples*, nations] to hear the wisdom of Solomon [ch. x. 1], from all the kings of the earth [*i.e.*, messengers, ambassadors, as in the next chapter], which had heard of his wisdom.

HOMILETICS.

Vers. 20—25.—*The Golden Age.* It has been cynically said that men always place the golden age in the past or in the future. Possibly they are not so far wrong after all. For, if our historian is true, there *has* been such a period in the history of the world. And if the Holy Gospel is true, there *will* be such a period hereafter. The reign of Solomon was the Augustan, the golden age, of Israel. The reign of Jesus, of which Solomon's empire was a foreshadowing, will be the golden age of the world. Let us then consider what light the first period—the past—throws upon the future ; in what respects, that is to say, the sway of Solomon is a type and prefigurement of the holy and beneficent rule of our Redeemer. Observe—

I. THE MONARCH. 1. *He was the wisest of men.* This was the root of the universal prosperity. He was *capax imperii ;* he had the understanding to judge that great people (ch. iii. 9). From a throne stablished in equity and intelligence (Psa. lxxii. 2) flowed a tide of blessing through the land. But " Messiah the Prince " is the Incarnation of Wisdom. He is " made unto us wisdom " (1 Cor. i. 30). In Him " are hid all the treasures of wisdom and knowledge " (Col. ii. 3). He is " the wisdom of God " (1 Cor. i. 24). 2. *He ruled in the fear of the Lord.* The precept of his father (2 Sam. xxiii. 3) was not forgotten (ch. iii. 6—9). Compare the account of Messiah's reign—the reign of the Branch of the root of *Jesse*—in Isaiah ii. 2—5. This " King shall reign in righteousness " (Isa. xxxii. 1).

II. THE EMPIRE. 1. *Its extent.* He had dominion from " the river to the border of Egypt," " from Tiphsah even to Azzah." The petty kings brought presents and did fealty. Now observe how Psalm lxxii., descriptive or prophetic of the reign of Solomon, is also prophetic of the reign of our blessed Lord. Of Him alone is it strictly true that " He shall have dominion from sea to sea," &c. (ver. 8), that " all kings shall fall down before Him," &c. True, His enemies do not yet " lick the dust" (ver. 9), for "we see not yet all things put under Him," but we know that all power is given to Him in heaven and in earth (Matt. xxviii. 18), and that "the kingdoms of this world" *shall* "become the kingdoms of our Lord and of his Christ" (Rev. xi. 15). 2. *Its duration.* Solomon's was a long reign, and would have been much longer (ch. iii. 14) had he been faithful. But He who shall possess "the throne of his father David" "shall reign over the house of Jacob *for ever*, and of his kingdom there shall be no end" (Luke i. 32, 33; cf. Dan. ii. 44; vii. 14, 27; Psa. cxlv. 13; Micah iv. 7).

III. THE SUBJECTS. 1. *Their number.* They were "many," "as the sand which is by the sea in multitude." Compare Dan. vii. 10, "ten thousand times ten thousand stood before him," and Rev. v. 11; vii. 9, "a great multitude which no man could number." 2. *Their character.* Solomon's sway extended over Gentiles as well as Jews (vers. 21, 24). A foreshadowing of the inclusion of Gentiles in the kingdom of Christ. In the one fold, two flocks (John x. 16). Compare Acts xxvi. 23; xxviii. 28; Rom. xi. 15; Ephes. iii. 6; ii. 14, &c. There are three particulars, however, in which the subjects of our Lord will differ from those of Solomon. (1) There will be no bondage, no forced labour, none to bear burdens. (2) The free labour of love will require no rest (ch. v. 14). The servants who serve Him "rest not day and night" (Rev. iv. 8), yet keep perpetual sabbath (Heb. iv. 9.) (3) All shall be holy. No Jeroboam shall "lift up his hand" against the Lord. He shall be all and in all.

IV. THE REIGN. 1. *It was peaceful* (ver. 24; cf. ch. v. 4 and 1 Chron. xxii. 9). In Messiah's reign they shall "beat their swords into ploughshares," &c. (Isa. ii. 4). Into His court "neither foe entereth nor friend departeth." He is the King and Prince of Peace (Heb. vii. 2). 2. *It was joyous and prosperous.* "Eating and drinking and making merry." "*Ibi festivitas sine fine*" (Augustine). And Athanasius speaks τῶν ἁγίων καὶ τῶν ἀγγέλων ἀεὶ ἑορταζόντων. The vine and the fig-tree may remind us of the tree of life with its twelve manner of fruits; the security (ver. 25) of the pillars in the temple of God (Rev. iii. 12). "In his days Israel shall dwell safely" (Jer. xxiii. 6; cf. Isa. xi. 6—9). That golden age lasted "all the days of Solomon" (ver. 23). That which is to come shall be coeternal with the endless life of the Son of God (Heb. vii. 16; John xiv. 19; Psa. xvi. 11).

Ver. 31.—"*The greatest, wisest, meanest of mankind.*" It is a spirited and glowing description which the historian here gives of Solomon's wisdom. We may believe that it was not without a pardonable pride that he recounted the rich endowments and the widespread fame of Israel's greatest monarch. But it is really one of the saddest chapters in the whole of Scripture—and one of the most instructive. Manifold as were his gifts, marvellous as was his wisdom, they did not preserve him from falling. It is a strange, shuddering contrast, the record of his singular powers and faculties (ch. iv. 29—34), and the story of his shameful end (ch. xi. 1—14) How came it to pass that a man so highly gifted and blessed of God made such complete shipwreck of faith and good conscience; that over the grave of the very greatest and wisest of men must be written, "Fallen, fallen, fallen, fallen from his high estate"? Let us consider (1) *The character of his wisdom;* and (2) *The causes of his fall.* As to (1), observe—

I. IT WAS UNPRECEDENTED AND HAS SINCE BEEN UNEQUALLED. The sages of Hebrew antiquity, the shrewd Arabians, the sagacious Egyptians, he has eclipsed them all. "Wiser than all men," such was the judgment of his contemporaries. And such is also the verdict of posterity. At the present day, among Jews, Christians, and Mohammedans, no fame equals his. Among the wise men of the world Solomon stands *facile princeps.*

II. IT WAS PRODIGIOUS. To the writer it seemed inexhaustible, illimitable. He can only compare it to "the sand that is on the sea shore;" and he could hardly use a more forcible illustration of its boundless and infinite extent.

III. IT WAS VARIED AND COMPREHENSIVE. It was both scientific and sententious. He was at once philosopher and poet. Nothing was too great and nothing too small for him. It is seldom that a man excels in more than one or two branches of knowledge, but Solomon was distinguished in all. He could discourse with equal profundity of the cedar and the hyssop, of beast and bird. It was lofty, it was wide, it was deep.

IV. IT WAS TRUE WISDOM. Not superficial, and not mere book learning. Book-worms are often mere pedants. Students often know little of the world and know less of themselves. But Solomon knew man (" The proper study of mankind is man") knew himself. He needed not the charge, γνῶθι σεαυτὸν. He was not one of the μετεωροσοφισταί whom the Attic poet justly ridicules (Aristoph. Nub. 360). His writings proved that he had studied the world, and was familiar with the heart.

V. IT WAS GOD-GIVEN WISDOM (ver. 29; cf. 3, 12, 28; Dan. ii. 21). Not "the wisdom of this world which is foolishness with God" (1 Cor. iii. 8), and which "descendeth not from above" (James iii. 15), but that which the Supreme wisdom teacheth. (Cf. Prov. ii. 6.) Solomon was truly θεοδίδακτος.

VI. IT WAS GOD-FEARING WISDOM. "The fear of the Lord," he says, "is the beginning of wisdom." (Cf. Prov. i. 7; ix. 10.) There is a wisdom (falsely so called) which dishonours and despises God. This did not Solomon's. The Proverbs point men to the Lord.

VII. HIS WISDOM STILL WARNS AND TEACHES THE WORLD. Some of the thousand and five songs (Pss. lxxii., cxxvi.) are still chanted by the Catholic Church. (It is significant, though, how few of this vast number remain to us. David was not as wise as Solomon, nor so prolific a writer, but his songs have survived in considerable numbers. They are among the greatest treasures of Christendom. Piety is before wisdom. "Knowledge shall vanish away," but "charity never faileth.") Some of his Proverbs are still read to the congregation. He still warns the young and the sensual (chs. ii.—vii.) He is fallen, but his words stand. Now turn we to

(2) *The causes of his fall.* How came this wisest of men, without fellow before or since, whose wisdom was so profound, so real, so boundless, whose wisdom came from God and led to God, and who though dead yet speaketh, how came *he* of all men to go astray? Was it not—

I. BECAUSE THE HEART WAS NOT KEPT. The intellect, *i.e.*, was developed and cultivated at the expense or to the neglect of the spiritual life. "His wives turned away his heart." But how came one of so much wisdom to let his wives turn it away? Because the wisdom had dwarfed and overshadowed the soul; because the moral did not keep pace with the intellectual growth, and it became flaccid and yielding. It is dangerous for wisdom to increase unless piety increases with it. The higher the tower, the broader should be its foundations. If all the weight and width is at the top, it will come to the ground with a crash. Even so, if wisdom is not to destroy its possessor, the basis of love and piety must be broadened. "Knowledge bloweth up, but charity buildeth up." The head of a colossus needs the trunk of a colossus to sustain it.

II. BECAUSE HIS OWN PRECEPTS WERE NOT KEPT. It was because he leaned to his own understanding that this giant form fell prostrate. It was because he forgot his warnings against the strange woman that he fell a prey to strange women. The keeper of the vineyards did not keep his own (Cant. i. 6). He was not true to himself, and he soon proved false to his God. After preaching to others, he himself became a castaway. A solemn warning this to every preacher and teacher that he should not do

> " As some ungracious pastors do,
> Show men the steep and thorny road to heaven,
> While, like a puffed and reckless libertine,
> Himself the primrose path of dalliance tread
> And recks not his own rede."

III. BECAUSE PRIDE POISONED HIS WISDOM AND PERVERTED HIS GIFTS. There was no decay of mental power; the force was unabated, but it was misdirected. Pride took her place at the helm. It is pride, not sensuality, accounts for his army of wives and concubines. But if pride brought them, pleasure kept them. And when he put his heart into their keeping, they turned him about at their will (cf. James iii. 3, 4). The heart carries the intellect along with it. (Here again compare his own words, Prov. xvi. 18, and iv. 23; cf. Dan. v. 20.) Magnificent Solomon, unequalled in wisdom, how art thou fallen from heaven! Aye, and if we could but draw aside the veil; if we could but visit the spirits in prison (1 Pet. iii. 19), we might perchance find among them one clothed of yore "in purple and fine linen" (Luke xvi. 19; cf. xii. 27), and who "fared sumptuously every day," and looking into the anguished face might find it was none other than the brilliant and illustrious son of David, the chosen type of the Messiah, the very wisest and greatest of mankind. "The wisest, greatest, *meanest* of mankind." We know of whom these words were spoken. But their true application is not to England's greatest chancellor, but to Israel's greatest king.

HOMILIES BY VARIOUS AUTHORS.

Vers. 20—25.—*A Prosperous Reign.* This chapter presents a general view of the prosperity of Solomon's reign, much of which was owing to the extraordinary glory of the reign of David. Such a rule as David's sowed seeds of blessing in the land which it was Solomon's privilege to reap. David united the kingdoms of Judah and Israel, and Solomon came into quiet possession of the completed commonwealth. David laid the foundation, Solomon developed the fabric and adorned it. Each succeeding generation inherits the good stored up for it by those that went before. Happy they who are the descendants of a noble ancestry. If it is true that "the sins of the fathers are visited on the children," &c., equally true is it that "the good men do lives after them." We all reap the fruits of the care and toil and suffering of our fathers. "Other men labour and we enter into their labours." The text suggests—

I. THE GRANDEUR OF A MULTITUDINOUS PEOPLE. "Judah and Israel were many, &c. What is the secret of the feeling of solemnity akin to awe with which we gaze upon a vast concourse of human beings? It is the fulness of life—not mere physical force, but thinking, emotional life, with all its latent capacities that impresses us. But think of a *great nation*—what a world of busy, many-sided life is here! What complex relations; what slumbering energies; what rich resources; what mines of undeveloped thought; what tides of feeling; what boundless possibilities of good or evil, of glory or of shame! Consider the mutual action and reaction of the individual and corporate life in such a nation; the conditions of its well-being; the tremendous responsibility of those who are set to guide its forces, to guard its interests, to control its destinies. We can understand the trembling of spirit Moses felt when he looked on the thronging host of Israel in the wilderness. "Wherefore layest thou the burden of all this people upon me?" &c. (Numbers xi. 11). So with Solomon—"Who is able to judge this thy so great a people?" (ch. iii. 9). Rulers who show that they are alive to the dread significance of their position claim our deepest sympathy. Well may we pray for them (1 Tim. ii. 2) that they may be inspired by the right spirit, prompted by purest motives, never allowed to fall into the sin

> "Of making their high place the lawless perch
> Of winged ambitions."

II. THE FAR-REACHING INFLUENCE OF A WISE AND RIGHTEOUS RULE. "And Solomon reigned over all kingdoms," &c. (ver. 21). These were tributary kingdoms. It was not the division of one great empire into many provinces, but the recognition by outlying principalities of the superior sovereignty of the Hebrew monarch. What was the cause of this wide-spread influence? Won by force of arms in David's reign, it was retained, probably, by force of good government and beneficent policy. Israel presented an example of a well-ordered state—entered, under Solomon, on a remarkable career as a commercial people—Solomon himself a royal merchant. Note his sagacity in "making affinity" with the king of Egypt (ch. iii.

1), and in his treaty with Hiram, king of Tyre (ch. v.) This was the secret of Solomon's influence. As far as we can judge, it was not so much the result of overmastering force, but of a policy by which the bonds of mutual confidence and helpfulness were strengthened. We are reminded that this is the real stability of any nation—the spirit of justice, integrity, beneficence that inspires it, coupled with the disposition to form friendly and helpful relations. The influence that arises from the display of military strength not worthy to be compared with this. " Righteousness exalteth a nation" (Prov. xiv. 34). " The throne is established by righteousness" (Prov. xvi. 12). Every nation is strong and influential just in proportion as its internal order and external relations are conformed to the law of righteousness.

III. THE PEACE THAT IS THE RESULT OF RIGHTEOUSNESS. "He had peace on all sides round about him" (ver. 24). This was the fulfilment of a prophecy that attended his very birth. David, the "man of war," yearned for a time of peace, and the yearning expressed itself in the names he gave his sons—Absalom, "the father of peace;" Shelomoh, Solomon, "the peaceful one." The peacefulness of Solomon's reign was the natural outcome of his own personal characteristics, and of the policy he adopted. " When a man's ways please the Lord, he maketh even his enemies to be at peace with him" (Prov. xvi. 7). False maxim of international life, " If you want peace prepare for war "—multiply the means and provocations of strife ! Maintain an attitude of distrust, defiance, menace ! Men have strange confidence in the pacifying effect of desolating force. They "make a solitude and call it peace," forgetting that tranquillity thus gained does but cover with a deceptive veil the latent seeds of hostility and revenge. How much better the Scripture idea, "The work of righteousness shall be peace," &c. (Isa. xxxii. 17), "The fruit of righteousness is sown in peace of them that make peace " (James iii. 18).

IV. THE SECURITY THAT SPRINGS FROM PEACE (ver. 25). "And Judah and Israel dwelt safely," &c.—this became almost a proverbial expression (2 Kings xviii. 31; Micah iv. 4; Zechariah iii. 10). Suggests the quiet enjoyment of the good of life, the fruit of honest labour, under the protection of impartial law. This is the result of peace. Often urged that war is an education in some of the nobler elements of national character; safeguard against luxury and indolent self-indulgence, &c. But may not these good results be bought at too terrible a price ? Are there no other fields for the healthy development of a nation's energies ?—no foes of ignorance, and vice, and social wrong, to say nothing of forms of beneficent world-wide enterprise, that call them forth in manly exercise ? It is the reign of peace that fosters the industries that enrich the life of a people, and the beneficent activities that beautify it. 'Tis this that " makes the country flourish and the city smile." The happy condition of things here described is said to have lasted through "all the days of Solomon ; " chiefly true of the earlier part of his reign. Sins and disasters involved the latter part in gloom. So far, however, we have in it a prophecy of the reign of David's " greater Son." Psa. lxxii. has its partial fulfilment in the days of Solomon ; but the grandeur of its prophetic meaning is realized only in the surpassing glory of His kingdom who is the true " Prince of righteousness and peace."—W.

Ver. 33.—*The voice of Nature speaking for God.* This is given as an example of the wisdom for which Solomon was justly famed. His information was at once accurate and far reaching. Nothing escaped the notice of his observant eye, nothing was too insignificant to deserve his attention. The " hyssop " which was remarkable neither for size nor beauty, neither for fragrance nor utility, as well as the noble " cedar," was the subject of his research and discourse.

I. THE GERM OF HIS KNOWLEDGE WAS FROM GOD. He was enriched with natural capacities above the average, as the preceding chapter shows. Men do differ widely in keenness of perception, in retentiveness of memory, in power of imagination, in love or dislike for the studies of natural science. A remembrance of this is of peculiar value to us in the training of children. The dullard in mathematics may prove the scholar in classics, &c. The wisdom of the Divine arrangement which makes differences between us in our natural tastes and capacities is seen in this, that it is on the one hand *a blessing to society*, enabling all spheres of life to be filled, and on the other *a means of culture* to character, by calling forth our sympathy, our forbearance, and our generosity in rejoicing over the triumphs of others.

II. THE GROWTH OF HIS KNOWLEDGE WAS FROM STUDY. Solomon did not have all the mysteries of nature unveiled to him by revelation. No "royal road to learning" existed then, or ever. His studiousness as a youth may be fairly inferred from his strenuous exhortations to diligence and his frequent rebukes of sloth. Out of the depths of personal experience he declared that the "hand of the diligent maketh rich"—in thought, as well as in purse. See also Proverbs x. 5 ; xix. 24 ; xxvi. 13, &c. Press home on the young the value of habits of diligence. Illustrate by examples from biography. It would be interesting to know with certainty the substance of Solomon's discourses. Probably he knew more than any other of his own day of horticulture, physiology, and kindred topics. But the reference is not so much to scientific treatises and orderly classifications as to the ethical use he made of the phenomena of nature. This may be inferred, partly from the fact that in those days, and in Eastern lands, this rather than that would be accounted "wisdom ;" and partly from such writings of his as are still extant—certain of the Psalms, the Canticles, and the Proverbs. Study the text in the light thrown by these books, and it will be seen that through Solomon's wisdom the voice of Nature spoke to his people for God, in the same fashion as in far nobler tones it spoke afterwards through Him who made the lilies whisper of God's care, and the fallow fields speak of Christian duty. Inanimate things and dumb creatures spoke to Solomon's people through him, and should speak to us.

I. THE CREATURES OF GOD SPEAK TO US OF DIVINE CARE. Solomon, like his father, could say, "The heavens declare the glory of *God;*" or like One greater than himself, "Consider the lilies of the field," &c. See how he speaks (Prov. xvi. 15) of the cloud of the latter rain that filled out the ears of corn ; of the dew upon the grass (Prov. xix. 12) ; of the gladness of nature, when the winter is past and the rain is over and gone (Cant. ii. 11—13). To see God's hand in all this is true wisdom. The phenomena are visible to pure intellect, but He who is behind them can only be " spiritually discerned." Many now are losing sight of God because the mental perception only is employed, and believed to be necessary, Once the world appeared to men as the expression of God's thought, the outcome of His will. Now some look on it as you may look on a friend who is not dead so far as natural life is concerned, but is worse than dead, because intelligence and will are gone, and he is an idiot ! May we be aroused by the Divine Spirit to yearn for the lost Father, for the vanished heaven.

II. THE CREATURES OF GOD SPEAK TO US OF HUMAN DEPENDENCE. Neither "hyssop" nor "cedar" can grow without Heaven's benediction, and of every "beast," and "fowl," and "creeping thing," and "fish," it may be said, "these all wait upon Thee." Man, with all his attainments and powers, cannot create a single element required by his life. He can use God's gifts, but they are God's gifts still; and because He is good, our Lord bids us learn the lessons of content and trust (Matt. vi. 25—34). We depend on these creatures in the natural world for food, clothing, shelter, &c., and they only live because God cares for them.

III. THE CREATURES OF GOD SPEAK TO US OF DAILY DUTIES. How often in Proverbs we are reminded of that. Agur, who had wisdom similar to that of Solomon, speaks of the diligence of the ant, of the perseverance of the spider, of the strength in union of the locusts, of the conscious weakness and provided shelter of the conies. Solomon speaks of the blessing that came to the keeper of the fig tree (Prov. xxvii. 18) as an encouragement to servants to be faithful and diligent. Adduce similar examples.

IV. THE CREATURES OF GOD SPEAK TO US OF MORAL DANGERS. Take three examples of this. 1. In Canticles ii. 15 Solomon alludes to "the little foxes who so stealthily approach and spoil the vines and their tender grapes" as illustrations of the small evils which desolate men's hearts and homes. Apply this. 2. Then in Proverbs xxiv. 30—34 he draws a picture of a neglected garden, grown over with thorns and nettles, and shows how looking on it he "received instruction," and warning against sloth. 3. Again turn to Proverbs xxiii. 32, where, speaking of intoxicating drink, he says, "at last it biteth like a serpent, and stingeth like an adder." It was in this way he referred to the animals and plants around him.

V. THE CREATURES OF GOD SPEAK TO US OF SOCIAL EVILS. In those days, as in other days, foolish favourites, and unworthy men, were exalted to places of trust and honour. Seeing it Solomon draws again on his observance of nature ; and having noted the disorder and injury caused by untimely storms, says, "As snow in summer, and as rain in harvest, so honour is not seemly in a fool " (Prov. xxvi. 1). Another example of this teaching occurs in Proverbs xxviii. 3. A heavy rain after long drought, raising the streamlets to floods, would sweep away the mud-built dwellings of the poor and the harvest already reaped ; and to those who had seen that the wise king said, " A poor man that oppresseth the poor is like a sweeping rain which leaveth no food."

VI. THE CREATURES OF GOD SPEAK TO US OF NOBLE POSSIBILITIES. Solomon saw growth around him on every side. The seed dropped in the crevice of a wall was not forgotten, but appeared in the " hyssop ; " and the sapling, which a child could break, at last became the great " cedar of Lebanon." God's benediction and man's toil developed life ; and the feeblest was not forgotten, the smallest not despised. We can imagine how from such facts Solomon would draw lessons of trust and hope.

IN CONCLUSION let us learn from the subject the following lessons—1. *Never be afraid of the teachings of natural science.* Show how geology, botany, astronomy, &c., are regarded by some Christians with terror, as if their influence would affect the spiritual truths revealed of God. Demonstrate the folly of this. Let theology recognize the sisterhood of science. 2. *Never become absorbed in pursuits which are merely intellectual.* The soul of man needs more than his intellect can win. The " hunger and thirst after righteousness " only a living God can satisfy. Use the suggestions of nature as the witnesses of God. 3. *Never neglect the wonderful works of God.* Many a frivolous life would be redeemed from vacuity and *ennui* if young people were trained to observe and take interest in the habits of animal life and the marvels of inanimate existence. Show the wholesomeness of such studies, as those of Charles Kingsley and others. But let us walk through this fair world as those who follow Christ, and then from the fragrant lilies and golden harvest fields He will speak to us of our Father in heaven.—A. R.

EXPOSITION.

CHAPTER V. 1—18.

SOLOMON AND HIRAM.—The somewhat detailed description which we have had in chapter iv. of Solomon's pomp and power and wisdom, is followed in chapters v. sqq. by an account of what, in Jewish eyes, was the great undertaking of his reign, and, indeed, the great glory of Hebrew history—the erection and adornment of the Temple. And as this was largely due to the assistance he received—both in the shape of materials and labourers from the Tyrian king, we have in the first place an account of his alliance with Hiram.

Ver. 1.—**And Hiram** [In vers. 10, 18, the name is spelled *Hirom* (חירום), whilst in Chronicles, with one exception (1 Chron.

xiv. 1, where the *Keri*, however, follows the prevailing usage), the name appears as *Huram* (חוּרָם). In Josephus it is Εἴρωμος. This prince and his friendly relations with the Jews are referred to by the Tyrian historians, of whose materials the Greek writers Dius and Menander of Ephesus (*temp.* Alexander the Great) availed themselves. According to Dius (quoted by Josephus contr. Apion, i. 17) Hiram was the son of Abibaal. Menander states that the building of the temple was commenced in the twelfth year of Hiram's reign, which lasted 34 years (Jos. Ant. viii. 3. 1 ; Contr. Ap. i. 18). Hiram is further said to have married his daughter to Solomon and to have engaged with him in an intellectual encounter which took the shape of riddles] **king of Tyre** [Heb. צֹר, *rock*, so called because of the rocky island on which old Tyre was built, sometimes called

מִבְצַר צֹר, the fortress of, or fortified Tyre (Josh. xix. 29; 2 Sam. xxiv. 7, &c.) The capital of Phœnicia. In earlier times, Sidon would seem to have been the more important town; hence the Canaanites who inhabited this region were generally called Zidonians, as in ver. 6] **sent his servants** [*legatos,* Vatablus] **unto Solomon** [The Vat. LXX. has here a strange reading, "*To anoint* Solomon," &c. The object of this embassy was evidently to recognize and congratulate the youthful king (the Syriac has a gloss, "*and he blessed him,*" which well represents one object of the embassy) and at the same time to make overtures of friendship. An alliance, or good understanding, with Israel was then, as at a later period (Acts xii. 20) of great importance to them of Tyre and Sidon. Their narrow strip of seaboard furnished no corn lands, so that their country depended upon Israel for its nourishment]; **for he had heard that they had anointed him king in the room of David his father** [*i.e.,* he had heard of the death of David and the accession of Solomon; possibly of the events narrated in chap. i.]: **for Hiram was ever** [Heb. *all the days : i.e.,* of their reigns; so long as they were contemporary sovereigns] **a lover of David.**

Ver. 2.—**And Solomon sent to Hiram.** [According to Josephus (Ant. viii. 2. 6), he wrote a letter, which together with Hiram's reply (ver. 8) was preserved among the public archives of Tyre. The account of 2 Chronicles ii., which as a rule is more detailed than that of the Kings, begins here. It does not notice, that is to say, the prior embassy of the Phœnician king, as the object of the chronicler is merely to narrate the measures taken for the erection of the temple], **saying** [The return embassy gave Solomon the opportunity to ask for the timber, &c., that he desired.]

Ver. 3.—**Thou knowest how that David my father could not build an house** [Hiram could not fail to know this, as his relations with David had been close and intimate. Not only had he " sent cedar trees and carpenters and masons " to build David's house (2 Sam. v. 11), but " they of Tyre brought much cedar wood to David " (1 Chron. xxii. 4) for the house of the Lord] **unto the name of the Lord** [*i.e.,* to be dedicated to the Lord as His shrine and habitation (cf. Deut. xii. 5, 11; and ch. viii. 18, 19, 20, &c.)] **for the wars** [Heb., *war.* As we have singular noun and plural verb, Ewald, Rawlinson, *al.* assume that *war* stands for *adversaries,* as the next clause seems to imply. Bähr and Keil, however, with greater reason, interpret, "for the war with which they surrounded him;" a construction (סָבַב with

double accusative) which is justified by Psa. cix. 3] **until the Lord put them under the soles of his feet** [until, *i.e.,* He trampled them down. The same image is found in some of David's psalms, *e.g.,* vii. 5; lx. 12; cf. Psa. viii. 6; xci. 13; Isa. lxiii. 3; Rom. xvi. 20; Eph. i. 22; Heb. ii. 8.]

Ver. 4.—**But now the Lord my God hath given me rest** [In fulfilment of the promise of 1 Chron. xxii. 9. David had had a brief rest (2 Sam. vii. 1), Solomon's was permanent. He was " a man of rest "] **on every side** [Heb. *round about,* same word as in ver. 3, and in 1 Chron. xxii. 9], **so that there is neither adversary** [Hadad and Rezon, of whom this word is used (1 Kings xi. 14, 23), apparently belonged to a somewhat later period of his reign] **nor evil occurrent** [Rather, " *occurrence,*" or " *plague* " (פֶּגַע), *i.e.,* " rebellion, famine, pestilence, or other suffering" (Bähr). David had had many such " occurrences " (2 Sam. xv. 14; xx. 1; xxi. 1; xxiv. 15).]

Ver. 5.—**And, behold, I purpose** [Heb. *behold me saying* (אָמַר, with infin. expresses purpose. Cf. Exod. ii. 14; 2 Sam. xxi. 16)] **to build an house unto the name of the Lord my God, as the Lord spake unto David my father, saying** [2 Sam. vii. 12, 13. He thus gives Hiram to understand that he is carrying out his father's plans, and plans which had the Divine sanction, and that this is no fanciful project of a young prince], **Thy son whom I will set upon thy throne in thy room, he shall build an** [Heb. *the*] **house unto my name.**

Ver. 6.—**Now therefore command thou that they hew me cedar trees out of Lebanon** [Heb. *the* Lebanon, *i.e.,* the White (*sc.* mountain). "It is the *Mont Blanc* of Palestine " (Porter); but whether it is so called because of its summits of snow or because of the colour of its limestone is uncertain. Practically, the cedars are now found in one place only, though Ehrenberg is said to have found them in considerable numbers to the north of the road between Baalbek and Tripoli. " At the head of Wâdy Kadisha there is a vast recess in the central ridge of Lebanon, some eight miles in diameter. Above it rise the loftiest summits in Syria, streaked with perpetual snow . . . In the very centre of this recess, on a little irregular knoll, stands the clump of cedars " (*Ibid.,* Handbook, ii. p. 584), over 6,000 feet above the level of the sea. It would seem as if that part of Lebanon where the cedars grew belonged to Hiram's dominion. " The northern frontier of Canaan did not reach as far as Bjerreh " (Keil), where the cedar grove is now. The idea of some older writers that the cedars belonged to Solomon, and that he only asked Hiram for artificers ("that they *hew* me cedar trees," &c.) is negatived by ver. 10. It is true that "all Lebanon" was given to Israel (Josh. xiii. 5), but they did not take it. They did not drive out the Zidonians (ver. 6; Judg. i. 31) or possess "the land of the Giblites" (ver. 5; Judg. iii. 3). It should be stated here, however, that the cedar of Scripture probably included other varieties than that which now alone bears the name (see on ver. 8)], **and my servants shall be with thy servants** [*i.e.*, sharing and lightening the work] : **and unto thee will I give hire for thy servants** [Solomon engaged to pay and did pay both Hiram and his subjects for the services of the latter, and he paid both in kind. See below, on ver. 11] **according to all that thou shalt appoint** [This would seem to have been 20,000 measures of wheat and 20 measures of pure oil annually, ver. 11] : **for thou knowest that there is not among us any that can skill** [Heb. *knoweth*, same word as before] **to hew timber like unto the Zidonians** [*Propter vicina nemora.*

Grotius, *Sidon* (Heb. צִידוֹן), means "fishing." See note on ver. 18. By profane, as well as sacred writers, the Phœnicians are often described by the name Zidonians, no doubt for the reason mentioned in the note on ver. 1. See Homer, Iliad vi. 290 ; xxiii. 743 ; Odys. iv. 84, 618 ; xvii. 424. Cf. Virg. Æn. i. 677, 678 ; iv. 545, &c. Gen. x. 15 ; Judg. i. 31; iii. 3 ; 1 Kings xi. 1, 33, &c. "The mechanical skill of the Phœnicians generally, and of the Zidonians in particular, is noticed by many ancient writers," Rawlinson, who cites instances in his note. But what deserves especial notice here is the fact that the Zidonians constructed their houses of *wood*, and were celebrated from the earliest times as skilful builders. The fleets which the Phœnicians constructed for purposes of commerce would ensure them a supply of clever workmen. Wordsworth aptly remarks on the part the heathen thus took in rearing a temple for the God of Jacob. Cf. Isa. lx. 10, 13.]

Ver. 7.—**And it came to pass, when Hiram heard the words of Solomon** [reported by his ambassadors], **that he rejoiced greatly** [see note on ver. 1. The continuance of the *entente cordiale* was ensured], **and said, Blessed be the Lord** [In 2 Chron. ii. 12, "Blessed be the Lord God of Israel that made heaven and earth." We are not warranted by the expression of the text in concluding that Hiram believed in the exclusive divinity of the God of Israel, or "identified Jehovah with Melkarth his god" (Rawlinson), much less that he was a proselyte to the faith of David and Solomon.

All that is certain is that he believed the Lord, as did most ancient nations ("*Der Polytheismus ist nicht ausschiesslich.* Bähr), to be one of the gods many. A belief in Jehovah as God was quite compatible with the retention of a firm faith in Baal and Astarte. It is also possible that he here adopts a language which he knew would be acceptable to Solomon, or the historian may have given us his thoughts in a Hebrew dress. It is noticeable that the LXX. has simply εὐλογητὸς ὁ θεὸς] **which hath given unto David a wise son** [Compare 1 Kings i. 48 ; ii. 9. The proof of wisdom lay in Solomon's fulfilling his wise father's purposes, and in his care for the worship of God. "Wise," however, is not used here in the sense of "pious," as Bähr affirms. In Hiram's lips the word meant discreet, sagacious. *He* would hardly recognize the fear of the Lord as the beginning of wisdom] **over this great people.**

Ver. 8.—**And Hiram sent to Solomon** [in writing, 2 Chron. ii. 11. It is instructive to remember in connexion with this fact that, according to the universal belief of antiquity, the use of letters, *i.e.*, the art of writing, was communicated to the Greeks by the Phœnicians. Gesenius, indeed, holds that the *invention* of letters is also due to them. See the interesting remarks of Mr. Twisleton, Dict. Bib. ii. pp. 866—868], **saying, I have considered the things which thou sentest unto me for** [Heb. *heard the things* (*i.e.*, message) *which thou sentest unto me*] : **and I will do all thy desire concerning** [Heb. *in*, *i.e.*, as to] **timber** [or *trees*] **of cedar** [Heb. *cedars*] **and timber of fir** [Heb. *trees of cypresses*. This is, perhaps, the proper place to inquire what trees are intended by the words אֶרֶז, and בְּרוֹשׁ, here respectively translated "cedar" and "fir." As to the first, it is impossible to restrict the word to the one species (*Pinus cedrus* or *Cedrus Libani*) which is now known as the cedar of Lebanon, or, indeed, to *any* single plant. That the *Cedrus Libani*, one of the most magnificent of trees, is meant in such passages as Ezekiel xxxi., Psa. xcii. 12, &c., admits of no manner of doubt. It is equally clear, however, that in other passages the term "cedar" must refer to some other tree. In Num. xix. 6, and Lev. xiv. 6, *e.g.*, the *juniper* would seem to be meant. "The cedar could not have been procured in the desert without great difficulty, but the juniper (*Juniperus oxycedrus*) is most plentiful there." (The "cedar" of our pencils, it may be remarked, is a kind of juniper—*Juniperus Bermudiana*.) In Ezekiel xxvii. 5, "they have taken cedars of Lebanon to *make masts* for thee," it is probable that the *Pinus*

Halepensis, not, as was formerly thought, the Scotch fir (*Pinus sylvestris*), is intended. The *Cedrus Libani* appears to be indifferently adapted to any such purpose, for which, however, the *Pinus Halepensis* is eminently fitted. But in the text, as throughout ch. v.—viii., the reference, it can hardly be doubted, is to the *Cedrus Libani*. It is true the wood of this species is neither beautiful nor remarkably durable. Dr. Lindley calls it the "worthless, though magnificent cedar," but the former adjective, however true it may be of English-grown cedar, cannot justly be applied to the tree of the Lebanon mountain. The writer has some wood in his possession, brought by him from the Lebanon, and though it has neither fragrance nor veining, it is unmistakably a hard and resinous wood. And it should be remembered that it was only employed by Solomon in the *interior* of the temple, and was there, for the most part, overlaid with gold, and that the climate of Palestine is much less destructive than our own. There seems to be no sufficient reason, therefore, for rejecting the traditional and till recently universal belief that the *Cedrus Libani* was the timber chosen for the temple use. Mr. Houghton, in Smith's Dict. Bib., vol. iii. App. A. p. xl., who speaks of it "as being κατ᾽ ἐξοχήν, the firmest and grandest of the conifers," says at the same time that "it has no particular quality to recommend it for building purposes ; it was probably therefore not very extensively used in the construction of the temple." But no other tree can be suggested which better suits the conditions of the sacred narrative. The *deodara*, which has found favour with some writers, it is now positively stated, does not grow near the Lebanon. It may be added that, under the name of *Eres*, the yew was probably included. The timber used in the palaces of Nineveh, which was long believed to be cedar, is now proved to be yew (Dict. Bib., art. "Cedar"). However, it is certain that אֶרֶז is a *nomen generale* which includes, at any rate, the pine, the cedar, and the juniper, in confirmation of which it may be mentioned that at the present day, "the name *arz* is applied by the Arabs to all three" (Royle, in Kitto's Cyclop., art. "Eres").

The Grove of Cedars now numbers about 450 trees, great and small. Of these about a dozen are of prodigious size and considerable antiquity, possibly carrying us back (as the natives think) to the time of Solomon. Their precise age, however, can only be a matter of conjecture.

The identification of the "fir" is even more precarious than that of the cedar. Celsius would see in this the true cedar of Lebanon. Others identify it with the juniper (*Juniperus excelsa*) or with the *Pinus Halepensis*, but most writers (among whom are Keil and Bähr) believe the evergreen cypress (*Cupressus sempervirens*) to be intended. Very probably the name *Berosh* comprehended two or three different species, as the cypress, the juniper, and the savine. The first-named grows even near the summits of the mountain. Bähr says it is inferior to cedar (but see above). According to Winer, it is well fitted for building purposes, as "it is not eaten by worms, and is almost imperishable and very light." It is certainly of a harder and closer grain, and more durable than the *Cedrus Libani*.

It shows the brevity of our account that Solomon has not mentioned his desire for "fir" as well as "cedar." This is disclosed in Hiram's reply, and in the parallel passage of the chronicler. It is also to be noticed that in the text the request for *materials* is more prominently brought to view, while in Chronicles the petition is for *workmen*.

Ver. 9.—**My servants shall bring them** [No word in the Hebrew; "Timber of Cedar," &c., must be supplied or understood from the preceding verse] **down** [It is generally a steep descent from the cedar grove, and indeed all the Lebanon district, to the coast] **from Lebanon unto the sea** [This must have been a great undertaking. The cedars are ten hours distant from Tripoli, and the road must always have been a bad one. ("What a road it is for mortals. In some spots it seems to have been intended for mountain goats only . . . . . It winds up sublime glens, and zigzags up rocky acclivities, and passes over stone-strewn terraces," &c. (Porter, Handbook, p. 583.) To the writer it appeared to be the most rugged and dangerous road in Palestine. It is possible that the timber was collected and floated at Gebal (Biblus. See note on ver. 18). Beyrout, the present port of the Lebanon, is 27 hours distant *viâ* Tripoli. But cedars would then, no doubt, be found nearer the sea. And the ancients (as the stones of Baalbek, &c., prove) were not altogether deficient in mechanical appliances. The transport of cedars to the Mediterranean would be an easy undertaking compared with the carriage of them to Nineveh, and we know from the inscriptions that they were imported by the Assyrian kings] **and I will convey them by sea in floats** [Heb. "*I will make* (or put) *them rafts in the sea*." This was the primitive, as it was the obvious, way, of conveying timber, among Greeks and Romans, as well as among Eastern races. The reader will probably have seen such rafts on the Rhine or other river] **unto the place which**

thou shalt appoint [Heb. *send*] **me** [In 2 Chron. ii. 16, Hiram assumes that this place will be Joppa, now Yâfo, the port of Jerusalem, and 40 miles distant from the Holy City. The transport over these 40 miles, also of most rugged and trying road, must have involved, if possible, a still greater toil than that from Lebanon to the sea] **and will cause them to be discharged there, and thou shalt receive them : and thou shalt accomplish** [Heb. *do*, same word as in ver. 8, and probably used designedly = " I will perform thy desire . . . and thou shalt perform my desire." There shall be a strict *quid pro quo*] **my desire, in giving food for my household** [Hiram states in his reply in what shape he would prefer the hire promised by Solomon (ver. 6). The food for the royal *household* must be carefully distinguished from the food given to the *workmen* (2 Chron. ii. 10). The fact that 20,000 cors of wheat formed a part of each has led to their being confounded (*e.g.* in the marginal references). It is noticeable that when the *second* temple was built, cedar wood was again brought to Jerusalem, *viâ* Joppa, in return for "meat and drink and oil unto them of Zidon" (Ezra iii. 7). The selection of *food* as the hire of his servants by Hiram almost amounts to an undesigned coincidence. Their narrow strip of cornland, between the roots of Lebanon and the coast—Phœnicia proper ("the great plain of the city of Sidon," Josephus, Ant. v. 3, 1) is only 28 miles long, with an average breadth of one mile—compelled the importation of corn and oil. Ezekiel (xxvii. 17) mentions wheat, honey, oil, and balm as exported from Palestine to the markets of Tyre. It has been justly remarked that the fact that Phœnicia was thus dependent upon Palestine for its breadstuffs explains the unbroken peace that prevailed between the two countries (Heeren. See Dict. Bib. ii. p. 865).

Ver. 10.—**So Hiram gave** [Heb. *kept giving, supplied*] **Solomon cedar trees and fir** [or cypress] **trees, according to all his desire.**

Ver. 11.—**And Solomon gave Hiram twenty thousand measures** [Heb. *cors*. See ch. iv. 22] **of wheat for food** [מַכֹּלֶת for מַאֲכֹלֶת] **to his household** [Rawlinson remarks that this was much less than Solomon's own consumption (ch. iv. 22). But he did not undertake to feed Hiram's entire court, but merely to make an adequate return for the timber and labour he received. And the consumption of *fine flour* in Solomon's household was only about 11,000 cors *per annum*] **and twenty measures of pure oil** [lit., *beaten oil, i.e.*, such as was

obtained by pounding the olives, when not quite ripe, in a mortar. This was both of whiter colour and purer flavour, and also gave a clearer light, than that furnished by the ripe olives in the press. See the authorities quoted in Bähr's Symbolik, i. p. 419] : **thus gave Solomon to Hiram year by year** [probably so long as the building lasted or timber was furnished. But the agreement *may* have been for a still longer period.]

Ver. 12.—**And the Lord gave** [Can there be any reference to the repeated "gave" of the two preceding verses ?] **to Solomon wisdom, as he promised him** (ch. iii. 12) **and there was peace** [one fruit of the gift. Cf. James iii. 17] **between Hiram and Solomon, and they two made a league together** [Heb. "*cut* a covenant." Cf. ὅρκια τέμνειν. Covenants were ratified by the slaughter of victims, between the parts of which the contracting parties passed (Gen. xv. 18 ; Jer. xxxiv. 8, 18, 19). Similarly σπονδή, " libation," in the plural, means "league, truce," and σπονδὰς τέμνειν is found in classic Greek.]

Ver. 13.—**And King Solomon raised a levy** [Marg., *tribute of men, i.e.*, conscription] **out of all Israel** [*i.e.*, the people, not the land—Ewald] **and the levy was thirty thousand men.** [That is, if we may trust the figures of the census given in 2 Sam. xxiv. 9 (which do not agree, however, with those of 1 Chron. xxi. 5), the conscription only affected one in *forty* of the male population. But even the lower estimate of Samuel is regarded with some suspicion. Such a levy was predicted (1 Sam. viii. 16).

Ver. 14.—**And he sent them to Lebanon, ten thousand a month, by courses** [Heb. *changes*] : **a month they were in Lebanon, and two months at home** [they had to serve, that is to say, four months out of the twelve —no very great hardship], **and Adoniram** [see on ch. iv. 6; xii. 18] **was over the levy.**

Ver. 15.—**And Solomon had threescore and ten thousand that bare burdens, and fourscore thousand hewers in the mountains.** [These 150,000, destined for the more laborious and menial works, were not Israelites, but Canaanites. We learn from 2 Chron. ii. 17, 18 that " *all* the strangers that were in the land of Israel " were subjected to forced labour by Solomon—there were, that is to say, but 150,000 of them remaining. They occupied a very different position from that of the 30,000 Hebrews. None of the latter were reduced to bondage (ch. ix. 22), while the former had long been employed in servile work. The Gibeonites were reduced to serfdom by Joshua (Josh. ix. 27), and the rest of the Canaanites as they were conquered (Josh.xvi.

10 ; xvii. 13 ; Judg. i. 29, 30). In 1 Chron. xxii. 2, we find some of them employed on public works by David. By the " hewers" many commentators have supposed that stone-cutters alone are intended (so Jos., Ant., viii. 2. 9) partly because stone is mentioned presently, and partly because חָצֵב is mostly used of the quarrying or cutting of stone, as in Deut. vi. 11 ; viii. 9 ; 2 Kings xii. 12, &c. Gesenius understands the word both of stone and wood cutters. But is it not probable that the latter alone are indicated ? That the word is sometimes used of wood-cutting Isa. x. 15 shows. And the words, "*in the mountain* " (בָּהָר) almost compel us so to understand it here. " The mountain" must be Lebanon. But surely the *stone* was not transported, to any great extent, like the wood, so great a distance overland and sea, especially when it abounded on the spot. (The tradition that the stone was quarried at Baalbek is quite unworthy of credence. It has no doubt sprung from the huge stones found there. " The temple was built of the beautiful white stone of the country, the hard *missal*" (Warren, p. 60.) It is true the number of wood-cutters would thus appear to be very great, but it is to be remembered how few comparatively were the appliances or machines of those days : almost everything must be done by manual labour. And Pliny tells us that no less than 360,000 men were employed for twenty years on one of the pyramids. It is possible, however, that the huge foundations mentioned below (ver. 17) were brought from Lebanon.]

Ver. 16.—**Beside** [without counting] **the chief of Solomon's officers** [Heb. *the princes of the overseers, i.e.*, the princes who acted as overseers, *principes qui praefecti erant* (Vatabl.)] **which were over the work three thousand and three hundred** [This large number proves that the " chiefs of the overseers " cannot be meant. Were all the 3,300 *superior* officers, there must have been quite an army of subalterns. But we read of none. In ch. ix. 23, an additional number of 550 " princes of the overseers " (same expression) is mentioned, making a total of 3,850 superintendents, which agrees with the total stated in the Book of Chronicles. It is noteworthy, however, that the details differ from those of the Kings. In 2 Chron. ii. 17 we read of a body of 3,600 " overseers to set the people a work," whilst in ch. viii. 10 mention is made of 250 " princes of the overseers." These differences result, no doubt, from difference of classification and arrangement (J. H. Michaelis). In Chron. the arrangement is one of *race, i.e.*, 3,600 aliens נֵרִים; cf. 2 Chron. ii. 18) and 250

Israelites, whilst in Kings it is one of *status, i.e.*, 3,300 inferior and 550 superior officers. It follows consequently that all the inferior and 300 of the superior overseers were Canaanites] **which ruled over the people that wrought in the work.**

Ver. 17.—**And the king commanded and they brought** [or *cut out, quarried* (Gesen.), as in Eccles. x. 9 ; see also ch. vi. 7 (Heb.)] **great stones, costly** [precious, not *heavy*, as Thenius. Cf. Psa. xxxvi. 8 ; xlv. 9 ; Esth. i. 4 in the Heb.], **stones and** [omit *and*. The hewed stones *were* the great and costly stones] **hewed stones** [or *squared* (Isa. ix. 10 ; cf. ch. vi. 36 ; vii. 9 ; xi. 12). We learn from ch. vii. 10 that the stones of the foundation of the *palace* were squared to 8 cubits and 10 cubits] **to lay the foundation of the house.** [Some of these great squared stones, we can hardly doubt, are found *in situ* at the present day. The stones at the south-east angle of the walls of the Haram (Mosque of Omar) are " unquestionably of Jewish masonry " (Porter, Handbook, p. 115). " One is 23 ft. 9 in. long ; whilst others vary from 17 to 20 feet in length. Five courses of them are nearly entire" (*ib.*) As Herod, in rebuilding the edifice, would seem to have had nothing to do with the foundations, we may safely connect these huge blocks with the time of Solomon. It is also probable that some at least of the square pillars, ranged in fifteen rows, and measuring five feet each side, which form the foundations of the Mosque *El Aksa*, and the supports of the area of the Haram, are of the same date and origin (cf. Ewald, Hist. Israel, iii. 233). Porter holds that they are " coeval with the oldest part of the external walls." Many of them, the writer observed, were monoliths. The extensive vaults which they enclose are unquestionably " the subterranean vaults of the temple area" mentioned by Josephus (B. J. v. 3. 1), and the " *cavati sub terra montes* " of Tacitus. It may be added here that the recent explorations in Jerusalem have brought to light many evidences of Phœnician handiwork.]

Ver. 18.—**And Solomon's builders and Hiram's builders did hew them, and the stone-squarers** : [the marg. *Giblites, i.e.*, people of Gebal, is to be preferred. For Gebal (=mountain) see Josh. xiii. 5 (" the land of the Giblites and Lebanon ") ; Psa. lxxxiii. 7 (" Gebal and they of Tyre ") ; and Ezek. xxvii. 9, where the LXX. translate the word *Biblus*, which was the Greek name of the city and district north of the famous river *Adonis*, on the extreme border of Phœnicia. It is now known as *Jebeil*. It has been already remarked that Tyre and Sidon, as well as Gebal, have Hebrew meanings. These are among the proofs of the practical identity of the Hebrew and Phœnician tongues. The Aramæan immigrants (Deut. xxvi. 5; Gen. xii. 5) no doubt adopted the language of Canaan (Dict. Bib., art. " Phœnicians "). Keil renders, "*even* the Giblites." He would understand, *i.e.*, that the Zidonian workmen were Giblites; but this is doubtful. The Giblites are selected, no doubt, for special mention because of the prominent part they took in the work. Gebal, as its ancient and extensive ruins prove, was a place of much importance, and lying as it did on the coast, and near the cedar forests, would naturally have an important share in the cutting and shipping of the timber. Indeed, it is not improbable that it was at this port that the land transport ended, and the rafts were made. A road ran anciently from Gebal to Baalbak, so that the transport was not impracticable. But as the forests were probably of great extent, there may have been two or three depôts at which the timber was floated] **so they prepared timber** [Heb. *the timber*] **and stones** [Heb. *the stones*] **to build the house.** [The LXX. (Vat. and Alex. alike) add here, "*three years.*" It is barely possible that these words may have dropped out of the text, but they look more like a gloss, the inference from the chronological statement of ch. vi. 1.]

HOMILETICS.

Vers. 7—12 compared with ch. xvi. 31 and ch. xviii. 4. *Tyre and Israel—a lesson on personal influence.* Twice in the history of Israel were its relations with the neighbouring kingdom of Tyre close and intimate. Twice did the Phœnician race exercise an important influence on the Hebrew people. In the days of Solomon the subjects of Hiram furnished men and materials to build a house to the name of the Lord. The Phœnicians were not only idolaters, but they belonged to the accursed races of Canaan, yet we see them here assisting the holy people, and furthering the interests of the true religion. But in the days of Ahab these relations were reversed. Then the kingdom of Ethbaal furnished Israel with a princess who destroyed the prophets of the Lord and sought to exterminate the religion of which the temple was the shrine and centre. In the first case, that is to say, we see Israel influencing Tyre for good; we hear from the lips of the Tyrian king an acknowledgment of the goodness of the Hebrew God; we see the two races combining to bring glory to God and to diffuse the blessings of peace and civilization amongst men. In the second case, we see Tyre influencing Israel for evil. No longer do the skilled artificers of Zidon prepare timber and stones for the Lord's house, but the prophets and votaries of Phœnician deities would fain break down the carved work thereof with axes and hammers. So far from rearing a sanctuary to Jehovah, they would root up His worship and enthrone a foul idol in the place of the Divine Presence. Such have been at different times the relations of Tyre and Sidon to the chosen race and the true religion.

Now why was this fatal difference? Why was the influence in one age so wholesome, in another so baleful? It may be instructive to mark the causes of this change. But observe, first—

I. It was not that the Phœnician creed was changed. In its essential features that was the same B.C. 1000 (*temp.* Solomon) and B.C. 900 (*temp.* Ahab). It was always idolatrous, always immoral, always an infamous cultus of the reproductive powers. The gods of Hiram were the gods of Ethbaal, and the rites of the latter age were also the rites of the former.

II. It was not that the law of the Lord was changed. The idolatry which it forbade at the first period, it forbade at the second. It never tolerated a rival religion; it always condemned the Phœnician superstition. *That* is, *semper eadem.*

III. It was not that Hiram was a proselyte. This was the belief of the divines of a past age, but there is no evidence in its favour.

We see then that it was no change in either of the religious *systems.* No; it was a change of *persons* made this difference. It was brought about by the personal influence of three or four kings—of Solomon, Jeroboam, Omri, Ahab. But before we trace the influence they respectively exercised, observe—

I. The wholesome relations between Hiram and Solomon, between Tyre and

ISRAEL, *i.e.*, WERE DUE TO THE PIETY OF DAVID. "Hiram was ever a lover of David." The timber he supplied for the temple was not the first he had sent (2 Sam. v. 11). The league between the two kings (1 Kings v. 12), and their joint undertakings (ch. v. 18; ix. 27), were the fruits of David's righteous dealings.

II. THE RELATIONS CONTINUED WHOLESOME AND BENEFICIAL SO LONG AS THE LAW OF THE LORD WAS KEPT. During David's reign, and the earlier part of Solomon's, the commerce of the two nations was to their mutual advantage. Then the Jew came into contact with idolatry unhurt. The soil was not ready for the baleful seed. At a later period (see Homily on ch. x. 22) it was otherwise.

III. THE LAW WAS NO SOONER VIOLATED THAN THE INFLUENCE OF TYRE BECAME HURTFUL. The Zidonian women in Solomon's harem were a distinct violation of the law (ch. xi. 1), and that trespass bore its bitter fruit forthwith (ch. xi. 7, 8).

The principal factors, consequently, in the change were these—

I. THE INFLUENCE OF SOLOMON. If he built altars for his Tyrian consorts, what wonder if the people learnt first to tolerate, then to admire, and at last to practise idolatry. Who can tell how much the frightful abominations of Ahab's days are due to the example of wise Solomon, to the influence of the builder of the temple?

II. THE INFLUENCE OF JEROBOAM. The cultus of the calves, though it was not idolatry, paved the way for it. That violation of the law opened the door for departures greater still. It was no great step from the calves to the groves, from schism to utter apostasy.

III. THE INFLUENCE OF OMRI. Nations, like individuals, do not become infamous all at once (*Nemo repente turpissimus fuit*). They have their periods and processes of depravation. Omri carried Jeroboam's evil work a step further; possibly he organized and formulated his system (Micah vi. 16). He exceeded all his predecessors in wickedness, and so prepared the way for his son's consummation of impiety.

IV. THE INFLUENCE OF AHAB. A second violation of the Jewish marriage law opened wide the gates to the pestilent flood of idolatries. The son of Omri weds the daughter of a priest of Astarte; and Phœnicia, once the handmaid of Israel, becomes its snare. Now the ancestral religion is proscribed, and the elect people lends itself to unspeakable abominations (1 Kings xvi. 32; cf. 2 Kings x. 26, 27; Rev. ii. 20). It may be said, however, that all this was the work of Jezebel, and due to her influence alone (1 Kings xxi. 25; cf. xviii. 13; xix. 2, &c.) That may be so, but it was only the example of Solomon, the schism of Jeroboam, and the apostasy of Omri made this marriage possible, or enabled Jezebel, when queen, to do these things with impunity. Hence learn—

I. THE POWER AND RESPONSIBILITY OF PERSONAL INFLUENCE. An idle word may destroy a kingdom. The Crimean war sprung out of the squabbles of a few monks over a cupboard and a bunch of keys. "There is not a child . . . whose existence does not stir a ripple gyrating onward and on, until it shall have moved across and spanned the whole ocean of God's eternity, stirring even the river of life and the fountains at which His angels drink." And our responsibility is increased by the fact that—

II. THE EVIL THAT MEN DO LIVES AFTER THEM. They go on sinning in their graves. Though dead, their example speaks. Witness Solomon and Jeroboam.

III. THE EVIL THAT KINGS DO AFFECTS WHOLE COUNTRIES. Their own kingdoms, of course, and neighbouring kingdoms too. It has been said that "the influence of one good man extends over an area of sixteen square miles." But who shall assign any limits to the influence of a wicked prince? It may plunge a continent into wars, and wars that shall last for generations, or it may steep it for ages in sensuality and superstition. Its issues, too, are in eternity. It is because of the *influence* of kings that we are so plainly commanded to pray for them (1 Tim. ii. 2; cf. Ezra vi. 10; Jer. xxix. 7).

IV. IN KEEPING OF GOD'S COMMANDMENTS IS GREAT REWARD. The perfect piety of David procured the friendship and help of Tyre. The disobedience of Solomon, Jeroboam, and Ahab led to the decay and dispersion of the nation and the destruction of their families.

V. TEMPTATION DISCIPLINES THE FAITHFUL SOUL, BUT DESTROYS THE SINNER. David took no harm from his commerce with Hiram, nor did Solomon in the days of his piety. A good man will choose the good and refuse the evil in a corrupt system. But the wicked will choose the evil and refuse the good. Ahab's relations with Tyre were altogether to his hurt. In David's loyal heart the evil seed found no lodgment; in Ahab's it found a congenial soil, and took root downwards and bare fruit upwards.

Ver. 17.—*Sure Foundations.* No city in the world has experienced so many vicissitudes as " the city of the Great King." The place of the " vision of peace " (or, "*foundation* of peace ") has known no peace. It has been sixteen times taken by siege since our blessed Lord's day, and conqueror after conqueror has cried, " Rase it, rase it, even to the foundation thereof" (Psa. cxxxvii. 7). It has been the carcase round which the Roman " eagles " have repeatedly gathered; it has been the battle-field of Saracen and Crusader; now the Christian has wrested it from the Moslem, and now the Moslem has torn it back from the Christian. The consequence is that it is a mound of ruins, a heap of *débris.* When the Anglican church was built, it was necessary to dig down some forty feet, through the accumulated rubbish of ages, to get a foundation. The Jerusalem of the past can only be reached by deep shafts. It is literally true that not one stone of the ancient city is " left upon another " (Matt. xxiv. 2). With ONE exception. Amid the wreck and havoc of war, amid the changes and chances of the world, the colossal foundations of Solomon remain undisturbed. His " great stones " are to be seen at the present day at the south-east angle and underneath the temple area (see on ver. 17). Everything built upon them has perished. Not a trace of tower or temple remains; nay, their very sites are doubtful. But " through all these great and various demolitions and restorations on the surface, its foundations, with their gigantic walls, have been indestructibly preserved " (Ewald). After the lapse of nearly three thousand years, " The foundation standeth sure."

Let us learn a lesson hence as to—I. *Christ.* II. *The Church of Christ.* III. *The doctrine of Christ and His Church.* We may see, then, in the Solomonic foundations of the Temple—

I. A PICTURE OF CHRIST. He compared Himself to the Temple (John ii. 19), and to the foundations of the Temple (Matt. xxi. 42). Yes, to these very *corner stones* which are still visible. It is remarkable that Psalm cxviii. 22—" The stone which the builders refused is become the head of the corner "—is cited by our Lord of Himself (Matt. xxi. 42), and is applied to Him by St. Peter (Acts iv. 11), while Isa. xxviii. 16, " Behold, I lay in Zion for a foundation a stone," &c.—words which were no doubt suggested by the great and precious stones of Solomon's building—are interpreted of Him both by St. Peter (1 Pet. ii. 6) and St. Paul (Rom. ix. 33). We have consequently " most certain warrants of Holy Scripture " for seeing in these venerable relics an image of the Eternal Son. He is the one foundation (1 Cor. iii. 11); the chief corner stone (ἀκρογωνιαῖος, Eph. ii. 20); He " abideth ever ; " " Jesus Christ is the same yesterday, to-day, and for ever " (Heb. xiii. 8, Gr.) That " sure foundation " can never fail. How many systems of philosophy, how many " oppositions of science " have " had their day and ceased to be "? How many proud empires have tottered to their fall; how many dynasties are extinct and forgotten? But the carpenter's Son still rules in the hearts of men, and the cross of Christ " towers above the wreck of time."

II. A PICTURE OF THE CHURCH OF CHRIST. As surely as the great corner stone images our Lord, so surely do the huge and strong foundations pourtray the Church of which He is the Founder. It is to the Church (ἐκκλησία ὑπο Θεοῦ τεθεμελιωμένη) those words refer, " The firm foundation of God standeth " (2 Tim. ii. 19, Gk.) The Church is " the pillar and ground of the truth; " it is " built upon the foundation of apostles and prophets" (Eph. ii. 20; cf. Rev. xxi. 14). And, like the foundations of the Temple, its base shall be stable and permanent. " The gates of hell shall not prevail against it " (Matt. xvi. 18). It is founded on a rock (*ibid.*)

> " Crowns and thrones may perish,
> Kingdoms rise and wane,
> But the Church of Jesus
> Constant will remain."

It was the boast of Voltaire that what it took twelve men to build one man should suffice to break down. But the Church is stronger in the hearts of men now than it was in the eighteenth century. And Voltaire's cry of impotent rage, *Ecrasez l'infâme*, seems farther than ever from its realization. Its enemies assert that Christianity has " destroyed two civilizations "—a striking admission of its strength and vitality. True, the Church has a legion of foes. But let us take courage. There is at Jerusalem a pledge and picture of her stability. Her fashions, her excrescences, her sects and schisms, like the buildings of the Holy City, shall pass away. But her foundation is sure.

III. A PICTURE OF THE DOCTRINE OF CHRIST AND THE CHURCH. As there are twelve foundations of the Church, so are there six foundation-truths, six " principles of the doctrine of Christ " (Heb. vi. 2). And of these it may justly be said, " Other foundation can no man lay than that is laid." Some of these doctrines may have been, or may hereafter be, more or less obscured—the " doctrines of baptism and of the laying on of hands " are often ignored or repudiated even now —but for long centuries the foundations of the Temple area have been hidden. Obscured or not, they shall never be shaken or removed. This " firm foundation standeth." The monoliths beneath the Mosque *El Aksa,* standing where Solomon and Hiram's builders placed them, are silent but eloquent pictures of the eternal and unchangeable truth of God. And if men build on the foundations of Christian doctrine, or on the one foundation of " the personal historical Christ" (Alford on 1 Cor. iii. 11), " wood, hay, stubble," *i.e.,* systems, more or less worthless, of their own, like the Temple of Jerusalem, these shall be destroyed by fire in the " day of visitation; " but the foundation shall remain unscathed, strong and sure and eternal as the God who laid it.

HOMILIES BY VARIOUS AUTHORS.

Vers. 2—6.—*The Temple.* Read also 2 Chron. ii. 1—10, where additional light is thrown on this transaction. It marks a period of extreme interest and importance in Hebrew history. It introduces us, by anticipation, to that which was the crowning glory of the reign of Solomon, for his name must ever stand connected with the magnificence of the first Temple, though it be but as a gorgeous dream of the far-distant past, which imagination strives in vain to reproduce with distinctness and certainty. Whether the Hiram who entered into this treaty with Solomon is the same as the Hiram who was the friend of David is a matter of doubt. Menander of Ephesus (quoted by Josephus) describes him as a man of great enterprize, a lover of architecture, noted for his skill in building and adorning the temples of the gods. And in this we have a valuable indirect confirmation of the Biblical history. Look at this purpose of Solomon to build a splendid temple to the Lord in two or three different lights.

I. IT EXPRESSES HIS DESIRE TO CARRY OUT THE GOOD DESIGNS OF HIS FATHER DAVID. Filial feeling prompted it. It drew the inspiration of its enthusiasm from the warmth of a filial heart. " Thou knowest how that David my father could not," &c. We are told why he " could not " (1 Chron. xxii. 7, 8; xxviii. 5). He had been " a man of war," and had " shed much blood." Noble purposes may be conceived in a time of discord and confusion; they can be actualized only in a time of rest. The hands must be free from the blood of men that would build a worthy dwelling-place for a righteous God. Nothing was more natural than that Solomon, under happier auspices, should resolve to do what his father had the " heart to do," but " could not." To how large an extent is human life a record of thwarted purposes ! A tale cut short before it is half told ; a laying of plans that are never worked out; a reaching forth towards fair ideals that men have not the power or the time to turn into realities. What can the high mission of each succeeding generation be but just to take up the good purposes that a previous generation failed to accomplish and develop them to their ripe issues? This is the real law of human progress. All honour to the son who, knowing what was truest and deepest in his father's heart, endeavours worthily to fulfil it.

II. IT IS THE SPONTANEOUS OUTCOME OF HIS OWN DEVOUT FEELING. Solomon never had the pure and lofty spirit of devotion that inspired the soul of David ; but as yet, at least, his religious sentiment is deep and true. A "house great and wonderful," dedicated to the Lord, in the royal city, will give it fitting public expression. All religious feeling instinctively seeks to body itself forth in appropriate forms. Forbidden as the Jews were to " make any likeness or image " of the great Object of worship (Exod. xx. 4), it was quite in harmony with the Divine dispensation of the time that the spirit of worship should robe itself in a grand symbolic garb. Solomon only sought to develop the service of the tabernacle into a system more imposing and enduring (2 Chron. ii. 4, 5). In every age symbolism has its place as the spontaneous and natural expression of religious thought and feeling. Let it be relied on as the means of *awakening* such thought and feeling, as the prescribed form in which it shall move—an artificial substitute for it—and it becomes a mockery and a snare. The magnificence of Solomon's design for the Temple indicated not only the fervour of his devotion, but the breadth of his view as regards the essential sacredness of all natural things. " The earth is the Lord's and the fulness thereof." All things beautiful and precious are turned to their true use when dedicated to Him. We cannot be too careful to give Him our richest and best. The true heart says, " I will not offer burnt offering to the Lord of that which doth cost me nothing." Let us not be more concerned for our own houses than we are for the Lord's. The history of the Temple, however, and of all ecclesiology, shows how easily the wealth of outward adornment in worship may become the grave of the spiritual and the veil of the Divine. In proportion as care for the symbolic form—the mere shrine of worship—has increased, the living reality—the worship of the Father "in spirit and in truth "—has passed away.

III. IT EXPRESSES HIS SENSE OF THE FACT THAT THE ACKNOWLEDGMENT OF GOD IS THE REAL STRENGTH AND GLORY OF A NATION. The Temple was to be dedicated "to the name of Jehovah"—the visible sign and symbol of the sovereignty of that name over the whole life of the people. There was worth in the sign just so far as that sovereignty was real. The Jewish commonwealth was a theocracy—the Temple the palace and throne of the great invisible King. Judaism was not the union of Church and State as two separate or separable powers, but their identification. No distinction between the political and ecclesiastical, the secular and spiritual spheres. The two were one. The ideal Christian nation is a theocracy in which Christ is king. Not made so by its institutions, but by the spiritual life that pervades it. True to its name only so far as the law of Christ is honoured in the homes of the people, moulds the form and habit of their social life, controls commerce, rules in Parliament, strengthens, ennobles, glorifies the Throne. Its Christian Churches are thus the very flower of a country's highest life.

> " Those temples of His grace,
> How beautiful they stand !
> The honour of our native place
> And bulwark of our land."

As the graveyard—where " the rude forefathers of the hamlet sleep "—tells of the vanity of all earthly things, how the pride and glory of man must one day moulder down to dust, so the church is the memorial of the unfading inheritance of truth and purity and love—the blessed fellowship of the redeemed—the " House of God, not made with hands, eternal in the heavens."

IV. IT EXPRESSES HIS DESIRE THAT ISRAEL SHOULD HAVE A CENTRE OF RELIGIOUS ATTRACTION AND BOND OF RELIGIOUS UNITY. The tabernacle had been the movable sanctuary of a wandering people, the Temple should be the resting-place of the Divine presence (Psa. cxxxii. 14). Hitherto there had been a divided worship, connected both with the tabernacle at Gideon and the ark in the city of David (1 Chron. xvi. 37—39). But in future all sacred associations are to be gathered up in the central glory of the Temple. One nation, one faith, one God, one sanctuary. But this localization of the highest forms of worship had its dangers. Men came to think of " the Holy Presence as belonging to the building, instead of the building as being hallowed and glorified by the Presence." Christ proclaims the infinite Presence, the impartial Love. " The hour cometh when ye shall neither in this mountain," &c. (John iv. 21). " One greater than the Temple is here "—in whom all its sacred symbols are fulfilled—the attractive centre and bond of union for redeemed souls of every age and nation. Our thoughts are led on to the glorious vision of the holy city of which it is written, " I saw no temple therein, for the Lord God Almighty and the Lamb are the temple of it" (Rev. xxi. 22).—W.

Ver. 5.—*The building of the Temple.* " Behold I purpose to build an house unto the name of the Lord my God." Every man has some special work given him by God. It is of the utmost importance that he should find out what that work is, if he would not make his life a failure and come short of the purpose of God for him. In the case of Solomon the great work given him to do was not to extend the boundaries of his kingdom, but to build the temple of the Lord. This he clearly understood, as is evident from his saying, " I purpose to build an house to the name of the Lord." This was to him the work of paramount importance. The building of the Temple was to give a religious centre to the theocracy. This was part of the Divine plan, a branch of the education of the people, by which God would prepare the way for the new covenant. The old covenant was essentially preparatory; it was " the shadow of good things to come " (Heb. x. 1). The Temple was to form a part of this preparation.

I. IT WAS A VISIBLE SYMBOL OF THE PRESENCE OF GOD WITH HIS PEOPLE. This was the only way in which such an idea could be brought home to men in the state of rude infancy in which they then were, and with their incapacity to apprehend directly spiritual graces. The material was thus the necessary medium of the spiritual.

II. The erection of a holy place for worship REMINDED MEN THAT THE EARTH WHICH THEY INHABITED WAS DEFILED ; it developed in them the sense of sin.

III. THE POSSIBILITY OF DRAWING NEAR TO GOD IN THIS HOLY PLACE pointed to the time of reconciliation, when every spot of a redeemed earth might be a place of prayer ; when there should be no longer one sanctuary for one nation alone, but when all the nations should have free access to God as worshippers in spirit and in truth. The fact that Solomon sought out workmen for the Temple, not only among the Israelites, but among the Gentiles, is prophetic, and prefigures the time when the multitude of worshippers shall be " of every kindred, and nation, and people, and tongue " (Rev. v. 9).

IV. THERE IS NOT A SINGLE CHRISTIAN LIVING WHO HAS NOT A TASK LIKE THAT OF SOLOMON TO FULFIL. Every Christian ought to say, " I purpose to build an house to the name of the Lord." (*a*) He must first become himself a living stone of the spiritual temple (2 Pet. ii. 51). (*b*) His body must be the temple of the Holy Ghost (1 Cor. vi. 19), his whole being a sanctuary (1 Cor. iii.) His house should be a house of prayer (Josh. xxiv. 15). Are not these human temples themselves the stones elect, precious, to be used by and by in that great heavenly temple which the Lord shall build and not man ? (2 Cor. v. 1.)—E. de P.

Vers. 7—12.—*Lessons from the conduct of a heathen prince.* Describe the condition of Tyre at this period, alluding to its commerce, its religious beliefs, its proximity to the kingdom of Solomon (the capitals being distant from each other about 122 miles), its monarchical institutions, as opposed to the usual republican government of Phœnician settlements—as exemplified in Carthage, the splendid daughter of Tyre, founded about 140 years after the building of Solomon's temple. Point out some of the effects of the intercourse between these two states, as suggested by Old Testament history. Suggest from this the responsibilities and the perils accruing to us as a Christian people, from the fact that our own destinies are so interwoven with distant and heathen nations. Allude to the fearlessness of Scripture in ascribing what is good and commendable to those whom the Jews generally scorned. Various examples may be given, *e.g.*, Abimelech king of Egypt, Cyrus, Hiram; and in the New Testament, Cornelius, Publius, &c. Compare the words of our Lord (Matt. viii. 11, 12).

The conduct of Hiram teaches us the following lessons.

I. THAT WE SHOULD REJOICE IN THE PROSPERITY OF OTHERS (ver. 7). Hiram was moved to joy, partly because of his love and admiration for David. It is an unspeakable advantage to have the position won by a father's toil, the affection and confidence deserved by a father's worth. In our material possessions, in our worldly occupation, in our ecclesiastical and, above all, our Christian relationships, how much of good has come from parentage! Contrast the possibilities of a lad, born of honoured parents, and therefore trusted till he proves untrustworthy, whose path in life is smoothed by the loving hands of those who care for him, for his father's sake, with the terrible disadvantages of the child of a convict, who is distrusted and ill-treated from his birth. Hiram was well disposed to Solomon for his father's sake. There were many reasons for jealousy. The two kingdoms adjoined each other, and national pride would be fostered by religious differences. It is easier to rejoice over the success of a distant trader than over the prosperity of a neighbour who is our competitor. Nor is it common for a heathen to be glad over the welfare of a Christian. Hiram was large-hearted enough to overlook barriers which were erected by the hands of rivalry and religious distinction.

II. THAT WE SHOULD FAIRLY CONSIDER THE DEMANDS OF OTHERS. "I have *considered* the things which thou sentest to me for" (ver. 8). The request of Solomon was bold. It would require sacrifice on the part of the Tyrians. They were asked to help in building a temple for another nation, and for the worship of One who was to them a strange deity. No prejudice, however, interfered with Hiram's fair consideration of Solomon's request; and as it was more fully understood, it seemed more and more feasible. How often prejudice prevents men from looking at a novel scheme for work, from welcoming a new expression of old truth, &c. A false patriotism sometimes refuses to see any excellency in another people. Sectarianism checks Christians in learning from each other. There is much presented to us which we cannot at once *welcome*, but at least it should be fairly *considered*. "Prove all things, hold fast that which is good."

III. THAT WHEN WE DO A KINDNESS, IT SHOULD BE DONE WITHOUT GRUDGING. "I will do *all* thy desire." It is not right to ask another for what is unreasonable, or to give to another what is unreasonable for him to expect. Sometimes to grant a request is easier than to refuse it, and we do what is asked to save ourselves trouble. Every demand should be weighed in the balance of equity. But if, after the test, it seems right to accede to it, we should not do it reluctantly, or partially, or murmuringly, lest we should mar the beauty of the act to others, and rob ourselves of the bliss of ministering to others in Christ's spirit. "Whatsoever ye do, do it heartily, as to the Lord, and not unto men," &c. (Col. iii. 23, 24). "Give, and it shall be given unto you; good measure," &c. (Luke vi. 38).

IV. THAT WE SHOULD RECOGNIZE AND RECOMPENSE THE ABILITIES OF THE HUMBLEST. In 2 Chron. ii. 13 we read that Hiram chose from amongst his subjects a skilful man, to be set over this business. Christians can serve their Lord in this way amidst their ordinary occupations. In the counting-house, or office, or factory the recognition and encouragement of diligence and skill may be a means of grace to employer and *employé*. We should devoutly recognize that knowledge, skill, capacity of any sort, are the gifts of God; and while we employ our own faithfully, we should, as opportunity serves, aid our fellow servants in the use of theirs.

V. THAT WE SHOULD ACKNOWLEDGE OUR MUTUAL DEPENDENCE. Solomon and Hiram were not independent of each other. It was for the good of these kings and of their peoples that they should be associated in this holy work. Solomon confessed, "There is not among us any that can skill to hew timber like unto the Sidonians" (ver. 6). Each nation, each individual has his own sphere to fill in the economy of God. No one of these can serve well in isolation. See St. Paul's teaching about the body and its members. Show how *nations* are mutually dependent, commercially and in their political relations. Point out the special responsibility of God's people when they are associated with heathen nations. Suggest the possibility that *each section of Christ's Church* may be doing its own appointed service, though all must feel that they are mutually dependent if the prayer of our Lord is to be fulfilled (John xvii. 21). Apply the principle to the *association of Christians* in Church fellowship, in evangelistic enterprize, in religious worship, &c., and show the benefits arising to the individual from the fact that he is one of many.

VI. THAT EACH SHOULD LOYALLY ACCEPT, AND HEARTILY DO, HIS OWN SHARE IN BUILDING THE TEMPLE OF THE LORD. (2 Chron. ii. 16.) Christians are likened to labourers in a vineyard, to servants in a household, to builders of a temple by our Lord and His apostles. In none of these spheres of activity is the work of all the servants alike in its publicity, in its honour, in its immediate effects, in its pleasantness, &c. Yet to every "good and faithful servant" the recompense will come; and he who shaped the stone in the quarry, or bore the burdens for more distinguished builders, will, in the great day, not lose his reward.—A. R.

EXPOSITION.

CHAPTER VI. 1—38.

SOLOMON'S TEMPLE.—The preparations for the building of the Temple having been related in the preceding chapter, the historian now proceeds to describe the edifice. He begins his narrative with a precise statement of the date of its erection (ver. 1); then follows (1) a description of the shape, size, and arrangement of the exterior (vers. 2—10), and (2) a detailed account of its internal fittings and adornments (vers. 15—35). The promise made to Solomon during its erection finds a place in vers. 11—13; while the vessels, &c., used in the Temple service are described in ch. vii. A parallel though briefer account, and one differing considerably in its arrangement, is found in 2 Chron. iii. iv.

The erection of this splendid sanctuary was no doubt the greatest event, both in Jewish and Gentile eyes, in the history of the Holy City. It made Jerusalem what it had not been till then, the religious capital. The stronghold of the Jebusites now became the shrine and centre of the Jewish system. We are not warranted, however, in believing that it shaped the name by which the city was known to the Greeks, Ἱεροσολυμὰ (Jos., B. J. 6. 10) and Ἱερὸν Σαλομῶνος (Eupolemus in Euseb. Præp. Ev.

ix. 34; see Stanley, "Jewish Church," ii. p. 193), being probably mere attempts to "twist Jerushalaim into a shape which should be intelligible to Greek ears" (Dict. Bib. i. 983).

We find a sufficient indication, however, of the profound importance which this undertaking assumed in Jewish eyes in the fact that four chapters of our history—and three of them of considerable length—are occupied with an account of the materials, proportions, arrangements, and consecration of this great sanctuary. To the historiographers of Israel it seemed meet that every measurement of the holy and beautiful house should be recorded with the greatest exactness, while the very vessels of service, "the pots and the shovels and the basons," were judged worthy of a place in the sacred page.

But these careful and detailed dimensions are not only proofs of the tender veneration with which the Jew regarded the Temple and its appointments; they are also (as Bähr has well shown, Symbolik, i. pp. 127, 128) indications and expressions of the belief that this house, so "exceeding magnifical," was for the Lord, and not for man. These exact measurements, these precise and symbolic numbers all point to a place for the Divine Presence; they are "the first requisite for every space and structure which has a higher and Divine destination, and they impart thereto the signature of the Divine " (Bähr). Indeed the very names *templum* and τέμενος (=a space measured off) are in themselves in some sort attestations to the ancient belief that the dignity of a temple of the Most High God required that the length and breadth and height, both of the whole and of its component parts, should be carefully recorded. It is this consideration explains a peculiarity of Scripture which would otherwise cause some difficulty; viz., the detailed and repeated measurements, and the almost rabbinical minuteness, not only of our author, but of Ezekiel and of the Apocalypse. When a " man with a measuring reed " (Ezek. xl. 3, 5; Rev. xi. 1; xxi. 15) appears upon the scene, we are to understand at once that the place is sacred ground, and that we are in the precincts of the temple and shrine of Jehovah.

At the same time it must be added here that, exact and detailed as is the description of this edifice, it is nevertheless so partial, and the account is, perhaps necessarily, so obscure as to leave us in considerable doubt as to what Solomon's Temple was really like. In fact, though "more has been written regarding the temple at Jerusalem than in respect to any other building in the known world" (Fergusson), the authorities are not agreed as to its broad features, while as to matters of detail they are hopelessly divided. On one point, indeed, until recently, there was a pretty general agreement, viz., that the house was "rectilinear and of box-form." But it is now contended that this primary and fundamental conception of its shape is entirely at fault, and that its sloping or ridged roof would give it a resemblance to the ark or to a tent. Nor have we the materials to decide between these conflicting views; in fact, nothing perhaps but drawings would enable us to restore the temple with any approach to accuracy. "It is just as easy to pourtray a living man from a tolerably well-preserved skeleton as to reproduce a building in a way which shall correspond with reality when we have only a few uncertain remains of its style of architecture in our posses-

sion " (Romberg and Steger, quoted in Bähr, "Bibelwerk," p. 49). And the difficulty is enhanced by the fact that the temple was *sui generis*. It was purely Jewish, so that no information as to its structure and arrangements can be derived from the contemporary architecture of Egyptians or Assyrians. In the absence of all analogies restoration is hopeless. It is well known that all the many and varied representations of different artists, based though they all were on the Scripture account (Exod. xxv. 31—37) of the seven-branched candlestick, were found to be exceedingly unlike the original, when the true shape of that original was disclosed to the world on the Arch of Titus. It is equally certain that, were a true representation of the temple ever to be placed in our hands, we should find that it differed just as widely from all attempted " restorations " of the edifice, based on the scanty and imperfect notices of our historian and Ezekiel.

The mention of Ezekiel suggests a brief reference to the temple, which he describes with so much precision and fulness in his fortieth and following chapters. What is its bearing on the description we have now to consider? Is it an account of the temple as it actually existed in or before his time; is it a plan or suggestion for its restoration (Grotius), or is it wholly ideal and imaginary? The first view, which long found favour with commentators, and which has still some advocates, is now pretty generally abandoned. For while many of Ezekiel's measurements, &c., correspond exactly with those of our historian, and while it may be conceded, therefore, that this delineation has a historical basis, there are features in the narrative which can never have been realized in any building, and which prove the account to be more or less ideal. For example. The outer court of his temple (Ezek. xlii. 16—20) would cover not only the whole of Mount Moriah, but more than the whole space occupied by the entire city of Jerusalem. He speaks again of " waters issuing out from under the threshold" (ch. xlvii. 1), and flowing down eastward to heal the pestilent waters of the Dead Sea, where a literal interpretation is manifestly impossible. And it is to be remembered that the prophet himself speaks of his temple as seen *in vision* (ch. xl. 2 ; xliii. 2, 3). The true account of this portraiture would therefore seem to be that, while it borrowed largely from the plan and proportions of Solomon's Temple, it was designed to serve as " the *beau ideal* of what a Semitic temple should be " (Fergusson, Dict. Bib. iii. p. 1460. In a paper in the " Contemporary Review," vol. xxvii. p. 978, Fergusson adopts the idea that it was designed to serve as a basis for the future restoration of the temple.)

Two other authorities, whose accounts have a direct bearing on the sacred narrative, must be mentioned here—Josephus and the Talmudic tract on the temple, called *Middoth* (*i.e.*, measures). Unfortunately, neither is of much avail for the illustration of the text we have now to consider. Josephus, too often unreliable, would seem to be especially so here. " *Templum aedificat*," says Clericus, " *quale animo conceperat non quale legerat a Salomone conditum.*" "Inconsistency, inaccuracy, and exaggeration are plainly discoverable in the measurements given by Josephus " (Conder, "Handbook to Bible," p. 368). " Wherever the Mishna is not in accord with Josephus the measurements of the latter are untrustworthy " (*ib.* p. 369). The writers of the Mishna, again, refer generally, as might be expected, to the temple of Herod, or confuse in their accounts the three temples of Solomon, Herod, and Ezekiel (Bähr). The student of temple architecture consequently derives but scant assistance in his work from the writings of uninspired historians.

Perhaps this is the proper place to remark on the close correspondence between temple and tabernacle. (See Fergusson, Dict. Bib. iii. p. 1455). In the first place, in plan and arrangement the two structures were identical. Each faced the east ; each had three parts, viz., porch, holy place, and holy of holies, while the side chambers of the temple (ver. 5) were analogous to the verandah formed by the projecting roof, or curtains, which ran round three sides of the tabernacle. Secondly, the measurements both of the whole edifice and of its component parts

were exactly double those of the tabernacle, as the following table will show :—

	TABERNACLE. cubits.	TEMPLE. cubits.
Entire length	40	80
„ width	20	40
„ height	15	30
Length of Holy Place	20	40
Width	10	20
Height	10	20
Length of Holy of Holies,	10	20
Width	10	20
Height	10	20
Width of Porch	10	20
Depth	5	10

The only exception to this rule is that of the side chambers, which (on the lowest story) were but five cubits wide, *i.e.*, they were identical in width with the verandah. It is held by some, however, that with the enclosing walls, they were ten cubits. If this were so, it follows that here again the same proportions are exactly preserved.

It will be clear from this comparison that the temple was constructed, not after any Egyptian or Assyrian model, but that it preserved the features and arrangement of the consecrated structure, the pattern of which was showed to Moses in the Mount (Exod. xxv. 9, 40 ; cf. Acts vii. 44 ; Heb. viii. 5), so that when " David gave to Solomon his son the pattern of the porch," &c., " and the pattern of all that he had by the spirit " (1 Chron. xxviii. 11, 12), the same arrangement and similar proportions were consciously or unconsciously preserved. The temple differed from the tabernacle only so far as a large house necessarily differs from a small tent.

It is also to be observed that every dimension of the temple was either *ten* cubits—the holy of holies was a cube of ten cubits—or a multiple of ten, just as the dimensions of the tabernacle are either five cubits or multiples of five. Now this decimal arrangement can hardly have been accidental. Not only had the Jews ten fingers, but they had ten commandments, and a system of tenths or tithes, and this number, therefore, was to them, no doubt, the symbol of completeness (" *Symbol der Vollendung und Vollkommenheit.*" Bähr,

Symbolik, i. p. 175), just as five was the sign of imperfection (ib. pp. 183—187). The very dimensions, consequently, of the house are a testimony to the perfections of the Being to whose service it was dedicated.

Nor is the recurrence of the number *three*, though by no means so marked, to be altogether overlooked. Considering its Divine original—that it was made after the pattern of things in the heavens—it is not wholly unworthy of notice that the building "had *three* compartments. . . . Each of the *three* sides was flanked by an aisle formed of *three* stories, and the holy of holies was of *three* equal dimensions" (Wordsworth). And if we cannot follow him further and see any significance in the fact that the "length was 3 × 30 cubits, and the height 3 × 10," we may still remember that this house was built, though Solomon knew it not, to the glory of the Triune God. Bähr, however, who also shows at some length how "the number *three* is everywhere conspicuous in the building" (p. 54), accounts for it on the ground that "three is in the Old Testament the signature of every true and complete unit" (*Was drei Mal geschieht ist das rechte Einmal; was in drei getheilt ist ist eine wahre Einheit*), so that practically three would signify here much the same as ten—it would stand as "the signature of the perfect unit, and so also of the Divine Being."

One remark more may be made here, viz., that in the temple or tabernacle we have the archetype of the Christian Church. The correspondence is so obvious as to strike the most casual observer. Porch, or steeple, nave, chancel, altar, side aisles, these have succeeded to, as they were suggested by, porch, temple of the house, oracle, mercy seat, side structure, of the Jewish sanctuary. Just as Christianity is built on the foundations of Judaism (see Homiletics), so has the Jewish temple furnished a model for the Christian; for, considering how closely the early Church fashioned itself after the pattern of Judaism, the resemblance can hardly be accidental.

Ver. 1.—**And it came to pass in the four hundred and eightieth year after the children of Israel were come out of the land of Egypt** [This date has been the subject of much controversy, which cannot even now be considered (*pace* Keil: "The correctness of the number 480 is now pretty generally admitted") as closed. Grave doubts are entertained as to its genuineness. Lord A. Hervey (Dict. Bib. vol. ii. p. 22) says it is "manifestly erroneous." Rawlinson considers it to be "an interpolation into the sacred text" (p. 515). And it is to be observed, 1. that the LXX. reads 440 instead of 480 years—a discrepancy which is suspicious, and argues some amount of incertitude. 2. Origen quotes this verse without these words (Comm. in S. Johann ii. 20). 3. They would seem to have been unknown to Josephus, Clem. Alex., and others. 4. It is not the *manner* of Old Testament writers thus to date events from an era, an idea which appears to have first occurred to the Greeks *temp.* Thucydides (Rawlinson). It is admitted that we have no other instance in the Old Testament where this is done. 5. It is difficult to reconcile this statement with other chronological notices both of the Old and New Testaments. For taking the numbers which we find in the Hebrew text of the books which refer to this period, they sum up to considerably more than 480 years. The time of the Judges alone comprises 410 years at the least. It should be stated, however, with regard to the chronology of the period last mentioned (1) that it only pretends to furnish round numbers—20, 40, and the like—and evidently does not aim at exactitude; (2) that there is good ground for suspecting that the periods are not always consecutive; that in some cases, *i.e.*, they overlap. We are not justified, therefore, because of the dates of the Judges in rejecting this statement. The question of New Testament chronology is somewhat more complicated. In Acts xiii. 20, St. Paul states the period between the division of Canaan, by Joshua (Josh. xiv. 1, 2), and the time of Samuel the prophet as 450 years (καὶ μετὰ ταῦτα ὡς ἔτεσι τετρακοσίοις καὶ πεντήκοντα ἔδωκεν κριτὰς κ.τ.λ.) But Lachmann, on the authority of A, B, C (and we may add א), considers the received text to be corrupt, and would place καὶ μετὰ ταῦτα after πεντήκοντα. Alford, however, treats this reading as "an attempt at correcting the difficult chronology of the verse," and says that "all attempts to reconcile" it with 1 Kings vi. 1 "are arbitrary and forced." If, then, the received text is to stand—and it is to be noticed that the reigns of the Judges, including Samuel, sum up exactly to the period mentioned by St. Paul, 450 years—the interval between the Exodus and the erection of the temple cannot well have been less than 99 or 100 years longer, *i.e.*, 580—Josephus makes it

592—instead of 480 years.　6. The chronology of Josephus — to which by itself, perhaps, no great weight is to be attached, agrees with St. Paul's estimate, and of course contradicts that of the text.　7. Nor does it seem to be a valid argument for the retention of the suspected words, that "the precision of the statement is a voucher for its accuracy." (Bähr, who adds, "Not only is the whole number of the years given, but also the year of the reign of the king, and even the month itself," for the genuineness of the later date, "*In the fourth year*," &c., is not questioned.) The remark of Keil that the building of the temple marked a new and important epoch in the history of the chosen people, and so justified an exceptional reference to the birth or emancipation of the nation, though undoubtedly true, will hardly avail much against the considerations alleged above. On the whole, therefore, I confess to the belief that these words are the interpolation of a later hand (of which we shall find traces elsewhere), though it would, perhaps, be premature, with only the evidence now before us, to exclude them from the text. It is certainly noteworthy that such destructive critics as Ewald and Thenius are satisfied as to their genuineness], **in the fourth year of Solomon's reign over Israel** [according to the chronology of Ussher, this was A.M. 3000], **in the month Zif** [*i.e.*, May. The word signifies *splendour*. The month was probably so called because of the brilliancy of its flowers (Gesen., Keil, *al.*)], **which is the second month** [This explanation is added because before the captivity the months (with the exception of *Abib*) appear to have had no regular names, but were almost always designated by numbers. (See, *e.g.*, Gen. vii. 11; 2 Kings xxv. 1). Only four pre-captivity names are recorded, and of these three are mentioned in connexion with the building of the temple, viz., *Zif* here and in ver. 37, *Bul* in ver. 38, and *Ethanim* in ch. viii. 2. It has hence been inferred that these names were not in general use, but were restricted to public documents, &c. (Dict. Bib. ii. 416), a supposition which, if correct, would account for the facility with which the old appellations were superseded by post-captivity names. The later name for this month was *Iyar* (Targum on 2 Chron. xxx. 2)], **that he began** [not in Heb.] **to build the house of** [Heb. *to*] **the Lord.** [The chronicler mentions the site (2 Chron. iii. 1), "In Mount Moriah, . . . in the threshing-floor of Ornan," &c. We know from the extensive foundations yet remaining that the preparation of the platform on which the temple should stand must have been a work of considerable time

and labour, and see Jos., Ant. viii. 3. 9, and Bell. Jud. v. 5. 1. We can hardly be wrong in identifying the remarkable rock known as the *Sakrâh*, over which the mosque of Omar (*Kubbet-es-Sakrâh*) is built—the "pierced rock" of the Jerusalem Itinerary—with the threshing-floor of Ornan. The reader will find an interesting paper on the site of the temple in "Scribner's Monthly," vol. xi. pp. 257—272. According to Mr. Beswick, whose measurements and conclusions it gives, the *porch* stood on the *Sakrâh*. Mr. Conder, however, urges strong reasons ("Tent Work," pp. 187—9) for placing the *Holy of Holies* on the rock. We should then "see the Holy House in its natural and traditional position on the top of the mountain; we see the courts descending on either side, according to the present slopes of the hill; we find the great rock galleries dropping naturally into their right places; and finally, we see the temple, by the immutability of Oriental custom, still a temple, and the site of the great altar still consecrated [?] by the beautiful little chapel of the chain." But see Porter i. p. 125; Pal. Explor. p. 4, also pp. 342, 343; "Our Work in Palestine," chs. viii. and ix. ; "Recovery of Jerusalem," ch. xii., &c. *Quot viatores, tot sententiae.*]

Ver. 2.—**And the house** [*i.e.*, not the whole structure, but the main building, exclusive of porch (ver. 3) and side chambers (ver. 5)] **which king Solomon built for the Lord, the length thereof was threescore cubits** [But what was the length of the cubit？ (אַמָּה) This unfortunately is by no means certain, as the Jews would seem to have had three different cubits. All the ancient measures, both Jewish and Gentile, were taken from parts of the body. Thus we find a "*finger-breadth*" (Jer. lii. 21), "*hand-breadth*" (1 Kings vii. 26), "*span*" (1 Sam. xvii. 24), and the Greeks had their δάκτυλος πούς and πῆχυς, and the Romans their *cubitus, pes, digitus,* &c. אַמָּה is used in its proper sense (*ulna*) Deuteronomy iii. 11. Probably at first it signified, like πῆχυς, the length from point of elbow to tip of little or middle finger. But it is obvious that this was an uncertain measure, and hence perhaps arose cubits of different length. According to Gesen. the cubit here mentioned, which was the older or sacred Mosaic cubit (2 Chron. iii. 3), was six palms, while that of Ezekiel (Ezek. xl. 5 ; xliii. 13), the royal Babylonian cubit, was seven, but on this as well as other points the authorities are very far from agreed. "The length of the cubit is one of the most knotty points of Hebrew archæology" (Dict. Bib. iii. p. 1736). There is a general *consensus* of opinion, however in favour of understanding the cubit here mentioned as measuring 18 inches. Fergusson (Dict. Bib. iii. 1451) considers this to be beyond question. It is certainly noteworthy that the measurements of Kings and Chronicles, of Ezra and Ezekiel, of Josephus and the Talmud, all agree, and we know that Josephus always uses the Greek cubit of 18 inches. Mr. Conder, however, maintains that the Hebrew cubit amounts to no more than *sixteen* inches. He says, "Maimonides tells us that the temple cubit was of 48 barleycorns, and any one who will take the trouble to measure barleycorns, will find that three go to the inch"—which gives 16 inches for the cubit. To this argument, which is not perhaps of much weight, he adds, what is of much greater moment, that "the Galilean synagogues, measured by it, give round numbers" (pp. 187—8)] **and the breadth thereof twenty cubits, and the height thereof thirty cubits.** [It thus appears that the temple was but a small—compared with many churches, a *very* small—building. But its purpose and object must be considered. It was not for assemblies of the people. The congregation never met *within* it, but the worship was offered *towards* it. It was a place for the Holy Presence, and for the priests who ministered before it.]

Ver. 3.—**And the porch** [אוּלָם, forepart, projection (*Vorhalle*, Gesenius). The porch was not a colonnade—that is called a "porch of *pillars*" (ch. vii. 6), but was formed by simply prolonging the side walls, and possibly the roof (see below). Bähr holds that it had only side walls and cieling, and was entirely open in front; and the fact that no mention is made of any door or opening, though the doors of the other parts of the edifice are all referred to (vers. 8, 31, 33), certainly favours this view, as also does the position of the pillars of ch. vii. 21] **before the temple of the house** [The house, or main building (ver. 2), had two parts. (1) "*The temple of the house*" (הֵיכָל = "spacious," hence "magnificent building," "palace," as in Prov. xxx. 28; Dan. i. 4. Gesen., Thes. i. 375). The same word is used of the tabernacle (1 Sam. i. 9), of the royal palace (1 Kings xxi. 1; 2 Kings xx. 18; Psa. xlv. 8, 15), and of heaven (2 Sam. xxii. 7, &c.) This was the *ναὸς par excellence*, and is called "the great house," because of its superior size and height, in 2 Chr. iii. 5. (2) *The oracle* (הַדְּבִיר) see on ver. 5. The two bore a rough resemblance to the nave and chancel of a Gothic church], **twenty cubits was the length thereof according to the breadth of the house** [The porch, *i.e.*, extended across the

entire front, or east end of the temple] **and ten cubits was the breadth** [*i.e., depth*] **thereof before the house.** [The height of the porch, of which no mention is made here, is stated in 2 Chron. iii. 4 as 120 cubits (say 180 feet), but there is surely some mistake in the figures. For (1) This is "unlike anything we know of in ancient architecture" (Fergusson). (2). A porch of such dimensions would surely have been called מִגְדָּל not אוּלָם (Thenius, Keil). (3) It is doubtful whether an erection of so great a height, with such a slender basis, would stand. It would certainly be out of all proportion. Towers are generally built about three times the height of the adjoining nave, but this would be six times as high, and moreover the porch did not taper to a point like a Gothic spire. It is much more probable, therefore, that there is a corruption of the text of Chronicles (see on 2 Chron. iii. 4)—errors in numbers are by no means infrequent—than that such a column could be erected to serve as a *porch*, or if erected—and this consideration appears to me to be decisive—could have been passed over by our author without notice. It is impossible, however, to say positively what the height of the porch was. Probably 30 cubits, the height of the house. Stanley characteristically puts it down as "more than 200 feet." It may be remarked here that Fergusson, following Josephus and the Talmud, contends that the temple had another building of the same height above it. See Dict. Bib. iii. p. 1456, and note on ver. 20.]

Ver. 4.—**And for the house he made windows of narrow lights.** [There has been much disputation over these words. The older expositors generally follow (as does the marg.) the Chaldee and Rabbins: "*windows broad within and narrow without;*" windows, *i.e.*, somewhat like the loopholes of ancient castles. The windows of the temple would then have resembled those of Egyptian sacred buildings. (It is not implied that there was any conscious imitation of Egypt, though Fergusson surely forgets the affinity with Pharaoh (ch. iii. 1), the trade with Egypt (ch. x. 28), and the favour with which some Egyptian fashions were regarded (Cant. i. 9), when he contends that the chosen people would never take the buildings of their ancestral enemy for a model.) But this meaning is not supported by the original (שְׁקֻפִים אֲטֻמִים), the literal interpretation of which is "*closed beams*" (cf. chap. vii. 4, 5), and which the most competent scholars now understand to mean "*closed or fixed lattices, i.e.*, the lattices or the temple windows were not movable, as in domestic architecture (2 Kings i. 2; xiii.

17 ; Dan. vi. 10). So Gesenius, De Wette, Keil, Bähr, *al*.]

Ver. 5.—**And against** [or *upon*, עַל ; they rested *on* the wall] **the wall of the house** [here meaning both temple and oracle : see below] **he built chambers** [Marg. *floors*. The Orig. is יָצוּעַ (Keri, יָצִיעַ) singular = *stratum* (יָצַע *stravit*, spread out). Symm. translates κατάστρωμα. Gesenius remarks that the word is used here and in ver. 10 in the masculine of the *whole* of the side structure, while in ver. 6 it is used in the feminine of the single stories. The floors bore this name, יָצוּעַ, because they were *spread upon*, not inserted into the walls. Rawlinson has evidently confounded this word with צֵלָע (see below) when he says, " The Hebrew word here used would be best translated a *lean-to*." Both words are translated alike "chambers" in the Authorized Version, but the first means *stories* or *floors*; the second may, perhaps, signify *lean-tos*] **round about,** against [It is doubtful whether אֵת is here, as commonly, merely the sign of the accusative, or is the preposition "*with,*" meaning "*in connexion with,*" *cum parietibus* (Seb. Schmidt), in which case its meaning would approach very closely to that of עַל above. Bähr remarks that עַל and אֵת are used elsewhere as almost synonymous, and refers to Psa. iv. 7 in connexion with Psa. lxvii. 2. Keil translates, " As for the walls " (*Anlangend die Wände*), but this gives us an unfinished sentence. It is probably an accusative, explicative of the preceding clause = " I mean the walls," &c., the singular, *wall*, having being used above. This additional clause] **the walls of the house round about** [would then mean that the term " house " is to be understood as including both temple and oracle (and excluding porch), as the next words define it], **both of the temple and of the oracle** [The floors, *i.e.*, ran round the south, west, and north sides of the building. Stanley aptly compares them to the little shops which nestle under the continental cathedrals; though the side aisles of some Gothic churches, viewed externally, would perhaps better represent their proportions] **and he made chambers** [צְלָעוֹת, literally, ribs, beams, (Gesenius); *Rippen* (Bähr). The design of the word is clearly to convey that the floors were " divided by partitions into distinct compartments " (Merz). According to Ezek. xli. 6 (where, however, the reading is doubtful) there were thirty-three of these side chambers; according to Josephus (Ant. viii. 3. 2) thirty. Thenius is probably not so far wrong when he sees in these chambers *bed-*

rooms. A sort of monastery would seem to have been attached to the temple. So many chambers could hardly have been required for the preservation of temple stores and utensils " (Keil), or of offerings (Ewald). Whatever their use, we can hardly suppose that they were wholly without light, though nothing is said about windows. They may have had " fixed lattices." It is to be remembered that the priests and Levites ministered " by night in the house of the Lord " (Psa. cxxxiv. 1)] **round about.**

Ver. 6.—**The nethermost chamber** [Heb. *floor*; cf. Ezek. xli. 6] **was five cubits broad** [It must be remembered that all the measurements are those of the interior], **and the middle was six cubits broad, and the third was seven cubits broad : for** [Explanation how these differences of size arose] **without** [*i.e.*, on the outside] **in the**

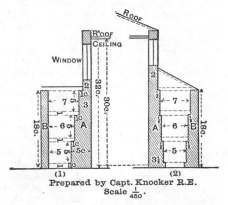

(1)   (2)
Prepared by Capt. Knocker R.E.
Scale 1/450.

wall of [Heb. omits] **the house** [main building—nave, and chancel] **he made** [Heb. *put*] **narrowed rests** [marg. " narrowings or rebatements." The word מִגְרָעוֹת means *lessenings, deductions; Absätze*, Gesen. (Thesaurus, i. 304), Bähr. The outside of the temple wall took the shape of three (or four) steps, and presented three ledges for the beams to rest upon. See below] **round about** [same word as in ver. 5. The recesses in the wall ran round the north, west, and south sides of the building; they were co-extensive, *i.e.*, with the flats or side-chambers], **that the beams should not be fastened** [Heb. *that no fastening*] **into the walls of the house.** [The meaning is perfectly clear, viz., that the timbers should not be let into the walls, (" they had not hold in the wall of the house," Ezek. xli. 6) ; but why this was forbidden is not quite so certain. According to Bähr, it was in order to preserve the great and costly stones of the temple intact ; but others, with greater probability, hold that it was because it appeared unseemly to have the side-chambers, which were for semi-secular purposes (cubicles, perhaps), made an actual part of the sacred edifice. Anyhow, it is clear that the beams rested on ledges made in the walls ; but whether in the temple wall only, or in the outer wall of the side structure also, is uncertain. The preceding sketch will not only illustrate the difference, but will help the reader to understand the description preceding. In drawing (1) rebatements are showed only in the temple or inner wall. In (2) they are showed in both walls. In (1) the edifice is represented with a flat ; in (2) with a span roof.

Keil decides in favour of the first arrangement (1), and Bähr says somewhat positively, " The outer wall of the structure had no rests." In fact, he suggests that the whole of this side building may have been of wood. It must be admitted that we *do* know that there were rebatements in the wall A, whereas nothing is said as to the outer wall B. It may also be reasonably alleged that the considerations of fitness and sacredness which forbade the insertion of the beams into the sanctuary wall would not apply to the outer wall, which was a part of the side structure only. Against this view, however, may be urged the extreme thickness of wall which this method of building would necessitate. For unless we suppose that the floor of the ground story rested on the rock, and so was quite detached from the building, we must suppose *four* rebatements, so that if the wall at the top were two cubits wide, it would be no less than six cubits (or nine feet) at the bottom. It is true that the walls of ancient buildings were of extraordinary thickness, but it must also be remembered that the temple was not fifty feet high. However, Ezek. xli. 9 suggests that the outside wall (B) may have been five cubits in thickness, and, if so, the inner wall would hardly be less. Fergusson, therefore, has some justification for putting each wall down as five cubits wide ; but on the whole, perhaps, the plan represented in (1) appears the more probable.

The historian here digresses for a moment to speak of the remarkable and, indeed, unprecedented way in which the temple was built. The stories were shaped and prepared beforehand in the quarry, so that there was nothing to do on their arrival in the temple area but to fit them into their place in the building.]

Ver. 7.—And the house, when it was in building, was built of stone made ready [Heb. *perfect*. This does not mean *unhewn*, though אֲבָנִים שְׁלֵמוֹת is undoubtedly used

in Deut. xxvii. 6 (cf. Exod. xx. 25) of unhewn or virgin stone ; and Gesenius would so understand the expression here. But the context seems rather to convey the idea that the stones were not shaped *on the spot*. It was apparently the belief of the ancients that stones of proper shape and size were provided in their bed by God (so Theodoret and Procopius.) It is inconceivable, however, that no dressing or preparation of any kind would be required ; an idea, moreover, which is contradicted by ch. v. 18. When Gardiner (in Bähr, American edition) quotes Keil (in his earlier work) as understanding " all unviolated stones of the quarry," he hardly does justice to that author, who straightway adds, " that is, not altogether unhewn stones . . . but stones that were so hewn and wrought in the quarry that neither hammer," &c. (see below). Similarly Thenius and Bähr] before it was brought thither [so the Authorized Version renders מַסָּע but mistakenly. It means, *the quarry* (Gesenius, Keil. For the construction, see Ewald, 289*a*, and Gesenius, Gram. ed. Rödiger, p. 170.) The verb נָסַע is used of quarrying in ch. v. 31 (Heb.) Where was this quarry ? The general idea is that it was in the Lebanon. And it is not to be denied that some of the massive substructions and corner-stones of the temple may have been brought from the mountain, along with the wood ; but the bulk of the stone, there can be no doubt, was found much nearer home. Some of it, according to the Mishna (*Middoth*, iii. 4), came from Bethlehem ; but we can hardly be mistaken in believing that for the most part it was quarried in Jerusalem itself, under the very temple rock, and out of the vast caverns recovered some years ago by Dr. Barclay (see his " City of the Great King "), the " Royal Caverns " of Josephus. See " Quart. Journal," Pal. Explor. Fund (No. vii.), pp. 373, 374, and cf. p. 34. There are unmistakable evidences of these extensive caverns having served as a quarry. Not only are the walls cut straight, but rude masses are left here and there to support the roof, and, what is still more convincing, there are stones more or less cut out of the rock, and incisions are made where stones are to be quarried. There was no reason why the workmen should go far afield for stone when they had it, and of very excellent quality, at their own doors]: so that there was neither hammer [Heb. *and hammers*. Keil understands " finished stones of the quarry, and hammer, and axe." But the word " was built " (נִבְנָה), coming as it does between " quarry " and " hammers," almost forbids this connexion] nor axe

[Heb. *the* axe] **nor any tool** [Heb. *every tool*] **of iron heard in the house, while it was building.** [The historian remarks on this, not only because it was so unusual, but with the evident idea that it was a fulfilment of the *spirit* of the law (Deut. xxvii. 5, 6), which required the *altar* to be of virgin stones, untouched by tool of iron. If the quarries are to be identified with the "Royal Caverns," it is easy to understand how the temple rose up in silence.

Ver. 8.—After recording this interesting and singular fact, the historian resumes his description of the side-building. **The door** [or entrance, doorway. פֶּתַח, as in ver. 31] **for** [Heb. *of*] **the middle chamber** [generally understood to mean "the middle side chamber of the lower story." But this is by no means necessary, for (1) צֵלָע may signify the *suite* of rooms, *i.e.*, the entire story or flat, as well as a single lean-to or compartment, and (2) הַתִּיכֹנָה is used in the next clause of the middle *story*. This has led Thenius, Keil, Ewald, Bähr, *al.* to substitute הַתַּחְתֹּנָה (following the LXX. and Targum), which would give the sense of "*lower story*" (as in Ezek. xli. 7). Bähr says this "must necessarily be read." That this emendation has much in its favour must be allowed, but it seems also certain that we get a perfectly clear meaning from the text as it stands, viz., that "the door (leading to) the middle floor was (on the ground floor) on the right side," &c. It is hardly likely that all the compartments on the ground floor had only one approach, and the doors which communicated with them may well have been passed over as requiring no special notice. But the historian feels it necessary to state how the second and third stories were reached, and the staircase which led to them causes him to speak of the position of the door which opened upon it] **was in the right side** [Heb. *shoulder*. This word (כְּתֵף) almost implies that the door was in the *external* wall of the side structure, not in the wall of the holy place (as Böttcher, *al.*) The fact that the floor-joists were not inserted into the temple walls, as being inconsistent with the dignity of the sanctuary, makes it almost a certainty that there was no direct communication between the building and its *dépendance*. It is very improbable that the walls of the house were anywhere broken through. The "right side" was the *south* side (chap. vii. 39), *i.e.*, the right, not as one faced the oracle, but, like the building, faced east. What was the exact position of the door, whether in the centre, or at either angle, it is impossible to say] **of the**

house: and they went up with winding stairs [לוּלִים is only found here and in 2 Chron. iii. The staircase was obviously unlike those of most Eastern buildings, within the side structure. Even if the outer wall was five cubits thick, of which we have no *proof*, it is very doubtful whether the staircase would or could be constructed within it] **into** [Heb. *upon*] **the middle chamber** [or story], **and out of the middle into the third.**

Ver. 9.—**So he built the house and finished it** [*i.e.*, the exterior (see on ver. 14)] **and covered** [*i.e.*, roofed, same word Deut. xxxiii. 21; Jer. xxii. 14; Hag. i. 4. There is no reference to the lining of cedar which was applied to the interior. That is described in ver. 15] **the house with beams and boards** [Heb. *rows, ranks*. The same word is used of soldiers 2 Kings xi. 8, 15] **of cedar.** [It has been universally held till quite lately that the roof was either vaulted (Thenius) or flat (Bähr, Keil). But Mr. Fergusson has alleged some reasons for believing that it was a span or gable roof. It is true that Oriental buildings almost invariably have externally flat (internally arched) roofs. In Palestine, because of the scarcity of timber, no other form is possible. But the temple, as we have seen, was constructed after the model of the tabernacle, and the latter, as the name almost implies, and as necessity would require, had a ridged roof (see Dict. Bib. iii. p. 1453). It does not *necessarily* follow, however, as Fergusson assumes, that the temple followed the tabernacle in this respect. It is obvious that when a "*house* was built unto the name of the Lord," the form of the tent might be abandoned as inappropriate. It is true that this shape would be consecrated to them by many centuries of use, but it is also possible that in a house it would strike them as altogether *bizarre*.]

Ver. 10.—**And then** [Heb. omits] **he built chambers** [Heb. *the* floor (הַיָּצוּעַ). The word (masculine) is here again used of the entire side structure] **against all the house, five cubits high** [*i.e.*, each story was five cubits (7½ feet). The three stories would altogether measure fifteen cubits, and of course something must be allowed for joists, floors, &c. The entire height of the side structure (exterior) would consequently be about 18 or 20 cubits. And as the house was internally 30 cubits high, the exterior measurement would probably be about 32 cubits. It has hence been inferred that between the side structure and the top of temple wall there would be a clear space of 12 or 14 cubits, in which the windows were inserted. But this is based on the assumption that the side structure had a *flat* roof, which is by no means certain. If the roof leaned against the walls of the house, with a low pitch, there would still be space amply sufficient for the clerestory windows. Rawlinson's diagram (p. 511), which gives 30 cubits as the height from basement to *ridge of roof*, and only allows 20 cubits for height of walls, practically makes the house 20 instead of 30 cubits high, for it is hardly likely that it had an open roof. In fact, we know that it had a cieling (ver. 14), which must have been at the height of 30 cubits (see the diagrams on p. 102. In (1) house and side structure are represented with flat, in (2) with ridged or sloping roofs), unless there was an upper chamber above the house, as to which see ver. 20. Rawlinson's diagram has this further defect, that he allows nothing for thickness of joists, floors, and cielings. If we allow one cubit for each floor, then, on his plan, there would be little or no room left for the windows. This verse is hardly to be considered as a repetition of ver. 5, the side structure being here mentioned in connexion with its height and the materials used in its construction] **and they rested on** [the meaning of the Heb. וַיִּאֱחֹז has been much disputed. It is uncertain what is the nominative, Solomon (as in וַיִּבֶן), or the "floor" (just referred to in קוֹמָתוֹ). Gesenius understands the former, and renders, "*he* covered the house," &c. Thenius, "*he* fastened the floor," &c. Keil adopts the latter alternative, "*it* held to the house with cedar beams." It may be urged against this rendering (as also against Thenius's) that beams which merely *rested* on the walls would hardly *bind* or *hold* the side structure to the main building. But it is almost impossible to decide between these interpretations. We may either render "he covered," &c. (with Chald., Vulg.) in which case ver. 10 would agree with ver. 9 (each, *i.e.*, would refer to the roofing; ver. 9 to roof of temple; ver. 10 to roof of side structure and its stories); or we may take the words to mean "it laid hold of, *i.e.*, rested on] **the house with timber of cedar.**

At this point the historian interrupts his description of the building to record the gracious promise made to the king during its erection. It should, perhaps, be stated that this (vers. 11—14) is omitted in the Vat. LXX. But it has every mark of genuineness.]

Ver. 11.—And the word of the Lord came to Solomon [probably through the prophet Nathan. It cannot well have been a direct communication, for the *second* direct revelation is mentioned in chap. ix. 2 (cf. iii. 5).

The original promise was made by Nathan (2 Sam. vii. 12). It seems exceedingly probable that the promise would be renewed through him if he were still alive] **saying,**

Ver. 12.—Concerning [or, *as to*. There is nothing, however, in the Hebrew] **this house which thou art in building** [כֹּנֶה. Cf. וַיִּבֶן, vers. 5, 9, 10] **if thou wilt walk in my statutes** [the connexion of ideas seems to be this, "Thou art doing well to build the house; thou art fulfilling my good pleasure (2 Sam. vii. 13); if thou wilt go on and in other matters wilt keep," &c. It is to be observed that this promise contains a faint note of warning. Possibly Solomon had already betrayed some slight tokens of declension], **and execute my judgments, and keep all my commandments to walk in them; then will I perform** [literally, *confirm*. Same word as in ch. ii. 3. The "word of the Lord" is the echo of the word of David] **my word with thee, which I spake unto David thy father** [*i.e.*, the word mentioned ch. ii. 4 and found 2 Sam. vii. 12 sqq.].

Ver. 13.—And I will dwell among the children of Israel, and will not forsake my people Israel [cf. Deut. xxxi. 6. A fresh element is here introduced into the promise, arising out of the erection of the temple. God had pledged His presence to the tabernacle (Exod. xxv. 8; xxix. 45; cf. Levit. xxvi. 11). And the temple was reared to be His dwelling-place (ch. viii. 13; 2 Chron. vi. 2). He now assures the royal builder that he will occupy it. "*Jehovah Shammah*" (Ezek. xlviii. 35). The covenant relation shall be more firmly established.

Ver. 14.— So Solomon built the house and finished it [though these words are a repetition of ver. 9, yet they are not without significance. Encouraged by the promise just made, he proceeded with the interior, of which the narrative henceforth treats. Ver. 9 speaks of the finishing of the shell.

Ver 15.—And he built [*i.e.*, *constructed, covered*] **the walls of the house within** [but not without also, as Stanley affirms, "Its massive stone walls were entirely cased in cedar, so as to give it the appearance of a rough log-house"] **with boards** [or beams (צְלָעֹות): same word as in vers. 5—8] **of** cedar [Heb. *cedars*. The practice of covering stone walls with a lining of wood, which in turn was ornamented with gold or colour (Jer. xxii. 14), seems to have had its origin in Phœnicia (Bähr), and may have been suggested to Solomon by his Zidonian workmen (Cf. 2 Chron. ii. 14], **both the floor of the house and the walls of the cieling** [This gives no sense and is against the Hebrew, which is as the marg.—"*from the floor* . . .

unto the walls," &c. The expression „walls of the cieling," though it may be *taken* to mean " the walls where they join the cieling," is peculiar, and the suggestion that for קִירוֹת *walls*, we should read קוֹרוֹת *beams*—the word of the parallel verse in 2 Chron.—has everything in its favour. The LXX. reads εὡς τῶν δοκῶν]: **and** [omit] **he covered them on the inside with wood** [This is apparently a mere repetition. The A. V. would lead us to suppose that a fresh particular was stated. We learn from 2 Chron. iii. 6 that not only were the walls, or their wooden lining, covered with plates of gold, "gold of Parvaim," but they were likewise ornamented with precious stones], **and he covered the floor of the house with planks of fir** [see on ch. v. 8].

Ver. 16.—**And he built twenty cubits on** [Heb. *from*] **the sides of the house both the floor and the walls** [Heb. as in ver. 15, "from the floor to the walls" (or beams). If קִירוֹת is a copyist's error, it is repeated here] **with boards of cedar** [He is now speaking of the wooden partition which separated the oracle from the temple of the house. At a distance of 20 cubits, measured along the sides from the west end of the house, he erected a cedar wall which reached from the floor to the cieling] **he even built them**] *i.e.*, the 20 cubits] **for it** [the house] **within** [The meaning is clear, though the construction is somewhat involved, viz., that he reared this partition inside the house to separate a portion for the oracle] **even for the oracle** [Heb. *an* oracle] **even for the most holy place** [Heb. *for the holy of holies*].

Ver. 17.—**And the house, that is, the temple before it** [or, *the anterior temple*. The portion of the structure before the oracle is sometimes called, as here, " the house;" sometimes (as in ver. 5) " the temple;" sometimes (as in ver. 4) " the temple of the house;" or, as here again, " the front temple," לִפְנָי is supposed to be an adjective formed from לִפְנָי. Thenius, however, supposes that דְּבִיר (*oracle*) has fallen out of the text. Our author now describes the division of the building into holy and most holy place] **was forty cubits long.**

Ver. 18.—**And the cedar of the house within** [lit. *cedar* (wood) *was placed against the house inside*] **was carved with knops** [Heb. *sculpture of gourds.* The sculpture is in apposition to cedar. The authorities are divided as to the kind of sculpture intended. Keil thinks they were *bassi relievi;* Bähr contends that, like those of the Egyptian monuments, they were sunken. פְּקָעִים

is generally assumed to be synonymous with פְּקָעֹת " squirting cucumbers" (2 Kings iv. 39, note). Bähr, however, justly observes that a deadly fruit, such as this is described to have been, was hardly likely to be employed in the decoration of the sanctuary, and he would render the word "buds." Keil thinks the gourds were oval ornaments, something *like* the wild gourd, which ran in rows along the walls. See the illustration, " Slab from Kouyunjik," Dict. Bib. ii. p. 49] **and open flowers** [lit. *burstings of flowers.* These words again are very variously interpreted. Thenius: *festoons of flowers;* Keil: *open flower buds;* Gesen.: *expanded flowers*]: **all was cedar; there was no stone seen.** [Really, the cedar was no more seen than the stone, for this in turn was overlaid with gold (ver. 22.)]

Ver. 19.—**And the oracle** [Heb. *an oracle.* Heb. דְּבִיר probably from דָּבַר *speak.* Sc Jerome, *oraculum;* and Aquila and Symm. χρηματιστήριον. Gesenius, Bähr, *al.*, however, interpret the word to mean the hinder part, *adytum*] **he prepared in the house within** [lit. *in the midst of the house within*, *i.e.*, between the Holy Place and the end structure] **to set there** [the principal purpose which the oracle served. תֵּת = תִתֵּן with repeated syllable. Cf. 1 Kings xvii. 14, *Keri*] **the ark of the covenant of the Lord.**

Ver. 20.—**And the oracle in the forepart** [or, *the interior* of the oracle. Keil, after Kimchi, maintains that לִפְנִי is the construct of the noun לִפְנִים. See ver. 29, where it clearly means *interior*, as its opposition to "without" shows. The A. V. yields no sense] **was twenty cubits in length, and twenty cubits in breadth, and twenty cubits in the height thereof** [that is to say, it was a perfect cube. When we consider that the oracle of the tabernacle was a cube of ten cubits and the Holy City (Rev. xxi. 16; cf. Ezek. xlviii. 8—35, especially ver. 20) is a cube of 12,000 furlongs, we cannot but regard these measurements as significant. To the ancients the square seemed the most appropriate shape to express the idea of moral perfection. The idea of the cube consequently was that of entire completeness, of absolute perfection. A little light is thrown on this subject by the use of τετράγωνος among the Greeks. See the quotation from Simonides in Plat. Protag. 334 A; Arist. Rhet. iii. 11; Eth. Nic. i. 10, 11, and compare the familiar " *totus teres atque rotundus.*" The height of the oracle (internally) being only twenty cubits, while that of the house was thirty (ver. 2), several questions of some interest suggest themselves for consideration. It is perhaps impossible in the present state of our knowledge to arrive at any very positive conclusions, but it may be well, nevertheless, if only to show in how much uncertainty the architecture of the temple is involved, to state them. First among them is this: Was the roof of the temple flat or ridged? (See above on ver. 9). (2) In either case, was the height of thirty cubits, or any uniform height, maintained throughout, or was the roof of the oracle some ten cubits lower than that of the house? The analogy of the tabernacle, of which the temple was a copy, would lead us to suppose that the ridge—if there was a ridge—of the entire building was level and unbroken, though the analogy of the Gothic church, which, we have already seen, is almost a reproduction of the temple, suggests that the oracle (like the chancel, and, it may be added, like the *adytum* of Egyptian temples) may possibly have had a lower roof. But (3), supposing the same height was maintained from end to end, to what use, if any, was the vacant space of ten cubits (15 feet) between cieling and roof of oracle applied? It has been held by some that there was a chamber here, but that it was empty, being formed, in fact, not for use, but in order to procure the cubical shape of the oracle. Others contend that this upper room, or one which ran the entire length of the building, was designed to serve as a receptacle for the reliques of the tabernacle, and they would identify it with the עֲלִיּוֹת (LXX. τὸ ὑπερῷον) of 2 Chron. iii. 9. And untrustworthy as Josephus is when not supported by independent evidence, it is worth mentioning here that both he and the Talmud "persistently assert that there was a superstructure on the temple equal in height to the lower part" (Fergusson, who, consequently, is of opinion that there undoubtedly was some such superstructure, as in the tomb of Darius, near Persepolis (see Dict. Bib. iii. pp. 1456, 1457), and that it was used for worship (2 Kings xxiii. 12), where see note). Bähr, however, argues forcibly against this idea. He says, *inter alia*, that there was no approach provided to these chambers; but our account is so manifestly imperfect that this argument is at the best a precarious one. He sees in the "upper chambers" (the Hebrew word is plural) the upper stories of the side structure. He agrees, however, with Ewald that there *was* a chamber over the oracle, but thinks it was unoccupied. Keil identifies this space with the "upper chambers" of 2 Chron. iii. 9, and upon the whole this appears to be the most feasible view. (4) How was the cieling, whether with or without this upper chamber,

and whether at the height of twenty or thirty cubits—how was it supported? For "no cedar beam could be laid across a space of twenty cubits without sinking in the centre by its own weight." Fergusson hence argues that the roof must have been carried on pillars—four in the sanctuary and ten in the hall. He remarks that they were used in the house of the Forest of Lebanon, where they were *less* suitable than here] **and he overlaid it** [lit. *made it shine*] **with pure gold** [marg. *shut up* (from סָגַר *clausit*). Cf. Job xxviii. 15 (Heb.) The same gold is described as טָהוֹר (Exod. xxv. 11) and טוֹב (2 Chron. iii. 8). It is called "shut up gold," not because it was *concealed* (κειμήλιον), but because of the exclusion of impure ingredients (Vulg. *aurum purissimum*). The lavish use of gold in the interior of the temple—its weight 600 talents (75,000 lbs.), its value almost incalculable—was not for mere display (for most of it was never seen except by the priests), but was symbolical of light and purity (Job xxxvii. 22, 23; Rev. xxi. 18), and stamped the place as the abode of Him who dwelleth in light (1 Tim. vi. 16). See Bähr *in loc.* The palace of the Lord must be "exceeding magnifical." The overlaying was not gilding, but *laminae* of gold were attached to the woodwork with nails. This art was probably derived from Egypt (Exod. xxv. 11, 13). Egyptian figures ornamented with gold plates are found both in the Louvre and British Museum. See Wilkinson, "Ancient Egyptians," ii. p. 233 sqq.) Rawlinson remarks that "such ornamentation was common in Babylon, in Assyria, and in Media." See Isa. xlvi. 6; Herod. i. 98; Layard, ii. 264. In addition to the gold, the house was garnished with precious stones (2 Chron. iii. 6). Cf. 1 Chron. xxix. 2, 8]; **and so covered the** [Heb. *an*] **altar which was of cedar.** [The italics in the A. V. lead us to suspect a mistranslation, and such it proves to be. What the writer means, supposing the present text to be retained, is, not that Solomon covered the cedar altar with gold, but that he overlaid the (stone?) altar with cedar. It is true the article is wanting, but this may perhaps be accounted for by the fact that the altar is now mentioned for the first time (Keil). It is much more probable, however, that the text has been slightly corrupted. The LXX. reads, καὶ ἐποίησε θυσιαστήριον (Cod. Alex. adds κέδρου), which proves that the Seventy had יַעַשׂ instead of וַיְצַף in their text. If so, the absence of the article is at once explained, and an unmeaning repetition in ver. 22 avoided. The mention of the altar—of course it is the altar of *incense* that is meant: the altar of burnt sacrifice was outside the building—in connexion with the oracle is significant. In ver. 22 it is called the "altar that (belonged) to the oracle," because it stood just outside it. In the tabernacle it was placed "before the vail" (Exod. xxx. 6; xl. 5, 26; Levit. xvi. 12—18), and it occupied this position because the incense burned upon it was offered before the Invisible Presence within. It is an argument in favour of the textual emendation suggested above that the altar in the tabernacle was of wood (Exod. xxx. 1), and that Ezekiel speaks of the "altar of wood" (ch. xli. 22), the altar of sacrifice being of earth, stones (Exod. xx. 24, 25), or brass (2 Chron. iv. 1). If we retain the Received Text we are almost compelled to believe that this altar was also of stone, as they would hardly cover a wooden altar with wood.

Ver. 21.—So [Heb. *And*. The ornamentation of the holy place is next mentioned] **Solomon overlaid the house** [as well as the oracle] **within with pure gold : and he made a partition by the chains of gold before the oracle** [These words are extremely obscure. The prevailing view is that of Gesenius, *al.*, that יְעַבֵּר ="he bolted," &c. But, if so, what did the chains bolt? Bähr says, the boards of the cedar partition, just as the bars fastened together the boards of the tabernacle (Exod. xxvi. 26—29). Gesen. himself (together with Keil, marg., *al.*) understands the *doors*, "he bolted the doors of the oracle," so as to keep them closed, except on the day of atonement. But the literal rendering is, "he carried over with chains of gold before the oracle," where nothing is said of either boards or doors. The more natural interpretation, therefore, would perhaps be: he carried on the gold plates of the house in chains of gold across the partition, and so fastened it to the side walls. Perhaps this was done to avoid any fracture of, or insertion into, the stonework]; **and he overlaid it** [What? Keil says, the cedar altar last mentioned at the end of ver. 20. But the altar has now dropped out of the reader's, and therefore presumably out of the writer's mind. It would be more natural to understand the words of the oracle just mentioned, but the adornment of the oracle has already been related (ver. 20), and it is hardly likely that having stated that it was covered with *pure gold* in one verse, he would mention that it was overlaid with *gold* in the next. It looks as if the cedar partition were referred to, the boards "before the oracle"] **with gold.**

Ver. 22.—**And the whole house he overlaid with gold** [This no mere repetition, *more Hebraico*, as Bähr and Keil would have us think. Something additional must surely be referred to, and 2 Chron. iii. 4 warrants us in understanding this statement to in-

clude the porch, the interior of which *was* gilded. Because the porch is elsewhere (ver. 3) distinguished from the "house," it does not follow that it can never be comprehended under that term] **until he had finished all the house : also** [Heb. *and*] **the altar that was by** [Heb. *to*. See on ver. 20] **the oracle he overlaid with gold.**

Ver. 23.—**And within the oracle** [The description now passes on to the mysterious symbolic figures which were placed in the holy of holies] **he made two cherubims** [As to the nature, composition, and significance of the cherubim, see notes on Exod. xxv. 19; xxxvii. 7. The only particulars which will require notice here are those in which the cherub of the temple differed from that of the tabernacle] **of olive tree** [Heb. *trees or wood of oil*. The oleaster (wild olive) is supposed to be intended, the proper name for the olive tree being זַיִת (Neh. viii. 15). The wood of the oleaster, which is firm, fine-grained, and durable, was used by the Greeks for the images of their gods (Winer). The cherubim of the tabernacle were of solid gold; those of the temple, on account of their great size (fifteen feet high) were necessarily of less costly material. But though of wood, yet the most durable and beautiful of wood, the olive, was employed in their construction. It is noticeable how olive wood is employed for the cherubim and doors of oracle, and for the posts of the temple doorway; the less precious cedar was used for lining the walls and for beams, &c., while for the floor and doors of house, the commoner cypress sufficed], **each ten cubits high.** [Half the height of the oracle. They occupied its entire width (ver. 24).

Ver 24.—**And five cubits was the one wing of the cherub, and five cubits the other wing of the cherub : from the uttermost part of the one wing unto the uttermost part of the other were ten cubits.** [As the four wings alone covered the whole extent of the oracle, each pair must clearly have been in contact on the body of the cherub.]

Ver. 25.—**And the other cherub was ten cubits ; both the cherubims were of one measure and one size** [or *shape*].

Ver. 26.—**The height of the one cherub was ten cubits, and so it was of the other cherub.** [The constant recurrence of the number ten, the symbol of completeness and perfection, is not to be overlooked.]

Ver. 27.—**And he set the cherubims within the inner house : and they stretched forth the wings of the cherubims** [The marg. reading, *the cherubim stretched forth their wings*, is altogether inadmissible], **so that the wing of the one touched the one wall, and the wing of the other cherub** touched the other wall, and their wings touched one another in the midst of the house. [In 2 Chron. iii. 10 we are told that the cherubim were of "image work" (the meaning of the Heb. word is unknown). We also learn that they "stood on their feet" and, unlike the cherubim of the tabernacle, which faced each other (Exod. xxvii. 9), faced the throne, i.e., the cedar partition, and the east. The object of this arrangement probably was to enable the wings to be stretched out across the sanctuary. In the tabernacle the wings were "spread out on high" (Exod. xxv. 20; xxvii. 9). In both cases the ark and mercy-seat were placed under the overshadowing wings (ch. viii. 6). There would be a clear space of eight or nine cubits between the bodies of the cherubim, and the ark only measured 2½ cubits (Exod. xxv. 10) in length and 1½ cubits in breadth. Unlike Ezekiel's cherubim (Ezek. chs. i. x; cf. Rev. iv. 7), these had apparently but one face. The cherub was not a simple, but a complex being, having no unalterable and fixed form. See Bähr, Symbolik, i. pp. 313, 314; Dict. Bib. vol. i. pp. 301—303.]

Ver. 28.—**And he overlaid the cherubims with gold.**

Ver. 29.—**And he carved all the walls of the house round about with carved figures of cherubims** [lit. openings, i.e., gravings or indentations of cherubim. פִּתּוּחִים is used of gravings in stone, Exod. xxviii. 11; xxxix. 6: in metal, xxviii. 36; xxxix. 30] **and palm trees and open flowers** [The open flowers may well have been lilies (ch. vii. 19, 22, 26). It is uncertain whether there were one or more rows of cherubim and palms. Keil, arguing from the analogy of Egyptian temples, contends for two or three rows, but it is doubtful how far the Israelites, notwithstanding their new and intimate relations with the country, would take Egypt and its idolatrous shrines for a model. Ezek. xli. 18 tends to show that the palm-trees alternated with the cherubs. The cherubim may have had two faces, such as he describes (ver. 19), the face of a man on the one side, and the face of a young lion on the other side; but if so, they must have differed in form from those of the oracle. Possibly the open flowers formed a border, or were sculptured in festoons, above, and the gourds (or buds) formed a border below (as in the Kouyunjik slab). But as to this the text is silent.

But while we are ignorant of the precise form and of the arrangement of these ornamental carvings, we are not wholly in the dark as to their symbolism. For everything in the temple, we may be sure, had a meaning. Let us inquire, then, into the significance of the cherubim, the palms, and the flowers.

1. *The Cherubim* have been regarded by some as symbols of the invisible Godhead, by others as "representations of the heavenly spirits which surround the Lord of glory and set forth psychical life at its highest stage" (Keil); but it seems best to view them as symbols of all animal life, including the highest and perhaps not excluding the thought of Him who is the source and spring of life, the *Anima animantium* (cf. ch. xii. 28). Hence they are spoken of as הַחַיּוֹת (Ezek. i. 5, 13, 15, &c.) "the living things" (compare τὰ ζῶα, Rev. iv. 6, 8, 9), and even as הַחַיָּה "the life" (Ezek. x. 14, 15, &c.) The cherubim consequently speak of the great animal kingdom before its Creator. "Creaturely being reaches its highest degree in those which have an *anima*, and among these, the lion, the bull, the eagle, and the man are the highest and most complete" (Bähr). These shapes, accordingly, were not inappropriate or unmeaning in a temple raised by the creature to the glory of the Creator.

2. Just as the cherubim speak of animal, so do the *Palms* of vegetable life. They are "the princes of the vegetable kingdom" (Linnæus). "Amongst trees there is none so lofty and towering, none which has such a fair majestic growth, which is so evergreen, and which affords so grateful a shade and such noble fruits—fruits which are said to be the food of the blessed in paradise—as the palm" (Bähr), who also adds that it is said to have as many excellent properties as there are days in the year, and cites Humboldt as designating it the "noblest of plants forms to which the nations have always accorded the meed of beauty." Judæa, he further remarks, is the fatherland of the palm, so much so that the palm in later days became the symbol of Palestine (as on the well-known coin with the legend *Judæa capta*). The palms, therefore, tell of the vegetable world, and of Him who fashioned its noble and graceful forms.

3. And very similar was the testimony of the *Flowers*. "Flowers and bloom have been, from ancient times to our own, the usual symbols of life-fulness. . . . So then by the flower-work, as well as by the cherubim and the palm-trees, was the dwelling of Jehovah, which was adorned therewith, designated as an *abode of life*" (Bähr). On the earthly dwelling-place of the Eternal, that is to say, were everywhere pourtrayed the various tokens of His Almighty power and goodness. And the significance of each is the same. "Thou hast created all things, and for thy pleasure they are, and

were created." They were graved] **within and without.** [These words, here and in ver. 30, are generally taken to mean "in the oracle and in the house." But it is worthy of consideration whether they do not rather signify, "in the house and in the porch." The latter was overlaid with gold (2 Chron. iii. 4). It is doubtful whether לַחִיצוֹן *on the outside,* can be applied to any part of the interior, and here its application would be to the *oracle* (Thenius)].

Ver. 30.—**And the floor of the house he overlaid with gold, within and without.**

Ver. 31.—**And for the entering of the oracle, he made doors** [which hung on golden hinges (ch. VII. 50] **of olive tree** [see on ver. 23)], **the lintel and side posts were a fifth part of the wall.** [The meaning of the Hebrew words has been much disputed. See Gesen. Thesaur, i. pp. 43—45. Gesen. himself interprets as A. V.: *crepido cum postibus erat quinta pars, i.e., quintam parietis partem occupabat.* The Rabbins: the "entablature with side posts and threshold formed a pentagon." But a pentagonal doorway is without example in Eastern architecture.

Thenius: "the strength (אַיל is generally taken as an architectural term = *crepido portae,* or entablature) of the posts was a fifth." Rawlinson: "the lintel was one-fifth of wall, and each door post one-fifth of its height;" in which case the doorway would of course be a square of four cubits. But perhaps the rendering of A. V. (with which Keil and Bähr also agree) is more natural. The meaning, consequently, would be that the entrance to the oracle, inclusive of the side posts which helped to form it, occupied one-fifth of the extent of the cedar partition. The entrance to the *house* (ver. 33) was one-fourth of the wall of the house.]

Ver. 32. — **The two doors also were** [Rather, perhaps, "And he made" is to be supplied from ver. 31, as Keil. Rawlinson remarks that such doors as these are characteristic of Assyrian gateways] **of olive tree: and he carved upon them carvings of cherubims and palm trees and open flowers, and overlaid them with gold, and spread** [וַיָּרֶד Hiph. of רָדַד] **gold** [Heb. *the gold*] **upon the cherubims and upon the palm trees** [The writer means, not that the carving alone was gilded—as Thenius thinks, who remarks on the effective contrast which the dark red cedar and the bright gold would furnish)—but that the gilding did not conceal the character of the carvings. It is clear from ver. 22 that "all the house" blazed with gold in every part. If the *floors*

were covered with gold, we may be sure both *walls* and *doors* would not be without their coating of the precious metal. Our author does not mention the curtain—it is clear that the doors would not dispense with the necessity for a vail—but the chronicler does (2 Chron. iii. 14). It was necessary in order to cover the ark (Exod. xl. 3, 21); hence it was sometimes called "the vail of the covering." But for this, when the doors were opened on the day of atonement, the priest in the holy place might have gazed into the oracle. See on ch. viii. 8. The doors opened outwardly (into the house). The vail was suspended within the oracle.]

Ver. 33.—**So also** [*i.e.,* similarly] **made he for the door** [or *entrance, doorway*] **of the temple posts of olive tree, a fourth** [Heb. *from a fourth*] **part of the wall.** It is uncertain whether we are to understand the "fourth part" of the height or of the breadth of the doorway, though the latter is probably meant. The height of the wall is variously estimated; generally at 30 (ver. 2), but by Rawlinson at 20 cubits. But the breadth is beyond dispute. It was 20 cubits. The doorway, consequently, would be five cubits wide. The effect of the preposition, "*from* a fourth," is probably this: The entrance with the side posts subtracted one-fourth from the space of the wall.

Ver. 34.—**And the two doors were** [As in ver. 32, the verb is to be supplied from the verse preceding. "And *he made* two doors, &c.] **of fir tree** [בְּרוֹשׁ see note on ch. v. 8]: **the two leaves** [lit. *ribs,* same word as in vers. 5, 8, 10] **of the one door were folding** [Heb. **rolling**], **and the two leaves** [קְלָעִים is probably a clerical error for צְלָעִים arising out of the עֵלַע in vers. 32, 35] **of the other** [Heb. *second*] **door were folding.** [It seems more natural to suppose that the leaves were formed by a vertical than by a horizontal division. Indeed, it is doubtful whether the word גָּלִיל would be applied to the latter arrangement. Keil objects to the former on the ground that the leaves would thus be only one cubit broad each, and the opening of one leaf, consequently, would be insufficient to admit of any person's passing through. But to this it may be replied (1) that the opening of *two* leaves would in any case form a sufficiently wide entrance, and (2) that it is not said that all the leaves were of uniform width. Besides, the other arrangement is without precedent in the public buildings of the East.]

Ver. 35.—**And he carved thereon cherubims and palm trees and open flowers** [The constant recurrence of the same forms is in itself a proof that they must have been significant], and covered them with gold fitted upon the carved work [Heb. *made straight upon the engraved work*. That is to say, the gold fitted closely to all the uneven and indented surface of the figures. Elsewhere, *laminae* were simply laid upon the level walls, &c.]

Ver. 36.—The description of the buildings concludes with a brief reference to the *enceinte* or court. And he built the inner court [The mention of an *inner* court, called in 2 Chron. iv. 9 the "court of the priests," presupposes, of course, the existence of an *outer* court. Our author does not mention this, but the chronicler does, under the name of "the great court," in Jer. xxxvi. 10, the former is called the "higher court," because it occupied a higher level] with three rows of hewed stone and a row of cedar beams. [These, it is thought, formed the enclosing *wall* of the court (the LXX. adds κυκλόθεν). The cedar beams were instead of copingstones. It has been supposed, however (J. D. Michaelis), that these three rows of stone, boarded with cedar, formed the *pavement* of the court. But the question at once suggests itself, Why pile three rows of stones one upon another merely to form a pavement, and why hew and shape them if they were to be concealed beneath a stratum of wood? It is a fair inference from 2 Chron. vii. 3, that the wall was low enough to permit men to look over it. Fergusson, on the contrary, argues that it must have been *twice* the height of the enclosure of the tabernacle, which would give us an elevation of ten cubits (Exod. xxvii. 18). It is worth suggesting, however, whether, the inner court being raised above the outer, which surrounded it, these stones may not have formed the retaining wall or sides of the platform. As the outer court had gates (2 Kings xi. 6; xii. 9; 2 Chron. iv. 9; xxiii. 5; xxiv. 8), it also must have had walls. From 2 Kings xxiii. 11; Jer. xxxv. 2; xxxvi. 10, we gather that there were various chambers in the forecourt. Such were certainly contemplated by David (1 Chron. xxviii. 12); but it is not recorded that Solomon built them. Nor have we any warrant, except the bare assertion of Josephus, for the belief that he built a colonnade or cloister on the east side, such as was

known to later ages by the name of "Solomon's Porch" (John x. 23; Acts iii. 11; v. 12). As to the dimensions of these spaces, we are left to conjecture. If, as in everything else, the dimensions of the tabernacle were doubled, then the court of the priests would measure 200 cubits from east to west, and 100 cubits from north to south. It should be stated, however, that in the temple of Ezekiel, the proportions of which, in the present instance, may well be historical, both courts are represented as perfect squares. Rawlinson inadvertently puts down the length (along the side of temple) at 100 cubits, and the breadth (ends of temple) at 200. The outer court would probably be twice as large as the inner, *i.e.*, 400 × 200 cubits. But all this is necessarily uncertain.]

Ver. 37.—In the fourth year was the foundation of the house of the Lord laid, in the month Zif [see on ver. 1].

Ver. 38.—And in the eleventh year, in the month Bul [בּוּל =rain. Hence Bul would be the month of rain (Gesen.) Keil understands it to signify produce (*proventus*), and sees in it the month of *fruits*. It extended from the November to the December full moon], which is the eighth month, was the house finished throughout all the parts thereof [Heb. דְּבָרָיו], and according to all the fashion of it [Heb. מִשְׁפָּטָיו]. So was he seven years in building it. [As Bul was the eighth month, and Zif the second, the house was precisely seven and a half years in building—a short period, if we consider the magnitude of the undertaking, but long enough, if we remember the enormous number of hands employed upon it, the preparations made by David, and the modest dimensions of the edifice (ver. 2). The commentators all cite Pliny's statement that all Asia was building the temple of Diana at Ephesus 200 years, but the cases are not at all parallel. We learn from 2 Chron. iii. 2, that it was on the *second* day of the month that the building was commenced. Bishop Wordsworth, who assigns seven years and *seven* months as the time occupied in this work, sees in this hebdomatic period an analogy to the seven days of the creation.]

HOMILETICS.

Vers. 2, 3, 20. — *Christianity built on the Foundations of Judaism.* The Jewish temple in its resemblance to the Gothic church is a not inapt illustration of the relations of Christianity to Judaism. The temple of Solomon was not only architecturally the exact reproduction on a larger scale, and in a

more permanent form, of the tabernacle of witness (see p. 98), it was also the
model and archetype of the sacred buildings of the Christian faith.   In appearance,
no doubt, it was somewhat different—the purposes for which the two edifices were
designed were different (p. 101), but the ground-plan and general arrangement
were the same (p. 99).   The porch, "temple of house," oracle, side chambers of
the one, correspond with the porch (or tower), nave, chancel, and side aisles of
the other.   Nor was this resemblance accidental.   The architects of earlier times—
times when men had not come to think that they most honoured Christianity by
going as far as possible away from Judaism, times when the first dispensation
was regarded as full of significance and guidance for the children of the second—
the architects of those days thought they would best serve the God of Jews
and Christians by adhering as closely as possible to the Divine " pattern which was
shewed in the mount," the pattern which had served for tabernacle and temple
alike.

Now this fact, that the *place* of Divine worship has been, in nearly all ages, built
after one model, may suggest the thought that the *principles* of Divine worship,
and indeed of religion, have been in all ages the same.   And for the good reason
that God and man, the worshipped and the worshipper, are in all ages the same.
If the successive generations of men who "went up to the temple to pray" went up
to an edifice *something* like ours, they also carried with them hearts, sins, sorrows,
needs, infirmities, *altogether* like ours.   The Gothic church, then, was modelled
after the Jewish temple.   Even so the Christian religion has been cast in the
mould of Judaism.   It is not a brand-new religion, utterly diverse from the dispensation which preceded it, but it is built on the old foundations.   Its proportions are
much statelier, its uses are much nobler, but still the Christian Church is the copy
of the Jewish, and Christianity is the child of Judaism.   There are some of our
cathedrals—York Minster, *e.g.*—which occupy the site, and parts of which follow
the outlines, of the old Saxon church of wood—another illustration of the relations
of our holy religion to the religion which it has replaced.   And that Christianity
was never designed to be destructive of Judaism, but was meant to be a development, an outgrowth and expansion of it, our Lord's words (Matt. v. 17) and His
apostle's (Rom. iii. 31 ; Col. ii. 17) clearly show.   The law, *i.e.*, was the outline of
which Christianity is the filling up and completion.   But observe : the filling up, if
it be true to its name, must keep within the lines of the sketch.

It is one of the tendencies of the age to throw over Judaism and its teaching (see,
e.g., "Scribner's Magazine," vol. xii. pp. 724 sqq., and the letters of Charles Dickens).
Men say they want " Christianity without Judaism. "   They speak of the latter as
a dead letter.   But surely it is an unworthy conception of the Supreme Wisdom
— the idea that a faith which was adapted to the men of one age has absolutely no
lessons or no guiding principles for the men of a later age, but must be cast aside
as wholly antiquated and effete.   A principle of *continuity* can be distinctly
traced operating in the kingdom of nature ; are we forbidden to believe that there
is any such law in the kingdom of grace ?   Let us now consider, then, in what
ways Christianity is built on the foundations of Judaism, and how the religion of
the New Testament follows the lines laid down in the Old.

I. The fundamental idea of Judaism was that of a VISIBLE CHURCH.   It was that
God had " taken a nation from the midst of another nation" (Deut. iv. 32—34) to
be a peculiar people to Himself, a "kingdom of priests, a holy nation" (Exod. xix.
5, 6).   His purposes of grace, *i.e.*, were to be manifested to the world through a
society.   Here, then, was a κλῆσις and an ἐκκλησία.   Precisely similar is the root
idea of our religion.   The Son of God came to found a Church (Matt. xvi. 18 ;
Ephes. ii. 20), to regenerate humanity through a brotherhood.   Behold the principle of continuity in this " great Church truth of God's word."   The very words
used of the Jewish people are transferred to the Christian Church (1 Peter
ii. 9 ; Rev. i. 6 ; v. 10).   The composition of the two societies was different (one
nation, all nations), the rites of admission were different (circumcision, baptism),
but the principle—a visible Church—was the same.   Every Jew was a priest.
Every Christian is the same.

II. The OFFICERS of the Jewish Church correspond with the officers of the Christian Church. "It is an apostolical tradition that what Aaron and his sons and the Levites were in the temple, that our bishops, priests, and deacons claim to be in the Church" (Jerome). No society can exist without at least (1) laws, and (2) officers. The Jewish Church had as its officers, high priest, priests, and Levites. The Christian Church has a great High Priest in the heavens (Heb. iv. 14), and its earthly officers are bishops, priests, and deacons. The analogy is not imperfect, for just as the high priest was of the order of the priests, so are bishops but superintending presbyters. The bishop is *primus presbyter;* the high priest was *summus sacerdos.* The Jewish Church had also its *prophets* (see Introduction, Sect. III., note), corresponding with the *preachers* of the Christian economy. A prophet need not be a priest; a preacher need not be a presbyter. Of course, the nature and functions of these officers of the two dispensations differ, as do the dispensations themselves, but the same outlines are preserved.

III. The SERVICES of the Christian Church are derived from the service of the Jewish synagogue. "Widely divergent as the two words and the things they represented afterwards became, the Ecclesia had its starting point in the Synagogue" (Plumptre). The earliest assemblies of Christians were composed of men who had worshipped in the synagogue (Acts xiii. 14; xiv. 1; xviii. 4, 26; xxii. 19. Cf. Luke iv. 16; John xviii. 20, &c.), and who, in default of directions to the contrary, naturally preserved under the new dispensation the form of worship to which they had been accustomed under the old. St. James, indeed (ch. ii. 1). speaks of the Christian assembly as a "synagogue." The use of fixed forms of prayer, the reading of the two lessons (Luke iv. 18; Acts xiii. 15, 27; xv. 21), and the cycle of lessons; the sermon or exposition (Acts xiii. 15; Luke iv. 21); the chanting of the Psalms of David; the very prayers for the departed which "have found a place in every early liturgy in the world" (Ellicott), all these have come to us from the synagogues of the Jews. The Catholic Church has not disregarded the principle of continuity. She has not thought fit to devise a liturgy of her own heart, or to disregard liturgical forms altogether. She has simply perpetuated, or adapted to its new and more blessed conditions, the form of service delivered unto her by the Jew.

IV. The PRINCIPLES of Christian worship are the principles of Jewish worship. It has been said that the true idea of *worship* as a *Divine service,* as the self-forgetting adoration of the ever-blessed God, was obscured, if not altogether lost, in the Church of England at least, during the seventeenth and eighteenth centuries. Men went to church—too often they go still—not for the service, but for the sermon; not for the glory of God, but for their own edification and instruction. It must not be supposed that it is here intended to depreciate edification. If men were perfect, the sermon might indeed be dispensed with. But so long as they are what they are, then those who have "any word of exhortation for the people" must "say on." But all the same, edification is not the *primary* reason for our assembling. The first Christians "came together to *break bread*" (Acts xx. 7), to "show the Lord's death" upon the Lord's day (Rev. i. 10). And God surely should ever come before man. Praise must take precedence either of prayer or preaching. The true idea of worship is the glory of God, not the profit of men. And if this idea *was* lost, or was obscured, it was because men ignored or despised the lessons and principles of Judaism. The worship of the temple, its psalms and sacrifices, its holocausts and hecatombs, all were designed for the glory and honour and worship of Jehovah—all were primarily to exalt and magnify the Incommunicable Name. And such should be the aim of all Christian worship. Our holy religion was never meant to dethrone the Deity, nor can Christians owe Him less, or less profound, adoration, than did Jews. Was *their* service solemn and stately? so should be ours. Did *they* never come before Him empty? neither should we. Was the altar, not the pulpit, the centre of their worship? the altar, not the pulpit, should be the centre of ours. The principles of Divine service know of no break. They are governed by the same law of continuity.

V. The SACRAMENTS of Christianity are founded upon the rites of Judaism.

Baptism (practised among the Jews before our Lord's time) takes the place of circumcision; the Lord's Supper of the Paschal Supper. Just as the rite of circumcision brought the Jewish child into the bond of the covenant, into the visible Church, so does baptism the Christian child; otherwise our children would be worse off than the children of the Hebrews. And as for the Lord's Supper, it was instituted in the very midst of the Passover (Luke xxii. 1, 7, 15—20), and was clearly designed to take its place. The rites of Judaism warrant our belief in a sacramental religion; they help to explain how it was that our Lord incorporated into His new and spiritual dispensation two outward and visible signs. The Law was full of these: the Gospel could hardly discard them altogether.

VI. The PRECEPTS and COMMANDMENTS of Judaism, again, "the law and the prophets," are not abolished, but fulfilled (Matt. v. 17; Rom. iii. 31) in Christianity. The Sermon on the Mount has given a new meaning to the covenant of Mount Sinai, even the ten commandments (Deut. iv. 13). Out of the law of the two tables has been developed the Christian law of love (Matt. xxii. 36—40; Luke x. 27; Rom. xiii. 8—10). The "new commandment" of Christ (John xiii. 34) is practically "the old commandment" which we had from the beginning (1 John ii. 7, &c.)

VII. And—to descend to minor matters—we might show how even the FESTIVALS of Christendom follow the lines of the Jewish feasts. True, Christianity has one blessed festival peculiar to itself—Christmastide, the feast of the Holy Incarnation— but the rest—Easter, Whitsuntide, Harvest Festival—correspond severally with the Jewish Passover, Pentecost, and Tabernacles. The *times* themselves are, perhaps, of no great moment—though the synchronism is remarkable—but the principles on which they are based, the principle, *e.g.*, of setting apart certain seasons for the commemoration of certain facts, or the acknowledgment of certain gifts, these are common to both dispensations. It is this principle which gave the Jew his sabbath: it is the same principle justifies, and indeed requires, the observance of the Lord's day. Christianity has not discarded the day of rest, though it observes the sabbath no longer. It has changed the day of rest into a day of worship, the seventh day into the first, the memorial of the creation into a memorial of the resurrection and redemption.

VIII. But it will be said, Surely Christianity is utterly unlike Judaism in one cardinal point, viz., it has no SACRIFICE. But is it so? Truly, we offer no longer either bullocks or goats. The Christian priest neither pours the blood nor burns the fat, but all the same he offers sacrifice (1 Peter ii. 5), the sacrifice of praise and thanksgiving (Heb. xiii. 15), the sacrifice of alms and oblations (Phil. iv. 18), the sacrifice of soul and body (Rom. xii. 1). Nor is that all. For observe: The Holy Supper in the Christian scheme, both as an offering, as a feast, and as a memorial, corresponds with the sacrifices of the law. For what, let us ask, was the meaning of all those sacrifices which the Jews "offered year by year continually"? They could not take away sin. They could not make the comers thereunto perfect. Why then were they offered? *One* reason was, that they might serve as memorials before God of the death of Christ. They were silent, but eloquent, reminders of Him who should put away sin by the sacrifice of Himself. Perhaps the Jew knew it not. Perhaps the high priest himself did not realize it, but *we* know that all those countless thousands of victims, offered year after year and century after century, were so many mute pleadings of the one priceless death. And as they spoke to the eternal Father of the Lamb who *should* die, precisely so do the bread and the wine of Christ's sacrament of love speak of the Lamb who *has* died. The fat and the blood were, the bread and the wine are, all ἀναμνήσεις (Num. x. 10; cf. Levit. xxiv. 7; Luke xxii. 19; 1 Cor. xi. 25; cf. Heb. x. 3). Our Lord Himself calls the wine "my blood of the new covenant" (τὸ αἷμά μου τῆς καινῆς διαθήκης), and we are surely justified, with many divines—John Wesley among them—in calling the Holy Eucharist "the Christian *sacrifice.*"

But sacrifice and sacrament have another point of contact. For some at least of the Jewish sacrifices, the peace offerings (see on ch. viii. 63—65) afforded a *feast* to the worshippers. In like manner, the sacramental species serve not only as a memorial of Christ's death (1 Cor. xi. 26), but they are also food to the faithful soul (1 Cor. x. 16, 17; Heb. xiii. 10; Matt. xxvi. 26; John vi. 54, 55). If, therefore, the Holy Communion is not a sacrifice, properly so called (inasmuch as there is no death), it has these marks of a sacrifice, that it is an oblation, a memorial, and a feast. And when we consider these remarkable analogies, we can hardly doubt that even the *sacrifices* of Judaism have their counterpart in the institutions of Christianity.

It was said by one of the Reformers that the man who can rightly distinguish between the Law and the Gospel should thank God and be assured that he is a true theologian. But theologians too often treat them as if they were antagonistic or irreconcilable, and one of the dangers to which the Reformed Churches are specially obnoxious is to forget the continuity of gospel and law: to forget that the Church is built on the foundation of the apostles *and prophets* (Ephes. ii. 20). If it is true that "*Vetus Testamentum in Novo patet*," it is also true "*Novum Testamentum in Vetere latet.*"

Ver. 19.—*The Ark of the Covenant of the Lord.* This temple of Solomon, so "exceeding magnifical," this "holy and beautiful house," "of fame and glory throughout all lands"—why was it built? what its primary purpose? It was above everything else a home for the ark (ch. viii. 1, 6), a place for the Divine Glory which hovered over it.

In this temple, unlike the shrines of Paganism, there was no statue, no similitude of a God. Here was no "image which fell down from Jupiter," no Baal or Asherah, no Apis or Osiris. We may imagine how this would impress the Phœnician workmen. We know how it impressed Pompeius and the Romans. There is deep significance in those words of the Roman historian: *Inania arcana, vacua sedes.* Nothing but the ark. And this ark, what was it? It was a coffer, a chest. It was nothing in itself; but it was meant to contain something. It was the casket of a rare jewel. "There was nothing in the ark, save the *two tables of stone*," &c. (ch. viii. 9). It was the "ark *of the testimony.*" So that the temple was properly and primarily the shrine and depository of the tables of the law graven with the "ten words," "the words of the covenant" (Deut. iv. 13).

Now we have just seen that the temple was the archetype of the Church: we have seen, too, that everything in Judaism has its analogue in Christianity. What, then, let us ask, was the significance of the ark? To what does it correspond in the new dispensation?

In the *Church,* to nothing. The "words of the covenant" are no longer kept in the dark. No; we now inscribe them on our chancel walls. In the "sanctuary" of the Gothic church the ten commandments are "writ large" for men to see.

But if Judaism was really the outline of Christianity, then there must be something in Christianity answering to that ark which was the core and centre of the Mosaic system. Certainly. But it is to be found, not in "temples made with hands," but in those other "temples" of the Christian faith, the bodies of believers, the temples of the Holy Ghost (1 Cor. iii. 16; vi. 19). The ark was the soul of Judaism. It may fittingly represent the souls which Christ has redeemed. Temple, ark, tables of the law—these severally correspond to the "body, soul, spirit" of the Christian man. Within the temple was the ark; within the ark the tables. Within the σῶμα is the ψυχή; within the ψυχή the πνεῦμα.

Nor is this so fanciful as it seems. For are not our bodies the "*temples* of the Holy Ghost"? And are not our hearts—*i.e.*, our inmost being, our spiritual part (1 Peter iii. 4)—the *fleshy tables* on which He writes His law? Yes, in the "new covenant" God writes His law in the heart, and puts it in the inward parts (see Jer. xxxi. 33; cf. Ezek. xi. 19, 20; 2 Cor. iii. 3). In the face of these scriptures, who can deny that the ark and its tables have their analogues in the New Testament?

Such, then, being the symbolism and significance of temple, ark, and tables of law, what are their lessons? Among others these:

1. *That God dwells within us.* No longer in temples made with hands, but "with him that is of a contrite and humble spirit" (Isa. lvii. 15). Did the She-

chinah brood over the mercy seat? Not less truly does God's Spirit dwell (Rom. viii. 9) and witness (ver. 16) with our spirit. Men say the Shechinah has left the world. On the contrary, It has enshrined Itself in the soul. *"Christ in you"* (Col. i. 27); God dwelling *in us* (1 John iv, 12); this is the last best gospel of our religion. The Old Testament, Neander says, tells of a God who is *for* man. In the Gospels we hear of Emmanuel, God *with* man. But the Epistles speak to us of God *in* man.

2. *That God writes His law upon us.* We have seen that in the Church there is neither ark nor tables of stone. It is because there is no need of either. This is the age of that "new covenant" of which the prophet spoke, when the finger of God should write the law upon the spirit, and when the *Bath Kol* should speak within. The laws of our country are so voluminous that no man can hope to know or to remember them, and their "glorious uncertainty" is proverbial. But God's law is but one (Rom. xiii. 9, 10; Heb. viii. 10; x. 16); and that sweet and blessed statute the Spirit graves within us. Now observe—

3. *The ark, led by God, conducted Israel to victory and rest.* In the journeyings of Israel the ark went before them (Num. x. 33). At the Jordan it opened a way for them (Josh. iii. 14—17). Before Jericho it led them on to victory (Josh. vi. 9—11). Even so the soul, guided and taught of God, passes safely through its pilgrimage, conquers its foes, and gains its heavenly rest. Let us yield ourselves to be "led by the Spirit of God" (Rom. viii. 14).

4. *The ark, led by man, conducted Israel to disaster and defeat.* When the Israelites, instead of following the ark, would *lead* it (1 Sam. iv. 3), it landed them in a "very great slaughter." It proved to be no *fetish*, as they had hoped; it only led them to a shameful death. "It is one thing to want to have truth on our side; another to want to be on the side of truth" (Whately). It is of no avail to have the commandments of God, unless we keep them; to know His will, unless we do it. And if we lean to our own understandings, the soul will make shipwreck. Reason, it is true, is "the *candle* of the Lord;" but revelation is the "*lamp* to our feet and the light to our path" (Psa. cxix. 105; cf. Prov. iii. 5, 6).

5. *The ark, the pride of Israel, on two occasions became its plague.* The men of Bethshemesh looked into it, and died. Uzzah put forth his hand to steady it, and was smitten for his error (2 Sam. vi. 7). So the ark teaches the much-needed lesson of reverence—reverence for God and the things of God. It also suggests that dishonour done to God, or disregard of His law, has a sure retribution. If we stifle our convictions or quench the Spirit's light, the law written within may hereafter become the "instrument to scourge us."

6. *In the second temple there was no ark.* A stone is said to have taken its place. The venerable relic of the wilderness life, the sacred chest, and its still more sacred contents, both perished in the sack of Jerusalem (2 Kings xxv. 9 sqq.) May we not see here a lesson against impenitence? Over how many souls may "Ichabod" be written? The ark of God is taken! The soul is led captive of the devil. The heart of flesh, the "fleshy tables" on which the Spirit loves to write, has given place to a heart of stone—a heart as cold, as hard, as senseless, as void of all grace and blessing as this stone which stood in the oracle in the room of the ark of the covenant of the Lord.

HOMILIES BY VARIOUS AUTHORS.

Ver. 1.—*The Purposes of the Temple.* The three chapters thus introduced describe the erection and dedication of Solomon's temple. Magnificent as the building was, architecturally and artistically, it deserves more consideration as that which was the divinely appointed centre of true worship. Its significance to Christians can hardly be overrated. This the Epistle to the Hebrews clearly shows. While it stood it was for all nations a witness for Jehovah; and now that in substance it has passed away, the spiritual truths it embodied are a heritage for us. Essentially it was one with the tabernacle, the erection and ritual of which were directly revealed by God on Sinai. Neither in principle nor even in minute detail were the directions of Jehovah about its construction to be disobeyed. From the ark of the covenant down to the hooks for the curtains the command ran, "See that thou make *all* things according to the pattern showed thee in the mount." There are far-reaching issues ever flowing from the smallest details of Divine law. Great meanings are wrapped by God in trifling things. (Give examples of this.) Solomon was right in superseding the tabernacle by the temple. The tent was suitable for the wandering life of an unformed nation, but the stately and stable temple for an organized people whose pilgrimage had ended. God's utterances both to David and Solomon, and the presence of the Shechinah on the day of consecration, prove that the erection of the temple was according to the will of God. The temple had meanings which no other building subsequently erected could have. It was "a shadow of good things to come." It symbolized much that was revealed in the person of Christ (Heb. ix. 11, &c.), and much that is now existing, not on earth, but in heaven (Heb. ix. 24, &c.) But, though its symbolism is a thing of the past, some of its purposes and uses are things of the present, known in the places set apart by Christian men for the worship of God. To some of those we now refer.

I. THE TEMPLE WAS A PLACE OF SACRIFICE (2 Chron. vii. 12). The sin-offering typified the atonement made by the Lamb of God, who once was offered for the sins of the world. This is the fact made known by the ministry of the Word and represented by the broken bread and outpoured wine of the Eucharistic feast. No time and no place can be more suitable than the sanctuary for the acknowledgment of sin, and the expression of faith. There each Christian sings—

> "My faith would lay her hand
> On that dear head of Thine."

II. THE TEMPLE WAS A PLACE FOR PRAYER AND PRAISE. Solomon used it thus (ch. viii.) Incense typified it. In Isaiah lvi. 7 we read, "My house shall be called a house of prayer, for all people." The Lord Jesus referred to this when the temple was used for other purposes (Matt. xxi. 13). Describe the *praise* of the temple. Many there understood the words, "Praise ye the Lord; for it is good to sing praises unto our God; for it is pleasant, and praise is comely." Show the advantages of *united* praise, the promises given to *combination* in prayer, *e.g.*, sympathies enlarged, weak faith invigorated by contact with stronger faith, &c.

III. THE TEMPLE WAS A PLACE FOR THE CONSECRATION OF PERSONS AND THINGS. There priests were set apart; there sometimes prophets were called (Isa. vi.); there dedicated things were laid before the Lord (2 Chron. v. 1). Show how in modern days this is still true of the assembly of God's people. Men are there roused to a sense of responsibility, and there consecrate themselves to the service of God. Resolutions and vows are made there which carry with them the impress of Divine approval. The cares of life, its purposes, its companionships are there made to appear in their Godward aspect. Through the worship of the sanctuary heavenly light falls on daily toil, and men learn to call nothing that God has cleansed common or unclean.

IV. THE TEMPLE WAS A PLACE FOR REMEMBERING THE LAW OF THE LORD. The temple was incomplete until the ark of the covenant was brought in; and "there was nothing in the ark save the two tables of stone which Moses put there at Horeb, when the Lord made a covenant with the children of Israel" (1 Kings viii. 9). Show the importance of organized Christian worship as a perpetual witness for the law of God. In the busy week there are temptations to forget it; to put expediency in the place of righteousness, &c. The whole tone of English society is raised by the faithful exhibition of God's requirements each sabbath day.

V. THE TEMPLE WAS A PLACE FOR THE UNION OF THE PEOPLE. The Psalms of the Ascents (Songs of Degrees) show this. The people overlooked their social distinctions and the tribes ignored their tribal jealousies when they ascended the sacred hill to unite as a nation in the worship of the one true God. Jeroboam was shrewd enough to see that it would be impossible for two separate kingdoms to exist while all the people met in the one temple. Hence the calves at Bethel and Dan, and hence in our Lord's day the temple on Gerizim. Show how in the Christian Church the rich and the poor meet together, and how essential Christian principle is to fuse together the various classes of society. There are many disintegrating forces at work—the capitalists and the working classes, for example, are seriously divided. Common meeting-ground cannot be found in the home, but in the Church. The recognition of the one Fatherhood precedes the realization of the one brotherhood. Christians are, unhappily, divided amongst themselves. Sectarianism has increased the division of society. Relief is to be found not in form, but in spirit; not in union, but in unity. As we worship together and work together, the oneness of which we dream may become a reality.

VI. THE TEMPLE WAS A PLACE FOR THE REVELATION OF GOD (see vers. 10, 11; 1 Chron. v. 13; vii. 2). His presence is not confined to any temple made with hands ; but wherever His people meet, there He reveals Himself as he does not do unto the world. "Where two or three are gathered together in My name there am I in the midst of them." It was when the disciples were assembled with one accord for prayer that the Holy Spirit came. So may our assemblies be blessed ; and sinners will find pardon, the careworn will find rest, the doubters will find faith, the weakly will find strength, and the despondent will find hope in the house of the Lord our God.—A. R.

Ver. 7.—*Building in silence.* This was due partly to the reverential feelings of those engaged in so holy a work. "The Lord is in his holy temple, let all the earth keep *silence* before him." If we are upbuilding Christian character in ourselves, or in our children ; if we are helping to rear the spiritual temple of God, such reverence, as opposed to thoughtlessness, flippancy, &c., should characterize us. The silence of the building was not only the outcome of devout feeling, but it was (like the temple itself) symbolical of spiritual truth; as we propose to show. A noble temple is being reared (1 Cor. iii. 16, 17; Eph. ii. 22; 1 Peter ii. 5). This temple is imperishable and unassailable ; that of Solomon's was pillaged (1 Kings xiv. 25; 2 Kings xii. 17), polluted by the unworthy (2 Kings xxi. 4—7), burnt by the enemy (2 Kings xxv. 9). The erection described in our text teaches us something of the work which is still carried on by the builders of the true temple.

I. THE BUILDERS OF GOD'S HOUSE ARE OFTEN DOING A SECRET WORK. Picture the workmen in the quarries, the moulders in the clay, the artist with his graving tool, &c. Their names were unknown, they were unrecognized by the multitudes who would worship in the temple they were helping to build. Illustrate from this the work of mothers influencing their children; of visitors to haunts of sin and sorrow, whose ministry of love is not known to their nearest friends; of literary men in obscure rooms who are influencing the destinies of a people, &c. Draw encouragement from this, *e.g.*, that we do not see all the good that is going on in England and abroad, in the Churches and outside them. So Elijah was cheered by the revelation that there were seven thousand in Israel who had not bowed the knee to Baal, when he thought he alone was left to witness for Jehovah. Refer to the Lord's teaching about the secret progress of His kingdom; the leaven hid in three measures of meal ; the seed cast into the earth and left buried by the man who sleeps and rises, unconscious that it is springing and growing up he knows not how.

II. THE BUILDERS OF GOD'S HOUSE DO VARIED WORK. Enumerate some of the different kinds of labour and of skill which were required for the temple. Show that the work varied in dignity, in arduousness, in remunerativeness, &c. None of it, however, was without its value or final effect. Describe the multitudinous forms of Christian activity, and the advantages of such diversity. It demands self-abnegation, it calls forth all graces and gifts, it makes one Christian dependent on another, and so evokes sympathy and gives place for co-operation, &c. Let none despise his own work, nor envy another his.

III. THE BUILDERS OF GOD'S HOUSE DO THEIR WORK WITH CAREFUL COMPLETE-

NESS. How exact the measurements, how perfect the finish of work, which only required to be brought together in order to make a complete whole. Piece joined piece in the woodwork, and every separate casting found its appropriate niche. Nothing but painstaking accuracy could have insured such a result. Yet probably no workman knew the whole design; he was only intent on finishing his own appointed work. Observe the carefulness of God in little things, whether in creation or in moral law. Small infringements of Divine ordinances bring lamentable results. Illustrate from the consequences of disobedience to natural law in pain, disease, &c. Argue from this to the higher in mental and moral spheres. Carelessness is not tolerated. How much less in concerns of the soul. Negligence is sin. "How shall we escape if we *neglect* so great salvation?" There must be care in laying the foundations of heavenly hopes (see Matt. vii. 24—27). Care also is required in doing work for our Lord. "But let every man take heed how he buildeth thereupon" (1 Cor. iii. 10—15).

IV. THE BUILDERS OF GOD'S HOUSE ARE MORE ANXIOUS FOR THOROUGHNESS THAN FOR NOISE. No sound of hammer or axe was heard to call the attention of passers by to the noble work going on; but all the inhabitants of the kingdom saw the effects of the quiet labour. Quietude is hard to obtain in the activities of the present day, yet God's servants must have it. Christ saw His disciples were excited, and said, "Come ye yourselves apart into the desert and rest awhile." Moses needed the solitude of Midian and of Sinai; Elijah the loneliness of Horeb, &c. Great souls are fashioned in silence. Our lonely times are our growing times. Exemplify by reference to a man laid aside by illness, to a mother or wife who is for a time absorbed in ministry to some invalid. The busy workers need quiet most. They wait on the Lord, and so renew their strength. Some of the best work done for Christ is silent. It is not proclaimed by large organization, or applauding crowds, but lies in the whispered counsel, the interceding prayer, &c.

V. THE BUILDERS OF GOD'S HOUSE WILL SEE THEIR LABOUR ISSUE IN THE DIVINE IDEAL. The work was widely distributed, secretly done, &c., but all was tending to an appointed end—the temple. The building existed in the mind of the master builder before it had material existence. So with God's work. A Divine purpose is controlling all, appointing all; and out of what seems confusion and contradiction He will bring forth "the new heaven and the new earth." Faithfully doing each one what lies to his hand, we shall all find that what we have done has its place and results; that our "labour is not in vain in the Lord." Forgotten and obscure workers will have their reward from Him who noticed the widow's mite, and gratefully accepted Mary's offering. We shall do more than we expect, if we do what we can.

VI. THE BUILDERS OF GOD'S HOUSE FIND THEIR REWARD IN THE GLORY OF THEIR GOD. Describe the temple—complete at last—resounding with songs of praise, crowded with worshippers, overwhelmed by the Divine presence—and use it as a type of the temple not made with hands, where the redeemed serve God day and night. The wish of God's noblest servant is that God may be glorified whether by life or by death.

Apply the idea of silent working to what God is doing in each Christian heart by the discipline of life and the influence of the Holy Spirit. It is felt within, but it is not known or heard without.—A. R.

Ver. 23.—*The Mystery of the Cherubim.* That the cherubim were symbolic no one denies. They are so often mentioned in Scripture that their meaning has been frequently discussed. Enumerate some of the opinions held. The view we accept is that *they were symbolic representations of redeemed humanity.* They were intended to inspire men with hope of redemption, from the day when the Lord placed them at the east of the garden of Eden, till the vision of John (Rev. xxi.) is fulfilled in the "new heavens and new earth," wherein the cherubim are no longer seen, having vanished before the reality they symbolically represented. In the cherubim we are reminded of the following—

I. THE PERFECTING OF HUMANITY. Some obscurity lingers about the forms of these beings. They are introduced in Genesis without a word of description ; and in Exodus (xxv. and xxxvii.) little is said beyond this, that they had "wings and faces." Turning to their visionary appearances—to Ezekiel and to John—there is variety in form. But whatever latitude there may be in detail, the leading form was always that of a *man*—*e.g.*, Ezekiel says (ch. i. 5), "they had the likeness of a man." With this, other creature forms were combined, viz., the lion, the ox, and eagle. These were selected for special reasons. They belonged to the noblest king-dom, that of animal life, as distinguished from that which was vegetable or mineral. They were amongst the highest after man in the nature of their life ; very different, for example, from sea-anemones, &c. They had loftier attributes than those of other creatures ; greater powers or wider usefulness. Hence, combined with the image of man to form the cherubim, they suggested the addition to him of the powers they specially represented. The lion, especially to the Hebrews, was a type of kingly *majesty* and glorious *strength*. Give quotations from Scripture. The eagle, with its keen vision and swift flight, was a type of *rapidity* of thought and movement (Deut. xxviii. 49 ; Job ix. 26 ; Prov. xxiii. 5). The ox, used in plough-ing, harrowing, carrying home the sheaves, and treading out the corn, represented patient and *productive activity*. In the cherubim all these were grafted on man—an ideal combination, to show that, though man was the highest creature of God (he alone having a moral and a rational nature), he could be, and would be, ennobled by having hereafter the powers bestowed, of which in creature life these animals were representatives. Show the Scripture evidence for expecting in heaven the faculties for knowing, for serving, for enjoying, which we have not here.

II. THE FULNESS OF LIFE. In Ezekiel and Revelation the cherubim are fre-quently spoken of as "the living ones" (*animantia, ζωα*). This expression is obscured in our translation by the unhappy rendering "beasts" (Rev. iv. 6), &c. The expression denotes *life* in its highest and most active form. In harmony with this, Ezekiel speaks of their "running and returning." John says, "they rest not day nor night." Though the cherubim in the temple and tabernacle were of necessity stationary, the same idea was there expressed by the outspread wings. The cherubim pointed on to the plenitude of life, Divine and spiritual, over which weari-ness should have no power, and towards which death would never approach. "I give unto them *eternal* life," &c. "I am come that they might have life, and that they might have it more abundantly," &c.

III. THE DWELLING WITH GOD. The cherubim were always associated with the Divine Presence. After man was driven from Eden, the cherubim was placed there to occupy the place he had forfeited ; where life was full, and where holiness was a necessity. When the tabernacle was constructed, all the inner curtains were inwoven with cherubic figures, and images of cherubim appeared on the sacred ark, which was the throne of Jehovah. This was repeated in the temple, as the passage before us shows ; for the magnificent cherubim, each ten cubits high, were stationed in the "oracle," the place where the Shechinah proclaimed God's presence. We must add, therefore, to the ideas we have dwelt on—this thought, that the life represented was life essentially connected with *God* Himself. Not only will the life of the future be full, but it will be holy. Holiness will be its essence. "The pure in heart shall see God." "Without holiness no man shall see the Lord." "Neither shall there enter into it anything that defileth," &c.

IV. THE BLISS OF THE FUTURE. A careful reading of Genesis iii. 24 shows that the "sword" and the "cherubim" were not only distinct, but had different functions. *The sword* "kept" the way to the tree of life, so that it was more accessible to fallen man. It was a symbol of repulsion and alarm. The cherubim "kept" the garden in a different sense. They did not defend it against man, but occupied it for man, and therefore gave to those who were shut out the hope of that which the promise of Jehovah had already announced. The presence of the cherubim said to fallen man : "This region of life is not destroyed, it is not given over to other creatures, but it is occupied and kept provisionally for you by a being in whom your nature predominates ; and hereafter, you yourself changed, enriched with new powers, restored by redemptive love to holiness, shall share Paradise regained." The means of realizing this became more clear as the ages rolled by. The hope that ideal humanity would inherit bliss did not die out, but the method of its fulfilment was unfolded in the Mosaic institutions. Not only did the cherubim in the oracle witness, as the cherubim in Eden had done, but once a year the high priest, as the representative of the people, went in, and stood with the cherubim in the presence of Jehovah. He entered not "without blood," but after atonement had been made for the sins of the people. Apply this to the truth revealed in the Epistle to the Hebrews. Show how Christ, who has atoned for the world's sin, has entered as our High Priest into the holiest of all, and how He has opened the kingdom of heaven to all believers. No wonder that in the Revelation "the Lamb that was slain" is depicted as being the object of heaven's praise; the link between man's guilt and God's mercy.

[For justification of this use of the cherubim, see Fairbairn's "Typology of Scripture."]—A. R.

Ver. 2.—The temple is described as " *the house which King Solomon built for the Lord.*" This idea of consecration ran through the whole plan of the building. Without having recourse to a minute and fanciful symbolism, we see clearly that everything is so disposed as to convey the idea of the holiness of God. IN THE CENTRE IS THE ALTAR OF SACRIFICE. The holy of holies, hidden from gaze by its impenetrable veil, strikes with awe the man of unclean heart and lips, who hears the seraphim cry from beneath their shadowing wings, "Holy, holy, holy, Lord God Almighty!" (Isa. vi. 3.) The temple of holiness is not the temple of nature of colossal proportions, as in the East, nor is it the temple of æsthetic beauty, as in Greece. It is the dwelling place of Him who is invisible, and of purer eyes than to behold evil (Hab. i. 13.) Hence its peculiar character. It answers thus to the true condition of religious art, which never sacrifices the idea and sense of the Divine to mere form, but makes the form instinct with the Divine idea. Let us freely recognize the claims of religious art. The extreme Puritanism which thinks it honours God by a contemptuous disregard of the æsthetic, is scarcely less mistaken than the idolatrous materialism which makes beauty of form the primary consideration. It was not for nothing that God made the earth so fair, the sky so glorious; and it was under Divine inspiration that the temple of Jerusalem was reared in such magnificence and majesty as to strike all beholders. Only let us never forget to seek the Divine idea beneath the beauty of the form. When we admire merely the beautiful, whether in a temple, as did the disciples, or in the great world of nature, the warning words of Christ fall upon upon our ear: "As for these things which ye behold, the days will come in the which there shall not be left one stone upon another" (Luke xxi. 6). "*Tous les cieux et leur splendeur ne valent pas le soupir d'un seul cœur.*" Love is the crowning beauty. It is like the precious vase of ointment which Mary of Bethany broke over the feet of Christ. Beauty is the fit associate of worship, so long as it is kept subordinate, and does not distract our minds from the higher spiritual realities of which it is but symbolic. Let us seek in the temple of nature the high and holy God, of whom it is said, that "the invisible things of Him are clearly seen from the creation of the world, being understood by the things that are made" (Rom. i. 19). Let us recognize His presence beneath the arches of the mediæval cathedral, among the memorials of a worship which we ourselves have left behind. Let us seek Him in the great monuments of Christian art, whether reared by poet, musician, painter, or sculptor. Let it be our aim to glorify Him in the forms of our worship, while we sedulously guard against the worship of the form, which is sheer idolatry. Such are the principles of Christian æsthetics, which are one branch of Christian morals. "The beautiful is the glory of the true," says Plato. When one corner of the veil which hides heaven from us is lifted, the Divine life shines forth in all its radiance of purity and beauty.—E. de P.

Vers. 37, 38.— *The Glorious House of the Lord.* In comparison with other sacred shrines of antiquity the temple of Solomon was small in its dimensions and brief in the time of its building. Nor will the mere fact of its material splendour account for the extraordinary interest with which it has ever been regarded — an interest in which Jew, Mohammedan, and Christian alike participate. The place it occupied, the part it performed in the religious history of the world, will alone account for this. If it is necessary to suppose any pre-existing model as suggesting the plan of its structure, it is to Assyria and not to Egypt, as some have thought, that we should look for such a type. But however this may be, it has a deep Divine meaning which raises it above comparison with any other temple that the hand of man has ever reared. Let us look on it now as the ancient symbol of the Church of the living God, that fellowship of new-born souls of whom St. Peter says, "Ye also as living stones are built up a spiritual house," &c. (1 Peter ii. 5). Note certain points of special interest in this analogy—those features of the temple which are suggestive of similar features in the spiritual fabric of the redeemed Church.

I. THE FIRMNESS OF ITS FOUNDATION. The threshing-floor of Araunah, the site of the temple, was part of the plateau on the top of Mount Moriah (2 Chron. iii. 1). Solomon, as we are told by Josephus, in order to enlarge the area, built massive walls on the sloping sides of the mountain, filling in the spaces with earth; and the foundations of these walls were composed of huge stones bedded and, as it were, mortised in the solid rock. How forcibly are we reminded of the word of Christ to Peter, "Upon this rock will I build my Church, and the gates of hell shall not prevail against it" (Matt. xvi. 18). Whatever the bearing of this word on the disciple himself may be, it is certain that it cannot refer to him apart from the grand confession he has just made—"Thou art the Christ, the son of the living God." Peter may be one of the great foundation stones, but Christ Himself is the solid, primary, unhewn Rock on which the fabric rests. Not so much any truth about Him, but *the personal Christ* in the grandeur of His being, the integrity of His righteousness, the strength and fidelity of his wondrous love, is the Church's firm foundation.

II. THE SILENT PROCESS OF ITS STRUCTURE. "There was neither hammer, nor axe, nor any tool of iron heard in the house while it was in building (ver. 7). This was probably in obedience to the prohibition recorded in Exodus xx. 26 and Deuteronomy xxvii. 5. It expressed the king's sense of the sanctity of the work. The tranquillity of the scene must not be broken by the clang of inharmonious sounds. "Like some tall palm, the noiseless fabric grew." The fact is suggestive. The building up of the Church of God is a silent, hidden process. Outward visible agencies must be employed, but the real constructive forces are out of sight. Truth works secretly and silently in the souls of men. "The kingdom of God cometh not with observation." Noise and show are out of harmony with the sanctity of it. Clamour and violence only hinder the work. Let us not mistake a restless, busy, fussy zeal for the externalities of Church life for true spiritual service. This is often in inverse ratio to the amount of real edification. The best machinery works with least friction and noise. The quiet, thoughtful workers, who move on steadily by the inspiration of their holy purpose, without much public recognition, may after all be the most efficient builders of the temple of God.

III. THE VARIETY OF THE AGENCIES BY WHICH THE WORK WAS DONE. Foreign power was enlisted in the service—Hiram and his artificers. Cedars from Lebanon, gold and silver and precious stones from Ophir and Parvaim, brass "without weight" from the foundries of Succoth and Zarethan—all were consecrated to it. So also with the spiritual fabric. The resources of the world are at the command of Him who rears it. "All things serve His might." All beings, with all their faculties, are at His disposal. All streams of human interest, and thought, and speech, and activity may be made tributary to the great river of His purpose. Our faith rests in the assurance that it is so—that just as our physical life is nourished by all sorts of ministries, near and remote, so the kingdom of truth and righteousness in the world is being built up by a vast variety of agencies which it is beyond our power to trace. All human affairs are but as the scaffolding within which the structure of God's great house is slowly rising to its completion. To this structure it is that the prophetic word, in its deepest meaning, may be applied, "The sons of strangers shall build up thy walls" (Isa. lx. 10). And in its final consummation shall be fulfilled the apocalyptic picture, "The kings of the earth do bring their glory and honour into it." (Rev. xxi. 22).

IV. THE MINGLED STRENGTH AND BEAUTY OF THE FABRIC. The blocks of stone were lined with cedar planks, and the cedar overlaid with plates of gold; the walls covered with carved "cherubims and palm trees and open flowers;" the brazen pillars crowned with "lily-work." The building was not of large dimensions, but wonderful for its combination of solidity and adornment, partaking of the firmness of the rocky mount on which it stood, glittering in the sunlight, the crowning glory of the royal city. How much more truly may we say of the spiritual temple, "Strength and beauty are in His sanctuary." There is no strength like that of truth and righteousness; no beauty like that of holy character :— strength drawn from Christ, the living Foundation, the reflected beauty of that purer heaven which is the eternal home of God.

V. THE ORDERLY ARRANGEMENT OF ITS PARTS AND APPURTENANCES. The temple was framed apparently after the model of the tabernacle, but with doubled dimensions and more enduring materials, and *that* was "after the pattern shown to Moses in the mount"—all regulated with regard to the due administration of the service of God. Courts, chambers, galleries, altars, lavers, utensils—all consecrated to some sacred use, or meant to enshrine some high symbolic meaning. The gathering up of a complex variety of parts in one grand structural unity. Such is the Church—an aggregate of various but harmonious and mutually helpful parts. "There are diversities of gifts and administrations and operations, but the same Spirit" (1 Cor. xii. 4). "All the building fitly framed together," &c. (Ephes. ii. 13). "The whole body fitly joined together and compacted by that which every joint supplieth," &c. (Ephes. iv. 16). It would seem necessary that the social religious life should assume some visible organized form; and though there may be no such form or forms ecclesiastical that can claim to have the stamp of distinct Divine approval, yet all are Divine so far as they minister to the general edification and preserve "the unity of the spirit in the bond of peace." They each and all have their place in the Divine order, if they help to fulfil the holy uses, and to heighten the glory of the great temple of the Lord.

VI. ITS SUBLIME DISTINCTION AS THE HABITATION OF GOD (see vers. 12, 13, &c.) This was but the repetition of a more ancient promise (Exod. xxv. 8 ; xxix. 45). And what are all these promises, with all the marvellous manifestations that verified them, but typical foreshadowings of the richer grace by virtue of which the Church becomes "the habitation of God through the Spirit"? "The Most High dwells not in temples made with hands;" His dwelling-place is the fellowship of redeemed souls.—W.

EXPOSITION.

CHAPTER VII. 1—51.

SOLOMON'S PALACES AND THE PREPARATION OF THE TEMPLE VESSELS.—The first twelve verses of this chapter constitute a break in the long account of the Temple, its furniture and its consecration. The historian having described the Temple buildings, before he passes on to speak of their contents, pauses for a moment to record a few particulars as to the building of the suite of palaces which next occupied Solomon's attention. The LXX., possibly following an older arrangement, but more probably (see next note) adopting an apparently more logical and methodical order, relegates this section to the end of the chapter.

Ver. 1.—**But Solomon was building his own house thirteen years** [There is no contrast implied between the time spent upon the temple and that occupied in the building of the palace, as the word "but" seems to suggest. The close connexion which exists in the original is interrupted by the division of chapters. In ch. vi. 38 we read, "So was he seven years in building it." Ch. vii. 1 then proceeds, "And he was building his own house thirteen years." The much longer period occupied in the erection of the royal palace is easily accounted for. In the first place, the buildings were much larger, and the undertaking altogether was a much more extensive one (ver. 2). Then, though seven years only were consumed in the actual building of the temple, yet preparations for the work had been made, both by David and Solomon, for a long time beforehand. Lastly, a special force of labourers would appear to have been employed on the temple, while it is probable that they wrought at the palaces in greatly diminished numbers. So that the longer period spent over his own house does not argue selfishness or worldliness on Solomon's part. On the contrary, it speaks well for his piety that he built the temple first and urged on that sacred work with so much vigour. The thirteen years date from the completion of the seven years of ch. vi. 38. That is to say, the building of the temple and palace together occupied twenty years, as is expressly stated in ch. ix. 10. It is therefore one of Stanley's reckless statements that the palace "was commenced at the same time as the temple, but not finished till eight years afterwards"], **and he finished all his house.** [By Solomon's "house" we are not to understand his private palace, or residence proper, alone (see ver. 8), but a range of palaces, more or less connected, including the "house of the forest of Lebanon" (ver 2), "the porch of pillars" (ver. 6), the throne-room or judgment hall (ver. 7), his own house and the house of Pharaoh's daughter (ver. 8). That all these are comprehended under the term "house" is evident from ch. ix. 1, 10, 15; x. 12, where Solomon's buildings are always spoken of as *two*, viz., "the house of the Lord " and the "king's house."

The situation of this string of palaces is by no means certain. Josephus says it stood over against (or opposite) the temple, which is highly probable; but this still leaves the question of site open, for the palace would be justly described as ἀντικρὺς ἔχων ναὸν, whether it stood west or south of the sanctuary. Ewald places it on the opposite ridge of Ophel, *i.e.*, on the south prolongation of the temple mount; while Fergusson, Bähr, &c., locate it on the north-east side of Zion, on the opposite side of the Tyropœan valley, and overlooking it and the whole city of David. Recent explorations seem to favour Ewald's view. See "Recovery of Jerusalem," pp. 319 sqq., and "Our Work in Palestine," p. 159 sqq. When we remember that the very site of *Zion* is disputed, it will not surprise the reader that questions of this kind should be involved in uncer-

tainty. And when it is further considered that the accumulated *débris* of Jerusalem at one point reaches a depth of 120 feet, it will be readily understood what ᴖbstacles stand in the way of their settlement.]

Ver. 2.—**He built also** [Heb. *and he built.* The A. V. rendering almost contradicts the view just advanced, viz., that the house of the forest of Lebanon was *part* of "all the house " (ver. 1)] **the house of the forest of Lebanon** [so called, not because it was a summer residence in Lebanon, as some have supposed, nor yet merely because it was built of Lebanon cedar, but because it displayed a perfect *thicket* or *forest* (יַעַר) of cedar pillars]; **the length thereof was one hundred cubits** [the temple proper was 60], **and the breadth thereof fifty cubits** [The temple was but 20. It does not follow that this space of 100 × 50 cubits was all roofed in, for it would seem as if the house was built round a courtyard. Rawlinson remarks that a roof of 75 feet is " much greater than is ever found in Assyria." But it is by no means certain that there *was* any such roof here], **and the height thereof thirty cubits** [the same as the temple], **upon four rows of cedar pillars** [How these were disposed of, or what was their number, it is impossible to say. Thenius says they were 400, but this is pure conjecture. The description is so meagre and partial that it is impossible to form a correct idea of the building. The remark made above (ch. vi. Introd. Note) as to the temple applies with still greater force to the palaces. " There are few tasks more difficult or puzzling than the attempt to restore an ancient building of which we possess nothing but two verbal descriptions; and these difficulties are very much enhanced when one account is written in a language like Hebrew, the scientific terms in which are, from our ignorance, capable of the widest latitude of interpretation, and the other, though written in a language of which we have a more definite knowledge, was composed by a person who could never have seen the building he was describing" (Fergusson, Dict. Bib. ii. p.658)], **with cedar beams** [כְּרֻתוֹת, *cut* or *hewn* beams] **upon the pillars.** [This palace, according to Fergusson, was " the great hall of state and audience" and the principal building of the range. But if it was this, which is very doubtful, for the throne was in the hall of judgment (ch. v. 7), it would seem to have served other purposes besides that of an audience-chamber. Among other things, it was certainly an armoury (ch. x. 17. Cf. Isa. xxii. 8). The Arab. Vers. calls it "the house of his arms." Possibly it was also the residence of the bodyguard (cf. xiv. 28 with x. 17). Bähr observes that the arrangement of the palaces accords with the Jewish conceptions of the kingly office. The first, the armoury, represents him in his militant character (1 Sam. viii. 20), the second in his judicial function (1 Sam. viii. 5, 6; 2 Sam. xv. 4; 1 Kings iii. 9), while the third shows him in his private capacity.]

Ver. 3.—**And it was covered** [or roofed] **with cedar above** [cf. vi. 9, 15] **upon the beams** [צְלָעוֹת lit., *ribs*, the word used in ch. vi. 5 of the *side chambers*, and in vi. 34 (in the masculine) of the *leaves* of the doors], **that lay on forty-five pillars, fifteen in a row.** [Rawlinson, al. are much exercised to reconcile this statement with that of ver. 2, which speaks of *four* rows, But the explanation is very simple, viz., that the "forty-five, fifteen in a row" does not refer to the pillars but to the side chambers or compartments (A. V., "beams"). The description is so very loose and general that positive statements are out of place, but the meaning certainly appears to be this, that there was a roofing of cedar over the *side chambers* (which rested upon the pillars mentioned in ver. 2) *forty-five* in number, fifteen in a row. It is true the Masoretic punctuation is against this view. It is also clear that the LXX. understood the numbers forty-five and fifteen to refer to the pillars, for they have essayed to cut the knot by reading *three* rows instead of "*four* rows," in ver. 2. Similarly the Arab. in ver. 3 reads *sixty* instead of forty-five; obviously another desperate attempt to solve the difficulty by a corruption of the text. But the solution suggested above is so simple and natural that we can hardly be wrong in adopting it. Bähr says positively that forty-five pillars could not have supported a structure 100 cubits by 50 cubits, " nor could the building have been named 'forest of Lebanon' from forty-five scattered pillars." It would follow, hence, that there were side chambers only on three sides of the building, as was the case in the temple. And if (as has been inferred from vers. 4, 5) a three-storied structure is here described; if, that is to say, the forty-five chambers were divided fifteen to a tier or story, it is highly probable that they would be distributed six to each long side and three to the rear (Bähr). This arrangement—a court surrounded by a colonnade and galleries—is still found in the East; as all travellers know. And in its favour it may be said that it is such as to have been suggested by the plan of the temple. The ground-plan is the same, with this difference, that a courtyard occupies the place of the temple proper.]

Ver. 4.—**And there were windows** [שְׁקֻפִים same word as in ch. vi. 4, i.e., *beams* or lattices. Keil understands, *beam layers;* and Bähr, *übergelegte Balken.* The LXX. has πλευρῶν] **in three rows** [or tiers. All we can say is that there is a possible reference to three stories formed by the three rows of beams], **and light** [lit., *outlook.* מֶחֱזָה probably means a wide outlook. LXX. χώρα, *aspectus, prospectus*] **was against light in three ranks** [Heb. *three times.* The meaning is that the side chambers were so built and arranged that the rooms had their windows exactly *vis-à-vis* in each of the three stories. Josephus explains, θυρώμασι τριγλύφοις, *windows in three divisions*, but this is no explanation of the words "light against light," &c. Fergusson understands the three outlooks to mean, first, the clerestory windows (that there was a clerestory he infers from Josephus (Ant., vii. 5. 2), who describes this palace as "in the Corinthian manner," which cannot mean, he says, "the Corinthian order, which was not then invented, but after the fashion of a Corinthian *oecus*, which was a hall with a clerestory"); (2) a range of openings under the cornice of the walls; and (3) a range of open doorways. But all this is conjecture.

Ver. 5.—**And all the doors and posts** [For מְזוּזֹת posts, Thenius would read מֶחֱזֹות *outlooks,* after ver. 4, which seems a natural emendation, especially as the LXX. has χώραι. We should then get the sense of "doors and windows"] **were square of beam.** [The word translated "windows" in ver. 4; the proper rendering is *beam,* and the meaning apparently is that all these openings were square in shape. Nothing is said about the height of the rooms, and as the commentators are not agreed whether there was one story or three, that can obviously be only matter of conjecture. Rawlinson, who thinks of but one hall, with three rows of windows, supposes, after Houbigant, that one row was placed in a wall which ran down the middle of the apartment. Such an arrangement, he observes, was found by Layard at Nimrud.]

Ver. 6.—**And he made a porch of pillars** [Heb. *the porch of pillars.* This was no doubt a covered colonnade, i.e., it had a roof but no sides. The pillars were its only walls. But here the question presents itself, Was this porch the vestibule of the house of the forest of Lebanon, just described? From the correspondence between its width and that of this palace, Rawlinson infers that it was (cf. ch. vi. 2, 3). Bähr believes it to have been the porch or entrance to the hall of judgment mentioned in the next verse, while Fergusson again assigns it an independent position, separate from either. The term *porch* (אוּלָם), the meaning of which is surely determined by its use in ch. vi., almost implies that it must have served as the entrance or vestibule to some building. But the size, and the fact that it had itself a porch (see below), favour the idea that it was an independent structure, though Rawlinson shows that "most of the Persepolitan porches had small pillared chambers at some little distance in front of them," and refers to the Egyptian *propylaea*. Keil argues that this *pillar hall*, as he calls it, stood between the house of the forest of Lebanon and the judgment hall. Bähr, as remarked above, sees in it the anterior part of the judgment hall, which latter, he adds, bore to it the same relation that the oracle did to the temple-house. He observes that as the ark was in the oracle, so the throne (ch. x. 18) found a place in the hall of judgment. This structure, therefore, with its porch, mentioned presently, would reproduce the main features of the temple arrangement. We see, consequently, that both the house of the forest of Lebanon and the porch of pillars followed in their outline the ground-plan of the temple. Nor is this at all surprising, considering that all these edifices probably had the same architect or designer]; **the length thereof was fifty cubits** [the length, *i.e.*, according to the view last advanced of the two divisions of the building, viz., the porch of pillars and the porch of judgment. But the correspondence of the length (or width—the same word is used of the width of the *temple* porch ch. vi. 3) of this porch with the width of the house of the forest of Lebanon is, to say the least, remarkable, and suggests that after all it may have been the porch of that building. If so, the resemblance to the temple would be still more striking], **and the breadth** [depth?] **thereof thirty cubits : and the porch** [Heb. *a* porch] **was before them** [*i.e.*, the pillars. The words can only mean that a smaller porch stood before the porch of pillars, or colonnade]: **and the other** [omit] **pillars** [*i.e.*, the pillars of the minor vestibule or fore porch] **and the thick beam** [Heb. *threshold*] **were before them.** [The broad threshold, approached by steps, and the pillars which it supported, together with the roof which covered them, formed the front part and approach to the larger porch or colonnade.]

Ver. 7.—**Then he made a porch** [or *the* porch] **for the throne where he might judge** [*i.e.*, it was at once audience-chamber (throne-room, ch. x. 18) and court of justice], **even the porch of judgment** [Stanley re-

marks that this "porch, or gate of justice, still kept alive the likeness of the old patriarchal custom of sitting in judgment at the gate." He then refers to the "gate of justice" at Granada and the "Sublime *Porte*" at Constantinople. It is, perhaps, not quite so certain that "this porch was the gem and centre of the whole empire," or that because it was so much thought of a similar but smaller porch was erected for the queen (ver. 8) ("Jewish Ch.," ii. p. 195)]: **and it was covered with cedar from one side of the floor to the other.** [Heb. *from the floor to the floor*, as marg. Gesenius understands these words to mean, "from one floor to the other," *i.e.*, to the cieling (the floor of the other story); in other words, the walls from bottom to top. So the Vulg., *a pavimento usque ad summitatem*, and Syr., *a fundamento ad coelum ejus usque*, which have led Thenius to suggest the reading עַד־קוֹרוֹת (unto the *beams*) instead of עַד הַקַּרְקַע. Keil thinks the cieling served as the floor of an upper story, built over the porch of judgment, but, as Bähr observes, no such upper story is even hinted at elsewhere. It seems to me that, on the whole, the A. V. rendering is to be retained, the meaning being that the whole space, both of wall and cieling, from one side of the floor to the opposite side, was covered with cedar.]

Ver. 8.—**And his house where he dwelt** [*i.e.*, his private residence. Not to be identified with the "house" of ver. 1. The term is here expressly restricted to his dwelling-house. There it as clearly includes all the several palaces] **had** [or *was*. The "court" is apparently in apposition to "his house." The words in italics, here as elsewhere, merely darken the sense] **another** [Heb. *the hinder*] **court within** [For the use of מִבֵּית לְ = *within*, compare ch. vi. 16; Num. xviii. 7, and see Gesen., Thesaur. i. 193] **the porch, which was of the like work** [*i.e.*, the walls were covered with cedar. The reference is clearly to materials, adornment, &c., not to size]. **Solomon made also an house for Pharaoh's daughter, whom he had taken to wife** [Heb. *he made also a house for . . . whom Solomon had taken, i.e.*, married], **like unto this porch.** [This would seem to have been the private residence of the queen, not the harem where all the wives and concubines (ch. xi. 3) were collected. It was evidently distinct from and behind the residence of the king, an arrangement which still prevails in Eastern palaces.]

Ver. 9.—**All these** [*i.e.*, buildings, palaces] **were of costly** [or precious ; cf. ch. v. 31

and vers. 10, 11] **stones, according to the measures of hewed stones** [lit., of *squaring* or *hewing*, same word in chs. v. 31 (Heb.), vi. 36, and Isa. ix. 9, &c. All the stones in these several buildings were shaped to certain specified dimensions], **sawed with saws** [גָּרַר is obviously an onomatopoetic word, like our *saw*. Gesenius cites σαίρω, *serro*, &c. The Egyptians, whose saws were apparently *all* single-handed, do not seem to have applied this instrument to stone, but part of a double-handed saw was found at Nimrud (Layard, p. 195, and Dict. Bib., art. "Saw"). That saws were in common use and were made of iron is implied in 2 Sam. xii. 31], **within and without** [It is not quite clear whether the meaning is that the two surfaces exposed to view, one within and the other without, the building were shaped with saws, or that the inner and hidden surface of the stone was thus smoothed as well as the exposed parts], **even from the foundation unto the coping** [or *corbels*. It is generally agreed (Gesen., Keil, Bähr) that the reference is to the "projecting stones on which the beams rest," though Thenius would understand *battlements* (Deut. xxii. 8) to be intended. But for these a different word is always used, and the LXX. γεῖσος signifies the projection of the roof, not an erection upon it], **and so on the outside toward the great court** [*i.e.*, the pavement of the court was of sawed stones (see ver. 12).]

Ver. 10.—**And the foundation was of costly stones, even great stones** [Bähr says, "Even the foundations which from without were not seen, were composed of these great stones." But the meaning evidently is that the foundation stones were larger than those reared upon them], **stones of ten cubits** [*i.e.*, ten cubits *long*, and of proportionate width, &c.], **and stones of eight cubits**. [The foundations of the palaces, consequently, were much less than those of the temple platform, some of which would measure 16 cubits. See note on ch. v. 17.]

Ver. 11.—**And above** [*i.e.*, upon the foundation stones just described] **were costly stones, after the measures of hewed stones** [It is implied here that the stones of the superstructure were less than those of the foundation. It is also implied that the former were more carefully smoothed and faced than the latter] **and cedars.** [Heb. *cedar.*]

Ver. 12.—**And the great court round about** [The palace, again like the temple, had two courts. The lesser is referred to in ver. 8, and was enclosed among the buildings. The great court probably surrounded the entire structure] **was** [enclosed by a wall] **with three rows of hewed stones, and a row of cedar beams** [The latter formed the coping. The wall of the court of the palace thus resembled that of the temple. See on ch. vi. 36. In all these coincidences we have tokens of the same designing hand], **both for the inner court of the house of the Lord.** [This sudden digression from the court of the palace to the temple is suspicious, and suggests either a mistranslation or corruption of the text. The historian evidently meant to say that the wall of the court, in its three rows of stones and its cedar coping, *resembled* the inner court of the temple; and, according to some grammarians (Gesen., Ewald), this meaning may well be conveyed by the text as it stands, ו in Hebrew serving sometimes to institute a comparison (Prov. xxv. 3, 12, 20 ; xxvi. 14, &c.) "As in the court," &c. But the instances just cited, being proverbs or apophthegms, are not strictly parallel with our text. It seems better, on the whole, however, to retain the text in this sense than to replace ו by כ, reading כלחצר or כחצר for ולחצר. כההצר (Horsley) is quite inadmissible, as the constr. case never has the art.], **and for the porch of the house.** [It is almost impossible to decide whether the porch of judgment (ver. 7) or the porch of the temple is here meant. The immediate context favours the latter. But this does not seem to have had any court or enclosing wall other than the inner court. Rawlinson decides for the porch of judgment, "which," he says, "had a planking of cedar over the stone pavement" (ver. 7). But ver. 7 (where see note) rather excludes than includes the pavement. The reference is probably to the "court within the porch," mentioned in ver. 8.]

After this brief account of the royal palaces, the author proceeds to mention the vessels, &c., used in the temple service, prefacing his description by a few words respecting the great Tyrian artist, by whom they were for the most part cast, and possibly designed also.

Ver. 13.—**And king Solomon sent** [rather, *had sent* (2 Chron. ii. 13)] **and fetched Hiram out of Tyre.** [This is our historian's brief version of the transaction which is recorded in 2 Chron. ii. 7—14. He has not mentioned before (ch. v. 6) Solomon's request for a master-builder. Hiram, like his namesake the king, is elsewhere (2 Chron. ii. 13 ; iv. 11, 16) called *Huram* or *Hirom* (ver. 40). See note on ch. v. 1. In the first of these passages the king calls him "Huram my father" (see note there) ; in the last he is designated "Huram his father." The title "Ab" (cf. Gen. xlv. 8, 41, 43 ; 2 Kings ii. 12 ; v. 13 ; vi. 21 ; cf.

viii. 9) shows the high esteem in which he
was held. It can hardly be, as some have
supposed, a proper name. It may signify
" counsellor," or master, *i.e.*, master-builder.
The Tyrians evidently regarded him with
some pride.]

Ver. 14.—**He was a widow's son of the
tribe of Naphtali** [In 2 Chron. ii. 14 he is
described as the " son of a woman of the
daughters of *Dan*." The discrepancy is
only apparent. For in the first place it is
not absolutely necessary to understand by
Dan the tribe of that name. It may well
refer to the town, formerly Leshem (Josh.
xix. 47), or Laish (Judg. xviii. 7, 27), colo-
nised by the Danites, and thenceforward
bearing their name (ver. 29), which was
situated within the borders of Naphtali.
If, however, it is preferred to see in the
" daughters of Dan " a tribal reference, we
may suppose (with Keil, *al.*) that the woman
was originally a Danite, but became, through
her first husband, " of the tribe of Naphtali." But the first explanation is the more
simple and obvious], **and his father was a
man of Tyre** [*i.e.*, Hiram was the son (not
stepson, or adopted son, as the Rabbins) of
a mixed marriage. In earlier times Laish
had but little intercourse with the Zidonians (Judg. xviii. 28). It is nowhere stated
that the inhabitants were of Phœnician
extraction ; nor can it be justly inferred
from this passage], **a worker in brass** [or
copper. Brass is a compound of copper
and zinc ; but נְחֹשֶׁת originally and strictly
signifies a pure metal (Deut. viii. 9 ; xxxiii.
25, &c. ; Job xxviii. 2). There were copper
mines in Palestine, and the art of working
this metal was known at a very remote
period (Gen. iv. 22, Heb., and see Wilkinson's "Ancient Egypt," vol. iii. p. 243 ;
and De Rougemont, "Age du Bronze," p.
180). In later times the word sometimes
denoted brass (χαλκός), or copper-bronze
(a mixture of copper and tin). Cf. Jer.
vi. 28. From 2 Chron. ii. 14 we learn that
Hiram was "skilful to work in gold and in
silver, in brass, in iron, in stone, and in
timber," &c. From the mention of brass
only in this passage, and in ver. 45, it has
been somewhat hastily concluded that " the
work that he personally did for Solomon "
was "limited to works in brass " (Rawlinson). It is, perhaps, safer to say that brass
only is mentioned here, because the following section treats exclusively of the brazen
ornaments, &c., of the sanctuary (Keil).
It would almost seem, however (see note on
ver. 48), as if he was not employed to make
the vessels of gold. Nor does this supposition really contradict the statement made
below, viz., that he wrought all Solomon's

work] : **and he was filled with wisdom, and
understanding, and cunning** [or *knowledge*,
as the same word is rendered Exod. xxxi. 3,
where similar language is used of Bezaleel.
It is noticeable, however, that the words
" filled with the spirit of God," used of the
Hebrew, are not applied to the Tyrian
workman] **to work all works in brass. And
he came to king Solomon** [probably with a
considerable number of assistants] , **and
wrought all his work.**

Ver. 15.—**For he cast two pillars of brass**
[The process of casting, as practised by the
ancients, receives considerable illustration
from the paintings of Thebes (see Wilkinson,
"Anc. Egypt." ii. pp. 234, 256; Kitto, "Daily
Bib. Illus." Sol. and Kings, pp. 72, 73)], **of
eighteen cubits high apiece** [Heb. *eighteen
cubits was the height of the one column*.
This was the height of the shaft (cf. 2 Kings
xxv. 17 ; Jer. lii. 21). To this must be added
the capital (vers. 16, 19), which measured five
(or, according to some, nine) cubits, and probably the pedestal. The pillars were hollow,
the metal being four finger breadths thick
(Jer. lii. 21). In 2 Chron. iii. 15 the height
is given as thirty-five cubits—a discrepancy
which has been variously explained. According to some writers (*e.g.*, Abravanel,
Movers, Wordsworth), this represents the
total length of the *two* pillars (each pillar
consequently being 17½ cubits) — an idea
which, perhaps, finds some slight support
in the word employed אֹרֶךְ *length*. Here it
is קוֹמָה *height*. By others it has been supposed that the total height of base, column,
and capital was thirty-five cubits, which, if
not incredible, is very improbable. Others
think it a part of that systematic reduplica-
tion of the heights of edifices by the
chronicler, of which we have already had
an instance in ch. vi. (where see note). But
the true explanation would seem to be that,
by a clerical error, thirty-five (לה) has been
substituted in the text for eighteen (יח).
So Keil and Bähr] : **and a line** [or *thread*]
**of twelve cubits did compass either of
them** [Heb. *the second column*] **about.** [It
must not be supposed, from the fact that
the height of the one column is given, and
the circumference of the other, that they
were dissimilar in height and breadth or
girth. There has probably been an accidental abbreviation of the full expression,
" Eighteen cubits was the height of the one
pillar, and eighteen cubits was the height
of the other pillar ; and a line of twelve
cubits compassed the one pillar, and a line
of twelve cubits compassed the other pillar."
It is just possible, however, that the peculiarity results from the actual system of

measurement employed in this case. As they were castings, it would be needless to measure both pillars, and so the length may have been ascertained from the first, and the breadth from the second. The columns would thus be about twenty-seven feet high, and about six feet in diameter.]

Ver. 16.—And he made two chapiters [or capitals] **of molten** [Heb. *poured*] **brass, to put upon the tops** [Heb. *heads*] **of the pillars : the height of the one chapiter was five cubits, and the height of the other chapiter was five cubits** [In 2 Kings xxv. 17 the height is given as three cubits ; but this is obviously a clerical error. See 2 Chron. iii. 15 ; Jer. lii. 22. A much more important question is whether the chapiter (כֹּתֶרֶת same word, akin to כֶּתֶר, crown) of four cubits mentioned in ver. 19 is to be understood as a part of this chapiter, or something additional and superposed, the entablature, *e.g.* The former appears the more probable. See note on ver. 19. But it is not a fatal objection to the latter view that it would make the entire chapiter, or both members, nine cubits high ; no less, that is, than one-half the length of the shaft. No doubt to modern ideas this appears wholly disproportionate ; but a double chapiter, bearing the same proportion to the shaft, is found in some of the buildings of Persepolis (Fergusson, Dict. Bib. iii. p. 1457). From the expression of vers. 41, 42, "the bowls of the chapiters" (cf. 2 Chron. iv. 12, 13 ; Jer. lii. 23), and the word "belly" (בֶּטֶן) in ver. 20, we gather that the chapiters were bowl-shaped, or bellied out something like the so-called "cushion capital" in Norman architecture.

Ver. 17.—And nets [Gesen., *lattice* ; Keil, *plait*. "It seems almost in vain to try and speculate on what was the exact form of the decoration of these celebrated pillars. The nets of checker-work, and wreaths of chain-work, &c., are all features applicable to metal architecture ; and though we know that the old Tartar races did use metal architecture everywhere, and especially in bronze, from the very nature of the material, every specimen has perished, and we have now no representations from which we can restore them" (Fergusson, Dict. Bib. *l.c.*)] **of checker work** [the Hebrew repeats the word : nets of *net-work*, or plaits of work of *plait*], **and wreaths** [or cords, twisted work, *i.e.*, festoons] **of chain work** [the wreathed or twisted festoon probably resembled a chain], **for** [or, *to, i.e.*, were on] **the chapiters which were upon the top of the pillars ; seven for the one chapiter, and seven for the other chapiter** [The LXX. having here δίκτυον, it is clear that the text they had read שְׂבָכָה "a net," and not שִׁבְעָה

"seven." Some, accordingly, would read, "a net for the one chapiter, and a net," &c. But there is no sufficient reason for the change. "This decoration consisted of seven twists arranged as festoons, which were hung round the capitals of the pillars" (Keil). The comparison with "chain work" was probably suggested by the fact that the intertwined threads, which crossed and re-crossed each other, bore a rough resemblance to the links of a chain.

Ver. 18.—And he made the pillars [There is evidently a confusion of the text here. Probably we should read, with some MSS. הרמנים, the *pomegranates* (so LXX.), instead of העמודים, or rather, we should *transpose* the two words, reading *pomegranates* where the Masoretic text has *pillars*, and *vice versâ*. "The pomegranate was one of the commonest ornaments of Assyria. . . . It is doubtful whether a symbolical meaning was attached to it, or whether it was merely selected as a beautiful natural form" (Rawlinson). Wordsworth characteristically sees in its many ripe seeds, "an expressive emblem of *fruitfulness* in *good works*." According to Bähr, it is an image of the law or covenant of Jehovah, and the seeds represent the separate commands (Symbolik, ii. 122, 123). In the tabernacle it was pourtrayed in works of divers colours on the hem of the robe of the ephod (Exod. xxviii. 33, 34 ; xxxix. 24). All the Scripture notices of this fruit prove its great abundance in Palestine (Num. xiii. 23 ; Josh. xv. 32 ; xxi. 25 ;—in the two last passages it appears as the name of a town—Cant. iv. 3, 13 ; viii. 2 ; Joel i. 12 ; Haggai ii. 9, &c.) It was also well known to the Egyptians (Num. xx. 5)], **and** [or *even*] **two rows round about upon the one network** ["The relation between the two rows of pomegranates and the plaited work is not clearly defined, but it is generally and correctly assumed that one row ran round the pillars below the plaited work and the other above" (Keil). The pomegranates, one hundred in number in each row (2 Chron. iii. 16), four hundred in all (2 Chron. iv. 13 ; Jer. lii. 23), would thus form a double border to the chain work], **to cover the chapiters that were upon the top, with pomegranates** [rather, *on the top of the pillars*, as the transposition mentioned above and the sense require] ; **and so did he for the other chapiter.**

Ver. 19. And the chapiters that were upon the top of the pillars [It is difficult to believe that these words, which are identical with those in vers. 16, 17, 18, can refer to a different — a second and superposed capital (Rawlinson), or to the entablature (Fergusson)] **were of lily work** [*i.e.*, *bassi-*

relievi in imitation of flowering lilies. Probably the bowl-shaped chapiter was treated as a full-blown lily, just as the capitals of Egyptian pillars took the form of the lotus. The molten sea was similarly treated (ver. 26). The lily (שׁוּשַׁן, from שׁוּשׁ, to be *white*), was undoubtedly an emblem of purity. Bähr observes that it may justly be named " the flower of the promised land," and that as the lotus was the religious flower of the Indian and Egyptian religions, so was the lily of the Jewish] **in the porch** [These words, בָּאוּלָם, are very obscure. Keil understands " as in the hall" (cf. κατὰ τὸ αὐλάμ, LXX.) But that idea would have been expressed by בָּאוּלָם, and nothing is said elsewhere about any lily-work in the porch (Bähr). Ewald, too, thinks the decoration of the porch is referred to, and holds that a description of this lily-work must once have preceded this statement, though it is now wanting. Thenius, *al.* suppose them to refer to the position of the pillars within the porch, and the "four cubits" mentioned presently, they take to indicate the diameter of the capitals. Wordsworth would render " *inside* or *toward* the porch," and understands that the lily-work was only on the *inside* of the pillars. It is, perhaps, impossible to arrive at any certain conclusion], **four cubits.** [This may either mean that of five cubits (which was the height of the entire capital), four, and these the upper four (ver. 22), were covered with lily-work, while one cubit at the bottom of the capital was ornamented with chain-work or festoons—we can hardly believe that nets, chains, and lily-work were all combined in the same space, or it may refer to the position of the pillars in the portico.]

Ver. 20.—**And the chapiters upon the two pillars** *had pomegranates* [Instead of the italics, Keil would supply *Hiram made*, but it is doubtful whether this is any improvement. We have already heard more than once that he made the chapiters. It is better to supply *projected* or *were*, as in the preceding verse. This verse is extremely obscure ; but its design *appears* to be to explain how the bowl of the chapiter projected above its base] **also above** [*i.e.*, above the neck, or lowest cubit, on which was the net and chain-work], **over against** [מִלְּעֻמַּת with two prefixes is a rare form] **the belly** [or " bowl" (ver. 41)] **which was by** [Heb. *beyond, on the other side of, i.e.*, as it appeared to a spectator standing below] **the network : and the pomegranates were two hundred in rows** [This agrees with the total

of four hundred, as given in ver. 42, and in 2 Chronicles, and with the " hundred round about" (*i.e.*, the number in each row) mentioned in Jer. lii. 23. We gather from this latter passage that ninety-six out of the hundred faced the four quarters, for this is apparently the meaning of רוּחָה, *windwards; see* Ezek. xlii. 16—18, not that the pomegranates could be " set in motion by the play of the wind," as Ewald confidently affirms. The remaining four pomegranates, of course, occupied the four corners. The necessary inference from this statement, viz., that this part of the capital was four-square, seems to have escaped the notice of the commentators] **round about upon the other chapiter.** [Some words have evidently dropped out of the Hebrew here, as in ver. 15. The text, no doubt, originally stood " two hundred in rows round about the one chapiter, and two hundred in rows round about upon the other chapiter." There has been no intentional compression—that is not the genius of the Semitic languages—but an accidental omission, occasioned by the recurrence of almost identical words.

Ver. 21—**And he set up the pillars in the porch** [We are now confronted by the much vexed questions, (1) What was the position, and (2) what the purpose, of these two columns? Were they *in* the porch, or before it? And were they architectural or monumental? Did they support the roof of the porch, or were they isolated and detached, after the manner of obelisks? I incline to the opinion of Bähr, that they stood *in* the porch, but that they formed no part of the building, *i.e.*, that they were not for any structural use, but simply for ornament. This appears to me, on the whole, to result from the following considerations : (1) The language used favours a position within the porch. We have here לָאֻלָם (="*at* or *in* the porch," perhaps *for* the porch, as Bähr), and in ver. 19 (where see note) בָּאוּלָם. And with this agree the expression of the Chron. "before (לִפְנֵי) the house," and "before (עַל־פְּנֵי) the temple" (2 Chron. iii. 15, 17). The pillars would, however, be "before the temple," whether they stood within or in front of the porch, and it may be safely allowed that the language of the historian is not *decisive* one way or the other. The prepositions of the text, however, seem to lend some support to Bähr's view. (2) We know that " the Phœnicians used *isolated* metal columns as sacred ornaments, so that Hiram would be familiar with such a mode of ornamentation " (Rawlinson). " Whenever in coins or histories we get a representation of a Phœnician temple, it always has a pillar or pillars standing within or before it" (Stanley). (3) It is extremely doubtful whether these columns, twenty-three feet in height, were adapted to serve as supports to the roof of the porch. The height of the latter has been variously estimated at twenty, thirty, and sixty cubits, and whichever estimate is preferred, the columns would appear to be of an unsuitable altitude. Fergusson says they *were* "appropriate to support the roof of the porch," but then he conceives the columns to be in all twenty-seven cubits high (see on ver. 19), and allows the remaining three cubits for the slope of the roof). But, as we cannot be certain either of the height of the porch or of the column, this is an argument of which very little can be made. (4) If the pillars were part of the building, they would almost certainly have been of the same material, *i.e.*, wood or stone. Their metallic composition is certainly an argument for their monumental character. It can hardly be alleged in favour of this view, however, that they are mentioned amongst the vessels or articles of furniture, for the historian might fittingly describe the pillars here, as being the principal of the "works in brass" which Hiram wrought, even if they did form the supports of the roof of the porch. Nor are we justified, considering the extreme brevity and the partial character of the description of the temple, in affirming that they would have been mentioned in connexion with the building, had they formed part of the edifice. (5) The remark of Stieglitz (cited by Bähr) that "it was their separate position alone which gave these pillars the impressive aspect they were designed to wear," lends some little support to this view. So also does (6) The fact that these columns, and these alone, received special names. "No architectural portion of the building received a name" (Keil). But this argument, again, is not to be unduly pressed, for to some it may seem that the names they bore would have a special propriety and an enhanced significance, if the columns contributed to the *strength* and *stability* of the edifice. The question, therefore, is one of considerable complexity, the more so, as it is maintained that it would be almost impossible to construct a roof thirty feet in width without some such pillars to support the beam (Fergusson); but the balance of evidence appears to favour the view that Jachin and Boaz were monuments erected in the porch, to dignify the sanctuary, and to symbolize the power and eternity of the Being to whom it was dedicated]: **and he set up the right pillar, and called the name thereof Jachin**

[*i.e.*, *he shall establish*, as marg. The name expressed the belief that God would preserve and protect the new fane. It is true that a Jachin is mentioned (1 Chron. ix. 10; xxiv. 17), as head of the 21st course of priests in the reign of David, while a Boaz was one of Solomon's ancestors, but the columns could hardly be named after them, or an private persons. Ewald suggests that they were named after "some favourites of the time, perhaps young sons of Solon on." The idea of Thenius that these names were engraved upon the pillars is not wh lly improbable, though of course it finds no support in the text] **and he set up the left pillar** [the left as one faced them from the house. The right hand is iden ified with the south in ver. 39], **and called the name thereof Boaz.** [Marg. *in it is strength*. Probably "*in Him, i.e.*, God, is its strength" (cf. Isa. xlv. 24). The thought of Jachin, "*He* will establish," is thus continued; and the two pillars pointed alike to the God of Israel as the true support and upholder of His sanctuary. The LXX. interpretation of these two names, Κατόρθωσις and Ἰσχύς (2 Chron. iii. 17), *success* and *strength*, though very far from literal, preserves their fundamental ideas.

Ver. 22.—**And upon the top of the pillars was lily work** [a repetition, in the Hebrew manner, of ver. 19. The "lily work," which probably involved two things, (1) that the capital had a rude resemblance to a "full blown lily-cup" (Bähr), and (2) that representations of the leaf of the lily are pourtrayed upon it (as in the cornice of Persepolis, an illustration of which will be found Dict. Bib. iii. p. 1457), was a not unfitting finial to the column, as it formed a sort of crown or chaplet upon it. The two pillars would thus resemble two giant plants, the column answering to the stalk, the capital to the flower. The ideas of architecture, it is well known, have very frequently been derived from the vegetable kingdom.

Ver. 23.—The writer now passes on to describe the brazen vessels made by Hiram for the temple use. **And he made a** [Heb. *the*] **molten sea** [so called on account of its unprecedented size and capacity. It was designed, like the laver of brass in the tabernacle (Exod. xxx. 18—20), to contain the water necessary for the ablutions of the priests. For its size and shape see below], **ten cubits from the one brim to the other** [Heb. *from his lip to his lip*] **round all about** [*i.e.*, *circular*], **and his height was five cubits** [this was the depth of the vessel, exclusive of its foot or base] : **and a line of thirty cubits did compass it round about.** [The historian obviously uses round numbers when he speaks of the diameter as ten

and the circumference as thirty cubits. If
the diameter was exactly ten, the circumference would of course be about 31½ cubits.
But the sacred writers seldom aim at precision.

Ver. 24.—**And under the brim of it round
about** [The edge of the laver was curved
outwards (ver. 26)] **there were knops** [see
note on ch. vi. 18. The text of 2 Chron.
iv. 3, בקרים (" the similitude, of *oxen*"), is
obviously a clerical error for פקעים (Keil),
but whether דמות is an interpolation may
well be doubted. Keil thinks it was introduced to explain the mention of oxen]
compassing [Heb. *surrounding*, some word]
it, ten in a cubit [It does not follow from
this that each gourd or knop was " a little
over two inches in diameter" (Keil), for they
may not have been in close contact, and,
moreover, the cubit was probably 18 inches],
**compassing the sea round about : the
knops were cast in two rows, when it was
cast.** [Lit., *two rows ; the knops were cast
in its casting.* The " brass," of which the
laver was composed, had been taken by
David from the cities of Hadarezer (1 Chron.
xviii. 8 ; 1 Sam. viii. 8, LXX.)]

Ver. 25.—**It stood** [Heb. *standing*] **upon
twelve oxen** [The import of the number
twelve is well explained by Bähr, Symbolik,
i. 201 sqq. Like *seven*, it is compounded out
of three and four. But the primary reference
here is to the twelve tribes], **three looking
toward the north, and three looking toward
the west, and three looking toward the
south, and three looking toward the east**
[So the tribes in the camp formed a square
round the tabernacle, three on each side—
east, south, west, and north (Num. ii.)] : **and
the sea was set above upon them, and all
their hinder parts were inward.** [The same
regard of the cardinal points (see Bähr,
Symbolik, i. 210 sqq.) has been noticed in
the pomegranates on the capitals of the two
columns. See note on ver. 20. Keil says
the feet of the oxen no doubt rested on
a metal plate, so that they were fixed and
immoveable; but this lacks proof. The
oxen would be immoveable in any case,
owing to the weight of the metal and the
water. All conjectures as to the height and
size of the oxen are necessarily of little
value.

Ver. 26.—**And it was a handbreadth thick**
[*i.e.*, three inches], **and the brim thereof
was wrought like the brim of a cup** [Heb.
and his lip like the work of the lip of a cup,
i.e., curved outwards], **with flowers of lilies**
[lit., " *a blossom of lily*." Keil understands
" ornamented with lily flowers," but the
strict interpretation—the " lily blossom "
being in apposition to " cup "—requires us
to refer the words to the shape rather than

to the ornamentation of the laver. The lip
was curved like a lily]: **it contained two
thousand** [In Chron. and by Josephus the
number is given as 3000. This may have
resulted, as Keil thinks, from confounding
ו and ג but it is suspicious that so many of
the numbers of the Chronicles are exaggerations. The common explanation of the
discrepancy, viz., that it held 2000 baths
" when filled to its ordinary height, but
when filled to the brim 3000 " (Wordsworth),
appears to me hardly ingenuous] **baths.**
[" The data for determining the value of
the bath or ephah are both scanty and conflicting " (Dict. Bib. iii. p. 1741). Josephus,
the only authority on the subject, says that
it equalled the Attic *metrêtês* (about 8½ gals.),
but it is very doubtful whether he was
" really familiar with the Greek measures "
(*ib.*) At any rate, if this statement is
correct, his other statement as to the shape
of the laver must be altogether erroneous,
since 2000 baths would equal 17,000 gals.,
and a hemispherical laver could not possibly
have contained more than 10,000. The
attempt has been made, on the assumption
that the sea was a hemisphere, as Josephus
affirms, to calculate from its capacity the
value of the bath, which in that case would
be about four gallons. But there is good
reason for doubting whether the laver was
hemispherical—such a shape would be ill
adapted to its position on the backs of
oxen—and some have maintained that it
was cylindrical, others that, like the laver
of the tabernacle, it had a foot (Exod. xxx.
18) or basin. The prevailing opinion of
scholars, however, appears to be that it was
30 cubits in circumference only at the lip,
and that it bellied out considerably below.
While the shape, however, must remain a
matter of uncertainty, we are left in no
doubt as to its purpose. It was " for the
priests to wash in" (2 Chron. iv. 6)—not, of
course, for immersing their whole persons,
but their hands and feet (Exod. xxx. 19, 21).
The priests (after Exod. iii. 5; Josh. v. 15,
&c.) ministered barefoot. It was, according to Rabbinical tradition, provided with
taps or faucets (Bähr). It has, however,
been held by some that the water issued
forth (as in the Alhambra) from the lions'
mouths. It is probable that a basin of some
sort was attached to it. Whether the laver
was filled by the hand or by some special
contrivance, it is quite impossible to say.
We know that provision was made for storing
water hard by. The present writer was privileged in 1861 to explore the great reservoir,
the *Bahr el Khebir*, still existing underneath
the Haram area, at a time when very few
Europeans had seen it (see Pal. Explor.
Fund, No. vii.; Barclay, " City of the Great

King;" Porter, Handbook, i. pp. 134, 138). The water was probably brought from Solomon's pools at Bethlehem, though "a fountain of water exists in the city and is running unto this day, far below the surface" ("Our Work in Palestine," p. 103). Tacitus mentions the *fons perennis aquae* and the *piscinae cisternaeque servandis imbribus.*

Ver. 27.—**And he made ten bases** [or *stands,* מְכוֹנוֹת, from כּוּן, *erectus stetit.* The description of both the bases and the lavers which they supported (vers. 27—39) is extremely obscure. We know, however, that the bases (as the name implies) were simply stands or pediments for the lavers] **of brass ; four cubits was the length of one base and four cubits the breadth thereof, and three cubits the height of it** [they were rectangular, or box-shaped, six feet square and four and a half feet high.

Ver. 28.—**And the work of the bases was on this manner** [Heb. *and this the work of the base*]: **they had borders** [מִסְגְּרֹת (from סָגַר, *clausit*) means strictly *enclosings, i.e., sides,* forming the stand. They were *panels,* because of the borders or ledges mentioned presently, but this was the accident of their construction. The translation " border" gives a totally wrong impression], **and the borders were between the ledges** [Heb. *the sides were between the borders, i.e.,* were enclosed by ledges or frames.

Ver. 29.—**And on the borders** [panels] **that were between the ledges were lions** [*i.e.,* figures or bas-reliefs of lions], **oxen, and cherubims** ["The lion and the ox are the two animal forms which occur most frequently in Assyrian decoration" (Rawlinson). They have also found a place through the cherubim, in the symbolism of Christianity]: **and upon the ledges there was a base above** [*i.e.,* there was a pedestal or stand (כֵּן ; see ver. 31) of some sort for the laver, upon the square basis]: **and beneath the lions and oxen were certain additions** [Heb. *wreaths, festoons,* לֹוְיָה (cf. Prov. i. 9), *corona*] **made of thin work.** [Heb. *pensile* or *hanging* work, מוֹרָד from יָרַד *descendit ;* Vulgate, *dependentia.* It would seem that on the panel, beneath the figures of animals, &c., were sculptured hanging festoons of flowers.

Ver. 30.—**And every base had four brazen wheels** [As the lavers were used for washing " such things as they offered for burnt offering" (2 Chron. iv. 6), and consequently would require to be continually emptied and refilled, they must of necessity be moveable, so that they could be taken, now to the sea, or other reservoir, now to the altar], **and plates** [Heb. *axles*] **of brass : and the**

four corners [Heb. *feet ;* פַּעַם signifies *step,* thence *foot,* and is here used of artificial feet. These were, no doubt, at the four corners, and served to raise the stand above the wheels, so that the foliage, &c., was not hidden] **thereof had undersetters** [Heb. *shoulders.* " The *bearings* of the axle " (Gesen.) must be meant. The bases had four feet, which apparently terminated in a sort of socket or fork, into which the axletrees were inserted] : **under the laver were undersetters** [Heb. *the shoulders*] **molten** [or cast], **at the side of every addition.** [Lit., *opposite to a man (i.e.,* each) *were wreaths.* The explanation of Keil is that " from the feet . . . there ascended shoulder pieces, which ran along the outside of the chest and reached to the lower part of the basin, which was upon the lid of the chest, and, as shoulders, either supported or helped to support it. " He thus understands the " shoulder " to extend from the foot, or axletree, to the bottom of the laver. But it seems quite as likely that these shoulders were *within* the stand; that they started from its upper corners, *i.e.,* "from under the laver" (as in the Hebrew), passed down along its inner angles, and emerged below—the stand may well have had no bottom—in the shape of feet or forks, which rested on the axletrees, and supported both stand and laver. Over against this internal shoulder-blade or support was placed externally a wreath. But Bähr despairs of arriving at any just and adequate understanding of this arrangement, and, in the absence of drawings, it is perhaps hopeless that we shall ever interpret the words with certainty.]

Ver. 31.—**And the mouth of it** [Heb. *his mouth.* I incline, with Keil, to think the mouth of the *laver* just mentioned (כִּיר masc.) is referred to rather than the *stand* (Thenius), which would require a fem. suffix] **within the chapiter** [By this we are, perhaps, to understand a round ornament, resembling the capital of a pillar, which stood in the centre of the dome-shaped covering (see ver. 35) of the stand, and on which the laver rested (so Keil, Bähr). Rawlinson says, " No commentator has given a satisfactory explanation of this passage "] : **and above** [Heb. *upwards*] **was a cubit** [*i.e.,* the neck or foot of the laver measured uniformly one cubit, in width apparently] : **but the mouth** [Heb. *and her mouth,* fem. This last-mentioned mouth is probably the mouth of the capital (fem.) The neck or mouth of the laver would appear to have been fitted into the mouth of the crown-shaped pedestal] **was round after the work of the base** [Heb.

stand-work, כֵּן here fixes the meaning of the word in ver. 29, *i.e.*, it decides it to be the substantive (Keil, after Chald.), not the adverb (as Thenius, Bähr, *al.*) a cubit and a half [so that the first mouth would fit easily into the second], and also upon the mouth of it [Heb. *her mouth*, that of the capital, which was external. The mouth of the laver was partially concealed] were gravings [Keil understands this of the carving of the *stand* already mentioned, ver. 29. But a *mouth* is mentioned, which the square stand lacked. Besides the word "also" points to additional carvings. I understand the chapter which formed the mouth of the stand to be meant] with [Heb. *and*] their borders, foursquare, not round. [*i.e.*, the capital had panels like the stand, and the former, like those of the latter, were square.]

Ver. 32.—And under the borders [*i.e.*, *panels*] were four [Heb. *the four*, *i.e.*, those mentioned in ver. 30] wheels ["The wheels reached no higher than that portion of the sides of the base which was ornamented with garlands" (Rawlinson). It would be more correct to say that the wheels did not cover *any* portion of the sides; they were *under* them] ; and the axletrees [Heb. *hands*, as holding the wheel to the base or stand. *Axletrees* is altogether misleading. The hands were the parts connecting the wheels and axles] of the wheels were joined to [Heb. *in*, as marg.] the base : and the height of a wheel was a cubit and half a cubit. [*i.e.*, 27 inches.]

Ver. 33.—And the work of the wheels was like the work of a chariot wheel [Heb. *the* chariot, *i.e.*, the ordinary chariot] : their axletrees [Heb. *hands*], and their naves [Gesenius understands *rims*. He derives גַב, *gibbus*, from גָּבַב, *curvatus est*], and their felloes [or *fellies*, as the word is now written. These are the parts which compose the circumference of the wheel ; but Gesen. translates *spokes*, because they are the joinings (חָשֻׁק *conjunxit*) of nave and rim], and their spokes [חִשֻּׁרִים Gesen. would render *naves*, because the spokes *collect* at that part], were all molten.

Ver. 34.—And there were four undersetters [It seems probable that this is not a repetition of ver. 30 (Rawlinson), but that the reference is to the upper part (cf. ver. 35) of the shoulder pieces, which, according to Keil's view, supported the laver] to the four corners of one base : and the undersetters were of the very base itself. [Heb. *from the base, its shoulders*. Whether these words mean that the shoulders projected from the base, that "they rose above the corners with a slight curve" (Keil), or

that they were cast with the base, *i.e.*, *from* the same mould, as in the next verse, it is impossible to say.]

Ver. 35.—And in the top [Heb. *head*] of the base was there a round compass [Probably "the base above" (ver. 29) or stand for the laver. This was apparently *arched* to the height of nine inches above the top of the base] of half a cubit high : and on the top of the base the ledges [Heb. *hands*. These can hardly be either "the hands of the wheels" (ver. 32) or the "shoulders" of ver. 30 or ver. 34, but what they were it is difficult to say. They may have been arms or projections supporting the laver] thereof and the borders thereof were of the same. [Heb. *from it, sc.*, of one piece or casting.]

Ver. 36.—For on the plates of the ledges [*hands*] thereof, and on the borders [*sides*, *panels*] thereof, he graved cherubims, lions, and palm trees, according to the proportion [Heb. *nakedness*, hence naked space, void. The meaning is that he filled all the spaces with carvings] of every one, and additions [wreaths, festoons] round about.

Ver. 37.—After this manner he made the ten bases : all of them had one casting, one measure, and one size.

Ver. 38.—Then made he ten lavers of brass : one laver contained forty baths [*i.e.*, about 340 gals., if we accept the account of Josephus, Ant. viii. 2. 9. But see on ver. 26] : and every laver was four cubits. [It is uncertain whether the height or the diameter is meant. Keil decides for the latter—and four cubits, the width of the sides of the stand, may well have been also the diameter of the basin—on the ground

that as "the basins were set upon (עַל) the stands," it can hardly refer to the height. But it is worthy of remark that "the height of all the other parts has been mentioned" (Rawlinson). See vers. 27, 32, 35, and without this particular we could not calculate the *entire* height, which, if the laver were four cubits, would be about thirteen feet. This surprising size is accounted for by remembering the height of the altar, to which the fat and other sacrificial portions had to be transferred from the laver] : and upon every one of the ten bases one laver. [Ten lavers would not be at all too many when we remember the prodigious number of victims which were occasionally offered.]

Ver. 39.—And he put five bases on the right side [Heb. *shoulder*] of the house, and five on the left side of the house [*i.e.*, on the south and north sides of the court of the priests] : and he set the sea on the right side of the house eastward over against the south. [This passage is decisive as to which was the right and which the left. The right side was the south. It was probably for convenience that the sea did not stand due east of the house, *i.e.*, between the porch and altar.]

Ver. 40.—**And Hiram made the lavers** [So the Rec. Text. But perhaps we ought to read סִירוֹת, *i.e.*, *pots*, here, as in ver. 45 and 2 Chron. iv. 11. This word is joined with shovels and basons, not only in these two passages, but also in Exod. xxvii. 3, 2 Kings xxv. 14, Jer. lii. 18; in other words, the appropriate term in this connexion would be "pots," while "lavers," having been just mentioned in ver. 38, would involve an idle repetition. Altogether, therefore, there can be little doubt that we should here read הסירות for הכירות. It is apparently the reading of the Chald., LXX., and some MSS. These "pots" were used, not for carrying away the ashes (Keil), but, as the name implies (סִיר, *effervescere*), for *boiling* the flesh of the peace offering (1 Sam. ii. 13, 14), **and the shovels** [these, again, as the name implies (יָע from יָעָה *abstulit; see* Gesen., Thesaurus, p. 607), were used for *taking away* the ashes from the altar (Exod. xxvii. 3 ; Num. iv. 14), **and the basons.** [The sacrificial bowls for receiving the blood of the victims (Exod. xxxviii. 3 ; Num. iv. 14).] **So Hiram made an end of doing all the work** [the writer now recapitulates the work of Hiram. The repetition may be due to the fact that the history was compiled from various lists and documents] **that he made king Solomon for** [Heb. omits the prep.] **the house of the Lord.**

Ver. 41.—**The** [Heb. omits the art. and reads *pillars, two*] **two pillars, and the two bowls of the chapiters that were on the top of the two pillars; and the two networks to cover the two bowls of the chapiters which were upon the top of the pillars.** [See on verses 16—20.]

Ver. 42.—**And four hundred pomegranates** [Heb. *the pomegranates,* 400] **for the two networks, even two rows of pomegranates for one network, to cover the two bowls of the chapiters that were upon the pillars** [Heb. *upon the face of the pillars*]. A chapiter could hardly be correctly described as עַל־פְּנֵי הָע. It is probable that this is a clerical error, and that we should read עַל־שְׁנֵי הָע (Bähr, Keil), "upon the *two* pillars." So LXX. ἐπ' ἀμφοτέροις κ.τ.λ. This is a more likely emendation than עַל רָאשׁ. It is true this latter is the reading of some MSS., and is followed by the Syr. and Vulg., but it can easily be accounted for, being a repetition of the last words of ver. 41, while

it fails to account, as the first-named emendation does, for the עַל־פְּנֵי.

Ver. 43. **And the ten bases and the ten lavers** [Heb. " *the bases, ten and the lavers, ten* "] **on the bases.** [See on vers. 27—37.]

Ver. 44.—**And one** [Heb. *the one*] **sea and twelve oxen** [Heb. *the oxen twelve*] **under the sea** [vers. 23—26].

Ver. 45.—**And the pots** [see on ver. 40], **and the shovels, and the basons, and all these vessels** [according to the *Keri*] **which Hiram made** [There is no mention of the altar, as in 2 Chron. iv. 1, possibly because it was not made by Hiram (Bähr)] **to** [rather, *for*] **king Solomon for** [Heb. omits] **the house of the Lord, were of bright brass.** [Marg. *made bright, i.e., polished* after casting.]

Ver. 46.—**In the plain** [Heb. *Ciccar, i.e.*, circle or circuit, the word used only of the Ghor or Jordan valley. This tract is called " *The Ciccar* " Gen. xiii., 11, xix. 17, &c. See Stanley, " Sinai and Palestine," App., § 12] **of Jordan** [in the Heb. this river (" *the* descender") always takes the art.] **did the king cast them, in the clay ground** [Heb. as marg. *in the thickness of the ground.* Whether the soil was made thick by stamping (Keil) it is impossible to say. It looks as if this site had been chosen because the soil was suitable] **between Succoth** [Gen. xxxiii. 17. It appears from Judg. viii. 5 that it lay east of the Jordan (*cf.* Josh. xiii. 27, where it allotted to the tribe of Gad) ; " and indeed it has been recovered, under its later name Tarala, at Tell Dar'ala, northeast of the Dâmieh ford " (Condor, p. 299). As Zarthan was almost certainly west of the Jordan, and as the casting—from the nature of the country must as certainly have been done to the west of the river, it is somewhat surprising to find a trans-Jordanic town mentioned as one of the landmarks defining the site. It is possible that there was a western Succoth—a place named *Sâkût* was discovered by Robinson and Van de velde, a few miles south of Bethshean ; but this name is radically different (Conder). It is, therefore, more probable that, being near the ford of the river, this place was so well known that it would serve better than any of the less familiar western towns to identify the site of the foundry] **and Zarthan.** [See note on chap. iv. 12.]

Ver. 47.—**And Solomon left all the vessels** *unweighed* [the interpretation of the A. V. italics is justified by the next clauses] **because they were exceeding many : neither was the weight of the brass found out.** [Marg. *searched.* So Gesen. *al.* This does not mean that the " brass for each vessel was not weighed out" (Bähr), but that the total weight of the metal was not, perhaps could not, be ascertained.]

The sacred record now proceeds to enumerate the vessels, &c., used *inside* the temple—those hitherto described having been for external use. These latter, as became the furniture of a house which blazed in gold, were all of gold, while the former were of brass. It would seem to be a fair inference, from the omission of Hiram's name, that he was not employed on the manufacture of these latter vessels.

Ver. 48.—**And Solomon made all the vessels which pertained unto** [neither word in Heb.] **the house of the Lord: the altar of gold** [the altar of incense. See on chap. vi. 20, 22] **and the table of gold** [The Heb. shows the meaning to be, He made the table out of gold, not "He made the golden table," as Keil. 2 Chron. iv. 8 (cf. ver. 19 and 1 Chron. xxviii. 16) speaks of ten tables] **whereupon the shewbread was.**

Ver. 49.—**And the candlesticks** [Exod. xxv. 31—37; xxxvii. 17—24. According to Jewish tradition, the seven-branched candlestick was preserved in the temple in addition to the ten named here] **of pure** [Heb. *shut*] **gold, five on the right side and five on the left, before the oracle** [" These are said to have formed a sort of railing before the vail, and to have been connected by golden chains *under* which, on the day of atonement, the high priest crept" (Dict. Bib. i. 249). The idea that the ten candlesticks rested on the ten tables mentioned in the Chronicles is entirely groundless. *Eleven* tables would in that case have been necessary (Bähr). Besides we are distinctly told that the tables were for the shewbread (2 Chron. iv. 19), not for the candlesticks], **with the flowers** [ornaments of the candlestick (Exod. xxv. 31)], **and the lamps** [the seven extremities of the candlestick which held the oil and the wicks (ver. 37). It is highly probable that the temple candlesticks were fashioned after that of the tabernacle], **and the tongs** [*ib.* ver. 38. Heb. *two takers*] **of gold.**

Ver. 50.—**And the bowls** [same word in Exod. xii. 22. The "dishes" of Exod. xxv. 29, and xxxvii. 16, with which Rawlinson identifies them, are expressed by a different word. He thinks they were for the oil—which the connexion would seem to imply —but they *may* have been for the blood], **and the snuffers** [Heb. *knives*, זָמָר, *carpsit*. The word is used of the pruning-hook in Isa. ii. 4; cf. Levit. xxv. 3. They served the purpose though they had not the shape of our snuffers], **and the basons** [same word as in vers. 40, 45. These latter, however, were of brass, while those of the text were of pure gold. According to 2 Chron. iv. 8, they were a hundred in number. As the root (זָרַק) signifies to *sprinkle*, they were probably either for the water or the blood of sprinkling. Keil thinks they were for the wine of the libations], **and the spoons** [כַּפּוֹת, lit., *palms* (of hands), hence used of shallow vessels (Exod. xxv. 29; Num. vii. 84, 86. The last cited passage (cf. vers. 14, 20, 26) shows that they were used for the incense (Lev. xxiv. 7, &c.), LXX. θυίσκαι], **and the censers** [or *snuffers, extinguishers*; marg. *ash-pans*. In Exod. xxv. 38 the word is translated *snuff-dishes*. In Num. iv. 14, xvi. 6, it signifies *censers*, which may well be the meaning here] **of pure gold; and the hinges** [or *sockets* of the hinges (Gesen., Keil)] **of gold, both for the doors of the inner house, the most holy place** [Heb. *for the holy of holies*], **and for the doors of the house, to wit, of the temple.** [These were evidently of inferior (not *pure*) metal.]

Ver. 51.—**So was ended all the work that king Solomon made for the house of the Lord. And Solomon brought in the things which David his father had dedicated** [marg. *holy things of David* (2 Sam. viii. 8, 10, 11; 1 Chron. xxii. 3, 14, 16; xxviii. 14—18). Cf. xxvi. 26—28] **; even the silver, and the gold, and the vessels, did he put among the treasures of the house of the Lord.** [So that all the store of precious metal and the brass that David had prepared was not absorbed in the decoration and furniture of the temple. There would seem to have been a considerable overplus, which was stored in the temple treasury.]

HOMILETICS.

Vers. 15—22.—*The Pillars of Brass.* If, as some think, the importance of any Scripture subject is to be gauged by the space assigned to it in the sacred page, then surely the fact that eight long verses of this chapter are occupied with the description of these two columns and their capitals proves, first, their importance in the eyes of Jewish writers, and, secondly, that they must have a significance for the minds of Christian readers.

But the importance of these monuments (which is also attested (1) by their *position*—in the very forefront of the temple—the first objects that would strike the eye of the beholder—and (2) by their *isolation*—they were apparently unconnected with the edifice and served a purpose of their own) is not due to what they were in themselves. No doubt they were regarded in that age as wonderful works of art. Probably they were the largest castings either accomplished or attempted up to that date. And from the minute details of their capitals, the chequer-work, chain-work, net-work, lily-work—details evidently recorded with some degree of pride and wonderment on the part of the historian—we may reasonably infer that there " were not the like made in any kingdom " (ch. x. 20). But it is not because of this that so much prominence is accorded to them in Scripture; it is because of their connexion with the temple. Their glory is reflected on them from the sanctuary. They are mentioned " because of the house of the Lord our God," of which they were the handmaids and ornaments. We are led, therefore, to inquire—

I. What meaning they had for the Jew?

II. What lessons they have for ourselves?

I. But in order to arrive at their *meaning*, we must first consider their *purpose*. We have seen that they were not structural, but monumental (note on ver. 21); in fact they served instead of an inscription upon the building. The Western world, with its love of the concrete, often stamps its great edifices with appropriate legends. But the children of the East have ever preferred the mystical teaching of symbolism. For them there has always been a charm in "the view of things half seen." And so the Jewish temple bore no letters on its front, but its representative pillars stood forth, embodiments in themselves of the ideas of the building, and silently proclaimed its object and character. And this is the teaching they had for the wise—

1. *That the temple was strong and firm and lasting.* Their very materials proclaimed this. They were not of perishing wood or stone, but of enduring bronze. Then, they were of unusual girth in proportion to their height, for whereas the shaft was 12 cubits in circumference, it was but 18 cubits high (Jer. lii. 21). The first impression they gave, consequently, would be that of strength, of fixity, and so they spoke, by their very character as well as by their names, of the *stability* of the house. It was no longer a tent (cf. Isa. xxxviii. 12), it was a house of cedar (2 Sam. vii. 2), it was a κτῆμα ἐς ἀεί. The two columns, that is to say, served instead of these two inscriptions, " *I have surely built thee a house to dwell in, a settled place for thee to abide in for ever*" (ch. viii. 13), and " *This is my rest for ever, here will I dwell, for I have desired it* " (Psa. cxxxii. 14).

2. *That its strength and stability were in God.* Of course this is an idea which symbolism could only express imperfectly. And yet it may be (as some have thought) that the brazen pillars would recall to some minds the pillar of cloud, the token of God's presence. And if we may see in the steeple a " silent finger pointing to the sky," then surely these erect columns may have carried men's thoughts upwards to the throne of God. But if not, the names, *Jachin, Boaz*, at any rate, witnessed for Him and proclaimed Him to all as the hope and stay of the new sanctuary. It was, therefore, as if in the place of pillars these superscriptions also had been conspicuous on the temple: for *Jachin*—" *God is in the midst of her; she shall not be removed;* " and for *Boaz*—" *Except the Lord build the house, they labour in vain that build it* " (Psa. cxxvii. 1. Note. This psalm is ascribed to Solomon. And these words *were* inscribed on the late Eddystone lighthouse).

3. *That it was the shrine of a holy God.* The two columns, standing as sentinels over the house, confronted all who came into its courts with the idea of *consecration.* We have seen that column and chapiter together bore a rough resemblance to a lily—the column the stalk, the chapiter the flower. Now the lily is the emblem of purity (see on ch. vii. 19). The " lily-work in the porch " proclaimed the house as belonging to the All-Holy One of Israel. The columns, therefore, in their esoteric symbolic language, spoke to the same effect as if these words had been blazoned on the temple's front (as on the high priest's mitre) : " *Holiness unto the Lord* " (Exod. xxviii. 36; xxxix. 30), or these, "*I the Lord your God am holy* " (Levit. xix. 2; xxi. 8).

4. *That it was for the worship of a holy people.* The chapters were fashioned after a lily-cup. The columns, *i.e.*, *blossomed* into purity under the shelter of the sanctuary, and so proclaimed that holiness was to be the *product* of the temple services and ritual. They served accordingly as *memoranda* both to priests and worshippers. It is said that on the front of the second temple words *were* inscribed, viz., these: "Know before whom thou art going to stand." In this first temple the two columns spoke to the same purport. To the priests they cried, "*Be ye clean that bear the vessels of the Lord*" (Isa. lii. 11); to the people they spoke, like the "fringe with the ribband of blue," "*Be ye holy unto your God*" (Num. xv. 38, 40).

5. *That it was for a people zealous of good works.* On the columns were 400 pomegranates. Pomegranates are said to be emblems of *fruitfulness*. If so, they taught the Hebrew worshipper this last lesson—they served instead of this inscription, "*Thou shalt not delay to offer the first of thy ripe fruits*" (Exod. xxii. 29); or this, "*He looked that his vineyard should bring forth grapes*" (Isa. v. 2).

II. But what lessons have Jachin and Boaz for ourselves? Do they not speak to us (1) *of the Church*, the "*pillar* and ground of the truth*" (1 Tim. iii. 15); (2) *of the Christian*, who shall be "a *pillar* in the temple of God?" (Rev. iii. 12.)

1. *Of the Church.* The lessons these brazen columns had for the Hebrew people, the same they have for ourselves, with this difference, that they also speak to us by their *fall*. They image forth the *stability* of the Church—that the gates of hell shall not prevail against it; that its *strength* is in God—its weapons are not carnal, but spiritual (2 Cor. x. 4; Matt. xxviii. 20; John xv. 4); that its object is *holiness* (Ephes. v. 27; i. 4; Titus ii. 12) and *fruitfulness* (John xv. 8; 2 Cor. ix. 10; Phil. i. 11). But they have an additional lesson for us, derived from their destruction. For why were these splendid works of art removed out of their place, broken up, and carried to Babylon? (Jer. lii. 17, 21.) It was because their lessons were unheeded, because the people were *not pure and holy* (Jer. xxii. 8, 9; v. 31; Acts vii. 43). And so we learn—not that the Catholic Church will "likewise perish:" that can never be (Matt. xvi. 18); of that it might be said, with a propriety of which the Latin poet was all unconscious, "Exegi monumentum *aere perennius*"—the columns lasted 423 years, the Church 1800 already—but that particular churches, if unfaithful, shall have their candlesticks removed out of their places (Rev. ii. 5). "If God spared not the natural branches," &c. (Rom. xi. 21).

2. *Of the Christian.* He may learn hence—(1) To be rooted and grounded in faith and love (Eph. iii. 17; Col. i. 23). (2) Not to be carried about by every wind of doctrine (Eph. iv. 14; James i. 6; note on ver. 20). (3) That "God is *our* refuge and strength" (Phil. iv. 13; Col. i. 11; 1 Peter v. 10). (4) That we are to "wear the white lily of a blameless life" (cf. 2 Peter iii. 14). (5) And to "bring forth much fruit," and (6) that if we overcome, we shall be pillars in the heavenly temple, not to be broken, or cast into the fire, or to share in the destruction of Babylon (Rev. xviii. 2), but to "go out no more for ever" (Rev. iii. 12).

Vers. 23, 24.— *The Molten Sea and the Brazen Lavers.* If the two pillars teach the lesson of purity, of personal holiness, how much more the sea and bases! For observe—

1. Sea and bases had the same end in view, viz., *purification.* The first was for the cleansing of the *priests.* The second for the cleansing of the *sacrifices* offered by the priests.

2. The extraordinary provision of water for the service of the temple. Underneath the temple area was a great reservoir (it is said to be some fifty feet deep), no doubt the same which exists at the present day, near the Mosque el Aksa (note on ver. 26). This was connected by an aqueduct (which can still be traced) with Solomon's Pools at Etham, near Bethlehem. Whether these great works were purely for the use of the temple, or whether the city also shared in their benefits, may be doubtful, but that the temple occupied the first place in the scheme is beyond all question. From this subterranean sea—whether by pipes or by the labours of the *Nethinim,* we cannot be certain—both molten sea and brazen lavers were filled.

But here a distinction must be made. The priests were *commanded* to wash, under pain of death (Exod. xxx. 19 sqq.; xxix. 4; xl. 30—32), but there was no such command with respect to the victims. No; the sacrifices would seem to have been washed because the Jewish mind instinctively felt that this was right and fitting. And that it *was* right and fitting is proved by the fact that the service was accepted, and here enjoys the Divine sanction. We should hardly have had twelve verses of Scripture devoted to the description of the lavers and their bases, had not God Himself approved of the washing of "the work of the burnt offering" (2 Chron. iv. 6, Heb.)

Hence we may learn—

I. That Christian priests *must* be washed.

II. That Christian sacrifices *should* be cleansed.

I. CHRISTIAN PRIESTS MUST BE WASHED. Here two questions arise. (1) *Who are Christian* PRIESTS? (2) *What is this* WASHING?

1. By *Christian priests* we may understand here all Christians. For all Christians *are* priests, precisely as all Jews were priests (cf. 1 Peter ii. 5, 9, with Exod. xix. 6). Of course, there is a priesthood among Christians, just as there was a priesthood among the Jews (see page 113). It is often said, and said truly, that the word ἱερεύς, *sacerdos*, is nowhere applied to the ministers of the New Testament; but the answer is that it *could* not have been so applied, so long as the Levitical priesthood existed, without risk of confusion. It is also true that the functions of the Christian presbyterate are very, very different from those of the Jewish priesthood; but all the same, if Christianity is filling up, and not the reversal or the negation of Judaism (Col. ii. 17; Matt. v. 17), then, assuredly, it must not only have its altar, (Heb. xiii. 10), but its priesthood. But let us understand the word here of the body of believers: for clearly, if we can prove that *all* Christians must be washed, how much more those who minister in holy things, and bear the vessels of the Lord? (Isa. lii. 11.)

2. By *Christian washing* we may understand, primarily, THE washing (κατ' ἐξοχήν) of the New Testament, "the washing of regeneration" (Titus iii. 5; cf. (1 Cor vi. 11; Eph. v. 26; Heb. x. 22; cf. vi. 2). For to all Christians is the command addressed, "Arise, and be baptized, and *wash away* thy sins" (Acts xxii. 16; cf. ch. ii. 38). Of all may our holy Lord be heard to say, "If I *wash* thee not, thou hast no part with me" (John xiii. 8; cf. iii. 5; Mark xvi. 16).

But is this all? Are we only to find here a lesson as to Christian baptism? Certainly not. For observe, (1) by baptism, the initial rite of our religion, men are *made* priests (Rev. i. 5, 6). (2) The washing of the priests was a washing of the *hands and the feet* (Exod. xxx. 19); and (3) it was to be *repeated* as often as they "went into the tabernacle of the congregation or" came near unto the altar (ver. 20; ch. xl. 32). Clearly, then, the "*one* baptism" of Christianity cannot respond to this exclusively. No; that rather corresponds to the washing of the whole person (Levit. xvi. 4, 24), which the Rabbins say was performed in the molten sea, or in its basin; but which may possibly have been performed in private. That there *was* such complete ablution on the part of the priests needs no proof; it is presupposed in the directions about the hands and feet. It would have been mockery to wash the extremities of the body, while the body itself remain unclean. But the priest who went to the temple pure might, perhaps, contract some defilement on the way; the exposed parts, the hands and the feet, might be stained and so become unfit for the service of the All-Holy. It was for this the molten sea was provided, and this helps to illustrate our Lord's words, "He that is washed needeth not save to wash his feet" (John xiii. 10). Even so we, though, as St. Paul says, we "*were* washed" (ἀπελούσασθε, aor.) "in the laver of regeneration," have sullied our baptismal robes in our passage through and contact with the world (James iii. 2), and need, day by day, cleansing and forgiveness (Matt. vi. 12). The text teaches, then, that we are unfit for the service of the Most Pure until we have washed our *hands* and *feet;* until, *i.e.*, we are purged from the soils and stains of this wicked world. Not only must "our bodies be washed with pure water," our "hearts" must also be "sprinkled from an evil conscience," before we can draw near with acceptance to

God (Heb. x. 22). "I cannot pray, but I sin; I cannot hear, or preach a sermon, but I sin; I cannot give an alms or receive the sacrament, but I sin; nay, I cannot so much as confess my sins, but my very confessions are still aggravations of them ; my repentance needs to be repented of, my tears want washing, and the very washing of my tears needs still to be washed over again in the blood of my Redeemer" (Bp. Beveridge).

What, then, let us now ask, is the "sea," what the "laver," for the washing away of these daily sins and defilements? It is a fountain of blood ("Not by water only, but by water and blood," 1 John v. 6); it is the other sacrament of our religion, the "blood of the new covenant shed for many for the remission of sins " (Matt. xxvi. 28). "The one baptism for the remission of sins " (Nicene Creed) cannot apply to the sins of later life. For this, other provision is needed, and in the mercy of God other provision is made in the sacrament of love and the ministry of reconciliation. (Cf. also Matt. xvi. 19; xviii. 18 ; John xx. 23 ; Matt. xxviii. 20.)

But here one word of caution may possibly be needful. It must not be supposed for a moment that there is any other source or ground of cleansing and forgiveness than the free, unmerited mercy of God in Christ; that there is any hope for the sinner except in the "full, perfect, and sufficient sacrifice, oblation, and satisfaction" once made by the one Saviour "for the sins of the whole world;" or that any rites or ordinances can have any virtue or efficacy apart from His meritorious death and His now victorious life. The sacraments are not, cannot be, the *sources* or the *grounds* of forgiveness, nor do they work like a charm—*ex opere operato*. But in the all-wise appointment of God, they are the *means* of grace, the *channels* through which His infinite mercy *ordinarily* flows (*gratia non ligatur mediis*) to the penitent and believing soul.

Nor must it be supposed that the generous provision made by God for the cleansing of all sin obviates the need for striving against sin (Heb. xii. 4). We are to "*cleanse ourselves* from all filthiness of flesh and spirit" (2 Cor. vii. 1). We are to "*purify ourselves*, even as He is pure" (1 John iii. 3). The priests of the Holy God must "live a clean life" (Wyclif).

II. CHRISTIAN SACRIFICES SHOULD BE CLEANSED. Here again two questions arise. (1) What are Christian *sacrifices?* (2) How can they be *cleansed?*

1. *Christian sacrifices.* Those which all Christian men are ordained to offer (1 Peter ii. 8) are these—(1) The living sacrifice of body and soul (Rom. xii. 1). (2) The sacrifice of praise and thanksgiving (Heb. xiii. 15). (3) The sacrifice of alms and oblations (Heb. xiii. 16; Phil. iv. 18).

2. The *Cleansing* of these sacrifices is that which takes place in a "pure heart and good conscience." It is a matter of motive, of *intention.* The quality of the sacrifice depends on the spirit of the sacrificer. It is a sacrifice, howsoever offered —there is such a thing as "the sacrifice of fools" (Eccles. v. 1)—but it may be, and often is, a maimed, or unclean, or unworthy sacrifice. If our praise, for example, be prompted by the love of music rather than the love of God ; if our alms be offered for the praise of men (Matt. vi. 1) and not "for His name's sake," then the sacrifice is unclean. The Christian priest, consequently, should "interrogate his heart "—"*Interroge viscera tua*" (Augustine)—before he enters on Divine service. It has been well said that we ought to wash our prayers and praises in our hearts before we put them into our lips. The customary "prayer before service" and the self-examination before communion (1 Cor. xi. 28), if made more real, would ensure the cleansing of the sacrifice. (Compare James i. 27.)

Ver. 46.—*The Clay Ground in the circuit of the Jordan.* These things are an allegory. These words suggest some thoughts as to the soil in which the King of Heaven moulds the vessels for *His* service (2 Tim. ii. 20, 21; Acts ix. 15; Rom. ix. 21, 23). They, too, are prepared in the *plain:* they are cast in the *clay ground.*

Observe (1) that both *pillars* and *vessels*, *i.e.*, Jachin and Boaz, as well as " the pots and the shovels and the basins," were cast in this same clay ground. In the two pillars we may fitly see for our present purpose emblems of those two "*pillars and* basements of the truth" (1 Tim. iii. 15), the Jewish and Christian churches;

in the vessels, emblems of those "*vessels* unto honour," the "messengers of the churches," Prophets, Apostles, Martyrs, &c. (2 Cor. viii. 23 ; Acts ix. 15). We shall find that the great Master Builder has prepared them all in the *plain ;* that all alike have been moulded in the *clay.*

As to the *plain,* the figure is obvious enough, and a few words will suffice to expound it. From the Mesopotamian immigrants into Palestine, the first fathers of the Jewish people, down to the peasants and fishermen of Galilee, aye, and to the poor monk, Luther, and the poor servitor, Whitfield, history constantly teaches the same lesson—that not many wise men or mighty or noble (1 Cor. i. 26) are the vessels chosen of Heaven to do God's work in the world. The apostles did not issue forth from "king's houses" (Matt. xi. 8). Just as "the gentle rain from heaven" leaves the mountains and descends into the vales, so does the grace of God ever condescend to men of low degree. Not "the princes of this world" (1 Cor. ii. 8), not its rich men (James ii. 6), but the "poor of this world" hath God chosen (ib. ver. 5). "Have any of the rulers or of the Pharisees believed on him?" (John vii. 48). No, it was the "common people"—the despised *amhaaretz*— "heard him gladly" (Mark xii. 37). The early adversaries of Christianity used to sneer at the humble origin and occupations of its champions, and the apologists would not and could not deny the charge.

Now as to the "*clay ground,*" observe that while the text gives this rendering, the margin has, "*thickness of the ground.*" It is not a distinction without a difference, for the latter rendering would import that the soil had been *made* thick, for the purpose of casting, by stamping or puddling. And which of these translations is the true one; whether, *i.e.,* the soil was naturally clayey—perhaps from the overflow of the Jordan (Josh. iii. 15, Heb.), perhaps from the springs which make much of the Jordan valley into a swamp (Conder, pp. 226—229)—or whether it was artificially prepared for castings, it is perhaps impossible to say. Nor need we wish to decide, since for our purpose both meanings are true. Whatever Hiram did, God casts His vessels, some in the clay, *i.e.,* in the most unpromising soil, with the most ungenial surroundings ; some "in the thickness of the ground," *i.e.,* in soil which has been trodden by the iron feet of the persecutor ; and some in both.

I. Let us now see how (1) THE CHURCHES—we regard them as two for our present purpose, though strictly the Christian ἐκκλησία is but the development of the Jewish (see p. 112)—and (2) THEIR MESSENGERS have both been prepared *in the clay ground.* But first, let us carry our thoughts to that foundry in the Jordan valley. We now assume that it was a bed of clay in which the castings were made. If so, it is probable this tract of land had hitherto laid waste. The ox had not drawn the plough through it ; it had yielded neither seed to the sower, nor bread to the eater ; the farmer had not planted it with olive or vine. And in a land so small—Palestine is about the same size as Wales—and so densely populated as the Holy Land ; in a country where every available yard was cultivated, and where even the steep hill sides were laid out in terraces to increase the acreage ; in a land, too, of great fertility (Deut. viii. 7–9)—for the whole realm was remarkably prolific, and "the plain of the Jordan" was the garden of the whole (Gen. xiii. 10)—this barren tract could not fail to be noticed. It had long been an eyesore, we may well believe, to the *fellahin* who tilled the neighbouring fields. The traveller who passed it on his way to the fords of the Jordan (Judg. viii. 5 ; xii. 6 ; Gen. xxxiii. 17) pronounced it unprofitable, and altogether it was "nigh unto cursing " (Heb. vi. 8).

And so it lay, century after century, a marsh, or piece of scrub, a blot on the landscape. Men thought it was irreclaimable. But now the temple is being built, the vessels of brass have to be cast, and through the length and breadth of Palestine they find no spot so suited to the purpose as the "clay ground between Succoth and Zarthan." Here shall the foundry be. And so from this despised and desolate tract the burnished brass went forth to adorn the temple of the Lord. Even so—

1. *The Jewish Church was moulded in the clay.* Where was it constituted? In the desert of Sinai, in the "great and terrible wilderness." In the Red Sea was its baptism (1 Cor. x. 2) ; at Horeb (lit., *dry ground*) it entered into the covenant. From the "backside of the desert," from the plain of *Râhah,* where "desolation

keeps unbroken sabbath; " from a "frozen tempest of black, weather-worn, rugged mountain peaks," the Hebrew Church went forth to witness for God. Nowhere, perhaps, under the whole heaven is there a more arid and rugged and desolate and uninhabitable land. Yet God chose it to be the school and training-ground of His Church.

2. *The Christian Church was cast in the clay.* Not in Greece, amid the schools of philosophy, not in Rome, among senates, and armies, and subject kings, but in Palestine, a despised corner of the empire, among Jews, who were hated of all men. And in what part of Palestine? Not in Jerusalem, among the scribes and doctors, but in the provinces, in "Galilee of the Goim." The question was often asked, Can any good thing come out of Nazareth? (John i. 46.) The answer was often given, " Out of Galilee ariseth no prophet" (John vii. 52). Surely this was clay ground. Yet there it pleased God to found the Holy Catholic Church. And this, which is true of the Church, is equally true of its vessels. For—

3. *The lawgivers and prophets of the Jewish Church were shaped in the clay.* Moses, it is true, was bred in the court, but he was not prepared there for his work. No, it was necessary for him to *leave* the court in order to become a "vessel meet for the Master's use." It was in this same desert of Sinai, amid the Bedouin, while keeping an Arab's flock, and leading a nomadic life, after forty years of solitude, that God appeared unto him. The lawgiver himself came from the clay. So did Elijah, the restorer of the law. He was a Gileadite. It was a wild, unsettled, semi-civilized, trans-Jordanic region gave to the world the greatest of the prophets. And he too must go into the desert, and must be trained for his work at Horeb—the *"dry ground"* (1 Kings xix. 8). And the same remark applies to nearly all the prophets, judges, &c. Occasionally we have a Jeremiah, the son of a high priest (Jer. i. 1), or a Daniel of the royal seed (Dan. i. 3), but more frequently a herdman, a gatherer of sycamore fruit (Amos vii. 14; 1 Kings xix. 19), or a captive by the river Chebar (Ezek. i. 3), rises up to speak for God.

4. *The apostles and preachers of Christianity were fashioned and prepared in clay ground.* (1) The founder of Christianity was well called a "root out of a *dry ground*" (Isa. liii. 2). "Is not this the carpenter's son?" (Matt. xiii. 55). "Jesus of Nazareth, the son of Joseph" (John i. 45). "How knoweth this man letters, having never learned?" (*ib.* vii. 15.) (2) The apostles, too, came from the fisherman's boat at Bethsaida (John i. 44), and from the receipt of custom (Matt. ix. 9) in Capernaum. Only one out of the entire college had studied in the schools (Acts xxii. 3). They were justly described as "ignorant and unlearned men" (*ib.* iv. 13). (3) And the same may be said of nearly all the early Christians and confessors. It was a most unpromising and unlikely soil in which the Church first took root. " Publicans and sinners." M. Renan has given a graphic description of the early Christians of Rome—a "longshore population," sleeping on the straw, " clad in malodorous stable slops," "smelling of garlic," "with fetid breath like that of ill-fed people," &c. It is not improbable that the bulk of the early Christians were men of this sort, tentmakers like Aquila, slaves like Onesimus, gaolers like him of Philippi, soldiers like those of Cæsar's household. And eighteen centuries have only served to establish more firmly the truth that "not many mighty," &c. It is curious and suggestive that so many of the saints of the Roman calendar are said to have been of noble birth. It is easy thus to glorify *dead* saints, but if, with Chateaubriand, we ask to see *living* ones, we frequently find them in the homes of the poor, and almost invariably amid cares, worries, temptations, hindrances, persecutions of every kind. The saints are still fashioned in the clay.

II. But let us now assume that this foundry of the Jordan valley was not a bed of natural clay, but that the soil had been prepared by stamping. We shall find that both (1) the Churches and (2) the messengers of the Churches have been prepared "in the *thickness of the ground,*" under the heel of persecution and oppression. And first of the *Churches.*

1. *The Jewish Church came out of the house of bondage.* " Out of the iron furnace" (Deut. iv. 20; 1 Kings viii. 51: cf. Exod. v.) " Dealt subtilly with our kindred, and evil entreated our fathers" (Acts vii. 19). It was among the *brick-*

fields—the thick Nile mud—of Egypt, and their hardships and oppressions, that God disciplined and prepared His people.

2. *The Christian Church has come out of great tribulation.* Its history begins with a shameful crucifixion, and it is a history written in blood, a history of "stripes" (Acts xvi. 23; 2 Cor. vi. 5), beatings (Acts v. 40), stonings (*ib.* vii. 59; xiv. 19), the sword (*ib.* xii. 2), "great persecution" (*ib.* viii. 1), and the like. Nero, Decius, Aurelian, Diocletian—what tragedies are connected with these names! Yet "the blood of the martyrs has been the seed of the Church," and in the reign of Constantine the empire awoke to find itself Christian. Persecution only evolved progress (Phil. i. 12, 13). And what is true of the pillars is also true of the vessels. For—

3. *The heroes of the Jewish Church passed through fire and sword.* Moses must flee his country, must learn obedience by the things which he suffered. Elijah—they sought his life (1 Kings xix. 10). Jezebel sought to slay the prophets of the Lord. Daniel is cast into the lions' den ; the Hebrew children into the fire; Jeremiah into the mire and clay (Jer. xxxviii. 6). Isaiah is sawn asunder (Heb. xi. 37). Zechariah is slain between the temple and the altar, &c. See Heb. xi. 34—38. What evidences of stamping are here! Surely the ground bears the marks of a struggle!

4. *The saints of the new dispensation have been made perfect through suffering.* For St. Paul, see 2 Cor. xi. 23—33, and remember that this list only extends, at the latest, to A.D. 58. That "chosen vessel" was first showed "what great things he must suffer" (Acts ix. 16). For the early Christians see Rev. ii. 10. 13; vi. 10; vii. 14, &c.; 1 Cor. iv. 13; 2 Cor. vi. 5—10. Polycarp, Augustine, Cyprian, Chrysostom—the time would fail me to tell of those bright vessels of grace, some in the dark ages, some in our own time, who were prepared for the ministry and the inheritance of the saints in "the thickness of the ground," and who, "after they had suffered awhile," were made perfect.

HOMILIES BY VARIOUS AUTHORS.

Ver. 21.—*Jachin and Boaz.* No features in Solomon's temple have given rise to so much controversy as these two famous pillars; the beauty of which Jewish writers are never tired of recounting. They were marvels of the glyptic skill for which the Phœnician workmen were distinguished. Homer speaks of such metallic work. In Il. xxiii. 741—744, he thus describes the prize assigned by Achilles for the foot race at the funeral of Patroclus—

> " A bowl of solid silver, deftly wrought,
> That held six measures, and in beauty far
> Surpassed whatever else the world could boast ;
> Since men of *Sidon*, skilled in glyptic art,
> Had made it, and *Phœnician* mariners
> Had brought it with them over the dark sea."

(See also his description of Menelaus' gift to Telemachus, Od. iv. 614—618.) Hiram, the Phœnician artificer, lent by the king of Tyre to Solomon, was specially skilled in such work (2 Chron. ii. 14). "In the plain of Jordan, in the clay ground between Succoth and Zarthan," he cast these two great bronze pillars, each $17\frac{1}{2}$ cubits high, with capitals five cubits high, adorned with pomegranates, and "nets of checker-work, and wreaths of chain-work." They were placed on the right and left of the porch of the temple, and probably were not obelisks, but were necessary as "pillars" to support the roof, which was thirty feet in width. That these were symbolic is evident from their names, which may be rendered, "Stability" and "Strength." The reference is not so much to the material building, but to the kingdom of God in Israel, which was embodied in the temple. They pointed then, and now, to the beauty and strength of the dwelling of God.

I. THE FASHIONING OF THE PILLARS. Made of bronze cast in the earth. None but the initiated would expect such an issue from such a process. Picture the anxiety of those in charge when the mould was constructed, when the metal was molten, &c. Apply to the anxiety and care of those rearing the spiritual temple. 1. *They were the product of human skill.* This skill was devoutly recognized as the gift of God. Compare ver. 14 with the description of Bezaleel's artistic "gifts." If wisdom of that kind is from God, how much more is the highest wisdom needed for the upbuilding of the true temple (1 Cor. iii. 12—17). Turn to the promises of the Holy Spirit to the apostles, and of wisdom to all who seek. Refer to times of difficulty and anxiety in which only this heavenly help could avail the teachers and rulers of the Church. Observe such expressions as that in which Paul speaks of himself as " a wise master builder." Indicate special gifts still required by those who succeed to this work. "If any man lack wisdom let him ask of God," &c. 2. *They were the result of marvellous diligence.* Years and generations of effort had made these artificers what they were, and now daily they applied themselves to their toil, nor was it without reward. Nothing great can be attained in this world without work. God has not made things pleasant by ordaining that the way to them should be easy, but He has made them precious by ordaining that the way should be hard. The hardships endured by miners, pearl divers, agricultural labourers, &c. The strenuous toil of the student, the man of business, the explorer, the scientist, &c. No wonder that in the highest sphere diligence is essential. It is required for the upbuilding of our Christian character; *e.g.,* " Give diligence to to make your calling . . . sure," &c. " Work out your own salvation," &c., " Not as though I had already attained," &c. Similar diligence is required by the Church for the evangelization of the world. Contrast the diligence shown in other pursuits with the indolence in this. 3. *They were the product of combined effort.* The wealth of Solomon was added to the skill of Hiram. Observe the diversity of workmen essential for the designing, moulding, fashioning, uprearing of these pillars. Each did his own work, did it heartily, completely. All was not equally honourable, easy, remunerative; yet none neglected his share of the toil. Speak of the millions now constructing God's spiritual temple; how the various races of men, how the differing sects of Christians, how the peculiar tastes and gifts of individuals, are rearing " the house not made with hands," " the habitation of God, through the Spirit."

II. THE SYMBOLISM OF THE PILLARS. 1. *Stability* (Jachin). In this the temple was a contrast to the tabernacle. Yet even the temple and all that was material of the old worship passed away to make room for the spiritual realities which abide eternally. In Hebrews (xii. 27) we read of "the removing of those things that are shaken, as of things that are made, that those things which cannot be shaken may remain." Show how, amidst the fall of empires, the Church has lived, in spite of all that evil powers could do (Matt. xvi. 18). Speak of the safety, for time and eternity, of those who are in Christ (John x. 28), &c. 2. *Strength.* The Church needs more than endurance, it wants vigour. Resistance must be supplemented by aggression. Far more than the Jewish Church the Christian Church is to be characterized by this. The apostles were not merely to hold their own, but to go " into all the world, and preach the gospel to every creature." Only the active Church, only the active Christian, has a robust and wholesome life. Let "Boaz" stand beside "Jachin." 3. *Beauty.* The lilies and pomegranates adorning the pillars not only showed that there should be beauty in the *worship* of God, and that the noblest art should be consecrated to Him, but symbolized the truth declared in Psa. xcvi. 6, "Strength and beauty are in His sanctuary." Strength needs beauty to adorn it. Beauty needs strength to support it. Illustration: the ivy clustering round the oak. Let the courageous man be gentle; the stalwart man tender; the sweet girl morally strong, &c. If we would have it so, we shall find those graces in the holy place of God, the sacred place of prayer, whether public or secret, for strength and beauty are in His sanctuary. Emblems of stability and strength, yet exquisite in their beauty, let Jachin and Boaz, in the porch of the temple, remind us of what God would see in the Christian Church, and in every Christian character.—A. R.

EXPOSITION.

CHAPTER VIII. 1—66.

THE DEDICATION OF THE TEMPLE. — The stately and impressive service with which the Temple, the character and contents of which have now been described, was dedicated, is related in this chapter, and divides itself into four sections. We have (1) the removal of the ark and Solomon's ascription of praise on the occasion (vers. 1—22). (2) The prayer of consecration (vers. 23—54). (3) The benediction of the congregation (vers. 55—61), and (4) the festal sacrifices which followed on and completed the dedication (vers. 62—66). The inaugural rites, it is clear, were on a scale corresponding with the magnitude and renown of the undertaking (1 Chron. xxii. 5).

SECTION I.—*The Removal of the Ark.*

Ver. 1.—Then [*i.e.*, when the work of the house of the Lord was practically ended, as stated in ch. vii. 51. But the precise date of the dedication is a matter of dispute and uncertainty. We know that it took place in the seventh month of the year, but of what year we cannot be so sure. Was it the same year in the *eighth* month of which (ch. vi. 38) the house was finished (Ewald)? Was the dedication, that is to say, one month anterior to the completion of the house and its appointments? Or are we to understand " the seventh month " to mean the Ethanim of the following year (Bähr)? are we to assign the dedication, that is, to a date eleven months after completion? Or, finally, are we to believe with the Vat. LXX. μετὰ εἴκοσι ἔτη (the LXX. text is here, however, in great confusion), that the temple was not dedicated until the palaces were also built (see ch. ix. 1—9); are we to hold, *i.e.*, that though finished and ready for use, it remained unused for a period of thirteen years (Thenius, Keil)? These are questions which we cannot perhaps answer with absolute certainty, but, to my mind, every consideration is in favour of the date first mentioned, *i.e.*, the seventh month of the eleventh year of Solomon's reign. It is true Bähr says that this opinion " needs no refutation," while Keil pronounces it "directly at variance with chap. vii. 51." But it is worth while to inquire whether this is so? And, first, as to the bearing of the passage just cited, " So was ended all the work which," &c., taken in connexion with ch.

viii. 1, " Then Solomon assembled," &c. To the cursory reader it appears no doubt as if this " then " must refer to the completion of the work of which we have just heard, and which was not effected until the eighth month of the year (ch. vi. 38). But (1) אָז though probably a mark of time (= *tunc*), is clearly a word of great latitude of meaning, and may apply as well to one month before completion (the time specified in ch. vii. 51) as to eleven months after ; and (2) it would be quite consistent with the *usus loquendi* of the sacred writers to describe the temple as finished, when in reality it was incomplete in a few minor particulars (*De minimis non curat scriptura*). Further more, if the temple was finished in every detail, and in all its furniture and appointments, in the eighth month, as we learn from ch. vi. 38, we may be perfectly sure it would or could be *practically* finished—finished so as to be ready for consecration—by the seventh month. Indeed, it is not an unreasonable presumption, that it hardly would be perfect and complete on the day of dedication. Those who have built or restored churches, not to speak of cathedrals, which would perhaps afford a closer analogy to the temple, know how extremely difficult, if not impossible, it is to have every detail finished and arranged for the day of consecration. Some few accidental omissions will have to be supplied afterwards, or experience will suggest certain alterations and improvements which have to be made. There is no inherent improbability, therefore, that the temple should be dedicated in the seventh month, though it was not finished לְבָל דְּבָרָיו until the eighth month, *i.e.*, three or four weeks later. And there was a strong reason why the dedication should take place at the earliest possible date. There had been a long period of preparation, extending back into the preceding reign (1 Chron. xxviii., xxix.); the dedication consequently had long been eagerly looked for; moreover, the erection had evidently been hurried forward, a prodigious number of labourers having been employed in order to expedite the work. It is almost inconceivable, therefore, that, after these energetic measures had been taken, either the king or the nation should have been content to wait thirteen years— nearly twice the time it had taken to build the temple—until the palaces, which were entirely independent and secular buildings, were also completed. If the great national sanctuary, which was the glory of the land, was ready for use, as we know it was, we can hardly believe, considering the natural eagerness and impatience of men, that the tribes of Israel, or their ambitious monarch, would, of their own choice, defer the consecration for an indefinite number of years. It would appear consequently that it is the view that the dedication was postponed for thirteen years "hardly needs discussion" (see below on ch. ix. 1). And the same considerations apply, though perhaps with diminished force, to their waiting one year. For if it be said that the delay was occasioned by the desire to connect the dedication with the feast of tabernacles, which was *par excellence the* feast of the year (הֶחָג) the answer is that it is more likely that the work would be hurried on by the employment of additional hands, if need be, or that the edifice would be consecrated, though not complete in all its details, at the feast of the eleventh year, than that, for the sake of one month, they should wait eleven months. And if the objection be raised that a feeling of religious awe would forbid the dedication of an imperfect building, or of a perfect building with imperfect arrangements, it is easy to reply that both building and furniture may have been practically complete, and may have been believed at the time to be perfect, but that the experience of the first few days suggested a few alterations or additions which threw the completion of the work in all its particulars into the eighth month. It is worthy of notice that Josephus distinctly states that the dedication was in the seventh month of the eighth year (Ant. viii. 4. 1)] **Solomon assembled** [יַקְהֵל. See Ewald, 233 *b*] **the elders of Israel and all the heads of the tribes, the chief** [Heb. *princes*] **of the fathers of the children of Israel.** [This great assembly (compare Dan. iii. 2) can hardly be said to have been suggested to Solomon by the precedent afforded by David (Keil), when bringing up the ark (2 Sam. vi. 1), for it was only natural that he should summon the representatives of the people to witness an event of such profound importance in the national history, as the dedication, after years of waiting (2 Sam. vii. 6—13), of a national sanctuary intended to supersede the tabernacle, at which for five centuries their forefathers had worshipped. And the more so, as they had been called together by David to consult about the erection (1 Chron. xxviii. 1), and had offered willingly of their treasures (*ib.* xxix. 6—9) towards its decoration. It is inconceivable, therefore, that the temple of the Jews could have been formally opened, except in the presence of the "elders and heads of the tribes." Nor can we (with Rawlinson) see a contrast between

the more popular proceedings of David, who "gathered together all the chosen men of Israel, *thirty thousand* (2 Sam. vi. 1), and the statelier, more aristocratic system of his son, who merely summons the chief men ;" for Solomon's "elders," &c. (Deut. xvi. 18; 1 Sam. xvi. 4 ; xxx. 26—31), may well have equalled David's "chosen men" in number. It is quite likely that there was more formality and stateliness in this latter case, but it was practically the same class of persons, *i.e.*, the leading men by birth, talents, or prowess, that were present on both occasions. In fact, it was the Jewish Church by representation] **unto King Solomon in Jerusalem, that they might bring up** [Heb. *to bring up*] **the ark of the covenant of the Lord** [so called because it contained the tables of the covenant which the Lord made with the children of Israel (ver. 9). The temple being really, or principally, a receptacle for the ark, the removal of this venerated relic to its place in the oracle is narrated first, as being of the first importance] **out of the city of David, which is Zion.** [Cf. 2 Sam. vi. 12, 17.]

Ver. 2.—**And all the men of Israel** [not all the heads of the tribes just mentioned (ver. 1), as Keil, but all who came to the feast, as every male Israelite was under obligation to do (Deut. xvi. 16)] **assembled themselves unto King Solomon at the feast** [the Heb. word הֶחָג (with the art.) always means the feast of tabernacles. The same word is used of the feast of passover (Exod. xiii. 15) and pentecost (*ib.* ver. 16), but "*the* feast" here can only mean that of tabernacles. As the "feast of ingathering" (Exod. xxiii. 16), as commemorating the deliverance from Egypt (Levit. xxiii. 43), and as peculiarly a social festival (*ib.* vers. 40—42 ; Num. xxix. 12 sqq.), it was the most joyous as well as the greatest (ἑορτὴ ἁγιωτάτη καὶ μεγίστη. Jos., Ant. viii. 4. 1) gathering of the year. (Compare the Jewish saying of a later date : "He who has never seen the rejoicing at the pouring out of the water of Siloam, has never seen rejoicing in his life.") It was doubtless for this reason that tabernacles was selected for the dedication. A special feast of dedication, however, was held for seven days before the feast of tabernacles proper commenced (see on ver. 65). It did not displace that great feast, however (Stanley), but simply preceded it. It is worthy of notice that Jeroboam selected the same feast (ch. xii. 32) for the inauguration of his new cultus. The idea of Josephus, that the feast of tabernacles "happened to coincide with the dedication" hardly seems probable] **in the month Ethanim** [variously interpreted to mean *gifts*, *i.e.*, fruits (Thenius), *flowing streams* (Gesenius)—it falls about the time of the early rains—and *equinox* (Böttcher)], **which is the seventh month.** [This is added because the month was subsequently known as Tisri (see on ch. vi. 1), or to show that "the feast" was the feast of tabernacles.]

Ver. 3.—**And all the elders of Israel came** [Not a mere repetition. The men who were summoned to Jerusalem (ver. 1) were all present, of their own accord, to witness the removal], **and the priests took up the ark.** [In the parallel account in 2 Chron. v. 4, we read that "*the Levites* took up the ark." But there is no contradiction, as has been too readily supposed. For ver. 7 of the Chronicles, "*the priests* brought in the ark," &c., confirms the statement of the text. And the explanation is suggested in ver. 5 of the same chapter, "These did the priests, the Levites (so the Heb.) bring up." Same expression in Josh. iii. 3. All the priests were Levites—Keil translates, "the Levitical priests"—and this somewhat singular expression is no doubt used to remind us that such was the case. Nor need it cause us any surprise to find the priests employed in this service. It is true that the ark was given into the charge of the Kohathite Levites (Num. iii. 30, 31) ; and it was their duty to bear it (*ib.* iv. 15 ; vii. 9 ; x. 21 ; cf. 1 Chron. xv. 2, 11, 12). But the real care and supervision of the ark always belonged to the sons of Aaron. It was their office, *e.g.*, to put on or take off the covering of the ark and of the vessels, which the Levites were forbidden directly to touch (Num. iv. 5—15). It was quite in accordance with the *spirit* of these provisions that Solomon now entrusted the carriage of the ark to the superior order. But more than that, Solomon was not without precedent to justify his choice. Indeed, we may see in his selection of the priests a minute mark of truth, amounting almost to an undesigned coincidence. For we find that on occasions of extraordinary solemnity — at the crossing of the Jordan, *e.g.* (Josh. iii. 6, 15, 17), and at the siege of Jericho (Josh. vi. 6), the *priests* had borne the ark (cf. 1 Sam. iv. 4 ; 1 Chron. xv. 11, 12). It was no doubt these familiar precedents guided Solomon, or the ecclesiastical authorities, in their selection of the priests on this occasion. A "settled place," a "house of cedars" (2 Sam. vii. 7), "having now been found for the ark" to abide in, after it had "dwelt in curtains" for 500 years, it was taking its last journey, and in order to mark this journey as exceptional, in order to show both the ark and the house the greater reverence, it was determined that it should be borne for the last time by the priests. Keil suggests that the ark may

have been uncovered, but this is very improbable. Why, we may ask, were coverings provided, and their use prescribed (Num. iv. 5—15), if they were to be arbitrarily dispensed with? He also adds that Levites were not allowed to enter the most holy place. But neither, it may be added, was this lawful for the priests. Levites and priests might enter that day, because the house was not then dedicated. The cloud (ver. 10) claimed it for God.

Ver. 4.—**And they brought up the ark of the Lord** [which had now been for nearly 40 years "in the tabernacle that David had pitched for it" on the Mount Zion (2 Sam. vi. 17)], **and the tabernacle of the congregation** [Heb. "the tabernacle of *meeting*" (Exod. xxix. 42, 46. See Dict. Bib. ii. p. 1414 ; Bähr, Symbolik, i. 80, 81). This had been for many years at Gibeon. (Cf. ch. iii. 4 ; 2 Chron. i. 3 ; 1 Chron. xvi. 39. See note on ch. iii. 4.) The tabernacle of Mount Zion is never called "the tabernacle of the congregation"—indeed, it is expressly distinguished from it, 2 Chron. i. 3, 4. The ark and the tabernacle were now reunited in the temple of Solomon, thus "marking the identity and continuity of the life and ritual of the Hebrew Church" (Wordsworth)], **and all the holy vessels that were in the tabernacle** [Perhaps the brazen altar. *Certainly* the altar of incense, the table of shewbread, the candlestick, and also the *brazen serpent* (Stanley)], **even those did the priests and Levites bring up.** [We are hardly justified in saying (as Keil, *al.*) that the Levites carried all but the ark. The text rather favours the view that the priests assisted in bringing up the tabernacle and its furniture. So 2 Chron. v. 5. Neither the tabernacle nor its vessels were designed for further use in the temple ; the latter had been replaced by vessels better suited to the enlarged sanctuary—they were simply preserved, so far as we know, as relics of the past, in the treasury or side-chambers.

Ver. 5.—**And king Solomon, and all the congregation of Israel, that were assembled unto him were with him, before the ark** [Prayers and sacrifices alike were offered *toward* the mercy seat (Psa. xxviii. 2 ; cf. Exod. xxv. 22)], **sacrificing sheep and oxen** [apparently the ark rested *en route* (cf. 2 Sam. vi. 13) whilst the sacrifices were offered. The object of the sacrifice was to testify the grateful joy of the people at the proximate realization of their hopes. There may have been also in the background the idea of averting the Divine anger, of making a propitiation for possible errors and imperfections in their service. There were tragedies connected with the removal of the ark in time past (1 Sam. iv. 17 ; vi. 19 ; 2 Sam.

vi. 7) which, we may be sure, were not altogether forgotten on this occasion] **that could not be told or numbered for multitude.** [Cf. 2 Sam. vi. 13. But the sacrifices on that occasion were on a much smaller scale (1 Chron. xv. 26). Josephus adds (Ant. viii. 4. 1), that a vast quantity of incense was burnt, and that men preceded the ark, singing and dancing, until it reached its destination].

Ver. 6.—**And the priests brought in the ark of the covenant unto his** [*i.e.*, *its.* But this word is never found in the A. V. It has come into use since the date of our translation] **place** [cf. ch. vi. 19] **into the oracle of the house, to the most holy place** [Heb. *holy of holies*], **even under the wings of the cherubims** [ch. vi. 27. Whether the ark stood with its length east and west, or north and south, it is somewhat difficult to decide. But see on ver. 8].

Ver. 7.—**For the cherubims spread forth their two wings over the place of the ark, and the cherubims covered** [יָסֹכּוּ from סָכַךְ, *texit*; hence סֻכָּה, *booth*; LXX. περιεκάλυπτον, *i.e.*, overshadowed and concealed. This word is of some importance as showing that the ark would thenceforward and always be in complete darkness, under the outstretched wings of the cherubim—a fact which suggests the true explanation of the following verse] **the ark and the staves thereof above** [Heb. *from above*].

Ver. 8.—**And they drew out** [It is uncertain whether יַאֲרִכוּ is transitive, as our A. V. renders it, and as in ch. iii. 14 = *lengthen*, in which case, however, it should almost be followed by אֵת, or intransitive, as in Exod. xx. 12 ; Deut. v. 16 ; xxv. 15, when the meaning would be, "*The staves were long*," but the latter rendering has the support of most scholars. As the oracle in the tabernacle was a cube of ten cubits, they cannot have been *more* than eight or nine cubits, and it is doubtful whether, the ark being only 2½ cubits, they would be so long. Their length is mentioned in order to account for the ends being seen. It is immaterial to the meaning of the passage, however, which interpretation we put upon this verb. If we adhere to the A. V. then we must understand that, as it was forbidden to remove the staves from the rings at the corners of the ark (Exod. xxv. 12—15), they drew the staves forward towards one end of the ark ; that they removed the staves altogether from the ark (Stanley) is a view to which the text lends no support] **the staves, that the ends** [Heb. *heads*. It is possible the ends of the staves were fitted with knobs. This would prevent their removal] **of the staves were seen out in**

[Heb. *from*] **the holy place** [Marg. *ark*, the word found in the Chron. v. 9. It is questionable, however, whether הַקֹּדֶשׁ is ever used, by itself, of the ark (Gesen., Thesaurus, s.v.) It may be used of the most holy place (see on ver. 10), but here it would appear to designate the הֵיכָל (ch. vi. 17), the body or "temple of the house" (Exod. xxvi. 33 ; Heb. ix. 2). Its meaning appears to be so defined by the next words] **before the oracle** [*i.e.*, a person standing *in* the holy place, but at the west end, near the entrance to the oracle (ch. vi. 31), could see the ends of the staves. Several questions of considerable nicety suggest themselves here. 1. What was the position of the ark ? Did it stand, that is to say, east and west, or north and south under the wings of the cherubim ? 2. What was the position of the staves ? Were they attached to the ends or to the sides of the ark ? 3. How could the ends of the staves be seen, and by whom and when—on the occasion of the dedication only or in later years ? 4. Why has our author recorded this circumstance? As to 1, the balance of evidence is in favour of the ark having stood north and south, in a line, that is, with the wings of the cherubim. For (1) only thus apparently could the cherubim have "covered the ark *and the staves thereof.*" (2) If it had been otherwise, the "cherubim overshadowing the mercy seat," presuming that they were retained in the temple, would have had an unequal and onesided position, for instead of being equally prominent, they would have stood, one with the back, the other with the face to the entrance and the holy place. (3) Had the ark stood east and west the projecting staves would surely have been in the high priest's way in the performance of his solemn functions (Levit. xvi. 12—15). That they served to guide him to the mercy seat is of course mere conjecture, and as such of no weight. 2. As to the staves, Josephus states (Ant. iii. 7. 5) that they ran along the *sides* of the ark, and this would appear to be the natural and proper arrangement. It follows hence again that they cannot have been more than eight or nine cubits long, inasmuch as they found a place between the bodies of the cherubim, which cannot have been more than nine cubits apart. 3. The explanation of the Rabbins is that the ends of the staves were not really *seen*, but that they projected into the curtain and so made two visible protrusions or prominences. But this view hardly satisfies the requirements of the text, and it assumes that the ark stood east and west, which we have found good reason to doubt. But even if this were so, it is doubtful whether the staves, so long as they remained in the rings, could be made to reach to the door of the oracle, unless indeed they were lengthened for the purpose. How then *were* they seen ? The following considerations may assist us to answer this question. (1) The oracle, of course, in its normal state was in perfect darkness (ver. 12). Once a year, however, a gleam of light was admitted, when the curtain was drawn partially aside to permit of the high priest's entrance. (2) When the curtain was drawn to one (probably the left) side, the light would fall, not on the ark, but on the ends of the staves projecting from the right or north end of the ark, which would thus be distinctly visible to the high priest. But (3) at this time the high priest was not alone in the holy place. It was not required that " there should be no man in the tabernacle of the congregation," except when the high priest went in to make an atonement for the *holy place* (Levit. xvi. 17). At an earlier stage of the service he would seem to have required assistance. According to the Mishna (*Yoma*), a priest held the basin of blood and stirred it to prevent coagulation, at the time of his first entry. Moreover (4) it is extremely doubtful whether the high priest can have drawn aside the curtain himself. Whether he entered three or four times on that day, at his first entry his hands were certainly full. If he carried " a censer full of burning coals of fire " . . . " and his hands (חָפְנָיו, *both fists*) full of sweet incense beaten small " (*ib.* ver. 12), it is clear that some other person must have drawn aside the veil for him. It is to this person, I take it, the priest who was privileged to draw aside the curtain, and possibly to others standing near—certainly to the high priest—that the ends of the staves were visible. Nor would a reverent look directed towards these objects—made originally for the Levites to handle — involve unhallowed curiosity. And if this were so, it would help to explain (4) the mention of this circumstance by our author. If it were a fact that year by year a gleam of light fell upon the staves, and if priest after priest testified of what he had seen, up to the time of writing (" unto this day; " see below), we can readily understand why a circumstance of so much interest should be recorded. And we have not an adequate explanation of its mention here, if we are to understand that the staves were seen on the day of dedication, when of course they must have been visible, and never afterwards, or that the staves were partially drawn out of their rings in order to show that the ark was now at rest], **and there they are unto this day.** [Same expression ch. ix. 21 ; xii. 19 ; 2 Kings

viii. 22. At the date of the publication of this book, the temple was of course destroyed (2 Kings xxv. 9), so that at *that* day the staves were *not* there. But the explanation is very simple. Our historian has copied the words he found in the MS. he was using.]

Ver. 9.—**There was nothing in the ark save the two tables of stone which Moses put there** [Exod. xxv. 16 ; xl. 20 ; Deut. x. 5. This statement appears to be at variance with Hebrews ix. 4, which mentions " the golden pot that had manna, and Aaron's rod that budded," as in the ark, along with " the tables of the covenant." And it is to be observed that, while our text excludes these relics from the ark (*temp.* Solomon), no other scripture save that just cited expressly includes them. In Exod. xvi. 34 and Num. xvii. 25 (Heb. A.V., xvii. 10) they are commanded to be laid up " before the testimony," words which no doubt may mean, as they were long interpreted to mean, " before the tables of testimony in the ark "—observe, the words are " before the *testimony*," not " before the *ark* "—but which are now generally thought to import " in front of the ark which contained the testimony." We know the book of the law was put " at the side (מִצַּד) of the ark " (Deut. xxxi. 26), and hence it is held by some that the golden pot, &c., occupied a similar position. It seems preferable, however, considering the distinct statement of St. Paul, or the author of the Epistle to the Hebrews, which, to say the least, embodies Jewish tradition, to adhere to the ancient interpretation that the golden pot of manna and Aaron's rod were in the ark. And this in no wise conflicts with the statement of the text, for these treasures might well have been removed by the Philistines, whose first thought, we may be sure, would be to open their new acquisition. It is not improbable, indeed, that the object of the men of Bethshemesh in looking into the ark was to see whether these treasures were still there. For if the golden pot ever was in the ark, we can hardly suppose it would escape the rapacity of the Philistines, who would leave the two tables of stone as things of no value. Indeed, it is just possible that the trespass offering, the golden mice, &c., were designed as a return for the golden pot which had been removed. And the statement of the text, "there was nothing," &c., almost implies that there *had* been something there at one time (see Alford on Heb. ix. 4). It seem probable, therefore, that the golden pot and Aaron's rod were originally deposited "before the testimony" *in* the ark ; that they were removed during its captivity (1 Sam. v., vi.) ;

and that the sacrilege was discovered at Bethshemesh (1 Sam. vi. 19). This last-mentioned episode explains how it came to be known that " there was nothing," &c. It is hardly likely after that memorable visitation that Solomon could have opened the ark and taken out the two relics, as Rawlinson suggests. Nor have we any warrant for the view that the mercy seat, with the cherubs, was removed to make way for a new lid without them, and so the interior of the ark was disclosed to view (Stanley)] **at Horeb** [See Exod. iii. 1; xvii. 6; xxxiii. 6; 1 Kings xix. 8. This name, which means *dry ground, desert*, would appear to have belonged to two or three different places in the wilderness. But as the name of the place where the law was given and the covenant with God made (Deut. iv. 10, 13) it became subsequently a *nomen generale* for the whole of the Sinaitic region (Dict. Bib. iii. p. 1326). Here the mount of the law is clearly meant] **when** [Heb. *which*, אֲשֶׁר is occasionally found in the sense of *quum*, as in Deut. xi. 6; Psa. cxxxix. 15; 2 Chron. xxxv. 20; cf. ch. ix. 10 (Gesen., Thes., s.v.)] **the Lord made a covenant** [Heb. *cut;* see note on ch. v. 12. בְּרִית is to be understood. Same ellipsis in 1 Sam. xx. 16; xxii. 8] **with the children of Israel when they came** [Heb. *in their coming*] **out of the land of Egypt.** [Exod. xxxiv. 27, 28; Deut. iv. 13.]

Ver. 10.—**And it came to pass, when the priests were come out** [Rather, *as the priests came out*] **of the holy place** [It has been supposed that " the holy " (הַקֹּדֶשׁ) is here put for the *most* holy place, as in Ezek. xli. 23. But this is not by any means the necessary interpretation. The cloud may obviously have filled the *entire* building only as the priests left it. It would seem, however, from verse 11 as if the priests, having left the *oracle*, were about to minister in the holy place], **that the cloud** [Observe the article; the well-known cloud which betokened the Divine presence. It had rested upon the tabernacle on the day that it was dedicated (Exod. xl. 34), had accompanied it in its journeys (*ib.* ver. 38), and had apparently been specially displayed at certain junctures in the history of Israel (Num. xii. 5, 10; xvi. 42; Deut. xxxi. 15). It was thus the acknowledged symbol of God's presence, and as such was a visible sign that He now accepted the temple, as He had formerly accepted the tabernacle, as His shrine and dwelling-place. It is hardly correct to identify the cloud with " the Shechinah of the Targums " (Rawlinson), for it is noticeable that the Targums never render " the cloud " or " the glory " by " the Shechinah." In fact, as regards the use of the word by Jewish writers, it would seem to be a periphrasis for God (Dict. Bib. iii. p. 1241). We may see in the cloud, however, the *seat* of the Shechinah (Kitto, Cyclopædia, iii. p. 821) **filled the house of the Lord.**

Ver. 11.—**So that the priests could not stand to minister because of the cloud** [They were overpowered by the manifestation, precisely as Moses had been before (Exod. xl. 35). It was at the moment when the singers and ·trumpeters, standing at the east end of the altar, began their service of praise—and the re-appearance of the priests may well have been the signal for them to begin (2 Chron. v. 13)—that " the house was filled with a cloud." Possibly the priests were about to burn incense. Evidently ministrations of some sort were intended and were interrupted. The exact correspondence with Exod. xl. 35 (cf. Ezek. xliv. 4) is not to be overlooked. The idea obviously is that the Divine approval vouchsafed to the tabernacle was now in turn granted to the temple], **for the glory of the Lord had filled the house of the Lord.** [Is the " glory of the Lord " identical with the cloud, or is something additional intended by these words? It is certainly noticeable that what ver. 10 says of the cloud—that it " filled the house—ver. 11 says of the glory. It is also true that there is no mention of any light or fire. And the " darkness " of ver. 12 might naturally seem to refer to the cloud, and therefore to exclude the idea of light. But surely the words כְּבוֹד יְיָ are to be interpreted here by their signification and use elsewhere, and we find " the glory of the Lord elsewhere mentioned as something distinct from the cloud. We must remember that what by day was a pillar of cloud, by night was a pillar of *fire* (Exod. xiii. 21, 22). In Exod. xix. 9, 16, the mention of the " thick cloud " is followed by the statement that " Mount Sinai was altogether on a smoke because the Lord descended upon it *in fire*" (ver. 18). Similarly, in Exod. xxiv., we are told that " the glory of the Lord appeared upon Mount Sinai, and the cloud covered it (the glory?) six days; and the seventh day He called unto Moses out of the midst of the cloud. And the sight of the glory of the Lord was like *devouring fire* " (vers. 16, 17). But perhaps the most decisive passage in this connexion is Exod. xl. 34, where we are told that " the cloud abode *upon* " the tent of meeting, while " the glory of the Lord filled the (interior of the) tabernacle." Compare Exod. xvi. 7, 10; Levit. ix. 6, 23; Num. xiv. 10; xvi. 19, 42. It would appear, therefore, that " the glory of the Lord " was not the cloud, but, as the word almost seems to imply, a "light from heaven above the brightness of the sun" (Acts xxvi. 13 ; cf. Rev. i. 14, 16). It is hardly necessary to add that the glory, though apparently resident in the cloud, was not always luminous; the cloud veiled it from the eyes of men.

Ver. 12. — **Then spake Solomon** [in a transport of emotion at the sight. The cloud and the glory proved that his pious work was accepted. These blessed tokens assured him that "the Lord was there" (Ezek. xlviii. 35) ; that the incomprehensible Godhead had entered the earthly shrine he had prepared, and would dwell there], **The Lord said that he would dwell in the thick darkness.** [Heb. עֲרָפֶל, lit., *darkness of clouds*. When did God speak of dwelling in dark cloud ? The reference, probably, is to Exod. xix. 9 ; xx. 21 , Deut. iv. 11 ; v. 22 (note that, in the three last cited passages, this same word is used, and in the last two in connexion with *cloud*, which would appear to be a practically synonymous term), but especially to Levit. xvi. 2, "I will appear in the cloud upon the mercy seat." Solomon had thus every warrant for connecting a theophany with the thick dark cloud. Cf. Psa. xviii. 11 ; xcvii. 2. The words cannot refer to "the holy of holies not lighted by windows" (Wordsworth).

Ver. 13.—**I have surely built** [Heb. *to build, I have built*] **thee a house to dwell in, a settled place for thee to abide in for ever.** [The temple was primarily, as already remarked, a shrine for the ark, between the cherubim of the mercy seat of which God dwelt. This was a מָכוֹן (from כּוּן, *statuit*), a settled place. The tabernacle was but a poor and transitory abode, partaking of the frailty of the shepherd's tent (Isa. xxxviii. 12). For עוֹלָמִים (αἰῶνες), cf. Isa. xxvi. 4 ; li. 9 ; Dan. ix. 24 ; Psa. cxlv. 13.

Ver. 14.—**And the king turned his face about** [He had been earnestly gazing toward the house where the cloud appeared. He now faced the congregation] **and blessed** [This word here, and in ver. 55, is used somewhat loosely. The blessing was in both cases addressed to God. The Hebrew king was not authorized to bless the people— that was the prerogative of the priests (Num. vi. 23; cf. Levit. ix. 22), and he is only said to bless here as felicitating, as wishing them a blessing. Dean Stanley ["Jewish Ch.," vol. ii. p 218) characteristically asserts that Solomon "performed the highest sacerdotal act of solemn benediction." But the same word is used in ver. 66, of the people blessing the king. "Did

the *people*," as Wordsworth pertinently asks, "also perform a priestly act? " The word is elsewhere used of *saluting*. See note on ver. 66, and Gesen. s.v.] **all the congregation of Israel : (and all the congregation of Israel stood)** ; [Heb. *were standing* (עָמַד) ; " *stood* " conveys the idea that the congregation rose as Solomon spoke, whereas they were standing already in the temple courts.

Ver. 15.—**And he said, Blessed be the Lord God of Israel** [ch. i. 48], **which spake with his mouth unto** [or, *concerning;* אֶל after verbs of speaking has the force of *de* (Gen. xx. 2 ; Jer. xl. 16 ; Psa. lxix. 27). **David my father** [The words were really spoken to Nathan], **and hath with his hand** [*i.e.*, power ; cf. Job xxxiv. 20 ; Acts iv. 28 ; xiii. 11 ; Ezra vii. 6] **fulfilled it** [the spoken word He has fulfilled in deed], **saying,** [The reference is to 2 Sam. vii., of which Solomon merely gives the substance. Much of what he says here is not recorded there.]

Ver. 16. **Since the day that I brought forth my people Israel out of Egypt, I chose no city out of all the tribes of Israel, to build a house, that my name might be therein** [The chronicler adds here, " Neither chose I any man to be ruler," &c. Probably our account comes nearer to the words actually spoken. The speech in the Chron. looks as if it had been somewhat amplified, though it only completes the sense (Rawlinson)], **but I chose David to be over my people Israel.** [Cf. Psa. lxxviii. 70. This psalm pursues much the same line of thought as this address.]

Ver. 17.—**And it was in the heart of David my father** [2 Sam. vii. 2 ; 1 Chron. xvii. 1] **to build an house for the name of the Lord God of Israel.**

Ver. 18.—**And the Lord said unto David my father** [Not, perhaps, *totidem verbis*. The Divine approval was implied in 2 Sam. vii. 11—16, and it may have been expressed at the same time. The narratives of Scripture are necessarily greatly condensed], **Whereas it was in thine heart to build an house unto my name, thou didst well that it was in thine heart.**

Ver. 19.—**Nevertheless thou shalt not build the house** [Wordsworth observes that it was filial reverence prevented Solomon's mentioning the *cause* of this prohibition, which, however, *is* mentioned with appropriate humility by David himself (1 Chron. xxii. 8)]; **but thy son that shall come forth out of thy loins, he shall build the house unto my name.** [2 Sam. vii. 11, 12. The recurrence of " the name " of the Lord is to be noticed (see vers. 16, 17, 18, 29, 43,

&c.) The *name* of God is the expression to man of His nature, attributes, &c.]

Ver. 20.—**And the Lord hath performed** [Same word as in ch. ii. 4. Lit., "hath raised up" (LXX. ἀνέστησε). Also same word as "risen up" (LXX. ἀνέστην) below, and as "set up" in 2 Sam. vii. 12. We might translate "established" throughout] **his word that he spake, and I am risen up in the room of David my father, and sit on the throne of Israel** [ch. i. 48], **as the Lord promised** [2 Sam. vii. 12], **and have built an house for the name of the Lord God of Israel** [*ib.* ver. 13].

Ver. 21.—**And I have set there a place for the ark, wherein is the covenant of the Lord** [Hence its name, "the ark of the covenant" (Exod. xxxiv. 28; cf. Deut. ix. 11)] **which he made with our forefathers when he brought them out of the land of Egypt** [vers. 9, 16].

SECTION II.—*The Prayer.*

The prayer of dedication, properly so called, now begins. This solemn and beautiful composition was probably copied by our author from the "Book of the Acts of Solomon" (1 Kings xi. 41), possibly from the "Book of Nathan the prophet" (2 Chron. ix. 29). It was evidently committed to writing beforehand, and would, no doubt, as a matter of course, be religiously preserved. The later criticism objects to its authenticity that the many references to the Pentateuch (compare ver. 12 with Exod. xix. 9; ver. 31 with Exod. xxii. 11, Levit. v. 1; ver. 33 with Levit. xxvi. 17, Deut. xxviii. 25; ver. 36 with Levit. xxvi. 25; ver. 50 with Levit. xxvi. 40, 42; ver. 51 with Deut. iv. 20, &c.) prove it to be of a later date. Ewald assigns it to the seventh century B.C.; but this is simply to beg the question of the date of the Pentateuch. It is obviously open to reply that these references only prove that the king was acquainted, as he was bound to be (Deut. xvii. 18), with the words of the law. It divides itself into three parts. The first (vers. 22—30) is general; the second (vers. 31—53) consists of seven special petitions; the last (vers. 50—53) consists of a general conclusion and appeal to God's covenant mercy.

Ver. 22.—**And Solomon stood** [*i.e., took his stand* (LXX. ἀνέστη). Not "was standing." It was but for a moment, however, for we find him presently kneeling (ver. 54;

2 Chron. vi. 13). The latter passage informs us that he both stood and knelt upon a "brazen scaffold," three cubits high] **before the altar of the Lord** [*i.e.*, the brazen altar of sacrifice. The platform or scaffold was "set in the midst of the court" (2 Chron. *l.c.*) All these rites took place in the open air. The king had no place *within* the edifice] **in the presence** [the word is not to be pressed to mean "*facing* the people." It is hardly likely he would pray towards the people—he was their προφήτης, *i.e.*, he spoke for them to God—or turn his back on the sacred Presence just manifested], **and spread forth his hands towards heaven:** [one attitude of earnest prayer thoughout the East, as may be seen at the present day amongst the Mohammedans. (See Lane's "Modern Egyptians," ch. iii., "Religion and Laws.") So completely was this posture identified with supplication that to "lift up the hands" came to be a synonym for prayer (Exod. ix. 29, 33; Psa. xliv. 20; cxliii. 6; Isa. i. 15; lxv. 2.)]

Ver. 23.—**And he said, Lord God of Israel, there is no God like thee** [Similar words are found in Exod. xv. 11; Psa. lxxxvi. 8, &c. They do not at all imply the existence of other gods, but are explained by other passages (*e.g.*, ver. 60; Deut. iv. 39, "the Lord He is God and *none else;*" 2 Sam. vii. 22; xxii. 32) as meaning that the God of Israel stands alone, and alone is God. It would be strange, indeed, if the people whose great *peculium* was the unity of the Godhead (Deut. vi. 4; Isa. xlii. 8) recognized other deities. Observe: Solomon begins his prayer with an act of *praise;* with a recognition at once grateful and graceful of God's past mercies (cf. Psa. lxv. 1, 2; Phil. iv. 6). *Exaudit Dominus invocantem, quem laudantem vidit*" (Augustine)], **in heaven above, or on earth beneath** [Josh. ii. 11], **who keepest covenant and mercy** [same words in Deut. vii. 9] **with thy servants that walk before thee with all their heart.** [Cf. ch. ii. 4.]

Ver. 24.—**Who hast kept with thy servant David my father** [Solomon sees in this a special pledge of God's faithfulness and truth] **that thou promisedst** [Heb. *spakest*, same word as below. The alteration in the A. V. obscures the connexion]: **thou spakest also** [Heb. *and thou spakest, i.e.*, "yea," or "for thou spakest"] **with thy mouth and hast fulfilled it with thine hand** [ver. 15, and ch. iii. 6. The completion of the house, following the establishment of Solomon upon the throne, was to him proof conclusive that the promise of 2 Sam vii. had received its fulfilment], **as it is this day.**

Ver. 25.—**Therefore now** [Heb. *And now.* The promise has been but partially fulfilled. The house is built; he now prays that the succession may be continued in David's line] **keep** [cf. ver. 24, " thou hast kept "] **with thy servant David my father that thou promisedst** [Heb. *spakest to*, as above] **him, saying** [The reference is of course to the great promise of 2 Sam. vii. 12—16], **There shall not fail thee a man in my sight to sit on the throne of Israel** [cf. ch. ii. 4], **so that** [marg., *if only.* As to the condition, see note on ch. ii. 4, and cf. ch. vi. 12, 13] **thy children take heed to** [Heb. *keep.* Same word as above. The repetition is suggestive. God's keeping His promise was contingent on *their* keeping His commandments] **their way, that they walk before me as thou hast walked before me.**

Ver. 26.—**And now, O God** [The LXX., Vulg., Syr., and Arab. read, *O Lord God*, as do many MSS. But the word is more likely to have been *inserted* (in conformity with vers. 23, 25) than to have been left out] **let thy word** [The Keri has *thy words.* Keil sees here a reference to "*all the words*" of 2 Sam. vii. 17; but this, especially when the reading is doubtful, is somewhat too remote], **I pray thee, be verified** [אָמֵן optative form. Gesen., Gram. 126. 2] **which thou spakest** [Psa. cxxxii. 14] **unto thy servant David my father.**

Ver. 27.—**But** [כִּי. Bähr refers for this use of the word to 1 Sam. xxix. 8; 1 Kings xi. 22; 2 Kings viii. 13; Jer. xxiii. 18] **will God indeed** [Heb. *verily;* same root as that of preceding verb, "*verified.*" The repetition shows the connexion of thought. " But can these words be verified? Will God verily," &c.] **dwell on the earth? behold the heaven and heaven of heavens** [Same expression Deut. x. 14. Cf. Psa. cxv. 16; cxlviii. 4; Isa. lxvi. 1. The Jewish belief respecting the *seven* heavens (see Wetstein on 2 Cor. xii. 2; Stanley, " Corinthians," *l.c.*) is of much later date, and a reference to it, or to the belief of some Rabbins in *two* heavens (after Deut. x. 14), is altogether out of the question. The " heaven of heavens " = "all the spaces of heaven, however vast and infinite" (Gesen., cf. Psa. cxlviii. 4). The analogy of " holy of holies " would, however, suggest that not *all* the heavens, but the *highest* heavens are intended] **cannot contain thee; how much less** [אַף כִּי : Ewald, 354 *c*] **this house that I have builded?** [Two points are to be noticed here. (1) Solomon never denies for a moment that the temple was a real habitation of Jehovah, or that a real presence was manifested there. He only denies that the Deity is *contained* in earthly temples (2) He had no un-

worthy ideas—such as were prevalent in that age—of God as a local deity, limited to space. The words clearly prove his grasp of the omnipresence and infinity of God. With this passage compare Psa. cxxxix. 7—10; Isa. lxvi. 1 (quoted in Acts vii. 49), and Acts xvii. 24.]

Ver. 28.—**Yet have thou respect unto the prayer of thy servant** [=the prayer I now offer, which is that thou wilt hear all future prayers offered here, mine and my people's] **and to his supplication, O Lord my God, to hearken unto the cry and to the prayer** [Three words are used here, תְּחִנָּה, תְּפִלָּה, and רִנָּה. The first (from הִתְפַּלֵּל, *precatus est;* see ver. 29) is apparently a general term for prayer; the second (from חָנַן, *propitius fuit*) is properly a cry for mercy; hence an earnest prayer or supplication; while the third signifies a joyful cry; hence a mournful cry or prayer] **which thy servant prayeth before thee to-day.**

Ver. 29.—**That thine eyes may be open** [This anthropomorphism does not conflict with what was said under ver. 27] **toward this house night and day** [not so much to watch over it as to see the worship and prayer offered there], **even toward the place of which thou hast said, My name shall be there** [cf. Ezek. xlviii. 35, and vers. 18. 19, 20, &c. When had God said this? Never, perhaps, in so many words. Keil says the reference is to 2 Sam. vii. 13 *implicite* (" He shall build an house for my name "), while Rawlinson thinks the " reference is not to any single text, but to the many passages in Deuteronomy where God speaks of a place which He will choose to 'set his name' there (Deut. xii. 5, 11, 18, &c.; xiv. 23; xv. 20; xvi. 2, &c.)" But it is very probable that a revelation was made to David respecting the sanctuary, the terms of which are not preserved to us. This is almost implied by Psa. lxxviii. 68; cxxxii. 10; 1 Chron. xxii. 1—passages which prove that David claimed to have Divine sanction for placing the temple on " Mount Zion." Psa. cxxxii. is unmistakeably Davidic, and embodies some features of the message of God (*e.g.*, the condition, ver. 12) not preserved in 2 Sam. vii.]: **that thou mayest hearken unto the prayer which thy servant shall make toward** [Marg. *in*, but Heb. אֶל supports the A. V. rendering. Now that God had revealed His presence in the temple, the Jew, wherever he might be, would, and as a matter of fact did, pray *towards* it (Dan. vi. 10; Psa. v. 7; Jonah ii. 4), just as the Mohammedan has his *Kibleh* in Mecca] **this place.**

Ver. 30.—**And hearken thou to the sup-**

plication of thy servant, and of thy people Israel, when they shall pray toward this place : and hear thou in heaven [Heb. *unto heaven*, אֶל־הַשָּׁמַיִם, a pregnant construction = hear the prayer that ascends unto heaven. The chronicler here, as elsewhere, simplifies the meaning by reading "from heaven," מִן־הַשּׁ] thy dwelling place [Here, and in vers. 39, 43, and 49, heaven is described as the true dwelling place of Deity. Confidently as Solomon believes that he has built a habitation for the Lord, he never dreams that the "Most High dwelleth not in temples made with hands" (Acts vii. 48; xvii. 4)] : and when thou hearest, forgive. [There is possibly a play of words here— שָׁמַיִם, שָׁמַעְתָּ].

With the next verse the special or particular supplications begin. Like those of the Lord's prayer, they are seven in number, and no doubt for the same reason, viz., because seven was the number of covenant, the number which expressed the relationship between the Lord and His people ("*die Signatur der Verbindung Gottes und der Welt*"—Bähr, Symbolik, i. 187 sqq.) In fact, to the Jew the number "seven" was something like the sign of the cross to a large portion of Catholic Christendom, for it spoke to him of God's covenant of mercy and peace.

And the first of the seven concerns *oaths*. The king implores the covenant-keeping God to watch over the covenants of words made in the now consecrated sanctuary, and to protect their sanctity by punishing the false swearer. There were cases in which the Mosaic law provided that an oath should be administered to suspected persons (Exod. xxii. 11; Levit. v. 1, 4, &c.) And there were other cases in which men of their own accord, for "an end of all strife," would make oath. Now every oath, whatever its form (Matt. xxiii. 16—22), is in reality an affirmation "by the God of truth" (Isa. lxv. 16); it is an appeal to the knowledge and power and justice of the Most High (Levit. xix. 12; Deut. vi. 13; x. 20; Isa. xlviii. 1; Jer. xii. 16; xliv. 26). A false oath, consequently, dishonoured the Divine name, and polluted the sanctuary dedicated to that name, and if it went unpunished, contradicted the principles and provisions of the dispensation of temporal punishments,

and so encouraged falsehood and impiety. God is here entreated, consequently, to take cognizance of the oaths sworn before His altar (ver. 31), and to be a swift witness against the false swearers (Mal. iii. 5). It is, perhaps, because of the direct dishonour which perjury offers to the Divine name that, as Bähr suggests, this prayer stands first among the seven, thus corresponding to the "Hallowed be Thy name" in the Lord's prayer, and to the third among the ten commandments.

Ver. 31.—If any man trespass [The force of the Hebrew (which begins somewhat abruptly) אֵת אֲשֶׁר (LXX. ὅσα ἂν ἁμάρτῃ) is probably, *As for that which*, or *in all cases in which*, i.e., *when* (as Ewald, 333 *a*). The chronicler, as usual, simplifies by reading אִם] against his neighbour, and an oath be laid [Heb. *and he* (the neighbour) *lay an oath*, i.e., prescribe a form of adjuration, such as that in Deut. xxi. 7] upon him to cause him to swear, and the oath come [This translation cannot be maintained. For in the Heb. there is no def. art., as there would be if אָלָה were noun and nominative; and, moreover, in that case the verb, to agree with the feminine noun, would be בָּאָה. And as no other meaning can be extracted from the words as they stand, we are driven to suspect a slight corruption of the text, either (1) the omission of וּ between the words, which in that case would have stood וּבָא וְאָלָה, and would mean, "*and he* (the accused) *come and swear*"—a conjecture which is supported by the LXX., καὶ ἔλθῃ καὶ ἐξαγορεύσῃ, or (2) the omission of the preposition בְּ, which would yield וּבָא בְאָלָה = *and he* (the accused) *enters into the oath*, an expression found in Neh. x. 29 and Ezek. xvii. 13] before thine altar in this house. [Despite the last words, the altar of sacrifice *before* the house is probably meant. This was *the* altar of the Jewish layman, and, moreover, it was one visible sign of the covenant. Psa. l. 5; Exod. xxiv. 6—8; cf. xx. 24. The altar which afforded shelter to the manslayer, in the same way lent sanctity to the oath. The practice of swearing by the altar (Matt. xxiii. 18) is of later date.

Ver. 32.—Then hear thou in heaven [Heb. *and thou, thou wilt hear the heavens*. The same expression, תִּשְׁמַע הַשָּׁמַיִם, is found in vers. 34, 36, 39. See Ewald, 300 *a*. Keil sees in it the adverbial use of the accusative. Most of the versions read "from heaven," as does the Chronicles and one MS.], and do [*i.e.*, act] and judge thy servants, condemning [Heb. *to make* (*i.e.*, prove) *wicked*] the wicked, to bring [Heb. *give*, same word as below] his way [*i.e.*, works, fruits] upon his head [cf. Ezek. ix. 10; xi. 21; same expression] and justifying [Heb. *to make righteous.* Cf. δικαιοῦν in N. T. and *justum facere*] the righteous [cognate words are used in both cases], to give him according to his righteousness.

The second special petition contemplates the case, which was morally certain to occur, of Hebrews taken captive in war and carried to a foreign land. To be separated from the commonwealth, the rites and the blessings of Israel, was one of the greatest calamities which could befal a Jew (Deut. iv. 27, 28; Levit. xxvi. 33; Psa. cxxxvii.), and as such Solomon gives it a prominent place in his prayer. The connexion, however, which some have imagined to exist between this prayer and the preceding, viz., that that referred to internal, this to external dangers, is too artificial to have found a place in Solomon's thoughts.

Ver. 33.—**When thy people Israel be smitten down before the enemy** [cf. Levit. xxvi. 7, 17; Deut. xxviii. 25. There is a constant reference to these two chapters throughout this prayer, or, if no direct reference to them, there are unmistakeable reminiscences of them], **because they have sinned against thee, and shall turn again to thee, and confess** [or *praise*. Psa. liv. 8 Heb.; cvi. 47; cxxii. 4] **thy name, and pray, and make supplication unto thee in this house.** [The marg. *towards* is a mistaken attempt at avoiding the difficulty which lies on the surface of the text, viz., that persons in a foreign land could not pray *in* the temple. But the king obviously is speaking here, not of those taken captive, but of the nation at large ("thy people Israel") by its representatives (cf. Joel ii. ii. 17), supplicating after its defeat. The idea of captives does not come in until the next verse. Under the term house the courts are obviously included (Acts ii. 46; Luke xviii. 10). Into the edifice the priests alone were admitted.

Ver. 34.—**Then hear thou in heaven, and forgive the sin of thy people Israel, and bring them** [*i.e.*, the captives of Israel, those carried off by the enemy. There is no thought here of the captivity of the *nation*—that is referred to in vers. 46—50— as the prayers to be offered *in* the temple prove. This petition is in exact accordance with the promises and threatenings of the law, for the former of which see Levit. xxvi. 40—44; Deut. xxx. 1—5; for the latter,

Levit. xxvi. 33; Deut. iv. 27; xxviii. 64 sqq.] **again unto the land which thou gavest unto their fathers.**

The third petition concerns the plague of *drought.* Just as rain, in the thirsty and sunburnt East, has ever been accounted one of the best gifts of God (Levit. xxvi. 4; Deut. xi. 11; Job v. 10, and *passim;* Psa. lxviii. 9; cxlvii. 8; Acts xiv. 17), so was drought denounced as one of His severest scourges (Levit. xxvi. 19; Deut. xi. 17; xxviii. 23, 24, &c.) This petition finds an illustration in the public supplications which are still offered in the East, and by men of all creeds, for rain.

Ver. 35.—**When heaven is shut up, and there is no rain, because they have sinned against thee; if they pray toward this place** [*toward*, because the inhabitants of the land everywhere would direct their prayers toward the holy oracle in Jerusalem (Psa. xxviii. 2)], **and confess** [*praise*] **thy name, and turn from their sin, when** [or *because*, כִּי] **thou afflictest them.** [LXX. ὅταν ταπεινώσῃς αὐτούς—Humbling should be the result of affliction.]

Ver. 36.—**Then hear thou in heaven** [see on ver. 32], **and forgive the sin of thy servants, and of thy people Israel, that thou teach them** [rather, *because thou art teaching them*, &c. The thought is, "Forgive, because they have learned the lesson Thy discipline of drought was meant to teach;" because the chastisement has fulfilled its purpose] **the good way** [1 Sam. xii. 23] **wherein they should walk, and give rain upon thy land, which thou hast given to thy people for an inheritance.**

The fourth petition refers to the various plagues mentioned in the law (Levit. xxvi.; Deut. xxviii.), as the punishment of apostasy or infidelity.

Ver. 37.—**If there be in the land famine** [Heb. *Famine should there be*, &c. The word is emphatic by position. Famine is denounced, Levit. xxvi. 20, 26; Deut. xxviii. 33], **if there be pestilence** [Levit. xxvi. 25; Jer xiv. 12; xxiv. 10; Amos iv. 10; Ezek. vi. 12, &c.], **blasting** [same word Gen. xli. 6; Amos iv. 9; Deut. xxviii. 22], **mildew** [lit. *paleness*, χλωρότης, Deut. *l. c.*], **locust, or if there be caterpillar** [It is uncertain whether חָסִיל, lit., *devourer*, here rendered "caterpillar," is not an adjective and an appellation of the locust = *devouring locust*. Deut. xxviii. 38 (יַחַסְלֶנּוּ הָאַרְבֶּה "the locust shall consume it") certainly favours this view.

But the Chron. and the Verss. distinguish it here (by the introduction of "and" between the two words) as a separate plague. It is also similarly distinguished, Joel i. 4 ; Psa. lxxviii. 46. Gesen. considers it to be a species of locust] ; **if their enemy besiege them in the land of their cities** [Heb. *his gates*, but "the land of his gates" hardly yields sense. It is noteworthy that the LXX. (with most of the Verss.) reads ἐν μιᾷ τῶν πόλεων αὐτοῦ. Thenius, consequently, to bring the Hebrew text into harmony, would substitute עיריו באחת for שעריו בארץ. Another suggested emendation is בארץ, בשעריו, "in the land, even in their gates." But it is doubtful whether any alteration is really required. "The land of their gates" (cf. "land of their captivity," 2 Chron. vi. 37 ; Jer. xxx. 10, &c.) may perhaps be interpreted the land where their gates (*i.e.*, fortified cities) are. The marg. "*Jurisdiction*"—the gate being the place of judgment (Ruth iv. 11; Prov. xxii. 22; 2 Sam. xv. 2)—is altogether out of the question] ; **whatsoever plague, whatsoever** [Heb. *every* plague, &c.] **sickness there be.**

Ver. 38.—**What prayer and supplication soever** [There is here a studied reference to the preceding words. Lit., *every prayer*, &c. We might render in ver. 37, "Whatsoever the plague," &c., and here, "Whatsoever the prayer," &c.] **be made by any man, or by all thy people Israel, which shall know every man the plague of his own heart** [Here again there is an unmistakeable reference to the "plague" (same word) of ver. 37. The plague of the heart is the inner smart of the conscience corresponding with and perhaps more painful than the smiting of the person. The meaning obviously is that the prayers will vary according to the various mental and physical sufferings of men], **and spread forth his hands** [see on ver. 22] **toward this house.**

Ver. 39.—**Then hear thou in heaven thy dwelling place, and forgive, and do, and give to every man according to his ways, whose heart thou knowest ; (for thou, even thou only, knowest the hearts of all the children of men ;)** [Jer. xvii. 10. Cf. ὁ καρδιογνώστης θεὸς (Acts xv. 8; also *ib.* i. 24).

Ver. 40.—**That they may fear thee all the days that they live in the land which thou gavest unto their fathers.** [Solomon anticipates that a godly fear will be the result of forgiveness and restoration. We find the same thought in Psa. cxxx. 4. The mercy and goodness of God *should* lead to repentance, but unhappily it not unseldom fails to do so.]

The fifth petition contemplates the prayers which foreigners, attracted by the fame of Jerusalem, of its religion and sanctuary could offer towards the house. The Gentiles who should visit Jerusalem would assuredly, with their polytheistic ideas and their belief in local or tribal deities, invoke the aid and blessing of the mighty God of Jacob. This mention of aliens from the commonwealth of Israel in the prayer of dedication, especially when viewed in the light of the exclusiveness and bigotry which characterized the Jews of later days, is especially to be noticed. As Rawlinson (*in loco*) observes, "Nothing is more remarkable in the Mosaic law than its liberality with regard to strangers." He then quotes Exod. xxii. 21; Levit. xxv. 35 ; Deut. x. 19 ; xxxi. 12 ; Num. xv. 14—16 ; and adds : "It is quite in the spirit of these enactments that Solomon, having first prayed God on behalf of his fellow countrymen, should next go on to intercede for the strangers," &c. The intercourse of the Hebrews at this period with foreign nations, and the influence they exercised on the Jewish thought and manners (see Stanley, "Jewish Ch." ii. Lect. xxvi.), are also to be remembered. These new relations with the stranger would no doubt have widened Solomon's views.

Ver. 41.—**Moreover concerning a stranger, that is not of thy people Israel, but cometh out of a far country for thy name's sake** [Solomon takes it for granted that such *will* come, and not without good reason, for the house was "exceeding magnifical" and destined to be "of fame and glory throughout all countries" (1 Chron. xxii. 5). And we can hardly doubt that in the visit of the Queen of Sheba we are to see one fulfilment of this anticipation. (Note the expression of ch. x. 1 "concerning the *name of the Lord*.") One who blessed God, as she did (ver. 9), would certainly pray towards the house. In the time of the *second* temple there were several instances of strangers (*e.g.*, Alexander the Great, Ptolemy Philadelphus, and Seleucus; see Keil *in loc.*) worshipping the God of Jacob in Jerusalem.

Ver. 42.—**(For they shall hear of thy great name** [Cf. Josh. vii. 9 ; Psa. lxxvi. 1; xcix. 3], **and of thy strong hand** [cf. Exod. vi. 6 ; xiii. 9 ; Deut. ix. 26, 29; cf. vii. 19. They had heard at a much earlier date (Exod. xv. 14; xviii. 1; Josh. v. 1). The reference is not so much to the marvels of the Exodus—that was long past—as to the wondrous works which Solomon assumes will hereafter be wrought], **and of thy** stretched out arm;) when he shall come and pray toward this house.

Ver. 43.—Hear thou in heaven thy dwelling place, and do according to all that the stranger calleth to thee for : that all people of the earth may know thy name [It is interesting to notice this foreshadowing of the inclusion of the Gentiles in the one fold. The same thought is found in some of the Psalms and in Isaiah, as St. Paul witnesses (Rom. xv. 9 sqq.) Cf. Psa. xxii. 27; lxxii. 11; lxxxvi. 9; xcviii. 3; cii. 15; cxvii. 1; Isa. xlix. 6; lii. 10] to fear thee, as do thy people Israel; and that they may know that this house, which I have builded, is called by thy name. [Heb. *that thy name is called* (or, *has been called*, נִקְרָא.
LXX. ἐπικέκληται) *upon this house, i.e.*, that God has taken this house for His habitation: that He dwells there, works, hears, answers there. Same expression, Jer. vii. 10, 11, 14; xxv. 29; Deut. xxviii. 10; Isa. iv. 1. In Num. vi. 27 we have, " they shall put my name upon the children of Israel." In Deut. xii. 5, and xvi. 6 (cf. 1 Kings xi. 36), we read of the place God has "chosen to put his name there."

So far the royal suppliant has spoken of prayers offered in or at the temple. He now mentions two cases where supplications will be offered by penitents far distant from the holy city or even from the Holy Land. And first, he speaks of the armies of Israel on a campaign.

Ver. 44.—If thy people go out to battle against their enemy, whithersoever [Heb. *in the way which*] thou shalt send them [These words clearly imply that the war, whether defensive or offensive (*i.e.*, for the chastisement of other nations), is one which had God's sanction, and indeed was waged by His appointment], and shall pray unto the Lord toward [Heb. *in the way of.* Same expression as above. The repetition is significant. " They have gone in God's way. They may therefore look the way of God's house for help." Executing God's commission, they might justly expect His blessing] the city which thou hast chosen, and toward the house that I have built for thy name.

Ver. 45.—Then hear thou in heaven their prayer and their supplication, and maintain their cause. [Heb. *do their judgments*, *i.e.*, secure them justice, defend the right. Same words, Deut. x. 18; cf. Psa. ix. 5, Heb.]

The last petition—the second of those which speak of prayers addressed towards the temple, or the Holy Presence which dwelt there, from a foreign land—contemplates as possible the captivity of the Hebrew nation. It has hence been too readily inferred that this portion of the prayer, at least, if not the preceding petition also, has been interpolated by a post-captivity writer. But there is really no solid reason for doubting its genuineness. Not only is it the *seventh* petition (see on ver. 31), but the captivity of Israel had been denounced as the punishment of persistent disobedience long before by Moses, and in the chapters to which such constant reference is made (Levit. xxvi. 33, 44; Deut. xxviii. 25, 36, 64; cf. iv. 27)—a fact which is in itself an indirect proof of genuineness, as showing that this petition is of a piece with the rest of the prayer. And when to this we add that the carrying of a conquered and refractory race into captivity was an established custom of the East, we shall be inclined to agree with Bähr, that "it would have been more remarkable if Solomon had *not* mentioned it."

Ver. 46.—If they sin against thee (for there is no man that sinneth not), and thou be angry with them, and deliver them to the enemy [Heb. *give them before an enemy*], so that they carry them away captives unto the land of the enemy, far or near;

Ver. 47. — Yet if they shall bethink themselves [Heb. as marg., *bring back to their heart.* Same phrase, Deut. iv. 39; xxx. 1. The latter passage, it should be noticed, treats of the captivity, so that Solomon, consciously or unconsciously, employs some of the very words used by Moses in contemplating this contingency. These repeated coincidences lead to the belief that the prayer was based upon and compiled from the Pentateuch] in the land whither they were carried captives, and repent, and make supplication unto thee in the land of them that carried them captives, saying, We have sinned, and have done perversely, we have committed wickedness. [This verse is full of *paronomasia*, הֶשֱׁוִבוּ ,נִשְׁבּוּ ,שָׁבוּ, &c. Words almost identical with this confession were used (Dan. ix. 5; Psa. cvi. 6) by the Jews in their captivity at Babylon, from which it has been concluded that this part of the prayer must belong to the time of the captivity. But surely it is, to say the least, just as likely that the Jews, when the captivity of which Solomon spoke befel them, borrowed the phrase in which their great king by anticipation expressed their penitence. Seeing in the captivity a fulfilment of his prediction, they would naturally see in this formula, which no doubt had been preserved in the writings of the prophets, a confession specially appropriate to their case, and indeed provided for their use.

Ver. 48.—**And so return unto thee with all their heart** [almost the words of Deut. xxx. ver. 2, as those in ver. 47 are of ver. 1], **and with all their soul, in the land of their enemies, which led them away captive** [observe the *paronomasia*—שבו is here used in two senses], **and pray unto thee toward** [Heb. *the way of*] **their land** [see Dan. vi. 10] **which thou gavest unto their fathers, the city which thou hast chosen, and the house which I have built for thy name.** [There is apparently a climax here, "land," "city," "house."]

Ver. 49.—**Then hear thou their prayer and their supplication in heaven thy dwelling place, and maintain their cause.** [Heb. *do their judgments*, as in ver. 45.]

Ver. 50.—**And forgive thy people that have sinned against thee, and all their transgressions wherein they have transgressed against thee, and give them compassion** [Heb. *to compassion* or *bowels* רְחָמִים=τὰ σπλάγχνα, 2 Cor. vi. 12; Phil. i. 8; ii. 1, &c.] **before them who carried them captive, that they may have compassion on them.** [For the fulfilment of this prayer, see Ezra i. 3, 7; vi. 13; Neh. ii. 6. Compare Psa. cvi. 46.]

In the three following verses we have a sort of general conclusion to the dedication prayer. It is hardly correct to say that these last words apply to all the preceding petitions—the plea "they are thy people" manifestly cannot apply in the case of vers. 41—43. On the other hand, as little are they to be limited to the persons last mentioned in vers. 46—50, though it is highly probable they were suggested by the thought of the captives. They are manifestly in close connection with the preceding verses.

Ver. 51.—**For they be thy people** [a citation or reminiscence of Deut. iv. 10], **and thine inheritance, which thou broughtest forth out of Egypt** [cf. vers. 21, 53. There is a constant recurrence throughout the Old Testament to this great deliverance, and with good reason, for it was the real birthday of the nation, and was also a pledge of future help and favour. God who had "wrought such great things for them in Egypt" could not well forsake them. Solomon's constant plea is that they are the elect and covenant race] **from the midst of the furnace of iron** [*i.e.*, a furnace for iron, heated and fierce as for smelting. Same phrase, Deut. iv. 20].

Ver. 52.—**That thine eyes may be open** [cf. ver. 29] **unto the supplication of thy servant, and unto the supplication of thy people Israel** [cf. vers. 28, 30], **to hearken unto them in all that they call for unto thee.**

Ver. 53.—**For thou didst separate them from** [Levit. xx. 24, 26; cf. Exod. xix. 5, 6] **among all the people of the earth, to be thine inheritance** [same expression, Deut. iv. 20; ix. 26, 29. This is no idle repetition of ver. 51. The idea of that verse is deliverance, of this election. Cf. Num. xvi. 9; viii. 14], **as thou spakest by the hand** [see note on ch. ii. 25] **of Moses thy servant** [Exod. xix. 5, 6; Deut. ix. 26, 29; xiv. 2], **when thou broughtest our fathers out of Egypt, O Lord God.**

In Chron. (ch. vi. 41, 42) the prayer ends somewhat differently. "Now therefore arise, O Lord God," &c.—words which are found in substance in Psa. cxxxii. 8—10. These two verses look like an addition, and were probably inserted by the chronicler to form a connecting link with ch. vii. 1—3 (Bähr). The LXX. has an extremely curious addition, said to be taken from the "Book of the Song." Stanley sees in its very abruptness and obscurity an evidence of its genuineness ("Jewish Ch." ii. 218).

Section III.—*The Concluding Blessing.*

The service of dedication concludes, as it commenced, with a benediction (ver. 14).

Ver. 54.—**And it was so, that when Solomon had made an end of praying all this prayer and supplication unto the Lord, he arose from before** [see note on ver. 22] **the altar of the Lord, from kneeling on his knees** [the first mention of this posture in the sacred history (Stanley). The Jews usually stood in prayer (Luke xviii. 11, 13)] **with** [Heb. *and*] **his hands spread up to heaven.**

Ver. 55.—**And he stood** [this does not necessarily imply that he drew nearer to the congregation, as Keil], **and blessed** [cf. 2 Sam. vi. 18, and see note on ver. 14. The words of blessing, which are presently given (vers. 56—61), prove that he did not assume priestly functions and put any blessing upon the people, Num. vi. 27] **all the congregation of Israel with a loud** [Heb. *great*] **voice, saying,**

Ver. 56.—**Blessed be the Lord, that hath given rest unto his people Israel, according to all that he promised** [a distinct reference to Deut. xii. 9, 10 (cf. iii. 20), where we read that when the Lord should have given rest to Israel, then a place for sacrifice, &c.,

should be appointed (ver. 11). That place is now dedicated, and the king sees in this circumstance a proof that the rest is now at last fully attained. The permanent sanctuary is a pledge of settlement in the land. The rest hitherto enjoyed (Josh. xxi. 44) had been but partial. Only under Solomon were the Philistines brought into complete subjection (1 Kings ix. 16), and hitherto the ark had dwelt in curtains] ; **there hath not failed** [Heb. *fallen;* cf. 1 Sam. iii. 19] **one word** [a clear reference to Josh. xxi. 45, as the preceding words are to ver. 44] **of all his good promise, which he promised by the hand** [cf. ver. 53] **of Moses his servant** [viz., in Levit. xxvi. 3—13, and in Deut. xxviii. 1—14, *i.e.,* in the chapters which are the sources of this prayer, &c.

Ver. 57.—**The Lord our God be with us, as he was with our fathers : let him not leave us, nor forsake us.** [Solomon insensibly glides again into prayer ; here for the presence of God, in ver. 59 for His help. There is probably a reference to Deut. xxxi. 6, 8 ; Josh. i. 5, where, however, "forsake" is represented by a different word.

Ver. 58.—**That he may incline our hearts unto him** [Psa. cxix. 26 ; cxli. 4], **to walk in all his ways** [ver. 25 ; ch. ii. 4. The condition on which God's blessing was insured was at this time printed on Solomon's mind], **and to keep his commandments, and his statutes, and his judgments** [see note on ch. ii. 3, to which ver. there is not improbably a reference], **which he commanded our fathers.**

Ver. 59. **And let these my words, wherewith I have made supplication before the Lord, be nigh unto the Lord our God day and night, that he maintain the cause of** [Heb. *to do the judgment of*] **his servant, and the cause of his people Israel at all times, as the matter shall require** [Heb. *the thing of a day in his day.* Same phrase Exod. v. 13 ; xvi. 4]:

Ver. 60.—**That all the people of the earth may know that the Lord is God, and that there is none else.** [See ver. 22. We have here a recurrence to the thought of ver. 43, which was evidently prominent in Solomon's mind. He hopes the house now dedicated will be fraught with blessing for the world, and that the Gentiles will come to its light. Cf. Isa. ii. 2, 3.]

Ver. 61.—**Let your heart therefore be perfect with the Lord our God** [An instructive commentary on these words is found in ch. xi. 4, where it is said of this Solomon, *"His* heart was not perfect," &c.—same words. Similarly, *ib.* vers. 3, 9 are a comment on the prayer of ver. 58. Having preached to others, he himself became a

castaway], **to walk in his statutes, and to keep his commandments, as at this day** [That day the nation proved its piety by the dedication of the house.

At the close of this prayer (omitted in Chron.), according to 2 Chron. vii. 1, " fire came down from heaven and consumed the burnt offering and the sacrifices, and the glory of the Lord filled the house," but Bähr rejects these words as an interpolation. He maintains, indeed, that the chronicler contradicts himself, for we can hardly think that the glory which we are told (ch. v. 14) had already filled the house, left it and then returned. It is certainly suspicious, and a much stronger argument against the words in question, that no mention of the fire is made by our author, for, brief as this history is, it is difficult to believe that so signal an interposition could have remained unnoticed, if it really occurred.

SECTION IV.—*The Festal Sacrifices.*

The ceremonial of dedication was followed, as would naturally be the case, by sacrifices on a scale of unusual grandeur. Apart from their religious use and significance, the sacrifices testified to the devotion of the giver, who on this of all days must not appear before the Lord empty, and they also afforded materials for the great and prolonged feast by which this auspicious event in the history of Israel must be commemorated.

Ver. 62. **And the king, and all Israel with him** [Another indication (see on ver. 2) that practically the whole Israelitish nation (*i.e.,* its males) assembled to witness this great function (ver. 65. But see on ch. xvi. 17). The words also prove that the sacrifices mentioned presently were offered by the people as well as by the king], **offered sacrifice before the Lord.** [See note on ch. ix. 25]

Ver. 63.—**And Solomon offered a sacrifice** [Solomon is mentioned as chief donor, and as the executive. But others shared in the gift] **of peace offerings** [Levit. vii. 11 sqq. This was especially the sacrifice of praise—it is called " the sacrifice of thanksgiving of his peace offerings," *ib.* vers. 13, 15. See Bähr, Symb. ii. 368 sqq. In the peace offering, the fat was burnt on the altar, but the flesh was eaten (ver. 15 ; cf. Deut. xii. 7), so that this form of offering was, in every way, adapted to a festival. The idea that " ox after ox, to the number of 22,000, and sheep after sheep, to the number of 120,000, were *consumed,*" sc. by fire (Stanley), is expressly excluded], **which he offered unto the Lord,** two and twenty thousand oxen, and an hundred and twenty thousand sheep. [It is very possible that these numbers have been altered in course of transcription, as is the case with numbers elsewhere, but there is no ground for suspecting exaggeration or mistake. For, in the first place, the Chronicles and all the Versions agree with the text, and, secondly, the numbers, compared with what we know of the sacrifices offered on other occasions, are not unduly large, nor were they such that (as has been alleged) it would be impossible to offer them within the time specified. If, at an ordinary Passover, a quarter of a million of lambs could be sacrificed within the space of two or three hours (Jos., Bell. Jud. vi. 9. 3), there can obviously have been "no difficulty in sacrificing 3000 oxen and 18,000 sheep on each of the seven days of the festival" (Keil). (But were not the sacrifices spread over fourteen days? ver. 65.) And it is to be remembered (1) that "profusion was a usual feature of the sacrifices of antiquity. . . . Sacrifices of a thousand oxen (χιλιόμβαι) were not infrequent. According to an Arabian historian (Kotobeddyn), the Caliph Moktader sacrificed during his pilgrimage to Mecca . . . 40,000 camels and cows and 50,000 sheep. Tavernier speaks of 100,000 victims as offered by the King of Tonquin" (Rawlinson, Stanley); and (2) that the context insists on the extraordinary number of victims. They were so numerous, we are told, that the brazen altar was quite inadequate to receive them (ver. 64). It has been already pointed out (note on ver. 62) that the people joined the king in the sacrifices. Indeed it is against not only ver. 62, but vers. 63, 65, to suppose that all the victims were offered by Solomon alone (Ewald, Stanley). If these numbers, therefore, include those offered by the people, we can the more readily understand them. For, by the lowest computation, there could hardly be less than 100,000 heads of houses present at the feast (Bähr, Keil), and if the numbers of David's census (2 Sam. xxiv. 9) may be trusted, there may very well have been four or five times that number, and on such an occasion as that, an occasion altogether without precedent, every Israelite would doubtless offer his sacrifice of thanksgiving—the more so as a large number of victims would be required for the purposes of the subsequent feast. And as to the impossibility of the priests offering so prodigious a number within the specified time (Thenius, al.), we have only to remember (1) that if there were 38,000 Levites (men over thirty years of age) in the time of David (1 Chron. xxiii. 3), or anything like that number, there must have

been at the very least at this period two or three thousand priests (Keil), and we can hardly think that at the dedication of so glorious a temple, in which they were so profoundly interested, many of them would be absent from Jerusalem. But if there were only *one* thousand present, that number would have been amply sufficient to perform all the priestly functions. For it was no necessary part of the priests' office either to slay the victim, or to prepare it for sacrifice—*that* any Israelite might do (Levit. i. 5, 6, 11 ; iii. 2, 8, &c.) ; the duty of the priest was strictly limited to " sprinkling the blood round about upon the altar " (Levit. iii. 2, 8 ; cf. i. 5), and burning the fat, the kidneys, &c., upon the altar (*ib*. iii. 5). It is clear, consequently, that there is no difficulty whatsoever as to the manual acts required of the priests. It only remains to notice one other objection, viz., that the people could not possibly have eaten all the flesh of these peace offerings. But here again the answer is conclusive, viz. (1) that it was not necessary that all should be eaten, for the law expressly provided that if any of the flesh remained over until the third day, it should be burnt with fire (Levit. vii. 15 ; xix. 6), and (2) no one can say what the number of people may not have been (see below on ver. 65), and (3) the sacrifices were spread over fourteen days.] **So the king and all the children of Israel dedicated the house of the Lord.**

Ver. 64.—**The same day did the king hallow the middle of the court** [*i.e.*, the entire area of the court of the priests (ch. vi. 36). Ewald (287 *g*) translates " the inner court." The whole space may have been regarded as " one huge altar " (Rawlinson), or temporary altars may have been erected all over the area. As already observed, this fact alone points to an enormous number of victims] **that was before the house of the Lord : for there he offered burnt offerings** [Heb. *the* burnt offerings, *i.e.*, either the usual daily burnt offerings (Num. xxviii. 3), or more probably, those appropriate to such a special function (Num. xxix. 13 sqq. ; cf. 1 Kings iii. 4)], **and meat offerings** [Heb. *the meat offering*. Both this and the preceding word (הָעֹלָה) are singular (generic) in the original], **and the fat of the peace offerings : because the brazen altar that was before the Lord** [*i.e.*, house of the Lord] **was too little to receive the burnt offerings, and meat offerings, and the fat of the peace offerings** [and yet it was 20 cubits (30 feet) square, and so would offer a surface of 100 (Keil 144) square yards].

Ver. 65.—**And at that time Solomon held a feast** [the necessary sequel to such a number of peace offerings (cf. ch. iii. 15). All the flesh that could he, must he eaten (Levit. xix. 5, 6)], **and all Israel with him, a great congregation** [see note on ver. 64. " All Israel " would hardly be an exaggeration], **from the entering in of Hamath** [the northern boundary of Palestine (Num. xxxiv. 8 ; cf. xiii. 31 ; Josh. xiii. 5 ; Judg. iii. 3 ; Ezek. xlvii. 16 ; Stanley, S. and P. p. 407; Dict. Bib. i. p. 644; Porter, pp. 620, 621] **unto the river** [Heb. נַחַל, *i.e.*, torrent bed, watercourse, *wâdy* (*river* is נָהָר). See Stanley, S. and P. pp. 14, 505, 506] **of Egypt** [*i.e.*, the southern limit of the Holy Land. See Num. xxxiv. 5 ; Josh. xv. 4, 47 ; 2 Kings xxiv. 7; Gen. xv. 18, where the word is נָהָר refers to the Nile. The Wady el Arîsh must be intended (Dict. Bib. vol. iii. p. 1046, 1047, and Gesen., Thesaurus, vol. ii. p. 872, Porter, p. 267)], **before the Lord our God, seven days and seven days, even fourteen days** [The two periods are thus distinguished, because they were properly distinct, the first being the feast of dedication, the second the feast of tabernacles. This is more clearly explained in 2 Chron. vii. 9, 10.]

Ver. 66.—**On the eighth day he sent the people away** [*i.e.*, on the eighth day of the *second* feast, the " three and twentieth day of the month " (*ib.*, ver. 10). The first impression is that the eighth day of the period of fourteen days is meant, but the context, to say nothing of the Chron., contradicts this. The feast of dedication began on the eighth day of the month Ethanim (ver. 2), and lasted until the fourteenth. The feast of tabernacles began on the fifteenth and lasted till the twenty-first. On the evening of the twenty-second, the " day of restraint " (Levit. xxiii. 36 marg.), he dismissed the people, who would depart to their homes next morning] : **and they blessed** [*i.e.*, felicitated, saluted (on taking leave). Cf. Prov. xxvii. 14 ; 2 Kings iv. 29 ; 1 Sam. xxv. 6, 14. Marg. *thanked.* See note on ver. 14] **the king, and went unto their tents** [*i.e.*, homes—an archaic expression, dating from the times of the desert wanderings. Josh. xxii. 4 ; Judg. vii. 8 ; 2 Sam. xx. 1 ; 1 Kings xii. 16] **joyful and glad of heart for all the goodness that the Lord had done for David his servant** [the real founder of the temple. Solomon had but carried out his ideas and had entered into his labours], **and for Israel his people.**

HOMILETICS.

Vers. 8—11.—*The Dedication of the Temple and its Teaching.* The eighth day of the seventh month of the year 1004 B.C., or, according to some, B.C. 1000, was one of the brightest days of Jewish history—

" a day in golden letters to be set
Among the high tides of the calendar ; "

for on that day the holy and beautiful house, which had been seven and a half years in building, for which preparations had been made for a much longer period (1 Chron. xxii. 5), and on which a force of some one hundred and sixty thousand workmen had been in different ways employed ; on that day of days this house of houses was solemnly dedicated to the service of Almighty God. Let us carry our thoughts back to that day ; let us join the procession ; let us try to realize the scene, for we may learn a lesson thence, first, as to the consecration of our churches, and secondly, as to the dedication of our souls and bodies to God.

It is an enormous concourse that is gathered in and about the holy city. From "the entering in of Hamath to the river of Egypt " (ver. 65) every town and hamlet had sent up its tale of men. No Israelite who *could* be present—and in the seventh month the labours of the field were well-nigh over—would be absent. We must not think of the heads of the tribes alone ; it is a nation keeps festival to-day. And such a nation, with such a history! And its glory culminates to-day in the dedication of its temple. What child of Israel, then, but would be there ?

With early morning all Jerusalem, and its neighbouring hills and valleys (Psa. cxxv. 2), was instinct with life. The Easterns always rise early, and that day was a high day. It is still early when the great procession is marshalled. At its head is " Solomon in all his glory." The dignitaries of the State, of the Church (ch. iv. 1—19) ; all are there. Their rendezvous is the Mount Zion ; their object to escort the ark of God, with all the honour they can render it, on its last journey, to its last resting-place. And so the white-robed priests (2 Chron. v. 12) take up the consecrated structure and bear it tenderly, yet proudly, to its home. To-day the Levites may not carry it. As at the Jordan (Josh. iv. 10), as at Jericho (Josh. vi. 4), as in Mount Ebal (Josh. viii. 33), so on its last journey it must be borne on the shoulders of priests. The procession—we cannot follow its course, for it is probable that, for the sake of effect, it would make a considerable *détour*, perhaps a circuit of the city; nor can we speak of its psalms—and we may be sure if psalms (Pss. xv., xxiv; 1 Chron. xvii. 7—36) were chanted at the removal of the ark, they would not be wanting at the dedication of the temple—or its sacrifices (ver. 5)—the procession (cf. 1 Kings i. 38) at last reaches the temple precinct; it passes through the gate; here the crowd is checked, but the priests and princes pass on; they reach the inner court; here the princes stop, but the priests pass on. The whole temple platform is now choked with worshippers, while thousands who cannot gain admittance witness the august ceremonial from without, many, no doubt, having found a coign of vantage on the Mount of Olives. The priests, with their precious burden, pass through the porch, pass through the holy place, pass through the veil into the thick darkness of the oracle. There they lay down the ark, the outward and visible sign of the covenant, under the overshadowing wings of the colossal cherubim. They leave it wrapped in darkness; they leave it to begin at once their ministrations before the new shrine. At this point of the ceremonial it had been arranged that priests and Levites, singers, trumpeters, and harpists should burst into a song of praise (2 Chron. v. 12, 13). But ere they can fully accomplish their purpose, the dedication has become a true *consecration*, for the awful cloud, the token of the Divine presence, the cloud which veiled " the glory of the Lord " has filled the house, and the priests cannot stand to minister. As at the dedication of the tabernacle (Exod. xl. 34) so now, the incommunicable Godhead has " come in a thick cloud " (Exod. xix. 3), and has driven them, as it drove Moses, from the sanctuary. The king, who sees the portent from without, recognizes at once that his and his father's hope is realized; that his and his people's offering is accepted; that his and their projects and labours are now crowned; and, overcome with joy, he cries, " I have surely built thee a house to dwell in, a settled place," &c.

> " Majestic silence! then the harp awoke,
> The cymbal clanged, the deep-voiced trumpet spoke,
> And Salem spread her suppliant hands abroad,
> Viewed the descending flame, and blessed the present God."

Such, in brief, was the dedication of this house. It is true prayers and sacrifices followed, but of these we cannot now speak particularly. The essential parts of the consecration were (1) the solemn and formal setting apart of the edifice by the king and the representatives of the people, to be the house of God, and (2) the formal entry—to use the language of men—by the Godhead, concealed under the thick cloud, upon His new shrine.

So that in this service, as in all true services, there were two parts, man's and God's. It was man's part to offer the house with appropriate ceremonial to the Most High; it was God's part to accept it with appropriate signs. Now both of these are commonly and correctly called *consecration*. It will be for our convenience, however, if we now call the first of these dedication and restrict the term consecration to the second. And, using the words in these senses, let us see in this imposing ceremonial a lesson, first, as to our *churches*. As to which, we learn:

I. THAT CHURCHES SHOULD BE FORMALLY DEDICATED TO GOD. For if a formal service of dedication was fitting in the case of the temple, how can it be inappropriate in the case of the church? Is the latter less worthy of care and reverent regard than the former? Is it built for objects of less importance, or objects less Divine? Is it less dear to God, or less truly "God's house," because man is admitted to a place therein? Or may men build houses for God and retain the ownership for themselves? " Can we judge it a thing seemly for any man to go about the building of an house to the God of heaven with no other appearances than if his end were to rear up a kitchen or parlour for his own use? Or, when a work of such a nature is finished, remaineth there nothing but presently to use it and so an end?" (Hooker.) Alas, that churches and chapels should ever have been offered—sometimes by public auction—to the pewholders, or dedicated by brass plates, &c., to the service of opulent parishioners. Too often have they become congeries of petty freeholds, temples of exclusiveness, God's house in nothing but name. But this could not have been if the true idea of *dedication* had not been obscured or lost.

II. How CHURCHES SHOULD BE DEDICATED TO GOD. This history tells us that it should be with all possible solemnity and stateliness. There may surely be a *procession.* If this was right for the Jew, it cannot be wrong for us. There may be processional *hymns*—the psalm which was acceptable in their lips cannot be unbecoming in ours; the dignitaries of the State may join the ranks, even "*kings* of the earth" may "bring their glory and honour into it" (Rev. xxi. 24); in fact, it cannot be too stately, provided it be done not for self-glorification but for the glory of God. For is not God the same now as then; is He not still a great king? And is not man the same? Does he not still owe the profoundest homage he can render to his Maker? And if it be heartfelt, why may it not be public? The history teaches that an august ritual befits the dedication of a church, and that, *inter alia,* there should be *sacrifices* (vers. 5, 62; cf. 2 Sam. xxiv. 24—we should not come before the Lord empty), *music* (2 Chron. v. 12, 13—the language of heaven, the one tongue that escaped confusion at the building of Babel), and that the book of the covenant should be borne (as it is in Germany, and as the ark was) in procession to its place. "These things the wisdom of Solomon did not account superfluous" (Hooker).

It is to be remembered here that our Lord by His presence sanctioned the observance of a feast of dedication (John x. 22).

III. THAT CHURCHES MUST BE CONSECRATED BY GOD. The bishop, or other officer, can only consecrate in the sense of dedicating—of setting apart from profane uses. And this is what the "consecration" of churches and churchyards really means—no more and no less (see Hooker, Eccles. Pol. v. 12. 6), If either is to be "*hallowed*" (ch. ix. 2), it must be by the Divine presence. The Moslems say that wherever their great Caliph Omar prayed is consecrated ground. We hold that holy ground (Exod. iii. 5) must derive its sanctity from the All-Holy. The God who filled the temple must also hallow the church.

IV. THAT CHURCHES SINCERELY DEDICATED TO GOD WILL BE CONSECRATED BY GOD. Was the Ineffable Presence granted to the temple? Then why not to the church also? God has no favourites, nor is His arm shortened. The Presence will not be *revealed,* but it will be *there;* none the less real, all the more real, because it is spiritual. It would be strange if, in the dispensation of the Spirit, we disbelieved in the presence of Him who fills heaven and earth, who is "in the midst of the seven candlesticks" (Rev. i. 13), and who has promised His presence to companies of "two or three" sincere souls (Matt. xviii. 20, *Ubi tres, ibi ecclesia*). Our churches indeed are "*sanctified* by the word of God and prayer" (1 Tim. iv. 5), and if there is no cloud, yet we may "behold the glory of the Lord" (2 Cor. iii. 18); but they receive their full and perfect consecration in the κοινωνία of Christ's body and blood (1 Cor. x. 16). Men forget that if there is not a Real Presence then there must be a real *absence.* Some will allow God to be present everywhere—*except* in His church and sacraments.

As to the *Christian life,* this dedication of the temple reminds us—

I. THAT OUR BODIES ARE TEMPLES OF THE HOLY GHOST (1 Cor. vi. 19; iii. 16, 17; 2 Cor. vi. 16). "God has built" the "temple of the body" (John ii. 21) to be His shrine (Rom. viii. 9, 11; 2 Cor. vi. 16; Eph. iii. 17).

II. THAT WE SHOULD DEDICATE THEM TO GOD (Rom. vi. 13, 19; xii. 1; 1 Cor. vi. 13 20; Matt. xxii. 21). This is done in baptism, may be done in confirmation, and must be done in conversion (the *turning to* God).

III. THAT IF WE DEDICATE THEM, GOD WILL CONSECRATE THEM. If we "open the door" (Rev. iii. 20; John xiv. 23) He will enter in and dwell there. We have but to give the heart—the innermost recess of the house, the *adytum*—to Him, and He will possess and glorify the whole body (Luke xi. 34, 36).

Chap. vi. ver. 7, and chap. viii. ver. 12.—*The Silence and the Darkness.* In the first of these passages we are told that the house, built for the habitation of the Most High, was reared in profound silence ; in the second, that the Most High Himself dwelleth in the thick darkness.

Now observe, first, that darkness stands in the same relation to sight that silence does to hearing. In the one, nothing is *seen ;* in the other, nothing is *heard.* And, secondly, that the cloud and the house were alike the shrine and the dwelling-place of Deity: the cloud the inner, the temple the outer abode. We learn, therefore, that the God who appears in the cloud (Levit. xvi. 2), and dwells in the thick gloom of the oracle, is One who shrouds Himself in silence and darkness. Hence, let us learn—

I. THAT HE IS A GOD THAT HIDETH HIMSELF (Isa. xlv. 15). "No man hath seen God at any time" (John i. 18 ; Matt. xi. 27 ; Deut. iv. 12). "Thick darkness is under his feet" (Psa. xviii. 9, Heb.) "Darkness is his secret place ; dark waters and thick clouds his pavilion" (ch. viii. 11 ; cf. Psa. xcvii. 2). And He hides Himself, not as Eastern kings have done (comp. Esther i. 14, and Herod. iii. 84), to enhance their renown and dignity, and to increase the awe and reverence of their subjects—*omne ignotum pro magnifico*—but because we cannot see His face and live (Exod. xxxiii. 20). "Whom no man hath seen or can see" (1 Tim. vi. 16). "Dwelling in the light which no man can approach unto" (*ib.*) Cf. Acts xxii. 11.

II. THAT WE CANNOT BY SEARCHING FIND OUT GOD (Job xi. 7). In one sense those are not so far wrong who speak of Him as "the Unknowable." The *Quicunque vult* describes Him as "Incomprehensible" (Latin, *immensus, i.c.,* immeasureable). Man cannot understand the mysteries of his own existence, how much less the being of the Godhead. If we could understand God, we should be intellectually equal with God (Gen. iii. 22). It is no argument against the doctrine of the Trinity, or the eternal generation of the Son, or the procession of the Holy Ghost, that each is a mystery. How could it be otherwise? We have "nothing to draw with, and the well is deep."

III. THAT HIS WAYS ARE WRAPPED IN DARKNESS. See Rom. ii. 33 ; Deut. xxix. 29 ; Eccles. xi. 5. His judgments are an abyss of which we cannot see the bottom (Psa. xxxvi. 6). His footsteps are not known (Psa. lxxvii. 19). As He dwells in the thick cloud, so are His judgments far above out of sight (Psa. x. 5). "It is the glory of God to conceal a thing" (Prov. xxv. 2). Hence it is that His dealings are often so mysterious and painful, because what He does we know not now (John xiii. 7). The disciples "feared when they entered into the cloud" (Luke ix. 34). "Now we know in part." We only see, it has been said, as it were, the underside of the carpet, and so life is a confused and meaningless mixture. It is not God's will that we should see the plan and pattern yet. (Cf. Col. i. 26 ; Ephes. iii. 9.)

IV. THAT HIS WORKS ARE WROUGHT IN SILENCE. He is Himself a God that keepeth silence ; Psalm l. 3, 21 recognizes this. If silence be golden, the Eternal has observed this golden rule. Men blaspheme Him, defy Him, challenge Him to smite them dead—as a well-known atheist is said to have done—&c., and He keeps silence. Amid "earth's many voices," amid its everlasting Babel, His voice is never heard. Similarly, He *works* in the silence. At the creation, "He spake and it was done." "God said, Let there be light, and there was light." Creation moves in silence. We speak of "the music of the spheres ; but it is but a beautiful conceit. On the contrary, "there is no speech, no language ; their voice is not heard" (Psa. xix. 3, Heb.) Much truer is that exquisite conception—

> "And nightly to the *listening* earth
> Repeats the story of her birth."

The fact is that,

> "In *solemn silence,* all
> Move round this dark terrestrial ball.'

And in silence, too, is this planet sustained and ordered.　How

> "silently the springtime
> Her crown of verdure weaves,
> And all the trees on all the hills
> Open their thousand leaves."

Or as another, not less beautifully, puts it—

> " Soundless as chariots on the snow
> The saplings of the forest grow
> To trees of mighty girth :
> Each nightly star in silence burns,
> And every day in silence turns
> The axle of the earth.

> " The silent frost, with mighty hand,
> Fetters the rivers and the land
> With universal chain ;
> And, smitten by the silent sun,
> The chain is loosed, the rivers run,
> The lands are free again."

But for the discordant din of men, and but for the voices of beasts and birds, this earth would be a temple of silence.　And it is in the silence that God reveals Himself.　Not in the great and strong wind, not in the earthquake, not in the fire, but in the still small voice (1 Kings xix. 12, 13).　"Let us be silent," says one, "that we may hear the whispers of the gods."　In the silence, too, His Church has grown.　His kingdom "cometh not with observation" (Luke xvii. 20).　As silently as the seed grows, day and night, in the soil ; as silently as the leaven works in the meal.　And in the silence our Holy Lord will come again—as a thief in the night, as a snare, as the lightning.

V. That all the earth should keep silence before Him (Hab. ii. 20).　It is not meant to preach here "the eternal duty of silence," nor that all worship should be "of the silent sort;" but that, in realizing the awful presence of God, men should be hushed into the profoundest awe.　When we do "take upon ourselves to speak unto our Lord," we should remember that "we are but dust and ashes" (Gen. xviii. 27).　Our finger on our lips, our lips in the dust.　It was this feeling, in part, led Solomon to build the temple in silence.　And the feeling which found this expression in act he has elsewhere translated in words (see Eccles. v. 1, 2).　It was with a similar feeling that our Lord acted (Mark xi. 16).　And it is significant that we read of "silence in heaven" (Rev. viii. 1).

VI. That God's work must be done in silence.　"All real work is quiet work. It must be unobtrusive if it is to be fruitful.　"The temple was *thrown down* with axes and hammers, and they that did it roared in the midst of the congregation (Psa. lxxiv. 4, 6), but it was built up in silence " (M. Henry).　A temple of the Lord, a temple of "living stones," is now being built.　"O God, that the axes of schism or the hammers of furious contention should be heard within Thy sanctuary" (Hall). It is because of our unseemly cries and wranglings, because of the clash of controversy and the shouts of heated partizans, that this temple has made such poor progress.　Not until we have been first hushed into *silence* can the headstone be brought forth with *shouting* (Zech. iv. 7).

Ver. 2; cf. vi. 16.—*The Holy of Holies and the Heaven of Heavens.*　Elsewhere (pp. 99, 112) we have spoken of the correspondence of the Jewish temple with the Christian Church.　But let us now trace a truer and higher resemblance. For the Epistle to the Hebrews tells us that the "holy places made with hands" are "the figures (ἀντίτυπα, *i.e.*, *copies*) of the true" (Heb. ix. 24).　The temple of Solomon, therefore, must correspond to things in the heavens.　It does this, first, in its structure ; secondly, in its furniture ; thirdly, in its services.

I. IN ITS STRUCTURE. The temple, we have seen, was a reproduction, on an enlarged scale, and in a more permanent form, of the tabernacle. And the tabernacle was fashioned after a heavenly pattern (Exod. xxv. 40; xxvi. 30; xxvii. 8; Heb. viii. 5). Thrice was Moses admonished to make it " according to the fashion which was showed him in the mount." It has been well said that earth is

> " But the shadow of heaven, and things therein
> Are to each other like."

But this is true in a special sense of the earthly and heavenly temples. Their resemblance is recognized in the very language used of the temple. " Heaven thy dwelling-place " is constantly found in close connexion with " this house " (ch. viii. 30, 34, 39, 43). The same word—*Zebul*—used of the temple in ch. viii. 13 is used of heaven in Isa. lxiii. 15. Compare also ver. 13, " a settled place for thee to dwell in," &c., with vers. 30, 39, 43, &c. (Heb.) The same word—*Haycal*—again, used of the temple in ch. vi. 5, 33; vii. 50; 2 Kings xxiv. 13, is elsewhere used of heaven (Psa. xi. 4; xviii. 7; xxix. 9, &c.) But can we *trace* the resemblance? Can we suggest any points of contact? Let us try, premising, first, that a " general analogy is all that we can look for" (Alford on Rev. viii. 3).

1. *The temple was tripartite* (see ch. vi. Introduction). It was composed of porch, holy place, and oracle (the side chambers were hardly integral parts of the structure; see note on ch. vi. 6). Now it is remarkable that though the Jewish fathers spoke of "seven heavens"—some held that there were two—Holy Scripture speaks of *three*, and three only. When St. Paul would describe the very dwelling-place of Deity, he calls it " the *third* heaven" (2 Cor. xii. 2). What are the three heavens—whether atmospheric (*nubiferum*), sidereal (*astriferum*), and angelic (*angeliferum*), or what—it does not concern us to say; it is enough for our purpose that there are three. And three, it must be remembered, is the number and signature of God.

2. *All the temple was God's dwelling-place.* It is a mistake to suppose that the oracle was the abode of God, the holy place the abode of the people. In the temple the people had no place. It was the "house of the great God" (Ezra v. 8); a palace for God, and not for man (1 Chron. xxix. 1). "As the whole house, so also each compartment . . . is called ' the dwelling-place '" (Bähr). Again, the holy place, as well as the entire sanctuary, is called the palace (ch. vi. 5 with 2 Kings xxiv. 13). The primary design of the temple, as of the tabernacle, was to afford a habitation for the ark and for Him whose covenant it contained.

3. *But the inner temple was God's shrine.* In the holy of holies, He was *revealed.* He dwelt "between the cherubim" (Exod. xxv. 22; 1 Sam. iv. 4; 2 Kings xix. 15, &c.) The word Shechinah, which is used to denote the Presence, is derived from *shachan,* "he dwelt." So it is in heaven. Heaven is God's throne (Isa. lxvi. 1; Acts vii. 49); but there is a "heaven of heavens," where He is revealed. True "the heaven and heaven of heavens" cannot contain Him, any more than the holy and the holy of holies, but in each He has His special habitation. Here again temple and temple not built with hands are alike.

4. *The temple blazed with gold and gems.* It was " exceeding magnifical " as the palace of the Godhead. Everything was appropriate to a great king. " Pure gold," " gold of Uphaz," cedar, olive wood, all was " for glory and beauty " (Exod. xxviii. 2). Compare the description of heaven in Rev. xxi. 9 sqq. Like a jasper stone (ver. 11); pure gold (vers. 18, 21); precious stones (vers. 19, 20); twelve pearls (ver. 21).

II. IN ITS FURNITURE. Observe: the furniture and appointments *outside* the house, in the court of the priests—brazen altar, molten sea, lavers, &c.—have no counterparts in heaven. They are " of the earth, earthy." In the holy place were the altar of incense, the table of shewbread, the ten candlesticks, &c. (ch. vii. 48—50). In the most holy place were the mercy-seat, the cherubim of glory, the ark, the golden censer, &c. And heaven has its golden altar (Rev. vi. 9; viii. 3; ix. 13), its incense (Rev. viii. 3, 4), its seven lamps (Rev. iv. 5; cf. Exod. xxvii. 23; Zech iv. 2). And for the table of shewbread, see Rev. xxii. 2. Or if it be said that the "table of the face" has no counterpart in heaven, we may reply that it is not needed, because His servants "see his face" and feast upon His presence (Rev. xxiv. 4). Similarly heaven has its mercy-seat—the Fount of Mercy dwells there—its cherubim and seraphim (Isa. vi. 2; Rev. iv. 7; cf. Ezek. i. 10), and its golden censer (Rev. viii. 3, 5). It has no ark—the covenant is writ in the heart of the Eternal, as He now writes it on the hearts of men (Heb. viii. 10). But it has its throne (Rev. iv. 2 *et passim*), and the ark was the throne of God (cf. Isa. vi. 2).

III. In its services. Here we must distinguish between (1) the service of the holy place, and (2) the service of the Holiest of all. As to the former, it must here suffice to say that it centred round the altar of incense. Morning and evening, year in, year out, incense was burnt upon the golden altar. And we have already seen that incense is offered in heaven. As to its meaning, lessons, &c., we have spoken elsewhere (pp. 199,200). Let us turn, therefore, to the worship of the most holy place. And here we observe—

1. *The cherubim of glory overshadowed the mercy-seat* (Heb. ix. 5). They were, as it were, choirs on either side of the place of the Presence. Now the cherubim were symbolical representations of all created existences (see note on ch. vi. 29) from the highest to the lowest. But especially did they shadow forth the highest forms of intelligence, the celestial beings who surround the Lord of glory; they were earthly counterparts of the heavenly seraphim (Isa. vi. 2), and so they pourtrayed, as far as was possible, the worship of the heavenly hosts. It is true they were silent—they could not be otherwise—but still they conveyed the idea of ceaseless contemplation, of the most profound and reverent homage, of awestruck adoration. Indeed, we only understand what they symbolized by comparing the shadow with the substance. For we find that heaven has its cherubim. The "four beasts (ζῶα) round about the throne, full of eyes before and behind" (Rev. iv. 6—8), are clearly the "very substance" of those things of which Isaiah's and Ezekiel's winged creatures (Isa. vi. 2; Ezek. i. 10; x. 14) were the likeness, and of which Solomon's cherubim were the copies. The silent, stately cherubim consequently were adumbrations of the mysterious hierarchy who ceaselessly praise the Un-created Light and lead the worship of the skies (Rev. iv. 8—11; v. 8, 9, 14), "raising their *Trisagion* ever and aye."

2. *The high priest entered the most holy place once a year.* The ceremonial of the day of atonement (Levit. xvi.) foreshadowed, as we are expressly told in Heb. ix., the entry of our great High Priest into heaven itself. The Jewish high priest, robed in spotless white vestments, passed through the veil of blue and purple and scarlet (Exod. xxvi. 31) into the holy oracle, with the blood of calves and goats, &c. Even so our unspotted Lord, "the High Priest of our profession" (Heb. ii. 1), passed through (not *into*, διεληλυθότα) the blue heavens (Heb. iv. 14) into the presence of the Eternal, with His own blood (ch. ix. 12). And as the high priest presented the tokens of death—as he sprinkled the blood (which is the life of the flesh) seven times before the mercy-seat eastward (Levit. xvi. 15), and so in figure pleaded the meritorious death of Him who should come to put away sin, so does our great High Priest present his pierced and wounded form—He stands before the throne as a "Lamb as it had been slain" (Rev. v. 6)—and pleads His passion, the death of One who *has* come, for the salvation and life of the world. It may be that, like the high priest, He utters no articulate words; it may be that, like him, He simply *appears* as the representative of man to *show* the tokens and pledges of atonement; or it may be that as the incense was burned when the blood was sprinkled, so His powerful intercession, of which the incense was a type, is joined to the silent pleading of His wounds. But whichever way it is, it is clear that the ritual of the holy of holies has its blessed counterpart in the ritual of the heaven of heavens.

Vers. 23—53.—*The Prayer of Dedication.* In how many and varied ways is Solomon a type of the Divine Solomon, the true Son of David (see pp. 63, 77, &c.) Even in this respect they are alike—that each has "taught us how to pray" (Luke xi. 1 sqq.)

For we may be sure that the Prayer of Dedication is for our instruction and *imitation,* otherwise it would hardly have been recorded, and recorded at such length, in Scripture. " After this manner therefore pray ye" (Matt. vi. 9).

I. LAYMEN MAY OFFER PUBLIC PRAYER. This is no monopoly of priests. The Hebrew king might not sacrifice or burn incense (2 Chron. xxvi. 18), but he might lead the prayers both of priests and people, and that on the greatest day in the history of Israel. Even so, though " we give not to our princes the ministering either of God's word or of the sacraments " (Art. xxxvii.), still we do not deny them any " prerogative which we see to have been given always to all godly princes in Holy Scripture " (*ib.*), and least of all the prerogative of prayer exercised by David, Solomon, Asa (2 Chron. xiv. 11), Jehoshaphat (*ib.*, xx. 5—12), and Hezekiah (*ib.*, xxx. 18—20). It was Constantine, a layman, presided at the Council of Nice.

II. KINGS SHOULD BE PROUD TO TAKE PART IN RELIGIOUS FUNCTIONS. Whatever divinity doth hedge them about, they are not greater or wiser than Solomon, and the proudest moment of *his* life was when he led the ark to its resting-place ; the happiest, when he " blessed all the congregation of Israel " (ver. 14). Never is king so great as when he takes his proper place before God. Alas! that religion should have ever been brought into such contempt that kings should be ashamed or afraid to be the " nursing fathers " of the Church (Isa. xlix. 23). Solomon's prayer is " a testimony that a wisdom which can no longer pray is folly" (Bähr).

III. PRAYER SHOULD BE PRECEDED BY PRAISE. It was not until Solomon had "blessed God " (ver. 15) that he prayed to God (vers. 23—53). " *Praemissa laude, invocatio sequi solet.*" This was the rule of the early Church (see Psa. lxv. 1, 2 for the scriptural order ; cf. Phil. i. 3, 4 ; iv. 6, and see Howson's Hulsean Lectures, No. iv., for the combination of thanksgiving and prayer in St. Paul's Epistles). And Solomon not only began but ended with blessing (ver. 56).

IV. TRUE PRAYER IS ASKING GOD FOR WHAT WE NEED. Not rhetorical display, not *sesquepedalia verba,* not a mere string of texts and hymns, but the simplest, humblest cry of the heart. Which of us has not heard prayers like the Pharisee's— without one word of prayer (*i.e.,* petition) in them? And how many prayers are made painful by their pretentiousness. Perhaps a child has been ordained our pattern (Matt. xviii. 2—4), that from it we should learn to pray. " In prayer it is better to have a heart without words than words without a heart " (Bunyan).

V. PRAYER SHOULD BE OFFERED FOR ALL SORTS AND CONDITIONS OF MEN. Not for self only. It is not "*my* Father," but " *our* Father." Perhaps *selfishness* is nowhere more conspicuous or more hateful than in our prayers. We are members one of another. It is in the Pharisee's prayer that we find so much " I." Notice how varied were Solomon's petitions, and cf. 1 Tim. ii. 1, 2, 8. Tennyson says—

> " For what are men better than sheep or goats
> That nourish a blind life within the brain,
> If, knowing God, they lift not hands in prayer
> Both for themselves and *those who call them friend ?* "

And he does not stop there, but adds that thus

> " the *whole round world*
> Is bound by golden chains around the feet of God."

This prayer of dedication was a veritable *Litany* (vers. 31, 33, 37, 41, 44, &c.)

VI. PRAYER SHOULD BE SCRIPTURAL, *i.e.,* conceived in the spirit and expressed in the words of Scripture. This prayer was pre-eminently so (see notes on vers. 22 sqq.) What St. Cyprian says of the Lord's prayer, " *Quanto efficacius impetramus quod petimus in Christi nomine, si petamus ipsius oratione,*" may suggest to us that that prayer is most likely to move God's hand which is based on God's Word. Supplication should be shaped by revelation.

VII. PRAYERS MAY BE LITURGICAL. The Scripture references, its artificial structure, and indeed its very preservation, prove that this prayer was a pre-composed form.   A form need not involve formalism.   All Christians use forms of *praise;* why not forms of *prayer?* (See Hooker, V. xxvi. 2. 3.)

VIII. OUTWARD FORMS ARE NOT TO BE DESPISED.   Solomon "kneeled upon his knees, with his hands stretched out towards heaven " (cf. Dan. vi. 10 ; Acts vii. 60 ; ix. 40 ; xx. 36 ; xxi. 5 ; Ephes. iii. 14, and, above all, Luke xxii. 41 and xxiv. 50. Also Psa. xxviii. 2 ; lxiii. 4 ; cxxxiv. 2).   Ritualism is a question of degree, for we all use *some* rites.   So long as we have bodies, we can never have a *purely* spiritual religion, but must " glorify God in our *bodies* and spirits " (1 Cor. vi. 20).   That forms have their foundation in human nature, and may be impressive and edifying, is proved by the fact that " no nation under heaven either doth or ever did suffer public actions which are of weight to pass without some visible solemnity " (Hooker, IV. i. 3), and for this reason, that

> " Sounds which address the ear are lost and die
> In one short hour ; while that which strikes the eye
> Lives long upon the mind : the faithful sight
> Graves on the memory with a beam of light."

It is only when forms usurp the place, or mar the reality, of spiritual worship (John iv. 24) that they are really reprehensible.

Vers. 62—66.—*The Feast on the Sacrifices.*   In this prodigious number of sacrifices—in round numbers 150,000 victims—3,000 oxen and 18,000 sheep for every day of the festival (Keil) ; five oxen and twenty-five sheep for every minute of each day (Thenius)—in this wholesale slaughter, which converted the court of the priests into one great shambles, and almost choked the sewers of the temple with blood, one feature is liable to be overlooked (note on ver. 64), namely, that all these sacrifices were "*peace* offerings," with the exception, of course, of the usual burnt offerings.   In all these—and king and princes and people alike brought their thousands—*all* was first given to God, but the bulk was given back by God to the sacrificers.   With the exception of the fat, &c., burnt on the altar, and the blood (which was the life), poured out at its base, and the customary portion of the priests (Levit. vii. 14, 21 ; 1 Cor. ix. 13), all the rest was carried home by the offerer to provide a *feast* for him and his family.   The peace offering was thus a social festival (*die feierliche und förmliche Mahlzeit* (Bähr, see his Symbolik, ii. 368 sqq.) And the same remark applies to the still greater number—a quarter of a million of paschal lambs offered year by year in later times.   The blood was sprinkled as a memorial before God, but the lamb was roasted entire to provide a supper for the household (Deut. xvi. 1—7).   In all these sacrifices God graciously entertained those who offered them with their own oblations—which He had first given them— at His own table.   And herein we have an illustration of God's gracious way of dealing with our gifts and offerings.   He accepts them at our hands, but gives them back for our use and enjoyment.   We present our sacrifice, and He spreads a banquet for our souls.   It is a curious circumstance, and one that shows how entirely this principle has been overlooked, that " sacrifice," which properly means " something made sacred," " consecrated," has come to be a synonym for " loss," "privation."   But this a true sacrifice can never be.   There is no such thing as giving at a loss to the Lord of all.   He insists on paying us back a hundred fold. All our offerings are in this sense peace offerings.   He sends us away laden with our own gifts, "joyful and glad of heart for all the goodness of the Lord " (ver. 66).   Let us now see how this holds good.

I. OF THE SACRIFICE OF THE DEATH OF CHRIST.   This is the one veritable sacrifice of the world.   Of all others it may be said, " Of thine own have we given thee." He alone "offered himself" (Heb. ix. 14).   " With his own blood " (ver. 12). Behold how this oblation comes back to us charged with blessing.   " *Once* offered to bear the sins of *many* " (ver. 28) ; " Having obtained eternal redemption for us " (ver. 12).   " By the obedience of one many are made righteous " (Rom. v. 19). Compare Heb. ii. 9, 10 ; xii. 2 ; Phil. ii. 6—11 ; and especially John x. 11, 17, and vi. 51.

II. OF THE SACRIFICE OF OUR BODIES (Rom. xii. 1). If in separating the body from common uses and yielding our bodies instruments of righteousness to God (Rom. vi. 13), we seem to suffer inconvenience, privation, &c., it is not really so. This sacrifice brings "joy and gladness of heart." Not unseldom are we conscious of the present gain. "Virtue is its own reward." The "testimony of the conscience" is no slight recompense. How great, for example, is the guerdon of purity!

> " So dear to Heaven is saintly chastity
> That when a soul is found sincerely so
> A thousand liveried angels lacquey her,
> Driving far off each thing of sin and guilt,
> And in clear dream and solemn vision
> Tell her of things that no gross ear can hear," &c.

There is a story told of George Herbert which shows how little sacrifices become great feasts. On his way to a musical gathering, he stopped by the way to help a poor waggoner out of the ruts. Arriving late and bespattered with mud, he was commiserated for the loss and inconvenience he had sustained. But he would not allow that it was loss. " The remembrance," he said, "will bring music into the heart at midnight."

III. OF THE SACRIFICE OF OUR ALMS. True, they *are* loss when given to serve self, or for the praise of men. "Verily I say unto you, they *have* (*i.e.,* e' haust, ἀπέχουσιν) their reward" (Matt. vi. 2). Such givers get what they bargained for; they receive " *their* good things" (Luke xvi. 25). But then there was no oblation to God. A Scottish laird having put a crown piece by mistake into the plate, asked for it back again. On being told that he might put what he chose in, but take nothing out, he said, "Well, well, I suppose I'll get credit for it in heaven." " Na, na," was the just reply, "ye'll only get credit for the penny." But if the alms be true offerings to God, then they have both a present and an eternal reward. Present, in hearing the widow's heart sing for joy, and in the blessing of him that was ready to perish" (Job xxix. 13) ; eternal, in that " God is not unrighteous to forget," &c. (Heb. vi. 10), and that a " cup of cold water only " shall in no wise lose its reward (Matt. x. 42). Such gifts are the truest and safest investments (Prov. xix. 17).

> "We lose what on ourselves we spend,
> We have as treasure without end
> Whatever, Lord, to Thee we lend."

There is on record an admirable prayer of Thomas Sutton, the pious founder of the Charterhouse, "O Lord, Thou hast given me a large estate, give me a *large heart.*" We cannot lose what we give away.

IV. OF THE SACRIFICE OF OUR OBLATIONS. We use "oblations" here in the liturgical sense of the word, *i.e.,* of the oblations of bread and wine in the Holy Communion. For these were anciently, and should be still, solemnly offered to God, as our thank-offerings, as a sort of first-fruits of His creatures. And now consider how they are given back to us. " The cup of blessing which we bless, is it not the communion (κοινωνία, the joint participation in) of the blood of Christ? the bread which we break, is it not the communion of the body of Christ? " (1 Cor. x. 16.) We have presented to the Divine Majesty bread and wine, and He gives us in return the body and blood of our Lord (*ib.,* xi. 24, 25).

V. OF THE SACRIFICE OF WORLDLY PROSPECTS, &c. Men often speak of the *sacrifices* they have had to make for the sake of their religion. And time was when great sacrifices were demanded; these are sometimes demanded still. But they involve no *loss,* no real and abiding injury. On the contrary, they are actually, and in the long run, a gain. " There is no man that hath left houses, or brethren, or sisters, or father, or mother, or wife, or children, or lands, for my sake and the gospel's, but he shall receive an hundredfold now in this time, houses, and brethren, and sisters, and mothers, and children, and lands, with persecutions; and in the world to come eternal life " (Mark x. 29, 30). On which

Bengel beautifully remarks that nature gives us each but one father and one mother, but the Church gives us many. (Cf. Rom. xvi. 13.) "What shall I do," said Amaziah, "for the hundred talents which I have given to the army of Israel?" "And the man of God answered, The Lord is able to give thee much more than this" (2 Chron. xxv. 9). Who had made more sacrifices than St. Paul? And yet who was it wrote of "having nothing, yet possessing all things?" (2 Cor. vi. 10). The man who had such loved and loving friends as Rom. xvi. proves him to have had, cannot be called poor. Well might he write, "I have all and abound" (Phil. iv. 18). The sacrifices he had made procured him a continual feast. It is the same with all our sacrifices. The Great King cannot receive gifts, but he must return them "according to his royal bounty" (1 Kings x. 13). The Greatest Giver in the world will never be outdone in generosity by king Solomon. (A beautiful illustration of the leading thought of this homily will be found in one of Mrs. Gatty's "Parables from Nature," called "The Circle of Blessing," 2nd series, 6th ed., pp. 5 sqq.)

HOMILIES BY VARIOUS AUTHORS.

Ver. 6.—*The Ark of the Covenant.* The ark was the heart of the temple. For it the shrine was erected. It was regarded as the throne of Jehovah. Hence the reverence with which it was approached. In itself the ark was not very remarkable. It was a chest $2\frac{1}{2}$ cubits long, and $1\frac{1}{2}$ cubits deep and broad, made of wood covered with gold; the lid, called "the mercy-seat," being of pure gold, having the cherubim at its ends. For its construction see Exod. xxv., where it is placed first as the most important of all the furniture of the tabernacle. Describe its connection with the people's entrance to Canaan, leading them through the Jordan, and heading the procession round Jericho. A superstitious sanctity was attached to it later. The outward symbol was supposed to have the efficacy which belonged only to that which it symbolized. It was carried into battle (1 Sam. iv.) under this delusion, but the ark could not save a people from whom God had withdrawn. Their superstition was rebuked by the defeat of the army, and the capture by the Philistines of the ark itself. Show how often in Church history the sign has been substituted for the thing signified, to the injury of God's cause. Though the superstitious belief in the ark was always rebuked, its sanctity was vindicated: by its avenging progress through the cities of Philistia, and by the punishment of Uzzah. Moreover, a blessing came with it to those who received it aright, e.g., to the house of Obed-Edom. The ark had been brought up to Jerusalem by David amid national rejoicing and placed in a tent prepared for it: now it found its abiding place in Solomon's temple. Throwing on the ark the light of the Epistle to the Hebrews, let us remind ourselves of certain religious truths to which it bore silent witness. These will be suggested by the contents of the ark, by its covering, by the mode of approaching it, and by its uses in worship.

I. THE ARK SUGGESTED THAT THE COVENANT RESTED ON LAW. The safe custody of the material tables of stone implied the moral observance of the precepts inscribed on them. "There was nothing in the ark save the two tables of stone," &c. (If we are to understand Heb. ix. 4 as asserting that Aaron's rod and the pot of manna were actually inside the ark, they had probably disappeared by Solomon's time.) The term "a covenant" is only used by way of accommodation, when applied to the relation between man and God. Such a "covenant" is merely a promise, which God makes dependent on the fulfilment of certain conditions; e.g., the promise after the flood is called a "covenant." So the covenant of Sinai was a promise on God's part, conditioned by the observance of the ten commandments on man's part. This was proclaimed by the presence of the tables of the law in the ark of the covenant. Show from Scripture and experience that bliss is conditioned by obedience. There is nothing lawless either in morals or in nature.

II. THE ARK PROCLAIMED THAT MERCY CAME BETWEEN MAN AND THE BROKEN LAW. "The mercy-seat" covered "the tables." The value of mercy was typified by the pure gold of the capporeth. Exhibit the necessity of mercy to men who are prone to evil and forgetful of good. Illustrate it from God's dealings with Israel, and Christ's goodness to His disciples. The publican struck the keynote of true prayer when he exclaimed, " God be merciful to me, a sinner ! " Compare Psalm li. Show how the sense of our want of mercy grows with our sensibility to the sinfulness of sin. Paul the apostle an example of this : " of sinners I *am* the chief."

III. THE ARK DECLARED THAT AN ATONEMENT MADE MERCY POSSIBLE. Describe the day of atonement; the sacrifice offered; the high priest entering the holy of holies with the blood which he sprinkled on the mercy-seat. Even he could only draw near to the mercy-seat after the sacrifice (compare Heb. ix.) " Without the shedding of blood there is no remission." Apply this to the sacrifice of " the Lamb of God," who was " wounded for our transgressions," whose " blood cleanseth from all sin." Describe him as the High Priest in the Holiest of all, having opened the way for all sinners to the abounding mercy of God.

IV. THE ARK ENCOURAGED MEN TO DRAW NEAR TO GOD. The law (represented by the tables) was broken ; but the mercy of God (represented by the capporeth) was revealed ; and the atonement (represented by the sprinkled blood) was provided ; so that God fulfilled His promise about the mercy-seat. " There will I *commune* with thee."

Apply the teaching of this subject to those conscious of guilt, burdened by sorrow, &c. " Let us, therefore, come boldly unto the throne of grace, that we may obtain mercy, and find grace to help in time of need."—A. R.

Vers. 10, 11.—*The Presence of the Lord in the House of the Lord.* The Shechinah, which is here referred to, was a most brilliant and glorious light, usually concealed by a cloud ; a fit emblem, therefore, of Jehovah, the God of light and of glory, who is veiled from His creatures. As the visible symbol of the Divine presence, " the pillar of cloud and fire," had gone before Israel in the wilderness, proving their guide and defence. Suddenly and mysteriously it appeared in the new temple of Solomon, at the festival of dedication, giving Divine sanction to the work, and assuring all beholders that Jehovah had made that His dwelling-place. Not only was the holy of holies filled with the cloud, but the holy place also, indeed, the whole building was permeated by it, so that all the building was henceforth holy. The signs of th Divine presence are different now, but the reality of it may be consciously felt. " Where two or three are met together in my name, there am I in the midst of them." The New Testament counterpart of this manifestation is found in the upper room on the day of Pentecost, when " suddenly there came a sound from heaven as of a rushing mighty wind, and it filled all the house where they were sitting " (Acts ii. 2). Compare these two manifestations : the splendour of the temple, with the poverty of the upper room ; the narrowness of national rejoicing, with the breadth of world-wide preaching, &c. Let us seek the changeless inward truth underlying the changeful outward form which embodies it.

I. THE PREPARATION FOR THE DIVINE PRESENCE. Read the account of that which, on the part of the people, had preceded this display. 1. *Sacred memories were recalled.* The worn tent, the ark, the holy vessels, had just been brought in (ver. 4), and glorious yet tender associations were connected with each. The revival of old impressions made in youth, &c., makes the heart sensitive to the Spirit of God. Give examples. 2. *Divine law was enthroned.* " Nothing in the ark save the two tables of stone " (ver. 9). Disobedience to God's commands, forgetfulness of them, unfits us for seeing Him. It deteriorates character, debases the heart. " Who shall ascend into the hill of the Lord ? he that hath clean hands and a pure heart," &c. 3. *God's claims were recognized.* By the completion of the temple, by the multitudinous sacrifices (ver. 5). The willingness to give ourselves up to God prepares us to see Him as *our* God. Not the intellectual research, but the reverent submission discovers Him. " Except ye be converted and become as little children, ye shall not enter the kingdom of heaven." " He that doeth the will of my Father shall know of the doctrine." " We beseech you, therefore, brethren, by the mercies of God, that ye present yourselves a living sacrifice,"

&c.   4. *Earnest prayers were offered.*   Solomon's prayer, which follows, was but the formal and public utterance of many secret prayers on the part of himself and others.   See how often he spoke to God about this building, and how often God spoke to him.   He and his people prayed above all things that the special glory of the tabernacle might be granted to the temple.   Now the prayers were answered.   "Ask and ye shall receive," &c.   The apostles expected the Holy Spirit ; but in order to receive the fulfilment of the Lord's promise, " they continued, with one accord, in prayer and supplication."

II. The effects of the Divine presence.   We do not refer to the special and immediate effects of the *cloud*, but to the moral and religious effect of the *presence* thus symbolized.   1. *It restored significance to old symbols.*   The ark had lost much of its sanctity in the eyes of the people, as the conduct of Uzzah showed. This naturally arose from its frequent removals, its uncovering, its capture by the Philistines, and most of all from the absence of the Shechinah.   Now the old veneration was restored to it, because its real significance was re-established. Apply this thought to churches, to their organizations, to their sacraments, &c. How often these are like the cloudless ark.   They want the realized presence of God to make them vivid with life.   2. *It testified to God's acceptance of the new building.*   Reverence and awe fell on all the worshippers.   True " consecration " arises from the signs of the Divine presence given to the faithful.   The conversion of a sinner, the uplifting of a fallen disciple, &c., these are the evidences we look for that worship and work, place and people, are accepted of God.   3. *It confirmed the faith of some, and inspired faith in others.*   From childhood they had been told of the appearance of the glory of the Lord in olden days.   Now, for the first time, they saw it, and doubt vanished before the light.   A great turning to God on the part of the unrighteous, or some similar spiritual evidence of the Divine power amongst us, would do more than all controversy to destroy scepticism.   4. *It proclaimed God's readiness to hear prayer.*   With what confidence Solomon could pray after this !   The realization that God is near us is our highest encouragement to speak to Him.   " Because he hath heard me in time past, therefore will I call upon him as long as I live."

If such be the glory and bliss of God's presence on earth, what will it be to stand before His throne in heaven ?—A. R.

Vers. 10, 11.—*The Glory-cloud.*—Never did Solomon appear so much " in all his glory " as on this memorial day of the dedication of the temple.   The solemnities of the service, the procession of the sacred ark from the city of David into its resting-place, the robed priests, the rapturous multitude, the unnumbered sacrifices, the music and the songs, must have formed altogether a marvellous spectacle.   But of all the incidents of the day none could be compared with that of the sudden appearance of the Shechinah—the glory-cloud.   This introduced a new supernatural element.   The rest was human—man's handiwork, man's worship, man's glory; this was Divine — the miraculous sign of the present and approving God.   It raises the scene above comparison with any similar scene in the history of any other nation.   Other peoples have reared their gorgeous temples, and kings and priests have gone in solemn pomp and circumstance to consecrate them. But what shrine has ever been honoured like this ?   Altars to false gods innumerable have been reared, but where has been the fire from heaven to kindle their sacrifices ?   Idol temples dedicated—where the radiant cloud of the Divine presence ?   The priests were too much dazzled by the shining splendour to continue their ministrations.   Solomon might well be filled with adoring wonder.   " But will God indeed ?" &c. (ver. 27).   Many Scripture examples of the way in which miraculous revelations of the presence of God overawe the spirits of men : Jacob at Bethel, Moses before the burning bush, Elijah at the mouth of the cave, the disciples of Christ on the Mount of Transfiguration, &c.   Solomon's, however, was not so much an emotion of fear, but of sacred reverence and glad surprise.   The appearance of the cloud set the seal of Divine acceptance on the temple and its service, linking it with all the glorious associations of the past—the climax and crown of a long series (900 years long, perhaps) of miraculous Divine manifestations. But look on it now as prophetic of a more glorious future, as imaging forth to the men of that age higher forms of Divine manifestation that in the fulness of time should come to pass.

I. THE INCARNATION OF CHRIST. When the eternal Son of the Father laid aside the "form of God," and took upon Him "the likeness of sinful flesh," He filled the temple of a human body with the Divine glory. God came to dwell in very deed "amongst men upon the earth." The Infinite Unseen submitted to the conditions of a finite visible personality. The Light insufferable, "which no man can approach unto," veiled itself in a cloud of mortal flesh. "We beheld his glory," &c. (John i. 14). When the second temple was being built, many of the people were troubled at the thought that it would be so inferior to the first. The old men who had "seen the first house" wept (Ezra iii. 12; Haggai ii. 3). But the prophets of the time were commissioned to comfort them with the assurance that, though the old symbolic grandeur was gone, the glory of the latter house should be greater than that of the former. It would contain no ark, no mercy seat, no Shechinah, no heaven-kindled fire, no Urim and Thummim, no prophetic spirit; "Ichabod" would be written on its walls. But a nobler Presence than had ever been seen on earth before would irradiate it in the coming time: "Behold I will send my messenger," &c. (Mal. iii. 1); "Yet once, it is a while, and I will shake the heavens," &c. (Haggai ii. 6, 7). Every time the Lord Jesus, "the brightness of the Father's glory," entered the temple—as a babe in His mother's arms, as a boy girding Himself for His "Father's business," as a man in the fulness of His Divine authority, purging it from defilement, expounding in it the law of acceptable worship, making it the centre of His beneficent healing ministry—He verified in some new form these prophetic words. The manifestations of the present Deity in the olden times "have no glory in this respect by reason of the glory that excelleth," even "the light of the knowledge of the glory of God in the face of Jesus Christ." Do we ask, "Will God in very deed dwell?" &c., the answer comes back to us, "Great is the mystery of godliness, God was manifest," &c. (1 Tim. iii. 16), "Immanuel, God with us" (Matt. i. 23). That outshining radiance in the temple was dazzling, almost repellent, deepening the sense of distance, creating fear; this Divine apocalypse is infinitely at ctive, gives unmistakable proof of sympathetic personal nearness, awakens grateful, trustful, and adoring love.

II. THE GIFT OF THE SPIRIT. The manifestation of God in the person of His Son was preparatory to the richer grace—the actual impartation of Himself by His Spirit to the individual souls of men (see Eph. iv. 8 sqq.; 2 Cor. vi. 16). The dispensation of the Spirit is the ultimate fact. In this God communicates Himself in the highest form of revelation, and the most intimate fellowship of which man is capable. The "dwelling" of the Holy Ghost in every new-born soul, in every assembly of true spiritual worshippers, in the "one body" of the universal Church, is prefigured in the scene before us. The day of the dedication of the temple finds its antitype in the "day of Pentecost." Place these manifestations side by side. As you trace the lines of comparison between them, how glorious does the Christian fact appear! The one was material in its nature—a bright and beautiful vision for the eye, appealing indirectly through the senses to the soul; the other intensely spiritual—a blessed overpowering influence, seizing at once on the minds and hearts of the people, the flowing in of a Divine life. And though there was something for the eye and ear, its form was such as to suggest most strikingly that living word of truth and holy fire of love which the heart alone can know. The one was diffuse, general, indiscriminate—a bright, scattered cloud filling the place;—the other was distinct and personal. The Spirit of God deals not with companies of men, but with isolated souls. There was a separate tongue of flame on the head of each. Not the *place* merely, but the *men*, each according to his own individuality, was "filled with the Holy Ghost." The one manifestation concealed more than it revealed. It was the sign of God's presence, but it made the people feel that He is indeed a "God that hideth himself." They could not really "behold his glory." They "saw through a glass"—a cloud—"darkly." The "dispensation of the Spirit," though it did not remove fleshly restrictions, brought in that blessed condition of things in which the soul has such a thrilling sense of Divine communion as scarcely to need any material help to the apprehension of it, and almost to forget the intervening veil. The one manifestation was local and exclusive, confined to the central shrine of Jewish worship, distinguishing the Jewish people from all the world besides; "to them belonged the glory." The grace of the Spirit is God's free gift to all mankind, "shed on us abundantly" (Joel ii. 28; Acts x. 45; Titus iii. 5). The Spirit is the exclusive possession of none of the churches, owns no human creed, or ritual, or ecclesiastical boundary rather than another, dwells with all who call upon the same redeeming Lord. The one manifestation was transitory, served a temporary purpose. The "glory" soon departed again, and returned to the heaven from whence it came. The other is an enduring reality. The Comforter, the Spirit of Truth, "abides with us for ever," the spring of an imperishable life, the pledge and prophecy of the unfading glory of God's unveiled presence.—W.

Vers. 17—19.—*The Unfulfilled Purposes of Life.* Men often take credit to themselves for the designs of others. An inventor is forgotten, having died in obscurity, while others make fortunes from that secret which he won by the sacrifices of ease, strength, and time. [Give other examples of the non-recognition by men of purposes and schemes which were unfulfilled by their originators.] Solomon showed himself to be truthful and magnanimous when, in the presence of his people, he ascribed to his father the inception of the building which now stood before them in its splendour. How much more ready is God, who knows the hearts of all men, to recognize and reward the unfulfilled longings of men to serve Him! Briefly indicate the reasons which made it unsuitable that David should personally do this special service (compare 2 Sam. vii. with 1 Chron. xxii. 8). He stood not alone in his disappointment, therefore the following thoughts which arise from considering it may help others to bear *the unfulfilled purposes of their lives.*

I. DAVID PROPOSED TO DO SOME GREAT THING FOR HIS GOD. We too often seek to effect great things for ourselves, or for our children, rather than for God. David wished to erect the temple. It was to be (1) an expression of his own gratitude for his election, protection, and exaltation. (2) A memorial to the people of the Divine goodness which had so wondrously constituted them as a nation. (3) A recognition that God was the centre of the nationality, as His temple was of the city. As to it all the tribes should repair, so to Him should all their hearts be turned. Suggest some of the tendencies which hinder men from indulging and accomplishing great purposes for God; *e.g.*, the love of money, self-indulgence, materialism, scepticism.

II. DAVID HAD IT IN HIS HEART TO DO MUCH FOR THE BENEFIT OF OTHERS. He lived for his people. He shrunk neither from the perils of war nor the anxieties of rule that they might become a strong and noble nation. He did not wish to build the temple for himself, but for them and their children. Had he been allowed to begin it (when alone he was able to do so) in extreme old age, he would probably never have seen its completion; but he was content that generations yet to come should have that as their place of worship. Rebuke the tendency of men to ignore their responsibility to posterity. Sometimes in national finance, in ecclesiastical arrangements, &c., the fact that the benefit would only lie in the future and not in the present, is enough to check effort and sacrifice. Who has not heard the question, "What has posterity done for us?" Show the fallacy of this reasoning, and its sinfulness, because of the selfishness and ingratitude it reveals. Indicate some of the blessings we enjoy as a nation, and as churches, from the labours and sacrifices of our predecessors who did not count even life dear to them.

III. DAVID WAS PREVENTED BY CIRCUMSTANCES FROM FULFILLING HIS PURPOSE. Wars, unsettlement, infirmities of age, &c., were some of these. They were beyond his control, but not beyond God's. Still the purpose was, as we have said, a right one. Give examples from modern life: *e.g.*, (1) The young man who longs to become a minister of God's truth, but is compelled to labour for the support of himself and others. (2) The Christian whose heart goes out with yearning over the lost, who lies a helpless invalid in some solitary room. (3) The child-disciple, stirred with noble enthusiasm, with splendid promise of future power in the Lord's kingdom, taken away in youth from the home and the world which seemed so sorely to want him, &c.

IV. DAVID MADE IT POSSIBLE FOR OTHERS TO DO WHAT HE COULD NOT DO. See an account given of the treasures he accumulated for the house of the Lord, the musical service he prepared, the plans for the building, &c. How unlike those who say, "if *I* cannot do this no one else shall;" or, with less selfishness, "*I* cannot do it, let others take all the burden if they are to have all the honour." Show how we can help others in doing their work, and so indirectly serve our God. It may not be possible for you to go abroad amongst the heathen; but you can support those to whom it is possible. Perhaps you cannot, from want of time, or suitability, teach the children or visit the sick; but you can invite others to do this, or encourage and sustain them in it.

V. DAVID'S NOBLE PURPOSE WAS FULFILLED BY HIS SON. This was God's design and promise (ver. 19). (1) *Encouragement to parents.* We live again in our children. "Instead of the fathers shall be the children," &c. By training a child for God, we may carry out, through him, the wish we could not execute. Parents multiply thus the possibilities of their own lives. Special encouragement here for weak and overburdened *mothers.* They cannot do public work for Christ, but through their children they can, *e.g.,* Eunice and Monica moved the world through Timothy and Augustine. (2) *Lesson to children.* What your parents used to do for God, you are to continue; what they could not do, you are to fulfil.

VI. DAVID'S UNACCOMPLISHED PURPOSE WAS RECOGNIZED AND RECOMPENSED BY THE LORD. "Thou didst well that it was in thine *heart.*" God knows what is in us of good as well as of evil. He approves the motive even when the effort fails. He sees the issue of every right purpose in all its width and depth. When Mary anointed her Lord she did more than she imagined; for she was the high priest anointing the Priest and King of Israel. In the day of judgment the righteous will be amazed at the issues and the rewards of their humble services, and with astonishment will ask, "Lord, when saw we thee?" &c. "And the king shall answer, and say unto them, Verily, I say unto you, inasmuch as ye have done it unto one of the least of these, my brethren, ye have done it unto me."—A. R.

Vers. 28.—*The Prayer of Dedication.* Describe the scene at the dedication of the temple. Note the fact that it is a king who leads his people to God's footstool. Show the influence of earthly rulers, who not only affect surrounding nations by their policy, but degrade or exalt the moral life of their people by their personal character, and by the tone of their court. Our reasons for thankfulness in the present reign. Contrast the influence of Victoria with that of Charles II. or George IV. Apply the same principle to other kings of men, *i.e.,* to rulers of thought in literature and science. How heavy the responsibility of those who use their kingliness to lead men from God into the dreariness of scepticism; how glorious the powers they may employ to exalt the Lord our God. Solomon is a proof that wisdom is better than knowledge. On this occasion he prayed as the representative and leader of others. A prayer so prominent in Scripture, so remarkable in circumstances, so acceptable to God, deserves consideration, that we may see its elements. It presents the following characteristics:

I. GRATEFUL ACKNOWLEDGMENT OF THE PAST. "In everything give thanks" (1 Thess. v. 18). "By prayer and supplication, with thanksgiving, make your requests known" (Phil. iv. 6). "It is a good thing to give thanks unto the Lord" (Psa. xcii. 1). "Bless the Lord, O my soul, and forget not all his benefits" (Psa. ciii. 2.) Notice the causes of Solomon's thanksgiving: (1) *God's goodness to his father* (ver. 24). Home blessings so wholly unmerited, so richly beneficial. (2) *Divine deliverance from bondage* (ver. 51). Egypt a type of sorrow, slavery to evil habit, &c. (3) *Separation and consecration for God's purposes* (ver. 53). The honour of this. Its responsibilities. Its signs. (4) *Rest and quietude* (ver. 56).

" He hath given rest unto his people Israel." The blessedness of peace to a country, exemplified by the contrast between Solomon's and David's reigns. The freedom from harassing anxieties experienced by many is from God. The rest of heart, which may be ours amidst the distresses of life, is from Him. "Peace I leave with you" (John xiv. 27). " Heart quiet from the fear of evil" (Prov. i. 33). See also 2 Cor. iv. 8. For all such blessings we should give God thanks.

II. CONFIDENCE IN THE PROMISES. (See ver. 29 as example.) Show how the patriarchs ever reminded God of His promises. Illustrate also from the pleadings of Moses and the prophets. Prove from Christ's own words that the promises are renewed and enlarged for us, and that only on them can our expectancy of blessing be founded. The utility of prayer cannot be demonstrated by reason, but by revelation. In the spiritual realm we know Divine laws by Divine declaration, the truth of which is confirmed by the experience of those who, *fulfilling the required conditions*, test them. " Ask and it shall be given you" (Matt. vii. 7) is a promise. But appended to it is the requirement of faith. " Without faith it is impossible to please God" (Heb. xi. 6). " According to your faith, so be it unto you." See also James i. 5—7 ; Matt. xxi. 22, &c.

III. ENLARGEMENT OF HEART (ver. 41, " moreover concerning a stranger," &c.) The prayer is remarkable on the part of a Jewish king. Give evidences of the narrowness and selfishness of the nation. We might expect this feeling in all its intensity on such an occasion as the consecration of this temple. But Solomon's sympathies overflowed national prejudices. The tendency of prayer is to enlarge the heart. Christians pray together who never work together. They who are nearest to God's throne are nearest to each other. As we pray, our yearnings go further afield, and we think kindly of the erring, pitifully of the lost, forgivingly of the wrong-doers.

IV. LONGING FOR THE GLORY OF GOD. Solomon's chief wish in regard to the temple is expressed in verse 60, " that all the people of the earth may know that the Lord is God, and that there is none else." Our Lord's prayer is like Solomon's in this, that it ends in an ascription of " the kingdom, and the power, and the glory," to God. So with all true prayer. It ends in praise. See how David, in the Psalms, prayed himself out of sadness into joy ; out of confession into thankfulness and praise. If we ask something for ourselves, or for others, it should be with the implied wish that it may be granted or withheld, as may be, for our welfare and God's glory. The yearning of each Christian should be that of the Lord Jesus, " Father, glorify thy name."—A. R.

Vers. 38, 39.—*The Praying King.* One of the most remarkable features of this scene of the dedication of the temple is the place occupied, the part performed, in it by Solomon himself. He is the central figure, the chief actor. Both priest and prophet give place to him. The dedicatory prayer is a spontaneous effusion of his own devout feeling, and it is he who pronounces afterwards the benediction on the people. He stands before us here as a true type of that greater " Son of David," who is our Prophet, Priest, and King. There is a great deal in the tone of this prayer that betokens a soul fully alive to the solemn and momentous meaning of what was taking place in Jerusalem that day. It is not, indeed, to the service of the ancient Jewish temple that we should look for the most perfect models of devotion. New Testament revelations multiply and strengthen immeasurably our motives to prayer, enlarge its scope, open to us new grounds of assurance in it. " One greater than Solomon " has taught us how to pray, and revealed to us the path to acceptance in the merit of His own mediation. But as the life of religion in the soul of man is essentially the same in all ages, so the principles involved in prayer as the expression of it are the same. Two such rudimentary principles appear in this passage, viz., the sense of need prompting the suppliant to look heavenwards, and the recognition of something out of himself as the ground of hope for acceptance.

I. THE SENSE OF NEED, &c. It is the " plague of the heart"—the burden resting heavy there, the haunting sense of want or sadness in the secret soul, coupled with some kind of faith in Divine power—that moves men to pray. All true

prayer is the utterance of these inward impressions. If much of our so-called praying were subjected to this test, it is to be feared that it would be found very hollow
and unreal, mere " words," a mere formal homage to custom—no deep, earnest,
irrepressible longing of the soul inspiring it.   Solomon begins to enumerate different calamities that may impel the people to pray, and then, as if overpowered
by the mere vague, distant imagination of these possibilities, he says, " Whatsoever
plague, whatsoever sickness," &c.   How soon are we lost in the attempt to realize
the manifold troubles of human life.   We can understand and sympathize with
individual griefs, but who can comprehend at all adequately the general sum of
human woe, and take the weight of it sympathetically upon himself ?   Every man,
however, knows where the universal evil specially touches himself.   " Every heart
knows its own bitterness."   And with God there is both an infinite acquaintance
with the whole and a special sympathy with each.   There are some griefs that you
lock up in your own bosom as secrets that none else must look upon.

> " Not e'en the dearest heart, and next our own,
>   Knows half the reasons why we smile or sigh."

But there is no grief you can conceal from Him.   He became in the person of His
Son " the man of sorrows and acquainted with grief," that we might feel how He
follows us, or rather, goes before us, in every path of suffering.   There is room in
the great fatherly heart of God for us all, with all our burdens, and we can never
measure the uplifting and sustaining power that comes to us by casting ourselves
and them upon it—" In everything by prayer and supplication," &c. (Phil. iv. 6, 7) ;
" Cast thy burden upon the Lord," &c. (Psa. lv. 22).   But this expression, " the
plague of his own heart," has a deeper meaning.   It opens to us all the dark sad
mystery of personal sinfulness, the moral disease that lurks within.   There are
times when the most careless, reckless spirit has glimpses of the unwelcome truth
that this, after all, is the deepest cause of its disquietude.   The multiform, mysterious evil of the world has its central root in the world's heart.   Something of
that "root of all bitterness" is in every human heart.   Here lies the fatal mischief.
It is not the tribulations of outward life, it is yourself you have most reason to
mourn over.   Not so much from them, but from something in yourself you have
need to pray to be delivered.   Christ always taught, by word and deed, the vital
connection between the external calamities and the internal "plague."   He took
upon Him our sicknesses and sorrows, not only to show us how they may be nobly
borne, but that He might bring His power as the Great Physician of souls to bear
upon the seat of our deadly disease, and by the efficacy of His blood might heal
and save us all.   Go penitently in His name to the mercy-seat with the "plague of
your heart," and you shall be redeemed from it.

II. THE RECOGNITION OF SOMETHING OUT OF ONE'S SELF AS THE GROUND OF HOPE.
This essential element in true prayer is suggested by the words, " And shall stretch
forth his hands towards this place."   An interesting view is here given us of the
relation of the temple to the individual religious life of the people.   It was intended
to be a witness to the unseen, a help to faith, an incentive to all holy thought and
feeling.   It stood through all the changes of time, the shifting lights and shadows
of the world around it, as an impressive symbol of the " everlasting covenant."   It
enshrined the " sure mercies of David."   Within its hallowed enclosure were
gathered the sacred historic records and relics, and the types and shadows of
" better things to come."   It told both of what God had done and what He had
promised—the monument of the glorious past, the prophecy of the brighter future.
There was deep meaning, then, in the suppliant " stretching forth his hands
towards that house," as expressive of the attitude of his soul towards that which it
symbolized.   When some lonely worshipper in a distant corner of the land, some
patient sufferer, some soldier in his agony on the field of battle, some captive, like
Daniel, in a strange country, directed his eyes towards the holy place, it was a
sort of pathetic appeal to God's own faithfulness, a silent but eloquent plea that He
would not forget His covenant, would fulfil the hopes that He Himself had

awakened, and not for their sakes alone, but for His own truth and mercy's sake, would hear and save. In all this the temple was a type of something nobler, diviner than itself. The temple was the shadow, the substance is in Christ. "In him are hid all the treasures," &c. The cross of Christ, in which all the promises are confirmed and sealed; the cross, which is both the altar of the Redeemer's sacrifice and the throne of His sovereignty, is the shrine of "truth and grace" to men. The glory alike of the past and of the future is centred, focussed there.

> " All the light of sacred story
> Gathers round its head sublime,"

and from it there streams forth an ever-brightening radiance into the ot erwise dark futurity. It stands the connecting link between heaven and earth, the meeting-place of God and man, the key to all human history, the basis of our immortal hope. Here, then, on this central object alike of Divine and human interest, must the eye of the suppliant be fixed. It is that pledge of Divine love and faithfulness, external to ourselves, embodied in the cross of Christ, that we must plead if we would find acceptance in our prayer. When God has thoroughly taught us what the "plague of our own heart" means, and has unveiled to us the blessed mystery of His mode of curing it, it will be the sustained habit of our life to stand as suppliants before Him " in the name of Jesus." Thus alone can we so link ourselves with the sanctities of a higher world as to make our common life Divine.—W.

Ver. 38.—The consecration of the temple was the grandest religious ceremony of the old covenant. It is important—

I. BECAUSE IT CENTRALIZES THE WORSHIP OF THE THEOCRACY.

II. BECAUSE IT SUPPLIES A TYPE OF THE SPIRITUAL TEMPLE which is to be reared in the Church and in every Christian soul. Solomon, as the king chosen of God, represents in this service of consecration the entire theocracy. The temple is essentially a house of prayer, as is manifest from the words of the consecration. " What prayer and supplication soever be made by any man, or by all thy people Israel, which shall know every man the plague of his own heart . . . hear thou in heaven." It is the sanctuary of the invisible God, and its gates stand open to the multitude, who come to worship and to offer sacrifice. Instead of a statue, such as was found in the idol temples, the priests of the true God place in their sanctuary the ark of the covenant, containing the law, the Divine expression of the holy will of God. The altar of sacrifice, placed in front of the sanctuary, reminds the people of their transgressions, while at the same time the sacrifice of the victims is prophetic of the future redemption. The consecrating prayer opens and closes with adoration. It spreads before God all the wants of the people, and asks from Him deliverance in every time of need (ch. ix. 3). It enumerates first temporal distresses, but the whole petition culminates in the ever-recurring pleading for forgiveness. This is the burden of the whole temple service, and this character is reproduced in Christian worship. In the time of its highest spirituality there were no properly consecrated Christian temples. *Aras non habemus* said Minutius Felix. A temple is nevertheless a necessity of worship; and we are free to recognize this apart from any superstitious notion, and remembering that while the heaven of heavens cannot contain the Most High, He yet condescends to dwell in the humble and contrite heart. There has been no longer a sanctuary in the old exclusive sense, since the blood was shed which has redeemed the whole earth to God. Our houses of prayer are not now more holy in themselves than our homes. Let us consecrate them by consecrating ourselves to God, and rendering to Him the worship which is His due—the sacrifice of our whole being. Let our prayers, like that of Solomon, begin and end with adoration, and let the burden of them be the expression of our repentance for sin. Let them have, like the prayer of the theocratic king, a breadth of intercession for the whole people of God, and let them lay at the foot of the cross the burden of the woes of humanity and the needs of the Church.—E. de P.

Vers. 41—43.— *The Stranger's Interest in the Temple.* Kindly human sympathy is one of the most marked characteristics of this prayer of Solomon. This is seen in the way in which he enters into various supposed conditions of need and suffering among his people ; takes the burden and the "plague" upon himself as if it were his own ; a true intercessor on their behalf. His royalty assumes here the aspect of fatherhood. The model king is one in heart and interest with those over whom he rules. We are reminded, too, that before the "mercy-seat" of God all human distinctions are lost. All suppliants stand on one common level, subject to the same dangers and necessities. All true prayer, therefore, is thus broad in its sympathies. But in this passage the king's supplications take a wider range than the needs of his own people. He pleads for the "stranger," the foreigner from a "far country." This is strictly in harmony with the Divine economy of the time, however much it may seem to be otherwise. It is remarkable how much there was in the Mosaic law that was expressly intended to enforce on the people a generous regard for those who were beyond their pale. They were commanded not to "vex a stranger" (Exod. xxii. 21), to relieve his poverty (Levit. xxv. 35), even to "love" him as "God loveth him in giving him food and raiment" (Deut. x. 18, 19), and all this in memory of the fact that they themselves were once "strangers in the land of Egypt." Strangers, moreover, were to be permitted to hear the solemn reading of the law in the "year of release" (Deut. xxxi. 12), and to offer sacrifices on the same conditions as themselves. "One law and one manner shall be for you and for the stranger that sojourneth with you" (Num. xv. 16). So that Solomon gave expression to the spirit of the dispensation to which he belonged when he thus prayed. Certain broad truths underlie this prayer—

I. JEHOVAH'S UNIVERSAL SOVEREIGNTY. He is the "God of the whole earth," and not merely of any particular portion of it (Isa. liv. 5). "Is he the God of the Jews only and not of the Gentiles?" (Rom. iii. 29.) "The God of the spirits of all flesh" (Num. xvi. 22). The whole Mosaic economy was built on the grand truth of the unity and absolute world-wide supremacy of Jehovah. The heathe according to their principle of local deities, might acknowledge the God of the ebrews as having authority over his own, but a Hebrew who should in any way recognize the gods of other nations and think of Jehovah merely as a national deity ould be a traitor to the commonwealth. The only living and true God can have no rival. The gods of the nations are idols, and "an idol is nothing in the world"—"a lying vanity," a vile "abomination." "The things which the Gentiles sacrifice they sacrifice to demons and not to God" (1 Cor. viii. 4, 5 ; x. 20). To "know God," to have "him whom they ignorantly worship" declared to them, is "eternal life" to men. The absence of this knowledge is death. The curse and misery of the world is that it "knows not its God." Solomon here dimly recognizes this truth ; and the case he contemplates is that of some child of the Universal Father in whom the sense of need has been awakened, "coming from a far country" to "seek the Lord, if haply he may feel after him and find him" (Acts xvii. 27, 28).

II. THE REPRESENTATIVE CHARACTER OF ISRAEL. They were a representative people in two respects. (1) Inasmuch as they were called to bear witness to the glory of the "great name" of Jehovah. His name is the symbol of His personality, the attributes of His being and character—spirituality, purity, righteousness, love, &c. Their mission was to make known to mankind the God who had revealed Himself in wondrous forms to them. How they failed to rise to the height of this mission their national history only too sadly tells. The utterances of the psalmists and prophets are full of the spirit of it, but all this was far above the comprehension of the great mass of the people. They utterly mistook the meaning of the distinction conferred upon them, and God taught them by the discipline of subjection and captivity the lesson that in the day of their national glory they failed to learn. In this mission as a witness Israel was a type of the Christian Church. Christ declared the Father's name to His disciples and He sent them forth on an errand like His own (John xvii. 18—26). How grand a vocation, to reflect the glory of His "great name" on the world's darkness, to say to the nations, "Behold your God!" (2) They were a representative people also in the sense that in their history God illustrated the general method and the uniform laws of His moral government. The "strong hand and the stretched out arm " here suggests the marvellous manifestation of Divine power that marked the career of the people from the beginning, the whole course of providential training and moral discipline through which they passed. But the principles on which God deals with one nation are the principles on which He deals with all. He is no "respecter of persons." The history of the " chosen people " unfolds His universal purpose and plan, illustrates unvarying laws, the conditions of all personal, social, and national life. And so it comes to pass that after every review of Israel's experiences we may say, " Now all these things happened unto them for ensamples," &c. (1 Cor. x. 11).

III. THE ATTRACTION OF THE TEMPLE FOR ALL LONGING HUMAN HEARTS AS THE SCENE OF GRACIOUS DIVINE MANIFESTATION. That which made it the centre of interest to pious Jews made it so also to earnest souls of other lands. The truth and mercy symbolized and enshrined there—promises, atoning sacrifices, benedictions—answered to universal needs of humanity. Solomon supposes a case in which the vague sense of this should lead the "stranger in a far-off land" to look with longing eyes, or to bend his steps, towards " the house over which God's name is called." We have no historical record of strangers actually worshipping in the first temple as they did in that built after the captivity ; but God said, " My house shall be called a house of prayer for all people " (Isa. lvi. 6, 7 ; Mark xi. 17) ; and there may have been many who, with a far-reaching hand of faith, " took hold of His covenant " as established there.

IV. THE RESPONSE GOD GAVE TO EVERY TRUE SUPPLIANT, WHOEVER HE MIGHT BE. " Hear thou in heaven thy dwelling-place," &c. This intercessory prayer, we may be sure, was answered. God does not awaken holy yearnings in any soul that He will not satisfy. " In every nation, he that feareth him," &c. The sovereignty that reigns over all lands is that of Almighty Love. There is room in the infinite Father's heart for all, even the far-off " stranger," and " the same Lord over all is rich unto all that call upon him."—W.

Ver. 49.—*Occasions for Prayer.* In the prayer of dedication Solomon suggests occasions on which it would be natural for men to turn to their God. The Divine Presence is constant, but our realization of it is not. Many require the shock of some unexpected or lamentable occurrence to rouse them to prayer. This effect, however, will only be seen in those who have, underlying their forgetfulness and sensuousness, an abiding (though sometimes inoperative) belief in God. This Israel for the most part had. Hence Solomon's belief that in their future times of distress and difficulty they would turn to Him who dwelt between the cherubims. Analyze the prayer, and see the following occasions suggested as those in which supplication would be natural.

I. WHEN MEN MAKE VOWS AND PROMISES. Compare ver. 31 with the ordinances of Moses (Exod. xxii. 7—9). The oath was taken in the presence of God, because the thought of Him as the Searcher of hearts would induce serious consideration and careful exactitude, and because He was tacitly invited by His providence to confirm or to punish the spoken word. Show how the principle, right in itself, became abused and vitiated, so that Christ condemned the practices of His day (Matt. v. 33—37). Learn from the ancient practice (1) *that our utterances should be made as by men conscious of the nearness of the God of truth.* Apply this to the immoralities of some business transactions, to the prevalence of slander in society, &c. (2) *That our resolutions should be formed in a spirit of prayer.* How vain the pledge and promise of amendment, unless there be added to the human resolve the help of God's providence in circumstances, and the grace of His Spirit in the heart ! Give examples of each.

II. WHEN MEN ARE INJURED OR DEFEATED BY THEIR ADVERSARIES. " When thy people Israel be smitten down before the enemy " (ver. 33). National defeat in war should lead to self-examination on the part of those smitten. Too often the investigation is applied only to material resources : incompetent officials are dismissed, weakened regiments are strengthened, new alliances are formed, &c. The mischief may lie deeper. Sometimes God is calling the people not to redeem national honour, but to seek national righteousness. The teaching of the verse may be applied figuratively to defeats suffered by Christian controversialists or by philanthropic workers, &c. Every check in onward progress is a summons to thought and prayer. " In the day of adversity consider." Illustrate by examples in Scripture, e.g., by the defeat of Israel at Ai, and its issues.

III. WHEN MEN ARE TREMBLING UNDER NATURAL CALAMITIES. Reference is made in ver. 35 to the withholding of rain; in ver. 37 to "famine, pestilence, blasting, mildew, locust, and caterpillar." Such troubles were sent in vain to bring the Egyptians to repentance. Compare those plagues with Elijah's message to Ahab, and with the threats of other prophets. Such statements as Deut. xi. 17 enshrine an abiding truth. In the long run the violation of God's laws do bring disasters of the very kind specified here. If the law of industry be violated, the harvests fail; if the law of mutual dependence be ignored by nations, commerce is crippled, and impoverishment comes; if the laws against self-indulgence, pride, ambition, &c., be defied, the spendthrift has the result in poverty, the proud nation in the miseries of war, &c. Even the disasters which are accounted "natural phenomena," then, should lead the wise-hearted to prayer, the sinful to penitence; and God will hear in heaven His dwelling-place, and answer and forgive. Show how, during the ministry of our Lord, the cripples, the blind, the diseased came to Him. Their misery made them feel their need of what He alone could give, and many of them became conscious of their spiritual wants from considering first the want that was physical. As they were thus led, so the Church has been which in the Old Testament was oppressed most by the earthly wants, and in the New by the spiritual. Those in the far country learn, by beginning to "be in want," that God is calling them to arise and return to Him.

IV. WHEN MEN ARE CONSCIOUS OF THEIR SIN. All through this prayer reference is made to sin and to the consequent necessity for pardon (vers. 38, 46—50). Point out the climax in ver. 47 : (1) "We have sinned"—have not kept in the ways of God—sin in its negative aspect; (2) "have done perversely"—acts of perversity; (3) "have committed wickedness"—the overwhelming passion which drives into corruption. The necessity of humble confession as an integral part of prayer from the lips of fallen man can readily be shown from Scripture. Examples of conscience of sin impelling to prayer seen in David (Psa. li.), the publican (Luke xviii. 13). " If we confess our sins, He is faithful and just to forgive us our sins, and to cleanse us from all unrighteousness" (1 John i. 9).

V. WHEN MEN ARE GOING FORTH TO CONFLICT IN GOD'S NAME. " If thy people shall go out to battle against their enemy whithersoever thou shalt send them," &c. (ver. 44). We must not forget that Israel was a theocracy. David, for example, spoke of his foes as being God's foes. So had it been with Moses, Joshua, &c. The consciousness of that gives almost superhuman power. " Man, being linked with Omnipotency, is a kind of omnipotent creature," says Bacon. Even when the belief that one is on God's side is false, the belief itself is an inspiration. Examples from history of such belief well or ill founded—Joan of Arc, the Puritans, &c. In actual war no nation can fairly put up this prayer unless the cause of war is that of which we can say, "whithersoever thou shalt send." No mistake need exist in reference to foes whom Christ came to destroy. The promise, "Lo ! I am with you," was the inspiration of the apostles as they confronted false philosophies, crass ignorance, brutal customs, degrading superstitions. Hence, if they were going forth to battle with such evils, the prayers of the Church went up on their behalf. Men were set apart for their Christian mission by prayer (give examples), and in their work they often turned to their intercessors, saying, " Brethren, pray for us !" Feeling our insufficiency to overcome the adversaries of the gospel, let us, like the apostles, " continue in prayer and supplication " till we are " endued with power from on high."—A. R.

Ver. 61.—*A Royal Benediction.* The prayer of Solomon is followed by a benediction. " He stood and blessed all the congregation," &c. (vers. 54, 55). But though he assumed for the time the priestly function, his utterance was not cast into the usual form of priestly benediction. It was rather an ascription of praise to the God who had fulfilled His promises and given rest to His people, and an exhortation to them that they on their part should follow that path of life in which alone they could hope to realize the further fulfilment of those promises, and enjoy the heritage of blessing that was theirs. Lessons are suggested here that are of force and value for all time.

I. THE RELATION BETWEEN TRUE PRAYER AND PERSONAL RIGHTEOUSNESS. Solomon felt that all the impassioned supplications that he had been pouring out before the Lord, and all the sympathetic enthusiasm of the people in these temple services, would be but a mockery unless he and they were prepared to walk with all fidelity in the way of God's commandments. They would soon be leaving the sacred shrine of worship. They could not always be amid the ecstatic and rapturous associations of the temple. They must go back to the matter-of-fact, prosaic world, to their posts of honour and responsibility, to the privacy of their homes, to their haunts of busy life, to their paths of commerce and of labour. Let them worship there. Let them dwell with God there. Let them embody there, in all the forms of practical virtue, the spirit of devotion that has inspired them amid these hallowed scenes. The "statutes and commandments" of the Lord had reference in great part to the due observance of the ritual of temple worship, but they also claimed, as much then as now, to control the whole spirit and conduct of human life in all its aspects. The relation between prayer and conduct is of a twofold character. They act and react the one on the other. True prayer sheds a hallowing influence over the entire field of a man's daily activity. When his soul has been face to face with God, absorbed in Divine communion, the inspiration of holy thought and feeling of which he has been conscious will inevitably betray itself in the way in which he acts when he mingles with the things and the beings of earth. The glory of heaven that has shone upon him cannot fail to be reflected in the beauty of his character and deed. A prayerful spirit is an earnest, pure, upright, loving spirit, and such a spirit will govern the whole form and method and aim of a man's life. Prayer solves difficulties, clears one's vision of the path of duty, draws strength from Divine sources for all toil and suffering, raises the tone and level of moral action, fortifies the spirit for any emergency, fills the heart with the peaceful joy of a better world. On the other hand, the conduct of life necessarily affects for good or ill the spirit and efficacy of prayer. If it is needful to pray in order that we may live as Christians, it is equally needful that we should live as Christians in order rightly to pray. The importance of prayer as one chief function of spiritual life doubles the importance of all our actions, because our prayers are so much as our doings are. According as we stand towards the world, with all the social relationships and duties that belong to our place in it, so do we stand before the mercy-seat. Think, for instance, how the beneficial effect of *family prayer* may be nullified by the prevailing spirit of family life. By the discord that may be allowed to reign in it, by its lack of the graces of mutual respect and loving self-sacrifice, by the worldliness of its associations, the meanness of its ambitions, the frivolity of its pleasures, the vanity of its cherished societies—how completely may the soul of domestic devotion be destroyed. Let a man be morally reckless in the intercourse and transactions of daily life, and all freedom, " boldness," gladness in prayer is at an end. Anything like loving, confiding converse with the " Father who seeth in secret" is impossible to him. If he cannot look without fear and shame in the face of his fellow man, how shall he dare to look in the face of God? The " heavens become as brass " above his head which no voice of prayer can penetrate. When Saul's heart is thoroughly set in him to do evil it is vain for him to inquire of the Lord. "The Lord answers him no more, neither by Urim, nor by prophet, nor by dream." Let there be a Divine unity and harmony in our life. Let our conduct in all human relationships show us to be what, in our hours of devotion, we seem to ourselves to be. Let it be our ambition every day " to live more nearly as we pray."

II. THE RELATION BETWEEN PRACTICAL VIRTUE AND THE STATE OF THE SECRET HEART. A man's heart must be "perfect with the Lord" before he can walk acceptably in the path of His commandments. The old legal economy was not after all so superficial as it seemed to be. God's commandment was "exceeding broad." Literal as the moral laws were, and formal as the ceremonial precepts, they touched at every point the life of the spirit within. "Moses describeth the righteousness which is of the law, 'That the man who doeth these things shall live by them" (Rom. x. 5), but the righteousness was not in the mere *doing*. David, the noblest representative of the spirit of the law, well knew that as it is from the fountain of the evil heart that all transgression proceeds, so from the purified heart springs all practical righteousness. "Create in me a clean heart, O God," &c. (Psa. li. 10). The glory of Christianity is that it not only recognizes this principle, but actually brings to bear on the heart the renewing, healing power. It cleanses the fountain of life within. The law could disclose the secret evil, convince of sin, rebuke, restrain, but it could not make men righteous. The gospel does. "Christ is the end of the law for righteousness," &c. (Rom. x. 4). "What the law could not do," &c. (Rom. viii. 3, 4). Keep your heart in habitual contact with the highest sources of spiritual inspiration—in familiar converse with Him who is the fountain of truth and purity and love. Watch over its most secret thoughts and impulses. Guard its sensibilities from the contaminations of the world and the hardening influences of life. Seek to preserve the freshness of its Divine affections and the integrity of its allegiance to Christ, if you would walk as He did, "in loveliness of perfect deeds."

III. THE BENEFICIAL INFLUENCE OF A SACRED MEMORY. "As it is this day." Solomon would have that day to dwell in their memories and hallow all their days. Times of special Divine manifestation and highest religious consciousness show us what we may be, what God would have us to be, what is the true level of our spirit's life.—W.

EXPOSITION.

CHAPTER IX. 1—9.

THE ANSWER TO SOLOMON'S PRAYER.— This chapter opens with an account of God's second appearance to Solomon. It must not be supposed, however, from the apparent close connexion of this relation with the preceding narrative, that it stands to it in equally close chronological order. It probably finds a place here because the historian has grouped together all the suitable materials in his possession which related to the temple. But see on ver 1.

Ver. 1.—**And it came to pass when Solomon had finished the building of the house of the Lord, and the king's house** [ch. vii. 1], **and all Solomon's desire which he was pleased to do** [By "desire" we are not to understand "pleasure buildings" (cf. vers. 10, 19). The chronicler gives the true meaning : "all that came into Solomon's heart." It is, however, somewhat doubtful what works are comprehended under this term. 2 Chron. vii. 11 limits it to the two great erections already described—"all that came into his heart to make *in* the house of the

Lord and in his own house." But it is by no means certain that our author intended the word to be thus restricted ; it is quite possible, *e.g.*, that some of the buildings mentioned below (vers. 15—19) are to be included. But another question of much greater importance presents itself here. In the Divine communication of vers. 3—9 there is constant and unmistakeable reference to the prayer of dedication (see especially ver. 3) ; in fact, this message is the *answer* to that prayer. It has been held, consequently, that the answer must have followed, if not immediately, yet soon after the petitions were uttered ; if so, the dedication must clearly have taken place, not on the completion of the temple (chap. vi. 38), but on the completion of the palace, &c. ; in other words, the temple must have been finished fully thirteen years before it was consecrated and occupied. Rawlinson suggests that the delay was perhaps occasioned by the circumstance that the furniture of the temple was not till then ready ; but ch. vi. 38, Heb., seems to state distinctly that *all* the vessels and appointments of the sanctuary were finished at the date there given. Reasons have been given elsewhere (see note on ch. viii. 1) in support of the position that the dedication cannot possibly have been delayed for so long a period, especially after the strenuous efforts which had been made to hurry on the undertaking. Nor does the text, when carefully examined, really require this hypothesis; indeed, it suggests some reasons for thinking that a considerable period must have intervened between the prayer and the response. For the tone of this response is unmistakeably foreboding, if not minatory. Vers. 6—9 contain a stern warning. But there was nothing, so far as we know, in the attitude of Solomon or of Israel at the time of the dedication to call for any such denunciation. At that time, as the prayer surely proves, Solomon's heart was perfect with the Lord his God. But the response has unmistakeably the appearance of having been elicited by signs of defection. The wide difference, consequently, between the spirit of the prayer and the tone of the answer suggests that some time must have elapsed between them, and so far supports the view that the dedication was not delayed until the palace, &c., was completed. And it is also to be remembered that the prayer of dedication had not been without acknowledgment at the time. The excellent glory which filled and took possession of the house was itself a significant and sufficient response. No voice or vision could have said more plainly, " I have heard thy prayer, I have hallowed this house." But when, some thirteen years later—about the very time, that is, when he was at the height of his prosperity, and when, owing to the completion of his undertakings, we might fear lest his heart should be lifted up with pride when Solomon and his court began to decline in piety and to go after other gods, then this merciful message opportunely refers him to the prayer which he was in danger of forgetting, and warns him of the consequences of the apostasy to which he was tending.]

Ver. 2.—**That the Lord appeared to Solomon the second time** [see on ch. vi. 11, and cf. xi. 9; Solomon had received a *message* during the building of the temple], **as he had appeared unto him at Gibeon** [*i.e.,* in a *dream* (ch. iii. 5)].

Ver. 3.—**And the Lord said unto him** [This message is given at greater length in 2 Chron. vii. 12—22. Vers. 13, 14, *e.g.,* contain a reference to that part of the prayer which related to drought and rain], **I have heard thy prayer and thy supplication** [These two words are found similarly united in Solomon's prayer, vers. 38, 45, 54], **that thou hast made** [Heb. *supplicated*] **before me; I have hallowed this house which thou hast built** [*sc.* by the manifestation described ch. viii. 11. Cf. Exod. xxix. 43: " the tabernacle shall be *sanctified* " (same

word) "by my glory." In 2 Chron. we read, " I have chosen this place to myself for a house of sacrifice," where, however, it is worth considering whether instead of the somewhat singular בֵּית זֶבַח the original text may not have been בֵּית זְבֻל, as in ch. viii. 13] **to put my name there** [ch. viii. 29; cf. vers. 16, 17, 18, 19; also Deut. xii. 11; Luke xi. 12] **for ever** [ch. viii. 13. As Solomon offered it, so God accepted it, in perpetuity. That the house was subsequently " left desolate " and destroyed (2 Kings xxv. 9) was because of the national apostasy (vers. 8, 9)], **and mine eyes and mine heart shall be there perpetually.** [In ch. viii. 29 Solomon asked that God's "eyes may be open . . . towards the house." The answer is that not only His eyes shall be open, but eyes and heart shall be *there* (Ephes. iii. 20; see Homiletics on ch. iii. 5);—the eye to watch, the heart to cherish it.]

Ver. 4.—**And** [Heb. *And thou*, emphatic] **if thou wilt walk before me as David thy father walked, in integrity of heart before me and in uprightness** [cf. ch. iii. 6, 14; xi. 34. David was not perfect, as our author tells us elsewhere (ch. xv. 5; cf. ch. i. 6; 2 Sam. xxiv. 10). His integrity consisted in his unvarying loyalty to the true God. Even when overcome by that fierce temptation (2 Sam. xi.) he never faltered in his allegiance to the truth. There was no coquetting with idolatrous practices; cf. Psa. xviii. 20—24], **to do according to all that I have commanded thee, and wilt keep my statutes and my judgments** [the echo of David's last words, ch. ii. 3, 4. It is probable, however, that the historian has only preserved the substance of the message. It is doubtful whether Solomon himself would remember the exact words]:

Ver. 5.—**Then I will establish** [same word as in ch. ii. 4, where see note. Surely he would remember this word as it would recall his father's charge to his mind] **the throne of thy kingdom upon Israel for ever** [this is the answer to the prayer of ch. viii. 26] **as I promised to David thy father, saying, There shall not fail thee a man upon the throne of Israel.** [2 Sam. vii. 12, 16; 1 Kings ii. 4; vi. 12; Psa. cxxxii. 12. But the primary reference is to ch. viii. 25; see Introduction, sect. III.]

Ver. 6.—**But if ye shall at all** [rather *altogether,* or *assuredly*] **turn from following me** [The A. V. entirely misrepresents the force of the Hebraism, *If to turn, ye shall turn,* which must mean completo, not partial, apostasy. Cf. 2 Chron. vii. 19, and 2 Sam. vii. 14, 15], **ye or your children** [as the promises of God are to us and our children (Acts ii. 39), so are His threatenings], **and will not keep my commandments and my** statutes which I [LXX. Μωυσῆς ; *Qui facit per alium*, &c.] have set before you, but go and serve other gods and worship them [Exod. xx. 5; Deut. v. 9; xiii. 2]:

Ver. 7.—**Then will I cut off Israel out of the land which I have given them** [Cf. Deut. iv. 26, 27; and for the fulfilment see 2 Kings xxv. 11, 21;] **and this house which I have hallowed for my name** [Jer. vii. 14] **will I cast out of my sight** [same expression, 2 Kings xxiv. 20]; **and Israel shall be a proverb and a byword among all people** [the exact words of Deut. xxviii. 37. Similar words in Isa. xiv. 4; Micah vi 16. Much the same punishment is denounced in Levit. xxvi. 14—38, and Deut. iv. 45, 63]:

Ver. 8.—**And at this house, which is high** [Heb. *And this house shall be high*, יִהְיֶה עֶלְיוֹן. Our translators were probably influenced by 2 Chron. vii. 21, the text of which is אֲשֶׁר הָיָה עֶלְיוֹן which would seem to be an emendation, designed to clear up the difficulty rather than an accidental variation of the text. But here the literal rendering is probably the truer, the meaning being "this house shall be conspicuous, as an example"—so the Vulg. *domus haec erit in exemplum*. The LXX. accords with the Hebrew text, ὁ οἶκος οὗτος ἔσται ὁ ὑψηλός, but the Syriac and Arabic read, "this house shall be destroyed." Keil sees in the words an allusion *implicite* to Deut. xxvi. 19, and xxviii. 1, where God promises to make Israel עֶלְיוֹן, and says "the blessing will be turned into a curse." The temple should indeed be "high," should be what Israel would have been, but it shall be as a warning, &c.; but this connexion is somewhat far-fetched and artificial. Thenius would read for עֶלְיוֹן, עִיִּים "ruins," after

Micah iii. 12; Jer. xxvi. 18; Psa. lxxix. 1; but it is hardly right to resort to conjectures, unsupported by a single version or MS., so long as any sufficient meaning can be extracted from the words as they stand, and no one can deny that "high" may surely signify "conspicuous." Cf. Matt. xi. 23], **every one that passeth by it shall be astonished.** [שָׁמֵם primarily means to be *dumb* with astonishment, Gesen., Thes. iii. p. 1435] **and shall hiss** [שָׁרַק, like "hiss," is an onomatopoetic word. It does not denote the hissing of *terror* (Bähr) but of derision; cf. Jer. xix. 8; xlix. 17; Job xxvii. 23; Lam. ii. 15, 16. Rawlinson aptly remarks, as bearing on the authorship of the Kings, that this is a familiar word in Jeremiah (see ch. xviii. 16; xxv. 9; xxix. 18; l. 13; li. 37, in addition to the passages cited above), and that the other prophets rarely use it. The fact that much of this charge is in Jeremiah's style, confirms the view taken above (note on ver. 4), that the *ipsissima verba* of the dream are not preserved to us. The author indeed could hardly do more than preserve its leading ideas, which he would naturally present in his own dress]; **and they shall say, Why hath the Lord done thus unto this land and to this house?** [Similar words Deut. xxix. 24, 25; Jer. xxii. 8.]

Ver. 9.—**And they shall answer, Because they forsook the Lord their God who brought forth their fathers out of the land of Egypt** [Based on Deut. xxix. 25. Solomon in his prayer referred repeatedly to this great deliverance, vers. 16, 21, 51, 53], **and have taken hold upon other gods and have worshipped them and served them; therefore hath the Lord brought upon them all this evil.**

HOMILETICS.

Vers. 1—9.—*The Second Appearance to Solomon.* "Behold the goodness and severity of God" (Rom. xi. 22). To Solomon goodness, to Israel severity.

I. The GOODNESS OF GOD is manifested—

1. *In revealing Himself to Solomon.* The greatest favour God can show us is to show us Himself; the greatest gift is to give us Himself.

> "Give what Thou wilt, without Thee I am poor,
> And with Thee rich, take what Thou wilt away."

"I will love him and will *manifest* myself unto him" (John xiv. 21). "I will come in to him and sup with him" (Rev. iii. 20). "We will make our abode with him" (John xiv. 23). There are no richer promises than these. Well may we exclaim, "*O altitudo!*" (Rom. xi. 33.) "O why should heavenly God to men have such regard!"

Yes, the riches, honour, glory, &c., given to Solomon were of small account compared with the good thoughts and high aspirations bestowed upon him. Riches are such third-rate blessings that God bestows them indiscriminately on the evil and the good. But noble resolves and high purposes—"courtliness and the desire of (true) fame, and love of truth, and all that makes a man"—these He reserves for His children. Solomon's riches and glory proved his ruin; the revelations he received were the true source of his greatness.

2. *In warning Solomon.* The very kindest thing a friend can do for us is to admonish us when we are going wrong. "Thou mayest be sure that he that will in private tell thee of thy faults is thy friend, for he adventureth thy dislike and doth hazard thy hatred" (Sir W. Raleigh). God showed this proof of love to Solomon. In the night watches, in the darkness and silence, away from the glamour and flattery of the court, the Divine voice was heard in his secret soul. And the *plainness* of the warning was a part of its mercifulness. The trumpet gave no uncertain sound (vers. 5—8). God set before him that day "life and good, death and evil" (Deut. xxx. 15). By one to whom such wisdom had been vouchsafed, warnings should have been unneeded. But they *were* needed—and they were mercifully granted. The good Shepherd goes "o'er moor and fell, o'er crag and torrent" to bring back the straying sheep.

II. The SEVERITY OF GOD is exhibited—

1. *In the punishment denounced against Israel.* "Cut off;" "cast out of my sight;" "a proverb and a byword;" "shall be astonished and shall hiss"—these are its terms. But observe: (1) None of these things needed to have befallen them. God had no pleasure in the death or dispersion of His elect people. It was their own fault if they were cut off. (2) These things were denounced in kindness to stay them in their sin and so to *prevent* their dispersion. These were the *sanctions* of that dispensation. "The law is not made for a righteous man, but," &c. (1 Tim. i. 9). (3) There was no disproportion or undue rigour in these penalties. What seems to us severity is really exact justice, or rather mercy, to the world. As Israel had been favoured above all peoples, so, in strict equity, should it be punished above all. "The glory, and the adoption, and the covenants," &c. (Rom. ix. 4), could not appertain to them without bringing with them "many stripes" for the disobedient. Those exalted to heaven shall be brought down to hell (Matt. xi. 23). It was necessary for *our* admonition that the chosen people should not afford the world the spectacle of a nation sinning unpunished (1 Cor. x. 11).

2. *In the punishment inflicted.* For how literally have these words been fulfilled! What an evidence of the truth of God the history of Israel supplies! This, at any rate, is no *vaticinium ex eventu.* "This day is this scripture fulfilled in your ears" (Luke iv. 21). "A proverb and a byword"—eighteen centuries at least testify to the truth of these words. "Cast out of my sight;" let the horrors of the siege of Jerusalem (see Jos., B. J. v. ch. x.—xiii., vi. *passim.* "Never," he says, "did any other city suffer such miseries") explain to us these words. And there is not a country of Europe, there is hardly a city, in which the history of the Jew is not traced in blood, written within and without in "mourning and lamentation and woe." Claudius expelled them from Rome (Acts xviii. 2); our Edward I. drove them out of Guienne and England. "Ivanhoe" gives some idea of their treatment in this country; but a romance could not record a tithe of the horrors of which Clifford's Tower in York or the Jews' house in Lincoln could tell. And yet it is allowed that they have always been treated more tenderly in England than in the rest of Europe. But even here, and down to the present day, the word "Jew" is too often a name of hate. In Servia, in Moldavia and Wallachia, they are still the objects of fierce persecution and not always unmerited obloquy. Even the "Anti-Semitic League," now (1880) being organized in Germany, is a part of the "severity" of God, a proof of the "sure word of prophecy." In Jerusalem, again, the metropolis of their race, they are accounted the filth and offscouring of all things. At the Greek Easter the refrain is often heard in the Church of the Holy Sepulchre, "O Jews, O Jews, your feast is a feast of apes." What a commentary, too, is the Jews' "place of wailing" on this scripture! The "holy and beautiful house" a desolation, the temple precincts trodden under-foot of the Gentiles! Conqueror after conqueror, pilgrim after pilgrim, has asked the question,

"Wherefore hath the Lord done thus?" &c., while the "ever-extending miles of gravestones and the ever-lengthening pavement of tombs and sepulchres" answer, "Because they have forsaken the Lord their God," &c. (ver. 9; Jer. xxii. 8, 9).

> "Tribes of the wandering foot and weary breast,
> When will ye fly away and be at rest?
> The wild dove hath its nest, the fox its cave,
> Mankind their country—Israel but the grave."

Application. Rom. ii. 21. In the history of the Israelitish nation we may see the principle of God's dealing with individual souls (see Keble's Occasional Papers, &c., pp. 435 sqq.) But we may also read in it a warning for the Christian Church (Rev. ii. 5).

HOMILIES BY VARIOUS AUTHORS.

Vers. 1—9.—*The Renewed Covenant.* This Divine manifestation was probably similar in form to that with which Solomon was favoured at the beginning of his reign, of which it is said, "In Gibeon the Lord appeared to Solomon in a dream by night" (ch. iii. 50). We have no means of judging as to the precise time of this occurrence; but the close connection of thought between what God here says to Solomon and the prayer at the dedication (seen most clearly in 2 Chron. vii. 14, 15) leads us to suppose that it took place immediately after that event. It illustrates:

I. THE FIDELITY OF GOD AND THE BLESSED RESULTS THAT ATTEND IT. God's faithfulness is seen (1) *in the answering of the prayer*—"I have heard thy prayer," &c. The vision was itself an instant and very gracious Divine response. All true prayer is heard. No pure breath of supplication, the incense of the heart, ever ascends to Heaven in vain. God does not disappoint the hopes and longings He has Himself awakened. As the vapours that rise from land and sea sooner or later return again, distilling in the silent dew, descending in fruitful showers upon the earth—not one fluid particle is lost—so every cry of filial faith that goes up to the great Father of all comes back in due time in some form of heavenly benediction. And more, the answer is often far larger and richer than our expectations. He "doeth exceeding abundantly," &c. (Eph. iii. 20). Solomon had prayed "That thine eyes may be open towards this house." God answers, "Mine eyes and mine *heart shall be there perpetually.*" The very heart of God dwells where His suppliant people are. This anthropopathic mode of speech is a gracious Divine accommodation to our human wants and weaknesses. God condescends to us that we may the better rise to Him. It is the necessarily imperfect yet most welcome expression of a sublime reality that we could not otherwise know. God has a tender "heart" towards us as well as an observant "eye." And wherever we seek Him with all our hearts there His heart responds to the throbbing of ours—a sympathetic personal Presence, meeting our approach, pitying our necessities, giving love for love. Note, too, the constancy of this grace—"for ever," "perpetually." "The gifts and calling of God are without repentance." Wherever He records His name there He "dwells." When He blesses, when He gives or forgives, it is "for ever." If the grace is cancelled, if the benediction is withdrawn, the fault is ours, not His. "Though we believe not, yet He abideth faithful; He cannot deny Himself" (2 Tim. ii. 13). (2) *In the repetition of the promise,* "If thou wilt walk before me," &c. (vers. 4, 5). The promise is reiterated as a sacred and inviolable engagement which God on His part will never break. "The sure mercies of David." All Divine promises are sure. We have but to place ourselves in the line of their fulfilment and all is well with us. They are steadfast as the ordinances of heaven and earth. Natural laws are God's promises in the material realm. Obedience to them is the sure path to physical well-being. Are His counsels in the moral and spiritual sphere likely to be less steadfast and reliable? Heaven and earth shall pass away, but the promises of His grace can never fail. "They stand fast for ever and ever, and are done in truth and uprightness" (Psa. cxi. 8).

II. THE INFIDELITY OF MAN AND THE FATAL CONSEQUENCES THAT FOLLOW IT. "But if ye shall at all turn from following me," &c. Here is a solemn note of warning, the presage of that guilty apostasy by which the Jewish people became in after years the most signal example to men and nations of the waywardness of human nature and the retributive justice of God. We are reminded that the faithfulness of God has a dark as well as a bright side to it. As the cloud that guided the march of the Israelites out of Egypt was light to them, but a source of blinding confusion and miserable discomfiture to their adversaries, so this and every other attribute of God bears a different aspect towards us according to the relation in which we stand to it, the side on which we place ourselves. Be true to Him, and every perfection of His being is a joy to you, a guide, a glory, a defence ; forsake Him, and they become at once ministers of vengeance. Even His love, in its infinite rectitude and purity, dooms you to the penalty from which there can be no escape. Whether in the physical or the spiritual realms, one feature of the very beneficence of God's laws is that they must avenge themselves. Learn here (1) *that all human loss and misery spring from forsaking God.* "If ye shall at all turn from following me, ye or your children," then shall all these woes come upon you. All sin is a departure from the living God. "My people have committed two evils, they have forsaken me," &c. (Jer. ii. 13). Adam cast off his allegiance to God when He listened to the voice of the tempter. Idolatry in its deepest root has this meaning (see Rom. i. 21—28). Every sinful life is a more or less in-tentional and deliberate renunciation of God, and its natural results are shame, and degradation, and death. The course of the prodigal in Christ's parable is a picture of the hopeless destitution of every soul that forsakes its home in God. "They that are far from thee shall perish" (Psa. lxxiii. 27). (2) *That according to the height of privilege so is the depth of the condemnation when that privilege is abused.* The very height of the "hallowed house" shall make the ruin the more conspicuous and the more terrible. There is no heavier judgment that God pronounces upon men than when He says, "I will curse thy blessings." The best things are capable of the worst abuse. And when the highest sanctities of life are violated they become the worst grounds of reproach and sources of bitterness. The greater the elevation, the deeper and more dreadful the fall. "Thou Capernaum, which art exalted to heaven," &c. (Luke x. 15). (3) *That one inevitable penalty of transgression is contempt and scorn.* "Israel shall be a proverb and a byword among all people." "He that passeth by shall be astonished and shall hiss." "When the salt has lost its savour it is henceforth good for nothing but to be cast out and trodden under-foot of men" (Matt. v. 13). The wicked may be in honour now, but the time is coming when they "shall awake to shame and everlasting contempt."—W.

EXPOSITION.

CHAPTER IX. 10—28.

SOLOMON'S BUILDINGS AND UNDERTAKINGS. —So far the historian has spoken exclusively of the two greatest works of Solomon's reign, the Temple and the Palace, and principally of the former. Even the message just related was, as we have seen, the response to the prayer offered when the temple was consecrated. But he now proceeds to mention other proofs of Solomon's greatness, and of the prosperity of his reign— doubtless because the glory of Israel then reached its climax, and the author would be tempted to linger over these details because of the dark contrast which his own time supplied—and this leads him to speak of the means by which all these enterprises were accomplished. The particulars here given are but fragmentary, and are grouped together in a somewhat irregular manner. It would seem as if both this account and that of the chronicler had been compiled from much more copious histories, each writer having cited those particulars which appeared to him to be the most interesting and important. But the design of the historian in either case is evident, viz., (1) to recount the principal undertakings of this illustrious king, and (2) to indicate the resources which enabled him to accomplish such ambitious and extensive designs. These latter were (1) the alliance with Hiram, which secured him the necessary materials (vers. 11—14); (2) the forced labour of the subject races (vers. 20—23); and (3) the voyages of his fleet (vers. 26—28).

Ver. 10.—**And it came to pass at the end of twenty years** [seven of which were occupied on the temple and thirteen on the palace (ch. vii. 1)], **when** [or, *during which*. LXX. ἐν οἷς ᾠκοδόμησε. This may well be the meaning of אֲשֶׁר בָּנָה, though אֲשֶׁר, *qui*, undoubtedly sometimes has the sense of *quum*] **Solomon had built the two houses, the house of the Lord and the king's house.** [Observe how all the palaces are regarded as one house. Note on ch. vii. 1.]

Ver. 11.—**(Now Hiram the king of Tyre** [Here we have a parenthesis referring us back to ch.v. 8—10] **had furnished Solomon with cedar trees and with fir trees and with gold** [The gold is here mentioned for the first time. No doubt Hiram's shipping had brought it in before the Jewish navy was built. It was this probably that led to the construction of a fleet] **according to all his desire), that then** [this is the apodosis to ver. 10] **king Solomon gave Hiram twenty cities** [really they were mere *villages*. "It is a genuine Eastern trick to dignify a small present with a pompous name" (Thomson). But עִיר is a word of very wide meaning] **in the land of Galilee.**

גָּלִיל lit., *circuit, region* (like *Ciccar*, ch. vii. 46), hence often found as here with the art. = *the region* of the Gentiles (Isa. ix. 1; 1 Macc. v. 15; Matt. iv. 15), so called because it was inhabited by Phœnicians (see 2 Sam.xxiv. 7, and Strabo, xvi. p.760), originally designated but a small part of the considerable tract of country later known as the province of "Galilee," viz., the northern part in the tribe of Naphtali (Josh. xx. 7; 2 Kings xv. 29; Isa. ix. 1. Cf. Jos., Ant. v. l. 18). It is easy to see why this particular region was surrendered to Hiram. (1) It was near his country (2 Sam. xxiv. 7); (2) the people were Phœnicians, allied to Hiram, but strangers to Solomon, both in race and religion; (3) Solomon could not with propriety alienate any part of Immanuel's land, or convey to a foreigner the dominion over the people of the Lord. Levit. xxv. 23 forbade the alienation of the land; Deut. xvii. 15 the rule of a stranger.

Ver. 12.—**And Hiram came out from Tyre to see the cities which Solomon had given him; and they pleased him not.** [Heb. *were not right in his eyes.* It has been con-

jectured that Hiram had hoped for the noble bay of Acco or Ptolemais (Milman, Rawlinson), but surely he had seaboard enough already. It was rather corn lands he would most need and desire. His disappointment is amply accounted for by the fact that the country assigned him was a hungry and mountainous, and therefore comparatively useless, tract. "The region lay on the summit of a broad mountain ridge" (Porter).]

Ver. 13.—**And he said, What cities are these which thou hast given me, my brother?** [Cf. chap. xx. 32. It would seem, at first sight, as if this form of speech was then, as now, the usage of courts. But the *Fellahîn* of Palestine, the "modern Canaanites," still address each other as "my father" or "my brother." See Conder,"Tentwork," p. 332]. **And he called them the land of Cabul** [The meaning of this word is quite uncertain. The LXX. reads Ὅριον, which shows that they must have read גְבוּל instead of כָבוּל; indeed, it is possible that the words have the same meaning (Gesen.) Stanley (S. and P. p. 364) thinks these cities formed the *boundary* between the two kingdoms, and refers to the use of ὅρια in Matt. xv. 21; Luke vi. 17, &c. According to Josephus, Χαβαλὼν is a Phœnician word, meaning *displeasing;* but his etymologies are to be received with caution, and Gesenius justly pronounces this a mere conjecture from the context. Thenius and Ewald regard the word as compounded of כ and בל = *as nothing;* Keil connects it with the root חבל, which would yield the meaning *pawned* or *pledged,* and hence concludes that this strip of territory was merely given to Hiram as a security for the repayment of a loan (see below on ver. 14); while Bähr derives it from כבל, an unused root, akin to the preceding = *vinxit, constrinxit,* and would see in it a name bestowed on the region because of its *confined* geographical position. He does not understand the word, however, as a term of contempt. "How," he asks, "could Hiram give the district a permanent name which contained a mockery of himself rather than of the land?" But the word was obviously an expression of disparagement, if not disgust, which, falling from Hiram's lips, was caught up and repeated with a view to mark not so much his displeasure as Solomon's meanness. But it is not necessary to find a meaning for the word, for it is to be considered that a city bearing this name existed at that time and in this neighbourhood (Josh. xix. 27), the site of which, in all probability, is marked by the modern *Kabúl,* eight miles east of Accho

(Robinson, iii. 87, 88; Dict. Bib. i. 237; Thomson, "Land and Book," i. 281, 511). It is possible, indeed, that it may have been one of the "twenty cities" (ver. 11) given to Hiram. And if this city, whether within or without the district of Galilee, were notorious for its poverty or meanness, or conspicuous by its bleak situation, we can at once understand why Hiram should transfer the name to the adjoining region, even if that name, in itself, had no special significance] unto this day. [See on ch. viii. 8.]

Ver. 14.—And Hiram sent [וַיִּשְׁלַח] must be understood as pluperfect, " Now Hiram had sent," referring to verse 11. This fact is mentioned to explain the gift of the cities, viz., that they were in payment for the gold he had furnished. The timber and stone and labour had been paid for in corn and wine and oil. See on ch. v. 11] to the king sixscore talents of gold. [This sum is variously estimated at from half a million to a million and a quarter of our money. (Keil, in loc., and Dict. Bib. iii. 1734. It equalled 3000 shekels of the sanctuary (Exod. xxxviii. 24—26). Keil, who, as we have seen, interprets Cabul to mean pledged, says somewhat positively that these 120 talents were merely lent to Solomon to enable him to prosecute his undertakings, and that the twenty cities were Hiram's security for its repayment. He further sees in the restoration of these cities (2 Chron. viii. 2, where see note) a proof that Solomon must have repaid the amount lent him. The " sixscore talents" should be compared with the 120 talents of ch. x. 10, and the 666 talents of ch. x. 14.]

Ver. 15.—And this is the reason [or manner, account, דְּבָר. Keil: " This is the case with regard to," &c. The historian now proceeds to speak of the forced labour. The LXX. inserts this and the next nine verses after ch. x. 22] of the levy [see on ch. v. 13, and xii. 18] which Solomon raised; for to build [The punctuation of the A.V. is misleading. The Hebrew has no break— "which Solomon raised for building," &c.] the house of the Lord and his own house and Millo [Heb. invariably, the Millo, as in 2 Sam. v. 9; 1 Kings xi. 27; 2 Kings xii. 20; 2 Chron. xxxii. 5; LXX. ἡ ἄκρα. The import of the word is much disputed, but Wordsworth has but slight warrant for saying that it means fortress. According to some it is an archaic Canaanitish term, " adopted by the Israelites when they took the town and incorporated into their own nomenclature" (Dict. Bib. ii. p. 367), an idea which finds some support in Judges ix. 6, 20. Mr. Grove would further see in it a name for Mount Zion, ἄκρα being the

invariable designation of that part of the city in the Maccabees. But see Jos., B. J. v. 4. 1; Ant. xv. 11. 5; and Porter, i. pp. 96, 109. Lewin (" Siege of Jerusalem," p. 256) identifies it with the great platform on which temple and palace alike were built. But the word yields a definite meaning in the Hebrew (=מִלּוֹא, "the filling in"). Gesenius consequently understands it to mean, a rampart (agger) because this is built up and filled in with stones, earth, &c. And the name would have a special fitness if we might suppose that it was applied to that part of the wall of Jerusalem which crossed the Tyropaeon valley. This ravine, which practically divided the city into two parts, would have been the weakest spot in the line of circumvallation, unless it were partly filled in—it is now completely choked up by débris, &c.—and protected by special fortifications; and, if this were done, and we can hardly doubt it was done (see on ch. xi. 27), Hammillo, " the filling in," would be its natural and appropriate name. And its mention, here and elsewhere, in connexion with the wall, lends some support to this view] and the wall of Jerusalem [We learn from 2 Sam. v. 9 that David had already built Millo and the wall. Rawlinson argues from chap. xi. 27 that these repairs had been " hasty, and had now—fifty years later—fallen into decay," and that Solomon renewed them. More probably the words indicate an enlargement of the Tyropaeon rampart, and an extension of the walls. See note there and on chap. iii. 1. Solomon, no doubt, wished to strengthen the defences of the capital, on which he had expended so much labour, and where there was so much to tempt the rapacity of predatory neighbours] and Hazor [For the defence of the kingdom he built a chain of fortresses "to form a sort of girdle round the land" (Ewald). The first mentioned, Hazor, was a place of great importance in earlier times, being the " head of all those (the northern) kingdoms" (Josh. xi. 10). It stood on an eminence—as indeed, for the sake of security, did all the cities of that lawless age (ib., ver. 13 marg.)—overlooking Lake Merom. It was at no great distance from the north boundary of Palestine, in Naphtali (Josh. xix. 36), and being favoured by position, it was strongly fortified—Hazor means fortress—and hence Joshua made a point of destroying it. It appears, however, to have speedily regained its importance, for in Judg. iv. 2, 17 we find it as the capital of Jabin, king of Canaan. It was selected by Solomon as the best site for a stronghold, which should protect his northern border, and as commanding the approach from

Syria. As it is not mentioned in ch. xv. 20, it would appear to have escaped in the invasion of Benhadad. Possibly it was too strong for him] and Megiddo [Josh. xii. 21; xvii. 11; Judg. v. 19. This place was chosen partly because of its central position—it stood on the margin of the plain of Esdraelon, the battle-field of Palestine, and the battles fought there prove its strategical importance, Judg. v. 19 (cf. 1 Sam. xxxi. 1); 2 Kings xxiii. 29; Judith iii. 9, 10—and partly, perhaps, because the high road from Egypt to Damascus passed through it. It dominated the passes of Ephraim (see Judith iv. 7). It has till recently been identified with *el-Lejjûn* (from *Legio*. Compare our *Chester*, &c.) (Robinson, ii. 116 sqq.; Stanley, S. and P., p. 347; Porter, 286, 287); but Conder ("Tent-work," p. 67) gives good reasons for fixing the site at the "large ruins between Jezreel and Bethshean, which still bears the name of *Mujedd'a*, i.e., on the eastern side of the plain] and Gezer [This commanded the approach from Egypt, and would protect the southern frontier of Solomon's kingdom. See Josh. x. 33; xii. 12; xxi. 21; Judges i. 29; 2 Sam. v. 25; 1 Chron. xx. 4. It stands on the great maritime plain, and is also on the coast road between Egypt and Jerusalem. The site was identified (in 1874) by M. Clermont Ganneau with *Tell Jezer*. The name means "cut off," "isolated" (Gesen.) "The origin of the title is at once clear, for the site is an out-lier—to use a geological term—of the main line of hills, and the position commands one of the important passes to Jerusalem" (Conder, p. 6).

The mention of Gezer leads to a parenthesis of considerable length (vers. 16—19). The question of the levy is put aside for the time, whilst the historian explains how it was that the king came to build Gezer. He then proceeds to mention the other towns built during the same reign.

Ver. 16.—For Pharaoh king of Egypt had gone up and taken Gezer and burnt it with fire [The total destruction of the place and its inhabitants by fire and sword looks more like an act of vengeance for some grave offence than like ordinary warfare], and slain the Canaanites that dwelt in the city [Though Gezer was allotted to Ephraim (Josh. xvi. 3) and designated as a Levitical city (ib., xxi. 21), the Canaanite inhabitants had never been dispossessed (Josh. xvi. 10; LXX. "Canaanites and Perizzites;" cf. Judg. i. 29), and they would seem to have enjoyed a sort of independence], and given it for a present [שִׁלֻּחִים, *dotatio*, dowry. It is the custom of the East for the husband to purchase his wife by a present (Gen. xxix. 18;

2 Sam. iii. 14, &c.); but in royal marriages a dowry was often given. "Sargon gave Cilicia as a dowry with his daughter. . . . Antiochus Soter gave his claims on Macedonia as a dowry to his step-daughter Phila, when she married Antigonus Gonatas. Coele-Syria and Palestine were promised as a dowry to Ptolemy Epiphanes, when he married Cleopatra, sister of Antiochus the Great," &c. (Rawlinson). Gezer being a *wedding* present, its conquest must have taken place years before the date to which the history is now brought down] unto his daughter, Solomon's wife.

Ver. 17.—And Solomon built Gezer [In the case of Gezer it was an actual rebuilding. But as applied to Beth-horon, &c., "built" probably means *enlarged, strengthened*] and Beth-horon the nether [mentioned in connexion with Gezer, Josh. xvi. 3 (cf. x. 10). It is deserving of mention that the two cities of Beth-horon still survive in the modern villages of *Beitûr el-tahta* and *el-fok*," names which are "clearly corruptions of Beth-horon "the Nether" and "the Upper" (Stanley, S. and P., p. 208). One lies at the foot of the ravine, on an eminence, the other at the summit of the pass. Like Megiddo and Gezer, this town, too, lay on a high road, viz., that between Jerusalem and the sea coast. The selection of Beth-horon for fortification by Solomon is also justified by history—three decisive battles having been fought here (see Josh. x. 10; 1 Macc. iii. 13—24, and Jos., Bell. Jud. ii. 19. 8. The object of the king in fortifying this place was to protect the uplands of Judah, Benjamin, and Ephraim against invasion from the Philistine plain. It is perhaps not unnoteworthy that, according to our author, it was Beth-horon the *nether* that Solomon "built," as this would naturally have suffered more than its loftier neighbour from war. According to 2 Chron. viii. 5, however, Solomon built Beth-horon the upper also.

Ver. 18.—And Baalath [probably the place mentioned in Josh. xix. 44, and therefore a town of Dan. By some it has been identified, but on wholly insufficient grounds —the mention of Tadmor immediately afterwards being the chief—with Baalbek. This is one of the names which prove how ancient and widespread was the worship of Baal (Gesen., Thesaurus, 225; Dict. Bib., i. 147, 148)] and Tadmor in the wilderness, in the land. [Whether this is (1) the famous Palmyra, or (2) Tamar, an obscure town of south Judah, is a question which has been much disputed. It should be stated in the first place that the *Cethib* has תמר, but the *Keri*, after 2 Chron. viii. 4, reads תדמר, as do all the versions; and secondly that a *Tamar* is mentioned Ezek. xlvii. 19 and xlviii. 28 a place which may well be identical with " Hazazon Tamar, which is Engedi " (2 Chron. xx. 2; cf. Gen. xiv. 7. In favour of (1) are the following considerations : (1) the statement of the chronicler that Solomon did build Palmyra (for of the identity of " Tadmor " with Palmyra there can be no reasonable doubt ; see Dict. Bib. iii. 1428). (2) The probability that Solomon, with his wide views of commerce, would seize upon and fortify the one oasis in the great Syrian desert in order to establish an *entrepôt* there (see on ver. 19). (3) The words " in the wilderness," which, of course, are eminently true of Palmyra. Against it, however, may be urged (1) that Tamar is much more likely to be changed into Tadmor than Tadmor into Tamar. (2) That this place is distinctly described as " in the land," which, *strictly*, Palmyra was not. But here it is to be observed that the chronicler omits these words, and that the Syriac, Arabic, and Vulgate render, " in the land of the wilderness." Keil says our text is manifestly corrupt, and certainly the expression is a singular one. Some would, therefore, alter בארץ into בְּאָדָם, or into בחמת (after 2 Chron. viii. 4). Both of the emendations, however, while undoubtedly plausible, are purely conjectural. Wordsworth, who thinks Palmyra is meant, says it is described as " in the land " to indicate that God had fulfilled his promise to extend *the land* of Solomon far eastward into the *wilderness* (Psa. lxxii. 9). And a Jewish historian, especially in the time of his country's decadence, might well recount how this great city had once been comprised within the boundaries of Israel. In favour of (2) are these facts : (1) That it is the reading of the text. It is said, however, that the ancient name of Tadmor was Tamar, and the place clearly owed its name to the *Palm* trees. But the name is always *Tadmor* in the Palmyrene inscriptions. (2) That this place was " in the wilderness," *i.e.*, of Judah. (3) That it was " in the land," and (4) that it was in close proximity to the places just mentioned. The evidence is thus so evenly balanced that it is impossible to decide positively between the two.

Ver. 19.—**And all the cities of store that Solomon had** [cities where the produce of the land was stored for the use of the troops or household, or against a season of scarcity (Gen. xli. 35; Exod. i. 11), or possibly (Ewald) they were emporiums for the development of trade. The fact that these store cities are mentioned in the same breath with Tadmor, is an argument for the identification of that place with Palmyra, which Solomon could

only have built as a means of gaining or retaining control over the caravan trade between the East and the Mediterranean. Cf. 2 Chron. xvii. 12; xxxii. 28, and Gen. xli. 48. They would seem to have been chiefly on the northern frontier, 2 Chron. viii. 4 (" in Hamath"); *ib.* ch. xvi. 4 speaks of " the store cities of *Napthali*." It should be remembered that Solomon had an adversary in Damascus], **and cities for his chariots, and cities for his horsemen** [Cf. ch. iv. 26. These were not so much fortresses (vers. 15—18) as places adapted to accommodate his cavalry, &c. For *horsemen* we should perhaps read *horses*. See note on ch. v. 6], **and that which Solomon desired to build** [Heb. *and the desire of Solomon which he desired*; cf. ver. 1. The use of the cognate verb refutes the idea that Solomon's " desire" is another name for pleasure-buildings or pleasaunces, as does also " desire" in ver. 11. It is certain, however, that such buildings were erected, and it is probable that they are referred to here] **in Jerusalem and in Lebanon** [It is highly probable that pleasure-houses were built in Lebanon (Cant. vii. 4, *passim*), for which Solomon may well have had a strong affection, and pleasure-gardens in Jerusalem (Eccles. ii. 4—7). See Stanley, pp. 197–199); and we may reasonably imagine (with Ewald) that in these latter he sought to grow specimens of the plants, &c., about which he " spoke' (ch. iv. 33 ; cf. Eccles. ii. 5). " It is a curious fact that in the ground hard by the ' fountains of Solomon' near Bethlehem, which exhibit manifest traces of an ancient garden, and where the intimations of Josephus would lead us to suppose that Solomon had a rural retreat, are still to be found a number of plants self-sown from age to age, which do not exist in any other part of the Holy Land " (Kitto, " Bib. Illus." vol. iv. p. 101). Some of Solomon's journeys to these favourite resorts, we can hardly doubt, are referred to in Cant. iii. 6—10; iv. 8 sqq.; vi. 11] **and in all the land of his dominion.**

Ver. 20.—**And all the people that were left of the Amorites, Hittites, Perizzites, Hivites, and Jebusites** [Judges i. 21—36 ; iii. 5; 1 Chron. xxii. 2] **which were not of the children of Israel.**

Ver. 21.—**Their children that were left after them in the land** [this is explicative of ver, 20], **whom the children of Israel also** [*also* is not in the Hebrew, and is meaningless] **were not able utterly to destroy, upon those did Solomon levy a tribute of bond service** [see on ch. v. 13, and cf. Judges i., *passim*, and 1 Chron. xxii. 2] **unto this day.**

Ver. 22.—**But of the children of Israel did Solomon make no bondmen** [see however ch. v. 13, 18. This service, though compulsory, was not servile. Bondage was forbidden, Levit. xxv. 39. The levy were treated as hired servants and had wages]; **but they were men of war, and his servants** [cf. ch. i. 9. Not only " officials of the war department" (Bähr) but officers of every kind], **and his princes** [these were the heads both of the military and civil services], **and his captains** [Heb. שָׁלִשָׁיו. LXX. τριστάται. Exod. xiv. 7 ; xv. 4 ; 2 Sam. xxiii. 8 ; 2 Kings ix. 25 ; x. 25, &c. These *third men* were really " a noble rank of soldiers who fought from chariots" (Gesen.), each of which would seem to have held *three* men, one of whom drove, while two fought : thence used of the body-guard of kings. That they formed a *corps*, and were not literally " captains," is clear from 1 Sam. xxiii. 8, &c.] **and rulers of his chariots, and his horsemen.**

Ver. 23.—**These were the chief of the officers that were over Solomon's work, five hundred and fifty, which bare rule over the people that wrought in the work** [see on ch. v. 16].

Ver. 24.—**But** [אַךְ, lit. *only*. Keil rightly connects the word with אָז below. " So soon as . . . then." Cf. Gen. xxvii. 30. This and ver. 25 are not interposed arbitrarily, as might at first sight appear, but refer to ch. iii. 1—4. The completion of the palaces rendered it no longer necessary or proper that Solomon's daughter should dwell in a separate house. The chronicler tells us that she had dwelt in David's palace on Mount Zion, and that Solomon was constrained to remove her, because he looked upon all the precinct as now consecrated (2 Chron. viii. 11)]. **Pharaoh's daughter came up** [עָלְתָה. Keil hence argues that the palace stood on higher ground than David's house. But this conclusion is somewhat precarious. The approach to the palace involved an ascent, but Zion was certainly as high as Ophel] **out of the city of David unto her house which Solomon** [Heb. *he*] **had built for her : then did he build Millo.** [Thenius infers from these words that Millo was a fort or castle for the protection of the harem. But there is no warrant for any such conjecture. In the first place, this wife would seem to have been lodged in her own palace apart from the other wives. 2. We can offer a better explanation of the word Millo (see ver. 15). 3. The word " then " may mean either (1), that when her palace was completed, Solomon then had workmen who were liberated and were employed on Millo (Keil), or (2), that when she vacated David's house, the building of Millo could be proceeded with.

Ver. 25.—**And three times in a year** [*i.e.*, no doubt at the three feasts, the times of greatest solemnity, and when there was the largest concourse of people. See 2 Chron. viii. 12. The design of this verse may be to show that there was no longer any offering on high places. It would thus refer to ch. iii. 2, as ver. 24 to ch. iii. 1] **did Solomon offer burnt offerings and peace offerings upon the altar which he built unto the Lord** [the chronicler adds, "before the porch"], **and he burnt incense.** [It has been supposed by some that Solomon sacrificed and burnt incense *propria manu*. According to Dean Stanley (" Jewish Ch." ii. pp. 220, 221), " he solemnly entered, not only the temple courts with sacrifices, but penetrated into the Holy Place itself, where in later years none but the priests were allowed to enter, and offered incense on the altar of incense." But this positive statement is absolutely destitute of all basis. For, in the first place, there is nothing in the text to support it. If Solomon ordered, or defrayed the cost of, the sacrifices, &c., as no doubt he did, the historian would properly and naturally describe him as offering burnt offerings. *Qui facit per alium facit per se*, and priests are expressly mentioned as present at these sacrifices (ch. viii. 6 ; 2 Chron. v. 7—14 ; vii. 2, 5). We have just as much reason, and no more, for believing that the king built Millo (ver. 24) with his own hands, and with his own hands "made a navy of ships " (ver. 26), as that he sacrificed, &c., *in propria persona*. And, secondly, it is simply inconceivable, if he had so acted, that it should have attracted no more notice, and that our historian should have passed it over thus lightly. We know what is recorded by our author as having happened when, less than two centuries afterwards, King Uzziah presumed to intrude on the functions of the priests (2 Chron. xxvi. 17—20) ; cf. 1 Kings xiii. 1), and we know what had happened some five centuries before (Num. xvi. 35), when men who were not of the seed of Aaron came near to offer incense before the Lord. It is impossible that Solomon could have disregarded that solemn warning without some protest, or without a syllable of blame on the part of our author. And the true account of these sacrifices is that they were offered by the king as the *builder of the temple*, and probably throughout his life, by the hands of the ministering priests (2 Chron. viii. 14). Thrice in the year he showed his piety by a great function, at which he offered liberally] **upon the altar** [Heb. *upon that, sc.* altar אֹתוֹ. See Gesen. Lex., p. 94 ; Ewald, Syntax, 333*a* (3)] **that was before the Lord.** [The altar of incense stood before the entrance to the oracle, the place of the Divine presence. See on ch. vi. 22]. **So he finished the house.** [Same word, but in the Kal form in ch. vii. 51. The Piel form, used here, may convey the deeper meaning, " he perfected," *i.e.*, by devoting it to its proper use. It was to be " a house of *sacrifice*" (2 Chron. vii. 12).

Ver. 26.—**And king Solomon made a navy of ships** [Heb. אֳנִי, a collective noun, *classis*. The chronicler paraphrases by אֳנִיּוֹת, plural. This fact finds a record here, probably because it was to the voyages of this fleet that the king was indebted for the gold which enabled him to erect and adorn the buildings recently described. (As to form, &c., of the ships, see Dict. Bib. ii. p. 1014). But no historian could pass over without notice an event of such profound importance to Israel as the construction of its first ships, which, next to the temple, was the great event of Solomon's reign] **in Ezion-geber** [lit., *the backbone of a man* (or *giant*). Cf. Num. xxxiii. 35; Deut. ii. 8; 2 Kings xiv. 22; 2 Chron. viii. 17. The name is probably due, like Shechem (see note on ch. xii. 25) to a real or fancied resemblance in the physical geography of the country to that part of the human body. Stanley (S. and P. p. 84) speaks of " the jagged ranges on each side of the gulf." *Akaba*, the modern name, also means *back*. 2 Chron. *l.c.* says Solomon went to Ezion-geber, which it is highly probable he would do], **which is beside** [Heb. אֵת = *apud* (Gesen., Lex. *s.v.*)] **Eloth** [lit., *trees* akin to Elim, where were *palm* trees (Exod. xv. 27; xvi. 1). The name is interesting as suggesting that Solomon *may have found some* of the timber for the construction of his fleet here. A grove of palm trees " still exists at the head of the gulf of Akaba" (Stanley S. and P. p. 20). Palms, it is true, are not adapted to shipbuilding, but other timber may have grown there in a past age. But see note on ver. 27. For Elath, see Porter, p. 40; Deut. ii. 8; 2 Sam. viii. 14 (which shows how it passed into the hand of Israel); 2 Kings viii. 20; xiv. 22; xvi. 6. It gave a name to the *Elanitic Gulf*, now the *Gulf of Akaba*], **on the shore** [Heb. lip] **of the Red sea** [Heb. *Sea of Rushes*. LXX. ἡ ἐρυθρὰ θάλασσα. The redness is due to subaqueous vegetation. " Fragments of red coral are for ever being thrown up from the stores below, and it is these coralline forests which form the true 'weeds' of this fantastic sea" (Stanley, S. and P. p. 83). There is also apparently a bottom of red sandstone (*ib.* p. 6, note). It is divided by the Sinaitic peninsula into two arms or gulfs, the western being the Gulf of Suez, and the eastern the Gulf of Akabah. The former

is 130 miles, the latter 90 miles long], **in the land of Edom.** [The subjugation of Edom is mentioned 2 Sam. viii. 14.]

Ver. 27.—**And Hiram sent in the navy his servants, shipmen that had knowledge of the sea with the servants of Solomon.** [The chronicler states (2 Chron. viii. 18) that he sent ships as well as servants, and it has been thought that ships were transported, in parts or entire, by land across the Isthmus of Suez, and there are certainly instances on record of the land transport of fleets. (Keil reminds us that Alexander the Great, according to Arrian, had ships transported—in pieces—from Phœnicia to the Euphrates, and that, according to Thucydides (Bell. Pelop. iv. 8) the Peloponnesians conveyed 60 ships from Corcyra across the Leucadian Isthmus, &c.) But this, especially when the state of engineering science, &c., among the Hebrews is taken into account, is hardly to be thought of. It is quite possible, however, that *timber* for shipbuilding was floated on the Mediterranean down to the river of Egypt, or some such place, and then transported either to Suez or to Akaba. Probably all that the chronicler means is that Hiram provided the materials and had the ships built. The Israelites, having hitherto had no fleet, and little or no experience of the sea, were unable to construct ships for themselves. And the Tyrians may have seen in the construction of a fleet for *eastern* voyages, an opening for the extension of their own maritime trade. Possibly in the first voyages Tyrians and Jews were co-partners.]

Ver. 28.—**And they came to Ophir** [It is perhaps impossible to identify this place with any degree of precision. The opinions of scholars may, however, be practically reduced to two. The first would place Ophir in India; the second in southern Arabia. In favour of India is (1) the three years' voyage (but see on ch. x. 22); (2) most of the other treasures brought back by the fleet, exclusive of gold, are Indian products. But against it is urged the important fact that no gold is now found there, south of Cashmere, whilst south Arabia was famed for its abundant gold (Psa. lxxii. 15; Ezek. xxvii. 22). On the other hand, it is alleged that in ancient times India was rich in gold (Ewald, iii. p. 264), and that there are no traces of gold mines in Arabia. The question is discussed at considerable length and with great learning by Mr. Twisleton (Dict. Bib. art. " Ophir "). He shows that it is reasonably certain (1) that the Ophir of Gen. x. 29 is the name of some city, region, or tribe in *Arabia*, and (2) that the Ophir of Genesis is the Ophir of the Book of Kings. And Gesenius, Bähr, Keil, *al.*

agree with him in locating Ophir in the latter country. Ewald, however, sees in Ophir "the most distant coasts of India," and it is probable that the Hebrews used the word somewhat loosely, as they did the corresponding word *Tarshish*, and as we do the words East and West Indies. They were not geographers, and Ophir may have been merely an emporium where the products of different countries were collected, or a *nomen generale* for " all the countries lying on the African, Arabian, or Indian seas, so far as at that time known" (Heeren). See on ch. x. 5], **and fetched from thence gold, four hundred and twenty talents** [The chronicler says 450. The discrepancy is easily accounted for, 20 being expressed by כ; 50 by נ. Wordsworth suggests that "perhaps thirty were assigned to Hiram for his help "] **and brought it to king Solomon.**

HOMILETICS.

Ver. 25.—*The Two Altars of Judaism*. This text is somewhat remarkable as bringing before us at the same moment the two altars of the Jewish Church—the great brazen altar of sacrifice and the golden altar of incense. The present is therefore, perhaps, a fitting place to study their use and significance.

For it is with good reason that they are here joined together. Though the ritual of the first was quite distinct from that of the second, yet each was an essential part of the same religious system; each was a centre of Hebrew worship. Moreover, the second was the complement of the first. Incense was the appropriate adjunct of sacrifice. And the two together formed practically the sum of the ordinary ceremonial of the children of the old covenant.

The altars themselves, however, will require but little notice, for they both alike derived their interest and importance from the purposes they served. The altar of sacrifice is not even mentioned by our historian in his account of the temple arrangements; while the chronicler dismisses it in a single verse. And neither the Kings nor the Chronicles describe the size, structure, &c., of the altar of incense. It is true the altar " sanctified the gift" (Matt. xxiii. 19; Exod. xxix. 37, 44), perhaps sanctified the incense also (but see Exod. xxx. 35—37), but all the same, the sacrifice and the incense, not the brazen or the golden altars, are the important and significant things. The two altars, that is to say, really bring before us the two questions of *Sacrifice* and *Incense*.

I. THE ALTAR OF SACRIFICE. But before we turn our thoughts to the sacrifices smoking on the altar, let us glance for a moment at the *altar* itself. Observe—

1. *Its position*. Outside the temple, the " house of sacrifice " (2 Chron. vii. 12 ; Matt. xxiii. 35), but in the court of the priests, and, therefore, exclusively for the service of the priests.

2. *Its dimensions*. It was fifteen feet high, and its top was a square of thirty feet (2 Chron. iv. 1). It was designedly high—the altar of the tabernacle was but four and a half feet high. It was high, despite the inconveniences resulting therefrom. The height required that a ledge or platform should be constructed round it; that a long slope or flight of steps should be ascended in order to reach it ; and that the lavers and sea should be high in proportion (ch. vii. 23, 25, 27, 38). Its great size and capacity—it presented a superficies of 900 square feet—was because of the great number of victims which were occasionally offered upon it at one time.

3. *Its horns*. These were no freak of the architect, but were of the essence of the structure, and of Divine obligation (Exod. xxvii. 2). The blood was put upon them (*ib.* xxix. 12 ; Levit. iv. 7, 18, 30, 34 ; viii. 15; ix. 9, &c.) ; the sacrifice, at least in early times, was bound to them (Psa. cxviii. 27) ; the suppliant for life clung to them (ch. i. 50 ; ii. 28, &c.) The altar was designed, that is to say, for sacrifice ; but it also served at the same time for sanctuary.

And now let us look at the *sacrifice*, at "the gift upon the altar." Observe—

1. *It is an offering*. Whatever the character of the sacrifice, burnt offering, sin offering, peace offering, meat offering, it was an offering, a gift. Whether whole bullocks were consumed, or only the fat, kidneys, &c., it had been first consecrated, devoted, given, to God. This is, perhaps, the primary idea of sacrifice. The victim must be presented before it could be immolated.

2. *It was ordinarily an offering made by fire* (1 Sam. ii. 28). The holy fire kindled by God (Levit. ix. 24), and which for long centuries was never suffered to go out (Levit. vi. 13), the element which at that time, and ever since, has been regarded in the East as an image of the Godhead, if not a sign of His presence, this consumed everything. The tongues of flame not only carried the smoke and smell of the sacrifice—hecatomb, holocaust, whatever it was—up into the blue sky and to the throne of God, but they, so to speak, devoured the victim; they feasted on the sacrifice.

3. *It was an offering of life.* Not only was this a matter of fact—that the victim was first slain, then offered on the altar, but this idea was expressed in the ritual of the sacrifice. The blood was poured out at the foot of the altar, or sprinkled on its horns, or borne into the most holy place. But the blood is the life of the flesh (Levit. xvii. 11), and hence the sprinkling of the blood was the core and centre of all sacrifice. (See Bähr, Symbolik, ii. pp. 199 sqq.) The very *separation* of the elements again—the blood poured in one place, the flesh or fat burnt at another—pictured death; for when the blood is withdrawn from the body death ensues. The consuming fire, too, spoke of death. So that in sacrifice men offered to God the most mysterious and precious of man's possessions and of God's gifts, the life, the ψυχή, which came from God and went back to God. It was an old and reasonable belief that the gods would have our nearest and dearest—see Tennyson's beautiful poem, "The Victim"—hence the gift to the altar was the life.

4. *It was an offering for life.* The full significance of sacrifice, we may readily believe, the Jew did not know. It is doubtful whether even the high priest comprehended the blessed meaning of those solemn rites in which he bore a part. But this they did know, that the life offered at the altar was an atonement for their life. The *lex talionis*, "an eye for an eye," &c. (Exod. xxi. 24), had taught them this. So had much of their expressive ceremonial, *e.g.*, the laying of the hands on the head of the victim, &c. (Levit. iii. 2; iv. 4, &c.) So above all had the express words of Scripture, "The life of the flesh is in the blood, and I have given it to you upon the altar for an atonement for your souls (Heb. *lives*, same word as above), for it is the blood that maketh atonement for the soul" (Heb. *through the life, sc.* of the blood) Levit. xvii. 11. They understood, that is, that sacrifice was not only eucharistic, but that it was also deprecatory and in some way expiatory. They hoped that it would somehow reconcile them and restore them to communion with God, *the* Life, the *Anima animantium.*

More than this, however, the Jewish worshipper did not see in the sacrifice. But for us who turn our gaze to Mount Moriah from the hill of Calvary, it has an additional significance. We may see in it—

5. *A picture of the offering of Jesus Christ.* An imperfect picture, no doubt—a shadow, a type, a parable, but still the outline is clear and distinct. We see here the priest, the victim, the altar, the mactation, the blood-pouring, the elevation, the death. As a *picture*, indeed, all sacrifice "showed the Lord's death" (1 Cor. xi. 26) much more vividly and touchingly than the Holy Communion does.

6. *A pleading of the death of Christ.* This is the crown and blossom of sacrifice. It was an ἀνάμνησις, a silent but eloquent memorial before God. Only thus can we adequately explain the elaborate sacrificial system of Moses. From any other point of view sacrifices are, as Coleridge confessed, an enigma. But see in them tokens, memorials, pleadings of the one vicarious death, and all is clear. Then we can comprehend why they should have offered thousands of victims "year by year continually." Every bullock, every sheep, was, though the worshippers knew it not, a mute reminder of the one sacrifice for sin. Each was a foreshadowing of *the* death; the death of Him who is "*the* life" (John xiv. 6); each spoke to the heart of God of the precious blood of Christ. Let us trace the parallel a little more in detail.

1. *The Altar prefigured the Cross.*

(1) *In its position.* The true altar of incense is in heaven. The altar of sacrifice was altogether of this world; it was in the truest sense "an altar of earth." But while outside the temple of heaven, the cross was yet in the court of the priests

for " Immanuel's land " was a sort of precinct or forecourt of the eternal sanctuary, and it was the home of a nation of *priests* (Exod. xix. 6). Hence we may learn (1) that sacrifice is only offered where there is sin, and (2) that the cross goes together with the kingdom (Rev. i. 5, 6); it is the altar of the Holy Catholic Church.

(2) *In its elevation.* Probably the altar was made high to give it due honour and prominence, or there may have been the thought of elevating the sacrifice towards heaven. But, whatever the reason, it struck the eye; every one saw that it was the centre and ornament and distinguishing mark of the court of the priests. Now the cross itself was probably raised but two or three feet above the ground— pictures generally represent it incorrectly—but it was planted on a hill. Conder (" Tent-work," pp. 196, 198) identifies Calvary with a rounded knoll, above a cliff or precipice some thirty feet high, near the Damascus gate), and it still—and this is the important thing—" towers above the wreck of time." It is still the glory and badge and attraction of Christ's people of priests. It was fitting, too, that He should be raised above earth who was from above (John iii. 31) ; that He should be suspended between earth and heaven who should reconcile earth to heaven.

(3) *The cross had no horns,* but it had *arms*—arms to which the victim was bound, arms which were stained with His blood, arms which offer shelter and sanctuary to the world.

> " Lord, on the cross Thine arms were stretched,
> To draw Thy people nigh," &c.

2. *The Sacrifice prefigured the Crucifixion.* It is hardly needful or possible here to point out in what manifold ways the various sacrifices of the Law fore-shadowed the oblation of Calvary. It must suffice to say here that this too was a voluntary offering (Heb. ix. 14), a *whole* offering (כָּלִיל—cf. Heb. x. 10, &c.), the grateful savour of which *ascended* (the idea of the word עֹלָה) to heaven (Gen. viii. 21 ; Ephes. v. 2); that the *life* was given (Matt. xx. 28) and *blood* poured (1 Peter i. 2) ; that the blood was poured for the remission of sins (Matt. xxvi. 28; Heb. ix. 22), and the life given for the life of the world (John vi. 51). It is for us to lay our hands on the head of the sacrifice, and the analogy is complete. We must bring no offering of our own merits, but must take refuge under the arms of the Cross—

> " Nothing in my hand I bring,
> Simply to thy Cross I cling."

It must not be supposed, however, that because sacrifices, properly so called, have ceased, because they have found their blessed fulfilment in " the one offering," " once for all " (Heb. x. 10, 14), therefore the *pictures* and *pleadings* of that offering have ceased also. On the contrary, the death of Calvary, which cannot be repeated, is for ever pleaded (Rev. v. 6) in the heavenly temple. In this sense it is a *continual* offering (Exod. xxix. 42). And it is also pleaded by the Church on earth. For the holy sacrament, like the sacrifice, tells of death, and of the same vicarious and victorious death. The sacrifice pleaded the merits of Him who should come ; the sacrament the merits of One who has come. The first was, the second is, an ἀνάμνησις of the death which won our life. (See Homiletics on ch. vi. pp. 114, 115.)

II. THE ALTAR OF INCENSE. It is often forgotten that Judaism had two altars. But who shall say that the altar of incense was less important or less gracious than that of sacrifice.

A few simple questions will perhaps best bring this subject of incense before us. Let us therefore ask—

1. *What was the incense ? It was* (see Exod. xxx. 34 sqq.) (1) *a confection of sweet spices;* a compound of the most fragrant and grateful products of the earth, which when burned emitted a pleasing odour. (2) *A perfume ordained of God.* Its constituents and their proportions were alike prescribed (*ib.* vers. 34, 35). These were to be " tempered (Heb. *salted*) together." Hence the scrupulous care with which it was prepared and preserved in the " house of Abtines." And hence the

probability that the story of thirteen ingredients (Jos., B. J. v. 5. 5) of the addition of cassia, cinnamon, &c., to the elements mentioned in the Law, is a Rabbinical fable. Such a confection would have been "strange incense." (3) *It was a perfume reserved for God* (Exod. xxx. 37, 38). None might be made for private use under pain of death (*ib.* ver. 38). Hence it was called "most holy" (Heb. *holy of holies*).

2. *Where was it offered?* In two places. Occasionally in the most holy place; usually on the golden altar which stood before that place. Hence this altar is spoken of as "before the Lord," and is called "the altar that belongeth to the oracle" (ch. vi. 22). It was clearly, therefore, and peculiarly an offering to God, whose throne was in the sanctuary, and whose palace was the temple. It was burnt before the Presence, whose seat was between the cherubim. Indeed, it is not improbable that it was only burnt *outside* the oracle, because the priests must not enter the most holy place. (The golden altar, as we have just seen, really "belonged to the oracle.") When the high priest *did* enter, on the day of atonement, the incense was burnt within the veil. And the Sadducees were accounted heretical because they contended that the incense might be kindled outside and then carried inside the holy of holies.

3. *When was it burned?* It was burned (1) *morning and evening.* When the lamps were trimmed at the break of day; when the lamps were lighted at the approach of night. Thus every little life—for our days are "lives in miniature"— was rounded off with incense. There was not a day for many hundred years but began and ended with this sweet service. (2) *With the morning and evening sacrifice.* It was bound up with the offerings of the great altar. "Mane, inter sanguinem et membra suffiebat, vesperi, inter membra et libamina" (Talmud, quoted by Lightfoot). "When the incense and prayers were finished, the parts of the victim were laid on the altar." So that the incense and the sacrifice were really parts of the same service. The two altars of Judaism presented their offerings to heaven at the same time. (3) *It was a "perpetual incense"* (Exod. xxx. 8), just as the sacrifice is called a continual burnt offering (*ib.* xxix. 42). The sweet perfume, we may remember here, never died out in the holy place. There was an everlasting fragrance, year in, year out, in the earthly abode of the heavenly King. (4) *It was offered together with prayer.* See Luke i. 10; Rev. v. 8; viii. 1—4; and Lightfoot, "Heb. and Talm. Exerc. on Luke i. 10."

4. *By whom was it offered?* (1) *By the priests.* Originally, it is believed, by the high priest exclusively, but subsequently a priest was chosen by lot (Luke i. 9) to perform this office each morning and each evening. And we are told that as this was esteemed the most honourable of all the functions of the priests, and as a blessing was thought to be attached to its performance, the lot was cast among those who were "new to the incense," *i.e.*, among those who had not offered it already. (2) *By the priests alone.* No function was more jealously guarded than this. On two memorable occasions (Num. xvi. 35—40; 2 Chron. xxvi. 16 sqq.) a terrible dispensation proclaimed that "no stranger, who was not of the seed of Aaron, should come near to offer incense before the Lord."

5. *Why was it offered?* Maimonides held that it was merely, or principally, designed to counteract the stench which would arise from the victims slain for the morning and evening sacrifice. Others have beheld in it merely a recognition of the majesty and sovereignty of God, and have seen its counterpart in the perfumes which were offered before the monarchs of the East (cf. Matt. ii. 11). But a moment's reflection will show that both these conceptions are miserably inadequate and unworthy. It is inconceivable that so prominent and essential a part of the Jewish system can have had no higher meaning or have no analogue in Christianity. It is universally admitted that the brazen altar and its sacrifices were full of symbolism. How can we think that while these prefigured Christ's death the golden altar and its incense foreshadowed nothing. No, they must have typified something, and something connected with the work of the eternal Son of God.

For observe, just as there is an altar raised on Calvary, just as there is a sacrificial altar of which we Christians eat (Heb. xiii. 10), so is there an altar in heaven (Rev. viii. 3). Nor will this surprise us if we bear in mind that the Mosaic worship was fashioned after the mode of the heavenly, and that the tabernacle and its furniture were made according to the pattern showed in the Mount.

What, then, did incense symbolize? Was it prayer? It has been very generally supposed (after Psa. cxli. 2) to be an emblem of prayer. But this is a view which reflection hardly justifies. For (1) prayer was offered at the *time of incense;* it was an invariable adjunct thereto, and we should hardly have the type and anti-type, the shadow and the substance, together. The type is only needed until the antitype takes its place. (2) Incense is said to be offered *with prayers* (Rev. v. 8), where the "which" (*αἵ*) would seem to refer to the "vials" (*φιάλας*) rather than to the θυμιαμάτων (ch. viii. 1—4). In the passage last cited, this is beyond doubt. The incense was to be *added to* (A. V. "offered"), and was therefore distinct from, the prayers of all saints.

No, the incense offered day by day, and century after century, prefigured the gracious *intercession of Christ,* that intercession through which alone our prayers are presented, which alone ensures their acceptance, and without which sinful man cannot draw near to God. When the high priest entered the oracle, as the representative of the congregation, the cloud of incense must cover him lest he should die. We have but to notice how close is the correspondence between type and antitype to be convinced that this is its true meaning. (1) His prayers are like the fragrant incense. In Him the Father is well pleased. And they are ordained of God. He is the "Anointed," the "Advocate with the Father," "the one Mediator." (There is a "strange incense," too—the mediation of saints and angels.) (2) He stands "before the throne," "at the right hand of God," "in heaven itself." (3) He "ever liveth to make intercession for us." The incense never dies out of the heavenly courts. When we pray, morning and evening, our Intercessor prays also. When we offer our sacrifices, He offers the incense at the same time. And He is also (4) our High Priest. When He passed through the heavens with His own blood to make atonement, the incense, to make intercession, was not forgotten. And if it be objected that in heaven the incense was offered by the elders (Rev. v. 8), or angels (*ib.* viii. 3), we may remember that the ministry at the golden altar, which strictly appertained to the high priest alone, was also shared by other ministers of the congregation, and the angels are "ministering spirits."

So that both the altars of Judaism speak to us of Christ: the one of His death, the other of His "endless life;" the first of the "one offering," the second of the ceaseless intercession. And between them they shadowed forth the fulness and completeness of our salvation. "We have an Advocate with the Father"—this is the gospel of the incense. "We have a great High Priest"—this is the evangel of incense and sacrifice alike.

HOMILIES BY VARIOUS AUTHORS.

Ver. 25.—*Solomon's Worship.* Our text appears at first sight to be introduced into this chapter in a superfluous and arbitrary manner. It is not without good reason, however, that this record of Solomon's religious worship stands between statements about his fortifications and his fleet. We have much to learn from the Old Testament method of blending the earthly with the spiritual, and of suffusing national enterprise with religion. The verse before us, read in connexion with the statement made in ch. iii. 2, indicates that, after finishing the temple, Solomon swept away the abuses, and remedied the defects which had prevailed. He had built the temple, and now would be the leader of his people in using it. He did not consider that the erection of an altar excused him from sacrificing on it. He was not one of those who will encourage others to devotion, while they neglect their own personal responsibility. Apply this to any who contribute to a society, but withold all personal service; or aid in the celebration of worship, while their own hearts are never engaged in it. If we compare the text with 2 Chron. viii. 12, 13, we see that it was not only on the national festivals (Passover, Pentecost, and Feast of Tabernacles), but on all occasions appointed by Mosaic law, that Solomon, through the priests, presented offerings before the Lord

No allusion is made here to expiatory sacrifices (the sin offering and the trespass offering) but these, of necessity, preceded those mentioned here. All the more fitly does the text represent what we should offer when we draw near to God, through the merits of the expiation already made for us by Him who became, on our behalf, a sin offering. This verse will answer the question of conscience, "*What shall I render unto the Lord ?*"

I. THE DEDICATION OF SELF. Burnt offerings were representative and not vicarious. They represented the dedication of himself to God on the part of the worshipper. St. Paul shows us this (Romans xii. 1), "I beseech you, therefore, brethren, by the mercies of God, that ye present your bodies a living sacrifice," &c. The appropriateness of the type can be easily shown by alluding to such points as these:—1. *The sequence of the burnt offering on the expiatory sacrifice.* No burnt offering was made until a previous sin offering had been presented. The worshipper must first be brought into covenant with God. Were the burnt offering presented first, the barrier of sin between man and God would be ignored, and the idea of an atonement would be denied. Our offering of ourselves is only acceptable through the previous sacrifice of Christ. 2. *The completeness of the burnt offering.* The sacrificer laid his hands on the victim, and then it was placed whole on the altar, its death signifying the completeness of the presentation of the man, body and soul, to the Lord. Show that God has the right to demand our whole selves ; not a share in affection and thought simply. 3. *The occasions for presenting the burnt offering.* (1) *Daily* (Exod. xxix. 38—42) to show that at no time are we "our own." (2) *Doubly on the sabbath* (Num. xxviii. 9, 10). The seventh day a time for special consideration and self-consecration. (3) *On great festivals* (Num. xxviii. 11 ; xxix. 39). Times of exceptional deliverance, enrichment, &c., are seasons for renewed self-dedication. Press home the entreaty of Rom. xii. 1.

II. THE GIVING OF THANKS. Peace offerings were of various kinds, but had the same meaning. They were a presentation to God of his best gifts, a sign of grateful homage, and at the same time afforded means for the support of God's service and His servants. Flour, oil, and wine were offered with the daily burnt offering. The show-bread was renewed each sabbath day. Special offerings were made on the sabbath and other festivals. The first-fruits were presented, and corn from the threshing-floor at the annual feasts, &c. (1) *All these were of a Eucharistic nature*, and teach us to render thanks and praise to God (Heb. xiii. 15). (2) *They betokened communion with God*, for in part they were eaten by the people in His presence. (3) *They aided in the sustenance of public worship.* The priests had the breast and shoulder. See the lesson Paul draws Phil. iv. 18. (4) *They ministered to the necessities of the poor.* Peace offerings constituted great national feasts. Give examples. Show Christ's care for the poor. Allude to such verses as Heb. xiii. 16. We express thankfulness to the Lord, and acknowledgment of His goodness, by distributing to others as they have need. "Inasmuch as ye have done it unto one of the least of these, my brethren, ye have done it unto me."

III. THE OFFERING OF PRAYER. "He burnt incense upon the altar." Incense was offered morning and evening (Exod. xxx. 7, 8), and on the great day of atonement (Levit. xvi. 12). The altar of incense stood before the holy of holies in the holy place, where only the priests could stand. Sacredness and sweetness were suggested by the incense, so carefully and secretly compounded, so exclusively used in the service of God. As a symbol it denoted prayer ; taken in its broadest sense, as the outflowing of the soul in adoration, prayer, praise toward God. Refer to Psalm cxli. 2, where prayer and incense are blended as reality and symbol ; to the smoke in the temple (Isaiah vi. 3 4) ; to the people praying while Zacharias was burning incense (Luke i. 10) ; to the prayers of the saints before the throne (Rev. v. 8 ; viii. 3, 4). 1. *Prayer should be reverent.* (The incense altar was close to the holy of holies, under the immediate eye of God.) 2. *Prayer should be constant.* (Incense was perpetual. "Pray without ceasing.") 3. *Prayer should be the outcome of self-dedication.* (Incense was kindled by a live coal from the altar of burnt offering.) 4. *Prayer is accepted through the merits of the atonement.* (The horns of the altar of incense were sprinkled with blood.)—A. R.

EXPOSITION.

CHAPTER X. 1—13.

THE VISIT OF THE QUEEN OF SHEBA.—The last words of the preceding chapter spoke of Solomon's fleet, of its voyages, and the treasures it brought home. The historian now proceeds to tell of one result to which these voyages led. The fame of the king and his great undertakings was so widely diffused, and excited so much wonder and curiosity, that a queen of Arabia came, among others, to see the temple and the palaces and the many marvels of Solomon's city and court. The prediction of Solomon's prayer (ch. viii. 42) has soon had a fulfilment.

Ver. 1.—**And when the queen of Sheba** [There is no good ground for doubting that by שְׁבָא we are to understand the kingdom of Southern Arabia (Yemen). It is true that while Gen. xxv. 3 (cf. 1 Chron. i. 32) speaks of Sheba, the son of *Joktan*, one of the colonists of southern Arabia, Gen. x. 7 and 1 Chron. i. 9 mention another Sheba, the son of *Cush*, and a doubt has arisen whether this was an Arabian or an Ethiopian princess, and it is alleged that she was the latter by Josephus, who calls her "queen of Egypt and Ethopia," and by some Rabbinical writers, and in the traditions of the Abyssinian church. But the kingdoms of Sheba (שְׁבָא) and Saba (סָבָא) are entirely distinct (Psa. lxxii. 10), the latter being the name both of the capital and country of Meroë, a province of Ethopia (Jos., Ant. ii. 10. 2); while the former in like manner designates both the chief city and also the kingdom of the Sabeans (Job i. 15). This tribe would seem to have grown richer and stronger than all the other Arabian peoples by means of its commercial enterprise, and it was especially famed for its gold, gems, and spices (Ezek. xxvii. 22 ; Jer. vi. 20 ; Isa. lx. 6; Joel iii. 8; Job vi. 19 ; Psa. lxxii. 10). It is noticeable that in both kingdoms government by female sovereigns was not uncommon (cf. Acts viii. 27) ; but it is very remarkable to find any country under the rule of a queen at this early date. (The idea that either of these lands was *always* governed by queens has no real basis.) The name of this princess, according to the Koran, was *Balkis*, according to Abyssinian belief, *Maqueda*. Whether she was a widow or virgin is unknown] **heard** [Heb. *hearing*. Doubtless through the Arab traders. The record of this visit,

following immediately upon the mention of the voyages (ch. ix. 26), is a grain of evidence in favour of locating Ophir in Arabia] **of the fame** (Heb. *hearing* ; cf. ἀκοή, which also means *the thing heard, report.* Compare ἀποκάλυψις, καύχησις, &c.] **of Solomon concerning the name** [Heb. לְשֵׁם, *i.e.*, "*in relation to, in connexion with,* the name," &c. No doubt it was the house he had built יְי לְשֵׁם (cf. chs. iii. 2 ; v. 17, 18 ; viii. 17, 18, 19, 20, &c.) had made him famous. But the expression is somewhat unusual, and these words are omitted by the chronicler.

Gesenius and Ewald, however, regard the לְ as instrumental, "the fame given him by the name," &c., as Judg. vii. 18; Ezek. xii. 12, &c., and Wordsworth compares the use of ἐν in Greek. The LXX. and other versions read "the name of Solomon and the name of the Lord." But the text is on every ground to be retained. The alliteration in this verse (probably accidental) is to be noticed. There is also a slight *paronomasia*] **of the Lord, she came to prove** (LXX. πειράσαι, *to test*)] **him with hard questions** [Heb. *in riddles* ; LXX. ἐν αἰνίγμασι. The Arabian mind has ever delighted in dark sayings, enigmas, &c., and extensive collections of these have been made by Burckhardt and others (see Keil *in loc.*) According to Dius (cited in Josephus, Contra Ap. i. 17. 18) Solomon also had dialectical encounters with Hiram and with Abdemon, or, according to Menander, a younger son of Abdemon, a man of Tyre.]

Ver. 2.—**And she came to Jerusalem** [a great undertaking in those days. Our Lord lays stress on this long journey, ἐκ τῶν περάτων τῆς γῆς, Matt. xii. 42 ; Luke xi. 31] **with a very great train** [Heb. *with a very heavy force or host* (חַיִל). Thenius understands the words of an armed escort, which may well have been necessary considering the countries through which she passed, and the treasures she carried. It would also be quite in the spirit of the age that the queen should be escorted by a band of her soldiers. But it is not so certain that this idea was in the historian's mind], **with** [not in Heb.] **camels** [2 Chron. ix. 1 has "*and* camels." But the word is here explicative of the חַיִל preceding (Keil). It does not, however, decide against an armed force, as camels would be in any case required. The camel was a familiar object to the Jews (Exod. ix. 3 ; Levit. xi. 4 ; Deut. xiv. 7, &c.); but such a procession as this would create great astonishment in Jerusalem, and we may imagine how the people would line the bazaars as she passed, and the acclamations with which they would greet the queen (cf. i. 40; Matt. xxi. 9) and her swart attendants] that bare spices [Heb. *balsams;* hence spices generally; LXX. ἡδύσματα. Exod. xxv. 6; xxxv. 28; Ezek. xxvii. 22. The perfumes of Arabia are proverbial (see Herod. iii. 107—113), and Yemen is the chief spice country (Dict. Bib. i. p. 91], and very much gold [Psa. lxxii. 15. Gold is not now found in Arabia, nor are there any traces of gold mines; but Strabo and Diodorus both state that it *was* found there, and, according to the latter, in nuggets of considerable size (Dict. Bib. i. p. 707). It is quite possible, however, that much of the "gold of Arabia" came to its emporiums from other lands. This particular present was doubtless brought by the queen because she had heard of the extensive use made of it by Solomon, and of the enormous quantities he required. "Strabo relates that the Sabeans were enormously wealthy, and used gold and silver in a most lavish manner in their furniture, their utensils, and even on the walls, doors, and roofs of their houses" (Rawlinson)] and precious stones [the onyx, emerald, and turquoise are still found in Arabia, and in former times the variety was apparently much greater (Plin., Nat. Hist. xxxvii.)]; and when she was come to Solomon, she communed with him of [Heb. *spake to him*] all that was in her heart. [The words are not to be restricted, as by Keil, to riddles. There may well have been, as the earlier interpreters supposed, *religious* discourse—*gravissimas et sacras quaestiones.*

Ver. 3.—And Solomon told her [הִגִּיד is used of solving riddles in Judges xiv. 13 (Bähr), and interpreting dreams Gen. xli. 24; Dan. v. 12] all her questions [Heb. *words*]; there was not anything hid from the king, which he told her not.

Ver. 4.—And when the queen of Sheba had seen all Solomon's wisdom, and the house he had built [ver. 5 compels us to understand this of the palace, not of the temple. Josephus says she was especially astonished at the house of the forest of Lebanon],

Ver. 5.—And the meat of his table [ch. iv. 22, 23], and the sitting [" The rooms of the courtiers in attendance" (Keil). But מוֹשַׁב may mean an *assembly* (Psa. i. 1), and possibly the queen saw them when gathered together for a meal] of his servants, and the attendance [Heb. *standing.* According to Keil," the rooms of the inferior servants." But ver. 8 appears to be decisive against this

view] of his ministers [*i.e.,* those who ministered to him. The word " servants" is, perhaps, to be understood of state officers, the word "ministers" of personal attendants (as in Acts xiii. 5, &c.) That the latter were an inferior class, the " standing " shows], and their apparel [cf. Matt. vi. 29. The rich and costly dress of Eastern courtiers and attendants is sometimes furnished by the king (Gen. xlv. 22; 1 Sam. xviii. 4; 2 Kings v. 5; Dan. v. 7; Esther v. 8; 1 Macc. x. 20. Cf. Chardin, "Voyage en Perse," iii. 230], and his cupbearers [By this word Keil would understand " drinking arrangements." But see 2 Chron. ix. 4, "cupbearers (same word) and *their apparel*"], and his ascent [עֹלָתוֹ. It is somewhat doubtful whether we are to interpret this word, *ascent,* or *burnt offering.* 2 Kings xvi. 18, 1 Chron. xxvi. 16, Ezek. xl. 26 make for the former, and the chronicler has

עֲלִיָּתוֹ which undoubtedly means " ascent." But all the translations understand the word of burnt offerings—the LXX. has καὶ τὴν ὁλοκαύτωσιν—and the word, " which occurs at least 300 times in the Bible," always (with one exception) signifies burnt offering. It is objected against this interpretation (1) that we should require the plural, *i.e.,* " burnt offerings;" but this is by no means certain, as the historian may refer to one particular holocaust (see ch. ix. 25) which the queen witnessed; and (2) that the sight of burnt offerings could not have caused her any astonishment (Keil). But their prodigious *number* may surely have done so; and we are certainly to understand that Solomon was remarkable for the scale of his sacrifices. Considering, however, that the word undoubtedly means " ascent" in Ezek. xl. 26, and that it is so paraphrased by the chronicler, it is perhaps safer to retain this rendering here]; there was no more spirit in her [same expression Josh. v. 1, and cf. ii. 11. For various legends as to this queen, see Stanley, " Jewish Ch." ii. pp. 234—236].

Ver. 6.—And she said to the king, It was a true report [Heb. *Truth was the word*] that I heard in mine own land of thy acts [or *words.* Same word as above and in the next verse] and of thy wisdom.

Ver. 7.—Howbeit, I believed not the words [" Fame, as it is always a blab, so ofttimes a liar" (Bp. Hall)] until I came, and mine eyes had seen it; and behold, the half was not told me; thy wisdom and prosperity exceeded the fame [Heb. *thou hast added wisdom and good to the report*] which I heard.

Ver. 8.—Happy [Heb. *O the happiness,*

as in Psa. i. 1; ii. 12; xxxiii. 12, &c.] **are
thy men** [LXX. *wives*, γυναῖκες]; **happy are
thy servants, which stand continually before thee** [see on ch. i. 2], **and that hear
thy wisdom.**

Ver. 9.—**Blessed be the Lord thy God**
[From this mention of the name of Jehovah,
taken in connexion with Matt. xii. 42, it has
been concluded that the queen became a
convert to the faith of Israel. But this
inference is unwarranted. Polytheism permitted, and, indeed, encouraged, a full
recognition of the gods many of the different races and regions. See on ch. v. 7,
and cf. 2 Chron. ii. 12 and Ezra i. 3.
Observe, too, it is " Jehovah, *thy* God."
And it is very significant that all her gifts
and treasures were for the king; none were
offerings to the temple] **which delighted
in thee** [cf. ch. v. 7], **to set thee on the
throne of Israel; because the Lord loved
Israel for ever** [a graceful and thoroughly
Oriental compliment. This visit was as
flattering to the pride of the chosen people
as to their king], **therefore made he thee
king, to do judgment and justice.**

Ver. 10.—**And she gave the king an
hundred and twenty** [Josephus says *twenty*]
talents of gold [Psa. lxxii. 15. " The rivers
still run into the sea; to him that hath
shall be given" (Bp. Hall). As to the *talent*,
see on ch. ix. 14], **and of spices very great
store** [Heb. *much exceedingly* (Ewald, 287 c.)
" The immense abundance of spices in
Arabia . . . is noted by many writers. Herodotus says that the whole tract exhaled an
odour marvellously sweet (iii. 113). Diodorus relates that the odour was carried out
to sea to a considerable distance from the
shore (iii. 46). According to Strabo the
spice-trade of Arabia was in the hands of
two nations, the Sabeans and Gerrhaeans,
whose profits from it were so enormous that
in his time they were the two wealthiest
nations on the face of the earth (xvi. 4. 19),"
Rawlinson], **and precious stones;. there
came no more such abundance of spices
as these which the queen of Sheba gave
to king Solomon.** [Josephus states (Ant.
viii. 6. 6) that the cultivation of the balsam
in Palestine dates from this visit; the
plant having been one of the queen's
gifts.

The two following verses form a sort of
parenthesis. In speaking of the gold and
gems brought by the Arabian queen, it
occurs to the historian to state that both of
these commodities were also brought in by
the fleet. Possibly, too, the mention of the
spices reminded him of the fragrant almug
trees brought from Ophir (Bähr). But it

would rather seem that they are included as
one of the chief products of the voyage.

Ver. 11.—**And the navy of Hiram also**
[*i.e.*, built and equipped by him, ch. ix.
26—28], **that brought gold from Ophir,
brought in from Ophir great plenty of
almug trees** [In 2 Chron. ii. 8; ix. 10, called
" algum-trees." The origin and meaning
of the word are alike uncertain. By some
(see Gesen., Thes. i. p. 93) the *Al* is supposed
to be the Arabic article, as found in *Al-coran,
Al-cohol, Ad-miral,* &c., but later authorities
(see, *e. g.*, Max Müller,"Science of Language,"
p. 214) lend no support to this view. " Celsius enumerates fifteen different trees, each
of which has been supposed to have a claim
to represent the almug tree of Scripture "
(Dict. Bib. iii. Appendix, p. vi.) It is now,
however, pretty generally agreed that the
red sandal-wood (*pterocarpus sandaliorus*,
Linn.; or, according to others, *santalum
album,* the white species) is intended—a tree
which grows in India and on the coast of
Malabar. It is said that in India sandal-
wood is called *valguha* (same root); and
Stanley sees in almug the " Hebraized form
of the Deccan word for sandal." Dr.
Hooker, however, (Dict. Bib. *l.c.*) regards
the question as still undecided], **and precious stones.** [Stanley remarks on the frequent references to gold and silver and
precious stones in the Book of Proverbs
(chs. i. 9.; iii. 14, 15; viii. 10, 11; x. 20;
xvi. 16, &c.), as one indication that it belongs to the age of Solomon.]

Ver. 12.—**And the king made of the almug
trees pillars** [lit., *props*. In 2 Chron. ix.
11 we have a different word, מְסִלּוֹת (cf.
Judg. xx. 31, 32; 1 Sam. vi. 12, &c.), there
translated *stairs*. The word in the text
מִסְעָד is ἅπαξ λεγ. Keil understands
" steps with bannisters;" Bähr (after
Jarchi) " tesselated pavements;" Gesenius,
" balusters;" Thenius, " divans;" Böttcher, " benches and similar moveables."
But was not the pavement already laid, and
of cedar; and would the sanctuary have
divans, &c.?] **for the house of the Lord, and
for the king's house, harps also and psal-
teries** [also mentioned together (Psa. lxxi.
22; cviii. 2; cl. 3). They were *stringed*
instruments, but their precise shape and
character is quite uncertain. One species
of sandal-wood, or of wood closely allied to
it, is said to have been much sought after for
musical instruments] **for the singers : there
came no such almug trees, nor were seen
unto this day.**

Ver. 13.—**And king Solomon gave unto
the queen of Sheba all her desire, whatsoever she asked, beside that which Solomon
gave her of his royal bounty.** [Heb. *ac-*

cording to the hand of king Solomon. The chronicler has, " beside that which she had brought unto the king." That is to say, in addition to the fitting presents which he made in return for her gifts, he freely gave her whatsoever she asked for. To ask for a coveted thing is no breach of Oriental propriety. The Ethiopian Christians find in these words (and considering the character of Solomon and the license of that age, perhaps not altogether without reason) a basis for their belief that she bore Solomon a son, Melimelek by name, from whom, indeed, the present sovereigns of Abyssinia claim to derive their descent.] **So she turned and went to her own country, she and her servants.**

Bishop Wordsworth has remarked (p. 44) that the record of this visit disappoints us. He says, "He (Solomon) answered her hard questions. He showed her his palace . . . but we do not hear that he invited her to go up with him into the house of the Lord,"

&c. Again: " The visit of the queen of Sheba seem to have been without any spiritual result." " In like manner," he adds, "we hear nothing of any attempt on Solomon's part to improve his friendship and commercial relations with Hiram into an occasion for communicating the better merchandise of Divine truth to the Sidonians." But surely this criticism overlooks the fact that Judaism was not a missionary religion, and that the chosen people had no sort of commission to convert the heathen. It is, no doubt, a mystery; but it is a fact, that for 2,000 years the light of God's truth was, by the counsel and purpose of God, restricted within the extremely narrow confines of Israel, and that the " fulness of the time," when the Gentiles should be "fellow-heirs," was distant from Solomon's day by a whole millennium.

HOMILETICS.

Vers. 1—13.—*The Queen of Sheba.* Well may the journey of this Eastern queen have a triple mention in the sacred page (1 Kings x. ; 2 Chron. ix. ; St. Matt. xii. ; St. Luke xi.), for it is almost, if not altogether, *sui generis.* We are so familiar with the story from our infancy that we often fail to realize its true character and proportions. A woman, a princess, an Arab queen, travels some three thousand miles in search of wisdom. We have read of long voyages undertaken and of great hardships endured by men who were in search of gold. Fable tells of the search for a *golden* fleece ; history tells of many voyages to a fancied *El Dorado,* but here only, and in the case of the Magi, do we read of a traveller who *brought* gold and sought *wisdom.*

And our Lord has honoured this history—this almost romantic story—by drawing *one* of its lessons with His own hand (Matt. xii. 42). But though He has there furnished the outline, He has left it for us to fill in the colouring. And the rest of the story He has left untouched ; the other lessons we have to gather for ourselves. We have, therefore, to consider, I. The journey of the queen. II. Her rich offerings to Solomon. III. Solomon's royal presents to her.

I. As to the JOURNEY—the one point noticed by our blessed Lord. He has reminded us (1) *of its character.* She came " from the ends of the earth." (2) *Of its purpose.* It was to " hear the wisdom of Solomon." Let us collect our thoughts round these two centres, the *nature* and *object* of this enterprise.

I. THE NATURE OF THIS JOURNEY. Four particulars must be borne in mind. (1) *The length of the way.* Presuming that Sheba was Yemen (see note on ver. 1), her capital would be at no great distance from Mocha or Aden, *i.e.,* it would be some fifteen hundred miles distant from Jerusalem. But ancient journeys are not to be measured by miles, but by hours. Now both the queen and her company travelled by camels, and the camel can only go, with any degree of comfort, at a walking pace, and, like other beasts of burden, must have occasional rests. Even if they had some " swift dromedaries" for the queen, the pace must have been regulated by the sumpter camels. We may be pretty sure, therefore, that the party would not travel, on the average, more than twenty miles a day, which would give something like seventy-five days for the journey to Jerusalem, and the same for the return. (2) *Its fatigues and hardships.* Eastern queens, even of the Sabeans, were not unacquainted with luxury (note on ver. 2), and the journey through the "great and terrible wilderness" would subject this lady to many discomforts. Camel-riding is very tiring; desert-travel profoundly wearisome. Whatever comforts her "very great train" might be able to procure her, nothing could alter the blazing sun overhead, the burning sands beneath, or the utter desolation and monotony of the desert. Those who have made the journey to Sinai will have some idea what the daily life of this party was like. (3) *Its perils.* "Perils of the wilderness" (cf. Psa. xci.; Deut. viii. 15), and "perils of robbers" alike. Her course lay through the land of Ishmael, whose "hand was against every man," and she carried with her large treasure—a tempting bait to the rapacious Bedouin. True, she had an armed escort, but that would not exempt her from dangers. Nor were these "perils by the way" all. She had left her kingdom without its head. An insurrection might be fomented against her (Luke xix. 14), or a usurper might snatch her crown. And all this was (4) *undertaken by a woman.* True, she was an Arabian, and therefore presumably hardy and patient, but all the same the sex of the traveller increases our admiration, especially when we consider the estimation in which women have generally been held in the East. And she was a queen, and left a court, left her fragrant country, "Araby the blest," to plod painfully and slowly over the desert reaches, till she came to the "city of the vision of peace."

II. THE PURPOSE OF THIS UNDERTAKING. Many sovereigns have left their homes at the head of "a very great train" both before and since her day, but with what different objects in view. They have swept across continents—the Rameses, the Shishaks, the Alexanders, the Tamerlanes of history, but not for wisdom. Theirs was no peaceful or kindly mission. Some, like Peter the Great, have visited foreign courts for the sake of advancing the commerce, &c., of their country. Some, like the Persian Shah recently, have travelled far to see the wonders of the world, and to taste of its pleasures; but she came to "prove Solomon with hard questions," to "commune with him of all that was in her heart," to

> "reason high
> Of providence, foreknowledge, will, and fate,
> Fixed fate, freewill, foreknowledge absolute."

It is clear that to her "*wisdom*" was "the principal thing," and she brought gold and *rubies* (Job xxviii. 18; Prov. iii. 15; viii. 11) to obtain it. She is like the "merchantman seeking goodly pearls." She has found one pearl of great price, and she will give all that she has to possess it. True, she *saw* the wonders of Solomon's court, but she came to *hear* his wisdom. She envied his courtiers, not because of their places, palaces, &c., but because they stood before him (ver. 8) and heard his words.

And our Saviour has said that this conduct will condemn the men of *His* generation. It were easy to show how. But it will be more to the point if we consider how it may condemn the men of our own time.

1. *Christ is "more* (πλεῖον) *than Solomon."* Solomon was the wisest of men; Christ was "the wisdom of God." Solomon, a great king; Christ, "King of kings and Lord of lords" (Rev. xvii. 4). Compare the Song of Solomon with the Beatitudes; the Proverbs with the Sermon on the Mount; Solomon's end and Christ's death. We should not dare to compare them had not He done it before. 2. *Christ is here.* No need to cross deserts or continents to find Him. "Say not in thine heart, Who shall ascend into heaven? (that is, to bring Christ down from above)," &c. (Rom. x. 6, 7). And say not, "True, He was present in those Galilean synagogues, in those streets of Jerusalem, but He is not *here.*" His own words affirm the contrary (Matt. xxviii. 20; xviii. 20, &c.) He is present everywhere.

> "One Spirit, His
> Who wore the platted crown with bleeding brows,
> Fills universal nature."

But more especially is he present in His Church, His word, His sacraments. 3. Christ has *come from the uttermost parts of the world* to us. It is not *we* who have to leave a kingdom. He has left His that he may "appoint unto us a kingdom."

> " Thy Father's home of light ;
> Thy rainbow-circled throne,
> Were left for earthly night,
> For wanderings sad and lone."

And yet men will not listen to Him, will not learn of Him. It is said that ninety-five per cent. of our labouring classes do not statedly attend any place of Christian worship. And of those who do, how many do His bidding? In the great assize all these will meet the Queen of the South. She will witness of the journey she took, of the sacrifices she made, of the risks she incurred, to sit at the feet of Solomon. She will tell of Solomon's "ascent," &c., and she will put to shame and everlasting contempt those to whom the words and wisdom, the sacrifice and ascension of the Lord were unholy or indifferent things (Heb. x. 29).

And not the Queen of the South alone. The kings of the East, Melchior, Jasper, Balthasar—so tradition calls them—they too came a long journey to see the child Christ. And how many pagans in Africa, in India, in the islands of the sea, have gone long miles just to hear one sermon from the passing missionary? Will not all these condemn the men of this generation?

III. HER OFFERINGS TO SOLOMON. It was the custom of those days to approach king, seer, &c., with a present (ver. 25 ; Psa. lxxii. 10 ; 1 Sam. ix. 7 ; Judg. vi. 18). And she did not come empty. We read of " camels bearing spices," of 120 talents of gold, &c. (ver. 10). Now observe: (1) *She gave of what she had.* Her country produced or imported gold; it produced spices and precious stones (note on ver. 2). Other visitors to Solomon gave garments, horses, &c. (ver. 25). These she had not, but she gave what she could (2 Cor. viii. 12). (2) *She gave what Solomon needed.* We know how much gold he required ; not for the temple only—that was apparently completed—but for his great and varied undertakings. She brought 120 talents of the " gold of Arabia "—literally the ransom of a province (ch. ix. 14). She brought spices—in ver. 15, we read of " the traffick of the *spice* merchants "—and precious stones—in 2 Chron. iii. 6 we find that Solomon garnished the house with these. So that, like Hiram, she helped to prepare a shrine for the Holy One of Israel. (3) *She gave generously.* Her munificence was unexampled—" very much gold " (ver. 2). " There came no more such abundance of spices," &c. (ver. 10).

And shall not her *gifts*, too, condemn our parsimony? For Christ, the Divine Solomon, has need of our spices and silver and gold. He too is building a temple (1 Peter ii. 5). He too plants store cities and treasures in His realm. He would have the whole round world girdled with Christian temples. He would make it one vast " Paradise " (Eccles. ii. 4, 5). And He needs our agency and our offerings. He wants the perfume of *sacrifice* on our part (Phil. iv. 18 ; Eph. v. 2 ; 2 Cor. ii. 15). The Queen of the South did not offer to Solomon of that which cost her nothing. But how seldom is the widow's mite offered to our king. " All these of their abundance have cast in," &c. (Luke xxi. 3). Compared with her gift how miserable are our subscriptions and offertories. Note : There is a striking similarity between her gifts and those of the Magi. Both too were offered to a king.

IV. SOLOMON'S GIFTS TO HER. She was not the loser either by her long journey or her costly presents. A prince like Solomon could not permit her to make sacrifices. *Noblesse oblige.* His generosity must exceed hers. So he gave her "all her desire," "whatsoever she asked" "according to the hand of the king" (ver. 13, Heb.) We see here a picture of the recompenses of our God. "According to his riches in glory" (Phil. iv. 19). "Exceeding abundantly above all that we ask or think" (Eph. iii. 20). "Ask and it shall be given you" (Matt. vii. 7). His gifts too are "according to the hand of a king," and what a king! He cannot remain in any man's debt. "A cup of cold water only" He will abundantly recompense.

HOMILIES BY VARIOUS AUTHORS.

Vers. 1—3.—*The Queen of the South.* This incident is remarkable as the only one in the reign of Solomon to which reference is made in the New Testament. Solomon is twice spoken of by our Lord in His recorded discourses. In one case his royal magnificence is declared inferior to the beauty with which God has clothed the "lilies of the field." "Even Solomon in all his glory was not arrayed like one of these" (Matt. vi. 29). Art can never vie with nature. What loveliness of form or hue that human skill can produce is comparable with that of the petals of a flower ? What is all the glory with which man may robe himself to that which is the product of the creative finger of God ? In the other case, it is the wisdom of Solomon that our Lord refers to, as having its wide-spread fame illustrated by the visit of the Queen of Sheba, and as being surpassed by the higher revelation of truth in Himself. "The queen of the south shall rise up in the judgment," &c. (Matt. xii. 42). The interest and importance of this incident is greatly heightened by its thus finding a place in the discourses of Christ. In itself there is no very deep meaning in it. It supplies few materials for high moral or spiritual teaching. The interchange of civilities between two Oriental monarchs is related by the historian with innocent pride, as setting forth the surpassing grandeur of the king whose reign was to him the golden age of his own nation's life. There is something of a romantic charm in it, too, that naturally gave rise to fanciful traditions being added to the biblical story. But beyond this it is an event of no great moment. This use of it, however, by our Lord lifts it out of the region of the commonplace, gives it other than a mere secular meaning, makes it an important channel of Divine instruction. Every name is honoured by association with His. Every incident becomes clothed with sacred interest when made to illustrate the relation of human souls to Him. Let us look at these two persons, then, in the light of the New Testament reference to their interview.

I. Solomon, in his wisdom, a type of the "greater" Christ. The distinctive personal characteristic of Solomon was his "wisdom." The fame of it is regarded by some as marking the uprising of a new and hitherto unknown power in Israel. Whence came this new phenomenon? We trace it to a Divine source. "The Lord gave unto David this wise son" (ch. v. 7). "God gave Solomon wisdom and understanding exceeding much" (ch. iv. 29). No doubt the extended intercourse with surrounding nations that he established was the beginning of a new life to Israel, bringing in a flood of new ideas and interests. This supplied materials for his wisdom but did not create it. It was not learnt from Egypt, or the "children of the East." It was a Divine gift, that came in response to his own prayer (ch. iii. 9). 1. One broad feature that strikes us in Solomon's wisdom is its remarkable versatility, the variety of its phases, the way in which its light played freely on all sorts of subjects. It dealt with the objects and processes of nature. It was a kind of natural science. He has been called "the founder of Hebrew science," the "first of the world's great naturalists." "He spake of trees, from the cedar tree," &c. (ch. iv. 33). One would like to know what the range and quality of his science really was ; but the Bible, existing as it does for far other than scientific purposes, does not satisfy our curiosity in this respect. It dealt with moral facts and problems —a true practical philosophy of life ; its proper ends and aims, its governing principles, the meaning of its experiences, its besetting dangers and possible rewards. It dealt with the administration of national affairs. This is seen in his assertion of the principle of eternal righteousness as the law by which the ruler of men must himself be ruled. His wisdom lay in the gift of "an understanding heart to judge the people and discern between good and evil," and the people "feared the king, for they saw that the wisdom of God was in him to do judgment" (ch. iv. 29). We are thus reminded of the unity of nature and of human life. Truth is one, whether in thought, feeling, or conduct, in things private or public, secular or spiritual. Wisdom is the power that discerns and utilizes the innermost truth of all things, finds out and practically applies whatever is essentially Divine. 2. Solomon's wisdom assumed various forms of expression : the Proverbial form, as in the "Book of Proverbs ; " the Poetic form, as in his "Songs" and "Psalms ; " the Socratic form, by question and answer, riddles—"dark sayings"—and the interpretation thereof. It is in this latter form that his wisdom here appears. Tradition says that Hiram engaged with him in this "cross questioning," and was worsted in the encounter; so here the queen of Sheba came "to prove him with hard questions," and "communing with him of all that was in her heart she found that he could tell her all her questions," &c. By all this we are led to think of "One greater than Solomon." (1) "Greater," inasmuch as He leads men to wisdom of a higher order. Solomon is the most secular of the inspired writers of the Old Testament. Divine things are approached by him, as it were, on the lower, earthly side. A prudential tone is given to the counsels of religion, and vice is set forth not so much as wickedness but as "folly." Think of the marked difference between the utterances of Solomon's wisdom and the sublime spiritual elevation of David's psalms. And when we come to Christ's teaching, what immeasurably loftier heights and deeper depths of Divine truth are here! Redemption, holiness, immortality, are His themes—the deeper "mysteries of the kingdom of heaven ; " "in him are hid all the treasures of wisdom and knowledge" (Col. ii. 3). (2) "Greater," inasmuch as the Divine fount of wisdom must needs be infinitely superior to any mere human channel through which it flows. Solomon was after all but a learner, not a master. His were but guesses at truth. Christ's were the authoritative utterances of the incarnate "Word." Solomon spoke according to the limited measure of the spirit of truth in him. Christ spoke out of His own infinite fulness. "God giveth not the Spirit by measure unto Him" (John iii. 34). Whence, indeed, did Solomon's wisdom come but from Him, the true fontal "Light that lighteth every man that cometh into the world"? The words that the wise in every age have spoken were but dim, dawning rays of the light that broke in a glorious day upon the world when He, the Sun of Righteousness, arose.

II. THE QUEEN OF SHEBA, IN HER SEARCH AFTER WISDOM, AS AN EXAMPLE FOR OURSELVES. All the motives that actuated her in this long pilgrimage from the far-off corner of Arabia we know not. Mere curiosity, commercial interest, personal vanity may have had something to do with it. But the words of the narrative suggest that it was mainly an honest thirst for knowledge, and specially for clearer light on highest matters of human interest. Learn (1) The nobility of a simple, earnest, restless search after truth. (2) The grateful respect which a teachable spirit will feel towards one who can unveil the truth to it. (3) The joyous satisfaction of soul that springs from the discovery of the highest truth. How much does such an example as this in the realms of heathen darkness rebuke the spiritual dulness and indifference of those who with the Light of Life shining gloriously upon them in the person of Christ refuse to welcome it, and walk in it! "Many shall come from the east and the west," &c. (Matt. viii. 11, 12).—W.

Vers. 1—13.—*The Queen of Sheba.* The suggestiveness of Solomon's intercourse with surrounding nations. His magnanimity was as remarkable as his magnificence. His broad policy stood out in striking contrast with the narrowness of some of his contemporaries and successors. It was one evidence of his divinely inspired wisdom. In some respects his enlightenment puts to shame modern diplomacy. Trace his relations with the king of Tyre and the queen of Sheba. These were not exceptionally treated by the wise-hearted ruler. His country was open to the commerce of surrounding peoples, and his court free to all who would live in amity with him. Indicate the typical nature of his kingdom—the golden age of God's people. Apply to the reign of Him who said, "A greater than Solomon is here!" Remarks on the position and the commerce of the land from which this great queen came.

Her conduct is full of suggestions for us—

I. HER COMING SHOWS THE PAINS THOSE SHOULD TAKE WHO ARE SEARCHING FOR TRUE WISDOM. The journey was long, arduous, costly. It may have raised opposition amongst the people she ruled. In spite of all she came. Give examples of men who in old time travelled far in search of wisdom, visiting schools of philosophy, astrologers, and sages, consulting oracles like that at Delphi. Not less is demanded of men in our days who investigate natural phenomena. Instances abound of travellers who have laid down life, as did Franklin and Livingstone, in journeys of discovery; of surgeons and physicians who have run personal risk to learn by crucial experiment a means of cure; of scientific discoverers who have sacrificed time and effort to make sure of one fact, or establish one law, &c. In contrast with all this how small the effort to win true riches, to know essential truth. Many are content with hearsay evidence. The queen of Sheba was not. At any cost she would see and know for herself. Perhaps it was with some remembrance of her visit that Solomon wrote Prov. ii. 3—5 : "If thou criest after knowledge, and liftest up thy voice for understanding; if thou seekest her as silver, and searchest for her as for hid treasures; then thou shalt understand the fear of the Lord, and find the knowledge of God." Compare this with the parable of the merchant seeking goodly pearls (Matt. xiii. 45, 46). See also Col. ii. 3.

II. Her confession expresses the feeling of those who have come to One greater than Solomon. "The half was not told me" (vers. 6, 7). St. Paul speaks of "the unsearchable riches of Christ; " of "the excellency of the knowledge of Christ," &c. In proportion as men really know Him, and live near Him, does He appear more winsome and worthy. Cite the utterances of such men as Bernard, Wesley, &c. Their words fall from our lips in song, yet they seem extravagant to us on our low level of religious life, and at our sad distance from Christ. Such bursts of praise we may use as tests of our devotion. Christ has not changed, but too often His people see Him from afar. Any one who is living near the Lord can say, "The half was not told me" of Thy love and glory.

III. Her offering suggests the presentation we should make to our King. Read verse 10. Draw out the parallel between this and the coming of the Magi (Matt. ii.), when they fell down and worshipped the child Jesus, and opened their treasures and presented to Him gifts—gold and frankincense and myrrh.

> " Say, shall we yield Him, in costly devotion,
>   Odours of Edom and offerings Divine ;
> Gems of the mountain, and pearls of the ocean,
>   Myrrh from the forest, or gold from the mine ?
>
> " Vainly we offer each ample oblation ;
>   Vainly with gifts would his favour secure ;
> Richer, by far, is the heart's adoration ;
>   Dearer to God are the prayers of the poor."

See Isa. i. 12 ; Psa. xl. 6, &c.

IV. Her entertainment reminds us of the welcome given by our Lord. 1. *Like Solomon* (ver. 3) *Christ answers our questions.* He knew His disciples "were desirous to ask Him," so they needed not even to frame their questions. Unspoken prayers are heard. 2. *Like Solomon* (ver. 5) *Christ reveals His glory.* The transfiguration, the last talk with the apostles, the apocalypse, &c. 3. *Like Solomon* (ver. 13) *Christ loads us with benefits.* Pardon, peace, strength, joy, &c.—of greater worth than gold and precious stones. These material, those imperishable.

Let the earnestness of this queen rebuke our sloth and unbelief. "The queen of the south shall rise up in the judgment with this generation, and shall condemn it : for she came from the uttermost parts of the earth to hear the wisdom of Solomon, and behold, a greater than Solomon is here" (Matt. xii. 42).—A. R.

EXPOSITION.

CHAPTER X. 14—29.

Solomon's wealth, pomp, and power.— The visit of the Queen of Sheba, in itself a striking proof of the fame and greatness of Solomon, is followed by a description of his revenues, his throne, and various other particulars of his wealth and magnificence, some of which are related here because they were the products of the voyages of that same fleet which had been the means of acquainting the queen with Solomon and his glory.

Ver. 14.—**Now the weight of gold that**

came to Solomon in one year [probably one particular and exceptional year, probably also the year of the queen's visit, not year by year (Wordsworth, *al.*), as the Vulgate (*per singulos annos*). One fleet only came home from its voyage after three years, and the gold would hardly weigh precisely 666 talents year by year] **was six hundred threescore and six talents of gold.** [The correspondence with the number of the beast (Rev. xiii. 18 ; cf. Ezra ii. 13) is in all probability not altogether accidental. It is possible, *i.e.*, that the number of the beast is a reminiscence of this number of talents. For we may surely see in this statement of Solomon's prodigious wealth an indication of his worldliness, the turning-point, perhaps, in his estrangement from God. " The love of money " may have been the root of all his evil. It is certainly remarkable that from this time forward his career is one of steady declension. It is also remarkable that while he is here represented to us as a " royal merchant," the mark of the beast is on the *buyers* and *sellers* (Rev. xiii. 17). But see " Expositor," May, 1881. It is, of course, possible that the number has been corrupted, but, on the other hand, it may have been recorded, partly because of the singularity of the sum total. The 666 talents include the receipts from all sources—taxes, tribute, and voyages—with the exception made presently (ver. 15). Rawlinson quotes Keil (in his earlier edition) as estimating this amount at £3,646,350. But in his later work, Keil puts it in round numbers at two and a half millions (17,000,000 thalers), while Mr. Poole calculates it at about £8,000,000. These widely varying figures are instructive, as showing that both estimates are little more than guesswork. We do not know the value of the Hebrew talent, nor, indeed, can it ever be rightly appraised until we know its purchasing power. The *denarius, e.g.,* is generally valued at 8½d. (or 7½d.) because it contained some 58 grains of pure silver, but its real *value* was nearer three shillings, inasmuch as it was a fair wage for a day's work on the land (Matt. xx. 2). In any case, it is clear that this sum should hardly be compared with the *annual* revenue of other Oriental empires, as by Rawlinson (see above).

Ver 15.—**Beside that he had of the merchantmen** [The root תּוּר signifies to *wander* or *travel about.* In Num. xiii. 16, 17, it is used of *spies.* It may here be applied to persons who travelled for purposes of trade ; but the versions differ very materially in their rendering of the word ; the LXX. understanding it of *tribute* (τῶν φόρων τῶν ὑποτεταγμένων) ; the Chaldee, Syriac, and Arabic of *artizans* ; the Vulgate of *ambassadors.* And the word is nowhere else used

of traders. For the construction, see Ewald 287*e*], **and of the traffick** [it is noteworthy that no such word is used before הַתָּרִים above] **of the spice** [not in Heb.] **merchants** [רָכַל is akin to רָגַל. Like the preceding word, the primary meaning is to *go about* (רֶגֶל *foot*) ; hence, to *trade.* It is probable that Solomon's great commercial enterprises were conducted for his own benefit, *i.e.*, that the merchants were little more than agents, who bought and sold for the king. Such is the custom of Eastern kings (Kitto)], **and of all the kings of Arabia** [הָעֶרֶב is very variously interpreted. According to Gesenius it means *foreigners*, and he would understand " foreign kings who made an alliance with the Israelites," and so the Chaldee. Keil: " the kings of the mixed population" (mentioned Exod. xii. 38. Cf. Jer. l. 37; Neh. xiii. 3). Perhaps the words are best explained by Jer. xxv. 24: " The kings of Arabia (עֶרֶב) and . . . of the mingled people (עֶרֶב) that dwell in the desert," *i.e.*, the desert of *Arabia deserta*, bordering on Palestine. The chronicler here gives us עֶרָב, *i.e.*, not the Arabia of the geographers, but the tract of country south and east of Palestine, as far as the Red Sea (Gesenius). No doubt these kings, who were great sheepmasters, paid their tribute in flocks of sheep and goats (2 Chron. xvii. 11 ; 2 Kings iii. 4], **and of the governors of the country.** [The word פַּחוֹת (cf. ch. xx. 24) is a foreign word, perhaps Sanskrit, apparently borrowed by the Jews from the Persians. It is used of Tatnai (Ezra v. 6), of Zerubbabel (Haggai i. 1), and of Nehemiah (Neh. v. 14). Probably our author, in whose day it was a familiar and well-understood word, substituted it for some older Hebrew designation. But the office and character of these " governors " is more difficult to define than the name. Rawlinson thinks that, in some parts of the empire, the kings —the " empire of Solomon," he observes, " was in the main a *congeries* of small kingdoms " — " had been superseded by governors." But it seems as natural to understand the term of the twelve prefects mentioned in chap. iv., who were " the governors of the land," or of similar officers in the different outposts of the kingdom. We know that the contributions which passed through their hands were furnished *in kind ;* hence, perhaps, it is that this income is distinguished from the gold of ver. 14.

Ver. 16.—**And king Solomon made two hundred targets** [צִנָּה, from a root which signifies *protect*, a large oblong shield, which covered the entire person (Psa. v. 12), θυρεός. *scutum.* See 1 Sam. xvii. 7, 41. The LXX. here reads δόρατα, *i.e.*, spears] **of beaten gold** [The authorities are divided as to the meaning of שָׁחוּט, here translated *beaten.* This rendering is supported by Bähr and Keil (after Kimchi), but Gesenius understands *mixed* gold. Rawlinson infers from the *weight* that the shields were only plated (shields were commonly made of wood, covered with leather). But whether they were solid or not does not decide the question whether the gold was pure or alloyed. " Shields of gold " are mentioned 2 Sam. viii. 7 ; 1 Macc. vi. 39] : **six hundred shekels** [Heb. omits *shekels*, as elsewhere, Gen. xxiv. 22; xxxvii. 28; Judg. viii. 26, &c. There were apparently two kinds of shekel, the Mosaic and the royal (for the latter see 2 Sam. xiv. 26). The former was twice as much as the latter, but there is no agree ment amongst commentators as to the weight or value of either. Nor can we be certain which is indicated here. Thenius decides for the former, and estimates the weight of the gold on each target to be 17½ lbs., and the value to be 6000 thalers (£900), or, according to Keil, 5000 thalers (£750). Keil, however, inclines to the belief that the royal shekel is meant, in which case the weight would be 9 lbs., and the value about £400. Bähr, however, estimates the gold at no more than £78 (523 thalers)] **of gold went to one target.**

Ver. 17.—**And he made three hundred shields** [portable shields (*peltas*, Vulgate) adapted for use in hand-to-hand encounters (2 Chron. xii. 9, 10 ; cf. 2 Sam. i. 21). That these were much smaller shields is clear from the text. These shields were borne by the royal body-guard on great occasions (ch. xiv. 27). They were taken away by Shishak (*ib.* ver. 26)] **of beaten gold ; three pound** [מָנֶה, μνᾶ, *mina.* As 2 Chron. ix. 16 has here 300 shekels, it follows that the *maneh* = 100 shekels. From Ezek. xlv. 12, however, it would seem that there were *manehs* of different value] **of gold went to one shield** [*i.e.*, half as much as to the target] ; **and the king put them in** [Heb. *gave them to*] **the house of the forest of Lebanon** [ch. vii. 2. They would certainly be suspended on the walls, but whether on the inside or the outside is not quite certain, and the text affords us no means of deciding. We know that elsewhere shields were suspended outside the walls of armouries, &c. " At Tyre the beauty of the place was thought to consist in the splendour and variety of the shields of all nations hung on its walls (Ezek. xxvii. 10, 11). In Rome the temple of Bellona was studded with them. In Athens, the round marks where

they hung can still be traced on the walls of the Parthenon. There were also arms hung round the walls of the second temple (Jos., Ant. xv. 11. 3)," Stanley. It is supposed that along with those made by Solomon were hung the shields taken by David from the Syrians, as according to 2 Sam. viii. 7, LXX., these latter also were carried off by Shishak. It has been inferred from Cant. iv. 4 that these also were 500 in number, and that the entire thousand were suspended on a part of the house of the forest of Lebanon known as the Tower of David ; cf. Isa. xxii. 8 ; Psa. xlvii. 9] .

The historian now proceeds to describe the great feature of another of Solomon's palaces. As the house of the forest of Lebanon was distinguished by the golden shields which emblazoned and glorified its walls, so was " the porch of judgment " (ch. vii. 7) by the chryselephantine throne.

Ver. 18.—**Moreover the king made a great throne** [Heb. *seat.* The use of a chair where the custom of the country is to squat on the ground, or to recline on a divan, is always a mark of dignity. See 2 Kings iv. 10 ; Prov. ix. 14] **of ivory** [Heb. *tooth.* Below in ver. 22 we have *elephant's tooth.* It is generally thought that this " throne of the house of David " (Psa. cxxii. 5) was of wood, veneered with ivory, as was the practice in Assyria (Rawlinson, " Ancient Monarchies," i. p. 463), and in the chryselephantine statues of the Greeks (Paus. ii. 4. 1; vi. 25. 4, &c.) Bähr says there is no more necessity for believing this throne to have been of solid ivory than the "ivory house " mentioned in ch. xxii. 39. Cf. Psa. xlv. 8 ; Amos iii. 15 ; vi. 4. But there is surely this difference between them, that the palace could not possibly be constructed entirely of ivory, whereas the throne might be, and some of the thrones of India have been (Rawlinson)], **and overlaid it with the best** [מוּפָז, from the root פָּז, *separavit* = *aurum depuratum.* The chronicler explains the word by טָהוֹר (2 Chron. ix. 17)] **gold.** [It is very unlikely that the gold entirely covered and concealed the ivory, especially if the latter was merely a veneer. Keil and Bähr consider that the gold was laid on the wood and the ivory inserted between the plates, but the text does not speak of over-laying with ivory, but of overlaying ivory with gold. And the presumption is that the ivory was solid. In the Greek statues both ivory and gold were applied in *laminae*, the former representing the flesh, the latter the drapery.]

Ver. 19.—**The throne had six steps** [" The characteristic feature in the royal throne was its elevation" (Dict. Bib. iii. p. 1493) ; cf. Isa. vi. 1], **and the top** [Heb. *head*] **of the throne was round behind** [same word ch. vii. 23, 24. Thenius and Bähr understand it of an arched or rounded canopy attached to the back ; Keil supposes that the back was arched or rounded in form]: **and there were stays** [Heb. *hands, i.e.,* arms] **on either side on the place of the seat** [see drawing of Assyrian throne in Layard's " Nineveh," ii. 301 ; Dict. Bib. iii. p. 1494], **and two lions** [probably of wood overlaid with gold. Cf. Jer. x. 3, 4] **stood beside the stays.**

Ver. 20.—**And twelve lions stood there on the one side and on the other, upon the six steps** [It is somewhat doubtful whether there were twelve or fourteen lions in all. Most commentators assume that there were fourteen, and the text will certainly bear that construction. But it is altogether more likely that there were twelve ; that is to say, that the two lions on the topmost step are the two mentioned in the preceding verse as " standing beside the stays," otherwise there would have been four lions on that step. And we all know that *twelve* had a significance such as could not attach to any other number (Bähr, Symbolik, i. 201—205 ; ii. 133, 423). It would signify that all the tribes had an interest in the royal house (cf. ch. xii. 16 ; 2 Sam. xx. 1) ; and a right of approach to the throne (cf. ch. xviii. 31). The lion, a familiar emblem of sovereignty among many nations, had an especial appropriateness in this case, as being the symbol of the tribe of Judah (Gen. xlix. 9 ; cf. Num. xxiii. 24 ; xxiv. 9). We are to see in them partly "symbols of the ruler's authority" (Keil), and partly, perhaps, they represented the twelve tribes as guardians of the throne. "The king mounted between figures of lions to his seat on the throne, and sat between figures of lions upon it" (Wordsworth). Thrones somewhat similar to this in character, but much less magnificent, are represented on the Assyrian monuments. The historian might justly add] : **there was not the like made** [Heb. *not made so*] **in any kingdom.**

Ver. 21.—**And all king Solomon's drinking vessels were of gold** [as were those of Assyria and Babylon. This lavish display of wealth was characteristic of Oriental courts. Rawlinson quotes Chardin's description of the splendour of the court of Persia, " *Tout est d'or massif*," &c., and adds, " Both Symes and Yule note a similar use of gold utensils by the king of Ava (Symes, p. 372 ; Yule, p. 84) "], **and all the vessels of the house of the forest of Lebanon were of pure gold** [סָגוּר ; see on ch. vi. 20.

LXX. χρυσίῳ συγκεκλεισμένα. This immense quantity of gold is quite paralleled in the accounts of profane writers. " Sardanapalus, when Nineveh was besieged, had 150 golden bedsteads, 150 golden tables, a million talents of gold, ten times as much silver, &c. (Ctesias, ap. Athenaeus, xii. p. 29). No less than 7170 talents of gold were used for the vessels and statues of the temple of Bel in Babylon. . . Alexander's pillage of Ectabana was estimated at 120,000 talents of gold," &c. (Bähr, *in loc.*)]; **none were of silver** [Heb. *none silver*. The Marg., " there was no silver in them," *i.e.*, they were unalloyed, is a misapprehension of the true meaning]: **it was nothing accounted of in the days of Solomon.**

Ver. 22.—**For** [Reason why silver was so lightly esteemed. It was because of the prodigious quantity both of gold and silver brought in by the fleet] **the king had at sea a navy of Tarshish** [It has been much disputed (1) whether this was a second fleet, or the same as that mentioned ch. ix. 26—28, as trading to Ophir, and (2) whether this fleet, if it were not the same, went to Ophir or to Tartessus in Spain. Keil and Bähr contend that there was but one fleet, first, because there is no mention of a second fleet at ch. ix. 28, and, secondly, because the cargoes were practically the same. I incline (with Rawlinson, *al.*) to think there were two separate navies, for the following reasons : (1) The expression " navy of Tarshish " (in 2 Chron. ix. 21 expanded into " ships *going to* Tarshish," which Keil and Bähr are compelled to set aside as a mistake on the part of the writer), taken in connexion with the following words, " with (עִם, *together with, as well as*) the navy of Hiram " (*i.e.*, as we conclude from ver. 11, the navy *manned*, or, it may be, *owned*, by Hiram) points to a separate fleet ; (2) the cargoes, so far from being the same, strike me as being altogether diverse. The Ophir fleet brought in "gold, almug trees, and precious stones." The navy of Tarshish " gold and silver, ivory, apes, and peacocks." See below. (3) Even if we understand here by the " navy of Hiram " a Phœnician fleet, still a second fleet is indicated. But this leads us to consider the destination of these ships. The term, " fleet of Tarshish," does not in itself prove anything, for the expression, " ships of Tarshish," is almost a synonym for " merchant vessels." In ch. xxii. 48 we read, " Jehoshaphat made ships of Tarshish *to go to Ophir*," and they " were broken at Ezion-geber " (cf. Psa. xlviii. 7 ; Jonah i. 3). It is probable that in Jewish lips the words were a *nomen generale* for all vessels going long voyages (Isa.

ii. 16; Psa. xlviii. 7; compare our "East Indiaman," "Greenlander "). But the words " in the sea," בַּיָּם, are most naturally understood of that ocean which the Jews called *par excellence* "*the* sea," or " the great sea " (Num. xxxiv. 6, 7), *i.e.*, the Mediterranean, though the term הַיָּם is undoubtedly used of the Red Sea, the Sea of Galilee, and the Dead Sea. And the more so as we know that the Tyrians had an extensive commerce with Tartessus, which was a great emporium of trade from the earliest times. Bähr objects that " no gold is found in Spain, but few peacocks, and little ivory ; " but Rawlinson, on the other hand, affirms that " Spain had the richest silver mines known in the ancient world, and had a good deal of gold also " (Plin., Nat. Hist. iii. 4), while " apes and ivory were produced by the opposite coast of Africa " (Herod. iv. 191. As to peacocks see below). And it is a powerful argument in favour of Tartessus that it is the plentifulness of *silver* in Solomon's days has suggested this reference to the fleet. For though silver "was found in the land of the Nabatæans, according to Strabo, xvi. 784 " (Keil), yet it was to Tartessus that the ancient world was chiefly indebted for its supplies of that metal. On the whole, therefore, it seems probable that a second fleet, trading with the Mediterranean seaports, is here described. And Psa. lxxii. 10 is distinctly in favour of this conclusion. When Ewald says (" Hist. Israel," iii. 263) that the Phœnicians would hardly tolerate a rival in the Mediterranean, he surely forgets that they had been admitted by the Jews to share the trade of Ophir] **with the navy of Hiram ; once in three years** [This period agrees better with a voyage to Spain than to Southern Arabia. And if we understand it of Spanish voyages, it removes one difficulty in the way of placing Ophir in Arabia. It has also been urged that " the Hebrews reckoned parts of years and days as whole ones " (Kitto) ; but this hardly would apply to the expression " *once* in three years "] **came the navy of Tarshish, bringing gold and silver, ivory** [Heb. *tooth of elephants*, LXX. ὀδόντες ἐλεφάντινοι. It is noteworthy that the name for elephant used here is derived from the Sanskrit (Gesen.), and an argument has been drawn hence in favour of placing Ophir in India, and of identifying the Tarshish fleet with the navy of Ophir. But such conclusions are extremely precarious. The name may have first come to the Jews from India, in which case it would be retained, from whatever quarter the commodity was subsequently derived. See Rawlinson, p. 546], **and apes** [קוֹף is in like manner identified by Gesenius, *al.*, with the Sanskrit *kapi*. Sir J. Emerson Tennant (" Ceylon," ii. p. 102) says " the terms by which these articles (ivory, apes, and peacocks) are designated in the Hebrew Scriptures are identical with the Tamil names by which some of them are called in Ceylon to the present day "], **and peacocks.** [So the the ancients interpret the original word, though some of the moderns would understand " parrots." But the root כבי appears in several Aryan tongues (cf. ταώς, from ταϝως, and *pavo*) as indicating the peacock (Gesen., Max Müller, *al.*) which originally came from India. Whether it was also found in Africa is uncertain. Aristophanes (Birds, 485) says, καλεῖται Περσικὸς ὄρνις. Wordsworth very justly sees in the mention of these curious beasts and birds a symptom of declension in simplicity and piety, a token that " wealth had brought with it luxury and effeminacy, and a frivolous, vainglorious love for novel and outlandish objects."

Ver. 23.—**So King Solomon exceeded all the kings of the earth for riches and wisdom** [Cf. ch. iii. 13. " There is something ominous of evil here. Riches are put *before* wisdom. This was not the case in the beginning of Solomon's reign (ch. iii. 11) " —Wordsworth.

Ver. 24.—**And all the earth sought to** [Heb. *sought the face* of] **Solomon, to hear his wisdom which God had put in his heart** [*i.e.*, mind. Cf. ch. iv. 34].

Ver. 25.—**And they brought** [Heb. *and these* (visitors were) *bringing*] **every man his present** [It is doubtful whether we are to understand by this word *tribute*, or *gifts*. The succeeding words, " a rate year by year," would seem to imply the former ; the fact that the visitors came not as subjects, but to " hear the wisdom," &c., the latter. Bähr understands that the presents " were repeated year by year, so highly had Solomon risen in estimation." But even this supposition does not explain the " rate"] **vessels of silver, and vessels of gold, and garments** [cf. Gen. xlv. 22 ; 2 Kings v. 26 ; Ezra ii. 69], **and armour** [rather, " *arms*, *weapons* " (Gesen.) Ewald understands *perfume* ; LXX. στακτὴν, *i.e.*, oil of myrrh], **and spices** [cf. ver. 10], **horses and mules** [see on ch. i. 33], **a rate year by year** [Heb. *the matter of a year in his year*].

The remaining verses of this chapter, which, in the account of the chronicler, find a place at the end of the first chapter of his second book, repeat some of the information already given in chs. iv. 26 and ix. 19, and furnish a few additional particulars as to the wealth and commerce of the king.

Ver. 26.—**And Solomon gathered together his chariots and horsemen, and he had a thousand and four hundred chariots** [these words have an important bearing on ch. iv. 26, where see note], **and twelve thousand horsemen.** [The question may suggest itself here, why did Solomon, who was a "man of peace," maintain such a formidable array of chariots and horsemen? For not only was it in contravention of Deut. xvii. 16 (cf. 1 Sam. viii. 11), but it was entirely unnecessary, especially for a nation inhabiting a hilly country like that of Israel. We find, consequently, that David, when he took a thousand chariots from Hadarezer (1 Chron. xviii. 4), only reserved for his own use one hundred of them, though he was at the time engaged in war. It may perhaps be said that this force was necessary to keep the tributary kings in due subjection. But it seems quite as likely that it was maintained largely for the sake of pomp and display. Solomon seems to have determined in every way, and at any cost, to rival and surpass all contemporary kings. The maintenance of this large force of cavalry is another token of declension], **whom he bestowed in the cities for chariots** (ch. ix. 19), **and with the king at Jerusalem.**

Ver. 27.—**And the king made silver to be in Jerusalem as stones** [an obviously hyperbolical expression], **and cedar trees made he to be as the sycamore trees** [the שִׁקְמָה is the συκομωρέα of the New Testament (Luke xix. 4), i.e., as the name imports, the fig-mulberry—the "sycamine tree" of Luke xvii. 6 would seem to denote the mulberry proper. Though now but comparatively rare in Palestine, it is clear that formerly it was very common (see, e.g., Isa. ix. 10, whence it appears that it was used for building purposes, and where it is also contrasted with the cedars). It was esteemed both for its fruit and its wood, so much so that David appointed a steward to have the supervision both of "the olive-trees and the sycamore trees in the Shefelah" (1 Chron. xxvii. 28). The sycamores of Egypt, which were used for the coffins of mummies (Dict. Bib. iii. p. 1394), are referred to in Psa. lxxviii. 47, in a way which bespeaks their great value. There is a good description of the tree in Thomson, "Land and Book," i. 23—25] **that are in the vale** [Same word as in 1 Chron. l.c. The Shefelah is a "broad swelling tract of many hundred miles in area, which sweeps gently down from the mountains of Judah ' to mingle with the bounding main ' of the Mediterranean" (Grove, Dict. Bib. iii. p. 1611). This "Low Country" extended from Joppa to Gaza. The translation "vale" is altogether misleading. Conder ("Tent-work," p. 5) describes it as "consisting of low hills, about five hundred feet above the sea, of white soft limestone," and adds that "the broad valleys among these hills . . . produce fine crops of corn, and on the hills the long olive groves flourish better than in other districts"—an incidental and valuable confirmation of the text. "The name Sifla, or Shephelah, still exists in four or five places round Beit Jibrîn" (Eleutheropolis), ib. p. 276] **for abundance.**

Ver. 28. — **And Solomon had horses brought out of Egypt, and linen yarn: the king's merchants received the linen yarn at a price.** [This is a difficult passage, and the difficulty lies in the word מִקְוֵה, here rendered "linen yarn." Elsewhere the word signifies, a congregation, or gathering, as of water (Gen. i. 10; Exod. vii. 19; Levit. xi. 36). Consequently, Gesenius (with Vatablus, al.) would here interpret, "company." "And the company of kings' merchants took the company (of horses) at a price." The great difficulty in the way of this interpretation is perhaps the paronomasia, which, though not altogether without precedent, would be formal and unusual in grave history. Somewhat similarly Bähr: "and as to horses . . . and their collection, the merchants of the king made a collection for a certain price," but this again is strained and artificial. Perhaps it is safer to see in the word the name of a place. The LXX. (similarly the Vulgate) renders, "from Egypt and from Thekoa," καὶ ἐκ Θεκουὲ, which Keil, however, contends is manifestly a variation of an older reading, καὶ ἐκ Κουὲ, "and from Kova." As to Koa or Kova, it is objected that no such place is mentioned elsewhere, and it is alleged that if it were a market for horses, or even if it were a frontier station, where the duties on horses were collected, we should surely have heard of it again. But this is by no means certain. Koa may well have been an insignificant post on the frontier which it was only necessary to mention in this connexion. Θεκουὲ certainly looks like an emendation, but it is to be remembered that although Tekoa (Amos i. 1; 2 Chron. xi. 6; xx. 20) was apparently an insignificant village, still it gave its name to a district; it was no great distance from the Egyptian frontier— it was some six Roman miles south of Bethlehem, according to Jerome (in Amos, Proem.), and it may have been the rendezvous of the Egyptian and Hebrew horse-dealers. The text would thus yield the following meaning: "And as for the export of Solomon's horses from Egypt and from Koa (or Tekoa), the king's merchants took them from Koa (or Tekoa) at a price."

Ver. 29. — **And a chariot** [including

perhaps the two or three horses (see note on ch. v. 6) usually attached to a chariot, and the harness. רֶכֶב is used (2 Sam. viii. 4; x. 18; Ezek. xxxix. 20) for *chariot and horses*] **came up and went out of Egypt for six hundred shekels of silver** [about £80 (Wordsworth, £35), but, as these figures show, the precise value cannot be ascertained with certainty. But it is quite clear that these amounts cannot have been the custom duty, or the profits after reckoning all expenses (Ewald) paid on chariots and horses, but must represent the actual price], **and an horse for an hundred and fifty : and so for all the kings of the Hittites.** [We can hardly see in these Hittites representatives of the seven nations of Canaan (Wordsworth, *al.*), though the term "Hittite" is sometimes undoubtedly used as a *nomen generale* for Canaanites (Josh. i. 4; Ezek. xvi. 3), for the Canaanitish tribes had been reduced to bond-service, the Hittites amongst them (ch. ix. 20). The word is probably used somewhat loosely of the semi-independent tribes bordering on Palestine, the *Khatti* of the Assyrian inscriptions (Dict. Bib. i. 819), with whom Solomon had a sort of alliance. It is a curious coincidence that we find horses and chariots associated in popular estimation with the Hittites, at a later period of the history (2 Kings vii. 6). Nor are we justified in supposing that these horses and chariots were furnished as cavalry to "Solomon's vassals, whose armies were at his disposal, if he required their aid" (Rawlinson), for the kings of Syria are mentioned presently, and some of these at least were enemies to Solomon. Probably all we are to understand is that neighbouring nations received their supply of horses from Egypt—the home of horses and chariots (Exod. xiv. 6; xv. 1; Deut. xvii. 16; Isa. xxxi. 1; Jer. xlvi. 2—4)—largely through the instrumentality of Solomon's merchants], **and for the kings of Syria** ["who became the bitterest enemies of Israel" (Wordsworth): one fruit of a worldly policy], **did they bring them out by their means.** [Heb. *by their hand they brought them out*, *i.e.*, they exported them through Solomon's traders.

HOMILETICS.

Vers. 14—29.—*The Decline and Fall of Solomon.* The fall of Solomon, in itself one of the most portentous facts in Scripture history (see Homiletics, pp. 78—80), is rendered doubly suggestive and admonitory by a consideration of the way in which it was brought about. It was not that he succumbed to some fierce onslaught of temptation; it was no terrible rush of passion—no sudden guilty love of "fair idolatresses," as some have held—wrought his ruin; on the contrary, his decline in piety was so gradual and slow as to be almost imperceptible. It is almost impossible—and this consideration alone is most instructive— to trace with certainty the steps which led to his downfall. The Arab tradition teaches that a little worm—no more—was, silently and unseen, gnawing at the staff on which this Colossus leaned, and that it was only when it broke and he fell that men discovered he was dead—an instructive parable of his moral and spiritual decay. We may well cry here—

" O fall'n at length that tower of strength
Which stood foursquare to all the winds that blew."

But it is much more pertinent to ask what brought that proud fortress to the ground. It would have sustained unshaken the blows of engines of war; it would have defied the hurtling storm and tempest, but it could not resist the gradual subsidence of its foundations, and so, while preserving a fair appearance almost to the last, it settled and settled, and at the last became a heap of ruins.

Let us trace, then, as best we can, that downward course which ended in the builder of the temple building altars to Baal; let us lay bare, if we can, this worm that was noiselessly but ceaselessly eating out his inner life. Perhaps we cannot discover all its hidden workings, but we can surely see some.

Up to the date of the dedication of the temple all would seem to have gone well. Unless the dedication prayer is, as some have affirmed, the composition of a later age, the prince who poured out his soul before God in those earnest and gracious words cannot have erred very far from the right way. And the message he received during the building of the temple confirms this view. It is a message not of warning but of encouragement. It is at the completion of the palaces that we discover the first certain token of defection. For it was then that the Lord appeared unto him the second time, and the communication then made was undeniably minatory. Its tone of threatening is inexplicable, except on the supposition that Solomon's "heart was not right with the Lord," &c. At this period, then, about the twenty-fourth year of his reign, the destroying worm was already at work.

Nor is it difficult to conjecture what was the first beginning of declension on Solomon's part. We find it in the erection of the palaces, or rather in the carnal mind and the self-love and the desire for ostentation which led to their erection. It is just possible that the building of these palaces was not, in itself, to be condemned. It is suspicious, no doubt, and argues selfishness and heartlessness, when, as in Russia, Turkey, &c., the huge and costly residences of the Crown contrast everywhere with the wretched hovels of the peasantry. And one would naturally expect the theocratic king to attain a higher level and to devote himself more to the advancement of his people's good than ordinary rulers. But it must be remembered that under Solomon the Jewish people enjoyed an unprecedented prosperity (ch. iv. 20, 21). The entire nation shared in the wealth and abundance of the court. We cannot be certain, consequently, that the palaces, *per se*, involved a departure from the law, the more so as some of them were necessary for purposes of state and justice (see on ch. vii. 7). But the matter appears in a very different light when we come to consider the way in which they were reared. Forced labour, on the part of the subject races at least, can no doubt be justified from Scripture (Josh. ix. 21 sqq.), at any rate, for the house of God (ver. 23), but not for the pleasure or aggrandisement of the monarch (1 Sam. viii. 11, 16). "It is not of the Lord of Hosts that the people shall weary themselves for *very vanity*" (Hab. ii. 13). And when we remember that Jeroboam was probably encouraged to rebel by seeing and hearing the murmurings of the house of Joseph (ch. xi. 28) of whose labours he was the overseer, and that this and similar burdens laid upon the people (ch. xii. 4) resulted in the revolt of the ten tribes, we can hardly suppose that Solomon completed his great undertakings (ch. ix. 15—19) without inflicting positive hardship and grave injustice on large numbers of his subjects. It is probable, indeed, that the woe pronounced against a later monarch (Jer. xxii. 13, 14) had not been unmerited by him. He had "used his neighbour's service without wages," &c. Possibly he had raised his forest of cedar pillars, &c., by the sweat and groans of his serfs. It was a common thing for Eastern autocrats to do, but when "Jedidiah" did it, the cries of the oppressed labourer went up "into the ears of the Lord of Sabaoth."

But whether the erection of the palaces was in itself wrong or not, and whether the raising of the "levy" (ch. ix. 15) was oppressive or not, there can be little doubt that the "proud look and high stomach" (Psa. ci. 5; cxxxi. 1, 2)—the very spirit which David had disclaimed—which prompted some of these understandings was altogether sinful. Solomon is now no longer the "little child" he once was (ch. iii. 7). Now that he has "strengthened himself," like his son after him, he begins to forget his God and to forsake His law (2 Chron. xii. 1). It has been promised him that he shall exceed all other kings in wisdom and riches and honour (ch. iii. 12, 13); but this is not enough for him, he must surpass them also in the outward tokens of wealth and power. His palaces, to begin with, must be greater than theirs. He no longer covets the best gifts (see Homiletics, p. 55). The fine gold is become dim.

Still, so far, there has been no deliberate, or perhaps even conscious, infraction of the law—only the worldly and selfish mind. He may well have argued that his state required this show of magnificence; that the Canaanites were ordained of God to hew wood and draw water at his pleasure. But this only shows how slight are the beginnings of evil; how fine sometimes is the line which divides right from wrong, and how easily our judgment is warped by our inclinations. It is the old story, *Homo vult decipi et decipiatur.*

It is impossible to say in what precise order the records of Solomon's reign are to be arranged, but it is probable that the next downward step is to be traced in the alliance in which he engaged with the Tyrians. We cannot blame him, of course, for the "league " of ch. v. 12. But for that, he could hardly have built the temple, to say nothing of the palaces. Whether he was justified, however, in having at sea " a navy of Tarshish *with the navy of Hiram*" (ch. x. 22) may well be doubted. For it was part of God's plan that the Jewish people should " dwell alone and not be reckoned among the nations " (Num. xxiii. 9). Their geographical position was one of almost complete isolation. They were not destined to be a great commercial country. Their land was to be the theatre of our redemption. Theirs were

> " those holy fields
> Over whose acres walked those blessed feet,
> Which eighteen hundred years ago were nailed
> For our salvation, to the bitter cross ;"

and it was no preparation for the Incarnation that it should become the home of " gripple merchants." Contact and copartnership with idolaters could hardly be for the advantage of the faith. Nor is it difficult to see that Solomon's commerce grew at the expense of his religion. Riches, proverbially a dangerous possession, were with him—wise though he was—a step towards utter ruin. All the time that his fleets were ploughing the main, that caravans of merchants were filling his store cities, that he was driving bargains with the Syrians and Hittites (ver. 29), leanness was spreading in his soul—he was becoming more and more a secular prince. It has been justly remarked that the mention of " apes and peacocks " (ver. 22), is a significant indication of the moral and mental deterioration which he was undergoing. To think that the wisest of men should find his pleasure in the antics of the one or the plumage of the other ; or that he, the viceroy of Jehovah, should import jibbering baboons and strutting fowls, if not for himself, for the outlandish women of his court. No, these " wide views of commerce," this partnership with the Tyrians, this influx of prosperity, has not been for Solomon's or Israel's good. Indeed, if we study the character of the average nineteenth century Jew, we may form a fair idea of what commercial enterprise and lust of gold did for Solomon, the first of Hebrew chapmen.

And yet this commerce, it is easy to see, may have been in its commencement unexceptionable. Possibly it was in part undertaken to provide gold for the embellishment of the temple. But it soon engendered, if indeed it was not engendered by, that " love of money which is the root of all evil." As Solomon grew richer he loved riches more. Ver. 23 is full of significance. " So Solomon exceeded all the kings of the earth *for riches and wisdom*." Time was when wisdom held the first place (ch. iii. 11). And so it came to pass that he who at first was " rich toward God," and who, like David his father, had only accumulated gold for the glory of the sanctuary, proceeded to " multiply silver and gold *to himself*" (Deut. xvii. 17). Even his drinking vessels were of pure gold (ch. x. 21). So that his commerce and its prodigious gains led at last to a distinct violation of the law. He has not ceased to serve God. He still sacrifices and burns incense three times a year (ch. ix. 25). But he is trying to serve God and mammon, and mammon has gained the mastery. It is probably mentioned as a circumstance full of significance, that the weight of gold that came to him in one year was *six hundred and sixty-six* talents (ver. 14). For as seven is the number of the covenant, so six marks a falling short of that covenant, and the first distinct violation of the covenant consisted in the multiplication of silver and gold.

And when a breach in the law was once made we are not surprised to hear presently that it was widened. *Facilis descensus Averni.* From the multiplication of the precious metals it was an easy step to the multiplication of horses. And here we see at once how Solomon's conscience has become seared, or he has learnt to disregard its warnings. He knew perfectly well that his " twelve thousand horsemen" were a violation of the law. And he could hardly excuse himself on the ground that they were required for purposes of defence. The hilly country of Palestine does not admit of their being deployed therein. It was partly because they could only be employed in *aggressive* warfare that they were forbidden. Whatever unction, therefore, he might lay to his soul as to his accumulation of gold, he could hardly think, if he thought at all, that his horses and chariots involved no sin. But they were necessary, he persuaded himself, to the state of so great and puissant a monarch, and he would have them. And so hardened was he, so careless of the commandment, that he actually established a market for horses on his southern frontier and supplied them to neighbouring kings, who presently employed them against the people of the Lord.

And yet, grave as was this disregard of law, it was but a worm that was at work in his soul—only self-love and self-confidence (cf. Isa. xxx. 1); only the lust of the eye and the pride of life. He is still the Lord's anointed : his lips distil know-ledge ; he still offers hecatombs, but his " heart is not right," &c.

And so the years passed by. To all outward appearance his glory and magni-ficence increased. It is very suggestive to consider how hollow was that prosperity which was the marvel of the world, and how that wisdom which was so renowned was foolishness with God. The court became more splendid, more voluptuous, more dazzling, but the man became year by year poorer and meaner and baser. It only needed one step more—and apparently he was not long in taking that—to complete his defection. The other monarchs of his time had their seraglios. It was necessary that he too should have an establishment of this kind, and he must have it even greater than theirs. He knew that the law forebade the multiplication of wives, but what of that ? He had violated the law already : he might just as well do it again. An obsolete precept, he may have argued, suited to primitive times, must not stand in the way of his pomp or his pleasures. And so the Lord's anointed gathered round him in the holy city a thousand strange, immodest women. His fleets and merchants brought him mistresses from every land. And *they* brought with them their foreign rites, and the effeminate king was taken captive by their charms, and they had their way, and nothing would suffice them but he must tolerate their religion, and what he did for one he must do for all, and—and so the end of sin and shame is reached, and the decline becomes a fall, and " the darling of Jehovah," the wisest of men, the representative of Heaven, the builder of the temple, the type of our Lord, builds altars to the " abominations " of Moab and Ammon " in the hill that is before Jerusalem " (ch. xi. 7).

This mournful history is full of admonition and instruction. It must suffice to indicate the following lessons :—

1. *A man may preach to others and yet be a castaway* (1 Cor. ix. 27). Solomon's Prayer (ch. viii.), Psalm (Psa. cxxvii.), and Proverbs should be studied in the light of his fall. " Thou therefore which teachest another, teachest thou not thyself ? " (Rom. ii. 21). Compare vers. 22, 23 with Prov. v.—vii. ; and remember the con-stant references to the " law " in the dedication prayer.

2. " *Nemo repente turpissimus fuit.*" " He that despiseth little things shall fall by little and little."

> "It is the little rift within the lute
> That by and by shall make its music mute."

3. " *Out of the heart of men proceed evil thoughts, adulteries, fornications,*" &c. (Mark vii. 21). It was not to an assault from without, it was to treachery within that Solomon yielded—Solomon who had said, " Keep thy heart with all diligence," &c.

4. " *The love of money is the root of all evil* " (1 Tim. vi. 10). May we not say, " Behold two kings stood not before him : how then shall we stand ? " (2 Kings x. 4). " Children, how hard it is for them that trust in riches," &c. (Mark x. 24). " Take heed, and beware of covetousness " (Luke xii. 15), " which is idolatry " (Col. iii. 5).

5. *The course of sin is downhill. Vires acquirit eundo.* The sinner is on an inclined plane ; and the gradient at first is almost imperceptible. Let us learn, too, " the deceitfulness of sin."

6. *Woman, made to be man's helpmeet, too often becomes his snare.* It is seldom that a man is ruined but a woman has had a share in it.

7. *Solomon was old at the time of his fall,* &c. (ch. xi. 4). Hot youth has its dangers and temptations ; but mature age has them also. David was not less than fifty when he fell. See p. 225.

EXPOSITION.

CHAPTER XI. 1—13.

SOLOMON'S DEFECTION. — The observant reader will have already remarked in this history some intimations of Solomon's approaching fall. Among these are, first, the repeated warnings which are addressed to him, especially in ch. ix. 6—9, and, second, his repeated transgressions of the law by which he ruled. We have already heard of the multiplication of silver and gold (ch. x. 14—25), in defiance of Deut. xvii. 17, and of the multiplication of horses (ch. x. 27—29), in disregard of ver. 16 of the same chapter. We now read how the ruin of this great prince was completed by the multiplication of wives. The historian obviously had the words of Deut. xvii. in his mind as he wrote. It is remarkable that the chronicler is altogether silent as to Solomon's fall, as he is also as to David's sin.

Ver. 1.—**But** [Heb. *And.* This chapter is a direct continuation of the preceding. LXX. καὶ ὁ βασιλεὺς κ.τ.λ. The polygamy was but a part of his worldliness, like the chariots, gold, &c.] **king Solomon loved** [The LXX. ἦν φιλογύνης is misleading. It is perfectly clear that it cannot have been mere sensuality led to this enormous harem. This is evident from (1) his time of life. It was "when he was old"—*i.e.*, when passions are *not* at their strongest—that his wives turned away his heart. (2) The number— if the numbers are to be trusted—of his wives. A thousand concubines cannot be kept for mere purposes of passion. (3) The large number of *princesses*, which shows that the object of this array of mistresses was to enhance his state and renown. As he exceeded other kings in glory, wisdom, and power, so must he excel them not only in armies, chariots, and horses, but also in the number of his wives. It is clear, therefore, that the "lust of the eye" and "the pride of life" had their part in this huge establishment. "The same consideration of state which leads a Western prince or noble to multiply horses, leads an Eastern prince to multiply wives, with often as

little personal consideration in the one case as in the other" (Kitto)] **many** [He is blamed for their number. This was against Deut. xvii. 17] **strange** [not merely *foreign*, though tnat is the primary meaning of the word, but strange as opposed to a lawful wife. Cf. Prov. v. 20; vi. 24; vii. 5, &c. No doubt the harlots in Israel were principally aliens] **women, together with** [וְאֶת־בַּת־כ׳] *i.e., praeter filiam Ph.* (Maurer). Pharaoh's daughter is regarded as his lawful wife] **the daughter of Pharaoh** [see note on ch. iii. 1], **women of the Moabites, Ammonites** [Heb. *Moabitesses,* &c. Perhaps these two nations are mentioned first because such alliances as these, though not forbidden in terms by the law, would nevertheless, from its spirit and bearing towards these races, be looked upon with especial disfavour. If the Ammonite or Moabite was not to be received into the congregation until the *tenth* generation (Deut. xxiii. 3) ; if the Israelite was not to seek their peace or prosperity all the days of his life (ver. 6), then the idea of inter-marriage with them must have been altogether repugnant to the Hebrew polity, as indeed we may gather from the book of Ruth], **Edomites** [Favourably distinguished (Deut. xxiii. 7) from the two preceding races. The Edomite was a "brother." His children of the *third* generation might enter into the congregation], **Zidonians** [Rawlinson thinks this word lends " some countenance to the tradition recorded by Menander (*ap.* Clem. Alex. 'Strom.' i. p. 386), that Solomon married a daughter of Hiram, king of Tyre." But such tradition was sure to arise ; the uxorious character of Solomon and his close relations with Hiram are quite sufficient to account for its growth. And a daughter of Hiram would hardly have been passed over without special mention], **and Hittites** [see on ch. x. 29].

Ver. 2.—**Of the nations concerning which the Lord said unto the children of Israel** [Of the nations just enumerated, the law *expressly* forbade marriage with the Hittites alone (Exod. xxxiv. 11—16; Deut. vii. 1—4), though the Zidonians are probably to be included, as being Canaanites (Gen. x. 15). But the *principle* which applied in the case of the seven nations of Canaan applied equally to all other idolaters. "They will turn away thy son from following me," &c. (Deut. vii. 4). The *spirit* of the law, consequently, was as much violated by an Edomite or Ammonite as by a Hittite alliance], **Ye shall not go in to them, neither shall they come in unto you** [much the same expression Josh. xxiii. 12. The historian does not cite any special Scripture, however, but gives the substance of several warnings], **for surely they will turn away your heart after their gods** [cf. Exod. xxxiv. 16]: **Solomon clave** [same word Gen. ii. 4] **unto these** [emphatic in Heb. "even to *these*," instead of cleaving to God (Deut. iv. 4; x. 20; xxx. 20, each of which has the same word as here), and despite the prohibitions of the law, &c.] **in love.**

Ver. 3.—**And he had seven hundred wives, princesses** [These may have been members of royal or princely houses of neighbouring nations. Evidently they enjoyed a distinguished rank], **and three hundred concubines** [Though not committed to a defence of the accuracy of the figures 700 and 300 (which are clearly *round* numbers), it must be said that the reasons alleged for reducing them (as from 700 to 70) are not of much weight. It is hardly correct, *e.g.*, to say (as Rawlinson) that the numbers are given in Cant. vi. 8 as "threescore queens and fourscore concubines," for it is obvious that too much importance must not be attached to an *obiter* statement ("there are threescore," &c.) in a poetical book, too, and one descriptive of Solomon's youth. The view of Ewald and Keil, again, that these numbers represent the sum total of the inmates of the harem at different periods of Solomon's long reign, rather than the number present at any one time—they would see in the numbers of Cant. *l.c.* a statement of the *average strength* of the *seraglio*—though not to be described as evasive, is certainly not the natural interpretation of the words. And these numbers, when we compare them with the establishments of other Eastern potentates, are not found to be at all incredible. The commentators all remind us that Dareius Codomannus, *e.g.*, took with him on his expedition against Alexander 360 *pellices*. Or if ancient history, as Rawlinson affirms, furnishes no strict parallel to these figures, the harems of modern Persia and Turkey at any rate have quite equalled that of Solomon. (See Bähr *in loc.*) It is true that Rehoboam had only 18 wives and 60 concubines (2 Chron. xi. 21), but then Rehoboam was not Solomon. If his harem was but a tithe of his father's, so also were his wealth and his power]: **and his wives turned away his heart.** ["Satan hath found this bait to take so well that he never changed since he crept into Paradise" (Bp. Hall).]

Ver. 4.—**For it came to pass, when Solomon was old** [As he was but sixty at the time of his death, "old" is here a relative term, and must mean "toward the close of his life," *i.e.*, when he was about 50 or 55], **that his wives turned away his heart after other gods** [The text does not limit Solomon's *polygamy* to the time of old age, but his idolatrous leanings. I say *leanings*, for it is doubtful to what extent Solomon himself took part in actual idolatry. Both Bähr and Keil—the latter in opposition to the views he held in 1846—not to speak of others, deny that he shared the idolatries of his wives, and the former labours hard, and on the whole, it seems to me, successfully, to prove that he was only guilty of *sanctioning* idolatrous worship in the vicinity of Jerusalem. His arguments, briefly stated, are these: (1) It is nowhere said that he "*served*" (עָבַד) other gods—the expression constantly used of the idolatrous kings; cf. xvi. 31; xxii. 53; 2 Kings xvi. 3, &c. (2) Neither the son of Sirach nor the Talmud nor the Rabbins know anything of his personal idolatry. (3) Had he formally worshipped idols, his sin would have been greater than that of Jeroboam—as to which, however, see on ch. xii. 29 sqq. (The "sin of Jeroboam" lay in "making Israel to sin," *i.e.*, in forcing his people into schismatic and unauthorized worship, rather than in any practices of his own.) (4) The expressions "his heart was *not perfect*," below, and "he went not *fully*" (ver. 6) are inconsistent with the idea of idolatry. Similarly Ewald says, "There is no evidence from ancient authorities that Solomon, even in advanced life, ever left the religion of Jahveh, and with his own hand sacrificed to heathen gods. All traces of contemporary history extant testify to the contrary" (vol. iii. p. 297). See, however, on ver. 5]: **and his heart was not perfect with the Lord his God** [It is instructive to compare with this the words of ch. viii. 61, "Let your heart be perfect," &c. Wordsworth remarks that "the defection even of Solomon from God through the influence of his strange wives is one of the best justifications" of the commands of Exod. xxxiv. 12—16; Deut. vii. 2—4, &c.], **as was the heart of David his father.**

Ver. 5.—**For Solomon went after** [Rawlinson observes that this expression, which is "common in the Pentateuch, always signifies actual idolatry." He cites Deut. xi. 28; xiii. 2; xxviii. 14; but it should be considered that in the two passages last cited the words are added, "*and served them.*" And the true explanation would seem to be that, though "it is not stated that Solomon himself offered sacrifice to these idols," yet "even the building of altars for idols was a participation in idolatry, which was irreconcilable with true fidelity to the Lord" (Keil). Bähr contends that the words "went after Ashtoreth," &c., no more involve personal service than the word "built" in ver. 7 involves personal labour; but both expressions show that he regarded these idolatries not only without disfavour, but with positive approval and practical encouragement. "It is not likely he could be so insensate as to adore such deities, but so far was the uxorious king blinded with affection, that he gave not passage only to the idolatry of his heathenish wives, but furtherance" (Bp. Hall). And the distinction, so far as the *sin* is concerned, between this and actual idolatry is a fine one. It is not implied, however, that Solomon ever discarded the worship of Jehovah. To the end of his reign he would seem to have offered his solemn sacrifices on the great altar thrice a year. But his heart was elsewhere (ver. 9).] **Ashtoreth the goddess of the Zidonians** [עַשְׁתֹּרֶת, 'Αστάρτη, probably connected with ἀστήρ, *stella*, and *star*, by some identified with the planet Venus, by others with the moon, is here mentioned for the first time in the singular (*Ashtaroth*, plural, is found in Gen. xiv. 5; Judg. ii. 13; x. 6; 1 Sam. vii. 4; xii. 10, &c.) With Baal, she divided the worship of the Phœnicians, the antiquity of which is evident from Gen. xiv. 5; Num. xxii. 41. It was really an impure cultus of the reproductive powers (see below on xiv. 23). Interesting proof of the existence of a temple of this goddess at Sidon is supplied by an inscription discovered there in 1855 (see Dict. Bib. i. 123)], **and after Milcom** [In Jer. xlix. 13; Amos i. 15, "Malcam," *i.e., their king.* According to Gesenius, the same as *Molech* (*i.e.*, the *king*) in ver. 7, though Ewald, Movers, Keil regard them as different deities. But it seems more probable that it was the same deity, worshipped (2 Kings xxiii. 10, 13) under different attributes. This is "the first direct historical allusion" to his worship in the Old Testament. A warning against it is found Levit. xx. 2—5. He was the fire-god, as Baal was the sun-god, and the sacrifices offered to him were those of children, who would seem to have not only "passed *through* the fire," but to have been burnt therein. Psa. cvi. 37, 38; Jer. vii. 31; xix. 5; Ezek. xxiii. 39, &c. See Dict. Bib. ii. 403] **the abomination** [*i.e.*, the hateful, detestable idol] **of the Ammonites.** [It has been suggested (Speaker's Commentary on Levit. xx. 2) that the children offered to Molech were children of incest or adultery, and we are reminded that Ammon was the child of *incest*. It must be remembered, however,

that we have no record of Jewish children passing through the fire to Molech before the time of Ahaz (Bähr, Keil).]

Ver. 6.—**And Solomon did evil in the sight of the Lord** [cf. Judg. ii. 11; iii. 7, &c.], **and went not fully** [לֹא מִלֵּא, *sc.* לָלֶכֶת A pregnant expression found also Num. xiv. 24; xxxii. 11, 12; Deut. i. 36] **after the Lord, as did David his father.**

Ver. 7.—**Then did Solomon build an high place** [see on ch. iii. 2] **for Chemosh, the abomination of Moab** [The meaning of "Chemosh" is uncertain. Gesenius suggests "Vanquisher"—Chemosh was the god of war. The mention of Ashtar-Chemosh on the Moabite stone "connects the Moabite religion with the Phœnician," where Ashtar is the masculine form of Astarte, and suggests that "Chemosh was connected with the androgynous deities of Phœnicia" (Speaker's Comm. on Num. xxi. 29). It is probable, in fact, that Chemosh, Baal, Ashtoreth, Molech, &c., were originally so many names of the one supreme God, worshipped under different attributes, and with various rites in different countries], **in the hill that is before Jerusalem** [see 2 Kings xxiii. 13. The hill is of course the mount of Olives. The altar would seem to have stood on the south peak, which is now known, as it has been for centuries past, as the *Mons Scandali*, or the *Mons Offensionis* (the Vulg. rendering of 2 Kings *l.c.*) See Robinson, i. 565,566], **and for Molech, the abomination of the children of Ammon.** [Ewald sees in these altars a wise religious tolerance ("Hist. Israel," iii. pp. 297, 298).]

Ver. 8.—**And likewise did he for all** [having done it for one, he must needs do it for all. "No hill about Jerusalem was free from a chapel of devils" (Hall)] **his strange wives, which burnt** [Heb. *burning*, Ewald, 335 *a*] **incense and sacrificed unto their gods.** [Observe, as bearing on the question of Solomon's apostasy, that Solomon *built* the altars; his wives *sacrificed*, &c. According to Keil, incense is here mentioned before sacrifice, because vegetable took precedence of animal offerings in the nature-worship of Western Asia (Bähr, Symbolik, ii. pp. 237 sqq.) But it is very doubtful whether this idea was in the mind of the writer.]

Ver. 9.—**And the Lord was angry with Solomon, because his heart was turned from the Lord God of Israel, which had appeared unto him twice.** [cf. iii. 5 and ix. 2. The anger arose partly from the exceptional favours which had been shown to him; cf. Amos iii. 2; Luke x. 12—15.]

Ver. 10.—**And had commanded him concerning this thing** [ch. ix. 6] **that he** should not go after other gods: but he kept not that which the Lord commanded.

Ver. 11.—**Wherefore the Lord said unto Solomon** [probably by a prophet, Ahijah or Iddo. There would hardly be a third appearance], **Forasmuch as this is done of thee** [Heb. *this was with thee*], **and thou hast not kept my covenant and my statutes, which I have commanded thee, I will surely rend** [*i.e.*, despite thy great power and magnificence, thy fortifications and munitions of war] **the kingdom from thee, and will give it to thy servant.** [Not merely *subject*, but *officer, employé*. This made the decree the more bitter. A " servant" should be heir to his glory. For a hireling Solomon's vast treasures had been prepared. This verse should be read in the light of Eccles. ii. 18.]

Ver. 12.—**Notwithstanding in thy days I will not do it** [The threatening had two gracious and merciful limitations, (1) The blow should not fall until after his death (cf. ver. 34; ch. xxi. 29; 2 Kings xxii.

20), and (2) the disruption should be but partial. There should be a " remnant " Rom. ix. 27; xi. 5, &c.] **for David thy father's sake** [*i.e.*, because both of David's piety and God's promise to him (2 Sam. vii. 13)] : **but I will rend it out of the hand of thy son.**

Ver. 13.—**Howbeit I will not rend away all the kingdom; but will give one tribe** [viz., Judah (ch. xii. 20, " the tribe of Judah only "). "Even the reservation of one tribe is called a gift " (Wordsworth) **to thy son for David my servant's sake, and for Jerusalem's sake which I have chosen.** [But for this provision, Jerusalem would have ceased to be the religious capital. When the sceptre departed from Judah, we may be sure that the " envy of Ephraim " would have demanded that the city of their solemnities should be placed elsewhere—at Shiloh, which for 400 years had been God's " bright sanctuary," or at Bethel, which from far earlier times had been a holy place. See on ch. xii. 29, 32.]

HOMILETICS.

Vers. 4—8.—*The Sin of Solomon.* Three questions will suffice to bring this subject before us. First, what was this sin? secondly, by whom was it committed? thirdly, when, and under what circumstances?

But first, it is well we should understand what this sin was *not.* (1) *It was not actual idolatry.* True, Solomon built the altars, but he built them for his wives (vers. 7, 8). The wisest of men never stooped so low as to " project his person " to dumb idols (note on ver. 4). To him, an idol was " nothing in the world " (1 Cor. viii. 4). That, of all things, was " vanity of vanities; " (2) *Nor was it the outcome of simple sensuality.* The wives who " turned away his heart," and to whom he " clave in love "—it was not passion but pride had collected them in such numbers under his palace roof. " His crowded seraglio was but one instance more of the sort of ambition which made him seek to surpass all men in his gardening, his agriculture, his treasures of gold," &c. (Keble). See on ver. 1. But when he had them, he must humour them, even in their idolatries. He was very far, we may be sure, from thinking that all religions were alike, which has been " the disease of some great wits; " but he flattered himself that he was tolerant and liberal, and as he claimed liberty of conscience, so he must concede it to others.

We see, then, that the essence of this sin was that having permitted himself, or purposes of state and pride and ostentation, the love of many strange women, he permitted them, and possibly some of his subjects also, to worship their false gods. And by so doing—

1. *He gave a direct sanction to superstition.* He may have argued, like some in later times and some who bear the Christian name, that these things, though nothing in themselves, were all very well for women, that the ignorant must have material objects of worship, &c. But it was not thus that the God of his fathers viewed the deed. This philosophic tolerance of other creeds, He called the teaching of falsehood. This liberality, in His sight, was " damnable uncharitableness "—the expression is Jeremy Taylor's—for it was leading poor souls away from the light and changing the truth of God into a lie (Rom. i. 25). It was " making the blind to wander out of the way " (Deut. xxvii. 18) in the worst possible sense of the words.

2. *He encouraged immorality and cruelty.* For it must never be forgotten what the " abominations " of these Semitic divinities were like. The idolatry of the East always involved impurity; hence its powerful hold on a nation like the Jews, for whom the worship of " silver and gold, the works of men's hands," could have had but little charm. Its " vile affections " (Rom. i. 26) were its chief attractions. And Solomon, who knew what the worship of Baal and Ashtoreth meant, who knew how unclean were their rites, and what painful and shameful sacrifices Molech and Chemosh demanded of their votaries, nevertheless gave the word, and presently the hills about Jerusalem were crowned with chapels of devils.

3. *He dishonoured the one true God.* For if " Polytheism is not exclusive," Monotheism, in the very nature of things, is and must be. Its basis, its fundamental conception, is that there are *not* " gods many and lords many." Its keynote is the *Shema Israel* (Deut. vi. 4), " the Lord our God is one Lord." It proclaims a " jealous God " who will not give His glory to another, nor His praise to graven images (Isa. xlii. 8). But Solomon robbed Him of His rights; of the exclusive sovereignty and the undivided authority which belonged to Him alone. By building idol altars he claimed homage for idol deities; before the eyes of the Lord's people, he thrust rivals and pretenders on to the Lord's throne, and degraded " the uncorruptible God into an image made like to corruptible man." (Rom. i. 23).

4. *He defied the Holy One of Israel.* For these altars of lust and cruelty were not built in a corner. They did not shrink from the light as in a past age; they were not frequented by *pagani.* They rose " on the hill that is before Jerusalem;" they fronted the altar of Jehovah; their priests were visible to the priests in the temple court; their smoke ascended to the sky along with the smoke of the daily sacrifice. If insult had been *designed*, it could hardly have been more open or obtrusive.

II. And by WHOSE permission, at whose bidding were these shrines of infamy erected? They were built by—

1. *The wisest of men.* In science (ch. iv. 33), in philosophy (*ib.* vers. 29—32), in self-knowledge (see Homiletics, pp. 78, 79). Cf. ch. iii. 12, 28.

2. *The most favoured and enlightened of men.* The Lord " appeared unto him twice " (ver. 9). His was " abundance of revelations " (cf. 2 Cor. xii. 7). To him it was said, " Ask what I shall give thee " (ch. iii. 5). This was *Jedidiah.* " There was no king like Solomon, who was beloved of his God, yet even him did outlandish women cause to sin " (Neh. xiii. 26).

3 *The builder of the temple.* To him had been granted the high honour which was denied to pious David. He had " found a place for the Lord, a habitation for the mighty God of Jacob " (Psa. cxxxii. 5). The golden altar, the brazen altar; he had planned and reared them both. And now he builds altars to " horrors " (see note on ch. xv. 13). " He that burneth incense, he blessed an idol " (Isa. lxvi. 3, Heb.)

4. *The teacher of the Church.* He was " that deep sea of wisdom which God ordained to send forth rivers and fountains of all Divine and human knowledge to all nations, to all ages; " he was " one of those select secretaries whose hand it pleased the Almighty to employ in three pieces of the Divine monuments of sacred Scriptures " (Bp. Hall). He is fallen, but his writings stand. He still preaches to others, though himself a castaway. There have been authors whose pestilent writings go on corrupting and destroying souls for ages after *they* have ceased to speak. But Solomon's is in some respects a sadder case than theirs. His writings have taught and blessed the world for nigh three thousand years after he himself fell into " utter wretchlessness of most unclean living."

5. *A man who warned others.* It is only when we study his fall in the light of his prayer and proverbs, with their many admonitions, that we realize how great a wreck he became and how appalling is the lesson of his fall. " Since the first man, Adam, the world hath not yielded either so great an example of wisdom or so fearful an example of apostasy, as Solomon " (Hall).

III. But WHEN was it, let us now ask, that Solomon fell into this deadly sin? At what period of his reign, and under what circumstances, did he sink to such depths of degradation ? Observe—

1. *It was not after sudden or special temptation* (see Homiletics, p. 216). We may truly say of him, "There hath no temptation taken you but such as is common to man." No Delilah, no Bathsheba wrought his ruin. It is instructive to compare ch. iv. 20—24 with the account of our Lord's temptation (Matt. iv. 3—11). Solomon was not tempted by hunger ; his "provision for one day was," &c. The enemy could not offer him " the kingdoms of the world and the glory of them : " he had them already (ch. iv. 21, 24; ch. x. *passim*); he could only use the common weapon of presumption, of spiritual pride, and it was by this that Solomon was slain.

2. *It was not after great trials or adversity.* His career, how unlike David's ! " Rest on every side." "Neither adversary nor evil occurrence " (ch. v. 4). " Eating, drinking, and making merry" (ch. iv. 20). Compare 1 Sam. chs. xviii.—xxx. And yet David stood and Solomon fell. What we call adversity (compare Jacob's " all these things are against me," Gen. xlii. 36) is often spiritual prosperity. "Tribulation" is a significant word. The *tribulum* was the threshing-sledge which separated the chaff from the grain. It is said by some that war is necessary for nations to preserve them from corruption and decay ; it is certain that peace is not always good for princes. The man of peace and rest, who was "not plagued like other men," has furnished the world with the most terrible example of apostasy. Well may the apostle bid us to " rejoice in tribulation also," to " count it all joy when," &c. (James i. 2).

3. *It was " when he was old."* St. Paul speaks of "youthful lusts," but old age has its special dangers and temptations. It was in the time of mature experience, when the hot blood of youth should have cooled, when he should have known the world and his wisdom should have been ripest, that his wives turned away his heart. Perhaps he presumed upon his exalted gifts and revelations. With age came self-confidence. It is thus that many strong cities have been taken. " *Praeruptum coque neglectum* " discloses the secret of their fall.

4. *It was when his riches had increased.* The greater his store, the leaner his soul. "It is easier for a camel," &c. (Matt. xix. 24). "The deceitfulness of riches " choked the word (Matt. xiii. 22). The Latin proverb which says that " every rich man is either a knave or the son of a knave " has some truth in it. Happy are those who have " neither poverty nor riches " (Prov. xxx. 8); happiest those who can say, " My riches consist, not in the abundance of my possessions, but in the fewness of my wants."

5. *It was when his prosperity was at its highest.* It was when he " waxed fat" that " Jeshurun kicked." It is when men " have eaten and are full " that they most need to " beware that they forget not the Lord their God " (Deut. viii. 10, 11). Observe, it was not until he had reached the very pinnacle of greatness and felicity that Solomon fell. " His prosperity, which even wise men find a constant wear and trial to the spirit, did him more harm than even his wisdom did him good" (Augustine). How appropriate that prayer, " In all time of our *wealth*, . . . good Lord, deliver us." " The food convenient which Agur prayed for is safer than the food abundant which even Solomon was surfeited with " (M. Henry).

6. *It was after his wives were multiplied.* Polygamy has ever been a snare to rulers. It is said that Scripture nowhere condemns it. If the letter does not, the spirit does. Scripture tells of the misery it has occasioned. Witness the families of Abraham, Jacob, Elkanah, and David. It was the immediate cause of Solomon's ruin. There are few partnerships which are so lightly entered into as the one which lasts for all life. And yet how completely is a man's honour, prosperity, and peace in his wife's keeping. " How many have we known whose heads have been broken by their own rib " (Bp. Hall). It is a quaint but true saying, " If a man would thrive, he must ask his wife." How strange that he who knew the priceless value of one true woman's love (Prov. xxxi. 10—31) should surrender himself to immodest and forbidden attachments. Can there be a reference to his thousand wives and concubines in those pessimist words of Eccles. vii. 26—28 ? " If one woman undid

all mankind, what marvel is it if many women undid one ? " (Hall.) " Thou didst bow thy loins unto women, and by thy body wast thou brought into subjection" (Ecclus. xlvii. 19).

7. *It was after repeated warnings.* He had had (1) the standing warning of Scripture (Deut. xvii. 16 sqq.), (2) the special warnings of his father David (1 Kings ii. 3, 4, and especially 1 Chron. xxviii. 9), (3) the supernatural warnings of God. (1 Kings iii. 14; vi. 12, 13; ix. 6, 7). And to these may surely be added (4) the repeated and emphatic warnings which he had himself addressed to others. But all these went for nothing. And so it is too probable his own words (Prov. xxix. 1) found a fulfilment in his own person. The saddest consideration of all is that this great preacher has unconsciously predicted his own fall, and passed sentence on himself. " Out of thine own mouth will I judge thee," &c. (Luke xix. 22).

HOMILIES BY VARIOUS AUTHORS.

Vers. 1—8.—*The Fall of a King.* Solomon was a king of men. Not only was he supreme civil ruler of his nation, he was also chief in wisdom and knowledge, and distinguished in the favour of God (Neh. xiii. 26). This moral royalty is open to all. The prize is nobler than that of the most glittering " corruptible crown." From this kingship Solomon fell, though he retained the throne of the nation. The rascal often lurks in the heart that is under an anointed face. Let us consider—

I. THE OCCASION OF THIS DELINQUENCY. 1. Solomon had *many wives.* (1) This was an invasion of God's order. That order was exhibited in Eden, when Eve stood singly by the side of Adam. Lamech was the first polygamist (Gen. iv. 19). He was, ominously, the fifth in descent from the fratricide Cain. (2) Moses tolerated polygamy, as he also suffered divorcements, not with approval of these customs, but rather in judgment upon the people for the hardness of their hearts (see Matt. xix. 3—9). (3) This principle will explain many Mosaic ordinations the observance of which was a burdensome yoke, and from which, by the mercy of Christ, we are happily released (Acts xv. 10, 11). Note : God's order cannot be invaded with impunity. It is our duty carefully to ascertain it, and faithfully to keep it. 2. His wives were *strange* women. (1) Not only were they foreigners, they were also idolaters. There is no proof that even Pharaoh's daughter was a proselyte. Solomon could have no spiritual sympathy with these without compromising his loyalty to Jehovah. (2) They were idolaters of those very nations against alliances with which the law of God was express (see ver. 2; Exod. xxxiv. 12—16; Deut. vii. 3, 4). The sin was therefore most flagrant. (3) The spirit of this inhibition still binds (see 1 Cor. vii. 39; 2 Cor. vi. 14). The reason for it is in the nature of things and must abide. Note : Many a man has had his heart pierced and his head broken by his own rib. 3. *David* had too many wives. (1) The example of David may have injuriously influenced Solomon. A large harem may have been a sign of grandeur ; but these kings ought to have been superior to such fashions (see Deut. xvii. 17). (2) The evils in the examples of good men are especially mischievous, for they are liable to be condoned into harmlessness ; the more readily so when to follow them is agreeable to natural inclination. (3) They are liable to be carried farther. If David had many wives, Solomon had very many. David's wives were chiefly daughters of Israel, but Solomon's were daughters of foreign idolaters. Amongst his 700 wives and 300 concubines, not one was good (see Eccles. vii. 28). Note : Good men should be especially watchful over their influence —parents, ministers, Sunday-school teachers, professors of religion.

II. THE PROGRESS OF THE EVIL. 1. *First the heart is set against the head.* (1) The earliest record here is that Solomon's *heart* was turned away. His head at first seems to have been clear, as Adam's also was, who, though in the transgression, yet was " not deceived " (1 Tim. ii. 14). But his heart, like that of Adam, was fatally susceptible to female influence. (2) It is a foolish thing in a wise man to trust his head when he gives his heart to evil. " Man at his best is vanity."

2. *Then the heart rules the head.* (1) This is the next stage and inevitable. This may be disputed long, but will assert itself in time. Observe well that when Solomon was " old " he so far yielded to the influence of his wives as to encourage and join in their idolatry. (2) Probably his vices made him prematurely old. Calmet supposes him to have been *eighteen* years old when he came to the throne, and he reigned *forty* years (ver. 42). Thus he could be only *fifty-eight* at his death. 3. *Finally the wise man becomes a fool.* (1) Behold this wisest of men trying to solve the impossible problem of serving Jehovah and Ashtaroth! He went not fully after the Lord his God as did David his father. (2) David indeed fell into grievous sin, but his offence was more directly against man; indirectly against God. Even then the offence *as against God* was the venom of his crimes (Psa. li. 4). But the sin of Solomon was against God directly. Note: Offences against society are denounced without mercy by men, while the mental rebellion of the unbeliever against God is even glorified as " honest doubt! " but the Bible is explicit that " He that believeth not shall be damned." (3) Behold this wise man further building a temple to Molech, the murderer, the devil, on the Mount of Olives, over against the temple of the Lord, the glorious work of his royal youth! Could folly go farther? (4) The mischief of Solomon's idolatry remained to the times of Josiah (see 2 Kings xxiii. 13). Who can say that it terminated even then? Eternity will declare.—M.

Vers. 9—13.—*The Anger of God.* This is the inevitable consequence of sin. Had God expressed no displeasure against Solomon, what mischief might not his example have wrought? The terrible judgments of the great day will have a most salutary effect upon the order and stability of the whole moral universe. If men sufficiently considered these things they would hesitate before they plunged into vices. Let us be admonished from this history as to—

I. HOW THE ANGER OF GOD IS PROVOKED. It is provoked—1. *By the turning away of the heart from Him.* (1) And justly so, for to do this is to outrage the highest propriety. God is everything that should engage the affections of an intelligent creature—" the perfection of beauty;" "the altogether lovely." (2) For to do this is the straight road to the deepest demoralization. Man is made in the image of God expressly that his nature may have its perfection in union and communion with Him. To turn away from God must lead to depravation evermore. This, in other words, is everlasting damnation. (3) Then let us keep our hearts (Prov. iv. 23). No diligence should be spared. Our life is in it. 2. By doing this *wantonly.* (1) It was an aggravation of Solomon's sin that *God had appeared* to him. Review the circumstances of the vision he witnessed before he set about the building of the temple (see ch. iii. 5—15). He could not have been wholly ignorant of the glorious character of God. (2) It was a further aggravation that God had appeared to him *twice* (ver. 9). Review the circumstances of the vision after the work of the temple was finished (see ch. ix. 1—9). Note: Privileges imply corresponding responsibilities. Note further: God keeps account of His favours conferred upon us, though we may forget them. He will remind us of them all in the great day of judgment. (3) It was an additional aggravation that he had been forewarned of the very evils into which he fell. And the promises of God to him had been so remarkably verified that he had the best reason to accept the truth of His admonitions. How slow of heart are the men to believe the inflexibility of Divine justice! (4) A *king* who exacts obedience from subjects, or a *master* who claims the obedience of servants, should be the last to forget his duty to God. Consider—

II. HOW THE ANGER OF GOD IS EXPRESSED. It is expressed—1. *In the severity of justice.* (1) The kingdom of Solomon was now doomed to be rent. He had divided his affections (between Jehovah and Molech), so are the affections of his subjects now to be divided. (2) A considerable portion of his kingdom is to be turned over to one of his servants. What a fitness there is in this judgment also! Solomon, the servant of God, rebelled against God; Jeroboam, the servant of Solomon, rebels against Solomon. (3) What a melancholy reversal! Time was when God loved Solomon (see 2 Sam. xii. 24 ; 1 Kings x. 9 ; Neh. xiii. 26). Severe is the fall from the height of a throne. From a vastly greater elevation is the fall of one cast from the bosom of God. (4) Behold how sin works ruin! It ruins individuals, families, nations. The anger of God is expressed—2. *With the mitigations of mercy.* (1) For the sake of David his father these judgments were not to come upon Solomon in his day. We little know the benefits or the evils entailed upon us by our forefathers. We should see that we entail not evils but benefits upon our descendants. (2) "For David's sake!" David, the beloved, was a type of Christ, for whose sake the entail of infinite mischief is cut off from his sons, and they are made heirs of inestimable blessings. (3) Even Rehoboam was to reap the benefit of the faithfulness of David. One tribe, the most important, was to be retained to him. The promises respecting the true son of David must be fulfilled. (4) "For Jerusalem's sake," also, mercy must rejoice upon judgment (ver. 13). The temple was there. The shechinah was there. Kingdoms are spared the severity of judgments in respect to the interests of religion in many ways little dreamed of by statesmen and rulers.—M.

Vers. 1—8.—*Solomon's Sin.* I. THE SIN. 1. Its *nature.* He not only aided his wives to continue their idolatrous worship, he himself participated in it. He went after strange gods, seeking their favour and observing their ordinances. The worship of Jehovah was not discarded, but delight in the true God was gone, and the flame of that loving zeal for God's commandments died away : his heart was not perfect with the Lord his God. The worship now offered in the temple was the lingering tradition of a brighter past, a thing of custom and outward necessity, and the heart was given to baser worships, sensuous and sensual. The soul had ceased to drink at the fountain of living waters, and was drinking at the fountain of death. Is our heart perfect with the Lord, our delight in His love, our hunger after His righteousness as deep as in the past? Do we offer a cold and formal worship to Him, while our heart warms into living interest and strong desire only at the world's shrines? 2. Its *guilt.* (1) God had given Solomon unparalleled wisdom, wealth, and power, and all were now turned against his Benefactor. All that fame and influence were used to glorify idolatry and lessen zeal for God's service. How often are God's gifts thus turned against Him! (2) The sin of Solomon became the sin of Israel (ver. 33). The responsibility of parents in regard to their children's attitude toward God—the responsibility of the leaders of thought and of society, of all of us, as to how we influence men in their attitude toward the things unseen and eternal. 3. Its *sadness.* It was his last work, the sin not of youth but of old age. The light which God had kindled did not flame out into eternal glory, but went out in eternal night. The seeds of sin and disaster were sown among his people, his life a wreck, his memory not a star to guide the wanderer in the darkness, but a warning beacon on the waste of death! The story of many a life besides : will it be the story of thine?

II. WHAT LED TO IT. 1. *Unregulated affections.* The wisdom of marrying only in the Lord. The danger of worldly alliances and worldly friendships. 2. *The despising of God's commandments* (see ver. 2, and Deut. xvii. 16, 17). The counsels of God were lightly esteemed. Many commands of God are to-day held to be antiquated and are quietly ignored. The directions of Scripture in regard to what are deemed minor things are set aside. The spirit of unbelief is there. For individuals and for churches it must prove a seed of sin and spiritual disaster. 3. *The human love displaced the Divine.* The spirit of disloyalty needed only a strong enough inducement to go further, and it found it here. To please his wives, altars to their gods were built on Mount Olivet, and then his own soul was taken in the snare of their abominations. The testimony which we are called to lift up in the face of all life away from God is safety for our own soul. It is hard to do it, but there is life in it for ourselves and, it may be, for others also.—U.

Vers. 9—13.—*God's Anger.* I. SINS ARE SET IN THE LIGHT OF PAST MERCIES. 1. *Solomon's idolatry is contrasted with the advantages conferred upon him.*

The Lord had appeared to him twice. The reality of God's existence and His personality had been engraven upon Solomon's soul. 2. *With the commandment given.* The Lord "had commanded him concerning this thing." The rebellion and ingratitude are both marked. Our sins are judged not only in themselves and their effects, but also in the light of what God has done and said to us. There is a baseness and an enmity in sin that will yet crush the sinful heart. Do we weigh sins in this way? Does our repentance read them thus? God's judgment will: "Forasmuch as this is done *of thee*," &c.

II. THE DIVINE JUDGMENT. 1. *Hopes frustrated.* Solomon may have excused his sin to himself because it conciliated neighbouring princes and nations and so strengthened his kingdom. But while he fancied himself building up, he was in reality casting down. Forgetfulness of God is forgetfulness of one's own good. 2. *Pride abased.* The dominion is given to a servant. There is not only loss but shame. There are first that will be last, and last first. 3. *Punishment reflects sin.* Solomon's rebellion and ingratitude are punished by rebellion and ingratitude. The kingdom is rent from him by a subject, and by one whom he had trusted and advanced (ver. 28). "Whatsoever a man soweth, that shall he also reap." As the wicked have shut out God, God will shut out them.

III. THE DIVINE MERCY. In God's chastisements there is ever a gateway of kindness through which we may pass up into His forgiveness and love. 1. *The judgment is delayed.* It was a heavy judgment that the kingdom should be rent from his son, but it would have been an added bitterness had his own day set in disaster and shame. 2. *The whole will not be taken even from his son.* His seed will still reign in Jerusalem. 3. *There is humbling even in the mercy.* It is done for David's sake and for Jerusalem's sake. Pride is crushed beneath God's mercy as well as beneath His judgment. We are pardoned for Christ's sake and His name's sake. In the midst of rebuke for iniquity there is mercy and life for lowly faith.—U.

Vers. 9, 10.—*The Downfall of Solomon.* The fall of Solomon has appeared to some commentators incredible. As to the fact itself, however, there can be no doubt. Nor is his fall so exceptional as many suppose. Others beside this king have had pious parentage, a religious education, a promising youth, extraordinary intellectual endowments, frequent warnings of their danger, and yet have failed and come short of the glory of God. Give examples. It is noteworthy that God saw Solomon's danger and warned him of it on the evening of that day upon which his religious devotion appeared most intense. The dedication of the temple was at once the zenith of the nation's glory, and of their king's highest attainments. Describe the Feast of Dedication; the song of the people—"Lift up your heads, O ye gates, &c.; the prayer of Solomon that this might be so; and the manifestation of the Divine Presence. Contrast this scene with the silence of the following night, in which the message of the Lord came, bidding him beware lest the emotion and resolve of the day should be evanescent (ix. 2). Our times of religious excitement are not our safest hours. Enthusiasm has its perils as well as its powers. Refer to Peter's eager protestation, and the Lord's word of caution, "Simon, Simon, behold, Satan hath desired to have," &c. (Luke xxii. 31). The sins which constituted Solomon's decadence—against which, through him, we are warned—appear to have been these:

I. SENSUALITY. His base self-indulgence grew upon him, as it does on any man. The life he lived was degrading to his manhood. Love became debased to lust, because it was divorced from purity. Physically, as well as morally, he became a wreck, and though not 60 years of age when he died, he was already weary, broken, and old (ver. 4). Some light may be thrown upon his downward progress by the books which bear his name, and which, if not written by him, were declarations of the experience he knew. If the Song of Solomon represents his bright youth, when love, though passionate, was undefiled, the book of Ecclesiastes is the outcry of his age, when all seemed "vanity and vexation of spirit," and when he tried once more painfully to lay the old foundation of the shattered fabric of his life

(Eccles. xii. 13). Compare him with Samson ; show how the indulgence of passion
destroys kingliness. Even such sin was not beyond pardon. It would have been
wel for Solomon had he returned to God, as his father had done (see Psa. li.)

II. EVIL COMPANIONSHIP (ver. 2). The Israelites were often warned against
marriage with the heathen. At times ordinary international intercourse was forbidden. Instances are given in which disobedience to this law of severance
brought terrible effects. Some companionship is essential to man. The hermit
must be a very imperfect Christian. John the Baptist was in the wilderness, but
Christ, whom we follow, was ever found in the haunts and homes of men. Yet
under the new dispensation the wise choice of companionship is insisted on, and
provided for. The twelve apostles were associated together, as well as separated
from others; and in their work they went forth by two and two. The Apostolic
Church presents a beautiful picture of fellowship (Acts ii.) It is amongst the wise-
hearted and devout that we are to find our friends. " Be ye not unequally yoked
together with unbelievers." The importance of this to the young, whose characters
are not yet formed. Hence responsibility rests on parents, who can encourage or
hinder acquaintances, and on young people themselves. He must have something
of Christ's wisdom and strength, and must be animated by His motives, who, like
Him, would be safe and useful amongst " the publicans and sinners."

III. EXTRAVAGANCE. The wealth of Solomon was enormous. The treasure
saved for him by David seemed inexhaustible, and the tribute from other peoples
(x. 25), the monopolies granted by the king (x. 28, 29), the importation of gold from
Ophir (ix. 28), &c., brought immense revenues. The king was proportionately extravagant. See the account given of his palaces, his gardens, and his retinue. No
country could long bear such a strain. Increased taxation was necessary, and this
was one of the causes of the break-up of the kingdom under Rehoboam. Show
in modern life the *temptations* to extravagance and ostentation; the *injury*
caused by these sins to a nation; the *moral perils* to which the extravagant are
exposed; the *diminution of help* to God's cause and to God's poor.

IV. OPPRESSION. He appears to have copied the Pharaohs not only in magnificence, but in disregard for human suffering. The Canaanites were reduced to the
position of helots; multitudes were torn from their homes to fell timber in the
forests, or hew stone in the quarries. Even the Israelites had to do forced labour.
Kings have responsibility to their people, as well as the people to their kings.
God's laws were violated by Solomon (Exod. xxii. 21; xxiii. 9). Show from history
the Nemesis of oppression. Indicate manifestations of the spirit of tyranny in
business, in homes, schools, &c.

V. IDOLATRY. Solomon erected temples to Ashtoreth, Milcom, and Chemosh.
Describe the idolatries specified. All idolatry sternly forbidden. The cultus of
these deities hideously cruel, dark, impure. Heathenism degrades man and dishonours God. Show the steps which led Solomon to the commission of such
egregious sin. (1) *He was broad in his views*, far advanced from the traditional
knowledge of the age, and often conversed with wise men of other creeds. Slowly
he lost his sense of the pre-eminence of the truth revealed to him. He saw what
was true in other systems, but meantime lost his horror at what was false in them.
This one of the special perils of our age; point it out. (2) *He wished all that was
connected with him to reflect his own magnificence.* It was not enough that his
wives and concubines should be at liberty to worship their idols; they must do it
splendidly, if at all, for his glory was concerned in their acts. (3) *He would please
and attract surrounding nations.* This partly for commercial ends, chiefly for
personal glory. Base motives lead to false policy, and false policy prepares for
national ruin.

CONCLUSION.—1. *The possibility of ruin to those whose religious advantages are
greatest.*

2. *The retribution heavier in proportion as the offence is aggravated by neglected warning.*—A. R.

Vers. 9—13.—*Solomon's Fall.* The dark omen that marred the brightness of

Solomon's second vision (ch. ix. 6) has come to be fulfilled. He was forewarned of danger and yet has fallen into it. The splendour of royal circumstance remained the same, but how completely has his true glory departed! "How is the gold become dim and the fine gold changed!" The smile of God that rested as glad sunshine on his head, has turned to "anger." The cause of the change is in the secresy of his own soul. The Scripture narrative is silent about the course of his inner life, the phases of thought and feeling through which he may have passed; so that this sudden note of discord in the midst of the harmony strikes us with something of sad surprise. Enough, however, is said to show that it was a moral change in the man himself. The Lord God of Israel had not changed in His purpose or method; it is Solomon whose "heart is turned from him." How far this was a fatal change, a real apostasy, we know not. We need not attempt to solve the purely speculative question as to whether he ever recovered from his fall; his later writings suggest at least the hope that it was so. Enough for us now to note the facts, to trace the causes, and learn the lessons. Certain broad principles of moral life are here strikingly illustrated.

I. THE TREACHERY OF HUMAN NATURE. Beneath the fairest exterior there may be latent germs of evil that only need outward incentives to develop themselves into disastrous issues. Even the inspirations of the highest wisdom and the raptures of religious emotion may have underlying them tendencies to the grossest forms of folly and the lowest deeps of sin and shame. Solomon was sincere enough in his earlier piety, but too little alive to the slumbering forces of evil that he bore within him. His moral history confirmed the truth of his own proverb: "He that trusteth in his own heart is a fool" (Prov. xxviii. 26). An Arab tradition says that in the staff on which he leaned there was a worm which was secretly gnawing it asunder. That worm was the hidden corruption of his moral nature. It is a solemn lesson: "Let him that thinketh he standeth take heed lest he fall." We can look upon no form of wrong-doing in others without being reminded that there is something akin to it in ourselves. Concealed in our own bosoms there is that which might possibly develop into similar issues. Our only security lies in the triumph of that gracious Divine power that can thoroughly purge the fountain of the heart, and destroy there the very germs of evil.

II. THE BASE USES TO WHICH THE HIGHEST ADVANTAGES OF LIFE MAY BE PERVERTED BY THE WAYWARD HEART. Solomon's greatness became the occasion and aggravation of his fall. His royal magnificence fostered "the lust of the eye and the lust of the flesh, and the pride of life." His consciousness of power degenerated into tyranny (1 Kings xii. 4; 1 Sam. viii. 11). The wealth of his emotional nature took the form of illicit love and boundless self-indulgence. His studious interest in Nature induced the dream of occult mysterious powers in material things, and the practice of magic arts. His intercourse with men of other nations led to his catching the infection of their idolatries, until at last the rival temples of Moloch, Chemosh, and Ashtaroth, with all their cruel and abominable rites, frowned darkly upon Olivet, over against the glorious house of the Lord on Mount Moriah. So fatally may the noblest personal endowments and the richest advantages of life foster the evil tendencies of the heart when once it has surrendered itself to their control. If it be true that "there is a soul of goodness in things evil," it is equally true that nothing is so good but that the spirit of evil may transform it into an instrument of moral injury. The fascinations of outward life are full of danger when that spirit lurks within. The wealth of a man's intellectual resources, the multitude of his possessions, the range of his influence, do but put into his hands the more abundant means of wrong-doing when his heart is not loyal to the good and true.

> "The fairest things below the sky
> Give but a flattering light;
> We must suspect some danger nigh,
> Where we possess delight."

This idea is not to be carried too far. Life would be intolerable on the principle of universal suspicion and distrust. The great Father of all would have His children use and enjoy freely the good of every kind that falls to their lot. But let them beware lest the spirit of evil, in some form of outward charm, through some secret avenue of soul or sense, should gain an entrance to the citadel of their heart, and "turn it away" from Him.

III. THE CERTAINTY OF DIVINE RETRIBUTIONS. Solomon cannot sin with impunity. His personal defection involves the throne in dishonour and the whole nation in discord and sorrow. He had been forewarned that it should be so, and the threatenings of God are as sure as His promises. What is God's "anger" but just the reverse side of that faithfulness that secures the purposes of His grace? What are His judgments but the severer methods of His holy love? An inexorable Nemesis tracks the path of the transgressor; not a mere blind fate—not a mere impersonal law of moral sequence—but a Divine will and power, pledged to vindicate the cause of eternal righteousness. It may follow him slowly, as with "leaden foot," but sooner or later it overtakes him. "Whatsoever a man soweth," &c. (Gal. vi. 7, 8). And though one only may sow the evil seed, how many, often, are the reapers! "The sins of the fathers are visited on the children," &c. No man can "perish alone in his iniquity." According to the range of his social relations so is the mischief his wrong-doing works. When the king falls, how many fall with him! The laws of God

> "must work their will,
> Whatever human heart may bleed;
> And more than they who do the ill
> Must suffer for the evil deed."

IV. THE MERCY THAT TEMPERS DIVINE JUDGMENTS. The execution of the sentence is both delayed and modified. Not in Solomon's own reign shall the thing be done; "nor shall the kingdom be wholly torn from his house" (vers. 12, 13). This is partly from tender regard for the sacred memory of David his father, and partly, we may believe, in mercy to himself, that space may be given him for repentance (see Psa. lxxxix. 30—37). We have here a type and example of the general method of God's ways. "In wrath he remembers mercy." Something of gracious forbearance is seen in the severest of His judgments. His chastisements are fatherly. And beneath the darkest providences and the sternest retributions there is the steady flow of a loving-kindness that endures throughout all generations, the strength of a covenant that shall never be broken.—W.

Vers. 9—13.—After the consecration of the temple Solomon reached the culminating point of his reign, both in a spiritual and temporal point of view. His fame and his dominion continued to increase. The Queen of Sheba came from the far East to pay him homage. From this summit of glory he had a sudden and shameful fall, and became all but an apostate. This son of David, whose high honour it was to have built and consecrated the temple of Jehovah, this heir of the promises on which hung the salvation of mankind, sank into idolatry. The causes of his fall were—1st, PRIDE: he forgot to give glory to God. 2nd, LUST: strange women enticed him after strange gods (ch. xi. 3). The fall of Solomon repeats in a manner the features of the first transgression. It began in the desire to be as God, and was consummated in the gratification of the flesh. Its emphatic warning to all God's people is, "Let him that thinketh he standeth, take heed lest he fall" (1 Cor. x. 12). Chastisement from God is the consequence of this fall. God had already warned Solomon that His most glorious promises were contingent on obedience to His commands. "If thou walk in my ways," &c. (ch. iii. 13, 14). God chastens Solomon because He loves him, and does not altogether take His mercy from him, since He still leaves the kingdom of Judah to his descendants. The book of Ecclesiastes, with its blending of bitterness and repentance, is perhaps the ripening fruit of this merciful severity.—E. de P.

EXPOSITION.

CHAPTER XI. 14—43.

SOLOMON'S ADVERSARIES.— As the historian has collected together in chs. vi., vii., viii. all the information he can convey respecting the *temple*, and in chs. ix., x. all the scattered notices respecting Solomon's *power* and *greatness*, so here he arranges in one section the history of Solomon's *adversaries*. It must not be supposed that the following records stand in due chronological order. The enmities here mentioned did not date from the delivery of the message of which we have just heard; on the contrary, the hatred and opposition of Hadad and Rezon began at an early period, though not the earliest (ch. v. 4), of Solomon's reign. It was only in his later life, however, that they materially affected his position and rule; hence it is that they are brought before us at this stage of the history, and also because they are manifestly regarded as chastisements for Solomon's sin.

Ver. 14.—**And the Lord stirred up an adversary unto Solomon, Hadad** [In ver. 17 written Adad, אֲדָד. Apparently this, like Pharaoh, was a title rather than a name. And, like Pharaoh, it is said to mean *the sun*. It was borne by a king of Edom in very early times, Gen. xxv. 15; xxxvi. 35, 39 (in the latter verse, as in ch. xxv. 15, Hadar is probably a clerical error for Hadad, as the name stands in 1 Chron. i. 30, 50, ר and ד being so very much alike. Gesenius, however, contends that Hadar is the true reading), and was also a favourite name with the kings of Syria, especially in the forms Benhadad, Hadadezer] **the Edomite: he was of the king's seed in Edom.**

Ver. 15.—**For it came to pass, when David was in Edom** [2 Sam. viii. 14. But the text is peculiar. Instead of "in Edom" we have "with Edom," אֶת־אֱדֹם, unless we take אֵת to be the mark of the accusative, which, however, there is no verb to govern. Keil interprets, "When David had to do with Edom." Bähr refers to 1 Chron. xx. 5, and Gen. xix. 4, but they are not strictly parallel; and it is possible that the text is slightly corrupt, as the LXX., Syr., and Arab. must have had בַּהֲכוֹת instead of בִּהְיוֹת before them "when David *smote* Edom." The LXX., *e.g.*, reads ἐν τῷ ἐξολοθρεῦσαι κ. τ. λ. It was only vicariously, however, that David *smote* Edom, or

was in Edom. According to 1 Chron. xviii. 12, *Abishai* slew 18,000 Edomites, while Psa. lx. (title) represents *Joab* as having slain 12,000 at the same time and place. The two brothers were both in high command, or Abishai may have been detailed by Joab to this service], **and Joab the captain of the host was gone up to bury the slain** [The commentators generally are agreed that these are the Israelites slain by the Edomites during an invasion of Israel, and not either the Edomites or Israelites slain in the valley of Salt], **after he had smitten** [rather, *that he smote*. This is the apodosis] **every male in Edom.** [This is, of course, hyperbolical (cf. "all Israel" below). It is clear that the whole Edomite nation did *not* perish. The words point to a terrible slaughter (cf. 1 Chron. xviii. 13) among the men of war. Possibly the cruelties of the Edomites (compare Psa. cxxxvii. 7; Obad. 10—14) had provoked this act of retribution, as to which see Deut. xx. 13.]

Ver. 16.—**For six months did Joab remain there with all Israel** [*i.e.*, the entire *army*, as in ch. xvi. 16, 17], **until he had cut off every male in Edom.**

Ver. 17.—**That Hadad fled** [This word excludes the idea that he was carried off in infancy by servants, something like Joash, 2 Kings xi. 2], **he and certain Edomites of his father's servants with him, to go into Egypt** [cf. Matt. ii. 13]; **Hadad being yet a little child.** [The words used of Solomon ch. iii. 7.]

Ver. 18.—**And they arose out of Midian** [a name of wide and somewhat varied significance. Midian embraces the eastern portion of the peninsula of Sinai (Exod. ii. 15, 21; iii. 1), and stretches along the eastern border of Palestine. The term has been compared with our "Arabia." And the indefiniteness arises in both instances from the same cause, viz., that the country was almost entirely *desert*. Midian would thus extend along the back or east of Edom. There is no need, consequently (with Thenius), to read מְעוֹן *i.e.*, their dwelling. It is noticeable, however, that the LXX. reads ἐκ τῆς πόλεως Μαδιὰμ, and some of the geographers do mention a city of that name on the eastern shore of the Elanitic gulf], **and came to Paran** [Elsewhere *Mount* Paran, Hab. iii. 3; Deut. xxxiii. 2; a desert and mountainous tract lying between Arabia Petræa, Palestine, and Idumæa (see Num. x. 12; xiii. 3, 27; 1 Sam. xxv. 1; Deut. i. 1), and comprehending the desert of Et Tih. It is difficult to identify it with greater precision, but it has been connected with the beautiful *Wâdy Feiran*, near Mount Serbal, in the Sinaitic range, which would agree fairly well with our narrative] : **and they took men with them out of Paran** [as guides through the desert, and possibly as a protection also], **and came to Egypt** [The direct route from Edom to Egypt would be across the desert of Et Tih—practically the route of the caravan of pilgrims from Mecca. But this does not settle the position of Paran, as the text seems to hint that the fugitives did not proceed direct from Edom. They may have taken refuge in the first instance amongst the tribes of Midian ; or they may have diverged from the straight course through fear], **unto Pharaoh king of Egypt** [This cannot have been the Pharaoh who was Solomon's father-in-law, for in the first place, the flight was in the time of David, and secondly, a prince who had aided and abetted these fugitives would hardly be likely to form an alliance with their great enemy. It may have been Psusennes II.] ; **which gave him an house, and appointed him victuals** [*i.e.*, certain cities or officers were charged with his maintenance, though, as his relations with the royal family were so extremely intimate (vers. 19—22), he may have been fed from the royal table], **and gave him land.**

Ver. 19.—**And Hadad found great favour in the sight of Pharaoh, so that he gave him to wife the sister of his own wife, the sister of Tahpenes** [LXX. θεκεμίνα. "No name that has any near resemblance to either Tahpenes or Thekemina has yet been found among those of the period " (Poole, Dict. Bib. iii. 1431). Rawlinson adds that the monuments of that age are extremely scanty] **the queen.** [Heb. גְּבִירָה the word generally used of the queen *mother* (as in ch. xv. 13). Here, and in 2 Kings x. 13, however, it is used of the queen consort.]

Ver. 20.—**And the sister of Tahpenes bare him Genubath his son** [otherwise unknown], **whom Tahpenes weaned in Pharaoh's house** [A significant token of his adoption into the royal family. The weaning, which generally took place in the second, sometimes third, (2 Macc. vii. 27) year, was clearly a much more *marked* occasion in the ancient East than it is among ourselves (Gen. xxi. 8 ; 1 Sam. i. 24)] : **and Genubath was in Pharaoh's household among the sons of Pharaoh.** [*i.e.* he was brought up in the Egyptian harem.]

Ver. 21.—**And when Hadad heard in Egypt that David slept with his fathers, and that Joab the captain of the host was dead** [It comes out very significantly here what a name of terror Joab's had been in Edom, and how deep was the impression which his bloody vengeance of a quarter of a century before had made] **Hadad said to Pharaoh,**

Let me depart [Heb. *send me away*], **that I may go to mine own country.** [Rawlinson cites Herod. iii. 132—137 ; v. 25, 35, 106, 107, to show that refugees at Oriental courts must obtain permission to leave them.]

Ver. 22.—**Then Pharaoh said unto him, But what hast thou lacked with me, that, behold, thou seekest to go to thine own country ?** [The natural inquiry of Eastern courtesy.] **And he answered, Nothing : howbeit let me go in any wise.** [Heb. *thou shalt surely send me away*. Rawlinson says, " There is a remarkable abruptness in this termination." But we must remember how unfinished, to our eyes, Scripture narratives constantly seem. There is no need, consequently, to suspect any accidental omission from the Hebrew text. The LXX., it is true, adds, " and Ader departed," &c., but this may be inferred from vers. 14, 25. And Hadad's persistent desire to depart, for which he assigns no reason, is suggestive of the thoughts which were stirring in his soul. " The keen remembrance of his native land, his lost kingdom, and the slaughter of all his house, gathered strength within him ; and all the ease and princely honour which he enjoyed in Egypt availed not against the claims of ambition, vengeance, and patriotism " (Kitto).]

Ver. 23.—**And God stirred him up another adversary** [almost identical with ver. 14], **Rezon the son of Eliadah** [Often identified with the Hezion of ch. xv. 18, but on insufficient grounds. Whether he was a usurper, who had dethroned Hadad (see Jos., Ant., vi. 5. 2), or an officer of Hadadezer's, who escaped either before or after the battle of 2 Sam. viii. 3—5, is uncertain. The following words agree equally well with either supposition], **which fled from his lord Hadadezer king of Zobah.**

Ver. 24.—**And he gathered men unto him, and became captain over a band** [either of rebels before or of fugitives after the defeat], **when David slew them of Zobah** [*Of Zobah*, not in Heb. " Them " must mean the Syrian army] : **and they went to Damascus, and dwelt therein** [As David put garrisons in Syria of Damascus (2 Sam. viii. 6), this must have been some time *after* the defeat of the Syrians. But Keil argues that it cannot have been in the middle or later part of Solomon's reign, inasmuch as Solomon must have been lord of Damascus, or he could not have built Palmyra. But it is not so incontrovertibly settled that Solomon did build Palmyra (see on ch. ix. 18) as to make this argument of much weight. And even if it were, we might still fix the reign of Rezon at an earlier period of Solomon's sway. See below], **and reigned.** [*i.e.*, the band or troop of Rezon, either in the confusion of the defeat, or in some subsequent time of anarchy, took possession of Damascus, and he, it would seem, usurped the crown. The word "reigned," however (plural), is somewhat remarkable. It may perhaps be accounted for by the plurals which precede it. The insertion of one "yod" (וימליכו for וימלכו) gives the sense "*they made him king*," which would certainly be preferable, if the emendation were not purely conjectural.

Ver. 25.—**And he was an adversary to Israel all the days of Solomon** [We are not compelled, however, to believe that his reign lasted "all the days of Solomon." This last expression is to be taken with considerable latitude. It is an Orientalism. At the time of ch. v. 4, neither Hadad nor Rezon was giving Solomon any trouble], **beside the mischief which Hadad did** [Heb. omits *did*. The construction of the Hebrew (see Ewald, 277d (2), 292b, note) is difficult. Literally, "and with the evil which Hadad," &c. (comp. ver. 1 of this chapter, "and with the daughter," &c., with Exod. i. 14, Heb.) The LXX. reconstructs the text, making the following words, "and he abhorred," &c., apply to Hadad; and altering Syria (ארם) into Edom (אדם) to suit. But it is far better to understand עשה (with our Authorized Version); *i.e.*, beside the mischief which Hadad *did* (or, "beside the mischief of Hadad," Ewald). "And he (Rezon) abhorred," &c. Hadad's enmity has already been described (vers. 17—22), and the historian has passed on to the case of Rezon. It is extremely unlikely that he should now suddenly recur exclusively to Hadad. It is very natural for him, on the other hand, in his account of Rezon, to remind us that all this was in addition to the mischief wrought by Hadad] : **and he abhorred** [Heb. *loathed*] **Israel, and reigned over Syria.**

Ver. 26.—**And Jeroboam** [Viewed in the light of their history, the names *Jeroboam* and *Rehoboam* are both instructive. The first means, "Whose people are many; " the second, "Enlarger of the people." The latter might almost have been bestowed in irony, the former by way of parody] **the son of Nebat** [The case of Jeroboam is now related at much greater length, not so much because of the importance of the rebellion at the time, as because of its bearing on the later history of Israel. It led to the disruption of the kingdom and the schism in the Church. It was the first great symptom of the decadence of the *power* of Solomon; of his decline in *piety* we have had many indications. We see in it an indication that the Hebrew commonwealth has passed its

zenith], **an Ephrathite** [*i.e.*, Ephraimite; cf. Judg. xii. 5; 1 Sam. i. 1. Ephraim was the ancient rival of Judah, and by reason of its numbers, position, &c., might well aspire to the headship of the tribes (Gen. xlix. 26; xlviii. 19; Deut. xxxiii. 17; Josh. xvii. 17)] **of Zereda** [Mentioned here only, unless it is identical with Zeredathah (2 Chron. iv. 17) or Zarthan (Josh. iii. 16; 1 Kings iv. 12) in the Jordan valley. That this place was apparently situate in the tribe of Manasseh, is no argument against the identification (Bähr), for an Ephrathite might surely be born out of Ephraim. It is, however, observable that Zereda has the definite article (similarly ἡ Σαρείρα in the LXX., but this place is located in *Mount* Ephraim), which Zarthan, &c., have not. Hence it is probably the same as the *Zererath* of Judg. vii. 22. In fact, some MSS. read צְרֵדָה there instead of צְרֵרָה and ר and ד are not only etymologically interchangeable, but are also extremely liable to be confused (see above on ver. 14)], **Solomon's servant** [*i.e.*, officer; cf. ver. 28], **whose mother's name was Zeruah** [*i.e.*, *leprous*. His mother's name is recorded, probably because his father, having died early, was comparatively unknown. But it is not impossible that the similarity either with *Zeruiah* (cf. ch. i. 7) or *Zererah* had something to do with its preservation. The people would not readily forget that Solomon's other great adversary was the son of Zeruiah. And we have many proofs how much the Jews affected the jingle of similar words], **even he lifted up his** [Heb. *a*] **hand** [*i.e.*, rebelled. Synonymous expression 2 Sam. xviii. 28, xx. 21. Observe, we have no history or account of this rebellion except in the LXX., but merely of the circumstances which led to it] **against the king.**

Ver. 27.—**And this was the cause** [or, *this is the account;* this is how it came about. Same words Josh. v. 4, and ch. ix. 15. We have here a long parenthesis, explaining the origin, &c., of Jeroboam's disaffection] **that he lifted up his hand** [Heb. *a hand*] **against the king. Solomon built Millo** [see on ch. ix. 15], **and repaired the breaches** [These words convey the impression that Solomon renewed the decayed or destroyed parts of the wall. But (1) סָגַר does not mean *repair*, except indirectly. It means he *closed*, *shut*. And (2) פֶּרֶץ sing, refers to *one* breach or opening. Moreover (3) it was not so long since the wall was built (2 Sam. v. 9). It could hardly, therefore, have decayed, and there had been no siege to cause a breach. We must understand the word, consequently, not of a part broken down, but of a portion unbuilt. We have elsewhere suggested that this was the breach in the line of circumvallation, caused by the Tyropæon valley, and that *the Millo* was the bank, or rampart which *closed* it. And to this view the words of the text lend some confirmation] **of the city of David his father.** [As Millo was built about the 25th year of Solomon's reign (ch. ix. 15), we are enabled to fix approximately the date of Jeroboam's rebellion. It was apparently about ten or twelve years before Solomon's death.

Ver. 28.—**And the man Jeroboam was a mighty man of valour** [same expression Judg. vi. 12 ; xi. 1 ; 1 Sam. ix. 1 ; 2 Kings xv. 20. In Ruth ii. 1 it hardly seems to imply valour so much as wealth (as A. V.) : **and Solomon seeing the young man that he was industrious** [Heb. *doing work*], **he made him ruler over all the charge** [Heb. *appointed him to all the burden*] **of the house of Joseph.** [The tribe of Ephraim, with its constant envy of Judah, must have been mortified to find themselves employed— though it was but in the modified service of Israelites—on the fortifications of Jerusalem. Their murmurings revealed to Jeroboam the unpopularity of Solomon, and perhaps suggested thoughts of overt rebellion to his mind.]

Ver. 29.—**And it came to pass at that time** [a general expression = " when he was thus employed "] **when** [Heb. *that*] **Jeroboam went out of Jerusalem that** [Heb. *and*], **the prophet Ahijah the Shilonite** [*i.e.*, of Shiloh, as is expressed ch. xiv. 2—4, where see notes. He too, therefore, was an Ephraimite (Josh. xvi. 5). This portion of the history is probably derived from his writings (2 Chron. ix. 29). We may be pretty sure that Nathan was now dead] **found him in the way ; and he** [*i.e.*, Ahijah. Ewald understands Jeroboam to be meant, and would see in the new garment his " splendid robe of office "] **ha d clad himself with a new garment** [שַׂלְמָה same word as שִׂמְלָה such transpositions of letters being common. The *simlah* was the outer garment (Gen. ix. 23 ; 1 Sam. xxi. 10, &c.), which served at night as a covering (Deut. xxii. 17). It was probably identical in shape, &c., with the camel's-hair *burnous*, or *abba*, worn by the Arabs at the present day (cf. Conder, pp. 318, 342), and being almost a square would lend itself well to division into twelve parts] ; **and they two were alone in the field** [*i.e.*, open country.]

Ver. 30.—**And Ahijah caught** [This English word almost implies that it was Jeroboam's garment (cf. Gen. xxxix. 12) ; but the original simply means " laid hold of."] **the new garment that was on him, and rent** [same word as in vers. 11, 12, 13] **it in twelve pieces.** [The first instance of an " acted parable " (Rawlinson).]

Ver. 31.—**And he said to Jeroboam, Take thee ten pieces : for thus saith the Lord, the God of Israel, Behold, I will rend the kingdom out of the hand of Solomon, and will give ten tribes** [Keil insists that " ten " is here mentioned merely as the number of completeness ; that, in fact, it is to be understood symbolically and not arithmetically. He further states that in point of fact the kingdom of Jeroboam only consisted of *nine* tribes, that of Simeon being practically surrounded by the territory of Judah, and so becoming incorporated in the southern kingdom. But surely, if that had been the idea in the prophet's mind, it would have been better expressed had he torn off *one* piece from the garment and given the rest, undivided, to Jeroboam (Bähr). And the reference to the number of the tribes is unmistakable. As to Simeon, we have no means of knowing what part that tribe, if it still existed, took at the division of the kingdom. See on ch. xix. 3. Its members had long been scattered (Gen. xlix. 7), and it gradually dwindled away, and has already disappeared from the history. But even if it had a corporate existence and *did* follow the lead of Judah, still that is not con - clusive on the question, for we know not only that the historian uses round numbers, but also that we are not to look for exact statements, as the next verse proves] **to thee.**

Ver. 32.—**But he shall have one tribe** [LXX. δύο σκῆπτρα. Some would understand " one tribe, in *addition to Judah*," but compare ch. xii. 20, " tribe of Judah," and see note on ver. 13. Possibly neither Judah nor Benjamin is here to be thought of separately. In ch. xii. 21, and 2 Chron. xi. 3, 23, they are *both* reckoned to Rehoboam. They might be regarded as in some sense one, inasmuch as they enclosed the Holy City (Seb. Schmidt), the line of division passing right through the temple platform. But it is perhaps safer, in view of ch. xii. 20, to understand the term of Judah, compared with which large and influential tribe " little Benjamin " was hardly deserving of separate mention] **for my servant David's sake, and for Jerusalem's sake** [see on vers. 12, 13], **the city which I have chosen out of all the tribes of Israel.**

Ver. 33.—**Because that they** [The LXX. has the singular throughout, and so have all the translations, except the Chaldee. But the plural is to be retained, the import being that Solomon was not alone in his idolatrous leanings ; or it may turn our thoughts to the actual idolaters—his wives —whose guilt he shared. The singular looks as if an alteration had been *made* to bring the words into harmony with the context, and especially with the concluding words of this verse, "David *his* father."] **have forsaken me, and have worshipped Ashtoreth the goddess of the Zidonians** [צדנין a Chaldee form. But many MSS. read צדנים], **Chemosh the god of the Moabites, and Milcom** [the LXX. has "their king the abomination," &c., καὶ τῷ βασιλεῖ αὐτῶν. See note on ver. 5], **the god of the children of Ammon, and have not walked in my ways, to do that which is right in mine eyes, and to keep my statutes and my judgments, as did David his father.**

Ver. 34.—**Howbeit I will not take the whole kingdom** [Rawlinson says the context requires "*aught* of the kingdom," and affirms that the Hebrew will bear this rendering. But he surely forgets that the Hebrew has the def. art. אֶת־כָּל־הַמַּמְלָכָה can only represent "*all* the kingdom, τὴν βασιλείαν ὅλην (LXX.) See Gesen., Thesau s.v. כֹּל d. It would certainly seem as if this verse should speak of Solomon's retaining the sceptre during his *lifetime*, and not of his retaining a *part* of the empire. But we may not go against the grammar] **out of his hand : but I will make him prince all the days of his life for David my servant's sake, whom I chose, because he kept my commandments and my statutes.** ["If Solomon break his covenant with God, God will not break his covenant with the father of Solomon" (Hall).]

Ver. 35.—**But I will take the kingdom out of his son's hand, and will give it unto thee, even ten tribes.**

Ver. 36.—**And unto his son will I give one tribe** [cf. ver. 32, note], **that David my servant may have a light alway before me** [The same expression is found in ch. xv. 4 ; 2 Kings viii. 19 ; 2 Chron. xxi. 7 ; and compare Psa. cxxxii. 17. Keil would explain it by 2 Sam. xxi. 17 ; but 2 Sam. xiv. 7, "my coal which is left," appears to be a closer parallel. The idea is not that of a *home* (Rawlinson), but *family, issue*. We speak of the *extinction* of a family (Bähr)] **in Jerusalem, the city which I have chosen me to put my name there.**

Ver. 37.—**And I will take thee, and thou shalt reign according to all that thy soul desireth** [We are not justified in concluding from these words that Jeroboam then had ambitious designs upon the throne (Keil). They rather mean, " as king, all thy desires shall be gratified " (cf. Deut. xii. 20 ; xiv.

26 ; 1 Sam. ii. 16 ; 2 Sam. iii. 21). Bähr paraphrases " thou shalt have the dominion thou now strivest for," but we have absolutely no proof that Jeroboam at that time had ever meditated rebellion. It is quite possible that the idea was inspired by this interview], **and shalt be king over Israel.**

Ver. 38.—**And it shall be, if thou wilt hearken unto all that I command thee** [cf. ch. iii. 14; vi. 12 ; ix. 4], **and wilt walk in my ways, and do that is right in my sight, to keep my statutes and my commandments, as David my servant did ; that I will be with thee** [cf. ch. i. 37, note], **and build thee a sure house** [cf. 2 Sam. vii. 11, 16; *i.e.*, a *family*, perhaps *dynasty*. Observe, however, there was no promise to Jeroboam, as there was to David, of an enduring *kingdom*. It was not God's design to take away the kingdom from David in perpetuity (ver. 39)], **as I built for David, and will give Israel unto thee.**

Ver. 39.—**And I will for this** [*i.e.*, the defection just described] **afflict the seed of David, but not for ever** [Heb. *all the days.* Cf. Psa. lxxxix. 28, 33, 36. This limitation, " not for ever," would seem to apply to the kingdom, for it was through the loss of their kingdom that the seed of David was afflicted. And if so, it promises, if not a restoration of the kingdom to the house of David, at any rate a renewal or continuance of God's favour. We may perhaps regard the promise as fulfilled in the subsequent history of the kings of Judah. Not only did the kingdom last for nearly 500 years, but the royal house of David maintained its position to the time of Zerubbabel. Nor is it to be overlooked that He "of whose kingdom there shall be no end " (Luke i. 33) was the son of David].

Ver. 40.—**Solomon sought the efore to kill Jeroboam.** [It is often assumed that Solomon's attempt on Jeroboam's life was the result of the prophecy of Ahijah. And our translation with its " therefore " favours this view. The Heb., however, has simply "*and* Solomon sought," &c. And these words connect themselves with ver. 26, " even he lifted up his hand," &c. With ver. 27 a parenthesis begins, explaining how it came about that Jeroboam rebelled. It is implied distinctly that it was because of Ahijah's prophecy. That prophecy, however, was in no sense a justification of treason or attack on Jeroboam's part. The fact that God had revealed His purposes was no reason why Jeroboam should forestall them. David knew and others knew that he was destined to be king, but he piously left it for God, in His own time and way, to place him on the throne. And Jeroboam's rebellion is the more inexcusable, because

Ahijah had expressly stated that Solomon was to retain the kingdom during his lifetime. However, "he lifted up his hand;" there was some overt act of rebellion, and Solomon, because of this, and not because of the prophecy (of which, indeed, he may never have heard), sought to slay him. Nor was the king without justification in so doing. Treason must be promptly suppressed, and treason against a benefactor (see ver. 28) is doubly hateful.] **And Jeroboam arose, and fled into Egypt** [cf. verse 17, and Matt. ii. 13. It was the natural place of refuge], **unto Shishak, king of Egypt** [Shishak is beyond doubt the Sheshonk I. of the monuments, and is the first of the Pharaohs who can be identified with certainty (see Dict. Bib. iii. p. 1288). The date of his accession appears to be somewhere between 988 and 980 B.C. As to his invasion of Palestine, see on ch. xiv. 25. His reception of Jeroboam almost proves that there has been a change of dynasty, and that the new Pharaoh was no friend to Solomon], **and was in Egypt until the death of Solomon.** [Compare again Matt. ii. 15.]

Ver. 41.—**And the rest of the acts of Solomon, and all that he did, and his wisdom, are they not written in the book of the acts of Solomon?** [The sources of this history are mentioned more specifically in 2 Chron. ix. 29.]

Ver. 42.—**And the time** [Heb. *days*] **that Solomon reigned in Jerusalem over all Israel was forty years.** [Josephus, here as elsewhere, doubles the figure, making his reign to have lasted *eighty* years. It is somewhat remarkable, but affords no just ground for suspicion, that each of the first three kings of Israel should have reigned just forty years. "Such numerical coincidences occur in exact history. Saosduchinus, Chiniladanus, and Nabopolassar, three consecutive kings of Babylon, reigned each twenty-one years" (Rawlinson).]

Ver. 43.—**And Solomon slept with his fathers** [see note on ch. ii. 10. For the later and often mythical accounts of Solomon, see Ewald, iii. pp. 318, 319. The question of his repentance is discussed by Keble, "Occasional Papers," pp. 416—434], **and was buried in the city of David his father; and Rehoboam his son** [So far as appears his only son. "Solomon hath but one son, and he no miracle of wisdom." "Many a poor man hath a houseful of children by one wife, whilst this great king hath but one son by any housefuls of wives" (Bp. Hall). It is worth remembering in this connection that Psa. cxxvii., which speaks of children as God's reward (ver. 3), is with good reason ascribed to Solomon] **reigned in his stead.**

HOMILETICS.

Vers. 31—35.—*The Punishment of Solomon's Sin.* We have lately traced the gradual declension in piety of this most puissant prince; we have seen him steadily sowing to the wind. The next thing Scripture records concerning him is the retribution which befel him. It is now for us to see him reaping to the whirlwind.

But in considering the recompenses of his sin, it is essential to remember—1. That we can only speak, because we only know, of the *temporal* punishment which attended him. It may be that was all. Possibly the flesh was destroyed that the spirit might be saved in the day of the Lord (1 Cor. vi. 5). It may be that, foully as he fell, he did not fall finally. but of this no man can be certain. There is every reason to think that the question has been "left in designed obscurity" (Keble, "Occasional Papers," pp. 392—434, where the subject is discussed at considerable length), that no one might presume. It may be, therefore, that he still awaits the just recompense of wrath in the day of wrath (Rom. ii. 5). 2. That if this temporal punishment does not strike us as severe—considering the enormity of his sin and the greatness of the gifts and privileges he had abused—it is partly because the temporal punishment was mitigated for his father's sake. The avenging hand could not smite Solomon without at the same time hurting David. We are expressly told that Solomon was maintained on the throne all his life, and that one tribe was given—the word implies that the gift was unmerited—to his son, for David's sake (vers. 34—36). If, therefore, we are tempted to think that the punishment was not exemplary, let us see in it an instance of God's "showing mercy unto thousands" (*sc.*, of generations, Exod. xx. 6)—a proof of the Infinite Love which "remembered David and all his afflictions" (Psa. cxxxii. 1). But such as it was, it was sufficient to teach us these two lessons at least. 1. "Be sure your sin will find you out" (Num. xxxii. 23). 2. "Whatsoever a man soweth, that shall he also reap" (Gal. vi. 7).

For this retribution was of two kinds. There was—I. THAT WHICH SOLOMON SUFFERED IN HIS OWN PERSON; and, II. THAT WHICH HE SUFFERED IN HIS FAMILY AND KINGDOM. Under the first of these categories the following penalties are to be ranked:

1. *His life was shortened.* Probably by the operation of natural laws. It is not suggested that he was directly smitten of God; it is quite possible that his rank voluptuousness destroyed his energies and induced premature decay. But all the same his days were cut short. Not only was long life the principal sanction of the dispensation under which he lived, but it had been expressly promised him as the reward of piety (ch. iii. 14). But his sun went down while it was yet noon. He was not sixty when the mandate went forth, "Remove the diadem, and take off the crown" (Ezek. xxi. 26). And if it be true, what Dr. Johnson said to David Garrick when the latter showed him his elegant house at Richmond, that great and rare earthly possessions "make deathbeds miserable," it must have cost Solomon a sharp pang to leave so soon his cedar palace and his chryselephantine throne.

2. *His life was embittered.* If, as is most probable, we have in the book of Ecclesiastes a chapter of his autobiography, it is clear that his glory brought him little satisfaction (ch. iii. *passim ;* v. 13; vi. 12; vii. 26); there was a worm at the root of all his pleasures. Of what avail were his houses, his gardens, his pools of water, &c., so long as he had not the heart to enjoy them?

> "It is the mind that maketh good or ill,
> That maketh wretch'd or happy, rich or poor,
> For some, that hath abundance at his will,
> Hath not enough, but seeks a greater store."

He knew nothing of "the royalty of inward happiness." How different St. Paul, "Having nothing, yet possessing all things," &c. (2 Cor. vi. 10). What a commentary on the "confessions" of Solomon, as they have been called, with their everlasting refrain, their *vanitas vanitatum,* is that confession of a man who suffered one long martyrdom of pain—the Baptist minister, Robert Hall—"I enjoy everything."

3. *He was tortured by remorse.* This is not expressly stated, but surely it may with good reason be inferred. For the wisest of men could not be so insensate, when he heard the message of doom (ch. xii. 2), as not to reflect how different his end was to be from his beginning; how fair the flower, and how bitter the fruit. Surely the cry he has put into others' lips would often rise from his own, "How have I hated instruction," &c. (Prov. v. 12).

4. *He was haunted by forebodings.* "This great Babylon" which he had builded, how soon should it be destroyed. The empire which he had consolidated should barely last his life. "One tribe"—how those words would ring in his ears! Then he had good reason, too, to fear that his son was one of the class he had himself described (Prov. x. 1; xv. 20; xvii. 25; xix. 13. Cf. Eccles. ii. 19), and no match for Jeroboam, of whose designs upon the throne he cannot have been ignorant (1 Kings xi. 26, 27). He had the mortification of knowing that his "servant" would enter into his labours. And to the prospect of dissensions within, was added the certainty of disaffection without. Hadad and Rezon were already on his border, and were only biding their time. The political horizon was indeed black and lowering.

5. *He was harassed by adversaries.* For it is clear from verses 14, 23, 26, that Solomon's enemies were not content to wait for his death. Damascus was a thorn in his side. Egypt was a hotbed of intrigues. The profound peace which he once enjoyed he had lost. The clouds of war were not only gathering, but some of them had burst. His throne of ivory and gold can have been but an insecure and uncomfortable seat for some time before he vacated it.

II. But men like Solomon think of posterity and of posthumous fame as much as of themselves. If every father has "given hostages to fortune," how much more vulnerable is a king in the person of his successor. Let us now trace the calamities which befel Solomon's house and kingdom.

1. *In the infatuation of his son.* Was there ever a political crisis so wofully mismanaged as that which marked Rehoboam's accession? A few pacific words, a graceful concession, and all would have gone well. But his brutal *non possumus* precipitated his downfall. It was enough to make Solomon turn in his grave. But it is for us to remember that "his mother's name was Naamah, *an Ammonitess*" (ch. xiv. 21, 31). And this is the result of multiplying *wives*.

2. *In the dismemberment of his kingdom.* The vast empire which Solomon had founded with so much care and pains, how short a time sufficed to tear it asunder. What a contrast between the "one tribe" with its barren territory, and the description of ch. iv. 20, 21. How had he spent his strength for naught, or rather for his slave Jeroboam, who inherited all the fairest and wealthiest portions of the realm. And this was the end of his land-hunger—that he was left with the desert of Judah.

3. *In the invasion of Shishak.* For he had not long slept with his fathers when the vast treasures which he had lavished on the palace of the Lord and his own palaces were carried away to Egypt. All the precious metals which David had accumulated, all the acquisitions of Solomon's fleets, all the royal offerings of the queen of Sheba and of tributary kings—gone to the sons of the stranger, to the swart children of Ham. He had amassed prodigious wealth, but it was for aliens and enemies. Not only the shields and drinking vessels, but the candlesticks, bowls, and the very *laminae* which had glorified the sanctuary, all fell to the invader. What a case of *Sic vos non vobis!* What would Solomon have said could he have foreseen Rehoboam's "Brummagem" shields, and the punctilious ceremony with which they were paraded and preserved? And this was the end of multiplying *silver and gold* to himself. He had put it all into a bag with holes (Haggai i. 6).

4. *In the demoralization of his people.* For the idolatries of Judah, the images, the groves, the Sodomites (ch. xiv. 23), were but the continuation and development of the idolatries which Solomon had inaugurated. His son did but reap the crop which himself had sown. Nay, so exact is the *lex talionis* that we presently find a *queen* of Judah erecting a "horror" for the most shameful of rites (see note on ch. xv. 13). And this was the result of building altars for his queens and princesses "on the hill that is before Jerusalem," that within a few years the Lord's people, whose was the law and the temple, &c., built them high places, &c., "on *every* high hill and under every green tree" (ch. xiv. 23).

5. *In the captivity of the nation.* For the dispersion and enslavement of the Jewish people, though only consummated some four centuries later, and though it was the retribution of a long series of sins, was nevertheless, in a sense, the result of Solomon's sin. That is to say, his sin was (as ch. ix. vers. 6, 7 show) the first beginning of that ever-deepening apostasy from the Lord, of which the captivity was, from the first, denounced as the punishment. Other princes no doubt followed in his steps and filled up the measure of iniquity, but the *Grand Monarque* of their race had first showed them the way. And so the people who had held sway even to the Euphrates were carried beyond the Euphrates, and those who had seen subject kings in their land became subjects in a foreign land (cf. Jer. v. 19). How full of instruction and warning is it that the captivity which Solomon foretold (ch. viii. 46) he should have done so much to precipitate. He predicted, *i.e.*, both his own and his nation's downfall.

6. But the *multiplication of horses*, that too, like the other sins, seems to have brought its own peculiar *Nemesis*. For whence, let us ask, came the army that pillaged Jerusalem, and carried off the treasures of the temple? It came in the footprints of the horses. First, the invasion of Solomon, and then the invasion of Shishak, "with twelve hundred chariots and *threescore thousand horsemen*" (2 Chron. xii. 3). And what came of the horses supplied to the Tyrians and Hittites? See ch. xx. 1 ("horses and chariots;" cf. ver. 25); ch. xxii. 31; 2 Kings vi. 15; vii. 6, &c. It is extremely probable that the cavalry he supplied to foreign kings became an instrument in their hands to scourge his own people. Nor is it wholly unworthy of notice that the murderer Zimri was "captain of *half the chariots*" (ch. xvi. 9). Assuredly, that unhallowed trade did not go unpunished.

Such, then, is the principal moral of this history: "Their sorrows shall be multiplied that hasten after another god " (Psa. xvi. 4). And among the additional lessons which this subject teaches are these: (1) That where much is given, much will be required; (2) That judgment begins at the house of God; (3) " He that knew his lord's will and did it not shall be beaten with many stripes; " (4) " *Every* transgression and disobedience shall receive its just recompense of reward; " (5) " If God spared not the natural branches," &c.

HOMILIES BY VARIOUS AUTHORS.

Vers. 14—25.—*Premonitions of Wrath.* Though the full weight of the judgment of God upon the sin of Solomon was not to come upon him in his lifetime, yet did he not, in this world, go altogether without punishment. The foreknowledge of the evils to come upon his family and people was in itself a heavy affliction. But in addition to this, the evening of his days was doomed to be disturbed. To this end— I. GOD STIRRED UP ADVERSARIES AGAINST HIM. 1. *In themselves these were inconsiderable.* (1) Hadad the Edomite ! What can he do ? He is indeed of the seed royal of Edom, but then Edom is tributary to Solomon, and Hadad i an exile in Egypt. (2) Rezon the Syrian ! What can he do ? He was only a captain under Hadadezer, king of Zobah, whom David defeated, and who fled with his men, over whom he seems to have acted as a chief of banditti. 2. *But they have been quietly acquiring influence.* (1) Hadad, who was a lad when he fled from David, has now attained to man's estate ; is in high favour with Pharaoh, and has become brother-in-law to the monarch of the Nile. (2) Rezon also, taking advantage of the apathy of Solomon, who is too much engaged in the seraglio to pay close attention to the affairs of his distant provinces, is already i Damascus and on the throne of Syria. 3. *With God behind them they are now formidable.* (1) The fly is a feeble creature, but let God send it forth as a plague, and Egypt is in agony. So Hadad, again amongst his Edomites, is by a competent Providence enabled to work " mischief" even to Solomon ! (2) Rezon also is in a position to gratify his abhorrence of Israel " all the days of Solomon," or to the end of those days. (3) Let us see the hand of God in all the events of life. Let the discernment of symptoms of His displeasure lead us to repentance and reformation. Let us never despise the day of small things, for the great hand of God ma be in it. It is difficult to distinguish the trifling from the momentous. II. HE STIRRED UP THOSE ADVERSARIES BY MEANS. 1. *They were reminded of the sufferings of their people.* (1) When David conquered Edom there was a fearful carnage. For six months Joab was engaged in cutting off all the males, until, no natives surviving, Israel had to bury the slain (vers. 15, 16). This slaughter was sufficiently dreadful, though it may only have extended to those old enough to bear arms. Hadad was not an infant then, but (נער קטן) a *little boy*—of sufficient age to see what was going on and make his escape with the servants. Rezon was of an age and in a position to estimate the miseries which the Syrians suffered when " David slew " them, which sufficiently accounts for the manner in which he " abhorred Israel." Wars are the cradles of resentments. (2) These terrible massacres have their justification in the sins of the people who suffered them. In executing the wrath of God upon Edom, David fulfilled the famous prophecy of Balaam (see Num. xxiv. 17—19). But in this David was the type of Christ, the true Star of Jacob and Prince of Israel, whose anger will sweep His enemies to extermination. 2. *They were persuaded that the opportunity was ripe for revenge.* (1) They heard that the warriors were dead (ver. 21). They were no longer paralyzed by the sound of the once terrible names of David and Joab. (2) As for Solomon, he never was a warrior. And now he is stupefied by idolatry, and enervated in the harem. (3) Consequently they put on a bold front, and from different points harassed and distracted Solomon, apparently with impunity. For the king of Israel knew that God was angry, and " conscience makes cowards of us all."

Who can afford to have God for his enemy ? Solomon could not afford it. Can we ? Who would not make peace with such an antagonist ? He proposes His own terms. Why do we not repent and believe the gospel ?—M.

Vers. 26—28.—*Jeroboam*. The words before us are interesting as the earliest notice of a character who made a considerable figure in Hebrew history. They bring before us—

I. THE OBSCURITY OF HIS ORIGIN. 1. He was an *Ephrathite of Zereda*. (1) The tribe of Ephraim was not obscure ; on the contrary, it was next in importance to Judah. But that importance was collective—arose from the multitude of its people. An individual Ephrathite would rather be lost in the multitude. (2) As to Zereda, so little was this place among the thousands of Ephraim that it is mentioned only here, and would have been forgotten but for Jeroboam. Note: Places derive notoriety from men. Men are greater than places. 2. He was the *son of Nebat and Zeruah*. (1) Of these persons we should not have heard but for the part their son played in history. How much of our reputation is adventitious! Unenviable is the notoriety gained through relationship with the devil. How truly glorious is that man who rejoices in the imputed righteousness of Christ! (2) Yet Nebat and Zeruah founded the reputation of Jeroboam. They had the moulding of the child which became the father of the man. This is the true reason for the association of their names with his. (3) In this view there is something judicial in this association of the names of parents and child. Their influence, though obscure, was sure, and now finds expression. What an expression will there be of obscure influences when the momentous resultants come out in the disclosures of the great judgment! 3. He was the *son of a widow*. (1) Why is this noted, but to suggest that through the death of Nebat the responsibilities of the home at Zereda early devolved upon Jeroboam? Thus, those executive powers which brought him under the notice of Solomon had early scope. How little we know of the purposes of Providence in the bereavements and afflictions of families! (2) Private afflictions are suffered for public uses. In suffering, let us not murmur, but listen to the voice of God, and pray that the dispensation may be sanctified.

II. HIS ADVANCEMENT TO POWER. 1. He became a *mighty man of valour*. (1) This fact is recorded, but not the stages by which he became so known. Many a struggle occurred which had no other record than in this resultant. The value of circumstances is expressed in resultants. Let us attempt to weave all the circumstances of our lives into a character of goodness that will endure for ever. (2) Jeroboam had an energetic spirit and probably a robust physique. These he inherited. Neither for genius nor good constitutions are we indebted to ourselves. We owe much to our ancestors. (3) But he cultivated his natural parts. Many are richly endowed by nature, but waste their endowments as an idle spendthrift wastes an inheritance. Our very faculties may become obliterated by disuse (Matt. xxv. 28). 2. *His abilities were discerned by Solomon*. (1) This is noted to have occurred in connection with the building of Millo, and the closing of, or to close, the breaches in the city of David (ver. 27). Possibly Jeroboam distinguished himself against Jebusites, or some other malcontents, or in closing those breaches in the face of the enemy. (2) Possibly the industry that attracted the notice of Solomon may have been simply in superintendence of improvements in the buildings at Millo and the fortifications. Providence finds opportunities for those who are ready to enter the opening door (Prov. xxii. 29). 3. *He was promoted to the charge over the house of Joseph*. (1) From an individual once lost in the multitude of this great house, he is now conspicuous before the multitude. His being an Ephrathite is now of importance to him. Let us never quarrel with circumstances, for we never know what may prove of service. (2) Being found diligent in a minor charge he is promoted to a major responsibility. So does God deal with His people (Matt. xiii. 12 ; xxv. 29). What is worth doing is worth doing well. 4. *Now he lifts his hand against his patron*. (1) Prosperity brings out the character. He is moved by ambition. Much would have more. He aspires to a throne. His success had encouraged this desire before he met Ahijah (see ver. 37). (2) He rebels against the author of his prosperity. Ambition smothers gratitude. How human! Is not this the case with all rebels against God? (3) How plainly we can see baseness when manifested by man toward his fellow ; but how slow we are to see this when ingratitude is toward God !

The obscurity of our origin is no bar to our advancement in the religious service of God. "Not many noble are called."—M.

Vers. 29—39.—*The Message of Ahijah.* As Jeroboam went out of Jerusalem with his commission from Solomon to rule as his lieutenant over the house of Joseph, meditating how he might use his fortune to construct a throne, he was met by Ahijah the Shilonite, who accosted him in a manner agreeable to his ambition. In the message of Ahijah we have—

I. A PROPHECY. 1. This was expressed in *sign.* (1) The Shilonite provided himself with a new garment. This was intended to symbolize the kingdom. The same sign had been similarly used before (see 1 Sam. xv. 27; xxiv. 5). Note: His people are the honourable clothing of a prince (see Prov. xiv. 28). (2) The garment was new. The kingdom of Israel was as yet young. Solomon was but the third monarch in succession. The garment was whole. So was the kingdom, as yet, unbroken. Note: The robe of Christ was seamless and woven throughout, which suggests the perfect unity which will appear in the subjects of His heavenly kingdom. Note further: That in His transfiguration, which symbolized His kingdom (see Matt. xvi. 28; xvii. 1), His raiment shined "as no fuller on earth could white it," suggesting the purity and glory in which the subjects of that kingdom are to shine (Matt. xiii. 43). (3) But the robe in the hands of the prophet, the messenger and representative of God, is now rent into twelve pieces, according to the number of tribes composing the kingdom, ten of which were given into the hand of Jeroboam. Note: God disposes. In its militant state the kingdom of Christ is subject to revolutions, but not so in its triumphant and heavenly state. 2. The prophecy also is expressed in *words* (vers. 31—39). (1) Thus the testimony is twofold. It appeals to the eye, also to the ear. (2) History verified the predictions to the letter. What a testimony to the truth of God is the harmony and correspondence of prophecy and history!

II. ITS REASONS. These are expressed and implied. 1. *The sin of Solomon is specified* (vers. 31, 33). (1) Solomon forsook the Lord. God never forsakes us unless we first forsake Him. Let us be admonished. (2) He worshipped idols. Ashtoreth, the impure Venus of the Zidonians; Chemosh, the abomination of the Moabites; and Milcom, or Moloch, the devil of the Ammonites, are put into competition with the God of Israel! Whoever is so foolish as to forsake God will surely become the dupe of devils. (3) We notice the plural pronoun, "*they* have forsaken Me," &c. Not Solomon and his wives, for these heathen women had never known God; but Solomon and the Israelites drawn away by his influence and example. Men seldom sin alone. Accomplices are involved with their leaders in a common retribution. (4) He forgat the good example of his father David. This is mentioned to his discredit. We are accountable to God for our advantages. For godly parents, godly ministers, opportunities. 2. *The piety of David is remembered.* (1) It is remembered in the mind of God. Let sincere Christians who are apt to be discouraged at their failures take comfort from the fact that God is more willing to remember our good endeavours than our failures. David in glory would know the blessedness of this. (2) It is remembered to the advantage of his offspring on the earth. The temporal judgments upon Solomon's sins were mitigated in consequence of David's piety. Would not David, in glory, have satisfaction in this? 3. *The Scriptures must be fulfilled.* (1) David was to have a light always before God in Jerusalem (Psa. cxxxii. 16, 17). The family of David must be preserved until Messiah comes to be the Light of the Gentiles. (2) As David was a type of Christ, so was Jerusalem, with its temple and shekinah, a type of His Church. Of this Church, Christ is the everlasting Light (see Isa. xxiv. 23; lx. 19, 20; Rev. xxi. 23). 4. *No mention is made of any goodness in Jeroboam.* (1) This omission is significant. It suggests that the Ephrathite was used only as the instrument of Providence for the punishment of sinners; and for this service had the reward of his ambition. Therefore the success of our desires in this world is no certain proof either of our goodness or of God's favour. (2) But in respect to his service God gave Jeroboam a glorious opportunity by goodness to make himself great like

David (see ver. 38).   What opportunities does God graciously vouchsafe to us!
Let us utilize them to the best possible account.—M.

Vers. 40—43.—*Solomon's End.*   There is peculiar interest attaching to the earlier
and later days of men who have made a figure in history.   Here we have the brief
record of the end of a character famed for wisdom above all mere men, upon which
we have sadly to meditate that—
I. HE SANK UNDER A DENSE CLOUD. 1. *His morning was very bright.* (1) From
his youth he was beloved of God.   In token of this he received from God the name
Jedidiah (2 Sam. xii. 24, 25).   Could any distinction be more glorious ?   Let the
young among us aspire to this distinction.   (2) When he came to the throne this
name was changed to Solomon, the *Peaceable.*   The wars of his father David were
everywhere so triumphant, that no adversary now appeared (ch. v. 4).   The love of
God brings peace.   (3) He was zealous and faithful in building the temple of the
Lord, which he devoted to God in a noble dedicatory prayer, and had an answer in
the descent of the holy fire upon the sacrifices, and in the Shekinah taking possession of the house.   Those who are beloved of God and rejoice in His peace are fit
agents for the building of the spiritual temple of the Lord.   (4) He was blessed by
God with extraordinary wisdom, not only in the arts of government, but also in
various walks of learning (1 Kings iii. 8—10 ; iv. 33).   The profoundest philosophers
have been godly men.   The boast of sceptics to the contrary is not sustained by
fact.   (5) He was inspired by God to contribute books to the sacred Scriptures.
The Chaldaisms which occur in the Ecclesiastes are not sufficient to wrest the
authorship of that book from Solomon, to whom the Jews have ever ascribed it ;
for these it may have acquired in passing through the hands of Ezra.   2. *But his
evening was very black.* (1) His reign extended over forty years, and a considerable
portion of that period he was under bad influences.   Pharaoh's daughter is thought
to have been a proselyte to Judaism, but of this there is no proof.   (2) This foreign
marriage was followed by about seven hundred more.   These were distinguished as
princesses (ver. 3).   Not that they were daughters of kings, but wives of Solomon,
of the second order, Pharaoh's daughter being queen.   Beside these were the three
hundred concubines.   Such a harem, in its number alone, was a plain violation of
the law (Deut. xvii. 17).   But he was still further guilty in making alliances with
heathen women (Exod. xxxiv. 16 ; Deut. vii. 3, 4).   (3) The very evils predicted
happened to Solomon ; through these he was drawn into the grossest idolatry (vers.
5—8).   (4) The last act recorded of him was that of seeking to kill Jeroboam, who
to avoid his resentment took refuge with Shishak, king of Egypt.   Shishak was
brother-in-law to Hadad, the Edomite adversary of Solomon, but not the father of
Solomon's wife, as some have supposed.   If, as the narrative suggests, this design
upon the life of Jeroboam was in consequence of his knowledge of the prophecy of
Ahijah, it was an evidence of extreme wickedness, for it was fighting against God.
It was the very sin of Saul against his father David.   And in this purpose he seems
to have persisted to his death ; for Jeroboam remained in Egypt until that event.
How fearful are the evils of apostasy !   How admonitory!
II. BUT IS THERE NO SUNSHINE IN THE CLOUD?   Some think they see it—1. *In
the promise of God to David.* (1) The promise referred to is recorded 2 Sam. vii.
12—17.   But was not Solomon, who was chastened with the rod of men by Hadad,
Rezon, and Jeroboam, the subject of the mercy of God, in that his family was continued in the throne of Judah?   In this he was distinguished from Saul, whose
succession was cut off.   (2) Unless this answer can be shown to be insufficient, the
Calvinistic argument based upon this text for the infallible final perseverance of the
saints is simply a begging of the question. 2. *In the Divine approval of the reign
of Solomon.* (1) The passage relied upon in this statement is 2 Chron. xi. 17.
But when the commencement of the rule of Rehoboam in Judah, for three years, is
commended as according to the example of David and Solomon, the allusion, as far
as Solomon is concerned at least, was to the manner in which he commenced his
reign.   (2) This is sufficient for the consistency of the text.   To make it prove more
would make it prove too much by committing God to the approval of what He has

elsewhere explicitly condemned. (3) Rehoboam, who as king of Judah, like his father Solomon, began his reign well, fell into the snare of Solomon in multiplying wives (see 2 Chron. xi. 21). 3. *In his authorship of the Ecclesiastes*, (1) The argument is that upon the message of God, by Ahijah, as is supposed (vers. 9—13), Solomon repented, and afterwards wrote this book, in which he confesses the vanity of his past life. (2) But the theory of his repentance upon that occasion ill consorts with the history of his seeking the life of Jeroboam, because he was destined to give effect to the burden of that message. True repentance will bear meet fruit (Matt. iii. 8). (3) The Ecclesiastes was more probably written before than after the apostasy of Solomon. The allusions to his experiences as " king over Israel in Jerusalem " may have been prophetic anticipations, which may explain the past tense, "*was* king," which is agreeable to the prophetic style. When all has been said that can be alleged to encourage hope in Solomon's end, the doubt is grave enough to instruct us that we must not presume upon God's mercy, and sin. Let us rather hope in His mercy, repent, and sin no more. Praise God for the Great Atonement!—M.

Vers. 14—25.—*The Divine Chastisements.* I. CHASTISEMENT IS MERCY. Though the judgment was kept back, Solomon was meanwhile made to feel the rod of correction. We may be forgiven and yet chastised—yea, chastised because we are forgiven. " Whom the Lord loveth He chasteneth, and scourgeth," &c. This, too, was mercy, for—1. *It was fitted to lead him to seek God in truth.* It is easier to feel and confess our folly and sin in adversity than when all is well with us, 2. *It revealed to him the kind of harvest he had prepared for his child.* He was now reaping the fruits of his father's fierce vengeance (see ver. 15). The story recorded on the page of Scripture was then on Israel's lips and in Solomon's thoughts. When God visits for sin, the iniquity of the past is remembered. Sins are seeds that produce harvests of trouble for those who come after us; and Solomon's reaping the fruit of his father's deeds must have set before him the legacy of judgment he was bequeathing to his own son. And yet Solomon does not seem to have been benefited. Are we reading the lessons of our chastisements? II. OUR ENEMIES ARE GOD'S INSTRUMENTS. 1. *When they assail us it is of Him.* The Lord stirred them up. They had been adversaries before, but they had hitherto been powerless to harm Israel (see ver. 4). But now in Solomon's fall the day of their opportunity came. Our foes are held as in a leash by God. Without His permission they can attempt nothing : when they are loosed it is of Him. They serve Him and in the truest sense serve us. In the midst of evil deeds and evil speech let us look past all to Him. 2. *God's restraining hand is still upon them.* Though Hadad and Rezon attempted more, they were not permitted to succeed. So far as they may serve us they are allowed to go, but no further.—U.

Vers. 26—43.—*The call to Jeroboam.* I. THE UNWEARIED EFFORTS OF GOD TO WIN MEN FOR RIGHTEOUSNESS. This is the beginning of the story of Jeroboam the son of Nebat, who made Israel to sin. 1. *He is met by mercy.* The widow's son is made king of Israel. 2. *By counsel and promise* (ver. 38). The seed is cast upon the stony ground and among the thorns, as well as upon the good soil. Learn—1. That, like the great husbandman, we should sow the seed of the kingdom everywhere ; though men may not hear, God is served and glorified in that offered mercy. 2. It is no proof that all is well with us, that we have been the recipients of God's goodness, or that His Word has touched and searched our heart : is there any fruit ? II. THE SPIRIT REQUIRED IN ORDER TO REAP LASTING BENEFIT FROM O HERS' DISASTERS. 1. *Sympathy with them in their suffering.* The judgment which is to fall upon Solomon and Israel is laid upon Jeroboam's heart. He went out clothed with a new garment, he returned with a handful of fragments, the symbol of the new kingdom and the effect of God's judgment. We cannot rightly enter into blessing springing from another's loss if we pass in with a light heart. 2. *Recognition of them as still objects of Divine mercy* (vers. 34, 36). The house of David was not to be utterly cast out. The love that smiles on us is still round them. 3. *Recognition that the gift we receive is from the hand of the same Master.* Blessing and judgment hang for him upon the same issues (vers. 33, 38). Only in lowliness and brotherliness can we rightly receive the gifts God sends us.

III. The impossibility of thwarting the Divine purpose (ver. 40). 1 *Solomon's attempt to remove the danger by slaying Jeroboam is defeated.* His life is guarded till his work is done. 2. *It only serves the Divine purpose.* Jeroboam's enmity is secured. He is sent down to Egypt and strengthened by alliance with a power unfriendly to Israel. Fighting against God, we only bind our cords the more firmly, we kick against the pricks. To humble ourselves under the mighty hand of God will bring us into the light of mercy: to contend with Him is destruction.—U.

Ver. 28.—*The Successful Man.* Among the "adversaries" of Solomon, Jeroboam was the most active. He raised sedition, or, in the words of Scripture, "lifted up his hand," against the king. He was of humble birth, but belonged to the most powerful tribe—Ephraim. His rise is described here. The fortifications of Millo underneath the citadel of Zion were being erected. Amongst those employed Jeroboam was noticed by the king as strong, skilful, and industrious. Ever on the outlook for talent, and with wisdom to discern it, Solomon made him superintendent of the tribute required in money and service of the tribe of Ephraim; a place of trust and profit. Jeroboam is a good example of worldly success, the subject for our consideration.

I. The elements of worldly success. 1. *Natural ability.* This belonged to the son of Nebat in large measure, as his subsequent history shows. Shrewdness, courage, self-reliance were his. These, and similar gifts, are unevenly distributed amongst men. Children at school are by no means equal in powers of attainment. In business, one man will make a fortune where another would not suspect a chance. Amongst the advantages of such inequality are these: that the higher and lower grades of work required by the world are alike done; and that room is given for the exercise of generosity, self-conquest, &c., in our social relations.

2. *Personal diligence.* With all Jeroboam's faults he was not idle. He did thoroughly and well what came to hand. This is the secret of success, both in student and business life. It rectifies the balance sometimes between men of unequal ability. The tortoise wins the race against the hare. The student conquers the genius. Where it is added to ability, success in life is certain. "Seest thou a man diligent in his business? he shall stand before kings: he shall not stand before mean men" (Prov. xxii. 29). "The hand of the diligent shall bear rule" (Prov. xii. 24). Examples: Abraham's servant; Joseph in Egypt, &c. Show how this is true in the higher sphere of the Christian life. "To him that hath to him shall be given," &c. He that is faithful with few things will become ruler over many.

3. *Kindly interest.* "Solomon saw the young man." This added an element of uncertainty to his prospects. It seemed a chance, but was under the rule of God, as the history shows. Diligence and fidelity should be ours, whether or no we have the notice of the earthly master, for the unseen King is ever watching us. We are to work with singleness of heart, as unto the Lord; to serve others "not with eye service as men pleasers," &c. Show the responsibility which rests on employers to develop, and encourage, and put to the best use the gifts of their *employés*. Promotion should follow merit.

II. The possibilities of worldly success. 1. *It is possible to defend others.* Jeroboam was known in future times of danger as the man who "enclosed the city of David." Higher possibilities than that belong to successful men. How they can guard those employed by them from disease, from moral contamination, from ignorance, &c. The responsibilities of landowners, manufacturers, &c.

2. *It is possible to lighten the burdens of others.* As ruler over the tribute, Jeroboam could alleviate or aggravate the burdens of the tribe. Point out what could be done by far-seeing, right-hearted statesmen to lessen the troubles of the poor, the miseries of subject races, the burdens of taxation, &c.

3. *It is possible to become ready for loftier rule.* He who was the overseer of

one tribe became the king of Israel.   The discharge of the duties of the former office made those of the latter less arduous.   Apply this to the preparation of men for the nobler rule of heaven, by the exercise of powers for God in the earthly sphere.

III. THE PERILS OF WORLDLY SUCCESS.   1. *Ingratitude.*   Jeroboam fostered ill-feeling against Solomon in Ephraim till he was expelled the kingdom.   Men often kick away the ladder by which they rose to fortune.   Give examples.   The wish to forget the past in which they wanted help, and to attribute to their own skill what came from the kindness of others, tempts to this.   Even poor parents have been left uncared for by prosperous children.

2. *Impatience.*   Jeroboam was to have the kingdom, as Ahijah told him, but he could not wait for Solomon's death.   His first exaltation and the words of the prophet aroused greed and ambition which would not be stayed.   A man who has known nothing but success is more impatient than are others at a disappointment or difficulty.   It is harder for him than for one trained in the school of adversity to say, "Not my will, but Thine be done."   His is seldom the "meek and quiet spirit" which is, in the sight of God, of great price.

3. *Rebellion against God.*   He heard from Ahijah's lips these words of God about Solomon—"I will make him prince all the days of his life;" yet during his life Jeroboam tried to dethrone him.   Compare this conduct with that of David towards Saul.   The contrast is the more remarkable because of the provocation David received, and because the son of Jesse, unlike the son of Nebat, had been actually anointed king.   He had no right to seize what God had promised to give. Jacob learnt this lesson in the house of Laban.   In this disregard, or defiance, of God was the germ of Jeroboam's ruin.   His rule was (like Solomon's) conditional on obedience to the Divine will (compare ver. 38 with ix. 4—6).   Stability depends on God; the seen on the unseen.   No cleverness, no diligence, no human help can bring lasting prosperity to a soul, or to a nation, which forsakes righteousness and forgets God.—A. R.

Vers. 29—36; chs. xiv. 21—31; xvi. 1, 2, 25, 26.—*The judgments of God on Judah and Israel from the death of Solomon to the time of Ahab.*   The separation of the people of God into two kingdoms was a punishment for the idolatry of Solomon; but from this punishment God brought forth good, for it was well that the pride of the Jews should not be fostered by unmixed prosperity.   It would have formed a far stronger barrier to the gospel in after times if it had not been thus early broken.

After the separation of the two kingdoms, idolatry more or less gross prevailed in both, with brief intervals of return to the worship of the true God.   This fearful moral declension is traceable to a great extent to the fall of Solomon.   Sin is thus always the parent of after evil.   He who rebels against God leaves behind him the influence of his example, and gives fresh force to the current of evil.   God made both kingdoms feel, during this period, repeated strokes of His chastising hand. Their history is a history of tears and blood.   Every fresh sin, the bitter outgrowth of former transgressions, becomes a source of new calamities.   The hard Asiatic tyranny of Rehoboam leads to the rending of the kingdom.   The erection of a half-pagan sanctuary entails upon Jeroboam and his race the catastrophes which issue in their ruin.

The history of the Jews during this period, therefore, presents the aspect of one long judgment of God, in which sin brings forth death and thus becomes its own punishment (James i. 15).   This is true also in the history of individuals; and we have in this fact one of the strongest evidences that we are under the government of a holy God.   Let us never forget that His holiness is at the same time love, and that through all the dark and sorrowful vicissitudes of our life He is carrying out His plan of mercy.   In spite of all its falls, its wanderings, and its woes, Israel did fulfil its preparatory mission.   If in the end the theocracy tottered to its fall, this failure also entered into the conditions of the Divine plan.   Israel was never treated by God, however, as a mere passive instrument.   God gave it repeated warnings, as, for example, by the mouth of the unknown prophet who was sent to Jeroboam to declare to him the judgments of God (ch. xiii.)—E. de P.

EXPOSITION.

CHAPTER XII. 1—24.

THE REVOLT OF THE TEN TRIBES.—With the reign of Rehoboam, on which our historian now enters, we begin the second great period in the history of the Hebrew monarchy, so far as it is related in these Books of KINGS. The first, which comprises the Augustan age of Israel, the short-lived maturity of the race in the reign of Solomon, has extended over forty years, from B.C. 1015 to B.C. 975. The second, which is the period of the existence of the two kingdoms of Israel and Judah side by side—that is to say, from the disruption to the carrying away of Israel into captivity—extends over two centuries and a half, viz., from B.C. 975 to B.C. 722, and is, with few exceptions, a period of steady and shameful decline.

And in giving his account of the division of the kingdom, our historian, *more suo*, confines himself to the recital of actual facts, and hardly speaks of their hidden causes. Yet the sixteenth verse of this chapter reveals to us very clearly one of the secret springs of the dissatisfaction which existed at the date of Rehoboam's accession, one of the influences which ultimately led to the disruption of Israel. Jealousy on the part of Ephraim of the powerful tribe of Judah had undoubtedly something to do with the revolution of which we now read. The discontent occasioned by Solomon's levies and the headstrong folly of Rehoboam were the immediate causes, but influences much deeper and of longer standing were also at work. The tribe of Ephraim had clearly never thoroughly acquiesced in the superiority which its rival, the tribe of Judah, by furnishing to the nation its sovereigns, its seat of government, and its sanctuary, had attained. During the two former reigns the envy of Ephraim had been held in check, but it was there, and it only needed an occasion, such as Rehoboam afforded it, to blaze forth. That proud tribe could not forget the glowing words in which both Jacob (Gen. xlix. 22—26, "the strength of my head") and Moses (Deut. xxxiii. 13—17)

had foretold their future eminence. They remembered, too, that their position—in the very centre of the land—was also the richest in all natural advantages. Compared with their picturesque and fertile possessions, the territory of Judah was as a stony wilderness. And for a long time they had enjoyed a certain superiority in the nation. In the time of Joshua we find them fully conscious of their strength and numbers (Josh. xvii. 14), and the leader himself admits their power (ver. 17). When the tabernacle was first set up, it was at Shiloh, in the territory of Ephraim (Josh. xviii. 1), and there the ark remained for more than three hundred years. And the pre-eminence of Ephraim amongst the northern tribes is curiously evidenced by the way in which it twice resented (Judg. viii. 1; xii. 1) campaigns undertaken without its sanction and co-operation. It and its sister tribe of Manasseh had furnished, down to the time of David, the leaders and commanders of the people—Joshua, Deborah, Gideon, Abimelech, and Samuel—and when the kingdom was established it was from the allied tribe of Benjamin that the first monarch was selected. "It was natural that, with such an inheritance of glory, Ephraim always chafed under any rival supremacy" (Stanley, "Jew. Ch." ii. p. 272). It was natural, too, that for seven years it should refuse allegiance to a prince of the rival house of Judah. Even when, at the end of that time, the elders of Israel recognized David as "king over Israel" (2 Sam. v. 3), the fires of jealousy, as the revolt of Sheba and the curses of Shimei alike show, were not wholly extinguished. And the transference of the sanctuary, as well as the *sceptre*, to Judah —for Jerusalem, whilst mainly in the territory of Benjamin, was also on the border of Judah—would occasion fresh heart-burnings. It has been supposed by some that Psa. lxxviii. was penned as a warning to Ephraim against rebellion, and to reconcile them to their loss of place and power; that, if so, it was not effectual, and that the jealousy endured at a much later date Isaiah xi. 13 shows. There had probably been an attempt on the part of Jeroboam the *Ephraimite* to stir up his and the neighbouring tribes against the ascendancy of Judah in the person of Solomon. That first attempt proved abortive. But now that their magnificent king was dead, now that the reins of government were held by his weak and foolish son, the men of Ephraim resolved, unless they could wrest from him very great concessions, to brook the rule of Judah no longer and to have a king of their own house. (The reader will find a very suggestive chapter on this subject in Prof. Blunt's "Undesigned Coincidences," pp. 162—174.)

Ver. 1.—**And Rehoboam** [see on ch. xi. 26, and compare the name Εὐρύδημος. The name possibly indicates Solomon's ambitious hopes respecting him. The irony of history alone emphasizes it. Eccles. ii. 18, 19 would seem to show that Solomon himself had misgivings as to his son's abilities. "As the greatest persons cannot give themselves children, so the wisest cannot give their children wisdom" (Hall). His mother was Naamah, an Ammonitess (ch. xiv. 31). It would appear from ch. xiv. 21, and 2 Chron. xii. 13, that he was 41 years of age at his accession. But this is, to say the least, doubtful. For (1) he is described in 2 Chron. xiii. 7 as being "young (נַעַר) and tender-hearted." (2) The LXX. addition to 1 Kings xii. 24 says he was *sixteen*; υἱὸς ὢν ἑκκαίδεκα ἐτῶν ἐν τῷ βασιλεύειν αὐτὸν. (3) It is hardly probable that Solomon, who was himself "young and tender" at his father's death, should then have had a son a year old. (4) Rehoboam's counsellors, who had "grown up with him," and were therefore of the same age as himself, are called "lads" (יְלָדִים, LXX. παιδάρια). To these reasons Rawlinson adds a fifth, viz., "that it is hardly likely that David would have permitted his son to marry an Ammonitess, which of course he must have done, if Rehoboam was born in his lifetime. But it should be remembered that David had himself married a foreign princess, Maachah, daughter of Talmai, king of Geshur (1 Chron. iii. 2). There is greater force in the remark that Solomon's marriages with Ammonite and Moabite women belong apparently to a later period of his life (ch. xi. 1). Altogether the evidence seems to point to a corruption of the text of ch. xiv. 21, &c., and it has been suggested that "forty-one" is there an error of transcription for "twenty-one," a mistake easily made, if, as is extremely probable, the ancient Hebrews, like the later, used the letters of the alphabet as numerals. Twenty-one would then be כא ; forty-one מא] **went to** [This journey was probably made soon after a prior coronation at Jerusalem. According to the LXX. addition, it was at least a year after his accession] **Shechem** [An old gathering place of the northern tribes (Josh. xxiv. 1). Its position, in the very centre of Palestine, fitted it for this purpose. ("Shechem may be considered the natural capital of Palestine," Conder, p. 16.) But it was perhaps primarily selected because it was the capital of Ephraim, not because it was a "national sanctuary of Israel" (Wordsworth), a title to which it has but little claim. It had once before furnished Ephraim with a king (Judg. ix. 2). We learn from Joshua xx. 7 that it was "in Mount Ephraim;" from Judges ix. 7 that it was under Mount Gerizim. To its position the place was, no doubt, indebted for its name. It is often said to be doubtful whether the place was named after Shechem, the son of Hamor (Gen. xxxiii. 18), or whether this prince took his name from the place. The latter is, no doubt, the correct view. For *Shechem* means strictly, not, as it is often translated, the "shoulder," but *dorsi pars superior*, or perhaps the space between the shoulder-blades (as is proved by Job xxxi. 22, "Let my shoulder fall," מִשִּׁכְמָה). Hence the word is found only in the singular (see Gesen., Thes. iii. p. 1407). Now any one who has seen the vale of Shechem (Nablûs) will hardly doubt that its name is due to its resemblance to this part of the body (compare "Ezion-geber," ch. ix. 26). The town lies in a valley between the two ridges of Ebal and Gerizim ; cf. Jos., Ant. iv. 8. 44. "The feet of these mountains where they rise from the town [to the height of 1000 feet] are not more than 500 yards apart." It is consequently one of the most striking and beautiful spots in Palestine, and the more so as its perennial supply of water clothes it with perpetual verdure. For its history see Gen. xii. 6 ; xxxiii. 18 ; xxxiv. ; xlviii. 22 ; Deut. xxvii. 4—12 ; Josh. xx. 7 ; xxi. 20 ; xxiv. 1, 25, 32 ; Judg. ix. ; &c. In the New Testament it has been supposed to appear under the form *Sychar* (John iv. 5), and this variation has been universally accounted for as a *paronomasia*, שֶׁקֶר meaning "a lie." But the recent survey has given us good reasons for identifying the place last named with 'Askar, a little village on the slope of Ebal, half a mile from Jacob's well and a little over a mile from Nablûs (Conder, pp. 40, 41)]: **for** [This word suggests that Rehoboam

had not "*selected* the capital of Ephraim to
be the scene" of his coronation (Rawl.)
but that he went thither *because* the northern
tribes claimed this concession. They demanded apparently that he should meet
them to receive their homage in the territory of Ephraim. It was a recognition of
the importance of the tribe, and there they
could the better urge their demands] all
Israel [That is, not the twelve tribes (Ewald),
but the ten, or their representatives. The
name of Israel was already identified with
the ten, or rather eleven, tribes (see 2 Sam.
ii. 9, 10, 17, 28). It is highly probable that
the comparative isolation of Judah from
the rest of the tribes (see Dict. Bib. vol. i.
p. 1157) had led to this result. Indeed, this
fact—that the term "Israel" was used of
the whole nation, *exclusive* of the tribe of
Judah—shows in a very significant way the
alienation of Judah from the rest] were
come to Shechem to make him king. [It
would certainly seem from these words as if
the ten tribes had then no settled idea of revolting. Kimchi sees in the very selection of
Shechem a proof that they were only "seeking an opportunity for transferring the
government to Jeroboam." Similarly Keil.
But the glories of Solomon's reign and the
traditions of the house of David would
surely make them hesitate, even if they
had heard of the prophecy of Ahijah the
Shilonite (ch. xi. 29), before they wantonly
broke away from Rehoboam. And the text
says expressly that they had assembled to
"make him king," *i.e.*, to accept him as
such, to anoint him (1 Chron. xii. 38 compared with 2 Sam. ii. 4; v. 3 shows that

הִמְלִיךְ is synonymous with מָשַׁךְ לְמֶלֶךְ, Keil),
after the example of Saul (1 Sam. ii. 15),
David (2 Sam. ii. 4; v. 3), and Solomon
(ch. i. 39; 1 Chron. xxix. 22). No doubt,
as the context shows, they intended to
stipulate for an alleviation of burdens, &c.,
and their selection of Shechem as the place
where they would render their allegiance
was a "significant hint" (Ewald. "The
very place puts Israel in mind of a rebellion," Bp. Hall) to Rehoboam. Their
putting forward Jeroboam as their spokesman—presuming for the present that the
received text of ver. 3 is to be retained, as
to which, however, see below—was a
further hint, or rather a plain indication,
that they did not mean to be trifled with.
It is not a proof, however, as Keil maintains, that they had already determined to
make the latter king, for they distinctly
said to Rehoboam (ver. 4), "Grant our
petition *and we will serve thee*." (Ewald,
who says "they had the fullest intentions
of confirming his power as king if their

wishes were granted," points out how this
fact makes against the received text,
according to which they had already summoned Jeroboam from Egypt.) It is clear
from this and the passages cited above that
the Jewish people at this period of their
history were accustomed, not indeed to
choose their king, but to confirm him in his
office by public acclamation.]
Ver. 2.—And it came to pass, when Jeroboam the son of Nebat [see on ch. xi. 26],
who was yet in Egypt [The usual, and indeed the necessary, interpretation, if we
retain our present Hebrew text, is that these
words refer, not as the context would lead
us to suppose, to the time indicated in vers.
1, 3, &c., but to the time of Solomon's
death. But see below], heard of it [The
words " of it," though not in the original,
are a fair and legitimate interpretation of
its meaning. Whether they are retained
or not, the natural and grammatical interpretation is that it was the visit to Shechem,
just before mentioned, of which Jeroboam
heard. But according to our received text,
Jeroboam was one of the deputation which
met king Rehoboam at Shechem. It has
been found necessary, consequently, to
understand the words of the death of
Solomon, which has been related in ch.
xi. 43. So the Vulgate, *Audita morte ejus.*
Similarly the LXX. Cod. Vat. inserts the
substance of this verse as part of ch. xi. 43.
(The Cod. Alex. follows the Hebrew.) But
this interpretation is surely strained and
unnatural] (for he was fled from the presence of king Solomon, and Jeroboam dwelt
in Egypt;) [The parallel passage in 2
Chron. x. has here, "And Jeroboam re-
turned from Egypt" (וַיָּשָׁב יְרֹ׳ מִמִּצְ׳) instead
of (וַיֵּשֶׁב יְרֹ׳ בְּמִצְ׳). And as some copies of the
LXX. have καὶ ἐπέστρεψεν Ἱεροβοὰμ ἐξ Αἰγύπ-
του and the Vulgate has "*Reversus est de
Aegypto*," Dathe, Bähr, *al.* would adopt this
reading here. It is true it involves but a
slight change, and it may simplify the construction. But no change is really required,
Bähr's objection, that in the text, as it
stands, we have an unmeaning repetition,
"He was still in Egypt . . . and Jeroboam
dwelt in Egypt," loses all its force if we
understand Jeroboam to have continued
his residence in Egypt (as the LXX. says
he did) after hearing of Solomon's death,
until summoned by the tribes to be their
leader. In any case the repetition accords
with Hebrew usage.]

Ver. 3.—That [Heb. *and*] they sent and
called him. And Jeroboam and all the
congregation of Israel came [It has been
held that this verse is largely an interpolation. The LXX. Cod. Vat. has simply,

"*And the people* spake unto king Rehoboam, saying." Of more importance, however, is the fact that it is at direct variance with ver. 20, which places the appearance of Jeroboam on the scene *after* the revolt of the tribes. Indeed, these two verses can only be brought into agreement by the questionable device of understanding the "all Israel" of ver. 20 very differently from the same expression in ver. 1. If, however, we follow in this instance the LXX., which omits the name of Jeroboam both here and in ver. 12 (and which thereby implies that he was not one of the deputation to Rehoboam, but, as ver. 2 states, was at that time still in Egypt), the difficulty vanishes. Ver. 20 then becomes the natural and logical continuation of vers. 2, 3. "And Jeroboam dwelt in Egypt. And they sent and called him [to the country.] . . . And when all Israel heard that Jeroboam was come again [at their summons] they sent and called him unto the congregation," &c. And in favour of the omission of Jeroboam's name is the fact that the Hebrew text, both in ver. 3 and in ver. 12, betrays some little confusion. In ver. 3, the *Cethib* has וַיָּבֹא and וַיָּבֹ in ver. 12, whereas the *Keri* has וַיָּבֹא in both cases. The words look, that is to say, as if a singular nominative had been subsequently introduced], **and spake unto Rehoboam, saying.**

Ver. 4.—**Thy father made our yoke** [see for the literal sense of the word, Num. xix. 2 ; Deut. xxi. 3, &c.; for its tropical use, Levit. xxvi. 13; Deut. xxviii. 48, &c.] **grievous** [Heb. *heavy*. Was this complaint a just one? It is one which occasions us some surprise, as the reign of Solomon had not only been glorious, but the people had apparently enjoyed the greatest plenty and prosperity (ch. iv. 20, 25; cf. viii. 66). Bishop Hall, Bähr, and other writers, consequently, who see in the fact that the ten tribes had chosen Jeroboam for their mouthpiece a settled determination on their part to revolt, affirm that their grievances were purely factitious. But we must not forget that, despite the unbroken peace (see Hall, "Contempl." ii. 136) and general prosperity and affluence, the people had had one burden at least to bear which is always galling and vexatious, the burden of a conscription. It is by no means certain, though it is constantly assumed, and is not in itself improbable, that the taxes and imposts had been heavy, the passages alleged in support of that view (ch. x. 15, 25; xii. 4, LXX.) being quite inconclusive. But while we have no right to speak of the "enormous exactions of the late king" (Stanley), we may be perfectly sure that

such an establishment as his (ch. iv. 22, 26) and such undertakings (ch.vi. 14, 22; iii. 1; vii.; ix. 26, 17, 18) would be extremely costly, and that their cost was not altogether defrayed by the presents of subject princes (ch. iv. 21; cf. x. 10, 14), the profits of the king's merchants (ch. x. 28), or the imports of the fleet (*ib.*, v. 21). But the people had certainly had to pay a more odious tribute, that of forced labour, of servile work (ch. iv. 6, Heb.; v. 14; cf. ch. ix. 21. מַס is almost always used of a tribute rendered by labour, Gesen.) It is quite true that Solomon was not the first to institute this; that David had exacted it before him (2 Sam. xx. 24); that the burden was one with which all subjects of the old-world monarchies, especially in the East, were familiar; and that in this case it had been imposed with peculiar considerateness (ch. v. 14). But it is none the less certain, when we consider the magnitude of Solomon's undertakings, and the number of men necessarily employed in executing them, that it must have involved some hardships and created much dissatisfaction; such results are inevitable in all conscriptions. "Forced labour has been amongst the causes leading to insurrection in many ages and countries. It alienated the people of Rome from the last Tarquin; it helped to bring about the French Revolution; and it was for many years one of the principal grievances of the Russian serfs" (Rawlinson). But we may find instances of its working perhaps as more Eastern, more closely illustrative of the text amongst the Fellahin of Egypt. "According to Pliny, 360,000 men had to work 20 years long at one pyramid" (Bähr). In the construction of the great Mahmoudieh canal, by Mehemet Ali, over 300,000 labourers were employed. They worked under the lash, and such were the fatigues and hardships of their life that many thousands died in the space of a few months (cf., too, Exod. i. 11 sqq.; ii. 23]: **now therefore make thou the grievous** [Heb. *hard, heavy*] **service of thy father, and his heavy yoke which he put upon us, lighter** [lit.," *lighten somewhat from*," &c.], **and we will serve thee.** [Their stipulations seem reasonable enough. Bähr, who says, "We cannot admit the complaint of too hard tribute-work to be well founded," and Keil, who maintains that "there cannot have been any well-grounded occasion for complaint," surely forget that both the aged counsellors (ver. 7) and also the writer of this book (vers. 13—15) manifest some degree of sympathy with the complainants.]

Ver. 5.—**And he said unto them, Depart yet for three days** [so as to afford time for counsel and deliberation. It has been assumed that both the old and young advisers of Rehoboam had been taken by him, as part of his retinue, to Shechem (Bähr). But it is quite as likely that some of them were summoned from Jerusalem to advise him, and that the three days' delay was in order to give time for their attendance. It is a long day's journey (12 hours) from Nablûs to Jerusalem. Three days, consequently, would just afford sufficient time for the purpose] **then come again to me. And the people departed.** [The peaceable departure, like the respectful demand, contradicts the idea of a settled purpose to rebel.]

Ver. 6.—**And king Rehoboam consulted with the old men** [According to Bähr," the זְקֵנִים are not old people, but the elders." No doubt the word is constantly used, as in the expressions, "elders of Israel," "elders of the city," &c. (cf. πρεσβύτεροι, *senatores* (from *senex*), *aldermen* = elder men), without any reference to age; but this is not the case here, as the strong contrast with "young men" (vers. 8, 13, 14) proves] **that stood before** [see on ch. i. 2] **Solomon his father** [among them, perhaps, were some of the "princes" of ch. iv. 2 sqq.] **while he yet lived, and said, How do ye advise that I may answer this people?**

Ver. 7.—**And they spake unto him, saying, If thou wilt be a servant unto this people this day, and wilt serve them** [Keil questions the propriety and expediency of this advice. He says, "The king could not become the עֶבֶד of the people without prejudicing the authority entrusted to him by God." But they do not propose that he should become their servant, except for one day, and then only in the sense of making reasonable concessions. What they mean is this: "If thou wilt brook for once to accede to their terms instead of dictating thine own," &c. The form of their answer was probably suggested by the temper of the king. They saw what was passing in his mind, viz., that he would fain play the autocrat, and that he resented it exceedingly that his subjects, just as he had begun to taste the sweets of royalty, should presume to parley with him; and they say in effect, "You think that they are reversing your relations, that they are making you, their sovereign, their servant. Be it so. It is but for one day. Then they will be your slaves for ever"], **and answer them** [*i.e.*, favourably; grant their request; cf. Psa. xxii. 22; lxv. 6], **and speak good words to them, then will they be thy servants for ever.** ["Thy servants," in oppo-

sition to "a servant" above; "for ever" in opposition to "this day."]

Ver. 8.—**But he forsook the counsel of the old men which they had given** [Heb. *counselled*] **him** ["We can easily imagine that their proposal was not very agreeable to the rash and imperious young king, in whose veins Ammonite blood flowed" (Bähr)], **and consulted with the young men** [see on ver. 1. "The very change argues weakness. .. Green wood is ever shrinking" (Hall)] **that were grown up with him** [possibly his companions in the harem], **and which stood before him** [*i.e.*, as his courtiers and counsellors (cf. ver. 6). The old men were the counsellors of *Solomon ;* the young men alone are spoken of as the ministers of Rehoboam.

Ver. 9.—**And he said unto them, What counsel give ye** [emphatic in the original] **that we** [It is noticeable how Rehoboam identifies these young men with himself. He employs a different expression when addressing the old men (ver. 6). The A. V. perhaps gives its force by the translation, "that *I* may answer," &c. ; lit., "to answer"] **may answer this people who have spoken to me, saying, Make the yoke which thy father did put upon us lighter?**

Ver. 10.—**And the young men that were grown up with him spake unto him, saying, Thus shalt thou speak unto this people** [There is a certain amount of contemptuousness in the expression (cf. St. John vii. 49)] **that spake unto thee** [The repetition, "speak, spake," is probably not undesigned. It suggests the idea of retaliation, or that it was a piece of presumption on their part to have spoken at all], **saying, Thy father made our yoke heavy, but make thou it lighter unto us** [lit., *from upon us*] **; thus shalt thou say unto them** [This iteration is expressive of determination and resentment. We may read between the lines, "I would make short work with them, and teach them a lesson they will not forget"], **My little finger** ["Finger" is not in the original, but the meaning is indisputable] **shall be** [or *is*, עָבָה, strictly, *was thicker*. The LXX. has simply παχυτέρα] **thicker than my father's loins.** [A figurative and perhaps proverbial expression. The sense is clear. "My hand shall be heavier than my father's, my force greater than his, my weakness even stronger than his strength." The counsel of the young men is full of flattery, which would be acceptable to a young king.

Ver. 11.—**And now whereas my father did lade you with** [or, lay upon you] **a heavy yoke, I will add to your yoke: my father chastised you with whips** [It is probable that the expression is not entirely figurative. It is quite possible that the levies of Amorites, Hittites (ch. ix. 20), &c., had been kept at their tolls by the lash], **but I will chastise you with scorpions.** ["The very words have stings" (Hall). It is generally held that there is here "no allusion whatever to the animal, but to some instrument of scourging—unless, indeed, the expression is a mere figure" (Dict. Bib. iii. p. 1161). Perhaps it is safer to understand it as a figure of speech, although the scorpion, unlike the serpent, is little like, or adapted to use as, a lash. Probably it was in the *pain* the whip caused that the resemblance lay (Rev. ix. 5). All the commentators mention that the later Romans used a whip called a "scorpio," and cite Isidore (Orig. 5, 27) in proof. Gesenius, Keil, *al.* understand "whips with barbed points, like the point of a scorpion's sting ;" the Rabbins, *Virgae spinis instructae;* others, the thorny stem of the egg-plant, by some called the "scorpion plant." Compare our use of the word "*cat.*" "The yoke and whips go together, and are the signs of labouring service (Ecclus. xxx. 26, or xxxiii. 27)" Bähr.]

Ver. 12.—**So Jeroboam and** [LXX. omits] **all the people came to Rehoboam the third day** ["Three days' expectation had warmed these smoking Israelites" (Hall)], **as the king had appointed, saying, Come to me again the third day.**

Ver. 13.— **And the king answered the people** [the omission of Jeroboam's name, though perhaps it cannot be pressed in argument, is noticeable] **roughly, and forsook the old men's counsel that they gave him.**

Ver. 14.—**And spake to them after the counsel of the young men, saying, My father made your yoke heavy, and I will add to your yoke: my father also chastised you with whips, but I will chastise you with scorpions.**

Ver. 15.— **Wherefore the king hearkened not unto the people, for the cause** [or course of events ; lit., *turn*] **was from the Lord** ["*Quem Deus vult perdere, prius dementat.*" God did not *inspire* Rehoboam's proud and despotic reply, but *used* it for the accomplishment of His purpose, the partition of the kingdom (cf. Exod. xiv. 4; Matt. xxvi. 24). God makes the wrath of man to praise Him], **that** [Heb. *in order that*] **he might perform his saying, which the Lord spake by** [Hob. *in the hand of;* cf. ch. xiv. 18; ii. 25, note] **Ahijah the Shilonite** [see on ch. xi. 11] **unto Jeroboam the son of Nebat.**

Ver. 16.— **So when all Israel saw that the king hearkened not unto them, the people answered** [Heb. *brought back word to ;* probably after some consultation amongst themselves] **the king, saying,**

What portion have we in David ? [Same expression as 2 Sam. xx. 1. The words, interpreted by this passage and 2 Sam. xix. 43, mean, "Since we have no kindness or fairness from David's seed, what is his house to us ? Why render homage to his son ? We receive nought from him, why yield aught to him ?"] **neither have we inheritance in the son of Jesse** [*i.e.,* "his tribe is not ours ; his interests are not ours." Bähr sees in the expression "son of Jesse" "an allusion to David's humbler descent," but surely without reason. It is simply a periphrasis for the sake of the parallelism. The rhythm almost elevates the words to the rank of poetry]: **to your tents, O Israel** [lit., *thy* tents, or dwellings ; *i.e.,* "Disperse to your homes (see ch. viii. 66 ; and cf. 2 Sam. xviii. 17 ; xix. 8 ; xx. 1), and prepare for war." אֹהֶל, which means primarily a "tent," has for its secondary meaning, "habitation," "home." This cry—the *Marseillaise* of Israel—probably had its origin at a time when the people dwelt in tents, viz., in the march through the desert (see Josh. xxii. 4 ; Num. i. 52 ; ix. 18 ; xvi. 26)]. **Now see to thine own house, David** [*i.e.,* let the seed of David henceforth reign over the tribe of Judah, if it can. It shall govern the other tribes no longer. "It is not a threat of war, but a warning against interference" (Rawlinson). רָאָה has the meaning of "look after," "care for." "David, the tribe father, is mentioned in place of his family" (Keil)]. **So Israel departed unto their** [lit., *his*] **tents** [see note on ch. viii. 66].

Ver. 17.— **But as for the children of Israel which dwelt in the cities of Judah** [*i.e.,* "the Israelites proper or members of other tribes, who happened to be settled within the limits of the land of Judah" (cf. ver. 23). A number of Simeonites were (Rawlinson) certainly among them (Josh. xix. 1—9). The term "children of Israel" is henceforward to be understood in its restricted sense (see on ver. 1). It cannot include the men of Judah], **Rehoboam reigned over them.**

Ver. 18. — **Then king Rehoboam sent Adoram, who was over the tribute** [Probably the same officer as the Adoniram of ch. iv. 6. For "Adoram," the LXX. and other versions read "Adoniram" here. It is curious that a person of the same name, Adoram (LXX. Adoniram), was over David's levy (2 Sam. xx. 24). That there was a relationship, and that the office had descended from father to son, can hardly be doubted, but whether two persons or three are indicated it is impossible to say. It is of course just possible, though hardly likely that one and the same person (Ewald) can have been superintendent of servile work under David, Solomon, and Rehoboam. It is generally assumed that the young king sent this officer "to treat with the rebels and to appease them, as Josephus expressly says" (Bähr). It seems quite as likely that he was sent to coerce them, or to collect the taxes, as a summary way of showing that the king meant to enforce his rights and was not moved by their words. For it is hardly probable that such a proud and headstrong prince as Rehoboam would stoop, especially after the confident threats which he had just uttered, to parley with rebels. Such a man, guided by such counsellors, and inflated with a sense of his own power and importance, would naturally think of force rather than of conciliation or concessions. He would be for trying his whips of scorpions. And if conciliation had been his object, it is hardly likely that he would have employed Adoram, the superintendent of the levy, a man who would naturally be obnoxious to the people, to effect it. Moreover the sequel—Adoram's tragical end—also favours the supposition that he was sent, not "to arrange some alleviation of their burdens" (Rawlinson), but to carry out the high-handed policy of the king]; **and all Israel stoned him with stones** ["With one exception, this was a bloodless revolution" (Stanley). It has been remarked that the practice of stoning is first heard of in the stony desert (Arabia *Petraea*). But in reality it is older than the date of the Exodus, as Exod. viii. 26 shows. And it is an obvious and ready and summary way of despatching obnoxious persons (cf. Exod. xvii. 4; 1 Sam. xxx. 6; 1 Kings xxi. 10). It is to this day a favourite method of the East for testifying hatred and intolerance], **that he died. Therefore king Rehoboam made speed** [So the LXX., ἔφθασεν. The Hebrew literally means, as margin, "*strengthened himself*." But the A. V. gives the practical force of the word. He bestirred himself; he lost no time; the death of Adoram showed him the danger of a moment's delay. "He saw those stones were thrown at him in his Adoram" (Hall).] **to get him up to his chariot, to flee to Jerusalem.**

Ver. 19.—**So Israel rebelled** [lit., *fell away* (marg.) The common secondary meaning of the word is to *transgress*. Its use here may perhaps suggest that their rebellion was not without sin] **against the house of David unto this day** (see on ch. viii. 8)].

Ver. 20.—**And it came to pass, when all Israel heard that Jeroboam was come again** [These words are hardly consistent with the idea that Jeroboam had been from the first the spokesman of "all Israel" in their

interviews with Rehoboam. If, however, the received text of vers. 3, 12 is retained (see on ver. 3), then we must understand the "all Israel" in ver. 1 of the *representatives* of the different tribes, and here, of the entire nation who had heard from its representatives, on their return to their homes (ver. 16), of the presence of Jeroboam in the country], **that they sent and called him unto the congregation** [Where and when this gathering was held we are not informed. Probably it was at Shechem, and soon after Rehoboam's flight. After the open and irreparable breach which they had made (ver. 18), the leaders of the tribes would naturally assemble at once to concert measures for their defence and future government], **and made him king** [by anointing. Note on ver. 1] **over all Israel** [This public and formal consecration of Jeroboam completed the secession of the northern tribes. Was this secession sinful? Bähr, Keil, and others, who start from the assumption that secession was determined upon even before Rehoboam came to Shechem, and that the complaints of the people respecting the grievous service to which they had been subjected by Solomon were groundless, naturally conclude that it was altogether treasonable and unjustifiable. But is this conclusion borne out by the facts? We may readily admit that the schism was not accomplished without sin: we cannot but allow that Israel acted with undue precipitation, and that Rehoboam, who was "young and tenderhearted," was entitled, for David's and Solomon's sake, as well as his own, to greater forbearance and consideration, and it is almost certain that both the "envy of Ephraim" and the ambition of Jeroboam largely influenced the result. At the same time, it is to be remembered that the division of the kingdom was ordained of God, and that the people had just cause of complaint, if not, indeed, sufficient warrant for resistance, in the arbitrary and insolent rejection of their petition by the young king. No law of God requires men to yield themselves up without a struggle to such cruel and abject slavery as Rehoboam threatened these men with. They judged—and who shall say unreasonably?—from his words that they had only tyranny and cruelty to expect at his hands, and what wonder if they stood on their defence? They are only to be blamed because they did more. But lawful resistance not uncommonly ripens into unlawful rebellion]: **there was none that followed the house of David, but the tribe of Judah only.** [This general statement is qualified immediately afterwards (ver. 21). The tribe of Benjamin, "the smallest of the tribes of Israel" (1 Sam. ix. 21), "*little*

Benjamin" (Psa. lxviii. 27), is here omitted as of comparatively small account. Exact precision has never characterized Oriental writers. There is no suspicion of untruth: it is the genius of the people to

"disdain the lore,
Of nicely calculated less and more.'

It may be added here that Edom remained under the sway of Judah until the reign of Jehoram (2 Kings viii. 20), just as Moab and other portions of Solomon's empire for a considerable period formed part of the new kingdom of Israel (2 Kings i. 1; iii. 4, 5).]

Ver. 21.—**And when Rehoboam was come to Jerusalem, he assembled all the house of Judah with** [Heb. *and*] **the tribe of Benjamin** [It is at first sight somewhat surprising that Benjamin, so long the rival of Judah, and which had so long resisted the rule of David, should on this occasion have detached itself from the leadership of Ephraim, its near and powerful neighbour, and a tribe, too, with which it had a sort of hereditary connexion. That a sort of jealousy existed at one time between the tribes of Benjamin and Judah, consequent, no doubt, on the transference of the sceptre from the house of Saul to that of David, is very evident. A thousand men of Benjamin constituted the following of the rebel Shimei, (2 Sam. xix. 17). The rising of Sheba the Benjamite, again (*ib.*, xx. 1), proves that the enmity and discontent were not even then subdued. But when the ten tribes fell away, Benjamin seems never to have faltered in its allegiance. The change is easily accounted for. It was the glory of Benjamin that Jerusalem, the joy of the whole earth, the civil and religious capital of the nation, was largely within its border. "The city of the Jebusite" was in the lot of Benjamin (Josh. xviii. 28). But it was also on the boundary line of Judah. This fact had, no doubt, brought the two tribes into close contact, and had given them interests in common, in fact had "riveted them together as by a cramp" (Blunt, pp. 167, 174, who traces "a gradual tendency of the ten tribes to become confederate under Ephraim," and a growing alliance and community of interests between Judah and Benjamin); and now Benjamin could not fail to see that separation from Judah would mean the loss of Jerusalem (which would be largely peopled by the men of Judah, David's tribe, and would be practically in their hands), while adhesion to Ephraim would not prevent the establishment of another sanctuary further north. The traditions of fifty years, consequently, and the common interest in the capital,

prevailed over hereditary ties and ancient feuds, and decided Benjamin to cast in its lot with Judah; the more so, as the heads of this tribe may have felt, after once furnishing Israel with its king, as jealous of Ephraim as they had once been of Judah. It must not be forgotten, however, that some portions of Benjamin, including Bethel, Gilgal, and Jericho, were incorporated in the northern kingdom (Ewald)], **an hundred and fourscore thousand chosen men** [the LXX. has ἑκατὸν καὶ εἴκοσι =120,000, but the larger number need create no astonishment. At the time of David's census, the men of Judah numbered—if the figures can be depended on —500,000, while Abijah could muster some 18 years afterwards an army of 400,000 (2 Chron. xiii. 3)], **which were warriors** [lit., *making war*], **to fight against the house of Israel, to bring the kingdom again to Rehoboam, the son of Solomon.** [It is characteristic of Rehoboam that he proposes forthwith to subdue the rebellious tribes by force. Probably he had no idea to what extent the tribes would prove disloyal.]

Ver. 22.—**But the word of God came unto Shemaiah** [This part of the history is probably derived from the "book" which this prophet wrote (2 Chron. xii. 15). When Keil describes him as "a prophet who is not mentioned again," he has surely overlooked 2 Chron. xii. 7, 8, where we find him prophesying with reference to the army of Shishak], **the man of God** [a common expression in the books of Kings. It rarely occurs in the other Scriptures. This designation is not altogether synonymous with "prophet." It is used, for example, of *angels* (Judg. xiii. 6, 8), of *Moses* (Deut. xxxiii. 1), and of *David* (2 Chron. viii. 14), and would embrace *any* minister or servant of God, while נָבִיא is restricted to the teaching order. There were *false* prophets, but no false men of God. It is also worth considering whether the name of prophet may not have been practically restricted to, or bestowed by preference on, those who had received a prophetic training, the "sons of the prophets" who had been taught in the schools. Cf. 1 Sam. x. 5—12; xix. 20; Amos vii. 14], **saying,**

Ver. 23.—**Speak unto Rehoboam, the son of Solomon, king of Judah, and unto all the house of Judah and Benjamin, and to the remnant of the people** ["the children of Israel" mentioned in ver. 17, where see note], **saying,**

Ver. 24.—**Thus saith the Lord, Ye shall not go up, nor fight against your brethren** [a timely reminder of the unity of the race, notwithstanding the division of the kingdom] **the children of Israel: return every man to his house: for this thing** [*i.e.*, the division, rupture] **is** [lit., *was*] **from me.** [A prophet of Judah now confirms what a prophet of Israel had already announced]. **They hearkened therefore unto the word of the Lord, and returned** [not "because they probably saw that a war with the numerically greater, and just now bitterly excited, ten tribes would bring them into a worse condition still" (Bähr), but because of the "word of the Lord." It was the remonstrance of the prophet alone restrained them. They knew their numerical inferiority before, but they nevertheless mustered for battle] **to depart** [a common Hebraism. The phrase in 2 Chron. xi. 4, יָשׁוּבוּ מִלֶּכֶת "they returned from going," was probably designed as an explanation], **according to the word of the Lord.**

At this point the Vat. LXX. inserts a long addition, which differs from, and indeed contradicts, the Hebrew text in some important particulars. Rehoboam is represented as 16 years of age (Heb. 40), as reigning 12 years (Heb. 17); his mother is Naanan (Heb. Naamah), and is the daughter of Ana, son of Nahash, king of Ammon. Jeroboam is described as son of Sarira, a harlot. He is appointed by Solomon superintendent of the levy of Ephraim, and builds for him a city Sarira, and also completes the circumvallation of Jerusalem. He has 300 chariots and aims at royalty. Solomon seeking to slay him, he flees to Shishak, king of Egypt, who treats him with distinction, giving him the sister of his own wife in marriage. Here his son

Abijah is born, when Rehoboam has been something like a year upon the throne. After his birth, Jeroboam asks a second time to be released: he returns to his own country, takes up his abode at Sarira, fortifies it, and gathers the tribe of Ephraim round him. Here Abijah falls sick, and the visit to the prophet, narrated in chap. xiv., takes place. The child dies; there is general mourning, after which Jeroboam goes to Shechem, and collects the tribes. Here the prophet Shemaiah (not Ahijah) tears a new garment in twelve pieces, gives him ten, and promises him the dominion over ten tribes. After which follow the events of vers. 5—24 of this chapter.

The great circumstantiality of this narrative has led some scholars—Dean Stanley among them—to prefer it before the Hebrew version. But its details will not bear careful examination, and there is little doubt that it is a compilation of later date. Its untrustworthiness has been well shown among others by Rawlinson, Speaker's Commentary *in loc.* But he omits to notice what is perhaps its strongest condemnation, viz., that this LXX. addition is in conflict with the LXX. (and Heb.) text of chap. xi. The account of Jeroboam's marriage with the sister of the queen, *e.g.*, is manifestly a variation of the history of Hadad (ch. xi. ver. 19; see also ver. 22). Nor does it harmonize with the preceding history of this chapter, as given by the LXX.

HOMILETICS.

Vers. 13—15.—*Judicial Infatuation.* It is impossible to read this history of the great rebellion, even at the present day, without a certain feeling of sadness. We see here a young prince, heir to one of the greatest empires of antiquity, the inheritor of an illustrious and unequalled name, with all the advantages which the glory and greatness of his father could give him, reaping the benefits of a long peace, his coffers full of money, his cities filled with all manner of store, his fleets ploughing the sea, his army guarding his frontier ; we see him wantonly flinging these singular advantages away from him, and absolutely courting his own destruction and the dismemberment of his kingdom. We see a position which has had but few, if any, parallels recklessly sacrificed for the lack of a few conciliatory words. It needed but the slenderest modicum of common sense and all would have gone well. He had but to stoop for one day in order to conquer for ever (ver. 7). But no ; we hear him instead hurling opprobrious words at the spokesmen of the ten tribes, and forthwith the land is ablaze with insurrection. He madly talks of the might of his little finger, of whips and scorpions, and from that hour his kingdom is divided ; the holy people are ranged under hostile banners, and the way is opened for the schism in the Church. We talk sometimes of men who dance on the edge of a volcano, and we have read of Nero fiddling while Rome was burning, but it may be questioned whether history affords a more pitiable instance of folly and infatuation than this. And it was such infatuation that we can hardly resist the conclusion that it was, somehow, retributive and judicial. " Who would not have looked any whither for the cause of this evil, rather than to heaven ? Yet the holy God challenges it to Himself " (Bp. Hall). " The cause was from the Lord."

It is well that we should understand, however, that this gross infatuation was only one out of many factors which produced the disruption. The division of the kingdom—the first act in the long drama of retribution for the sin of Solomon—was to a large extent the natural result of the rule and policy of Solomon. No doubt of all the causes of revolt the prophecy of Ahijah was the most influential. It was that " beginning " which, as Aristotle sagely remarks, is often the larger half. Possibly but for that, Israel's " winter of discontent " would have been " made glorious by the summer sun " of the accession of a young prince. Probably but for that, Jeroboam would never have " lifted up his hand against the king." But we must not shut our eyes to the fact that the people had had a " heavy yoke " to bear. Rehoboam himself confessed to this (ver. 14). It is idle to say that their demands betray a foregone conclusion to revolt. The contrary is distinctly implied in verses 4, 7. Nor is it the fact that the rebellion was wholly due to the jealousy of Ephraim, for that proud tribe had readily acquiesced in the supremacy of Judah during the reign of David. Indeed, the rebellion is almost inexplicable, except on the supposition that the people had suffered real hardships, and carried heavy burdens during Solomon's reign. Men do not soon forget the glories of such an empire as his, and do not wantonly tear it asunder, and reduce it to impotence, unless they have had substantial grievances. But in this case, so many were their grounds of disaffection that, remembering that Jeroboam, who no doubt appeared to them in the light of a champion and tribune of the people, was in reserve, should they need his services, it only needed the infatuation of Rehoboam to kindle the smouldering embers of discontent into a flame.

And when we see in this inconceivable infatuation the *immediate* cause of the disruption, we must still remember how it was that Rehoboam came to be capable of such egregious folly. Are we to suppose that he was expressly blinded for the occasion ? Is it implied that, like Saul, an evil spirit from the Lord troubled him, or that, like Ahab, he was the victim of heaven-sent delusions ? Is it not rather enough to believe that he was simply left to himself, to be the sport of his own folly and pride ? His infatuation would still be judicial, if we saw in it, not the strange perversity of a moment, but the spontaneous outcome of his birth and education. Indeed, in that case, it would be still more conspicuously the just and appropriate retribution for his father's sin. It was because of Solomon's foreign wives, and the idolatries which, with his sanction, they practised, that Solomon's empire was to be torn from his son (chap. xi. 33). And now we find that the dismemberment of this empire was brought about by the son of one of these strange women—the child of an unregenerate Ammonitess. It has been said that " every great man is the son of his mother." * The same remark might be made of every great fool. It was probably because Naamah was what she was that Rehoboam was what he was. " The two worst men in my parish," said a clergyman, " are what their mothers have made them." We could not expect much character, not to speak of wisdom, in Solomon's mistresses, who were chosen for their charms, and whose cloistered life, amid the intrigues, and follies, and pettinesses of the harem, did not fit them to be the mothers of kings. What knowledge of the world or of men, what honour, what common sense could we hope to find in one brought up under such influences ? The bearing of Rehoboam is precisely the bearing we should expect as the result of the training of an Eastern harem. It appears, consequently, that we may justly regard his infatuation as judicial, not so much in the sense of being inspired

---

* " Règle générale, à laquelle du moins je n'ai guère vu d'exceptions, *les hommes supérieurs sont tous les fils de leur mère.*"—*Michelet.*

for the moment, but as being the natural consequence of his parents' folly and sin. But let us now consider what shape this same infatuation took; let us separate it into its constituent parts, that we may the better understand Rehoboam's character, and see the workings of his mind. Observe—

I. HIS ENTIRE UNCONSCIOUSNESS OF DANGER. There were not wanting, to those who could read the signs of the times, many indications of peril. It was a " significant hint " that Shechem had been selected for his coronation ; that the tribes insisted on a conference ; that instead of acclamations he was met with stipulations. It was a presage of danger that their first words to Solomon's son, to David's grandson, were of a " heavy yoke " and a grievous burden. It was still more ominous that Jeroboam had already raised the standard of revolt, and that this arch-rebel—according to the received text, but see on vers. 3, 20—was present among the malcontents. Even if he had not at that time been recalled from Egypt, still Rehoboam knew full well that he was there, and ready to rebel again if opportunity offered. All these were mutterings of the coming storm, and no one who was not a fool could have failed to perceive their import.

II. HIS VACILLATION AND IRRESOLUTION. Bishop Hall observes that his stipulating for three days in which to consider their demand was the only word he spoke which argued wisdom. Matthew Henry, on the other hand, thinks that it was " impolitic to take time to consider," and it may well be doubted whether this was not really a false and dangerous move. Had he bluntly refused all concessions and laid hands on the ringleaders, it is very probable that such a display of energy would have quelled the spirit of insurrection. Or had he graciously and instantly promised a redress of their grievances, he would have preserved his crown. But this delay was dangerous. It set them a-thinking what they would do in case of a refusal. A Fabian policy has saved some states, no doubt ; but how many has it destroyed ? And if, as has been suggested (on ver. 5), the object of the three days' delay was that he might summon his young companions to his side, its unwisdom is still more apparent.

III. HIS PRIDE AND OBSTINACY. It was pride, not mental incapacity, led him to reject the counsel of the old men and seek for further advice. It was because it went against the grain to be a " servant," even for one day. That they should have presumed to ask concessions, or to parley with him at all, was an offence in his eyes. It is easy to read his vexation between the lines. With his high-flown notions of Divine right, with the characteristic contempt of an autocrat for the masses, it was mortifying to find his subjects bandying words with him. We may be pretty sure that, had the old men advised " whips of scorpions," &c., we should have heard of no further consultation. The pride of Solomon and the pretensions of Naamah reappear in their son.

IV. HIS FOLLY. This, which is conspicuous all the way through, is especially manifest in (1) his turning to the young men for advice, and (2) in his taking it in preference to that of the old men. We might also instance the threats to which he stooped, and the mission of Adoram, but these come more appropriately under—

V. HIS INSOLENCE AND DEFIANCE. Had he wished to provoke a rebellion, he could not have taken more effectual means to secure the end. " I will add to your yoke." " I will chastise you with scorpions." What cry could he possibly expect in return, except a war-cry, such as he presently hear ? If he had meant to punish, he should surely have held his tongue and used his hands. To boast of what he would do is like the Chinese warrior, who thinks to disperse his enemies by a ferocious shout. And to send Adoram, not to make overtures of peace—Rehoboam's folly would hardly go so far as to select him for such a mission—but, as it would seem, to collect tribute or to make a show of his authority, why, if he had designed to make the breach irreparable, and to stamp out the last faint hope of reconciliation, he could not have done more. It was the act of a spoilt child, it was the coming out in the flesh of what was bred in the bone.

Amongst the lessons this history teaches are these: (1) The sins of the fathers are visited upon the children, and that by the operation of so-called natural laws. (2) That God uses the folly, as well as the wrath, of man to praise Him. (3) That if a fool be brayed in a mortar with a pestle, yet will not his foolishness depart from him, (4) That the mother has the marring or the making of her child in her hands. (5) That,

> " A pebble in the streamlet's source,
> Hath turned the course of many a river;
> A dewdrop on the baby plant,
> Hath warped the giant oak for ever."

HOMILIES BY VARIOUS AUTHORS.

Vers. 1—5.—*The Dead and the Living.* "The king is dead; long live the king!" This paradox expresses an important truth. Bathsheba recognized it when David on his deathbed promised her that Solomon, her son, should succeed him on the throne, and she said, "Let my lord king David live for ever" (ch. i. 31).

I. SOLOMON IS DEAD. 1. *His active form is no longer seen.* (1) He "slept with his fathers" (ch. xi. 43). He has stiffened into a corpse. Perfectly passive now ! What a moral! The doom of all. Work while it is day. (2) He was "buried in the city of David his father." He had a royal funeral. But all this state was simply to *bury him*—to put him out of sight. Much wisdom is *buried alive* in state display. (3) Jeroboam may now return from Egypt. The protection of Shishak is no longer needed. Human wrath has its limitations. Not so Divine wrath (see Matt. x. 28). 2. *Where is the disembodied spirit?* (1) Not extinct. Not in stupor. The term "sleep" relates to the body. It anticipates for it an *awaking*—a resurrection. (2) Stirring in the world of spirits as it stirred when embodied in this world of matter. (3) What a world is that! How populous! How darkly veiled! yet how interesting to us who are on our way thither!

II. BUT HE SURVIVES IN REHOBOAM. This fact is the ground of—1. *Rehoboam's claim to the throne.* (1) He is Solomon's representative. This is more than a law phrase. Had he not been the son of Solomon he would not have been invited to Shechem. We inherit responsibilities. (2) Solomon lives in Rehoboam with a potency to move "all Israel." See the nation from Dan to Beersheba, under this influence, streaming down to Shechem. 2. *The nation's suit to the claimant.* (1) In this *they* recognise the claim of Solomon's representative to the crown. (2) Also that he may likewise oppress them as Solomon had done (see ch. iv. 7, 22; ix. 15). From Solomon's oppressions they seek of Solomon, in Rehoboam, relief. (3) How history verifies prophecy (see 1 Sam. viii. 10—18).

III. SO SURVIVING, HIS INFLUENCE IS MODIFIED. 1. *A new individual appears.* (1) Rehoboam is not the facsimile of Solomon. He is indeed the son of a wise man; but the son, not of his wisdom, but of his folly. His mother was an Ammonitess. This fact is emphasised, according to the Hebrew style, by being stated and restated (ch. xiv. 21, 31). (2) His character is the resultant of the influences of Solomon, of Naamah, and of those which also flowed into the current of his life during the apostasy of his father. He became the impersonation of these various moral forces. (3) The influence of Solomon in Rehoboam, therefore, is considerably modified. Parents are to a large extent responsible not only for their own direct influence upon the character of their children, but also for the contemporary influences to which they allow them to be exposed. 2. *New relationships have therefore to be formed.* (1) The people suffered the imposts of Solomon while he lived. They grew upon them by degrees, and brought with them a system of vested interests. The whole system became so crystallized around the person of the king that it was difficult to obtain relief. (2) Now Solomon is dead all this is loosened, and the opportunity is given for the nation to remonstrate. They are prompt to improve it. (3) Jeroboam is not only present now, which he would not have been had Solomon lived, but is made the spokesman of the people. (4) Rehoboam confesses the force of these altered circumstances in listening to the suit, and taking time to deliberate upon the nature of his reply. The value of influences is a most profitable subject for Christian consideration; present—posthumous (see 2 Peter i. 15).—M.

Ver. 6—11.—*Israel's Magna Charta*. The question submitted to Rehoboam at Shechem concerned the constitution of the monarchy. Hitherto there had been no constitution defining the rights of the people and limiting the power of the crown. Rehoboam took three days to deliberate upon the people's Bill of Rights, and in that interval took counsel. The old men who stood before Solomon advised concession, while the young ones, who had grown up with him, recommended resistance. Wisdom was with the ancients.

I. LIMITED MONARCHY IS BEST FOR THE PEOPLE. 1. *Because it recognises their rights*. (1) The people do not exist for the king. They may be governed as a republic without a king. (2) But the king exists for the people. Where no people are there can be no king. (3) For a king, therefore, to use the people simply for his own aggrandisement and ignore their rights is preposterous (Jer. ii. 14). 2. *It respects their happiness*. (1) Since the people collectively are of more importance than an individual monarch, the haughty bearing of a monarch is out of place. So the sages counselled Rehoboam to " serve " the people and " speak good words to them." (2) The interests of a good king will be bound up with the happiness of his subjects, and he cannot reasonably object to a constitution that will recognise this community of interests.

II. IT IS BEST ALSO FOR THE PRINCE. 1. *It encourages his virtues*. (1) It does this by limiting his extravagance. Solomon would have been far happier had his people been saved the charge of building palaces for, and sustaining in state, seven hundred princesses and three hundred concubines. (2) For what would be necessary to sustain his rank a constitutional king might trust the good sense of his people. At Shechem they did not seek exemption from taxation, but relief from its excesses. They knew that it would not be to the credit of a great people to pauperise their prince. 2. *It gives stability to his throne*. (1) " They will be thy servants for ever." Such was the manner in which this was expressed by the sages. It will be their *interest* to be so. *Gratitude* also will bind them. The loyalty of love is stronger and more enduring than that of fear. This is the loyalty which the gospel claims, and the constancy of the subjects of the kingdom of Christ is witnessed in a million martyrdoms. (2) Who rules over a loving people may be tranquil. He need not fear the poniard of the assassin. (This is the paradise of tyrants!) He will have the joy of ruling over a happy nation. The typical constitutional monarch is the father of his people.

III. ADVOCATES OF TYRANNY SCORN TO REASON. 1. *The young counsellors give no reasons*. (1) This method they leave to the ancients. For reasons they substitute smart speech. " Thus shalt thou say unto them, My little finger shall be thicker than my father's loins." Pertness too often has displaced reason. (2) Why should reasons be given by one who claims a Divine right to act as he pleases? 2. *But may there not be a benevolent autocracy?* (1) Certainly. And if this can be guaranteed, together with competent wisdom, then there is no better government. For is not this the very idea of the government of God? (2) But who can guarantee this in human kingdoms? The people certainly are as likely to know what is for their welfare as the majority of their kings. (3) What if the autocrat should prove a fool? What if he should prove a devil? Would not a kingdom in this case be a hell upon earth? (4) Rehoboam seems to have combined the satanic and the foolish. Lost the greater part of his kingdom; reigned over the remnant wickedly. Christians should pray for their rulers. They should bless God for their liberties.—M.

Vers. 12—15.—*Infatuation*. " Whom the gods mean to destroy they first infatuate." Such was the observation of a heathen philosopher ; and it is true, only that the infatuators are devils, and God permits. The text furnishes a case in point. What but infatuation could have prompted Rehoboam to have acted so insanely? It is seen—

I. IN HIS REFUSAL TO HEARKEN TO THE PEOPLE. 1. *They assembled to honour him*. (1) He was invited to Shechem to meet them that they might crown him. (2) They promised to serve him as they had served his father. They had a reservation, but—2. *Their reservation was not unreasonable.* (1) They had suffered what they called a " grievous yoke " of taxation and servitude, of which they desired a relaxation. Had they not a right to demand this? Did the people exist to be the slaves of their kings? (2) They did not ask to be released from all taxation and service. They acknowledged the duty of sustaining the legitimate burdens of the state. Why, then, did he not hearken?

II. IN THE ANSWER HE GAVE THEM. 1. *Respecting his father's administration.* (1) He owned that his father had ruled with rigour ; that he had made their yoke heavy. He put it even stronger than the complainants; that he had " chastised them with whips." (2) Might he not rather have softened it to them? He could have reminded them that Solomon had created their commerce ; that their commerce had so enriched them that they might bear the taxes ; that his wisdom had made the nation great and respected ; that he had built their temple ; that they had something for their taxes in great public works. (3) But he lacked, not only the wisdom of his father, but also the feelings of a good son. 2. *Respecting his own.* (1) He declares that he will rule them more oppressively than his father did; that he will increase their burdens and sting them with " scorpions "—knotted whips armed with iron points. (2) These rough and hard words were paraded and rendered more offensive by the rough and hard manner (ver. 13). (3) How gratuitous was this insolence ! What but infatuation could have prompted it? It is seen—

III. IN THE CIRCUMSTANCES ATTENDING THE ANSWER. 1. *It was deliberately given.* (1) It could not claim the excuse of being uttered thoughtlessly in haste, for ho had taken three days to consider it. (2) In taking these three days the tyrant betrayed the fool. It gave the people time to confer and agree upon a policy. 2. *It was advisedly given.* (1) He did not speak without counsel. He had taken the advice of the wits with whom he had been brought up. (2) He had also consulted the sages who had been schooled in the wisdom of Solomon, and he might have acted upon it but did not. (3) He left God out of his counsels, though his Shechinah was still in the temple. 3. *He trusted in his fortune.* (1) He was the son of Solomon. Probably the only son. We read of no other; had there been one he would probably have been mentioned as a rival who would keep the nation united. (Note : population is not increased by polygamy. Hosea iv. 10.) Rehoboam, therefore, presumed upon the strength of his claim to the throne. (2) Even the presence of Jeroboam at the head of the remonstrants did not shake his confidence in his fortune. He could scarcely have been ignorant of the message of God to his father, and the corresponding prophecy of Ahijah. But what are the words of Jehovah to this son of Naamah the Ammonitess, whose national god was Molech? (3) But the Providence he ignored is seen in the infatuation that ignored it. The cause, the (הבס) *revolution,* was from the Lord (ver. 15.) " They that lose the kingdom of heaven throw it away as Rehoboam did his, by their own wilfulness and folly " (Matthew Henry). Miserable is the infatuation that imperils the salvation of the soul.—M.

Vers. 16—20.—*The Revolution.* The unconciliatory, insulting, insane conduct of Rehoboam in rejecting the Bill of Rights of the people of Israel provoked a revolution in the state. This is recorded in the text, in which we learn that—

I. IT COMMENCED WITH THE REJECTION OF THE KING. 1. *This act was done in haste.* (1) By his hesitation at such a time, under such circumstances, to listen to their grievances, the people saw that Rehoboam was a tyrant. They accordingly availed themselves of the three days he took to consider his reply, to concert their measures, and were therefore ready for action. (2) They soon " saw that the king hearkened not." He left them in no doubt, for he took high ground at once. And they were as prompt in their resolution. 2. *It was done in anger.* (1) This is seen in the manner in which the leaders of the people mingle their advice to their constituents with their answer to the king (ver. 16). (2) Also in the promptness with which the people acted upon the advice. " So Israel departed unto their tents." 3. *But their anger carried them too far.* (1) Why include David in their resentment? *Had they* no inheritance in the son of Jesse? Would they have said so when David delivered them from the hand of Goliath? How fitful is the passion of the multitude! How soon are good men forgotten! (2) In rejecting David did they not forsake the Lord who gave them David and his seed for ever by a covenant of salt? (2 Chron. xiii. 5—8.) (3) In rejecting David, in whom was the promise of Messiah, did they not go far towards rejecting Christ? See Stephen's argument, Acts vii. (4) Were they not impolitic in this? In so rejecting David they alienated from their cause the great tribe of Judah. Wrong is never truly politic. (5) In their hot haste they do not consult God, either by urim or by prophet (Hosea viii. 4).

II. IT WAS COMPLETED IN THE CROWNING OF JEROBOAM. 1. *Between these acts there was an interval.* (1) While in their tents the Israelites were still open to consider. They were as yet committed to no policy for the future. Time and reflection might have shown them that their anger had been carried too far. (2) Wise counsel now might have brought before them the evils of a division in the nation. Thus they would be weakened in the presence of the heathen. And in case of differences with Judah difficulties might arise in respect to their religious duties. For their temple was in the dominion of Judah. They may, therefore, be liable to temptations to irreligion, if not to idolatry. (3) While in their tents they were likewise still open to negotiations. Reasonable concessions now from Rehoboam might bring them back to their allegiance. 2. *But Rehoboam's folly hastened the sequel.* (1) He sent among them "Adoram, who was over the tribute." Adoram, from his office, was odious to them, for the taxes he had collected were the very ground of their complaint. Thus the infatuation of the king was as conspicuous in his choice of an ambassador as in that of his counsellors. (2) The haste with which this was done aggravated the evil. It was done while he was yet in Shechem, before his return to Jerusalem. If Adoram was commissioned then to collect taxes, Rehoboam lost no time in producing his scorpion. (3) Irritated as they were, this act roused their resentment to fury, and "all Israel stoned" Adoram to death. 3. *They now completed the revolution.* (1) Rehoboam, in terror of his life, mounted his chariot, and fled to Jerusalem. So ignominiously ended his threatening words! (Prov. xi. 2; xvi. 18; xvii. 19; xviii. 12.) (2) Israel, now free from the embarrassment of the monarch's presence proceeded at once to crown Jeroboam. (3) But in all this there is no consultation with the Lord; yet to the letter are the predictions of Ahijah verified. There is a Providence in human affairs. Prophecy makes this evident. Wicked men are, in their very waywardness, unconsciously made the instruments of that Providence in bringing punishment upon themselves.—M.

Vers. 21—24.—*The Message of Shemaiah.* In the order of Providence the words of the prophet Ahijah became so far translated into history, that ten of the tribes of Israel had revolted from the son of Solomon and had made the son of Nebat their king. Rehoboam, unwilling to lose so important a portion of his kingdom, was now mustering a formidable army to reduce them to submission. At this juncture the word of the Lord came to Shemaiah. Let us consider—

I. THE MESSAGE. 1. *It was the word of Jehovah.* (1) So it is worthy of all respect. It is the word of Infinite Wisdom and Knowledge. It is the word of the Supreme Arbiter. (2) God does not speak immediately to men upon ordinary occasions. Indirectly He speaks to us evermore and in a million voices. (3) Happy is that people among whom the voice of God is heard. This was eminently the happiness of Israel. It was a sad day in Israel when there was "no open vision" (1 Sam. iii. 1). 2. *It came by the hand of Shemaiah.* (1) God spake "in divers manners." By audible voice, as from Sinai; by urim, as in the temple; by dream; and by prophet, as in the present case. (2) Ahijah was a man of God. Such in general were the prophets. But sometimes it pleased God to use persons of equivocal character;—Balaam, Pharaoh, Nebuchadnezzar, Caiaphas (John xi. 49—52). 3. *It came to the whole community.* (1) To Rehoboam. He was first mentioned as the head. Also because he was the principal cause of the mischief which he now sought to repair. (2) To Judah and Benjamin. These tribes were so united as to be viewed as "one tribe," and are unitedly called "Judah." The temple was actually within Benjamin's boundary. (3) To the remnant of the people. These consisted of priests and Levites, and godly people out of all the tribes who were unwilling to separate themselves from the house of David (2 Chron. xi. 13—16). 4. *It commanded peace.* (1) They were not to fight with their brethren. The case must be extreme that can justify a civil war. What miseries must have ensued if 180,000 warriors of Judah had encountered a corresponding army of Israel! (2) They were to submit to a revolution which was from the Lord. Not that God was the author of it, but permitted to be brought about by the king and his people for the punishment of their wickedness. "What is brought about in the course of God's providence is considered and spoken of as done by Him as a general would say that he drew the enemy into a snare, which he had only laid in his way" (Julius Bate).

II. ITS RECEPTION. 1. *They hearkened to the word.* (1) They recognized it as the word of God. Shemaiah was known to be a "man of God." His message also agreed to that of Ahijah, the fulfilment of a part of which pledged the fulfilment of the remainder. (2) To resist now would be to fight against God. This would be a hopeless business. But is not this the attitude of every sinner? 2. *They returned to their houses.* (1) The remnant of Israel were naturally glad to be spared the horrors of a war with their brethren. (2) So were the people of Judah and Benjamin. People are generally averse to war unless stirred up to it by their rulers. What a responsibility rests with war-makers! (3) Rehoboam is powerless without the people. He is now thoroughly cowed. The discipline was good for him. This was seen in the next three years of his reign. It were well if all men recognised God's word when it comes to them. We have God's word written in the Scriptures of truth. Do we take it home to guide and control our conduct?—M.

Vers. 12—16.—*The rending of the kingdom.* The name of Rehoboam is remarkable as seen in the light of the facts of his history. The "enlarger of the kingdom" becomes the chief instrument in its disruption. The one strong nation, the throne of which he inherited from his father, is changed by his folly into two comparatively weak and distracted kingdoms, which maintain towards each other an attitude of perpetual jealousy and strife. The revolt of the ten tribes was a calamity from the ill effects of which the land never recovered. Both politically and religiously the unity of the chosen people was hopelessly broken, and the career of each separate division became henceforth one of ever deepening corruption. The northern kingdom was governed for two hundred and fifty years by a succession of men who followed only too closely in the steps of "Jeroboam, the son of Nebat, who made Israel to sin." Their reigns were little else than a story of crime and bloodshed and confusion. And though the history of Judah was not quite so dark, it tells very much the same tale. Few of its kings were wholly free from the prevalent wickedness. The efforts of the noblest of them, aided by all the moral influence of a long line of inspired prophets, were powerless to arrest the downfall of the state; till at last, after three hundred and eighty years, it sunk into the shame and misery of the Captivity. How can it be said of all this, that "The cause was from the Lord"? Look (1) at the human element, (2) at the Divine element, in this transaction. It is full of meaning for every age.

I. THE HUMAN ELEMENT. The rending of the kingdom was not a sudden event that came without warning. As in all such cases, a variety of circumstances prepared the way for it. There were slumbering sources of mischief, certain conditions of thought and feeling, specially old jealousies between the tribes of Ephraim and Judah, that made it inevitable. But having regard to the nearer occasions, note—(1) How the seed of evil sown in one generation bears deadly fruit in the next. Trace the calamity back to the time when Solomon's heart first began to turn from the Lord. The root of it lay in his idolatry, and in the oppressions into which his luxury led him. That idolatry undermined the deepest foundation of the nation's unity in its loyalty to Jehovah, the Great Invisible King; that tyranny violated the public sense of righteousness, which is the strength of every nation, and kindled a smouldering fire of discontent, which was sure, when occasion served, to burst into a flame.   So true is it that the evil, as well as the good, men do "lives after them." Through the subtle relations that exist between man and man, generation and generation, the possible influence of any form of wrong-doing can never be measured.   It spreads in widening circles.   As in the line of individual history every man reaps what he sows—

> "Our deeds still travel with us from afar,
> And what we have been makes us what we are"—

so in the line of succeeding generations.   Germs of evil sown by the fathers spring up among their children.   There is a conservation of moral forces as of material. Let a corrupting power be once set in motion, and, though hidden for awhile, it is sure to appear again in some riper and more extended form.   The nation retains its visible unity under Solomon, but when the charm of his personal reign is over, the disintegrating work that has been going on beneath the surface is made manifest.   (2) The danger there is in following the prompting of foolish inexperience and headstrong self-will.   Rehoboam was wise in taking counsel of his advisers in this emergency.   His folly lay in listening to those who flattered his vanity, rather than those whose prudence was a safer guide ; and in supposing that, whether the discontent that urged the plea of oppression was reasonable or not, heavier oppression would cure it.   It is a familiar picture of human life that we have here.   "Days should speak, and multitude of years teach wisdom" (Job xxxii. 7) ; but how often is the counsel of youthful incompetence followed because it is more agreeable.   There is a time to resist as well as to yield ; but experience shows that the pride that refuses all reasonable concession, and perhaps adds insult to wrong, defeats its own end.   To stoop is often to conquer.   To humble one's self is the way to be exalted.   Imperious self-will rushes blindly to its own ruin.   Kindly human sympathy and generous self-abandonment win honour and power.   "He that would be great among you," &c. (Matt. xx. 26, 27).

II. THE DIVINE ELEMENT.   This is seen in two respects.   (1) So far as these events were the result of the wrong-doing of men, God ordains the laws by virtue of which that result comes to pass.   All sin is a defiance of the Divine Authority. But the sovereignty of God is proclaimed in the very disasters that follow it and avenge it.   What is the punishment of sin but an assertion, in a form that cannot be avoided, of the authority against which it is a rebellion?   We can no more avert the penalty that treads on the heels of transgression than we can escape from our own shadow, or change the course of nature, and that because we cannot get beyond the reach of God.   The law that governs it is backed by all the forces of Omnipotence.   It is but a phase of the Will that is "holy and just and good." Learn to look through all the wayward and uncertain forms of human action to the majesty of that Eternal Righteousness that "cannot be mocked," but will vindicate itself in unfailing sequences of reward and punishment.   (2) Evil as these events and doings may be, God works out through them His own all-wise purposes.   The principle involved in this may be profoundly mysterious to us, but the fact is too manifest to be denied.   Jeroboam may have been utterly wrong in the spirit that moved him, taking advantage of tribal jealousy for the purposes of his own ambition ; and yet he did but fulfil the Divine decree expressed through Ahijah the Shilonite (ch. xi. 29 seq.), and even through the prediction of the patriarch Jacob, which gave to Joseph the ascendancy and declared that the seed of Ephraim should "become a multitude of nations."   Rehoboam's high-handed policy was without excuse, and yet he and his foolish counsellors were but ministers of the Divine purpose, maintaining God's choice of the house of David, and helping to fulfil the prophecy that the "sceptre should not depart from Judah until Shiloh come."   All history is full of illustrations of the way in which God makes the evil of the world, in itself essentially at variance with His will, to serve Him. All streams of human folly and wrong, wandering and tortuous as they may be, become tributary to the great river of His purpose, "He maketh the wrath of man to praise Him." The highest example is the sacrifice of Jesus, man's iniquity working out the world's redemption. "Him, being delivered by the determinate counsel and foreknowledge of God, ye have taken, and by wicked hands," &c. (Acts ii. 23). The final verification of this truth belongs to the time when, out of all the sin and strife and sorrow of the ages, God shall bring forth the glorious triumph of His gracious sovereignty, the "gathering together into one of all things in Christ."—W.

Vers. 13, 14.—*Rehoboam's Folly.* Such madness is scarcely credible in the son of Solomon. These two kings present a remarkable contrast. Solomon at twenty years of age is the wisest man of his times, Rehoboam his son, at forty, is unfit to rule himself or his people. Wisdom is not by descent, but is the gift of God. Describe the scene in the chapter: the visit of Rehoboam to Shechem, probably with a view to conciliate the ten tribes; the complaint of the people; the two councils of the king; the maddening effect of his reply. The study of small and foolish men is advantageous, as well as the study of the great and wise, that by their follies we may be warned. Rehoboam's faults lie on the surface, as would be natural in so shallow a character as his. A careful study of the chapter reveals to us the following.

I. REHOBOAM'S FEEBLENESS OF CHARACTER. We should expect of one who succeeded to the throne in the prime of his life some clear notions of the policy he would pursue. Brought up in a court to which the rulers of other peoples came (ch. x. 24), over which the wisest king of that age ruled, he was rich in natural advantages. He could also have discovered for himself the condition of the people, their causes of complaint, &c. Had he given himself to such thought he would have been prepared for prompt and resolute action on his accession. Instead of this he seems helpless; turns now to these and now to those for counsel, and has not even enough wisdom to weigh the value of advice when it is given. "Unstable as water, thou shalt not excel," is a law of far-reaching application. Amongst the virtues we should inculcate in our children is that of sober self-reliance. It may be fostered in the home with safety and advantage. Trust a child with something which he is free to use or abuse, in order to test him, and develop in him this grace. Probably Rehoboam had been brought up in the harem, and so had the heart of a child, with the years of a man. All gifts must be exercised to increase their value. "A double-minded man is unstable in all his ways," and an example of this lies before us.

II. REHOBOAM'S CONTEMPT OF EXPERIENCE. He consulted the old advisers of Solomon, it is true, but clearly for the look of the thing only. Directly after speaking with "the responsible ministers of the crown," he turned to the courtiers, who were far less able to advise in such a crisis. Job says, "With the ancients is wisdom; and in length of days understanding." This is not always true. A man may be old without being wise, he may go through many experiences without being experienced. Still, other things being equal, a long study of affairs gives knowledge and discretion. It would clearly be so, with men chosen by the wise Solomon. Besides, those who have already won their honours are more disinterested than those who are ambitiously seeking to win them; and those whose reputations are high are more careful to guard themselves against folly than those who have no reputation to lose. [Found on such principles the duties of submission to authority, of reverence to age, &c., which are the essentials of a happy home and of a peaceful society.]

III. REHOBOAM'S RESORT TO THE FOOLISH. The answer of the young men showed their folly. That such a spirit should exist is a proof that in the later years of Solomon the people about him had sadly deteriorated. (1) These were the boon companions of Rehoboam, and knowing his haughty temper they flattered him to the top of his bent. (2) They were courtiers brought up amid the luxuries of the splendid reign just ended, and knew little or nothing of the condition of the people. For these and other reasons they were of all others the most unfit to give counsel in this crisis. [Give examples from history of kings ruined by their favourites.] We should always suspect those who gratify our vanity, or seek to further our lower pleasures. Show the evils which arise, especially to weak characters, from foolish associates. " He that walketh with wise men shall be wise, but a companion of fools shall be destroyed." " Forsake the foolish, and live." " Blessed is he that walketh not in the counsel of the ungodly, nor standeth in the way of sinners, nor sitteth in the seat of the scornful."

IV. REHOBOAM'S BOASTFULNESS OF HIS POWER. " My little finger shall be thicker than my father's loins." A proverbial expression to denote that his power was greater than his father's. Such bragging is no sign of courage. At the first outbreak of rebellion, this boaster " made speed to get him up to his chariot, to flee to Jerusalem." A strong character expresses itself not in great words, but in great deeds. The boastful Peter fails, the silent John stands firm. The Pharisee is rejected, the publican justified. " He that humbleth himself shall be exalted, and he that exalteth himself shall be abased."

V. REHOBOAM'S ABUSE OF HIS AUTHORITY. " My father made your yoke heavy, and I will add to your yoke," &c. This was not the speech of one who felt himself to be a shepherd of God's flock, but of one who assumed despotic authority. This was never permitted to a king of Israel, nor is it intended by God that any man should thus rule. It would be an evil to the ruler himself as well as to his people. Least of all is it to be tolerated in the Christian Church. The highest in ecclesiastical office are forbidden to be " lords over God's heritage," but are to be " examples to the flock." Christ said, " The kings of the Gentiles exercise lordship over them . . . but ye shall not be so " (Luke xxii. 24—29).

VI. REHOBOAM'S NEGLECT OF PRAYER. How differently he began his reign from his father! Solomon went first to God ; Rehoboam went hither and thither for counsel, but never turned to God at all. How often we act thus in our temporal perplexities, in our theological difficulties, &c. How sadly we forget the words, " If any of you lack wisdom let him ask of God," &c. (Jas. i. 5—8). Throw the lurid light of this story on Proverbs i., and make personal application of the warning given there.—A. R.

Ver. 16.—*The Revolt.* This was the song of the insurrection. It is the *Marseillaise* of Israelitish history. We heard it first after the revolt of Absalom (2 Sam. xx. 1). It appears to have originated with " Sheba, the son of Bichri, a Benjamite." The revolt described in our text was more serious, beginning as it did the ruin of Solomon's splendid kingdom. All such national events (the wars of the Roses, the civil war of the sixteenth century, the revolution of 1688, the French Revolution of the last century, &c.) are worthy of study. Moral causes lie at the root of them all, and the hand of God is over them all. The moral and Divine are more clearly revealed in Old Testament history ; hence in part its value. In tracing this great revolution to its causes, we do not forget, though we do not dwell upon, two factors to which our attention is called by Scripture—(1) the design of God, and (2) the ambition of Jeroboam. We must remember, however, in regard to the former that God expressly declared that He would base future events on the king's obedience or disobedience to His law. And as to the ambitious designs of Jeroboam, they would all have been futile if (as God had foreseen) there had not been popular discontent, combined with princely folly. What, then, were the ultimate causes of the event described ?

I. TRIBAL JEALOUSY. This had always existed. Ephraim and Judah had specially displayed it. The jealousy of Ephraim had asserted itself both against Gideon and Jephthah (Judg. viii. 1 ; xii. 1). The pride of this tribe was fostered by such facts as these : Joshua sprung from it, Samuel was born within its borders, Saul was of Benjamin, hereditary with Joseph ; its geographical position gave it power, &c. Hence, till David's time, the leadership of the nation was practically in the hands of Ephraim. He reigned seven years over Judah before he could obtain supremacy over the other tribes. He dealt wisely with those who belonged to Ephraim, selecting some of them for special favour, &c. Solomon, however, aggravated the discontent by his oppression towards the close of his reign, so that Rehoboam had no easy task before him. All was ripe for revolt. 1. *National strength is impossible without national unity* Clans must lose their jealousies if they would become a strong people. The severance of the rich from the poor, the hostility between capital and labour, the disaffection of any section of the people must be a source of weakness, a sign of decadence. 2. *The Church's power is sapped by sectarian hostility.* There may be diversity in modes of work and worship, but amongst all Christians should be unity of spirit. " There are diversities of operations, but the same spirit." Each tribe may march through the wilderness with its own banner, but all must find their one centre in the Divine presence, and seek their one Canaan as a land of rest. Isaiah foretells the day when " Ephraim shall not envy Judah, and Judah shall not vex Ephraim " (ch. xi. 13).

II. HEAVY TAXATION. It affected the people's wealth, and still more painfully their personal labour. A more foolish step than that which Rehoboam took could scarcely be imagined. He sent to appease the people " Adoram, who was over the tribute ; " the very man who represented the oppression they resented ! *Quem Deus vult perdere, prius dementat.* Show how extravagance, disregard of the rights of others, unjust demands, carelessness of the interests of dependants, lead to disaster—in homes, in business, in national and ecclesiastical affairs. Illustrate this from history ; the decline and fall of the Roman Empire ; the dissolution of the formerly vast dependencies of Spain, &c. So if a *Church* demands too much, as Rome does, she loses all. The intelligent men of Roman Catholic countries are sceptics.

III. RELIGIOUS INDIFFERENCE. That this existed is evident from the ease with which Solomon set up the worship of Ashtoreth, Milcom, and Chemosh ; and from the fact that Jeroboam, directly after the revolt, erected the calves at Bethel and Dan. J. D. Michaelis and others have sought to justify the people in their rebellion, but there can be no doubt that so far as they were concerned the revolt was criminal. Neither in this nor in any other act of man does higher causality affect the morality of an act. They were anxious about the decrease of taxation, but not about the removal of idolatry. To them it mattered little whether Jehovah were worshipped or not. But it was to represent Him, to fulfil His purpose, to preserve His truth, that the kingdom existed. Indifference to God is destructive of the stability of human hopes, of the kingliness of human character, of the peace and security of human kingdoms. Christ has come into the world to arouse it from indifference, that all men may go out to greet Him as " King of kings, and Lord of lords." If you lose the kingdom of heaven it is because, like Rehoboam, you throw it away. The lost opportunity never came to him again. He was forbidden to try to recover by force what he sacrificed by folly (ver. 24). Over him and over many a man the lament may be heard, " Oh that thou hadst known, even thou, at least in this thy day, the things which belong unto thy peace, but now they are hid from thine eyes."—A. R.

Vers. 1—20.—*The accomplishment of the predicted judgment.* I. DANGERS OFTEN COME DISGUISED. 1. *It was a time of joyous expectation.* Nothing betokened the nearness of rebellion and disaster. All Israel had come to Shechem to make him king. There was no dispute about the succession, and no unwillingness to own the sway of the house of David. All was hopeful. Danger may lurk in joy like a venomous insect in a flower. 2. *The people's request was reasonable.* Rehoboam could shield himself under no plea of Divine right. David was appointed to shepherd Israel, and the people had a right to protest against their burdens. 3. *Their demand seems to have been urged with moderation.* There was as yet no determination to rebel. The issue lay with the king. It was to bear the stamp of his mind as well as theirs. There are moments that face us with a sudden demand to manifest the spirit that is in us and to make or mar our future. Should the demand come to thee to-day, what mark would be left, what work would be done?

II. A DANGER WISELY MET. 1. *The importance of the juncture was felt and owned.* He took time for consideration. A good decision is nothing the worse of a calm review : a bad one needs it. 2. *He sought counsel.* We are helped by the light of others' judgment, but above all we need the direction of God.

III. THE BEGINNING OF DISASTER. 1. *A grave defect.* Among all that is said of these three days there is no mention of his inquiring of the Lord, or lifting up one cry for guidance. There is pride and passion in us which only God can subdue : these retained are worse than all our foes ; they can only harm us through the enemies we harbour within our breast. 2. *The counsels of wisdom are rejected* (vers. 7, 8). 3. *The counsels of folly accepted* (vers. 8—11). He was seeking for the reflection of his own proud, vengeful thought, and he now found it in the advice of those who were like-minded. What we need is not the strengthening of our own judgment, but its correction by the utterance of love and righteousness and truth.

IV. FOLLY'S HARVEST. 1. *The shame of rejection and desertion* (ver. 16). 2. *His last attempt to assert his authority defeated* (ver. 18). 3. *His ignominious flight.* He who might have won a kingdom has to flee for his life. 4. *The separation of the ten tribes completed* (vers. 19, 20). If Rehoboam had fled from the evil which was in himself, he would not have required to flee from his people. We give birth to the terrors which pursue us. There is but one flight possible from loss and death—the flight from sin.—U.

Vers. 21—33. I. AN ERROR THAT COULD NOT BE REPAIRED (vers. 21—24). Rehoboam had zeal and strength behind him in his attempt to bring back the tribes by force. One hundred and eighty thousand men responded to his call; but all were dispersed at the lifting up of God's hand. The attempt was forbidden, 1. *Because of the ties of kindred.* These were forgotten by Rehoboam when he threatened the people with a heavier yoke. Tyranny is possible only in the denial of the brotherhood of man. It was forgotten now as he gathered his hosts together. Wars are impossible in the recognition of the brotherhood of man. This is God's word to the nations, to England as to the rest : " Ye shall not . . . fight against your brethren." 2. *Because the loss was of God.* " This thing is from Me." These two thoughts assuage anger and beget repentance ; they who are against us are our brethren, and the blow is from our Father's hand. Our mistakes are permitted, and we eat their bitter fruit in God's righteous judgment. Keep the way of love and lowly dependence on God. Every other is full of mistake and irreparable loss.

II. THE BLINDNESS OF WORLDLY POLICY (vers. 25—33). Judged from a merely human standpoint, Jeroboam showed commendable foresight, and took effectual precautions against a great and possible danger. Yet he did not look far enough or high enough. The range of his vision did not embrace the mightiest of all forces. It shut out God, and every step he took ensured the destruction of the power he sought to guard, 1. *His fear was unbelief.* There did seem to be a danger in the recourse of the tribes to Jerusalem, but he had God's promise that He would build him a sure house if he would do that which was right in God's sight (xi. 38). Do not our fears go right in the face of the promises of God ? 2. *It was base forgetfulness of God's mercy.* The Lord had fulfilled part of what He had said. The very circumstances in which the fear arose (the possession of the kingdom) were thus its answer. Our fears not only deny God's promises, but also the testimony of the past. Unbelief and ingratitude are the first steps in the path of sin (Rom. i. 21). 3. *His defiance of God.* When unbelief has shut Him out of the heart, His commandments are lightly esteemed. To suit the exigencies of state, God's ordinances were overturned, other holy places were set up, the commandment against image-worship broken, the priesthood and the feast-time changed. Jeroboam's sin lives still in our statecraft, in the conduct of our business, &c. God's purpose regarding us and the world is nothing ! His commandments are the only things that with safety can be disregarded ! 4. *His misdirected ingenuity.* He cleverly takes advantage (1) of the jealousy of the tribes. Why should Jerusalem be the only holy place, or Levi the one servant of God ?

(2) He only repeats the sin, and quotes the words, of Aaron, and the fathers (Exod. xxxii. 4). (3) He uses places already consecrated, Bethel by Jacob's vision and altar, and Dan, the shrine of Micah's image (Judg. xviii. 30). (4) He hides zeal for his own safety under the plea of care for the people's convenience (ver. 28). Misused ability cannot shield from God's judgment. In every step he took he was the more surely sealing his own doom, and ensuring the final extinction of his people. "Be not deceived, God is not mocked."—U.

EXPOSITION.

CHAPTER XII. 25—33.

THE ESTABLISHMENT OF THE KINGDOM OF ISRAEL, AND THE SCHISM IN THE CHURCH.— The historian, after describing the great rebellion of the Jewish people, proceeds, in the rest of this chapter, to relate the measures which the new king took to secure his position. These were both external and internal. The external means were the erection of fortresses ; the internal, the provision of new sanctuaries, priests, and ordinances.

Ver. 25.—**Then Jeroboam built** [*i.e.*, *re-built* or *fortified*, בָּנָה naturally has both meanings] **Shechem** [see on ver. 1 and on ch. xiv. 1] **in Mount Ephraim** [The *Har-Ephraim*, or mountain *district* of Ephraim (in Josh. xi. 16 called the "Mountain of Israel ; " cf. Josh xvii. 15—18 ; Judg. iv. 5 ; x. 1 ; 1 Sam. i. 1), is "the central mass of the hills of Palestine, nearly equidistant from the northern and southern boundary of the whole country" (Stanley, S. and P., p. 229), and the richest and most beautiful part of the land. "The tower of Sichem had been burnt down by Abimelech and the tower of Penuel had been destroyed by Gideon, Judg. viii. 17 " (Keil). The *city* of Shechem had been destroyed at the same time as the tower, but had no doubt been rebuilt, at least in part, otherwise it could hardly have been selected for Rehoboam's coronation. It was naturally Jeroboam's first care to strengthen his position by fortifying his capital, and the more so as this city would be particularly obnoxious to Rehoboam as the scene of the revolution ; but why he should at the same time have rebuilt Penuel—Ewald thinks the seat of government was placed here—is not at first sight so obvious, as it lay beyond the Jordan (Gen. xxxii. 22, 30 ; xxxiii. 17) and was therefore presumably outside the circle of hostilities, should such arise. Probably it was because this was the gate to his Trans-Jordanic territory. A tower commanding the fords of the Jordan would secure Reuben, Gad, &c., against invasion from Judah. It is also not unlikely that Jeroboam, who was the great castle builder of that age, had some fears of " hostile attacks from the north and north-east " (Keil), or thought of " the caravan road which led over Gilead to Damascus " (Wordsworth), and of which he would wish, for the sake of his revenue, to retain the control], **and dwelt therein** [He made it his first residence and capital]; **and went out from thence** [*i.e.*, when he had secured one fortified city. He could hardly be certain as yet which side some of the tribes would take. It is also possible that some of the workmen who had built Shechem were afterwards employed on the fortification of Penuel], **and built Penuel.** [Bähr says, " There is no doubt that he built these fortifications by tribute labour, like Solomon." But is this quite so certain ? The people after the revolt would naturally conclude that Rehoboam, of whose proud temper they had had such proof, would want to wreak his vengeance on the city which had rejected him, and the instinct of self-defence would lead them at once to rebuild their walls. And the new-born kingdom would also earnestly desire to possess a suitable capital. Thus their self-interest and enthusiasm alike would obviate the necessity for a conscription.]

Ver. 26.—**And Jeroboam said in his heart, Now shall the kingdom return to the house of David** [It needed much less prescience than Jeroboam seems to have possessed to perceive that fortresses and armies would be of no avail for the defence of his realm, so long as Jerusalem remained the one sanctuary of the land. He clearly foresaw that if the people went up thither, as in time past, three times a year, to keep the feasts, the religious sentiment would in time reassert itself and sweep him and his new dynasty away. With one religion, one sanctuary, one priesthood, there could not long be two kingdoms. People who had so much in common would, sooner or later, complete the unity of their national life under a common sovereign. And we find, indeed, that so powerful were the attractions of the temple, and the religious system of which it was the centre, that "the priests and Levites that were in all Israel," together with the more devout laity, fell away to Rehoboam (2 Chron. xi. 13, 16), while the speech of Abijah on Mount Zemaraim (2 Chron. xiii. 11), proves that others as well as Jeroboam were well aware that the old religion and the new kingdom could hardly co-exist.]

Ver. 27.—**If this people go up to do sacrifice** [Heb. *sacrifices*] **in the house of the Lord at Jerusalem** [as the law of Moses ordained (Deut. xii. 11, 14; xvi. 6, 11)], **then shall the heart of this people turn again unto their lord** [The Syriac omits this word. The LXX. has πρὸς Κύριον καὶ κύριον αὐτῶν], **even unto Rehoboam king of Judah** [When Wordsworth remarks that Jeroboam "here acknowledges Rehoboam as the 'lord' of the people," he surely forgets that these are not the actual *words* of Jeroboam, but the thoughts which the historian supposes him to have had (ver. 26)], **and they shall kill me** [as they would do, if they wished to return to Rehoboam's rule. Their first offering would be the head of the usurper, 2 Sam. xx. 20, 21; cf. 2 Sam. iv. 7], **and go again** [lit., *turn again*, same word as above] **to Rehoboam king of Judah.**

Ver. 28. — **Whereupon the king took counsel** ["With his counsellors, or the heads of the nation who had helped him to the throne" (Keil). Bähr understands, " he reflected about it alone" (*et excogitato consilio*, Vulgate), alleging that so important a circumstance as the concurrence of the heads of the people in changing the system of worship would not have been passed over in silence. But while the text does not perhaps imply any formal deliberation with the elders, it is reasonable to suppose that Jeroboam, who owed his position to popular election, and who was far too sagacious not to follow the example of Rehoboam (vers. 6, 9), would summon others to advise him as to this critical and momentous step. Wordsworth refers to Isa. xxx. 1, and says that "Jeroboam is the image and pattern of Machiavellian politicians." "Next to Ahithophel, I do not find that Israel yielded a craftier head than Jeroboam's " (Hall)], **and made two calves** [It is generally held that these were in imitation of, or were suggested by, the "golden calf" of Aaron (Exod. xxxii. 2), and the close resemblance of Jeroboam's words (below), in inaugurating this new *cultus*, to Aaron's have been thought to prove it. But surely it has been overlooked that Jeroboam could hardly be so shortsighted and unwise as deliberately to reintroduce a worship which had provoked the "fierce wrath " (ver. 12) of God, and had

nearly resulted in the extermination of the Jewish race. For of course neither Jeroboam nor his people could have forgotten the stern condemnation which Aaron's calf-worship had received. The molten image ground to powder, the ashes mixed in the drink of the people, the slaughter of three thousand worshippers, &c., would assuredly have lived in the memories of the nation. A more impolitic step, consequently—one more certain to precipitate his ruin, by driving the whole nation into the arms of Judah — Jeroboam could not have taken, than to attempt any revival or imitation of the forbidden cultus of the desert. And it is as little likely that the worship of the calves was derived from the worship of Apis, as practised at Memphis, or of " Mnevis, the sacred calf of Heliopolis " (Stanley), though with both of these Jeroboam had recently been in contact. It would have been but a sorry recommendation in the eyes of Israel that the first act of the new king should be to introduce the hateful idolatry of Egypt into the land; and every consideration tends to show that the calf-worship was not, and was not intended to be, idolatry, such as the worship of Egypt undoubtedly was. It is always carefully distinguished from idol-worship by the historians and prophets. And the idea which Jeroboam wished to give his subjects was clearly this—that, so far from introducing new gods or new sanctuaries, he was merely accommodating the old worship to the new state of things. He evidently felt that what he and his house had most to fear was, not the armies of Rehoboam but the ritual and religious associations of Jerusalem. His object, if he were wise, must therefore be to provide a substitute, a counterfeit worship. "I will give you," he virtually says, " at Bethel and Dan, old sanctuaries of our race long before Jerusalem usurped their place, those visible emblems of the heavenly powers such as are now found only in the temple. You too shall possess those mysterious forms which symbolize the Invisible, but you shall have them nearer home and easier of access." There can be little doubt, consequently, that the " calves" were imitations of the colossal cherubim of Solomon's temple, in which the ox or calf was probably the *forma praecipua* (ch. vi. 23).] **of gold** [Hardly of solid gold. Possibly of wood covered with gold plates, *i.e.*, similar to the cherubim (ch. vi. 23—28); probably of molten brass (see ch. xiv. 9, and cf. Psa. cvi. 19), overlaid with gold; such images, in fact, as are described in Isa. xl. 19], **and said unto them, It is too much for you** [This translation, *pace* Keil, cannot be maintained. Nor can it be said that " the exact meaning of the original is doubtful" (Rawlinson), for a study of the passages where this phrase, רַב־לָכֶם occurs (see, *e.g.*, Deut. i. 6; ii. 3; iii. 26; and cf. Gen. xlv. 28; Exod. ix. 28; 2 Sam. xxiv. 16; 1 Kings xix. 4) will convince the reader that it must be rendered here, "It is enough"—*i.e.*, "you have gone long enough to a city which only owes its present position to the ambition of the tribe of Judah, and which is a standing testimony to your own inferiority; henceforth, desist." We have an exact parallel in Ezek. xliv. 6; where the Authorized Version renders, "Let it suffice you." The LXX. supports this view by rendering ἱκανούσθω ὑμῖν throughout. Vulgate, *nolite ultra ascendere*, &c.] **to go up to Jerusalem: behold thy gods** [rather "god," for Jeroboam had no idea of introducing polytheism. It is true he made *two* calves because of his two sanctuaries, but each was designed to represent the same object—the one God of Israel. The word is translated "gods" in Exod. xxxii. 1, 4, 8, 23, 31; but as the reference is in every case to the one calf, it should be translated "god" there also. In Nehemiah's citation of the words (ch. ix. 18), the word is unmistakably singular. "*This* is thy god," &c. The words are not "*exactly* the same as the people used when setting up the golden calf" (Bähr). Jeroboam says, "*Behold*," &c.], **O Israel, which brought thee up out of the land of Egypt.** [It is at first sight somewhat difficult to resist the view, which is generally entertained, that Jeroboam, of set purpose, cited the *ipsissima verba* of the Israelites in the desert (Exod. xxxii. 4). But a little reflection will show that it is much more difficult to believe that a monarch, circumstanced as Jeroboam was, could at the very outset of his career have acted in the teeth of history, and have committed the gross blunder, not to say wanton outrage, of deliberately connecting his new cult with the calf-worship of the desert. He can hardly have dared, that is, to say, "This is no new religion, for this very form of worship our fathers used formerly in the desert, under the guidance of Aaron himself" (Seb. Schmidt, followed by Keil, *al.*) unless both he and his people alike—which is inconceivable—were ignorant of their nation's history recorded in Exod. xxxii. 19—35. It has been argued by some that this action of Jeroboam and the ready compliance of the ten tribes, prove that the Pentateuch cannot then have been written. But, as Hengstenberg (cited by Wordsworth) rejoins, the same argument would lead to the conclusion that the Bible could not have been written in the dark

ages, or, we might add, even at the present day. He can hardly have claimed, that is to say, to be reintroducing the calf-worship, which God had so emphatically reprobated, unless he designed an open defiance of the Most High, and wished to shock all the religious instincts and convictions of his people. It is much more natural, consequently, to suppose, considering the very frequent recurrence, though sometimes in slightly different shapes, of the formula "the Lord thy God, which brought thee out of the land of Egypt" (Exod. xx. 2; xxix. 45, 46; Levit. xix. 36; xxiii. 43; xxv. 38; xxvi. 13, 45; Num. xv. 41; xvi. 13; xx. 16; Deut. v. 6, 15; vi. 12; viii. 14; ix. 26; Josh. xxiv. 6, 17; Judg. vi. 8; 1 Sam. viii. 8; x. 18; 1 Kings viii. 21, &c.) that the correspondence is accidental, the more so as Jeroboam does not quote the exact words, and that he has used a phrase which was constantly in their ears, insisting thereby that his calves were emblems of the God of their race, the God whose great glory it was that He had taken their nation out of the midst of another nation, &c. (Deut. iv. 34), and delivered them from a thraldom with which, perhaps, the tyranny of Rehoboam is indirectly compared. Or if there *was* any reference to the golden calf, it must have been depreciatory, as if to say, "*That* was rank idolatry, and as such it was punished. That calf was an image of Apis. My calves are cherubic symbols, symbols such as He has Himself appointed, of the Great Deliverer of our race. Behold thy God, which really brought thee up," &c.]

Ver. 29.—**And he set the one in Bethel, and the other put he in Dan.** [Two considerations seem to have influenced Jeroboam in his choice of these sites. First, both these places were in some sort sanctuaries already. Bethel was already a *makôm*, or holy place, in the days of Abraham; was consecrated by the visions and altar of Jacob (Gen. xxviii. 11—19; xxxi. 13; xxxv. 1, 7, 15), and by the ark having been there (Judg. xx. 26—28, Heb.; cf. Jos., Ant., v. 2. 10). And though Dan (Josh. xix. 47; Judg. xviii. 29; xx. 1) can hardly have had as sacred a character as the "house of God and the gate of heaven" (Gen. xxviii. 17) had, still it had its shrine and its schismatic priesthood. A grandson of Moses (Judg. xviii. 13, true reading) had ministered there, and his sons were the priests of Dan still. Secondly, these localities would suit the convenience of his subjects, being respectively at the southern and northern extremities of the kingdom. And this, no doubt, was one reason why Dan was chosen in preference to other places, such as Shiloh, which, though more sacred, were less conveniently situated. A sanctuary at Dan would save the northern tribes many tedious journeys. It should be remarked that Bethel properly belonged to Benjamin (Josh. xviii. 13, 22), though it was also on the border of Ephraim; and it has been suggested that it was Jeroboam's selection of this place as a seat of the calf-worship decided the tribe of Benjamin to follow the lead of Judah. But the narrative seems to imply that their choice had been made at an earlier period (ver. 21), and the city would seem to have been long in the possession of the house of Joseph (Judg. i. 22). It is now known as *Beitin*, and is one of the most naked and dreary spots in Palestine. "The place seems, as it were, turned to stone; and we can well imagine that the patriarch found nothing softer than a stone for his pillow." Conder, p. 252, who suggests that from the time of Abraham Bethel was a מָקוֹם, a sacred *place* merely (Gen. xxviii. 11), and distinct from the adjoining *city* of Luz (ver. 19).]

Ver. 30.—**And this thing became a sin** [It *was* in itself sinful, for it both set at nought the express prohibition of the Decalogue (Exod. xx. 4), and also disregarded the one sanctuary of God's choice (Deut. xii. 5). And it led to other sins, *e.g.*, the intrusion of a schismatic and irregular priesthood, and the performance of un-authorized rites, and to "an ever-deepening corruption of the national faith" (Ewald). Cf. Hosea viii. 5; xiii. 2. But the meaning is, it became an occasion of sin to the people ("*Quod fuit postea causa gravissimi peccati*" —Vatab.) Jeroboam "*made Israel to sin*" (ch. xiv. 16; xv. 26, &c.) It is difficult to conceive, in the face of these and similar words, how any one can seriously maintain that "the church of Israel was the national church" (Stanley, ii. 264)]: **for the people went to worship before the one even unto Dan.** [The people frequented both sanctuaries; why, then, is that at Dan especially mentioned? Some (Rawlinson, *e.g.*) have suggested that the text is here corrupt, and that we should read, "before the one to Bethel, and before the other to Dan." According to others, "the one" (הָאֶחָד) refers to the double הָאֶחָד ("the one," "the other"); cf. ver. 29. They would interpret, that is, "the people went to both, even to the distant Dan" (Bähr, Thenius). Keil would force the text and understand, "the people, even unto Dan," *i.e.*, the people throughout the whole kingdom. Similarly, Wordsworth. Ewald understands "before the one" to mean כְּאֶחָד *i.e.*, "*as one*," *sc.* man. On the whole it is better to take the words as they stand, literally. It is quite conceivable that,

at first, the people resorted almost exclusively to the Danite sanctuary. Having been for long years a seat of worship, and having probably its "house of high places," or temple (see below), already built, it would naturally be in a position to receive worshippers some time before Bethel was prepared for that purpose. Jeroboam's offering in person at Bethel (ver. 32) which marks the inauguration of his new ritual there, may have been partly designed to attract worshippers to a shrine, which, as being nearer Jerusalem, or for some other reason, was neglected. But the verse is patient of another interpretation. It may intend to convey that the rebellious tribes, in their defiant disregard of the old order of things, the order now represented by a hostile kingdom, went *en masse* to the opposite point of the compass, even to the unhallowed and hitherto despised sanctuary of the Danites. The LXX. (Vat.) addition here is noticeable, "And they forsook the house of the Lord."]

Ver. 31.—**And he made an house of high places** [See on ch. iii. 2, and cf. 2 Kings xvii. 29. It is often assumed (Keil, Rawlinson, *al.* after Josephus) that Jeroboam built *two* temples for his cherubim, and the statement of the text, that he built one, is explained on the ground that the historian contrasts the "house of high places" with the "house of the Lord." Ewald, too, after 2 Kings xvii. 29, 32, understands the words as *plural*. But is it not more probable that a chapel or sanctuary already existed at Dan, where an irregular priesthood had ministered for more than four hundred years? This verse would then refer exclusively to Jeroboam's procedure at *Bethel* (see next verse). There he built a temple and ordained a number of priests, but Dan had both already. We know that the Danite priests carried on the calf-worship to the time of the captivity (Judg. xviii. 30). This "house of high places" has grown in Ewald's pages into "a splendid temple in Canaanite style"], **and made priests of the lowest of the people** [Heb. מִקְצוֹת "*from the ends*," *i.e.*, from all classes, *ex universo populo* (Gesen.), and not, as the writer explains presently, from the tribe of Levi alone. Gen. xix. 4, Judg. xviii. 2, Ezek. xxxiii. 2, prove this to be the correct interpretation of the word. Rawlinson, who remarks that "Jeroboam could have no motive for specially selecting persons of low condition," does not thereby dispose of the A. V. rendering, for the historian might mean that *some* of Jeroboam's priests were of the lowest stamp, because he could find no others, or because he was so little scrupulous as to take them. "Leaden priests are well fitted to golden deities" (Hall)], **which were not of the sons of Levi.** [Jeroboam would doubtless have been only too glad to have retained the services of the Levitical priests, but they went over in a body to Rehoboam (2 Chron. xi. 13). The statement of ver. 14, that " Jeroboam and his sons " had " cast them out," suggests that they had refused to take part in his new cult and that thereupon he banished them, and, no doubt, confiscated their possessions. The idea of Stanley, that " following the precedent of the deposition of Abiathar by Solomon, he removed from their places the whole of the sacerdotal order," is a wild conjecture for which Scripture affords not the slightest warrant.]

Ver. 32.—**And Jeroboam ordained a feast in the eighth month, on the fifteenth day of the month, like unto the feast that is in Judah** [*i.e.*, the Feast of Tabernacles, which was held on the 15th of the *seventh* month (cf. ch. viii. 2). This was the great feast of the year, and, as the feast of harvest or ingathering, the most joyous. See on ch. viii. 1. Had Jeroboam provided no counter attraction to this great festive gathering in Judah he might have found it a formidable temptation to his subjects. The reason usually given for the alteration of the time —in defiance of the law, which expressly fixed it in the seventh month (Levit. xxiii. 34, 39, 41)—is that the eighth would be more generally convenient in the north, where the harvest or vintage was a month later (Then., Keil), as affording more time for the ingathering. In favour of this view is the consideration that the Jews not unfrequently had to intercalate a month—a second Adar— into their year, because of the season being a late one. Some of the older commentators, *e.g.*, Vatab., think this time was chosen as the anniversary of his accession, but this is pure conjecture, and such an association would be contrary to the genius of the Hebrew people. Keil maintains that Jeroboam's design was to " make the separation, in a religious point of view, as complete as possible." But we can hardly be expected to believe that he altered the *month*, for the sake of creating a distinction, but " retained the *day* of the month, the fifteenth, for the sake of the weak who took offence at his innovations" (Keil). The day was retained, as Bähr points out, because, the months being lunar, the fifteenth was the day of the full moon], **and he offered** [Heb. as marg., " *and he went up*," *i.e.*, ascended the altar ; LXX. ἀνέβη. (Keil contends that וַיַּעַל means "and he sacrificed," but this translation is without precedent. Ver. 33, " and he went up *to burn incense*," is decisive as to the meaning.) The altar was always raised. It was prob-

ably approached by a slope, as Exod. xx. 26 forbade steps, though it is by no means certain that they were not used even in Solomon's temple, and Jeroboam probably would have no scruples on such a minute point of ritual. It has been thought (Kitto, iv. 147) that he was moved to officiate in person by the precedent of the Egyptian kings, who exercised priestly functions ; but it is much more probable that he was guided by the example of Solomon at the dedication of the temple] **upon** [*i.e.*, he stood upon the ledge or platform (called in the A. V. "compass," Exod. xxvii. 5) in the middle of the altar] **the altar. So did he in Bethel** [*i.e.*, the feast was held at one centre only, and at Bethel alone the king offered in person. But I venture to suggest that instead of בָּהּ, "*so did he*," &c., we should read כִּי. The LXX. seem to have had this word before them—ἐπὶ τὸ θυσιαστήριον ὃ ἐποίησεν ἐν βαιθήλ. And not only does this slight change bring the Hebrew into harmony with the LXX., but it also simplifies the construction. "He went up upon the altar which he made to sacrifice unto the calves which he made." The very tautology is instructive, as suggesting that altar, calves, and priests were all of Jeroboam's making, not of God's ordaining. The use of כִּי as a relative (=אֲשֶׁר) is strictly grammatical], **sacrificing** [marg., *to sacrifice*] **unto the calves that he had made : and he placed in Bethel** [Dan being already provided with its priesthood] **the priests of the high places** [*i.e.*, of "the house of high places" (ver. 31). Or it may be a contemptuous designation of Jeroboam's irregular priests] **which he had made.**

Ver. 33.—**So he offered** [Heb. *went up*, as before. This verse is really the introduction to the history of the next chapter] **upon the altar which he had made in Bethel the fifteenth day of the eighth month, even in the month which he had devised** [Josephus (Ant. viii. 8. 5) seems unaware that this new feast was kept at a different date from the true Feast of Tabernacles. But these words are decisive] **of his own heart** [The Cethib has מִלִּבַּד by which Maurer and Keil understand מִלְּבַד ("*seorsum.*" But qu.) But the Keri מִלִּבּוֹ is every way to be preferred, So LXX., ἀπὸ καρδίας αὐτοῦ. Similarly, Neh. vi. 8] ; **and ordained** [rather, *kept, celebrated*] **a feast unto** [Heb. *for*] **the children of Israel : and he offered** [*went up*] **upon the altar, and burnt incense** [Heb. *to burn*, &c. The context seems to imply that it was not incense, or not incense only, but the sacrifice, or sacrificial parts of the victim, that the king burned. See on ch. xiii. 3 (רֵשָׁן). And this meaning is justified by Lev. i. 9, 17 ; 1 Sam. ii. 16 ; Amos iv. 5, where the same word is used. It cannot be denied, however, that the word is generally used of incense, and it is very probable that both this and sacrifices were offered by Jeroboam on the same altar (cf. ch. xi. 8). We may perhaps see in Jeroboam's ministering in person, not only the design to invest the new ordinance with exceptional interest and splendour, but also the idea of encouraging his new priests to enter on their unauthorized functions without fear. The history, or even the traditions, of Nadab and Abihu (Lev. x.) and of Korah and his company (Num. xvi. 40), and the threatenings of the law (Num. xviii. 7, 22, cf. 2 Chron. xxvi. 20), may well have made them hesitate. To allay their fears the king undertakes to offer the first of the sacrifices. And that their fears of a Divine interposition were not groundless the sequel shows.]

HOMILETICS.

Ver. 30.—*The Sin of Jeroboam.* What was this sin, of which, from this time forward, the historian has so much to say? It is mentioned more than twenty times in Scripture. It casts its dark shadow across fifteen reigns of the kings of Israel. Its baleful influences were felt for more than two and a half centuries. It was the prime cause (2 Kings xvii. 21–23) of that captivity from which the ten tribes have never returned. Surely we ought to know what it was. And as one help to a right conclusion, let us first clearly understand what it was *not.*

I. IT WAS NOT THE SIN OF REBELLION. There may have been sin in the way in which the rupture with Judah was brought about (see 2 Chron. xiii. 6, 7), though that is by no means certain (notes on vers. 19, 20). But even if Israel was set upon rebellion, and even if Jeroboam had rudely and wickedly precipitated the revolt, that cannot be " the sin " of which he is here and elsewhere accused. For, in the first place, *later* kings could not be held responsible for Jeroboam's conduct at the time of the disruption, *i.e.*, they could not commit *that* sin of Jeroboam ; and, secondly, the disruption itself was ordained of God (ch. xi. 31 sqq. ; xii. 15 ; 2 Chron. xi. 4). Verse 15, too, is decisive. " The cause was from the Lord." Those who sate on Jeroboam's throne, consequently, no less than the successors of Solomon, reigned *de jure Divino.* The former equally with the latter were the anointed of Heaven (2 Kings ix. 3, 6). It was the Lord " raised up " (ch. xiv. 14) Baasha (ch. xv. 28, 29), Zimri (ch. xvi. 12), Jehu (2 Kings ix. 6), and the rest.

II. IT WAS NOT THE SIN OF GOING AFTER OTHER GODS. If this were the sin referred to here it would probably have been called " the sin of Solomon," for Solomon is twice charged with that sin (ch. xi. 4, 10), whereas Jeroboam never went after Baal, or Ashtoreth, or Milcom. It is true the calves are once called " other gods " (ch. xiv. 9), but they are only so called in derision, and in ch. xvi. 31 the sin of Jeroboam is expressly distinguished from the worship of other gods. It was probably Jeroboam's boast (see note on ver. 28), not that he was instituting a new religion, or setting up a rival Deity, but that he was worshipping the one true God in a more rational and primitive way. See Jos., Ant. viii. 8. 4. And that the calf-worship was not idolatry, properly so called, is clear from this consideration, that " the sin of Jeroboam " is confined to the kingdom of Israel. Not one of the kings of Judah is ever taxed with it. And yet it was in Judah, and not in Israel, that idolatry prevailed. Of the kings of Israel, only Ahab and his two sons were guilty of idolatry ; whereas of the kings of Judah only five set their faces against it. Yet the non-idolatrous kings of Israel are constantly charged with Jeroboam's sin, and the idolatrous kings of Judah never. Polytheism, therefore, it cannot have been.

III. IT WAS NOT THE SIN OF IMAGE WORSHIP. The calves were not made to be worshipped, any more than the cherubim of Solomon's temple. Nor do we read that they received Divine worship. " The people went to worship *before the one,*" &c. The Scripture, it is true, calls them " molten images," but Jeroboam doubtless said they were symbols of the heavenly powers, designed (like the images of the Roman Communion) to be helps to devotion, and they are nowhere called " idols," or "horrors," or "statues." We entirely misconceive Jeroboam's purpose, and discredit his sagacity, if we think that he had the worship of Apis or Mnevis or any similar idol in his mind. The last thing that would occur to him would be to set up a purely pagan system amongst such a people as the Jews. His was not the sin of idol worship. What, then, was it?

I. IT WAS THE SIN OF HERESY. For "heresy" in the original meaning of the word simply implied an arbitrary *selection* of doctrines or practices—αἵρεσις = *a choosing*—instead of dutifully *accepting* those which God has enjoined. This is precisely what Jeroboam did. Instead of taking and handing down to his successors, whole and undefiled, the "faith once delivered," he presumed to modify it; to adapt it, as he thought, to the new order of things, &c. His heresy was threefold.

1. *He chose his own places of worship.* God had ordained that there should be one sanctuary for the whole nation. Both the law of Moses and the history of Israel alike taught that the religious centre of the nation should be one. From an early age it was predicted that God would choose Himself a place to put His name there (Deut. xii. 13, 14; xiv. 23). And this Divine choice had been recently and unmistakably made. He "chose not the tribe of Ephraim, but chose the tribe of Judah, the Mount Zion which He loved." And He built His "sanctuary," &c. (Psa. lxxviii. 67—69; cf. Psa. cxxxii. 13, 14). At the dedication of this sanctuary this choice had been publicly proclaimed (ch. viii. 10, 11; 2 Chron. vii. 2, 12, 16). The whole nation then understood that God had "chosen Jerusalem to put His name there." And Jeroboam was aware of this, and was also aware that the division of the kingdom was to make no difference as to the oneness or the position of the sanctuary. To prevent misconception he was twice reminded in the message of Ahijah, his charter to the crown, that Jerusalem was "the city which God had chosen out of all the tribes of Israel" (ch. xi. 32, 36). It was to be in the future, as it had been in the past, the one place of incense and sacrifice. And that Jeroboam knew it, his own thoughts (ch. xii. 26, 27) reveal to us. "If this people go up to do sacrifice in the *house of the Lord at Jerusalem*." He is quite clear, then —indeed, he could not be otherwise—as to the place of God's choice. But that place, he argues, will not do for him. Political considerations demand that he shall find a religious centre elsewhere. So he "takes counsel," and decrees *ex mero arbitrio* that Israel shall have three holy places instead of one, and that Bethel and Dan shall henceforward divide the honours hitherto enjoyed by Jerusalem.

2. *He chose his own modes of worship.* Though the way in which God should be approached had been prescribed, though every detail of the Divine service had been ordered beforehand, and though he had been warned against adding aught to it or diminishing aught from it (Deut. iv. 2; xii. 32), yet he decided otherwise. Perhaps he persuaded himself that he had good reasons for it; but all the same he *chose* otherwise than God had chosen. Though Exod. xx. 4, &c., forbade the making of graven images, yet he "made molten images" (ch. xiv. 9). Though the law decreed that the sons of Aaron alone should offer sacrifice and burn incense, yet he determined to play the priest himself, and also "made him priests of the lowest of the people." *Sic volo, sic jubeo,* &c.

3. *He chose his own times of worship.* Nothing could have been more positively fixed than the date of the Feast of the Tabernacles. It was to be "the fifteenth day of the seventh month" (Levit. xxiii. 34, 39). But this was not the day of Jeroboam's "choice." He "devised" a month "of his own heart; " he consulted, perhaps he thought, his people's convenience; but was there ever heretic yet that was not full of arguments, when all God asks is obedience?

> "In religion
> What dangerous error, but some sober brow
> Will bless it and approve it with a text,
> Hiding the grossness with fair ornament."

II. IT WAS THE SIN OF SCHISM. It is not without reason that in the Litany "heresy and schism" are coupled together, for the latter springs out of the former (Justin Martyr quotes as one of the sayings of our Lord ἔσονται σχίσματα καὶ αἱρέσεις (cf. 1 Cor xi. 18). Jeroboam's arbitrary *choice* led to a *division* in the Jewish Church. Let us briefly consider in what way the breach in the national unity, hitherto so close and conspicuous, was effected.

1. *1 he one centre of unity gave place to three centres of division.* Hitherto, three times a year (cf. ix. 25) all the males of Israel, from Dan to Beersheba, had gathered round one altar. Thither, "the tribes went up, the tribes of the Lord." Now, instead of going, even *from Dan*, the people went to worship before the calves "even *unto Dan*." The ten tribes turned their backs on Jerusalem, and sought, some of them, a sanctuary at the opposite point of the compass. Nor did those who worshipped at Bethel afford a less striking proof of disintegration, for that sanctuary was within sight of the temple mount. The two pillars of smoke ascending day by day from rival altars, but twelve miles apart, proclaimed to all that there was a " schism in the body."

2. *The one priesthood of Aaron shared its ministry with the priests of Jeroboam.* No longer were offerings brought exclusively to the sons of Levi, but " whosoever would" might burn the incense and sprinkle the blood. The schism was accentuated by the appointment of a new order of men, with vested interests in the perpetuation of division.

3. *The one ritual of Divine obligation was travestied by rites and ceremonies of human appointment.* If the breach was widened by the intrusive priesthood, it was deepened by the unauthorized and forbidden cultus of the calves. The stranger, who came out of a far country for God's name's sake (ch. viii. 41, 42), to pray toward the house, found himself in the presence of rival systems, each claiming to be primitive and true, but differing so widely that he would go home to his own land, doubting whether both were not false. He would say, as others have said since, that before men compassed sea and land to make proselytes, they had better agree among themselves.

4. *The one Feast of Tabernacles appointed of God was parodied by a Feast devised of man.* That feast, the most joyous of the year, had once been the greatest manifestation of religious unity which Israel afforded. It was the very "dissidence of dissent" when the feast of the seventh month was straightway and ostentatiously followed by a feast of the eighth month, celebrated but a few miles distant. It was the culminating proof of διχο—στασία.

III. THE SIN OF KORAH (Num. xvi.) This has been already twice referred to, as a part of the heresy and as a factor in the schism. But it may well stand by itself as a substantive part of the sin. It was just as great a violation of the Divine law to use the ministry of unauthorized persons as to worship at shrines of man's choosing or with ordinances of man's devising.

This, then, was " the sin of Jeroboam." It was not rebellion, not idolatry, but the worship of the true God in unauthorized places, with unauthorized rites, and by unauthorized ministers. Nor did it make it less a sin that it seemed to prosper. The church of Jeroboam straightway became the church of the majority. At the time of the captivity it could boast of some antiquity (Judg. xviii. 30; 2 Kings xvii. 16). But all the same God put His brand upon it. Three miracles (1 Kings xiii.) were wrought as a testimony against it. The voices of the prophets were raised to condemn it (Hosea, *passim;* Micah vi. 16, &c.) But from year to year and reign to reign it flourished, and bore its baleful fruit, and then, after the schism had lasted two hundred and fifty years, while the kingdom of Judah, despite its idolatries, still retained for 135 years longer its place in the covenant land, the ten tribes were carried away to the cities of the Medes, were " scattered beyond the river," and disappeared from the page of history.

And has this sin no lessons ? has its punishment no warnings for ourselves ? If, as some seem to think, we may pick and choose our doctrines at pleasure ; if the Scripture *is* of private interpretation ; if we are at liberty each one to set up his own dogmas against the *quod semper, quod ubique, quod ab omnibus* of the Catholic Church ; or if there is no such thing as schism : if it is never mentioned or never reprobated in the New Testament; if the Babel of sects—there are over one hundred of them in this England of ours—is according to the plan and purpose of our Lord ;

or if, again, the "form of sound words," the *depositum fidei*, the creeds of the undivided Church, have no authority: if they can be added to by the autocrat of Rome, or diminished from by any state, or sect, or teacher; or, finally, if there is no such thing as a "mission" of Christ's ministers; if any man may take this honour to himself; if those who have never been *sent* themselves may nevertheless *send* others—then this history is void of all meaning. But if, on the other hand, Christianity is the child of Judaism, and the Christian Church the inheritor of the principles of the Jewish; if that church is One and Catholic and Apostolic; if the faith was once for all (ἅπαξ) delivered to the saints; if our Lord Christ sent His apostles even as the Father had sent Him (John xx. 21), if they in turn "ordained elders in every city" (Titus i. 5; cf. 2 Tim. ii. 2), and by laying on of hands (Acts xiii. 3); if the tactual succession is not a mere piece of priestly assumption—then assuredly the history of Jeroboam's sin is full of meaning, and "very necessary for these times." And the prominence accorded to it in Scripture, the twenty references to its working—we can understand it all when we remember that "whatsoever things were written aforetime were written for our learning," and that the Spirit that moved the prophets foresaw the manifold heresies and schisms of Christendom.

HOMILIES BY VARIOUS AUTHORS.

Vers. 25—27.—*Jeroboam's Despondency.* "Uneasy lies the head that wears a crown." Jeroboam's ambition was to be a king, and God gave him his desire. This was to punish Solomon and his house for their apostasy, and the men of Israel who had been led away in it. The sequel proved that the ambition of Jeroboam also brought its punishment, for he soon found his throne the reverse of a comfortable seat.

I. HIS FAITH IN HIS PEOPLE WAS SHAKEN. 1. *They seem to have become restive under his rule.* (1) This was likely to be the case. Their complaint against the house of David was the pressure of their burdens. But these could not be lightened when two kings had to be maintained instead of one; when a court had to be supported by a greatly diminished constituency. (2) They had to create a capital worthy of the kingdom. So Jeroboam set about building Shechem, which was a ruin; for, two centuries before, it had been demolished by Abimelech (Judg. ix. 45). The cost of this, including that of the palace there, appears to have been so disagreeable, that Jeroboam, for his tranquillity, shifted his court to Penuel, on the east of the Jordan. (3) Penuel now stood in need of improvements. It had suffered at the hands of Gideon nearly three centuries before, when the tower was destroyed (Judg. viii. 17). A second palace here was not likely to ease their burdens. (4) Then their ability to pay taxes was reduced; for their commerce, created in the days of Solomon, seems to have declined. This would not improve their temper. 2. *He therefore became gloomily apprehensive.* (1) He feared that, having now discovered that their burdens were no lighter, they might reflect that they had done wrong in throwing off allegiance to their legitimate sovereign, and that the "kingdom would return to the house of David." (2) Further, that this disposition must be encouraged by their visits to Jerusalem for religious purposes (Deut. xvi. 16, 17). They would then see that neither Shechem nor Penuel, as capitals, could compare with Jerusalem. (3) And he feared that a counter revolution must imperil his life, for Rehoboam would demand this as a condition of their reconciliation. But the true cause of his despondency was that—

II. HE HAD FORGOTTEN TO TRUST IN GOD. 1. *Had he no assurance in the words of Ahijah?* (1) Did not Ahijah give him ten pieces of the rent garment? Did he not accompany the sign with assuring words? (Chron. xi. 37.) Has not this part of the prophecy been fulfilled? (2) Is it not, therefore, in the power of Jeroboam to perpetuate his throne by faithfully serving God? (Chron. xi. 38.) The fulfilment of the former part of the prophecy surely pledges the latter. (3) Ah, but this promise is conditional! So are all God's promises. If we comply not with the conditions we shall infallibly forfeit the kingdom of heaven. 2. *But he was moved by ambition rather than piety.* (1) Had he complied with the holy conditions, instead of apprehending mischief to his throne from the visits of his subjects to Jerusalem, it would be the other way. For the more they learnt to love and serve God, the more loyal must they be to a godly king. (2) But he felt in his soul that he had not so complied : nor had he any disposition to repent ; therefore, instead of seeking help in God, as he should have done, he trusted to his own wicked policy. There is no real happiness without God. The very pinnacle of human ambition is a throne : yet without God is there no happiness here. " What shall it profit a man if he gain the whole world and lose his own soul ? "—M.

Ver. 28.—*Jeroboam's Calves.* Unbelief is the root of all mischief. Had the king of Israel believed God, he would have obeyed Him ; then he would have been under no temptation to set up a spurious religion to the confusion of his family and people. But what did he mean by these calves ?

I. They were intended to be images of the God of Israel. 1. *So he describes them in the text.* (1) " These are thy Elohim, O Israel." Our English Bibles give the word " God " without the capital G, as though the purpose of Jeroboam were to lead the people away from the true God. This, indeed, was the effect, but that it was the design may well be doubted. (2) He further identifies the Elohim represented in them as having brought them up out of the land of Egypt. This expression is equivalent to saying that the Elohim he would remind them of in these figures was the same who wrought all the miracles of the Exodus. (3) We must not be misled by the words, " Behold thy Elohim," or " These *are* thy Elohim," as though he wished to impose these calves upon them as the very Elohim who wrought all the wonders of their miraculous history. For this is a Hebraism for *similitudes* (see Gen. xli. 27; Dan. ii. 38; 1 Cor. x. 4). Note : Romanists impose their monstrous transubstantiation upon those who have not discerned this. 2. *His error was a reproduction of Aaron's.* (1) This will be clear from a comparison of the text with Exod. xxxii. 4. (2) Aaron could not, under the very shadow of the Shekinah, and within hearing of the voice of thunder from Sinai, have intended to substitute his calf for the very Elohim. (3) But that he only intended it as an emblem of the true God is placed very clearly before us in the words following (Exod. xxxii. 5, 6), in which the feast celebrated before his calf is called a " feast of Jehovah." 3. *Yet this was idolatry.* (1) Idolatry may consist of worshipping the creature instead of the Creator. This the Romanist does when he worships the wafer. (2) Or it may be substituting some imagination of his heart for the God who has miraculously revealed Himself, and whose revelations concerning Himself are written in Holy Scripture. Such were the idealizations of the ancient (and also modern) heathen. (3) Or it may consist in attempting to worship the true God through unauthorised images (see Exod. xx. 4). This was the case with Aaron, also with Jeroboam. It is likewise the case with the Romanist, who uses crucifixes, and images and pictures of the Persons of the Trinity.

II. But why did he make calves ? 1. *He had the cherubim in his mind.* (1) These had the visage of a calf. They had, indeed, also the visages of a lion, of a man, and of an eagle. But the whole figure terminated in the foot of a calf (Ezek. i. 7). (2) Jeroboam's calf probably had also associated with it the other visages of the cherubim; so probably had Aaron's, for they respectively call their image by the plural name Elohim (אלהים). The single image at Bethel is also called calves (עגלים) in the plural, which suggests a plurality of visages, though not necessarily visages of calves, for the whole emblem appears to have been designated by this name. 2 *But the cherubim were emblems of the Holy Trinity.* (1) The calf or young bull, which by the ancients was taken for an emblem of fire, stood here for the first Person of the Godhead. (See Bate's " Critica Hebræa," under עגל and כרוב ; also his learned " Inquiry into the Occasional and Standing Similitudes of the Lord God in the Old and New Testaments.") (2) The lion was the symbol of light, and stood for the second Person. With the face of the lion that of the man was constantly associated, foreshadowing the assumption of the manhood into the Godhead by that blessed Person. (3) And the eagle, the emblem of air, stood for the Holy Spirit. (4) These, therefore, are called the *cherubim*, or *similitudes of the Great Ones*, from םיבר *Great Ones*, and כ *like*. 3. *Micah's teraphim were like Jeroboam's calves.* (1) They were a compound or plural image like the cherubim, and used like them (see Judg. xvii. 5, xviii. 5). (2) Michael was a worshipper of the true God, and so was Laban, who also used teraphim (see Gen. xxxi. 19, 30, 37, 49). (3) Compare also 1 Sam. xix. 13; Ezek. xxi. 21; Hosea iii. 4. (4) The *cerberus* of the pagans, with its plurality of heads, was a corruption, and the name of that monster keeps up the sound, of the original Hebrew *cherubim*. How subtle is the spirit of idolatry! We cannot keep too close to God's Word.—M.

Vers. 28—33.—*Jeroboam's Sin.* The king of Israel, moved by personal ambition instead of zeal for God, fearing lest his people, in going to Jerusalem to worship, should see reason to regret having rent the kingdom, took counsel to prevent this. The result was the development of the policy described in the text. It was cunning—

I. IN THE KIND OF WORSHIP IMPOSED. 1. *As to its objects.* (1) It purported to be the worship of the God of Israel. Essentially the same with the worship at Jerusalem. Thus it conciliated favour. Had it been the worship of any god of the nations, opposition would have been provoked. (2) Yet was it idolatry. So in like manner is much of the worship of modern times which passes under the name of Christianity. Satan does not lose his identity by transforming himself into an angel of light. 2. *As to its modes.* (2) Its images were imitations of the cherubim. Such also were the teraphim. And as God was said to *dwell in*, not "between" (שׁכן is to *inhabit*), the cherubim, so Jeroboam directed his dupes to seek the God of Israel *in* his calves. (2) With these were associated altars, for sacrifice and incense, like those in the temple; and the victims would be clean animals proper for sacrifice; the incense also would be similar to that burnt in Jerusalem. (3) He had a Feast of Tabernacles, which is described in the text as "like unto the feast that is in Judah." Only that he altered the date as well as the place from the fifteenth day of the seventh month to the corresponding day of the month following. It is significantly noted, "which he had devised of his own heart" (see Num. xv. 39). He was a forerunner of another character who has not hesitated to "change times and laws" (Dan. vii. 25). 3. *As to its ministers.* (1) His priests were Levites, where he could get them. In this he seems to have succeeded at Dan. For the descendants of Jonathan, who was of the family of Aaron, appear to have fallen in with his designs (see Judg. xviii. 30). (2) But it was different at Bethel. Here the Levites, it is to be hoped, had too much principle to serve his calves. So "he made priests of the lowest of the people." (3) Amongst these he officiated himself. Morally he was indeed amongst the lowest of the people, notwithstanding his position as king. This, unhappily, was not sufficiently discerned. The wicked do not understand (Dan. xii. 10).

II. IN THE PLACES CHOSEN FOR THAT WORSHIP. 1. *Dan was chosen with sagacity.* (1) This was a city in the north, whose Canaanitish name was Laish, but which, when conquered by the Danites, received the name of their father (Judg. xviii. 29—31). This would be convenient to the people living so distant from Jerusalem. (2) Besides, from its founding, this city was sacred to the worship of God through the medium of teraphim. This was about the time of Joshua's death when Phinehas ministered at the tabernacle at Shiloh (compare Judg. xx. 27, 28). From these very teraphim, when they were in the house of Micah, God gave responses to Jonathan the priest. (3) For the teraphim of Micah, which were carved blocks covered with *silver*, Jeroboam substituted one of his calves, which was covered with *gold;* otherwise there does not appear to have been any material change in the worship there. So the prejudices of the people would not be shocked. 2. *Bethel also was chosen with sagacity.* (1) This was in the southern part of the kingdom, to accommodate those who might otherwise go to

Jerusalem through convenience of distance. How adroitly do the wicked place their snares! (2) This place, too, had a memorable history. It was the scene of the vision of the ladder and renewal of the covenant with Jacob, in token of which the patriarch vowed to the Lord, anointed a pillar, and built an altar (Gen. xxviii. 19, 20 ; xxxi. 13 ; xxxv. 1, 7). It was one of the stations of Samuel, and a place to which, in his days, the people were accustomed to go up to worship (1 Sam. vii. 16 ; x. 3). (3) Here, accordingly, Jeroboam fixed his head-quarters, and built a pretentious temple, or "house of high places" (ver. 31).

Thus practically did Jeroboam say, with another purpose in his heart, "It is too much for you to go up to Jerusalem." Beware of religion made easy ; it may land you in perdition. Beware of imitations of Divine things. Keep rigidly to the Word of God.—M.

Vers. 26—28.—*The Sin of Jeroboam.* This passage describes the act which is so often referred to with horror, in the books of Kings and Chronicles, as "the sin of Jeroboam, the son of Nebat." To an irreligious man like himself, nothing would appear more natural or politic than this conduct. He had been driven into Egypt by Solomon, had there married Pharaoh's daughter, and become familiar with the worship of Apis and Mnevis. Now he had returned, and found himself the ruler of the ten tribes, the first king of the separate "kingdom of Israel." Recognizing as he did the religious tendencies and memories of his people, he saw that the national assemblies for worship in the temple at Jerusalem would, sooner or later, unite the tribes again under one king. Hence his action. Looking at his conduct (1) from the earthward, and (2) from the heavenward side, we see that his policy was at once shrewd and sinful.

I. THE SHREWDNESS OF JEROBOAM'S POLICY. (1) *It was an appeal to tribal independence.* In effect he said, "Why should you men of Ephraim be dependent for your worship on Judah? Why should your tribute go to support their temple? Let us have a place of our own." This argument has been repeated by demagogues in every land and age. Class has been set against class, nation against nation, Church against Church, by this spirit. Show some of the advantages of recognizing our interdependence. (2) *It was an appeal to self-indulgence.* "It is too much for you to go up to Jerusalem." Point out instances in which religious teachers have condescended to such base suggestions as this ; *e.g.,* the theology that declares self-conquest nothing, that makes faith the executioner, instead of the sustainer of morality ; the teaching that will offer "indulgences" to those of sinful habit ; the worship that pleases a sensuous taste, but demands no intelligent thought, &c. 3. *It was an appeal to former memories.* He made *Shechem* his capital, a place associated with Abraham and Jacob, and afterwards assigned to the Levites, and made a free city. He erected one of the calves at *Bethel,* a holy place on the borders of Benjamin and Ephraim (see Gen. xxxii.). No doubt his design was to conciliate those who were proud of past history. 4. *It was a bold attempt to deceive the devout.* He pretended that it was the old worship re-established ; that Jehovah was really represented by the calves : "These be thy gods (the old gods) that brought thee out of the land of Egypt." Not the first or last time in which the prince of darkness has appeared as an angel of light. Shrewd as was the policy, it was not perfectly successful even during his reign. The best people emigrated to Judah (like the Huguenots to England), to enrich another kingdom by work and wealth ; and the prophets and many of the priests were roused to hostility. Even had it succeeded, however, such policy deserved to be branded with infamy. Principle must never be sacrificed to expediency. Success never condones wrong-doing with God.

II. THE SINFULNESS OF JEROBOAM'S POLICY. 1. *It revealed his utter distrust of God.* See the promise that had been given him (ch. xi. 38) : "I will build thee a sure house." He could not believe it. He would trust his own skill rather than God's favour. So had it been with Saul and Solomon. The path of simple obedience is strait and narrow, and "few there be that find it." "Do My will and trust Me," is the lesson of life, but we are slow to learn it. Many professing

Christians consider religion inappropriate to business competition and to political movements. In this they resemble the son of Nebat. 2. *It violated the fundamental law of the Decalogue.* If the first command was not actually broken, the second was, necessarily. Had these calves merely been the outward symbols of Jehovah, they were amongst the forbidden "images." Jeroboam knew this. He remembered the calf Aaron made, for his words were an echo of those of the first high priest. He knew that only the intercession of Moses then saved the people from destruction, yet again he defiantly disobeyed. Show the peril of allowing images, crucifixes, banners, the elements in the sacrament, &c., to take a false position in Christian worship. Even if the initiated worship God through these, they break (in spirit) the second command; while the more ignorant are with equal certainty led to the violation of the first. 3. *It involved and necessitated other sins.* (1) The people worshipped in the place God had not chosen, as He had chosen the temple. (2) They had no ark of the covenant on which rested, and because of which was promised, the real presence of God. (3) The priests were chosen by the king in opposition to the ordinance of God (vers. 31, &c., ex *universo* populo. (4) The national feast of tabernacles was changed from the seventh month (Levit. xxiii. 34) to the eighth, not only because the harvest was later in the north than in the south of Judah, but to widen insidiously the breach between the kingdoms. So in all ages and in all spheres one sin leads to another. It would be better to die as Abigail (ch. xiv. 13) than to reign as Jeroboam.—A. R.

Vers. 26—30.—*The Golden Calves.* Jeroboam here earns for himself that name of evil repute—"the son of Nebat, who made Israel to sin." As the leader in the revolt of the ten tribes he was simply fulfilling a Divine purpose. "The thing was from the Lord,"—the ordained penalty of Solomon's transgression (ch. xi. 31, 33). But this setting up of the golden calves, this only too successful attempt to sever the sacred bond that bound the people of the whole land in one common allegiance to the temple and the great invisible King who sat enthroned there, bore a widely different character. This was not "from the Lord." It was wholly evil. "The thing became a sin," and the sin of Jeroboam became the prolific source of sin in Israel through all succeeding generations (see ch. xiv. 7—16). This transaction illustrates—

I. THE FATAL PERVERSITY OF A LAWLESS AMBITION. This was Jeroboam's ruin. God, by the prophet Ahijah, had promised to establish him in the kingdom on certain conditions (ch. xi. 38). There was no wrong in the mere fact of his seeking to verify this prediction. His sin lay in the nature of the means he adopted. He thought it needful in order to his having a "sure house" that the people should be kept from going up to sacrifice at Jerusalem. In other words, he would strengthen *his* house at the expense of doing deep dishonour to the "*House of the Lord.*" His own petty kingship was more to him than the Infinite Majesty of Jehovah. Thus we see how a carnal ambition (1) is subject to needless fears; (2) trifles with or defies a power that it finds to be infinitely stronger than itself; (3) thinks to secure its ends by means that actually defeat them; (4) is deceived by its seeming successes. History is full of examples of the way in which men have sought power for themselves, either by the abuse or the degradation of things sacred, or have thought to serve ends right in themselves by unrighteous means. This was one form of Satanic temptation to which our blessed Lord was subject. "All these things will I give thee," &c. (Matt. iv. 8, 9), and his professed followers have too often fallen before it.

II. THE ARTIFICE OF A WICKED PURPOSE. This is seen in the way in which Jeroboam practised craftily upon the religious sentiment of the people in the service of his own ambitious designs. (1) He pandered to their idolatrous propensities. The "golden calves" may have been intended as a memorial rather than a representation of the Deity. But they were too suggestive of the base, sensuous worship of Egypt, and violated the second commandment if not the first. (2) He made pretence of consulting their ease and convenience. "It is too much for you," &c. (3)

He took advantage of the sacred associations of Bethel and Dan, as if the place would hallow the proceeding.   (4) He instituted a priestly order as a substitute for the Levites.   (5) He ordained festivals that should rival those of Judah and Jerusalem.   In all this, while affecting to do honour to the traditions of religion, he struck a fatal blow at the religious unity and integrity of the nation, turning the highest sanctities of its life into an occasion of sin.   How forcibly are we reminded that iniquity assumes its most hateful form when it prostitutes to its own ends things sacred and Divine.   Satan is never so Satanic as when he wears the garb of "an angel of light."   The most detestable of all vices is hypocrisy.   More deadly injury has been done to the cause of religion by its false friends than its bitterest enemies could ever inflict.

III. THE DISASTROUS EFFECTS OF WICKEDNESS IN HIGH PLACES.   Jeroboam's wicked policy perpetuated and multiplied in Israel the evils of which the rending of the kingdom at first had been the penalty.   With few exceptions all the kings that followed him "did evil in the sight of the Lord," and the record of their reigns is little else than a story of crime and bloodshed and misery.   Moreover, the leprosy of idolatry spread from the throne down through all classes of the people until the kingdom of Israel was completely overthrown and the ten tribes were carried captive into Assyria.   Such are the woes that fall on a land when its princes are corrupt and reprobate.   So true is it that "they that sow to the wind shall reap the whirl-wind."—W.

EXPOSITION.

CHAPTER XIII. 1—10.

THE TESTIMONY OF GOD AGAINST THE CALF WORSHIP.—We have in this chapter, which some commentators consider to be derived from a different source from the narratives which precede and follow it—the expression of ver. 32, "the cities of Samaria," according to them, proving it to be of a later date, while the style and colouring of the story suggest that it embodies a tradition current in the time of the compiler—an account of certain circumstances of profound significance which marked the inauguration of Jeroboam's first great feast—for the close connexion with ch. xii. shows that it is "the fifteenth day of the eighth month" that is here described. The chapter divides itself into two sections, the first (vers. 1—10) containing the public testimony of the prophet of Judah against the schismatic worship, the second (vers. 11—32) his subsequent perversion and his tragical death.

Ver. 1.—And, behold, there came a man of God [see on ch. xii. 22. The "man of God" is throughout carefully distinguished from the "prophet." Josephus calls the former Jadon, probably the Grecized form of Iddo, עִדּוֹ, which appears as יֶעְדּוֹ Ia'do, in the Keri of 2 Chron. ix. 29. Iddo, however, notwithstanding his "visions against

Jeroboam the son of Nebat" (2 Chron. ix. 29), it cannot have been, for he survived to the reign of Abijah, and indeed wrote a "story" (Heb. Midrash, i.e., Commentary) of that reign, whereas this man of God died forthwith. For a similar reason, we cannot believe it to have been Shemaiah, the historian of the reign of Rehoboam (2 Chron. xii. 5, 15)] out of Judah [whither, as a rule, both priests and prophets would seem to have retreated (2 Chron. xi. 14, 16). It is clear, however, that the migration of the latter was not so general as that of the former. In ver. 11 we find a prophet at Bethel; in ch. xiv. Ahijah is still at Shiloh, and at a later day we find schools of the prophets at Bethel, Jericho, &c. (2 Kings ii. 3, 5). Stanley says with truth that "the prophetical activity of the time . . . is to be found in the kingdom, not of Judah, but of Israel," but omits to add that it was because the northern kingdom more especially needed their ministry. It was just for this reason that Ahijah and others remained at their posts.] by [Heb. in, same word as in vers. 2, 9, 17, 20, 32, &c. Similarly, 1 Sam. iii. 21. The בְ is not merely instrumental, but, like the ἐν of the N. T., denotes the sphere or element. " By the word" would imply that he had received a Divine communication ; " in the word," that his message possessed him, inspired him, was "in his heart as a burning fire shut up in his bones" (Jer. xx. 9)] the word of the Lord unto Bethel [It is worth remembering that the new sanctuary at Bethel would probably be visible from the temple

(Porter, p. 219; Van de Velde, ii. 283), so that this function was an act of open defiance]: **and Jeroboam stood by** [Heb. *upon*. See on ch. xii. 32, 33. It is the same occasion] **the altar to burn incense** [or to burn the fat, &c., of the sacrifice. See on ch. xii. 33. This altar was clearly, *pro hac vice*, an altar of burnt offering; not an altar of incense, as is proved by the next verse.]

Ver. 2.—**And he cried against the altar in the word of the Lord, and said, O altar, altar, thus saith the Lord** [This apostrophe of the altar is very striking and significant. It is as if the prophet disdained to notice the royal but self-constituted priest; as if it were useless to appeal to him; as if his person was of little consequence compared with the religious system he was inaugurating, the system of which the altar was the centre and embodiment]; **Behold a child shall be born unto the house of David, Josiah by name** [This particular mention of the Reformer by name was formerly regarded, as by many it is still, as a remarkable instance of prophetic foresight. But the tendency of late, even amongst orthodox theologians, has been to doubt the authenticity of these two words, on the ground that it is unlike Scripture prophecy in general to descend to such details, which rather belong to soothsaying than prediction. Prophecy concerns itself not with names, times, and similar particulars, but with the " progressive development of the kingdom of God in its general features " (Keil). It is not for a moment denied that the prophet could just as easily, speaking "in the word of the Lord," have mentioned the *name* of Josiah, as the circumstance that a son of the house of David would utterly destroy the worship of calves. But it is alleged that the latter prediction is quite in accordance with Scripture usage, and the former altogether contrarient thereto. The case of Cyrus (Isa. xliv. 28; xlv. 1), it is true, is an exception to the rule, unless כֹּרֶשׁ (which means *the sun*) is, like Pharaoh and Hadad, a name of office, a title of the Persian kings. The instances of Isaac (Gen. xvii. 19) and Solomon (1 Chron. xxii. 9) are not parallels, as in both these cases the name was highly significant, and each was mentioned, not by way of prophecy, but as a direction to bestow that name on a child shortly about to be born. And it is certainly noticeable—though the argument *e silentio* is necessarily a precarious one—" that where this narrative is again referred to (2 Kings xxiii. 15—18) there is no allusion to the fact that the man of God had prophesied of Josiah *by name* " (Rawlinson). On the whole, therefore, it seems probable that the two words יֹאשִׁיָּהוּ שְׁמוֹ

were no part of the original prophecy, but a marginal note which in course of time found its way accidentally into the text. The idea of Keil, that " Josiah " is mentioned here not as a proper name, but as an appellation, "he whom Jehovah sustains," is hardly worthy of serious consideration. It may be allowed, however, that the *meaning* of the name affords some slender reason for its mention]; **and upon thee shall he offer** [lit., *sacrifice*] **the priests of the high places** [see on ch. xii. 32] **that burn incense upon thee, and men's bones** [Heb. *bones of man, i.e.*, human bones. Nothing could more completely foreshadow the future desecration of the altar. The presence in the congregation of a living man who had merely touched a dead body and had not been purified, defiled the tabernacle (Num. xix. 13), how much more the dead body itself, burnt on the very altar. The Samaritan who once strewed the temple with human ashes (Jos., Ant. xviii. 2. 2) knew that he took the most effectual way to pollute it] **shall be burnt** [Heb. *shall they burn*] **upon thee.** [For the fulfilment, see 2 Kings xxiii. 20, " At the ground of this judgment, as of the whole theocratic law, lies the *jus* talionis " (Keil, 1846).]

It is worthy of note how completely this brief protest proclaimed to Jeroboam the utter and shameful overthrow, both of his political and religious systems. A child of the rival house of David should stand where *he* then stood, his successors extinct or powerless to prevent him, and should cover this new cultus with disgrace and contempt. The man of God, he must have felt, has proclaimed in few words the fall of his dynasty, the triumph of his rival, and the failure of all his schemes.

Ver. 3.—**And he gave a sign** [The Heb. מוֹפֵת rather signifies a *portent* (τέρας, *miraculum, prodigium*) than a *sign*, the proper word for which is אוֹת. The word occurs repeatedly in the Pentateuch, where it is rendered *wonder*, or *miracle*, by our translators (Wordsworth). Signs had, of course, been given before (Exod. iv. 30; vii. 9; 1 Sam. xii. 17; &c.) but hardly in such *immediate* attestation of a special message. From this time forward such signs are not infrequent (Isa. vii. 14; xxxviii. 8; 2 Kings xix. 29). They mark the decline of faith (Matt. xii. 39). As to the need at this crisis for some miraculous token, see Homiletics. The fitness of this particular sign is obvious] **the same day, saying, This is the sign which** [Rather *that*; אֲשֶׁר = *quod*. The A. V. rendering hardly makes sense. Nor does it agree, as Rawlinson seems to think, with the LXX., which reads τοῦτο τὸ ῥῆμα ὃ ἐλάλησε κύριος, &c.] **the Lord hath spoken** [*i.e.*, by me. "This is the proof that my message is from Him, and is no idle threat." Wordsworth sees in this sign "a proof vouchsafed by God Himself to the man of Judah, as well as to Jeroboam, that he was really sent by God," &c. But surely a man who came "in the word of the Lord," and cried, "Thus saith the Lord," wanted no proof that "he was doing God's bidding" (see 1 Cor. xiv. 22)] ; **Behold, the altar shall be rent and the ashes** [strictly, *fat ashes.* דֶּשֶׁן ; properly, "fatness" (see Judg. ix. 9 ; Psa. lxiii. 5. πιότης, LXX.), is the fat of the sacrifice, which was burnt upon the altar, mixed with the ashes that consumed it] **that are upon it shall be poured out.** [The sign, a partial destruction of the altar, and the scattering of the sacrifice, was admirably calculated to presage its ultimate and final and ignominious overthrow. The idea favoured by Stanley ("Jewish Ch." ii. 280) that this prediction was fulfilled "if not before, at least" in the time of Amos, when the altar was destroyed by an earthquake shock (Amos ix. 1; cf. iii. 14), does not seem to take account of ver. 5.]

Ver. 4.—**And it came to pass when king Jeroboam** [The A. V. follows the LXX. The Heb. omits "Jeroboam"] **heard the saying of the man of God, which had cried against the altar in Bethel, that he put forth his hand** [instinctively. His first thought was, not to wait and see whether the promised sign was given, but to seize and punish the man who had dared thus to denounce and thwart him. And we may imagine how extremely mortifying this interruption must have been to him. It threatened the complete frustration of his policy at the very moment when it seemed certain of success] **from the altar** [the ledge or platform, *i.e.*, where he stood. He did not leave it, but shouted his commands to his servants], **saying, Lay hold on him.** ["Arrest him," "let him not escape." One word in the Heb.] **And his hand, which he put forth against him, dried up** [Possibly the result of paralysis or tetanus (Ackermann in Bähr). It was like the "withered hand" of the New Testament (Matt. xii. 10, &c.) deprived of feeling and vital force, as the next words show], **so that he could not pull it in again to him.** [It was not only powerless to punish, it was punished. "Now stands the king of Israel, like some antique statue, in a posture of impotent endeavour" (Hall). This was a warning to the king, not so much against his unauthorized and schismatical rites, as against his attempt to

avenge himself on the messenger of God (Psa. cv. 14, 15).]

Ver. 5.—**The altar also was rent** [by the same invisible power, and probably at the same moment], **and the ashes poured out from the altar, according to the sign which the man of God had given by the word of the Lord.**

Ver. 6.—**And the king** [humbled and alarmed by the judgment he had experienced in his own person] **answered and said unto the man of God, Intreat now** [The Heb. is very expressive—"*Smooth* or *stroke the face.*" It is an expression which occurs several times. See especially Exod. xxxii. 11 ; 2 Kings xiii. 4 ; 2 Chron. xxxiii. 12 ; Prov. xix. 6] **of the Lord thy God** [*i.e.*, whose messenger thou art. "Jeroboam, conscience-stricken, does not dare to call Jehovah his own God" (Wordsworth). This was probably the case, yet surely it is an inference not warranted by the text. The expression, "The Lord thy God," is of constant occurrence, especially when a "man of God" is addressed; cf. ch. xvii. 12 ; xviii. 10], **and pray for me** [This sudden change in his bearing shows how much Jeroboam was frightened. The sight, too, of the king humbly supplicating the prophet who a moment before had protested against the calf-worship was calculated to make an impression on the minds of the people], **that my hand may be restored me again. And the man of God besought** [lit., *stroked the face of*] **the Lord, and the king's hand was restored him, and became as it was before.**

Ver. 7.—**And the king said unto the man of God, Come home with me, and refresh thyself** [with food, ablutions, &c. (Gen. xviii. 4, 5 ; xix. 2 ; Mark vii. 3, &c.) We are hardly justified in seeing in these words (with Bähr and Keil) an attempt to "gain the prophet over to his side by friendliness," and to render his threat harmless in the eyes of the people. The king doubtless may have hoped that it would "blunt the edge of the prophet's denunciation of his schismatical altar" (Wordsworth); but this was not the object, or not the sole object, with which the invitation was given. Jeroboam could not possibly have done less, after the signal service the man of God had rendered him, than invite him to his palace. Eastern courtesy alone (Gen. xviii. 4 ; xix. 2 ; xliii. 24, &c.) would require him to offer hospitality to his benefactor. And he could scarcely hope that any hospitalities would either neutralize the impression which the recent miracles had made, or win over to his side one who had a direct commission from the Most High to oppose him. With more reason, Wordsworth cites 1 Sam. xv. 30,

"Honour me now, I pray thee, before the elders of my people." A feeling of gratitude may have *prompted* the invitation, while the king at the same time was very sensible of the advantages which would accrue to himself if it were accepted], **and I will give thee a reward.** [The services, especially of seers and prophets, were invariably requited in the East with presents, as are those of Judges, Kadis, Kaimakams, and other officers at the present day (see ch. xiv. 3; Gen. xxiv. 53; xxxiii. 11; xliii. 11; Num. xxii. 17; Judg. iii. 17; vi. 18; xiii. 15; 1 Sam. ix. 7, 8; xii. 3; 2 Kings v. 5, 15; viii. 8, 9).]

Ver. 8.—**And the man of God said unto the king, If thou wilt give me half thine house** [cf. Num. xxii. 18, of which, however, there is hardly a reminiscence. Obviously, half the contents or wealth of thy house], **I will not go in with thee, neither will I eat bread nor drink water in this place.**

Ver. 9.—**For so was it charged** [Heb. *he, sc.* the Lord, *charged me*] me by [Heb. *in*] the **word of the Lord, saying, Eat no bread, nor drink water** [Participation in food—the "eating salt"—is in the East a token of friendship and affinity; a sign of close communion and fellowship. The prophet's refusal to participate was consequently a practical and forcible disclaimer of all fellowship, a virtual excommunication, a public repudiation of the calf-worshippers.

Cf. 1 Cor. v. 11, "With such an one, no, not to eat." As Corn. à Lapide, "*Ut ipso facto ostenderet, Bethelitas idololatras adeo esse detestabiles, et a Deo quasi excommunicatos, ut nullum fidelium cum iis cibi vel potus communionem habere velit*"], **nor turn again by the same way that thou camest.** [The object of this command was not "simply to test the obedience of the prophet" (Rawlinson), nor yet that no one might "force him to a delay which was irreconcilable with his commission" (Keil), for that was practically executed, but to avoid as far as possible—what, indeed, happened in spite of these precautions—his being traced and followed. Because of this provision, the old prophet (ver. 10) was reduced to ask, "What way went he?" But the charge, we can hardly doubt, was also designed to serve another purpose, viz., to warn the prophet against doing what he did presently—against returning to Bethel. When he was followed, and when he was told of a revelation commanding his return, he should have remembered, among other things, that it had clearly been part of God's purpose, as evidenced by the explicit instructions given him, that he should not be followed. This alone should have led him to suspect this old prophet of deceit.]

Ver. 10.—**So he went another way, and returned not by the way that he came to Bethel.**

HOMILETICS.

Vers. 2, 3, 8.—*Protest and Excommunication.* The sin of Jeroboam, the schism which he inaugurated in person at the first feast of tabernacles held in Bethel, was not consummated without protest. When the king, possibly in the "golden garments" of the priesthood, mounted the altar platform and stood before the vast multitude assembled to witness this first great function of the new *régime,* a messenger of God, sent from Judah, the seat of the true religion, lifted up his voice and witnessed against these irregular and impious proceedings, against the unsanctified altar, the unhallowed sacrifice, and the intrusive priesthood. It must have been pretty clear beforehand that any protest addressed to Jeroboam, who had devised and elaborated this corruption of Mosaic worship, would be unavailing, but nevertheless it must be made. It was probably in part because Jeroboam was beyond the reach of remonstrance that the warning was addressed to the altar itself. In other words, it was made for the sake of the people rather than of their king. They should be mercifully, and therefore distinctly, taught that this calf-worship had not and could not have the sanction of the Most High. Whether they would hear, or whether they would forbear, they should see that God had not left Himself without witness; they should know that at this crisis there had been a prophet amongst them. The breach should not be made without due warning of its sinfulness and its consequences. "For a testimony unto them" the man of God addresses the dumb altar, the sign and centre of the new system, and proclaims not only its overthrow but the destruction of Jeroboam's house and the defeat of all his schemes.

And as, under such circumstances, mere threats, of whatsoever character and by whomsoever spoken, would have had but little weight without " signs following," the message straightway receives the confirmation of a miracle. That the man of God " came from Judah " was in itself reason enough why the men of Israel should not listen to him, unless he compelled their attention by prodigies. " A partizan," they would say, " perhaps a hireling of Rehoboam, it was natural such a one would prophecy evil of the Northern Church and kingdom," and so his words would have been unheeded, even if his life had been spared. Besides, one who professed to come as he did, " in the word of the Lord," they had a right to ask for his credentials, and those credentials could only be miraculous. Had not Moses and Aaron " wrought signs and wonders in the land of Egypt, before Pharaoh and all his servants?" Had not Samuel, too, supported his message by a portent ? (1 Sam. xii. 18.) If the denunciation of the schism, consequently, was not to be inoperative, he must " give a sign " the same day.

And to these " two witnesses "—"the " sure word of prophecy " and the " sign following "—the rashness and impiety of Jeroboam procured the addition of a third, or rather of *two* more—silent, but eloquent attestations, each of them, that the prophet had not spoken in his own name. For, enraged at this bold, this most unwelcome and sinister interruption of his ritual, and fearing the effect of this brave protest on his audience and the thousands of Israel to whom the news would ultimately come, and forgetting at the moment the sacred character of the speaker and the unseen panoply which protected him, he stretches forth his hand intuitively, as if to detain the prophet, and thunders his commands to the attendant soldiery to arrest him. But that hand, really raised against the Most High, suddenly becomes rigid and power-less, and he must needs stoop to beg the prophet's prayers that it may be restored to him again. And so it came to pass that the heretic king furnished in his own person, much against his will, two powerful proofs that the " man of God " did indeed speak the word of God and was supported by the power of God. It is thus that God makes the wrath of man to praise Him.

Such, then, was the PROTEST, in word and deed, which marked the first great service of the schismatic Church. But that was not all. The protest was to be followed by an INTERDICT. The man of God was commissioned at the same time to put the city and inhabitants of Bethel under a ban. He was to treat them as *lepers*, as so tainted with heresy, so polluted and unclean in the sight of God, that he could neither eat of their bread nor drink of their cup. For this was clearly the object of the injunction, " Eat no bread nor drink water there ; " it was to show that all who participated in this unhallowed worship were thenceforward to be treated by Divine command as heathens and publicans. And to the children of the East this public disclaimer of fellowship, this practical excommunication, would have a significance such as with our altered conditions of society we can hardly conceive, though the " Boycotting" of our own time may help us to under-stand its operation. Every citizen of Bethel, every worshipper of the calves, would feel himself branded as unclean. The " scarlet letter " which the Puritans of New England printed on the bosom of the adulteress hardly involved a greater stigma. It was for this reason, therefore, that when the king bade the man of God to his palace and promised him a royal recompense for the service he had rendered him, the latter flung back his invitation in his face, and swore that half the king's house would not tempt him to eat of his dainties. Jeroboam, and his people through him, should learn that if they would persist in their wanton defiance of Divine law; if they *would* have two churches and three sanctuaries where God had decreed there should in either case be but one ; if they would sacrifice before the works of their own hands, and by ministers of man's ordaining, and at times of man's devising, then the pious Hebrews who preserved inviolate the ancient faith should wipe their hands of them, and treat them as renegades and aliens from the common-wealth of Israel.

The lessons of this history are manifold. Two, however, occupy a position of pre-eminence above the rest.

1. *That corruptions of religion are not to be consummated without* PROTEST *on the part of the Church.* That Christianity, as well as Judaism, should have its

heresies and schisms was distinctly foretold by St. Paul himself (1 Cor. xi. 19 ; Acts xx. 29, 30). But if they are inevitable, because of the frailty of our nature and the hardnesss of our hearts, they are none the less sinful, and it is none the less our duty to strive and to witness against them. If God did not suffer that first great schism to pass unreproved, can we do better, or do less, than follow His example ? It may be said that *we* cannot always distinguish between heresy and orthodoxy —that we "call our doxy orthodoxy, and other people's doxy heterodoxy," and this is quite true. But individual opinion is one thing and the teaching of the Church another. Has the Church, then, no teaching office ? Is she or is she not " the pillar and ground of the truth" ? Has she or has she not the promise of our Lord's guidance and illumination ? (Matt. xviii. 17, 18; xxviii. 20.) Or can the Church universal err ? (Matt. xvi. 18.) Is her " *Quod semper, quod ubique,*" &c., no test of truth ? It is not for the private Christian to claim any infallibility, but it is for the Church to say what is in and what is against her *depositum fidei.* And furthermore it is her duty, in her synods and by her officers, to protest against all corruptions of the faith. " A man that is a heretic . . . reject," Titus iii. 10 ; cf. ch. i. 9—11 ; 1 Tim. vi. 3—5 (" From such withdraw thyself "); Rom. xvi. 17 ; Matt. xviii. 17 ; 3 John 9, 10; Gal. i. 8; ii. 11. The Christian verity is not less dear to God than was the teaching of Moses. The preacher is as much bound to preserve the faith whole and undefiled as was the prophet. And it is idle to say, as it sometimes is said, that mere protests are worse than useless. They may not avert a schism—this protest did not—but they may have their use nevertheless, as this had. Or if they are entirely futile as regards others, they are not forgotten of God. Besides, who shall say that success or non-success is to alter the standard of Christian duty ? It is surely something to be able to say, whatever the issue, *Liberavi animam meam.* It is to be remembered that God knew beforehand that this *His* protest, though enforced by signs and wonders, would be comparatively unavailing.

2. *That certain crimes against morality and religion are still to be visited by* EXCOMMUNICATION. Not the excommunication of bell and book and candle—*that* finds no place in Holy Scripture—but social excommunication such as that described to us in this history. Indeed, there is also an ecclesiastical excommunication which must sometimes be wielded. There are persons with whom we have no right to eat and to drink at the Table of our Blessed Lord—persons who must be repelled at any cost from Holy Communion, lest we should indirectly make ourselves " partakers of other men's sins " (1 Tim. v. 22). When John Wesley once proposed to give a note of admission to the Lord's Table to a man of dubious character, Henry Moore, one of his preachers, bluntly said that if that man were admitted he should refuse to attend. " Sir," said Wesley, " I should attend even if the devil came to Holy Communion." " So should I," was the answer; " but not if John Wesley gave him a note of admission." For it is obvious that the Eucharist, the closest rite of fellowship—the rite which makes and proclaims us members one of another (Rom. xii. 4, 5)—if knowingly administered to the "notorious evil-liver," is a virtual condoning of his sin ; it is equivalent to bidding him God speed (2 John 10, 11), and so it makes the Church " partaker of his evil deeds." " Therefore put away from among yourselves that wicked person " (1 Cor. v. 13). But our history points rather to social than ecclesiastical interdict. And it must be distinctly understood that the refusal to eat and drink with notorious and incorrigible evil-livers is a part of Christian duty (see 1 Cor. v. 9—11 ; 2 Thess. iii. 14, 15; Matt. xviii. 17). We are not permitted to know them and to treat them like other men. The story of St. John's hurriedly leaving the bath because of the presence there of the heretic Cerinthus, is one for which the so-called tolerance of the age can only afford a contemptuous smile ; but the age is often wiser in its own conceit than Christ and His apostles. Only let us remember, if we must treat any as heathens and publicans, how Christ treated the penitent publicans (cf. Luke xv. 1, 2); and then let us not shrink from discharging this painful duty both to our country, our Church, and our God. Among the secondary lessons of our story are these:

1. *That right shall triumph in the long run.* The schism throve for 250 years,

but the altar was ultimately dishonoured and overthrown. The Reformer who should desecrate it with bones of men was already appointed in the counsels of God. Even so, sooner or later, " every plant which my heavenly Father hath not planted shall be rooted up " (Matt. xv. 13). " If this work be of men, it will come to nought " (Acts v. 38).

> " Our little systems have their day,
> They have their day and cease to be."

Magna est veritas, &c. The Babel of sects cannot last for ever.

2. *The ministers of God are secure so long as they do their duty.* Jeroboam, with the ten tribes at his back, was powerless against the unprotected missionary. " He reproved kings for their sakes, saying . . . Do my prophets no harm " (Psa. cv. 14, 15). The stars shall fall from their courses before a hair of their heads shall be injured. Cf. Dan. iii. 27; vi. 22; 2 Kings i. 10, &c. But it may be objected, " The saints and messengers of God have often been brutally outraged and murdered " (Heb. xi. 35—37). True, but who shall say that they were not then most secure ? " Through much tribulation we must *enter into the kingdom of God* " (Acts xiv. 22). It was when Stephen was martyred that he saw " Jesus standing"—*i.e.*, to help—" at the right hand of God." It has been suggested that it was when St. Paul was stoned and taken up for dead (Acts xiv. 19) that he was caught up into Paradise (2 Cor. xii. 4). *Sic iter ad astra.*

3. *The wicked cannot dispense with the prayers of the saints.* " Entreat the face of the Lord thy God and pray for me " (cf. Exod. ix. 28; Num. xii. 2, 13; Acts viii. 24). How often has this history repeated itself; and what a foreshadowing of the world to come ! Here was one of the synagogue of Satan worshipping at the prophet's feet, &c. (Rev. iii. 9). Observe, too, it is the part of a man of God to answer threats with prayers. " They are mine adversaries, but I, prayer " (Psa. cix. 4, Heb.; cf. Psa. xxxv. 13 sqq.) It is the very best way of overcoming evil with good.

4. *Men are often more concerned about their sufferings than about their sins.* Jeroboam's entreaty is, not that his sin may be forgiven, but that his hand may be restored. How many pray, " Heal my body; " how few, " Heal my soul, for I have sinned against thee " (Psa. xli. 4). The plague of head or hand extorts more cries for mercy than the plague of the heart (ch. viii. 38).

5. " *Law and order cannot be violated with impunity by any ruler under any religious pretext* " (Maurice). The rent altar teaches the lesson of Psa. ii. 2—5: " Those betray themselves that think by any sin to support themselves." . . . " He promised himself that the calves would secure the crown to his family, but it proved they lost it " (M. Henry).

6. *Let the ministers of God beware of bribery.* " Come home with me and I will give," &c. The device of Jeroboam for silencing and conciliating the prophet has often been tried since, and with fatal success. How many men's mouths have been stopped by a sop—by place or pension, nay, by an insignificant present. Men know well—the enemy of man knows well—that the preacher finds it hard to reprove a benefactor. The writer once heard an influential person boasting that he had silenced his clergyman's remonstrances and appeals by a present of game ! The world has a shrewd suspicion that the clergy are not incorruptible; that they, like others, have their price. Let us be on our guard against *social* corruption. How sinister the influence of some *homes* on the younger clergy. The cordial " Come home with me " was to them a snare of Satan. With the State clergy how strong the temptation to sacrifice independence for a benefice; with Nonconformists, to speak smooth words lest the congregation should " stop the supplies." The man of God thus speaks to all ministers of God.

HOMILIES BY VARIOUS AUTHORS.

Vers. 1—3.—*The Fire of Jehovah.* Jeroboam went to inaugurate his feast of tabernacles at his principal temple in Bethel, and to give effect to the ceremonies officiated in person as high priest. Then, as he stood by the altar, censer in hand, he was confronted by the word of the Lord. A man of God from Judah denounced the altar in the words before us, which contain a very remarkable prophecy; and he authenticated his message by a miraculous sign. (Compare Mark xvi. 20.) The subject teaches—

I. THAT GOD SEES THE END FROM THE BEGINNING. 1. *This is evinced in His works of creation.* (1) There is foresight in the constitution and adjustments of the framework, and in the motions, of the orbs. (2) Also in the *anticipatory instincts* of animals—storing of food, provisions for young. Moths deposit their eggs upon leaves, not used by themselves as food, but proper to sustain the larvæ. (3) And in the *anticipatory faculties* of man. Intelligent foresight in business, in politics, in science, in religion. 2. *It is evinced in prophecy.* (1) Great outlines of the world's history pre-written there (see Gen. ix. 25—27; Dan. vii.). (2) Particular example here. (Compare this with 2 Kings xxiii. 15—20.) The facts here were attested—By the Jews, on whose behalf they were ordered—By the Ephrathites, who would have impugned their authority if they could. 3. *This example is too circumstantial to have been accidental.* (1) The child was to be of the house of David. Who but God could foresee that the house of David should occupy the throne of Judah at a distance of 356 years? (2) Who but God could foresee that Bethel would then have passed from the kings of Israel under the dominion of Judah? (See 2 Chron. xiii. 19.) (3) Who but God could foresee that at a distance of 340 years a child should be born to the house of David, bearing the name of *Josiah*, who should in due time do these things? (4) Who else could anticipate, even when Josiah received his name, that the grandson of the wicked Manasseh, and son of the no less wicked Amon, should come to the throne, and with pious zeal bring these things to pass? Note: Such prescience as God displayed in this prophecy, and such providence as He evinced in its accomplishment, encourage faith. They assure us that our very names are in His book (Phil. iv. 3). They encourage prayer.

II. THAT HE WILL CONFRONT THE SINNER IN JUDGMENT. 1. *The message to Jeroboam was to this very effect.* (1) He bore His testimony against the altar. It had been consecrated, after a fashion, by the king, but God would desecrate it. The bodies of its priests were to be sacrificed upon it, and the bones of men were to be burnt upon it (ch. xiii. 2). God will accept no will-worship—no worship ordered after the policy of statesmen. (2) In the demolition of the altar, not only is the religion connected with it doomed to be overthrown, but the judgment involves its votaries—the king, his priests, his people. (3) The testimony was strong. The man of God cried aloud. He did not quail in the presence of the king amidst his friends. God's messengers should never cringe nor quail. God's word can never fail. 2. *These things were an allegory.* (1) Many of the wonderful narratives of Holy Scripture may be thus understood. We have the famous example, Gal. iv. 21—31. (2) Here Jeroboam, like all other leaders in apostasy, was a forerunner of *the* Antichrist. As the religion of the "man of sin" is a caricature of the religion of Christ, so was that of Jeroboam a parody upon the Mosaic. (3) Josiah was a type of Christ, the true Son of David. (Compare Isa. vii. 14.) Warning and mercy come before destruction. The army of Judah was stayed from crushing Jeroboam (ch. xii 24), and in the mission of the man of God there was mercy in the warning. Let the sinner be admonished not to refuse the gospel.—J. A. M.

Vers. 4—6.—*The Man of Sin.* When the man of God predicted the confusion of the political religion of Jeroboam, and gave the sign that the altar at Bethel should be rent and its ashes poured out, the pride of the king who stood there as a priest was mortified, and his resentment was manifested as described in the text.

I. JEROBOAM WAS A TYPICAL SINNER. 1. *He transgressed God's law*—(1) In making *images*. The law forbad this (Exod. xx. 4, 5). But he made two golden calves. Note: Images of God must be caricatures, and God will not be mocked, solemnly or otherwise, with impunity. How many frightful caricatures of Deity has the "man of sin" perpetrated! (2 Thess. ii. 3—12.) (2) In multiplying *altars*. Legal worship was limited to one altar "in the place which the Lord should choose" (Deut. xvi. 16). This was to keep before men the one only Mediator (John xiv. 6; 1 Tim. ii. 5). Therefore other altars than that at Jerusalem were "altars unto sin" (Hos. viii. 11). (3) In creating *priests*. According to the law, none but sons of Aaron had a Divine vocation to the priesthood (Exod. xxx. 7, 8; 2 Chron. xxvi. 18; Heb. v. 4). According to the gospel, Christ is sole Priest. Jeroboam, an Ephrathite, invaded the law-principle, making himself high priest, and making subordinate priests of the lowest of the people. 2. *He did so impudently*. (1) His sin was not of ignorance, for he had access to the Scriptures; but it did not serve his purpose to refer to them. (2) Prophecy was particularly distasteful to him, for his doom is written there. Jeroboam had this from the lips of Ahijah, and now has it from the man of God from Judah. Beware of the spirit that would discourage a study upon which God has pronounced a blessing (Rev. i. 3). (3) The spirit of his religion was *political*. He would not have troubled himself with it had he not political ends to serve (ch. xii. 26—29). And to carry out these he dissembled: "It is too much for you to go to Jerusalem!"

II. HIS DOOM ALSO WAS TYPICAL. 1. *He was confronted by the word of God*. (1) With this the man of God from Judah withstood him at his altar. So by the word of the Lord, and especially with the spirit of prophecy, has the man of sin been confronted by Waldenses, Paulikians, Hussites, Lutherans, and such-like men "from Judah." (2) But against this testimony he invoked the civil power under his usurped control (ver. 4). The *spirit* of persecution was there. The modern Jeroboam carried it further (Dan. xii. 21 ; Rev. xiii. 7; xvii. 6). 2. *He was humbled by the power of God*. (1) His hand was withered ; his power to persecute was paralyzed. How powerless is the hand of man when arrested by the hand of God! Behind the political restraints which now hold the persecuting hand of our enemies we must discern the invisible hand of God. (3) The altar, then, was cloven, and the ashes of the spurious sacrifices poured out as with contempt. This also was effected by the same invisible hand. Who can resist the might of God? (4) Constrained by these judgments, he confessed the finger of God, and entreated the man of God to pray for the restoration of his hand (see Exod. x. 16, 17; Num. xxi. 7 ; Matt. v. 23, 24). 3. *Yet he persisted in his sin*. (1) His humiliation was selfish. It was the creature of his terror and suffering, so it was transient. (2) True repentance is of a loftier principle, and is enduring. It is a life, as faith also is a life. (3) Instead of using his restored hand to demolish his high places, he used it to repair the altar at Bethel, and persisted in his sin (vers. 33, 34 ; 2 Chron. xiii. 20). But Josiah executed the judgments of prophecy in due time. So will the modern Jeroboam and his monstrous organization of sin perish in the fires of the judgment (Dan. vii. 10, 11 ; 2 Thess. ii. 8). Note: Let those come out of Babylon who would escape her plagues.—J. A. M.

Vers. 7—10.—*The Man of God*. We may view "Jeroboam the son of Nebat, who made Israel to sin," as the "man of sin" of his time, and a forerunner of *the* Antichrist of more modern times (2 Thess. ii. 3). In contrast to him we have to consider the "man of God," in which character this prophet who confronted Jeroboam at Bethel, is described. The instructions under which he acted teach us how a saint should behave amongst workers of iniquity.

I. HE MUST HOLD NO FELLOWSHIP WITH THEM. 1. *He must not eat and drink with them*. (1) For this was anciently a profession of fellowship. Hence the Hebrews in Egypt would not eat with the Egyptians (Gen. xliii. 32). The Jews would not eat with the Samaritans (John iv. 9) ; and they were shocked to see

Jesus eating with publicans and sinners (Matt. ix. 11).   For the same reason Christians were forbidden to eat with ungodly persons (1 Cor. v. 11 ; see also Rom. xvi. 17 ; 2 Thess. iii. 6, 14 ; 2 Tim. iii. 5 ; Jas. iv. 4 ; 2 John 10).   (2) The law of distinction between clean and unclean meats set forth not only the duty of avoiding fellowship with moral uncleanness, but also with those who are morally unclean ; for the unclean animals represented " sinners of the Gentiles " while the clean stood for the " holy people " of Israel (Acts x. 14, 34, 35).   (3) The eating of the forbidden fruit in Eden at the instigation of the serpent, who also seems to have eaten of it first, expressed fellowship with Satan !   As the trees of Eden were *sacramental*, it may have expressed a *covenant* with the Evil One !   Those who ate together were understood to stand to each other in a *covenant* relationship (Gen. xxxi. 43—46).   (4) In this light the Christian Eucharist sets forth the covenant fellowship, that we have, first, with Christ, and secondly, with those who are in such fellowship with Him (see, in this light, John vi. 53—56).   2. *He must refuse their presents*.   (1) Some think Jeroboam's offer to " reward " the man of God was to give him a *bribe*.   This is not evident.   Yet good men are liable to be tempted with bribes, but should stoutly refuse them (1 Sam. xii. 3 ; Job xv. 34).   (2) The king's intention was to do honour to the man of God, according to a constant custom in the East (see 1 Sam. ix. 7 ; 2 Kings v. 15).   The word מתת here translated " reward," would have been better rendered " gift," as in many other places it is.   But such a gift or present, if accepted, would express friendship, and therefore, coming from the hand of an arch idolator and schismatic, it must be declined.   (3) Good men must be careful how they accept favours from the wicked, lest in doing so they may compromise to them their independence, or come unduly under their influence (see Gen. xiv. 23 ; xxiii. 13—16 ; 2 Kings v. 16).

II. HIS INTERCOURSE WITH THEM SHOULD BE BRIEF.   1. *While serving God he is safe*.   (1) His very testimony for God commits him to a course of conduct consistent with it.   This element of moral strength is lost to those who hide their light under a bushel.   (2) He has a right to claim God's help (Matt. x. 19, 20 ; xxviii. 20).   2. *But it is perilous longer to remain*.   (1) The very disposition to remain amidst circumstances with which we should have no sympathy argues weakness which should alarm.   (2) He lays himself open to temptation.   He may find the " king " disposed to honour him.   Some are foolishly susceptible to flattery from the great ones of this world.   The man of God should be proof against this (ver. 8).   (3) He may be taken at a disadvantage.   Being away from the influence of godly friends. Having now no claim to special help from God.   3. *But why must he return by another way ?*   (1) Not only did the man of God give a sign, but he was also himself a sign (see Ezek. xii. 11 ; xxiv. 24 ; Zech. iii. 8, margin).   As Jeroboam was the sign of the man of sin, this prophet was, at least in his instructions, a typical " man of God."   (2) In coming from Judah, where God was purely worshipped in His temple, to Ephraim, where " altars were made unto sin," he would personate that moral lapse into which Ephraim had fallen.   (3) In his speedy return from Ephraim to Judah, after deprecating the sin of the place, he would represent to the Ephrathites what God expected from them, viz., repentance and reformation.   (4) But the way back to God is not precisely the reversal of the way from Him.   Adam fell by sin of his own and was turned out of Eden, but must return by the righteousness of another (Gen. iii. 24).   Our way back to God is the " *new* and living way opened in the blood of Jesus."—J. A. M.

Vers. 1, 2.—*The Nameless Prophet*.   Jeroboam's inauguration of the high place at Bethel was an imitation of Solomon's dedication of the temple at Jerusalem. Like Solomon, he chose the feast of tabernacles as the season for this ceremony, although he daringly altered the date of the feast from the seventh month to the eighth.   Describe the scene : the crowds of people, the new-made priests, the gorgeous shrine, the conflicting feelings of the worshippers.   None dared to oppose the king, and at the expected moment he stepped forward to burn incense before the calf.   Just then one, who had been till then unnoticed, pressed to the front of the crowd.   He came from the neighbouring kingdom of Judah.   In words of terrible invective he delivered the message of the Lord. Who was he ? Josephus (Ant., viii. 8. § 5) identifies him with Iddo the seer. There is no proof of this. He was one of the many servants of Jehovah who have done their work without emblazoning on it their name. Like John the Baptist, he was content to be " a voice crying " out a testimony for God. In considering the service rendered in his day by this NAMELESS PROPHET let us look at the following :

I. HIS MESSAGE. 1. *Its Divine origin.* " He cried . . . in the word of the Lord." A remarkable expression. It represents the word as the sphere in which he lived, the atmosphere he breathed. A sense of the Divine presence, a confidence in the Divine call, a certainty of the Divine message, characterized him. This was a sign of the true prophet. Compare with this the call of Samuel, the announcements of Elijah, the commission of Isaiah, &c. To some the declarations of God's will came fitfully. Prophecy was never a constant possession of a servant of God. There was a tidal flow of inspiration, the law of which we know not. So was it with the miraculous powers of the Apostles. 2. *Its definite nature* (ver. 2). The very name of the coming avenger is mentioned more than three hundred years before Josiah's birth. It was foretold that the priests would be sacrificed on the altar at which they had insulted God. The *lex talionis* is the ground of this, as of other theocratic laws. It reminds us that the sinner is destroyed by his own sin ; that punishments are not arbitrary, but are the legitimate issues of crime against God. It was further announced that the bones of the dead would be taken from the graves and burnt on the altar, so that the place of idolatry might be defiled and dishonoured. See Num. xix. 16. For fulfilment of prophecy read 2 Kings xxiii. 15—20. 3. *Its merciful design.* In ch. xii. 24 we read that God forbade the advance of the army of Judah on Jeroboam. Instead of carnage he sends this message. He willeth not the death of a sinner, but would rather he should turn from his wickedness and live. Suggest the warnings God now sends to rouse us to thought and penitence.

II. HIS COURAGE. It was a bold thing to venture amongst the people at a time when they were full of hatred to Judah, and of unwillingness to be reminded of Jehovah ; and to face the king, who was a man of despotic and resolute temper, in the very pride of his royal strength. But in the presence of them all the prophet's cry arose, " O altar, altar, thus saith Jehovah," &c., as if the stones would listen more readily than the people. Give examples of similar courage being displayed by men who have had the consciousness they were speaking for God ; *e.g.*, Moses before Pharaoh, Elijah before Ahab, John the Baptist before Herod, Peter and John before the Sanhedrim, Paul before Felix. From church history, too, such examples as that of Ambrose, John Knox, &c., may be cited. Show how requisite courage is now to genuine fidelity to conviction, amongst sceptical or sinful associations.

III. HIS CREDENTIALS. A sign was given there and then. The altar was cleft in twain, and the ashes were poured out. For the significance of the latter see Levit. xvi. 3, 4. Point out the credibility of supernatural signs as attesting supernatural revelations. Refer to the miracles of Christ, of which He said, " Believe me for the very works' sake." See also Mark xvi. 20 ; Acts ii. 43. Indicate the nature of the credentials which the world may fairly demand of Christian men in the present day ; and show how far we fail in giving these, and the causes of our failure.

IV. HIS SAFETY. Amidst all the perils encircling him he was " kept by the power of God." The hand that would have slain him was withered ; the man who cursed his message besought his prayers. " Man is immortal till his work is done." When God's servants die, it is because they have fulfilled the purpose of their lives. They have many enemies, but God can disable all their foes. The path of duty is the path of safety. Illustrate this from the records of the Christian Church ; Luther at Worms, &c. 1. *Learn to listen for God's message.* He would make you His " voice." 2. *Learn to dare anything in God's name.* The rarity of Christian chivalry. 3. *Learn to trust in God's protection.* " He that dwelleth in the secret place of the Most High shall abide under the shadow of the Almighty." 4. *Learn to pray even for your persecutors.* Compare ver. 6 with Matt. v. 44.—A. R.

Ver. 6.—*The King confronted by the Prophet.* Jeroboam is not allowed to pursue his iniquitous career without solemn Divine rebuke and warning. Though Rehoboam has been forbidden to attempt forcibly to suppress the revolt of the tribes (ch. xii. 24), a "man of God out of Judah" is sent sternly to denounce the rival altar, and to give the sacrilegious king something like a symbolic forewarning of the disasters that should surely befall him. The scene, described here with so much simplicity and dramatic force, is full of moral instruction.

I In the person of the king we see THE HELPLESSNESS OF A WICKED MAN IN THE HANDS OF AN OFFENDED GOD. The physical associations and the mental conditions here presented are alike suggestive of this. It is a striking picture of restrained infatuation and impotent rage. 1. *The king's withered arm* tells how God can in a moment turn the strength that is used against Him to weakness. "When thou with rebukes dost correct man for iniquity," &c. (Psa. xxxix. 11). 2. *The rent altar* suggests the certain frustration, sooner or later, of the purposes and plans of those that are at enmity with God. "The Lord bringeth the counsel of the heathen to nought," &c. (Psa. xxxiii. 10). "If this counsel or this work be of man," &c. (Acts v. 38). 3. *The king's inability to pray for himself* reminds us how God sometimes forsakes those who forsake Him, so that it seems utterly vain for them to call upon Him. Many a man has felt like Saul, "I am sore distressed, and God is departed from me," &c. (1 Sam. xxviii. 15). 4. *His appeal to the prophet to intercede for him* is typical of the way in which ungodly men are often contrained by force of circumstance to seek succour from those whom they have despised. "The wheel of fortune turns and lowers the proud," and they are placed, perhaps, at the mercy of the very men whom they once scorned and injured. Such are the penalties that God often inflicts on those who trifle with His authority and defy His power. Such is the curse that falls upon "presumptuous sin."

II. The behaviour of the prophet presents A FINE EXAMPLE OF MORAL DIGNITY AND CONSCIOUS STRENGTH. See here—(1) The courage of a man who knows that God is on his side. The prophets of old, conscious of a more majestic Presence and a higher Sovereignty, never trembled before the face of wicked kings. The fear of God casts out all other fear. "Be not afraid of them that kill the body," &c. (Luke xii. 4, 5). "If God be for us," &c. (Rom. viii. 31). (2) The magnanimity of one who feels that he is called to witness for God among men. The prophet will not take advantage of the king's helpnessness; rather responds at once to his appeal. He who is inspired by God's Spirit will not return scorn for scorn, or retaliate an attempted injury, but rather use for beneficent ends the power that he possesses. "Lord, wilt thou that we command fire to come down from heaven and consume them?" "Ye know not what manner of spirit ye are of," &c. (Luke ix. 54, 56). (3) The efficacy of the prayer of a righteous man. The withered arm is restored, and though this had no happy moral effect, as might have been expected, on Jeroboam, the whole transaction, in which mercy was thus blended with judgment, vindicated the honour of Jehovah, and established afresh His sovereign claim to the allegiance alike of king and people.—W.

Vers. 1—10.—I. THE PRETENSIONS OF ERROR DEEPEN ITS SHAME. The idolatrous altar was being solemnly consecrated. The people's eyes were dazzled with the splendour of the priestly and regal display. Jeroboam himself stood by the altar to offer incense. And then the cry arose which arrested every ear and thrilled through every soul. 1. *The attempt to give importance to the new idolatry only broadened the mark for God's rebuke:* it simply lent emphasis to His condemnation. They had come to consecrate, and had really come to attend upon God while He desecrated the work of their hands. Heathenism in its splendour thus rebuked by the preaching of the cross, Rome by the light of the Reformation. 2. *The agent by whom God's glory was vindicated.* The insignificance of the poor, weary, travel-stained man deepened their disgrace. "God hath chosen the weak things of the world to confound the things which are mighty."

II. THE DOOM OF IDOLATROUS WORSHIP. 1. *The altar will be desecrated.* The place will be made an abomination and horror. Sin's judgment will in the end be sin's destruction. 2. *The sin will be wiped out in the blood and shame of those who have wrought it.* The priests will be offered upon the altar, the bones of its worshippers burned upon it. The world's sin will be ended in God's fiery judgment upon the sinful. 3. *The certainty of God's purpose.* Centuries intervened between the prediction and the fulfilment, but all was arranged. The time was fixed, the avenger named. There is no uncertainty in God's mind regarding the end of iniquity. The decree has been recorded, the time fixed, THE MAN named by whom He will judge the world in righteousness. 4. *The sign meanwhile given.* The altar was rent and its ashes poured out. The wrath revealed from heaven now is proof that all God's purpose shall be fulfilled.

III. MAN'S INABILITY TO CONTEND WITH GOD. 1. *The withered arm.* The arm outstretched in eager, wrathful command to arrest the man of God, withered in the very attitude. It was the emblem of his house and of his people; they were withered in the attitude of rebellion against God. 2. *The prophet's safety.* He needed none to shield him. God protects all those who serve Him. 3. *Jeroboam's humiliation.* He turns from idol and altar and priests, and requests the prophet's intercession with Jehovah. 4. *His arm is restored at the prophet's request,* and he thus bears in his person another token that the word he has heard is from God. It is the story of God's contest with darkness and wrong to-day.

IV. SEPARATION ESSENTIAL FOR TESTIMONY. Jeroboam's hospitality and reward were alike refused. The prophet was even forbidden to return by the same way: he was not to enter even into acquaintance with men who were sinning so deeply against God. Unless there be separation our testimony is a sham. Our life unsays our speech. If we will speak God's word to the sinful, our attitude must reveal their distance from God and the peril in which they stand. If our own heart be filled with holy fear it may pass from us to them.—J. U.

EXPOSITION.

CHAPTER XIII. 11—34.

THE DISOBEDIENCE AND DEATH OF THE MAN OF GOD.—The seduction of the man of God, who has borne such fearless witness against Jeroboam's ecclesiastical policy, and his tragical end, are now narrated, partly because of the deep impression the story made at the time, but principally because these events were in themselves an eloquent testimony against the worship of the calves and the whole ecclesiastical policy of Jeroboam, and a solemn warning for all time against any, the slightest, departure from the commandments of God. The very unfaithfulness of this accredited messenger of the Most High, and the instant punishment it provoked, became part of the Divine protest against the new *régime*, against the unfaithfulness of Israel; whilst the remarkable manner in which these occurrences were recalled to the nation's memory in the reign of Josiah (2 Kings xxiii. 17, 18) made it impossible for the historian of the theocracy to pass them over without notice.

Ver 11.—**Now there dwelt an old prophet** [Heb. *a certain* (lit. *one*) *old prophet.* For this use of אֶחָד (=τις) cf. 1 Kings xx. 13; xix. 4] **at Bethel** [It is at first somewhat surprising to find one of the prophetic order residing here, at the very seat and stronghold of the apostasy, especially after what we read in 2 Chron. xi. 13—16, that the priests and Levites, and it would seem all devout worshippers of the Lord God of Israel, had left the country, and had gone over to Rehoboam. For we cannot suppose that a sense of duty had kept this prophet at his post (see note on ver. 1). The fact that he remained, not only in the kingdom, but at its ecclesiastical capital; that he stood by without protest when the schism was being effected, and that, though not present himself at the sacrifice, he permitted his sons to be there, is a sufficient index to his character. It is quite possible that strong political sympathies had warped his judgment, and that he had persuaded himself that the policy of Jeroboam was necessitated by the division of the kingdom, which he knew to be from the Lord, and which one of his own order had foretold. Or it may be that, despite his better judgment, he had gone with his tribe and the majority of the nation, and now felt it difficult to withdraw from a false position. Or, finally, he may have taken the side of Jeroboam because of the greater honours and rewards that prince had to bestow (see on ver. 18). There is a striking similarity between his position and action and that of Balaam]; **and his sons** [The Heb. has *son;* The LXX., Syr., and Vulg., *sons.* It is quite true that a "very slight change in the Hebrew text would bring it into accordance with the Septuagint here" (Rawlinson, similarly Ewald), but it would be against sound principles of textual criticism to make it. It is much more likely that the LXX. and other versions *have* been altered already, and that the plural has been introduced here because it is uniformly found in the later narrative. "*His son*" (בְּנוֹ), as the *lectio ardua*, is therefore to be retained. The use of the singular indicates that one of them was at first the principal speaker. Perhaps one hastened home with the news before the rest. The sons of the prophet are not to be confounded with "the sons (*i.e.*, disciples) of the *prophets*" (2 Kings ii., iii., iv., *passim*); not merely because "the latter would scarcely have witnessed the golden calf-worship" (Bähr), but also because they would have been differently designated] **came and told him all the works** [Heb. *work*] **that the man of God had done that day in Bethel: the words which he had spoken unto the king, them they** [observe the plural] **told also to their father.** [It is quite clear that the virtual excommunication which the man of God had pronounced had made as great an impression as the signs which he had showed. The interdict was a matter which came home to the Bethelites, as an affront to the whole community.]

Ver. 12.—**And their father said unto them, What way went he?** [The question shows that the old prophet throughly understood the import of those "words," and that his first thought was that the interdict must be removed at any cost.] **For his sons had seen** [Heb. *and his sons saw*, or *showed.* LXX. δεικνύουσιν. Similarly most of the versions. A very slight change in the vowel points וַיִּרְאוּ for וַיַּרְאוּ would give this sense] **what way the man of God went which came from Judah.**

Ver. 13.—**And he said unto his sons, Saddle me the ass.** [This prompt and seemingly abrupt command—though we cannot be sure that all the conversation is here reported—shows his instant resolve to follow. These are the words of one who had made up his mind, *coûte que coûte*, to bring the man of God back.] **So they saddled him the ass: and he rode thereon.**

Ver. 14.—**And he went after the man of**

God and found him sitting under an oak [Heb. *the* oak; *i.e.*, the well-known oak. Possibly there was but one, or one of great size, in the neighbourhood—such trees are comparatively rare in Palestine. Possibly also this tree became well known from these events. It is singular that in another place (Gen. xxxv. 8) we read of "the oak" (אַלּוֹן) of Bethel, whilst in Judg. iv. 5 we read of the "palm tree" (תֹּמֶר) of Deborah, between Ramah and *Bethel.*" And it is not at all improbable, seeing that in 1 Sam. x. 3 we read of the terebinth (אֵלוֹן) of *Tabor*—in the A. V. rendered "*plain* of Tabor"—which Ewald ("Hist. Israel," iii. 21; iv. 31) considers to be only a dialectic variation of *Deborah*, and remembering the great age to which these trees attain, that the same tree is referred to throughout. The word here used, it is true, is אֵלָה (which is generally supposed to indicate the terebinth, but is also "used of any large tree" (Gesenius), and which, therefore, may be used of the אֵלוֹן of Bethel. Both names are derived from the same root (אוּל *fortis.* Cf. Amos ii. 9), and both indicate varieties—*what* varieties it is not quite clear—of the oak. Some expositors have seen in this brief rest the beginning of his sin, and certainly it would seem against the *spirit* of his instructions to remain so near a place (see note on ver. 16) from which he was to vanish speedily, and, if possible, unperceived. In any case the action betrays his fatigue and exhaustion], **and he said unto him, Art thou the man of God that camest from Judah? And he said, I am.**

Ver. 15.—**Then he said unto him, Come home with me** [Heb. *Come with me to the house*] **and eat bread.** The sting was in the tail of this invitation. If he would partake of food, he would thereby remove the ban and so neutralize one part of his mission.]

Ver. 16.—**And he said, I may not** [Heb. *am not able to*] **return with thee, nor go in with thee: neither will I eat bread nor drink water with thee in this place.** [The translation "*in that place*" adopted by Wordsworth (after the Vulgate, *in loco isto*) does not agree with the Hebrew. And it is not required by the context. The tree was probably at no great distance from the town.]

Ver. 17.—**For it was said to me** [Heb. *a word to me*] **by** [Heb. *in*] **the word of the Lord, Thou shalt eat no bread, nor drink water there, nor turn again to go by the way that thou camest.**

Ver. 18.—**He said unto him, I am a**

prophet also as thou art; and an angel (Bähr observes that "he does not venture to say that Jehovah spake to him, but says an angel did." Is it not more probable that the angel was mentioned, partly for the purpose of giving an air of circumstantiality and reality to his story, and partly to convey the idea of his having a superior authority for his message? A communication through a celestial messenger would seem to have been regarded as a higher form of revelation than a subjective communication to the mind of the prophet. Cf. Acts vii. 53; Heb. ii. 2; Luke i. 13, 29; Acts xxvii. 23, &c. Observe, the prophet speaks presently of "the word of Jehovah"] spake unto me by [Heb. *in;* same expression as in ver. 17] the word of the Lord, saying, Bring him back with thee into thine house that he may eat [Heb. *and he shall eat*] bread and drink water. But he lied to him. [These last words are inserted parenthetically; hence there is no "but" in the Heb. The true character and designs and motives of this "old prophet" have long been a *crux interpretum* (see Hall, Contempl., ii. 151—3.) Some, including Josephus and most Jewish commentators, have supposed him to be altogether a false and lying prophet, such as are found plentifully later on in the history (ch. xxii. 6; Jer. xxviii. 1); but against this is the fact that he was undoubtedly the channel of a Divine communication (ver. 21). The real difficulty, no doubt, lies in the fact that one by whom the Spirit of God spake to man should have acted so base a part as he did. But it must be remembered (1) that he did not know what a terrible judgment his lie would bring upon "the man of God;" (2) that truth had not the place in the Jewish scheme which it has in Christian morals; (3) that the gift of prophecy is compatible with much moral imperfection on the part of the prophet—the cases of Balaam and Caiaphas will occur to all— and (4) that this man was constrained to prophesy almost in spite of himself; he was compelled, *i.e.*, to proclaim his own falseness, and to announce the punishment of the man he had himself deceived. It is also to be considered that this lying prophet, like those of ch. xxii. 22, accomplished the purpose of God, which was to make the man of God a *sign* to the men of that generation. Cf. Isa. xx. 3; Ezek. xii. 6; xxiv. 24. In this latter consideration, indeed, lies the key to the history. The *object* the old prophet had in view it is not so difficult to divine. He hears that the prophet of Judah has refused the hospitality of King Jeroboam, and has put the city of Bethel and the new cultus under a virtual ban by refusing to eat bread in the place, or to hold any communication

with the inhabitants, himself among the rest, although he has taken no part, even by his presence, in the ceremonial of the day. He naturally feels himself condemned and aggrieved by this conduct. A *prophet* would feel the interdict much more keenly than the people, and there can be little doubt that this man, who had been trying to serve two masters, was deeply mortified by the excommunication pronounced against him. He resolves, therefore, to rehabilitate himself in his own estimation and that of his neighbours, by bringing back the man of God to eat and to drink, and so in effect to remove the interdict, at any cost. If he succeeds, he will make the whole city, and especially the sovereign, whose policy has been so emphatically condemned, his debtor; while by accomplishing what the *king* had failed to effect, he will at once heal his wounded pride and secure a position of influence in the new kingdom. If it was the hope of temporal advancement had detained him at Bethel, he now sees, as he thinks, an easy way to its attainment; if it was an ardent sympathy with the new state of things, he sees before him an opportunity of expressing it in a most practical and serviceable way.]

Ver. 19.—So he went back with him, and did eat bread in his house, and drank water [cf. ver. 10].

Ver. 20.—And it came to pass, as they sat at the table [cf. Ps. lxxviii. 30. He is taken in the act, "even in the blossoms of his sin"], that the word of the Lord came unto the prophet that brought him back.

Ver. 21.—And he cried [same word as in ver. 2. He who denounced the "sin of Jeroboam" is now denounced in turn] unto the man of God that came from Judah, saying, Thus saith the Lord, Forasmuch as thou hast disobeyed the mouth of the Lord, and hast not kept the commandment which the Lord thy God commanded thee.

Ver. 22.—But camest back, and hast eaten bread and drunk water in the place, of the which the Lord did say to thee, Eat no bread, and drink no water; thy carcase [rather *corpse*; "carcase" is now a term of disparagement, of which, however, there is no idea in the Hebrew] shall not come unto the sepulchre of thy fathers. [The desire, common in a greater or less degree to all mankind, to rest after death amongst *kindred* dust, was especially strong in the Jew. It is evidenced by the common euphemism "he was gathered *unto his fathers,*" and by the provisions of Abraham (Gen. xxiii. 4), Jacob (Gen. xlvii. 29; xlix. 29—31), and Joseph (Gen. l. 25). See also the words of Barzillai (2 Sam. xix. 37; and compare

2 Sam. ii. 32). This denunciation did not necessarily imply a violent death (as Keil, al.) or even a speedy death, but it prepared the man of God for some untimely end.]

Ver. 23.—**And it came to pass, after he had eaten bread, and after he had drunk, that he saddled** [*i.e.*, the prophet of Bethel; the "man of God" would seem to have come on foot. See below] **for him the ass, to wit, for the prophet whom he had brought back.** This translation is inadmissible. For not only is the term "prophet" throughout this narrative restricted to the prophet of Bethel (the prophet of Judah being always spoken of as "the man of God,") but the expression here used הַנָּבִיא א'ה' is also twice used (vers. 20, 26) of the same prophet. He is characterized there, that is to say, as "the prophet which brought him back;" it is hardly likely, therefore, that the same words are here to be interpreted, "the prophet whom he brought back." The mistake has arisen from the proximity of לוֹ ("for him") to לַנָּבִיא ("to" or "for the prophet"). But the לוֹ is here indicative of possession (the dative of the possessor), as in 1 Sam. xiv. 16, "the watchmen to," *i.e.*, *of*, "Saul," and *ib.* xvi. 18, "a son to Jesse" (cf. Gen. xiv. 18 Heb.; 1 Kings v. 29 Heb.; Ruth ii. 3 Heb.) We must therefore render "He (the old prophet, but this is not absolutely certain; the "man of God" *may* be understood) saddled for him (the man of God) the ass of the prophet which brought him back." The man of God had been delayed by his return to Bethel, and the prophet, out of pity, lends or gives him his ass. Not merely, it is probable, for the sake of speeding him on his way, but that he might have some living thing with him on a journey which he had so much cause to dread.

Ver. 24.—**And when he was gone** [Heb. *and he went*], **a lion** (Lions were evidently numerous in Palestine in former days, though they are now extinct. This is proved by the names of places, such as *Laish*, *Lebaoth*, &c., and by the constant reference to them in Scripture. They had their lairs in the forests, one of which existed near Bethel (2 Kings ii. 24), and especially in the thickets of the Jordan valley (Jer. xlix. 19; Zech. xi. 3)] **met** [Heb. *found*. The primary meaning of מָצָא is, no doubt, "found accidentally," "came upon" (εὗρεν, *invenit*), but it is often used of finding after a search (1 Sam. ix. 4, &c.), and it should be remembered that this is the word used in vers. 14, 28] **him by** [*in*, as below] **the way, and slew him: and his carcase was cast in the way** [road,

highway, ver. 25], **and the ass stood** [Heb. *standing*] **by it, the lion also stood** [*standing*] **by the carcase.** [These particulars are mentioned to show that his death was no accident, or chance, but a visitation of God. There are probably but few persons who have not felt that this summary punishment was marked by extreme severity; the more so, as the prophet was cruelly deceived, and that by a brother prophet, who claimed to have received a subsequent revelation, and whom, consequently, it appeared to be a duty to obey. And when it is observed that the really guilty person, the prophet of Bethel, so far as appears, escaped all punishment, and by his lie secured for himself respect for his remains, we seem to have a case of positive hardship and injustice. As I have discussed the question at some length elsewhere (Homil. Quart., vol. iv. pp. 214—221), it must suffice to say here that the difficulty is at once removed if we remember that although the Jewish dispensation was one of temporal recompenses, yet all the same there *is* a judgment hereafter. No doubt the man of God was punished for his disobedience, for inexcusable disobedience it was. It is quite true that he was solemnly assured that an angel had appeared to revoke his commission, but for this he had only the word of a stranger, of one, too, with whom he had been commanded "not even to eat." He had "the word of the Lord:" that is to say, the voice of God, borne in upon his soul, forbidding his return, and the word of an irreligious stranger, who gave no "sign the same day" in proof of his mission, authorizing it. There can be no doubt which he ought to have followed, the more so as the command he had himself received was so remarkably explicit and decisive (ver. 9); so decisive that we can hardly suppose he would have deviated from it, had not the pains of hunger and thirst pleaded powerfully in favour of the pretended revelation of the Bethelite prophet. Indeed, it is hardly too much to say that he eagerly welcomed this cause for returning. It is impossible, therefore, to acquit him of disobedience. Nor is it difficult to see that the consequences of this disobedience were serious. It was not as if he had disregarded a mere *positive* obligation, the only object of which was to test his obedience (Rawlinson); he had acted in a way calculated to destroy the moral effect of his mission. He had been employed not only to testify publicly against the calf-worship, but also to lay the city and the new sanctuary of Jeroboam under an interdict, and by his return that interdict lost much of its force. His eating and drinking, small matters in themselves, were full of significance. Indeed, he did in one way precisely what Jeroboam and his people were doing in another—he forsook the plain commands of God for the ordinances of men ; he listened to the tempter and ate the forbidden fruit ; and so it came to pass that, instead of witnessing against disobedience, he himself set them the example of disobedience. It is the story of the Fall over again ; and therefore death, the punishment of the Fall, befell him. But before we say that his punishment was too severe, let us remember what, by the mercy of God, that primal punishment has become. It has been turned into a blessing. It has given us the incarnation, redemption, eternal life. We forget that death is not necessarily an evil—is in reality a blessing. One of the heathen has said that if we only knew what the future life was like, we should not be content to live. To this " man of God " it must surely have been gain to die. If the flesh was destroyed, it was that the spirit might be saved (1 Cor. v. 5). Only because we forget that death is the gate of life do we complain of the severity of his doom. And as to the lying prophet who wrought all this mischief escaping retribution—which, by the way, he did not do, for assuredly he must have had a life-long remorse—it is overlooked that the day of retribution has not yet arrived. There is for him a judgment *to come*. It may be said that the Jew did not know of this—that the future life had not then been revealed. That is quite true, and for that very reason this visitation would make all the deeper impression on their minds. To this must be added that the man of God did not die merely or principally because of his sin, but " that the works of God might be made manifest in him." His death was necessary in order that his mission might not be altogether invalidated. His miserable end—as it must have seemed to them—would surely speak to the inhabitants of Bethel and to all Israel and Judah, for long years to come, as to the sure vengeance awaiting the disobedient, whether king, prophet, priest, or people. Though dead " he cried against the altar of Bethel." And the sacred narrative (vers. 26—32) affords us some ground for hoping that the " old prophet " became penitent for his sin. It is noteworthy that he joins his testimony to that of the man of God. Thus, this tragedy extorted even from *him* a warning against disobedience (ver. 26), and a confirmation of the prophecy against the altar of Bethel (ver. 32).]

Ver. 25.—**And, behold, men passed by, nd saw the carcase cast in the way, and** the lion standing by the carcase : and they came and told it in the city where the old prophet dwelt. [This was precisely what God had designed. By this means, the very disobedience and death of the man of God became a part of the protest against the new rites. " For if the partaking of food against the commandment of God, though the result not of indulgence, but of deceit, brought so great a punishment upon a righteous man, what sort of chastisements would befall those who had left their Maker and were worshipping senseless images " (Theodoret.)]

Ver. 26.—**And when the prophet that brought him back from the way heard thereof, he said, It is the man of God, who was disobedient** [Heb. *rebelled ;* same word as in ver. 21] **unto the word** [Heb. "*mouth*," as in ver. 21] **of the Lord : therefore the Lord hath delivered him unto the lion, which hath torn** [Heb. as marg., *broken*. The word " is very expressive, for the lion kills with one blow " (Thenius)] **and slain him, according to the word of the Lord, which he spake unto him.**

Ver. 27.—**And he spake to his sons, saying, Saddle me the ass. And they saddled him.**

Ver. 28.—**And he went and found his carcase cast in the way, and the ass and the lion standing by the carcase : the lion had not eaten the carcase nor torn** [Heb. *broken*, as in ver. 26] **the ass.**

Ver. 29.—**And the prophet took up the carcase of the man of God, and laid it upon the ass** [*i.e.*, the one standing by], **and brought it back : and the old prophet came to the city, to mourn and to bury him.** [The mourning is specially mentioned, because in the East professional wailers were and are employed at funerals. The Jew, no less than the Greek and Roman, esteemed it a great misfortune and disgrace to be deprived of decent burial : Isa. xiv. 19 ; Jer. xxii. 19 ; and especially 2 Kings ix. 10.]

Ver. 30.—**And he laid his carcase in his own grave** [Matt. xxvii. 60. This was a mark of profound respect (Ruth i. 17 ; Gen. xxiii. 6)] ; **and they mourned over him, saying, Alas, my brother.** [A customary formula in lamentation (Jer. xxii. 18). It hardly implies that " he was mourned and buried as a relative of the family " (Bähr). Seeing that the old prophet was responsible for his death, he could hardly have done less. " It is a cruel courtesy to kill a man and then help him to his grave " (Hall).]

Ver. 31.—**And it came to pass, after he had buried him, that he spake to his sons, saying, When I am dead, then bury me i** the sepulchre [Palestine, being of lime-stone formation, has a large number of caves. These, enlarged and adapted, were everywhere used for interments. ("The whole cliffs on its southern side [Hinnom] are honeycombed with tombs," Porter). In three sides of the cave vaults (*loculi*), each large enough to hold a body, were recessed in the rock, the entrance being closed by a slab of stone (see Conder, pp. 85, 96, 118, &c.) In the so-called "tombs of the kings" and "prophets" we have such sepulchres on a large scale. A Paper on the Tombs of Palestine will be found in the Quarterly Statement of the Palestine Exploration Fund, p. 66 sqq. It appears from 2 Kings xxiii. 17 that a pillar was erected to mark this prophet's resting-place] wherein the man of God is buried; lay my bones beside his bones. [That is to say, "Bury me in the cell next to his" (Rawlinson). But it is not absolutely certain that this arrange-ment (of *loculi*) obtained at this early period. The bodies may have been in much closer contact. See 2 Kings xiii. 21. The LXX. adds here, "That my bones may be saved with his bones;" an obvious gloss, founded on 2 Kings xxiii. 18. This request throws some light on the yearning desire of the modern Jew to rest as near as possible to the bodies of the saints. See Porter, i. p. 145.]

Ver. 32.—For the saying which he cried by the word of the Lord against the altar in Bethel, and against all the houses of the high places [At that time there would seem to have been but two "high places." Keil sees "a prophetic element in these words." He thinks the old prophet foresaw that such sanctuaries would be multiplied. Rawlinson gathers, "from the mention of the *great* high place in 1 Kings iii. 4, that there were many lesser high places in the land," which, no doubt, was the case at the date of Solomon's accession. It is probable, how-ever, that many of these, if not all, would be deserted when the temple was built. And it is most reasonable to suppose that in these, as in the following words, the his-torian has represented the prediction or affirmation of the old prophet in the lan-guage of his own time] which are in the cities of Samaria. [Obviously, these exact words cannot have been used by the prophet of Bethel, for Samaria dates its existence and *name* from the reign of Omri (1 Kings xvi. 24). The compiler of the Kings pro-bably found the term in the documents which he used, or possibly, as already sug-gested, translated the prophet's meaning into the language of a later day] shall surely come to pass.

Ver. 33.—After this thing [calculated though it was to make a deep impression and to furnish a solemn warning] Jeroboam turned not from his evil way. "Some hand was found that durst repair the altar God had rent" (Matthew Henry). According to Josephus, the old prophet now explained away the miracles of the prophet of Judah, alleging that the altar had fallen because it was new and the king's hand had become powerless from fatigue (Ant.,viii. 9, § 1)], but made again [Heb. "*returned and made.*" The tautology is significant. He returned not from his sin, but returned to it] of the lowest [see on ch. xii. 11] of the people priests of the high places : whosoever would [Heb. *pleased*], he consecrated [Heb. *filled his hand.* In the consecration of Aaron and his sons, and possibly of their successors also, the portions of the victim which were usually burned upon the altar, together with the right shoulder or leg, which was the priest's portion, and three cakes of un-leavened bread, were put into the hands of the candidates for the priesthood, and waved before the Lord before they were offered on the altar (Exod. xxix. 22—26 ; Levit. viii. 25—28). To "fill the hand" consequently became a synonym for con-secration] him [It would almost appear, from the extreme readiness with which Jeroboam ordained his priests, that few candidates offered themselves for the office. In one respect, however, he exacted more from the candidate than did the law. For whereas the latter required "one bullock and *two* rams" (Exod. xxix. 1, &c.), he demanded one bullock and *seven* rams as the offering on consecration (2 Chron. xiii. 9], and he became one of the priests [Heb. *and he became priests*, &c. So the Chaldee. LXX. καὶ ἐγένετο ἱερεύς] of the high places.

Ver. 34.—And this thing [Heb. "in this thing :" בַּדָּבָר. Cf. 1 Chron. vii. 23 ; ix. 33] became sin unto the house of Jeroboam, even to cut it off, and to destroy it from off the face of the earth [ch. xv. 29. The forfeiture of the crown would bring in its train, almost as a matter of course, the destruction of his family (ch. xiv. 10—14). And we are taught here that both events are to be regarded, under the dispensation of temporal rewards and punishments, as the recompenses of his impiety; of that daring schismatic policy which, in all its branches, betrayed a complete disregard of the terms of the covenant, and which was persevered in contemptuous defiance of the repeated warnings of God.]

HOMILETICS.

Vers. 21 sqq.—*The Man of God and the People of God.* The morning of that fifteenth day of the eighth month, that black day in the Hebrew Kalendar, that birthday of division, was hardly more memorable or eventful than the evening. In the morning the Bethelites saw the signs of the man of God; in the evening they saw in him a sign, a parable, and a terrible warning. The lesson of the rent altar and the rigid hand was followed by the lesson of the lion and the ass and the rigid corpse. Truly, of that day it might be truly said, " The evening and the morning were one day."

For we may be sure, when the old prophet came back from his quest of the body, and brought with him that melancholy burden, swinging across the ass, the men of Bethel, who had already heard from wayfarers of the tragedy, would crowd the streets or lanes—for Bethel was probably little more than a village—to meet him, and would gaze, hushed and awestruck, into the dumb and helpless face of the man whose words and deeds had that day been so full of power. There was not a child that night but would leave his play to stare in silent wonder, or with whispered question, on the corpse. Of that sad funereal procession, the words which, near a thousand years later, described the entry of a living Prophet into an adjoining city, might justly be used, " All the city was moved, saying, Who is this?" (Matt. xxi. 10.) Nor would the language which described the effect of that same Prophet's death a few days later be less applicable here, " All the people that came together to that sight, beholding the things which were done, smote their breasts and returned" (Luke xxiii. 48).

Let us now suppose, however, for the sake of bringing out the lessons of this narrative, that there were some in the crowd—as on the first feast-day there may well have been—strangers in Bethel (cf. John xii. 20; Acts ii. 5—11), who did not understand the things which were come to pass there that day. Let us join them, as they go, carried by the stream, to meet the body; let us listen to their questions, and to the answers they receive. We shall not gather all the truth from the discourse we overhear, but we shall learn at all events one lesson which this tragedy had for the men of that time.

Now the first question which would rise to these strangers' lips, as they came upon the body, borne by the patient ass, which was the one terrified witness of the catastrophe, would be, " Who is this?" They think, perhaps, it is some peasant who has been slain as he tilled his fields, or some itinerant chapman who has been murdered on his journey. But the bystanders speedily undeceive them. They tell them that this is " a man of God who came from Judah." His name, it may be, is unknown to them, but not his deeds. They relate, with breathless excitement, not unmixed with fear, how a few short hours ago he was amongst them; how on the morning of that very day he had confronted their king as he was in the act of sacrificing, had denounced his innovations, had foretold the overthrow of his policy and dynasty, and had then wrought wonderful works in attestation of his mission. The strangers listen with steadily increasing wonderment. Had this man been " a murderer whom vengeance suffered not to live," or a sinner above all men that dwelt in Bethel, they could have understood it. Such a one, however he might have met his end, would only have received the just reward of his deeds, but " a man of God," a man who wrought miracles, a favourite of Heaven!—they cannot comprehend it, and they, as excited as their informants, hurriedly ask how he has come by his death.

" A lion slew him," is the answer. It is true no human eye saw the deed, but there can be no doubt as to the manner of his death. Then they tell how wayfaring men that afternoon had seen a strange sight, a corpse cast in the way— *whose* corpse they knew not—and an ass and a lion standing as joint sentinels over it, &c. And then the strangers would understand that this man of God had died by the visitation of God. They would remember that the " teeth of evil beasts" were one of the plagues denounced in the law, and they would wonder, and they would ask, what this messenger of the Most High, this miracle-worker, could have done between morning and evening to bring this terrible judgment down upon his head.

And this was a question which only the old prophet could rightly answer, and he had answered it already. He had told his sons and neighbours that afternoon, when first he heard of this tragedy, that it was the punishment of disobedience (ver. 26). Not improbably he proclaimed it again to the crowd which awaited his return. "*He* had been charged," he would say, as they stood gazing on the helpless corpse, "to lay our city under a ban; he had been commanded to eat no bread, to drink no water here. And he came back, and he ate bread and he drank water in my house; therefore it is that 'the lion hath torn him and slain him, according to the word of the Lord'" (ver. 26).

And so the men of Bethel, and the strangers among them—and thousands of strangers would be present in Bethel at that time—would understand that this man, albeit a prophet, and a doer of wondrous works, had paid the penalty of his partial disobedience with his life. They would perceive that God had not spared His own elect messenger. They would see that the man who had been commissioned to protest against Jeroboam's will-worship, who had courageously faced the king in his might, and had stood like an Athanase against the world, had received judgment without mercy when he overstepped the commandment of his God. And they would assuredly be reminded, some of them at least, how sinful and how dangerous must be that departure from the law which they had that day seen instituted amongst themselves. And as one by one they dropped off, and, deeply awed and impressed, returned to their tents or booths, the one thought which above all others filled their minds would be this—how sure and swift and terrible was the recompense of disobedience.

But if these strangers, in their perplexity, proceeded to make further inquiries, as they may well have done; if they asked what could have led such a man as this to set at nought the plain commandment of God : if they discovered from the old prophet, or his sons, or others, the circumstances of his sin ; if they learned that this man of God had resisted the entreaties of the king, had obeyed his own instructions to the letter, and had only come back and eaten bread on the solemn assurance of this old prophet himself that an angel from heaven had distinctly reversed his commission; if they understood that it was because he had taken this man at his word and trusted to his good faith, as they themselves would have done in like circumstances, that he had been induced to return ; and that because of this, and nothing else, this ambassador of the Most Merciful had died by the stroke of a wild beast, we may imagine what their astonishment and horror would be like. "Who shall deliver us," they would cry, "out of the hand of this mighty God?" And it is probable that at first they would find it difficult to see wherein his sin lay, and to disentangle the right and the wrong in his conduct. They would say, and rightly, that he was much more sinned against than sinning. It would seem to them that the really guilty party escaped unpunished, whilst his innocent victim paid to the uttermost farthing. And it is possible that some found, at least for a time, in this episode, as some in later days have done, a riddle which they could not read. But its meaning could not be lost upon them all; if it had been, the Divine purpose in this visitation would have been defeated. It may be the old prophet himself expounded its lessons ; it may be that "such as set their heart to seek the Lord"—and we may be sure that Jeroboam's innovations had occasioned the gravest misgivings and fears in many minds—found them out for themselves. But in any case some would not be long in discovering that *these things were an allegory.* "As hieroglyphics," says Lord Bacon, "preceded letters, so parables were more ancient than arguments." May we not add that *acted* parables were still more ancient than *spoken* ones. A Tarquin, striking off the heads of the tallest poppies, belongs to the beginnings of history. This was the age when men not only gave signs, but *were* such themselves (Isa. xx. 3 ; Ezek. xxiv. 24; Matt. xii. 39, 40). The death of the "*man* of God" accordingly was a parable, an object-lesson of the most impressive kind as to the doom of the unfaithful *people* of God. In his end, men might see a fore-shadowing of their nation's, if it should persevere in the worship of the calves.

For they would assuredly remember, as they pondered this history, that as this prophet of Judah was a *man* of God, precisely so was Israel the *people* of God (ch. viii. 43, 52, 66; xiv. 7; Levit. xxvi. 12; Deut. xxvi. 18). As he was to other men, so was Israel to other nations. Was he elect of God and precious? So were they. Had he a mission? So had they. Had God spoken to him? He had also spoken to them, and moreover, had given them a charge not unlike his. For it is to be also considered that God had plainly spoken to Israel on this very subject of Divine worship. At the very threshold of the Decalogue, at the head of "the words of the covenant," stood the charge, "Thou shalt have none other gods but me. Thou shalt not make to thyself any graven image," &c. And it is to be noted here that these words stand side by side with the formula, "I am the Lord thy God, which brought thee out of the land of Egypt"—the very words which Jeroboam had cited in instituting his new mode of worship; the very cry which had been raised before when Israel made its *first* golden calf (Exod. xxxii. 8). It is almost certain, therefore, that these initial words of the covenant had been lately and forcibly recalled to their minds. But in any case they could not be ignorant that their forefathers had been expressly charged to make no similitude, no graven or molten image (Levit. xxvi. 1; Deut. iv. 16, 25; v. 8; xxvii. 15, &c.) And this commandment, too, like the message of that morning, had been confirmed with signs following. The blackness, darkness, tempest, trumpet, fire, all these had attested that revelation of God's will. It might possibly occur to some of their minds, therefore, that when the first protest against a corrupt following of the true God was raised, He "gave a sign the same day."

Such, then, was the commandment given to Israel. It was as explicit, as authoritative as that which this dead prophet had recently received. But of late a new teacher had appeared amongst them, in the person of their king, who presumed to countermand this law of the Almighty. We are not told, indeed, that Jeroboam claimed to be prophet as well as priest, but we find him acting as one, and received as one. It is hardly likely that *he* laid claim to any revelation from on high. He was not the man to pretend to visions of angels. It was his contention that he was reverting to the old form of religion, but that was all. At the same time, he was the great false prophet of the Old Testament. Just as Moses was the giver of the law, just as Elias was its restorer, so was Jeroboam its depraver. Precisely what the lying prophet taught the man of God, that had he taught the people of God, viz., that God's command was somehow abrogated. Prophet of Bethel and priest-king of Bethel were alike in this, that each met the Divine, "*Thou shalt not,*" with the human, "*Thou shalt.*" There was this difference between them, that the first inculcated disobedience to but one command, whilst the second contravened a whole system; but this very divergence would make the parallel all the more impressive. "If," they would argue, "if a prophet, a doer of signs and wonders, died without mercy because he listened to the voice of a brother prophet—who swore that he had received a revelation concerning him—and so was betrayed into breaking one commandment, of how much sorer punishment shall those be thought worthy who at the mere word of their king, albeit he claimed no spiritual authority, and acted from political motives only, reject the gracious covenant of heaven, confirmed by many signs, and go after false gods," &c. There were some, no doubt, would see in the corpse borne to its burial that day a foreshadowing of the more terrible judgment then hanging over their own heads.

And so we find this prophet of Judah has not lived or suffered in vain. His death, like that of Samson, wrought even more effectually than his life. He was set forth as it were appointed to death (1 Cor. iv. 9). He silently and unconsciously mirrored forth the sin and the punishment of a disobedient people.

It now only remains for us to indicate briefly how the analogy between man of God and people of God received its completion in the punishment which befell the latter. The punishment of the prophet was death; of the people, whose sin was much greater, death and superadded infamy. We see this—

1. *In the case of Jeroboam's house.* For the family of the deceiver was the first to suffer. As in the case of the man of God, "swift retribution" followed upon sin. And what retribution! The death and destruction of the race. He himself was smitten of God. His seed was suddenly cut off. The sword of Baasha was as swift as the lion's paw. Only one of his children "came to the grave." The rest were devoured of beasts and birds. (Cf. ch. xiv. 11 with ch. xiii. 28.)

2. *In the case of his intrusive priests.* If they escaped a violent death, their remains experienced disgrace worse than death (ver. 2). Here prophet and priests stand in contrast. The respect accorded to his ashes was denied to theirs.

3. *In the case of the entire people.* For the captivity, foretold in ch. xiv. 15, was the death of the kingdom, and the death-knell of the people. The ten tribes soon lost their corporate existence. And what agonies preceded that dissolution! (See Jer. lii.; Lam. *passim;* Pss. lxxiv., cxxxvii.) The people to death, the land to lions! (2 Kings xvii. 25.) Could the analogy be much closer?

But indeed the analogy does not end there. *De te fabula narratur.* The Christian Church has inherited the place, the privileges, the responsibilities of the Jewish people. If that Church, or if the individual Christian be unfaithful or disobedient, let them see their own fate glassed and pourtrayed in that of the disobedient prophet. "If God spared not the natural branches," &c. "I will remove thy candlestick out of his place." "Shame and everlasting contempt."

The Two Prophets. We have already considered the principal lesson which this strange history had for that time. Let us now indicate some of the lessons which it has for all time. The text, to borrow Bishop Ridley's phrase, "shall lead us by the hand;" we will record them as we find them set down in the story. And first let us contemplate the OLD PROPHET. Observe—

1. *It was the false prophet that was old.* Age should bring wisdom (Job. xxxii. 7; ch. xii. 7), and piety. But see Homiletics, p. 225. The old king (ch. xi. 4) and the old prophet alike remind us that there is "no sinner like an old sinner."

2. *It was only the false teacher that was styled a prophet.* Probably because he alone had been taught in the schools. He was, so to speak, in the prophetical succession. The man of God was an irregular, though not self-constituted messenger. But observe, when God employs an irregular, He authenticates his mission with a sign. And consider, too, the unworthiness of ministers argues nothing against the office or the succession. See Art. XXVI.

3. *The old prophet was in Bethel.* "Where Satan's seat is" (Rev. ii. 3). But God had not fixed the bounds of his habitation. What wonder if, like him who "pitched his tent toward Sodom" (Gen. xiii. 12), he fell into temptation and sin? The old prophet, in his way, has "lifted up his eyes and beheld the plain of the Jordan, that it was well watered everywhere." He has remained here to worship the rising sun. Conscience bade him go. Convenience made him stay.

4. *The old prophet tries to serve two masters.* Though Jeroboam sets up molten images, a sanctuary, a priesthood, he raises no protest. But when Jeroboam burns incense and sacrifices, he does not sanction the proceeding by his presence. But he compromises the matter by sending his sons. "*Video meliora proboque, Deteriora sequor.*" "He that wavereth is like a wave of the sea driven with the wind and tossed" (James i. 6). The temporiser soon finds difficulties in his path. Those who try to gain both worlds generally contrive to lose both. After the conduct of ver. 18, he could not respect himself; and after the prophecy of ver. 32, he could expect no advancement from the king.

5. *The old prophet stoops to lies.* And yet he was a true prophet. A preacher of righteousness, yet he practised deceit. Baalam has been called "a strange mixture of a man." This prophet's character and conduct were equally strange. But, alas! it is a common thing to find men's example differing widely from their precept; to find insight without holiness, light without love. Prophetic gifts do not imply piety. It is no new thing for God's ministers to fall into sin.

6. *The old prophet slays a man of God.* It was his tongue, not the lion's paw, really slew a man more righteous and better than he. A prophet is the instru-

ment of a murder (cf. John viii. 44). "What shall be given unto thee, or what shall be done unto thee, thou false tongue?" (Ps. cxx. 3.) Let us take care lest we destroy *with our meat* one for whom Christ died (Rom. xiv. 15). Let us remember—

> "What guilt, what grief may be incurred
> By one incautious, hasty word."

Now let us turn to the MAN OF GOD. Observe—

1. *The man of God believes every word.* He was not altogether without excuse. False prophets were not as plentiful as they afterwards became. He was unprepared for such unblushing deceit. We should probably have done the same. Yet we have had manifold warnings (Matt. vii. 15; xxiv. 11.; Acts xx. 29; 1 John iv. 1; 1 Tim. iv. 1, &c.) We have been taught that if "an angel from heaven preach any other gospel unto us," it is at our peril we listen (Gal. i. 8). We have been reminded that "Satan himself is transformed into an angel of light" (2 Cor. xi. 14).

2. *The man of God is deceived by lies.* It is a favourite device of the enemy. He is the "father of lies" (John viii. 44). It was thus he deceived our first parents. That weapon has answered so well that he plies it again and again (cf. 2 Cor. iv. 4; 2 Thess. ii. 11).

3. *The man of God goes back to Bethel.* This faithful and courageous servant, who had defied the king, who had refused his dainties and rewards, &c., does not endure to the end. "Let him that thinketh he standeth," &c. "Whosoever shall keep the whole law and offend in one point he is guilty of all," because he is guilty of disobedience. "Evil is wrought by want of thought." The commands of God must be kept in their entirety.

4. *The man of God is denounced by the prophet.* Those who lead us into sin are the first to tax us with it afterwards. The deceiver turns upon his victim. We get scant comfort from companions in sin. "What is that to us? See thou to that" (Matt. xxvii. 4).

5. *The man of God hears his doom in silence.* "He was speechless." "I became dumb and opened not my mouth, for it was thy doing." "Being convicted by their own conscience" (John viii. 9).

6. *The man of God dies without mercy.* Though a prophet, the teeth of an evil beast avenge his disobedience. Judgment begins at the house of God (1 Pet. iv. 17). The teacher shall receive the greater condemnation (James iii. 1). "Many stripes" are for those who knew and did not. "The wages of sin is death."

7. *Yet his corpse is not mangled or dishonoured.* It was partly for our admonition that he died. He was ordained to be a sign to that generation. Therefore, though deceived, he was not forsaken. The lion and the ass keep watch over his remains. "Precious in the sight of the Lord is the death of his saints." "A bone of him shall not be broken." "Let no man move his bones" (2 Kings xxiii. 18). His honourable funeral (cf. Isa. liii. 9; Matt. xxvii. 60) and the respect subsequently paid him show that he was no castaway.

And now that we have considered the prophet of Bethel and the prophet of Judah separated by deceit and death, let us see them for a moment reunited.

1. *In their testimony.* For to the witness of the man of God against the altar of Bethel was added the unwilling, and therefore powerful, witness of the old prophet (ver. 32). Jeroboam has gained nothing by the death of the man who had denounced him and his rites. Though dead, he speaks, and speaks as he could never have done in life. And now "one of themselves, even a prophet of their own," has been constrained to echo and enforce his testimony. The king has now the testimony of two unimpeachable witnesses against his impious proceedings.

2. *In their grave.* "Lay my bones beside his bones." Like Balaam, this old prophet would "die the death of the righteous." "Gather not my soul with sinners" (Psa. xxvi. 9) is his cry. "*Sit anima mea cum illo.*" He will take his chance with the man of God rather than with the king. "I had rather be," says one, "with Origen wherever he is than with Justinian and Theodora wherever they are." "In death they were not divided."

But how different their lot in life. The deceived dies; the deceiver lives. The lion which slew the comparatively innocent man of God would not touch the lying prophet. Though old, he is spared to grow older, while the other's sun went down at noon. What an illustration this of the strange confusion of this present life (cf. Pss. lxix., lxxiii., &c.); what a proof of a life to come, where each shall receive his just recompense of reward! To the Jew, suckled in a creed of temporal rewards, &c., this history would present some anxious problems, all of which are clear since our Prophet, Priest, and King "brought life and immortality to light."

HOMILIES BY VARIOUS AUTHORS.

Vers. 11—19.—*The Old Serpent again.* As the ways of the serpent are tortuous so are those of Satan. If he cannot effect his purposes by moving in one direction he will move in another, and thus by crooked ways he advances (Isa. xxvii. 1; Psa. cxxv. 5). He had already tempted the man of God by means of the schismatic king, and failed; his next work is to see what influence an old prophet may have upon him. So versatile are his devices that it is our wisdom to be ever on the alert. Observe the adroitness with which he lays his plans. His astuteness is seen—

I. In CHOOSING HIS INSTRUMENTS. These were—1. "*The sons of the old prophet.*" (1) They were near the altar. Whether by the contrivance of Satan, or that, finding them there, he made them his tools, is not revealed. Or whether they were there out of curiosity, or sympathy with the apostasy, is not revealed. But they were there—on the devil's ground. We must keep from that if we would escape mischief. (2) They were witnesses of the words and works of God. So, might have been rebuked for sympathy with evil and admonished to separate themselves from it. They also saw the way the man of God took in returning to Judah. (3) They lost no time in reporting to their father, urged, unconsciously to themselves, by Satan. We cannot always tell when we are prompted by the devil, or when he uses for his purposes our natural promptings. We should pray God to spare us the humiliation of serving Satan's purposes. 2. *The old prophet himself.* (1) He was an "old" prophet, or had been a prophet in the old time before the apostasy of Jeroboam. Probably he had backslidden from God; for, though he did not appear at Bethel, he allowed his sons to be there. Had he not lost his old fire would he not have lifted his voice against the national sin? Backsliders from God become the devil's dupes. (2) The energy of Satan is seen in the promptness of this old prophet's action. He quickly got information. He lost no time in the pursuit. The sluggishness of age was shaken off under the excitement of the devil's spur. (3) But what was the old man's motive? Probably the desire to display that hospitality which the Easterns cultivated so carefully, mingled with a curiosity to know more about the wonders the man of God was commissioned to discover. But Satan's motive was very different. Beware that your motives become not subservient to those of the devil. Let your motives be pure and godly.

II. In USING THEM. 1. *See the stratagem in Eden, repeated.* (1) Had Satan tempted Eve in his proper character he would have failed (1 Tim. xi. 14). So the man of God was proof against the solicitations of the king whom he discerned to be the "man of sin" of his time. (2) Satan therefore concealed himself under the sleek, lustrous form of a serpent, and deceived our mother. Then transferring himself to the fallen Eve, under her lovely disguise, overcame Adam. So, enshrining himself in the old prophet, he vanquished the "man of God." Beware of Satan's disguises. Especially beware of the religious devil. (3) The offence, again, was *eating.* In Eden it was eating the forbidden *thing.* Note: The place may be right, the thing wrong. At Bethel it was eating in the forbidden *place.* Note: The thing may be right, the place wrong. 2. *See the spirit of the devil.* (1) The spirit of *cruelty.* The old prophet knew that the man of God was forbidden to eat in Bethel, yet he importuned him to eat bread with *him.* Cruelty is no less real because sheathed in professions of kindness. Over-indulgent parents are their children's cruelest enemies. (2) The spirit of *treachery.* The man of God had refused a king:

will he withstand a prophet? (Jer. xxiii. 13; Amos ii. 11.) (3) The spirit of *lies* (ver. 18). Now is Satan transformed into an angel of light. Could the old prophet have been himself thus deceived? He deceived the man of God. Beware of the devil of hospitality. Perhaps the man of God the more readily yielded being weak with fatigue and fasting (compare Matt. iv. 2—4). No example, save that of Jesus, may be followed implicitly.—J. A. M.

Vers. 20—22.—*The Voice of Reproof.* No man of God will deliberately sin against God (John viii. 44; 1 John iii. 9; v. 18). But the good are liable to be surprised or deceived into transgression (James i. 13—15; 1 John i. 1, 2). We must be ever on our guard against the "wiles" and "depths" of Satan. For lack of vigilance this man of God fell into the snare, and we see here how he was reproved.

I. HE SINNED AGAINST THE WORD OF JEHOVAH. 1. *This is evident upon the face of the narrative.* (1) He came out of Judah "by the word of Jehovah." Cried against the altar at Bethel " in the word of Jehovah." Gave the sign upon the altar "by the word of Jehovah" (vers. 1, 2, 5). (2) He professed that his instructions not to eat in Mount Ephraim, but to return to Judah by another road, were by the same word. Professed to the king (ver. 9); to the old prophet (ver. 17). 2. *But could not God revoke or modify His word?* (1) Certainly. He did so to Abraham (see Gen. xxii. 11, 12). What had been might be. (2) Upon the recognition of this principle the old prophet proceeded, and so far was the man of God from disputing it that he was taken in the snare (vers. 18, 19). 3. *Wherein, then, was his fault?* The revocation here came not with the evidence of the command. The command was immediately from " the mouth of the Lord" (ver. 21). The revocation came immediately from the mouth of the old prophet. Note: We are responsible for the proper use of reason in religion. (2) Faith in the word of the Lord must be implicit. The Bible is that word. The evidence that it is such is conclusive—external, internal, collateral. (3) Other voices must not be allowed to replace this. The voice of " nature," of " reason," of the " Church." We listen implicitly to these at our peril.

II. BY THE WORD OF JEHOVAH HE WAS REPROVED. 1. *This came to the man of God himself.* (1) The reading of the text would lead us to conclude that it came to the old prophet. The words אשר השיבו here rendered, " who brought him back," are in verse 23 construed, " whom he had brought back," and might be so construed here. Josephus asserts that the word of the Lord here came to the man of God; and so does the *Arabic.* In the 26th verse we are assured by the old prophet that this word of the Lord came to the man of God. (2) According to this view it was " Jehovah " who " cried unto the man of God," viz., from heaven as He called to Abraham (Gen. xxii. 11). So, coming to himself, as the command did in the first instance, he had not to weigh contradictory testimonies from the old prophet, but was left without a doubt. God brings home sin with demonstration. 2. *It came to him in the ripeness of his transgression.* (1) " As they sat at table." Conscience reproves the sinner in the very act of sin. This is the voice of God in the soul. But here was an external voice to which the internal voice responded. Conscience responds to the word or law of God. (2) It came to all who were at the table. To the old prophet as well as to the man of God. His conscience, too, would respond to the voice of God. To the sons of the old prophet, if present, there would also be a voice. What will our emotions be when in the day of judgment all the mischief to which we have been accessories will be discovered? 3. *It was terribly severe.* (1) He is doomed to die. " Sin, when it is finished, bringeth forth death." We all die in consequence of sin entailed. But here is an actual " sin unto death " (1 John v. 16). (2) He is doomed to die *abroad.* The mention of his carcase not coming to the sepulchre of his fathers implied a violent death away from home. Possibly the manner of his death may have been made known to him (compare ver. 26; ch. xx. 36). The word of God is not violated with impunity. What will be the case of those who seldom take pains to consult it?—J. A. M.

Vers. 23—29.—*The Visitation of Judgment.* The man of God from Judah, deceived by the old prophet of Ephraim, ate and drank in that land of apostasy. This was a disobedience to the word of the Lord, and a complicity in the abominations he was sent to denounce. For this he heard the Divine voice of reproof, and went forth to suffer accordingly, as detailed in the text.

I. THE SEQUEL VERIFIED A REMARKABLE PROPHECY. 1. *Review the prophecy.* (1) Ver. 22. He was, therefore, doomed to die away from his home; and, presumably, by violence. (2) With what solemn feelings would he see his ass saddled with the prospect of such a journey! Ought not our feelings also to be solemn to whom death is certain, though the moment and the manner be unknown? 2. *Note the fulfilment.* (1) Vers. 29, 30. He was met and slain by a lion, and his corpse was cast in the way. There was a spectacle for all passengers! What an evil thing is sin! (2) Thus suffered for disobedience a "man of God." The sanctity of his profession did not protect him from sin, neither can it protect him from punishment. So neither, the dignity of his office. So neither, the service he had rendered to God (see 1 Cor. ix. 27; 2 Cor. xiii. 5, 6). (3) Judgment begins at the house of God, but falls more terribly upon the wicked (1 Peter iv. 17, 18). They may well tremble before "Him that can destroy both soul and body in hell." (4) The man of God came not to the sepulchre of his fathers, yet was mourned over by one who had been a snare to him, but to whom he had been made a blessing. There are strange reciprocities.

II. THE FULFILMENT WAS ATTENDED BY REMARKABLE SIGNS. 1. *Miracle controlled the instincts of animals.* (1) The lion was moved, not by thirst for prey, but by revenge. But this revenge was the Lord's. The animal had suffered nothing from the hand of the man of God. (2) Instinct was otherwise controlled. For here were the lion and the ass together watching the carcase. The ass did not fly from the face of the lion; neither did the lion molest the ass. (3) Nor was this strange witnessing the accident of a momentary surprise. It was maintained while certain passengers, who first observed it, journeyed to the city and reported it; and until, in consequence, the old prophet, divining its import, came upon the scene. 2. *Here let us admire the Divine resources.* (1) He that moved upon the instincts of the lion and the ass was the same who made the representatives of the animal creation defile before Adam to receive their names; who brought them into the ark of Noah; restrained the lions from injuring Daniel; the same who, in the days of His flesh, dwelt among the wild beasts in the wilderness, and who controlled the movements of fishes in the depths (Mark i. 13; Matt. xvii. 27; Luke v. 4—7). This power over the instincts of the lion and ass is but a sample of corresponding dominion over every department of nature. And the resources of this power are the resources of justice and mercy. 3. *But what is the mystical meaning of the signs?* (1) The death of the man of God was judgment for his complicity with the sin of Ephraim in eating and drinking in that polluted place. So it was the last of the series of warnings to Jeroboam before the abandonment of his house to destruction (see ver. 33). (2) The lion that inflicted the penalty was the symbol of Judah, of its royalty, and especially of Shiloh, in whom that royalty culminated. Hence Messiah is described as the "Lion of the tribe of Judah" (see Gen. xlix. 9, 10; Rev. v. 5). Of this glorious Lion, Josiah was to be a type. Messiah visits the sin of Ephraim in the apostasy of the son of Nebat, and the sin of Judah for complicity in its abominations (see Hosea v. 14). So in like manner will He strike down the forms of apostasy extant in these latter times. (3) The ass was the symbol of Issachar (Gen. xlix. 14, 15); but not of Judah; for it is difficult to justify the translation in verse 11, which is better rendered, "and him shall the peoples obey; binding up the shoots of the vine, and the branches of the choice vine." (4) As the ass stood as a witness of this judgment of God upon the sin of Jeroboam, and then carried the carcase away to be buried, so "Baasha, the son of Ahijah, *of the house of Issachar,*" destroyed and put out of sight the house of Jeroboam, fulfilling the prophecy of Ahijah the Shilonite (ch. xv. 27—30). How manifold is the wisdom of God! How deep are His judgments!— J. A. M.

Vers. 30—34.—*The Law of Extremity.* God has made us free to choose or refuse good or evil. Will cannot be coerced and yet be free ; coercion here, therefore, would be destruction. But while God does not compel us to choose the right, He induces by gracious promises, and admonishes by alternative penalties. Still we remain free to elect the good with its blessings, or the evil with its entailments of misery. But so loth is He to see His creatures wretched that He has opened a way of repentance and reformation for sinners. In this, mercy is carried to the extreme limit which consists with the welfare of the universe, which must ever depend upon the order and harmony of righteousness. At this point there comes in the law of extremity ; and the sinner passing it has to encounter "judgment without mercy."

I. THE OLD PROPHET SOUGHT MERCY. 1. *His conduct expressed repentance.* (1) He went out for the corpse of the man of God, and brought it to his home, discerning the hand of God in the judgment. Looking now upon that ghastly form of death he saw his own sad work. He had caused a mischief he could not now repair. How inadequately men estimate beforehand the consequences of their wrong-doing ! (2) He decently interred the body in his own grave. This was the only reparation now within his power for the injury he had caused. But how inadequate ! What a bitter thought ! (3) He "mourned over him, saying, Alas, my brother!" This exclamation (הוֹי אָחִי) was the refrain of a lamentation (see Jer. xxii. 18). Ward, in his "Manners and Customs of the Hindoos," gives two specimens of such lamentations. There are frequent allusions to these in the prophets (see Jer. xxx. 7; Ezek. vi. 11; Joel i. 15 ; Amos v. 16, 17; Rev. xviii. 10—19). With the old prophet this was more than a conventional mourning. He mourned for himself before God. 2. *His conduct also expressed faith.* (1) He commanded his sons, when he died, to lay his bones beside those of the man of God. He believed him to be a man of God in reality, notwithstanding this single act of disobedience for which he had suffered death. There are "sins unto death," viz., of the body, which do not involve the final death of the soul. He desired to be with him in the resurrection. The concern of the ancients respecting the disposition of their bodies after death arose out of their faith in a resurrection (see Gen. l. 24—26; Exod. xiii. 19; Heb. xi. 22; see also 2 Kings xiii. 20, 21). (2) He gave as the reason of his command the faith he had in the certainty of the prophecy of the man of God (ver. 32). And in further testimony of his faith put an inscription on the tomb (see 2 Kings xxiii. 17). He desired to be associated in death with the denouncers of Jeroboam's sin rather than with those involved in that sin. Nor would he be identified in the judgment with perverters of true worship. (3) By this faith his bones were spared when those of the priests and votaries of Jeroboam were burnt upon the altar by Josiah (see 2 Kings xxiii. 19). By a corresponding faith shall we be saved from the judgments of the more illustrious Son of David upon the man of sin of the mystical Babylon.

II. BUT JEROBOAM ENCOUNTERED THE EXTREMITY OF WRATH. 1. *He disregarded the goodness of God.* (1) The conditional promises by the hand of Ahijah were very gracious (ch. xi. 37—39). What a magnificent opportunity he had ! But he missed it. (2) What opportunities have we wasted ? Who can estimate their value ? No opportunity of glorifying God should escape us. 2. *He disregarded his remonstrances.* (1) The judgments upon Rehoboam were lessons to him. The same God who in them visited the sins of Solomon had also set him upon the throne of Israel, and would deal with him upon the same principles. But he sinned against this admonition. (2) Then came the warning from the man of God at the altar. That God was in this warning was left without doubt by the signs (vers. 3—6). These staggered him for a moment; but there was no true repentance. (3) Then came the final warning in the death of the man of God for being implicated, though by a deception, in his sin. This also was shown to be from God by miraculous signs (ver. 64). But this also he disregarded (ver. 33). (4) Now, therefore, the law of extremity must take its course. He and his house are devoted to destruction (ver. 34). This last warning was written in letters of blood. God gave it to Him at the expense of His own servant. And He warns us at the expense of His own Son ; and if we finally reject Christ the extremity of mercy is spurned, and we must encounter the extremity of wrath.—J. A. M.

Vers. 18, 19.—*Lead us not into temptation, but deliver us from evil.* The miraculous element in this chapter is, with many, a reason for its rejection. The same reason might lead us to reject the story of our Saviour's life, and deny the possibility of supernatural revelation. If miracles and signs ever occurred they would be likely to do so at the time described in this chapter. Idolatrous practices were being set up. Many who had been worshippers of Jehovah had been seduced. Worldly policy, social influences, moral enervation, following on the extravagant prosperity of Solomon's reign, and an inherent tendency to sensuous worship, were all combining to induce the people to put away all belief in Jehovah. Then, if ever, He would fitly reveal His power, as He did at the later crisis when Elijah faced the false prophets on Carmel. The effect on Jeroboam was *nil*, but the godless had warning, and the secret worshippers of the Lord still left in Israel were encouraged. The story of the temptation and fall of this prophet, who at least delivered one message with fidelity, is tragic and suggestive. After reading it we have left with us the following thoughts :

I. THAT A STRONG TEMPTATION HAD BEEN RESISTED. Jeroboam had failed to reach the prophet by violence, but resolved to overcome him by craft. Terrible as had been the effect of Jehovah's wrath (ver. 4), the king's conscience was not stirred. His heart was not touched, though his arm was withered. Hence he did not ask the prophet to pray that his sin might be forgiven, but that his arm might be restored. Immediately after, with a show of civility and gratitude, he invited him to his house. Clearly this was not in order to honour the prophet, but to weaken the effect of his message. The people had heard it, and had been moved by it ; but if they saw the messenger going down in seeming friendship with their king, this would diminish, perhaps destroy, the effect of his words. Lest this should happen, the prophet had been forbidden to enter any house. As the representative of Jehovah, he was to show that God would not dwell amongst the people. Firmly, therefore, he rejected the invitation of the king, saying, "If thou wilt give me half thine house, I will not go in with thee, neither will I eat bread nor drink water in this place," &c. The temptation was resisted ; the victory won. Give illustrations of similar moral conquests. A young man tempted to impurity says, "How can I do this great wickedness, and sin against God?" Another sits silent among the scorners, and cannot be induced to join or smile with them, &c. There are times when we are specially able to resist : *e.g.*, when we come fresh from the influences of a Christian home ; when we are feeling the impression of an earnest sermon ; when we are made serious by the death of a dear friend. Under such influences many obey the command, "Resist the devil, and he will flee from you ! "

II. THAT A NEW TEMPTATION WAS SUCCESSFUL. (Read vers. 11—19.) (1) *What were the motives of this old prophet of Bethel?* Probably he was not a false prophet, though these existed ; as tares amongst the wheat, as Judas among the apostles. Nor must he be charged with the malignant wish to bring this man to his death. Picture him as one who knew his Lord's will, but did it not. He had been silent, instead of protesting against the impiety of Jeroboam, and now felt rebuked by this daring stranger. To entertain him might reinstate him in his own good opinion, and in the eyes of the people. Hence he gives the invitation, and when it is resisted another sign of his moral decadence appears, and he tells a lie about receiving a message from the Lord. (2) *How came this temptation to succeed?* Not improbably there was some self-complacency in one who had just resisted the king successfully, and a sense of false security which is indicated by his resting under the terebinth instead of pressing on homewards. Observe here 1. *The conquest of one evil may only bring on the assault of another ; e.g.*, when sensuality is repressed, scepticism may arise and prevail. We sometimes forget that it is not a momentary but a life-long conflict we have to wage. If the Egyptians are drowned, the Amorites and Canaanites await us. A gross sin fails to conquer us, but a subtle sin may lead us to bitter bondage. We can never say to our soul, "Take thine ease;" but always, and everywhere, must listen to the command, "Watch, and pray, lest ye enter into temptation." 2. *Lingering near scenes of temptation may imperil us fatally.* Had the prophet not rested he might not have been overtaken, but would have crossed the border line of the two kingdoms. As the moth flutters round the candle, so do some hover about sin. They read of vices which they think they would never commit, and choose associates unlike what they mean to be, and yet dare to pray, "Lead us not into temptation." He who "standeth in the way of sinners," as one half inclined to join them, may at last "sit in the seat of the scorners," as one who has united with them. "Avoid it, pass not by it," &c. (Prov. iii. 15).

III. THAT A TRIVIAL ACT OF DISOBEDIENCE WAS A GREAT SIN. It seemed a small offence to go home with a brother prophet; but observe that he was in no doubt as to the will of God. He was not really deceived by that lie about the angel's message. He knew that he was forbidden to enter any house, and that the reason for that inhibition was weighty : he knew further that God would not contradict Himself, or alter His command, yet his sensuous wish for food and rest prevailed. An act may seem trifling, but the principle involved in it may be momentous. So it was in Eden. To eat the fruit, or to leave it untouched, might appear a question of small consideration ; but man's decision of it, "brought death into the world, and all our woe." It is in trifles that we test the willingness of our children's obedience. If they refuse to do an unimportant act because to do it would be to disobey us, we are more satisfied with their sensitive loyalty than if the act were notoriously evil. To sin for the sake of a passing pleasure is morally worse than to sin for the sake of a kingdom, for the temptation is less.

IV. THAT A TRAGIC PUNISHMENT WAS INFLICTED. (Read vers. 23—25.) Note the points which marked out this event as the result of God's displeasure, and not of accident ; *e.g.*, that it was foretold (vers. 21, 22), and that the lion did not kill the ass, nor eat the dead body. Show how Jesus Christ used the judgments of God, as recorded in the Old Testament, for purposes of moral and religious instruction. Sin merits punishment. "We are sure that the judgment of God is according to truth, against them which commit such things," &c. (Rom. ii. 2—5). In the consciousness of frequent disobedience let the prayer arise, "God be merciful to *me* a sinner." —A. R.

Vers. 20—22.—*The Disobedient Prophet.* The "old prophet," though here employed as the medium of a Divine message, had acted falsely towards his "brother" ("he lied unto him," ver. 18). The fact that he was content to remain in the land under the rule of Jeroboam was against him. As the Levites had been supplanted by a base priesthood, so the prophets in Israel would seem to be a degenerate race. It must have aggravated the bitterness of the remorse the "man of God" felt, that the prophet who had dealt so treacherously with him should be commissioned to pronounce the Divine sentence on his transgression. His case seems altogether a hard one. How shall we explain it ? What lessons does it teach ?

I. THE INFLEXIBILITY OF A DIVINE COMMAND. The command had been given clearly and positively (ver. 9), and He who gave it had in no way revoked it. The reasons for it remained as they were. The man of God greatly erred in giving more weight to the report of an angelic message delivered to another than to the clear voice of "the word of the Lord" in his own soul. "God is not a man, that he should lie; nor the son of man, that he should repent" (Num. xxiii. 19), and His commands can be abrogated only by others that are equally explicit and authoritative.

II. THE DANGER OF PARLEYING WITH THE TEMPTER. The integrity of the man of God was imperilled as soon as he began to listen to the persuasion that would lead him astray. The first deliverances of conscience are generally right, and we run great moral risk when we begin to question them. He who had resisted the allurements of the king yields to those of the seeming prophet. Moral evil is always most fascinating when it assumes a sacred disguise, and the false "prophet" is the most plausible and dangerous of all tempters.

III. THE GUILT OF DISOBEDIENCE. "To obey is better than sacrifice," &c.

(1 Sam. xv. 22, 23). The spirit of disobedience is the root of all practical iniquity. "By one man's disobedience many were made sinners" (Rom. v. 19). A seemingly trifling offence may thus, especially under certain circumstances, have an important meaning, and entail fatal consequences out of all proportion to its outward form. It is on this principle, that every act of wilful wrong is a violation of the spirit of obedience, that St. James says, "Whosoever shall keep the whole law, and yet offend in one point, he is guilty of all" (James ii. 10).

IV. THE TEMPORAL PENALTIES THAT FOLLOW THE SIN EVEN OF GOOD MEN. The "man of God" may have been at heart a true prophet, and may have received in another world the eternal reward of the true prophet; but his transgression involved him in a violent death, and he was denied the privilege, so much desired by every Hebrew, of having his body laid in the "sepulchre of his fathers." Sin may be pardoned and yet punished. The temporal penalty may be inflicted though Divine mercy cancels the eternal. David's sin is forgiven, but his child must die (2 Sam. xii. 13, 14). Christ is "the propitiation for our sins," and His blood "cleanseth us from all sin," but He promises us no immunity from the ill effects, the shame and loss and pain and sorrow in which our sin may in this world involve us.—W.

Vers. 11, 12.—*The Tempter.* I. THE PROPHET'S SIN AND DOOM. Evil is never wanting in emissaries. It finds them among the so-called followers of God as well as in the world. *This was*—1. *a prophet.* The possession of privileges does not ensure salvation. Balaam took the wages of unrighteousness. "Many will say to me in that day, Lord, Lord, have we not prophesied in thy name?" &c. Is our own life on a level with the place God has given us? If not, we may be among those whose influence and suggestions place stumbling-blocks in the path of God's children. 2. *He dwelt at Bethel,* without testifying against its sin, and unmoved by fear of God's judgment. How many who know God's will and have declared it to others remain in Bethel still! 3. *His instant resolve.* The very story of the prophet's obedience led him to tempt the man of God. His own religion was not like this, and this must therefore be either hypocrisy or delusion. Had the king's request not been made publicly it might have been acceded to. There must be a weak point somewhere, and he will try to find it. Lower life is ever suspicious of a higher, and is anxious to prove that it is not higher. The prophets in Bethel are ever on the watch to break the credit of the men of God from Judah. Is thine the spirit of the learner or of the scorner? Does the higher life judge thee and fill thee with desire to press upward, or only with angry suspicion and desire to show it is no better than thine own? They who are of the wicked prophet's spirit still do his work.

II. THE FALL OF THE MAN OF GOD, 1. *How the tempter found him.* He sat, weary and faint, resting under the shadow of the tree. The invitation to eat bread had more power there than before in Bethel. The tempter knows his opportunity. In times of weakness and need we should hide ourselves in the joy and strength of God. 2. *The weapons he uses.* When an appeal to appetite fails, he professes his oneness with him and uses falsehood. "I am a prophet also as thou art, and an angel spake unto me," &c. To eat bread in Bethel with a prophet did not seem quite the same thing as eating with the idolatrous king; nor does fellowship with those who profess to know God, but yet remain in communion with the world, seem the same thing as fellowship with the world itself. It is thus that the testimony of the Church against idolatry and iniquity has so largely ceased. And then there is Scripture for every concession. "An angel spake unto me . . . but he lied unto him." A worldly Church ensnares where the world itself cannot. 3. *The fatal neglect.* God was as near to him as He could be to his tempter, and he might have inquired of Him. But in the weakness of the flesh he desired to have it so. There is only one preservative from spiritual shipwreck—a *sincere* desire to know what the Lord saith, and a determination to follow that only.

III. HIS DOOM. (Vers. 20—22.) 1. *It was uttered as he sat at meat.* Conviction found him in his sin, and the food he had desired became as wormwood and gall to him. 2. *It came from the lips of his seducer.* We do not rise in the world's estimation through compliance with its desires. As God used the lying prophet so will He use the men of the world for the humbling of those who yield before their temptations. 3. *The penalty.* Death in the land where he had sinned. His carcase, buried in Bethel, declared the truth his obedience should have impressed. God will judge His unfaithful servants. If not glorified in their service, He will be glorified in their punishment.—J. U.

Vers. 23—34.—*Judgment and its result.* I. MERCY DISPLAYED IN THE MIDST OF JUDGMENT. The sin may have been forgiven though the chastisement fell. 1. *His body was preserved from dishonour.* The lion's ferocity was bridled; the prophet's body was neither eaten nor torn; he guarded the remains from the fowls of the air and the beasts of the field. (1) Though God chastises His erring people, He will not utterly cast them away. (2) The fiercest instruments of His vengeance can go only so far as He permits them. 2. *The message he had borne received added weight by his punishment.* In his humiliation God was exalted. The circumstances showed that the blow was from the hand of God, and the question was no doubt raised in many a heart, if the Lord has so punished His servant's error, what will Israel's judgment be? 3. *He still preached in his grave.* He was buried near the altar, and over his tomb was graven the story of his mission and his fate (2 Kings xxiii. 17).
II. THE PUNISHMENT OF UNFAITHFULNESS. When all has been said that can be of the attendant mercy, the judgment still stands out in terribleness. The prophet still preached, but the cry came up from the dark pathway of death. His place was not among the vessels of mercy, but among the vessels of wrath. If we eat in idolatrous Bethel, even though it be in ignorance, God's hand will find us. He punishes now in spiritual leanness, and that again leads to deeper judgment; in the falling away of our children into indifference and worldliness and sin, and will not God demand their blood at our hand? God will have perfect compliance in regard to the conduct of His own worship; He demands "a pure offering." Are we making His word our only law? Whose altar are we serving, Jehovah's or Jeroboam's?
III. BETHEL'S ANSWER TO GOD'S WARNINGS. 1. *The prophet's fear.* (1) He owned God's servant. He cared for his body, mourned over him with the cry, "Alas my brother!" placed him in his own tomb and had his own bones laid beside those of the man of God. (2) He lifted up again God's testimony (ver. 32). The beginning of a better thing in Bethel is ever after this fashion: the honouring God's servants, cleaving to them, and continuing their work. 2. *The king's unconcern.* We are not told that he did anything worse than he had done before; he simply "*returned* not from his evil way." And this became sin to his house, to cut it off and to destroy it, &c. To bring upon ourselves God's judgments we need do no more than turn a deaf ear to His warnings.—J. U.

EXPOSITION.

CHAPTER XIV. 1—20.

THE DEATH OF JEROBOAM'S SON.—The protest of the prophet of Judah, the signs which supported it, and above all the solemn visitation, with its strange portents, which straightway followed it, having alike failed to arrest Jeroboam (ch. xiii. 33) in his high-handed and shameless depravation of the true religion, we now read of the retribution which came upon his family, and which began with the sickness and death of

his firstborn. We can hardly regard this as a part of the discipline designed to reform the king, and so avert the schism, for the narrative distinctly conveys the impression that Jeroboam's day of grace was past, and that judgment was already begun. Moreover, these events would seem to belong to a much later period than that of which the preceding chapter treats—a period, indeed, not far distant from the close of Jeroboam's reign. He then heard, as was fitting, from the venerable prophet who had been God's messenger to announce to him his future reign over the ten tribes, that the death of the youth whom he had destined to succeed him was but the beginning of sorrows, and foreshadowed the speedy and shameful extinction of his family (ver. 14). He too, like Solomon, has sown to the wind and now reaps to the whirlwind. This section is omitted in the Vat. LXX.

Ver. 1.—**At that time** [or *about* (בְּ) *that time*. The king is now settled at Tirzah (ver. 17). In ch. xii. 25 we left him residing at Shechem. The time referred to is that somewhat indefinite period mentioned in ch. xiii. vers. 33, 34. These opening words clearly connect the sickness with Jeroboam's impenitence. What led the king to move his Court to Tirzah, Shechem being, as we have already seen, not only the capital of Ephraim, but "the natural capital of Palestine," "its central situation, its accessibility, and its wonderfully fine water supply" giving it "advantages not enjoyed by any other city in the land" (Conder), we are not told; but it is interesting and instructive to find that it has one conspicuous disadvantage as a capital, viz., that it is "commanded by a hill on either side so close to the town, that the old geographer, Marino Sanuto, in the fourteenth century, considers the place to be untenable by any military force, because stones might be rolled down upon the houses, from either Ebal or Gerizim" (Conder, p. 16. Cf. Judg. ix. 36). It is very probable that this consideration suggested the transfer, of which Ewald despaired of discovering the cause (" Hist. Israel," iv. 23)] **Abijah** [Rawlinson sees in the name, which means "Jehovah is his father," an indication that Jeroboam "did not intend to desert the worship of Jehovah." But the name was probably bestowed long before the schism, possibly in Egypt. It is more likely that it connects itself, if with anything, with the message of Jehovah to him (ch. xi. 28). But the name was not uncommon—it was borne by a son of Rehoboam (ver. 31; compare *Ahijah*, below), and inferences from names must necessarily be precarious] **the son of Jeroboam fell sick.** [The historian undoubtedly means us to see the finger of God in this sickness. This was one of the penalties of disobedience (Deut. xxviii. 22, 58—61; Exod. xxiii. 25].

Ver. 2.—**And Jeroboam said to his wife** [Conscious that his proceedings would merit Ahijah's reproof, he is afraid to go in person. And his wife—if in this particular we may trust the LXX., an Egyptian princess—could be more readily disguised. The com-

mission was too delicate to be entrusted to a stranger. "None might know it but his own bosom, and she that lay in it" (Bp. Hall). Jeroboam evidently suspected that this sickness was punitive, and he would not have others think so too], **Arise, I pray thee, and disguise** [lit., *change*. The word suggests that the disguise was to be effected by a change of *garments*. "She must put off her robes and put on a russet coat" (*ib.*) Possibly the queen was not unknown to the prophet (ver. 4)] **thyself, that thou** [Observe the archaic form אַתִּי for אַתְּ, which latter the Keri would substitute, quite needlessly, here] **be not known** [Heb. *and they* (*i.e.*, those whom she met, not the prophet only) *shall not know that thou art, &c.*] **to be the wife of Jeroboam; and get thee to Shiloh** [the modern *Seilûn*. "There is no site in the country fixed with greater certainty than that of Shiloh" (Conder, p. 44. See Judg. xxi. 19). The identification, however, was only effected in 1838. Conder gives some interesting particulars which lead him to believe that we can identify the very site of the tabernacle. For its history, see Josh. xvi. 5; xviii. 1—10; Judg. xviii. 31; xxi. 19; 1 Sam. iv. 3; Jer. xli. 5. Presuming that Tirzah is to be identified with *Teiasir* (see on ver. 17) Shiloh would be over thirty miles' distant—more than a day's journey to the queen, as the road involves some toilsome climbing] : **behold, there is Ahijah the prophet** [see on ch. xi. 29. Shiloh was probably the birthplace, as well as the residence, of Ahijah. It was in the territory of Ephraim (Josh. xvi. 6), and at no great distance from Bethel. We can only explain Ahijah's continued residence there, after the migration of the God-fearing Israelites to the southern kingdom, not by his great age, but by the supposition that, having been concerned in the transfer of the kingdom to Jeroboam, he felt it a duty to stay and watch his career. And the time has now come when he can be useful. His relations with Jeroboam had apparently so far been good. He had not protested, so far as we know, against the calf-worship, but then God had sent another prophet to do that], **which told me that I should be king** [Heb. *he spake of me for king*] **over this people.** [So that he had already proved himself a true prophet, and so far a prophet of good.]

Ver. 3.—**And take with thee** [Heb. *in thine hand*] **ten loaves** [Ten would seem to have been a usual number (1 Sam. xvii. 18). On the subject of gifts or fees to prophets, judges, &c., see on ch. xiii. 7], **and cracknels**, as marg. The original word נִקֻּדִים (בָּקַד *pupugit*) means "pricked," or "spotted." It is the word translated "mouldy" in Josh. ix. 5, 12, where Gesenius would render "crumbs." Mouldy bread would hardly be taken as a present. These cakes, according to the LXX., Cod. Alex., were for the prophet's *children*] and a cruse [*i.e.*, leather bottle. בַּקְבֻּק *Bakbûk*, is clearly an onomatopoetic word, suggested by the bubbling noise of liquids in emptying] of honey [Spices and other delicacies were often given as presents, and honey was a special product of the country (Exod. iii. 8; Deut. viii. 8; 2 Sam. xvii. 29. The honey sent by Jacob to Joseph was probably "honey of grapes"). The present was purposely a poor one, for the sake of maintaining the deception; *i.e.*, it was a part of the disguise], and go to him: he shall tell thee what shall become of [Heb. *be to*] the child. [At first it strikes us as strange that Jeroboam merely asks what the result will be. He does not petition, that is to say, as in ch. xiii. 6, for a cure. But we find the same peculiarity, which some would explain by the fatalism of the East, in 2 Kings i. 2, and ch. viii. 9. In the present instance, however, no such explanation is needed. For (1) Jeroboam could hardly ask a favour of a prophet of Jehovah, or hope that it would be granted if he did, and (2) if, as he feared, the sickness was judicial, it would be useless to ask for healing. The infatuation which insisted on a disguise for the purpose of deceiving the prophet, who nevertheless was believed to be able to divine the issue of the sickness, is very characteristic, and has had many parallels since.

Ver. 4.—And Jeroboam's wife did so, and arose, and went to Shiloh, and came [probably on the second day] to the house of Ahijah. But [rather *Now*] Ahijah could not see; for his eyes were set [Heb. *stood*. Same word as in 1 Sam. iv. 15. Cf. Gen. xxvii. 1. In *amaurosis* the pupil is set, and does not contract with the light. A partial paralysis of the optic nerve is common in extreme old age] by reason of his age. [Heb. *for hoariness, i.e.* old age.]

Ver. 5.—And the Lord said unto Ahijah [the attempted deceit was frustrated by a direct revelation, the same which disclosed the fate of the child. "God laughs in heaven at the frivolous fetches of crafty politicians" (Hall)]. Behold, the wife of Jeroboam cometh to ask a thing of thee for her son [or *concerning* אֶל, properly "to," *ad*, has the meaning of *de*, after verbs of speaking. Cf. Gen. xx. 2; 1 Sam. iv. 19, &c.; Jer. xl. 16. Gesenius remarks on the similar use of εἰς in the New Testament: Acts ii. 25; Eph. v. 32]; for he is sick: thus and thus [cf. Judg. xviii. 4; 2 Sam. xi. 25. זֶה is a

form of זֹאת] shalt thou say unto her, for it shall be, when she cometh in, that she shall feign herself to be another woman [Heb. *make herself strange*].

Ver. 6. And it was so, when Ahijah heard the sound [Heb. *voice*] of her feet as she came in [בְּאָה should strictly be plural, in agreement with רַגְלֶיהָ *feet*. It is in the singular, probably because the writer is thinking of the woman. But see Ewald, 317 *a*, and cf. 1 Sam. iv. 15] at [Heb. *in*] the door, that he said, Come in, thou wife of Jeroboam; why feignest thou thyself to be another? [Heb. *makest thyself strange*, as in ver. 5] for [the Heb. "*and*" brings out the meaning much better, which is, "Thou art cleverly playing a part, and *I* all the while have a message," &c.] I am sent to thee with heavy [same word as in ch. xii. 13; there translated *rough*] tidings. [Heb. omits. For the construction see Ewald, 284 *c*.]

Ver. 7.—Go, tell Jeroboam, Thus saith the Lord God of Israel, Forasmuch as I exalted thee from among the people [compare 2 Sam. xii. 8; Psa. lxxviii. 70; 1 Kings xvi. 2], and made thee prince over my people Israel. [God still claims dominion over Israel, despite the schism. They are still His people, and He is still their God],

Ver. 8.—And rent [same word as in the former prophecy of Ahijah, ch. xi. 30, 31] the kingdom away from the house of David, and gave it thee: and yet thou hast not been as my servant David [who had been proposed to Jeroboam as his example, ch. xi. 38. This name, as that of a prince of the rival house, would now be almost hateful to Jeroboam], who kept my commandments, and who followed me with all his heart [cf. ch. xi. 33, 38; xv. 5], to do that only which was right in mine eyes;

Ver. 9.—But hast done evil above all that were before thee [perhaps preceding *kings* are not meant, so much as judges— *judices et duces Israelis* (Le Clerc). Kings, however, are not excluded. Both Saul and Solomon had sinned (1 Sam. *passim;* 1 Kings xi. 5, 6), though neither had set up an organized idolism and "made Israel to sin"] : for thou hast gone and made thee other gods [in defiance of the decalogue (Exod. xx. 4). Jeroboam, no doubt, insisted that his calves were not idols, but cherubic symbols. But God does not recognize this distinction. Practically they were "other gods," and so they are here called derisively], and molten images [the word is used of the golden calf, Exod. xxxii. 4, 8. See also Exod. xxxiv. 17; Deut. ix. 12; Judg. xvii. 3, 4. The "other gods" and the "molten images" are but two names for the same thing, viz., the calves of Bethel and Dan], **to provoke me to anger** [This was the result, not, of course, the object of Jeroboam's idolatrous worship], **and hast cast me** [The order of the Hebrew stamps the "me" as emphatic, "*and* ME *hast thou cast,* &c.] **behind thy back** [This strong expression only occurs here and in Ezek. xxiii. 35. It forcibly expresses Jeroboam's contemptuous disregard of God's revealed will. In Psa. l. 17, Neh. ix. 26, we have somewhat similar phrases]:

Ver. 10.—**Therefore, behold, I will bring evil upon the house** [The punishment fell on the house (ch. xv. 29), not, however, to the exclusion of the prime offender (2 Chron. xiii. 20 ; cf. ch. xxi. 29). The reader will observe that the judgments denounced against Jeroboam's sin, like all those of the Old Testament, are temporal. The recompense to come is completely ignored. These severe retributions are calculated and proportioned precisely as if there were no hereafter] **of Jeroboam, and will cut off from Jeroboam him that pisseth against the wall** [This phrase, which Rawlinson observes is confined to the period from David to Jehu, is by him, and generally, understood to mean "every male." (It is found in 1 Sam. xxv. 22 ; 1 Kings xvi. 11 ; xxi. 21 ; and 2 Kings ix. 8.) But it is noteworthy, as Gesenius has remarked, that this is not a habit of Eastern men. Every traveller in Egypt will confirm the remark of Herodotus (ch. ii. 35) on this subject, and the same applies to Palestine ; *i.e.,* the men sit down for this purpose, covered with their garments (Judg. iii. 24 ; 1 Sam. xxiv. 3). Some, consequently, have been led to suppose that the reference is to the *dog,* but animals would hardly share in the destruction of the royal house. Gesenius is probably right when he interprets it of *boys.* Thus understood, it lends additional meaning to the passages where it occurs. It expresses extermination, root and branch, man and boy], **and him that is shut up and left in Israel** [A proverbial expression (Deut. xxxii. 36 ; 1 Kings xxi. 21 ; 2 Kings ix. 8), and involving some play upon words. It evidently means "men of all kinds," but as to the precise signification of the terms "shut up" and "left," there has been much difference of opinion, some (1) interpreting them to mean respectively *married* and *single* (so Keil, *al.*); others (2) *bond* and *free* (Gesen. *al.*); others (3) *precious* and *vile;* and others again (4) *minors* and *those of age.* (So Bähr, "All the male descendants, even the *minors,* were threatened with destruction.") On the whole perhaps (2) is preferable], **and will take away the remnant** [Heb. "*exterminate after*" (Gesen.) or

"*sweep after*" (Keil). The first rendering is the more literal. The "after" is explained, not as Bähr ("as often as a new scion arises I will take it away"), but by the fact that one who expels another *follows after* him (Gesen.)] **of the house of Jeroboam, as a man taketh away dung** [cf. 2 Kings ix. 37 ; Job xx. 7 ; Jer. viii. 2 ; ix. 22 ; xvi. 4. This word expresses the loathing and contempt with which they would be treated], **till it be all gone.**

Ver. 11.—**Him that dieth of Jeroboam** [Heb. *to* Jeroboam, *i.e.,* belonging to, of the house of. "*Of* Jeroboam," conveys the idea of his *seed.* It is possible that his *wife* shared in the general doom], **in the city shall the dogs eat; and him that dieth in the field shall the fowls of the air** [Heb. *heavens,* as in Gen. i. 26 ; ii. 19 ; vii. 23, &c.] **eat** [This was a terrible threat to a Jew— that the dead body should fall a prey to dogs and wild beasts. Cf. Psa. lxxix. 2 ; Jer. vii. 33 ; xvi. 4 ; xxxiv. 20 ; Ezek. xxix. 5, &c. For him it had a factitious horror, because of the threatening of Deut. xxviii. 26 ; cf. Rev. xix. 17, 18. It was, therefore, the climax of disgrace and misfortune ; the greatest dishonour that could be offered to the dust and to the memory. Hence the threat of David (1 Sam. xvii. 46 ; cf. ver. 44) ; hence the devotion of Rizpah (2 Sam. xxi. 10), and the complaint of the Psalmist (Psa. lxxix. 2). Cf. Homer, Iliad i. 4, 5.

" Whose limbs, unburied on the naked shore,
   Devouring dogs and hungry vultures tore."

Dogs, it is well known, are the scavengers of Eastern cities. They exist there in great numbers, and in a semi-savage state, and the carcases of animals and carrion of all sorts are left for them to consume, which they do most effectually, roaming the streets all night (Psa. lix. 6, 14) in search of garbage. Vultures and other birds of prey perform a similar office in the open country (Job xxxix. 29, 30 ; Matt. xxiv. 28)] **: for the Lord hath spoken it.**

Ver. 12.—**Arise thou therefore, get thee to thine own house : and when thy feet enter into the city, the child** [Heb. *then* the child. This is the force of the]] **shall die.** [This was "the sign that the Lord hath spoken" (ch. xiii. 3). The death of the child at the precise moment of the return should serve as an earnest and foretaste of the doom just denounced.]

Ver. 13.—**And all Israel shall mourn for him** [no doubt he was heir to the throne] **and bury him** [mentioned to heighten the contrast. He should be the one exception to the rule of ver. 11] **: for he** [Heb. *this*] **only of Jeroboam shall come to the grave, because in him there is found** [Heb. *was*

found] **some** [Heb. *a*] **good thing** [The
idea is not merely that he was an amiable
youth, but the words imply some degree of
piety, and almost suggest that he dissented
from his father's ecclesiastical policy. "The
Rabbins have a fable that he disobeyed his
father's command to hinder people travelling to Jerusalem to keep the feasts, and
that he even removed obstructions in the
road" (Bähr)] **toward the Lord God of
Israel in the house of Jeroboam.**

Ver. 14.—**Moreover** [Heb. *and*] **the Lord
shall raise him up a king over Israel, who
shall cut off the house of Jeroboam** [for the
fulfilment, see ch. xv. 29] **that day: but
what? even now.** [Rawlinson only expresses a general feeling when he says that
" no satisfactory sense can be obtained from
the Hebrew text," and suggests that it is
corrupt or defective. The passage, no
doubt, is one of extreme difficulty, and inasmuch as the MSS. and Versions lend us
no aid to its interpretation, affords scope for
conjecture. The explanation I venture to
submit may, I hope, contribute—it can
hardly do more—to the elucidation of the
text. I observe that in ver. 13 זֶה is used of
Abijah, "this one alone," &c. I assume that
it has the same import here, viz., " this one
to-day," *i.e.*, "this one dies or is cut off
to-day,"הַיּוֹם being understood,as constantly,
adverbially, = *hodie* (see, *e.g.*, Gen. iv. 14;
xxii. 14; 1 Kings ii. 24). It would be a
natural reflection to the prophet who had
just been speaking of the excision of the
house of Jeroboam, "one perishes to-day,
judgment is already begun," *i.e.* As to the
rest, for עַתָּה I would read אַתָּה, which has
practically the same sound, and for which,
consequently, עַתָּה is sometimes substituted
by the transcriber, as in ch. i. 18, 20, and
understand " And what wilt thou also do?"
i.e., what will become of thee also ? It is
quite possible (ver. 11) that Jeroboam's wife
perished in the wholesale destruction of his
house, as it is clear from the severe punishment assigned to her (ver. 12) that she must
have shared in his sin. The readiness with
which she lent herself to this deceit (ver. 4)
also favours the supposition that she had
approved his policy. She would then have
survived her husband only two years.
Keil's explanation, " cut off the house of
Jeroboam *this day*," appears contrary to
actual fact, while to interpret "*that* day"
(with the A. V.) is contrary to Hebrew
grammar.]

Ver. 15.—**For** [Heb. *And*. The prophet
now proceeds to state the share of the
people in the punishment. They had
acquiesced in the wicked innovations of
Jeroboam and had joined in the worship of

the calves] **the Lord shall smite Israel, as
a reed** [קָנֶה *κάννα, canna,* cane] **is shaken**
[The construction is pregnant, viz., " shall
smite Israel so that it shall be shaken as a
reed," &c. (cf. Luke vii. 24). " The image is
very striking, for Israel was brought so low
that every political influence bore it along "
(Thenius)] **in the water, and he shall root
up** [same word as in Deut. xxix. 28; Jer.
xxiv. 6] **Israel out of this good land, which
he gave to their fathers, and shall scatter
them beyond the river** [*i.e.*, the Euphrates;
see on ch. iv. 24. This is the first clear
prophecy of the captivity foreshadowed by
Moses (Deut. iv. 27; xxviii. 25, 36, 63, 64),
and by Solomon (ch. viii. 46—50). For
its fulfilment, see 2 Kings xvii. 6; xviii.
11, &c.], **because they have made their
groves** [Heb. *their Asherahs, i.e.*, images of
Astarte. The translation " grove " after the
LXX. ἄλσος, Vulg. *lucus*, is now abandoned.
It is clear some sort of idol is intended by
the term. This is evident from ver. 23,
where it is said the Asherahs (A.V. *groves*)
were built " under every green tree " (cf. 2
Kings xvii. 10); from ch. xv. 13 (where see
note); from 2 Kings xxiii. 6, which tells
how Josiah " brought out the Asherahs out
of the house of the Lord," and from the
connexion in which the word is found with
" molten images, carved images," &c. (ver.
23; 2 Chron. xxxiii. 19; xxxiv. 3, 4; cf.
also Judg. iii. 7; 1 Kings xviii. 19). They
were doubtless effigies of Ashtoreth, made
of wood (Deut. vii. 5; cf. 2 Kings xxiii. 6),
planted erect in the ground (Deut. xvi. 21),
and were consecrated to her impure and
revolting worship. It is clear from this
passage that the frightful impurities of the
Canaanitish races had subsisted in the new
kingdom by the side of the new *sacra*. They
had probably revived under Jeroboam's rule,
having apparently been in abeyance since
the time of Gideon], **provoking the Lord to
anger.** [Ch. xiv. 22; xv. 30; xxi. 22; 2
Kings xvii. 11, 17; xxii. 17; Deut. iv. 25;
xxxii. 16, 21; Judg. ii. 12; Psa. lxxviii. 58.

Ver. 16.—**And he shall** [or, *that he should*]
**give Israel up because of the sins of Jero-
boam, who did sin, and who made Israel
to sin.** [These words became almost a formula (ch. xv. 33, 34; xvi. 2, 19, &c.)]

Ver. 17.—**And Jeroboam's wife arose, and
departed, and came** [possibly she lingered
for some time on the road, dreading to
return] **to Tirzah** [Identified by Robinson
and Van de Velde (Narrative, ii. 334, 335),
with *Tellûzah*, or *Talûse*, a place in the
mountains, six miles north of Shechem.
See Josh. xii. 24. Both these writers admit,
however, that if this is indeed Tirzah, "all
traces of royalty have disappeared." " With
the exception of a few sepulchral caves,

subterranean granaries, wells, and old hewn stones, nothing of ancient Tirzah remains in Talûse." Conder recognizes the name in the modern *Teiûsir*—a village near Jezreel, in the Great Plain—which "contains the exact letters of the Hebrew word, though the two last radicals are interchanged in position." "The beauty of the position, . . . the ancient remains, and the old main road from the place to Shechem seem to agree well with the idea of its having once been a capital" ("Tent-work," p. 57). Some of its "numerous rock-cut sepulchres," he thinks, may be the tombs of the early kings of Israel. It was famed for its beauty (Cant. vi. 4), and for this reason, perhaps, among others (see on ver. 1) was selected by Jeroboam for his residence. It is not certain that it had taken the place of Shechem as the political capital]: **and when she came** [the Hebrew is much more graphic. "She came to . . . and the child died"] **to the threshold of the door** [Heb. *house*], **the child died.** [This statement seems at first sight to contradict that of ver. 12, which says the child should die as she entered the *city*. But the palace may have been on the edge of the city (Rawl.), or the "city" may have been little more than the palace.]

Ver. 18.—**And they buried him** [see on ver. 13]; **and all Israel mourned for him, according to the word of the Lord, which he spake by the hand** [see on ch. ii. 25] **of his servant Ahijah the prophet.** [It was a token of the righteous judgment of God that the same prophet who announced Jeroboam's exaltation predicted his fall.]

Ver. 19.—**And the rest of the acts of Jeroboam, how he warred** [see ver. 30; 2 Chron. xiii. 2], **and how he reigned, behold, they are written in the book of the chronicles of the kings of Israel.** [As to this work, see Introduction, Section VI. The exact title is "the book of the words (or matters) of the days," *i.e.*, the record of daily occurrences.]

Ver. 20.—**And the days which Jeroboam reigned were two and twenty years** [Bähr remarks that the exploits of this long reign find no mention in Scripture; the historian dwells exclusively on the sin, the consequences of which were of so much greater moment]: **and he slept with his fathers** [Jeroboam's end would appear to have been untimely. After his defeat by Abijah, we are told, "the Lord struck him, and he died," which may either mean that he died by a lingering disease (2 Chron. xxi. 18, 19) or more suddenly (2 Sam. xii. 15), but which certainly implies that he died "by the visitation of God." I have suggested elsewhere (Homil. Quart. IV., p. 257) that the "stroke" was not improbably his son's death, which was at once so tragical and such a bitter foretaste of judgment to come. He may have "warred and reigned" (ver. 19) *after* this event. He may also have steadily drooped to his grave], **and Nadab his son reigned in his stead.**

HOMILETICS.

Vers. 1—20.—*Abijah and Ahijah.* Perhaps there is no single section of this book more full of lessons, and lessons of the most varied kind, than this. Let us try to gather something of what God has strawed with so liberal a hand.

1. "*At that time* (ver. 1) "—the time of ch. xiii. 33. The sickness of the child distinctly connects itself with the father's persistence in sin (see Deut. vii. 15; xxviii. 22, 61). The hard and impenitent heart treasures to itself wrath (Rom. ii. 5). Warnings (ch. xiii.) have been unheeded: it is now the time for judgment. "If we sin wilfully," &c. (Heb. x. 26, 27). *Deus habet suas horas et moras.* As "the fulness of time" gave us a Redeemer, so it will give us a Judge.

2. "*Abijah, the son of Jeroboam, fell sick*" (*ib.*) Observe—(1) The pious son sickened, and died; the impenitent father and the worthless brother lived." Then sickness is no invariable proof of God's displeasure. "Behold, he whom thou lovest is sick" (John xi. 3; cf. Heb. xii. 6). "Whom the gods love, die young." The fable of Ganymede is full of significance.

> "Te rapuit coelum, tales nam gaudet habere
> Illustres animas degeneresque fugit."

> "Tis ever thus, 'tis ever thus with all that's best below,
> The dearest, noblest, loveliest are always first to go;
> The bird that sings the sweetest, the pine that crowns the rock,
> The glory of the garden, the flower of the flock.

> "'Tis ever thus, 'tis ever thus with creatures heavenly fair,
>   Too finely framed to bide the brunt more earthly creatures bear;
> A little while they dwell with us, blest ministers of love,
>   Then spread their wings we had not seen, and seek their home above."

See also Longfellow's poem of "The Reaper and the Flowers." (2) Sickness spares none. "Neither his dignity as a *prince*, nor his age as a *young* prince, nor his interest with heaven as a *pious* prince could exempt him from sickness" (M. Henry). As to the purpose of sickness, see Homiletics, pp. 12, 13. Perhaps this child, in whom was *some* good thing, only needed the discipline of sickness to make him fruitful in *every* good work. "After ye have *suffered* awhile, make you perfect," &c. (1 Peter v. 10). (3) The sickness of his son, while it was a judgment on Jeroboam, was a warning to Israel. "A cloud and darkness" to the one; it gave light to the other (Exod. xiv. 20).

> "Let us be patient! These severe afflictions
>   Not from the ground arise,
> But oftentimes celestial benedictions
>   Assume this dark disguise."

3. "*Get thee to Shiloh*" (ver. 2). But Shiloh was not one of his sanctuaries. Why not to Bethel? There were *his* priests and prophets (see on ch. xxii. 6). But Jeroboam only does what many more have done since. He has one religion for health, another for sickness. Like Joab, he turns in adversity to the altar which he scorned in prosperity. He would fain share the consolations of those to whose admonitions he never listened. This sending to Ahijah is one result of the sickness of Abijah.

> "'There is no God,' the foolish saith,
>   But none, 'there is no sorrow;'
> And nature oft, in time of need,
>   The cry of faith will borrow.
> Eyes that the preacher could not school
>   By wayside graves are raised,
> And lips say, 'God be pitiful,'
>   Which ne'er said, 'God be praised.'"

4. "*There is Ahijah the prophet*" (*ib.*) Whom he has never troubled since the day when "he spake of him for king" (ch. xi. 31). "Yet did not the chief butler remember Joseph, but forgat him" (Gen. xl. 31). The ministers of Christ may well be content if they are sent for in times of sorrow and sickness. "Lord, *in trouble* have they visited thee" (Isa. xxvi. 16). We think scorn of those who only come near us when they want something. But how often do we serve God thus?

5. "*Disguise thyself, that thou be not known to be the wife of Jeroboam*" (*ib.*) Was ever grosser infatuation than this? Jeroboam, the most astute of politicians, the Machiavelli of the Old World, thinks that a prophet who can peer into futurity cannot penetrate his flimsy disguises. It never occurs to him that "the seer" can see through a woman's veil. Ahithophel is not the only statesman whose wisdom has been turned into foolishness (2 Sam. xv. 31). What an illustration does this history afford of that saying of the Temanite, "He taketh the wise in their own craftiness" (Job v. 13; 1 Cor. iii. 19).

6. "*He shall tell thee what shall become of the child*" (ver. 3). A strange object for such a journey. It is not, "what *to do* for the child;" still less, "what to do for the *sin*;" but simply, what should be the issue of the sickness. But that, time would show. It needed no ghost, no prophet to declare that. *Che sara sara.* Probably Jeroboam despaired of obtaining more. There are petitions "which for our unworthiness we dare not ask." Despair is not uncommonly the end of presumption. "Sin makes such a strangeness between God and man, that the guilty heart either thinks not of suing to God, or fears it" (Bp. Hall). Or was it fatalism prompted this inquiry? It has often been remarked that unbelief and

superstition are very near of kin. Man cannot divest himself of all belief. Head and heart alike "abhor a vacuum." Those who will not believe in one God shall be the victims of strong delusions, and shall believe a lie (2 Thess. ii. 11).

> "Hear the just law, the judgment of the skies,
> He that hates truth shall be the dupe of lies;
> And he that will be cheated to the last,
> Delusions strong as hell shall bind him fast."

Witness Julian the Apostate, Lord Herbert of Cherbury, Robert Owen, and many more. The Chinese people the air with demons and spirits of the dead. Infidel France thinks it unlucky to travel on a Friday. "There was never wicked man that was not infatuate" (Hall).

7. "*His eyes were set*" (ver. 4). Yet "having his eyes open" (Num. xxiv. 4). Reason is "the candle of the Lord." Revelation is a "light to the feet, and a lamp to the path." Inspiration is as "eyes to the blind." "Visions of the Almighty need not bodily eyes, but are rather favoured by the want of them" (Henry). The eye is but the instrument of vision. Eyes of flesh are not the organs of the spirit.

8. "*I am sent to thee with heavy tidings*" (ver. 6). Compare Ezek. xiv. 4. "I the Lord will answer him that cometh according to the multitude of his idols." Heavy tidings for heavy transgression. The sentence should be proportionate to the sin. "Whatsoever a man soweth," &c.

9. "*I exalted thee from among the people*" (ver. 7). It was Jeroboam's abuse of the singular favours he had received, and his forgetfulness of Divine benefits, that so much enhanced his sin. Cf. ch. xi. 9; 1 Sam. xv. 17 ("When thou wast little in thine own sight"); 2 Sam. xii. 8, 9; Psa. lxxiii. 10 ("Took him from the sheepfolds," &c.); Luke xii. 48 ("Unto whomsoever much is given," &c.); *ib.*, x. 15 ("Exalted to heaven, thrust down to hell"). It is well to remember the rock whence we were hewn, and the hole of the pit whence we were digged (Isa. li. 1).

10. "*Other gods and molten images*" (ver. 9). Men often disguise their sins under specious names. "Cherubic symbols" was perhaps Jeroboam's name for his calves. He would not allow that they were images or idols. Josephus happily reproduces the language he held to his subjects: "I suppose, my countrymen, you know that every place hath God in it," &c. (Ant. viii. 8. 4). But God calls things as they really are. Longfellow truly says that "things are not what they seem." But they *are* what they seem to the Omniscient.

11. "*And rent the kingdom away from the house of David*," &c. Note the contrast between this language and the discourse which Ahijah held with Jeroboam once before. That meeting was full of promises; this message is full of upbraidings. Then God declared that He *would* rend the kingdom; here He complains that He has done so, and done so in vain. Then He proposed David as Jeroboam's pattern—his name is mentioned six times—here He accuses the king of contemning that example. There He speaks of a "sure house;" here, of "taking away the remnant of the house," "as a man taketh away dung." Yet "the gifts and calling of God are without repentance." It is Jeroboam's sin has made this difference.

12. "*I will bring evil on the house of Jeroboam, and will cut off*," &c. Compare ch. xii. 27. "And they shall kill me." So the very means which Jeroboam took to secure his throne procured its overthrow. "The engineer is hoist with his own petard." If he could but have trusted God his kingdom would have lasted. But he must needs prop it up himself, with rotten supports, and leaning on these he brought it speedily to the ground.

13. "*When thy feet enter into the city the child shall die*" (ver. 12). For the second time does a prophet give Jeroboam a sign the same day. And the second sign was hardly less significant than the first. For the mother was, in some sense, the cause of her child's death. Her step on the threshold was the signal for the severance of his "thin-spun life." It was not only a foretaste, consequently, of the doom awaiting the entire house; it was also a shadowing forth of the cause of that destruction. The sins of the father were visited upon the children.

14. *"And all Israel shall mourn for him"* (ver. 13). The most, and the most genuine, tears are shed over the graves of children. (Is it that many of us, as we grow older, become less lovely and engaging, less desirable as companions?) Yet of this child it might justly have been said, "Weep ye not for the dead, neither bemoan him" (Jer. xxii. 10). For (1) he was taken away from the evil to come (ver. 11). (2) He escaped the butchery of Baasha. And he escaped, too, the danger of contamination and moral ruin. His life was not unduly shortened. Life is to be measured not by the beats of the pulse, but by the life-work we have accomplished. "He being made perfect in a short time fulfilled a long time."

> " It may be by the calendar of years
> You are the elder man ; but 'tis the sun
> Of knowledge on the mind's dial shining bright
> And chronicling deeds and thoughts that makes true time."

(3) The " good thing toward the Lord God of Israel" was an earnest of better things to come. "Little faith can enter heaven." "A little grace goes a great way with great people." "Those that are good in bad times and places shine very bright in the eyes of God. A good child *in the house of Jeroboam* is a miracle of Divine grace " (Henry).

15. *"For the Lord shall smite Israel"* (ver. 15). For if Jeroboam had "made Israel to sin," Israel had loved to have it so (ch. xii. 30). He could not have had his calves and sanctuaries without priests; and calves, sanctuaries, and priests would have been useless without worshippers. But as the king, so the people. Jeroboam was but a sample of many thousands of his subjects. As the chief offender, he was the first to suffer, and suffered most. But the nation that had shared his sin must suffer in its measure and turn.

16. *"Beyond the river"* (*ib.*) The judgments of God are governed by a *lex talionis*. Not only "an eye for an eye and a tooth for a tooth," but, "Like as ye have forsaken me, and served strange gods in your land, so shall ye serve strangers in a land that is not yours" (Jer. v. 19).

17. *"And Jeroboam's wife arose, and departed, and came to Tirzah"* (ver. 17). It is hardly possible to realize the horror with which the princess, still wearing her disguise, heard the doom of her house, and who shall attempt to describe the agonies of that journey home. Rizpah, the daughter of Aiah (2 Sam. xxi. 10 sqq.), has been called the *Mater Dolorosa* of the Old Testament, but the title equally belongs to Jeroboam's wife. But why, let us ask, does *she* suffer such things? Why must this sword pierce her soul? Was it not because of her share in the sin? As she is included in the sentence against the house (ver. 11, Heb.), it is probable that she had aided and abetted her husband in his irreligious and schismatic policy. And now she must drink of his cup: she must be the first to taste its bitterness; she must bring death to one child and tell of disgrace worse than death to the rest.

18. *"And they buried him"* (ver. 18). In Tirzah the beautiful (Cant. vi. 4), great lamentation was made over him. And indeed his seemed to be a case for tears. The heir to the throne, he was never to ascend it. The possessor of singular gifts and advantages, he was never to exercise the former or enjoy the latter. Had he lived, he might have effected a reformation, and suppressed the calf-worship. But now the grave closes over him, and he is no more seen. What a proof this of a life to come! Otherwise there would be injustice with God, inequality in His dealings with men. "But the righteous live for evermore, their reward also is with the Lord." "We fools counted his life madness and his end to be without honour. How is he numbered among the children of God, and his lot is among the saints " (Wisdom v. 4, 5, 15).

HOMILIES BY VARIOUS AUTHORS.

Vers. 1—3.—*The Impenitent Seeker.* The day of judgment will come at the end of the world, when the heavens and earth shall be burnt up (2 Thess. ii. 7—10; 2 Peter iii. 7). But this has its prelude in a season of judgments which overtakes the sinner in this life. Jeroboam, having sinned away his day of grace, had now entered into such a season. But of this he seems to have been doubtful. Hence learn—

I. THAT THE SINNER MAY BE SURPRISED IN HIS SEASON OF JUDGMENTS. 1. *That there are such seasons is evident.* (1) Witness the great deluge (Gen. vi. 11—13). Also the rain of fire on the cities of the plain (Gen. xix. 13). The overthrow of nations. Signal visitations upon notorious sinners (Exod. ix. 13—15; 1 Sam. xxviii. 15—19). (2) Such were presages of the awful judgment to come (Matt. xxiv. 37—39; 2 Peter ii. 4—6; Jude 5—7; Rev. xviii. 4). 2. *But all afflictions are not such retributions.* (1) Some are entailed upon us through the fall, and alike affect the penitent and impenitent (Gen. iii. 16—18; Job v. 17; 1 Cor. x. 13). (2) Some come to us through the wickedness and blundering of those around us. Many suffer, irrespective of their character, as when a ship is wrecked through the drunkenness of the master. (3) Some are appointed or permitted for disciplinary and educational purposes. These are often amongst our greatest blessings. (4) Sometimes we suffer for the benefit of others—vicariously. When this is voluntary it is very Christ-like (see Psa. xxii. 11; Col. i. 24). (5) Under all these we have a refuge in God (Psa. ix. 9, 13; xlvi. 1). 3. *These may be confounded.* (1) Had Jeroboam known that the mercy of God had reached its limit, and that the season of retribution had set in, he might have spared his queen her journey to Shiloh. (2) But what else could he have expected? Was he not obstinately wedded to his sins? Had he not before him the history of Saul? (1 Sam. xxviii. 15—19.) (3) Men still, in our day, presume upon the mercy of God to their destruction. Eminently the case with those who defer repentance. Learn further—

II. THAT A SINNER MAY SEEK THE LORD TO NO GOOD PURPOSE. This happens— 1. *When the end sought is unprofitable.* (1) Such was the case with Jeroboam. His inquiry should have been, not, "What shall become of the child?" but, "How may the anger of God be averted?" (Compare 2 Sam. xii. 16, 17.) But he was not prepared to repent of his sin. (2) His inquiry was one of curiosity as to the future. Similar curiosity was manifested by Saul under similar circumstances. It is unseemly for a sinner to pry into Divine mysteries rather than seek the salvation of his soul. 2. *When the spirit of the seeker is improper.* (1) He did not, indeed, seek his calves (compare 2 Kings i. 2). He rather sought Ahijah, because the spirit of prophecy was with him (ver. 2). But he had no such faith in his calves. (2) Why, then, did he not renounce them? He had reasons of worldly policy against this (see ch. xii. 26—28). He was therefore a deceiver of the people. Hence he would have his queen disguise herself. So several of the Popes were known to have been infidels. (3) So were he and his dupes doomed to perish together (see Matt. xv. 14; 2 Thess. ii. 9—12; 1 Tim. iv. 1, 2). 3. *When the manner of the search is unworthy.* (1) He paid a respect to the man of God. This was the meaning of his present (see 1 Sam. ix. 7, 8). Hence such gifts are called blessings (see Gen. xxxiii. 10, 11; Judg. i. 15; 1 Sam. xxv. 17; xxx. 26, marg.; 2 Kings v. 15). (2) Even Jacob would eat of his son's venison before he proceeded to bless him (see Gen. xxvii. 4, 19, 25, 31; see also 1 Kings xvii. 11). (3) So are God's blessings and sacrifices offered to Him commonly associated (see Gen. viii. 20—22; ix. 1—17). All His blessings come to us through the sacrifice of Christ; and especially so when we, by faith, present Christ to Him. (4) But here was no sacrifice; and the value of the gift was small. What were a few loaves, a few cakes, and a cruse of honey as a gift from a king! (Compare 2 Kings v. 5; viii. 9.) The meanness of his present was another reason why he would have his queen disguised.

What an argument for early piety is here! Surrender to Christ before you are overtaken by a season of judgments. How admonitory is this subject to the effect that prayer should be true; that we should seek the right thing, in the right spirit, and in the right manner!—J. A. M.

Vers. 4—6.—*Spiritual Vision.* When the season of retributions set in upon Jeroboam, and his son Abijah was smitten with sickness, he sent to the prophet Ahijah the Shilonite to inquire of the word of Jehovah, what should become of the child. He was unwilling it should be publicly known that, in such an emergency, he had recourse to the prophet of the Lord rather than to his calves (compare 2 Kings i. 2). He accordingly entrusted this delicate business to his wife, and enjoined that she should disguise herself. The text evinces how futile were these expedients. Note—

I. SIN SEEKS DISGUISES. 1. *Truth needs none.* (1) It is naturally open. "He that doeth truth cometh to the light." (2) It has nothing to be ashamed of. It is self-consistent, harmonious, lovely. (3) It ought to be displayed; its influence is elevating (Phil. ii. 15, 16). The saint who hides his light wrongs his race. (4) Churches are constituted that Christians should, to the best advantage, witness for Christ. They are the candlesticks (see Matt. v. 14—16; Rev. i. 20). Note: Christians should discourage the eccentricity that would lead them away from the Churches. 2. *It is otherwise with sin.* (1) It is naturally close. The sinner has as instinctive an aversion to the light as the owl and the bat, his types. (2) It has everything to be ashamed of. It is self-contradictory, discordant, frightfully and monstrously ugly. (3) It ought, by the impenitent sinner, to be concealed. For *he* could only desire to disclose it in order to infect and demoralize others. (4) But the true should drag it to the light, that its deformity might be seen, abhorred, and execrated.

II. GOD SEES THROUGH ALL DISGUISES. 1. *Nature itself teaches this.* (1) He that formed the eye, can He not see? (Exod. iv. 10—12; Psa. xciv. 9.) (2) He that formed the mind, can He not perceive? (1 Chron. xxviii. 9; Psa. vii. 9; Prov. xv. 11; Rev. ii. 23.) 2. *It is evinced in the visions of prophecy.* (1) How far-reaching are those visions! The end was seen from the beginning. The instalments fulfilled certify the remainder. (2) How deep their insight into the secret workings of the heart! The secret ambition of Jeroboam, when he was yet the servant of Solomon, was read by Ahijah (ch. xi. 37). Now he sees through the disguise of the queen and reads its motives. 3. *This should be considered.* (1) How foolish are disguises where God is concerned! And where is God not concerned? (2) Those who would deceive God only deceive themselves. (3) What disclosures will the day of judgment make! (1 Cor. iii. 13; iv. 5.) What a day of trembling to the hypocrite!

III. GOD CAN OPEN THE EYES OF THE BLIND. 1. *Literally.* (1) Miracles upon the sight were occasionally wrought in ancient times (Gen. xix. 11; 2 Kings vi. 18). (2) Many such were wrought by Christ. 2. *Spiritually.* (1) The prophets were gifted with spiritual vision. They were therefore called *seers.* Their prophecies were called *visions.* (2) Such vision had Ahijah. His natural sight had now failed him (ver. 4), yet he saw Jeroboam's queen before she came into his presence, saw through her disguises, and discerned the purpose of her visit. (3) Spiritual vision is not exclusively the privilege of prophets. (*a*) God gives this to the sinner when He discovers to him the exceeding sinfulness of sin. God strips him of the disguises by which he would deceive himself, and exhibits his own life-likeness to his conscience. (*b*) God gives it to believers, when He witnesses His pardon and their adoption, to their spirits. (See Acts xxvi. 17, 18; Eph. i. 18.) Have your eyes been opened? Pray God that Satan may never succeed in throwing his dust into them.—J. A. M.

Vers. 7—11.—*Hard Tidings.* Such is the character given by the prophet to the matter of the text (ver. 6). What we translate "*heavy* tidings" is, in the Hebrew, as in the margin, *hard*. The uses of the word (קשה) in several places suggest that it should be here taken as indicating retributive judgments merited by one who had hardened his heart in sin. Observe—

I. PRIVILEGES INVOLVE RESPONSIBILITIES. Thus—1. *Special favour calls for special gratitude.* (1) Jeroboam was "exalted from among the people." He was "an Ephrathite of Zereda," an obscure place, mentioned once, and that only in connection with his birth (ch. xi. 26). The names of his parents also had remained in obscurity but for the figure he cut in history. (2) He was made "prince" over the "people of God." This was a splendid distinction. A people is great, not through its number or the extent of its territories, but from its virtues (see Deut. vii. 6 ; xiv. 2; xxvi. 18, 19). What an influence has that people exerted upon human destinies ! (3) The kingdom rent from the house of David was given to him. Jeroboam, then, was placed in succession to that David who had led the armies of Israel to victory ! Also to that Solomon who had built the temple, and who, in the earlier part of his career, filled the world with the fame of surpassing wisdom ! 2. The favoured are *compared* with their *peers.* (1) Jeroboam was a *compeer* to David. Both were lifted from humble station—David from the sheep, Jeroboam from the army (ch. xi. 28). Both ascended the throne of Israel—founded dynasties. (2) But how do they *compare?* "David kept the commandments of God"—followed Him "with all his heart." This did not Jeroboam. Melancholy record, he did *nothing* for God ! 3. They are *contrasted* with their *peers.* (1) Jeroboam "had done evil above all that were before him." More than Saul, who never worshipped idols. More than Solomon, who did not make Israel to sin. (2) Jeroboam made "other gods ; and " (or *even*) "molten images." Note : He intended his calves to represent the God of Israel ; but the God of Israel Himself calls them "other gods." So are the images of Antichrist other gods though baptized with Christian names. This was worse than the idolatry of Solomon. The caricaturing of the true God is more offensive to Him than the worshipping of His creatures. Let the worshippers of barbarous pictures of the Holy Trinity, in which the Almighty is pourtrayed as a decrepit old man, and such-like, seriously consider this. (3) Jeroboam is described as having "cast" the God of Israel "behind his back." What a startling figure ! How descriptive of the sin of those who now neglect God !

II. RESPONSIBILITIES ABUSED PROVOKE JUDGMENTS. Amongst these may be mentioned—1. *The bitter sense of wasted opportunity.* (1) Jeroboam is reminded that he once had the grand chance of making for himself a "sure house like David " (see ch. xi. 38). What golden opportunities may *we* not have wasted ! (2) That though the more glorious chance was missed and lost, he had then a gracious season of warnings, which also he let slip. (See events recorded ch. xiii.) This respite improved *might* have averted, and *would* have mitigated, the severity of the judgments impending (compare ch. xxi. 29). 2. *The knowledge that the day of vengeance has set in.* (1) An admonition of such a day was *implied* in the earlier prophecy of Ahijah, in the judgments then denounced against the house of David for the sin of Solomon (ch. xi. 30—38). (2) This admonition was *declared explicitly* in the message of the man of God from Judah, and solemnly impressed by the signs attending and following (ch. xiii.) (3) Now Ahijah announces that these judgments are *taking effect.* But even now, had Jeroboam come to God in the spirit of repentance, though his sin is "unto death," yet might he save his soul. It is hard now to break a chain so riveted as that is by which he has bound himself. No repentance being evinced, the knell of doom sounds forth like the echoes of the closing door of Noah's ark, which announced mercy fled and wrath begun. 3. *The severity of the sentence.* (1) The honour of the house of Jeroboam is to be brought down to ignominy. (2) The carcases of members of this family are to be consumed by carrion-feeders. Such are the swords of the wicked (compare Gen. xv. 11 ; Jer. xxxiv. 18—20). Whether by the sword of Baasha, or *literally,* after that sword had done its part, the words of Ahijah came true (see ch. xv. 29). "The doom of the house of Jeroboam was a figure of that of the house of this man of sin (see Rev. xix. 17, 18). God knows the proud afar off. But He gives grace to the humble.—J. A. M.

Vers. 12—14.—*The Reprobate's Doom.* In the queen of Jeroboam we see a remarkable messenger. For she went as messenger from a king and returned as messenger from a prophet. Her message in the first instance was simple, but in her return twofold. She brings a message to the king, and with it a message also to the nation. The message to the king brings—

I. HEAVY TIDINGS RESPECTING ABIJAH. 1. *As to the issue of his illness.* (1) "The child shall die." This is a direct answer to the question with which the royal messenger was charged (ver. 3). Here was the withering of a limb of Jeroboam's family answering to the sign of the withering of his arm (see ch. xiii. 4). (2) The king does not now ask for the restoration of the child as he had done for the restoration of his arm (ch. xiii. 6). He did not even ask, in time, that the judgment might be averted. How could he, without repenting of his sin? Note: The descents of depravity, like those of natural gravitation, are in accelerating degrees. (3) This judgment is the signal that the season of retributions has now fairly set in. What a horror to wake up to such a conviction! "Be sure your sin will find you out." 2. *As to the near approach of his death.* (1) "When thy feet enter into the city." Every step of the queen's advance over that twelve miles from Shiloh to Tirzah measured a stride of death towards his victim. Do we sufficiently realize the fact that this is the case with us in passing through the journey of life? (2) What must have been the conflict in the heart of the queen? Maternal affection would urge her steps with speed that she might see her son alive. Yet was it a race with death; and death was first at the palace. That monster overtakes the swiftest. If he passes one it is to strike another, and so that the recoil of his sting may wound the trembling heart. 3. *As to the circumstances attending.* "All Israel shall mourn for him and bury him;" but for him only of the royal family, "because in him there is found some good thing towards the Lord God of Israel." Hence learn (1) God's punishments are discriminative. He does not overlook the good in the evil. (2) Yet the good suffer with the evil. Abijah dies for the sin of his father. Christ dies for the sin of the world. But in His death is life to the believer. (3) Still the good suffer for their good. They are taken away from evil to come. Had Abijah lived he might have been drawn into his father's sin. God often takes them soonest whom He loves best. (4) The evil suffer in the good. Jeroboam had reason to mourn the loss of the best of his family. So had Israel, since the succession would now open to a wicked prince. Note: We should pray for the preservation of virtuous and useful lives. Especially so when such are found in seats of power and influence.

II. HEAVY TIDINGS RESPECTING HIS SURVIVORS. 1. *They are devoted to extermination.* (1) This as a general fact was already known. (2) It is now published with additional circumstance. The agent that shall effect it is one who shall himself mount the throne of Israel. (3) This was fulfilled to the letter (see ch. xv. 27—30). 2. *Judgment will come speedily.* (1) Some think this exclamation of the prophet, "But what? Even now" arose from his having seen that this would be the case. (2) So it proved. Within two years Jeroboam died. He was succeeded by Nadab, who two years later was slain by Baasha. In that time also, and by the same hand, the predicted extermination was completed. (3) "The wicked do not live out half their days." This is true of dynasties as of individuals. The dynasty of Jeroboam lasted only four and twenty years.—J. A. M.

Vers. 15—16.—*The Future of Israel.* The vision of the Shilonite concerning the house of Israel, now before us, seems to have come upon him suddenly. We think the exclamation, "But what? Even now!" was the half-involuntary expression of the surprise of this new revelation. This utterance should, then, have stood at the beginning of verse 15 rather than at the end of the verse preceding. The connecting particle "For," with which verse 15 now opens, favours this view. The new vision describes the then future calamities of Israel, together with their provoking causes.

I. HE WAS HENCEFORTH TO BE TROUBLED IN HIS OWN LAND. He is there to stagger and tremble under the stroke of God—1. "*As a reed is shaken in the water.*" (1) The reed is a figure of *frailty*. Rabshakeh, in describing the inability of the Egyptians to support Hezekiah against the Assyrians, compares them to a bruised reed (2 Kings xviii. 21; Isa. xxxvi. 6; see also Ezek. xxxix. 6). Contrariwise, our Lord, asserting the stability and vigour of John Baptist, said that he was *no* "reed shaken with the wind" (Matt. xi. 7). In derision of the royalty of Jesus the soldiers put a reed in His hand for a sceptre (Matt. xxvii. 29). Subsequent history bore emphatic testimony to the instability and feebleness of Ephraim. (2) The reed is " shaken in the water." This element is at once a symbol of *trouble* and of *people* (see Psa. lxix. 17; Rev. xvii. 15). So disquiet, arising from popular tumults and civil war, is suggested. And did not this become fact? The frequent changes of dynasty kept the nation in perpetual broils. These evils were aggravated by wars with their brethren of Judah. 2. *As a reed shaken by the wind.* (1) This is not asserted, but implied, since reeds shake in water when moved by winds. And foreign influences had much to do with the troubles of Israel. (2) Foreign idolatries introduced by Solomon's wives were at the root of the troubles. (3) The wars between Israel and Judah brought foreign armies upon the scene— Egyptians, Syrians, and Assyrians. By these rough winds the troubles were aggravated.

II. THEN TO BE SCATTERED IN THE LANDS OF STRANGERS. 1. *A captivity of Israel is foretold.* (1) The settlement of the people in Canaan is frequently described in Scripture under the figure of the planting of a vine there (see Psa. lxiv. 2; lxxx. 8; Jer. ii. 21; xi. 17). (2) This is now to be reversed. "He shall root up Israel out of this good land which he gave to their fathers." Suppose the vine had feeling; what a painful process! 2. *Also the region of their dispersion.* (1) " I will scatter them beyond *the river,*" *i.e.*, the Euphrates, for thus, by emphasis, this river is ever distinguished in Scripture (see Gen. xv. 18; compare Deut. xi. 24 with 1 Kings iv. 21 and Psa. lxxii. 8). (2) This river also stands for the *Assyrians,* through whose territory it flowed. Their armies invading Israel are likened to the Euphrates rising and overflowing its western bank (see Isa. viii. 7). (3) How literally was all this accomplished (see 2 Kings xv. 29; xvii. 6, 18).

III. THESE VISITATIONS WERE TO EXPRESS THE ANGER OF GOD. 1. *First provoked by their Canaanitish idolatries.* (1) These are represented here by " their groves." The word *Asherah* (אשרה, אשירה) occurs thirty-nine times, and is everywhere translated *groves,* yet it may well be doubted whether this is its meaning. For take the next occurrence after that in our text, viz., ver. 23 of this chapter: How could a grove be built under a green tree? How could a grove be made in the house of the Lord? (See 2 Kings xxi. 7; xxiii. 6.) (2) These Asheroth, or Ashcrim, appear to have been images made of wood, cased in metal, perhaps fashioned like goats, which were worshipped with abominable rites. They were popular Canaanitish divinities, and for this reason to be execrated by Israelites (see Exod. xxxiv. 13; Deut. xvi. 21). (3) But for all this they fell into the snare of worshipping together with the Baalim, or Bulls, and other Canaanitish idols (Judg. iii. 7; vi. 25; 1 Kings xviii. 19). 2. *Then by their complicity in the sin of Jeroboam.* (1) This addition to their earlier idolatries filled up the measure of their iniquity. For it completely alienated them from the worship of Jehovah in His temple. (2) They forsook the Lord, so He threatens to "give up Israel for the sin of Jeroboam," as He had also given up the house of Jeroboam to judgment.— J. A. M.

Vers. 17—18.— *Death and Mourning.* With a heavy heart the queen of Jeroboam moved along the road from Shiloh to Tirzah, and received the salute of death at the threshold of the palace. This sad event was soon followed by a state funeral and by a public mourning. In all this note how—
I. SORROW TARNISHES HUMAN SPLENDOUR. 1. *Survey this palace of Tirzah.* (1) This is not the only palace of Jeroboam. Soon after his promotion to the crown of Israel we find him building a palace at Shechem. That commemorated the event of his elevation; for there those circumstances occurred which gave rise to it (see ch. xii.) (2) But this palace did not long satisfy the royal ambition. We

find the king presently engaged in building a second at Penuel, in the tribe of Gad, eastward of Jordan (ch. xii. 25). Those who come suddenly to fortune commonly affect great splendour. (3) Now we find him occupying a third. This probably was the most magnificent. It is situated in a place famous for its beauty in the days of Solomon (see Song vi. 4). From this it had its name (תרצה), which signifies *pleasantness.* Doubtless the palace was in keeping with the place, for it was preferred as the royal residence until its destruction by fire (ch. xvi. 18). 2. *Behold in this paradise a corpse!* (1) Death has smitten Abijah, the best and most promising of the royal family. What a scene of grief when the mother, arrived from Shiloh, entered that chamber! What a dense gloom would rest on the household! In that solemn moment how vain must earthly splendour have appeared! (2) And does not sorrow still mingle with all earthly scenes! Why, then, should we not rather set our affections upon things above? (3) Wealth cannot bribe death. The King of Terrors enters the palace of royalty as certainly as he enters the cottage of poverty. To the great this enemy is even more formidable than to the humble, for they have more to leave. The acquisitions of the worldling, therefore, are only giving point and venom to the sting of death.

II. IT HAS RELIEFS AND AGGRAVATIONS. 1. *The reliefs are the fruits of virtue.* (1) The public mourning would be a solace to the royal family. A king might provide a pompous funeral for his son, but he could not command the heart of the nation to mourn (2) This public mourning was a tribute to the virtues of the prince (see ver. 13). (3) There was pure comfort in the reflection that the spirit of the pious youth is away from a world of sin, in the companionship of saints and holy angels. 2. *The aggravations are the fruits of sin.* (1) How the grief of Jeroboam must have been embittered by the fact that this bereavement came not as a messenger of mercy to him, but as a visitation of judgment! (2) How it must have alarmed him to know that it was but the first of a series of judgments destined to issue in the extermination of his house! (3) The very virtues of the prince first taken, in this view, became an aggravation, for he is removed as too good a prince for so wicked a people, and to make way for the succession of a wicked prince to punish them.—J. A. M.

Vers. 19, 20.—*The Review.* The text reminds us—

I. THAT THE SEASON OF DEATH IS A TIME FOR REFLECTION. 1. *In presence of a corpse the giddiest pause.* (1) This is seen when an ordinary funeral passes along the streets, in the sombre countenances of the bystanders, if not in more special tokens of respect. It is more evident still when the deceased may have been an acquaintance or a relative. But most so in the very house of mourning, where the relics are seen shrouded in their pallor and immobility. (2) What trains of thought are started! (a) What a mystery is death! (b) What a mystery is life! (c) What a mystery is futurity!—the spirit world—the resurrection—the judgment—heaven—hell. (d) Are we prepared to encounter the inevitable? Who can forecast the moment? (e) Why should we defer the needful preparation? 2. *When a monarch dies a nation thinks.* (1) This is so under ordinary conditions. The social position occupied is so elevated that the event is conspicuous to all. What a leveller is death! In this article all claim kindred, the prince and the beggar (Prov. xxii. 2). (2) But Jeroboam's death was by the stroke of God (2 Chron. xiii. 20). Such a conspicuous judgment was fitting to the man of sin (see Isa. xi. 4; 2 Thess. ii. 8; Rev. xix. 15). How alarmingly would such a death speak to workers of iniquity! (3) The demise of Jeroboam opened the succession to Nadab, who, without the genius of his father, followed in his iniquities. 3. *But the virtuous only are lamented.* (1) Jeroboam was buried. He *did* come to the sepulchre "with his fathers." And he may have had the formality of a *family* mourning. His household may have gone barefoot, wept, torn their clothes, smote on their breasts, lay on the ground and fasted, as the custom was. (2) But there was no *national* mourning. The public mourning for Moses and Aaron lasted thirty days, that for Saul seven (Num. xx. 29; Deut. xxxiv. 8; 1 Sam. xxxi. 13).

For Abijah, a pious prince of the house of Jeroboam, there was a national mourning, though he never came to the throne ; but for Jeroboam, after a reign of twenty-two years, no mourning ! (Ver. 13.) (3) What a contrast—the apathy of the nation, now at the close of their experiment at king-making, to the enthusiasm at its commencement (ch. xii. 20) ! How seldom do revolutionists adequately consider the end ! They often anticipate a paradise and find a hell.

II. THAT WE SHOULD, THEREFORE, SO LIVE THAT SUCH REFLECTIONS MAY PROVE GRATEFUL. To this end our policy should be—1. *Pure.* (1) Such was not the policy of Jeroboam. When his people became restive under his rule, and he feared they would return to Rehoboam, instead of looking to God, he forsook Him and made Israel to sin. (2) The policy of purity is the policy of faith. Faith in God— in Christ—in truth. 2. *Peaceable.* (1) Peace is kin to purity (James iii. 17). God made peace for Jeroboam before he had departed from Him (see ch. xii. 21—24). So does He still undertake for His people (Prov. xvi. 7). (2) Wars are born of evil lusts (James iv. 1). When Jeroboam forsook the Lord, then commenced an embroilment in hostilities from which he was never free. First with Rehoboam (ver. 30), then with Abijah (2 Chron. xiii). 3. *So shall we avoid disaster.* (1) By pursuing an opposite policy Jeroboam brought disaster upon *himself.* His body was smitten by God. There is no evidence of any repentance to the saving of his soul. (2) He brought disaster upon his *family.* The best of his sons died prematurely for his sin. Two years later he perished himself. Still two years later and his race became exterminated with violence. (3) He brought disaster upon his *people.* Impatient of taxation under Rehoboam, they made him king, but got no relief, having to build palaces and sustain wars. And by their complicity in his idolatry they filled up the measure of their iniquity and incurred the anger of God, which involved them in the miseries of foreign invasion and captivity. What profit is there in a crown that is retained by the policy of sin ? The whole world is dearly purchased with the loss of the soul. J. A. M.

Ver. 13.—*Early Piety in an Unexpected Place.* (A Sermon to Young People.) Jeroboam had married in Egypt a princess named Ano. She was the elder sister of Tahpenes, the wife of Shishak, king of Egypt. Their home had been gladdened by the birth of a child, whom they brought with them on Jeroboam's return to his own tribe and country. This child, Abijah, on whom their affections and the hopes of the people were fixed, was stricken by illness, and seemed likely to die. Then the parents turned to the Lord in their trouble, for the calves at Bethel and Dan, they knew, were powerless to help them. [Note the frequency with which those who in theory deny God, or in practice forget Him, seek His help in their time of fear and grief.] They would not send to the temple at Jerusalem for several reasons ; but Jeroboam remembered the old prophet, Ahijah, who had spoken to him in the field some years before (ch. xi. 29—31), and foretold that he should rule over the ten tribes of Israel. Accordingly, Queen Ano secretly set out for Shiloh (the ancient sanctuary), where, in a humble home, the prophet lived. She disguised herself as a poor woman, and took a present such as a peasant would offer—ten loaves, two rolls for the children of the prophet, a bunch of raisins, and a jar of honey. Jeroboam hoped he might, by this deceit, get a word of hope about the dying boy, for he knew that he could not expect comfort from Ahijah, because he had grievously disobeyed his command. He feared, therefore, that if the man of God recognized Ano he would rebuke this sin. The attempt was vain. The prophet, nearly blind though he was, knew by revelation who was coming. Terrible were the words of doom he uttered about the house of Jeroboam ; and the only gleam of comfort for the parents was that in Abijah "there was found some good thing towards the Lord God of Israel," so that he should not have the curse of living to see and share the woe and shame which were coming. Abijah gives us an example of piety which is worthy of consideration, especially by the young.

I. ABIJAH'S PIETY WAS EARLY. 1. *Define piety.* It is right disposition toward God, resulting from the secret influence of God's Holy Spirit. It reveals itself in desires after what is good, and pure, and true ; in resolutions to seek these ; in prayers, through which the heart pours out its love and longing towards God. This should be more natural to us than to Abijah. He knew of God's power, we know of His love. He had heard of the Shekinah; we have heard of Jesus Christ, who says, "He that hath seen me hath seen the Father." Children ran to Jesus once, and found rest and gladness in His love; why not now? 2. *Describe early piety.* Show how it is cultivated, hindered, and revealed. Urge upon parents and teachers the importance of expecting it. We overlook the "blade," and then wonder we do not see later "the full corn in the ear." If we accept the teaching of Jesus Christ, it is evident that a child is naturally more likely than an adult to enter His kingdom. To *be* a child is a necessity; to "*become* a child" is an arduous struggle, and sometimes a sore humiliation. The door of mercy is so low that children can most easily pass through it. Happy is the home which is adorned by the presence of a child-disciple. There are those now estranged from God who may have a fulfilment of the words, "a little child shall lead them."

II. ABIJAH'S PIETY WAS SINCERE. 1. *Some good thing was* IN *him*—that is, in his heart. It was not something put on and off, like a garment; but an abiding principle, influencing the thoughts as well as the life. Nothing is more offensive to God than pretended piety. The long-faced visage which never smiles, the cant phrases which express what cannot really be honestly felt by a child, are hideous to man and God. 2. *This good thing was "toward the Lord God of Israel."* It reminds us of the phrase, "repentance towards God, and faith in the Lord Jesus Christ." We may turn from sin to *respectability*, but that is not repentance towards *God*. We may love to do right things because they please men, but this is not piety towards God. "The Lord seeth not as man seeth; for man looketh on the outward appearance, but the Lord looketh on the heart" (1 Sam. xvi. 7).

III. ABIJAH'S PIETY WAS DISCERNIBLE. "It was *found* in him." 1. *God saw it.* He spoke of it to His servant Ahijah, as of something He rejoiced to find. God is ever looking for what is good, in the world and in your heart. Though the world is corrupt, and men have done abominable works, the Lord looks down from heaven to see if there are any that understand and seek God. See Psa. xiv. 1, 2. Compare this with the Lord's parables of the woman seeking the lost piece of silver, and of the father going out to look for and meet the returning prodigal. Not only your faults and sins, but your good wishes and holy thoughts and silent prayers are recognized by God. 2. *Man saw it.* Ahijah did not proclaim his piety—that would have been offensive, especially in a child—but it was "found" in him. He was so young that he could take no active part in the service of God, and was unable publicly to oppose his father's idolatry; but his parents, and the courtiers, and the servants must have been sometimes shamed by his earnest eyes. A noiseless violet makes the hedgerow fragrant. It bewrays itself by its sweetness.

IV. ABIJAH'S PIETY WAS UNEXPECTED. He belonged to the house of Jeroboam, who made Israel to sin. His mother was probably still a heathen; his father was ambitious, cruel, and irreligious, and, so far as we know, this little boy alone, in all the court, loved the "God of Israel." His piety was the more conspicuous on this account, just as the stars are brightest when the sky is dark, and the cedars are most beautiful when surrounding trees are leafless. Describe the position of children in a godless home, with irreligious companions, &c. Even there it is not impossible to love and serve the Lord.

CONCLUSION. *It seems at first sight, especially to children, a strange reward that was given to Abijah—to die young.* But there were peculiar reasons for this. He was delivered from a sinful world, a distracted country, and evil influences; nor did he ever see those dear to him murdered and dishonoured. He was "taken away from the evil to come." If the veil were rent, and we could see the heavenly home in its beauty and sinlessness, we should understand what Paul meant when he said, "To depart and to be with Christ is far better." Every parent whose child dies in the Lord may hear amidst his sobs the words of Jesus, "Suffer the little children to come unto me, and forbid them not, for of such is the kingdom of heaven."

" Little one, precious one,
Summoned away,
Ere life's uprising sun
Dawned into day,
Gone from thy mother's arms,
Gone to the Saviour's breast,
Safe from life's rude alarms,
Blissful thy rest."   A. R.

Vers. 17, 18.—*The Dead Child*. Following the order of events as they appear
in the Hebrew text rather than in the Septuagint, we regard this as the first of the
calamities that befell the house of Jeroboam, until it became extinct on the death of
Nadab (ch. xv. 29), as the penalty of his transgression in violating the religious
unity of the nation. So soon was he made to feel that he was in the grasp of a
Power that could not be mocked or trifled with, and against which it was vain for
him to rebel. The narrative is full of touching interest, and has many points of
moral teaching. It illustrates—

I. THE TENDERNESS OF NATURAL AFFECTION EVEN IN A BAD MAN. We have no
reason to doubt that genuine parental feeling prompted both Jeroboam and his wife
in their appeal to the prophet. One cannot but sympathize with them in their
distress at the fatal sickness of their child. Human nature in its deepest degradation is not altogether lost to the touches of tender emotion. The thrill of parental
love may be found in hearts so debased and hardened that nothing else can move
them. The most ferocious savage will defend his own, and " barbarous people " are
capable of " showing no little kindness " even to strangers (Acts xxviii.) But in
many cases there is no real moral worth in these affections and amenities. They
can scarcely be called " redeeming qualities." Parental feeling is often little else
than an animal instinct. It may exist side by side with the most grovelling passions and the most complete moral obliquity. Jeroboam loved his child, and yet,
in proud self-will and impious defiance of the Divine authority, he could secure his
own carnal ends at the cost of the utter spiritual degradation of the people.

II. THE BLINDNESS OF A SINFUL INFATUATION. The king flies in his distress to
the prophet whom he has long slighted and ignored. He sought no counsel from
him in the setting up of the golden calves at Dan and Bethel. But now, as if he
had himself fulfilled all the conditions of the Divine promise, he thinks to get from
the prophet a word to confirm his hope of a " sure house " (ch. xi. 38). Such is the
folly of human nature. When the shadow of adversity falls on men they try, with
something like a superstitious impulse, to get consolation from religious sources
which, in the time of their prosperity, they neglected and despised. But what could
Jeroboam expect from the oracle of a God whom he sinned against so grievously but
" heavy tidings " respecting his child ? He bids his wife " feign herself to be another
woman ; " but how could he dream that a prophet, who had power to read the
future, would not be able to penetrate the false disguise ? Thus, when men's hearts
are " set in them to do evil " do they resort to vain subterfuges, and flatter themselves with a delusive hope. Thus do they often rush blindly on their own condemnation and ruin ; provoking, and even antedating, the very calamities they have
so much cause to dread.

III. THE CURSE OF SIN ON THE SACRED RELATIONSHIPS OF LIFE. It is terribly
expressive of the hatefulness, in God's sight, of Jeroboam's impiety that the very
flower and crown of his house should be thus stricken—the fairest and the best,
the one who seemed likely to justify his name Abijah (" Jehovah is my Father ")
—because already in his young heart there was found " some good thing towards
the Lord God of Israel." So is it often in the course of human history. The evil
men do comes back to them, not only in divers forms of retribution, but often in
the form of penalties that pierce them in the tenderest part. The dearest ties of
life are broken. Or they see their own moral deformity reflected in those whom
they would fain shield from its bitter consequences. Or their brightest hopes are
withered at the root, and that which might have been, and was intended to be, the
source of the purest earthly joy becomes the occasion of keenest sorrow.

IV. THE BLENDING OF AN ELEMENT OF MERCY WITH GOD'S SEVEREST JUDGMENTS. We see here how the innocent suffer with the guilty. The iniquity of the fathers is visited upon the children (Exod. xx. 5). Yet to the child himself, in this instance, it was a gracious visitation. (1) He was emphatically "taken from the evil to come." (2) His incipient piety was recognized and crowned by this translation to a happier sphere. (3) It was his special privilege to die a natural and not a violent death—the only one of the house of Jeroboam who should "go to the grave in peace." Thus in the darkest Divine judgment there is a gleam of mercy. There is "light in the cloud." It has a "silver lining." The sufferings of innocent children, and the fact that so large a proportion of the human race die in infancy, are dark mysteries to us. But even here we see the dispensation of an all-wise Love, remembering Him who said, "It is not the will of your Father in heaven that one of these little ones should perish" (Matt. xviii. 14). "Suffer the little children to come unto me, and forbid them not; for of such is the kingdom of God" (Mark x. 14).—W.

Vers. 1—20.—*Affliction and judgment.* I. THE STRICKEN KING. Abijah seems to have been heir to the throne, and to have been alike the king's and the people's hope. The father's heart was touched: the king saw the dynasty threatened, to establish which he had ventured so much. The voice of God, against which the ear was closed, will be heard again in the quietness of the sick chamber, in the silence of death. God follows us through deepening sorrows, if haply we may turn ere we are overwhelmed by the waters of destruction.
II. THE RESORT FOR HELP. 1. *His trouble drives him towards God.* It is meant to do this. It is the touching of God's hand that we may look up and live.

> "Eyes which the preacher could not school
> By wayside graves are raisèd,
> And lips cry, 'God be pitiful,'
> Which ne'er said, 'God be praisèd.'"

2. *He is drawn by the remembrance of past mercy.* "Behold, there is Ahijah the prophet, who told me that I should be king over this people." The remembrances of mercies are cords to draw back straying hearts to God. The thought of what God has done makes a holy place for faith, and rears an altar whence may rise the incense of accepted prayer. 3. *His hope is defeated by his own deceit.* "Disguise thyself, that thou be not known as the wife of Jeroboam." He thought he might find help without owning and yielding his sin. How many prayers are like Jeroboam's embassy! Men wish to find mercy and yet cling to their sinful life, and imagine that because their wicked practices are kept behind their back they are not there in God's sight! 4. Gifts (ver. 3) could not make up the lack of a true, penitent heart.
III. THE LORD'S ANSWER. 1. *Disguise is impossible before God* (vers. 5, 6). We can conceal nothing from Him; and one word of His ("Come in, thou wife of Jeroboam!") is enough to rend every veil of pretence from the soul and overwhelm it with shame. We may now close the ears to the voice of accusing conscience, but we go onward, as she went, to where the Judge will name us. 2. *God's name.* "The Lord God *of Israel.*" Not only will the covering be torn from the sinner's heart and life; God will be revealed. He is the mighty avenger of those who have been seduced and sinned against. 3. *Jeroboam's ingratitude* (vers. 7—9). He was taken from among the people, and yet he had shown no anxiety to discharge aright the duties of the high office committed to him. (1) Human patterns were despised ("Thou hast not been as my servant David"). (2) God Himself was cast behind his back. 4. *The doom.* (1) There was deepest dishonour for *him.* His house was overthrown and removed as the vilest refuse. (2) There was destruction for his people. For the impenitent and all who are led by them there is, and can be, only utter and eternal ruin.
IV. THE SHADOW OF FALLING JUDGMENT (vers. 17—20). 1. *Abijah's death.* The light of the home, the hope of the land, is taken. 2. *Jeroboam's death.* "The Lord struck him and he died" (2 Chron. xiii. 20). The clear intellect and the strong

hand are smitten and removed. Slowly but surely the word advances to its accomplishment. Are there no shadows of judgment on thy path? Have no words come true that make thy heart tremble because of those other words which God's lips have also spoken?—J. U.

EXPOSITION.

CHAPTER XIV. 21—31.

THE REIGN OF REHOBOAM.—Ver. 21.—**And Rehoboam, the son of Solomon, reigned in Judah. Rehoboam was forty** [or twenty. See on ch. xii. 1] **and one years old when he began to reign, and he reigned** [this reign is related at greater length in 2 Chron. xi., xii.] **seventeen years** [cf. ch. xv. 1] **in Jerusalem, the city which the Lord did choose** [cf. ch. xi. 36; Psa. lxxviii. 68; Neh. i. 9] **out of all the tribes of Israel** [cf. 2 Chron. vi. 6; 2 Kings xxi. 7] **to put his name there.** The historian reminds us that Jerusalem was by God's appointment the religious centre of the land; that Bethel and Dan were no sanctuaries of His choosing; and that, however much the realm of Rehoboam was restricted, he still reigned in the capital of God's choice. It is possible the words have some reference to the next verse, and imply that, though it was the holy city, yet even there they fell away from God (Bähr). **And his mother's name was Naamah** [or, according to the LXX., Naanan. See on ch. xii. 24], **an** [Heb. *the*, *i.e.*, the well-known] **Ammonitess.** [The name of the mother is given with every king of Judah, principally because of the position of influence she occupied in the kingdom. See on ch. ii. 13, and ver. 31 below.]

Ver. 22.—**And Judah did evil in the sight of the Lord** [not, however, before the *fourth* year of Rehoboam's reign. For the first three years the nation remained steadfast in the faith, and the kingdom was greatly strengthened and consolidated. The defection commenced when Rehoboam began to feel himself secure (2 Chron. xii. 1). It is to be observed, however, that the historian says "Judah" (not Rehoboam) "did evil," &c. It is probable that a considerable section of the *people* approved of the idolatrous practices introduced in the preceding reign, and that Rehoboam was unable to repress them. It was his misfortune to have to reap the bitter fruits of Solomon's unfaithfulness], **and they provoked him to jealousy** [Heb. *made him jealous*. Same word, Exod. xx. 5; xxxiv. 14; Num. v. 14. The words of the covenant proclaimed the Lord a "jealous God." This is of course anthropomorphic language. The nation was regarded as the bride of Jehovah, and God is said to be made jealous, because idolatry was unfaithfulness to Him. The worship of Baal and Ashtoreth, it must be remembered, involved unutterable *immoralities*, hence the special fitness of the word, which is only used of idolatry of one kind or other] **with their sins which they had committed** [Heb. *sinned*] **above all that their fathers had done.**

Ver. 23.—**For they also** [*i.e.*, they as well as the ten tribes] **built them high places** [*i.e.*, houses of high places. See on ch. iii. 2 and xiii. 32] **and images** [Heb. *pillars* or *statues* (מַצֵּבוֹת; LXX., στήλας). These were, no doubt, originally memorial pillars or stones, erected to commemorate some Divine manifestation, and with no thought of idolatry (see Gen. xxxi. 13; xxxv. 14, 20; xxviii. 18). But the Canaanites erected pillars, which were also statues or images, to their god, Baal. Hence we read of the "image" (מַצְבָה) of Baal (2 Kings iii. 2; x. 26, 27; cf. xviii. 4; xxiii. 14); and hence also we find such images frequently mentioned side by side with the so-called "groves," *i.e.*, the "Asherahs" (ver. 15; Exod. xxxiv. 13; Deut. vii. 5; xii. 3; xvi. 21, &c.) Both the *Mazzebah* and the *Asherah*, consequently, was an upright pillar or post, but the former was of stone, the latter of wood; the former dedicated to Baal, the god of nature, of generation; the latter to Ashtoreth, the goddess of nature and productive power. The gradual transition of the memorial pillar into the Baal statue is hinted at in Levit. xxvi. 1. It is observable that these idolatrous and immoral rites seem to have found a home in Judah before they were introduced into Israel **and groves** [*Asherahs*, idols; see on ver. 15. This verse proves conclusively that the translation "grove" is a mistaken one] **on every high hill, and under every green tree.** [The phrase is from the Pentateuch, Deut. xii. 2; cf. Jer. ii. 20; iii. 6; Hosea iv. 13. "Probably the evil example of Maachah, his favourite wife (2 Chron. xi. 20—22), whose idolatrous tastes were displayed under Asa (2 Chron. xv. 16), was not without a pernicious effect on Rehoboam" (Wordsworth).]

Ver. 24.—**And there were also Sodomites** [קָדֵשׁ, a collective noun = הַקְּדֵשִׁים (ch. xv. 12) = consecrated persons or devotees, because they were set apart to the service of

Astarte, the *Dea Syria*. It is clear from Deut. xxiii. 18 (Heb.) that *male* prostitutes are here spoken of, the name of the female being קְדֵשָׁה. The former is described in ver. 19 *l.c.* as a *dog*, the latter as a *whore*] **in the land** [cf. ch. xv. 12. It is highly probable that these infamous persons were of Canaanite or Phœnician origin (this being a Phœnician superstition, Movers, " Phöniz." i. 671), but it is somewhat precarious to found an assertion to that effect on these last words (as Bähr)], **and** [Heb. omits *and*] **they did according to all the abominations of the nations** [see Levit. xviii., xx.; Deut. xviii. 9—12] **which the Lord cast out before the children of Israel.** [" Here we see a reason for God's command, requiring the extirpation of the Canaanites " (Wordsworth).]

Ver. 25.—And it came to pass in the fifth year [that is, two years after king and people forsook the law of the Lord (2 Chron. xii. 1). Retribution seems to have overtaken Judah sooner than Israel. They had the less excuse, and they seem to have plunged deeper into idolatry and immorality (see Homiletics, p. 335)] **of King Rehoboam, that Shishak king of Egypt** [to whom Jeroboam had fled (ch. xi. 26, 40)] **came up against Jerusalem.** [This expedition is related with somewhat more of detail in 2 Chron. xii. 2—4. For Shishak, see ch. xi. 40. It was in the twentieth year of his reign that Shishak, once Jeroboam's protector and friend, invaded Palestine. It has been conjectured (Ewald, *al.*) that he was incited so to do by Jeroboam, and that the two kings waged war against Judah in concert (see on ver. 30). But as to this Scripture is silent; and moreover, if Jeroboam summoned Shishak to his assistance, it is certain that his own kingdom did not altogether escape invasion; and it is perhaps more probable that the divided and weakened state of the country seemed to promise the Egyptian king an easy capture of Jerusalem, of the treasures of which he had doubtless heard. It is well known that a record of this expedition exists in the sculptures and inscriptions of the great temple at Karnak. The *bassi relievi* of the temple wall contain over 130 figures, representatives, as the names on the shields show, of so many conquered cities. Amongst these are found three of the " cities for defence " which Rehoboam had built, viz., Shoco, Adoraim, and Aijalon (2 Chron. xi. 7—10), while many other towns of Palestine, such as Gibeon, Taanach, Shunem, Megiddo, &c., are identified with more or less of probability. One feature in the list is remarkable, viz., the number of Levitical and Canaanite cities—cities of *Israel*

—which Shishak is said to have conquered. The usual inference is that such cities, although in Jeroboam's dominions, had nevertheless held out against his rule—the former for religious reasons; the latter, perhaps, in the effort to recover their independence. Mr. Poole, however (Dict. Bib., art. " Egypt "), accounts for the names on the supposition that Shishak directed his forces against the northern as well as the southern kingdom, and certainly this seems to agree better with the facts. It is hardly likely that Jeroboam, with the army at his command, would tolerate so many centres of disaffection in his midst. Besides, the Levites, we are told, had migrated in a body to Judah; and the Canaanites at this period can hardly have been in a position to defy any Hebrew monarch. The silence alike of our historian and of the chronicler as to the invasion of Israel is easily accounted for by the fact that Judah bore the brunt of the war.]

Ver. 26.—And he took away the treasures of the house of the Lord [The historian omits to mention the interposition of Shemaiah (2 Chron. xii. 5—8). The account of the Chronicles is altogether much fuller], **and the treasures of the king's house; he even took away all** [rather, " *and everything* (*sc.* that he could lay his hands on) *he took away*." The spoil must have been enormous] : **and he took away all the shields of gold** [cf. ch. x. 17] **which Solomon had made.**

Ver. 27.—And king Rehoboam made in their stead brazen shields [lit., shields of brass or copper; a striking token of the decadence of the kingdom; cf. ch. ix. 28 ; x. 22. " He changed his father's religion, as his shields, from gold to brass " (Hall)], **and committed** [Heb. *appointed*] **them unto the hands of the chief of the guard** [Heb. *commanders of the runners* (see on ch. i. 38)], **which kept the door of the king's house.** [Cf. 2 Kings xi. 6. The functions of the body-guard were very varied. A primary duty was, obviously, to supply sentinels and attendants for the palace.]

Ver. 28.—And it was so, when the king went unto the house of the Lord, that the guards [*runners*] **bare them** [Whatever idolatries Rehoboam tolerated or encouraged, it is clear that he maintained the temple worship with great pomp and circumstance. The state visits of the Sultan to the Mosque may perhaps be best compared with these processions. Ewald sees in this circumstance a proof of Rehoboam's vanity. The brazen shields were " borne before him in solemn procession, as if everything were the same as before "], **and brought them back into the guard chamber**

[Heb. "*chamber of the runners*." Solomon's golden shields were kept "in the house of the forest of Lebanon" (ch. x. 17). These shields of brass were of so little value that the guard chamber sufficed for their custody.

Ver. 29.—**Now the rest of the acts of Rehoboam, and all that he did, are they not written in the book of the chronicles of the kings of Judah?** [See on ver. 19.]

Ver. 30.—**And there was war** [cf. 2 Chron. xii. 15, "wars." Keil argues from the prohibition of war by Shemaiah (ch. xii. 23) that this must mean "hostility, enmity." But מִלְחָמָה surely implies more than angry feelings or a hostile attitude; and it is highly probable that, even if there were no organized campaigns, a desultory warfare was constantly carried on on the borders of the two kingdoms. It is also possible that Jeroboam took a part in the war of Shishak] **between Rehoboam and Jeroboam all their days.**

Ver. 31.—**And Rehoboam slept with his fathers** [The same formula as in ch. ii. 10; xi. 43; xv. 8, 24, &c. It is used of nearly all the kings of Judah], **and was buried with his fathers** [These words go to prove, against Gesenius, that the phrase "slept (lit., *lay down*) with his fathers" is not to be interpreted of Sheol, but of the grave; see on ch. ii. 10] **in the city of David. And his mother's name was Naamah, an Ammonitess.** [Same words as in ver. 21. The repetition can hardly be, as Bähr, Wordsworth, al., imagine, designed, in order to show that the worship of Moloch was brought by her to Jerusalem (ch. xi. 7), and that she exercised a sinister influence upon her son. As she is twice called "the Ammonitess" it can hardly be doubted that she was one of the "Ammonitesses" (ch. xi. 1, Heb.) who turned away Solomon's heart; and it is also certain that Rehoboam did not inherit his folly from his father. At the same time these words are more easily accounted for on the supposition that the historian found them in this position in one or more of the documents from which he compiled his history. It is also to be remembered that some of these chronological statements are manifestly by a later hand, and have been transferred from the margin to the text. See on ch. vi. 1.] **And Abijam** [elsewhere called *Abijah* (2 Chron. xii. 16; xiii. 1), or *Abijahu* (2 Chron. xiii. 21, Heb.) Some MSS. have Abijah here. The variation is not easily accounted for except as a clerical error. The supposition of Lightfoot that the name was designedly altered by the historian to avoid the incorporation of the sacred JAH into the name of a bad man is too fanciful, the more so as Abijam was by no means an exceptionally bad king. It is, however, approved by Bähr and Rawlinson. But it is as little probable that Abijam is the original form of the name (Keil). The form *Abijahu*, the LXX. 'Αβιού, and the analogy of *Abiel* (1 Sam. ix. 1) all make against this idea. On the whole, it is more likely that Abijam results from an error of transcription, ה and the final ם being easily confounded] **his son reigned in his stead.**

HOMILETICS.

Ver. 25.—*The Invasion of Shishak.* Three years after the death of David, the foundations of the temple, the glory of that age—some have called it *orbis miraculum*, the marvel of every age—were laid. Four years after the death of Solomon his son—some forty years, that is to say, after its foundation, three and thirty years after its completion, according to some only twenty years after its dedication—the treasures of that temple, its gold and gems, were carried off by an invader. A short time after his accession, again, Solomon made alliance with the strongest and proudest of the empires of that age, with Egypt, and a Hebrew, one whose forefathers were Pharaoh's bondmen, was gladly recognized as great Pharaoh's son-in-law. A short time after his death, this same Egyptian kingdom is become an assailant of Solomon's son, and Pharaoh is turned to be the oppressor and plunderer of his realm. For a great part of Solomon's reign it was the boast of the people that an Egyptian princess occupied one of his splendid palaces in Jerusalem, but he has not been long dead before those same palaces are rifled by Egyptian princes, and Jerusalem is environed by the legions of Shishak.

And yet that temple, the magnificence of which has been so short-lived, which was hardly completed ere it was despoiled, was built to the name of the Lord, and as a habitation for the mighty God of Jacob. And as such it was accepted by Him. That house had had a greater glory and consecration than of gold and precious stones, for "the glory of the Lord had filled the house of the Lord" (ch. viii. 11). Why, then, is it, we may well ask, as the men of that age would ask, that it is so soon left comparatively desolate? Cannot the Deity to whom it was dedicated protect it against spoliation. Or have His worshippers provoked Him to anger, so that He has "abhorred his sanctuary," and "delivered his glory into the enemies' hand"?

For we may be quite sure that there was a profound reason for this profound dishonour and disgrace. We cannot account for the fact that the temple of the Lord, the "house of the great God" (Ezra v. 8), was stripped bare and left a wreck within a few years of its erection, on the supposition that a chance happened to it, and that it only suffered as other shrines have done from the vicissitudes of fortune and the impartial, inevitable havoc of war. "*In rebus bellicis*," it has been said, "*maxime dominatur Fortuna*." But if we feel at liberty to interpret other histories by a theory of chance, that idea must be excluded in thinking of *God's* people. If their history was fortuitous, then the Old Testament is a delusion. No; we may not be able always to trace the finger of God in profane history, but it will be passing strange if we cannot recognize it here.

Now the *immediate* cause of the invasion was, no doubt, the divided and therefore weakened state of the kingdom. We might have been tempted to think that Jeroboam had summoned his patron Shishak to his aid, had we not proof that Israel as well as Judah suffered from this campaign. And of course it *is* possible that Jeroboam instigated a war which ultimately extended to his own kingdom. But it is obvious that Shishak would need no invitation to attack Jerusalem. The fame of its immense treasure is quite sufficient of itself to account for his advance. So long as it was guarded by the armies of Solomon it was secure. But Rehoboam, whose troops would not number a third of his father's, and who was paralyzed by the hostility of Israel crouching like a wild beast on his northern border, offered an easy prey to a general with 1,200 chariots and 60,000 horsemen, and "people without number" under his command.

We see, then, that it was the treasures of the Holy City—the vast accumulation of the precious metals—which excited the cupidity of the Egyptians, while their defenceless state suggested the idea of seizing them. Observe here—

I. THE RETRIBUTION OF SOLOMON'S SIN. 1. *Of his greed and pride.* He has "multiplied silver and gold to himself" only to provoke an invasion of his territory and the humiliation of his people. If he had obeyed the law; if he had been content to embellish the house of the Lord and leave the palaces alone; if his overweening pride and his insatiable thirst for fame had not prompted him to amass treasures which excited universal attention, it is probable that Judah would have escaped invasion. In this case "pride has gone before destruction." The very magnitude of his treasures led to their dispersion.

2. *Of his idolatry.* We have already seen how this sin (ch. xi. 5—8) was punished by the partition of his realm. In the plunder of his palaces, provoked and made possible by that division, we see a further recompense of his outrage and defiance of the Almighty. The hills on which his idol altars were erected now swarmed with idolaters, assembled not to sacrifice, but to slay. We are reminded here of the retribution which befell the Jerusalem of a later day. On one of the hills before Jerusalem the Jews raised a cross—they crucified the Prince of Life. On all the hills that are round about Jerusalem, the Romans raised crosses, the crosses of His murderers (Jos., Bell. Jud. v. 11. 1).

3. *Of his multiplication of horses.* For it is to be remembered from what quarter the retribution came. There is an exquisite judicial propriety in an invasion from Egypt, and an invasion of chariots and horses. This was *re-taliation* in the proper sense of the word ; it was like for like. Why, there was almost a beaten track made for those same chariots by the horses and chariots which Solomon had imported in such prodigious numbers. Literally the trade horses paved the way for the horses of war. This illegal traffic had long since familiarized Egyptian charioteers with the shortest way to the Holy City.

4. *Of his multiplication of wives.* Solomon's lawful wife came from Egypt. Had he been true to her, he would probably have been true to his Lord God (ch. xi. 3), and so his realm would have escaped invasion. It is a kind of Nemesis

for the wrong done to his Egyptian consort that his harem was plundered by Egyptians. There are those who connect Napoleon's fall with the repudiation of Josephine. The "judge of the widow" (Psa. lxviii. 5) is also the avenger of the injured and dishonoured wife (Heb. xiii. 4). Human laws seldom take cognizance of these, the deepest of wrongs, but the cry of the heart-broken woman goes up into the ears of One who has said, " *I* will repay."

II. The punishment of Rehoboam's folly and sin. 1. *Of his obstinacy.* For in the first place, but for his infatuation, humanly speaking, the kingdom would have escaped division, and the land would have escaped invasion. That infatuation, it is true, was the product of his breeding and his training, but that consideration does not wholly exonerate him from blame. No man can charge his parents or surroundings with his sin. The law does not excuse the thief on the ground that from infancy he has been taught to steal. Rehoboam was a free agent, and ought to have acted otherwise, and doubtless he knew it when it was too late.

2. *Of his pride.* It was his pride had rejected all compromise, and had prated of scorpions, &c. It had been humbled once in the dismemberment of his realm. It must be humbled again in the spoliation of his palaces. For observe, it was when he " had strengthened himself" (2 Chron. xii. 1) that Shishak came to prove his weakness. St. Paul is not the only one who has had to learn the lesson, " When I am *weak*, then am I strong." It is extremely probable that this vain-glorious prince, after losing most of his realm, still piqued himself on the abundance of his treasures. His trust was in his shields of gold. So he must be reduced to shields of pinchbeck.

3. *Of his infidelity.* " He forsook the law of the Lord" (2 Chron. *l.c.*) Much as his father had done before him. " What the old sing," says the German proverb, " the young chirp." That is to say, he still worshipped Jehovah (ver. 28 ; cf. ch. ix. 25), but he sanctioned, or did not suppress, idolatry. The son of an Ammonitess, he would find it difficult to trample on the gods of his mother (ch. xi. 5), and he was probably too much afraid of another insurrection to stamp out the abominations of vers. 23, 24.

III. The recompense of Israel's idolatries. Though the chronicler informs us that Rehoboam " forsook the law and *all Israel with him*," yet it seems probable from vers. 22, 24, " *And Judah* did evil," &c., that he rather followed than led his people. He could hardly fail, at first, to see that his strength lay in a rigid adherence to the law ; that his policy was one of piety. The Levites and others who streamed into Judah, shocked by the innovations of Jeroboam, cannot fail to have suggested that his *rôle* was orthodoxy. It is probable, therefore, that it was not until a large section of his people, infected with the superstitions and vices they had learned in Solomon's reign, clamoured for the tolerance of shameful shrines, that he yielded to idolatry. Ver. 25 seems to connect the invasion directly with the people's sin. But for the high places and images. &c., the land would have been spared this humiliation. It is to be carefully noted that, so long as king and people served the Lord, Shishak was held back from attacking them. Hence we understand why Judah receives earlier and greater stripes than Israel. It was Jeroboam made Israel to sin. It was Judah made Rehoboam to sin. The guilty people, accordingly, are punished by the invasion of their land and the spoliation of their treasure ; the guilty king by the destruction of his house. And here again, let us observe, how significant that the chastisement should come from Egypt. Time was when God had punished the idolatries of Egypt through the instrumentality of the Jewish people (Exod. vii.—xiv.) Now the tables are turned, and Egypt is employed to avenge the idolatries of Judah. This was the first time that an Egyptian army had crossed their border—the first time, indeed, that the land had sustained the brunt of any invasion. It was the Sodomites and the like had drawn forth those swords from their scabbards. What a contrast between Exod. xiv. and 1 Kings xiv. Israel, who then " saw the Egyptians dead upon the sea-shore," now feels the grip of Pharaoh at his throat, and the iron of Pharaoh in his soul.

HOMILIES BY VARIOUS AUTHORS.

Vers. 21—24.—*The Sin of Judah.* Having discoursed of Jeroboam and the kingdom of Israel, the sacred historian now returns to Rehoboam and the sister kingdom of Judah. To have found a better state of things here would have been refreshing, but in this we are disappointed. How fearful was the moral state of the whole world in those days!

I. JUDAH HAD FALLEN INTO THE GROSSEST IDOLATRY. 1. *He had multiplied high places.* (1) High places were not necessarily for idolatry. They were proper to the worship of the true God in patriarchal times. (2) Even after God had chosen Jerusalem to put His name there, the patriarchal use of high places was upon special occasions sanctioned by Him (see ch. xviii. 38). (3) In Judah there was little need for these, since the extremity of the kingdom was not very remote from Jerusalem. The distance to Beersheba would be about forty British statute miles. (4) But the high places of Judah were mainly designed for idolatry. Hence their association in the text with " images and groves " and rites of Sodomites and other Canaanitish abominations. 2. *He had built many temples.* (1) The term (מצבות) here translated " images " is elsewhere commonly rendered *pillars* (see Gen. xxviii. 18; xxxi. 51; xxxv. 20; Exod. xxiv. 4; Isa. xix. 19). It is far from evident that this word is ever used for any image or figured thing. In places where it is construed " images," *pillars* would give as good sense (see Exod. xxiii. 24; 2 Kings x. 26, 27). Marginal readings bear this out (see Deut. vii. 5; xvi. 22). (2) It is probable these pillars were distributed in ranks, as those of the Druids at Stonehenge and Abiry, to serve as temples in which the powers of the material heavens were worshipped. 3. *He had enshrined idols in these.* (1) The Asherim (אשרים) are here evidently misrendered " groves; " for how could groves be planted " under every green tree " ? (See Homily on vers. 15, 16, *supra*.) (2) They were idols apparently in figure like goats. For Jeroboam " ordained him priests for the high places and for the devils (שעירים *goats*), and for the calves which he had made " (2 Chron. xi. 15). Here we have no mention of *Asherim;* of *goats*, however, we have mention. But when Josiah destroyed these things, there is mention of the *Asherah*, but no mention of the *goat* (compare 2 Kings xxiii. 15). The Asherah destroyed by Josiah appears, then, to be the goat which Jeroboam had set up. (3) These Asherim, or Asheroth—for they appear to have been male and female idols—were supposed to convey blessings to their worshippers, and hence their name (from אשר to *proceed*, to *bless*). 4. *His idolatry was attended with shocking rites.* (1) They were the very abominations for which the land had spewed out the Canaanites as with abhorrence (see Levit. xviii. 28; xx. 22, and contexts). (2) Conspicuous amongst these were the Sodomites, whose orgies were intimately connected with the Asherim, and to encourage which the women wove hangings (see 2 Kings xxiii. 7). How fruitful in inventions is the wickedness of the heart! (Eccles. vii. 29.)

II. FOR HIS DEGENERACY HE WAS WITHOUT EXCUSE. 1. *He had Jerusalem for his capital.* (1) This was the city chosen of God out of all the tribes of Israel to put His name there. The temple of Jehovah was there, and the Shekinah of Jehovah was in it. (2) Every appliance for acceptable worship was there at hand. The altars were there; the priesthood was there; the appointed assemblies, festival and ferial, were there. (3) They sinned, therefore, " before the face of the Lord," as in His very presence. Even more so than Israel, who could not now claim Jerusalem for his capital, though he was still bound to go there to worship. Let us remember that God is ever near us; this thought will restrain our truancy. 2. *He had a son of David for his king.* (1) The mother of Rehoboam, indeed, was an Ammonitess. This is emphatically (twice) mentioned. She was one of those strange women who had turned the heart of Solomon from the right way. The abomination of her country was Milcom or Molech, whose rites were most ferocious and demoralizing. (2) But against these influences were noble traditions on the other side. His father, in the beginning of his reign, was illustrious in wisdom and zeal for the God of Israel. The memories of his grandfather were glorious. To this must be added the most material circumstance that the Covenant was with his house; for Messiah Himself was to be the Son of David. (3) These things were not without their influence. For three years after the revolution under Jeroboam, Rehoboam governed Judah in the fear of God, and so established his throne (see 2 Chron. xi. 17). (4) When, after this, Rehoboam " forsook the law of the Lord," his subjects should have dissuaded him and, if necessary, resisted him. But they went "with him" (2 Chron. xii. 2). (5) To such excesses did they go that they " sinned above their fathers in provoking the Lord to jealousy."—J. A. M.

Vers. 25—31.—*The Entailments of Sin.* During the three first years of his reign in Judah, Rehoboam walked in the steps of Solomon and David, enjoyed peace, and became established in his throne. Afterwards he gave himself up to idolatrous abominations, and brought evil upon himself and upon his people. The entailments of their sin were—

I. TROUBLE. 1. *There was continual war between the kingdoms.* (1) While they remained faithful to God they had peace. God interposed to preserve peace by the hand of Shemaiah (ch. xii. 21—24). (2) But when they forsook the Lord, they soon got to strife, which continued as long as the kings lived (ver. 30). This strife was also handed down to their successors. (3) Thus sinners become God's instruments to punish one another. So it is seen to this day in the contentions and litigations of individuals. Men are slow to see the hand of God. 2. *Shishak aggravated the mischief.* (1) The influences which brought him upon the scene may be discerned. Hadad, who occasioned so much trouble to Solomon, was Shishak's brother-in-law. Shishak was thus disposed to give asylum to Jeroboam when he fled for his life from Solomon. Shishak now conspires with Jeroboam to ruin Rehoboam. (2) The array brought against Judah by Shishak was formidable (see 2 Chron. xii. 3). It would have been crushing had not Rehoboam and his people, in their extremity, humbled themselves before God (2 Chron. xii. 7). (3) But they still had to feel the smart of their sins.

II. FORFEITURE. 1. *In war there is always loss.* (1) Necessarily there is the forfeiture of *peace.* Who can estimate the value of peace? Perfect peace is the resultant of perfect harmony as the white light is composed of all the colours in the iris. (2) There is the loss of *property.* Labour is the source of wealth: the labour withdrawn from industry to wage war is so much loss of wealth. The soldier also is a consumer. When he does not provide for his own sustenance, the labour of others must be taxed to feed him. (3) There is the loss of *life.* War is seldom bloodless. Often the slaughter is fearful. Wellington is reported to have said that the calamity next in severity to a defeat is a victory. 2. *Shishak despoiled the temple of its treasure.* (1) The booty here was enormous. The spoils of David's victories were there; also the accumulations of Solomon's peaceful commerce. (2) The shields of gold that Solomon had made are particularly mentioned. It is added that Rehoboam had brazen shields made to replace them. How sin reduces the fine gold to brass! 3. *Shishak also rifled the palace.* (1) The treasures here also were immense. Perhaps there never was such plunder as this in human annals. (2) Rehoboam handed down a diminished inheritance to his son. By his folly he alienated ten tribes of his nation from his kingdom. Abijam likewise succeeded to a kingdom greatly impoverished. He became heir also to embroilments. The entailments of sin pursue the spirit into the invisible world. Forfeiture. Trouble.—J. A. M.

Vers. 21—31.—*Unfaithfulness and its rebuke.* I. JUDAH'S SIN. 1. *The nature of the transgression.* The grossest idolatry was set side by side with the pure worship of God. The temple and its services were still His (ver. 28), but on every high hill and under every green tree were the images and altars of the false gods. The preservation of the pure worship of God is no proof that all is yielded which God demands. The heart may be full of the world's idolatries, of its covetousness and lust and manifold sin. 2. *Its enormity.* (1) It was wrought *in Jerusalem,*

" the city which the Lord did choose," &c., and this, too, in the face of the defection of the ten tribes. It is high treason against Jehovah when those whom He has called and honoured are faithless to the trust committed to them. It is the darkest crime against God and man to betray the last earthly refuge of the truth. (2) It was done after an interval of repentance and religious zeal (2 Chron. xi. 17; xii. 1). They had known and yet forsaken the better way. (3) Their idolatry was more unrestrained and daring than any that Israel had ever known (ver. 22). 3. *Its fruits* (ver. 24). Errors in worship become vices in life. The soul that is cut off from the fountain of life must needs break out into corruption.

II. JUDAH'S CHASTISEMENT. It inflicted deep humiliation and loudly proclaimed God's indignation. 1. *It was inflicted by an old and beaten foe.* Their temple songs, celebrating the ancient triumph over "Rahab," must have deepened their shame. 2. *The holy city and the temple itself were spoiled.* God loathed their holy things. We need not marvel that rationalism and infidelity are rampant in a faithless, worldly Church. It is God's way. Israel's idolatry is punished by Egypt's triumph. 3. *It left its mark in enduring poverty* (vers. 26—28). The splendour passed away from the royal pomp, and doubtless also from the temple service. The nation and Church which Egypt has spoiled, whose faith has been shaken by doubt, or swallowed up in unbelief, have lost their strength and glory. They are but the shadows of what a true and pure faith once made them.—J. U.

EXPOSITION.

CHAPTER XV. 1—24.

THE REIGNS OF ABIJAM AND ASA, KINGS OF JUDAH.

The Reign of Abijam.

Ver. 1. — **Now in the eighteenth year of king Jeroboam, the son of Nebat, reigned Abijam** [see note on ch. xiv. 31. It is implied in 2 Chron. xi. 20—22 that he was not the first-born among Rehoboam's twenty-eight sons, but the eldest son of the favourite wife. As he left behind him thirty-eight children (2 Chron. xiii. 21) at his decease, some three years later, he must have been of considerable age at his accession. This consideration rather favours the idea that Rehoboam was "*forty* and one years old when he began to reign" (*ib.*, xii. 13)] **over Judah.**

Ver. 2.—**Three years** [The Alex. LXX. says δεκαεξ, *sixteen*. The "three years" are not to be interpreted strictly. As he ascended the throne in the eighteenth and died in the twentieth year of Jeroboam's reign, he cannot have completed three years. But it does not follow that "he cannot have reigned much more than two years" (Rawlinson, and similarly Keil). He may have reigned all but three] **reigned he in Jerusalem. And his mother's name was Maachah** [in 2 Chron. xiii. 2 called *Michaiah*, Heb. *Michajahu*. That the same person is meant is proved as well by the context as by 2 Chron. xi. 21, where the name is given as here. Keil (cf. Dict. Bib. ii. 162) ascribes the discrepancy to an error of the copyist; but the names are so unlike in the original as to discountenance this assump-

tion. I venture to suggest that *Michajahu* was the significant form—the word means "Who is like Jehovah?"—which the name Maachah, "oppression," borne by the Geshurite princess who married David (2 Sam. iii. 3) assumed when she joined the *Lord's* people, and embraced, as no doubt she would do, the religion of Jehovah. Such a change would be quite in accordance with the genius and traditions of the Semitic races (Gen. xvii. 5, 15; xxx. *passim;* xxxii. 28; xli. 45; Exod. vi. 3, &c. Cf. 2 Kings xxiii. 34; xxiv. 17; Hosea i. 4, 6), and there may well have been special reasons in this case, apart from the piety of David, why it should be made. For the name Maachah appears to have been taken from the town and district of that name near Geshur— a part of Syria was called *Syria Maachah* (1 Chron. xix. 6; cf. 2 Sam. x. 6—8). In 2 Sam. xx. 14, 15 we read of a district of *Beth Maachah*—and it not improbably witnessed to unhappy memories. How natural it would be that David's bride should take a name of better omen and of a religious import, and how natural that the grand-daughter who bore her name should be called by that name in both its forms. Since writing the above, I find that a somewhat similar idea has occurred long since to others. Both Kimchi and Jarchi hold that she had two names. It is supposed by some that she assumed the name *Michaiah*, as more dignified, on becoming queen. Wordsworth thinks that Michaiah was her real name, and that it was degraded into Maachah when she was deposed for idolatry. This latter view dovetails with the one suggested above. It would be quite in accordance with Jewish usages and habits of thought that the name which had been changed into *Michaiah* when the grandmother became a proselyte, should be changed back into *Maachah* when this princess apostatized], **the daughter** [rather, grand-daughter. בַת includes all female descendants, as אֵם (see ver. 10) all ancestresses] **of Abishalom.** We can hardly doubt that Absalom, the son of David, is meant here. We have (1) the express statement of 2 Chron. xi. 21, "Rehoboam loved Maachah, the daughter of *Absalom*," &c. (2) The fact that two of Rehoboam's other wives were of the family of David, which shows that it was part of his policy to marry the daughters of that house. (3) The mother of Absalom was named Maachah (2 Sam. iii. 3). (4) The name is so uncommon—in fact, it is ἅπαξ λεγ—that another person can hardly be intended. Moreover, the variation in spelling is extremely slight. It has been held, however, that a different person is designated by the name, principally because Absalom had but one daughter whose name was Tamar (2 Sam. xiv. 27), whereas Abijah's mother is said to have been the daughter of Uriel of Gibeah (2 Chron. xiii. 2). But this difficulty admits of an easy solution. Tamar was doubtless married to Uriel, and Maachah was the fruit of this marriage. And with this explanation agrees the account of Josephus (Ant. viii. 10, 1).

Ver. 3.—**And he walked in all the sins of his father, which he had done before him** [sins, *i.e.*, from the theocratic standpoint. See ch. xiv. 22, 25. It does not appear that either Abijah or Rehoboam was a vicious man, and from his pious language on Mount Zemaraim (2 Chron. xiii. 10—12) we should certainly have thought that Abijah was a god-fearing prince. But ver. 13 proves that he had no doubt had sanctioned idolatry, and this was no doubt his principal sin, as the next words explain]: **and his heart was not perfect with the Lord and his God, as the heart of David his father** [the words used of Solomon, ch. ii. 4].

Ver. 4.—**Nevertheless** [כִּי *but, sed, sondern,* Gesen. 393] **for David's sake did the Lord his God give him a lamp** [Better than margin, *candle.* The word is "always used figuratively of progeny." See note on ch. ii. 26; and of 2 Sam. xxi. 17; Job xviii. 5, 6; Psa cxxxii. 17] **in Jerusalem, to set up his son after him, and to establish Jerusalem** [But for David's piety, that is to say, his family would have been dethroned, if not destroyed, as was that of Jeroboam (1 Kings xiv. 10), of Baasha (ch. xvi. 2), of Ahab (2 Kings x. 11), &c. Abijah was

the third prince of that line who had permitted idolatrous worship, so that that dynasty had richly deserved to forfeit its position. The stability of the family of David on the throne for nearly 400 years, amid all the changes and chances of that period, and whilst in Israel there were "nine changes of dynasty within 250 years" is, as Rawlinson remarks, very "difficult to account for on mere grounds of human reason"]:

Ver. 5. **Because** [אֲשֶׁר, here causative for אֵת יַעַן. Comp. *quod*] **David did that which was right in the eyes of the Lord, and turned not aside from anything that he commanded him all the days of his life, save only in the matter of Uriah the Hittite.** [2 Sam. ii. 4. But this last clause is not found in the LXX., and such a statement was more likely to be inserted by transcribers, having first appeared in the margin as a gloss, than to be omitted, had it ever formed part of the text. And in support of this view it may be alleged that (1) the matter of Uriah was by no means David's only sin, and (2) it is not the manner of our writer thus to qualify his words. See next verse.]

Ver. 6.—**And there was war between Rehoboam and Jeroboam all the days of his life.** [Practically identical with ch. xiv. 30, where see note. Thenius thinks the insertion of the words were due to the carelessness of some copyist, and Bähr admits that our present text is possibly not the original one. For *Rehoboam,* some MSS., with the Syriac and Arabic, read *Abijah,* but this is clearly an emendation, which in turn begets another repetition (ver. 7), and there is really no need either to alter or suspect the text. Such repetitions are quite in accordance with Eastern usage, and Rehoboam here stands for the house of Rehoboam, or the cause and kingdom which Rehoboam represented. The object of mentioning his name can hardly be "to remind the reader that Abijam inherited this war from his father" (Rawlinson), for it was only on Rehoboam's death that the slumbering hostility blazed out into actual war. That there was warfare between Abijam and Jeroboam we know not only from ver. 7, but from 2 Chron. xiii. 3—20 also.

Ver. 7.—**Now the rest of the acts of Abijam and all that he did, are they not written in the book of the chronicles** [see note on ch. xiv. 29. The marginal reference to 2 Chron. xiii. misleads the casual reader] **of the kings of Judah? And there was war** [not only hostility, but open war (Vulgate, *praelium*), hence the repetition] **between Abijam and Jeroboam.**

Ver. 8.—**And Abijam slept with his fathers; and they buried him in the city of David** [This fact alone should negative Lightfoot's theory as to his name; see note on ch. xiv. 31] : **and Asa his son reigned in his stead.**

The Reign of Asa.

Ver. 9.—**And in the twentieth year of Jeroboam king of Israel reigned Asa** [Gesen. interprets the name to mean "physician"] **over Judah.** [This reign is related at much greater length in 2 Chron. xiv.—xvi. We are there told of the Ethiopian invasion, of the prophecies of Azariah and Hanani, of the league with Syria, &c.]

Ver. 10.—**And forty and one years reigned he in Jerusalem** [Corn. à Lapide points out that Asa saw *eight* kings of Israel on the throne, Jeroboam, Nadab, Baasha, Elah, Zimri, Tibni, Omri, and Ahab]. **And his mother's** [or grandmother's, as margin] **name was Maachah, the daughter of Abishalom.** [The same words as in ver. 2, and the reference can hardly be to a different person. Bähr indeed questions whether אֵם can here stand for grandmother, (1) because in every other case it designates the king's *mother*, (2) Because the mother of the king, and not the grandmother, enjoyed the dignity and position of *Gebirah* (ver. 13; 2 Chron. xv. 16). Some would read for Abishalom, *Uriel of Gibeah;* others, strengthened by the *Michaiah* of 2 Chron. xiii. 2, think the historian mistaken in mentioning the name of Abijam's mother (ver. 2; 2 Chron. xi. 21) as *Maachah.* The difficulty by no means admits of a ready solution, but perhaps the best explanation is that the grandmother, Maachah, Rehoboam's favourite wife, retained her position, possibly by force of character, or because Asa's mother was dead. It is not certain, however, that if the latter had lived she would have displaced Maachah, of whose influence and imperious temper we have several indications ; *e.g.,* in the appointment of her son, though not the first-born, to succeed his father, and in her open maintenance of idol-worship, and above all in the fact that she was publicly deposed by Asa.

Ver. 11.—**And Asa did that which was right in the eyes of the Lord, as did David his father.** ["It is a wonder how Asa should be good, of the seed of Abijam, of the soil of Maachah " (Hall).]

Ver. 12.—**And he took away the Sodomites** [see on ch. xiv. 24, and Rom. i. 23—27. It appears from ch. xxii. 46 that this abomination was not wholly suppressed] **out of the land, and removed all the idols** [גִּלּוּלִים from גָּלַל *volvit.* A term of contempt (see

Deut. xxix. 17, where it is coupled with "abominations; " Ezek. xxiii 37) ; but whether the word is to be interpreted by גֵּל a ball of *dung*, in which case these idols (*Dei stercorei*) would have a designation like Beelzebûl (" the lord of dung "), or with גַּל a heap of stones (Gen. xxxi. 46, 48), *Dei lapidei*, is uncertain. Keil would translate *logs*, Gesenius *trunks, stocks*, which from being *rolled* might well bear this name] **that his fathers had made.**

Ver. 13.—**And also Maachah his mother, even her he removed from being queen** [Rather, *queen-mother. Gebirah*, as already pointed out on ch. ii. 19, answers to the *Sultana Valide.* The Vulgate reads, *Ne esset princeps in sacris Priapi.* Wordsworth reminds us of the position which the queen-mother Atossa holds in the *Persae* (vers. 159—850). A queen consort is hardly possible in a polygamous household ; see Kitto, iv. 177] **because** [Heb. *which*, as in ver. 5] **she had made an idol** [מִפְלֶצֶת from פָּלַץ *terruit*, signifies an object of fear, *formido*—not *pudendum*, a thing of shame, as the Rabbis and others have held, *i.e.*, a phallic image (*simulacrum obscoenum*, Jerome), but *horrendum.* The devout Jew could not but regard such objects with horror] **in a grove** [Heb. *for* (*i.e.*, to serve as) *an Asherah.* See note on ch. xiv. 15, 23. Asherah is not the name of the *goddess* (= Astarte), as Wordsworth thinks, but of the image], **and Asa destroyed** [Marg. *cut off*, Heb. simply *cut*, which here must mean *cut down*. The image was, no doubt, planted erect in the ground] **her idol** [*horror*, as above], **and burnt it** [this shows that it was made of wood] **by the brook Kidron.** [Cf. Exod. xxxii. 20. Here, as in ch. xvii. 3 (where see note), our translators have been unable to adhere strictly to the original "*in* the brook," &c., from not knowing that נַחַל, which primarily means " brook," also means " watercourse," *wâdy.* It is probable that the *brook* was at this time flowing, and that the ashes of the wooden Asherah were cast into it ; but the burning also took place in the *Wâdy*, or valley. We read of another similar burning in 2 Kings xxiii. 4, 6 ; but in this case the ashes were either carried to Bethel or cast upon the graves, to defile them. It is a fair inference that on this latter occasion the Kedron was dry. The valley, " the fields of the Kedron " (ver. 4 *l.c.*), is conveniently placed for such a purpose.]

Ver. 14.—**But the high places** [evidently such as are referred to in ch. iii., *i.e.*, unauthorized shrines of Jehovah ; cf. 2 Kings xiv. 4] **were not taken away** [lit., *de-*

parted not. Yet we read in 2 Chron. xiv. 3, that Asa "*took away* the high places (cf. ver. 5). But it is clear, even from 2 Chron. xv. 17, that *all* of them were not removed, and the discrepancy arises from the well-known Eastern idiom of putting the whole for the part, of which we have instances in Gen. vii. 19; Exod. ix. 25, &c. Cf. ver. 32; 2 Kings xix. 35, and see below. Asa probably aimed at removing all, and he may have removed all out of the *cities* (2 Chron. xiv. 5), but some remained in the country districts or in remote places. Or he may have swept them away for a short time, and they may have been stealthily and gradually re-introduced. It may be interesting to remark here that down to the present day the *cultus* of the high places exists—under a modified form, it is true—in Palestine. Every traveller will remember the *Mukâms* which crown almost every hill. The religion of the Fellahîn, though nominally Mohammedan, is really, like that of China, a worship of the dead. "In almost every village of the country a small building, surmounted by a whitewashed dome, is observable, being the sacred chapel of the place; it is variously called Kubbeh, "dome," Mâzor, "shrine," or Mukâm, "station," the latter being a Hebrew word, used in the Bible for the places of the Canaanites (Deut. xii. 2). . . . Just as in the time of Moses, so now the position chosen for the Mukâm is generally conspicuous. . . . This Mukâm represents the real religion of the peasant" (Conder, pp. 304 sqq.)]: **nevertheless Asa's heart was perfect with the Lord all his days**. [We have here a notable instance of the Oriental exaggeration just referred to. For the very same expression is used by the chronicler (2 Chron. xv. 17), who in the next chapter (ch. xvi. 7—12) tells us of Asa's unfaithfulness in his old age.]

Ver. 15.—**And he brought in the things which his father had dedicated** [Heb. *the holy things of his father*. These were probably the spoils Abijah had taken in his war with Jeroboam (2 Chron. xiii. 18)], **and the things which himself had dedicated** [These were probably the spoils of the Ethiopians (2 Chron. xiv. 15; cf. xv. 11)], **into** [the Hebrew omits this word. Keil says that "house" is an accusative governed by "brought"], **the house of the Lord, silver, and gold, and vessels.**

Ver. 16.—**And there was war between Asa and Baasha king of Israel all their days.** [This statement must be compared with 2 Chron. xiv. 1, 6, from which we gather that during the first ten years of Asa's reign there cannot have been *war*, properly so called, between them. Indeed, it would seem from 2 Chron. xv. 19, xvi. 1, that it

was not until the 36th year of Asa's reign that it first broke out. But these numbers have clearly not escaped corruption (see note there), as at the date last mentioned Baasha must have been dead (cf. ver. 33 below). It is probable that war is to be taken here, as elsewhere (cf. xiv. 30), in the sense of hostility, and in any case we have here another instance of the hyperbolical habit of the Eastern mind.]

Ver. 17.—**And Baasha, king of Israel, went up against Judah** [This statement probably refers to the reconquest of the three cities which Abijah had taken from Jeroboam (2 Chron. xiii. 19), as Ramah could hardly have been rebuilt whilst Bethel remained in the hands of Judah], **and built Ramah** [Heb. *the* Ramah, *i.e.*, "the elevation," or "high place." Now *er Râm* (=the height), in Benjamin (Josh. xviii. 25; Judg. xix. 13, 14), five miles distant from Jerusalem, near the frontier of the two territories, and also then, as now, on the great north road. It was the key, consequently, to both kingdoms. Hence the struggles to possess it, vers. 21, 22; 2 Chron. xvi. 1, &c.], **that he might not suffer any to go out** [Heb. *not to give any going out*, &c.] **or come in to Asa, king of Judah.** [The object of Baasha in fortifying this place is evident. It was not merely to have an advanced post as a menace to Jerusalem (Rawlinson), but primarily, by its command of the high road, to prevent his subjects from falling away to the kingdom of Judah, or even from going up to Jerusalem to worship; in fact, to isolate Judah and to blockade its capital. That there was a great defection to Asa at this time we know from 2 Chron. xv. 9. This was an exodus which Baasha felt must be checked. Blunt (" Coincidences," pp. 176—8) has happily shown from 2 Chron. xvi. 6, &c., how the primary object must have been to "stop the alarming drainage of all that was virtuous out of their borders." Rawlinson sees in the fortification of this place "the first step towards a conquest of the southern kingdom." But as to this the text is silent, or rather it assigns an entirely different reason.]

Ver. 18.—**Then Asa took all the silver and the gold that were left** [LXX. τὸ εὑρεθὲν, which Rawlinson thinks points to a corruption of our text. He says, "The Jewish treasuries should now have been tolerably full," because (1) of the long peace (2 Chron. xiv. 1—6), and (2) the "very much spoil" they had taken from the Ethiopians (*ib.*, ver. 13). Compare ver. 15 above. But the historian has in mind the depletion of the treasury by Shishak (ch. xiv. 26). It is true there was nothing "left" on that occasion, but the treasures since accumulated are referred to under this term. It may be the phrase is not strictly accurate, but the LXX. reading looks suspiciously like an emendation] **in the treasures of the house of the Lord, and the treasures of the king's house, and delivered them into the hand of his servants : and king Asa sent them** [cf. 2 Kings xvi. 8. For this act of faithlessness he was reproved by Hanani the seer (2 Chron. xvi. 7) : "O Asa, where was thy piety, while thou robbedst God to corrupt an infidel for the slaughter of the Israelites?" (Hall)] **to Ben-hadad** ["the son of the sun" (see note on ch. xi. 23). Three kings of Damascus at least bore this name, viz., this king, his son (ch. xx. 1), and the son of Hazael (2 Kings xiii. 24)], **the son of Tabrimon** [the name means, *Good is Rimmon*, as to which deity see note on 2 Kings v. 18], **the son of Hezion** [by some identified with Rezin (ch. xi. 23), but on insufficient grounds] **king of Syria, that dwelt at Damascus** ["The centre of the Aramaean power west of the Euphrates" (Ewald)], **saying,**

Ver. 19.—**There is a league** [Rawlinson would render, "Let there be a league . . . as there was," but the A.V. is equally good. Asa claims that a league does exist, and, in fact, has never been broken] **between me and thee, and between my father and thy father** [Syria would seem to have been the first of the possessions of Solomon to regain its independence (ch. xi. 24). Its friendship would naturally be sought by Judah, as a counterpoise, perhaps, to the alliance between Israel and Egypt (Ewald)]: **behold, I have sent unto thee a present** [elsewhere a *bribe*. Psa. xv. 5 ; xxvi. 10 ; 1 Sam. viii. 3] **of silver and gold ; come and break** [Heb. *come, break now*, ה cohortative] **thy league with Baasha king of Israel, that he may depart from me.** [Heb. *go up from upon me.*]

Ver. 20.—**So** [Heb. *and*] **Ben-hadad hearkened unto king Asa, and sent the captains** [or *princes ;* same word as in ch. xxii. 31 ; cf. xx. 24] **of the hosts which he had against the cities of Israel, and smote Ijon** [now represented by *Tell Dibbin*, a mound near the north end of the *Merj 'Ayûn* (which probably preserves the name), a "meadow of fountains," a few miles north-west of Dan. This hill would offer a commanding site for a stronghold, and traces are found there of a large and ancient city (Robinson, iii. p. 375 ; Dict. Bib., i. p. 863], **and Dan,** [near the northern extremity of Palestine (ch. iv. 25 ; 1 Sam. iii. 20, &c.) Now certainly identified with *Tell el Kadi* the "hill of the Judge" (which preserves the *meaning* of the name), near the main source of the

Jordan. The Tell, apparently an extinct crater, is covered with ruins. Stanley, S. and P., p. 395—6. Thomson, "Land and Book," i. p. 320. Van de Velde, ii. p. 420. The situation is described as superb, and the country as extremely fertile. This is the last mention of the place in Scripture. Retribution has soon fallen on one of the centres of Jeroboam's schism], **and Abel-beth-maachah** [now known as *Abil el Kamh* (Robinson, iii. p. 372 ; but see Stanley, S. and P., p. 390, note 6 ; Thomson, i. p. 324. Rawlinson argues from 2 Sam. xx. 14 that there were originally *two* towns, but ver. 15 leads us to question the present text of ver. 14. Ver. 19 shows it to have been a place of considerable importance. In 2 Chron. xvi. 4. it is called *Abel Maim*, "the meadow of the waters," not only, it is probable, because of the lake, but of the huge marsh, the *Ard el Huleh*, which drains into it (see Stanley, *l.c.*) All these towns are in the neighbourhood of Lake Huleh (Merom), and all being in the extreme north, bore the brunt of the invasion. The name *Maachah* is to be noticed in connection with ver. 2], **and all Cinneroth** [in Num. xxxiv. 11 ; Deut. iii. 17, *Cinnereth ;* in the New Testament, *Gennesaret.*" "The expression 'all Cinneroth' is unusual, and may be compared with 'all Bithron,' probably like this, a district and not a town" (Grove, Dict. Bib., i. p. 330). It is the district on the western shore of the lake of Galilee, north of Tiberias, which gave its name to the adjoining sheet of water. A *city* Chinnereth, perhaps the capital of the district, is mentioned Josh. xix. 35], **with** [עַל not uncommonly has this meaning. Cf. Gen. xxxii. 12 (Heb.), "the mother *with* the children ;" Exod. xxxv. 22, "men *with* women.] **all the land of Naphtali.** [Not only were the fortresses of Naphtali just mentioned smitten by the Syrians, but they laid waste all the surrounding district.]

Ver. 21.—**And it came to pass, when Baasha heard thereof, that he left off building of Ramah** [He could not prosecute it when he had enemies on every side. He at once assumes the defensive], **and dwelt in Tirzah.** [Ch. xiv. 17. He retired to his capital. It is not implied that he had entertained the idea of dwelling at Ramah.]

Ver. 22.—**Then king Asa made a proclamation** [Heb. *made all to hear*] **throughout all Judah ; none was exempted** [Heb. *none free*], **and they took away** [Heb *took up*] **the stones of Ramah, and the timber thereof, wherewith Baasha** [It is noticeable that it is generally "king Asa," but never "king Baasha"] **had builded ; and king Asa built with them Geba of Benjamin**

[Sometimes "*the* Geba," *i.e.*, *height;* in Josh. xviii. 24, *Gaba;* now *Jeba*, only 45′ north-east of Ramah. This was the northern limit of the southern kingdom (2 Kings xxiii. 8). It occupied a striking position, standing on a rocky knoll on the south side of the great gorge of Michmash (now known as the *Wâdy Suweinît*), a " great crack or fissure in the country, with vertical precipices some 800 feet high " (Conder, p. 254; cf. Dict. Bib., i. p. 658 and Porter, i. p. 214). As Geba would command the pass, it is easy to understand why Asa fortified it, the more so as this defile " appears to have been more than once the meeting-place between the Jews and their enemies " (Conder)], **and Mizpah.** [Heb. *the* Mizpah, *i.e.*, *watch-tower* (Gen. xxxi. 49). The name points to an eminence, but it is remarkable that while so many sites of minor importance have been recovered, this old gathering-place of the tribes (Judg. xxi. 1; 1 Sam. vii. 5; x. 17—25), and the seat of Gedaliah's government (Jer. xl. 6), cannot be identified with certainty. It has been conjectured that it is now represented by the commanding eminence of *Nebi Samwil* (Robinson, ii. p. 328; Van de Velde, ii. p. 53), but Stanley (S. and P., ii. p. 213—4) and Grove (Dict. Bib., ii. p. 389) argue in favour of Scopus, and " the survey has done little to throw light on this question " (see Conder, pp. 257—9). It is to be hoped that the " pit," or well, which Asa made (Jer. xli. 9), probably " to provide Mizpah with a plentiful supply of water in case of a siege " (Ewald), may yet be brought to light.

Ver. 23.—**And the rest of all the acts of Asa, and all his might** [see 2 Chron. xiv., xv.], **and all that he did, and the cities which he built** [during the peace in the earlier part of his reign (2 Chron. xiv. 5, 6)], **are they not written in the book of the chronicles of the kings of Judah ? Nevertheless** [Heb. *only*. There was one exception to his otherwise happy and prosperous reign] **in the time of his old age** [see notes on ch. i. 1; xi. 4. " Old age " means here, as there, the end of life. Asa cannot well have been more than fifty. It was in the 39th year of his reign (2 Chron. xvi. 12) that this disease attacked him] **he was diseased in his feet.** [It is generally supposed that this disease was the gout. In the Chronicles (*l.c.*) he is reproached for seeking " not to the Lord but to the physicians." We must remember what the art of medicine at that day was like (see Kitto, " Daily Bib. Illus.," iv. p. 195 sqq.), and that the Jews regarded sickness and healing as alike the *immediate* acts of God.

Ver. 24.—**And Asa slept with his fathers, and was buried with his fathers** [" in his own sepulchre which he had made for himself " (2 Chron. xvi. 14, which also notices " the bed filled with sweet odours," in which he was laid and the " very great burning " made for him)] **in the city of David his father: and Jehoshaphat his son reigned in his stead.**

HOMILETICS.

Vers. 11—26.—*The Reign of Asa.* Though this prince reigned forty and one years—a longer period than any of his predecessors, and, with two exceptions, a longer period than any of the kings who came after him—yet his reign, so far as it is recorded here, may be summed up in few words. " Happy is the nation," it has been said, " which has no history." But happier still the nation whose history, like that of Judah in the time of Asa, may be comprehended under these two heads —*internal reforms*, and *external discipline*.

I. INTERNAL REFORMS. Two questions present themselves for consideration here. First, What were Asa's reforms? Secondly, In what way were they accomplished?

1. His reforms were practically of two kinds: (*a*) *Moral*, and (*b*) *Religious*. It is not implied that he either put morality before religion, or believed that the one could be separated from the other. It may be a question in these days—it is at least hotly disputed—whether morality can long support itself without a religious basis and religious sanctions; but it was no question in that dark age, or for many hundred years afterwards. Then it was a choice between the one true religion and the most shameful immoralities practised under the name of religion. All that is meant here, therefore, is that Asa's reforms resulted in purging and raising the tone of public morality by suppressing the idolatry which sanctioned and consecrated impurity.

(1) *The moral reformation* is suggested to our minds by the words " He took away the Sodomites out of the land " (ver. 12). What an abyss of corruption does this one brief sentence reveal to us. " It is a shame even to speak of those things

which" were "done of them in secret" (Eph. v. 12). And this among the holy people, the bride of the Lord! No wonder that Asa's first effort was directed against these horrible enormities. This suppression of the Sodomites was a first step towards—

(2) *The religious reformation.* He next "removed all the idols that his fathers had made." "His fathers." Solomon, as well as Rehoboam and Abijah. Probably none of the three had himself reared idol shrines. But all the three had, to say the least, permitted idolatry, and connived at it. It was sin enough that they had not vigorously and promptly suppressed it. They were, each in his turn, the representative of the mighty God of Jacob. What were they doing that they permitted any rivalry between the bestial gods of the heathen and the Holy One of Israel? But probably we see here the bitter fruits of Solomon's sin—so true it is that "the evil that men do lives after them." When that powerful prince had once granted to foreign deities and shameful superstitions a footing in Immanuel's land, it was more than his comparatively feeble successors could do to dislodge them. The people loved to have it so, and neither Rehoboam nor Abijah was strong enough to say them nay. Thus did Solomon, down to Asa's days, yes, and down to the time of the captivity (2 Chron. xxxvi. 14), go on sinning in his grave.

And let us notice here an instructive contrast between Asa and Solomon. It was the wise king, the most magnificent of the monarchs of the earth, at the height of his prosperity, and towards the end of a long and peaceful reign, built altars for the abominations of neighbouring nations. It was a young prince, unknown to fame, with no special gifts or endowments, with a restricted dominion, and encompassed with difficulties, who was the first to stem this tide of sin and shame with which his great ancestor had flooded the land. "The first last, and the last first." Compare 1 Cor. i. 27—29. Wealth has greater dangers than adversity.

2. But let us now consider the way in which these great reforms were brought about.

(1) *He began at the right place.* "Even Maachah his mother he removed," &c. The *Gebirah*, the first lady in the land, whose conduct would of course be an example to all the women of his realm (Esther i. 17, 18), was deposed from her lofty station. The history of Israel shows repeatedly how the country took its tone, as indeed every country must do, more or less, from the court. It is not only in dress that the queen sets the fashion. The Japanese have a striking proverb, "Fish begin to stink at the head." If the court be corrupt, profligate, irreligious, the commonalty will soon follow suit, for we all imitate our superiors. In this sense is that word true, *corruptio optimi pessima.* It would consequently have been of little use for Asa to put down idols elsewhere had he tolerated them in the harem, the nursery of his successors. This hydra could not be slain by hewing its feet, or piercing its body; it was only mortal in its *head.* Maachah's "horror" must be destroyed or idolatry will live and flourish. Moreover, in beginning with her, Asa shows that he appraised aright the power of female influence. He might have realized that those who "rock the cradle, rule the world." The sinister influence of the harem had ruined Rehoboam; it should not ruin Jehoshaphat. Here, again, let us mark the contrast between the conduct of Asa and that of Solomon; between the cases of Maachah and Naamah. Solomon built idol altars for his wives: Asa burnt the idol of his mother. The strong king was brought into subjection by weak and foolish women; the weak king humbled and degraded the proudest and strongest woman of her time. The former could not resist the blandishments of one of his many foreign mistresses when she petitioned for the gods and rites of her native country; the latter was deaf to the entreaties of his mother when she prayed to retain, not her idol, but her place. It must have cost him an effort to deal with the queen-mother who had exercised so great an influence in former reigns. It has been said that the devil often "comes to a man in the shape of his wife and children" (J. Hinton), and truly a man's real foes are not unfrequently those of his own household. Just as their flattery is the most insidious and mischievous (Whately), so are their faults too often considered venial, and their sins, when manifest, are the hardest to reprove (cf. ch. i. 6; 1 Sam. iii. 13). These are the

"hand" and the "eye," which cause men to offend, and which they must cut off or pluck out and cast from them (Matt. v. 29 sqq.) Hence the charge of Deut. xiii. 6 sqq., cf. Matt. x. 37.

And the moral effect of this act, the public deposition of the queen-mother, can hardly be over-estimated. It showed the country that the king was in real earnest; that he was no respecter of persons; that no idolatry could expect tolerance at his hands. Probably but for this he could neither have taken away the Sodomites nor removed the idols. Possibly it was because neither Rehoboam (see 2 Chron. xi. 21) nor Abijam dared to deal with the idolatries of Maachah, who would seem to have been a woman of imperious will, that these foreign superstitions had defiled the land so long. Asa struck at their root in removing her from being queen.

(2) *He did not stop half-way.* He destroyed "with both hands earnestly" (Micah vii. 3). He not only cut down her idol, he burnt it in the valley of the Kedron. There was no place left her for repentance. He had burnt his ships behind him; had destroyed the nests, so that the rooks might not return. This public burning, witnessed, no doubt, by crowds of spectators, spoke louder than any words or ordinances could do. When they saw the "horror" reduced to ashes, and the ashes cast into the brook, they could have no doubt as to the purpose of their king. They would remember how Moses had acted before (Exod. xxxii. 20).

(3) *He did what he could.* It is no reproach to him that "the high places were not removed" (ver. 14), for the chronicler (chs. xiv. 5; xv. 12, 13, 17), as well as our author, testifies that this was no fault of his. "His heart was perfect all his days." He did what in him lay, and his service was accepted accordingly (2 Cor. viii. 12). "The fleetest horse cannot escape from its tail."

(4) *His reformation was followed by a restitution.* It was not merely destructive, as too many so-called reforms have been. (1) He gave up to the sacristy of God the silver and gold he had taken from the Ethiopians. It was his happiness to restore to it some of the treasure of which it had been denuded in the reign of Rehoboam. (Observe: When idolatry came in, the treasures went out of the land. When idolatry was expelled, prosperity returned. Godliness has the promise of the life that now is.) His, consequently, was no cheap reform. He offered of that which cost him something (2 Sam. xxiv. 24). He might have converted his spoil into drinking vessels of pure gold (ch. x. 21), but he surrendered it to the service and keeping of the Most High. (2) He induced his people to dedicate *themselves* anew to the Lord (2 Chron. xv. 12 sqq.; cf. 2 Cor. viii. 5). This was the crown and blossom of his reformation. "They sware unto the Lord with a loud voice."

And, as the fruit of this righteous policy, we find that he enjoyed, for a part of his reign at least, (1) *quietness* (2 Chron. xiv. 1), "The Lord gave him rest" (ver. 6) —the effect of righteousness is quietness and assurance (Isa. xxxii. 17); (2) *prosperity* (ver. 7), and (3) *growth*, in the shape of a large accession of God-fearing, law-abiding subjects. "They fell to him out of Israel in abundance when they saw that the Lord his God was with him." Not all the numerical superiority of Israel, not all its fruitful territory, availed against the attraction of a realm, in one sense a rival kingdom, where respect for God's law promised security, liberty, and peace.

But let us now observe that these reforms and this courageous piety did not exempt him from—

II. EXTERNAL TROUBLES. The quiet only lasted ten years His fenced cities did not save him from invasion. He had to encounter, first, the invasion of Zerah (2 Chron. xiv. 9), and secondly, the aggression of Baasha (1 Kings xv. 17). He may have been tempted to think when that overwhelming host of swart barbarians marched against him that his piety profited him nothing. He may have argued, when he saw the fortress of Ramah threatening his very capital—the city God had chosen to put His name there that God made no difference between the righteous and the wicked, between His faithful people and the calf-worshipping Israelites. But observe : both these troubles were really blessings in disguise. Afflictions and adversities may be either punitive or disciplinary. Solomon's were of the former, Asa's of the latter class. For (1) when Asa had learned his own weakness, and learnt whither to look for help (2 Chron. xiv. 11)—lessons both of them of singular blessed-

ness—the Lord smote the Ethiopians. This invasion resulted in the enrichment
of the country. The spoil was enormous. And the victory ministered, not to
pride, but to piety (*ib.*, xv. 8). (2) The only result, so far as we know, of the
menaces of Baasha was that that king drew upon himself an invasion of Syrians
(in which it is to be observed, Dan, one of the seats of the calf-worship, was smitten),
and Asa gained two fortresses as a protection against future inroads (ver. 22). It is
true that Asa betrayed a want of faith in taking the consecrated gold and silver
wherewith to bribe the northern barbarians (2 Chron. xvi. 7, 8), and that he was
chastised for the deed (ver. 9), but, all the same, his generally "perfect heart" was
rewarded by more than deliverance. If he ever cried with Jacob, "All these
things are against me," he must have subsequently exclaimed with Joseph, "Ye
thought evil against me, but God meant it unto good" (Gen. l. 20). His troubles
must have taught him this lesson, "Many are the afflictions of the righteous, but
the Lord delivereth him out of them all" (Psa. xxxiv. 19).

And so we see in the dangers and assaults which this reformer underwent proofs
of the loving discipline of God—trials intended for *his* reformation and for the
chastening of his country. It is difficult at first sight to see how so brutal and
hateful a thing as war can ever be for the good of any people, especially when we
remember that a "victory is the next worst thing to a defeat." But those have
some reason on their side who tell us that war is the purgatory of nations, and that
battles in the moral are something like thunderstorms in the physical world.
There are victims in either case—what hecatombs of victims in some cases—but
the atmosphere is all the clearer afterwards. The campaign of Zerah probably
taught him and his people to bridle their ambition, and to leave their neighbours
alone; it certainly taught Asa and Israel to trust in the Lord and to cling closer
to Him. They learned that "Providence does" *not* "always help the biggest
battalions"—that everything turns on the blessing of God. * They proved the
truth of that promise, "Five of you shall chase an hundred, and an hundred of you
shall put ten thousand to flight," &c. (Levit. xxvi. 8). Psalm xx. might have been
penned with reference to this war. It certainly breathes the spirit of that time.
"*Deo adjuvante*"—this is its keynote. And this, too, is the burden of Asa's
prayer (2 Chron. xiv. 11), of Azariah's prophecy (*ib.*, xv. 2 sqq.), of Judah's praises
(vers. 12, 14, 15).

It has been remarked that in the history of the covenant people we may see
pourtrayed the trials, deliverances, &c., of the covenant soul (Keble). And
certainly the prosperous reign of Asa is a picture of what a truly Christian life
involves. Happy are those whose lives, in their main features, may be thus
characterized : "Internal reforms," "external discipline." The three things which,
Luther said, made the minister also make the man, "Prayer, meditation, and
temptation." The idols must be utterly abolished by "the expulsive force of a
new affection;" "the horror," the fear and horrible dread that possesses the
unreconciled, must be cast out by perfect love; "everything that defileth" must
be consumed by its ardent flames; the heart must be "dedicated," and then the
loving correction of God will do the rest, and after we have suffered awhile, in
the battle of life, in the chamber of sickness (ch. xv. 23), will make us perfect
(1 Peter v. 10), and grant us "quietness and assurance for ever."

Ver. 22.—*Church and Dissent.* The building and subsequent demolition of
Ramah—its building by Baasha to check the defection of his subjects to the
southern kingdom and the Jewish Church ; its removal by Asa in order that the
highway to Judah and the temple of Jerusalem might be open to returning
schismatics—this incident may serve to introduce a comparison between the
kingdom of Asa and the kingdom of Christ; or rather, the history and relations of
the *two* kingdoms of Palestine after the schism may suggest some thoughts as to
the proper attitude and relations of the Catholic Church towards her separated
children.

And that our view of those relations, so far as it is disclosed to us by this history,

* "In Gottes Segen ist alles gelegen."

may not be partial and incomplete, it is proper that we should begin the survey, not with the accession of Asa, but some two decades earlier; in fact, with the commencement of the schism. And we may learn—

I. THAT IT IS NOT TO BE WONDERED AT THAT HERESY SHOULD BE STRONG AND AGGRESSIVE. Ten tribes worshipped the calves; only two were faithful to the Lord. Jeroboam's novelties carried "all Israel" away after them. Even so "the churches of Jerusalem, Alexandria, Antioch, and Rome have erred" (Art. xix.) Donatists, Montanists, Arians, Apollinarians—how many were the sects of the first days! And now, out of the two hundred millions of Christendom, how many are there whom with the profoundest sorrow we must pronounce either heretical or schismatical. And no wonder, for

> "The search for truth is not one half so pleasant,
> As sticking to the views we hold at present."

Most of our schisms have had their origin in pride and emulation; most of our heresies spring out of our corrupt human nature. It is every way pleasanter to *choose* among doctrines than to take them as revealed by God.

II. THAT THERE MUST, NEVERTHELESS, BE NO FIGHTINGS AMONGST CHRISTIANS. The armies of Judah were solemnly forbidden to attack those of Jeroboam (ch. xii. 24). Though a host of near two hundred thousand armed men had mustered for battle, yet they must "return every man to his house." They were reminded that the children of Israel were their "brethren," and that the division in the kingdom— not that in the *Church*—was ordained of God. A special messenger is entrusted with a special revelation (ver. 22) to prevent the unseemly spectacle of brethren, the children of the same Father, meeting in the shock of battle. And observe that, though there was undoubtedly war at a later period between the divided branches of the Hebrew family (ch. xiv. 30; xv. 6, 16, &c.; 2 Chron. xiii. 3), yet it is by no means certain that these wars ever had the Divine sanction. Observe, too, that hostility and antagonism, short of actual organized warfare, is here described as "war" (ch. xiv. 30, note). Now may we not justly infer—what, indeed, is certain on other grounds—that, whatever their heresies, there must be no *hostilities* between the divided sections of the Christian family? There have been "wars and fightings" amongst them, it is true, but this is against the will and prayer of their head (John xvii. 21; xiii. 35; cf. 1 Cor. i. 11; xi. 18; James iv. 1). For they are "brethren" (Matt. xxiii. 8) by a much closer bond than were the Jews. Spiritual ties are far more real and binding than those of flesh, of mere matter (Matt. xii. 48, 49; Rom. xvi. 13; Titus i. 4; Philem. 10). And if it was unseemly and unnatural for Jew to lift up hand against Jew, how much more for members of the same body (Eph. v. 30; Rom. xii. 5), professors of the same gospel of love? And not only the hand, but the tongue. There must be no stabbing and wounding of brethren by words any more than by swords. "There is nothing," says Whichcote, "more unnatural to religion than contentions about it." Christians have fighting enough to do without falling upon each other. There are the common enemies of the Christian life—the world, the flesh, and the devil. There are the enemies of the faith, the hosts of devilry, and uncleanness, and unbelief, and indifference. It is well when disputing about "modes of faith" that we should remember that there are untold millions of men still worshipping cows and even demons. It is well, too, that we should consider that we are none of us infallible, and may easily confound friends and foes. It has been justly said that many of our disputes are like that midnight conflict at Syracuse, where each party mistook the watchword of the other, and all was hopeless confusion (Stanley.) We must "contend earnestly for the faith once for all delivered," &c., it is true, but there are two ways of doing that. "It is not the actual differences of Christians that do the mischief, but the mismanagement of those differences" (P. Henry). "Nous avons eu assez de *polémique*," said a French ecclesiastic; "il nous reste à avoir un peu d'*irenique*."

III. THAT THERE MUST BE NO SACRIFICE OF TRUTH OR COMPROMISE OF PRINCIPLE FOR THE SAKE OF CONCILIATING HERETICS. Asa, like Rehoboam, was only too glad to welcome deserters from Jeroboam's Church and kingdom; his action with respect to Ramah proves that. But neither of them ever thought of accommodating the worship or polity of Jerusalem to suit the wishes or prejudices of the schismatic Israelites. To neither of them did it occur to allow that calf-worship was right worship; neither would admit that there was any true Church but that of Judah, or any sanctuary but that of Jerusalem; neither could or would recognize the orders or ministrations of Jeroboam's man-made priests. In fact, it would have been impolitic, as well as unfaithful, to have done so. It was because Judah was true to its convictions, and consistently repudiated the schism, and stood resolutely on the old paths, that such numbers of pious Israelites came over to its side. Even so now, nothing but harm can come of sacrificing one iota of principle for the sake of the union of Christendom. We may be branded as illiberal and bigots if we ask for the credentials of every *soi-disant* minister of Christ; if we deny the name of "Church" to each of the manifold sects and societies of human origin; if we repudiate an unorganic Christianity, a religion of mere emotionalism. But all the same, we have no right to exercise a spurious charity and to give what is not ours; we have no right to surrender one jot of Catholic truth for the sake of conciliating outsiders. That would be indeed to "make a solitude and call it a peace." In that way our religion might soon be watered down so that truth and life and efficacy would all be gone, and the thin residuum would be stale, flat, and unprofitable. Only the infidel could ultimately gain by such a process. Our answer, then, to the separatist must be this: "All that thou desirest of me I will do, but this thing I may not do." Deeply as we desire unity, we dare not purchase it at such a price. "*Amicus Plato, amicus Socrates, sed magis amica veritas.*"

IV. THAT THERE MUST BE NO CALLING IN THE AID OF UNBELIEVERS AGAINST SEPARATED BRETHREN. This was done more than once in Jewish history, but the result was always disastrous. If Jeroboam called in the aid of Shishak against Rehoboam, he suffered himself, as we have seen (note on ch. xiv. 25), from the Egyptian invasion. Nor was Asa's appeal to Ben-hadad less ill-advised. In the first place, it betrayed a lack of faith in God; then (2) he had to rob the Lord's treasury of the gifts he had recently dedicated thereto; and (3) the bands of Syria, having once tasted the sweets of conquest, were ever afterwards threatening or ravaging (chs. xx., xxii.; 2 Kings v. 2; vi. 8, &c.) the Holy Land. Asa's son, Jehoshaphat, found it necessary, as he thought, to join forces with those of Israel against this very power which Asa invoked. And how often have Christians pursued the same policy. How often have the armies of the Ottomans, *e.g.*, been employed by Christians against Christians. The cannon by means of which Constantinople was taken were cast by Christian engineers. For four centuries have Mussulman legions been largely officered by Christian renegades, and recruited from Christian lands—Albania, Wallachia, &c. The "unspeakable Turk" has only been tolerated in Europe because of the divisions of Christendom. And is not the same thing being done in another way at the present time? There are Christians who think it right to make common cause with atheists, secularists, &c., against their brethren. If the example of Asa (2 Chron. xvi. 7—9) is not decisive against such a proceeding, surely that of Jehoshaphat (*ib.*, xix. 2) and Amaziah (*ib.*, xxv. 6—10) prove that we should neither help, nor seek help from, the ungodly. The result of such alliances, as Asa found to his cost, will be, "From henceforth thou shalt have wars." The mercenaries we have hired against one another will end by doing battle against all who bear the Christian name. The Britons who called in the Saxons to their aid presently found their new allies settled in their homes and themselves driven forth into the wilderness.

V. THAT NO OBSTACLES MUST BE RAISED IN THE PATH OF REUNION. That this should be done by the separatists need cause us no surprise. Baasha could not *afford* to have the highway to Judah open. His occupation would be gone if the breach were healed and the nation or the Church again became one. And, alas! there are similar "vested interests" in the perpetuation of division amongst Christians. But just as it was Asa's care to pull down the frontier fortress of Ramah, just as the stones and timber were carried away bodily by the labour of all his subjects, so should it be the great concern of the Church and of every Christian to remove the barriers which separate those for whom Christ died. The national Church, for example, should be as wide and comprehensive as possible. Sects must of necessity have narrow and restricted boundaries; for their *raison d'etre* is almost invariably to be found, not in the propagation of error, but in the assertion of some forgotten or neglected truth, which they have made their *peculium*, and treat as if it were the sum total of revelation to the neglect of the " proportion of faith." But why should we multiply our tests and articles of membership ? The Apostles' Creed was thought to embody everything of necessity to salvation in the first age of the Church; and when at a later period truth had become mixed with error, the Nicene symbol was still the only test of the Christian layman. Why should it not be a sufficient test of Catholicity now ? Why must we refine and define, and so make intercommunion almost impossible ?

> " Must it be Calvin, and not Christ ?
> Must it be Athanasian Creeds,
> Or holy water, books, and beads?
> Must struggling souls remain content
> With councils and decrees of Trent ? "

It is partly because we have built Ramahs round our Zion that our schisms are so many. We have insisted on forcing our shibboleths on those who could not receive them, forgetting that, however true any dogma may be in itself, still, if it is not of necessity to be believed, and we make it an essential part of our system of doctrine, it may straightway become a source of discord and division. There are many such barriers and obstacles of our own creation—sometimes in the shape of practical abuses—which require to be removed, and no Christian should be " exempt " from the work of " building silver bridges for flying enemies and golden bridges for returning friends."

VI. THAT, INSTEAD OF RAISING BARRIERS BETWEEN BRETHREN, WE SHOULD STRENGTHEN OUR DEFENCES AGAINST THE COMMON ENEMY. The stones and timber of Ramah, Asa used to build Geba of Benjamin and Mizpah. Thereby the road to Jerusalem was left open to friends, whilst these two fortresses commanded it against foes. Against Baasha, if he would wage war against his kinsmen ; against the Assyrian at a later date (Isa. x. 28, 29). And is there no lesson for Christians here ? Too often they are fighting amongst themselves about the " infinitely little " —about the date of Easter, about unleavened bread, about the " five points," about lights and vestments, about wafer bread, or about unfermented wine in the Holy Communion—while the enemy is marshalling his forces. Intemperance, sensuality, devilry in every form, are destroying the Church's children by thousands, and her watchmen the while are fencing with each other. The siege of Jerusalem (Jos., Bell. Jud. v. 1) is reproduced amongst ourselves. The enemy is thundering at our gates, and the Church is paralyzed by factions. We keep raising barricades in the streets of Zion whilst hostile legions are swarming on the adjoining heights. We have our Geba, our Mizpah to build, and we perversely build Ramahs instead.

VII. THAT A HOUSE DIVIDED AGAINST ITSELF CANNOT STAND. First Samaria, then Jerusalem fell before the enemy. Christianity is now comparatively powerless for aggressive purposes; indeed, it hardly keeps pace with the population; and its enemies are asking how much longer it can stand on its defence. *Divide et impera*, thus have many empires fallen. True, the Catholic Church cannot perish, but national Churches have fallen again and again. There has been some talk amongst the Brahmins of sending a mission to England. And we may see in France, in Germany, a foreshadowing of what is in store for us here. " The class which has recently attained supreme political power is alienated from Christianity in its present forms." Are the Church and the sects alike to be broken up one by one ? Or shall we lay aside our " fratricidal dissensions," and combine against the legion of foes—Atheism, Agnosticism, Socialism, and the rest ? Of one thing we may be sure, that as long as our " unhappy divisions " last we shall never win England, much less the world, for Christ.

HOMILIES BY VARIOUS AUTHORS.

Vers. 1—8.—*The succession of Abijam* to the throne of Judah appears to have had one limiting principle, viz., that the successor should be of the house and lineage of David (see 2 Chron. xiii. 8). Within this limit it seems—

I. IT WAS DETERMINED BY THE WILL OF THE REIGNING KING. 1. *The principle of primogeniture was not considered.* (1) Else Abijam could not have ascended the throne: for he had elder brothers, sons of Mahalath and Abihail, and we know not how many besides (see 2 Chron. xi. 18—21). (2) These were deliberately set aside by the choice of the king. The reason given for that choice is arbitrary. Rehoboam " loved Maachah, the daughter of Absalom, above all his wives," and therefore he " made Abijah, the son of Maachah, the chief ruler among his brethren: for he thought to make him king" (2 Chron. xi. 22, 23). (3) For this he had precedent. We have no proof that Rehoboam was not the only son of Solomon; but Solomon was a younger son of David (see 2 Sam. iii. 2—5; xiii. 13, 14), and was preferred before his elder brethren upon the designation of his father (see ch. i. 13, 32—35). 2. *Abijam represented Rehoboam by walking in his sins.* (1) He recognized the God of Israel. This he did formally in his address to Jeroboam before engaging him in battle (see 2 Chron. xiii. 4—12). So did Rehoboam recognize the God of Israel (see 2 Chron. xii. 10—12). (2) "But his heart was not perfect with the Lord his God, as the heart of David his father." David never followed idols; but Rehoboam forsook not the sins of Solomon, and Abijam forsook not the sins of Rehoboam. (3) Their mixed worship was like that of the Samaritans of later times, who "feared the Lord and served their own gods " (2 Kings xvii. 32). If this was not worshipping other gods " *before* the Lord," it was worshipping them " *beside* Him" (see 2 Cor. vi. 16). Yet—

II. THE CHOICE OF REHOBOAM HAD THE DIVINE SANCTION (ver. 4). 1. *Primogeniture, therefore, cannot plead Divine right.* (1) Else would not God have set aside the choice of Rehoboam in favour of his elder son, or rather, of the representative of the elder son of David? (2) David himself was a younger son in the family of Jesse. And if we go back to earlier times, Judah, a younger son, was preferred before Reuben, in the family of Jacob. Jacob himself was chosen to the prejudice of Esau, and Isaac before him to the prejudice of Ishmael. (3) God had His own reasons for confirming the election of Rehoboam, which, however, were different from those which moved the king. 2. *God had respect to His servant David.* (1) " Because David did that which was right in the eyes of the Lord." He had no complicity with idolatry, but worshipped the one true God with pure delight. When away from the courts of the Lord he longed for them with vehement desire. What a worthy example! How it rebukes the half-day worshippers of modern times! (2) He failed only " in the matter of Uriah." That was a foul blot. How sad so grand a life should have been so darkly blurred! (3) Yet " his heart was perfect with the Lord his God." For he heartily repented of that sin, and was forgiven (see 2 Sam. xii. 13; Pss. xxxii. 1—5; li.) God giveth liberally and upbraideth not. 3. *Therefore for David's sake Abijam reigned.* (1) " That he might always have a lamp "—a man of his line. Abijam was a son of David by an unbroken male descent, and also by a female descent. " His mother's name was Maachah, the daughter of Abishalom." *Abishalom* is written " Absalom " in 2 Chron. xi. 21. Maachah was the *daughter* of Absalom as Abijam was the *son* of David, viz., as being descended from him. Her father's name was " Uriel of Gibeah," who appeared to have married a *daughter* of Absalom, who left no son (2 Chron. xiii. 2). She bore the name of her grandmother, who was " Maacah, the daughter of Talmai, king of Geshur " (2 Sam. iii. 3). (2) Christ is the true lamp of David (see Psa. cxxxii. 17). For His sake the line of David must be preserved. (3) The lamp, too, must shine in Jerusalem. " God gave him a lamp in Jerusalem, to set up a son after him, and to establish Jerusalem." The Redeemer must come to Zion, there to turn away iniquity from Jacob. So before the Romans destroyed Jerusalem, and the family of David had lost their genealogies, Jesus came and became an expiatory sacrifice for sin.—J. A. M.

Vers. 9—15.—*Reformation.* The moral condition of Judah was fearful when Asa came to the throne. The apostasy of Solomon had inaugurated a retrogression which was aggravated in the reigns following, so that for three generations the abominations of the heathens were increasing. The condition of Israel was even worse, under the system introduced by Jeroboam, to which the successors of that monarch tenaciously held. When the Holy Land was in such a state of degeneracy, what was the condition of the world at large! There was, therefore, the greatest need for reformation.

I. OF THIS ASA BECAME THE SUBJECT AND SPECIMEN. Reformations have ever been inaugurated by individuals who have embodied and exemplified their principles. Witness Luther in Germany, Knox in Scotland, &c. Such also was Asa. 1. *He " did that which was right in the eyes of the Lord."* (1) To do right in the eyes of the world is praiseworthy. For wicked men "know better;" and they have keen vision to discover inconsistencies in professors of religion (see Phil. ii. 15 : 1 Pet. ii. 11—15). (2) To do right in the eyes of good men is a higher commendation. They have a purer light, and consequently a finer appreciation of moral qualities. Things which the world will allow they cannot approve. (3) But to do right in the " eyes of the Lord " is the highest praise. He reads the heart—surveys the motives—requires " truth in the inward parts." What a searching vision shall we pass under in the day of judgment! If that vision approve us now we shall then have nothing to fear. 2. *In this he is compared with David.* (1) David never followed idols. The one blur of his life was the matter of Uriah, of which he heartily repented. Who amongst us has nothing to repent of? (2) David's loyalty to God was sincere and fervent. What a warm spirit of piety breathes in the Psalms! Are they not, even in our gospel age, a fine vehicle for spiritual worship? (3) David was a prophet. This Asa was not. He had the grace, not the gifts, of the founder of his house. Gifts are not equally within the reach of all; graces are. 3. *Such commendation was eminently creditable to Asa.* (1) He stands out in remarkable contrast to his father. Abijam was wicked; Asa was good. The influence of the father was vicious; the son resisted it and was virtuous. (2) Asa's mother seems to have died early, for Maachah, the daughter of Absalom, who was his grandmother, is here mentioned as his mother. Under the influence of Maachah, Abijah developed badly; notwithstanding that evil influence Asa developed well. (3) We must not ignore, but fully recognize, individual moral responsibility. The will cannot be compared to a pair of scales which is mechanically moved by weights.

II. OF THIS ALSO HE BECAME THE INSTRUMENT. This is God's order (1 John i. 3). What he felt he tried to promote. 1. *Beginning with his own house.* (1) He removed the idols which his father had made. He felt especially bound to do this in order to cut off the entail of sin from his house. (2) He frowned also upon the idolatry of his grandmother. " She made an idol in a grove " (מפלצת לאשרה) *a glory for an Ashere.* The word is used for *terribleness* or *majestic glory* Jer. xlix. 16. Setting an image in the cloud of glory was setting it on an ark or chariot of cherubim to be worshipped. (See Psa. l. 3, where נשערה is used for the cloud of glory about Jehovah.) Asa demolished this *nimbus,* or glory, together with the Ashere, or idol, and probably threw the ashes into the Kedron in contempt (compare Deut. ix. 21; 2 Kings xxiii. 12; 2 Chron. xv. 16). (3) Furthermore, he removed Maachah from being queen (dowager). He thus merited the commendation of Levi (see Deut. xxxiii. 9; see also Math. x. 37). 2. *Then influencing the nation.* (1) He removed the Sodomites out of the land. What prosperity can there be in any state where public immorality is tolerated by the magistrates? (2) He destroyed the high places of idolatry with their altars and idols, in the country and in the cities (see 2 Chron. xiv. 3, 5). (3) The high places used in the worship of Jehovah after the fashion of the patriarchs, he spared. For this he is but lightly censured;

to have limited the ordinances of public worship to the temple would have been the more excellent way. (4) He encouraged the worship of Jehovah (see 2 Chron. xiv. 4). Not by precept only, but by example also. He dedicated to the Lord the things which his father had vowed, but either neglected to pay or died before he could carry his purpose into effect. Also the spoil which he himself had taken from the Ethiopians (see 2 Chron. xv. 11, 12). Where the heart of God's people is loyal the treasuries of His house will be full.—J. A. M.

Vers. 16—24.—*The War Policy of Asa.* "Forty and one years reigned he in Jerusalem" (ver. 10). The evil kings of Judah were about as numerous as the good, but their reigns were shorter. "The wicked do not live out half their days." But though the reign of Asa was long and glorious, his war policy with Baasha was not creditable.

I. THE OBJECT WAS RIGHT. 1. *The war was provoked by the enemy.* (1) Baasha was the aggressor (ver. 17). War is such a fearful evil that whoever provokes it is greatly culpable. (2) Therefore on Asa's part it was defensive. If human war is ever defensible it is when defensive. 2. *It was provoked by impious intention.* (1) Asa had set his heart upon the reformation of true religion, in which he was blessed by God with peace and prosperity (2 Chron. xiv. 1—7). (2) The more pious Ephrathites were attracted in great numbers to Jerusalem to join in the pure worship of the temple; and the reformation was influencing the northern kingdom (2 Chron. xv. 9). (3) Baasha now feared, as Jeroboam did when he set up his calves (ch. xii. 26—28), that his people would return to the house of David. To prevent this he proceeded to fortify the frontier town of Ramah (2 Chron. xvi. 1). (4) This was to coerce the Ephrathites to transgress the law of God (see Deut. xii. 11; xiv. 23—26; xvi. 2). To resist this persecution was as pious in Asa as the persecution was impious in Baasha.

II. THE MEANS WERE WRONG. 1. *They were human.* (1) Asa did not rely upon the Lord. This was the less excusable since God had wrought such signal deliverance for him from the vast multitude of the Ethiopians (see 2 Chron. xiv. 9—15). What was the host of Baasha compared with that army? (2) He did not even inquire of the Lord. Had God sanctioned his recourse to Ben-hadad then had he been blameless. (3) Though in other particulars he had listened to the advice of Azariah, the son of Oded, with blessed advantage, yet in this he had disregarded that advice (see 2 Chron. xv. 1, 2). 2. *They were unworthy.* (1) What right had he to engage a heathen to fight with his brethren? (2) What right had he to bribe a heathen to break his covenant (ברית *purification*) with Baasha, in which the blood of sacrifice had been sprinkled to express his *purity* of intention, as we now take the sacrament? What opinion could the heathen form of the religion of one who could offer a bribe for such a purpose? (3) What right had he to take the treasure of the temple for such a purpose?

III. THE SUCCESS WAS PARTIAL. 1. *The end was answered.* (1) The Syrians attacked Israel in the north. The news of this drew Baasha away from Ramah (vers. 20, 21). (2) This gave Asa the opportunity to demolish the fortifications in progress so as to open the road Baasha sought to close. He also removed the material so that the road might be kept open. (3) The material was useful to him in building Geba of Benjamin and Mizpah. 2. *But the price was too great.* (1) He missed an opportunity of spoiling the Syrians as he had spoiled the Ethiopians. This fact is revealed, though by what means Providence purposed to have brought it about is not disclosed (2 Chron. xvi. 7). (2) The treasures of the temple and of the palace were therefore needlessly alienated. (3) His brethren in "Ijon, and Dan, and Abel-beth-Maachah, and all Cinneroth," or Gennesaret, "with all the land of Naphtali," were exposed to the horrors of the Syrian invasion. The heart of Israel would be alienated from Asa in consequence, and the reformation hindered. (4) Asa's own heart became hardened, else he would not have imprisoned Hanani, and oppressed some of his people (who probably sympathized with the prophet). (5) And he inherited the judgment of wars to the end of his days. Also a disease in the feet, respecting which he sought to "physicians rather than the Lord" (2 Chron. xvi. 10, 12).

Note : Asa's blunders followed upon his prosperity. Few abide this test. Loss of spirituality and religious zeal accompanies the growing worldly prosperity of churches !—J. A. M.

Vers. 1—8.—"*Beloved for the father's sake.*" I. THE STORY OF A MISUSED OPPORTUNITY. Even in a three years' reign much might have been done. Israel had its troubles, the past its lessons of wisdom; but there was no ear to hear the one, and no heart to attempt redress of the other. 1. *The secret of failure.* (1) *He was content with things as he found them.* It is not said that he introduced any new idolatries : " He walked in all the sins of his father, which he had done before him." The sin and responsibility of those who continue to walk in the paths of sinful, though general and time-honoured, customs, and who do not forsake the idolatries and iniquities of their fathers. (2) *His love was not set upon God.* The worship of Jehovah was still continued. Abijah had experienced the signal mercy of God (2 Chron. xiii.) His heart might have been won, but it " was not perfect with the Lord his God as the heart of David his father." There was no thirsting after God, no delight in the sense of the favour which is life, and the loving-kindness which is better than life. The love of God the only source of work for God. 2. *The sinful was also a troubled reign :* "there was war," &c., and it was war with brethren. 3. *The opportunity was soon ended :* " he reigned three years." Opportunities abused may be soon removed. The life which sin has marred death may swiftly seal.

II. A RIGHTEOUS LIFE AN UNDYING POWER WITH GOD. " For David's sake did the Lord his God give him," &c. Our good does not die with us or with our generation. The memory of it dwells, and prevails, with God. 1. The sinful king has a son to succeed him, and one whom God directs and blesses. 2. The city is preserved and the flood of evil driven back—" to establish Jerusalem." God's promises, our prayers, and our purposes are alike remembered. They bloom amid our dust. Our love and loyalty to God will fall in blessing upon ages yet to come.

III. SIN LEAVES ITS STAIN ON THE FAIR RECORD OF A RIGHTEOUS LIFE. " Save only in the matter of Uriah the Hittite." God will not wink at or cloak our iniquity. Is there any matter of which thou and all will hear when the books are opened ? If there be, is it not a call for humiliation and for prayer ?—J. U.

Vers. 9—24.—" *Zeal without trust.*" AN OPPORTUNITY RECOGNIZED AND USED. The need of the time was manfully met. Brought up in an idolatrous home, he nevertheless saw that this sin was sapping the foundation of the nation's stability and strength, and he set himself to root it out. 1. *The land was cleansed from filthy abomination,* from legalized, and even sanctified, sin (" And he took away the Sodomites," &c.) The nation that legalizes sin will reap corruption and shame : that which suppresses it by righteous enactment will pass up into purity and strength and truest glory. 2. *He put down idolatry with unflinching faithfulness.* He " removed ALL the idols *which his father had made.*' " And also Maachah his mother, even her he removed from being queen," &c. Neither reverence for the dead not fear of the living was suffered to stand in the way of his obedience to God. It is easy to condemn sin in the abstract. It is hard to stand face to face with him who is its servant and say, " Thou art the man." Is our faithfulness after the pattern of Asa's ? 3. *His failure was one of ability, not of will* (ver. 14). We may not be able to accomplish all we desire, or that is needful, but if our heart be " perfect with the Lord " all is well. 4. *He did not keep back the Lord's portion.* The " silver and gold and vessels," which his father and he himself had vowed, were brought into the Lord's house. His faithfulness was shown *in what he gave* as well as in what he condemned.

II. THERE MAY BE ZEAL FOR GOD WITHOUT PERFECT TRUST IN GOD. The man of action is not always a man of prayer. 1. *Baasha's attempt* (see 2 Chron. xvi. 7, &c.) The danger was great, but to the politician there seemed a way out of it. He was not shut up to God's help, as in the invasion by the Ethiopian king, and therefore God was not sought. (1) Forsaking the path of trust, he entered the crooked ways of worldly policy. He bribed Ben-hadad to break faith with Baasha. How often is self-help stained with meanness and unrighteousness! (2) God does not always forsake His people when they forsake Him. Asa's plan succeeded. The fortress that was being built against him became two for him. If unbelief was so blessed, what mercies might have crowned faith! 2. *The disease which embittered his latter days.* "Nevertheless in the time of his old age he was diseased in his feet." Here, again, his faith was tried and found wanting. "In his disease he sought not to the Lord but to the physicians" (2 Chron. xvi. 12); and he found no relief. There is a limit to God's forbearance even with His people. How much is there of our weakness and trouble and distress over which the words are written, "Ye have not, because ye ask not"!—J. U.

Ver. 14.—*Religious sincerity.* A beautiful flower often springs from the midst of corruption. The more we realize the moral condition of Asa's surroundings the more we wonder at the grace which made him what he was. His father was Abijam (or Abijah), the second king of Judah, of whom it is said, "He walked in all the sins of his father, which he had done before him." His education appears to have been entrusted to Maachah, his grandmother, a daughter of Absalom the rebel, and herself a gross idolatress. The remembrance of these facts makes the statement respecting this young prince the more surprising—"Asa did that which was right in the eyes of the Lord, as did David his father." An independent spirit and a resolute will must have been coupled with his piety. [Show from this the possibility of triumphing over the most adverse circumstances by those who sincerely seek to serve God.] It is not, however, to his manly resolution, to his vigour, or to his political wisdom that our attention is specially called by the text, but to his RELIGIOUS SINCERITY.

I. RELIGIOUS SINCERITY ASSERTS ITSELF IN REFORMING ZEAL (vers. 12, 13). It was only twenty years since the death of Solomon, yet irreligion and vice had corrupted the nation. Evil spreads more rapidly than good in a fallen world. The deadly fungus springs up in a night, the fruit-tree grows slowly to perfection. A half-hearted or timid man would have been content to worship Jehovah himself, and thus silently rebuke the idolatry of his people; but Asa, being an earnest man, could not content himself with any *laissez faire* principle. With a strong hand he would put down evil wherever he could reach it. Often in God's sight to leave evil alone, unrebuked, and uncombated is to share the guilt of those who commit it. It is the spirit of Cain, and not of Christ, that asks, "Am I my brother's keeper?" Asa's reforming zeal contains lessons to rulers, to employers, to parents, indeed to all who can mould the circumstances of others. See, therefore, how it made itself felt. 1. *Opportunities for sin were diminished.* Ver. 12 implies that there were those in Judah who made a traffic of vice. Corrupt themselves, they corrupted others. There are places in Christian cities which should be swept away by the strong hand of law. 2. *Incentives to sin were destroyed.* The idol referred to (in ver. 13) is literally "the horror." The obscene rites connected with its cultus will not bear investigation. Suffice it to say that this so-called worship provoked to vice of the most hideous kinds. Against provocations and incentives to sin how earnestly should parents guard their children, and masters and mistresses their servants. Impure literature is in the forefront of these; not only that which offends by its grossness, but that which secretly stains by its suggestions. 3. *Influences for sin were removed.* Sometimes vice is made popular by leaders of fashion or of policy. The unrighteousness of a clever man, the impurity of a leader in society are woefully far-reaching in their effects. Maachah, the queen-mother, was one of the most potent in Asa's court, was his near relation, his early instructress; yet, with as much wisdom as courage, "he removed her from being queen," and destroyed her idol publicly and shamefully. It might be said that he was indebted to her, that she was aged and should be respected, or that she could not live long, and might therefore be tolerated. Such pleas would not avail with a man whose "heart was perfect with the Lord." (Apply this.)

II. RELIGIOUS SINCERITY PROCLAIMS ITSELF BY CONFIDENCE IN GOD. This confidence was at the heart of Asa's courage. Read our text in the light of the fuller history of the king (given in 2 Chron.), and see how his confidence displayed itself. 1. *He found rest in God in peril.* Many adversaries would be raised by a reformation which was ruthless in its rigour. Idolatrous priests, the party led by Maachah, &c., would rebel; but Asa was not perturbed. God was his refuge and strength. 2. *He offered prayer to God in his difficulty.* As an example read 2 Chron. xiv. Describe the incursion of the Ethiopian host, and this prayer of the king, "Lord, it is nothing with thee to help, whether with many, or with them that have no power: help us, O Lord our God, for we rest on thee, and in thy name we go against this multitude." A victory followed which was unique in the history of God's people. Conquest waits on prayer in every struggle with evil. 3. *He consecrated himself and his people to God after their deliverance* (see ver. 15, and compare with it 2 Chron. xv.) He renewed the covenant, and afresh dedicated all he possessed to the Lord. So he deserved the high commendation, "Asa's heart was perfect with the Lord all his days." It remains yet to be observed that—

III. Religious sincerity may be associated with imperfect service. *He failed to remove the high places.* This Hezekiah and Josiah did. To leave them was to provide a way of return to the idolatrous practices he had put down. Beware of leaving lesser sins unconquered, after victory has been attained over grosser crimes.—A. R.

EXPOSITION.

CHAPTER XV. 25—XVI. 28.

The reigns of Nadab, Baasha, Elah, Zimri, and Omri, kings of Israel.—After bringing up the history of the kings of Judah, which has engaged his pen since ch. xiv. 21, to the date of the death of Asa, our author goes back some forty years to record the contemporary history of the kingdom of Israel, with which the rest of this book, the last thirteen verses alone excepted, is occupied. On the other hand, none of these reigns are even noticed by the chronicler, who only refers to the history of Israel, so far as it is inextricably connected with the object of his work; in other words, so far as is necessary to explain or illustrate the reigns of the kings of Judah.

Ver. 25.—And Nadab [= *liberal*] the son of Jeroboam began to reign [Heb. *reigned*] over Israel in the second year of Asa king of Judah, and reigned over Israel two years. [The reigns of these five kings of Israel are related with great brevity. It was not the object of the author to chronicle secular history—for this he refers us to "the books of the days"—he is only concerned with the events of their reigns in so far as they relate to the kingdom of God.]

Ver. 26.—And he did evil in the sight of the Lord, and walked in the way of his father [Jeroboam begat all his sons, save one, "in his own likeness"], and in his sin wherewith he made Israel to sin. [*I.e.*, not the rebellion, but the schism (chs. xii. 30; xiv. 16; cf. vers. 30, 34; xvi. 2, 13, 19, &c.; see Homiletics, p. 274). All the successors of Jeroboam, it is clear, either thought themselves compelled, by the exigencies of their position, to adhere to his ecclesiastical policy, or found themselves more and more entangled in its toils.]

Ver. 27.—And Baasha the son of Ahijah [not the prophet of that name (ch. xiv. 2), who was an Ephraimite, whereas this Ahijah was], of the house of Issachar [This fact is perhaps mentioned to distinguish the father of Baasha from the prophet. Or it may owe its insertion to the insignificance of this tribe (Gen. xlix. 14, 15) up to this date. *This* change of dynasty, unlike the last, was in no way connected with tribal jealousies. Baasha owed his elevation to his own abilities or to his unscrupulous daring], conspired [The word implies associates. There was a plot formed for Nadab's assassination] against him: and Baasha smote him at Gibbethon [= *eminence*. In the tribe of Dan (Josh. xix. 44) and a Levitical city: one of the four assigned to the Levites in the territory of that tribe (*ib.*, xxi. 23). It has not been identified. Evidently it was on the border of Philistia. Some would connect it with the modern *Mejdel*, a little to the north of Ascalon. The reader will observe how large a number of the names of towns indicate their elevation. The cities of those days were set on a hill. It was dangerous to build in the plain], which belonged to the Philistines [Blunt suggests ("Coincidences," p. 181) that it was because the place had been deserted by the Levites, in the general exodus to Judah, that the Philistines availed themselves of the opportunity to seize and fortify it. But the divided and consequently weakened state of the kingdom would of itself have encouraged them to throw off the yoke of Israel (Ewald)]; **for Nadab and all Israel laid siege to Gibbethon.**

Ver. 28.—**Even in the third year of Asa** [We have here (as in ch. xvi. 8, 23) a conspicuous instance of the Hebrew habit of counting parts of years as entire years. It is obvious that if Nadab succeeded to the throne in the *second* (ver. 25) and died in the *third* year of Asa, he cannot have reigned two full years] **king of Judah did Baasha slay him** [As the assassination took place during the siege, it is extremely probable that Baasha, like Omri, was the captain of the host], **and reigned in his stead.** [Probably Nadab had showed himself quite unequal to the task of governing, of which reading the army was in that age a principal function (1 Sam. viii. 20). It is just possible that in the occupation of Gibbethon by Philistines we have a proof of his feebleness and incapacity. Anyhow, when the strong hand of Jeroboam is removed, the fruits of the rebellion at once begin to appear. The contempt and defiance which Jeroboam had showed towards constituted authority are now manifested towards his successor. Baasha only takes a leaf out of Jeroboam's book (ch. xi. 26).]

Ver. 29.—**And it came to pass, when he reigned, that he smote all the house of Jeroboam; he left not to Jeroboam any that breathed** [Same expression in Josh. xi. 14; cf. Deut. xx. 16. Males and females alike were destroyed; see ch. xiv. 11], **until he had destroyed him, according unto the saying of the Lord, which he spake by his servant Ahijah the Shilonite** [ch. xiv. 10. It is not implied that it was *because* of this prophecy that Baasha exterminated the house of Jeroboam. It is probable that, so far from setting himself to fulfil it, he knew nothing about it, and, as he thought, merely took effectual measures for his own security. His seat could never be safe, so long as one of Jeroboam's house survived. Grotius aptly cites, with reference to these wholesale murders, the saying, νήπιος ὃς πατέρα κτείνας, υἱοὺς κατέλιπε]:

Ver. 30.—**Because of the sins of Jeroboam which he sinned, and which he made Israel to sin, by his provocation wherewith he provoked the Lord God of Israel to anger.** [Cf. ch. xvi. 2, 7, 13, 26, &c.]

Ver. 31.—**Now the rest of the acts of Nadab, and all that he did, are they not written in the book of the chronicles of the kings of Israel?**

Ver. 32.—**And there was war between Asa and Baasha king of Israel all their days.** [Verbatim as ver. 16, where see note. Several commentators suggest that this latter statement was copied from the chronicles of Israel, and that of ver. 16 from those of Judah. It is held by others, however, that for Baasha we should here read *Nadab*, and in favour of this view is the fact that the reign of Nadab is still under consideration, the history of Baasha only beginning with the following verse.]

Ver. 33.—**In the third year of Asa king of Judah began Baasha the son of Ahijah to reign** [Practically a repetition of ver. 28. These iterations are thoroughly in accord with Eastern usage (cf. vers. 26, 30, 34; ch. xvi. 1, 7, &c.)] **over all Israel in Tirzah, twenty and four years.**

Ver. 34.—**And he did evil in the sight of the Lord, and he walked in the way of Jeroboam, and in his sin wherewith he made Israel to sin.**

CHAPTER XVI.

This division of chapters, immediately after the commencement of the narrative of the reign of Baasha, is somewhat unfortunate, inasmuch as it obscures the close connexion between the sin of Baasha and the prophecy which it provoked. The idea the historian would convey is clearly this —the analogy between the dynasty of Jeroboam and that which supplanted it, (1) in their sin, (2) in the denunciation of each by a prophet, and (3) in the punishments which followed their sins—an analogy so close that the prophet Jehu almost employs the *ipsissima verba* of his predecessor, Ahijah.

Ver. 1.—**Then the word of the Lord came to Jehu, the son of Hanani** [Hanani is mentioned in 2 Chron. xvi. 7—10 as having admonished Asa, and as having been thrown into prison for so doing. Both he and his son would seem to have belonged to the kingdom of Judah. We find the latter in 2 Chron. xix. 2 a resident in Jerusalem, and protesting against the alliance between Jehoshaphat, whose historian he became, and whom, consequently, he must have survived (2 Chron. xx. 34), and Ahab. He is mentioned in the verse last cited as "made to ascend on the book of the kings of Israel" (see Introduction, p. xiii.) His prophetic career must have extended over at least half a century] **against Baasha, saying,**

Ver 2.—Forasmuch as I exalted thee out of the dust [cf. ch. xiv. 7 ; 2 Sam.vii. 8 ; Psa. lxxviii. 70. These words assuredly point to a lowly origin. He may well have risen from the ranks], **and made thee prince** [The original word is used of leaders of various degrees, comprehending even the king : ch. i. 35 ; 1 Sam. ix. 16 ; x. 1 ; cf. Dan. ix. 25] **over my people Israel** [There is no approval implied here of the means by which Baasha had raised himself to the throne. All that is said is that he had been an instrument in God's hands, and owed his throne to God's sanction and ordering. Even his conspiracy and cruelties had been overruled to the furtherance of the Divine purpose], **and thou hast walked in the way of Jeroboam, and hast made my people Israel to sin, to provoke me to anger** [better *vex*, one word] **with their sins ;**

Ver. 3.—Behold, I will take away [Heb. *exterminate ;* same word as in chs. xiv. 10 (where see note) ; xxi. 21 ; xxii. 47, &c.] **the posterity of** [Heb. *after*] **Baasha, and the posterity of** [*after*] **his house, and will make thy house like the house of Jeroboam the son of Nebat.** [Cf. ch. xv. 29; xxi. 22, &c.]

Ver. 4.—Him that dieth of [Heb. *to ;* see note on ch. xiv. 11] **Baasha in the city shall the dogs eat ; and him that dieth of his in the fields shall the fowls of the air eat.** [It may be these words, like those of the next two verses, were almost a formula, but if so, it is noticeable that precisely the same formula was used of Jeroboam a few years before, and Baasha knew well how it had been accomplished. "All the prophets in succession have the same message from God for the same sins" (Wordsworth).]

Ver. 5.—Now the rest of the acts of Baasha, and what he did, and his might [as to which see ch. xv. 17—21. He could hardly have given a stronger proof of his might than by fortifying a post but five miles distant from Jerusalem. Keil, however, would interpret the word, both here and in ch. xv. 23, of his energy and strength in government. Better Bähr, *tapfere Thaten.* Ewald hence infers that Baasha was "a man of distinguished bravery"], **are they not written in the book of the chronicles of the kings of Israel ?**

Ver. 6.—So Baasha slept with his fathers, and was buried in Tirzah [cf. ch. xv. 21, 33. This place is twice mentioned as his residence], **and Elah his son reigned in his stead.** [It is perhaps more than a mere coincidence that this uncommon name, *Elah* ("terebinth," see note on ch. xiii. 14), is also the name of the great valley (1 Sam.

xvii. 2, 19 ; xxi. 9) near to Gibbethon, where Baasha was proclaimed king.]

Ver. 7.—And also by the hand of the prophet Jehu, the son of Hanani, came the word of the Lord against Baasha [This does not refer, as some have thought, to a second prophecy on Jehu's part, but is rather explicative of ver. 2. Rawlinson thinks the object of the historian herein was to point out that Baasha was punished for the "murder of Jeroboam [?] and his family," as well as for the calf-worship. Keil and Bähr hold that it is designed to guard against a perversion of ver. 2, "I made thee prince," &c., from which it might be inferred that he was commissioned of God to murder Nadab. But it is simpler to suppose that his primary idea was to convey, by this repetition, which no doubt is derived from a different source from the statement of ver. 2, that Baasha was visited *by God* for his various sins. It was no chance that happened to him. The excision of his house, like that of Jeroboam, was distinctly foretold], **and against his house, even for all the evil that he did in the sight of the Lord, in provoking him to anger with the work of his hands** [ver. 2 ; note the coincidence with ch. xv. 30, in connexion with the next words. Bähr explains "the works of his hands" as idols, *Dii factitii,* after Deut. iv. 28, but this appears somewhat far-fetched], **in being like the house of Jeroboam, and because he killed him** [*i.e.*, Nadab].

The Reign of Elah.

Ver. 8.—In the twenty and sixth year of Asa, king of Judah, began Elah, son of Baasha, to reign over Israel, two years [cf. ch. xv. and see note on ch. xv. 28].

Ver. 9.—And his servant [Not only "subject," as Rawlinson, but officer. The same word is used of Jeroboam ; ch. xi. 26, note. We may almost trace here a *lex talionis.* Baasha was Nadab's "servant," as Jeroboam was Solomon's] **Zimri** [From the occurrence of this name among those of the descendants of Jonathan (1 Chron. viii. 36), it has been supposed (Stanley) that this was a last effort of the house of Saul to regain the throne], **captain of half his chariots** [רֶכֶב as in ch. ix. 19 ; x. 26. The violation of the law of Deut. xvii. 16 brings its own retribution], **conspired against him** [precisely as Elah's father had "conspired" (ch. xv. 27) against Nadab], **as he was in Tirzah, drinking himself drunk in the house of Arza, steward of** [Heb. *which was over ;* cf. chs. iv. 6 ; xviii. 3 ; 2 Kings x. 5 ; xviii. 37] **his house in Tirzah.** [Several points present themselves for notice here. First, the example of Jeroboam has clearly had its full influence on the nation. "The Lord's anointed " is no longer had in reverence, as in the days of David (1 Sam. xxiv. 6, 10 ; xxvi. 9, 16 ; 2 Sam. i. 14), nor is it accounted a sin to grasp at the crown. (2) Zimri only does what Baasha had done before him. That prince was "hoist with his own petard." (3) Elah would seem to have been a dissolute and pusillanimous prince. His place was clearly with his army at Gibbethon (ver. 15 ; cf. Jos., viii. 12. 4). And as clearly it was *not* in the house of one of his subjects, even the intendant of his palace. " An Oriental monarch . . . is precluded by etiquette from accepting the hospitality of his subjects " — Rawlinson, who further remarks that the low tastes which we here find Elah indulging "had probably been formed before his father was exalted *out of the dust.*" As probably they were inherited direct from his father. Anyhow, they led to his destruction. It is clear that Elah's want of character, like Nadab's, suggested the conspiracy of Zimri. (4) It is extremely probable, though not absolutely certain, as Bähr affirms, that Arza was one of the conspirators, and that the wretched prince had been decoyed to his house and made drunk, with a view to his murder there.]

Ver. 10.—And Zimri went in [cf. Judg. iii. 20 ; 2 Sam. iv. 7] and smote him and killed him, in the twenty and seventh year of Asa king of Judah, and reigned in his stead. [Cf. ch. xv. 28 and 2 Kings xv. 23. It is curious how it happened three times in the history of Israel that "the only powerful prince in a new dynasty was its founder, and after his son and successor reigned two years, the power passed into other hands " (Ewald).]

The Reign of Zimri.

Ver. 11.—And it came to pass when he began to reign, as soon as he sate on his throne, that he slew all the house of Baasha [see note on ch. xv. 29. The LXX. Vat. omits the rest of this verse and the first clause of ver. 12]: he left him not one that pisseth against a wall [*i.e.*, not a boy. See ch. xiv. 10 note], neither of [Heb. *and*]

his kinsfolks [The יֹּאֵל is strictly the person to whom (1) the right of redemption (Levit. xxv. 26 ; Ruth, *passim*) and (2) the duty of avenging blood (Num. xxxv. 19) belonged. And this being the next-of-kin (Ruth ii. 12, 13), the word came to mean *near relative, kinsman,* as here ; cf. Ruth ii. 20. All the same, it discloses to us Zimri's object, which was to destroy the avenger of blood. And it shows (in connexion with

ver. 16) that none of Baasha's children, if he had other children, had gone to the war], nor of his friends. [Zimri went a step farther than Baasha had gone. He was not content with extirpating the royal family, but put to death the partizans of the ho use, all who would be likely to sympathize with Elah or to resent his murder.]

Ver. 12.—Thus did Zimri destroy all the house of Baasha, according to the word of the Lord which he spake against Baasha, by [Heb. *in the hand of*] Jehu the prophet [Vers. 1, 7 ; cf. ch. xv. 29. The analogy is now complete],

Ver. 13.—For [אֶל corresponds with the עַל of ver. 7 = *propter;* cf. chs. xiv. 5 ; xxi. 22] all the sins of Baasha, and the sins of Elah his son, by which they sinned, and by which they made Israel to sin, in provoking the Lord God of Israel to anger [the formula of ch. xv. 30, &c.] with their vanities. [The calves, not idols, are referred to here. Cf. Deut. xxxii. 21 ; 1 Cor. viii. 4. The same idea is embodied in the word *Bethaven;* Hosea iv. 15 ; v. 8.]

Ver. 14.—Now the rest of the acts of Elah, and all that he did, are they not written in the book of the chronicles of the kings of Israel ?

Ver. 15.—In the twenty and seventh year of Asa king of Judah did Zimri reign [The same word elsewhere translated in A. V. *began to reign.* It is really an aorist = succeeded to the throne] seven days in Tirzah. And the people were encamped [Heb. *encamping*] against Gibbethon, which belonged to the Philistines. [It has at first sight a suspicious look that two kings of Israel, within an interval of about twenty-five years, should have been slain by conspirators during a siege of this place. But when the narrative is examined, its probability and consistency become at once apparent. Stanley assumes that the siege lasted over the whole of this period, but it is more likely that when Baasha found himself king, he discovered that he had domestic matters enough upon his hands, without a foreign war, and so he raised the siege. It is very probable that he feared opposition such as Zimri and Omri subsequently experienced. And his wars with Asa and with Syria may well have prevented his renewing the undertaking. On the accession of Elah, however, with the usual ambition and impetuosity of youth, it was decided to recommence the siege and to win this city back for Israel. But the fate of Nadab, and the consequent ill omen attaching to the place would not be forgotten, and this, as well as his voluptuous habits, may have deterred the *fainéant* Elah from besieging it in person, while the conspiracy which marked the former siege may at the same time have suggested to Zimri and others the thought of conspiring against Elah.]

Ver. 16.—**And the people that were encamped heard say, Zimri hath conspired, and hath also slain the king : wherefore all Israel** [obviously, all the army. Cf. ch. xii. 1, 16, 18] **made Omri, the captain of the host, king over Israel that day in the camp.** [It was hardly likely they would submit to the usurpation of Zimri. Not only had he occupied a subordinate position, but his murder of all Elah's friends must have made him a host of enemies in the camp. It was the natural thing for them, therefore, to turn to Omri. He had the advantage of being in possession. The captain of the host stood next to the king (2 Kings iv. 13 ; 2 Sam. v. 8 ; xix. 13 ; xx. 23), and twice stepped into his place (2 Kings ix. 5). This history has many parallels in that of the Roman empire.]

Ver. 17.—**And Omri went up from Gibbethon** [" The expression, ' went up,' accurately marks the ascent of the army from the Shephelah, where Gibbethon was situated, to the hill country of Israel, on the edge of which Tirzah stood " (Rawlinson)], **and all Israel** [see on ver. 16] **with him, and they besieged Tirzah.** [It is probable that they arrived before the city on the sixth or seventh day after the assassination of Elah. This period would just allow sufficient time for the news of the conspiracy to travel to Gibbethon and for the march of the army.]

Ver. 18.—**And it came to pass, when Zimri saw that the city was taken** [the meaning is probably that which Josephus gives : " When he saw that the city had none to defend it," or possibly, " when he saw that a breach was made "], **that he went into the palace** [אַרְמוֹן citadel, fortress, from אָרַם *altus fuit.* So Gesen., Keil, Bähr, *al.* The palace, no doubt, consisted of a string of buildings (ch. vii. 2—9) of which this was the highest and strongest part. Ewald thinks that the harem—a word which has almost the same radicals—or women's apartment, is meant—the *most secluded* portion of the great palace (Josephus understands it to mean " the inmost part "), and hence infers, as also from 2 Kings ix. 31, that the women of the palace had willingly submitted to the effeminate murderer of their lord, and that even the queen-mother had made advances towards him (vol. iv. p. 36). But, as Bähr remarks, there is nothing of this in the text, and Zimri's desperate act rather shows daring and contempt of death than effeminacy or

sensuality. And 2 Kings xv. 25 (cf. Psa. cxxii. 7) seems to point to a stronghold rather than a seraglio] **of the king's house, and burnt the king's house** [probably the palace which Jeroboam had built. Ewald thinks it was this structure gave Tirzah its reputation for beauty ; Cant. vi. 4] **over him with fire** [According to the Syriac, the besiegers set fire to the palace. Similarly Jarchi. But the text is decisive. The parallel deed of Sardanapalus will occur to all readers. Rawlinson also refers to Herod. i. 176, and vii. 107], **and died.** [This word is intimately connected with the verse following. But there is no need to rearrange the verses. The text, as it stands, conveys clearly enough that Zimri's tragical death was a retribution for his sins. Bähr remarks that of Elah and Zimri we learn nothing, apart from the fact that they held to the sin of Jeroboam, except how they died.]

Ver. 19.—**For his sins which he sinned in doing evil in the sight of the Lord, in walking in the way of Jeroboam, and in his sin which he did, to make Israel to sin.** [It is quite clear that in his reign of one week Zimri cannot have done much to show his complicity in the schism of Jeroboam, and it is probable that the sacred writer means that his character and antecedents were such as to prove that all his sympathies were with the irreligious party. Bähr thinks that he had "formerly displayed much partiality for the calf-worship." But it is quite as likely that the idea in the historian's mind was that all these events were the bitter fruits of Jeroboam's misguided and impious policy, into the spirit of which, Zimri, like his predecessors, had been baptized. It is interesting to remember here the aspect these repeated revolutions and assassinations would wear to the kingdom of Judah, then enjoying quietness and prosperity under Asa. We cannot doubt for a moment that they were regarded as so many manifestations of the righteous judgment of God, and as the outcomes of that spirit of insubordination and impiety which, in their eyes, had brought about both the division of the kingdom and the schism in the church.]

Ver. 20.—**Now the rest of the acts of Zimri** [We see here the tendency of the historian to express himself in formulae. He checks himself, however, and does not add " and all that he did," &c.], **and his treason that he wrought** [Heb. *his conspiracy which he conspired.* Though this was all there was to tell of him, yet no doubt it would be recorded at greater length by the historians of the day. We can hardly suppose that the " books of the words of the days " would dismiss so striking an event in a few sentences], **are they not written in the book of the chronicles of the kings of Israel ?**

The Interregnum.

Ver. 21.—**Then were the people of Israel divided into two parts : half of the people followed** [lit., *was after*. Same expression 2 Sam. ii. 10 ; cf. ch. i. 7] **Tibni the son of Ginath** [Who he was, or why he was set up in opposition to Omri, it is impossible to say. It has been supposed that the army was divided in its preferences, and that part of the soldiery wished to make Tibni king, and this is perhaps the most probable conjecture. It is to be considered that the *entire* army was not encamped before Gibbethon. Nor are vers. 16, 17 fatal to this view, as Bähr maintains, because " all Israel " there clearly means all the army under the command of Omri. It is hardly likely that Tibni was set up by the people of Tirzah, after the death of Zimri, to continue the struggle. The only thing that is certain is that, the hereditary principle being overthrown, the crown appeared to be the legitimate prize of the strongest ; and Tibni, who may have occupied a position of importance, or have had, somehow, a considerable following, resolved that Omri should not wear it without a fierce contest], **to make him king** [Omri had been already made king, *i.e.*, anointed, ver. 16] ; **and half followed Omri.**

Ver. 22.—**But the people that followed Omri prevailed against the people that followed Tibni the son of Ginath** [It appears, however, from the following verse that the struggle lasted four years] : **so Tibni died** [According to Jos., Ant. viii. 12. § 5, he was slain by the conqueror. The LXX. has here a curious and probably genuine addition. " And Thabni died, *and Joram his brother at that time*], **and Omri reigned.** [The jingle of the Hebrew words is probably designed.]

The Reign of Omri.

Ver. 23.—**In the thirty and first year of Asa king of Judah began Omri to reign over Israel, twelve years** [As Omri was proclaimed king in the twenty-seventh and died in the thirty-eighth year of Asa (cf. vers. 15, 29), he cannot in any case have reigned twelve *full* years ; whereas if his reign is to be dated, as it is here, from the thirty-first year of Asa, it is obvious that he would only have reigned seven, or, according to the Jewish mode of reckoning, eight years. Rawlinson proposes to get over the difficulty by rearranging the text. He would attach the first clause of this verse

to ver. 22, and read, " And Omri reigned in the thirty-first," &c. But to this there are two serious objections. First, that ver. 23, as it now stands, only follows the usual formula with which a new reign is announced (cf. vers. 8, 15, 29) ; and, second, it is extremely doubtful whether any prose sentence in the Hebrew ever begins as ver. 23 would then do, " *Reigned Omri* over Israel twelve years." Such a sentence would certainly be quite alien to the *usus loquendi* of our author. We are therefore reduced to the conclusion either (1) that the text here, as in some other instances (ch. vi. 1 ; 2 Kings i. 17 ; cf. iii. 1 ; xiii. 1, 10, &c.), has suffered at the hands of a reviser, or (2) that the numbers have been corrupted in transcription ; or (3) that the historian expresses himself in a somewhat confused way. Of these suppositions perhaps (1) is the most likely. Anyhow, it is clear that the twelve years of Omri's reign are to be counted not from the thirty-first, but from the twenty-seventh year of Asa, *i.e.*, from the date of Zimri's death (see vers. 10, 15, 29). The confusion has arisen from the fact that it was not until Tibni was slain, after four years of conflict, that Omri became *sole* ruler] : **six years reigned he in Tirzah.**

Ver. 24.—**And he bought** [*i.e.*, after the six years just mentioned. During the four years of anarchy Omri would seem to have retained possession of the capital which he had taken (ver. 18) on Zimri's death. But the palace being burnt and the defences perhaps weakened by the siege, he determined, rather than rebuild it, to found a capital elsewhere] **the hill Samaria** [Heb. *Shomerôn*, called by Herod *Sebaste*, whence its modern name *Sebustieh*. In his selection of Samaria for the seat of government, Omri acted with singular judgment. It has been said that " Shechem is the natural capital of Palestine," and no doubt it enjoys a commanding position and great advantages, but Samaria has even superior recommendations. It is a site with which no traveller can fail to be deeply impressed. Even Van de Velde, who says, " I do not agree with Dr. Robinson and other writers who follow him that the mountain of Samaria presents so admirable a combination of strength, fertility, and beauty, that the like is hardly to be found in Palestine " (vol. i. pp. 374, 375), nevertheless readily allows its superiority to Tirzah, and remarks on the strength of its position. " Many travellers have expressed a conviction that the spot was in most respects much preferable to the site of Jerusalem " (Kitto). It is a large oval or oblong mound, with a level surface, adapted for buildings, with steep sides to make its position im-

pregnable, and surrounded by an amphitheatre of hills. " Samaria is in a position
of great strength . . . and must before the invention of gunpowder have been almost impregnable. It stands some 400 feet above
the valley, the sides of the hill being steep
and terraced in every direction for cultivation, or perhaps for defensive purposes . . .
broad and open valleys stretch north and
south, and the hill is thus almost isolated,"
Conder, p. 47, who adds, "Strategical reasons may be supposed to have dictated the
choice of the capital of Omri, for on the
north the hill commands the main road to
Jezreel over a steep pass, on the west it
dominates the road to the coast, and on the
east that to the Jordan" (p. 49). Grove
(Dict. Bib. iii. 1099) speaks of "the singular
beauty of the spot," and Stanley (" Jewish
Church" ii. p. 284) justly sees in the selection
of this spot a proof of Omri's sagacity. But
perhaps the best proof is that which the
subsequent history supplies. Shechem and
Tirzah had each been tried, and each in
turn had been abandoned. But Samaria
continued to be the capital so long as the
kingdom lasted] of Shemer for two talents
of silver [variously estimated at £500 and
£800. This purchase, obviously of the
freehold, *i.e.*, in perpetuity, was in contravention of the law of Levit. xxv. 23. David
had bought the threshing-floor of Ornan, but
that was (1) from a Jebusite, and (2) for a
high religious purpose (2 Sam. xxiv. 24). It
has been suggested that this purchase may
have inspired Ahab with the idea of buying
the vineyard of Naboth], and built on [Heb.
built] the hill, and called the name of the
city which he built, after the name of
Shemer, owner of the hill, Samaria. [It is
not improbable that the vendor bargained
that the land should retain his name (cf.
Psa. xlix. 11). The reluctance of the
Israelite to part with his patrimony, even to
the king, is brought out very strikingly in
ch. xxi. Shemer, in selling his choice par-
cel of land for a capital, might well wish to
connect his name with it. The fact that
שֹׁמְרוֹן means *watch-mountain* (Gesen.), and
that we should have expected a name formed
from Shemer to take the form *Shimrôn*—
Shomerôn would strictly imply an original
Shomer—is not by any means a proof that our
historian is at fault in his derivation. For, in
the first place, the names Shomer and Shemer
are used of the same person in 1 Chron. vii.
32, 34. And secondly, nothing would be
more in accordance with Jewish ideas than
that Omri, in naming the hill after its
owner, should give a turn to the word which
would also express at the same time its
characteristic feature. A pun, or play upon
words, was the form which wit assumed

amongst the Semitic races (as, indeed, is the
case still, see Conder, p. 301), and the form
Shomerôn would at once perpetuate the
memory of Shemer, and express the hope and
purpose of Omri. It is a curious fact that
the later Samaritans did play upon this very
word, representing themselves as *guardians*
(שֹׁמְרִים) of the law (Ewald). The Greek
form of the name, Σαμάρεια, would seem to
have been derived through the Chaldee
שָׁמְרָיִן as found in Ezra iv. 10, 17.]

Ver. 25.—**But Omri wrought evil in the
eyes of the Lord, and did worse than all
that were before him.** [It has been thought
that Micah vi. 16 ("the statutes of Omri,
&c.") points to a fresh departure from the
Jewish faith ; to the organization of the
calf-worship into a regular formal system,
or to " measures for more competely iso-
lating the people of Israel from the services
of the house of the Lord at Jerusalem"
(Kitto).

Ver. 26.—**For he walked in all the way
of Jeroboam the son of Nebat, and in his
sin wherewith he made Israel to sin, to
provoke the Lord God of Israel to anger
with their vanities.**

Ver. 27.—**Now the rest of the acts of
Omri which he did, and his might that he
showed** [Not only in the war with Tibni,
but certainly in the subjugation of the
Moabites, of which mention is made in the
recently discovered *Moabite stone*. He may
well have had other wars, which, like this,
have escaped notice in Scripture. If the
king of Syria spoke truly (1 Kings xx. 34),
the war with that power had been extremely
disastrous. Yet the Assyrian inscriptions
prove that Omri's name was more widely
and permanently known in the East than
those of his predecessors or successors.
Samaria, for example, down to the time of
Tiglath-Pileser, appears as *Beth Khumri*,
the "house of Omri ;" Athaliah, the daughter
of Ahab, is called a daughter of *Omri ;* and
Jehu appears in the *Black Obelisk Inscription* as " the son of Omri " (Rawlinson,
" Hist. Illus. of O. T.," pp. 111—12). It is
perhaps an evidence of " his might " that
his dynasty retained the throne to the third
generation], **are they not written in the
book of the chronicles of the kings of
Israel ?** [Vers. 26, 27 are an exact repetition, *mutatis mutandis*, of ch. xiii. 14 ; cf.
xv. 30.]

Ver. 28.—**So Omri slept with his fathers,
and was buried in Samaria** [After the example of earlier kings, he found a grave in
his capital city ; cf. chs. ii. 10 ; xi. 43 ; xiv.
31 ; xvi. 16]: **and Ahab his son reigned in
his stead.**

HOMILETICS.

Ver. 29.—*The Punishment of Jeroboam's Sin.* We have already considered the true character of Jeroboam's sin (pp. 274 sqq.) It now remains for us to observe, first, the punishment which it provoked, and secondly, its workings in later generations. And its punishment was so great and so varied that it will of itself occupy the rest of this homily.

But let us remember, in the first place, that there were two parties to this sin. Jeroboam sinned himself and also " made Israel to sin." King and people alike were involved in the schism. If the one suggested it, the other embraced it. Originating with the former, it was approved and perpetuated by the latter. There were two parties, consequently, to the punishment. That was impartially shared between sovereign and subjects. We have to consider, therefore—

I. THE RETRIBUTION WHICH BEFELL THE ROYAL HOUSE.

II. THE RETRIBUTION WHICH OVERTOOK THE PEOPLE AT LARGE.

I. And in considering the pain and loss in which this sin involved those who sate upon the throne of Israel, we must discriminate between Jeroboam and his successors. Jeroboam was the prime, but not the only offender. If he was the author, subsequent kings were continuators of the schism. And as he had his punishment, so they had theirs. Let us therefore take account first of the sorrows and sufferings of the heresiarch, *Jeroboam.* Amongst these were the following:

1. *The foreknowledge that his kingdom would be overthrown.* This dismal foreboding must have clouded all his reign, for it dated from the day of that first sacrifice at Bethel. Then he learnt that a child of David's house should cover his schemes and memory with disgrace. He knew that the dynasty he had founded should not endure, and moreover that *he* was the author of its ruin, and he knew that others knew it too. " Uneasy lies the head that wears a crown." What shall we say of the crowned head disquieted by such forebodings as these?

2. *The foretaste of the destruction of his family.* As he had learnt from the man of God of the triumph of his rival and the dishonour of his priesthood, so he learnt from Ahijah of the excision of his family. This ambitious prince knew that his posterity would be swept away like dung, would be devoured like carrion. And he was assured of this, not only by prophetic word and by signs following, but he had an earnest thereof in the death of his firstborn. He knew that that was but " the beginning of the end." It was a sharp pang, but it was the lightest part of his punishment (ch. xiv. 13).

3. *Remorse and vexation.* He could not fail to compare the two messages of Ahijah (chs. xi. 31—39; xiv. 7—16). The first gave him dominion over ten tribes. The second left him neither subject nor survivor. God *had* promised to " build him a sure house." God now threatens him and his with annihilation. And why this change? He knew why it was. " The gifts and calling of God are without repentance." It was because of the calves (ch. xiv. 9). How he must have repented that piece of folly and faithlessness : how he must have cursed his infatuation—the more inexcusable, as he had the example of Solomon before him. It is possible that this remorse was so poignant that it shortened his days; that it was thus " the Lord struck him, and he died " (2 Chron. xiii. 20).

4. *The shameful murder of his family.* We can readily believe that a *parvenu* like Jeroboam, a servant who had raised himself to the throne, would have been content to suffer for the rest of his days, if thereby he could have averted the dishonour of his name and the destruction of his posterity—of all evils the greatest in the eyes of a Jew. But no; he foresaw that butchery awaited his nearest and dearest, and he had not slept long in his grave before the knife of Baasha was at his children's throats. And this murder of his posterity, though after the manner of Eastern despotisms, would seem to have been marked by circumstances of peculiar cruelty (ch. xvi. 7). It was so truculent that it brought down vengeance on the instrument. Our history gives no details, but it is easy to picture the divans dripping with blood, the corridors choked with the corpses of Jeroboam's wife and

children. The annals of Turkey and other Eastern kingdoms would supply many illustrations of this deed.

5. *His own untimely end.* For he died by the visitation of God—by a *stroke* of some kind or other. He may have perished like Antiochus Epiphanes, like Sylla, like Herod, like Philip of Spain. Or, like our Henry the First, he may have never smiled again after his son's death, but steadily drooped to his grave. Somehow his life was cut short. "The wicked shall be silent in darkness."

Such, then, was the fourfold penalty which Jeroboam paid for his sin. Let us now consider the punishment which befell his successors, who "walked in his way" and "departed not" from his heresy. We may trace it—

1. *In the shortness of their reigns.* Nadab, Elah, Ahaziah, all reigned two years. Zimri one week. None of the kings of Israel reigned like David and Solomon, or like Asa and other kings of Judah. In the 250 years that the kingdom of Israel lasted, nineteen kings occupied the throne, as against eleven kings of Judah. Asa saw seven kings in turn rise and fall during his reign ; Uzziah saw six ; and we have but to remember that long life was one of the principal sanctions of the Mosaic dispensation to be assured that these brief reigns were a manifestation of the righteous judgment of God.

2. *In the revolution and assassination which often closed them.* In these 250 years the dynasty was changed no less than seven times, and we know what a change of dynasty meant, in that and a later age. It was one of its traditions that "the man was a fool who when he slew the father spared the children." Six times this tragedy of Tirzah was repeated. Once an unhappy prince, to escape the butchery awaiting him, devoted himself and his household to the flames. Once seventy ghastly heads, in two heaps at the city gate, witnessed to the work of extermination.

II. But now let us note the share of the people in this dispensation of suffering. What befell the priests who ministered at Dan and Bethel—what the worshippers who resorted thither ? They or their children suffered these six penalties at least.

1. *Misgovernment.* Of the kings of Israel there was not one who did not " do evil " in the sight of the Lord. By which we are not only to understand that he worshipped the calves ; oppression, exactions, intolerable cruelties may be comprehended under the words. The case of Naboth (ch. xxi.) was probably not the only one of its kind. We may be sure, too, that when Elah was drinking himself drunk, injustice was being practised in his name. Incapacity—on the part of the king—may have been the cause of some insurrections, but oppression is a much more probable reason. We know what Rome was like when the purple fell to military adventurers. Probably Israel fared no better at the hands of its Baashas, Omris, and Menahems. What suffering a change of dynasty involved on the people we may gather from 2 Kings xv. 16. An Eastern kingdom at the best was a despotism, at the worst a devildom.

2. *Civil war.* The four years' struggle between Omri and Tibni and their respective partisans, which was a war to the death (ch. xvi. 22), entailed no less miseries on the country than civil war always does. Lands ravaged, homesteads fired, women violated—these were some of its incidents. It has been said that no one can give any adequate description of a battle. What shall be said of a battle lasting over four years? for in a country not so large as Yorkshire civil strife would mean unceasing conflict.

3. *Invasion.* (1) By Abijah (2 Chron. xiii. 4), (2) by Shishak, (3) by Syria, (4) by Assyria. Shishak was primarily appointed to chastise Judah, Syria was the lash of Israel. Observe that in the invasion of ch. xiii. 4, 19, Bethel was captured by the men of Judah, whilst in that of ch. xv. 20, Dan—Jeroboam's other shrine— was among the first to suffer. The priests of Dan and the inhabitants of the surrounding territory, the worshippers at its temple, bore the brunt of Ben-hadad's invasion. But the bands of Syria were always invading the land (ch. xx; 2 Kings vi.) And many a "little maid" (2 Kings v. 2) was carried off to dishonour.

> "Many a childing mother then
> And new-born baby died."

What a picture of the horrors of war have we in 2 Kings viii. 12. Yet such horrors must have been of common occurrence in Israel. And they culminated in the sack of Samaria and the captivity of the nation.

4. *Loss of territory.* Israel was "cut short" (2 Kings x. 32). In 2 Kings i. 1 (cf. iii. 5) Moab rebels. Syria, its great adversary, was once an appanage of Israel. Now Israel is made a dependency of Assyria (2 Kings xv. 19, 20).

5. *Famine.* It was the Lord called for this (2 Kings viii. 1). It was one of His "sore judgments" (Ezek. xiv. 13, 21). And it would seem to have been almost chronic in Israel (cf. chs. xvii. 1, 12; xviii. 2; 2 Kings iv. 38; vi. 25 sqq.; vii.; viii. 1). And the terrible straits to which the people were reduced thereby may be inferred from 2 Kings vi. 25, 29; cf. Deut. xxviii. 56, 57.

6. *Captivity.* For the carrying away beyond Babylon into the cities of the Medes was part of the reckoning for Jeroboam's sin, and for the allied sin of idolatry (ch. xiv. 15; 2 Kings xvii. 22, 23). The "carrying into captivity"—these are familiar words on our lips. But which of us can form any conception of the untold, unspeakable miseries which they cover? The gangs of prisoners tramping to Siberia give us but a faint idea. "Hermann and Dorothea" is a tale of modern times, and the flight it pictures conveys no just impression of the horrors of a wholesale transportation. When the land was swept as with a drag net (cf. 2 Kings xxi. 13, and compare Herod. iii. 149, vi. 31, where the manner in which the Persians carried away the population of some of the Greek islands is described), and the entire population marched in gangs across the burning plains, under brutal and lustful overseers—men in comparison with whom a "Legree" would be mildness itself—we may imagine some of the horrors of that journey. Nor did those sufferings end in the land of their captivity. Before the people was absorbed amongst the neighbouring nations, and so effaced from the page of later history, we may be pretty sure they paid a constant tribute of suffering for their sin. *Vae victis*, this was the unvarying law of ancient warfare, and the exiles of Assyria proved it in their own persons. Two hundred and fifty years after the schism, the seed sown by Jeroboam was still reaped in cruelty and agony and blood.

Ver. 2.—*The Working of Jeroboam's Sin.* The punishment which Jeroboam's sin brought down upon himself, his successors, and his people, was not its worst part. Its influences upon others, the lessons of disobedience and defiance taught by that malign example, were even more disastrous. Let us now trace, as far as we can, its workings; let us see how the leaven of the calves leavened the whole lump.

1. *He begat a son in his own likeness.* "The evil that men do lives after them"—it lives in their *children;* it is inwrought into their constitution. As a rule, the child reproduces the character of the parent, the moral traits, quite as closely as the physical. There are exceptions—Abijah was one—but they help to prove the rule. He was the only exception in the house of Jeroboam (ch. xiv. 3). *Fortes creantur fortibus et bonis,* and the converse is equally true. Nabab, and the other children of that house, not only practised the lessons they had learned in Jeroboam's school, but they reproduced in their own persons the self-will, the impatience of control, and the other faults and vices of their father. What wonder if "Nadab did evil in the sight of the Lord"? he only "walked," as the next words remind us, "in the way of his father" (ch. xv. 26).

2. *He begat a spirit of lawlessness and insubordination among his people.* There are not a few indications of demoralization and corruption in Israel, corresponding with the depravation of religion. The very revolutions, which followed one after another, are in themselves a proof of this. The chronic disaffection and the periodical upheavings of society in the northern kingdom, especially when contrasted with the quietness and security of Judah, can only be accounted for by the influences of the court. North and south were of one blood, and lived under one sky. It was because the former had been taught disobedience and disregard of constituted authority, it was because the sense of reverence and duty had been weakened by the action of Jeroboam, that it became like a reed shaken in the water—so often rebelled against its sovereigns. Jeroboam had accustomed them

to play fast and loose with the commandments of Heaven; what wonder if they made small account of their obligations to their earthly king?

3. *He taught Baasha, Zimri, and Omri to lift up their hands against the king.* Just as David's religious veneration for the person of the "Lord's anointed" tended to make his throne and that of his successors the more secure, so did Jeroboam's rebellion (ch. xi. 26) afford an example of aggression to later ages. His subjects were not likely to believe in the "divinity that doth hedge a king." Why should they scruple to grasp at the crown if it came within their reach? Why was Nadab more sacred than Rehoboam? Why should the son of Baasha, again, have more respect than the son of Solomon?

4. *He taught his subjects, indirectly, to hold life cheap.* There had been two changes of dynasty before Baasha had learned from him to attack the king and to exterminate his family, but both of these had been, so far as the royal family was concerned, bloodless. David never thought of slaying the children of Saul. His inquiry was, "Is there not yet any of the house of Saul that I may show the kindness of God unto him?" (2 Sam. ix. 3.) And when "Israel rebelled against the house of David," they never contemplated a massacre of Solomon's harem, or even of insolent Rehoboam. But observe the change in succeeding revolutions. "He left not to Jeroboam any that breathed" (ch. xv. 29; cf. xvi. 11; 2 Kings x. 11). Why this thirst of blood? It is because Jeroboam has returned from Egypt, and his godless proceedings have depraved public morality, and the restraints of law have been enfeebled, and men have grown more reckless and desperate (ch. xvi. 18, 24). It is clear to the most cursory reader that a daring impiety characterizes the whole period from Jeroboam to Hoshea, and for this "the sin of Jeroboam" is mainly responsible. That was the "first step" which makes the rest of the road easy.

5. *He entailed his sin upon his successors.* Of each of the kings of Israel do we read that he "walked in the way of Jeroboam, and in his sin which he did," and we wonder, perhaps, how it was that not one of these nineteen kings, sprung as many of them were from different lineages, had the courage and the piety to retrace his steps, and revert to the primitive faith and mode of worship. But a little reflection will show that this, under the circumstances, was well-nigh an impossibility. For Jeroboam had made the calf-worship an integral part of the national life. It was so intertwined with the existence of Israel as a separate people, that to abandon it would be to repudiate all the traditions of the kingdom, and tacitly to acknowledge the superiority of Judah. Any king attempting such a reformation would appear to be a traitor to his country. The attempt would have provoked a second schism. No, it was clear to each monarch at his accession, if he reflected on the subject at all, that the calf-worship *must go on.* The *damnosa hereditas* which he had received he must transmit. There was no place for repentance.

6. *He paved the way for idolatry.* Already, in ch. xiv. 15, we find the "groves" following directly upon the calves, the images of Asherah upon the images of Jehovah. Ahab and Jezebel are not wholly responsible for the abominations of Baal and Ashtaroth. It was the daring innovations of Jeroboam had prepared the minds of men for this last and greatest violation of the law. "Man does not become base all at once." The plunge into wholesale idolatry would have been impossible, had not the deep descent to the calf-worship been traversed first. *Pecati poena peccatum.* That, too, begets children in its own likeness. Those who despised the "tabernacle of witness" in the wilderness were given up to take up "the tabernacle of Moloch and the star of the god Remphan" (Acts vii. 42, 43). If men will not have God in their thoughts, He gives them over to a reprobate mind (Rom. i. 28).

7. *We see his hand in the building of Jericho.* It was Hiel, a *Bethelite,* braved the curse and rebuilt the walls and reared the gates of the city of palm trees. Here we see the influence of a prior violation of law. Whether he acted in ignorance of law, or defiance of law, it is to Jeroboam's sin the deed owed its perpetration. The law might well be forgotten which had been so completely ignored. And the subject had been encouraged to violate it by his sovereign.

8. *We hear his voice in the curses of the children of Bethel.* Where but at Bethel would children have dared thus to revile a prophet of the Lord? The children only reflected the impiety and hatred of their parents. And from whom had these latter learned their hatred but from the king, who "made an house of high places" there, and inaugurated the schismatic worship with his own hands? From the day when a man of God laid the city under an interdict, the prophets of Jehovah must have been unpopular at Bethel, and as the time passed by, and the breach was widened, passive dislike ripened into open scorn and hatred, and a new prophet, of whose powers they had had no experience, could not pass by without insult and defiance.

The Jews have a saying, that in all the scourgings, plagues, and chastisements which they have endured, there is not one but has in it an ounce of the dust of the golden calf which Aaron made. The saying holds equally good of the calves which Jeroboam made. There is not one of the troubles which befell both the crown and the kingdom, not one of the bitter sufferings which the ten tribes endured, but had its starting-point in the sin of Jeroboam.

HOMILIES BY VARIOUS AUTHORS.

Vers. 25—34.—*The Seed of Evil-doers.* 1. The subject before us furnishes illustration of the following propositions, viz.:

I. WICKED ARE THE SEED OF THE WICKED. 1. There is a sense in which this is *generally* true. (1) Jeroboam "made Israel to sin." Nadab "did evil in the sight of the Lord and walked in the way of his father, and in his sin whereby he made Israel to sin." (2) Baasha murdered Nadab and usurped his throne. Then he exterminated the whole house of Jeroboam. In this he fulfilled the words of Ahijah the Shilonite. Yet was it not out of zeal for God, but to serve his own selfish ambition. So under the same evil promptings he continued in the sin of Jeroboam (ver. 34). And his son after him walked in his steps. (3) Do we not still find that those who loyally serve God are children or grandchildren of godly persons? "The seed of the righteous is blessed." (4) This is the rule, but not without its exceptions; else missions to the heathen, abroad and at home, would be hopeless, which, thank God, they are not. 2. There is a sense in which this is *universally* true. (1) "Seed" is not always reckoned according to the flesh. "The children of the promise are counted for the seed" (Rom. ix. 8; see also the reasoning, Rom. ix. 13—18). (2) Thus God can, out of the very stones, raise up children to Abraham. Gentile believers in Christ are such (see Matt. iii. 9; Gal. iii. 26, 29). (3) In this sense all are not Israel who are of Israel. Descendants of Abraham who follow not his true faith and good works are not his seed (see John viii. 37, 40; Rom. ii. 28; ix. 7; Gal. vi. 15). (4) As the good, whether sprung from evil or good ancestors, are the seed of God; so are the wicked, whether sprung from evil or good ancestors, the seed of the devil (see Gen. iii. 15; John viii. 44; 1 John iii. 8). So are the wicked, without exception, the seed of the wicked.

II. THE TRIUMPHING OF THE WICKED IS SHORT. 1. *How brief was the reign of these kings!* (1) "The days which Jeroboam reigned were two and twenty years" (ch. xiv. 20). But this was little more than half the term of Asa's reign (ver. 10). (2) Nadab "reigned over Israel two years." This was really but a portion of two years, for, according to the usage of Scripture, a year entered is reckoned as if completed. He "began to reign over Israel in the second year of Asa," and "in the third year of Asa" did Baasha slay him (vers. 25, 28). (3) Baasha reigned "twenty and four years," still little more than half the time of Asa's reign. This son of David sat upon the throne of Judah long enough to see eight kings upon the throne of Israel, viz., Jeroboam, Nadab, Baasha, Elah, Zimri, Tibni, Omri, and Ahab. In these he witnessed no less than five dynasties! 2. *How little happiness had they in their rule!* (1) Sin brings the vexation of an evil conscience, with its attendant disquiet, suspicion, and fear. (2) Also the vexation of an angry Providence. They that take the sword take the blade with the haft. The wars of these ever-changing dynasties left little room for repose. (3) How difficult for men to learn that worldly ambition and vexation are sisters; that abiding happiness is found only in the ways of God!

III. THE END OF THE WICKED IS DESTRUCTION. 1. *This is written in history.* (1) It is recorded in the history of these kings. Jeroboam in person died upon his bed, but in his family his light was extinguished in blood. Baasha in like manner died on his bed, but in his family he too perished by the sword. (2) These examples are but samples of history at large—sacred, secular. 2. *It is also written in prophecy.* (1) We meet with it in the alternatives to the conditions of salvation. (2) This destruction follows the spirit into the invisible world, and is a "much sorer punishment" than that which terminates in natural death. (3) The judgments upon the wicked recorded in history are but figures of the more terrible doom threatened in prophecy.—J. A. M.

Vers. 25—34.—*God's threatenings find at last a complete fulfilment.* I. THE LAST STEP IN A CAREER OF REBELLION AND FOLLY. Nadab might have been warned. His way to the throne was opened up by God's judgment in the removal of Abijah. He must have heard of the Divine threatenings; he might have seen the evil results of his father's sin. But in the face of all these things he adopted the sinful policy of his father. 1. *"He did evil in the sight of the Lord."* His heart and life were estranged from God and righteousness. This is the explanation of all that follows. Contempt of the claims of revelation, and rebellion against God are but the revelation to men of a heart and life which have already grieved and provoked God. 2. *He continued in a path already dark with the frown of God :* "and walked in the way of his father." The son who continues in his father's sin may incur thereby a deeper guilt than his. The iniquity of it may not have been at first so fully manifested. It might have been considered and abandoned in the shadow of the father's death. As the ages roll on sins manifest themselves, and the nation which will not turn from them seals itself for destruction. Are there sins with us the evil of which we know to-day as we did not know before? Then the guilt of their retention is greater than that of their first commission. 3. *He resolutely pursued a path which meant destruction, not for himself only, but for an entire people :* "and in his sin wherewith he made Israel to sin." It was nothing less than an attempt to rob God of His chosen people, and them of Him, in order that the house of Jeroboam might reign in safety. The terrible selfishness and the murderous heart of sin! II. THE JUDGMENT. 1. *He was smitten in the midst of his army.* The host of his warriors could not save him. There is no place where God's hand cannot reach us. 2. *He was slain, not by the Philistines, but by one of his own servants.* Treachery and rebellion were visited with fitting punishment. The strict justice of the Divine vengeance. His judgments are *repayments :* "I will repay." 3. *The Divine threatening literally fulfilled* (ver. 29). God's words against sin are not lightly spoken. The end is hid from us, but His eye is resting, while He speaks, upon the woe.—J. U.

Ch. xv. 33—xvi. 7.—*Unrighteous Zeal.* I. SMITERS OF THE SINFUL ARE NOT NECESSARILY RIGHTEOUS (ch. xv. 33, 44). 1. *Baasha's crime.* Behind the slaughter of his master and his master's house lay the threatening of God. The Divine decree seemed to legalize the crime. But God's command did not come to *him*, nor was he moved by righteous indignation against the sins of the house of Jeroboam. He served his own passions, and it was sin to him before God, "because he killed him." The iniquity of those who rush in to smite wrong and hypocritically veil their hatred and spite and greed under the plea of zeal for God and righteousness (Rom. ii. 1). 2. *His evil life.* "He did evil in the sight of the Lord." State reforms are impossible for men whose own heart refuses God's yoke. Our work can never rise higher than the level of our life. There is also a spiritual law of gravitation : the streams of our influence can only flow downward. 3. *His hurtful reign.* He "walked in the way of Jeroboam," &c. He may have condemned Jeroboam's sin in regard to the calves, &c.; but when begirt with the same state exigencies he continued the course he himself had punished with death. It is easy to condemn the sins of others. God has nobler work for us: it is, when surrounded by their temptations to triumph over them, and to serve not by words only but by deeds.

II. GOD'S MESSAGE TO BAASHA (ch. xvi. 1—7). 1. *His exaltation was of God.* "I exalted thee out of the dust." The throne was not secured by his wickedness. The Lord had stilled opposition and given him success. 2. *It was great and unlooked for.* His tribe had no claim to the throne, and his own place among his people was a mean one. But God had, step by step, advanced him, and was now enabling him to reign in peace. The Lord's help is not withheld from those who do not know and do not serve Him. "Despisest thou the riches of His goodness and forbearance and long-suffering, not knowing that the goodness of God leadeth thee to repentance?" (Rom. ii. 4.) 3. *The return made to God.* He had changed nothing. Israel was still being led down the path of darkness and judgment, "to provoke Me to anger with their sins." Every higher interest was sacrificed to the policy of keeping the ten tribes separated from the other two. Statesmen out of office condemn that which, when in office, they are afraid to change. And how many are there who are neglecting the trusts God has committed to them. Once they said, "If *we* had only place or wealth, &c., God would be served and men blessed." These have been given and what has been done? Has the vow been performed? 4. *Baasha's punishment worse than Jeroboam's.* "I will take away the posterity of Baasha *and the posterity of his house*" (see ver. 11, "Neither of his kindred nor of his friends"). The Divine justice is shown in the differing penalties of sin.— J. U.

Vers. 1—7.—*Jehu's Prophecy.* Jehu was a prophet and the son of a prophet. Of his father Hanani we read in 2 Chron. xvi. 7—10, where it is recorded to his honour that he suffered imprisonment for the fidelity of his testimony against Asa. This son was worthy of such a father. His testimony before Baasha, a man of desperate resolution and unscrupulous irreligion, was admirably courageous. We hear of him again after an interval of forty years (see 2 Chron. xix. 2; xx. 34). In his prophecy here—

I. HE RECITES THE CRIMES OF BAASHA. These were—1. *That he "walked in the way of Jeroboam."* This implies (1) that he was influenced by a like ambition. An ambition to be great in the eyes of men—to be a king. (See ch. xi. 37.) (2) That to compass this he resorted to unscrupulous measures. He rebelled against his king. He rebelled against his God. 2. *That he made the people of the Lord to sin.* (1) To make any people, or person, to sin is a great crime. And who can sin only to himself? Directly or indirectly sin must exert an influence beyond. (2) To make God's covenanted people to sin is a higher crime. The oath upon them is violated. The salt of the earth, too, loses its savour, and the world is left to putrefy. (3) To make God's people to sin, not as by accident, but of set purpose, is the highest crime. This Baasha did in upholding Jeroboam's calves—the "work" of men's "hands" (ver. 7). He did this fearing, as Jeroboam had feared, that if the people went to Jerusalem to worship they might repent of their rebellion against the house of David. For the same reason Baasha opposed the reformation under Asa, and to this end set about the building of Ramah (see 2 Chron. xvi. 1). 3. *That he thereby provoked the anger of the Lord against them.* (1) This expressed itself in the incessant wars by which they were shaken "as a reed is shaken in the water" (ch. xiv. 15). (2) This is laid at the door of Baasha. His house is implicated with him. Jehu, therefore, had a message also to his house (ver. 7). 4. *And because he killed Jeroboam.* (1) This, however, he did not, *in person.* Jeroboam died on his bed (ch. xiv. 20). (2) But, *in his house,* he slew him (ch. xv. 27—29). A man lives in his posterity; when his posterity are destroyed or exterminated, he is extinct. (3) Perhaps the words "because he killed *him*" might be fairly rendered "because he killed *it,*" viz., the *house* of Jeroboam. This anyhow is the meaning (see ch. xv. 27, 29). The notion that he killed *Jehu* is inconsistent with the records of history, which bring Jehu upon the scene again in the days of Jehoshaphat.

II. HE UTTERS THE JUDGMENTS OF THE LORD. 1. *The posterity of Baasha was to be taken away.* (1) His own. He was to have no male representative. (2) That of his house. His female as well as male issue was to be destroyed. He was to be utterly rooted out. 2. *History repeats itself.* (1) It does this because crime must provoke appropriate punishment. God recognizes the *lex talionis*—eye for eye, tooth for tooth. (2) The house of Baasha being like to that of Jeroboam, the doom is similar. As Baasha executed the judgment of the Lord upon the house of Jeroboam, another aspirant to royalty is to execute the judgment of the Lord upon the house of Baasha. Note 3. *There are posthumous punishments.* (1) Baasha was as great a criminal as any of his house, yet he came to his grave in peace and honour. He died on his bed and was buried in state. Must there not be a future reckoning and retribution? (2) Baasha is punished in the extermination of his house. But this judgment came upon him after his decease. How could that affect *him* unless there be a future state? (3) The same inference follows from the judgment upon the bodies of his posterity after their decease. What matter would it be to him or them to have their bodies eaten by dogs or by vultures when the life was gone, unless the spirits survived? (4) How such things react upon the disembodied spirit is a mystery. "There are many things in heaven and earth that do not enter into our philosophy."—J. A. M.

Vers. 8—14. *The House of Baasha.* The character of Baasha is drawn in the paragraphs immediately preceding, which also contain an account of his end, which was better than he deserved, and suggests the reality of a future retribution. His family so fully followed in his steps that we have no mention of an Abijah amongst them, "in whom was found some good thing towards the Lord God of Israel" (see ch. xiv. 13). The judgment of God upon this wicked house is written in the words before us. We have to reflect upon—

I. THE DEPRAVITY OF THE HOUSE OF BAASHA. 1. *The prophecy of Jehu came to them as a warning.* (1) Such is the nature of this class of prophecies. The threatenings of God, like His promises, are conditional. So, had they repented, the judgments denounced would have been removed or moderated. (2) Of this principle the Scriptures furnish many illustrations. Take, *e.g.*, the argument of Abraham's prayer for Sodom and its success (Gen. xviii. 23—32). See the effect of the contrition of Ahab (ch. xxi. 27—29). How the judgment of the Lord upon Nineveh was averted through their humiliation before God (Jonah iii., iv.). (3) This prophecy, therefore, came in mercy, as a respite, to give space for repentance. Else judgment might have fallen without remonstrance, as it did in the issue. By timely repentance and reformation let us seek to avert all threatened judgments. 2. *But here was no repentance.* (1) Elah walked in the steps of his father. He followed the sin of Jeroboam. Their idolatries are called "vanities." The gods they worshipped could neither profit nor help them. "Happy is that people whose God is the Lord." Miserable, those whose gods are vanities! (2) Moreover, Elah abandoned himself to sensuality. See him in Tirzah, a palace beautifully situated (Cant. vi. 4), where he might have found innocent and rational enjoyment. But there he is in the apartments of Arza, his *major domo*, drunk! What a condition for a king! (3) What a condition for a nation, to be ruled by such a king! The Ephrathites had reason to repent of their revolution. They did not improve upon the house of David. Revolutionists have generally found their dreams of a political Paradise illusory. (4) The wisdom of Christians would be to make the best of the political system they may inherit, and pray for the speedy coming of the kingdom of Christ. This was the spirit of Paul's exhortations, even when such a monster as Nero ruled the kingdoms of the world (see Rom. xiii. 1; 1 Tim. ii. 1, 2; Tit. iii. 1; also 1 Pet. ii. 13, 17).

II. THE INSTRUMENTS OF THE JUDGMENTS OF GOD. 1. *The wicked follow their own devices.* (1) Zimri had an ambition to reign. Such an ambition is not uncommon. Few can ascend the throne of a kingdom. But there are tyrants on the

magisterial bench, in the factory, in the shop, in the mansion, in the college.   (2)
Zimri had also a desperate resolution to bend circumstances to his object.   His
rank as a cavalry officer, commanding half the chariots of Elah, gave him access to
the palace.   There, finding his lord helplessly drunk, he sacrificed gratitude and
duty, and struck the fatal blow.   What a warning to drunkards!   Death is especially
terrible when it surprises the sinner in his sin (see Luke xxi. 34).   (3) With infernal
promptitude Zimri proceeded to slaughter the whole of the seed royal.   In the
massacre he involved also the "kinsfolk and friends," so as to leave no rival to
contest the throne.   (4) But how little did he dream, after wading through this sea
of blood, that his reign should be limited to a single week!   How disproportionate
was the end to the means!   If men could duly estimate the end, how it would lead
them to hesitate over the employment of the means!   2. *But the providence of
God is over all.*   (1) God foresaw everything.   This is evident in the word of
prophecy.   And He so controlled the actors that the results answered the ends of
justice.   This also is evident in the same word.   (2) But this did not excuse the
wickedness of the executioners.   God allows the wicked to punish each other for
Him.   So makes He the wrath of man to praise Him (see 2 Kings ix. 31).   (3)
He has better work for His saints.   To bless is more congenial to them than to
destroy.   The ambition of the spiritual is too noble to be satisfied with an earthly
crown, or to pay its price.—J. A. M.

Vers. 8—20.—*A Divine judgment and its instrument.*   I. THE JUDGMENT.   1. *It
was delayed in God's long-suffering.*   Baasha had reigned nearly twenty-four
years; Elah nearly two.   The Lord is swift to bless but slow to strike.   He has no
delight in a sinner's death.   Do we remember that God's long-suffering to-day is
not forgetfulness or indifference, but the restraining of infinite love?   2. *It came
upon him in his sin.*   The army was in the field, but he was not there.   He was
deaf to the calls of duty and honour.   He had lost his self-respect; he "was
drinking himself drunk in the house" of his chamberlain.   And now in a moment
pleasure was swallowed up in terror, the misused life in death.   The suddenness
of God's judgments: "at such an hour as ye think not," &c.   3. *Its extent.*   It was
not less than was predicted.   His kindred and his friends were cut off and their
offspring (ver. 11).   Every word was fulfilled.   God's threatenings are not exaggerations meant to frighten us away from sin; *they are descriptions.*   God's eye is
resting on the woe which is hid from us, and His words are those of perfect truth
and tenderest love.

II. THE INSTRUMENT.   1. *Zimri was his servant.*   He had trusted and advanced
him.   Again we notice how ingratitude and rebellion against God are repaid in
kind.   If there be no love and truth toward God in us, let us not be surprised if we
find these wanting in others toward us.   2. *Though his deed fulfilled God's word,
it was not of God:* "he sinned in doing evil in the sight of the Lord;" it was
"treason that he wrought."   That which punishes evil may itself be sin.   God's
shield was withdrawn from around the house of Baasha, and an ambitious, cruel
heart was allowed to work its will upon them.   It is no justification of our act that
the nation or persons against whom it is done were wicked and deserved their fate;
the question remains, Were we righteous in inflicting it?   3. *The scourge was soon
broken and cast away.*   He reigned but seven days.   In slaying the king he was
but ending his own life; in entering the palace gained by blood, he was laying himself upon his funeral pyre.   The cup we covet may be a cup of death.   Take God's
way, and bide God's time: He will give that which is good.—J. U.

Vers. 15—22.—*The Kingdom of Men.*   Though "the Most High ruleth in the
kingdom of men," yet is He not responsible for the principles by which such
kingdoms are actuated.   For these are in striking contrast to those which shall
obtain in the "kingdom of God."   In the kingdom of men as represented in the
specimen before us we encounter—
I. FOLLY.   1. *True religion is pure wisdom.*   (1) It is the "wisdom of God"
revealed—*outwardly*, in His word—*inwardly*, by being written by His Spirit in

the heart. (2) To encourage this is man's highest wisdom. Godliness has promise of this life—of that to come. 2. *False religion is supreme folly.* (1) It is in some respects even worse than no religion. It is more than a negation in respect to truth; it is pertinacious antagonism to truth. (2) It is folly in relation to the highest interests of man. It demoralizes in the proportion of its ascendancy. It forfeits the heaven it professes to seek. It aggravates the hell it professes to avoid. (3) It expresses itself in vanity. What more vain than the idols of the heathen? The very forms of those idols evince the monstrosity of folly. Witness a monkey or an onion for a God; a fish with a man's head; a satyr; a griffin! (see Deut. xxxii. 21; Isa. xli. 29.) 3. *Of such folly was the kingdom of Israel flagrantly guilty.* (1) The calves with which they so deeply sinned were introduced by the kingcraft of Jeroboam. (2) They are maintained by the kingcraft of all his successors, of whatever dynasty. Even Zimri, who only reigned seven days, and in those days was occupied in exterminating the house of Baasha, yet found time to pronounce himself in their favour. (3) What a substitute for the Lord God of Israel who brought them up out of the land of Egypt!

II. RESTLESSNESS. 1. *Witnessed in frequent dynastic changes.* (1) The house of Jeroboam lasted twenty-four years. This gave place to that of Baasha, which lasted twenty-six. Zimri wore the crown seven days. Then came a four years' struggle for it between Omri and Tibni. At length "Tibni died and Omri reigned." 2. *These changes represented strong passions.* (1) There was the impatience of the rule of the house of David which resulted in the revolution in favour of Jeroboam. Yet so little did they benefit by the change, that when Baasha destroyed that house they accepted, without a murmur, the rule of the regicide. (2) But when Zimri treated the house of Baasha as Baasha had treated that of Jeroboam, they did not accept the second regicide. They now evinced some sense of right and wrong; but it was a wayward sense. There was no inquiry after the will of God. The army set up Omri, their general; but the civilians, apparently, chose Tibni. Here was a confusion which lasted until the death of one competitor. 3. *These commotions were sanguinary.* (1) The division of the nation into two kingdoms induced civil war. (2) Civil war also attended the treason of Zimri. For the army was occupied with the siege of Gibbethon when the news of this treason reached them, which determined them to raise the siege and invest Tirzah instead. The capture of Tirzah was not unbloody. A desperate character like Zimri would not tamely yield, when, rather than fall into the hands of Omri, he burnt the palace over his head and perished in the flames. (3) The competition for the crown between Omri and Tibni protracted the civil war four years. Omri is not said to have resigned until the "thirty-first year of Asa, whereas Zimri's treason occurred in the twenty-seventh year of Asa," upon which Omri was chosen by the army. (Compare vers. 15 and 23.) The difference here is about four years.

III. CRIME. 1. *Foremost under this head is idolatry.* (1) We mentioned this under the head of "folly," but it is not thereby removed from the category of "crime." Idolatry is the grossest and most direct insult to the living God. (2) Hence no crime is in Scripture more heavily denounced and more signally obnoxious to punishment. 2. *Next comes the capital crime of murder.* (1) As idolatry is the highest affront to God, so is murder the greatest offence against man. (2) The crown of Israel was deeply stained with the blood of murder—with that of the house of Jeroboam; with that of the house of Baasha. (3) Suicide also disgraced these violent times. And the note is significant that in his suicide Zimri perished "for his sins which he sinned in doing evil in the sight of the Lord, in walking in the way of Jeroboam, and in his sin which he did to make Israel to sin" (vers. 18, 19). Note: Men with their own hands may punish their sin.

What a contrast is the kingdom of God! Its principles are peace, righteousness, and joy. Of this those have the earnest who in heart accept Jesus as their Melchisedec.—J. A. M.

Vers. 21—34.—*Change without improvement.* I. OMRI'S INDEBTEDNESS TO DIVINE GOODNESS. 1. *His success against Zimri* (vers. 15—25). The traitor fell before him almost without a struggle. 2. *Against Tibni.* Israel was equally divided, yet his life was preserved and the kingdom given to him. Men pass up to place and means and influence through a pathway which, if it is only looked back upon and considered, is full of power to touch the heart and bow it under the will of God. Do we read the story of our past, and let it touch us with the tale of God's marvellous mercy?

II. HIS SIN. 1. *His hardness of heart.* Not only was he blind to God's mercy. He passed up unawed through the midst of the terriblest judgments and the most marked fulfilment of God's threatenings. Neither the goodness nor the severity of God was allowed to touch him. 2. *He " did worse than all that were before him."* He was a man of energy and worldly wisdom. Both were bent to strengthen his power. He went further than Jeroboam, who seduced Israel, for he seems to have compelled them (see the mention of Omri's statutes, Micah vi. 16) to sacrifice before the calves. Great talents, if joined to a selfish, hardened heart, only carry men further away from God.

III. HIS SIN'S FRUIT (vers. 29—34). 1. *In his son's character and reign.* (1) "He did evil in the sight of the Lord *above all that were before him.*" (2) It was possible only to an Ahab to set Jezebel—the great enemy of God and His people—upon the throne of Israel. (3) It was not enough to worship the calves of Bethel and Dan. He must turn wholly away from the God of Israel and worship Baal. 2. *In the people's contempt of Jehovah.* Hiel's act was done in the face of Israel, yet it was not forbidden; its commission awakened no fear. The man was left childless, yet judgments so harrowing and fulfilments of prophecy so marked had no effect upon his own soul. The legislation that blots out God's ordinances delivers a people over to darkness and judgment.—J. U.

Vers. 23—28.—*Omri's Reign.* After a four years' contest with Tibni, the son of Ginath, for the crown of Israel, the followers of Omri prevailed over the adherents of his rival. The issue, then, was that "Tibni died and Omri reigned." Whether Tibni died in battle, or whether, when his followers were overcome, he was taken and put to death, is not written; but the record illustrates how in the revolutions of the wheel of fortune the fall of one makes way for the rise of another. Let us now view this new monarch—

I. IN HIS PALACES. 1. *" Six years reigned he in Tirzah."* (1) This was once a lovely palace. Beautiful for its situation like Jerusalem (Cant. vi. 4), and beautified during the reign in it of all the earlier kings of Israel. For it was the third and last palace built by Jeroboam, the first of these kings, to which he removed from his palace at Penuel. (2) But it was now damaged by fire. When Zimri shut himself up in it as his defences were driven in by the forces of Omri in the siege of the city, he set it on fire and perished in the conflagration. Thus in a moment the labour of years was demolished. Destruction is easier than construction. This principle also holds in morals. (3) Still for six years Omri held his court in this city. Whether he occupied a portion of the palace which escaped the flames, or resided temporarily elsewhere in the city, is not revealed. The omissions of Scripture are instructive. Things of minor importance must not be allowed to divert attention from momentous things. 2. *Six years he reigned in Samaria.* (1) The origin of this new capital is here recorded (ver. 24). Seven hundred pounds of our money seems a small price for a hill considerable enough to be the site for the capital of a kingdom. (Compare 1 Chron. xxi. 25 : 600 shekels of gold = £1,095.) Perhaps Shemei was animated by public spirit when he disposed of his hill for so trifling a sum. Perhaps he did so to perpetuate his name. His motive is withheld from us. Herein also is instruction. We are not judges of the motives of our fellows. God surveys the motives of all hearts. (2) Henceforth Samaria figures prominently in the history of Israel. It gives its name to the middle portion of Canaan. Tirzah, Penuel, Shechem, are henceforth little heard of. Men give importance to places rather than places to men. The importance even of heaven will be rather that of its inhabitants than of its situation. Learn the paramount value of spiritual qualities.

II. AT THE ALTAR. 1. "*He walked in all the ways of Jeroboam.*" (1) This means that he encouraged the worship of the calves, if not that he even appeared at the altar as high priest (see chs. xii. 33; xiii. 1). (2) It means further that he was moved by the same state policy. He desired to keep his people from Jerusalem lest they should repent of their revolution from the house of David. (3) Note: Satan has his opportunities. While the pride of Israel smarted under the insolence of Rehoboam, Jeroboam could impose his calves upon them. Had he missed that opportunity, it might have been impossible afterwards to have effected his purpose. Omri could not have done it. We should be wise as serpents, viz., in avoiding the snare of the devil, in availing ourselves of our opportunities for good. 2. *He " did worse than all that were before him.*" (1) He "made Israel to sin" as Jeroboam did, persuading them to halt at Bethel or visit Dan, for that Jerusalem was too far from them. Persuading them also that his calves were images of the true God (see ch. xii. 28). (2) He bound them by *statute* to worship the calves (compare Micah vi. 16). In this he went farther than Baasha, who had set about building Ramah to prevent the people from going to Jerusalem (2 Chron. xvi. 1).

III. IN HIS EXIT. 1. *He " was buried.*" (1) He had a state funeral. Money might procure that. He left a son to succeed him on the throne who would pay this public respect to his remains. (2) How variously is the same subject viewed by men in the flesh, and by the inhabitants of the spiritual world! The funeral of the corpse is the event upon earth; the destiny of the spirit is the event yonder. 2. *He " slept with his fathers.*" (1) This expression does not mean that he was buried with them in their sepulchre, for Omri was buried in Samaria, a city which had no existence in the days of his fathers. Of Baasha also it is said that he "slept with his fathers, and was buried in Tirzah" (ver. 6), though there is no evidence that any of his fathers were buried in Tirzah. (2) It seems to import that he died upon his bed, as the generality of mankind finish their course. This expression does not appear to be used when any die by the hand of violence as a judgment of the Lord upon their sin. (3) Yet a violent death was deserved by Omri, as it was also by Baasha and Jeroboam, who, like him, came peacefully to the grave. They laid up sin for their posterity (see Job xxi. 19). But are they thus to escape the punishment of their own iniquity? Surely there must be a "judgment to come!"—J. A. M.

EXPOSITION.

CHAPTER XVI. 29—34.

THE REIGN OF AHAB.—With the accession of Ahab a new main section of our history begins—the section which has its close in the destruction of the house of Omri by Jehu, as related in 2 Kings x. And this reign is recorded at unusual length; in fact, it occupies nearly all the remaining portion of this volume, whereas the reigns of preceding kings have in several instances been dismissed in a few verses. It owes this distinction to the ministry of the great prophet Elijah by which it was marked, and, indeed, was profoundly influenced; but this ministry, it must be remembered, was necessitated by the critical circumstances of the time. It may be that "every age thinks itself a crisis," but no one can fail to see that this was one of the veritable turning-points of Jewish history. One of the real "decisive battles of the world"—that between the Lord and Baal—was then fought out. No wonder that our historian felt constrained to chronicle at length the transactions of a reign so pregnant both with good and evil for the people of the Lord and for the faith with which they had been put in trust. Indeed, the same guiding principle which led him to devote so many of his pages to the reign of Solomon, when the theocratic kingdom was at its highest, impelled him to linger over the reign of Ahab when religion was at its lowest ebb. The secular historian, too often like the sun-dial which "counts no hours save those serene," draws a veil over the time of his country's decadence, or touches its misfortunes with a light hand. It is only in the inspired records that we have an impartial register both of the glory and shame of a commonwealth.

Ver. 29.—**And in the thirty and eighth year of Asa king of Judah** [see notes on ver. 23] **began Ahab** [" Father's brother." The name is apposite. He was Omri's *alter ego* in impiety] **the son of Omri to reign over Israel : and Ahab the son of Omri reigned over Israel in Samaria twenty and two years.**

Ver. 30.—**And Ahab the son of Omri** [The repetition is noticeable. It is possible that the preceding verse has been revised by a chronologer. The LXX. text is much more condensed] **did evil in the sight of the Lord above all that were before him.** [The same words are used of his father in ver. 25. It is not difficult to see in what way Ahab's rule was worse even than Omri's. The latter had gone beyond his predecessors in the matter of the calf-worship. See note on ver. 25. But the calf-worship, however it may have deteriorated in process of time—and it is the tendency of such systems to wax worse and worse—was nevertheless a cult, though a corrupt, and unauthorized, and illicit cultus, of the one true God. Under Ahab, however, positive idolatry was established and fostered—the worship of foreign and shameful deities.]

Ver. 31.—**And it came to pass, as if it had been a light thing for him** [Heb. as marg. *was it a light thing ?* Ewald (362 a) explains this to mean "*because* it was." But it seems better to understand, " was it such a light thing . . . that he must needs also ? " &c.] **to walk in the sins of Jeroboam the son of Nebat** [*i.e.*, the sins of heresy and schism], **that he took to wife Jezebel** [="Without cohabitation," "chaste," Gesenius, who compares it with *Agnes*. It is hardly the original of Isabella] **the daughter of Ethbaal** [="With Baal." The Greek form 'Ιθόβαλος or Εἰθώβαλος, found in Jos., Ant. viii. 13. 1 ; cf. Contr. Ap. i. 18, suggests as its original אִתּוּ בַּעַל *i.e.*, " with him is Baal." In either case the name well became him, for, according to Menander (*apud* Jos. *l.c.*), he was *the* priest of Astarte, who gained for himself the throne of the Zidonians by the assassination of Pheles. He is further said to have reigned thirty-two years, and to have lived sixty-eight years. He would therefore be thirty-six years old at the time of his accession. It does not appear that (Keil) he was the brother of Pheles. Pheles, however, was certainly a fratricide. (Rawlinson reminds us that Jezebel was great-aunt to Pygmalion and

Dido.) This statement helps to explain Jezebel's fierce and sanguinary character, and at the same time accounts for her great devotion to the gods of her country, and for her determined efforts to establish their impure rites in her husband's kingdom. It was only what one would expect from the child of such a parent] **king of the Zidonians** [This alliance, it is extremely probable, was made for purely political reasons, as a counterpoise against the active, ambitious, and encroaching power which had arisen in Damascene Syria. The army which had already humbled Omri (ch. xx. 34) could not fail to be a source of danger to Tyre], **and went and served Baal** [Heb. *the Baal, i.e.*, the lord or master ; cf. ὁ κύριος. The name appears among the Babylonians as Bel (Isa. xlvi. 1)—Greek βῆλος. Reference has already been made to the frequent recurrence of the word in different compound names, and in different parts of Palestine, as showing how widespread must have been his worship at an earlier age. We are also familiar with the word in the names Hannibal, Hasdrubal, &c. Baal was the supreme male god of the Canaanitish races, as Ashtoreth was their great female divinity. The former was regarded, not only as the possessor, but as the generator, of all], **and worshipped him.**

Ver. 32.—**And he reared up an altar for Baal in** [Heb. omits *in ;* cf. ch. xv. 15, &c.] **the house of Baal** [A temple, we can hardly doubt, of considerable splendour. Jezebel would not be satisfied with less], **which he had built in Samaria** [According to 2 Kings iii. 2, x. 27, he also raised a pillar (A. V. *image*) in the house of Baal. We learn from Dius and Menander that Hiram had raised a golden pillar to Baal in Tyre. Perhaps Ahab may have copied this. But it is probable that this image, which represented the generative powers of nature, was an essential part of the impure worship of Baal. The house and its contents alike were destroyed by Jehu (2 Kings x. 27).

Ver. 33.—**And Ahab made a grove** [Heb. *an Asherah, i.e.*, image of Astarte, a female figure corresponding to the male effigy just described. See note on ch. xiv. 23] ; **and Ahab did more to provoke the Lord God of Israel to anger than all the kings of Israel that were before him.**

Ver. 34.—**In his days did Hiel the Bethelite** [Observe the form בֵּית הָאֱלִי, and see note on ch. ii. 8. It is noticeable that it was reserved for a man of *Bethel* to commit this act of impiety. It was to such results the worship of the calves contributed] **build** [*i.e., rebuild, fortify*, as in ch. xii. 25 ; cf. ch. ix. 17. It is clear from Judg. iii. 13 and

2 Sam. x. 5 that it had not been entirely uninhabited. But the Arab village was now converted into a town with gates and bars] Jericho [We learn from Josh. xviii. 21 that Jericho then belonged to Benjamin. It had evidently passed, however, at this date into the possession of Israel. It has been suggested that the transference took place in the reign of Baasha (Rawlinson). But it would seem that from the very first, parts of Benjamin (notably Bethel, Josh. xviii. 13) belonged to the northern kingdom. See Ewald, "Hist. Israel," iv. 2, 3. It is not quite clear whether the rebuilding of Jericho is mentioned as a proof of the daring impiety of that age and of the utter contempt with which the warnings of the law were treated, or as showing the ignorance and consequent disregard of law which prevailed. But, on the whole, it seems to be implied that Hiel knew of the threatening of Joshua, and treated it with defiance. It has been suggested that the rebuilding had really been instigated by Ahab, and for his own purposes, hoping thereby to "secure to himself the passage across the Jordan" (Keil), but the text affords but slight warrant for this conjecture]: **he laid the foundation thereof in Abiram his firstborn** [*i.e.*, at the cost of, in the life of, Abiram], **and set up the gates thereof in his youngest son Segub, according to the word of the Lord** [Josh. vi. 26], **which he spake by Joshua the son of Nun.** [The exact fulfilment of the prophecy is mentioned, as showing that even in those dark and troublous times God did not leave Himself without witness, and that law could never be violated with impunity.]

HOMILIES BY VARIOUS AUTHORS.

Vers. 29—33; ch. xvii. 1.—Ahab represents the culminating point of the perversity of the kingdom of Israel. At once more able and more profane than his predecessors, he fostered to an unprecedented degree the corruption of morals, private and public injustice, and idolatrous practices. Ahab, prompted by Jezebel, became the more dangerous enemy of the cause of God. At this period of the national history arose the greatest of the prophets, Elijah, who well bore out his name—the strength of God—and who was the faithful type of John the Baptist, the immediate forerunner of Christ. In the coming of Elijah at such a crisis, we have an illustration of a general and permanent rule of God's kingdom. The excess of evil calls out the strongest manifestations of good. Never was the power of Satan more rampant than at the time when the Son of God appeared upon earth. So in the end of time, the day of Antichrist will be also the day in which Christ will intervene most directly in the great drama of history. Let us not, then, yield to a hopeless pessimism when the powers of darkness seem to be let loose, for the two following reasons:

I. The letting loose of evil brings its own condemnation. By showing its true nature it passes sentence on itself, and brings to maturity all the seeds of death latent within it. Ahab, casting off all restraints and rushing recklessly on his ruin, writes his own condemnation.

II. An Ahab always calls forth an Elijah. Whenever the army of God seems on the verge of defeat, its Divine leader takes the direct command. Reflections like these may reinforce our courage in view of the giant evils of our own day.—E. de P.

Vers. 30—33.—*Moral Ruin through Moral Weakness.* This was the turning-point in the history of the kingdom of Israel. Till now the people had professedly worshipped Jehovah under the symbol of the calf. Now idolatry of a grosser kind was avowedly set up as the national religion, on a scale of great magnificence. The text, therefore, is worthy of our study as the record of an event of deep historic significance, but we propose to consider it as a suggestive example of the way in which a man of moral weakness may be betrayed into the worst depravity, to the undoing of himself and others. We learn the following lessons from Ahab's life, of which a summary is given here:

I. That a foolish choice may result in lasting dishonour. Ahab's marriage was the cause of his ruin. Jezebel, his wife, was the daughter of Ethbaal, who had been the high priest of Astarte, but was led by his ambition and unscrupulousness to usurp his brother's throne. Her parentage and her surroundings would have been a sufficient warning to a prudent king. But besides these Ahab had the Divine law before him (Exod. xxiv. 16), which distinctly forbade union with the Canaanites. Such a marriage was unprecedented in the kingdom of Israel, and was the more fatal because of the character of the queen, the Lady Macbeth of Scripture. She was reckless and licentious, fanatical and cruel, with a temper as vindictive as her will was resolute. Her husband became a mere tool in her hands. He could not foresee all the issues of his choice, but he knew the choice was sinful. Show from this—illustrating by example—1. *How one wrong step leads to another.* This marriage to the establishment of idolatry. Indicate the nature of the false religion set up. 2. *How companionship influences character.* The stronger moulding the weaker. "A companion of fools shall be destroyed." 3. *How personal fascination may cause men to swerve from rectitude.* Jezebel's fascinating power was regarded as witchery and became proverbial (Rev. ii. 20). 4. *How young people should be warned against unholy alliances.* Marriage makes or mars character, hope, and blessedness (2 Cor. vi. 14). "Be ye not unequally yoked together with unbelievers."

II. THAT EASY GOOD NATURE MAY PROVE THE SOURCE OF DEEP DEGRADATION. Ahab was not destitute of good feelings and right impulses. Had he been firm instead of pliable, and resolutely refused to gratify the queen by the establishment of idolatry, he might, with God's help, have neutralized the effect of the false step he had taken. But he was of a yielding nature, while she was resolute; and so, like Samson, he lost his kingliness. Point out the special dangers of those who are kindly and genial. Their unwillingness to disoblige, their wish to be popular, their dread of derision, their love of ease and pleasure, &c., may have fatal issues.

III. THAT BRILLIANT TALENTS WILL NOT COMPENSATE FOR MORAL WEAKNESS. This king was gifted with military skill, with artistic taste, &c., but these could not help him in the hour of spiritual conflict. Give examples from history of the careers of clever but unprincipled men, their meteoric success, their future punishment, here or hereafter; *e.g.*, Napoleon I. Many men of genius have been ruined by drunkenness, and often high education has served only to alter the form and increase the influence of the sin. The clever forger is worse than the common thief; the viciousness of a leader of society does more injury than the licentiousness of an ignorant peasant.

IV. THAT ARCHITECTURAL SPLENDOURS AND MILITARY VICTORIES ARE NOT PROOFS OF NATIONAL PROSPERITY. Describe Ahab's magnificent buildings, his ivory house, his daring restoration and fortification of Jericho, his palace and park in Jezreel, which became to Samaria what Versailles once was to Paris. Show how often in history such costly expenditure has been a sign of decay. Extravagance and luxuriousness are omens of ruin to a people. "The Decline and Fall" of the Roman Empire is an abiding illustration of this. Nor will successful wars give stability to a kingdom. Ahab's victories were great military achievements, but of what avail to him and to his house? "The throne must be established in *righteousness.*"

V. THAT AMPLE POSSESSIONS DO NOT CONTENT AN UNQUIET HEART. In Jezreel, the perfection of taste, Ahab was wretched, because he wanted Naboth's vineyard. (Read that story.) It is not in the power of earthly things to satisfy a hungering soul. The richest man is not content if he has only his riches, nor will any addition to them give him satisfaction. "Take heed, and beware of covetousness: for a man's life consisteth not in the abundance of the things which he possesseth" (Luke xii. 15). "Blessed are they that hunger and thirst after righteousness, for they shall be filled." God "satisfieth the longing soul, and filleth the hungry soul with goodness."

VI. THAT PARTIAL REPENTANCE DOES NOT AVERT GOD'S PUNISHMENT OF SIN. Ahab "put sackcloth upon his flesh, and fasted, and lay in sackcloth, and went softly," when he heard Elijah's final threat; but, though this first sign of penitence was graciously encouraged by a promise, the change went no further He dreaded punishment, but his heart did not turn from sin, and therefore, though he disguised himself in the battle, the arrow "shot at a venture" was winged by Divine retribution to his heart. God is our Judge, as well as our King. For the impenitent there will be no escape. In vain will they " call on mountains and rocks to fall on them, and hide them from the wrath of God." Now in this day of mercy, God calls on all to repent, and find pardon and hope in Him, who has come " to seek and to save that which was lost."—A. R.

Vers. 29—33.—*Ahab's wickedness.* The evil genius of the son of Omri appeared— I. IN HIS WALKING IN THE SINS OF JEROBOAM. 1. *In this, probably, he encouraged his father.* (1) He appears to have been associated with Omri in the kingdom. Omri reigned twelve years—viz., six in Tirzah, and six in Samaria; but his reign commenced " in the thirty-first year of Asa " (ver. 23). This would bring the close of his reign to the second year of Jehoshaphat, whereas in the text we read that " in the thirty and eighth year of Asa, king of Judah, began Ahab, the son of Omri, to reign over Israel." Hence it is evident Ahab must have been four or five years associated with his father in the throne. (2) The extreme wickedness with which Omri is charged was probably owing to Ahab's evil influence; for the " statutes of Omri " seem to have been inspired by the " counsels of Ahab " (see Micah vi. 16). So the note that " he sinned above all that were before him " is alike applied to the father and son (see verses 25, 30). And the leading influence of Ahab may explain why we commonly read of the " house of Ahab " rather than of the house of Omri. Parents are often demoralized by wicked children. 2. *He did not alter his course after his father's death.* (1) The sin of Jeroboam was perpetuated in Israel down to the time of their captivity. The captivity seemed necessary to break its power over them. Judgment is the last resource of mercy. (2) The same reasons of state continued to influence the successive rulers of the nation. Reasons of state are too often more potent than reasons of piety and righteousness. Else we had been spared the discredit of wicked wars, wicked laws, wicked trading.

II. IN HIS MATRIMONIAL ALLIANCE WITH JEZEBEL. 1. *She was a pronounced idolater.* (1) She was a Zidonian, and for any Israelite to marry one of that nation were a violation of the law of God (Exod. xxxiv. 11—16; Deut. vii. 3; Josh. xxiii. 11—13). For a king of Israel to do this was the more reprehensible. Office brings responsibilities. (2) These people were worshippers of strange gods, and in particular of Baal. Hence the name of this queen (איזבל), which may be derived from איזה, *where?* and בל, a contraction of בעל, *Baal,* thus: *Where is Baal? q.d.,* a seeker of Baal. Hence also her father's name (אתבעל), *Ethbaal,* which Gesenius construes to denote, " *Living with Baal, i.e.,* enjoying the favour and help of Baal." 2. *Such alliances have ever proved demoralizing.* (1) The giants (נפלים), *monsters,* viz., in wickedness, perhaps, rather than in stature, whose violence provoked the judgment of the deluge, were the issue of marriages between the " sons of God," or holy race of Seth, and the " daughters of men," or profane descendants of Cain (Gen. vi. 1—4). (2) Solomon's heathen wives and concubines made a fool of the wisest of men, and brought his house and nation into infinite trouble (ch. xi. 1—13). (3) The history of this alliance also was most disastrous. 3. *For typical reasons also they were forbidden.* (1) The marriage union should represent the union between Christ and His Church (Eph. v. 32). Therefore a husband, that he may justly represent Christ, is bound to be holy; and so is his wife, that she may suitably represent the Church. (2) Should the reverse happen, then is the woman an emblem of an apostate Church, of which the husband represents the Antichristian head (see 1 Cor. vi. 15, 16). Jezebel, accordingly, is viewed in this light in the imagery of the Apocalypse (see Rev. ii. 20).

III. IN HIS ENCOURAGEMENT GIVEN TO BAAL AND ASHERE. 1. *To Baal.* (1) To this god he built a temple in Samaria. This was the more audacious since, being placed in his capital, it seemed to vie with the temple of the Lord in the capital of Judah. (2) To Baal also he reared an altar there. This, of course, meant a service of priests and sacrifices. (3) Furthermore he himself worshipped Baal. Thus he gave the influence of his position to the encouragement of this idolatry.

That influence was therefore also given to discourage the pure worship of the God of Israel. 2. *To Ashere.* (1) This word is construed " grove " in the text as elsewhere. But a little reflection will teach us that groves do not spring up in a day. Beside, it is not here said that Ahab *planted* (נטע), but that he *made* (עשה) the Ashere. (2) The Ashere was a Canaanitish idol, probably of the figure of a goat, in the worship of which there appear to have been very abominable rites.

No wonder, then, the anger of the Lord should be provoked. If we would not provoke it we must avoid the spirit of idolatry. This spirit is shown in the love of illicit things. Also in excessive love of lawful things.—J. A. M.

Ver. 34.—*The Temerity of Hiel.* In discussing this subject we have to consider—

I. " THE WORD OF THE LORD WHICH HE SPAKE BY JOSHUA THE SON OF NUN." The record of this word is found in Josh. vi. 26. And the questions now arise—1. *Why did God thus curse Jericho?* (1) That its desolate condition might be a standing testimony to His abhorrence of the wickedness of the place. So abandoned were that people to idolatry that Rahab the hostess alone was accounted worthy of being saved. And " all her kindred "—(כל־משפחותיה)—all her *families*—the word is plural; families, viz., on her father's and mother's side, both were given to her (Josh. vi. 23). Note: The faith of an individual is not only a personal blessing, but also a blessing to his family, to his nation, to the world, in time, in eternity. (2) That it might be a standing sign prophetic of judgments to come. (*a*) Jericho was the first city which offered resistance to the people of God; and it was proper it should stand forth as a figure of the last city that shall offer resistance, viz., Great Babylon. (*b*) As Jericho was compassed about six days before it fell, so is Great Babylon destined to last until the beginning of the seventh age of prophetic chronology. (*c*) As Jericho fell at the seventh blast of the trumpet, so at the sounding of the seventh Apocalyptic trumpet will Great Babylon come into remembrance before God. (*d*) As Rahab, through the righteousness of faith, escaped the plagues of war and fire which destroyed the city, so are the people of God urged to come out of Babylon lest they partake her plagues also of war and fire. 2. *Why did God thus curse the rebuilder of Jericho?* (1) Consider the import of the curse. His eldest son was to perish by a judgment of Heaven as soon as the work commenced; and if, notwithstanding the judgment, he persisted in the undertaking, he should see the death of his youngest son. It is thought the intermediate members of his family would also perish as the work advanced. That the curse involved the penalty of *death* is evident, since the curse upon the city meant the death of its inhabitants (see Josh. vi. 17). The law of God also expresses that devoted things must die (see Levit. xxvii. 29). (2) The curse, then, came to keep up the testimony for God against sin; also to be a public sign of the judgment upon Babylon to come. Whoever would remove such a testimony must be a man of determined wickedness, and therefore deserving execration. Let us beware how we oppose or discredit any faithful testimony for Christ.

II. THE TEMERITY OF HIEL TO ENCOUNTER THIS MALEDICTION. 1. *The historical fact is before us.* (1) He did build Jericho. Not only did he lay the foundation, but he also set up the gates. Resolution and persistency are fine qualities when they are concerned with truth and goodness. But it was otherwise here. (2) He paid the penalty accordingly. When he laid the foundation his first-born Abiram perished. This did not deter him. So when he set up the gates " his youngest son Segub " was smitten. 2. *But what could have possessed him?* (1) The general answer to this question is, that the spirit of wickedness possessed him. No godly man could be so rashly defiant. Even reputable men of the world would shrink from such an audacious undertaking. The respect for sacred things manifested by such unconverted men encourages the hope that they may yet seek His grace and mercy. Hiel must have been a hardened sinner to have attempted this. (2) A more particular answer is suggested. (*a*) He was a " Bethelite." This expression may mean that he was born in Bethel, though this is not clear. It suggests rather that he was wedded to the sin of Jeroboam; for Bethel was the head-quarters of that apostasy. There Jeroboam placed one of his famous calves. There he built an altar. There also he built a temple. There his priests congregated, and there he, in person, officiated as high priest. The service of the calves would so harden the heart of Hiel as to prepare him to disregard the curse of Jehovah. (b) Then, he lived in the days of Ahab. These were days of fearful degeneracy. For Ahab provoked the Lord by wickedness more than all that had been before him. Hiel might argue that if Ahab could thus outrage the law of the God of Israel and survive, so might his own children survive, though he should transgress the adjuration of Joshua. It is dangerous to do evil because others have done it, apparently, with impunity. (c) The curse was denounced a long time ago. Since then five centuries and a half had passed away. Time weakens memory with men, and when man has a purpose to serve, he may argue that this also is the case with God. But He that remembers mercy for ever also remembers justice and judgment. Let us not deceive ourselves. Let us pray God to bring our sins to our remembrance, that we may repent of them before Him, for with Him they are never forgotten till forgiven.—J. A. M.

EXPOSITION.

CHAPTER XVII. 1—24.

ELIJAH AND THE GREAT DROUGHT.—The picture which the historian has just drawn of the shameless idolatry and the gross degeneracy of the earlier part of Ahab's reign forms a fit prelude to an account of the ministry of the great prophet Elijah, which occupies this and several succeeding chapters; for the two stand together in the closest connexion. It was only the unprecedented corruption of that age which necessitated such a mission, and a mission armed with such credentials as his. It will be obvious to the most cursory reader that the narratives comprised in the remaining portion of this book and the earlier part of 2 Kings are of a very different character from those which have so far been before us. The ministry of Elijah and Elisha alike is little more than a series of miracles. Of their words comparatively few are recorded; we hear of little but the signs and wonders that they wrought. And on this ground— because it is miraculous—this portion of our history is summarily discarded by many recent writers, not as wholly unhistorical, but as mythical ; as containing, indeed, many germs of truth, and as having a basis of fact, which, however, has been distorted into its present legendary shape by the credulity and fancy of a later age, or by the half-unconscious exaggeration of some poetico-prophetic writer. But without entering upon the question of miracles generally,

for which this is not the place, two remarks may be hazarded here. First, that the narrative is so sober, so circumstantial, so full of touches which have every appearance of having been painted from the life, that were it not for its supernatural element, the most destructive critic would never have thought of questioning its veracity. Secondly, that if miracles are ever allowable or conceivable, if there ever have been occasions in the history of our race when we might concede to the Necessary Being the liberty which we ourselves possess, of varying the so-called order of nature, or of impressing a visible purpose upon its forces, then assuredly the time at which we have now arrived, the beginning of Ahab's reign, was such an occasion. It is quite true that no new revelation was then given to the world. Neither Elijah nor Elisha, as Ewald has observed, "originated anything essentially new," but the task assigned them was one which needed supernatural support and attestation, no less than the promulgation of a new law or gospel. It was their work, at the very darkest hour in the spiritual history of Israel, when a determined effort was being made to stamp out the faith of God's elect, when the nation chosen of God to be the depositary of His truth was fast lapsing into heathenism, and more, into unutterable abominations, it was their work to witness for God and truth and purity. If God's purposes of grace to our world, which had been ripening from age to age, were not now to be frustrated ; if the one lamp which cast a ray on the world's thick darkness was not to be utterly extinguished, then, as far as we can see, God must send special messengers, and arm them, in token of their mission and authority, with superhuman powers. The age demanded the messenger; the messenger must have credentials ; the credentials could only be miraculous. If it is objected, therefore, against our history that it contains a mass of miracles, our answer is that the crisis necessitated them, and that only miracles would have availed to accomplish the moral and religious reformation which Elijah is allowed on all hands (see, *e.g.*, Ewald, " Hist. Israel," iv. 63) to have wrought ; that only signs such as he was commissioned to show would have sufficed, in that age, to counteract the influences of such a princess as Jezebel and of such a propaganda as her eight hundred and fifty priests ; to rescue the world from corruption, and to preserve to distant generations the treasury of truth and hope with which the Jewish people had been entrusted by the Most High. " The times," says Bishop Hall, were fit for Elijah, and Elijah for the times. The greatest prophet is reserved for the worst age. Israel had never such an impious king as Ahab, nor such a miraculous prophet as Elijah." " The profusion of God's miraculous working in Elijah was due to the exorbitant wickedness of the rulers of Israel at that time, which required an extraordinary manifestation of God's Divine power, in order to recover His people from the ruin and misery into which they had fallen " (Bishop Wordsworth).

The grandeur of the *character* of Elijah, however, has been universally recognized, and not least by those who have disputed his miracles. Indeed, it may well be questioned whether the intellect and conceptions of that or a much later age were adequate to create such a character and personality as his, a character which has profoundly impressed men of all ages and of all creeds. The glowing panegyric of the son of Sirach (Ecclus. xlviii.) need only be hinted at here. The colossal proportions he assumes in the traditions and belief of the Mohammedans is well known. " Omnium suae aetatis pro-

phetarum facile princeps; et si a Mose discesseris, nulli secundus," is the testimony of an illustrious Jew (Abravanel). "The grandest and most romantic character that Israel ever produced " is the verdict of a brilliant writer amongst ourselves (Stanley). His highest praise, however, is that "in the New Testament no prophet is mentioned and extolled so frequently as Elijah " (Bähr). Nor must it be forgotten here that he it was who was chosen to appear with Moses in glory at our Lord's transfiguration, and to speak of the exodus He should accomplish in Jerusalem (Luke ix. 31).

The chapter divides itself into four parts. In ver. 1 we see Elijah standing before Ahab and denouncing the drought; in vers. 2—7 we find him hiding in the Wâdy Cherith and fed by the " Orebim ; " in vers. 8—19 he is resident at Zarephath, feeding the widow and her house; in vers. 17—24 he restores the widow's son to life and health.

Ver. 1.—**And Elijah** [This name, which appears both as אֵלִיָּהוּ, and, less frequently, אֵלִיָּה, means *my God is Jehovah.* It is so singularly appropriate to the man who bore it, and so exactly expresses the idea of his life and the character of his work (see especially ch. xviii. 39), that it is difficult to resist the belief that it was assumed by him. This is certainly more probable than that it was due to the prescience of his parents. It may, however, mark their piety and hopes, and may have influenced the life of their son. Cf. 1 Chron. iv. 10], **the Tishbite** [So he is called without any further designation in ch. xxi. 17; 2 Kings i. 3, 8, &c. The presumption is altogether in favour of תִּשְׁבִּי being the name of his birthplace. Cf. ch. xi. 29], **who was of the inhabitants of Gilead** [The interpretation of these words is much disputed. The Heb. stands הַתִּשְׁבִּי מִתֹּשָׁבֵי גִלְעָד. It will be observed that the first and second words have the same radicals, and it has been hence inferred that they cannot mean " two entirely distinct things " (Rawlinson, *al.*), and that either the Masoretic pointing must be set aside, when the words would yield the meaning, " Elijah, the Tishbite of Tishbe of Gilead," or they must be interpreted," Elijah, the stranger of the strangers of Gilead." But it is by no means certain that the current interpretation is not the best. Such a play upon words as it involves is not at all uncommon in Hebrew. The meaning would then be that Elijah, who was, if not by birth, by domicile, of Tishbe, was one of the strangers —תּוֹשָׁב is found in the sense of πάροικος, *inquilinus*, in Gen. xxiii. 4 ; Exod. xii. 45 ; Levit. xxii. 10 ; xxv. 35, 47, &c.—or immigrants who had settled in Gilead. The only objection to this rendering—apart from the identity of radicals just mentioned—is that we should have expected to find תִּשְׁבֵּי written *plene*, as the word always is elsewhere. It is alleged by Keil, Bähr, *al.*, however, that the *stat. constr. plur.* may well be an exception to the rule, and in support of this view it may be mentioned that the cognate word, יוֹשֵׁב, is constantly found in the *constr. plural* as יֹשְׁבֵי (see Gesen., Thes. 635). It is clear, then, that the usual interpretation is by no means to be lightly set aside. It is certainly preferable to the rendering, "Elijah the stranger," &c., for we have no proof that הַתִּשְׁבִּי can bear this meaning. In favour of the alternative rendering "the Tishbite of Tishbe," it may be said that it has the support of the LXX., ὁ ἐκ Θεσβῶν, and of Josephus (Ant. viii. 13. 2), ἐκ πόλεως Θεσβώνης τῆς Γαλααδίτιδος χώρας. Nor is it any weighty objection to this view that we now here read of a Tishbe in Gilead : as for the matter of that, we have no undoubted traces of any such place *west* of the Jordan ; the passage in Tobit (ch. i. 2, LXX.), which is often alleged as proving that there was a Tishbe in Galilee, and from which Gesenius, Bähr, Keil, &c., conclude that this must be the Tishbi here referred to, being too uncertain to permit us to build any positive conclusions thereupon. See Dict. Bib. iii. pp. 1489, 1516. In any case —and it is perhaps impossible to decide positively between this and the rendering of the A. V.—it is clear that Elijah, even if born in Galilee (but see John vii. 52, for the belief of the Jews), was trained for his work in Gilead. It was, therefore, a rugged, unsettled, half-civilized, trans-Jordanic region gave to the world the greatest of its prophets. In this respect he was like Moses (Exod. iii. 1), and his antitype the Baptist (Luke i. 80). " The fact that this mission was entrusted not to a dweller in royal city or prophetic school, but to a genuine child of the deserts and forests of Gilead, is in exact accordance with the dispensations of Providence in other times" (Stanley)] **said unto Ahab** [The abrupt way in which Elijah appears upon the scene without a word of introduction or explanation is certainly remarkable. Ewald observes that "his first entry within the province of the history seems almost as unique and inexplicable as his final disappearance." " Elijah comes in

with a tempest, and goes out with a whirlwind " (Hall). But there is no sufficient ground for believing (Thenius, *al.*) that a part of our history which described some of his antecedents has been lost to us, or that our text merely recites the *issue* of a long conference which Elijah had held with Ahab, for other prophets of this period, Ahijah, Shemaiah, Jehu, are introduced to us in a similar manner, though it must be allowed that their respective ministries were of very different proportions and importance from Elijah's. This sudden appearance, however, is thoroughly characteristic of the man. He presently disappears just as suddenly (ver. 5. Cf. xix. 3 ; 2 Kings i. 8). It was thought by some in that age that he was borne hither and thither by the Spirit of God (ch. xviii. 12), and men of a later time caught this as one of his prominent characteristics (Ecclus. xlviii. 1 12). Hence, too, the traditions of a still later period, according to which he was " the fiery Phinehas returned to earth, or an angel hovering on the outskirts of the world," Stanley], **As the Lord God of Israel liveth** [This formula here occurs for the first time, and it is full of meaning. It asserts first that Jehovah, not Baal, is the God of Israel, and it suggests, in the second place, that he is the *living* God, such as Baal was not, and that though ordinarily He keeps silence, He is one who can make His power felt], **before whom I stand** [*i.e.*, " Whose I am and whom I serve" (Acts xxvii. 23). Cf. ch. xviii. 15. The slaves of the East stood before their masters. See note on ch. i. 28, and cf. 1 Sam. iii. 1 ; Luke i. 19. Elijah claims to speak in God's name, and as His ambassador], **there shall not be dew nor rain** [Observe the order of the words. Dew is perhaps put first as more essential to vegetable life. Elijah only denounces a plague already threatened in the law as the punishment of idolatry (Deut. xi. 16, 17 ; xxviii. 23 ; Levit. xxvi. 19). He came forward as the vindicator and restorer of the law] **these years** [An indefinite period. Its duration depended on Elijah's word, and that again on the penitence, &c., of the people. It was because of the obduracy of king and people that it lasted so long] **but according to my word.** [The idolatrous priests no doubt claimed for Baal the dominion over nature and absolute control over the clouds and rain—a power which, it may be worth observing, the monks of the convent of St. Katherine at Sinai, where Elijah was, are thought to possess by the Arabs of the Sinaitic peninsula. Elijah directly challenges them to a trial of strength. It was as if he had said, " The God that answereth by rain, let him be God." **On the fitness** of this miracle, both as a sign and as a punishment, see "Homil. Quart." v. 100, 101. " To Eastern and Southern nations, where life and water go always together, where vegetation gathers round the slightest particle of moisture and dies the moment it is withdrawn, . . . the withholding of rain is the withholding of pleasure, of sustenance, of life itself" (Stanley). " My word" is somewhat emphatic, " *Nisi ego, et non alius vir . . . dixero*" (Seb. Schmidt). No doubt there is a special reference to the prophets of Baal. Their inability to remove the ban would prove the impotency of their god. Elijah had *asked* for the supernatural powers which he here claims (James v. 17, 18).]

Ver. 2.—**And the word of the Lord came unto him, saying** [cf. ver. 8; ch. xviii. 1; xxi. 17; 2 Kings i. 3],

Ver. 3.—**Get thee hence, and turn thee** [for the construction (*dat. commodi*) cf. Gen. xii. 2; xxii. 2; Cant. ii. 11] **eastward** [This he must do, whichever side of the Jordan, east or west, the brook Cherith was, for his interview with Ahab had probably taken place at Samaria. But the word would be specially appropriate, if the Cherith was beyond Jordan. Ewald, indeed, holds that our text is decisive on this point], **and hide thyself** [Heb. *be hid*, *i.e.*, lie hid, Niphal. It does not seem to have occurred to the prophet that such a calamity as he had denounced against the country almost made his disappearance from the scene a necessity, or if it did, he still waited for instructions. Cf. ver. 9; ch. xviii. 1, &c. Not merely was his flight necessary in order to escape persecution or punishment—the search which Ahab instituted for him in part explains his disappearance—but to avoid importunity. It would have been morally impossible for him, though a man of inflexible will (Bähr) to dwell among the people, while the land groaned under the terrible burden which he had laid upon it, and which he alone was able to remove. His life would not have been safe—see ch. xviii. 4—and the ordeal would have been intolerable. And ch. xix. 2 shows that the prophet's nature had its weaker side. Wordsworth observes that Elijah's escapes and departures into unknown places are "faint resemblances of the mysterious vanishings of our blessed Lord, after He had delivered some of His Divine messages which excited the anger of the people;" Luke iv. 29; John viii. 59; x. 39] **by** [Heb. *in*] **the brook**

[Heb. נַחַל; *i.e.*, *watercourse, wâdy*. This word has two meanings. Its primary meaning is *torrent;* its secondary and, from the

fact that the torrents of the East are for the most part dried up during the greater part of the year, its common meaning is *torrent-bed*, or ravine, valley. Both meanings are brought out here. Elijah should *dwell in* and *drink of* the נַחַל. Cf. ch. xv. 3] **Cherith** [The word means *separation*, a name which may possibly indicate that it was extremely secluded, or it may have been a boundary line of some sort. Tradition identifies the brook Cherith with the *Wâdy-el-kelt, i.e.*, the great valley, west of the Jordan, which debouches into the Ghor, half a mile south of Jericho, and Robinson and Porter pronounce in its favour. Van de Velde (ii. 310, 311) suggests the *Wâdy Fasael*, a few miles to the north. But it is much more probable that it is to be sought in the region east of the Jordan, where, indeed, Eusebius and Jerome place it. It is extremely doubtful whether the Wâdy-el-kelt, or any Cis-Jordanic ravine, would afford sufficient privacy. Probably Jericho was already rebuilt. As we cannot decide with certainty, we may reasonably conjecture that it is to be sought in Elijah's own country of Gilead, and probably in the *Wâdy Alias, i.e.*, at no great distance from *'Abara* (Conder, "Tent-work," p. 230), the Jordan ford nearly opposite Bethshan, where, indeed, an old tradition places it] **that is before** [Nothing positive can be concluded from עַל פְּנֵי. In Gen. xvi. 12; xxiii. 19; xxv. 18; Josh. xviii. 14, &c., it means eastward. But this meaning is gathered from the context] **Jordan.** [The Cherith was clearly *one* of the lateral valleys which run into the Ghor. It is just possible that the name may be recovered by the survey of the country east of the Jordan, which is now (1880) being organized.]

Ver. 4.—**And it shall be that thou shalt drink of the brook** [There was clearly nothing miraculous about the supply of *water*. No miracle was wrought even to continue the supply, ver. 7] ; **and I have commanded** [cf. ver. 9; Isa. v. 6; Amos ix. 3, &c.] **the ravens to feed thee there.** [Despite the general agreement of scholars that by עֹרְבִים we *must* understand "ravens," I think probability favours the meaning *Orbites, i.e.*, inhabitants of Orbo. In support of the received rendering is the very powerful consideration, that it is the interpretation of all the versions (except the Arabic) and of Josephus, who, beyond all question, represented the belief current in his own time (Ant. viii. 13. 2). It is also certain that elsewhere in Scripture we find some of the inferior animals supernaturally constrained to effect God's purposes, both of mercy and of judgment (1 Kings xiii. 24;

2 Kings ii. 24 ; Dan. vi. 22 ; 2 Peter ii. 16), though never, it must be said, in so rational and methodical a way. Nor can it rightly be contended that the words " I have commanded," צִוִּיתִי, imply human agency, for elsewhere we find the Almighty *commanding* (same word) the serpent (Amos ix. 3) and the clouds (Isa. v. 6 ; Psa. lxxviii. 23). It is not, however, a sufficient account of this narrative to say that the prophet merely helped himself to the food which the ravens, whose *habitat* was in the Wâdy Cherith, brought, day by day, to their nests and their young. For, not to insist on the words, מְבִיאִים לוֹ, *bringing to him* (ver. 6), the expressions " bread (or *food*, לֶחֶם) and flesh," and " morning and evening " certainly point to something more than such a fortuitous supply. Whether the *Orebim* were " ravens " or not, they certainly acted in an intelligent and rational way: they brought food, that is to say, to the *prophet*, and they brought it for months together with unfailing regularity. But against this view the following considerations may be urged. 1. It is hardly in accord with God's *usual* way of working, that he should employ birds of the air and those unclean (Levit. xi. 15 ; Deut. xiv. 14) and ravenous birds, to feed and succour His saints, rather than men or angels. Of course, no one who does not altogether repudiate the supernatural will deny for a moment that the Almighty *could*, had it seemed good to Him, have sustained His prophet by the instrumentality of ravens, just as easily as by any other means. But it appears to be almost a fixed principle of His dealings with men, not to resort to miracles when ordinary means will suffice ; or if He does employ miracles, they are never *bizarre* or fantastic ; they are *not* such as to suggest the idea of fable or legend ; they are invariably the simplest and directest means to the end. And it is submitted that this prolonged and methodical ministry of ravens is altogether unlike God's method of procedure on other occasions. It was an angel succoured Hagar and Ishmael in their need (Gen. xvi. 7). It was an angel fed Elijah himself, a few years later (1 Kings xix. 5, 6). They were angels who ministered to our blessed Lord after His long fast (Matt. iv. 11). But God's " chief means," it is always to be remembered, " is man." And it is to be carefully observed that when, about this very time, not one, but one hundred prophets were threatened, just as Elijah was, with death, no miracle was wrought to save their lives or to supply their wants, but they were fed by human agency, with bread and water (ch. xviii. 13). But it is still more signifi-

cant that elsewhere in this narrative, which is characterized by the profoundest sobriety and reticence, there is what we may almost call a studied absence of the miraculous element. No miracle is wrought to protect Elijah against Jezebel, but he must consult for his own safety by flight. He is sent to the brook Cherith, because there is *water* there ; in other words, God chose that hiding place in order to obviate the necessity for a miracle. And when the water of the brook dries up, no miracle is wrought to prolong the supply, but the prophet, at the risk of detection, must go forth and seek it elsewhere. And at Zarephath he is fed, not by ravens, but by human agency—by a widow woman. It is true a miracle appears to have been wrought, but the narrative has so little idea of effect and gives so little prominence to the supernatural that even that is doubted. To put the interpretation of " ravens, " consequently, on the word עֹרְבִים, provided it will yield any other meaning, appears to be to do violence to the spirit of the context, and to the tenour of Scripture generally. 2. It is somewhat difficult to believe that such a prodigy as this, so altogether unique and irregular, would not have been mentioned, had it really happened, elsewhere in Scripture. The absence of all reference thereto is remarkable, when we consider how constantly the ministry of Elijah and its lessons (Luke iv. 25, 26 ; ix. 54 ; James v. 17 ; Rev. xi. 5, 6) are referred to in the New Testament ; but when we observe what an admirable and unequalled illustration of God's providential care this incident would have supplied to some of our Lord's discourses, and notably to that of Luke xii. 22 sqq., this silence becomes almost suspicious. 3. Despite the practical unanimity of the versions, the interpretation " ravens " has been disputed from very early times. St. Jerome among Christians, Rabbi Judah Hakkodesh and Kimchi amongst Jews—these are but some of those who have repudiated this rendering. 4. A very slight change in the vowel points—עֲרָבִים instead of עֹרְבִים—yields the meaning " Arabians. " That a fugitive would readily find, not only shelter but sustenance among the Bedouin, whose generous hospitality and loyalty to strangers is proverbial, is obvious, and we know that about this time some Arab tribes had dealings with the Jews (2 Chron. xvii. 11) ; but without any change at all, a sufficient meaning may be extracted from the word. For we find that somewhere in the *Ciccar*, or plain of the Jordan, off which the Wâdy Cherith lay, was a rock Oreb (עֹרֵב, Judg. vii. 25), apparently east of the Jordan (Judg.

viii. 1), but in any case, at no great distance from Bethabara (John i. 28). Now Bethabara has been identified, almost to a certainty (Conder, " Tent-work," pp. 229—232) with the modern 'Abarah (i.e., passage or ferry), " one of the main fords of the Jordan just above the place where the Jalûd river, flowing down the valley of Jezreel and by Beisân, debouches into Jordan." But we learn from an ancient and independent source, the Bereshith Rabba (see Dict. Bib. ii. 464), that in the neighbourhood of Beisân, i.e., Bethshean, there was anciently a town named Orbo, עֲרְבוֹ—a word, it is to be observed, which preserves the radicals of עוֹרֵב transposed. We may safely assume that these two places, Orbo and Oreb, were identical; that the former was the representative at a later day of the latter, or was the shape which the name assumed when bestowed on the hamlet, as distinct from the rock. The inhabitants of this place would, of course, be called עֹרְבִים, just as the inhabitants of Ziph were known as Ziphim (1 Sam. xxvi. 1), or the men of Zidon as Zidonim (1 Kings v. 6). We find, consequently, that this word, which means "ravens," also designates the inhabitants of a village near Bethshean, and probably east of the Jordan; that is to say, in or near Elijah's native country of Gilead. And with this agree the testimonies of Rabbi Judah and Jerome already referred to. The former held that the Orebim were not ravens at all, but inhabitants of Orbo or the rock Oreb, while the latter says, with equal positiveness, Orbim, accolae villae in finibus Arabum, Eliae dederunt alimenta. It only remains for us to notice the perfect naturalness and consistency of the narrative thus interpreted. Elijah is bidden to go eastward; to hide in the Wâdy Cherith, where he would be among tribesmen or friends. For water, there is the brook; for food, the Orbites, whose name would be familiar to him, and whom he may have known, are commanded to feed him. He goes; he is received with Arab hospitality; the Eastern law of Dakheel, by which any man at any time is entitled to throw himself upon the mercy and protection of another, ensures his safety. The Orebim minister assiduously to his wants. Every morning before the dawn, every evening after dark, they bring him bread and flesh.]

Ver. 5.—**So he went and did according unto the word of the Lord: for** [Heb. and] **he went and dwelt by** [Heb. in] **the brook Cherith, that is before Jordan.**

Ver. 6.—**And the ravens brought** [Heb. bringing] **him bread and flesh in the morning, and bread and flesh in the evening**

[the Vat. LXX. has " bread in the morning and flesh in the evening." It has been objected that this verse is fatal to the view advanced above—that the עֹרְבִים were not birds but men—that no men would have " come regularly twice a day, . . . thus giving themselves needless trouble and increasing the chance of detection, when they might easily have left him a supply for several days" (Rawlinson). But if we may believe that the prophet was, if not among kinsmen or friends, yet among the pastoral, semi-nomadic people of Gilead, a people, that is to say, like the Bedawin in their instincts and customs, it is easy to understand that having taken him under their protection, they would make a point of visiting him regularly, not only to show him all possible honour, as a person endued with supernatural powers (cf. ch. xviii. 7, 13), but to afford him some measure of sympathy and companionship. And we can then see a reason for the morning and evening being mentioned. Their visits would be made in the twilight, which is really longer in the East than is generally supposed]; **and he drank** [Hebrew drinks. The Heb. future often has the force of an imperfect, and expresses continued or repeated action] **of the brook.**

Ver. 7.—**And it came to pass after a while,** [Heb. at the end of days. Not necessarily post annum. The words no doubt have this force elsewhere, Levit. xxv. 29; Judg. xi. 40; xvii. 10; 1 Sam. xxvii. 7, &c.; but in all these cases, the meaning is not resident in the words themselves, but in the context. It is impossible to say how long Elijah remained in the Wâdy. All we can be sure of is that he must have been more than two years, out of the three and a half, at Zarephath. See on ch. xviii. 1] **that the brook dried up, because there had been no rain in the land.** [גֶּשֶׁם, imber, signifies heavy rain. The word used in ver. 1 is מָטָר, rain of any kind.]

Ver. 8.—**And the word of the Lord came unto him, saying,**

Ver. 9.—**Arise, get thee to Zarephath** [Cf. Obad. 20. The name points to furnaces or workshops for the refining of metals, צָרַף, liquavit. LXX. Σαρεπτὰ; cf. Luke iv. 26. It is now represented by an insignificant village, Surafend, which, however, preserves the original name. It lies still, as no doubt it did then, on the high road between Tyre and Sidon, and on the shore. The prophet would thus be in the lion's den, in the very heart of the dominions of Ethbaal. See Porter, ii. 397. Stanley (S. and P. p. 268) shows how the memory of this visit still lingers in the traditions of the neighbourhood], **which belongeth to Zidon** [Sidon is visible from a spot a quarter of an hour distant. "The dependence of Sarepta on Sidon is indicated in the inscriptions of Sennacherib, where it is mentioned as belonging to Luliya, king of Sidon," Rawlinson], **and dwell there: behold, I have commanded a widow woman there to sustain thee** [In considering these words the generally destitute condition of the widow of the East should be borne in mind (Acts vi. 1 ; 1 Tim. v. 3—5, &c.) We gather from Luke iv. 25, 26, that it was for her sake as well as his that the prophet was sent thither. Matt. xv. 21—28 tells of another Syro-Phoenician woman.]

Ver. 10.—**So he arose and went to Zarephath** [It does not follow that his route lay over the "White Promontory," or Ladder of Tyre, the way our Lord took when He "departed into the coasts of Tyre and Sidon" (Matt. xv. 21). If his place of concealment was anywhere near 'Abara, or Bethshean, it is probable he would keep east of the Jordan, as far as Banias or Dan, where the river is fordable, and whence a road leads direct to Sidon. He would thus avoid Tyre]. **And when he came to the gate of the city** [the ruins of Surafend are still very considerable (see Thomson,"Land and Book," i. 235) and prove it to have been a place of importance, a town with gates and walls. "Gate," however, is used somewhat loosely in the O. T.—of the *entrance* to a village, or even of the place of concourse and of judgment], **behold, the** [Heb. *a*. He did not yet know that this was *the* widow to whom he was sent. Her replies to his requests first informed him that this was the object of his search] **widow woman was there** [Heb. *behold there, a widow woman*] **gathering of sticks** [This was not a promising sign. It only proved her poverty]: **and he called to her, and said, Fetch me, I pray thee, a little water in a vessel** [Heb. *the* vessel. Bähr understands the drinking-cup that Elijah had brought with him from the Wâdy Cherith ; but surely it is extremely improbable that he would carry either cup or bottle with him. "*The* vessel" probably imports the ordinary vessel used for the purpose—the "potter's earthen bottle" (Jer. xix. 1). That this was used for fetching water, we know from Isa. xxx. 14], **that I may drink.**

Ver. 11.—**And as she was going to fetch it** [The gift of water to the thirsty is always regarded as a sacred duty in the East. "Never yet during many years' residence in Syria and many a long day's travel, have I been refused a draught of water by a single individual of any sect or race. The Bedawy in the desert has shared with me the last drop in his water-skin" (Porter). It is clear

that the water supply of Phoenicia had not entirely failed. "The fresh streams of Lebanon would retain their life-giving power long after the scantier springs of Palestine had been dried up, " Stanley] **he called to her, and said, Bring me, I pray thee, a morsel of bread** [The request for *food* will soon reveal to him whether this is the widow woman who is to sustain him] **in thine hand.** [Bähr would understand here, "Give me a morsel of the bread which thou hast in thine hand"—*einen Bissen des Brodes das du besitzest*—and he has the LXX., ψωμὸν ἄρτου τοῦ ἐν τῇ χειρί σου, to support him. But it is fatal to this view

(1) that the verb is לְקַחִי—the same as already used in the request for water (ver. 10), and (2) that there is no article before bread. "*The* bread in thine hand" would have been clear, but the words as they stand can only mean, "Bring me, together with the water *in the* vessel, a morsel of bread *in thine* hand." Besides, "in thy possession" would probably have been expressed by "*under* thine hand," as in 1 Sam. xxi. 3, 4, 8, though "in the hand" *is* found in Eccles. v. 13 ; Ezra vii. 25, in a somewhat similar sense.]

Ver. 12.— **And she said, As the Lord thy God liveth** [Bähr, Keil, *al.* conclude from this formula that the woman was a worshipper of the God of Israel. Bähr is extremely positive on this point, affirming that, had she been a heathen, the words would have been positively hypocritical, and more, that Elijah would never have been sent (Luke iv. 26) to an idolater. He further suggests that possibly she was an Israelite by birth, who had been married to a Phoenician. But all this is extremely doubtful. In the first place, it is noteworthy that the words are, "Jehovah *thy* God," words which show that she recognized Elijah, perhaps by his Jewish face, probably by his prophetic dress (2 Kings i. 8) as a worshipper of Jehovah. But had she also been the same, it is probable that she would have said "*my* God," for that form would not only have given greater force to her obtestation, but would have established a bond of sympathy—such as Jews in a foreign land were only too glad to recognize —between them. And the remark that it is hypocrisy to swear by a god in whom one does not believe is disposed of by the consideration that she may well have believed in the Lord as well as in Baal. See note on ch. v. 7. The Tyrians knew nothing of monotheism], **I have not a cake** [מָעוֹג, the synonym of עֻגָּה (ver. 13), the smallest kind of bread. It was baked in the ashes ; hence the LXX. ἐγκρυφίας. We gather from this pitiful disclosure that the famine had already extended to Phoenicia, as it naturally would do, considering how dependent that co untry was on Israel for its breadstuffs; see note on ch. v. 9, 11. Josephus (Ant. viii. 13, 2) cites Menander as attesting to a year's drought in the reign of Ethbaal], **but an handful of meal in a** [Heb. *the*] **barrel** [רַכ, probably connected with *cadus*, *cadeau*, &c.; bucket, pail], **and a little oil in a cruse: and, behold, I am gathering two sticks** [*i.e.*, a few sticks (Gesenius). We may compare the German idiom *ein Paar* and our "two or three." But "*two*" in this sense occurs nowhere else in the Bible —"two or three" is found in 2 Kings ix. 32; Isa. xvii. 6; Amos iv. 8. According to Roberts, the word is constantly used for "few" by the natives of India. This widow was evidently reduced to the greatest extremities], **that I may go in and dress it for me and my son** [The LXX. has τέκνοις here and in ver. 13, and τὰ τέκνα in ver. 15. Bähr contends that Elijah first learnt from these words—the mention of a son and the absence of any mention of her husband—that he was addressing a "widow woman." But we read Gen. xxxviii. 14, 19, of "*garments* of widowhood" (cf. Deut. xxiv. 17), and ver. 10, "a widow woman," &c., almost implies that Elijah from the first recognized her as such], **that we may eat it, and die.**

Ver. 13.—**And Elijah said unto her** [This looks at first like a further test. But it is pretty clear that the prophet now knew that the widow of whom God had spoken was before him], **Fear not; go and do as thou hast said** [Heb. *according to thy word*] **but** [Heb. *only, however*]: **make me thereof** [Heb. *thence, i.e.*, of the oil as well as the meal. The former took the place of butter. Bread was sometimes baked in oil] **a little cake first, and bring it unto me, and after make for thee and thy son.** [The "first" and "afterwards" are emphatic by position. When Bähr says that Elijah would never have made this demand, and that still less would the widow have paid any attention to it, had she been a heathen, he appears to forget the words that followed (ver. 14). When one in the garb of a prophet swore, as this man did, by the sacred name, a heathen, with the belief of the heathen in miracles, might well be persuaded that the word was truth. Elijah's manner alone would carry conviction with it.]

Ver. 14.—**For thus saith the Lord God of Israel** [The words, "God of Israel," if anything, favour the supposition that he was speaking to one who was not of Israel. See on ver. 1. There the words were addressed

to one who was denying the God of Israel] **The barrel of meal shall not waste, neither shall the cruse of oil fail, until the day that the Lord sendeth** [Heb. *giveth*. For תֵּת see note on ch. vi. 19] **rain upon the earth.** [Heb. *on the face of the ground*. Like expression ch. xviii. 1; Gen. ii. 5. It has been said that there is not a syllable here to imply a miracle, and it has been contended that this Sareptan household was sustained for over two years simply by the blessing of God on the use of natural means. But clearly, if there was nothing else, there was supernatural knowledge on Elijah's part. And it cannot be denied that the literal construction of the words points to a "supernatural and inexplicable multiplication of food" (Rawlinson), similar to those of which the Gospels tell. It is just possible that this was a figure of speech, which practically meant no more than the necessaries of life should somehow be provided, directly or indirectly, by God. Nor is this view effectually negatived, as Bähr contends, by Luke iv. 26; but, in view of 2 Kings iv. 44, Matt. xiv. 15—21, xv. 32—38, it is extremely improbable. It is curious how many miracles of Elijah and Elisha foreshadowed those of our blessed Lord.

Ver. 15.—**And she went and did according to the saying of Elijah** [the echo of ver. 13, "Go and *do according to thy saying*"]: **and she, and he,** [or *he and she*, according to Chethib] **and her house** [probably her friends or poor relatives who came to partake of her plenty (Bähr)], **did eat many days.** [Heb. *days, i.e.*, an indefinite period. See note on ver. 7. The word does not refer to the first baking (ver. 13), but it is to be explained by the next verse.

Ver. 16.—**And** [Omit. This verse is explicative, not additional] **the barrel of meal wasted not, neither did the cruse of oil fail, according to the word of the Lord, which He spake by** [Heb. *by the hand of*] **Elijah.** [Having received a prophet in the name of a prophet, she received a prophet's reward. (Matt. x. 41, 42). Stanley suggests that our Lord, when He spoke of the "cup of cold water," may have had this incident in his mind.

Ver. 17.—**And it came to pass after these things, that the son of the woman, the mistress of the house, fell sick; and his sickness was so sore, that there was no breath left in him.** [Does this mean that he was dead? Keil thinks it perfectly clear that it does. Bähr is as firmly persuaded that it does not. He justly remarks (1) that the same expression occurs in Dan. x. 17 (cf. 1 Kings x. 5) where it does not imply death. (2) That as the text does not say, "and he died," we must conclude that it did not mean to say it. (3) Verses 18, 20 do not necessitate the belief that he was dead (see below). (4) Josephus, who was not afraid of the miraculous, has interpreted the words thus: ὡς καὶ τὴν ψυχὴν ἀφεῖναι καὶ δόξαι νεκρον. To this it may be added that נְשָׁמָה simply means *breath*, and that where it is desired to convey the idea of *life*, additional words are used (as in Gen. ii. 7, "the *breath* of life; Gen. vii. 22, "the *breath* of the spirit of life." Cf. Job xxvii. 3, Prov. xx. 27 (where the intelligence or reason appears to be meant), Eccles. iii. 21. It must be confessed also that the statement, "his sickness was so sore," &c., is quite *apropos* and intelligible, if we may understand that he lay in a state of *coma*, but would be an extremely roundabout way of affirming that he was dead.

Ver. 18.—**And she said unto Elijah, What have I to do with thee** [Heb. *what to me and thee*. Same formula, Judg. xi. 12; 2 Sam. xvi. 10; 2 Kings iii. 13; Matt. viii. 29; John ii. 4. It means, "What is there between us?" or practically, "What have I done?" "Is this the result of my association with thee? Must such sorrow befal me because thou art with me?" Bähr], **O thou man of God**? [This woman, if a Phœnician, was evidently familiar with the titles borne by the Hebrew prophets (ch. xii. 22; xiii. *passim*; Judg. xiii. 6, 8). Nor is this to be wondered at. The intercourse between the two nations had been very considerable] **art thou come unto me to call my sin** [not necessarily any "special sin in her past life,"] **to** remembrance [her idea evidently is that the prophet by residing with her, seeing her life, &c., had become acquainted with her sinfulness, and had called it to the remembrance of the Almighty. She does not mean that he had recalled it to *her* mind, but that he had been the מַזְכִּיר or remembrancer of God. Cf. Gen. xl. 14; Ezek. xxi. 28; Jer. iv. 16] **and to slay my son**? [Observe, she does not speak of him as slain.]

Ver. 19.—**And he said unto her, Give me thy son. And he took him out of her bosom,** [the age of the child may hence be roughly inferred] **and carried him up into a loft** [Heb. הָעֲלִיָּה *the* upper chamber. LXX. τὸ ὑπερῷον. *Loft* is most misleading. The upper room "was often [rather, *always*] the best apartment in an Eastern house" (Rawlinson). It was sometimes the guest-chamber (Luke xxii. 11, 12), and, from the uses to which it was put, must have been large (Acts i. 13; ix. 39; xx. 8; 2 Kings i. 2). Thomson (L. & B. i. 235) infers from the fact that the widow's house had an upper room, "that

the mode of building in Elijah's time and the custom of giving the *'alliyeh* to the guest were the same as now; also that this poor widow was not originally among the poorest classes (who have no *'alliyeh*), but that her extreme destitution was owing to the famine"], **and laid him upon his own bed.** [It may be doubted whether the verb יַשְׁכִּבֵהוּ lit., *made him to lie down*, would be used of a corpse.]

Ver. 20.—**And he cried unto the Lord, and said, O Lord my God, hast Thou also** [*i.e.* in addition to the misery and suffering brought through me upon my country] **brought evil upon the widow with whom I sojourn, by slaying** [Heb. *to slay*. Wordsworth partly bases his conclusion that the child was dead on the inexact translation of the A. V.] **her son**?

Ver. 21.—**And he stretched himself** [marg. *measured* himself, but Gesenius holds that *stretch out* is the primary meaning of the root] **upon the child** [cf. 2 Kings iv. 34. The commentators are again at variance as to whether these words imply the use of natural means or not. Those who hold that the child was dead naturally adopt the negative, and some (Keil, Rawlinson, *al.*) compare with it the action of our Lord in the case of the blind, deaf and dumb (Matt. ix. 35; Luke vii. 14; John ix. 6, 7). But surely the circumstances and the purpose alike, in these latter cases, were entirely different. The object of the touch, of anointing the eyes, &c., in these cases of healing, appears to have been to awaken a sufficient faith—without which "He could do no miracle" (Matt. xiii. 58)—in men whose infirmities of blindness, deafness, &c., prevented their attaining faith through the ordinary channels of seeing and hearing the merciful and gracious Son of man. But here the child, if not dead, was senseless. We are driven, therefore, to the belief that the prophet "used rational means for warming and revivifying" the child, "not with the hope that of themselves they would prove effectual, but in the sure confidence that God, in answer to his weeping supplication, would impart supernatural force to the natural human agencies," Bähr] **three times** [Not only in his prayer but also in this triple repetition do we recognize Elijah's profound conviction that only by the Almighty power of God could the child be restored, and that whatever means were used, God alone could make them effectual. For three is the number and signature of the Godhead—" die eigentlich göttliche Zahl, die Signatur des göttlichen Wesens" (Bähr, Symb. i. 143). Hence it is, *inter alia*, that "the calling upon the name of Jehovah in the old covenant "—he might have added, "and in the new;" cf. Mark xiv. 39, 41; 2 Cor. xii. 8—"was a threefold act:" Psa. lv. 17; Dan. vi. 10, 13; Num. vi. 24–26; Isa. vi. 3 (Bähr). The correspondence with 2 Cor. xii. 8 is very striking] and cried unto the Lord, and said, O Lord my God, I pray Thee [Heb. now] let this child's soul come into him [Heb. *upon his inside*; עַל is here, as elsewhere, used for אֶל] again. [Though נֶפֶשׁ, here translated " soul," constantly means "life," yet it by no means settles the question whether the child was really living or dead. For (1) the primary meaning of the word is " breath " (Gesen., Thesaurus, *s. v.*), and (2) the words might with perfect propriety, even if we interpret " life " or " soul," be used of one who lay in a lifeless and inanimate condition. Massillon's graphic language (vol. i. p. 91, ed. 1838), showing the contrast between Elijah's procedure and that of our blessed Lord (Luke vii. 14; viii. 54; John xi. 43), is worth citing here: " Elie ressuscite des morts, il est vrai; mais il est obligé de se coucher plusieurs fois sur le corps de l'enfant qu'il ressuscite; il souffle, il se rétrécit, il s'agite; on voit bien qu'il invoque une puissance étrangère; qu'il rappelle de l'empire de la mort une âme qui n'est pas soumise à sa voix, et qu'il n'est pas lui-même le maître de la mort et de la vie: Jesus-Christ ressuscite les morts comme il fait les actions les plus communes; il parle en maître à ceux qui dorment d'un sommeil éternel, et l'on sent bien qu'il est le Dieu des morts comme des vivants, jamais plus tranquille que lorsqu'il opère les plus grandes choses."]

Ver. 22.—**And the Lord heard the voice of Elijah; and the soul of the child came into him again, and he revived** [or *recovered*. Cf. 2 Kings i. 2; viii. 8].

Ver. 23.—**And Elijah took the child, and brought him down out of the chamber into the house** [Probably the עֲלִיָּה was reached by an *outside* staircase, and did not directly communicate with the lower rooms. Cf. Matt. xxiv. 17; Mark ii. 4; 2 Kings ix. 13] **and delivered him unto his mother: and Elijah said, See, thy son liveth.**

Ver. 24.—**And the woman said to Elijah, Now by this** [Heb. *this.* Gesenius interprets עַתָּה זֶה *just now.* Similarly Bähr, *nunmehr*] **I know that thou art a man of God** [not that she had doubted it before. See ver. 18. In the face of what Elijah had done for her, she could not doubt it. All that she means is that this is a great fresh proof of his mission], **and that the word of the Lord in thy mouth is truth.** [This last word אֱמֶת from which Amittai (Jonah i. 1) is formed, perhaps gave rise to the tradition that this boy was afterwards known as the prophet Jonah. Amittai was held to have been this widow's husband.

HOMILETICS.

Ver. 1.—*The Mission and Ministry of Elijah.* The appearance on the arena of Israel's history of such a champion as Elijah, armed with such high credentials, wielding such supernatural powers, marks a crisis in the history of God's ancient Church. We have but to see him, to hear him for one moment, to know that a great struggle is impending. God, like Nature, which is but a name for God, " does nothing in vain." Such high powers as his foreshadow great issues. Four points consequently may well engage our attention, viz., the man, his mission, his message, his ministry.

I. THE MAN. 1. *He was a wild man* (Gen. xvi. 12; Heb. *a wild-ass man*). Abraham has been called an "Arab sheykh." We have in Elijah a veritable Bedawy, if not by birth or tribe, by training and in character. The rough sheepskin (ch. xix. 13), the shaggy hair (2 Kings i. 18), the marvellous bodily endurance (ch. xviii. 46), the careful avoidance of the city, the flight into the desert (ch. xix. 4), the whole bearing of the man suggests to us the child of the wilderness. He, the greatest of the prophets, one of the "first three " of those born of women, has the exterior, the instincts, the heart of an Ishmaelite. He was thus a fit successor of Moses, the shepherd of Horeb, who in the very haunt and home of the Bedawin, was trained for his high vocation; he was meet to be the forerunner and pattern of the Baptist who was bred in the desert, clad in Arab dress, and fed with Arab food (Matt. iii. 1, 4). It is impossible to understand the man and his work unless this be borne in mind. The gaunt dervish who one day strode into the presence of the king and lifted up his sinewy arm and denounced the great drought; the shaggy, long-haired sheykh, who single-handed faced the hierarchy of Baal, and knew no fear, his were the asperities, the privations, the scant fare, the primitive, semi-nomadic life of a Gileadite. The sweet uses of adversity had moulded this man for the crisis. Our great chancellors, it has been said, come to us from the garret : the desert has ever been the school of the greatest prophets. The rugged, unsettled pasturages of Bashan were a meet nurse for a prophetic child. This champion was cast " in the clay ground " (see p. 142).

2. *He was a man of like passions with ourselves* (James v. 17). An " earthen vessel " (2 Cor. iv. 7). " In all points tempted like as we are," and *not* "without sin " (Heb. iii. 15). The Bible never pictures men as perfect. The *phronema sarkos* remains even in the regenerate.

II. HIS MISSION. Consider—1. *Whence it was derived.* He was not taught of men (Gal. i. 12, 17). He was ἰδιώτης καὶ ἀγράμματος. The God who separated him from his mother's womb called him by His grace (*ibid.* v. 15). He was an extra-ordinary messenger for a great emergency. But observe ; when God employs such messengers, men whose mission is derived directly from on high, the " signs of an apostle " are wrought by them. We are not to listen to an angel from heaven, unless he shows us his credentials. We have a right to ask of those who run without being sent to show us a sign. When the missionary Dr. Wolff told one of the Eastern bishops that the " Lord had sent him," the prelate not unreasonably asked him for a display of his powers. If God should send us an Elias again, He will give us at the same time a sign from heaven.

2. *When it was conferred.* It was (1) When iniquity abounded. When Hiel had built Jericho ; when Ahab had raised a temple for Baal ; when Jezebel had gathered round her an army of false prophets ; when the faith of God's elect was in jeopardy. The darkest hour is ever before the dawn. *Cum duplicantur lateres, venit Moses.* " Man's extremity is," &c. " Israel was sore wounded when God sent them this balm *from Gilead* " (Henry). (2) When ordinary means were insufficient. There were true priests in Jerusalem ; there were " sons of the prophets," it is probable, in Bethel and Samaria ; there were seven thousand faithful ones in Israel ; but what were these against such a queen as Jezebel, against such a propaganda and such a system as hers ? It was then no longer a question of heresy or schism, of calves or cherubim, of Jeroboam's or Jehovah's priests ; the very existence of the Church was at stake. Elijah was summoned to the court ; he was armed with " power to shut heaven that it rained not in the days of his prophecy " (Rev. xi. 6), with power to call down fire to devour his enemies, and the like, because only thus could the elect people be stayed from throwing themselves into the arms of an organized pro-stitution ; from yielding themselves, body and soul, to the whoredoms and witch-crafts of " that woman Jezebel ; " because only thus could the light of truth, the one lamp which illumined the world's darkness, be preserved from utter extinction.

III. HIS MESSAGE. It was a denunciation of immediate drought, one of the most terrible calamities that can befal an Eastern land. In Palestine, animal as well as vegetable life is directly dependent on the rain. Not only do the showers which irrigate the land feed the springs, but they are carefully stored up in cisterns for daily use. It is only as compared with the arid wastes of Egypt that the Holy Land could be called " a land of brooks and waters, of fountains and depths," &c. (Deut. viii. 7). And it is also described by the same writer as a land that " drinketh water of the rain of heaven " (*ibid.* xi. 11). Consequently rain, everywhere a prime necessity of existence, is doubly indispensable in Palestine. The rainfall of Jerusalem is on the average three times as great as that of London. It is clear, consequently, that this message threatened a terrible plague, that it portended long and protracted suffering. There are some who will not hear of the " terrors of the Lord," who would never have them mentioned in the pulpit. Yet pain and privation are among the first sanctions of God's law, and we have the authority of many eminent divines for saying that more men are won to God and right by fear than by love. It sounds fine and philosophic to speak of fear as an unworthy motive, but men forget what an unworthy animal is man. Besides, this drought was a part of the punishment, and was admirably adapted to serve as a punishment for apostasy. It was meet that men who practically denied the living God should be practically reminded of their dependence on Him. It was well that those who held Baal to be lord of nature, should be left to discover his impotence (cf. Judg. x. 14; Jer. xiv. 22). "Are there any of the vanities of the heathen that can give rain ? " And it was a punishment this, which penitence might avert. Moreover, it was the penalty foretold in the law (Deut. xxviii. 23). Elijah was not left to scatter plagues at his pleasure. Like an earlier prophet, he could not "go beyond the word of the Lord to do less or more " (Num. xxii. 18). Of himself, he could do nothing (*ibid.* v. 33). His message was, " As the *Lord* liveth." If the rain should only come "according to his word," it was because his word was God's word. If his prayer for the drought had been answered (James v. 17), it had first been inspired. He speaks here as the minister, not the master. He is the willing, patient slave of Jehovah. "Before whom I stand."

IV. HIS MINISTRY. From this initial message let us turn to his ministry as a whole. And it presents to our view these broad features—

1. *It was exercised in silence.* How few are Elijah's recorded words, and those few are the utterances of but five or six occasions. He was *not* "mighty in word." He had no sooner delivered his first brief message than he disappears, and for three years and a half Israel hears him no more. He speaks for a moment: he is dumb for a triennium. And when he reappears, it is but for a day. That one day's ministry ended, he is again hidden from our view. Thrice more he reappears in the history, but each time it is but for a day, and then he goes into the silent heavens, and save on the night of transfiguration, speaks to men no more. How like to the revelations of God to man. He "keepeth silence (Psa. l. 3). He too hideth Himself. "He spake and it was done." How unlike the everlasting chatter of some of our later prophets. " Ministers," it is sometimes said, "are mere talkers." Elijah proclaims the dignity, if not " the eternal duty, of silence." "All real work," some one has said, " is quiet work." How many of our sermons, full of sound and fury, leave not a trace behind them. But the silent Elias accomplished the regeneration of his country.

2. *It was a ministry of deed.* There was no need for him to speak. The works that he did bore witness of him. Declamation, argument, remonstrance, would have been absurd. The time for that was past. And he had actions to speak for him. Surely there is a lesson for Christ's ministers here. It is true they cannot work wonders like Elijah ; and it is also true that they are sent to "preach the Word," to reprove, rebuke, exhort, &c. ; but we are reminded here that a fruitful ministry must be one of *action.* Words, however eloquent, in the long turn count for less than a holy life. The age, however it may hanker after sensationalism, is nevertheless suspicious of all talk. Why is it that our holy religion has but such an indifferent hold on the masses of our countrymen? One reason is that while we "point to heaven," we do not always "lead the way." " *Cujus vita contemnitur, ejus praedicatio despicitur.*" The life of their parish priest is the only Bible many Englishmen ever read, and alas, what a smeared and blotted page that sometimes is. And those who do hear our sermons have learned to discount them. They know full well that words are cheap, and that emotion, and even unction, can be simulated. They often wonder how much of our discourse we really believe and practise ourselves, and they turn to our lives for an answer. That familiar paradox, consequently, is full of truth and meaning, that, "in preaching, the thing of least importance is the sermon." It was well said that *actio*—action in the truest sense of the word, not gesture or manner, but conduct—is the first, second, and third great essential of eloquence (see " Guesses at Truth," ii. pp. 146 seqq.) A French ecclesiastic, the Abbé Mullois, has laid it dowh, as one of the canons of preaching, that "to address men successfully, they must *be loved much.*" "Nothing influences others so much as character. Few people are capable of reasoning, and fewer still like the trouble of it; and besides, men have hearts as well as heads. Hence, consistency, reality, ever-present principle, shining through the person in whom they dwell, and making themselves perceptible, have more weight than many arguments, than much preaching " (Heygate, " Ember Hours "). It is Baxter

who speaks of clergymen who " cut the throats of their sermons by their lives ; " but there are many who, without doing this, invalidate their words by their actions. It is well for us to remember that personal character is the best preparation for the pulpit. " *Facta, non verba;* " this is, and will be increasingly, the demand of the age upon the prophetic order. " *Non magna eloquimur sed vivimus.*" This must be more and more the response of the ministry.

3. *It was brave and fearless.* On three occasions this court preacher took his life in his hand (ch. xvii. 1; xviii. 2; xxi. 19). On one occasion he seems to have quailed (ch. xix. 3), but even then it does not appear that he fled from any present duty, or, like Jonah, declined any commission. His ministry as a whole was boldly discharged as in the presence of the Eternal, " Before whom I stand." He saw none other than his Master. Like another preacher before royalty, Massillon, he spoke as if he saw Death standing at his elbow. Like Daniel, he knew that his God could deliver him. The fear of man is cast out when we realize the presence of God (Isa. li. 12, 13).

4. *It was seemingly a failure.* If others did not think so, he did. We know that no work, really and truly done for God, can be wasted (Isa. lv. 11) ; but we are often tempted to think it is. But it must be such work as will stand the trial by fire (1 Cor. iii. 13). It has been strikingly said, " If any man's work is a failure, the probability is that it is because he is a failure himself." Still, it is for our comfort to remember, in times of depression, that the greatest of the prophets saw little or no fruit of his labours. He was persuaded that even the unexampled miracles that he wrought were of little or no avail (ch. xix. 10). We find that when there were seven thousand secret followers of the Lord God, Elijah thought himself left alone. And indeed the state of Israel, even after the ordeal of Carmel, might well lead him to take the gloomiest and most despairing view of the situation. Jezebel pursues her infamous way. The son of Ahab sends to consult a foreign oracle, and ignores the God of Israel. The fire must come down a second time and burn up the idolaters instead of the bullock and the altar. But all the same, we know that his work was not in vain. Nor can ours be, if done like his. We have nothing to do with immediate successes. " One man soweth, another reapeth." Nor is success in any shape mentioned in our instructions. That is God's part, not ours. We have but to sow the seed, He must make it grow. The world worships success — or what it calls success—and the greatest of ministries—Elijah's, Jeremiah's, Ezekiel's, our blessed Lord's—were all failures from a worldly point of view.

Vers. 3—7.—*The Solitary Place.* We have just seen that it was from the wilderness that Elijah went forth into the busy, wicked world, and to the anxious, dangerous work of a prophet. He, like his antitype, was in the desert " until the time of his showing unto Israel" (Luke i. 80). There, in secret communion with God, he had gained strength for the encounter; there he had meditated over the grievous apostasy of his people, and had " vexed his righteous soul from day to day with their evil deeds " (2 Pet. ii. 8). And there, as he " prayed earnestly that it might not rain," the word of the Lord came to him and burned in his bones (Jer. xx. 9), and bore him into the presence of the king (Amos iii. 8). But it is now for us to observe that no sooner had he entered upon his ministry, and delivered his first brief message, than he was sent into the desert—it may be, the same desert— again. The word of the Lord straightway bids him turn eastward and hide in the brook Cherith. Now the word *Cherith* means *separation.* This section conse- quently may fittingly speak to us of the need of separation, of the uses of solitude and retirement in the discipline of the saints. From Elijah's separation from his work and the world we may glean some lessons as to our own. Observe—

1. *Solitude was necessary to Elijah's safety.* He must hide or lose his head. When Jezebel cut off the prophets of the Lord (ch. xviii. 13), we may be sure he would not be spared. Was it not because of him indeed that the others were attacked ? Had his dwelling been with men, the messengers of Ahab would assuredly have found him and slain him (ch. xviii. 10). So it is sometimes neces- sary, for the life of our souls, that we should flee into the desert. It is at our peril

that we stay in Sodom. We must "escape to the mountain." It may be from some enchantress, whose whoredoms and witchcrafts are as cruel as Jezebel's; it may be from companions whose snares are more perilous than Ahab's sword; it may be from a society hardly less pestilent than that of Israel. There are times when our only safety is in flight. Those hermits who buried themselves in the Thebaid, or who burrowed in the rocks of the Wâdy Feiran, the world has only a smile for their folly, and it is no doubt true that God would have us leaven the world, not leave it. But it would have been well if some had, for a time at least, followed their example. How many souls have perished because they would not enter into their chambers and shut their doors and hide themselves until the indignation be overpast (Isa. xxvi. 20); because they had not the courage to disappear for a while, if only into their closets. "He that wilfully stands still to catch dangers, tempteth God instead of trusting him."

2. *Solitude was necessary to his soul's health.* It is remarkable how God's elect messengers, each in his turn, have been sent "apart into a desert place to rest awhile" (Mark vi. 31). Moses must spend forty years in the great and terrible wilderness; must spend forty days and forty nights in Horeb, the Mount of God. Elijah himself only emerges from the Cherith to go to another hiding-place at Zarephath, and from Zarephath he passes almost directly to the same wilderness and the same mount where Moses was. The Baptist's life was almost divided between the desert and the prison. St. Paul must learn his gospel in Arabia. And our Holy Lord, He must begin His ministry by a forty days' fast, and from time to time must seek a quiet place to rest and pray. All men who are much before the world need their times of retirement. In the "loud stunning tide of human care and crime" it is difficult to hear the whispers of God in the soul. Now the voices of nature, such as men hear in solitude, are among the voices of God. Nature has been called "God's great green book."

> "One impulse from a vernal wood
> May teach you more of man,
> Of moral evil and of good,
> Than all the sages can."

"There are two books," says Sir Thomas Browne, "from whence I collect my divinity. Besides that written one of God, another of his servant nature, that universal and public manuscript that lies expansed unto the eyes of all." And is not every tree, every leaf, in its way a mute witness for God and purity? It is remarkable that the greatest crimes and brutalities are committed in those districts of this country where men can have neither nature nor solitude—in the dens of Liverpool, amid the cinder heaps of the Black Country, in the dingy pit villages of Durham. It is only in quiet, under the silent stars, amid the purple heather, by the murmuring brook, or in the inner chamber, that we can know ourselves and our God. The "Ancient Mariner's" conception of his "wide, wide sea"—

> "So lonely 'twas, that *God Himself*
> Scarce seemèd there to be,"

fine though it is, contradicts the experience of the saints, who have found that it is precisely the profoundest solitude that is instinct with His presence.

And now let us consider how God calls us all in turn to a brook Cherith. (1) He calls us to separation from sin. The Church is a Cherith. Baptism is a "water of separation," the token and pledge of our renunciation of world and flesh and devil, of our admission into the family of God. While in the world, we may not be of it. Our calling is to holiness (1 Pet. i. 15; 1 Thess. iv. 7; 2 Tim. i. 9). We are to be sacrifices (Rom. xii. 1), and the root idea both of holiness and of sacrifice is a separation to God. (2) Sometimes He calls us to a chamber of sickness, sometimes to the very "valley of the shadow of death." How often is bodily sickness for the soul's health! That vale of separation becomes a vale of blessing; the *Cherith* leads to a *Berachah* (2 Chron. xx. 26; cf. Psa. lxxxiv. 6). What a school of the heart has that enforced solitude often proved! See Homiletics, p. 13. (3) Nor must we forget here the *Retreat*—those opportunities for meditation and prayer, happily revived amongst us of late years. The name may possibly be Romish, but the thing is sensible and scriptural enough—a voluntary retirement for a short period from the world that we may hear and think only of the things which make for our peace. The saying still holds good, "He goeth before you into Galilee "— a retired mountain place it was (Matt. xxviii. 16)—" *there* shall ye see him."

3. *Elijah's retirement was for the ultimate welfare of Israel.* So long as he remained amongst them, the people would have looked to him as the author of their calamities, or would have cried to him to avert them. His disappearance afforded them leisure to examine themselves and face their sins, and left them only God or Baal to cry to. It is sometimes well that the prophet should keep silence. *Deus habet suas moras.* It is not always that He stretches out his hands all day long to the disobedient and gainsaying. Having spoken by Elijah to Ahab and Israel, now He and His prophet must withdraw into the darkness, and the drought must do its silent work. And there are times, too, when Christ's ministers must be silent. When the Gadarenes besought our Lord to depart out of their coasts, He straightway took them at their word (Matt. viii. 34; ix. 1; cf. ch. xxiii. 38, 39). The apostles were to shake off the dust of their feet against the city that received them not, and to depart from it (Matt. x. 14), and they did so (Acts xiii. 51). When the Jews counted themselves unworthy of eternal life, Paul and Barnabas turned to the Gentiles (Acts xiii. 46). When the churches of Asia fell and repented not, their candlestick was removed out of its place (Rev. ii. 5). Their loss is our gain. "These things were written for our admonition."

Vers. 4—7.—*The Food of the Saints.* We have just seen the prophet in his solitude. Let us now consider the manner in which he was sustained there. His needs were supplied in two ways, partly by natural, partly by supernatural means. No miracle was wrought to give him water. He must make his home in the wâdy and drink of the rivulet that flowed past his feet. It was there, and he must help himself to it. But with his food it was quite different. He could not find that, and so it was brought to him; it was provided him by God. For even if it was not laid at his feet morning and evening by ravens—and we have soon reason to think that it was not—even if it was furnished him by the villagers of Orbo, his tribesmen and friends, or by the loyal and hospitable Arabs who roamed over the adjoining region, still it was supplied by the ordering and special Providence of God. For it is as much a supernatural work to control, by an unseen Power, the minds of men as the instincts or habits of birds. If we get rid of the ravens we do not get rid of the miracle. It is clear, consequently, that he was sustained in part by natural, in part by superhuman agency. Now our food, like his, is, though in a different way, natural and supernatural. We use the terms in the popular sense, for who shall say that all food is not supernatural. True, it comes to us by what we call " natural processes," in what we call the " order of Nature; " but it is obvious that the so-called "laws of Nature " are only " statements of the observed course of Nature, or the uniform results of known physical causes ending in some prime cause or causes not merely physical" (Sir E. Beckett, " Origin of the Laws of Nature "). Nature only means what is fixed, settled, uniform (Bp. Butler). But, using the words as they are used in common parlance, part of our sustenance, the supply of our bodily wants is, for the most part natural; and another part, the satisfaction of our spiritual necessities, is for the most part supernatural. Our needs, that is to say, are supplied something like Elijah's were. Let us trace the resemblance a little more in detail, and let us see first how it holds good of our

I. BODILY SUSTENANCE. We learn from this history—

1. *That we must use the means within our reach.* Not even for His elect messenger, the greatest of the prophets, does God work an unnecessary miracle. " Dieu n'agit pas par des volontés particulières " (Malebranche). No doubt God could have supplied his drink just as easily as his daily bread, in an extraordinary way, but He would not. No; in a valley debouching into the Jordan was a stream, fed

from some hidden source, such as the snows of Hermon, or springing from the roots of the hills of Gilead, and the prophet must seek it, and take up his abode near it. What do we learn from this but that God "will have our endeavours concur to our preservation," a truth somewhat roughly, but strikingly, put in the Puritan *mot d'ordre*, "Trust in God, and keep your powder dry." It is no real kindness to do for Elijah what he can do for himself. There are lands where daily bread is to be had without care or labour; where a man has but to put forth his hand and take the bread-tree fruit and eat and be satisfied, but that is said to be a doubtful boon. It is found that the natives of those lands will not work, and their life, which should be full of high endeavour, which should aim, if at nothing more, at "making two blades of grass grow where only one grew before," is wasted in basking in the eternal sunshine. The primæval law, "In the sweat of thy brow thou shalt eat bread," though we call it a curse, is really a blessing. "Six days shalt thou labour" is as much a Divine command as the command to rest on the seventh. It is God decrees, "If any man will not work, neither shall he eat" (2 Thess. iii. 10). The imperious necessity to provide our daily bread is one of the springs which keeps the world in motion: it is the salt which keeps our life from stagnation and corruption. It is in vain we cry to Jupiter for help. God has given us fields and seed. He gives us rain and sunshine; it is for our good that we should do the rest.

2. *That then God will supply what is lacking.* When we have done our best we may justly look to Him to give what we cannot get. And this He will do. "Thy bread shall be given thee, and thy waters shall be sure" (Isa. xxxiii. 16). "Never have I seen the righteous forsaken, nor his seed begging their bread" (Psa. xxxvii. 25). In the barren wilderness, He gave bread from heaven. "In the days of famine, they shall be satisfied" (Psa. xxxvii. 19). What a commentary on these words does this history furnish! Elijah had "called for a famine on the land" (ch. xviii. 2; Luke iv. 25), and had "broken the whole staff of bread" (Psa. cv. 16); but he himself had enough and to spare. God spreads for him "a table in the wilderness" (Psa. lxxviii. 16), and almost "in the presence of his enemies" (Psa. xxiii. 5). The stars shall fall from their courses, but he shall have enough. It has been thought by some that the ravens brought him bread and flesh from Ahab's own table. It would have been so, had it been necessary. If he was supplied with food by human instrumentality, it was none the less by God's command. And this is God's ordinary way of hearing "the prayer of the poor destitute;" he puts it into the hearts of others to help. "God works by means, and the chief means is man" (Bossuet).

3. *That God gives us our bread daily.* Elijah only received a small supply of food at once. Though he had no lack, he had no profusion. He had "daily bread"—for "morning and evening are one day" (Gen. i. 5)—and no more. Even he must walk by faith and learn to "take no thought for the morrow." And daily bread is all that is promised us; all that we are taught to pray for (Matt. vi. 11). And that, perhaps, because a day is a life in miniature; each day is rounded by dawn and dusk, by sleep and darkness, into a perfect little life. Whether the birds brought him food or not, he and they received it alike, τὸν ἐπιούσιον ἄρτον, the bread of a day in its day. The lesson of the manna (Exod. xvi. 20) is taught us again by the brook Cherith.

4. *That God guarantees us necessaries, not luxuries.* Elijah's fare was frugal. "Water, bread, and flesh" (cf. Isa. xxxiii. 16). As a rule, He gives us food "exceeding abundantly above all that we can ask or think." How prodigious is the variety of our food, how lavish its supply! What rich provision has the Eternal Goodness made for the gratification of our tastes. Fish, flesh, fowl, fruits, —the list is endless. And of the flesh or fruits, again, how many *genera*, and in the *genera* how many *species*, and in the species what countless *varieties*. Lavish profusion marks His gifts. But all the same he *covenants* to give us less than the fare of Cherith, even bread and water. "God gives order for competency, not for wantonness" (Hall).

II. SPIRITUAL FOOD. But we are now to consider that "man doth not live by bread alone, but by every word," &c. (Deut. viii. 3; Matt. iv. 4). The saints have meat to eat of which the world knows nothing (John iv. 34). Elijah had other food than that which the ravens brought him. In giving "daily bread," God does not forget man's spiritual part, even if he forgets it in his prayer for bread. And God supplies the soul's needs by laws not unlike those which govern the supply of material food.

1. *We must use the means of grace.* The treasury of the Church contains an abundant provision. There are "living waters," there is "super-substantial bread," there is word and sacrament, prayer and psalm. But we must come to the waters and drink (John vii. 37; Rev. xxii. 17). Our faith needs something to feed upon, and it is in vain we ask for miracles, so long as we do not use means. If we want to love God more, we must seek to know God, through His word and works, better. If we want to be more like Christ, we must be more with Christ, in His word and ordinances, for it is "association produces assimilation." There is a tendency to decry the *means* of grace. There is a religion which is wholly subjective, which seeks its growth and expansion in everlasting self-introspection or mystical contemplation of the Divine perfections. But "Thou shalt drink of the brook." True, the channel is nothing—*Annus non ager, facit fructum*—but a channel. It is God must fill it, but if God has dug it, it is presumption to discard it.

> "The means that Heaven yields must be embraced,
> And not neglected; else if Heaven would
> And we will not, Heaven's offers we refuse."

2. *If we are debarred from the means of grace, God will give grace without means.* It is a blessed truth, *gratia non ligatur mediis.* We may not dispense with them, but God can, and does. He did so in the oft-cited instance of the dying thief. *He* was saved without sacraments, but St. Paul was not (Acts xxii. 16). And how often have the saints and martyrs, cut off, amid fierce persecutions, from the communion of the saints, found their deserts or their cells glorified by direct communion with God. Matthew Henry quaintly says that "if we cannot go to the house of the Lord, we can go to the Lord of the house." The Church of England proclaims that there may be a true Eucharist without the elements (*vide* The Communion of the Sick, 3rd Rubric). But it is only when we are deprived of the means that we can justly expect God to dispense with them. He has commanded His ministers to feed His Church (Acts xx. 28; 1 Peter v. 2); He has given them word and sacrament, bread and wine, wherewith to nourish it; but He is independent both of means and ministers.

3. *Supplies of grace are granted day by day.* Our soul's bread is a daily bread. Every day we ask for forgiveness, for grace (Matt. vi. 11); and as our days, so our strength shall be (Deut. xxxiii. 25). If we have not morning and evening prayer in the Church, we may have it in the house. And morning and evening may be sanctified by the Word of God and prayer, in private. Each may find a Cherith in the closet; each receive there his portion of meat in due season.

4. *Grace is given without measure.* God does not promise luxuries, because they are often hurtful. But there is no over-indulgence here. It is significant how excess in wine is contrasted with being filled with the Spirit (Ephes. v. 18). One cannot drink too deep of the living waters (John vii. 38). They are given freely (Rev. xxii. 17).

Vers. 8—16.—*The Furnace of Trial.* The village of Zarephath appears to have borrowed its name from the furnace or furnaces created there for the *smelting* of metals. See note on ver. 9. A great lexicographer interprets the word to mean, a "workshop for the melting and refining of metals." But that name might with scarcely less propriety have been bestowed upon it from the circumstances recorded in this section. It was a veritable furnace for men; a place of assay and refining both for the prophet and the widow with whom he lodged. "Surely . . . there is a place for gold where they fine it" (Job xxviii. 1).

I. IT WAS A PLACE OF TRIAL FOR ELIJAH. In connexion with it he was subjected to the following trials of his faith and courage—

1. *He had to leave his hiding place.* For months he had dwelt safely in the deep, sequestered, peaceful wâdy. That he must hide there, and hide so long, showed how great was the danger to which he was exposed. But now he is commanded to quit his asylum, to go forth into the world, to run the risk of recognition, of betrayal, of death; and to do so, we cannot doubt, would cost him a struggle, and put his faith in God to the proof.

2. *He had to seek a home in Zidon.* How those words would strike upon his ears, "Which belongeth unto Zidon"! Zidon was the capital of Ethbaal. The father of Jezebel, his implacable enemy, held sway there. It was like going into the lion's den. His feeling would be something like that of David's men, "Behold, we be afraid here in Judah: how much more then if we come to Keilah" (1 Sam. xxiii. 3). Of all hiding places, that would seem to him to be the most to be dreaded. How can he escape detection *there?* He might well have taken fright, as at a later period, and have fled further into the desert. Or he might have petitioned, like Lot (Gen. xix. 20), to be allowed to find some other refuge. But he did neither. "He arose and went to Zarephath." He was "strong in faith, giving glory to God" (Rom. iv. 20).

3. *He had to be sustained by a widow woman.* The position and circumstances of the Eastern widow are to be remembered here. The seclusion in which Oriental women live makes its difficult for a widow to find a livelihood, even if there were work for her to do. And we have only to consider what the position of widows amongst ourselves would be, if there were no such things as investments, no means of putting out money to usury (Deut. xxiii. 19). Hence the repeated injunctions to remember the widow (*ibid.* xiv. 29; xvi. 11, 14; xxiv. 17, 19—21; Job xxiv. 21; xxix. 13; Psa. cxlvi. 9). Hence the special provision for widows in the early Church (Acts vi. 1; 1 Tim. v. 4—9). The widow was an object for charity, and needed sustenance. And now Elijah learns that by a widow he is to be sheltered and sustained. And this widow a foreigner, probably an idolater—an alien both in race and religion. Surely there was a trial both of his faith and of his obedience here.

4. *He finds the widow in the extremest poverty.* He encounters her "gathering of sticks." That in itself was not an encouraging sign. Next he hears from her lips that her cupboard is empty. She has not food for herself, much less for a stranger. "A handful of meal," a "little oil," this is all her store. She who was to sustain his life is herself ready to die. But he knows in whom he has believed. He "argued not against Heaven's will." He did not "bate a jot of heart or hope." "Make me a little cake first." He is assured that "they shall not be ashamed in the evil time, and in the days of famine they shall be satisfied" (Psa. xxxvii. 9). He knows that "God will not suffer his word to fail, nor alter the thing that is gone out of his lips" (Psa. lxxxix. 34).

5. *He is immured in her house for two years.* Those two years were years of banishment from his country and his work. Three years and a half had he to wait, and most of the time in a strange land, ere his recal; cut off, "not from life, yet from usefulness, which is the end and comfort of life." Which of us would not have been impatient, or, like the Baptist in his fortress-prison, tempted to think God had forgotten us? And he knew that all this time his people were suffering. We think it strange if a servant of God is laid aside for a few months from his ministry. But the greatest of the prophets was silenced, was buried alive, for the mystical period of forty and two months, for "time and times and half a time" (Rev. xi. 2, 3; xii. 6, 14). "When we cannot work for God we must sit still quietly for him" (Henry). "They also serve who only stand and wait."

6. *His presence there is no protection against sickness.* Of the three inmates of the cottage home, one sickens and droops to his grave. This sickness causes us no surprise, but it did Elijah (ver. 20); and that because he lived under the dispensation of temporal rewards. Sickness was then regarded as, and it often was, the scourge of the Almighty (Deut. vii. 15; xxviii. 61; cf. 1 Cor. xi. 30). It was a trial, consequently, of Elijah's faith. It looked as if the hand of the Lord was gone out against him. It seemed as if he was to be always the author of misfortune ("Hast thou *also,*" &c.); as if the widow by whom he had been housed, and who had hidden him at the risk of her life, was to be requited with cruel punishment for her good deed. But let us now see in Zarephath

II. A FURNACE OF TRIAL FOR THE WIDOW. It was this in two ways—

1. *A stranger demands a share of her last meal.* Or, rather, he demands the first share. "Make me a little cake first." Now consider her position. She is reduced to her last morsel. So sore is the famine that she and her son, after they have eaten this meal together, are about to lie down and wait for death. They must have suffered hunger enough already; they must have dreaded the hunger even unto death which awaited them. At this moment a stranger suddenly appears before her, and says he must eat first. It is true that he wears the aspect of a prophet, and appeals to the Lord God of Israel, but prophets were often deceivers (chs. xiii 18; xxii. 12), and foreign gods could be expected to show her no favour. And at home, her own flesh and blood, the son of her womb, stretches out his skinny fingers, attenuated by famine, and cries for all she has to give. Moreover, if this prophet could multiply food, as he professed to be able to do, why should he ask her for bread? Was it reasonable that she should part with her last morsel on the strength of such a promise? "Charity begins at home." "Let the children first be filled." "Shall I take my bread and my water and give it to one that I know not whence he is" (1 Sam. xxv. 11)? Thus she might justly have argued. We could not have wondered had the ordeal been too great for her; had she kept fast hold of her children's bread and denied it to "dogs." But, like that other Syro-Phoenician woman (Matt. xv. 21 sqq.), her faith was equal to the test; she "went and did according to the saying of Elijah." And, therefore, of her also it might justly be said, "I have not found so great faith, no not in Israel."

2. *Her son falls sick and lies apparently lifeless.* The tie between a mother and an only son is, perhaps, the closest and tenderest of all blood relationships; and it has been remarked that it is peculiarly strong and sacred in the East. "The only son of his mother and she was a widow" (Luke vii. 12): who does not feel the pathos of these words? And the tie would be all the stronger in this case because they had suffered together; because he had been given back to her from the jaws of death (ver. 12). It is said by some that we value things in proportion to what they have cost us, and on this principle they would explain the deep love of the mother for her offspring. Goethe's mother used to say that "she and her Wolfgang had always clung to each other, because they had been *young* together;" but to have hungered together, to have, hand in hand, looked Death in the face, to have soon the spectre retreating, surely this communion in suffering, this συμπάθεια, this *compassio*, would beget a much profounder sympathy. And now this boy, whose life had been miraculously preserved, is so sick that there is no breath left in him. What could this fond and anxious mother think? Was the prophet who had given them bread unable to defend them from sickness? Or was this God's recompense for her hospitality? She might have had hard thoughts of God, or unworthy thoughts of the prophet. It is a wonder she held fast her integrity. But she only thought hardly of herself. It must be, she argued, a judgment for her sin. The man of God had read her life; had brought her sin to the remembrance of his Master (ver. 18). It never occurs to her, strong as was the temptation, to arraign God's providence. But her faith and patience must have been sorely tried.

It now remains for us to consider how these assays of faith, which have given to this Phoenician workshop its fame and immortality, were "more precious than of gold that perisheth, though it be tried with fire" (1 Peter i. 7). In that workshop God Himself sat "as a refiner and purifier of silver."

It is said that when the crucible, the fining pot for silver (Prov. xvii. 3), is put into the furnace, the chymist has a sure and ready test of its purity; a means of knowing when his long processes have accomplished their object. When he sees his *face reflected* in the glowing and untarnished metal, he knows that the purification is complete.

It was that Elijah and his hostess might learn to know God, might be transformed into the image of God, that they experienced this two years' purgation in the furnace. It was that the dross might be purely purged, and the tin taken away (Isa. i. 25) ; that they might be changed into the image of their Creator (Col. iii. 10 ; 2 Cor. iii. 18).

Now the historian does not record the results of this assay, except incidentally. But we can clearly see that the faith of Elijah and the widow alike grew stronger by the exercise. How much Elijah gained ; how the discipline told on his subsequent career ; how the trying of his faith wrought patience (James i. 3), we cannot now discover. But we can see that it resulted in the widow's conversion, or in the confirmation of her faith, and in the glory and praise of God (ver. 24). And that is not all. Its issues are in eternity. The cross was the forerunner of the crown (James i. 12).

HOMILIES BY VARIOUS AUTHORS.

Ver. 1.—*Elijah.* In this sudden manner the Tishbite is introduced, upon which Bishop Hall remarks, "He comes in with a tempest who went out with a whirlwind." And Lamartine says, "Recalling his life and his terrible vengeance, it seems as if this man had the thunder of the Lord for a soul, and that the element in which he was borne to heaven was that in which he was brought forth." Let us consider—

I. HIS PRESENCE. 1. *It is awful in its vagueness.* (1) It was of the inhabitants of Gilead—"The hard, stony region," south of the river Jabbok. This was one of the wildest parts of the Holy Land. The awful scenery of that district harmonized well with the ruggedness of the spirit of this prophet. John the Baptist first appeared in a wilderness. Out of a wilderness Jesus came up when He entered upon His public ministry (Matt. iii. 1; Luke iv. 1, 14, 15). (2) He is distinguished as the Tishbite. Calmet says Tishbe was a city beyond Jordan in the tribe of Gad, and in the land of Gilead. Gesenius, from Relandi, mentions Tishbe as "a town of Napthali." Could there have been two Tishbes ; and were the words "Of the inhabitants of Gilead" added to distinguish? (3) "The Tishbite," we incline to think, was a name of office or commission. It designates Elijah as the *Converter* (תשבי from שב to turn). In this he resembled John the Baptist, whose commission also was to preach *repentance.* (See Matt. xi. 13, 14; xvii. 12; Luke i. 17.) When Elijah comes again "before the coming of the great and dreadful day of the Lord," it will be in his character of *Tishbite* or *Converter*, viz., "to turn the heart of the fathers to the children, and the heart of the children to their fathers." (See Matt. iv. 5, 6). 2. *It is awful also in its intensity.* (1) His name (אליהו) some interpret to be, "My God Jehovah is he," others, "God is my strength." In either case it reminds us of God, and God is the very centre of all reality. (2) Elijah brings us into the very presence of God also by the manner in which he announces himself. "As Jehovah liveth, before whom I stand." In this way also the angel Gabriel announced himself to Zacharias, and that too when he revealed the coming of the Baptist. (See Luke i. 19.) It is probable Elijah, like John the Baptist, also was a priest, and the expression under review may intimate this. (Compare Deut. x. 8.) About 940 years after this, Elijah, with Moses, in a remarkable manner stood, in the presence of Jehovah, in the mount of transfiguration (Matt. xvii. 1—3). (3) This declaration of the *living* God was appropriately timed. For the calves or young bulls of Jeroboam, and the bulls and goats of Sidon established through the influence of Jezebel, had so occupied public attention that He was forgotten. Lamentable is the substitution of death for life !

HIS FAITH. 1. *It is bold in its assertion.* (1) "There shall be neither dew nor rain." The material elements which mechanically produce dew and rain were worshipped by the Phoenicians, and now by the Israelites, while the God that made them was forgotten. Is not this the very error of modern atheistic physicists? They worship Baal, Ashtoreth, and Ashere under other names, and ridicule faith and prayer. But Elijah asserts the *living* God as superior to *nature*, who will restrain both dew and rain, and so make the gods to worship him. (See Deut. xi. 16, 17; Jer. xiv. 22.) (2) "There shall be neither dew nor rain *these years.*" Dew and rain, according to the course of nature, may be withholden for days, for weeks, even, in rare cases, for months; but not for years. When therefore for "three years and six months" these meteors were awanting, the phenomenon was supernatural. 2. *The qualification is no less remarkable*—"But according to my word." (1) Unless divinely authorized to say this, such a declaration would be most presumptuous. And the inevitable failure of the prediction would cover the pseudo-prophet with ridicule and confusion. (2) But Elijah was a genuine man. He spoke under the inspiration of Jehovah before whom he stood. Such inspiration makes all the difference between presumption and faith. This is just the distinction made by James, who describes Elijah's faith as (ἐνεργουμενη) *inwrought persuasion* of a righteous man (James v. 16). Faith is the gift of God. 8. *The directness is admirable.* (1) This address is to Ahab. It comes not to him as a hearsay, but with the highest authenticity. The inspired messenger of God is above kings. (See Jer. i. 10.) (2) It is fearlessly delivered. When a man is conscious that he stands before Jehovah he may use great freedom of speech. The courage of the lion is in the heart of faith. Elijah was a man of faith because he was a man of prayer. It is an encouragement to our faith to know that "Elias was a man of like passions as we are" (James v. 17).—J. A. M.

Vers. 2—6.—*Resources of Providence.* When the heavens are shut up by the word of the Lord, what will become of the prophet who declared that word? Will he not suffer from the drought in common with the sinners on whose account the dew and rain are restrained? Will he not be exposed to the rage of an idolatrous king and queen whose humbled gods cannot, in this crisis, vindicate themselves? Will not a demoralized populace resent their sufferings upon the man of God? God knows all, and is equal to all, emergencies.

I. HE HAS RESOURCES FOR THE PROTECTION OF HIS SERVANTS. 1. *He could defend Elijah in the midst of his enemies.* (1) The power that had shut up the heavens could surely do this. The elemental fire which now scorched the earth, He could cause to fall upon the heads of any who would threaten his servant. (See 2 Kings i. 10—15.) (2) Without recourse to violence, he could dispose the hearts of men to respect His messenger, as afterwards He did. (See chap. xviii.) But this was not now His way. 2. *He has also places of refuge for His servants.* (1) If there be a valley secluded from human intrusion God knows it. In the courses traversed by the brook Cherith Elijah may safely hide. These recesses lay "eastward" from Samaria, where probably the prophet had encountered the king; and eastward from the Jordan, for this is the import of the phrase "before Jordan." Probably this seclusion was in his own wild district of Gilead. (2) Ahab will not suspect that Elijah is here; for how could he possibly subsist in such a desolate region. Water he might find in the streams of the mountains; but where can he get bread from bald rocks in time of drought? (Matt. xiii. 5, 6.) 3. *Into such asylums He can guide His saints.* (1) "The word of the Lord" came to Elijah. Christ is that Word (John i. 1—14). He was the MEMRA of the Targums—that personal Word, who "appeared" to patriarchs and prophets. See Gen. xv. 1.; xxviii. 20.) He will be ever with his people guiding them into safety. (2) "The word of the Lord came unto him *saying*," or expressing His wisdom in human vocables. To Elijah the direction was, "Get thee hence," &c. To all He comes in the promises and precepts of holy Scripture. (3) Those who believe and obey God's Word, as Elijah did, are in safe keeping. They need never fear the combinations of wickedness against them.

II. HE HAS RESOURCES ALSO FOR THEIR SUPPORT. 1. *Their water is sure.* "Thou shalt drink of the brook." (1) There was refreshment for the body. The stream of that brook continued to flow for a whole year. Such is supposed to be the import of (ימים) *days*, when there is nothing to limit it (as in ver. 7, marg.; see also ver. 15, marg.; Gen. iv. 3). (2) His soul meanwhile was refreshed, as, by faith, he realized the wells of salvation which flow from the Word of the Lord.

(See Psa. xlvi. 4; John iv. 14; vii. 37—39; Rev. xxii. 17.) 2. *Their bread shall be given.* "I have commanded ravens to feed thee there. (1) What an unlikely thing! Ravens were unclean creatures (Levit. xi. 15). They are insect-feeding, carrion-eating birds, themselves fed by special providence of God. (See Job xxxviii. 41; Psa. cxlvii. 9.) (2) Yet God *could* do it; for the instincts of all creatures are in His hands. He restrained hungry lions from harming Daniel; instructed a fish how to behave to Jonah; and another to lift a piece of silver from the bottom of a lake and then fasten upon a hook. "Is anything too hard for the Lord?" (3) But *would* He do it? Would He employ an unclean creature to feed His servant? He might have His own reasons even for this. Elijah sustained for three years and a half in the wilderness was a type of the Christian Church nourished by the word of God for three and a half prophetic years (Rev. xii. 6, 14). Babylon the great, from whose face the Church had to fly, was the mystical Jezebel, as the true Church was the mystical Elijah. But in this Church the destruction of clean and unclean creatures had no place. (See Acts x. 15, 28; xv. 7—11.) Might not this gospel have been foreshadowed in the manner in which Elijah was fed? 3. *But is it certain that ravens were employed?* (1) He might have been fed by *Arabians?* For the word (ערבים) translated "ravens" also denotes *Arabians.* (See it so used in the singular, Isa. xiii. 30; Jer. iii. 2; Neh. ii. 19; and in the plural as here, 2 Chron. xxi. 16: xxii. 1.) And Gilead bordered upon that tract of country more especially described in Scripture as Arabia. (2) Or he might have been fed by *merchants.* For this word also designates merchants. (See Ezek. xxvii. 9, 27.) If Israelitish merchants supplied the prophet's needs, then probably would they be of the seven thousand who scorned to bow the knee to Baal (ch. xix. 18), and so would not discover his hiding place to Ahab. (3) Or he might have been sustained by certain inhabitants of Oreb, a rocky place beyond Jordan. (See Judg. vii. 22; Isa. x. 26.) This opinion is favoured by Jerome, who says, "The Orbim, inhabitants of a town on the confines of the Arabs, gave nourishment to Elijah." (See more in A. Clarke.) (4) Whether by ravens, Arabians, merchants, or people of Oreb or Orbo, matters little; God can spread a table in the wilderness. He can give us the bread of the day in the day —"bread and flesh in the morning, and bread and flesh in the evening." Necessary things are sure; luxuries we may dispense with. The greatest luxury to the wise and good is the feast upon the spiritual food which accompanies faithful obedience to God (John iv. 32—34).—J. A. M.

Vers. 7—9.—*The Widow of Zidon.* Towards the close of Elijah's year of seclusion, to use the words of Dr. Macduff, "the brook began to sing less cheerily; once a full rill or cascade, which, night by night, was wont to lull the prophet of Israel to sleep, it becomes gradually attenuated into a silver thread. In a few days it seems to trickle drop by drop from the barren rock, until, where pools of refreshing water were before, there is nothing now left but sand and stones." It is time for the prophet to look to God for further direction; and in response to his prayer, "the word of the Lord came unto him, saying, Arise," &c. How different are the resources of the believer from those of the worldling! When the Cherith of the worlding fails he has nothing further to look to, but when from the believer one comfort is withdrawn another is at hand (Psa. xxxvii. 19). Let us meditate upon—

I. THE COMMAND OF GOD TO THE WIDOW. 1. *She is to sustain the prophet of the Lord.* (1) What an honour is this! For two years and a half to entertain the man that "stands before Jehovah," at whose word the clouds are sealed or the windows of heaven opened! (See ver. 1 and xviii. 41.) The man whose prayer was to bring fire down upon the sacrifice on Carmel to the confusion of idolatry! (ch. xviii. 38.) Who was to bring the same element down upon the soldiers of Ahaziah! (2 Kings i. 10—12). Who was destined to ride alive into the heavens in a chariot of fire! (2 Kings ii. 11). Who was destined, many centuries later, to appear in glory with Messiah on the mount of transfiguration! (Matt. xvii. 3). And who is yet to come before the great day of judgment to gather back the children of Israel from their dispersion! (Mal. iv. 5, 6). (2) How could she hope for such distinc-

tion? A poor widow, so poor that she has no servant and no fuel in her house!
A widow with her son, both at the point of death! A stranger, and a stranger of
Zidon too—the land of Baal—and the land of the wicked Jezebel! Note: God's
ways are not as our ways. He brings unlikely things to pass. How little do we
know what may be the thoughts of His heart concerning us! 2. *But how is she to
accomplish this?* (1) Unbelief might murmur at such a requisition. It might
charge God foolishly as a tyrant requiring brick where he had not supplied straw.
Those who shrink from Church work because of fancied incompetence fall into this
error, neglecting to trust God.   (2) It is enough that God has commanded.
His commands are promises. (See Exod. iii. 10—12; Judg. vi. 14.) See how the
meal and oil are multiplied in the hands of the widow. The more difficult
(humanly considered) the undertaking, the more gloriously will the excellency
of the power of God appear. (See 2 Cor. xii. 9.) Attempt great things for God.
Expect great things from God.
    II. The reasons of the command. 1. *Elijah needed succour.* (1) The brook
is dried up. Now is the time to test the prophet's faith. But he is a man of
prayer, so is familiar with God. Those who best know God have most confidence
in Him. Let us be much in prayer. (2) Then " the word of the Lord came."
Man's extremity is God's opportunity. In no strait let us despair of help while we
keep a single heart. God knows all things. He can do whatever He will.
2. *The woman needed succour.* (1) She too had come to extremity—to the last
handful of meal. What a touching spectacle is that widow at the gate of Zarephath
gathering a few sticks to prepare the last meal for herself and her son! (2) Had
she not prayed? No doubt; and most sincerely. She was evidently a believer in
the God of Israel. Jehovah was not unknown in the land of that Hiram who
" was ever a lover of David," and so materially aided Solomon in building the
temple (1 Kings v.)   (3) But then she was not an Israelite to whom " were the
promises." So in addressing Elijah her words are, " As the Lord *thy* God liveth."
She believes in the " living God," but cannot presume to call Him *her* God. (See
Rom. ix. 4.) What right had a poor stranger of Zidon to look for any special
consideration from the Lord? (4) " He giveth grace unto the humble." He that
reads the heart saw that she would believe if only she had a promise to authorize
her faith. He accordingly gave her the opportunity which she seized and improved. (See Acts x. 1—6.) Let us act up to our light, and God will guide us into
all the truth. 3. *But were there no widows in Israel?* (1) Upon the best
authority we know that there were " many," and as needy as this Zidonian. In
the severity of such a famine deaths from starvation were no rare occurrence.
(2) But the same authority informs us that there were none so worthy as this
widow of Sarepta (Levit. iv. 24—26). No widow in Israel would have received the
prophet as this widow received him. The moral is that if we would have special
favour of God we must have special faith to receive it. Let us ever be in that
attitude of whole-hearted consecration to God which will make us eligible for any
service he may be pleased to promote us to. To be permitted to do anything for
God is an unspeakable honour.—J. A. M.

Vers. 10—16.—*The Barrel of Meal.* In the East the people kept their corn in
earthen jars to protect it from insects which swarm in the heat of the sun. What
in our translation is called a " barrel " (כד) was one of these vessels. The store in
this case was run low; there was but a " handful " left; yet this was so multiplied
by the power of God that three persons found at least in it sufficient provision for
two and a half years. Let us inquire—
    I. How its condition became known. 1. *Elijah came to Zarephath in quest
of the widow.* (1) Such were his instructions (vers. 8, 9). But was there only one
widow in this city of " smelting furnaces " (comp. ch. vii. 14), this hive of industry,
this centre of population? How, then, is he to discover the right one? (2) God
knows her, and that is enough for the prophet. The Word of the Lord who came
to him at Samaria and at Cherith will now guide him. (See Isa. xlii. 16.)
(3) Let us follow the light we have and God will give us more. So was Abraham's

faithful servant guided to Rebecca (Gen. xxiv.) 2. *He found her at the gate of the city.* (1) She was there on an errand of her own, viz., to gather a few dry sticks to kindle a fire to cook her last meal in this world. (2) She was there also, though unknown to herself, on an errand from God. She was commanded to sustain the prophet of Israel. (3) Yet these two errands harmonize. God uses man's purposes to work out His own. Man proposeth; God disposeth. 3. *He readily identified her.* (1) He asked her for water, which, with admirable promptitude, she went to fetch. This was the sign by which Abraham's servant identified Rebecca (Gen xxiv. 14). The cup of cold water has its promise of reward (Matt. x. 42). (1) Then he asked for bread, which further request opened the way for the whole truth, " As the Lord thy God liveth, I have not a cake, but," &c. (ver. 12). From these words it is evident that she recognized Elijah, at least as an Israelite, and probably as the prophet of Israel; for he was a person of pronounced individuality. His profusion of hair, probably, placed Elisha in such contrast to him that Elisha was mocked as a " bald head." (Comp. 2 Kings i. 8, and ii. 23.)

II. How ITS RESOURCES WERE MAINTAINED. 1. *By the miracle-working power of God.* (1) " The barrel of meal wasted not, neither did the cruse of oil fail, according to the word of the Lord which he spake by Elijah." This supplied not only the guest but the widow and her son for two years and a half. As Bp. Hall remarks, " Never did corn or olive so increase in the growing as these did in the using." (2) This miracle was similar to that of the manna. The oil was used as butter for the meal, and the taste of the manna was like fresh oil (Num. xi. 8). Also to Christ's miracles of the loaves. (3) The lessons are the same. The miracles all teach that "man lives not by bread alone, but by the word of God." That this spiritual food is the gift of God. That it differs essentially from the bread that perishes. Not only is it imperishable, but it multiplies in the using, grows as it is dispensed. How delightful were the spiritual feasts of that two years and a half in the widow's dwelling! (See Rev. iii. 20.) 2. *Through the faith of the widow.* (1) She was predisposed to believe. God saw this, else He had not honoured her with His command to sustain his prophet. (See Luke iv. 24—26.) Let us ever live in that moral fitness to be employed by God. (2) This disposition was encouraged. She waited for something to justify her faith in God, and she got it: " And Elijah said unto her, Fear not; go and do as thou hast said," &c. (vers. 13, 14). She knew that the word of the Lord was with Elijah And this instruction to make first a little cake for the prophet was according to God's order. (See Num. xv. 20, 21.) (3) She proved the genuineness of her faith by her works. " She did according to the saying of Elijah." By works faith is perfected. And God justified the faith that justified him.—J. A. M.

Vers. 17, 18.—*The Reproaches of Death.* In verse 15 we read that the widow and her household did eat of the multiplied meal " *days* " (מִים), a term which is by some Hebraists understood, when used without qualification, to denote a *year*. So the phrase with which the text opens, " And it came to pass *after* these things," imports that the miracle of raising the widow's son occurred " after " Elijah had been one year in her house. The " things " to which this miracle succeeded were the earlier signs of the presence of God with the prophet, meanwhile the widow read the bereavement her own way.

I. SHE SAW THE HAND OF GOD IN IT. 1. *She attributed it to Elijah.* " Art thou come unto me, to slay my son." (1) Not, however, under any notion of unkindness to her in the heart of the prophet. For (*a*) had she not, and her son with her, been saved from death by famine in connexion with his sojourn in her house? (*b*) The heavenly conversation they must have had during the year would preclude such an idea. (2) Yet here is the fact; and it is written for our learning. The incidents in Scripture, given under Divine inspiration, are therefore to be very particularly noted. They cannot be too carefully or too prayerfully studied. 2. *She attributed it to him as a " man of God."* (1) This was not, in her estimation, an ordinary case of death. The circumstances surrounding it were all extraordinary.

(2) At least she saw that it was intended by God for some high purpose. She was right. We should not be wrong so to regard ordinary providences. All God's purposes are high. All His providences are important. His providence is in everything. Life therefore is no stale thing.

II. SHE READ HIS REPROACHES IN IT. "Art thou come to call my sin to my remembrance?" 1. *We should never forget that we are sinners.* (1) Whatever reminds us of God should remind us of sin. For all sin is, directly or indirectly, against Him; and this is the gravest side of the offence (Psa. li. 4; Luke xv. 21). (2) Death especially should remind us of God, before whose tribunal it conducts us. So it should especially remind us of sin, for it is its wages appointed by God. 2. *The remembrance, however, will affect us variously according to our moral state.* (1) Sin, in the first instance, is called to the remembrance of all that they may hate it and forsake it. (2) To those who have endeavoured to do this, it is still called to remembrance, that they may trust in Christ for forgiveness and salvation. (3) To the justified it is called to remembrance that they may praise God for His mercy. In this sense sin will be remembered even in heaven. (See Rev. v. 9; vii. 9, 17.)

III. SHE CONNECTED THESE REPROACHES WITH THE PRESENCE OF ELIJAH. "What have I to do with thee, O thou man of God?" &c. 1. *Why did she do this?* (1) Prophets were sent usually to reprove, and denounce judgments. Hence the coming of Samuel to Bethlehem inspired the magistrates and people with alarm. (See 1 Sam. xvi. 4.) This bereavement, therefore, might suggest to the widow her sin in general, or some particular sin, though not clearly defined to her as yet. (2) Or it might have brought home to her some imperfection in the service of God which she had not previously sufficiently considered. Had she adequately appreciated the great privilege of having such a guest? (3) Was there not in this a confession that she was unworthy of such an honour, and a desire implied that she should be made worthy, lest otherwise his continued presence must become an occasion of judgments? Was not the expression of Peter, with whom Jesus lodged, of similar import when the divinity of the Master was brought vividly before him by the miraculous draught of fishes, and he exclaimed, "Depart from me, for I am a sinful man, O Lord?" (Luke v. 8). 2. *Did she not here recognize a great truth?* (1) What sanctifications and consecrations Levites, and more especially sons of Aaron, needed, who had to draw near to God; and how perilous to them, even then, were their approaches to that sacred presence! (Exod. xxviii. 43; Levit. viii. 35; xv. 31; xvi. 2, 13; xxii. 9; Num. iv. 15; xvii. 13). (2) How clean should they be who bear now the vessels of the Lord! How careful unsanctified persons should be not to tamper with holy things! Witness the judgments upon Uzzah and Uzziah. (See 1 Sam. vi. 19; 2 Sam. vi. 7; 2 Chron. xxvi. 19, 20.) The sanctification now required is moral, of which the ceremonial was the type. (3) All shall have to appear in the very presence of the Judge. How shall we stand then? Let us now prepare for that solemnity.—J. A. M.

Vers. 19—24.—*The Sign of the Widow's Son.* Here is a touching scene—a poor widow pressing to her bosom the corpse of her only child, while in the agony of her bereaved soul, addressing Elijah, she says, "What have I to do with thee, O thou man of God? art thou come to call my sin to my remembrance, and to slay my son?" Now note the words of the text: "And he said unto her, Give me thy son," &c. In this history we have—

I. AN EXAMPLE OF THE POWER OF FAITH. Behold here—1. *The spirit of faith.* (1) He had confidence in God before he prayed. This is evident from the manner in which he asked the widow for the corpse. He did not tell her what he intended; but, on the other hand, neither did he express any hesitation as to the comfort she might expect. (2) This confidence must have been divinely authorized, else it would have been presumption which, instead of conciliating the favour, would have awakened the displeasure of God. (3) This was what Elisha and the sons of the prophets called "the Spirit of Elijah," *i.e.*, the Spirit of God abiding with him. (See 2 Kings ii. 9, 15.) 2. *The prayer of faith.* (1) He recognized the hand of God in the bereavement: "Hast thou also brought evil upon the widow with whom I sojourn by slaying her son?" He calls it "evil," yet attributes it to God. Moral evil God cannot perpetrate, but evil which comes in the form of affliction or punishment is a very different thing. (See Job ii. 10; Isa. xlv. 7; Amos iii. 6; John ix. 1—3.) (2) He entreated God to restore the child's life. "He cried unto the Lord." Here is the "fervency" which characterizes "effectual" prayer. (3) He entreated Him confidingly: "O Lord *my* God." This appealing to God in the *possessive* expresses a loving trust in a Covenant-Friend. (See Levit. xxvi. 12; Jer. xxxi. 33; 2 Cor. vi. 16; Heb. xi. 16; Rev. xxi. 3.) (4) Hence his success. "The Lord heard the voice of Elijah." He saw in Elijah those moral qualifications which make it fitting that He should answer prayer. So the prophet was able to restore the child alive to his mother. 3. *But what example is this for us?* (1) Elijah's success in prayer was not because he was a prophet. James replies to this objection when he assures us that "Elias was a man subject to like passions as we are." For this is the ground on which he proceeds to lay down the broad principle, viz., that "the effectual fervent prayer of a righteous man availeth much" (James v. 16; see also Acts xi. 24). (2) Therefore *we* also *may* be moved by the Holy Ghost; and we *must* be so moved if we would pray effectually. True faith is "of the operation of God" (Luther's prayer for the recovery of Myconius instanced in Krummacher). (3) But how may we know that we are so influenced? God will make it plain as one of the secrets of holy communion with Him (Psa. xxv. 14; John vii. 17; xv. 15). When we are free from selfish desire, and above all things seek God's glory, there is little danger of being led astray. (4) The widow was no prophetess, but she also was an example of faith. (See Heb. xi. 35.) Witness her recognition of God, and the readiness with which she gave her son from her bosom at the prophet's request. Her faith was honoured as well as his.

II. A PROPHETIC SIGN. 1. *So the widow interpreted it* (ver. 24). (1) It authenticated Elijah as a "man of God." Not only that he was a good man, but that he was a prophet of the Lord. (2) Consequently "that the word of the Lord in his mouth" was no sham. (Comp. ch. xxii.) Spurious prophets could not give miraculous signs. 2. *Such signs were parables.* The question, then, is, what did this parable teach? (1) Could it be a sign that the drought would be removed which had now lasted two years, working fearful ravages, and must, if continued long, destroy the nations visited? For the "word of the Lord in the mouth of Elijah" did encourage the hope that rain should come upon the earth (ver. 14). The coming of rain would be a national resurrection. (2) Could it be a pledge of the resurrection of the dead at the last day? The gospel has thrown floods of illustration upon this subject, but in old times it was obscure. This miracle taught the separate existence of the soul. Also that the disembodied spirit may and shall be reunited to its organic companion. (3) Why did Elijah stretch himself upon the child? He was a type of Christ. So he made himself like the dead to foreshow that Christ by dying in our room should give us life. This He does morally. Also physically, viz., in the resurrection of the body. (Comp. 2 Kings iv. 34; John xi. 43—45; Acts xx. 10.) Is there any correspondence between the "three times" mentioned in the text and the "three times" in which our Lord prayed for the removal of the cup of His suffering? (Matt. xxvi. 44).—J. A. M.

Ver. 1.—*The Messenger of Jehovah.* Stanley is justified in describing Elijah as "the grandest and most romantic character that Israel ever produced" (S. &. P., p. 328). He appears suddenly, and disappears miraculously. Hence imagination has had scope. Some Rabbins believed that he was Phineas, the grandson of Aaron, and others that he was an angel from heaven. The impression his ministry made upon the mind of the people re-appeared again and again after the lapse of centuries. When, for example, the miracles of our Lord aroused the wonder of the people, many said, "It is Elias." Such a character and work as were his deserve careful study. Describe the social and religious condition of the kingdom of Israel after Ahab's accession and marriage with the dauntless, fanatical, idolatrous Jezebel. Never was reformation more called for, and never were supernatural works more necessary as the credentials of a Heaven-sent ambassador. Our text presents for our consideration—I. *A messenger from a forsaken God*, and II., *A message for an apostate people*.

I. A MESSENGER FROM A FORSAKEN GOD. Ahab was congratulating himself on the success of his policy. It had been greater than he could have expected. The old faith and fervour of the people had died out so completely that they were quiet under the bold introduction of Baal and Ashtoreth. The Sidonians were linked with the kingdom of Israel against Syria. Scarcely a protest had been heard against these political and religious movements. Suddenly there appeared before the king and queen, perhaps as they were enthroned in their ivory palace, Elijah the Tishbite; rough in appearance, as he was bold in utterance. Above the ordinary height, of great physical strength, a girdle round his loins, and a sheepskin cloak over his brawny shoulders, his long thick hair streaming down his back, he was even in appearance a memorable man; and there was something very startling in this his sudden dash into the royal presence, to thunder out his curse, and the rebuke which no doubt preceded it. His appearance may be compared to the flash of lightning that for a moment makes everything which was before in darkness vividly distinct. Some points are worthy of note. 1. *The obscurity of his origin.* The Tishbite means the "converter," and would fitly describe his work. The endeavour to discover a town of such name in Palestine appears to have failed. The phrase, "from the residents of Gilead," does not necessarily imply that he was an Israelite. He may have been an Ishmaelite or a heathen by birth. It was designed that obscurity should thus hang over his origin. To the people he would seem to come all the more directly from God. The human element was overshadowed by the Divine. Show the mightiness of secret forces in nature, in thought, and in the kingdom of God. 2. *The signs of his fitness.* A rough man was needed to do rough work. The settler in the backwoods wants the strong sharp axe to effect a clearing, before more delicate implements are required. Elijah had his constitutional strength and courage fostered by his surroundings. Gilead was a wild, unsettled country compared with Ephraim and Judah. Instead of stately palaces and flourishing towns, it boasted tent villages and mountain castles; and desperate and frequent were the fights with surrounding freebooters. (See 1 Chron. v. 10, 19—22. Compare with it "Rob Roy," chap. xix.) The Gileadites were to Israel what the Highlanders, a century back, were to the Lowlands. Amid scenes of conflict, of loneliness, probably of poverty, this strong character was moulded. Compare with Moses in Midian, with John the Baptist in the wilderness. God gives each servant the right training for the service appointed for him both on earth and in heaven. 3. *The secret of his strength.* His name, Elijah, and his formula, "as the Lord God of Israel liveth," indicate it. An overpowering conviction that Jehovah lived, that He was near, that He was the God of this people, and that He would assert His supremacy over all false gods is implied in the verse. This is the secret of spiritual strength in all ages. The disciples were weak when Jesus was on the mount of transfiguration, strong when He returned; they were despondent after the crucifixion, exultant at Pentecost. The revelation of God's presence and power is what all Churches now need. 4. *The completeness of his consecration.* "Before whom I stand." This he said, not with a sense of God's nearness only, nor of His favour, but to express that he was the Lord's consecrated servant, through whom and by whom he might do what He willed. *Standing* is an attitude of attention, expectancy, readiness. So in ancient Scripture servants are represented as all standing looking towards the king, with loins girded, eyes intent, ready to do his will. Note: We cannot stand before the Lord until we have knelt before Him in penitence and humility and prayer. This Elijah had done in Gilead.

II. A MESSAGE FOR AN APOSTATE PEOPLE. "There shall not be rain nor dew these years, but according to my word." We assume here the credibility of miracles and content ourselves with indicating the suitability of this to its purpose. 1. *This was revealed in prayer.* Elijah had "prayed earnestly that it might not rain" (James v.) He felt that such a chastisement would move the hearts of the people, and turn their thoughts towards God, as it ultimately did. The prayer was the offspring of God's Spirit. The human utterance was the echo of the Divine will. The mystery of prayer is revealed (1 John v. 14, 16). 2. *This was a response to the challenge of Baal-worship.* The productive powers of nature were adored under the idolatrous symbol. Here they were shown to be dependent on the unseen God. All natural laws are. They are the expressions of the Divine will. It was in vain to cry, "O Baal, hear us!" 3. *This man would affect all classes of the people.* They had shared the sin, and therefore must share the penalty. The loftiest are not beyond God's reach, the lowliest are not hidden from God's notice. The tiny garden of the peasant was cursed, as well as the splendid park of the king. National sin brings national calamities. The message, not to some, but to all, is, "Repent, and be converted." 4. *This was associated with estrangement from God.* It was to be "according to the word" of His servant. The change would be foreseen and foretold, not by the false priests, but by the praying prophet. The curse came because of sin, as had been proclaimed by the law. (See Levit. xxvi. 19; Deut. xi. 16; xxviii. 23.) It was removed on repentance (1 Kings xviii.) *Listen to the message God still sends to men, bidding them root out idolatry from every nation and from every heart.* May the God of Israel, before whom they stand, prosper all His messengers!—A. R.

Vers. 2—4.—*Strange Provision in a Sad Necessity.* The miracles associated with the ministry of Elijah and Elisha have led some to deny the historical credibility of the Books of Kings. It should be remembered that great miracles were rendered necessary by a great and general apostasy. It was essential to the survival of true faith that Jehovah should indicate His unseen sovereignty. In Israel such attestation was more required than in Judah, where the sanctuary and the priesthood, in the worst times, testified for God. This passage sets before us I. *Silent suffering.* II. *Divine deliverance.* III. *Restful retreat.* Each of which points we will consider.

I. SILENT SUFFERING is implied by all that we know of the prophet's circumstances. The famine he had foretold had come; and he shared the privations of the people. Others might have kindness shown them, but there was none for this man. Regarded as the cause of the calamity, he was an accursed outcast. Upon such a temperament the steady persistent pressure of hunger and hatred would tell severely. He would feel pity for others—for the poor dumb beasts, for the innocent children—and would be tempted to ask, "Was I right in praying for this, and bringing this woe on the people?" Meantime he was himself suffering the rigours of famine, and no chariot of fire came to bear him away from the desolated land. Like Samson, it seemed as if he had shaken the house, and was bringing destruction on himself as well as on the idolators. Yet not a word of complaint. He was sustained by the conviction that he had done right, and that God would see to the issues. Apply the teaching from this to occasions on which men are still called upon to do God's will, to utter God's truth, regardless of consequences. Sometimes we are able to "count the cost," and then we should do so. But often this is impossible. The love of Christ may constrain us to do, or to say, something which will place us in unexpected difficulties. Illustrate by Peter's zeal, which prompted him to step out of the boat upon the sea. He was terrified at a result he had not taken into calculation; but he was perfectly safe, for he was going towards Christ. Exemplify by instances from ordinary life—*e.g.*, an assistant in business refuses to tell a lie, or to act one, and loses his situation. A daughter confesses her love to Christ, and finds her home a place of torment, &c. The one thing that can support us in such circumstances is the humble, yet confident, conviction that we have done what God willed. And often from those straits He delivers us in the most unexpected way, before we ask Him, as He delivered Elijah.

II. DIVINE DELIVERANCE. 1. *It was unexpected.* No one would have imagined, and some cannot now credit the means adopted. The ravens have been a sore offence to critics. Discuss some of their theories—that they were merchants, Arabians, &c. The difficulties are not removed by the interpretations suggested, nor do they seem warranted by the text. Had men brought food to the hidden prophet, Ahab would soon have discovered his whereabouts; nor would they be likely to bring food twice daily, when a store might have been conveyed with only one risk. The supernatural is always startling, but to those who reject materialism it is not incredible. If God notices a sparrow fall, and if diseases obey Him, as soldiers obey their general (Matt. viii. 8—10), this feeding by the ravens might well be. God often uses strange instruments to effect His purposes. Give examples from Scripture and history. Even the plans and the deeds of the wicked are under His control. All things work His will. 2. *It was revealed.* " The word of the Lord came to him." It comes to us. Sometimes the inward impulse after prayer impels us to take God's way ; and sometimes all other paths are closed, and of the one left open Providence says, "This is the way, walk in it." Are we seeking to know *God's* will about ourselves ? Are we concerned that our way should be His choice, and not our own ? " In all thy ways acknowledge him, and he shall direct thy paths."

III. Restful retreat. Describe the wild ravine of the Kelt, which Robinson and Stanley identify, with some probability, as the Cherith. The precipitous rocks, in places 500 feet high, the caverns in the limestone, in one of which the prophet hid, &c. Such a man needed quiet. He had it afforded to him again in Horeb. No great activity for God can be worthily sustained without much waiting on Him. In this retreat Elijah had two sorts of provision. 1. *Daily bread.* It is only that which we are taught to expect, and pray for. The daily reception of blessing teaches us our constant dependence. The manna fell every morning, and could not be hoarded for the future. Daily strength, too, is given for daily duties. 2. *Quiet communion.* All nature would speak to Elijah of his God. The brook would whisper of the water of life; the birds would celebrate the care of God, &c. In the world around him, in secret converse with his own heart, and in earnest prayer to the God of Israel, before whom he stood, Elijah would get refreshment and strength for coming conflict and conquest. Refer to the invalid, to the aged, to the little children, as those to whom God gives a time of quiet, to prepare them for the future service.

1. *Expect God's deliverance whenever you are in the path of duty.* 2. *Be content that God should work in His own way.* 3. *Seek to have a spirit of contentment, and a heart that is* " *quiet from the fear of evil.*"—A. R.

Ver. 16.—*The Widow's Cruse.* Describe this incident in the life of Elijah. Show some of the ADVANTAGES which arose from his visit to Zarephath ; *e.g.,* 1. *It was a means of blessing to himself.* He found a true worshipper of Jehovah even in the coasts of Tyre, where, under the rule of Jezebel's father, one was least to be expected. This would strengthen his faith, and it would keep alive his hope that his work in Israel would "not be in vain in the Lord." We may sometimes assure ourselves of the vitality of Christianity by witnessing its effects among the heathen. A visit to the South Sea islands would prove a tonic to debilitated faith. 2. *It was a means of blessing to the widow.* Not only was she kept alive in famine for the prophet's sake, but she received spiritual blessing. Christ refers to Elijah's visit as a sign of the care God had, even under the old dispensation, for the heathen peoples, where He left not Himself without witness. (Compare Luke iv. 25.) Show that as Elijah turned from Israel to Zidon, so the apostles turned to the Gentiles (Acts xviii. 6). Learn from the story the following general lessons :—

I. That God provides for the necessities of His servants. In the famine He had already made provision for Elijah at Cherith, and now that the supply there had failed, other resources were opened. Not always in our way, but in some way, He answers the prayer, " Give us this day our daily bread." He does not promise luxuries or wealth, but our "bread shall be given to us, and our water shall be sure." We are not to be anxious about our future, but are to remember that it is in the hands of God. It is said of our food and raiment, that our "heavenly father knoweth that we have need of these things." When a child is at home he learns his lessons, obeys the rules of his parents, &c., but he has no care about the food he will want on the morrow. He never dreams but that it will be provided. Such should be our spirit, whatever may be our powers of productive work. We are diligently and earnestly to do whatsoever our hands find to do, feeling certain that "they who seek the Lord shall not want any good thing." The Israelites followed the cloud, though it led them into the wilderness, with the conviction that God was leading them; and when it was necessary He provided manna in proportion to their wants. If God does not ignore our temporal necessities, He will certainly not fail to supply our spiritual wants. In the Father's house there is bread enough and to spare. This we may prove on earth, but its highest fulfilment will be seen in heaven, where the Lamb, who is in the midst of the throne, shall feed us.

II. That God uses what men would despise. With limitless resources, we should have imagined that God would miraculously create what was required, disregarding "the handful of meal" and the little oil left in a cruse. Not so, however. There is no waste in the Divine economy. The breath of men, the exhalations of plants, the refuse cast into the field, or into the sea, the rising mist, the falling shower, are all accounted for, and have a purpose to fulfil, a work to do. There is no physical force which becomes utterly extinct, though it passes from one form of manifestation to another. Motion passes into heat, heat into electricity, &c., in an endless cycle. The economy of force asserts itself everywhere under the rule of God. This, which is proclaimed by science, is constantly illustrated in Scripture. It is the same God who worketh all in all. If manna is given to the Israelites, it ceases directly the people can eat of the corn of the country. The supernatural rises out of the natural. The miraculous provision for Elijah was not a new creation, but an increase of what already existed; and in the use of this there was no prodigality or waste. Compare with Christ's miracle of the feeding of the five thousand. After showing that He had infinite resources, He said to His disciples, "Gather up the fragments that remain, that nothing be lost."

III. That God reveals our way step by step. Picture Elijah sitting by the brook Cherith, watching its waters becoming shallower day by day under the drought. He knew not what he should do next, but he waited, and trusted, and prayed; and when the brook was dried up, "the word of the Lord came unto him, saying, Arise, get thee to Zarephath," &c. God does not reveal the future to us, but draws across it an impenetrable, or at most a semi-transparent veil. We know not with absolute certainty what a day may bring forth. The advantages of this are evident—1. *It saves us from sorrow and from sin.* (1) *From sorrow*, because if we foresaw all that we should have to endure, if we knew the day of our death, the extent of our losses, &c., our burden would be greater than we could bear. "Sufficient unto the day is the evil thereof." (2) *From sin*, because we should grow absorbed in worldly occupations if we were certain life would be long; or become despondent and spiritless in work if we knew it would be short. 2. *It fosters in us the graces of trust and prayer.* If we know nothing of the future ourselves, and cannot feel confident about our own plans, we are led to confide in Him who foresees what is before us, and to ask Him in prayer for daily guidance and support.

IV. That God rewards our consecration of what we have to Him. It was a *generous* act towards a stranger, a *pious* act towards a servant of Jehovah, to fetch for Elijah the water which was now so costly, and to be willing to share with him what appeared to be her last meal. "There is that scattereth, and yet increaseth." Even in temporal affairs this is true. Hoard seed in the springtime, and you cannot be enriched; scatter it, and the harvest will come. Give to the poor in the name of their Lord, and you will not fail of reward—either here or hereafter. We are to give, however, not for the sake of applause or recompense, but "as unto the Lord," to whom we owe all that we have. This woman not only gave to the prophet, but gave to him *in the name of a prophet*, and therefore "received a prophet's reward" (Matt. x. 40—42). May He who commended the widow when she gave her two mites so accept our gifts and services, and so approve our motives, as at last to say, "Inasmuch as ye have done it unto one of the least of these, my brethren, ye have done it unto me!" (Matt. xxv. 40.)—A. R.

Ver. 21.—*Prayer for the Dead.* The portrait of the widow of Zarephath is remarkably natural. Her calmness in speaking of the trouble that was only threatened (ver. 12), is contrasted with her agony when trouble actually comes (ver. 18). She believed in Jehovah though in a heathen kingdom ; yet there was a blending of superstition with her faith. She supposed that God might have overlooked her sin, had it not been that He was present with His prophet in her home ; and she confounded discipline with retribution. The latter was the mistake of the barbarians at Melita. (Compare Acts xxviii. 4.) See also our Lord's teaching, Luke xiii. 4. The death of this child is to be explained on the principle which asserted itself in the blindness of the man whom Jesus cured (John ix. 3), or in the illness of Lazarus, concerning which our Lord said, "This sickness is not unto death, but for glory of God" (John xi. 4). Rembrandt has depicted the scene brought before us in this chapter. In a roughly built upper room the dead child lies upon the bed ; one hand rests upon his breast, while the other has fallen heavily at his side, giving a wonderful idea of the weight of death. Elijah stands on the further side of the bed with his rugged, earnest face upturned towards heaven and his hands clasped in an agony of supplication as he says, "O Lord my God, I pray thee let this child's soul come into him again !" This event was not intended to be wondered at as a prodigy, nor was it merely to benefit the widow, but for all time has spiritual significance. With this belief we see in it—

I. AN EMBLEM OF SPIRITUAL DEATH. The child had died suddenly, or Elijah would have been told of his illness. His death was real, and was more than the insensibility of Eutychus (Acts xx. 10). We say that a thing, susceptible of life, is *dead* when it cannot receive what is essential to its growth and well-being ; *e.g.*, a tree is dead when it is no longer able to absorb the nutriment without which it must fade, and ultimately fall. An animal is dead which can no longer breath air or assimilate food. The mind is dead—as is that of an idiot—when it receives no true mental impressions. The soul is dead which is insensible to spiritual influence. As it is possible to have physical without mental life, so it is possible to have mental without spiritual life. "Spiritual death" is not a mere figure of speech. It may be illustrated by the condition of this child. The food provided for him was useless now, the tenderest words of his mother were unheeded, and the voice that so lately was musical with laughter was silent. Similarly the spiritually dead are indifferent to God's provision, unconscious of their own possibilities, irresponsive to the Father's voice. "Except a man be born again he cannot enter the kingdom of God." "He that hath not the Son hath not life." "Dead in trespasses and sins." "Come from the four winds, O breath, and breathe upon these slain that they may live."

II. AN EXAMPLE OF INTERCESSORY PRAYER. A man of Elijah's strong nature would have strong affections, and we can imagine how intensely he had come to love this child. On hearing of his death he could only say to the distracted mother, "Give me thy son," and then carried him up to his own room, and cried to God in an agony of prayer. 1. *It was offered in solitude.* Not even the mother was there. Such intense crises in life must be met alone. Jesus Christ was wont to "depart into a solitary place" to pray. Understanding our needs He said, "When thou prayest, enter into thy closet, and shut to the door, and pray to thy Father which seeth in secret." "Jacob was left alone" when he wrestled with the angel. Compare Elijah's miracle with that of the Lord, who, when He went into the room where Jairus' daughter lay dead, "suffered no man to go in," beyond those who were one with Him in sympathy and prayer. 2. *It was peculiarly definite.* There was one want in his heart, one cry on his lips. Our prayers too often are meditations on the Divine attributes, or general confessions, and thanksgivings. If our King asked "What is thy petition ?" we should sometimes be at a loss for an answer. Pray for one grace, for one unbelieving friend, &c. 3. *It was intensely earnest.* Elijah could not be denied. His was not a speech, but a cry. He looked for the awakening, and flung himself on the dead in an agony of earnestness as if he would infuse his own warmth and life. The touch was similar to that of Peter, when he took the cripple by the hand (Acts iii. 7)—not the *cause* of blessing, but the medium of blessing. The Divine power works through the human agency.

III. AN EARNEST OF TRUE RESURRECTION. Elijah could not give life, but he could

ask God for it. Nor can we arouse to new life by preaching, though God can do so
through preaching. Our words are only the media through which the Holy Spirit
works. The Atlantic cable is useless except as the message is flashed forth by mysterious unseen power. This distinguishes the miracles of our Lord Jesus from
those of His servants. (Compare Luke vii. 14 with Acts iii. 12—16.) There is a
resurrection wherein saints shall be raised by the power of God to a life of immortality, the promise and pledge of which we have in the resurrection of Christ, who
is the "firstfruits of them that sleep." There is also a spiritual resurrection, to
which Paul refers when he appeals to Christians as those "risen with Christ; and
of this, as well as of that, is there an illustration in our text. Raised to newness of
life we, like the child Elijah prayed for, have to live for awhile in the old sphere.
The prophet gave the child to his mother. Jesus restored Lazarus to his sisters,
the young man at Nain to his mother, and the ruler's daughter to her parents; and
so to us, who have "passed from death unto life," He says, "Return to thine own
house, and show how great things God hath done for thee." This miracle constrained the widow to accept as God's truth the declaration of His servant (ver. 24).
How much more reason have we, who believe in the supernatural works of His
Son, to say, "We know that thou art a teacher come from God; for no man can do
these miracles that thou doest, except God be with him!"—A. R.

Vers. 1—6.—*Elijah the Tishbite.* One of the noblest of the noble figures that
cross the stage of Old Testament history appears before us here. Few names have
such a halo of glorious associations surrounding them as that of Elijah. The
mystery of his origin, the grandeur of his mission, his physical and moral
characteristics, the peculiar nature of his miracles, his wonderful translation and
reappearance with Moses at the time of our Lord's transfiguration, together with
the place that he occupies in the last utterances of inspired prophecy, and in the
anticipations of the Jewish people—all combine to invest the person of this great
prophet with a peculiar and romantic interest. This opening chapter in the story
of his prophetic ministry is full of instruction. Note—

I. HIS ABRUPT APPEARANCE. There is nothing actually unique in this. Other
prophets of the age are introduced thus suddenly (Ahijah, Jehu, Shemaiah, &c.)
But considering the circumstances of the time it is remarkable. 1. *It proclaims
God's continued interest in, and sovereignty over, Israel as well as Judah.* The
revolt of the ten tribes had not broken the bond between Him and them, or
altered the fact of His supremacy. Nor had their religious defection nullified His
purpose of mercy. 2. *It is called forth by a dread moral crisis.* The seed sown
by Jeroboam was fast developing its most deadly fruits. The Baal worship brought
in by Ahab and Jezebel was a far worse "abomination" than the worship of the
calves. A cruel persecution was raging, the prophets of the Lord were being slain,
and it seemed as if the true religion would perish out of the land. 3. *It was a revelation of irresistible power.* The worship of Baal was essentially the worship of
power; probably the productive power of nature. Here is the messenger of Him
"to whom all power belongeth," that great unseen Power that can arrest the order
of nature, seal up the fountains of heaven, wither those resources of earth on which
the life alike of man and beast depends. We are reminded of the various ways in
which God may see fit to fulfil His sovereign purposes. All powers, human and
material, are at His command. "All things serve his might." In the darkest
hour in the history of church or nation, let us believe that still "the Lord
reigneth." Let us trust Him to "plead his own cause," and vindicate the claims
of truth and righteousness.

II. HIS PERSONAL DIGNITY. It is the dignity of one who sustains a special
relation towards "the living God." His name implies this: "Jehovah is my
God." And this solemn asseveration, "As the Lord God of Israel liveth, *before
whom I stand,*" is suggestive of the dignity (1) of personal fellowship; (2) face to
face vision; and (3) Divine proprietorship; (4) consecrated servitude. One would
think the old Jewish tradition were true. It sounds like the voice of an angel.
But lofty as this utterance is. majestic as is the relation towards the Divine Being

which it indicates, it has its Christian counterpart. Think of St. Paul's words : "There stood by me this night the angel of God, *whose 1 am and whom I serve*" (Acts xxvii. 23). This is not an exclusive, exceptional dignity. We may all in our measure share it. And as no earthly position sheds any real glory upon a man except so far as he recognizes a Divine element in it, fills it as before God with holy fear ; so there is no work or office of common life which may not be ennobled by this feeling. We stand there before God as His servants to do that very thing. "Such honour have all his saints."

III. His COURAGE. It is the courage of one who knows that God is with him, that he is the messenger of the Divine will, the instrument of a Divine purpose, the channel of Divine strength. He boldly confronts Ahab, "not fearing the wrath of the king," bearding the lion in his den. Does not mingle with the people, antedating their sufferings by spreading among them the evil tidings, but goes straight to him who is the fountain-head of the mischief and can avert the calamity by his repentance. Such is the brave spirit with which God fills his heroes. Whether in the defiance of danger, or the endurance of suffering, it is the sense of God—a Divine inspiration, Divine support—that has ever been the spring of the noblest form of courage. "Greater is he that is in you," &c. "If God be for us," &c. "Be not afraid of their terror, but sanctify the Lord God in your heart," &c. This is the principle—the solemn fear of God taking possession of a man casts out all other fear ; in the sense of the sovereignty of a Divine claim, he fears nothing but the dread of being unfaithful to it. Now this brave spirit was not kindled in the breast of Elijah all at once. Such a moral phenomenon is not the birth of an hour or a day. We may believe that it was developed in him gradually among the mountains of Gilead—a fitting scene for the nurture of such a moral constitution as his. The fire burned within him as he mused on the degradation of his country. St. James speaks of the fervency of Elijah's prayer: "He prayed earnestly that it might not rain," &c. (James v. 17). No doubt the withholding of the rain was given as a "sign" in answer to his prayer; but after all, may we not regard his prayer most as the means of preparing him to be the prophet and minister of this great "sign"? Not that the order of nature was placed at the caprice of a poor, frail mortal; but that he, "a man of like passions with us," was able in the fervour of his faith and prayer to rise up and lay hold on the strength of God, to read the purpose of God, reckoned worthy to become the agent in the execution of that purpose. The historic incident is not so far removed as it may seem to be from the range and level of our common life. Heaven gives back its answer to suppliant faith. As regards the fellowship of the human soul with the mind and with the power of God, it must ever be true that "the effectual fervent prayer of the righteous man availeth much."

IV. His EXTRAORDINARY PRESERVATION. A type of the providential care that God will ever exercise over those who are faithful to Him in the path of duty and of trial. Whether "ravens" or "wandering Arabians" were the instruments in his preservation, it little signifies, so that we recognize the positive Divine interposition. And what is the supply of our daily wants but the fruit of a perpetual Divine interposition? "Give us this day our daily bread." Walk uprightly before God, be true to Him in all the sacred responsibilities of life, and trust in Him to provide (Matt. vi. 33).—W.

Ver. 16.—*Entertaining a Stranger.* We naturally ask why Elijah should have been sent at this crisis to Zarephath. The fact that it lay so near to the birthplace of Jezebel, and in the very home of the Baal worship, may have had something to do with this. It might be a safer place of retreat for the prophet than it seemed to be, for Ahab would scarcely dream of following him there. But other reasons are suggested by the use our Lord makes of this incident (Luke iv. 25, 26). The prophet was not "accepted in his own country," but found a confiding welcome and generous hospitality at the hands of an alien. God rebuked the proud unbelief of His own people by making this poor lone widow, in the midst of her idolatrous associations, the instrument of His purposes. And thus that early age had its foreshadowings of the grace that should hereafter be bestowed on the Gentiles. The lessons of the narrative lie upon the surface.

I. GOD'S SURE GUARDIANSHIP OVER HIS SERVANTS. Elijah is perfectly safe under the shield of Divine protection, as safe in the region of Sidon as he was by the brook Cherith. He who commanded the ravens to feed him can put it into the heart and into the power of the Phoenician woman to do the same. When one resort fails He can provide another. He causes one and another to fail that He may show how boundless His resources are. There is absolutely no limit to the possibilities of God's sustaining and protective power. "He shall give his angels charge concerning thee." The angels of God are many and various. There is nothing which He cannot make to be the instrument of His purpose, the vehicle of His power. And He causes them to wait in duteous ministry on those whom He has called to high and holy service in His kingdom. God has a grand mission for Elijah to accomplish in Israel and will take care that he shall be able to fulfil it. "Man is immortal till his work be done."

II. THE HONOUR GOD PUTS ON THE LOWLY. We see here not only the Divine preservation of Elijah, but a special act of grace towards the woman of Zarephath. It was a signal honour to have been thus singled out from the crowd for such a Divine visitation, to be used as an important link in the chain of great public events, to have her name handed down to future ages as the "woman of Sarepta," whose glory it was to "entertain a prophet in the name of a prophet and receive a prophet's reward." And in this there was not merely a providential arrangement of outward circumstances, but a gracious influence exerted on her own soul; for God lays His sovereign hand not only on the course of external events, but on the secret springs of moral life. Her readiness to respond to the prophet's appeal was from Him. Poor and humble as she was His eye was upon her for good. "He regarded the low estate of his handmaiden." Thus has God often put distinction upon those who might least have expected it. Let none think themselves beneath His notice, or too insignificant to be made by Him the instrument of some high and holy purpose. "Though the Lord be high, yet hath he respect unto the lowly" (Psa. cxxxviii. 6).

> " He hears the uncomplaining moan
> Of those who sit and weep alone."

The forlorn and desolate, if only they walk humbly and reverently before Him, are the objects of His tenderest regard. He is nearer to them than He seems to be, and often has surprising grace in store for them. The poor widow casts her two mites unnoticed into the treasury, but He to whom the secrets of all hearts are open clothes her with honour above all the rich pretentious people who only gave what they so well could spare. The sinful woman, in self-forgetting devotion, pours her rich ointment on the head of the incarnate Love ; captious onlookers see no glory in her deed, but a word from Him crowns it with an everlasting halo of world-wide fame (Matt. xxvi. 13; Mark xii. 43, 44).

III. THE REWARD OF TRUSTFUL AND OBEDIENT FAITH. The poor widow " showed her faith by her works, and by works was her faith made perfect." At the prophet's word she drew freely from her scanty store, and " the barrel of meal wasted not, neither did the cruse of oil fail." The reward of her faith came in the form of a miracle similar to that of Christ's multiplication of the loaves and fishes to feed the hungry multitude. It surpasses our comprehension, but is not more wonderful than the mysterious process that is ever going on in the building up of the tissue of plants and of the animal frame. Shall not the Power that is perpetually chang- ing the elements of earth and air and water into nourishing food for man and beast be able to increase " the meal and the oil" as it pleases? The true life of faith is one of " patient continuance in well-doing," coupled with calm dependence on that ever-active power. Of the righteous God says, " Bread shall be given him," &c. (Isa. xxxiii. 16). " In the day of famine they shall be satisfied " (Psa. xxxvii. 19). Christ did not mock us when He taught us to pray to our Father in heaven,

"Give us this day our daily bread." Tread faithfully the path of duty, and "He that ministereth seed to the sower will both minister bread for your food, and multiply your seed sown, and increase the fruits of your righteousness" (2 Cor. ix. 10).—W.

Vers. 17—24.—*Life from the Dead.* The miracles wrought by Elijah or associated with his name were for the most part of the nature of severe judgments, and present the person of the lowly prophet in a stern and terrible light before us. But the two miracles that mark the opening of his career were miracles of mercy, and show that there was another side to his character, one that was tenderly sympathetic and humane. Having at first brought hope and a new lease of life to the starving mother and her child, he now lifts the dark shadow of death from off the desolated home and turns its sorrow into joy. This narrative has a peculiarly pathetic interest, and is suggestive of lessons that touch the deepest realities of human life. It naturally divides itself into two parts, in which we see (1) the sadness of death and (2) the joy of restoration.

I. THE SADNESS OF DEATH. That the child was really dead we cannot doubt. "There was no breath left in him." The gleam of hope in the poor widow's condition was suddenly beclouded, and a strange, yet not altogether unnatural, revulsion of feeling took possession of her breast. Thus does an unexpected calamity, especially perhaps when it takes the form of personal bereavement, often work for a while a sad change in the attitude of the soul. 1. *It darkens the whole horizon of life*—quenches the light of other joys. The abundance of meal and oil, and the honour of the prophet's presence are as nothing while the child lies dead in the house. There are sorrows which seem utterly to blot out the sunshine of one's existence, and to be aggravated rather than relieved by the joys that accompany them. 2. *It creates resentment against the supposed, or perhaps the real, author of it.* "What have I to do with thee, O thou man of God?" The prophet, who had proved himself so beneficent a friend, is regarded as an enemy. 3. *It is a severe test of one's faith in God.* This woman, it may be, was in an intermediate state of mind between blind devotion to the old idolatries and the full acceptance of the faith of Israel. How rude a check did this event seem to give to her progress into clearer light! Thus is the faith of men often sorely tried by the adversities of life. This is part of their Divine purpose. The "fiery trial" seems "strange at first, but the meaning and reason of it are revealed afterwards." Happy they whose faith, in spite of the severe strain put upon it, holds fast to the living God—too deeply rooted in the soul to be torn up by any sudden sweeping blast. 4. *It awakens the sense of sin.* "Art thou come to me to bring my sin to remembrance?" It is significant that the thought of her own sin should be her first thought. The calamity brought this to her remembrance because it seemed to her a sign of God's remembrance of it. Learn that though particular afflictions are not always to be connected with any particular transgression as their cause (John ix. 2, 3), yet all sorrow must be traced ultimately to its source in moral evil. It is a true instinct that leads us to think of our sins in times of adversity. Whenever affliction comes to us it should produce tenderness of conscience and call forth the prayer, "Show me wherefore thou contendest with me," in order that if there be any secret wrong in ourselves that demands this severe discipline we may have grace to fight against it and cast it out.

II. THE JOY OF RESTORATION. The behaviour of Elijah is beautifully expressive of his deep human sympathy, and also of the intimacy of the relation between himself and God as a man of prayer and the instrument of the Divine energy. Having special regard to the nature and effect of this miracle of restoration, observe that—1. *It is typical of the beneficent ministry of Christ.* In Him the power of God came, as it never had before, into healing contact with the frame of our diseased and dying humanity. He took our nature upon Him that He might effectually cure its infirmities and sicknesses. "Virtue" continually went forth from Him. He was the great health-restorer and life-giver; and as all the healing ministries of former ages had anticipated His coming, so all true philanthropy since has caught its highest inspiration from the constraint of His love and the force of His example. 2. *It is prophetic of the future glorious resurrection.* We see here one of the many witnesses that gleam out amid the obscurity of the olden times to the truth that God would surely one day " bring life and immortality to light," while it points us on to the time when, " at the voice of the son of God, all that are in their graves shall come forth." " Then shall be brought to pass the saying that is written, Death is swallowed up in victory " (Isa. xxv. 8; 1 Cor. xv. 54). 3. *It illustrates the joy of a soul that for the first time is made fully conscious of the gracious presence and power of God.* " Now by this I know that thou art a man of God," &c. There is a tone of deep satisfaction in these words. It is the satisfaction that springs from the discovery of Divine truth and the vivid sense of God. There is no satisfaction of which the soul of man is capable that can be compared with this. The end of all forms of Divine manifestation— prophetic visitations, miracles, providences, &c.—is this. We reach the highest joy possible to us upon earth when we can say with St. John, " We know that the Son of God is come, and hath given us an understanding, that we may know him that is true, and we are in him that is true, even in his son Jesus Christ. This is the true God and eternal life " (1 John iv. 20).—W.

Vers. 1—6.—*Elijah's Advent and Service.* I. THE GREAT PROPHET. 1. *His name:* Elijah, my God (is) Jehovah. It was a symbol of his spirit. It expressed his judgment of Israel's idolatry and the choice which with his soul's whole strength he had made of God. Light and fidelity are the only foundations of any true work for God or man. 2. *His origin.* The words (" of the inhabitants," &c.) seemed to indicate that he belonged to none of the tribes of Israel. (1) His mission was prophetic of that of the Gentiles. Israel, forsaking God, were to feel that God was also forsaking them (Rom. x. 19). The very meanness of the origin of God's faithful ones lends power to their testimony. (2) It proved the infinitude of God's resources. Ahab and Jezebel might slay His prophets; they could not arrest the progress of His work. From the most unthought-of quarter there arises a mightier than all whose lives had been taken. The power of a devoted life to make the world feel the impossibility of its prevailing in its contest with God. 3. *His attitude toward God.* " Before whom I stand." He was the Lord's servant. He lived for Him. His eye rested on Him. The whole man stood girded for prompt, unquestioning obedience. This is the spirit of all true service. Is God as real to us ? Do we thus stand before Him?

II. HIS MESSAGE. 1. *The judgment.* It was that predicted from of old as the chastisement of Israel's idolatry (Deut. xi. 17). The land was to be consumed by drought. The blessings which God withholds from the soul that forsakes Him are imaged in those withheld from the land. There is " neither dew nor rain." The refreshment, the rich consolation, once imparted by the word or found in prayer, are no longer known. The stimulating of loving zeal after what is nobler and purer has ceased. 2. *Through whom it fell :* " According to my word." Those who reject God will be judged by man. God will still confront them in their fellows. God is magnified in His servants. The kingly power and priesthood of believers in their relation to the world.

III. HIS RETIREMENT. 1. *It served God.* Ahab and Israel were left face to face with Him. Man disappeared that the eye might rest on God alone. There are times when He is best served by silence. Many words often undo the effect of the homethrust dealt by a few. 2. *It was his safety.* He was shielded from Ahab's anger. We may be hid by affliction from the power of our great foe. Temptation and danger may have been darkening the path that lay before us when God led us aside and made us rest awhile with Him. 3. *It prepared him for after service.* He was taught God's unfailing power and care. His wants were provided for though no man knew of his dwelling place; and that by the most unlikely instruments. He learned how fully he might trust God. He to whom God is thus revealed will not fear the face of man.—U.

Vers. 7—16.—*Divine Care.* I. THE ENDLESSNESS OF GOD'S RESOURCES. 1. *The brook failed;* and one essential of life could no more be had there. But it was only that this wondrous provision might give place to greater marvels. When means are threatened, the heart sinks; but He who has provided these for a season knows of the failure; and He who sent to Cherith can send elsewhere. One channel of help fails only that the soul may be quickened by a fresh revelation of God's kindness. 2. *He was sent to what seemed to be the most dangerous of all places*—to the territory of Jezebel's father. And yet the very unlikelihood of his seeking shelter there increased his safety. God's path can only be trod by faith, but that faith is soon changed to praise. 3. *He was sent to a most unlikely quarter.* The hostess whom the Lord had chosen was a widow and one who possessed sufficient to furnish only one more meal for herself and her child. But here again faith was to break forth into praise. God's power is infinite, and the meanest as well as the mightiest may be used to glorify Him. II. THE REWARD OF OBEDIENT FAITH. 1. *For Elijah.* He went undoubting; he sought the city, and lo, *at the gate* (ver. 10) he met his hostess. Those who act on God's promises will meet with the revelation of His truth and graciousness. 2. *For the woman* (vers. 11—16). It was her last meal. Love of her child and her own hunger must have made it hard to obey, but the seed she sowed in faith yielded a thousandfold. God's call to sacrifice for His service, for honesty and truth, is the path to plenty not to loss. 3. *For both.* The woman entered a new world. The unseen was unveiled; she knew God. Elijah found in a heathen land a home which God had sanctified. The communion of faith glorifies all human relationship.—U.

Vers. 17—24.—*Affliction and its Fruits.* I. THE DISCIPLINE OF TRIAL. 1. *It is no proof of God's anger.* Sorrow darkens the homes of God's beloved. This was a home of faith and ministering love. Affliction is no more proof of wrath than is the farmer's ploughing of his field. To him, with his eye upon the future harvest, it is only the needful preparation of the soil. And the great Husbandman, with His eye upon the eternal glory, must open up a bed within the soul's depths for the seed of life. 2. *God's blow may be very heavy.* Her son, her only child, is taken. God's plough sinks deep that His work may be rightly done. The very greatness of our anguish is a measure by which we may gauge the greatness of the Lord's purpose and of the love which will not suffer us to miss the blessing. II. THE FRUITS IT YIELDS. 1. *It reveals our need.* She may have been conscious daily of the goodness of God and yet been blind to the fact that she needed more than she had yet received. God now awakens her (1) to the sense of her unworthiness: "What have I to do with thee?" (2) to the remembrance of her transgressions: "Art thou come to call my sins to remembrance?" The darkness of trouble is the shadow of guilt. There is discipline because there is need of salvation. Sins may be pardoned, but God must open up a gulf between the soul and them. The time of trouble is meant to be a time of heart-searching and of confession. 2. *It stirs up to prayer.* Elijah's heart was poured out in bold expostulation and earnest entreaty (vers. 20, 21). In the sharpness of our need our cry gains strength; we press, in our urgency, into the Divine presence. These times open up a way to God by which we find ready access ever after. 3. *It leads to the vision of God's glory.* "And the Lord heard," &c. (ver. 22). The prayer was followed by a revelation of God's power such as till then man had never seen: the dead was raised. "Ask and ye shall receive." The soul that *asks* will see God's salvation and be filled with the light of the Divine glory. 4. *It deepens trust.* "Now by this I know," &c. (ver. 24). When man's need meets God's help, the soul is bound to Him by the strongest ties.—U.

Vers. 1.—7.—*First Preparation of Elijah for his great Mission.* After Elijah's first appearance before Ahab to announce to him the Divine visitation of sterility and dearth which was to come upon the land as the chastisement of his sin, the prophet was sent away into a solitary place to prepare himself for his great and solemn

mission, which was to overthrow idolatry and vindicate the worship of the true
God. This work of preparation was divided into two great periods. 1. The
preparation of the desert. 2. The lonely life of the prophet in the house of the
widow of Sarepta.

The Desert was, from the time of Moses to the days of John the Baptist, the
great school of the prophets. These men of God were trained for their work: 1.
By being brought face to face with their sacred mission in all its greatness, and
free from the prejudices and petty influences of human society. There they could
steadfastly contemplate the Divine ideal, undistracted by the rude realities of man's
fallen condition. 2. There they were also cut off from all human aid, left to test
their own strength, or rather to prove their own utter weakness, and, overwhelmed
with the sense of it, to cast themselves wholly on Divine strength. Thus they
received directly from God, as did Elijah, the supplies by which they lived, and
realized the conditions of absolute and immediate trust in Him. Coming forth from
this discipline of the desert, they were enabled to say with Paul, " When I am
weak, then am I strong " (2 Cor. xii. 10). 3. This loving converse of the prophets
with their God brought them into closer fellowship, more intimate union, with Him.
Thus they came forth from the desert, like Moses from the Mount of Sinai, bearing
unconsciously upon them the reflection of His glory. As St. Paul says, " We,
beholding as with open face the glory of the Lord as in a mirror, are changed into
the same image from glory to glory, even as by the Spirit of the Lord " (2 Cor.
iii. 18). Considerations like these have a fit application to the pastor, who ought
to be much in solitary communion with God, in order to be raised above the compromises of principle so common in society, and to get his whole nature permeated
with Divine strength. Every Christian soul has in like manner a prophet's mission,
and ought therefore often to seek the desert solitude, in which the Invisible is
brought near, and to frequent those sacred mountain tops of prayer, where the
disciple, like the Master, renews his strength (Luke v. 16).—E. de P.

Vers. 7—24.—*Second Preparation of Elijah.* Elijah passed through his second
phase of preparation under the humble roof of the widow of Sarepta. He is in the
right attitude for gaining a holy preparedness for his work, for he has placed
himself absolutely and directly under the guidance of God. When the word of God
comes to him, he is ready to arise and go whithersoever it bids. Thus was Christ
" led of the Spirit " to commence His public ministry (Matt. iv. 1); and throughout
His whole course He recognized the same unfailing guidance. The purpose of
God in sending Elijah to the poor widow was to show him, before he entered on
the great conflict with idolatry, that he had at his disposal a Divine power which
nothing would be able to resist. Elijah was, so to speak, to prove his arms, far
from human observation, BY A PASSAGE OF DEEP PERSONAL EXPERIENCE. Hence
the double miracle of the barrel of meal and the cruse of oil always full. Hence,
yet more distinctly, that glorious miracle of the raising of the widow's son by the
prophet. This miracle had no witnesses ; nor must we marvel at this. God does
not perform miracles to fascinate onlookers ; He does not make a spectacle of His
marvellous working. His glory is sufficiently magnified in the deliverance of a
humble believer, like the widow of Sarepta, and in the qualification of the prophet
for his mission. Jesus Christ refused to work any miracles for show, and the
sublimest manifestations of His power were reserved for humble hearts and lowly
dwellings. Elijah has learnt to know the strength of God which is in him; he has
proved it in the secresy of his soul. He has a full assurance that it will be manifested in him when he stands before Ahab, no less mightily than in the obscurity
of the widow's house. This intimate personal experience of the grace of God is of
incomparable value to His servants. If we would have Divine strength to use in
the great conflict with sin around us, we must prove its miraculous energy in our
private life. And let us remember also that our homes may be the scene of the
mightiest manifestations of the grace of God, and of the most signal providential
deliverances, if only our hearts be open to Him in humility and love, like the heart
of the widow of Sarepta.—E. de P.

EXPOSITION.

CHAPTER XVIII. 1—46.

ELIJAH'S RETURN AND THE ORDEAL OF MOUNT CARMEL.—The preceding chapter having been exclusively occupied with the fortunes of Elijah during his enforced absence of three and a half years from the land of Israel, we are left to conjecture what the course of events in the northern kingdom during this period of drought and suffering must have been. But it is not difficult to picture in our minds the steadily increasing alarm and distress which the solemn ban he had pronounced must have occasioned. At one time, it may be, especially if the prophet up to that period had been unknown, both king and people, under the malign influence of Jezebel, professed to regard his threatening with contempt, the more so as the priests of Baal would not fail to assure them of the protection and blessing of "the Lord" of nature. But as the months and years passed by, and neither dew nor rain fell—as the heavens were brass and the earth iron—and the pastures languished, and the fruits of the earth failed, and the cisterns became dry, and man and child and beast began to suffer the extremities of thirst, we cannot doubt that the tone and temper of the country underwent a great change. At first, threats had been freely uttered against Elijah, who was perversely regarded as the author of all this misery, and that and the neighbouring countries were scoured to find him. Moreover, reprisals were made on the system which he represented, by a fierce persecution of the prophetic order, of which he was recognized as the head. But it is probable that when the drought lasted into the third and fourth year, and when absolute ruin and death stared the country in the face, that then defiance had given place to dread and regret in every bosom, save, perhaps, that of the queen and the sycophants who ate of her table. The conviction was steadily gaining possession of the minds of all Israel that Baal and Ashtoreth were vanities, and that the Lord alone made the heavens and covered them with clouds. The great drought, and the manifold sufferings which it entailed—suffer-

ings which the animated description of the prophet Joel (ch. i.) enables us to realize—were doing their work. The heart of the people was being slowly turned backward, and in the third year of his sojourn at Zarephath the time was ripe for Elijah's return, which our author now describes, together with the striking results which followed it. In the first fifteen verses, we have the meeting of Elijah and Obadiah ; in vers. 16—20, the meeting of Elijah and Ahab ; vers. 21—38 describe the ordeal of Mount Carmel ; vers. 39, 40, its immediate results; while the remainder of the chapter depicts Elijah's prayer for rain, the bursting of the storm, and the return to Jezreel.

Ver. 1.—**And it came to pass after** [This word is wanting in the Heb. except in a few MSS.] **many days that the word of the Lord came to Elijah in the third year** [From what date is this "third year" to be counted ? The *prima facie* view is that the words refer to "these years" mentioned in ch. xvii. 1, *i.e.*, to the date of the announcement of the drought, and this is the interpretation of the Rabbins and some of the moderns. But it is almost fatal to this view that the duration of the drought is distinctly stated in the New Testament to have been "three years and six months" (Luke iv. 25 ; James v. 17). It is every way better, therefore, to connect the words with ch. xvii. 7, *i.e.*, with the date of the sojourn at Zarephath. It follows hence that the prophet spent about one year in the Wâdy Cherith, and two and a half in the house of the widow], **saying, Go, show thyself** [Heb. *be seen*] **unto Ahab; and I will send** [Heb. *give*] **rain upon the earth.** [Heb. *on the face of the ground.* Cf. xvii. 14.]

Ver. 2.—**And Elijah went to show himself unto Ahab. And** [or *Now*. It would, perhaps, have been better to begin a new verse here, as this is the beginning of a parenthesis, explanatory of the circumstances under which king and prophet met. It was this famine led to Obadiah's encountering Elijah on the road] **there was a sore famine in Samaria.** [The effect of a three years' drought would be to reduce the entire people to the verge of starvation. The severity of the famine was no doubt mitigated, as on a former occasion (Gen. xli. 57), by the importation of corn from Egypt.]

Ver. 3.—**And Ahab called** [Rather, *had called.* "The verbs וַיִּקְרָא, וַיְהִי, &c. (vers. 3, 4, 5, 6), carry on the circumstantial clauses" (Keil).] **Obadiah** [This name is almost as remarkable as Elijah's, or would be, if it were not more common. It means "servant of Jehovah." Compare the modern Arabic *Abdallah.* Although borne by one who " feared the Lord greatly " (ver. 3), and " from his youth " (ver. 12), it occurs too frequently (1 Chron. iii. 21 ; vii. 3 ; viii. 38 ; ix. 16 ; 2 Chron. xvii. 7 ; xxxiv. 12 ; Ezra viii. 9 ; Obad. i., &c.) to justify the belief that it was assumed or bestowed as an indication of his character (Rawlinson)], **which was the governor of his** [Heb. *over the*] **house.** [See note on ch. iv. 6, and cf. ch. xvi. 9. Rawlinson says it " tells in favour of the monarch's tolerance that he should have maintained an adherent of the old religion in so important an office." But it is just as probable that it was *because* of his religion that he occupied this post of trust. Ahab could depend on his fidelity and conscientiousness]. (**Now Obadiah** [here begins a second parenthesis within the first] **feared** [Heb. *was fearing*] **the Lord greatly.**

Ver. 4.—**For it was so, when Jezebel cut off the prophets of the Lord** [Our author now instances a proof of Obadiah's devotion. The incident to which he refers is otherwise unknown to us, nor can we refer it with certainty to its proper place in the history. But it is extremely probable that this work of extermination was begun as an act of reprisals for the drought denounced by Elijah. Ver. 13 almost implies that it had taken place during his absence. We see here, consequently, an additional reason for his flight (cf. ch. xix. 2). These " prophets " are the same as those elsewhere called the " sons of the prophets, *i.e.,* members of the prophetic schools ; cf. 2 Kings ii. 3, 5, 7, &c.] **that Obadiah took an hundred prophets** [This would lead us to suppose that the great majority escaped. But see ver. 19 and ch. xxii. 6. That we find so large a number still in the land, notwithstanding the exodus (2 Chron. xi. 16), and the steady growth of impiety, shows that God had not left Himself without witnesses], **and hid them by fifty** [Keil would insert a second חֲמִשִּׁים as do some MSS. (Gardiner), and as in ver. 13. Such a word might easily be omitted in transcription, it is true. But " *proclivi lectioni,*" &c.] **in a cave** [Heb. *the* cave ; but LXX. ἐν σπηλαίῳ. Similarly in ver. 13. What is the force of the article here it is somewhat difficult to say. It has been suggested that these caves were in the sides of Mount Carmel ; there are large caves under the western cliffs (Stanley) ; more than two thousand, according to others ; " often of great length and extremely tortuous " (Dic. Bib. i. p. 278) ; but this is mere guesswork, as Palestine, being

of limestone formation, abounds in caverns. See Stanley, S. and P. pp. 151, 52. From the earliest times we find men—outlaws and the like—taking up their abode therein. Cf. Josh. x. 17 ; Judg. vi. 2 ; 1 Sam. xxii. 1 ; Ezek. xxxiii. 27 ; Heb. xi. 38. Probably the division into two companies was partly for the sake of security (see Gen. xxii. 8), and partly for the sake of convenience. The greater the number to be fed, the greater the chance of detection. Compare also Jacob's precautions Gen. xxxii. 8], **and fed them with bread** [or, *food*] **and water.**) [It is to be observed, as bearing on ch. xvii. 4—6, that these hundred prophets, though preserved by the special providence of God, were nevertheless maintained through human agency and by natural means.

Ver. 5.—**And Ahab said** [*had said*] **unto Obadiah, Go into** [Heb. *in*] **the land, unto all fountains** [Heb. *places of fountains.* Cf. with מַעְיָן from עַיִן, מָאוֹר from אוֹר &c.] **of water, and unto all brooks** [*wâdies* ; see on ch. xvii. 3]: **peradventure we may find grass to save the horses and mules alive** [It has been inferred from Ahab's concern for his stud that he viewed the sufferings of his subjects with comparative indifference, or at least regarded them as of altogether secondary importance. But this is a too hasty conclusion. His subjects were, for the most part, as well able to find water for themselves as he was for them, and he might safely trust to their instinct of self-preservation to do their best to meet the emergency. But the dumb cattle, confined to the stall, could not act for themselves. Hence this expedition in search of fodder], **that we lose not all the beasts.** [Marg. *that we cut not ourselves off from,* &c. But this rendering, and still more that of the text, misinterprets the force of the Hiphil נַכְרִית. The literal translation is, " *That we may not have to cut off from (i.e.,* a portion of, מִן partitive, as in ver. 13 below, מִנְּבִיאֵי).* What Ahab means is that, unless they soon find fodder, they will have to slaughter a portion of their animals. So Bähr, *Und nicht von dem Vieh (einen Theil) umbringen müssen.* Similarly Keil.]

Ver. 6.—**So they divided the land between them to pass throughout it** [" This personal inspection by the king and one of his chief officers marks the extreme straits to which the Israelites were now reduced " (Rawlinson). The difference, however, between an Eastern and an European monarch must not be overlooked. " None (of the emirs of Arabia or the chiefs of central Asia) think it beneath them to lead an expedition in search of grass or water " (Kitto)]: **Ahab** went one way by himself [Heb. *alone*. Rawlinson says, "This does not mean that either Ahab or Obadiah was unaccompanied by a retinue," but it *may* very well mean that (לְבַד, *solus*; LXX. μόνος; Bähr *allein*. Cf. ver. 22), if, indeed, it must not necessarily mean it; and ver. 14 certainly implies that Obadiah at least was unattended], and Obadiah went another way by himself.

Ver. 7.—And as Obadiah was in the way, behold, Elijah met him [Heb. *to meet him*]: and he knew [*i.e.*, recognized. Same word, Gen. xxvii. 23; xlii. 7, &c.] him, and fell on his face, and said, Art thou that [Heb. *this*, probably used adverbially (like *hic*) for *here* =בָּזֶה] my lord Elijah? [The humble obeisance and the terms in which he addresses him alike show the profound reverence with which Obadiah regarded him, as well he might do, considering the terrible power he wielded. The whole land was, so to speak, at his mercy.]

Ver. 8.—And he answered him, I am [Heb. *I*]: go, tell thy lord, Behold, Elijah is here. [The last two words are not in the Hebrew, and the sentence is much more graphic without them.]

Ver. 9. And he said, What have I sinned, that thou wouldst deliver [Heb. *that thou art giving*] thy servant into the hand of Ahab, to slay me?

Ver. 10.—As the Lord thy God liveth [Obadiah uses precisely the same adjuration as the widow of Zarephath, ch. xvii. 12. But then, though Jehovah was undoubtedly his God, He was in a more special and intimate manner Elijah's God. The oath corresponds well with the prophet's name], there is no nation or kingdom, whither my lord hath not sent to seek thee [Keil says the hyperbole is to be explained by the "inward excitement and fear" of the speaker. But the Orientals use similar exaggerations in their calmest moments. All that is meant is that all neighbouring and accessible courts had been communicated with. This search for Elijah shows that Ahab regarded *him* as the author of the drought, and did not recognize it as sent by God. The belief in occult and magical powers has always held possession of the Eastern mind]: and when they said, He is not there [Heb. *Not, and he*, &c.]; he took an oath [LXX. ἐνέπρησε, which has been thought by some to point to acts of vengeance. But more probably it is a clerical error, perhaps for ὥρκισε, or ἐνώρκισε. On the frequency of oaths in that age see on ch. i. 51] of the kingdom and nation, that they found thee not.

Ver. 11.—And now thou sayest, Go, tell thy

lord, Behold, Elijah is here. [Heb. *Behold, Elijah*. Obadiah echoes the words of ver. 8.]

Ver. 12.—And it shall come to pass, as soon as I am gone from thee, that [Heb. *I shall go from thee, and*] the Spirit of the Lord shall carry thee whither I know not [These words, which literally translated are "*shall lift thee up upon where*," &c., are to be explained by 2 Kings ii. 16, "lest the Spirit of the Lord hath taken him up" (same word) "and *cast him upon some mountain*," &c. Seb. Schmidt, Wordsworth, *al.* think that such a transportation must have already occurred in the history of Elijah, but the sudden, mysterious disappearance and the long concealment of the prophet is quite sufficient to account for Obadiah's fear. Compare Acts viii. 39. The words do suggest, however, that it had been believed by some that the Lord had hid Elijah, and it is not improbable that during his long absence rumours had often gained credence that he had been seen and had suddenly disappeared, just as later Jews have held that he "has appeared again and again as an Arabian merchant to wise and good Rabbis at their prayers or in their journeys" (Stanley)]; and so when I come and tell [Heb. *and I come to tell*] Ahab, and he cannot find thee, he shall slay me [This is just what a prince like Ahab, or any prince who was under the guidance of a Jezebel, would do, out of sheer vexation at losing his prey when so nearly in his grasp]: but [Heb. *and*] I thy servant fear the Lord from my youth. [Obadiah's meaning clearly is not that he, "as a God-fearing man and a protector of the prophets, cannot have any special favour to expect from Ahab" (Keil; similarly Ewald),but that it was hard that one who was a steadfast worshipper of Elijah's God should be slain for his sake. It is extremely unlikely that Ahab knew of Obadiah's having protected the prophets. He could hardly have maintained him in his post had he known that the steward of the palace had thwarted the designs of his queen.]

Ver. 13.—Was it not told my lord what I did when Jezebel slew the prophets of the Lord, how I hid an hundred men of [Heb. *from*] the Lord's prophets by fifty in a cave, and fed them with bread and water? [Stanley happily calls Obadiah "the Sebastian of this Jewish Diocletian."]

Ver. 14.—And now thou sayest [="This is to be the reward of my devotion, is it?"]. Go, tell thy lord, Behold, Elijah is here: and he shall slay me.

Ver. 15.—And Elijah said, As the Lord of hosts liveth, before whom I stand [This formula should be compared with that of ch. xvii. 1. The repetition is suggestive as exhibiting the *habit* of the man. He was the ready and patient slave of Jehovah. The צְבָאוֹת is apparently introduced not so much to "elevate the solemnity of the oath" (Keil, Bähr)—for surely Elijah would wish to make the affirmation of ch. xvii. 1 as strong and solemn as possible—nor yet to convey the meaning that "it is not Baal or Ashtaroth who are the rulers of the heavenly bodies" (Wordsworth), for Obadiah knew that perfectly well, but because it was thus better adapted for a believer. In addressing Ahab it suited Elijah's purpose better to give prominence to the idea that Jehovah was "the God of *Israel*"], **I will surely show myself unto him to-day.**

Ver. 16.—**So Obadiah went to meet Ahab, and told him: and Ahab went** [Very readily, it would seem. Anything was better than suspense and famine. And Elijah's very return contained in it a promise of rain] **to meet Elijah.**

Ver. 17.—**And it came to pass, when Ahab saw Elijah, that Ahab said unto him, Art thou he** [Rather, *here:* same words as in ver. 7. "Do I at last see thee again? Hast thou ventured into my presence?"] **that troubleth Israel?** [Heb. *thou troubler of Israel.* For the word (עָכַר) see Gen. xxxiv. 30; Josh. vi. 18; vii. 25; Prov. xi. 17; 1 Sam. xiv. 29. When Rawlinson says that this charge of troubling Israel has "never been before brought against any one but Achan," he apparently forgets the passage last cited. "My father hath troubled the land." Wordsworth paraphrases, "Art thou the Achan of Israel?" but it is very doubtful whether this thought was in Ahab's mind.]

Ver. 18.—**And he answered, I have not troubled Israel; but thou, and thy father's house** [It has been supposed that Ahab "hoped to abash the Tishbite, perhaps to have him at his feet suing for pardon" (Rawlinson). If so, he must have completely misjudged his man. And why the prophet should sue for pardon, when he was so clearly master of the situation, it is difficult to imagine. It is quite as likely that Ahab expected denunciation and defiance such as he now provokes], **in that ye have forsaken the commandments of the Lord, and thou** [The change from plural to singular is instructive. Preceding kings and the people at large had broken God's commandments by the calf-worship, but Ahab alone had introduced the Baal-cultus into the land] **hast followed** [Heb. *goest after*] **Baalim.** [The plural may either refer to the various names and forms under which Baal was worshipped—Baal-Berith, Baal-Zebub, &c. (Bähr, *al.*)—or more prob-

ably to the various images or statues of this god set up in the land (Gesenius). "This boldness, this high tone, this absence of the slightest indication of alarm, seems to have completely discomfited Ahab, who ventured on no reply," &c. (Rawlinson). It is probable that, though he put on a bold front, he was from the first thoroughly cowed.

Ver. 19.—**Now therefore send, and gather to me all Israel** [*i.e.*, by representation, the heads of the people, elders, &c. Cf. ch. viii. 2, 65; xii. 16, 18; xvi. 16, 17] **unto Mount Carmel** [Heb., as almost always, *the Carmel*, *i.e.*, the park. Cf. 1 Sam. xxv. 1—5. It is "the park of Palestine." It is indebted for this name to the luxuriant vegetation—"the excellency of Carmel" (Isa. xxxv. 2)—which clothes its southern slopes (Porter, p. 371; Stanley, S. and P. pp. 352—54, and App. p. 14; Van de Velde, i. pp. 317, 318). It is now generally called *Mar* (*i.e.*, Lord or Saint) *Elyas*, after the great prophet. No one who has seen the locality can have any doubts as to which part of the mountain was the scene of the sacrifice, or can fail to be struck with the singular fitness of the place to be the theatre of this thrilling history. Carmel is rather a ridge than a mountain, some twelve miles in length. Its western (or strictly N.N.W.) extremity is a bold headland, some 600 feet in height, which dips almost directly into the waters of the Mediterranean. Its highest point, 1728 feet above the sea level, is about four miles from its eastern extremity, which, at an elevation of 1600 feet, rises like a wall from the great plain of Esdraelon. It is at this point, there can be no question, we are to place the scene of the burnt sacrifice. The identification has only been effected in comparatively recent days (1852), but it is beyond dispute. Not only does the Arab name which it bears—*El Murahka*, "*the Burning*," or "*Sacrifice*"—afford striking witness to the identity, but the situation and surroundings adapt themselves with such wonderful precision to the requirements of the narrative as to leave no reasonable doubt in the mind. For (1) it is a sort of natural platform, or pulpit, raised 1000 feet above the adjoining plain, and therefore well calculated to afford a view of the proceedings, or at least of the descent of the Holy Fire, to spectators of all Israel. The flame would probably be seen by Jezebel in her palace at Jezreel. This eminence is visible from Nazareth, some twenty miles away. "There is not a more conspicuous spot on all Carmel than the abrupt, rocky height of El Murahka, shooting up so suddenly on the east" (Van de Velde, i. pp. 322, 323). "The summit . . . commands the last view of the sea behind and the first view of the great plain in front" (Stanley). In fact, it was in its way just as well adapted for the solemn vindication of the law which took place there as *Jebel Sufsafeh* was for the giving of the law. (2) A sort of plateau near the summit—the table-land where the altars were built, &c.—would accommodate a vast number of spectators (ver. 21). (3) There is a spring of water close at hand—less than 100 yards distant —and a spring which is said to flow even in the driest seasons, which would supply the water of which we read in vers. 4, 33—35. Josephus (Ant. viii. 13, 5) says it came from the fountain. (4) The sea, though not visible from the plateau itself, is seen from a point some 300 feet higher, a detail which accords admirably with the account of vers. 42—44. It may be added that the place is still held sacred by the Druses, and reverenced by " Jews, Christians, Moslems, and Bedouin as the site of these miracles of Elijah " (Thomson). The traveller, consequently, cannot doubt for a moment, as he stands on the table-land of *El Murahkah* and looks across the great plain to Jezreel and the heights of Galilee and Samaria, that he is on the very spot sanctified by the descent of the heavenly fire. It should be added, as explaining the selection of Carmel by Elijah, that its situation is central and convenient ; that it is near the sea, from whence the rain-clouds would come ; that it is easy of access from Jezreel ; and that it was not only a holy place from earlier times (cf. 2 Kings iv. 23), but also had its altar of Jehovah, an altar, no doubt, in constant use when the people "sacrificed and burnt incense on the high places," but which had in later days fallen into neglect, and was now broken down. It was every way, therefore, a most appropriate locality for the public vindication of the despised and outraged law of God. " No place could be conceived more fitted by nature to be that wondrous battle-field of truth " (Tristram in Wordsworth)], **and the prophets of Baal** [so called not because they were *Weissager und Verkünder* (Bähr) of the god, nor yet because they were teachers and emissaries of his religion, but because of the prophetic frenzy (ver. 28) into which they worked themselves (Keil)] **four hundred and fifty, and the prophets of the groves** [Heb. *of the Asherah*, *i.e.*, of Astarte, not " grove," as Rawlinson. See note on ch. xiv. 15] **four hundred** [Rawlinson remarks that " the number 400 seems to have been one especially affected by Ahab." He reminds us that we find 400 prophets at the close of his reign (1 Kings xxii. 6), and also remarks on " the prevalence of the number 40 in the religious systems of the Jews (Exod.

xxxvi. 24, 26 ; Deut. xxv. 3, &c.)" But when it is remembered that Baal's prophets were 450, and the prophets of ch. xxii. 6 were *about* 400 men, the solitary instance of the 400 prophets of Astarte—who, by the way, were Jezebel's rather than Ahab's ministers —affords but a slender basis for his conclusion], **which eat at Jezebel's table.** [Heb. *eaters of.* There is nothing in the Hebrew to imply that they sat with her at the same board ; and it is certain that this would be altogether repugnant to Eastern ideas of propriety. All that is meant is that they were fed by her bounty. See note on ch. ii. 7.]

Ver. 20.—So Ahab sent unto all the children of Israel, and gathered the prophets together unto Mount Carmel. [" The persecuting king became a passive instrument in the hand of the persecuted prophet " (Stanley). His ready compliance with Elijah's request, notwithstanding the bitter hatred of the man which he had just betrayed, is easily explained. It was not so much that " he bowed before the spiritual supremacy of the prophet, which impressed him " (Bähr), as that he hoped, from his reappearance, that he was now about to speak the word (ch. xvii. 1) and give rain upon the earth, and Ahab was willing to take any measures which would conduce to that result. It would take some days to collect the representatives of the tribes.]

Ver. 21.—And Elijah came unto all the people [He is concerned not so much with the king as the people of the Lord. His object was not " to prove that Ahab and not he had troubled Israel," but to prove that Jehovah and not Baal was God. There is abundant room on the plateau, or " wide upland sweep " (Stanley), above referred to, to accommodate a large concourse of people], **and said, How long halt ye between two opinions ?** [This is a faithful and felicitous rendering. But it must be remembered that " halt " is used in the sense of " limp." Vulg. *Usquequo claudicatis in duas partes.* The same word is used in ver. 26 of the swaying, tottering dance of the Baal prophets.] **If the Lord be God** [Heb. *if Jehovah the God*], **follow him** [Heb. *go* (*i.e.*, walk straight) *after him*]: **but if Baal, then follow him. And the people answered him not a word.** [Not only were they awed by the presence of the king and the priests of Baal on the one side, and of Elijah on the other, but they were " convicted by their own consciences," and so were speechless (Matt. xxii. 12).]

Ver. 22.—Then said Elijah unto the people, I, even I only, remain [Heb. *I, I am left alone.* Cf. Gen. xxxii. 24 ; LXX. μονώ-τατος] **a prophet of the Lord** [Thenius

hence concludes that the "hundred prophets" of whom we read in vers. 4, 13 had
been discovered in their hiding place and
had been put to death. But this by no means
follows from Elijah's statement here or in
ch. xix. 10 (where see note); and we know
that the schools of the prophets had not
ceased to exist (2 Kings ii. 3, 5, 7; cf. 1
Kings xxii. 8). All that Elijah says is that
he *stood that day alone* as a prophet of
Jehovah. "I only remain *in the exercise of
the office* of a prophet" (Rawlinson). The
rest might well hesitate, after the fierce
persecution which they had undergone, to
face the king and their bitter enemies, the
Baal prophets. It must be remembered
that Elijah had had no opportunity of communicating with them, and he may have
been quite ignorant as to what number had
remained steadfast and true. One thing he
knew, that he alone was left to prophesy,
and to confront the whole hierarchy of the
false God]; **but Baal's prophets are four
hundred and fifty men.** [It is clear, not
only from the silence of this verse and of
ver. 25, respecting them, but still more from
the fact that they escaped in the general
slaughter (ver. 40), that the prophets of
Astarte were not present, and the natural
inference is that either Jezebel had forbidden their presence or that they shrank
from the ordeal. The LXX. inserts "and
the prophets of the grove, four hundred,"
but the words are evidently added from
ver. 19. The Baal prophets would doubtless
have been only too glad to do the same, but
they were under the immediate command of
the king. It is not certain that they had
any forebodings of evil, or dreaded reprisals
on Elijah's part, but they had had proof
conclusive of his power and of their impotence. We must remember that all through
the triennium prayers and sacrifices had,
no doubt, been constantly offered with a
view to procure rain. We learn from
Menander (Jos., viii. 13. 2) that even in
Phoenicia supplication had been made for
rain by Ethbaal.

Ver. 23.—**Let them therefore give us two
bullocks; and let them choose one bullock
for themselves, and cut it in pieces** [same
word Exod. xxix. 17; Levit. i. 6, 12; Judg.
xx. 6], **and lay it on wood** [Heb. *the woods*],
and put no fire under [Heb. *and fire they
shall not set to*]: **and I will dress** [Heb.
make, עָשָׂה, like ποιεῖν in the LXX., is constantly used in a sacrificial sense = *offer*.
Cf. Exod. xxix. 36, 38, 41; Levit. ix. 7;
xv. 15; Judg. vi. 19, &c. This is to be remembered in interpreting our Lord's τοῦτο
ποιεῖτε, κ.τ.λ. (Luke xxii. 19)] **the other
bullock, and lay it on wood** [*the* wood],

and put no fire under [*and fire I will not
set to*]:
Ver. 24.—**And call ye on the name of
your gods** [As Elijah is still addressing the
people, not the prophets of Baal (see ver.
25), this change of person is significant.
He sorrowfully assumes that they have
taken Baal and Astarte for their gods], **and
I will call on the name of the Lord : and the
God that answereth by fire, let him be God.**
[Heb. *he* shall be *the God, i.e.,* the true God
and their God. Cf. ver. 39. Not only was
a "sign from heaven" (Mark viii. 11) ever
esteemed a more powerful and direct proof
of Divine energy—perhaps as being less
liable to be counterfeited, and as excluding
the idea of the operation of infernal powers
(Matt. xii. 24)—but it must be remembered
that Baal claimed to be the Sun-god and
Lord of the elements and forces of nature;
while Jehovah had already, according to the
law, identified Himself with this token
(Levit. ix. 24; 1 Chron. xxi. 26; 2 Chron.
vii. 1). Indeed, this sign had a double fitness as a test of the true religion. It would
not only put the *powers* of the rival deities
to the proof; it would also at the same
time decide which of the rival systems of
worship was acceptable to the Supreme
Being. It is observable that there is no
mention of rain. We might have expected,
after the long drought, that this would be
the test. But that could not be promised
until the Lord had first been recognized as
God.] **And all the people answered and
said, It is well spoken.** [Heb. *Good the word.*
They accepted Elijah's proposition, but whether eagerly or reluctantly it is difficult to
say. The Hebrew merely conveys that they
admitted its fairness and reasonableness.

Having gained the assent of the people,
for whose verdict he and the Baal prophets
were now contending, and who were, consequently, entitled to be consulted as to the
sign which would satisfy them, he turns to
the band of 400 prophets, who, probably in
all the bravery of their sacrificial vestments
(2 Kings x. 22), occupied a separate position
on the hill top, between the king and the
people, and repeats his proposal to them.

Ver. 25.—**And Elijah said unto the prophets of Baal, Choose you one bullock for
yourselves, and dress** [or *offer*, as in ver.
23] **it first; for ye are many** [Heb. *the
many*. Every pre-eminence and advantage
which he gives to them will make his
triumph, when it comes, all the greater. It
is quite possible that he meant again to hint
at their immense superiority in point of
numbers. But no doubt he was only too
glad to find a reason for their taking the

lead. "He is anxious that their inability shall be fully manifested before he shows his own power" (Rawlinson). Whether the idea was also present in his mind that they "could prepare their victim in a much shorter time than he could prepare his" (*ib.*) is by no means so certain; **and call on the name of your gods** [or *god, i.e.,* Baal], **but put no fire under.** [The repetition (cf. ver. 24) shows that the ordeal was proposed separately to the people and the prophets.]

Ver. 26.—**And they took the bullock which was given them** [Heb. *which he* (or *one*) *gave; i.e.,* they declined to choose], **and they dressed it, and called on the name of Baal from morning even until noon, saying, O Baal, hear us** [Heb. *answer us.* Same word as below. They thought they would be heard for their much speaking. **But there was no voice** [Heb. *and not a voice*], **nor any that answered. And they leaped** [or *limped.* Same word as that translated " halt " in ver. 21. Gesenius thinks the word is " used scornfully of the awkward dancing of the priests of Baal." But it seems more natural to understand it as descriptive of what actually occurred, *i.e.,* of the reeling, swaying, bacchantic dance of the priests, which was probably not unlike that of the dancing dervishes or the Indian devil-worshippers of our own time] **upon** [or *near, i.e., around*] **the altar which was made.** [Heb. *he,* that is, *one made,* עָשָׂה impersonal. But some MSS. and most versions read עָשׂוּ].

Ver. 27.—**And it came to pass at noon, that Elijah mocked** [or *deceived*] **them, and said, Cry aloud** [Heb. *with a great voice*]: **for he is a god** [*i.e.,* in your estimation. "Here is one of the few examples of irony in Scripture " (Wordsworth)] ; **either he is talking** [the marg. *he meditateth* is preferable. Cf. 1 Sam. i. 16; Psa. cxlii. 3. But the word has both meanings (see 2 Kings ix. 11), fairly preserved in the LXX., ἀδολεσχία αὐτῷ ἐστι], **or he is pursuing** [Heb. *for he hath a withdrawal, i.e.,* for the purpose of relieving himself. A euphemism. Cf. Judg. iii. 24 ; 2 Sam. xxiv. 3. Stanley attempts to preserve the *paronomasia,* שִׂיחַ, שִׂיג, by the translation, " he has his head full " and " he has his stomach full "], **or he is in a journey** [the thrice repeated כִּי must be noticed. It heightens the effect of the mockery], **or peradventure he sleepeth** [Though it was noon, it is not clear that there is a reference to the usual midday *siesta* of the East], **and must be awaked.**

Ver. 28.—**And they cried aloud** [Heb. *in a great voice,* as above. It was not that they took Elijah's words *au sérieux,* but his scorn led them to redouble their efforts, if only to testify their faith in their god. The

frantic cries of the Greek Easter (see Porter, i. 168; Condor, 176—178) in Jerusalem, the prayers of the pilgrims for the descent of the holy fire, may help us to realize the scene here described], **and cut themselves** [cf. Deut. xiv. 1; Jer. xvi. 6 ; xli. 5 ; xlvii. 5] **after their manner** [Keil quotes from Movers, Phöniz. i. pp. 682—83, a description of the religious dances offered to the *Dea Syria.* " A discordant howling opens the scene. Then they rush wildly about in perfect confusion, with their heads bowed down to the ground, but always revolving in circles, so that the loosened hair drags through the mire ; then they begin to bite their arms, and end with cutting themselves with the two-edged swords which they are in the habit of carrying. A new scene then opens. One of them, who surpasses all the rest in frenzy, begins to prophesy with sighs and groans," &c. In the " Contemporary Review," vol. xxvii. pp. 371 sqq., Bishop Caldwell has graphically described the devil-dances of Southern India—a description which may be read with profit in this connexion. One sentence may be transcribed here : " He cuts and hacks and hews himself, and not unfrequently kills himself there and then." Kitto mentions " the furious gashes which the Persians inflict upon themselves in their frantic annual lamentation for Hossein." Rawlinson says this was also common among the Carians and Phrygians] **with knives** [Heb. *swords*] **and lancets** [Heb. *lances, spears.* The A. V. is misleading. The instruments they used were weapons of heavy-armed troops. For רְמָחִים, see Num. xxv 7 ; Judg. v. 8; Jer. xlvi. 4], **till the blood gushed out upon them.** [Heb. *until the shedding of blood upon them.* It is perfectly clear that their faith in Baal was sincere and profound. Making due allowance for the fact that they were under the eyes of their king and patron, and of representatives of the entire people, it is still impossible to doubt their sincerity. Some of them, it is probable, were Phoenicians. "Of one thing I am assured—the devil-dancer never shams excitement " (Caldwell).]

Ver. 29.—**And it came to pass, when midday was past** [Elijah allowed them all the time he could, consistently with the great work he had himself to do, which would absorb all the rest of the day], **and they prophesied** [Notice the striking coincidence with the description of the worship of Ashtoreth given above. We are not to think of vaticinations, but of frenzied cries, &c. It is not clear, however, that any fresh element in their worship is intended, as Keil imagines. Their service as a whole, seeing they were *prophets,* would be called a "prophesying," and the word, consequently, may merely mean "they pursued their calling," "they cried and prayed," &c.] **until the time of the offering** [Keil and Rawlinson would translate, "until *towards* the time," &c. There is certainly some indefiniteness in the words עַד לַעֲלוֹת, *until* [the hour] *for placing, &c.*, but we may well believe that their dances and cries continued up to the moment of Elijah's prayer (ver. 36)] **of the evening sacrifice** [Heb. *the Minchah, i.e.*, the meat offering or unbloody sacrifice. In Gen. iv. 3—6 the word would appear to be used of any offering; but at a later day it was restricted to bloodless offerings, and was opposed to זֶבַח. Cf. Psa. xl. 7; Jer. xvii. 26. Directions as to the offering of the Minchah are given, Exod. xxix. 38—41; Num. xxviii. 3—8. The evening sacrifice was probably offered then, as it certainly was at a later day, at the ninth hour. Cf. Acts iii. 1; x. 3, 30, and see Jos., Ant. xiv. 4. 3. Wordsworth thinks this synchronism very significant, as suggesting that the true worship of God was that of the temple in Jerusalem], **that there was neither voice, nor any to answer** [as in ver. 26], **nor any that regarded.** [Heb. *and not attention.* The LXX. has a curious variation and addition here : " And Elijah the Tishbite said to the prophets of the idols, Stand back; I will now make ready my offering."]

Ver. 30.—**And Elijah said unto all the people** [He has now done with the priests. They have had their opportunity; his turn is come], **Come near unto me.** [Hitherto they had gathered round the altar of Baal, and some, it may be, had joined their prayers to those of the priests (ver. 24). In ver. 21, he "drew near"—same word—to them. Now they must stand round the altar he is about to build. He will have "eye-witnesses and ear-witnesses" (Keil). There must be no suspicion of imposture.] **And all the people came near unto him. And he repaired the altar of the Lord that was broken down.** [It has been already suggested that this altar may have dated from the time when there was no house built unto the name of the Lord. But it is just as likely that it had been restored, if not raised, by some of the "seven thousand who had not bowed their knees unto Baal," or by some of the faithful remaining in Israel after the calf-worship and the hostility between the two kingdoms had made worship at Jerusalem an impossibility. Anyhow we can hardly be mistaken in holding that this was one of the "altars" (ch. xix. 10) "thrown down" by command of Ahab or Jezebel. Elijah's repairing it was an act

of profound significance. It showed him as the restorer of the law and the true religion.]

Ver. 31.—**And Elijah took twelve stones** [This number, too, was full of significance. Not only would it carry back their thoughts to the giving of the law (Exod. xxiv. 4; xxviii. 21), and to their fathers' entrance into the promised land (Josh. iv. 3, 9), but it would remind them of the essential unity of the people, notwithstanding the division of the kingdom. The act was thus a protest against the schism. We cannot hold with Keil, Wordsworth, *al.* that it was "a practical declaration on the part of the prophet that the division of the nation *into two kingdoms* was at variance with the will of God," because we are distinctly told that that division was "from the Lord" (ch. xii. 15). But it was certainly a witness against a divided Church, and a reminder of the unity of the race], **according to the number of the tribes of the sons of Jacob, unto whom the word of the Lord came** [Gen. xxxii. 28], **saying, Israel shall be thy name.** [He thus protests against the exclusive assumption of the name of Israel, and the exception of the southern kingdom from the glorious heritage and calling of Israel, by the ten tribes. But we cannot follow Bähr in the belief that Jacob received "from Jehovah the name of Israel," *i.e.*, the "soldier of God," because he commanded his house to "put away the strange gods" (Gen. xxxv. 2, 10 sqq.), or that Elijah would teach that "only those who did as Jacob did had a claim to his name." The great idea is that the people are *one*, and are the Lord's.]

Ver. 32.—**And with the stones** [the twelve he had chosen out of the ruins. Cf. Exod. xx. 25] **he built an altar in the name of the Lord** [not "by the command of Jehovah" (Bähr), but rather as the minister and for the service of Jehovah, or, as Keil. "by the authority and for the glory of Jehovah." Nor is it certain that "he called, as he built it, on the name of Jehovah, and so dedicated it to His service" (Rawl.) See Gen. xii. 8; xiii. 4; xxxiii. 20; xxxv. 7]: **and he made a trench** [or *channel*, 2 Kings xviii. 17; Isa. vii. 3; xxxvi. 2; Ezek. xxxi. 4. The word implies that it was for holding the water, not for keeping off the people] **about the altar, as great as would contain two measures of seed** [Heb. *as the inside* (lit., *house*) *of two seahs of seed.* These words have been variously interpreted. Keil, with Thenius and Wordsworth, understands that "the trench was so large that you could sow two seahs of seed upon the ground which it covered." But apart from the fact that בַּיִת must refer to capacity rather than superficial extent, one does not measure a trench, as Bähr observes, by the ground which it covers, but by its depth. He would follow Gesenius in understanding that the trench was so deep as to hold two seahs of seed; *i.e.*, as deep as the grain measure containing two seahs. The סְאָה was the third of an ephah. Cf. Jos., Ant. ix. 4. 5, and the σάτα τρία of Matt. xiii. 33.]

Ver. 33.—**And he put the wood in order, and cut the bullock in pieces, and laid him on the wood** [Rawlinson says " He obeyed, that is, all the injunctions of the law with respect to the offering of a burnt sacrifice (see Levit. i. 3—9), and adds, " He thus publicly taught that all the ordinances of the law were binding on the kingdom of Israel." But it is very probable that the priests of Baal had done the same things. All sacrifice involved such manual acts. Cf. Gen. xxii. 9, where the same word עָרַךְ is used. No doubt the prophet did everything in an orderly and regular way; but the people could hardly learn a lesson of obedience from such elementary acts as these, and the less so as the law provided that the sacrifice should be offered only " by the *priests*, the sons of Aaron " (Levit. i. 8), and Elijah's ministrations, consequently, might seem to warrant or condone the ministrations of Jeroboam's intrusive priesthood. That they did not lend any *real* sanction to those irregularities is clear, however, to us. For, in the first place, priests were not to be had, all having long since left the kingdom. In the second place, the higher commission of the prophet embraced within itself the authority for all necessary priestly acts. Cf. 1 Sam. xvi. 2. Elijah acted, as Grotius well observes, *jure prophetico, minoribus legibus exsolutus, ut majores servaret*], and said, **Fill four barrels** [Heb. כַּדִּים. Cf. ch. xvii. 12. It designates the ordinary water-pitcher, generally carried then, as now, by women: Gen. xxiv. 14—20; Judg. vii. 16; Eccles. xii. 6] **with water, and pour it on the burnt sacrifice, and on the wood** [The water, as already remarked, was doubtless brought from the adjoining spring (though it is clear from ver. 40 that the Kishon was not dry, and Thomson thinks that its sources, and particularly the fountain of *Saadieh*, furnished the supply). " In such springs the water remains always cool, under the shade of a vaulted roof, and with no hot atmosphere to evaporate it. While all other fountains were dried up, I can well understand that there might have been found here that superabundance of water which Elijah poured so profusely over the altar" (Van de Velde, i. p. 325).]

Ver. 34.—**And he said, Do it the second time. And they did it the second time.**

[Heb. *Repeat, and they repeated.*] **And he said, Do it the third time. And they did it the third time.** [See note on ch. xvii. 21.]

Ver. 35.—**And the water ran round** [Heb. *the waters went round*] **about the altar, and he filled the trench also** [*i.e.*, the trench, which was only partially filled with the water of the twelve כַּדִּים, he now filled to the brim] **with water.** [The object of these repeated drenchings of the victim and altar was to exclude all suspicion of fraud. It would almost seem as if tricks not unlike that practised year by year at the Greek Easter at Jerusalem were familiar to that age. Some of the fathers expressly state that the idolatrous priests of an earlier time were accustomed to set fire to the sacrifice from hollow places concealed beneath the altar, and it was an old tradition (found in Ephrem Syrus, and Chrysostom) that the Baal prophets had concealed a man for that purpose beneath their altar, but that he had died from suffocation (Stanley). Bähr, however, sees in these 3 × 4 vessels of water a symbolical act. The significance of this combination, he says, is unmistakable (cf. " Symbolik" i. pp. 150, 169, 193, 205), though we cannot be certain as to the precise meaning of the prophetic act. His only suggestion is that it points to abundance of rain as the reward of keeping the covenant (Deut. xxviii. 12, 23). But all this is extremely precarious, and the more so as the pitchers may have been filled any number of times before the trench was full.]

Ver. 36.—**And it came to pass at the time of the offering of the evening sacrifice** [see note on ver. 29], **that Elijah the prophet** [this designation of Elijah is unusual. Cf. Mal. iv. 5. Elsewhere he is " the Tishbite," or the " man of God "] **came near, and said, Lord** [Heb. *Jehovah.* Not only does the sacred name stand at the head of his prayer, it is also mentioned thrice (LXX. four times)] **God of Abraham, Isaac, and Israel** [Two things are to be noticed here: first, that this formula had only once before been used, and that by God Himself, before the giving of law, at the burning bush. It was when God revealed Himself in *flaming fire* that He had proclaimed Himself the God of Abraham, &c. Secondly, that the variation " *Israel* " is made designedly (cf. ver. 31), not only to proclaim the Lord as the " God of Israel " (cf. ch. xvii. 1), but also to suggest that the name and privileges of Israel belonged to all the sons of Jacob. The LXX. adds, " Hear me, O Lord, hear me this day by fire "—most of which is clearly borrowed from the next verse], **let it be known this day that thou art God in**

Israel [according to ver. 24, " the God that
answereth by fire, &c.], **and that I am thy
servant, and that I have done all these
things according to thy word.** [LXX. διὰ
σὲ. Not only the earlier proceedings of the
day, but the three years' drought, &c. Keil
would include the miracle about to be performed, but the people could hardly doubt
that that, when done, was done according
to the Divine word. It is interesting to
compare with these words ch. xvii. 2, 3, 8,
16, 24, and ch. xviii. 1, all of which mention
the " word of the Lord."]

Ver. 37.—**Hear me, O Lord** [*Jehovah*],
hear me [or *answer me;* same word as in
vers. 24, 26, and 29], **that this people
may know that thou art the Lord God**
[Rather, " *that thou, Jehovah, art the God.*"
Same expression as in ver. 24, " let him be
the God "], **and that thou hast turned
their heart back again.** [Cf. Mal. iv. 5, 6 :
" He (" Elijah the prophet ") shall turn the
heart of the fathers," &c. He speaks as if
the miracle were already wrought (cf. John
xi. 41), and the people already repentant.
His prayer is that they may understand
that the prodigy about to be performed was
wrought for their conversion.]

Ver. 38.—**Then the fire of the Lord**
[*Jehovah*. Not lightning, but supernatural
light and heat emanating from God Himself. Cf. Levit. ix. 24 ; 1 Chron. xxi. 26 ;
2 Chron. vii. 1 ; Heb. xii. 29] **fell, and consumed** [Heb. *ate up, devoured*] **the burnt
sacrifice, and the wood, and the stones** [*in
calcem redigit*, Cler.], **and the dust** [Bähr
translates *die Erde*, and understands this to
be the earth with which the altar of twelve
stones had been packed. Similarly Rawlinson. But it is very doubtful whether עָפָר
pulvis, could be used in this sense. It may
mean *dry* earth, but this altar had been
deluged with water], **and licked up** [לָחַךְ is
clearly onomatopoetic, like our *lick;* Germ.
lecken ; Gr. λείχω, &c. It expresses well
the action of *tongues* of flame] **the water
that was in the trench.**

Ver. 39.—**And when all the people saw it,
they fell on their faces** [As in Levit. ix. 24 ;
2 Chron. vii. 3 ; cf. Num. xxii. 31 ; Josh. v.
14 ; Rev. xi. 16. They recognized in the
fire, that is to say, the token of the
Divine Presence]: **and they said, The Lord**
[*Jehovah*. The connexion of this verse
with the three verses preceding is obscured
by our translation], **he is the God; the
Lord, he is the God.** [The echo of ver. 24.
The Hebrew words are the same. Stanley
remarks that it is as if (by a slight inversion)
they turned " the name of the prophet himself into a war-cry, 'Eli-Jah-hu.' "]

Ver. 40.—**And Elijah said unto them,**

**Take the prophets of Baal; let not one of
them escape.** [Elijah's promptitude is extremely striking. The people had hardly
recovered from their terror and awe before
he proceeds to judgment. The narrative
has the air of truth, and was doubtless
reduced to writing by an eye-witness.] **And
they took them : and Elijah brought them
down** [Heb. *caused them to go down, i.e.,*
had them brought down. He could but
lead the way, as they numbered 450] **to the
brook** [*Wâdy*. " Like most of the so-called
'rivers of Palestine,' the perennial stream
forms but a small part of the Kishon "
(Grove)] **Kishon** [" Tortuous," now called
Nahr el Mukatta, the " river of slaughter."
See Thomson, L. and B. ii. pp. 140, 141 ;
Porter, pp.383—4; Dict. Bib. ii.p.45. It flows
directly under Carmel], **and slew them there.**
[Obviously, he merely superintended the
slaughter. That he slew them all with his
own hand is altogether out of the question.
Nor is it clear that " sword in hand he stood
over them " (Stanley). Josephus rightly explains : " they slew the prophets at Elijah's
instigation." It is almost certain, from
their resorting to the Kishon for this purpose, that it was not quite dry at the time.
Their blood would mingle with its waters,
and the flood which the " great rain " would
presently produce (cf. Judg. v. 21) would
carry their corpses down to the sea. It has
often been supposed that the mound near
the Kishon, known as *Tell el Cassis*, " the
mound of the priests," derives its name
from this slaughter of the prophets of
Baal. But Conder (p. 90) remarks that
" Kassîs is the word applied to a Christian
priest, and the word Kohen or Kamir would
more naturally be expected if there was any
real connexion with the idolatrous priests
of Baal."]

This action of the prophet Elijah in instituting this wholesale slaughter in the hour
of his triumph has been repeatedly arraigned
and denounced, but most unjustly. According to some, it was an act of gross fanaticism and cruelty ; others have seen it in a
wild and terrible *vendetta* for the murder
of the Lord's prophets. By some, indeed,
it has been justified on the principles of the
lex talionis (Exod. xxi. 24, &c.); on the
ground, that is to say, that the men who
had instigated Jezebel in her attempted extermination of the prophetic schools had
merited extermination in their turn. But
it is a fatal objection to their view, first,
that we not only have no proof, but no
reason for thinking, that it was at their

instigation that the queen "cut off the prophets of the Lord;" and, secondly, that it is not clear that she succeeded in her sanguinary purpose, or that many lives were sacrificed to her fury. And Elijah's action needs no such lame apologies. As the Lord's prophet, as the vindicator and restorer of the law, there was no other course open to him. If the Mosaic law was then written, and this very incident is one of the proofs that it *was* then written; if, however it had fallen into contempt or desuetude, it was still binding upon Israel; and if Elijah was justified in executing its provisions, and was required to execute them, however repugnant they might be to his inclinations (Deut. xxvii. 26; Gal. iii. 10), then he could not have done otherwise than he did. For it was an essential part of that law, it was an obligation that was laid, not once or twice, but on three separate occasions (Exod. xxii. 20; Deut. xiii.; xvii. 2—7), on the Jewish people, it was a duty they were to perform, however distressing and harrowing it might be (Deut. xiii. 6—9), to provide that the worshipper of false gods, and especially the teacher of such worship, should be put to death. It was primarily, of course, the duty of the authorities, of the theocratic king and his subordinates, to execute these injunctions. But the king of that age was corrupt and powerless—nay, was himself idolatrous. So great was the depravity of the time that the false prophet enjoyed the favour and protection of the court, and the true prophet was everywhere being hunted to death. The execution of this law, consequently, could not be expected from the king. It must be executed, if at all, in spite of him, and in disregard of his protests. It was only Elijah, therefore, could put it into force, and Elijah only in the hour of his triumph. And the *jus zelotyparum*, the right claimed by every faithful Jew to execute vengeance, after the example of Phinehas (Num. xxv. 11), upon any gross breach of the Divine law committed in his presence, was not his only warranty; he held a commission, higher than the king's, as the prophet of the Most High. He had just proved that the Lord He was God. It was now for him to prove that God's law was no dead letter. It was

for him to cut off the men—some of them renegades from the faith of Israel, some of them foreign missionaries introduced into the land—who had corrupted his countrymen, and threatened the very existence of the true religion. It is necessary, therefore, for those who challenge his conduct in this respect, who call him sanguinary, vindictive, &c., to settle their account with the law which he obeyed, and, indeed, with Him who has approved this deed, and has forewarned us that He too will act in like manner (Luke xix. 27). For this terrible retribution is by no means an exceptional or isolated act, in contrast to the general spirit of that dispensation; on the contrary, it is in thorough accord with the system out of which it sprung. We gain nothing, therefore, by repudiating this one transaction. For clearly, in the first place, it was allowed and approved of God, who otherwise would hardly have answered the prayer which Elijah presently offered, and (2) other similar acts have distinctly received Divine commendation (Exod. xxxii. 25—28; Num. xxv. 7—13; 2 Kings i. 9 sqq.) It is true that the spirit of Elias was not the spirit of Christianity (Luke ix. 56), but it is forgotten how different was the dispensation of Elijah from that of the New Covenant. In that age idolaters must receive their just recompense of reward, because the judgment *to come* had not then been revealed; because justice must be measured out to men in this life. We do not avenge idolatry or irreligion now with fire and sword, not because the thing is any the less sinful, but because the duty has been taken out of our hands; because our religion instructs us to leave it to Him who has said, "Vengeance is Mine," &c. It is perhaps worth remarking here that there is nothing in this history half so dreadful as might be seen on a thousand battle-fields— and those not battle-fields for truth and right — on which, nevertheless, Elijah's critics have learned to look with complacency. It may, however, be objected to this view that the punishment denounced by the law was stoning (Deut. xiii. 10; xvii. 5). But surely it is easy to see why, in this particular, the law was not kept. It was simply that the exigency of the occasion did not permit of its being kept. It was because the 450 traitors to God and their country could not be stoned within the few hours that remained before the night closed in and the multitude dispersed, that a more speedy punishment, that of the sword, was adopted. And it would have been a sacrifice of the spirit of the law to the letter had some few false prophets been stoned and the rest thereby been afforded the opportunity to escape, and, under Jezebel's protection, to renew their efforts against truth and morality and religion.

Ver. 41.—**And Elijah said unto Ahab, Get thee up** [It is clear from the word עֲלֵה that the king had gone down with the crowd to the Kishon. Curiosity had perhaps impelled him to witness the slaughter which he was powerless to prevent. And no doubt he had been profoundly awed by the portent he had just witnessed], **eat and drink** [It is hardly likely that there was aught of derision in these words. It is extremely probable that the excitement of the ordeal was so intense that the king had barely tasted food all day long. Elijah now bids him eat if he can, after what he has witnessed. There is now, he suggests, no further cause for anxiety or alarm. The people being repentant (vers. 39, 40), and the men who have brought a curse on the land being cut off, the drought can now be abated (cf. 2 Sam. xxi. 1, 6, 14). The next words assign the reason why he should eat and drink. It is a mistake, however (Ewald, Rawlinson), to suppose that he was bidden to "eat of the feast which always followed a sacrifice," for this was a whole burnt offering and had been entirely consumed (ver. 38). It is probable that the attendants of the king had spread a tent for him upon the plateau, and had brought food for the day along with them]; **for there is a sound of abundance of rain** [Heb. *for a voice of a noise*—הָמוֹן; cf. *hum*, an onomatopoetic word—*of rain*. Gesenius and Keil think that the prophet could already hear the sound of the drops of rain, but if so, it was only in spirit (cf. ver. 45). The words may refer to the rise of the wind which so often precedes a storm, but it is more probable that Elijah speaks of signs and intimations understood only by himself. This was the "word" of ch. xvii. 1.]

Ver. 42.—**So Ahab went up to eat and to drink. And Elijah went up to the top** [Heb. *head*] **of Carmel** [It is clear from ver. 43 that this was not the actual summit,

nor can it have been, as Bähr supposes, the outermost promontory towards the sea, unless he means the foot or slope of that ridge or promontory, for from this רֹאשׁ the sea was not visible. It also appears from the עֲלָה of ver. 44 that this point must have been at a lower elevation than the plateau where the altar had stood and where Ahab's tent was]; **and he cast himself down upon the earth** [Same word 2 Kings iv. 34, 35, of Elisha's prostration upon the dead child. But if Elijah "stretched himself full length" upon the earth, as the Easterns constantly do in prayer (see Thomson, i. 26, 27) it was but for a moment, as we presently find him kneeling], **and put his face between his knees.** ["The Oriental attitude of entire abstraction" (Stanley). The posture witnessed to the intensity of his supplication.]

Ver. 43.—**And said to his servant** [of whom we now hear for the first time. It is an old tradition that this was none other than the son of the Sareptan, who was afterwards known as the prophet Jonah (Jerome, Praef. in Jonam). See note on ch. xvii. 24], **Go up now, look toward** [Heb. *the way of*] **the sea.** [It is a striking confirmation of the theory which identifies *El Murahkah* with the scene of Elijah's sacrifice that the sea, though not visible from the plateau itself, is from the crest of the hill, a few feet higher. Van de Velde writes, "On its west and north-west sides the view of the sea is quite intercepted by an adjacent height. That height may be ascended, however, in a few minutes and a full view of the sea obtained from the top." Similarly the latest authority, Mr. Conder: "The peak is a semi-isolated knoll with a cliff some forty feet high, looking south-east. . . . The sea is invisible, except from the summit, and thus it was only by climbing to the top of Carmel, from the plateau where the altar may have stood, that the prophet's servant could have seen the little cloud," &c.] **And he went up, and looked, and said, There is nothing. And he said, Go again seven times.** [Cf. Josh. vi. 15—20; 2 Kings v. 14; Matt. xviii. 21; Psa. cxix. 164. The idea here is that of sufficiency, of completion, rather than, as elsewhere, of covenant. And yet it must be remembered that Elijah was only praying for what God had already promised to grant (ver. 1). This earnest prayer for rain under these circumstances suggests that the former prayer "that it might not rain" (James v. 17) had also been inspired of God. But it is worth considering whether Elijah's attitude was not one of reverent and assured expectation, as much as of prayer. When Rawlinson says that "the faithfulness and patience shown [by the servant] in executing this order without a murmur, imply devotedness of no common kind," he surely forgets that the drought had lasted for three years and a half, and that the servant had that day seen the fires of God descend at Elijah's prayer. It is inconceivable, under such circumstances, that any man could murmur.]

Ver. 44.—**And it came to pass at the seventh time, that he said, Behold, there ariseth a little cloud out of the sea, like a man's hand.** [כַף lit., *palm*, hollow of hand. Cf. Luke xii. 54, "When ye see the cloud (Gr. τὴν νεφέλην) arise out of the west, straightway ye say, There cometh a shower; and so it is." "Still in autumn the little cloud comes up like a man's hand and swells till huge thunder pillars are piled black and high above the mountains" (Conder). But it is not in Palestine alone that a little cloud on the horizon is frequently the harbinger of rain]. **And he said, Go up** [see note on ver. 42], **say unto Ahab, Prepare thy chariot** [Heb. *bind*], **and get thee down** [Keil, Stanley, and others assume that Ahab's chariot was waiting at the foot of the mountain. But it is to be noticed that the command to harness the horses precedes that to "go down." The writer *rode* down from *El Murahkah* to the plain, and it is quite conceivable that the royal chariot may have conveyed Ahab to the plateau of sacrifice and have waited for him there], **that the rain stop thee not.** [After heavy rain (גֶּשֶׁם) the Kishon, which "collects the whole drainage of this large basin" (Conder), the Great Plain, soon becomes an impassable swamp (Judg. v. 21), "I can tell you from experience that in wet seasons it (the Wâdy) is extremely muddy, and then the Kishon causes great tribulation to the muleteers. Rarely indeed do they get over it without some of their animals sticking fast in its oozy bottom" (Thomson, L. and B. ii. p. 218).]

Ver. 45.—**And it came to pass in the meanwhile** [Heb. *unto thus and unto thus*, *i.e.*, till now and then (cf. Exod. vii. 16; Josh. xvii. 14). Gesen., Bähr, *al.* support the rendering of the A. V. Ewald, Keil, *al.* understand "while the hand is being moved hither and thither," *i.e.*, very speedily. The practical difference is not great], **that the heaven was black with clouds and wind, and there was a great rain.** [" The cry of the boy from his mountain watch had hardly been uttered when the storm broke upon the plain " (Stanley). " The

storm " [over " the dark slate-coloured ridge of Carmel," witnessed by Conder in 1872] " burst suddenly, the rain descending with violence, hissing on the ground, as if not able to come down fast enough, and accompanied with gusts of wind, thunder, and lightning."] **And Ahab rode, and went to Jezreel.**

Ver. 46.—**And the hand of the Lord was on Elijah** [Same expression 2 Kings iii. 15; Ezek. i. 3; iii. 14; viii. 1; xxxiii. 22; cf. also Exod. ix. 3; Judg. ii. 15; Ruth i. 13; Acts xi. 21; xiii. 11. Some of the commentators understand the words of Divine *guidance*, some of a supernatural strengthening. There is no need to exclude either interpretation. An impulse from on high impelled him to "gird up his loins" and go with the king; a strength not his own sustained him whilst "he ran," &c. The distance across the plain to Jezreel is about fourteen miles; the royal chariot would drive furiously, and whatever fleetness and endurance the prophet had acquired in the wilds of Gilead, it seems hardly likely that, after the fatigues and excitement of that day, he would have been able, without the hand of the Lord upon him, to keep ahead of the chariot horses], **and he girded up his loins** [*i.e.*, gathered round his waist the *abba*, or "mantle"—the אַדֶּרֶת (cf. ch. xix. 13, 19; 2 Kings ii. 13, 14) was so-called from its ample size—which would otherwise have impeded his movements. Probably this, apart from the girdle, was his sole garment. (See Dict. Bib. vol. ii. p. 232)], **and ran before Ahab** [Thomson (vol. ii. p. 227) mentions an interesting illustration of this incident which he witnessed. The forerunners of Mohammed Ali Pasha " kept just ahead of the horses, no matter how furiously they were ridden, and in order to run with the greatest ease they not only girded their loins very tightly, but also tucked up their loose garments under the girdle." But such a spectacle is of common occurrence in the East. Kitto remarks that the *Shatirs* of Persia keep pace with ease with their masters' horses. They also are tightly girded. His object was apparently twofold. First, to honour the sovereign whom he had that day humbled in the presence of his subjects. The great prophet, by assuming the lowly office of a *foot*-man, or forerunner (see note on ch. i. 5), would give due reverence to the Lord's anointed, like Samuel on a somewhat similar occasion (1 Sam. xv. 30, 31). Secondly, he may have hoped by his presence near the king and court to strengthen any good resolves which the former might have made, and to further the work of reformation which he could not but hope the proceedings of that day would inaugurate. That this tribute of respect would be grateful to Ahab, who hitherto had only regarded Elijah as an adversary, it is impossible to doubt. And that Elijah believed he had struck a death-blow to the foreign superstitions fostered by the court, and especially by the queen, is equally certain. It is not clear, as Bähr assumes, that his servant accompanied him on the road. He may have rejoined him later on in the day or night] **to the entrance** [Heb. *until thou comest to.* The Arab aversion, which Elijah is supposed to have shared, to entering cities, has often been remarked. But there were other and deeper reasons why he should not adventure himself within the city. Probably the same guiding hand which led him to Jezreel impelled him to lodge out-side the walls. It was impossible to say what Jezebel, in her transports of rage, might do. After such a day, too, any prophet would shrink from familiar contact with men and from the strife of tongues] **of Jezreel.** [Ahab had a palace here (ch. xxi. 1). But Samaria was still the capital, and so remained till the captivity (ch. xxii. 37; 2 Kings xv. 13, 14; xvii. 5, 6). The selection of Jezreel as a royal residence is easily accounted for. It stands on " a knoll 500 feet high " (Conder), overlooking both the plain of Esdraelon and the valley of Jezreel. In fact, it is the finest situation in the " Great Plain." Hence perhaps its name "the sowing-place of God." See Stanley, S. and P. pp. 336 sqq.; Porter, p. 353; Dict. Bib. vol. i. p. 1080; Van de Velde, vol. ii. p. 370.]

HOMILETICS.

Vers. 3, 4.—*The Governor of Ahab's House.* There are few things in these books of Scripture more surprising and suggestive than the position of Obadiah in the palace of Ahab. Consider—

I. THE AGE. We have seen that during this reign (ch. xvi. 30, 33; xxi. 25), and especially in the capital city of Samaria (ch. xvi. 32), the wickedness of Israel had reached its zenith. From the accession of Jeroboam, and the schism which followed it, the northern kingdom had steadily gone from bad to worse, till its apostasy and impiety culminated under the malign influences of Ahab and Jezebel. Their joint reign marks a new departure in the religious history of the ten tribes. Hitherto men had worshipped the God of their fathers, though in an irregular and unauthorized way, and idolatry, though not unknown, had not been open and unblushing. Now, however, the whole nation, with but few exceptions, abandoned itself to the licentious worship of Phoenician gods, and the ancestral religion was proscribed, its altars were overthrown, and a determined effort was made to stamp out its prophets and professors.

II. THE PLACE. We should expect, consequently—what Elijah really believed to be the case (ch. xix. 10)—that to find a pious man we must search the land as with a lantern. We should expect to find some Abdiels, "faithful among the faithless found," but we should look for them away from the haunts of men, in " caves and dens of the earth," in the brook Cherith, or the cottage of Zarephath, or wandering about " in sheepskins and goatskins," &c. (Heb. xi. 37, 38). But we should hardly hope to find them in the cities of Israel, in the broad light of day, in conspicuous positions, and least of all should we look for them in Samaria, where Satan's seat was, the fortress and citadel of Baal.

Or if we were so sanguine, notwithstanding the godlessness of the times and the genius of the place, as to count on some saints in Samaria, we should never betake ourselves to the great men (Jer. v. 5); we should go in search of piety in the cottages of the poor. We should never dream of finding any followers of the Lord occupying an exalted station, living under the shadow of the palace, or in close contact with the determined and unscrupulous queen.

III. HIS POSITION. But if we were assured that even in Ahab's palace, under the same roof with Jezebel, a devout and steadfast servant of Jehovah was to be found, we should certainly have expected to find him in some insignificant servitor, some poor retainer of the place. That any high official, that a minister of state could retain his piety in that cesspool of corruption, that hotbed of idolatry and immorality, and at the very time that Jezebel was cutting off the Lord's prophets, would seem to us altogether out of the question. " What communion," we should ask, "hath light with darkness ? or what part hath he that believeth with an infidel ? "

IV. His piety. Yet we find that Obadiah, the intendant of the palace of Samaria, the trusted and faithful minister of Ahab, the "third ruler in the kingdom," " feared the Lord greatly" (ver. 3), and, though surrounded by Baal-worshippers, never bowed the knee to Baal; though risking his life by his devotion to Jehovah, yet served Him truly, and succoured His prophets.

We have a parallel to this, and a still more striking instance of piety under the most adverse and discouraging circumstances in the New Testament. We have something like it, indeed, in the case of Daniel and the three Hebrew children ; something approaching it in the case of Joanna, the wife of Chuza, Herod's steward (Luke viii. 3) ; but we find a still closer analogue in the saints of Cæsar's household (Phil. iv. 22).

When we remember that the saints of Rome were the talk, the admiration, the patterns of the early Christian Churches " throughout the whole world " (Rom. i. 8) ; that among the saints of Rome, those of the palace or of the barracks (Phil. i. 13) attached to Cæsar's palace on the Palatine, were conspicuous, at least (ch. iv. 22) for their charity, for the crowning Christian grace of φιλαδελφία, the stamp and seal royal of the saints (John xiii. 35 ; 1 John iv. 20) ; when we remember, too, that this was in Rome, at that period the very worst city in the world, the resort—their own writers being witness—of all the knaves and charlatans and libertines of the empire ; that this was in the year A.D. 63, when the palace of the Cæsars was occupied by Nero, of all those born of women perhaps the meanest, basest, most infamous, most profligate ; that this Nero was murderer of brother, murderer of mother, of wife, of paramour ; persecutor and butcher of the Christians, sworn foe of goodness and purity in every shape, patron and abettor of every kind of abomination, according to some the " Beast " of the Apocalypse ; when we consider that under his roof, in the pandemonium which he had created around him, *saints* were found, meek followers of the unspotted Christ, we cannot but be impressed with the fact that the wisdom of God has preserved for our encouragement two conspicuous instances—one under the Old Dispensation, one under the New—of fervent piety living and thriving in a palace under the most adverse circumstances, amid the overflowings of ungodliness. And these facts may suggest the following lessons :

1. "*Let every man, wherein he is called, there abide with God*" (1 Cor. vii. 20, 24). The temptation to desert our post, because of the difficulties, seductions, persecutions it affords, is peculiarly strong, because it presents itself under the garb of a religious duty. We think we shall " one day fall by the hand of Saul " (1 Sam. xxvii. 1). We fear the temptation may be too strong for us, and we consult, as we fancy, only for our safety, in flight. But we forget that " every man's life is a plan of God;" that we have been placed where we are by Him, and placed there to do His work. We forget also that His " grace is sufficient" for us ; that with every temptation He can make a way to escape (1 Cor. x. 13) ; that He will not suffer us to be tempted above that we are able to bear; and that flight under such circumstances must be mere cowardice and faithlessness. It was a great mistake of the hermits and the religious of a past age to leave the world because it was so wicked, for this was to take the salt out of the earth, and to leave it to corruption. If the men who alone can leaven society shut themselves up in a cloister or a study, it is simply leaving it to the devil to do his worst. This is not to fight, but to flee. Except these abide in the ship, how can it be saved ? (Acts xxvii. 31.) It is egregious selfishness to hide our candle under a bushel, lest perchance the blasts of temptation should extinguish it. Obadiah was called by the providence of God to be governor of Ahab's house. The post must have been one of extreme difficulty, of constant trial and imminent peril. We see from vers. 10, 14 the kind of man he had to deal with, and how, from day to day, he carried his life in his hand. But he did not desert the state of life into which it had pleased God to call him. He considered that he was there for some good purpose ; that he had a work to do which only he could do, and he resolved to stop and do his duty. Perhaps he remembered the ruler of Pharaoh's house, and the deliverance *he* wrought for Israel (Gen. xlv. 7, 8).

Anyhow, he waited and endured, and at length the opportunity came. When Jezebel would exterminate the Lord's prophets, then the steward of the palace understood why he had been placed in that perilous and responsible position. It was that he might save much people alive (Gen. l. 20). Then he did what, perhaps, only he could have done—took a hundred of the Lord's prophets, hid them in two caves, and fed them with bread and water.

2. *The saints make the best servants.* It is scarcely less strange to find Ahab employing Obadiah than to find Obadiah serving under Ahab. Some have seen herein a proof of the king's tolerance, but it is much more like a proof of his sagacity. Whether he knew of Obadiah's faith may be uncertain, but we may be sure that he had proved his fidelity. It was because Obadiah was " faithful in all his house " that he was retained in this position. It was not to Ahab's interest to have a Baal-worshipper at the head of his retainers. Bad men do not care to be served by their kind. They pay piety and probity the compliment—such as it is—of encouraging it in their dependants and children. They find, as Potiphar did, as Darius did, that the God-fearing bring a blessing with them (Gen. xxxix. 5). For if there is no special benediction of their basket and store, of their fruit and fold (Deut. xxviii. 4, 5), yet they are guarded against peculation and waste (Luke xvi. 1). How many, like Ahab, have found that those who share their sins or pleasures cannot be entrusted with their goods ; that if they would have faithful servants, they must have God-fearing ones. (See Krummacher, i. secs. 145—149.)

3. *It is only the power of God could keep men holy in Ahab's or Nero's palace.* Coleridge has somewhere said that there are two classes of Christian evidences— Christianity and Christendom ; the system in itself, its pure morality, its beneficent teachings, and its results, its conquests, and achievements in the world. For it is altogether beyond the power of human nature to work the moral changes which Christianity has wrought either to convert men or to preserve them from falling. That a man who is notorious in his neighbourhood, the talk and terror of the country side, a chartered libertine, an *âme damnée*, or even like St. Paul, a persecutor and injurious ; or like Augustine, or John Newton ; that such an one should be suddenly stopped, transformed, ennobled, should preach the faith which he once persecuted—this is very difficult to account for on human grounds. And that men with every temptation to sin, everything to lose and nothing to gain by godliness, worldly interest, pride, passion, shame, everything combining against religion— that these should, nevertheless, denying ungodliness and worldly lusts, live soberly, righteously, and godly (Titus ii. 12) in the Sodom around them—this is no less a miracle of Divine grace. The influences that preserved an Obadiah, a St. Paul, a Pudens, and Linus, and Claudia (2 Tim. iv. 21) must have been from above. We know only too well what human nature, unassisted by grace, is capable of. We know it tends inevitably, not to bear a rich crop of virtues, but, like the cereals, to degenerate, to run to seed. In Socrates and Seneca—" half-inspired heathens "— we see it at its best, and yet how wide the gulf between Nero's preceptor and the saints of Nero's household. When we see our nature, planted in a hotbed of grossness and profligacy, nevertheless yield the " peaceable fruits of righteousness," then we know that the hand of the great Husbandman must, if silently and unseen, yet assuredly, have been at work.

4. *If religion held its own in Ahab's or in Nero's court, it will hold its own and win its way anywhere.* How can we ever despair of our religion so long as we have such proofs that it is the "power of God unto salvation"? Society, both in England and on the continent of Europe, may be very godless ; it may be changing for the worse ; we may be preparing for an outbreak of Communism, Nihilism, Materialism, Atheism ; the masses in our large towns may be very brutal and besotted and animal, may be utterly estranged from religion in every shape ; but, whatever England is like, and whatever Europe is like, its state is nothing like so desperate as was that of Rome under Nero. The savages to whom we send our missionaries, again, no doubt they are debased, sensual, apathetic, or even hostile to our religion ; but are they really worse, is their case more hopeless, than that of Ahab's or Nero's subjects ? And if the days of persecution are not ended ; if in

China, and Melanesia, and Turkey the sword is still whetted against the Christian, can we find among them all a more truculent persecutor than Jezebel, a more savage and unprincipled inquisitor than Tigellinus. But we cannot pretend that our sufferings are anything like theirs. No longer are the prophets hunted like partridges; no longer are they clad in the skins of wild beasts, or dipped into cauldrons of pitch; no longer do we hear the sanguinary cry, *Christianos ad leones*. And yet, despite those terrible mockings and scourgings, those agonies in the amphitheatre, those privations in the caves, religion, in Samaria and in Rome alike, held its ground. In Israel, seven thousand true-hearted confessors would neither be tempted nor terrified into bowing the knee to Baal. In Italy, the blood of the martyrs was the seed of the Church; neither Nero, nor Decius, nor Diocletian could hinder the onward march of Christ's baptized host, and now it is matter of history how one day the empire woke up to find itself Christian.

5. *If men could be saints in Ahab's and Nero's palace, they may be saints anywhere.* How constantly do men plead the adverse circumstances in which they are placed as a reason why they cannot serve God. Sometimes it is a godless street or wicked hamlet; sometimes it is an irreligious household or infidel workshop; or their trade is such, their employers or associates are such, that they cannot live a godly life. But the example of Obadiah, the example of those saints of the Praetorium, convicts them of untruth and of cowardice. They cannot have greater temptations or fiercer persecutions than befell those Roman Christians. If *they* proved steadfast, and lived in sweetness and purity, which of us cannot do the same wherever we may be placed?

6. *The saints of Ahab's and Nero's courts shall rise up in judgment with this generation, and shall condemn it.* In a wicked city, in an impure court, through fire and blood, they kept the faith. Christianity is now established in the land. Kings are its nursing fathers. Its holy rites are celebrated freely and openly. Yet how many dishonour or deny it! how many are ashamed of their religion! With what shame will they meet the brave confessors of the past! They will need no condemnation from their Judge (Matt. xii. 41; John v. 45).

Vers. 17—20.—*The King and his Master.* For three and a half years king and prophet have not met (Luke iv. 25). For three and a half years, forty and two months, twelve hundred and sixty days (Rev. xi. 2, 3; xii. 6; xiii. 5; Dan. vii. 25), the mystical period of persecution and blasphemy, the plague of drought has afflicted the land. But now the time—God's "fulness of time"—has arrived for its removal. The time to favour Israel is come, and king and prophet meet again. It was an anxious moment for each of them. It was a critical moment in the history of the Church. Let us mark their words; let us observe how they bear themselves; we shall surely learn something from their carriage and discourse.

I. *The king goes to meet the prophet.* Elijah would seem to have waited in the place where Obadiah left him until Ahab appeared. He is not going to take the place of a suppliant. Subject though he is, he is Ahab's superior. He has a commission higher and nobler than the king's. It is his task to reprove the king; hence, in a manner, he summons him before him. The proud monarch who has scoured all lands in search of him must now humble himself to go before the prophet. "Behold Elijah."

II. *Ahab fears to meet Elijah.* It is true he is the first to speak, and accuses the prophet of troubling the land; but we may well believe that, despite his brave words when Jezebel was at his side, and the cheap courage he manifested when he had the court and the priests of Baal at his back, he must have looked forward to this meeting with something like dismay. He had good cause for misgivings and fears. First, he was to encounter a true prophet, and one vested with supernatural powers. Of one thing he could have no doubt, as to the "sure word of prophecy" in Elijah's lips. No less than the Sareptan, he had proved that the word of the Lord in Elijah's lips was truth (ch. xvii. 24). "*He* spake and it was done." He had denounced a drought, and it had come to pass, a drought beyond all precedent, a drought which still cursed the country, and was at that moment taxing its resources (ver. 5). And of another thing Ahab must have been equally certain, that this drought was no chance which had happened him. The coincidence between the word and the event negatived that idea. He must see in it the finger of God; he must recognize in the prophet the power of God. But (2) the man for whom he had been searching over hill and dale, in town and hamlet, in his own and in adjoining lands, now proposes a meeting. Clearly, then, *he* is not afraid. He almost compels an interview—"I will show myself unto him to-day." (3) Even if Ahab ascribed his power to magic or witchcraft, still men tremble in the presence of a sorcerer. We cannot wonder, therefore, if his courage almost failed him, and if he looked forward to the meeting with something like dread. But he remembers his imperious consort; he thinks how full of threatening and fury he himself has been, and he feels he must put on a bold front; he must carry himself proudly; he must tax the prophet with wrong-doing. And so, when at last they meet, the king is the first to speak. "Art thou here?" he cries, almost frightened at the sound of his own voice. "Art thou here, thou troubler of Israel?" Words have often served to conceal men's thoughts, often been a veil to hide their abject fears.

Now, we have heard words like these, we have read of them in other mouths than Ahab's. It is a common charge against the prophets and people of God. The saints are always in the wrong. It is always they who "turn the world upside down" (Acts xvii. 6, 8); always they who "do exceedingly trouble our city" (*ib.*, xvi. 20). Our Lord was accused of sedition. The first Christians were called "enemies of the human race." All manner of evil is said against them falsely. Ahab only speaks "after his kind." He saw that Elijah had been instrumental in bringing down the drought and the terrible famine which accompanied it. He never pauses to ask what moved Elijah to call for a drought; what caused Elijah's God to send it. The herald is accused as the cause of the war. "There is nothing new under the sun." The same charge is made, and with the same unreason and perversity at the present day. The lamb must have fouled the stream, whichever way it flows. If the Baptist comes neither eating nor drinking, they say, "He hath a devil." If the Son of man comes eating and drinking, they say, "Behold a gluttonous man and a winebibber." If we pipe, they will not dance: if we mourn, they will not lament (Matt. xi. 16 sqq.)

III. *Elijah denounces the king to his face.* "I have not troubled Israel, but thou," &c. "The righteous are bold as a lion." There is no trace of fear in these words. The truth has nothing to fear. And the truth it was then, and is now, that the trouble and suffering of the world spring out of sin, out of forgetting and forsaking God. If men will leave Him out of their thoughts and lives, their sorrows cannot but be multiplied (Psa. xvi. 4). It is like leaving the sun out of our solar sytem—the world would revert to primæval chaos. The French revolution shows the result of the negation of God. Communism and Nihilism do the same. "There is no peace to the wicked." But not only do they "pierce *themselves* through with many sorrows," but they trouble *Israel* (Eph. vi. 16), the peaceful people of God. But for them this world would be a Paradise. It is they who make wretched homes and broken hearts. It is they who necessitate our armies, our police, our gaols, our poor rates. It is they who sometimes make us wonder, with some of the ancients, whether this earth is not really a place of punishment. But for them, and the confusion and misery they cause, men would never ask "whether life is worth living;" still less conclude that "the greatest good is never to have been born into the world, and the next to die out of it as soon as possible." We are entitled, therefore, like Elijah, to denounce the godless and the vicious as the enemies of society, as conspirators against the world's peace and prosperity. "The only common disturber of men, families, cities, kingdoms, worlds, is sin." It is one of the arguments for our holy religion that, sincerely practised, it ensures "the greatest possible happiness of the greatest possible number." It is the brand of Atheism that it brings trouble, uncleanness, selfishness, suffering, at its heels.

IV. *The king endures the upbraiding of the prophet.* To Elijah's "Thou art the man," he makes no reply. He is taxed with the ruin of his country, and is speechless. His courage has soon evaporated. He who would accuse Elijah cannot defend himself. Though anointed king, he is weak and helpless (2 Sam. iii. 39), and owns his subject his superior. How soon have they changed places! Ahab has been hunting for the prophet's life, has been vowing vengeance upon him if found. Now he has found him, and he trembles before him. And this because conscience has made him a coward. He knows in his inmost heart that Elijah has spoken the truth; that God is on his side; and he is afraid of him, just as Saul, giant and king though he was, was afraid of the stripling David. And men are still afraid of a true saint of God. They regard him with almost a superstitious dread. Sometimes it is fanaticism they fear; but sometimes it is the holiness which condemns their sinfulness (Luke v. 8).

V. *The king obeys the prophet's commands.* Elijah might be king from the commands he issues. "Send and gather to me"—observe "to me"—"all Israel unto Mount Carmel, and the prophets of Baal," &c. Did Ahab know why they were wanted? Did Elijah then tell him of the ordeal by fire? It is extremely improbable. It is probable that, though Ahab hoped for rain, still he anticipated no good to his or Jezebel's prophets from this meeting. He would have disobeyed this command if he dared. But he has found his master, and it is in the uncouth, untutored Gileadite. We are reminded of Herod and John, of Ambrose and Theodosius, of Savonarola and Lorenzo de' Medicis, of Mary of Scots and John Knox. At Elijah's bidding, his posts go throughout the land. The prophet has had a triumph already. Truth and the consciousness of right, and the power of God's presence, have proved greater than sceptre and crown.

Vers. 21—40.—*Israel's Conversion.* It has been remarked elsewhere that in the history of the Israelitish people we may see pourtrayed the trials and experiences of a Christian soul.

And not only is that true of this history as a whole, but it also holds good of various periods of that history, of various crises in the nation's life. It holds good of that great crisis recorded in this chapter. For from the conversion of Israel on the day of Carmel, we may gather some lessons as to the true doctrine of conversion, the conversion of a *man* from sin to righteousness, from the power of Satan unto God. From the turning of *their* heart back again (ver. 37), we may learn something as to the change to be wrought in our own. Let us consider, therefore—
1. What it was. 2. How it was accomplished. 3. What were its results.

I. WHAT IT WAS. It was—
1. *A change of mind.* It was a μετάνοια, a change of thought and view. Of course it was more than this, but this it was pre-eminently and primarily. On that day of the Lord's power (Psa. cx. 3) the views of king and people were altered. The king and court—and Ahab was not without his ministers and courtiers to witness the ordeal—had many of them believed in Baal, and served him. It is true some had wavered (ver. 21) between Baal and Jehovah; but the people as a whole had held Baal to be Lord and God, prince of nature, source of life, not to the exclusion of Jehovah, but along with Him. The first thing for them to learn, consequently, was that an "idol is nothing in the world;" that Baal was no more than a log (ch. xv. 12), a senseless stock, powerless for good or evil. It is clear that Elijah's first object was to demonstrate before this great convocation on Carmel the absolute impotence and nothingness of their idol deities. He had been proving for three years past and more that Baal had no dominion over the clouds; that he could not discharge that primary function of a God, viz., to control the course of nature, and give his votaries rain from heaven and fruitful seasons (Levit. xxvi. 4; Deut. xi. 17; 1 Sam. xii. 17; 1 Kings viii. 36; Psa. lxviii. 9; Jer. v. 24; Joel ii. 23; Amos iv. 7; Acts xiv. 17). And now he offers to prove that Baal has as little power over the fire, that recognized emblem and property of God (Gen. iii. 24; Exod. xix. 18; Levit. ix. 24; Deut. iv. 36); only known to men, according to an ancient tradition, because it had been stolen from heaven. He will also prove that the Lord whom he serves can give both fire and rain; and by these facts he will gain their understandings, the assent of their minds to the

conclusion that the Lord alone is God. This was his first task, his main object. And this is the first step towards the conversion of a soul—that it should "*know* the only true God and Jesus Christ," &c. At the basis of conversion lies the knowledge of God and of self. There is a knowledge which "bloweth up;" while "charity buildeth up" (1 Cor. viii. 1). There is also a γνῶσις which is life eternal. He is the converted man who can say, "We have *known* and believed the love that God hath to us" (1 John iv. 16). It was a favourite saying of St. Theresa that if men really knew God, they could not help loving and serving Him. By nature they do not know Him; they have false and unworthy ideas of Him; they think Him to be altogether such an one as themselves (Psa. l. 21), because the devil, the "slanderer" (διάβολος), who is not only the "accuser of the brethren" before God (Rev. xii. 10; Job i. 9), but also the accuser of God before the brethren (Gen. iii. 5), poisons their minds against God, traduces and misrepresents Him, so that the opening of the eyes (Acts ix. 18; xvi. 14; xxvi. 18; Luke xxiv. 45; Eph. i. 18), the enlightening of the mind, the shining of the glorious gospel of Christ in the darkened heart (2 Cor. iv. 4, 6)—this is the beginning of our conversion. A conversion which rests, not on knowledge, but emotion, cannot be real and lasting.

2. *A change of affection.* Believing Baal to be God, they had yielded him their homage, their service. The heart, for the most part (Rom. vii. *passim*), goes with the understanding. If the latter be firmly persuaded, the former is enlisted. "As he thinketh in his heart, so is he" (Prov. xxiii. 7). Those who regarded Baal as their helper and benefactor could not help reverencing and loving him (ch. xix. 18; cf. Job xxxi. 27). But when they learnt his impotence; when they saw that they had been deceived (Acts viii. 9); when it was forced upon them that these things were dumb idols, lying vanities, and that the Lord alone had made them, sustained them, blessed them, then there was a strong revulsion of feeling; their heart was turned back again; their affections went forth to Him whom they had slighted and wronged. And so it is in our conversion. It is not a purely intellectual process; it stirs the lowest depths of the heart. When a man realizes that God is not hate, but love; that he is a Father, not a hard master; that the devil has deceived him and enslaved him, while promising him liberty; that the world has cheated him, and its pleasures have mocked him, it would be strange indeed if this apocalypse did not affect the whole man; if the knowledge did not lead at once to loathing and love; loathing for the enemy who has played us so false and slandered our gracious Father; love for Him who first loved us, and sealed His love by pain and sacrifice. And with the new-born love there will be compunction; grief that we have grieved the Eternal Love. This is what we call repentance. It is a part of the μετάνοια.

3. *A change of conduct.* If the head does not always carry the heart with it, the heart always controls and governs the man. It is the mainspring of our nature. The heart is the helm that turns the ship "whithersoever the governor listeth" (James iii. 4). We have no record, indeed, of any permanent change in the religious life of Israel, and it has been too readily assumed that all the congregation that witnessed the descent of the fire, and confessed their belief in Jehovah, straightway lapsed into paganism. But it is clear that, for a time at least, there was a change in their conduct. The readiness with which they slew the priests of Baal shows it. Indeed, without this there would have been no conversion at all. For that word, though constantly used in a purely conventional and non-natural sense—to express, in fact, a mystical change in the man, a peculiar conscious transition which the heart is supposed to experience—really describes a change in the life and conduct (Acts xv. 3; Luke xxii. 32; Matt. xviii. 3; James v. 19). The secret inner change the Scripture always calls "repentance" (Matt. ix. 13; Luke xv. 7; Acts xx. 21; Rom. ii. 4; Heb. vi. 6, &c.) Conversion is the outward and visible change resulting from the former, and corresponding with it. Hence St. Peter's words, "Repent and be converted" (Acts iii. 19). This conversion of Israel was not an emotion, an experience, an ecstasy, but a change from Baal-worship to Jehovah-worship; from impurity and devilry (Deut. xxxii. 17; 1 Cor.

x. 20) to righteousness; it was a turning "from idols to serve the living and true God" (1 Thess. i. 9).

II. How was this conversion brought about?

1. *By the ministry of a prophet.* The appeal of Elijah (ver. 21) had some influence; the works he wrought—he was a prophet of deed—had much more. He was God's messenger to turn the disobedient to the wisdom of the just (Luke i. 17). We are reminded here of the place which the ministry of the word occupies in the New Dispensation. "How shall they hear without a preacher?" "We preach unto you that ye should turn from these vanities," &c. (Acts xiv. 15). No one says that a preacher is indispensable, but no one can deny that he is God's ordinary instrument for the conversion of men (1 Cor. i. 18, 21).

2. *By the chastening of God.* The drought and the famine prepared their stubborn hearts for Elijah's appeal, and disposed them to decision. At another time he might have addressed Israel in vain. And sorrow and pain, privation and bereavement are still not unfrequently found to dispose the rebellious mind to hear the message of God. "When thy judgments are in the earth, the inhabitants of the world will learn righteousness" (Isa. xxvi. 9; cf. ver. 16).

3. *By the terrors of the Lord.* It is the "still small voice" wins most for God; but the wind and earthquake and fire have their preparation work to do. The law preceded the gospel, and even the gospel has its stern threatenings. Apostolic preaching did not overlook the terror of the Lord (2 Cor. v. 11). We can hardly doubt that fear played some part in the conversion. As on a former occasion, the giving of the law (Exod. xx. 18), so at this solemn vindication of the law, "the people were afraid by reason of the fire" (Deut. v. 5). Why, then, should we call that common which God hath cleansed? Why discard an instrument which God has sanctioned?

4. *By a supernatural token.* For the fire was *the* turning-point in this conversion. It was at the awful "sign from heaven," this evidence of a Divine Presence, that the great cry arose, "The Lord, He is the God." The bones were dry until the breath came into them. And may not this remind us that there is a supernatural element in our conversion too? Man cannot change himself. Only by the power of the Holy Spirit, the Spirit which descended in *fire* (Acts ii. 3; Matt. iii. 11), can the eyes be opened, the heart softened, repentance wrought, or true and lasting conversion to God be accomplished. This is the dispensation of the Spirit. It is His to convince of sin (John xvi. 8), to testify of Christ (John xv. 26), to renew the heart (Titus iii. 5), to give peace and joy (Gal. v. 22).

5. *After prayer to God.* Not only the prayer of vers. 36, 37, offered before the restored altar of God (ver. 30); Elijah had prayed for many years. The discipline of drought was an answer to his prayer. Nor can we think that he was alone in his petitions. The seven thousand would assuredly pray for the regeneration of their country. The triumph of Carmel is the answer to those cries of God's elect (Luke xviii. 7). And prayer is still one of the instruments of our conversion. It is significant how prayer is mentioned in connection with the example of Elias, and with conversion in James v. 17—20. Nor is the mention of prayer in connection with St. Paul's conversion less instructive (Acts ix. 11). It is one step the soul takes towards God; and by persevering in prayer the goal is reached, for "Every one that asketh, receiveth" (Matt. vii. 8). Whosoever shall *call* on the name of the Lord shall be saved (Acts ii. 21). A prayer of half a dozen words once sufficed for justification (Luke xviii. 14).

6. *It was the result of a sudden decision.* "How long halt ye?" &c. He will have them make up their minds one way or the other. It is better to be cold than lukewarm (Rev. iii. 16). We cannot serve two masters. How many conversions are deferred because men will not look facts in the face! That is all the preacher asks of them. "If there is a God, then serve Him. If there is a judgment, then prepare for it." Decision of character is necessary to the great change. When the prodigal says, "I will arise," the first step has been taken. And "it is only the first step that costs."

III. WHAT WERE ITS RESULTS? It is well to ask this question, for some forget that conversion is not the end, but the beginning. It is the entrance on the life of reconciliation and obedience; it is the door to sanctification and perfection. This conversion was (1) evidenced by—

1. *Obedience.* The law enjoined that the false prophet should be put to death (Deut. xii. 1—11). The sin of seducing the Lord's people was so heinous that it merited a capital punishment. It has been objected against Elijah that, in the massacre of these 400 men, he displayed a sanguinary and revengeful spirit. But it would have been strange if he, the restorer of the law, had ignored one of its provisions. We should have suspected this conversion had the false prophets been spared. "This sacrifice was no less pleasing to God than that other." For the true convert sets himself to do God's will. Whatever grace and favour God may have showed him cannot release him from the discharge of duty. He must still "keep the commandments" if he would enter into life (Matt. xix. 17). Obedience is the touchstone of conversion (Luke vi. 46; John xiv. 21).

2. *Watchfulness.* No doubt one reason why the false prophets were put out of the way was that they might no longer be able to tempt God's people. The convert will be careful to avoid all occasions of sin; he will cut off the right hand that causes him to offend. He will keep himself that the wicked one touch him not (1 John v. 18). If strong drink has been his snare, he will abstain; whatever his besetting sin, he will put it away. But (2) it was followed by—

3. *Blessing.* After the conversion came the rain, and a renewal of prosperity and plenty (James v. 18). Not until the people had turned to Him with all their hearts, could He "be jealous for his land, and pity his people" (Joel ii. 12, 18). The drought, the punishment of apostasy, was removed on their repentance. Once more the thirsty land drank in the grateful showers; once more a plentiful rain refreshed God's inheritance, and the land brought forth its increase (James v. 18)— a picture this of the blessings which attend the reconciled soul. "Rivers of living waters." "The water of life freely." "The fruit of the Spirit." "The peaceable fruits of righteousness."

Vers. 41—45.—*Effectual Fervent Prayer.* It is pre-eminently in the matter of *prayer* that Elijah is proposed to us as an example in the New Testament. From the long list of Hebrew saints and worthies *he* has been selected by St. James (v. 17, 18) to prove and illustrate the proposition that "the prayer of a righteous man availeth much in its working" (ver. 16, Revised Version). His prayers for *drought* are not mentioned by our historian, but his prayer for *rain* may not unreasonably be supposed to be referred to in the account of vers. 42—45. Let us notice its more prominent features.

1. *It was the prayer of a righteous man.* The prayers of unrighteous men are sometimes heard (Luke xviii. 14; 2 Chron. xxxiii. 19), but only their prayers for grace and pardon. The intercessions of the wicked for others are of no avail, any more than the prayers of the impenitent for themselves. "If I regard iniquity in my heart, the Lord will not hear me" (Psa. lxvi. 18). Common sense teaches that God is not likely to grant the requests of impenitent rebels. "To the wicked God saith, What hast thou to do" with intercession? "Get thee to the prophets of thy father," &c. (2 Kings iii. 13). "Go and cry unto the gods which ye have chosen" (Judg. x. 14). But "he will fulfil the desire of them that fear him" (Psa. cxlv. 19).

2. *It was the prayer of a man of like passions with us.* We are not to think that Elias stood on a pedestal apart from the rest of his kind. He is not pictured to us, as are the heroes of so many biographies, as perfect. We are not sure that that great "day of Carmel" passed without sin. We are quite sure that he betrayed fear and unbelief in his flight, impatience and discontent in the desert. Yet his prayers availed much. Let us, therefore, though compassed about with infirmity, and stained with many sins of ignorance and imperfection, come boldly to the throne of grace.

3. *It was fervent.* "He prayed with prayer" (προσευχῇ προσηύξατο), says St. James. His attitude reveals its fervency—it was that of complete self-abstraction, of intense

inward entreaty. We must seek "with all the heart" (Psa. cxix. 2; Jer. xxiv. 7). Seeking *early* (Prov. i. 28; viii. 17; Psa. lxiii. 1; lxxviii. 34; Isa. xxvi. 9) does not mean seeking in youth, but seeking eagerly, intently. Compare the expression, "rising up early," &c. (Jer. vii. 13; xxv. 3, 4; xxvi. 5; xxxv. 15, &c.) Some one has said that there are not many persons who really and truly *pray* half a dozen times in their lives. We offer up formal or lukewarm petitions, and then marvel that we receive no answers. Prayer must be ἐκτενής (Luke xxii. 44). It is not that God is hard to persuade; it is that He will have us mean what we say. There is no difficulty with Him. We are straitened in ourselves.

4. *It was persevering.* He was not daunted by the laconic "nothing" (Heb. *not aught*) of his servant. "Go again seven times." It is not enough to pray; we must "pray and not faint" (Luke xviii. 1; Eph. vi. 18; Col. iv. 2). We must "diligently seek him" (Heb. xi. 6). St. Paul besought the Lord thrice (2 Cor. xii. 8), after the example, it is probable, of our Blessed Lord (Matt. xxvi. 44). Compare the example of Abraham (Gen. xviii. 23 sqq.) Daniel prayed three times a day (Dan. vi. 10). The "seven times" of Elijah means that he will pray until the covenant God hears his petitions (cf. Levit. iv. 6, 17; viii. 11; xiv. 16).

5. *It was touching God's kingdom.* This is the proper subject for our prayers (Matt. vi. 33). We may have doubts whether some of the blessings we would fain crave are good for us, but we always ask "according to his will" when we pray, "Thy kingdom come." Our prayers for rain or fine weather are often selfish. Elijah only desired the drought, only supplicated for rain, as a means of influencing Israel and advancing God's work. It is partly the selfishness of our prayers which has led men to question the efficacy of all prayer. If men want to have their own way with the elements, or to make God's power further their private ends, is it strange if He declines to hear them? If we are to "obtain our petitions," we must "ask those things that please him."

6. *It was believing.* He never doubts the promise of ch. xviii. 1. He has already announced the rain to Ahab, before he prays for it. Similarly our Lord gave thanks at the grave of Lazarus: "I thank thee that thou hast heard me" (John xi. 41), just as if the dead man had already come to life again. We must ask in faith (James i. 6, 7; Matt. xxi. 21, 22; Mark ix. 23). No wonder if God does not hear the petitions of the man who doubts whether God is, or is the rewarder of those who seek Him. Before we pray we should at least be clear that there is One who hears and can help us. Unbelief makes God a liar.

7. *It was humble.* "Cast himself down upon the earth." What self-abasement before God! And he was heard in that he feared (Heb. v, 7). God has respect unto the lowly, and giveth grace to the humble (James iv. 6; 1 Peter v. 5; Psa. ix. 12; x. 17).

8. *It was in the Holy Ghost* (Jude 20). This prayer was first inspired. Elijah would never presume to ask either for drought or rain, unless the prayer had been put into his heart. As he mused in the wilds of Gilead over the apostasy of Israel, and vexed his righteous soul with the news of the Baal-worship, he felt constrained to cry to God, as we find His saints constantly doing, to awake, to make bare His arm, to vindicate His outraged honour. And what could he pray for, except that God would enforce the penalties He had Himself denounced? His prayer for drought is the outcome of his zeal for God's law, with which God had Himself inspired him. And we, too, are promised supernatural help and guidance in our prayers (Rom. viii. 26, 27; Jude 20).

9. *It availed much.* It opened the windows of heaven. "There was a great rain." It gave life to those who were sitting in the shadow of death. "The earth brought forth her fruit." The desolate land became as Eden. Man and beast drank and lived.

10. *It availed immediately.* While he was yet speaking, God heard (Isa. lxv. 24). If that word is ever true, *Bis dat qui cito dat*, it was true of this occasion. Indeed, the answer almost anticipated the prayer (ch. xviii. 1, 41). God is more ready to give than we to pray.

HOMILIES BY VARIOUS AUTHORS.

Vers. 1—6.—*The Cry for Life.* For three years and six months the heavens were as brass. Throughout the summers the sun glared and flamed in a cloudless sky, and the temperature, even at night, never sank to the dew-point. Throughout the winters, if the temperature reached that point, the elements were so boisterous that no dew could settle upon the herbage, and the winds carried the aqueous vapour away to other lands. In the absence of dew and rain, vegetation, excepting only that near rivers or fringing streams fed from the deepest springs, was scorched and blasted. The mortality, therefore, amongst animals was frightful, and men suffered incredible things. The agony of distress had now risen to such a pitch that throughout the land there was one earnest, plaintive cry for life.

I. Some cried for life to nature. 1. *Such was the case with Ahab.* (1) He had worshipped Baal, the fire of nature. But Baal was now punishing his votaries. Such is the manner in which the "god of this world" repays his dupes. (2) Yet did not Ahab repent of his folly. For, instead of seeking the living God, who was proving Himself the superior of Baal, he divides the land between himself and the governor of his house, to search for herbage. (3) Note also the heartlessness of the idolater. He is more concerned for his *stud* than for his *people.* "Peradventure we may find grass to save the *horses* and *mules* alive, that we lose not all the *beasts.*" 2. *He was a specimen of a class* (1) His queen was of the same way of thinking. She had been brought up to worship Baal. She had a masculine temper and swayed the mind of her husband. (2) The courtiers and the majority of the nation, who thought more of court fashion than of the holy service of Jehovah, bowed the knee to Baal.

II. Others cried for life to God. 1. *Of this number was Elijah.* (1) He recognized God as above nature, when he announced that there would be a departure from the ordinary course of nature in the withholding of dew and rain for successive years. Still he recognizes this when he shows himself to Ahab, believing that God would now give rain (ch. xvii. 1; xviii. 1, 2). (2) He recognized God as above nature before these assurances, for he received them in answer to faithful prayer (see James v. 17, 18). This is not mentioned in the history, but implied in his character as a man of God. Note: A man of God is a man of prayer. 2. *Obadiah also was of this number.* (1) He "feared the Lord greatly." This arose from the strength of his faith. We cannot fear that in which we do not believe. (2) His faith was fruitful in good works. He screened one hundred of the Lord's prophets from the violence of Jezebel, and sustained them. "Bread and water," like "daily bread" in the Lord's prayer, is an expression for things needful for the body. And in thus sheltering and nourishing the servants of God, Obadiah hazarded not only the loss of his situation, but also of his head. (3) One who feared the Lord greatly after this fashion would pray to Him. *Piety* would move him to it. *Patriotism* also would move him at this juncture. 3. *There were many more who cried to God.* (1) There were the "prophets of the Lord" preserved by Obadiah, and doubtless others also who escaped the vigilance of Jezebel. These would cry *to God* for life. (2) And if there were so many prophets, or sons of the prophets, there would be a considerable number of devout persons in Israel notwithstanding the abounding apostasy (see ch. xix. 18). There is a great deal of goodness where men little expect to find it.

God is the source of life, not only to the body, but also to the soul. Let us seek to Him for life.—J. A. M.

Vers. 7—16.—*The Servant of the Lord.* Such is the meaning of Obadiah's name; and so truly descriptive of his character is it that we may take him as a typical servant of God.

I. He feared the Lord from his youth. 1. *Piety is not natural.* (1) On the contrary, we inherit a depraved heart (Gen. v. 3; Psa. li. 5; Rom. v. 12; Eph.

ii. 3). (2) And this depravity is complete (Gen. vi. 5; Isa. i. 5, 6; Rom. iii. 9—19).
(3) Life is only tolerable through the meliorating influences of the " gospel of the
grace of God." To these must be attributed whatever seems good in unconverted
men (Rom. i. 28—32). 2. *Grace is free.* (1) All are *directly* the subjects of its
illuminations, restraints, and encouragements (John i. 9 ; 1 Cor. xii. 7). (2) Some
are *indirectly* specially favoured. Being surrounded by Christian influences.
Being children of godly parents. (3) These opportunities, if duly improved, will
infallibly lead to salvation (Titus ii. 11—14). 3. *Those who fear God from their
youth have great advantages.* (1) They have not given evil habits time to consolidate into rigidity. Time is necessary to this, for habits are strengthened by
repetition. The hard crystallization of bad habits renders the conversion of old
sinners very difficult. Therefore, how few are such conversions, comparatively !
(2) They have a splendid opportunity of founding a strong character of goodness.
When the habit of resisting temptation is formed, it becomes more and more
natural and easy to resist. Hence, like Obadiah, who " feared the Lord from his
youth," they will come to fear Him " greatly."

II. HE FEARED THE LORD GREATLY. See the manifestation of this in his—1.
Respect for the ambassador of God. (1) He "knew Elijah." Probably he had
been present when the prophet warned the king that his fire-god would be made
to punish his votaries in the absence of dew and rain (ch. xvii. 1). The godly,
having sympathy with the ministers of God, are quick to recognize them. (2) He
" fell on his face before him." This was the form of a most respectful salutation.
He honoured in him that God whose ambassador he was. Obadiah feared the
Lord too greatly to give to any creature the homage due to God alone. (3) He
addressed him reverently, " My lord Elijah." And he spoke of himself as " thy
servant." This was proper on his part ; but we note how Elijah transferred the
style to Ahab—" Go tell *thy lord,* Behold, Elijah is here." 2. *Kindness to the
servants of God.* (1) Through the sin of Jeroboam the priests and Levites went
into Judah (see 2 Chron. xi. 13, 14). To supply their lack in Ephraim, prophets'
colleges were established. The students in these colleges were called " sons of the
prophets " (see 2 Kings ii. 3, 5, 7). (2) These, together with their masters, or
" fathers," were probably the objects of Jezebel's resentment when Elijah could
not be found. They are called " prophets of the Lord " (ver. 13 ; compare ch.
xxii. 35, 36, 11). (3) At the time of that persecution Obadiah sheltered and fed
one hundred of these. This he did at the hazard of his life. Because he feared
the Lord greatly, he feared not the wrath of the king (compare Heb. xi. 23, 27).
3. *Faith in the power of God.* (1) He believed that Jehovah might raise a wind
that could carry Elijah away from the power of Ahab. He doubtless knew that
Enoch had been translated into the heavens, and may have known of examples of
translations from one locality to another, not recorded in the earlier Scriptures
(compare 2 Kings ii. 11—16 ; Ezek. iii. 14; Acts viii. 39). (2) A being who could
do such wonders, and whose power was now terribly manifest in the drought, was
greatly to be feared (see Matt. x. 28; Luke xii. 5). (3) But while God is of all
enemies the most formidable, He is an Almighty Friend.

III. HE FAITHFULLY SERVED HIS KING. 1. *God-fearing men make good citizens.*
(1) Wicked as Ahab was, he preferred Obadiah to the courtiers of Jezebel in the
high office of chamberlain. (2) This is not a solitary case. Joseph over the house
of Pharaoh. Daniel in the house of the kings of Babylon. Christians were in the
household even of Nero. (3) The qualities of a servant of the Lord—truth,
honour, diligence—are those sought after for places of trust. " Godliness is profitable unto all things " (1 Tim. iv. 8 ; Isa. lviii. 14). 2. *God preserves them in their
faithfulness.* (1) Service in a licentious court Obadiah would not have chosen.
But he is in it and maintains his integrity. They that fear the Lord need not go
out of the world. (2) They have a testimony for God. (3) They have opportunities
of serving the servants of the Lord.

Let us not murmur at our providential lot. God can change it if He see fit.
If He does not change it, then He has a purpose in it which we should endeavour
to fulfil.—J. A. M.

Vers. 17, 18.—*The Troubler.* Elijah, who during the terrible drought was concealed, now, at the word of the Lord, came forth to show himself to Ahab, as God was about to give rain. What a meeting! One of the worst of kings with one of the noblest of prophets. What confrontings will there be in the great day of judgment! Here each charges the other with being the troubler of Israel. Observe, then—

I. THAT THE WICKED SEEK TO MALIGN THE GOOD. 1. *Ahab accused Elijah.* (1) He assumed that all the horrors of the famine were the work of the prophet, and therefore sought to slay him. How many precious lives, in all ages, have been sacrificed to the theories of tyrants. (2) This persecutor was terribly in earnest. He sought the prophet in Israel. Then in neighbouring kingdoms. He even took an oath of the kingdoms that they did not shelter him. It were well for the world if men were as earnest in good as they are in evil. (3) But God can hide His servants from the fury of their adversaries. In the solitudes of Cherith. In the stir of Zarephath. (4) Now Ahab accuses the prophet to his face. But see how his courage cools in the presence of the man of God. He frames his accusation mildly in the form of a question, "Art thou he that troubleth Israel?" Conscience makes tyrants tremble. 2. *He found a pretext.* (1) Theorists can easily find pretexts for tyranny. Ahab seized upon Elijah's words (ch. xvii. 1), and drew his own inference. (2) As these words were verified to the letter, the tyrant saw, or affected to see, his theory confirmed. This kind of reasoning is very common. (3) Why did he not accuse God? Elijah acted as the servant of God. He feared to do this in *form,* though he did it in *fact* (see Prov. xiv. 31; Matt. x. 40—42; xxv. 40, &c.; Acts v. 39; ix. 1—15; Heb. vi. 10). 3. *He had a motive.* (1) Why did not Ahab accuse himself? His conscience no doubt did this for him. (2) But he could not afford publicly to bear the odium of having brought the miseries of the famine upon his people. (3) Therefore he shifts the responsibility on to the shoulders of the prophet. How essentially does the spirit of the lie enter into all sin!

II. TRUTH COMES HOME IN DUE TIME. 1. *Goodness will be vindicated.* (1) It may suffer long under the reproaches of liars. This is permitted because God is long-suffering. He makes the trial a blessing to "those who are exercised thereby." (2) But God is jealous for His servants. Therefore the triumphing of the wicked is but for a season. If the vindication takes not place in this world it certainly will in the next. (3) Elijah had his opportunity. He repudiated the imputation of Ahab. Good men are true patriots. The trial on Carmel settled the question. 2. *Sin will be shamed.* (1) Let it only be brought home, and it will cover the sinner with confusion. (2) "Thou and thy father's house" have troubled Israel "in that ye have forsaken the commandments of the Lord." Complicity in the sin of Jeroboam is specified here. This sin was a breach of the first and second commandments of the decalogue. It was also a forsaking of the Levitical law, which prescribed ceremonies that were but parodied in Ephraim. This offence was carried to its height in the statutes of the house of Ahab which were those of Omri (see Micah vi. 16). (3) "And *thou* hast followed Baalim." This was a sin introduced by Ahab himself, no doubt prompted by Jezebel. The way of error is from bad to worse.

Sin is the troubler of humanity. It invaded the tranquillity of Eden and broke it up. It brought down judgments of God upon individuals and communities. Upon Cain. Upon the antediluvians. Upon the cities of the plain. Upon Israel. It has provoked wars, in whose wake came pestilences and famines. It troubles the abyss of hell.—J. A. M.

Vers. 19—21.—*Christ or Belial?* Here is a curious phenomenon. A monarch, who had searched all kingdoms for a prophet that he might reek anger upon his life, now sought out and confronted by that prophet, and submitting to his orders to call an assembly of the nation! How God can turn about the hearts of princes! Conspicuous in this vast concourse are the idolatrous priests with gnashing teeth. Elijah stands alone undaunted, a witness for Jehovah, and, appealing to the multitude, he accuses them of unworthy hesitation between irreconcilable services.

I. WHY HESITATE IN SEEKING HAPPINESS ? 1. *No joys can compare with the heavenly.* (1) There are, indeed, sad professors of the true religion. (*a*) Some are constitutionally melancholy. This is a disease which certainly is not aggravated by the sense of the favour of God. (*b*) Some have false views of religion. They caricature it into a sepulchral thing. They do it injustice. (*c*) But the case most common is that sad professors do not experience what they profess. They halt between Jehovah and Baal—between Christ and Belial. In fashion. In friendships. In pursuits. So conscience stings them sore. (2) When religion is true there is the best reason for joy. (*a*) It brings emancipation from the slavery of sin. (*b*) Deliverance from the tyranny of Satan. (*c*) Adoption into the family of God. (*d*) Heirship to everlasting life. The true heir has the title-deeds of his inheritance in his heart (Eph. i. 13, 14 ; 2 Cor. v. 4, 5). Thus does he antedate the very bliss of heaven (Luke xvii. 21 ; Eph. i. 3). 2. *If sinners be not sad, the more shame.* (1) For sin degrades the man below the brute. As far below as the powers of a man are superior. The degradation of a devil would be impossible to a brute. If a man can be transformed into a compound of swine and devil and not be sad, this is the climax of depravity. (2) Sin is perfidy to infinite love. Such ingratitude can only be reconciled with the absence of sadness upon the ground of the most shameful perversity. (3) The sinner is befooled by Satan. In his reflective moods he must loathe himself; but Satan whirls him away from his reflections into some mad dance, and drowns the voice of his conscience in some boisterous laugh. So the fool still befooled exults in his folly. O shame !

II. WHY HESITATE IN SEEKING SALVATION ? 1. *Life is the determining period.* (1) It is the seed-time for the reaping in eternity. The yield then will be according to the sowing now. In quality : " After its kind." Also in quantity. (2) Therefore the young have a splendid opportunity. They have time in their favour. " How long shall ye ? " 2. *Procrastination is precarious work.* (1) " How long (פסח) hop ye ? "—this word denotes the passing over from one place to another—" between two opinions." It is used scornfully of the awkward leaping of the priests of Baal, in ver. 26. As the squirrel hopping from branch to branch may miss its footing and fall, so may the halting sinner hop into ruin. (2) Consider the uncertainty of life. Read the gravestones. How enormous is the mortality amongst the young ! Unroof hell ! (3) Consider the solemnities of eternity. The freshness and vividness of memory in the disembodied state. What a preparation for the day of judgment !

III. FOR INDECISION THERE IS NO DEFENCE. " The people answered him not a word." But there are motives to evil when there are no good reasons. Such are— 1. *Conjugal influence.* (1) Ahab's heart was estranged from God by the influence of Jezebel. His predecessors suffered from the same cause. Notably so Solomon. (2) Beware of contracting ungodly matrimonial alliances. Remember the famine in Samaria. The same God still " ruleth in the kingdom of men." 2. *The smile of favour.* (1) Idolatry was favoured at court. The priests of Ashere feasted " at Jezebel's table." Mean-spirited Israelites sought court favour at the expense of the favour of God. (3) True worshippers were persecuted. Elijah had to hide himself at Cherith and Zarephath. The sons of the prophets had to hide in the caves of Obadiah. To keep a whole skin many hesitated. Will you encounter the frown of God to escape the sneer of an old companion ? 3. *The force of example.* (1) Elijah stood alone as the prophet of the Lord. He had with him a handful of laymen. Obadiah was conspicuous amongst them. If the prophets fed by Obadiah had issued from their caves, they did not stand forth on Carmel in their official character. (2) The pronounced idolaters were a larger company. There were the prophets of Baal four hundred, and the prophets of Ashere four hundred and fifty, with a proportionate following. (3) Still " the people " were vacillators. These were the majority. The power and influence of numbers were with the moderate people who would fain keep good terms with God and the devil. The halters are still the majority. How few amongst the multitude of the wicked have resolved in heart and soul that they will go to the devil! It is time you made up your mind one way or the other. How long halt ye ?—J. A. M.

Vers. 22—24.—*The Test of Fire.* Elijah had appealed to the people on their inconsistency in hesitating between services so widely different and so utterly irreconcilable as those of Jehovah and Baal. He got no response. "The people answered him not a word." Then he proposed the test of fire to determine which was worthy. The conclusiveness of such an appeal could not be challenged; so the people with one voice answered, "It is well spoken."

I. THE TEST WAS UNEXCEPTIONABLE. 1. *For Baal was the fire-god.* (1) His name designates him as the *lord* or *ruler*. It comes from the verb (בעל) to *own* or *possess*, to be *master of*. But the sun, from its splendour and central position, accounted the visible lord in the material heavens, was their Baal. Sanchoniathon says the Phoenicians thought the sun to be the only lord of heaven, calling him *Beelsamen*, which in their language is *lord of heaven*. In "Beelsamen" we at once recognize the Hebrew בעל שמים. (2) Baal was the *fire* or body of the sun, rather than its *light*. So in 2 Kings xxiii. 5 we find Baal (בעל) distinguished from (שמש) the *solar light*. (See Parkhurst under שמש.) Parkhurst points out that the Runic or Islandic BAAL signifies *fire*, the Saxon BAEL, and BAEL-FYR, a *burning pile*, a *pyre*, a *bonfire*. Probably our *bonfire* is simply a corruption of *Bael-fyr*. (3) The image of this idol was a *bull*. This animal was by the ancients regarded as the emblem of *fire*. The similitude seems to have been in its red colour, in the curled hair upon its forehead giving the idea of flame, in the horns budding with its head suggesting the darting of rays of light from the sun. In Tobit (i. 5) we read of "the heifer called Baal." We have the name of this god still preserved in our English *bull*. 2. *The controversy was whether Baal was independent of Jehovah.* (1) His worshippers claimed this for him. (2) Elijah maintained the opposite. And with cogent reason, for during three years and six months Jehovah made Baal punish his votaries. (3) Now the prophet proposes the further test of a sudden miracle. If Baal be god, if he be independent of Jehovah, let him come down and consume the sacrifice offered to him. If he cannot, then why should he be worshipped? If Jehovah can send fire on his sacrifice, then is He manifestly Lord of Baal, and should be so acknowledged. (4) That suitable acknowledgment of God which such a miracle demands, implies—(*a*) Recognition of His almighty providence and lordship over the material and moral universe. (*b*) The engagement of all our powers in His worship and service.

II. SO WAS THE MANNER OF THE TEST. 1. *The prophets of Baal had precedence.* (1) Not because Baal was entitled to it, for that would be a concession of the argument, but because they were many. Elijah stood alone the prophet of the Lord, while the idolatrous prophets were 850 men. (2) They were to provide the sacrifices. They were wealthy. Elijah was poor. They could not object to the test when the sacrifices were of their own selection. 2. *The experiment was to be fair.* (1) Not only might the priests of Baal choose their bullock, cut it in pieces after their approved method, lay it on the wood of the altar; but they must "put no fire under." Else where would be the proof of the ability of Baal? Under some heathen altars holes were dug in which fire was concealed, which communicating with the altar set the wood on fire to make the simple people believe that the sacrifice was consumed by miraculous fire. This Elijah would not permit. (2) Ordinarily the sacrifices offered to Baal were offered in fire; and sometimes human sacrifices were so offered. "They built the high places of Baal to burn their sons with fire, for burnt offerings" (Jer. xix. 5). The Phoenician Baal seems to have been identical with the Ammonite Molech. "They built the high places of *Baal* which are in the valley of the son of Hinnom, to cause their sons and their daughters to pass through the fire to *Molech*" (Jer. xxxii. 35). (3) Ashtaroth also were virtually the same as "Baalim," under which plural term are included diversified Baals, as Baal Peor, &c.; and so in ver. 25 the prophets of Baal are said to have (אלהים) " gods," in the plural. (4) These had their various images, in some of which the man and bull came into union. The Assyrian man-bull so conspicuous in the Nineveh marbles, is probably one of these.

Let us bless God for our Christianity. It is pure light. Compared with it other systems are dark with ignorance, superstition, and error. It is supreme benevolence. Happy is its contrast to the characteristic cruelties of idolatry.—J. A. M.

Vers. 25—29.—*The Failure.* When the appeal of Elijah to the people had gained their applause, he had the prophets of Baal at his command. The test he had proposed was so fair that they could not reasonably object to it, and the voice of the people rendered it impossible for them to evade the trial. The prophet of the Lord accordingly pressed the matter home upon his adversaries in the words of the text. They were obliged to proceed to the trial which ended in their discomfiture.

I. THEIR PRAYER WAS EARNEST. 1. *They began early.* (1) Everything seems to have been in readiness soon after daybreak; so that almost as soon as their Apollo looked out of the eyelids of the morning the cry arose, "O Baal, hear us!" (2) Worshippers of Jehovah should not be less zealous. The early morning was chosen by His devoted servants (see Gen. xix. 27; xxii. 3; Exod. xxiv. 4; Job i. 5; Psa. v. 3; lix. 16; lxxxviii. 13; Mark i. 35). Such exercises will be a noble preparation for the day. 2. *They persisted.* (1) They continued their supplications until noon. As the sun rolled upwards in the heavens their hopes rose. As it neared the zenith they felt it was now or never, and 850 voices in full chorus cried, "O Baal, hear us!" (2) Even when the noon point was turned and their god was sinking in the west, still they urged their suit, adding to their entreaties frantic gestures and mingling their own blood with their sacrifice. (3) Idolatry is essentially cruel, and in this contrasts strongly with the service of Jehovah (see Levit. xix. 28; Deut. xiv. 1). The cruel penances of Rome are kindred to those of Baal's servants. "The devil is a murderer." Of bodies. Of souls. (4) Persistency should mark the servants of God. Jacob wrestled all night with the angel at Penuel, and at daybreak prevailed. The parable of the importunate widow was given to impress this lesson. We should ask *until* we receive. (5) How blessedly has persistency been rewarded! Ministers have seen this; parents; Sunday-school teachers, tract distributors.

II. BUT IT WAS MISDIRECTED. 1. *Their god was contemptible.* (1) He was destitute of the attributes they ascribed to him. The sun, though a glorious body, is but matter. It has no more intelligence than a flint. How the intellects as well as the eyes of men are dazzled with splendour! (2) How different is the true God! He is a Spirit—invisible—omniscient—omnipresent—omnipotent—holy—just—good. He claims, and should receive, the homage of all our faculties. 2. *Their worship, therefore, was ridiculous.* (1) So Elijah thought when he stung them with mockery. "He is a god!" (כי אלהים הוא) he is a supreme god! Here is a fine stroke of irony. This weapon of rhetoric was used by our Lord— "Art thou a master in Israel and knowest not these things?" (2) "He is *talking*." He is so stunned with the thunder of his own voice and with the voices of his associates in the pantheon that he cannot hear the ordinary voices of mortals. Therefore "cry aloud." Or "he is (שׂיח) *meditating*" (margin)—in a brown study, in a reverie—and must be roused. (3) "Or he is pursuing," or "hath a pursuit." He is so engaged with some other matter that he cannot hear your feeble voice. What sort of god is yours? (4) "Or he is in a journey"—so far away that your prayer will be useless unless you can cry aloud. (5) "Or peradventure he sleepeth and must be awaked." You must first raise a clamour about his ears to arouse him, or you pray in vain. How doubtful must be the success of any worship paid to such a god! 3. *Ridicule was righteously applied.* (1) It should never be substituted for reason, as too often it is. It is a favourite weapon with sceptics who are at a loss for an argument. (2) But where reason is wasted upon stupidity then it is fitting. Elijah was silent from sunrise till noon, when the experiment had a fair trial and failed. Then he rallied the idolaters with a ridicule that was full of argument. (3) When evening set in they gave up the contest in despair. There is an evening coming in which all contests with Jehovah shall so terminate. —J. A. M.

Vers. 30—35.—*The Preparation.* As the time of the evening sacrifice approached, Elijah left the priests of Baal prophesying in despair. Satan, if permitted, could have brought fire down (see Job i. 12, 16; Rev. xiii. 13, 14); but God restrained him. The people were now convinced that Baal was not able to hear his priests; so they drew round Elijah, and observed the order in which he proceeded with his preparation.

I. HE REPAIRED THE ALTAR OF THE LORD. 1. *Then there had been an altar of the Lord on Carmel.* (1) Some great man, as Abraham or Samuel, had built an altar there. Its relics remained a memorial of the piety of earlier times. Influence for good or evil is posthumous. (2) This mount was, in consequence, reputed as holy. Perhaps this determined Elijah in his choice. Holy *places* were formerly more important than they are under this spiritual dispensation (see Mal. i. 11; John iv. 20—24; 1 Tim. ii. 8). 2. *But this altar had been "broken down."* (1) Not only had it fallen into decay, but it had suffered from the hand of violence. Probably this was one of the sad evidences of the wicked zeal of Jezebel. It was significant of the apostasy of the times (see ch. xix. 14; Rom. xi. 2, 3). Idolatry was in favour at court; courtiers therefore favoured it; so did the multitude who followed the fashions. (2) Such influences still are potent. Idolatrous fashions in dress. In furniture. Even in religion. 3. *Elijah would not use the altar used by the priests of Baal.* (1) The service of Jehovah must be pure. It must not be contaminated by the remotest connection with idolatrous abominations. Let us search our hearts (see 2 Cor. vi. 15—18). (2) In repairing the disused altar of Jehovah, Elijah showed that his was no new religion, but that of the fathers of the nation. So he significantly rebuked the apostasy. 4. *Twelve stones were employed in the repairs.* (1) This was "according to the number of the sons of Jacob, unto whom the word of the Lord came, saying, Israel shall be thy name." This was done to show that, though *ten* of the tribes had separated from the house of David, still, in worship there should be no division (see Gen. xxxii. 28; Exod. xxiv. 4; Josh. iv. 5, 20). (2) "The twelve stones being for the twelve tribes were the mystical body of Him who was their sacrifice and altar both, or who offered His own body, and suffered in it, and who was promised to be accepted in the name (ישראל) *Israel*, i.e. (ישר) *pleasing to, right with*, or *upright before* (אל) *the Lord*" (see Matt. iii. 17). *But* (3) It was also prophetic of the healing of all schisms in the mystical body of Christ in the happy time to come (see Ezek. xxxvii. 21, 22). (4) All this the prophet did "in the name of the Lord" (ver. 32). By His direction; therefore with notable significance. For His glory. And since God so expressly authorized such a deviation from the Levitical law, does it not indicate that that law had its principal value in its typical teaching, and that when the antitypes came it should pass away? (See Col. ii. 22; Heb. viii. 13.)

II. HE PREPARED THE SACRIFICE. 1. *"He put the wood in order."* (1) Why did he not dispense with the wood? The celestial fire certainly did not need it, for it fell upon the sacrifice before it touched the wood, and was so fervent that nothing could stand before it. Stones and dust could no more resist it than wood. Had the wood been intended for fuel, would the prophet have overflowed it with water? (2) The order was usual in sacrifices. It was observed for typical purposes. The holocaust was a type of Christ, our Sacrifice, who, when consumed in the holy fires of the Godhead on the altar of Calvary, was laid on the wood of the Cross. 2. *He poured water upon the sacrifice.* (1) He poured it in great quantity and with much deliberation, for in preparing the altar he dug a trench to receive the overflow (vers. 32—35). The water probably came from a deep well-spring in the mountain side rather than from the Kishon. The Mediterranean seems out of the question. Josephus states the well to have been the source (Ant. viii. 13). (2) It was conveyed in four barrels, and these were filled and emptied three times, thus making *twelve.* Here again we meet with the number of the tribes of Israel.

The order, viz., in sets of four three times repeated, was that of the stones in the high priest's breastplate, upon which were engraven the names of the tribes.   (3) Could this sign be intended to show that a plentiful rain would shortly come upon all Israel?   And further, that it should come through the repentance of the people for whose sin it had been withholden?   That it should come through the return of the people from the altar of Baal to that of Jehovah?   If so, then in this sign the gospel also is preached to us.   We too must be saved from spiritual drought and death through repentance towards God and faith in Christ.—J. A. M.

Vers. 36—40.—*The Triumph.*   While Elijah completed his preparations for offering up his sacrifice, the prophets of Baal, who had failed to vindicate their religion, were hoping that the servant of Jehovah likewise might fail.   It was matter of history that Jehovah had answered by fire.   (See Gen. iv. 5; Levit. ix. 24; Judg. vi. 21; 1 Chron. xxi. 26.)   About a century before this that fire came from heaven which was still kept burning upon the altar at Jerusalem (2 Chron. vii. 1). But Carmel is not Jerusalem; and Jehovah has not promised to record His name here.   And, should Elijah fail, then would they fall upon him and destroy him. Yet, on the other hand, he is an extraordinary servant of Jehovah; his word concerning the rain and dew has come true; so may his confidence respecting this answer of fire be honoured.   Such thoughts flashed through their minds; but the moment has arrived; the preparations are complete.   Now observe—
I. THE PRAYER.   1. *It is offered at the time of the evening sacrifice.*   (1) The stated evening sacrifice is now on the temple altar.   Elijah holds communion with that altar.   He, too, though on Carmel, is a true worshipper of the God of David. There are differences in religious worship sanctioned by God which must not be accounted schism.   Protestant Nonconformists are not necessarily schismatics. (2) It is the "hour of prayer."   Prayer should ascend with the sacrifice; Christ should be in all our supplications.   The hour of prayer was the "ninth hour" (Acts iii. 1), that hour in which Jesus "cried with a loud voice, and yielded up his spirit" (Matt. xxvii. 50).   So in submission must we yield up our spirits with his in prayer to God.   2. *It pleads for the honour of God.*   (1) It reminds Him of His covenant.   "Jehovah Elohim of Abraham, Isaac, and of Israel."   With these patriarchs He had established His covenant.   They knew nothing of Baal's covenants.   (2) "Let it be known this day that thou art God in Israel."   Let those who will not acknowledge Thee be confounded.   (See Josh. ii. 11.)   Let those who repent be reconciled to Thy favour.   (3) "Let it be known this day in Israel that I am thy servant, and that I have done all these things at thy word."   Else to have so acted would have been the height of presumption.   But with the authority of God mistrust would have been presumption.   We are bound to believe the promises of God.   3. *It sues for mercy to the penitent.*   (1) "Hear me, O Jehovah, hear me, that this people may know that thou art Jehovah Elohim;" that Thou art the self-existent, covenant-keeping God.   (2) "And that thou hast turned their heart back again."   The blessings of the covenant are conditioned upon faith. Without repentance there is no true faith.   (3) How few are the words of this prayer!   No vain repetitions.   How wide the contrast with the clamour of Baal's priests!
II. THE RESPONSE.   1. *Then the fire of the Lord fell.*   (1) There was no mistake about it.   It was indeed the "fire of Jehovah"—miraculous fire; for it worked downwards, contrary to the ordinary operation of fire, which works upwards.   The sacrifice was soon consumed.   Then the wood.   The water was licked up.   The very stones and dust were vitrified and volatilized.   (2) The destruction of the altar pointed to the pleasure of God that patriarchal high places should be removed, and that all Israel should henceforth worship at the Levitical altar of the temple at Jerusalem.   This is the last instance on record in which God accepted a sacrifice offered on a patriarchal altar.   (3) But where now is Baal?   Is not that celestial fire which was worshipped as a god completely in the hands of Jehovah?   2. *The demonstration was irresistible.*   (1) "When all the people saw it they fell upon their faces."   Here was an act of reverence towards God.   It was the sign also of

their renunciation of Baal. (2) This confession in symbol was accompanied by a corresponding confession in words. "And they said, Jehovah, he is the Elohim; Jehovah, he is the Elohim." Words are signs of a fuller expression. (3) But words must be followed up by deeds. The prophets of Baal have now to be sacrificed. The law required this. (See Deut. xiii. 1—11.) They were accordingly slaughtered by the brook Kishon. Thus was returned upon their heads the slaughter of the prophets of the Lórd. (See vers. 4, 13.) (4) The retribution was complete. Some are of opinion, because the "prophets of Baal" only are mentioned, that the 400 prophets of Ashere were absent and escaped. But this does not follow, for the prophets of Ashere might be included under the designation "prophets of Baal," as Saul's sons are included in his name. (See 1 Sam. xxxi. 8—13; 2 Sam. xxi. 13.) The prophets of Ashere certainly were present. (See vers. 19, 20; also ch. xix. 1.) Let us confess the Lord. In *signs:* observing His sacraments and ordinances of worship public and private. In *words:* confessing Him before men upon all fitting occasions. In *deeds:* bringing forth the fruits of good living, and sacrificing the idolatries that would lead us astray.—J. A. M.

Vers. 41—46. *The Sound of Rain.* The fire has fallen upon the sacrifice of Elijah. The people are convinced, renounce Baal, confess Jehovah supreme, and evince their sincerity by slaying the idolatrous priests. Now there is "a sound of abundance of rain."

I. THIS WAS THE SOUND OF SALVATION. 1. *Rain was salvation to the nation.* (1) Three years and six months of drought brought it to the point of extinction. The heavens were brazen; the earth was scorched. The people were blackened with excessive heat, and worn with want. Their numbers were thinned by death; survivors moved like skeletons on the edges of their graves. (2) To such the sound of rain is tidings of life. Let it come, and soon, in such a climate as Palestine, vegetation will burst into verdure. There will be "seed for the sower and bread for the eater." 2. *It was a sign of spiritual blessings.* (1) The kingdom of nature was constituted to furnish apt similes of the kingdom of grace. The blooming of the desert after rain is a familiar figure of spiritual revival. (See Isa. xxxv.; lv. 10—13.) (2) The descent of rain is a figure of the descent of the Holy Spirit upon the receptive soul (Isa. xxxii. 15). Water, a purifier, refresher, vitalizer, fittingly sets forth His energies; and as these are *active*, so in baptism the element should come *upon* the person as rain upon the passive earth. (See Acts ii. 3, 4, 17, 32; x. 44—48.) 3. *Revivals have their premonitions.* (1) The sound comes before the rain. It is heard in the branches of trees, and in the waves of seas and lakes. So is a coming revival discerned in the Church by emotion under the word, interest in religious services public and private, and increased evangelistic activity. (2) This is first heard by the spiritual. Elijah was the first to hear the sound of the coming rain. It begins in the higher heavens before it reaches the earth. Those who are much in prayer have the sensitive ear to *hear* "afar off." (Compare 2 Peter i. 9.)

II. THE CONDITIONS HAD BEEN FULFILLED. 1. *Sin was repented.* (1) The people saw the impotence of Baal. He could not answer for himself. They were now convinced of their folly in submitting to such a delusion. So it must be with every sinner whose eyes are opened. (2) They destroyed the authors of their delusion. They slew the prophets of Baal. Not one escaped. So in the most complete manner must our evil lusts be slain. No power must be left to them to lure us from the truth again. 2. *Christ was accepted.* (1) Elijah must show himself to Ahab as a condition of rain (ver. 1). Ahab so far accepted him as to submit to his directions. But Elijah was a type of Christ, without whose revelation of Himself to us we can have no spiritual grace. (See ch. xvii. 1.) (2) Elijah was a type of Christ in his *person.* His name (אליה and אליהו) is "My God Jehovah," or, "Whose God is he," expresses the union of God and man in Christ. (3) He was a type of Christ also in his *office.* All prophets were types of the One Great Prophet. Elijah, who was remarkable amongst the number, eminently so. (4) He, too, united with his office of *prophet* the functions of the *priest.* He offered up the sacrifice on Carmel. In this sacrifice the people accepted Jehovah as their covenant God. So must we likewise accept God in Christ. In token of their communion with Jehovah they appear to have feasted on the sacrifices. With the burnt offering there were doubtless peace offerings, for these were usual accompaniments, upon which the worshippers feasted. This was the *eating* and *drinking* to which Elijah moved Ahab (ver. 42). (5) Elijah also was a type of Christ in his character of *Intercessor.* While Ahab and his people were partaking of the peace-offerings, "Elijah went up to the top of Carmel, and cast himself down upon the earth, and put his face between his knees." He bowed reverently in prayer with his head towards the ground—an attitude still observed in the East. So Christ, in the heights, makes intercession for us. 3. *The blessing came.* (1) While Elijah interceded he sent his servant to look for the signs of the coming blessing. In this parable, in which the prophet is still the type of Christ, his servant stands for the *Church*, whose duty it is to look for the fruits of the Redeemer's pleadings. Are we thus looking? (2) The servant went, and went again and again before he witnessed any sign, in which the lesson to us is that while Christ pleads we must never be discouraged, but " hope to the end." (3) At the *seventh* time the promise appeared in a cloud as of a man's hand rising out of the sea, which was to be followed by others in rapid succession until the heavens were " black with clouds and wind," and the thirsty earth was visited with copious showers of refreshing rain. This was prophetic of that *seventh* time, or " fulness of time," when the hand of God shall act *in the sea,* or among all nations, and raise that " plentiful shower " which shall *refresh His weary inheritance* (Psa. lxviii. 9). Meanwhile Elijah sent his servant to Ahab, saying, " Harness the horses, and get thee down, that the rain stop thee not." (4) Now the parable is changed. Ahab, the king of Israel, after the destruction of the prophets of Baal, riding as in triumph, and attended by the blessings of heaven, is the type of Christ. So Elijah runs before him in the spirit and power of God. The Baptist accordingly came "in the spirit and power of Elias," as the forerunner of Christ, in His first advent, to establish His *spiritual* kingdom. But Elias, *in person*, will be His harbinger when He comes again, in the fulness of His blessing, to establish a *visible* and everlasting kingdom (Mal. iv. 5).—J. A. M.

Vers. 7—16.—*Obadiah.* It is a proof of the extremity of distress to which the land had been reduced by famine that the king himself with one of his highest officers, the governor of his household, should have gone forth on this expedition in search of water and pasturage. The reverence the person of Elijah inspired is seen in the behaviour of Obadiah towards him when they met. The brief notice we have of this man is highly instructive.

I. His FIDELITY. His name, Obadiah, "servant of Jehovah," is suggestive of the strength of his religious character. And it was probably no vain boast that he had always sustained it (ver. 12). It may seem strange that so good a man should have been willing to remain in the service of such a king, and of a state so demoralized and disorganized by the spirit of idolatry. But note—1. *Religious fidelity wins respect even from those whose own life is most at variance with it.* Ahab must have known that his servant remained true to the God of his fathers, and his being continued in such a post was a testimony to his moral and practical worth. Like Joseph in the court of Pharaoh, and Daniel in Babylon, " the Spirit of God was in him," and the king could find none more worthy of his trust. The fear of God is after all one of the highest qualifications for the secular businesses and responsibilities of life, and " when a man's ways please the Lord he maketh even his enemies to be at peace with him " (Prov. xvi. 7). 2. *It is often a noble thing to stand at the post of duty, however uncongenial the moral atmosphere may be.* We have no reason to believe that Obadiah retained his position by any kind of moral laxity. He did not violate his conscience in maintaining his secular allegiance. Naaman the Syrian, in the zeal of his new devotion to the God of Israel, asked a dispensation of forgiveness if he should bow with his master in the house of Rimmon (2 Kings v. 18), but we have no evidence even of such a compromise as this in the case of Obadiah.   There are times when religious principle itself dictates that men should refuse to relinquish positions of peculiar danger and difficulty ; but when fidelity to an earthly master is absolutely incompatible with fidelity to God, an upright spirit will not long hesitate.   3. *God may have some great purpose for His servant in such a case to fulfil.*   Obadiah's mission may have been to mitigate as far as possible the horrors of the famine, to save as he did the lives of the sons of the prophets (ver. 13) ; to exert, perhaps, some kind of restraining influence over the conduct of the king.   At all events the presence of such a man in one of the high places of the land would be a standing proof that God had not utterly abandoned His people.   Every situation in life has its grand opportunities ; when there is no possible way of turning it to good account we may well forsake it.

II. HIS FEAR.   " What have I sinned ? " &c.   Faithful as Obadiah was, there was an element of timidity in his nature.   He shrank from the risk the commission of the prophet imposed on him.   His timidity has two aspects.   1. *So far as it meant distrust of Ahab it was natural.*   He knew only too well his capricious and despotic temper, and could not rely either on his justice or his clemency.   "The tender mercies of the wicked are cruel" (Prov. xii. 10).   "Let me not fall into the hands of man," &c. (2 Sam. xxiv. 14).   2. *So far as it meant distrust of Elijah or of the protective providence of God it was wrong.*   Could he think that the prophet would abuse his confidence, or that God would be unmindful of him, and after allowing him, for no fault of his own, to be involved in danger, would leave him to his fate ?   This shows weakness, and was unworthy of the character he bore.   The best of men have their seasons of weakness, and fail sometimes under the pressure of unwonted circumstances to maintain the very virtues for which they are most distinguished.   The meek-spirited Moses is impetuous ; the saintly David falls a prey to grovelling passion ; the brave Peter proves a coward.

III. THE TRIUMPH OF HIS FIDELITY OVER HIS FEAR.   The solemn asseveration of Elijah (ver. 15) rouses the braver spirit in him, and he responds to the call and goes to meet Ahab.   When there is true nobility of character in a man, a word, a flash of light upon the realities of the situation, will often be enough to move him to put forth all his strength and shake off the spell of meaner feeling that may for a while have fallen upon him.—W.

Ver. 21.—*A solemn alternative.*   It must have been by special Divine direction that Elijah was moved thus to put the relative claims of God and of Baal to a public test.   The command to gather the priests and people together on Carmel was one that Ahab, defiant as he was, dared not resist.   We may suppose these words to have been uttered just before the crisis of the tragedy, when the people were waiting in breathless silence and suspense upon the issue.   Nothing is more impressive than a pause like this before some expected catastrophe.   The prophet improves it by making one brief pointed appeal to the judgment and conscience of the people.   "How long ? " &c.   His voice of stern, yet sorrowful, rebuke must have struck deep into many hearts ; but "they answered him not a word."   "Halting between two opinions " was probably a true description of the mental condition of the great mass of the people.   Some, no doubt, were blind devotees of the reigning idolatry ; others consented to its rites, and practised them through fear of the penalty of resistance, or in hope of some form of secular reward.   But the greater part of them were just in this state of moral hesitancy, leaning sometimes to one side and sometimes to the other, swayed by the influences that happened to be strongest upon them at the time.   It was the fatal defect of their national character, the sad heritage of earlier days—the "forty years' provocation in the wilderness."   What have we here but a true picture of religious indecision ?   Learn from the prophet's remonstrance—

I. THE RESPONSIBILITY OF EVERY MAN AS REGARDS HIS OWN RELIGIOUS OPINIONS. That the people are rebuked for "halting between two" implies their power and obligation to decide.   "Opinions," mental judgments, convictions (marg. "thoughts"), these are the root from which the fruits of all religious feeling and action grow.   Here lies the secret guiding and formative power of a man's life. "As a man thinketh in his heart, so is he." It is thought that inspires affection, moulds character, guides the will, determines conduct, rules the man. We cannot well exaggerate the importance of the relation thought bears to the highest interests of our being. But how are these "thoughts" of ours determined? Every man's religious ideas and beliefs, say some, are determined for him by a thousand influences over which he has no control—by early education, by the books that fall in his way, by human associations, native temperament, conformation of brain, &c. There is a measure of truth in this that we dare not ignore. These things have a great deal to do with the matter, and the fact should modify our judgment of the mental position of others in relation to religious truth, and teach us to watch carefully the bearing on ourselves of such influences. Many of us owe our Christian beliefs far more than we imagine to the force of favouring circumstances. We may well thank God that it is so; for as we mourn to think how many things there are that tend to distort the truth and hide it from man's eyes, so we rejoice that there should be so many channels through which the Light of Life may find its way into the soul. But however this may be, God holds every one of us under obligation to think for himself, judge for himself, believe for himself; to use with uprightness of spirit all the means within his reach for the formation of right opinions, to welcome and follow the light that shines from heaven upon his way.

II. The duty of a practical carrying out of one's own honest convictions. "If the Lord be God, follow him." The startling "sign" that was about to be given them was intended to decide this grave alternative. "The God that answereth by fire, let him be God." It was great condescension in Jehovah to suffer His claims to be thus put in seeming competition with those of Baal. But the prophet would have the decision of the people to spring from real conviction, and that conviction to be based on sufficient proof. And then let it be a practical decision—final, conclusive, manifest. Let there be an end to all this miserable vacillation, this shameful subserviency to the leading of Ahab and Jezebel and the Baal priesthood, this dark dishonour done to the God of Israel by the multiplication all over the land of heathen groves and altars. All true religious thoughts and opinions have reference to a true life. They are hollow and worthless unless consummated in this. "Faith without works is dead being alone" (James ii. 17). A heavy condemnation rests on those who "profess that they know God, but in works deny him" (Titus i. 16). It is a fatal inconsistency to believe in a God and yet not "follow Him." Have you true religious ideas and convictions? Translate your thinking into life.

III. The urgency of the need for this practical decision. "How long?" &c. We may suppose that the prophet was not only impressed with the tardiness of that generation in declaring once for all for the service of Jehovah, but with the memory of the weary provocation of the past, When will Israel be true and steadfast in her allegiance to her God and King? It is in every respect unreasonable, unmanly, and infinitely perilous to allow the question of your religious position to remain unsettled.—W.

Ver. 21.—*Religious Indecision.* Describe the gathering of the people upon Mount Carmel: the suffering they had endured from the long-continued drought; the eager expectancy of the secret worshippers of Jehovah, and the reappearance of Elijah the prophet; the general readiness to obey the summons to witness a decisive contest, &c. *The descent into national idolatry had been gradual.* One step had made the next easy, and sometimes inevitable, till now the chosen nation was in the deepest degradation. Of this many of them were scarcely conscious. They had followed the example set by the court without remonstrance and without reflection. *The opportunity for consideration had come at last.* Elijah abruptly threw himself into the current of national life—like a gigantic rock in the stream, which cannot itself be stirred, but whose presence must make itself felt, and may divert the stream into another channel. *The test he proposed to the people was obviously fair;* indeed, it appeared to give every advantage to the worshippers of Baal. It was not fire but rain that the thirsty land required; but had he said, "The God that answereth by *rain*, let him be God," Baal's priests might argue that it was not water but fire that their God could rule. Elijah would fight the idol on his own chosen ground. Show how often advantage seems to be given to God's adversaries, as if they were allowed to make out the best cause they could, yet all to no effect. The wisdom of the world was left to the Church's foes. The people were not asked to do what was rrational, but were to have evidence, and this evidence was to be adapted to their ensuous character. Religion appeals to a man as to a rational being. The sin with which Elijah charged the people on Carmel was *religious indecision*, which we now consider.

I. THE CONDITION OF INDECISION. 1. *It implies some enlightenment on religious subjects.* Many heathen exist even in a Christian land. Living under the shadow of our sanctuaries, they are profoundly ignorant of God, of His claims, and of His gospel. They are not halting "between two opinions," for they have no opinion about a religious life, but are decided in their godlessness. Such was not the condition of Israel, nor of their modern representatives. There is no want of intellectual knowledge of scriptural truth complained of here. 2. *It implies contradiction between theory and practice.* The Israelites would not have denied the Divine interpositions of the past, and many would have admitted that the temple at Jerusalem was originally the true place for worship, &c. Like some in Crete, in Paul's days, "they profess that they know God, but in works they deny him." 3. *It implies dissatisfaction with present condition.* They were like men longing for something which they have not yet resolved to seek. So at Athens, some who heard Paul felt that his words were so wise and weighty that they exclaimed, "We will hear thee again of this matter." They were moved by transient feeling, like Felix (Acts xxiv. 25) and Agrippa (Acts xxvi. 28). To all such comes this protest against vacillation.

II. THE CAUSES OF INDECISION. 1. *Want of thoughtful consideration.* Many speculate about religion who have never yet cried, "What must I do to be saved?" A busy life diverts them from earnest thought, their powers being absorbed in worldly affairs. Or a frivolous habit of mind may prove their bane. 2. *Deficiency of personal courage.* It would require courage under Jezebel's rule to become worshippers of Jehovah. Give instances of the difficulties which beset earnest men in modern life, the necessity sometimes arising for true heroism on the part of those who would follow Christ. 3. *Tendency to procrastination.* To-day is devoted to that which is evident to the senses, to-morrow to that which concerns the soul. Examples:

III. THE CONSEQUENCES OF INDECISION. 1. *Increase of difficulties.* Evil habits grow in strength. The simple spray of ivy can be gathered by a child's hand, but after the growth of years, though it is killing the tree, you cannot tear it off. A worldly man who is now impervious to good never meant to be what he is, but he expected that when the stress of making his position was over he would have time and inclination to attend to affairs of the soul. Imperceptibly God seems to have "given him over to a reprobate mind, because he did not choose to retain God in his knowledge." 2. *Loss of opportunity.* Even if it were easier to decide for God next year, it would be madness to delay. "Boast not thyself of to-morrow," &c. Read the parable of the Rich Fool—Luke xii. 3. *Irreparable ruin.* If God's opportunity is lost, it will not be re-created after death. See how Christ spoke of Capernaum, of Chorazin, and of Jerusalem. "But now they are hid from thine eyes." "He that is filthy, let him be filthy still." In face of such penalties press home the question on the undecided, "How long halt *ye* between two opinions?" —A. R.

Ver. 44.—*Elijah's Prayer for Rain.* The wonders which accompanied the ministry of Elijah were not meaningless prodigies. Those who question the wisdom of miracles should remember that the condition of those for whom they were intended rendered them necessary. Sensuous men must learn through their senses, and worshippers of material force must be met by physical displays of power. We do not try to instruct a child by an essay, or to convince a savage by a syllogism. God could speak directly to the devout patriarchs; but when the worshippers of Baal were to know that there was a living God, they saw the fire from heaven, and heard the bursting of a storm after years of drought. Idolatry had just been swept away by a whirlwind of popular execration. The time had therefore come for the curse to be removed. Elijah with a premonition of the distant rain bade king and people eat of the sacrificial feast, while he went up the mountain to pray. Six times his servant ascended the loftiest peak of Carmel, and came back to say that there was no sign of change; but the seventh time, gazing over the blue expanse of the Mediterranean, he saw a cloud tiny as a man's hand, which was the pledge of answered prayer, for soon the heavens were "black with clouds," and over the thirsty land there was "a great rain." In dealing with events of Old Testament history, we must guard ourselves against giving a fanciful interpretation which cannot be reasonably justified; but we must not forget, on the other hand, that such incidents reveal great principles which run through the whole economy of God, in the moral as well as in the physical world.

I. THE SPIRITUAL SIGNIFICANCE OF THE BLESSING SOUGHT. The New Testament justifies us in regarding the rain which Elijah prayed for as a type of the Holy Spirit, without whom our hearts are barren, and the moral world is dead. See, for instance, how boldly the writer of the Epistle to the Hebrews evolves from the tabernacle what those who constructed it little imagined. Take as another example the allusion which Paul makes to the rock in the wilderness, in which he says emphatically, "That rock was Christ." Recall passages in which the descent of the Spirit is likened to the falling of rain and the distilling of dew. Points of analogy : the grounds on which the heavenly blessing is withheld; the misery that follows its absence ; the preparation and prayer for its coming ; the subsequent fertility of the barren land, &c. The sins of our age are not unlike those of Elijah's time, though they are less gross in form. The enervating luxuries of civilization, the indifference of many to the decline of religion, the deification of force and of lust, are examples. There has been a forsaking of the Lord on the part of His people, and hence this barrenness of good, in spite of all our toil ; because there is a withholding of the gracious influences of the Divine Spirit. May He "come down as rain upon the mown grass, and as showers that water the earth."

II. THE SPIRITUAL PREPARATION FOR THE BLESSING PROMISED. 1. *Self-forgetfulness.* Elijah was personally provided for, and would lack nothing. His heart bled, however, for the suffering people. For them he prayed. We want more of such soul-burdening on the part of parents and pastors. 2. *Reformation.* By the execution of the false prophets, Elijah had done all that in him lay to put away evil. Sins are obstacles in the way of descending blessings. We cannot win the Holy Spirit by good conduct, but we may hinder His work by our sin. Sin is a bar across the sluice-gates of benediction, and must be removed or broken before the dry channel can be flooded. 3. *Prayer.* It is in the Epistle of James that we are told that Elijah's prayers brought both the drought and the rainfall. The fact that the prophet heard the sound of abundance of rain stimulated his supplication, and did not prevent it. He did not argue that God would send the storm whether he prayed or not, but believed that the reception of blessing was inseparably connected with the offering of prayer. Similarly the Holy Spirit was promised to the disciples, but they met to pray till He came. "Ask, and you shall receive." 4. *Watchfulness.* Elijah was so sure of God's fidelity and goodness that he sent his servant seven times to look for the faintest sign of rain. We need watchfulness for the following reasons : (1) *The answer to prayer does not always come when and how we expect it.* *E.g.,* we ask for holiness, and God sends an illness, in which our murmuring closes our heart against the very blessing that is then nearing us. Or we pray for spirituality, and have the possibility of it presented to us in some unexpected joy, which too often makes us more worldly than grateful. Or we entreat God for the salvation of our child ; and because we do not watch, we fail to recognize the sign and pledge of the Holy Spirit's work in the child's eager questioning and simple prayer. (2) *The answer to prayer may be long delayed.* Elijah was not discouraged even by the sixth repetition of the despairing phrase, "There is nothing." Yet on that very day his one earnest cry had instantaneously brought down fire from heaven. How often like the Psalmist we say, "Hath God forgotten to be gracious?" "Wait on the Lord, wait patiently for him." (3) *The answer to prayer may begin in what seems trifling.* A cloud the size of a man's hand, hardly describable on the horizon, was enough to transfer Elijah's prayer into praise. Little in itself, it was the beginning of a glorious blessing. The baptism of the Holy Spirit will not suddenly fill the world with worshippers; but it will be seen, perhaps, in the turning to God of one lad, who shall prove the Elijah of his age; or in the new light given to one who has long been under the shadow of doubt; or in some holy resolve, some noble thought that shall presage blessing to the world. Slight and insignificant as it may seem, gratefully welcome it, and still hope, and wait, and pray, till He " come and rain righteousness upon us."—A. R.

Vers. 21—40.—*The God that answereth by fire.* I. ISRAEL'S SIN (ver. 21). 1. *Its nature :* indecision, a want of whole-hearted devotion; "How long halt ye ? " &c. They tried to combine both worships, bowing before Jehovah in secret, and publicly before Baal in the assemblies commanded by the court. There are two who contend to-day for our devotion and service—the world and God (1 John ii. 15). The world has its rewards and demands; God has His. 2. *Its folly.* Both cannot be served. What we build in obedience to one we cast down in obedience to the other. "If the Lord be God, follow him," &c. 3. *The necessity for its abandonment.* The messenger sent to announce blessing (ver. 1) must first convince of sin and secure its removal. The blessings of God stand at the door, but they can enter only as our sins are cast out. II. THE CHALLENGE (vers. 22—24). 1. *A false test rejected.* Baal seemed triumphant. Elijah stood alone, the prophets of Baal were many, and yet the cause had still to be decided. The pretensions of a faith are not established by numbering its adherents and weighing their influence. Truth has often stood alone, and may stand alone again. 2. *The true test proposed.* Baal's claims and Jehovah's are put to the proof. There is wrath against the land; which will remove the cause of it ? By which will the sin offering laid upon the altar be accepted and the iniquity be removed? That test which alone met Israel's need could alone prove Israel's God. 3. *The true test accepted.* "And all the people answered and said, It is well spoken." Israel's answer will yet be the cry of all nations. The heart of the world will yet acknowledge the true God's work. III. THE DECISION (vers. 25—39). 1. *Baal tried and found wanting.* (1) The first choice was given to the priests of Baal. The world has had time enough to prove the truth of its pretensions, and to show whether it can meet man's need. The sacrifice has long lain upon its altar. (2) The earnestness of the false prophets. The failure is not due to lack of effort on the part of the world's votaries. There is no path which has not been trod to find whether the world has aught to satisfy the cry of man's soul; there is no sacrifice it has called for that has been withheld. (3) Their perseverance. Midday, the hour of the sun's might, was past, yet still they cried and cut themselves, &c. The boundless faith and unwearied efforts of the world's worshippers. (4) The failure. The sacrifice lay unconsumed upon the altar, lay still there hastening to corruption, when the darkness fell and the priests lay weltering in their blood. 2. *God tried and proved.* (1) God's altar built in the face of the world's discomfiture (vers. 29, 30). It was reared about the time of the *evening* sacrifice. "In the fulness of the times." "After that in the wisdom of God the world by wisdom knew not God, it pleased," &c. (1 Cor. i. 21). The vanity of the world's way was proved ere Christ was manifested. (2) The altar was one on which God had been served before (" He repaired the altar of the Lord which was broken down "). What was lost in the first is restored in the second Adam. The accepted sacrifice must be offered upon a perfect manhood. (3) God proved to the uttermost (33—35). There is nothing where that sacrifice is set which the fire of God will not kindle and change into the glory into which that sacrifice itself is lifted. (4) The answer. The fire fell; the accepted sacrifice went up in living flame which kindled all things round it—wood, stones, dust, water. We cannot test God in His own way without receiving an answer which will lift from the heart's depths the cry, "The Lord, he is God."

IV. THE JUDGMENT OF THE FALSE PROPHETS. The manifestation of God's glory is the hour of sin's overthrow.—J. U.

Vers. 41—46.—*The return of blessing.* I. ELIJAH'S ASSURANCE OF GOD'S MERCY. "There is a sound of abundance of rain," but it was only as yet a sound in *the prophet's* ear. 1. *The ground of the assurance.* (1) God had promised (ver. 1), He would therefore fulfil His word. (2) The preliminary work which He had sent him to do was accomplished. The people's heart was turned. Their sin was washed away. The curse would surely, then, be also removed. We build a still mightier trust on God's consistency. "He that spared not his own son," &c. 2. *The use he made of it.* "He said unto Ahab," and through him to all Israel, " Get thee up," &c. The work of the believer is to comfort God's people, and strengthen their expectation of good.

II. HIS PREVAILING WITH GOD. 1. *The assurance of God's mercy does not exclude prayer.* "Ahab went up to eat and drink," but "Elijah went up to the top of Carmel." The worldling may expect good and know nothing of supplication; not so with the man of God. Expectation is but encouragement to prayer. The desire that the blessing might come at once and cause the seed of faith to spring up in the people's hearts, made earnest prayer more necessary to Elijah than the refreshment which his body craved. 2. *The utter lowliness of the true worshipper.* "He cast himself down upon the earth." His face was hid. The man who stands nearest God is the lowliest of all God's worshippers. 3. *His importunity.* He did not cease till his prayer was granted. Again and again was the servant sent till the small cloud was seen.

III. HIS ATTEMPT TO PREVAIL WITH MAN. 1. *His message to Ahab* (" Prepare," &c.) *showed his care for the king.* He was a foe to the sin, but not to the man. 2. *He honoured him.* He "ran before Ahab to the entrance of Jezreel." The mighty prophet became the erring king's servant. The ministers of God must seek to win the sinful as well as to smite their sin. Hatred and contempt will neither advance God's cause nor man's well-being.—J. U.

Vers. 1—46.—*Elijah and the Prophets of Baal.* Elijah is now prepared for his work. He who had sent him into the desert now commands him to enter into open conflict with idolatry. God makes His will known to him in two ways.

I. BY AN INWARD IMPULSE.

II. THROUGH HIS MEETING WITH THE YOUNG OBADIAH, the protector of the prophets, and the faithful servant of God in the midst of the impure court of Ahab. Let it be ours to seek such a twofold assurance of the will of God. Let us not rest satisfied with an inward impulse, lest we be led astray by an illusive mysticism; let us watch also the indications of Providence. The wisdom that cometh down from above is not a blind leading; it can give a reasonable explanation of its motives. It learns to read the will of God at once in the book of the heart and in that of Providence. In his decisive interview with Ahab, Elijah shows us how we are to contend with the idolatry which is always at the root of every doctrine hostile to God. 1. The first element of strength is *his manly and indomitable courage.* To the king's insolent question, "Art thou he that troubleth Israel?" he replies, "I have not troubled Israel, but thou and thy father's house, in that ye have forsaken the commandments of the Lord, and thou hast followed Baalim" (ver. 18). He only will be victorious in the battle for the right who does not fear to denounce, without flinching, the sin of his people, and to say, like John the Baptist to the mighty ones, whether in the realm of society or of science, "It is not lawful for thee" (Matt. xiv.) Wherever sin is, the witness for truth and righteousness must first strike home to the conscience before attempting to convince the mind. 2. Everything in the language of Elijah breathes *a full assurance of victory.* He knows that he has on his side that strength of God which he has proved. To believe that we shall be

victorious is already to have half won the battle. 3. Elijah's irresistible weapon is
prayer. "Hear me, O Lord, hear me ; that this people may know that thou art
the Lord God, and that thou hast turned their heart back again" (ver. 37). If we
now look away from Elijah himself to the plan he proposed to pursue in his warfare
against idolatry, we shall see that no better is possible for us to-day. He does not
multiply arguments in dealing with his adversaries; he meets them on the common
ground of experience. He gives practical rather than theoretical demonstration of
the power of God. Here are the priests of Baal assembled on Mount Carmel. On
their side are the people, the favour of the king, the confidence of the public.
Elijah stands alone, and yet he feels he is not alone, for God is with him. The
heaven, closed for long months against the fertilizing rain, in punishment of the
perverseness of Israel, seems a vault of iron and brass. Will it ever melt again,
and spread life in soft reviving showers over the land ? In vain Ahab has sent his
servants up and down throughout the country ; the water springs have all failed.
The one question in all hearts is, What intercession may avail to draw down the rain
once more from heaven ? Elijah offers a challenge full of bitter irony to the priests
of Baal. May he not lawfully do so, as the messenger of Him of whom it is said
that "He shall laugh at the mighty ones who exalt themselves against him"?
(Psa. ii. 4.) In vain the priests cry, and leap, and cut themselves with stones, in
their savage rites ; there comes no answering voice from their deaf and dumb idol.
But at the prayer of Elijah the heavens re-open, and his God reveals Himself in the
glory of His power. Champions of the true God, the God of the gospel, defend it,
as Elijah did, against the insolent idolatry of materialism, or of the pantheism
which sets up an idol as monstrous as the Baal of old. Be bold, like Elijah, in
showing the idolaters how deeply they have fallen. Believe in the victory of your
cause ; use the invincible weapon of prayer; and to those who have vainly sought
the living water in the broken cisterns of earth (Jer. ii. 13), show the heavens
opened and the gracious rain descending upon all broken hearts, and bringing the
blessings of a full redemption. Give to our generation this conclusive practical
evidence. Meet the positivism of the infidel with the positivism of the Christian.
This is the surest means of casting down the idol into the dust, without having
recourse to that exterminating sword which the prophet of the old covenant was
commanded to draw upon the idolatrous priests. We live under another dispensation, and ours is that sword of the Spirit which only wounds to heal.—E. de P.

EXPOSITION.

CHAPTER XIX. 1—21.

ELIJAH'S FLIGHT. THE THEOPHANY OF
HOREB AND THE CALLING OF ELISHA.—We
can readily understand with what a sense
of humiliation and shame the weak and
excited king, who must have been awed and
impressed by the strange portent he had
witnessed, would recount the day's proceedings to his imperious and headstrong consort, and with what intense mortification
and rage she must have heard of the triumph
of the proscribed religion and of the defeat
and death of the priests of Baal. One might
almost have expected that the testimony of
an eye-witness, and that her husband, to
the greatness and completeness of Elijah's
victory ; that his unprejudiced, and indeed

unwilling, account of the sacrifices, of the
descent of the heavenly fire, of the cries it
wrung from the people, &c., would have
brought conviction to her mind and taught
her how useless it was to kick against the
pricks. But there are eyes so blinded (2
Cor. iv. 4) and hearts so steeled against the
truth that no evidence can reach them, and
this fierce persecutor of the prophets had
long been given over to a reprobate mind.
She listens to his story, but her one thought
is of revenge.

Ver. 1.—**And Ahab told Jezebel all that
Elijah had done, and withal how he had
slain** [Heb. *and all which he had slain.*

The construction, if it were not for the כָּל
would be usual enough. As that word is
omitted in some MSS. and versions, it is

possible it has been inserted by a tran-scriber, mechanically, from the אֶת כָּל־אֲשֶׁר preceding] **all the prophets,** [*sc.*, of Baal, all who were present] **with the sword.**

Ver. 2.—**Then Jezebel sent a messenger unto Elijah** [The prophet, wrapped in his abba, was seemingly about to spend the night in the open air, possibly at the gate, or in the plain. There, in the darkness, the messenger found him, Bähr assumes that this message had Ahab's sanction; *i.e.*, that he must have known of it and was too weak to prevent it. But it is just as likely that it was sent without his privity. On the evening of *that* day he would be afraid to threaten one vested with such tremendous powers as Elijah had just proved himself to possess], **saying** [Here the LXX. inserts "If thou art Eliou and I Jezebel"], **So let the gods** [As אֱלֹהִים is here found with a plural verb, it is rightly assumed that the reference is to the divinities of Phoenicia or of paganism generally. Besides, Jezebel would hardly swear by the one God of Elijah and of Israel. The LXX., however, has ὁ θεός], **do to me, and more also** [Heb. *and so let them add.* See on ch. ii. 23. Stanley appositely recalls to our minds "the tremendous vows which mark the history of the Semitic race, both within and without the Jewish pale, the vow of Jeph-thah, the vow of Saul, the vow of Hanni-bal." Rawlinson remarks that this oath was "familiar in the mouths of kings about this time" (1 Kings xx. 10 ; 2 Kings vi. 31). But it was a standing formula in Israel at all times. See Ruth 1. 17 ; 1 Sam. iii. 17 ; &c.], **if I make not thy life as the life of one of them by to-morrow about this time.** ["That queen consort, it seems, was, in effect, queen regent" (Henry). What in-duced the queen to send this message ? For it is obvious that if she really meant to slay Elijah, she took the very means to defeat her purpose by thus forewarning him of her intentions. Some of the older exposi-tors (see, *e.g.*, Hall, vol. ii. p. 396) have seen in the act a proof of her blind infatua-tion, of that infatuation which God often employs to defeat the machinations of wicked men, and this view is not to be lightly rejected. That she fully meant what she said is hardly to be doubted. But later writers, including Keil, Bähr, and Words-worth, see in the threat nothing more than a scheme for ridding herself of the presence of Elijah. They argue that, finding herself unable to put him to death, partly because of the impression he had made upon the people, and partly, too, because of the ascendancy he had just gained over the king, she resolved, by threatening him with

instant death, to give him an opportunity for flight. But this view hardly takes suffi-ciently into account the exasperation, the blind unreasoning hate, or the reckless and desperate character of the queen. It must be remembered that this message was despatched, not after she had had time for thought and calculation, but on the spur of the moment, as soon as she had heard of the massacre of the priests of Baal. That night she could do nothing, nor perhaps could she see her way clearly to compass his death on the morrow. But she will have him know that he is not going to escape her, and that, whatever the effect on her husband, *she* is unconquered and un-relenting. She does not stop to argue that he may take the alarm and flee. But she must gratify her impotent rage forthwith by threatening him with death the next day.]

Ver. 3.—**And when he saw that** [Heb. *and he saw and arose*, &c. But the LXX. has καὶ ἐφοβήθη, and the Vulgate *timuit*, and it is to be observed that this meaning, "*and he feared*," can be extracted from this word וַיַּרְא without any change of radicals, for the full form יִירָא is occasionally abbreviated into יָרֵא ; see 1 Sam. xviii. 12 ; xxi. 13 ; 2 Kings xvii. 28. A few MSS. have here וַיִּירָא and it certainly suits the context better. Bähr, who interprets, "he saw how matters stood," *i.e.*, that she meant him to flee, is not justified in asserting that this expression would require an accusative of the person feared. (See, *e.g.*, Gen. iii. 10 ; xv. 1 ; xviii. 15.) Both he and Keil further-more object to this interpretation that it is contrary to actual fact, neither of them being willing to allow that Elijah was afraid. Bähr says it is inconceivable that the man who had that day faced alone king and priests and the entire people should have become all at once afraid of a bad woman, and he explains Elijah's flight as caused by the discovery that he could not carry on his work of reformation, and by the absence of any intimation (like that of ch. xviii. 1) that he was to stay and hazard his life. But apart from the fact that we are distinctly told that he "went *for his life*" (cf. vers. 4, 10), and that his flight seems to have been instant and hurried, history tells of many great souls, hardly less brave than Elijah's, which have succumbed to a sudden panic. Anyhow, it is evident that for the moment Elijah had lost faith in God, otherwise he would certainly have waited for the "word of the Lord," which had hitherto invariably guided his movements (ch. xvii. 2, 8; xviii. 1). No doubt other emotions besides that of fear were struggling in his breast, and prominent among these was the feeling of profound disappointment and mortification. It is clear that he had hoped that the "day of Carmel" would turn the heart of the entire nation back again (ch. xviii. 37), and the great shout of ver. 39, and the subsequent execution, at his command, of the men who had deceived and depraved the people, might well justify the most sanguine expectations. We can readily imagine, consequently, how, especially after the excitement and fatigues of that day, the threatening and defiant message of the queen would seem the death-blow of his hopes, and how, utterly dispirited and broken down, he lost all trust, all faith, and, while fleeing for his life, "requested for himself that he might die" (ver. 4)], **he arose, and went for his life** [Keil is compelled, by his refusal to allow that Elijah was actuated by fear, to render these words, "went to commit his soul to God in the solitude of the desert." But the meaning is settled for us by the like expression in 2 Kings vii. 7; nor does Jer. xliv. 7 lend any support to Keil's view. Gesenius compares τρέχειν περὶ ψυχῆς. Od. ix. 423. The A. V. exactly represents the meaning], **and came to Beer-sheba** [Gen. xxi. 31; xxvi. 33. The southern boundary of Palestine (Josh. xv. 28; 2 Sam. xxiv. 7; Judg. xx. 1; 1 Chron. xxi. 2, &c.), allotted to the tribe of Simeon (Josh. xix. 2), which tribe, we gather from this passage (see also 2 Chron. xix. 4), was now absorbed in the southern kingdom. (See note on ch. xi. 31.) Wordsworth suggests that "perhaps he resorted to Beer-sheba in order to strengthen his faith with the recollection of the patriarchs who had dwelt there," &c. But if that had been his object, a journey to the place was hardly necessary, and it is clear that he only passed through it on his way to Mount Sinai. "Beer-sheba was about 95 miles from Jezreel"—Rawlinson, who adds that Elijah cannot have reached it till the close of the second day. But we must remember that his pace would be regulated by the powers of his servant, probably a mere lad (LXX. παιδάριον), so that it is hardly likely he could travel day and night without stopping to rest], **which belongeth to Judah** [It is part of Keil's argument in proof that Elijah did not flee from fear of Jezebel, that, had such been the case, he would have remained in the kingdom of Judah, where he would have enjoyed the protection of Jehoshaphat. But it is by no means certain that this prince, considering his close alliance with Ahab (ch. xxii. 4; cf. xviii. 10; 2 Kings viii. 18; 2 Chron. xviii. 1), would have sheltered the prophet. Indeed, it is remarkable, as Blunt has well pointed out (Coincid.

pp. 183, 184), that the prophet *never* took refuge in the southern kingdom. At one time he found a sanctuary beyond the Jordan; at another in the kingdom of Tyre, but never in the realm of Jehoshaphat. When he does come in haste to Beer-sheba, "it is after a manner which bespeaks his reluctance to set foot within that territory, even more than if he had evaded it altogether." The reason partly was, no doubt, as Wordsworth says, that his mission was to idolatrous Israel. Judah had both priests and prophets of its own], **and left his servant** [There is no warrant for the assertion (Stanley) that "one only of that vast assembly remained faithful to him, the Zidonian boy of Zarephath." The identity of this boy with the servant is by no means certain; nor is the defection of the people at all proven] **there.** [Probably because he wished to be alone with God; possibly because the boy was then too exhausted to go further, and there was no reason why he should be subjected to the uncertainties and privations of desert life; hardly for the security of both (Blunt). It is perhaps implied, however, that the kingdom of Judah, though not a safe abode for him, would be for his servant. When we remember that this servant never rejoined him, but that presently Elisha took his place, we can scarcely help wondering whether he was afraid to accompany Elijah any longer (cf. Acts xv. 38).]

Ver. 4.—**But he himself went a day's journey into the wilderness** [Cf. Gen. xxi. 14, 21; Jer. ix. 2; Rev. xii. 6. Beer-sheba stands on the fringe of the desert of *Et-Tih*. It was not for the sake of security alone that the prophet plunged into the "great and terrible wilderness." It is probable that from the first, "Horeb, the mount of God," was in his thoughts. He may well have seen that he was destined to be a second Moses; that he was raised up to assert and enforce the covenant of which Moses was the mediator. We have seen already that he cites the words spoken to Moses at the bush (ch. xviii. 36); that to him as to Moses there was granted an apparition of fire; we now find him rejected as Moses had been before him (Acts vii. 25, 35). How natural that, like Moses, he should flee into the land of Midian, to the place where God had spoken with Moses face to face. Wordsworth reminds us that the Jewish Church, by its cycle of lessons, suggests a comparison between the Law Giver and the Law Restorer], **and came and sat down under a** [Heb. *one;* see note on ch. xiii. 11] **juniper tree** [The רֹתֶם, here found with a feminine numeral (Keri, masculine), in ver. 5 with a masculine, is not the *juniper*, but the plant now known to the Arabs as *retem*, *i.e.*, the *broom* (*genista monosperma*, or *G. raetam*), "the most longed-for and most welcome bush of the desert, abundant in beds of streams and valleys, where spots for camping are selected, and men sit down and sleep in order to be protected against wind and sun" (Robinson, Pal. vol. i. p. 203). It does not, however, afford a complete protection (Thomson, L. and B. vol. ii. pp. 436, 437). Every traveller remarks on its abundance in the desert; it gave a name, *Rithmah*, to one of the stations of the Israelites (Num. xxxiii. 18. Cf. Stanley, S. and P. pp. 20, 79). Its roots are still used by the Bedouin, for the manufacture of charcoal (cf. Psa. cxx. 4, "coals of *rethem*"), which they carry to Cairo] : **and he requested for himself** [Heb. *asked as to his life*, accusative of reference] **that he might die** [Again like Moses, Num. xi. 15; Exod. xxxii. 32] ; **and said, It is enough** [or, *Let it be enough*. LXX. ίκανού-σθω. See note on ch. xii. 28] ; **now, O Lord, take away my life** [" Strange contradiction ! Here the man who was destined not to taste of death, flees from death on the one hand and seeks it on the other." Kitto] ; **for I am not better than my fathers.** [These words clearly reveal the great hopes Elijah had formed as to the result of his mission, and the terrible disappointment his banishment had occasioned him. Time was when he had thought himself a most special messenger of Heaven, raised up to effect the regeneration of his country. He now thinks his work is fruitless, and he has nothing to live for longer. Keil concludes from these words that Elijah was already of a great age, but this is extremely doubtful.]

Ver. 5.—**And as he lay and slept** [" While death was called for, the cousin of death comes unbidden" (Hall)] **under a** [Heb. *one*] **juniper tree, behold, then** [Heb. הִנֵּה *this;* "behold here," *siehe da*, Gesen.], **an angel** [Heb. *messenger;* the same word as in ver. 2, but explained in ver. 7 to be a messenger of God. Cf. Gen. xvi. 9; xxi. 17] **touched** [Heb. *touching*] **him, and said unto him, Arise and eat.** [Probably he had eaten little or nothing since leaving Jezreel. Food was now what he most needed. This circumstance suggests that the profound depression betrayed in his prayer (ver. 4) was largely the result of physical weakness.]

Ver. 6.—**And he looked, and, behold, there was a cake** [same word as in ch. xvii. 13] **baken on the coals** [Heb. a *cake of stones*, or *coals*. LXX. ἐγκρυφίας. The thin, flat bread of the East, especially among the nomadic desert tribes, is constantly baked in a rude

oven, constructed in the sand or soil. A little hollow is made ; sometimes it is lined with stones to retain the heat ; fuel, often the root of the *genista*, is placed upon it and kindled, and when the sand or stones are sufficiently hot, the embers are raked to one side, and the dough is placed in the oven, where it is sometimes covered with the ashes. Hence the Vulgate calls it *sub-cinericius panis*], **and a cruse of water at his head** [*i.e.*, the place of his head. Marg. *bolster*. The word is almost used as a preposition. Cf. 1 Sam. xix. 13 ; xxvi. 7]. **And he did eat and drink, and laid him down again.** [Heb. *returned and laid down.*]

Ver. 7.—**And the angel of the Lord came again the second time, and touched him** [*i.e.*, to awaken him. It was the food was to strengthen him], **and said, Arise and eat** [Probably he had eaten but little the first time, for sorrow and weariness] ; **because the journey is too great for thee.** [The LXX. ὅτι πολλὴ ἀπὸ σοῦ ἡ ὁδός and the Vulgate *grandis enim tibi restat via*, which Bähr follows, seem hardly so true to the Hebrew idiom as the A. V. rendering. Keil cites Vatablus, *iter est majus quam pro viribus tuis*. It is very improbable that (Rawlinson al.) the journey to Horeb was now suggested to him for the first time by the angel.]

Ver. 8.—**And he arose, and did eat and drink, and went in the strength of that meat forty days and forty nights** [Cf. Exod. xxiv. 18; xxxiv. 28; Deut. ix. 9, 25 ; Jonah iii. 4; Matt. iv. 2; Acts i. 3. But the primary reference is perhaps to the "forty days and forty nights" which Moses spent in Horeb, during which he "neither did eat bread nor drink water" (Deut. ix. 9), or to the forty years during which Israel was sustained in this same desert with "angels' food" (Psa. lxxviii. 25). It is noteworthy how both Moses and Elias were precursors of our Lord in a forty days' fast. "The three great fasters met gloriously on Tabor" (Hall). It is not implied that it took the prophet the whole of this time to reach Horeb, which is only distant from Beersheba some 130 miles. "There are eleven days' journey from Horeb, by the way of Mount Seir to Kadesh Barnea" (Deut. i. 2). It is of course possible that he wandered aimlessly hither and thither during this period, but it seems better to understand the words of the whole of his desert sojourn] **unto Horeb the mount of God.** [See note on ch. viii. 9. It is just possible that Horeb was already known as "the mount of God" at the time God appeared to Moses there—the whole of the Sinaitic peninsula was sacred in the eyes of the Egyptians; but it is more probable that this designation is used in Exod. iii. 1

proleptically, and that it was bestowed on
the Mount of the Law because of the
special revelation of the Godhead there
(Exod. iii. 6; xix. 3, 11, 18; Deut. i. 6;
iv. 10; v. 2, &c.)]

Ver. 9.—**And he came thither unto a cave**
[Heb. *the* cave. LXX. τὸ σπήλαιον. Many
commentators identify this with "the clift
of the rock" where Moses was concealed
while the Lord "passed by" (Exod. xxxiii.
22), and the use of the same word, עָבַר
in ver. 11 certainly favours this view. But
is it clear that the clift (נְקָרָה *fissure*) was a
cave ? Ewald understands "the cave in
which at that time travellers to Sinai
commonly rested." It is perhaps worth
remembering that a part of the desert,
though at some distance from Horeb, bears
at this day the name of *Maghârah*, or cave.
But there is a "narrow grot" pointed out
by tradition as the abode of Elijah, on the
side of Jebel Musa. "There is nothing to
confirm, but there is nothing to contradict,
the belief that it may have been in that
secluded basin, which has long been pointed
out as the spot. . . . No scene could be
more suitable for the vision which follows"
(Stanley). There is, however, one formidable
difficulty in the way of this identification,
viz., that the cave is only just large enough
for a man's body, which does not agree with
ver. 13], **and lodged** [לוּן means strictly to
pass the night. It is possibly connected
radically with לַיְלָה] **there; and, behold, the
word of the Lord came to him** [Not "in
vision as he slept" (Rawlinson). He could
not "go forth" in his sleep. That he was
to go forth "on the morrow" is equally
unlikely see ver. 11, note], **and he said
unto him, What doest thou here, Elijah ?**
[Many writers, Bähr and Keil among them,
will not allow that there is aught of reproof
in this question, or that Elijah had in any
way erred in his hasty flight. The former
asks how it comes to pass that the angel,
instead of reproving him, succoured and
strengthened him (vers. 6, 7), if he was
acting in faithlessness or disobedience. But
surely it does not follow that God denies all
grace and sustenance to His elect servants
even if they do, in a moment of despair,
forget or distrust Him. Elijah may have
been strengthened for this very journey,
because God would meet with him and
teach him the lessons of patience and trust
he needed to learn, at the "mount of God"
itself. And his answer, especially when
contrasted with that of ver. 14 (where see
note), certainly betrays, not only irritation
and despair, but a "carnal zeal which
would gladly have called down the ven-

geance of the Almighty upon all idolaters"
(Keil). The question in itself, it is true,
does not necessarily impart censure—it
might merely mean, "What wouldst thou
learn of me?" But when it is remembered
that the prophet had been *sent* to every
other destination by the "word of the
Lord," and that he had left Jezreel without
any such word—left it in terror and bitter
disappointment and sheer distrust of God—
it does look as if the words conveyed a
gentle reminder that he had deserted the
post of duty, and had no right to be there.
So Clericus, "*Quasi Deus diceret nihil esse
Eliae negotii in solitudine, sed potius in locis
habitatis, ut illic homines ad veri Dei cultum
adduceret.*"]

Ver. 10.—**And he said, I have been very
jealous** [Cf. Num. xxv. 11, which the prophet may have had in his mind. But the
jealousy of Phinehas was in harmony with
that of God (ver. 13)] **for the Lord God of
hosts** ["The title of *Lord God of hosts* is first
heard in the mouth of Elijah the prophet,
who had been very jealous for Jehovah in
opposition to Baal and Ashtaroth [Ash-
toreth?] the Phoenician deities; cf. 2 Kings
xxiii. 5, 'Baal, the sun, and moon, and
planets, and all the host of heaven'"
(Wordsworth)]: **for the children of Israel
have forsaken thy covenant** [he had memories of the covenant all around him],
thrown down thine altars [cf. ch. xviii. 30,
note. It is clear that many altars, similar
to that on Carmel, had been built, and had
been overturned], **and slain thy prophets
with the sword** [If the "hundred prophets"
of ch. xviii. 13 escaped, of which we cannot be certain, others did not]; **and I, even
I only, am left** [See note on ch. xviii. 22. It
must be confessed that the *prima facie*
view is that the prophets had been well-
nigh exterminated. But we must take into
account the deep despondency with which
Elijah spoke, and remember the correction
which his words received (ver. 18)]; **and
they seek my life, to take it away.** [The
commentators are hopelessly divided as to
the spirit and temper with which these
words were spoken. Bähr, as before, is very
positive that there is no complaint or murmuring against God on Elijah's part. He
contends that the prophet has been led to
Sinai simply by the earnest longing for a
disclosure concerning the dealings of God,
and for instructions as to his future conduct;
and this view has the support of other
weighty authorities. But it is extremely
difficult to resist the conclusion that we
have here at the least a "tacit reproof that
God had looked on so quietly for such a
length of time, and had suffered things to
come to such an extremity" (Keil). St.

Paul speaks of him as pleading with God against Israel (ἐντυγχάνει τῷ θεῷ κατὰ τοῦ Ἰσραήλ. Rom. xi. 2), and certainly represents the χρηματισμός he received as a correction. And the idea which this verse, taken in connexion with the prophet's flight (ver. 3) and his prayer (ver. 4), leaves on the unbiassed mind certainly is that in his zeal for God he resented not only the growing corruption of the age, but above all the frustration of his efforts to stay it. What burdened and vexed his righteous soul was that in the very hour of victory, when the people had confessed that Jehovah alone was God, he, the one solitary witness for the truth, should be driven from his post to escape as best he might, and to leave the covenant people to the baneful influence of Jezebel and her army of false prophets. It is the cry which we hear over and over again in the Old Testament, the complaint of the silence and apparent indifference of God, of the persecution of the righteous, and the impunity of evil-doers.]

Ver. 11.—And he said, Go forth [The LXX. inserts αὔριον, which, however, is destitute of authority, and was probably inserted from Exod. xxxiv. 2, to explain the difficulty which the prophet's apparent disregard of this command creates], and stand upon the mount before the Lord. And, behold, the Lord passed by [Heb. *passeth by*. Only used here and in Exod. xxxiii. 22; xxxiv. 6 of the Divine Being. The beatific vision must be transient. An abiding presence, a שֶׁבֶת, was more than man could bear. So Bähr. As Elijah does not seem to have gone forth from the cave until he heard the still small voice (ver. 13), some would take the participle עֹבֵר which is probably employed as more graphic, as a *future*, i.e., "the Lord will pass by," and this is the interpretation of the LXX.; ἰδοὺ παρελεύσεται κύριος· καὶ ἰδοὺ πνεῦμα μέγα. κ.τ.λ. The effect of this re-arrangement of the text would be that the words, "And behold the Lord passing by," must be taken as a part of the message, "Go forth," &c., and not as a statement of what happened. That statement would then begin with the next words, "And a great and strong wind," &c. But in that case we might have expected "For behold," &c., or the "And behold" would have come before "a great and strong wind," &c. It is also to be considered—and this seems to me decisive that the words "rent," "break," &c., are also participles, which it would be unnatural to divorce from the participle preceding], and a great and strong wind [Such as was not uncommon in that region. The approach to Sinai from the west is known as *Nukb-Hâwy*, "the

pass of the *winds*." Elsewhere we find the *Wâdy-el-Burk*, or "valley of lightning." These phenomena—the tempest, fire, &c.—would be all the more awful and impressive because of the surrounding desolation and the utter solitude] rent the mountains, and brake in pieces the rocks before the Lord; but the Lord was not in the wind [Heb. *not in the wind Jehovah*]: and after the wind an earthquake [Once before (Exod. xix. 18) an earthquake accompanied the descent of God upon the same mountain. The desert of Sinai, with the exception of the *Hammam Pharoun* and other hot springs, affords no traces of volcanic action. "Everywhere there are signs of the action of water, nowhere of fire" (Stanley). But רַעַשׁ properly means (compare *rauschen*, *rush*) a crashing noise (Job xxxix. 24; Isa. ix. 4), and the mysterious sounds of Jebel Musa have often been remarked (see Stanley, S. and P. pp. 13, 14)]; but the Lord was not in the earthquake:

Ver. 12.—And after the earthquake a fire [For the association of tempest, earthquake, fire, &c., as punishments of God, see Isa. xxix. 6, and Psa. xviii. 7, 8. "Fire" may well signify lightning (Job i. 16; Exod. ix. 23). For a vivid description of a thunderstorm at Sinai, see Stewart's "Tent and Khan," pp. 139, 140; *ap.* Stanley, "Jew. Ch.," vol. i. p. 149] : but the Lord was not in the fire : and after the fire a still small voice. [Heb. *a voice of gentle silence*. דְּמָמָה an onomatopoeic word, is allied to our word *dumb*. Very similar expression Job iv. 16. What was the object and meaning of this succession of signs? First, let us remember that Elijah was the prophet of *deeds*. He taught his contemporaries not by word but by act. He is here taught in turn by signs. There passes before him in the mountain hollow, in the black and dark night, a procession of natural terrors—of storm, and earthquake, and fire. But none of these things move him; none speak to his soul and tell of a present God. It is the hushed voice, the awful stillness, overpowers and enchains him. He is to learn hence, first, that the Lord is a God "merciful and gracious, long-suffering, and abundant in goodness and truth" (Exod. xxxiv. 6); and secondly, that as it has been with himself, so it will be with others; the name of the Lord will be proclaimed in a voice of gentle silence (*ib.*, ver. 5). The weapons of His warfare, the instruments of religious progress, must be spiritual, not carnal. Not in fire and sword and slaughter, but by a secret voice speaking to the conscience, will God regain His sway over the hearts of Israel. (See Homiletics.) The striking similarity between this theophany and that which Moses saw in the same place, or at no great distance from it, must not be overlooked, for this constitutes another link between law-giver and law-restorer. The proclamation of Exod. xxxiv. 3, 7 is the best exponent of the parable of vers. 11, 12. To each was the vision of God granted after a faithful witness against idolatry, and after a slaughter of idolaters; each was in a clift of the rock; in either case the Lord *passed by*; the one was taught by words, the other rather by signs, but the message in each case was the same—that judgment is God's strange work, but that He will by no means clear the guilty (cf. ver. 17).]

Ver. 13.—**And it was so, when Elijah heard it, that he wrapped his face in his mantle** [Like Moses, Exod. iii. 6.; cf. xxxiii. 20 ; xxxiv. 33 ; 2 Cor. iii. 13 ; Isa. vi. 1, 2. This mantle (see note on ch. xviii. 46) was probably a sheepskin. The LXX. calls it μηλωτή (cf. Heb. xi. 37). In Zech. xiii. 4 we find that the prophets wore a mantle of *hair*], **and went out, and stood** [Same words as in ver. 11. It was the still small voice, apparently, that first brought him to obey the command there given. He would perhaps be afraid to issue from the shelter of his cave during the tempest and the earthquake, which may have followed directly after the instruction to go forth was given. Possibly there was a lesson for him here also, viz., that amid the din and excitement and torture of drought and famine and fire and blood the commands of God are less likely to be heard in the soul and obeyed, than in the hour of peace and stillness. The drought and famine and sword have their work to do, even as the tempest and the earthquake have theirs ; but it is by the voice of mercy and love that the hearts of men are turned back again. " Not in the strong east wind that parted the Red Sea, or the fire that swept the top of Sinai, or the earthquake that shook down the walls of Jericho would God be brought so near to man as in the still small voice of the child of Bethlehem" (Stanley)] **in the entering in of the cave.** [He hardly obeyed the letter of the command of ver. 11 even then. Does not this point to a rebellious and unsubdued heart ? Is it not a confirmation of the view taken above, that he fled to Horeb, full of bitter disappointment and murmuring against God ; and that the purpose of this revelation was not only to teach him as to God's dealings with men, but also to school and subdue his own rebellious heart?] **And, behold, there came a voice unto him** [The expression is different from that of ver. 9. There we read of the " word of the Lord," here of a " voice." But this is

not to be identified with the " still small voice" of ver. 12], **and said, What doest thou here, Elijah ?** [As in ver. 9.]

Ver. 14.—**And he said, I have been very jealous for the Lord God of hosts : because the children of Israel have forsaken thy covenant, thrown down thine altars, and slain thy prophets with the sword ; and I, even I only, am left ; and they seek my life, to take it away.** [Verbatim as in ver. 10. What are we to understand from this repetition of the former answer ? Has the lesson of this theophany been lost upon him ? Has he failed to grasp its significance ? It is probable that he only partially understood its meaning, and it certainly looks as if he still felt himself an injured and disappointed man ; as if the recollection of the way in which his work had been frustrated still rankled in his soul. But though the words are the same, it is possible, and indeed probable, that the *tone* was entirely different ; that instead of speaking, as he had spoken before, querulously and almost defiantly, he now, catching his inspiration from the still small voice, speaks with bated breath and profound self-humiliation. The facts are the same. He repeats them, because they and they alone explain why he is there, and because he cannot see as yet how they are to be remedied. But he is now conscious of a misgiving as to the wisdom and piety of his course. He feels he has acted hastily and faithlessly, and has wanted to do God's work in his own rough way. He will go back, if it be God's will ; he will be content to wait God's time, and to follow His leading. The commission which is straightway given him almost proves that he had experienced a change. It implies that he is now fitted for his high ministry.]

Ver. 15.—**And the Lord said unto him, Go, return on thy way** [Heb. *to thy way*, as in Gen. xix. 2 ; xxxii. 2 ; Num. xxiv. 25, &c.] **to the wilderness of Damascus** [The construct case with ה local. Keil refers to Deut. iv. 41 ; Josh. xii. 1 ; and Ewald 216 *b*. This cannot mean " through the desert to Damascus," for he could not possibly go any other way, nor yet " to the desert (through which he had just come) to Damascus," for he was then in the heart of the desert. He was to find a hiding-place —we find the king of Damascus at war with Ahab, ch. xx.—or possibly a sphere for work, —he would be near Hazael—in the rugged desert which stretches south and east of the Syrian capital. (See Stanley, " Sinai and Palestine," p. 410 ; Porter's " Five Years in Damascus," vol. ii. p. 254 sqq.) Here, too, the prophet would be at no great distance from his own country. See on ch. xvii. 3]: **and**

when thou comest, anoint [Heb. *and thou shalt come and anoint.* LXX. καὶ ἥξεις καὶ χρίσεις. Tho A. V. increases the difficulty. In the Hebrew the *time* of the anointing is indefinite. This commission has long been a *crux interpretum.* For neither Hazael, nor Jehu, nor Elisha, so far as we have any record, was ever *anointed* by Elijah. Elisha was *called* by him to the prophetic office. Hazael, it is barely possible, may have been anointed secretly, like David (1 Sam. xvi. 2, 13), but all that we gather from Scripture is, that he was called in an indirect way, and certainly not anointed, by Elisha (2 Kings viii. 12—15). Jehu was certainly anointed, but it was neither by Elisha nor Elijah (2 Kings ix. 1, 6), but by one of the sons of the prophets. All we can say, consequently, is that the command was obeyed *in the spirit,* and no doubt in the best possible time and way. There may have been good reasons, of which we know nothing, why Elijah should devolve the appointment of the two kings upon his successor, and we can readily understand that the word "anoint" was, as in Judg. ix. 8, Isa. lxi. 1, never meant to be construed literally. For in the first place, we have no record elsewhere of the anointing of any *prophet;* and secondly, it is remarkable that when Elijah might so easily have anointed Elisha, he did nothing of the kind. It is clear, therefore, that he understood the word to mean "appoint." And the root idea of anointing, it must be remembered, was the *setting apart* for the service of God (Exod. xxix. 6). Hence it was (Bähr) that vessels (Exod. xxx. 26 sqq.), and even stones (Gen. xxviii. 18), were anointed. And when we find that these three persons were set apart sooner or later, and in different ways, to fulfil the high purposes of God, that ought to suffice us. The author of this history clearly found no difficulty in reconciling this account and that of 2 Kings viii., ix. It has also been objected to this charge (Rawlinson) that it is no "explanation or application of the preceding parable." But this is precisely what it appears to have been intended to be. The prophet is here taught by word much the same lesson that had been conveyed by signs, in the preceding vision. No doubt there are additional particulars—the vision dealt only with principles, the charge descends to details and prescribes duties—but still the great lesson that souls are to be won, that God's kingdom is to be advanced, not by wrath and vengeance, by fire and sword, but by meekness and gentleness, through the reason and the concience, is proclaimed. Hazael and Jehu, each was God's instrument to punish; each was like the sweeping storm or the devour-ing fire, each was an engine of destruction; but by neither of these were the hearts of men turned to the Lord. It was the sword of Elisha, the sword of his mouth (cf. Isa. xi. 4; xlix. 2; Rev. i. 16; ii. 16), should constrain men to hide their faces and humble themselves before God] Hazael [the *seer of God.* This name, viewed in connection with Elijah's vision of God, is noticeable] **to be king over Syria:**

Ver. 16.—**And Jehu** [*Jehovah is he.* The name was as appropriate as Elijah's] **the son** [*i.e.,* descendant, probably grandson (2 Kings ix. 2, 14). Nimshi may have been a person of more importance than Jehoshaphat] **of Nimshi shalt thou anoint to be king over Israel** [The prophet thus learns that the house of Omri is to share the fate of the dynasties which had preceded it. Jezebel's triumph is not to endure] **: and Elisha** [*My God is salvation.* This name, borne by the successor of Elijah, "My God is the Lord," looks like a fresh revelation of God's nature and purpose of grace] **the son of Shaphat** [*Judge*] **of Abel-meholah** [The mention of his abode, Abel-meholah, "the meadow of the dance" (cf. ch. iv. 12; Judg. vii. 22), a town in the Jordan valley, at no great distance from Beth-shean, almost implies that he was hitherto unknown to Elijah. It is to be observed that no such addition follows the mention of Hazael or Jehu] **shalt thou anoint to be prophet in thy room.** [So far from Elijah's work being fruitless, or from the prophetic order being extinguished, provision is now made for his successor.]

Ver. 17.—**And it shall come to pass, that him that escapeth the sword of Hazael** [See 2 Kings viii. 12, 28; x. 32; xiii. 3, 22] **shall Jehu slay** [2 Kings ix. 24—33; x. *passim.* Cf. Isa. lxvi. 16] **: and him that escapeth from the sword of Jehu shall Elisha slay.** [Elijah might reasonably interpret the commission to "anoint" Hazael, &c., as a figure, seeing there is an undoubted figure of speech here. Elisha was a man of peace. His sword was the "sword of the Spirit, the word of God." It was by "the breath of his lips he slew the wicked" (Isa. ii. 4; 2 Thess. ii. 8; Hosea vi. 5). Not only are vers. 16, 17 an interpretation, in some sort, of the vision, but they are an answer to Elijah's complaint (vers. 10, 14). The "children of Israel" who had forsaken the covenant should be punished by Hazael (cf. 2 Kings viii. 12, "I know what thou wilt do unto the *children of Israel,*" and cf ch. x. 32); the king and queen who had thrown down the altars and slain the prophets should be slain, one by the sword of Syria, the other at the command of Jehu; while to his allegation that the prophets were extinct and he was left alone is opposed the ordination of a successor, and the mention of the "seven thousand" in ver. 18.]

Ver. 18.—**Yet I have left me** [So St. Paul, Rom. xi. 4, κατέλιπον; but the LXX. (καταλείψεις) and all the versions translate the word as future, as in the margin, *I will leave*, and so the ꝉ conversive seems to require. See Gesen., Gram. § 124—26] **seven thousand** [not so much a round as a symbolical number—"the ἐκλογή of the godly" (Keil). "The remnant according to the election of grace" (Rom. xi. 5). It is like the 144,000 and the 12,000 of Rev. vii. 4—8. The prominent idea is perhaps this: Though the children of Israel have forsaken My covenant, yet I have kept and will keep it. It also suggests how the still small voice had been speaking in the silence] **in Israel, all the knees which have not bowed unto Baal, and every mouth which hath not kissed him.** [We gather from Job xxxi. 26, 27 that it was customary to kiss the hand to the idol, or object of worship, and from Hosea xiii. 2 to kiss the image itself. Most of the commentators adduce Cicero *in Verrem* iv. 43, where he speaks of the statue of Hercules at Agrigentum, the lips and chin of which were a little worn by the kisses of devotees.]

Ver. 19.—**So he departed thence, and found** [Nothing can be concluded from this word as to previous acquaintance] **Elisha the son of Shaphat, who was ploughing** [It was in the winter, consequently (Prov. xx. 4. See Conder, p. 328). "Elisha is found not in his study, but in the field : not with a book in his hand, but the plough" (Hall). **with twelve yoke of oxen** [Heb. *ploughing twelve yoke*, from which Ewald gathers that he was ploughing twelve yoke of land— צֶמֶד like *jugum*, is used as a measure of land in 1 Sam. xiv. 14, Isa. v. 10—and was then at work on the twelfth and last. But the meaning of the "twelve yoke" here is surely settled by the "yoke of *oxen;*" cf. ver. 21 and see below] **before him** [This word also points to animals, not land. The twelve pair of oxen, it is generally thought, are mentioned to show that Elisha was a man of substance. It is not certain, however, that all the twelve belonged to him. See next note], **and he with the twelfth** ["I have seen more than a dozen ploughs thus at work. To understand the reason of this, several things must be taken into account. First, that the arable land of nearly all villages is cultivated in common; then that Arab farmers delight to work together, partly for mutual protection, and partly from their love of gossip," &c. Thomson, L. and B. i. 208] : **and Elijah passed by**

him [Heb. *to him*. The idea that he may have "crossed the stream of the Jordan" (Rawlinson) is extremely improbable. The current is strong, and it is not everywhere fordable, especially in winter], **and cast his mantle upon him.** [Heb. *to him* אֵלָיו. But LXX. ἐπ᾽ αὐτόν. Already, it would seem, the rough hairy mantle had come to be recognized as the garb of a prophet (cf. Zech. xiii. 4). "The prophet's cloak was a sign of the prophet's vocation" (Keil). To cast the cloak to or upon Elisha was therefore an appropriate and significant way of designating him to the prophetic office. "When Elijah went to heaven Elisha had the mantle entire" 2 Kings ii. 13 (Henry). The Germans use the word *mantel-kind* of an adopted child.]

Ver. 20.—**And he left the oxen** [As, being the last in the line, he could do, without stopping the others. It is probable too that, Elisha being the last, Elijah's action would not have been observed by the rest], **and ran after Elijah** [It is clear that Elisha both understood the act, and made up his mind at once. No doubt he too had long sighed and prayed over the demoralization of his country and the dishonour done to his God. Elijah, after casting the mantle, strode on, leaving it for Elisha to take or reject it. The latter soon showed his choice by *running* after him], **and said, Let me, I pray thee, kiss my father and my mother, and then I will follow thee. And he said unto him, Go back again** [Heb. *go, return*] : **for what have I done to thee ?** [There is not a word of reproof here, as Wordsworth and Rawlinson imagine. Indeed, it would have been strange if there had been. A greater readiness to obey the prophetic summons, Elisha could not well have showed. Forthwith, as soon as he realized his call, "he left the oxen and ran after" his new master. True, he asks permission—and why should he not ? for "grace is no enemy to good nature"— to give a parting embrace to the father and mother to whom he owed his life, and whom he had been required by God to honour. But there is no proof of "a divided heart" here. If he had begged to be allowed to stay and *bury* his mother and father (St. Luke ix. 59—61) it might have been otherwise. But he suggests nothing of the kind. He says : "One kiss, one farewell, and then I will follow thee." It is a complete mistake, consequently, to interpret Elijah's words to mean, "Go, return to thy ploughing, for why shouldst thou quit it ? . . . Thou canst remain as thou art" (Rawlinson). Their true meaning, as evidenced by the sequel (ver. 21), clearly was, "Go back and kiss them ; why shouldst thou not ? *For* what have I done to thee? I have summoned thee to follow me. But I have not required thee to repudiate thine own flesh and blood."]

Ver. 21.—**And he returned back from him** [Wordsworth is not warranted in affirming that Elisha " did *not* go back and kiss," &c. The text rather implies that he did], **and took a yoke** [Heb. *the yoke.* Cf. ver. 19] **of oxen, and slew them** [Heb. *sacrificed;* LXX. ἔθυσε. But the word, though generally restricted to sacrificial acts, primarily means " to slay " simply, as here, and in Gen. xxxi. 54; 1 Sam. xxviii. 24; 2 Chron. xviii. 2; Ezek. xxxix. 17. There was no altar there, and the flesh of a sacrifice was never boiled], **and boiled their flesh** [Heb. *boiled them, the flesh*] **with the instruments of the oxen** [the plough, yoke, &c. The plough of the East is extremely rude and slender, but the yoke, shaft, &c., would afford a fair supply of wood. The scarcity of timber may have had something to do with this application of the " instruments of the oxen ; " but it is much more important to see it in a symbolical act, expressive of Elisha's entire renunciation of his secular calling. He would henceforth need them no longer. Cf. 1 Sam. vi. 14; 2 Sam. xxiv. 22], **and gave unto the people** [Not only the servants or peasants who had been ploughing with him, but possibly his neighbours and friends. This was a farewell, not a religious feast. Cf. Luke v. 29, where Levi makes a "great feast " on the occasion of his call], **and they did eat. Then he arose, and went after Elijah, and ministered unto him.** [*i.e.*, became his attendant, as Joshua had been the minister of Moses (Exod. xxiv. 13 ; Josh. i. 1), and as Gehazi subsequently became servant to him. See 2 Kings iii. 11: "Elisha . . . which poured water on the hands of Elijah; " and cf. Acts xiii. 5.]

HOMILETICS.

God and the Man of God. This chapter lends itself more readily to textual than to topical treatment.

Ver. 1.—"*And Ahab told Jezebel all that Elijah had done.*" Was there no word, then, of what *God* had done? Did he think that Elijah, by his own power or holiness, had brought down fire from heaven? Or if Elijah brought it, was there no thought of Him who sent it? But it is an every-day experience that men will think of anything, talk of anything but their Maker. They do not " like to retain God in their thoughts " (Rom. i. 28). Perhaps Ahab was afraid in the presence of Jezebel to connect the awful portent with the name of the Lord. That would be tantamount to confessing before her that the Lord He was God (ch. xviii. 24). Jezebel, therefore, may think it was magic if she will. Men are not unseldom cowards in religion, even before their own wives and children. How blessed it is when husband and wife rehearse to each other the righteous acts of the Lord ; how doubly blessed when the believing husband wins and saves the unbelieving wife (1 Cor. vii. 14, 16). Then marriage is a sacrament indeed.

"*And . . . how he had slain all the prophets,*" &c. There was no need to tell her that, at least that night. This communication shows that Ahab's heart was unchanged, otherwise he would have practised a discreet reserve. He must have known full well what the effect of those dark tidings would be. Had he wished for her conversion, he would surely have waited till the morning light. That would have given the other tidings he had brought a chance to work repentance. To speak of the death of the prophets would be to fill her with ungovernable rage. It was charity to hold his peace. That was " a time to keep silence."

Ver. 2.—"*Then Jezebel sent a messenger.*" Not, as we might have expected, to sue for forgiveness, but to threaten reprisals. "She swears and stamps at that whereat she should have trembled" (Hall). There is no hate like a woman's, no wickedness like hers. They never do things by halves.

> " Men differ at most as heaven and earth,
> But women, best and worst, as heaven and hell."

This woman will not be persuaded though one rose from the dead (Luke xvi. 1). The fiery sign was lost upon her (" Faith cometh by hearing, not by apparitions "). Ahab witnessed the execution of the priests and was too much awed to prevent it. Jezebel only hears of it, and straightway vows vengeance against its author. " Adam was not deceived, but the woman being deceived was in the transgression " (1 Tim. ii. 14).

" *The gods do so*," &c. This is like much of the profane swearing that we hear, " full of sound and fury, signifying nothing." It costs very little to invoke factitious deities. " The gods she sware by could do her no harm." They had not been able to save their own prophets. Cf. Judg. vi. 31.

" *If I make not thy life*," &c. The enemies of God's Church and prophets are always chained, and sometimes are infatuate too. They cannot " go beyond the word of the Lord to do less or more " (Num. xxii. 18). " The king's heart is in the hand of the Lord . . . he turneth it whithersoever he will " (Prov. xxi. 1). " He taketh the wise in their own craftiness " (1 Cor. iii. 19), and turns the counsel of an Ahithophel into foolishness (2 Sam. xv. 31). The *wrath* of man is made to praise Him (Psa. lxxvi. 10). " Her threat preserved him whom she meant to kill." " It were no living for godly men if the hands of tyrants were allowed to be as bloody as their hearts " (Hall).

Ver. 3.—" *He arose and went for his life.*" Elijah, the intrepid apostle of Carmel, who had met the king without fear and faced the four hundred Baal prophets, and stood alone *contra mundum*, is seized with panic fear. The champion of the morning becomes the coward of the evening. We may well exclaim here, *Quantum mutatus ab illo !* well ask, " Lord, what is man ? " Some have called man a demigod; have seen in him " the peer of the angels." " What a piece of work," says Hamlet, " is man ! how noble in reason ! how infinite in faculties ! in form and moving how express and admirable ! in action how like an angel ! in apprehension how like a god ! " In Elijah we see man at his best. He was one of the " first three." He is distinguished even from his brother prophets by the work he was called to do, by the powers with which he was entrusted, by the grace given to him, the care taken of him, the triumphant end granted to him. But how weak and unworthy does this elect messenger of God now appear. " Should such a man as I am flee ? " (Neh. vi. 11.) " How are the mighty fallen ! " How completely he is the sport of circumstances ; how full of contradictions his conduct. At one moment he flees for his *life;* at the next he requests for himself that he may *die.* " Doth he wish to be rid of his life because he feared to lose it ? " (Hall.) Yesterday strong in faith, fearing neither man nor devil ; to-day trembling before a woman, wretched and despairing. But more than that, we find him impatient, petulant, proud, arraigning the providence and wisdom of God. " Take away my life," this is the cry of a mortified ambition ; of one who cannot trust himself in God's hands any longer. " I am not better than my fathers." What do these words reveal, but that he *had* thought himself better than they ; that he had been " exalted above measure through the abundance of revelations " ? (2 Cor. xii. 7.) And this is Elijah, the restorer of the law, the express ambassador of heaven. It is well said that he was " a man subject to like passions as we are " (James v. 18). " I have seen an end of all perfection." Here is humanity at its best, and how poor and weak it is. If man is " the glory " he is also " the scandal of the universe."

> " Chaos of passions, passions all confused,
> Still by himself abused or disabused,
> Created half to rise and half to fall,
> Great lord of all things, yet a prey to all :
> Sole judge of truth, in endless error hurled,
> The glory, jest, and riddle of the world."

Ver. 5.—" *Behold, an angel touched him.*" So that he was watched and guarded, even while he slept. His impatience and faithlessness have not diminished the loving care and tenderness of God. " He knoweth our frame." His very sleep was ordained in mercy. Observe the contrast between the pity and love of God and the childish repining and discontent of the man of God ! Observe, too, how God uses the ministry of angels ! Compare Matt. iv. 11 ; Luke xxii. 43 ; Acts xxvii. 23 ; v. 19 ; xii. 8. " Are they not all ministering spirits ? " (Heb. i. 14.) " No wilderness is too solitary for the attendance of those blessed spirits." " While he slept, his breakfast is made ready for him by those spiritual hands."

> " How oft do they their silver bowers leave
> To come to succour us that succour want!
> How oft do they with golden pinions cleave
> The flitting skyes, like flying pursuivant,
> Against fowle fiendes to ayd us militant!
> They for us fight, they watch, and dewly ward,
> And their bright squadrons round about us plant;
> And all for love and nothing for reward.
> O why should heavenly God to men have such regard? "

Ver. 6.—" *A cake baken on the coals*," &c. Not only was the prophet protected, he was provided for by the angel. What a commentary on that verse, " He giveth it to his beloved while they sleep "·(Psa. cxxvii. 2, Heb.) And does not God give us all food in like manner? While the farmer sleeps, the seed springs and grows up, he knoweth not how (Mark iv. 27). Our Keeper neither slumbers nor sleeps (Psa. cxxi. 4). Observe also how God prepares a table in the wilderness. It is not the first time He has given angels' food in the desert (Psa. lxxviii. 25; Neh. ix. 21; Deut. viii. 16).

Ver. 7.—" *Arise and eat*." Though this was supernatural food, so far as we can see miraculously provided, and in any case of preternatural efficacy, yet it must be taken and eaten in the ordinary way. Elijah might have been endued with strength for his desert journey without the aid of any material elements. The angel's touch or even the word of the Lord would surely have sufficed (Judg. vi. 21; Ezek. ii. 2; iii. 24; Luke vii. 7). Instead of which a cake is baken on the coals, and he must rise and eat thereof, eat thereof *twice*. God works by means, and it is for man to use them. It is presumption to expect God to dispense with them because He *can* do so.

Ver. 8.—" *Went in the strength of that meat*," &c. It is very noticeable how many miraculous feedings we have in Holy Scripture. Not only does the New Testament record a feeding, now of five thousand with five loaves, now of four thousand with seven loaves (Matt. xv. 9, 10); not only is one or other of these mentioned by all four evangelists (Matt. xiv. 17; Mark vi. 38; Luke ix. 13; John vi. 9; Matt. xv. 36; Mark viii. 6); but the Old Testament, in addition to such narratives as those of 1 Kings xvii. 14 sqq.; 2 Kings iv. 1—6, 42 sqq., tells of a miraculous supply of food which extended over forty years (Exod. xvi. 14—35; Deut. viii. 3, 4, 16). Is not all this to teach us that man doth not live by bread alone? (Deut. viii. 3.) Are they not rehearsals, adumbrations of the great mystery of our religion, of the true " bread from heaven which giveth life unto the world"? (John vi. 32 sqq.) We too are journeying to Horeb, the mount of God. The home of our souls is the " mountain of myrrh and the hill of frankincense " (Cant. iv. 6). And the journey is too great for us. Without Divine aid, without soul food, we shall " faint by the way." But God has provided for us a gracious *viaticum*, a meat which the world knows not of, flesh which is meat indeed, blood which is drink indeed (John vi. 55).

Ver. 9.—" *The word of the Lord came to him*." Though he had not merited such a favour, for he had acted without that word when he fled. True, he fled to the desert, so far as we can see, that he might hear what God would say concerning him, but he had no right to presume that He who had not spoken at Jezreel would speak at Sinai. But God never deals with us as we deserve, or as we deal with one another. " If thou, Lord, shouldest mark iniquities, O Lord, who shall stand? " (Psa. cxxx. 3.) " If they break my statutes . . . then will I visit their transgression with the rod . . . nevertheless, my loving-kindness will I not utterly take from him," &c. (Psa. lxxxix. 31—33). " Thou hast played the harlot with many lovers; yet return again to me, saith the Lord" (Jer. iii. 1). If the word did not come to us when we stray, how could we be reclaimed? God must take the first step (John vi. 44).

" *What doest thou here, Elijah?*" It is more than doubtful whether there was any audible voice (see ver. 12). God spoke through the *conscience*. And this is still the organ used by the Holy Ghost. Have *we* never heard this question in our secret souls? perhaps when we stood in the way of sinners, or sat in the seat of the scornful. We should do well to put it repeatedly to our own hearts. "*Bernarde, ad quid venisti ?*"—it was thus that the greatest saint of the Middle Ages often tried his motives and conduct.

Ver. 10.—"*I have been very jealous.*" We often confound zeal for our own ends and purposes with zeal for God; often misread our own motives. Jehu cried, "Come and see my zeal for the Lord" (2 Kings x. 16); "but Jehu took no heed to walk in the law of the Lord God of Israel," &c. (vers. 29, 31). Saul's "zeal for the children of Israel and Judah" (2 Sam. xxi. 2) procured the impalemant of seven of his sons. St. Paul bears witness of the Jews, that "they have a zeal of God, but not according to knowledge," and testifies of himself, "concerning zeal, persecuting the Church" (Phil. iii. 6; cf. Acts xxvi. 9, 11). We can understand the cynical warning. *Surtout, point de zéle,* when we remember what crimes have been committed in its name. The spirit of Elias, the spirit of fire and sword (2 Kings i. 10; 1 Kings xix. 1), is not the spirit of our Lord or His Church (Luke ix. 55, 56). There was not improbably in this complaint something of the resentment which James and John felt when the Samaritans did not receive them. Was it not in part pique at his rejection by Israel led to Elijah's intercession against them? (Rom. xi. 2.) It is true, he begins, "They have rejected thee," but he ends, "They have rejected me" (1 Sam. viii. 7). And our lamentations over the non-success of our ministry, are they inspired by the dishonour done to God, or the indifference manifested towards ourselves? There may be both pride and temper in the complaint, "He followeth not us" (Mark ix. 38).

Ver. 11.—"*Stand . . . before the Lord.*" Only thus can we know ourselves, and self-knowledge must be our first aim. "*E caelo descendit, γνῶθι σεαυτόν.*" "In thy light shall we see light." We compare ourselves with pigmies when we compare ourselves with others (2 Cor. x. 12). It is only in the presence of our Maker that we learn our nothingness and sinfulness. "Now mine eye seeth thee. Wherefore I abhor myself, and repent in dust and ashes" (Job xlii. 5, 6). "Beholding the glory of the Lord, we are changed into the same image" (2 Cor. iii. 18).

Ver. 12.—"*A still small voice.*" The terrors of the Lord awe the soul; His love melts and wins it. What the law could not do, the gospel has done (Rom. viii. 3). Christ draws men unto Him by the sweet attraction of His cross (John xii. 32). The lightnings and thunders, the trumpet and the voices of Sinai, do not move the world as do the seven last words of the Crucified. "Not in the wind that parted the Red Sea, or the fire that swept the top of Sinai," was God brought so near to man, "as in the ministrations of Him whose cry was not heard in the streets, as in the still small voice of the child at Bethlehem" (Stanley). This parable may be compared with the familiar fable which tells how storm and sun strove together for the mastery. The former made the traveller wrap his garments more closely about him; the latter made him cast them aside. Love is more powerful than fear, and that because "love is of God." Judgment is His strange work. "God loves to make a way for Himself by terror, but He conveys Himself to us in sweetness" (Bp. Hall)—a truth well brought out in Theodore Monod's exquisite hymn—

> "Yet He found me: I beheld Him
>   Bleeding on the cursèd tree;
> Heard Him pray, 'Forgive them, Father;'
>   And my wistful heart said faintly,
>   'Some of self, and some of Thee.'
>
> "Day by day His tender mercy
>   Healing, helping, full and free;
> Sweet and strong, and, ah! so patient,
>   Brought me lower, whilst I whispered,
>   'Less of self, and more of Thee.'
>
> "Higher than the highest heavens,
>   Deeper than the deepest sea,
> Lord, Thy love at last hath conquered;
>   Grant me now my spirit's longing,
>   'None of self, and all of Thee.'"

Ver. 13.—" *Wrapped his face in his mantle*." He was afraid to look upon God (Exod. iii. 6; cf. Gen. iii. 10, "I hid myself"). "Conscience makes cowards of us all." Besides, no man can see His face and live (Exod. xxxiii. 20). The beatific vision is too much for our poor mortality, too much for the angelic powers (Isa. vi. 2). It is in mercy that God is veiled from our view. The seeing God as He is belongs to the times of restitution (Matt. v. 8; Heb. xii. 14; Rev. i. 7; xxii. 4; 1 Cor. xiii. 12).

Ver. 14.—" *I have been very jealous*," &c. The same question, and precisely the same words in reply. But everything was not the same. The man and the manner were alike changed (cf. 1 Sam. x. 6). He has heard the "still small voice," and it has hushed his own. How true it is, "It is not the words we say, but the manner and spirit in which we say them, gives them their force and significance."

Ver. 15.—" *Go, return*." This is God's answer to the question, "What doest thou here?" "Thou hast now no business here. Thou hast a work to do elsewhere. Thou art not left alone, nor has God ceased to watch over and care for His Church. His ministers of wrath are already nominated; it is for thee to call them to their work." Which of God's servants has not desponded like Elijah? Who has not been tempted to think his work a failure? Who has not had to complain of a gain-saying and disobedient people? How many have been induced to desert their posts? But no man's work *can* be a failure unless he is a failure himself. Our work is to witness, whether men will hear or whether they will forbear. If they forbear, who shall say that that work is not successful? And it may be suggested here that work is often the very best remedy for despondency and doubt. The diligent soul has no time for self-torture. Its eye is fixed on others. There is a quaint legend which tells how, some years after the event, St. Thomas was again troubled with agonizing doubts as to our Lord's resurrection. He sought the apostles, and began to pour his soul's troubles into their ears. But first one, then the other, looked at him in astonishment, and told the unhappy doubter that he was sorry for him, but really he had so much to do he had no time to listen to his tale. Then he was fain to impart his woes to some devout women. But they, as busy as Dorcas and in like employment, soon made him understand that they had no leisure for such thoughts as these. At last it dawned upon him that perhaps it was because they *were* so busy that they were free from the doubts by which he was tortured. He took the hint; he went to Parthia; occupied himself in preaching Christ's gospel, and was never troubled with doubts any more.

Ver. 18.—" *Yet have I left me seven thousand*." There is always a remnant (Rom. xi. 4, 5). The gates of hell cannot prevail against the Church. God has His secret ones, unknown to men. The number of the elect must be accomplished. (Rev. vii. 4). The prophets have been too much given to pessimist views. "God's faithful ones are often his hidden ones" (Psa. lxxxiii. 3).

> "Yet in fall'n Israel are there hearts and eyes,
> That day by day in prayer like thine arise,
> Thou know'st them not, but their Creator knows."

Archbishop Ussher used to say to say that in the great Assize, if the King should set him on His right hand, three things would surprise him. First, to find himself there; secondly, to find that numbers of whose salvation he had always been confident were not there; thirdly, to find that thousands of whose salvation he had always despaired were there after all.

Ver. 19.—" *Found Elisha . . . ploughing*." God never calls an idle man. "If ye have not been faithful in the unrighteous mammon, who will commit to your trust the true riches?" (Luke xvi. 11.) The man who will not plough by reason of the cold (Prov. xx. 4), if he put his hand to the gospel plough, will presently look back (Luke ix. 62), and go not to the work (Acts xv. 38). The apostles were called from their ships, their nets, the receipt of custom, &c., none from the market-place or the street corners. They only exchanged one department of God's work for another, for "the man who makes two blades of grass grow where only one grew before is a fellow-worker with God." *Laborare est orare.* "An honest calling in the world does not at all put us out of the way of our heavenly calling." "In all labour is profit."

Ver. 20.—"*He left the oxen.*" No service without sacrifice. Sometimes it is only ships and nets (Mark i. 20), sometimes it is houses and lands, father and mother, wife and child (Matt. xix. 29).

"*Go back again.*" Why should he not kiss his father and mother? "For God commanded, saying, Honour thy father and mother," and it is not for the greatest of the prophets to make the commandment of God of none effect (Matt. xv. 4—6). Religion developes and intensifies the domestic affections. Ties of flesh become stronger and closer when cemented and consecrated by grace. It would be strange if the religion of love made husband or wife, parent or child, love each other less.

Ver. 21.—"*Took a yoke of oxen and slew them.*" He has done with earthly pursuits. He burns his ships behind him. It would be well for the Church of Christ if her ministers acted in like manner. The temptation to eke out a scanty income by trade, especially among missionaries, must be great; but a man cannot be half a clergyman, and must not be entangled with the affairs of this life. Some of the Swiss pastors have become hotel-keepers, but if they have been the gainers, religion has not. Of all masters, religion and business are the two which can least be served together.

HOMILIES BY VARIOUS AUTHORS.

Vers. 1—8.—*Elijah's Prayer for Death.* How erratic have been the movements of this prophet! Our first introduction to him is at the court of Ahab, whence, as soon as he utters his prophecy, he is away to Cherith in the east, among the wilds of Gilead. Next we find him in the north, at Zarephath of Zidon. Then he meets Obadiah, probably in the plain of Esdraelon, whence he passes over to Carmel in the west. From Carmel he runs before Ahab's horses to the entrance of Jezreel. The next day finds him on his way to Beersheba in the extreme south of Judah. The day following he is pushing his way into the wilderness of Sinai, where we now find him under a shrub, requesting for himself that he may die. Let us consider—

I. THE OCCASION OF THIS PRAYER. 1. *Jezebel had threatened his life.* (1) Ahab had reported to his queen what Elijah had done at Carmel, and in particular recounted how he had slain all the prophets. In this statement we notice two capital faults. He did not recount what *Jehovah* had done; he did not properly distinguish the "prophets" slain as idolatrous and false. The gospel may be variously preached. (2) Instead of reflecting and repenting, Jezebel was filled with resentment, and resolved upon the destruction of Elijah. Miracles will not do more than reason with a corrupt and prejudiced heart. (See Luke xvi. 31; John xii. 10, 11.) (3) She accordingly sent messengers to Elijah with an oath, declaring that within twenty-four hours she would revenge upon his life the slaughter of her priests. Wickedness is not always politic: by giving him this notice she gave him an opportunity to escape. 2. *To save his life he fled.* (1) Was this wrong? Some have blamed him for it because he did not first ascertain the will of God. Had he no voice of God in the instinct of self-preservation? Had he no voice of God in the providence which apprised him of his peril? Would he not have tempted the Lord his God to have waited for another voice? Had he remained and forfeited his life, would he not have been to blame? God gives us our reason, and if we follow its light, together with that of an upright conscience, we shall do well. (2) But who can say that Elijah had no direction from the word of the Lord? Certainly there was a plan for his journey recognized by the angel with which he was familiar (see ver. 7). The distance from Beersheba to Horeb was about 150 miles. (3) In his flight he came first to Beersheba, where he was under the protection of Jehoshaphat, king of Judah, who feared the Lord. There he left his servant in safety, and might have abode himself in safety had he not acted under the promptings of inspiration to proceed alone into the wilderness. (3) *Alone with God he asks to die.* (1) The Hebrew phrase is, "He requested *for his life* that he might die." There is life in death to the righteous. (2) "It is enough." This is the language of disappointment. He looked for better fruit of his ministry than he found. He thought, Surely this demonstration on Carmel will extinguish idolatry; but he finds Jezebel swearing against his life, and apparently in a position to carry out her purpose. "Now, O Lord, take away my life; for I am not better than my fathers." I am no more useful here than they have been who are gone hence. Let me join them.

II. THE ANSWERS GIVEN TO IT. 1. *They come in the form of physical refreshment.* (1) Elijah's prayer was evidently uttered under the influence of physical exhaustion and discomfort. His sitting under the "juniper" is mentioned, not to suggest that he derived comfort from an ample shade, but rather to show how little shelter he could find. The word (רתם) is construed as in the text by the Hebrews, by Jerome, and the Vulgate; yet it is rather the *genista* (*broom*), a shrub with yellow flowers which grows in the desert, and which has its name (from רתם *to bind*) from the *toughness* or *tenacity* of its twigs, which were used for *withes.* Not only was he wayworn with his journey and exposure to the sun, but faint also for want of food and drink. (2) The answer came to his prayer, therefore, in the blessing of refreshing sleep. Out of this also he was seasonably aroused by an Angel to find a cake on the coals (as bread is sometimes baked in the East) and a cruse of water at his bolster. God knows our frame, pities us, and makes due allowance for our frailties. When we find our spirits in a morbid state let us look to our health. Hygiene may come, even to the soul, as an angel of God. 2. *They came to him in spiritual blessing.* (1) The refreshment which Elijah received was *supernatural* in its *source.* The bread and water came to him with the word and touch of the Angel-Jehovah (מלאך יהוה). This was no common angel, but one of the Persons of the Godhead. (2) It was *supernatural* also in its *effects* (ver. 8). In these he is brought intimately into association with Moses and Jesus. (Compare Exod. xxxiv. 28; Deut. ix. 9, 18; Matt. iv. 2.) It is also noteworthy how these three appear in glory together on the holy mount. (See Luke ix. 30, 31.) The spiritual life we derive from God's word is set forth in the mystery of the manna which for *forty* years nourished the people of God in this wilderness. It is also set forth in that new life of Jesus in which after His resurrection He appeared to His disciples during *forty* days. (See Rom. vi. 11; Gal. ii. 20.)—J. A. M.

Vers. 9—18.—*Elijah at Horeb.* Elijah went in the strength of the refreshment he had received from the Angel-Jehovah a forty days' journey to Horeb. He was now on holy ground. It was the "mount of God" on which Moses had seen the Angel-Jehovah in the bush, and was within sight of Sinai, memorable for the giving of the law. On Horeb he lodges in a cave, perhaps the very recess from which Moses witnessed the Shechinah (see Exod. xxxii. 22), and here becomes the subject of Divine communications and revelations. Consider now—

I. HIS INTERCESSION AGAINST ISRAEL. 1. *Observe the occasion.* (1) The question came to him by the word of the Lord, "What doest thou here, Elijah?" In answer to this he urged what Paul calls his "intercession against Israel" (Rom. xi. 2, 3). Wherever we are it behoves us to ask ourselves what business we have here. Everywhere our first business is to glorify God. (2) This question is thought to suggest that Elijah might have been more profitably employed elsewhere. But did he not come here after receiving supernatural strength from God Himself expressly for this journey? (See vers. 7, 8.) (3) Rather must we not look upon his journey in the light of a parable, showing how God abandons those who refuse to be reformed? (Compare Jer. ix. 2.) In this view we can see how Elijah acted in "faith" in this journey; for Paul seems to allude to him in Hebrews xi. 38. 2. *The matter of the accusation.* (1) The view now given harmonizes with this, the substance of which is the prophet's great jealousy for the Lord God of hosts, whose honour had been outraged by the apostasy of the children of Israel. Here is no confession of that unworthy timidity with which Elijah has been, we think, too hastily charged. Nor had he any rebuke from God for such supposed dastardliness, which doubtless he would have received had he deserved it. He is here because he cannot abide in the land of Israel, where Jehovah was commonly insulted. (2) He recounts the particulars of his grief. " For the children of Israel have forsaken thy covenant"—have substituted false Elohim for Thee; "thrown down thine altars"—attempted to abolish Thy worship; "slain thy prophets with the sword"—to provide against any revival of the pure religion of their fathers; "and I, even I only, am left; and they seek my life to take it away." Of what use, then, could he be to such a people? (See Hosea iv. 17.) (3) The motive of this intercession to God against Israel is not personal revenge, but zeal for Jehovah. And though we are bound, as Christians, to love our enemies, that does not say that we are to love the enemies of God. There is a spurious charity in high favour which the Scriptures do not sanction. (See 2 Chron. xix. 2; Psa. cxix. 19; cxxxix. 21; Luke xiv. 26.) Beware of that charity which has complicity with sin. (4) The repetition of the answer when a second time the question was put evinces the deep sincerity of the prophet's soul.

II. THE ANSWER OF GOD UNTO HIM. 1. *This was first given in symbol.* (1) To witness the vision he was caused to stand on the mount before the Lord. Probably this was the place where Moses stood on a similar occasion (see Exod. xix. 9, 16). We should have the Rock of Ages for our foundation when we witness visions of God. All shall witness them in the judgment of the great day. (2) Terrible signs immediately followed upon the passing by of Jehovah. (*a*) First, "a great and strong wind rent the mountains, and brake in pieces the rocks before the Lord." Here was a sign of wrath upon the rulers and people, through *invasion*. (Compare Jer. iv. 11—13; Ezek. vi. 2; Amos iv. 1). (*b*) "And after the wind an earthquake." This is a sign of *revolution*, whether in things civil, ecclesiastical, or both. (Compare Psa. lxviii. 8; Rev. vi. 12; xvi. 18). (*c*) "And after the earthquake a fire." This is the symbol of *judgments* more immediately from *God* (see Deut. iv. 24; Psa. xviii. 12—14; lxvi. 12; Jer. xlviii. 45). (3) But the Lord was in none of these. Judgments are a strange work to Him. They are necessary to the order of His government, but not congenial to His nature. "He *delighteth* in mercy." So the Lord was in the "still small voice" which followed. The gentle voice of the gospel follows the law which came with the uproar of the elements, and *God is in it.* So Elijah wrapped his face in his mantle. (Compare Exod. iii. 6; Isa. vi. 2.) 2. *It was afterwards expounded in words.* (1) Elijah, the intercessor against Israel, and therefore the impersonation of anger against sin, was to return to Israel by way of Damascus, where he was to "anoint Hazael to be king over Syria." In Hazael now we must look for the "strong wind" that was to come up and make havoc upon the mountains and rocks of Israel. (Compare 2 Kings viii. 12, 13; x. 32, 33; xiii. 3.) (2) "Jehu the son of Nimshi" was Elijah to "anoint to be king over Israel." Here was the instrument of the "earthquake" of revolution. (See 2 Kings ix. 1—3.) Not only did Jehu bring a signal destruction upon the whole house of Ahab; he brought down judgment also upon the worshippers of Baal (2 Kings x. 28). (3) "Elisha the son of Shaphat" was this impersonation of righteous anger to "anoint to be prophet" in his room. Here is God's instrument of "fire." His words are to be swords of flame. So "it shall come to pass that him that escapeth from the sword of Hazael shall Jehu slay; and him that escapeth from the sword of Jehu shall Elisha slay." No sinner can escape the fire of God's word. (4) But the "still small voice" of the gospel of mercy has its triumphs. "Yet I have left me seven thousand in Israel," &c. God has His faithful "hidden ones" (Psa. lxxxiii. 3). No wonder Elijah should cover his face with reverent gratitude at the discovery of that sealed company in whose midst was JEHOVAH-SHAMMAH! (Ezek. xlviii. 35; Rev. vii. 13—17.)—J. A. M.

Vers. 19—21.—*The Call of Elisha.* After the visions of Horeb, and in pursuance of the commission there received, Elijah returned from the wilderness and re-entered the land of Israel. Whether he went round by Damascus, and in his course anointed Hazael to be king over Syria, as Samuel had anointed David long before he ascended the throne of Israel, we are not informed. It is not necessary for the fulfilment of his instructions (ver. 15) to suppose that he did so; for prophets are said to *do* things which they *predict*. (See Jer. i. 10; Ezek. xliii. 3; Rom. iv. 17.) The reason is that their predictions are sure to be accomplished; and upon the same principle a true faith in the promises of God is said to be the "substance" or subsistence of "things hoped for" (Heb. xi. 1). It is certain that *Elisha* made provision for the anointing of Jehu; *Elisha* also informed Hazael that he should be king over Syria (see 2 Kings viii. 13; ix. 1—3). The call of Elisha was by the hand of *Elijah*.

I. THE CALL OF ELISHA WAS FROM GOD. 1. *Elijah threw his mantle over Elisha.* (1) The prophet's mantle was the symbol of his office. It seems to have been the skin of an animal, or composed of some hairy material (see 2 Kings i. 8; Zech. xiii. 5; Isa. xx. 2; Matt. iii. 4). In allusion to this, perhaps, the popes invest their cardinals with the *pallium*—a cloak or *pall* made of wool. (2) The mantle of Elijah thrown upon Elisha was the sign that he was to "follow him," to be his servant first, and eventually to be his successor. The mantle, accordingly, came fully into the possession of Elisha when his "master" was "taken from his head" (2 Kings ii. 3, 13). (3) The "spirit of Elijah" then "came upon Elisha." So essential to a prophet is the Spirit of God that prophets themselves are called "spirits." False prophets also are called "spirits," but for an opposite reason (see ch. xxii. 22, 23; 1 Cor. xiv. 32; 1 John iv. 1, 2). 2. *Elijah acted under Divine direction.* (1) After he had asked for himself that he might die, God expressly commissioned him to anoint "Elisha the son of Shaphat of Abel-Meholah" to be "prophet in his room" (ver. 16). The true minister is God's gift. (2) God knew the qualities of Elisha. The manner in which he received the call proved him to be a true man. God's order is, first "grace," then "apostleship" (see Rom. i. 5). Those persons deceive themselves who, being destitute of godliness, affect apostleship (see Psa. l. 16). Nor can apostleship abide where grace is forfeited (Acts i. 25). (3) Elijah found Elisha, not in the schools of the prophets, but ploughing in the field. The spirit of prophecy will not be tied down to human institutions, however venerable and respectable.

II. THE RESPONSE OF ELISHA WAS TO GOD 1. *He accordingly renounced the world.* (1) He had something to sacrifice. The "twelve yoke of oxen" indicate prosperity. The glimpse we get of his home is sufficient to discover comfort and happiness. Everybody has something to give up for God. (2) At the call of God he gave up all. Instantly he "left the oxen and ran after Elijah." There should be no hesitation in entering upon the service of God. Elisha did not go home to *ask* but to *take* leave of his parents. For the authority of God is above that of parents. His proposal to return to his home was not a pretext for delay, else he would have merited the censure of our Lord (see Luke v. 29; ix. 61, 62) The completeness of his renunciation of the world was expressed in his sacrificing the oxen together with the gear. Ministers, in particular, should be free from the entanglements of this life (see Matt. x. 9, 10; 1 Cor. ix. 14; 2 Tim. ii. 4). 2. *He followed Elijah.* (1) He had something to encounter. The life of a prophet was not without its privations and discomforts. And in following Elijah, whose life was threatened with an oath by Jezebel, he would expose himself to her malignity. The offence of the cross has not ceased. (2) He encountered all cheerfully. Elijah responded to his request to let him kiss his father and mother before following him, saying, "Go, return; for what have I done to thee?" This answer was intended to throw upon Elisha the consideration of all that was involved in his call, so that his choice might be intelligent and free. He was not long in counting the cost. God had predisposed his heart (see Psa. cx. 3). Soon we find him pouring water upon the hands of Elijah—lovingly serving the servant of his Lord (2 Kings iii. 11).

Observe: 1. Elisha, though evidently a great man at Abel-Meholah, could handle the plough. There is no disgrace in honest labour. It is even honourable. 2. While in pursuit of his business he was called of God. Business will not be honest if it prevent us from hearing God's voice. 3. He returned to kiss his father and mother and make a farewell feast with his household before following Elijah. Natural affection and social endearments, within proper limits, are respected by religion. 4. Elisha's parents do not seem to have hindered him. Those parents incur fearful responsibilities who, under worldly influences, hinder their sons from responding to a call of God to enter His ministry.—J. A. M.

Vers. 1—18.—*The Desponding Prophet.* A marvellous change has come over Elijah. It is difficult to imagine a more complete contrast than is presented by his moral attitude in this and the previous chapters. He who just before has so boldly confronted the proud king, and defied the priests of Baal, standing without fear before his flaming altar, and sternly carrying out the judgment of God on the corrupters of His people, is now filled with dismay, and flies from the post of duty and of danger. So unstable are the grandest forms of human virtue, and so weak are the noblest of men when God is pleased for a while to leave them to themselves. Consider (1) The prophet's state of mind. (2) The way in which God deals with him. I. THE PROPHET'S STATE OF MIND. It is one of deep despondency. Fear of the queen's revenge is not enough of itself to explain it. There is disappointment at the apparent result of the events of the previous day, weariness of life, disgust at the condition of the land, a sense of powerlessness before the difficulties of his position, perhaps doubt as to the wisdom of what he has done. He speaks and acts as a dispirited, broken-hearted man. Note some of the manifest causes of this despondency. We can never thoroughly understand the feelings of a man unless we take into account the sources and occasions of them, and try to put ourselves in his place. 1. *Physical exhaustion.* His bodily frame was worn and weary. His animal spirits had had a great strain upon them, and now suffered a corresponding relapse. Unwonted exertion of strength was followed by unwonted weakness. The relation that exists between the state of the body and the state of the mind is very mysterious, but very real. The elation or depression of our religious feeling depends far more on mere physical conditions than we often imagine. A diseased body will often cause a dark cloud to come over the spirit's firmament; much that is morbid in the religious thoughts and emotions of good men needs to be dealt with by the physician of the body rather than of the soul. 2. *Loneliness.* He was without the companionship and sympathy of those who would share his labours and perils. " I, even I only, am left, and they seek my life to destroy it." It is a single-handed conflict in which he is involved. There are none to stand by him, none whom he can trust. Such isolation is the severest possible test of fidelity. As the rock never appears more majestic than when seen standing alone, with the ocean billows rolling round it, so with one who is ",faithful found among the faithless," cut off from all natural and human supports, isolated in a surrounding sea of indifference or iniquity. (Think of *Paul:* " At my first answer no man stood with me, but all forsook me," 2 Tim. iv. 16; above all *the Christ.* " I have trodden the winepress alone, and of the people there was none with me," Isaiah lxiii. 3.) Supernatural help will often come for special emergencies, and will make the soul sublimely independent of external aid; but it is hard to carry on a long, patient conflict with difficulties *alone.* 3. *Want of success.* His ministry seems all in vain. His words are but as the dreams of the false prophets. The solemn testimony given on Carmel has passed away without effecting any real change in the condition of things. The fire that consumed his sacrifice has gone out. Righteous vengeance has been inflicted on the idolatrous prophets, and the Kishon has swept away their blood. The drought has done its work, and the rain has returned upon the land. And now all seems to be going on just as it was before. Ahab and Jezebel are as hostile and treacherous and full of cruel hate as ever; and as for the people, there is no kind of security for their constancy to their recent vows. Surely he is living his sad life in vain ! That dreariest of all thoughts to a man of high and holy purpose—that his labour is utterly fruitless—sweeps like a withering wind through his soul, and he wishes he were dead. " O Lord, take away my life, for I am no better than my fathers." 4. *The sense of having forsaken the post of responsibility.* It may have been a natural impulse that moved him to " fly for his life," but no wonder his despondency deepened as he lost himself in the solitudes of the wilderness. His was the inward disquietude which will always be the penalty of a man's having weakly or wilfully deserted the path of duty. When good men place themselves in a false position, they must expect the shadow of some morbid condition of feeling to fall upon their spirits. When the hands of those who ought to be busy about some work for God are idle, their hearts are left a prey to all sorts of evil influences. Religious activity is one of the main secrets of religious health. What is our grand business in this world but just to battle against the weaknesses of our own nature, and the force of adverse circumstances? And when the difficulties of our position gather thickest about us, then is the time to cast ourselves most fearlessly on the Divine power that will enable us to overcome them and listen to the voice that says, "Be thou faithful unto death, and I will give thee the crown of life."

II. GOD'S WAY OF DEALING WITH HIM. Taking a general view of the Divine method, we see that each successive step is wisely adapted to the prophet's need. 1. *Physical refreshment.* An angel is sent with food for the nourishment of his exhausted frame; not to talk with him, not by remonstrance or persuasion to chase away his morbid feelings, but to feed him. The disease of the mind is to be cured by first removing the weakness of the body, which was one of its causes. It is a suggestive incident. Our physical nature is as truly an object of Divine thought and care as the spiritual. God will not fail to supply the meaner wants of His children. The beneficent ministries of His providence are ever auxiliary to the higher purposes of His grace. 2. *A significant revelation of the Divine presence and power.* The remarkable phenomena described in the eleventh and twelfth verses no doubt had a symbolic meaning. The wind, the earthquake, and the fire were emblems of the conspicuous and extraordinary manner in which Elijah probably expected the work of God to be carried on. The "still small voice" that followed taught him that God's chosen way of working was rather one that is calm and noiseless. The stirring events that had recently taken place were only preparatory to the silent but mightier energy of His spirit working through the voice of the prophet. We are apt to over-estimate the power of that which "cometh with observation." Why should the wind, and the fire, and the earthquake be God's only instruments? Is He not equally in the gently-dawning light, the soft-whispering breeze, the silent, secret forces of nature? Your path of usefulness may be obscure, your influence unobserved, its issues slowly developed. But be not disheartened. Remember the "still small voice" breathing in the ear of the prophet at the mouth of the cave when the tumult was over, and learn that it is by a feeble instrument and a quiet, patient process that God will accomplish His grandest work in the moral sphere. This is the method of the world's Redeemer. "He shall not cry nor lift up, nor cause his voice to be heard in the streets, &c. (Isa. xlii. 2, 3, 4). 3. *Words of rebuke and encouragement.* "What doest thou here, Elijah?" "Go, return on thy way." "Yet have I left me seven thousand in Israel," &c. Thus does God reprove him for the faithlessness that lay at the root of his despondency. If the veil that hid the secret life of Israel could at that hour have been uplifted, he would have seen how little real reason there was for it. Seven thousand living witnesses might have come forth from their obscurity to show that his work was not in vain. We little know what God is doing beneath the surface, at the secret heart of society, when appearances seem most unfavourable. Let us be true to ourselves and to Him, doing faithfully the work He has given us to do in storm or in calm, and leave it to Him to bring about the glorious issue. "Be ye therefore steadfast, immovable," &c. (1 Cor. xv. 58).—W.

Ver. 19—21.—*The Call of Elisha.* It was by an express Divine command that Elijah summoned Elisha to the prophetic office (ver. 16). And yet we may discern a purely human element in this. He did it by the impulse of natural feeling. Stern, rugged, self-reliant as he was, he needed sympathy and companionship. He yearned for the society of a kindred spirit. He could not bear to live alone. Whether he had any previous personal knowledge of Elisha we know not; but it is certain that, totally different as the two men were, he found in him a faithful friend and servant. And scanty as the materials of the narrative may be, there is enough to show how deep and tender an affection existed between them. Note in reference to this call—

I. THE SOVEREIGNTY OF THE DIVINE CHOICE. No indication is given as to why Elisha particularly should have been called to this office. So it has generally been in the case of those who, in the olden times, were raised up to occupy distinguished positions in the development of the Divine plan. (Abraham, Moses, Saul, David, &c.) So was it in Christ's choice of the inner circle of His disciples; as when to the sons of Zebedee mending their nets, and to Matthew at the receipt of custom, He said, "Follow me." But the elections of God are never arbitrary and capricious. He chooses whom He will to be the instruments of His purpose, "taking one of a city and two of a family" as it pleases Him (Jer. iii. 14). But there is always some deep and sufficient reason for this, though we may not be able to trace it. Every man who has done any great work for God in the world has been more or less deeply impressed with this sense of a special Divine call and commission. And it has given a dignity to his bearing and strength and courage to his spirit that nothing else could give. Every true Christian finds highest inspiration in the thought that God has singled him out from the crowd and summoned him to the service of a consecrated life. "Ye have not chosen me, but I have chosen you, and ordained you," &c. (John xv. 16).

II. THE SACRED PERSONAL RELATION IT ESTABLISHED BETWEEN THE PROPHET AND HIS SERVANT. Elijah's throwing his "mantle" upon him as he passed by was a symbolic act indicative of this. It was the sign of their common prophetic vocation, the seal and bond of the new relation existing between them. It betokened—
(1) some kind of adoption to sonship. "My Father, my Father" (2 Kings ii. 12).
(2) A transference of the responsibility of the prophetic work. (3) The impartation of the same spirit, even the "double portion" of the first-born (2 Kings iii. 9, 10). We see here something dimly typical of the relation Christ sustained towards His chosen apostles. "As thou hast sent me into the world, even so also have I sent them," &c. (John xvii. 18, 19). Some such relation subsisted between Paul and his "dearly beloved son" Timothy. "As a son with the father he hath served with me in the gospel" (Phil. ii. 22). "Wherefore I put thee in remembrance," &c. "Hold fast the form of sound words," &c. (2 Tim. i. 6, 13). The thought becomes proverbial when we speak of the "mantle" of a great leader falling upon his successors. One of the chief ends of a noble life is answered when others take up the work that it left unfinished, and catch the spirit of its example; nothing more sacred than the spiritual bond thus established.

III. THE COMPLETENESS OF ELISHA'S SELF-SURRENDER. Natural feeling for a moment throws an obstacle in the way. "Let me, I pray thee, kiss my father and my mother." It was a hard task for him at once to loosen himself from family ties, and relinquish the comforts of what was probably a prosperous pastoral life, and cast in his lot with the wandering prophet. Elijah's answer seems to disown the exercise of any undue constraint upon him, and simply leaves him free to choose. But the loyalty of his spirit to the Divine authority soon settles the alternative, and after an act expressive of his entire abandonment of the associations of his former life, "he arose and went after Elijah and ministered unto him." We are reminded of the way in which Christ called on men to surrender their all and follow Him (Luke ix. 57—62). Fidelity to Him demands complete self-sacrifice. The strongest fascinations, and even the dearest ties of earth, will give way to the realized sovereignty of His claims. "He that loveth father or mother more than me is not worthy of me" (Matt. x. 37).—W.

Ver. 4.—*The Causes of Despondency.* Human character is more complex than many imagine. Its elements are so diverse, and sometimes so contradictory, that only God can fairly judge it. The biographies of Scripture and the subtleties of our own hearts combine to enforce the lesson, "Judge not, that ye be not judged." We should have placed in the foremost rank the disciple who first acknowledged the divinity of our Lord, and we should have cast him out of the Church who denied his Lord with oaths and curses; yet both the one and the other were the outcome of the same character. Never was contradiction more complete than in Elijah. One day he leads a whole nation in penitence, the next he flees to save his life, as one who has thrown up all hope of Jehovah's cause. None but the pitiful and patient Father-God would have judged him aright; nor was Elijah the last to say, " Thy gentleness hath made me great." We are reminded that it is difficult to judge ourselves as well as others. On Carmel, Elijah might have thought himself invincible, and in Horeb an unmitigated coward, but he was neither. Varieties of mood must not be too much considered. They do not afford a fair index to character. We are not infidels because we pass through a phase of doubt, we are not reprobates because we are deeply conscious of sin, nor are we Christians because we enjoy a religious service. A sad and frequent experience of religious life, that of *despondency*, is set before us here, and we will seek to discover its causes.

I. REACTION AFTER EXCITEMENT. Great natures are peculiarly subject to this. The impulse which impels to a noble act has a rebound proportioned to its intensity. Peter and John the Baptist stand beside Elijah as exemplars of this fact. From it arises the special peril of revivalistic services. Excitement has its place and power in the advance of Christ's kingdom, but we must not substitute spasmodic feeling for steady growth.

II. EXHAUSTION OF PHYSICAL AND NERVOUS ENERGY. Even the gigantic strength of Elijah underwent a terrible strain on Carmel. Anxiety, enthusiasm, burning zeal, exultation combined to agitate him, and these were doubtless preceded by many days and nights of passionate, agonizing prayer. God's provision for the prophet—the sleep that came over him, as over a tired child, the food prepared by angel hands—prove that this was recognized.

Show the mutual dependence of body and mind. Neither the equable temperament of some Christians nor the excitability of others is due always to the presence or absence of Divine grace. Good food, fresh air, and change of scene would do more than religious exercises to restore tone to some who are despondent. The neglect of sanitary laws is a sin. There was far-reaching wisdom in Paul's declaration, " I keep the body under."

III. ABSENCE OF SYMPATHY. " I am left *alone*." " I *only* am left." Such was the burden of Elijah's cry. This is a special source of despondency to missionaries surrounded by the heathen. It affects also multitudes who are not so literally alone. They may have many Christians around them, but in their special work, in their peculiar difficulty, they can find none to help, or even to understand them. " Alone in a crowd " is a true description of many a disciple of Christ, who is thinking his own thoughts and fighting his own foes. Show from this the wisdom of the provision God has made in Church fellowship. Point out the causes which tend to make such communion unreal or unhelpful. Urge the cultivation of sympathy with young disciples, with obscure workers, &c.

IV. INFLUENCE OF DOUBT. The confidence of the prophet on Carmel had broken down. Jezebel had not been cowed by the sudden revulsion of popular feeling. She doubted its permanence, and at all events resolved that she would not lose heart, so Ahab and his courtiers were reassured when she swore to have revenge on Elijah. The prophet thought now that he had been too sanguine—that the one chance had come and gone without effect. Doubt paralyzed him. Doubt of God's willingness to forgive plunges the penitent into despondency. He would scarcely venture secretly into a crowd to touch the hem of Christ's garment. Doubt of God's readiness to hear and answer prayer keeps the Christian from the light of His countenance, &c.

V. INVISIBILITY OF ANTAGONISTS. Elijah could face his visible foes on Carmel without quailing—indeed, he dared to taunt them at the risk of being torn to pieces— but against this vague feeling of despair he could not hold his own. Moral battles are the hardest to fight. He who can grapple with what is tangible sometimes fails when called on to " wrestle not with flesh and blood, but with principalities, and powers, and the rulers of the darkness of this world." Some would rather run the risk of being condemned hereafter, as wicked and slothful servants, than have the certainty of being sneered at now as those who are " righteous overmuch."

VI. Enforced inactivity. Elijah's opportunity for vigorous action seemed over. He was cast in upon his own thoughts. Few could bear it less patiently than he. The man who can dare and do anything finds it specially hard to wait and to suffer. Similar temptation to despondency comes to those who are laid aside by illness, or removed from a happy sphere of service. But that is the time to wait on the Lord, and so "renew our strength."

Conclusion. *In all hours of despondency remember that He who knew the agony of Gethsemane and Calvary pities us, and feels for us.* "We have not a High Priest who cannot be touched with the feeling of our infirmities," &c.—A. R.

Ver. 9.—*A Question from God for the consideration of Man.* Elijah was fleeing from peril and from work, but he could not flee from God. The Father seeth in secret. No man is out of His sight, no feeling eludes His vigilance (Psalm cxxxix.) Christ knew the plans of His foes (Matt. xii. 25). He understood the unexpressed wants of the sinful (Matt. ix. 2). He heard the secret conversations of His followers (Mark ix. 33), and lovingly answered their unspoken questions (John xvi. 19). In this story God's pity is as conspicuous as His knowledge. Refreshed by the provision given by unseen hands, Elijah went to Horeb, a place sacred in its associations and lonely in its grandeur. There, hidden in a cave from the wrath of Jezebel, the voice of Jehovah reached him, saying, "What doest thou here, Elijah?"

I. The question came to a prophet in his hour of despair. This Divine interposition on his behalf teaches us the means God uses to bring us out from our despondency. The prophet was delivered from his depression by learning the following lessons: 1. *That God was near.* Whatever the sin that needs pardon, the weakness that wants conquering, the doubt that wants unravelling, there is no fear of the issue if we can consciously bring it to God. Elijah was saved because he dared tell Jehovah all that was in his heart. Moses sometimes was compelled to leave his work to the elders, that he might speak to God face to face. The disciples "went and told Jesus" their grief and their triumph. Aye, and the Master Himself nerved Himself for work and for suffering by prayer—on the mountain or in the garden. Satan says, Give up prayer till your difficulties are removed. Christ says, "Come unto me, all ye that labour, and are heavy laden, and I will *give* you rest." 2. *That success was assured.* Elijah thought he stood alone. but the Lord said, "Yet I have left me seven thousand in Israel," &c. Success was not where the prophet had looked for it. The crowds on Carmel had not been radically changed, but the secret worshippers of God had been strengthened by his heroism. So in the Lord's ministry, the nucleus of the Church was not found in the applauding multitudes on Olivet, but in the few faithful ones in the garden of Gethsemane. Our work may be greater than we think. No word or work for Christ fails of its reward. "For as the rain cometh down, and the snow from heaven, and returneth not thither, but watereth the earth, and maketh it bring forth and bud, that it may give seed to the sower and bread to the eater: so shall my word be that goeth forth out of my mouth: it shall not return unto me void, but it shall accomplish that which I please, and it shall prosper in the thing whereto I sent it." 3. *That work was waiting* (ver. 15). Elijah was not to remain in the cave, any more than the disciples were to dwell on the mount of transfiguration. For his own sake and for the good of others he was to be up and doing. If you would be saved from brooding, despondency, and doubt, throw yourselves into the work of God. Do with all your might what your hands find to do: and your service will restore tone to your mind, and bring hope to your heart, and prepare you to hear the "Well done, good and faithful servant."

II. This question came to a man in a false position. "What doest thou *here*, Elijah?" The inquiry should pursue others who have fled to caves in which they would fain hide themselves from responsibility. 1. *It comes to the impenitent, in the cave of concealment.* They say, "Doth God know?" He sees the secret sin. He knows the iniquity of that which society applauds, and the day is coming when excuses shall be stripped off, and wickedness discovered Before that terrible day, when "the secrets of all hearts shall be disclosed," come to the feet of a pardoning God. 2. *It comes to the penitent in the cave of despondency.* To all such God says, "Come now, and let us reason together." 3. *It comes to the indolent in the cave of sloth.* Years of profession unrelieved by a single act of service or sacrifice call for repentance. 4. *It comes to the sorrowful in the cave of murmuring* "Lift up the hands which hang down," &c. Suffer your Redeemer to bring you out of the horrible pit, and "put a new song into your mouth, even praise unto our God."

CONCLUSION. The Lord speaks to all. "To-day if ye will hear his voice, harden not your hearts."—A. R.

Vers. 12.—*The still small Voice.* Describe the stupendous scenes amidst which Elijah stood. A wind came shrieking up the mountain ravines, unseen yet instinct with secret force ; an earthquake made the solid ground heave and reel; fire glared from heaven, like that which had fallen on the sacrifice at Carmel, or on a subsequent occasion consumed the captains and soldiers of Ahaziah. Amidst this war of the elements the prophet was unmoved by fear ; indeed, probably a wild exultation filled his heart as he saw this stormy reflection in nature of the conflict within him. (Compare Shakespeare's splendid description of King Lear in the storm.) The uproar in nature was succeeded by a solemn calm ; and as Elijah waited for the next marvellous display of Divine power, "a still small voice" broke the silence, and the prophet knew that it was the voice of God. He who till now had been undaunted and unmoved, now reverently covered his face with his mantle, and bowed in humble worship in the felt presence of Him before whom angels veil their faces. This strange and weird experience evidently had reference to the work which Elijah had attempted, and over which he was now so despondent. When he learnt that the Lord was not in the wind, the earthquake, or the fire, he reflected that permanent religious reformation might not result from the material signs of Divine power, displayed in the withholding of the rain, the raising of the dead, or the fall of fire on Carmel, but from the more quiet testimony of his own devout life, and from the fidelity of the "seven thousand who had not bowed the knee to Baal." In effect, the message to him and to us was this : "Not by might, nor by power, but by my Spirit, saith the Lord." We are taught, in the first place—

I. THE SPIRITUAL WEAKNESS OF WHAT SEEMS MIGHTY. "The Lord was not in the wind, ... in the earthquake, ... in the fire." Let us exemplify this truth—1. *By the experience of Elijah.* He had done many mighty works, but the people were startled rather than reformed. No radical and abiding change had been effected. "The wind" may represent the drought, both in its coming and in its ceasing; "the earthquake," the raising of the child from the dead ; and "the fire," the answer to prayer on Carmel. It was not these wonders which could change the heart of the people, but "the still small voice" speaking within for God. 2. *By the miracles of judgment.* Take the plagues of Egypt as specimens. Marvellous enough they were, but in the result "Pharaoh's heart was hardened." 3. *By the penalties of the law.* Show from the history of Israel, and from the comments made on it in the Epistles, the powerlessness of the law to put away sin. The fear of punishment may check the outward manifestation of sin, but in itself does not conquer innate sinfulness. If a child does not love his father, no orders, however stringently enforced, will make him happy. It was not John the Baptist, but Jesus Christ, who was the world's Redeemer. 4. *By the events of Providence.* Illness, the dread of death, a startling bereavement, a national calamity, &c., do not convert men, unless through them or after them "the still small voice" is heard. Men may be driven to alarm, to murmuring, to despair, perhaps to suicide; but their hearts are still rebellious under the influence of trouble. It is not the storm, but the voice of Jesus in the storm, saying, "It is I," that brings rest to those who welcome Him.

II. THE SPIRITUAL STRENGTH OF WHAT SEEMS FEEBLE. The still small voice, which only a listening man could hear, was more Divine and more mighty than all Elijah had witnessed before. There was all the difference between God's *power* and God's *presence.* " The Lord was not in the fire," but His was the still small voice; concerning which we observe—1. *It follows on preparation.* Elijah had heard so much, had been so startled into keen listening for the wonderful, that he did not fail to hear this. So the miracles which had not converted the people had made them ready for Elisha and the school of the prophets. Similarly John preceded Jesus. It is thus in personal experience. The earthquake did not convert the jailer at Philippi, but it aroused him to ask, " What must I do to be saved ? " Trouble does not save a man, but it may make him ready to listen to the words of life. Some must lose all before they find all in God. 2. *It reminds of secret forces.* The most mighty are silent in nature and in grace; *e.g.*, gravitation is far more tremendous than volcanic agency. 3. *It typifies the influence of the Holy Spirit.* " He shall convince the world of righteousness," &c. How secretly He melts the heart to repentance, faith, and obedience, and changes the whole current of affection and thought. 4. *It whispers of the love of Christ.* He forced none into His kingdom, but won all His subjects man by man. Not His reproaches, but His look of love, broke the heart of Peter into penitence, after the denial. Paul's inspiration was found not in applause or success, but in this—that he could ever say, " The love of Christ constraineth me."

CONCLUSION. *Wait for no resistless influences,* for no startling events ; but listen to the " still small voice " which speaks within, testifying of your deep necessity and Christ's glorious redemption.—A. R.

Vers. 1—8.—*The Prophet's Despair.* I. ELIJAH'S WEAKNESS. 1. *His disappointment.* With the hand of the Lord upon him he had come to Jezreel (ch. xviii. 46). Was it not because a further success for God awaited him there ? Could Carmel's wonders and the mercy of God in the rain now flooding the earth be resisted ? Jezebel's message, displaying only determined and increased hostility, rudely dispels the dream. The blighting of the long-expected fruit of prayer and waiting and mightiest effort is worse to bear than all the hardships which went before. Other trials may depress, but under this the spirit is utterly broken. 2. *His flight.* He shows no trust in Him who was mightier than Jezebel. He flees to the south of Judah. Even there it does not seem to him that he is in safety, and he goes a day's journey into the wilderness; but neither at Jezreel nor at Beersheba does he seek direction from the Lord. The overthrow of hope is also the overthrow of faith. Ceasing to hope in God we cease to wait on God. 3. *His prayer.* (1) Its inconsistency. He had fled for his life, and now he prays God that he may die. We are not fittest for heaven when we are most tired of earth. We must " enter his gates "—the gates of the city that hath foundations—" with praise," not with complaints and accusations. (2) Its unbelief. God's work is abandoned as impossible ; nothing remains for Him but to take back the life of His defeated servant ! Many a noble heart besides has lifted up the same cry of despair. The noblest of mankind are nothing when once the fire of trust is quenched in the soul. " The just shall live by faith ; " when faith dies, every good and noble thing dies with it.

II. HOW GOD BINDS UP THE BROKEN-HEARTED. 1. *He gives rest.* " He lay and slept." Even in the desert to which we flee unbidden, God gives shelter and rest. " For so he giveth his beloved sleep." 2. *He imparts strength for the onward way to where light will break upon the darkness and a new mission will be given.* Elijah is fed once and again with angel food, and in the strength of it goes " forty days and forty nights unto Horeb, the mount of God." We are revived with tender heavenly ministrations : we see His goodness in the land of the living, and pass onward to the place where we shall meet with Him and hear His voice.—J. U

Vers. 9—18.—*Elijah at Horeb.* I. HOW GOD DEALS WITH THE DESPAIRING. 1. *Elijah's mistake.* Because Jezebel's enmity remained unsubdued the struggle was at once given over as hopeless ; " and he came thither unto a cave, and lodged there." The same mistake is made by those who labour on with unexpectant toil, whose wrestling with God is given up, whose feeble thought and listless tones proclaim their hopelessness : by those who have laid down the work to which

God called them—preachers in retirement or in other spheres, teachers, &c.—and those who have ceased to strive against their own sin. 2. *God's remedy.* (1) The heart is searched. "What doest *thou here*, Elijah?" A prophet in the desert? A living man illumined with the light of the knowledge of God, a companion of rocks and stones and solitude; and death and sin crying to be visited with the rebuke of God, and hearts fainting for lack of His light and consolations? Was it for this God endowed and called thee? A word for those who have left the vineyard; for those who have not yet entered; for the worldly and the sinful. To hear this voice is preparation for entering the path of life and of service. Till it be heard there is no possibility of either. (2) Unbelief is unveiled. When God's voice is heard, and the reasons for the wilderness flight are named, it is seen that He has been shut out of sight. He mentions his own zeal, and Israel's sin, but of God there is nothing said. It is unbelief alone which can kill prayer and earnest, hopeful toil. It was only when Peter ceased to gaze on Jesus that the stormy waves engulfed him. If we are in the wilderness, forgetfulness of God has set us there.

II. THE PATH OF DELIVERANCE FOR THE HOPELESS. 1. *The vision of God.* Elijah's thoughts of God's way were corrected. (1) God was not in the whirlwind, or the earthquake, or the fire. What had failed to turn Israel and subdue Jezebel was not what was really God's power unto salvation, but what Elijah erroneously conceived to be this. We despair because certain methods, influences, arguments fail; but they can only fail because God is not *in them.* (2) God was in the still small voice that awoke within the heart. The power which now held and searched the prophet's own soul was the manifestation of what was power for the souls of others. 2. *The recognition of ourselves as only part of the manifold agency of God.* Other hands as well as his were to carry on the work of judgment and of mercy (vers. 15—17). To feel our brotherhood with the servants of God fills us with joy and power. 3. *The assurance that God never works in vain* (ver. 18). The results may be hid from us, but they are known to Him.—J. U.

Vers. 19—21.—*The Prophet's Call.* I. THE CALL TO SERVICE. 1. *Where it found him*—in the field engaged in laborious, careful toil. The Master chooses servants for higher trusts who have been faithful in lower. 2. *How it came.* The mantle cast upon him was a sign of adoption. It was a call to share the prophet's home and love. Elijah was to find a son in the newly-called servant of God, and Elisha a father in the great prophet of Israel. We pass into God's service through union with His people.

II. INDECISION REBUKED (ver. 20). 1. *The request.* He "ran after Elijah," yet with entreaty for permission to go back and kiss father and mother. The new ties and the old were both binding him, and the vain attempt was made to comply with both. God's call must from the first have the mastery. The seeming severity which we are called upon to exercise will yield fruits of joy. God, fully chosen, will be fully known; and the breaking of lower ties may preach the claims of God to those we love best. 2. *The answer.* "Go back again, for what have I done to thee?" The gift neglected is taken away. As we value it and sacrifice for it, in that measure is it given to us. Treat God's grace as nothing, and to you it becomes nothing.

III. THE CHOICE MADE. 1. *The past was broken with.* His own yoke of oxen were slain, the instruments of his toil consumed. 2. *It was done with gladness.* He made a feast for the people. 3. *He took the place which God meanwhile assigned him.* "Then he arose, and went after Elijah, and ministered unto him." Humble, loving companionship with God's people is preparation for taking up their work. J. U.

Vers. 4—21. *Return of Elijah to the Desert.* It is well for us to recognize that the great servants of God are men like ourselves, that they were formed of the same clay, and that they share our infirmities. Elijah had no time to magnify himself after his triumph on Mount Carmel. It was at this very moment God allowed him to pass through the most terrible mental conflict. Led into the bare and arid solitudes of Horeb, he fell into a state of depression bordering on despair, and, throwing himself down under a juniper tree in the wilderness, he cried, "O Lord, now take away my life!" (Ver. 4.) A spiritual crisis like this comes in the life of most men of God, and may be explained by two reasons. 1. There is a spiritual necessity for it. The man of God who has gained the first great victory is apt to think that it is decisive and final, and that he may now cease to fight. And behold, the evil that was vanquished yesterday lifts up its head again, and the conflict has to be begun anew. "I have been very jealous for the Lord God of hosts; for the children of Israel have forsaken thy covenant" (ver. 10). 2. This painful crisis is permitted by God, who will not have His servants uplifted in their own eyes, even by the most splendid triumphs of the cause which it is their honour to maintain. This is the explanation of the mysterious thorn in the flesh with which St. Paul was buffeted (2 Cor. xii. 7). This is the cause of the momentary despondency of John the Baptist, which prompted that utterance of a faltering faith, "Art thou he that should come?" (Matt. xi. 3.) To the same source we may trace the anguish of Luther in the Wartburg. He who is pleased thus to exercise the soul of His children is Himself their only efficient Comforter. God raises His downcast servant Elijah by means of a glorious vision. The Lord is not in the wind, not in the earthquake; these are but the symbols of His awful majesty. He is in the still small voice, which whispers the name afterwards to be proclaimed to the whole world by the beloved disciple, and written in letters of blood upon the cross: "*God is love*" (1 John iv. 16). Let us not forget, however, that if God is not in the stormy wind and earthquake, these manifestations of His severity necessarily preceded the manifestation of that love which is His true essence. It was needful that the reed which had presumed to lift up itself against God should be bent, that the hard heart, like the stone, should be broken in order that the still small voice might gain an entrance to it. Repentance must come before the deliverance and joy of pardon. It is by this path through the desert that God leads every soul of man; it was thus that He led His servant Elijah. His overwhelming anguish of soul was like the whirlwind which prepared the way for the soft whisper of heavenly peace. This desert of spiritual desolation is to be made to blossom like the rose under the reviving breath of the Lord (Isa. xxxv. 1). Elijah comes forth from it with renewed strength and courage, after the wholesome discipline of humiliation, a witness to us of the truth of the Divine assurance uttered by the lips of Christ Himself: "Blessed are they that mourn, for they shall be comforted" (Matt. v. 4).—E. de P.

EXPOSITION.

CHAPTER XX. 1—43.

THE INVASIONS OF ISRAEL BY THE SYRIANS AND THEIR RESULTS.—The insertion of this chapter, which contains an account of two invasions of Israel by the hosts of Syria, and of the utter defeat of the latter, and which therefore constitutes a break in the history of Elijah, which has occupied the historian up to the end of ch. xix., and which is resumed with ch. xxi.—the insertion of this twentieth chapter in this place is apparently due to the compiler of these records, who seems to have adopted this arrangement as the more chronological. It is not absolutely certain, however, that we owe this disposition of his materials to the

original compiler, as the Vatican LXX., which sometimes appears to represent an older and purer text, places ch. xx. after ch. xxi., thereby concluding the history of Elijah—so far as it was comprehended in the reign of Ahab—before entering on the subject of the Syrian wars. It is not improbable, consequently, that this latter was the original order; and it is quite certain that the account of Elijah's ministry, of which ch. xxi. forms a part, is of a piece with ch. xix., and by the same hand, and is by a different hand from the author, or authors, of chaps. xx. and xxii. Ch. xxii. 1 also supplies a reason why that chapter should follow ch. xx. There seems, moreover, to be a close connexion between ch. xxii. and the denunciation of ch. xx. 42. But the present arrangement evidently dates from very early times.

Ver. 1.—**And Ben-hadad** [See on chs. xi. 14 and xv. 18. The LXX. uniformly spells the name *Ader* (υἱὸς Ἄδερ). The form אֲדַד is found in ch. xi. 17, and ד and ר are frequently interchanged; cf. Gen. xxv. 15, xxxvi. 39 with 1 Chron. i. 30, 46. We learn from ver. 34 that this prince was the son of a Syrian king who had conquered some of the cities of Israel, but we cannot nevertheless be certain that he was the son of that Ben-hadad (ch. xv. 18) who invaded Israel in the reign of Baasha (Ewald). See on ver. 34.] **the king of Syria gathered all his host** [See note on ch. x. 2, where we have same word] **together: and there were thirty and two kings with him** [Evidently these were vassals, not allied powers. The number alone proves that they must have been petty princes or chieftains of Hittite tribes, ruling over very limited districts and all acknowledging the suzerainty of the king of Damascus, all paying tribute (ch. x. 25), and furnishing a contingent in time of war. "The Assyrian inscriptions show that this country was, about the period in question, parcelled out into a number of petty kingdoms," &c. (Rawlinson. See "Records of the Past," vol. xii. p. 20)], **and horses, and chariots** [Heb. *horse and chariot;* cf. ver. 21 and chs. i. 5; x. 26; xvi. 9, &c. Both are collective nouns. We see here the fruit and retribution of Solomon's irreligious policy (ch. x. 29 and Homiletics, p. 216). "A king who has been probably identified with this Ben-hadad brought into the field against Assyria nearly 4000 chariots" (Rawlinson)]: **and he went up and besieged Samaria, and warred against it.** [The object of this expedition was clearly to humble and to plunder the kingdom of Samaria. It would almost appear, from the *animus* of the Syrian king and the studied offensiveness of his messages, as if Ahab or Israel must have given him dire offence. But Ben-hadad was clearly a vain and overbearing and tyrannical prince, and the only crime of Israel may have been that it was independent of him, or had refused to do him homage.]

Ver. 2.—**And he sent messengers to Ahab king of Israel into** [Heb. *to.* It is not clear that they entered the city. They may have delivered their message to the king, or to his representatives at the gates or to the people on the walls (2 Kings xviii. 18, 27)] **the city, and said unto him, Thus saith Ben-hadad,**

Ver. 3.—**Thy silver and thy gold is mine** [Heb. *mine it is*]; **thy wives also and thy children** [Nothing reveals Ben-hadad's object

more clearly than the mention of Ahab's wives. When we consider how jealously the seraglio of an Eastern prince is guarded, and how the surrender of the harem is a virtual surrender of the throne (2 Sam. xvi. 21, 22; note on ch. ii. 22), and certainly a surrender of all manhood and self-respect, we see that his aim was to wound Ahab in his tenderest point, to humble him to the lowest depths of degradation, and possibly to *force* a quarrel upon him], **even the goodliest** [The LXX. omits this. Bähr says the word can only apply to the sons, and that it must mean the most eminent young men of the city—not Ahab's children—whom Ben-hadad demanded as hostages. But against this is (1) Ahab's answer, "All that I have," &c.; (2) the fact that Ben-hadad obviously meant insult and plunder; and (3) the language of ver. 7, where see note], **are mine.** [Heb. *mine are they.* Rawlinson would explain this excessive demand of the Syrian king by the assumption that when it was made the siege had already lasted a long time, and that the people were now reduced to the greatest straits, circumstances which the historian, with the characteristic brevity of the sacred writers, omits to mention. But really no such supposition is needed. The overwhelming force which Ben-hadad had at his back would, in his eyes, justify any demands. And the *prima facie* view of ver. 2 is that the messengers were sent on the first approach of the army, or rather at the beginning of the siege.]

Ver. 4.—**And the king of Israel answered and said, My lord, O king, according to thy saying, I am thine, and all that I have.** [Much has been written about Ahab's pusillanimous acquiescence in these disgraceful terms, &c. But it is not absolutely clear that he ever meant to surrender either wives or children to the invader. All that is certain is that he judged it wise, in the presence of the enormous force arrayed against him, to make every possible concession, to adopt the most subservient tone, and to cringe at the feet of Ben-hadad. But all the time he may have hoped that his soft answer would turn away wrath. It is very far from certain that had Ben-hadad sent to demand the wives and children which Ahab here seems willing to yield to him they would have been sent. When Ben-hadad threatens (ver. 6) a measure which involved much less indignity than the surrender of the entire seraglio to his lusts, Ahab stands at bay. Allowance must be made for the exaggerations of Eastern courtesy. The writer was entertained in 1861 by Jacob esh Shellabi, then sheykh of the Samaritans, who repeatedly used words very similar to these. "This

house is yours," he would say; never meaning, however, that he should be taken at his
word.]

Ver. 5.—**And the messengers came again,
and said, Thus speaketh Ben-hadad, saying,
Although** [Heb. כִּי. According to some of
the grammarians, this is merely the Hebrew
equivalent of the ὅτι *recitantis*. But the
כִּי אִם of the next verse suggests that there
must be a connexion between the two, and
that the second emphasizes the first, much
as in the A. V.] **I have sent unto thee, saying, Thou shalt deliver me thy silver, and
thy gold, and thy wives, and thy children.**
[Our translators have often sacrificed force
to elegance by disregarding the *order* of the
Hebrew, which here, *e.g.*, is " *Thy silver and
thy gold . . . to me thou shalt give them.*"]

Ver. 6.—**Yet I will send my servants unto
thee to-morrow about this time** [This proposal was definite and immediate, the first
demand was vague and general. "In the
first Ahab was to send what he thought fit
to give; in the second, Ben-hadad's servants
were to take into their own hands whatsoever they thought fit to sieze" (Wordsworth)], **and they shall search thine house,
and the houses of thy servants; and it
shall be, that whatsoever is pleasant in**
[Heb. *the desire of*] **thine eyes** [The LXX.
and some other versions have a plural
suffix—*their eyes*. But the Hebrew text is
to be preferred. The object of Ben-hadad
was to couch his message in the most offensive and humiliating terms, and "the desire
of *thine* eyes" would be likely to cut deeper
and wound more than "the desire of *their*
eyes"], **they shall put it in their hand, and
take it away.** [If Ahab ever hoped by his
abject submission to conciliate the Syrian
king, he now finds that his words have had
just the opposite effect. For all that the
latter concluded from it was that Ahab was
one upon whom he might trample at pleasure, and this servility encouraged Ben-
hadad to renew his demands in a still more
galling and vexatious form. This second
message discloses to us still more plainly
the royal bully and braggart, and shows us
what the "comity of nations" in the old
world was often like.]

Ver. 7.—**Then the king of Israel called
all the elders of the land** [Bähr remarks
that this expression, compared with "the
elders of the *city*" (ch. xxi. 8, &c.), suggests either that these nobles, as the highest
officials, had their residences at the court, or
upon the approach of Ben-hadad had be-
taken themselves thither with their treasures.
Rawlinson builds on this slender basis the
conclusion that the council of elders which,
he says, belonged to the undivided kingdom,

had been continued among the ten tribes,
had an important place in the government,
and held regular sittings at the capital]
**and said, Mark, I pray you, and see how
this man** [or *fellow*. The הַזֶּה expresses
either hatred or contempt. Cf. ch. xxii.
27; Luke xxiii. 2, 18, &c.] **seeketh mischief** [the purport of Ahab's address is
not, "Ben-hadad is not satisfied with
my treasures; he wants yours also" (Bähr),
for there is no reference whatsoever to *their*
property, but, "See how he is determined
on our ruin. Nothing short of our destruction will suffice him. He is bent on
provoking an encounter, that he may
plunder the city at pleasure." The salient
word is the [רָעָה]: **for he sent unto me for
my wives, and for my children** [LXX. περὶ
τῶν υἱῶν μου. This shows clearly that " the
most eminent young men " cannot be meant
in ver. 3], **and for my silver, and for my
gold: and I denied him not.** [What these
words mean depends on what ver. 4 (where
see note) means. It is difficult to conceive
that any monarch could gravely proclaim
his own shame to his counsellors; could
confess, that is, that he had consented to
surrender his children and concubines without a struggle.]

Ver. 8.—**And all the elders and all the
people** [not only, *i.e.*, the inhabitants of
Samaria (Keil), but also those who had fled
thither for refuge. It is not implied that
they were formally consulted, but at such a
crisis, when nothing could be done, humanly
speaking, without their support, it was
natural that they should express their
opinion] **said unto him, Hearken not unto
him, nor consent.** [Lit., *thou shalt not consent*. אַל is the equivalent of μή, *ne*, and לֹא
of οὐ, *non*. Cf. Amos v. 5, and Ewald 350 *a*.]

Ver. 9.—**Wherefore** [Heb. *and*] **he said
unto the messengers of Ben-hadad, Tell
my lord the king** [He still employs the
same obsequious language as in ver. 4], **All
that thou didst send for to thy servant at
the first I will do: but this thing I may**
[Heb. *can*] **not do** [At first sight it appears
as if Ahab objected to the search (ver. 6),
i.e., plunder, of his house and capital much
more than to the surrender of his wives to
shame and of his children to slavery. But
we must remember that a man is ready to
promise almost anything in his extremity,
and that we do not know what construction
he put, or would have claimed to put, upon
Ben-hadad's first demand, had that monarch
consented to revert to these conditions, or
by what means he hoped to evade it]. **And
the messengers departed, and brought him**
[Ben-hadad, not Ahab, as Rawlinson

imagines] **word again.** [Not the "word re-lated in the next verse" (Rawlinson), but the message just recorded.]

Ver. 10.—And Ben-hadad sent unto him, and said [These words would be quite superfluous, if the oaths of which we now hear were the "word" of ver. 9], **The gods do so unto me, and more also** [see notes on ch. ii. 23; xix. 2], **if the dust of Samaria shall suffice for handfuls** [The meaning of שְׁעָלִים *pugilli*, is fixed by Isa. xl. 12, and Ezek. xiii. 19] **for all the people that follow me.** [Heb. *that* are *in my feet*. Same expression Judg. iv. 1C; v. 15; 1 Sam. xxv. 27; 2 Sam. xv. 17, &c. This thoroughly Oriental piece of bluster and boasting, which was intended, no doubt, to strike terror into the hearts of king and people, has been variously interpreted, but the meaning appears to be sufficiently clear. Ben-hadad vows that he will make Samaria a heap of dust, and at the same time affirms that so overwhelming is his host, that this dust will be insufficient to fill the hands of his soldiers. Rawlinson compares with it the well-known saying of the Trachinian to Dieneces, that the Median arrows would obscure the sun (Herod. vii. 226), but 2 Sam. xvii. 13 is still more apposite.]

Ver. 11.—And the king of Israel answered and said, Tell him, Let not him that girdeth on his harness boast himself as he that putteth it off. [This proverb consists of *four* words in the Hebrew. The commentators cite the Latin, *Ne triumphum canas ante victoriam*, but proverbs to the same effect are found in most languages.

Ver. 12.—And it came to pass, when Ben-hadad [Heb. *he*] **heard this message** [Heb. *word*], **as he was drinking, he and the kings in the pavilions** [Heb. *booths*. The word shows that, in lieu of tents, kings and generals on an expedition sometimes used leafy huts, like those of Israel (Levit. xxiii. 34, 42). Such booths, it is said, are still erected on military expeditions in the East], **that he said unto his servants, Set yourselves in array** [Heb. שִׂימוּ one short, decisive word. His indignation and astonishment were too great for more. We might perhaps render "Form." Cf. 1 Sam. xi. 11; Josh. viii. 2, 13; Job i. 17; Ezek. xxiii. 24. It cannot mean οἰκοδομήσατε χάρακα (LXX.)] **And they set themselves in array** [or *formed*. Again one word, which is more spirited and graphic, and conveys that the command was instantly obeyed] **against the city.**

Ver. 13.—And, behold, there came a prophet [Heb. *one prophet*. Cf. ch. xiii. 11. According to Jewish writers, this was Micaiah, son of Imlah, but ch. xxii. 8 negatives this supposition. This is another

proof that *all* the prophets had not been exterminated. Where Elijah was at this time, or why he was not employed, we have no means of determining. Bähr says that he was "least of all suited for such a message," but not if he had learned the lesson of ch. xix. 12. At the same time, it is to be remembered that he invariably appears as the minister of wrath. It may also be reasonably asked why this gracious interposition was granted to the kingdom of Samaria at all. Was not this invasion, and would not the sack of the city have been, a just recompense for the gross corruption of the age, for the persecution of the prophets, &c.? But to this it may be replied that Ben-hadad was not then the instrument which God had designed for the correction of Israel (see ch. xix. 17; xxii. 31; 2 Kings x. 32), and furthermore that by his brutal tyranny and despotic demands, he had himself merited a chastisement. The city, too, may have been delivered for the sake of the seven thousand (ch. xix. 18; 2 Kings xix. 34. Cf. Gen. xviii. 26 sqq.) But this gracious help in the time of extremity was primarily designed as a proof of Jehovah's power over the gods of Syria (cf. vers. 13, 28; ch. xviii. 39; 2 Kings xix. 22 sqq.), and so as an instrument for the conversion of Israel. His supremacy over the idols of Phoenicia had already been established] **unto Ahab king of Israel, saying, Thus saith the Lord, Hast thou seen all this great multitude?** [cf. ver. 10. "In Ben-hadad's wars with the Assyrians, we sometimes find him at the head of nearly 100,000 men" (Rawlinson).] **Behold, I will deliver it into thine hand this day; and thou shalt know that I am the Lord.** [This explains to us the *motif* of this great deliverance.]

Ver. 14.—And Ahab said, By whom? And he said, Thus saith the Lord [Observe the repetition. He is careful to give special prominence to the sacred name, as the only help in trouble (Psa. xx. 1, 5, 7, &c.)], **Even by the young men** [or *servants*—נַעֲרֵי has both meanings, corresponding with παῖς (cf. Gen. xxxvii. 2; 2 Kings v. 20; viii. 4] **of the princes of the provinces.** [The local governors (cf. chs. iv. 7; x. 15), on the approach of Ben-hadad, had apparently fled to the capital. Whether these "young men" were their "pages" (Thenius), or even were "young lads" (Ewald) at all, or, on the contrary, a "select body of strong young men" (Bähr), the body guard of the various governors (2 Sam. xviii. 15) (Von Gerlach), may be doubtful; but when Bähr says that Ahab would not have consented to appoint weak boys to lead the van, at least without remonstrance, he must have forgotten that *all* the ordinary means at

Ahab's disposal were equally insufficient, and that in themselves 200 or 2000 tried veterans would have been just as inadequate a force as 200 pages. The agency by which the victory was won was purposely weak and feeble (*per turbam imbellem*), in order that the work might be seen to be of God (cf. Judg. vii. 2; 1 Cor. i. 27, 29). And this consideration makes against the supposition that the attacking body was composed of tried and skilful warriors.] **Then he said, Who shall order** [Heb. *bind;* we speak of "*joining* battle"] **the battle?** [The meaning is—not, "who shall command this force," but, "which side shall begin the fray?"] **And he answered, Thou** [*i.e.*, thy band of young men shall make the attack.]

Ver. 15.—**Then he numbered** [or *reviewed* (cf. Num. i. 44 sqq.; iii. 39—43)] **the young men of the princes of the provinces, and they were two hundred and thirty-two** [cf. 2 Chron. xiv. 11; Psa. xxxiii. 16; Deut. xxxii. 30, &c. LXX. διακόσια τριάκοντα. Theodoret remarks that by this band—230, as he understood it—Almighty God would destroy the hosts of thirty and two kings. The numbers may have been recorded because of the correspondency]: **and after them he numbered all the people, even all the children of Israel, being seven thousand.** [This number is of course to be understood, unlike that of ch. xix. 18, literally. And the context (cf. ver. 19) shows that this was the number of fighting men. But this small army can hardly fail to create surprise, especially if we compare it with the statistics of the soldiery of an earlier age (2 Sam. xxiv. 9; 1 Chron. xxi. 5; 2 Chron. xiii. 3; xiv. 8). It is true this was not strictly an army, but a garrison for the defence of the capital. But it looks very much as if, under the feeble rule of Ahab, the kingdom of Israel had become thoroughly disorganized. "The position of Jarchi is that of a true Rabbi, viz., that the 7000 were those who had not bowed the knee unto Baal (ch. xix. 18)," Bähr.]

Ver. 16.—**And they went out at noon.** ["At the time when Ben-hadad, haughty and confident, had given himself up with his vassals, to the table, news of which had probably been received in the city" (Bähr). But it seems at least equally probable that the noon hour was selected either in obedience to the unrecorded directions of the prophet, or as being a time for rest and sleep, as it still is in the East.] **But Ben-hadad was drinking himself drunk in the pavilions, he and the kings, the thirty and two kings that helped him.** [Strong drink would seem to have been a besetment of the monarchs of that age (cf. ch. xvi. 9; Prov. xxxi. 4; Dan. v. 1 sqq.; Esther i. 10;

vii. 2; Hab. ii. 5). It can hardly have been to "mark his utter contempt of the foe," Rawlinson, who compares Belshazzar's feast (Dan. v. 1—4) when besieged by Cyrus. But Ben-hadad was the besieger. We are rather reminded of Alexander's carouse at Babylon.]

Ver. 17.—**And the young men of the princes of the provinces went out first; and Ben-hadad sent out** [Or *had sent out.* Possibly, the unusual stir in the city, the mustering of the troops, &c., had led to his sending out scouts before the young men issued from the gates. The LXX., however, has "And they send and tell the king of Syria," which Rawlinson thinks represents a purer text. But it looks like an emendation to avoid the difficulty, which is removed by translating וַיִּשְׁלַח as pluperfect], **and they told him, saying, There are men come out of Samaria.** [Heb. *men went forth*, &c.]

Ver. 18.—**And he said, Whether they be come out for peace** [*i.e.*, to negociate or to submit], **take them alive; or whether they be come out for war, take them alive.** [We may trace in these words, possibly the influence of wine, but certainly the exasperation which Ahab's last message had occasioned the king. So incensed is he that he will not respect the rights of ambassadors, and he is afraid lest belligerents should be slain before he can arraign them before him. Possibly he meant that they should be tortured or slain before his face.]

Ver. 19.—**So these young men of the princes of the provinces came out of the city, and the army which followed them.** [*i.e.*, the 7000. They "came out" after the young men.]

Ver. 20.—**And they slew every one his man** [The LXX., which differs here considerably from the Hebrew, inserts at this point καὶ ἐδευτέρωσεν ἕκαστος τὸν παρ' αὐτοῦ. Ewald thinks the Hebrew text ought to be made to correspond, and would read וַיַּכּוּ אִישׁ אִישׁוֹ *i.e.*, each repeatedly killed his man, as in 1 Sam. xiv. 16]: **and the Syrians fled** [When a few had fallen, utter panic seized the rest. The separate kings, with their divided interests, thought only of their own safety. It was a *sauve qui peut.* "The hasty and disordered flight of a vast Oriental army before an enemy contemptible in numbers is no uncommon occurrence. Above 1,000,000 of Persians fled before 47,000 Greeks at Arbela" (Rawlinson). The very size of such hosts, especially where the command is divided and where the generals are drunk or incapable, contributes to their defeat]; **and Israel pursued them: and Ben-hadad the**

king of Syria escaped on an horse [Thenius suggests that this was a chariot horse, the first that presented] **with the horsemen.** [Heb. *and horsemen; sc.*, escaped with him (Keil). He had an escort in some of his fugitive cavalry.]

Ver. 21.—**And the king of Israel went out** [It looks as if Ahab had remained within the city until the defeat of the Syrians was assured], **and smote** [LXX. καὶ ἔλαβε, *and captured*] **the horses and chariots** [*i.e.*, the cavalry and chariotry; cf. ver. 1], **and slew the Syrians with a great slaughter.** [Heb. *in Syria a great, &c.*]

Ver. 22.—**And the prophet** [obviously the same prophet] **came to the king of Israel, and said unto him, Go, strengthen thyself** [both as to army and to city], **and mark, and see what thou doest** [" Take every precaution. Don't think that the danger is past"] : **for at the return of the year** [in the following spring. There was a favourite time for campaigns (2 Sam. xi. 1), viz., when the rainy season was past. Several late wars, notably those of our own armies in Africa and Afghanistan, have been considerably influenced by the seasons. And the wars of ancient times were almost universally summer raids. " Sustained invasions, lasting over the winter, are not found until the time of Shalmaneser " (2 Kings xvii. 5; xviii. 9 10, Rawlinson)] **the king of Syria will come** [Heb. *cometh*] **up against thee.**

Ver. 23.—**And the servants of the king of Syria said unto him** [naturally anxious to retrieve their character and obliterate their disgrace], **Their gods are gods of the hills** [All pagan nations have believed in local deities, *Dii montium, dii nemorum, &c.* (see 2 Kings xviii. 33—35; xix. 12, 13). Keil accounts for this belief—that the gods of Israel were mountain divinities, by the consideration that the temple was built on *Mount* Moriah, and that worship was always offered on " *high* places." Kitto reminds us that the law was given from Mount Sinai, and that fire had recently descended on Mount Carmel. " In Syrophoenicia, even mountains themselves had Divine honours paid to them " (Movers, Phoen. i. 667 sqq.) But it is enough to remember that Samaria was a hilly district, and that the courtiers must find some excuse for the defeat]; **therefore they were stronger than we; but** [Heb.

(וְאוּלָם) often well rendered but not in this instance) by the LXX. οὐ μὴν δὲ ἀλλά] **let us fight against them in the plain, and surely we shall be stronger than they.** [This counsel, which apparently rests on religious grounds alone, was, it is probable, really dictated by the practical consideration

that in the plain the Syrians would be able to deploy their chariots—a most important arm of their service—in a way which they could not do in the valleys round Samaria. See ch. xvi. 24, note. Moreover, the Israelites would lose the advantage of a strong position and the cover of their fortifications if they could be induced to meet them in the " great plain," or on any similar battle-field.]

Ver. 24.—**And do this thing. Take the kings away, every man out of his place, and put captains** [Same word as in ch. x. 15, where see note] **in their rooms.** [Not so much because (Bähr) the kings only fought through compulsion, for they appear to have been in complete accord with Ben-hadad (vers. 1, 12, 16), as because of their incapacity and divided interests and plans. The captains would presumably be selected because of their valour, military skill, &c.; the kings would owe their command to the accident of birth, &c. Moreover, an army with thirty-three leaders could not have the necessary solidarity. Bähr assumes that the removal of the kings would involve the withdrawal of the auxiliaries which they contributed. But this does not appear to have occurred to Ben-hadad's advisers when they said, " put captains *in their rooms.*" If the auxiliaries were withdrawn, what were the thirty-two captains to command ?]

Ver. 25.—**And number thee an army, like the army that thou hast lost** [Heb. *that is fallen from thee*, not as marg., *that was fallen.* For the form מֵאוֹתְךָ see Ewald, 264 *b*)], **horse for** [Heb. *as*] **horse, and chariot for chariot : and we will fight against them in the plain, and surely we shall be stronger than they. And he hearkened unto their voice, and did so.**

Ver. 26.—**And it came to pass at the return of the year, that Ben-hadad numbered the Syrians** [Heb. *Syria*], **and went up to Aphek** [As the word signifies " fortress," it is only natural that several different places should bear this name, and the commentators are not agreed as to which of them is here intended. Keil and Bähr identify it with the Aphek hard by Shunem (1 Sam. xxix. 1; cf. xxviii. 4), and therefore in the plain of Esdraelon, while Gesenius and Grove—the latter because of its connection with הַמִּישׁוֹר *the plain*, a word applied, κατ' ἐξοχήν, to the plain in the tribe of Reuben (Deut. iii. 10; iv. 43; Josh. xiii. 9, 16, 17, 21, &c.)—would see in it the Aphek east of the Jordan, the *Apheca* of Eusebius, and perhaps the place mentioned 2 Kings xiii. 17 (where, however, see note). This trans-Jordanic Aphek is now represented by the village of *Fik*, six miles east of the sea of Galilee, and standing, as Aphek must have then stood, on the high road between Damascus and Jerusalem. On the whole, the balance of probability inclines to the latter. It would follow hence that the Israelites, emboldened by their victory of the preceding year, had crossed the river to meet the enemy], **to fight against Israel.** [Heb. *to the war with Israel.*]

Ver. 27.—**And the children of Israel were numbered** [lit., *numbered themselves.* Hithpael], **and were all present** [Rather, *and were provided with food,* כּוּל=to nourish. The Alex. LXX. inserts καὶ διοικήθησαν. Vulgate *acceptis cibariis.* Marg. *were victualled.* This word of itself suggests that they were at a distance from their capital or other city], **and went against them** [Heb. *to meet them*] : **and the children of Israel pitched before them like two little flocks**

חֲשִׂיף strictly means *separated.* It is rightly translated " *little* flocks " (not "flocks," Rawlinson), because the idea is that of two bands of stragglers separated from the main body of the flock. So the Vulgate, *duo parvi greges caprarum;* but LXX., δύο ποίμνια αἰγῶν. Ewald thinks the " *two* flocks " points to an auxiliary force furnished by Jehoshaphat, fighting with Israel. He also thinks *goats* are mentioned to convey the exalted position of the camp upon the hills. Flocks of goats as a rule are smaller than those of sheep, the former being more given to straying] **of kids** [lit., *she-goats.* " These flocks pasture mostly on the cliffs, and are smaller than the flocks of sheep " (Bähr)] ; **but the Syrians filled the country.** [The whole plain swarmed with their legions in striking contrast to the two insignificant bodies of Israelites.]

Ver. 28.—**And there came a man of God** [Whether this is the same person as the "prophet" of vers. 13, 22, is not quite clear. The difference in the designation (see on ch. xiii. 1 and p. 303) would lead us to suppose that a different messenger was meant. It is true the Hebrew has the article " *the* man of God" (LXX. ὁ ἄνθρωπος τοῦ θεοῦ), but הָאֱלֹהִים אִישׁ (see Judg. xiii. 6; Deut. xxxiii. 1) is often hardly distinguishable from the same words without the article, **and spake** [Heb. *said,* same word as below] **unto the king of Israel, and said, Thus saith the Lord, Because the Syrians** [Heb. *Syria,* but with a plural verb] **have said, The Lord is God of the hills, but he is not God of the valleys, therefore will I deliver all this great multitude into thine hand, and ye shall know that I am the Lord.** [It was partly for the instruction of Israel, and to confirm their wavering faith

in Jehovah (see ver. 13), that this deliverance was wrought. But it was also that neighbouring nations might learn His power, and that His name might be magnified among the heathen.]

Ver. 29.—**And they pitched one over against the other** [Heb. *these opposite these*] **seven days.** [The Syrians, despite their overwhelming numbers, appear to have been afraid to attack, and the Israelites were naturally reluctant, despite the promise they had received, to join battle with so great a host]. **And so it was, that in the seventh day the battle was joined** [Heb. *the war drew near.* It may have been by the direction of the man of God that the Israelites attacked on the seventh day, or the precedent of Jericho (Josh. vi. 15) may have influenced their leaders; or the number seven, properly the mark and signature of the covenant, may have come to be regarded superstitiously—in fact, as a lucky number (cf. Isa. lxv. 11; Esther iii. 7] : **and the children of Israel slew of the Syrians an hundred thousand footmen in one day.** [This prodigious slaughter may well create surprise. That two comparatively small companies should be able, physically, to slay, with the rude weapons of that age, 100,000 warriors, fighting for their lives, seems hardly credible. It is probable, therefore, that the numbers here, as elsewhere, have been exaggerated in the course of transcription. Another explanation of the difficulty has, indeed, been *suggested* by Bähr, viz., that וַיַּכּוּ may signify here, as it undoubtedly does elsewhere, " defeated," " put to flight " (see Gen. xiv. 5; 1 Sam. xiii. 4, &c.) And the Hebrew at first sight seems to favour this idea, for it may be rendered literally, *they smote Syria, a hundred thousand, &c.* The 100,000 would then represent the entire strength of the Syrian infantry. But the mention of the "footmen" and of "one day" alike suggests that it is of slaughter, not dispersion, that the historian speaks.]

Ver. 30.—**But the rest** [Plainly those not *slain.* It cannot mean those not *defeated*] **fled to Aphek** [It is clear that this fortress was then in the possession of the Syrians, as they took refuge within its walls], **into the city; and there a wall** [Heb. *the* wall, *i.e.,* the city wall] **fell upon twenty and seven thousand of the men that were left.** [The Hebrew implies that these were practically all who survived the battle. הַנּוֹתָרִים is the word translated above, "the rest." We have here surely an exaggeration, even more obvious than that of ver. 39. For even if we suppose an earthquake, it is difficult to believe that the walls of a place like

Aphek could bury so large a number in their ruins. Rawlinson suggests that the Syrians at the time were "manning the defences in full force," and that the earthquake "threw down the wall where they were most thickly crowded upon it;" but the question arises whether it is possible to mass 27,000 men upon any part of a wall, or all the walls, especially of an ancient village fortress. Thenius hints that the fall of the wall may have been occasioned by the Israelites undermining it during the night, but it seems hardly likely that so small a force could undertake operations of that kind against so formidable a body of troops. Keil objects to this view on another ground, viz., that its object is to negative the idea of a Divine interposition. But the text does not ascribe the fall of the wall to any such interposition, and we know that the sacred writers are not slow to recognize the finger of God whenever it is exerted.] **And Ben-hadad fled, and came into** [Heb. *to*] **the city** [*i.e.*, Aphek. Rawlinson interprets this statement to mean that he "fled from the wall, where he had been at the time of the disaster, into the inner parts of the city," but this is extremely doubtful. Observe the words, "fled *and came* to the city"—words almost identical with those used of the fugitives above], **into an inner chamber.** [Heb. *into a chamber within a chamber*, as in ch. xxii. 25. This cannot mean "from chamber to chamber," as marg. It is to be observed that חֶדֶר alone signifies properly an *inner* chamber. See Gen. xliii. 30; Judg. xvi. 9, 12. Rawlinson thinks that a *secret* chamber may be meant "a chamber in the wall, or one beneath the floor of another."]

Ver. 31.—**And his servants** [Possibly the very same men who (ver. 23) had counselled this second expedition] **said unto him, Behold now, we have heard that the kings of the house of Israel are merciful kings** [As no doubt they were when compared with contemporary pagan sovereigns]: **let us, I pray thee, put sackcloth on our loins** [in token of humiliation and contrition. שַׂק is identical, radically, with σάκκος, *saccus*, and our *sack*], **and ropes upon our heads** [*i.e.*, round our necks. To show how completely they were at Ahab's mercy. Bähr shows that this custom still exists in China, but the well-known story of the citizens of Calais, after its siege by Edward III., supplies a closer illustration], **and go out** [Heb. *go*] **to the king of Israel** [It would appear from the language of ver. 33 as if Ahab's army was now besieging the place. He himself may have kept at a safe distance

from it]: **peradventure he will save thy life.** [LXX. *our* lives, τὰς ψυχὰς ἡμῶν.]

Ver. 32.—**So they girded sackcloth on their loins, and put ropes on their heads, and came to the king of Israel and said, Thy servant Ben-hadad saith, I pray thee, let me live.** [Compare with this abject petition for life the arrogant insolence of vers. 6, 10. The tables are indeed turned.] **And he said, Is he yet alive ? he is my brother.**

Ver. 33.—**Now the men did diligently observe whether anything would come from him, and did hastily catch it** [Heb. *and the men augured*—נָחֵשׁ *divinavit.* Cf. Gen. xliv. 15; Levit. xix. 26; 2 Kings xvii. 17. LXX. οἰωνίσαντο. Vulgate *acceperunt pro omine*—*and hasted and made him declare whether from him*, the meaning of which is sufficiently clear, viz., that the men took Ahab's words, "He is my brother," as a speech of good omen, and immediately laid hold of it, and contrived that the king should be held to it and made to confirm it. The only difficulty is in the word וַיַּחְלְטוּ which is ἅπαξ λέγ. The Talmud, however, interprets it to mean, *declare, confirm ;* in the Kal conjugation and the Hiphil would therefore mean, *made him declare.* The LXX. and Vulgate, however, have understood it otherwise, taking חָלַט as the equivalent of חָלַץ *rapuit.* The former has ἀνελέξαντο τὸν λόγον ἐκ τοῦ στόματος αὐτοῦ, and the latter *rapuerunt verbum ex ore ejus.* They would seem also to have read instead of הַדָּבָר מֵ'הַמֶּמֶנּוּ (Ewald). The law of *dakheel* (see Layard, N. and B. pp. 317—319), by which Rawlinson would explain this incident, seems to be rather an usage of the Bedouin than of any civilized nations] : **and they said, Thy brother Ben-hadad. Then said he, Go ye, bring him. Then Ben-hadad came forth to him** [out of his hiding-place and out of the city]: **and he caused him to come up into the chariot.** [A mark of great favour (compare Gen. xli. 43), and of reconciliation and concord (cf. 2 Kings x. 15).]

Ver. 34.—**And Ben-hadad said unto him, The cities, which my father took from thy father, I will restore** [We can hardly see in these words "the terms of peace which he is willing to offer as the price of his freedom" (Rawlinson), because he was absolutely at Ahab's mercy, and was not in a position to make any stipulations ; but they express Ben-hadad's idea of the results which must follow the conquest. His utter defeat would necessitate this reconstruction of their respective territories, &c. We cannot be quite certain that the cities here referred to are those enumerated in ch. xv.

20, as taken by Ben-hadad's armies from Baasha. For Baasha was not the father, nor even was he the "ancestor" (as Keil, later edition) of Ahab, but belonged to a different dynasty. At the same time it is quite conceivable that a prince in Ben-hadad's position, in his ignorance or forget-fulness of the history of Israel, might use the word "father" improperly, or even in the sense of "predecessor." We know that אָב had a very extended signification. Keil and Bähr, however, think that we have a reference to some war in the reign of Omri (cf. ch. xvi. 27), which is not recorded in Scripture. And the words which follow make this extremely probable, inasmuch as in Baasha's days Samaria had no exist-ence] ; **and thou shalt make streets** [חֻצוֹת lit., *whatever is without;* hence streets, spaces, quarters] **for thee in Damascus, as my father made in Samaria.** [The com-mentators are agreed that a permission to establish bazaars or quarters, in which the Hebrews might live and trade, is here con-ceded]. **Then said Ahab** [These words are rightly supplied by our translators. The meaning would have been quite clear had the Hebrews been familiar with the use of quotation marks. For lack of these, all the versions ascribe the words to Ben-hadad], **I will send thee away with this covenant. So he made a covenant with him, and sent him away.**

Ver. 35.—**And a certain man** [Heb. *one man;* cf. ch. xiii. 11, note] **of the sons of the prophets** [Here mentioned for the first time, though the prophetic schools prob-ably owed their existence, certainly their development, to Samuel. The בְּנֵי הַנּ׳ are of course not the children, but the pupils of the prophets. For this use of "son," cf. 1 Sam. xx. 31 ("a *son* of death"); 2 Sam. xii. 5; Deut. xxv. 2; Matt. xxiii. 15; 1 Kings iv. 30; Ezra ii. 1; John xvii. 12, and Amos vii. 14. Gesenius refers to the Greek ἰατρῶν υἱοί, ῥητόρων υἱοί, &c., and says that among the Persians "the disciples of the Magi are called, "*Sons* of Magi." The word, again, does not neces-sarily imply youth. That they were some-times married men appears from 2 Kings vi. 1, though this was probably after their collegiate life was ended. As they were called "sons," so their instructor, or head, was called "father" (1 Sam. x. 12)] **said unto his neighbour** [or *companion.* Another *prophet* is implied. It was because this "neighbour" *was* a prophet that his dis-regard of the word of the Lord was so sinful, and received such severe punishment], **in the word of the Lord** [see on ch. xiii. 1], **Smite me, I pray thee.** [Why the prophet,

in order to the accomplishment of his mission—which was to obtain from Ahab's own lips a confession of his deserts—why he should have been smitten, *i.e.*, bruised and wounded, is not quite clear. For it is obvious that he might have sustained his part, told his story, and obtained a judg-ment from the king, without proceeding to such painful extremities. It is quite true that a person thus wounded would perhaps sustain the part of one who had been in battle *better*, but the wounds were in no way necessary to his disguise, and men do not court pain without imperious reasons. Besides, it was "in the word of the Lord" that these wounds were sought and received. It is quite clear, therefore, that it cannot have been merely to give him a claim to an audience with the king (Ewald)—he could easily have simulated wounds by means of bandages, which would at the same time have helped to disguise him—or that he might foreshadow in his own person the wounding which Ahab would receive (ch. xxii. 11), for of that he says nothing, or for any similar reason. The wounding, we may be quite sure, and the tragical circum-stances connected therewith, are essential parts of the parable this prophet had to act, of the lesson he had to teach. Now the great lesson he had to convey, not to the king alone, but to the prophetic order and to the whole country, the lesson most necessary in that lawless age, was that of implicit unquestioning obedience to the Divine law. Ahab had just transgressed that law. He had "let go a man whom God had appointed to utter destruction;" he had heaped honours on the oppressor of his country, and in gratifying benevolent im-pulses had ignored the will and counsel of God (see on ver. 42). No doubt it seemed to him, as it has seemed to others since, that he had acted with rare magnanimity, and that his generosity in that age, an age which showed no mercy to the fallen, was unexampled. But he must be taught that he has no right to be generous at the ex-pense of others; that God's will must be done even when it goes against the grain, when it contradicts impulses of kindness, and demands painful sacrifices. He is taught this by the prophetic word (ver. 42), but much more effectively by the actions which preceded it. A prophet required to smite a brother prophet, and that for no apparent reason, would no doubt find it re-pugnant to his feelings to do so; it would seem to him hard and cruel and shameful to smite a companion. But the prophet who refused to do this, who followed his benevolent impulses in preference to the word of the Lord, died for his sin—died forthwith by the visitation of God. What a lesson was this to king and country—for no doubt, the incident would be bruited abroad, and the very strangeness of the whole proceeding would heighten the impression it made. Indeed, it is hardly possible to conceive a way in which the duty of unquestioning obedience could be more emphatically taught. When this prophet appeared before the king, a man had smitten and wounded him, disagreeable and painful as the task must have been, because of the word of the Lord; whilst a brother prophet, who declined the office because it was painful, had been slain by a wild beast. It is easy to see that there was here a solemn lesson for the king, and that the wounding gave it its edge.] **And the man refused to smite him.**

Ver. 36.—**Then said he unto him, Because thou hast not obeyed the voice of the Lord, behold, as soon as thou art departed from me, a lion** [Heb. *the lion*, perhaps the lion appointed already to this office, or one that had lately been seen in the neighbourhood] **shall slay thee. And as soon as he was departed from him, a** [Heb. *the*] **lion found him** [same word as in ch. xiii. 24, where see note], **and slew him.** [For the same sin as that of "the man of God (ch. xiii. 21, 26), viz., disobedience (Deut. xxxii. 24; Jer. v. 6), and disobedience, too, under circumstances remarkably similar to those. In fact, the two histories run on almost parallel lines. In each case it is a prophet who disobeys, and disobeys the "word of the Lord;" in each case the disobedience appears almost excusable; in each case the prophet appears to be hardly dealt with, and suffers instant punishment, whilst the king escapes; in each case the punishment is foretold by a prophet; in each case it is effected by the instrumentality of a lion. And in each case the lesson is the same that God's commands must be kept, whatever the cost, or that stern retribution will inevitably follow.]

Ver. 37.—**Then he found another man, and said, Smite me, I pray thee. And the man smote him, so that in smiting he wounded him.** [Heb. *smiting and wounding.* This last particular is apparently recorded to show how promptly and thoroughly this "other man," who is not said to have been a prophet, obeyed the charge. Probably he had the fate of the other before his eyes.]

Ver. 38.—**So the prophet departed, and waited for the king by the way, and disguised himself with ashes upon his face.** [Rather, *a bandage upon his eyes.* אֲפֵר there can be no doubt, denotes some sort of covering (LXX. τελαμών), and is probably the

equivalent of עָפָר. Ashes cannot be put on the *eyes*, and even on the head would be but a poor disguise. This bandage was at the same time in keeping with the prophet's *rôle* as a wounded man, and an effective means of concealment. It would almost seem as if this prophet was personally known to the king.]

Ver. 39.—**And as the king passed by, he cried unto the king** [in his capacity of supreme judge; see on ch. iii. 9]: **and he said, Thy servant went out into the midst of the battle** [*i.e.*, the recent battle]; **and, behold, a man turned aside** [סָר; cf. ch. xxii. 43; Exod. iii. 3; xxxii. 8. But Ewald, *al.* would read, סַר *prince* or *captain* (properly שׂר), a change which certainly lends force to the apologue, and makes the analogy more complete. Only such an officer was entitled to give such an order. Moreover, just as a common soldier ought to obey his captain, so should Ahab have obeyed God. But as our present text yields a good and sufficient meaning, we are hardly warranted in making any change], **and brought a man unto me, and said, Keep this man: if by any means he be missing, then shall thy life be for his life, or else thou shalt pay** [Heb. *weigh.* There was then no coinage. Payments were made by means of bars of silver or gold] **a talent of silver.** [A considerable sum—about £400. "The prisoner is thus represented to be a very important personage" (Thenius). There is a hint at Ben-hadad. Ewald holds that the wounds represented the penalty inflicted instead of the talent which a common soldier naturally could not pay.]

Ver. 40.—**And as thy servant was busy** [Heb. *doing.* The LXX. περιεβλέψατο ὁ δοῦλός σου, and the Vulgate *dum ego turbatus huc illucque me verterem*, have led some critics to urge the substitution of פֹּנֶה *turning*, or שֹׁעֶה *looking*, for עֹשֶׂה *doing*, in the text. But no alteration is needed] **here and there** [or *hither and thither*—the ה is generally *local*—as in Josh. viii. 20. But sometimes it is merely *demonstrative*, "here and there," as in Gen. xxi. 29, Dan. xii. 5, and so it may be understood here (Gesenius)], **he was gone** [Heb. *he is not*]. **And the king of Israel said unto him, So shall thy judgment be; thyself hast decided it.** [Cf. 2 Sam. xii. 5—7, Ahab has himself pronounced that his judgment is just, and what it shall be.]

Ver. 41.—**And he hasted, and took the ashes away from his face** [Heb. *removed the covering from upon his eyes*]; **and the king of Israel discerned him that he was of the prophets.** [That is, he was one of the prophets who were known to him. The face alone would hardly have proclaimed him a prophet. And the prophet's dress would of course have been laid aside when the disguise was assumed.]

Ver. 42.—**And he said unto him, Thus saith the Lord, Because thou hast let go** [Heb. *sent away;* same word as in ver. 34. This is an indirect proof that those were the words of Ahab] **out of thy hand** [Heb. *out of hand*—same idiom in 1 Sam. xxvi. 23—*i.e.,* power, possession. Cf. Gen. xxxii. 12; Exod. xviii. 9; Num. xxxv. 25] **a man whom I appointed to utter destruction** [Heb. *a man of my devoting.* Cf. Isa. xxxiv. 5; Zech. xiv. 11. It is the word used of the Canaanites and their cities, Deut. ii. 34; vii. 2; Josh. viii. 26; x. 28; and it gave a name to the city *Hormah,* Num. xxi. 3; xiv. 45. Ben-hadad, therefore, was doomed of God], **therefore thy life shall go for** [Heb. *be instead of*] **his life, and thy people for his people.** [By the *lex talionis.* It was probably because of this denunciation (cf. ch. xxii. 8) that Josephus identifies this prophet with Micaiah, the son of Imlah, "whom Ahab appears to have imprisoned on account of *some* threatening prophecy" (Rawlinson). See ch. xxii. 9, 26. For the fulfilment of this prediction see ch. xxii. It has seemed to some writers as if Ahab were here very hardly dealt with for merely gratifying a generous impulse, and dealing magnanimously with a conquered foe. Indeed, there are commentators who see in his release of the cruel and insolent tyrant a "trait which does honour to the heart of Ahab." But it is to be remembered, first, that Ahab was not free to do as he liked in this matter. His victories had been won, not by his prowess, by the skill of his generals, or the valour of his soldiers, but by the power of God alone. The war, that is to say, was God's war: it was begun and continued, and should therefore have been ended, in Him. When even the details of the attack had been ordered of God (ver. 14), surely He should have been consulted as to the disposal of the prisoners. The prophet

who promised Divine aid might at any rate have been asked—as prophets constantly were in that age (ch. xxii. 5, 8)—what was the "word of the Lord" concerning Israel's overbearing and inveterate enemy. But Ahab, who had himself played so craven a part (vers. 21, 31), and who had contributed nothing to these great and unhoped-for victories, nevertheless arrogated to himself their fruits, and thereby ignored and dishonoured God. Secondly, if he had so little regard for his own private interests as to liberate such a man as Ben-hadad, he ought, as trustee for the peace and welfare of Israel, to have acted differently. The demand of ver. 6 should have revealed to him the character of the man he had to deal with. And lastly, he was acting in defiance of all the principles and precedents of the Old Testament dispensation. For one great principle of that dispensation was the *lex talionis.* The king was the authorized dispenser of rewards and punishments, not only to wicked subjects but to aggressive nations. It was his duty to mete out to them the measure they had served to Israel. And the precedents were all in favour of putting such wretches as this Ben-hadad to the sword (Josh. x. 26; Judg. vii. 25; 1 Sam. xv. 33). If he had been the first oppressor who fell into the hands of Israel, Ahab might have had some excuse. But with the fate of Agag, of Adoni-bezek, of Oreb and Zeeb, in his memory, he ought at any rate to have paused and asked counsel of God before taking Ben-hadad into his chariot and sending him away with a covenant of peace, to reappear at no distant period on the scene as the scourge of the Lord's people.]

Ver. 43.—**And the king of Israel went to his house heavy and displeased** [Heb. *sullen and angry;* same words ch. xxi. 4], **and came to Samaria.** [The order of this verse suggests that the house was one in or near Aphek, in which the king was lodged after the battle—on which this interview, therefore, followed closely—and that shortly afterwards he left it for his capital.]

HOMILETICS.

Vers. 1—43.—*The Purgatory of Nations and Kings.* The two invasions of Israel by the armies of Syria, and their defeat by the finger of God, may suggest some lessons as to God's dealings with *nations,* and with oppressive and tyrannical kings.

Two considerations must, however, be borne in mind here. First, that the present age, unlike the Mosaic, is not a dispensation of *temporal* rewards and punishments. It is true that even now men *do* receive a rough sort of retribution, according to their deserts, from the operation of natural laws; but that retribution is uncertain and indirect. Sometimes vengeance overtakes the wrong-doer, but as often as not he escapes scathless. The Jewish economy, however, had absolutely none but temporal sanctions. A "judgment *to come*" formed no part of its system. It dealt with men as if there were no hereafter. It taught them to expect an exact and proportionate and immediate recompense ; an eye for an eye, and a tooth for a tooth. It preached an ever-present Deity, the true King of the country, visiting every transgression and disobedience with its just recompense of reward (Heb. ii. 2). And so long as that economy was practised in its integrity, so long, either through the immediate dispensations of God, or the mediate action of the authorities who represented Him, did vice and crime, extortion and oppression, infidelity and apostasy, receive their just deserts. But with the advent of our Lord, and His apocalypse of life and immortality, all this was changed. We no longer look for temporal judgments because we are taught to wait for the judgment-seat of Christ. It is only within very narrow limits that we expect to see vice punished or virtue rewarded. It causes us no surprise, consequently, to find even the tyrant and oppressor escaping all the whips and stings of vengeance. We know that he will not always escape ; that though " the mills of God grind slowly, yet they grind exceeding small," and that he and all such as he will surely satisfy the inexorable claims of Justice hereafter.

But there is apparently one exception—and this is the second consideration—to this general rule. If the individual is not judged here, the nation is. For nations, as such, have no existence apart from this life present. In the kingdom of the future, nationalities have no place (Col. iii. 11). " Mortals have many tongues, immortals have but one." If, then, men are ever to be dealt with in their corporate capacity, they must, and as a matter of fact they do, receive their reckoning here. It surely is not difficult to trace the finger of God in the history of Europe as well as of Israel, of modern as of ancient times. In our own generation have not both Austria and Prussia paid in blood for the spoliation of Denmark? Have not the United States suffered for their overweening pride and greed and reckless speculation? Has not France paid a heavy forfeit for the corruption, the profligacy, the secularity which marked the latter years of the Empire? Has not England, too, had to lament her intermeddling? have not her late reverses suggested to many minds the painful thought that the hand of the Lord is gone out against her? Is she not suffering at this moment for her past misgovernment of Ireland? Is not Turkey, by the agonies of dissolution, expiating the uncleanness and injustice of the last four centuries ? Yes, it should be clear that whatever arraignment awaits the individual hereafter, the community, the nation, receives its requital and acquittance here.

And if this be so, it is obvious that the king, the representative of the country, or the sovereign power, who is responsible primarily for the action of the community, will have a share, and by far the largest share, in whatever good or evil befalls it. On him primarily does the disgrace and blow of a disaster fall. It is not always true that " the kings make war and their subjects have to pay for it," for the king, in case of defeat, pays the heaviest toll of all. And though there is no one to call him to an account for internal misgovernment, yet even that does not go unrecompensed, as the history of Rome, of Russia, of Turkey, of England shows. We are warranted in looking, consequently, for the punishment of aggressive nations and tyrannical kings in this present age.

Now this chapter describes two invasions of the territory of Israel, and two successive defeats of the invaders. In the invasions we see the punishment of Israel and of Ahab ; in the defeats the punishment of Syria and Ben-hadad. Let us inquire, in the first place, what each had done to provoke and deserve his respective chastisement.

1. THE INVASIONS. That these were punishments hardly needs proof. For can any land be overrun with a horde of barbarians, such as the Syrians and their confederates, the Hittite chieftains, were, without widespread and profound suffering ? We know what invasion means in modern times, when warfare is conducted with some approach to humanity, but what it meant in the Old World and the Orient, we are quite unable to realize. It is idle to say that the Syrians were defeated in the end. Who shall picture to us what the thousands of Israel suffered during the

advance, possibly during the retreat, of that unwieldy and rapacious host, certainly during the occupation of the country ? " Before them the garden of Eden, behind them a desolate wilderness" (Joel ii. 3). Fire, rapine, famine, these three fell sisters marched in their train. The invasions, then, though repelled, would entail prodigious loss and suffering on the people. It would not compensate the Jewish farmer for the loss of his corn and oil and wine, still less the Jewish father for the dishonour of his daughters, to know that the siege was raised, that the king had fled to an inner chamber, that thousands of their enemies lay buried under the walls of Aphek. No, each invasion was nothing short of a national calamity, and we do well to ask what it was had provoked this chastisement. It was—

1. *The sin of the people at large.* The sin of Israel at this epoch was idolatry. The sin of Jeroboam had already received, in part at least, its recompense. A Syrian invasion in a preceding generation (ch. xv. 20) had wasted the territory of Dan. But the calf-worship was continued, and vile idolatry was now associated with it. It is true this had been fostered, if not introduced, by Jezebel, but it is impossible to acquit the people of blame. The pleasant vices of the Phoenician ritual were sweet to their taste. They loved to have it so. Justice demanded, consequently, that they should share in the punishment. Idolatry had already procured the investment and spoliation of Jerusalem ; it now accounts for the march of the Syrians and the siege of Samaria, the centre of the Baal-worship. This is the third time that a foreign army has appeared before a polluted shrine. " How can they expect peace from the earth who do wilfully fight against heaven ? "

2. *The sin of its rulers.* We have just seen that Ahab and Jezebel were primarily responsible for this last great apostasy. It was Jezebel really who "reared up an altar for Baal," &c. (ch. xvi. 32), though Ahab was a facile instrument in her hands. We find, consequently, that king and queen were the first to suffer, and suffered most. It is easy to picture the abject wretchedness and despair to which Ahab was reduced by the insolent messages of the northern barbarian. Those were indeed days of trouble and rebuke and blasphemy. The iron must have entered into his soul as he found himself utterly without resources, at the mercy of one who showed no mercy, but absolutely gloated over his misery. Nor did Jezebel escape her share of torture. She had to face the prospect of being handed over, with the other ladies of the harem, to the will of the brutal, sensual, drunken despot who was thundering at their gates. Had her hair turned white, like that of another queen, in one night, we could not have wondered at it. Strong-willed, desperate woman that she was (2 Kings ix. 31), she must have known too well how cruel are the tender mercies of the wicked not to have trembled. It is clear, therefore, that that prince and princess reaped some fruit of their doings in this life.

But it may be said that this reign of terror did not last long, and that despair was speedily succeeded by the joy and triumph of victory. But the victory was not one which could afford unmixed satisfaction, either to king or people. It was not won by their prowess. It was of such a kind that all boasting was excluded. In the first place, they owed it to a prophet of the Lord—one of the order whom Jezebel had persecuted. It would therefore heap coals of fire upon Ahab's head. Secondly, it was achieved by a handful of boys. His trained veterans had to follow their lead and enter into their labours. It was therefore more of a humiliation than a glory for his arms. It left him, in the presence of his people, a helpless debtor to that God whose altars he had overthrown ; to that prophet whose companions he had slain.

Such were the immediate causes of the invasion. Two others, which were more remote, must be briefly indicated.

3. *The unwisdom and unbelief of Asa.* He it was who first taught the Syrians that the way to Samaria lay open to them, and that the spoils of the country repaid the cost and trouble of invasion (ch. xv. 18, 19).

4. *The impiety of Solomon.* The horses and chariots furnished by that great prince to the "kings of the Hittites and the kings of Syria " (ch. x. 29) now overrun the great plain and stream into the valleys of Samaria. The Syrians owed the

most important arm of their service (vers. 1, 25) to the disobedience of the Lord's anointed. The two-and-thirty subject princes had once been the vassals of Solomon (ch. iv. 21). We now turn to—

II. THE DEFEATS. If this prodigious host was really called together to chastise the idolatries of Israel, it seems strange that it was not allowed to effect its purpose ; that in the very hour of victory it was utterly and irretrievably defeated. But the explanation is not far to seek. Its advance was the punishment of Ahab's sin ; its dispersion the punishment of Ben-hadad's. " Well may God plague each with other who means vengeance to them both." And Ben-hadad's sin consisted in—

1. *Defiance of God.* The battles of the Old World, as this chapter shows, were regarded as the contests of national deities. The defeat of Pharaoh was a judgment upon the gods of Egypt (Exod. xii. 12). It was to altars, hecatombs, incantations that Balak looked for help (Num. xxii., xxiii.) It was the mighty gods of Israel that the Philistines feared (1 Sam. iv. 7, 8). And we know how Goliath (*ib.*, ch. xvii. 45) and Sennacherib alike (Isa. xxxvii. 23) defied the living God. And when we see Ben-hadad swearing by his gods (ver. 10), when we find his courtiers accounting for their first defeat by the belief that the gods of their adversaries were gods of the hills only, we perceive at once that this war was regarded on Syria's and Israel's part alike (ver. 28) as a trial of strength between the deities whom they respectively worshipped. The defeat, consequently, was primarily the punishment of Ben-hadad's blasphemy (Isa. xxxvii. 29).

2. *Wanton insolence and cruelty.* We constantly find the instruments used of God for the punishment of Israel, punished in their turn for their oppression of Israel. We have instances in Judg. iii. ; iv. 3, 22 ; vi. 1 ; cf. vii. 25 ; 2 Chron. xxxii. 21 ; Isa. x. 5—12, 24 sqq.; xiv. 4 sqq. ; Obad. x. 28. When king or army exceeded their commission, when they trampled on the foe, they straightway provoked the vengeance which they were employed to minister. It would have been strange if such overbearing brutality as Ben-hadad's (vers. 3, 6, 10) had gone unreproved.

3. *Overweening pride.* He was so intoxicated with the greatness of his army, with the praises of his courtiers and allies, that he thinks, Nebuchadnezzar-like, that neither God nor man can withstand him. His haughtiness comes out very clearly in his messages (vers. 3, 6), in his scorn of his adversaries (vers. 16—18), in the passionate outburst with which he receives Ahab's reply (ver. 10). " The proud Syrian would have taken it in foul scorn to be denied, though he had sent for all the heads of Israel." And pride provokes a fall (Prov. xvi. 18 ; xxix. 23 ; cf. 2 Chron. xxxii. 26 ; Isa. xvi. 6, 7 ; Obad. iv.) The highest mountain-tops draw down on themselves the artillery of the skies. Pride stands first on the list of the " seven deadly sins," because self-worship is the most hateful form of idolatry, the most obnoxious to the Majesty of Heaven.

4. *Drunkenness.* Like another invader, he transgressed by wine (Hab. ii. 5 ; cf. Dan v. 2, 23). His revels in the thick of the siege reveal to us the man. It would have been, in Jewish eyes especially, a glaring injustice if such a man, while employed to chastise the sins of others, had escaped all chastisement himself. And his two-and-thirty confederates were like him. They had aided and encouraged him ; they drank with him (ver. 16), and they fell with him (ver. 24).

It only remains for us now to observe how exact and exemplary was the punishment which overtook king and princes and the entire army—for the army, no doubt, had shared the views and vices of its commanders. The defeat of the entire host was not occasioned by the sin of its leader alone, any more than the invasion was provoked by the sin of Ahab alone. In the day that God visited the sin of Ben-hadad, He visited also the sin of Syria. In the first place, the drunkenness of the leaders brought its own retribution. It involved the demoralization of the soldiery. With such besotted and incapable heads, they were unprepared for attack, and fell an easy prey to the vigorous onslaught of the 232 youths. The size of the host, again, contributed to make the disaster all the greater. And what but pride and cruelty had dictated the assembling of such an enormous array, merely to crush a neighbour kingdom ? And their pride was further humbled by the circumstances of their defeat. It was to their eternal disgrace that a handful of men, of boys rather, unused to war, foemen quite unworthy of their steel, had routed and dispersed them ; that their innumerable army had melted away before " two little flocks of kids." What a contrast to the proud boasting of ver. 10! Even the manner of Ben-hadad's escape, his hurried, ignominious flight on the first horse that offered ; his cowering abjectly in a corner of an inner chamber, this helped to sink him to a lower pitch of shame. The cavalry that was to accomplish such great things ; he is thankful for one of its stray horses to bear him away from the field of slaughter. The walls of Aphek, again, avenged his threats against the walls of Samaria. And the kings who had flattered him and encouraged his cruel projects, they too received a meet recompense, not only in the defeat, but in their summary degradation from their commands ; while the courtiers who suggested the second expedition expiated their folly by the miseries and indignities which they suffered. It was a pitiful end of a campaign begun with so much of bluster and fury, and threatening ; that procession of wretched and terrified men, with " sackcloth on their loins, and ropes on their heads." Nor did the losses of Syria end with the battle or the earthquake ; the king voluntarily cedes a part of the territory which his father had won by his valour from Israel, and returns to his capital with a decimated army, a tarnished fame, and a restricted realm. His gluttonous desire for pillage, his forcing a quarrel upon Israel, his defiance of the Almighty, have been punished by the forfeiture of all he holds most dear.

It has more than once been remarked that the history of Israel has its lessons for the individual soul. But it also speaks to nations and kings. This chapter proclaims that neither any people nor its rulers can forget God with impunity ; that disregard of His laws is sure to bring down His judgments ; that the purgatory of nations is in this life present ; that, while the individual awaits a judgment to come, the community is judged now, by sword, and famine, and pestilence ; by invasion and defeat; by loss of fame and territory ; by bad harvests and crippled trade. Corporate bodies and communities may " have no conscience," but they will prove sooner or later, as Assyria and Babylon, as Medes and Persians, as Greeks and Romans, as Russia and Turkey, as France and Germany have proved, that " verily there is a reward for the righteous; verily there is a God that judgeth in the earth" (Psa. lviii. 11).

But this history has other lessons than those which concern nations and kings. Some of these we may glean as we pass along.

Ver. 1.—" All his host . . . thirty and two kings . . . horses and chariots." It has been remarked that it is not easy to account for this expedition. Was it that Ahab had refused to do fealty? or had he offered some personal affront to the Syrian king? Nay, may we not find explanation enough in the fact that Ben-hadad, having an enormous host at his command, must find something for it to do? Large standing armies are constantly the cause of war. Preparations for war in the interest of peace (si vis pacem, &c.) are so manifestly paradoxical that who can wonder if war, and not peace, is the result? Let Europe beware of its bloated armaments. It is natural for statesmen to wish to have something to show for the cost of their maintenance.

Ver. 3.—" Thy silver . . . is mine." A conspicuous instance this of that law of old time—

> " the simple plan
> That they should take who have the power,
> And they should keep who can."

But is our modern warfare so very different in principle ? Why may kings remove landmarks any more than peasants ? Why may a Ben-hadad, an Alexander, a Napoleon cry, " Your lands or your life," without reproach, and yet the footpad who plays at the same game on the highway is hanged for it ? Why should what is plain " stealing " in private life be called " conveying " or " annexing " when practised on a larger scale?

Ver. 4.—" I am thine." " Wisely doth Ahab, as a reed in a tempest, stoop to this violent charge." "It is not for the overpowered to capitulate." Besides, who know what the "soft answer" might effect? If smooth words could do no good, rough ones would certainly do much harm. The meek always have the best of it, and so inherit the earth.

Ver. 9.—"*This thing I may not do.*" "Better die than live in disgrace," says the Greek proverb. The king of Samaria was in a similar strait to those four logical lepers who, a few years later, in another siege, lay at the gate of the city (2 Kings vii. 4). He could but die in any case, and he might perchance live if he stood on his defence. Even a worm will turn when trod upon. We should think scorn of Ahab, had he not made a stand for his life and wife and children.

Ver. 10.—"*The gods do so to me,*" &c. How often has the swearer to eat his words. The hero *does;* he never talks of what he will do. "Victory is to be achieved, not to be sworn." This vulgar fashion of calling upon God to do *oneself* some hurt thus appears to be of great antiquity. But it always proceeds from those who have very little belief in God at all. The profane swearer is practically an infidel, so far as the gods he invokes are concerned. An Italian workman was once reproved in a Roman studio for the oaths which he swore by the sacred name of *Gesù.* "Oh," said he boldly, "I'm not afraid of Him at all." Then, lowering his voice to a whisper, he added, "I'll tell you what I'm afraid of: it is His blessed mother." He never swore by the Deity he believed in.

Ver. 12.—"*Set yourselves in array*" (Heb. שִׂימוּ). The command was prompt and decided enough. But observe, he himself went on drinking (ver. 16). This helps to explain his defeat. He was a man of words only. The successful generals —it is a trite saying—are those who say "Come," not "Go."

Ver. 13.—"*There came a prophet.*" *O altitudo!* For years past the prophets have been proscribed, hunted, harried to death. Yet in his darkest hour, when other refuge fails him, Ahab finds a prophet at his side. God bears no grudges. It is sufficient to give us a claim upon His help that we are helpless (Psa. lxviii. 5 ; Hosea xiv. 3). He "comforteth" (*i.e.,* strengtheneth, *con fortis*) "those that are cast down" (2 Cor. vii. 6). "Who can wonder enough at this unweariable mercy of God? After the fire and rain, fetched miraculously from heaven, Ahab had promised much, performed nothing, yet God will again bless and solicit him with victory; one of those prophets whom he persecuted shall comfort his dejection with the news of deliverance and triumph." This act of grace should have proved that the Lord was God, and that the prophet was His messenger. It is not in man to act thus.

"*Thou shalt know that I am the Lord.*" "Not for thy righteousness or the uprightness of thine heart dost thou go in to possess their land, but for the wickedness of these nations," &c. (Deut. ix. 4, 5). The drought, the fire, the great rain, none of these had convinced the king and queen. Will deliverance from the jaws of death move them? Will they believe in a God of battles? Will they recognize His finger in a superhuman victory?

Ver. 15.—"*The young men . . . were two hundred and thirty-two.*" "Not by might nor by power" (Zech. iv. 6). God's host is ever a little flock (cf. Judg. vii. 2—7 ; 2 Chron. xx. 12 ; 1 Cor. i. 27—29). The "weak things" were chosen then, as subsequently, "that no flesh should glory in his presence." God never departs from that rule. The "carpenter's son," the "fishermen," the "unlearned and ignorant men" —it is the same principle underlies His choice in every case.

Ver 16.—"*Drinking himself drunk . . . he and the kings.*" Of strong drink it may justly be said, "Many strong men have been slain by her" (Prov. vii. 20). "It is not for kings to drink wine" (*ib.,* xxxi. 4). Nor is it for warriors. Alexander, conqueror of the world, was conquered by wine. Our great generals of modern times have been abstainers. The march to Coomassie, to Candahar was effected without the aid of intoxicants. The Russian soldiers in the Crimea were drugged with *vodka,* but it did not prevent their defeat.

Ver. 18.—"*Take them alive.*" "Security is the certain usher of destruction. We have never so much cause to fear as when we fear nothing" (cf. Dan. v. 1, 30; Luke xvii. 27 ; 1 Thess. v. 3).

Ver. 20.—" *They slew every one his man.*" It is thus the world must be won for Christ. Mohammed had two fixed ideas : first, to make converts ; second, to make his converts *soldiers.* And every Christian is a soldier of the Cross, enlisted at his baptism into the Church *militant.* By personal, individual effort are Churches built up and believers added to the Lord. So it was in the first days. "Andrew findeth his own brother Simon." "Philip findeth Nathanael" (John i. 41—45).

Ver. 23.—" *Their gods are gods of the hills.*" It is no uncommon thing to find men laying the blame of their misfortune on God. We smile at those poor pagans who beat their wooden gods with sticks, or those Italian villagers who, a few weeks ago (Sept., 1881), threw the image of their patron saint into a well, and set upon their parish priest, because their prayers for rain remained unanswered ; but the same thing, slightly varied in shape, is often done amongst ourselves. "Bad luck" is held responsible for many of the failures for which we have only ourselves to thank. That "everybody is against him" is often the cry of the man who has no enemy but himself. The idle scoundrel who has wife and children generally accuses *them* of being the causes of his misfortunes ; if he has no such scapegoats, he will lay the blame on God's providence. He never remembers that he himself was "drinking himself drunk" at the hour for action.

Ver. 22.—" *Go strengthen thyself.*" Though God had delivered him once and would deliver him again (ver. 28), yet Ahab must consult for his own safety. While trusting in God, he must keep his powder dry. The same prophet who has announced deliverance by a band of youths, wholly inadequate to cope with the Syrians, now bids him look well to the defences of the country. *Aide-toi et Dieu t'aidera;* this is the purport of his message.

Ver. 29.—" *Seven days.*" Compare the " seven thousand " of ver. 15, and Josh. vi. 4, 15, 16. He hath commanded His *covenant* for ever (Psa. iii. 9 ; cf. 1 Chron. xvi. 15 ; Psa. lxxxix. 28, 34). By this act, Israel (1) showed that they remembered the works of the Lord, His wonders of old time; and (2) they reminded Him of His holy covenant (Luke i. 72—74).

Ver. 30.—" *A wall fell,*" &c. (Cf. Acts xxviii. 4 ; Hab. ii. 11). " A dead wall in Aphek shall revenge God on the rest that remained." Where they sought shelter and thought themselves secure, they found death (cf. Amos v. 19 ; ix. 3 ; Psa. cxxxix. 7—10 ; Luke xix. 40).

Ver. 31.—" *The kings of Israel are merciful kings.*" How true is that of the true King of Israel. He is the very fount of mercy (Exod. xxxiv. 7; Num. xiv. 18; Pss. xxv. 10; c. 5; ciii. 17; cxxx. 7). We often picture Him as "less merciful than His image in a man." But let us do Him this dishonour no more. It is " His property always to have mercy." Is He less clement than an Ahab ? Is His heart less tender to penitent rebels ? " Behold now, we know that the King of Heaven, the God of Israel, is a merciful God ; let us put sackcloth upon our loins, and strew ashes upon our heads, and go meet the Lord God of Israel, that he may save our souls."

Ver. 34.—" *I will send thee away,*" &c. On another occasion such conduct as this was commanded (2 Kings vi. 22, 23). Why, then, was it sinful now ? Precisely because it was *not* commanded; because God intended the opposite (ver. 42). It was not clemency, it was culpable weakness to send this overbearing despot, who had already cost Israel so dear, to send him to his home, there to renew his plots against the people of God. As well might the magistrate compassionate the burglar, or the garotter, and instead of shutting him up in prison, send him into the streets, to be the plague of society. The king, like the magistrate, is trustee for the commonwealth. He has no right to gratify his benevolent instincts at the expense of the community. Still less right had the theocratic king, the representative of Heaven, to liberate, *ex mero arbitrio,* a tyrant whom God had manifestly given into his hands. " Charity cannot excuse disobedience." He had proved Ben-hadad twice, yet he asks for no material guarantees. He neither consults nor remembers his deliverer.

Ver. 40.—" *Thyself hast decided it.*" So shall *our* judgment be. " Out of thine own mouth," &c. (Luke xix. 22). How many will stand self-condemned, condemned by their own precepts, condemned by the sentences they have passed upon others, by the measure they have exacted from others, &c.

Ver. 43.—"*Heavy and displeased.*" Cf. Pss. xvi. 4; xxxii. 10. "Uneasy lies the head that wears a crown." Life out of God brings only disappointment. The most magnificent of kings found it vanity and vexation of spirit. The things of earth cannot satisfy the soul of man, the soul made for God. History has preserved for us a striking testimony to this truth in the confession of Abdalrahman, caliph of Spain. "I have now reigned," he wrote, "fifty years in victory or peace; beloved by my subjects, dreaded by my enemies, and respected by my allies. Riches and honours, power and pleasures, have waited on my call, nor does any earthly blessing appear to have been wanting to my felicity. In this situation I have numbered the days of pure and genuine happiness which have fallen to my lot: they amount to *fourteen!* O man, place not thy confidence in this present world."

HOMILIES BY VARIOUS AUTHORS.

Vers. 1—11.—*The Spirit of War.* In human histories so much is made of brilliant uniforms, scientific discipline, skilful manœuvres, exploits, surprises, and successes, that readers are carried away with "the pomp and circumstance" of so-called "glorious war." In the text we have the other side; and we are reminded of the appeal of James: "From whence come wars and fightings among you? Come they not hence, even of your own lusts that war in your members?" (James iv. 1.) Conspicuous amongst these is—

I. THE SPIRIT OF WAR. We see this—1. *In Ben-hadad's message* (ver. 3). (1) We do not understand this to be a demand from Ahab for the actual surrender to Ben-hadad of his "silver" and "gold," "wives" and "children." Else it would be difficult to see any material difference between this first message and that which followed (ver. 6). (2) The meaning seems to be that Ben-hadad would hold Ahab as his vassal, so that Ahab should retain his wealth, wives, and children only by the sufferance and generosity of his superior. He would have the king of Israel reduced to the condition of the "thirty and two kings" who, with their subjects and fortunes, appear to have been at his service (compare ver. 12 with ver. 24). 2. *In his confident boasting.* (1) He boasts of the vastness of his army. "All the people that follow me." The Hebrew is given in the margin, "at my feet," suggesting *subjection* and *submission.* (2) Of the certainty and ease with which such an army may carry victory. "The gods do so to me and more also if the dust of Samaria shall suffice for handfuls for all the people that follow me." They need not be content with handfuls of dust when they can fill their hands with the most valuable things in Samaria. (3) This was the boasting which Ahab rebuked by the use of what had probably been a proverbial expression: "Let not him that girdeth on his harness boast himself as he that putteth it off." This caution might be profitably considered by those who are engaged in spiritual conflicts: "Be not high-minded, but fear."

II. THE SPIRIT OF INJUSTICE. This we see—1. *In Ben-hadad's requisitions.* (1) In those of his first message right is outraged. "*Thy* silver and gold are *mine.*" Taking this demand in the sense of Ahab's coming under *villenage* to Ben-hadad, the claim was iniquitous. Man has rights of property and freedom, which, unless they are forfeited to law by crime, should ever be held most sacred. The injustice of slavery is horrible. (2) The second message went even farther. It threatened open robbery. Robbery not only of the monarch, but of his subjects also. A starving wretch who steals a loaf of bread may be convicted as a felon; but a warrior who plunders kingdoms—a Napoleon—is glorified as a hero! But how will these weigh together in the balances of the sanctuary? 2. *In his principles of appeal.* (1) *Justice* is not named. How often *is* justice named in warfare where it has no place! The Syrian king was more outspoken than many modern war-makers. (2) *Mercy* is quite out of the question. Yet in modern times wars against savages have been trumpeted as benignities, because of the civilization which, it is presumed, will follow in their wake! (3) Ben-hadad did not live in these favoured times, so the one principle to which he appeals is *might*. "He *has* the men," and he *will have* "the money too!" In this he has had too many successors in the kingdoms of *civilization*. (4) Not only must the covetousness of the king be gratified; so also must the host "at his feet;" and since the "dust of Samaria" will not satisfy them, Samaria must be *sacked* and *pillaged*. One injustice begets another.

III. THE SPIRIT OF CRUELTY. This appears—1. *In the provocations.* (1) Observe the "putting" of Ben-hadad's requisitions. No attempt is made to spare the feelings of Ahab, but, on the contrary, the language is studiously framed to lacerate. "Whatsoever is pleasant in *thine* eyes"—note, not what is pleasant in the eyes of the spoilers—"they shall put it in their hand and take it away." (2) Witness also the peremptoriness. "To-morrow about this time." 2. *In the struggles.* (1) Men are in conflict. This is not a strife of elements without feeling, which is terrible enough, but of flesh and blood and nerves with exquisite sensibilities, with susceptibilities of acute pain and suffering. (2) The combatants are *armed.* That they may put each other to torture they are provided with swords, spears, arrows; and in these days of civilization, with fire-arms of various kinds. Elephants, camels, horses, and other animals are pressed into the dreadful service. (3) Survey the battle-field after the strife. Men and animals dead and dying, mingled; gaping wounds; mangled limbs, sickening horrors! What pictures of cruelty are here! (4) Reflect upon the homes plunged into grief and poverty entailed through the loss of bread-winners; and add the sequel of pestilences and famines. Surely we should pray for the advent of that peaceful reign of righteousness which is promised in the Scriptures of prophecy.—J. A. M.

Vers. 12—21.—*The hand of God.* The notable answer of the king of Israel to the insolent king of Syria, "Let not him that girdeth on the harness boast himself as he that putteth it off," came to Ben-hadad when he was drinking wine with the thirty and two kings that followed him. He at once gave orders to his servants to set themselves in battle array. While the enormous host which "filled the country" (see vers. 25, 27) disposed itself to attack the city, the men of Israel, who were but a handful, naturally trembled for the issue. At this juncture God interposed in the manner related here, and thereby asserted the general truths, viz.—

I. THAT GOD RULES IN THE DESTINIES OF MEN. 1. *Here He showed His hand.* (1) He sent a prophet. Jarchi says it was Micaiah, the son of Imlah, while others think it was Elijah in disguise; but it is useless to speculate on this point. We are more concerned with the purport of His message, which was to promise victory to Israel, and to indicate how that victory should be organized, so that in the issue Jehovah might be acknowledged. (2) The hand of God was seen not only in the prophet's foreknowledge of events, but also in the *wisdom* of the adjustments by which they were to be brought about. For the victory was organized according to instructions of the prophet, purporting also to be from the Lord. Who but the Lord could have foreseen that at noon Ben-hadad and his kings would be so drunken as to be unfit and indisposed to take their posts of command? Who else could have foreseen that Ben-hadad would have been so foolish as to order the sortie to be *taken alive?* For thereby the Syrians were put to a disadvantage, which enabled the "young men of the princes of the provinces" and those who followed them to slay "every one his man," and throw the invading host into confusion. (3) The power of God also was evident when the disparity of numbers is considered. An army of seven thousand Israelites could never, without supernatural aid, have demoralized and routed the formidable hosts of Syria. (4) And that God was in this victory could not be reasonably doubted, since this was not an extraordinary event by itself, but one of a series of such events; therefore it could not have been an accident. It was preceded by three years of drought which began and ended according to the "word" of Elijah, with the miracle on Carmel. 2. *By so showing His hand He evinced that He is ever working.* (1) When events are ordinary, men are disposed to see in them *natural* causes only; but extraordinary events force upon their consideration the fact of a superior agency behind these causes. (2) This truth is the more evident when the ordinary are recognized in the extraordinary. Thus God ordered the battle. He appointed the general, disposed the attack which was to assure the victory, and timed everything so to fit in with circumstances as to bring about the promised result. (3) With God there is no essential difference between things ordinary and extraordinary. It is simply a question of *proportions.* For natural causes are all *second* causes, and would have no existence but for the *First Cause.* A miracle is but the *unusual* action of the First Cause upon the second causes; but in the *usual* action, God is none the less present and necessary to the result.

II. THAT HE RULES IN RIGHTEOUSNESS AND MERCY. 1. *He humbles the proud in righteousness.* (1) Defeat in any case is humiliation. To Ben-hadad after his confident boasting it was eminently so. He would remember the lesson, "Let not him that girdeth on his harness boast himself as he that putteth it off." Let us observe it. (2) The manner was an aggravation of the defeat. It was accomplished by two hundred and thirty-two "young men of the princes of the provinces," who are by some thought to have been a militia raised by provincial magistrates, and by others, with perhaps better reason—for the number seems too small to answer the former description—the attendants of such of those princes as were then in Samaria. It was intensely humiliating that a company of such combatants should rout a formidable army. God makes the weak confound the mighty. (3) Ben-hadad would be mortified to think how his overweening confidence, together with his drunkenness, had directly contributed to his humiliation. He was too drunk to appear at the head of his army, but not too drunk to find his way to the cavalry to facilitate his flight. "There is but one step from the sublime to the ludicrous!" 2. *He shows long-suffering in mercy.* (1) The judgment upon Ben-hadad was mercy to Ahab. It delivered him from the hand of a cruel oppressor. It gave him another warning and space for repentance. (2) Did Ahab deserve this? Certainly not, while he submitted to be led by Jezebel, and that notwithstanding his experience of the drought and the miracle on Carmel. God is long-suffering in mercy. (3) But there were "seven thousand in Israel, all the knees which had not bowed unto Baal, and every mouth which hath not kissed him." Jarchi would identify these with the "seven thousand" mentioned in verse 15. Probably some of that seven thousand went to compose this, and for their sakes it may have been that God had so signally interposed. Let us never lose sight of God. Let us discern His hand in nature, providence, grace. Let us never provoke His justice by pride, by rebellion. Let us respect His long-suffering by repentance. Let us throw ourselves upon His mercy for salvation, for help. —J. A. M.

Vers. 22—30.—*Wisdom in Counsel.* No man is so wise that it may not be to his advantage to consider advice; but in listening to advice we may be led astray. There are two classes of advisers, viz., those who are influenced by the "wisdom of this world," and those who are influenced by the "wisdom from above." Of both we have examples in the text.

I. THE WISDOM OF THIS WORLD IS A WISDOM OF EXPEDIENCY. 1. *It is not destitute of sagacity.* (1) It has its maxims of *prudence.* (a) Ben-hadad's counsellors would not have him underrate his enemy. The army they advise him to raise for the invasion of Israel must not be inferior to that which had been lately vanquished (ver. 25). Let us not underrate our spiritual foes. (b) Neither would they have him underrate the quality of his soldiers. They do not admit that his army was fairly *beaten,* but speak of "the army that *thou hast lost,*" or "that *fell from thee.*" In this also they were right, for if God had not helped

Israel the Syrians would not have been routed. In all our spiritual conflicts let us fight under the banner of Jehovah. (2) It has its lessons of *experience*. (*a*) Ben-hadad's counsellors lay emphasis here—"And do this thing, Take the kings away, every man out of his place." Why remove the kings? Because in the last war they were "drinking themselves drunk" when they should have been at their posts, and the army, without officers, became confused and demoralized. Trust not the kings again (see Pss. cxviii. 9; cxlvi. 3). (*b*) "Put captains in their rooms." Let the army be commanded by men of ability and experience. Pageants are of no use in times of exigency. 2. *But its sagacity is mingled with folly.* (1) Because the *motives* of the wicked are vicious. (*a*) In his former war Ben-hadad's impulse was *pride*. The insolence of his demands evidenced this (vers. 3, 6). But what wisdom is there in pride? (*b*) Though mortified by defeat, that pride remained, and was now moved by the spirit of revenge: "Surely we shall be *stronger* than they." But what wisdom is there in resentment? (*c*) Beyond these base feelings the desire for plunder seems to have moved the Syrian. But where is the wisdom in a king becoming a common robber? (2) Because they put themselves into conflict with the Almighty. (*a*) The Syrians formed an unworthy idea of the Elohim of Israel when they localized and limited Him to the hills. Palestine is a hilly country, and its cities and high places were generally on hills; and probably in the hill country of Samaria the cavalry and chariots of Syria were of little service. (See Psa. xv. 1; xxiv. 3; lxxxvii. 1; cxxi. 1.) (*b*) In the proposal to give Israel battle in the plains the Syrians now set Jehovah at defiance.

II. THE WISDOM FROM ABOVE IS THE WISDOM OF TRUTH. 1. *It is far-reaching.* (1) God sees the end from the beginning. We should therefore seek His counsel and guidance. (2) He forewarns His people. He sent His prophet to the king of Israel to inform him that the king of Syria would come up against him at the return of the year. He forewarns us of the things of eternity. 2. *It is prudent.* (1) The prophet advised Ahab to prepare for the event. "Go, strengthen thyself, and mark, and see what thou doest." We should ever deport ourselves as in the presence of spiritual foes. (2) God helps those who help themselves. 3. *It is un-erring.* (1) Events foreshown by God will surely come to pass. (2) According to the advice of the prophet, "at the return of the year," viz., "at the time when kings go forth to battle" (see 2 Sam. xi. 1; 1 Chron. xx. 1), probably answering to our *March*, which has its name from *Mars*, the god of war, Ben-hadad "went up to Aphek to fight against Israel." There were several cities of this name: one in the tribe of Asher (Josh. xix. 30); another in Judah (1 Sam. iv. 1); a third in Syria (2 Kings xiii. 17). The last is probably that referred to here. 4. *It is profitable.* (1) This follows from its other qualities. The guidance which is "prudent," "far-reaching," and "unerring" must be "profitable." (2) But further, those who follow that guidance so commend themselves to God that He directly interposes in their behalf. There was a faithful "seven thousand" in Israel (ch. xix. 18). (3) If in conflict with those who prefer a worldly policy, they not only have God on their side, but they have Him with them against their enemy. (4) God helped Ahab against Ben-hadad, not that Ahab deserved it, but that Ben-hadad had to be punished (ver. 28. See also Ezek. xxxvi. 22). The "two little flocks of kids" could not have slain in one day "one hundred thousand men" unless God had helped them. The hand of God also was in the falling of that wall by which "seven and twenty thousand" perished.

Let us faithfully pursue the policy of right. Let us never permit the expediency of a moment to swerve us from this. Truth abides.—J. A. M.

Vers. 30—43.—*False Mercy.* The first army with which Ben-hadad invaded Israel was defeated with "great slaughter," and the king saved himself by flight. The defeat of the second was even more complete, when 127,000 men were destroyed and the king had to surrender at discretion. But Ahab, for his false mercy in sparing the life of Ben-hadad, brought judgment upon himself and upon his people.

1. MERCY IS FALSE WHEN IT OPPOSES THE RIGHTEOUSNESS OF GOD. 1. *That*

righteousness dooms the incorrigible to death. (1) "The wages of sin." The incorrigible will certainly find this in the "damnation of hell" (Psa. ix. 17). (2) Their time also in this life is shortened either by the sword of the magistrate or by the judgment of God. They get sufficient space for repentance; but the space so given, if misimproved, aggravates the terror of their death. Protracted probationary existence under such conditions, therefore, becomes a doubtful mercy. (3) It is also the reverse of mercy to their contemporaries, because the influence of the wicked is mischievous. It is, therefore, a considerate judgment that they do "not live out half their days" (Psa. lv. 23). (4) The difference between good and evil cannot be too strongly marked. The good must have no fellowship with the wicked. In eternity their separation is complete (Matt. xxv. 46; Luke xvi. 26). The more perfect the separation here, the more of heaven upon earth will the good enjoy; and the more of hell upon earth, the wicked. 2. *Ben-hadad was obnoxious to that doom.* (1) He was guilty of the highest crimes against humanity. In his offensive wars he was not only a public robber, but also a wholesale murderer. But murder at least is held to be a capital crime (see Gen. ix. 5; Exod. xxi. 12, 14; Levit. xxiv. 17. See also Matt. xxvi. 52; Rev. xiii. 10). (2) He was guilty likewise of the highest crimes against God. He was not only a gross idolater, but also a blasphemer of Jehovah. He localized and limited Him as "Elohim of the hills" and defied Him in the plains. But such blasphemy also was punishable with death (Levit. xxiv 11—16). (3) He committed all these offences in the land of Israel, where they were capital crimes, and the God of Israel delivered him into the hand of Ahab that he might suffer the penalty. 3. *But Ahab opposed his mercy to the righteousness of God.* (1) But is there no mercy for the penitent? Certainly there is. In repentance there is no encouragement to evil; on the contrary, in it evil is condemned. Faith in Christ is the perfection of repentance since therein only can we be effectually delivered from sin. Repentance must be genuine. (2) Ben-hadad's repentance was not genuine. His servants "girded sackcloth on their loins, and put ropes on their heads, and came to the king of Israel, and said, Thy servant Ben-hadad saith, I pray thee, let me live." (Sir John Froissart relates that the inhabitants of Calais acted in a similar manner when they surrendered their city to Edward III. in 1346). All this was intensely mortifying to Ben-hadad, whose tone was so different when he thought himself in the position of a dictator (see vers. 3—6). The haughtiest in prosperity are often the meanest in adversity. (3) But here is no show of repentance towards God. He confesses that he deserves to be hanged for invading the land, but not a word about his blasphemy against the Elohim of Israel. Yet Ahab granted him his life.

II. THOSE WHO SHOW SUCH MERCY ENCOUNTER THE JUDGMENT OF GOD. 1. *Because thereby they encourage evil.* (1) If sin be committed with impunity it will soon lose its character. Men are naturally inclined to sin, and are restrained chiefly by fear of its penalties. If these are remitted, offences against the law of God will come to be justified. (2) The estimate of goodness would consequently be lowered, for we judge of qualities by contrasts. Heaven is seen in its strongest light as the antithesis of hell. Remove from sin its sinfulness, and goodness will be distorted into weakness or folly. (3) Such confounding of right and wrong must be fatal to all law and order, and tend to inaugurate the wildest confusion and the deepest misery. All this flows from the principle of false or indiscriminate mercy. 2. *Hence Ahab was held to be an accomplice with Ben-hadad.* (1) He had an unworthy sympathy with this blaspheming monarch. "Is he yet alive? He is my brother." "Brother king, though not brother Israelite. Ahab valued himself more on his royalty than on his religion" (Henry). Would Ben-hadad have called Ahab his *brother* had *he* been victorious? (2) "He caused him to come up into the chariot." This was a sign of cordial friendship (see 2 Kings x. 15, 16). "The friendship of the world is enmity against God." So instead of imposing terms, he accepted those proposed by Ben-hadad (ver. 34). (3) "So he made a covenant with him and sent him away." The form of these covenants was to cut a sacrifice in twain, and the persons entering into the compact walked between the pieces and were sprinkled, together with the articles of agreement, with the blood, to express that if they

failed to fulfil their pledge God might treat them as the sacrifice had been treated.
3. *Ahab in consequence was doomed to die.* (1) This was signified to him by
another prophet. He is by the Jews supposed to have been Micaiah, and with
some reason perhaps (compare ch. xxii. 8). (2) This prophet, after the example
of Nathan (2 Sam. xii.), made Ahab pronounce his own sentence (vers. 37—42). In
the doom of the prophet who, for disobedience to the word of the Lord in not smiting his fellow, was destroyed by the lion, Ahab could also read his doom for not
obeying the word of the Lord when he should have smitten Ben-hadad to death (vers.
35, 36). (3) The prophecy came true. Ahab was slain fighting against the Syrians
to recover Ramoth in Gilead (ch. xxii. 35). And by the hands of the Syrians, under
Hazael, the children of Israel suffered severely (see 2 Kings viii. 12 ; x. 32, 33). (4)
In anticipation of these things Ahab "went to his house heavy and displeased."
Heavy at the tidings and *displeased* with the prophet. It would have been more
to his advantage had he gone to the house of God in contrition for the sins of his
wicked life.—J. A. M.

Vers, 1—21.—*Veiled Mercies.* I. AHAB'S EXTREMITY (vers. 1—11). God's goodness
to the froward is shown by His bringing them into circumstances where they may
prove and know Him. The clouds they "so much dread are big with mercy." 1.
The land is overrun and the capital besieged. The fruit of sin is difficulty and disaster. The land and the life which will not acknowledge God will know at last what
it is to be bereft of His protecting care and the ministrations of His goodness. These
are the *eternal* portion only of those whom they raise and bless. 2. *His degradation* (vers. 2—4). In his own city he has to listen and assent to the terms that rob
him at one stroke of all that is dearest and best. The foe has no mercy, and Ahab
neither strength nor dignity. Those who forsake God, and shut themselves out
from the experience of His truth and mercy, will prove the vanity of every other
trust. 3. *His helplessness* (vers. 5—11). (1) Compliance with Ben-hadad's first
demands does not save him from further degradation. Those who rely only on the
world's compassion lean on a reed which will break and pierce them. (2) Ahab's
defiance (ver. 11) was an appeal to chance. He had no clear confidence that
Ben-hadad's threatenings would come to nothing. Forgetfulness of God is weakness
for the battle of life, and darkness amid its dangers. Are we remembering Him ?
Are we stirring ourselves up to lay hold on God ?
II. GOD'S HELP (vers. 12—21). 1. *Its compassionateness.* The help came unsought, and when, indeed, there was no thought of seeking it. How often has He
thus prevented us with the blessings of His goodness ! 2. *Its timeliness.* The
final attack was about to be made (ver. 12). The progress of the siege had no
doubt alarmed Ahab, and led to negotiation. Now it needed but one more effort
and the Syrian hosts would be surging through the streets of Samaria. Within the
city there was only a terrible fear, or dull, defiant despair. But now, as the blow
is about to fall, the shield of God sweeps in between. The Lord knows His time
to help, and, by helping, to reveal Himself and bind us to Him. 3. *Its fulness.*
(1) Israel is glorified. The weakest part of the army achieves the victory. (2)
Ahab is honoured (ver 14). The victory is gained under the leadership of the man
whom God might have righteously destroyed. (3) The triumph is complete
(vers. 20, 21), Ben-hadad a fugitive, and his army a prey. The glory of God is
manifested most of all in His mercy. We cannot contemplate our deliverance from
danger and the fulness of our triumph in Christ without feeling upon our soul the
recreative touch of the hand of God.—J. U.

Vers. 22—43.—*Resisted Mercy.* I. GOD MULTIPLIES HIS BENEFITS TO THE SINFUL
(vers. 22—30). Ahab makes no public acknowledgment of God's mercy, nor, so far
as appears, has it been suffered to change in any way his attitude towards Jehovah;
yet God crowns him with loving-kindnesses. 1. *Delivered from one danger, he is
warned of another.* " Go, strengthen thyself, and see what thou dost," &c. The
enemy, baffled for the time, will return again. The intimation was a call not only to
prepare his hosts and strengthen his cities, but, beyond all else, to seek His face who

had delivered him already, and was able to deliver him again.   We are warned of dangers that we may strengthen ourselves in God.   There is love in the warning, and vaster love in the offered strength.   2. *When the danger comes he is assured of success* (ver. 28).   The most needful preparation had been neglected; Ahab had not sought God.   But God again seeks *him*.   Mark the unwearied, all-forgiving love of God. 3. *The Lord fights for him.*   In vain did the Syrians change their ground and remodel their army.   In vain did they surround with their myriads the two small bands of Israel.   They are given as stubble to the swords of Israel, and the very walls of the city into which they flee for safety become their destruction.   God's hand is so marked in His deliverances, that the sinful cannot fail to see the wondrous love that is behind them.   They bring us face to face with "the depths of the riches" of His mercy.   4. *The purpose of the mercy.*   "Ye shall know that I am the Lord."   It is the revelation of God, and is meant to be the birth-hour of the soul.   The goodness of God may be mentioned with seeming gratitude, but it has been barren of result unless it has brought us into the presence of the King.   The Divine Love has blessed us in vain unless it has become the light of the Lord's face.

II. How THE MERCY WAS MADE OF NO EFFECT.   To Ahab the mercy brought only deeper condemnation.   It will be more tolerable for Tyre and Sidon in the day of judgment than for Chorazin and Bethsaida, which saw the goodness of God in Christ, and yet repented not.   1. *The mercy was frustrated by prayerlessness.* Though warned of the danger, he does not with lowly confession of sin and un-worthiness implore God's direction and help.   There is no breaking up of the fallow ground that it may receive the blessing as the seed of joy and life in God.   2. *By thanklessness.*   When the blessing came it might still have saved him.   The benefits with which God had loaded him might have bowed him in lowly acknow-ledgment of his multiplied iniquities and long impious rebellion.   The goodness of God leads us to repentance only as we pass in before the Lord through the gates of praise.   3. *By blindness to the indications of God's will.*   The multitude slain in the battle, the falling of the wall upon those who escaped, the overthrowing of every defence till the king, the head and centre of the whole evil, was reached, might have shown that God purposed to make an end for the time of the Syrian power, and give a full deliverance to Israel.   The fruit of the victory was blighted by Ahab's blindness and folly.   To co-operate with God in working out our own salvation, we must read and faithfully fulfil His purpose.   4. *By vanity and worldly policy.*   He enjoys for a brief moment the power which God has given, becomes the benefactor and brother of the man whom the Lord had doomed, and makes a covenant with him.   The trust which God had desired should wholly rest upon Himself he reposes in his foe.   The hour of prosperity, which should be our covenant-time with God, is too often made the occasion for worldly alliances, which lead us to forget Him and all we owe to Him.

III. MERCY FRUSTRATED BEARS FRUIT IN JUDGMENT (vers. 35—43).   1. *The message came through swift and stern judgment.*   Disobedience meant death (vers. 35, 36).   The Divine threatenings come to us through terrible judgments. 2. *Ahab was self-condemned.*   The voice of conscience is on God's side.   "If our heart condemn us," &c.   3. *His own life should answer for the life he spared.* Letting go God's enemy, and keeping back his hand from God's righteous though terrible work, he destroyed himself.   No cross, no crown.   The awful price which a soul must pay for present ease and pleasure: "He that loveth his life shall lose it." 4. The shadow of God's wrath swallows up the worldling's peace (ver. 43); and it falls ever deeper till the end come.—U.

Ver. 40.—*The Neglected Opportunity.*   Ben-hadad II. was seeking his revenge for a defeat inflicted on him the preceding year by the Israelitish army, led by a band of 232 young noblemen.   He had disciplined his army, and re-officered it, no longer allowing money or family influence to supersede military skill.   Every-thing that organization could accomplish or superstition dictate (ver. 23) had been done, but all proved in vain; for the contest was not simply between Ben-hadad and

Ahab, but between the heathen and the living God who had been blasphemously challenged. Describe Ben-hadad's successful appeal to Ahab after the defeat. Why was it not commendable (as it was, for example, after the siege of Calais) to spare the vanquished? Because the motive was not pity, but policy; and the criminal allowed to escape had avowedly fought as Jehovah's foe. It is sometimes "expedient that one man should die for the people." Ben-hadad's death would have been the salvation of Ahab, who in the next war fell mortally wounded; it would have ensured a lasting peace, as this was the campaign of the Syrian king, rather than of the Syrian people; and it would have seriously shaken the confidence of the heathen in their gods. The king let his prisoner go to his own undoing. It was this sin which was now rebuked. Picture Ahab returning from the field flushed with victory. He is accosted by a man who has been sitting wounded and dusty beside the road. He is a disguised prophet, probably Micaiah, acting a parable. Says he, in effect: "I have come from the battle. In the hour of victory, the captain, whom I acknowledge I was bound to obey, gave me in charge a prisoner of note, saying that if he escaped my life should answer for it. I admit that I failed, though not designedly; but while thy servant was busy here and there he was gone. Ought I to suffer for that slight negligence?" And when Ahab answered, "Yes," the disguise was flung off, and the daring prophet appeared, saying, "In pronouncing my doom, thou hast pronounced thine own." [Read vers. 42 and 43.] The prophet set before the king a picture of his neglect of opportunity which is worthy of our study. We observe—

I. THAT OPPORTUNITY IS GIVEN OF GOD. "There is a time for every purpose under heaven." Examples: (1) *In the operations of nature.* There is a suitable time for the gathering of fruit. It may not come when you wish it or expect it; but neglected then, the fruit is spoiled. A farmer may in the spring be "busy here and there" with other things, and so neglect to sow his seed. The opportunity does not recur. (2) *In the cultivation of mind.* The indolent schoolboy never gets again the leisure and opportunity for study; and if he did, his capacity for acquiring knowledge has decreased. Contrast the flexibility of mind of the lad with that of the man in middle life. (3) *In the acquisition of material good.* Energy, promptitude, and diligence displayed at a critical moment make a man a millionaire. "There is a tide in the affairs of men which, taken at the flood, leads on to fortune," &c. (4) *In the consecration of life.* No father is content with the physical beauty of his child if mentally he is dead—an idiot; nor is our heavenly Father satisfied to see mental vigour accompanied by spiritual death. He looks for a change, which is a passing from death unto life, and for this He gives opportunity. Observe, secondly—

II. THAT OPPORTUNITY IS GRANTED TO ALL. If you would discover this, (1) *Consider your outward circumstances.* The helpfulness of a Christian home; inherited tendencies; direct religious teaching; exemplars of holy life; recognition of God at the family altar; services frequented from childhood. If these leave you unblessed, they leave you under heavier condemnation. Soon the home may be broken up, and the encouragements to good may vanish, and with unavailing regret you will say, "As thy servant was busy here and there, they were gone." (2) *Consider your inward condition.* There are seasons when it is easier to avail ourselves of religious advantages. *Youth* is such a season, for then impulses are generous, susceptibilities are tender, affections free. Under the influence of *bereavement* or *personal illness* religious convictions are experienced. In and through these the Holy Spirit works. Such a time may be like the morning twilight which brightens into day, or like the evening twilight that deepens into night. Beware of letting convictions slip!

III. THAT OPPORTUNITY IS NEGLECTED BY MANY. Two causes of this may be suggested: (1) *The pressure of business.* The man on the battle-field was busy enough, but he failed to remember his special charge. Nothing he did was wrong in itself, but it became a wrong when it led to the neglect of obvious duty: and if his life was sacrificed because of that neglect, the advantage gained by other activity was of no value. Apply this, and show the difficulty in the way of meditation and prayer, created by the multitudinous claims upon our activity. (2) *The effect of frivolity.* Some people are "busy here and there" in another sense. You never know where to find them. Their character is indeterminate: their information is incomplete; their work is wanting in persistence and thoroughness; and their whole life is frittered away, they scarcely know how. Each day comes to such an one, saying, " Here is something for you to do for God, something for you to think of for your spiritual good ;" and, having delivered its message, the day falls back into the darkness of night. Again and again the message comes in vain, until the last day approaches, then vanishes, and eternity is at hand! The work is left undone; and over the lost opportunity he can only say, " While thy servant was busy here and there, it was gone."

CONCLUSION.—1. *Apply to Christians who are neglecting work for God.* 2. *Apply to the careless who are neglecting decision for God.*—A. R.

EXPOSITION.

CHAPTER XXI.—1—29.

THE STORY OF NABOTH. THE DOOM OF AHAB'S HOUSE. HIS PENITENCE.—Ver. 1.— **And it came to pass after these things** [These words are omitted in the Vat. LXX., which, as before remarked, transposes chs. xx. and xxi. See introductory note, ch. xx], **that Naboth** [" Fruit," " produce " (Gesen). Wordsworth sees in him a type of Christ, cast out of the vineyard (Matt. xxi. 39) and slain] **the Jezreelite** [The Alex. LXX. here, and throughout the chapter, reads ὁ Ἰσρα- ηλίτης. Josephus (Ant. viii. 13. 8) says that Naboth was of illustrious family] **had a vineyard, which was in Jezreel** [See note on ch. xviii. 46], **hard by the palace** [LXX. *threshing-floor.* Stanley (Dict. Bib. vol. ii. p. 454), arguing from this word, would reject the Hebrew text of this narrative, which places both the vineyard and the plot of ground (2 Kings ix. 25, 26) in Jezreel, and would locate the vineyard on the hill of Samaria, in the " void place " of ch. xxii. 10] **of Ahab king of Samaria.** [It is clear from these last words that Jezreel had not replaced Samaria as the capital. It was a " palace " only that Ahab had there. No doubt the beauty of the situation had led to its purchase or erection. As Jezreel is only twenty-five miles distant from Samaria, it is obvious that it might be readily visited by the court.]

Ver. 2.—**And Ahab spake unto Naboth, saying, Give me thy vineyard** [The prediction of Samuel (1 Sam. viii. 14) is being realized], **that I may have it for a garden of herbs** [as in Deut. xi. 10; Prov. xv. 17], **because it is near unto** [Heb. *beside*] **my house: and I will give thee for it a better vineyard than it: or** [Heb. omits *or*], **if it seem good to thee** [Heb. *if good in thine eyes*], **I will give thee the worth of it in money.** [Heb. *I will give to thee silver, the price of it.* See note on ch. xx. 39. Whatever Ahab's moral

weakness, he was certainly a prince of some enterprize. Ch. xxii. 39 speaks of the " cities " which he built. And the palace of Jezreel would seem to have been erected by him. This vineyard was to be one of his improvements.]

Ver. 3.—**And Naboth said to Ahab, The Lord forbid it me** [Heb. *Far be it to me from Jehovah.* These words reveal to us, first, that Naboth was a worshipper of the Lord —otherwise he would hardly have used the sacred name, and that to Ahab, with whom the servants of the true God had found but scant favour ; and, secondly, that he looked upon the alienation of his patrimony as an act displeasing to the Lord, and as violating the law of Moses (Levit. xxv. 23 sqq. ; Num. xxxvi. 7 sqq.) We have instances of the sale of land to the king in 2 Sam. xxiv. 24—but that was by a Jebusite—and in ch. xvi. 24], **that I should give the inheritance of my fathers unto thee.** [" The preservation of the נַחֲלָה was for every covenant-keeping Israelite a matter not merely of piety towards his family and his tribe, . . . but a religious duty " (Bähr). It is clear, however, that the restraints of the old Mosaic law began to be irksome in that latitudinarian age. Many of its provisions were already regarded as obsolete.]

Ver. 4.—**And Ahab came into his house** [At Samaria, as we gather from vers. 18, 14, 16, &c.] **heavy and displeased** [Heb. *sullen and angry* ; same words as in ch. xx. 43. Ewald thinks that we have here a clear reference to that passage] **because of the word which Naboth the Jezreelite had spoken to him: for** [Heb. *and*] **he had said, I will not give thee the inheritance of my fathers. And he laid him down upon his bed** [Rawlinson understands this to mean the couch on which the Orientals recline at meals. And מִטָּה *is* used with this meaning in Esther i. 6 Ezek. xxiii.

41, and elsewhere. But "*his* bed" seems rather to point to his private chamber ; see on ver. 5], **and turned away his face** [The Vulgate adds *ad parietem.* Cf. 2 Kings xx. 2 ; from which place it may have been unconsciously introduced here], **and would eat no bread.** [Keil contends that " this childish mode of giving expression to his displeasure shows very clearly that Ahab was a man sold under sin (ver. 20), who only wanted the requisite energy to display the wickedness of his heart in vigorous action;" but whether this is a just inference from these words may well be questioned. It rather shows that so little did he meditate evil that he accepted the refusal of Naboth as conclusive, and gave way to childish grief.

Ver. 5.—**But Jezebel his wife came to him, and said unto him, Why is thy spirit so sad** [same word as in ver. 4], **that thou eatest no bread ?** [It would seem that the queen missed him from the banqueting hall—he can hardly, therefore, have lain down on one of the divans or couches therein—and went to his bedroom to inquire the reason.]

Ver. 6.—**And he said unto her, Because I spake unto Naboth the Jezreelite, and said unto him, Give me thy vineyard for money** [Heb. *silver*]; **or else, if it please** [Heb. *delight*] **thee, I will give thee another vineyard for it : and he answered** [Heb. *said*], **I will not give thee my vineyard.** [Ahab does not mention the reason which Naboth assigned for his refusal. But Naboth's reasons were nothing to him, and he had hardly given them a second thought.]

Ver. 7.—**And Jezebel his wife said unto him, Dost thou now govern** [Heb. *make;* LXX. ποιεῖς βασιλέα] **the kingdom of Israel ?** [There is no question expressed in the Hebrew which stands, " *Thou* now makest the kingdom over Israel." The commentators generally, however, understand the words—as the LXX, and the A. V.—as an ironical question, " Art thou ruler in aught but name ? " though some take it as an imperative : " Do thou now exert authority over the kingdom of Israel." And on the whole, this latter interpretation appears to be preferable. " Do thou now play the king. Make thy power felt. Give me the requisite authority. I will," &c.] **Arise, and eat bread** [or *food*], **and let thine heart be merry** [Heb. *good;* same words 1 Sam. xxv. 36] : **I** [This word is emphatic. " If *thou* wilt do thy part, *I* will do mine."] **will give thee** [no need to buy it] **the vineyard of Naboth the Jezreelite.**

Ver. 8.—**So she wrote letters** [Heb. *writings*] **in Ahab's name, and sealed them with his seal** [The use of the seal, for the pur-

pose of authentication, is of great antiquity. Some of the Egyptian signets are more than 4,000 years old. Their use in the age of the patriarchs is attested by Gen. xxxviii. 18 and xli. 42 ; their importance is proved by the text, by Esther iii. 10 ; viii. 2, 8, 10 (cf. "Herod," iii. 128) ; Dan. vi. 17 ; Jer. xxxii. 10, 54 ; Hag. ii. 23, &c. Whether this seal—which does not necessarily prove that those who used it could not write— was impressed upon the writings themselves according to the modern practice of the East, or upon a piece of clay (Job xxxviii. 14), which was then attached to the letter by strings, we have no means of knowing. The use of Ahab's seal affords a strong presumption that he was privy to her designs (Bähr), but of this we cannot be absolutely certain], **and sent the letters unto the elders** [see Deut. xvi. 18] **and to the nobles** [same word Neh. ii. 16 ; iv. 13 ; Eccles. x. 17] **that were in his city, dwelling** [or *inhabitants*, as in ver. 11] **with Naboth.**

Ver. 9.—**And she wrote in the letters, saying, Proclaim a fast** [The object of this ordinance was to give the impression that the city was labouring under, or threatened with, a curse, because of some undiscovered sin (2 Sam. xxi. 1 ; Josh. ix. 11 ; Deut. xxi. 9), which must be removed or averted by public humiliation. Cf. Joel i. 14 ; ii. 12 ; 1 Sam. vii. 6 ; 2 Chron. xx. 3)], **and set Naboth on high among the people.** [Heb. *at the head of the people.* Keil, *al.* interpret, " bring him into the court of justice, as defendant before all the people." And certainly הוֹשִׁיבוּ here, and in the next verse— where it is used of the witnesses (cf. ver. 13)—means, *make to sit;* which looks as if judicial procedure were intended. But "at the *head* of the people "rather suggests that in the public assembly, which marked the fast (Joel ii. 15), Naboth was assigned the most distinguished place. The reason for this is obvious, viz., to give a colour of impartiality to the proceedings. As Grotius, *Ne odio damnasse crederentur, quem ipsi honoraverunt.* It would also accord with the popular idea of retributive justice that Naboth should be denounced in the very hour of his triumph and exaltation. Josephus, however, says that it was because of his high birth that this position was assigned him.]

Ver. 10.—**And set two men** [according to the provisions of the law (Deut. xvii. 6, 7 ; xix. 5 ; Num. xxxv. 30). "Even Jezebel bears witness to the Pentateuch" (Wordsworth). Josephus speaks of *three* witnesses], **sons of Belial** [*i.e.*, worthless men. This use of the word "son" (cf. Psa. lxxxix. 22, " son of wickedness"), which is one of the commonest idioms of the East, throws some light on the expression "sons of the prophets" (see ch. xx. 35, note; cf. Deut. xiii. 13; Matt. xxvi. 60)], **before him** [confronting him], **to bear witness against him, saying, Thou didst blaspheme** [Heb. *bless;* cf. Job i. 5, 11; ii. 5; LXX. εὐλόγησε. The Lexicographers are not agreed as to how this word, the primary meaning of which is to *kneel,* hence to *pray,* to *bless,* came to signify *curse* or *biaspheme.* According to some, it is an euphemism, the idea of cursing God being altogether too horrible for the Jew to express in words; whilst others derive this signification from the fact that a curse is really a *prayer* addressed to God; and others, again, account for it by the consideration that a person who *bids farewell* to another sometimes does so in the sense of dismissing and *cursing* him. Anyhow, it is noticeable that the word "blessing" is sometimes used with a similar meaning amongst ourselves] **God and the king** [God and the representative of God in Israel are here coupled together, as in Exod. xxii. 28. To curse the king was practically to curse Him whose vicegerent he was (cf. Matt. xxiii. 18—22). Hence such cursing is called blasphemy and was punishable with death (Deut. xiii. 11; xvii. 5; 2 Sam. xvi. 9; xix. 21; and see on ch. ii. 43, 44)]. **And then carry him out** [*i.e.,* out of the city (cf. Levit. xxiv. 14; Acts vii. 58; Luke iv. 29; Heb. xiii. 12). "*Locus lapidationis erat extra urbem, omnes enim civitates muris cinctae paritatem habent ad castra Israelis*" (Babyl. Sanh.)], **and stone him** [the legal punishment for blasphemy (Levit. xxiv. 16)], **that he may die.** [The terrible power accorded to "two or three witnesses," of denouncing a man to death, accounts for the prominence given to the sin of bearing false witness (Exod. xx. 16; xxiii. 1; Deut. xix. 16). It found a mention in the Decalogue.]

Ver. 11.—**And the men of his city, even the elders and the nobles who were the inhabitants in his city, did as Jezebel had sent unto them** [Their ready compliance shows not merely the "deep moral degradation of the Israelites" at that period, but also the terror which the name of Jezebel inspired], **and as it was written in the letters which she had sent unto them.** [That she did not hesitate to put her infamous command into writing shows the character of the woman.]

Ver. 12.—**They proclaimed a fast, and set Naboth on high among the people.**

Ver. 13.—**And there came in** [Heb. *came.* The assembly was probably held *al fresco.* From the word אֶמֶשׁ, A. V. *yesterday,* but

strictly, *yesternight,* Stanley suggests that the trial took place by night. But the word is often used in the wider sense of "yesterday" (Gesenius)] **two men, children of Belial, and sat before him: and the men of Belial witnessed against him, even against Naboth, in the presence of the people** [The whole congregation was interested in a charge of blasphemy. If unpunished, the guilt rested on the congregation. Hence the provision of Deut. xxiv. 14. By the imposition of hands they testified that the guilt of the blasphemer thenceforth rested upon his own head], **saying, Naboth did blaspheme God and the king. Then they carried him forth** [Heb. *made him to go forth*] **out of the city, and stoned him with stones, that he died.** [It appears from 2 Kings ix. 26 that the children of Naboth, who otherwise might have laid claim to their patrimony, were put to death at the same time, and probably in the same way; cf. Josh. vii. 24, 25; Num. xvi. 27. This was the rule of the East (Dan. vi. 24). The principle of visiting the sins of the parents upon the children seems to have been carried to an excess, as we find Joash (2 Kings xiv. 6) instituting a more merciful rule.]

Ver. 14.—**Then they sent to Jezebel** [clearly she was not at Jezreel], **saying, Naboth is stoned, and is dead.** [Stanley observes that it is significant that this announcement was made to her and not to Ahab. It appears from ver. 19 that the corpses both of Naboth and his children were left to be devoured of dogs.]

Ver. 15.—**And it came to pass, when Jezebel heard that Naboth was stoned, and was dead, that Jezebel said to Ahab, Arise, take possession** [or *inherit, succeed to;* same word Gen. xxi. 10; Deut. ii. 24; Jer. xlix. 1. The possessions of a person executed for treason were *ipso facto* forfeited to the crown. There was no law prescribing this, but it followed the principles of the Mosaic code. Just as the goods of the idolater were devoted as *cherem* to the Lord (Deut. xiii. 16), so those of the traitor reverted to the king. So Keil] **of the vineyard of Naboth the Jezreelite, which he refused to give to thee for money** [there is a proud malicious triumph in these words. "He refused, simple fool, to sell it. Now thou canst have it for nothing. I have discovered a better plan than buying it"]: **for Naboth is not alive, but dead.**

Ver. 16.—**And it came to pass, when Ahab heard that Naboth was dead, that Ahab arose up** [According to the LXX., his first act was to rend his clothes and put on sackcloth. Afterwards "he rose up," &c.] **to go down** [The "Great Plain, on the margin of which Jezreel stands, is at a much lower level than Samaria, which is in the mountain district of Ephraim"] **to the vineyard of Naboth the Jezreelite, to take possession of it.** ["Behind him—probably in the back part of his chariot—ride his two pages, Jehu and Bidkar (2 Kings ix. 26)," Stanley. But the expression "riding in pairs after Ahab" (A.V. "rode together after") does not make it certain that they were in the same chariot. Indeed, they may have been on horseback. This was apparently (2 Kings ix. 26) on the day after the murder.]

Ver. 17—**And the word of the Lord came to Elijah the Tishbite, saying** [As in ch. xvii. 1, 8; xviii. 1],

Ver. 18.—**Arise, go down** [Bähr hence concludes that Elijah was at this time in a mountain district. But wherever he might be, this word would probably be used of a journey to the plain of Esdraelon] **to meet** ["The word used 1 Sam. xvii. 48 of David going out to meet Goliath" (Stanley). But the same word is used (*ib.*, ch. xviii. 6) of the women going out to meet Saul, and indeed it is the usual word for all meetings. We cannot hence infer, consequently, that Elijah went forth as if to encounter a foe] **Ahab king of Israel, which is in Samaria** [*i.e.*, whose seat is in Samaria; who rules there. There is no need to understand the word of the territory of Samaria]: **behold, he is in the vineyard of Naboth, whither he is gone down to possess it.** [The words imply that Elijah found Ahab—strode into his presence —in the vineyard; not that he was there already when the royal chariot entered it (Stanley).]

Ver. 19.—**And thou shalt speak unto him, saying, Thus saith the Lord, Hast thou killed** [הֲרָצַחְתָּ, a rare and expressive word. We might render, *slaughtered*], **and also** [this word suggests that Jezebel's programme, which he had accepted, was fast being accomplished. But in the very hour of its completion it should be interrupted] **taken possession? And thou shalt speak unto him, saying, Thus saith the Lord** [For the repetition, see on ch. xx. 13, 14], **In the place where dogs** [LXX. αἱ ὕες καὶ οἱ κύνες] **licked the blood of Naboth shall dogs lick thy blood** [according to the *lex talionis*, as in ch. xx. 42], **even thine.** [Heb. *even thou.* The LXX. adds, "And the harlots shall bathe in thy blood." For the construction see Gesen., Gram. § 119. 3; and cf. Gen. xxvii. 34; Prov. xxiii. 15; Psa. ix. 7. Thenius contends that there is a contradiction between this ver. and ch. xxii. 38 (together with 2 Kings ix. 25) which is absolutely insuperable. But as Bähr ob-

serves, "How thoughtless our author must have been if in two consecutive chapters— *i.e.*, on the same leaf, as it were—he had inadvertently inserted direct contradictions." And the following considerations will show that the discrepancy is only apparent. (1) The sentence here pronounced against Ahab was, on his repentance, stayed in its execution. God said distinctly, "I will not bring the evil in his days," and as distinctly added that He would "bring the evil in his *son's days, upon his house*" (ver. 29). And (2) with the prophecy, as thus modified, the facts exactly record. The body of Jehoram was "cast into the portion of the field of Naboth the Jezreelite" (2 Kings *l.c.*). And if it be objected (3) that our historian sees in the death of Ahab *in Samaria* (ch. xx. *l.c.*) a fulfilment of this prophecy, the answer is that that death was a *partial* fulfilment of Elijah's words. The repentance of Ahab, having secured him immunity from this sentence, his subsequent folly and sin (cf. ch. xxii. 27) nevertheless brought down upon him a judgment of God strikingly similar, as we might expect it would be, to that originally denounced against him, which was now reserved for his son. In other words, the prophecy was fulfilled to the letter in the person of his son, but it had a secondary fulfilment in its spirit on himself].

Ver. 20.—**And Ahab said to Elijah, Hast thou found me** [Not merely, "Hast thou found me out? hast thou surprised me in the very act?" though this meaning is not to be excluded, but also, "Has thy vengeance overtaken me?" מָצָא is used in this sense 1 Sam. xxiii. 17; Isa. x. 10; Psa. xxi. 9. Ahab is so conscience-stricken by the sudden apparition of Elijah, whom in all probability he had not seen or heard of since "the day of Carmel," and by his appearance on the scene at the very moment when he was entering on the fruit of his misdoing, "in the very blossom of his sin," that he feels that judgment is already begun], **O mine enemy?** [No doubt the thought was present in Ahab's mind that Elijah had ever been opposed to him and thwarting him, but he does not dream (Von Gerlach, in Bähr) of justifying himself by ascribing Elijah's intervention to personal hatred towards himself. The sequel shows that he was thoroughly conscious of wrong-doing.] **And he answered, I have found thee: because** [not because I am thine enemy, but because] **thou has sold thyself** [or *sellest thyself, i.e.,* surrenderest thyself wholly. The idea is clearly derived from the institutions of slavery, according to which the bondservant was wholly at his master's disposal and was bound to accomplish his will. Whether "the practice of men selling themselves into slavery" (Rawlinson) existed in that age may perhaps be doubted. We have the same thought in 2 Kings xvii. 17, and Rom. vii. 14] **to work evil in the sight of the Lord.** [We can readily gather from these words why the doom was denounced against Ahab, who had but a secondary share in the crime, rather than against Jezebel, its real perpetrator. It was because Ahab was the representative of God, God's minister of justice, &c. If he had not himself devised the death of Naboth; if he had, which is possible, remained in ignorance of the means by which Jezebel proposed to procure him the vineyard, he had nevertheless readily and gladly acquiesced in her infamous crime after its accomplishment, and was then reaping its fruits. And because he was the king, the judge, who, instead of punishing the evil-doer, sanctioned and approved the deed, and who crowned a reign of idolatries and abominations with this shameful murder, the prophetic sentence is directed primarily against him.]

Ver. 21.—**Behold, I will bring evil upon thee, and will take away thy posterity** [Heb. *exterminate after thee*. See note on ch. xiv. 10. Ahab knew well the meaning of these words. He had before him the examples of Baasha and Zimri], **and will cut off from Ahab** [Heb. *to Ahab*] **him that pisseth against the wall, and him that is shut up and left in Israel** [see on ch. xiv. 10].

Ver. 22.—**And will make thine house like the house of Jeroboam the son of Nebat** [cf. ch. xv. 29], **and like the house of Baasha the son of Ahijah** [ch. xvi. 3, 11],

for [אֶל used in the sense of עַל, as elsewhere] **the provocation wherewith thou hast provoked me to anger** [ch. xiv. 9; xvi. 7, &c.], **and made Israel to sin.**

Ver. 23.—**And of Jezebel** [Heb. *to Jezebel*. LXX. τῇ Ἰεζάβελ. But we cannot be sure that she also received a message of doom

from Elijah, as לְ like אֶל after verbs of speaking sometimes has the meaning of, *concerning*. Cf. Gen. xx. 13; Psa. iii. 3; Judg. ix. 54; 2 Kings xix. 32. Moreover, if the denunciation had been direct, it would have run, "The dogs shall eat *thee*," &c. See also ver. 27] **also spake the Lord** [Probably at the same time. Certainly by the same prophet (2 Kings ix. 36). Elijah's words to Ahab appear to be only partially recorded (*ib.*, ver. 26)], **saying, The dogs shall eat Jezebel** [see on ch. xiv. 11] **by the**

wall [חֵל same word as חֵיל, is used of the *strength* and defences of a town, *sc.* its forti-

fications, and especially of the *ditch* or moat before them. Cf. 2 Sam. xx. 15. The LXX. render by προτείχισμα or περίτειχος, the Vulgate by *antemurale*. "There is always in Oriental towns a space outside the walls which lies uncultivated and which is naturally used for the deposit of refuse of every kind. Here the dogs prowl, and the kites and vultures find many a feast" (Rawlinson). In 2 Sam. xxi. 12 we find the bodies of Saul and Jonathan impaled in the open space (A. V. "street") of Bethshean. This heap of refuse—for such the place soon becomes—is called in the Arabian Nights "the mounds" (Stanley)] **of Jezreel.** [Retribution should overtake her near the scene of her latest crime (2 Kings ix. 36). By this the just judgment of God would be made the more conspicuous.

Ver. 24.—**Him that dieth of Ahab in the city the dogs shall eat; and him that dieth in the fields shall the fowls of the air eat.** [See on ch. xiv. 11; xvi. 4. Stanley, forgetting that the phrase is almost a *formula*, thinks that "the large vultures which in Eastern climes are always wheeling aloft under the clear blue sky doubtless suggested the expression to the prophet." "The horizon was darkened with the visions of vultures glutting on the carcases of the dead, and the packs of savage dogs feeding on their remains, or lapping up their blood."]

Ver. 25.—**But** [Heb. *Only*] **there was none like unto Ahab, which did sell himself to work wickedness in the sight of the Lord** [as in ver. 20], **whom Jezebel his wife stirred up** [or as Marg., *incited*, instigated and urged to sin. Cf. Deut. xiii. 7 Heb.; Job xxxvi. 18].

Ver. 26.—**And he did very abominably in following idols** [Heb. *to go after the idols*. For the last word see on ch. xv. 12], **according to all things as did the Amorites.** [Heb. the Amorite—the word is always singular—here put as a *nomen generale* for the seven nations of Canaan. Cf. Gen. xv. 16; 2 Kings xxi. 11; Exek. xvi. 3; Amos ii. 9, 10. Strictly the term Amorite, *i.e.*, *Highlander*, is in contrast with Canaanite, *i.e.*, dwellers in the *lowlands;* see Num. xiii. 29; Josh. v. 1. But the word is used interchangeably with Canaanite (cf. Deut. i. 44 with Num. xiv. 45, and Judg. i. 10 with Gen. xiii. 8), Hittites (Judg. i. 10 with Gen. xxiii. 2, 3, 10), Hivites (Gen. xlviii. 22 with Gen. xxxiv. 2), and Jebusites (Josh. x. 5, 6, with Josh. xvii. 63, &c.) The ethnical and geographical ideas of the Jews were never very precise. The idolatries of the seven nations had lingered, as we might expect, amongst the Zidonians, whence they were re-introduced into the kingdom of Samaria—one fruit of disobedience to the command of

Deut. vii. 1—5, &c.], whom the Lord cast out before the children of Israel [Deut. ii. 34 ; iii. 8, &c.]

Ver. 27.—And it came to pass, when Ahab heard those [Heb. *these*] words [vers. 21—24, and others not recorded], that he rent his clothes [cf. 2 Sam. xiii. 19; Job i. 20 ; ii. 12 ; Jer. xxxvi. 24, &c.], and put sackcloth upon his flesh [ch. xx. 31; 2 Kings vi. 30 ; Joel i. 8 ; 2 Sam. xxi. 10, Heb.], and fasted, and lay [*i.e.*, slept] in sackcloth, and went softly. [All these were signs of contrition and humiliation (ver. 29). The " going softly "—Josephus says he went barefoot—is especially characteristic of the subdued and chastened mind.]

Ver. 28.—And the word of the Lord came to Elijah the Tishbite, saying, [It is not clear that this mitigation of the sentence was *announced* to Ahab],

Ver. 29.—Seest thou how Ahab humbleth himself before me ? [The repentance, if it was not profound, or enduring, was nevertheless, while it lasted, sincere. The Searcher of hearts saw in it a genuine self-abasement. And " He will not break the bruised reed nor quench the smoking flax ; " Isa. xlii. 3 ; Matt. xii. 20.] Because he humbleth himself before me, I will not bring the evil [There is a manifest reference to ver. 21, where the same words are used] in his days ; but in his son's days [There is no injustice here—no threat of punishment against the innocent instead of the guilty—as might at first sight appear. For in the first place, God knew well what the son would be, and in the second place, if the son had departed from his father's sins he would have been spared (Ezek xviii. 14 *sqq.*) ; the sentence would have been revoked. Judgment was deferred to give the house of Ahab another chance. When Ahab lapsed into sin, he suffered in his own person : when his sons persisted in sin, excision befell the family] will I bring the evil [ver. 19] upon his house [ver. 22].

HOMILETICS.

Vers. 1—15.—*The Martyrdom of Naboth.* History tells of few crimes of its kind more flagitious, more cruel and cold-blooded than this. Here we see that spectacle which one of the ancients said was dear to the gods—a just man suffering shameful wrongs with dignity and patience : we see a man because of his fidelity to God and His law judicially done to death by the representative of God, by the authority appointed to execute the law.

And just as the crime has few parallels, so has the history few equals in point of graphic force and quiet pathos. It is like one of those sketches by the hand of a master, which set us wondering to see how much effect can be produced, and how much meaning conveyed, by a few broad lines and touches. We see in the first place the king, from his palace lattices, or from his garden slopes, casting hungry, envious eyes on the rich vineyard of his neighbour. He must have it at any cost. The residence is incomplete without it. We then hear him making overtures to the sturdy owner. There is a smile upon his face. His words are smoother than butter. Nothing could be fairer, as it seems at first, than his proposals. Surely Naboth will do well to sell or exchange on such liberal terms as these. But we find him straightway shrinking in pious horror from the idea. There is nothing to soften or modify his blunt and abrupt refusal. He cannot, he will not, do this thing and sin against God. We see a cloud of vexation gather on the king's brow. He is foiled. The project on which he has set his heart he cannot realize. With a mortified scowl, a look in which suppressed rage and bitter disappointment are equally blended, he terminates the interview and hurries to his palace, while Naboth, strong in the consciousness of right, but not without misgivings as to the issue, goes to tell his story to his wife and children at home.

And now the scene changes. We are admitted to a room, a bedroom of the palace of Samaria. We see on an ivory couch, in an ivory house (ch. xxii. 29), or in a chamber ceiled with cedar, and painted with vermilion (Jer. xxii. 14), a man whose soul is so vexed and troubled that he can eat no bread, that he has a word for no one, but turns his face sullenly to the wall. Can this be the king of Israel? can this be Ahab, whose recent victories over the Syrians have rung through many lands ? It is Ahab indeed. The great conqueror is a slave to himself. By his side there stands his dark, malignant, Phoenician consort. We hear his pitiful, almost childish, complaint, that he cannot have the vineyard he so much covets, and we straightway see a look of something like scorn upon her face. We hear her almost contemptuous rejoinder, " Art thou, then, so helpless, so utterly without resources, as to lie here and grieve like a spoilt child ? Is it for nothing that thou art a king, or art thou king in name only ? If thou art baffled, I am not. Arise, and eat bread. Banish dull care and give thyself up to feasting. I will give thee the vineyard of this wretched peasant."

The next tableau introduces us to another chamber of this same royal residence. The king may keep his bed if he will, but the queen is up and doing. The scribes are now writing at her command. She it is who dictates the words, who stamps the writings with the king's seal. The scribe's hand may well tremble as he pens the infamous decree, for the letter consigns Naboth to death ; but she knows no fear, has no scruples. The letters are despatched, the royal posts carry their sealed orders to Jezreel, and the murderess sits down to eat and drink, and rises up to play.

Again the scene changes. We find ourselves in a village convocation. The elders of Jezreel, the officers of the royal borough, have proclaimed a fast. Their town has incurred the wrath of God, and they must find out and expiate the sin. Naboth is there. He fears this meeting bodes him no good, but he is compelled to attend. He finds himself, to his great surprise, set " at the head of the people." But who shall picture the astonishment and pain in this man's face, when there rise up in that assembly, two miserable varlets who swear that he, Naboth, the humble servant of the Lord, the man who has honestly striven to keep the law, even against his king, has committed a horrible breach of law, has blasphemed God and the anointed of God. He thinks, perchance, at the first, that the charge is so utterly reckless and improbable, that none of these his neighbours, who know him so well, and have known him from his youth up, will entertain it for a moment. But he is speedily undeceived. He finds that he has not a chance with them, that all steel their faces and hearts against him. He perceives that there is a conspiracy against him. In vain he protests his innocence ; in vain he appeals to his blameless life. His cries and those of his wife and children are alike unheeded. In a trice he is condemned to die the death of the blasphemer.

And now we find ourselves hurried along by a tumultuous crowd. We pass through the city gate, we reach the open space outside the walls. So far, Naboth has hardly realized that they are in earnest, so suddenly has the thing come upon him. Surely it is some grim jest that his neighbours play upon him. It cannot be that he is to die, to look for the last time on the faces of those he loves, on his native fields, on the blessed light of the sun. But if he has any lingering hopes of deliverance they are rapidly dispelled. He sees them making preparations for his execution. They are going to stone him on the spot. " O God in heaven!" he thinks, "is it for this I have kept Thy law ? Is this agony and death the reward of mine integrity ? Must I then die, when life is so sweet ! Is there no power to rescue me out of the jaws of the lion ? Has God forgotten me ? or will He look on it and require it?" (2 Chron. xxiv. 22.) It is true the history says nothing of any such thoughts, of any prayers, appeals, entreaties, threatenings; but the history, it must be remembered, is but an outline, and that outline it is left for us to fill up. And we cannot doubt that Naboth had some such thoughts as these. But whatever they were, they were speedily brought to a close. " The king's business required haste." Time for reflection would mean time for repentance. The witnesses speedily divest themselves of their *abbas;* they lay them down at the feet of the elders ; they take up stones and rush upon him. At the first blow he quivers from head to foot with a great throb of pain, but blow follows fast upon blow ; he sinks senseless ; the blood streams from his wounds ; the dear life is crushed out of him, and Naboth's name and the names of his sons are added to those on the glory roll of the noble army of martyrs.

But it is now for us to ask what led to this shameful deed. There were five parties to this tragedy—Naboth, the king, the queen, the elders, the witnesses. Let us see how each of these contributed, though in very different ways, to this diabolical result. We shall thus see how Naboth, who was murdered in the name of law and religion, was a martyr to law and religion. And let us consider—

1. *The piety of Naboth.* For it was his religion brought this doom upon his head. He had but to comply with the request of the king—and what loyal subject would not wish to gratify the Lord's anointed?—and all would have gone well. So far from being stoned, he would have been honoured and rewarded. And that request seemed so reasonable. There was no attempt at robbery or confiscation. The king offered an ample equivalent; a better vineyard than it, or bars of silver which could buy a better. Was he not perverse and wrong-headed to let a scruple stand in the way? We should not have done so. No; but is not that precisely because we have not the steadfast piety of Naboth? There is no reason to think that he was not loyal. Doubtless he would have been glad to oblige his king. But there were two considerations stood in the way. First, his duty to God; secondly, his duty to his forefathers and to his posterity. His duty to God. For God's law said, "The land shall not be sold for ever" (Levit. xxv. 23); it laid down that every child of Israel should "cleave to the inheritance of the tribe of his fathers" (Num. xxxvi. 7). And Naboth knew this, and Ahab knew it. But to the latter the law was a dead letter; to the former it was a living reality. To him there was no God but one, no will to be considered in comparison with His. If Naboth could but have consented to do as others had done (ch. xvi. 24), he would have kept his life. But he could not. He "did not fear loss, but sin." It was a crime against Jehovah, and he would not consent. Moreover it was—though perhaps this thought had comparatively little influence with him—a wrong to his ancestors and to his posterity. For generations past, ever since it was allotted to his first father, had that vineyard been in his family. It had been transmitted through a long line to him. It was his duty to transmit it intact to those who came after him, and he would do it. It was for these reasons—sentimental reasons some would call them—that Naboth died, because of his belief in a living God, and because he kept His law, and especially the first and fifth commandments of the Decalogue.

2. *The impiety of Ahab.* Just as the action of Naboth arose out of his belief, so did that of Ahab spring out of his practical unbelief—an apt illustration of the close connexion between our faith and our practice. This crime had its beginning, its *fons et origo*, in idolatry. It was because Ahab worshipped gods many and lords many that his allegiance to the Divine law was shaken. The law of Baal, he argued, did not forbid the alienation of land—why should the law of Jehovah? The root of this sin, therefore, like the root of all sin, was unbelief. And its blossom was a direct violation of the Decalogue. Out of the breach of the first commandment sprang violations of the sixth, eighth, ninth, and tenth. Just as Naboth, the believer in the one true God, stands out conspicuously as a keeper of the ten words, so do all the other parties in the tragedy stand convicted of violating them. It was primarily the tenth commandment that Ahab set at nought. He had no right to set his heart upon that vineyard, which the great King had given to another. And a breach of law was the less excusable in his case, insomuch as he was the guardian of law and was acquainted with its provisions (Deut. xvii. 18). Of all men, he should have been the last to defy or disregard it. But it is only when we consider that when his subject, to whom he should have been an example, set him an example, and refused to participate in his sin, that then, so far from repenting and praying that the thought of his heart might be forgiven him, he mourns and repines that he was not allowed to consummate it—it is only when we consider this that we realize its true character. His was a sin against light and knowledge; a sin against his helper and benefactor (ch. xx. 13, 28); a sin in spite of manifold warnings; a sin which led to blacker sin still. He coveted an evil covetousness to his house. That "love of money" was a root of false witness, of foul murder. And in this estimate of Ahab's sin it is assumed that he neither knew nor sanctioned Jezebel's designs. If he gave her the royal seal with the least idea of the malignant purpose to which she would apply it, he was virtually an accessory before the fact, and so was guilty of murder and robbery. And even if he was ignorant of her intentions, still the

readiness with which he reaped the fruits of her crime makes him a partaker in her sin. It is a common saying that the "receiver is as bad as the thief." And he must have known that "Jezebel could not give this vineyard with dry hands."

3. *The depravity of Jezebel.* Great as Ahab's guilt was, it was altogether eclipsed by that of his wife. At her door lies the real sin of the murder. The hands that accomplished it were not so guilty as the heart that suggested it and the mind that planned it. Ahab broke the tenth, Jezebel the sixth, eighth, ninth, and tenth commandments. Covetousness, false witness, murder, confiscation, she stands convicted of them all. But what lends its most hideous feature to her sin is the consideration that she, the sworn foe of the law of Jehovah, availed herself of its forms to compass Naboth's death. Was ever such black-hearted ingenuity as hers? We can fancy her laughing in her sleeve at the crafty use she made of the hated system of the Jews. We can see her shaking her finger at Naboth and saying "Simple fool! thou hast stood out for the law; thou shalt have a surfeit of it this time." It is possible that she rejoiced at the base part to which she commits the elders of Jezreel. If they will cling to their austere and gloomy creed, she will make them carry out its provisions. To this shameful murderess it added zest to her sin that she scored a triumph against the followers and the law of the God of Israel. We must also observe the evident satisfaction, the malicious triumph, with which she hears of Naboth's death. So far from feeling the least compunction, she hurries with the good news to her husband. Her part, so far as we know, is absolutely without a parallel of all the daughters of our first mother. What name is there so deservedly infamous as hers?

4. *The corruption of the elders.* We may readily acquit them of liking the task entailed upon them. They could not embark on that course of crime without many qualms of conscience and secret self-upbraidings. But the name of Jezebel inspired so much terror that they dared not resist her will. Their sin was, first, that they feared man more than God. It was unbelief at bottom; they had more faith in the finger of the queen than in the arm of the Almighty. They argued, as the Turkish peasant does, that the queen was near and God was a long way off. It was, secondly, that they abused their office. In defiance of law (Exod. xxiii. 2, 6; Deut. xvi. 19), they wrested judgment and condemned the innocent (Deut. xxvii. 19, 25), and so they share with Jezebel the guilt of the murder. It is idle to plead the constraint put upon them, to say that they would have died had they resisted her; they *should* have died rather than slay the innocent. But for their complaisance, the queen might have been baffled. One might reasonably expect *elders* —the "judges and officers" of the land (Deut. xvi. 18)—to answer, "We ought to obey God rather than man." History tells of many judges who have withstood the corrupt commands of their sovereign. During the Mohammedan rule in Spain one of the caliphs took forcible possession of a field belonging to one of his subjects. This man, as a forlorn hope, stated his grievance before the kadi, a man renowned for his integrity, and the kadi promised to bring his case before the king. Loading his mule with a sack of earth which he had taken from the stolen field, he strode into the presence of the prince, and asked him to be so good as to lift the sack of earth to his shoulders. The caliph tried to comply with his request, but the burden proved too heavy for him; he could not move, still less carry, it. "Wretched man!" cried the judge, "see what thou hast done. Thou canst not carry one mule's burden of the earth of this field of which thou hast deprived thy subject. How, then, canst thou hope to sustain the whole field on thy shoulders in the dreadful day of judgment?" The appeal was successful; the prince made immediate restitution and rewarded the judge. But nothing of this kind did the elders of Jezreel. They only feared for their skins. They argued that one or the other must die, and if so it must be Naboth. And so *he* died, and *they* bore the stain of blood upon their souls.

5. *The perjury of the witnesses.* It is hardly correct to describe their sin as perjury. It was much more than that. It was actual murder also. As witnesses, they had to cast the first stone—to take the principal part in the execution. Even without this they were guilty of murder, for it was upon their testimony that

Naboth was condemned to die. They share with the elders, consequently, the guilt of violating the sixth and ninth commandments. But they were "sons of Belial" to begin with. They were not ministers of God; still less were they the "Lord's anointed." And they were but instruments in the hand of others. The elders were the hand; the queen was the head.

It is clear, then, that Naboth's death was a true martyrdom. He died a victim to his faith in God and his obedience to law. He was a witness (μάρτυς), consequently, for God no less than Elijah or Elisha. Like Elijah, he was a public vindicator of the law, and he sealed his witness with his blood. He died because he would not deny it; because others, its guardians and executors, violated and abused it.

But if any deny his right to be enrolled in the army of martyrs, it only needs to compare his end with that of the protomartyr Stephen, and indeed with that of our blessed Lord. The analogy could not well be closer. 1. The same passions and influences were at work in each case. It was unbelief and pride and covetousness occasioned the death of Naboth. These were the forces arrayed against our Lord and against Stephen. Was there a coveted vineyard in one case? so there was in the other (Luke xx. 14, 15). 2. The tribunals were equally corrupt. The Sanhedrim was the counterpart of the elders; the council of Jerusalem of that of Jezreel (Matt. xxvi. 59; Acts vi. 12). 3. The princes of this world occasioned the death of Naboth; the princes of this world took counsel against the Christ (Acts iv. 26, 27), and crucified the Lord of glory (1 Cor. ii. 8). 4. The charge was the same in every case, viz., blasphemy (Matt. xxvi. 65; Acts vi. 13). The variation is extremely slight: "God and the king" in one case; "against Moses and God" in another (Acts vi. 11). 5. The charge was made in each instance by men who were conspicuously law-breakers (John xvii. 19; Acts vii. 53), and it was made in the name of law (John xix. 7; Acts. vi. 14). 6. The means used to compass the death were alike in every case, viz., false witness (Matt. xxvi. 59, 60; Acts vi. 11, 13). 7. Each of these three martyrs suffered without the gate (Acts vii. 58 : Heb. xiii. 12). Like Naboth, Stephen was stoned; like Naboth, our Lord would have been stoned if the Jews had had the power (John xviii. 31), and if the counsel of God had not willed otherwise (Acts iv. 28). 8. There is indeed one difference, and that is suggestive. The martyrs of our religion prayed for their murderers (Luke xxiii. 34; Acts vii. 60); the martyrs of Judaism could only cry, "The Lord look on it and require it" (2 Chron. xxiv. 22). The blood of the covenant speaks better things than the blood of Naboth.

Vers. 17—24.—*Divine Retaliation.* We have just seen Naboth martyred because of his fidelity to law; we have seen him murdered by men who in the name of law violated all the laws of God and man.

Now the dispensation under which these men lived promised a present recompense, a temporal reward, to obedience, and it denounced temporal punishment against "every transgression and disobedience." We may imagine, consequently, how this tragedy would strike the men of that age. They would see in it a direct failure of justice. They would ask whether there was a God that judgeth in the earth. They would look, and especially the God-fearing amongst them, in utter perplexity and distress on this conspicuous instance of the triumph of force and wrong. "What is the Almighty," they would be tempted to ask," that we should serve him? and what profit should we have if we pray unto him?" (Job xxi. 15.) They would be tempted to think that "in keeping of his commandments there was *no* reward; yes, even tempted to say in their hearts, "There is no God" (Psa. liii. 1).

It would have been strange, therefore, if such a red-handed, cold-blooded murder had passed unnoticed and unavenged; if the dogs had been left to feast on the remains of Naboth, and Ahab had been suffered to enter on his vineyard without protest. But this was not to be. The men of Jezreel had not seen the last act in the tragedy. They must learn that "no reckoning is brought in the midst of the meal; the end pays for all;" they must be taught to count no man happy before his death. They must be reminded that there is a prophet in Israel, and a God of

Israel who will by no means clear the guilty. And so Elijah, the great restorer of the law, stands forth to avenge the death of Naboth, the law-keeper, at the hands of law-breakers.

"Arise, take possession of the vineyard of Naboth, which he refused to give thee for money, for Naboth is not alive, but dead." Did the king stop to ask how this death had been brought about? Did he know the shameful crime that had been committed in his name, and under his palace walls? He must have known something of it, if not all. Even if he thought it prudent to ask no questions, still he would remember the significant promise of ver. 7; he would have some suspicions of the purpose for which the royal seal was required; and it would be clear to him, even if he did not know the exact circumstances, that somehow Jezebel had compassed Naboth's death. It was clear to him that this vineyard was bought at the price of blood.

But he will not let such considerations as these hinder his enjoyment of it. All he thinks of or cares for is this, that the vineyard is his and he can enter upon it at once. He *will* enter upon it at once. His chariot shall bear him to the spot. He will view his new property that day; he will begin his garden of herbs forthwith.

The citizens of Jezreel, the "elders," and "children of Belial" amongst them, see the royal chariot crossing the plain, breasting the hill, entering the city. They know full well what is its destination. There is hardly a child in the city but guesses the king's errand. It causes them no surprise when the chariot and its escort pass on to the vineyard of Naboth. But they shall learn, and through them all Israel shall learn, that there is a just God in heaven, and that even the king is responsible to a Higher Power; and they shall know that God Himself is against the evildoer, and shall render to every man according to his works (Prov. xxiv. 12; Matt. xvi. 27; 2 Tim. iv. 14).

For who is this that strides up to the king as he stands in the coveted vineyard, and shapes his projects concerning it? It is a prophet—the dress proves that; a glance shows that it is the dreaded, mysterious prophet Elijah. "Behold Elijah" (ch. xviii. 8, 11) is on their lips. Whence has he come? Since the day of Carmel he has been hidden from their view. They had often wondered why he had so suddenly disappeared; whether he was still alive; whether the Spirit had cast him upon some mountain or into some valley (2 Kings ii. 16); whether he was hiding among foreigners as he had done before. And now he is amongst them again. And Jehu and Bidkar at least (2 Kings ix. 25), and probably others with them, presently understand the reason of his sudden reappearance. "Hast thou killed," he thunders forth, "and also taken possession?" They see the guilty look on Ahab's face; they note his ashy paleness; they observe how he trembles helplessly from head to foot. Then they hear the terrible doom—and their ears tingle, as Elijah's impassioned words fall upon them—"Thus saith the Lord, In the place where dogs licked the blood of Jezebel shall dogs lick thy blood, even thine." They hear, and Ahab hears, that for him a death as cruel and shameful as Naboth's is reserved; that, king though he is, he shall come to the dogs at the last. But more: they presently learn that for his children, born in the purple and delicately nurtured, there remains a reckoning; that their blood must be shed, their bodies torn of beasts, like those of Naboth's sons. Nor shall proud Jezebel, the prime mover in this murder, escape. In the open space before the city wall the dogs which devoured the flesh of Naboth shall feast upon her dead body. All this was spoken in the broad day, before king and retinue, by a prophet whose words had never fallen to the ground. The king is *found out;* he is taken red-handed in the blossoms of his sin. Yesterday the crime, to-day the sentence. We may compare the feelings of that group standing in the vineyard with those of that surging crowd who saw Robespierre standing under the guillotine to which he had consigned so many hundreds of Frenchmen. "Aye, Robespierre, there is a God." We may imagine how they stood for a while transfixed to the spot; how, when Elijah had hurled his words at the king, he strode away and left them to rankle in his mind. But the thing was not done in a corner, and it could not be kept secret. As the chariot returns to Samaria the townsman in the street, the peasant in the field, perceive that something untoward has happened. The news of Elijah's reappearance spreads like wildfire; his scathing words are passed from lip to lip; every town and hamlet soon knows that Naboth is avenged; it knows that with what measure king and queen meted to him it shall be measured to them again.

The lessons which this public manifestation of the righteous judgment of God had for the men of that age, and some of which it has still, may be briefly stated in the words of Scripture. Among them are these:

1. "The eyes of the Lord are in every place beholding the evil and the good" (Prov. xv. 3) ; God *doth* know, and there *is* knowledge in the Most High (Psa. lxxiii. 11; cf. Psa. xi. 4).

2. "Verily there is a reward for the righteous; verily he is a God that judgeth in the earth" (Psa. lviii. 11). "Thou beholdest mischief and spite, to requite it with thy hand" (Psa. x. 14).

3. "Be sure your sin will find you out" (Num. xxxii. 23).

4. "Though hand join in hand, the wicked shall not be unpunished" (Prov. xi. 21).

5. "I will come near to you in judgment, and I will be a *swift witness* against the sorcerers, and against the adulterers, and against false swearers, and against those that oppress the hireling in his wages, the widow and the fatherless, and that turn aside the stranger from his right, and fear not me, saith the Lord" (Mal. iii. 5).

6. "Whoso sheddeth man's blood, by man shall his blood be shed" (Gen. ix. 6).

7. "Life for life, eye for eye, tooth for tooth, hand or hand, foot for foot, burning for burning, wound for wound, stripe for stripe" (Exod. xxi. 23—25). "God loves to punish by retaliation" (Hall).

Vers. 28, 29.—*Divine Relentings.*—If we were to seek the Scriptures through for a proof that God's "property is always to have mercy," and that judgment is His strange work, where should we find a more striking and eminent one than in this relenting towards Ahab? Consider—

I. AHAB'S SIN. In this respect "there was none like him." He "sold himself to work wickedness." It was not because of Naboth's murder alone that the sentence of vers. 19—22 was pronounced against him; it was for the varied and accumulated sins of a reign of twenty years. Among these were—

1. *The sin of schism.* He continued the calf-worship (ch. xvi. 31). He kept "the statutes of Omri." Despite the warnings of prophets and of history, he maintained the shrines, sacrifices, priests, of Bethel and Dan.

2. *The sin of his marriage.* "Was it a light thing to walk in the way of Jeroboam that he must take to wife Jezebel" (ch. xv. 31 Heb.), in direct violation of the law (Deut. vii. 1—3), in disregard of the example of Solomon? To place such a woman, daughter of such a house, on the throne of Israel was to insult the true religion, and to court its overthrow.

3. *The sin of idolatry.* (Ch. xvi. 32.) Samaria had its house of Baal, its altar for Baal. He did very abominably in following idols (ch. xxi. 26).

4. *The sin of impurity.* This was involved, as we have already remarked, in the idolatry of that age. "Ahab made an Asherah" (ch. xvi. 32). Indeed, it is to the impurities of Canaanitish worship that the words just cited (ver. 26) refer. The abominations of the Amorites are not to be named amongst Christians.

5. *The sin of persecuting the prophets.* It is very possible that Ahab himself was no persecutor, but Jezebel was, and he should have restrained her (1 Sam. iii. 13). He was directly responsible for her deeds. She owed her power, place, and influence to him.

6. *The sin of releasing the persecutor of God's people.* The pardon and favour he accorded to Ben-hadad are mentioned as a part of the provocation wherewith he provoked the Lord (ch. xx. 42). It sprang out of his forgetting God. He ignored altogether God's will and pleasure in the matter. See p. 492.

7. *The sin of slaying Naboth and his sons.* For with this crime Ahab is charged. "Hast *thou* killed?" "I have seen yesterday the blood of Naboth . . . and I will

requite *thee* " (2 Kings ix. 26).   Perhaps he flattered himself that that sin lay at Jezebel's door.   If so, he is soon undeceived.

Such was Ahab's sevenfold sin.   Consider—

II. ITS AGGRAVATIONS.   It enhanced his guilt that—

1. *He was the Lord's anointed.* He was the head of the Jewish Church. *Fidei Defensor* — this was the highest function of a true king of Israel.   His very position reminded him of the gracious and marvellous history of his fathers.   To him it was granted to be the representative of heaven to the chosen people.   How great the sin when the champion of the faith became its oppressor, when the " nursing father " of the Church depraved and prostituted it.

2. *He had witnessed miracles.*   The drought, the fire, the rain, all these signs and tokens had been wrought in his presence.   Unto him they were showed that he might know that the Lord He was God (Deut. iv. 35, 36 ; cf. 1 Kings xviii. 39).   Did ever king hear the voice of God as he had done ?

3. *He had been miraculously helped and delivered.* Cf. 2 Chron. xxvi. 15.   If he gave no heed to the signs, he should have been moved by the victories God had granted him. These were plain proofs that the Lord alone was God (ch. xx. 13, 28).

But neither plagues, nor signs, nor victories moved that rebellious heart.   He is scarce home from his Syrian compaigns, to enjoy the fruit of his success, than he lends himself to fresh sin, to murder and oppression.   He, the executor and guardian of law, connives at the murder of a law-abiding subject.   Let us now consider—

III. HIS REPENTANCE.   Now that he is found out and denounced, like Felix, he trembles.   As Elijah stands over him, and announces the doom of his house, he sees a horrible vision of blood and slaughter.   The garden of herbs he has pictured dies away from his view.   He sees in its stead his own mangled body cast into the plot of ground where he was then standing.   He sees his hands, his feet, his face gnawed by the curs of the adjoining city.   He sees his proud consort stripped of her silk attire, suffering a like indignity in the neighbouring ditch.   He sees his children, the fruit of his body, stretched in the streets of the town, or in the open champaign, a feast for the jackal and the carrion crow.   " Like the house of Jeroboam," " like the house of Baasha," he knew the horrors involved in these words. A horrible dread overwhelms him.   He is smitten by sudden compunction. He must get away from this cursed spot at once.   He might *then* have justly said to his charioteer, " Turn thine hand and carry me away, for I am wounded " (ch. xxii. 34). An arrow from Elijah's lips has pierced his harness through.   He mounts his chariot, it bears him through the plain, bears him to his palace—no longer " heavy and displeased," but utterly crushed and terrified.   Again he steals to his bedchamber, and turns his face to the wall and eats no bread.   In vain the queen assays to laugh him out of his fears.   No instruments of music can charm his melancholy, no physicians can minister to that mind diseased.   He cannot banish that vision from his thoughts. It haunts him like a nightmare. Can he not avert the doom ?   Can he not make his peace with Heaven ?   He has but lately forgiven a cruel and persistent enemy ; is there no forgiveness for him ?   He will make the effort.   He too will " gird sackcloth on his loins, and put a rope on his head," and go to the great king of Israel.   He rises from his couch a sadder and a wiser man. He rends his kingly robes and casts them from him ; he assumes the garment of humiliation, he fasts, he prays, he goes softly.   It is true his penitence was neither profound nor enduring (ch. xxii. 8, 26), but it was undoubtedly—

1. *Sincere while it lasted.* It is a mistake to call it the " shadow of a repentance." There was real contrition—not only fear of punishment, but also sorrow for his sin. We may be sure that, like a former king of Israel, his cry was, " I have sinned against the Lord " (2 Sam. xii. 13).

2. *Open and public.*   His queen, his courtiers, saw the sackcloth, marked the hushed voice, the downcast eye, and knew what it meant (ver. 29).   " *Seest thou how Ahab ?* " &c., implies that it was notorious.   The crime was known of all men ; the sorrow and humiliation must be the same.

3. *Marked by restitution.* The Scripture does not say so, but it does not need

to say so. There could be no real repentance, certainly no relenting, on God's part so long as Ahab kept the vineyard. His prayers would have been unheeded so long as there was a lie in his right hand. A "penitent thief" has always restored the theft. Ahab could not recall Naboth to life. But he could surrender the vineyard to the widow, and we may be sure he did so.

But this repentance, this self-abasement was observed, was carefully watched outside the palace. As day by day, with contrite heart and bowed head and soft footstep, the miserable king moved among his retainers, the merciful God and Father of the spirits of all flesh beheld his returning prodigal, yearned over him, ran to meet him. He who will not break the bruised reed nor quench the smoking wick welcomed the first faint tokens of contrition. The sentence of doom shall be deferred. The same voice which just now thundered, "Hast thou killed?" &c., is now hushed into tenderness. "Seest thou," it says, "seest thou how Ahab humbleth himself before me? Because," &c. (ver. 29). Ahab receives—

IV. PARDON. And this pardon, it is to be observed, was—

1. *Instant.* The rebellion had lasted for years. The forgiveness follows on the heels of repentance. While he was speaking God heard. Cf. Dan. x. 12.

2. *Free and full.* If Ahab's repentance, that is to say, had been lasting, the sentence would have been reversed so far as he was concerned. It was not finally reversed because of his subsequent sin and that of his sons. The guilt of innocent blood, no doubt, could only be purged by the blood of him that shed it (Num. xxxv. 33), and it is to be remembered that Jezebel was never included in the pardon. But it is probable that God, to "show forth all long-suffering," would have spared the king and his sons, if they had turned from their evil way.

3. *Conditional.* "*Dum se bere gesserit.*" This provision is always understood, if not expressed.

4. *Forfeited.* When Ahab turned like a dog to his vomit, then the sword which had been sheathed awhile leapt again from its scabbard, and he was suddenly destroyed, and that without remedy.

HOMILIES BY VARIOUS AUTHORS.

Vers. 1—4.—*Covetousness.* Amongst the arguments used by Samuel to discourage the people of Israel from desiring a king, he said, "He will take your fields, and your vineyards, and your olive-yards, even the best of them." We have in the verses before us a notable example of the truth of this forecast, understanding covetousness in a bad sense.

I. DESIRE, IN THE ABSTRACT, IS NOT COVETOUSNESS. 1. *It is the principle of exchanges.* (1) If persons had no desire to possess anything beyond what they have acquired, there would be no motive to trade. Of the virtuous woman it is said, "She considereth a field and buyeth it: with the fruit of her hands she planteth a vineyard" (Prov. xxxi. 16). (2) All commerce is founded upon the desire to make exchanges. 2. *But commerce is fruitful in blessings.* (1) There are evils connected with trading, viz., where dishonest practices come into it. But these are intrusions; and they are denounced as "illegitimate" and "uncommercial." (2) Genuine commerce gives profitable employment to thought and labour. (3) It brings the countries and peoples of the wide world into correspondence. Thereby it enlarges our knowledge of those countries, their peoples and products, and otherwise stimulates science. (4) It encourages philanthropy. Relief is afforded for distresses through famines, floods, fires, earthquakes; and religious missions are organized. 3. *Desire, well directed, should be encouraged.* (1) To be absolutely without desire for things evil would be a happy state. Therefore this state should be earnestly desired. (2) There is also the positive desire to be Christ-like. This can scarcely be too vehement. (3) Ahab does not seem to have signalized himself in either of these directions.

II. ILLICIT DESIRE IS COVETOUSNESS. 1. *We should not desire what God has forbidden.* (1) Herein Ahab was wrong in desiring the vineyard of Naboth. It was the " inheritance of his fathers," transmitted in the family of Naboth, from the days of Joshua, and it would have been unlawful for him to part with it (Levit. xxv. 23 ; Num. xxxvi. 7). (2) Ahab was wrong in tempting Naboth to trangress the commandment of the Lord. He should never have encouraged a desire, the gratification of which would involve such a consequence. (3) It was a pious act in Naboth, who, doubtless in things lawful would be pleased to gratify the king, to have indignantly refused to gratify him here. " *The Lord forbid it me* that I should give the inheritance of my fathers unto thee." He had his tenure from the Lord. He looked upon his earthly inheritance as a pledge of a heavenly. 2. *This rule requires the study of God's word.* (1) It is of the utmost moment to us to be acquainted with the will of God. This he has revealed in the Scriptures. (2) In cases of transgression we cannot plead ignorance when we have the Bible in our hands. Neither can we shift now our responsibility on to our teachers. (3) Do we make proper use of our Bibles ? Do we *study* them ? Do we read them *prayerfully* ? We must not sell the moral inheritance we have received from the past.

III. INORDINATE DESIRE IS COVETOUSNESS. *Some things are lawful without limit.* Such are the direct claims of God. (1) The *love* of God. We may love Him with all our heart. We cannot love Him too much, or too much desire His love. (2) The *service* of God. This, indeed, is another form of love ; for love expresses itself in service (John xiv. 15, 23 ; Rom. xiii. 10 ; Gal. v. 14 ; 1 John v. 3). (3) The *knowledge* of God. To love and serve God perfectly we must have a perfect knowledge of Him according to our capacity. We cannot too ardently desire this knowledge. (4) If Ahab had loved, served, and known God with perfect desire, he would have found such satisfaction as to have rendered it impossible for him to have sulked as he did because he could not obtain Naboth's vineyard. When God is absent there is a restless void; nothing can satisfy an unholy spirit. 2. *Other things are lawful in measure.* (1) Otherwise they would interfere with the direct claims of God. The creature must not be put into competition with the Creator. " Thou shalt have none other gods *beside* me." (2) Desire for sensible and temporal things must not displace the desire for things spiritual and eternal. To love the inferior preferably to the superior is to deprave the affections. (3) It would have been lawful for Ahab to have purchased a lease of the vineyard of Naboth at a fair price, leaving it in the power of Naboth to have redeemed it ; and for it to revert to Naboth or his heirs in the jubilee (Levit. xxv. 23—28). But this desire to possess it, even under these conditions, could not be justified if a refusal should lead him to go home " heavy and displeased " and sicken with chagrin. Ahab's discontent brought its own punishment. He was a king, yet discontented. Discontent is a disease of the soul rather than of the circumstances.—J. A. M.

Vers. 5—14.—*A Sinful Nation.* Time was when the Hebrew nation was great and respected, " a praise in the earth " for kings wise and honourable, for magistrates upright and noble, and for a people faithful and true. But how completely is all this changed ! A more pitiable picture of national depravity could scarcely be drawn than that presented in the text. Here we have—

I. AN INIQUITOUS PALACE. 1. *The king is utterly unprincipled.* (1) See him " heavy and displeased," sick with rage and chagrin, lying in bed in a sulk, his face turned away, refusing to eat. And what for ? What dreadful calamity has befallen him ? Simply that he could not have the vineyard of Naboth for a garden of herbs ! (2) But, to make things worse, he could not have it without inducing Naboth to transgress God's law (see Levit. xxv. 23). Naboth had too much respect for the law to yield. Ahab was really sulking against God ! (3) What a model king is this ! How could he expect his subjects to be law-abiding when he showed them this example ? What a royal soul to take it thus to heart that in addition to his kingdom he cannot have this vineyard ! 2. *His queen is a " cursed woman."* (1) Such is the style in which she is described by Jehu (2 Kings ix. 34). She seems never to have failed in any incident of her life to justify this description. (2) Now she promises to give Ahab the vineyard of Naboth. Thus she encouraged his evil humour, instead of pointing out to him, as she should have done, his folly.

(3) She will accomplish this by an act of cruel and treacherous despotism scarcely to be paralleled in history (vers. 8—10). She makes her pliant husband her accomplice, using, with his consent, his seal of state, as probably she had done before when she destroyed the prophets of the Lord (ch. xviii. 4), to give authority to the missive of death. She engaged in this business all the more readily because Naboth appears to have been one of the " seven thousand " who would not bend to Baal.

II. AN UNSCRUPULOUS MAGISTRACY. 1. *Their servility is horrible.* (1) Not a voice of any noble or elder in Jezreel is raised in protest against the order from the palace to have Naboth murdered. With eyes wide open—for the sons of Belial are not found for them ; they have themselves to procure these wretches—they proceed to give effect to the dreadful tragedy. (2) What motive can influence them ? They are afraid of Jezebel. They knew her power over Ahab, and they knew the cruelty and vindictiveness of her nature was nerved by more than masculine resolution. (3) But where was their fear of God ? 2. *It is aggravated by treachery.* (1) Naboth was one of their number. Is not this suggested in the words, " the elders and nobles that were in the city, *dwelling with Naboth* " ? Then is there no voice of neighbourly friendship to speak for Naboth ? No voice is raised. (2) If one voice found courage surely others would take courage, and it might be found in the sequel that the sense of justice would be represented by such numbers and influence that even Jezebel might hesitate to reek vengeance upon them. But not a voice was raised. 3. *The treachery is aggravated by hypocrisy.* (1) The tragedy opens with a fast. This is proclaimed ostensibly to avert from the nation the judgments of God supposed to have been provoked by the crimes of Naboth. How much more fitting had it been proclaimed to avert the judgment provoked by the crimes of Naboth's murderers ! (2) The accusation is, "Thou didst blaspheme God and the King". (ברכת אלהים ומלך), which by some is rendered, " Thou hast *blessed* the false gods and Molech." Parkhurst says, " The Lexicons have absurdly, and contrary to the authority of the ancient versions, given to this verb (ברך) the sense of *cursing* in the six following passages: 1 Kings xxi. 10, 13 ; Job i. 5, 11 ; ii. 5, 9. As to the two first, the LXX. render ברך in both cases by ευλογεω, and so the Vulgate by bendico, *to bless*. And though Jezebel was herself an abominable idolatress, yet, as the law of Moses still continued in force, she seems to have been wicked enough to have destroyed Naboth upon the false accusation of *blessing the heathen Aleim* and *Molech*, which subjected him to death by Deut. xiii. 6 ; xvii. 2—7." (3) What abominable cruelties have been perpetrated under the name of religion !

III. A DEMORALIZED PEOPLE. 1. *Sons of Belial are at hand.* (1) There seems to have been no difficulty in procuring men so lost to truth and mercy that they will readily swear away the life of a good citizen. Nor is this to be wondered at when the whole magistracy are sons of Belial, no better than those they suborned. Jezebel saw no difficulty in procuring such. The nobles and elders of Jezreel found none. (2) The sons of Belial no doubt were paid for their services. The " consideration " is not mentioned. What will not some men stoop to for gain ! What will they hazard in eternity ! And for what a trifle ! 2. *No voice is raised for justice.* (1) Naboth has no hearing in his defence. The sentence given, he is hurried away to be stoned to death. (2) His family are sacrificed along with him (see 2 Kings ix. 26). This was on the principle that the family of Achan had to suffer with him (Josh. vii. 24). But how different are the cases ! (3) Unless the family of Naboth had perished with him, the vineyard would not have fallen to the crown. This would be an objection to Jezebel hiring sons of Belial to assassinate Naboth, for Naboth's heirs would still have to be disposed of. Melancholy is the condition of the nation in which right is sacrificed to might. " Sin is a reproach to any people."—J. A. M.

Vers. 15—24.—*Divine Inquisition.* Ahab lost no time in reaping the fruit of Jezebel's wickedness. The next day, after the murder of Naboth and his family, we find him taking possession of the coveted vineyard (see 2 Kings ix. 26). But in all this dark business there was an invisible Spectator, whose presence does not seem to have been sufficiently taken into the account.

I. GOD IS AN OMNISCIENT OBSERVER. 1. *He inspects all human actions.* (1) He was present in the palace looking upon the king of Israel as he sulked and sickened upon his bed. His eye also was full upon Jezebel as she proposed her ready cure for the monarch's chagrin. "Thou God seest *me*." (2) He was present in that court of justice when the honest Naboth was "set on high among the people." He witnessed the sons of Belial as they swore away the lives of a worthy family. He looked into the faces of the "nobles" and "elders" of Jezreel who suborned these perjurers. "Thou God seest *me*." (3) He was a spectator at the place of execution. He saw the steadiness of Naboth's step, and noted well the bearing of his sons as they came forth to suffer for righteousness. And the swelling of every muscle of those who hurled the stones was measured by His piercing vision. "Thou God seest *me*." 2. *He surveys all human motives.* (1) He clearly discerned the abominable hypocrisy of Jezebel's "fast." It was proclaimed ostensibly to avert from the nation Divine judgments provoked by the alleged blasphemy or idolatry of Naboth. The *vineyard* of Naboth had more to do with it than his crime. It is "a new thing in the earth" to see Jezebel jealous for the honour of Jehovah! (2) He knew why the sons of Belial publicly perjured themselves, and accurately estimated the price for which they sold the lives of honourable citizens. He also estimated the cowardly fear of Jezebel's wrath, rather than encounter which the magistrates carried out her wicked instructions. "Nobles" and "elders" they were accounted by men; perjurers, murderers, and dastards they were accounted by God. (3) He nicely weighed the motive which nerved the muscle of every man who lifted a stone against the life of Naboth. If any were misled by the hypocrisy of the authorities, and thought they "did God service" when they cast the stones, their sincerity was recognized; and those who were not deceived were also known. 3. *Nothing is forgotten before Him.* (1) As He sees the end from the beginning so does He see the beginning from the end. (2) Let us never forget that God never can forget. Every action of our lives is present with Him—so every word—so every thought and intent of the heart. Therefore—

II. GOD IS A SUPREME JUDGE. 1. *He makes sin bitter to the sinner.* (1) The acquisition of the vineyard, the murders notwithstanding, was at first so pleasing to Ahab that it cured his sickness, and he "rose up to go down to the vineyard of Naboth the Jezreelite, to take possession of it." And this is often the first effect of the gratification of covetousness. (2) But how transient is the unworthy satisfaction! It is soon succeeded by a season of reflection. The sudden apparition of Elijah upon the scene filled Ahab with alarm. His conscience now brought his guilt home, and before Elijah uttered a word, the king exclaimed, "Hast thou found me, O mine enemy?" This was the language of mingled hatred and fear (see Gal. iv. 16). The presence of the good is a silent and effective rebuke to the wicked. (3) The enormity of Ahab's guilt was brought home to him by the questions, "Hast thou killed, and also taken possession?" He has killed, for by taking possession he sanctions the means by which his title is made out (see Job xxxi. 39; Jer. xxii. 13, 14; Hab. ii. 12). (4) God's Holy Spirit still, by means of the word of prophecy, if not by the lips of living prophets, carries guilt to the consciences of sinners, and fills them with remorseful shame. 2. *He conveys judgments in His providence.* We read this principle in the denunciations uttered by Elijah. (1) Upon Ahab. "In the place where dogs licked the blood of Naboth shall dogs lick thy blood, even thine." This was fulfilled (see ch. xxii. 38). But how "in the place?" for Naboth suffered near Jezreel. Jezreel is, generally, called Samaria, being like Bethel, one of the "cities of Samaria" (see ch. xiii. 32). So in verse 18, the vineyard of Naboth is said to be in Samaria. The passage is more clearly thus translated: "And the word of Jehovah came to Elijah the Tishbite, saying, Arise, go down to meet Ahab the king of Israel, who is in Samaria; behold, at the vineyard of Naboth, whither he is gone down to take possession of it." (2) Upon the family of Ahab (vers. 21, 22, 24). This was a reprisal for the family of Naboth sacrificed with him (see 2 Kings ix. 26). All was to the letter accomplished (see 2 Kings ix., x.) (3) Upon Jezebel. The "cursed woman" is signally execrated (ver. 23). The retribution was as signally accomplished (see 2 Kings ix. 36). (4) This law of retribution in the judgments of Providence is not limited to sacred history. Orestes recognized it when he said to Ægisthus—

> " Go where thou slew'st my father,
> That in the selfsame place thou too may'st die."

It may be read in every full and accurate history. 3. *He will finally judge the world.* (1) For Naboth and his family have yet to be vindicated. Providence has vindicated their reputation; but they have to be vindicated in person also. To this end all parties concerned in their murder will have to stand face to face, with their hearts exposed to the clear light and sensible presence of Omniscient Justice. What defence can the sons of Belial then set up? The magistrates? Jezebel? Ahab? (2) What a day of vindications will that be to all the righteous! What a day of confusion to all the wicked! Everything will be righteously adjusted in that final sentence (Matt. xxv. 34, 41, 46).—J. A. M.

Vers. 25—29.—*Ahab's Repentance.* After the terrible sentence pronounced by Elijah upon Ahab for his enormities follows this account of his repentance. The record teaches—

I. THAT THERE IS REPENTANCE FOR THE VILEST. 1. *Ahab answered this description.* (1) He " wrought wickedness." So have we all. But his was evil of no common order. "He did very abominably in following idols, according to all things as did the Amorites, whom the Lord cast out before the children of Israel." (See Gen. xv. 16; 2 Kings xxi. 11.) (2) He wrought this wickedness " in the sight of the Lord," as the Amorites did not, for they had not the religious privileges of an Israelite. Ahab in particular had signal proofs of the presence of God. The shutting and opening of the heavens, to wit, together with the miracle on Carmel. Where much is given much is required. (3) He had " sold himself " to work this wickedness. (See Rom. vii. 14.) He was slave to Jezebel—slave to Satan. He drudged hard in his serfdom. (4) None of his predecessors had gone so far wrong. " There was none like unto Ahab " (see ch. xvi. 33). Jeroboam had "made Israel to sin," and Omri, at the instigation of Ahab, made "statutes " to confirm that sin. (See Micah vi. 16.) Ahab went further, and established the worship of Baal, with its attendant abominations of Ashere. (See ch. xvi. 29—33.) (5) He was in the worst company. He had married a " cursed woman," and submitted to be led by her into the extremes of wickedness. "Whom Jezebel his wife stirred up." Under her instigation he consented to a wholesale massacre of the sons of the prophets; and now she makes him her accomplice in the murder of Naboth, with its attendant atrocities. 2. *Yet Ahab took God's message to heart.* (1) He believed the terrible sentence, as he had good reason to do, for it came by the hand of Elijah. In all his former experience he had found that the word of the Lord in Elijah's mouth was truth. (2) Now, with his death vividly before him, and the fearful doom of his house—all the fruit of his crimes—these crimes live up again, and pass in formidable order before his eyes. (See Psa. l. 21.) Conspicuous amongst the spectres that would move before him would be those of the newly murdered Naboth with his children. (3) This ghastly phantasmagoria would be to him a premonition of the solemnities of the final judgment in which the thousands injured, whether in body or soul, by his bad conduct and influence, would cry to God's justice for vengeance upon the royal culprit. 3. *He humbled himself accordingly.* (1) Before Jehovah. He " rent his clothes " in token of deep grief. (See Gen. xxxvii. 34; Job i. 20; Ezra ix. 3.) " He put sackcloth upon his flesh, and fasted, and lay in sackcloth, and went softly." Here were all the signs of deep contrition before God. They were symbols of the prayer of the heart for mercy. (2) Before men. To put on sackcloth he laid aside those robes of state in which he had prided himself. Instead of moving with his former kingly tramp he now "went softly." (Compare Isa. xxxviii. 15.) He moved with the timid step of a culprit. (3) Who will say his repentance was not genuine? God did not say so. He afterwards, indeed, professed to " hate " a faithful servant of God (ch. xxii. 8). But what does this prove? Simply that he afterwards *relapsed* into sin. And it admonishes us not to presume upon any dogma of infallible final perseverance, but, by the help of God, to " work out our own salvation with fear and trembling."

II. THAT THERE IS MERCY FOR THE PENITENT.   1. *God observed the repentance of Ahab.* (1) He observed it before man had. He saw its first motions in the depths of his heart. He saw the prodigal " while yet a great way off " (Luke xv. 20). (2) Doubtless He graciously encouraged these motions so that they ripened into confession. And does not the goodness of God still lead men to repentance, even the vilest ? 2. *He called the attention of Elijah to it.* (1) To the prophet he said, " Seest thou how Ahab humbleth himself before me." This was an encouragement to the man of God. His labour was not in vain. Ahab required some moral courage to humble himself before Jehovah in the presence of Jezebel. (2) God in His goodness directs His servants to those who are penitent that they may minister words of encouragement to them. Ananias was sent to Saul (Acts ix. 11). 3. *He extended His mercy to the suppliant.* (1) " Because he humbleth himself before me, I will not bring the evil in his days : but in his son's days will I bring the evil upon his house." The mercy is not a reversal of the mischief, neither was the repentance. The mischief is done, and cannot be reversed. Early piety is therefore earnestly to be desired that the mischief of an evil life may be avoided. (2) It was a substantial benefit nevertheless. (*a*) To Ahab personally. It was something to be spared the pain of witnessing the judgments of God upon his wicked house ; but, what is still more considerable, this mercy contained a promise respecting the world to come ; for, and especially in prophecy, things visible are signs or portents of things spiritual. (*b*) It was also a benefit to his nation. For after this, probably, came the war with Ben-hadad, in which God interposed in a very remarkable manner on behalf of His people. In the Septuagint, which translation was made from much older copies of the Hebrew Bible than any now extant, this chapter and that here before it change places ; and the order in the Septuagint is also followed by Josephus. (3) This fact is very important, for it shows also where the backsliding of Ahab commenced. It was evidently in the false mercy which he showed to Ben-hadad. After this relapse God forsook him and handed him over to evil spirits and lying prophets, who wrought his ruin. " He that endureth to the end shall be saved."—J. A. M.

Vers. 1—24.—*The Progress of Sin.* This chapter describes one of the blackest crimes which ever blotted the page of history. The description is so graphic that we seem eye-witnesses of the tragedy, and so suggestive that we can understand the motives and feelings of the principal actors. Naboth has been blamed sometimes for refusing what appeared a reasonable request—that he would sell a piece of land to his rightful king at a fair price. It is evident, however, that he was not only acting within his right, but that he could not have assented to the proposal without breaking the Divine law given by Moses. The paternal inheritance might only be sold in extreme poverty, and then on the condition that it might be redeemed at any time ; and, if not previously redeemed by purchase, it reverted to the original owner at the year of jubilee (Levit. xxv. 13—28). With Naboth it was not the dictate of churlishness, but of conscience, to refuse the proposal of the king. Nor was Ahab's guilt the less because the crime was suggested by Jezebel. He might be deficient in nerve and inventiveness, but he was not in iniquity. Let us trace him in this his hideous downfall, that none of us may be " hardened by the deceitfulness of sin." Our subject is the PROGRESS OF SIN.   We see here—

I. POSSESSIONS LEADING TO COVETOUSNESS. His stately palace and park at Jezreel did not content him. With greedy eye he looked on this tiny plot of free-hold, and resolved to have it. It is not in the power of material possessions to satisfy man. The rich man must be richer still ; the large kingdom must extend itself yet further ; the great business must crush the small competitors, &c. How often this leads to wrongs wrought on the poorer and weaker ! " The love of money is the root of all evil." " Take heed and beware of covetousness, for a man's life consisteth not in the abundance of things that he possesseth."

II. COVETOUSNESS LEADING TO DISCONTENT. "He laid himself down upon his bed, and turned away his face, and would eat no bread." Disappointed of that which he coveted he could find no pleasure in that which he already possessed. Show how easily a discontented habit of mind may be formed, and how it embitters everything. Thankfulness, gladness, and hope are strangled by this serpent sin. The necessity of watching against the rise of this in our children.

III. DISCONTENT LEADING TO EVIL COUNSEL (ver. 7). Ahab was just in the right condition to welcome anything bad. On an ordinary occasion he might have repelled this hideous suggestion. Satan watches his opportunity. His temptations are adapted to our age, our social position, our mood of mind. What would fail to-day may succeed to-morrow. What the youth would spurn the old man may welcome, &c. "Watch and pray, lest ye enter into temptation." It is an evil thing to have a bad counsellor always near you. Let that thought guard us against unholy associates.

IV. EVIL COUNSEL LEADING TO LIES (ver. 10). The fast was a hypocritical device to prepare the minds of the people for the death of Naboth. Its appointment pre-supposed that there was a grievous offence committed by some one, which the community was to mourn. Their suspicions would be ready to fasten on any man who was suddenly and boldly accused by two independent witnesses. The scheme was as subtle as it was sinful. Give examples of the use of deceit and lies in modern life for the purpose of making money, advancing social interests, &c. Show the sinfulness of this.

V. LIES LEADING TO MURDER (ver. 13). Not only was Naboth killed, but his children also (2 Kings ix. 26). Hence the property would revert to the king. It was a cold-blooded murder. Few worse are recorded in history. Seldom is this most heinous crime committed until the way has been paved for it, as here, by lesser sins. Exemplify this.

VI. MURDER LEADING TO RETRIBUTION. Read Elijah's bold and terrible denun-ciation of the crime on the very soil of the coveted vineyard (vers. 20—24). Retribution may linger long, but it comes at last. In the light of many a startling discovery we read the words, "Be sure your sin will find you out."

CONCLUSION.—"Cleanse thou me from secret faults: keep back thy servant also from presumptuous sins," &c.—A. R.

Vers. 27—29.—*Partial Penitence.* Such was the effect of Elijah's message delivered in the vineyard of Naboth. The fearless courage of the prophet had again asserted itself, and once more the king quailed before his terrible words of denunciation. The subject is the more worthy of study because the deceitfulness of the human heart is here laid bare by "the searcher of hearts." If we under-stand Ahab, we shall better understand ourselves.

I. THE DECEITFUL NATURE OF AHAB'S HUMILIATION. We shall show that there was a mixture of the good and evil, of the true and false. 1. *It originated in a true message.* No phantom of his own brain, no utterance of a false prophet misled Ahab; but the declaration of a man who, as he knew by experience, spoke truly, and spoke for God. He dared not refuse credence to the message, but that his heart was unchanged was shown in his continued hatred to the messenger (1 Kings xviii. 17; xxi. 20). In all ages the word of God has been "as a fire," and as a "hammer" (Jer. xxiii. 29). Give examples. The Ninevites, the Jews at Pentecost, &c. It has "pleased God, by the foolishness of preaching, to save them that believe." 2. *It asserted itself in fasting and tears.* These would be natural signs of distress. In themselves they were no evidence of sincerity. It is easier to put on the outward than to experience the inward. There is always danger of letting the visible supersede the invisible, though it is only of value as the honest expression of conviction. Leaves and blossoms may be tied around a dead branch, but that does not make it live. (The perils of Ritualism.) Even under the Old Dispensation this was understood. Samuel said, "To obey is better than sacrifice," &c. David exclaimed, "Thou desirest not sacrifice," &c. (Psa. li. 16, 17; see also Micah vi. 8; Isa. i. 11). Compare the words of our Lord, "Moreover when ye fast, be not as the hypocrites, of a sad countenance; for they disfigure their faces, that they may appear unto men to fast." 3. *It consisted in terror, not in turning.* Ahab was thoroughly alarmed, but imagination rather than conscience was at work within him. He did not forsake his idols, nor give up Naboth's vineyard, nor abandon his self-confidence. See next chapter, which narrates his dealings with Micaiah. Evidently there was no change of heart or of life; nor had his present feeling any abiding influence. He was like those who are alarmed at the thought of hell, not at the thought of sin. They shrink from punishment, but not from guilt. Examples. The drunkard weeping maudlin tears over his poverty; the detected wrong-doer thrown out of employment; the sinner who believes himself to be at the point of death, &c. True repentance makes us feel and act differently towards sin and towards God.

II. The Divine notice of Ahab's humiliation. 1. *It did not escape the Divine search.* God looks down from heaven to see if there were any that do *good.* He rejoices to find not the evil that must be punished, but the feeble germs of good that may be encouraged. (Compare Psa. xiv. 2.) Even such a sinner as Ahab (ver. 25) was not disregarded when he showed the faintest signs of repentance. God would foster them lovingly, as He fosters the seed sown in the warm earth. The prodigal is seen "when yet a great way off." Even the first beginnings of righteousness were commended by our Lord: "Jesus, beholding him, loved him," &c. 2. *It led to the mitigation of the Divine punishment.* Ahab's feeling was real as far as it went. The postponement of punishment was to give opportunity for more genuine repentance. Had that revealed itself, the judgment would have been averted. Compare this with our Lord's washing the feet of Judas, though He knew he was about to betray Him. "The goodness of God leadeth to repentance." See how ready God is to meet those who may return to Him (Acts ii. 38; Joel ii. 12—14). [Note.—We ought to notice and encourage what is right even in those who are not what they should be, commending it whenever it is possible.] 3. *It failed to win a reversal of the Divine judgment.* A temporary repentance may be followed by a temporary reprieve; but final salvation must be preceded by true repentance. If the heart is not turned from sin, it cannot be turned from hell. "Godly sorrow worketh repentance to salvation, not to be repented of; but the sorrow of this world worketh death." Not only must evil be expelled, but good must enter; for if the heart is left "empty, swept, and garnished" by self-reformation, the evil spirits will return. Good must supersede evil; Christ must supplant sin; the Holy Spirit must conquer the evil spirit. (Compare Acts xi. 17, 18.)

A partial penitence gained reprieve, and much more will *a thorough repentance gain justification.* As Trapp says, "If the leaves of repentance be so medicinal, much more the fruit."—A. R.

Vers. 1—4.—*First Steps in the Path of Crime.* I. Unbridled desire. 1. *The spirit in which Ahab came.* He came down to Jezreel not to present a thank-offering to God for recent deliverance, nor to inquire what might be done to meet the wishes or improve the condition of the people. Had he come thus, paths of usefulness would have opened up before him, and, instead of the dark memory of guilt, he would have left behind him blessing and praise. God and man were alike shut out, and self was set up as that which alone was to be regarded and served. Such a spirit not only stands open to temptation; it invites it. Right aims shut out is half Satan's victory. 2. *How the temptation presented itself.* He was about to make improvements upon the palace, and his eye fell on Naboth's vineyard. This made into a garden of herbs would secure greater privacy and allow other improvements to be carried out. As he looked only upon his own things the advantages of the acquisition were magnified, the fire of desire was kindled and fanned into even fiercer flame. A selfish spirit is ready to be set on fire by the slightest spark of evil suggestion. There was much in God's recent goodness, much also in the necessities of Israel, to raise Ahab above so small a care. The spirit of selfish discontent, which "never is, but always to be, blest," makes thankfulness and service alike impossible. If it rule us we are already set in the way of sin. From the spot on which we stand a hundred dark paths branch out—envies, jealousies, false-hood, dishonest dealing, mean lying artifices, thefts, murders. When tempted to set the heart on what we have not, let us come back into the midst of the good which God has given, and say that if He see it to be best for us, that will be given too. 3. *How the object was pursued*. All restraints were cast aside. Ahab's offer (ver. 2) seems at first sight most generous. But it shut out of sight (1) the ties which bound Naboth to his inheritance, and (2) the duty he owed to God. The Israelite could not alienate his lot even when pressed by direst necessity. It might be parted with for a time, but it returned again to its rightful owners at the year of jubilee. Ahab's offer was a temptation to Naboth to think lightly of God's arrangements and to despise his birthright.

II. MISDIRECTED ANGER. "Ahab came into his house heavy and displeased," not with himself, but with Naboth. His anger was not against his sin, but against the man who had rebuked it. He might have stood and said, "I have sinned. I have abused my position. I have been caring for my own good, and not for theirs over whom God has set me." But he took the side of his sin against the truth. He that struck at that struck him. When God meets us as He then met Ahab, we must either return humbled and penitent into the right way, or withstand Him and pass into deeper darkness.—U.

Vers. 5—14.—*Sin's friendships, and what they lead to.* I. THE SINFUL FIND MANY HELPERS. Ahab seems to have done all that he was able or cared to do. He had tempted Naboth and failed, and the matter seemed to have come to an end. But where Ahab stops, Satan's servants meet him and carry on the work. Jezebel prevails on him to tell the story, and the elders of Jezreel and its sons of Belial are ready to do their part also, to give him his desire and steep his soul in crime. The man who is casting away means and character and health and eternal life will find friends to take the part of his worse against his better self, and agents enough to aid him in accomplishing his sinful will. It is vain to think of arresting a career of vice merely by change of place. Satan has his servants everywhere.

II. THE MISUSE OF INFLUENCE. There is much that may be admired in Jezebel's conduct. However false she was to others, she was true to her own. With tender-ness, which lends a peculiar grace to a strong, regal nature like hers, she approaches the moody monarch. Under the warm sunshine of loving sympathy the bands which bind the burden to his soul melt away. It is laid down and exposed to view. But however góod the impulses which incite the wicked to action, their feet take to the paths of sin. 1. *Her sympathy becomes fierce championship of wrong.* There is love for Ahab, but no consideration for Naboth, and no regard to the voice of justice and of God. How much human love to-day is after the pattern of Jezebel's—narrow, selfish, unjust! The home is everything; the world outside has no claims, sometimes not even rights! Others are regarded with pleasure as they favour those we love; with aversion and hatred so soon as they oppose them, or even stand in their way. Homes are meant to be training schools for God's sons and daughters, where they may learn to be patient, forbearing, less exacting, able to make allowances for difference of disposition and of judgment, and so pass out able to do a brother's, sister's part in the great world around them. But Jezebel's affection frustrates God's plan and arms the home against the world it was meant to serve. 2. *She goads him on to greater sin.* She blames him not for setting his heart so upon a trifle, but for letting the matter rest where it did. She reminds him of his might and Naboth's weakness: "Dost thou now govern?" &c. How often does the sympathy of the wicked daringly recommend what the heart had feared to think, and this too with reproaches of weakness, of wrongs and slights left unavenged! Instead of quenching the fire of hate, they fan it into fiercer flame. 3. *She bears him onward into crime* (vers. 7—10). Ahab's very weakness would have prevented him shedding Naboth's blood, but her subtle brain and indomitable will supply what is needful to steep his soul in guilt. How many dark stains have been in this very way fixed upon the page of history! How much genius and talent have thus served, and are serving now, the devil's purpose!

III. THE EVIL WROUGHT BY TIME-SERVERS (vers. 11—15).   There is nothing to relieve the baseness of the elders and nobles of Jezreel. They were not impelled by misguided affection to avenge a fancied wrong. They could not even plead ignorance. They were behind the scenes and arranged for the trial. It was murder of the deepest dye—murder done under the guise of zeal for the offended majesty of God. They had one of the grandest opportunities of shielding innocence and rebuking wickedness in high places. They had only to say they could not lend themselves to such a deed. But these do not stand alone. The greatest crimes in history have been wrought in this very way. Is there no place to-day over which "Jezreel" might well be written? Are there no men and no causes frowned upon, not because that in themselves they deserve such treatment, but because they are not in favour, and it will not pay to befriend them? Are there none who will use their influence in favour of a good cause when it is safe to do so, but who will be looked for in vain when it sorely needs to be befriended? There may be no crime wrought now in this land such as was then done in Israel; but should the time come, these are the men who will do as the elders and nobles did then. The spirit is the same, and in the like circumstances it will bear the same fruit.—U.

Vers. 15—29.—*Guilt and Mercy.* I. TO ENJOY THE FRUITS OF SIN IS TO TAKE ITS GUILT. "Hast *thou* killed?" &c. It is not said that Ahab knew of the plot. The plain inference is that he did not. *Jezebel* wrote to the elders, and to her the tidings were sent that the deed was done. But if Ahab did not know before, he knew after. Knowing how it had been procured he nevertheless received it, and heard as he stood there the word of the Lord : "Hast *thou killed*, and also taken possession?" There are men, for example, who could not pass their days in the vile drink traffic. They could not sleep at night for thought of the wives and mothers and children whose misery had pleaded in God's sight against them and their work. The thought of the souls they had helped to lead down into the eternal darkness would terrify them. But they can pocket the gains of that very trade; they can receive the higher rent which their property secures because it is let to the sellers of drink, and live in quietness, and sit at the Lord's table, and die in good esteem, and go forth to meet—what? the same judgment as the publican! Your reputable merchant may not lie and cheat; but if the young men that serve behind his counters do so, and if he knowingly pockets the gains of such baseness, he is equally guilty in God's sight. To take the fruit of falsehood and oppression and wrong is to stain our souls with their guilt. "Thus saith the Lord, In the place where dogs licked the blood of Naboth shall dogs lick thy blood, *even thine.*" "Behold I will bring evil upon thee," &c. (vers. 21—24).

II. WHAT IT MEANS WHEN A MAN FINDS THE TRUTH HATEFUL. Ahab's question, "Hast thou found me?" &c., was a self-revelation. There were many to whom Elijah's presence would have been like that of an angel of God; but to Ahab it is as the shadow of death. And the explanation was, "Because thou hast sold thyself to work evil in the sight of the Lord." It is only *to death* that the truth is a savour of death. He was sin's bondman. For the gratification of evil desire he had sold himself to work Satan's will, and now in his attitude to God's servant he was owning Satan still as master. It is easy to listen with approval, and with pleasure even, when other men's sins are dealt with; but when our own are touched—when we are met with our feet standing in Naboth's vineyard, what is our attitude toward the truth? Is it anger or submission? Whom do we own as master, Satan or God?

III. THE RICHES OF GOD'S MERCY (vers. 25—29). 1. *The greatness of Ahab's sin.* He had outstripped all who had gone before him, great as their sins had been; "but there was none like unto Ahab," &c. 2. *The inadequacy of his repentance.* It was no doubt sincere, but it did not go far enough. It was fear of judgment, not loathing of sin. 3. *The fulness of the Divine compassion.* Verses 25 and 26 might well have been a prelude to the record of full and speedy vengeance, and especially so in view of the unsatisfactory nature of his sorrow. But it is the introduction to the story of mercy. All that sin—sin of deepest dye—will not prevent God running forth to meet Ahab so soon as he *begins* to turn to Him. That sorrow, shallow though it was, God had marked and accepted. " Seest thou how Ahab ?" &c. God is not a stern, relentless Judge. Father's heart has never yearned over child as God's over us.—U.

Ver. 20.—*Naboth's Vineyard.* The robbery and murder of Naboth form one of the darkest episodes in the story of Ahab's life. We see that idolatry and persecution were not the only crimes into which Jezebel seduced him. Indeed, such iniquities never stand alone. They would naturally be the parents of many more. He was probably guilty of many such acts of cruel wrong during his wicked career. This is related to show how completely he had " sold himself to work evil in the sight of the Lord." Let us think of (1) his sin, (2) his punishment, (3) his remorse.

I. His sin. It had many elements of moral wrong in it, and is not to be characterized by any one particular designation. 1. *Avarice.* Large and rich as his royal domain was, he envied Naboth the possession of his little vineyard. 2. *Oppression.* It was a wicked abuse of power. " Might " to him was " right." 3. *Impiety.* Ahab must have known that he was tempting Naboth to the violation of an express Divine command (Num. xxxvi. 7). 4. *Abject moral weakness.* This is seen in his childish petulance (ver. 4) and in his mean subserviency to the imperious will of Jezebel. 5. *Base hypocrisy*, in subjecting the injured man to the decision of a mock tribunal. Crimes like this generally present various phases of evil thought and feeling; and when they attempt to cover themselves with a false veil of rectitude, it only tends to deepen immeasurably our sense of their iniquity.

II. His punishment. The prophet was assuming his true function in pronouncing this swift judgment on the cruel wrong that had been committed. His calling was to proclaim and enforce the laws of eternal righteousness, to vindicate the oppressed, to rebuke injustice, and that not least, but rather most of all, when it sat enthroned on the seats of authority and power. Note respecting this punishment. 1. *Its certainty.* Ahab could not really be surprised that his " enemy had found " him, for that " enemy " was but the instrument of a God to whom " all things are naked and opened." " The eyes of the Lord are in every place, beholding the evil and the good," and the transgressor can never escape His righteous judgment. " Be sure your sin will find you out " (Num. xxxii. 23). 2. *Its correspondence with the crime.* " In the place where the dogs licked the blood of Naboth," &c. (ver. 19). The principle involved in this has often been a marked feature of the Divine retributions. " Whatsoever a man soweth," &c. (Gal. vi. 7, 8). " They have sown the wind, and they shall reap the whirlwind " (Hosea viii. 7). 3. *Its delay.* The sentence was fully executed only in the person of his son Joram (2 Kings ix. 25, 26); but this in no way alters the character or lessens the terribleness of it as a punishment upon *him.* Especially when we remember what an instalment of the full penalty was given in the violence of his own death (ch. xxii. 34—37). " Because sentence against an evil work is not executed speedily, therefore the heart of the sons of men is fully set in them to do evil " (Eccles. viii. 11). But when, space being thus given them for repentance, they abuse it, they do but " treasure up wrath for themselves against the day of wrath," and, falling under the righteous vengeance of God, they do not escape " till they have paid the uttermost farthing." Thus did Ahab inherit the woe pronounced on him who thinks to secure any good for himself by iniquity and blood (Hab. ii. 12). Ill-gotten gain always brings with it a curse.

III. His remorse (ver. 27). It can scarcely be called repentance. It may have been sincere enough so far as it went, and for this reason God delayed the threatened punishment; but it was wanting in the elements of a true repentance. It was the compunction of a guilty conscience, but not the sacred agony of a renewed heart. It sprang from sudden alarm at the inevitable consequences of his sin, but not from a true hatred of the sin itself. It soon passed away, and left him still more a slave to the evil to which he had " sold himself " than he was before. " For godly sorrow worketh repentance to salvation not to be repented of: but the sorrow of the world worketh death " (2 Cor. vii. 10).—W.

EXPOSITION.

CHAPTER XXII. 1—53.

THE EXPEDITION OF AHAB AND JEHOSHA-
PHAT AGAINST RAMOTH-GILEAD. THE DEATH
OF AHAB. THE REIGNS OF JEHOSHAPHAT
AND AHAZIAH.

Ver. 1.—**And they continued** [rather,
rested. Heb. *sate, dwelt.* Cf. Judg. v. 17.
The LXX. has ἐκάθισε, sing.] **three years
without war** [The Hebrew explains the
"rested"—*there was not war,* &c. See Ewald,
286 *g.* The three years (not full years,
as the next verse shows) are to be
counted from the second defeat of Ben-
hadad; the history, that is to say, is resumed from ch. xx. 34—43. Rawlinson
conjectures that it was during this period
that the Assyrian invasion, under Shalmaneser II., took place. The Black Obelisk tells us that Ahab of Jezreel joined a
league of kings, of whom Ben-hadad was
one, against the Assyrians, furnishing a
force of 10,000 footmen and 2000 chariots;
see "Hist. Illust." pp. 113, 114. The common danger might well compel a cessation
of hostilities] **between Syria and Israel.**

Ver. 2.—**And it came to pass in the third
year** [Of the peace; not after the death of
Naboth, as Stanley], **that Jehoshaphat the
king of Judah came down** [The journey to
Jerusalem being invariably described as a
"going up," one from Jerusalem to the
provinces would naturally be spoken of as a
"going down"| **to the king of Israel.** [For
aught that appears, this was the first time
that the monarchs of the sister kingdoms
had met, except in battle, since the disrup
tion, though the marriage of Jehoram, son
of Jehoshaphat, with Athaliah, the daughter
of Ahab and Jezebel, had taken place some
years before this date (2 Chron. xviii. 1, 2).
It is probable that it was the growing power
of Syria had led to this affinity and alliance.]

Ver. 3.—**And the king of Israel said unto
his servants** [During the visit. It seems
likely that Jehoshaphat went down to
Samaria by Ahab's invitation, and that the
latter then had this campaign in view. The
chronicler says that Ahab "incited," or
"stirred him up" (same word as in ch.
xxi. 25) to go with him to battle. Ahab
was unable to contend single-handed, and
without Divine assistance which he could
not now look for—against Syria; and saw
no means of compelling the execution of
the treaty which Ben-hadad had made with
him (ch. xx. 34), and which he appears to
have shamelessly broken, except by the help
of Jehoshaphat, whose military organiza-

tion at this time must have been great, and,
indeed, complete (2 Chron. xvii. 10—19).
It is in favour of this view that Ahab entertained him and his large retinue with such
profuse hospitality. The chronicler, who
dwells on the number of sheep and oxen
slain for the feast, intimates that it was
this generous reception "persuaded" Jehoshaphat to join in the war], **Know ye
that Ramoth in Gilead** [Generally, as
below (vers. 4, 6, &c.), "Ramoth-Gilead,"
i.e., of Gilead. See note on ch. iv. 13.
This "great frontier fortress was, in the
hands of Syria, even after many reverses,
a constant menace against Israel" (Stanley)]
is ours [*i.e.,* it was one of the cities which
Ben-hadad had promised to restore (ch.
xx. 34). This shows that, as we might
expect from a man of Ben-hadad's overbearing yet pusillanimous character, he
had not kept good faith. Though so long a
time had elapsed, it was still in his hands],

and we be still [חָשִׁ֑ים is onomatopoetic,
like our "hush." Marg. rightly, *silent from
taking it.* The word conveys very expres-
sively that they had been afraid of making
any movement to assert their rights, lest
they should attract the attention and anger
of their powerful and incensed neighbour],
**and take it not out of the hand of the king
of Syria?** [It is hardly likely that Ahab
could have forgotten the warning of ch.
xx. 42. It is probable that Ben-hadad's
flagrant disregard of his treaty engagements
determined him to run all risks, especially
if he could secure the help of the then
powerful king of Judah.]

Ver. 4.—**And he said unto Jehoshaphat,
Wilt thou go with me to battle to Ramoth-
Gilead?** [It is probable this question was
asked with some misgivings. Such an
alliance was altogether new, and Ahab
might well wonder how the idea would
strike a pious prince like Jehoshaphat.
That the latter ought to have refused his
help, we know from 2 Chron. xix. 2.] **And
Jehoshaphat said to the king of Israel, I am
as thou art** [Heb. *as I as thou*], **my people
as thy people, my horses as thy horses.**
[From the ready and unreserved way in
which he at once engages in this war, we
may safely conclude that he, too, had
reason to fear the power of Syria. Probably
Ben-hadad, when he besieged Samaria (ch.
xx. 1), had formed the idea of reducing the
whole of Palestine to subjection. And
Jehoshaphat would remember that Ramoth-
Gilead, where the Syrian king was still en-

trenched, was but forty miles distant from Jerusalem. Bähr holds that horses are specially mentioned " because they formed an essential part of the military power" (Psa. xxxiii. 16, 17 ; Prov. xxi. 31). It is true that in a campaign against the Syrians they would be especially useful (see on ch. xx. 1.) ; but they receive no mention at the hands of the chronicler, who reads instead of this last clause, " And we (or I) will be with thee in the war."]

Ver. 5.—And Jehoshaphat said unto the king of Israel, Inquire, I pray thee, at [This word is redundant] the word of the Lord to-day. [בַּיוֹם hardly conveys that "he asks to have the prophets called in at once," " lest Ahab should consent in word and put off the inquiry in act " (Rawlinson); but rather means, " at this crisis," "under these circumstances." This request agrees well with what we learn elsewhere as to Jehoshaphat's piety (2 Chron. xvii. 4—9 ; xix. 5—7, &c.) And, remembering how Ahab's late victories had been foretold by a prophet, and had been won by the help of Jehovah, Jehoshaphat might well suppose that his new ally would be eager to know the word of the Lord.]

Ver. 6.—Then the king of Israel gathered the prophets [Called by Micaiah " his prophets" (ver. 22), and "thy prophets" (ver. 23)] together, about four hundred men [From the number (cf. ch. xviii. 19) it has been concluded that these were "the prophets of the groves," i.e., of Astarte, who escaped the massacre of the Baal prophets (ch. xviii. 40). Others have supposed that they were prophets of Baal. But both these suppositions are negatived (1) by the fact that Jehoshaphat asks Ahab to "inquire at the word of Jehovah," and (2) that these prophets profess to speak in the name and by the Spirit of Jehovah (vers. 11, 12, 24). Moreover (3) Ahab would hardly have insulted Jehoshaphat by bringing the prophets of Baal or Astarte before him (Waterland in Wordsworth). And yet that they were not true prophets of the Lord, or of the " sons of the prophets," appears (1) from ver. 7, where Jehoshaphat asks for a "prophet of the Lord ; " and (2), from ver. 20 sqq., where Micaiah disclaims them, and is found in direct opposition to them. The only conclusion open to us, consequently—and it is now generally adopted—is that they were the priests of the high places of Bethel and Dan, the successors of those whom Jeroboam had introduced into the priestly office. It need cause us no surprise to find these priests here described as "prophets" (cf. Jer. xxii. 13 ; Ezek. xiii. 1), and as claiming prophetic gifts, for the priests of

Baal bore the same name (ch. xviii. 19, 22, &c.), and apparently pretended to similar powers. "No ancient people considered any cultus complete without a class of men through whom the god might be questioned " (Bähr). The existence of so large a number of prophets of the calves proves that the inroads of idolatry had by no means destroyed the calf-worship. If its priests were so many, its worshippers cannot have been few], and said unto them, Shall I go against Ramoth-Gilead to battle, or shall I forbear ? And they said, Go up; for the Lord [אֲדֹנָי It is very significant that at first they hesitate to use the ineffable name. It was probably this circumstance excited Jehoshaphat's suspicions. It has been said that the reason why he was dissatisfied with this answer is unexplained ; but when we remember how careful the true prophet was to speak in the name of Jehovah (chs. xiv. 7 ; xvii. 1,14; xx. 13, 14, 28), we can hardly doubt that it was their mention of "Adonai "occasioned his misgivings. The chronicler gives the word as Elohim] shall deliver it [LXX. διδοὺς δώσει, shall surely give it] into the hand of the king.

Ver. 7.—And Jehoshaphat said, Is there not here a prophet of the Lord [Heb. Jehovah] besides [i.e., in addition to these soi-disant prophets. He hardly likes to say bluntly that he cannot regard them as inspired, but at the same time hints clearly that he cannot be satisfied as to their mission and authority], that we might inquire of him ?

Ver. 8.—And the king of Israel said unto Jehoshaphat, There is yet one man [Cf. ch. xviii. 22], Micaiah [The name (=Who is like Jehovah ?) is as appropriate to the man who bore it as Elijah's name was to him (ch. xvii. 1 ; cf. xviii. 39). But it is not an uncommon name in the Old Testament—it is borne by eight different persons. Compare Michael, "Who is like God ?"] the son of Imlah [The chronicler writes the name Imla, יְמְלָא], by whom we may inquire of the Lord [Ahab evidently had wished Jehoshaphat to understand that the prophets already consulted were prophets of Jehovah, as no doubt they claimed to be. One of them bore a name in which the sacred Jah formed a part]: but I hate [שָׂנֵאתִי (cf. odi), have learned to hate] him [Ahab had good reasons for not caring to consult a man whom he had put into prison (see ver. 26, and compare Matt. xiv. 3), because of his reproofs or unwelcome predictions. Josephus, and Jewish writers generally, identify Micaiah with the nameless prophet of ch. xxi. 42]; **for he doth not prophesy good concerning me, but evil.** [The chronicler adds כָּל־יָמָיו ; *i.e.*, persistently, throughout his whole career. Ahab insinuates that Micaiah is actuated by personal dislike. The commentators refer to Homer. Il. iv., 106—108.] **And Jehoshaphat said, Let not the king say so.** [He does not mean that the prophet cannot say just what he will, but suggests that Ahab is prejudiced against him. Perhaps he suspected that there might be a very different reason for Micaiah's sinister predictions.]

Ver. 9.—**Then the king of Israel called an officer** [Heb. *one eunuch.* So the LXX., εὐνοῦχον ἕνα. So that Samuel's forebodings have been realized (1 Sam. viii. 15, marg.) Probably, like Ebed Melech, *the Ethiopian* (Jer. xxxviii. 7), he was a foreigner; possibly a prisoner of war (Herod. iii. 49; vi. 32). Deut. xxiii. 1 suggests that even such a king as Ahab would hardly inflict this humiliation upon an Israelite. From 1 Chron. xxviii. 1, Heb., we gather that even David's court had its eunuchs, and we may be sure that Solomon's enormous harem could not be maintained without them. In later days we find them prominent in the history, and occupying important positions under the king (2 Kings viii. 6; ix. 32; xxiii. 11; xxv. 19; Jer. xxix. 2; xxxiv. 19; lii. 25, &c. Cf. Gen. xxxvii. 36)], **and said, Hasten hither Micaiah the son of Imlah.**

Ver. 10.—**And the king of Israel and Jehoshaphat the king of Judah sat each on his throne** ["Oriental kings had portable thrones, which they took with them upon their journeys" (Herod. vii. 212. Layard, "Nineveh and Babylon," p. 150) Rawlinson], **having put on their robes** [As a council of state was to be held, the kings put on their official vestments. בְּגָדִים simply means "coverings," "clothes," but that the special royal dress is here intended is clear, as Bähr observes, from Levit. xxi. 10. This gathering of prophets and counsellors seems to have followed the banquet. When Jehoshaphat expressed his readiness to go to war, Ahab appears to have forthwith convened this assembly, in order that the matter might be put in train at once. Ewald says a review of the troops was designed, but of this the text knows nothing] **in a void place** [Heb. *a threshing-floor.* See note on ch. xxi. 1. The "floor" implies not only a vacant space, but an exalted position. Ordinarily, it would not be enclosed within the city walls, nor does it appear that this floor was] **in the entrance** [The Hebrew has no preposition; simply פֶּתַח which would be more correctly rendered "*at* the entrance." The town gate was the great place of concourse (2 Kings vii. 1). Here, too, justice was dispensed. See Ruth iv. 1; 2 Sam. xv. 2; xix. 8; Pss. lxix. 12; cxxvii. 5; Deut. xxi. 19; Gen. xix. 1; xxiii. 10; Amos v. 12, 15, &c.] **of the gate of Samaria; and all the prophets prophesied before them.** [They continued their prophesyings even whilst Micah was being summoned. Or the reference may be to the prophesyings of ver. 6.

Ver. 11.—**And Zedekiah** [This name = "Justice of Jehovah," is one of the proofs that these cannot have been prophets of Baal, as Stanley and others suppose] **the son of Chenaanah** [= "Canaanitess." But we gather from 1 Chron. vii. 10 that this, like Shelomith, was a man's name. The Benjamite there mentioned may be identical with the father (or ancestor) of Zedekiah] **made him** [Rawlinson would translate "*had* made him." He says that the horns must have "been made previously, in expectation of some such occasion as that now afforded him." But it is quite conceivable that during the prophesyings, which clearly lasted some time, the idea occurred to Zedekiah, and it would not take long to put it into execution] **horns of iron** [Thenius understands that these were iron spikes held on the forehead. But the reference is clearly to the horns of a bullock, and the appropriateness of the prophetic act is only manifest when we remember that Ephraim is compared to a bullock (Deut. xxxiii. 17), and, more, that Moses spake beforehand of the strength of his horns, and predicted that with them he should "*push the people* together to the ends of the earth." Not only, that is to say, was the horn a familiar Oriental symbol of power (1 Sam. ii. 1, 10; 2 Sam. xxii. 3; Pss. lxxxix. 24; xcii. 10; Dan. vii. 21; viii. 8, &c.), but it was identified in a peculiar manner with the powerful tribe of Ephraim; in other words, with the kingdom of Israel. This symbolical act was not necessarily an imitation of the action of Ahijah (ch. xi. 30). Such acted parables were not uncommon among the prophets (2 Kings xiii. 15; Isa. xx. 2; Jer. xiii. 1; xix. 10; xxxii. 9 sqq.; Ezek. iv., v.; Acts xxi. 11)] : **and he said, Thus saith the Lord** [Heb. *Jehovah.* He now uses the sacred name; no doubt because of Jehoshaphat's demand, ver. 7], **With these shalt thou push** [the word of Deut. xxxiii. 17] **the Syrians, until thou have consumed them.**

Ver. 12.—**And all the prophets prophesied** [Heb. *were prophesying*] **so, saying,**

Go up to Ramoth-Gilead, and prosper [a Hebraism for "thou wilt prosper." Gesenius, Gram. § 127. 2, cites parallels in Gen. xlii. 18; Prov. xx. 13; Psa. xxxvii. 27; Job xxii. 21; Isa. viii. 9; xxix. 9, and reminds us that in the Latin *divide et impera* we have the same idiom]: for the Lord [all speak in His name now, hoping thus to satisfy the king of Judah] shall deliver it into the king's hand.

Ver. 13.—And the messenger that was gone [or *went*] to call Micaiah, spake unto him, saying, Behold now, the words of the prophets declare good unto the king with one mouth [Heb. *one mouth good to the king.* The messenger may possibly have had instructions to seek to conciliate Micaiah. In any case he thinks it well to tell him of the unanimity of the prophets. His testimony, he suggests, will surely agree with theirs] : let thy word, I pray thee, be like the word of one of them, and speak that which is good. [Heb. *speak good.*]

Ver. 14.—And Micaiah said, As the Lord liveth, what the Lord saith unto me, that will I speak. [We are forcibly reminded of the answer of Balaam, Num. xxii. 18, 38. And we may see not only in the suggestion of this messenger, but also in Ahab's belief (ver. 8), that Micaiah could prophesy at pleasure, a striking correspondence with the ideas of Balak (*ib.* v. 6, 17). Instead of regarding the prophet as being merely the mouthpiece of Deity, he was believed in that age to have a supernatural influence with God, and to be entrusted with magical powers to shape the future, as well as to foretell it.]

Ver. 15.—So he came to the king. And the king said unto him, Micaiah, shall we go against Ramoth-Gilead to battle, or shall we forbear? [Same words as in ver. 6. There is an apparent studied fairness in this repetition. It is as if Ahab said, "Despite his prejudice against me, I will not attempt to influence his mind. I only deal with him as with the rest."] And he answered him, Go, and prosper : for the Lord shall deliver it into the hand of the king. [As Ahab's inquiry is the echo of the question of ver. 6, so is Micaiah's response identical with the answer of the prophets. He simply echoes their words, of which, perhaps, he has been informed by the eunuch. There was an exquisite propriety in this. The question was insincere ; the reply was ironical (cf. ch. xviii. 27). Ahab is answered "according to the multitude of his idols" (Ezek. xiv. 4). He wishes to be deceived, and he is deceived. No doubt Micaiah's mocking tone showed that his words were ironical; but Ahab's hollow tone had already proved to Micaiah that he

was insincere ; that he did not care to know the will of the Lord, and wanted prophets who would speak to him smooth things and prophesy deceits (Isa. xxx. 10).]

Ver. 16.—And the king said unto him, How many times shall I adjure thee that thou tell me nothing but that which is true in the name of the Lord ? [Rawlinson concludes from these words that "this mocking manner was familiar to Micaiah, who had used it in some former dealing with the Israelite monarch." But we must remember that Ahab's words were really addressed to Jehoshaphat. He is so manifestly playing a part, that we need not assume that he is strictly truthful. His great desire evidently is to discredit Micah's predictions, which he clearly perceives, from the bitter and ironical tone of the latter, will be adverse to him.]

Ver. 17.—And he said [We may imagine how entire was the change of tone. He now speaks with profound seriousness. Thenius sees in the peculiarity and originality of this vision a proof of the historical truth of this history. "We feel that we are gradually drawing nearer to the times of the later prophets. It is a vision which might rank amongst those of Isaiah or Ezekiel" (Stanley)], I saw all Israel scattered upon the hills, as sheep that have not a shepherd : and the Lord said, These have no master : let them return every man to his house in peace. [The last words are illustrated by the command of ver. 31 ; compare ver. 36. We may also picture the effect these words would have on the assembly at the city gate. For, however much they might be inclined to discredit Micaiah's words, and however much the reckless, unreasoning war-spirit might possess them, there were none who did not understand that this vision portended the dispersion of the Israelite army and the death of its leader. King and people had been constantly represented under the figure of shepherd and sheep, and notably by Moses himself, who had used these very words, "sheep without a shepherd" (Num. xxvii. 17 ; cf. Psa. lxxviii. 70, 71 ; Isa. xliv. 28; Jer. xxiii. 1, 2 ; Ezek. xxxiv. *passim*. It is observable that Micaiah's vision, like Zedekiah's parable, borrows the language of the Pentateuch. Coincidences of this remote character are the most powerful proofs that the Pentateuch was then written.]

Ver. 18.—And the king of Israel said unto Jehoshaphat, Did I not tell thee that he would [Heb. *say to thee, He will*, &c.] prophesy no good concerning me but evil ? [It is clear that Ahab had understood perfectly the purport of Micaiah's words. He now appeals to them as a proof of the latter's malice.]

Ver. 10. **And he said, Hear thou** [in 2 Chron. xviii. 18, *Hear ye*] **therefore** [The LXX. has οὐχ οὕτως, whence it would almost appear that they had the text לֹא כֵן before them (Bähr). But לָכֵן is every way to be preferred. It is emphatic by position, and the meaning is, " Since you will have it that my words are prompted by malice, hear the message I have for you," &c.] **the word of the Lord. I saw the Lord** [It is not implied (Wordsworth) that he had any direct and objective vision of God, such as Moses (Exod. xxxiv. 5), Elijah, or St. Stephen. He here declares what he may have seen in dream or trance. (Cf. Rev. i. 10 ; iv. 2 ; Isa. vi. 1 ; Ezek. i. 1.) It was a real but inner vision (Keil). In its interpretation the caution of Peter Martyr is carefully to be borne in mind ; *Omnia haec dicuntur ἀνθρωποπαθῶς*] **sitting on his throne** [It was natural for some of the commentators to see in these words a reference to the two kings then sitting in their royal apparel, each upon his throne. But it is very doubtful whether any such thought was present in the mind of the speaker, who simply relates a vision of the past], **and all the host of heaven** [The celestial powers, cherubim, angels, archangels, who surround the Lord of glory. That there can be no reference to the sun, moon, and stars, notwithstanding that these are called " the host of heaven" in Deut. iv. 19, xvii. 3, is clear from the next words. The expression is to be explained by Gen. xxxii. 1, 2] **standing by him** [עָלָיו ; for the meaning, see Gen. xviii. 8] **on his right hand and on his left.** [The resemblance of this vision to that of Isaiah (ch. vi. 1—8) must not be overlooked.]

Ver. 20.—**And the Lord said, Who shall persuade** [Same word in Exod. xxii. 16, Heb. ; Judg. xiv. 15 ; xvi. 5 ; Prov. i. 10, &c.; in all of which instances it is translated "entice." Compare with this question that of Isa. vi. 8.] **Ahab, that he may go up and fall at Ramoth-Gilead ?** [The meaning is that Ahab's death in battle had been decreed in the counsels of God, and that the Divine Wisdom had devised means for accomplishing His purpose.] **And one said on this manner, and another said** [Heb. *saying*] **on that manner.** [Bähr again quotes from Peter Martyr: " *Innuit varios providentiae Dei modos, quibus decreta sua ad exitum perducit*, and adds that in this vision "inner and spiritual processes are regarded as real phenomena, nay, even as persons."]

Ver. 21.—**And there came forth a spirit** [Heb. *the spirit*. By some, especially of the earlier commentators, understood of the evil spirit. But the view now generally adopted (Thenius, Keil, Bähr) is that " the spirit of prophecy" is meant, " the power which, going forth from God and taking possession of a man, makes him a prophet (1 Sam. x. 6, 10; xix. 20, 23). The נָבִיא is the אִישׁ הָרוּחַ (Hosea ix. 7) " Bähr. This power is here personified], **and stood before the Lord, and said, I** [emphatic in the Hebrew] **will persuade** [or entice] **him.**

Ver. 22.—**And the Lord said unto him, Wherewith ?** [Heb. *By what?*] **And he said, I will go forth, and I will be a lying spirit** [Heb. *a spirit of a lie*. Cf. Zech. xiii. 2 ; 1 John iv. 6] **in the mouth of all his prophets.** [His prophets, not God's. Cf. 2 Kings iii. 13.] **And he said, Thou shalt persuade him, and prevail also : go forth, and do so.**

Ver. 23.—**Now therefore, behold, the Lord hath put a lying spirit in the mouth of all these thy** [Cf. ὁ οἶκος ὑμῶν, Matt. xxiii. 38] **prophets** [This statement, especially to those who have taken the narrative literally, and who have seen in " the spirit" either one of the angels of God, or Satan himself, has presented almost insuperable difficulties. The main difficulty lies in the fact that the Almighty and All Holy is here made to give His sanction to deceit and lying, for the purpose of tempting Ahab to his death. We have precisely the same difficulty, though, if possible, more directly expressed in Ezek. xiv. 9 : " If the prophet be deceived . . . I the Lord have deceived that prophet." Cf. Jer. xx. 7 ; 1 Sam. xvi. 15. But this difficulty vanishes if we remember that this is anthropopathic language, and is merely meant to convey that God had "taken the house of Israel in their own heart," because they were " estranged from Him through their idols" (Ezek. xiv. 5). Ahab wished to be guided by false prophets, and the justice of God decreed that he should be guided by them to his ruin. Sin is punished by sin. " God proves His holiness most of all by this, that He punishes evil by evil, and destroys it by itself" (Bähr). Ahab had chosen lying instead of truth : by lying—according to the *lex talionis*—he should be destroyed. The difficulty, in fact, is that of the permission of evil in the world ; of the use of existent evil by God to accomplish His purposes of good], **and the Lord** [not I alone, ver. 18] **hath spoken** [*i.e.*, decreed] **evil concerning thee.**

Ver. 24.—**But Zedekiah the son of Che-**

naanah [Rawlinson holds that he was a sort of coryphaeus of the false prophets. It is more probable that, having put himself forward on a former occasion (ver. 11), he now feels specially aggrieved at Micaiah's blunt assertion, that he and the rest have been possessed by a spirit of lies] **went near, and smote Micaiah** [A thoroughly natural touch. But the whole narrative has every mark of naturalness and veracity. It is easy to see how enraged Zedekiah would be at the slight cast upon his prophetic powers. Apparently this gross indignity elicited no protest or word of displeasure from either of the kings. Micaiah, like Elijah, was left alone], **on the cheek** [cf. Job xvi. 10; Lam. iii. 30; Luke vi. 29; and above all Matt. xxvi. 67; Luke xxii. 64; Acts xxiii. 2. Herein Micaiah had "the fellowship of sufferings" (Phil. iii. 10) with our blessed Lord. Rawlinson thinks that his hands would be bound, but this is extremely improbable. In that case Ahab could hardly have asked him to prophesy (ver. 15), or if he did, Jehoshaphat would know beforehand what to expect], **and said, Which way** [Heb. *What*, or *where*. The chronicler supplies "way," thereby bringing the expression into unison with ch. xiii. 12; 2 Kings iii. 8; Job xxxviii. 24] **went** [Heb. *passed, crossed*, עָבַר] **the Spirit of the Lord** [These words are important, as showing that the speaker had not identified "the spirit" of ver. 21 with the evil spirit: Job. i. 6 sqq.] **from me to speak unto thee?** [It is pretty clear from these words, in connexion with ver. 23, that Zedekiah had been conscious of an inspiration, of a spirit not his own, which impelled him to speak and act as he did. We must not attach too much importance to a taunting and passionate speech, but its meaning appears to be: I have spoken in the name and by the spirit of Jehovah. Thou claimest to have done the same. How is it that the Spirit of God speaks one thing by me, another by thee? Thou hast seen (ver. 19) the secret counsels of Heaven. Tell us, then, which way, &c.

Ver. 25.—**And Micaiah said, Behold, thou shalt see** [Keil understands, "that the Spirit of the Lord had departed from thee." But the meaning rather appears to be, "Thou shalt see which was a true prophet." He does not answer the insolent question, but says, "Thou wilt alter thy mind in the day," &c. With this may be compared our Lord's words, Matt. xxvi. 64. He also manifests our Lord's spirit (1 Peter ii. 22 sqq.) "as if the Great Example had already appeared before him" (Bähr)] **in that day when thou shalt go into an inner chamber** [see note on ch. xx. 30] **to hide thyself.** [When was

this prediction fulfilled? Probably when the news of the defeat reached Samaria, or on the day after Ahab's death. Jezebel would almost certainly take summary vengeance upon the false prophets who were responsible for her husband's death and the reverses of the army. Or if she did not, the prophets had good reason to fear that she would, and would hide accordingly.

Ver. 26.—**And the king of Israel said, Take** [Sing. *Take thou*. This command was probably addressed to the eunuch mentioned in ver. 9] **Micaiah, and carry him back** [Heb. *make him return*. This shows clearly that he had come from prison] **unto Amon the governor** [שַׂר *chief;* same word in chs. iv. 2; xi. 24; xvi. 9; Gen. xxxvii. 36; xl. 9, 22, &c. The "chief of the city" is also mentioned 2 Kings xxiii. 8; cf. Neh. xi. 9] **of the city** [who would naturally have charge of the town prison. Probably the prison was in his house. Cf. Gen. xl. 3; Jer. xxxvii. 20], **and to Joash the king's son.** [Thenius supposes that this prince had been entrusted to Amon for his military education, and refers to 2 Kings x. 1. But in that case he would hardly have been mentioned as associated with him in the charge of so important a prisoner. Whoever Joash was, he was a man in authority. It is curious that we find another prophet, Jeremiah, put into the prison of Malchiah, the son of the king (A. V. *the son of Hammelech;* same expression as here), Jer. xxxviii. 6; cf. xxxvi. 26. Some have seen in this designation a name of office, and Bähr thinks that "Joash was not probably a son of Ahab, but a prince of the blood." But when we remember what a number of sons Ahab had (2 Kings x. 1), no valid reason can be assigned why Joash should not have been one of them. He may have been billeted upon Amon, and yet associated with him in the government of the city.]

Ver. 27.—**And say** [Heb. *thou shalt say*], **Thus saith the king, Put this fellow in the prison** [Heb. *house of the prison*. Bähr thinks that Micaiah had formerly been in arrest under Amon's charge, and now was to be committed to the prison proper. But more probably the words mean, "put him in the prison again." His superadded punishment was to be in the shape of prison diet. It is probable that it was owing to the presence of Jehoshaphat that Micaiah escaped with no severer sentence], **and feed him with bread of affliction** [or *oppression*, לַחַץ *pressit;* cf. Exod. iii. 9; Num. xxii. 25; 2 Kings vi. 32], **and with water of affliction** [Josephus (Ant. viii. 15. 4) relates that after Micaiah's prediction the king was in great suspense and fear, until Zedekiah deliberately smote him, in order to show that he was powerless to avenge an injury as the man of God did (ch. xiii. 4), and therefore no true prophet. This may be an "empty Rabbinical tradition" (Bähr), but we may be sure that Ahab did not hear Micaiah's words unmoved. He had had such convincing proofs of the foresight and powers of the Lord's prophets that he may well have trembled, even as he put on a bold front, and sent Micaiah back to the prison house], **until I come in peace.** [This looks like an effort to encourage himself and those around him. But it almost betrays his misgivings. He would have them think he had no fears.

Ver. 28.—**And Micaiah said, If thou return at all in peace, the Lord hath not spoken by me. And he said, Hearken, O people** [Rather, *O nations. Audite, populi omnes*, Vulgate. He appeals, so to speak, to the world], **every one of you.** [It is a curious circumstance that these same words are found at the beginning of the prophecy of Micah (ch. i. 2). The coincidence may be purely accidental, or the words may have been borrowed by the prophet, not, indeed, from our historian, but from some record, the substance of which is embodied in his history. Micah lived about a century and a half after Micaiah; about a century before the Book of Kings was given to the world.

Ver. 29.—**So the king of Israel and Jehoshapat the king of Judah went up to Ramoth-Gilead to battle.** ["By the very network of evil counsel which he has woven for himself is the king of Israel led to his ruin" (Stanley). We can hardly doubt that Jehoshaphat at least would have been well content to abandon the expedition. After the solicitude he had manifested for the sanction of one of the prophets of Jehovah, and after that the one who had been consulted had predicted the defeat of the army, the king of Judah must have had many misgivings. But it is not difficult to understand why, notwithstanding his fears, he did not draw back. For, in the first place, he had committed himself to the war by the rash and positive promise of ver. 4. In the next place, he was Ahab's guest, and had been sumptuously entertained by him, and it would therefore require some moral courage to extricate himself from the toils in which he was entangled. Moreover, he would have subjected himself to the imputation of cowardice had he deserted his ally because of a prophecy which threatened the latter with death. The people around him, again, including perhaps his own retinue, were possessed with the spirit of battle, and treated the prophecy of Micaiah with con-

tempt, and it would be difficult for him to swim alone against the current. It is probable, too, that he discounted the portentous words of Micaiah on account of the long-standing quarrel between him and Ahab. And, finally, we must remember that his own interests were threatened by Syria, and he may well have feared trouble from that quarter in case this war were abandoned. Rawlinson suggests that he may have conceived a personal affection for Ahab; but 2 Chron. xix. 2 affords but slender ground for this conclusion.]

Ver. 30.—**And the king of Israel said unto Jehoshaphat** [At Ramoth-Gilead, on the eve of the battle], **I will disguise myself** [same word ch. xx. 38] **and enter** [The margin, "when he was to disguise himself," &c., is quite mistaken. The Hebrew has two infinitives; lit., *to disguise oneself and enter;* a construction which is frequently employed to indicate an absolute command. Cf. Gen. xvii. 10; Exod. xx. 8; Isa. xiv. 31; and see Ewald, 328 c. "The infinitive absolute is the plainest and simplest form of the voluntative for exclamations" (Bähr). It agrees well with the excitement under which Ahab was doubtless labouring] **into the battle.** [It is not necessary to suppose with Ewald, Rawlinson, al., that he had heard of Benhadad's command to his captains (ver. 31). It is hardly likely that such intelligence could be brought by spies, and there would be no deserters from the Syrian army to that of the Jews. It is enough to remember that Micaiah's words, "these have no master," could not fail to awaken some alarm in his bosom, especially when connected with the prophecy of ch. xx. 42. He will not betray his fear by keeping out of the fray—which, indeed, he could not do without abdicating one of the principal functions of the king (1 Sam. viii. 20), and without exposing himself to the charge of cowardice; but under the circumstances he thinks it imprudent to take the lead of the army, as kings were wont to do (2 Sam. i. 10), in his royal robes. He hopes by his disguise to escape all danger]: **but put thou on thy robes** [LXX. τὸν ἱματισμόν μου. "*My* robes." "We can neither imagine Ahab's asking nor Jehoshaphat's consenting to such a procedure. Jehoshaphat had his own royal robes with him, as appears from ver. 10" (Rawlinson). If this LXX. interpretation could be maintained it would lend some colour to the supposition, otherwise destitute of basis, that Ahab by this arrangement was plotting the death of Jehoshaphat in order that he might incorporate Judah into his own kingdom. It is clear, however, that Ahab then had other work on his hands, and it is doubtful whether even he was capable of such a pitch of villainy. What he means is, either (1) that the Syrians have a personal enmity against himself (ver. 31), whereas they could have none against the king of Judah ; or (2) that Jehoshaphat's life had not been threatened as his own had. "These words וְאַתָּה לְבַשׁ are not to be taken as a command, but simply in this sense : Thou canst put on thy royal dress, since there is no necessity for thee to take any such precautions as I have to take" (Keil). Do they not rather mean that Jehoshaphat should be the recognized leader of the army in which Ahab would serve in a more private capacity?] **And the king of Israel disguised himself, and went into the battle.**

Ver. 31.—**But the king of Syria commanded** [rather, *had* commanded. These words are of the nature of a parenthesis. "Now the king," &c. צִוָּה is so rendered in 2 Chron. xviii. 30] **his thirty and two captains** [mentioned in ch. xx. 24. It does not follow, however (Wordsworth), that these very men had been spared by Ahab] **that had rule over his chariots** [Heb. *chariotry*. Another indication that the chariots were regarded as the most important arm of the Syrian service], **saying, Fight neither with small nor great, save only with the king of Israel.** [This Orientalism, translated into Western ideas, means, "Direct your weapons against the king." What Ahab had done to provoke such resentment is not quite clear. Rawlinson supposes that Ben-hadad's "defeat and captivity were still rankling in his mind, and he wished to retaliate on Ahab the humiliation which he considered himself to have suffered." But it is impossible to see in Ahab's generous conduct towards him a sufficient reason for the fierce hatred which these words disclose. It is much more probable that some affront had subsequently been offered to the Syrian monarch, possibly in the shape of the reproaches which Ahab may have addressed to him on account of his retention of Ramoth-Gilead, and the gross violation of the treaty of ch. xx. 34. It is also possible that he hoped that the death of Ahab would terminate the war (Bähr).]

Ver. 32.—**And it came to pass when the captains of the chariots saw Jehoshaphat, that they said, Surely** [אַךְ, not *only* (Bähr, Keil), but *certainly* ; cf. Gen. xliv. 28 ; Judges iii. 24 ; 2 Kings xxiv. 3] **it** [Heb. *he*] **is the king of Israel. And they turned aside** [Cf. ch. xx. 39, same word. The Hebrew inserts עָלָיו.

The chronicler reads יָסֹבּוּ *they surrounded him*, instead of יָסֹרוּ ; and the LXX. has ἐκύκλωσεν in both places. But the Syrians can hardly have actually closed round the king, and the alteration might easily be made in the course of transcription] **to fight against him** [according to their instructions] : **and Jehoshaphat cried out.** [This cry has been very variously interpreted. According to some, it was his own name that he ejaculated, which is possible, if the command of ver. 31 was known in the allied army. According to others, it was the battle-cry of Judah, which, it is said, would be familiar to the Syrians, and which would rally his own soldiers round him. The Vulgate, no doubt influenced by the words of 2 Chron. xviii. 31, "And the Lord helped him, and God moved them to depart from him," interprets, *clamavit ad Dominum*. That it was a cry for Divine help is the most probable, because it is almost an instinct, especially with a pious soul like Jehoshaphat, to cry to God in the moment of danger. That he had doubts as to whether the course he was pursuing was pleasing to God, would make him all the more ready to cry aloud for mercy the moment he found himself in peril. But it may have been merely a cry of terror. It must be carefully observed that the Scripture does not say that it was this cry led to his being recognized and spared.]

Ver. 33.—**And it came to pass, when the captains of the chariots perceived** [in what way we are not told. But Ahab would be known to some of them, ch. xx. 31] **that it was not the king of Israel, that they turned back from pursuing him.**

Ver. 34.—**And a certain man** [Heb. *a man*. It was natural for some of the Rabbins to identify this archer with Naaman —the tradition is found in Josephus. But it is directly contrary to the spirit of the narrative to attempt to identify him. As it was a chance arrow, so it was by an unknown archer] **drew a bow at a venture** [Heb. *in his simplicity*, *i.e.*, with no intention of shooting Ahab : not knowing what he was doing. That this is the meaning is clear from the use of the words in 2 Sam. xv. 11], **and smote the king of Israel between the joints of the harness** [The marg., *joints and the breastplate*, comes nearer the Hebrew. But it is clear that the rendering *joints*, notwithstanding that it has the support of Gesenius and others, is a mistaken one. "In the joints" we can understand, but "between the joints and the coat of mail," gives no sense. It is obvious that הַדְּבָקִים like הַשִּׁרְיָן following, must signify some portion of the armour, and the meaning of the verb דָּבַק, adhaesit, leads us to conclude that "the hanging skirt of parallel metal plates—hence the plural"—(Bähr) is intended. The coat of mail only covered the breast and ribs. To this a fringe of movable plates of steel was *attached* or *fastened*, hence called דְּבָקִים. So Luther, *Zwischen den Panzer und Hengel.* One is reminded here of the Parthian arrow which wrung from Julian the Apostate the dying confession, "Thou hast conquered, O Galilean." Cf. Psa. vii. 13, 14]: **wherefore he said unto the driver of his chariot, Turn thine hand** [or, according to the Chethib, *hands.* The charioteers of Palestine, like those of Egypt and Assyria, or those of modern Russia, held a rein in each hand. Same expression 2 Kings ix. 23. The meaning is "turn round"] **and carry me out of the host; for I am wounded.** [Heb. *made sick.* The king probably felt his wound to be mortal, as a wound in such a part, the abdomen (cf. 2 Sam. ii. 23; iii. 27; xx. 10), would be. Vulgate, *graviter vulneratus sum.* How far an arrow in such a place could penetrate, we may gather from 2 Kings ix. 24; cf. Job xvi. 13. And he was seemingly anxious that the army should not know it, lest they should be discouraged. They would soon discover it if he remained with the host; he can fight no longer; his wound needs attention; hence this command. It is quite possible that the charioteer, in the din and confusion of battle, may not have observed that his master was wounded. The arrow had not struck any part of the armour.]

Ver. 35.—**And the battle increased** [Heb. *went up.* Marg. *ascended.* The tide of warfare rose higher and higher. Both Keil and Bähr think that the image is taken from a swelling river, and cite Isa. viii. 7. The object of this verse is to explain how it was that the king's request was not complied with] **that day: and the king was stayed up in his chariot** [Heb. *made to stand.* LXX. ἦν ἑστηκώς. He was supported in his chariot by some of his servants, and maintained in an erect posture. Chariots were destitute of seats. According to Thenius and Keil, he maintained himself erect, by his own strength. But the word is passive] **against the Syrians** [Heb. *in the face of the Syrians.* נֹבַח, *coram.* His back was not turned to them, as he had desired. The idea that he was in any way fighting against the Syrians is altogether foreign to the text. It is at first sight somewhat difficult to reconcile this statement with the direction given to the charioteer in the preceding verse, and

some have been led, though without sufficient warrant, to conclude that Ahab left the field, had his wound bound up, and then returned to take his part in the battle. But the explanation is very simple. As the battle increased, it became impossible to comply with the king's desire. So thick was the fight that retreat was impossible. Hence the wounded king, who would otherwise have sunk down to the bottom of the chariot, had to be "stayed up in the presence of the Syrians." This circumstance may also account for the fact that he died at even. Had it been possible to remove him and staunch his wounds, he might have lingered for some time. As it was, he bled to death. It is not clear, therefore, that "his death was kingly" (Kitto), or that we must concede to Ahab "the credit of right princely fortitude on this occasion" (Rawlinson). He would have left the host could he have done so. It was his servants propped up the dying man in his chariot, to encourage the army. What a picture for an artist—the king with the pallor of death spreading over his face, the anxious faces of the attendants, the pool of blood, the sun sinking to the horizon, &c.], **and died at even: and the blood ran out of the wound** [Heb. *the blood of the wound poured*] **into the midst** [Heb. *bosom*; LXX. κόλπον, the hollow part, or "well." The same word is used of the concave part of the altar] **of the chariot.**

Ver. 36.—**And there went a proclamation throughout the host** [Heb. *And the shouting passed over in the camp.* Gesenius will have it that רִנָּה must mean a "joyful cry," and would see the cause of joy in the cessation of hostilities and the permission to return home] **about the going down of the sun** [According to the chronicler (ch. xviii. 34), it was at sunset that the king died. It seems natural, therefore, to connect this shout with his death. But the approach of night would of itself put an end to the battle. It does not appear that Israel had been utterly defeated, or had suffered great loss. But "they had no master"], **saying, Every man to his city, and every man to his own country** [or *land*].

Ver. 37.—**So the king died** [The LXX. makes this to be a part of the proclamation, ἕκαστος εἰς τὴν . . . γῆν ὅτι τέθνηκεν ὁ βασιλεύς, which involves a very slight change in the Hebrew text, כי מת המלך instead of וימת המלך and gives a better sense. It has already been stated that the king died. Such repetitions however are common in Hebrew, and this reading has almost the look of an emendation] **and was brought** [Heb. *came*. The A. V. is against the grammar. As "came" would be a strange word to use of a dead man, it is highly probable that instead of ויבא we should read ויבאו with the LXX. καὶ ἦλθον] **to Samaria; and they buried the king in Samaria** ["with his father," ch. xvi. 28].

Ver. 38.—**And one washed the chariot in** [or *at ;* Heb. עַל] **the pool of Samaria.** [Nearly all Eastern cities had their tanks or pools, often outside the city gate. Jerusalem has several of these, and we read of one at Hebron (2 Sam. xiv. 12) and Gibeon (*ib.* ii. 13). Cf. Cant. vii. 4. The Hebrew word בְּרֵכָה is preserved in the modern Arabic *Birkeh*]; **and the dogs** [The LXX. has *the swine and the dogs*. The mention of swine is hardly likely to have been omitted, had it formed part of the original text] **licked up his blood** [cf. ch. xxi. 19, note. According to Josephus, the chariot was washed "in the fountain of *Jezreel*." The alteration would appear to have been made to avoid the difficulty occasioned by the discrepancy between the statement of the text, and that of ch. xxi. 19], **and they washed his armour** [So the Chaldaic and the Syriac. But this translation is now abandoned, (1) because it is contrary to the usage of the language to make זֹנוֹת the object ; and (2) because that word occurs in the Old Testament only in the sense of *harlots* (Bähr). The true meaning is that given by the LXX., καὶ αἱ πόρναι ἐλούσαντο. רָחַץ does not require any object such as " chariot," or " corpse," for it is found in the sense of bathe (intrans.) in Exod. ii. 5; Num. xix. 19 ; Ruth iii. 21; 2 Kings v. 10. Bähr reminds us that harlots are elsewhere associated with dogs (Deut. xxiii. 19 ; Rev. xxii. 15). This fact is mentioned as a proof of the just judgment of God. Even if these harlots were not prostitutes devoted to the service of the Phoenician deities, whose cultus Ahab had sought to establish in Israel, still the result of his religious policy had been the spread of prostitution. It is a fine example of the *lex talionis*. " He which is filthy, let him be filthy still"]; **according unto the word of the Lord which he spake** [the reference is to ch. xxi. 19].

Ver. 39.—**Now the rest of the acts of Ahab, and all that he did, and the ivory house which he made** [So called because it was adorned with ivory. See on ch. xi. ; and cf. Amos iii. 15 ; Psa. xlv. 8; Cant. vii. 5. Rawlinson cites several passages from Greek and Latin authors to prove that ivory was anciently applied, not only to furniture, but to the doors and walls of houses], **and all the cities that he built** [Probably Jezreel was one, but we have no information concerning them. The fact that he did build cities, however, is one proof of Ahab's enterprize. He was not weak in all particulars], **are they not written in the book of the chronicles of the kings of Israel ?**

Ver. 40.—**So Ahab slept with his fathers; and Ahaziah** [" Whom Jehovah upholds." The name suggests that, notwithstanding his idolatries, Ahab cannot have completely abandoned the worship of the Lord] **his son reigned in his stead.**

Reign of Jehoshaphat.

Ver. 41.—**And Jehoshaphat** [" Whom Jehovah judges"] **the son of Asa began to reign over Judah in the fourth year of Ahab king of Israel.** [The historian now resumes for a moment the history of Judah, which has dropped out of notice since ch. xv. 24, where the accession of Jehoshaphat was mentioned. His reign, which is here described in the briefest possible way, occupies four chapters (xvii.—xx.) of 2 Chron.]

Ver. 42.—**Jehoshaphat was thirty and five years old when he began to reign; and he reigned twenty and five years in Jerusalem. And his mother's name was Azubah the daughter of Shilhi.**

Ver. 43.—**And he walked in all the way of Asa his father** [Apart from his alliance with the house of Ahab, and the troubles in which it involved him, his reign was alike pious and prosperous. Like Asa's, it was distinguished by internal reforms, and by signal deliverances from foreign enemies]; **he turned not aside from it** [as Asa was tempted to do in his old age], **doing** [Heb. *to do*] **that which was right in the eyes of the Lord : nevertheless the high places were not taken away** [Heb. *departed not*, as in ch. xv. 14 ; 2 Chron. xv. 17 ; 2 Kings xii. 4, Heb. ; xiv. 4, Heb. But see 2 Chron. xviii. 6. The discrepancy is the exact parallel of that between 1 Kings xv. 14 and 2 Chron. xiv. 3; or between this latter passage and 2 Chron. xv. 17. And the explanation is the same, viz., that an effort was made to remove the high places, which was partially, and only partially, successful] ; **for the people offered and burnt incense yet in the high places** [cf. ch. iii. 2].

Ver. 44.—**And Jehoshaphat made peace with the king of Israel.** [One great feature of his reign was this : that the hostility which had lasted, even if it sometimes slumbered, between the two kingdoms for seventy years, from the date of their separation to the time of Asa's death, gave way to peace and even alliance. Judah now recognized the division of the kingdom as an accomplished fact, and no longer treated Israel, even theoretically, as in rebellion. It is probable that the marriage of Jehoram and Athaliah was at once the fruit of, and was intended to cement, this good understanding (2 Chron. xviii. 1). It is hardly likely (Bähr) that the peace was the result of the union of the two families. From the analogy of *ib.* xix. 2; xx. 37; cf. 1 Kings xvi. 31; 2 Kings iii. 14, we should conclude that the marriage at any rate was ill-advised and displeasing to God. Bähr sees in it a step on the part of Jehoshaphat towards realizing the union of the two kingdoms under the supremacy of Judah. He thinks that we cannot otherwise account for this complete change of front.]

Ver. 45.—**Now the rest of the acts of Jehoshaphat, and his might** [as in ch. xv. 23, xvi. 27, &c. It is noticeable that this word is not used of Ahab, notwithstanding his wars and victories] **that he showed** [see 2 Kings iii. 9 sqq.; 2 Chron. xvii. 12 sqq. His judicial reforms are hardly referred to here], **and how he warred** [*ib.* chs. xviii., xx.], **are they not written in the book of he chronicles of the kings of Judah?**

Ver. 46.—**And the remnant of the Sodomites, which remained in the days of his father Asa** [It appears hence that Asa's removal of the religious prostitutes (ch. xv. 12), like that of the high places, had been but partial], **he took** [Heb. *exterminated*] **out of the land.**

Ver. 47.—**There was then no king in Edom: a deputy** [בָצָב, same word as in ch. iv. 7. It is implied that this officer was appointed by the king of Judah (Wordsworth)] **was king.** [This fact is mentioned to show how it was that Jehoshaphat was able to build a fleet at Ezion-Geber, in the territory of Edom (ch. ix. 26). That country would seem to have regained its independence very soon after Solomon's death (ch. xi. 14), but would also appear from the text, and from 2 Kings viii. 20, 22, to have been again made subject to Judah, probably by Jehoshaphat himself; see 2 Chron. xvii. 10, 11.]

Ver. 48.—**Jehoshaphat made** [The Chethib has עֶשֶׂר *ten*, obviously a clerical error for עָשָׂה *made*] **ships of Tharshish** [see note on ch. x. 22] **to go to Ophir** [In 2 Chron. xx. 36, *Tharshish* is read for Ophir. Wordsworth holds that two separate fleets are intended, but this is most improbable] **for gold** [Evidently the great prosperity of his reign had suggested to him the idea of emulating Solomon's naval exploits, and of

reviving the commerce of his people with the East] : **but they went not** [Heb. *it went not*] . **for the ships were broken** [Probably they were dashed by a storm against the rocks which "lie in jagged ranges on each side," Stanley] **at Ezion-Geber.**

Ver. 49.—**Then said Ahaziah the son of Ahab unto Jehoshaphat, Let my servants go with thy servants in the ships. But Jehoshaphat would not.** [But we are told in 2 Chron. xx. 37 that the ships were broken, according to a prophecy of Eliezer, the son of Dodavah, because Jehoshaphat *had* joined himself with Ahaziah. The explanation is that the fleet had been built by the two kings conjointly, and manned by the subjects of Jehoshaphat exclusively; and that, after the disaster, Ahaziah proposed either to repair the injured vessels, or to construct a second fleet, which should then be partly manned by sailors of the northern kingdom, "men probably accustomed to the sea, perhaps trained at Tyre" (Rawlinson). This proposal was declined by the king of Judah, not so much on account of the "reflection on his subjects' skill contained in it," as because of the prophecy of Eliezer, and the evidently judicial disaster which had befallen the fleet already built.]

Ver. 50.—**And Jehoshaphat slept with his fathers, and was buried with his fathers in the city of David his father: and Jehoram his son reigned in his stead** [2 Chron. xxi.]

Reign of Ahaziah.

Ver. 51.—**Ahaziah the son of Ahab began to reign over Israel in Samaria the seventeenth year of Jehoshaphat king of Judah, and reigned two years over Israel.** [Parts of two years; 2 Kings iii. 1; and cf. i. 17 and viii. 16. It is suggested that Jehoram was associated with his father in the government of Judah from the date of the expedition against Ramoth-Gilead, and this is not improbable. But it has been already remarked that these chronological notices appear to have undergone a revision which has sometimes resulted in confusion.]

Ver. 52.—**And he did evil in the sight of the Lord, and walked in the way of his father** [ch. xvi. 30—33; cf. 2 Kings iii. 2] **and in the way of his mother** [The powerful influence of Jezebel, even after Ahab's death, is hinted at here. It was to her that *idolatry* owed its position in Israel], **and in the way of Jeroboam the son of Nebat** [the calf-worship and idolatry existed side by side], **who made Israel to sin.**

Ver. 53.—**For he served Baal, and wor-**

shipped him, and provoked to anger [or *vexed*] the Lord God of Israel, according to all that his father had done. [The termination of this book at this point could hardly be more arbitrary if it had been made by accident. These verses are closely connected with 2 Kings ch. i. The division here obscures the connexion between the sin of Ahaziah and the judgments which it provoked.]

HOMILETICS.

Vers. 1—40.—*The Death of Ahab and the Defeat of Israel.* This chapter is almost entirely occupied with an account of the death of Ahab, and of the circumstances which preceded and attended it. The earlier portion of the chapter, which contains the prophesyings of the false prophets and the vision of Micaiah, is only recorded because of its bearing on the death of the king, and the dispersion of his army.

And the prominence accorded to Ahab's end only corresponds with the space assigned to his reign. That reign was so full of evil for Israel that it occupies a fourth part of this entire book. It was meet, therefore, that the death which avenged it should be recorded with proportionate detail. For the battle of Ramoth-Gilead was the final payment—so far as this world is concerned—for the sins of two and twenty years.

But it is to be observed in the first place that Ahab's repentance (ch. xxi. 29), as the penitence begotten of fear often is, was but shortlived. Had it lasted, we had not read of this tragical death. How soon the king shook off his impressions we know not, but we do know that—thanks to the natural weakness of his character, still further enfeebled by years of self-indulgence and submission to a stronger will than his own; thanks to the evil genius (ch. xxi. 25) ever at his side to stifle good resolves and to steel his heart against the true religion; thanks to the impious system to which he found himself committed, and the toils of which he found it impossible to break, this unhappy king steadily lapsed into his old sins. It "happened unto him according to the true proverb, "The dog is turned to his vomit again" (2 Peter ii. 22).

And it is also to be considered here that Israel had gone hand in hand with him in his downward course. Had the king's career been one of steadily increasing demoralization? so had that of the people. The death of Naboth affords sufficient proof of this. The ready compliance of the elders, the alacrity with which they perpetrated that judicial murder, shows to what a moral depth the example of the court and the idolatry around them had plunged the holy nation. No; king and queen had not sinned alone, and justice required they should not suffer alone. Nations and their rulers, as we have already seen, receive a reckoning in this life; how much more the *covenant* people and the *Lord's* anointed? Placed as they were under a direct law of *temporal* punishments and rewards, it would have been strange, indeed, if such a reign as this had gone unrecompensed. But so far from that, they have already received part reckoning for their sin. The three years drought, the famine, the terrible Syrian invasions, have avenged a part of their idolatries and immoralities; but there still remains a long score of guilt to be expiated in shame and suffering and blood.

And here it may be well to remind ourselves what were the sins which awaited a settlement under the walls of Ramoth-Gilead. They were five in number. (1) The calf-worship—the hereditary sin of the northern kingdom, the sin of Jeroboam; (2) the worship of Baal with the prostitution which accompanied it—the sin primarily of Jezebel and her Phoenician following, but shared in by almost the entire nation; (3) the determined persecution of the prophets and the virtual proscription of the ancient faith; (4) the release of the Syrian king in disregard of God's will—the sin of Ahab and his captains; and (5) the murder of Naboth in defiance of all law—the sin of the rulers and elders. It may be thought that the two last were peculiarly Ahab's or Jezebel's sins, and that the people had no part in them; but this is a mistaken view. No doubt he and his infamous consort had by far the largest share in all the four, and therefore they received, as we shall see presently, by far the severer punishment. But just as the people worshipped at the shrines which the king supported, just as they practised the abominations which he had introduced, so had they approved his policy towards Ben-hadad—see the words of ch. xix. 42, "thy *people* for his people"—and the guilt of innocent blood, as we know (Num. xxxv. 33 ; Deut. xxi. 7 ; 2 Sam. xxi.) rested on the community until it had been cleansed in blood. It is clear, then, that at the time when this chapter opens, king and people, though in very different degrees, were chargeable with the sins of schism, of idolatry, of unfaithfulness to God, of murder. It is now for us to observe how these things were expiated.

Now there are two principles which underlie all God's retributive dealings with his ancient people. First, that sin is left, or made to bring its own penalties. *Per quod quis peccat, per idem quoque plectitur idem.* Secondly, that the penalty is ever correspondent with the sin. This latter is what we commonly call the *lex talionis.* We have had instances of the working of both of these laws, but especially of the latter, in the earlier portions of this history. We shall find the same laws in operation here.

For consider—I. By what means Ahab was led to death and Israel to defeat. II. By what instruments these punishments were inflicted. III. In what way they were signalized as the chastisements of sin.

I. In considering the INFLUENCES which moved Ahab to war, and which led to his destruction, we must assign the first place to—

1. *The perfidy of Ben-hadad.* No doubt it rankled in Ahab's breast that, after he had dealt so magnanimously with a prostrate foe, after he had treated an insolent invader with unexampled generosity, and after a solemn covenant had been made betwixt them, it rankled in his soul that a Syrian garrison, in spite of all embassies and remonstrances, should hold the Jewish fortress of Ramoth-Gilead and thus offer a standing menace to Israel and Judah alike. But did it never occur to him that the conduct of Ben-hadad was but the counterpart of his own? He too had forgotten his benefactor and deliverer, to whom he was bound by solemn covenant; *he* still maintained a garrison of idolatrous priests in the heart of Immanuel's land. Ben-hadad's breach of faith was no greater than his own. Probably, he never thought of this when he debated whether he should go up against Ramoth-Gilead. He would remember, however, that he had only himself to blame for this act of perfidy, and he would devoutly wish he had dealt with the oppressor as he had deserved; he would perhaps think that it only served him right for his weakness and sin. We see, however, that he is paid back in his own coin, that the measure he has meted to God is measured to him again. The sin of three years before gave the first impulse to war and death.

2. *The lies of the false prophets.* It is hardly likely that Ahab would have engaged in this war but for the unanimous verdict of the four hundred prophets in its favour. We see in Micaiah's vision that a "lying spirit" was the principal means employed to procure his fall (ver. 22). But what were these prophets, and how came they to prophesy thus? One thing is certain, that they were *not* prophets of Jehovah, and another thing is also clear, that whether they were prophets of Baal, or, as is most probable, prophets of the calves, the false system which Ahab had supported became through them a means of his destruction. The schism or the idolatry, as the case may be, is bearing its bitter fruit. He has sown to lies, he reaps to delusions. It is a conspicuous instance of the just judgment of heaven that Ahab is lured to his death by the impostors he had cherished and patronized. "He that hates truth shall be the dupe of lies." The sin of the calves too brings its own retribution.

But how was it, it is worth asking, that these four hundred sycophants came to counsel him thus? Was it not that they took their cue from him, and prophesied what they knew would please? They saw that the king had already made up his mind—for his resolution was taken before they were summoned (vers. 4, 5), and they thought it wisest to swim with the stream. It may be they were guided by other and inscrutable impulses (ver. 23), and were constrained, they knew not how, to prophesy as they did; it may be they honestly mistook the *vox populi* for the *vox Dei*, but probably the working of their minds was this: "The king wishes it. Jehoshaphat assents to it. The people are set upon it. We should be going against common sense and our own interests to resist it."

And so the king was a second time paid in his own coin. Those martial prophecies had been minted in his own brain. He wished for lies and he had them. His own passions and pride were reflected, were echoed, in the voices of his four hundred soothsayers. It is the case of which both sacred and profane history supply so many examples, *Homo vult decipi et decipiatur*. It is thus God deals with deceivers still. He leaves them to be deceived, to be the prey of their own disordered fancies. It is notorious how men find in the Bible what they *wish* to find there; how all unsuspectingly they read their own meanings into the words of Scripture; how they interpret its injunctions by the rule of their own inclinations. "He feedeth on ashes; a deceived heart hath turned him aside that he cannot deliver his soul, nor say, Is there not a lie in my right hand?" (Isa. xliv. 20). "Ephraim is joined unto idols: let him alone" (Hosea iv. 17).

3. *The silence of the Lord's prophets.* Why was it, we cannot help asking here, why was it that there were no true prophets present, at this crisis in the history of Israel, to step forth and warn the king against this undertaking? Why were the four hundred deceivers left to have their own way? We see here the fruit of persecution, the recompense of those fierce dragonnades which Jezebel had maintained against the prophetic order. Of the men who might have interposed to prevent this disastrous expedition, some were dead, others were banished; king and queen had wickedly silenced them. They now reap the fruit of those repressive measures. Their curses come home to roost. Elijah might have saved king and country, but he is hiding from the wrath of Jezebel, or is withdrawn by God from the arena of history. Micaiah the son of Imlah foresaw the end, but Ahab had imprisoned him, and could not brook to take his advice, and had persuaded himself that his admonitions were the outcome of personal enmity. It is true *this* prophet was not silent, but plainly foretold defeat and death; but Ahab was in a manner bound not to regard his warnings. He had told Jehoshaphat it would be so. It would look like cowardice to be influenced by *his* vaticinations. And so he is left to the prophets of his choice: no hand is raised to stop him: he goes straight into the jaws of death, the victim of his own folly and cruelty and sin.

II. The INSTRUMENTS of retribution were—

1. *The king whom Ahab had wickedly spared.* We have already seen in what the sin of sparing the tyrant Ben-hadad consisted (p. 492). It is now for us to observe that this foolish and impious deed brought its own peculiar Nemesis. It was Ben-hadad himself who said, "Fight neither with small nor great, but with the king of Israel only." Ahab's ill-advised clemency procures his own destruction. With base natures, it only needs that we should put them under obligations which they cannot possibly discharge, in order to provoke their bitter enmity. But it is much more material to observe here that in Ben-hadad's conduct we may see a parable of the cruel revenge which a cherished sin will often take on those who have once conquered and then trifled with it. The devil that was cast out returns bringing with him seven other devils more wicked than himself (Matt. xii. 45). We are constantly as tender to the sins which tyrannized over us as was Ahab to Ben-hadad. Instead of slaying them—hewing them in pieces before the Lord—we leave the roots of bitterness in the heart's soil, and they spring up and trouble us. It is like that peasant of whom we have all read, who found a viper in the field, benumbed with the winter's cold, and put the venomous beast into his bosom to warm it back into life. The first use it made of its restored power was to wound and destroy its benefactor. How dearly have we often paid for our pleasant vices!

2. *The Syrians who were once subjects of Israel.* It is well to remember here that these enemies who gave Ahab his death-wound at Ramoth were once under the heel of Israel (2 Sam. viii. 6). Now we see their relations reversed. Syria has now become the standing oppressor of the chosen people. We have already pointed out some of the steps which led to this result. The sin of Solomon (see p. 223) and the unfaithfulness of Asa alike were factors in the change. But the most influential

reason was the godlessness of Ahab. But three years ago Syria lay at his mercy; its power was completely broken. But Ahab, so far from learning that the Lord was God (ch. xx. 13, 28), had ignored the Lord, and acted as if his own might had gotten him the victory. How fitting that these same Syrians should be the instruments to scourge him.

3. *An unknown, unconscious archer.* The arrow that pierced Ahab's corselet was shot "in simplicity," without deliberate aim, with no thought of striking the king. It was an unseen Hand that guided that chance shaft to its destination. It was truly "the arrow of the Lord's vengeance." (Cf. 2 Kings xii. 17.) It would be deeply instructive could we know the thoughts of that unhappy king, as with the arrow in his side, and the blood draining from his wound, and forming a sickening pool in the well of the chariot, he was stayed up those wretched weary hours until the sunset against the Syrians. Surely he knew at last that "the Lord was God" (ch. xviii. 39; xx. 13, 28). His cry would now be, "Thou hast found me, O my enemy." He would think, it may be, of Elijah's and Micaiah's prophecies; he would think of Naboth's bleeding and mangled corpse; he would think, above all, that his sin had found him out, and that Jehovah had conquered. He had fought all his life for Baal, but it was in vain; he had been kicking against the pricks; he had been wrestling not with flesh and blood, but with an Invisible, Irresistible, Omnipotent God, and now he is thrown, cast down never to rise again.

III. It now only remains for us to consider the CIRCUMSTANCES of Ahab's death. These were of so portentous and exceptional a character as to mark it—

1. *As a direct visitation of God.* The army, that day defeated, the contingent of Judah, the citizens of Samaria, the subjects of both kingdoms, could not think that a mere chance had happened to Ahab when they remembered (1) That this death had been distinctly foretold. Not once or twice, but three times had a prophetic voice foreshadowed for him a sudden and shameful end (ch. xx. 42; xxi. 19; xxii. 17, 28). Moreover, Micaiah, the last of these monitors, had staked his reputation as God's prophet on the fulfilment of his prediction of disaster. And his oracle had not been spoken in secret; he had appealed to the entire assembly gathered round the two kings—and the flower of Israel and Judah alike were there—and even to neighbouring nations (ver. 28, Heb.), to be witnesses of his words, and those words were fresh in their memories. (2) How the king met his death. For it was of course known to the army that Ahab had disguised himself, whilst Jehoshaphat had put on his robes. After the sinister prophecy of Micaiah, we may be sure that the allied armies would watch, with the gravest anxiety, for the issue. They would perceive that the king himself was not without his fears; they would wonder whether his disguise would procure his escape. And when at the end of the day they learnt that Jehoshaphat who had been arrayed like a king, and who on that account had been exposed to imminent peril, had escaped unhurt, whilst their king, who had never been recognized, had been pierced by a chance arrow between the joints of his harness and mortally wounded, was there one but would see the finger of God in this death? Surely if the Psalmist's words were then written, they would occur to their minds, "Whither shall I go from thy spirit, and whither shall I flee from thy presence?" &c. (Psa. cxxxix. 9—12), or that other Psalm, "God shall shoot at them with a swift arrow; suddenly shall they be wounded" (Psa. lxiv. 7), and the result would be that all men would fear and declare the work of God (*ib.* ver. 9), and confess that this was His doing. The fugitives who stole away in the dark and black night to their homes, like sheep without a shepherd, would have learnt one lesson at least that day, viz., that there was "a God that judgeth in the earth."

2. *As God's appropriate recompense for the sins of that age.* We have already seen how this history puts its stamp of reprobation on (1) the calf-worship, inasmuch as by the prophets the calves the king was beguiled into this enterprize. But the sin of Jeroboam was not the special sin of Ahab's reign. On the contrary, the calf-worship was rather overshadowed and eclipsed by the frightful idolatries, which had so much greater fascination for the evil heart of unbelief. It was the characteristic of that reign that the unclean rites of Baal and Astarte, the abominations of the Amorites, were re-established in the land. We see in Ahab's death (2) the requital

of his share in that sin (ch. xvi. 31, 32). The idolatry which had desolated the church was avenged by a horde of idolaters ravaging the land and slaying the arch-idolater in battle. There is a rough *lex talionis* here. (Cf. Jer. v. 19.) If they *would* have idolatry they should taste the tender mercies of idolaters. On that field were the predictions of Moses (Deut. xxviii. 25), Samuel (1 Sam. xii. 25), and Solomon (1 Kings viii. 33) fulfilled.

(3) But a recompense still more exact and conspicuous attended the impurities which Ahab had practised under the name of religion. He had filled the land with prostitutes. What a proof of the just judgment of God it was that these infamous persons added dishonour to his death! He had maintained them through life: he should be associated with them in his end. The harlots bathed in the pool that was reddened with his blood (vers. 38, Heb.)

(4) Nor was the connexion of Ahab's death with the sin of releasing Ben-hadad any less conspicuous. What meant that strange malignant command, " Fight . . . only with the king of Israel ? " Was it not that the Syrian king, on whom Ahab would not execute vengeance, had become, in the counsels of God, an instrument of vengeance, a minister to execute wrath, against the anointed of the Lord ? " Thy life shall go for his life "—it was thus that every religious mind would interpret so singular and, considering the circumstances (chap. xx.), so otherwise inexplicable a word of command. It was as if Ben-hadad had proclaimed that his mission primarily was to settle the long arrearages of justice with that wicked Ahab.

(5) How the murder of Naboth was avenged that shameful day, it is hardly necessary to point out. There was a strict retaliation—wound for wound, stripe for stripe, blood for blood, dishonour for dishonour. There were many, besides Jehu and Bidkar, who would recall the fierce threatening of the Tishbite (ch. xxi. 19) ; many, besides priests and prophets, would remember the axiom of their law, "blood defileth the land," &c. (Num. xxxv. 33), or would think on that day of the so-called " precept of Noah," " Whoso sheddeth man's blood, by man shall his blood be shed " (Gen. ix. 6). The elders of Jezreel, yes, and Jezebel herself, understood that Naboth's blood had cried from the ground, and that the cry had come up into the ears of the Lord of Sabaoth. It was His foot that was dipped in the blood of His enemies (Psa. lxviii. 23).

And this ignominious death—in what sharp contrast it stands with the indolent, luxurious, sensual life ! " The ivory house that he made," what an irony we may see in those words! " Shalt thou reign, because thou closest thyself in cedar. . . . He shall be buried with the burial of an ass," &c. (Jer. xxii. 15, 19). The cities he built, the victories he won, how poor and empty do these exploits seem as we stand by the pool of Samaria, and see the livid, blood-stained corpse dragged from the chariot ! The Latin poet asks what all his pleasures, travels, knowledge, can avail a man who has to *die* after all ; but the question presents itself with tenfold force when life's fitful fever is followed by such a sleep, by such a dream, as Ahab's. " It had been good for that man if he had not been born " (Matt. xxvi. 24).

And the death of Ahab was followed by the dispersion of his army. When the proclamation rang through the host, " Every man to his country," and when the serried ranks precipitately broke up, and horseman and footman fled for his life, then the share of Israel in the sins of Ahab and Jezebel was in part expiated. There was not a man but knew why " the children of Israel could not stand before their enemies." " There is an accursed thing in the midst of thee, O Israel." (Josh. vii. 12, 13). Baal had troubled them, had made of the heights of Ramoth a very valley of Achor.

HOMILIES BY VARIOUS AUTHORS.

Vers. 1—8.—*Bad Company.* According to the order of the chapters in the LXX., which is probably the original or true order, chapter xx. should immediately precede this. Then, after the history of the war between Ahab and Ben-hadad, this chapter opens naturally : " And they continued three years without war between Syria and

Israel." In the third year of this peace Jehoshaphat visited Ahab; and from this visit arose serious events, which are admonitory to us that we should avoid the company of the wicked.

I. BAD COMPANY COMPROMISES CHARACTER. 1. *It injures morals.* (1) The earlier career of Jehoshaphat was faultless. He is highly commended for his faithfulness to God and zeal against idolatry (2 Chron. xvii. 1—6). (2) His first fault was sanctioning the marriage of his son Jehoram with Athaliah the daughter of Ahab (2 Kings viii. 18, 26). (3) This led the way to the further fault of that friendly visit to Ahab mentioned here, for which he was rebuked by "Jehu the son of Hanani the seer" (2 Chron. xix. 2). (4) Yet once again we find him falling into a similar snare. He agreed with Ahaziah the son of Ahab, a wicked scion of a wicked house, jointly to equip a fleet at the port of Ezion-Geber, on the Red Sea, to sail to Ophir for gold. In this also he incurred the anger of the Lord and suffered the loss of his fleet (ver. 48; 2 Chron. xx. 35—37). Note: A fault is like a seed, fruitful "after its kind." A fault once committed prepares the way for a repetition. 2. *It damages reputation.* (1) Reputation is character as estimated by men. This estimate may or may not be just; for men may judge wrongly through ignorance of circumstances which would put a new complexion upon conduct. Therefore judgments should be charitable, and not too hastily formed. (2) But it is a maxim among men, generally true, that "you may know a man by his friends." Friendships involve sympathies. It had been better for Jehoshaphat's reputation had he never made affinity with the wicked house of Ahab. (3) This principle will apply to books. Hence the kindred maxim, "You may see a man in his library." It is bad enough when the newspaper shuts up the Bible; it is worse when the Bible is neglected through preference for sensational fictitious literature. 3. *It impairs influence.* (1) This follows. Character is influence. Reputation is influence. Advice will be readily received from a genuine man, which coming from an artificial character would be spurned. (2) What a power for good or evil is moral influence! See the evil exemplified in Israel under Ahab and Jezebel. See the good in Judah under Jehoshaphat. Lessons: Let your character be true. Jealously guard your reputation. Look to these for the sake of your influence.

II. BAD COMPANY COMPROMISES HAPPINESS. Because—1. *Happiness is involved in character.* (1) This truth is abundantly illustrated in sacred history. Examples are furnished in the text. Secular history teaches this truth. Everyday experience evinces it. (2) Yet is it difficult so to convince individuals of this as to lead them to abandon sin and throw their energies wholly into the blessed service of God. Happiness is proportionate to the completeness of consecration. This consecration cannot be reconciled with the friendship of the world (James iv. 4). 2. *Goodness is grieved in it.* (1) Jehoshaphat was not long in the company of Ahab before his ear was offended by horrible words. "I hate him." Whom did Ahab hate? Micaiah, the faithful prophet of the Lord. Does not this look like a declaration of hatred against the Lord? (See Prov. xiv. 31; xvii. 5; Zech. ii. 8.) (2) Why does Ahab hate Micaiah? "For he doth not prophesy good concerning me, but evil." Because he does not falsify the truth of God to flatter me. Because he does not play the devil to please me, as these four hundred do! Note: Hatred to God means love to Satan. (3) Such sentiments were distressing to the feelings of Jehoshaphat. To the revulsion of his righteous soul he gave expression (but too feeble) in the remonstrance, "Let not the king say so." The conversation of such as are in sympathy with evil will offend the good in proportion to their pureness. 3. *It leads the most wary into trouble.* For the persuasions of the wicked are subtle. (1) In presence of Jehoshaphat "The king of Israel said unto his servants, Know ye that Ramoth in Gilead is ours, and we be still, and take it not out of the hand of the king of Syria?" It was a considerable city in the tribe of Gad on the other side Jordan, and one of the cities of refuge. It was one of the cities which Ben-hadad, by the letter of his covenant, was bound to restore (see ch. xx. 34). The cause of Israel was obviously just. (2) Then turning to Jehoshaphat, Ahab said, "Wilt thou go with me to battle at Ramoth-Gilead?" To which, carried away with the obvious justice of the cause, Jehoshaphat responded, "I am as thou art, my people as thy people, my horses as thy horses." This was too strong a compliment to Ahab and his people, and the response was too ready. We may not champion every just cause. It may be wrong to champion a good cause in wicked company. (3) Bethinking himself, as a godly man should do, "Jehoshaphat said unto the king of Israel, Inquire, I pray thee, at the word of the Lord." A good man seeks to take God with him, and so long as he abides in this holy company he is safe. But let him beware that he be not persuaded by the wicked to forsake it. (4) Ahab was equal to the occasion. He had four hundred prophets ready with one mouth to pronounce for the war, and that, too, in the name of the Lord. This hireling company, however, did not satisfy Jehoshaphat, yet he fell into their snare. He should have availed himself of the opportunity to withdraw given him in the prophecy of Micaiah; but, under the spell of Ahab's evil influence, he went to the battle and got into trouble. There is no safety in the company of the wicked. 4. *It provokes judgments of God.* (1) The good partake in the plagues of their wicked associates. Jehoshaphat barely escaped, through the mercy of God, with his life; and he suffered the loss of many of his people (see Rev. xviii. 4). The fly that keeps aloof is not entangled in the spider's web. (2) The good incur Divine judgments for their own sin. The sin of friendship with the enemies of God. The sin such friendship must infallibly occasion. Such was the experience of Jehoshaphat (see 2 Chron. xix. 2). Such will be yours. Avoid it.—J. A. M.

Vers. 9—14.—*The False and the True.* There would be no counterfeit coin if there were no sterling; so neither would there be false prophets if there were no true. Because there are both, their qualities have to be tested, that we may refuse the spurious and value the genuine (see Jer. xxiii. 38). To this end let us consider—
I. TESTS WHICH MAY NOT BE TRUSTED. 1. *The test of profession.* (1) Ahab's prophets "prophesied." That is to say (a) They used modes usual with prophets to procure information from Heaven. These were sacrifice, prayer, music (see 1 Sam. x. 5, 6; 2 Kings iii. 15), and, when time permitted, fasting. (b) They used modes usual with prophets to communicate the information when received. "Zedekiah, the son of Chenaanah, made him horns of iron: and he said, Thus saith the Lord, With these shalt thou push the Syrians, until thou have consumed them" (cf. Jer. xxvii. 2; xxviii. 13). The "horn" was the symbol of a king (see Dan. vii. 24; Rev. xvii. 12). These were "two," to represent Ahab and Jehoshaphat, Israel and Judah. They were of "iron" to express strength (see Dan. ii. 40). The prophecy was that, aided by Jehoshaphat, Ahab should push the Syrians to destruction. (2) They prophesied "in the name of the Lord." Some think because their number corresponded to that of the prophets of Ashere (ch. xviii. 19) these were the same, having escaped when the prophets of Baal were slain at the brook Kishon (ch. xviii. 40). If so, then their profession on this occasion was designed to deceive Jehoshaphat (see Jer. xxiii. 30). (3) Anyhow there was profession enough, but it was hollow, and proved conclusively that profession must not be taken as a test of truth. 2. *The test of numbers.* (1) Here were "four hundred" who prophesied professedly in the name of the Lord. Against this number Micaiah the son of Imlah stands alone; yet the truth of God is with him against the multitude. "Truth is not always to be determined by the poll. It is not numbers, but weight, that must carry it in the council of prophets" (Bishop Hall). (2) This instance does not stand alone. The majority was in the wrong against Noah. Elijah was in the minority on Carmel, but he was right. Jesus had the whole Jewish Church against Him, though He was Truth itself. 3. *The test of unanimity.* (1) The four hundred were united against Micaiah. Sometimes there is unanimity of this kind against a common object, where otherwise there is little agreement. Herod and Pilate made friends in opposition to Jesus. (2) But these prophets were agreed among themselves. They all seem to have followed the leadership of Zedekiah. "And all the prophets prophesied so, saying, Go up to Ramoth-Gilead, and prosper: for the Lord shall deliver it into the king's hand." 4. *How does this argument bear upon the authority of the Church?* (1) It is pleaded that the

Church, which is practically understood to be the clergy in council, has authority to bind the conscience in matters of faith. The arguments relied upon to sustain this view are generally based upon claims of profession, numbers, and agreement. (2) On the other hand, the definition of the Church is questioned, and the claims are refused as insufficient for their purpose, since by them Ahab's prophets might prove themselves true!

II. TESTS WHICH MAY BE TRUSTED. 1. *The witnesses should be honest.* (1) Ahab's prophets were interested in their testimony. They enjoyed the patronage of the king, and they said what they knew would gratify him. Their testimony, therefore, is open to suspicion. (2) Micaiah, on the contrary, had nothing to gain, but everything to lose, in taking his course. He knew the temper of the king. He was importuned by the king's messenger to concur with the king's prophets. He had already suffered for his faithfulness, for he seems to have been brought from the custody of Amon, in whose prison he had probably lain for three years. By flattering Ahab he might now obtain release, but by taking an opposite course he could only expect to go back to jail. Probabilities also were against him, for in the last two battles, Ahab, without the aid of Jehoshaphat, worsted the Syrians. Should the king of Israel now "return in peace" what may Micaiah expect? (3) Nothing but the consciousness that he was uttering the truth of God could account for the son of Imlah deliberately encountering all this. And only upon this ground could he hope for any favour from God. Suspicion, therefore, as to the honesty of Micaiah is out of the question. (4) But can it be pleaded that the honesty of the ecclesiastics who framed the decrees of councils is beyond suspicion? In decreeing the infallibility of the bishop of Rome, *e.g.*, were they disinterested, when they knew how pleasing to him would be the reputation of such an attribute, and when they knew what patronage and power to injure were vested in his hands? 2. *They should have miraculous authentication.* (1) It is easy to say, "Thus saith the Lord," but not so easy to evince it. The four hundred could *say* it, but they could show no miracle to *prove* that they spoke from God. (2) It was otherwise with Micaiah. For, with the Jews, we presume he was that prophet who "prophesied evil concerning Ahab," and authenticated his message by the sign of the lion destroying his fellow for disobedience (cf. ver. 8 with ch. xx. 35—43). (3) Clergy in council may claim Divine authority for their decrees, but unless they can verify their claim by adequate signs they presume when they impose. 3. *Their testimony should be agreeable to the word of God.* (1) "Micaiah said, As the Lord liveth, what the Lord saith unto me, that will I speak." The one question for us in these days is this: Is the testimony agreeable to the Bible? This we know by infallible proofs to be the word of God. "But," it is objected, "the Bible needs authoritative interpretation, and who is to interpret but the Church?" To which we may answer, And the Church still more needs authoritative interpretation, and who is to interpret but the Bible? The authority of the Bible is admitted; that of the Church is in question. (2) The right of private judgment must be maintained. For the exercise of this right we shall every one of us give account of himself unto God. That ill-defined thing, the Church, cannot release us from this obligation. We cannot put our judgment and conscience into commission.—J. A. M.

Vers. 15—23.—*Micaiah's Prophecy.* It is evident from the text and from ver. 8 that this was not the first time Ahab and Micaiah had met. The Jews suppose, apparently with reason, that Micaiah was that prophet who, when Ahab sent Ben-hadad away with a covenant, said to the king of Israel, "Thus saith the Lord: Because thou hast let go out of thine hand a man whom I appointed to utter destruction, therefore thy life shall go for his life, and thy people for his people" (see ch. xx. 35—43). In considering the prophecy of Micaiah now before us, we notice—

I. THAT IT IS PREFACED WITH A SALLY OF IRONY. 1. *He answers the king in the words of his prophets.* (1) Cf. vers. 6, 12, 15. (2) These words are equivocal. "The Lord shall deliver *it* into the hand of the king." What king? "The king" may mean either Ahab or Ben-hadad. What? This is not clear; for the word "it" is supplied. Is it Ramoth-Gilead or something else that is to be delivered into the hand of the king (of Israel)? or is it the king of Israel or something else to be delivered into the hand of the king (of Syria)? What kind of prophecy is this? (3) The utterance of these prophets resembles those of the heathen oracles, the following appropriate samples of which are given by A. Clarke: "The Delphic oracle spoke thus of Crœsus, which he understood to his own destruction: '*Crœsus, Halym penetrans, magnam subvertet opum vim;*' which is to say, 'If you march against Cyrus, he will overthrow *you*,' or '*you* will overthrow *him*.' He trusted in the *latter*, the *former* took place. He was deluded, yet the oracle maintained its credit. So in the following: '*Aio te, Æacida, Romanos vincere posse. Ibis redibis nunquam in bello peribis.*' Pyrrhus, king of Epirus, understood by this that he should conquer the Romans, against whom he was making war; but the oracle could be thus translated: 'The Romans shall overcome thee.' He trusted in the former, made unsuccessful war, and was overcome; and yet the juggling priest saved his credit. The latter line is capable of two opposite meanings: 'Thou shalt go, thou shalt return, thou shalt *never perish* in war,' or, 'Thou shalt go, thou shalt *never* return, thou *shalt perish* in war.'" 2. *But he repeats those words with significant expression.* (1) The bare repetition, with proper emphasis, of the equivocal words of the false prophets would be a fine stroke of irony. But when to emphasis were added tone, gesture, play of feature, the irony would become very keen. (2) This sarcasm of Micaiah is worthy to compare with that of Elijah (see ch. xviii. 27). "Go and prosper." This assurance of thy prophets is vague enough to encourage the confidence of a simpleton! 3. *God uses terrible rhetoric in His wrath.* (1) Irony and sarcasm are fitting weapons to be wielded against those who have neither conscience nor reason (see Prov. xxvi. 3—5). Ahab was a man of this class. Witness the logic of his hatred (ver. 8). He felt the sting (ver. 16). (2) These weapons are formidable in the hands of the Almighty (see Psa. ii. 4, 5; xxxvii. 13; Prov. i. 24—32; Eccles. xi. 9; Mal. ii. 17 and iii. 1; Rom. ii. 1—9).

II. THAT IT COMPARES FAVOURABLY WITH THAT OF HIS COMPETITORS. 1. *Its burden is the reverse of equivocal.* (1) There is in sacred prophecy a double sense, but the sound is certain. It is not a dubiousness but a manifoldness of meaning, a development, an evolution, such as we find in a seed that opens first into the blade, then into the ear, and eventually into the full corn in the ear. (2) This prophecy of Micaiah gave a distinct answer to the question of Ahab (ver. 13). The advice was to forbear. These "sheep." The sheep is not a creature fitted for battle. They have "no shepherd." Their king, deserted by the Spirit of God, has not the qualities of a shepherd. Therefore "Let them return every man to his house in peace." (3) But the advice contains a prophecy. It is to this effect: their king who ought to be their shepherd, shall fall at Ramoth-Gilead, and his people shall be like sheep, "scattered upon the mountains" by the power of the enemy (compare Zech. xiii. 7). 2. *The vision shows that all worlds are under Divine control.* (1) "I saw the Lord sitting on his throne." Here was a comparison with the scene before him, described ver. 10. Ahab and Jehoshaphat are enthroned as kings on the earth; but there is a King in the heavens immeasurably above them. (2) "And all the host of heaven standing by him on the right hand and on the. left." The host of heaven *stood* while Jehovah *sat*. They awaited His commands. Those on His "right hand" probably to render services of *benevolence;* those on His "left," services of *judgment.* (3) Then comes in another kind of agency (vers. 20—23). This scene is analogous to that described in the Book of Job (see Job i. 6; ii. 7). Things in heaven, things in earth, things under the earth, all serve the purposes of Divine Providence (see Job xii. 16; 2 Thess. ii. 11, 12; Rev. xx. 7, 8). (4) The waywardness of Ahab showed how fully he was under the control of the spirit of falsehood. This is seen in his senseless resentment against Micaiah. Turning to Jehoshaphat, he said, "Did I not tell thee that he would prophesy no good concerning me, but evil?" as if Micaiah's own utterances could control the providence of God. Then turning to his officers he had Micaiah marched back to the prison where Ahab knew he could find him (cf. ver. 8 with vers. 26, 27). Let us give due heed to the more sure word of prophecy.—J. A. M.

Vers. 24—29.—*The Argument of Wickedness.* The Bible is a book of texts because it is a book of types. It does not profess to give full histories, but refers to public records for these (see Josh. x. 13; 2 Sam. i. 18; 1 Kings xi. 41; 1 Chron. ix. 1). Inspiration selects from histories typical or representative incidents to bring out the principles of the grace and truth of God. In the scene before us we have types of wickedness in Zedekiah and Ahab, the one ecclesiastical, the other civil, which may be profitably studied in the arguments they use contending with Micaiah, the representative of the truth of God. These arguments are—

I. RAGE AGAINST THE TRUTH. The reason is obvious, viz., because the truth is the worst that can be said of the wicked. 1. *It is the worst that can be said of their character.* (1) It shows up their *selfishness.* The one object of Ahab was that "good" might be prophesied *for him.* To gain this he sold himself to his four hundred liars. These liars, to gain the patronage of Ahab, sold their consciences. Because Ahab could not gain flattery from Micaiah, he hated him. (2) It shows up their *folly.* For what was the selfishness of Ahab but self-deception? The patronage of liars could not convert falsehood into truth, neither could the persecution of a true man convert truth into falsehood. Zedekiah, in deceiving Ahab, deceived his own soul. All sin is folly. (3) It evinces their *degradation,* for it proves them to be the dupes and serfs of infernal spirits. Can degradation go lower? 2. *It is the worst that can be said of their doom.* (1) The wicked are to be destroyed in *time.* Ahab in particular was to fall at Ramoth-Gilead. From that battle he was "not to return in peace." Zedekiah was to "go into an inner chamber to hide himself," as Ben-hadad had done (ch. xx. 30), and there to meet his fate. While to the righteous death is an entrance to glory, it is the "king of terrors" to the wicked (see 1 Cor. xv. 55—57). The sting is here: (2) The wicked are to be destroyed in *eternity.* The alarm with which the ancients received predictions of maltreatment to their corpses arose from their apprehension that it presaged a posthumous retribution upon the soul. The dogs licking the blood of Ahab would suggest that devils would not only be the instigators but also the instruments of his ruin. (3) Who can estimate the horrors of damnation? The truth will prove to be the worst that can be said of the lost. Is it wonderful, then, that the wicked should abhor the truth? 3. *They are therefore constrained to hypocrisy.* (1) For their own sakes they have to play the hypocrite. They conceal their selfishness and affect generosity, conscious that were their base soul-hunger to come honestly to the day, they would become odious. They hide their folly and affect wisdom lest they should suffer contempt. (2) For the sake of society wicked men are hypocrites. Were they to be honestly known to each other, respect and confidence would be at an end; in fact, society would be impossible. There are no friendships in hell.

II. THE RESENTMENT OF VIOLENCE. 1. *The logic of the wicked is weak.* (1) Zedekiah's speech was pertinacious: "Which way went the Spirit of the Lord from me to speak unto thee?" He assumed what Micaiah had not conceded, that he *ever had* the Spirit of the Lord. Micaiah had declared him, on the contrary, to have been influenced by a "spirit" of a very different description. Zedekiah also denied what he should have disproved, viz., that Micaiah *had* the Spirit of the Lord. (2) Ahab wanted a prophet of the God of truth to tell lies to please him. He found four hundred to tell him lies, professedly in the name of the Lord. But the one honest man who told him the truth he imprisoned, because the truth did not please him. Yet the truth was what he adjured him to tell. What reason is there in all this? (3) What sinner is there in our day who can clear himself of folly? (See Prov. xiii. 19; 1 Cor. iii. 19.) 2. *The strength of the wicked is tyranny.* (1) The reason of Zedekiah was in his fist (ver. 24). "Which way?" From the fist to the cheek? The coward us d this argument with a council of four hundred ecclesiastics about him, and the civil power in reserve. So was Jesus insulted (see Matt. xxvi. 57—68). So were the Protestant confessors. False prophets have ever been the worst enemies of the true. Micaiah did not return the blow, but referred the decision to God. True prophets wield other than carnal weapons. (2) The reason of Ahab was in his bribes and prisons. Micaiah could not be cajoled as the four hundred were, therefore " the king of Israel said, Take Micaiah, carry him back unto Amon the governor of the city, and to Joash the king's son, and say, Thus saith the king, put this fellow in prison, and feed him with bread of affliction, and with water of affliction, until I come in peace." (3) But truth is not vanquished thus. How confident was Ahab that he should "come in peace"! And this is that Ahab who three or four years before so sagaciously said to Ben-hadad, "Let not him that girdeth on his harness boast himself as he that putteth it off." Persistency in sin does not sharpen men's wits. Time vindicates truth. To this vindicator Micaiah called the attention of the people (ver. 29). (4) But where was Jehoshaphat? He was silent when he should have spoken for the prophet of God. See the influence of bad company. "So the king of Israel, and Jehoshaphat the king of Judah went up to Ramoth-Gilead." Alas, Jehoshaphat!—J. A. M.

Vers. 30—38. *Lessons of the Battle.* After disposing of Micaiah by sending him to prison with hard fare as the reward of his faithfulness, Ahab and Jehoshaphat gathered their forces and set out together to fight for the recovery of Ramoth-Gilead. The events of the day show—

I. THAT PROPHECY MAY TEND TO ITS OWN FULFILMENT. 1. *Micaiah's words influenced Ahab's conduct.* (1) Though Ahab had imprisoned the prophet he could not shake off the influence of his prophecy. So with a view to obviating its effect he proposed to disguise himself. He speaks of himself in the third person (ver. 30), thus (התחפש), "He will [strip] disguise himself"—a form of speech, perhaps, considered suitable to an action in which he was to appear as a third person. To complete the deception, if we follow the LXX., he induced Jehoshaphat to put on his (Ahab's) robes. (a) Note the subtlety of the wicked. Ahab's proposal to Jehoshaphat was ostensibly to give him the post of honour in commanding the army. This, too, may have suggested the use of the third person in speaking of himself. Ahab's real purpose was to divert from himself the fury of the battle; and probably he hoped Jehoshaphat might be slain. In that case his son-in-law would succeed to the throne of Judah, and he might be able so to manage him as to serve his own purposes. (b) In all this we see the danger of bad company. We see it likewise in the sad fact that Jehoshaphat should become a party to a contrivance to falsify the word of God! (2) But how useless are disguises when the providence of Omniscience is concerned! Ahab might hide himself from the Syrians, but he could not hide himself from God. Neither could he hide himself from angels and devils, who are instruments of Divine Providence, ever influencing men, and even natural laws, or forces of nature. Note: No disguise will avail to evade the scrutiny and retributions of the judgment-day. (3) Yet by his disguise Ahab, unwittingly, helped the prophecy. "The king of Syria commanded his thirty and two captains that had rule over his chariots, saying, Fight neither with small nor great, save only with the king of Israel." Suppose Ahab had been in Jehoshaphat's place, and had fallen into the hands of the captains, what would have become of the words of Elijah? (See ch. xxi. 19.) But as things worked out these words became literally true. 2. *They also influenced the conduct of the Syrians.* (1) The Syrians would be aware of the prophecy of Micaiah dooming Ahab to fall at Ramoth-Gilead. For in a country about the size of North Wales, Samaria being distant from Ramoth-Gilead only thirty miles, the news of this public meeting of kings and contest of prophets could not be a secret. Ahab would facilitate the publication of the encouragement he had from the four hundred, to strike terror into the Syrians; but where the news of his encouragement went the words of Micaiah also would travel. (2) Probably this intelligence determined the Syrians to "fight only against the king of Israel," in which they would have the God of Israel with them, the formidableness of whose hostility they had experienced in the last two battles (compare 2 Chron. xxxv. 21, 22). To this Jehoshaphat probably was indebted for the sparing of his life, for "God moved the Syrians to depart from him" (see 2 Chron. xviii. 31). And probably they were influenced by it to agree to the proclamation to disband, when the death of Ahab became known (cf. vers. 17, 36). 3. Note a remarkable illustration of this principle in the zeal of Jehu in exterminating the house of Ahab (see

2 Kings ix. 25, 26; x. 10, 11, 16, 17). Those who are "looking for," are thereby "hastening the coming of the day of God" (see 2 Peter iii. 12).

II. THAT NEVERTHELESS THE HAND OF GOD IS IN IT. 1. *This was evident in the case of Ahab.* The purpose of Ben-hadad, should Ahab have fallen into his hands, is not recorded. Would he return Ahab's compliment of releasing him with a covenant? Would he show Ahab how he ought to have treated him? (2) But God had other means than the captains of Ben-hadad to accomplish His purpose. "A man drew a bow at a venture (marg. "in his simplicity") and smote the king of Israel between the joints and harness." A simpleton brings down a king! (See Prov. i. 32.) God guided the arrow to the opening in the joints of the armour, as He guided the pebble from the sling of David into the frontals of Goliath. No armour is proof against the shafts of Divine vengeance. (3) The hand of God also was seen in the sequel. The prophecies of Elijah and Micaiah seem to be in conflict. The one speaks of the dogs licking the blood of Ahab at "Samaria;" the other of Ahab falling at "Ramoth-Gilead." Who but God could so order events that there should be no conflict here? "The blood ran out of the wound into the midst (Heb. bosom) of the chariot;" perhaps more correctly, "into the bosom of the charioteer," on which the king leaned. "And *one* washed the chariot;" or rather, "And the driver washed himself in the pool of Samaria, and the dogs licked his blood" *i.e.*, the blood of Ahab which fell from the bosom of the driver. "And the things they washed." For זנות denotes the *several kinds of things*, being derived from זן, a *kind* or *species*. Before the person and things defiled with blood were permitted to enter the city, they were to be washed; and the dogs licked up the blood that fell from the driver's bosom, and off the things, as they lay to be washed (see Psa. lxviii. 23). (4) But were not the words of Elijah "In the place where the dogs licked the blood of Naboth" (viz., Jezreel) "shall dogs lick thy blood, even thine"? But in the context there, the vineyard of Naboth is said to be in Samaria (see ch. xxi. 18, 19), because Jezreel, like Bethel, was one of the "cities of Samaria" (see ch. xiii. 32). In the very vineyard of Naboth did the blood of Ahab flow from the veins of his son (see 2 Kings ix. 25, 26). The providence that accomplished is no less admirable than the omniscience that predicted. 2. *This was also evident in the case of Jehoshaphat.* (1) Micaiah did not say that the king of Judah should fall at Ramoth-Gilead; but his prophecy did intimate that he would be of little use to the army. The word (אדנים) in ver. 17 rendered "master" is plural, and evidently associates Jehoshaphat with Ahab. When Ahab was wounded to death and Jehoshaphat had fled for his life, the people had "no masters," so the proclamation soon followed which determined "every man to his house in peace." (2) Jehoshaphat's danger lay in his being assimilated to Ahab. He should never have said, "I am as thou art" (ver. 4), then would he not have been persuaded to don Ahab's robes. By the influence of his company Jehoshaphat was becoming morally like him, and therefore was in danger of sharing his miserable fate (see Prov. xiii. 20). (3) To avoid this danger he had to become himself again. "He cried out" [to Jehovah] (see 2 Chron. xviii. 31); and thus was discovered to the captains, who would expect to hear Ahab cry rather to Baal. The hand of God was evident in his deliverance; and this he might read as a parable assuring him that his future safety must lie in his renouncing evil companions and returning to the piety of his earlier years.—J. A. M.

Vers. 39, 40, 51—53.—*Survival.* After the account of Ahab's death and burial, and of the manner in which the dogs of Samaria fulfilled the prophecy of Elijah, the earlier verses of our text follow. In the first of these the reader is referred to the archives of the nation for an account of the "rest of the acts" and works of this monarch, viz., those to which inspiration was not here specially directed. In the second, the succession of Ahaziah is mentioned. With these verses, because of the unity of the subject, we associate the three verses referring to the reign of Ahaziah, with which the chapter closes. Taking the latter first in order, we see—
I. THAT AHAB SURVIVED IN AHAZIAH. 1. *This was legally true.* (1) "So Ahab slept with his fathers; and Ahaziah his son reigned in his stead." In law, a

man is said to "live in his heirs." He is never legally dead while he has an heir. There is a good reason for this. Ahaziah would never have mounted the throne of Israel unless his father had been there before him. He reigned in the posthumous influence of Ahab. His representative. (2) When a man is what is called "the architect of his own fortune," he is said to have had "no father." But in this language the fact is ignored that, under Providence, this "architect" is indebted to his ancestry for his existence, for his faculties, and for the circumstances which he may have seized and moulded into this "fortune." 2. *It was also morally true.* (1) In Ahaziah the vices of Ahab were reproduced. "He did evil in the sight of the Lord, and walked in the way of his father." The bad example of his father wrought its influence into his character, and thus Ahab survived in Ahaziah. (2) The record descends to particulars. "He walked in the way of his father, and *in the way of his mother.*" Here not only is Jezebel reproduced in Ahaziah, but Ahab's sin in marrying Jezebel also survives. "And in the way of Jeroboam the son of Nebat, who made Israel to sin." Here is not only the posthumous influence of Jeroboam, but also of the sin of Ahab in perpetuating it. "For he served Baal, and worshipped him." The establishment of this Canaanitish abomination was due to Ahab and Jezebel, and they infamously survive in its perpetuation. (3) Note (*a*) A Church is not the more true for being established. Here were two State Churches which were, in the Biblical sense, atheistic. (*b*) For concurrent endowment, whatever may be said for its expediency, there can be no moral defence. 3. *But there was no necessity for this.* (1) Legal representation is an accident over which we have no control. It is a notable truth that men have influences in spite of themselves, and that these also are posthumous. (2) But *moral* representation is in a different category. Ahaziah might have reigned in Ahab's stead without imitating his vices. "Jehoram the son of Ahab," *e.g.*, "wrought evil in the sight of the Lord; but *not* like his father, and like his mother; for he put away the image of Baal that his father had made" (2 Kings iii. 2). (3) Ahaziah should have been admonished by the history of the judgments of God upon the house of Jeroboam. He should have taken the warning given in the judgments of God on the sins of his father. His guilt, therefore, was upon his own head, and he suffered accordingly. He reigned two years. God makes short work with some sinners. His death was provoked by his perversity (see 2 Kings i. 3, 4). We see further—

II. THAT AHAB SURVIVES IN HISTORY. 1. *He survived in secular history.* His acts and works were written in the chronicles of his nation. (1) Amongst these were mentioned "all the cities that he built." Perhaps this building of cities simply meant the construction of fortifications for their defence. Whether they reflected credit or discredit upon his memory we cannot pronounce. A man may do a great deal of work to very little profit. (2) The chronicles mentioned "the ivory house which he made." This palace had its description probably from the quantity of that valuable substance used in its ornamentation. But this does not seem to have been to his honour. A kingdom impoverished through famines, wars, and idolatries was in no position to bear the cost of such a piece of luxurious and selfish vanity. Amos accordingly denounces this work of pride (Amos iii. 15). (3) The survival of Ahab in secular history was a consequence of his social position. The masons and carpenters, whose skill brought the works of Ahab to perfection, had no mention there. Social *status* is a talent from God, for the right use of which men are accountable. 2. *He survives in sacred history.* (1) The sacred history consists of selections from the secular under the guiding influence of Divine inspiration, with a view to illustrating the principles of the providence, truth, and grace of God. To illustrate such principles is the noblest end of writing. So of reading. What quantities of trash, in which the claims of God are ignored, is both written and read! (2) In these selections the notices of the wicked are generally brief. Perhaps no wicked man has a larger share of the sacred writings occupied with his acts than Ahab. Such acts are not agreeable to the Spirit of God. But in the hands of inspiration they are made an influence for good. They are recorded, apparently, because of their relation to the actions of prophets and good men. They are made to serve as a dark background to show up to admiration virtuous qualities, and to be made themselves odious in the contrast. The principles of the wicked should only be studied to be shunned. So God brings good out of evil. (3) The sacred records have survived the secular. "The book of the chronicles of the kings of Israel" has long since perished. The sacred records have come down to our times. In these, after a lapse of nearly thirty centuries, Ahab survives. But for these his name would not be known. Note (a) the Providence which has preserved the Scriptures evinces their Divine authenticity. (b) Things are permanent as they stand related to the everlasting God. (c) The posthumous influence points to the immortality of man.—J. A. M.

Vers. 41—50.—*Jehoshaphat.* These words give a summary of the life of this king of Judah, and faithfully record, as the Scriptures do to admiration, the good and the bad, as these will be considered in the judgment of the great day. Consider—

I. THE PRAISE OF JEHOSHAPHAT. 1. *He came of a good stock.* (1) He was " of the house and lineage of David." The traditions of that house were in many respects a glorious inheritance. David was a "man after God's own heart." In no instance was he found inclining to idolatry. (2) He was the son of Asa. Of his mother we have this significant mention : "And his mother's name was Azubah, the daughter of Shilhi. And he walked in the ways of Asa his father, and departed not from it, doing that which was right in the sight of the Lord." This suggests the healthiness of his mother's moral influence. The reference here to Asa, too, is highly honourable. (3) The blessing of pious parents is inestimable. It works beneficially in example, in precept, in solicitude. This last is most effectual in prayer to God. Those who are favoured with godly parents should praise God evermore. Wicked children of pious parents are doubly culpable. 2. *He improved his advantages.* (1) He " walked in the ways of Asa his father." These were ways of righteousness. Let the children of godly parents now ask themselves whether they walk in the good ways of their ancestors. (2) He " turned not aside from it." He showed no favour to idolatry. The note which follows is no impeachment of the truth of this statement : "Nevertheless the high places were not taken away ; for the people offered and burnt incense yet in the high places." The high places that Jehoshaphat spared were those in which the true God was worshipped in accordance with the usage of patriarchal times (see 2 Chron. xxxiii. 17). (3) He went farther than Asa in the work of reformation :—"The remnant of the Sodomites which remained in the days of Asa his father he took out of the land." The parallel place to this in the Chronicles is : " And his heart was lifted up in the ways of the Lord : moreover he took away the high places and the groves (אשרים) out of Judah " (2 Chron. xvii. 6 ; xix. 3). By removing the Sodomites we understand that he demolished their shrines, their Asherim, their instruments of pollution. When the nests are destroyed the rooks fly. 3. *This was to his praise.* (1) Others, similarly placed, failed to make this good use of their advantages. Jehoram, his own son, may be mentioned in sad contrast to him. Several of his ancestors had scandalously departed from the godly ways of their father David. Men will be justified or condemned in the light of such comparisons in the last great day (see Luke xi. 31, 32). (2) God rewarded him with prosperity (2 Chron. xvii. 4, 5). He had an army—probably an enrolled militia—of 1,100,000 men. The Philistines, Arabians, and Edomites were subject to him. The note here, that " there was then no king in Edom : a deputy was king," which prefaces the account of his fleet at Ezion-Geber, was designed to explain how Jehoshaphat was able to have a fleet at a port which belonged to Edom (see ch. ix. 26), viz., because he appointed the viceroy in Edom which was tributary to him (see Gen. xxvii. 29, 37 ; 2 Sam. viii. 14).

II. THE BLAME OF JEHOSHAPHAT. This seems all to have been connected with the "peace " which he made "with the king of Israel." It appears to have commenced with—1. *The marriage of his son.* (1) Jehoram, the eldest son of Jehoshaphat, and with his consent, took Athaliah, the daughter of Ahab and Jezebel, to be his wife. Jehoshaphat's heart was lifted up with the abundance of his "riches and honour," and "joined affinity with Ahab" (see 2 Chron. xviii. 1). He became too great to be content with an humble match for his son, and sacrificed godliness to grandeur. He has many imitators in this. (2) Unequal yoking has ever been prolific in mischief. Athaliah inherited the evil spirit of both her parents, and she led away the heart of Jehoram from God to his ruin. The object of this marriage was to build up the house of Jehoshaphat, but it well-nigh proved its ruin (see 2 Chron. xxii. 10, 11). God is the builder of families (see 2 Sam. vii. 11, 27; 1 Kings ii. 24; xi. 38; Psa. cxxvii. 1). 2. *His friendship with Ahab.* (1) This evil grew out of the marriage. The peace between Israel and Judah, which in the abstract was a benefit, was probably a condition of the marriage. But the friendship between Jehoshaphat and Ahab which followed, was too intimate for the good of the king of Judah's soul. (2) Evils beget evils. This friendship led to Jehoshaphat helping Ahab in his war against Syria, and had nearly cost Jehoshaphat his life. It also sullied his reputation, for he was persuaded into it by Ahab against the voice of Micaiah. This friendship exposed Jehoshaphat to the reproof of the prophet Jehu (2 Chron. xix. 2). 3. *His friendship with Ahaziah.* (1) This son of Ahab was no more a companion fit for Jehoshaphat than Ahab. For Ahaziah "walked in the way of his father, and in the way of his mother, and in the way of Jeroboam the son of Nebat, who made Israel to sin: for he served Baal and worshipped him, and provoked to anger the Lord God of Israel, according to all that his father had done." (2) Yet Jehoshaphat formed a trade alliance with Ahaziah. They jointly fitted out a fleet at the port of Ezion-Geber, on the Red Sea, to sail to Ophir for gold. But for this God rebuked him, and "the ships were broken" in the port (see 2 Chron. xx. 35—37). Let no money consideration, no gold of Ophir, induce godly young men to enter into trade partnerships with the ungodly. (3) This judgment of God had a salutary effect upon Jehoshaphat. For when Ahaziah would renew the attempt at Ezion-Geber, Jehoshaphat declined (ver. 49). Let us be careful never to repeat a blunder.—J. A. M.

Vers. 1—28.—*Crime brings its own punishment.* I. THE WICKED RUSH UPON DESTRUCTION. 1. *Ahab provokes the war in which he himself will perish.* The peace which had lasted so long might have continued. Every day it was prolonged was a day placed between him and death; and yet with his own hand he brings to an end the period of grace. How often are the calamities of the wicked invoked by themselves, and are the fruit of their own rashness! 2. *It came as the prompting of the deepest wisdom.* Jehoshaphat's presence afforded the opportunity of forming a league to which success seemed certain. The selfish cunning of the sinful becomes a snare to them. 3. *He closes his ear against God's deterring counsel.* (1) When asked to inquire of God, he brings those only who will speak the things that accord with his own determination. The false prophets are called, but not the true. (2) When compelled to bring Micaiah from the prison (see ver. 26, "carry him *back* unto Amon," &c.), he endeavours to prevent Jehoshaphat being moved by his words. Micaiah is his enemy, therefore a prophecy of good is not to be expected from *him.* (3) When warned he will not be hindered, but defies God, who would save him, by insulting and persecuting His servant (ver. 27). II. THE FALSE PROPHETS. 1. *They bind the cords which are leading a sinful soul to death.* The word which they profess to speak for God is a word which it pleases the king to hear. It is the echo of his own desires (ver. 6). There are those who by voice and pen proclaim a new gospel. It is no longer sought to lead up the world to God and thus reconcile it to Him. It is boldly declared that the reconciliation is already effected. God has come down to it. There is no anger and no threatening and no terrible shadow of judgment. There is nothing but goodness and love. They are the false prophets of to-day, and these do for the men of their generation what those did for Ahab. 2. *Their blasphemy.* When a prophet of *Jehovah* was asked for (ver. 7), they who have hitherto spoken only of Adonai do not scruple to take the name of the Highest into their lips (vers. 11, 12). We do not escape the false prophets when we appeal from their speech concerning the

God of nature to His revealed will, the word of the Lord. They meet us there. It is in vain we seek to rest upon the plainest words; they are explained away. Hell is a superstitious dream, and the cross of the disciples of Christ a mere figure of speech, with no hard, stern reality behind it. 3. *They are possessed by a spirit of falsehood* (vers. 21—23). Their position is more a punishment of past sin than conscious transgression. They speak with honesty of a sort, but it is out of their heart's darkness. They were willing to be deceived, and they have been deceived. They did not wish to know God as He is, and they have been left with the god of their own imagination. In which school are we, that of the false prophets, or of the true? 4. *They smite the true servants of God.* Zedekiah's blow preceded the king's judgment. It proved nothing but his own soul's distance from God. It was the act of a man provoked by zeal for his own honour. He who had been moved by zeal for God's honour would have stood in silent awe of that terrible but certain judgment which the man was braving.

III. THE TRUE SERVANT OF GOD. 1. *In a corrupt court his is no welcome presence* (ver. 8). The distance between Ahab and God was reflected in that which separated him from the speaker of God's word. Continued faithfulness, if it may not win, must be repelled and hated. " Woe unto you when *all* men speak well of you; for so," &c. 2. *The necessity laid on him to declare the whole counsel of God* (ver. 14). He cannot turn to the right hand or the left; the world's wealth cannot bribe him, its power and cruelty cannot terrify him. What king or people desire to hear, or courtly prophets or current creeds have said, weighs nothing with him. He cannot speak in God's name aught save what *God has said.* 3. *His message.* He speaks first in easily discerned irony (vers. 15, 16). It was an intimation to the king that he desired to hear no prophecy that would run counter to his inclinations. Then, when he is solemnly appealed to, a picture is presented (ver. 17) of the smitten, shepherdless people, which might well have touched even Ahab's heart. Next king and people are led up to the throne of God. The servant and his words are forgotten in the revelation of his Master. Even the false prophet's utterances are turned to account; they and the reliance which the king is placing on them are part fulfilment of the Divine vengeance. There was deeper tenderness and truer love for Ahab in that one breast than in all the four hundred. 4. *The greatness of all true service for God.* There is a glory about that despised, persecuted man before which that of both kings pales. It is a glory which nothing can tear from the loyal heart, and which shines the brighter amid the world's darkening hate. It is a glory which may be our own.—U.

Vers. 29—40.—*The Certainty of God's Threatenings.* I. AHAB'S ATTEMPT TO ELUDE THE DIVINE VENGEANCE. 1. *His apprehension of coming evil.* If Micaiah's words were not the words of God, why should he take precautions? His heart gives the lie to his own unbelief; the words cling to him. The bold refusal to listen to God's word is no assurance that the soul will not afterwards be shaken by a fearful looking for of judgment. 2. *His ungenerousness* (ver. 30). " I will disguise myself; but put thou on thy robes." The effect of the counsel was necessarily to concentrate the enemy's attention upon Jehoshaphat. Sin not only makes a man a coward, it robs him of nobleness. 3. *The immediate effect of Ahab's stratagem.* Ben-hadad's arrangements for the capture or slaughter of Ahab were rendered of no avail. The captains could not find the man they sought. A momentary success often attends the plans of those who endeavour to flee from God. 4. *The chance shot.* The success of Ahab's device only served to make the blow come more plainly from the hand of God. Ben-hadad's purpose could be baffled, but not His. There is no escape from God.
II. THE FULFILMENT OF GOD'S WORD. 1. *He fell at Ramoth-Gilead* (ver. 20). 2. *"Israel was scattered upon the hills," and the command was given to return* (vers. 17, 36). 3. *The dogs licked Ahab's blood* (ch. xxi. 19), not in Jezreel, indeed, because the judgment then pronounced was that of the overthrow of the dynasty. This was delayed on account of Ahab's repentance, and happened, as predicted, "in his son's days" (ch. xxi. 29). But the personal part of the prediction, "The dogs

shall lick thy blood, even thine," was not revoked. There are prophecies both of
evil and of good, within the range of which we set ourselves. God's words are
touching us, and will likewise be literally fulfilled.—U.

Vers. 41—53.—*Two Life Stories.* I. JEHOSHAPHAT'S. 1. *He prolonged the good
influence of his father's reign.* Judah's thought was still kept under the light of
truth, and its life more fully led into the ways of God: he completed his father's
reforms (ver. 46). The continuance of God's work anywhere is as important as
the origination of it. 2. *He was consistent.* "He turned not aside from it." He
did not merely begin well; over his whole reign there rested the Divine approval;
he did "that which was right in the eyes of the Lord." The life which is ever
sinning, repenting, forgetting, achieves nothing. It is like a plant uprooted and
planted again, to be again uprooted, &c., and which, even should its life be preserved, will never bear fruit. It is like " a backsliding heifer," and with such a life
the great Husbandman's work cannot be carried on. 3. *There was failure as well
as success in his career.* "Nevertheless the high places were not taken away."
He had endeavoured to remove them (2 Chron. xvii. 6). But " the people offered
and burnt incense yet in the high places." The mightiest efforts in the great warfare with darkness leave something for other hands to do, and must till He come
who alone can perfect all things. 4. *He sought to be at peace with his brethren*
(ver. 44). He went further in this, indeed, than he ought to have done (2 Chron.
xix. 2), but the desire for peace was laudable. 5. *He humbled himself under God's
rebuke* (compare vers. 48, 49 with 2 Chron. xx. 35—37). At first he had been beguiled into fellowship with the idolatrous king of Israel without reflecting upon the
danger which lay in it for himself and his people. But when God had manifested
His displeasure, nothing could make him renew the confederacy. The judgment
might mistake, but the heart was loyal to God.

II. AHAZIAH'S. 1. *A sinful life.* "He did evil in the sight of the Lord." With
such a life there was no possibility of blessing for his people. The roots of his usefulness were destroyed. To do, we must first of all become. Our work cannot rise
above the level of our life. 2. *A disastrous policy* (vers. 52, 53). He continued
the work of Israel's destruction. The departure made by Jeroboam and perfected
by Ahab and Jezebel, he accepted in its full rejection of Jehovah. He did not go
beyond them, he simply did "according to all that his father had done," but in
doing this his sin was of the deepest dye. His father had been judged, but God
was still braved, and Israel was led still nearer to destruction. We may only continue what others have begun; but if we pay no heed to the proofs of God's anger,
and take no thought of the inevitable results of the policy we pursue, our persistence
may be one of the deepest crimes against God and man.—U.

Ver. 34.—*The Pierced Armour.* This occurred during the third campaign of
Ben-hadad against Israel. Micaiah had forewarned Ahab against the danger he
incurred, and was cast into prison for his pains. The warning was, however, taken
sufficiently to heart to induce the king to disguise himself. Describe the expedient
adopted, and its remarkable failure. Ahab was in many respects a typical sinner.
He was an idolater, a persecutor, impenitent, though sometimes touched; and in
the plenitude of power he fell. We see here—

I. A MAN ARMED AGAINST GOD. True he was fighting against the Syrians, but as
he girded on his armour he remembered and defied the words of the prophet.
His ominous prophecy should not be fulfilled, he would yet come back safe and
victorious to put Micaiah to death, and with this determination he put Jehoshaphat
in command, and clad himself with proof armour. In spirit, therefore, he was
fighting not only against the hosts of Syria, but against the word of God. Hence
let us depict one who is armed *against* God. Reverse the description St. Paul gives
(Eph. vi.) of one armed *by* God. The impenitent sinner represented by Ahab
defends himself. 1. *By false hopes* (Deut. xxix. 19, 20). These constitute his
" helmet," which wards off true thoughts of self and sin. He blindly trusts in
Divine mercy, while sin is unrepented. forgetting that " a God all mercy is a God

unjust" (Young).   "There is none other name given under heaven whereby we may be saved," &c.   "How shall we escape, if we neglect so great salvation?"   2. *By a hardened heart.*   This is his "breastplate."   A man impenitent is a man lost.   Some are "past feeling," their consciences are "seared as with a hot iron," and God gives them over to their "hardness of heart," and to an "impenitent mind."   "Who has hardened himself against God, and prospered?"   We may become "hardened by the deceitfulness of sin."   3. *By defiant words.*   There is a tongue which is set on fire of hell.   Adduce examples.   Ahab defied Micaiah.   4. *By an unbelieving mind.*   The king questioned the truth of the prophet's message. He had more confidence in his own past success and in his military skill than in the declaration of a man who knew something of God but nothing of war.   Unbelief ever prevents the inflowing of Divine goodness.   Jesus "could do no mighty works because of their unbelief."   5. *By a dumb spirit.*   No asking for pardon, no cry for mercy rose from Ahab's heart, or it would not have proved too late; for the Lord is "not willing that any should perish."

II. A MAN STRICKEN BY GOD.   The chance arrow of the Syrian archer fulfilled the Divine purpose.   1. *By the arrow of conviction.*   God's word is sharp and powerful, and pierces even to the dividing asunder of soul and spirit, and is a discerner of the thoughts and intents of the heart.   (1) *It may be shot unwittingly,* as the archer drew at a venture not knowing what he might hit.   Let our words for God be pointed, and be winged by faith, and He will see that they hit the mark. (2) *It may touch the one vulnerable spot.*   That arrow pierced "between the joints of armour" otherwise proof.   So David's stone would have fallen powerless on the greaves or the breastplate of the giant of Gath.   God, who knows our hearts, tries every avenue.   Through our reason, through our affections, through our conscience, His word seeks to find its way.   2. *By the arrow of judgment.*   (1) *It was foretold* (ver. 28).   Ahab ran the risk.   So do they who continue in sin after hearing of "a certain fearful looking for of judgment and fiery indignation, which shall devour the adversaries."   (2) *It was inevitable.*   All disguise and precaution were unavailing.   The justice of God sooner or later reaches the right man.   (3) *It was terrible.*   The weak, sensuous man, whose promise had sometimes been so fair, fell in a moment from kingship, from life, and from hope.   "He that being reproved hardeneth his neck, shall suddenly be destroyed, and that without often remedy."—A. R.

HOMILETICAL INDEX

TO

THE FIRST BOOK OF KINGS

II KINGS

EXPOSITION AND HOMILETICS BY

G. RAWLINSON

HOMILIES BY VARIOUS AUTHORS

C. H. IRWIN   J. ORR

D. THOMAS

THE SECOND
BOOK OF THE KINGS

—◇—

INTRODUCTION

—◇—

THOUGH the two Books of the Kings "were originally and are really but one work, by one writer or compiler," and though most of the points which need to be touched on in an "Introduction," being common to both books, have been already treated in the Introductory section prefixed to the Commentary on 1 Kings, still there seem to be certain subjects more particularly connected with the Second Book, which require a more general and consecutive treatment than is possible in a running commentary on the text; and the consideration of these will form, it is hoped, a not superfluous or unwelcome "Introduction" to the present volume. These subjects are, especially, (1) "the difficulties in the Chronology," and (2) "the interconnection between sacred and profane history during the period of the Israelite monarchy."

I. DIFFICULTIES IN THE CHRONOLOGY.

The difficulties in the chronology attach almost exclusively to the Second Book. In the First Book we find, indeed, that portions of years are counted for years in the estimates given of the length of kings' reigns, and that thus there is a tendency in the chronology to exaggerate itself—a tendency which is most marked where the reigns are shortest. But the synchronisms which enable us to detect this peculiarity are a sufficient safeguard from serious error; and it is not difficult to arrange in parallel columns the Jewish and the Israelite lists in such a way that all or almost all the statements made in the book are brought into harmony; e.g. Rehoboam reigned seventeen *full* years (ch. xiv. 21), when he was succeeded by Abijam, whose first year was parallel with the eighteenth of Jeroboam (ch. xv. 1), and who reigned three full years (ch. xv. 2), dying and being succeeded by Asa in Jeroboam's twentieth year (ch. xv. 9). Jeroboam, having reigned twenty-two years *incomplete* (ch. xiv. 20), died in Asa's second year, and was succeeded by Nadab (ch. xiv. 25), who reigned parts of two years, being slain by Baasha in Asa's third year (ch. xv. 28). Baasha held the throne for twenty-four *incomplete* years, his accession falling in Asa's third, and his death in Asa's twenty-sixth year (ch. xvi. 8). Elah's "two years" (ch. xvi. 8) were, like Nadab's and Baasha's, *incomplete*, since he ascended the throne in Asa's twenty-sixth, and was killed by Zimri in Asa's twenty-seventh year (ch. xvi. 15). At the end of a week Zimri was slain by Omri, and a struggle followed between Omri and Tibni, which lasted four years —from Asa's twenty-seventh year to his thirty-first (ch. xvi. 23). Omri's reign was reckoned by some to begin at this time, by others to have begun upon the death of Zimri. It is from this earlier event that his "twelve years" are to be dated, and those years are again *incomplete*, since they commenced in Asa's twenty-seventh, and terminated in his thirty-eighth year (ch. xvi. 29). Ahab's "twenty-two years" (ch. xvi. 29) should, apparently, be twenty-*one*, since they ran parallel with the last four years of Asa and with the first seventeen of Jehoshaphat. The entire period from the accession of Rehoboam and Jeroboam to the death of Ahab and accession of Ahaziah in the seventeenth year of Jehoshaphat was seventy-eight years.

TABULAR VIEW OF THE CHRONOLOGY OF 1 KINGS.

Year before Christ.	Year of the Davidic kingdom.	King of all Israel.	
1012	41	SOLOMON, 40 years (1 Kings xi. 42)	
		Kings of Judah.	Kings of Israel.
972	81	Rehoboam, 17 years (1 Kings xiv. 21)	Jeroboam, 22 years (1 Kings xiv. 20)
955	98	Abijam, 3 years (1 Kings xv. 2)	18th year of Jeroboam (1 Kings xv. 1)
952	101	Asa, 41 years (1 Kings xv. 10)	20th year of Jeroboam (1 Kings xv. 9)
951	102	2nd year of Asa (1 Kings xv. 25)	Nadab, 2 years (1 Kings xv. 25)
950	103	3rd year of Asa (1 Kings xv. 28)	Baasha, 24 years (1 Kings xv. 33)
927	126	26th year of Asa (1 Kings xvi. 8)	Elah, 2 years (1 Kings xvi. 8)
926	127	27th year of Asa (1 Kings xvi. 10, 21)	Zimri (1 Kings xvi. 10) / Tibni (1 Kings xvi. 21) / Omri (1 Kings xvi. 21), 12 years (1 Kings xvi. 23)
922	131	31st year of Asa (1 Kings xvi. 23)	Omri alone (1 Kings xvi. 23)
915	138	38th year of Asa (1 Kings xvi. 29)	Ahab, 22 (21?) years (1 Kings xvi. 29)
911	142	Jehoshaphat (1 Kings xxii. 41)	4th year of Ahab (1 Kings xxii. 41)
895	158	17th year of Jehoshaphat	Ahaziah (1 Kings xxii. 51)

The chronology of the Second Book of Kings is far more complicated. The following are some of its difficulties. 1. Two dates are given for the accession of Jehoram of Israel, viz. the second year of Jehoram of Judah (ch. i. 17), and the eighteenth year of Jehoshaphat (ch. iii. 1). 2. Jehoram of Judah is said to have begun to reign in the fifth year of his father Jehoshaphat (ch. viii. 16), and also in the fifth year of Jehoram of Israel, which was the twenty-second year of Jehoshaphat. 3. Jehoahaz, son of Jehu, is said (ch. xiii. 1) to have ascended the throne in the twenty-third year of Joash of Judah; but as Joash ascended the throne in the seventh of Jehu (ch. xii. 1), and Jehu reigned no more than twenty-eight years (ch. x. 36), the true year of the accession of Jehoahaz must have been (as Josephus says it was) Joash's twenty-first. 4. Amaziah's first year is made to run parallel with the second year of Joash of Israel (ch. xiv. 1); but if the reign of this Joash began in the thirty-seventh year of his namesake of Judah (ch. xiii. 10), and if this monarch reigned altogether forty years (ch. xii. 1), Amaziah cannot have succeeded him till Joash of Israel's fourth year. 5. Azariah is said to have begun to reign in the twenty-seventh year of Jeroboam II. (ch. xv. 1); but if Amaziah lived fifteen years only after the death of Joash of Israel (ch. xiv. 17), Azariah should have succeeded him in Jeroboam's sixteenth year. 6. Zachariah's accession, which seems (ch. xiv. 29) to be placed directly after his father's death, should have fallen in Azariah's twenty-fifth or twenty-sixth year; but it is placed in his thirty-eighth (ch. xv. 8); so that an interregnum of eleven or twelve years, whereof Scripture gives no hint, and which is very unlikely, has to be interpolated (Clinton, 'Fasti Hellenici,' vol. i. p. 325) between the son's reign and the father's. 7. Jotham is given in one place a reign of sixteen years (ch. xv. 33), while in another (ch. xv. 30) his twentieth year is spoken of. 8. Hoshea's accession is placed (ch. xv. 30) in the twentieth year of Jotham—regarded by some as the fourth year of Ahaz, and again (ch. xvii. 1) in the twelfth year of Ahaz. 9. Hezekiah's first year is said to have been the third of Hoshea (ch. xviii. 1), but his fourth year is made Hoshea's seventh instead of his sixth, and his sixth year Hoshea's ninth (ch. xviii. 9, 10) instead of his eighth. 10. Altogether, the years of the Israelite monarchy, from the accession of Ahaziah to the captivity of Hoshea, are made to amount to a hundred and fifty-nine, while those of the Judæan monarchy for the same period amount to a hundred and eighty-three, or an addition of twenty-four.

The difficulties are increased if we compare the sacred chronology for the period with the profane. The Assyrian annals place an interval of a hundred and thirty-two years only between the taking of Samaria and a year in the reign of Ahab, while the scriptural numbers make the interval, at the lowest computation, a hundred and sixty years, and at the highest a hundred and eighty-four. By the Assyrian annals Hezekiah's expedition against Sennacherib took place in the twenty-first year after the fall of Samaria; by the present scriptural numbers (ch. xviii. 10, 13) it took place in the eighth year afterwards.

It is evident that any attempt to restore the true chronology must be to a large extent conjectural, and almost arbitrary. Some of the scriptural numbers must be altered, or else suppositions must be made for which there is no warranty. Still, a commentator is almost forced to take some definite view, and, so long as he allows that his view is merely put forward tentatively and provisionally, he is not open to censure. No apology would therefore seem to be needed for the following tabular conspectus of the probable chronology of the period between the accession of Ahaziah of Israel and the fall of Samaria:—

Year before Christ.	Year of the Davidic monarchy.	Kings of Judah.	Kings of Israel.	Contemporary kings.		
				Egypt.	Assyria.	Babylon.
895	158	17th year of Jehoshaphat	Ahaziah, 2 years		Asshur-nazir-pal	
894	159	18th year of Jehoshaphat	Jehoram, 12 years (2 Kings iii. 1)	Kings of the twenty-second dynasty		
890	163	JEHORAM, 8 years	5th year of Jehoram of Israel (2 Kings viii. 16)			
883	170	AHAZIAH, 1 year	12th year of Jehoram of Israel (2 Kings viii. 25) JEHU, 28 years			
882	171	Athaliah, usurper, 6 years				
876	177	JOASH, 40 years	7th year of Jehu (2 Kings xii. 1)			
856	197	21st year of Joash (Josephus, 'Ant. Jud.,' ix. 8. § 5)	JEHOAHAZ, 17 years		Shalmaneser II.	
840	213	37th year of Joash of Judah (2 Kings xiii. 10)	JOASH, 16 years	Kings of the twenty-third dynasty		Babylon generally under Assyria
837	216	AMAZIAH, 29 years	4th (not 2nd) year of Joash (2 Kings xiv. 1)			
824	229	15th (or rather 14th) year of Amaziah (2 Kings xiv. 23)	JEROBOAM II., 41 years (more probably 53 years)		Shamas-Vul	
809	244	AZARIAH, 52 years	27th (really 16th) year of Jeroboam II. (2 Kings xv. 1)		Vul-nirari	
771	282	38th year of Azariah (2 Kings xv. 8)	ZACHARIAH, 2 years			
770	283	39th year of Azariah (2 Kings xv. 17)	MENAHEM, 10 years (perhaps 11)	Later kings of the twenty-third dynasty	Pul (?)	
759	294	50th year of Azariah (2 Kings xv. 23)	PEKAHIAH, 2 years			
758	295	52nd year of Azariah (2 Kings xv. 27)	PEKAH, 20 (rather 27) years (2 Kings xv. 27)		Tiglath-pileser II.	
757	296	JOTHAM, 16 years	2nd year of Pekah (2 Kings xv. 32)	Pian-khi (?)		Nabonassar,
742	311	AHAZ, 16 years	17th year of Pekah (2 Kings xvi. 1)	Bocchoris		Nadius, Chinzirus,

Year before Christ.	Year of the Davidic monarchy.	Kings of Judah.	Kings of Israel.	Contemporary kings.		
				Egypt.	Assyria.	Babylon.
730	323	12th year of Ahaz (2 Kings xvii. 1)	HOSHEA, 9 years	So, or Sabaco		Tiglath-pileser (Porus)
727	326	HEZEKIAH, 29 years	3rd (really 4th) year of Hoshea (2 Kings xviii. 1)		Shalmaneser IV.	Shalmaneser IV. (Elulæus)
724	329	4th year of Hezekiah (2 Kings xviii. 9)	7th year of Hoshea: Samaria besieged (2 Kings xviii. 9)	Sibache, or Sevechus		
722	331	6th year of Hezekiah (2 Kings xviii. 10)	9th year of Hoshea: Samaria taken (2 Kings xviii. 10)		Sargon	Sargon (Arkeanus)

After the termination of the Israelite monarchy by the capture of Samaria in B.C. 722, the difficulties of the chronology become much less, chiefly from the absence of those exact synchronisms which have constituted the main difficulty in the period between the accession of Ahaziah and the Israelite captivity. Such exact synchronisms as occur (ch. xxiv. 12; xxv. 2, 8, and 27) show in general a remarkable agreement between sacred history and profane, while the vaguer ones (ch. xx. 12; xxiii. 29; xxiv. 1) are also quite consonant with the accounts given to us by secular historians. The only serious difficulty which meets us is the date in ch. xviii. 14, which assigns the first expedition of Sennacherib against Jerusalem to Hezekiah's *fourteenth* year, or B.C. 714, whereas the Assyrian annals place it in Sennacherib's fourth year, which was B.C. 701, or thirteen years later. This date is best regarded as an interpolation a marginal gloss which has crept into the text, and which was the mere conjecture of a commentator. The event itself probably occurred in the twenty-seventh year of Hezekiah's reign.

The subjoined table will complete the chronology of the Davidic monarchy, and may be regarded as scarcely presenting any doubtful points or uncertainties—

Year before Christ.	Year of the Davidic monarchy.	Kings of Judah.	Contemporary kings.		
			Egypt.	Assyria.	Babylon.
722	331	6th year of Hezekiah		Sargon (B.C. 722—705)	Merodach-Baladan (B.C. 722—710)
714	339	14th ditto: Hezekiah's illness (2 Kings xx. 6)		Sennacherib (B.C. 705—681)	Bel-ibni (B.C. 704—701)

Year before Christ.	Year of the Davidic monarchy.	Kings of Judah.	Contemporary kings.		
			Egypt.	Assyria.	Babylon.
701	352	27th year of Heze-kiah: Hezekiah attacked by Senna-cherib (2 Kings xviii. 13—xix. 36)	Tirhakah (B.C. 701—667)		
					Asshur-nadin-sum (B.C. 700—681)
698	355	MANASSEH, 55 years (2 Kings xxi. 1)		Esarhaddon (B.C. 681—668) Asshur - bani-pal (B.C. 668—626)	Esarhaddon (B.C. 681—668) Saul-Mugina (B.C. 668—648) Chiniladanus, or Asshur-bani-pal (?) (B.C. 648—626)
			Mi-ammon-nut Psamatik I. (about B.C. 650—610)		
643	410	AMON, 2 years (2 Kings xxi. 19)			
641	412	JOSIAH, 31 years (2 Kings xxii. 1)			Nabopolassar (B.C. 626—605)
623	430	18th year of Josiah: celebration of Pass-over (2 Kings xxiii. 23)		Assyrian em-pire ends about B.C. 617	
610	443	Battle of Megiddo (2 Kings xxiii. 29) JEHOAHAZ, 3 months	Neco (B.C. 610—595)		
609	444	JEHOIAKIM, 11 years (2 Kings xxiii. 36)			Nebuchadnez-zar (B.C. 605—562)
598	455	JEHOIACHIN, 3 months (2 Kings xxiv. 8)			
597	456	ZEDEKIAH, 11 years (2 Kings xxiv. 18)	Psamatik II. (B.C. 595—590) Hophra (B.C. 590—565)		
586	467	End of reign.			Evil-Merodach (B.C. 562—560)

II. INTERCONNECTION BETWEEN SACRED AND PROFANE HISTORY DURING THE PERIOD OF THE ISRAELITE MONARCHY.

At the commencement of the monarchy, during the reigns of David and Solomon, the great world-power was Egypt. Assyria, which had exercised an extensive sway in Western Asia from about B.C. 1300 to B.C. 1070, in the latter part of the eleventh century B.C. passed under a cloud, and did not emerge from it until about B.C. 900. Egypt, on the other hand, about B.C. 1100, began to increase in strength, and soon after B.C. 1000, resumed her *rôle* of Asiatic conqueror under the Sheshonks and Osarkons. It is quite in accordance with these facts that, in the first period of the Israelite monarchy, from the accession of David to the usurpations of Jehu and Athaliah, the historical Scriptures contain no mention at all of Assyria,[1] which lay entirely without the sphere of Hebrew influence, having lost all its authority over any part of the tract west of the Euphrates. Egypt, on the contrary, comes once more to the front. Unmentioned in the history from the date of the Exodus to the accession of Solomon, she then reappears as a power friendly to Israel, and anxious to make alliance with the new kingdom which has been established at no great distance from her borders. Who the Pharaoh was who gave his daughter to Solomon (1 Kings iii. 1), and with her the city of Gezer as a dowry (1 Kings ix. 16), is uncertain; but there can be no doubt that he was one of the kings of Manetho's twenty-first dynasty, and it is probable that he was one of the later kings, either Pinetem II., the last but one, or Hor-Pasebensha, the last. The union of the two royal houses led to much intercourse between the two peoples, and a brisk trade was established between Palestine and the valley of the Nile, which included a large importation of Egyptian horses and chariots into Palestine, and even into Syria (1 Kings x. 28, 29), where the Hittite kings purchased them. Political refugees passed from one country to the other without question (ch. xi. 17—19), and sometimes those from Asia obtained considerable influence at the Egyptian court.

The twenty-first Egyptian dynasty was succeeded by the twenty-second, probably somewhat late in the reign of Solomon. The new dynasty continued the policy of receiving Asiatic refugees, and Sheshonk (or Shishak), the first monarch, gave an asylum to Jeroboam (1 Kings xi. 40) not many years before Solomon's death. There was nothing in this to disturb the relations between the two countries; but when Jeroboam, after the death of Solomon, returned to Palestine, and the two rival kingdoms of Judah and Israel were established side by side in a relation of mutual hostility, Egypt could not well remain friendly to both. Not unnaturally she leant to the state which was the larger, and appeared to be the more powerful of the two, and which had, moreover, been founded by the Israelite refugee to whom she had given an asylum, and who had probably lived in Egypt on terms of personal intimacy with the reigning monarch.[2] Accordingly, the great expedition of Shishak into Asia (2 Chron. xii. 2—4) in Rehoboam's fifth

---

[1] In the Psalms there is one mention of Assyria (Assur) which may belong to this time (see Ps. lxxxiii. 8). David's Syrian conquests, perhaps, brought him on one occasion into contact with the Assyrians (2 Sam. x. 15—18).

[2] The Septuagint 'Additions to Kings' have not the authority of history, but they show what the Alexandrian Jews believed to have been Jeroboam's position at the court of Shishak (see the additions to 1 Kings xii. after ver. 24)

year, which is recorded on the walls of the temple at Karnak,[1] appears to have been undertaken, in great part, in the interest of Jeroboam, whose hands were thereby greatly strengthened against his adversary. Rehoboam became for a time an Egyptian tributary (2 Chron. xii. 8); and though the *Yuteh malk* of the Karnak inscription may not especially designate him,[2] yet the war was certainly directed mainly against the Judæan kingdom, and resulted in its degradation. Sheshonk had probably entertained designs of wider conquest, and he actually subjected many of the Arab tribes in the trans-Jordanic region, and in the tract between Egypt and Palestine; but his military ardour was not sufficient to urge him to further efforts, and it was left for one of his successors to invade Asia with a greater force (comp. 2 Chron. xiv. 9 with xii. 3) in the hope of sweeping all before him.

Zerach the Ethiopian, who in the eleventh year of Asa (2 Chron. xiv. 1, 9) made an expedition into Palestine at the head of an army of a million men, is probably identical with Osarkon[3] (*Ua-sar-ken*) II., the great-grandson of Sheshonk I., and the fourth king of the twenty-second Manethonian dynasty. Zerach's army consisted of Cushites and Lubim (2 Chron. xvi. 8), as Sheshonk's (Shishak's) did of Cushites, Lubim, and Sukkyim (2 Chron. xii. 3). He invaded Judæa in the south, and marched upon Jerusalem by the way of Mareshah. Here, however, Asa met him, with forces not much exceeding half the number of his adversary's, and defeated him in a pitched battle—one of the most glorious in all Hebrew history—entirely discomfiting his host and pursuing it to Gerar, on the extreme south of Palestine, and returning with an immense spoil to Jerusalem. The Egyptian aspirations after Asiatic conquests were crushed by this terrible blow; and it was not till the advance of Assyria menaced Egypt herself with conquest that the soil of Palestine was again trodden by an Egyptian army.

Assyria's advance to greatness, which commenced about B.C. 900, upon Egypt's decline, is not noticed so early in the scriptural narrative as might have been expected. We find by the Assyrian annals that the contact of Assyria with the northern kingdom began as early as the reign of Jehu, if not even in that of Ahab. An "Ahab," described as "Ahab of Samhala" or "Sirhala," is engaged in battle with Shalmaneser II. about B.C. 854, and suffers defeat.[4] But chronological considerations render it extremely doubtful whether the person thus designated can have been the son of Omri. Jehu, however, seems certainly to have come within the sphere of Shalmaneser's influence, and to have been induced to send him presents, which Shalmaneser regarded as a tribute,[5] not later than the year B.C. 842,

---

[1] See Mr. Reginald Stuart Poole's article on "Shishak" in Smith's 'Dictionary of the Bible,' vol. iii. pp. 1293, 1294.

[2] Max Müller, in the 'Proceedings of the Society of Biblical Archæology' for December 6, 1887, pp. 81—83.

[3] Ewald, 'History of Israel,' vol. iv. p. 51, Eng. trans.

[4] G. Smith, 'Eponym Canon,' p. 108; Rawlinson, 'Ancient Monarchies,' vol. ii. p. 103, 2nd edit.

[5] 'Eponym Canon,' p. 114.

according to the Assyrian chronology. Assyria was at this time pressing especially upon the Syrian states, the Hamathites, Hittites, Syrians of Damascus, and Phœnicians. Shalmaneser contended successively with the Benhadad who preceded Hazael on the Damascene throne, and with Hazael himself; his reign, according to the Assyrian reckoning, extended from B.C. 860 to B.C. 825.[1] His attacks, and those of his successor, Shamas-Vul (B.C. 825—810), may have advantaged the Israelites by weakening the Damascene kingdom, which was at this time their principal adversary (see ch. x. 32, 33; xii. 17, 18; xiii. 17—25).

The advance of Assyria, though not uncheckered by defeats, continued, without serious interruption, until, in the reign of Menahem (B.C. 770—760), an actual invasion of the northern kingdom took place under a monarch called Pul (ch. xv. 19; 1 Chron. v. 26), who put the land to a tribute of a thousand talents of silver. The native monuments make no mention of this Pul, for he can scarcely be Tiglath-pileser, who took the name and reigned as Pulu (Pul or Porus) in Babylon for two years (B.C. 729—728) before his decease in B.C. 727; since Pul is distinguished from Tiglath-pileser both in Kings (ch. xv. 19, 29) and in Chronicles (1 Chron. v. 26), and moreover Tiglath-pileser's first year was B.C. 745. It seems most probable that the Pul who attacked Menahem was a pretender to the throne of Assyria, contemporary with Asshur-dayan III. (B.C. 771—753), in whose time we hear of several revolts, and midway in whose reign three copies of the Eponym Canon draw a line, the usual sign of the commencement of a new reign.[2] Pul may have been acknowledged as King of Assyria by a portion of the nation from B.C. 763, where the line is drawn, to B.C. 758, when peace is said to have been restored to the land; and during this interval may have made the expedition mentioned in ch. xv. 19.

Of the expedition of Tiglath-pileser against Pekah King of Israel, which resulted in the conquest of the trans-Jordanic territory, and the captivity of the Reubenites, the Gadites, and the half-tribe of Manasseh (1 Chron. v. 26; comp. ch. xv. 19), the Assyrian annals contain a fragmentary account, as well as of the war between the same monarch and Rezin King of Damascus, mentioned in ch. xvi. 9. Tiglath-pileser appears in his inscriptions as a great and warlike monarch, who re-established the military supremacy of Assyria over Western Asia after a period of depression. He seems to have ascended the throne in the year B.C. 745, and to have reigned from that date until B.C. 727—a space of eighteen years. In the earlier part of his reign he seems to have invaded Judæa, probably from the Philistine plain, and to have been engaged for some time in a war with a king of Judah whom he calls Azariah, but who must apparently have been either Jotham or Ahaz. This war, which is not mentioned in Scripture, had no important result; but in a little time it was followed by another which greatly increased the influence of Assyria in the Palestinian region. Ahaz now certainly occupied the Judæan throne, while that of Samaria was held

---

[1] 'Eponym Canon,' pp. 59, 60. [2] Ibid., pp. 48, 63.

by Pekah, and that of Damascus by Rezin. The northern kings were anxious to form a Syrian confederacy against Assyrian aggression, and invited Ahaz to join them; but, that monarch declining, they resolved to put him down, and give his kingdom to a creature of their own, a certain Ben-Tabeal (Isa. vii. 6), who is thought to have been a Damascene.[1] Under these circumstances, Ahaz invoked the aid of Tiglath-pileser against their common enemies (ch. xvi. 7), and a war followed, which lasted apparently three years (B.C. 734—732). Tiglath-pileser's first efforts were against Rezin. After several battles in the open field, wherein the Assyrian arms were successful, he forced the Syrian king to take refuge within the walls of Damascus, which he then besieged and took.[2] Rezin fell into his hands, and was slain (ch. xvi. 9); several of his generals were impaled on crosses; the country was ravaged; the unarmed inhabitants seized, and the mass of them carried away as captives.[3] The war was then carried from the Damascene territory into that of Samaria, which was entered upon the north and upon the east, and treated much as the Damascene had been. The captivity of Israel commenced. Assyria extended her territory from the Lebanon and the Hamathites' country, to the hills of Galilee and the coast of the Dead Sea. Judæa, under Ahaz, became her tributary,[4] as did Moab, Edom, and Ammon.[5] In Samaria a new king was set up in the person of Hoshea, who murdered Pekah, with the connivance of the Assyrian monarch.[6]

The Assyrian records agree with Scripture in making a Shalmaneser (Shalmaneser IV.) the successor of Tiglath-pileser,[7] though they do not represent Shalmaneser (as Scripture has generally been supposed to do) as the conqueror of Samaria. They give to this king a reign of five years only, from B.C. 727 to B.C. 723, and represent him as a warlike monarch, engaged in a series of military expeditions; but the notices of him which have come down to us are extremely scanty and fragmentary, and throw little light on the biblical narrative. We learn, however, from Phœnician sources,[8] that Shalmaneser's wars were at any rate in the neighbourhood of Palestine, since we are told that he overran all Phœnicia, took Sidon, the continental Tyre, and Akko, and even attacked the island Tyre with a fleet manned chiefly by Phœnician sailors. His enterprises seem to have been cut short by a domestic revolution, headed by the great Sargon, who drove Shalmaneser from the throne, probably put him to death, and mutilated his annals.

---

[1] Ewald, 'History of Israel,' vol. iv. p. 158.
[2] G. Smith, 'Eponym Canon,' p. 121.   [3] Ibid.; comp. ch. xvi. 9.
[4] Ch. xvi. 8; comp. ch. xviii. 7 and 'Eponym Canon,' p. 124, where Ahaz seems to be mentioned as a tributary under the name of "Jehoahaz."
[5] 'Eponym Canon,' p. 124, lines 60, 61.
[6] In ch. xv. 30, the murder of Pekah is assigned to Hoshea; but in the annals of Tiglath-pileser ('Eponym Canon,' p. 123, line 17) that monarch appears to have represented it as his own act. He certainly made Hoshea king.
[7] See the 'Eponym Canon,' p. 65.
[8] Menand. Eph. ap. Joseph. 'Ant. Jud.,' ix. 14.

Sargon claims as his first act the conquest of Samaria, from which he says that he carried off 27,290 captives.[1] He is, perhaps, the king intended in ch. xvii. 6 and xviii. 11 ; and he obtains distinct mention in Isa. xx. 1. Hezekiah seems to have revolted from him (ch. xviii. 7) ; but he was successful in most other quarters. He put down a rebellion in which Hamath, Arpad, Zimirra, Damascus, and Samaria were combined, about B.C. 720, defeated an Egyptian army, and took Raphia and Gaza in the same year, conquered Ashdod in B.C. 711, and Babylon in B.C. 710 ; invaded Edom in B.C. 707, and established his authority over Cyprus and over some of the islands of the Persian Gulf about the same time.[2] In his reign the Assyrian empire advanced itself to the borders of Egypt, and from thenceforth until about B.C. 650 the two countries were engaged in almost perpetual hostilities, Judæa and Syria furnishing for the most part the battle-ground between the contending forces. Sargon's first adversary was a certain Sibache,[3] who is probably identical with the Shabak or Shabatok of the hieroglyphics, the Sabaco of Herodotus,[4] and the So or Seveh[5] of Scripture (ch. xvii. 4). He afterwards contended with a monarch whom he calls the King of Meroë,[6] who is perhaps Tirhakah, perhaps Shabatok. After reigning seventeen years, Sargon died, and was succeeded on the Assyrian throne by the world-famous Sennacherib, the most widely known, if not really the greatest, of Assyrian monarchs.

It was in the middle of the reign of Sargon—about B.C. 714 or 713—that the first contact occurred between Judæa and Babylon. A native prince, named Merodach-Baladan, rose in insurrection against the Assyrians on the death of Shalmaneser, and succeeded in re-establishing Babylonian independence for a short space.[7] Threatened by Sargon, and anxious to strengthen himself by alliances, this king sent, about B.C. 714, an embassy into Palestine, under the pretence of congratulating Hezekiah on his recovery from his severe illness (ch. xx. 12). The ambassadors were received with favour, and shown all Hezekiah's treasures (ch. xx. 13) ; and it is most likely that an alliance was concluded ; but a few years later, B.C. 710, Sargon marched an army into Babylonia, defeated Merodach-Baladan, and expelled him from the country, took Babylon, and, following the examples of Tiglath-pileser and Shalmaneser, established himself as king. The Canon of Ptolemy calls him Arkeanos (equivalent to Sarkina), and assigns him the space from B.C. 710 to B.C. 705. It was in this latter year that Sargon died.

The death of Sargon and the accession of the untried Sennacherib gave the

---

[1] 'Eponym Canon,' p. 125, line 24.

[2] See 'Ancient Monarchies,' vol. ii. pp. 141—147.

[3] 'Eponym Canon,' pp. 125, 126; Oppert, 'Inscriptions des Sargonides,' p. 22; Sir H. Rawlinson, *Athenæum*, No. 1869, p. 534.

[4] Herod., ii. 137.

[5] The proper pointing of the word סוא in ch. xvii. 4 is probably סֶוֵא, and not סוֹא.

[6] 'Eponym Canon,' p. 128, line 61 ; p. 130, line 36.

[7] Oppert, 'Inscriptions des Sargonides,' p. 28.

signal for a series of revolts. In Babylonia several pretenders arose,[1] and after a time Merodach-Baladan re-established himself as king; but he only wore the crown for six months. In B.C. 702 Sennacherib drove him out, recovered the country to Assyria, and placed a viceroy upon the Babylonian throne.[2] The next year he made his great expedition into Syria, Phœnicia, and Palestine, chastised Sidon and other Phœnician towns which had thrown off the Assyrian yoke, took Ascalon and Ekron, defeating a force of Egyptians and Ethiopians, which had come to help the people of the latter city, and then overran Judæa, and attacked Jerusalem. "Because Hezekiah King of Judah," he says, "would not submit to my yoke, I came up against him, and by force of arms and by the might of my power I took forty-six of his strong-fenced cities, and of the smaller towns which were scattered about I took and plundered a countless number. And from these places I captured and carried off as spoil 200,150 people, old and young, male and female, together with horses and mares, asses and camels, oxen and sheep, a countless multitude. And Hezekiah himself I shut up in Jerusalem, his capital, like a bird in a cage, building towers round about the city to hem him in, and raising banks of earth against the gates, so as to prevent escape. . . . Then upon this Hezekiah there fell the fear of the power of my arms, and he sent out to me the chiefs and the elders of Jerusalem, with thirty talents of gold, and eight hundred talents of silver, and divers treasures, a rich and immense booty. . . . All these things were brought to me at Nineveh, the seat of my government, Hezekiah having sent them by way of tribute, and as a token of submission to my power."[3] The close accord of this entire account with the notice contained in the Second Book of Kings (ch. xviii. 13—16) is very striking. The "fenced cities" are the first object of attack; then Jerusalem is threatened; Hezekiah is shut up in the place (comp. 2 Chron. xxxii. 2—8); then submission is made; a sum of money in gold and silver is paid for a ransom; even the number of the talents of gold is the same in both narratives. The only discrepancy is with respect to the silver, in which Sennacherib may include all that he carried off from the country. Finally, the invading host retires, the siege is broken up, and peace restored between the countries. One serious difficulty alone presents itself—viz. the date of the expedition in the present Hebrew text. This is given as "the *fourteenth* year of Hezekiah," or eight years only after the capture of Samaria. But in the fourteenth year of Hezekiah, B.C. 714, Sargon was still upon the throne; the Assyrian arms were engaged in Media and Armenia; and there was no Assyrian expedition into Palestine.[4] Sennacherib's invasion cannot possibly have taken place until B.C. 705, nine years later, for not till then did he ascend the throne;[5] and by his annals[6] it appears not to have actually taken place till his fourth

---

[1] Polyhistor. ap. Euseb., 'Chron. Can.,' i. 5. § 1.
[2] 'Ancient Monarchies,' vol. ii. p. 157.
[3] Sir H. Rawlinson, in 'Ancient Monarchies,' vol. ii. pp. 161, 162.
[4] See 'Eponym Canon,' p. 66.   [5] Ibid., p. 67.
[6] Ibid., pp. 131—136; comp. 'Ancient Monarchies,' vol. ii. p. 158.

year, B.C. 701. The date, therefore, in ch. xviii. 13 must be an error; and the choice would seem to lie between regarding it as a corruption—"fourteenth" for "twenty-seventh"—and viewing it as the marginal note of a commentator which has crept into the text.

After an interval (2 Chron. xxxii. 9), which may not have exceeded a few months, and which certainly cannot have exceeded a year or two, Sennacherib attacked Hezekiah for the second time. It probably vexed him that he had not insisted on occupying Jerusalem with a garrison, and he may also have received fresh provocation from Hezekiah, if that monarch had made an application to Egypt for aid, as he seems to have done (ch. xviii. 24; Isa. xxx. 1—4). At any rate, Sennacherib proceeded once more to threaten Jerusalem, sent a force against it under three of his chief officials (ch. xviii. 17), attempted to stir up disaffection among the soldiers of the garrison (ch. xviii. 17—36), and announced his intention of coming against the city in person and "destroying it utterly" (ch. xix. 10—13). At the same time, he laid siege to various towns in Southern Palestine, and contemplated invading Egypt, where Tirhakah was collecting an army to oppose him (ch. xix. 9). But at this point of his career his ambition received a signal check. In a single night, silently and suddenly—as the Jews believed, by the direct action of the Almighty[1] (ch. xix. 35; 2 Chron. xxxii. 21; Isa. xxxvii. 36)—almost his whole army was destroyed; and nothing remained for him but to relinquish his hopes of further conquest in the south-west, and to make a hurried retreat to his capital (ch. xix. 36).

The later years of Sennacherib were inglorious. In B.C. 694 Babylonia revolted from him, and succeeded in re-establishing its independence. Between this date and his death the only expeditions which can be probably assigned to him are one into Cilicia and another into Edom.[2] He certainly made no attempt to recover the laurels which he had lost in Palestine and on the borders of Egypt, but allowed Manasseh in Judæa, and Tirhakah in the valley of the Nile, to remain unmolested. Domestic troubles probably occupied the later portion of his reign, which was terminated by his murder in 681 B.C. (ch. xix. 37), after he had held the Assyrian throne for the space of twenty-four years.

Sennacherib's murder is not distinctly mentioned in the Assyrian records, but Esarhaddon appears as his son and successor, and there are traces[3] of this prince having had at first to contend for the crown with his half-brothers, Adrammelech and Sharezer (ch. xix. 37). The scene of the conflict was Armenia; and after it was over, Esarhaddon appears to have

---

[1] The catastrophe has been attributed to the simoom (Milman, 'History of the Jews,' vol. i. p. 307), to a plague (Gesenius, Winer, etc.), to a sudden storm (Vitringa, Stanley), and even to a night attack of the enemy (Michaëlis); but the words of the narrative distinctly point to that silent, sudden extinction which English law calls "the visitation of God."

[2] 'Ancient Monarchies,' vol. ii. pp. 175—177.   [3] Ibid., p. 186.

made an expedition into Syria, where Sidon had revolted,[1] and, after crushing the revolt, to have established his authority over the whole of Phœnicia, Palestine, and the adjacent countries. Manasseh, the weak son of Hezekiah, was at this time forced to become a tributary and subject-monarch, as were also the kings of Edom, Moab, and Ammon, of Tyre, Gebal, and Arvad, of Gaza, Ekron, Ascalon, and Ashdod.[2] Assyria's dominion was at once extended and consolidated, and the way was paved for aggressions upon Egypt, which began about B.C. 672, in Esarhaddon's ninth year.[3]

The offence given by Manasseh to his sovereign, on account of which he was arrested and carried captive *to Babylon* (2 Chron. xxxiii. 11), may be probably assigned to the reign of Esarhaddon, who alone of all the Assyrian kings maintained a residence in that city. And we may conjecture that his restoration to his kingdom (2 Chron. xxxiii. 13) had a connection with Esarhaddon's Egyptian projects, since it would have been only prudent to secure the fidelity of Jerusalem before the perils of an Egyptian campaign were affronted. Esarhaddon carried on war with Tirhakah successfully between B.C. 673 and B.C. 670; but in B.C. 669 or 668 the fortune of war turned against him, and Tirhakah once more established his authority over the whole of Egypt.[4]

It is somewhat remarkable that Scripture makes no mention of Esarhaddon's son and successor, Asshur-bani-pal, who mounted the Assyrian throne in B.C. 668, and reigned till B.C. 626. This prince must have been contemporary with Manasseh for twenty-five years, with Amon, and with Josiah. In the early part of his reign he made at least two expeditions against Egypt, and must have repeatedly passed through Palestine at the head of powerful armies.[5] In his later years he warred successfully with Elam, Babylon, Armenia, Phœnicia, and Arabia. It was about the middle of his reign that the decline of Assyria began. A great Scythic invasion swept over Western Asia, and spread everywhere ruin and desolation.[6] Assyria's distant dependencies, Egypt, Palestine, Lydia, detached themselves. Before she had time to recover from her depressed condition, her conquest was taken in hand by the combined Medes and Babylonians.[7] Nineveh fell about B.C. 616, or a little earlier,[8] and Western Asia became a field wherein rival ambitions met and collided. Media, Babylonia, Lydia, and Egypt, all of them sought to profit by the downfall of the great power so long dominant over the Oriental world, while even such petty states as Judæa took the opportunity to aggrandize themselves (ch. xxiii. 15—20; 2 Chron. xxxiv. 6).

So far as Judæa was concerned, the world-powers which took the place

---

[1] 'Eponym Canon,' p. 137.   [2] Ibid., p. 139, lines 13—18.   [3] Ibid., p. 69.
[4] Ibid., p. 202.   [5] 'Ancient Monarchies,' vol. ii. pp. 201—203.
[6] Herod., i. 103—106; comp. 'Ancient Monarchies,' vol. ii. pp. 221—228.
[7] Herod., i. 106; Abydenus ap. Euseb., 'Chron. Can.,' i. 9; Polyhistor. ap. eund., i. 5.
[8] The Assyrian Eponym list continues down to B.C. 617 ('Eponym Canon,' p. 71).

of Assyria, and strove to establish their domination in the place of hers, were Babylon and Egypt. Egypt appears to have anticipated her rival. As early as the reign of Psamatik I. she recommenced aggressions upon Asia by persistent attacks upon the strongest of the Philistine cities, the famous Ashdod,[1] and about B.C. 610, under Neco, the son and successor of Psamatik, she invaded Syria in force, defeated Josiah at Megiddo,[2] overran Judæa, Phœnicia, and Syria as far as Taurus and the middle Euphrates, and made herself mistress of the entire region between the borders of Egypt and the great city of Carchemish. Neco held possession for some years of this rich and interesting region, recovering thus the hold upon Asia which had been possessed a thousand years earlier by the great monarchs of the eighteenth dynasty—the Thothmeses and Amenhoteps. Then, however, Babylon bestirred herself. Nabopolassar, the prince who, in conjunction with the Median monarch Cyaxares, had attacked and destroyed Nineveh, became independent King of Babylon from the moment of Assyria's downfall; but it took him some time to establish his authority over the tract lying between Babylon and Carchemish, though probably he claimed a dominion over all the western provinces of the Assyrian empire from the first. Neco's conquest he viewed as a rebellion which must be crushed;[3] but it was not till the year B.C. 605, when he was already becoming enfeebled by old age, that he found himself in a position to carry the Babylonian arms into the far West, and attempt the chastisement of the "rebel." Even then he had to give up the notion of proceeding against his enemy in person, and to depute the task of subjugation to his eldest son, the crown prince, Nebuchadnezzar. Nebuchadnezzar, in B.C. 605, led the Babylonian forces from the capital to Carchemish (now Jerabus), and there engaged the troops of Neco in the great battle[4] which destroyed Egypt's last hope of maintaining her Asiatic supremacy, and installed Babylon in the position of the dominant power of South-Western Asia. From her defeat at Carchemish Egypt never recovered. She made some feeble efforts under Apries (Pharaoh-Hophra) and Amasis to effect Phœnician and Cyprian conquests;[5] but the results were trivial, and in a short time she collapsed utterly. Babylon, on the other hand, carried all before her. Nebuchadnezzar conquered Elam, Syria, Phœnicia, Judæa, Edom, Ammon, Moab, Egypt. In his long reign of forty-three years (B.C. 605—562) he seems not to have met with a reverse. The Babylonian empire under his sway attained to an extraordinary degree of prosperity. Jehoiakim, having "become his servant" in B.C. 605 (ch. xxiv. 1), revolted from him in B.C. 602, and was deposed (2 Chron. xxxvi. 6) and probably put to death by him (Jer. xxii. 19; xxxvi. 30) in B.C. 598. Jehoiachin, his son, was then set up as king, but within three months (ch. xxiv. 8) displeased his lord paramount, who deprived him of his throne, and carried

---

[1] Herod., ii. 157.
[3] Berosus, 'Fr.,' 14.
[5] Herod., ii. 161, 182.

[2] Ch. xxiii. 29; comp. Herod., ii. 159.
[4] See Jer. xlvi. 2—17; and Berosus, *l. s. c.*

him captive to Babylon in B.C. 597 (ch. xxiv. 10—15). Still, Judæa was allowed to maintain its semi-independence. Zedekiah, uncle to Jehoiachin, received the crown at the hands of Nebuchadnezzar (ch. xxiv. 17), and swore fealty to him (2 Chron. xxxvi. 13); but after a short time he too began to contemplate revolt, made an alliance with Egypt (Ezek. xvii. 15), and in B.C. 588 openly declared himself independent of his suzerain (ch. xxiv. 20). Nebuchadnezzar was not slow to accept the challenge. He at once marched against Jerusalem, and laid siege to it. Apries (Hophra), the Egyptian monarch, made one attempt to come to the assistance of his ally (Jer. xxxvii. 5); but the attempt failed, either through the defeat of his army or through his own want of resolution.[1] In B.C. 586, after a siege of eighteen months, the end came. A breach was made in the northern wall of the town, and a lodgment effected within the defences (Jer. xxxix. 2, 3). Zedekiah fled, but was pursued and made a prisoner, blinded, and carried to Babylon (Jer. xxxix. 4—7). Jerusalem surrendered itself; the temple, palace, and chief houses were burnt (ch. xxv. 9); and the bulk of the population, all except the very poor, were carried off into Babylonia as captives. The history of the entire Israelite monarchy thus ends. From the accession of Saul to the destruction of Jerusalem by Nebuchadnezzar was a period of five hundred and seven years, which was divisible into three portions : (1) from the accession of Saul to that of Rehoboam—the period of the undivided monarchy—a space of a hundred and twenty years, from B.C. 1092 to B.C. 972; (2) from the accession of Rehoboam in Judah and of Jeroboam in Israel to the fall of Samaria—the period of the two parallel kingdoms—a space of two hundred and fifty years, from B.C. 972 to B.C. 722; and (3) from the destruction of the Israelite kingdom to the final captivity of Judah, a period of a hundred and thirty-seven years, from B.C. 722 to B.C. 586 inclusive. During the first period Israel's fortunes were connected with those of Egypt; during the second, partly with Egypt but mainly with Assyria; during the third, to some extent with both Egypt and Assyria, but mainly with Babylon. Most, if not all, of the points of contact between Israel and these nations during the period treated of have been touched on in these pages, and the result would seem to be a remarkable general harmony and agreement between the sacred records and the profane, together with a certain residuum of difficulties, for the most part connected with the chronology. On these it is not improbable that future discoveries may throw further light; though it is, perhaps, too much to expect that all difficulties will be ultimately swept away. It does not seem to be the general way of God's providence to make everything plain to us. "The trying of faith worketh patience," and without it patience would never "have her perfect work," nor would faith itself be deserving of those encomiums and that "good report" which it obtains throughout the Christian Scriptures.

---

[1] Josephus says that he was defeated ('Ant. Jud.,' x. 7. § 3). Jeremiah's words (Jer. xxxvii. 7) seem rather to imply a retreat without a battle.

THE SECOND
BOOK OF THE KINGS

EXPOSITION.

CHAPTER I.

Vers. 1—18.—THE REVOLT OF MOAB. THE ILLNESS, IMPIETY, AND DEATH OF AHAZIAH. The narrative of the Second Book of Kings follows on that of the First Book in the closest possible sequence. The history of Ahaziah's reign begins in 1 Kings xxii. 51, and is carried on, without any real break or pause in the sense, to ch. i. 18. How the two books came to be divided at this point is quite inexplicable. The division is most unhappy. Not only does it, without apparent reason, draw a strong line of demarcation in the middle of a reign; but it separates what it was evidently the intention of the writer most closely to connect —viz. the sins of the monarch and their punishment. Ahaziah began his reign by openly showing himself a devotee of Baal— by "walking in the way of his father *and in the way of his mother*," the wicked Jezebel: therefore calamity immediately smote him—first Moab rebelled, threw off the Israelite yoke, and re-established its independence; and then, within a short space, Ahaziah himself met with an accident which produced a dangerous illness. The writer relates barely the former fact, but enlarges on the latter, which gave occasion for one of the most remarkable of the miracles of Elijah.

Ver. 1.—Then Moab rebelled; literally, *and Moab rebelled*, but with an idea, not merely of sequence, but of consequence. The "Moabite Stone," discovered in 1869, throws considerable light on the character and circumstances of this rebellion. Moab had, we know, been subjected by David (2 Sam. viii. 2), and had been very severely treated. Either in the reign of Solomon, or more probably at his death, and the disruption of his kingdom, the Moabites had revolted, and resumed an independent position, which they had maintained until the reign of Omri. Omri, who was a warlike monarch, the greatest of the Israelite monarchs after Jeroboam, after settling himself firmly upon the throne of Israel, attacked the Moabite territory, and in a short time reduced it, making the native king, Chemosh-gad, his tributary. At the death of Omri, Ahab succeeded to the suzerainty, and maintained it during his lifetime, exacting a tribute that was felt as a severe "oppression" (Moabite Stone, line 6; comp. ch. iii. 4). The death of Ahab in battle and the defeat of his army encouraged Mesha, who had succeeded his father, Chemosh-gad, to raise the standard of revolt once more, and to emancipate his country after a period of subjection which he estimates roughly at "forty years." The "Stone" is chiefly occupied with an account of the steps by which he recovered his territory. **After the death of Ahab.** Probably, as soon as he heard of it. In Oriental empires the death of a brave and energetic monarch is constantly the signal for a general revolt of the subject peoples. They entertain a hope that his successor will not inherit his vigour and capacity.

Ver. 2.—Ahaziah fell down through a lattice; rather, *through the lattice*. It is implied that the upper chamber had a single window, which was closed by a single *lattice*, or shutter of interlaced woodwork. The shutter may have been insufficiently secured; or the woodwork may have been too weak to bear his weight. Compare the fall of Eutychus (Acts xx. 9), where, however, there is no mention of a "lattice." **Was sick;** *i.e.* "was so injured that he had to take to his bed." **Inquire of Baal-zebub the god of Ekron.** As a worshipper of Baal, bent on walking in the evil way of his father and of his mother (1 Kings xxii. 52), Ahaziah would naturally inquire of some form of the Baal divinity. Why he chose "Baal-zebub the god of Ekron," it is impossible to say. Perhaps Baal-zebub had at the time a special reputation for giving oracular responses. Perhaps the Ekron temple was, of all the ancient sites of the Baal-worship, the one with which he could most readily communicate. Philistia lay nearer to Samaria than Phœnicia did, and of the Philistine towns Ekron (now *Akir*) was the most northern, and so the nearest. "Baal-zebub" has been thought by some to be equivalent to "Beel-samen," "the lord of heaven"—a divine title well known to the Phœnicians; but this view is etymologically unsound, since *zebub* cannot possibly mean "heaven." "Baal-zebub" is "the lord of flies"—either the god who sends them as a plague on any nation that offends him (comp. Exod. viii. 21—31), or the god who averts them from his votaries and favourites, an equivalent of the Greek Ζεὺς ἀπόμυιος, or the Roman "Jupiter Myiagrus," flies being in the East not unfrequently a terrible plague. The Septuagint translation, Βααλ-μυῖαν, though inaccurate, shows an appreciation of the true etymology. **Of this disease;** rather, *of this illness* (ἐκ τῆς ἀρρωστίας μου ταύτης, LXX.).

Ver. 3.—**The angel of the Lord.** It would be better to translate, with the LXX., *an angel* (ἄγγελος, not ὁ ἄγγελος). An angel had appeared to Elijah on a previous occasion (1 Kings xix. 5, 7). **Elijah the Tishbite** (comp. 1 Kings xvii. 1; xxi. 17, 28; ch. i. 8; and for the meaning of the expression, *hat-Tishbi*, see the comment on 1 Kings xvii. 1). **Arise, go up.** Elijah was, apparently, in the low tract of the Shefelah, or in Sharon, when the messengers started, and was thus commanded to "go up" and meet them, or intercept them on their journey before they descended into the plain. God would not have the insult to his majesty carried out. **Is it not because there is not a God in Israel?** rather, *Is it that there is no God at all in Israel?* The double negative is intensitive, and implies that the king's consultation of Baal-zebub, god of Ekron, is a complete and absolute denial of the Divinity of Jehovah. To consult a foreign oracle is equivalent to saying that the voice of God is wholly silent in one's own land. This was going further in apostasy than Ahab had gone (see 1 Kings xxii. 6—9).

Ver. 4.—**Now therefore.** The word translated "therefore" (לָכֵן) is emphatic, and means "for this reason," "on this account."

Because Ahaziah had apostatized from God, God sentenced him to die from the effects of his fall, and not to recover. It is implied that he might have recovered if he had acted otherwise. **And Elijah departed;** *i.e.* quitted the messengers, showing that his errand was accomplished—he had said all that he was commissioned to say.

Ver. 5.—**And when the messengers turned back;** rather, *when the messengers returned;* i.e. when they reached the presence of Ahaziah, he perceived at once that they could not have been to Ekron and come back in the time. He therefore inquired of them, **Why are ye now turned back?** "Why have ye not completed your journey?"

Ver. 6.—**There came a man.** It is not likely that the messengers did not know Elijah by sight. He was too prominent a person in the history of the time, and too remarkable in his appearance, not to have been recognized, at any rate by some of them. But they thought it best to keep back the prophet's name, and to call him simply "a man" (*'ish*)—perhaps actuated by good will towards Elijah, perhaps by a fear for their own safety, such as had been felt by Obadiah (1 Kings xviii. 8—14).

Ver. 7.—**What manner of man was he?** literally, *what was the manner of the man?* What was his appearance? Were there any marks about him by which he might be recognized and known? Ahaziah may have already suspected that the man who had denounced woe on him would be the same who had denounced woe on his father (see 1 Kings xxi. 20—22).

Ver. 8.—**A hairy man;** literally, *a lord of hair* (בַּעַל שֵׂעָר). Some take the meaning to be that he was rough and unkempt, with his hair and beard long; and so the LXX., who give ἀνὴρ δασύς. But the more usual explanation is that he wore a shaggy coat of untanned skin, with the hair outward. Such a garment seems certainly to have been worn by the later prophets (Zech. xiii. 4; Matt. iii. 4), and to have been regarded as a sign of their profession. But there is no positive evidence that the dress had been adopted by Isaiah's time. **Girt with a girdle of leather.** Generally the Israelites wore girdles of a soft material, as linen or cotton. The "curious girdle" of the high priest's ephod was of "fine twined linen," embroidered with gold, and blue, and purple, and scarlet (Exod. xxviii. 8). Girdles of leather, rough and uncomfortable, would only be worn by the very poor and by the ascetic. Elijah may have adopted his rough and coarse costume, either to show contempt for things earthly, as Hengstenberg thinks; or as a penitential garb indicating sorrow for the sins of the people, as Keil supposes; or simple to chastise and subdue the flesh, as other ascetics. It is Elijah the Tishbite. The description given is enough. The king has no longer any doubt. His suspicion is turned into certainty. There is no living person but Elijah who would at once have the boldness to prophesy the death of the king, and would wear such a costume as described. Elijah is, of course, his enemy, as he had been his father's "enemy" (1 Kings xxi. 20), and will wish him ill, and prophesy accordingly, the wish being "father to the thought." It is not improbable that Elijah had withdrawn himself into obscurity on the accession of Ahaziah, or at any rate on his exhibition of strong idolatrous proclivities (Ewald), as he had done on more than one occasion from Ahab (1 Kings xvii. 10; xix. 3—8). Ahaziah may have been long wishing to arrest and imprison him, and now thought he saw his opportunity.

Ver. 9.—**The king sent unto him a captain of fifty.** "Captains of fifties" were first instituted in the wilderness by the advice of Jethro (Exod. xviii. 21—25). Though not expressly mentioned in the military organization of David, they probably formed a part of it, and so passed into the institutions of the kingdom of Israel. **With his fifty.** Some recognition of Elijah's superhuman power would seem to have led Ahaziah to send so large a body. His doing so was a sort of challenge to the prophet to show whether Ahaziah or the God whom he represented was the stronger. The circumstances recall those of the "band of men and officers from the chief priests and Pharisees" (John xviii. 3), which was sent, "with swords and staves," to arrest another righteous Person. **He sat on the top of a hill**; literally, on the top of the hill (ἐπὶ τῆς κορυφῆς τοῦ ὄρους, LXX.). The high ground where Elijah had met the messengers (ver. 3) seems to be intended. When they were gone, the prophet took his seat on the highest point, conspicuous on all sides, so avoiding any attempt at concealment, and awaiting the next step that the king would take, calmly and quietly. **He spake unto him, Thou man of God.** The captain is thought by some to have spoken ironically; but there is no evidence of this. The address is respectful, submissive. The miraculous powers of Elijah (1 Kings xvii. 22; xviii. 38) were probably known to the officer, who hoped by the tone of his address to escape the prophet's anger. In the same spirit he avoids issuing any command of his own, and prefers simply to deliver the king's command—**The king hath said, Come down.**

Ver. 10.—**And Elijah answered . . . let fire come down.** The LXX. render, καταβήσεται πῦρ—"fire will come down;" and so some moderns, who are anxious to clear

the prophet of the charges of cruelty and bloodthirstiness which have been brought against him. But there is no need of altering the translation. Elijah undoubtedly "commanded fire to come down from heaven" (Luke ix. 54), or, in other words, prayed to God that it might come down, and in answer to his prayer the fire fell. The narrative may be set aside as an embellishment of later times, having no historical foundation, by those who (like Ewald) deny that miracles are possible; but, if it be accepted, it must be accepted as it stands, and Elijah must be regarded, not as having merely prophesied a result, but as having been instrumental in producing it. We must judge Elijah, not by the ideas of our own day, but by those of the age wherein he lived. He was raised up to vindicate God's honour, to check and punish idolatry, to keep alive a faithful remnant in Israel, when all the powers of the earth were leagued together to destroy and smother true religion. He was an embodiment of the Law—of absolute, strict, severe justice. The fair face of mercy was not revealed to him. Already, at Carmel, he had executed the Divine vengeance on idolaters after an exemplary fashion (1 Kings xviii. 40). Now, Ahaziah, the son of the wicked Jezebel, had challenged Jehovah to a trial of strength by first ignoring him, and then sending a troop of soldiers to arrest his prophet. Was Elijah to succumb without an effort, or was he to vindicate the majesty and honour of Jehovah? He had no power of himself to do either good or harm. He could but pray to Jehovah, and Jehovah, in his wisdom and perfect goodness, would either grant or refuse his prayer. If he granted it, the punishment inflicted would not be Elijah's work, but his. To tax Elijah with cruelty is to involve God in the charge. God regarded it as a fitting time for making a signal example, and, so regarding it, he inspired a spirit of indignation in the breast of his prophet, who thereupon made the prayer which he saw fit to answer. The judgment was in accordance with the general tone and tenor of the Law, which assigns "tribulation and anguish to every soul of man that doeth evil" (Rom. ii. 9), and visits with death every act of rebellion against God. **There came down fire.** Josephus says that the "fire" was a flash of lightning (πρηστήρ), and so the commentators generally.

Ver. 11.—**Again also**; rather, *and again* (see the Revised Version). **He answered and said**; rather, *he spoke and said* (ἐλάλησε καὶ εἶπε, LXX.). **Come down quickly.** The king has grown impatient. It is conceivable that the death of the first captain with his band of fifty had been kept from him, and that he was only aware of an unaccountable delay. He therefore changes his order from " Come down " to " Come down *quickly*."

Ver. 13.—**A captain of the third fifty;** rather, *the captain of a third fifty* (see the Revised Version). This captain went up— *i.e.* ascended the hill on which Elijah was still seated, and there **fell on his knees,** or bowed himself down, before the prophet, as suppliants were wont to do, beseeching his compassion. The fate of the two former captains had become known to him by some means or other, and this induced him to assume an attitude, not of command, but of submission. He acknowledged that the prophet held his life and the lives of his fifty men at his free disposal, and begged that they might **be precious in his sight,** or, in other words, that he would spare them. What response Elijah would have made, had he been left to himself, is uncertain. But he was not left to himself. An angel of God again appeared to him, and directed his course of action.

Ver. 15.—**Go down with him: be not afraid of him;** *i.e.* " descend the hill with him— have no fear of him, accompany him to the presence of the king; do my will, and there shall no harm happen unto thee." **And he arose, and went down.** Elijah showed no hesitation, no fear, no undue regard for his own personal safety. He had been contending for God's honour, not for his own advantage. Now that God bade him contend no more, but yield, he complied promptly, and ceased all resistance.

Ver. 16.—**He said unto him;** *i.e. Elijah* said to the *king.* Introduced into the royal presence, as a prisoner, perhaps fettered and chained, the prophet in no way lowered his tone or abated from the severity of his speech. Distinctly, in the plainest possible words, he warned the monarch that his end approached—he would never quit the bed whereon he lay, but, *because* he had insulted Jehovah by sending to consult the god of Ekron, would surely die. Apparently the king, abashed and confounded, released the prophet, and allowed him to go his way. **Thus saith the Lord.** Elijah rehearses the words of the message which he had sent by the first of the three captains (see ver. 6)— Thus saith the Lord, **Forasmuch as thou hast sent messengers to inquire of Baal- zebub the god of Ekron, is it not because there is no God in Israel to inquire of his word?** Therefore thou shalt not come down off that bed on which thou art gone up, but shalt surely die. God's determinations are unalterable.

Ver. 17*a*.—**So he died according to the word of the Lord which Elijah had spoken.** Not only did he die in consequence of his fall without once quitting his bed, but his

death was, as Elijah had said, a judgment on his sin in sending to consult Baal-zebub.

REIGN OF JEHORAM.

Ver. 17*b*. — **And Jehoram** — or, *Joram,* LXX., " whom Jehovah exalts; " another evidence that Ahab did not regard himself as having abandoned altogether the worship of Jehovah (see the comment on 1 Kings xxii. 40)—**reigned in his stead** ("his brother," אחיו, has probably fallen out after " Jeho- ram," and requires to be inserted in order to give force to the last clause of the verse) **in the second year of Jehoram the son of Jehoshaphat King of Judah.** In ch. iii. 1 it is said that Jehoram, the son of Ahab and brother of Ahaziah, began to reign over Israel in the eighteenth year of Jehoshaphat himself. The apparent discrepancy is recon- ciled by supposing that Jehoshaphat asso- ciated his son Jehoram in the kingdom in his seventeenth year, when he was about to enter upon the Syrian war, so that the eighteenth year of Jehoshaphat was also the second year of Jehoram. It is certain that association was largely practised in Egypt at a date long anterior to Jehosha- phat, and David's proclamation of Solomon as king was an association, so that the expla- nation is not untenable. On the other hand, the difficulties of the chronology of 2 Kings are so numerous and so great as to defy com- plete reconciliation, and to lead to a suspicion that the numbers have either suffered ex- tensive corruption, or have been manipulated by an unskilful reviser (see Introduction, p. iii.). **Because he had no son;** *i.e.* because he, Ahaziah, had no son, he was succeeded by his younger brother, Jehoram.

Ver. 18.—**Now the rest of the acts of Ahaziah which he did.** These may have included some months of warfare against Mesha, King of Moab, who seems to have rebelled at the very beginning of Ahaziah's reign (ver. 1 and ch. iii. 5). Mesha's war of independence consisted of a succession of sieges, whereby he recovered one by one the various strongholds in his territory, which were occupied by the Israelites—Medeba, Ataroth, Nebo, Jahaz, Horonaim, and others —expelling the foreign garrisons, rebuild- ing or strengthening the fortifications, and occupying the cities by garrisons of his own. On one occasion, at the siege of Nebo, he declares that he killed seven thousand men. He found in the town a place of worship containing vessels, which he regarded as " vessels of Jehovah" (Moabite Stone, line 18); these he took, and dedicated them to Chemosh, the special god of Moab. How much of the war fell into the reign of Aha- ziah, and how much into that of Jehoram his brother, is uncertain. **Are they not** written in the book of the chronicles of the kings of Israel? Mesha's stone is a striking testimony to the *contemporary* record of historical events by the Palestinian monarchs of the time, which has sometimes been doubted.

HOMILETICS.

Vers. 1—18.—*The short reign of Ahaziah: his sins, and their punishment.* For homiletic purposes we must attach to this chapter the last three verses of the First Book of the Kings. We find in that passage a short but very complete account of the general character of Ahaziah's sins; we find in this chapter a tolerably full account of one great act of sin, and a clear declaration of the manner in which that act and his other sins were punished. It will be well to consider separately (1) the sins; (2) their aggravations; and (3) their punishment.

I. THE SINS. These were three in number: (1) walking in the way of Jeroboam the son of Nebat (1 Kings xxii. 52), or maintaining the calf-worship—the hereditary will-worship of the northern kingdom, introduced by Jeroboam, the first non-Davidic king, and thenceforth continued uninterruptedly by each successive Israelite monarch; (2) walking in the way of his father—neglecting the worship of Jehovah, persecuting his prophets, practically proscribing the old religion, and probably ruling with harshness and cruelty; and (3) walking in the way of his mother—"serving Baal and worshipping him" (1 Kings xxii. 53), maintaining the Phœnician sensualistic cult, which Jezebel had introduced from Zidon (1 Kings xvi. 31), and which was of a most demoralizing and debasing character. It was, primarily, under this third head that the special act of sin fell which forms the main subject of ch. i.

II. THEIR AGGRAVATIONS. Ahaziah might have been expected to have learnt wisdom by experience, to have taken to heart the warning furnished by his father's life and death, and *at least* to have avoided the sins which had brought down upon the king and upon the kingdom so terrible a blow, so signal and severe a punishment. But, on the contrary, he went beyond his father in the great sin for which his father was punished, viz. apostasy from Jehovah to Baal. Ahab had always been half-hearted in his irreligion—he would, and he would not; he strove to combine an acknowledgment of Jehovah with a practical devotion to his rival; he gave both his sons names which placed them under the protection of Israel's true God; he at one time "humbled himself before Jehovah," and "fasted, and lay in sackcloth, and went softly" (1 Kings xxi. 27, 29); he consented to inquire of a prophet of the Lord at the request of Jehoshaphat (1 Kings xxii. 9); he had no dealings, that we know of, with the foreign Baalistic temples or oracles which abounded in Phœnicia and Philistia, and thus did not, at any rate, parade his contempt of Jehovah in the eyes of the adjoining nations. Ahaziah acted differently. He was a consistent, thorough-faced, out-and-out idolater. Jehovah was nothing to him; Baal was everything. We ought, perhaps, to view it as some extenuation of his sin that he would naturally be influenced to some extent by his mother, whatever her character, and that the strong, firm, and fierce character of Jezebel would naturally influence him to a large extent. But men are not mere creatures of circumstances; they have the power to resist influences no less than to yield to them, and are bound to consider the nature of the influences surrounding them, and to resist such as they perceive to be bad. There is no evidence that Ahaziah offered any resistance at all to Jezebel's influences. He was the weak son of a wicked mother, and simply "walked in her way." As Ewald says, he "exhibited a far more decided inclination than Ahab had done to all sorts of heathenish superstitions" ('History of Israel,' vol. iv. p. 77, Eng. trans.). He made a parade of his Baalistic leanings. He was obdurate and persistent, and despised warning after warning. A cruel hardness of heart, quite equal to his mother's, is shown in his exposing to probable death a second and a third body of fifty men, rather than submit to Elijah, and own himself in the wrong. Thus he would appear to have reached, in his comparatively short life, a deeper depth of moral evil than his father in his longer one.

III. THEIR PUNISHMENT. The revolt of the subject kingdom of Moab was the first punishment which befell the apostate king. He had to determine, on ascending the throne, what line he would take in religious matters—whether he would maintain or abolish the Baal-worship, whether he would maintain or abolish the worship of the calves, whether he would persecute or protect the adherents of the Jehovistic religion. He decided to " walk in the way of his father and of his mother," and at once the first blow fell. Moab revolted, and was successful. The mere attempt at revolt might have happened in any case, for Mesha would naturally have seized such an opportunity as the death of Ahab under such circumstances offered. But the God of battles determines success or failure, and Mesha's unbroken series of victories (Moabite Stone, lines 9—33) were the consequence of Ahaziah's guilt. As usual, " for the king's offence the people bled." Seven thousand Israelite warriors were destroyed in one siege ; the women and children were taken prisoners, and "devoted to Ashtar-Chemosh." There was widespread and extreme suffering. This should not surprise us. There is a solidarity between a king and his people, which unites them almost indissolubly in their fortunes and in their sins. The people follow the king's example, and, partaking in his guilt, naturally and justly partake in his punishment (see the homiletics on 1 Kings xxii., pp. 542, 543). The king's second punishment was personal. It was permitted that an accident should befall him. Sitting in an upper chamber, *i.e.* in one not upon the ground floor, which had a latticed window, opening out probably on a garden, he rashly leant against it, when the fastenings or the woodwork gave way, and he was precipitated to the ground. The hurt received was serious, and forced him to take to his bed, where he lay probably in much pain and discomfort. Here was an opportunity for considering his ways, for asking himself what was amiss in them, for mourning over the sins which he had committed (1 Kings xxii. 52, 53), and renouncing them and turning away from them. God's judgments are sent to lead men to repentance. Prolonged lying on a sick-bed is especially favourable to meditation, self-examination, self-condemnation, penitence. But Ahaziah was obdurate. He thought nothing of the goodness of God in sparing his life, for the fall might well have been instantaneously fatal ; he thought nothing of God's mercy in giving him a time for reflection and amendment. He was merely impatient of his affliction, and anxious to have done with it. And in his impatience and obduracy he added sin to sin. Ignoring Jehovah and his prophets, through whom it was always possible to "inquire of the Lord " (1 Kings xxii. 5—28), he makes his appeal to Baal. It is an ostentatious appeal. He sends a public embassy to consult the Baal of a foreign town. Then his final punishment is decreed. Hitherto his life had hung in the balance—his fate had been in the hands of him with whom are the issues of life and death. Now his own act had shut the gate of mercy. The sentence went forth from the mouth of God's prophet, " Thou shalt not come down off that bed on which thou art gone up, but shalt surely die." Cut off in his youth, childless (ver. 17), he pays the fitting penalty of obstinate persistence in sin, and, after weeks or months of suffering, "goes to his own place." He " whom Jehovah upholds " becomes " he whom Jehovah destroys "—destroys after a short reign of little more than a year—a reign disgraceful to himself and disastrous to his country.

Vers. 9—16.—*The " spirit we are of "—the old dispensation and the new.* I. THE SPIRIT OF THE OLD DISPENSATION. The spirit of the Law was strict, stern, inexorable justice. "Cursed be the man that maketh any graven or molten image. . . . Cursed be he that setteth light by his father or his mother. . . . Cursed be he that removeth his neighbour's landmark," etc. (Deut. xxvii. 15—26); " He that curseth father or mother, let him die the death " (Exod. xxi. 17); " Eye for eye, tooth for tooth, hand for hand, foot for foot, burning for burning, wound for wound, stripe for stripe " (Exod. xxi. 24, 25); " He that smiteth a man, so that he die, shall surely be put to death " (Exod. xxi. 12); "He that smiteth his father or his mother, shall surely be put to death " (Exod. xxi. 15); "He that stealeth a man, and selleth him, shall surely be put to death " (Exod. xxi. 16); "Thou shalt not suffer a witch to live " (Exod. xxii. 18); " Whosoever lieth with a beast shall surely be put to death " (Exod. xxii. 19); " He that sacrificeth unto any god, save unto the Lord only, he shall be utterly destroyed" (Exod. xxii. 20), etc. Man was so far gone from original righteousness, had so corrupted and depraved himself, that only by the strictest possible system, by the most solemn warnings, the most awful threats, and the sternest possible execution of the threats when the occasion came, could wickedness be repressed, crime prevented from becoming rampant, mankind be reclaimed, society saved. Hence the severity of the Mosaic code, the frequency of the penalty of death, and the strictness with which the penalty was in almost every case exacted. The first idolatry was punished by the death of three thousand by the sword (Exod. xxxii. 28). Nadab and Abihu, for offering strange fire, were destroyed by fire from heaven (Lev. x. 1, 2). When Korah, Dathan, and Abiram rebelled against Moses, the earth gaped and swallowed them up (Numb. xvi. 32). The iniquity of Peor was avenged by the slaughter of all the heads of the people (Numb. xxv. 4, 5). The sin of Gibeah cost the lives of twenty-five thousand Benjamites (Judg. xx. 46). Elijah, in calling down fire from heaven upon the minions of an idolatrous tyrant sent to arrest him for declaring to their master the sentence of Jehovah, was but acting in the general spirit of the Law, which regarded all opposition to Jehovah as deserving of death, and looked upon the inspired prophets of God as the ministers of an avenging righteousness. From time to time some signal display of Jehovah's anger against rebels and his power to punish them was requisite to preserve among the people any respect or reverence at all for true religion; and Elijah deemed that the time for such a display was now come. That the fire fell at his word showed that he had judged aright, and that his will reflected the Divine will and was in unison with it.

II. THE SPIRIT OF THE NEW DISPENSATION. The new dispensation opened with the proclamation of "peace on earth, good will toward men" (Luke ii. 14). The curses of the Law were replaced by the Beatitudes" (Matt. v. 3—10). The gentle and tender Jesus destroyed nothing but a single senseless tree (Matt. xxi. 19). He went about doing good. He was "sent to heal the broken-hearted, to preach deliverance to the captives, and recovering of sight to the blind, to set at liberty them that were bruised, to preach the acceptable year of the Lord" (Luke iv. 18, 19). When men rose up against him, when his life was attempted, before his hour was come, he was content by an exertion of his miraculous power to withdraw himself, to pass through their midst, and go his way. On one occasion he himself pointed the contrast between the two dispensations in the most distinct and remarkable manner. It was when he and his disciples were proceeding on a journey through this very district of Samaria, where Elijah had shown forth the justice of God, that his disciples, James and John, the "Sons of Thunder," as they were called, desired to repeat the Tishbite's act for the punishment of some Samaritans who would not permit him to enter their village. "Lord," they said, "wilt thou that we command fire to come down from heaven, and consume them, even as Elias did?" But they little knew the Master they addressed. Jesus "turned and rebuked them, and said, Ye know not what manner of spirit ye are of. For the Son of man is not come to destroy men's lives, but to save them. And they went to another village" (Luke ix. 51—56). "It was," remarks Archbishop Trench, "as if he had said, 'Ye are mistaking and confounding the different standing-points of the old and new covenants, taking your stand upon the old—that of an avenging righteousness, when you should rejoice to take it upon the new—that of a forgiving love'" ('Notes on the Miracles,' ch. iv. p. 36, note). The spirit of the Christian dispensation is seen especially in such commands as the following: "Resist not evil but whosoever shall smite thee on thy right cheek, turn to him the other also" (Matt. v. 39); "Love your enemies, bless them that curse you, do good to them that hate you, and pray for them which despitefully use you and persecute you" (Matt. v. 44); "Be kindly affectioned one to another with brotherly love; in honour preferring one another" (Rom. xii. 10); "Recompense to no man evil for evil" (Rom. xii. 17); "Avenge not yourselves, but rather give place unto wrath: for it is written; Vengeance is mine; I will repay, saith the Lord. Therefore if thine enemy hunger, feed him; if he thirst, give him drink: for in so doing thou shalt heap coals of fire upon his head. Be not overcome of evil, but overcome evil with good" (Rom. xii. 19—21).

HOMILIES BY VARIOUS AUTHORS.

Vers. 1—4.—*Seeking after strange gods: its cause and consequence.* We are here introduced to a kingly home. All the pomp of royalty is there. But it is not a happy home. To begin with, there is *sickness* in that home. Royalty, or rank, or riches cannot keep sickness out. Ahaziah had been looking through the window of his chamber, or, as some think, leaning over the frail baluster of wicker-work which ran round the roof on the inner or courtyard side, when the lattice-work gave way, and he was precipitated into the court beneath and seriously injured. But there are homes of sickness that are nevertheless happy homes. The sufferer is happy; the other members of the family are happy. Why? Because they all know that Jesus is there. They hear his voice saying, "It is I: be not afraid." They took Christ into their house when all was going well with them, and they find that he does not leave them when sickness comes. But it was not so with Ahaziah. How a man will bear sickness depends a good deal on what his life and character have been when he was in health. This is true physically. It is true also in a moral and spiritual sense. The bad man is generally afraid of sickness. Yes; for he is afraid of death. What about Ahaziah's previous history? We have it summed up in the closing verses of 1 Kings. " He did evil in the sight of the Lord, and walked in the way of his father, and in the way of his mother, and in the way of Jeroboam the son of Nebat, who made Israel to sin: for he served Baal, and worshipped him, and provoked to anger the Lord God of Israel, according to all that his father had done." Oh! the tremendous influence of a bad example. Ahaziah was in alarm about this illness. He wanted to know if he was to recover. He had forsaken God when in health; perhaps he does not think that God would hear him now. Or perhaps he has been so hardened in sin that he really believes his heathen god can help him. So he sends messengers to inquire of Baal-zebub at Ekron, whether he would recover of his disease.

I. THE CAUSE OF SEEKING AFTER STRANGE GODS. What is the secret of that idolatry which in all ages has taken such a hold of the human heart? Why is it that such a people as the Hebrews, descended from one who lived so entirely under the power of the invisible God as Abraham did—they who in their Passover had a constant reminder of God's existence and power, and in their ten commandments a constant reminder of his mind and will,—why is it that they so far forgot God as to sink into the degrading worship of the heathen deities? Or, to bring it more home to ourselves and our own surroundings, why is it that men and women who know that Christ died for them, who therefore know the priceless worth of their immortal souls, who bear in the very name of Christian a constant reminder of the Son of God, and who have in the precepts of the gospel the highest code of morality ever taught to man,—why is it that they too forget God, reject his mercy, set at nought his counsels, and will have none of his reproof? Why is it that in our Christian land so many are living in practical heathenism? Why are they so few who read the Bible, and, of those who do read it, so few who obey its teachings? Why so many thousands who never enter the house of God? Why is it that a really religious daily newspaper it is almost impossible to find, while nearly all our daily newspapers largely devote themselves to advance the interests of the theatre, the race-course, and the betting-ring? Truly it may be said that our nation has gone after strange gods. What is the secret of it all? Largely this, *the love of what is seen, more than of what is unseen.* This is at the root of all idolatry. It is this that makes men such an easy prey to sin. They are absorbed in the interests and pleasures of the body only. They forget the interests of the immortal soul. They live for the present, but neglect the future. They live for self, but neglect God. They lay up treasure on earth, but have no treasure in heaven. We see this love of what is seen—this going after strange gods—*in much of the philosophy of the present day.* Men deny God, the God of the Bible, the intelligent, wise, powerful, provident, holy, loving Creator of the universe. And what do they substitute for him? A mere negation. At best matter or force. Here plainly they are absorbed in what is seen. They make a god of matter. They forget that only mind could produce mind, only soul could produce soul, that only an intelligent Being could produce the order and control the workings of the universe. Strange gods, indeed—gods of which they have no certainty—they set up in place of the God of our Christian faith. We see this love of what is seen operating also *in the case of the money-lover.* It is not wrong to acquire wealth, provided it is rightly won and rightly used. But there are many *who make a god of money.* It occupies all their thoughts while they are awake. When they are asleep, they dream of it. Even the sabbath, supposed to be devoted to the worship of God, is often devoted to meditations on money and how to get it. Yet even for the present life there are things more precious than money. Men who sacrifice everything for money soon find that they have lost things which money cannot buy.

> " The world with stones instead of bread
> My hungry soul has always fed :
> It promised *health ;* in one short hour
> Perished the fair but fragile flower.
> It promised *riches ;* in a day
> They made them wings and flew away.
> It promised *friends ;* all sought their own,
> And left my widowed heart alone."

And then what shall we say of the folly of those who, while making ample provision for this short life, have made none for the life that is to come? " What shall it profit a man, if he shall gain the whole world, and lose his own soul ?" Let us beware of making a god of money. We see the same love of what is seen *entering even into the Church of God.* There is too much tendency, even in the Christian Church, to worship earthly rank, to attend to the rich and neglect the poor. How often have our Churches made a god of custom, of the traditions of men, of public opinion, of expediency and worldly policy! Images and pictures are set up to aid in the worship of him of whom it is said that " God is a Spirit : and they that worship him must worship him in spirit and in truth."

II. THE CONSEQUENCE OF SEEKING AFTER STRANGE GODS. " But the angel of the Lord said to Elijah the Tishbite, Arise, go up to meet the messengers of the King of Samaria, and say unto them, Is it not because there is not a God in Israel, that ye go to inquire of Baal-zebub the god of Ekron ? Now therefore thus saith the Lord, Thou shalt not come down from that bed on which thou art gone up, but shalt surely die." The strange deity that Ahaziah sought after had not served him much. Strange gods have never been much help to those who seek after them. They have not helped the heathen nations, but their degrading and demoralizing worship has always been a source of weakness and decay. It is the same with all the strange gods that men serve everywhere—with all the passions and desires to gratify which they spend their energies and time. We read of King Ahaz that he turned away from the true God to serve the gods of Damascus, because Syria enjoyed prosperity. He said, " Because the gods of the kings of Syria help them, therefore will I sacrifice to them, that they may help me." " But," says the Bible narrative, " they were the ruin of him, and of all Israel " (2 Chron. xxviii. 23). How many a man has done like Ahaz—turned his back upon God, and found that the strange gods whom he served proved to be his ruin! Many a man has lived without God when in health, who was very glad to seek him when sickness came and death was drawing nigh. It is told of a sceptic called Saunderson, who was a great admirer of Sir Isaac Newton's talents, but who made light of his religion when in health, that when on his death-bed he was heard to say, in mournful entreaty, " God of Sir Isaac Newton, have mercy on me!" But, as many a one has found, it may be too late then to seek the Lord. Such are the consequences of seeking after strange gods. The same message which was sent to Ahaziah will one day be sent to us—this part at least : " Thou shalt not come down from that bed on which thou art gone up, but shalt surely die." The way to prepare for that message is to accept the messages of life. The way to prepare for sickness is to serve God while in health. —C. H. I.

Vers. 5—16.—*Fire from heaven.* Ahaziah's messengers were intercepted by Elijah. They brought back to Ahaziah the fearless prophet's announcement of his doom. Elijah's message was God's message. He began it by " Thus saith the Lord." The statement that Ahaziah would surely die was in reality the sentence of him who knows the future of every life, and in whose hand is the breath of every human being, be he peasant or be he king. But such a terrible sentence had not brought Ahaziah to his senses. He does not begin to set his house in order. He does not prepare to meet his God as a guilty but penitent sinner. No; but when the messengers tell him of the strange interruption they had met with, recognizing at once from their description that it was Elijah the Tishbite who had stopped them, he is filled with anger and defiance. He has defied God when in health ; now he defies him from a bed of sickness. He sends forth a captain with a company of fifty men to lay hold upon the prophet. It was not the first time Elijah's life had been threatened by royal sinners. When a man is fearless in rebuking sin, he must expect the hatred of impenitent sinners. Smooth words may win a fleeting popularity, but the friendship of this world is enmity against God. Popularity is dearly bought that is obtained at the sacrifice of truth, of conscience, and of duty. But Elijah's life is safe in the hands of the Master whom he serves. Once before God had vindicated his own honour and Elijah's faithfulness by sending fire from heaven to consume his sacrifice. In a similar manner now he defends Elijah and punishes his enemies. The incident is one which presents some difficulties. The study of it suggests many useful lessons.

I. FIRE FROM HEAVEN IS AN ACT OF JUSTICE. It may appear to some that these first two captains and their fifties were hardly dealt with. Some one may say, "It was their duty to obey. They were only executing the king's orders. They were not responsible for the message which they brought from the king to Elijah. It was hard, then, that they should suffer for doing that which it was their duty to do." These are very plausible statements. Let us examine them a little more closely. Let us remember that man is not a mere machine. Every man has an immortal soul, coming from God, going back to God, and accountable to God for its actions. There is such a thing as individual personal responsibility. No external circumstances, no position in life, can ever take away that responsibility. These captains and their men were bound to do their duty to their king. Yes; but not in defiance of the Law and power of God. Where the will of man or the word of man comes into conflict with the will or Word of God, then it is the duty of every human being to say, "We ought to obey God rather than men." These officers and soldiers were really encouraging Ahaziah in his guilt. They knew that he was an idolater. They knew that he was a worshipper of Baal. They knew that the man whom he was sending them to arrest was a servant of the most high God, and his foremost living prophet. They knew of the sentence which had already been pronounced against Ahaziah. Yet here, at his bidding, they go forth as the instruments of his defiance against the living God. They were sharers in his guilt—*participes criminis*. They were personally guilty before God. We can never shift our own responsibility on to the shoulders of others. It did not make Adam's guilt less that he accused Eve, or Eve's guilt less that she accused the serpent. They were intelligent beings, with the power of free choice. Our plain duty is, if we are in any position or business which requires us to violate the Law of God, at once to give it up. God says, "Them that honour me I will honour." Moreover, *they had already been warned of the sin and danger of resisting God*. They knew how the prophets of Baal had been slain. They knew how Elijah's prophecy—in other words, God's sentence—against Ahab had come true, that where the dogs licked the blood of Naboth, there they would lick the blood of Ahab, and they knew that a similar doom was foretold against Jezebel. Yet in spite of all these warnings they went forth against the prophet of God. So the sinner has many warnings. How often God's Word and God's messenger have called him to repentance! Perhaps by sickness and suffering he has had reminders of approaching death. By sudden bereavement he has been reminded that " in such an hour as ye think not the Son of man cometh." Let him beware of turning a deaf ear to the warning voice. "See that ye refuse not him that speaketh." Further, when we are considering the justice of this fire from heaven, let us remember that *the life of God's most useful servant was at stake*. It is pretty certain that Ahaziah, when he sent for Elijah, wanted to take his life. It is pretty certain also that, had Elijah gone with either of the first two captains, his life would have been in danger. It was only after the third time of sending that God said to Elijah, "Be not afraid of him." It was only then, perhaps, that Ahaziah realized the uselessness of fighting against God. We hold by the principle that life should not be recklessly sacrificed. But if we are disposed to speak of this incident as reckless sacrifice of life, let us remember what hundreds of lives have been imperilled and sacrificed more than once, even for the sake of a single British subject. No right-minded person would condemn the sending forth of soldiers—many of them to certain death—in such a case as that of Abyssinia, where the lives of British subjects were in danger, or that of the attempted rescue of General Gordon. Before we can cherish a suspicion of injustice against the dealings of God, let us be sure that we have right and reason on our side. A full examination of all the circumstances will generally banish even such a suggestion from our minds. But, then, there are many cases where we cannot possibly understand or know all the circumstances. In such a case, is it not the only course we can take to bow in submission to the all-wise will of God? "Shall not the Judge of all the earth do right?" For all these reasons I conclude that the fire which came down from heaven upon these soldiers was an act of justice.

II. FIRE FROM HEAVEN IS AN ACT OF NECESSITY. More than one reason has already been suggested why this fire from heaven was necessary. It may have been necessary in defence of the prophet's life. It may have been necessary in vindication of the power and honour of God; for it took place at a time of almost universal idolatry and Baal-worship on the part of Israel. This, however, we may be sure of, that, whether we can see the necessity for it or not, *fire from heaven is necessary, or God would not send it.* There are three uses which fire serves in the natural world, for which analogies may be found in the spiritual world. These are *purifying, destroying*, and *testing*. We need the *cleansing fires* to purify us in the spiritual life. Perhaps we are becoming too worldly, too much engrossed with the things of this life, laying up for ourselves treasures upon earth. Perhaps we are making an idol of some earthly object of our affection. Perhaps we are becoming spiritually proud. Perhaps we compare ourselves favourably with others, and think how much better we are than they. Then our heavenly Father may think it wise to purify us from such dross as this. And so he calls us to pass through the furnace of affliction, or adversity, or sickness. Thus he humbles us. Thus he keeps us mindful that we are but dust. Thus he keeps us mindful of our dependence upon him. Then the *destroying fire* is needed in the moral and spiritual world, as well as in the natural world. It was a necessary part of the Divine government that Sodom and Gomorrah should be destroyed. They were a moral plague-spot. The festering limb must be cut off if the body is to be saved. So also Herculaneum and Pompeii were destroyed when they too became a centre of moral degradation and corruption. Would it be any wonder, would it be any injustice, if the fire of God would come down from heaven and burn up some of the moral plague-spots of modern times? Would not the world be vastly the better if the gambling-hells and drinking-hells and hells of immorality were burnt up in one vast conflagration? And if they are spared, and if the moral corrupters of others are spared, will it be any better for them in that day when "the fearful, and unbelieving, and the abominable, and murderers, and whoremongers, and sorcerers, and idolaters, and all liars, shall have their part in the lake which burneth with fire and brimstone: which is the second death"? Then there is *the testing fire*. This also is necessary in the spiritual world. "Wherein ye greatly rejoice," says the Apostle Peter, "though now for a season, if need be, ye are in heaviness through manifold temptations, that the trial of your faith, being much more precious than of gold that perisheth, though it be tried with fire, might be found unto praise and honour and glory at the appearing of Jesus Christ" (1 Pet. i. 6, 7). If there were no trials and difficulties, there would be no test, no proof of our faith. And then the time is coming when the fire—the searching, testing fire of God's judgment—shall try every man's work of what sort it is. If our life is built up on Christ, then out of the *purifying* fire it will come clearer and brighter, from the *destroying* fire it will suffer no harm, and from the *testing* fire it will come forth to honour and glory. "Then shall the righteous shine forth as the sun in the kingdom of their Father" (Matt. xiii. 43).

III. FIRE FROM HEAVEN IS NOT INCONSISTENT WITH THE DIVINE MERCY. Here we may consider a difficulty which some have raised. When Jesus, on his way to Jerusalem, passed through a village of the Samaritans, the people there would not receive him, "because his face was as though he would go to Jerusalem." The disciples, in anger, asked him if they should command fire to come down from heaven, as Elijah did, and consume them. The answer of our Saviour was, "Ye know not what manner of spirit ye are of. For the Son of man is not come to destroy men's lives, but to save them" (Luke ix. 51—56). Now, the question which some have asked is this—Does not Christ here condemn the action of Elijah? A careful study of the narrative before us would at once dispose of such a question as that. It is said here, "*The fire of God came down from heaven.*" Even if this were not stated, it is obvious that Elijah of himself had no power to bring down fire from heaven, unless with God's sanction and assistance. But a great many commentators and preachers, who would not go the length of saying that Christ condemned Elijah, seem to suggest that he condemned *his spirit, as unsuited to gospel times.* Even for this suggestion I do not think there is any warrant. Our Saviour condemned the disciples for a spirit of vindictiveness and revenge, which probably was intensified by the feeling of prejudice and animosity which existed against the Samaritans. He also stated that he was not come to destroy men's lives, but to save them. His work, *then,* was one of salvation. But those who rejected his salvation were certainly to perish. More than once Christ in the clearest manner teaches this. "Except ye repent, ye shall all likewise perish." He foretells the doom of Jerusalem. He foretells the terrible agony of lost souls, who shall go away into everlasting fire; "there shall be the wailing and the gnashing of teeth." The action of retributive justice, therefore, is perfectly consistent with mercy toward the sinner. The consuming fire may be part of a merciful and loving purpose toward the world at large. *In the particular case before us, we see that mercy was exhibited as well as justice.* The third captain, who showed a humble spirit, and apparently some regret at the work he had to do, was mercifully spared the fate which had fallen upon the other two. While we speak of the consuming fire of God's justice, we would speak also of mercy for the penitent, of forgiveness, full and free, for every anxious soul, for every returning wanderer. "Believe on the Lord Jesus Christ, and thou shalt be saved."—C. H. I.

Vers. 1—8.—*Worldly royalty and personal godliness.* "Then Moab rebelled against Israel," etc. The two Books of Kings, which form but one in the most correct and ancient edition of the Hebrews, whilst they constitute a very strange and significant history, are fraught with much moral and practical suggestion. These verses bring under our notice two subjects of thought—worldly royalty in a humiliating condition, and personal godliness truly majestic.

I. WORLDLY ROYALTY IN A HUMILIATING CONDITION. 1. Here is a king in *mortal suffering.* "And Ahaziah fell down through a lattice in his upper chamber that was in Samaria, and was sick." Nature has no more respect for kings than for beggars; her laws treat them as ordinary mortals. 2. Here is a king in *mental distress.* On his bed of suffering the king's mind was most painfully exercised as to what would be the issue of his bodily suffering. He sends messengers to the idols in order to ask whether "I shall recover of this disease." No doubt the fear of death distressed him, as indeed it distresses most. 3. Here is a king in *superstitious darkness.* He had no knowledge of the true God, no enlightened religious feeling, and he sent his messengers to an idol—the god of flies—to know whether he should recover or not. What a humiliating condition for royalty to be in! And yet it is a condition in which kings and princes are often found. The other subject of thought here is—

II. PERSONAL GODLINESS TRULY MAJESTIC. Elijah is an example of personal godliness, though, in a worldly sense, he was very poor, and his costume seemed to be almost the meanest of the mean. "He was a hairy man, and girt with a girdle of leather about his loins." But see the majesty of this man in two things. 1. In *receiving communication from heaven.* "But the angel of the Lord said to Elijah the Tishbite." A truly godly man is ever in correspondence with Heaven; his "conversation is in heaven." 2. In *reproving the king.* "Is it not because there is not a God in Israel, that thou sendest to inquire of Baal-zebub the god of Ekron?" The thing called *religion* in many countries is just strong enough to reprove the poor, but too weak to thunder reproof into the ear of the corrupt and pleasure-seeking monarchs. In his reproof he pronounces on him the Divine judgment, "Thou shalt not come down off that bed on which thou art gone up, but shalt surely die."

CONCLUSION. Which is the better, do you think—a throne or a godly character? Fools only prefer the former; the man of sense, thoughtfulness, and reflection would say the latter.—D. T.

Vers. 9—18.—*Man in three aspects.* "Then the king sent unto him a captain of fifty," etc. In this paragraph we have man in three aspects.

I. MAN RUINED THROUGH THE CONDUCT OF OTHERS. The messengers which the king sent to Elijah—fifty each time on three different occasions—were all, except the last fifty, destroyed by lightning. This awful judgment came upon them, not merely on their own account—although, like all sinners, they had forfeited their lives to eternal justice—but as messengers of the king. Throughout the human race, in all races and times, there are found millions groaning under the trials and sufferings brought on them by the conduct of others. In this world the innocent suffer for the guilty; the "fathers eat sour grapes, and the children's teeth are set on edge."

II. MAN EMPLOYED AS THE EXECUTOR OF DIVINE JUSTICE. These hundred men, messengers from the king, were struck down by Elijah at the command of God. There was no personal vengeance in the act. Elijah was used as the organ of Heaven. God's plan in this world is to *punish* as well as to *save man by man*. How was Pharaoh punished, and the Canaanites, etc.? By man. Sinful nations are punished, often by worthless kings and ruthless despots.

III. MAN STEPPING INTO THE PLACE OF THE DEAD. The King Ahaziah dies; Jehoram steps into his place. "So he died according to the word of the Lord which Elijah had spoken. And Jehoram reigned in his stead." "One generation cometh, and another passeth away." Places, positions, and the various offices of life are no sooner vacated by death than they are stepped into by others. Thus the world goes on, and the dead are soon forgotten. The greatest man on earth to-day is but a mere bubble on the great river of human life; he sparkles for a moment, and is lost for ever in the abyss.—D. T.

Ver. 1.—*The revolt of Moab.* (On this cf. ch. iii.) Moab, one of the conquests of David (2 Sam. viii. 2), perhaps regained its independence after the death of Solomon, and, if the Moabite Stone can be trusted, was again subdued by Omri, Ahab's father. Now, on the occasion of the death of Ahab, it renewed the attempt to throw off the Israelitish yoke. 1. The original conquest had been not unstained by cruelty. These things burn into the memory of peoples. 2. The rule of Omri and Ahab had been most oppressive (ch. iii. 4). Nothing else could be expected from these godless monarchs. "The tender mercies of the wicked are cruel" (Prov. xii. 10). Half the rebellions and revolutions in the world have their origin in oppression and misgovernment. 3. Ahab and Israel had just sustained a severe defeat, that viz. at the hands of the Syrians (1 Kings xxii.). This weakened the Israelitish power, and gave a favourable opportunity for revolt. Those whom we hold in subjection by force, not love, cannot be blamed if they take the earliest opportunity to get rid of our yoke. 4. Israel and Moab were divided by religion. This is the deepest ground of severance among peoples. Nationalities based on different religious faiths constantly tend to fall asunder. Any unity in which they are held can be only external. The federation of the race can only be accomplished on the basis of the worship of the One Jehovah, and the one Lord Jesus Christ. 5. God used these revolts as a means of chastisement (cf. 1 Kings xi. 23). Under David, the greatest theocratic ruler, the kingdom was built up, consolidated, extended. The revolt from God, both in Judah and Israel, was signalized by the revolt of dependencies. Will our own Britain hold its foremost position among the nations, or will its greatness too decay, and its power be shorn by successive breaking off of its colonies? The answer, we believe, will depend very much on its fidelity to God.—J. O.

Vers. 1—8.—*Ahaziah's sickness.* Son of a doomed house (1 Kings xxi. 29), Ahab's successor on the throne reigned for two inglorious years. His evil character is described in the words, "He walked in the way of his father, and in the way of his mother, and in the way of Jeroboam the son of Nebat, who made Israel to sin" (1 Kings xxii. 52). A weak ruler, he was probably the mere tool of his mother Jezebel, whose worst qualities he inherited. In determined idolatry, open defiance of Jehovah, and vindictive persecution of God's servants, as shown by his attempt on the life of Elijah, he is the true child of the "cursed woman" (ch. ix. 34). Even on his death-bed he shows no such compunction as occasionally visited his father Ahab (1 Kings xxi. 27). Undeterred by examples and warnings, he "hardened his neck" in a way which led to his being "suddenly destroyed" (Prov. xxix. 1).

I. THE FATAL FALL. The *fainéant* king came to his end in a manner: 1. Sufficiently *simple*. Idly lounging at the projecting lattice-window of his palace in Samaria

—perhaps leaning against it, and gazing from his elevated position on the fine prospect that spreads itself around—his support suddenly gave way, and he was precipitated to the ground, or courtyard, below. He is picked up, stunned, but not dead, and carried to his couch. It is, in common speech, an accident—some trivial neglect of a fastening—but it terminated this royal career. On such slight contingencies does human life, the change of rulers, and often the course of events in history, depend. We cannot sufficiently ponder that our existence hangs by the finest thread, and that any trivial cause may at any moment cut it short (Jas. iv. 14). 2. Yet *providential*. God's providence is to be recognized in the time and manner of this king's removal. He had " provoked to anger the Lord God of Israel " (1 Kings xxii. 53), and God in this sudden way cut him off. This is the only rational view of the providence of God, since, as we have seen, it is from the most trivial events that the greatest results often spring. The whole can be controlled only by the power that concerns itself with the details. A remarkable illustration is afforded by the death of Ahaziah's own father. Fearing Micaiah's prophecy, Ahab had disguised himself on the field of battle, and was not known as the King of Israel. But he was not, therefore, to escape. A man in the opposing ranks " drew a bow at a venture," and the arrow, winged with a Divine mission, smote the king between the joints of his armour, and slew him (1 Kings xxii. 34). The same minute providence which guided that arrow now presided over the circumstances of Ahaziah's fall. There is in this doctrine, which is also Christ's (Matt. x. 29, 30), comfort for the good, and warning for the wicked. The good man acknowledges, " My times are in thy hand " (Ps. xxxi. 15), and the wicked man should pause when he reflects that he cannot take *his* out of that hand. 3. *Irremediable*. From the bed to which he had been carried up, the king was never to rise. The injury he had received was fatal. Yet a little space was given him—even him—for repentance. His fall might have produced immediate death. These few remaining days, when the sands were running out, were, however, only to demonstrate further his incorrigibility of nature.

II. THE MESSAGE TO EKRON. A sick-bed, with the possibility of the sickness proving fatal, tests most men. It tested Ahaziah. We note in his behaviour the following instructive facts : 1. *He was moved to apply to some god*. Not, indeed, in hope of a cure, but only to obtain information as to the issue of his illness. He sent to consult an oracle, not to ask a blessing. But even in this there is seen the desire for supernatural help, for direct intercourse with the invisible, which men so often feel in their hour of trouble. It was a dark hour for Ahaziah. Life hung in the balance, and he shrank from death with a great dread. He could not wait for the verdict of events, but would fain wrest the secret from a heathen shrine. Piety can afford to leave the issue in God's hands. Impiety dare not do this, and can find no comfort save in the assurance of recovery. 2. *He did not apply to Jehovah*. Was there not a God in Israel to inquire of? Ahaziah knew very well that there was, and that there were prophets, like Micaiah and Elijah, who would tell him the truth. It need not be questioned that it was an evil conscience, and that only, which kept him from applying to Jehovah. He knew how impiously he had behaved towards Jehovah. He perfectly well understood what kind of reception he would receive from the prophets, and in what language they would address him. He anticipated the nature of the sentence they would pronounce. He dared not, therefore, inquire of the Lord. So when men, in their distress, feel impelled to go to God, they are often held back by the remembrance of past wickedness. They know, if they come, it must be with changed hearts and the renouncing of evil deeds, and for this they are not prepared. 3. *He applied to the god of Ekron*. Baal-zebub—"lord of flies," as the word means. The oracle of this god had probably some local repute, which led him to select it. Here comes in the element of superstition. The craving after the supernatural in human nature is not to be stilled, and, if it cannot be gratified in a lawful, it will seek gratification in some unlawful way. Saul, forsaken of God, turned to the witch of Endor (1 Sam. xxviii. 6, 7). " A notorious infidel like Philippe Egalité, though in other respects a man of ability, could yet try to presage his fate by the sort of cup-augury involved in examining the grounds of coffee." The Roman world, in the time of the apostles, was not more characterized by its educated scepticism than by the influx into it of every kind of superstition (cf. Farrar's ' St. Paul,' ch. xix.; Conybeare and Howson, ch. v.). In our own day, multitudes professing disbelief in God's revelation turn with eager credulity to the delusions of spiritualism. It was to supersede unlawful modes of consulting the invisible world that God gave "the sure word of prophecy" (Deut. xviii. 9—22).

III. THE UNEXPECTED MEETING. The messengers speed on their way to the shrine of Baal-zebub at Ekron, but their steps are soon to be arrested. Here we notice: 1. *A new task for Elijah.* "The angel of the Lord said to Elijah the Tishbite, Arise, go up to meet the messengers of the King of Samaria." The medium of communication is, perhaps, the historical angel of the covenant—he of whom God had said, "Provoke him not, for he will not pardon your transgressions, for my Name is in him" (Exod. xxiii. 21). The Divine side of the calamity which had befallen Ahaziah comes to light in this message by the prophet. Ahaziah had forgotten God, but God had not forgotten him. He is the "jealous God" (Exod. xx. 5), who takes the vindication of his honour into his own hands. 2. *A surprise for the messengers.* Elijah's appearances partake everywhere of the nature of a dramatic surprise. He comes no one knows whence; he departs no one knows whither. His personality was impressive—"a hairy man, and girt with a girdle of leather about his loins" (ver. 8). Suddenly he confronts the messengers, and puts to them the ironic question, "Is it not because there is not a God in Israel that ye go to inquire of Baal-zebub the god of Ekron?" It is rare that, in fleeing from the path of duty, we do not meet God in the way in some form. Balaam on his journey to the King of Moab; Jonah fleeing from the presence of the Lord to Tarshish; Elijah himself when he fled to Horeb, hearing the voice of the Lord, "What doest thou here, Elijah?" (Numb. xxii. 22; Jonah i.; 1 Kings xix. 9). 3. *Evil tidings for Ahaziah.* The messengers need go no further. The information they sought at Ekron was given them, unasked, from a surer source. An oracle had spoken, but not the one to which they were sent. Ekron's reply was anticipated by Jehovah's: "Now therefore thus saith the Lord, Thou shalt not come down from that bed on which thou art gone up, but shalt surely die." Unhappy monarch! God hath spoken, and no other can reverse it (Numb. xxiii. 20).

IV. THE RETURN TO THE KING. There was that in the appearance, manner, and language of this man who had crossed their path like an apparition which convinced the messengers that God had spoken through him. They accordingly returned at once to the sick king. A few words of explanation sufficed to put him in possession of the circumstances. A guilty conscience is swift to comprehend in such matters. With unerring precision the king's thoughts interpreted the riddle of the mysterious prophet. "What manner of man was he which came up to meet you, and told you these words?" "It is Elijah the Tishbite." Ahaziah knew what that meant. His feelings would be those of his father Ahab when he exclaimed, "Hast thou found me, O mine enemy?" (1 Kings xxi. 20). The appearance of Banquo's ghost at the banquet was not more terrible to Macbeth than this crossing of his path by Elijah was to Ahaziah at that moment. His sins had found him out. However long the lane of wickedness may be, we may be sure the Avenger stands at the end of it.—J. O.

Vers. 9—16.—*The prophet of fire.* The act of Elijah, in calling down fire from heaven on his enemies, is thus remarked upon by Dean Stanley, with reference to Christ's allusion to it in the gospel (Luke ix. 51—56). "When the two apostles appealed to the example of Elijah 'to call down fire from heaven,' he to whom they spoke turned away with indignation from the remembrance of this act, even of the greatest of his prophetic predecessors" ('Jewish Church,' vol. ii. p. 258). We cannot endorse this remark. Jesus, indeed, gently rebuked his disciples, telling them they did not know what manner of spirit they were of, and reminding them that the Son of man was not come to destroy men's lives, but to save them. But he did not mean to imply that the spirit which Elijah showed was, in its own time and place, *wrong*. It was a pure and holy zeal for God's honour, and God sanctioned it by sending the fire. Only there was a *better* and *higher* spirit—the spirit of love and grace in Christ; and it was by this the disciples of Christ ought to have been actuated. What was congruous with the old dispensation was not necessarily congruous with the higher spirit of the new. Christ may have intended to suggest also that the disciples were mistaken in thinking that their spirit was exactly that of the Old Testament man of God. He was moved solely by regard for God's honour; in their case personal anger and resentment probably gave an impure tinge to their passion.

I. BEDCHAMBER REVENGE. It is pitiable to see this sick king, within a few hours of his death, instead of humbling himself in repentance, stretching out his puny arm to do battle with God in the person of his messenger. If he must die, he is resolved that Elijah shall die also. This resolve is: 1. *A sign of character.* It shows the thoroughly hardened and irreligious nature of the man. There are no limits to a sinner's madness in warring against God. 2. *An act of infatuation.* Knowing what he did of the prophet's history, he might have understood that his enterprise was hopeless. He may have reasoned that, as the blood of prophets had been spilt before (1 Kings xviii. 4), so it might be spilt again. But he was now crossing a prophet in the direct discharge of his duty, and was thus, in a sense, giving a direct challenge to God. " Woe unto him that striveth with his Maker ! Let the potsherd strive with the potsherds of the earth " (Isa. xlv. 9). A knowledge of the perilousness of the task in which he was embarking is shown in the fact that a band of fifty men is sent to arrest one prophet (cf. John xviii. 3). If a band was necessary, it could only be because Elijah had supernatural aid to rely on; and, if he had that aid, no amount of force could overcome him. 3. *A trace of evil influence.* It is the spirit of Jezebel which breathes in this Heaven-defying resolution. The queen-mother had not forgotten her yet unfulfilled threat, "So let the gods do to me, and more also, if I make not thy life as the life of one of them by to-morrow about this time" (1 Kings xix. 2). There were old scores to pay off against Elijah, and this wicked woman was no doubt there to strengthen her son in his resolution to pay them.

II. ELIJAH ON THE HILL. The band that was sent to apprehend Elijah found him seated on the top of a hill. Observe: 1. *The solitary grandeur of his situation.* The situation was characteristic. We may say of Elijah what Wordsworth says of Milton, his "soul was like a star, and dwelt apart." He is a strange, solitary figure from first to last—stern, rugged, unconquerable. 2. *His moral fearlessness.* The appearance of Ahaziah's soldiers inspired him with no terror. He had apparently waited in the neighbourhood where he met the messengers, and did not now retreat. Strong in his sense that God was on his side, he did not fear what man could do to him (Ps. cxviii. 6). 3. *His invisible protection.* The result showed how entirely Elijah was justified in his confidence. "The angel of the Lord," who had sent him on his mission, " encamped around him " (Ps. xxxiv. 7), and kept him from all evil. Those who are engaged in Divine work can confidently rely on Divine protection. Not till they had "finished their testimony " was the beast allowed to kill the witnesses (Rev. xi. 7). The mountain on which Elijah sat was no doubt as "full of horses and chariots of fire " as the hill of Samaria was in after-days for the protection of Elisha (ch. vi. 17). What could bands of fifties avail against one thus defended ?

III. THE CAPTAINS AND THEIR FIFTIES. 1. *The first captain.* Clothed with a little brief authority, this first captain, accompanied by his fifty men, approaches Elijah, and orders him to surrender. (1) The terms of his summons : " Thou man of God, the king hath said, Come down." In the same breath in which he acknowledges him to be a servant of Jehovah, he demands his submission to the wicked King of Israel. *Le roy le veult*—the king wills it. Thus poor, paltry, human authority ventures to assert itself against the authority of the King of kings. No uncommon thing, it must be said, in history. In the extravagance of its conceit, too often has royal authority presumed to set itself above the law of heaven, and to dragoon, imprison, and coerce those who chose to obey God rather than man. Nor have tools ever been wanting to carry out these infamous behests. (2) A lurking fear. Notwithstanding his bravado, the officer was not without his own fear of Elijah. He does not boldly mount the hill to secure his prisoner, but stands at a respectful distance, and summons him to " come down." The wicked often inwardly fear the righteous at the very time when they boast most loudly of having them in their power. (3) The answer of fire. This insolent summons to Elijah, in his character of "man of God," was a direct challenge to Jehovah to vindicate his own honour, and that of his insulted servant. The insult was wanton and public, and must be as publicly met. Elijah met it by invoking God, if he was truly his servant, to send down fire from heaven to consume this blustering captain and his myrmidons. As before, in the contest with Baal's prophets, his prayer was granted, and the answer came by fire (1 Kings xviii. 21—39). " Elijah will let him know that the God of Israel is superior to the King of Israel, and has a greater power to enforce his commands " (Matthew Henry). Thus at length, gospel dispensation though it is, will fire descend from heaven to consume the hosts of the ungodly (Rev. xx. 0). **2.** *The second captain.* One example of this kind should have been enough. But when men are inspired by fury and hate of God, above all, when it is not their own lives they are risking, they are not easily deterred. As if this first defeat but added fuel to the king's anger, the order goes forth for another band to be equipped, and sent to take the prophet. The captain who received the mandate had no choice but to obey, and military pride may have led him to suppress any outward show of misgiving. But it must have been with no small quaking of heart that he set out on this now doubly perilous service. Still Elijah sits on his hill, and, putting as bold a front on matters as he can, the second captain, in the king's name, repeats the summons to come down. "O man of God, thus hath the king said, Come down quickly." Elijah from his height returns the former answer; and once again the thunderbolt descends, and scatters the bodies of this second fifty at the hill's foot beside the first. **3.** *The third captain.* Not even yet will the king own the folly of resistance. Like Pharaoh in conflict with Moses, each new calamity but seems to harden him the more. A third captain is despatched with the same peremptory orders to seize the recalcitrant prophet. (1) But this captain is wiser than his predecessors. He does what few in his position could help doing—accepts a lesson from experience. He abandons the insolent tone of previous captains, and, falling on his knees before Elijah, sues for peace. "O man of God, I pray thee, let my life, and the life of these fifty thy servants, be precious in thy sight." He sees the folly of flinging away his life, and the lives of his men, to please a foolish king in a contest as wicked as it was vain. (2) This prayer robs his mission of its offensiveness, acknowledges God's supremacy, and shows that Elijah's life is in no danger. The angel of the Lord accordingly says to Elijah, "Go down with him: be not afraid of him." By this timely humbling of himself, the third captain (*a*) saved the lives of himself and his men; (*b*) obtained what the former captains could not obtain by their bullying, viz. that Elijah should go with him. No fire descended from heaven upon him, for God takes no pleasure in the wanton destruction of human life. And not only was his life spared, but he was saved from the king's anger, by Elijah consenting to accompany him. He was a living example of the truth, "God resisteth the proud, but giveth grace unto the humble" (Jas. iv. 6).

IV. THE WORD OF DOOM CONFIRMED. Brought, not as a prisoner, but as a conqueror, to Ahaziah's bedchamber, Elijah repeated in person the terrible message he had formerly sent by the messengers. "Thou shalt not come down off that bed on which thou art gone up, but shalt surely die." It is the word of doom, and as such Ahaziah cannot but hear it. This is all he has made of his futile attempts to fight against God—to hear that doom confirmed by the very prophet whose head he had vowed to bring to the dust. The counsel of the Lord, it alone stands; the imagination of the sinner perishes. It is from Christ's own lips that those who now fight against him and despise his gospel will hear their final sentence.—J. O.

Vers. 17, 18.—*Unwritten history.* Ahaziah died, and Jehoram his brother succeeded him. "The rest of his acts" were written "in the book of the chronicles of the Kings of Israel;" but Scripture has not preserved them. Why should it? What was there in the records of that brief and evil existence to entitle the memory of it to live? "The memory of the just is blessed; but the name of the wicked shall rot" (Prov. x. 7). Enough is written to hold him up to after-ages as an example of the certainty of retribution. Then Scripture buries him with the epitaph, "So he died according to the word of the Lord which Elijah had spoken."—J. O.

EXPOSITION.

CHAPTER II.

Vers. 1—25.—THE REMOVAL OF ELIJAH FROM EARTH, AND SOME EARLY MIRACLES OF ELISHA. The great prophet of Israel was to have a departure from earth as marvellous as his life had been. Ewald's words, though not intended in an historical, but only in a literary sense, embody very forcibly what the humble believer may accept as the actual *rationale* of the occurrence related in vers. 1—12: "An earthly career which had no equal in the purity of its devotion to the service of Jehovah, and was at the same time consummated by such powerful efforts to promote the kingdom of God, could only have a corresponding close. It ceases before the very eyes of men, only to be taken up into the realm of pure spirit, that is, to heaven, there to carry on its work with less disturbance, and with greater power; and at that moment heaven itself descends to earth, to take to itself that spirit which is already entirely its own. And so a fiery chariot with fiery horses comes down from heaven and bears Elijah in the tempest up to heaven" ('History of Israel,' vol. iv. pp. 109, 110, Eng. trans.). In Ewald's view, the narrative is pure imagination, the beautiful conception of one who greatly admired the Tishbite, and invented for him an end in ideal harmony with his life. But may not Omnipotence sometimes work out ideal harmonies in the actual matter-of-fact universe? And is it "advanced criticism," or sound criticism at all, to take a professed history, and pick and cull from it certain portions as absolute facts, quite indubitable (see p. 107, note 2, *ad fin.*), while rejecting other portions, which have exactly the same external testimony, as pure fictions absolutely devoid of the slightest historical foundation?

The record of Elisha's early miracles (vers. 13—24) prepares the way for the position which Elisha is to occupy in the next section of the history, under the Israelite monarchs, Jehoram, Jehu, Jehoahaz, and Jehoash. On Elisha falls the mantle of Elijah (ver. 13), and with it a portion of his spirit, sufficient to enable him to carry on the prophetic office with vigour and steadfastness.

Ver. 1.—**And it came to pass, when the Lord would take up Elijah into heaven.** The subject is introduced as one of general notoriety, the writer professing rather to give the exact details of a well-known fact, than to relate a new fact unknown to his readers. "When the time came," he means to say, "for Elijah's translation, of which you, my readers, all know, the following were the circumstances under which it took place." The fact itself was deeply impressed on the Jewish consciousness. "Elias," says the Son of Sirach, "was taken up in a whirlwind of fire, and in a chariot of fiery horses"

(Ecclus. xlviii. 9). He was ranked with Enoch, as not having seen death (Josephus, 'Ant. Jud.,' ix. 2. § 2), and was viewed as "continuing in heaven a mysterious life, which no death had ever interrupted, whence he was ready at any time to return to earth" (Ewald, 'History of Israel,' vol. iv. p. 113). The scribes thought that he was beyond all doubt to make his appearance upon the earth in person, before the coming of the Messiah (Matt. xvi. 10). **By a whirlwind.** *Sa'ărah* is not so much an actual "whirlwind" as a storm or atmospheric disturbance (συσσεισμός, LXX.). It is a word which only occurs here in the historical Scriptures. **That Elijah went with Elisha from Gilgal.** Elijah had become to Elisha what Joshua was to Moses (Exod. xxiv. 13)—his "minister," or regular attendant, from the time of his call at Abel-meholah (1 Kings xix. 21). Elijah had no fixed residence, but moved from place to place as the Spirit of God suggested. His wanderings had now brought him to Gilgal (probably *Jiljilieh*, near Nablous), one of the most ancient sanctuaries of the land (1 Sam. x. 8; xi. 15, etc.), celebrated in the history of Saul and Samuel.

Ver. 2.—**And Elijah said unto Elisha, Tarry here, I pray thee; for the Lord hath sent me.** Elijah makes three efforts to rid himself of the presence of his faithful attendant (see vers. 4 and 6), either really desirous to pass in solitude the few remaining hours of his earthly life, for he knows that his end is approaching (vers. 9, 10), or for the purpose of testing his fidelity and affection. Under ordinary circumstances, the servant would naturally have obeyed his lord, and submitted to a temporary separation; but Elisha has a presentiment, or something stronger than a presentiment, of what is impending (vers. 3, 5), and will not be induced to accelerate by a single moment the time of the last parting. He will remain with his master, ready to do him all needful service, until the end. **To Bethel.** Bethel was the spiritual centre of the kingdom of the ten tribes. There may have been many reasons why Elijah should visit it once more before he quitted the earth. He may have had directions to leave, consolation to give, words of warning to speak. We must not suppose that the narrative before us is complete. **And Elisha said unto him, As the Lord liveth, and as thy soul liveth.** These were ordinary forms of earnest asseveration with the Israelites, generally used separately (Judg. viii. 19; Ruth iii. 13; 1 Sam. i. 26; xiv. 39; xvii. 55; xix. 6; xx. 21; 2 Sam. iv. 9; xi. 11, etc.); but on occasions of special solemnity united, as here and in 1 Sam. xx. 3; xxv. 26; ch. iv. 30). The prophet is not to be blamed for using them, since the command, "Swear not at all," had not yet been given. I will not leave thee. The resolve indicates strong attachment, deep fidelity, combined, perhaps, with a reasonable curiosity to see how the end would be brought about. So they went down to Bethel. The expression, "went *down*," shows that the Gilgal of ver. 1 is not that of the Jordan valley, but the mountain-city between Sichem and Bethel.

Ver. 3.—**The sons of the prophets that were at Bethel.** (On the expression, "sons of the prophets," see the comment upon 1 Kings xx. 35.) The institution of the "schools of the prophets," or theological colleges where young prophets were brought up, is usually assigned to Samuel, one of whose habitual residences for a part of the year was Bethel (1 Sam. vii. 16). Probably he had established a "school" there which continued to this time. **Came forth to Elisha, and said unto him.** The students did not venture to address the master himself, who was a person of too much dignity to be intruded on; but sought out the servant, to give him a warning of what their prophetic instinct assured them was about to happen. **Knowest thou that the Lord will take away thy master from thy head** (*i.e.* from his position as teacher and master) **to-day?** There was, perhaps, something a little officious and self-assertive in this question. They might have felt sure, if they had been properly modest, that Elisha would have at least as much prophetic instinct and foresight as themselves. Hence he answers them with something of rebuke: **And he said, Yea, I know it**—literally, *I too know it*—**hold ye your peace**; or, "Hush—do not chatter about what is so sacred; do not suppose that you are wiser than any one else; be a little modest and a little reticent."

Ver. 4.—**And Elijah said unto him, Tarry here, I pray thee.** The first trial of Elisha's fidelity is followed by a second. The master suggests his tarrying at Bethel, the sacred centre, where he will have the company of the "sons of the prophets," and will not be companionless, as perhaps he would have been at Gilgal. He himself is ordered to take a second journey, longer and rougher than the first. **For the Lord hath sent me to Jericho.** Will it not be better that Elisha shall spare himself the long and rugged descent from the high-land of Ephraim to the deep gulley of Jordan, and remain with the friends who have sought him out, while his master accomplishes the remainder of his journey alone? **And he said, As the Lord liveth, and as thy soul liveth, I will not leave thee.** Absolute unchangeableness of resolution is best shown by absolute unchangingness of speech. Elisha, therefore, simply repeats his previous words. And

the master once more yields. So they came to Jericho.

Ver. 5.—**And the sons of the prophets that were at Jericho came to Elisha, and said unto him, Knowest thou that the Lord will take away thy master from thy head to-day?** And he answered, Yea, I know it: hold ye your peace. At Jericho, too, as well as at Bethel, there was a school of the prophets, though the two places were not more than about twenty miles apart. This would seem to imply the existence of a large number of such seminaries at this period. No doubt, when the secular power was most strongly opposed to true religion, the prophetical order had to make increased efforts to raise its numbers and multiply its schools. The prophets of Israel, it must be remembered, were, after the withdrawal of the priests and Levites (2 Chron. xi. 13, 14), the sole teachers of the people in true religion.

Ver. 6.—**And Elijah said unto him, Tarry, I pray thee, here; for the Lord hath sent me to Jordan.** Elijah makes a third effort to detach his follower from him, or a third trial of his fidelity. He is ordered, not to a town, where his follower might find lodging and refreshment and companionship, but into the open country—to the Jordan. And then, who can say whither? Will it not be best for Elisha to leave him now, and not continue a wandering which threatens to be endless? But the follower is staunch; nothing daunts him; and he makes the same reply as before. **And he said, As the Lord liveth, and as thy soul liveth, I will not leave thee. And they two went on.**

Ver. 7.—**And fifty men of the sons of the prophets went, and stood to view.** It is a harsh judgment to blame the "sons of the prophets" for an idle and shallow curiosity in merely "standing" at a distance "to view" the wonderful event, which Elisha was determined to witness as closely, and associate himself with as intimately, as possible. For the sons of the prophets to have approached nearer, and hung on the skirts of Elijah, would have been an impertinence. Elisha's persistence is only justified by his strong affection, and the special office which he held, of attendant minister. The fifty students showed a courteous sense of what was due to the prophet's desire of seclusion by not pressing on his footsteps, and at the same time a real interest in him, and a reasonable curiosity, by quitting their college and "standing to view" on some eminence which commanded a prospect of the lower Jordan valley. There were many such eminences within a short distance of Jericho. **And they two stood by Jordan.** At length all other human companionship was shaken off—"*they two*" stood, side by side, on the banks of the sacred stream, which had played so important a part, and was still to play so far more important a part, in the theocratic history. All the world, except their two selves, was remote—was beyond their ken; the master and the servant, the prophet of the past and the prophet of the coming generation, were together, with none to disturb them, or interfere between them, or separate them. Jordan rolled its waters before their eyes, a seeming barrier to further advance; and Elisha may naturally have looked to see the final scene transacted in that "plain below a plain," the Jordan bed, sunk beneath the general level of the Ghor, green with lush grass and aquatic plants, and with beds of reeds and osiers, but squalid with long stretches of mud and masses of decaying vegetation, brought down from the upper river, and with rotting trunks of trees torn from the banks higher up. But the end was not yet. Jordan was to be crossed, and the ascension to take place from the plain whence Moses, when about to quit earth, had made his ascent to Pisgah.

Ver. 8.—**And Elijah took his mantle** (the LXX. have τὸν μηλωτήν); the sheep-skin cape or capote, which covered his shoulders. **And wrapped it together**; rather, *and rolled it up* (εἴλησε, LXX.); so that it resembled in some degree a rod or staff. **And** [with this he] **smote the waters**; consciously imitating the act of Moses when he "stretched out his hand over the Red Sea" (Exod. xiv. 21), and divided its waters asunder. **And they were divided hither and thither, so that they two went over on dry ground.** The parallelism with the miraculous acts of Moses and Joshua (Josh. iii. 13) is obvious, and allowed even by those who view the acts themselves as having no historical foundation (Ewald, 'History of Israel,' vol. iv. p. 111, note, Eng. trans.). It was intended that Israel should regard Elijah and Elisha as a second Moses and Joshua, and should therefore yield them a ready obedience. If miracles are impossible, *cadit quæstio*; exegesis of Scripture, and even reading of Scripture, may as well be put aside. But if they are possible, and have a place in the Divine economy, here was a worthy occasion for them. The powers of the world were arrayed against the cause of true religion and so against God; the cause was about to lose its great champion and assertor, Elijah; a weaker successor was about to take his place;—without some manifest display of supernatural might the cause of religion would evidently have lost ground, perhaps have been ruined altogether. It pleased God, therefore, just at this time, to grant that signs and wonders of an extraordinary character should be done by the hands of his servants Elijah and Elisha, that a halo of mystic glory should encircle them, for the better sustentation of his own cause against his adversaries, for the exaltation and glorification of his faithful ones, and for the confusion and dismay of those who were opposed to them. Now, surely, if ever, was there a *dignus vindice nodus*, justifying a miraculous interposition.

Ver. 9.—**And it came to pass, when they were gone over, that Elijah said unto Elisha, Ask what I shall do for thee, before I be taken away from thee.** Elijah knows that the time is growing now very short. He will soon have left the earth. A yearning comes over him, before he goes, to leave his faithful follower, his trusty, persevering adherent, some parting gift, some token of his appreciation, some sign of his love. What does his "minister" desire? Let him ask what he will, and his master will, if it be possible, grant it. **And Elisha said, I pray thee, let a double portion of thy spirit be upon me.** Elisha's request has been variously explained. The older commentators regarded him as having asked for twice as much spiritual and prophetical power as Elijah had possessed; and this interpretation is certainly favoured by the reply of Elijah, as recorded in the next verse. But it is objected (1) that Elisha's modesty would prevent him from asking so much; and (2) that double the spirit and power of Elijah certainly did not rest upon him. This latter fact is quite undeniable. As Keil says, "It is only a quite external and superficial view of the career of Elisha that can see in it a proof that double the spirit of Elijah rested upon him" ('Commentary on Kings,' *ad loc.*). To one who looks beneath the surface, and regards something besides length of life and number of miracles, Elisha is a very faint and feeble replica of Elijah. Ewald's judgment is here correct: "Elisha is great only so far as he continues and carries out with more force than any other man of his time the work which Elijah had begun with new and wonderful power . . . he did not possess any such intensity of inward power as his master" ('History of Israel,' vol. iv. p. 82, Eng. trans.). Accordingly, Ewald, rejecting the old explanation, suggests one of his own—that Elisha asked for "*two-thirds* of Elijah's spirit" (ibid., p. 81); but this would be a very strange and unusual request, even if the Hebrew could be made to mean it. Who ever asks for two-thirds of a thing? The third explanation, to which most modern commentators incline (Keil, Thenius, Patrick, Clarke, Pool, Böttcher), is that Elisha merely requested that he might receive twice as much of Elijah's spirit as should be received by any other of the "sons of the prophets." He made a reference to Deut. xxi. 17, and asked for the "double portion" (literally, "double mouthful") which was the right of an eldest son. The only objection to this view is Elijah's answer (see the next verse).

Ver. 10.—**And he said, Thou hast asked a hard thing;** literally, *thou hast been hard in asking (ἐσκλήρυνας τοῦ αἰτήσασθαι*, LXX.). Perhaps the "hardness" of the request was in the thing asked, not in the quantity of the thing. Had Elisha asked for anything that Elijah had it directly in his power to give, as for his mantle, or his blessing, or his prayers in the other world, to grant the request would have been easy. But he had asked for something that was not Elijah's to give, but only God's. Elijah could not bequeath his spirit, as a man bequeaths his property; he could only pray God that Elisha's pious request might be granted. Nevertheless, **if thou see me when I am taken from thee, it shall be so unto thee; but if not, it shall not be so.** Our translators have thought to clear the sense by inserting "nevertheless" and "when I am." But the inserted words would be better away. As Elijah cannot either grant or refuse a request for a spiritual gift, which it is not in his power to bestow, he is divinely instructed to give Elisha a sign, by which he shall know whether God grants his prayer or not. The sign of acceptance is to be his actually seeing his master's translation. Probably the chariot and horses were not visible to the natural human eye, any more than the angelic hosts were who compassed Elisha himself about at Dothan (ch. vi. 17).

Ver. 11.—**And it came to pass, as they still went on, and talked** (comp. Luke xxiv. 50, 51). The antitype answers to the type in little details as well as in the general outline. **That behold, there appeared a chariot of fire, and horses of fire.** God's "angels are spirits, and his ministers *a flaming fire*" (Ps. civ. 4). When the eyes of Elisha's servant were opened, and he saw the angelic host that protected his master, it appeared to him that "the mountain was full of horses and chariots *of fire* round about Elisha" (ch. vi. 17). Material fire is, of course, not to be thought of. But the glory and brightness of celestial beings, when made visible to man, has some analogy with fire, or at any rate brings the conception of fire before the mind. The historian doubtless reports the account which Elisha gave of what he saw on this memorable occasion. **And parted them both asunder; and Elijah went up by a whirlwind into heaven;** literally, *and Elijah went up in a storm into the heavens.* There is no mention of a

"whirlwind;" and "the heavens" are primarily the visible firmament or sky which overhangs the earth. Elijah, like our Lord, rose bodily from the earth into the upper region of the air, and was there lost to sight. Three only of the seed of Adam—Enoch, Elijah, Jesus—have passed from earth to heaven without dying.

Ver. 12.—**And Elisha saw** it (comp. ver. 10). The condition was fulfilled which Elijah had laid down, and Elisha knew that his request for a "double portion" of his master's spirit was granted. **And he cried, My father! my father!** It was usual for servants thus to address their masters (ch. v. 13), and younger men would, out of respect, almost always thus address an aged prophet (ch. vi. 21; xiii. 14, etc.). But Elisha probably meant something more than to show respect. He regarded himself as Elijah's specially adopted son, and hence had claimed the "double portion" of the firstborn. That his request was granted showed that the relationship was acknowledged. **The chariot of Israel, and the horsemen thereof;** *i.e.* the best earthly defence of Israel. "In losing thee," he means, "we lose our great protector—him that is more to us than chariots and horsemen—the strength of Israel, against both domestic and foreign foes." The sight of the fiery chariot and horses may have determined the imagery, but they are not spoken of. Note the substitution of "horsemen" for "horses," and comp. ch. xiii. 10, where the same expression is used in reference to Elisha. **And he saw him no more.** Elijah passed beyond Elisha's ken. So far as we can gather from the expressions employed, no cloud received him (Acts i. 9), but he gradually vanished from sight. **And he took hold of his own clothes, and rent them in two pieces;** an action marking extreme horror or extreme grief—here the latter (comp. Gen. xxxvii. 29; 2 Sam. xiii. 19; Job i. 20; ii. 12, etc.).

Ver. 13.—**He took up also the mantle of Elijah that fell from him, and went back, and stood by the bank of Jordan;** literally, *the lip of the Jordan;* that is, the brink of the stream, at the point, probably, where he and his master had crossed it.

Ver. 14.—**And he took the mantle of Elijah that fell from him, and smote the waters**—imitated, *i.e.*, the action of Elijah (ver. 8), as Elijah had imitated the action of Moses at the passage of the Red Sea—**and said, Where is the Lord God of Elijah?** The present Hebrew text reads, "Where is the Lord God of Elijah, *even he?*" the last two words being emphatic; but the emphasis scarcely appears to be needed. Hence the translators have very generally detached the two words from Elisha's question, and, attaching them to the succeeding clause, have rendered it, **And when he also had smitten the waters;** but the position of the vau conjunctive, after אַף־הוּא and before יַכֶּה, makes this division of the clauses impossible. It has therefore been proposed by some to read אֵפוֹא, "now," for אַף־הוּא, "even he" (Houbigant, Thenius, Schultz, Böttcher, Dathe), and to translate, "Where *now* is the Lord God of Elijah?" Is he still here, with me, or has he withdrawn himself from earth with his prophet, and left me alone to my own unaided strength? This gives a good meaning, but is perhaps too bold a change. The LXX. had evidently our present Hebrew text before them, and, as they could make nothing of it, transcribed it into Greek characters, Ποῦ ὁ Θεὸς Ἠλιοῦ ἀφφώ; **they parted hither and thither: and Elisha went over.** God showed, *i.e.*, that he was still with Elisha by enabling him to repeat Elijah's last miracle, and thus gave him an assurance that he would be with him thenceforth in his prophetic ministry.

Ver. 15.—**And when the sons of the prophets, which were to view at Jericho** (see ver. 7), **saw him, they said, The spirit of Elijah doth rest on Elisha.** It is not quite clear upon what grounds the sons of the prophets came to this conclusion. Probably they had seen the passage of the Jordan by the two prophets, the disappearance of Elijah, and the return of Elisha across the stream in a way which they may have suspected to be miraculous. But the Jordan is four or five miles distant from the city of Jericho, and their apprehension of the various circumstances would be incomplete, and more or less vague. Perhaps there was something in Elisha's appearance and expression of countenance which impressed them, and appeared to them to mark his exaltation to a higher dignity and spiritual position. **And they came to meet him, and bowed themselves to the ground before him;** thus acknowledging him for their master, as they had been wont to acknowledge Elijah.

Ver. 16.—**And they said unto him.** Thenius suggests that Elisha first related to them what had befallen his master; but the impression left by the narrative is rather that *they* began the conversation, being aware of Elijah's disappearance, which in that clear atmosphere they may have distinctly perceived, though the ascension may not have been visible to them. Keil thinks that they saw the ascension, but supposed that the body, after being taken up a certain height into the air, would necessarily fall to earth, and that they wished to find it and bury it. But the natural interpretation is that they thought the prophet had been "caught away" by a Divine influence, as Philip the evangelist was in later times

(Acts viii. 39), and would be found somewhere alive, as Philip "was found at Azotus." **Behold now, there be with thy servants fifty strong men;** literally, *sons of strength*; i.e. stout, active persons, capable of climbing the rough and precipitous rocks among which they thought that Elijah might be cast. **Let them go, we pray thee, and seek thy master: lest peradventure the Spirit of the Lord hath taken him up, and cast him upon some mountain, or into some valley.** On either side of the *ciccar*, or Jordan plain, are rugged districts, consisting of alternate rocky mountain slopes and narrow gulleys, or water-courses, dry during the greater part of the year. The sons of the prophets think that Elijah has been carried by the Spirit of God into one or other of these mountain tracts, and wish to search them. **And he said, Ye shall not send;** or, *do not send;* meaning, "it will be useless—you will find nothing—it is not as you suppose."

Ver. 17.—**And when they urged him, till he was ashamed, he said, Send;** literally, *when they urged him until shame;* which some expound to mean, "until *they* were ashamed to press him any more" (Gesenius, Winer, Keil); but others, with more reason, "until *he* was ashamed to persist in his refusal" (ἑὼς οὗ ἠσχύνετο, LXX.). It is always a hard thing for one man to refuse the repeated and earnest request of a multitude. When Elisha said, "Send," he had not in the least changed his mind; he only meant to say, "Send, then, if you insist upon it, to satisfy *yourselves*, not *me*. There is no harm in your sending." **They sent therefore fifty men; and they sought three days, but found him not.** The result bore out the advice and anticipations of the prophet. It was simply *nil*. No trace was found of the aged seer who had been translated from earth to heaven.

Ver. 18.—**And when they came again to him, (for he tarried at Jericho,) he said unto them, Did I not say unto you, Go not?** The prophet was not above vindicating the propriety of his past conduct. He waited at Jericho until the fifty men returned from their vain search, and then reminded them that his advice to them had been not to start on a useless errand. The ministers of God *have* to vindicate themselves, because God's honour is concerned in their being without reproach.

Vers. 19—25.—The historian passes to the record of some of Elisha's minor miracles, belonging to the time whereof he is writing, and helping to explain the position of dignity and respect which he is found to occupy in the next chapter (vers. 11—14).

The miracles showed his twofold power, both to confer benefits and to punish.

Ver. 19.—**And the men of the city**—*i.e.* the inhabitants of Jericho; probably the civic authorities, having heard of the recent miracle—said unto Elisha, **Behold, I pray thee, the situation of this city is pleasant, as my lord seeth.** According to the unanimous voice of travellers, the situation of Jericho (now *Eriha*) is charming. Lying on a broad plain which is traversed by an abundant river, at the point where one of the main wadys debouched from the Judæan upland upon the low country, shaded by groves of palm trees (Deut. xxxiv. 3) and fig-mulberries (Luke xix. 4), the air scented with aromatic shrubs, opobalsam, myrobalanum, and the like, facing the Orient sun, and commanding a wide prospect both across and also up and down the Ghor, with the mountains of Moab in the distance, Jericho was, no doubt, even before the miracle of Elisha, a "pleasant" place. But—there was one drawback—**the water is naught, and the ground barren.** Bitter and brackish springs, of which there are many in the Jordan valley, gushed forth from the foot of the mountains, and formed rivulets, which ran across the plain towards the Jordan, not diffusing health and fertility, but rather disease and barrenness. Untimely births, abortions, and the like prevailed among the cattle which were fed in the neighbourhood, perhaps even among the inhabitants of the locality, and were attributed to the bitter springs, which made the land "miscarrying" (ἀτεκνουμένη, LXX.). It was the prayer of the men of Jericho that Elisha would remove this inconvenience.

Ver. 20.—**And he said, Bring me a new cruse.** Impurity must be cleansed by means that are wholly clean and pure. The prophet called for an absolutely *new* cruse, one that had been put to no use at all, and therefore could not have been defiled. **And put salt therein.** Salt, which physically would be most unapt to heal an unwholesome stream already holding too much salt in solution, is selected doubtless as emblematic of purity, being that by which corruption is ordinarily prevented or stayed. Under the Law every offering was to be purified by salt (Lev. ii. 13). The same symbolism is still employed under the gospel (see Matt. v. 13; Mark ix. 49; Luke xiv. 34). **And they brought it to him.**

Ver. 21.—**And he went forth unto the spring of the waters, and cast the salt in there.** The "spring" intended is supposed to be that now called *Ain-es-Sultân*, "the spring of the Sultan," which is the only copious source near the site of the ancient Jericho. The modern town lies at a distance of two miles from it. Ain-es-Sultân is described as "a large and beautiful fountain of sweet and pleasant water" (Robinson, 'Researches,' vol. ii. p. 384), and as "scattering, even at the hottest season, the richest and most grateful vegetation over what would otherwise be a bare tract of sandy soil." The other springs of the neighbourhood are mostly brackish. **And said, Thus saith the Lord, I have healed these waters; there shall not be from thence**—*i.e.* from the waters—**any more death or barren land;** rather, *or miscarrying.*

Ver. 22.—**So the waters were healed unto this day, according to the saying of Elisha which he spake.** It was not a mere temporary, but a permanent, benefit which Elisha bestowed upon the town.

Ver. 23.—**And he went up from thence unto Bethel.** The ascent is steep and long from the Jordan valley to the highlands of Benjamin, on which Bethel stood, probably one of not less than three thousand feet. The object of Elisha's visit may have been to inform the "sons of the prophets" at Bethel (ver. 8) of the events that had befallen Elijah. **And as he was going up by the way**—*i.e.* by the usual road or pathway, for, in the strict sense of the word, roads did not exist in Palestine—**there came forth little children out of the city.** "Little children" is an unfortunate translation, raising quite a wrong idea of the tender age of the persons spoken of. On the other hand, Bishop Patrick's assertion that the words are to be "understood of adult persons, who had a hatred to the prophet," is quite untenable. *Naârim ketanaim* would be best translated (as by our Revisers in the margin) "young lads"—boys, that is, from twelve to fifteen. Such mischievous youths are among the chief nuisances of Oriental towns; they waylay the traveller, deride him, jeer him—are keen to remark any personal defect that he may have, and merciless in flouting it; they dog his steps, shout out their rude remarks, and sometimes proceed from abusive words to violent acts, as the throwing of sticks, or stones, or mud. On this occasion they only got as far as rude words. **And mocked him, and said unto him, Go up, thou bald head! go up, thou bald head!** It has been maintained that the scoff of the lads contained an allusion to the ascension of Elijah (Patrick, Pool, Clarke), of which they had heard, and was a call upon Elisha to follow his master's example in quitting the world, that they might be no longer troubled with him. But it is not at all apparent that the lads even knew who Elisha was—they would probably have jeered at *any* aged person with whom they had fallen in; and by "Go up" they merely meant "Go on thy way;" the force of their jeer was not in the word *'alêh*, but in the word *kêrêach*, "bald head." Baldness was sometimes produced by leprosy, and then made a man unclean (Lev. xiii. 42—44); but the boys probably flouted the mere natural defect, in which there was no "uncleanness" (Lev. xiii. 40, 41), but which they regarded as a fit subject for ridicule. Their sin was disrespect towards old age, combined, perhaps, with disrespect for the prophetical order, to which they may have known from his dress that Elisha belonged.

Ver. 24.—**And he turned back, and looked on them;** rather, *and he looked behind him, and saw them,* as in the Revised Version. The boys, after the manner of boys, were following him, hanging upon him, not daring to draw too near, hooting him from behind, as ill-bred and ill-intentioned youths are apt to do. **And cursed them in the name of the Lord.** The action cannot be defended from a Christian point of view—Christians have no right to curse any one. But we can well understand that, under the old covenant, a prophet newly installed in office, and commencing his ministry, might deem it right to vindicate the honour of his office by visiting such conduct as that of these misguided youths with a malediction. Under the Law God's ministers were required to curse the disobedient (Deut. xxvii. 14—26). Elisha could not tell what would be the effect of his curse. It could have no effect at all excepting through the will and by the action of God. **And there came forth two she-bears out of the wood;** or, *the forest;* i.e. *the* forest, which, as all knew, lay within a short distance of Bethel, and was the haunt of wild beasts (see 1 Kings iii. 24). **And tare forty and two children of them.** It is not said how far the lads were injured, whether fatally or not. But the punishment, whatever its severity, came from God, not from the prophet, and we

may be sure was just. For "shall not the Judge of all the earth do right?" A severe example may have been needed under the circumstances of the time, when a new generation was growing up in contempt of God and of religion; and the sin of the lads was not a small one, but indicated that determined bent of the will against good, and preference of evil, which is often developed early, and generally goes on from bad to worse.

Ver. 25.—**And he went from thence to Mount Carmel.** Ewald thinks that Carmel was, on the whole, the main residence of Elijah, and "through him became a special prophetic locality" ('History of Israel,' vol. iv. p. 68). If so, we may account for Elisha's visiting it on this occasion by his desire to communicate the facts of Elijah's removal from earth to those who had been his intimates in that quarter. **And from thence he returned to Samaria.** Elisha does not imitate the wild, half-savage life and almost constant seclusion of his master. He "prefers from the first the companionship of men," fixes his home in the capital of his country, Samaria (ch. v. 9; vi. 32); is a friendly counsellor of the king (ch. vi. 9), and highly honoured by him (ch. viii. 4); his whole life, indeed, is, compared with that of Elijah, one of ease and tranquillity. But, though living "in the world," he is not "of the world." As Ewald says, "In spite of all the seductions to which he was abundantly exposed through the great consideration in which he was held, he retained at every period of his life the true prophetic simplicity and purity, and contempt for worldly wealth and advantages" ('History of Israel,' vol. iv. p. 83). He is thus, far more than Elijah, a pattern for Christian ministers, especially for such as are highly placed, who will do well to follow his example.

HOMILETICS.

Vers. 1—10.—*Preparation for our departure from earth.* Abnormal as was the mode of Elijah's departure from the earth, his conduct in prospect of departure may be to some extent a lesson to Christians. Note—

I. His RESIGNATION. No murmur escapes him; he shows no unwillingness to depart, no clinging to earth, no fear of removal, no shrinking from entrance on the unseen world. When God determines that the objects with which he has been placed upon the earth are accomplished, and that the Divine purposes will now be best carried out by other agents, he is quite ready to go, satisfied to depart, content that God should do with him as seemeth him good. Occupied with listening intently to the Divine voice which speaks within him, and executing its mandates, he moves from place to place, as ordered, indifferent where he is or what toils he undergoes, so that to the last he may faithfully perform the Divine will.

II. His ABSORPTION IN DIVINE CONTEMPLATION AND MEDITATION. The things of earth concern him no more. He moves on in a holy calm, wrapt in pious thought, not even speaking, except in rare snatches, to his attached follower. The unseen world, the coming change, the things of heaven, occupy him. He does not address, perhaps he scarcely sees, the "sons of the prophets," who come forth to take their last look on the great teacher of the day. The time is too solemn a one for greetings, or conversations, or even exhortations. He does not seek to "improve the occasion," as shallower spirits might have done. In silence he goes his way, his mind fixed on God and the things of God—things ineffable, inexpressible—which "eye hath not seen, nor ear heard, neither hath it entered into the heart of man" to conceive, but which are revealed in flashes to the soul about to depart, and give it a foretaste of the final "joy of the Lord."

III. His CONSIDERATION, DESPITE HIS ABSORPTION, FOR HIS ATTACHED FOLLOWER. Nothing is more common than for persons, in the near prospect of death, to be wholly occupied with themselves, and to have no consideration at all for others—to lose them out of sight, to forget them. Elijah, though wrapt in holy contemplation, is constantly mindful of his follower. Three times he suggests that his attendance is not necessary, and that he should spare himself the toil and trouble of tedious journeys (vers. 2, 4, 6). Finally, he invites him to ask whatever boon he pleases, with an implied pledge that, if it be within his power, he will grant it. The boon asked is one not directly in his power to grant; but he does not refuse it on that account. He consults God secretly as to the Divine will with respect to it, and obtains an answer which sustains the spirit of his follower, and makes the moment of his bereavement one also of comfort and triumph to him.

Vers. 2—12.—*Faithful friendship.* Though Elisha is said to have "ministered" to Elijah (1 Kings xix. 21), and to have "poured water on his hands" (ch. iii. 11), yet he was far more Elijah's friend than his servant. There was no broad difference of rank between the two to hinder this. Rather Elisha was, in original worldly position, the higher of the two. The glimpse we get of his early home in 1 Kings xix. 19—21 is indicative of comfort and wealth. In education and manners he must have been quite Elijah's equal. A friendship, in the proper sense of the term, was thus possible between them, and seems to have existed, and to have been warm and true. It was a friendship, however, in which a certain disparity was recognized on either side—the φιλία καθ' ὑπεροχὴν of Aristotle. Elijah was the elder man of the two; he had, when the two became acquainted, the higher social position, being familiar with the court at the time when Elisha was a mere well-to-do farmer; and, as the recognized head of the prophetical order, he had a *quasi*-ecclesiastical position far higher than that which Elisha occupied during his lifetime. The French proverb says, "Dans les amitiés il y a toujours un qui aime, et l'autre qui est aimé;" and, under the circumstances, it was natural that the attachment should be warmest on Elisha's side. 1. Elisha shows his attachment by that continuous ministry which caused him to be designated as "Elisha, which poured water on the hands of Elijah" (ch. iii. 11)—that constant waiting upon the great prophet, and unceasing service, which lasted from the casting of the mantle at Abel-Meholah to the ascent in the chariot and horses of fire. 2. He shows it by his determination to see the last of his friend, to remain in his company as long as he possibly can. 3. He shows it very remarkably by the sympathy which he displays with Elijah's mood on the journey from Gilgal to the plain east of Jordan, the silence which he keeps, the brief replies which he makes, the care which he takes that his master's meditations shall be kept free from disturbance. 4. Finally, he shows it by his deep grief when the hour of parting comes; the exclamation forced from him, "My father! my father!" and the violent rending of his clothes *into two pieces*, which was something very different from the conventional rending of ordinary mourners. As David and Jonathan furnish the scriptural model for a friendship between equals, so Elijah and Elisha may properly be regarded as the model for a friendship between unequals, both equally constant, but perhaps not both equally loving—one the protector, the director, the benefactor, the teacher, the master, the guide; the other the dependent, the scholar, the servant, the faithful devotedly attached follower, admirer, almost slave; bound together in a lifelong bond always becoming more and more close, and presented to us, not merely to awaken in us a passing interest, but to stir us under suitable circumstances to imitation.

Ver. 9.—*Desire for spiritual exaltation.* The Apostle Paul exhorts his converts to "covet earnestly the best gifts" (1 Cor. xii. 31). Selfishness can intrude everywhere; and no doubt there may be a selfish desire for high spiritual gifts and powers, merely to promote our individual glorification. We must be on our guard, not only against the more vulgar forms of selfishness, but also against those rarer and more recondite forms of it which constitute the special temptations of minds not accessible to low motives of the ordinary kind. It is, perhaps, difficult for us, in all cases, to discern our own motives; but an honest wish to discern them will go a long way towards enabling us to arrive at the truth. Desire for spiritual exaltation is noble, pure, and right—

I. When our motive is to be of greater use to others. In this case our wish will be for the gifts which tend most to the good of others—for the power to edify, for the power to console, for the power to convert the wicked, for the power to strengthen the upright. We shall not desire to be clever, or eloquent, or logical, or deeply learned; but to be able to win souls to Christ. We shall not be concerned about other persons' estimates of us; we shall not want their admiration, or their praise, or even their good opinion; but we shall want to see some fruit of our ministerial labours, some increase of earnestness and spiritual-mindedness amongst those who are committed to our charge, some improvement in their habits, some greater zeal, some warmer devotion, some higher spirit of self-sacrifice.

II. When our motive is the greater glory of God. God is glorified in the perfection of his creatures; and desire of spiritual exaltation is right when we really and truly desire it for this end. But it is hard to know when this is the case. Great saints, no doubt, have attained to such a condition, and have longed to reach nearer and nearer to spiritual perfectness, not from any selfish motive, but purely to do more honour to God, to glorify him in their souls and spirits, which are God's. But so few attain to this spiritual height, that a man can scarcely be justified in assuming to himself that he has reached it. We shall do well to suspect our own motives; to keep strict watch upon ourselves, to be on our guard against the insidiousness of self-seeking. Ascetics in all ages, and some in the present age who do not affect any remarkable strictness or severity of life, but call themselves searchers after occult science, or after the higher wisdom, or esoteric Buddhists, or by some other similar outlandish name, and profess to be seeking high spiritual perfection as their own highest good, do not for the most part seek to conceal the selfishness of their aims, or pretend to be actuated either by the wish to benefit others or the desire to promote the glory of God. Their self-training and self-culture begin and end in self, and have nothing noble, or grand, or admirable about them; but, if they are insincere, are a cloak for ordinary vulgar self-seeking, and, if they are sincere, are the result of a delusion cast on them by Satan.

Vers. 14—24.—*The signs of a teacher sent from God.* No man is entitled to assume the position of a teacher sent from God of his own mere motion, or without some external authorization. "How can men preach, except they *be sent?*" (Rom. x. 15). Where an organization has been established by Divine agency, human authorization, the mission of those to whom the power of mission has been assigned, is sufficient. But where there is no such established Church system, the commission has to be given directly by God, and can only be attested to man by the accompaniment of miraculous powers. Miraculous operations may be of three kinds: (1) τέρατα, mere "wonders," suspensions of or departures from the ordinary course of nature; (2) ἰάματα, "cures," works of mercy, miraculous interpositions for the benefit of mankind at large, or of certain persons; and (3) φθοραί, "destructions," miraculous hurts to persons or things, withering up of limbs, smitings with leprosy, or with palsy, or with death itself. It has often been remarked that our Lord's miracles were predominantly of the second kind. The same may be said of Elisha's. But as, in the providence of God, it was thought fitting that our Lord, besides his numerous miracles of mercy, should work some mere wonders, as walking on the sea, passing through closed doors (John xx. 19), ascending up in his human body to heaven; and should also work at least one miracle of destruction, the withering up of the barren fig tree through his curse; so also Elisha's mission was attested by miracles of all three kinds. First of all, he exhibits a "wonder" by dividing Jordan; then he works a miracle of mercy, by healing the bitter waters; thirdly, by his curse, he brings about a miracle of destruction, or at least of serious injury, through the she-bears tearing the children. He is thus shown forth to his nation as God's accredited messenger, endowed with miraculous power of each kind, and therefore entitled to speak to them with full and complete authority.

HOMILIES BY VARIOUS AUTHORS.

Vers. 1—8.—*Parting visits.* Here, through the telescope of Scripture story, we are permitted to witness the closing scene of a great life. Let us draw near and look carefully at what happens there, for the like of it only happened once before—and of that we have little record—and it has never happened since. Only two men, Enoch and Elijah, went straight from earth to heaven without passing through the valley of death. It was true of Elijah as well as of Enoch, that "he walked with God." It is a solemn time, surely, in a man's life when he knows that his earthly journey is drawing to a close, that the shadows of death are closing in upon him, and that eternity is opening up before him. It is well for those who, like Elijah, are ready to depart. "Eye hath not seen, nor ear heard, neither have entered into the heart of man, the things which God hath prepared for them that love him." It is a solemn time, too, *for those who are left behind.* What anxious questioning! What possible doubts about the future! What eagerness to look behind the veil and penetrate the darkness which hides the loved one from our view! How happy those who by the eye of faith can see their departed ones entering through the gates into the city, to be for ever with the Lord! It is quite evident that God had conveyed to Elijah some intimation of the fact that he was so soon to be taken away from earth. The sons of the prophets were aware of it, and Elisha knew it also. *But Elijah seems to have felt no personal anxiety at the thought.* Many hundred years after this, when John Knox—the Elijah of Scotland—was on his death-bed, he said to those who stood around him, "Oh, serve the Lord in fear, and death shall not be terrible unto you!" Something like this was Elijah's experience. He had been faithful to God's cause and commands during his life, and now he was not afraid that God would forsake him at its close. *How, then, did Elijah spend the few hours that remained to him before he entered into the presence of his Maker?* Some there are who would like to spend those hours in peaceful contemplation alone with God. Elijah was himself a man of contemplative disposition. He loved to be alone with God. His "soul was like a star, and dwelt apart." And yet, with all this, the active was stronger in him than the contemplative; or rather, the two were so well balanced that the one was a help to the other. From his hours of solitude and communion with God he drew inspiration and strength for his stern conflicts with men and sin. If he was a man of contemplation, he was also a man of action. And so we find him spending the greater part of his closing hours *in busy activity and usefulness*—visiting the schools of the prophets. Is there not a lesson here? Ought we not to imitate Elijah in redeeming the time, in working while it is day? *Do you want to spend your last hours well?* If so, you should spend every day as you would like to spend your last. One day a lady asked John Wesley how he would spend that day if he knew it was to be his last. She doubtless expected some rules for pious meditation and seclusion. His answer was, "Just, madam, as I intend to spend it;" and then he proceeded to tell her what his busy programme of work was for the day. Oh, that we could all say *that* every day, that if it was to be our last we would spend it just as we intend to spend it! We ought to be able to say it, for *any* day may be our last. No doubt there are many whom God lays aside by age, or infirmity, or suffering for weeks, or months, or years before he calls them home. *They cannot spend their closing hours in what is usually called work for Christ, though they may be really working for him by their patience in suffering, by their faith and hope, by their words of counsel to others. But so long as God gives us health and strength to work for him, then it is best to do as Elijah did—to live in harness to the last. Notice the *scene of Elijah's closing labours.* He visited the schools of the prophets, the colleges or institutions where young men were trained for their future work of teaching others the truths of religion. It was *amongst the young* his last hours were spent. Elijah felt the importance of these colleges. He realized that the young were the hope of the Church. Hence he would devote to them his last, and probably his best, hours. He would give them words of counsel and exhortation—words that, under such circumstances, few of them would ever forget. *There is a lesson here for us all.* Parents need to realize more the importance of personally instructing their children. They need to take more interest in the kind of education they receive. They need to be more careful about the companions with whom they permit their children to associate. Not merely parents, but all members of the Christian Church, should take a deeper interest in the education of the young. How little our people know, as a rule, about our theological colleges! and how little encouragement do those labouring in them receive from the Church as a whole! Elijah's closing hours were spent *in active work*, and that active work consisted in *visiting among the young*. Such were his *parting visits.*—C. H. I.

Ver. 9.—*A parting request.* After visiting the schools of the prophets at Bethel and Jericho, which were both on the west side of Jordan—the side nearest Jerusalem, the side nearest Europe—Elijah, accompanied by Elisha, crossed over to the other side, that is, the east side of Jordan, the side nearest the centre of Asia. Why was this? Elijah was a Tishbite, of the inhabitants of Gilead, on this east side of Jordan. Like the mountaineer of Switzerland, or the Highlander of Scotland, he was brought up amid the mountains of Gilead. Like them, he was fearless and brave. And he would seem also to have had all the love of the Swiss or the Highlander for his native hills. He wishes to end his earthly life where it had first begun. Perhaps in the dim distance he can see the spot where nestles the home of his childhood. His life has been a stormy one, and now, ere he leaves it for the peaceful life of heaven, he takes one last fond, lingering look at the quiet home of earth. The friends of his youth are gone. Those whom he knew in childhood have forgotten him. But by his side there is a faithful friend who forsook home and friends for his sake and the sake of the truth of God. Elijah was not a rich man. Silver and gold he had none. But he was one of those who could say, " As sorrowful, yet alway rejoicing; as poor, yet making many rich." Such as he had, he wanted to give to his friend. " And it came to pass, when they were gone over, that Elijah said to Elisha, Ask what I shall do for thee, before I be taken away from thee. And Elisha said, I pray thee, let a double portion of thy spirit be upon me." As Solomon, when he came to the throne, asked not for riches, or honour, or long life, but for a wise and understanding heart, so Elisha also realized what was of most importance for a minister of God, for a teacher of others. *Character is the best gift.* You may give your children a good education, you may store up a fortune for them, but if they have not a good character, all else is useless and worse than useless. *The spirit of Elijah*—that was just what a minister of God needed then, and what the minister of the gospel needs still. *The spirit of Elijah* was a spirit of fidelity to duty, a spirit of faithfulness in rebuking sin, a spirit of fearlessness and courage in the presence of opposition and danger, and at the same time also a spirit of tenderness and love. Such a spirit every Christian worker should seek to possess. And just as Elisha sought to obtain a *double* portion of it to qualify him for his responsible and prominent position, so also, the minister of Christ needs to be doubly endowed with the Spirit of God. He who would lead and teach others must be doubly spiritual, doubly wise, doubly careful, doubly holy, doubly zealous and scrupulous for the honour and cause of Christ. *The spirit of Elijah* was *needed then*, and it is *needed still. The sins of his time are the sins of our own time.* There are the same immorality, the same covetousness, the same forgetfulness of God, the same absorption in the concerns and pleasures of the present world. We need more men with the spirit of Elijah, who will be faithful to God and conscience at any cost, who will rebuke sin in high places and in any place—the sins of royalty and rank as well as the sins of the poor. How much indecision and worldliness and timidity and time-serving there are on the part of many professing Christians! We need more men with the spirit of Elijah, to ask, " Who is on the Lord's side? " and to cry aloud to the faltering, weak-kneed, half-hearted Christians, "How long halt ye between two opinions?. If the Lord be God, follow him; but if the world be your god, follow it." Elisha's *parting request* is a request which we might all appropriately make in prayer to God, that a double portion of Elijah's spirit may rest upon us.—C. H. I.

Vers. 11, 12.—*Parted friends.* Elijah seems to have had a desire to avoid a final parting. Either for that reason, or to try Elisha's devotion, he urged him to tarry first at Gilgal, and afterwards at Bethel. But in vain. Elisha remained with him to the last. What hours of emotion those must have been for Elisha! How he put away from him the very mention of his friend's departure! When the sons of the prophets asked him if he knew that God was going to take away his master from his head that day, he answered, in words of natural impatience, "Yes, I know it; hold ye your peace." Their words were a thoughtless intrusion on his grief, an unintentional probing of his keen emotions. And so it was as if he said, "Don't talk to me about it." "Talking of trouble makes it double." And when they had passed over Jordan, and still walked on, *what a talk that was!* Those who have ever sat by the bedside of a dying friend know what such moments are. The time seems all too short. So much is to be said. So many questions to ask. So many counsels to be given. So many wonderings as to what it will all be like when next we meet. But the sharp, decisive moment comes at last. Strange forms fill the sky. They draw near to the earth. They are chariots and horses of fire. They touch the earth. Elijah enters, and suddenly, in a whirlwind, is lost to mortal sight. Elisha stands a moment like one in a dream. Then, recovering himself, and gazing after his beloved leader's vanishing form, he cries, "My father! my father! the chariot of Israel, and the horsemen thereof!" He felt, in the poignancy of his grief, as if the strength of Israel had been that day taken from it. But he soon resigns himself, and passes on, to carry on Elijah's work. So, too, will the Christian think of his departing friend.

> " Sleep on, beloved, sleep, and take thy rest,
> Lay down thy head upon thy Saviour's breast;
> We love thee well, but Jesus loves thee best:
> Good night! "

When friends are parted by death, perhaps the one who remains wonders *why one was taken, and the other left.* Perhaps you were not prepared to die. Perhaps you had done but little for your Master, and he wanted you to do some more for him. He gave you another chance. If God spares our lives, if he raises us up again from a bed of sickness, we may be assured that there is a gracious purpose in it all. But Elijah not only passed out of mortal sight. It is recorded that *he went up into heaven.* There is no word of an intermediate state. On through the pearly gates, on through the strains of heavenly music, on into the presence of the King. "Let me die the death of the righteous, and let my last end be like his." Let me live as Elijah lived, and I shall—even though I pass through the valley of the shadow of death—enter as Elijah entered into that house of many mansions, that home eternal in the heavens, that "city that hath foundations, whose Builder and Maker is God."—C. H. I.

Vers. 13—18.—*The beginning of Elisha's work.* I. DIVINE POWER TESTED. Elisha wanted a token that God's presence and power were with him. To obtain this he used Elijah's mantle as he had seen Elijah use it. He smote the waters, and said, "Where is the Lord God of Elijah?" We learn from this a twofold lesson. 1. *The best way to prove the power of Divine grace is to exercise the gifts we have.* "Neglect not the gift that is in thee." We shall not accomplish much in the world if we stand gazing up into heaven.

> "We may not make this world a paradise
> By walking it together with clasped hands."

2. *All effort should be accompanied by prayer.* Elisha knew that the mantle of Elijah was of little use, unless the Lord God of Elijah was with him. "Apostolical succession" profits little if there be not also the baptism of the Holy Ghost. If we would succeed in our business, we must look for the Divine guidance, help, and blessing. "Except the Lord build the house, they labour in vain that build it."

II. THE DIVINE PRESENCE MANIFESTED. "When he had smitten the waters, they parted hither and thither: and Elisha went over." If we had faith to undertake great things for God, then we might expect great things from God. Are we attempting as much as we might for our Lord? Are we putting his Divine promises and power to the test? Have we not his own assurance, "Lo, I am with you alway, even to the end of the world"? Why should our efforts be so feeble, when we have all the resources of Divine grace at our disposal? The Divine presence was manifest not only to Elisha himself, but to the sons of the prophets also. When they saw him, they said, "The spirit of Elijah doth rest on Elisha." If we are walking with God, abiding in Christ, the evidence of it will soon be manifest in our lives.

III. DIVINE PURPOSES DOUBTED. Although, as we have seen above, the sons of the prophets knew that Elijah was to be taken from them, yet they were slow to believe in his actual removal. They asked Elisha's permission to send fifty strong men to seek for Elijah, "lest peradventure the Spirit of the Lord hath taken him up, and cast him upon some mountain, or into some valley." Elisha knew how vain it was, and forbade an expedition so futile. But in response to their urgent and repeated entreaties he gave them permission to send. After the exploring party had been searching for Elijah for three days in vain, they at length gave up the quest and returned to Jericho. So the human heart is ever reluctant to submit to God's purposes. Because we cannot see the meaning of some good man's removal, we think it was ill-timed. Yet God's work does not depend upon the human instruments whom he uses. No doubt there is something beautiful and pathetic about this affection of these young men for their old teacher. But when he was gone, why spend their time in profitless brooding over his loss, instead of showing his spirit, and fulfilling his desires by throwing themselves heartily into their work under Elisha? The Church of Christ best shows its regard for the workers of the past and for their work, not by standing still where they have left off, but by carrying forward and improving the work they have begun. There are ever new conditions of life opening up, and these must be considered as well as the memories of the past.—C. H. I.

Vers. 19—22.—*The waters healed.* A beautiful city was Jericho. It stood in the midst of a small but luxuriant plain. Fig trees and palm trees, and wheat, aromatic flowers and plants, grew there in great profusion. A few miles distant rolled the river Jordan, "the most interesting river on earth," and in the background lay the rugged hills of Quarantana. Jericho, too, had a famous history. It was the first city to which the Israelitish spies came when they set out to view the land of promise. It was the first city taken by the Israelites, when its walls fell down as they were compassed about by the priests and people of Israel. Five hundred years after that its walls were rebuilt, in the days of Ahab, by Hiel the Bethelite, who suffered the judgment pronounced by God against the man that would rebuild them (1 Kings xvi. 34). Yet despite their history and their beautiful surroundings, the inhabitants of Jericho were not happy. The city, rich in so many natural advantages, lacked one of the most important of all necessities of a large town—pure water. *The water was diseased or bad,* and its badness seems to have affected even the fertile land. The men of the city tell Elisha that the water is bad and the ground barren. (The word translated "barren" really means in the original that the ground cast its fruit or did not bring its fruit to perfection.) Beautiful Jericho with its bad water is like many another place on earth. Many a city is fair without, but all corrupt within. Many a mansion, outwardly gorgeous, is full of wretchedness within. Many a man who presents a smiling face to the world has the canker of a guilty conscience gnawing at his heart. Those who are wrong and want to get set right may find some thoughts of comfort and hope in the passage before us. It points us to Jesus, the only One who can set all right and keep all right. "Thus saith the Lord, I have healed these waters."

Notice here SOME WATERS THAT NEED HEALING, AND CHRIST'S POWER TO HEAL THEM. 1. *There are waters of sin.* Men may dispute about the universality of the Deluge in the days of Noah. But here is a flood about whose universality there is no doubt. The Gulf-stream has a well-defined course. But the stream of sin is everywhere. Certain forms of disease are peculiar to certain countries. But the disease of sin is found in every land. (1) *There are corrupt currents in our national life.* Our political parties are far from being what they ought to be. Compared with those concerned in the government of other countries, perhaps our statesmen may stand high. But compared with the requirements of God's Law, compared with the standard which ought to be required of those who would legislate for a Christian nation, how far short they come! We may thank God for a Christian queen, but who will say we have a Christian legislature? There are Christian men in it, no doubt. But, alas! what an absence of Christian principle in many of the representatives of our people! Some of them notorious atheists. Some of them trampling on the most sacred laws of God and man; and yet—what a mockery!—the professed lawmakers of the nation. What laws in the interests of the Sunday observance, in the interests of morality, in the interests of sobriety and temperance, could we expect from lawgivers who care for none of these things? *Truly our political life needs to be purified.* We need a reformed parliament in the highest and best sense. (2) *There are corrupt currents in our social life.* Perhaps, after all, our legislature is but a fair reflection of our national life. No community that was decidedly Christian would return an avowed atheist as its representative. No community that had a high standard of morality would return men notorious for their wickedness. And then *the condition of the press* also affords an index to the state of public religion and morality. What vile rubbish is circulated in the form of the novel! What corrupting abominations in the shape of newspapers issue from the London press! The same demoralization and degradation which in heathen lands and in ancient Israel were wrought by the worship of idols, are now being wrought by the circulation of bad literature. The immense circulation which some of the worst of these publications have reached affords an unhappy indication of a low standard of public morality. (3) *There are corrupt currents in our commercial life.* Those who are engaged in business know well that it is so. Customers too often attempting to defraud those who supply them with what they need. Sellers too often attempting to defraud those who buy their goods. Those who are in the employment of others robbing them with one hand while they take their pay with the other. There is a curse upon all ill-gotten gain, that all the excuses of the world, all the benedictions of the wicked, never can undo. Wealth gotten by dishonesty or fraud, wealth gotten at the temporal, moral, or spiritual expense of others, is a foul stream, that will bring its blight upon the whole life, and leave it smeared with slime. 2. *How are these corrupt currents to be cleansed? How is this foul stream to be purified?* Ah! there is only One who can do it. Laws will not do it. Good resolutions will not do it. *Jesus is the great Healer.* He pours in the fresh stream of water of life upon the diseased currents of the world. (1) *He works through his Word.* As Elisha cast the salt into the bad water of Jericho, so Jesus casts the purifying influence of the gospel into the polluted stream of human life. He brings its influence to bear upon the conscience and the heart, alarming men by the fear of death and the terrors of the judgment, and winning them by the still small voice of kindness and of love. (2) *He works also through his people.* Christians are to exercise a purifying influence upon the world's life. "Ye are the salt of the earth," are the words of Jesus. The full force of this statement is only realized when we remember that in the natural world salt is the great antidote against corruption. To withhold salt from a prisoner used to be, in the dark ages, the most cruel way of bringing about a slow and gradual death, and that under its most loathsome form. Hence it is that the ocean is, as it has been called, "the chemical bath of the world." It is the *salt* that is in it which is its chief preservative against corruption, and not only so, but which renders it such a source of life and health. Now, just what the salt is to the sea, and what the salt was to the waters of Jericho, Christians are to be to the life of the world. They are not to lose their savour by not exercising an influence upon the world. *Then* the world is pretty sure to exercise an influence upon *them.* No; but they are to carry with them into all the relationships of life the teachings of the gospel and the Spirit of Christ. Here is the practical work which Christians have to do in reference to the corrupt currents of which we have been speaking. Every grain of salt exercises an influence, small though it may be. Exercise what influence you have as citizens to secure that public positions shall be filled with Christian men. Resist the spread of impure and vicious literature, and counteract it so far as you can by helping to circulate books and newspapers and magazines of a healthy and moral tone. Let your influence in business and in social relationship be on the side of Christ and purity and truth. 3. *Is there one in whose heart and life the stream of sin is still flowing unchecked and unchanged?* What have those waters of sin done for you that you thought so pleasant to the taste? Have they never been bitter waters? Have you never suffered the penalty of sin's consequences? Have you never startled at the whisper of an accusing conscience? Has not sin left its blight upon your life? Have you not found, like the men of Jericho, that though the outward surroundings of your life are pleasant, yet the current of your desires and pleasures is only bringing evil with it, and your life is barren of any good or useful fruit? If you think, as some do, that you can yet make it all right by your own exertions, you are making a great mistake. You can never undo the past. Christ alone can give you forgiveness through his blood. Go to him and ask his mercy. Go to him and ask his help to overcome temptation, to conquer old habits, to get rid of old associates. How happy the moment when you hear the Saviour of the world, the Son of God, your future Judge, saying to you, " Thy sins be forgiven thee; go in peace "! What moment in the sinner's experience on earth can compare with that when he hears a voice from heaven saying, " Thus saith the Lord, *I have healed the waters* "? 4. *But even God's people sometimes need a healing of the waters too.* The Christian, too, needs a purifying from sin's corrupting influence. Let the salt of the Divine Word be freely used by God's children, that it may exercise its purifying, preserving influence upon their spiritual life. Our lives would be far holier, far purer, far happier, far more fruitful than they are, if we kept our minds more in contact with the influence of the Word of God. 5. *And then there are the bitter waters of sorrow.* Trial and suffering will always be bitter to the taste. But he who is the " Man of sorrows, and acquainted with grief " knows how to sweeten the bitter cup. Many a tried and troubled Christian has experienced that, " though no chastisement for the present seemeth to be joyous, but grievous, nevertheless *afterward* it yieldeth the peaceable fruit of righteousness to them that are exercised thereby." Many a time our most bitter trial proves to be our sweetest blessing. We fear as we enter into the cloud, but we see a new vision of Jesus there, and before all is over we learn to say, " Master, it is good for us to be here." The salt of God's Word, here also, has power to purify the diseased waters of unbelief and to sweeten the bitter waters of affliction. In all our troubles we may hear the voice of Jesus saying, " *I have healed the waters.*" 6. To every one who has experienced the healing power of Jesus the exhortation may be given—*Be a sweetener of life for others.* Is there *strife* between neighbours, between brethren, between fellow-Christians? Don't do anything to embitter it. Rather seek to be at peace and to cultivate peace with all men. " Blessed are the peacemakers: for they shall be called the children of God." Are there persons known to you in *poverty?* Try to sweeten life for them by giving them a little of your comforts. Are there *young persons*, lonely, and far from home and friends? Try to sweeten life for them by a little kindness and attention. Are there some known to you who are going down the broad way to *destruction?* Give them some message from God's Word, spoken in kindness, that may help, as the salt at Jericho, to purify the muddy current of their life. Learn of Jesus how to do good to others. And though *you* may but cast in the salt into life's bitter waters, he will bless your efforts, and you will hear him say, " Thus saith the Lord, *I have healed the waters.*"—C. H. I.

Vers. 1—14.—*The departure of good men.* " And it came to pass, when the Lord would take up Elijah into heaven." Two subjects are here presented for notice—

I. THE DEPARTURE OF A GOOD MAN FROM THE EARTH. Death is a departure from the world; it is not an extinction of being, but a mere change in its mode. There are two facts concerning Elijah's departure which mark the departure of all men. 1. The *time* is of God. " It came to pass, when the Lord would take up Elijah." There is an appointed time for man on the earth; when the hour is up, he must go, not before or after. Elijah's time had come. There are no accidental deaths, no premature graves. " *Thou* turnest man to destruction; " " Thou takest away his breath." 2. The *manner* is of God. Elijah was to be taken away by a " whirlwind." That was the method God appointed for him. He takes men away by various methods, sometimes by devastating winds, sometimes by scathing lightnings, sometimes by boisterous billows, sometimes by accident or starvation, sometimes by prolonged disease, etc. All that is with him. We are not the creatures of chance. He " careth for us; " for each, for all.

II. THE POWER OF GOODNESS IN A GOOD MAN'S DEPARTURE. See what a grand spirit Elijah displays in the immediate prospect of his exit. 1. A spirit of *calm self-possession.* When Elijah knew of the solemn event awaiting him, how calmly he talked to

Elisha, and wended his way to Bethel, according to the Divine commandment! There was no excitement or perturbation. He moves and talks with a majestic calmness. Religion alone can give this peace. " He will keep him in perfect peace whose mind is stayed on him." 2. A spirit of strong *social interest*. See how it affected Elisha. How tenderly and strongly he felt bound to him! Elisha says, " As the Lord liveth, and as thy soul liveth, I will not leave thee." He repeated this thrice., And when the sons of the prophets spoke to him about it he said, " Hold ye your peace." As if he had said, " I cannot bear to hear it." .No doubt these sons of the prophets and all who came under the godly influence of Elijah felt thus bound to him. There is no power by which one man can link another so closely and mightily to him as the power of goodness. Goodness is a mighty magnet. 3. A spirit of *far-reaching philanthropy*. Elijah goes to Bethel, but wherefore? Probably to deliver a valedictory address to the " sons of the prophets." They were in college there, in the college, perhaps, which Elijah himself had founded. Would that his address had been reported! His great solicitude was that these young men should hand down the religion of God to the men of coming times. The spirit of genuine religion is not a narrow spirit, a spirit confined to a Church, a country, or a period, but a spirit that embraces in its loving sympathies the spiritual interests of the race.—D. T.

Vers. 15—22.—*The proper spirit for theological students.* " And when the sons of the prophets which were to view at Jericho," etc. The " sons of the prophets " were theological students, and they here manifest a spirit which may be considered alike becoming and necessary in all those who are set apart to study the revelations of God.

I. Here is a SPIRIT OF REVERENCE. " And when the sons of the prophets which were to view at Jericho saw him, they said, The spirit of Elijah doth rest on Elisha. And they came to meet him, and bowed themselves to the ground before him." Being convinced by the fact that Elisha had performed the same marvel that Elijah had— divided the waters of Jordan—that he was a Divine prophet, they bowed in reverence before him. Though, perhaps, they knew that Elisha was taken from the plough, the manifestation of the Divine in him inspired them with solemn awe. He who has in him most of the Divine should be the most reverenced. Reverence is an essential qualification for a student. The volatile and the frivolous, however superior in intellect, and however persistent their investigations, will never reach a true know- ledge of God. Nothing is more incongruous, nothing more distressing to the eye of earnest men, than the spirit of irreverence in theological halls. Biblical students should see in their tutors so much of the Divine as to cause them to bow in reverence before them. True reverence is neither superstition nor sadness.

II. Here is a SPIRIT OF INQUIRY. These students earnestly desired to know what had become of Elijah, and they urged Elisha to send out fifty strong men in quest of him. No man will ever get true knowledge unless he has in him the spirit of earnest inquiry. The deepest cry of the student's soul should be, " Where shall wisdom be found? and where is the place of understanding? " This spirit was *strong* in these " sons of the prophets " on this occasion. They so " urged " Elisha to send forth in quest of Elijah that, we are told, Elisha was " ashamed " to refuse them. But although the spirit of inquiry is essential to a student, and its earnestness is to be commended, it is often, alas! defective. It was so now. 1. It was *wrongly directed*. They had a wrong apprehension ; they imagined that the body of Elijah had been borne up to " some mountain," or " cast into some valley." Perhaps all science begins with an hypothesis, but the hypothesis is vain unless it have some foundation. There was no foundation for the supposition of these " sons of the prophets." Inquiry should start from facts. 2. It was *unsuccessful*. The fifty men went forth according to the students' request, and searched for " three days, but found him not." It is useless to search for subjects beyond our reach. You cannot find in the Bible what is not there, such as scientific systems.—D. T.

Vers. 23—25.—*Ridicule.* " And he went up from thence unto Bethel: and as he was going," etc. These verses lead us to consider ridicule in three aspects.

I. As INFAMOUSLY DIRECTED. 1. Directed against an old man on account of his *supposed personal defects*. " Go up, thou bald head! " This meant, perhaps, " Go up, as Elijah has gone, if thou canst; we want to get rid of thee." Though baldness of the head is not always a sign of age, Elisha was undoubtedly far advanced in years. Nothing is more contemptible or absurd than to ridicule people on account of constitutional defects, whether of body or mind. Direct the shafts of ridicule, if you like, against defects of moral character, against vanity and pride, sensuality, but never against constitutional defects,—that is impious; for no man can make one hair white or black, or add a cubit to his stature. 2. Directed against an old man of *most distinguished excellence.* Elisha was a man of God, and everything concerning him shows manifestations of a godly character. To ridicule a good man is not only more impious, but more absurd, than to laugh to scorn the very sun in its brightness. 3. Directed against a man *engaged in a mission of mercy.* He was Heaven's messenger of mercy to his country. He came to Bethel to bestow wise counsels on the sons of the prophets in their seminary, and to bless all who would listen to his counsels. How often has ridicule been thus infamously directed! Christ himself was once its victim; ay, its chief victim. "They that passed by wagged their heads." They put on him a "crown of thorns."

II. MALEVOLENTLY INSPIRED. The animus in this ridicule was that of an intolerant religion. There were two schools of religion in Bethel, two rival sects; one was the religion of the true God, and the other that of idolatry. One of Jeroboam's calves was there established as the object of worship. There is no malevolence so inveterate and ruthless as that inspired by false religion and rival sects. Perhaps these children had not this infernal passion to any extent, but were the mere instruments of their intolerant parents. Probably their parents sent them out now to meet the prophet, and put the very words into their mouths, taught them by what notes, grimaces, and attitude they should ring them out. This ridiculing the men of God was one of the crying sins of Israel. "They mocked the messengers of God, and despised his words, and misused his prophets." These children were but the echoes and the instruments of their parents' religious malignant intolerance.

III. TERRIBLY PUNISHED. "And he turned back, and looked on them, and cursed them in the name of the Lord. And there came forth two she-bears out of the wood, and tare forty and two children of them." 1. They were punished by the *will of the prophet.* He "cursed them." Perhaps there is no arrow more poignant than that of ridicule. One might have thought, however, that one of Elisha's moral strength and stature would not have felt it at all, especially when directed by children. But he knew their ridicule was but the ridicule of their mothers and fathers, and perhaps of the townspeople in general, who were all about him; and his righteous indignation was kindled. The more loving a man is the more fierce his wrath rages when set on fire. The "wrath of the Lamb" is the most tremendous wrath in the universe. 2. They were punished by the *justice of God.* The prophet's indignation was righteous, and, because it was righteous, the justice of God sanctioned it by causing "two she bears out of the wood to tear forty and two children of them." This was a tremendous homily of Divine justice to the whole population—a sermon that would thunder in the hearts of the fathers, the mothers, and the neighbours.

CONCLUSION. Take care how you use your faculty of ridicule. It is a useful faculty in its place. *Satire is the east wind of thought.* Scorching sarcasm has withered to the roots many a noxious weed; satire has humbled to the dust, has struck to the earth, many a proud and haughty soul. Elijah used it on Carmel's brow, Job used it to his arrogant friends, and Paul to the conceited members of the Corinthian Church. Ridicule, rightly inspired and directed, is

> "A whip of steel, that can as with a lash
> Imprint the character of shame so deep,
> Ev'n in the brazen forehead of proud sin,
> That not eternity shall wear it out."
>
> (Randolph.)

D. T.

Vers. 1—6.—*Preparative to translation.* The time had come when the Lord would take Elijah up in a whirlwind into heaven. It was a singular honour to be put upon a singularly great and good man. No case had happened like it since the days of

Enoch—that other great prophet, who maintained a witness for God amidst the all but universal wickedness of antediluvian times (Jude 14). No other would happen till the ascension of Christ. We observe—

I. THE PROPHET'S MOVEMENTS. It is to be remarked concerning these that they were: 1. *Directed by the Spirit of the Lord.* "The Lord hath sent me to Bethel;" "The Lord hath sent me to Jericho;" "The Lord hath sent me to Jordan." But this was true of Elijah's life throughout. "He was as if constantly in the hand of God. 'As the Lord liveth, before whom I stand,' was his habitual expression—a slave constantly waiting to do his master's bidding" (Stanley). He had grown so entirely into the habit of taking his direction from God, that his life was already half unearthly. The invisible world was more real to him than the visible. Thus he was inwardly prepared for translation. To merge one's will in God's is already to be living a heavenly life on earth. Elijah was in this a forerunner of Christ (John v. 19). 2. *Directed to the schools of the prophets.* From Gilgal Elijah was sent first to Bethel, then to Jericho, then to Jordan, at two of which places were seminaries or communities of "the sons of the prophets." His last movements thus took the form of a farewell visit to these seats of prophetic instruction. It was these schools of the prophets, with Elisha at the head of them, that were to retain and perpetuate his influence after he was gone. He had doubtless had much to do with the organization and fostering of them, and he appears amongst his disciples once more, in their various centres, ere he departs. If he did no more, he would leave with each, at least, a parting blessing. The blessing of a dying believer is ever to be valued (Gen. xlviii., xlix.; Deut. xxxiii.). It was in the act of blessing his disciples that Jesus "was parted from them, and carried up to heaven" (Luke xxiv. 51). 3. *A sign of approaching removal.* The prophetic atmosphere is electric. Elijah knows that he is to be removed; Elisha knows it (vers. 3, 5); the sons of the prophets have some intimations of it. These rapid, yet purposeful, movements from place to place portend the coming change. Like the restlessness of birds on the eve of migration, they tell that Elijah is not long to be on earth.

II. ELIJAH AND ELISHA. Elisha stands nearer to Elijah than any other (ch. iii. 11). He is found here in his company at Gilgal. A study of the relations between the prophet and his destined successor, in view of the approaching departure of the former, is full of interest. 1. *Elijah's desire for solitude.* Once, twice, and a third time Elijah requested Elisha to tarry behind, and leave him to go whither he was sent alone. (1) In the expression of this desire we can trace a very natural craving of a man in his position. The sense of awe in connection with what was about to take place, which made Elisha himself desire not to talk of it (vers. 3, 5), would, in a far intenser measure, indispose Elijah to have his private thoughts disturbed. (2) But the request was of the nature of a test to Elisha. It gave him the opportunity of saying whether he would go or stay. It drew out the qualities of his nature, which showed that he was *fit* for such a privilege as that of seeing Elijah taken up. It is not every one who has the spiritual meetness for being a witness of sacred scenes. Jesus took only Peter, James, and John with him to the Mount of Transfiguration, into the house of Jairus, and into the recesses of Gethsemane. 2. *Elisha's determination to follow Elijah.* Elisha was not to be baulked of his determination to see the last of what should befall his beloved master. "As the Lord liveth, and as thy soul liveth," was his reply on each occasion, "I will not leave thee." In this speaks: (1) Affection for Elijah. The nearer came the hour for parting with him, the more precious was his society. He could not bear the thought of losing one moment of the time that yet remained for converse. It is only when dear friends are either actually taken away or on the point of being taken from us, that we realize how invaluable is the boon of their presence. (2) A desire to see the wonders of God's working. It was no vain curiosity which prompted Elisha to go with Elijah, but a rational wish to see the crown of glory put on a career that had already received so much honour. He wished to see the completion of one of God's great works. He felt that it could not but teach him more of God, thrill and inspire him with more zeal for service, fix past impressions of Elijah on his soul, and altogether leave lasting results in his nature, to witness this "great sight." Therefore he would not miss it. (3) A hope of blessing. Could he but see Elijah as he was taken from him, something whispered that he could not fail to bring away a blessing from the sight. And so it happened (vers. 10, 15). 3. *Perseverance rewarded.* Elisha's importunity prevailed. He and Elijah went on together. Mostly perhaps in silence, but latterly, at least, in converse (ver. 11). There is a holy boldness in seeking a blessing—the spirit of Jacob, "I will not let thee go except thou bless me" (Gen. xxxii. 26), which never fails of its reward.

III. ELISHA AND THE SONS OF THE PROPHETS. At each new centre, as the travellers went on, bands of "the sons of the prophets" came forth to Elisha, and said, "Knowest thou that the Lord will take away thy master from thy head to-day?" His answer, as befitted one who felt the unspeakable sacredness of the event in prospect, was, "Yea, I know it; hold ye your peace." There is a time to speak, and a time to be silent (Eccles. iii. 7), and this was the hour for silence. Speech would jar on the solemnity of the occasion. The deeper experiences of life are to be meditated upon, rather than much spoken about. The tongue has great power over the heart. The effects of many a solemn hour have been dissipated by unseasonable talk about them.—J. O.

Vers. 3, 5, 7.—"*The sons of the prophets.*" It is surely instructive to find, even in godless Israel, these numerous bands of young men, congregated under prophetic oversight, and receiving sacred instruction. The origin of "schools of the prophets" seems traceable to Samuel (1 Sam. xix. 20). But the order took a new impulse under Elijah. "The companies of the prophets now reappear, bound by a still closer connection with Elijah than they had been with Samuel. Then they were 'companies, bands, of prophets;' now they are 'sons, children, of the prophets;' and Elijah first, and Elisha afterwards, appeared as the 'father,' the 'abbot,' the 'father in God,' of the whole community" (Stanley). In the development and fostering of these communities, we see Elijah working with an eye to the future. He takes care that the fruits of his reforming labours shall not be lost, but shall be handed down to after-generations. He provides for the *preservation* and *propagation* of his influence. We do well to take a leaf out of his book, and study like means for the creation and consecration of godly influence. Wherever men have desired to perpetuate their principles they have formed schools, clubs, guilds, associations, colleges, and by means of these their teachings have been spread abroad. The infidel clubs of the last century, *e.g.*, spread the principles which led to the French Revolution. The prophetic schools seem to have devoted themselves largely to sacred history, poetry, and music; but taught the pupils also to labour in honest occupations for self-support. Any mode of binding together and instructing the youth of our time, which shall combine religious training and sound education with an inculcation of the principles of honest independence, deserves every support.—J. O.

Vers. 7—15.—*Elijah taken up.* The translation was to take place on the eastern side of Jordan. Dean Stanley quotes the remark, "The aged Gileadite cannot rest till he again sets foot on his own side of the river."

I. CROSSING JORDAN. 1. *The fifty disciples.* "On the upper terraces, or on the mountain heights behind the city, stood 'afar off,' in awe, fifty of the young disciples; 'and they two stood by Jordan'" (Stanley). Of all the prophetic company, Elisha alone was permitted to accompany the master. The others do not seem to have ventured to ask. But they did not feel themselves precluded from reverentially standing at a distance, to observe what might take place. They did not witness the translation, but they saw the waters divided. There may be neophytes in spiritual experience, who are unqualified for the reception of God's grander revelations, but even to these, "standing to view," God will reveal his power in some measure. 2. *The stream divided.* The river flows between the travellers and the further bank, but Elijah hesitates not a moment. As if his conscious nearness to eternity had already raised him above natural conditions—had given him the faith and power before which natural obstacles are non-existent—he rolled his mantle together, and "smote the waters, and they were divided hither and thither, so that they two went over on dry ground." A miracle! Truly, but there are situations in which miracles seem almost natural. When men are on the point of being taken up bodily to heaven, we need not wonder if "therefore mighty works do show forth themselves" in them (Mark

vi. 14). Natural laws are fixed only till, in the grasp of a higher influence, they become flexible, and bend and yield. This miracle is a repetition of an earlier one (Josh. iii. 14—16), and, on a lesser scale, of an earlier still (Exod. xiv. 21, 22).

II. ELISHA'S REQUEST. 1. *Encouragement to ask.* Elisha had "stood the trial of his unchangeable fidelity and perseverance," and Elijah now said to him, when they had gone over Jordan, "Ask what I shall do for thee, before I be taken away from thee." Elijah did not put himself in place of God. He probably expected Elisha to ask for a parting blessing, or for some other favour which it was in his own power to grant—at most to prefer a request which God might grant through him. A greater than Elijah said to his disciples, when he was about to be taken from them, "Hitherto have ye asked nothing in my Name: ask, and ye shall receive" (John xvi. 24). 2. *A bold petition.* Elisha was not slow to avail himself of the opportunity given. He had in view the position he would be called to occupy as the successor of Elijah, and his request took the form of a prayer for a double portion of Elijah's spirit. He "coveted earnestly the best gifts" (1 Cor. xii. 31). He asked, like Solomon, not for any earthly good or glory, but for spiritual endowment for his great office (1 Kings iii. 5—14). Or rather, he asked for the office itself, with the spiritual endowment which accompanied it—for there is no reason to suppose that hitherto Elisha was a prophet, or more than the servant of a prophet. The "double portion," by general consent, is to be taken in the sense of Deut. xxi. 17; *i.e.* the two portions of a firstborn son, in comparison with the portions received by the other sons. Viewing certain features of the ministry of Elisha—its longer duration, the number and character of its miracles, etc.—we might almost think that Elisha had received literally "a double portion" of the spirit of Elijah, *i.e.* as some have held, twice as much. But this is not the meaning, and reflection will convince us that, with all his eminence, Elisha is a lesser prophet than Elijah—less forceful, original, creative. 3. *The decisive sign.* Elijah replied that Elisha had asked "a hard thing"—one which there might be a difficulty in granting. To designate a prophet, and bestow on him the prophetic spirit—especially in exceptional measure—belongs only to God; and the grounds of his action in such high matters are not for man to prejudge. There was, however, a natural probability that it would be God's will to designate Elisha as heir of the prophetic gift, and a sign was given by which it might be known whether it was or not. If Elisha saw Elijah when he was taken from him, he might conclude that his prayer was answered—possibly because it was only in an exalted, that is prophetic, state of mind that the vision could be had (cf. ch. vi. 16); if he saw nothing, God had not answered it. There is "a vision and a faculty Divine," which is the surest token of answer to a prayer for God's Spirit. Christ's parting legacy to his disciples was his Spirit; and in this, not one, but all, may richly share (John xiv. 16, 17; xv. 26; xvi. 13—15). We do well to realize, like Elisha, that it is not by might nor power of our own, but only by God's Spirit, that we are fitted for any great work in his service.

III. CHARIOTS OF FIRE. 1. *The media of translation.* As the two went on, and talked, suddenly there appeared a chariot of fire, and horses of fire, and Elijah was parted from Elisha, and went up by a whirlwind into, or towards, heaven. (1) There was an actual appearance to Elisha's vision of fiery chariot and horse. It is wholly against the text to explain this, as Bähr does, by mere figure of speech, even though Elisha afterwards uses this metaphor of Elijah (ver. 12). (2) It remains doubtful whether the representation is that of a chariot which conveys Elijah to heaven, or of a host of chariots and horses which surrounds him as he ascends. The word is commonly used as a collective (cf. ch. vi. 17), and probably denotes "chariots." In this case, the heavenly chariots appear, but the actual mode of Elijah's ascent is by the whirlwind. (3) At most, Elisha's vision could only follow Elijah's ascent for some little way upwards, till, perhaps, as in the case of the Saviour, "a cloud received him out of his sight" (Acts i. 9). The realm to which Elijah was taken is not situated in the material heavens, so that, by traversing so much space, he could arrive at it. The change that passed over him, which culminated in his reception into the invisible world, was after a fashion unknown—possibly at present incomprehensible—to us. (4) We must hold, however, that Elijah was really taken in the body to heaven. Bähr's supposition that he was simply whirled away, and disappeared from earth, perhaps undergoing some secret death and burial as Moses did (for this seems to be his idea), is too much akin to the error of the disciples who sent out fifty strong men to seek for him among the hills (vers. 16, 17). It was not Elisha's view, and has no support in the narrative. 2. *The lessons of the translation.* Besides being a signal honour put upon a great servant of God, and a striking Old Testament anticipation of the ascension of Christ, it gave to the Israelites, in midtime of their history, a powerful confirmation of the fact of immortality. "The impression made by the history of Enoch, that 'God took him,' is marked by the repetition of the word as to the ascension of Elijah" (Pusey). It is noteworthy, also, that the immortality typified by these cases is an immortality in the body. We believe, if careful examination of passages is made, it will be found that it was in this form, that is, as connected with a resurrection, and not as an abstract immortality of the soul in Sheol, which had no attractions for the Hebrew mind, that the hope of immortality was entertained by believing Hebrews (cf. Job xiv. 12—15; xix. 25—27; Ps. xvi. 10; xvii. 15; xlix. 14, 15; Matt. xxii. 31, 32; Heb. xi. 13—22. See also the able discussion of this subject in Fairbairn's 'Typology of Scripture,' vol. i. pp. 352—361, 3rd edit.). 3. *Elisha's lament.* As Elijah was parted from him, and taken up, Elisha broke out into loud lament: "My father, my father! the chariot of Israel, and the horsemen thereof." This no more implies that Elisha did not believe that his master was being taken up to heaven, than the mourning of Christians for the loss of some revered teacher or guide implies doubt as to his eternal happiness. It is the sense of personal loss, and of loss to the world, which prevails on these occasions. Elisha did not overestimate the value of Elijah to Israel—more than chariots and horsemen—and we cannot overestimate the worth to a nation of the presence and labours of the servants of God in it. The religion of a nation is its best bulwark, and those who do most for religion are those who serve their country best. Armaments without God in the midst are of poor avail.

IV. THE FALLEN MANTLE. Elisha had seen the prophet ascend, and he knew that his request was granted. He accordingly picked up the mantle of Elijah, which had fallen from him, and which he rightly regarded as a symbol of the new spirit with which he was to be endowed. Popular speech embodies the thought of this passage when it figures succession to greatness as the descent of the mantle of the great man upon his successor. 1. *Test of the new power.* Elisha's possession of the "spirit and power of Elias" was soon to be tested. The Jordan waters again rolled between him and his destination, but, invoking Divine power in the words, "Where is the Lord, the God of Elijah, even he?" he smote the waters with the wonder-working mantle, and, as before, they divided apart. 2. *Acknowledgment of the new power.* The "sons of the prophets" still "stood to view" at Jericho, and when they saw the prophet's deed, and still more, perhaps, when they looked on his person, to which inspiration lent a new grandeur and dignity, they said, "The spirit of Elijah doth rest on Elisha." Then they bowed to the ground before him, and acknowledged him master. (1) The Spirit of God in a man readily betrays its presence. (2) Where the Spirit of God manifestly possesses a man, others will not be slow to make acknowledgment of the fact, and to yield him appropriate honour. (3) It is mainly the possession of this Spirit which entitles a man to obedience in the house of God.—J. O.

Vers. 16—18.—*Seeking the translated.* It is plain from this passage that, while the prophets of Jericho knew from Divine intimations that Elijah was to be parted from them, they did not understand the full meaning of their own revelations. They still clung to the belief that the parting might only be temporary—that, as on other occasions, the Spirit of God had caught him up, and carried him away to some place, where, by searching, he might be found (cf. 1 Kings xviii. 10—12). They desired, therefore, permission to send out fifty strong men to look for him among the mountains and valleys. Elisha knew better, but, as they persisted, he allowed them, for the satisfaction of their minds, to send. When they had sought for three days, and found him not, they returned, and Elisha said, "Did I not say unto you, Go not?" One result of the search, in any case, would be to set doubts at rest and confirm Elisha in his position of authority.

I. IT IS THE MARK OF A GREAT MIND THAT IT DISTINGUISHES BETWEEN THE TEMPORARY AND ACCIDENTAL, AND THE PERMANENT AND FINAL. In this Elisha's superiority is seen to the "sons of the prophets." He took in at once the essence of the situation. He knew that it was useless to seek further for Elijah—that he was parted from them for ever. They dwelt on formal resemblances to previous disappearances—on the accidents of the event; Elisha penetrated to its real meaning. The same mark of distinction between superior and inferior minds appears in all departments. Paul was a notable example of this power to distinguish between substance and accident—between what was temporary and what was final ; while his opponents in the Christian Church exhibited the opposite defect. Apply to creed, ritual, Church-government, etc.

II. This defect in insight often leads to much needless trouble. It caused, in this case, three days of needless search. It is often the occasion of dispute, division, delay in executing reforms, fruitless experiments to attain impossible ends. All are not like the children of Issachar, "men of understanding of the times, to know what Israel ought to do" (1 Chron. xii. 32). Men go about, holding on by, or seeking the revival of, that which has served its day, and is being left behind.

III. A circuitous way of attaining to certainty is better than no way at all. These sons of the prophets satisfied themselves at length, though after much useless trouble. It was well they did so, since they could not otherwise be assured. There are direct ways to certainty which the better class of minds perceive, but which are like roads shut to others. These must take a more laborious and circuitous route. We see this, e.g., in Christian evidences. The other apostles were satisfied, but Thomas had to put his fingers in the print of the nails, etc. (John xx. 24—29). The need of bearing with man's weaknesses and imperfections, and of allowing him to reach conviction by the way he is capable of, explains much that seems circuitous in God's government of the world.—J. O.

Vers. 19—22.—*The healing of the spring.* This first miracle is a fitting introduction to—in some respects a symbol of—the whole ministry of Elisha. In contrast with his predecessor, Elisha was a gentle, beneficent power in Israel. His miracles, like those of Christ, were, with two exceptions only (in this like Christ also), miracles of mercy, not of judgment. He is the "still small voice" coming after the whirlwind, the earthquake, and the fire (1 Kings xix. 11, 12). He is as Melancthon to Elijah's Luther; we may even say, with reverence, as the "Son of man" to Elijah's John the Baptist. Unlike Elijah, he is not a child of the desert, but a man of the city. He came "eating and drinking" (Matt. xi. 19). He mixed with the people; lived a homely life; was the friend and counsellor of kings. Of all this, his first deed of mercy is the image.

I. The rebuilt city and the unhealed spring. 1. *The city and its curse.* The city was Jericho. After the curse pronounced on it by Joshua (Josh. vi. 26), it had lain in ruins till the reign of Ahab, when it was rebuilt by Hiel the Bethelite, at the cost of his eldest and youngest sons' lives (1 Kings xvi. 34). 2. *The unhealed spring.* The city was rebuilt, but the spring on which its prosperity then, as ever since, depended, remained unhealed. The situation of the city was pleasant, but the water was bad, and the land "miscarried," i.e. the water had a deleterious effect on those with child. 3. *The heart and its issues.* How striking an image is this rebuilt city, with its unhealed spring, of godless civilizations, founded on self-will and defiance of God's counsel (Gen. iv. 17), often stately and imposing, yet ending in vanity, because no means exist to cure the spring of the corrupt human heart! "Of republican Athens, of imperial Rome, it might well be said, 'The city was pleasant.' In both there was learning, genius, high civilization, the cultivation of the fine arts to an extent that has made the Elgin marbles, for example, the wonder of the world. But 'the water was naught, and the ground was barren,' because there was the absence of true religion. No country whatever can in the highest sense prosper without it" (Rev. T. H. Howat). Politics, literature, art, science, material civilization, will dwindle and decay unless a pure stream can be made to flow from the people's heart; for "out of it are the issues of life" (Prov. iv. 23).

II. The prophet's healing of the spring. The case of the city of Jericho was brought under the notice of Elisha by the men of the city—a lesson to us not to fail to improve our spiritual opportunities. 1. *The means of cure.* The means by which Elisha effected the cure of the unwholesome waters were exceedingly simple. He obtained "a new cruse"—new, and therefore free from all defilement, and in this was put some salt. The salt appears here as the symbol of what is uncorrupt and purifying. There lay in it no natural virtue to heal the water—a circumstance which made the miracle more conspicuous. 2. *The Agent in the cure.* In casting the salt into the spring, Elisha spoke in the name of the Lord, and attributed, as was right, all the power to him. "Thus saith the Lord, I have healed these waters." The miracle looks back to an earlier wonder—that of the healing of the bitter waters at Marah, where God declared, "I am the Lord that healeth thee" (Exod. xv. 26). One act of mercy lays the foundation for expecting a second. 3. *The effect of the cure.* There was not to be from thence (the spring) any more death or barrenness. The result of Elisha's word was that "the waters were healed unto this day." "Down to the present hour all travellers to Palestine—Robinson, Dean Stanley, Professor Porter—speak in glowing terms of the cool, sweet, and pleasant waters of the 'Fountain of Elisha.' The soil is extensively cultivated. Sugar-yielding canes are plentiful. Fig trees abound on all sides" (Howat). All which things may again be interpreted as a parable. The gospel is the new cruse, and in it is the healing salt—the word of truth—which, cast into the diseased spring of the human heart, heals and purifies its waters; yet is the effect not wrought by the natural action of the truth, apart from the Divine and omnipotent operation of the Holy Spirit, who works through human means, yet is himself the efficient Agent in all conversion. The work is of God, and the effects are incalculable. "Old things are passed away; behold, all things are become new" (2 Cor. v. 17). The most marvellous influence is exerted by Christianity on the spring, not only of private, but of public and social life; and State as well as Church is blessed. Christianity is the salvation of peoples—the source of true national as well as of individual well-being.—J. O.

Vers. 23—25.—*The mockers at Bethel.* This miracle, in contrast with the preceding, is one of judgment. Its apparent severity has made it a stumbling-block to many. The deed is one in "the spirit of Elias" in the harsher sense, and leaves a painful impression. But the painful aspect of the miracle need not be made greater than it is, nor must it be overlooked that the occasion was one when some display of the "severity of God" was necessary.

I. NATURE OF THE SIN. Elisha, going up to Bethel, was assailed by a band of young people from the city, who mocked him, and said to him, "Go up, thou bald head!" 1. *The mockers.* These were not, as the text might lead us to infer, "little children" of six or seven years of age, but "young lads," boys and young men, who had come to the age of responsibility. They came out of Bethel—once a patriarchal sanctuary, but now a focus of Israelitish idolatry—and had evidently been trained in utter ungodliness. 2. *The mocking.* Either Elisha was actually bald—in which case there was added to profanity the ridiculing, so common to boys, of a physical defect— or, as some have thought, "bald head" is a synonym for "leper," this being one of the signs of that disease. In either case there was manifested a spirit, contracted probably from their elders, of bitter hatred of the pure religion of Jehovah, and reviling of its prophets and professors. Levity, ridicule, and profane reviling of the pious and their ways is something on which God must always put the brand of his stern disapprobation.

II. AGGRAVATIONS OF THE SIN. These must be considered in forming a fair judgment on the case. They enable us also better to draw out the lessons of the offence. There was: 1. *Dishonour to a sacred place.* Bethel means "the house of God." It was one of the places where God had recorded his name (Gen. xxviii. 16—19). Now it was Beth-aven, "the house of the idol" (Hos. x. 5). The jeering outburst of impiety of these young men of the city was only a symptom of the iniquity which abounded in it. God was dishonoured in a holy place. 2. *Dishonour to a sacred person.* Elisha was God's prophet, and, in some sense, the living representative at that time of the prophetic order. In him, mockery was heaped on all God's servants, and on true religion in general. He was known and eminent as the successor of Elijah, and probably it was on this account that he was singled out for these hostile manifestations. 3. *Dishonour to a sacred subject.* It is not certain, but it is the view of some, that in the words, "Go up, thou bald head!" there is allusion to the recent translation of Elijah. Sacred places, sacred persons, and sacred things are all to be honoured, and contempt poured on any of them is insult done to God.

III. PUNISHMENT OF THE SIN. After bearing the contumely for a time, Elisha, doubtless by God's inward direction, turned round, and pronounced a curse on these youthful mockers. The curse was God's, not his, as shown by the effect immediately given to it. "There came forth two she-bears out of the wood, and tare forty and two of them." How many escaped we are not told, nor whether all these forty-two were actually killed. But as connected with Elisha's curse, the event was an awful and unmistakable warning, both to those who escaped and to the population of the city. Had these she-bears issued from the wood without the previous word of Elisha, no one would have wondered at forty-two of this band of youths being attacked and slain. It would have been a "calamity." Here the event is the same, and it is the same Providence which is concerned, only the hidden reason of the dispensation comes to light. The whole incident teaches in a very emphatic manner the responsibility of youth. "I take this story as teaching us what I think we very much need to be taught, namely, that the faults of our youth, and those which are most natural to us at that age, are not considered by God as trifling. . . . You may hear grown-up people talk in a laughing manner of the faults which they committed at school, of their idleness, and their various acts of mischief, and worse than mischief. And when boys hear this, it naturally makes them think it really does not matter much whether they behave well or ill—they are just as likely to be respectable and amiable men hereafter. I would beg those who think so to attend a little to the story in the text" (Dr. Arnold, quoted by Rev. T. H. Howat).—J. O.

Ver. 25.—*Carmel.* Elisha, after his endowment with the prophet office, retired for a time to his master's old haunt at Carmel, and then returned to Samaria. So Paul, after his conversion and call to the apostolic office, retired to Arabia (Gal. i. 17). 1. *Retirement as a means of preparation for active duty.* The need of retreat, of private communion with God, of time to digest the lessons of the past, of reflection and meditation. 2. *Active work as the fruit of retirement.* Retirement is not to degenerate into monkery.—J. O.

EXPOSITION.

CHAPTER III.

Vers. 1—27.—THE GENERAL CHARACTER OF JEHORAM'S REIGN OVER ISRAEL. HIS WAR WITH MOAB.

Ver. 1.—**Now Jehoram the son of Ahab began to reign over Israel in Samaria the eighteenth year of Jehoshaphat King of Judah.** This note of time is not quite in accordance with the chronology of 1 Kings, which gives Jehoshaphat a reign of twenty-five years (1 Kings xxii. 42), Ahab one of twenty-two years (1 Kings xvi. 29), and Ahaziah one of two years (1 Kings xxii. 51), and makes Jehoshaphat's first year run parallel with Ahab's fourth (1 Kings xxii. 41), since thus Ahab's death-year would be Jehoshaphat's nineteenth, and Jehoram's accession-year, at the earliest, Jehoshaphat's twentieth. The difficulty may be removed by assigning to Ahab a reign of twenty instead of twenty-two years. On the mode of reconciling the statement of this place with that of ch. i. 17, that Jehoram of Israel began to reign in the second year of Jehoram of Judah, see the comment upon that passage. **And reigned twelve years.**

Ver. 2.—**And he wrought evil in the sight of the Lord**—as did every other king of Israel both before him (1 Kings xiv. 16; xv. 25, 34; xvi. 13, 19, 25, 30; xxii. 52) and after him (ch. viii. 27; x. 31; xiii. 2, 11; xiv. 24; xv. 9, 18, 24, 28; xvii. 2)—**but not like his father, and like his mother**—*i.e.* Ahab and Jezebel, the introducers of the Baal-worship into Israel—**for he put away the image of Baal that his father had made.** It had not been said previously that Ahab had actually set up an image of Baal, but only that he had "built him a house in Samaria, and reared him up an altar," and that he "served him and worshipped him" (1 Kings xvi. 31, 32). But an image of the god for whom a "house" was built was so much a matter of course in the idolatrous systems of the East, that it might have seemed superfluous to mention it. The actual existence of the image appears later, when its destruction is recorded (ch. x. 27). It seems that Jehoram, at the commencement of his reign, took warning by the fates of his father and brother, so far as to abolish the state worship of Baal, which his father had introduced, and to remove the image of Baal from the temple where it had been set up. The image, however, was not destroyed—it was only "put away."

Ver. 3.—**Nevertheless he cleaved unto the sins of Jeroboam the son of Nebat, which made Israel to sin; he departed not therefrom.** The maintenance of the calf-worship was, no doubt, viewed as a political necessity. If the two sanctuaries at Dan and Bethel had been shut up, the images broken, and the calf-worship brought to an end, there would, as a matter of course, have been a general flocking of the more religious among the people to the great sanctuary of Jehovah at Jerusalem; and this adoption of Jerusalem as a spiritual centre would naturally have led on to its acceptance as the general political centre of the whole Israelite people. Israel, as a separate kingdom, a distinct political entity, would have disappeared. Hence every Israelite monarch, even the Jehovistic Jehu, felt himself bound, by the political exigencies of his position, to keep up the calf-worship, and maintain the religious system of Jeroboam the son of Nebat.

Vers. 4—27.—THE WAR WITH MOAB. The historian goes back to the origin of the war. He had already, in ch. i. 1, mentioned the revolt of Moab at the death of Ahab; but he now recalls his readers' attention to the fact, and to some extent explains it and accounts for it. Moab had been treated oppressively—had been forced to pay an extraordinarily heavy tribute—and was in a certain sense driven into rebellion (vers. 4, 5). Jehoram, when he came to the kingdom, determined to make a great effort to put the rebellion down, and to re-establish the authority of Israel over the revolted people. His relations with Jehoshaphat of Israel were so close that he had no difficulty in persuading him to join in the war. He was also able to obtain the alliance of the King of Edom. Thus strengthened, he made no doubt of being successful, and confidently invaded the country (vers. 6—9). The course of the war is then related (vers. 10—27).

Ver. 6.—**And King Jehoram went out of Samaria the same time**—literally, *the same day*—and **numbered all Israel**; rather, *mustered* or *reviewed* (ἐπεσκέψατο, LXX.) all Israel. "Numbering" was forbidden (1 Sam. xxiv. 1), and is not here intended, the verb used being פָּקַד, and not מָנָה.

Ver. 7.—**And he went and sent to Jehoshaphat the King of Judah, saying.** Je-

hoshaphat had originally allied himself with Ahab, and had cemented the alliance by a marriage between his eldest son, Jehoram, and Athaliah, Ahab's daughter (ch. viii. 18; 2 Chron. xviii. 1). He had joined Ahab in his attack on the Syrians at Ramoth-Gilead (1 Kings xxii. 4—36), and had thereby incurred the rebuke of Jehu the son of Hanani (2 Chron. xix. 2). This, however, had not prevented him from continuing his friendship with the Israelite royal house; he "joined himself with Ahaziah" (2 Chron. xx. 35), Ahab's successor, and though their combined naval expedition met with disaster (1 Kings xxii. 48), yet he still maintained amicable relations with the Israelite court. Jehoram, therefore, confidently sought his active help when he made up his mind to engage in a war with Moab. **The king of Moab hath rebelled against me: wilt thou go with me against Moab to battle? And he said, I will go up: I am as thou art, my people as thy people, and my horses as thy horses.** Compare the answer which the same king had made to Ahab, when requested to join him in his attack on the Syrians (1 Kings xxii. 4). The words were probably a common formula expressive of willingness to enter into the closest possible alliance. Jehoshaphat, it appears from 2 Chron. xx. 1—35, had, a little before this, been himself attacked by the united forces of Moab and Ammon, and brought into a peril from which he was only delivered by miracle. It was, therefore, much to his advantage that Moab should be weakened.

Ver. 8.—**And he said, Which way shall we go up?** Jehoram asked Jehoshaphat's advice as to the plan of campaign. There were two ways in which Moab might be approached—the direct one across the Jordan and then southward through the country east of the Dead Sea to the Arnon, which was the boundary between Moab and Israel; and a circuitous one through the desert west of the Red Sea, and across the Arabah south of it, then northwards through Northern Edom, to the brook Zered, or Wady-el-Ahsy, which was the boundary between Moab and Edom. If the former route were pursued, Moab would be entered on the north; if the latter, she would be attacked on the south. Jehoshaphat recommended the circuitous route. **And he answered, The way through the wilderness of Edom;** probably for two reasons: Edom, though under a native king, was a dependency of Judah (1 Kings xxii. 47), and on passing through the Edomite country, an Edomite contingent might be added to the invading force; Moab, moreover, was more likely to be surprised by an attack on this quarter, which was unusual, and from which she would not anticipate danger.

Ver. 9.—So the King of Israel went as leader of the expedition, he is placed first—and the King of Judah—the second in importance, therefore placed second—and the King of Edom—the third in importance, therefore placed last. It is to be remarked that, when Edom was last mentioned, she was ruled by a "deputy," who received his appointment from the King of Judah (1 Kings xxii. 47). Now, apparently, she has her own native "king." The change is, perhaps, to be connected with the temporary revolt of Edom hinted at in 2 Chron. xx. 22. And they fetched a compass of seven days' journey. The distance from Jerusalem, where the forces of Israel and Judah probably united, to the southern borders of Moab by way of Hebron, Malatha, and Thamara, which is the best-watered route, and would probably be the route taken, does not much exceed a hundred miles; but its difficulties are great, and it is quite probable that the march of an army along it would not average more than fifteen miles a day. And there was no water for the host. The confederate army had reached the border of Moab, where they had probably expected to find water in the Wady-el-Ahsy, which is reckoned a perennial stream (Robinson, 'Researches,' vol. ii. p. 488); but it was dry at the time. All the streams of these parts fail occasionally, when there has been no rain for a long time. And for the cattle that followed them; rather, *for the beasts that followed them* (see the Revised Version). The baggage-animals are intended (see ver. 17).

Ver. 10.—And the King of Israel said, Alas! that the Lord hath called these three kings together, to deliver them into the hand of Moab! Jehoram first assumes, without warrant, that the expedition is one which Jehovah has sanctioned, and then complains that it is about to fail utterly. As he had made no attempt to learn God's will on the subject at the mouth of any prophet, he had no ground for surprise or complaint, even had the peril been as great as he supposed. God had not "called the three kings together;" they had come together of their own accord, guided by their own views of earthly policy. Yet God was not about to "deliver them into the hands of Moab," as in strict justice he might have done. He was about to deliver the three kings from their peril.

Ver. 11.—But Jehoshaphat said, Is there not here a prophet of the Lord, that we may inquire of the Lord by him? The Israelite monarch despairs at once; the Jewish monarch retains faith and hope. Undoubtedly he ought to have had inquiry made of the Lord *before* he consented to accompany Jehoram on the expedition. But one neglect of duty does not justify persist-

ence in neglect. This he sees, and therefore suggests that even now, at the eleventh hour, the right course shall be taken. It may not even yet be too late. And one of the King of Israel's servants—*i.e.* one of the officers in attendance on him—answered and said, Here is Elisha. Apparently, Jehoram was not aware of Elisha's presence with the army. He had to be enlightened by one of his attendants, who happened to be acquainted with the fact. We may suppose that Elisha had joined the army "at the instigation of the Spirit of God" (Keil), God having resolved to rescue the Israelites from their peril by his instrumentality, and at the same time to show forth his glory before the people of Moab. The son of Shaphat (comp. 1 Kings xix. 16, 19), which poured water on the hands of Elijah; *i.e.* who was accustomed to minister to Elijah's wants, and to attend upon him.

Ver. 12.—And Jehoshaphat said, The word of the Lord is with him; that is, "he is a true prophet; he can tell us the will of God." It is impossible to say how Jehoshaphat had acquired this conviction. Elijah's selection of Elisha to be his special attendant (1 Kings xix. 19—21) was no doubt generally known, and may have raised expectations that Elisha would be the next great prophet. Jehoshaphat *may* have heard of the miracles recorded in ch. ii. At any rate, he appears to have been firmly convinced of Elisha's prophetic mission, and to have accepted him as the authorized exponent of God's will at the time. So the King of Israel and Jehoshaphat and the King of Edom went down to him. Prophets were commonly summoned into the king's presence, or, if they had a message to him, contrived a meeting in some place where they knew he would be. That the kings should seek Elisha out and visit him was a great sign both of the honour in which he was held, and also of the extent to which they were humbled by the danger which threatened them.

Ver. 13.—And Elisha said unto the King of Israel, What have I to do with thee? get thee to the prophets of thy father, and to the prophets of thy mother. Despite Jehoram's self-humiliation, Elisha regards it as incumbent on him to rebuke the monarch, who, though he had "put away the image of Baal which his father had made," still "wrought evil in the sight of the Lord," and "cleaved to the sins of Jeroboam the son of Nebat" (ch. ii. 2, 3). Jehoram must not be allowed to suppose that he has done enough by his half-repentance and partial reformation; he must be rebuked and shamed, that he may, if possible, be led on to a better frame of mind. "What," says the prophet, "have I to do with thee? What common ground do we occupy? What is there that justifies thee in appealing to me for aid? Get thee to the prophets of thy father"—the four hundred whom Ahab gathered together at Samaria, to advise him as to going up against Ramoth-Gilead (1 Kings xxii. 6)—"and the prophets of thy mother," the Baal-prophets, whom Jezebel, who was still alive, and held the position of queen-mother, still maintained (ch. x. 19)—"get thee to *them*, and consult *them*. On them thou hast some claim; on me, none." And the King of Israel said unto him, Nay: for the Lord hath called these three kings together, to deliver them into the hand of Moab. A most soft and meek answer—one well calculated to "turn away wrath." "Nay," says the king; "say not so. Let not that be thy final answer. For it is not I alone who am in danger. We are *three* kings who have come down to thee to ask thy aid; we are all in equal danger; have respect unto them, if thou wilt not have respect unto me; and show them a way of deliverance."

Ver. 14.—And Elisha said, As the Lord of hosts liveth, before whom I stand, surely, were it not that I regard the presence of Jehoshaphat, the King of Judah, I would not look toward thee, nor see thee. Jehoshaphat's conduct had not been blameless; he had twice incurred the rebuke of a prophet for departures from the line of strict duty—once for "helping the ungodly" Ahab at Ramoth-Gilead (2 Chron. xix. 2); and a second time for "joining himself with Ahaziah to make ships to go to Ophir" (2 Chron. xx. 36; comp. 1 Kings xxii. 48). Even now he was engaged in an expedition which had received no Divine sanction, and was allied with two idolatrous monarchs. But Elisha condones these derelictions of duty in consideration of the king's honesty of purpose and steady attachment to Jehovah, which is witnessed to by the authors both of Kings (1 Kings xxii. 43; ch. iii. 11) and Chronicles (2 Chron. xvii. 3—6; xix. 4—11; xx. 5—21, etc.). He "regards the presence of Jehoshaphat," and therefore consents to return an answer to the three kings, and announce to them the mode of their deliverance. The adjuration wherewith he opens his speech is one of great solemnity, only used upon very special occasions (see 1 Kings xvii. 1; ch. v. 16), and adds great force to his declaration.

Ver. 15.—But now bring me a minstrel. A player on the harp seems to be intended. Music was cultivated in the schools of the prophets (1 Sam. x. 5; 1 Chron. xxv. 1—3), and was employed to soothe and quiet the soul, to help it to forget things earthly and external, and bring it into that ecstatic condition in which it was most open to the reception of Divine influences. As David's harping refreshed Saul, and tranquillized his spirit (1 Sam. xvi. 23), so the playing of any skilled minstrel had a soothing effect on those possessing the prophetic gift generally, and enabled them to shut out the outer world, and concentrate their whole attention on the inward voice which communicated to them the Divine messages. And it came to pass, when the minstrel played, that the hand of the Lord came upon him. By "the hand of the Lord" is meant the power of the Spirit of God, the Divine effluence, whatever it was, which acquainted the prophets with the Divine will, and enabled them to utter it.

Ver. 16.—And he said, Thus saith the Lord, Make this valley full of ditches; rather, *full of pits* (βοθύνους, LXX.). The object was to detain the water which would otherwise have all run off down the torrent-course in a very little time.

Ver. 17.—For thus saith the Lord, Ye shall not see—*i.e.* perceive—wind, neither shall ye see rain. Wind and rain usually go together in the East, especially when there is sudden heavy rain after a time of drought. What Elisha promises is a heavy storm of wind accompanied by violent rain, which, however, will be at such a distance that the Israelites will see nothing of it, but whereof they will experience the effects when the torrent-course that separates them from the Moabite country suddenly becomes a rushing stream as the rain flows off down it. Their "pits," or trenches, will retain a portion of the water, and furnish them with a sufficient supply for their wants. It was necessary that the storm should be distant, that the Moabites might know nothing of it, and so fall under the delusion (ver. 23) which led to their complete defeat. Yet that valley shall be filled with water. Travellers tell us that, in certain circumstances, it takes but ten minutes or a quarter of an hour for a dry water-course in the East to become a raging torrent quite impassable. That ye may drink, both ye, and your cattle—*i.e.* the animals which you have brought with you for food—and your beasts; *i.e.* your beasts of burden, or baggage-animals. Animals, except camels, suffer from drought even more than men, and die sooner. The Israelites do not appear to have ever employed camels.

Ver. 18.—And this is but a light thing in the sight of the Lord. God, the Author of nature, has full control over nature, and it is an easy matter for him to produce at will any natural phenomenon. It is otherwise when the stubborn element of the human will is brought into play. Then difficulty may arise. He will deliver the Moabites also into your hand. It would be better to translate, *he will also deliver* (see the Revised Version).

Ver. 19.—And ye shall smite every fenced city, and every choice city. The LXX. omit the second clause, perhaps because they could not reproduce in Greek the assonance of the Hebrew, where the words for "fenced" and "choice" (מִבְצָר and מִבְחוֹר) have nearly the same sound. **And shall fell every good tree.** It has been said that the Law forbade this, and argued (1) that Elisha did not here utter a command, but only a prediction (Pool), not bidding the Israelites to cut down the trees, but only telling them they would do so; (2) that Elisha intentionally excepted the Moabites from the merciful provision of the Law (Deut. xx. 19, 20), having authority to do so, and regarding the Moabites as exceptionally wicked (Keil); and (3) that the Mosaic Law was not observed under the kings, and that Elisha himself had forgotten the provision about fruit trees (Geddes). But a careful examination of the passage in Deuteronomy will show (1) that there is no general prohibition of the cutting down of fruit trees, but only a prohibition of their being cut down *for siege works;* (2) that the prohibition rests on prudential, not on moral, grounds, and is thus practically limited to cases where the conquest of the country attacked, and its occupation by the conquerors, are looked forward to. The words are, "When thou shalt besiege a city, . . . thou shalt not destroy the trees thereof by forcing an axe against them: *for thou mayest eat of them.*" The destruction of the fruit trees in an enemy's country was a common feature of the wars of the period, and was largely practised, both by the Assyrians and the Egyptians (see Layard's 'Monuments of Nineveh,' first series, pl. 73; second series, pl. 40; 'Nineveh and Babylon,' p. 588; and 'Records of the Past,' vol. ii. pp. 5, 51, etc.). **And stop all wells of water.** The stoppage of springs and wells was another common practice in ancient times, often employed against enemies and aliens. The Philistines stopped the Hebrew wells in the days of Isaac (Gen. xxvi. 18). Hezekiah stopped the springs of water outside Jerusalem, when he expected to be besieged by the Assyrians (2 Chron. xxxii. 3, 4). The Scythians, when Darius invaded their country, stopped all their own wells as they retired before him (Herod., iv. 120). Arsaces III. partly stopped, and partly poisoned, the Persian wells in his war with Antiochus the Great (Polyb., x. 28. § 5). The practice was regarded as quite legitimate. **And mar every good piece of land with stones;** literally, *grieve every good piece of land.* To clear the stones off a piece of ground was the first step towards preparing

it for cultivation in the stony regions on either side of the Jordan. The clearance was generally effected by collecting the stones into heaps. When it was wished to "mar the land," the stones were there to be spread over it afresh.

Ver. 20.—And it came to pass in the morning, when the meat offering was offered— *i.e.* about sunrise, which was the time of the morning sacrifice—**that, behold, there came water by the way of Edom.** The Wady-el-Ahsy drains a portion of Southern Moab, and also a considerable tract of Northern Edom. The nocturnal storm had burst, not in the Moabite country, where it would have attracted the attention of the Moabites, but in some comparatively distant part of the Idumæan territory, so that the Moabites were not aware of it. Josephus says that the storm burst at a distance of three days' journey from the Israelite camp ('Ant. Jud.,' ix. 3. § 2); but this can only be his conjecture. **And the country was filled with water.** By "the country" (*ha-arets*) must be meant here the bed or channel of the water-course. This was suddenly filled with a rushing stream, which, however, rapidly ran off, leaving the water-course dry, excepting where the pits had been made by the Israelites. But this supply was ample for the army.

Ver. 21.—And when all the Moabites heard that the kings were come up to fight against them. The Hebrew has no pluperfect tense; but the verbs have here a pluperfect force. Translate, *When all the Moabites had heard that the kings were come up to fight against them, they had gathered all that were able,* etc. The muster of the troops had long preceded the storm. **They gathered all that were able to put on armour;** literally, *there had been gathered together all that girded themselves with girdles;* i.e. all the male population of full age. **And upward—***i.e.* and all above the age when the girdle was first assumed—**and stood in the border;** took up a position near the extreme border of their territory, on the northern bank of the Wady-el-Ahsy.

Ver. 22.—And they rose up early in the morning, and the sun shone upon the water, and the Moabites saw the water on the other side as red as blood. The red hue of the water is ascribed by Ewald to "the red tinge of the soil" in the part of Edom where the rain had fallen ('History of Israel,' vol. iv. p. 88); by Keil, to "the reddish earth of the freshly dug trenches," or pits ('Commentary on 2 Kings,' p. 305); but the only cause of the redness mentioned either in Kings or in Josephus is the ruddy hue of the sunrise. A ruddy sunrise is common in the East, more especially in stormy weather (see Matt. xvi. 3); and the red light, falling upon the water in the pits, and reflected thence to the opposite side of the wady, would quite sufficiently account for the mistake of the Moabites, without supposing that the water was actually stained and discoloured. The Moabites concluded that the red-looking liquid was blood, from knowing that the wady was dry the day before, and from not suspecting that there had been any change in the night, as the storm which had caused the change was at such a distance.

Ver. 23.—**And they said,- This is blood.** Even Ewald recognizes here " a historical background for the narrative." The idea of such a mistake could scarcely have occurred to a romancer. **The kings are surely slain, and they have smitten one another.** There were rivalries and jealousies subsisting between Judah, Israel, and Edom, which made it quite possible that at any time open quarrel might break out among them. Edom especially was, it is probable, a reluctant member of the confederacy, forced to take her part in it by her suzerain, Jehoshaphat. The Moabites, moreover, had recently had personal experience how easily the swords of confederates might be turned against each other, since their last expedition against Judah (2 Chron. xx. 1—25) had completely failed through such a sudden disagreement and contention. **Now therefore, Moab, to the spoil.** If their supposition were correct, and the kings had come to blows, and the hosts destroyed each other, Moab would have nothing to do but to fly upon the spoil, to strip the slain, and plunder the camp of the confederates. A disorderly rush took place for this purpose (see Josephus, ' Ant. Jud.,' ix. 3. § 2).

Ver. 24.—**And when they came to the camp of Israel, the Israelites rose up.** The first rush of the main body would be upon the camp, where they would expect to find the richest spoil. It was near at hand; and the occupants kept themselves concealed in it, expecting the disorderly attack which actually took place. They then " rose up," and fell upon the crowd of assailants, who were off their guard, and expecting nothing less. A confused rout followed. **And smote the Moabites, so that they fled before them.** Josephus says, " Some of the Moabites were cut to pieces ; the others fled, and dispersed themselves over their country." **But they went forward, smiting the Moabites even in their country.** There are two readings here, יבו and ויכו. The former is to be preferred, and is to be pointed וַיְּבוֹ (for וַיְּבוֹא, as in 1 Kings xii. 12). This gives the meaning of the text. The marginal translation follows the Keri וַיְּכוּ, which is (as Keil says) " a bad emendation."

Ver. 25.—**And they beat down the cities**

—*i.e.* destroyed them, levelled them with the ground—**and on every good piece of land cast every man his stone** (see ver. 19 and the comment *ad loc.*), **and filled it** [with stones]. **And they stopped all the wells of water, and felled all the good trees** —*i.e.* the fruit trees, δένδρα ἥμερα (Josephus)—**only in Kir-haraseth left they the stones thereof** ; literally, *until in Kir-haraseth*—i.e. in Kir-haraseth only—*left he the stones thereof.* He (*i.e.* the commander, or the army) went on destroying and levelling the cities, *until* he came to Kir-haraseth, which proved too strong for him. There he was obliged to leave the stones untouched. Kir-haraseth, which is not mentioned among the early Moabite towns, nor even upon the Moabite Stone, and which is therefore thought to have been a newly constructed fortress (Ewald), was, in the later times, one of the most important of the strongholds of Moab (see Isa. xv. 1; xvi. 7, 11; Jer. xlviii. 36). It was sometimes called Kir-Moab, " the fortress of Moab." At what time it got the name of Kerak is uncertain ; but we find it spoken of as Kerak-Moab by Ptolemy (about A.D. 150), and by Stephen of Byzantium (about A.D. 530). It was a place of much importance in the time of the Crusades. The situation is one of great strength. The fortress is built upon the top of a steep hill, surrounded on all sides by a deep and narrow valley, which again is completely enclosed by mountains, rising higher than the fort itself. It is undoubtedly one of the strongest positions within the territory anciently possessed by the Moabites. **Howbeit the slingers went about it, and smote it.** Ewald thinks that by " slingers " are meant, not mere ordinary slingers, but persons who worked more elaborate engines, as catapults and the like (' History of Israel,' vol. iv. p. 89, note, Eng. trans.). He is undoubtedly correct in saying that " all sorts of elaborate modes of attacking fortifications were very early known in Asia ; " but it is very questionable whether the Hebrew word used (הַקַּלָּעִים) can mean anything but " slingers " in the usual sense. The LXX. translate by σφενδονῆται. The situation is one which would allow of " slingers," in the ordinary sense, sending their missiles into the place, and grievously harassing it.

Ver. 26.—**And when the King of Moab saw that the battle was too sore for him**—*i.e.* that he could not hope to maintain the defence much longer, but would be forced to surrender the fortress—**he took with him seven hundred men that drew swords, to break through even unto the King of Edom.** Perhaps he regarded the King of Edom as the weakest of the three confederates, and the least likely to offer effectual resistance ;

perhaps he viewed him as a traitor, since Edom had been his ally a little earlier (2 Chron. xx. 10, 22), and wished to wreak his vengeance on him. **But they could not.** The attempt failed; Edom was too strong, and he was forced to throw himself once more into the beleaguered town.

Ver. 27.—**Then he took his eldest son, that should have reigned in his stead**—the throne of Moab being hereditary, and primogeniture the established law (cf. Moabite Stone, lines 2 and 3, "My father reigned over Moab thirty years, and I reigned after my father")—**and offered him for a burnt offering.** Human sacrifice was widely practised by the idolatrous nations who bordered on Palestine, and by none more than by the Moabites. A former King of Moab, when in a sore strait, had asked, "Shall I give my firstborn for my transgression, the fruit of my body for the sin of my soul?" (Micah vi. 7); and there is reason to believe that a chief element in the worship of Chemosh was the sacrifice of young children by their unnatural parents. The practice rested on the idea that God was best pleased when men offered to him what was dearest and most precious to them; but it was in glaring contradiction to the character of God as revealed by his prophets, and it did violence to the best and holiest instincts of human nature. The Law condemned it in the strongest terms as a profanation of the Divine Name (Lev. xviii. 21; xx. 1—5), and neither Jeroboam nor Ahab ventured to introduce it when they established their idolatrous systems. The King of Moab, undoubtedly, offered the sacrifice to his god Chemosh (see Moabite Stone, lines 3, 4, 8, 12, etc.), hoping to propitiate him, and by his aid to escape from the peril in which he found himself placed. His motive for offering the sacrifice **upon the wall** is not so clear. It was evidently done to attract the notice of the besiegers, but with what further object is uncertain. Ewald thinks the king's intention was to "confound the enemy by the spectacle of the frightful deed to which they had forced him," and thus to "effect a change in their purposes" ('History of Israel,' vol. iv. p. 90); but perhaps it is as likely that he hoped to work upon their fears, and induce them to retire under the notion that, if they did not, Chemosh would do them some terrible injury. **And there was great indignation against Israel: and they departed.** It seems necessary to connect these clauses, and to regard them as assigning cause and effect. The deed done aroused an indignation against Israel, which led to the siege being raised. But an indignation on whose part? Keil thinks, on God's. But could God be angry with Israel for an act of the King of Moab, which they had no ground for anticipating, and which they could not possibly have prevented? especially when the Israelites had done nothing to cause the act, except by carrying out God's own command to them through his prophet, to "smite every fenced city and every choice city" (ver. 19). The indignation, therefore, must have been human. But who felt it? Probably the Moabites. The terrible act of their king, to which they considered that Israel had driven him, stirred up such a feeling of fury among the residue of the Moabite nation, that the confederates quailed before it, and came to the conclusion that they had best give up the siege and retire. They therefore departed **from him**— i.e. the King of Moab—**and returned to their own land;** severally to Edom, Judæa, and Samaria.

HOMILETICS.

Vers. 1—3.—*Half-repentances not accepted by God.* Jehoram was better than his father and his mother, very considerably better than his brother (1 Kings xxii. 52, 53). He "put away the image of Baal that his father had made," lowered the Baal-worship from the position of the state religion to that of (at the most) a tolerated cult, and professed himself a worshipper of Jehovah. But his heart was not whole with God. He "cleaved unto the sins of Jeroboam the son of Nebat, and departed not therefrom." At Dan and Bethel the golden calves still received the homage of both king and people; priests, not of the blood of Aaron, offered the sacrifices of unrighteousness before the insensible images; and ritual practices were maintained which had no Divine sanction. Jehoram's reformation stopped half-way. He repented of what Ahab and Jezebel and Ahaziah had done, but not of what Jeroboam had done. His was a half-hearted repentance.

I. HALF-HEARTEDNESS IS FROM FIRST TO LAST CONDEMNED BY SCRIPTURE. "How long halt ye between two opinions? if the Lord be God, follow him: but if Baal, then follow him" (1 Kings xviii. 21); "Oh that there were such an heart in them, that they would fear me, and keep *all* my commandments *always!*" (Deut. v. 29); "I call heaven and earth to record this day against you, that I have set before you life and death, blessing and cursing: therefore choose life" (Deut. xxx. 19); "No man can serve two masters, . . . ye cannot serve God and mammon" (Matt. vi. 24); "Whosoever shall keep the whole Law, and yet offend in one point, he is guilty of all" (Jas. ii. 10); "I know thy works, that thou art neither cold nor hot: I would that thou wert cold or hot. So then because thou art lukewarm, and neither cold nor hot, I will spue thee out of my mouth" (Rev. iii. 15, 16). God's true servants are those whose heart is whole with him (Ps. lxxviii. 37), who are "faithful in *all* his house" (Numb. xii. 7), who "fear him, and walk in *all* his ways, and love him, and serve him with *all* their heart and *all* their soul" (Deut. x. 12).

II. HALF-HEARTEDNESS CONTAINS WITHIN ITSELF THE GERMS OF WEAKNESS AND OF FAILURE. "A double-minded man is unstable in all his ways" (Jas. i. 8). Changefulness, vacillation, infirmity of purpose, inconsistency, half-repentances, half-resolves, are sure to result in failure and inability to effect anything. No policy is successful unless it is thorough. No character is calculated to impress others, or carry through any important work, or leave its mark on the world, but one that is firm, strong, sincere, consistent, thorough-going. Half-measures are of little service. Half-resolves are almost worse than absence of all resolve. Half-repentances stand in the way of real change of heart and amendment of life. Half-hearted rulers are apt to "ordain something good here and there, or abolish something bad, while they perceive still more which their duty would require them to remove, but they cannot bring themselves to do it, from motives of policy which are not pure, or pleasing to God" (Lange). Such half-heartedness, while it angers God, is not even expedient, with respect to men, in the long run.

Vers. 4, 5.—*Rebellion not to be entered upon with a light heart.* We are not sufficiently acquainted with the position of Moab under Israel, or with the extent of the Moabite resources, or with the grounds of just complaint which they may have had, to determine whether this particular rebellion was justifiable or no. But we can clearly see from the narrative that rebellion is a very grave matter, one to be very carefully considered, and only to be adventured upon under a combination of circumstances that very rarely occurs.

I. THERE MUST BE GREAT AND SERIOUS GRIEVANCES. Whether the tribute exacted by Israel from Moab was excessive and unduly burdensome, or even absolutely intolerable, depends on the actual wealth of the country in flocks and herds, which is a point whereon we have no sufficient information. But it is clear that a tribute may be excessive; nay, may be so oppressive as to justify revolt. There is a point beyond which a country's resources cannot be strained, and no subject people is bound to wait until the last straw has broken its back. Systematic insult and injury, determined misgovernment without prospect of alleviation, severe oppression, absolutely exhaustive taxation, are grievances against which a subject people may fairly rebel, and appeal to the arbitrament of arms. But the weight of the grievances endured is not the only factor in the equation.

II. THERE MUST ALSO BE A REASONABLE PROSPECT OF SUCCESS. Probably ten rebellions have been crushed for one that has succeeded. It is difficult to calculate chances beforehand; and hope is apt to "tell a flattering tale." To have a good cause is certainly not enough, fortune being too often on the side, not of justice and right, but of "big battalions." No cause could be much better than that of the gladiators who revolted under Spartacus; but Rome crushed them, and quenched the flames of their rebellion in blood, within the space of two years from the time of its breaking out. The war of the Fronde was equally justifiable from a moral point of view; but it was hopeless from the first, and ought never to have been adventured on. On the other hand, the rebellion of the Jews against Antiochus Epiphanes, and that of the Swiss against Gessler, which might well have seemed hopeless to those who initiated them, succeeded. The issue in every case is in the hand of God, with whom, as Judas Maccabæus said, "it is all one to deliver with a great multitude or a small company; for the victory of battle standeth not in the multitude of an host, but strength cometh from heaven" (1 Macc. iii. 18, 19). Still, in every case, probabilities ought to be seriously weighed, consequences thoughtfully considered. In nine cases out of ten, it is better to "bear the ills we have than fly to others that we know not of." War is such a terrible evil, the source of such incalculable mischief and wretchedness, that almost everything should be borne before the appeal is made to it.

III. THERE SHOULD BE A REASONABLE CONVICTION THAT THE ADVANTAGES OF SUCCESS WILL OUTWEIGH THE EVILS OF THE STRUGGLE NECESSARY FOR ACHIEVING IT. An oppressed nationality will, perhaps, always expect this to be the case, and will turn a deaf ear to those who urge the prudential consideration. But it may be worth attending to nevertheless. It will be too late, if the discovery be made after the struggle is over, that "le jeu ne valait pas la chandelle." A nation may, after long years of bitter conflict, shake off a foreign yoke, but may emerge from the strife so weakened, so exhausted, so impoverished, that its new life is not worth living. The evils of the struggle are certain; the benefits of independence are problematical. Subject nationalities should consider well, before they break into revolt, not only the chances of success, but the probable balance of loss and gain supposing that ultimately success is achieved.

Vers. 6—12.—*Faith and unfaith tested by danger and difficulty.* Jehoshaphat and Jehoram are associates, allies, brothers-in-arms. They are united in one cause, have one object, one aim. And they fall into one and the same danger and difficulty. A failure of water at the spot where they had fully expected to find it brings them and their armies into peril of almost instant destruction. But how differently are they affected under the same circumstances! Jehoram at once despairs, sees no way out of the difficulty, has no plan, no counsel, to suggest. Far from flying to God for succour, he only thinks of him to reproach him. Jehovah, he says, has called three kings together, only to deliver them into the hand of Moab. The reproach is as unfounded as it is useless. Jehovah had not called the three kings together. He had not been consulted on the subject of the expedition, and he had not spoken. The three kings had come together of their own free will, and of their own mere motion. And Jehovah was not about to deliver them into the hand of Moab, but was about to give them a great victory over Moab—a victory which would prevent Moab from causing any further trouble for half a century (ch. xiii. 20). But Jehoram, being the embodiment of unfaith, is blind, hopeless, and helpless. It is otherwise with Jehoshaphat, who all his life "has prepared his heart to seek God" (2 Chron. xix. 3). Danger and difficulty draw forth what is best in him, rouse him out of a sort of trance of religious indifference into which he had fallen, and cause him to fall back upon Jehovah as the only sure Refuge in time of trouble, and to ask, "Is there not here a prophet of the Lord, that we may inquire of the Lord by him?" Jehoshaphat's faith makes him both hopeful and helpful. He suggests a course which leads to a happy result. But for him, so far as appears, the danger might have terminated in disaster.

Vers. 13—19.—*The servant of God in the presence of the great of the earth.* Three lessons may be learnt from the conduct of Elisha before the confederate kings.

I. A LESSON OF ZEAL FOR GOD. Elisha does not allow himself to be abashed by the earthly grandeur and dignity of his visitors, or to be rendered yielding and complaisant by the compliment which they have paid him in seeking him out, instead of summoning him to their presence. As the servant and minister of God, he is always in a grander presence than theirs (" As the Lord God liveth, *before whom I stand,*" ver. 14); and as God's mouthpiece he is entitled to be approached, even by the most exalted of human dignitaries, as a superior. Out of zeal for God he asserts himself, and adopts a tone of rebuke, remonstrance, and almost contempt, which would have ill befitted a subject, had he not been acting in the capacity of God's prophet and representative.

II. A LESSON OF FEARLESSNESS. Oriental kings are not accustomed to rebuke, and are apt to resent it. They have despotic, or *quasi*-despotic power, and can visit with very severe pains and penalties those who provoke them. Ahab imprisoned Micaiah the son of Imlah, and fed him with "the bread of affliction and the water of affliction " (1 Kings xxii. 27); Jezebel sought Elijah's life (1 Kings xix. 2); Joash was privy to the murder of Zechariah the son of Jehoiada (2 Chron. xxiv. 20). In openly rebuking Jehoram, his sovereign, on account of his idolatry, Elisha showed a boldness and a fearlessness that were at once surprising and admirable. He evidently "did not fear what flesh could do unto him" (Ps. lvi. 4).

III. A LESSON OF PREPAREDNESS FOR DIVINE EFFLUENCES. Elisha, having exhibited his zeal for God and his fearlessness of man, had finally to address himself to the special needs of the occasion. Three kings had applied to him to know the will of God with respect to a certain difficult conjuncture. He did not yet know it. How could he bring himself into the frame of mind best fitted to receive an effluence from on high? He regarded music as, under the circumstances, the best preparation. His example teaches us (1) that music has religious uses; (2) that it is of the utmost importance to prepare ourselves, if we would have the Divine Spirit speak to our own spirits. Men often complain that they derive no benefit from sacramental and other ordinances. May not the reason be that they do not prepare themselves aright? The Holy Spirit will not enter into our hearts unless they are made ready for his august presence.

Vers. 21—25.—*God's enemies rewarded after their deserving.* Whether or no the Moabites were, humanly speaking, justified in their attempt to shake off the Israelitish yoke, and re-establish their independence, at any rate they were, as a nation, distinctly hostile to Jehovah and his laws, and must be counted as among God's enemies. Their Chemosh cannot be reckoned as an adumbration of the true God; he is rather an adumbration of the evil and malignant spirit. A people that delights in human sacrifice, and offers to its deities tender and innocent children, drowning their cries with the loud din of drums and tom-toms, must have depraved its conscience by long persistence in evil, and departed very far indeed from original righteousness. Moab, moreover, had, from the time of Balak, determinately set itself at once to oppose the Israelites, whenever opportunity offered, by armed force, and also to corrupt and deprave them morally and religiously. The Moabites had recently made what seems to have been an entirely unprovoked attack upon Jehoshaphat, and had stirred up the Ammonites and Edomites to do the same (2 Chron. xx. 1—18). They had already suffered one chastisement for this wrong-doing, at the hand of God (2 Chron. xx. 22—24); but God's anger against them was not yet fully appeased. The rebellion on which Mesha had adventured led now to a further chastisement—Moab was ravaged from one end of the country to the other, the towns were taken and demolished, the fruit trees cut down, the good land "marred," only Kir-haraseth was left unharmed; and even there the inhabitants suffered greatly. Moab was severely punished; but, as usually, God's justice was tempered with mercy. She was not crushed; she was not destroyed. If we may believe Mesha, she gradually recovered and rebuilt her towns. After fifty years of depression she was able to resume her raids into the land of Israel (ch. xiii. 20), and it was not till the establishment of the Roman supremacy over the East that, having filled up the measure of her iniquities, she ceased to exist as a nation.

HOMILIES BY VARIOUS AUTHORS.

Vers. 1—3.—*The continuity of evil.* How hard it is to get rid of the power of evil! Ahaziah had sought after strange gods. He had served Baal with all his corruptions. Jehoram his brother, who succeeds him, is a little better. "He put away the image of Baal which his father had made." Perhaps he was frightened by Ahaziah's fate as the consequence of his sin, and by the fire from heaven which had consumed the two captains and their fifties for their defiance of the Most High. But still "he cleaved unto the sins of Jeroboam the son of Nebat, who made Israel to sin." Both Ahaziah and Jehoram had been trained in evil by their father and mother. The whole land had been contaminated by the influence of Ahab and Jezebel. How true are the poet's words, "The evil that men do lives after them"! *Beware of leaving evil influences behind you.*—C. H. I.

Vers. 4—12.—*Forgetting God, and its results.* We see from these verses how very partial was Jehoram's reformation. He put away the image of Baal, but he experienced no change of heart. Outward observances of religion, outward conformity to God's Law, are of little use, if the heart is not right within. Observe how Jehoram shows his entire forgetfulness or disregard of God.

I. BY HIS MUSTERING OF THE PEOPLE. The King of Moab had risen in rebellion against him. What is Jehoram's first act? Is it to seek help or guidance from God? No; he goes forth and musters all Israel. He relied for safety upon the strength of his army. He forgot "the chariots of Israel, and the horsemen thereof." He forgot the judgments that had come upon Ahaziah for his disregard of God.

II. BY SEEKING HUMAN HELP AND GUIDANCE. He goes and seeks the help of Jehoshaphat King of Judah. "Wilt thou go up with me to battle?" From him also he seeks *guidance*. "Which way shall we go up?" There is no word of turning to *God* for direction. How very like the manner in which we act still! We seek guidance anywhere but from God. We ask of public opinion, of men of the world, of godless neighbours, "Which way shall we go up?" No wonder that our plans are so often failures, and that anxiety and trouble fill our hearts. Far better that we should turn to the Lord, as Moses did, and say, "If thy presence go not with us, carry us not up hence." *Where God's guidance is not sought, God's blessing cannot be expected.* So Jehoram found. He and Jehoshaphat were joined by the King of Edom, and, as the three kings and their armies journeyed through the wilderness, there was no water for the host and for the cattle that followed them. *Jehoram thinks of God then.* He remembers there is such a thing as an overruling providence. But how does he think of him? Only to throw upon God the blame of his own actions. He says, "Alas! that the Lord hath called these three kings together, to deliver them into the hand of Moab!" So we have heard men blame God for the consequences of their own acts. Like Jehoram, they will have none of God's counsel, they follow their own way, and then they grumble at God because he lets them eat of the fruit of their own way, and be filled with their own devices. Then, in their trouble and difficulty, Jehoshaphat inquires for a prophet of the Lord. Jehoram never thought of it. Elisha is discovered, and the three kings do not wait to send for him, but go down in person, and together, to consult with him. What a beautiful testimony that is which Jehoshaphat bears to Elisha, "The word of the Lord is with him"! That was the secret of Elisha's power.—C. H. I.

Vers. 13—15.—*Elisha and the minstrel.* When the kings come down to see him, at first Elisha is filled with just indignation. He rebukes the King of Israel for his godlessness, and says, "What have I to do with thee? get thee to the prophets of thy father, and to the prophets of thy mother." And then, when Jehoram repeats his profanity of throwing the blame upon God, Elisha protests that, but for the presence of Jehoshaphat King of Judah, he would have nothing more to do with him. But he has God's people to think of, and God's message, and so, in order to calm his mind and bring him into a fit state to deliver God's message, he says, "Bring me a minstrel" (the Hebrew word means one who played upon the harp). "And it came to pass, when the minstrel played, that the hand of the Lord came upon him." And then Elisha delivers to them that command of God by obeying which the armies obtained at once refreshing and safety, strength and victory. We learn here—

I. THE USE OF MEANS IN GENERAL. The kings had not taken the right way to obtain success. In setting out on their expedition they had used no means to obtain God's guidance. They trusted on the arm of flesh, and leaned to their own understanding. Then at last, when in a difficulty, in distress for want of water, and in danger of being defeated by their enemies, they think *then* of some means of obtaining God's help. It was no harm for them to look to the state of their armies, and to take the best military advice they could get, provided they had first of all sought direction from God. But this they had not done. Elisha acts very differently. He seeks to put his mind into a fit state to receive and deliver God's message. 1. *We ought to use means to bring our souls into fellowship with God.* There are few persons, no matter how godless, no matter how worldly, who do not cherish the hope of getting to heaven and being with God hereafter. But when are they going to prepare for heaven? Many professing Christians lead practically godless lives. They seldom or never read the Word of God. They never pray to God—in any real sense of the word, at least. Are they in a fit state to enter God's heaven? When, then, is the preparation to be made? Death-bed preparation is a rare thing, and at best a very mean thing, though one would rather see a poor sinner turning to his God at the eleventh hour than not at all. Unless

you are converted, you are *never* fit to enter heaven. " Prepare to meet thy God."
Use the means which God has given you to obtain the salvation of your soul. Strive
to enter in at the narrow door. Look to Jesus as your Saviour. Search the Scriptures,
for in them eternal life is to be found. They are able to make you wise unto salvation.
Go where you will get blessing. Here is one means which Christ himself recommends
to every sinner, " *Come unto me,* all ye that labour and are heavy laden, and I will
give you rest." *The same exhortation is applicable to Christian people.* Use the means
to bring your souls into fellowship with God, to obtain the touch of God's hand. Use
every means to promote the spiritual life of yourselves and others. How important
for parents and children is the observance of family prayer! Many a conversion, many
a consecration of a young life to God, can be traced to the words read, to the earnest
pleadings offered up, at the family altar. Happy that home where God-fearing parents

> " . . . their secret homage pay,
> And proffer up to heaven the warm request
> That he who stills the raven's clam'rous nest,
> And decks the lily fair in flow'ry pride,
> Would in the way his wisdom sees the best
> For them and for their little ones provide;
> *But chiefly in their hearts with grace Divine preside.*"

2. *We ought to use also the best means for carrying on God's work.* The Church
must not despise the use of means. What progress is made in facilities for carrying
on the business of the world! What rapid communication! What gigantic efforts
made to push commercial enterprises! And is the Church of Christ to be the only
body that is asleep? Is there no need for activity, for earnestness, for *push*, in the
concerns of eternity? While immortal souls are perishing, while so many fields are
white to harvest, ought we not to be up and doing? There are methods that it is no
advantage for the Church to adopt. But the Church of Christ should avail itself of
every lawful means to advance the Redeemer's kingdom. It should use the press far
more than it does. It should advertise far more than it does. *It should do anything
and everything in the way of enterprise that will bring the gospel to the people, and
that will bring the people to the gospel.* It must go out into the streets and lanes of
the city, to the highways and hedges of the country, and compel the people to come in.
The Church that knows best how to use the means which modern civilization has
placed at its disposal, is the Church that will do most, with God's blessing and the
presence of his Spirit, to advance the kingdom of Christ. We must seek to use everything and win everything for Jesus. Some persons say that ministers are so often
talking about money. There is so much money devoted to the service of the devil
and of sin and of pleasure every week, that it is the minister's duty to try to win a
little of it for Christ. If he spoke about it every Sunday it would not be one whit too
often. Let us use the means if we want to win the world for Jesus. Let us not think
that anything will do for him. Let us not give to the Lord that which costs us
nothing.

    II. THE USE OF MUSIC IN PARTICULAR. When Elisha said, " Bring me a minstrel,"
it was because he believed the harper's music would be *a real help* to him in experiencing
God's presence and in doing God's work. And he was right. For "it came to pass,
when the minstrel played, that the hand of the Lord came upon him." There are many
uses of music in the Christian life. 1. *Music is an inspiration for work and warfare.*
Why is it that our regiments go forth to battle accompanied by their bands of music?
Is it not that they may be inspirited and cheered by martial and triumphant strains?
Is there no place, then, for inspiring music in the Christian life? Are there not times
when our spirits flag, and we are easily discouraged? At such times how inspiriting
is a joyful song of praise! 2. *Music is also a soother of the spirit.* So it was here in
Elisha's case. So it was in the case of King Saul. When David played before him
on his harp, the evil spirit went from him, and the troubled mind became at peace.
We read also in the account of the Last Supper of our Lord, just before his agony at
Gethsemane and on the cross, that " when they had sung an hymn, they went out to
the Mount of Olives." Who can doubt that the spirits both of Master and disciples
were soothed and tranquillized as their hearts and voices joined together in the hymn
of praise? 3. *Music is largely the occupation of the redeemed in heaven.* St. John

tells us in the Revelation, " And I heard the voice of harpers harping with their harps: and they sung as it were a new song before the throne, and the four living creatures, and the elders : and no man could learn that song but the hundred and forty and four thousand,'which were redeemed from the earth." The sweetest earthly music we have ever heard, the largest and best-trained chorus of human voices, will give us but a faint conception of the sweetness and grandeur of the heavenly music. Mozart or Mendelssohn, Handel or Beethoven, never in their loftiest flights conceived a strain so thrilling as the song around the throne of God. Considering, therefore, the power of music, considering the uses to which it may be put on earth and the help it renders to true devotion, considering the place assigned to it in heaven,—it may fairly be claimed that *music should be more cultivated by the Christian Church*. While we do not go to church for a musical performance, we should have in our churches the very best music it is possible to have. It is often the very worst. The best music ought not to be left to the service of the devil and of the world. To preach the gospel is our great work. Yes; but there is no special merit in preaching the gospel unless you try to get the people to come and hear it. There is really no reason why we should not preach the gospel, and have attractive services and bright music at the same time. Martin Luther said, " One of the finest and noblest gifts of God is music. This is very hateful to the devil, and with it we may drive off temptations and evil thoughts. *After theology, I give the next and highest place to music.* It has often aroused and moved me so that I have won a desire to preach. We ought not to ordain young men to the office of preacher, if they have not trained themselves and practised singing in the schools." Luther was not far wrong. Our congregations should devote more time to the *practice and preparation* of congregational psalmody. Young ladies, young men, with musical gifts and accomplishments—why not consecrate them to the service of Jesus ?

" Sing at the cottage bedside;
   They have no music there,
And the voice of praise is silent
   After the voice of prayer.

" Sing of the gentle Saviour
   In the simplest hymns you know,
And the pain-dimmed eye will brighten
   As the soothing verses flow.

" Sing! that your song may silence
   The folly and the jest,
And the ' idle word ' be banished
   As an unwelcome guest.

'' Sing to the tired and anxious—
   It is yours to fling a ray,
Passing indeed, but cheering,
   Across the rugged way.

" *Thus, aided by his blessing,*
   The song may win its way
Where speech had no admittance,
   And change the night to day."

C. H. I.

Vers. 16—25.—*The valley full of ditches.* Two troubles had come upon Israel at this time. The kings of Israel, Judah, and Edom were gone forth to battle against the King of Moab. Strife is an evil between nations or individuals. It takes years for a nation to recover from the devastating effects of war. Terrible is the destruction of life and property which war causes. To the horrors and perils of war in this case was added a fresh difficulty. Their armies, passing through the desert, had no water to drink. Under the burning heat they suffered fearfully from thirst. We know how greatly our own troops suffered from lack of water in Egypt and the Soudan. Dr. Livingstone, in his travels, has given us an idea of what it is to be without water in the desert. When he saw his children almost perishing of thirst before his eyes, he had a new idea of the value of water. It was no wonder, then, that, with the soldiers weak and languishing from thirst, with no water either for them or for their horses and cattle, they began to despair and regard defeat as certain. But the Prophet Elisha was sent for, as we have seen, and, on being consulted by the kings of Israel and Judah, he said, "Make this valley full of ditches. For thus saith the Lord, Ye shall not see wind, neither shall ye see rain; yet that valley shall be filled with water, that ye may drink, both ye, and your cattle, and your beasts. And this is but a' light thing in the sight of the Lord: he will deliver the Moabites also into your hand." We have here—

I. A STRANGE COMMAND. "Make this valley full of ditches." 1. *It was a strange command that ditches should be dug in a desert place.* But so it is also in the spiritual kingdom. God often chooses the most unlikely places and the most unlikely persons for the operations of his grace. Is it not a fact that, in thinking of the spread of the gospel, and in engaging in Christian work, we are too much guided by human calculations? We judge too much by outward appearances. We forget that God's ways are not as our ways, nor his thoughts as our thoughts. People have sometimes refused to give to certain missions because they did not think there was any use in sending the gospel to the particular people for whom the mission was intended. Is God's arm shortened that it cannot save? It is time for us as Christian Churches and as Christian people to work wherever God gives us the opportunity, even though it should be in the most unlikely and unpromising sphere. God calls us, wherever we are, to dig up wells in the valley. 2. Further, *it was a strange command, because there was no appearance of rain at the time, and there was no river at hand from which the wells could be supplied.* Why dig wells when you don't know where the water is to come from? We live in a utilitarian age. Men like to have a reason for everything. They like to be assured of a return for their labour. Consequently, even professedly Christian men are disposed to question the utility of many of God's commands. Why rest on the sabbath more than on any other day? Why attach any peculiar sanctity to the sabbath? Why not worship God at home, or walk in the fields, instead of going to church? We might show the benefit to the nation of religious observances and of religious teaching. We might show the benefit to the individual of assembling with others for devotional exercises instead of merely worshipping God in private or even in the home. But it is enough here to notice that God has *commanded* these duties. That ought to be enough to convince any intelligent being, any religious being. God gives no command for which there is not a good reason. I may not see the reason. I may not see the benefit that will result from it. But I am convinced by reason, by conscience, by history, by human experience, that whatever the command may be, a real benefit follows the obedience of it, and real unhappiness and suffering the disobedience of it. 3. One other thought this strange command of God suggests—*God wants us to be fellow-workers with him.* God could have sent the water and provided a place of storage for it without the assistance of the Israelites here. But he does not choose to do so. He says, "Make the valley full of ditches." When modern missions to the heathen first began to be spoken of about a century ago, those who advocated them were met on every side, and in many a church, from pulpit and from pew, from prelate and from presbyter, with the objection that God could save the heathen without their instrumentality. It is obvious that those who reasoned thus about God's method of converting the world had read their Bible to very little purpose. We find human agency, as a rule, accompanying Divine grace. Christ's own command is clear, "Go ye therefore, and teach all nations, . . . and, lo! I am with you alway." How do we stand in regard to the commands of God? Is there any command that we are deliberately and constantly disobeying? It ought to be the daily prayer of every Christian, "Make me to go in the path of thy commandments; for therein do I delight."

II. SUBMISSIVE FAITH. It is clear from the narrative that the men of Judah did as God had commanded them, and made the valley full of ditches. These Hebrew soldiers gave a good example of submissive practical faith. 1. They might have reasoned— *Better to be going forth against our enemies than to be wasting our time digging these trenches.* So men reason when they hurry forth to their work in the morning without waiting to give God thanks for the rest of the night, and to ask his blessing upon the work of the day. Is it any wonder that the life is so dry, and that things so often seem to go wrong, when we do not take time to dig up wells for God's blessing? Is it any wonder that the Churches are so unfruitful, that conversions are so infrequent, that revivals are so rare, that there is not more spiritual power in the preaching of the Word, that the influence exercised upon the world around us is so slight, when, with all the attention to congregational machinery and church order, there is so little attention to congregational prayer? It is a fine sight to look at the great engines of a steamer when in motion, and admire the beautiful mechanism of cylinder and crank and piston. But all that elaborate and powerful machinery would be utterly useless unless the steam was there to set it in motion. Let us have our church machinery and organization as perfect as may be, but let us remember that the secret of power is *behind and beyond it all.* "Not by might, nor by power, but by my Spirit, saith the Lord." The Hebrew soldiers did not think the time lost which they spent in preparing the way for God's blessing. 2. They might have reasoned—*Better to move further on where we shall have water than to spend our labour in this desert place.* So Christians are sometimes disposed to reason. Ministers grow weary of seeing no fruit of their labours. Sunday-school teachers grow weary of their class. But if all the workers in God's vineyard had reasoned in that way, and abandoned any sphere of labour because it seemed unfruitful or because they were weary of waiting, the gospel would have made very little progress in the world. 3. They might have reasoned—*If we're to be saved, we shall be saved. It is not likely that digging up trenches in the valley will deliver us out of the hands of the Moabites.* So the sinner reasons when he is urged to believe on the Lord Jesus Christ. Satan, for his soul's destruction, prompts him with objections to the plan of salvation. But objections to the plan of salvation can no more alter it than any suggestions which a man of science might make could alter the course of nature. The way of salvation is clear. "Believe on the Lord Jesus Christ, and thou shalt be saved." Is it not better for us, as these soldiers did, to take God's plan, to believe that whatever he commands is for our good, to accept his loving offers of salvation purchased for us by the precious blood of his beloved Son, and to yield ourselves to him as willing servants, doing the will of God from the heart?

III. STREAMS OF REFRESHING AND SAFETY. "And it came to pass in the morning, when the meat offering was offered, that, behold, there came water by the way of Edom, and the country was filled with water." Not more eagerly do the weary watchers watch for morning than those languid soldiers watched for the coming of the water. It was a welcome sight. So it is with the blessings of the gospel. "Blessed are they that hunger and thirst after righteousness: for they shall be filled."

> " As dew upon the tender herb,
>   Diffusing fragrance round,
> As showers that usher in the spring
>   And cheer the thirsty ground,—
> So shall his presence bless our souls,
>   And shed a joyful light,
> That hallowed morn shall chase away
>   The sorrows of the night."

And then also the streams that filled the trenches proved to be *streams of safety.* When the Moabites arose in the morning, and looked over to the place where the Israelites were encamped, they only saw the glare of the sun upon the water as red as blood. They had probably no idea that water could be there. And so they said, "This is blood; the kings are surely slain, and they have smitten one another." They thought they had nothing to do but plunder the deserted camp of the Israelites, and the result was that the Israelites gained an easy victory, and were delivered out of the hand of their enemies. It is the same with the blessings of the gospel. *The gospel which satisfies also saves the soul.* And it satisfies because it saves. Herein all human religion and philosophies fail. They may point out a high ideal, but they give us little help to attain it. They may point out the evil of sin, but they cannot strengthen us to overcome it or deliver us from its power. And all they can offer us is only for the present life. But the gospel not only puts before us the high ideal, but enables us through Divine grace to attain to it. It not only shows us the guilt of sin, but it points us to the cleansing blood. It not only shows us the evil of sin, but gives us the victory over it through Christ Jesus our Lord. It not only gives us blessings for the present life, but secures to all who believe on the Lord Jesus Christ the life of heaven, life with God, life that shall never end. *Make the valley full of ditches.* Open your heart to receive this satisfying, saving gospel. Children of God, if you want God's blessing to flow in upon you in reviving, refreshing streams, prepare the way for it. *Dig up wells in the desert.* Value your Sundays, your opportunities for private prayer, the house of God, the prayer-meeting. You need them all to refresh your souls and to revive your spiritual life amid the parching, chilling influences of the world. And then in your short life do what you can to *make channels through which blessings may flow to others.* In this aspect, what a privilege it becomes to help missions, to build churches and schools, and to take part in every effort for the benefit and enlightenment of others! You may never see the streams of blessing flow, but at any rate *you will have dug the channels for them.* Such labour is not in vain in the Lord.—C. H. I.

Vers. 26, 27.—*The heartlessness of heathenism.* 1. *Heathenism blights the natural affections.* Christianity honours and sanctifies them. 2. *Heathenism disregards human life.* What sacrifice of life by cannibalism, under the car of Juggernaut, in the suttees of India! What disregard of human life in the exposure of Chinese infants, in the aged and the sick left alone to die on the banks of the Indian rivers! Christianity has changed all this. It takes high views of human life. The body is the dwelling-place of an immortal soul. Care for the sick and for the dying is due to the influences of the gospel. Where are the hospitals, the philanthropic movements, of heathenism or of agnosticism? Even for the comforts of the present life we owe much to Christianity.—C. H. I.

Vers. 1—5.—*Evil—the same in principle, though not in form.* "Now Jehoram the son of Ahab began to reign over Israel," etc. Two subjects are here illustrated.
I. THAT WHILST THE FORMS OF EVIL MAY CHANGE, THE PRINCIPLE MAY CONTINUE RAMPANT. "And he [that is, Jehoram] wrought evil in the sight of the Lord; but not like his father, and like his mother." His father and mother worshipped Baal, but the very "image" of the idol "that his father had made he put away." But notwithstanding that "he cleaved unto the sins of Jeroboam." Observe: 1. *Though the existing generation sins not in the form of the preceding, their sin is not less sin on that account.* The forms in which barbarians and our uncivilized ancestors sinned appear gross and revolting to us; nevertheless, our sins are not the less real and heinous in the sight of God. Our civilization hides the revolting hideousness, but leaves its spirit perhaps more active than ever. Your father's prominent sin, perhaps, was that of drunkenness, but though you touch not the inebriating cup, you sin in other forms—the forms, perhaps, of vanity, avarice, ambition, etc. 2. *That mere external reformations may leave the spirit of evil as rampant as ever.* Jehoram "put away the image of Baal," but the spirit of idolatry remained in him in all its wonted force. "He cleaved unto the sins of Jeroboam the son of Nebat, which made Israel to sin; he departed not therefrom." This is ever true. Religiously, you may destroy a superstitious organization, and yet leave the spirit of religious superstition, intolerance, and pride, even more vigorous than ever, to assume other forms. So of political institutions. You may destroy this form of government or that, monarchical or democratic, and yet leave the spirit in which these forms work, vital and vigorous to manifest itself in other forms.
II. THAT WHILST SIN MAY ONLY BE IN THE FORM OF NEGLECT OF DUTY, IT MAY IN THE CASE OF ONE MAN ENTAIL SERIOUS EVILS ON POSTERITY. "And Mesha King of Moab was a sheepmaster, and rendered unto the King of Israel a hundred thousand lambs, and a hundred thousand rams, with the wool. But it came to pass, when Ahab was dead, that the King of Moab rebelled against the King of Israel." Moab was a tributary to the kingdom of Israel, and contributed largely to its revenue, not in cash, but in cattle, or in wool, but not the less valuable on that account. But now a rebellion had broken out, and a serious revolt was threatened. Why was this? Matthew Henry ascribes it to the neglect of Ahaziah, the former king, the brother of Jehoram. He made no attempt to avoid such a catastrophe. Ah! sins of omission entail serious evils. The neglect of one generation brings miseries on another. The neglect of parents often brings ruin on the children. Negative sins are curses. "We have left undone the things we ought to have done;" and who shall tell the result on all future times?—D. T.

Vers. 6—12.—*Worldly rulers—men in trial seeking help from a godly man.* "And King Jehoram went out of Samaria the same time, and numbered all Israel," etc.

I. Here we have WORLDLY RULERS IN GREAT TRIAL. "And King Jehoram went out of Samaria the same time, and numbered all Israel. And he went and sent to Jehoshaphat the King of Judah, saying, The King of Moab hath rebelled against me." The revolt of Moab threatened the ruin of Jehoram and his empire, and he, smitten with alarm, numbers, or rather, musters, all Israel, and hurries to Jehoshaphat to seek his aid. They, with their armies, go forth to meet in battle their enemy on a seven days' journey, enduring the privation of water for themselves and their cattle. At the end of their journey, disheartened and exhausted, they reached a crisis of terrible anxiety and danger. Worldly rulers have their trials. "Uneasy lies the head that wears a crown." What terrible ends in past ages kings have come to! and to-day all the thrones of Europe seem to be tottering to their fall. Providence destines that a man who aspires to the highest office must pay a terrible price for it. The trials of high office, added to the natural trials of man as man, are often overwhelming. Here we have worldly rulers in great trial—

II. SEEKING HELP FROM A GODLY MAN. "But Jehoshaphat said, Is there not here a prophet of the Lord, that we may inquire of the Lord by him? And one of the King of Israel's servants answered and said, Here is Elisha," etc. Mark the cry, "Is there not here a prophet of the Lord?" The question is answered, and the three kings—those of Israel, of Judah, and of Edom—go in earnest quest of him. They "went down to him." This: 1. Proved their *instinctive belief in the existence of one God, the Maker and Manager of worlds.* Man always, in overwhelming distress, turns away from his systems and theories, and looks up to the Everlasting One. 2. Proved their *faith in the power of a truly good man with that God.* This is common; sceptics and worldlings on their death-beds are continually sending for those to visit them whom they believe to be men of God. The evil must ever bow before the good. What an illustration we have of this in the case of the two hundred and seventy-five men on board the ship tossed in the dangerous tempest on her way from Cæsarea to Rome, with the Apostle Paul on board! Paul was a poor prisoner in chains, and the passengers were made up of soldiers and merchants and men of science; but to whom did they look in the turmoil? Paul, who at the outset, when "the south wind blew softly," was nothing in that vessel, became the moral commander during the tempest. Amidst the wild roaring of the elements, the cries of his fellow-voyagers, the crashes of the plunging ship, the awful howl of death, in all he walked upon the creaking deck with a moral majesty, before which captain, merchant, soldier, and centurion bowed with loyal awe. So it has ever been; so it must ever be. The good show their greatness in trials, and in their trials, the evil, however exalted their worldly position, are compelled to appreciate them. How often do the world's great men on death-beds seek the attendance, sympathies, counsel, and prayers of those godly ones whom they despised in health! —D. T.

Vers. 13—27.—*Aspects of a godly man.* "And Elisha said unto the King of Israel, What have I to do with thee?" etc. Elisha was confessedly a godly man of a high type, and these verses reveal him to us in three aspects.
I. AS RISING SUPERIOR TO KINGS. When these three kings—Jehoshaphat the King of Judah, Jehoram the King of Israel, and the King of Edom—approached Elisha, was he overawed by their splendour? or was he elated by their visit? No. He was no *flunkey;* no true man ever is. Here are his sublimely manly words, "What have I to do with thee?" 1. *He rebukes Jehoram for his idolatry.* "Get thee to the prophets of thy father, and to the prophets of thy mother." "In your prosperity you Israelite kings have been serving these false gods, and you have despised me as the servant of the true God. Why come to me now in your distress? Go and try what they can do for you." What courage in this poor lonely man, thus calmly to confront and honestly to rebuke a monarch! Ah me! where is this courage now? The loudest professors of our religion in these times will too often crouch before kings, and address them in terms of fawning flattery. 2. *He yields to their urgency out of respect to the true religion.* "And Elisha said, As the Lord of hosts liveth, before whom I stand, surely, were it not that I regard the presence of Jehoshaphat the King of Judah, I would not look toward thee, nor see thee." Jehoshaphat was pre-eminently a godly man (2 Chron. xvii. 5, 6), and that influenced the great Elisha to interpose on his behalf. "Them that

honour me I will honour," saith the Lord. A godly **man is the** only true independent man on this earth; he can "stand before kings" and not be ashamed, and rebuke princes as well as paupers for their sins. Whither has this spirit fled? We are a nation of sycophants. Heaven send us *men*!

II. As PREPARING FOR INTERCESSION WITH HEAVEN. What these kings wanted was the interposition of Heaven on their behalf, and they here apply to Elisha to obtain this; and after the prophet had acceded to their request, he seeks to put himself in the right moral mood to appeal to Heaven, and what does he do? "But now bring me a minstrel. And it came to pass, when the minstrel played, that the hand of the Lord came upon him." Probably his mind had been somewhat ruffled by the presence of these kings, especially at the sight of Jehoram, the wicked and idolatrous king, and before venturing an appeal to Heaven he felt the need of a devout calmness. Hence he called for music, and as the devout musician sounded out sweet psalmody on his ear, he became soothed and spiritualized in soul. The power of music, especially the music which is the organ of Divine ideas, has in every age exerted a soothing and elevating influence on the human soul. By the harp David expelled the evil spirit from the heart of Saul. "Buretti declares music to have the power of so affecting the whole nervous system as to give sensible ease in a large variety of disorders, and in some cases to effect a radical cure: particularly he instances sciatica as capable of being relieved by this agency. Theophrastus is mentioned by Pliny as recommending it for the hip gout; and there are references on record by old Cato and Varro to the same effect. Æsculapius figures in Pindar as healing acute disorders with soothing songs."

> "Music exalts each joy, allays each grief,
> Expels diseases, softens every pain,
> Subdues the rage of poison and of plague,
> And hence the wise of ancient days adored
> One power of physic, melody, and song."

Luther taught that the "spirit of darkness abhorred sweet sounds."[1] There is a spiritual mood necessary in order to have intercourse with Heaven, and this mood it is incumbent on every man to seek and retain.

III. As BECOMING THE ORGAN OF THE SUPERNATURAL. (1) Through him *God made a promise of deliverance.* "For thus saith the Lord, Ye shall not see wind, neither shall ye see rain," etc. (vers. 17—19). (2) Through him *God effected their deliverance.* "And when they came to the camp of Israel, the Israelites rose up and smote the Moabites," etc. (vers. 24, 25). Thus the Almighty made this godly man both to *foretell* and *fulfil* his plans. We would remind those who are sceptical of this, and who perhaps ridicule the idea of man becoming the organ of Divine power: 1. That there is nothing *antecedently improbable* in this. God works through his creatures; since he created the universe he employs it as his agent. What wonders he works through the sun, the atmosphere, etc.! Science teaches that even through worms he prepares the soil of this earth to produce food for man and beast.[2] But inasmuch as man is confessedly greater than the material universe—for he is the offspring of the Infinite, and participates in the Divine nature—it cannot be absurd to regard him in a pre-eminent sense as an organ of the supernatural. 2. *Biblical history* attests this. Moses, Christ, and the apostles performed deeds that seem to us to have transcended the natural. A morally great man becomes "mighty through God." God has ever worked wonders through godly men, and ever will.—D. T.

Vers. 1—3.—*Jehoram; or, qualified evil.* The successor of Ahaziah was Jehoram, another son of Ahab and Jezebel. It is said, however, concerning him, that, though he did evil, it was not like his father and mother, for he removed from its place the image of Baal which they had impiously set up. Nevertheless, he upheld the worship of the calves—the distinguishing sin of the northern kingdom.

I. THERE ARE DEGREES IN SIN. Some go greater lengths in transgression than others. It is right and dutiful to note even distinctions of this kind, and give every one his due. We may be thankful when even a less form of evil is substituted for a

---

[1] See Jacox's 'Secular Annotations' on Medicamental Music.
[2] See Darwin's 'Vegetable Mould and Earth-Worms.'

worse one. The impartiality and discrimination of the Bible, even among those whose actions it must condemn, is a proof of its fidelity.

II. PARTIAL REFORMS ARE POSSIBLE WHICH DO NOT TOUCH THE ROOT OF SIN. Jehoram so far profited by the experience of his predecessors that he withdrew his countenance from the Baal-worship. This was a real reform, and he gets credit for it. So, many men take certain steps in the direction of reform—breaking off particular evil habits, intemperance, perhaps, or profane swearing—who yet get no further. They are able to do this. It is gratifying to see them do it. But it leaves the root of the matter untouched.

III. QUALIFIED EVIL IS EVIL STILL. The foundation of Jehoram's character was still evil—" he wrought evil in the sight of the Lord." This is the great fact which God looks at, and in the light of which he judges us. Herod "did many things" to please John the Baptist, but his bad heart remained unchanged (Mark v. 20). The cardinal necessity of the heart is renewal—regeneration—the founding of the life on a spiritual basis.—J. O.

Vers. 4, 5.—*King Mesha's rebellion.* The general causes of this rebellion are considered on ch. i. 1. The victories recorded on the Moabite Stone as achieved by the favour of Chemosh belong probably to the earlier stages of the revolt. They can hardly have followed the crushing destruction of vers. 24, 25. Prior, also, to the expedition of this chapter, must be placed the attempt to overwhelm Jehoshaphat by the combined forces of the Moabites, Ammonites, Edomites, etc. (2 Chron. xx.), which seems to be the invasion described in Ps. lxxxiii. The language alike of the history and of the psalm in the description of that invasion—which, like the present struggle, ended in supernatural defeat—shows how dangerous an enemy an independent kingdom of Moab would have been to Judah, and how necessary it was, in the interests of the covenant nation, that this rival power should, on its first upspringing, be effectually broken. Jehoram's action was overruled to bring about this effectual humbling of Moab, though, for his own humiliation, Moab does not seem ever to have been brought again under the yoke of Israel. Great as were the severities of the war, they were not greater than Moab, as a conquering power, meted out to others (see Moabite Stone), and would still have meted out had she been victor.—J. O.

Vers. 6—8.—*The alliance of the three kings.* No time was to be lost, if the King of Israel was to check the progress of this formidable rebel, who, from the inscription on his stone, appears to have had some remarkable successes.

I. JEHORAM'S PROPOSAL. 1. Jehoram's first step was to muster for the expedition the whole army of Israel. His trust was in chariots and horses. How little they could do for him, apart from God's help, was soon to be made manifest. 2. He next sent a message to Jehoshaphat, inviting him to accompany him. This shows, at least, that he took a sufficiently serious view of the difficulty of his enterprise. He did not enter on it lightly. Perhaps also he had the inward feeling that it would be likelier to go well with him if this godly king were on his side. A wicked man is always glad when he can get a good one to lend his countenance to any of his doings.

II. JEHOSHAPHAT'S CONSENT. This was at once and freely given. Jehoshaphat had refused partnership with Ahaziah (1 Kings xxii. 49). But: 1. Jehoram was a man of less impious character. 2. The war seemed just. 3. He had to secure the safety of his own kingdom. This had already been menaced, and would no doubt be menaced again, if Mesha continued his victorious career. 4. There was further the unfortunate bond of kinship—Jehoram's sister Athaliah being married to Jehoshaphat's son. Entanglements with the wicked lead into many a snare. Jehoshaphat's chief error was in deciding on his own responsibility, and not doing first what he was glad enough to do after—"inquire of the Lord." How many troubles we often get into through simply neglecting to seek Divine guidance! Secular things ought to be made the subjects of prayer as much as spiritual things. "In everything by prayer and supplication," etc. (Phil. iv. 6).

III. THE WAY BY EDOM. Which way would they take? Jehoshaphat urged that they should go by the wilderness of Edom, that is, round the foot of the Dead Sea. This route would be the longer, but it enabled Moab to be attacked from a safer side, and had the further advantage that it would secure to the allies the services of the deputy-king of Edom, who, as a vassal of Jehoshaphat, could not refuse to accompany them (1 Kings xxii. 47; ch. viii. 20). The Edomites had, indeed, but lately joined in the confederacy against Judah, but they were now probably burning to be avenged on the Moabites, who, in that expedition, had proved to be their worst enemies (2 Chron. xx. 23). Thus providence overrules the passions of men to work out its own ends.—J. O.

Vers. 9—17, 20.—*Man's extremity is God's opportunity.* This expedition, begun without consulting God, soon landed the allies in dire straits. I. THE STRAITS OF THE ARMY. 1. *The failure of water.* The host must have been a large one, and they had much cattle with them for sustenance. For some reason, the journey occupied seven days, and the desert was waterless. They were in the same distress that the Israelites were in centuries before under Moses (Exod. xvii. 1—3; Numb. xx. 1—5); but they had not the same right to rely on Divine help. When, at the end of seven days, they arrived at a valley where water might be looked for—probably "the brook Zered" (Deut. ii. 13)—their condition became desperate. 2. *God's hand recognized.* Jehoram recognized, when it was too late, that it was not Moab who was fighting against him in this expedition, but God. "Alas! that the Lord hath called these three kings together, to deliver them into the hand of Moab!" (1) How readily God can humble man's pride, and bring to nothing his best-laid schemes! We are reminded of Napoleon's march against Moscow, and of the annihilation of his army by the severities of a Russian winter. (2) God's hand is often recognized in trouble, when it is not in prosperity. (3) God frequently leads men into distress, that they may be convinced of their folly in neglecting him, and may be led to seek his help (Ps. cvii.). II. THE APPEAL TO ELISHA. 1. *Jehoshaphat's inquiry.* The King of Israel abandoned himself to despair, but Jehoshaphat asked, "Is there not here a prophet of the Lord, that we may inquire of the Lord by him?" Had he inquired of the Lord at the beginning, he would not now have been in this difficulty. But: (1) It was better to inquire late—if haply it might not be too late—than not to inquire at all. A good man only needs to be convinced of his errors to endeavour to repair them. A touch of the rod of chastisement turns back his heart to God, whom he may have been forgetting. To whom else shall he go? God alone can help. (2) Even the sinner, if convinced that God is contending with him, should not delay repentance through remembrance of past sins. If he has never prayed before, let him do it now. But, alas! repentances of this kind are too often insincere—the mere fruit of present fear—and are not followed up by change of life. 2. *The three kings and the prophet.* (1) Jehoshaphat's question elicited the fact that Elisha the son of Shaphat was in the camp or near it. It was a servant of the King of Israel that gave this information, so that even in this ungodly king's household there were some true worshippers (cf. 1 Kings xviii. 3, 4). This servant, though in a humble position, did the greatest service possible to his king and nation. But for his information, the armies of three kingdoms might have been annihilated. In like manner, it was "a little captive maid" who directed Naaman to the prophet (ch. v. 2, 3). (2) Jehoshaphat felt at once they had the right man—"The word of the Lord is with him." Pretenders, false prophets, hypocrites, are of no avail when real trouble comes. It is the genuine prophet that is needed then. Elisha must have followed the camp by Divine direction, to give this aid in the hour of extremity—another evidence that the events of this expedition, like all other events, were being shaped by an overruling Providence. (3) The kings at once repair to Elisha. They did not ask him to come to *them*, but, as suppliants, "went down" to him. It was a strange sight—the three kings standing before this prophet of the Lord, whom, at other times, two of them at least would have disdained to consult. But it was now felt that Elisha alone stood between them and death. He, the man of God, was, like his master before him—"the chariot of Israel, and the horsemen thereof"—under God, the protector and salvation of the nation. There come seasons when religion gets the homage paid to it which its importance at all times deserves. 3. *Help only for the sake of Jehoshaphat.* Elisha's spirit seems to have been strangely perturbed by the visit of these three kings. He was roused in part by scorn at a king like Jehoram, who ordinarily paid no respect to religion, coming to ask his aid in the pinch of physical distress. It is Elijah's fire which glows in him for the moment, as he sternly asks, "What have I to do with thee?" and bids the humbled monarch get him to the prophets of his father (the calves'-prophets) and the prophets of his mother (the Baal-prophets), to see what they could do for him. But Jehoram knew that the prophets of the calves or of Baal could in that extremity give him little help. He deprecates Elisha's anger, only to be told that, but for the sake of Jehoshaphat, the prophet would neither look towards him nor see him. (1) It is character, not rank, which God regards. Jehoram harps upon the string that, if nothing is done, "three kings" will perish. He seems to fancy, with the French lady, that God will think twice before casting off persons of that quality. But Elisha undeceives him. Only because the good Jehoshaphat is in the company will God show any mercy to him. (2) The ungodly often reap great benefits from association with the good. Jehoram now found this to his advantage. (3) There will come a time of exposure for all "refuges of lies." Elisha laid bare the folly of trusting to the idol-prophets, and Jehoram felt the truth of his rebuke. So will it be with all vain imaginations (Isa. xxviii. 14—18).

III. THE DIVINE DELIVERANCE. 1. *Holy minstrelsy.* The discomposed state of Elisha's mind was not fitted for the reception of "revelations of the Lord." If God would speak, passion must be stilled. To this end, he called for a minstrel, that by the soothing, subduing effect of sacred melody, his soul might be restored to a calm condition. It is a wonderful power that resides in music; we do well in God's service to take advantage of it. "The noblest passages in 'Paradise Lost' were composed as Milton's daughter played to her father on the organ." Music gives wings to the soul, reveals to it the existence of a world of harmony, touches and harmonizes it to like "fine issues." 2. *A labour of faith.* As the minstrel played, the hand of the Lord came upon Elisha, and he gave directions to make the valley full of trenches. As yet there was not the slightest sign of water, nor would there be any. The work was to be done in entire dependence on the word of God that water would be sent. This is faith—acting on God's bare word of promise. All that night the labourers toiled, and when the morning came, the valley was seamed with trenches, and studded with pits, to hold the yet invisible supply of the life-giving water. 3. *Streams from Edom.* In the morning, true to the Divine promise, the wished-for water came. (1) It came without visible sign. The people who looked for it saw neither wind nor rain, but simply "there came water by the way of Edom, and the country was filled with water." Yet there is no necessity for supposing a supernatural creation of water, for God does not work without means, when means are available. The bursting of a waterspout, or heavy rains, at some distance, would give rise to the phenomenon. There was doubtless a providential preparation for the deliverance, as there was a providential design in the distress. (2) It came at the time of the morning oblation. The deliverance was thus connected with the service in the temple—Jehovah's true sanctuary. As it was for Jehoshaphat's sake the deliverance was granted, so a token was now given that it was the religion of Judah to which God had respect. The hours of prayer are fit seasons for the conferring of blessing (cf. Dan. ix. 21). (3) It came in great abundance. When God gives he gives plentifully. "The country was *filled* with water." It is so with the supply God has given for the thirst of the world—those living waters of which we do so wisely to drink (John vii. 37, 38). Such events as these pledge to us the fulfilment of Divine promises (Isa. xliv. 3). The psalmist says, "The rain also filleth the pools" (Ps. lxxxiv. 6).—J. O.

Ver. 10.—*An evil conscience.* "And the King of Israel said, Alas! that the Lord hath called these three kings," etc.! 1. Trouble awakens the evil conscience. 2. The evil conscience takes the darkest view of the actions of God. 3. The evil conscience is glad to shelter itself by associating with others. (See excellent remarks in Krummacher.)—J. O.

Vers. 18—27.—*The defeat of Moab.* This also was foretold by Elisha as a mercy from the Lord, in comparison with which the supply of water was "a light thing." If these are God's "light things," surely we need not fear to ask from him all that we require. Our sin is, not in asking too much, but in asking too little (John xvi.

24). "He is able to do exceeding abundantly above all that we ask or think" (Eph. iii. 20).

I. LOST THROUGH ILLUSION. The manner in which the defeat of the Moabites was brought about is very remarkable. The defeat was caused: 1. *Through illusion.* Their forces—"all that were able to put on armour, and upward"—were mustered on the mountains opposite, ready for battle on the morrow. As the morning sun rose, its red beams, falling on the pools of water in the valley, gave the water the appearance of blood—an effect to which the red soil may have contributed. This startling appearance the Moabites—who knew nothing of the unlooked-for supply of water—interpreted in their own way. They said, "This is blood," and concluded—remembering a recent experience of their own (2 Chron. xx.)—that the attacking forces had fallen out, and destroyed each other. 2. *Through over-haste and over-confidence.* The cry was at once raised, "Moab, to the spoil!" and, casting aside all precautions, the people flew down, to find themselves in the power of their enemies. How many defeats are sustained in life from the same causes! We eagerly snatch at first appearances, which are often so deceptive; we hurry to the fray, without taking due precautions or counting the cost; we are confident in our strength or numbers as sufficient to bear down all opposition, if by chance we should be surprised. Therefore we fail. God often snares men through their own illusions. Haman went to Esther's banquet under the illusion that it was the road to highest honour, and found it the way to death (Esth. v. 11, 12; vii.). Of the wicked it is said, "For this cause God shall send them strong delusion, that they should believe a lie" (2 Thess. ii. 11).

II. THE MERCILESS PURSUIT. The passage describing this pursuit is a terrible illustration of the severities of war. They were, perhaps, under the circumstances, not needless severities, but they are none the less extreme and painful to think of. (1) The Moabites were pursued into their own country, and cut down in the pursuit. (2) The cities were levelled to the ground. (3) The good land was made useless by every man casting on it a stone, till it was covered with stones. (4) Even fruit trees were cut down, and wells stopped. (5) There remained only the city of Kir-haraseth, which, on its elevated plateau, defied direct assault; but it they besieged, while the slingers, taking their station on the surrounding eminences, galled it with their missiles. The words of the prophet in ver. 19 are perhaps prediction, not command, but it may be inferred that he gave the policy pursued his sanction. The object was so effectually to cripple the power of Moab that it would not be able to lift up the head for many a day to come. 1. The most direct lesson we can learn from the passage is the dreadfulness of war. Wherever or however waged, wars are a source of incalculable misery. Even just wars entail a loss of life, a destruction of wealth, and a waste of the means of production and of human happiness, which may well make the heart of the lover of his species sicken. 2. An indirect lesson to be gleaned from ver. 25 is the power of little things—"every man his stone." By each man bringing but a single stone, the ground was covered, and the end aimed at attained. The power was wielded here for destruction, but it may be wielded as well for good. Each doing his individual part—though that in itself is little —great results will be achieved. 3. We do well to carry into moral warfare the same thoroughness as is here displayed in physical warfare. Not content with operating on individuals, let us strike at causes and sources—stopping the wells of poisonous influence, etc.

III. THE LAST TRAGIC ACT. The war was brought to a sudden and unlooked-for termination. 1. *The fearful sacrifice.* Beaten into his last stronghold, driven to desperation, the King of Moab, having made an unsuccessful sortie with seven hundred men, resolved on an act which, he rightly judged, would strike horror into the hearts of his enemies, while it might also propitiate his god. He took his eldest son, the heir to his throne, and offered him up for a burnt offering on the wall. (1) The fact that he performed the sacrifice upon the wall would seem to show that he had in view as much the effect to be produced on the spectators as the possible effect to be produced on Chemosh. (2) The deed was awful and inhuman—perhaps, from Mesha's point of view, not without its nobler and patriotic side—but in itself most detestable. We have need to be thankful for a purer religious faith, which teaches us that God does not delight in such unnatural and cruel acts (Micah vi. 6—9). 2. *Repulsed by horror.* "There was," we read, "great indignation against [or, 'upon'] Israel: and they departed from him, and returned to their own land." The meaning seems to be that the ghastly act produced a universal horror, which turned into indignation against Israel as the original authors of the expedition which had so dreadful an end. There is an element of superstition in all men, and sudden revulsions of feeling, caused by an act that powerfully impresses the imagination, are not uncommon. The Israelites themselves so far sympathized with the emotion of horror which brought upon them the indignation of the Moabites, of neighbouring tribes, perhaps also of the Edomites and others among their own allies, that they gave up the thought of proceeding further. This seems a more natural explanation than either (1) that the indignation meant is that of Jehovah; or (2) that it is the wrath of Chemosh (!); or (3) the subjective horror of the Israelites themselves.—J. O.

EXPOSITION.

CHAPTER IV.

Vers. 1—44.—TYPICAL MIRACLES WROUGHT BY ELISHA. *General introduction.* The miracles of this chapter are all of them miracles of mercy. The first and last consist in the multiplying of food, and thus belong to the same class as our Lord's feeding the four and the five thousands, and Elijah's increasing the meal and oil of the widow of Zarephath (1 Kings xvii. 10—16). It serves no useful purpose to ask *how* miracles of this class were wrought. The inspired writers have not told us; and our own thoughts upon the subject can at the best be mere unfounded conjectures. The rationalistic attempts which have been made to solve the mystery exhibit a weakness and feebleness that are absolutely puerile (see Bähr, 'Commentary on Kings,' vol. ii. p. 46, Eng. trans.). The second miracle is the resuscitation of a dead person, and belongs, consequently, to the very narrow class of such recoveries—of which in the Old Testament there are three only (see 1 Kings xvii. 17—23; here; and ch. xiii. 21). The third miracle consists in rendering fit for man's use that which was previously unfit, not by human skill or science, but by miracle; and is analogous to the act of Moses whereby the waters of Marah ceased to be bitter (Exod. xv. 25), and to that other act of Elisha himself, whereby the waters of Jericho were healed (ch. ii. 19—22). It is evidently the object of the writer or compiler of 2 Kings to collect in this place the principal, or at any rate the most noted, of the miraculous acts of the great prophet who succeeded Elijah, and so to preserve them from oblivion. This object, which he began to set before himself in ch. ii. 13,

continues to be pursued, and forms a link uniting the various narratives together, up to ch. viii. 6.

Vers. 1—7.—1. *The multiplication of the widow's oil.*

Ver. 1.—**Now there cried a certain woman of the wives of the sons of the prophets unto Elisha, saying.** We learn from this that the "sons of the prophets" were not merely, all of them, college students, but included fathers of families, who cannot have lived a cloistered life, but must have had separate homes for themselves and their families. Such persons may still have taught in the prophetical schools, as do the married tutors and professors of modern universities. **Thy servant my husband is dead.** Elisha had, it seems, known her husband, who had been his "servant," not literally and in deed, but in will and heart, *i.e.* always ready to serve him. She recalls this fact to his memory, to predispose him in her favour. **And thou knowest that thy servant did fear the Lord.** Here was a second ground for Elisha's interference—the woman's husband had been a God-fearing man, one who not only acknowledged Jehovah, but worshipped him in spirit and in truth. There is a Jewish tradition, or legend, that the woman's husband was the Obadiah of 1 Kings xviii. 3—16, but no dependence can be placed on it. Obadiah, the "governor of Ahab's house," can scarcely have been one of the "sons of the prophets." **And the creditor is come to take unto him my two sons to be bondmen.** In primitive communities, men borrowed upon their personal credit, and the primary security for debt was regarded as being their own persons, the value of their labour, and that of those dependent on them. In Greece and Rome, originally, as in the Hebrew community, borrowers ordinarily raised money by pledging their persons, and, if they could not pay when the debt became due, went into servitude with their children. The Mosaic Law presupposes this state of things, and permits its continuance, but in two respects interferes to modify it: (1) by requiring that the service exacted shall not be severe (Lev. xxv. 43, 46), but such as was commonly rendered by hired servants (Lev. xxv. 39, 40); and (2) by limiting the period of service to the date of the next jubilee year (Lev. xxv. 40, 41). In the instance brought here under our notice, it would seem that the creditor had not proceeded to claim his rights until the debtor died, when he enforced them against the man's children (comp. Neh. v. 1—8).

Ver. 2.—**And Elisha said unto her, What shall I do for thee?** Elisha acknowledges at once the call upon him to do something for the woman. This is, no doubt, in part, because she is a widow. Widows were, in the Law, especially commended to the attention and care of the faithful. As Bähr says, "It is a well-known feature of the Mosaic Law, one which is distinctly prominent, that it often and urgently commands to succour the widows and the fatherless, and to care for them (Exod. xxii. 22—24; Deut. xiv. 29; xxiv. 17, 19; xxvi. 12; xxvii. 19). They are mentioned as representatives of the forsaken, the oppressed, and the necessitous as a class (Isa. x. 2; Jer. vi. 6; xxii. 3; Zech. vii. 10; Mal. iii. 5; Baruch vi. 37). It is especially emphasized and praised in Jehovah, that he is the Father and Judge (*i.e.* Protector of the rights) of the widows and the fatherless (Deut. x. 18; Ps. lxviii. 5; cxlvi. 9; Isa. ix. 17, etc.). Neglect and contempt of them are counted among the heaviest offences (Ps. xciv. 6; Job xxii. 9; Ezek. xxii, 7); just as, on the other hand, compassion and care for them is a sign of the true fear of God, and of true piety (Job xxix. 12; xxxi. 16; Tobit i. 7; Jas. i. 27)." Elisha could also gather from the tone of the woman's address that she, like her late husband, was God-fearing. **Tell me, what hast thou in the house?** Hast thou anything, that is, which thou canst sell, and so pay the debt? **And she said, Thine handmaid hath not anything in the house, save a pot of oil;** literally, *save an anointing of oil;* i.e. so much oil as will suffice for one anointing of my person.

Ver. 3.—**Then he said, Go, borrow thee vessels abroad of all thy neighbours, even empty vessels; borrow not a few.** God stints not in his gifts (Isa. lv. 1). When he offers them, men should take advantage of the offer *largely*, in the same spirit in which it is made (see below, ch. xiii. 19).

Ver. 4.—**And when thou art come in, thou shalt shut the door upon thee and upon thy sons.** The miracle was to be performed secretly. Attention was not to be called to it—perhaps because otherwise the prophet would have been overwhelmed with applications

from others; perhaps because the act was not a mere mechanical one, but required that, during its performance, the hearts of the woman and of her sons should be lifted up in prayer and adoration and thankfulness to God for the mercy which he was bestowing. Interruption from without would have interfered with the frame of mind which was befitting the occasion. Compare our Lord's secret performance of many miracles. **And shalt pour out into all those vessels**—*i.e.* those which thou shalt have borrowed—**and thou shalt set aside that which is full;** *i.e.* as each vessel is filled, it shall be removed and set aside, and one of the empty vessels substituted—that the pouring might be continuous.

Ver. 5.—**So she went from him, and shut the door upon her and upon her sons**—*i.e.* obeyed exactly the prophet's orders—**who brought** the vessels to her; **and she poured out;** literally, *they bringing the vessels to her, and she pouring out.* The *modus operandi* had been left to the woman and her sons, and was thus arranged and ordered, so that there was no confusion nor hurry.

Ver. 6.—**And it came to pass, when the vessels were full, that she said unto her son, Bring me yet a vessel.** It did not occur to her that all the vessels had been already filled; so she asked her son for another, that she might fill it. **And he said unto her, There is not a vessel more;** *i.e.* all the vessels that we have in the house are full; there remains no empty one. **And the oil stayed.** God will not have waste. If the oil had continued to flow, it would have fallen on the floor of the house, and have been of no service to any one. Therefore, when all the vessels were full, there was a sudden stoppage.

Ver. 7.—**Then she came and told the man of God;** *i.e.* Elisha (comp. vers. 9, 16, 21, 22, etc.). She did not feel entitled to make use of the oil which she had got by his instrumentality without first telling him and receiving his directions respecting it. The prophet gave them with all plainness and brevity. **And he said, Go, sell the oil, and pay thy debt, and live thou and thy children of the rest.** The oil in the vessels was more than sufficient for the discharge of the debt. The prophet directs the woman to sell the whole, and, after satisfying the claim of her creditor with part of the money, to support herself and her children on the remainder.

Vers. 8—37.—2. *The promise of a child to the Shunammite woman, and the restoration of the child to life.*

Ver. 8.—**And it fell on a day, that.** The expression seems to be archaic. It occurs only here and in the opening chapters of the Book of Job (i. 6, 13; ii. 1). The most literal 'rendering would be, *and the day came when.* **Elisha passed to Shunem.** Shunem was a village of Galilee, situated in the territory assigned to Issachar (Josh. xix. 18). It is reasonably identified with the modern *Solam,* at the south-eastern foot of the Gebel Duhy, or "Little Hermon," a "flourishing village encompassed by gardens" (Porter), and "in the midst of the finest corn-fields in the world" (Grove), on the edge of the Plain of Esdraelon. Elisha, in his progression to different parts of the northern kingdom, happened to come on one occasion to Shunem. **Where was a great woman.** Houbigant strangely translates, "a *tall* woman," maintaining that a woman would not be called "great" in the sense of "wealthy" during her husband's lifetime; but no other commentator has accepted his view. The meaning seems to be that she was a woman of substance, one well-to-do, perhaps one that had brought her husband the bulk of his wealth. **And she constrained him to eat bread;** *i.e.* she invited him in as he passed her house, and would take no denial. Compare Lot's pressing hospitality, as related in Gen. xix. 1—3. **And so it was, that as oft as he passed by, he turned in thither to eat bread.** Elisha, it appears, had frequent occasion to pass through Shunem on his way from Carmel to visit the cities of Galilee, or *vice versâ.* It became his habit, on these journeys, to eat his meals at the house of the rich Shunammite. Hence arose a kindly feeling on both sides and a close intimacy.

Ver. 9.—**And she said unto her husband, Behold now, I perceive that this is an holy man of God.** Not all the *soi-disant* men of God were truly religious and God-fearing. In Elisha's time, as in all others, there were among the teachers of religion some who were "wolves in sheep's clothing." The Shunammite woman, after a certain length of acquaintance, came to the conclusion that Elisha deserved the title which he commonly bore, was truly a "man of God," a real devoted servant of Jehovah. She therefore wished to do more for him than she had hitherto done. **Which passeth by us continually;** *i.e.* who passes through our village, and has his meals with us so frequently.

Ver. 10.—**Let us make a little chamber, I pray thee, on the wall.** Thenius understands "a walled chamber," which he supposes to have been "built upon the flat roof of the house;" but it is more probable that a small addition to the existing upper chamber of the house is meant—a tiny room resting partly upon the wall of the house, partly projecting beyond it, balcony fashion. Such sleeping-chambers are common in Oriental dwellings. **And let us set for him**

there a bed, and a table, and a stool, and a candlestick; rather, *a bed, and a table, and a chair, and a lamp*—the necessary furniture of an apartment which was to be used, not only ; as a sleeping-chamber, but also for retirement, for study, and perhaps for literary composition. **And it shall be, when he cometh to us, that he shall turn in thither.** In the intervals between his active ministrations, a prophet would naturally desire quiet retirement, security from interruption. He would need to reflect, to meditate, to pray, perhaps to write. The Shunammite's proposal shows, not only kindness, but thoughtfulness and appreciation.

Ver. 11.—**And it fell on a day, that he came thither, and he turned into the chamber, and lay there;** *i.e.* slept there, passed the night there.

Ver. 12.—**And he said to Gehazi his servant.** Gehazi is here mentioned for the first time. He seems to have been Elisha's "servant" in a lower sense than Elisha had been Elijah's. Still, his position was such that on one occasion (ch. viii. 4, 5) a king of Israel did not disdain to hold a conversation with him. **Call this Shunammite. And when he had called her, she stood before him;** *i.e.* before Gehazi. Elisha communicates with the woman through his servant, or at any rate in his presence, probably to prevent any suspicion of impropriety arising in the mind of any one. The prophet of the Lord must not be evil spoken of.

Ver. 13.—**And he said unto him, Say now unto her, Behold, thou hast been careful** —literally, *anxious*—for us with all this care—or, *anxiety;* i.e. thou hast taken all this trouble in lodging both me and my servant, and in attending on us: what is to be done for thee ? or, *What is there that thou wouldest have done for thee ?* Is there anything that we can do for thee in return ? **Wouldest thou be spoken for to the king ?** Elisha assumes that he has credit at court, and offers to use it in the Shunammite's favour, if she has any request to prefer. We see something of his influence in ch. vi. 9—12, 21—23; viii. 4—6. **Or to the captain of the host ?** *i.e.* the person whose authority and influence was next to that of the king. **And she answered, I dwell among mine own people;** *i.e.* "The court is nothing to me. I want nothing from it. I have no wrong to complain of, no quarrel with any of my neighbours, so as to need the help of one in power. I dwell peaceably among them. They are 'my own people'—friends or dependents." The reply is that of one perfectly content with her position. Perhaps she aims at impressing on Elisha that she has had no selfish motive in what she has done for him, but has merely wished to honour God in his prophet.

Ver. 14.—**And he said**—he, Elisha, said to Gehazi—**What then is to be done for her?** If the woman will suggest nothing herself, can Gehazi suggest anything? Has he heard her express any wish? Does he know of any boon that would be welcome to her? Evidently the woman's disinterestedness has increased the prophet's desire to do something for her. **And Gehazi answered, Verily she hath no child, and her husband is old.** It does not appear that the woman had made any complaint or exhibited any special anxiety on the subject of offspring. But Gehazi knows· that to be barren is regarded by all Hebrew women as a reproach, that it exposes them to scorn and contumely (1 Sam. i. 6, 7), and that offspring is universally, or all but universally, desired. He therefore assumes that the Shunammite must wish for it. And Elisha accepts his suggestion without a moment's hesitation.

Ver. 15.—**And he said, Call her. And when he had called her, she stood in the door;** rather, *the doorway.* The same word in Hebrew stands both for "doorway" and for "door." It would seem that the woman came at once on being called, but, out of modesty and respect, would not advance beyond the entrance of the apartment.

Ver. 16.—**And he** — *i.e.* Elisha — **said, About this season, according to the time of life**—rather, *when the time comes round;* literally, *revives;* i.e. about this time next year—**thou shalt embrace a son;** *i.e.* "a son shall be born to thee, whom thou wilt embrace, as mothers are wont to do." **And she said, Nay, my lord, thou man of God, do not lie unto thine handmaid.** Like Sarah, the woman was incredulous; she could not believe the good tidings, and thought the prophet was only raising hopes to disappoint them. Her words, "Do not lie unto thy servant," are less harsh in the original, being merely equivalent to the "Do not deceive me" of ver. 28.

Ver. 17.—**And the woman conceived, and bare a son at that season that Elisha had said unto her, according to the time of life;** rather, as the Revised Version gives the passage, *the woman conceived, and bare a son at that season, when the time came round, as Elisha had said unto her.* The event was exactly as predicted; the child was born at the same season of the ensuing year.

Ver. 18.—**And when the child was grown** —not grown *up,* for he was still a "child" (vers. 30, 31, 35, etc.), but grown to be a boy, perhaps four or five years old—it fell **on a day, that he went out to his father to the reapers.** The corn-fields about Shunem attract the admiration of travellers. The husband of the Shunammite, the owner of several, was in one of them, superintending the cutting of his corn by the reapers; and

the boy joined him there, as he had probably often done before. Country children delight in watching the various operations of the farmstead.

Ver. 19.—**And he said unto his father, My head, my head.** Sunstroke was common in Palestine (Ps. cxxi. 6; Isa. xlix. 10; Judith viii. 2, 3), and would be most frequent and most fatal at the time of harvest. The cry of the child is at once most touching and most natural. **And he said to a lad;** literally, *to the lad*—probably *the* lad who had attended the "young master" to the field. **Carry him to his mother;** *i.e.* take him indoors, and let his mother see to him. No wiser directions could have been given.

Ver. 20.—**And when he had taken him, and brought him to his mother, he sat on her knees till noon.** It was in the morning, therefore, that the child received his sunstroke—an unusual, but not an unknown, occurrence. In the East the sun often becomes intensely hot by ten o'clock. **And** then **died.** There is no ambiguity here, no room for doubt; the child not only became insensible, but *died.* The historian could not possibly have expressed himself more plainly.

Ver. 21.—**And she went up, and laid him on the bed of the man of God.** One cannot be certain what thoughts were working in the poor bereaved mother's heart; but probably she entertained some vague notion that the prophet might be able to resuscitate her child, and thought that, until his presence could be obtained, the next best thing was to place the child where the prophet's presence had lately been. Elijah had placed on his own bed the child whom he restored to life (1 Kings xvii. 19); and the fact may have been known to the Shunammite. She certainly did not expect mere contact with the bed to resuscitate her child. **And shut the door upon him.** Either that the body should not be disturbed, or rather that the death should not be known. It is clear that, from whatever motive, the woman wished to conceal the death of the child until she had seen what Elisha could do for her. She neither told her husband nor the servant who accompanied her. **And went out;** *i.e.* quitted the prophet's apartment, closing the door as she quitted it.

Ver. 22.—**And she called unto her husband, and said, Send me, I pray thee, one of the young men, and one of the asses.** She "called to her husband" from the house, without calling him into the house, expressing her desire to visit Elisha, without stating the object of her visit, and asked for the necessary riding-animal and escort. The nearest part of Carmel was at least fourteen or fifteen miles from Shunem, so that she could not walk. **That I may run**—*i.e.* hasten

—to the man of God. "Man of God" was evidently the designation by which Elisha was known in the house (vers. 16, 21, 25). And come again; i.e. return home before nightfall.

Ver. 23.—And he said, Wherefore wilt thou go to him to-day? it is neither new moon nor sabbath. The husband demurred; he saw no occasion for the journey. It was not either "new moon" or "sabbath" —times when evidently the prophets conducted services, which were attended by pious persons from the neighbourhood: what could she want of Elisha? He had evidently no idea that the child was dead. Probably he had not realized to himself that he was in any danger. And she said, It shall be well. She uttered the single word shalôm, literally, "peace," but used, like the German gut, or the English "all right," to content an inquirer without giving him a definite answer. And the husband accepted her assurance, and did not press for an explanation. The ass and the servant were placed at her disposal without more words.

Ver. 24.—Then she saddled an ass; rather, then she saddled (i.e. "caused to be saddled") the ass—the particular animal which her husband had placed at her disposal. And said to her servant, Drive, and go forward; i.e. "set the ass in motion, and then proceed steadily forward." In the East, each donkey has its driver, who sets it in motion, and regulates its pace. The rider leaves all to him. Slack not thy riding for me—rather, slacken me not the riding (Revised Version), or, slacken not my riding; i.e. "do not lessen the pace of my riding"—except I bid thee.

Ver. 25.—So she went and came unto the man of God to Mount Carmel. Carmel was to Elisha what Gilead had been to Elijah in his early days—a place for solitary retirement and meditation, where, free from disturbance, he might hold communion with nature and with God. It was not usual for his disciples to intrude upon him there, except at stated times, when gatherings were held at his residence for edification and for worship. And it came to pass, when the man of God saw her afar off—literally, over against him; i.e. coming towards him (ἐρχομένην, LXX.)—that he said to Gehazi his servant, Behold, yonder is that Shunammite. The prophet knew her at a distance, probably by her attire and carriage. We may gather, from her husband's words in ver. 23, that she was one of those who had been accustomed to attend the gatherings on new moons and sabbaths.

Ver. 26.—Run now, I pray thee, to meet her, and say unto her, Is it well with thee? is it well with thy husband? is it well with the child? Elisha feels that there must

be something the matter, to account for the Shunammite's coming to him so unexpectedly. His anxiety is aroused, and, in his impatience to know what has happened, instead of waiting for the woman's arrival, he bids his servant run, and ask what is the matter. Some misfortune, he supposes, must have happened either to her, or to her husband, or to the child. And she answered, It is well. She gave, as before to her husband (ver. 23), the ambiguous answer, "Peace," intending thereby merely to put off Gehazi, and not explain herself to any one but his master.

Ver. 27.—And when she came to the man of God to the hill—rather, the mountain; i.e. Carmel, where Elisha's residence was— she caught him by the feet (comp. Matt. xviii. 29; Mark v. 22; vii. 25; Luke viii. 41; John xi. 32). It has always been usual in the East to embrace the feet or the knees, in order to add force to supplication. But Gehazi came near to thrust her away. He regarded the act as one unduly familiar or unduly importunate, and interfered to protect and release his master. And the man of God said, Let her alone; for her soul is vexed within her. Elisha would not have the woman disturbed. He saw that she was in deep distress, and, if there was anything unseemly in her action according to the etiquette of the time, excused it to her profound grief and distraction. The ordinary mind is a slave to conventionalities; the superior mind knows when to be above them. And the Lord hath hid it from me, and hath not told me. God had not informed Elisha, by inward miraculous illumination, of the illness of the child, or its death, or the wild hopes stirring in the afflicted mother's mind, which induced her to make her long and troublesome journey. We need not feel surprised at this. There is always a limit to the miraculous; and facts that may be learnt by a little inquiry are but rarely communicated supernaturally.

Ver. 28.—Then she said, Did I desire a son of my lord? did I not say, Do not deceive me? The woman does not directly reveal her grief. Great sorrow is reticent, cannot endure to put itself into words. But she sufficiently indicates the nature of her trouble by the form of her reproach. "Did I ask for a son? Did I make complaint of my childlessness? Had I been importunate, and obtained my son of thee by much asking, I would not have complained. But I did not ask. I did not even snatch greedily at the offer. I demurred. I said, 'Do not deceive me.' But now thou hast done worse than deceive me. Thou hast kept the word of promise to the ear, and broken it to the hope. It is greater misery to have a child and lose him, than never to have had one at all." All this, and more, seems to be involved in the woman's words. And the prophet fully understood their meaning.

Ver. 29.—**Then he said to Gehazi, Gird up thy loins, and take my staff in thine hand, and go thy way: if thou meet any man, salute him not; and if any salute thee, answer him not again.** The object of all these injunctions is haste. Lose not a moment. Go as quickly as thou canst to the house where the child lies. Spend no time in greetings on the way. Slack not. Tarry not. **And lay my staff upon the face of the child.** What effect the prophet expected from this act, we are not told. Gehazi appears to have expected that it would at once cause a resuscitation (ver. 31); but there is no evidence that the prophet participated in the expectation. He may have done so, for prophets are not infallible beyond the sphere of the revelations made to them; but he may only have intended to comfort and cheer the mother, and to raise in her an expectation of the resuscitation which he trusted it would be allowed him to effect.

Ver. 30.—**And the mother of the child said, As the Lord liveth, and as thy soul liveth** (comp. ch. ii. 2, 4, 6), **I will not leave thee.** Apparently, the woman supposed that Elisha intended to do nothing more, but trust the child's recovery to such virtue as might inhere in his staff. But her own resolution was long ago taken—she would be content with nothing less than bringing the prophet face to face with her dead child. She "will not leave" him till he consents to accompany her to her home. **And he arose, and followed her;** as, no doubt, he had intended from the first.

Ver. 31.—**And Gehazi passed on before them, and laid the staff on the face of the child; but there was neither voice, nor hearing.** Gehazi did as he had been told, executed his mission faithfully; but there was no apparent result. The child was not roused by the staff being placed across his face. All remained still and silent as before. Although on some occasions it has pleased God to allow miracles to be wrought by the instrumentality of lifeless objects, as when Elisha's bones resuscitated a dead man (ch. xiii. 21), and when virtue went out from the hem of our Lord's garment (Mark v. 25—34), and still more remarkably, when "handkerchiefs or aprons from the body of Paul were brought unto the sick, and the diseases departed from them, and the evil spirits were cast out of them" (Acts xix. 12); yet the instances are, comparatively speaking, rare, and form exceptions to what may be called the usual Divine economy of miracles. Miracles are, as a general rule, attached in Scripture

to intense unwavering faith—faith, sometimes, in those that are the objects of them, almost always in those that are the workers of them. The present case was not to be an exception to the general rule, the circumstances not calling for an exception. The power of faith was to be shown forth once more in Elisha, as not long previously in Elijah (1 Kings xvii. 19—23); and Israel was to be taught, by a second marvellous example, how much the effectual fervent prayer of a faithful and righteous man avails with the Most High. The lesson would have been lost had the staff been allowed to effect the resuscitation. Wherefore he—*i.e.* Gehazi—**went again to meet him**—*i.e.* Elisha—**and told him, saying, The child is not waked.** It is clear from this, that Gehazi had expected an awakening; but there is nothing to show what the prophet himself had expected. We are certainly not entitled to conclude, with Peter Martyr, that "Elisha did wrong in attempting to delegate his power of working miracles to another;" or even, with Starke, that "Elisha gave the command to Gehazi from overhaste, without having any Divine incentive to it."

Ver. 32.—**And when Elisha was come into the house, behold, the child was dead, and laid upon his bed** (comp. ver. 21). The child remained where his mother had laid him.

Ver. 33.—**He went in therefore, and shut the door upon them twain**—that he might not be interrupted during his efforts to restore the child's life (comp. ver. 4)—**and prayed unto the Lord.** Probably his heart had been lifted up in inarticulate prayer from the time that he realized the calamity which had befallen the Shunammite; but now he went down on his knees, and lifted up his voice in outspoken words of prayer.

Ver. 34.—**And he went up, and lay upon the child, and put his mouth upon his mouth, and his eyes upon his eyes, and his hands upon his hands;** following the example set him by his master and predecessor, Elijah (1 Kings xvii. 21). The idea may in both cases have been to fit the body for reinhabitation by the soul (see ver. 22), through the restoration of warmth to it. **And he stretched himself upon the child;** *i.e.* brought his flesh as close as he could to the flesh of the child, covering the body and pressing on it, to force his own bodily warmth to pass into it. The word used, וַיִּגְהַר, is different from that in 1 Kings xvii. 21, which is יִתְמֹדֵד, and implies a closer contact. **And the flesh of the child waxed warm.** Elisha's efforts had an effect; the child's body was actually warmed by them.

Ver. 35.—**Then he returned, and walked in the house to and fro;** literally, *once to* *and once fro;* took, *i.e.,* a single turn up and down the large room adjoining his bed-chamber—scarcely with any remedial object, but as men do when they are in distress and doubt. **And went up, and stretched himself upon him**—*i.e.* repeated his former act, laying himself upon the child, and warming it—**and the child sneezed seven times**—showing the recovery of suspended respiration—**and the child opened his eyes;** *i.e.* came to himself.

Ver. 36.—**And he called Gehazi, and said, Call this Shunammite;** *i.e.* tell her to come here. No time was to be lost in restoring the child to his mother, now that he was alive again. **And when she was come in unto him, he said, Take up thy son;** *i.e.* lift him up, take him in thine arms, feel him to be all thine own once more.

Ver. 37.—**Then she went in, and fell at his feet, and bowed herself to the ground;** in acknowledgment of the boon conferred on her. In the East such prostrations are common, and denote at once gratitude and humility. **And took up her son, and went out.** (On some later circumstances in the life of the woman, see ch. viii. 1—6.)

Vers. 38—41.—3. *The healing of the unwholesome pottage.*

Ver. 38.—**And Elisha came again to Gilgal;** *i.e.* revisited Gilgal, where he had been previously with his master (ch. ii. 1), either casually, or perhaps on one of his regular circuits (Keil) to visit the schools of the prophets. **And there was a dearth in the land**—probably the dearth again mentioned in ch. viii. 1—**and the sons of the prophets** were **sitting before him.** Some translate "the sons of the prophets *dwelt with him*" (Vulgate, Luther, Bishop Horsley); but our version is probably correct. The LXX. give ἐκάθηντο; and Ezek. viii. 1; xvi. 1; xxxiii. 31; with Zech. iii. 8, show that שבים לפני may have the meaning of "sitting in the presence of a person." **And he said unto his servant, Set on the great pot**—*i.e. the one* great pot that there would be in the house—**and seethe pottage for the sons of the prophets.** Even in a famine there would be some vegetables produced on which life might be sustained.

Ver. 39.—**And one went out into the field to gather herbs.** One of the sons of the prophets, probably, went out into the neighbouring country, and looked about for any wild fruits or vegetables that he could see anywhere. **And found a wild vine.** Not a wild grape vine (*Vitis labrusca*), the fruit of which would have been harmless, but some cucurbitaceous plant, with tendrils, and a growth like that of the vine. **And gathered thereof wild gourds.** The exact kind of gourd is uncertain. Recent critics

have mostly come to the conclusion that the vegetable intended is the *Cucumis agrestis* or *Ecbalium elaterium,* the "squirting cucumber" of English naturalists. This is a kind of gourd, the fruit of which is egg-shaped, has a bitter taste, and bursts when ripe at a slight touch, squirting out sap and seeds. The main ground for this conclusion is etymological, פקעת being derived from פקע, "to crack" or "split." Another theory, and one which has the ancient versions in its favour, identifies the "gourd" in question with the fruit of the colocynth, which is a gourd-like plant that creeps along the ground, and has a round yellow fruit of the size of a large orange. This fruit is exceedingly bitter, produces colic, and affects the nerves. **His lap full;** as many as he could carry in the *sinus,* or large fold, of his *beged,* or shawl. **And came and shred them into the pot of pottage: for they knew** them **not;** *i.e.* the sons of the prophets, who stood by and saw them shred into the pot, did not recognize them, or did not know that they were unwholesome.

Ver. 40.—**So they poured out for the men to eat. And it came to pass, as they were eating of the pottage, that they cried out and said, O thou man of God, there is death in the pot.** Either the bitter flavour alarmed them, or they began to feel ill effects from what they had swallowed, which, if it was colocynth, might very soon have produced stomach-ache or nausea. Rushing, therefore, at once to the worst possible supposition, they concluded that they were poisoned, and exclaimed, "O man of God, there is death in the pot!" "If eaten in any large quantity," says Keil, "colocynths might really produce death." **And they could not eat thereof;** *i.e.* they could not continue to eat the pottage—all stopped eating.

Ver. 41.—**But he said, Then bring meal.** Elisha seems not to have hesitated for a moment. Prompt measures must be taken, if poisoning is even suspected. He has meal brought—not that meal has any virtue in itself against colocynth, or against any other deleterious drug. But he acts, now as always, under Divine direction, and is instructed to use meal on this occasion, as he used salt in healing the waters of Jericho. The meal, as Keil observes, "might somewhat modify the bitterness and injurious qualities of the vegetable," whatever it was, but "could not possibly take them entirely away. . . . The meal, the most wholesome food of man, was only the earthly substratum for the working of the Divine effluence which proceeded from Elisha, and made the noxious food perfectly wholesome." **And he cast it into the pot; and he said, Pour out now for the people**—*i.e.* the assembled company of sons of the prophets—**that they** may eat. And there was no harm in the pot. Such as had faith in Elisha, and continued to eat of the pottage, found no ill result. What they ate did them no harm.

Vers. 42—44.—4. *The feeding of a hundred men on twenty loaves.*

Ver. 42.—**And there came a man from Baal-shalisha.** "Baal-shalisha" is reasonably identified with the "Beth-shalisha" of Eusebius and Jerome, which they place twelve Roman miles north of Diospolis, or Lydda (now Ludd). By "north" we must probably understand "north-east," since the "land of Shalisha" lay between the territories of Ephraim and Benjamin (1 Sam. ix. 4). The position thus indicated would not be very far from the Gilgal (*Jiljilieh*) of ch. ii. and iv. 38. **And brought the man of God bread of the firstfruits.** It is clear that the more pious among the Israelites not only looked to the prophets for religious instruction (ver. 23), but regarded them as having inherited the position of the Levitical priests whom Jeroboam's innovations had driven from the country. The firstfruits of corn, wine, and oil were assigned by the Law (Numb. xviii. 13 ; Deut. xviii. 4, 5) to the priests. **Twenty loaves of barley.** The "loaves" of the Israelites were cakes or rolls, rather than "loaves" in the modern sense of the word. Each partaker of a meal usually had one for himself. Naturally, twenty "loaves" would be barely sufficient for twenty men. **And full ears of corn ;** *i.e.* a few ripe ears of the same corn as that whereof the bread was made. Ears of corn were offered as firstfruits at the Passover (Lev. xxiii. 10), and were regarded as the most natural and becoming tokens of gratitude for God's harvest mercies. **In the husk thereof ;** rather, *in his bag,* or *in his sack* (see the Revised Version). And he said, Give unto the people—*i.e.* to the sons of the prophets who dwelt at Gilgal—that they may eat.

Ver. 43.—**And his servitor said, What, should I set this before an hundred men ?** The servant felt that the quantity was quite insufficient, and thought it absurd to invite a hundred men to sit down to a meal which would not satisfy a fifth of the number; but Elisha repeated his command. **He said again, Give the people, that they may eat.** This time, however, he added an explanation of the proceeding: for thus saith the Lord, They shall eat, and shall leave thereof. God had supernaturally intimated to him that the quantity of food would prove ample for the hundred men ; they would show that they had had enough by leaving some of it. And the result was as predicted.

Ver. 44.—**So he set it before them, and they did eat, and left thereof, according to the word of the Lord.** We are not expressly told how the miracle was wrought, whether by an augmentation of the quantity of the food supernaturally produced, or by a lessening of the appetites of the men, as Bähr supposes. But the analogy of our Lord's miracles of feeding the multitudes, whereof this is a manifest type, makes it probable that in this case also there was a miraculous increase of the food. The object of the writer in communicating the account is certainly not merely to show how the Lord cared for his servants, but to relate another miracle wrought by Elisha, of a different kind from those previously related. He is occupied with Elisha's miracles through this entire chapter and through the three next.

HOMILETICS.

Vers. 1—7.—*The seed of the righteous never forsaken by God.* The whole ground of appeal on which the poor widow relies, and which proves so entirely adequate, is the fidelity to God of her deceased husband. "Thy servant my husband is dead ; and thou knowest that thy servant did fear the Lord" (ver. 1). She assumes that Elisha is on this account almost bound to interfere on behalf of the man's two sons, who are in danger of being carried into slavery. And Elisha allows the validity of her claim, and straightway comes to their relief. The example may well recall the emphatic words of the psalmist, which the minister and director cannot too strongly impress on anxious and doubting mothers, "I have been young, and now am old; and yet saw I never the righteous forsaken, nor his seed begging their bread" (Ps. xxxvii. 25). A blessing rests upon the seed of the righteous—

I. BY DIVINE PROMISE. "I the Lord thy God am a jealous God, visiting the iniquity of the fathers upon the children unto the third and fourth generation of them that hate me ; and *showing mercy unto thousands of them that love* me, and keep my commandments" (Exod. xx. 5, 6); "The mercy of the Lord is *from everlasting to everlasting* upon them that fear him, and his righteousness *unto children's children*" (Ps.

ciii. 17); "The children of thy servants shall continue, and their seed shall be established before thee" (Ps. cii. 28).

II. BY THE SYMPATHY INVOLVED IN GOD'S FATHERHOOD. After God all fatherhood (πᾶσα πατρία) in heaven and earth is named (Eph. iii. 15). As a Father, he sympathizes with all fathers, knows their hearts, understands their longings, is tender towards their tenderness. Them that love him he will love, and will reward them where they would most wish to be rewarded, in their children. The seed of the righteous may often, does often, wander into devious ways, depart from righteousness, provoke God, draw down upon himself God's chastisements; but in the end how seldom does he wholly fall away, completely forget the lessons of his youth, the example of godly parents, the precepts so carefully instilled into his mind in early life, day by day and year by year! how seldom does he become a blasphemer, or an unbeliever, or an utterly hardened reprobate! How often, on the other hand, does he recover from grievous falls, returns to God, repent, amend, and "do the first works"! God's tender care not only saves the children of the righteous from begging their bread, or falling into utter destitution, but watches over their spiritual welfare, and in a thousand ways checks their wanderings, weans them from their evil courses, and at last brings them to himself.

Vers. 8—37.—*Godliness has, to a large extent, the promise of this life, as well as of the life to come.* The "good Shunammite" and her husband are examples of the union, which is more common than men are apt to allow, between piety and prosperity. They have nothing heroic about them, nothing out of the common. They are substantial middle-class people, dwelling in a quiet country-side, farming on a moderate scale, with a comfortable house of their own, dwelling contentedly amid their labourers and their country neighbours. But they are not rendered selfish or worldly minded by their prosperity. They feel and admit the claims of religion upon them. In Elisha they recognize a "man of God;" first, it would seem, officially. As the official representative to them of the Most High, they regard him as entitled to kindness and hospitality. They press upon him their good offices, insist on his taking his meals with them, "constrain him to eat bread" (ver. 8). When by degrees they have become acquainted with his character, they recognize in him something more—they "perceive that he is a *holy* man of God" (ver. 9). Like is perceived by like. It takes some holiness to perceive and recognize holiness. And the perception raises a desire for greater intimacy. Like desires like. It will be a blessed thing if they can persuade the prophet, not merely to take an occasional meal in their house, but to be an occasional inmate—to rest there, to sleep there. So the woman proposes to her husband to build the prophet a sleeping-chamber; and he readily consents, apparently without a murmur (ver. 10). He is neither jealous, nor stingy, nor ill-natured. The woman has her way, and her kindly nature is gratified by the frequent presence of the godly man, whose ministrations she attends on sabbaths and holy days (ver. 23). And now her piety, which has been wholly disinterested, receives an earthly reward. The disgrace of barrenness is, at the prophet's intercession, removed from her, and she obtains the blessing of offspring. Nay, more. Though death removes her offspring, he is restored to her, rendered doubly precious by having seemed to be for ever lost. The well-deserved prosperity of herself and husband culminates in this happy restoration, which puts the finishing touch to the earthly bliss that had lacked only this crowning joy. And so it is in life generally. Not only the proud and ungodly, but the godly also, are "rewarded after their deserving" (Ps. xciv. 2). Many virtues, *e.g.* honesty, sobriety, industry, prudence, have a natural tendency to draw to their possessor a considerable share of this world's goods; as the opposite vices, dishonesty, drunkenness, idleness, imprudence, have a natural tendency to disperse such goods when possessed and prevent their accumulation. Goodness, on the whole, secures the respect and esteem of other men, and the respect and esteem of our fellows tends in various ways to our worldly advantage. Men place more trust in the godly than in the ungodly, and situations of trust are, for the most part, situations of profit. Nor must we omit the consideration of the Divine blessing, which always rests upon the godly, in fact, and is sometimes openly manifested. "The eyes of the Lord are upon the righteous, and his ears are open unto their cry: but the face of the Lord is against them that do evil" (Ps. xxxiv. 15, 16); "No good thing will God withhold from them that walk uprightly" (Ps. lxxxiv. 11).

And the entire result is that, upon the whole, even in this life, right conduct, goodness, piety, have the advantage over their opposites, and that happiness and misery are distributed, even here, very much "according to men's deserving"—not, of course, without exceptions, even numerous exceptions—but still predominantly, so that the law holds good as a general one, that "godliness hath the promise of this life." Our blessed Lord went so far as to say, "There is *no man* that hath left house, or brethren, or sisters, or father, or mother, or wife, or children, or lands, for my sake, and the gospel's, but he shall receive an hundredfold *now in this time*, houses, and brethren, and sisters, and mothers, and children, and lands, with persecutions; and in the world to come eternal life" (Mark x. 29, 30).

Vers. 27—31.—*Limits to inspiration.* Many men seem to suppose that the prophetical inspiration, the Divine *afflatus*, whatever it was, which God vouchsafed in times past to his prophets, apostles, and evangelists, was absolutely unlimited—a sort of omniscience, at any rate omniscience on all those subjects on which they spoke or wrote. But Scripture lends no sanction to this supposition. "Let her alone," says Elisha to Gehazi; "for her soul is vexed within her: *and the Lord hath hid it from me*, and *hath not told me*" (ver. 27). Ignorance of the future would also seem to underlie the instructions given to Gehazi in ver. 29. And there are, in point of fact, limitations to every prophet's knowledge even with respect to the things concerning which he writes or speaks. "Now, behold," says St. Paul, "I go bound in the spirit unto Jerusalem, *not knowing* the things that shall befall me there" (Acts xx. 22). And again, "Now concerning virgins *I have no commandment of the Lord*: yet I give my judgment, as one that hath obtained mercy of the Lord to be faithful" (1 Cor. vii. 25). The apostles spoke much of the coming of Christ to judgment, but "of that day and of that hour knoweth no man" (Matt. xxiv. 36). Prophetic knowledge was always partial, limited. To Isaiah the return from Babylon, the establishment of Christ's kingdom upon earth, and the final triumph of Christianity, were blended together into a single vision of glory from which the chronological idea was absent. Ezekiel probably did not know whether the temple which he described (xl.—xliv.) was to be spiritual or material. Zechariah knew that a day would come when there would be "a fountain opened to the house of David and to the inhabitants of Jerusalem for sin and for uncleanness;" but the nature of the fountain was, apparently, not revealed to him. The prophets always "saw through a glass darkly," "knew in part" and prophesied in part; had not even a full knowledge of the meaning of their own words. We must therefore not look in the inspired writings for an exactness and accuracy and completeness to which they make no pretence; we must not claim infallibility for the *obiter dicta* of apostles or evangelists; we must not be surprised at occasional slips of memory, as the quotation of "Jeremy" for "Zachary" (Matt. xxvii. 9), or at little discrepancies, as the various readings of the title on the cross, or at other similar imperfections. The Divine element in Scripture does not exclude the presence also of a human element; and the human element cannot but show traces of human weakness, human ignorance, human frailty. The trifling errors that a microscopic criticism points out in the sacred volume no more interfere with its illuminating power, than do the spots seen by astronomers on its surface interfere with the light of the sun, or slight flaws with the magnificence and splendour of a unique diamond. The Bible is God's Word, the most precious treasure that man possesses, even although it be true that "we have this treasure in earthen vessels" (2 Cor. iv. 7).

HOMILIES BY VARIOUS AUTHORS.

Vers. 1—7.—*The widow's oil increased.* This simple and touching story is one of those many narratives which make the Bible a book for every one, and a book for everyday life. The individual is never lost in the nation or the race. It is so in actual fact. Our own personal needs and struggles and anxieties are of more importance and interest to us than the struggles of a nation or the general well-being of the human race. It is the same in the Bible. The Bible is partly a history of nations, and particularly of the Jewish nation. But it is much more a history of individuals.

It is this that makes it such a book of universal comfort and instruction. We can all find something in it that suits ourselves. As we read of the men and women whose lives are recorded in it, we learn more from their faith and their failings, from their temptations and their victories, than we could from any abstract discourses about the benefit of virtue and the evil of vice. We learn that they were men and women of like passions with ourselves. We learn that the temptations they conquered we can conquer by the help of the same Spirit; that the trials they endured we can endure; and that the faith and holiness to which they attained are within our reach also. And then how homely and how practical the Bible is! Its heroes and heroines do not live in a Utopia. It shows them to us under very much the same conditions as we live under still. It shows them to us in their homes and at their business, in their loves and in their married life, at the plough and in the fishing-boat, at the marriage-feast and at the funeral. Perhaps we think it hard to be religious in our business, in society, or amid the petty cares and worries of our daily life. The Bible shows us men and women living under the same conditions, and yet living so much in the fear of God and the presence of eternity that they triumphed over their distractions, and, whilst in the world, were not of it. Such a glimpse of everyday life we obtain in the narrative before us. We learned some valuable lessons from the palace of King Ahaziah; we may learn quite as important ones from the humble home of a prophet's widow.

I. INNOCENT SUFFERING. There is a good deal of suffering in the world. Many suffer *innocently*. But not all those who think they suffer innocently are really innocent. Here, however, there appears to be a case of really innocent suffering. It is a poor widow who comes to tell Elisha her tale of want and woe. Her husband had been one of "the sons of the prophets"—a word that was used in a general sense to signify those who were pupils of the prophets, trained by the prophets. He had unfortunately got into debt. How he was led into it we are not told. He was a God-fearing man. It was not, therefore, through dissipation or sin. But it may have been through his own imprudence or improvidence. Or it may have been through some unexpected loss, or through failure on the part of others to meet their liabilities to him. At any rate, he died in debt, and his poor widow is the sufferer. 1. This incident, and there are many like it happening every day, *shows us the folly and danger of getting into debt.* One of the worst features of it is that so often the innocent—the wife or children who perhaps know nothing at all of the debt—have to suffer for the folly or the dishonesty of others. We need to have a more awakened conscience on this subject of using money which really is not our own. As a matter of worldly policy and prudence, it is a great mistake. As a matter of morality, it is very doubtful indeed. How many of the tremendous crashes which have taken place in the commercial world are the result of men living beyond their means! They made too large demands upon the future. They incurred liabilities which they had no means of meeting. And in many cases debt proves to be a temptation to dishonesty. I have yet to learn the difference between the dishonesty of the man who gets a month's imprisonment for a petty theft, and the dishonesty of many who are legally protected in their crime by the strange device of the bankruptcy court. Not that every bankrupt is dishonest. But many who are thus protected are. We want a clearer and a cleaner public conscience on this question of debt. 2. *There is a word here also for creditors.* The creditor in this story was a regular Shylock. He wanted his pound of flesh. He would be satisfied with nothing less. Mark the utter heartlessness and cruelty of the man. He knew the poor widow was unable to pay. There were no goods and chattels that he could seize, or none worth seizing, so he actually came to make her two sons his slaves. Even the slightest touch of humanity might have led him to content himself with *one* of the sons. He might have left the other to be the solace and support of his widowed mother. But no. There is no mercy, no pity, in his hard and selfish heart. He must have the two sons to satisfy his claim. Now, the Scripture, while it countenances lending to those who are in want, and while it commands the payment of debts, recommends the exercise of mercy and humanity in exacting this payment. For instance, in Exodus it is said, " Ye shall not afflict any widow, or fatherless child. If thou afflict them in any wise, and they cry at all unto me, I will surely hear their cry; and my wrath shall wax hot, and I will kill you with the sword; and your wives shall be widows, and your children fatherless" (Exod. xxii. 22—24). And in Deut. xxiv. 17 we have a similar command. We learn here in all the relationships of life to mingle mercy with justice. Too often in the keen competition of life, and in the race for wealth, the finer feelings become blunted. If you are a Christian, it is your duty to imitate the spirit and precepts of Jesus. Whether you are a Christian or not, you are responsible to God for the way you act towards your fellow-men. Always consider the circumstances of the case. Where it is possible, be specially careful of the widow and the fatherless and the orphan. God has a special care for them, and he will avenge their cause on the persecutor and the oppressor.

II. ACTIVE FAITH. The poor widow had nothing in her house save a pot of oil. She was not as well off as the widow of Zarephath, to whom Elijah came; she had not even a handful of meal in the barrel. The olive oil was used as butter with the flour or meal. Dr. Kitto says it is indeed a remarkable fact that poor people in Israel, who are reduced to the last extremity, have generally a little oil left. Yet in this extremity, with this jar of oil as her sole possession, what does the prophet tell her to do? To go and borrow empty vessels of all her neighbours, and to borrow just as many as she could get. Was it not a strange command? *Empty* vessels! Why not borrow *vessels with something in them?* No; for that would have been to get deeper into debt. *Empty* vessels. The fact of bringing empty vessels into her house implied that she had something to fill them with. *This just shows the greatness of the woman's faith.* She trusted God's prophet. She knew that he would not deceive her or bid her do anything for which there was not a good reason. She trusted God's power. She knew that God was able, in his own way and in his own time, to supply all her need. We need to learn a similar faith. *We need it for our temporal affairs.* We need to trust God that he can and will and does supply the daily wants of his people. What though the purse is empty? God can send the means to fill it.

> "It may not be my time;
> It may not be thy time;
> But yet in his own time the Lord will provide."

We need to learn similar faith—a faith that shows itself not in idleness but in action—*in regard to spiritual things.* We may see but empty vessels before us. God is able to fill them. He does it very often by making us labourers together with him, as he did in this case of the widow and her sons. A respected Sunday-school teacher tells that when he first went to teach in a mission Sunday school in one of our large cities, he said to the superintendent, "Where is my class?" He could see no class for him to teach. The superintendent's answer was, "You'll have to go out and gather a class." He did so, and soon had a large and attentive class of lads gathered in by his own exertions from the streets. Don't you know of any empty vessels that would be better if they were filled with the love of Christ and the grace of God? Are there no empty vessels in your own homes? Are there no empty vessels round about you where you live— hearts that are without God and without hope, lives that are utterly destitute of any aims or usefulness? If you know of such, will you not try to bring them under the influence of the gospel? *This woman showed a strong faith, for she had doubtless to face the ridicule and difficulties and questionings of her neighbours.* They probably laughed at a woman borrowing vessels when she had nothing to fill them with. We must learn not to mind what people will say of us when we are doing God's work. There are some people who object to everything. There are some people who are always raising difficulties. Those who raise the difficulties and make the objections are generally those who do the least and give the least. Never mind them. Make sure that your work is God's work. Consider it prayerfully and carefully before you undertake it. And then, having made sure that it is God's work, so far as you can get light upon your path, turn not aside to the right hand or to the left. Trust in God to carry you and your work safely through, and to crown your labours with success. "The fear of man bringeth a snare; but he that putteth his trust in the Lord shall be safe."

III. ABUNDANT BLESSING. The woman was well rewarded for her unquestioning faith. So long as she continued pouring from her little jar of oil, so long the oil continued to flow until all the vessels were full. She could have filled more vessels if she had had them. But when there were no more vessels to be filled, the oil ceased to flow. At any rate she had enough to sell for the payment of her debt, and to provide herself and her sons with a temporary support. We learn here that *our blessings may be limited by our capacity to receive.* There is no limit to God's love. There is no limit to his power to bless. He gives in overflowing measure, far beyond our expectations, far beyond our deservings. But then we may stint the blessing for ourselves by not being in a fit state to receive it. We see constantly in Scripture and in the history of the Christian Church that there are certain conditions under which larger spiritual blessings may be expected, and certain conditions which may hinder these blessings. 1. *We may hinder our blessings by want of faith and expectation.* Had Abraham persevered in prayer, he might have won the salvation of Sodom even on account of righteous Lot alone. On a later occasion Elisha was displeased with King Joash for his want of faith in shooting the arrows. The king only smote thrice upon the ground, and Elisha said, "Thou shouldest have smitten five or six times; then hadst thou smitten Syria till thou hadst consumed it: whereas now thou shalt smite Syria but thrice." How often we hinder our blessings because we do not persevere in prayer! 2. *We may hinder our blessings by not making a right use of those we have got.* "To him that hath shall be given, and from him that hath not shall be taken away even that which he seemeth to have." There is no waste in God's kingdom. He will not give further blessings to those who are neglecting or misusing the privileges they have got. Let us see to it that we are in a fit state to receive God's blessing. "If we regard iniquity in our hearts, the Lord will not hear us." Let us empty ourselves of worldliness and selfishness and sin, if we are to expect God to fill us with his Spirit. A word to Christians. Search your heart, examine your own life, and see if there is anything that hinders the Divine blessing. Give up that besetting sin; give up that godless society; put away that pride, or hatred, or love of the world, or evil temper, out of your heart, and then you may expect God to bless you and make you a blessing. Then you will be *a vessel meet for the Master's use.* A word to the unrepenting. Why go away once more without Christ? Why go away empty from the house of God? All fulness dwells in Christ—fulness of pardon, fulness of grace and strength. Thirsty, unsatisfied soul, draw near to the feet of Jesus. Repent, and ask of him, and he will give you the living water.—C. H. I.

Vers. 8—17.—*Kindness requited.* I. GOOD MEN CARRY THEIR GOODNESS WHEREVER THEY GO. The Shunammite's words are a testimony to the character of Elisha. "I perceive that this is *a holy man of God,* which passeth by us continually." Elisha's conduct and conversation showed him to be a holy man of God. It was evident that God was with him, and that he lived near to God. He did not leave his religion behind him at home. Wherever he was, he took his religion with him. A lesson for modern Christians. There is not much reality in our religion if we do not confess it amongst strangers just as much as where we are known. The inward character is shown by the outward acts. "Cœlum, non animum, mutant, qui trans mare currunt." It is evident that Elisha was a man of studious habits. The furniture which the Shunammite placed in his room shows this. The stool or chair and the table were intended to afford him facilities for study. He who will teach others must store his own mind with knowledge. Paul exhorted Timothy to give attention to reading. The minister and the Sunday-school teacher need constant study to equip themselves for their important work.

II. GOOD MEN CARRY A BLESSING EVERYWHERE. Their goodness benefits others as well as themselves. "The holy seed shall be the substance thereof." Some there are who bring evil wherever they go. One bad man, one wicked woman, may corrupt a whole community. Some are the perpetual occasions of strife, discord, unpleasantness, unhappiness. What an unenviable character! Oh to be like him who "went about every day doing good"!

III. KINDNESS TO GOOD MEN IS NEVER LOST. This Shunammite treated Elisha kindly because he was a servant of God, and the God whom he served rewarded her for her kindness to his servant. "Give, and it shall be given unto you." She lost nothing, but gained much, by her generosity and hospitality, by the trouble she took to provide a resting-place for the prophet. "He that receiveth a prophet in the name of a prophet shall receive a prophet's reward; and he that receiveth a righteous man in the name of a righteous man shall receive a righteous man's reward."—C. H. I.

Vers. 18—37.—*Death and restoration.* This is a touching story. It is a story for children. It is a story for parents. It is a story for every one. The circumstances of this little boy's death were peculiarly sad. He had been an unexpected gift of God to his parents. His mother had not sought for him; but God sent her a son as a reward for her kindness to his servant, and in answer to the prophet's prayer. Perhaps when this sudden stroke came upon her, and she watched the little fellow pine away and die in her arms, the poor mother felt a little disposed to murmur at the strange providence. She no doubt wondered why God had tried her thus, to send her a child entirely unexpected and unasked by her, and then—when he had reached that most interesting age, when he was able to run merrily to and fro, when his childish prattle filled the house with gladness, and when his parents' affections had begun to twine themselves about him—*then* to take him from her! She may not, perhaps, have had hard thoughts of *God*, but, with all the faith and patience which she afterwards showed, she certainly was a little disposed to blame Elisha. For we find her saying to him, when she went to tell him of her trouble, " Did I desire a son of my lord? did I not say, Do not deceive me?" But God's hand was in it all, as she soon learned. Perhaps she was beginning to make an idol of this child, and God took this way of reminding her that the child was *his*, that on earth there is none abiding, and that he himself should have the supreme homage of the human heart. Ah yes, she knew something of God's love before, but she never would have known half so much of it but for this trial. The sunshine is beautiful; but sometimes in a time of continued drought we learn that the world would not get on with perpetual sunshine. We are positively glad to see the clouds and the rain. If we could only learn the same lesson for our spiritual life! The sunshine is sweet, but the clouds have their uses too.

> " No shattered box of ointment
> We ever need regret,
> For out of disappointment
> Flow sweetest odours yet.
>
> " The discord that involveth
> Some startling change of key,
> The Master's hand resolveth
> In richest harmony."

We have here—

I. A BELIEVING MOTHER. We see her strong faith in God in that answer which she gave to Gehazi. At Elisha's command he asked her, " Is it well with thee? is it well with thy husband? is it well with the child?" And she answered, " *It is well.*" Not a woman of many words, this. But a woman of great thoughts, of practical faith, of heroic patience. 1. *It was well with the child.* She had no doubt of that. She knew less about the hereafter than we do. She did not know what we know about him who is the Resurrection and the Life, who was himself dead and is alive again. She did not know what we know about heaven—about the angels' song and the pearly gates and the golden streets. But this she felt assured of, that there was a hereafter; that, though the body died, the soul still lived; that her child was with God, and that, therefore, it was well with him. 2. *It was well with her husband. It was well with herself.* Yes, although sorrow had entered their home, still she could feel and say that it was well all round. She could have anticipated Paul in his unfaltering assertion, for " we know that all things work together for good to them that love God, to them who are the called according to his purpose." Calmly and confidently, even though perhaps her tears were falling while she spoke, she uttered the single Hebrew word which means " *It is well.*" *Thank God for believing mothers.* A mother's faith in God has rescued many a son from the very grasp of hell itself. How many an eminent servant of God has owed his conversion to the prayers of a believing mother! St. Augustine and John Newton are well-known instances. *A word here to bereaved parents.* You too may have watched a dear child droop and die. Perhaps you murmured rebelliously under your affliction. Learn to look away behind the veil, into that happy land of which perhaps your darling sang—and as you look there surely you cannot but say, "It is well—it is well with the child." *A word here to all parents.* Can you say, as you think of your children one by one, "It is well with the child"? If they should die in infancy, it certainly is well with them. But your children of maturer years, who are growing up into manhood and womanhood—*how is it with them?* Are there not some in your household that you know are still unsaved? O parents, can you rest until you win them for Christ? It is right to give them a good education. But the most important concern of all is the salvation of their immortal souls.

II. A DEAD CHILD BROUGHT TO LIFE. All dead children will be brought back to life. The body only dies; the soul lives for ever. This little one, however, was brought back to the life of earth. Perhaps God thought that this poor mother had been sufficiently tried. Perhaps he wanted to give even then some proofs of the possibility of a resurrection. It was an exceptional act then. It is not to be expected by bereaved parents now. They can only say with David, "I shall go to him, but he shall not return to me." *Is it not better so?* Could we wish them back again? Look upon them in that bright land where Jesus is, and where the angels are, where their little feet are never weary, where their little faces are always bright and happy, where their little bodies shall nevermore be racked by pain or enfeebled by sickness, where their minds shall never know another thought of sin, and tell me if you would bring them back to this world of wickedness, of temptation, of sickness, and of sorrow? Surely not. Surely they were taken away from the evil that is to come. To depart and be with Christ is far better. 1. *Notice the means of this child's revival.* (1) *First of all, there was prayer.* "And when Elisha was come into the house, behold, the child was dead, and laid upon his bed. He went in therefore, and shut the door upon them twain, and prayed unto the Lord." So it must be in all efforts for the revival of dead souls. Parents must have recourse to prayer if they would see their children converted. We want more praying families; we want more praying Churches. Nothing but the Spirit of God can make the dry bones to live. If our work is to last, it must be done in prayer. (2) Then, again, observe that *Elisha used the means to bring about an answer to his prayers.* He asked for a certain blessing, and he showed that he expected an answer. *He stretched himself upon the child,* that his body might communicate heat to that of the child, and his breath upon the child's mouth encouraged the returning vitality. It is God's method of converting the world, of quickening dead souls. It is the Spirit of God that alone can quicken a dead soul. But he uses human instrumentality. *He uses living Christians.* The apostles were men on fire with the Holy Ghost and with zeal for souls, and therefore their labours were blessed. The reason there are so few conversions, the reason the Church has so little influence upon the world compared to what it might have, is that too often the Church itself is worldly, seeking for temporal position and worldly gain, and that Christians show too little of the spirit of their Master. They have a name to live, but are dead. But it is wonderful what one or two living Christians can effect in a congregation, in a community, even throughout the world. 2. *Notice also the signs of this child's revival.* "The child sneezed seven times, and the child opened his eyes." It was enough. Elisha did not wait for the child to speak. He did not wait for him to walk. He recognized the unmistakable signs of life, and at once he restored the child to his sorrowing mother. Christians ought to watch for signs of spiritual life as the result of their labours and their prayers. They should not be discouraged if there seems but little fruit. Do not discourage the slightest indication of a desire on the part of any one to turn from sin and come to Christ. Encourage those who may be seekers after God, groping feebly after the truth, struggling, perhaps, with their difficulties and doubts. What souls have you been the means of bringing from death into life?—C. H. I.

Vers. 38—41.—*Death in the pot: a sermon to young men.* These young men were very nearly being poisoned. There was a famine in the land. Elisha came to Gilgal, where there was a school or college of young men in training for the sacred office of teaching others. Perhaps they were not skilled in the art of making the most of the vegetables which grew round about them, and were badly off for food. Elisha ordered his servant to put on the great pot, and make some pottage, or thick broth, for the hungry students. One of the young men went out to gather herbs for the purpose.

There is a species of wild gourd or melon, called *Cucumis prophetarum*, which is common in the hill country, and which, when green, is sliced and boiled as a vegetable. But in the plains near Gilgal there is a plant extremely similar in appearance, but very different in its qualities. It was probably this—the *colocynthus*, or squirting cucumber —that is called the "wild gourd" in this chapter, and that the young men gathered and sliced down into the large pot of broth (see Thomson, 'The Land and the Book'). When the pottage had been poured out, the young men began to eat of it, but, alarmed by its bitter taste, and probably suspecting then that poisonous herbs had been put into it, they cried out to Elisha, "O thou man of God, there is death in the pot!" From this incident we may show that, while there is many an enjoyment, many a course of conduct, as pleasant to the eye and apparently as safe as those poisonous herbs appeared to be, yet there is need for caution. "There is death in the pot." "There is a way that *seemeth* right unto a man, but the end thereof are *the ways of death*."

I. THIS MAY BE SAID OF FRAUDULENT PRACTICES. "*There is death in the pot.*" They nearly always begin in ways that seem perfectly safe and harmless. A man takes a little from his employer's desk, intending to return it again. But in nine cases out of ten he never returns it. He has touched what is not his own. The brand of the thief is on his brow and the curse of the thief is on his life. A young man who had been well brought up went from home to enter a bank in a large city. It was noticed, when he returned home, that he was beginning to dress very extravagantly. Each time he returned, some fresh extravagance was noted. He had already begun to spend money faster than he made it, for his salary was but small. He was a smart young man, and would soon have got on well in his business, for he was a general favourite. But in a foolish hour he began to abstract some of the bank money. Little by little it went on, until his defalcations were very considerable. At last he was discovered, dismissed in disgrace from the bank, and it was only the intervention of an influential friend of his family that prevented his arrest. He broke his mother's heart, and brought down his father's grey hairs with sorrow to the grave. Fraudulent practices may be very often traced to the habit of *gambling* or *betting*. This was testified once more quite recently in London by Mr. Vaughan, the Bow Street magistrate, on a charge which came before him. There was a cashier in the receipt of a salary of £150 a year, with prospects of advance. For eight or nine years he had filled his post creditably; but having got behind in his home expenses, he took a few shillings, and invested them in betting. As he was lucky, from taking shillings he proceeded to pounds; and having once started, he found that it was impossible for him to stop. He had always the hope of winning some day by a stroke of luck, and of thus being able to pay back again the sums which he had embezzled. But the "luck" never came, and he had at last to confess to his employers that he had defrauded them to the extent of £250. "I wish," said Mr. Vaughan, "that the clerks in mercantile houses would come to this court, and see what I see, and hear what I hear. This is only one of a multitude of cases in which prisoners have confessed that their robberies are entirely due to betting. *I regard it as a curse to the country.*" Beware of dishonesty in any form. "There is death in the pot." It means death to a man's reputation, death to his worldly prospects, death to his peace of mind, for he must live in constant terror of discovery; and if he should escape discovery and judgment upon earth, how can he endure the thought of that day when the secrets of every life shall be disclosed, and when he shall stand condemned at the judgment-seat of God?

II. THIS MAY BE SAID ALSO OF PRACTICES OF IMPURITY. "*There is death in the pot.*" Temptations to it abound on every side. A corrupt press sows broadcast its demoralizing stories, with its suggestive pictures. The theatre, with its brilliant lights and strains of sweetest music—so often dedicated to the service of the devil—lures men into the way of the tempter, and into the den of the destroyer. It appears an innocent, harmless amusement. But "there is death in the pot." For one who comes unscathed and safe out of the theatre, there are scores who come out of it morally and spiritually the worse for its influence. Let men say what they like about the influence of the drama as a teacher of morals—and there is nothing to be said against the drama in itself—is there a single case of a man made better by going to the theatre? *Where is he? Let him be produced.* And even if one or two could be produced, what would they be as a testimony in favour of the theatre, compared to the testimony against it of the thousands it has ruined? "It might do good, but never did." Beware of impurity in any form: Beware of impure books, impure songs, the impure jest, impure companions. "There is death in the pot." There is no sin that brings a more speedy or more terrible retribution in this life, than impurity of thought or deed. In a diseased body and a diseased mind it leaves its deadly marks. The impure man is a walking sepulchre. He is digging his own grave. Above all, he is destroying all hope of entering that pure and holy heaven where God is, and into which there shall in no wise enter anything that defileth.

III. THIS MAY BE SAID ALSO OF HABITS OF INTEMPERANCE. *"There is death in the pot."* We need not take an extreme position on the subject of alcohol any more than on any other subject. But it is right that, as intelligent beings, with a reason and a conscience, as Christian men and women with God's Word to guide us, we should look facts in the face. Medical opinion is often resorted to by those who make too free in their use of alcohol. Let us hear the latest and best medical opinion on the subject. At the last meeting of the British Medical Association (Dublin, 1887), one of the most interesting papers was the report of a special committee which had been appointed by the association to inquire into the connection of disease with habits of intemperance. Here are some of the conclusions which the committee, after most careful investigation, arrived at: "(1) That habitual indulgence in alcohol beyond the most moderate amounts has a *distinct tendency to shorten life*, the shortening being on the average fairly proportional to the degree of indulgence; (2) that the strictly temperate who have passed the age of twenty-five live on the average at least *ten years longer* than the intemperate." Is not this an important proof of our statement? "Habitual indulgence in alcohol beyond the most moderate amounts has a distinct tendency to shorten life." The man who drinks alcohol to any considerable extent is slowly killing himself. "There is death in the pot." If we turn from the assembly of doctors to the experience of everyday life, we get similar proofs. What terrible madness and infatuation drink causes! What fearful havoc it has made! What hopes it has blighted! What homes it has wrecked! What lives it has ruined! There is death in the cup of intoxicating drink, as many a man has proved when it has been too late. But absence of wrong-doing will never make you right. As Elisha cast the meal into the pot, wholesome and nourishing food in place of the deadly poison, so be it yours to fill your mind with the teaching of God's Word, and your life with holy and useful deeds. The great Teacher is Jesus Christ. Ask him to enter into your life, to purify your heart and your desires. Ask him for time and for eternity to save your soul.—C. H. I.

Vers. 42—44.—*The loaves multiplied.* I. THE PROPHET PROVIDED FOR. It was a time of famine. "But they that fear the Lord shall not want any good thing." Elisha received a thank offering from the people—"bread of the firstfruits, twenty loaves of barley, and full ears of corn." *The objection to a paid ministry has no warrant in the Word of God.* Old Testament and New alike encourage provision for the wants of God's ministers. Jesus said, "The labourer is worthy of his hire." Paul said, "They that preach the gospel should live of the gospel." It is impracticable and inconvenient that men should be preachers of the gospel, with all the preparation which that work requires, and pastors of the flock, with all the attention which this requires, and at the same time be burdened with the toil and anxiety of providing for their own temporal support and that of their families, if they have them.

II. THE PEOPLE FED. We see here: 1. *Elisha's unselfishness.* He had freely received; now he freely gives. In that time of famine he might have thought it prudent to store up for himself the supply of food he had received. But no. He trusts God for the future. His first thought is of others who were hungry round about him. "Give unto the people, that they may eat." There is need for more of this unselfishness, considerateness, thoughtfulness. How many of those who have abundance forget to think of those who are in want! 2. *The Divine power exercised.* God owns his servants, not only by supplying their wants, but by giving power to their word. Oh that every minister of Christ would realize this! What a new power it would give to his work! what a new stimulus to his earnestness! When we think of the greatness and responsibility of our work, we may well ask, "Who is sufficient for these things?" But when, on the other hand, we think of the Divine power which works along with the faithful minister, we may well say, "I can do all things through Christ which strengtheneth me." He can help us to break among our people the bread of life, and bless it abundantly in the breaking.—C. H. I.

Vers. 1—7.—*A prophet's widow and a prophet's kindness.* "Now there cried a certain woman of the wives of the sons of the prophets unto Elisha," etc. There are two subjects of thought in these verses.

I. A PROPHET'S WIDOW IN DISTRESS. "Now there cried a certain woman of the wives of the sons of the prophets unto Elisha, saying, Thy servant my husband is dead; and thou knowest that thy servant did fear the Lord: and the creditor is come to take unto him my two sons to be bondmen." This poor woman had not only lost her husband, and was left with a bleeding heart—left lonely and desolate in a cold world, but was left in great poverty. Her husband was not only a good man, one "who did fear the Lord," but a "prophet," a religious teacher, one engaged in disseminating *Divine* ideas amongst men. It seems that he not only died poor, but died in debt. Even now a large number of ministers are unable to make provision for their wives and children in case of their death. Some of the most enlightened, thoughtful, and really useful ministers are amongst the poorest. Observe: 1. *That poverty is not necessarily a disgrace.* It is sometimes the result of inflexible honesty and moral nobility. 2. *That the best lives here are subject to trials.* It is reasonable to infer that this widow was a good woman—one who, like her departed husband, "did fear the Lord;" and yet see her distress! The afflictions of the good are not penal, but disciplinary. 3. *That avarice feeds cruelty.* "The creditor is come to take unto him my two sons to be bondmen." The debt she owed, which, we may imagine, could not have been very large, her heartless creditor insisted on being discharged at once, and demanded her two sons to become slaves to him in order to work out the debt. The avaricious world is heartless; even in London hundreds are dying on every side of starvation. 4. *That provision should be made for the widows of ministers.* The incomes of very many ministers in England to-day are not sufficient to enable them to make provision for their wives and children in case of their death. Churches which have committees for sending out missionaries, for distributing Bibles (which are cheap enough now), and for distributing tracts, which are often calumnies on Christianity, ought certainly to see that provision is made for the future of their ministers' families.

II. A PROPHET AT WORK TO RELIEVE A BROTHERS' WIDOW. In her distress instinct tells her where to go, and she goes to Elisha, not only a man who knew her husband, but one of kindred experiences and sympathies. To him she "cried." Her appeal was really an unintentional compliment to Elisha. The greatest compliment a man can offer is an opportunity for contributing to a truly deserving object. When a man's compeers rank him amongst those whose meanness has become patent, Charity ignores him. In her benign mission she marches by him in stately silence, as one whom society has placed in the branded category of sordid souls. See how Elisha helps this widow. 1. *Promptly.* "And Elisha said unto her, What shall I do for thee? tell me, what hast thou in the house?" He did not want arguments or testimonials, etc., but with a beaming generosity he virtually said, "Tell me your condition, and I will do my utmost to serve you." He set to work at once. Having told him she had nothing in her house but one "pot of oil," he says to her, "Go, borrow thee vessels abroad of all thy neighbours, even empty vessels; borrow not a few." She obeys his behest, goes amongst her neighbours, and borrows all the vessels, and then, according to his directions, she closes the door upon herself, and upon her sons, and begins to pour out into each vessel a part of the little pot of oil which she had, and as she poured every vessel she had collected became full to the brim. The more she poured the more came, until she lacked vessels to hold it. A symbol this of all benevolent virtues—the more they are used the more they grow. So, indeed, with all the faculties of the soul under the influence of true generosity; right giving is the way to the most precious getting. All this, of course, indicates on Elisha's part supernatural assistance. 2. *Effectively.* "Then she came and told the man of God [Elisha]. And he said, Go, sell the oil, and pay thy debt, and live thou and thy children of the rest." Oil was one of the commoditics Judæa traded in (Ezek. xxvii: 17).   She would,'therefore, have little difficulty in disposing of this oil, which no doubt was of the best description.   The proceeds were to go first to the satisfaction of her heartless creditor, and then to the permanent relief of herself and family.

CONCLUSION.   Matthew Henry's remarks are good: " Let those who are poor and in distress be encouraged to trust God for supply in the way of duty.   ' Verily thou shalt be fed,' but not feasted.   It is true we cannot now expect miracles, yet we may expect mercies if we wait on God and seek him.   Let widows particularly, and prophets' widows in a special manner, depend upon him to preserve them and their fatherless children alive; for to them he will be a Husband and a Father.   Let those whom God hath blessed with plenty use it for the glory of God, and under the direction of his Word; let them do justly with it, as this widow did, and serve God cheerfully in the use of it; and, as Elisha, be ready to do good to those that need them—be eyes to the blind, and feet to the lame."—D. T.

Vers. 8—17.—*Hospitality.*   " And it fell on a day, that Elisha passed to Shunem," etc.   In these verses there are two very interesting subjects of a practical character.

I. HOSPITALITY RIGHTFULLY EMPLOYED.   The object of the hospitality was Elisha the prophet, and the author of it is called here " a great woman." [1]   The account given is very clear and sententious.   "And it fell on a day, that Elisha passed to Shunem, where was a great woman; and she constrained him to eat bread.   And so it was, that as oft as he passed by, he turned in thither to eat bread."   Observe : 1. *The hospitality was very hearty.*   "She constrained him to eat bread."   She did not give Elisha a mere formal invitation, nor was she urged to it by pleadings on his behalf, either by himself or others.   It was spontaneous and hearty, worthy of "a great woman."   It was so hearty that Elisha felt authorized, " as oft as he passed by," to enter and " eat bread." On his prophetic mission he would be constantly journeying, and often passing the house, and as often as he did so he felt there was a hearty welcome for him inside, and entered.   2. *The hospitality was shown to a poor but godly man.*   The woman " said unto her husband, Behold now, I perceive that this is a holy man of God, which passeth by us continually."   Conventional hospitality welcomes to its table the respectable only, and the more respectable in a worldly sense the more welcome.   But genuine hospitality, as in the case before us, looks out for the poor and deserving, and constrains them to enter and be fed.   " When thou makest a feast, call not thy brethren, nor thy kinsmen, nor thy rich neighbours; lest they also bid thee again, and a recompense be made thee. But when thou makest a feast, call the poor, the maimed, the lame, and the blind." 3. *The hospitality involved considerable trouble and expense.*   This " great woman" said to her husband, "Let us make a little chamber, I pray thee, on the wall; and let us set for him there a bed, and a table, and a stool, and a candlestick."   She did not say to her husband, "Entertaining him will put us to no inconvenience or expense, therefore let us invite him."   No, she calculated upon some inconvenience and cost ; a little chamber would have to be built, quiet and suitable for a man of spiritual thoughtfulness and devotion.   And then some furniture, too, would have to be procured— " a bed, and a table, and a stool, and a candlestick."   The hospitality that involves no outlay is common, but is a counterfeit, nay, a misnomer.   The accommodation this woman offered to Elisha, it must be borne in mind, included that of his servant Gehazi—he shared the provisions and the apartments of his master.

II. HOSPITALITY NOBLY REWARDED.   Elisha, instead of being insensible to the great generosity of his hostess, glowed with gratitude that prompted a strong desire to make some return, and " said to Gehazi his servant, Call this Shunammite. . . . And he said unto him, Say now unto her, Behold, thou hast been careful for us with all this care; what is to be done for thee ? "   His offer : 1. *Implies his consciousness of great power with man.*   "Wouldest thou be spoken for to the king, or to the captain of the host?" Though poor himself, he had influence with the rich; and though too independent in soul to ask of them a favour for himself, he could do it for others.   Her answer to his generous offer is expressive of the calm self-respect, unmercenariness, and dignity of a " great woman."   She answered, " I dwell among mine own people."   As if she had said, " We are provided for; we neither aim at nor need preferment."   2. *Implies his*

[1] See *Homilist*, vol. xxxviii. p. 289.

consciousness of his power with God. He finds out, through his servant Gehazi, that the one great thing on earth that they desired most, and would most appreciate, was a family; a child would brighten their hearth and gladden their hearts. This, through his wonderful power with Heaven, Elisha obtains for them. Thus the Almighty himself acknowledged the hospitality which this woman had shown to his faithful prophet. "Be not forgetful to entertain strangers: for thereby some have entertained angels unawares."

CONCLUSION. Dinings out and social banquets are common enough amongst us, but hospitality of the true sort is, it may be feared, somewhat rare—the hospitality described by Washington Irving, which "breaks through the chill of ceremonies, and throws every heart into a glow." There is an emanation from the heart in genuine hospitality that cannot be described.—D. T.

Vers. 18—31.—*Great trials.* "And when the child was grown," etc. This paragraph suggests three general observations.

I. That great trials OFTEN SPRING FROM GREAT MERCIES. With what rapture we may suppose did this woman welcome her only child into the world, and with what care and affection did she minister to his health and enjoyments! It was her greatest earthly prize. She would sooner have parted with all her property, and even, perhaps, with her husband, for he was an old man, than lose this dear boy of hers. Yet she does; death snatches him from her embrace. "And when the child was grown, it fell on a day, that he went out to his father to the reapers. And he said unto his father, My head, my head. And he said to a lad, Carry him to his mother. And when he had taken him, and brought him to his mother, he sat on her knees till noon, and then died." Though the boy was dead, the woman did not seem to lose hope; her maternal love would not allow her to realize the terrible fact at once. She first lays him on the bed in the chamber which she had built for the prophet; then she calls to her husband, and entreats him to send a servant with one of the asses, that she might fly with swiftness to Elisha. When her husband suggested some difficulty about her going just at that time, she replied, "It shall be well." "Then she saddled an ass, and said to her servant, Drive, and go forward; slack not thy riding for me, except I bid thee. So she went and came unto the man of God to Mount Carmel." This was a journey of about five or six hours. Distance is nothing when the traveller's heart overflows with emotion. How frequently it happens that from our greatest blessings our greatest trials spring! 1. *Friendship* is a great blessing. One true friend, whose soul lives in ours and ours in him or her, is of priceless worth. Yet the disruption of that friendship may strike a wound into the heart that no time can heal. 2. A *sanguine temperament* is a great blessing. It drinks in largely of the beauties of nature; it paints the future with the brightest hopes, and stimulates the energies to the greatest enterprises. All the best productions of the human species have sprung from such temperaments. But what trials it brings, in frustrated plans, blighted purposes, and extinguished hopes! But life abounds with illustrations of the fact—the greater the blessings we enjoy, the greater agony felt in their loss.

II. That great trials SHOULD BE PATIENTLY ENDURED. In this great trial this woman seems wonderfully resigned. In reply to a difficulty which her husband suggested in setting out for the journey, she said, "It shall be well." And when Gehazi, the servant of Elisha, on her approach to the prophet, asked her, "Is it well with thee? Is it well with thy husband? Is it well with the child?" she answered, "It is well." "Though I left my dear boy a corpse at home, and my heart bleeds, I feel it is all ' well;' it is the dispensation of a Father all-wise and all-loving. I bow to his will." A state of mind so magnanimous as this under great trial is the duty of all, and the sublime privilege of the holy and the good. Thus Job felt, "The Lord gave, and the Lord hath taken away; blessed be the Name of the Lord." Thus our great Example felt when overwhelmed with immeasurable distress he said, "Not my will, but thine be done."

> "Thy way, not mine, O Lord,
>   However dark it be;
> Lead me by thine own hand,
>   Choose out the path for me.

> "Smooth let it be or rough,
>   It will be still the best;
> Winding or straight it matters not,
>   It leads me to thy rest."

III. That great trials MAY HAVE A BLESSED END. The end of this woman's great trial was the restoration of her dead child to life. This was brought about: 1. *In connection with her own efforts.* If she had remained at home, and not sped her way to the prophet at Carmel, her boy in all probability would, it would seem, have remained a corpse, and would have had to be buried for ever out of her sight. When she reached him, see how earnestly she pleads: "And when she came to the man of God to the hill, she caught him by the feet," etc. 2. *By the power of God through Elisha.* In the following verses we have a representation of the way in which this was brought about. God helps man by man. All our trials might have a blessed end. "Our light affliction, which is but for a moment, worketh for us a far more exceeding and eternal weight of glory." Yes; whilst "we look not at the things that are seen," the result, under God, depends upon ourselves.—D. T.

Vers. 32—37.—*The relation of prayer to secondary causes.* "And when Elisha was come into the house, behold, the child was dead," etc. The death of the Shunammite's son, as we have seen in the preceding verses, was in many senses to her a very severe trial—a trial from which we have inferred that *great trials often spring from great mercies; that great trials should be patiently endured;* and *that great trials might have a blessed end.* By prayer Elisha now raised the woman's dead boy to life. See what Elisha did here.

I. HE PRAYED TO THE LORD. "Let this child's soul come into him again."

II. HE PUT HIMSELF INTO DIRECT CONTACT WITH THE CHILD. Mouth to the child's mouth, eyes to the child's eyes, hands to the child's hands, as if he transfused all the vital magnetism of his own nature into the person of the dead child.

III. HE PERSEVERED WITH THE EFFORT. Until the child's flesh waxed warm, and the child sneezed with the breath of new life.—D. T.

Vers. 38—44.—*Ministries to man, good and bad.* "And Elisha came again to Gilgal: and there was a dearth in the land," etc. Elisha had returned to Gilgal, the seat of a school of the prophets; he had come thither once more on his yearly circuit, and during the famine which prevailed in the land. As the students sat before their master, he discerned in their emaciated forms the terrible effects upon them of the famine. In the narrative we discover the action of several ministries, or events with which men are visited more or less in passing through this sublunary state.

I. Here is the ministry of SEVERE TRIAL. "There was a dearth in the land." To be destitute of those provisions which are essential to the appeasement of hunger and the sustentation of life is undoubtedly one of the greatest trials. Such destitution is of two kinds—the *avoidable* and the *unavoidable.* The former is common. Tens of thousands of people in this country, which so abounds with wealth, are, alas! subject to the trial of this destitution every day. But men bring this destitution on themselves. To the heartless cupidity of one class of men, and the indolence, extravagance, and intemperance of another, the poverty which is rampant in England to-day must be ascribed. The latter kind of destitution, viz. the *inevitable,* is that recorded in these verses; it arose out of the sterile condition into which the land was thrown. This was the destitution which now prevailed in Israel; it afflicted all, the good and the bad. In truth, Nature knows of no moral distinctions; she treats kings and paupers, the righteous and the wicked, alike.

II. Here is the ministry of GROSS IGNORANCE. In order to allay the ravenous hunger of his pupils, Elisha said to his servant, "Set on the great pot, and seethe pottage for the sons of the prophets. And one went out into the field to gather herbs, and found a wild vine, and gathered thereof wild gourds, his lap full, and came and shred them into the pot of pottage: for they knew them not. So they poured out for the men to eat. And it came to pass, as they were eating of the pottage, that they cried out, and said, O thou man of God, there is death in the pot. And they could not eat thereof." Whatever were the herbs which the servants gathered it matters not;

they were nauseous and pernicious. "The sons of the prophets," says Matthew Henry, "it would seem, were better skilled in divinity than philosophy, and read their Bibles more than their herbals." What they put into the pot tended to produce death rather than to strengthen life. Every day men are afflicted through the gross ignorance of themselves and others. Through ignorance men are everywhere putting "death in the pot," in a *material* sense. The cook, the doctor, the brewer, the distiller, how much death do they bring into the "pot" of human life! Through ignorance, too, men are everywhere putting "death in the pot" in a *spiritual* sense. Calvinistic dogmas, unauthorized priestly assumptions, etc., how much death do they bring into the spiritual "pot" of life! Man's ignorance of God and his claims on the soul, its nature, its laws, and the necessary conditions of true spiritual progress, is the minister of death.

III. Here is the ministry of HUMAN KINDNESS. "And there came a man from Baal-shalisha, and brought the man of God bread of the firstfruits, twenty loaves of bread, and full ears of corn in the husk thereof." Whoever this man was (for no description is given of him save the place of his residence), he was a Heaven-inspired philan-thropist. Mercy, the highest attribute of heaven, was in him, and he left his home and came forth to minister to the needs of his suffering race. Thank God for that kindness which has survived the Fall, and still lives in human hearts. The most precious ministry on earth is this: it feeds the hungry, clothes the naked, heals the diseased, wipes away the tears of human sorrow; it is, indeed, Christ in human flesh. For he was then in the world, though the world knew it not.

IV. Here is the ministry of SUPERNATURAL POWER. Supernatural power through Elisha comes to the relief of these sufferers. The supernatural was manifested in two ways. 1. In counteracting the death-tendency of what was in the pot. "But he said, Then bring meal. And he cast it into the pot; and he said, Pour out for the people, that they may eat. And there was no harm in the pot." A supernatural power is required to counteract the pernicious in life. If the Almighty allowed evil to take its course freely and fully, death would run riot and reduce the whole race to extinction. The supernatural was manifested also: 2. In increasing the supplies of life. Elisha commanded his servant to distribute amongst his starving pupils the provisions which the man that came from Baal-shalisha had brought. To this the servant replied, "What, should I set this before a hundred men? He said again, Give the people, that they may eat: for thus saith the Lord, They shall eat, and shall leave thereof. So he set it before them, and they did eat, and left thereof, according to the word of the Lord." As the pot of oil increased in the pouring, so the provisions increased in the eating. It has been said of old of God, that he will abundantly bless the "provisions of his people, and satisfy the poor with bread." It is true that moral goodness, truth, and justice, skill, prudence, and diligence, have a tendency to increase everywhere the provisions of human life, and they are doing so every day. But in this case there seems to be the exertion of a power transcending the human. However this may be, that which we call the supernatural is nothing more than the natural. As Nature herself is immeasurably beyond our comprehension, transcends our conceptions, for us to speak of the supernatural implies the arrogation of an intelligence which we do not possess.—D. T.

Vers. 1—7.—*The miracles of Elisha: the pot of oil.* The next few chapters relate a number of the miracles of Elisha—all of them works of mercy.

I. THE WIDOW'S TROUBLE. The story told in these verses is one of sore distress. It is a story: 1. *Of bereavement.* A poor woman, widow of one of "the sons of the prophets," cried to Elisha, "Thy servant my husband is dead." We learn from this that the prophetic communities were not monastic. Marriage was permitted, and members of the fraternity had houses and families of their own. But this poor woman's husband had recently died. She had to face the difficulties and fight the battles of life alone. We are in presence of one of the minor tragedies of life —little thought of, because not uncommon. 2. *Of debt.* Her husband had been pious—"Thou knowest that thy servant did fear the Lord"—but his affairs had been left in confusion at his death, or, having no means of subsistence, the family had sunk into dependence on a creditor since his decease. A man may be good, and yet imprudent. On the other hand, misfortunes may overtake the best-intentioned, and reduce them from affluence to poverty. It is, however, a sad thing when the head of a household dies, and leaves to his struggling family an inheritance of debt. This is a contingency to be by every legitimate means guarded against. The Rev. C. H. Spurgeon, commenting on the text, "Take no thought for the morrow," etc. (Matt. vi. 34), began by announcing, " I insured my own life last week, and have thus been able to carry out the injunction of the text, and not to be over-anxious for the morrow, for much undue care and anxiety that I had is now laid aside, secure in the knowledge that my forethought has provided for my loved ones." 3. *Of bondage*. The creditor to whom the debt was due showed himself merciless, and, as the law permitted, was about to take as slaves the two sons of the woman (Lev. xxv. 39). It mattered little to the hard-hearted creditor that his debtor had "feared the Lord," that the two sons were the only remaining comforts of the widow, and that, with "patience," they might have "paid him all" (Matt. xviii. 29). He must have his own. It was forbidden to a creditor, to whom a fellow-Israelite was sold, to "compel him to serve as a bond-servant," and to "rule over him with rigour" (Lev. xxv. 39, 43). But an unscrupulous man would pay little heed to these injunctions. Altogether, the picture is a sad one. Happily, the poor woman knew where to come with her tale of grief. She remembered the " Father of the fatherless " and the " Judge of the widow" (Ps. lxviii. 5), and, when every earthly avenue of help was closed, poured her sorrows into the ear of God's prophet.

II. The directions of Elisha. As the representative of One who had specially declared himself the Friend of "the fatherless and widow" (Deut. x. 18), Elisha could not turn a deaf ear to the widow's plaint. A sympathetic interest in the bereaved and distressed is at all times a duty of God's ministers. 1. *He inquired as to her possessions*. " Tell me, what hast thou in the house ? " God's help takes its starting-point from what we already have. The widow had but "one pot of oil"—oil for anointing; but this was made the basis of what was to be done. So Elijah founded his miracle on the widow of Zarephath's " handful of meal in a barrel, and a little oil in a cruse " (1 Kings xvii. 12), and Christ his on the lad's " five barley loaves, and two small fishes " (John vi. 9). The lesson is that what means of help we have are to be made use of to the utmost before supernatural aid is invoked. 2. *He bade her prepare for a liberal experience of God's goodness*. " Go, borrow thee vessels abroad of all thy neighbours, even empty vessels ; borrow not a few." She was to expect large things of the Lord. Her task in collecting the vessels was, like the digging of the trenches in the last chapter, emphatically a work of faith (ch. iii. 16, 17). God does not stint us in answer to our prayers. His word rather is, " Open thy mouth wide, and I will fill it " (Ps. lxxxi. 10). If our faith will but trust him, he will astonish us with his liberality. 3. *He enjoined secrecy*. " When thou art come in, thou shalt shut the door upon thee and upon thy sons, and shalt pour out," etc. This was too sacred a work to be made a vulgar wonder. To receive the full benefit of the blessing, the inmates of the house were to be alone, in privacy, their thoughts and spirits undisturbed. Jesus enjoins the cultivation of secrecy in religion (Matt. vi. 1—18). He often forbade the blazoning abroad of his miracles (Matt. viii. 4, etc.). The parading of religious experiences takes the bloom off them.

III. The multiplying of the oil. 1. *The oil multiplied*. The widow and her sons did as directed, and, as they poured the oil into the borrowed vessels, it still increased till the vessels were full. The element of miracle here is very notable, but we are not entitled to expect such miracles at the present day. But the pledge of Divine help in distress implied in such a miracle remains to us, and God will honour every draft on his promises made by faith, basing itself on such deeds as this. A singular incident in proof is recorded by Krummacher in his remarks on this miracle ('Elisha,' lect. v.). It might almost be said that there is a multiplying power in the Divine blessing, apart from miracle (Ps. xxxvii. 16). 2. *The oil stayed*. When the vessels were full, the widow said to her son, " Bring me yet a vessel." There was not, however, a vessel more. Then the oil stayed. Had there been more vessels, it would have flowed on. The sole limit of the supply was the limit of their capacity to receive. We are not straitened in God ; we are straitened only in ourselves. 3. *The oil sold*. The news being brought to Elisha, he ordered the grateful woman—poor no more—to sell the oil, and pay her debt, and live, she and her children, of the rest. The debt was not repudiated; it was paid. God would put the stamp of his approval on honesty. The whole incident teaches us the lesson of trusting God in every time of need. When have the righteous been forsaken, or their seed seen begging bread (Ps. xxxvii. 25)? If we can trust in God for temporal supplies, much more may we for our spiritual supplies (Phil. iv. 19).—J. O.

Vers. 8—17.—*The lady of Shunem* : 1. *A son given.* The scene of this exquisite story is the town of Shunem, on the slope of Little Hermon, one of the eminences looking down on the rich and extensive plain of Jezreel. I. RECEIVING A PROPHET IN THE NAME OF A PROPHET. In this town dwelt a wealthy lady, wife of a man who had large possessions in land—the Boaz of that district. The first part of the story is a beautiful instance of the consecrated use of wealth. 1. *Elisha observed.* Shunem lay in Elisha's route in passing to and fro, probably on his visits to the schools of the prophets. The lady of Shunem did not at first know him, but his appearance, as he passed and repassed, attracted her attention. She saw, from the gravity, benevolence, and distinction of his aspect, that he was "a holy man of God." She felt an interest in him, first as a wayfarer, then as a man of piety. It is well when even our outward deportment is such that others are compelled to take knowledge of us that we have been with Jesus (Acts iv. 13). 2. *Elisha welcomed.* The immediate impulse of the pious lady was to show hospitality to the traveller. (1) This illustrates her own piety. It was because she feared God that she was moved to show this kindness to his servant. Piety often lingers in rural districts when wickedness is rampant in the cities. One marked manifestation of piety is reverence for, and hospitable treatment of, God's saints (Matt. x. 40—42 ; xxv. 34—46). Elisha was received " in the name of a prophet " (Matt. x. 41). (2) It illustrates also her natural benevolence of heart. Had this lady not been naturally of a benevolent disposition, accustomed to act hospitably and generously, she would not so readily have thought of constraining Elisha " to eat bread." St. Paul notes it as the mark of a godly woman, " if she have lodged strangers " (1 Tim. v. 10). 3. *Elisha a customary guest.* When once Elisha had found his way to this good lady's house, it would be alike a pleasure to him and a satisfaction to his hostess " to turn in thither " every time he passed through Shunem. The more the Shunammite saw of the prophet, the more she reverenced and desired to serve him. With the inventiveness of a mind that " deviseth liberal things " (Isa. xxxii. 8), it soon occurred to her to make permanent arrangements for his comfortable reception. Her husband, to whom she proposed her plans, entered heartily into them. Unlike the churlish Nabal (1 Sam. xxv.), he was willing to give of his wealth for a prophet's entertainment. A chamber, accordingly, was fitted up on the wall for Elisha's private use, and there he abode, and could feel at home, whenever he passed that way. How beautiful the large and unstinted generosity, the wise forethought, the warm consideration for another's comfort, displayed in this incident ! This wise and unselfish use of wealth is the true secret of obtaining enjoyment out of it. II. A PROPHET'S REWARD. We are called to notice : 1. *The prophet's gratitude.* It was not with hope of reward that the Shunammite had done her acts of kindness, but Elisha was none the less anxious to show his sense of her generosity by doing her some service in return. He bade Gehazi his servant call her, and say to her, " Thou hast been careful for us with all this care; what is to be done for thee ? " A grateful spirit well becomes a servant of God (2 Tim. i. 16—18). There is none whose gratitude we should so much desire to have as that of " righteous men." They may not, like Elisha, have interest with kings and courts, but ¡they have interest with Heaven. God rewards for their sake. Their prayers and intercessions are worth more than silver and gold. 2. *The Shunammite's humility.* (1) Elisha's first proposal was, " Wouldst thou be spoken for to the king, or to the captain of the host ? " His influence at court, since the victory over the Moabites, was probably very great. It is not clear what exactly he supposed the king could do for her that the Shunammite was likely to desire; for it could not be thought, least of all by Elisha, that life in Samaria, and a position in Jehoram's court, even though attended by wealth and honour, was an advantageous exchange for her present rural felicity. A case did arise, however, later on, in which it was of benefit to her to " be spoken for to the king" (ch. viii. 1—6). To many minds such a proposal as Elisha's would have had supreme attractions. To be "presented at court" is, in many circles of fashion, the acme of ambition—to gain titles, honours, royal recognitions, the *summum bonum* of existence. (2) It was different with this Shunammite. Her wise and beautiful and unambitious answer was, " I dwell among mine own people." She had no desire to exchange her simple country life at Shunem, surrounded by those who knew and loved her, for any grander station king or captain could give her. In this she judged rightly. The elements of happiness are probably found in their greatest perfection in such a quiet country existence, with the means of doing good to others, as this lady enjoyed. They are emphatically not to be found in the sphere of court-favour and court-patronage—too often the sphere of sycophancy, intrigue, faction, backstairs influence, miserable jealousies and spites, which reduce life to the emptiest, vainest show. 3. *The prophet's reward.* What, then, was to be done for the Shunammite? (1) Gehazi, with the shrewdness of a man of the world, struck on the right idea. "Verily she hath no child, and her husband is old." Perhaps he had ere this heard the lady lament her want of offspring. It was the one cross of her otherwise contented and happy life. Her husband, like Elkanah, might console her with the words, " Am not I better to thee than ten sons?" but her warm, motherly heart, overflowing as it was with kindness to others, yearned for a child of her own on whom to lavish its riches. Without this boon, however she might feel the duty of resignation, existence remained incomplete. It is rare but that some cross, if it be but one, is mingled with our blessings, if only to teach us that existence here is not the be-all and end-all. (2) Elisha saw at once the propriety of Gehazi's suggestion, and confident in the Divine readiness to give effect to his word, he called the Shunammite, and announced to her the joyful fact that, with the revolving months, she should embrace a son. The intimation astounded her, as well it might. It so entirely transcended her hopes and expectations, that she could hardly believe in its realization. " Nay, . . . thou man of God," she said, " do not lie unto thine handmaid;" as if she was afraid he was trifling with her, trying some experiment upon her feelings, or otherwise deluding her. Her words were not really those of unbelief, but of faith asking for greater assurance. When her mind had time to take in the full extent of Elisha's promise, inexpressible joy would chase the last trace of doubt from her soul. (3) The event happened as predicted, and a son was born. We learn that those who show kindness to God's people shall not go without their reward (Matt. x. 41, 42). The reward may not come in the form they anticipate, but it will come in the way that is best for them, and will generally be above all that they ask or think (Eph. iii. 20), God's power, "which calleth those things which be not as though they were" (Rom. iv. 17), will do marvels for us, if only we have faith to receive his promise.— J. O.

Vers. 18—37.—*The lady of Shunem:* 2. *The son taken and restored.* A lapse of several years occurs in the story, during which time the child had grown, till he was able to go out to his father to the harvest-field.

I. THE UNEXPECTED STROKE. 1. *A boyhood of promise.* Everything combined to invest this Shunammite's son with interest, and to make him the idol of his parents' heart. He was an only son, the son of his father's old age, a child of promise—almost of miracle. He would be the joy and delight of his home, a constant wonder, an unceasing study. He was his father's, not less than his mother's, favourite, as seen by the way in which the child runs out to him in the field. Great hopes would be built on him, and it might be thought that these could hardly fail to be realized. From the manner in which he had been given, God might seem pledged to preserve him from the ordinary dangers of childhood. He lived—so it might be fancied—a charmed life, and could not fall a victim to disease and trouble as other children did. Alas! the contrary was soon to be shown. 2. *The child smitten.* The manner of the playful child's seizure is simply and naturally told. The boy is sporting among the reapers, when suddenly he exclaims, " My head, my head!" The father is by his side, and orders him to be carried home to his mother. He thinks, apparently, only of some passing illness. The heat has proved too much for him. The mother's instinct more surely divines the fatal character of the stroke. She does not even lay him on his bed, but, taking him on her knees, holds him there in an agony of terror and affection, boding the worst. How great a mother's love! The father is sought in the hour of play; the mother's knee is the place in sickness. At noon the child dies. 3. *The child dead.* (1) It is not an unexampled thing for children to be taken away as suddenly and pathetically as this Shunammite's son was. Many a parent's bleeding heart can tell of similar wounds. The suffering and death of little children is one of the "dark things" of Providence. Often it is the brightest and most promising that is taken, and the removal is sometimes as sharp, startling, and unlooked-for as in the case here described. Yesterday, nay, at morn, the mother had her child by her, happy, winsome, full of mirth and frolic; at noon he is snatched from her embrace for ever. (2) The special mystery in the case of this Shunammite's son is that he was a child of promise. Had not God given her this son—given him without her seeking—and how could he now, without manifest injustice, snatch him away from her again in this ruthless manner? Was there not, in this way of dealing, a breaking of promise with her, something arbitrary, capricious, unfair? So to her wild, whirling thoughts, it may have seemed. God's ways are, in truth, often very mysterious. Yet in the present instance may not the very fondness of these doting parents for their child help to explain something of the darkness of God's dealing with them? God never binds himself to an unconditional continuance of our blessings. There was danger, just because this child was held so dear, of the parents' centring all in it—forgetting, in their feeling of the security of their possession, that the gift still hung on the will of the Giver. To recall them to a sense of their dependence, or, if this is rejected, then, as in Abraham's case, to perfect the faith of this Shunammite through trial, the gift is for the time withdrawn. (3) The child is dead, and with almost unnatural composure, the stricken mother rises from her seat, bears the child's body aloft to the prophet's chamber, lays it on the bed, and goes out, locking the door behind her. She tells neither servants, husband, nor any one else, of what has happened. Her husband was still in the field, and she must have put off any inquiries he made with evasive answers. A great mystery hung over this unlooked-for bereavement, and as only the prophet can solve that mystery, to the prophet she will go.

II. THE JOURNEY TO CARMEL. 1. *On the way.* (1) The lady sends to her husband for an ass, and a young man to accompany her, that she may "run" to the prophet, and come again. She gives no explanation, for in her heart she no doubt cherished hope that her mission would not be in vain. She clung to the promise of God (cf. Heb. xi. 17—19). In the hour of trouble, nothing lightens the gloom like a promise to hold by. (2) The husband's surprised question, "Wherefore wilt thou go to him to-day? it is neither new moon, nor sabbath," shows that it was Elisha's custom to hold religious assemblies on the sabbath days, to which the godly in Israel resorted. This is an interesting side light on the practice of the time. Weekly assemblies were not provided for in the Law, but where love to God is in the heart, it needs no law to bring believers together (Mal. iii. 16). (3) The journey was made in haste. "Slacken not the riding." Such errands brooked no delay. When one is earnest in pressing for a blessing, no obstacles will be allowed to stand in the way. Neither in service of God, in seeking blessing from God, nor in pursuit of holiness, should we be tempted to "slacken" our endeavours (Phil. iii. 13, 14). 2. *Meeting Gehazi.* From afar, from his dwelling on Carmel, Elisha saw the hard riding of the lady whom he recognized as the Shunammite. With an instant presentiment that something was wrong—though nothing had been revealed to him (ver. 27)—he bade Gehazi hasten, and inquire concerning herself, her husband, and her child, if it were "peace." To him, however, she was in no wise minded to open up her heart. She but curtly replied, as she had before done to her husband (ver. 23), "It is peace." With all her deep affliction, she had not surrendered faith. She felt that God was trying her, but though "faith and form" were sundered in the night of fear, she had courage to believe that it would yet be "well." Her comfort was not in the well-being of her child with God, but in the hope that he would be restored to her. With the new light the gospel has given, Christians can say of their dear lost children, "It is well," though they have no hope of beholding them again on earth (see sermons and pieces in Logan's 'Words of Comfort;' especially sermon by C. H. Spurgeon on this text, 'Infant Salvation,' p. 117, 9th edit.). 3. *At Elisha's feet.* (1) Arrived in the prophet's presence, the bereaved mother cast herself in mute grief and supplication at his feet. With singular inappreciation of the delicacy of the situation, Gehazi approached to thrust her away. But Elisha perceived how deeply her soul was "vexed" within her, though as yet he could not divine the cause. There is a silence which is often more eloquent than speech. God does not need our words to tell him what we want; he can read even the "groanings that cannot be uttered" (Rom. viii. 26). This mourner took her trouble to the right place. (2) By-and-by she found words, which in form were words of expostulation, "Did I desire a son of my lord? did I not say, Do not deceive me?" In reality she was recalling to the prophet that it was his own word which had promised her this child. She was telling him in effect that the child was dead, and supplicating his help to prevent his original promise being completely cancelled. God is pleased that we should plead his promises with him. He bids us "put him in remembrance" (Isa. xliii. 26); like Job, "fill our mouth with arguments" (Job xxiii. 4). He will honour his own word, for "his gifts and calling are without repentance" (Rom. xi. 29).

III. THE CHILD RESTORED. 1. *Gehazi's failure.* Anxious to lose no time in doing what he was confident it was the will of God should be done, Elisha directed his servant, who could so much more quickly than himself, to speed forward, and lay his staff upon the face of the child. He was neither to allow time to be wasted, nor his thoughts to be distracted, by saluting any one on the way. ("The King's business required haste;" 1 Sam. xxi. 8; cf. Luke x. 4.) Gehazi did as he was commanded, but "there was neither voice nor hearing." The staff did not work the wonder—was never intended to do so; it was only a symbol of the prophetic authority under sanction of which the deed was to be wrought. There have been many speculations as to the cause of Gehazi's failure, some supposing that Elisha had stepped beyond his province in presuming to delegate this power to another; others, that the failure was a designed rebuke to Gehazi; others, that this was a new trial of the Shunammite's faith. But surely the simplest explanation is also the most probable. Gehazi was sent in good faith, but the deed was not one to be wrought by magic, but by the concurrence of faith and prayer. Elisha's prayers accompanied his messenger, but the defects in Gehazi's own spiritual nature proved too serious for the work he had to do. God would not act through such an instrument. Even when Elisha came upon the scene, it was not without difficulty that he accomplished the miracle. His foresight in this was limited, even as in the matter of the child's death the fact was "hid" from him. 2. *Elisha's success.* The Shunammite had refused to leave Elisha, and now, as they journeyed onward, Gehazi met them, announcing, "The child is not awaked." Elisha himself now took in hand the task in which Gehazi had failed. (1) He went into the room where the child was, shut the door "upon them twain," and prayed. The prophet and the dead are alone together, but God is there too. Elisha attacked the problem from its spiritual side. His first object was to get his own soul into a spiritual frame, and to secure God's approval of his efforts. He believed, like his master Elijah, in the virtue of "effectual fervent prayer" (Jas. v. 16). Such preparations are necessary if we would accomplish the greater miracle of raising the spiritually dead. Prayer attains its highest power when "secret" (Matt. vi. 6). (2) Divinely directed in answer to his prayer, Elisha now stretched himself upon the body of the child, placing his mouth on his mouth, his eyes on his eyes, his hands on his hands, etc. (cf. 1 Kings xviii. 21), and a first stage in restoration was accomplished—"the flesh of the child waxed warm." We can give no explanation whatever of the *rationale* of this procedure, which yet in some way unknown may have made Elisha a co-agent in the work of restoration. If life was not absolutely extinct—a supposition countenanced by the fact that decomposition does not seem, even at the distance of many hours, to have set in (Bähr)—some reason might be seen for it. (3) Elisha now arose, walked for a time to and fro, perhaps to increase animal heat, more probably in an energetic bracing of mind and spirit to overcome remaining obstacles to the power of faith, then renewed his former position of contact with the child. Life gradually reasserted its power; the child sneezed once, again, seven times; then opened his eyes, and was restored to his parent. The lessons from this concluding part of the story are: (1) Prayer conjoined with appropriate action does not fail of its reward. (2) The duty of perseverance. (3) Some spiritual tasks are more difficult than others (Mark ix. 29). (4) In the case of the Shunammite, the victory of faith. (5) The ease with which Christ wrought his miracles as compared with these laborious exertions of Elisha—a proof of the superior greatness of his power.—J. O.

Vers. 38—41.—*The deadly pottage.* Two other remarkable, though more briefly related, works of Elisha are narrated in the closing verses of this chapter. Both have to do with " the sons of the prophets" at Gilgal; both relate to a time of famine; and one is an Old Testament anticipation of a signal miracle of Christ. The first is the healing of the deadly pottage.

I. THE PROPHETIC COLLEGE. We are transported to Gilgal, and gain a glimpse into the interior of the prophetic school. 1. *Religious instruction.* Elisha is there, and "the sons of the prophets" are "sitting before him," receiving his instructions. There is dearth of temporal provision, but none of spiritual. The usual exercises of instruction and devotion go on, as if plenty reigned. 2. *Religious fellowship.* The famine has not sufficed to break up the little community, but has drawn the members of it—as trial should always do—closer together. They have a common table. They "dwell together in unity" (Ps. cxxxiii. 1). Elisha, like a good captain, shares the hardships of his army. God's people are sometimes brought into difficulty enough, but the effect should only be to strengthen the bonds of brotherly love. 3. *Religious order.* There are orderly arrangements. Elisha is not only preceptor, but director of the temporal affairs of the community. All obey him, as all appeal to him when trouble arises. The invisible Head of the community is Jehovah. On him they rely with confidence, when every other source of help fails.

II. DEATH IN THE POT. The great pot is set on to seethe pottage in, and one goes out to gather herbs to eke out the scanty supply. 1. *The poisonous gourd.* Attracted by some wild creepers, the messenger gathers therefrom a lapful of gourds, which he mistakes for gourds of a similar appearance that are edible. The plants he had gathered were in reality poisonous. He brought them home, and they were shred into the pottage. We may learn two lessons. (1) The danger of being deceived by appearances. Things often are not what they seem. The most plausible errors are those which bear a superficial resemblance to great truths. We need to have our " senses exercised to discern both good and evil" (Heb. v. 14). To the true vine there correspond many wild vines; to the gourds that nourish and satisfy, many fair but poisonous imitations. (2) The best intentions may lead to sad mistakes. The important point to be noticed here is that our intentions, however good, cannot prevent things from acting according to their real nature. The person who gathered the gourds thought them innocuous, but they produced their poisonous effects all the same. " Sincerity " does not exonerate us from the consequences of our actions; at least it cannot prevent these consequences following. Poisonous principles are as harmful in their influence when promulgated in ignorance, as when diffused with the fullest knowledge of their deadly character. " They knew it not " does not suffice to alter the nature of facts. 2. *The timely discovery.* The pottage was no sooner tasted than the peculiar flavour and felt effects discovered to those eating it that there was something amiss. The cry was raised, " O thou man of God, there is death in the pot!" (1) One poisonous ingredient had destroyed the value of much wholesome food. It did not require that all the elements in the pottage should be unwholesome; it was enough that this one was. Through it the whole mixture was rendered deadly. It is not uncommon to defend a system by pointing to the numerous truths which it contains. But one vital error blended with these truths may give the whole a fatal quality. The gospel itself may be adulterated with specious lies which destroy its power for good. (2) It is well when there is timely discovery of evil. It is better when, as here, those who have made the discovery resolve to partake no more of the poisoned dish. " They could not eat thereof." But many, in moral things, who know, who at least have been warned, that there is "death in the pot," go on eating of it. There is death in the *intoxicating* pot, yet many will not refrain.

III. THE POTTAGE HEALED. Elisha had within himself a monition what to do. He said, " Bring meal." The meal was brought, and cast into the pottage, and the evil was at once cured. There seems no reason for using the meal except that it was customary to accompany these prophetic miracles with an outward symbolical act; and the meal, as a symbol of what was wholesome and nutritious in food, was as appropriate a medium as any to be used. We get this idea—that the unwholesome is to be displaced by the wholesome. If the bane is to be destroyed, we must use as antidote that which is of opposite character. As a work of God's power, the miracle was a pledge to the prophets of God's ability and readiness to help them in every time of need. The simplest means can be made effectual if God blesses it.—J. O.

Vers. 42—44.—*The twenty barley loaves.* This miracle foreshadows Christ's acts of multiplying the loaves (Matt. xiv. 15—21; xv. 32—39, etc.).

I. THE GIFT OF LOAVES. In a time of great need in the little society, there came a man from Baal-shalisha, bringing with him twenty barley loaves and a quantity of fresh corn. This welcome gift was: 1. *Prompted by a religious motive.* It was "bread of the firstfruits." The religious dues were ordinarily paid to priests and Levites, but in the state of religion in Israel, this good man thought that he kept the spirit of the Law best by bringing his loaves and corn to Elisha and his pupils. The act is proof (1) of his genuine piety; (2) of his religious good sense; (3) of his habitual conscientiousness in discharge of duty. He did not conceive that "dearth in the land" freed him from the obligation of the firstfruits. Would that every *Christian* had as high and conscientious a standard in religious giving! We may suppose that the man was further moved in part by a benevolent desire to be of service to Elisha and the prophets. In that case he would be no loser by his kindness. 2. *Providentially timed to meet a pressing necessity.* From the point of view of Elisha and his friends, the visit of the man of Baal-shalisha was a signal interposition of Providence for their relief. Their supplies were exhausted, and they had been praying and hoping for a door of help to be opened to them. Just then this anonymous donor from Baal-shalisha comes in with his bread. It was as direct a case of Divine provision as when the ravens brought bread and flesh to Elijah at the brook Cherith (1 Kings xvii. 6). God's ways of providing for his people are endless in their variety. Many instances are on record of help sent in just as wonderful a way to those in need as this passage exhibits.

II. THE MIRACULOUS INCREASE. Precious as these twenty barley loaves were, they formed, after all, but scant provision for a hundred hungry men. The prophet had, however, warrant from God to convert them into the sufficiency required. 1. "*Thus saith the Lord.*" "Give unto the people," said Elisha, "that they may eat." When Gehazi objected that there was not enough for all the company, the prophet repeated his command, adding, "For thus saith the Lord, They shall eat, and shall leave thereof." A "thus saith the Lord" suffices to overcome all objections. What can it not accomplish? It made the worlds at first; it gave the Israelites manna in the wilderness; it brought water from the rock; it had but a little before multiplied the widow's oil. If we have this warrant for anything we are told to do, we need not hesitate to attempt it. 2. *The people fed.* Accordingly, when the bread was served out, it was found to be sufficient for all. It is curiously supposed by some that the miracle was not in the multiplication of the bread, but in causing the portions received to satisfy hunger. The analogy of the other miracles by multiplication, not in the Gospels alone, but in these very histories (1 Kings xvii. 12—16; ch. iv. 1—7), is against this. We see in the provision made (1) a blending of providence and miracle. An appreciable quantity of the bread provided was furnished by the man of Baal-shalisha; God made this sufficient by a direct act of power. Another illustration of the variety of the Divine methods. The one thing certain is that those who trust him *will* be provided for (Ps. xxxiv. 9, 10). We do well to see in it also (2) an image of the true, God-given, spiritual bread, which God brings to us in our spiritual need, and by which he satisfies our spiritual hunger (John vi. 26—58).—J. O.

EXPOSITION.

CHAPTER V.

Vers. 1—27.—THE CURE OF NAAMAN'S LEPROSY. HIS GRATITUDE; AND THE SIN OF GEHAZI. The historian continues his narrative of Elisha's miracles, commenced in ch. ii., and gives in the present chapter a very graphic and complete account of two which were especially remarkable, and which stood in a peculiar relation the one towards the other. One was the removal of leprosy; the other, its infliction. One was wrought on a foreigner and a man of eminence; the other, on a Hebrew and a servant. The second was altogether consequential upon the first, without which the occasion for it would not have arisen. The two together must have greatly raised the reputation of the prophet, and have given him an influence beyond the borders of the land of Israel ; at the same time extending the reputation of Jehovah as a great God through many of the surrounding nations.

Ver. 1.—**Now Naaman, captain of the host of the King of Syria.** The name "Naaman" is here found for the first time. It is thought to be derived from that of an Aramæan god (Ewald), and appears in the later Arabic under the form of *Nomân*, in which shape it is familiar to the students of Arabian history. Benhadad, who had been wont in his youth and middle age to lead his armies into the field in person (1 Kings xx. 1—20 ; xxii. 31 ; 'Ancient Monarchies,' vol. ii. p. 103), seems now in his old age to have found it necessary to entrust the command to a general, and to have made Naaman captain of his host. Compare the similar practice (ibid., p. 101) of the Assyrian monarchs. **Was a great man with his master, and honourable**— rather, *honoured*, or *held in esteem* (τεθαυμασ- μένος, LXX.)—**because by him the Lord had given deliverance**—literally, *salvation*, or *safety* (σωτηρίαν, LXX.)—**unto Syria.** Probably he had commanded the Syrian army in some of its encounters with the Assyrians, who at this time, under Shalmaneser II., were threatening the independence of Syria, but did not succeed in subjecting it. **He was also a mighty man in valour**—*gibbôr haïl*, commonly translated in our version by " mighty man of valour," does not mean much more than " a good soldier "—but he was **a leper.** Leprosy had many degrees. Some of the lighter kinds did not incapacitate a man for military service, or unfit him for the discharge of court duties (ver. 18). But there was always a danger that the lighter forms might develop into the severer ones.

Ver. 2.—**And the Syrians had gone out by companies** ; or, *in marauding bands.* No peace had been made after Ahab's expedition against Ramoth-Gilead. Hostilities, therefore, still continued upon the borders, where raids were frequent, as upon our own northern border in mediæval times. **And had brought away captive out of the land of Israel a little maid.** The marauding expeditions of ancient times had for one of their main objects the capture of slaves. In Africa wars are still carried on chiefly for this purpose. **And she waited on Naaman's wife.** Either Naaman had led the expedition, and this particular captive had been assigned to him in the division of the booty,

or she had merely passed into his possession by purchase, and thus become one of his wife's attendants.

Ver. 3.—**And she said unto her mistress, Would God my lord were with the prophet that is in Samaria !** literally, *Oh that my lord were before the prophet who is in Samaria !* Elisha had a house in Samaria (ch. vi. 32), where he resided occasionally. **For he would recover him of his leprosy.** The " little maid " concludes from her small experience that, if her master and the great miracle-working prophet of her own land could be brought together, the result would be his cure. She has, in her servile condition, contracted an affection both for her master and her mistress, and her sympathies are strongly with them. Perhaps she had no serious purpose in speaking as she did. The words burst from her as a mere expression of good will. She did not contemplate any action resulting from them. " Oh that things could be otherwise than as they are ! Had I my dear master in my own country, it would be easy to accomplish his cure. The prophet is so powerful and so kind. He both could and would recover him." Any notion of her vague wish being carried out, being made the ground of a serious embassy, was probably far from the girl's thought. But the " bread cast upon the waters returns after many days." There is no kind wish or kind utterance that may not have a result far beyond anything that the wisher or utterer contemplated. Good wishes are seeds that ofttimes take root, and grow, and blossom, and bear fruit beyond the uttermost conception of those who sow them.

Ver. 4.—**And one went in, and told his lord, saying.** " One went in " is a possible translation ; but it is simpler and more natural to translate " he went in," *i.e.* Naaman went in, and told his lord, Benhadad, the King of Syria. **Thus and thus said the maid that is of the land of Israel.** Being " of the land of Israel," her words had a certain weight—she had means of knowing—she ought to know whether such a thing as the cure of leprosy by the intervention of a prophet was a possible occurrence in her country.

Ver. 5.—**And the King of Syria said, Go to, go** ; rather, *Go, depart* ; i.e. lose no time ; go at once, if there is any such possibility as the maiden has indicated. " We see," Bähr says, " from the king's readiness, how anxious he was for the restoration of Naaman." **And I will send a letter unto the King of Israel.** Letters had been interchanged between Solomon and Hiram, King of Tyre (2 Chron. ii. 3—11), a century earlier ; and the communications of king with king in the East, though sometimes carried on orally by ambassadors, probably took place to a large extent by means of letters from a very early date. Written communications seem to have led to the outbreak of the war by which the foreign dynasty of the Hyksos was driven out of Egypt, and the native supremacy re-established ('History of Ancient Egypt,' vol. ii. pp. 199, 200). Written engagements were certainly entered into between the Egyptian kings and the Hittites at a date earlier than the Exodus (ibid., pp. 291, 310). Benhadad evidently regards the sending of a letter to a neighbouring monarch as a natural and ordinary occurrence. **And he—** i.e. Naaman—**departed, and took with him ten talents of silver**—reckoned by Keil as equal to 25,000 thalers, or £3750; by Thenius as equal to 20,000 thalers, or £3000—**and six thousand pieces of gold.** "Pieces of gold" did not yet exist, since coin had not been invented. Six thousand shekels' weight of gold is probably intended. This would equal, according to Keil, 50,000 thalers (£7500); according to Thenius, 60,000 thalers (£9000). Such sums are quite within the probable means of a rich Syrian nobleman of the time, a favourite at court, and the generalissimo of the Syrian army. Naaman evidently supposed that he would have, directly or indirectly, to purchase his cure. **And ten changes of raiment** (comp. Gen. xlv. 22; Hom., 'Od.,' xiii. 67; Xen., 'Cyrop.,' viii. 2. § 8; 'Anab.,' i. 2. § 29; etc.). The practice of giving dresses of honour as presents continues in the East to this day.

Ver. 6.—**And he brought the letter to the King of Israel, saying.** The hostile relations between Syria and Israel would not interfere with the coming and going of a messenger from either king to the other, who would be invested with an ambassadorial character. **Now when this letter is come unto thee.** We must not suppose that we have here the whole letter, which, no doubt, began with the customary Eastern formalities and elaborate compliments. The historian omits these, and hastens to communicate to us the main point of the epistle, or rather, perhaps, its main drift, which he states somewhat baldly and bluntly. **Behold, I have therewith sent Naaman my servant to thee, that thou mayest recover him**—literally, *and thou shalt recover him*—**of his leprosy.** The letter made no mention of Elisha. Benhadad assumed that, if the King of Israel had in his dominions a person able to cure leprosy, he would be fully cognizant of the fact, and would at once send for him, and call upon him for an exertion of his gift or art. He is not likely to have comprehended the relations in which Kings of Israel stood towards the Jehovistic prophets, but may probably have thought of Elisha "as a sort

of chief magus, or as the Israelitish high priest" (Menken), whom the king would have at his beck and call, and whose services would be completely at his disposal.

Ver. 7.—**And it came to pass, when the King of Israel had read the letter, that he rent his clothes.** In horror and alarm (comp. 2 Sam. xiii. 19; 2 Chron. xxxiv. 27; Ezra ix. 3; Jer. xxxvi. 24). He concluded that once more (see 1 Kings xx. 7) the Syrian monarch was determined to find a ground of quarrel, and had therefore sent to him an impossible request. **And said, Am I God, to kill and to make alive?** To "kill" and to "make alive" were familiar expressions in the mouth of the Israelites to designate omnipotence (see Deut. xxxii. 39; 1 Sam. ii. 6). Recovering from leprosy was equivalent to making alive, for a leprous person was "as one dead" (Numb. xii. 12) according to Hebrew notions. **That this man doth send unto me to recover a man of his leprosy.** The king evidently does not bethink himself of Elisha, of whose great miracle of raising the dead to life (ch. iv. 34—36) he may not up to this time have heard. Elisha's early miracles were mostly wrought with a certain amount of secrecy. **Wherefore consider, I pray you, and see how he seeketh a quarrel against me.** The king misjudged Benhadad, but not without some grounds of reason, if he was ignorant of Elisha's miraculous gifts. Benhadad, when seeking a ground of quarrel with Ahab, had made extravagant requests (see 1 Kings xx. 3—6).

Ver. 8.—**And it was so**—or, *it came to pass*—when Elisha the man of God (see ch. iv. 7, 16, etc.) **had heard that the King of Israel had rent his clothes, that he sent to the king, saying, Wherefore hast thou rent thy clothes?** The king's act was public; his complaint was public; he wished his subjects to know the outrageous conduct, as he viewed it, of the Syrian king (comp. 1 Kings xx. 7, where Ahab similarly calls attention to the strait in which he is placed). Thus the rumour went through the town, and reached the ears of the prophet, who therefore sent a message to the king. **Let him come now to me;** i.e. let Naaman, instead of applying to thee, the earthly head of the state, the source of all human power, which is utterly unavailing in such a case, apply to me, the source of spiritual power, the commissioned minister of Jehovah, who alone can help him under the circumstances. **And [then] he shall know that there is a prophet in Israel;** i.e. he shall have swift and sure demonstration, that God "has not left himself without witness," that, "in spite of the apostasy of king and people, the God who can kill and make alive yet makes himself known in

Israel in his saving might through his servants the prophets" (Bähr), of whom I am one.

Ver. 9.—**So Naaman came with his horses and with his chariot.** The Syrians had had chariots, and used horses to draw them, from a remote date. The Hyksos, who introduced horses and chariots into Egypt, though not exactly a Syrian people, entered Egypt from Syria; and in all the Syrian wars of the Egyptians, which began about B.C. 1600, we find their adversaries employing a chariot force. In one representation of a fight between the Egyptians and a people invading Egypt from' Syria, the war-chariots of the latter are drawn by four oxen; but generally the horse was used on both sides. Syria imported her horses and chariots from Egypt (1 Kings x. 29), and, as appears from this passage, employed them for peaceful as well as for warlike purposes. There was a similar employment of them from a very early time in Egypt (see Gen. xli. 43; 1.9). **And stood at the door of the house of Elisha.** Elisha was at this time residing in Samaria, whether in his own house or not we cannot say. His abode was probably a humble one; and when the great general, accompanied by his cavalcade of followers, drew up before it, he had, we may be sure, no intention of dismounting and entering. What he expected he tells us himself in ver. 11. The prophet regarded his pride and self-conceit as deserving of a rebuke.

Ver. 10.—**And Elisha sent a messenger unto him.** Elisha asserted the dignity of his office. Naaman was "a great man" (ver. 1), with a high sense of his own importance, and regarded the prophet as very much inferior to himself. He expected to be waited on, courted, to receive every possible attention. Elisha no doubt intended very pointedly to rebuke him by remaining in his house, and communicating with the great man by a messenger. But there is no ground for taxing him with "priestly pride," or even with "impoliteness" on this account. He had to impress upon the Syrian noble the nothingness of wealth and earthly grandeur, and the dignity of the prophetic office. He did not do more than was requisite for these purposes. **Saying, Go and wash in Jordan seven times.** Elisha speaks, no doubt, "by the word of the Lord." He is directed to require of Naaman a compliance with a somewhat burdensome order. The nearest point on the course of Jordan was above twenty miles distant from Samaria. Naaman is to go thither, to strip himself, and to plunge into the stream seven times. The directions seem given to test his faith. They may be compared with that of our Lord to the blind man, "Go, wash in the pool of Siloam," and, in another point of view, with that given to Joshua (Josh. vi. 3—5), and that of Elijah to his servant (1 Kings xviii. 43). To repeat a formal act six times without perceiving any result, and yet to persevere and repeat it a seventh time, requires a degree of faith and trust that men do not often possess. **And thy flesh shall come again to thee, and thou shalt be clean.** The scaly leprous scurf shall fall off and reveal clean flesh underneath. Thy body shall be manifestly freed from all defilement.

Ver. 11.—**But Naaman was wroth, . . . and said.** Not unnaturally. As a "great man," the lord on whose arm the king leant, and the captain of the host of Syria, Naaman was accustomed to extreme deference, and all the outward tokens of respect and reverence. He had, moreover, come with a goodly train, carrying gold and silver and rich stuffs, manifestly prepared to pay largely for whatever benefit he might receive. To be curtly told, "Go, wash in Jordan," by the prophet's servant, without the prophet himself condescending to make himself visible, would have been trying to any Oriental's temper, and to one of Naaman's rank and position might well seem an insult. The Syrian general had pictured to himself a very different scene. **Behold, I thought, He will surely come out to me, and stand, and call on the Name of the Lord his God, and strike his hand over the place, and recover the leper;** rather, *take away the leprosy* (ἀποσυνάξει τὸ λεπρόν, LXX.). Naaman had imagined a striking scene, whereof he was to be the central figure, the prophet descending, with perhaps a wand of office, the attendants drawn up on either side, the passers-by standing to gaze —a solemn invocation of the Deity, a waving to and fro of the wand in the prophet's hand, and a sudden manifest cure, wrought in the open street of the city, before the eyes of men, and at once noised abroad through the capital, so as to make him "the observed of all observers," "the cynosure of all neighbouring eyes." Instead of this, he is bidden to go as he came, to ride twenty miles to the stream of the Jordan, generally muddy, or at least discoloured, and there to wash himself, with none to look on but his own attendants, with no *éclat*, no pomp or circumstance, no glory of surroundings. It is not surprising that he was disappointed and vexed.

Ver. 12.—**Are not Abana and Pharpar, rivers of Damascus, better than all the waters of Israel? may I not wash in them, and be clean?** The "rivers of Damascus" are streams of great freshness and beauty. The principal one is the Barada, probably the Abana of the present passage, which, rising in the Antilibanus range, and flowing through a series of romantic glens, bursts finally from the mountains through a deep gorge and scatters itself over the plain. One branch passes right through the city of Damascus, cutting it in half. Others flow past the city both on the north and on the south, irrigating the gardens and orchards, and spreading fertility far and wide over the Merj. A small stream, the Fidjeh, flows into the Barada from the north. Another quite independent river, the Awaaj, waters the southern portion of the Damascene plain, but does not approach within several miles of the city. Most geographers regard this as the "Pharpar;" but the identification is uncertain, since the name may very possibly have attached to one of the branches of the Barada. The Barada is limpid, cool, gushing, the perfection of a river! It was known to the Greeks and Romans as the Chrysorrhoas, or "river of gold." We can well understand that Naaman would esteem the streams of his own city as infinitely superior to the turbid, often sluggish, sometimes "clay-coloured" (Robinson, 'Researches,' vol. ii. p. 256) Jordan. If leprosy was to be *washed* away, it might naturally have appeared to him that the pure Barada would have more cleansing power than the muddy river recommended to him by the prophet. **So he turned and went away in a rage.**

Ver. 13.—**And his servants came near, and spake unto him, and said, My father.** Naaman's attendants did not share his indignation, or, if they did, since servants in the East are apt to be jealous of their masters' honour, had their feelings more under control; and they therefore interfered with mild words, anxious to pacify him, and persuade him to follow the prophet's advice. "My father" is a deferential and, at the same time, an affectionate address, not unnatural in the mouth of a confidential servant (comp. ch. ii. 12). There is thus no need of any alteration of the text, such as Ewald (יֹב for אָבִי) or Thenius (אָם for אָבִי) proposes. It must be admitted, however, that the LXX. seem to have had יֹב in their copies. **If the prophet had bid thee do some great thing**—"had set thee," *i.e.,* "some difficult task"—**wouldest thou not have done it? how much rather then,** [shouldest thou perform his behest] **when he saith to thee, Wash, and be clean?** The reasoning was unanswerable, and took effect. Naaman was persuaded.

Ver. 14.—**Then went he down;** *i.e.* descended into the deep Jordan valley from the highland of Samaria—a descent of above a thousand feet. The nearest route would involve a journey of about twenty-five miles. **And dipped himself seven times in Jordan**—

i.e. followed exactly the prophet's directions in ver. 10—**according to the saying of the man of God: and his flesh came again like unto the flesh of a little child**—literally, *of a little lad*—**and he was clean.** Not only was the leprosy removed, but the flesh was more soft and tender than that of a grown man commonly is. It was like the flesh of a boy.

Ver. 15.—**And he returned to the man of God, he and all his company.** It is not always seen what this involved. It involved going out of his way at least fifty miles. At the Jordan, Naaman was on his way home, had accomplished a fourth part of his return journey; in three more days he would be in Damascus, in his own palace. But he feels that it would be an unworthy act to accept his cure and make no acknowledgment of it, having turned away from the prophet "in a rage" (ver. 12), now, without apology, or retractation, or expression of regret or gratitude, to return into his own country under the obligation of an inestimable benefit. His cure has wrought in him, not merely a revulsion of feeling from rage and fury to thankfulness, but a change of belief. It has convinced him that the God of Elisha is the God of the whole earth. It has turned him from a worshipper of Rimmon into a worshipper of Jehovah. He must proclaim this. He must let the prophet know what is in his heart. He must, if possible, induce him to accept a recompense. Therefore he thinks nothing of an outlay of time and trouble, but retraces his steps to the Israelite capital, taking with him all his company, his horses and his chariots, his gold and silver and bales of clothing, and numerous train of attendants. **And came, and stood before him;** *i.e.* descended from his chariot, and asked admittance into the prophet's house, and was received and allowed an audience—a striking contrast with his previous appearance before the house, in expectation that the prophet would come down and wait upon him. **And he said, Behold, now I know that there is no God in all the earth, but in Israel.** This is an acknowledgment of the sole supremacy of Jehovah on the part of a heathen, such as we scarcely find elsewhere. The general belief of the time, and indeed of antiquity, was that every land had its own god, who was supreme in it—Baal in Phœnicia, Chemosh in Moab, Moloch in Ammon, Rimmon in Syria, Bel or Bel-Merodach in Babylon, Amun-Ra in Egypt, etc.; and when there is an acknowledgment of Jehovah on the part of heathens in Scripture, it is almost always the recognition of him as *a* god—the God of the Jews or of the Israelites, one among many (see Exod. x. 16, 17; ch. xvii. 26; xviii. 33—35; 2 Chron. ii. 11; Dan. ii. 47;

iii. 29; vi. 20, etc.). But here we have a plain and distinct recognition of him as the one and only God that is in all the earth. Naaman thus shows a greater docility, a readier receptivity, than almost any of the other pious heathens who are brought before us in Scripture. Balaam and Cyrus alone equal him. **Now therefore, I pray thee, take a blessing**—*i.e.* "a present"—**of thy servant.** Heathens were accustomed to carry presents to the oracles which they consulted, and to reward those from which they received favourable responses with gifts of enormous value (see Herod., i. 14, 50, etc.). The Jewish prophets did not generally object to such free-will offerings. Naaman therefore quite naturally and reasonably made the offer. He would have contravened usage had he not done so.

Ver. 16.—**But he said, As the Lord liveth, before whom I stand, I will receive none.** Elisha regards it as best, under; the circumstances, to refuse the offered recompense. It was not compulsory on him so to act; for the precept, " Freely ye have received, freely give" (Matt. x. 8), had not been yet uttered. Pious Israelites commonly brought gifts to the prophets whom they consulted (1 Sam. ix. 7, 8; 1 Kings xiv. 3). But, in the case of a foreigner, ignorant hitherto of true religion, whom it was important to impress favourably, and, if possible, win over to the faith, Elisha deemed it advisable to take no reward. Naaman was thus taught that Jehovah was his true Healer, the prophet the mere instrument, and that it was to Jehovah that his gratitude, his thanks, and his offerings were due. **And he urged him to take it; but he refused.** Contests of politeness are common in the East, where the one party offers to give and even insists on giving, while the other makes a pretence of declining; but here both parties were in earnest, and the gift was absolutely declined.

Ver. 17.—**And Naaman said, Shall there not then, I pray thee, be given to thy servant two mules' burden of earth?** Naaman does not state what he intends to do with the earth; and the critics have consequently suggested two uses. Some suppose that he intended to make the earth into an altar upon which he might offer his sacrifices; comp. Exod. xx. 24, where an altar of earth is spoken of (Bähr and others). But the more general opinion (Thenius, Von Gerlach, etc.) is that he wished to spread the earth over a piece of Syrian ground, and thereby to hallow the ground for purposes of worship. The Jews themselves are known to have acted similarly, transferring earth from Jerusalem to Babylonia, to build a temple on it; and the idea is not an unnatural one. It does not necessarily imply

the "polytheistic superstition" that every god has his own land, where alone he can be properly worshipped. It rests simply on the notion of there being such a thing as " holy ground" (Exod. iii. 5)—ground more suited for the worship of God than ordinary common soil, which therefore it is worth while to transfer from place to place for a religious purpose. **For thy servant will henceforth offer neither burnt offering nor sacrifice [as meat offerings or firstfruits] unto other gods, but unto the Lord.** It is implied that Naaman had been hitherto a polytheist. Not much is known of the Syrian religion, but, so far as can be gathered, it would seem to have been a somewhat narrow polytheism. The sun was the supreme god, and was worshipped ordinarily under the name of Hadad (Macrob., 'Sat.,' i. 23). There was also, certainly, a great goddess, the "Dea Syra" of the Romans, whom they identified with Cybele and with their own "Bona Dea," a divinity parallel with the Ashtoreth of the Phœnicians, and the Ishtar of the Assyrians and Babylonians. Whether there were any other distinct deities may be doubted, since Rimmon is possibly only another name of Hadad (see the comment on ver. 18). Adonis is simply "Adonai," ;*i.e.* " my Lord," an epithet of the Supreme Being.

Ver. 18.—**In this thing the Lord pardon thy servant.** Naaman is not prepared to be a martyr for his religion. On returning to Damascus, it will be among his civil duties to accompany his master to the national temples, and to prostrate himself before the images of the national deities. If he declines, if (like an early Christian) he will not enter " the house of devils," much less bow down before the graven image of a false god, it may cost him his life; it will certainly cost him his court favour. For such a sacrifice he is not prepared. Yet his conscience tells him that he will be acting wrongly. He therefore expresses a hope, or a prayer, that his fault, for a fault he feels that it will be, may be forgiven him—that Jehovah will not be "extreme to mark what is done amiss," but will excuse his outward conformity to his inward faith and zeal. That **when my master goeth into the house of Rimmon.** Rimmon is probably derived from *rum* (רום), "to be high," and means "the exalted god," according to the gloss of Hesychius—'Ράμας, ὕψιστος θεός. It is wrongly connected with רמּוֹן, "a pomegranate," and should rather be compared with the Arabic *Er Rhaman*, "the Most High." The royal name, "Tab-Rimmon" (1 Kings xv. 18), contains the root, as does also the local name (Zech. xii. 11), "Hadad-Rimmon." This last word gives rise to the suspicion that Hadad and Rimmon are merely two names of the same deity, who was called "Hadad" or "Hadar" as bright and glorious, "Rimmon" as lofty and exalted. To worship there, and he leaneth on my hand. Either Naaman's leprosy must have been recent, and he refers to the king's practice in former times, or there must have been far less horror of leprosy among the Syrians than there was among the Hebrews. And I bow myself in the house of Rimmon—before the image, or at any rate before the supposed presence of the god—when I bow down myself in the house of Rimmon, the Lord pardon thy servant in this thing. The repetition of the clause indicates Naaman's anxiety on the subject.

Ver. 19.—And he said unto him, Go in peace. Elisha declared neither that God would nor that he would not forgive Naaman his departure from the path of strict right. He was not called upon to give an answer, since Naaman had not put a question, but had only expressed a wish. His "Go in peace" is to be taken simply as "wishing the departing Syrian the peace of God upon the road." So Keil, rightly. So he departed from him a little way. Naaman left the presence of Elisha, quitted Samaria, and had gone a short way on his homeward journey when Gehazi overtook him. Ver. 19 is closely connected with ver. 20.

Ver. 20.—But Gehazi, the servant of Elisha the man of God, said (see ch. iv. 12—36 for the position held towards Elisha by Gehazi), Behold, my master has spared Naaman this Syrian. Gehazi either honestly thinks, or at least persuades himself, that a Syrian ought to be, not spared, but spoiled, as being a foreigner and an enemy. In not receiving at his hands that which he brought (see ver. 5). Gehazi may not have known how much it was, but he had seen the laden animals, and rightly concluded that the value was great. But, as the Lord liveth, I will run after him, and take somewhat of him. "As the Lord liveth" seems a strange phrase in the mouth of one who is bent on lying and on stealing. But experience teaches us that religious formulæ do drop from the lips of persons engaged in equally indefensible proceedings. This is partly because formulæ by frequent use become mere forms, to which the utterer attaches no meaning; partly because men blind themselves to the wrongfulness of their actions, and find some excuse or other for any course of conduct by which they hope to profit.

Ver. 21.—So Gehazi followed after Naaman. A company of travellers in the East, even though it consist of the retinue of a single great man, will always contain footmen, as well as those who ride on horses or in

chariots, and will not travel at a faster pace than about three miles an hour. Thus Gehazi, if he went at his best speed, could expect to overtake, and did actually overtake, the cavalcade of Naaman. He probably overtook them at a very short distance from Samaria. And when Naaman saw him running after him. Gehazi was pressed for time. He could not start at once, lest he should make it too plain that he was going in pursuit of Naaman; and he could not absent himself from the house too long, lest his master should call for him. He had, therefore, at whatever loss of dignity, to hurry himself, and actually "run after" the Syrian. Naaman, either accidentally looking back, or warned by some of his train, sees him, recognizes him, and is only too glad to respond to his wishes. He lighted down from the chariot to meet him. An act of great condescension. As Bähr notes, "Descent from a vehicle is, in the East, a sign of respect from the inferior to the superior;" and Naaman, in lighting down from his chariot, must have intended to "honour the prophet in his servant" ('Commentary on Kings,' vol. ii. p. 55). But such honour is not commonly paid, and thus the act of Naaman was abnormal. And said, Is all well? The words admit of no better translation. Seeing Gehazi's haste and anxious looks, Naaman suspects that all is not well, that something has happened since he left the prophet's house, and accordingly puts his question, הֲשָׁלוֹם—Rectene sunt omnia? (Vulgate).

Ver. 22.—And he said, All is well. Gehazi's reply was, "All is well." There has been no accident, no calamity—only a casual circumstance has caused a change in my master's wishes, which I am sent thus hurriedly to communicate to thee. My master hath sent me, saying, Behold, even now (i.e. just at this time) there be come to me from Mount Ephraim two young men of the sons of the prophets. The details are added to give a greater air of truthfulness to the story. Give them, I pray thee, a talent of silver, and two changes of garments; i.e. a change apiece, and a talent between them—rather a large sum in respect of the pretended occasion, but a trifle compared with the amount which Naaman had expected to expend (ver. 5), and probably very much less than he had recently pressed upon the prophet (ver. 16). Gehazi had to balance between his own greed on the one hand, and the fear of raising suspicion on the other. His story was altogether most plausible, and his demand prudently moderate.

Ver. 23.—And Naaman said, Be content, take two talents; rather, consent, take two talents. Do not oppose thyself to my wishes

—consent to receive double what thou hast asked. Naaman is anxious to show his gratitude by giving as much as he can induce the other side to accept. He suggests two talents, probably because the strangers who are said to have arrived are two. **And he urged him.** Gehazi must have made some show of declining the offer. **And bound two talents of silver in two bags**—*i.e.* put up two talents separately in two bags, closing the mouth of the bag in each case by "binding" it round with a string—**with two changes of garments**—as asked for (ver. 22)—**and laid them upon two of his servants.** If the Hebrew silver talent was worth £375 as Keil supposes, or even £300 as Thenius reckons, it would be pretty well as much as an ordinary slave could carry, being somewhat over a hundredweight. **And they bare** them **before him;** *i.e.* they—the servants—bare the two sacks of money before him—Gehazi.

Ver. 24.—**And when he came to the tower;** rather, *to the hill* (Revised Version). Some well-known eminence at a little distance from the Damascus gate of Samaria must be intended. Here Gehazi stopped the slaves, and took the money from them. It was important for his purpose that they should not be seen re-entering the city, as that would have occasioned remark, and might naturally have led to inquiry. **He took** them—*i.e.* the bags—**from their hand** —*i.e.* from the hands of Naaman's servants —**and bestowed** them **in the house;** *i.e.* by himself or deputy brought them to Elisha's house, and there hid them away. **And he let the men**—Naaman's servants—**go, and they departed.** They hastened, no doubt, to rejoin their master.

Ver. 25.—**But he went in, and stood before his master.** Gehazi, lest his absence should be noticed, as soon as he had put away the money, sought his master's presence, entering the room casually, as if he had been busied about the house. He was met at once, however, by the plain and stern question which follows. **And Elisha said unto him, Whence** comest thou, **Gehazi?** literally, *Whence, Gehazi?* A short, stern, abrupt question. **And he said, Thy servant went no whither.** There was no help for it. One lie necessitates another. Once enter on the devious path, and you cannot say whither it will conduct you. To deceive and plunder a foreigner of a hostile nation probably seemed to Gehazi a trifle, either no sin at all, or a very venial sin. But now he finds himself led on to telling a direct lie to his master, which even he could not have justified to himself.

Ver. 26.—**And he said unto him, Went not mine heart** with thee? There is no "with thee" in the original; and the words

have been taken in quite a different sense. Ewald regards לבי, "my heart," as designating Gehazi, and meaning "my loved one, my favourite disciple." "Thou hast denied that thou wentest any whither; but did not my favourite disciple in truth go forth, when the man turned again from his chariot, as Naaman did?" (ver. 21). But no parallel instance can be adduced of any such use of לבי, which is altogether too strong a term to be applied to a mere favourite servant. The irony, moreover, of the term under the circumstances would be too great. Maurer's interpretation of לבי by "my prophetic power" (my prophetic power had not departed from me) is no better, since it requires הלך to be taken in two different senses in the two most closely connected clauses of vers. 25 and 26. Altogether, our version would seem to be the best rendering that has been suggested. It accords with the Septuagint, with Theodoret, and with the Vulgate; and it gives a satisfactory sense: "Did not my spirit go forth with thee when thou wentest forth, etc.? Was I not present in spirit during the whole transaction?" **When the man turned again from his chariot to meet thee?** (see ver. 21). Is it **a time to receive money, and to receive garments, and oliveyards, and vineyards, and sheep, and oxen, and menservants, and maidservants?** The prophet follows Gehazi's thoughts, which had been to purchase, with the money obtained from Naaman, olive yards, and vineyards, and sheep, and oxen, etc.; and asks—Was this a time for such proceedings? Keil well explains, "Was this the time, when so many hypocrites pretend to be prophets from selfishness and avarice, and bring the prophetic office into contempt with unbelievers, for a servant of the true God to take money and goods from a non-Israelite . . . that he might acquire property and luxury for himself?" It was evidently a most unfit time. As Thenius says, "In any other case better than in this mightest thou have yielded to thy desire for gold and goods."

Ver. 27.—**The leprosy therefore of Naaman shall cleave unto thee;** *i.e.* "As thou hast taken his goods, thou shalt also take his leprosy, which goes with them." A just Nemesis. **And unto thy seed for ever.** The iniquity of the fathers is visited upon the children. Gehazi, however, could avoid this part of the curse by not marrying. **And he went out from his presence a leper as white as snow.** There were many forms and degrees of leprosy (Lev. xiii. 2—46). Gehazi's was of the most pronounced kind. And it fell on him suddenly, as her leprosy fell upon Miriam (Numb. xii. 10), complete at once, so that there could be no further aggravation of it. The lesson should be taken to heart, and should be a warning to us, both against lying and against covetousness.

HOMILETICS.

Vers. 1—19.—*The lessons taught by the story of Naaman.* "The story of Naaman," says Menken, "is a worthy part of the history of those revelations and manifestations of the living God which, in their connection and continuation through many centuries, and in their tendency towards one goal and object, were designed to plant upon earth the knowledge and the worship of the true God! But it offers besides to our consideration *a rich store of reflections,* in which neither heart nor understanding can refuse a willing participation." Among the lessons, or "reflections," would seem to be the following.

I. No EARTHLY HAPPINESS WITHOUT ALLOY. Naaman, as far as external prosperity went, had all that he could desire. 1. He was "captain of the host of the King of Syria," commander-in-chief, *i.e.,* of all the national forces. He held a great position, involving high rank, vast patronage, considerable emolument, and a place in the thoughts of men next to that of the king. 2. He was "a great man with his master"—high in the royal favour—able to obtain any boon that he desired, and advance all whom he cared to patronize. 3. He was also "a mighty man of valour," or rather "a good tried soldier," approved by deeds of arms to the nation, and enjoying his own confidence and self-respect. But on all this there was one drawback. Naaman "was a leper." And so it is generally. "Everywhere, where there is or seems to be something great and fortunate, there is also some discordant 'but,' which, like a false note in a melody, mars the perfectness of the good fortune. A worm gnaws at the root of everything pertaining to this world; and everything here below contains the germs of death in itself" (Menken). Life is full of compensations. There is no misery without alleviation; no low estate without some gleam of joy or hope to brighten and glorify it; and also no happiness without some concomitant annoyance or discomfort. Now it is domestic trouble, now an unhappy turn of mind, now a recollection of some sin in the past, now an anticipation of some calamity in the future. But, perhaps most frequently, it is ill health, some form of bodily suffering. Naaman's affliction was of the most grievous kind—leprosy! a disease at once painful, unsightly, disgusting, and regarded as a disgrace.

II. SOLACE AND HELP COME TO US FROM THE MOST UNEXPECTED QUARTERS. A "little maid," a foreigner, a captive, a slave, accidentally introduced into his household, and occupying a very humble place in it, perhaps almost unknown by sight to the great lord of the mansion, who has something better to do than to take notice of his wife's attendants,—this little maid, humble as she is, and apparently of the least possible consequence, initiates the entire series of events which form the substance of the narrative. She sees her master's sufferings; she is touched by them; she longs to have them assuaged; and she bethinks herself of a possible cure of them. "Would God my lord were with the prophet that is in Samaria!" Perhaps it was a mere vague wish, a thought that rose in the mind, and was uttered without the slightest idea that action would be based on it. But our lightest words may have effects of which we never thought. The "little maid's" gentle aspiration fell on some ear which took note of it; inquiry was made; hope was aroused; and finally action followed. The small accident of an Israelite maid, who knew of Elisha's power to work miracles, being a member of his wife's household, and giving utterance to her feelings of compassion, led on to the great general's cure, and to the glorification of the Name of Jehovah throughout the Syrian nation. The mouse in the fable gave aid which was of the most vital importance to the lion. We can never tell from what humble friend or dependant we may not receive help in trouble, by precious hints or suggestions, or by effectual fervent prayers, which may be of inestimable service to us.

III. THE GREAT OF THE EARTH A POOR STAY AND SUPPORT. Neither Benhadad King of Syria, nor Joram King of Israel, were really of any help to Naaman in his trouble. Benhadad meant well; but his letter to the King of Israel confused the plain issue, and was not of the slightest practical service. Joram had to acknowledge himself utterly powerless (ver. 7), and, but for the prophet's interference, would probably have represented to the King of Syria that there was no more help to be obtained for Naaman in Israel than in his own country. Great civil personages are rarely fit to take the lead in matters which even touch upon religion. They place far too much trust in the cunning devices of mere human policy, and far too little in the force of religious principle and the overruling providence of God. The Magi did not help Christ by bringing him their gifts of gold and frankincense and myrrh. They did but draw Herod's attention to him, and bring his infant life into peril. Herod Antipas did not help John the Baptist. He "heard him gladly" (Mark vi. 20), but imprisoned him, and ultimately put him to death. The advice of the psalmist is excellent, "Put not your trust in princes; . . . for there is no help in them" (Ps. cxlvi. 3).

IV. OUR BEST HELP FROM RELIGION AND ITS MINISTERS. Naaman might have returned to Damascus in the same condition in which he left it, unhelped, unaided, uncured, but for the existence, and for the action taken by, a minister of God. Men often jeer at ministers, deride them, deny the use of them, call them idlers and super-numeraries, and declare their belief that the world would get [on quite as well, or much better, without them; but in times of difficulty and danger, and especially in the time of sickness, they are apt to have recourse to them. A Belshazzar in difficulty seeks to Daniel (Dan. v. 13), a Naaman to Elisha, a Theodosius to Ambrose, a guilty sinner to his parish priest or to the nearest godly minister of his acquaintance. Ministers, it is true, do not now heal diseases; and it is fitting that in sickness the physician should be called in, to begin with. But when the physician can do no more, when he declares the resources of his art exhausted, when death draws near us, then there are but few who despise the aid of the previously contemned servant of God, but few who are not glad to have a minister of God at their bedside, and to receive from his hands the last consolations of religion. How many have been brought by ministerial aid to die in peace and joy, who without it would have lain for days tortured with doubts and fears and misgivings! How many have even been snatched at the last moment like brands from the burning, brought through ministerial influence, even on their death-beds, to a repentance not to be repented of! It is well not to trust beforehand to a death-bed repentance, but to set our house in order while we are still in health. But the example of the thief on the cross shows that, even under the very shadow of death, the mercy of [God is not exhausted. A death-bed repentance is always possible; and in bringing it about the assistance to be derived from an experienced minister can scarcely be over-estimated.

V. THE NATURAL MAN A POOR JUDGE OF GOD'S METHODS OF SALVATION. "I thought," said Naaman, "he will surely come out to me," etc. Naaman had made up his mind what the prophet's method would be. He had his own notions concerning the fitness of things, and the mode in which Divine help, if it came at all, would come to him. When his expectations were disappointed, as human expectations on such a subject are likely to be, he was offended, and "turned and went away in a rage" (ver. 12). Do not many turn from religion altogether on similar utterly insufficient grounds? They "thought," if God gave a revelation at all, he would give it in this or that way—by a voice from heaven speaking with equal force to all, with the accom-paniment of a continuous display of miracles, by the mouth of an immaculate priesthood, or in some way quite different from that in which it has pleased God to give it; and, being disappointed in their expectation, they reject the whole matter, refuse to have anything to do with it, "turn and go away in a rage." "I thought" is all-powerful with them. Well does Menken observe, "This 'I thought' is the most mighty of all mighty things upon earth, and even if it is not the most ruinous of all ruinous things, it is yet certainly the most unfortunate of all unfortunate ones. This 'I thought' brought sin and misery and death into the world ; and it prevents redemption from sin and death in the case of thousands ! These thousands, if they perish in their opinion, will begin the next life with 'I thought.'"

VI. SECOND THOUGHTS OFTEN THE BEST. It is never too late to amend. To pride one's self on absolute consistency and unchangingness is the height of folly in a being who is not, and knows he is not, omniscient. Our first thoughts must often be mis-taken ones, and in such cases it is at least possible that our second thoughts may be better. Moreover, second thoughts may be suggested from without, and may come from those who are far wiser than ourselves. Naaman showed his good sense in giving up his original intention and adopting the advice of his servants. To have persisted for consistency's sake would have been foolish obstinacy, and would have resulted in his remaining a leper and an idolater to the day of his death.

VII. A TIME FOR ALL THINGS—A TIME TO GET, AND A TIME TO LOSE. "The labourer is worthy of his hire." Ministers cannot live on air any more than other people. There is a time when, and there are circumstances under which, it is lawful for them to receive such an amount of this world's goods as they need, or even such an amount as is offered to them. For any surplus which they receive beyond their needs they are trustees, bound to expend such surplus as they deem best for the honour of God and the benefit of man. Prophets were entitled to accept gifts of those who consulted them (1 Sam. ix. 7, 8), and Elisha himself took without hesitation the twenty loaves from the man of Baal-shalisha. But when Naaman made his offer, Elisha felt that it was "a time to lose." He had to show that "the gift of God could not be purchased with money;" he had to impress it on an ignorant but intelligent heathen, that Jehovah was a God not like other gods, and that his prophets were men not like other men. He had to teach the doctrine of free grace. His example should be a lesson to ministers, that not every gift, even though it be offered by a willing heart, ought to be accepted. There are times when a minister should decline a testimonial, an augmentation of stipend, the donation of a new pulpit, or a new organ, and when he should be glad to "lose" them for the furtherance of higher objects.

VIII. GRATITUDE FOR TEMPORAL BLESSINGS BEST SHOWN BY OUR TURNING TO GOD. When Naaman found that the prophet would receive no gift at his hand, he acquiesced, and resolved to show his gratitude for the great blessing which he had received in another way. He would thenceforth offer neither burnt offering nor sacrifice unto any other god, but only unto the Lord (ver. 17). It was a noble resolve. It might offend his sovereign, it might hamper his promotion, it might deprive him of court favour. Still, he did not hesitate; he made the resolution, and he proclaimed it. Whether he kept it faithfully or no, we are not told; we know nothing of his after-life; the curtain drops on him as he departs to his own country. But, so far as the history is carried, it shows him faithful and true. He bears off his two mules' burden of earth. He means no more to worship Rimmon. He will acknowledge and worship one God only, Jehovah. There may be weakness in the compromise with conscience which he proposes in ver. 18; but it is a pardonable weakness in one bred up a heathen. At any rate, he does right, and sets us a good example, in his resolute turning to Jehovah, as the true Source of the blessing which he has received, and as therefore deserving henceforth of all his worship and all his gratitude.

Vers. 20—27.—*The lessons taught by the sin and punishment of Gehazi.* Gehazi's is a sad case, but a not unusual one; the case of a person brought into close contact with a high form of moral excellence and spirituality, who, instead of profiting by the example, wilfully casts it aside, and adopts a low standard of life and conduct—a standard which always tends to become lower. The first lesson to be learnt from his case is this—

I. IF CONTACT WITH EXCELLENCE FAIL TO RAISE US, IT WILL SINK US, IN THE MORAL SCALE. The two disciples closest to our Lord seem to have been St. John and Judas Iscariot. The one leant upon Jesus' breast; the other dipped with him habitually (τὸν βάπτοντα μετ᾽ ἐμοῦ ἐν τῷ τρυβλίῳ) in the dish (Mark xiv. 20). The one was exalted to a spirituality rarely attained by man; the other sank to such a condition that his Lord said of him, he "is a devil" (John vi. 70). Both elevation and degradation are equally natural. The one comes from the imitation of the high example before us; the other from resisting the impulse to such imitation. If we resist impulses to good, we do ourselves irreparable harm; we blunt our consciences, harden our hearts, render ourselves less sensitive to good influences for ever after. And the longer the contact with goodness continues, the higher the exaltation, or the lower the deterioration, of our nature. Gehazi had been for years Elisha's servant. He had been on the closest terms of intimacy with him. He had witnessed his patience, his self-denial, his gentleness, his kindness, his zeal for Jehovah. But the only effect had been to harden him in evil. He had grown proud and contemptuous, as shown by his calling Naaman "this

Syrian" (ver. 20), a swearer (ver. 20), covetous, untruthful, careless of his master's honour, secretive (ver. 24), shameless. He had no sense of God's watchful eye and continual presence, no respect or love for his master, no care for what Naaman and the other Syrians would think of him. He thus did as much as in him lay to ruin his master's projects, and to lower him in the esteem of those whose good opinion he knew his master valued. Another lesson to be drawn from the narrative is the following :—

II. ONE SIN LEADS ON TO ANOTHER BY A SEQUENCE WHICH IS ALMOST INEVITABLE. Gehazi begins with covetousness. He cannot see the great wealth of Naaman, the wedges of silver and gold, and the large bales of rich stuffs, without a keen desire to obtain possession of a portion. He hopes that his master will spoil the Syrian, and not spare him ; in that case he may contrive to get a share in the advantage. His master's refusal, no doubt, seems to him mere folly, quixotism—almost madness. He sets his clever wits to work, and soon frames a scheme by which his master's intentions shall be frustrated. The scheme, as any scheme must under such circumstances, involves him in lying ; nay, in a whole heap of lies. He tells a circumstantial tale in which there is not a single word of truth. The tale runs glibly off his tongue, and easily deceives the foreigner, who is not of a suspicious temper. Gehazi is completely successful, obtains even more than he had ventured to ask ; hides it away without any difficulty, and thinks that all is over. But all is not over. " Whence comest thou, Gehazi ? " sounds in his ears ; and he must either confess all or, directly and unmistakably, lie to his master. *Of course*, the lie is resolved upon ; his previous conduct has so demoralized him, that we cannot even imagine him to have hesitated. The direct falsehood to his master, which he would fain have avoided, has to be uttered : " Thy servant went no whither." *Facilis descensus Averni.* The only security against a moral decline as grievous as Gehazi's is not to enter upon it, not to take the first step. *Principiis obsta.* Check evil tendencies at once, and the fatal sequence need never be entered upon. Gehazi's punishment has also its lesson. He had gained his coveted wealth ; the prophet could not take it from him. He was a rich man, and might carry out all his far-reaching schemes of proprietorship, and lordship over others. But what will it all profit him, if he is to be, to the end of his days, a leper ? The apples of Sodom, so " fair to view," are felt and known to be worthless, when they " turn to ashes on the lips." So was it with him ; and so is it, commonly, with those who pursue a course similar to his. The prosperity acquired by fraud has within it a taint of rottenness. There is " a little rift within the lute "—a drawback of some kind or other, which deprives the prosperity of all its value, and makes the wealthy prosperous man a miserable wretch. If he escape external calamity, he will, at any rate, not escape the worm of remorse, which will eat into his heart, and poison his cup of pleasure.

HOMILIES BY VARIOUS AUTHORS.

Vers. 1—3.—*The captive Israelitish maid.* There are four personages that stand out with special prominence in this chapter, from each of which important lessons may be learned. These are—the little Hebrew maid ; Naaman, the commander-in-chief of the Syrian army ; the Prophet Elisha ; and Gehazi, the prophet's servant. We shall speak first of the little maid.

I. THIS LITTLE MAID DID NOT FORGET HER RELIGION WHEN SHE WENT FROM HOME. We see that, though in a foreign land, she still thought of her fathers' God and of his prophet. That is an important lesson in these days, when travelling has become so common. The motto with a great many professing Christians seems to be that when they are at Rome, they must do as Rome does. When they travel on the continent, they keep the continental Sunday, just as if the same God was not looking down upon them there as at home, just as if the Lord's day was not the Lord's day everywhere, and as if there were not good Christian people on the continent who valued the day as a day of rest and worship. Mr. Ruskin wrote some pointed words lately in reference to the way Christian people seem to forget their religion when they go abroad. He asked them to count up their expenditure on railway fares and sight-seeing, on guides and guide-books, on luxuries and photographs ; and then to ask themselves how much they had spent in donations to the poor Churches of France and Belgium, or of the Waldenses in Italy. Happily, all travellers are not like this. Many Christian tourists like to find a Sunday blessing, and to hear a word of refreshing, in some little country church among the hills of Scotland or of Switzerland, or in the quiet chapel amid the pleasure-seeking crowds of Paris. But how many there are who lock up their religion when they turn the key in their house-door, and, however careful they may be of taking guide-books and other provisions for the journey, never dream of putting a Bible in the trunk! No matter where we go, let us take our religion with us, as Joseph took his into Egypt, as Daniel took his into Babylon, as this little Hebrew maid took hers into Syria. *This little maid had strong inducements to give up her religion.* No doubt it would have pleased her master and mistress if she had worshipped their gods. They might have said that her worship of any other God was an impertinence, a sort of suggestion that they were doing wrong. But she listens to the voice of conscience and of duty rather than to the voice of worldly policy and expediency. *It is a message to all who are in the employment of others.* Never sacrifice principle for place. Never sacrifice the favour of God for the favour of man. Your employer pays for your labour; he does not buy your conscience. If ever attempts are made to tamper with your conscience, be it yours to answer, " We ought to obey God rather than man." Trust God for the consequences. Trust him to provide for you. "In all thy ways acknowledge him, and he shall direct thy paths."

II. This little maid did not render evil for evil. She had been torn from her home and from her native land by the rude hands of Syrian soldiers. Perhaps her father had fallen beneath the enemy's sword. Yet we do not find her cherishing a spirit of vindictiveness or revenge. Instead of rejoicing to see her captor suffer, she pities him. She longs that he may be healed of that terrible and loathsome disease. Have we never exulted in the sufferings of others? Have we never felt a secret thrill of gratification when some misfortune has befallen one with whom we were at variance? Such a spirit, the spirit of revenge, however natural it may be, is not the spirit of Christ. He bids us do unto others as we would wish them to do unto us. The Christ-like spirit is to love our enemies, to bless them that curse us, to do good to them that hate us, and to pray for them that despitefully use us and persecute us.

III. This little maid was but young; yet, by doing what she could, she became a blessing to others. She did not say to herself, "I am but young; there is nothing I can do." She did not wait for some great thing to do. But she just did the work that lay nearest her. She saw a way in which she might be useful, and she took the opportunity at once. She said to her mistress, "Would God my lord were with the prophet that is in Samaria! for he would recover him of his leprosy." That was all. She just told of where the blessing of health was likely to be found. 1. *This is a lesson for young people, for the children.* None of you is too young to do something for Jesus. Jesus has some work for every one of you to do. It may be his work for you that you should conquer some sinful passion, some evil habit. It may be his work for you that you should stand up for him and his Word among bad companions; or that by your own quiet and gentle life, and loving disposition and kind deeds, you should show how good it is to be a Christian. Do the work that lies nearest. If you are at school or college, and find your studies irksome, and long to get free to work at your own will and pleasure; if you are learning your business, and find it a drudgery;— remember that just here Christ has a work for you to do. These difficulties have to be mastered. Master *them*, and then you will show your fitness for mastering far greater difficulties. "He that is faithful in that which is least is faithful also in much." 2. *It is a lesson for young and old.* What are you doing to be a blessing to others? Is there not some sick person to whom you might read, some poor family that you might visit occasionally with some of the comforts of life, some tempted one to whom you might speak a word of help and encouragement, some backslider to whom you might speak a word of kindly warning, some careless, godless one whom you might urge to flee from the wrath to come? And if you can do but little for the sinner and the godless yourself, perhaps you can do as the little maid did—*tell them where blessing is to be found,* and invite them to come to the house of God. There is no need for rivalry between different Christian communities. There are godless people enough to fill all the places of worship, if only Christian people would stir themselves and go out into the streets and lanes, into the highways and hedges, and, by the power of irresistible persuasion, compel them to come in. Don't trouble yourself by thinking of your own fitness or unfitness. Are you willing to be of use in Christ's work? Are you anxious to be a blessing to others? That is the great question. If so, Jesus will do the rest. He will make you a vessel unto honour, sanctified, meet for the Master's use.

IV. THE SECRET OF THIS LITTLE MAID'S FAITHFULNESS AND USEFULNESS WAS HER STRONG AND SIMPLE FAITH. She could be faithful *to* God, because she believed *in* God. She believed that God would take care of her when she was faithfully serving him. She could be useful to others because, though she was a captive and had no means to help them, she knew of One who had. *She had faith in God.* She knew that God was with Elisha, and therefore she had no doubt about Elisha's success. Yes; it is *faith* we want, if we are to be useful. We *say* we believe a great many things. But *how* do we believe them? Where is our faith in God's promises shown in our patience under difficulties and trials and discouragements? Where is our faith in God's promises shown by our liberality to his cause? Where is our faith in God's promises shown by our work done for Christ? If our faith in God is real, it will show itself in every detail of our daily life; it will overflow in acts of usefulness and love.—C. H. I.

Vers. 4—19.—*Naaman the Syrian.* This case of Naaman is an illustration of the imperfection that there is in all things human. Naaman was commander-in-chief of the Syrian army. Not only so, but he had seen service. He had won his spurs in active warfare. He had led his troops to victory. "By him the Lord had given deliverance to Syria." Hence, as we read, "he was a great man with his master, and honourable." No doubt he had been greeted on his return from battle, as victorious generals were greeted then and are greeted still, with the triumphant shouts of a joyful and exultant multitude. His cup of happiness was almost full. But there was one element of trouble that mingled with his joy. "But he was a leper." That little word "*but*," how significant it is! We should all be happy, but for something. Our plans would all be successful, but for something. We should all be very good, but for some inconsistency, some failing, some besetting sin. Here is a very good man, but he has such a bad temper. There is a very kind woman, but she has such a bitter tongue. Here is a very good man, but he is so stingy and so selfish. Here is a man who would be very useful in the Church of Christ, but he is so worldly minded. Here is a good preacher, but he doesn't just practise what he preaches. These little "buts" have their uses. They keep us, or they *ought* to keep us, humble. We ought not to be very proud of ourselves, we ought not to be very hard on others, when we think of that ugly sin of our own. But most of all, these "buts" ought to be the means of driving us, as Naaman's leprosy was the means of driving him, nearer to God. That almighty hand can alone weed the evil forces out of our nature, and bring us into conformity to his own heavenly likeness.

I. NAAMAN'S PRIDE. Kings sometimes, like other people, do stupid things. The Hebrew maid had spoken of the *prophet* that was in Israel, as being able to cure her master of his leprosy. But the King of Syria sends a letter to the *King* of Israel, saying, "I have sent Naaman my servant unto *thee*, that *thou* mayest recover him of his leprosy." The King of Syria may have meant nothing more than this, that the King of Israel might bring about Naaman's recovery by sending him to the prophet; but the King of Israel took the words as an attempt to pick a quarrel with him, and rent his clothes in anger and passion. Very often great and destructive wars have arisen from much more trifling causes—from the folly or incapacity, the rashness or stubbornness, the pride or the passion, of rulers. How thankful we should be for a wise and prudent sovereign, when we think how much harm a foolish sovereign can do! After Elisha heard of the King of Israel's absurd and childish display of anger and dismay, he sent to him, saying, "Wherefore hast thou rent thy clothes? let him come now to me, and he shall know that there is a prophet in Israel." So Naaman came with all the pomp and grandeur of a great Oriental general, and stood at the door of Elisha's house. Elisha is not overawed by this display of magnificence. He does not hasten forth and make a humble obeisance to the man of rank. He knew what respect was due to authority and station; but just then he had to do with *Naaman the man, with Naaman the leper*, and not with Naaman the general. As the servant of God, it is his duty to benefit Naaman's soul as well as his body, *and the first thing he must do is to humble him.* Naaman's leprosy was an enemy to his happiness. But he had a far worse enemy in his own heart. That was pride. How hard it was to expel it we shall see. Elisha did not go himself to speak to Naaman, but sent a messenger. That was bad enough for Naaman's pride. And this was the message that he sent: "Go and wash in Jordan seven times, and thy flesh shall come again to thee, and thou shalt be clean." That was worse. How keenly Naaman felt it we see in his action and his words. He turned away from the place in a rage, perhaps swearing at his servants to get out of his way, and said, "Behold, I thought, He will surely come out to me, and stand, and call on the Name of the Lord his God, and strike his hand over the place, and recover the leper." His leprosy had not humbled his pride. Here he was—come all the way from Syria just for the one purpose of getting cured; and yet he turns away from the only person who could cure him, because he does not pay him sufficient court, and does not flatter his vanity. How unreasonable was Naaman's pride! How unreasonable is pride in any one! And yet it is a common failing. There are very few of us without a little of it. Bishop Hooker says, "Pride is a vice which cleaveth so fast unto the hearts of men, that if we were to strip ourselves of all faults, one by one, we should undoubtedly find it the very last and hardest to put off." *What have any of us to be proud of?* Has the *sinner* any reason to be proud? He is walking on the broad way that leadeth to destruction. Not a journey, not a prospect, to be proud of, certainly! Has the *saint* any reason to be proud? Surely not. It is by the grace of God he is what he is. "Not of works, lest any man should boast." No true child of God has ever had a proud heart. Look at the humility of the Apostle Paul. Early in his Epistles he speaks of himself as "the least of the apostles;" later on he calls himself "less than the least of all saints;" while the latest description he gives of himself is "the chief of sinners." Such was Paul's estimate of his own character, the more he looked at it in the light of God's holy Law, and in the light of the cross of Jesus. The longer he lived, the more humble he became. "God resisteth the proud, but giveth grace to the humble." Away, then, with pride! Away with pride of riches! away with pride of rank! away with pride of learning! away with pride of beauty in the face that is made of clay! away with pride from every Christian heart! away with pride from the house of God! away with pride from all departments of Christian work! away with pride towards our fellow-men! Let us follow in the footsteps of him who was meek and lowly in heart.

II. NAAMAN'S CURE. Observe *the simplicity of the cure.* "Go and wash in Jordan seven times, and thy flesh shall come again to thee, and thou shalt be clean." It was the very simplicity of the cure that was the stumbling-block to Naaman. So it is with the sinner still. The simplicity of the gospel offer prevents many a one from accepting it. The servants of Naaman expressed this weakness of the human heart when they said, "My father, if the prophet had bid thee do some great thing, wouldest thou not have done it?" The simple thing, strange though it may seem, is often the hardest to do. The great thing, the thing which costs most labour, in which there is most room for our own effort, is the thing which many find it easiest to do. This is one of the reasons why the heathen religions, and the Roman Catholic religion, have so strong a hold upon the human heart. Their religion is justification by works. They afford large scope for human exertions, for penances, for pilgrimages. There is scope for good works in Protestantism too, in true Christianity. "Be careful to maintain good works," says the apostle. "We are his workmanship, created in Christ Jesus unto good works." But good works are the result, and not the cause, of our justification. We can never by any pilgrimages, by any penances, by any fastings, work out a salvation, a righteousness, for ourselves. "Not by works of righteousness which we have done, but according to his mercy he saved us, by the washing of regeneration and renewing of the Holy Ghost, which he shed on us abundantly through Jesus Christ our Saviour." Was it not a foolish thing for Naaman, a poor, miserable leper, with his life a burden to him, to be questioning the method of his cure? Is it not a foolish thing for any sinner, with death at every moment staring him in the face, and a dark and hopeless eternity yawning before him, to question God's plan of salvation? A man who is seized with a dangerous illness does not spend a whole day in discussing what remedies the physician has ordered, but, if he has common sense, he uses the remedies at once. *Sinner, the cure for your disease is a simple one.* " Believe on the Lord Jesus Christ, and thou shalt be saved." *It is the only one.* " There is none other Name under heaven given among men whereby we can be saved," except the Name of Jesus. Naaman, at last, persuaded by his servants' entreaty, believed the prophet's promise, and acted in obedience to his instructions. He went and washed in Jordan, and, as the prophet said, he was made whole. God promises to every sinner that if you believe on the Lord Jesus Christ you shall receive everlasting life. Did you ever know God's promise to fail? Why, then, should you hesitate, as a lost soul, to take the way of salvation provided for you through the mercy of God and the infinite love of Christ?

> " There is a fountain filled with blood
>   Drawn from Immanuel's veins;
> And sinners, plunged beneath that flood,
>   Lose all their guilty stains.

> " The dying thief rejoiced to see
>   That fountain in his day;
> And there may I, though vile as he,
>   Wash all my sins away."

III. NAAMAN'S GRATITUDE. Naaman's marvellous cure made him a believer in the God of Israel. He returned to Elisha with gratitude in his heart. How different the spirit in which he now approaches the prophet! No longer proud and haughty, waiting at the door for Elisha to come out to him, he enters the prophet's house, and humbly stands before him. He shows a spirit of gratitude to God and to his prophet. He asks Elisha to give him a quantity of earth, that he may raise an altar unto the God of Israel, saying that he will henceforth sacrifice to no other god. You whom God has raised up again from beds of sickness—have you shown in any practical way your gratitude to him? *Do you ever count up your mercies* when you calculate how much you will subscribe to some religious object? If you did, there would not be much difficulty in clearing off church debts. We are, all of us, every day we live, dependent on God's mercy and bounty. In his hand our breath is. " In him we live, and move, and have our being." Many of us are saved sinners, redeemed through the precious blood of Christ. What have we done to show our thankfulness to God, who called us out of darkness into his marvellous light? Naaman, though a changed man and no longer an idolater, was still *wanting in decision.* He asked to be pardoned for bowing in the temple of the god Rimmon, when his master, the king, went in to worship there. Some have thought that Elisha's answer, " *Go in peace,*" gave permission to Naaman to go through this outward form of idolatry. But the prophet did not mean this at all. His words were but the Eastern form of saying " good-bye." He neither condemned nor approved Naaman's action. He left it as a matter for his own conscience. And so it must be in many things. We cannot lay down hard-and-fast lines for others. Beginners in the Christian life, especially, should be tenderly dealt with. But while we make every allowance for Naaman, who had spent all his life in heathenism, let us not imitate him in his want of decision. He owed allegiance to a higher King than to the King of Syria. In matters of conscience, let no man be our master but Christ. Let us never sacrifice principle for expediency, or obey the call of popularity rather than the call of duty. A far higher example is that of John Knox, who, when rebuked for his outspoken words before Queen Mary and her council, said, " I am in the place where I am demanded of conscience to speak the truth; and therefore the truth I speak, impugn it whoso list."—C. H. I.

Vers. 20—27.—*Elisha and Gehazi.* We shall, perhaps, derive most profit from the study of these two characters if we look at them together, as they are here set before us, in sharp and striking contrast.

I. CONTRAST THE COVETOUSNESS OF THE ONE WITH THE UNSELFISHNESS OF THE OTHER. 1. Look, first of all, at *Elisha's unselfishness.* It is a sublime picture. We hardly know which to admire most—*Elijah* as he stands forth alone in rugged grandeur to confront the prophets of Baal; or *Elisha*, as in quiet simplicity and sincere forgetfulness of self he stands there before Naaman, and gently puts away from him the general's tempting gift.   Of the two, I think Elisha's was the harder and therefore more heroic deed.   Look at the temptations which he must have felt.   The fame of him had spread into Syria, so much so that this haughty general, the foremost man in all Syria except its king, comes to him to be healed of his leprosy.   The King of Syria himself sends a letter with his general.   And now, when, at Elisha's bidding, Naaman has washed in Jordan, and become cured, was it not a strong temptation to the prophet to take glory and honour and reward for himself?   Naaman wanted to give him rich remuneration.   He presses it upon him.   " Now therefore, I pray thee, take a blessing of thy servant."   Listen to the answer : " As the Lord liveth, before whom I stand, I will receive none."   Again Naaman urges him to take the gift, and once more and finally the prophet refuses.   And why?   Did he think there was any harm in taking a gift?   Not at all.   At other times he was quite content to be dependent on the bounty of others.   St. Paul tells us that " even so hath the Lord ordained that they which preach the gospel should live of the gospel."   Elisha had no objection to the gift as such, and even if he did not want it for himself, he could have made good use of it. *Why, then, did he refuse it ?*   (1) In the first place, *he thought of the honour of his God.* Elisha knew well that it was not *his* word or by *his* power that Naaman had been healed, but by the power of the living God.   He wanted Naaman to think, not of the prophet, but of the prophet's God.   So St. Peter acted when he and St. John had healed the lame man at the Beautiful gate of the temple.   He said to the people, " Why look ye so earnestly on us, as though by our own power or holiness we had made this man to walk ?" and then proceeded to point out to the people the benefit of faith in Christ. So it will be with every true servant of Christ.   He will seek to point men to his Master, and not to himself.   (2) Again, *he thought of the honour of his religion.*   He doubtless felt that if he had taken Naaman's gift, Naaman might afterwards have said, " Well, these prophets of Israel, who call themselves followers of the true God, are no better than our own heathen priests.   They follow their calling just for the money that it brings."   Elisha knew that that was not true.   He knew that he might lawfully take the gift, and yet be influenced by far higher motives, in the service of God.   But he felt that, though all things are lawful, all things are not expedient.   Oh that all God's people were equally solicitous about the honour of Christ's cause and kingdom!   How careful we should be lest by our worldliness, our inconsistencies, our thoughtlessness, we bring reproach upon the religion we profess!   (3) Further, *Elisha thought of the honour of his country.*   Israel had, at that time, been defeated by Syria.   Elisha felt that it would be an humiliating thing for him—a Hebrew—to take a gift from one of the conquering nation, and especially from him who had perhaps been the leading general in the war against the Jewish people.   Evidently that was what he meant when he said to Gehazi afterwards, " Is it a time to receive money, and to receive garments, and oliveyards, and vineyards, and sheep, and oxen, and menservants, and maidservants ? " The time of his country's disgrace and defeat was not a time for him to indulge in luxury and display.   There is room for more Christian patriotism in the present day— a patriotism that shall rest the honour of its country on the industry, morality, and uprightness of its people, and that shall see in every departure from these virtues a cause of humiliation and shame.   (4) Finally, *Elisha thought also of the good of Naaman.*   He wanted not only to benefit his body, but his soul also.   Therefore he avoided everything that might put a stumbling-block in his way.   And we see how well he succeeded.   Naaman, from what he had seen of Elisha, the prophet of the true God, and from what he had seen of God's power, resolved that he would never sacrifice to any other god but to the God of Israel.   If we would benefit others, our own hearts must be right with God.   There must be no doubt about our sincerity, no uncertainty about our motives.   We see in all this how little Elisha thought of self.   He had a great opportunity, and he used it well.   He had a strong temptation presented to him, and he resisted it.   It is a splendid instance of unselfishness, a splendid illustration of the power of Divine grace.   2. How different from all this *the covetousness, the selfishness, of Gehazi!*   The honour of his God, the honour of his religion, the honour of his country, the good of Naaman—none of these things ever cost him a thought.   In *his* mind self is the one all-absorbing, overmastering consideration.   Even his master's honour is of little value in his eyes.   Elisha had refused to take Naaman's gift, yet Gehazi runs after him, and says that his master has sent him to ask for money and clothes, just as if he was so fickle as not to know his own mind, and so mean as now to send and beg that which but a little time before he had sturdily declined. Gehazi's greed for money had blunted all the finer feelings of his nature. No wonder that our Saviour said, "Take heed and beware of covetousness." No wonder that Paul said, "The love of money is a root of all evil." All kinds of sins result from the love of money. We have an illustration of it in Gehazi's case. We have illustrations of it every day. How often men grow rich, but do not grow better! Sometimes increasing wealth has the strange effect of *decreasing liberality*. Sometimes increasing wealth brings with it increase of pride. Sometimes increasing wealth has made men more worldly. Instead of seeking to serve Christ *more* with their increased opportunities and increased influence, *they serve him less.* Thank God if with increasing wealth he has given you increasing grace. Thank God if he has enabled you to *give* the more, the more you got. Thank God if with increasing wealth you have kept a cool head, a warm heart, a steady hand, a clear conscience, and the friends of your youth. To those who are beginning life we would earnestly say, *Beware of covetousness.* Don't imagine that to be rich is the be-all and end-all of life. There are some things which money cannot buy. There are some things which money cannot do. Money can't keep death away from the door. Money cannot purchase the pardon of sin, or obtain for a single soul admission into heaven. "We brought nothing into this world, and it is certain we can carry nothing out." But we are not therefore to despise money. Get all the money you can, provided you get it honestly, provided you do not sacrifice your soul's interests because of it, and provided that, when you have it, you spend it well. Make a good use of your money in your lifetime. "Make to yourselves friends of the mammon which the unrighteous worship, that, when ye fail, they may receive you into everlasting habitations."

II. CONTRAST THE DECEITFULNESS OF THE ONE WITH THE STRAIGHTFORWARD HONESTY OF THE OTHER. There was nothing two-faced about Elisha. He did not say one thing with his lips, and think the very opposite in his heart. When Jehoram, King of Israel, after his idolatry and his sins, got into difficulties at the time that he and the other two kings went forth against the King of Moab, he then sent for Elisha. But Elisha does not meet him in any fawning, flattering spirit. He at once rebukes him for his sins. He says, "What have I to do with thee? get thee to the prophets of thy father, and to the prophets of thy mother." In the same way he treats Naaman as one whose pride needs to be humbled. Though he might have offended Naaman by refusing to take his gift, he plainly tells him, "As the Lord liveth, before whom I stand, I will receive none." What a contrast to this blunt, straightforward honesty is the two-faced deceitfulness of Gehazi! Observe how one sin brings another with it. He first of all *coveted the money and the raiment,* when he heard Elisha refuse Naaman's present. Then *covetousness leads to deception and lying.* He ran after Naaman's chariot, and invented a false story that some young men had come to Elisha, and that he wanted money and clothing for them. His guilt was doubly great, because he was Elisha's trusted servant or steward, and because he probably had other servants under him. And then he lies, not only to Naaman, but to his master, when he says, "Thy servant went no whither." Oh, the baseness, the wickedness, of deceit! And yet how much of it is practised in the world! *How much of it in the social relationships of life!* What sham friendships! What hollow civilities! Whited sepulchres and social shams! How much of it *in the commercial* world! What barefaced adulteration! What cheating of customers! What false statements—known to be false—about the value of goods! Sometimes there are revelations—great failures, gross frauds. But what an immense amount of deceit goes on that is never heard of! Many deceive or act dishonestly just up to the limit of detection, just as if God's eye was not on them all the time. To say, "Every one does it," as an excuse for deceit or dishonesty in a business, is no reason why a Christian man should do it, why any man should do it. God's eye sees. His command is clear, "Thou shalt not steal." Thou shalt not put forth thine hand to take what is not thine own. The man who robs his customers, the man who plunders or purloins from his employers, even though he may be respectable in the eyes of the world, is as much a thief in the sight of God, and perhaps far more guilty, than the poor boy who steals a loaf in his hunger and want. Deceit and dishonesty never can bring a blessing. "Be sure your sin will find you out." We have many instances in history of the fearful consequences of even a single act of deceit. The one great stain upon the memory of Lord Clive, the hero of Plassey, and one of the greatest men who ever administered British rule in India, is his single act of deception practised on an Indian prince. The words which Lord Macaulay has written on this subject are so important and so true, that they are well worth repeating: "Clive's breach of faith," he says, "was not merely a crime, but a blunder. We don't know whether it be possible to mention a state which has on the whole been a gainer by a breach of public faith. The entire history of British India is an illustration of this great truth, that it is not prudent to oppose perfidy to perfidy—*that the most efficient weapon with which men can encounter falsehood is truth.* During a long series of years, the English rulers of India, surrounded by allies and enemies whom no engagement could bind, have generally acted with sincerity and uprightness, and the event has proved that sincerity and uprightness are wisdom. *English valour and English intelligence have done less to extend and preserve our Oriental empire than English veracity.* All that we could have gained by imitating the doublings, the evasions, the fictions, the perjuries, which have been employed against us, is as nothing compared with what we have gained by being *the one power in India on whose word reliance can be placed.*" Covetousness and deceit are injurious to personal happiness, to the order and peace of society, and to the welfare and prosperity of the nation. It is the gospel of Christ that alone has proved itself capable of grappling with these evils, and banishing these vices from the human heart. It teaches us not to think of self merely, but of others also. It teaches us to " put away lying, and to speak every man truth with his neighbour." · To spread the gospel of Christ is the best way to promote social and commercial morality, to promote confidence between man and man, and to hasten the coming of that time when there shall be peace on earth and good will to men. Let the love of Jesus fill your heart, and flow out into your life, and then you will not intentionally do a wrong to any one, in thought, in word, or in deed.—C. H. I.

Vers. 1—27.—*History of Naaman's disease and cure, illustrative of certain forces in the life of man.* " Now Naaman, captain of the host of the King of Syria, was a great man with his master," etc. Naaman, in a worldly point of view, was a great man— one of the magnates of his age. But he was the victim of a terrible disease. " He was a leper." Leprosy was a terrible disease—*hereditary, painful, contagious, loathsome,* and *fatal.* In all these respects it resembled sin. Naaman's disease and his cure, as here sketched, manifest certain *forces* which have ever been and still are at work in society, and which play no feeble part in the formation of character and the regulation of destiny. Notice—

I. The force of WORLDLY POSITION. Why all the interest displayed in his own country, and in Israel, concerning Naaman's disease? The first verse of this chapter explains it. " Now Naaman, captain of the host of the King of Syria, was a great man." Perhaps there were many men in his own district who were suffering from leprosy, yet little interest was felt in them. They would groan under their sufferings, and die unsympathized with and unhelped. But because this man's worldly position was high, kings worked, prophets were engaged, nations were excited, for his cure. It has ever been a sad fact in human history that men magnify both the trials and the virtues of grandees, and think but little of the griefs and graces of the lowly. If a man in high position is under trial, it is always " a great trial," of which people talk, and which the press will record. If he does a good work, it is always " a great work," and is trumpeted half the world over. This fact indicates: 1. The *lack of intelligence* in popular sympathy. Reason teaches that the calamities of the wealthy have many mitigating circumstances, and therefore the greater sympathy should be toward the poor. 2. The *lack of manliness* in popular sympathy. There is a fawning servility, most dishonourable to human nature, in showing more sympathy with the rich than with the poor in suffering.

II. The force of INDIVIDUAL INFLUENCE. " And the Syrians had gone out by companies, and had brought away captive out of the land of Israel a little maid; and she waited on Naaman's wife. And she said unto her mistress, Would God my lord were with the prophet that is in Samaria! for he would recover him of his leprosy. And one went in, and told his lord, saying, Thus and thus said the maid that is of the land of Israel." This little girl, who had been torn from her native country, and carried into the land of strangers by the ruthless hand of war, told her mistress of a prophet in Israel who had the power to heal lepers. This led the King of Syria to persuade Naaman to visit Judæa, and to give the leprous captain an introduction to the king, who, in his turn, introduced him to the prophet, who effected his healing. The influence of this little slave-girl should teach us three things. 1. The *magnanimity of young natures*. Though she was an exile in the land of her oppressors, instead of having that revenge which would have led her to rejoice in the sufferings of her captors, her young heart yearned with sympathy for one of the ruthless conquerors. A poor child, a humble servant, a despised slave, may have a royal soul. 2. *The power of the humblest individual*. This poor girl, with her simple intelligence, moved her mistress; her mistress, the mighty warrior; then Syria's king was moved; by him the King of Israel is interested; and then the prophet of the Lord. Thus the little maid may have been said to have stirred kingdoms. No one, not even a child, "liveth to himself." Each is a fountain of influence. 3. The *dependence of the great upon the small*. The recovery of this warrior resulted from the word of this captive maid. Some persons admit the hand of God only in what they call great events! But what are the great events? "Great" and "small" are but relative terms. And even what we call "small" often sways and shapes the "great." One spark of fire may burn down all London.

III. The force of SELF-PRESERVATION. "And the King of Syria said, Go to, go, and I will send a letter unto the King of Israel. And he departed, and took with him ten talents of silver, and six thousand pieces of gold, and ten changes of raiment. And he brought the letter to the King of Israel, saying, Now when this letter is come unto thee, behold, I have therewith sent Naaman my servant to thee, that thou mayest recover him of his leprosy." It would seem that Naaman at once consulted Benhadad, King of Syria, on the subject suggested by the captive maid, and, having obtained an introduction to the King of Israel, hurried off, taking with him "ten talents of silver," etc.—great wealth—which he was prepared to sacrifice in the recovery of his health. The instinct of self-preservation is one of the strongest in human nature. "Skin for skin, yea, all that a man hath will he give for his life." Men will spend fortunes and traverse continents in order to rid themselves of disease, and prolong life. This strenuous effort for recovery from disease reminds us of: 1. The *value of physical health*. This man had lost it, and what was the world to him without it? Bishop Hall truly says of him, "The basest slave in Syria would not change skins with him." Health—this precious blessing—is so lavishly given, that men seldom appreciate it till it is lost. 2. The *neglect of spiritual health*. This man was evidently morally diseased—that is, he neither knew of the true God nor had sympathy with him. He was a moral invalid. A worse disease than leprosy infected his manhood and threatened the ruin of his being. Yet there is no struggling here after spiritual recovery. This is a general evil.

IV. The force of CASTE FEELING. "And the King of Syria said, Go to, go, and I will send a letter unto the King of Israel." Why did the King of Syria send Naaman with the letter to the monarch of Israel? Was it because he was given to understand that the king would work the cure? No; for mention was made by the captive girl of no one who could effect the cure but "the prophet that is in Samaria." Or was it because he thought that Israel's monarch would discover the prophet, and influence him on behalf of the afflicted officer? No; for in his royal letter he says, "Behold, I have . . . sent Naaman my servant to thee, that *thou* mayest recover him of his leprosy." Why, then? Simply because of caste feeling. He, forsooth, was too great to know a prophet— too great to correspond with any one but a king. What was a prophet, though full of Divine intelligence, and nerved with Divine energy, compared even to a soulless man if a crown encircled his brow? 1. Caste feeling *sinks the real in the adventitious*. The man who is ruled by it so exaggerates external things as to lose sight of those elements of moral character which constitute the dignity and determine the destiny of man. He lives in bubbles. 2. Caste feeling *curtails the region of human sympathies*. He who is controlled by this feeling has the circle of his sympathies limited not only to what is outward in man, but to what is outward in those only in his own sphere. All out- lying his grade and class are nothing to him. 3. Caste feeling is *antagonistic to the gospel*. Christ came to destroy that middle wall of partition that divides men into classes. The gospel overtops all adventitious distinctions, and directs its doctrines and offers its provisions to man as man.

V. The force of GUILTY SUSPICION. "And it came to pass, when the King of Israel had read the letter, that he rent his clothes, and said, Am I God, to kill and to make alive, that this man doth send unto me to recover a man of his leprosy? Wherefore consider, I pray you, and see how he seeketh a quarrel against me." The construction that the monarch put upon the message of his royal brother was, instead of being true and liberal, false and ungenerous. He ascribed evil motives where there were none, and saw malignant intentions where there was nothing but a good-natured purpose. All this springs from that *suspicion* which is a prevalent and disastrous evil in the social life of this world. Where this suspicion exists, one of the two, if not the two, following things are always found. 1. *A knowledge of the depravity of society.* The suspicious man has frequently learnt, either from observation, testimony, or experience, or from all these together, that there is such an amount of falsehood and dishonesty in society as will lead one man to take an undue advantage of another. However, whether he has learnt this or not, it is a lamentable fact, patent to all observant eyes. 2. *The existence of evil in himself.* The suspicious man knows that he is selfish, false, dishonest, unchaste, and he believes that all men are the same. If he were not evil, he would not be suspicious of others, even though he knew that all about him were bad. An innocent being, I trow, would move amongst a corrupt age without any suspicion whatever. Being destitute of all bad motives himself, he would not be able to understand the corrupt motives of others. On the other hand, were society ever so holy, a bad man would still be suspecting all. An unchaste, selfish, fraudulent man would suspect the purity, the benevolence, and the integrity of angels, if he lived amongst them. The greatest rogues are always the most suspicious; the most lustful husbands are always the most jealous of their wives, and the reverse. Well has our great dramatist said, "Suspicion haunts the guilty soul." A miserable thing truly is this suspicion. Heaven deliver us from suspicious people! Suspicion is the poison of all true friendship; it is that which makes kings tyrants, merchants exactors, masters rigorous, and the base-natured of both sexes diseased with a jealousy that shatters connubial confidence, and quenches all the lights of connubial life.

VI. The force of REMEDIAL GOODNESS. Though the king could not cure, there was a *remedial* power in Israel equal to this emergency. That power Infinite Goodness delegated to Elisha. God makes man the organ of his restorative powers. It was so now with Elisha. It was pre-eminently so with Christ. It was so with the apostles. The redemptive treasure is in "earthly vessels." The passage suggests several points concerning this remedial power. 1. It *transcends natural power.* "When Elisha the man of God," etc. The monarch felt his utter insufficiency to effect the cure. Natural science knew nothing of means to heal the leper. Supernatural revelation reveals the remedy through Elisha. Herein is an illustration of Christianity. No natural science can cure the leprosy of sin; it tried for ages, but failed. 2. It *offends human pride.* "So Naaman came with his horses," etc. Naaman came in all the pomp of wealth and station to the prophet's door, expecting, no doubt, that Elisha would hurry out to do him honour. But a true man is never moved by glitter. He did not even go out to meet the illustrious visitor, but sent a messenger to bid him go to the Jordan, and there wash. But both the unbending independency of the prophet, and the simple method he prescribed, so galled the proud heart of the Syrian warrior, that he "was wroth, and went away, and said, Behold, I thought, He will surely come out to me," etc. Herein is an illustration of Christianity. It strikes at the root of pride, and requires us to become as "little children." 3. It *clashes with popular prejudices.* "Are not Abana and Pharpar, rivers of Damascus, better than all the waters of Israel? may I not wash in them, and be clean?" It is common for men to regard that which belongs to themselves and to their country as the "better"—*our* children, *our* family, *our* sect, *our* class, *our* nation, are "better." This man's prejudice said, "Abana and Pharpar;" the prophet said, "Jordan;" and this offended him. "And he went away in a rage." Herein, again, is an illustration of Christianity. Human prejudices prescribe this river and that river for cleansing, but the gospel says, "Jordan." 4. It *works by simple means.* "And his servants came near, and spake unto him, and said, My father, if the prophet had bid thee do some great thing, wouldest thou not have done it? how much rather then when he saith to thee, Wash, and be clean?" The means to Naaman seemed to be too simple to answer the end he sought. Had there been some severe regimen, or some painful operation, or some costly expenditure, he would have accepted it more readily; but "to wash," seemed too simple. The means of spiritual recovery are very simple. But men desire them otherwise. Hence vain ceremonies, pilgrimages, penances, prolonged fastings, and the like. "Believe, . . . and thou shalt be saved," says God; man wants to do something more. 5. It *demands individual effort.* "Then went he down, and dipped himself seven times in Jordan according to the saying of the man of God." Naaman had to go down *himself* to the river, and to dip *himself* seven times in its waters. His restoration depended upon his individual effort. And so it is in spiritual matters. Each man must believe, repent, and pray, for himself. There is no substitution. 6. It is *completely efficacious.* "His flesh came again like unto the flesh of a little child." The means employed for this leper's cure fully answered the end. Every vestige of the disease was gone, and he was restored to more than the vigour of his former manhood. Herein once more, "Believe, . . . and thou shalt be saved."

VII. The force OF A NEW CONVICTION. "And he returned to the man of God," etc. Observe: 1. The *subject of* this new conviction. What was the subject? That the God of Israel was the *only* God. This new conviction reversed his old prejudices and the religious creed of his country. It was not reasoning, it was not teaching; *experience* had wrought this conviction into his soul. He *felt* that it was God's hand that healed him. 2. The *developments* of this new conviction. A conviction like this must prove influential in some way or other. Abstract ideas may lie dormant in the mind, but convictions are ever operative. What did it do in Naaman? (1) It evoked gratitude. Standing with all his company before the prophet, he avowed his gratitude. "Now therefore, I pray thee, take a blessing of thy servant." Just before his cure he had anything but kindly feelings towards the prophet. He was full of "rage." New convictions about God will generate new feelings toward man. (2) It annihilated an old prejudice. Just before his cure he despised Israel. Jordan was contemptible as compared with the rivers of Damascus. But now the very ground seems holy. He asks of the prophet liberty to take away a portion of the earth. "Shall there not then, I pray thee, be given to thy servant two mules' burden of earth?" A new conviction about God widens the soul's sympathies, raises it above all those nationalities of heart that characterize little souls. (3) It inspired worship. "Thy servant will henceforth offer neither burnt offering nor sacrifice . . . but unto the Lord." His whole nature was so flooded with gratitude to God who had healed him, that his soul went forth in holy worship. Through the force of this new conviction, he felt as St. Paul did when he said, "What things were gain to me, those I counted loss."

VIII. The force of ASSOCIATES. Naaman had been in the habit of worshipping "in the house of Rimmon," with his master the king. This, probably, he had done for years with other officers of the state. The influence of this he now felt counteracting the new conviction of duty. He felt that, whilst it would be wrong for him to go there any more, yet he could not but go. "In this thing the Lord pardon thy servant," etc. Loyalty and gratitude towards the king contributed much to prevent him renouncing all connection with the house of Rimmon. How often do our associations prevent us from the full carrying out of our convictions! It ought not to be so. "He that loveth father or mother," etc. It is somewhat remarkable that the Prophet Elisha, instead of exhorting Naaman to avoid every appearance of idolatry, said to him, "Go in peace." The prophet, perhaps, had faith in the power of Naaman's conviction to guard him from any moral mischief.

IX. The force of SORDID AVARICE. Gehazi is the illustration of this. In his case we have: 1. *Avarice eager in its pursuits.* "But Gehazi, the servant of Elisha," etc. He saw, as he thought, a fine opportunity for his greed, and he eagerly seized it. "I will *run* after him." Avarice is one of the most hungry passions of the soul. It is never satisfied. Had the avaricious man, like the fabled Briareus, a hundred hands, he would employ them all in ministering to himself—Dryden calls it

"A cursed hunger of pernicious gold."

It is that passion that makes all men like Gehazi "*run.*" Men are everywhere out of breath in their race for wealth. 2. *This avarice is in one associated with the most generous of men.* He was the servant of Elisha, who, when Naaman offered some acknowledgment of his gratitude to him, exclaimed, in the most solemn way, "As the Lord liveth, before whom I stand, I will receive none." One would have thought that association with a generous soul like this would have banished every base sentiment from Gehazi's heart. But when it once roots itself in the soul, it is the most inveterate of lusts. The history of modern enterprises shows us numerous examples of men who, from early life, have been in association with ministers, churches, religious institutions, and in some cases have themselves been deacons, chairmen of religious societies, and the like, whose avarice has so grown, in spite of all those influences, as to make them swindlers on a gigantic scale. 3. *This avarice sought its end by means of falsehood.* "My master hath sent me," etc. This was a flagrant falsehood. Avarice is always false. Its trades are full of tricks; its shops of sophistries. All its enterprises employ the tongue of falsehood and the hand of deceit.

X. The force of DISTRIBUTIVE JUSTICE. There is justice on this earth as well as remedial goodness, and Heaven often makes men the organ as well as the subject of both. Elisha, who had the remedial power, had also the retributive. Here we see retributive justice: 1. *Detecting* the wrong-doer. "And Elisha said unto him, Whence comest thou, Gehazi?" etc. Justice has the eyes of Argus; has more than the eyes of Argus—it sees in the dark. It penetrates through all fallacies. "The eyes of the Lord run to and fro, beholding the evil and the good." 2. *Reproving* the wrong-doer. "Is it a time to receive money," etc.? An old expositor has quaintly put it, "Couldest thou find no better way of getting money than by belying thy master, and laying a stumbling-block before a young convert?" His avarice was a thing bad in itself, and bad also in seizing an opportunity which should have been employed for other and higher ends. 3. *Punishing* the wrong-doer. "The leprosy therefore of Naaman shall cleave unto thee," etc. He had money of the leper, but he had his disease too. In getting what he considered a blessing, he got a curse as well. Wealth avariciously gotten never fails to bring a curse in some form or other. If it does not bring leprosy to the body, it brings what is infinitely worse, the most deadly leprosy into the soul, and often entails injuries on posterity.—D. T.

Vers. 1—7.—*The story of Naaman:* 1. *The disinterested maiden.* The story of the great Syrian captain, who was healed of his leprosy and brought to the knowledge of the true God through the instrumentality of a captive Hebrew maid directing him to Elisha, is one of the most beautiful, as it is one of the richest in gospel suggestion, of the narratives of the Old Testament. Our Lord refers to it in his discourse at Nazareth, as showing that it is not always the direct possessors of privileges who know best how to take advantage of them. "Many lepers were in Israel," etc. (Luke iv. 27).

I. THE GREAT MAN'S LEPROSY. The story opens by introducing us to Naaman, the captain of the host of the King of Syria. 1. *So much, and yet a cross.* On this distinguished man Fortune seemed to have lavished her utmost favours. He was (1) high in rank, "captain of the host;" (2) great in honour, "a great man with his master;" (3) successful in war, "honourable, because by him the Lord had given deliverance unto Syria;" (4) distinguished for personal bravery, "a mighty man of valour." The expression quoted above, "The *Lord* had given deliverance," etc., shows how far the Hebrews were from regarding Jehovah as a merely national Deity. His providence extended to other nations as well. It was he, not Rimmon, who had given Syria her victories. Naaman had thus wealth, honour, the favour of his sovereign, the admiration of the people—everything that men commonly covet. Yet (5) "he was a leper." This spoiled all. It was the cross in his lot; the drop of gall in his cup; the worm at the root of his prosperity. It made him such that, as has been said, the humblest soldier in his ranks would not have exchanged places with him. Few lives, even those which seem most enviable, are without their cross. The lady of Shunem has wealth, comforts, a loving husband; but she is childless. It does not take much sometimes to dash our earthly happiness, to take the golden light out of life. Because it is so, we should seek our happiness in things that are enduring. "He builds too low who builds beneath the skies." 2. *The cross a mercy in disguise.* As it proved, this grief of Naaman's became his salvation. It brought him under the notice of the little

Hebrew maid, led to his visit to Elisha, ended in his cure and his conversion to the faith of the God of Israel. He was one who could say, "It is good for me that I have been afflicted" (Ps. cxix. 71). How often are seeming crosses and trials thus over-ruled for good! "Men see not the bright light which is in the clouds: but the wind passeth, and cleanseth them" (Job xxxvii. 21). The evangelical application of the story is aided by the fact that leprosy is so impressive a type of sin—insidious, pro-gressive, corrupting, fatal.

II. THE SLAVE-GIRL'S ADVICE. It was God's design to show mercy to Naaman, for his own glory, as well as for a testimony that the Gentiles were not outside the scope of his grace. The instrument in accomplishing that design was a little Hebrew maid. 1. *Her presence in Naaman's house.* She had been taken in a marauding expedition, and brought to Syria as a captive. Sold, perhaps, like Joseph, in the slave-market, she had been purchased as an attendant for Naaman's wife. Her presence in the great captain's household was thus: (1) providential, even as was Joseph's residence in the house of Potiphar; (2) sad, for she was torn from her own land and friends, and the thought of their sorrow at her loss would add to hers; yet (3) designed for blessing. It not only gave her the opportunity of doing good to her master, but no doubt ulti-mately turned to her own great advantage. Another example of how the things which seem all "against us" (Gen. xlii. 36) are often for our good (comp. Gen. l. 20). 2. *Her helpful suggestion.* Slave though she was, the little maid was in possession of a secret which the great Naaman did not know, and which was worth "thousands of gold and silver" (Ps. cxix. 72) to him. She dropped a hint to her mistress, "Would God my lord were with the prophet that is in Samaria!" etc. Her suggestion was indicative of: (1) Pity. Though a slave, her heart was tender, even towards her master. She was grieved for his affliction. She yearned to see him recovered. Her "would God!" is almost a prayer for his recovery. (2) Fidelity. It is told of Joseph that he was faithful as a servant in the house of his master the Egyptian (Gen. xxxix. 2—6). This little maid, though a "servant under the yoke" (1 Tim. vi. 1), yet "counted her master worthy of all honour" (1 Tim. vi. 1). She served, "not with eye-service, as men-pleasers," but "in singleness of heart," "with good will doing service" (Eph. vi. 5—7), though her lord was an alien, and might seem to have little claim upon her gratitude. As a good servant should, she desired his prosperity in mind, body, and estate. In this was shown (3) her disinterestedness. In her position it need not have been wondered at if she had secretly rejoiced at her master's affliction. But her heart cherished no resentment. Anticipating the gospel, she sought to return good for evil (Matt. v. 44). We learn from this part of the story (1) that even the humblest may be of essential service to those above them. Most of all is this the case when they possess the knowledge of the true God. A hint dropped may guide the spiritual leper to the fountain of healing. (2) The young, too, should take encouragement. In their several stations they may be greatly used for good. (3) We should do to others the utmost good we can, even though they are our enemies.

III. THE ARROGANT KING'S EPISTLE. The news of what the little maid had said soon spread abroad, and came first to the ears of Naaman, then to the ears of the King of Syria (Benhadad?). 1. *The King of Syria's epistle.* The monarch valued his general, and was ready to take any steps to further his cure. Accordingly, he indited a letter, and sent Naaman with it, with much pomp and state, to the King of Israel (Jehoram?). He sends: (1) With the arrogance of a victor. The tone of his communication to the monarch at Samaria was unmistakably of the nature of command. It haughtily announces that he has sent Naaman to him, and requires that he shall recover him from his disease. There lurks in the letter a reminder of the defeat at Ramoth-Gilead (1 Kings xxii.). (2) With the ignorance of a heathen. He writes to the rival ruler as if it lay in *his* power to kill and to make alive. He probably thought that the king had only to command, to compel Elisha to serve him in any way he pleased. Hence, without mentioning Elisha, he lays the whole responsibility of seeing that his captain is cured on the shoulders of Jehoram. He has the notion—common enough to monarchs—that kings should be supreme in religion as in everything else. He thinks that God's prophets must take their commands from whoever chances to occupy the throne. (3) With the munificence of a sovereign. If there was haughtiness in the tone of his letter, he did not at least send his officer without abundant rewards. He bore with him ten talents of silver, six thousand shekels of gold, and ten changes of raiment. These enormous sums were, no doubt, thought certain to purchase the cure. Another heathenish idea, akin to the modern notion that anything can be bought with money. Elisha taught him differently when the cure was accomplished (ver. 16). Simon Magus would have bought even the power to communicate the Holy Ghost with gold (Acts viii. 18, 19). There are blessings which are beyond the reach of money, and yet can be had "without money and without price" (Isa. lv. 1). 2. *The King of Israel's distress.* When the King of Israel read the communication, he was both indignant and distressed. As he viewed the letter, it was: (1) A request for the impossible. "Am I God, to kill and to make alive, that this man doth send unto me to recover a man of his leprosy?" This was, at any rate, a frank acknowledgment of his own helplessness. It sets in a stronger light the Divine character of the cure by Elisha. (2) An attempt to force upon him a quarrel. His interpretation of the letter was not unnatural. Yet it was mistaken. We do well to be careful in forming judgments and imputing motives. (3) An attack upon his weakness. It was this that distressed him so much. He did not feel able to make war against the King of Syria, and therefore he resented the more keenly this attempt (as he conceived it) to drive him into a corner.—J. O.

Vers. 8—19.—*The story of Naaman: 2. The suggestive cure.* The cure which Naaman came to seek was, nevertheless, obtained by him. We have here—

I. THE INTERPOSITION OF ELISHA. Naaman was on the point of being sent away, when Elisha interposed. God's prophet vindicates God's honour. 1. *Elisha sends to the king.* "He sent to the king, saying, Wherefore hast thou rent thy clothes?" etc. His words were: (1) A rebuke of faithlessness. The king was not God, to kill and to make alive; but was there not a God in Israel who could? Had he already received no proofs of this God's power? Wherefore, then, had he rent his clothes? How much of our despondency, fear, despair, arises from want of faith in a living God! (2) An invitation to seek help in the right quarter. "Let him come now to me." The proof that there was a prophet, and behind the prophet a living, wonder-working God, in Israel, would be seen in deeds. Why does the sinner rend his clothes, and despair of help? Is Christ not able to save? Does he not invite him to come? 2. *Naaman comes to Elisha.* (1) He seeks cleansing. (2) Yet with unhumbled heart. His horses and chariot drive up to Elisha's door. The great man has no thought of descending to ask the prophet's blessing. He waits till he comes out to him. He is the man of rank and wealth, whom Elisha should feel honoured in serving. But Elisha does not come out. Not in this spirit are cures obtained at the hand of God. Naaman must be taught that gold, silver, horses, chariots, rank, avail nothing here. To be saved the highest must become as the humblest. Pride must be expelled (Phil. iii. 7, 8).

II. THE MODE OF CURE. 1. *Elisha's direction.* Instead of himself appearing, Elisha sent a messenger to Naaman, directing him to wash seven times in Jordan, and he would be clean. The means of cure was: (1) Simplicity itself. Nothing could be simpler or more easy than to bathe seven times in Jordan. Any leper might be glad to purchase cleansing by plunging in a river. God's way of salvation by Christ is characteristically simple. It involves no toilsome pilgrimages, no laborious works, no protracted ceremonies. "Believe in the Lord Jesus Christ, and thou shalt be saved" (Acts xvi. 31). (2) Symbolical. Jordan was the sacred stream of Israel; bathing was the Levitical mode of the purification of a leper (Lev. xiv. 8, 9); seven was the sacred number. Leprosy, as the type of sin, was fitly cleansed by these purificatory rites. That which answers to the bathing in the spiritual sphere is "the washing of regeneration, and of renewing of the Holy Ghost" (Titus iii. 5). (3) In its very simplicity, fitted to humble the proud heart. As we are immediately to see, it humbled Naaman. It did not strike him as a sufficiently great thing to do. Thus many are offended by the very simplicity of the gospel. It seems treating them too much like children to ask them simply to believe in the crucified and risen Saviour. Their intellectual eminence, their social greatness, their pride of character, are insulted by the proposal to efface themselves at the foot of the cross. 2. *Naaman's anger.* "Naaman was wroth, and went away." The causes of his anger were: (1) His expectations were disappointed. He thought the prophet would have shown him more respect; would have employed impressive words and gestures; would have given the cure more *éclat.* Instead of this, there was the simple command to wash in Jordan. What a down-come from the imposing ceremonial he expected! Men have their preconceived ideas about religion, about salvation, about the methods of spiritual cure, which they oppose to God's ways. They say with Naaman, "Behold, I thought, He will surely" do this or that. The Jews rejected their Messiah because he was " as a root out of a dry ground " (Isa. liii. 2); they rejected Christianity because its spiritual, unceremonial worship did not accord with their sensuous ideas. Others reject the gospel because it does not accord with the spirit of the age, is not sufficiently intellectual, philosophical, or æsthetical. God reminds us, "My thoughts are not your thoughts," etc. (Isa. lv. 8). (2) He was required to submit to what seemed to him a humiliation. He was told to bathe in the waters of Jordan, a stream of Israel, when there were rivers as good, nay, better, in his own country, to which, if bathing was essential, he might have been sent. "Are not Abana and Pharpar, rivers of Damascus," etc.? It seemed like a studied slight put upon his native rivers, an intentional humiliation put upon himself, to require him to go and bathe in this local stream. How often does wounded pride rebel at the simple pro- visions of the gospel, because they involve nothing that is our own, that reflects glory on self, or allows glory to self! This is the very purpose of the gospel. "Where is boasting, then? It is excluded" (Rom. iii. 27). Things are as they are, "that no flesh should glory in his presence " (1 Cor. i. 29). When Christ's atonement is extolled, the cry is, "Have we not rivers, Abanas and Pharpars, of our own?" "Naaman came with his mind all made up as to *how* he was to be healed, and he turned away in anger and disgust from the course which the prophet prescribed. He was a type of the rationalist, whose philosophy provides him with *à priori* dogmas, by which he measures everything which is proposed to his faith. He turns away in contempt where faith would heal him" (Sumner). 3. *Naaman's obedience.* Thus a second time the blessing was nearly missed—this time through his own folly and obstinacy. But, fortunately, a remonstrance was addressed to him, and he proved amenable to reason. (1) The remonstrance of his servants. They, looking at things through a calmer medium, and with less of personal pique, saw the situation with clearer eyes. They addressed him soothingly and affectionately. They touched the core of the matter when they said, "My father, if the prophet had bid thee do some great thing, wouldest thou not have done it?" It was Naaman's *pride* that had been offended. But they pointed out to him, in very plain terms, the folly of his conduct. Was it not a cure he wanted? And if it was, then, surely, the simpler the means prescribed the better. Why quarrel with the conditions of cure because they were so simple? The same reasoning may be applied to the gospel. It is the simplicity of its arrangements which is the beauty of it. If men really wish to be saved, why quarrel with this simplicity? Surely the simpler the better. Would men not be willing to do "some great thing" to obtain peace with God, pardon of sin, renewal and purity of heart? How much more, then, when it is said, "Wash, and be clean"? (2) The washing in Jordan. Naaman's ire had cooled. He felt the force of what his servants urged. He might prefer Abana and Pharpar, if he liked; but it was Jordan the prophet had named. If he did not choose to submit to bathe in this river, he must go without the cure altogether. "Neither was there salvation" (Acts iv. 12) in any other river than this one. This decided him. He went down without further parley, bathed seven times in Jordan as directed, and, marvel of marvels, "his flesh came again like unto the flesh of a little child, and he was clean." So speedy, sure, and complete was the reward of his obedience. As effectual to procure salvation and spiritual healing is the look of faith to Jesus, the appropriation of the merit of his blood, the spiritual baptism of the Holy Ghost.

III. NAAMAN'S GRATITUDE AND PIETY. What joy now filled the heart of the newly cleansed Naaman! How clearly he saw his former folly! How glad he was that he had not allowed his anger to prevail against the advice of his servants and his own better reason! At once he returned to Elisha; and it was very evident that his heart was overflowing with gratitude, and that he was a changed man. Like the leper in the Gospel, he returned "to give glory to God" (Luke xvii. 17, 18). Gratitude is most becoming in those who have received great mercies from God. Salvation awakens joy; gratitude prompts to consecration—not in order to salvation, but as the result of it, man becomes "a new creature" (2 Cor. v. 17). We observe: 1. *His acknowledgment*

of God. " Behold, now I know that there is no God in all the earth, but in Israel."
This is not a comparative statement, but an absolute one.   Naaman is convinced that
the gods of the heathen are nullities, and that the God of Israel is the only true God.
He was brought to this acknowledgment through the great miracle God had wrought
upon him.   It is God's mighty acts in and for men which give the best evidence of his
existence.   2. *His offer of reward.*   It was no longer the heathenish notion of purchase, but a pure motive of gratitude, which led Naaman to press the wealth he had
brought upon Elisha.   The prophet, however, had no desire for his goods.   With an
emphatic asseveration, he declared that he would accept nothing.   (1) He must keep
his act free from the possibility of misconception.   (2) A miracle of God must not be
vulgarized by being made the occasion of money presents.   (3) Naaman's instruction
must be completed by teaching him that money gifts do not pay for spiritual blessings.
Yet Naaman's motive was a right one.   It is right also that, from the motive of gratitude, we should consecrate our wealth to the Lord's service.   3. *His determination to
worship.*   If he cannot persuade Elisha to accept gifts, he himself will become a suppliant, and ask a favour from the prophet.   He entreats that he may be permitted to
take with him two mules' burden of earth of the Holy Land, that he may form an
altar for the worship of Jehovah ; for he is resolved henceforth to worship him only.
This was granted.   His altar would connect his sacrifices with the land which God had
chosen as the place of his special habitation.   Real religion will express itself in acts of
worship.   It will not content itself with cold recognition of God.   It will build its
altars to Jehovah, in the home, in the closet, in the church, and in the chief places of
concourse.   4. *His religious scruple.*   One point alone troubled him.   In attending his
royal master, it would be his duty to wait on him in his state visits to the temple of
Rimmon, and, as his master leaned on his hand in bending before that idol, he would
be under the necessity of seeming to bend before it, and yield it obeisance also.   He
asked that the Lord might pardon him in this thing.   Elisha bade him go in peace.
(1) His act was not really worship, nor did he mean it to pass for such either before
the king or the other worshippers.   (2) " An idol is nothing," and, if he understood
that clearly, his conscience would not be " defiled " (1 Cor. viii. 4—7).   There is need
for great care, even in outward acts, lest they expose the doer to misconception, or hurt
the consciences of others.   Life, however, is woven of intricate threads, and it is impossible but that in public, social, and official positions the Christian will sometimes find
himself in situations of all the concomitants of which he can by no means approve.   It
will not do to say of those that it is his duty at all hazards to come out of them ; for it
is frequently through his duty that he is brought into them, and to escape them entirely
he would require to " go out of the world " (1 Cor. v. 10).   If active participation in
anything sinful is sought to be forced on him—as if Naaman were required actually to
bow the knee in worship to Rimmon—then he must refuse (Dan. iii.).—J. O.

Vers. 20—27.—*The story of Naaman : 3. Gehazi's falsehood.*   In Elisha's company
we might have expected only honour, integrity, truthfulness.   But the society of the
good will not of itself make another good.   Hypocrisy can cover a foul interior.   A
fair outward seeming can cloke a heart ruled by very evil principles.   In the first
apostolic band there was a Judas.   In Elisha's service there was a Gehazi.   The sin of
both was covetousness.   The offspring of covetousness in Gehazi's case was hypocrisy
and falsehood.

I. COVETOUSNESS PROMPTING FALSEHOOD.   1. *His reproach of his master.*   When
Naaman was gone, Gehazi indulged in reflections on his master's conduct.   It did not
at all commend itself to him.   " Behold, my master has spared Naaman this Syrian,
in not receiving at his hands that which he brought," etc.   Such generosity seemed
absurd.   It was a chance missed which might never come again.   Fantastic scruples
were all very well, but when they led to the loss of a fortune, they were greatly to be
reprobated.   What scruple need there have been in any case about spoiling a foreigner ?
Covetousness generally sees only the money consideration.   When great gain is at
stake, the man is held to be a fool who allows religious or sentimental considerations, or
even ordinary moral scruples, to stand in the way.   2. *His covetous determination.*   If
his master has acted foolishly, he will not imitate his example.   It is not yet too late,
with a little art, to repair the damage.   He will hurry after the Syrian, and obtain

something from him. "As the Lord liveth"—mark the profane mixing up of religion and impiety—"I will run after him, and take somewhat of him." Morality goes down before the greed of gain. 3. *His unblushing falsehood.* (1) Naaman beheld Gehazi running after him, and was delighted to think that he might, after all, have the opportunity of serving Elisha. He alights from his chariot—a different man now than when his stately equipage "stood" at Elisha's door—and asks eagerly, "Is all well?" (2) Gehazi, in reply, tells him an unblushingly invented falsehood. There had come two young men of the sons of the prophets from Mount Ephraim, and Elisha had sent to entreat for them a talent of silver and two changes of raiment. The finish of this style of falsehood, and Gehazi's subsequent hypocrisy, speak to considerable practice in the art of deceit. Such ready audacity, so great perfection in the arts of lying and concealment, are not attained at the first attempt. No man becomes a rogue quite suddenly. Elisha was probably no more deceived in the character of Gehazi than Jesus was in the character of Judas, who was secretly "a thief," and "had the bag, and bare what was put therein" (John xii. 6).

II. GRATITUDE DICTATING LIBERALITY. The willing response made by Naaman to what he took to be Elisha's request is the bright side of this otherwise discreditable incident. 1. He doubled what was asked. "Be content, take two talents." He was glad to get an opening for forcing some acknowledgment of his gratitude on Elisha. 2. He sent two of his servants back with the sacks of silver and the raiment. What he did, he did handsomely. He gave every token he could of his desire to oblige Elisha. 3. Gehazi relieved the servants when they came near the house, and had the treasure smuggled into the house, and safely hid. This was the part of the business in which there lay some risk of detection; but it was securely managed, and Gehazi no doubt breathed a sigh of relief when he saw the valuables carefully stowed away. His treasure was as safely concealed as Achan's wedge of gold, and two hundred shekels of silver, and goodly Babylonish garment (Josh. vii. 21). But it was to prove as great a curse. Meanwhile, light in conscience, glad in heart, and pleased at having been permitted to bestow even this small gift (comparatively) on Elisha, Naaman sped on his way home. He probably never knew how he had been deceived.

III. JUSTICE DECREEING PENALTY. Gehazi's act, however, skilfully concealed as it was from human view, was not to remain unpunished. God knew it. Gehazi had forgotten this. God is the one factor which the wicked leave out of their calculations, and he is the most important of all. David was careful to conceal his crime with Bathsheba; but it is written, "The thing that David had done displeased the Lord" (2 Sam. xi. 27). 1. *Gehazi's hypocrisy.* He went calmly in, and stood before his master, as if nothing had happened. There is, as above stated, a perfection in this villainy which shows that it was not a first offence. But there comes a point when men's sins find them out. They gain courage by repeated attempts, and by-and-by take a step too far. What they think is their master-stroke proves their ruin. 2. *Elisha's challenge.* What had happened had not been "hid" from Elisha. The Lord had showed it to him. His heart had gone with Gehazi, and he had seen Naaman turning from his chariot to meet him. He now challenged him with his conduct. He: (1) Exposed his falsehood. Gehazi answered boldly to the question, "Whence comest thou?" "Thy servant went no whither." Then Elisha told him what he knew. We can imagine the servant's conscience-stricken look and speechless confusion at this discovery. Let sinners consider how they will face the disclosures of the judgment-day, and what they will answer (Eccles. xii. 14; Rom. ii. 16; Col. iii. 25). We have a parallel instance of exposure, with an even severer punishment, in the case of Ananias and Sapphira (Acts v. 1—11). (2) Unveiled his inmost motives. "Is it a time"—in connection with a work of God so great—"to receive money, and to receive garments, and oliveyards, and vineyards," etc. These were the things Gehazi intended to purchase with his money. His mind was running out in grand plans of what he would do with his treasures. A miracle such as had been wrought should have filled him with very different thoughts. Elisha lays bare the covetous root of his disposition. God reads to the bottom of our hearts (Heb. iv. 12; Rev. ii. 23). Gold is valued by covetous men for what it will bring. It is a further development of avarice when it comes to be loved for its own sake. 3. *The judgment of leprosy.* By a just retribution, the leprosy of Naaman, which had been taken from him from miracle, is now by miracle put on Gehazi and his seed for ever (cf

Exod. xx. 5). There is a symmetry—a relation of fitness—often observable in God's retributions (Gen. ix. 6; Judg. i. 7; Esth. vii. 9, 10; Matt. vii. 2; xxvi. 52, etc.), Little would Gehazi's wealth delight him with this loathsome and accursed disease upon him. Men make a wretched bargain who for wealth's sake barter away peace with God, purity of conscience, inward integrity, and their soul's honour. They may obtain gain, but they are smitten with a leprosy of spirit which is their ruin. Covetousness in the heart is already a leprosy. The outward leprosy, in Gehazi's case, was but the external sign of what internally already existed.—J. O.

EXPOSITION.

CHAPTER VI.

Ver. 1—ch. vii. 20.—FURTHER MIRACLES WROUGHT BY ELISHA. The historian relates first a (comparatively) private miracle wrought by Elisha in the vicinity of Jericho, for the benefit of one of the "sons of the prophets" (vers. 1—8). He then tells us briefly of a series of public miracles which brought Elisha into much note and prominence. War, it appears, had again broken out in a pronounced form between Israel and Syria, Syria being the aggressor. The Syrian monarch prepared traps for his adversary, encamping in places where he hoped to take him at a disadvantage. But Elisha frustrated these plans, by addressing warnings to the King of Israel, and pointing out to him the various positions occupied (vers. 8—12), which he consequently avoided. When this came to the ears of the King of Syria, he made an attempt to obtain possession of Elisha's person —an attempt which failed signally (vers. 13—23), owing to the miraculous powers of the prophet. Benhadad, some time after this, made a great expedition into the land of Israel, penetrating to the capital, and laying siege to it. The circumstances of the siege, and the escape of the city when at the last gasp, are related partly in the present chapter (vers. 24—33), partly in the next.

Ver. 1.—And the sons of the prophets said unto Elisha, Behold now, the place where we dwell with thee—literally, *before thee*—**is too strait for us.** The scene of this miracle is probably the vicinity of Jericho, since both Gilgal and Bethel were remote from the Jordan. The "school of the prophets" at Jericho, whereof we heard in ch. ii. 5, 19, had increased so much, that the buildings which hitherto had accommodated it were no longer sufficient. A larger dwelling, or set of dwellings, was thought to be necessary; but the scholars would make no change without the sanction of their master. When he comes on one of his circuits, they make appeal to him.

Ver. 2.—Let us go, we pray thee, unto Jordan. Jericho was situated at some little distance from the Jordan, on the banks of a small stream, which ran into it. Along the course of the Jordan trees and shrubs were abundant, chiefly willows, poplars, and tamarisks (see Josephus, 'Bell. Jud.,' iv. 8. § 3; Strabo, xvi. 2. § 41). It would seem that the Jordan thickets were unappropriated, and that any one might cut timber in them. **And take thence every man a beam.** The meaning is, "Let us *all* join in the work, each cutting beams and carrying them; and the work will soon be accomplished." **And let us make us a place there.** They propose to build the new dwelling on the banks of Jordan, to save the trouble of conveying the materials any long distance. **Where we may dwell. And he answered, Go ye.** Elisha, *i.e.*, approved the proposal, gave it his sanction and encouragement.

Ver. 3.—And one said, Be content, I pray thee, and go with thy servants. One of the number was not satisfied with the prophet's mere approval of the enterprise, but wished for his actual presence, probably as securing a blessing upon the work. **And he answered, I will go.** Elisha approved the man's idea, as springing from piety and faith in God. He, therefore, raised no difficulty, but at once, in the simplest manner, acceded to the request. There is a remarkable directness, simplicity, and absence of fuss in all that Elisha says and does.

Ver. 4.—So he went with them. And when they came to Jordan—*i.e.* to the river-bank—**they cut down wood.** They set to work, each felling his tree, and fashioning it into a rough beam.

Ver. 5.—But as one was felling a beam— *i.e.* a tree, to make it into a beam—**the axe-head;** literally, *the iron.* We see from Deut. xix. 5 that the Hebrews made their axe-heads of iron as early as the time of Moses. They probably learnt to smelt and work iron in Egypt. **Fell into the water.**

The tree must have been one that grew close to the river's edge. As the man hewed away at the stem a little above the root, the axe-head flew from the haft, into which it was insecurely fitted, and fell into the water. The slipping of an axe-head was a very common occurrence (Deut. xix. 5), and ordinarily was of little consequence, since it was easily restored to its place. But now the head had disappeared. **And he cried, and said, Alas, master!**—rather, *Alas, my master!* or, *Alas, my lord!*—for it **was borrowed**; rather, *and it was a borrowed one.* The words are part of the man's address to Elisha. He means to say, "It is no common misfortune; it is not as if it had been my own axe. I had borrowed it, and now what shall I say to the owner?" There is no direct request for help, but the tone of the complaint constitutes a sort of silent appeal.

Ver. 6.—And the man of God said, Where fell it? And he showed him the place. And he cut down a stick, and cast it in thither; and the iron did swim. Two natural explanations of this miracle have been attempted: (1) that Elisha passed a piece of wood underneath the axe-head, which he could see lying at the bottom of the river, and then lifted it up to the surface (Von Gerlach); (2) that he thrust a stick or bar of wood through the hole in the axe-head, made to receive the haft, and so pulled it out (Thenius). But both explanations do violence to the text; and we may be sure that, had either been true, the occurrence would not have been recorded. The sacred writers are not concerned to put on record mere acts of manual dexterity.

Ver. 7.—Therefore said he, Take it up to thee. And he put out his hand, and took it. Elisha does not take the axe-head out of the water himself, but requires the scholar to do it, in order to test his faith. He must show that he believes the miracle, and regards the iron as really floating on the top of the water, not as merely appearing to do so.

Ver. 8—ch. vii. 20.—PUBLIC MIRACLES OF ELISHA (resumed).

Ver. 8.—Then the King of Syria warred against Israel. It may seem strange that, so soon after sending an embassy to the court of Samaria, and asking a favour (ch. v. 5, 6), Benhadad should resume hostilities, especially as the favour had been obtained (ch. v. 14); but the normal relations between the two countries were those of enmity (ch. v. 2), and a few years would suffice to dim the memory of what had happened. The gratitude of kings is proverbially short-lived. **And took counsel with his servants**—i.e. his chief officers—**saying, In such and such a place** (comp. 1 Sam. xxi.

2) **shall be my camp;** or, *my encampment.* תַּחֲנֹת appears to be "a noun in the form of the infinitive." It does not occur elsewhere.

Ver. 9.—And the man of God—i.e. Elisha, who at the time was "*the* man of God"(κατ' ἐξοχήν)—**sent unto the King of Israel**—Jehoram, undoubtedly (see ver. 32)—**saying, Beware that thou pass not such a place; for thither the Syrians are come down.** Some translate, "Beware that thou *neglect* not such a place, for thither the Syrians *are coming* down;" but our version is probably correct, and is approved by Bähr and Thenius. Elisha did not suffer his hostile feeling towards Jehoram personally (ch. iii. 13; v. 8; vi. 32) to interfere with his patriotism. When disaster threatened his country, he felt it incumbent on him to warn even an ungodly king.

Ver. 10.—And the King of Israel sent to the place. Recent commentators (Keil, Thenius, Bähr) mostly suppose this to mean that Jehoram sent troops to the place pointed out by the prophet, and anticipated the Syrians by occupying it. But it agrees better with the prophet's injunction, "Beware that thou *pass* not such a place," to suppose that he merely sent out scouts to see if the place were occupied or no, and finding, in each case, Elisha's warning true, he avoided the locality. **Which the man of God told him and warned him of, and saved himself there, not once nor twice;** *i.e.* repeatedly; at least three several times, perhaps more.

Ver. 11.—Therefore the heart of the King of Syria was sore troubled for this thing. Keil says, "The King of the Syrians was *enraged* at this;" but סָעַר exactly expresses "trouble," "disturbance," not "rage," being used of the tossing of the sea, in Jonah i. 11. **And he called his servants, and said unto them, Will ye not show me which of us is for the King of Israel?** Benhadad not unnaturally suspected treachery among his own subjects. How otherwise could the King of Israel become, over and over again, aware of his intentions? Some one or other of his officers must, he thought, betray his plans to the enemy. Cannot the others point out the traitor?

Ver. 12.—And one of his servants said—i.e. one of those interrogated, answered— **None, my lord, O king;** literally, *Nay, my lord, the king*—meaning, "Think not so; it is not as thou supposest; there is no traitor in thy camp or in thy court; we are all true men. The explanation of the circumstances that surprise thee is quite different." **But Elisha, the prophet that is in Israel**—compare "*the* man of God" (ver. 9); so much above the others, that he is spoken of as if there were no other—**telleth**

the King of Israel the words that thou speakest in thy bedchamber: literally, *in the secret place of thy bedchamber*. How the Syrian lord knew this, or whether he merely made a shrewd guess, we cannot say. Elisha's miraculous gifts had, no doubt, become widely known to the Syrians through the cure of Naaman's leprosy; and the lord, who may possibly have been Naaman himself, concluded that a man who could cure a leper could also read a king's secret thoughts without difficulty.

Ver. 13.—And he—*i.e.* Benhadad—said, Go and spy where he is, that I may send and fetch him; *i.e.* "Send out spies to learn where Elisha is at present residing, that I may despatch a force to the place, and get him into my power." The object was scarcely "to find out, through Elisha, what the King of Israel and other princes were plotting against him in their secret counsels" (Cassel), but simply to put a stop to Elisha's betrayal of his own plans to Jehoram. And it was told him, saying, Behold, he is in Dothan. The spies were sent, and brought back word that, at the time, Elisha was residing in Dothan. Dothan, the place where Joseph was sold by his brethren to the Ishmaelites (Gen. xxxvii. 17), lay evidently not very far from Shechem (Gen. xxxvii. 14), and is placed by Eusebius about twelve miles north of Samaria. In the Book of Judith (iv. 6; vii. 3) it is mentioned among the cities bordering the southern edge of the Plain of Esdraelon. Modern travellers (Van de Velde, Robinson) have reasonably identified it with the present *Dothân*, a tel, or hill, of a marked character, covered with ruins, and from the foot of which arises a copious spring, to the south-west of Jenin, between that place and Jeba, a little to the left of the great road leading from Beisan (Scythopolis) to Egypt.

Ver. 14.—Therefore sent he thither horses, and chariots, and a great host; rather, *and a strong force*. The expression, חַיִל כָּבֵד, is used by the historical writers with a good deal of vagueness—sometimes of a really great army, sometimes merely of a large retinue (1 Kings x. 2) or of a moderate force (ch. xviii. 17). We must assign it its meaning according to the context. And they came by night, and compassed the city about. A night march was made, to take the prophet by surprise, and the city was encompassed, that it might be impossible for him to escape.

Ver. 15.—And when the servant of the man of God was risen early—he had, perhaps, heard the arrival of the Syrian forces during the night, and "rose early" to reconnoitre—and gone forth, behold, an host compassed the city both with horses and

chariots; rather, *an host compassed the city, and horses, and chariots*. A force of footmen, a force of horsemen, and a chariot force, are intended (comp. ver. 14). And his servant said unto him, Alas, my master! how shall we do? Though the servant could not know that it was Elisha's person which was especially sought, yet he was naturally alarmed at seeing the city invested by a hostile force, and anticipated either death or capture, which last would involve the being sold as a slave. Hence his "Alas!" and his piteous cry, "How shall we do?" Can we, *i.e.* in any way, save ourselves?

Ver. 16.—And he—*i.e.* Elisha—answered, Fear not: for they that be with us are more than they that be with them. Elisha did not need to *see* the forces arrayed on his side. He *knew* that God and God's strength was "with him," and cared not who, or how many, might be against him (comp. Ps. iii. 6, "I will not be afraid for ten thousands of people, that have set themselves against me round about;" and Ps. xxvii. 3, "Though an host should encamp against me, my heart shall not fear: though war should rise against me, in this will I be confident"). His confidence reminds us of that shown by Hezekiah (2 Chron. xxxii. 7) on the invasion of Sennacherib.

Ver. 17.—And Elisha prayed, and said, Lord, I pray thee, open his eyes, that he may see. If the prophet's servant was to be reassured, he must be made to *see* that help was at hand; he would not have found rest or peace in the mere assurance that God was nigh, and would keep his prophet from harm. His mental state required something like a material manifestation; and hence Elisha prays that he may be permitted to behold the angelic host, which everywhere throughout creation is employed at all times in doing the will of God, and accomplishing his ends (comp. Gen. xxviii. 12; xxxii. 2; Ps. xxxiv. 7; lxviii. 17; Dan. vii. 10, etc.). The prayer is granted. And the Lord opened the eyes of the young man; and he saw: and, behold, the mountain was full of horses and chariots of fire round about Elisha. As the earthly force, which had alarmed Elisha's servant, was a force mainly of horses and chariots, so the heavenly force revealed to his eyes was made to bear the same appearance. But the heavenly chariots and horses were "of fire"—glowed, *i.e.* with a strange unearthly brightness (see the comment on ch. ii. 11).

Ver. 18.—And when they came down to him. Keil and others suppose this to mean that the Syrians "came down" to Elisha; but, if they were in the plain that surrounds the hill whereon Dothan was built, as appears from ver. 15, they would have had to *ascend* in order to reach Elisha, not to *descend*. We must, therefore, with F. Meyer, Thenius, and Bähr, translate, "When they [Elisha and his servant] came down to *them* [the Syrians]"—either changing אֵלָיו into אֲלֵיהֶם, as Thenius does, or understanding אֵלָיו to refer to the "host" (חַיִל) of the Syrians. Elisha prayed unto the Lord, and said, Smite this people, I pray thee, with blindness. Not literal blindness, or they could not have followed Elisha's lead, and marched a distance of twelve miles to Samaria; but a state of confusion and bewilderment, in which " seeing they saw, but did not perceive" (compare the "blindness" of the men of Sodom, in Gen. xix. 11). And he smote them with blindness according to the word of Elisha.

Ver. 19.—And Elisha said unto them, This is not the way, neither is this the city. This was clearly "an untruthful statement" (Keil), if not in the letter, yet in the intent. Elisha meant the Syrians to understand him to say, " This is not the way which ye ought to have taken if ye wanted to capture the Prophet Elisha, and this is not the city (Dothan) where you were told that he was to be found." And so the Syrians understood him. In the morality of the time, and, indeed, in the morality of all times up to the present, it has been held to be justifiable to deceive a public enemy. Follow me, and I will bring you to the man whom ye seek. But he led them to Samaria. It could only be through the miraculous delusion for which Elisha had prayed, and which had been sent, that the Syrians believed the first comer in an enemy's country, followed him to the capital without hesitation, and allowed him to bring them inside the walls. But for the delusion, they would have suspected, made inquiries of others, and retreated hastily, as soon as the walls and towers of Samaria broke on their sight.

Ver. 20.—And it came to pass, when they were come into Samaria, that Elisha said, Lord, open the eyes of these men, that they may see. And the Lord opened their eyes, and they saw; and, behold, they were in the midst of Samaria. Their delusion was dispelled—they returned to their proper senses, and, seeing the size and strength of the town, recognized the fact that they were in Samaria, their enemy's capital, and so were helpless.

Ver. 21.—And the King of Israel said unto Elisha, when he saw them, My father. In his joy at the deliverance of so large a force of the enemy into his hands, Jehoram forgets the coldness and estrangement which have hitherto characterized the relations between himself and the prophet (ch. iii. 11—14; v. 8), and salutes him by the

honourable title of "father," which implied respect, deference, submission. Compare the use of the same expression by Joash (ch. xiii. 14), and the employment of the correlative term "son" (ch. viii. 9) by Benhadad. Shall I smite them? shall I smite them? The repetition marks extreme eagerness, while the interrogative form shows a certain amount of hesitation. It is certain that the Israelites were in the habit of putting to death their prisoners of war, not only when they were captured with arms in their hands, but even when they surrendered themselves. When a city or country was conquered, the whole male population of full age was commonly put to death (Numb. xxxi. 7; 1 Sam. xv. 8; 1 Kings xi. 15; 1 Chron. xx. 3, etc.). When a third part was spared, it was from some consideration of relationship (2 Sam. viii. 2). The Law distinctly allowed, if it did not even enjoin, the practice (Deut. xx. 13). Jehoram, therefore, no doubt, put his prisoners of war to death under ordinary circumstances. But he hesitates now. He feels that the case is an extraordinary one, and that the prophet, who has made the capture, is entitled to be consulted on the subject. Hence his question.

Ver. 22.—And he answered, Thou shalt not smite them. The prophet has no doubt. His prohibition is absolute. *These* prisoners, at any rate, are not to be slain. "The object of the miracle," as Keil says, "would have been frustrated, if the Syrians had been slain. For the intention was to show the Syrians that they had to do with a prophet of the true God, against whom no human power could be of any avail, *that they might learn to fear the Almighty God*" ('Commentary on 2 Kings,' p. 327, Eng. trans.). There was also, perhaps, a further political object. By sparing the prisoners and treating them with kindness, it might be possible to touch the heart of the King of Syria, and dispose him towards peace. Wouldest thou smite those whom thou hast taken captive with thy sword and with thy bow? rather, *Wouldest thou be smiting those*, etc.? *i.e.* "Wouldest thou, in smiting these persons, be smiting those whom thou hadst made prisoners in war, so as to be able to justify thy conduct by Deut. xx. 13? No; thou wouldest *not*. Therefore thou shalt not smite them." Set bread and water before them. "Bread" and "water" stand for meat and drink generally. Elisha bids Jehoram entertain the captive Syrians hospitably, and then send them back to Benhadad. That they may eat and drink, and go to their master.

Ver. 23.—And he prepared great provision for them. Jehoram followed the directions of the prophet, carrying them out, not in the letter merely, but in the spirit. He entertained the captives at a grand banquet (Josephus, ' Ant. Jud.,' ix. 4. § 3), and then gave them leave to depart. And when they had eaten and drunk, he sent them away, and they went to their master. So the bands of Syria came no more into the land of Israel. The Syrian raids, which had hitherto been frequent, perhaps almost continuous (ch. v. 2), now ceased for a time, and the kingdom of Israel had a respite. Bähr supposes that the raids were discontinued simply " because the Syrians had found out that they could not accomplish anything by these expeditions, but rather brought themselves into circumstances of great peril" ('Commentary on Kings,' vol. ii. p. 69). But the *nexus* of the clause, " So the bands," etc., rather implies that the cessation was the consequence of Jehoram's sparing and entertaining the captives.

Ver. 24—ch. vii. 20.—*The siege of Samaria by Benhadad.*

Ver. 24.—**And it came to pass after this—** probably some considerable time after, when the memory of Jehoram's kind act had passed away—**that Benhadad king of Syria gathered all his host.** A contrast is intended between the inroads of small bodies of plunderers and the invasion of the territory by the monarch himself at the head of his entire force. **And went up.** However Samaria was approached from Syria, there must always have been a final ascent, either from the Jordan valley or from the Plain of Esdraelon. **And besieged Samaria.** Josephus says that Jehoram was afraid to meet Benhadad in the open field, since his forces were no match for those of the Syrian king, and therefore at once shut himself up within his capital, without risking a battle. The walls of Samaria were very strong.

Ver. 25.—**And there was a great famine in Samaria.** It was Benhadad's design to capture the place, not by battering down its walls with military engines, but by blockading it, and cutting off all its supplies, as Josephus tells us (*l. s. c.*). **And, behold, they besieged it, until an ass's head was sold for fourscore pieces of silver, and the fourth part of a cab of dove's dung for five pieces of silver.** The ass, being an unclean animal (Lev. xi. 4), would not be eaten at all except in the last extremity, and the head was the worst and so the cheapest part; yet it sold for " eighty pieces " (rather, shekels) of silver, or about £5 of our money ; as in the Cadusian famine mentioned by Plutarch (' Vit. Artaxerx.,' § 24), where an ass's head was sold for sixty drachmas (about forty shillings). " Dove's dung " is thought by some to be the name of a plant; but it is better to understand the term

literally. Both animal and human excrement have been eaten in sieges (Josephus, ' Bell. Jud.,' v. 13. § 7; Cels., ' Hierobot.,' ii. p. 233), when a city was in the last extremity.

Ver. 26.—**And as the King of Israel was passing by upon the wall.** The wall of Babylon is said to have been so broad at the top that a four-horse chariot could turn round on it (Herod., i. 179). All ancient cities had walls upon which a great part of the garrison stood, and from which they shot their arrows and worked their engines against the assailants. From time to time the commandant of the place—the king himself, in this instance—would mount upon the wall to visit the posts, and inspect the state of the garrison, or observe the movements of the enemy. **There cried a woman unto him.** Houses sometimes abutted on the wall of a town (see Josh. ii. 15; 1 Sam. xix. 12, etc.), and women sometimes took part in their defence (Judg. ix. 53), so that in visiting the posts a commandant might be brought into contact with women. **Saying, Help, my lord, O king**, rather, *save*, i.e. " preserve me from perishing of hunger."

Ver. 27.—**And he said, If the Lord do not help thee.** This is probably the true meaning. The king is not so brutal as to "curse" the woman (ἐπηράσατο αὐτή τὸν Θεόν, Josephus, ' Ant. Jud.,' ix. 4. § 4); neither does he take upon himself to tell her that God will not save her (Maurer). He merely refers her to God, as alone competent to do what she asks. **Whence shall I help thee?** Whence, *i.e.*, dost thou suppose that I can save thee? **Out of the barnfloor, or out of the winepress?** Dost thou suppose that I have stores of food at my disposal? An overflowing barnfloor, where abundant corn is garnered, or a winepress full of the juice of the grape? I have nothing of the kind ; my stores are as much exhausted as those of the meanest of my subjects. I cannot save thee.

Ver. 28.—**And the king said unto her, What aileth thee?** Probably, as Bähr suggests, the woman explained to the king that she did not appear before him to beg food, but to claim his interposition as judge, in a case in which she considered herself to be wronged. Such an appeal the king was bound to hear ; and he therefore asks, " What aileth thee?" *i.e.* " What is thy ground of complaint?" Then she tells her story. **And she answered, This woman said unto me, Give thy son, that we may eat him to-day, and we will eat my son to-morrow.** Compare the prophecy in Deuteronomy, " The tender and delicate woman among you, which would not adventure to set the sole of her foot upon the ground for delicateness and tenderness, her eye shall be evil **towards** the husband of her bosom, and toward her son, and toward her daughter, and toward her young one that cometh out from between her feet, and toward her children which she shall bear: for she shall eat them for want of all things secretly in the siege and straitness, wherewith thine enemy shall distress thee in thy gates" (xxviii. 56, 57). There is historical testimony that the prophecy was three times fulfilled; viz. (1) in Samaria on the present occasion; (2) in Jerusalem during the last siege by Nebuchadnezzar (Lam. iv. 10); and (3) in Jerusalem during the last siege by Titus (Josephus, 'Bell. Jud.,' vi. 3. § 4). In modern sieges surrender is made before the population is driven to such straits.

Ver. 29.—**So we boiled my son** (comp. Lam. iv. 10, "The hands of the pitiful woman have *sodden* their own children"), **and did eat him: and I said unto her on the next day, Give thy son, that we may eat him: and she hath hid her son.** Some have supposed that the woman concealed her child in order to consume it alone; but it is more probable that, when the time came for carrying out her agreement, she found that she could not give it up, and hid it in order to save it.

Ver. 30.—**And it came to pass, when the king heard the words of the woman, that he rent his clothes.** In horror and consternation at the terrible state of things revealed by the woman's story (comp. ch. v. 7). **And he passed by upon the wall, and the people looked.** It is better to translate, with our Revisers, (*Now he was passing by upon the wall;*) *and the people looked;* or, *and, as he was passing by upon the wall, the people looked.* **And, behold,** he had **sackcloth within upon his flesh.** Jehoram had secretly assumed the penitential garment, not a mere sign of woe, but a constant chastisement of the flesh. He wore sackcloth next his skin, no one suspecting it, until, in the exasperation of his feelings at the woman's tale, he rent his robe, and exposed to view the sackcloth which underlay it. We are scarcely entitled to deny him any true penitential feeling, though no doubt he was far from possessing a chastened or humble spirit. Poor weak humanity has at one and the same time good and evil impulses, praiseworthy and culpable feelings, thoughts which come from the Holy Spirit of God, and thoughts which are inspired by the evil one.

Ver. 31.—**Then he said, God do so and more also to me, if the head of Elisha the son of Shaphat shall stand on him**—*i.e.* "continue on him"—**this day.** The form of oath was a common one (comp. Ruth i. 17; 1 Sam. iii. 17; xxv. 22; 2 Sam. xix. 13; 1 Kings ii. 23; xix. 2, etc.). It was an

imprecation of evil on one's self, if one did, or if one failed to do, a certain thing. Why Jehoram should have considered Elisha as responsible for all the horrors of the siege is not apparent; but perhaps he supposed that it was in Elisha's power to work a miracle of any kind at any moment that he liked. If so, he misunderstood the nature of the miraculous gift. In threatening to *behead* Elisha, he is not making himself an executor of the Law, which nowhere sanctioned that mode of punishment, but assuming the arbitrary power of the other Oriental monarchs of his time, who regarded themselves as absolute masters of the lives and liberties of their subjects. Beheading was common in Egypt, in Babylonia, and in Assyria.

Ver. 32.—**But Elisha sat in his house, and the elders sat with him; and the king sent a man from before him.** It is best to translate, *Now Elisha was sitting in his house, and the elders were sitting with him, when the king sent a man from before him.* Elisha had a house in Samaria, where he ordinarily resided, and from which he made his circuits. He happened to be sitting there, and the elders of the city to be sitting with him, when Jehoram sent "a man from before him," *i.e.* one of the court officials, to put him to death. The "elders" had probably assembled at Elisha's house to consult with him on the critical situation of affairs, and (if possible) obtain from him some miraculous assistance. **But ere the messenger came to him, he said to the elders, See ye how this son of a murderer hath sent to take away mine head?** Elisha was supernaturally warned of what was about to take place—that an executioner was coming almost immediately to take away his life, and that the king himself would arrive shortly after. He calls the king "this son of a murderer," or rather "this son of *the* murderer," with reference to Ahab, the great murderer of the time, who had sanctioned all Jezebel's cruelties—the general massacre of the prophets of Jehovah (1 Kings xviii. 13), the judicial murder of Naboth (1 Kings xxi. 9—13), the attempt to kill Elijah (1 Kings xix. 2)—and had, by a fierce and long-continued persecution, reduced the worshippers of Jehovah in Israel to the scanty number of seven thousand (1 Kings xix. 18). Jehoram had now shown that he inherited the bloodthirsty disposition of his father, and had justly earned the epithet which Elisha bestowed on him. **Look, when the messenger cometh, shut the door, and hold him fast at the door.** Keil renders the last clause, "force him back at the door;" the LXX. "press upon him in the doorway"— παραθλίψατε αὐτὸν ἐν τῇ θύρᾳ—they were not to allow him to enter the apartment. Is not the sound of his master's feet behind him? Elisha adds this as a reason why the elders should stop the messenger. He could not in a general way have expected them to resist the king's will as declared by his representative; but he might reasonably ask a short respite, if the king was just about to arrive at the house, to confirm the order that he had given, or to revoke it.

Ver. 33.—**And while he yet talked with them**—*i.e.* while Elisha yet talked with the elders, endeavouring probably to persuade them to stop the messenger—**behold, the messenger came down unto him: and he said.** The narrative is very compressed and elliptical. Some suppose words to have fallen out (as אליו) ויאמר אחריו after אליו); but this is unnecessary. The reader is expected to supply missing links, and to understand that all happened as Elisha had predicted and enjoined—that the messenger came, that the elders stopped him, and that the king

shortly arrived. The king was, of course, admitted, and, being admitted, took the word, and said, **Behold, this evil is of the Lord; what—rather, *why*—should I wait for the Lord any longer?** Jehoram had, apparently, to some extent repented of his hasty message, and had hurried after his messenger, to give Elisha one further chance of life. We must understand that they had been in communication previously on the subject of the siege, and that Elisha had encouraged the king to "wait for" an interposition of Jehovah. The king now urges that the time for waiting is over; matters are at the last gasp; "this evil"—this terrible suffering which can no longer be endured—"is of the Lord," has come from him, is continued by him, and is not relieved. What use is there in his "waiting" any longer? Why should he not break with Jehovah, behead the lying prophet, and surrender the town? What has Elisha to say in reply?

HOMILETICS.

Vers. 1—7.—*Mutual love and help the best bond of religious communities.* "Behold, how good and joyful a thing it is, brethren, to dwell together in unity! It is like the precious ointment upon the head, that ran down unto the beard, even unto Aaron's beard, and went down to the skirts of his clothing; like as the dew of Hermon, which fell upon the hill of Zion" (Ps. cxxxiii. 1—3). In religious communities it has been too often the practice to govern by fear. An autocratic authority has been committed to, or assumed by, the head, who has exacted from all the other members an entire, absolute, and unreasoning obedience. Vows of obedience, of the most rigid character, have been taken; and it has been inculcated on all that the sum total of virtue lay in obeying, without a murmur or a question, every order issued by the superior. An iron rule has characterized such institutions, and a cold, unloving temper has prevailed in them. How different is the picture drawn in the beautiful passage before us! How sweet and pleasing is the community-life of Elisha and his prophet-disciples! Though bound by no vow of obedience, they undertake nothing without their master (vers. 2 and 3). They require an enlargement of their dwelling-place, but they will not commence it without his sanction. Even his sanction is not enough; they ask his presence, his superintending eye, his guiding mind. And he complies willingly, cheerfully. No trouble is too much for him. "Go ye," he says; but when they object and plead, "Be content, I pray thee, and go with thy servants," he at once consents, and says, "I will go." He goes, he looks on with sympathy, he guides, he aids. At the first touch of misfortune, his sympathy blossoms into help. How charming is the childlike confidence and communicativeness of the disciple, who, on losing his axe-head, immediately reveals his loss to the master, and tells him why it was so especially grievous to him—"And it a borrowed one!" And how admirable the kindness and fellow-feeling, which uttered no reproach, made no suggestion of carelessness or of stupidity in selecting a tree so near the stream, but thought only of finding a remedy. Natural means being unavailing, the prophet deems the occasion no unsuitable one for the exercise of his miraculous powers, which he is as willing to exert on behalf of a humble prophet-student as on that of a great Syrian general. The terms on which Elisha and his disciples live are evidently those of mutual confidence and affection, of protection and fatherly care on the one hand; of appeal, regard, and childlike love on the other; and the result is a community which it is delightful to contemplate, and which increases and flourishes, in spite of the contempt and persecution of the world-lover, so that its place is "too strait for it."

Vers. 8—23.—*Wicked men vainly attempt to outwit God.*   Benhadad, after the miracle wrought upon his favourite Naaman, had abundant reason to know that Israel was the people of God, and enjoyed special Divine protection and superintendence. Had he been truly wise, he would have laid aside his hostile designs against the nation, and have made it his endeavour to cultivate friendly relations with them, and, if possible, secure their alliance.   But true wisdom is a plant of rare growth, while its counterfeit, cunning, is a weed that grows rankly at all times and everywhere.   Benhadad resolved to have recourse to craft against the Israelites, and thought perhaps that, while the protection of their God would not fail them in a pitched battle, he might be able in petty engagements, by means of ambushes and surprises, to snatch an occasional victory.   But his plan failed egregiously.   God enabled his prophet to foresee where each ambush would be placed; and each time he warned Jehoram of the snare, which was thereupon easily avoided.   Craft and cunning were of no avail against the wisdom which is from on high—the Divine foreknowledge, of which the prophet was made in some measure partaker.   Benhadad then bethought him of a new device.   He would capture the prophet, and thenceforward his plans would be undetected, and the success which he had expected from them would follow.   How simple and easy it must have seemed!   The prophet moved about from city to city, teaching the faithful, and was now in one place, now in another.   What could be easier than to make inquiry, and learn where he was residing at any particular time, and then to make a sudden inroad, surround the place, occupy it, and obtain possession of his person?   Such seizures of individuals have been planned many hundreds of times, and have generally been successful.   Had Benhadad had only human enemies to deal with, there can be little doubt that his plans would have prospered.   He would have outwitted the prophet, and would have got him into his power; but it was necessary that he should also outwit God.   Here was a difficulty which had not presented itself to his mind, and which yet surely ought to have done so.   What had frustrated his efforts previously?   Not human strength; not human wisdom or sagacity; but Divine omniscience.   God had enabled Elisha to show the King of Israel the words which he spake in the secrecy of his bedchamber.   Why should he not grant him a foreknowledge of the new design?   Or why should he not enable the prophet in some other way to frustrate it?   There are ten thousand ways in which God can bring the counsels of men to no effect, whenever he pleases.   Benhadad ought to have known that it was God, not merely the prophet, against whom he was contending, and that it would be impossible to outwit the Source of wisdom, the Giver of all knowledge and understanding.   But men in all ages have thought (and vainly thought) to hoodwink and outwit God.   1. The first dwellers upon the earth after the Flood were divinely commanded to spread themselves over its face and "replenish" it (Gen. ix. 1). They disliked the idea, and thought to frustrate God's design by building themselves a city and a tower as a focus of union (Gen. ix. 4).   But God "came down," and confounded their language; and so "scattered them abroad from thence upon the face of all the earth" (Gen. ix. 8).   2. Isaac sought to outwit God, and frustrate his preference of Jacob over Esau (Gen. xxv. 23), by giving his special blessing to his firstborn; but God blinded him, and caused him to be himself outwitted by Rebekah and Jacob, so that he gave the blessing where he had not intended to give it (Gen. xxvii. 27—29).   3. Pharaoh King of Egypt at the time of the Exodus, thought to frustrate God's designs respecting his people by a long series of delays and impediments, and finally by shutting them up into a corner of the land, whence apparently they had no escape unless by an absolute surrender; but God gave them a way of escape across the Red Sea, which removed them wholly from his control.   4. Jonah thought to outwit God, when commanded to warn the Ninevites, by flying from Asia to the remotest corner of Europe, and there hiding himself; but God counteracted his schemes and made them of no avail.   5. Herod the Great thought to outwit God, to preserve his kingdom, and to make the advent of Christ upon earth unavailing, by a general massacre of all the young children to be found in Bethlehem (Matt. ii. 16); but the warning given by God to Joseph and Mary confounded his counsels, and made the massacre futile.   6. Men have, in all periods of the world's history, endeavoured to hoodwink God by professing to serve him, while they offered him a formal, outward, and ceremonial observance, instead of giving him the true worship of the heart.   But

God has not been deceived; he "is not mocked;" he readily discerns the counterfeit from the genuine, and rejects with abhorrence all feigned and hypocritical religiousness. Every attempt of man to cheat his Maker recoils on his own head. "The foolishness of God is wiser than men; and the weakness of God is stronger than men" (1 Cor. i. 25). We cannot deceive him. "All things are naked and opened unto the eyes of him with whom we have to do" (Heb. iv. 13).

Vers. 16, 17.—*The spirit-world, and the power to discern it.* The little episode of the alarm felt by Elisha's servant, and the manner in which Elisha removed it, teaches us principally three things.

I. THE REALITY, AND PERPETUAL PRESENCE, AROUND US AND ABOUT US, OF THE SPIRIT-WORLD. The existence of an order of spirits intermediate between God and man, who are closely connected with man, and play an important part in the Divine government of the world wherein we live, is an essential part of the scheme of things set before us in the Scriptures. "The doctrine of angels," as it has been called, is this: "That there lives in the presence of God a vast assembly, myriads upon myriads of spiritual beings (Ps. lxviii. 17; Dan. vii. 10), higher than we, but infinitely removed from God, mighty in strength, doers of his word, who ceaselessly bless and praise God, wise also, to whom he gives charge to guard his own in all their ways, ascending and descending to and from heaven and earth (Gen. xxviii. 12, 13; John i. 51), and who variously minister to men, most often invisibly. All these beings are interested in us and in our well-being. When our earth was created, 'all the sons of God burst forth into jubilee' (Job xxxviii. 7) in prospect of our birth, who were to be their care here, their fellow-citizens hereafter in bliss. At the giving of the Law on Mount Sinai, they were present in myriads. When God vouchsafed his presence on Mount Zion, and the holy place became a new Sinai, 'twice ten thousand angels, yea, thousands many times repeated' (Ps. lxviii. 17) were there. They are present with God, witnessing the trials of our race (Job i. 6; ii. 1; 1 Kings xxii. 19). Their love for man is indicated by the charge given to them when they are set to destroy the guilty in Jerusalem, 'Let not your eye spare, neither have pity' (Ezek. x. 5), as though they would have pity, only that they must needs be of the same mind with God. There is a distinction, or gradation of ranks, among the members of the heavenly host—Cherubim, seraphim, archangels, principalities, powers" (abridged from Pusey's 'Daniel the Prophet,' pp. 517—524). It is irrational to'explain away as embellishment or poetic imagery a representation of the actual condition of things in God's universe, which is so frequent, so all-pervading, so harmonious, and, it may be added, so consistent with what we should have naturally expected apart from revelation.

II. THE PERPETUAL REALIZATION OF THIS PRESENCE BY THOSE POSSESSED OF FAITH. There is no reason to believe that Elisha saw the angels that compassed him round, with his bodily eyes. But he knew that they were there. He was sure that God would not desert him in his peril, and had such a confident faith in "the doctrine of angels," that it was as if he could see them. And so it was with David. "The angel of the Lord," he says, "encampeth round about them that fear him, and delivereth them" (Ps. xxxiv. 7). So with Hezekiah, who, when Sennacherib invaded his land, "spake comfortably to the people, saying, Be strong and courageous, be not afraid nor dismayed for the King of Assyria, nor for all the multitude that is with him: for *there be more with us than with him*" (2 Chron. xxxii. 7). Judas Maccabæus had probably the same faith when he uttered the words, "It is no hard matter for many to be shut up in the hands of a few; and with the God of heaven it is all one, to deliver with a great multitude, or a small company: for the victory of battle standeth not in the multitude of an host; but *strength cometh from heaven*" (1 Macc. iii. 18, 19). St. Paul realized the continual angelic presence when he declared, "We are made a spectacle unto the world, and to angels, and to men" (1 Cor. iv. 9). The author of the Epistle to the Hebrews realized it when he told the Jewish converts, "Ye are come unto Mount Zion, and unto the city of the living God, the heavenly Jerusalem, and to *an innumerable* company of angels" (Heb. xii. 22). St. John the divine realized it, when he gave the angels a large share in all the later judgments that should befall the earth, and made them dispensers of the blessings and of the wrath of God (Rev. vii. 1—xx. 3). If the doctrine has been at any time obscured, it has been when faith wavered, and there was a tendency to confine the supernatural within the narrowest possible limits. It was easy to suggest that the expression, "the angels of God," was a periphrasis for God himself, and that he had no need to act, and therefore probably did not act, by intermediaries. But the faith of the Church has always been different. The festival of St. Michael and All Angels has been generally celebrated from a very ancient date; and the Collect for that festival has borne witness to the perpetual ministration of angels, not only in heaven, but also upon earth, and to the part borne by them in the succour and defence of God's people.

III. THE POSSIBILITY OF A MANIFESTATION OF THE PRESENCE IN QUESTION TO THE BODILY SENSES OF THOSE WHOSE FAITH IS TOO WEAK TO APPREHEND IT. Elisha's servant did not see a vision. It was not his mind only that was impressed. His bodily eyes beheld an appearance as of chariots and horses of fire (ver. 17), which was based on the objective reality of the actual presence of an angelic host upon the hill whereon Dothan was situated. The prophet prayed that his eyes should be opened, and his prayer was granted. "The Lord opened the eyes of the young man, and he saw." Physicists are probably right in saying that what is absolutely immaterial cannot be seen by the optic nerve. But we are nowhere told that angels are absolutely immaterial. It is the belief of many philosophers that all finite spirits are attached to bodies of some kind or other—bodies more or less volatile and ethereal. We can readily conceive that the optic nerve may, by an increase of its sensitiveness, be made to see these; and in this way we may account, not only for the wonderful sight beheld on this occasion by Elisha's servant, but for the many other appearances of angels to men and women recorded in Scripture (Gen. iii. 1; xix. 1—15; xxxii. 24—30; Judg. vi. 11—22; 2 Sam. xxiv. 16, 17; 1 Kings xix. 5—7; Isa. vi. 6; Dan. vi. 22; ix. 21; x. 16—21; Zech. i. 11—19; iv. 1, etc.; Luke i. 11—19, 26—38; ii. 9—13; John xx. 12; Acts v. 19; viii. 26; xii. 7—10; Revelation, *passim*). Miraculously, power is given to the optic nerve which it does not ordinarily possess, and it is enabled to see beings actually present, who under ordinary circumstances are invisible to it.

Vers. 24—33.—*Half-heartedness.* Jehoram was altogether half-hearted in his religion. He "halted between two opinions." While he paid a certain amount of respect to Elisha, as the prophet of Jehovah, he nevertheless allowed the worship of Baal to continue in the capital (ch. x. 18—28), if not elsewhere, and maintained the calf-worship also at Dan and Bethel (ch. iii. 3). He had suffered himself to be guided by Elisha in respect of the Syrian prisoners captured by the prophet (ver. 23), and had evidently been in communication with him on the subject of the present siege, had probably been exhorted by him to repentance, and promised that, if he would wait upon Jehovah, in due time there should be deliverance. The prophet's words had made some impression on him; he had to a certain extent turned to God, had put sackcloth upon his loins, not ostentatiously, but secretly (ver. 30), had borne the privations of the siege without murmuring, had refused to surrender the town, and looked to Jehovah to deliver it. But there was no depth in his penitence, no surrender of the heart and the will to God, no firm and rooted faith in God's truthfulness, and in the certain accomplishment of his promises. His repentance was but a half-repentance. A single incident of the siege, a horrible one certainly, but yet not without a parallel in other sieges and in shipwrecks, shattered the whole fabric of his repentance and his resolution, turned him against the prophet and against Jehovah, caused him to threaten the prophet's life, and to make up his mind that he would follow his own course, and not wait for the Lord any longer (ver. 33). He thus revealed the true state of his heart and soul, showed his spiritual unsoundness, revealed himself as one whose character was rotten at the core, who had never turned to Jehovah in sincerity and truth. What wonder, then, that God had not granted the deliverance promised to true faith and true penitence, that a half-repentance had not availed with him? So it had been with Ahab (1 Kings xxi. 27; xxii. 34); so it would always be with all those who, after Jehoram's example, should be half-hearted in religion, should at once "fear the Lord, and serve their own gods" (ch. xvii. 33)—own for masters both God and mammon. A half-repentance is useless. Nothing avails but to turn to God with all the heart and all the soul and all the strength. God hates waverers. To such he says, "I know thy works, that thou art neither cold nor hot: I would thou wert cold or hot. So then because thou art lukewarm, and neither cold nor hot, I will *spue thee out of my mouth*" (Rev. iii. 15, 16).

Ver. 32.—*Princes may be resisted when they are bent upon wrong-doing.* There was a time when princes were flattered, by being told that they "could do no wrong;" that "a divinity hedged them in;" that their subjects were bound to render them, under all circumstances, an absolute and unqualified obedience. But this is certainly not scriptural teaching. The higher powers are to be obeyed in their lawful commands, but not in their unlawful ones. When Pharaoh, King of Egypt, commanded the midwives to put to death all the male children borne by the Hebrew women, "the midwives feared God, and *did not as the King of Egypt commanded them*, but saved the men children alive" (Exod. i. 17); and God rewarded them for so acting: "Therefore God dealt well with the midwives; . . . and because they feared God, he made them houses" (Exod. i. 20, 21). So now Elisha, the prophet of God, bids the elders resist the king's messenger—"hold him fast," and not let him execute the king's commands. Again, the higher powers, the great council of the Sanhedrin, commanded Peter and John, shortly after the Day of Pentecost, "not to speak at all nor preach in the Name of Jesus" (Acts iv. 18); to whom the apostles replied, "Whether it be right in the sight of God to hearken unto you more than unto God, judge ye. For we *cannot but speak* the things which we have seen and heard" (Acts iv. 19, 20). Resistance to lawful authority, when it commands unlawful acts, is an important part of a Christian man's duty, and ought to be inculcated just as much as obedience to lawful authority when it commands lawful acts.

HOMILIES BY VARIOUS AUTHORS.

Vers. 1—7.—*An early theological college; its life and lessons.* Our theological colleges, where young men are trained for the office of the Christian ministry, do not receive from the Christian public that attention and sympathy which they deserve. More interest ought to be taken in education generally. The Church should show more interest in Sunday-school work. If office-bearers and parents in every Christian land would visit the Sunday school occasionally, and hear the children repeat their lessons and sing their hymns, it would do themselves good, and it would be a great encouragement to those who are engaged in the important work of Sunday-school teaching. The work of our theological colleges is to a great extent different from that of other places of education. The very nature of the studies is such that the general public could not be expected to take much interest in them. But there are other ways of showing an interest in our colleges besides actually entering a college class-room, or listening to a professor's lecture. Occasionally, a rich member of the Church leaves a considerable sum to found a scholarship or a bursary; but how little is done by the members of the Church generally! Yet all the members of the Church are interested in having not only a godly, but also a well-educated ministry.

I. There was industry in that college. These students in Elisha's college knew how to work, and *they were not above doing their own work*. They had not reached that high state of civilization when manual labour is considered a disgrace. Their house, which was college and students' residence all in one, had become too small for them. So they said to Elisha one day, "Let us go, we pray thee, unto Jordan, and take thence every man a beam, and let us make us a place there, where we may dwell." It was an enactment of the Jewish religion that every boy, no matter what his position, should be taught some handicraft. The Jewish Talmud says, "What is commanded of a father toward his son? To circumcise him, to teach him the Law, and to teach him a trade." Thus we find that the Apostle Paul, who had sat at the feet of Gamaliel, and was a distinguished scholar, was also a tentmaker. Even when a preacher of the gospel, he laboured with his own hands for his support. It is not generally the custom now for ministers of the gospel to follow any other calling. It is found more convenient that they should devote themselves entirely to the work of the ministry, for all men have not the genius of the Apostle Paul. It is true that the missionaries of certain Missionary Societies all learn a trade, and most of them support themselves by their own exertions at farming or other work. But this also has been found very undesirable, and it has been under serious consideration to abandon the custom altogether. But whether they engage in manual labour or not, all ministers and all students for the ministry should be, as these students in Elisha's time were, industrious in their work. In whatever calling we are engaged, let us cultivate habits of industry. Let us remember the apostle's injunction to be " diligent in business, fervent in spirit, serving the Lord."

II. THERE WAS DISCIPLINE IN THAT COLLEGE. These young students, excellent and well-conducted as they no doubt were, did not think they might do as they liked or go where they liked. They came to Elisha, and asked his consent to their proposal. And so it should be in all the relationships of life. " Order is Heaven's first law." There should be discipline in the family, discipline in the Church, discipline in the Sunday school, discipline in the nation, and regard for constituted authority. Dr. Arnold of Rugby once said to his assembled scholars, when there had been some disorder in the school, and he had expelled several boys, " It is *not* necessary that this should be a school of three hundred, or of one hundred, or of fifty boys ; but it *is* necessary that it should be a school of Christian gentlemen." No wonder there is disregard for authority in the nation when it is not properly taught or insisted on in the home. The Christian Church should be a model of order. Order should characterize its services, its management, its work. "Let all things be done decently and in order."

III. THERE WAS KINDNESS IN THAT COLLEGE. What pleasant and brotherly relations between the prophet and his pupils ! He could be stern with the haughty Naaman ; he could severely rebuke the covetous, lying Gehazi ; but he knew how to unbend among his innocent-hearted students. He had evidently already won their affections. *It was a good sign of both him and them that they asked him to accompany them.* And now he shows his kindly nature once more by going with them at their request. So it ought to be with all Christians. We hardly think enough of Christ's command that we should love one another. What friendly relations there should be between professors and students, between ministers and their people, between parents and children, between teachers and scholars, between employers and employed, between masters and servants ! *Authority is never weakened by kindness.* Some employers, some teachers, seem to think it adds to their dignity and to their influence to be stern to those beneath them. They make a great mistake. The most respected professors are those who treat their students as brothers, and not as inferiors. The most respected employers are those who are kind and courteous and considerate to those in their employment. Kindness does not weaken influence ; it increases it. Oh ! to be filled with the spirit of Christ, who made himself of no reputation, and took upon himself the form of a servant. Kindness and humility are twin sisters.

IV. THERE WAS GROWTH IN THAT COLLEGE. Under the influence of such a teacher as Elisha, the number of students increased so much that the place became too small for them, and it was necessary for them to build a new school of the prophets. Let me see growth in a Church and I shall believe in its life. A stone does not grow, because it has no life. A tree grows, because there is life in it. If you see that a tree has ceased to grow, to put forth new leaves in the spring-time, you know that it is dead. A Church that is not growing must be a lifeless Church. If you are a living Christian, let the signs of it be manifest in the growth of your Christian graces.

V. THE PRESENCE OF GOD WAS THERE. This was shown in the miracle which Elisha wrought of causing the iron to swim. It was not by his own power. He was only the instrument in the hand of God, and God owned his efforts, for he was engaged in God's work. This last feature of that theological college was the best of all. God's presence was in the midst of it. Without that, of what use would have been their industry or their discipline? Without that, would there have been such bonds of kindness? Without that, would there have been such evidences of growth ? " Except the Lord build the house, they labour in vain that build it." Without that, what a mockery it would have been for them to have looked forward to be the teachers of others in the truths of religion ! What a mockery for any man to enter a pulpit and speak about the love of Jesus, who is himself a stranger to that love ! What a mockery for any man to speak about the grace of God, who has never experienced it in his own heart and life! The late Rev. Dr. Cooke of Belfast once said that "*an educated ministry is desirable, but a converted ministry is essential.*"—C. H. I.

Vers. 8—16.—*God's presence with his people.* There has been a sudden change in the horizon of Elisha's life. From the quiet work of cutting down trees and building a college, he is suddenly called upon to stand a siege from a Syrian army. These changes do come in the lives of most of us. Health suddenly changes into sickness. Friendship suddenly changes into hostility. Wealth suddenly changes into poverty. Such changes will come in the life of the believer and in the history of the Church of God. At one time all seems bright; the next moment the prospect seems dark and discouraging. It is well to be prepared for such changes when they come. The true servant of God will heed them very little. He lives not under, but above, the things of earth.

> " As some tall cliff that lifts its awful form,
> Swells from the vale, and midway cleaves the storm,
> Though round its breast the rolling clouds are spread,
> Eternal sunshine settles on its head."

So it was with Elisha. Wherever you find him, he always seems the same. On the present occasion the circumstances were such as to strike terror to the stoutest heart. Elisha's servant trembled at the sight that met him when he rose that morning and looked forth from the city walls. A mighty host, with horses and chariots, encompassed the city round about. It was an unexpected attack. No forces were within the city to defend it against such a mighty host. Elisha was the only one whom the besieging army wanted. In the desire for self-preservation, it was not unlikely that the inhabitants of Dothan might give him up to the enemy, and thus turn away the invader from their gates. From a human point of view it was no wonder that Elisha's servant said, "Alas, my master! how shall we do?" There was no terror in Elisha's face, no panic in his heart, at this startling news. What calmness, what courage, what sublime confidence there is in that answer of his, "Fear not: for they that be with us are more than they that be with them!" *And what was the secret of his confidence?* The one reason of Elisha's confidence and calm was that God's presence was with him. What a beautiful fulfilment of that promise, "Thou shalt hide them in the secret of thy presence from the pride of man; thou shalt keep them secretly in a pavilion from the strife of tongues"! We learn from this story—

I. God's presence with his people is not generally realized by their enemies. It was so on the occasion before us. The King of Syria commenced another war against Israel. He held, as we should say, a council of war, and consulted with his generals concerning the arrangements for the campaign. He thought, by skilful strategy, to take the King of Israel unawares. But all his plans and manoeuvres were thwarted in some mysterious way. The King of Israel seemed to know all his movements with more certainty than a clever player at a game of skill might anticipate the moves of his opponent. Several times in this way the King of Israel saved himself. At last the King of Syria began to be suspicious. There must be a traitor in the camp. Some of those enjoying the king's confidence must be revealing his plans to the enemy. And so he asks, "Will ye not show me which of us is for the King of Israel?" The King of Syria was an able general; but like another great general of modern times, Napoleon the Great, there were some forces that he did not take sufficient account of. The race is not always to the swift, nor the battle to the strong. There are other things than military skill and big battalions to be thought of in going forth to battle. When Edward, the English king, came forth to view the Scottish troops before the battle of Bannockburn, he was astonished at the small force waiting on foot to receive the attack of his mighty army. But they were putting their trust in the God of battles, and presently he saw the unusual sight of the whole Scottish army, as their custom was, kneeling down and offering a short prayer to God. "Believe me," said the general who rode by his side, "yon men will win or die." Of that unseen Power, in whose hands are the issues of battle, the Syrian king took no account. *He did not realize that God's presence was with his people.* Is not this the mistake which the enemies of God's people have made in all ages? It was the mistake of the persecutors and oppressors of Israel. It was the mistake of those who persecuted the Reformers of England, Scotland, France, and Switzerland. It was the mistake which Pharaoh made when he refused to let the children of Israel go. It was the mistake which Herod made when he thought to crush the new kingdom that was yet to arise, by slaughtering the helpless babes in Bethlehem and its neighbourhood. It was the mistake which Nero made in his persecutions of the Christians at Rome. It was the mistake which Louis XIV. of France made when he revoked the famous Edict of Nantes. It is the mistake which the Roman Curia has made in all ages, in thinking to crush out civil and religious liberty by the tortures of the Inquisition, by the martyrdoms of the scaffold and the stake, by the massacres in the Waldensian valley, by the *autos-da-fé* of Spain. *The same thing may be said of the unbeliever and the sceptic.* They have not realized that the presence of the living God is with his Church and in the midst of her, and that he, in his own way and in his own time, can vindicate his own truth. How often, during these eighteen hundred years, has the unbeliever exulted in what he has called the overthrow of Christianity! and yet how vain and foolish the boast has proved to be! Voltaire boasted that with one hand he would overthrow the Christianity which it had required twelve apostles to build up. " At this day, the press which he employed at Ferney to print his blasphemies is actually employed at Geneva in printing the Holy Scriptures." May we not still say, as we think of the enemies of the truth, the enemies of virtue, the enemies of religion, and as we listen to their audacious boasts, "He that sitteth in the heavens shall laugh; the Lord shall have them in derision"?

II. GOD'S PRESENCE WITH HIS PEOPLE IS NOT REALIZED BY MANY AMONGST THEMSELVES. Elisha's servant, no doubt, believed in God. If any one had denied God's presence with his people, he would doubtless have firmly asserted it as his belief. Yet when the time came to put his belief to a practical test, we see how slight a hold it had taken of him. When he went forth in the morning and saw the horses and chariots and the mighty host encompassing the city round about, he said to Elisha, "Alas, my master! how shall we do?" Do *you* never feel a sensation like Elisha's servant? You believe you are a child of God, you believe that God takes care of his people, yet perhaps there are times when you are unduly anxious about your business, and allow yourself to be weighed down by foolish and causeless fears. How many are alarmed by the thought of sickness in themselves or in their families, and nervously ask, "What shall we do?" Oh that we would learn to realize God's presence with us! "My times are in thy hand." In the same way, how many professing Christians are there who do not sufficiently realize *God's presence in his Church!* How much more active we should be, how much more earnest in Christian work, if we realized that God is working with us! With what power a minister ought to preach if he could only remember to say with John the Baptist, "There cometh One mightier than I after me"! Then how many are *easily discouraged by difficulties*. Some are always saying when they see a difficulty in the way, "What *shall* we do?" "Who will roll us away the stone?" Some are always imagining difficulties and foreseeing them at the very beginning of a work. This spirit of timidity, of fear, is a great hindrance in Christian work. Half-belief is almost as bad as no belief, in this respect. Half-heartedness in religious work is one of the greatest hindrances to its success. In this, as in everything else, the maxim holds good, "Whatsoever thy hand findeth to do, do it with thy might." The *half-hearted ten* out of the twelve spies sent to view the promised land frightened the Israelites from going up, and nearly caused God, in his righteous anger at their unbelief, to disinherit them altogether. *The half-hearted inhabitants of Galilee* prevented the blessing of the Saviour of men resting upon them, for we read that "he did not many mighty works there because of their unbelief." *The half-hearted followers of Christopher Columbus* nearly prevented him from discovering America. There is no room for half-heartedness in religion. There is a loud call for decision and firmness both in belief and in conduct.

III. GOD'S PRESENCE WITH HIS PEOPLE IS ALWAYS REALIZED BY HIS TRUE SERVANTS. The King of Syria did not realize that God's presence was with his people, and he was at his wits' end to know how to circumvent them. Elisha's servant did not realize that God's presence was with himself and his master; and how panic-stricken he was at the danger that seemed to threaten them! But there was one man for whom the armies of the King of Syria had no terror, to whom difficulties brought no dismay, and that was *the man who lived near to God*, and realized that God was near to him. Hence it is that we find Elisha saying, " Fear not: for they that be with us are more than they that be with them." So it has been with God's true servants in all ages. They have realized that God's presence was with them, and in the strength of that one idea they have surmounted the greatest difficulties, braved the most terrible dangers, met fearlessly the most overwhelming opposition, and accomplished tasks that to the worldly eye seemed almost incredible. Look at *Abraham*. He went forth from his native land, " not knowing whither he went." And why? Because he knew that God was with him. Look at *Nehemiah*. An exile from his native land, he undertook the wonderful enterprise of rebuilding the walls of Jerusalem. He had plenty of opposition. But he went on with his work in spite of the ridicule and attacks of Sanballat and his companions. And what was the secret of his determination and perseverance? You have it in his answer to Sanballat, " The God of heaven, *he will prosper us;* therefore we his servants will arise and build." This year (1888) is the anniversary of two great events in British history—two great deliverances which illustrate in a marvellous way God's presence with his people. It is the three hundredth anniversary of the defeat of the Spanish Armada, which took place in 1588. Yet it was not English ships or English power that really turned away that invasion from our shores; but the winds and waves of him who holdeth the sea in the hollow of his hand. It is also the two hundredth anniversary of the revolution of 1688. And while we should never use such anniversaries as the occasion of displaying a vindictive or unchristian spirit towards those who differ from us, yet in the interests of truth, in the interests of true Anglicanism, in the interests of civil and religious liberty, it is most desirable that these two great events should be rightly and piously commemorated. One thing they illustrate very clearly, and that is, that however dark the prospects of God's people seem to be, and however overwhelming seem the forces arrayed against them, he is able to banish every cloud and to give them the victory over all their enemies.

> " God is our Refuge and our Strength,
>   In straits a present Aid;
>   Therefore, although the earth remove,
>   We will not be afraid."

One or two practical applications. 1. *It is well to be on God's side.* In a time of danger or of trouble, a great many people expect God to be on their side, who have never taken any pains to show themselves on his side. If you want to have the unspeakable advantage of God's presence with you in your time of difficulty or danger, the most important question you could now ask yourself is, " Am I on God's side?" 2. A word to those who are God's people. *Undertake great things for God.* Remember that you have unlimited resources at your command. We should be ashamed of how little we are attempting to do for God, when we have the inexhaustible treasury of Divine grace to help us. 3. *Never suffer yourself to be daunted or depressed by difficulties.* The greater the difficulties, the greater should be the determination of the Christian. " Let courage rise with danger." Luther sang his most stirring songs of praise and hope and courage in the darkest moments of his life. Those who have God with them can afford to sing amid the darkness.—C. H. I.

Vers. 17—23.—*Eyes closed, and eyes opened.* I. EYES CLOSED. 1. *The young man's eyes were closed.* He did not see the horses and chariots of fire that were round about Elisha. He did not realize that deliverance was at hand. How many like him are blind to the power of God, to the providences of God! How many are quick to see anything that concerns their temporal advantage, but slow to see that which concerns their immortal souls! How many see no beauty in Christ! 2. *The Syrians' eyes were closed.* This was a judicial act of God in response to Elisha's prayer. So there is a spiritual judicial blindness. " Seeing they shall see, but not perceive; hearing they shall hear, but shall not understand." It is a spiritual law which has its analogies in the natural world. If we neglect to use any of our bodily powers, the power itself is soon lost. Similarly, mental or spiritual powers, if neglected, will soon become useless. Let us be careful that we use the privileges and opportunities and talents which God has given us, lest they be taken from us altogether. " To him that hath shall be given," that is, to him that hath made a good use of his talents; "and from him that hath not" —from him that has so neglected his talents that they are practically not *his*—" shall be taken away even that which he hath."

II. EYES OPENED. 1. *The Syrians' eyes were opened to see their true condition.* Instead of being a victorious army, with Elisha a captive in their hands, they find that he has them in his power, and has led them into the midst of Samaria and into the presence of the King of Israel. They then saw how defenceless and how helpless they were. That is the first step in the path of salvation. The first step for a sinner is to see his need. So with Bunyan's pilgrim. The first thought that led him to set out on his journey was the feeling of his utter helplessness. " Sir, I perceive by the book in my hand that I am condemned to die, and after that to come to judgment (Heb. ix. 27); and I find that I am not willing to do the first (Job xvi. 21), nor able to do the second (Ezek. xxii. 14)." " Lord, show me myself." 2. *The young man's eyes were opened to see that deliverance was at hand.* " The Lord opened the eyes of the young man ; and he saw : and, behold, the mountain was full of horses and chariots of fire round about Elisha." This is the second step in the sinner's salvation. Having seen his need, he next needs to see the Saviour. " Behold the Lamb of God, which taketh away the sin of the world!" Have *you* seen your true condition, your spiritual need ? Have *you* seen your need of Jesus as your Saviour?

" When free grace awoke me, by light from on high,
Then legal fears shook me, I trembled to die;
No refuge, no safety in self could I see—
Jehovah Tsidkenu my Saviour must be.

" My terrors all vanished before the sweet Name;
My guilty fears banished, with boldness I came
To drink at the fountain, life-giving and free —
Jehovah Tsidkenu is all things to me."

III. THE POWER OF PRAYER. Elisha's prayers prevailed three times in this short narrative. There may be some one known to us whose eyes are closed, who is spiritually blind. Have we brought the case to God in prayer ? Is it a wandering son ? " Lord, I pray thee, open his eyes, that he may see." Is it a wayward daughter ? a godless friend ? We may not reach them by our words ; *but we can reach them by our prayers.*

IV. THE POWER OF DIVINE GRACE. Elisha did not exult in his triumph over his enemies. He did not take advantage of their helplessness. They had come to take him captive, perhaps to take away his life ; but he heaps coals of fire on their head. The King of Israel wanted to smite them. But Elisha reminds him (according to one view) that it was not customary to smite even captives taken in war: how much less should he smite those who had been put within his power, not by any exertions of his own, but by the miraculous interposition of God ! On the contrary, Elisha recommends that they should be well treated and well fed. This was done. And what was the consequence ? " So the bands of Syria came no more into the land of Israel." *This little act of kindness had turned away their wrath.* What an example for us to imitate toward those who treat us ill ! " Be not overcome of evil, but overcome evil with good."—C. H. I.

Vers. 24—33.—*Samaria besieged.* I. A CITY IN DISTRESS. Once more the people of Samaria were in great straits. A besieging army was at their gates, and, most terrible of all, the horrors of famine were within their walls. They were reduced to the greatest extremities. The women were actually beginning to cook and eat their own children. Whichever way they looked, the prospect was dark. To open the gates to the Syrians meant death or captivity. And the longer they remained within their walls, the more certainly death and starvation stared them in the face. *See here the evil result of forsaking God.* To such extremities they had brought themselves by their own sins. They had forsaken the living God, and now their false gods were not able to help them in the day of their calamity. It is an evil day in a man's history when he turns his back upon God's Word, upon God's commandments, upon God's Son. As it often happens, *their calamities had hardened their hearts and blinded their eyes.* There was one man in their midst who had often before proved a wise counsellor and friend. They had Elisha, the man of God, in their city—the man who, by counselling them to make the valley full of ditches, had delivered the Moabites into their hands; the man, too, who had revealed Benhadad's secrets, and smitten the Syrian army with blindness. But they had forgotten all that. Instead of looking to Elisha for guidance or help, they blame him for all their troubles. How often does it happen that, when people get into difficulties, they throw the blame upon others! When troubles and difficulties come upon us, our first business should be to search our own hearts and lives, and see whether the trouble may not be of our own causing.

II. A PROPHET IN DANGER. The king was a partaker in the wickedness of the people. He encouraged the prevailing idolatry. Now he shares their suffering. But he never thinks of looking to God for deliverance. He never thinks of humbling himself before God, and confessing his sins. On the contrary, he shows a disposition to cast the blame both on God and on his prophet. When the poor woman in her hunger and distress called to him for help, he answered, "If the Lord do not help thee, whence shall I help thee? out of the barnfloor, or out of the winepress?" Though he wore sackcloth, the outward sign of mourning or penitence, there was no sign of inward penitence or humility in his heart. How blind and infatuated he is in his anger and defiance! He threatens to take away the prophet's life. Jezebel had once said to Elijah, "So let the gods do to me and more also, if I make not thy life as the life of one of them [the prophets whom she had slain] by to-morrow about this time." So here Jehoram says, "God do so and more also to me, if the head of Elisha the son of Shaphat shall stand on him this day." Even Jezebel's threat had apparently more reason for it than Jehoram's. Elijah had undoubtedly slain the prophets of Baal. But in this case Elisha was innocent of any charge. Jehoram quite gratuitously holds him responsible for the famine in Samaria, and threatens to take away his life. But man proposes and God disposes. Although Elisha is in danger, he is never in dismay. When the king's messenger came to take off his head, Elisha bade the elders to hold the messenger fast at the door till the king himself, who was close behind, should arrive. Elisha had had dealings with Jehoram before. He would hear his sentence from the king himself, if at all. Well for those who, like Elisha, live near to God. "Serve the Lord in fear," said John Knox on his death-bed, "and the flesh will not fear death." Dangers do not distress them; death brings no dismay. "Yea, though I walk through the valley of the shadow of death, I will fear no evil: for thou art with me; thy rod and thy staff they comfort me."—C. H. I.

Vers. 1—7.—*A Church-extension enterprise.* "And the sons of the prophets said unto Elisha, Behold now, the place where we dwell with thee is too strait for us," etc. If there were a Church in Israel at all, the schools of the prophets undoubtedly constituted a part of that Church. They were a communion of godly men. The brief narrative, therefore, may fairly be regarded as a record of a Church-extension enterprise, and as such four things are observable—things that all who contemplate such enterprises should ponder and imitate.

I. This Church-extension enterprise was STIMULATED BY THE PRINCIPLE OF GROWTH. The old sphere had become too narrow for them, they had outgrown it. "And the sons of the prophets said unto Elisha, Behold now, the place where we dwell with thee is too strait for us." The numbers who came to listen to Elisha and the increase of students required greater accommodation than the whole place could afford. This is a principle on which all Church-extension, should proceed; but in these modern times it is sometimes not only ignored, but outraged. Although statistics show that the churches and chapels in England fall miserably short of the accommodation necessary for the whole population, it is three times greater than is required for the number of attendants. On all sides empty churches and chapels abound, millions of money contributed for religious purposes lie as the "one talent," wrapped in a napkin, unused. And yet still, almost every religious denomination seems to feel that the building of new churches is its grand mission. The fact is that church-building has, in many cases, become a business speculation. One church should grow out of another; the grain of mustard seed will create its own organism, multiply its own branches, and propagate its vitality.

II. This Church-extension enterprise was CONDUCTED IN A MANLY MANNER. 1. *The best counsel was sought before a step was taken.* These sons of the prophets went to Elisha and said, " Let us go, we pray thee, unto Jordan." Though they were young, perhaps with all the stirring impulses of youth, they were conscious of their need of counsel, and they sought it. In these modern times in England—we speak from extensive experience—churches and chapels are often built from ignorant zeal and a spirit of rivalry. How unmanly is this! 2. *Each man set to honest work in the matter.* " Let us go, we pray thee, unto Jordan, and take thence every man a beam, and let us make us a place there, where we may dwell." Matthew Henry quaintly says, "When they wanted room they did not speak of sending for cedars, and marble stones, and curious artificers, but only of getting every man a beam, to run up a plain hut or cottage with." Each man, it would seem, felled his beam, carried and adjusted it. How right, manly, and honest all this! They never thought of putting up a grand place at other people's expense. Ah me! how far we are fallen in spirit from them! To erect modern churches and chapels, what means do we use? Fawning entreaties, addressed to moneyed ignorance and stupidity, bazaars with their questionable procedures, their displays, their raffles, and their flirtations.

III. This Church-extension enterprise ENCOUNTERED DIFFICULTIES UNEXPECTED. " And when they came to Jordan, they cut down wood. But as one was felling a beam, the axe-head fell into the water : and he cried, and said, Alas, master! for it was borrowed." Why this distress of the woodman? Was it because the axe was borrowed and he had not the wherewith to pay, or because he was checked in his operation? Perhaps both were reasons for his distress. The former I trow the greater. In all worthy enterprises on this earth difficulties crop up unawares. Perhaps the best enterprises encounter the greatest difficulties. "The race is not to the swift, nor the battle to the strong." But difficulties are in truth blessings in disguise. They challenge the courage and rouse the forces of the worker. They bring out his manhood. They are to the true worker what tempests are to young trees—they deepen the roots and strengthen the fibres. Besides, there is no consciousness of virtue in doing that which involves no struggle.

IV. This Church-extension enterprise OBTAINED SUPERNATURAL HELP WHEN NEEDED. When the man who had lost his axe was crying out in distress, Elisha, the "man of God said, Where fell it? And he showed him the place. And he cut down a stick, and cast it in thither; and the iron did swim. Therefore said he, Take it up to thee. And he put out his hand, and took it." Elisha here, by raising the axe and making the iron swin, overcame a law of nature—the law of gravitation. Up to this point in this enterprise there does not seem to have been any supernatural interposition. They prosecuted their journeying, they cut down the timber, they carried their beams, all by their own natural skill and force. They did not require supernatural aid. But now one of them did, and it came. We must not expect any special power from heaven to do that which we have the natural force to accomplish ourselves. " As thy day, so thy strength shall be."—D. T.

Vers. 8—23.—*The King of Syria and Elisha.* "Then the King of Syria warred against Israel," etc. In these sixteen verses we have four subjects worth looking into —wickedness thwarted, timidity dispelled, supernatural power manifested, and revenge overcome.

I. WICKEDNESS THWARTED. The King of Syria had determined on an enterprise of bloodshed and wickedness. He had made all arrangements, fixed on the place for his camp. "In such and such a place shall be my camp." But Elisha thwarted the bloody purpose of the Syrian king by informing the Israelitish monarch, Jehoram, of the very place where the Syrians had determined to encamp. His words are, "Beware that thou pass not such a place; for thither the Syrians are come down." The king attended to the prophet's directions, "and saved himself there, not once nor twice." Terrible was the disappointment of the Syrian monarch. "The heart of the King of Syria was sore troubled for this thing; and he called his servants, and said unto them, Will ye not show me which of us is for the King of Israel? And one of his servants said, None, my lord, O king: but Elisha, the prophet that is in Israel, telleth the King of Israel the words that thou speakest in thy bedchamber." Observe: 1. That wicked men are most secretive in their purposes. It would seem that the plans of the King of Syria's bloody enterprise were known only to his most confidential officers, and that they were revealed to them in his bedchamber. There, and perhaps there only, did he detain them, and perhaps with closed doors and soft whisperings. Wicked men, in order to get on in the world, are bound to be secretive. And the more wicked they are, the more necessary for them is this secretiveness. Were dishonest doctors, lawyers, tradesmen, merchants, statesmen, to be open and candid, revealing all that is nefarious in their aims, they would fall into poverty and universal contempt. The good alone can afford to be open and candid; the wicked are bound to be hypocrites if they would live. 2. That none of their purposes are so secret as to escape the notice of Almighty God. How came Elisha to know them? He was far away from the monarch's bedchamber— away in Israel. It was Elisha's God who made the communication to him. Solemn thought. There is One who knoweth what is in man—in every man. He reads all secrets; he "understandeth our thoughts afar off." 3. The revelations of a wicked man's secrets will frustrate his designs. It did so in the case of this king.

II. TIMIDITY DISPELLED. When the Syrian monarch learnt that Elisha was in Israel, he despatched a spy to find him out; and when he discovered that he was in Dothan, "he sent thither horses, and chariots, and a great host: and they came by night, and compassed the city about." All this struck a panic into the heart of Elisha's servant, and he cried out, "Alas, my master! how shall we do?" How did Elisha relieve his servant of this terrible fear? By assuring him that there were more on their side than on the side of their enemies. "Fear not: for they that be with us are more than they that be with them." This assurance he gave not merely with words, but by ocular demonstration. "And Elisha prayed, and said, Lord, I pray thee, open his eyes, that he may see. And the Lord opened the eyes of the young man; and he saw: and, behold, the mountain was full of horses and chariots of fire round about Elisha." It is generally supposed that the reference is here to angels "that excel in strength;" they are in truth the body-guard of the good. They are more in their number than our foes, superior in their power, in their invincible determination, in their authority too. But to see them we must have our spiritual eyes open as the prophet's eyes were now. Faith in the wonderful resources which Heaven has provided for the good will dispel all fear.

III. SUPERNATURAL POWER MANIFESTED. Supernatural power is here manifested: 1. In opening the eyes of the prophet's servant. 2. In bringing under his notice the mountain which was full of horses and chariots of fire. 3. In smiting with blindness the army of Syria. "And when they came down to him [that is, the Syrian army], Elisha prayed unto the Lord, and said, Smite this people, I pray thee, with blindness. And he smote them with blindness according to the word of Elisha." These armed legions, whose eyes were glaring with vengeance before, were now in midnight darkness. In this state Elisha becomes their guide and conducts them to Samaria, and when they had come there another supernatural act was performed in the restoration of their sight, and then they beheld their terrible position. "Behold, they were in the midst of Samaria," in the hands of the King of Israel.

IV. REVENGE OVERCOME. The King of Syria, hearing that Elisha had revealed his murderous plan to the monarch of Israel, and had thus thwarted the purpose and the plan of his campaign, was fired with indignation, and sent to Dothan "horses, and chariots and a great host: and they came by night, and compassed the city about." How furiously we may suppose revenge flamed in every member of the army, as well as in the soul of their royal master, as they "compassed the city about"! And this feeling would no doubt be intensified when they found that Elisha had betrayed them into the hands of their enemies. They were in the midst of Samaria, within the very grasp of the King of Israel, and at his mercy. How would Elisha advise the King of Israel to treat these revengeful legions now? "And the King of Israel said unto Elisha, when he saw them, My father, shall I smite them? shall I smite them?" What was the prophet's advice? Did he say, "Destroy them"? No. He answered, "Thou shalt not smite them." Did he say, "Spare their lives, but make them slaves, take them into captivity and make them beasts of burden"? Did he say, "Deprive them of all food, and starve them to death"? No; he said, "Set bread and water before them, that they may eat and drink, and go to their master. And he prepared great provision for them: and when they had eaten and drunk, he sent them

away, and they went to their master." What was the result of this generous treatment? Did they go away with the old passion of vengeance burning in them? Away
to reorganize themselves in greater numbers and with greater force to make another
attack? No. Here is the result: "So the bands of Syria came no more into the land
of Israel." The magnanimous kindness extinguished the flames and paralyzed the arms
of revenge, so that they came no more into the land of Israel. This is the Divine way,
nay, the *only* way, of conquering our enemies. Evil can only be overcome by good.
The most glorious victory over an enemy is to turn him into a friend.—D. T.

Vers. 15—17.—*Invincible helpers of the good.* "And when the servant of the
man of God was risen," etc. The context illustrates two circumstances too frequently
overlooked, but ever demanding the recognition and study of mankind. 1. *The value
of a good man to his country.* The Syrian monarch makes war with Israel; his
counsels are formed, his arrangements are complete, and sanguine are his hopes of
victory. But there is a good man in Israel—Elisha—who reads the hidden purpose
of the Syrian despot, sounds the alarm, puts his country on its guard, invokes Heaven,
and thus confounds the wily stratagems and thwarts the murderous purposes of the
foe. "So the bands of Syria came no more into the land of Israel." True piety
is the source of true patriotism; its prayers and prophecies are the sure "defences" of
nations. This idea is dawning on the world now; and in coming periods will blaze
in broad daylight on mankind. We shall one day see that the victories of truth and
prayer were the only victories that ever served the interest of any nation, and that
many a pious man, who lived in obscurity and died under oppression, conferred greater
blessings on the commonwealth than those statesmen and warriors whose patriotism
has been emblazoned in history and sung in verse. The context illustrates: 2. *The
source of a wicked man's weakness.* Why did not this Syrian tyrant succeed in his
plans? The words which one of his servants addressed to him explain the cause:
"Elisha, the prophet that is in Israel, telleth the King of Israel the words that thou
speakest in thy bedchamber." His projects would not bear the light. As a principle,
wicked men would seldom, if ever, realize their ends were there a prophet to unveil
their hearts, and publish all the selfish, sensual, dishonest, and blasphemous thoughts
that transpire in the hidden chamber of their souls. Wicked tradesmen, lawyers, statesmen, and others succeed only as they conceal their hearts from public view. Let some
prophet, like Ezekiel of old, break open the barred door of their "chamber of imagery,"
and expose the hideous forms "portrayed upon the wall," the impious works that are
wrought "in the dark," and forthwith they will lose all public sympathy, patronage,
and support. O my soul, cherish thou thoughts that shall bear a prophet's fiery
glance—principles that will glow, bloom, and look attractive in the daylight; and
purposes that will commend thee to the Divine consciousness of brother spirits, and to
the favour of the Everlasting. I proceed to state, with the utmost brevity, a few
general truths suggested by the incident before us.

I. THAT THE GOOD ARE OFTEN PLACED IN CIRCUMSTANCES TO REQUIRE SUPERHUMAN
HELP. Elisha and his servant were, at this time, at Dothan. The Syrian king, enraged
with the prophet for frustrating his military designs on Israel, sends "horses, and
chariots, and a great host" in pursuit of him. The mighty army "came by night, and
compassed the city about." Early in the morning the prophet's servant beheld the
armed and ruthless multitude drawn up around the city. Here were enemies
which the prophet himself could not subdue, perils from which his unaided power
could not extricate himself. Faint symbol this of the spiritual enemies that surround
our dwellings! True, in these days, the antagonists of the good are not so outwardly
visible as they were in times that are past. The *great enemy* does not send forth his
host now garbed in the attire of the persecutors. They appear not amongst us in the
grim and savage forms of the Julians and the Neros, the Maximins and the Diocletians;
they assume an habiliment more consonant with the tastes of this civilized era. Their
forms fascinate rather than terrify. They seek to draw rather than to drive. But
still, are they any less deadly in their aim, or formidable in their power, because they
change their garb, drop the sword, and stretch out the hand of false friendship? It is
not the plundering of our property nor the wounding of our bodies that injures us most,
but the corrupting of our souls. The awakening within our spiritual natures of an impure

suggestion may work a far more fearful ruin than incarcerating us in dungeons, or sending us to the martyr's stake and flames. I call those *forces* mine enemies that are unfavourable to my spiritual interests. Whatever dims my inner vision, and tends to veil from me the sublimities of the "unseen;" whatever deadens my sensibility to duty, and interferes with the free and vigorous play of my faculties; whatever draws me from the eternal future, and links me to the transient present; whatever cools, materializes, and contracts my sympathies, and keeps me more in connection with the contingent than the absolute; whatever depresses me in my struggles to reach that ideal of perfection dimly portrayed in my soul, but drawn out in abiding loveliness in the life of Jesus; whatever forces act thus, I call, with emphasis, my foes. And do not such foes surround us? Tell me of a period when "sinful lusts," which "war against the soul," were more potent and active than now? Our civilization is little more than a perfection in those arts that minister to the senses, pander to the appetites, and gratify the desires of the flesh. When did worldliness ever wield a more wide and mighty sway? When were the votaries of mammon so numerous and enthusiastic in their devotions? The deepest cry of the age seems to be, "My soul thirsteth for gold." When did corrupt literature scatter over the social soil the seeds of error, impiety, and licentiousness to such an extent as now? We are as truly hemmed in by antagonistic forces as was Elisha by the horses and chariots and hosts than encompassed him at Dothan. As we glance at them, the impression of the prophet's servant comes to us, "Alas, master! what shall we do?" We require the help that Elisha had—help from without—from Heaven.

II. That Heaven has provided helpers for men superior to all antagonists. "And he answered, Fear not: for they that be with us are more than they that be with them." It is generally supposed that the reference is here to the angels "that excel in strength," and that *they* were the horses and chariots of fire that came to the prophet's help. Angels are the hosts of God, and "the body-guard of the good"—"ministering spirits, sent forth to minister unto the heirs of salvation." This doctrine is so antecedently probable, so clearly revealed in Scripture, and so generally believed, as to require no evidence. It is to their *superiority* that our attention is now called.

1. *They are "more" in number than the foe.* If we confine our attention to merely what we see in this world, we shall conclude that the agents of evil are the more numerous. A wider survey of the general realm of spiritual being, as suggested by philosophy, and as revealed in the Bible, presents an opposite view. As malformations in nature are few compared with symmetrically organized existences, so evil spirits are few compared with the good. The great cities, principalities, and hierarchies of the universe are loyal subjects of the great King, and zealous agents in promoting his will; it is but a little province that has here and there thrown off its allegiance. Hell is but a withered leaf in the waving forest of life—a flickering meteor in the starry vault of being. It is our happiness to know that evil is the exception in the universe; good is the rule. Thus evil exists as a contingency—it might or might not be; but good exists by an absolute necessity—it is and must be, because God is and must be. 2. *They are "more" in the instrumentalities they wield.* The agents of evil are not only fewer in number, but inferior also in their armour. Falsehood, selfishness, wrong,—these are their miserable weapons; and are they not weakness compared with truth, love, right, the weapons of the good? Ay; they can no more stand before them than "dry stubble" before the raging fire—the gloom of the night-heavens before the rising sun. The history of the world gives many instances of one man, with truth and right on his side, subduing countries under the reign of falsehood and wrong. 3. *They are "more" in their invincible determination.* The *power* of a moral intelligence in any operation will not be entirely or chiefly determined by the instruments he employs, but by the strength of the purpose under which he acts. A man with a weak purpose, however great his advantages, will not do much. Now, the agents of evil can have no invincible purpose, for the obvious reason that their consciences—whose sanctions can alone give invincibility—are not on their side. Just as far as any being is under the influence of evil, he must be fickle and fearful. "The wicked flee when no man pursueth: but the righteous are bold as a lion." 4. *They are "more" in the authority under which they act.* The Bible teaches that the angels of evil are under the control of one master-spirit of darkness—"the prince of the power of the air;" but those of the good are

under the authority of the Infinite. His Spirit inspires them, his will they obey, his energy is their strength. Satan, the master of the evil spirits, is himself the creature and slave of God. The moral usurper cannot move or breathe but by the permission of *him* who "maketh his angels spirits, and his ministers a flame of fire." Truly, then, my pious friend, however great the spiritual foes, thy helpers are greater. To the eye of sense, indeed, thou seemest to wrestle against fearful odds. Wealth, fashion, customs, influence, worldly maxims, habits, and even numbers, seem against thee; but "fear not: for they that be with us are more than they that be with them." Open the eye of faith, and look beyond the boundary-line of sense, and thou shalt see that the great "mountain" of universal being is "full of horses and chariots of fire round about" thee.

III. THAT THE SUPERIOR HELPERS OF THE GOOD ARE ONLY SEEN BY SOME. Elisha saw the celestial helpers, but his servant saw them not—saw nothing but the enemy. The one, consequently, stood calm amidst the gleaming and rattling weapons of the Syrian army, the other was all perturbation and alarm. Thus men under similar circumstances receive different impressions. The event which overwhelms one with alarm inspires another with hope and heroism. The reason of this is that some have eyes to see only the evil in things, others to see the good as well. Why is this? Why is it that all men cannot see the spiritual helpers that surround them? Several reasons might be assigned. 1. There is the *tendency to judge after the senses*. The majority of men, like the servant of the prophet, see only with the physical eye. Although true philosophy shows that all things that come within the cognizance of the senses are shadows, not substances—semblance, not essence, they reversely consider the visible and tangible only as real. Spirits, therefore, which lie beyond the line of sense, and which are the living creatures in all the "wheels" of human events, and in all the forms of matter, are never practically realized, and often theoretically ignored. 2. There is *the habit of referring everything to secondary causes*. This habit allows no room for God, nor for spiritual interpositions, but in a miracle. What is regular it calls natural; what is miraculous alone is Divine. It sees God in holding the sun over Gibeon, and the moon in the valley of Ajalon, but sees nothing of him in rolling these stupendous bodies, age after age, in their spheres, with an undeviating regularity, and a swiftness incalculable. I say nothing of the irrationality of this habit, nor of its prevalence, of which there can be no question. All I say is that, since God helps us by natural laws, this habit manifestly prevents men from seeing the helpers he sends. 3. There is also a *gloominess of disposition*. This is sometimes a cause. There are men who will not see good. They hear no music in the harp of love; they see no brightness in the unclouded sky of noon. On this earth, even when robed in its summer beauty or laden with autumnal wealth, they sing, or rather groan—

> "Lord, what a wretched land is this,
> That yields us no supply!"

The horses and chariots of mercy may move around them as celestial guards, yet they cry, "All these things are against me." 4. There is *want of sympathy with God*. Strong and earnest sympathy with a being always induces the mind to bring that Being near—near to the inner eye and heart. By this law we bring the distant near—cross oceans and continents. Yes; from worlds beyond the grave the imagination wafts the loved one home to our inmost breasts; and we see the form and hear the voice again. Had we this sympathy with God and holy spirits, we should set them always before us. Jesus had it, and he said, "Ye leave me alone; and yet I am not alone, because the Father is with me."

IV. THAT TO SEE THESE SUPERHUMAN HELPERS ONLY REQUIRES THE OPENING OF THE EYES. "Lord, I pray thee, open his eyes." The outward world is to us according to our five senses. Had we fewer, it would be less than it is; or, if more, it would be greater. There are, probably, properties in the material system which we have at present no sense to discover; or, peradventure, there may be senses closed up within, that will one day be developed, and make this old world a new thing to us. But, likely as this may be, the existence of a sense in the soul for seeing spiritual existences is more probable. I am not disposed to pronounce all who have stated that they have seen such beings to be either fanatics or impostors. The *à priori* wonder is, not that they should be seen, but that they are not more generally perceived. We are related to the material world, and we have senses to discern material existences. We are, confessedly, more intimately and solemnly related to the spiritual; and is it not natural to expect that we should have a sense to see spiritual beings? Were such a sense to be opened within us, as the eye of the prophet's servant was now opened, what visions would burst upon us! The microscope gives to us a new world of wonders; but were God to open the spiritual eye, what a multitude of worlds would be revealed! Ah, my sceptic brother! deniest thou a spiritual world? Where is thy reason? Wilt thou plead the fact that thou hast never seen a spiritual existence? This, assuredly, will not serve thee. Wilt thou permit a deaf man to deny that a thunderstorm ever rent our cloudy atmosphere, because he has never heard the terrific roar; or a blind man to deny that a rainbow has ever spanned these skies, because he, forsooth, has never seen the beauteous arch? Why, then, shouldest thou deny a spiritual world? Before the eyes of the prophet's servant were opened, he might have denied the existence of these helpers. When his master spoke to him of them, he might have said within himself, "Has my master lost his reason, or is he dreaming? I see nothing on the mountain but the Syrian host." All at once, however, his eyes were opened, and what a scene burst upon him! "The mountain was full of horses and chariots of fire round about Elisha." Even so it will be with thee, my friend: ere many days shall pass, God will open thine eyes; and that spiritual world in which thou art now living, and whose existence thou deniest, will burst in awful sublimity upon thine astonished soul!—D. T.

Vers. 24—33.—*Subjects worth considering.* "And it came to pass after this, that Benhadad king of Syria gathered all his host, and went up, and besieged Samaria," etc. These verses, brimful of the wicked and the horrible, press the following subjects on our attention.

I. THE INHUMANITY OF WAR. "And it came to pass after this, that Benhadad king of Syria gathered all his host, and went up, and besieged Samaria. And there was a great famine in Samaria: and, behold, they besieged it, until an ass's head was sold for fourscore pieces of silver, and the fourth part of a cab of dove's dung for five pieces of silver." The inhumanity of the Syrian king and his host in invading Samaria is seen in the shameful disregard of the kindness which the Samaritans had previously shown them. In the preceding verses we read that the Samaritans had not only allowed them to escape entire destruction when they were at their mercy, but, at the interposition of Elisha, supplied them with abundant provisions to appease their hunger and to invigorate their frames. Notwithstanding this, they now came to work ruin on their very saviours. War has no gratitude, no sense of right, no sentiment of kindness; often it dehumanizes human nature, transforms the man into a fiend.

"How all minor cruelties of man
Are summed in war, conclusive of all crimes!"
('Festus.')

II. THE TERRIBLENESS OF HUNGER. To such absolute destitution did these ruthless warriors reduce the inhabitants of Samaria, that not only did the ravenous hunger drive them to obtain food from the "ass's head" and from "dove's dung," but from human flesh—mothers from the children of their womb. "And as the King of Israel was passing by upon the wall, there cried a woman unto him, saying, Help, my lord, O king. And he said, If the Lord do not help thee, whence shall I help thee? out of the barnfloor, or out of the winepress? And the king said unto her, What aileth thee? And she answered, This woman said unto me, Give thy son, that we may eat him to-day, and we will eat my son to-morrow. So we killed my son, and did eat him," etc. Here is a tragic tale, a tale that makes the heart quail, and the nerves quiver with horror. Hunger in itself is a blessing, it implies health and stimulates to action; it is in truth the mainspring that keeps the human machinery of the world in action. But when it becomes intense and unappeasable, it sets all moral commandments at defiance, it will break through stone walls, shatter thrones, and break up empires. It is among the primary duties of rulers to keep the hunger of the people appeased. Alas! everywhere in England we hear its groans; may not these groanings be the mutterings of nature before the volcanic eruption?

III. The misdirection of passion. The tale of the famishing woman, and the revolting scenes he beheld, pierced the heart of the King of Israel. His feelings at first seem to have been those of great humiliation and deep sympathy. "And it came to pass, when the king heard the words of the woman, that he rent his clothes." But they soon became those of raging wrath against Elisha. "Then he said, God do so and more also to me, if the head of Elisha the son of Shaphat shall stand on him this day." If Elisha had, from a malign spirit, really brought all this distress upon the Samaritan people, this wrath might have been justified. Anger against wrong is right. But it was not Elisha that brought the calamities; it was themselves—their idolatries, their sins. Elisha was their greatest friend. The misdirection of human indignation is no uncommon evil. How often men are angry with one another without a cause! Passion misdirected put to death the Son of God himself.

IV. The calmness of goodness. Whilst all these revolting scenes were taking place, and the king burning with rage against Elisha, was resolving on his destruction, where was Elisha? "But Elisha sat in his house, and the elders sat with him." With his disciples, fellow-citizens, and "elders" Elisha sat, without anxiety or alarm. Mark: 1. It was not the calmness of *servile submission*. Though he knew the threat of the king, he had no idea of making an apology or seeking to appease unreasonable indignation, or yield with stoicism to his fate. No. Whilst he sat calmly, the pulse of manhood throbbed stronger in every vein, and when he heard the king's messenger approach the door of his house, he said to the elders, "See ye how this son of a murderer hath sent to take away mine head?" It is grand to hear men give others their proper title, even though they be kings. Were all men thus honest, many of those who are now called "right honourables" would be "right abominables." 2. It was not the calmness of *irresolution*. It was not a state of unnerved indifference; on the contrary, there was in it a resolute power. "Look, when the messenger cometh, shut the door, and hold him fast at the door." For the man's own sake hold him, do not let him contract crime by committing murder. Probably at this moment Elisha saw the king himself hurrying towards him, to revoke his murderous decree. Conscious goodness is always calm. He is "kept in perfect peace whose mind is stayed on the Lord." 3. It was the calmness that *conquers*. The king himself, it would seem, was soon at the door. He had relented, and hurried to prevent the execution of his murderous command. "And while he yet talked with them, behold, the messenger came down unto him: and he said, Behold, this evil is of the Lord; what should I wait for the Lord any longer?" This utterance is that of the king, and it would seem it was a response to the prophet's exhortation to "wait for the Lord." And he means to say, "This evil is not from thee, Elisha, but from the Lord, and it is hopeless; 'what should I wait for the Lord any longer?'" It is not likely that such a humiliating utterance as this would have fallen from the lips of the king, had he met Elisha in a state of furious excitement. No doubt it was the moral majesty of calmness that struck the heart of the monarch.—D. T.

Vers. 1—7.—*The borrowed axe.* This is another of Elisha's miracles of aid. The story belongs to the same class of acts as those related in ch. ii. 19—22; iv. 1—7, 38—44.

I. The axe-head needed. The first verses present us with a picture of expansion and extension. The place where "the sons of the prophets" dwelt or "sat" before Elisha, at Jericho, had become too strait for them. Elisha's influence was evidently telling on the nation. The religious movement represented by the prophetic schools was growing in force and volume. It is encouraging to hear of growth and progress in the Church. We note: 1. *The prophets faced their situation.* "Behold now, the place where we dwell with thee is too strait for us." They did not stand still, and endeavour to accommodate their increased numbers to the old conditions. They showed a spirit of enterprise, of advance, in correspondence with their altered needs. This was true wisdom. The Church must adapt herself to new needs, to altered circumstances, to the conditions of progress, if she is to hold her ground. "Enlarge the place of thy tent," etc. (Isa. liv. 2). 2. *They were willing to put forth needful effort.* "Let us go, we pray thee, unto Jordan, and take thence every man a beam," etc. They were prepared to do what was necessary to bring about the changes required. They had the two conditions of successful work—unity of spirit, and individual willingness. They were to work together for a common end, and each man was to do his separate part. The individual wood-cutter could accomplish little. Unitedly, they could easily make a place for their common accommodation. 3. *They desired Elisha to go with them.* "Be content, I pray thee, and go with thy servants." Elisha was the bond of their community. They desired neither to act without his sanction nor to go where he could not accompany them. The Church, in her changes, must abide by fundamental truth, and do nothing which would exclude the Master.

II. THE AXE-HEAD LOST. Elisha's sanction given, the band of prophets was soon busy at Jordan, cutting down trees, and preparing for the new building. Then occurred the mishap and loss which gives its name to the story. As one was felling a beam, the axe-head flew off, and fell into the deep part of the river. It was a borrowed axe, and the man's lamentations were instant and sincere. Mishaps will occur in the best undertakings. 1. *He had lost what a neighbour had lent him.* The property was not his own. It had been lent him, probably at his own request, and in the spirit of neighbourly good will. Such neighbourly acts are pleasing to think of. But the more willingly the axe had been lent him, the more did the loser now regret the mishap which had befallen it. It is well that neighbours should be ready to lend; but the incident also shows the danger of borrowing. We should seek to be as independent of others as we can; then, if misfortune does befall us, what we lose is at least only our own. 2. *He could not replace the loss.* Had he been able to do so, he would not have required to borrow. The "sons of the prophets" were good men, but poor men. An axe-head was a small thing, but it meant much to the user, and perhaps not less to the original owner. It is a spirit of conscientiousness which speaks in the man's lament. He held the axe as a trust, and desired earnestly to return it. It is good to see men "faithful in that which is least" (Luke xvi. 10). 3. *He could no longer do his part of the work.* The axe-head was indispensable for the cutting down of his beam. He had the handle, but it was of no use without the iron. This also grieved him. Anything that incapacitates a man for bearing his part in the building work of God's kingdom will be a sorrow to him.

III. THE AXE-HEAD RECOVERED. The indirect appeal made to Elisha in the words, "Alas, master! for it was borrowed," was not in vain. It was a case in which Elisha might be expected to help, and he did so. In the miracle we see: 1. *Human agency.* There is a remarkable blending of the Divine and the human in the whole transaction. Elisha asked, "Where fell it?" It might have been thought that if he had the power to bring the iron to the surface, he would also be able to tell where it fell. But the man had to show him the place. Then, when the iron swam, Elisha said, "Take it to thee." And the man put out his hand and took it. 2. *Expressive symbol.* The miracle, as usual, was accompanied by a symbolical action. A stick was cut down, and thrown into the water. The act was only an expressive way of saying, "Let the iron swim as this stick does." Its sole function was to direct attention to the supernatural result. 3. *Almighty power.* "The iron did swim." There was here, not the alteration of the properties of iron (else it would be iron no longer), but the introduction of a new cause, which counteracted the natural effect of gravity, and raised the iron to the surface. Nature is but an instrument in the hand of God, and can be bent by him to his own purposes. The lesson of the incident is to trust God for help even in what we might be tempted to call the small things of life. The loss of an axe-head may seem a trivial circumstance to call for an interference with the laws of the universe. But with God there is no great and little. We can make known *all* our wants to him, with assurance of being helped.—J. O.

Vers. 8—23.—*A bootless invasion.* The chronic hostility which subsisted between the Israelitish and the Syrian kingdoms soon broke out again in war. In this, as in other instances, Syria was the aggressor. The invaded kingdom was delivered, not through "the sword and the bow" (ver. 22) of its king, but once more through the interposition of Elisha.

I. FRUSTRATED PLANS. 1. *Royal strategy.* The war which the King of Syria commenced was intended to be carried on, not by battle in the open field, but by a series of surprises, caused by the planting of ambuscades at convenient spots. It was cunning more than strength that the king relied on. He "took counsel with his servants" as to the best method of carrying out his plans. Men are apt to overvalue cunning. It plays a large part in the conduct of worldly, especially of political and military, affairs. 2. *The failure of plans.* If the plotters were "profound to make slaughter" (Hos. v. 2), God was deeper than the plotters, "a rebutter of them all" (Hos. v. 2). This was the element Benhadad left out of his calculations. Everything that passed in the king's council-chamber was revealed by God to Elisha, who told it to the King of Israel. What was spoken "in the ear" in Damascus was proclaimed "upon the housetops" in Samaria (Luke xii. 3). Thus the King of Israel saved himself "not once or twice." The wicked greatly err when they say, "How doth God know? and is there knowledge in the Most High?" (Ps. lxxiii. 11). Not one of their plans but is "naked and opened" (Heb. iv. 13) to him. With a knowledge and skill infinitely beyond theirs, he can easily bring the cunningest of their schemes to nought. This is the comfort and safety of those who trust God, and are under his special care. 3. *The secret discovered.* The King of Syria's chagrin at the continual frustration of his schemes was great. He could account for it in no other way than that some of his own servants habitually betrayed his counsels. They who have God to fight with must lay their account for many disappointments and troubles. At last the real state of the case was made known to him by one who had learned the facts about Elisha. It was a startling discovery to make, that the things which he spoke in his bedchamber were accurately told by Elisha to his enemy, the King of Israel. None of us would like to be thus supervised in our secret doings by our fellow-men. How little we reflect that, in sober fact, we are being thus morally supervised by the living God! Elisha's name would be well known in Syria since the healing of the famous captain.

II. INVISIBLE DEFENCE. If Elisha was the medium of discovering his plans, the only practicable course for the King of Syria to pursue was to secure the person of the prophet, and so stop further communications with the King of Israel. Benhadad might have reflected that, if all his plans were known to Elisha, this plan would be known too, and Elisha could easily escape. But wicked men do not, as a rule, reflect on the folly of their opposition to God. The king, having ascertained that Elisha was at Dothan, sent an expedition to arrest him. 1. *The encompassing host.* The force despatched against Elisha was "a great host," far exceeding the captains of fifties with their fifties who were sent to arrest Elijah (ch. i.). Benhadad put trust in chariots and horses (Ps. xx. 7). Yet why so great a company to take one prisoner, if no supernatural arm was there to fight for him? And if God was Protector, what would even this great host avail? Another proof of the inward uncertainty with which this enterprise was entered upon is seen in the fact that the host surrounded the city "by night." Combined with the worldly man's belief that physical force is irresistible, there is the lurking fear that it may not prove irresistible after all. 2. *The trembling servant.* Awaking early the next morning, and going forth, the servant of Elisha saw, to his dismay, the city compassed about with both chariot and horse. His cry, as he rushed back to report the fact to his master, was, "Alas, my master! how shall we do?" Thus apt are men to judge of a situation purely by the standard of sense. The material factors are nearly the only ones looked at. Things are esteemed to go well or ill with us according as the *natural* situation looks favourable or the reverse. It is the constant aim of Bible-teaching to lift us above this point of view—to give us a higher one. 3. *The invisible protectors.* Elisha prayed that the young man's eyes might be opened, and then he saw the mistake he was committing. "The mountain was full of horses and chariots of fire round about Elisha." No wonder that, in this moment of apparent danger, Elisha was full of calm trust. Knowing Benhadad's designs, he might have escaped had he desired, but with the forces of the invisible King interposed between him and his enemies, he did not feel even this to be necessary. Not less confidently, in seasons of danger from ungodly men, may the believer commit his way unto the Lord. It may not be given him to see the symbols of invisible protection, but not the less surely can he depend that "the angel of the Lord encampeth round about them that fear him, and delivereth them" (Ps. xxxiv. 7). He can say with David, "I will not be afraid of ten thousand of people that have set themselves against me round about" (Ps. iii. 6). They can do him no further harm than God sees meet to allow. They that are for him are more than they that be against him.

III. GOOD FOR EVIL. 1. *The supernatural blindness.* Descending from the neighbouring heights, on which they had encamped during the night, the Syrians now approached to take Elisha. He, on his part, prayed the Lord, "Smite this people, I pray thee, with blindness." The prayer was granted, though the word means rather confusion and dazedness of mind, than absolute deprivation of sight (Gen. xix. 11). Their movements became aimless, and Elisha, going up to them, said, "This is not the way, neither is this the city: follow me, and I will bring you to the man whom ye seek." There is the appearance of falsehood in this speech only if we forget that the men were in a mental maze, and probably were actually going aside both from the way and the city in their attempted search for it. Elisha, in promising to bring them to the man whom they wanted, undertook no more than he performed. Only when the Lord opened their eyes, they found they were, not in Dothan, but in Samaria. This is one way in which God frequently discomfits wicked men, pouring confusion into their counsels. They "grope for the wall, like the blind, and grope as if (they) had no eyes: (they) stumble at noonday as in the night; (they) are in desolate places as dead men" (Isa. lix. 10). They are granted the desires of their hearts, but after a fashion of God's own; and in such a way as to lead to their final discomfiture (2 Sam. xv. 31). 2. *The King of Israel's proposal.* It seemed at first as if this great multitude of the Syrians had been led like sheep into the slaughter-house. They were now in the King of Israel's power, and for what end could Elisha have brought them there but that the king might smite them? The king himself was nothing loth. In eager tones, he urged Elisha to be permitted to destroy them. The policy of slaughter is always an easy one. It might seem sanctioned by Old Testament precedents. Probably, however, even in the Old Testament, there is no example of the divinely sanctioned extermination of a multitude who were not captives in lawful war. This is the point Elisha urges in reply. If the king smote this multitude, would he be smiting those whom he had taken with his sword and bow? He would not. God had delivered these captives into his hands, and with other ends than that he should destroy them. 3. *Elisha's magnanimous counsel.* Elisha showed the King of Israel "a more excellent way" (1 Cor. xii. 31). Let him set bread and water before them, that they might eat and drink, and go to their master. Here, surely, in the Old Testament, breathes the spirit of the New. It is Christ's precept of doing good to enemies, of returning good for evil, of seeking to overcome evil with good. The King of Israel behaved more nobly in this way than if he had shed the blood of these captives. God has no pleasure in the unnecessary effusions of blood. An instance of similar clemency to captives took place in the reign of Pekah, at the instigation of the Prophet Oded (2 Chron. xxviii. 9—15). The King of Israel did as Elisha desired, and the captives were first entertained, then sent back. So generous a deed should have evoked a friendly spirit in Benhadad, but at most it only did so for a time. We are not, however, to be discouraged from acting rightly, because those to whom we show kindness do not appreciate our action.—J. O.

Vers. 24—33.—*The siege of Samaria.* Unwarned by the failure of previous attempts, Benhadad was soon engaged in a new war on Israel. The fresh invasion was made the occasion of a fresh deliverance, more wonderful than any of the preceding, but not before Samaria had been reduced to the most desperate straits.

I. THE HORRORS OF A SIEGE. 1. *The city invested.* The King of Syria advanced with his army, and struck a direct blow at the capital of the country. Samaria was the key of the situation. In it was the king, the court, the Prophet Elisha, the whole state of royalty. If it could be forced to capitulate, the entire land would be at the mercy of the invader. Benhadad, accordingly, surrounded the city, and, having cut off all supplies, waited till famine compelled it to surrender. The method of siege is common in warfare. Nothing could more awfully illustrate the helplessness of human beings when deprived of the use of the ordinary productions of nature. We depend on God for daily existence, and do not realize it. 2. *The fearful famine.* With no supplies coming in, the stock of food in Samaria was soon utterly exhausted. We are reminded of the terrible distress in such famous sieges as those of Londonderry in 1689, and Paris in 1870. What in ordinary circumstances would have been deemed unfit for human food, nay, loathed, was eagerly seized upon, and famine prices were gladly paid for it.

"An ass's head was sold for fourscore pieces of silver," etc. Hunger is one of the most commanding of appetites. "In every land and in every age the first and most interesting question the majority of men have to practically solve is, 'How are we to get bread?' Man's social, moral, and spiritual welfare turns to an incalculable extent on that question. Throughout all history, sacred and profane, this great want has been swaying and moulding as a first power the nations of men. Hence the significance of the petition in the centre of the Lord's prayer, 'Give us this day our daily bread.' It may seem at first sight a comparatively small petition, overshadowed and dwarfed by the great, spiritual petitions both before and after it; but he who knew what was in man, knew what a powerful influence the question of daily bread had upon his whole life and welfare; and when we ourselves consider what a power it is in the world, we see something of the reason for placing such a petition in the centre of a model of prayer" (F. Ferguson). 3. *Natural affection destroyed.* The shocking episode narrated in vers. 26—29 illustrates the previous remarks (cf. Deut. xxviii. 53—57). The king was stopped when passing by on the wall by a woman appealing to him for help. With not unnatural bitterness he replied, "If the Lord do not help thee, whence shall I help thee?" Was it out of the empty barnfloor, or the dry winepress? He then inquired into her complaint, and heard from her her revolting tale. A woman had proposed to her that she should give her son for food to them both that day, and she would give *her* son next day. The complainant had fulfilled her part of the bargain, and now the second woman had hidden her son. One asks—Could human nature, in its direst extremity, ever descend to such revolting deeds? Alas! the instances in history are not few. We have reason to thank God for his goodness in preserving us from such extremity and such temptation.

II. GUILT LAID AT THE WRONG DOOR. 1. *The token of humiliation.* The woman's dreadful story, revealing such depths of horror in the city, stung the king to the heart. His first act was to rend his clothes, and, as the people looked, they saw that secretly he had been wearing sackcloth upon his flesh. The commentators, perhaps, hardly do justice to Jehoram in this act. The next verse shows that his religion did not go very deep; but various circumstances suggest that there was a measure of sincerity in his penitence. He had evidently thus far listened to the counsels of Elisha, and tried to "wait on the Lord" for deliverance. He does not show badly in his sympathy with the people. The very secrecy of his wearing of sackcloth distinguishes it from the act of an ostentatious formalist. He probably, like his father Ahab, really "humbled" himself for a time, "and went softly" (1 Kings xxi. 27, 29). If, in his outburst of passion, he uttered a threat of death against Elisha, it appears to have been no sooner spoken than it was repented of, and he hastened after his messenger to counteract it. It is good when God's chastisements lead to humiliation of the soul. We can at least make Jehoram an example in the unostentatiousness of his exercises of penitence (Matt. vi. 16—18). 2. *The threat and its reception.* Carried away by his anger and his feeling of the intolerableness of the situation, the king swore an oath that that very day the head of Elisha should be taken from him. It was a wicked and inexcusable utterance. The reasons of it may be thus assigned: (1) Elisha had apparently urged him to patience and repentance, assuring him that help would come. That hope had been disappointed. (2) He fixed the responsibility of the delay of help on Elisha, as one who had power with God, and had not exercised it. (3) He was angry with God himself, and was moved to wreak his vengeance on God's ministers. Had he properly considered the matter, he would have reflected that Elisha, like himself, could but present his desires to God, and wait God's time; that the prophet had unweariedly been doing this, and was the one hope and saviour of the people; and that, if guilt lay at any one's door, it was his own wickedness, and that of his associates, that was bringing these calamities upon the nation. Wicked men, however, are seldom willing, except in a very limited degree, to take home guilt to themselves. They will blame God, their fellows, their spiritual counsellors, any one but themselves, for their miseries. It is a very different picture we have of Elisha. He sits composedly in his house, with the elders of Samaria around him, no doubt exhorting them and strengthening them to wait on God. By that prophetic *clairvoyance* of which we have so many instances, he knew of the king's threat as soon as it was uttered, and bade the elders shut the door against this messenger of "the son of a murderer," and detain him till the king himself came. 3. *Why wait longer on the Lord?* Jehoram soon arrived, and his first words to Elisha were, "Behold, this evil is of the Lord; what should I wait for the Lord any longer?" That he had departed from his threat may be presumed from Elisha answering him as he did. But his words show his radical misconception of religion. To wait on the Lord was not a duty to be done from regard to its own rightness and propriety. It was, he thought, a means to an end. If benefits were to be gained from it, it was to be done; if not, it was to be set aside. Service of God which springs from this principle is not true service. It is disguised self-interest. It has no real spring of love, devotion, or worship. The spirit is kindred with that of the fetish-worshipper, who prays to his gods for rain, and beats them if he does not get it. But why blame Jehoram, as if he were specially impious? Does not the same spirit show itself in multitudes among ourselves? While the sun shines on them they are willing enough to be religious. If adversity comes, there is unbelief, murmuring, impatience, rebellion at the Divine ordering. "Shall we receive good at the hand of God, and shall we not receive evil?" (Job ii. 10). It is not enough to acknowledge that evil is from the Lord, we must humble ourselves under his hand, submit to him, own the justice of his dealings, and seek to profit by his chastisements. We must not faint, or grow unbelieving, but be assured that, in protracting the hour of deliverance, God is but waiting to make the deliverance more signal and glorious (Heb. xii. 5—11).—J. O.

EXPOSITION.

CHAPTER VII.

Vers. 1—20.—THE SIEGE OF SAMARIA (*continued*): THE DELIVERANCE.

Vers. 1, 2.—The separation of these verses from the preceding narrative is most unfortunate. They are an integral part of it, and form its climax. In answer to the king's attempt upon his life, and hasty speech in which he has threatened to renounce Jehovah, Elisha is commissioned to proclaim that the siege is on the point of terminating, the famine about to be within twenty-four hours succeeded by a time of plenty. There is thus no reason for the king's despair or anger.

Ver. 1.—**Then Elisha said, Hear ye the word of the Lord.** This was a very solemn exordium, well calculated to arrest attention. It must be remembered that the prophet's life was trembling in the balance. The executioner was present; the king had not revoked his order; the elders would probably have suffered the king to work his will. All depended on Elisha, by half a dozen words, changing the king's mind. He therefore announces a Divine oracle (comp. 2 Chron. xiii. 4; xv. 2; xx. 20; and for the exact expression, see Isa. i. 10; xxviii. 14; xxix. 5, etc.; Jer. ii. 4; vii. 2, etc.). **Thus saith the Lord, To-morrow about this time** shall **a measure**—literally, *a seah*—**of fine flour** be sold **for a shekel.** The "seah" was probably about equal to a peck and a half English, the shekel of the time to about half a crown. Thus no extraordinary

cheapness is promised, but only an enormous fall in prices from the rate current at the moment (ch. vii. 25). Such a fall implied, almost necessarily, the discontinuance of the siege. Jehoram appears to have accepted the prophet's solemn asseveration, and on the strength of it to have spared his life, at any rate till the result should be seen. **And two measures**—literally, *seahs*—**of barley for a shekel, in the gate of Samaria.** The gates, or rather gateways, of Oriental towns were spacious places, where business of various kinds was transacted. One at Nineveh had an area of above two thousand five hundred square feet. Kings often held their courts of justice in the city gates. On this occasion one of the gates of Samaria seems to have been used as a corn-market (comp. vers. 17—20).

Ver. 2.—**Then a lord on whose hand the king leaned**; rather, *the lord*, or *the captain*, as the word שָׁלִישׁ is commonly translated (Exod. xiv. 7; xv. 4; 2 Sam. xxiii. 8; 1 Kings ix. 22; ch. ix. 25; x. 25; xv. 25; 1 Chron. xi. 11; xii. 18; 2 Chron. viii. 9). (For the habit of kings to lean on the hand of an attendant, see above, ch. v. 18.) **Answered the man of God, and said, Behold, if the Lord would make windows in heaven, might this thing be?** The king makes no reply; he waits for the result. But the officer on whose arm he leans is not so reticent. Utterly incredulous, he expresses his incredulity in a scoffing way: "Could this possibly be, even if God were to 'make windows in heaven,' as he did at the time of the Flood (Gen. vii. 11), and pour through them, instead of rain, as then, a continual shower of fine meal and corn?"

Disbelief is expressed, not only in the prophetic veracity of Elisha, but in the power of God. Hence Elisha's stern reply. **And he said, Behold, thou shalt see it with thine eyes, but shalt not eat thereof.** At once a threat and a warning. If the thing was to be, and the lord to see it and yet not profit by it, the only reasonable conclusion was that his death was imminent. He was thus warned, and given time to "set his house in order," and to repent and make his peace with the Almighty. Whether he took advantage of the warning, or even understood it, we are not told.

Vers. 3—16.—The mode in which Elisha's prophecy of relief and deliverance was fulfilled is now set forth. Four lepers, excluded from the city, and on the point of perishing of hunger, felt that they could be no worse off, and might better their condition, if they deserted to the Syrians. They therefore drew off from the city at nightfall, and made for the Syrian camp. On arriving, they found it deserted. The entire host, seized with a sudden panic, had fled, about the time that they began their journey. The lepers' first thought was to enrich themselves by plunder, but after a while it occurred to them that, unless they hastened to carry the good news to Samaria, inquiry would be made, their proceedings would be found out, and they would be severely punished. So they returned to the capital, and reported what they had discovered. Jehoram, on receiving the news, feared that the Syrians had prepared a trap for him, and declined to move. He consented, however, to send out scouts to reconnoitre. The scouts found evident proof that the entire army had actually fled and was gone, whereupon there was a general raid upon the camp and its stores, which were so abundant that Elisha's prophecy was fulfilled ere the day ended.

Ver. 3.—**And there were four leprous men at the entering in of the gate;** or, *at the entrance to the gate-house.* Lepers were forbidden by the Law to reside within cities (Lev. xiii. 46; Numb. v. 3). They were thrust out when the disease developed itself, and forced to dwell without the walls. No doubt their friends within the city ordinarily supplied them with food; and hence they congregated about the city gates. **And they said one to another, Why sit we here until we die?** In the extreme scarcity, it is probable that no food was brought to

them, the inmates of the city having barely enough wherewith to sustain themselves (ch. vi. 25). Thus they were on the point of perishing.

Ver. 4.—**If we say, We will enter into the city, then the famine is in the city, and we shall die there.** The lepers were certainly not at liberty to enter the city when they pleased; but perhaps they might have managed, in one way or another, to return within the walls. They ask themselves, however, "Cui bono?" What will be the use of it? The famine is inside the town no less than outside. If they entered the city, by hook or by crook, it would only be to "die there." **And if we sit still here, we die also;** rather, *if we remain here,* or, *if we dwell here.* Lepers, excluded from a city, are in the habit of building themselves huts near the gateways. "The lepers of Jerusalem, at the present day, have their tents by the side of the Zion gate" (Keil, *ad loc.*). If the leprous men remained where they were, death stared them in the face equally. **Now therefore come, and let us fall unto the host of the Syrians.** Let us, *i.e.,* fall away from our own side, desert them, and go over to the enemy (comp. ch. xxv. 11; Jer. xxxvii. 13, 14; xxxix. 9; lii. 15). **If they save us alive, we shall live; and if they kill us, we shall but die;** *i.e.* we cannot be worse off than we are, even if they kill us; while it may be that they will be more merciful, and let us live.

Ver. 5.—**And they rose up in the twilight.** Most certainly in the *evening* twilight, as soon as the sun was down (see ver. 9). Had they set off in the daytime, the garrison would have shot at them from the walls. **To go unto the camp of the Syrians: and when they were come to the uttermost part** —*i.e.* the most advanced part, that which was nearest to Samaria—**of the camp of Syria, behold, there was no man there.** The camp was empty, deserted. Not a soul was anywhere to be seen.

Ver. 6.—**For the Lord had made the host of the Syrians to hear a noise of chariots, and a noise of horses, even the noise of a great host.** קוֹל, voice, is used for noises of any kind (see Exod. xx. 18; Ps. xlii. 7; xciii. 4; Jer. xlvii. 3; Ezek. i. 24; iii. 13; Joel ii. 5; Nah. iii. 2), though generally for those in which the human voice preponderated. A noise like that of chariots and of horses and of a great host (חַיִל גָּדוֹל) was borne in upon the ears of the Syrians about nightfall of the day on which Jehoram had determined to put Elisha to death; and, as they expected no reinforcements, they naturally concluded that succour had arrived to help their enemy. How the noise was produced it is impossible to say. Natural causes are insufficient; and the writer evidently regards the event as miraculous: "The *Lord had made* the host of the Syrians to hear a noise," etc. Nothing can be more weak and irrelevant than to remark, with Bähr, "There are instances, even nowadays, that people in certain mountainous regions regard a rushing and roaring sound, such as is sometimes heard there, as a sign of coming war." The Syrians thought they heard the actual arrival of a vast army. **And they said one to another, Lo, the King of Israel hath hired against us the kings of the Hittites.** This supposition has been thought "strange," almost inexplicable. "No such nation as the Hittites any longer existed," says Mr. Sumner ('The Books of the Kings,' vol. ii. p. 72, Eng. trans.). But the Assyrian records of the ninth and eighth centuries B.C. make it evident, not only that the Hittites still existed at that date, but that they were among the most powerful enemies of the Ninevite kings, being located in Northern Syria, about Carchemish (Jerabus) and the adjacent country. It is also apparent that they did not form a centralized monarchy, but were governed by a number of chiefs, or "kings," twelve of whom are mentioned in one place (G. Smith, 'Eponym Canon,' p. 112). It was no very improbable supposition on the part of the Syrians that Jehoram had called in the aid of the Hittite confederacy, and that they had marched an army to his assistance. **And the kings of the Egyptians.** "The plural, *kings* of the Egyptians," says Keil, "is not to be pressed. It is probably occasioned only by the parallel expression, 'kings of the Hittites.'" But Egyptian history shows us that about this date Egypt was becoming disintegrated, and that two or three distinct dynasties were sometimes ruling at the same time, in different parts of the country—one at Bubastis, another at Thebes, a third at Tanis, occasionally a fourth at Memphis (see "Ancient Egypt," in 'The Story of the Nations,' p. 311). The writer thus shows a knowledge of the internal condition of Egypt which we should not have expected. **To come upon us;** *i.e.* to fall upon us from the north and from the south at the same time. In their panic, the Syrians did not stop to weigh probabilities, or to think how unlikely it was that such a simultaneous attack could have been arranged between powers so remote one from the other.

Ver. 7.—**Wherefore they arose and fled in the twilight.** At the very time when the lepers were drawing off from the gate of Samaria to fall away to them (see ver. 5). **And left their tents, and their horses, and their asses, even the camp as it was.** Partly, perhaps, in mere panic; partly to induce a belief on the part of the enemy that they had not quitted their camp. So

Darius Hystaspis, when he began his retreat from Scythia (Herod., iv. 135), left his camp standing, and the camp fires lighted, and the asses tethered (see ver. 10), that the Scythians, seeing the tents and hearing the noise of the animals, might be fully persuaded that his troops were still in the same place. Asses were the chief baggage-animals in many ancient armies. **And fled for their life.** Thinking that, if they waited till dawn, the Israelite allies, Hittites and Egyptians, would exterminate them.

Ver. 8.—**And when these lepers came to the uttermost part of the camp.** The narrative, begun in ver. 3, is here taken up from the point where it was broken off in ver. 5, and the phrase there used is repeated, to mark the connection. **They went into one tent, and did eat and drink.** The first necessity was to satisfy the cravings of their appetite, as they were well-nigh starving. Then their covetousness was excited by the riches exposed to view in the tent. **And carried thence silver, and gold, and raiment.** Oriental armies carried with them vast quantities of the precious metals, in the shape of gold and silver vases, goblets, dishes, as well as in collars, chains, furniture, and trappings. Herodotus says (ix. 80) that, when the camp of Mardonius at Platæa fell into the hands of the Greeks, there were found in it "many tents richly adorned with furniture of gold and silver, many couches covered with plates of the same, and many golden bowls, goblets, and other drinking-vessels. On the carriages were bags containing gold and silver kettles; and the bodies of the slain furnished bracelets and chains, and scimitars with golden ornaments—not to mention embroidered apparel, of which no one made any account." The camp of the Syrians would scarcely have been so richly provided; but still it contained, no doubt, a large amount of very valuable plunder. **And went and hid it.** The lepers had no right to the pick of the spoil. It belonged to the nation, and it was probably the king's right to apportion it. The lepers had to conceal what they appropriated, lest it should be taken from them. **And came again, and entered into another tent, and carried thence also, and went and hid it.** Plundering thus probably, not two tents only, but several. At last, either covetousness was satiated or conscience awoke.

Ver. 9.—**Then they said one to another, We do not well.** It was a tardy recognition of what their duty required of them. As Grotius says, "Officium civium est ea indicare, quæ ad salutem publicam pertinent." Their fellow-countrymen in the city of Samaria were perishing of hunger, mothers eating their children, and the like, while they employed hour after hour in collecting and hiding away their booty. They ought, as soon as they had satisfied their hunger, to have hurried back to the city and spread the good news. **This day is a day of good tidings, and we hold our peace;** *i.e.* we keep silence, and do not proclaim them, as we ought. **If we tarry till the morning light, some mischief will come upon us;** rather, *punishment will fall on us;* we shall suffer for what we have done—a very reasonable supposition. **Now therefore come, that we may go and tell the king's household.** The "king's household" means the court, the medium through which the king was ordinarily approached.

Ver. 10.—**So they came and called unto the porter of the city;** *i.e.* to the guard of the gate nearest them. The word שֹׁעֵר, "porter," or "gate-man," is used *collectively.* **And they told them, saying, We came to the camp of the Syrians, and, behold, there was no man there, neither voice of man, but horses tied, and asses tied, and the tents as they were.** The horses and asses within a camp were always "tied," or tethered, as we see from the monumental representations of Egyptian camps (Rawlinson, 'History of Ancient Egypt,' vol. i. p. 476), and also learn from historians (Herod., iv. 135). It is somewhat surprising that the horses were left behind, as they would have expedited the flight had they been saddled and mounted. But this was, perhaps, overlooked in the panic.

Ver. 11.—**And he called the porters; and they told it to the king's house within;** rather, *and the porters* (or, *gate-keepers*) *called out and told it,* etc. יִקְרָא may be a plural *before* its subject; or the true reading may be יִקְרְאוּ, which is found in some manuscripts.

Ver. 12.—**And the king arose in the night, and said unto his servants, I will now show you what the Syrians have done to us. They know that we be hungry; therefore are they gone out of the camp to hide themselves in the field.** Jehoram, knowing of no reason for the flight of the Syrians, suspected a not uncommon stratagem. He supposed that the enemy had merely gone a little way from their camp, and placed themselves in ambush, ready to take advantage of any rash movement which the Israelites might make. So Cyrus is said to have entrapped and slaughtered Spargapises, the son of Tomyris, together with a large detachment, in his last war against the Massagetæ (Herod., i. 211). His supposition was not unreasonable. **Saying, When they come out of the city, we shall catch them alive, and get into the city.** A double advantage might be expected to follow—those who quitted the town to plunder the camp would be surrounded and

made prisoners, while the town itself, left without defenders, would be captured. Compare the capture of Ai by Joshua (Josh. viii. 3—19), when the chief part of the garrison had been enticed out of it.

Ver. 13.—**And one of his servants answered and said, Let some take, I pray thee, five of the horses that remain.** One of Jehoram's "servants," *i.e.* of the officers attached to his person, suggested that a small body of horse (four or five) should be sent out to reconnoitre. The besieged had still some horses left, though apparently not many. Note the phrase, "five of the horses *that remain.*" The majority had died of want, or been killed to furnish food to the garrison. (**Behold, they are as all the multitude of Israel that are left in it**—*i.e.* in Samaria—**behold, I say, they are even as all the multitude of the Israelites that are consumed**); *i.e.* they will run no more risk than the other troops who remain in the city, for these, too, "are consumed," *i.e.* are on the point of perishing. Supposing that they fall into the enemy's hands, it will go no harder with them than with the "multitude" which is on the point of starvation. **And let us send and see.** We can do nothing until we know whether the siege is really raised, or whether the pretended withdrawal is a mere *ruse.* We must send and have this matter made clear.

Ver. 14.—**They took therefore two chariot horses**; literally, *two chariots of horses;* i.e. two chariots, with the accustomed number of horses, which (with the Israelites) was two, though with the Assyrians and Egyptians it was frequently three. The employment of chariots instead of horsemen is remarkable, and seems to indicate that with the Israelites, as with the Egyptians, the chariot force was regarded as superior to the cavalry for practical purposes. **And the king sent after the host of the Syrians, saying, Go and see.** The advice of the king's "servant" was taken; a couple of chariots were sent out to reconnoitre.

Ver. 15.—**And they went after them unto Jordan.** The charioteers, finding the camp really empty, discovering no ambush, and coming upon abundant signs of a hasty and perturbed flight, followed upon the track of the fugitives until they reached the Jordan, probably in the vicinity of Beth-shan, which lay on the ordinary route between Samaria and Damascus. Convinced by what they saw that the Syrians had really withdrawn into their own country, they pursued no further, but returned to Samaria. **And, lo, all the way was full of garments and vessels, which the Syrians had cast away in their haste.** Cloaks, shawls, shields, and even swords and spears, would be cast away as *impedimenta*—hindrances to a rapid flight.

These strewed the line of the retreating army's march. And the messengers returned, and told the king. Gave a full and complete account of what they had seen.

Ver. 16.—**And the people went out, and spoiled the tents of the Syrians.** The whole population of Samaria, with one accord, quitted the town, and flung themselves upon the spoil—the rich garments, the gold and silver vessels, the horses and asses, of which mention had been made previously (vers. 8—10). At the same time, no doubt, they feasted on the abundant dainties which they found in the tents. Having satisfied their immediate wants, they proceeded to lay in a store of corn for future use, and crowded tumultuously into the gate, where the corn found in the camp was being sold. **So a measure of fine flour;** rather, *and a measure,* etc.—**was sold for a shekel, and two measures of barley for a shekel, according to the word of the Lord** (see ver. 1).

Ver. 17.—**And the king appointed the lord on whose hand he leaned to have the charge of the gate.** Anticipating disorder, unless special care were taken, through the probable eagerness of the people to purchase the corn which was offered to them at so moderate a rate, Jehoram appointed the officer on whose arm he had leant when he visited the house of Elisha (see ver. 2), to have the charge of the gate, and preside over the sale. Probably there was no thought of the post being one of danger. **And the people trode upon him in the gate, and he died.** It has been questioned whether the death was accidental (Bähr), and suggested that the eager and famished people resisted his authority, and violently bore down his attempts to control them. But there is nothing in the text that is incompatible with an accidental death. Such deaths are not uncommon in dense crowds

of anxious and excited people. **As the man of God had said, who spake when the king came down to him.** The varieties of reading here do not affect the general sense. The writer's intention is to lay special stress on the fulfilment of Elisha's prophecy; and to emphasize the punishment that follows on a lack of faith. The concluding passage of the chapter is, as Bähr says, "a finger of warning to unbelievers."

Ver. 18.—**And it came to pass as the man of God had spoken to the king, saying, Two measures of barley for a shekel, and a measure of fine flour for a shekel, shall be to-morrow about this time in the gate of Samaria.** The otiose repetition of almost the whole of ver. 1 can only be explained as a mode of emphasizing, and so impressing upon the reader two main points: (1) Elisha's prophetic powers; and (2) the dreadful consequences that follow on scornful rejection of a message from God (see the comment on ver. 2).

Ver. 19.—**And that lord answered the man of God, and said, Now, behold, if the Lord should make windows in heaven, might such a thing be? And he said, Behold, thou shalt see it with thine eyes, but shalt not eat thereof** (see the comment on the preceding verse).

Ver. 20.—**And so it fell out unto him;** *i.e.* the prophecy was exactly fulfilled. The lord, being appointed to keep order in the gate where the corn was sold, "saw with his eyes" (ver. 2) the wonderful fall of prices within the short space of twenty-four hours, which Elisha had prophesied; but "did not eat thereof"—did not, in his own person, obtain any benefit from the sudden plenty, since he perished before he could profit by it. **For the people trode upon him in the gate, and he died** (see the comment on ver. 17).

HOMILETICS.

Vers. 1, 2, and 17—20.—*The sin of the scoffer, and its punishment.* Unbelief may be involuntary, and so neither incur guilt nor deserve punishment. St. Paul "obtained mercy" notwithstanding his bitter persecution of the early Christians, "because he did it ignorantly in unbelief" (1 Tim. i. 13). Modern sceptics are, no doubt, in many cases unable to believe, their eyes being blinded through their education, through ingrained prejudice or invincible ignorance. But to scoff at religion must be at all times a voluntary act; and it is an act which Holy Scripture views as in the highest degree blamable. In the instance here recorded, where Elisha, rising up in all the majesty of God's prophet, and addressing himself to king, nobles, and elders, solemnly required them to "hear the word of Jehovah," and then proclaimed with a voice of authority the raising of the siege and the speedy conversion of the existing scarcity into abundance, it indicated extreme effrontery and contempt for holy things, to take the word, when the king himself was silent, and utter a scoff, questioning the power as well as the truthfulness of God. The "lord" was clearly puffed up with a high opinion of his own wisdom, enlightenment, and knowledge of the world and its ways, and perceiving no probability of the change prophesied, of which there was indeed at the time no sign, thought himself entitled, not only to disbelieve the announcement, but to pour contempt upon it. "It is too often the case that high-born and apparently well-bred men, at court, take pleasure in mockeries of the Word of God and of its declarations, without reflecting that they thereby bear testimony to their own inner rudeness, vulgarity, and want of breeding" (Bähr). They think it a proof of their own cleverness and superiority to superstitious terrors, to mock and ridicule what they know to be reverenced by others. For the most part God allows them to escape punishment in this world, but now and then he signally vindicates his honour in the sight of all, by a manifest judgment upon the scoffers. An Elymas the sorcerer is struck blind (Acts xiii. 11) suddenly, an Arius perishes in the dead of night, or an Israelite "lord" suffers the penalty due to his rash words by being "trampled underfoot." God can at any time "arise to judgment," and "reward the proud after their deserving." Let men see to it that they provoke him not by "speaking unadvisedly with their lips." If they cannot receive his Word and hold fast his truth, let them at least "keep still silence," refrain themselves, and not draw down his vengeance upon them by profane scoffs and idle jesting.

Vers. 3—15.—*The plenitude of God's power to deliver from the extremest dangers.* It is impossible to conceive a peril greater than that of Samaria at this time. The Syrians were masters of all the open country. They had for months surrounded the town and strictly blockaded it. The store of provisions within the walls was almost wholly exhausted, and there was no possibility of obtaining a supply from without. Jehoram had no ally who could be expected to come to his aid. Human wisdom, as personified in the "lord on whose hand the king leaned," might well view the end as certain, not seeing from what quarter deliverance could possibly come. But man's extremity is God's opportunity. With God nothing is impossible. Nothing is even hard. He has a thousand resources. He can send forth his angel into a camp at nightfall, and in the morning they shall be "all dead men" (ch. xix. 35). He can make brothers-in-arms to fall out, and turn their swords one against another (2 Chron. xx. 23). He can send a groundless panic upon the largest and best-appointed host, and cause them to flee away and disappear, "like the chaff of the summer threshing-floor." He can make two men, like Jonathan and his armour-bearer (1 Sam. xiv. 6—16), victorious over a multitude. "A thousand shall flee at the rebuke of one," if God so wills it. Panic he can cause in a hundred ways. "It is only necessary that in the darkness a wind should blow, or that water should splash in free course, or that an echo should resound from the mountains, or that the wind should rustle the dry leaves, to terrify the godless, so that they flee as if pursued by a sword, and fall though no one pursues them" (Lev. xxvi. 36). In the present case, the Syrians heard a sound, how caused we know not, and instantly imagined that a danger threatened them, which could only be escaped by immediate flight. Israel had hired against them, they thought, two armies, one of Egyptians and the other of Hittites; the armies had arrived, and would fall upon them at dawn of day. So they hastily fled in the darkness, casting away arms and vessels and garments as they went (ver. 15), and leaving behind them their camp standing, with all its stores intact, its flour and barley, its gold and silver, its rich raiment, its war-horses and beasts of burden. The Samaritans were called upon to do nothing—they had but to "stand still, and see the salvation of God" (Exod. xv. 13). In one day, without any exertion of their own, their deliverance was complete. And so it is with God always.

I. GOD HAS POWER TO DELIVER FROM ALL EARTHLY PERILS. In an hour, in a moment, if he pleases, God has power to deliver: 1. From disease. He can cleanse the leper; give sight to the blind; heal malignant ulcers; infuse strength and vigour into the palsied; make plague, or fever, or any other mortal sickness to pass away. 2. From poverty. He can cause the poorest man to find a treasure, or put it into the heart of a rich man to leave him one, or so bless his little store that it becomes abundance (ch. iv. 1—7), or give him favour in the sight of a monarch (Esth. vii. 6—11), or put the wealth of thousands at his disposal (Acts iv. 34—37). 3. From oppression. He can destroy or cast down the oppressor, cut him off suddenly, release his victims, break the chains from off their neck, "lift them up out of the mire, and set them with the princes of his people." 4. From shame. He can raise from the dungeon to the palace (Gen. xli. 14; Dan. vi. 23—28); can make men ready to worship one whom a moment before they denounced as a murderer (Acts xxviii. 3—6); can "set on thrones" those who have been treated as "the offscouring of all things" (1 Cor. iv. 14).

II. GOD HAS ALSO POWER TO DELIVER FROM SPIRITUAL PERILS.   1. He can preserve from the power of Satan, "deliver from the evil one," quench all his fiery darts, abate his pride, rescue men from his dominion when they seem on the point of submitting to it.   2. He can deliver from the guilt of sin; can accept atonement; can put away men's sins from them, so that, "though they were as scarlet, they shall become white as snow; though they were red like crimson, they shall be as wool" (Isa. i. 18).   3. And he can deliver from the power of sin.   He can "strengthen the weak hands, and confirm the feeble knees" (Isa. xxxv. 3), can take away the evil out of men's hearts, and put his Holy Spirit within them; can enable them to resist the temptations of the world, the flesh, and the devil; can make of them "new creatures."   God, and God alone, can do this; and to him we must look for this deliverance; to him we must pray for this deliverance; to him, when we have obtained it, we must be eternally grateful for this deliverance.   "Thanks be to God for his unspeakable Gift!"

Vers. 4—11.—*Afflictions may alienate men from God instead of bringing them near to him.* This truth is remarkably exemplified in the conduct and reasonings of the lepers.   Here are four poor men, severely afflicted by a malady which was reckoned to come, more directly than most others, from God's hand, whom we should have expected to find humbled and softened by it, more God-fearing, more tender and compassionate towards their fellow-men, than the generality.   But the reverse is the case with them. Instead of submitting themselves to God in their wretchedness, and hanging upon him, and looking to him for succour, they are sunk in a dull discontent, well nigh reckless and desperate.   It is scarcely possible that they had not heard how Elisha preached a miraculous deliverance, and urged the king not to surrender the city, but "wait for Jehovah" (ch. vi. 33).   Yet of deliverance they have not the slightest expectation; they are as unbelieving as the proud "lord" of the court; if they remain with their countrymen, they hold that they must certainly die.   So they resolve not to remain, but to go over to the enemy.   No feeling of shame restrains them—it does not seem even to occur to them that there is any disgrace in desertion.   They are impelled by motives which are purely egoistic—what is *their* best chance?   Whether their countrymen will be damaged by its becoming known that they have now no food for their lepers, they either do not inquire or they do not care.   What weighs with them is that, if they go over, they may possibly save their wretched lives; if they do not, they have, they think, no chance at all.   It may be said that "self-preservation is the first law of nature;" but not self-preservation at all costs.   Death is preferable to dishonour. The lepers take their departure, and reach the Syrian camp.   Here an extraordinary surprise befalls them; the camp, which they had expected to be full of Syrian soldiery, is empty—there is not a man left in it (ver. 5).   All its wealth, all its stores, are open to the first comer.   How do the lepers act under these strange circumstances?   Again in a purely selfish spirit.   That they should fall upon the food, and "eat and drink" (ver. 8), was natural, and no one will blame them so far, though it would have been nobler to have at once hurried back, and proclaimed the glad tidings to the famished city.   But, having satiated their appetites, they are not content.   Covetousness is stirred up by what meets their gaze, and they must proceed to enrich themselves by carrying off and securing a quantity of objects in silver and gold (ver. 8).   When doubt begins to stir in their minds as to the propriety of this proceeding, it is not conscience that awakens, or regard for their fellow-citizens that moves them, but mere consideration for their own interests—"If we tarry till the morning light, we shall find punishment" (marginal rendering).   Thus, from first to last, the lepers are an example of mean and grovelling selfishness—such selfishness as poverty too often engenders, as misfortune intensifies, and to which the sense of belonging to a despised class lends a peculiar bitterness.   Their calamities have in no way brought the lepers near to God, or induced them to cast their care upon him, but have hardened and brutalized them.   We may learn from this—

I. THAT, THOUGH AFFLICTIONS ARE SENT FOR OUR GOOD, WE SHALL GET NO GOOD FROM THEM UNLESS WE RECEIVE THEM IN A RIGHT SPIRIT; *i.e.* submissively, resignedly, even gratefully, as intended to benefit us.

II. THAT, IF WE EXTRACT NOT FROM THEM THE SWEET USES FOR WHICH THEY WERE MEANT, WE SHALL BE APT TO GET FROM THEM IRREPARABLE HARM—the irreparable harm of a lowering of our moral tone, and an alienation of our souls from their Creator.

Vers. 12—15.—*Unseasonable distrust.* Humanly speaking, Jehoram's distrust of the report of the lepers was not *unreasonable.* Such a stratagem as that which he suspected was often practised in the wars of the ancient world, with great advantage to one side and great loss to the other. But his distrust, though not unreasonable, was *unseasonable* from the point of view of faith and belief in God. Elisha having just announced such an inversion of the actual state of things as could only be brought about in an extraordinary way, the occurrence of something extraordinary was to be expected. Jehoram ought to have been on the look out for some strange intelligence; and that which the lepers brought him was in such complete accordance with the tenor of Elisha's prophecy, that a very moderate degree of faith would have sufficed to make him receive it gladly, joyfully, and without any mistrust. He would then have shortened the sufferings of his people by a day, which must have been lost by the despatch of the two chariots to reconnoitre; and he might, perhaps, have saved the life of his "lord," whose dreadful death may have been caused by the impatience of a famished multitude too long restrained from sallying forth. Men are apt to be mistrustful; and it is generally just at the wrong time. They are sanguine and over-confident when it would have been well to suspect, suspicious and over-circumspect when there is no need of doubt or circumspection. God calls them to the kingdom that he has prepared for men, and bids them "come, buy and eat; yea, come, buy wine and milk without money and without price" (Isa. lv. 1); and they hang back, hesitate, delay, as if they were about to be entrapped. A bold impostor invites them to adopt his shibboleth, and trust in it for salvation—they listen eagerly, hang on his words, are persuaded, and join the Mormons or the Peculiar People. Rash youth boasts as it girds on its armour, and looks for an easy victory over sin and Satan, over the world, the flesh, and the devil. Timid old age faints and is weary, and despairs of winning through and "persevering to the end," though God has brought it so far upon its way. It is well to mistrust one's self; it is faithless to mistrust God. He who has borne us up hitherto on eagles' wings will still bear us up. He "fainteth not, neither is weary." He "will not leave us, nor forsake us."

HOMILIES BY VARIOUS AUTHORS.

Vers. 1, 2, with 12—20.—*The unbelieving lord.* Elisha interrupts the king's evil design by a prediction of plenty in Samaria. His mention of a fixed time doubtless induced the king to wait until he should see if the prophecy was fulfilled. "Thus saith the Lord, To-morrow about this time shall a measure of fine flour be sold for a shekel, and two measures of barley for a shekel, in the gate of Samaria." It was a bold statement to make, for *there was no human likelihood of its fulfilment.* If the next day had proved Elisha to be a deceiver, no doubt he would have been torn limb from limb by the infuriated and hungry populace. But Elisha makes not the statement on his own authority, but uses the words, "Thus saith the Lord." One of the king's principal courtiers, on whose arm he leaned, could not conceal his scorn and incredulity. "Behold, if the Lord would make windows in heaven, might this thing be?" Observe, his statement is not "If the Lord would make windows in heaven, this thing *might be.*" He doesn't even admit that. It is a question expressing entire impossibility. "Even if the Lord would open windows in heaven, *is it at all likely* that such a thing as this would happen?" But what seemed impossible to him was possible with God. The prophet warned him that he would suffer for his unbelief. "Behold, thou shalt see it with thine eyes, but shalt not eat thereof." As it was predicted, so it came to pass. During the night, the Lord caused the Syrian army to hear a great noise, like the noise of horses and chariots and a mighty host, and they fled in terror, leaving their camp with all their possessions and provisions behind them. Four lepers, going out of the city in the evening twilight, discovered the deserted camp. They brought back the news to the beleaguered city. At first, a stratagem was feared ; but by-and-by in wild eagerness for food and plunder, the famished citizens rushed forth. The unhappy lord, who had doubted the prophet's message and the promise of God himself, was trodden upon at the gate and died. From this striking and tragic story we may learn—

I. UNBELIEF MAY HAVE REASON, APPARENTLY, ON ITS SIDE. This courtier might have given many plausible reasons for doubting the prophet's message. 1. *He might have disputed the prophet's right to speak in the name of God at all.* He might have said, "How do I know that this man is speaking the truth?" though even there Elisha had already given pretty tangible proof of his credibility and trustworthiness. The faithful minister of Christ need not mind the sneers of men, provided God has owned his work, and set his heavenly seal upon his ministry. 2. Or he might have said, " *The thing is utterly incredible.* It is utterly impossible. Where is flour to come from in such plenty as to supply this whole city of Samaria? There has been a besieging army around our walls for many days. They have desolated and plundered the country round about. Where is the food to come from, even if there was any one to bring it to us? And we know of no friendly army that is coming to raise the siege or cut its way through the serried ranks of the Syrians." All these would have been very natural thoughts to pass through that courtier's mind. No doubt they were the very reasons, or some of them, which led him to disbelieve Elisha's message. Probably, if he had stated his reasons to the people, he would have got a hundred to agree with him for every one who believed Elisha. No doubt they all looked upon Elisha as a fanatic and an enthusiast. *They,* to all appearance, had common sense, had reason on their side. And yet it turned out to be one of those many cases in which " God hath chosen the foolish things of this world to confound the wise, and the weak things to confound the mighty." Unbelief can be very plausible. Unbelief nearly always appears to have reason on its side. There is not a doctrine of the Bible against which the most plausible arguments might not, and have not, been advanced. Even Scripture itself can be quoted in support of unbelief and sin. "The devil can cite Scripture for his purpose." *Good arguments are not necessarily a proof of the truth or justice of a case.* This needs to be remembered in an age when many arguments are urged against the truth of Christianity. What plausible reasons have been urged against the main truths of the Christian religion! Take *the Deity of Christ,* for example. How plausible are the arguments which human reason can bring forward against the doctrine of the Trinity and the Divinity of Christ! And yet of what value are such arguments when placed side by side with our Lord's statement, "I and my Father are one;" with the statement of the Apostle John, "The Word was with God, and the Word was God;" or with the statement of the Apostle Paul, that " in him dwelleth all the fulness of the Godhead bodily"? In the same way the most plausible arguments can be, and are being, brought against the *atoning nature of Christ's death,* although we have the clear statements of God's Word that "he bore our sins in his own body on the tree," and Christ's own statement that he laid down his life for the sheep. Over and over again it has been asserted that *the Gospel miracles* are incredible. Over and over again the most plausible arguments have been brought against future punishment, although we have the clear and emphatic statements of our Lord Jesus Christ himself on the subject. Unbelief may have reason, apparently, on its side.

II. OUR REASON IS NO TEST OF POSSIBILITY. Our ideas are no test as to what is possible or impossible. Our minds are limited in their range. How often in the march of scientific discovery and invention it has happened that things which seemed impossible in one century were proved to be possible in the next! It is not yet three hundred years since Galileo was condemned to imprisonment by the Inquisition for asserting that the earth moved round the sun. Even our own Sir Isaac Newton, little more than two hundred years ago—the man who discovered the force of gravitation, and invented the first reflecting telescope—was assailed with such abuse on propounding his discoveries, that he actually determined on suppressing the third book of the ' Principia,' which contains the theory of comets. And what shall we say of the invention of the steam-engine by James Watt, scarcely a hundred years ago—an invention which has revolutionized our manufactures, and made possible a speed of locomotion by land and sea that would have been ridiculed as impossible only a few years ago? Every discovery of science, every invention in the useful arts, has at first been scorned as an impossible dream, then laughed at as impracticable, and finally accepted when it became impossible to deny the truth of the one or the usefulness of the other. *The impossibilities of to-day turn out to be the possibilities of to-morrow.* It is well to remember this, that, because we are unable to conceive of something taking place, it does not therefore follow that it is impossible. The fact is, that when we say anything is "impossible," we just mean that *we cannot conceive it.* But, as has already been shown, this is no reason why a doctrine or statement may not be true, or why a certain occurrence may not take place. We may have never known anything of the kind to occur before; but that is no proof that a thing is impossible, though in the minds of many people it is the only argument. What has never occurred before, may occur yet. There are discoveries in science still undreamed of in our advanced philosophy. There are inventions yet to be conceived which, if to-day we could hear of them, we might pronounce the wild ravings of a fanatic. *There are infinite resources in the hand of him who rules the world.* Who are we, that we should limit God? Who are we, that we should set bounds to his power? Who are we, that we should set bounds to his justice on the one hand, or to his mercy on the other? Must we not bow in deep humility before all the problems that affect his dealings with men, and say, "Shall not the Judge of all the earth do right?" Must we not reverently accept whatever he has been pleased to reveal in his own Word of his Divine purposes and plans, no matter what our reason may say?

III. THE DANGEROUS CHARACTER OF UNBELIEF. We have seen how unreasonable this courtier's unbelief was. Not only so, but it was *injurious.* So unbelief in a professing Christian is injurious to himself and to others. It hinders his own usefulness. It hinders the progress of the gospel. It hinders the success of Christian work. It is the Achan in the camp, the canker of Christian life and power, the chilling blight of the Christian Church. What an age of deadness in the Church of Christ in England, Scotland, and Ireland, was the eighteenth century, the age of moderatism, the age of indifference and rationalism! What an absence of missionary enterprise! What an absence of evangelistic effort! As Churches and as individuals, we should pray to be delivered from unbelief, and to be filled with living, working, all-conquering faith. Mr. Spurgeon says, in his remarks on this passage, that if we are hindering God's work by our unbelief, it may happen to us as it happened to this nobleman, that God may see fit to take us out of the way. He says that he has remarked, "that when any truly good man has stood in God's way, God has made short work with him. He has taken him home, or he has laid him aside by sickness. If you will not help and will hinder, you will be put aside, and perhaps your own usefulness will be cut short." If you have not faith enough in the power of the gospel, if you have not faith enough in the promises of God, if you have not faith enough in the power of prayer, then be in earnest in asking for more faith—such faith as will stand firm in the day of temptation, of trial, of conflict, of opposition. Never say to yourself about any Christian work, "If the Lord would make windows in heaven, might such a thing be?" An affectionate word to the unbeliever, to the sinner. *Unbelief is dangerous.* Christ speaks of unbelief as *a sin.* He says of the Holy Spirit that "he will convince the world of sin, because they believed not on me." Men may call it a hard doctrine, but there it is. "He that believeth not is condemned already, because he hath not believed in the Name of the only begotten Son of God." Is there anything hard in that? The offer of salvation is made to every one. It is so plain that there can be no mistake about it. If there had been any other way, any other Saviour, men might plead uncertainty. But they are plainly told, "neither is there salvation in any other." Those who believed not the warnings in the days of Noah, perished. Their day of grace was long, but they neglected it. So with the Israelites whose bones lay whitening in the wilderness. "They entered not in because of unbelief." Oh, how terrible that unbelieving courtier's doom: "Thou shalt see it with thine eyes, but shalt not eat thereof"!—C. H. I.

Vers. 1, 2.—*A Divine teacher and a haughty sceptic.* "Then Elisha said, Hear ye the word of the Lord; Thus saith the Lord, To-morrow," etc. Here are two objects not only to be looked at, but to be studied.

I. A DIVINE TEACHER. "Then Elisha said, Hear ye the word of the Lord; Thus saith the Lord, To-morrow about this time shall a measure of fine flour be sold for a shekel, and two measures of barley for a.shekel, in the gate of Samaria." Elisha was inspired and commanded by the Almighty God to make a proclamation to a starving population. The famine was still prevailing. The shadow of death darkened the sky, and his freezing breath was in the air, and men were shivering on the confines of the grave. Thus, when things seemed to be at their worst, Elisha appears as a messenger of mercy from Heaven, declaring that on the next morning there would be an abundance of provision obtainable in the gate of Samaria. Two circumstances connected with this promise will apply to the gospel. 1. It was *a communication exactly suited to the condition of those to whom it was addressed.* People were starving, and the one great necessity was food, and here it is promised. Mankind are morally lost; what they want is spiritual restoration, and the gospel proclaims it. 2. It was *a communication made on the authority of the Eternal.* "Thus saith the Lord." That the gospel is a Divine message is a truth too firmly established even to justify debate. By the gospel, of course, I do not mean all the tracts of which the book we call the Bible is composed, but the Divine biography of Christ as recorded by his four biographers.

II. A HAUGHTY SCEPTIC. "Then a lord on whose hand the king leaned answered the man of God, and said, Behold, if the Lord would make windows in heaven, might this thing be?" Here is one of the most contemptible of all classes of men—a courtier, a sycophant in relation to his king, a haughty despot in regard to all beneath him. When he heard the prophet's deliverance, he, forsooth, was too great a man, and thought himself, no doubt, too great a philosopher, to believe it. It was the man's *self-importance* that begat his incredulity, and this, perhaps, is the parent of all scepticism and unbelief.—D. T.

Vers. 3—8.—*The force of will.* "And there were four leprous men at the entering in of the gate," etc. Here we have—

I. MEN INVOLVED IN THE MOST WRETCHED CONDITION. "There were four leprous men at the entering in of the gate." Of all the diseases which afflict mankind none is more painful, loathsome, and disastrous than leprosy. It was the scourge of the Hebrew race. Moses minutely describes the appearance of this malady, and gives clear and forcible rules to govern the medical treatment of it. Fat and blood and other particles of diet which excite or aggravate constitutional tendencies to diseases of the skin, were strictly forbidden to the Jews. There are many points of analogy between leprosy and sin.

II. Men in the most wretched condition FORMING A RESOLUTION. "They said one to another, Why sit we here until we die? If we say, We will enter into the city, then the famine is in the city, and we shall die there: and if we sit still here we die also. Now therefore come, and let us fall unto the host of the Syrians: if they save us alive, we shall live; and if they kill us, we shall but die." Emaciated and wretched as might have been their bodily condition, their moral nature had sufficient stamina left to make a resolution. Mind is often more active in physical disease than in physical health. Pain whips all the faculties into action, marshals all the forces of the soul. Truly wonderful is the power of the human will. Let no man justify mental indolence and moral inertia by pleading his bodily troubles. But how often this is done! How often do you hear men say, "We can do nothing because of the circumstances in which we are placed"! The "cannot" of such is their "will not," and the "will not" is their own choice.

III. Men ACTING OUT THE RESOLUTION formed in the most wretched condition. These four poor starving leprous men not only formed a resolution, but they worked it out. "And they rose up in the twilight, to go unto the camp of the Syrians." In giving practical effect to their resolution, two results followed. 1. *Difficulties vanished.* Their great dread was of the Syrians, but as they approached the Syrian camp, "Behold, there was no man there." Wherefore had they fled? Here is the answer: "For the Lord had made the host of the Syrians to hear a noise of chariots, and a noise of horses, even the noise of a great host. And they said one to another, Lo, the King of Israel hath hired against us the kings of the Hittites, and the kings of the Egyptians, to come upon us. Wherefore they rose and fled in the twilight, and left their tents, and their horses and their asses, even the camp as it was, and fled for their life." By what force were these Syrians scared away? Not the force of the rough elements of nature, or the force of armies, but the force of terrible ideas—ideas that made them hear the noise of the rattling chariots and the tramping steeds of war, that had no existence. But these ideas, albeit, were ideas from God. "The Lord had made the host of the Syrians to hear a noise." God often frightens wicked men by ideas. "God can," says Matthew Henry, "when he pleases, dispirit the boldest and most brave, and make the stoutest heart to tremble. Those that will not fear God, he can make to fear at the shaking of a leaf." Before a strong resolution, apprehended difficulties frequently vanish into air. Where there's a will there's a way, even though it be over rugged mountains and surging floods. A man's "I will" has a power in it mighty as the forces of nature, ay, mightier, for it can subordinate them. "If thou hast faith as a grain of mustard seed, thou shalt say to this mountain, Be thou removed," etc. 2. *The object was realized.* What these poor starving leprous men deeply needed and sought was provisions to appease the cravings of hunger and to reinvigorate their waning life. And they got them. "And when these lepers came to the uttermost part of the camp, they went into one tent, and did eat and drink, and carried thence silver, and gold, and raiment, and went and hid it," etc. Thus they gained even more than they sought; they not only gained food, but wealth.

CONCLUSION. Learn here the wonderful moral force of the human mind. It possesses a power to make resolutions under the most trying external conditions, and the power to work them out successfully. The fiat "I'll try" has wrought wonders in human history, is working wonders now, and so it ever can. Well does Dr. Tulloch say, "Everything yields before the strong and earnest will. It grows by exercise. It excites confidence in others, while it takes to itself the lead. Difficulties before which mere cleverness fails, and which leave the irresolute prostrate and helpless, vanish before it. They not only do not impede its progress, but it often makes of them stepping-stones to a higher and more enduring triumph."—D. T.

Vers. 9—11.—*The right and the prudent.* "Then they said one to another, We do not well," etc. These verses record the conference which these four lepers had with one another after they had succeeded in working out their resolution to go unto the "host of the Syrians;" and in this conference we discover—

I. THE RIGHT. "They said one to another, We do not well: this day is a day of good tidings, and we hold our peace." The silver and the gold which they had discovered they had hidden away; and now, perhaps, conscience told them it was not right. It is not right for us to conceal the good we have discovered, or to appropriate it entirely to our own use; let us communicate it. The distribution of good is right. Every man should be "ready to communicate." The monopoly of *material* good is a huge wrong, and the crying sin of the age. Legislation will have to deal with this social abomination sooner or later; it is crushing the millions to the dust. Monopolies must be broken up; the wants of society and the claims of eternal justice demand it. What is truly "glad tidings" to us we should proclaim to others. The rays of joy that fall over our own lives we should not retain, but reflect.

II. THE PRUDENT. Whether these poor men felt it was right to communicate to others the tidings of the good they had received or not, they certainly felt it was prudent. "If we tarry till the morning light, some mischief will come upon us: now therefore come, that we may go and tell the king's household." Accordingly they acted. "So they came and called unto the porter of the city: and they told them, saying, We came to the camp of the Syrians, and, behold, there was no man there, neither voice of man, but horses tied, and asses tied, and the tents as they were. And he called to the porters; and they told it to the king's house within." Not to do the right thing must cause some "mischief"—mischief not only to the body, but to the soul as well, to the entire man. There is no prudence apart from rectitude. What is wrong in moral principle is mischievous in conduct. He who is in the right, however outvoted by his age, is always in the majority, for he has *that* vote which carries all material universes and spiritual hierarchies with it. Right is infallible utilitarianism.—D. T.

Vers. 12—16.—*The help that comes to distressed men from without.* "And the king arose in the night," etc. These verses suggest a few thoughts concerning the help that sometimes comes to distressed men from *without.* The best help that a man can get in any case is from *within*—from a right working of his own faculties, independence on his Maker. Still, help from without is often most valuable. There are three kinds of human helpers without. 1. Those that help men *by their will*. These are men, the chosen of the race, who lay themselves out for philanthropic service. 2. Those that help men *against their will*. It often turns out, as in the case of Joseph's brethren, that our enemies really serve us. 3. Those that help men *irrespective of their will*. We are helped in many ways by those who know and care nothing about us. We come into possession of their knowledge, inventions, property. The property of the men of the last age is ours to-day. Such is the kind of help which the Syrians now rendered the Israelites, and we offer three remarks concerning this help.

I. IT WAS NEEDED. The men of Samaria were in the utmost distress, and the king arose in the night and sent forth two of his servants (ver. 12) in pursuit of the Syrians to see what had happened. As they approached the spot they found that the Syrians had departed, but had left their property behind. " And the way was full of garments and vessels, which the Syrians had cast away in their haste." Thus in the height of their distress they found relief. It is often so in passing through life; often so in individual as well as in social life. In the greatest extremity help appears. When the cloud is darkest a beam of light breaks on it.

II. IT WAS UNDESERVED. Did these Samaritans deserve help? By no means. They were nearly all idolatrous and worthless people. They merited condign punishment, everlasting ruin. This is true of all men as sinners. Whatever help we receive is utterly undeserved. " It is of the Lord's mercies that we are not consumed."

III. IT WAS UNEXPECTED. They went forth longing for food, but quite uncertain whether they would find any. They found that the enemy had fled, and in their haste had left provisions behind. " So a measure of fine flour was sold for a shekel." Are not all men, in the providence of God, constantly receiving *unexpected* favours? The choicest blessings come when least expected.—D. T.

Vers. 17—20.—*God's promise realized and his truth vindicated.* " And the king appointed the lord on whose hand he leaned to have the charge of the gate," etc. We have here an instance of two things.

I. GOD'S PROMISE REALIZED. In the first verse of this chapter Elisha had said, " Hear ye the word of the Lord; Thus saith the Lord, To-morrow about this time shall a measure of fine flour be sold for a shekel." The morrow had come, and here is the fine flour and the barley being sold in the gate of Samaria. Here is the Divine promise fulfilled to the letter. God is ever faithful who hath promised. If a being makes a promise, and it is not fulfilled, it must be for one of three reasons—either because he was insincere when he made the promise, or subsequently changed his mind, or met with unforeseen difficulties which he had not the power to surmount. None of these can be applied to the all-truthful, unchangeable, all-seeing, and almighty God.

II. GOD'S TRUTH VINDICATED. The haughty courtier said to the prophet yesterday, when he was told that a measure of fine flour would be sold for a shekel, " If the Lord would make windows in heaven, might this thing be?" As if he had said, " Do not presume to impose on me, a man of my intelligence and importance. The intellectual rabble may believe in you, but I cannot." Whereupon the prophet replied, " Thou shalt see it with thine eyes, but shalt not eat thereof." And so it came to pass. Here are the flour and the barley, and there lies dead the haughty sceptic. " And so it fell out unto him: for the people trode upon him in the gate, and he died." Truth has ever vindicated itself, and will ever do so. Men's unbelief in facts does not either destroy or weaken facts; the facts remain. Though all the world deny the existence of a God, moral obligation, and future retribution, the facts remain.—D. T.

Vers. 1, 2.—*The unbelieving lord.* The spirit of despair had taken possession of Jehoram. It was at this point that Elisha interposed with his promise of deliverance.

I. PREDICTED DELIVERANCE. Elisha made what must have seemed an incredible announcement. 1. The city was at that moment suffering the extremest horrors of famine. By the same hour on the morrow food would exist in plenty. 2. Such food as was then obtainable was of the coarsest, most loathsome, and most revolting nature. By to-morrow they would be dieting on fine flour and barley in abundance. 3. Their disgusting food was only to be had at famine prices. To-morrow a measure of fine flour would be sold for a shekel, and two measures of barley for a shekel. 4. To-day they were fast beleaguered. To-morrow flour and barley would be sold in the open gates of Samaria. After this, " is anything too hard for the Lord ? " (Gen. xviii. 14). If men will not seek him, God leaves them to feel the extremity of their own helplessness before he interposes. Then he shows himself " plenteous " in mercy (Ps. ciii. 8). Who can doubt that, if king and city had sought God earlier with sincere hearts, the deliverance would have come sooner ? Thus by his own frowardness does the sinner stand in the way of his own good.

II. RATIONALISTIC DOUBT. The spirit of incredulity, which must have been in many minds when Elisha made this surprising announcement, found expression in the utterance of the captain on whose hand the king leaned, " Behold, if the Lord would make windows in heaven, might this thing be ? " 1. *The author of this sceptical scoff was a person in high rank.* The atmosphere of a court, and the position of a courtier, are not favourable to the development of piety. They are more apt to develop, as here, a worldly, sceptical, cynical spirit, with small faith in God, virtue, and truth. Piety is to be looked for rather in the cottages than in the palaces of a people, though there are notable exceptions. " Not many mighty," etc. (1 Cor. i. 26). 2. *The language is that of scornful incredulity.* It is the speech of a rationalist. Judged by the standards of sense and of natural reason, the sudden access of plenty which Elisha predicted was impossible. If the Lord opened windows in heaven, it might be looked for, but not otherwise. And who expected help from that quarter? Thus the worldly wise lord reasoned, sneering at Elisha's word as the imagination of a heated brain. He is the type of all rationalists. Interpositions from heaven are the last things they are disposed to believe in ; and in any case they will not believe God's Word unless they can see how it is to be fulfilled, and on what natural principles the unusual event is to be explained. As in the present case there was no possibility of help from within the city, and no prospect of the Syrians leaving when the city was just about to fall within their power, and no evidence that food in such abundance could be obtained at a day's notice even if they did leave, Elisha's promise could only be assigned to the category of delusion. The spirit of faith is the opposite of this. It takes God at his word, and leaves *him* to find out the means of accomplishing his own predictions.

III. THE PUNISHMENT OF UNBELIEF. Elisha entered into no argument. He left his word to be proved or disproved by the arbitrament of time. But he told the great lord who—so much wiser than Elisha—had scoffed at its fulfilment, what the penalty of his unbelief would be. He would see the promised plenty indeed, but he would not eat of it. Is not this the fate of every unbeliever? God's word stands sure ; it comes to pass in due time ; but the intellectualist, the scoffer, the doubter, the man who was too wise to believe, finds himself shut out from participation in the blessing.—J. O.

Vers. 3—11.—*The four lepers.*

"God moves in a mysterious way,
His wonders to perform."

Speculation might have exhausted itself in vain in conjecturing how Elisha's prediction was to be accomplished. Nevertheless, the wonder was performed by a series of events as simple as it was unlooked for.

I. A POLICY OF DESPAIR. 1. *The lepers at the gate.* We are first introduced to four lepers at the entering in of the gate. They were outside, and had hitherto subsisted by food handed out or thrown to them from within. But now the famine in the city made such assistance impossible, and the four men were dying of hunger. Poor, pitiable objects, the last persons to whom any one would have thought of looking for a glimpse of hope on the situation within the walls. Yet these despised lepers were to be, in a sense, the saviours of the city. We cannot but reflect on the humble and seemingly unlikely instruments God often chooses to accomplish his ends. He puts the "treasure in earthen vessels " (2 Cor. iv. 7). As if to abase human pride, he purposely selects instrumentalities which the wisdom of man would scorn. 2. *Dire alternatives.* Brought face to face with death, the poor lepers are forced to the earnest consideration of their position. What could they do? If they stay where they are they must die, and if they enter the city they must die. There remains the alternative, only to be contemplated as a last resource, of going over to the camp of the enemy. This has been put off as long as possible; but it appears now to be the only course which affords them any chance of life. Suppose the Syrians kill them, they are no worse off than before; if the Syrians take pity on them and save them alive, they shall live. The chance of life may be faint, but it is the only one left, and better than none. When men are in earnest, a very slight probability suffices them to act upon. They discover the truth of Butler's axiom that " probability is the guide of life." Did these men not act rationally in allowing even a slight probability to turn the balance of their action? How should it be otherwise when we deal with spiritual things? A man is in doubt as to the existence of God, as to the reality of a future life, etc. It may seem to him that the evidence for these truths amounts to no more than probability. He perhaps makes this an excuse for dismissing the consideration of them from his mind. But ought he not to give weight to this probability in action? In another way the doubter may take a leaf from the lepers' book. If he remains where he is, he perishes, for atheism can hold out to him no other hope. But if, on the ground even of a slight balance of probability, he acts on the lines of Christ's religion, he can be no worse than he is, while, if that religion is true (we speak only from his standpoint), he obtains eternal advantage. Or is the doubter one who does not question the truth of the gospel, but only questions his own right to appropriate its provisions? Let such a one imitate Esther, who, with the words on her lips, "If I perish, I perish" (Esth. iv. 16), went in to Ahasuerus. Let him cast himself on Christ, and leave himself there. He will find, like Esther, that he does not perish. 3. *The Divine will and the human will.* In these consultations among themselves, the lepers were moved only by the consideration of their own misery. They neither knew of Elisha's prediction, nor had any thought of aiding to fulfil it. Yet all the while they were working out God's secret counsel. They were, while seeking their own ends, the unconscious instruments of a higher will than their own. Thus are we all. Man's passions, ambitions, wants, follies, sins even, are subordinated in providence to the fulfilling of all-wise, comprehensive purposes, of which the immediate actors have no glimpse. "The counsel of the Lord standeth for ever; the thoughts of his heart to all generations" (Ps. xxxiii. 11).

II. THE DESERTED CAMP. 1. *An astonishing discovery.* At nightfall, in pursuance of their purpose, the lepers betook themselves to the camp of the Syrians. It was the evening of the day on which Elisha had made his promise. Of the hope then held out they were ignorant, but they were to be the first to make the discovery that deliverance had been wrought. It would be with fear and trembling that they approached the well-appointed tents, and the very silence that everywhere prevailed would strike them at first with new awe. But now an astonishing state of things revealed itself. The camp was there—that camp so lately astir with military life—but not a soul was to be seen in it. Absolute stillness reigned throughout the tents; or, if sounds were heard, they were only those of the horses and asses which were left without masters. Thus near may our salvation be to us, and we know it not. 2. *The flight of the Syrians.* The explanation of the state of things which the lepers discovered is given in vers. 6, 7. The Syrians themselves may in later years have told the story, or it may have been got from Elisha, whose prophetic gift gave him the knowledge of what had taken place. The Syrians, it appears, had heard strange noises—sounds as of chariots and horses and of a great host; and, smitten with sudden panic, believing that the Hittites or Egyptians had brought help to the Israelites, they at once abandoned everything and fled. The panic was of supernatural intensity, as the sounds were of supernatural origin. The mind of man, no less than external natural conditions, is in the hand of God. He can smite with " madness, and blindness, and astonishment of heart" (Deut. xxviii. 28); can make men the sport of their own imaginations and delusions. Such penalties are threatened against the wicked. 3. *Dividing the spoil.* The first impulse of the lepers, when they discovered that the camp was literally empty, was to supply their own wants. We can fancy them rubbing their eyes, and wondering if what they beheld was not all a dream. There around them, as if in some region of enchantment, were food and drink in abundance, with gold, silver, raiment, and valuables of every kind.

They were stunned with their good fortune, and wandered about from tent to tent, eating and drinking, and carrying out the good things they saw, to hide them. We can compare with the surprise of these lepers the joy of the soul on its first discovery of "the unsearchable riches of Christ" (Eph. iii. 8). How infinite, grand, and varied the provision found in him, the riches of salvation, the supply for spiritual wants, the treasures for the enrichment and beautification of the soul! and how wondrously and unexpectedly these burst upon the view when God "reveals his Son" in us (Gal. i. 16). At first the absorbing concern is for one's self—the engrossing thought is to appropriate what is necessary for our own life. But this stage, as in the case of the lepers, soon passes by, and gives place to another less selfish.

III. THE BRINGERS OF GOOD TIDINGS. 1. *Self-rebuke.* Four leprous men alone in that great camp, and a city near at hand perishing of hunger: it was a strange situation. The lepers themselves began to feel they were not acting rightly in delaying to carry the news of this astonishing plenty to their famine-stricken brethren. "We do not well," they said: "this is a day of good tidings, and we hold our peace." Does not every mind feel that their words were just? Would it not have been selfishness unspeakable had they continued to think only of themselves, and delayed to carry the good tidings to their friends in the city? Acting thus selfishly, might they not justly fear that some "mischief" would come upon them? And did they not at length do right in saying, "Now therefore come, that we may go and tell the king's household"? The application is obvious to our own duty as those who possess the saving knowledge of the true God, and of Jesus Christ his Son. "We do not well," if we withhold it from those who are perishing for lack of this knowledge (Hos. iv. 6). How many are in this condition! The whole heathen world, and ignorant multitudes are around us. "It is a day of good tidings:" shall we not make these good tidings known? "Freely ye have received, freely give" (Matt. x. 8). "Shall we whose souls are lighted," etc.? 2. *Bearing good news.* The lepers delayed no more, but hastened to the gate of the city, and told their wonderful story to the porter, who told it to others, who carried it to the king's house. Thus, from one to another, the news spread. It was not reckoned any drawback to it that they were lepers who brought it.—J. O.

Vers. 12—20.—*The good news verified.* The tidings brought by the lepers were so astounding that it was natural there should at first be some hesitation in acting on them. I. THE KING'S SUSPICIONS. Jehoram was roused in the night-time, but his mood was distrustful and desponding. He was convinced that the Syrians were but playing him a trick. Their apparent retreat was a piece of strategy to get the Israelites out into the plain. Then they would fall on them and destroy them. "I will now show you what the Syrians have done to us," etc. 1. *Distrust of man.* The suspicious disposition of the king accords with his general character. It has been noticed that Jehoram presents himself throughout the history as a man of moody, changeful, unreliable nature. "When the prophet leads the enemy into his hands without a blow, he becomes violent, and is eager to slaughter them all; then, however, he allows himself to be soothed, gives them entertainment, and permits them to depart in safety. At the siege of Samaria, the great distress of the city touches his heart. He puts on garments which are significant of grief and repentance, but then allows himself to be so overpowered by anger, that, instead of seeking the cause of the prevailing misery in his own apostasy and that of the nation, he swears to put to death, without delay, the man whom he had once addressed as 'father.' Yet this anger also is of short duration. He does not hear the promise of deliverance with scorn, as his officer does, but with hope and confidence. Then, again, when the promised deliverance is announced as actually present, he once more becomes doubtful and mistrustful, and his servants have to encourage him and push him on to a decision" (Bähr). It is shown by the present instance how a suspicious, distrustful disposition often outwits itself. One could not have blamed Jehoram for being cautious; but his habit of mind led him to go beyond caution, and to conclude for certain that the news brought was false, and that the Syrians were attempting a deception. Had he been left to himself, he would have rested in that conclusion, and inquired no further. Yet he was wrong, and the Syrians had actually fled. An excess of scepticism thus frequently leads those who indulge it astray. Jehoram was so accustomed to diplomacy, to intrigue, to strategy, that he thought of no other explanation of the facts related to him. By his moody unbelief he nearly missed the blessing. 2. *Distrust of God.* There was more than distrust of man in Jehoram's suspicions; there was likewise distrust of God. Had his attitude to God's promise, as conveyed through Elisha, been one of faith, he would at once have recognized that this which was told him was its fulfilment. He would have remembered Elisha's word; he would have perceived how precisely this report fitted into it; he would at least, before dismissing the lepers' story, have felt it his duty to consult Elisha, and ask him for his guidance. It was his unbelief which gave the dark tinge to his reflections. Are we not often guilty of similar distrust? We offer prayers, and, when the answer comes, we are astonished, and can hardly believe (Acts xii. 15, 16). Our unbelief darkens God's providence to us, and prevents us from seeing his gracious hand.

II. VERIFICATION OF THE FLIGHT. 1. *The servants' counsel.* The servants on this, as on other occasions, showed themselves wiser than their lord (Exod. x. 7; ch. v. 13). One of them gave him sound advice. The report they had received was, surely, at least worth inquiring into. Let him send some of the chariot-horses that remained (they were very few, and, like the remnant of the people of Israel, wasted with starvation, so that, at the worst, no greater evil could befall them than already existed), and let the charioteers bring word of the true state of the case. How many rash criticisms, hasty condemnations, unwise delays, would be avoided, if men would but act upon the principle "go and see"! The practical instincts are often sounder in the common people than in their lordly superiors. 2. *The king's messengers.* The king did as his servant suggested, and the chariots, two in number, were sent forth. The camp was found deserted, as the lepers had said, but, to make sure, the messengers continued their tour of inspection along the road leading to Jordan. The evidences of hasty flight were indubitable. "All the way was full of garments and vessels, which the Syrians had cast away in their haste." There was now no further doubt, so "the messengers returned, and told the king." They had seen, and believed: how much better had the king trusted the word of the Lord, and believed, though he had not seen (John xx. 29)! When men are fleeing for their lives, they willingly leave all behind them. It should moderate our sense of the value of earthly treasures when we see how, in an emergency, they are so little recked of. A day will come when the proudest and haughtiest would gladly part with all they have for a single smile from the face of him who sits upon the great white throne (Rev. vi. 15, 16; xx. 11). 3. *God's word fulfilled.* Thus it came about that, in a manner wholly unprecedented and unlooked for, the prediction of Elisha was fulfilled. The starving people found themselves set free from their besiegers, and, crowding out to the deserted tents, regaled themselves on the abundance of provision the Syrians had left. The store of the Syrian host was at their disposal, and a measure of fine flour was sold for a shekel, and two measures of barley for a shekel. "Wisdom is justified of her children" (Matt. xi. 19). Those are always found right at last who repose implicit trust in God's Word. Worldly men may laugh at them; rationalists will mock them; the astute in this world's affairs will count them hare-brained and foolish; but the event justifies them. The principle of verification holds as true in religion as in science. What we now accept in faith will ultimately be verified by sight. The difference between religion and science is that the latter refuses to act till it has received the verification (though even this is subject to qualification); the former trusts God, acts, and *awaits* the verification.

III. FATE OF THE MOCKER. There remained to be fulfilled the word which Elisha had spoken, that, though the king's officer who had scoffed at the promise should see the predicted plenty, he would not eat thereof. This word also was verified in a remarkable, but seemingly accidental, way. This officer was appointed to superintend the sale of provisions in the gateway, but the pressure of the frantic crowd was so great that he was trodden underfoot and died. How simply, yet how accurately, was the prophet's forecast fulfilled! 1. The incident is another evidence that even seeming "accidents" do not lie outside the providence of God. 2. It teaches men the folly and danger of mocking at God's Word. 3. It shows the certainty of God's threatenings being fulfilled. 4. It illustrates the end of the ungodly—*seeing* the fulfilment of God's promises of mercy, but not permitted to *enjoy.*—J. O.

EXPOSITION.

CHAPTER VIII.

Vers. 1—29.—THE SEQUEL OF THE STORY OF THE SHUNAMMITE. THE KILLING OF BENHADAD BY HAZAEL; AND THE WICKED REIGNS OF JEHORAM AND AHAZIAH IN JUDAH.

Vers. 1—15.—Elisha is still the *protagonistes* of the historical drama. The writer brings together in the present section two more occasions of a public character in which he was concerned, and in which kings also bore a part. One of the occasions is domestic, and shows the interest which Jehoram took in the miracles of the prophet, and in those who were the objects of them (vers. 1—6). The other belongs to Syrian, rather than to Israelite, history, and proves that the influence of Elisha was not confined to Palestine (vers. 7—15).

Vers. 1—6.—*The sequel of the story of the Shunammite.*

Ver. 1.—**Then spake Elisha unto the woman, whose son he had restored to life.** There is no "then" in the original, of which the simplest rendering would be, "And Elisha spake unto the woman," etc. The true sense is, perhaps, best brought out by the Revised Version, which gives the following : *Now Elisha had spoken unto the woman,* etc. The reference is to a time long anterior to the siege of Samaria. **Saying, Arise, and go thou and thine household, and sojourn wheresoever thou canst sojourn: for the Lord hath called for a famine.** A famine is mentioned in ch. iv. 38, which must belong to the reign of Jehoram, and which is probably identified with that here spoken of. Elisha, on its approach, recommended the Shunammite, though she was a woman of substance (ch. iv. 8), to quit her home and remove to some other residence, where she might escape the pressure of the calamity. He left it to her to choose the place of her temporary abode. The phrase, "God hath *called for* a famine," means no more and no less than "God has determined that there shall be a famine." With God to speak the word is to bring about the event. **And it shall also come upon the land seven years.** Seven years was the actual duration of the great famine which Joseph foretold in Egypt (Gen. xli. 27), and was the ideally perfect period for a severe famine (2 Chron. xxiv. 13). Many of the best meteorologists are inclined to regard the term of "seven years" as a cyclic period in connection with weather changes.

Ver. 2.—**And the woman arose, and did after the saying of the man of God.** It is a satisfaction to find that there was yet faith in Israel. There were still those to whom the prophet was the mouthpiece of God, who waited on his words, and accepted them as Divine commands whereto they were ready to render immediate and entire obedience. It is conjectured by some that the woman had become a widow, and fallen into comparative poverty; but the narrative gives no indication of this. Even opulent persons have to migrate in times of severe dearth. **And she went with her household, and sojourned in the land of the Philistines.** Philistia was a great grain country (Judg. xv. 5), and, though not altogether exempt from famine, was less exposed to it than either Judæa or Samaria. The soil was exceedingly fertile, and the vapours from the Mediterranean descended upon it in dews and showers, when their beneficial influence was not felt further inland. The Shunammite may have had other reasons for fixing her residence in the Philistine country; but probably she was chiefly determined in her choice by its proximity and its productiveness. **Seven years.** As long, *i.e.*, as the famine lasted (see the last clause of ver. 1).

Ver. 3.—**And it came to pass at the seven years' end, that the woman returned out of the land of the Philistines.** She stayed no longer than she could help. Her own land, where she could have the ministrations of a "man of God" (ch. iv. 23), was dear to her; and no sooner had the famine abated than she returned to it. **And she went forth to cry unto the king for her house and for her land.** During her prolonged absence, some grasping neighbour had seized on the unoccupied house and the uncultivated estate adjoining it, and now refused to restore them to the rightful owner. Widows were especially liable to such treatment on the part of greedy oppressors, since they were, comparatively speaking, weak and defenceless (see Isa. x. 2; Matt. xxiii. 14). Under such circumstances the injured party would naturally, in an Oriental country, make appeal to the king (comp. 2 Sam. xiv. 4; 1 Kings iii. 16; ch. vi. 26, etc.).

Ver. 4.—**And the king talked with Gehazi;** rather, *now the king was talking with Gehazi,* as in the Revised Version. The king, *i.e.*, happened to be talking with Gehazi at the moment when the woman came into his presence and "cried" to him. It has been reasonably concluded from this, that chronological order is not observed in the portion of the narrative which treats of

Elisha and his doings, since a king of Israel would scarcely be in familiar conversation with a leper (Keil). It may be added that Gehazi can scarcely have continued to be the servant of Elisha, as he evidently now was, after his leprosy. He must have dwelt "without the gate." **The servant of the man of God.** That a king should converse with a servant is, no doubt, somewhat unusual; but, as Bähr notes, there is nothing in the circumstance that need astonish us. It is natural enough that, having been himself a witness of so many of the prophet's marvellous acts done in public, Jehoram should become curious concerning those other marvellous acts which he had performed in private, among his personal friends and associates, with respect to which many rumours must have got abroad; and should wish to obtain an account of them from a source on which he could rely. If he had this desire, he could scarcely apply to the prophet himself, with whom he was at no time on familiar terms, and who would shrink from enlarging on his own miraculous powers. "To whom, then, could he apply with more propriety for this information than to the prophet's familiar servant"— an eye-witness of most of them, and one who would have no reason for reticence? Oriental ideas would not be shocked by the king's sending for any subject from whom he desired information, and questioning him. **Saying, Tell me, I pray thee, all the great things that Elisha hath done.** Miracles are often called "great things" (נְדֹלוֹת) in the Old Testament, but generally in connection with God as the doer of them (see Job v. 9; ix. 10; xxxvii. 5; Ps. lxxi. 19; cvi. 21, etc.).

Ver. 5.—**And it came to pass, as he was telling the king how he**—i.e. Elisha—**had restored a dead body to life.** This was undoubtedly the greatest of all Elisha's miracles, and Gehazi naturally enlarged upon it. As an eye-witness (ch. iv. 29—36), he could give all the details. **That, behold, the woman, whose son he had restored to life, cried to the king for her house and for her land.** The coincidence can scarcely have been accidental. Divine providence so ordered matters that, just when the king's interest in the woman was most warm, she should appear before him to urge her claim. At another time, Jehoram would, it is probable, have been but slightly moved by her complaint. Under the peculiar circumstances, he was deeply moved, and at once granted the woman the redress for which she asked. **And Gehazi said, My lord, O king, this is the woman, and this is her son, whom Elisha restored to life.** The Shunammite was accompanied by her son, now a boy of at least ten or eleven years old—the

actual object of Elisha's miracle. The king's interest in the woman would be still more roused by this circumstance.

Ver. 6.—**And when the king asked the woman, she told him;** rather, *and the king made inquiry of the woman, and she answered him.* The extent of the inquiries is not indicated. They may have included questions concerning the miracle, as well as questions concerning the woman's claim to the land and house, and the evidence which she could produce of proprietorship. **So the king appointed unto her a certain officer**— literally, *a certain eunuch,* or *chamberlain*— an officer of the court, who was in his confidence, and would give effect to his directions—**saying, Restore all that was hers, and all the fruits of the field since the day that she left the land, even until now.** The order was, that not only was the Shunammite to receive back her house and estate, but that she was also to have "the mesne profits"— *i.e.* the full value of all that the land had produced beyond the expense of cultivation during the seven years of her absence. English law lays down the same rule in cases of unlawful possession for which there is no valid excuse.

Vers. 7—15.—*Elisha's visit to Damascus, and its consequences.* It has been usual to connect this visit of Elisha's to Damascus with the commission given to Elijah many years previously, to anoint Hazael to be king over Syria (1 Kings xix. 16). But it is certainly worthy of remark that neither is Elijah authorized to devolve his commission on another, nor is he said to have done so, nor is there any statement in the present narrative, or elsewhere that Elisha anointed Hazael. It is therefore quite possible that Elisha's journey was wholly unconnected with the command given to Elijah. It may, as Ewald imagines, have been the consequence of disorders and dangers in Samaria, growing out of the divergence of views between Jehoram and the queen-mother Jezebel, who still retained considerable influence over the government; and Elisha may have taken his journey, not so much for the sake of a visit, as of a prolonged sojourn. That he attracted the attention both of Benhadad and of his successor Hazael is not surprising.

Ver. 7.—**And Elisha came to Damascus.** It was a bold step, whatever the circumstances that led to it. Not very long previously the Syrian king had made extraordinary efforts to capture Elisha, intending either to kill him or to keep him confined as a prisoner (ch. vi. 13—19). Elisha had subsequently helped to baffle his plans of conquest, and might be thought to have caused the disgraceful retreat of the Syrian army from the walls of Samaria, which he had certainly prophesied (ch. vii. 1). But Elisha was not afraid. He was probably *commissioned* to take his journey, whether its purpose was the anointing of Hazael or no. **And Benhadad the King of Syria was sick.** Ewald supposes that this "sickness" was the result of the disgrace and discredit into which he had fallen since his ignominious retreat, without assignable reason, from before the walls of Samaria; but Benhadad must have been of an age when the infirmities of nature press in upon a man, and when illness has to be expected. He was a contemporary of Ahab (1 Kings xx. 1), who had now been dead ten or twelve years. **And it was told him, saying, The man of God is come hither.** Elisha seems to have attempted no concealment of his presence. No sooner was he arrived than his coming was reported to Benhadad. The Syrians had by this time learnt to give him the name by which he was commonly known (ch. iv. 7, 21, 40; v. 20; vi. 6, 10; vii. 2, 18) in Israel.

Ver. 8.—**And the king said unto Hazael.** It is implied that Hazael was in attendance on Benhadad in his sick-room, either permanently as a chamberlain, or occasionally as a minister. According to Josephus ('Ant. Jud.,' ix. 4. § 6), he was "the most faithful of the king's domestics" (ὁ πιστότατος τῶν οἰκετῶν). We cannot presume from ver. 12 that he had as yet distinguished himself as a warrior. **Take a present in thine hand, and go, meet the man of God.** It was usual, both among the heathen and among the Israelites, for those who consulted a prophet to bring him a present (see 1 Sam. ix. 7; 1 Kings xiv. 3). Hence, mainly, the great wealth of the Delphic and other oracles. Naaman (ch. v. 5) had brought with him a rich present when he went to consult Elisha in Samaria. **And inquire of the Lord by him, saying, Shall I recover of this disease?** The miracles of Elisha had had at any rate this effect—they had convinced the Syrians that Jehovah was a great and powerful God, and made them regard Elisha himself as a true prophet. Their faith in their own superstitions must have been at least partially shaken by these convictions. It was by these and similar weakenings of established errors that the world was gradually educated, and the way prepared for the introduction of Christianity. There was very early among the Syrians a flourishing Christian Church.

Ver. 9.—**So Hazael went to meet him**—

i.e. **Elisha—and took a present with him;** literally, *in his hand;* but we must not press this expression. "In his hand" means "under his control." The present was far too large to be carried by an individual. It consisted **even of every good thing of Damascus**; *i.e.* of gold and silver and costly raiment, of the luscious wine of Helbon, which was the drink of the Persian kings (Strab., xv. 3. § 22), of the soft white wool of the Antilibanus (Ezek. xxvii. 18), of *damask* coverings of couches (Amos iii. 12), perhaps of Damascus blades, and of various manufactured articles, the products of Tyre, Egypt, Nineveh, and Babylon, which her extensive land trade was always bringing to the Syrian capital. **Forty camels' burden.** Not as much as forty camels could carry, but a gift of such a size that it was actually placed on the backs of forty camels, which paraded the town, and conveyed in a long procession to the prophet's house the king's magnificent offering. Orientals are guilty of extreme ostentation with respect to the presents that they make. As Chardin says, "Fifty persons often carry what a single one could have very well borne" ('Voyage en Perse,' vol. iii. p. 217). The practice is illustrated by the bas-reliefs of Nineveh and Persepolis, which furnish proofs of its antiquity. One present-bearer carries a few pomegranates; another, a bunch of grapes; a third, a string of locusts; a fourth,'two small ointment-pots; a fifth, a branch of an olive tree, and the like (Layard, 'Monuments of Nineveh,' second series, pls. 8, 9, etc.). It is not unlikely that a single camel could have carried the whole. **And came and stood before him, and said, Thy son Benhadad King of Syria hath sent me to thee, saying**—Benhadad seeks to propitiate Elisha by calling himself his son, thus indicating the respect he feels for him (comp. ch. vi. 21; xiii. 14)—**Shall I recover of this disease?** Nothing was more common in the ancient world than the consultation of an oracle or a prophet in cases of disease or other bodily affliction. Two questions were commonly asked, "Shall I recover?" and "How may I recover?" So Pheron of Egypt is said to have consulted an oracle with respect to his blindness (Herod., ii. 111), and Battus of Cyrene to have done the same with respect to his stammering (ibid., iv. 155). It was seldom that a clear and direct answer was given.

Ver. 10.—**And Elisha said unto him, Go, say unto him, Thou mayest certainly recover.** The existing Masoretic text (אָמַר־לֹא חָיֹה תִחְיֶה) is untranslatable, since *ĕmár-lo* cannot mean, "say not," on account of the order of the words; and *lo* cannot be joined with *khayíh thikhyah,* first on account of the makkeph which attaches it to *ĕmár,* and secondly because the emphatic infinitive is in itself affirmative, and does not admit of a negative prefix. The emendation in the Hebrew margin (לֹו for לֹא), accepted by all the versions, and by almost all commentators, is thus certain. Our translators are therefore, so far, in the right; but they were not entitled to tone down the strong affirmative, *khayih thikhyah*, "living thou shalt live," or "thou shalt surely live," into the weak potential, "thou mayest certainly recover." What Elisha says to Hazael is, "Go, say unto him, Thou shalt surely live;" *i.e.* "Go, say unto him, what thou hast already made up thy mind to say, what a courtier is sure to say, Thou shalt recover." **Howbeit the Lord hath showed me that he shall surely die.** If Hazael had reported the whole answer to Benhadad, he would have told no lie, and thus Elisha is not responsible for his lie.

Ver. 11.—**And he settled his countenance steadfastly**—literally, *and he settled his countenance and set it;* i.e. Elisha fixed on Hazael a long and meaning look—**until he**—*i.e.* Hazael—**was ashamed;** *i.e.* until Hazael felt embarrassed, and his eyes fell. It may be gathered that the ambitious courtier had already formed a murderous design against his master, and understood by the peculiar gaze which the prophet fixed upon him that his design was penetrated. **And the man of God wept.** There flashed on the prophet's mind all the long series of calamities which Israel would suffer at the hands of Syria during Hazael's reign, and he could not but weep at the thought of them (see the next verse).

Ver. 12.—**And Hazael said, Why weepeth my lord?** While inwardly contemplating an act of audacious wickedness in defiance of the prophet's implied rebuke, Hazael preserves towards him outwardly an attitude of extreme deference and respect. "**My lord**" was the phrase with which slaves addressed their masters, and subjects their monarchs (see ch. v. 3; vi. 12, etc.). **And he answered, Because I know the evil that thou wilt do unto the children of Israel: their strongholds wilt thou set on fire, and their young men wilt thou slay with the sword, and wilt dash their children, and rip up their women with child.** The prophet does not intend to tax Hazael with any special cruelty. He only means to say, "Thou wilt wage long and bloody wars with Israel, in which will occur all those customary horrors that make war so terrible—the burning of cities, the slaughter of the flower of the youth, the violent death of children, and even the massacre of women in a state of pregnancy. These horrors belonged, more or less, to all Oriental wars, and are touched on in Ps. cxxxvii. 9; ch.

xv. 16: Isa. xiii. 16, 18; Hos. x. 14; Nah. iii. 10; Amos i. 13, etc. The wars of Hazael with the Israelites are mentioned in ch. x. 32, 33; xiii. 3—7; and Amos i. 3, 4.

Ver. 13.—**And Hazael said, But what, is thy servant a dog, that he should do this great thing?** This rendering is generally allowed to be incorrect. The true sense, which is well represented in the Septuagint (Τίς ἐστιν ὁ δοῦλός σου, ὁ κύων ὁ τεθνηκὼς, ὅτι ποιήσει τὸ ῥῆμα τοῦτο;), is—"But what is thy servant, this dog, that he should do so great a thing?" Hazael does not accuse Elisha of making him out a dog in the future, but calls himself a dog in the present. "Dog" is a word of extreme contempt—"the most contemptuous epithet of abuse" (Winer), as appears, among other places, from 1 Sam. xxiv. 14 and 2 Sam. xvi. 9. Hazael means to say—How is it possible that he, occupying, as he does, so poor and humble a position as that of a mere courtier or domestic (οἰκέτης, Josephus), should ever wage war with Israel, and do the "great things" which Elisha has predicted of him? **And Elisha answered, The Lord hath showed me that thou shalt be king over Syria.** Elisha explains how it would be possible. Hazael would not continue in his poor and humble condition. Jehovah has revealed it to him that the mere courtier will shortly mount the Syrian throne.

Ver. 14.—**So he departed from Elisha, and came to his master; who said to him, What said Elisha to thee? And he answered, He told me that thou shouldest surely recover.** This, as already observed, was giving half Elisha's answer, and suppressing the other half. The *suppressio veri* is a *suggestio falsi;* and the suppression was Hazael's act, not Elisha's. Had Hazael repeated the whole of Elisha's answer—"Say unto him, Thou shalt surely recover; howbeit the Lord hath showed me that he shall surely die"—Benhadad might have been puzzled, but he would not have been deceived.

Ver. 15.—**And it came to pass on the morrow, that he took a thick cloth.** *Macber* is a cloth of a coarse texture—a mat, or piece of carpeting. It has here the article prefixed to it (*ham-macber*), which implies that there was but one in the sick-room. We may conjecture that it was a mat used as a sort of pillow, and interposed between the head-rest (so common in Egypt and Assyria) and the head (compare the *c'bir* of 1 Sam. xix. 13). **And dipped it in water.** The water would fill up the interstices through which air might otherwise have been drawn, and hasten the suffocation. A death of the same kind is recorded in the Persian history entitled 'Kholasat el Akhbar,' which contains (p. 162) the following passage: " The malik ordered that they should place a carpet on Abdallah's mouth, so that his life was cut off." And spread it on his face, so that he died. It has been supposed by some commentators, as Luther, Schultz, Geddes, Boothroyd, that Benhadad put the wet *macbêr* on his own face for refreshment, and accidentally suffocated himself; but this is very unlikely, and it is certainly not the natural sense of the words. As "Hazael" is the subject of "departed" and "came" and "answered" in ver. 14, so it is the natural subject of "took" and "dipped" and "spread" in ver. 15. Ver. 11 also would be unintelligible if Hazael entertained no murderous intentions. Why Ewald ('History of Israel,' vol. iv. p. 93, Eng. trans.) introduces a "bath-servant," unmentioned in the text, to murder Benhadad for no assignable reason, it is difficult to conjecture. And Hazael reigned in his stead. The direct succession of Hazael to Benhadad is confirmed by the inscription on the Black Obelisk, where he appears as King of Damascus (line 97) a few years only after Benhadad (*Bin-idri*) had been mentioned as king.

Vers. 16—24.—THE WICKED REIGN OF JEHORAM IN JUDAH. At this point the writer, who has been concerned with the history of the kingdom of Israel hitherto in the present book, takes up the story of the kingdom of Judah from 1 Kings xxii. 50, and proceeds to give a very brief account of the reign of Jehoshaphat's eldest son, Jehoram, or (by contraction) Joram. His narrative has to be supplemented from 2 Chron. xxi., which contains many facts not mentioned by the writer of Kings.

Ver. 16.—And in the fifth year of Joram the son of Ahab King of Israel, Jehoshaphat being then King of Judah; literally, *and of Jehoshaphat King of Judah*. The words are wanting in three Hebrew manuscripts, in some editions of the Septuagint, in the Peshito Syriac, in the Parisian Heptaplar Syriac, in the Arabic Version, and in many copies of the Vulgate. They cannot possibly have the sense assigned to them in our version, and are most probably a gloss which has crept into the text from the margin. Jehoram the son of Jehoshaphat King of Judah began to reign. Jehoram's reign was sometimes counted from the seventeenth year of his father, when he was given the royal title, sometimes from his father's twenty-third year, when he was associated, and sometimes from his father's

death in his twenty-fifth year, when he became sole king (see the comment on ch. i. 17 and ch. iii. 1).

Ver. 17.—Thirty and two years old was he when he began to reign; and he reigned eight years in Jerusalem. The eight years seem to be counted from his association in the kingdom by his father in his twenty-third year. He reigned as sole king only six years.

Ver. 18.—And he walked in the way of the kings of Israel, as did the house of Ahab; *i.e.* he introduced into Judah the Baal and Astarte worship, which Ahab had introduced into Israel from Phœnicia. (On the nature of this worship, see the 'Commentary on the First Book of Kings,' p. 374.) The "house of Ahab" maintained and spread the Baal-worship, wherever it had influence. Ahaziah, the son of Ahab, championed it in Israel (1 Kings xxii. 53); Jehoram, his brother, allowed its continuance (ch. x. 18—28); Jehoram of Judah was induced by his wife, Athaliah, the daughter of Ahab, to countenance it in Judæa; Athaliah, when she usurped the throne upon the death of her son Ahaziah, made it the state religion in that country. "Evil communications corrupt good manners." The alliance of the two separated kingdoms, concluded between Jehoshaphat and Ahab (1 Kings xxii. 2—4), had no tangible result beyond the introduction into Judah of the licentious and debasing superstition which had previously overspread the sister country. For the daughter of Ahab was his wife. In ver. 26 Athaliah, the wife of Jehoram, is called "the daughter of Omri;" but by "daughter" in that place must be meant "descendant" or "granddaughter." Athaliah has been well called "a second Jezebel." And he did evil in the sight of the Lord. The wicked actions of Jehoram are recorded at some length in Chronicles (2 Chron. xxi. 2—4, 11—13). Shortly after his accession he put to death his six brothers—Azariah, Jehiel, Zechariah, Ahaziah (?), Michael, and Shephatiah—in order to "strengthen himself." At the same time, he caused many of the "princes of Israel" to be executed. Soon afterwards he "made high places in the mountains of Judah, and caused the inhabitants of Jerusalem to commit fornication" (*i.e.* to become idolaters), "and compelled Judah thereto." That the idolatry which he introduced was the Baal-worship is clear, both from the present passage and from 2 Chron. xxi. 13.

Ver. 19.—Yet the Lord would not destroy Judah for David his servant's sake. The natural punishment of apostasy was rejection by God, and on rejection would, as a matter of course, follow destruction and ruin. God had declared by Moses, "If thou wilt not hearken unto the voice of the Lord thy God, to observe to do all his commandments and statutes, which I command thee this day; all these curses shall come upon thee. . . . The Lord shall send upon thee cursing, vexation, and rebuke, in all that thou settest thine hand unto for to do, *until thou be destroyed*, and until thou perish quickly; because of the wickedness of thy doings, whereby thou hast forsaken me. The Lord shall make the pestilence cleave unto thee, *until he have consumed thee from off the land*, whither thou goest to possess it. The Lord shall smite thee with a consumption, and with a fever, and with an inflammation, and with an extreme burning, and with the sword, and with blasting, and with mildew; and they shall pursue thee *till thou perish*. And thy heaven which is over thy head shall be brass, and the earth that is underneath thee shall be iron. . . . The Lord shall cause thee to be smitten of thine enemies; thou shalt go out one way against them, and flee seven ways before them: and thou shalt be removed into all the kingdoms of the earth. . . . Thou shalt become an astonishment, a proverb, and a byword, among all nations whither the Lord shall lead thee" (Deut. xxviii. 15—37). The apostasy of Jehoram, and of the nation under him, was calculated to bring about the immediate fulfilment of all these threats, and would have done so but for a restraining cause. God had made promises to David, and to his seed after him (2 Sam. vii. 13—16; Ps. lxxxix. 29—37, etc.), which would be unfulfilled if Judah's candlestick were at once removed. He had declared, "If thy children forsake my Law, and walk not in my statutes, . . . I will visit their offences with the rod, and their sin with scourges. Nevertheless my loving-kindness will I not utterly take away, nor suffer my truth to fail. My covenant will I not break, nor alter the thing that is gone out of my lips; I have sworn once by my holiness that I will not fail David." If he had now swept away the Jewish kingdom, he would have dealt more hardly with those who clave to David than with those that broke off from him. He would not have shown the "faithfulness" or the "mercy" which he had promised. He would have forgotten "the loving-kindnesses which he sware unto David in his truth" (Ps. lxxxix. 49). Therefore he would not—he *could* not —as yet "destroy Judah," with which, in point of fact, he bore for above three centuries longer, until at last the cup of their iniquities was full, and "there was no remedy." **As he promised him to give him alway a light, and to his children.** There is no "and" in the original. Translate—

As he promised him to give him always a light in respect of his children, and compare, for the promise of "a light" (1 Kings xi. 36; xv. 4; and Ps. cxxxii. 17).

Ver. 20.—**In his days Edom revolted from under the hand of Judah.** Edom had been conquered by Joab in the time of David, and had been treated with great severity, all the males, or at any rate all those of full age, having been put to death (1 Kings xi. 15, 16). On the death of David, Edom seems to have revolted under a prince named Hadad, and to have re-established its independence. It had been again subjected by the time of Jehoshaphat, who appointed a governor over it (1 Kings xxii. 47), and treated it as a portion of his own territories (ch. iii. 8). Now the yoke was finally thrown off, as had been prophesied (Gen. xxvii. 40). Edom became once more a separate kingdom, and was especially hostile to Judah. In the reign of Ahaz the Edomites "smote Judah" and carried away many captives (2 Chron. xxviii. 17). When the Chaldæans attacked and besieged Jerusalem, they cried, "Down with it, down with it, even to the ground!" (Ps. cxxxvii. 7). They looked on with joy at the capture of the holy city (Obad. 12), and "stood in the crossway, to cut off such as escaped" (Obad. 14). After the return from the Captivity, they were still Judah's enemies, and are especially denounced as such by the Prophet Malachi (i. 3—5). In the Maccabee wars, we find them always on the Syrian side (1 Macc. iv. 29, 61; v. 3; vi. 31; 2 Macc. x. 15, etc.), doing their best to rivet the hateful yoke of the heathen on their suffering brethren. As Idumæans, the Herodian family must have been specially hateful to the Jews. **And made a king over themselves.** The king mentioned in ch. iii. 9, 26 was probably a mere vassal king under Jehoshaphat.

Ver. 21.—**So Joram went over to Zair.** Naturally, Joram did not allow Edom to become independent without an attempt to reduce it. He invaded the country in full force, taking up a position at a place called Zair, which is not otherwise known. Zair (צָעִיר) can scarcely be Zoar (צֹעַר), which, wherever it was, was certainly not in Edom; and it is hardly likely to be a corruption of "Seir" (שֵׂעִיר), since the utterly unknown צעיר would scarcely be put by a copyist in the place of the well-known שׂעיר. Moreover, if Mount Seir were intended, it would probably have had the prefix הר, as in 1 Chron. iv. 42; 2 Chron. xx. 10, 22, 23; Ezek. xxxv. 2, 3, 7, 15. "Seir" alone is poetical rather than historical, especially in the language of the later books of the Old Testament. **And all the chariots with him;**

or, *all his chariots* (Revised Version). The
article has the force of the possessive
pronoun. **And he rose by night, and smote
the Edomites which compassed him about.**
Josephus understands the writer to mean
that Joram made his invasion by night, and
smote the Edomites on all sides ('Ant.
Jud.,' ix. 5. § 1); but it seems better to
suppose, with most modern commentators,
that the meaning is the following: Soon
after Joram invaded the country, he found
himself surrounded and blocked in by the
Edomite troops, and could only save himself
by a night attack, which was so far successful that he broke through the enemy's lines
and escaped; his army, however, was so
alarmed at the danger it had run, that it
at once dispersed and returned home. **And
the captains of the chariots;** *i.e.* the captains
of the Edomite chariots. They too were
"smitten," having probably taken the chief
part in trying to prevent the escape. **And
the people fled into their tents;** *i.e.* dispersed
to their homes. Compare the cry of Jeroboam (1 Kings xii. 16), "To your tents, O
Israel!"

Ver. 22.—**Yet Edom revolted;** rather, *and
Edom revolted;* or, *so Edom revolted.* Joram's
attempt having failed, the independence of
the country was established. **From under
the hand of Judah unto this day.** The
successes of Amaziah and Azariah against
Edom (ch. xiv. 7, 22) did not amount to
reconquests. Edom continued a separate
country, not subject to Judæa, and frequently at war with it, until the time of
John Hyrcanus, by whom it was subjugated.
"Unto this day" means, at the most, until
the time when the Books of Kings took
their present shape, which was before the
return from the Captivity. **Then Libnah
revolted at the same time.** Libnah was
situated on the borders of Philistia, in the
Shefelah, or low country, but towards its
eastern edge. Its exact position is uncertain; but it is now generally thought to
be identical with the modern *Tel-es-Safi,*
between Gath and Ekron, about long.
34° 50' E., lat. 31° 38' N. It had been an independent city, with a king of its own, in
the early Canaanite time (Josh. x. 30; xii.
15), but had been assigned to Judah (Josh.
xv. 42), and had hitherto remained, so far
as appears, contented with its position. Its
people can scarcely have had any sympathy
with the Edomites, and its revolt at this
time can have had no close connection with
the Edomite rebellion. Libnah's sympathies
would be with Philistia, and the occasion
of the revolt may have been the invasion
of Judæa by the Philistines in the reign of
Jehoram, of which the author of Chronicles
speaks (2 Chron. xxi. 16), and in which
Jehoram's sons were carried off.

Ver. 23.—**And the rest of the acts of Joram,
and all that he did, are they not written in
the book of the chronicles of the kings of
Judah?** Some of these acts are recorded in
our present Second Book of Chronicles;
e.g. his execution of his brothers and of
many nobles (2 Chron. xxi. 4); his erection
of high places (2 Chron. xxi. 11); his persecution of the followers of Jehovah (2 Chron.
xxi. 11); his reception of a writing from
Elisha, which, however, had no effect upon
his conduct (2 Chron. xxi. 12—15); his war
with the Philistines (2 Chron. xxi. 16) and
with the Arabs (2 Chron. xxi. 16); his loss
of all his sons but one during his lifetime;
his long illness, and his painful death
(2 Chron. xxi. 18, 19). But the 'Book of
the Chronicles of the Kings of Judah' was
a work on a larger scale than the extant
Book of Chronicles, and probably went into
much greater detail.

Ver. 24.—**And Joram slept with his
fathers.** Joram died after an illness, that
lasted two years, of an incurable disease of
his bowels. No "burning" was made for
him, and there was no regret at his death.
**And was buried with his fathers in the city
of David;** *i.e.* in the portion of Jerusalem
which David built; but, according to Josephus ('Ant. Jud.,' ix. 5. § 3) and the
author of Chronicles (2 Chron. xxi. 20), not
in the sepulchres of the kings. **And Ahaziah
his son reigned in his stead.** Ahaziah is
called "Jehoahaz" in 2 Chron. xxi. 17, by
an inversion of the two elements of his
name, and "Azariah" in 2 Chron. xxii. 6,
apparently by a slip of the pen.

Vers. 25—29.—**The Wicked Reign of
Ahaziah in Judah.** The writer continues
the history of Judah through another reign
—a very short one—almost to its close. He
describes the wickedness of Ahaziah, for the
most part, in general terms, attributes it to
his connection with the "house of Ahab,"
and notes his alliance with Joram of Israel
against the Syrians, and his visit to his
brother monarch at Samaria, which led on
to his death.

Ver. 25.—**In the twelfth year of Joram
the son of Ahab King of Israel.** In ch. ix.
29 the year of Ahaziah's accession is said
to have been Joram's *eleventh* year. It is
conjectured that he began to reign as viceroy to his father during his severe illness in
Joram's eleventh year, and became sole king
at his father's death in the year following.
**Did Ahaziah the son of Jehoram King of
Judah begin to reign;** *i.e.* begin to be full
king.

Ver. 26.—**Two and twenty years old was
Ahaziah when he began to reign.** The

writer of Chronicles says, "two and forty" (2 Chron. xxii. 2), which is absolutely impossible, since his father was but forty when he died (see ver. 17, and comp. 2 Chron. xxi. 5, 20). Even "two and twenty" is a more advanced age than we should have expected, since Ahaziah was the youngest of Jehoram's sons (2 Chron. xxi. 17); he must therefore have been born in his father's nineteenth year. Yet he had several elder brothers (2 Chron. xxi. 17; xxii. 1)! To explain this, we have to remember (1) the early age at which marriage is contracted in the East (twelve years); and (2) the fact that each prince had, besides his wife, several concubines. That Joram had several appears from 2 Chron. xxi. 17. **And he reigned one year in Jerusalem. And his mother's name was Athaliah, the daughter of Omri King of Israel.** There is something very remarkable in the dignity and precedence attached to Omri. He was, no doubt, regarded of a sort of second founder of the kingdom of Israel, having been the first monarch to establish anything like a stable dynasty. His "statutes" were looked upon as the fundamental laws of the kingdom, and were "kept" down to the time of its destruction (Micah vi. 16). Foreigners knew Samaria as *Beth-Khumri*, or "the house of Omri." He is the only Israelite king mentioned by name on the Moabite Stone (line 5), and the earliest mentioned in the inscriptions of Assyria. Even Jehu, who put an end to his dynasty, was regarded by the Assyrians as his descendant, and known under the designation of " Yahua, the son of Khumri" (Black Obelisk, epig. ii.). Athaliah, the daughter of Ahab, is called "the daughter of Omri," not only in the present passage, but also in 2 Chron. xxii. 2.

Ver. 27.—**And he walked in the way of the house of Ahab.** Compare what is said of Ahaziah of Israel in 1 Kings xxii. 52, 53, and of Jehoram of Judah in the present chapter (ver. 18). What is specially intended is that Ahaziah kept up the Baal-worship introduced by his father into Judah. **And did evil in the sight of the Lord, as did the house of Ahab: for he was the son-in-law of the house of Ahab ;** literally, *for he was related by marriage to the house of Ahab.* חתן is any relation by marriage, not " son-in-law " in particular (see Exod. iii. 1, and the comment on the place).

Ver. 28.—**And he went with Joram the son of Ahab to the war against Hazael King of Syria in Ramoth-Gilead.** Some translate, *and Joram himself went ;* but this is a very rare use of את, and one which would be unnatural in this place—for why "Joram himself," when "Joram" alone would have been quite sufficient?—and still more unnatural in 2 Chron. xxii. 5, where the same phrase occurs. It is best, therefore, to follow our translators, who are in accord both with the Septuagint and with the Vulgate. Ahaziah followed the example of his grandfather Jehoshaphat, who had accompanied Ahab to Ramoth-Gilead (1 Kings xxii. 29), to fight against the Syrians in the time of Benhadad. That the city was still disputed shows the importance which it possessed in the eyes of both parties. **And the Syrians wounded Joram.** It appears that Hazael, soon after his accession, with the ardour of a young prince anxious to distinguish himself, made an expedition against Ramoth-Gilead, which had been recovered by the Israelites between the death of Ahab and the time of which the historian is now treating. Joram went to the relief of the town with a large force, and, being received within the walls, maintained a gallant defence (ch. ix. 14), in the course of which he was wounded severely, though not fatally. Thereupon he and his brother king quitted the town and returned to their respective capitals, leaving a strong garrison in Ramoth-Gilead under Jehu and some other captains. Joram needed rest and careful nursing on account of his wounds, and Ahaziah would naturally withdraw with him, since he could not serve under a mere general.

Ver. 29.—**And King Joram went back to be healed in Jezreel.** Jezreel was more accessible from Ramoth-Gilead than Samaria. It lay in the plain, and could be reached without travelling over any rough or mountainous country. It was also the usual place to which the court retired for rest and refreshment—the Versailles or Windsor of Samaria, as it has been called. **Of the wounds which the Syrians had given him at Ramah, when he fought against Hazael King of Syria.** "Ramah" is another name for "Ramoth-Gilead" or "Ramoth in Gilead," which is the full name of the place. The word means "high," "elevated," and is cognate to *Aram.* **And Ahaziah the son of Jehoram King of Judah went down to see Joram the son of Ahab in Jezreel.** Ahaziah would probably take the route by way of Jericho, the Jordan valley, and the Wata el Jalud, and would consequently begin his journey by the rapid *descent* from Jerusalem to Jericho. **Because he was sick ;** *i.e.* unwell, wounded.

HOMILETICS.

Vers. 1—6.—"*All things work together for good to them that love God.*" The piety of the Shunammite had been sufficiently shown in the previous record left us of her (ch. iv. 8—37). The sequel of her story indicates how, in a wonderful way, events and circumstances seemingly fortuitous and unconnected work together for the advantage and happiness of one who lives virtuously, and seeks in all things to serve God and advance the cause of religion. "The series of incidents," it has been well said, "forms a marvellous web of Divine dispensations" (Bähr).

I. THE FAMINE. This lies at the root of the whole. If God had not ordained a famine upon the land—"called for it," and brought it about—none of the other incidents would have been possible. The woman would not have lost her property, would have had no occasion to "cry" to the king, and would have come into no personal contact either with him or with Gehazi.

II. THE PROPHET'S WARNING. The prophet, when so terrible a calamity as a seven years' famine impended over the land, might well have given all his thoughts to the general sufferings of the people, and have forgotten individuals. But God's providence determines otherwise. Elisha bethinks himself of the Shunammite, albeit she is but a unit in the vast mass of suffering humanity, and warns her of the coming evil, bidding her quit the land and sojourn elsewhere. This advice, which she follows, is the second link in the chain.

III. THE COINCIDENCE OF THE KING'S DESIRE TO LEARN MORE ABOUT ELISHA WITH THE RETURN OF THE WOMAN TO HER OWN LAND. It was, humanly speaking, a pure accident that the curiosity of the king with respect to Elisha happened to be aroused just as the famine was over, and the woman, having returned from Philistia into the land of Israel, found her estate occupied by another. It was another accident that she bethought herself of appealing to the king, instead of having recourse to any other remedy.

IV. THE COINCIDENCE OF GEHAZI BEING SPEAKING OF HER CASE EXACTLY AS SHE MADE HER APPEARANCE. Gehazi had scores of miracles to relate, and might have been discoursing of any one of them; but events were so ordered that it was of her child's resurrection that he was telling the king, and not of any other miracle, when she came into the royal presence. This coincidence it was which so interested the king in her, that he at once gave the order for restoring her estate to her.

We may learn from the entire narrative, (1) that our lives are divinely ordered; (2) that nothing happens to us by mere chance; (3) that events which seem to us, at the time when they happen, of the least possible importance, may be necessary links in the chain which Divine providence is forging for the ordering of our lives, and for the working out through them of the Divine purposes.

Vers. 7—9.—*The power of calamity to bend the spirit of the proud.* Benhadad had hitherto been an enemy of Jehovah and his prophets. He had sought Elisha's life (ch. vi. 13—20), and, when baffled in his design to seize his person, had made a bold attempt to crush and destroy the whole Israelite nation. But now God had laid his hand upon him; he was prostrated on a sick-bed; and lo! all was altered. The mighty monarch, so lately glorying in his strength, and, in his own opinion, infinitely above any *soi-disant* prophet, is brought down so low that, on hearing of Elisha's having come voluntarily to his capital, instead of seizing him, he sends him a humble embassy. Hazael, a high officer of the court, is bidden to "take a present in his hand, and go meet *the man of God*, and inquire of Jehovah by him—Will the king recover from his disease?" The present is a rich one, made by Oriental ostentation to appear even grander than it is in reality. Forty camels bear their burden to the prophet's door, and bring him "every good thing of Damascus," without let or stint. The great king calls himself Elisha's son—"Thy son Benhadad has sent me to thee" (ver. 9). Never was there a more complete reversal of human conditions. The hunted enemy is now felt to be the best friend; is courted, flattered, propitiated both by act and word. The proud king grovels in the dust, is content to be the prophet's son and servant, does him obeisance morally, and hangs upon his words as those of one with whom are the issues of life and death! And so it is with the proud and mighty generally. (1) A Pharaoh despises Jehovah, and asks, "Who is the Lord, that I should obey his voice and let Israel go? I know not the Lord, neither will I let Israel go" (Exod. v. 2); but in a little time the same Pharaoh has to rise up in the dead of the night, and to call for Jehovah's servants, Moses and Aaron, and to entreat them to go forth from among his people, both they and the children of Israel, and go, serve Jehovah, as they had said; also to take their flocks and their herds, as they had said, and to be gone; and to "*bless him also*" (Exod. xii. 31, 32). (2) An Ahab lets loose the dogs of persecution against the people of God, destroys the prophets of Jehovah, and sells himself to work evil in the sight of the Lord; but, when boldly rebuked and threatened with calamity, all his pride forsakes him, and he rends his clothes, and puts sackcloth upon his flesh, and fasts, and lies in sackcloth, and goes softly (1 Kings xxi. 27). (3) A Manasseh turns from God to worship Baal, and does after all the abominations of the heathen, and builds again the high places, and rears up altars for Baal, and uses witchcraft, and sets up a carved image in the house of God, and sheds innocent blood very much till he fills Jerusalem from one end to another (ch. xxi. 16), and does worse than the heathen whom the Lord destroyed before the children of Israel, even causing Isaiah (according to the tradition) to be sawn asunder; but calamity smites him, the captains of the host of the King of Assyria take him, and put hooks in his mouth, and chains upon his limbs, and carry him captive to Babylon to the King of Assyria—then all his pride falls away from him like a cast-off garment, and in his affliction he beseeches the Lord his God, and humbles himself greatly before the God of his fathers, and prays to him, and makes supplication, and is forgiven, and thenceforth serves Jehovah (2 Chron. xxxiii. 11—16). The pastor who has under his charge proud, tyrannical, oppressive persons, who scorn rebuke, and think to ride roughshod over their fellow-men, may wait with a good hope for the hour of sickness or calamity, which sooner or later, unless in the case of sudden death, comes to all. He will find the Benhadad of the sick-room a very different person from the Benhadad of the camp, or of the court, or of the mart, and one much more open to admonition. Hardness, stubbornness, self-reliance, can scarcely survive, when the weakness of decay and the helplessness of acute sickness have supervened. He need not despair, however cruel, oppressive, and injurious to others the man's earlier life may have been. If a Benhadad could humble himself, if an Ahab could repent and "go softly," if a Manasseh could turn to God and obtain pardon, there must be a possibility of repentance even for the most hardened sinners.

Vers. 10—15.—*Hazael and Elisha.* The contrast is striking between the two characters here brought for the first and last time into contact. In Hazael we have—

I. THE CRAFTY SCHEMER, cunning and treacherous, who sees in his master's calamity his own opportunity; who feels no gratitude for past favours, no pity for present weakness and suffering, no compunction at playing a double part; who has no horror of crime, no dread of the enduring infamy which attaches to the assassin and the traitor. Hazael is wise in a certain sense—he is clever, audacious, skilful in devising means to ends, secret, determined, unscrupulous. He contrives a mode of death which will leave no trace of violence, and may appear accidental, if suspicion arises that it has not happened in the ordinary course of nature.

II. THE MAN OF BLOOD. Hazael is altogether cruel and unsparing. He reaches the throne through blood. As king, he deluges Israel in blood, "cutting the nation short, and smiting them in all their coasts" (ch. x. 32); "destroying them, and making them like the dust by threshing" (ch. xiii. 7). We must view him as a born soldier, never so happy as when engaged in a campaign, now resisting the attacks of Assyria on his northern border ('Ancient Monarchies,' vol. ii. p. 364), now attacking the Philistines (ch. xii. 17), almost constantly warring with his immediate neighbours the kings of Israel, once even threatening Judah, and "setting his face to go up to Jerusalem" (ch. xii. 17) in the hope of taking it.

III. THE SUCCESSFUL WARRIOR. Hazael succeeded in repulsing the Assyrians, and maintaining his independence, notwithstanding all their efforts to conquer him. He reduced Israel to a species of semi-subjection (ch. xiii. 7). He compelled even Judæa to purchase peace at his hands (ch. xii. 18). He was, on the whole, the most warlike of all the early kings of Syria; and, though he suffered one great defeat at the hands of the Assyrian king, Shalmaneser II., yet he issued from the struggle unsubdued, and left his dominions intact to his son and successor, Benhadad III.

In Elisha, on the other hand, we have—

I. THE WISE, CLEAR-SIGHTED, SINGLE-MINDED, HONEST ADVISER. Elisha has no cunning, no art, no special cleverness. But he can read character; he can see through Hazael's designs. Whether king, or noble, or common person applies to him for advice, he uses the same simplicity, counsels each as seems to him for the best, and seeks to gain nothing for himself by the advice which he gives them. His plainness offends Naaman (ch. v. 12); his firmness enrages Jehoram (ch. vi. 31); his penetration disconcerts Hazael (ch. viii. 11); but he cares nothing how men may receive his words. It is a Divine message that he delivers, and deliver the message he must and will, in simple plain language, whether men will hear or whether they will forbear.

II. THE MAN OF PEACE. Elisha's character is eminently peaceful and conciliatory. He weeps at the thought of those horrors which war causes almost of necessity (ch. viii. 11). Once only do his counsels lead on to an engagement (ch. iii. 16—24); mostly he contrives that perils shall be averted without the shedding of blood (ch. vi. 18—22; vii. 6—15). He will not allow the prisoners that he has made to be put to death, or in any way ill treated (ch. vi. 22, 23). He seeks to check Hazael's murderous propensities by a look which he cannot misunderstand (ch. viii. 11).

III. THE PROPHET AND TEACHER. The office of the prophet was to rebuke sin, as Elisha did (ch. iii. 13, 14), to sustain faith, to train up fresh prophets, to teach the faithful (ch. iv. 23), to announce God's will to king and people, and to execute commissions with which God specially entrusted him. Elisha never failed in the performance of any of these duties. Cast upon a dark time, when a debasing superstition, imported from a foreign country, had full possession of the court and had laid a strong hold upon the country, he faithfully upheld Jehovah and Jehovah's laws before backsliding kings and "a disobedient and gainsaying people." To Elisha principally it was owing that true religion still maintained itself in the land against the persecutions of Jezebel and her sons, and that, when the dynasty of Omri came to an end, there was still a faithful remnant left, which had not bowed the knee to Baal, but had clung to Jehovah under all manner of difficulties. If Elisha left no *great* prophet to succeed him, it was probably because great men are not made to order, and God's providence did not see fit to continue the succession of first-rate prophetical teachers, which had been raised up to meet the extreme danger of the introduction and maintenance of a false state religion by apostate kings.

When two such characters are brought into contact, the natural result is mutual repulsion. Hazael is ashamed that Elisha should read him so well; and Elisha weeps when he thinks of the woes that Hazael will inflict upon Israel. Outward respect is maintained; but the two must have felt, when they parted, that they were adversaries for life, bent on opposite courses, with opposed principles, aims, motives; not only the servants of different gods, but antagonistic in their whole conception of life and its objects, sure to clash if ever they should meet again, and, even if they should not meet, sure to be ever working for different ends, and engaged in thwarting one the other.

Vers. 16—27.—*The power of bad women for evil.* All the evil wrought, all the irreligion, all the licentiousness and depravity, and almost all the misery suffered during the reigns of Ahab, Ahaziah, and Jehoram in Israel, and of Jehoram and Ahaziah in Judah, were caused by the machinations and influence of two wicked women—Jezebel and her daughter Athaliah. Jezebel, a proud imperious woman, born in the purple, a "king's daughter," and extraordinarily strong-minded and unscrupulous, obtained a complete ascendancy over the weak and unstable Ahab, and must be viewed as the instigator of all his wicked actions. With Ahab's connivance, she "slew the prophets of the Lord," persecuted the faithful, set up the worship of Baal and Ashtoreth in Samaria, introduced into Israel the unchaste rites of the Dea Syra and of Adonis, threatened the life of Elijah and drove him into banishment, contrived the judicial murder of Naboth, and imparted to Ahab's reign that character of licentiousness and bloody cruelty which gives it its sad pre-eminence above all others in the black list of Israel's monarchs. Nor did Jezebel's evil influence stop here. She outlived her husband by some thirteen years, and during that period was the evil genius of her two sons, Ahaziah and Jehoram. Ahaziah she completely perverted (ch. xxii. 52, 53). Over Jehoram she had less influence; but to her we must ascribe it that during his reign the Baal-worship continued in the capital (ch. x. 25—27) and in the country districts (ch. x. 21), though he himself took no part in it (ch. iii. 2). Athaliah, though without the strength of mind and will which characterized her mother, resembled her, as a faint *replica* resembles a strongly painted portrait. Married to Jehoram of Israel, a weak prince, she had little difficulty in establishing her ascendancy over him, and becoming his chief adviser and counsellor (ver. 18). It was under her direction that Jehoram "made high places in the mountains of Judah, and caused the inhabitants of Jerusalem to commit fornication, and compelled Judah thereto" (2 Chron. xxi. 11), or, in other words, established the Baal-worship in Judah and Jerusalem, and forced the inhabitants to embrace it. Over Ahaziah, her son, who was but two and twenty at his accession, her influence was naturally greater. He seems to have been a mere puppet in her hands (2 Chron. xxii. 3—5). With a boldness worthy of her mother, Athaliah, on the death of her son Ahaziah, murdered all his half-brothers, and seized the sovereign power, which she held for six years—a unique feature in the history of the Jews. The Baal-worship was now made to supersede the worship of Jehovah in the temple on Mount Zion, and Mattan, the chief of Baal, was installed in the place previously occupied by the Aaronic high priest (2 Chron. xxiii. 17). Jehovah-worship was forbidden, persecuted, and probably ceased, except in secret; and the kingdom of Judah was, so far as appearances went, apostate. Such were the evils wrought by these two ambitious and wicked women. The history of the world, though it can furnish no exact parallels, has many cases more or less similar. Semiramis may be a myth, but Queen Hatasu in Egypt, Queens Atossa and Parysatis in Persia, Olympias in Greece, Messalina and Poppæa Sabina in Rome, Catharine de Medici, and Catherine Empress of Russia, in modern Europe, were women equally imperious, equally determined, and the prolific causes of equal mischief. It would seem that, in the female nature, where the natural impulses are so largely towards good, if these are perverted and Satan allowed the mastery, there is no longer any let or restraint; the passions become ungovernable, the will as iron, the heart hard and unrelenting; evil has unresisted sway, and the result is something even more fearful and terrible than the wickedness of the worst man. *Corruptio optimi pessima.* Woman's function in the world is to be soft and tender, to smooth down man's roughnesses, to pacify and soothe and mitigate; if she abnegates these functions, and assumes the man's duties of ruling and repressing and bending to her will the stubborn necks of others, she runs counter to her proper nature, and becomes a monstrosity. There is no saying to what lengths of profligacy, cruelty, and other wickedness she may not go. She is worse than a wild beast, and may do infinitely more evil. She may utterly corrupt a society, or she may deluge with blood a continent. She may ruin the country to which she belongs and bring its fairest provinces to desolation. She may stir up hatreds, set class against class, and cause a civil war that shall cost the lives of hundreds of thousands. The only security against all this mischief is for woman not to desert her sphere, but to remain within it, working for God, and doing the good which she was designed to do.

HOMILIES BY VARIOUS AUTHORS.

Vers. 1—6.—*The Shunammite's land restored.* The Bible has a good deal to say about the land question. There is one memorable passage in Isaiah (v. 8): "Woe unto them that join house to house, that lay field to field, till there be no place, that they may be placed alone in the midst of the earth!" There is another memorable passage in the Epistle of St. James: "Behold, the hire of the labourers who have reaped down your fields, which is of you kept back by fraud, crieth: and the cries of them which have reaped are entered into the ears of the Lord God of Sabaoth." If such denunciations of oppression and wrong had been remembered, we should have had less of socialistic combinations and less of agrarian crime. In this passage we have—

I. A COMMAND OBEYED. Elisha's command seemed a hard one. This woman of

Shunem was to arise with her household, and leave her home and farm for seven years. He told her, indeed, that there was to be a famine in the land. But she might have wanted more proof. She might have said, " Well, I shall wait till I see some signs of the famine. It is a great hardship to have to get up in this way and leave my home, without any immediate reason. What if Elisha's fears should turn out to be untrue? May not the famine be as bad anywhere else ? " So men often reason when God gives them some command or points out to them the way of salvation. Lot lingered, when urged to depart out of Sodom, though the very angels of God had come to warn him of his doom. So men linger still, when urged to flee from the wrath to come. They linger, though every day is bringing them nearer to eternity. They linger, though they know not the day nor the hour when the Son of man may come. Whether it be the path of salvation or the path of Christian service which God calls us to tread, let us not linger, let us not hesitate to obey, but, like this woman of Shunem, let us do at once what God commands.

II. LOSS INCURRED. This woman actually did suffer by her prompt obedience. She escaped the famine, indeed, but she lost her land. On this subject Dr. Thomson says, in 'The Land and the Book,' "It is still common for even petty sheikhs to confiscate the property of any person who is exiled for a time, or who moves away temporarily from his district. Especially is this true of widows and orphans, and the Shunammite was now a widow. And small is the chance to such of having their property restored, unless they can secure the mediation of some one more influential than themselves. The conversation between the king and Gehazi about his master is also in perfect keeping with the habits of Eastern princes; and the appearance of the widow and her son so opportunely would have precisely the same effect now that it had then. Not only the *land*, but all the *fruits of it* would be restored. There is an air of genuine verisimilitude in such simple narratives which it is quite impossible for persons not intimately familiar with Oriental manners to appreciate, but which stamps the incidents with undoubted certainty." *We may incur loss from a worldly point of view by obeying a command of God.* But which do we prefer—worldly gain or a conscience at peace with God ? Which loss is greater—the loss of a few pounds, or the loss of our heavenly Father's smile ? Even if we do lose by it—it is best to do the will of God, to follow in the footsteps of Jesus.

III. QUESTIONS ASKED. We are not told what led to this remarkable conversation which Jehoram had with Gehazi. Perhaps the time of famine had humbled him. Perhaps he was becoming penitent for his threat of taking Elisha's life. Perhaps it was mere idle curiosity. But at any rate, here is the King of Israel inquiring of Gehazi, " Tell me, I pray thee, all the great things that Elisha hath done." Gehazi, at this time, loved to think and speak of Elisha. He had been a good master to him. His deeds were worth recording. And so Gehazi proceeds to tell the story of Elisha's mighty deeds. 1. *We ought to be ready to answ*. *questions about our Master.* They may proceed from curiosity, from wrong motives. Never mind. Our answer, given in a Christian spirit, may be the means of disarming ridicule. It may be an opportunity for us to tell the old, old story of the cross. 2. *We ought not to be ashamed of our Master.* He is " the chiefest among ten thousand . . . and altogether lovely." His Name is above every name. The Name, the life, the works, the words, of Jesus ought to be a favourite theme with us.

IV. RESTITUTION MADE. When God's time comes, how very easily he can fulfil his purposes ! Gehazi had just reached that part of his story where Elisha restored the Shunammite's son to life, when, to his astonishment and delight, the Shunammite herself appeared on the scene. She came with her petition to the king that he would cause her house and land to be restored. Gehazi, not, perhaps, very regardful of courtesy or etiquette, calls out in the fulness of his joy, " My lord, O king, this is the woman, and this is her son, whom Elisha restored to life." The king, whose feelings had already been touched by the pathetic narrative of the little lad carried home from the harvest-field to die, touched also by the entreaty of the woman for the restoration of her lost property, and perhaps recognizing the hand of Providence in the remarkable events of that day, gives orders that not only her land, but the fruits of it from the day she left, should be restored to her. That was wholesale restoration and restitution. Who shall say it was unjust? What a disgorging there would be, if all who have taken money or land from others by unlawful means, all who have extorted unjust rents, were compelled to restore their ill-gotten gains! The Shunammite had not suffered, after all, by her obedience. "No one hath forsaken houses, or lands, or father, or mother, or friends, . . . but he shall receive an hundredfold more in this life, and in the world to come life everlasting."—C. H. I.

Vers. 7—15.—*Elisha, Hazael, and Benhadad.* The present interview between Elisha and Hazael arose out of Benhadad's illness. Benhadad heard that Elisha had come to Damascus, and he sent Hazael to inquire of the Lord by him if he would recover of his disease. It is wonderful how ready men are to forsake God when they are well, and to seek his help when they are in sickness or trouble. When he was well, the King of Syria "bowed himself in the house of Rimmon," but now, in his time of weakness and anxiety about his life, he sends to inquire of the God of Israel. Elisha's answer to Benhadad's question was evidently an enigma. "Go, say unto him, Thou mayest certainly recover: howbeit the Lord hath showed me that he shall surely die." Elisha looked steadfastly into Hazael's face. Did Hazael understand the enigma or not? Why, then, are such signs of confusion in his face? Why does his eye fail to meet the prophet's gaze? Why does his cheek grow pale? Why that uneasy twitching of the mouth? Yes. Elisha's suspicions—and perhaps also the hints which God had given him—are confirmed. It was true that Benhadad *might* recover. His illness was not mortal. And yet his death was certain, and Hazael's conscience told him that he was already a murderer in his heart. As Elisha thinks of all the trouble and suffering that shall come upon Israel through Hazael's instrumentality, he can no longer restrain his feelings. He bursts into tears. When Hazael asks him why he weeps, it is then that the prophet tells him all the cruelties which he will perpetrate upon God's people. This tale of horrors called forth the question from Hazael, "What is thy servant, this dog, that he should do this great thing?" It was only then that Elisha showed him that he knew that murder was already in his mind. He quietly says, "Behold, the Lord hath showed me that thou shalt be king over Syria." Hazael then went back to Benhadad, and gave him an answer very different from that which Elisha had really given to him. Instead of giving him the whole message, he gives him merely a part, tells him that he shall recover, omits that it has been revealed to the prophet that he shall surely die. *The morrow came; and on the morrow Hazael was a murderer.* Despite all his protestations of weakness and inability to do "great things," he—the king's trusted servant—betrays his master's confidence and takes away his life. Taking a thick cloth and dipping it in water, he spread it upon the king's face, either when he was asleep, or under pretext of cooling and refreshing him, so that the breathing was stopped and the king died. Terrible succession of falsehood, treachery, and murder. We learn from this incident—

I. THE POSSIBILITIES OF EVIL IN THE HUMAN HEART. Many persons deny the depravity of human nature. They deny the story of the Fall. They object to such ideas, and regard them as theological dogmas, and the mere creations of narrow, hard, illiberal minds. But these truths of the fall of man and the depravity of human nature are something more than theological dogmas. They are facts of experience—painful, indeed, and humiliating to human pride, but facts nevertheless. And here it may be stated that to believe in the fall of man and the depravity of human nature is quite consistent with the deepest human sympathy and love. To believe in the possibilities of evil that there are in the human heart is quite consistent with believing in its great possibilities of good. The Bible, which teaches man's fall, teaches also that man was made in the image of God, and that it is possible yet for that lost and faded image to be restored. The Bible, which tells man that he is a sinner, helpless, condemned, perishing, tells him also that, in the infinite mercy of that God against whom he has sinned, a way of salvation has been provided; that the Saviour is the Son of God himself; that we may have "redemption through his blood, even the forgiveness of sins;" and that "whosoever believeth on him shall not perish, but have everlasting life." It is *for our own good* that we should know what possibilities of evil there are in the unregenerate heart. What use is it to say, "Peace! peace!" when there is no peace? What avails it for the watchman to cry, "All's well!" if the enemy are not only at the gates, but actually within the city? He who would help men to do the right and overcome the wrong must faithfully point out to them the possibilities of evil that are within their own heart. Who that knows human nature, that knows the facts of history, can doubt that such possibilities exist? Look at Hazael, hitherto the faithful, trusted servant, stooping over the bedside of his master, and calmly and deliberately taking away his life. He had the ambition to be King of Syria, and he wades to the throne through his master's blood. Who that knows what crimes men will commit when under the influence of covetousness, intemperance, hatred, or some other passion— men who otherwise would have shrunk from the very mention of such acts—can doubt the possibilities of evil within the human heart? *There are possibilities of evil even in good men.* The old nature is not taken away. "When I would do good," said St. Paul, "evil is present with me, so that how to perform that which is good I find not." "For I see a law in my members, warring against the law of my mind, and bringing me into captivity to the law of sin." What, then, is the difference between a Christian and an unregenerate man? There are possibilities of evil in them both, but the Christian strives against the evil, whereas the unregenerate man yields to sin and loves it. The Christian may fall, but if so, he is filled with penitence. The Christian will have his faults, but, if so, he acknowledges them and seeks help to forsake them. "Faults!" says Thomas Carlyle, in his lectures on 'Hero-Worship,' "the greatest of faults is to be conscious of none." Yes; there are possibilities of evil, there are actualities of evil, in the best of men. Christ might still say to an assembly of even his own disciples, "Let him that is without sin cast the first stone at a fallen sister or an erring brother."

II. The DANGER OF IGNORING THESE POSSIBILITIES. Hazael did not become a murderer all at once. The old Latin saying is, *Nemo repente fit turpissimus*—"No one becomes suddenly very wicked." It is true. Perhaps a few years before this if any one had told Hazael that he would be a murderer, he would have been highly indignant. Even now he asks, "What is thy servant, this dog, that he should do this great thing?" It is uncertain whether this exclamation of Hazael refers only to Elisha's prophecy about the cruelties he would perpetrate on Israel, or whether it refers also to the suggestion of Elisha that he was to be the murderer of Benhadad. If it refers to the murder of the king, then the exclamation would express surprise at the idea of his venturing to lift his hand against his master. If it only refers to the subsequent cruelties which he was to commit, it shows in any case that Hazael did not know of what he was capable. Shakespeare's representation of Brutus when meditating the murder of Julius Cæsar, to which he had been incited by other conspirators, throws light upon Hazael's feelings.

> "Since Cassius first did whet me against Cæsar
> I have not slept.
> Between the acting of a dreadful thing
> And the first motion, all the interim is
> Like a phantasma, or a hideous dream:
> The genius and the mortal instruments
> Are then in council; and the state of a man,
> Like to a little kingdom, suffers then
> The nature of an insurrection."

It is, indeed, a dangerous thing to tamper with temptation. There is that affinity between the evil which is in our own heart and the temptations which are without, that there is between the gunpowder and the spark. It is wisdom to keep the sparks away. It is wisdom to keep away from the temptation.

> "Vice is a monster of so hideous mien,
> As, to be hated, needs but to be seen;
> Yet, seen too oft, familiar with her face,
> We first endure, then pity, then embrace."

It is "fools" who make a mock at sin. It is a foolish thing to make light of the guilt of sin in God's sight. It is a foolish thing to make light of the power of sin in our own hearts. "Lead us not into temptation."

III. There is only one SAFEGUARD AGAINST THESE EVIL TENDENCIES IN OUR OWN HEARTS: THAT SAFEGUARD IS THE GRACE OF GOD. Of the power of that grace Hazael knew nothing. Temptation upon temptation came crowding into his mind. *The first was the great ambition to be king.* He has yielded to that long since. It has taken complete possession of his mind. Then there came *the temptation to carry a false message to his master,* who had reposed such confidence in him. He yielded to that. Then there came *the temptation to take away his master's life.* It was a strong one, no doubt. There was but that weak, helpless king, upon a bed of sickness, between him and the throne. One little act, which no one would suspect, and the object of his ambition would be attained. But if he had resisted the other temptations, this one might never have assailed him at all, or, if it had, he would easily have resisted it. *The reason of his fall was the want of a sufficient force within.* We need something more than human to conquer the Satanic power of sin.

> " What but thy grace can foil the tempter's power?"

Hazael had *no restraining power* to check his own evil tendencies, *no resisting power* to stop the temptation at the door, ere it entered and took possession of his heart. He seems to have had a feeling of shame, as when he became confused before Elisha's steady glance. But shame, by itself, with no other superior influence to sustain it, is easily vanquished. Lust, covetousness, ambition, intemperance,—every one of these is able to put shame to flight. The *immoral* man—he has long since trampled on shame. The miser, the *covetous* man—he will stop at nothing that will increase his possessions. The *ambitious* man—he will not allow shame to hinder him in the desire for power and place. The *drunkard*—shame has long since ceased in his besotted mind; no blush is seen upon his bloated face. No; if we are to resist evil, if we are to conquer sin, it must be in some power stronger than poor human nature can supply. Hazael did not know that power. He trusted in his own sense of shame, in his own sense of what was right, and that failed him. He who had said, "What is thy servant, this dog, that he should do this great thing?" on the morrow took his master's life. Contrast Hazael's exclamation with Joseph's when he was tempted : "How can I do this great wickedness, and sin *against God?*" Ah! there was something there to which Hazael was a stranger. There was the personal presence of a personal God; there was the fear of offending that holy God; there was the fear of grieving that loving heavenly Father who had watched over Joseph when his brethren had forsaken him, and who had provided for all his wants. Hazael's feeling is more like that of Peter, "Though all men forsake thee, yet will not I"—the expression of wounded pride, of boastful self-security. Yet Peter fell into the very sin of which he had expressed such horror only a few hours before. It is not such self-confidence, but a humble feeling of our own weakness and an attitude of entire dependence upon God, that will really keep the door barred against temptation.

One or two practical applications. 1. *Be on your guard against the beginnings of evil.* If you yield to one temptation, no matter how small and insignificant it may be, others are sure to follow in its wake. 2. *Be charitable toward the faults and failings of others.* When we know what possibilities of evil there are in our own hearts, how can we have the presumption to sit in judgment upon others? If others have fallen and we are secure, perhaps it was because we were not exposed to the same temptations. We are to consider ourselves, lest we also be tempted. 3. If you have not yet experienced the forgiveness that is in Christ Jesus and the power of Divine grace, *seek them now!* Let it be your earnest prayer, "Create in me a clean heart, O God, and renew a right spirit within me." If you would be safe from the possibilities of evil that are in your own heart, and from the temptations of a godless world, then your prayer should be now and always, "Lead me to the Rock that is higher than I."—C. H. I.

Vers. 1—6.—*Topics for reflection.* "Then spake Elisha unto the woman, whose son he had restored to life," etc. In these verses we have an illustration of the reward of kindness, the ignorance of royalty, and the influence of godliness.

I. THE REWARD OF KINDNESS. "Then spake Elisha unto the woman, whose son he had restored to life, saying, Arise, and go thou and thine household, and sojourn where-soever thou canst sojourn : for the Lord hath called for a famine; and it shall also come upon the land seven years. And the woman arose, and did after the saying of the man of God: and she went with her household, and sojourned in the land of the Philistines seven years." Through Elisha this Shunammite woman obtained three great favours: (1) the restoration of her son (ch. iv.); (2) direction for herself and family to leave their old home during the seven years' famine; and then, when she returned from the land of the Philistines, where she had sojourned seven years; (3) the restoration of her old home, which had either fallen into the hands of covetous persons, or been confiscated to the crown (ver. 6). These are confessedly signal favours; but why were they rendered? Undoubtedly on account of the kindness which this woman had manifested to Elisha, as recorded in the fourth chapter (vers. 8—10). She had shown him great hospitality, built a chamber for him in her own house, furnished it, and boarded and lodged him for a considerable time. Here, then, is the *reward of kindness*. Observe: 1. *Kindness should always awaken gratitude*. The very consti- tution of the human soul and the moral laws of God as revealed in Christ show this. Yet, alas! so far away has the human soul gone from its pristine state that real grati- tude for favours is somewhat rare. So much so, indeed, that it often turns out that the person on whom you bestow the greatest favours turns out to be your opponent and foe. Seneca has truly said that "were ingratitude actionable, there would not be in the whole world courts enough to try the causes in." So common is it that it is almost a maxim that, if you would alienate a man from you, you should bestow on him favours. Shakespeare has compared it to the cuckoo—

> "The hedge-sparrow fed the cuckoo so long
> That it had its head bit off by its young."

2. *Gratitude will always requite favours*. The man who receives favours without some practical acknowledgment is an ingrate. "A man," says L'Estrange, "may as well refuse to deliver up a sum of money that is left him in trust, without a suit, as not to return a good office without asking."

> "He that has nature in him must be grateful;
> 'Tis the Creator's primary great law,
> That links the chain of beings to each other,
> Joining the greater to the lesser nature,
> Trying the weak and strong, the poor and powerful,
> Subduing men to brutes, and even brutes to men."
>
> (Madan.)

II. THE IGNORANCE OF ROYALTY. When the Shunammite woman had returned from the land of the Philistines, she made application to the king for the restoration "of her house and for her land," whereupon "the king talked with Gehazi the servant of the man of God, saying, Tell me, I pray thee, all the great things that Elisha hath done." Now, mark the ignorance of this King of Israel. He was so ignorant of Elisha—the man who had been working such wonders in his country, delivering such sublime truths, and rendering such high service to the state, that he here inquires of the prophet's servant concerning him. "It was to his shame," says Matthew Henry, "that he needed now to be informed of Elisha's works, when he might have acquainted himself with them as they were being done by Elisha himself." Shame! that kings should be ignorant of the morally best and greatest men in their kingdom! Yet they have always been so, especially if the men, as in Elisha's case, lived in poverty. They know all about the moral pigmies that live in splendid palaces, bear high-sounding titles, are lords of castles, and owners of broad acres. Such, they not only know, but will honour with their visits, consort with them, shoot with them, etc. But to go into the obscure home of a truly great man who blesses the country with his soul- quickening thoughts, and holds fellowship with Heaven, they would no more think of doing, than of travelling to the moon. Will it be always thus? Heaven forbid!

III. THE INFLUENCE OF GODLINESS. When the king heard from Gehazi what Elisha had done, "his majesty" (as we say) granted the woman her request. "And when the king asked the woman, she told him. So the king appointed unto her a certain officer, saying, Restore all that was hers, and all the fruits of the field since the day that she left the land, even until now." It was the involuntary influence of Elisha that disposed the monarch to do all this. Who shall tell the good that even the *involuntary* influence of a godly man communicates to his age? The voluntary influence of a man's life—that is, the influence he exerts by intention and conscious efforts—is truly insignificant compared with that stream of unconscious influence that goes forth from him, not only at all times through his life, but even after he has quitted this mundane sphere. "Though dead, he yet speaketh." "As a little silvery ripple," says Elihu Burritt, "set in motion by the falling pebble, expands from its inch of radius to the whole compass of the pool, so there is not a child—not an infant Moses—placed however softly in his bulrush ark upon the sea of time, whose existence does not stir a ripple gyrating outwards and on, until it shall have moved across and spanned the whole ocean of God's eternity, stirring even the river of life and the fountain at which his angels drink."—D. T.

Vers. 7—16.—*Striking characters.* "And Elisha came to Damascus," etc. We have here—

I. A DYING KING. "Benhadad the King of Syria was sick." Benhadad, for his age and country, was a great king, rich and mighty, but now he is on his dying-bed. Kings die as well as others. Observe: 1. This dying king *was very anxious.* What was he anxious about? Not about any great spiritual interest concerning himself or others, but concerning his own physical condition. "Shall I recover of this disease?" This was the question he wanted Elisha to answer. Not, you may be sure, in the negative. Knowing some of the wonders that Elisha had performed, he in all likelihood imagined he would exert his miraculous power on his behalf, and restore him to life. All men more or less fear death, kings perhaps more than others. If ungodly, they have more to lose and nothing to gain. 2. His anxiety *prompted him to do strange things.* (1) It was strange for him to ask a favour from the man whom he had so long regarded as his enemy. We read (ch. vi. 14, 15) that this Benhadad had sent to Dothan "horses, and chariots, and a great host: and they came by night, and compassed the city about," in order to capture this lonely prophet. What a change is this! Dying hours reverse our judgments, revolutionize our feelings, bring the lofty down. (2) It was strange for him to ask a favour of a man whose religion he hated. Benhadad was an idolater; Elisha was a monotheist, a worshipper of the one true God. Now, in dying, all the king's idolatrous thoughts have taken wing, and the one God appears as the great reality, and to the servant of that one God he sends, urging a favour. (3) It was strange for him to make costly presents to a poor lonely man. "The king said unto Hazael, Take a present in thine hand, and go, meet the man of God, and inquire of the Lord by him, saying, Shall I recover of this disease? So Hazael went to meet him, and took a present with him, even of every good thing of Damascus, forty camels' burden, and came and stood before him," etc. What is the wealth, the grandeur, the crown, the sceptre, of the mightiest monarch to him when he feels himself dying? He will barter all away for a few short hours of life.

II. A PATRIOTIC PROPHET. "The man of God wept." Elisha, forecasting the king's death, and knowing the wickedness of this Hazael who was to succeed to the throne, smitten with patriotic tenderness, looked so "steadfastly" into the eye of Hazael that he blushed with shame, and the prophet broke into tears: "The man of God wept." But why did he weep? "Why weepeth my lord?" said Hazael. "And he answered, Because I know the evil that thou wilt do unto the children of Israel: their strongholds wilt thou set on fire," etc. This was the overwhelming misery that the prophet foresaw would befall Israel, when this wretched courtier, his interrogator, would take the throne. As Christ foresaw the coming doom of Jerusalem, and wept over it, so Elisha saw the horrors approaching Israel, and broke into tears. The loving sympathies of a godly man are not confined to men or places, but spread over the ages, and flow down to bless posterity.—D. T.

Vers. 17—24.—*Lessons from the life of Jehoram.* "Thirty and two years old was he [Jehoram] when he began to reign," etc. This is a short fragment of a king's history —the history of Jehoram. Brief as it is, it contains many practical truths.

I. THAT PIETY IS NOT NECESSARILY HEREDITARY. Parents, as a rule, transmit their physical and intellectual qualities to their children, but not their moral characters. Jehoram was a bad man and a wicked king, but he was the son of Jehoshaphat, who was a man of distinguished piety, and reigned wisely and beneficently over Israel for twenty-five years. Of him it was said that "the more his riches and honour increased the more his heart was lifted up in the ways of the Lord" (2 Chron. xvii.

5, 6). He caused the altars and places of idolatry to be destroyed, and the knowledge of the Lord to be diffused throughout the kingdom, and the places of ecclesiastical and judicial authority to be well filled (2 Chron. xvii. 9). But how different was his son! One of the first acts of his government was to put to death his six brothers, and several of the leading men of the empire. It is here said that "he walked in the way of the kings of Israel, as did the house of Ahab." He regulated his conduct by the infamous "house of Ahab," and not by the religious house of his father. He was in truth a murderer, an idolater, and a persecutor. But whilst piety is not *necessarily* hereditary—not necessarily, because children are moral agents—what then? Are parents to do nothing to impart all that is good in their character to their children? Undoubtedly, no! They are commanded to "train up a child in the way it should go" when it is young. And where their power is rightly employed, there is, if not invariable, yet general, success. Where the children of godly parents turn out to be profligate and corrupt, as a rule some defect may be found in the parental conduct. How often eminent ministers of the gospel, and in the main good men, are guilty of neglecting, to a greater or less extent, the parental oversight and religious training of their children! Even in the life of Jehoshaphat we detect at least two parental defects. 1. *In permitting his son to form unholy alliances.* This good man, Jehoshaphat, formed a league with Ahab against Syria, contrary to the counsel of Micaiah (2 Chron. xviii.). For this the Prophet Jehu censured him severely. In consequence of this alliance his son married the daughter of this infamous Ahab, and the matrimonial connection with such a woman, idolatrous, corrupt, and the daughter of Jezebel, had, no doubt, a powerful influence in deteriorating his moral character. 2. *In granting his son too great an indulgence.* He raised him to the throne during his own lifetime. He took him into royal partnership too soon, and thus supplied him with abundant means to foster his vanity and ambition. Ah, me! how many parents ruin their children for ever by over-indulgence!

II. THAT IMMORAL KINGS ARE NATIONAL CURSES. What evils this man brought upon his country! It is said that "in his days Edom revolted from under the hand of Judah, and made a king over themselves. So Joram went over to Zair, and all the chariots with him: and he rose by night, and smote the Edomites which compassed him about, and the captains of the chariots: and the people fled into their tents," etc. Through him the kingdom of Judah lost Edom, which "revolted" and became the determined enemy of Judah ever afterwards (Ps. cxxxvii. 7). Libnah, too, "revolted at the same time." This was a city in the south-western part of Judah assigned to the priests, and a city of refuge. But these revolts are but specimens of the tremendous evils that this immoral man brought upon the kingdom. It has always been so. Wicked kings, in all ages, have been the greatest curses that have afflicted the human race.[1] God said to Israel of old, "I gave thee a king in mine anger" (Hos. xiii. 11). And the gift, on the whole, it must be confessed, has been a curse to mankind; and that because few men who have attained the position have been divinely royal in intellect, in heart, in thoughts, in aims, in sympathies. What does Heaven say of wicked kings? "As a roaring lion, and a raging bear; so is a wicked ruler over the poor people." When will the world have true kings?—such a king as is described in the Book of Proverbs, as one "that sitteth in the throne of judgment," and who "scattereth away all evil with his eyes"? He is one who sees justice done. He does not rule for the interest of a class, but for the good of all. His laws are equitable. Partialities and predilections which govern plebeian souls have no sway over him.

> "He's a king,
> A true right king, that dare do aught save wrong,
> Fears nothing mortal but to be unjust;
> Who is not blown up with the flattering puffs
> Of spongy sycophants; who stands unmoved,
> Despite the jostling of opinion."

III. THAT DEATH IS NO RESPECTER OF PERSONS. 1. *Death does not respect a man's position, however high.* "And Jehoram slept with his fathers, and was buried." Jehoram was a king, yet death struck him down, and he "was buried with his fathers." Palaces are as accessible to death as paupers' huts. Attempted resistance in the former.

---

[1] See 'New Book of Kings,' by Davidson, M.A. (Reeves and Co., Fleet Street).

however skilfully organized, would be as futile as in the latter. Death cares nothing for kings; crowns, diadems, sceptres, courtiers, and pompous pageantries are only as dust in his icy glance. 2. *Death does not respect a man's character, however vile.* Jehoram was a bad man, and utterly unfit to die; but death waits not for moral preparation. When we remember what evils wicked men, especially wicked kings, work in the world, death must be regarded as a beneficent messenger. The psalmist saw mercy in the destruction of despots. He "overthrew Pharaoh and his host in the Red Sea: for his mercy endureth for ever." "To him which smote great kings, and slew famous kings: for his mercy endureth for ever" (Ps. cxxxvi.). There is mercy for the race in their destruction. When such demons in human flesh are cut down, the world breathes more freely, a load is rolled from its heart, obstacles are swept from its path of progress. When the Pharaohs are overwhelmed, the human Israel can march on to promised lands.

CONCLUSION. Parents, cultivate personal religion, and endeavour with all earnestness to transmit it to your children. Kings, seek to understand and to embody the ideal of true kingship, be royal in moral character. All, stand in readiness for the approach of death.—D. T.

Vers. 1—6.—*The Shunammite and her lands.* This narrative is the sequel to the history of the Shunammite in ch. iv. It furnishes another instance of how God cares for and rewards his people.

I. ELISHA'S WARNING. In chronological order this narrative seems to precede the cure of Naaman, while Gehazi was still the servant of the prophet. A famine of long duration was about to descend on the land, and Elisha gave timely warning to the Shunammite to take refuge somewhere else. 1. *The good are often sharers in the calamities of the wicked.* This famine was no doubt sent on Israel as a punishment for sin. God's prophet foretold it, as Elijah had foretold the drought in the days of Ahab (1 Kings xvii. 1). Famines and similar calamities do not come uncalled for. They are instruments used by God in his moral government (Ezek. xiv. 21; Amos iv.). And in the distresses brought upon the world by sin God's people are often sharers. The innocent are involved in the sufferings of the guilty (Ezek. xxi. 3, 4). This lady of Shunem, now probably a widow, is compelled, by the approach of famine, to abandon home and lands and rural comfort for a sojourn among idolaters. 2. *The good, notwithstanding, are marvellously protected amidst the calamities of the wicked.* It was God's mercy to this Shunammite, who in former days had befriended his prophet, which now led to her being warned beforehand. God's rewards for kindness shown to his servants are not soon exhausted. It was sad to be involved in the famine, but it would have been sadder had she not received this warning to withdraw in good time. Thus God, by a special providence, cares for and watches over the interests of his people. He guides their steps, and is a Shield to them from trouble. 3. *The good are provided for amidst the calamities of the wicked.* The Shunammite was directed to sojourn with her household wherever she could find a refuge. She believed the word of the man of God, obeyed it, and went to sojourn in the land of the Philistines. There she abode for the seven years that the famine lasted, and during that period was sufficiently provided for. It was an act of faith on the part of the Shunammite to take this step, for she had nothing to go upon in regard to this famine but the prophet's bare word. That, however, was held sufficient, and she left all to do as he had bidden her. God's people are always safe in acting on his commands. When Elijah was sent to hide by the brook Cherith, the ravens were "commanded" to feed him; and when he was told to go from there to Zarephath, a widow woman was similarly "commanded" to sustain him (1 Kings xvii. 4, 8). As God provided for Jacob and his household in Egypt in a time of famine, so he prepares a provision for all his people who humbly trust him. "They that seek the Lord shall not want any good thing" (Ps. xxxiv. 10).

II. THE SHUNAMMITE'S RETURN. At length, through the ceasing of the famine, the way was open for the Shunammite to come back. Her return was: 1. *After long exile.* Seven years had she been absent from the land of Jehovah. During that period she had lived amidst Philistine surroundings. Her spirit must often have been grieved at the idolatrous and heathenish sights she witnessed; for what moral communion could she have with the worshippers of Dagon? Nor could she now, as of old, saddle her ass, and repair to the prophet on sabbaths and new moons for consolation and instruction. Exile of this sort would be painful to her spirit, as it was to that of the psalmist (Ps. xlii. 4, 6). God in his providence often thus deprives his people for a time of the privilege of ordinances, perhaps through sickness, perhaps through removal to new scenes, perhaps through the interposition of direct obstacles. There was in the Shunammite's case a famine of the Word as well as of bread. These things try faith, and operate to the quickening of spiritual desire. 2. *To meet a new trial.* The Shunammite came back to her home, to find that, in her long absence, her house and lands had been alienated from her. Probably, as deserted by their owner, they had become the property of the crown (ver. 6). Or some neighbouring proprietor may have possessed himself of the abandoned fields. In any case, it was a sore discovery for the Shunammite to make, on her return, that she could no longer obtain her own. The trial of coming back seemed almost greater than that of going away. Might not the same providence that had cared for her in Philistia have watched over her possessions at home? It was God who had called her thence: might he not have secured that, when she returned, she would get her own? The issue of this trial should encourage believers not too readily to distrust the Almighty. It came to be seen that God *had* been caring for her in her absence—had, so to speak, been putting out her lands at interest for her, so that, when they were restored, she "received her own with usury" (Matt. xxv. 27).

III. THE SHUNAMMITE'S APPEAL. The most striking part of the story is yet to come. Having no other remedy, the Shunammite appealed to the king, as first magistrate, to restore to her her lands. "She went forth to cry unto the king for her house and for her land." We note concerning her appeal: 1. *Its justice.* The Shunammite had a good and just cause. Kings and magistrates are set to administer justice. Yet it is possible that, but for the circumstances next narrated, the impoverished lady might have cried long enough before her possessions were restored to her. It is difficult to get the holders of unlawfully acquired property—especially in land—to yield up again their title to it. The cry of the poor does not always penetrate, as it should do, to the ear of justice. 2. *Its providential opportuneness.* It is God's prerogative to maintain the cause of the oppressed (Ps. ix. 4, 9, 10), and he was preparing the way for this cause being heard. The circumstances are remarkable, showing how entirely all events are in the hand of God, how what we call accidental conjunctures are really providences, and how, without overriding human freedom, all things, even the most ordinary, are working together for good to those who love him. (1) It happened that, just as the Shunammite approached, her son being with her, to present her prayer, the king and Gehazi, Elisha's servant, were talking together of the wonderful works of the prophet. "Tell me, I pray thee," said the king, "all the great things that Elisha hath done." Jehoram, though a wicked man (ch. ix. 22), had yet, as we have formerly seen, a certain susceptibility to good in him. His was a divided nature. He had a reverence and respect for Elisha; he knew the right; he took pleasure in hearing of Elisha's wonderful deeds. Yet he never took God's Law truly into his heart. How many are like him (Ezek. xxxiii. 30—33)! (2) In particular, Gehazi was relating to the king how Elisha had restored the dead son of the Shunammite to life. How singular, we say, that this should have been the subject of conversation at that very moment! But it was God who ordered that this should come about. We find a very similar instance in the case of King Ahasuerus in the Book of Esther. He could not sleep, and ordered the chronicles of his kingdom to be read before him. It was the night when Haman's plot was ripe for the destruction of Mordecai, but the passage read was that which told how Mordecai had made known a conspiracy against the king's life. This saved him, and led to Haman's own destruction (Esth. vi.). The wheels within wheels in God's providence are truly marvellous. He lifts up one and casts down another by the simplest possible means. (3) As Gehazi was speaking, the Shunammite and her son stood before them, and cried to the king. No doubt in great surprise, Gehazi said, "My lord, O king, this is the woman, and this is her son, whom Elisha restored to life." The ear of the king was now effectually gained. 3. *Its success.* The woman, being asked to state her plea, did so, and her request was at once granted. Not only were her house and land restored to her, but recompense was made for all the fruits of the field since the day she had left it. Thus she received back in abundance all she possessed. She not only got justice, but generosity. How good it is to be a friend of God! "If God be for us, who can be against us?" (Rom. viii. 31). With him for our Advocate, what need we fear? Having given this woman the greater gift, in reward for her kindness to his prophet, he does not withhold from her any lesser gift. So may the believer reason, if God "spared not his own Son," etc. (Rom. viii. 32).—J. O.

Vers. 7—15.—*Elisha and Hazael.* Elisha had come to Damascus, probably sent thither by God to carry out in spirit the commission given long before to Elijah (1 Kings xix. 15).

I. BENHADAD'S MESSAGE. 1. *Its occasion.* "Benhadad the King of Syria was sick." Royal rank affords no protection against the invasions of disease. Nor is the thought of death less alarming to the monarch than to the peasant. Benhadad's heart trembled as he reflected on the possible issues of his trouble, and he gladly availed himself of the opportunity of Elisha's presence in Damascus to send a messenger to him. His conduct is in striking contrast with Ahaziah's (ch. i.). That Israelitish king, forsaking the God of Israel, sent to inquire at an idol shrine at Ekron. Benhadad, though a Syrian and a worshipper of Rimmon, turns in his sickness from Rimmon to Jehovah. 2. *The messenger.* The person sent was Hazael, one of Benhadad's great courtiers. Hazael was a very different kind of a man from Naaman. He was a bold, bad, ambitious intriguer, who was already cherishing deep thoughts of crime against his master. Yet Benhadad seems to have trusted him. How unreliable are the friendships of the wicked! Men flatter with their tongue, but in their hearts are malice, falsehood, and selfish, ambitious designs (Ps. v. 9). 3. *The message.* Hazael came to Elisha with great pomp. He brought a present borne on forty camels. If lavish wealth could buy a favourable answer from Jehovah, surely now it would be obtained. But God is no respecter of persons; still less does he bestow favour for bribes. We may be sure that, as in a former case (ch. v. 16), Elisha touched nothing of all this wealth that was brought to him. Accompanying the present was a message from the king: "Thy son Benhadad hath sent me to thee, saying, Shall I recover from this disease?" For those to whom this world is all, such a question is of very terrible moment. Well may they cling to life who have nothing beyond to hope for.

II. THE INTERVIEW WITH HAZAEL. 1. *Elisha's exposure of Hazael's motives.* As Hazael stood before Elisha, the prophet's clear vision read to the depths of his soul. Hazael was evidently speculating on the possibilities of his master's death, and had private designs upon the throne. When once the idea of making himself king had occurred to him, he was not the man to let the ambitious project readily drop again. The thought of removing the king by violence had no doubt flashed upon him, but he waited to learn whether the sickness would prove fatal before he framed a settled purpose. Elisha showed by his answer that he read the whole character of the man. "Go, say unto him, Thou shalt certainly recover"—that was the truth as regards the sickness; then he added, "Howbeit the Lord hath showed me that he shall surely die." Hazael's guilty thoughts would furnish the explanation. We do well to remember that there is nothing we can conceal from the Searcher of hearts. "All things are naked and opened unto the eyes of him with whom we have to do" (Heb. iv. 13). Our thoughts, even in their most inchoate condition, are known to him. He understandeth our thoughts "afar off" (Ps. cxxxix. 2). 2. *Elisha's prophecy of Hazael's barbarities.* Did Elisha approve of Hazael's designs, and mean to give them Divine sanction? We are able to answer this by noting his subsequent conduct. (1) He settled his face steadfastly, and looked with a fixed gaze at Hazael till the latter was ashamed. Then Elisha wept. Elisha stood before Hazael as a kind of outward conscience. He revealed Hazael to himself, but at the same time condemned the thoughts which he saw in his mind. It was a holy, earnest gaze which Elisha turned on Hazael—a look of reproval, of sorrow, of holy pain; and Hazael felt that it was so when he blushed under it. (2) When Hazael asked concerning his weeping, Elisha became more explicit, and told him of the awful barbarities he would inflict on Israel. The picture was so dreadful that even Hazael, with apparent sincerity, asked, "Who is thy servant, this dog, that he should do this great thing?" Hazael, like many others, was not aware of the possibilities of his own heart. A certain measure of crime he knew himself to be capable of, but he thought that other iniquities were beyond him.   Once on the downward grade, however, there is no point at which a sinner can be sure of stopping.   One crime leads with a fatal facility to a worse.   The heart grows hardened, and things are done which, at an earlier stage, might have been thought impossible.   It is told of Robespierre that, in the beginning of his career, he was almost driven distracted by the thought of having sentenced a man to death.   The greatest criminals were once innocent children, and at one period of their lives would have shuddered at the deeds they afterwards calmly perpetrated.   The only safe course is to resist the beginnings of evil.   3. *Elisha's announcement of Hazael's greatness.*   Elisha's final announcement to Hazael was, "The Lord hath showed me that thou shalt be king over Syria."   The prophet announces the fact, which indeed fulfilled a Divine purpose regarding Hazael (1 Kings xix. 15), but announces it without approval of the particular means by which that purpose would be realized.   Jacob would have received the blessing in God's time and way, though his mother Rebekah had not counselled deceit as a means of obtaining it; and the kingdom would have come to Hazael, also in God's good time and way, though he had kept his hands free from crime.

III. A PALACE MURDER.   If Elisha's words did not arrest the guilty purpose which was shaping itself in Hazael's mind, they could only have the contrary effect of inflaming his ambition.   Like Macbeth with the witches' salutation ringing in his ears, he felt himself a child of destiny, and took speedy means to fulfil his destiny.   1. *He deceived the king.*   He repeated, in the letter of them, Elisha's words, "Thou shalt surely recover;" but said nothing 'of the context, which gave the words so terrible a significance.   The king was assured that his disease was not mortal, which was true; but he was left in the dark as to the declaration that he should nevertheless surely die.   2. *He slew the king.*   Next day, probably while Benhadad slept, Hazael took a thick quilt, and, dipping it in water, spread it over the king's face, and suffocated him.   He thus fulfilled the prediction that he should be King of Syria.   He "had his reward."   But was it worth the crime?   What could compensate for a soul stained with the sin of treachery and murder?   Of Banquo it was prophesied that he would be lesser than Macbeth, yet greater; not so happy, yet happier.   Would the same not have been true of Hazael had he been content to remain Benhadad's faithful officer, instead of climbing to the throne in this hateful fashion?   What, after all, is there so much to envy in the state of kings, that a soul's peace should be bartered to acquire it?   Surrounded by false friends; served by courtiers ready at any moment to turn against him if it serves their interests better; envied even by those who flatter him; exposed to the peril of assassination,—the monarch is almost more to be pitied than the humblest of his subjects.   Hazael had but exchanged his own pillow for a more thorny one.   "Uneasy lies the head that wears a crown."—J. O.

Vers. 16—29.—*Two kings of Judah.* (On the chronology, see Exposition.) The reigns of Jehoram and Ahaziah are black spots in the history of Judah.

I. JEHORAM, SON OF JEHOSHAPHAT. We may notice concerning this ruler: 1. *He had a pious father.* We may quote Thomas Fuller's quaint comments on this part of the Saviour's genealogy: "Lord, I find the genealogy of my Saviour strangely checkered with four remarkable changes in four immediate generations. (1) 'Rehoboam begat Abiam;' that is, a bad father begat a bad son. (2) 'Abiam begat Asa;' that is, a bad father a good son. (3) 'Asa begat Jehoshaphat;' that is, a good father a good son. (4) 'Jehoshaphat begat Joram;' that is, a good father a bad son. I see, Lord, from hence, that my father's piety cannot be entailed; that is bad news for me. But I see also that actual impiety is not always hereditary; that is good news for my son." 2. *He made an evil marriage.* "The daughter of Ahab"—Athaliah—"was his wife." In sanctioning this union of his son with the house of Ahab Jehoshaphat grievously erred. Jehoshaphat's whole policy of keeping up friendly relations with Ahab was a mistake, destined to bear bitter fruit in his family and his kingdom. No considerations of political expediency should have tempted him¦ to allow a marriage of the heir of his throne with a daughter of the infamous Jezebel. Rulers have even yet to learn that the sacrifice of religious and moral considerations to state policy is in the end the greatest impolicy. Marriage is a relation which cannot be too carefully entered into. Yet it is often the relation which is entered into most thoughtlessly,

Pecuniary, social, or family considerations are allowed to determine a step which ought never to be taken except on grounds of real affection and moral and spiritual affinity. Athaliah's entrance into the royal household of Judah had a disastrous effect on its future. She was a true child of the Israelitish Jezebel, and reproduced her character in all its essential features. Bold, bad, energetic, unscrupulous, ambitious, her influence over her husband was wholly for evil. And he seems to have yielded himself entirely up to it. 3. *He walked in evil ways.* "He walked in the way of the kings of Israel," etc. The connection of this with his marriage is indicated in the words, "For the daughter of Ahab was his wife." To that malign influence is probably to be attributed the great crime with which his reign began—the slaughter of his six brethren, with many of the princes (2 Chron. xxi. 2—4). The other evils of his reign are indicated by the Chronicles—tempting and compelling the people to idolatry, etc. (2 Chron. xxi. 11, 13). 4. *He was mercifully dealt with for the sake of David.* Grieved though God was with his conduct, he would not destroy Judah, having pledged himself to David to perpetuate his line. The descendants of holy men and women do not know how much of God's mercy and forbearance they often owe to their ancestral connection. God spares them for their fathers' sakes (Rom. xi. 28). 5. *Yet his sins brought heavy disasters on the kingdom.* God did not destroy Judah, but he punished it. As the wickedness of the Israelitish kings was punished by the revolt of Moab (ch. i. 1), so the sins of Jehoram were visited by a series of calamities which fell upon the nation. The revolt of Edom, of Libnah, invasions of the Philistines, Arabians, etc., broke in upon and desolated the land (2 Chron. xxi. 16, 17). Only when rulers and people were fearing the Lord could it be said, "Also in Judah things went well" (2 Chron. xii. 12). Things cannot go well when men's hearts are bent on wickedness. God is against us, and troubles rise thick on every side. The revolt of Edom is the only calamity referred to in detail in the text. Jehoram seems to have attempted to suppress the rebellion, but, being encompassed by the enemy, had great difficulty in cutting his way through, and escaping. The loss of Edom was a permanent one. 6. *He came to a miserable end.* He went down to his death visibly under a cloud of Divine wrath, and amidst the contempt, if not the execrations, of his people. God smote him, the Chronicler tells us, with a painful and incurable disease, and he died, despised and unlamented (2 Chron. xxi. 18, 19). He was buried in Jerusalem, but not in the tomb of the kings. Presumptuous transgressors are rightly visited with judgments of exceptional severity (cf. Acts xii. 23). It is the memory of the just that is blessed, but the name of the wicked shall rot (Prov. x. 7).

II. AHAZIAH, SON OF JEHORAM. 1. *A short but evil reign.* Ahaziah, who reigned but one year, was the youngest son of Jehoram, the elder having been slain in the wars with the Arabians (2 Chron. xxii. 1). His reign was evil, like his father's. In this case it is said expressly that Athaliah and others of her kindred were his counsellers to do evil (2 Chron. xxii. 3, 4). A mother's influence is even more potent than a father's. But when both parents go partners in open wickedness, it is no wonder if a son follows their example. 2. *A fateful visit.* Ahaziah and Jehoram of Israel were speedily to meet their end together. The Chronicler says " the destruction of Ahaziah was of God by coming to see Joram " (2 Chron. xxii. 7). Jehoram had been wounded in a campaign against Hazael at Ramoth-Gilead, and was now at Jezreel to be healed of his wounds. Thither Ahaziah repaired to visit him, and there both kings were slain by Jehu. The visible providence of God is again seen in this visit. His hook is in the nose of the sinner; he leads him wherever he will (2 Kings xix. 28).—J. O.

EXPOSITION.

CHAPTER IX.

Vers. 1—37.—THE ANOINTING OF JEHU. HIS MURDER OF JEHORAM AND AHAZIAH. THE DEATH OF JEZEBEL.

Vers. 1—10.—Elisha is still the primary figure in the historical drama; but at this point his personality merges in the general account of the kingdom of Israel, which it is one of the objects of the writer to trace from beginning to end. Elisha here performs his last public act, being commissioned, and carrying out his commission, to transfer the kingdom of Israel from the unworthy dynasty of Omri, which on account of its persistent idolatry has fallen under Divine condemnation, to a new dynasty, that of Jehu, which will, at any rate, check the worst excesses of the prevalent idolatrous system, and maintain the Jehovah-worship as the religion of the state. The position recalls that of Saul and David at the original institution of the monarchy, but has many special points which differentiate it from that conjuncture. The circumstances called on Jehu for prompt action; there was no such immediate call upon David. Jehu's public proclamation as king laid him open to a charge of high treason; David's secret anointing placed him in no such danger. History never repeats itself *exactly*, and its events have severally to be judged by a consideration of all their circumstances, without much reference to any former *quasi*-parallel historical passage.

Vers. 1—10.—*The anointing of Jehu.*

Ver. 1.—**And Elisha the prophet called one of the children of the prophets;** *i.e.* one of the students in one of the prophetical schools which he superintended. There is no indication that the individual chosen for the mission stood to Elisha in any peculiar relation. A rabbinical fancy, scarcely to be called a tradition, makes him "Jonah, the son of Amittai." **And said unto him, Gird up thy loins, and take this box of oil;** rather, *this flask of oil.* Oil and ointments were commonly kept in open-mouthed jars, vases, or bottles, made of stone, glass, or alabaster, as appears from the remains found in Egypt and Assyria. Many of the bottles are earlier than the time of Elisha. **In thine hand, and go to Ramoth-Gilead.** Ramoth-Gilead lay across the Jordan, in the proper territory of Gad. It had been seized and occupied by the Syrians in the reign of Ahab; and the possession had been maintained till recently. Joram, however, had recovered it (Josephus, 'Ant. Jud.,' ix. 6. § 1, Ἤδη γὰρ αὐτὴν ᾑρήκει κατὰ κράτος), and had left a strong garrison in the place when he retired to Jezreel.

Ver. 2.—**And when thou comest thither, look out there Jehu the son of Jehoshaphat the son of Nimshi.** Jehu had been in a high position under Ahab (ver. 25), and had been pointed out to Elijah, by Divine revelation, as the future King of Israel (1 Kings xix. 16). Elijah had been bidden to anoint him king, but apparently had

neglected to do so, or rather had devolved the task upon his successor. Meantime Jehu served as a soldier under Ahaziah and Jehoram, Ahab's sons, and attained such distinction that he became one of the captains of the host (*infra*, ver. 5), according to Josephus (*l. s. c.*) the chief captain. Jehu was commonly known as "the son of Nimshi" (1 Kings xix. 16; ch. ix. 20), either because, his father having died young, he was brought up by his grandfather, or perhaps simply "because Nimshi was a person of more importance than Jehoshaphat." **And go in**—*i.e.* seek his presence, go into his quarters, wherever they may be, have direct speech with him—**and make him arise up from among his brethren** (comp. vers. 5 and 6). Jehu's "brethren" are his *brother*-officers, among whom Elisha knows that he will be found sitting. **And carry him to an inner chamber.** Persuade him, *i.e.*, to quit the place where thou wilt find him sitting with the other generals, and to go with thee into a private apartment for secret conference. Secrecy was of extreme importance, lest Joram should get knowledge of what was happening, and prepare himself for resistance. Had he not been taken by surprise, the result might have been a long and bloody civil war.

Ver. 3.—**Then take**—rather, *and take*—**the box of oil**—rather, *the flask of oil*—**and pour it on his head.** Compare the consecration of Aaron to the high-priestly (Lev. viii. 12), and of Saul (1 Sam. x. 1) and David (1 Sam. xvi. 12) to the kingly office. The oil used was the holy anointing oil of the sanctuary (Exod. xxx. 25)—τὸ ἅγιον ἔλαιον, as Josephus says. **And say, Thus saith the Lord, I have anointed thee king over Israel.** This is an abbreviated form of the actual message, which is given in its entirety in vers. 7—10. The writer of Kings avoids all needless repetitions. **Then open the door**—the conference was to be with closed doors, that no one might either hear or see what took place—**and flee, and tarry not.** The Divine message delivered, all would have been done that needed to be done. There would be nothing to wait for. So the young man was to depart with the same haste with which he had come.

Ver. 4.—**So the young man, even the young man the prophet**—the repetition of *han-na'ar* is doubtful, since it is not found either in the Syriac or in the Septuagint—**went to Ramoth-Gilead.**

Ver. 5.—**And when he came, behold, the captains of the host were sitting**—either "sitting in council," or, at any rate, collected together in one place, not engaged in any active work, but seated—**and he said, I have an errand**—literally, *a word*—**to thee, O captain.** Probably he knew Jehu by sight, and looked at him as he spoke; but, as he addressed no one by name, there might be a doubt who was intended. Jehu, therefore, causes the doubt to be resolved by his question. **And Jehu said, Unto which of all us? And he said**—*i.e.* the young man the prophet answered—**To thee, O captain.** Jehu was thus singled out as the object of the message—the person to whom alone it was addressed, and whose special attention was, consequently, required to it.

Ver. 6.—**And he** (Jehu) **arose, and went into the house.** Jehu left his seat, rose up, and led the way, from the court, where he had probably been sitting with the other generals, into the house which adjoined the court. The messenger followed; and the two were together, alone. **And he**—*i.e.* the messenger—**poured the oil on his head**—as directed (ver. 3)—**and said unto him, Thus saith the Lord God of Israel;** literally, *Thus saith Jehovah, God of Israel.* Jehovah's name is emphatically put forward, in contrast with the name of Baal, as that of the true God of Israel; and appeal is made to Jehu, as to one whose God is Jehovah, and who will accept as authoritative a message emanating from him. **I have anointed thee king over the people of the Lord,** even **over Israel;** literally, *over the people of Jehovah, over Israel.* Practically, the people is, in the main, "the people of Baal" (ch. x. 19—21), but theoretically and by covenant it is "the people of Jehovah"—his "peculiar people" (Deut. xiv. 2), chosen by him out of all the nations of the earth to be his own.

Ver. 7.—**And thou shalt smite the house of Ahab thy master.** This is plainly a command, not a prophecy. Jehu is expressly ordered by God to "smite," *i.e.* destroy utterly, the whole house of Ahab. This command he carried out (vers. 24, 33; ch. x. 1—11); and his obedience to it obtained for him the temporal reward that his children to the fourth generation should sit on the throne of Israel (ch. x. 30). Yet still his conduct in destroying the house of Ahab is spoken of by the Prophet Hosea as a sin, and God declares, by Hosea's mouth, that he will "avenge the blood of Jezreel upon the house of Jehu" (Hos. i. 4). It is naturally asked—"How could Jehu's shedding this blood, at God's command and in fulfilment of his will, be a sin?" And it is rightly answered, "Because, if we do what is the will of God for any end of our own, for anything except God, we do in fact our own will, not God's. It was not lawful for Jehu to depose and slay the king his master, except at the express command of God, who, as the supreme King, sets up and puts down earthly rulers as he wills. For any other end, and done otherwise than at God's express command, such an act is sin. Jehu

was rewarded for the measure in which he fulfilled God's commands, as Ahab, ' who had sold himself to work wickedness,' had yet a temporal reward for humbling himself publicly, when rebuked by God for his sin, and so honouring God, amid an apostate people. But Jehu, by cleaving, against the will of God, to Jeroboam's sin (ch. xi. 29, 31), which served his own political ends, showed that, in the slaughter of his master, he acted, not as he pretended, out of zeal for the will of God (ch. x. 16), but served his own will and his own ambition only. By his disobedience to the one command of God, he showed that he would have equally disobeyed the other, had it been contrary to his own will or interest. He *had no principle of obedience.* And so the blood which was shed according to the righteous judgment of God, became sin to him that shed it in order to fulfil, not the will of God, but his own" (see Dr. Pusey's ' Minor Prophets, with a Commentary,' p. 9, col. 1). **That I may avenge the blood of my servants the prophets.** Comp. 1 Kings xviii. 4 and xix. 14. Elijah believed *all* the prophets of Jehovah, except himself, to have been either slain or banished under Ahab, as we see from 1 Kings xviii. 22 and xix. 10, 14. **And the blood of all the servants of the Lord.** There had evidently been a general persecution of the followers of Jehovah, and not merely a persecution of the prophets. It was only after a number of martyrdoms that the followers of Jehovah in Israel were reduced (1 Kings xix. 18) to the scanty number of "seven thousand." **At the hand of Jezebel.** Jezebel was at the bottom of all the persecutions. Sometimes she took matters into her own hands, gave her own orders, and saw them carried out (1 Kings xviii. 13; xxi. 8—14). At other times she was content to "stir her husband up" (1 Kings xxi. 25) and incite him to evil courses.

Ver. 8.—**For the whole house of Ahab shall perish: and I will cut off from Ahab him that pisseth against the wall, and him that is shut up and left in Israel** (see the comment on 1 Kings xiv. 10). While the exact force of the phrases used is doubtful, the general intention to embrace in the sentence all Ahab's posterity cannot be doubted.

Ver. 9.—**And I will make the house of Ahab like the house of Jeroboam the son of Nebat.** Jeroboam's house had been "cut off," smitten, destroyed, till not one of his posterity was left, about seventy years previously (1 Kings xv. 29), by Baasha, "because of his sins which he sinned, and which he made Israel sin, by his provocation wherewith he provoked the Lord God of Israel to anger" (1 Kings xv. 30). The far greater sin of Ahab could not be visited with less severity. **And like the house of Baasha the** son of Ahijah. As the whole house of Jeroboam had been cut off for its idolatries, so the house of Baasha, which succeeded to the throne, was removed even more speedily, Baasha himself and all his posterity being swept from the earth by Zimri, who "smote him and killed him," and succeeded him (1 Kings xvi. 11). The house of Ahab had had a double warning of the fate in reserve for those who deserted the religion of Jehovah, but had disregarded both warnings alike, and had provoked God yet more than their predecessors, by introducing a novel and degraded form of idolatrous worship.

Ver. 10.—**And the dogs shall eat Jezebel in the portion of Jezreel.** This had been previously prophesied by Elijah (1 Kings xxi. 23; ch. ix. 26, 27). To an Israelite, and even to a Phœnician, it was an awful threat; for both nations alike buried their dead carefully in deep-dug graves or rocky receptacles, and both regarded the desecration of a corpse as a grievous calamity ('Records of the Past,' vol. ix. pp. 112, 114). The dog was to the Hebrews, and to the Orientals generally, an unclean animal, and to be devoured by dogs would have been viewed as a fate which, for a queen, was almost inconceivable. **And there shall be none to bury** her. Jezebel had no one sufficiently interested in her fate to watch over her remains. Rizpah, the daughter of Aiah, had kept watch over the bodies of the seven sons of Saul, and suffered neither the birds of the air to rest on them by day, nor the beasts of the field by night (2 Sam. xxi. 10); and in Greece, if we may believe the poets, life had been risked, and actually forfeited, to save a near relative from similar ignominy (Soph., 'Ant.,' lines 245—743). But "Jezebel had none to bury her." When she was ejected from the palace window (ver. 33) and fell to the ground, and was trodden under foot by Jehu's chariot-horses, no one came forth from the palace to give the bruised and wounded corpse such tendance as was possible. There was entire neglect of the body for (probably) some hours; and, during these, the catastrophe occurred which Divine foresight had prophesied, but which human malice had not intended (see vers. 34—37). **And he opened the door, and fled.** The young man the prophet obeyed to the letter the injunctions which Elisha had given him (ver. 3). The moment that he had executed his errand, he fled.

Vers. 11—22.—*Conspiracy of Jehu against Jehoram.*

Ver. 11.—**Then Jehu came forth to the servants of his lord.** After the young man the prophet had made his precipitate retreat, Jehu, too, quitted the inner chamber, and "came forth"—returned to the place where he had been sitting with "the servants of

his lord"—the other captains of the host (ver. 5)—and rejoined their company. **And one said unto him, Is all well?** One of the other captains of the host took the word, and asked, in the ordinary phraseology of the time, "Is it peace?" (comp. vers. 17, 18, 19, 22)—or, in other words, "Is all right?" "Is all well?" The sudden appearance and disappearance of the messenger had evidently created an impression that all was *not* well. **Wherefore came this mad fellow to thee?** He did not suppose the man to be actually mad. He calls him "this wild fellow"—"this scatterbrain," on account of the haste and strangeness of his conduct; but he quite expects to hear that there was "method in the madness," and that the communication had some serious import. **And he**—*i.e.* Jehu—**said unto them, Ye know the man, and his communication.** Jehu suspected that the whole scene had been arranged beforehand; that Elisha and the young prophet and the captains of the host were in league, and had concerted a way of offering him the throne. He may have had reason to regard the captains as disaffected towards Jehoram, though this does not appear at all distinctly in the very brief narrative.

Ver. 12.—**And they said, It is false.** There was no rudeness in the reply. It merely denied that Jehu's supposition was correct. There had been no collusion between the spiritual and temporal authorities. The captains had no knowledge of the young prophet's errand. **Tell us now.** "Tell us," *i.e.*, "what the young prophet said, since we are completely in the dark upon the subject." **And he said, Thus and thus spake he to me, saying, Thus saith the Lord, I have anointed thee king over Israel.** Jehu declared to them without any reserve all that the young prophet had said to him. He accepted their declaration that they were not in league with him, and then gave them an exact account of all that had occurred. He left it for them to determine what, under the circumstances, they would do.

Ver. 13.—**Then they hasted, and took every man his garment, and put it under him on the top of the stairs.** Kings were honoured by the spreading of garments in their way, that their feet might not touch the dusty ground (Matt. xx. 8). The captains of the host, without hesitation, acclaimed Jehu king on the strength of the prophetical announcement, made his cause their own, and joined in his rebellion. It is reasonably conjectured (Bähr) that "a deep dissatisfaction with Joram must have prevailed in the army," though whether the dissatisfaction arose from the idolatry of the house of Ahab, or from Joram's withdrawal from the war, may be doubted. Jehu, on the other hand, was evidently highly esteemed. The captains threw themselves with ardour into his cause, and extemporized a sort of enthronement. As often in an Oriental house, an external staircase led from the court to the upper story or to the roof. This they carpeted with their *begeds*, or outer cloaks, and, seating him on the top stair, saluted him as actual king. The expression, *el-gerem ham-ma'alôth*, is not literally, "on the *top* of the stairs," but rather "on the stairs *themselves*." Naturally, however, the captains would emplace him upon the topmost stair. **And blew with trumpets.** This was a recognized part of the ceremonial of a coronation (see 2 Sam. xv. 10; 1 Kings i. 39; ch. xi. 14). **Saying, Jehu is king.**

Ver. 14.—**So Jehu the son of Jehoshaphat the son of Nimshi** (see the comment on ver. 2) **conspired against Joram.** It is not meant that there was a secret conspiracy previous to the prophet's coming, but that, by the open acts which followed on his coming, Jehu and the captains were guilty of a "conspiracy." **Now Joram had kept Ramoth-Gilead;** rather, *now Joram was keeping Ramoth-Gilead.* Joram, in his capacity of chief ruler, was keeping, *i.e.* defending, Ramoth-Gilead against the Syrians with the bulk of his forces. **He and all Israel, because of Hazael King of Syria;** since Hazael wished to win the city back, and would have done so, had it not been stoutly defended. The writer speaks of Joram as the defender, though he was absent, because the defence was made under his orders. Then, to prevent misunderstanding, he repeats what he had already said in ch. viii. 29 with respect to Joram's wounds, and his retirement to Jezreel to be healed of them.

Ver. 15.—**But King Joram was returned to be healed in Jezreel of the wounds which the Syrians had given him, when he fought with Hazael King of Syria** (see the comment on ch. viii. 29). **And Jehu said, If it be your minds.** As soon as he is proclaimed king, Jehu addresses himself to the captains, and proposes a policy. He does not venture to assume a tone of authority, or of imperative command, since he is still but a pretender, and not "established in the kingdom." "If it be your minds," he says; *i.e.* "If you agree with me, and have nothing to urge against my proposal. **Then let none go forth** nor **escape from the city**—literally, *let no escaper go forth from the city*—equivalent to *let no one quit the city*—**to go to tell it in Jezreel.** This is the important point. Secrecy was absolutely essential. If the revolt had got wind—and a single messenger might have carried the news—the whole attempt might have failed, or only have succeeded after a long and bloody civil war. All Jehu's efforts were bent on keeping his revolt secret until he himself announced it to the astonished king (see ver. 22).

Ver. 16.—**So Jehu rode in a chariot, and went to Jezreel; for Joram lay there.** We must understand that the captains came into Jehu's views, acknowledged the necessity of secrecy, and took precautions against the departure of any one, openly or secretly, from the city. Jehu, with a moderate troop or company (שֶׁמֶץ), sets out, perhaps on the very day of his enthronement, and hastens with all speed to Jezreel, bent on arriving there before any suspicion has arisen of revolt or rebellion. His great object was to surprise Joram, and to kill or capture him before he could take any steps to organize a defence. Probably the force which accompanied him was wholly a chariot force. **And Ahaziah King of Judah was come down to see Joram** (see ch. viii. 29, and the comment *ad. loc.*). Ahaziah, it must be remembered, was Joram's nephew, as well as his ally in the war against Syria. It was natural that he should visit his uncle when he was wounded, even if the wounds were not very serious.

Ver. 17.—**And there stood a watchman on the tower in Jezreel;** literally, *and the watchman stood on the tower in Jezreel.* The watch-tower on the south-east, towards Ramoth-Gilead, is intended. There were probably others in other directions; but the writer is not concerned with them. Each watch-tower had its *one* watchman, who gave warning if anything unusual caught his attention. **And he spied the company of Jehu as he came.** *Shiph'ah* is generally "abundance," "multitude" (Deut. xxxiii. 19; Job xxii. 11; Isa. lx. 6), but seems here to designate a "band" or "company" of moderate size. It is a somewhat rare word. **And said, I see a company.** The watchman gave notice to those whose business it was to inform the king, that a band or company of men was approaching the city. **And Joram said, Take an horseman, and send to meet them, and let him say, Is it peace?** Joram apprehended no danger. If the "company" had been a band of Syrians, or other enemies, coming in hostile fashion, the watchman would have worded his warning differently. The king probably concluded that he was about to receive tidings from the seat of war, and meant to ask, "Is the news good or bad—peaceful or the contrary?" No blame attaches to him for not taking alarm at once.

Ver. 18.—**So there went one on horseback to meet him, and said, Thus saith the king, Is it peace? And Jehu said, What hast thou to do with peace? turn thee behind me.** Jehu chooses to accept the messenger's words as if they were his own, and not those of the king. "What does it matter to such a one as thee, a mere common man, whether my tidings are peaceful or the contrary? I shall not tell thee my errand. Turn and follow in my train." The messenger had no choice but to obey. An attempt at flight would have led to his being seized or slain. **And the watchman told, saying, The messenger came to them, but he cometh not again.** The watchman evidently thought his not returning suspicious, and reported it at once. Joram should now have taken alarm, but he did not. He appears to have had no notion that any danger could be approaching.

Ver. 19.—**Then he sent out a second on horseback.** Persistency in a course shown by experience to be futile was characteristic of the sons of Ahab and Jezebel (compare the conduct of Ahaziah, as described in ch. i. 9, 11, 13). **Which came to them, and said, Thus saith the king, Is it peace?** Exactly the same inquiry as before, and no doubt in the same sense (see the comment on ver. 17). Jehu, addressed with the same words, thinks it sufficient to give the same answer. His object is to lose no time, but to reach the king as quickly as possible. **And Jehu answered, What hast thou to do with peace? turn thee behind me.**

Ver. 20.—**And the watchman told, saying, He came even unto them, and cometh not again.** A still stranger circumstance, and one still more suspicious. The second messenger could only have been sent out because the king disapproved the detention of the first. Whoever, therefore, had detained the second messenger must be consciously acting in opposition to the wishes of the king. **And the driving is like the driving of Jehu the son of Nimshi.** It is not meant that Jehu was driving his own chariot (which great men never did, ch. xxii. 34), and drove in a furious manner, but that the "company" was being urged forward at an unusual pace, in a reckless and hot-headed way. The watchman conjectured, therefore, that Jehu must be leading them, since he had a character for impetuosity. **For he driveth furiously;** or, *madly*—"like a madman" (Keil)—"præcipitanter" (Vatabl.). The LXX. translate ἐν παραλλαγῇ—which has, perhaps, the same meaning (comp. Eur., 'Hipp.,' 935; Lysias, Fr., 58).

Ver. 21.—**And Joram said, Make ready**—rather, *harness*; literally, *attach*—i.e. "attach the horses to the chariot—**and his chariot was made ready**—literally, *and one attached*, or *harnessed*, *his chariot*—**and Joram King of Israel and Ahaziah King of Judah went out, each in his chariot.** The uncle and the nephew went out together, still, as it would seem, unapprehensive of any danger, though the circumstances were certainly such as might well have aroused suspicion. Joram

was probably anxious to know the reasons which had induced the captain of his host to quit his post at Ramoth-Gilead. Ahaziah probably accompanied him out of politeness, though he too may have been curious to learn the news. If any disaster had overtaken the army of Israel, the safety of Judah might also be endangered. "Tua res agitur, paries cum proximus ardet." **And they went out against Jehu**—rather, *to meet Jehu*—εἰς ἀπαντὴν ᾿Ιοὺ (LXX.); see the Revised Version—**and met him in tho portion of Naboth the Jezreelite.** Humanly speaking, this was accidental. The "portion of Naboth," or his plot of ground, lay outside the south-eastern gate of the city, at no great distance from the walls; and it happened that Joram and Jehu met within its limits. Had the king started a little sooner, or had Jehu made less haste, the meeting would have taken place further from the town, and outside the "portion of Naboth." But Divine providence so ordered matters that vengeance for the sin of Ahab was exacted upon the very scene of his guilt, and a prophecy made, probably by Elisha, years previously, and treasured up in the memory of Jehu (ver. 26), was fulfilled to the letter.

Ver. 22.—**And it came to pass, when Joram saw Jehu, that he said, Is it peace, Jehu?** Still the same question is asked; but we cannot be sure that it is asked in exactly the same sense. Something in the aspect of Jehu, and in his furious haste, may by this time have alarmed the king. Or possibly he may be merely repeating the question put through his messengers, and still unanswered, "Is all well with the army or no? Has there been any disaster?" Jehu, at any rate, chooses to understand his vague phrase in the former sense, as if he had asked, "Is it peace between thee and me?" and answers in the negative. **And he answered, What peace, so long as the whoredoms of thy mother Jezebel and her witchcrafts are so many?** literally, *so long as the whoredoms of thy mother Jezebel and those many witchcrafts of hers continue.* By "whoredoms" are meant idolatries, as so frequently in Scripture (Lev. xix. 29; xx. 5; Jer. iii. 2, 9; xiii. 17; Ezek. xvi. 17; xx. 30; xxiii. 11, etc.; Hos. ii. 2; iv. 12; v. 4; Nah. iii. 4, etc.); by "witchcrafts" all those magical practices which were so common at the time in Egypt, Assyria, and Babylonia, and no doubt also in Phœnicia, and which were so strictly forbidden by the Mosaic Law (Exod. xxii. 18; Deut. xviii. 10). Besides the Baal-worship, Jezebel had introduced these unhallowed practices into the kingdom of Israel. Jehu reproaches Joram with allowing them, and declares that there can be no peace between him and his master under such circumstances,

Having gained his object and got within bowshot of the unsuspecting monarch, he throws off the mask and declares uncompromising hostility. "No man could use such terms of the queen-mother who was willing any longer to be a subject."

Ver. 23—26.—*Murder of Jehoram by Jehu.*

Ver. 23.—**And Joram turned his hands, and fled.** Joram made his charioteer turn the chariot suddenly round, and fled by the way by which he had come. "Turning the hands" is turning the chariot round by means of the hands; and Joram is said to have done that which he caused to be done. **And said to Ahaziah, There is treachery, O Ahaziah.** *Mirmah* is "deceit" or "fraud" of any kind, and here is not ill rendered by "treachery." Jehu's conduct was not justified by the mission given him (vers. 6—10), which certainly did not authorize him to commit a treacherous murder.

Ver. 24.—**And Jehu drew a bow with his full strength.** This meaning is scarcely contained in the Hebrew, which merely says that Jehu "filled his hand with his bow," that is to say, took his bow into his hands for the purpose of using it. **And smote Jehoram between his arms;** *i.e.* directed an arrow against Jehoram with so true an aim, that it struck him in the middle of the back between his shoulders. **And the arrow went out at his heart.** This was quite possible, for the heart lies towards the centre of the chest, not wholly on the left side. It is not necessary to suppose an oblique wound. **And he sank down in his chariot.** Jehoram fell into the "well," or body, of the chariot, and there lay, the chariot being brought to a stand.

Ver. 25.—**Then said Jehu to Bidkar his captain;** literally, *his thirdsman;* Koil renders "his aide-de-camp," probably one of those who was in his chariot with him—**Take up, and cast him in the portion of the field of Naboth the Jezreelite.** "Take up the body," *i.e.* "and cast it into the plot of ground which once belonged to Naboth the Jezreelite, and was forfeited to the crown at his death (1 Kings xxi. 15), and taken possession of by Ahab" (1 Kings xxi. 16). The reason for the order follows. **For remember how that, when I and thou rode together after Ahab his father, the Lord laid this burden upon him.** The LXX. have μνημονεύω, "I remember;" but the Hebrew text is זכר, not אזכר "Remember" (imperative mood) is the correct translation. Jehu recalls his captain's recollection to an occurrence which was deeply impressed upon his own. "When thou and I rode together after Ahab" probably means "when we two stood behind Ahab in his chariot." The Assyrian sculptures usually represent the monarch as attended by two body-guards, who ride in the

same chariot with him, standing up behind him, and often interposing their shields to protect his person. In this near proximity Jehu and Bidkar would hear any speech which was addressed to Ahab. By a "burden" is meant a sentence of punishment (comp. Isa. xiii. 1; xv. 1; xvii. 1; etc.; Nah. i. 1, etc.).

Ver. 26.—**Surely I have seen yesterday the blood of Naboth** (comp. 1 Kings xxi. 19, where the same idea of retribution is expressed, though in different words). Jehu, after the lapse of fourteen or fifteen years, naturally had forgotten the exact words used. **And the blood of his sons.** The execution of Naboth's sons had not been mentioned previously; but, under the rude jurisprudence of the age (ch. xiv. 6), sons were usually slain with their fathers. And, unless they had been removed, Ahab could not have inherited the vineyard. **Saith the Lord; and I will requite thee in this plat, saith the Lord.** This was the gist of the prophecy, which ran as follows: "*In the place* where dogs licked the blood of Naboth shall dogs lick thy blood, even thine." **Now therefore take** and **cast him into the plat of ground, according to the word of the Lord.** The evil prophesied against Ahab had been formally and expressly deferred to his son's days on Ahab's repentance (cf. 1 Kings xxi. 29).

Vers. 27—29.—*Murder of Ahaziah.*

Ver. 27.—**But when Ahaziah the king of Judah saw** this, **he fled by the way of the garden house.** As soon as Ahaziah saw Jehu shoot his arrow, he too took to flight; not, however, in the same direction as Joram, but southwards, towards his own land. If "garden house" is the right translation of בֵּית הַגָּן, we can say no more than that it was probably one of the lodges of the royal demesne, which lay south-east and south of Jezreel, whereof nothing more is known. But it is quite possible that we ought to translate, with the LXX., "by the way of Beth-Gan"—ἔφυγεν ὁδὸν Βαιθ-γάν. In this case "Beth-Gan" would be a village or town, probably identical with En-gannim, which lay at the foot of the hills bounding the Plain of Esdraelon, nearly due south of Jezreel (Zerin), and which is now known as Jenin (see the Map of Western Palestine, by Mr. Trelawney Saunders, compiled from the surveys of the Palestine Exploration Fund, where Ahaziah's flight is well traced. **And Jehu followed after him, and said, Smite him also in the chariot;** rather, *in his chariot,* not in that of Jehoram, since the two kings rode respectively in their own chariots (ver. 21). It was a bold step in a pretender not yet settled upon the throne to provoke the hostility of a neighbouring country by murdering its monarch; but Jehu probably thought he had more to fear from Ahaziah himself, who had been on such close terms of friendship with Jehoram, than from any probable successors. He, therefore, finding him in his power, pursued after him and slew him. From a religious point of view he could justify the act; since the commission given to him (ver. 7) was to smite all the house of Ahab, and Ahaziah was Ahab's grandson. And they did so **at the going up to Gur, which is by Ibleam.** The "ascent of Gur," מַעֲלֵה־גוּר, was probably the rising ground between the southern edge of the Plain of Esdraelon and the place known as "Ibleam," or "Bileam" (1 Chron. vi. 70), which is reasonably identified with the modern *Bir-el-Belameh*, two miles south of Jenin. Here the steep ascent necessarily delayed the chariot, and Ahaziah's pursuers gained upon him, approached him, and wounded him. **And he fled to Megiddo.** Wounded at the ascent of Gur, and despairing of making his way through the rough mountainous country which lay between him and Jerusalem, Ahaziah suddenly changed his route, perhaps thereby baffling his pursuers, and, skirting the hills, had himself conveyed to Megiddo (*Ledjun*), where he died, either of his wounds, or through some fresh violence on the part of Jehu (see 2 Chron. xii. 8, 9). The reconciliation of 2 Chron. xii. 8, 9 with the present passage is difficult, but not wholly impossible. Perhaps the Chronicler means by "Samaria" the kingdom, not the town.

Ver. 28.—**And his servants carried him in a chariot to Jerusalem.** No king of the house of David had as yet been buried elsewhere than in the rock-hewn sepulchre which David had constructed for himself and family at Jerusalem. As soon, therefore, as Ahaziah was dead, his attendants conveyed his dead body in a chariot to the Judæan capital. Jehu did not oppose, having no quarrel with the dead. **And buried him in his sepulchre;** *i.e.* in the particular excavation, or *loculus,* which he had prepared for himself. Jewish, like Egyptian, kings seem to have made it their business to see to the construction of their tomb as soon as they mounted the throne. Thus Ahaziah, though he had reigned but a year (ch. viii. 26), had already prepared himself a sepulchre. His "servants" buried him in it. **With his fathers in the city of David** (comp. 1 Kings xi. 43; xiv. 37; xv. 8, 24; xxii. 50; ch. viii. 24).

Ver. 29.—**And in the eleventh year of Joram the son of Ahab began Ahaziah to reign over Israel.** In ch. viii. 25 the accession of Ahaziah is placed in Joram's twelfth, instead of his eleventh, year. The slight discrepancy is sufficiently explained by the double reckoning of a king's "first year,"

familiar to chronologists, either (1) from the date of the accession to the end of the current civil year; or (2) from the date of the accession to the same day in the ensuing year.

Vers. 30—37.—*Death of Jezebel.*

Ver. 30.—**And when Jehu was come to Jezreel.** Some commentators suppose that Jehu did not engage personally in the pursuit of Ahaziah, but, leaving that to a portion of his retinue, pushed on with all haste to Jezreel, where Jezebel was, "the originator of all the mischief." But it is certainly more natural to understand (with Keil and Josephus) that Jehu himself pursued. The pursuit to Ibleam, where Ahaziah was mortally wounded, and the return to Jezreel, need not have occupied more than about three hours. **Jezebel heard** of it. She would naturally be the first to hear. On the death of her son, which must have ǀbeen plainly seen from the walls of Jezreel, she became practically the chief authority in the place, and indeed in the kingdom. Jehoram's sons were probably minors. **And she painted her face;** literally, *and she put her eyes in antimony;* i.e. she adorned her eyes with the dark dye which has always been fashionable in the East, and which is still used at the present day. The dye is spread both on the upper and the lower eyelids. It at once increases the apparent size of the eye, and gives it unnatural brilliancy. The Oriental nations, Babylonians, Assyrians, Medes, Persians, were acquainted with the practice from very early times; and it is not surprising that it was known to Jezebel. What was her exact object in applying it is more doubtful. The older commentators, who are followed by Ewald, suppose that she intended to "summon up all her seductive fascinations in order to tempt and conquer Jehu;" but more recent writers (Bähr, Keil, and others) argue that her probable age renders this incredible, since she had already a grandson who was twenty-three years of age (ch. viii. 26), and must therefore have been herself at least fifty. But, if we remember that Cleopatra was forty when she held Antony as her slave and hoped to captivate Augustus, it would seem to be not altogether beyond the bounds of possibility that a Phœnician princess of fifty may have thought that, by the use of art, she might render herself a captivating personage. There is, at any rate, no evidence that "putting the eyes in antimony" was an ordinary or a fitting preparation for meeting death in a way worthy of a queen. Ewald's view has, therefore much to commend it to our acceptance. Jezebel, trusting in the charms and the fascination which had been so potent over Ahab, may have imagined that she had still enough beauty left to capture

Jehu, provided she increased her natural attractions by a careful use of all the resources of art. **And tired her head.** Phœnician statues of goddesses have their hair arranged in long pendent curls, and bear on their heads a small conical cap with a ribbon wreathed round the base. The artists probably had queens and princesses as their models. There is no evidence that false hair was worn in Phœnicia, either by men or women. **And looked out at a window.** Windows, sometimes open, sometimes latticed, were common in Oriental houses from the earliest times. They mostly looked into the court round which a house was commonly built; but some few were in the external wall of the building; and through these new arrivals might be reconnoitred. Jezebel "looked out," partly to see, but perhaps still more to be seen.

Ver. 31.—**And as Jehu entered in at the gate, she said, Had Zimri peace, who slew his master?** This is a possible meaning of Jezebel's words, and it has among its advocates—Luther, De Wette, Maurer, and Dathe, besides our own translators. But so defiant an utterance is quite incompatible with an intention to captivate and conciliate. Probably, therefore, we should understand the queen either as saying affirmatively, "Peace to thee, Zimri!" (or, "Hail, Zimri!") "slayer of thy lord," or else as asking, "Is it peace" (*i.e.* "Is it peace now between thee and me?"), "Zimri, slayer of thy lord?" In either case, Zimri is an honorific appellation, recalling the fact of another Israelite general, who had revolted, slain his master, and reigned as king.

Ver. 32.—**And he lifted up his face to the window, and said, Who is on my side? who?** Whatever Jezebel's intention, Jehu yielded not a jot; he was deaf to her flatteries, blind to her seductions. He had made up his mind for "war to the knife" before he embarked upon his enterprise, and the feeble attempts of a queen whose part was played out, whose age he knew, and whom he no doubt regarded as an old woman, had no power on him. Instead of responding to her blandishments, he took a stern and hard line. He would not see her privately. He summoned to his aid the menials of the palace—the eunuchs—those on whom beauty has least influence. "Who is on my side? who?" he exclaimed (literally, "Who is with me? who?"): thus calling on the court servants to desert their masters, the guards to turn their swords against their employers, the menials to consummate an intra-palatial revolution. We cannot deny to Jehu the credit of vigour, promptness, audacity, talent to seize on the opportunity of the moment, and to make the most of it; but he must ever present himself to us as

the rough soldier, with no courtesy, with no chivalry, bent on accomplishing his own ends, and shrinking from no deed of blood, no precedent *pessimi exempli*, if thereby his ends might be brought about. **And there looked out to him two or three eunuchs.** Eunuchs had become an integral part both of the Jewish and of the Israelite courts from the time of David (1 Chron. xxviii. 1). They are an institution which almost necessarily accompanies polygamy; and they had long held high office in Egypt, in Babylon, and in Assyria. A position outside nature, at variance with all men's natural feelings and aspirations, of necessity depraves the character, weakens the moral principle, and ends by debasing the class. In Oriental history, the lowest, vilest part is always played by the eunuchs of the palace, who are ever ready to take part in any intrigues, in any conspiracies, and who seem to be almost wholly devoid of the ordinary feelings of humanity. The eunuchs who "looked out" to Jehu were probably the *chief* eunuchs of the palace, who had authority over the others, and indeed over the court officials generally.

Ver. 33.—**And he said, Throw her down.** A splendid example of the wicked man's prompt and bold and unscrupulous decision. A queen, a queen-mother, always more tenderly regarded than an ordinary queen-regnant, a princess in her own right (see ver. 34), daughter of a neighbouring and powerful potentate, settled in her kingdom for over thirty years, the most powerful person in the state during that entire period, backed up by the numerous and dominant party of her co-religionists, she is to Jehu nothing but a wicked woman who is in his way; she inspires him with no awe, she does not even touch him with any feeling of respect. "Throw her down." History presents no parallel to such an indignity. Kings and queens had been, time after time, removed by violence; their lives had been taken; they had been transplanted to another sphere of being. But the open casting forth from a window of a crowned head by the menials of the court, at the command of a usurper, was a new thing, unprecedented, unparalleled. It must have been a shock to all established notions of propriety. In commanding it Jehu showed his superiority to existing prejudice, his utter fearlessness, and his willingness to create a new precedent, which might seriously shake the monarchical principle. **So they threw her down.** There appears to have been no hesitation. The boldness of Jehu communicated itself to those whom he addressed; and the eunuchs violently seized the person of the queen, and precipitated her from the window to the ground below. She fell on the road by which the palace was approached, and lay there bleeding and helpless. **And some of her blood was sprinkled on the wall.** As she fell, some portion of her body struck against the wall of the palace, and left splashes of blood upon it. There were probably some projections from the wall between the window and the ground. **And on the horses.** As her body struck the projections, a bloody shower spurted from it, which fell in part upon the horses that drew Jehu's chariot. **And he trode her underfoot.** Like Tullia (Liv., i. 48), Jehu had his chariot driven over the prostrate corpse, so that the hoofs of his horses, and perhaps his own person, were sprinkled with the royal blood. Compare the passage of Livy, " Ameus, agitantibus furiis, Tullia per patris corpus carpentum egisse fertur, partemque sanguinis ac cædis paternæ cruento vehiculo, contaminata ipsa respersaque, tutisse ad penates suos virique sui." It is not often that royal corpses, unless in the heat of battle, have received such treatment.

Ver. 34.—**And when he was come in**— *i.e.* when Jehu had established himself in the royal palace—**he did eat and drink, and said.** His first care was to refresh himself —to order a banquet to be served, and to satisfy his appetite with food and drink. Not till afterwards did he bethink himself of the bloody corpse of his late queen and mistress, lying on the cold ground uncared for and untended, exposed to scorn and ignominy. When the thought occurred to him, it brought about a certain amount of relenting. **Go, see now this cursed woman.** He calls Jezebel ;"a cursed woman," not inappropriately. She had brought a curse on her husband, on her sons, and on her grandsons; she had been the evil genius of two countries, Israel and Judah; she had been the prime mover in a bloody persecution of the worshippers of Jehovah ; and was the true original source of the present revolution, which was to result in the deaths of so many others. **And bury her: for she is a king's daughter.** As queen-mother, Jehu, it seems, would not have regarded Jezebel as entitled to burial; but as daughter of Eth-Baal, King of the Zidonians (1 Kings xvi. 31), and so a princess born, he allowed her claim. Perhaps he feared lest further insult to the corpse might provoke the resentment of the Phœnician monarch, and draw down upon him that prince's hostility.

Ver. 35.—**And they went to bury her: but they found no more of her than the skull, and the feet, and the palms of her hands.** "The harder parts of the human frame " (Stanley); perhaps also the less palatable, since cannibals say that the palm of the human hand is excessively bitter. Dogs in Oriental countries are ever prowling about, especially in the vicinity of towns, on the look-out for food, and will eat flesh or offal of any kind. They have been called "the scavengers of the East," and the phrase well describes them. Dean Stanley saw "the wild dogs of Jezreel prowling about the mounds where the offal is cast outside the gates of the town by the inhabitants."

Ver. 36.—**Wherefore they came again, and told him.** The men whom he had sent to bury Jezebel returned, and told the king what they had found. The narrative woke another chord of memory which had hitherto slept. **And he said, This is the word of the Lord, which he spake by his servant Elijah the Tishbite.** The prophecy referred to is doubtless that recorded in 1 Kings xxi. 23. It is, however, here expanded, either because Jehu's recollection was not exact, or because the record in 1 Kings is abbreviated. The great point of the prophecy is common to both records, viz. that the dogs should eat Jezebel at Jezreel, on the scene of her iniquities. **Saying, In the portion of Jezreel shall dogs eat the flesh of Jezebel.** It is not quite clear what is meant by the "portion" (חֵלֶק) of Jezreel. Probably there is no allusion to the "portion" (חֶלְקָה) of Naboth (vers. 25, 26). Rather the same is meant as by חֵל in 1 Kings xxi. 23, viz. the cultivated space or "portion " of land outside the wall of the town (see the comment on that passage).

Ver. 37.—**And the carcase of Jezebel shall be as dung upon the face of the field** (comp. Ps. lxxxiii. 10 ; Zeph. i. 17; Jer. ix. 22 ; xvi. 4, etc.). The expression was proverbial. **In the portion of Jezreel** (see the comment on the preceding verse); so **that they shall not say, This is Jezebel.** The fragments of the body were so scattered that there could be no collective tomb, no place whereat admirers could congregate and say, " Here lies the great queen—here lies Jezebel." To rest in no tomb was viewed as a shame and a disgrace.

HOMILETICS.

Vers. 1—10.—*The prophet and the prophet-disciple—the duties of direction and of obedience.* The time had come for a great change—a " great revolution," to use the words of Ewald. The first dynasty of Israel which had shown any indications of stability was to be swept away, and another still more stable dynasty was to be established. That the will of God might be soon and recognized in the matter, its initiation was entrusted to the regular expounders of the Divine will—the prophets. Elisha, we may be sure, received express directions how to act; and the directions included a delegation of certain most important duties to another. Thus two persons are concerned in the great initiative scene; and the conduct of each is worthy of attention, and, under given circumstances, of imitation. Consider—

I. ELISHA AS DIRECTOR. 1. Elisha has made up his mind; there is no hesitation about him, no instability of purpose; he knows what he has to do, and is wholly bent on doing it. 2. His directions are clear, definite, unmistakable. There is no ambiguity in any of them. He prescribes a fixed and clearly defined line of conduct, which his subordinate is to carry out. He wastes no time on the consideration of accidents or contingencies. A certain work is to be done; and his subordinate is to do it in the simplest and most direct way.

II. THE PROPHET-DISCIPLE AS SUBORDINATE AGENT. 1. The prophet-disciple accepts the subordinate position readily, cheerfully, without reluctance. He is content to obliterate himself, and to play the part of a tool or instrument. 2. His obedience is exact, perfect. Whatever he has been ordered to do, he does; and he does no more. He is not officious, as so many zealous servants are; he does not seek to better his instructions. 3. His errand done, he disappears, sinks back into obscurity. We hear of his making no claim either on Elisha or on Jehu. The greatest political transaction of the day had proceeded from his initiative; but he asks no reward, he makes no boast. His work done, he vanishes, and we hear no more of him.

God's work has still to be carried on in the world by two sets of persons—directors and executants. It will be well or badly done, according as the lines here marked out are kept to or departed from. That wonderful efficiency which none can fail of admiring in the working of so many institutions within the Roman communion is traceable in a great measure to the fact that both directors and executants act in the spirit that animated Elisha and the prophet-disciple.

Vers. 11—24.—*Political revolutions justifiable under certain circumstances.* In a general way, revolution, resistance to constituted authority, rebellions, risings against the civil power, seem to be condemned, or at any rate discountenanced, by the teaching of Scripture, whether in the Old Testament or the New. They arise, for the most part, from human ambitions, from lust of power, from greed, from unrestrained passions, from selfishness; they involve in their course untold sufferings to large numbers; they issue commonly in a condition of social and political life, not better, but worse, than that from which they sprang. "Let every soul be subject to the higher powers;" "Fear God: honour the king;" "Ye must needs be subject, not only for wrath, but for conscience' sake," are precepts of wide application and of great force, deriving additional weight from the fact that, when they were uttered, a Nero occupied the throne. Still, their force may be overstrained. Scripture does not require, under all circumstances, an absolute and entire submission to the civil rulers, but justifies resistance, and allows of the resistance being pushed, in extreme cases, to rebellion. Examples are : 1. The resistance offered by David, first to Saul, and then to Ishbosheth. According to human law, Ishbosheth was the legitimate ruler, against whom David rebelled (2 Sam. ii. 1—10). 2. The rebellion of Jeroboam (1 Kings xii. 12—20). 3. The present instance—the rebellion of Jehu. 4. The rebellion of the Maccabee princes, related in the first and second Books of the Maccabees, which enlist our sympathy strongly in their behalf, and are set before her members by the Church "for example of life, and instruction in morals." If we ask, "When is rebellion justifiable?" the answer would seem to be—

I. IN THE LAST RESORT, WHEN THE NATION MUST OTHERWISE BE IRRETRIEVABLY INJURED. In Jehu's case "a family was on the throne which had introduced a licentious worship, had fostered it, and had persecuted the older and purer religion, which, if it had not succeeded in taking so firm a hold upon the people as to bind them to purity and virtue, at any rate had not been itself a deeply corrupting influence. The mischief had spread so far that it was time to try the last and severest measures, or to give up the contest entirely. The indictment was made out against the ruling house of corrupting the national honour, and undermining the national existence, of depriving the nation of a religion whose spirit was pure and elevating, and giving it one whose spirit was corrupting and licentious " (Bähr). In the case of the Maccabees, a foreign power, dominant over the country by right of conquest, had formed the design of completely sweeping away the Jewish religion and substituting for it the Greek, or rather the Syrian, polytheism and idolatry. The crisis was even more terrible than that in Jehu's time, the danger more pressing and greater. In both these cases the nation seems to have waited with the utmost patience, until there was no other remedy. Either a convulsion had to be faced, or the national religion, the national morality, and the national self-respect, would have been swept away. The nation in each case preferred revolution to submission ; and the sympathies of the sacred writers evidently go with them in their choice.

II. WHEN THERE IS A FAIR PROSPECT OF SUCCESS IF A STAND IS MADE. *Nemo tenetur ad impossibilia.* If the force on the side of authority is overwhelming, if the national spirit opposed to it is weak and faint, if there is no reasonable hope that resistance may be effectual and save the nation from the evils suffered and apprehended, then, whatever their reluctance, though it be "pain and grief to them," patriots are bound to restrain themselves and to remain quiescent. As Plato says, they must shelter themselves under a wall while the storm rages ; they must be content to keep themselves pure, as the seven thousand, who had not bowed the knee to Baal, did in Ahab's reign ; they must wait for better days. If, however, there be a fair chance of success, if it be reasonable to hope that the yoke which is doing deadly hurt to the nation may be thrown off, then no considerations of their own convenience or ease, no fear of blame, no shrinking from disturbance, or even bloodshed, should deter patriotic souls from initiating the struggle by which alone their country can be saved. Desperate diseases require desperate remedies. If Elisha and Jehu had waited with folded hands for Joram and Jezebel to work out their wicked will, the Baal-worship would have been riveted upon the northern, perhaps even upon the southern, kingdom. If the Maccabee family had submitted to the agents of Antiochus Ephiphanes, and failed to raise the standard of revolt, Judaism would have been merged in heathenism, and have perished from the earth. It may be added that if, in our own country, no resistance had been offered to James II., but his commands had been submitted to and carried out, then Great Britain would have been recovered to the Roman obedience, and the witness to a purer Christianity than that of Rome, which has been held up to the world by the English Church during the last two centuries, would have been extinguished and crushed, with what loss to the nation, to Europe, and to the world generally, it is impossible to estimate.

Vers. 25—37.—*Retribution may be long in coming, but it comes at last.* Even a heathen could say, " Raro antecedentem scelestum deseruit pede pœna claudo " (Horace, ' Od.,' iii. 2, lines 31, 32). Yet throughout all history evil-disposed men have persisted in wicked and cruel conduct, just as if it was not only possible, but probable, that retribution would be escaped. The lesson thus needs continually to be impressed on men, that, sooner or later, retribution *must* come—that there is no escape from it. Retribution must come—

I. BECAUSE GOD RULES THE UNIVERSE, AND GOD IS JUST. Disbelief in retribution is essentially atheistic. It implies either that there is no God, or that God is without one or more of those attributes which make him God. A just God must have the will to punish ; an omnipotent God must have the power to punish. If a so-called God did not punish sin, he must be either not just, or not omnipotent, or not either ; but then he would not be God. As Bähr says, "A God without vengeance, *i.e.* who cannot and will not punish, is no God, but a divinity fashioned from one's thoughts."

II. BECAUSE GOD HAS DECLARED THAT IT SHALL COME, AND GOD IS TRUE. God has said to each man, through his conscience, that he will punish sin. Remorse and regret, the dissatisfaction of a guilty conscience, are such punishment begun. In his Word God has expressly declared that he "will reward every man according to his works" (Ps. lxii. 12; Prov. xxiv. 12; Matt. xvi. 7; Rom. ii. 6; 2 Tim. iv. 14); that he "will by no means clear the guilty" (Exod. xxxiv. 7); that "indignation and wrath, tribulation and anguish, shall be on every soul of man that doeth evil " (Rom. ii. 8, 9). Nothing is more plainly taught in the whole of Scripture, from the beginning to the end, than requital, retribution, condign punishment. Ahab's case is singular, not in the general principle, but only in the exact correspondence between the sin and its punishment. Such correspondence is rare and abnormal; but it does occur from time to time, and, when it occurs, there is something about it that is most impressive and striking. When the author of proscription, Marius, is himself proscribed; when the dethroner of kings, Napoleon I., is himself dethroned; when the inventor of conspiracies, Titus Oates, falls a victim to an invented conspiracy; when Robespierre and Danton, who have ruled by the guillotine, perish by the guillotine;—"poetic justice," as it has been called, is satisfied, and the world at large is forced to recognize and acknowledge that requital has taken place in a signal way.

III. BECAUSE ANY NEGATIVE INSTANCE THAT CAN BE PRODUCED WILL ONLY SHOW A DELAY, NOT AN ABROGATION OF THE SENTENCE. Infinite time is at the disposal of the Almighty. Men are impatient, and, if retribution does not overtake the sinner speedily, are apt to conclude that it will never overtake him. But with the Almighty "one day is as a thousand years, and a thousand years as one day." The important thing to be borne in mind is the end; and the end will not be reached till " the judgment is set, and the books are opened" (Dan. vii. 10), and men are "judged out of those things which are written in the books, according to their works" (Rev. xx. 12). Punishment may be long in coming—the ungodly may continue during their whole lifetime in prosperity. But there remains a future. Where the heathen felt and said, " Raro," the Christian will say, " *Nunquam* antecedentem scelestum deseruit pede poena claudo."

HOMILIES BY VARIOUS AUTHORS.

Vers. 1—37.—*The deaths of Jehoram and Jezebel; or, the Divine law of retribution.* King Jehoram was lying sick at Jezreel of the wounds he had received in battle from the Syrians. Ahaziah King of Judah had come down to visit him, and, as they conversed together, the watchman upon the city wall brought tidings of an armed company approaching. Jehu, at the head of them, was by-and-by recognized by his furious driving. He had already been proclaimed king in Ramoth Gilead, but Jehoram knew nothing of this. He suspected some ill news, however, and he and Ahaziah drove out with their two chariots to meet Jehu. *And where was it that they met?* Jehu had good reason to know the place. So had Jehoram. About twenty years before, another memorable meeting had taken place there. Jehoram's father, Ahab, had coveted Naboth's vineyard. Jehoram's mother, Jezebel, had brought about Naboth's death by a process of false swearing against him. Naboth was dead, and Ahab, accompanied by his two captains, Jehu and Bidkar, rode out to take possession of that vineyard whose owner the queen had murdered. But his sin had found him out. Elijah, the messenger of God, met him there. And there, in that vineyard which he had procured through covetousness, envy, treachery, and bloodshed, Ahab was compelled to listen to his doom. Terrible words they were indeed for a king to hear. "Thus saith the Lord, In the place where dogs licked the blood of Naboth shall dogs lick thy blood, even thine." And Jezebel, the instigator of the crime, was not forgotten. "The dogs shall eat Jezebel by the wall of Jezreel." And now, in that very place, stained with the blood of Naboth, Jehu meets Jehoram, the son of Ahab the murderer and the king. The blood of Naboth cries to Heaven for vengeance. Jehoram was little better than his father. He too "cleaved unto the sins of Jeroboam the son of Nebat, who made Israel to sin." He forsook the true God and served other gods. No doubt his conscience smote him and his spirit failed him, as he asked of Jehu, "Is it peace?" But there was not much time left him to prepare to die. Jehu's words were few, and his actions quick as thought. With his full strength he drew his bow and sent his arrow straight to Jehoram's heart. It was then that the words of Elijah, spoken twenty years before in that very place, flashed back upon his mind, and he caused the lifeless body of Jehoram to be cast into the field of Naboth the Jezreelite. But Jehu's work of vengeance is not yet done. Jezebel's long career of wickedness had hardened her heart and blinded her to her danger. As Jehu rode into the city, she sat at her window in her best attire, as if to defy him, and greeted him with the sneering question,

"Had Zimri peace, who slew his master?" But Jehu is not a man to be trifled with. He finds willing helpers in her own servants. At his command they threw her down into the street, and she—the adulteress and the murderess, the woman whose name has become proverbial as a symbol of everything that is bad—is trampled under the horses' feet, and once more the doom of Heaven is fulfilled: "In the portion of Jezreel shall dogs eat the flesh of Jezebel." We learn from this narrative some important lessons.

I. SIN, NOT REPENTED OF, MUST BE PUNISHED. This is a law of nature. It is a fact of history. It is the very essence of morality. It is the very essence of justice. It is at the basis of social order in a nation. It is at the basis of the moral government of the universe. Those who transgress *the law of nations*, those who transgress the laws of honesty or of morality, those who take away the life, or the property, or the character of others, must be made to suffer for it. This is necessary, that justice may be vindicated. It is necessary, in order that property and person and character may be safe. It is necessary, in order that other evil-doers may be deterred from crime. Even under our own national law, we feel that there is something wrong when an evil-doer escapes. We feel that it has a bad effect upon the community when crime goes unpunished. Now, what is *sin* in the Bible sense? *Sin is the transgression of the Law.* It is a transgression of a far higher law than the law of nations, of that law on which the well-being of all nations depends—the eternal Law of God. The Law of God is at the foundation of all true well-being and happiness in every nation and in every age. "This do, and thou shalt live." "The commandment is holy, and just, and good." It is, therefore, in the interests of every nation, it is in the interests, not of one generation of men merely, but of those who shall come after them, that those who transgress the Divine Law should suffer for it. *Every violation of a Divine law must be followed by its corresponding punishment.* "Whatsoever a man soweth, that shall he also reap." Look at your own lives in the light of this great truth. Are there any sins in your lives unrepented of? Then be assured that the punishment, if it has not yet come, awaits you. Sins against God, against God's Law, against God's sabbath; sins against our fellow-man—sins of unfair dealing, sins of evil-speaking, or other and grosser sins; every one of these, if not repented of, is sure to bring its corresponding punishment. "Be sure your sin will find you out."

II. PUNISHMENT MAY BE DELAYED, BUT IT IS NONE THE LESS SURE. There is an old Irish proverb, "The vengeance of God is slow, but sure." We have many illustrations of that in history. It was long after Jezebel's great crime before her punishment overtook her. When the Israelites were journeying through the wilderness, the Amalekites treated them with great treachery and cruelty, falling upon them in the rear, and when they were faint and weary. It was not until four hundred years afterwards that the sentence against Amalek was executed: but it was executed at last. We may kill our enemies, we may seek to destroy all traces of our crime, but *we can never destroy the memory and the guilt of it by any acts of ours.* Charles IX. of France was led, by the importunity of another Jezebel, Mary de Medicis, to kill Admiral Coligny, who was the great leader of the French Protestants. For a long time he refused, but at last he consented in the memorable words, "Assassinate Admiral Coligny, but leave not a Huguenot alive in France to reproach me." That was the origin of the Massacre of St. Bartholomew. Having killed Coligny, he did not want any of his friends to remain to bear witness against him. How anxious men are to destroy all traces of their crime! And yet how vain all such efforts are! There is One whose eye sees every act of human life. We may escape the judgment of men, but we cannot escape the judgment of God. *If not here, then certainly hereafter*, every sin, not repented of, will receive its due reward. "For we must all appear before the judgment-seat of Christ; that every one may receive the things done in his body, according to that he hath done, whether it be good or bad."

III. THERE IS OFTEN A RESEMBLANCE BETWEEN THE PLACE AND MANNER OF THE SIN AND THE PLACE AND MANNER OF THE PUNISHMENT. 1. It was *at Naboth's vineyard* that the great sin of Ahab's house had been committed. There, too, at Naboth's vineyard, Jehoram, Ahab's son, was slain. It was *outside the walls of Jezreel* that the dogs licked the blood of Naboth. There, too, the dogs licked the blood and ate the flesh of Jezebel his murderess. It would seem as if this was part of the Divine Law of retribution. One reason for it would appear to be that *it fixes unmistakably the connection between the sin and its punishment.* Robespierre, the famous French revolutionist, literally choked the river Seine with the heads of those whom he sent to the guillotine. But the day came when the death-tumbrel containing himself was trundled along the streets of Paris to the selfsame fatal axe, amid the shouts and execrations of the multitude. Cardinal Beaton condemned to death George Wishart, one of the first of the Scottish Reformers, and watched him burning at the stake, while he himself reclined on rich cushions on the walls of his castle at St. Andrew's. Three months afterwards the cardinal himself was put to death, and his dead body was hung by a sheet from the very battlements whence he had looked at the execution of Wishart. *There is something more than accident in such things.* There is the vivid impression intended to be made on people's minds, that "whatsoever a man soweth, that shall he also reap." 2. *The same is true of the resemblance between the manner of the sin and the manner of the punishment.* Jezebel's murder of Naboth was treacherous and ignominious. She herself was put to death in a treacherous and ignominious way. "With what measure ye mete, it shall be measured to you again." Jacob cruelly deceived his aged father Isaac when he was blind and feeble. What a pointed retribution it was when he was afterwards cruelly deceived by his own sons in their statements about Joseph! Haman was hanged on the gallows which he had made for Mordecai. One of the most terrible instances of this truth, that as we have treated others we shall be treated ourselves, is the case of Charles IX. of France, referred to above. He consented to the Massacre of St. Bartholomew. He caused the streets of Paris to run with the blood of the Huguenots. He died at the age of twenty-four: and what a death! French historians of the highest order say that he was in such agony of remorse that he literally sweated blood. The blood that oozed from his own body caused him to think of those whose blood he had so freely shed, and he cried out in his last hours about the massacre of the Huguenots. Horrible! Yes; but there is a deep and solemn truth underlying all this. It is a truth that should have practical result upon every life. "With what measure ye mete, it shall be measured to you again." If your sin is public, most likely your punishment will be public. Men who commit commercial frauds—that is, sins against public confidence and trust—they ought to suffer, and they do suffer, public exposure. If your sin is secret, your punishment will also most likely be secret. They who sin against the laws of health suffer in an impaired constitution. They who sin by speaking evil about others most likely will have many to speak evil about themselves. Standing there by Naboth's vineyard, and thinking of the envy, covetousness, and murder, of which it reminds us, and their terrible consequences, let us hear the blood of Naboth and the blood of Naboth's house crying to us from the ground, "With what measure ye mete, it shall be measured to you again." Such, then, is the Divine law of retribution. But God, who is just, is also merciful. He willeth not the death of a sinner, but rather that he should turn from his wickedness, and live. We have looked at the way of his justice. Let us look also at the way of his mercy. It is the way of the cross. "God so loved the world, that he gave his only begotten Son, that whosoever believeth in him should not perish, but have everlasting life." *If you reject God's mercy, there is only the other alternative—God's retributive justice.*—C. H. I.

Ver. 1—ch. x. 36.—*The history of Jehu.* "Then Jehu came forth to the servants of his lord," etc. Jehu was the son of Jehoshaphat and the grandson of Nimshi. He was one of the monsters of history. The leading facts of his revolting life will be found in this and the following chapter. His history furnishes—

I. A REVOLTING EXHIBITION OF HUMAN DEPRAVITY. He was ruthlessly and craftily cruel. He shot Jehoram dead in his chariot. "And Jehu drew a bow with his full strength, and smote Jehoram between his arms." He commanded Jezebel, who was looking out of a window as he drove up, to be thrown down, and in her fall she was fatally injured, and her body was trodden down by the feet of horses, and afterwards consumed by dogs (ver. 36). He then proceeded to exterminate the family of Ahab. He addressed letters to those who had the care of his sons (no less than seventy in number), and proposed to them to select the fittest of them, and place him on the throne of his father. This they declined to do (through fear of

Jehu), but promised to do anything else that might be required. Accordingly Jehu directed them to bring the heads of Ahab's sons the next day to Jezreel, and they were sent in two baskets. He directed them to be emptied out in two heaps at the gate of the city, and to remain there over night. The next morning he ordered a general slaughter of all Ahab's family and adherents in the town of Jezreel. He then set out for Samaria, and, meeting on his way a party of forty-two persons, all of the family of Ahaziah, he seized and slew them (ch. x. 1—13). Pursuing his malignant cruelty, on his arrival at Samaria, he cuts off every branch of the house of Ahab that he can find (ch. x. 17). To effect this, with an infernal craftiness, he ordered all the worshippers of Baal throughout the land to assemble, as if he desired to join them in united worship. All having assembled, without the absence of a single man, he caused every one to be put to death (ch. x. 20—28). Here is a fiend in human form; and, alas! he is but a specimen of those monsters in human history who, in almost every age and land, have revelled in the blood and slaughter of their fellow-men. Such characters as these declare in thunder that men have fallen from their normal state. For who can believe that Infinite Purity and Benevolence would create characters of this class? All sin is an *apostasy*.

II. A DISTRESSING MYSTERY IN THE GOVERNMENT OF GOD. That a just God should allow such men to become kings, and should even place them on a throne over the destinies of millions, is a mystery at which we stand aghast. That the merciful Father should permit men to be murderers one of another confounds us with amazement. Yet this has been going on everywhere through the millenniums of human history. Verily "clouds and darkness are round about him." "His way is in the sea, and his path in the great waters," etc.

III. A MIGHTY ARGUMENT FOR FUTURE RETRIBUTION. Were we to believe that this state of things is to continue for ever, that there is no retributive period before us, when there will be a balancing of human accounts and a settling of human affairs, religion, which is supreme love to God, would be out of the question. He who could prove to me that there is no future state of retribution would destroy within me all the possibilities of religion. But the concurrent belief of mankind, the universal cries of conscience, and the declarations of the gospel assure us that there is a reckoning day to come. "We must all appear before the judgment-seat of Christ." "I saw, and behold a great white throne," etc.

IV. A PROOF OF THE SUPREME NEED OF A MORAL REGENERATOR. What can alter the character of such men as this Jehu, and put an end to all the cruelties, tyrannies, frauds, and violence, that turn the world into a Pandemonium? Philosophy, literature, civilization, legislative enactments, ceremonial religions? No; nothing short of a power which can *change the moral heart*. "Marvel not that I say unto you, Ye must be born again." The gospel is this regenerating power. Thank God, One has come into this world who will "create a new heaven and a new earth, wherein dwelleth righteousness."—D. T.

Vers. 1—14.—*Jehu made king.* The word of the Lord to Elijah, that Jehu should be anointed king (1 Kings xix. 16), was now to be fulfilled. The delay in the fulfilment is perhaps to be attributed to Ahab's repentance (1 Kings xxi. 29). God bore long with this wicked house, and did not cut it off till the cup of its iniquity was full. The execution of God's threatenings may be long postponed, but, like his promises, his threatenings never fail in the end to be fulfilled (2 Pet. iii. 9).

I. THE MESSENGER DESPATCHED. 1. *He was sent by Elisha.* On Elisha had fallen the mantle of Elijah, and to him belonged the task of executing Elijah's unfulfilled commissions. We must distinguish throughout this history between the motives which actuated Jehu in his conspiracy against Ahab, and the providential purpose which, as God's instrument, he was raised up to fulfil. That is to be read from the standpoint of the prophet. Israel was a people called into existence for the purpose of being a witness for the true God amidst surrounding heathenism. It owed its existence and possession of the land of Canaan to Jehovah. From him it had received its polity; to him it was bound in solemn covenant; the fundamental laws of its constitution required undivided allegiance to him. The penalties which would follow from disobedience were but a counterpart of the blessings which would flow from obedience.

The first great sin of the nation was in the setting up of the calves under Jeroboam. For adherence to this unlawful form of worship two dynasties had already perished (ver. 9). But with the accession of the house of Omri a new development in evil took place (1 Kings xvi. 31, 32). The worship of the Phœnician Baal was introduced; God's prophets were relentlessly persecuted, and, under the influence of Jezebel, the moving spirit of three reigns, corruption had spread far and near throughout the realm, and had penetrated even to Judah. Jehoram at first showed a better spirit (ch. iii. 2), but he must afterwards have yielded to the superior influence of his mother, for Baal-worship was restored, and had the prestige of court example (ver. 22; ch. x. 21). Under these circumstances, it was folly to hesitate, if Israel was to be saved. "Here the question of the justifiableness of rebellion against a legitimate dynasty, or of revolution in the ordinary sense of the word, cannot arise. The course of the house of Ahab was a rebellion against all law, human and Divine, in Israel" (Bähr). Even in ordinary earthly states, the right of revolution when religion, liberty, morality, and national honour can be saved by no other means, is universally conceded. But revolution here was not left to dubious human wisdom. The initiative was taken by Jehovah himself, acting through his prophet, and express Divine sanction was given to the overthrow of Ahab's house. 2. *His responsible commission.* The person chosen by Elisha to convey God's call to Jehu, and anoint him king, was one of the sons of the prophets. The anointing was to be in secret; hence the choice of a deputy. No value attaches to the tradition that the messenger was the future Prophet Jonah. Of his personality we know nothing more than is here told. He was an obscure individual, yet he set in motion a train of events of the most tragic significance. A child's hand may suffice to explode a mine. This messenger Elisha ordered to take a flask of the holy oil, and go to Ramoth-Gilead, where Jehu was. When he found the son of Nimshi, he was to retire with him into the innermost apartment, and anoint him King of Israel in the name of Jehovah, then he was to "open the door, and flee, and tarry not." 3. *The spirit in which he was to execute it.* It was a clear, unmistakable, but terribly serious and important message this prophetic disciple was entrusted with; and it is instructive to notice the manner in which he was directed to perform his task. "Gird up thy loins," etc., said Elisha. He was to prepare at once for action; he was to make no delay on his errand; he was faithfully to execute the commands given to him; when his work was done, he was directly to leave the spot. In God's service there is to be no lingering, or looking back, or turning from side to side, or dallying on the field of duty. The powers of body and soul are to be braced up for the doing of the "one thing" given us to do. "Girding up the loins of your mind," says an apostle (1 Pet. i. 13). Promptitude, speed, fidelity, stopping where the command of God stops,—these are invaluable qualities for doing God's work.

II. JEHU ANOINTED. 1. *The messenger's arrival.* Jehoram had returned to Jezreel to be healed of wounds received from the Syrians, and Jehu was at this time in command of the army at Ramoth-Gilead. The city itself had previously fallen into the hands of the Israelites. When the messenger arrived, he found the captains of the host sitting together in some house or court, and he at once addressed Jehu with the words, "I have an errand to thee, O captain." Jehu put the question, "Unto which of all us?" and the answer was, "To thee, O captain." The call of God may come to us at unexpected times and in surprising ways. It may come through others, or its voice may be heard in providence. There are general calls which God gives "to us all," and there are special calls to the individual. In whatever way the call of God is made known to us, we do well to give attentive heed to it. 2. *The act of anointing.* Jehu's anointing was to take place secretly. The messenger was to take him into an "inner chamber," and there make known his errand. We are reminded that it is generally in silence and secrecy that God gives men their summons to their peculiar life-work. No time was wasted. The young man, trembling, excited, no doubt, at the thought of the perilous deed he was performing, and at the awful nature of the message he had to deliver, had no sooner got Jehu in private than he poured the oil from his flask upon his head, and said, "Thus saith the Lord God of Israel, I have anointed thee king over the people of the Lord, even over Israel." There is involved in this brief announcement the truths: (1) That royal authority is from God. He sets up kings and puts down kings (Dan. ii. 21). Those only who rule by his sanction and with his favour are legitimate rulers. (2) Israel was a people of the Lord. Only God, therefore, had the right to appoint its rulers, and to determine the limits within which royal power should be exercised. It was by their setting at nought of all the limits of a theocratic constitution that Ahab and his house had forfeited the throne. (3) Jehu was made king by the direct act of God. God had taken the kingdom from Ahab's house and given it to him. It followed however, that if he, in turn, departed from God's commandments, he would incur the same fate. 3. *The terrible charge.* The prophet next declared to Jehu the terrible duty imposed upon him as the executor of God's judgments. It was certainly work from which any man might shrink, though to Jehu it does not seem to have been repugnant, as paving his own way to the throne. We notice: (1) The ground of the judgment: "That I may avenge the blood of my servants the prophets," etc. "Precious in the sight of the Lord is the death of his saints" (Ps. cxvi. 15). Whoso touches them, touches him (Acts ix. 4). He will not allow the least injury done to them to pass unavenged (Matt. xviii. 6). (2) The range of the judgment: "The whole house of Ahab"—king, queen-mother, the royal household, every one, great and small, having in him the accursed blood. It was a root-and-branch extermination that was decreed. (3) The terribleness of the judgment. Dreadful as this execution was, it was in accordance with the ideas of the time. In some sense it was a necessary concomitant of such a revolution as Jehu was about to bring about. From the Divine side it was justified as an act of vengeance against a wicked house. Ahab's house did not fall without warning, for it had already the doom of Jeroboam's and Baasha's dynasties to warn it from evil courses. Special signs of the Divine wrath were to attend the end of Jezebel, the prime instigator of Ahab's wickedness. It was foretold that the dogs would eat Jezebel in the portion of Jezreel, and there would be none to bury her. How fearful a thing it is, as shown by these examples, to fall into the hands of a living God (Heb. x. 31)! Great persecutors have often met a terrible end.

III. JEHU PROCLAIMED. 1. *Jehu and his captains.* The whole circumstances of the prophet's visit had been so strange, his appearance had been so wild, and his calling out of Jehu for a private interview so remarkable, that the captains who had witnessed the scene were naturally much astonished. Their first question, accordingly, when Jehu reappeared among them, himself somewhat agitated, and his hair streaming with the oil which had been poured upon it, was "Is it peace? Wherefore came this mad fellow to thee?" Men under any spiritual excitement seem "mad fellows" to profane minds (Hos. ix. 7; Acts xxvi. 24; 2 Cor. v. 13); but there may have been something in this messenger's dishevelled appearance—the result of his haste—his eager, hasty manner, and the strange fire that burned in his eye, which gave them the impression of one not altogether accountable for his actions. His hasty flight at the end of the interview would add to their surprise. Jehu, in reply, sought to evade explanation. His words, "Ye know the man, and his communication," mean either, "You have taken a right estimate of him as a madman, and therefore need not concern yourself with what he said;" or, "You are yourselves at the bottom of this trick, and know very well wherefore he came." The latter is, perhaps, the better sense, and may indicate that Jehu wished to sound his companions before going further. Their eager, "It is false; tell us now," shows how greatly their curiosity was aroused. Jehu thereupon told them frankly what had happened. 2. *Jehu proclaimed king.* The response on the part of the captains was immediate. Jehu must already have been a general favourite, or the proposal to make him king would not have met with such easy acceptance. As with one accord, the captains threw off their upper garments, spread them on the stairs, made Jehu mount above them, and, blowing the trumpets, forthwith proclaimed him king. Would that when God comes declaring to men the anointing and exaltation of " another King, even Jesus," his words found as ready a response!—J. O.

Vers. 14—37.—*Jehu as avenger.* No sooner is Jehu proclaimed king than, with characteristic decision, he gives orders that no one be permitted to leave the city to carry news to Jehoram; then, mounting his chariot, he drives off furiously to Jezreel. Whatever Jehu did, he did "with all his might" (Eccles. ix. 10). It is this vigorous decision of character which made him so suitable an instrument in executing God's vengeance on the house of Ahab.

I. JEHU'S APPROACH TO JEZREEL. 1. *The watchman's announcement.* In the far distance the watchman on the tower of Jezreel beholds a company of horsemen rapidly approaching. What can it portend? The report is brought to the king, who unsuspiciously sends out a messenger on horseback to inquire. Towers and watchmen are for the protection of a city and its inhabitants. But "except the Lord keep the city, the watchman waketh but in vain" (Ps. cxxvii. 1). And if the Lord decrees the destruction of a city, or of those in it, towers and watchmen will do little to protect them. 2. *Successive messengers.* These verses are chiefly interesting as illustrating the character of Jehu. The messenger sent by Jehoram soon reaches the company, and asks, "Is it peace?" The idea probably is, "What tidings from the field of battle?" Jehu does not even answer him civilly, but, with a rude "What hast thou to do with peace?" he orders him to turn behind him. A man this who will brook no delay, submit to no curb, endure no check, in his imperious course. He sweeps obstacles from his path, and bends them to his will. This messenger returns not, and a second, sent out from the king, meets a like reception, and is also compelled to ride behind. 3. *Jehu recognized.* At length the horsemen are near enough for the watchman to get a closer view, and he has no difficulty in recognizing the furious driving of the leading figure as the driving of Jehu. It is familiar to all that character imprints itself on manner. Physiognomy, walk, gesture, handwriting even, are windows through which, to an observant eye, the soul looks out. Hypocrisy may create a mask behind which the real character seeks to hide itself. But hypocrisy, too, has characteristic ways of betraying its presence, and the mask cannot always be kept on. If we wish habitually to appear true, we must be true.

II. JEHORAM AND AHAZIAH SLAIN. 1. *The fateful meeting.* On learning that Jehu was approaching, King Jehoram, now convalescent, prepared his chariot, and, accompanied by Ahaziah of Judah, went out to meet his captain. (1) The two encountered at the portion of Naboth the Jezreelite. Strange coincidence, only, as we shall see below, more than coincidence. As the chariots meet, the king puts the anxious question, "Is it peace, Jehu?" Alas! the day of peace is over; it is now the day of vengeance. (2) Jehu throws no disguise over his intentions. With his usual vehement abruptness he at once bursts forth, "What peace, so long as the whoredoms of thy mother Jezebel and her witchcrafts are so many?" Jehu was right: there can be no peace in a state when the foundations of religion and morality are everywhere subverted. When fountains of immorality are opened at head-quarters, their poisonous influence speedily infects the whole nation (Hos. iv. 5). They who are responsible for the subversion of righteousness in a state, must bear the penalty. (3) Jehoram needed to hear no more. He saw at a glance the situation, and with a shout, "Treachery, O Ahaziah!" he turned and fled. But there was no grain of pity in Jehu. With fierce promptitude he seizes his bow, fits one arrow to the string, and, taking sure aim, smites the flying king right through the heart. Jehoram falls—is dead. 2. *Blood for blood.* The tragedy thus transacted was in the immediate neighbourhood of Naboth's vineyard. On that very spot, or near it, Naboth's own blood had been shed (1 Kings xxi. 13), and, as this verse shows (ver. 26), not his alone, but the blood of his sons. Thither, after the murder, Ahab went down to take possession of the vineyard, and there, when he arrived, he found Elijah standing, waiting to denounce upon him the doom of blood. This was not all, for among those who rode with Ahab that day were two of his captains, one of them Bidkar, the other this Jehu, who heard the prophetic announcements against Ahab and his family (1 Kings xxi. 19—24). Ahab himself was subsequently spared, but the doom predicted against him had now fallen on his son: "In the place where dogs licked the blood of Naboth shall dogs lick thy blood, even thine" (1 Kings xxi. 19). That prophecy, probably, had never altogether left the mind of Jehu, but now it came home to him with fresh force as he saw it actually fulfilled by his own hand. Bidkar, too, as it chanced, was there, and Jehu recalled to him the prophetic oracle. Then, to give it literal accomplishment, he bade Bidkar give orders that the corpse of Jehoram should be thrown into the plat of ground which formerly belonged to Naboth. Startling correspondences often thus occur between sin and its mode of punishment. When they occur in fiction, we speak of them as instances of "poetic justice." But poetry, in this as in other cases, is "unconscious philosophy," and is not opposed to truth. Its truth in such representations lies rather in seizing and bringing to light actual laws in the moral government of the world. There is a singular tendency in events in history to fold back on each other—even dates and places presenting a series of marvellous coincidences. 3. *A partner in doom.* The King of Judah had, the moment the alarm was given, sought his own safety. He fled " by the way of the garden house "—was it the " garden of herbs," into which Naboth's vineyard had been converted (1 Kings xxi. 2)? But in vain. The peremptory Jehu allows nothing to escape his vigilance, and immediately he is on Ahaziah's track. His command was, " Smite him also in the chariot," and this was done, " at the going up to Gur, which is by Ibleam." Ahaziah continued his flight to Megiddo, where he died. A slightly different account of the manner of his death is given in 2 Chron. xxii. 9. Whatever the precise circumstances of the death, we cannot but see in it (1) a righteous retribution for his own sins; and (2) an example of the end of evil association. Through his mother Athaliah, daughter of Jezebel, he was brought into close and friendly relations with the court of Samaria, and, sharing in the crimes of Ahab's house, shared also in their fate. It was his visit to King Jehoram which immediately brought down this doom upon him.

III. THE FATE OF JEZEBEL. 1. *Her daring defiance.* When Jehoram had been slain, the end of Jezebel, the prime mover and presiding spirit in all the wickedness that had been wrought in Israel, could not be far distant. Jezebel perfectly apprehended this herself, for, on hearing that Jehu had come to Jezreel, she prepared to give him a defiant reception. While one loathes the character of the woman, it is impossible not to admire the boldness and spirit with which she faces the inevitable. Her proud, imperious nature comes out in her last actions. She paints her eyelids with antimony, tires her head, and adorns her person, as if she was preparing for some festal celebration. Then she plants herself at the window, and, when Jehu appears, assails him with bitter taunting words. " Is it peace, thou Zimri, thy master's murderer? " she mockingly asked. What a power for evil this woman had been in Israel! What a power, with her strong intellect and will, she might have been for good! 2. *Her ghastly end.* If Jezebel thought, by this show of imperious defiance, to produce any effect on Jehu, perhaps to disarm him by sheer admiration of her boldness, she had mistaken the man. Jehu's impetuous nature was not to be thus shaken from its purpose. He quickly brought the scene to a conclusion. " Who is on my side? who? " he cried, lifting up his eyes to the windows. Two or three eunuchs, no friends of Jezebel, and anxious only to please the new ruler, gave the needful sign. " Throw her down," was the pitiless order; and in another instant the painted Jezebel was hurled from the palace window, and, dashed on the ground, was being trodden by the hoofs of the horses. Pitiless herself, she now met with no compassion. One who had shed much blood, and rejoiced in it, her own blood was now bespattered on the wall and on the horses. Jehu had no compunctions, but, fresh from the dreadful spectacle, entered the palace, and sat down to eat and drink. But the climax was yet to come. As if even he felt that, vengeance being now sated, some respect was due to one who had so long held sway in Israel, he bade his servants " Go, see now this cursed woman, and bury her: for," he said, " she is a king's daughter." The servants went, but soon returned with a shocking tale. Attracted by the scent of blood, the prowling city dogs had found their way into the enclosure, and, short as the time had been, all that remained of haughty Jezebel was the skull, and feet, and palms of the hands, strewn about the court. 3. *A prophecy fulfilled.* Such was the dreadful end of this haughty, domineering, evil woman. Possibly even Jehu could not restrain a shudder when he heard of it. He had not thought of it before, but now he recalled the close of that awful prophecy of Elijah to Ahab, " The dogs shall eat Jezebel by the wall of Jezreel " (1 Kings xxi. 23), the terms of which had been repeated to him by Elisha's messenger, (ver. 10). That word of God had been fulfilled with ghastly literalness. Would that men would lay to heart the lesson, and believe that all God's threatenings will be as certainly fulfilled!—J. O.

EXPOSITION.

CHAPTER X.

Vers. 1—36.—THE REIGN OF JEHU OVER ISRAEL.

Vers. 1—28.—The revolution initiated by the destruction of Joram and Jezebel is here traced through its second and its third stages. The immediate question, after Joram's death, was—Would any member of his family rise up as a claimant of the throne, and dispute the succession with Jehu? Ahab had seventy male descendants, all of them resident in Samaria: would there be any one among their number bold enough to come forward and assert his hereditary right? Jehu regarded this as the most pressing and imminent danger, wherefore his first step was to challenge such action, and either precipitate it or crush it. In vers. 1—11 is related the action taken by him, so far as the descendants of Ahab were concerned, and his success in ridding himself of all rivals possessed of so strong a claim. Vers. 12—14 relate his dealings with another body of Ahab's relations, belonging to the neighbouring kingdom of Judah. In vers. 15—28 an account is given of the still more bloody and more sweeping measures by which he cowed the party opposed to him, and firmly established his dynasty in the Israelite kingdom.

Vers. 1—11.—*The destruction of the seventy sons of Ahab.*

Ver. 1.—**And Ahab had seventy sons in Samaria.** By "sons" we must understand "male descendants." Most of the "seventy" were probably his grandsons (see ver. 3); some may have been great-grandsons. They lived in Samaria; since Samaria was the principal residence of the court, Jezreel being simply a country palace—the "Versailles," as it has been called, or "Windsor" of the Israelite kings. **And Jehu wrote letters, and sent to Samaria, unto the rulers of Jezreel.** "Jezreel" is almost certainly a corrupt reading. The "rulers of Jezreel" would be at Jezreel; and, if Jehu wished to communicate with them, he would not need to "write." Had any chance taken them to Samaria—a very improbable circumstance—they would have had no authority there, and to address them would have been useless. Jehu's letters were, no doubt, addressed to *the rulers of Samaria;* and so

the LXX. expressly state (ἀπέστειλεν ἐν Σαμαρείᾳ πρὸς τοὺς ἄρχοντας Σαμαρείας); but the reading "Jezreel" can scarcely have arisen out of "Samaria" (יזרעאל out of שמרון), since the difference of the two words is so great. Most probably the original word was "Israel" (ישראל), which is easily corrupted into "Jezreel" (יזרעאל). The rulers of Samaria, the capital, might well be called "the rulers of Israel." **To the elders;** rather, *even the elders.* Not distinct persons from the "rulers," but the same under another name (see 1 Kings xxi. 8, 13; and compare the Revised Version). **And to them that brought up Ahab's** children —*i.e.* the tutors, or governors, under whose charge they were placed—**saying**—

Ver. 2.—**Now as soon as this letter cometh to you.** In the East at this time, and in most parts of it to the present day, letters can only be sent by special messengers. There is no public post. Kings and private individuals must equally find persons who will undertake to carry and deliver their despatches. Even the post organized by Darius Hystaspis was not one that went daily, but only one kept ready for the king to use when he had occasion for it. **Seeing your master's sons are with you.** "Your master's sons" must mean Joram's sons; by which we learn that, unlike his brother Ahaziah (ch. i. 17), Joram had male offspring who survived him, and were now with the rest of Ahab's descendants, at Samaria. **And there are with you chariots and horses, a fenced city also, and armour;** literally, *the chariots, and the horses, a fenced city also, and the armour.* The main chariot force of the country, and the chief arsenal, containing both armour and arms, were naturally at Samaria, the capital, and might thus be regarded as at the disposition of the Samaritan municipality. Jehu scornfully challenges them to make use of their resources against him. He is quite ready for a contest. Let them do their worst. The LXX. have "fenced cities" (πόλεις ὀχυραί) instead of "a fenced city;" but the existing Hebrew text is probably right. Samaria was the only fortified town in their possession.

Ver. 3.—**Look even out the best and meetest of your master's sons, and set him on his father's throne.** "Choose," *i.e.,* "among the sons of Joram the strongest, the boldest, and the ablest, and make him king in his father's room; take him for your leader against me; do not hesitate and beat about the bush; but at once make up your minds, and let me know what I have to

expect." **And fight for your master's house.**
There had been a civil war before the
dynasty of Omri succeeded in settling itself
on the throne (1 Kings xvi. 21, 22). Jehu
believes, or affects to believe, that there will
now be another. He does not deprecate it,
but invites it. Probably he felt tolerably
confident that the garrison of Samaria, even
if called upon by the municipality, would
not venture to take up arms against the
army of Ramoth-Gilead, which had declared
itself in his favour. Still, supposing that
it did, he was not fearful of the result.

Ver. 4.—**But they were exceedingly afraid.**
They were men of peace, not men of war—
accustomed to discharge the duties of judges
and magistrates, not of commandants and
generals. They could not count on the
obedience even of the troops in Samaria,
much less on that of any others who might
be in garrison elsewhere. They would naturally have been afraid of taking up arms
under almost any circumstances. What,
however, caused them now such excessive
fear was probably the tone which Jehu had
adopted—his " scornful challenge," as it has
been called. He evidently entertained no
fear himself. He dared them to do that
which he pretended to recommend them to
do. They must have felt that he was laughing at them in his sleeve. **And said, Behold,
two kings stood not before him: how then
shall we stand?** The kings intended are
Joram and Ahaziah, who had confronted
Jehu, and had met their deaths. What
were *they* that they should succeed where
" two kings " had failed ? The argument was
fallacious, and a mere cloak for cowardice.
The two kings had been taken by surprise,
and treacherously murdered. Their fate
could prove nothing concerning the probable issue of a civil war, had the "princes"
ventured to commence it. It must be admitted, however, that the chance of success
was but slight.

Ver. 5.—**And he that was over the house**
—*i.e.* the officer in charge of the royal
palace (comp. 1 Kings iv. 6)—**and he that
was over the city.** There would be a single
" governor of the city "—not the commandant of the garrison, but the chief civil ruler,
nearly corresponding to a modern " mayor "
(see 1 Kings xxii. 26). **The elders also**
(comp. ver. 1). The " governor " of a town
was assisted by a council of "elders." **And
the bringers up** of the children (see the
comment on ver. 1). **Sent to Jehu, saying,
We are thy servants, and will do all that
thou shalt bid us; we will not make any
king.** Jehu's letter had the effect which
he intended, of making the authorities of
Samaria declare themselves. They might,
perhaps, have temporized, have sent an ambiguous answer, or have sent no answer at

all, and have let their action be guided by
the course of events. But, taken aback by
Jehu's directness and plainness of speech,
it did not occur to them to be diplomatic;
they felt driven into a corner, and compelled to make their choice at once. Either
they must resist Jehu in arms or they must
submit to him. If they submitted, they had
best (they thought) do it with a good grace.
Accordingly, his letter produced a reply,
more favourable than he can possibly have
expected—" They were his servants," or
" his slaves," ready to do all his pleasure ;
they would not set up a king, or in any
way dispute his succession ; they submitted
themselves wholly to his will. **Do thou**
[they said] **that which is good in thine eyes ;**
i.e. " take what steps thou pleasest to confirm thyself in the kingdom."

Ver. 6.—**Then he wrote a letter the second
time to them, saying** ; rather, *a second time.*
The reply of the Samaritan authorities gave
Jehu an opportunity, of which he was not
slow to take advantage. They might have
been contented with their negative response,
" We will not make any man king ; " but
they had gone beyond it—they had departed from the line of neutrality, and had
placed themselves unreservedly on Jehu's
side. " We are thy servants," they had
said, " and will do all that thou shalt bid
us." It is always rash to promise absolute
obedience to a human being. To volunteer
such a promise, when it is not even asked,
is the height of folly. **If ye be mine**—
as they had said they were, when they
called themselves his " slaves "—**and if ye
will hearken unto my voice**—*i.e.* obey me,
do as I require—**take ye the heads of the
men your master's sons, and come to me to
Jezreel.** The Samaritan authorities were
ordered to bring the heads with them, that
they might be seen and counted. In the
East generally, the heads of rebels and pretenders, by whatever death they may have
died, are cut off, brought to the sovereign,
and then exposed in some public place, in
order that the public at large may be certi-
fied that the men are really dead (comp. 1
Sam. xxxi. 9). **By to-morrow this time.** As
Jezreel was not more than about twenty
miles from Samaria, the order could be executed by that time. It necessitated, however, very prompt measures, and gave the
authorities but little time for consideration.
**Now the king's sons, being seventy persons,
were with the great men of the city, which
brought them up** (comp. ver. 1).

Ver. 7.—**And it came to pass, when the
letter came to them, that they took the king's
sons, and slew seventy persons.** Having
committed themselves by their answer to
Jehu's first letter, the Samaritan great men
seemed to themselves to have no choice, on

receiving his second, but to allow themselves to become the tools and agents of his policy. They accordingly put the seventy princes to death without any hesitation, though they can scarcely have done so without reluctance. **And put their heads in baskets.** Thus concealing their bloody deed as long as they could. In the Assyrian sculptures, those who slay the king's enemies carry the heads openly in their hands, as though glorying in what they have done. **And sent him** them **to Jezreel.** Jehu had bidden them to *bring* the heads to him; but this was a degradation to which they did not feel bound to submit. They therefore *sent* the heads by trusty messengers.

Ver. 8.—**And there came a messenger, and told him, saying, They have brought the heads of the king's sons. And he said, Lay ye them in two heaps at the entering in of the gate until the morning.** Thus all who entered into the town or quitted it would see them, and, being struck by the ghastly spectacle, would make inquiry and learn the truth. "The gate" was also a general place of assembly for the gossips of the town and others, who would soon spread the news, and bring together a crowd of persons, curious to see so unusual a sight.

Ver. 9.—**And it came to pass in the morning, that he went out, and stood, and said to all the people, Ye** be **righteous.** Not an ironical reproach to those who had brought the heads—"Ye consider yourselves righteous, yet this bloodshed rests upon you;" much less a serious declaration (Gerlach) that now at last the sins of idolatrous Israel were atoned for; but an argument *ad captandum*, addressed to the crowd of spectators whom the unwonted spectacle had brought together, "Ye are just persons, and capable of pronouncing a just judgment; judge, then, if I am the wicked person which men generally consider me." **Behold, I conspired against my master, and slew him: but who slew all these?** I confess to one murder; but here are seventy murders. **And who is guilty of them?** Not I, or my party, but the trusted adherents of the Ahabite dynasty, the rulers placed by them over the capital, and the governors to whom they had entrusted the royal children. Does not this show that all parties are weary of the Ahabites and of their system? Does it not clear me of any private or selfish motive, and indicate the desire of the whole nation for a change, civil and religious—a change which shall entirely subvert the new religion introduced by Jezebel, and fall back upon the lines of that maintained by Elijah and Elisha?

Ver. 10.—**Know now that there shall fall unto the earth**—*i.e.* "perish," "come to nought"—**nothing of the word of the Lord,** **which the Lord spake concerning the house of Ahab.** As the accomplishment had gone so far, it was safe to predict, or at any rate Jehu felt emboldened to predict, that the entire prophecy of Elijah would be fulfilled to the letter. The whole house of Ahab would perish—it would be made like the house of Jeroboam the son of Nebat, and like the house of Baasha the son of Ahijah (1 Kings xxi. 23), and its adherents would share its fate. **For the Lord hath done that which he spake by his servant Elijah;** *i.e.* "has requited Ahab in the portion of Jezreel; has caused dogs to eat the flesh of Jezebel; and has begun the destruction of his house. The inchoate fulfilment of prophecy was always felt to be the strongest possible argument for its ultimate complete fulfilment.

Ver. 11.—**So Jehu slew all that remained of the house of Ahab in Jezreel, and all his great men, and his kinsfolks;** rather, *and Jehu slew.* Encouraged by his past success, having killed Jehoram, Ahaziah, and Jezebel, having secured the adhesion of the chief men in Samaria, and effected the destruction of all those who might naturally have claimed the succession and involved him in civil war, Jehu proceeded to greater lengths. He "slew all that remained of the house of Ahab in Jezreel"—the princesses probably, as well as the princes—and further put to death all the leading partisans of the dethroned dynasty, the "great men," perhaps even those who had worked his bloody will at Samaria, and the intimate friends and supporters of the house—the מְיֻדָּעִים, as they are here called—not relatives, but "intimate acquaintances." **And his priests.** This expression causes a difficulty, since the destruction of the Baal-priests is related subsequently (vers. 19—25). It has been suggested to understand by כֹּהֲנִים, not "priests," but "high state officers" (Bähr)—a meaning which the word is thought to have in 2 Sam. viii. 18 and 1 Kings iv. 5. But this signification of כֹּהֵן is scarcely an ascertained one. Perhaps the same persons are intended as in ver. 19, the present notice of their death being a mere summary, and the narrative of vers. 19—25 a full statement of the circumstances. **Until he left him none remaining;** *i.e.* until the entire Ahabite faction was blotted out.

Vers. 12—14.—*The massacre of the brethren of Ahaziah.*

Ver. 12.—**And he arose and departed, and came to Samaria;** rather, *went on his way to Samaria* (ἐπορεύθη εἰς Σαμάρειαν, LXX.). Having arranged matters at Jezreel as his interests required, and secured the adhesion of the Samaritan "great men," Jehu now set out for the capital. The narrative from this point to ver. 17 is of events that happened to him while he was upon his road. **And as he was at the shearing-house in the way.** Between Jezreel and Samaria was a station where the shepherds of the district were accustomed to shear their flocks. The custom gave name to the place, which became known as Beth-Eked (Βαιθακάθ, LXX.; *Beth-Akad*, Jerome), "the house of binding," from the practice of tying the sheep's four feet together before shearing them. The situation has not been identified.

Ver. 13.—Jehu met with the brethren of Ahaziah King of Judah. The actual "brethren" of Ahaziah had been carried off and slain by the Arabians in one of their raids into Palestine, as we learn from 2 Chron. xxi. 17; xxii. 1; the youths here mentioned were their sons (2 Chron. xxii. 8), and therefore Ahaziah's nephews. **And said, Who are ye?** Travellers in a foreign country were always liable to be questioned, and were expected to give an account of themselves (see Gen. xlii. 7—13; Story of Saneha, line 38; Herod., ii. 159, etc.). The princes were thus not surprised at the inquiry, and readily answered it. **And they answered, We are the brethren of Ahaziah; and we go down to salute the children of the king.** There is something abnormal and needing explanation in this visit. *Forty-two* princes, with their retinues, do not, under ordinary circumstances, start off on a sudden from one capital, on a complimentary visit to their cousins at another. Perhaps Ewald is right in surmising that, "at the first report of disturbances in the kingdom of the ten tribes, they had been sent off by Athaliah to render any assistance that they could to the house of Ahab in its troubles" ('History of Israel,' vol. iv. p. 100, Eng. trans.). In this case their answer must be regarded as insincere. Falling in with an armed force stronger than their own, they *pretended* ignorance of the revolution that had taken place, and sought to pass off their hostile purpose under the pretence of a visit of compliment. But the pretence did not deceive Jehu. **And the children of the queen.** The queen-mother, Jezebel, is probably intended. Her rank entitled her to special mention.

Ver. 14.—And he said, Take them alive. And they took them alive, and slew them. The brevity of the narrative leaves many points of it obscure. It is impossible to say why the order was given, "Take them alive," when, immediately afterwards, they were massacred. Perhaps Jehu at first intended to spare their lives, but afterwards thought that it would be safer to have them put out of his way. It must be borne in mind that they were descendants of Ahab. **At the pit of the shearing-house;** rather, *at*

the well of Beth-Eked. Probably the bodies were thrown into the well (comp. Jer. xli. 7). **Even two and forty men.** It is this number which makes the idea of a visit of compliment incredible. **Neither left he any of them.** The Greeks said, Νήπιος, ὃς πατέρα κτείτας παῖδας καταλείπει; and the general Hebrew practice was to give effect to the teaching conveyed by the maxim (see Josh. vii. 24, 25; ch. ix. 26; xiv. 6).

Vers. 15—17.—*Jehonadab the son of Rechab associated by Jehu in his acts.*

Ver. 15.—And when he was departed thence, he lighted on Jehonadab the son of Rechab. Between Beth-Eked and Samaria Jehu fell in with the great Kenite chief, Jehonadab, the founder of the remarkable tribe and sect of the Rechabites (Jer. xxxv. 6—19). Jehonadab is mentioned only here and in the passage of Jeremiah just quoted; but it is evident that he was an important personage. His tribe, the Kenites, was probably of Arab origin, and certainly of Arab habits. It attached itself to the Israelites during their wanderings in the Sinaitic desert, and was given a settlement in "the wilderness of Judah," on the conquest of Palestine (Judg. i. 16). Jehonadab seems to have been of an ascetic turn, and to have laid down for his tribe a rule of life stricter and more severe than any known previously. He required them not merely to dwell in tents, and, unless under the compulsion of war, never to enter cities, but also to abstain wholly from the use of wine, and to have neither house, nor field, nor vineyard (Jer. xxxv. 8—10). Gautama, between three and four centuries later, enjoined a somewhat similar rule upon his disciples. It is indicative of much strength of character in either case, that so strict a rule was accepted, adopted, and acted upon for centuries. On the present occasion, Jehu, it would seem, desired the sanction of Jehonadab to the proceedings upon which he was about to enter, as calculated to legitimate them in the eyes of some who might otherwise have regarded them with disapproval. Jehonadab had, no doubt, the influence which is always wielded by an ascetic in Oriental countries. **Coming to meet him.** This expression tells us nothing of Jehonadab's intent. The meeting may have been merely a chance one. **And he saluted him, and said to him, Is thine heart right, as my heart is with thy heart?** literally, *he blessed him*; but the word used (*barak*) has frequently the sense of "to salute" (see 1 Sam. xiii. 10; xxv. 14; ch. iv. 29, etc.). Jehu's inquiry was made to assure himself of Jehonadab's sympathy, on which no doubt he counted, but whereof he was glad to receive a positive promise. Jehonadab must have been known as a zealous servant of Jehovah, and might therefore be assumed to be hostile to the house of Ahab. **And Jehonadab answered, It is.** Unhesitatingly, without a moment's pause, without the shadow of a doubt, the Kenite chief cast in his lot with the revolutionist. Heart and soul he would join him in an anti-Ahab policy. **If it be, Give** me **thine hand.** The Hebrews did not clench agreements, like the Greeks and Romans, by grasping each other's hands. Jehu merely means to say, "If this is so, if thou art heart and soul with me in the matter, put out thy hand, and I will take thee into my chariot." Jehu intended at once to do honour to the Kenite chief, and to strengthen his own position by being seen to be so familiar with him. **And he—** i.e. Jehonadab—gave him—i.e. Jehu—**his hand; and he took him up to him into the chariot.** There was always room in a chariot for at least three or four persons—the charioteer and the owner of the chariot in front, and one or two guards behind.

Ver. 16.—**And he said, Come with me, and see my zeal for the Lord.** Jehonadab must have understood that some further measures were about to be taken against the family and adherents of Ahab. He evidently approved of all that Jehu had already done, and was willing to give his countenance to further severities. He probably did not know exactly what Jehu designed; but he must have been able to make a tolerably shrewd guess at what was impending. **So they made him ride in his chariot.** Perhaps וַיַּרְכִּבוּ should be changed into וַיִּרְכַּב, which seems to have been the reading of the LXX., who translate, by ἐπικάθισεν αὐτὸν ἐν τῷ ἅρματι αὐτοῦ, "he made him ride in his chariot."

Ver. 17.—**And when he came to Samaria, he slew all that remained unto Ahab in Samaria, till he had destroyed him.** Seventy male descendants of Ahab had been already destroyed in Samaria (vers. 1—7). It seems unlikely that the city can have contained any other members of his house excepting females. Did Jehu now destroy the daughters of Ahab resident in Samaria, with their families? The masculine form used—הַנִּשְׁאָרִים—does not disprove this. **According to the saying of the Lord, which he spake to Elijah** (comp. ver. 10, and see also the comment on ch. ix. 7).

Vers. 18—28.—*Jehu destroys the worshippers of Baal, and puts an end to the Baal-worship.*

Ver. 18.—**And Jehu gathered all the people together, and said unto them, Ahab served Baal a little; but Jehu shall serve him much.** Hitherto the revolution had borne the appearance of a mere dynastic change, like those introduced by Baasha (1 Kings xv. 27—29), Zimri (1 Kings xvi.

9—12), and Omri (1 Kings xvi. 17—19), and had had none of the characteristics of a religious reformation. Probably, as yet, no suspicion had touched the public mind that Jehu would be a less zealous worshipper of Baal than his predecessor. The outburst against Jezebel's "whoredoms" and "witchcrafts" (ch. ix. 22) would be known to few, and might not have been understood as a condemnation of the entire Baalistic system. The "zeal for Jehovah" whispered in the ear of Jehonadab (ver. 16) had been hitherto kept secret. Thus there was nothing to prevent the multitude from giving implicit credence to the proclamation now made, and looking to see the new reign inaugurated by a magnificent and prolonged festival in honour of the two great Phœnician deities, Baal the sun-god, and Ashtoreth or Astarte the famous "Dea Syra." Such festivals were frequently held in Phœnicia and the rest of Syria, often lasting over many days, and constituting a time of excitement, feasting, and profligate enjoyment, which possessed immense attraction for the great mass of Asiatics.

Ver. 19.—**Now therefore call unto me all the prophets of Baal, all his servants, and all his priests.** In Phœnicia, it would seem, as in Egypt and among the Jews, "prophets" and "priests" were distinct classes of persons. The Egyptians called the priest *ab*, the prophet *neter hon*, literally, "servant of God." They held the priest in the greater honour. In Phœnicia, on the contrary, judging from the scanty notices that we possess, prophets appear to have taken precedence of priests, and to have had the more important functions assigned to them (see 1 Kings xviii. 19—40; xxii. 6). Let none be **wanting**—literally, *let not a man fail*—**for I have a great sacrifice to do to Baal.** Like the other gods of the heathen, Baal and Ashtoreth were worshipped chiefly by sacrifice. The sacrifice was sometimes human, but more commonly a sacrificial animal, such as a bull, a ram, or a he-goat. In the greater festivals several hundreds of victims were offered; and their flesh was served up at the banquets by which the festivals were accompanied. **Whosoever shall be wanting, he shall not live.** His absence would be regarded as an act of contumacy verging on rebellion, and so as deserving of capital punishment. **But Jehu did it in subtilty, to the intent that he might destroy the worshippers of Baal.** "Subtilty" was characteristic of Jehu, who always preferred to gain his ends by cunning rather than in a straightforward way. Idolaters were by the Law liable to death, and Jehu would have had a perfect right to crush the Baal-worship throughout the land, by sending his emissaries everywhere, with orders to slay all whom they found engaged in it. But to draw some thousands of his subjects by false pretences into a trap, and then to kill them in it for doing what he had himself invited them to do, was an act that was wholly unjustifiable, and that savoured, not of the wisdom which is from above, but of that bastard wisdom which is "earthly, sensual, devilish" (Jas. iii. 15). Jehu's religious reformation did not succeed, and it was conducted in such a way that it did not deserve to succeed. A little more honest boldness, and a little less frequent resort to subterfuge and craft, might have had a different result, and have been better both for himself and for his people.

Ver. 20.—**And Jehu said, Proclaim a solemn assembly for Baal.** The word translated "solemn assembly" is the same which is applied to the great feasts of Jehovah among the Israelites in Lev. xxiii. 36; Numb. xxix. 35; Deut. xvi. 8; 2 Chron. vii. 9; Neh. viii. 18; Isa. i. 13; Joel i. 14; ii. 15; and Amos v. 21. Originally, it signified a time of repression, or abstention from worldly business; but it had probably grown to mean a day when worldly business was suspended for the sake of a religious gathering. Such gatherings had no doubt been held from time to time in honour of Baal; and Jehu's proclamation consequently excited no distrust. **And they proclaimed it.** No opposition was made to the king's wish. No Jehovist party showed itself. The "solemn assembly" was proclaimed for some day in the near future, when all the people had been apprised of it.

Ver. 21.—**And Jehu sent through all Israel;** i.e. through the whole of his own kingdom, from Dan on the north to Bethel on the south. **And all the worshippers of Baal came, so that there was not a man left that came not.** Duty and inclination for once coincided. The king's command made it incumbent on them, they would argue, to attend; and attendance would, they supposed, result in a time of excitement and enjoyment, which they were not disposed to miss. The death-penalty threatened for non-attendance (ver. 19) was scarcely needed to induce them all to come. **And they came into the house of Baal.** Ahab had erected a temple to Baal in Samaria shortly after his marriage with Jezebel (1 Kings xvi. 22). Like the other temples of the time, in Judæa, in Egypt, and in Phœnicia, it was not a mere "house," but contained vast courts and corridors fitted for the reception of immense numbers. **And the house of Baal was full from one end to another;** literally, *from brim to brim;* i.e. brimful—"metaphora sumpta a vasibus humore aliquo plenis."

Ver. 22.—**And he said unto him that was over the vestry.** The word translated "ves-

try" (מֶלְתָּחָה) occurs only in this place; but its meaning is sufficiently ascertained, first, from the context, and secondly, from the cognate Ethiopic *altah,* which means "a linen garment." *Linen* garments were regarded as especially pure, and were generally affected by the priests of ancient religions, and preferred by the worshippers. Heathen temples had almost always "vestries" or "wardrobes" attached to them, where garments considered suitable were laid up in store. **Bring forth vestments for all the worshippers of Baal.** It may be doubted whether "*all*" the worshippers of Baal" could have been supplied with robes out of the temple vestry, which would ordinarily contain only vestments for the priests. But Jehu may have had the supply kept up from the robe-room of the palace, which would be practically inexhaustible. The gift of garments to all comers, which was certainly not usual, must have been intended to render the festival as attractive as possible. **And he brought them forth vestments.** The keeper of the wardrobe obeyed the order given him, and supplied vestments to all the worshippers.

Ver. 23.—**And Jehu went, and Jehonadab the son of Rechab, into the house of Baal.** Keeping up the pretence that he was a devotee of Baal, anxious to "serve him much" (ver. 18), Jehu himself entered the sacred edifice, together with Jehonadab the son of Rechab, whom he wished to have as a witness to his "zeal for the Lord" (ver. 16). Having entered, he addressed the multitude, or the chief authorities among them, requiring that they should exercise extreme vigilance, and make it quite certain that none but true followers of Baal were present. **And said unto the worshippers of Baal, Search, and look that there be here with you none of the servants of the Lord, but the worshippers of Baal only.** Jehu's real object was undoubtedly to save the lives of any "servants of Jehovah" who might incautiously have mixed themselves up with the Baal-worshippers, out of curiosity, or to have their share in the general holiday. That he should have thought such a thing possible or even probable indicates the general laxity of the time, and the want of any sharp line of demarcation between the adherents of the two religions. He cleverly masked his desire for the safety of his own religionists under a show of keen anxiety that the coming ceremonies should not be profaned by the presence of scoffers or indifferent persons. His requirement was in the spirit of that warning which the heathen commonly gave before entering upon the more sacred rites of their religion—"Procul este, profani."

Ver. 24.—**And when they went in—rather,**

when they had gone in; i.e. when the whole multitude of Baal-worshippers, priests and people, had entered within the precincts of the temple—**to offer sacrifices and burnt offerings.** The priests officiate, but the offerings are regarded as conjointly made by priest and people. **Jehu appointed four score men without.** Josephus says ('Ant. Jud.,' ix. 6. § 6) that they were the most trusty men of his body-guard, which is likely enough. They were no doubt also known to Jehu as attached to the worship of Jehovah. **And said, If any of the men whom I have brought into your hands escape,** he that letteth him go, **his life shall be for the life of him** (comp. 1 Kings xx. 39). Gaolers were commonly put to death if a prisoner committed to their charge escaped them (see Acts xii. 19; xvi. 27).

Ver. 25.—**And it came to pass, as soon as he had made an end of offering the burnt offering.** It has been concluded from this that Jehu "offered the sacrifices *with his own hand,* as though he were the most zealous of Baal's adorers" (Ewald, 'History of Israel,' vol. iv. p. 100); but the conclusion does not follow necessarily from the expression used. The suffix ו in כְּכַלֹּתוֹ may be used indefinitely, "when *one* finished," or "when *they* finished;" or Jehu may be said to have made the offerings, because he furnished the victims, not because he immolated them with his own hand. Throughout heathendom, wherever there were priests, it was the duty of the priests to slay the victims offered. **That Jehu said to the guard**—literally, *to the runners* (see the comment on 1 Kings i. 38) —**and to the captains**—*i.e.* the officers in command of the guard—**Go in, and slay them; let none come forth.** We must suppose that some guarded the doors, while others advanced into the crowd and struck right and left. The unarmed multitude seems to have made no resistance. **And they smote them with the edge of the sword**— *i.e.* cut them down unsparingly, smote and slew till none were left alive—**and the guard and the captains cast** them **out.** This is generally understood to mean that all the bodies were thrown by the guards out of the temple. Dean Stanley says, "The temple was strewn with corpses, which, as fast as they fell, the guard and the officers threw out with their own hands" ('Jewish Church,' vol. ii. p. 188). But it is not apparent why they should have taken this trouble. Perhaps Bähr is right in suggesting that no more is meant than that the guard and the officers thrust the bodies out of their way, as they pressed forward to enter the sanctuary which contained the sacred images. **And went to the city of the house of Baal.** "They made their way," as Ewald says, "into the inner sanctuary, the enclosure of which rose

like a lofty fortress—עִיר originally meant "fortress"—where Baal was enthroned, surrounded by the images of his fellow-gods" ('History of Israel,' *l. s. c.*). It is to be remembered that the assembled multitude occupied the court or courts of the temple, within which, in a commanding position, was the "house" or "sanctuary"—perhaps reserved for the priests only.

Ver. 26.—**And they brought forth the images out of the house of Baal**; rather, *the pillars* (see the comment on 1 Kings xiv. 23). It was a special feature of the Phœnician worship to represent the gods by στῆλαι or κίονες, which appear to have been conical stones, or obelisks, destitute of any shaping into the semblance of humanity (see Tacitus, 'Hist.,' ii. 3; Damasc. ap. Phot., 'Bibliothec.,' p. 1063; Max. Tyr., 'Diss.,' xxxviii. p. 384). The Phœnicians acknowledged several deities besides Baal, as Ashtoreth, Melkarth, Dagon, Adonis or Tammuz, El, Sadyk, Esmun, and the Kabiri. The "pillars" brought forth may have represented some of these deities, who might all of them be "contemplar" deities with Baal; or they may have been "Baalim," *i.e.* forms and aspects of Baal, each the object of some special cult (see Movers, 'Phönizier,' § 674). **And burned them.** The "pillars" in this instance were probably, not of stone, but of wood.

Ver. 27.—**And they brake down the image of Baal**; rather, *they brake in pieces the pillar of Baal.* The representation of Baal, the main *stele* of the temple, being of stone or metal, could not be destroyed by fire, and was therefore broken to pieces (comp. ch. xxiii. 14). **And brake down the house of Baal**—*i.e.* partially ruined it, but still left portions of it standing, as a memorial of the sin and of its punishment—a solemn warning, one would have thought, to the people of the capital—**and made it a draught-house unto this day**; made it, *i.e.*, "a depository for all the filth of the town" (Stanley); comp. Ezra vi. 11; Dan. ii. 5; iii. 29; and for the word "draught" in this sense, see Matt. xv. 17. Such a use was the greatest possible desecration.

Ver. 28.—**Thus Jehu destroyed Baal out of Israel.** The measures taken were effectual; the worship of Baal was put down, and is not said to have been revived in the kingdom of the ten tribes. Moloch-worship seems to have taken its place (see ch. xvii. 17).

Vers. 29—31.—*Jehu's shortcomings.*

Ver. 29.—**Howbeit from the sins of Jeroboam the son of Nebat, who made Israel to sin, Jehu departed not from after them.** It was a crucial test of Jehu's faithfulness to Jehovah; would he maintain the calf-worship of Jeroboam or not? With whatever intent the worship had been set up by its author, the curse of God had been pronounced against it by the chief prophet of the time (1 Kings xiii. 2), and his word had been attested as from heaven by two miracles (1 Kings xiii. 4, 5). Jehu ought to have known that the calf-worship, if not as hateful to God as the Baal-worship, at any rate was hateful, was a standing act of rebellion against Jehovah, and laid the nation under his displeasure. But, while his own interests were entirely detached from the one, they were, or at least would seem to him to be, bound up with the other. The calf-worship was thought to be essential to the maintenance of the divided kingdom. Abolish it, and all Israel would "return to the house of David" (1 Kings xii. 26—30). Jehu was not prepared to risk this result. His "zeal for Jehovah" did not reach so far. Thus his "reformation of religion" was but a half-reformation, a partial turning to Jehovah, which brought no permanent blessing upon the nation. To wit, **the golden calves that were in Bethel, and that** were in Dan. The erection of the calves (1 Kings xii. 29) was the initial sin, their worship the persistent one. (On the nature of the calf-worship, see the comment on 1 Kings xii. 28, and compare the 'Speaker's Commentary' on the same passage.)

Ver. 30.—**And the Lord said unto Jehu**—scarcely by direct revelation, rather by the mouth of a prophet, most probably of Elisha, as Thenius supposes—**Because thou hast done well in executing** that which is right **in mine eyes.** In making himself the executor of God's will with respect to the house of Ahab, and utterly destroying it, as he had been commanded (ch. ix. 7), Jehu had "done well;" he had also done well in putting down the worship of Baal, and slaying the idolaters, for the destruction of idolaters was distinctly commanded in the Law (Exod. xxii. 20; xxxii. 27; Numb. xxv. 5). These acts of his are praised; but nothing is said of his motives in doing them. They were probably to a great extent selfish. And **hast done unto the house of Ahab all that was in mine heart** (see ch. ix. 24—37; x. 1—7, 11, 14), **thy children of the fourth** generation **shall sit on the throne of Israel.** External obedience was suitably rewarded by an external, earthly honour—the honour of having his dynasty settled upon the throne during five generations, and for a period of above a hundred years. No other Israelite dynasty held the throne longer than three generations, or for so much as fifty years. The "children" or descendants of Jehu who sat upon the throne after him were Jehoahaz, his son, Jehoash or Joash, his grandson, Jeroboam II., his great-grandson, and Zachariah, son of Jeroboam II., his great-great-grandson.

Ver. 31.—**But Jehu took no heed to walk in the Law of the Lord God of Israel with all his heart.** Jehu's character is thus summed up by Dean Stanley: "The character of Jehu is not difficult to understand, if we take it as a whole, and consider the general impression left upon us by the biblical account. He is exactly one of those men whom we are compelled to recognize, not for what is good or great in themselves, but as instruments for destroying evil, and preparing the way for good; such as Augustus Cæsar at Rome, Sultan Mahmoud II. in Turkey, or one closer at hand in the revolutions of our own time and neighbourhood. A destiny, long kept in view by himself or others—inscrutable secrecy and reserve in carrying out his plans—a union of cold, remorseless tenacity with occasional bursts of furious, wayward, almost fanatical zeal; —this is Jehu, as he is set before us in the historical narrative, the worst type of a son of Jacob—the 'supplanter' ... without the noble and princely qualities of Israel; the most unlovely and the most coldly commended of all the heroes of his country" ('Lectures on the Jewish Church,' vol. ii. p. 289). The estimate is lower than that formed by most other writers; but it is not far from the truth. **For he departed not from the sins of Jeroboam, which made Israel to sin** (comp. ver. 29).

Vers. 32—36.—*Jehu's wars, length of reign, and successor.*

Ver. 32.—**In those days the Lord began to cut Israel short.** It is certainly not stated in direct terms that the ill success of Jehu's foreign wars was a punishment on him for his continued maintenance of the calf-idolatry; but the juxtaposition of vers. 31 and 32 naturally raises the idea, and constitutes a strong presumption that it was in the writer's mind. The "theocracy" under the kings was carried on mainly, as the writer of Chronicles clearly saw, by the bestowal of worldly prosperity and military success on good kings, and the accumulation of misfortunes and military disasters on bad ones (see 2 Chron. xii. 5—12; xiii. 4—18; xiv. 2—15; xv. 2—15; xvii. 3—5. etc.). By "cutting Israel short"—literally, "cutting off in Israel"—is probably meant the conquest of certain portions of the territory. Hazael resumed the war which Benhadad had so long waged, and gained numerous successes. **And Hazael smote them in all the coasts of Israel;** or, *along their whole frontier* (Bähr). The frontier intended is, of course, that on the north and east, where the Israelite territory was conterminous with that of Syria.

Ver. 33.—**From Jordan eastward.** The territory west of the Jordan was not attacked at this time. Hazael's expeditions were directed against the trans-Jordanic region, the seats of the three tribes of Reuben, Gad, and Manasseh. This tract was far easier of access than the other, and was more tempting, being the richest part of Palestine. The region comprised all the land of Gilead —*i.e.* the more southern region, reaching from the borders of Moab on the south to the Hieromax or Sheriat-el-Mandhûr upon the north, the proper land of the Gadites, and the Reubenites, and [a portion of] the Manassites—together with Bashan, the more northern region, which belonged wholly to Manasseh—from Aroer (now *Arair*), which is by the river Arnon—the *Wady-el-Mojeb*, which was the boundary between Israel and Moab (Numb. xxi. 13, 24), both in the earlier and (Isa. xvi. 2) in the later times—even Gilead and Bashan. There is other evidence, besides this, that Hazael was one of the most warlike of the Syrian kings. We find him, on the Black Obelisk of Shalmaneser II., mentioned as a stubborn adversary of the Assyrian arms. In the seventeenth campaign of Shalmaneser, a great battle was fought between the two monarchs. Hazael brought into the field more than twelve hundred chariots, but was defeated, and obliged to retreat, his camp falling into the hands of the enemy ('Records of the Past,' vol. v. p. 34). Four years later Shalmaneser invaded Hazael's territory, and took, according to his own account (ibid., p. 35), four cities or fortresses belonging to him. He does not claim, however, to have made him a tributary; and by his later annals it is evident that he avoided further contest, preferring to turn his arms in other directions. (On Hazael's campaign in Philistia, and designs against Jerusalem, see the comment upon ch. xii. 17, 18.)

Ver. 34.—**Now the rest of the acts of Jehu, and all that he did, and all his might.** This last phrase is remarkable, considering that Jehu's wars, after he became king, seem to have been entirely unsuccessful ones, that he lost a large portion of his dominions to Syria, and (as appears by the Black Obelisk) paid tribute to the Assyrians ('Records of the Past,' vol. v. p. 41). "Might" has been ascribed by the writer of Kings only to Baasha and Omri among previous Israelite monarchs, and only to Asa and Jehoshaphat among previous Jewish ones. "*All* his might" has only been used of Asa. We must probably understand, that, although defeated, Jehu gained much distinction, by his personal prowess and other military qualities, in the Syrian wars, and was reckoned "a mighty man of valour" in spite of the ill success of his wars. **Are they not written in the book of the chronicles of the kings of Israel?** (see the comment on ch. i. 18).

Vers. 35, 36.—**And Jehu slept with his fathers: and they buried him in Samaria. And Jehoahaz his son reigned in his stead. And the time that Jehu reigned over Israel in Samaria** was **twenty and eight years.** Twenty-eight years was a long reign for an Israelite king, only exceeded by one other king in the entire list, viz. Jeroboam II., who is said in ch. xiv. 23 to have reigned forty-one years. The kings of Judah were longer lived.

HOMILETICS.

Vers. 1—7. *The fear of man a stronger motive with the wicked and worldly than the fear of God.* Revolutions subject to severe trial most of those who occupy high stations at the time of their occurrence. Such persons have to determine, at very short notice for the most part, the line which they will pursue, the side which they will embrace, and the lengths to which they will go in their support of it. In making their choice they are apt to think less of what they ought to do than of what their worldly interests require them to do. They "are in a strait betwixt two"—on the one hand is the fear of man, on the other the fear of God. The one ought to prevail; the other commonly does prevail. Let us consider a little why this is so.

I. REASONS WHY THE FEAR OF GOD IS WEAK. 1. The wicked and worldly, who form, alas! the vast mass of mankind, do not generally even so much as realize the existence of God. They may not be absolute atheists, but practically they do not have God in their thoughts. 2. Those who believe in God and have *some* fear of him view him as distant, and his vengeance as a thing that may come or may not. He is merciful, and may be propitiated; he is compassionate, and may not be "extreme to mark what is done amiss." Men hope that he will forget their misdeeds, or forgive them for his Son's sake, or accept a tardy repentance as compensating for them and blotting them out. 3. Some view God as altogether benevolent and beneficent, and therefore as incapable of punishing men, forgetting that, if he is kind, he is also just, and, if he is forgiving, he is also jealous. They take their idea of God, not from what is revealed concerning him in Scripture, but from their own imaginations respecting him—imaginations which are echoes of their wishes.

II. REASONS WHY THE FEAR OF MAN IS STRONG. 1. Man is visibly present, and has a power to injure and punish which cannot be doubted. 2. Man's vengeance falls heavily and speedily. It is rarely delayed; and it is often of great severity. 3. It consists of pains and penalties which are more easily realized than those which God threatens. We know very well what is meant by the death of the body, but what the death of the soul may mean is obscure to us. 4. If we offend men, it is very unlikely that they will forgive us. Most men regard clemency as a weakness, and exact "the uttermost farthing" from those who, they think, have injured them.

Under these circumstances, the fear of man prevails. The rulers of Samaria, challenged by Jehu either to raise the standard of revolt against him, or definitely to embrace his cause, and mark their adhesion to it by embruing their hands in blood, must have balanced in their minds for a time the two alternatives—should they consent to slay, without offence alleged, seventy persons obnoxious to the powers that were, undeterred by fear of Divine vengeance, to escape the anger of Jehu? or should they brave his anger, and refuse to engage in the massacre required of them, out of regard for the Law of God (Exod. xx. 13), and through fear of the vengeance denounced by God upon such as contravened it (Gen. ix. 6)? They yielded to the lower, but more immediate, fear, and submitted themselves to be mere tools in Jehu's hands, because they feared man rather than God. Having made up their minds that their forces were insufficient to contend with those of Jehu, they put themselves at his disposal, and consented to do all that he required of them. So, constantly, in civil struggles, parties have put before them the alternative of following conscience and embroiling themselves with the civil authorities, or of defying those authorities, keeping their conscience clear, and observing the strict Law of God in the matters whereon they have to exercise a choice. Sometimes, as in the case of the Girondists, the better part is taken—duty, truth, virtue, are preferred to expediency, and martyrdom, a glorious martyrdom, is for the most part the consequence; but generally the result is different— expediency carries the day, and the sad spectacle is seen of men sacrificing their principles to their immediate interest, and consenting to wade through crime if they may preserve their worthless lives by so doing.

Vers. 8—11.—*The wicked have small regard for their helpers and confederates.* Jehu had made the authorities of Samaria his tools. He had required of them the performance of a wicked and bloody act, such as despotism has rarely exacted from its instruments. Seventy persons to be slain in the course of a few hours—for no offence, for no state necessity except to smooth the path of a usurper! And the seventy persons for the most part boys and youths, some probably infants, and these defenceless ones entrusted to the care and protection of those who were now called upon to take their lives! It was a tremendous burden to cast on men not previously his partisans, not bound to him by any interchange of good offices and benefits—rather, under the circumstances, his natural opponents and adversaries. Yet they took the burden on themselves; they accepted the miserable task assigned to them—they accepted it, and carried it out. No doubt they thought that by so doing they had bound the king to them, made him their debtor, and laid him under an obligation which he would not be slow to acknowledge. But the deed once done, the deaths once accomplished, and immediately the instigator of the crime turns against his accomplices. "Ye are righteous," he says to the crowd which has gathered together to gaze at the heads of the victims—"ye can discern aright; now judge between me and these murderers. I slew my master—I killed one man, a political necessity compelling me: *but who slew all these?*" He holds up his friends and allies, without the least compunction, to the popular odium. He entirely conceals the fact that he himself has been at the root of the whole matter, has conceived the massacre, and commanded it (ver. 6). He contrasts the terrible deed of blood, which has horrified all who have heard of it, with his own comparatively small crime, and claims to have his light offence condoned, overshadowed as it is by the heinous deed of the Samaritans. We do not know whether by his speech he provoked any popular outbreak. At the least, he turned the tide of popular disfavour from himself to his confederates, and left them to answer, as best they might, the serious question, "Who slew all these?" It is worth the preacher's while to impress on men the frequency of such conduct on the part of the persons who conceive evil designs, but must have tools to execute them. There is no solidarity among those who are confederates in wickedness. We hear of "honour among thieves;" but it is often "conspicuous by its absence." Monarchs engaged in plots denounce and disgrace their agents, when the plots fail, even sometimes permitting their execution; ministers are conveniently oblivious of the services rendered by those who win elections by intimidation and bribery; even "head-centres" are apt to look coldly on the work done by "ratteners" or "moonlighters," and, instead of commending and rewarding them, are rather anxious to disclaim all complicity in their actions. If the poor tools knew beforehand how little benefit they would derive from their wicked violence, what small thanks they would get from those who set them on, and how ready these last would be, on any difficulty arising, to leave them in the lurch, they would scarcely lend themselves to the purposes of their instigators. It is one of the weaknesses of the kingdom of evil that its agents do not keep faith one with another. It would weaken the kingdom still more if the conviction were general that this is so, and that the subordinate agents who work out an end have little to look for in the way of reward or encouragement from their employers.

Vers. 15—23.—*Jehu and Jehonadab—the man of the world and the recluse ascetic.* Worldly policy often finds it advisable to call to its aid the sanctions of religion, and the support of those who stand high in popular estimation as religionists of more than ordinary strictness and sanctity. It is comparatively seldom in the East that a political revolution is effected without the assistance of a dervish or a mollah of high reputation for strictness of life, who throws over a questionable movement the halo of his reputed holiness. In the present instance we have, on the one hand—

I. JEHU, THE MAN OF THE WORLD, versed in the ways of courts, experienced in affairs both civil and military, a good general, popular with his brother-officers, prompt in action, decided, not overburdened with scruples, and at the same time subtle, inclined to gain his ends by cunning and artifice rather than by force. Circumstances have brought him to the front, and put the direction of a politico-religious movement into his hands; but the situation is not without its risks and dangers. Jehu, if he does not absolutely require, cannot but welcome, and feel his position strengthened by, any spiritual support. From the time that he took action, he had not received, and he did not dare to invite, the co-operation of Elisha. He could not expect that Elisha would approve the proceedings on which he was bent, involving, as they did, a large amount of falsehood and dissimulation. All the more, therefore, must he have rejoiced when help appeared from another quarter—help on which it is scarcely possible that he can have reckoned. Over against Jehu stands—

II. JEHONADAB THE SON OF RECHAB, a chief whose position is abnormal and peculiar. The tribe of the Rechabites, whose sheikh he was, was a branch of the Kenites, Midianitish Arabs apparently, settled at the time of the Exodus in the Sinaitic peninsula. The Kenites, or some of them, had accompanied the Israelites during a large part of their wanderings in the wilderness, and had been of great assistance to them (Numb. x. 29—32; 1 Sam. xv. 6); in return for which they were allowed to settle in Southern Judæa (Judg. i. 16) and other parts of the Holy Land (Judg. iv. 11). They retained, however, their nomadic habits, and were a wandering people, like our gipsies, in the midst of the settled inhabitants of Palestine. When the Rechabite tribe fell under the chieftainship of Jehonadab, he appears to have bound them down by stricter rules than they had previously observed, and to have required of them an austerity of life whereof there have been few examples in the history of nations (Jer. xxxv. 6, 7). They were to dwell in tents, avoid cities, drink no wine, and cultivate no land. Jehonadab must himself have been a recluse and an ascetic, or he would never have instituted such a "rule." He had probably the same sort of reputation as now attaches to a Mohammedan *santon* or *fakir*, and represented to the mind of his tribe, and even to numbers among the Israelites, the strict devout religionist, whose accession to a party or a cause stamped it at once with a high moral and religious character. Jehu needed Jehonadab; but there was not much to attract Jehonadab to Jehu. He would seem to have lent Jehu his countenance simply from a regard for the honour of Jehovah, and a detestation of the Baal-worship. But he would, perhaps, have done Jehovah more honour had he held himself aloof from the crafty schemer who disgraced the cause of true religion by lies and treachery.

Vers. 29—33.—*Half-heartedness punished by God as severely as actual apostasy from true religion.* The temper of the Laodiceans is no uncommon one. Men may even think that they have a "zeal for the Lord" (ver. 16), and yet show by their acts that it is a very half-hearted zeal—a zeal that goes a certain length, and then stops suddenly. There is no reason to doubt that Jehu honestly disliked, nay, perhaps detested, the religion of Baal. It was an effeminate, sensual, weakening, debasing system, which a rough soldier might well view with abhorrence. Jehu was honest and earnest in his opposition to it, as he showed by the measures which he took to put it down. They were no half-measures—they stamped out the religion, for the time at any rate (ver. 28). But with this destructive process his zeal terminated. He did not go on to consider what he could do to reintroduce and stimulate the true worship of Jehovah. Had his thoughts moved in this direction, he would have been brought face to face with the calf-worship, and would have had to consider seriously the question of its maintenance or abolition. But this question probably never presented itself to his mind. He was not possessed by any real love of God, or desire to worship him in spirit and in truth. Had he been, he would have called in the advice and help of Elisha, and taken counsel with him as to what was best to be done. But this is exactly what he does not do. He comes into no contact with Elisha. After delivering his one great attack upon Baalism, he rests upon his oars, and is "neither cold nor hot" (Rev. iii. 15). Consequently, punishment falls upon him. Hazael "smites him in all his coasts." While the apostate Ahab and his dynasty had maintained the kingdom, on the whole, without serious loss or diminution of power, Jehu loses province after province to Syria, is deprived of all his trans-Jordanic territories, and induced to submit to the indignity of paying tribute to Assyria. God punishes his lukewarmness as severely—may we not say more severely than Ahab's open rebellion?

HOMILIES BY VARIOUS AUTHORS.

Vers. 1—11.—*Ahab's sons put to death.* Jehu's commission is to cut off utterly the whole house of Ahab. Like a moral plague was the iniquity of Ahab's house. Every member of it, by heredity, by example, by association, shared the guilt of Ahab and Jezebel. There is a good moral reason for the extermination of such a nest of evil-doers. But Jehu was not troubled with many scruples or difficulties. He had got a certain work to do, and he did it. We have here—

I. FAITHLESS SERVANTS. The general corruption and demoralization were manifest in the way in which Ahab's sons were treated by the elders of Samaria, and those that brought up Ahab's children. It was no zeal for what was right, no particular hatred of what was wrong, that caused them to yield so complaisantly to Jehu's real wish. Jehu, indeed, satirized them to their face. He made it appear as if he really wanted them to defend their master's children and fight for their master's house. It would not have been unnatural to expect this from them. But they were sore afraid. Not only were they willing, in their craven cowardice, to surrender Ahab's children to Jehu, to let him work his own will on them, but they actually slew them with their own hands, and sent their heads to Jehu. *Where there is unfaithfulness toward God, there will be unfaithfulness in the relations between man and man.* Fickleness is a characteristic of the world's friendships. Deception is a characteristic of the world's business. But the Christian will be faithful to duty, to conscience, to God. "He sweareth to his own hurt, and changeth not" (Ps. xv. 4).

II. THE UNFAILING WORD. "There shall fall unto the earth nothing of the word of the Lord, which the Lord spake concerning the house of Ahab: for the Lord hath done that which he spake by his servant Elijah." Every judgment of God which was threatened upon Ahab's house was fulfilled. God's judgments upon Israel—how literally and fully have they been fulfilled! Every judgment pronounced against sin is sure of certain and complete fulfilment. *So also God's promises will be fulfilled.* Not a single promise of God was ever broken. Why, then, should any of us doubt his word, his willingness to receive, his power to save, his desire to pardon? "Come now, and let us reason together, saith the Lord: though your sins be as scarlet, they shall be as white as snow; though they be red like crimson, they shall be as wool."—C. H. I.

Vers. 12—14.—*Ahaziah's brethren put to death.* Fresh from the scene of retribution and bloodshed at Jezreel, Jehu is now on his way to Samaria. At the shearing-house on the way he meets the brethren of Ahaziah King of Judah. Ahaziah himself had already perished at Jehu's hands for his companionship with Jehoram. And now his brethren, not warned by Ahaziah's fate, go down "to salute the children of the king and the children of the queen." Jehu's vengeance on Ahab's house was searching and complete. He had already slain at Jezreel not only Ahab's kinsfolk, but his great men and his priests—all who in any way showed favour or encouragement to Ahab. In the same spirit he now puts to death these brethren of Ahaziah because of their relationship and sympathy with Ahab's house. Note here—

I. The results of evil companionship. "The companion of fools," says the wise man, "shall be destroyed." These brethren of Ahaziah might have pleaded that they were doing no harm. But the house of Ahab was notorious for its wickedness. It had been singled out for the terrible retribution of God. To keep up friendship with men and women so wicked was to become a partaker of their crimes. The old Latin proverb was *Noscitur a sociis*—"A man is known by the company he keeps." If we would avoid the fate of the wicked, let us avoid their fellowship. "Enter not into the path of the wicked, and go not in the way of evil men. Avoid it, pass not by it, turn from it, and pass away." "Blessed is the man that walketh not in the counsel of the ungodly, nor standeth in the way of sinners, nor sitteth in the seat of the scornful."

II. The result of unheeded warnings. The brethren of Ahaziah had already got a warning in the fate which had befallen their brother. But notwithstanding this, they went on to their own destruction. So men act every day. 1. *God's Word warns them, but in vain.* They laugh to scorn the message of the gospel that urges them to accept salvation, and to flee from the wrath to come. They act as the people in the days of Noah, who disregarded the warnings of that faithful, patient preacher, and knew not till the flood came and swept them all away. 2. *God's providences warn them, but in vain.* Sudden deaths remind them of life's uncertainty. Perhaps for a day or two they are impressed; and then they become engrossed with the world again. If one were to speak to them about their soul, they would say, "Go thy way for this time; when I have a convenient season, I will call for thee." 3. *God's judgments warn them, but in vain.* The intemperate man, the immoral man, the dishonest man, infatuated with evil desires, go on in their sinful courses, notwithstanding the ruin and misery, the premature deaths, the unhappy lives, the degradation and disgrace, which so many have suffered in consequence of these sins. "See that ye refuse not him that speaketh."—C. H. I.

Vers. 15—31.—*The zeal of Jehu, and its lessons.* Jehu is now going up to Samaria with the resolve to destroy the prophets of Baal firmly rooted in his heart. On his way he meets Jehonadab the son of Rechab. This Jehonadab was the founder of the Rechabites. It was he who commanded his children to drink no wine, to build no houses, and plant no vineyards, but to live in tents all their days—a command which was so scrupulously obeyed by their descendants that the Lord instructed the Prophet Jeremiah to hold them up as an example of obedience to the Jews in after-years; and with this obedience God was so much pleased that he made the promise that Jonadab the son of Rechab should not want a man to stand before him for ever. It was this simple-minded, temperate, self-denying man whom Jehu met in his career of vengeance and ambition, and whom doubtless he wanted to associate with himself in order to give a measure of respectability to his further proceedings. He invited him into his chariot, and said, "Come with me, and see my zeal for the Lord."

I. There was much that was good about Jehu's zeal. From the day that Jehu got his work to do, he lost no time in the doing of it. He was eminently a man of action. That he had good qualities no one can doubt. There are many things that are attractive about Jehu. He was a brave and fearless soldier. *Decision, earnestness, promptness, thoroughness,*—these were the chief features of his character. His decided character impressed itself on every detail of his life. When he was still far off from Jezreel, the watchman upon the city wall was able to distinguish him in the dim distance by the way he drove his horses. "The driving is like the driving of Jehu the son of Nimshi; for he driveth furiously." He did not waste many words. When the messengers of King Jehoram rode out to meet him with the question, "Is it peace?" his answer to one after the other of them, without reining in his horses for a moment, was, "What hast thou to do with peace? turn thee behind me." Neither did he waste words when he came to deal with Jezebel and Jehoram. He knew that in such work as he was engaged there is danger in delay. We may learn much from what was good in Jehu's character. Zeal itself is a grand thing. It is men of zeal who have revolutionized the world. Moses was a man of zeal. So was Elijah. So was Daniel. So was St. Paul. So was Martin Luther. So was John Knox. All these men were mocked at as fools and fanatics and enthusiasts in their time. But every one of those men has left his mark for good upon the history of the world. We may say the same of such enthusiasts as William Wilberforce and John Howard, and, to come to more modern times, as Plimsoll, the sailors' friend. It is the world's enthusiasts that have been its greatest benefactors. Yes; we want more zeal; we want more enthusiasm. It is the fashion amongst many to sneer at enthusiasm, and to mock at zeal. But let those who mock at enthusiasm show what they can do compared with what the enthusiasts have done. Give me the man who has an enthusiasm about something. Give me the man who thinks that life is worth living, and that there is something worth living for. Let it be study, let it be business, let it be one of the learned professions,—the man who has enthusiasm in his work is the man that is most likely to succeed. If there is any one who should show enthusiasm, it is *the Christian*. Who should be so full of zeal? Who has so much cause to rejoice with joy unspeakable and full of glory? Who can point to such a leader as the great Captain of our salvation? What example so inspiring as the example of Christ? What name is such a watchword as the precious Name of Jesus—the Name above every name? Who can look forward to such a prospect as that which awaits the faithful Christian? "Be thou faithful unto death, and I will give thee the crown of life." Who has such resources at his disposal as the Christian for work and conflict? Zeal! surely the Christian ought to overflow with zeal. Zeal! when he thinks of his Saviour and his cross. Zeal! when he thinks that heaven with all its glory awaits him. Zeal! when he thinks of the welcome from the King. Zeal! when he thinks how short his time is here. Zeal! when he thinks of the perishing and needy all around him. Yes; it is well to have within your heart the glow and fire of Christian zeal. What if the careless and the callous, the godless and the worldly, mock? You have a heart, you have a hope, you have a strength, that is above their shallow sneers. And, having Christian zeal, let it not spend itself in mere sentiment, profession, or words. But let it show itself in action prompt and decisive, in earnestness and thoroughness of life. "Whatever ye do, do it heartily, as unto the Lord, and not unto men."

II. THERE WAS MUCH THAT WAS WRONG, AND THERE WAS SOMETHING WANTING, IN JEHU'S ZEAL. 1. *There was much that was wrong mingled with Jehu's zeal.* (1) In the first place, there was *boastfulness*. "Come with me, and see my zeal for the Lord." The man who thus parades his good deeds is lacking in one of the first elements of true goodness and usefulness, and that is humility. Yet there has been a good deal of that kind of zeal for God in all ages. The Pharisees considered themselves very zealous for the Law of God, but they sounded a trumpet before them when they gave their alms, and loved to pray standing at the corner of the streets. We have not the sounding of the trumpet nowadays in the same form, but we have other ways of making known our generous and philanthropic acts. There is nothing wrong in these acts being made known. On the contrary, a public acknowledgment of charitable and religious contributions is necessary to guard against fraudulence and deceit. It is of use also to remind others of their duty and stimulate them, perhaps, to greater liberality. But when we give our alms in order that we may be known to have given them—"to be seen of men"—we give from a wrong motive—we do that which Christ condemned. It is the same with all branches of Christian work. And it seems to be one of the dangers of modern Christian life that there is too much temptation to boast of mere numbers in our Churches, or of so much money accumulated, or of so many converts made.

Too many Christian workers act like Jehu when he said, " Come with me, and see my zeal for the Lord." True Christian work is far quieter than this. (2) There was something worse than boastfulness in Jehu's zeal. *There was cruel treachery and deceit.* When he came to Samaria, he gathered all the people together and said, " Ahab served Baal a little ; but Jehu shall serve him much." Then, under the pretence of offering a great sacrifice to Baal, he assembled all the worshippers of Baal in the temple of that false deity, and, having thus unfairly and deceitfully entrapped them, caused them to be put to death. It was an act of deceit for which there was no excuse. Matthew Henry truly observes, " God's service requires not man's lie." What a contrast to Elijah's honest, outspoken conduct when he, single-handed, confronted the prophets of Baal, and put their god and his God to the test ! No cause will ever prosper, no matter how much zeal may be manifested in it, if it is built up by the treachery and deceit of those who are at the head of it. Let us never so far accommodate ourselves to the false morality of our time as to do evil that good may come. God can, and does, bring good out of evil. But those who do the evil must suffer for it, according to that Divine law of retribution which was so plainly and terribly fulfilled in the case of Ahab and Jezebel. 2. In addition to all this, *there was something wanting in all Jehu's zeal.* He had not the love of God in his heart. He had indeed obeyed God's command and fulfilled his commission *in one particular direction*, but the ruling motive in his actions would seem to have been personal ambition. It was no hatred of idolatry as such that caused him to destroy the worship of Baal. Perhaps it was because it was a foreign worship. It certainly was not his zeal for the pure worship of God, because we read, " Howbeit from the sins of Jeroboam the son of Nebat, who made Israel to sin, Jehu departed not from after them, to wit, the golden calves that were in Bethel, and that were in Dan " (ver. 29). And again, " But Jehu took no heed to walk in the Law of the Lord God of Israel with all his heart " (ver. 31). We may learn here that a man may have the outward form of godliness without the power of it. He may appear to be a foremost worker in the cause of religion, and yet have no religion in his own heart. He may even appear to be a great religious reformer, and yet he may be utterly destitute of any personal reformation of character. *Jehu was able to pull down, but he built nothing up.* Why? Because his own character and life were not founded on the rock. He had not begun at the beginning—the fear of God and the Law of God. " He took no heed to walk in the Law of God with all his heart." See to it that your goal springs from a right motive, and that it works in ways of which God will approve.

III. NOTE HERE SOME LESSONS ABOUT GOD'S DEALINGS. 1. *God often makes use of even godless men.* Perhaps you start at this. Yes; but it is true. *He uses them for certain purposes.* There are some things which do not require a high kind of character. So God sometimes uses even wicked men to be the executioners of his judgments. The kings and nations whom he used to execute his judgments upon Israel were by no means righteous themselves. Many of them were grossly corrupt. But they were the rod in his hand to chasten and punish his offending people. We might give many illustrations from history. To take one only. King Henry VIII. of England was far from being a model man, yet God in his all-wise providence used his quarrel with the pope to be the means of furthering and establishing the Reformation in England. It was in the time of Henry VIII. that for the first time the papal supremacy in England was overthrown. 2. *God gives such agents of his justice and providence their own reward.* We find this in the case of Jehu. For the good he had done, God rewarded him. He had set his heart on the throne, and God gave it to him. The measure of our desires is very often the measure of our blessings. If we set our ambition on earthly rank, or riches, or honour as our chief good, we shall very likely get them. But in getting them we shall perhaps lose something that is far better worth having. " What shall it profit a man, if he shall gain the whole world, and lose his own soul ? " 3. *For God's work of salvation, he uses consecrated men.* Jehu was of use as a destroyer, as an image-breaker, but he was no national or moral reformer in the true sense. He was of no spiritual benefit to others. For such work God uses only those who themselves have received spiritual blessing. *There is a limit to the extent and to the ways in which he will use godless men.* Even David—God's own servant, who had repented of his sins—was not permitted to build a house to his Name, because his hands were stained with blood; he had been a man of war all his days. David was permitted to provide and store up the material, but to Solomon, David's son, was given the great honour of building a temple to the God of Israel. If we want to be of use in God's service, we must be thoroughly consecrated to God. We must be vessels meet for the Master's use. "Their hands must be clean, who bear the vessels of the Lord." It is personal character that gives power for God's service. It is personal character that gives fitness for God's fellowship here and hereafter. "Except a man be born again, he cannot see the kingdom of God." "Follow peace with all men, and holiness, without which no man shall see the Lord."—C. H. I.

Vers. 1—14.—*Destruction of Ahab's house.* Jehu was not a man to do things by halves. Whatever matter he had in hand, he pushed with unhesitating feet to his goal. His motto was, "If it were then done when 'tis done, then 'twere well it were done quickly." This vigorous determination is a feature in his character worthy of commendation. It is not so clear that the craft and guile he employed in securing his ends were, even from an Old Testament standpoint, justifiable. I. THE CRAFTY MESSAGE. No small amount of craft, as this chapter shows, mingled with Jehu's headlong zeal. 1. *The seed royal in Samaria.* The direct posterity of Ahab—here called Ahab's sons—amounted to seventy persons. Some may have been his own children, others the children of Jehoram, or of his other sons. They resided at Samaria, and were under the care of nobles responsible for their education and up-bringing. On them, too, the judgment of God was to fall. In itself it was a common Oriental practice for the founder of a new dynasty to put to death the descendants and blood-relations of his predecessor (cf. 1 Kings xv. 29; xvi. 11; ch. xi. 1; xxv. 7). This was to protect the new ruler from blood-vengeance. In the present case the destruction was by direct command of Heaven. The principle of corporate responsibility for sins committed is recognized and acted on throughout the Old Testament (see Mozley's 'Ruling Ideas of the Old Testament'). It embodies a truth of permanent validity (Matt. xxiii. 34, 35). Nevertheless, a pathos attends a fate like that of Ahab's sons. "Whirled down," as Carlyle says of other unfortunates, "so suddenly to the abyss; as men are, suddenly, by the wide thunder of the mountain avalanche, awakened not by *them*, awakened far off by others!" 2. *The crafty letter.* Having struck his first blow, Jehu lost no time in delivering his second. But instead of openly advancing to Samaria, and demanding the surrender of the seventy sons, he proceeds by guile. His policy was, not to put the nobles and elders in Samaria in opposition to him, but to gain them to his side. His further object was to implicate those persons in his deeds, by making them the direct agents in the slaughter of Ahab's sons. The manner in which he accomplished these ends shows no little skill. He first sends a letter to the great men in the capital, offering them a challenge to open war. He recounts to them their advantages—the presence of their master's sons, a fortified city, horses, chariots, armour, etc.; then bids them select the one of Ahab's descendants whom they think most suitable, and make him king, and fight for their master's house. This put the nobles in the dilemma, either of getting up an improvised resistance to Jehu, or of making unconditional submission. No time was given them to consider. They must decide at once, and that, in circumstances like theirs, meant only submission. 3. *The submissive reply.* The course taken by the nobles and elders was what Jehu anticipated. A terrible panic took possession of them. They saw how vain it was to attempt war with the most popular and energetic general in the army, backed as he was by the support of other captains. They had no head, and, notwithstanding Jehu's sarcastic list of their advantages, no proper means of defence. The fact that two kings—not to speak of Jezebel—had already fallen before this "scourge of God" added to their dismay. With the unanimity of despair, "he that was over the house, and he that was over the city, the elders also, and the bringers up of the children," indited a humble epistle, sent it to Jehu, and put themselves entirely in his hands, offering to do whatever he bade them. Necessity is a terrible tyrant. How many things men yield to force and fear which they would not yield to reason or persuasion! II. THE TREACHEROUS MASSACRE. 1. *The new demand.* Jehu took the leaders at their word, and sent them the conditions of his acceptance of their submission. If they were his, and would hearken to his voice, the proof of allegiance he would require of them would be that they bring to him by the same hour to-morrow the heads of their master's sons. The requisition was peremptory, the time given brief, and they had already committed themselves by promising obedience to whatever Jehu wished. Their case was a hard one; nevertheless, the act they were called upon to perform was, from their side, a revolting and treacherous one. 2. *Ahab's sons slain.* Hateful as the requirement was, the nobles and elders of Samaria, now that they had come to terms with Jehu, do not seem to have shown any hesitation in carrying it out. The sons of Ahab had been entrusted to their care; they had no quarrel with them; they did not profess to be moved by any regard for a command of God; yet now that policy and their own safety dictated that their charges should be given up to death, they acquiesced without a murmur. This shows the weakness of moral feeling in the ruling classes of Samaria. It shows how utterly rotten were all the bonds that bound man to man. The willingness with which the men of Jezreel swore away Naboth's life at Jezebel's command (1 Kings xix.) was one instance, and here is another. "Put not your trust in princes, nor in the son of man" (Ps. cxlvi. 3). Political morality is of the weakest fibre. For some paltry interest men will turn their backs to-morrow on the most sacred professions of to-day. They will forswear the closest friendships, stoop even to the lowest treachery. 3. *Jehu's public appeal.* That very evening apparently, the heads of Ahab's sons were brought to Jehu in baskets. He bade them be piled in two heaps at the entrance of the gate until the morning. Then, standing in the gateway, he called the people to witness that the leaders in Samaria were as deeply incriminated as he. They, the people whom he addressed, were "righteous," *i.e.* clear from blood-guiltiness, and might be disposed to judge him severely for his acts of the previous day. He acknowledged that he had conspired against his master, and had slain him; but—pointing to the pyramids of heads—who had slain all these? In truth, he went on to aver, not any of them were guilty, for this was but the fulfilment of the word of the Lord which he had spoken by Elijah. (1) Jehu was right in his averment, "Know now that there shall fall to the earth nothing of the word of the Lord." Many demonstrations of that fact have been given. We do well to impress the truth upon our minds. (2) It is a common thing for men to shield themselves from the consequences of their acts by pleading that others are as guilty as they are. This, however, will not justify them.

III. AHAZIAH'S BRETHREN. A further act in the tragedy of the destruction of Ahab's house took place at a certain shearing-house on the road to Samaria. Thither forty-two brethren (kinsmen) of Ahaziah had come down on their way to pay a pleasure visit to their relations, the princes at the capital. They were apparently as yet unaware of the revolution that had taken place. It was, however, to prove a costly visit to them. Jehu, fresh from his work of blood, encountered them at the shearing-house, and, on ascertaining who they were, had them all put to death on the spot. Their bodies were cast into the pit of the place. In pursuit of their pleasures, how many, like Ahaziah's brethren, have found themselves overtaken by death! The way of pleasure is, for many, the way of death—the way to the pit of destruction.—J. O.

Vers. 15—28.—*Destruction of the worshippers of Baal.* The plans of Jehu were already assuming larger shape. He had now a scheme in view for rooting Baal entirely out of the land.

I. THE MEETING WITH JEHONADAB. 1. *A helpful ally.* While relying mainly on his own promptitude and energy, Jehu had a shrewd eye to whatever would help to strengthen his position before the people. Hasting to Samaria in his chariot, he met a man of much reputation for sanctity—Jehonadab the son of Rechab. As a protest against the corruption and luxury of his time, Jehonadab had withdrawn from life in cities, and had laid upon his sons a vow that they would drink no wine, neither build houses, nor plant vineyards, but would dwell in tents all their days (Jer. xxxv. 6, 7). To get this man of ascetic virtue on his side would, Jehu felt, greatly fortify his claims. It would give colour and repute to his proceedings. Jehu at once sounded Jehonadab as to his feelings in regard to him, and finding that Jehonadab's heart was as his heart, he extended his hand to the anchorite, and took him up with him into his chariot. It is noticeable how anxious men who make no pretensions to godliness often are to get the countenance and approval of good men for their deeds. Hypocrisy has been called the homage which vice pays to virtue, and this desire for the approval of a holy man is, in another form, the tribute of worldly policy to the superior power of character. 2. *Zeal for the Lord.* "Come with me," said Jehu, "and see my zeal for the Lord." (1) Of Jehu's "zeal," in itself considered, there could be no question. Zeal was his most prominent characteristic. His zeal is seen in his eager haste to attain his ends, in his scouting of difficulties, in the thoroughness with which each piece of work is accomplished, in the quickness and skill of his devices. Such zeal is in large measure a natural endowment—a thing of temperament. Still, it is an essential to success in practical undertakings, spiritual as well as worldly. The man who gets on is the man who does not let the grass grow beneath his feet, who is an enthusiast in what he takes in hand. "It is good to be zealously affected always in a good thing" (Gal. iv. 18). (2) More doubtful is the quality of Jehu's zeal "for the Lord." Ostensibly it was God's will Jehu was carrying out; outwardly it was God's work he was doing. He may even have persuaded himself into the belief that he was honestly and disinterestedly serving God's ends. But the result showed that, in serving God, it was really his own ends Jehu was serving. His zeal was impure. It was largely inspired by selfish ambition, by considerations of policy, by the thought of the reward to himself. It was impure also in its admixture of craft and worldly expediency. Had the same service been proposed to Jehu without any apparent material advantages to himself, his zeal would not have been so easily evoked. (3) Similarly, how much that passes for "zeal for the Lord" in this world is of the same impure nature! How much of it is inspired by sectarian rivalry, by party spirit, by the desire to make "a fair show in the flesh" (Gal. vi. 12), by self-interest and worldly policy! How largely is it alloyed with human passion and intrigue! Truly we do well to examine ourselves. Zeal is to be tested, not by its passing and spasmodic exhibitions, but by its power of endurance amidst good report and evil report. 3. *The end of Ahab's house.* When Jehu reached Samaria with Jehonadab, he made an end of all that remained of the family of Ahab—the word of the Lord by Elijah being thus completely fulfilled.

II. THE FEAST TO BAAL. 1. *Jehu's proclamation.* Hitherto Jehu had acted without giving to any one much explanation of his motives and designs. He had denounced to Jehoram Jezebel's idolatries and witchcrafts; he had whispered to Jehonadab of his "zeal for the Lord;" but to the eye of the crowd his proceedings bore only the complexion of an ordinary political conspiracy. Having established himself upon the throne, the stage was clear for the revelation of his own intentions. And great dismay must have spread through the ranks of all those who looked for a revival of true religion from the downfall of Ahab's house, when the first public manifesto of the new king proclaimed him an enthusiastic worshipper of Baal. "Ahab," were his words, "served Baal a little; but Jehu shall serve him much." If Ahab's service of Baal was reckoned little, what was to be expected from one who would serve him so much more? It was certain that, whatever Jehu did, he would do it with abounding zeal. If he took up Baal's cause, there was no saying to what lengths he would carry it, or what severities he would employ to crush rival worships. Terrible disappointment would seize the hearts of the worshippers of Jehovah; and the servants of Baal, who had thought their cause destroyed, would be correspondingly elated. It is good neither to be unduly uplifted nor too heavily cast down at unexpected turns in public affairs. Those who rely for the success of their cause on the favours of great men are apt to be sorely disappointed. 2. *The deluded assembly.* It seemed at the first as if Jehu were to be every whit as good as his word. His proclamation not only included a declaration of his fixed intention to worship Baal, but gave effect to that intention by summoning a great assembly of the prophets, priests, and servants of Baal, to be held in the house of Baal at Samaria. A day was set apart, and the assembly was proclaimed throughout all Israel. The king was to offer a great sacrifice, publicly ratifying his avowal of allegiance to the heathen god. From all parts of the land the worshippers of Baal come trooping up, and the spacious courts of the great "house of Baal" were filled to overflowing. As if to give the highest possible *éclat* to the occasion, Jehu first ordered vestments to be produced from the temple or palace robe-chamber, and given to the worshippers; then he caused search to be made that none but servants of Baal were present. The worshippers of Baal were charmed; yet in truth they were there as sheep gathered together for the slaughter. All this, we are told, "Jehu did in subtilty, to the intent that he might destroy the worshippers of Baal." It is impossible to condone this flagrant hypocrisy, which even went the length of offering up a sacrifice to the false god. How unlike the open challenge of Elijah, who gave orders, indeed, for the destruction of Baal's prophets, but only after they had been publicly convicted of imposture (1 Kings xviii.)! We must not do evil, even that good may come. We see, however, how sometimes the wicked are on the very brink of their destruction when their hearts are most lifted up (Esth. v. 11, 12; Ps. lxxiii. 18—20). Things are not always what they seem. It is no uncommon thing to see the haters of truth given up to believe a delusion, that they may be destroyed.

III. BAAL ROOTED OUT. 1. *The guards posted.* While the festal throng is rejoicing within, eighty strong guards are posted without by the wily Jehu, to secure that none shall escape. To the captains and guard are committed the task of actual slaughter. 2. *Jehu's sacrifice.* Proceeding to the interior, Jehu takes part in the various solemnities. At length the worship reaches its climax in the offering of the great burnt offering of the king. This, as remarked above, was an act not to be justified. It showed how little Jehu understood the spiritual nature of God, or was sincerely desirous of serving him, when he could bring himself to promote God's cause by going through this idolatrous farce. Is it, however, worse than many other things that are professedly done in the Name, and ostensibly for the honour, of God? 3. *A promiscuous slaughter.* When the festivity was thus at its height, Jehu gave the word, and, the soldiers entering, an indiscriminate and merciless slaughter took place. Not one of Baal's worshippers was allowed to escape. It was a fearful massacre, but seems effectually to have rooted Baal-worship out of the land. The slaughter of the deluded votaries was followed by the breaking down of the house of Baal, with its pillars, images, etc. The retribution in itself was righteous, and shadows forth the terrible, sudden, and overwhelming ruin that shall yet overtake all God's enemies. But the deed of vengeance is sadly stained with human passion, deceit, and wrong.—J. O.

Vers. 20—36.—*The reign of Jehu.* Under this head we note—
I. JEHU'S REWARD. 1. *Four generations on the throne.* Jehu had outwardly fulfilled the commission given him by God, and had wrought a great deliverance for Israel. This public service God acknowledged by the promise that his sons should sit upon the throne to the fourth generation. The service was outward, and the reward was outward. Approval of Jehu's deeds did not extend to approval of every detail in his conduct. The limit—"fourth generation"—already implies that Jehu was not all he should have been, and anticipates that his sons would not be morally better, else the line would have been continued. 2. *The stain of blood.* Jehu had shed much blood. Guilt could not be imputed to him in this, so far as he was acting under an express Divine command. He "delivered his soul" (Ezek. xxxiii. 9), however, only if this Divine command furnished the actual motive of his conduct. If the Divine mandate but covered designs of selfish ambition, the stain of blood came back on him. Hence the different judgment passed on these deeds in Hos. i. 4, "I will avenge the blood of Jezreel upon the house of Jehu." In 2 Kings Jehu's acts are regarded on their outward side, while in Hosea they are considered on their inner and spiritual side. His real character was made apparent by his subsequent deeds. He obeyed God only so far as he could at the same time serve himself. He would willingly have shed the same amount of blood to secure the throne for himself, had there been no Divine command at all. It hence became impossible to exonerate him from a measure of blood-guiltiness. By making himself one with Ahab in his sins, Jehu fell back to the position of an ordinary manslayer.

II. JEHU'S FAILURE. 1. *His sin.* Generally it is affirmed that, after his elevation to the throne, "he took no heed to walk in the Law of the Lord God of Israel with all his heart," and particularly it is charged against him that he did not remove the golden calves of Jeroboam. He continued that idolatrous and schismatic worship at Bethel and at Dan. This means that his "zeal for the Lord" stopped short at the point needed for the consolidation of his own power. Once seated on the throne, with no more blood of Ahab's house to shed, he became indifferent to religious reform. The self-will that underlay his pretended zeal for God thus became apparent. It seemed to him politically prudent to keep up the division of the kingdoms by perpetuating the calf-worship of Jeroboam; so, though he knew it was wrong, he refrained from interfering with it. We see in this the distinction between true and false zeal. True zeal for God is careful above all things to walk in God's ways. It honours his commandment above considerations of expediency. It is not spasmodic, but persists in well-doing. False zeal, on the contrary, is fitful and wilful. It is moved when self-interest, or private passion, or inclination, or the praise of men, coincides with the Divine command; it throws off the mask when religion and interest point in opposite directions. It is time alone can test the quality of zeal. 2. *His punishment.* We find that after his declension Jehu suffered severe losses of territory. Hazael and the Syrians pressed in, and took from him most of the land on the east side of Jordan. It is not difficult to connect the two things as cause and effect. Had Jehu remained faithful to God, it is not to be thought that he would have suffered these losses. Because he did not remain faithful, he was scourged more severely than perhaps another man would have been. He was raised up to punish others, and, foreseeing his declension, an instrument had been prepared to punish him (ch. viii. 12). When God was against him, his generalship and valour were of no avail. We are thus taught that true self-interest and irreligion do not coincide. Jehu sought his own ends, and, as a politic ruler, thought it wiser to disobey God than to run the risk of putting down a popular idolatry. The result showed how short-sighted his calculations were. The wisest course, even for our own interests, is to do what God requires.

Nothing more is told of the twenty-eight years' reign of Jehu. He was buried in Samaria, and his son Jehoahaz succeeded him.—J. O.

EXPOSITION.

CHAPTER XI.

Vers. 1—21.—REVOLUTION IN JUDAH, FOLLOWING THE REVOLUTIONARY MOVEMENTS IN ISRAEL. REIGN OF ATHALIAH OVER JUDAH. CONSPIRACY OF JEHOIADA, AND DEATH OF ATHALIAH.

Vers. 1—3.—On learning the death of Ahaziah (ch. ix. 27), Athaliah, daughter of Ahab and Jezebel, the queen-mother, murders all her grandchildren (except the youngest, Joash, who is secreted by his aunt, Jehosheba) and seizes the kingdom. No resistance is made to her, and she retains the sole authority for six years. The worship of Baal, introduced by Jehoram into Judah, and supported by Ahaziah (ch. viii. 27), is maintained by her (ch. xi. 18).

Ver. 1.—**And when Athaliah the mother of Ahaziah saw that her son was dead.** (On Athaliah, see the comment upon ch. viii. 18.) She was married to Jehoram, son of Jehoshaphat, probably in the lifetime of his father, to cement the alliance concluded between Ahab and Jehoshaphat against the Syrians (1 Kings xxii. 2—4). She inherited much of her mother Jezebel's character, obtained an unlimited ascendancy over her husband, Jehoram, and kept her son Ahaziah in leading-strings. It was unquestionably through her influence that Jehoram

was prevailed upon to introduce the Baal-worship into Judah (ch. viii. 18; 2 Chron. xxi. 5, 11), and Ahaziah prevailed upon to maintain it (ch. viii. 27; 2 Chron. xxii. 3, " He also walked in the ways of the house of Ahab: *for his mother was his counsellor to do wickedly* "). On the death of Ahaziah, she found her position seriously imperilled. The crown would have passed naturally to one of her grandchildren, the eldest of the sons of Ahaziah. She would have lost her position of *gebirah*, or queen-mother, which would have passed to the widow of Ahaziah, the mother of the new sovereign. If she did not at once lose all influence, at any rate a counter-influence to hers would have been established; and this might well have been that of the high priest, who was closely connected by marriage with the royal family. Under these circumstances, she took the bold resolution described in the next clause. **She arose and destroyed all the seed royal.** She issued her orders, and had all the members of the house of David on whom she could lay her hands put to death. The royal house had already been greatly depleted by Jehoram's murder of his brothers (2 Chron. xxi. 4), by Arab marauders (2 Chron. xxi. 17), and by Jehu's murder of the "brethren" of Ahaziah (ch. x. 14); but it is clear that Ahaziah had left several sons behind him, and some of his "brethren" had also, in all probability, left issue. There may also have been many other descendants of David in Judah, belonging to other branches of the house than that of Rehoboam. Athaliah, no doubt, endeavoured to make a clean sweep, and get rid of them all.

Ver. 2.—**But Jehosheba** ("Jehoshabeath," Chronicles; "Josabethé," Josephus). **The daughter of King Joram, sister of Ahaziah**—half-sister, according to Josephus ('Ant. Jud.,' ix. 7. § 1), the daughter of Joram by a secondary wife, not by Athaliah—**took Joash the son of Ahaziah, and stole him from among the king's sons** which were slain. As aunt of the royal children, Jehosheba would have free entrance into the palace, and liberty to visit all the apartments. She did not dare openly to oppose Athaliah's will, but contrived secretly to save one of the intended victims, the smallest of them, an infant of a year old ($\pi\alpha\iota\delta\acute{\iota}o\nu$ $\acute{\epsilon}\nu\iota\alpha\acute{\upsilon}\sigma\iota o\nu$, Josephus). His tender age, probably, moved her compassion, and induced her to select him from the rest. **And they hid him, even him and his nurse.** The order in the Hebrew is, "even him and his nurse, and they hid him," which clears the sense. Jehosheba stole away Joash and his nurse, and they, *i.e.* Jehosheba and the nurse together, hid him between them. **In the bedchamber;** rather, *in the chamber of mattresses*—a room in the palace where mattresses, and perhaps coverlets, were stored. Chardin notes ('Works,' vol. iii. p. 357) that there is usually such a room in an Oriental palace, which is only used as a store-chamber, and not as a dwelling-room. **From Athaliah, so that he was not slain.** Athaliah's servants may not have been very anxious to carry out her cruel orders to the uttermost, and may have made no very careful search.

Ver. 3.—**And he was with her**—he, *i.e.* Joash, was with her, *i.e.* Jehosheba, his aunt—**hid in the house of the Lord;** *i e* the temple. We learn from Chronicles (2 Chron. xxii. 11) that Jehosheba was married to Jehoiada, the high priest, and would thus have ready access to the temple. We must suppose that, after a few days' concealment in the "chamber of mattresses," Jehosheba found an opportunity of transferring him, with his nurse, to a chamber in the temple, where he was thenceforward nourished and brought up. There were various chambers in the temple used for secular purposes, as we learn from 1 Kings vi. 5—8 and Neh. xiii. 5—9. **Six years** (comp. ver. 21 and 2 Chron. xxiv. 1). **And Athaliah did reign over the land.** It is difficult to realize all that this implies. It cannot mean less than that for six years Baalism was triumphant in Judah—the temple was allowed to fall into decay (ch. xii. 5)—a temple to Baal was erected in Jerusalem itself, to supersede the temple of Jehovah (ch. xi. 18); and a high priest appointed to be a rival to the successor of Aaron. Whether persecution was indulged

in, as under Jehoram (2 Chron. xxi. 11), is uncertain; but the servants of Jehovah were at any rate under a cloud, slighted, contemned, held as of small account. Perhaps we may conclude, from the position occupied by Jehoiada, and from the powers which he was able to exercise when he determined on revolt (ver. 4; 2 Chron. xxiii. 1, 2), that Athaliah, during her six years' reign, was to some extent held in check by a Jehovistic party, which she knew to exist, and which she did not dare openly to defy. Thus she left Jehoiada (apparently) in possession of the temple, of its treasures and its armoury (ver. 10); she allowed the temple service to continue (2 Chron. xxiii. 4—7); she permitted the priests and the Levites to serve in their regular "courses" (2 Chron. xxiii. 8); she let the fortress of the eastern city—for the temple was always a fortress—remain in her enemies' hands. Still, the time was evidently one "of trouble, and of rebuke, and blasphemy:" the oppressed worshippers of Jehovah were greatly discontented; and the nation generally was ripe for a counter-revolution, so soon as the signal was given by an authority whom they could trust.

Vers. 4—16.—*Conspiracy of Jehoiada.* After waiting, impatiently we may be sure, for six long years, and seeing the young prince grow from an infant to a boy of seven years of age, Jehoiada deemed that the time was come to venture on an effort. It was necessary for him to make his arrangements beforehand with great care. His first step was to sound the captains of the royal guard. To these men, five in number (2 Chron. xxiii. 1), he sent secretly, and invited them to confer with him in the temple on important business. Finding them well disposed to adopt his views, he revealed to them the fact that Joash had escaped the massacre of Ahaziah's sons, and was still living, even allowing them to see him. The result of the interview was that they put themselves at Jehoiada's disposal, and agreed to take their orders from him (ver. 4). Jehoiada then proceeded to his second step. Either distrusting the body-guard which the captains commanded, or regarding it as insufficient in numbers, he gave them orders to visit the various cities of Judæa, and collect from them a strong force of Levites and other trusty persons, and bring them to Jerusalem (2 Chron. xxiii. 2), where he would give them their orders. This was done successfully, and, as it would seem, without in any way rousing the suspicions of Athaliah. A day was fixed for proclaiming Joash king; the guard and the Levites were skilfully disposed about the temple and the palace; the king was brought up, crowned, anointed, and saluted as monarch, with noisy acclamations (ver. 12). The noise was heard in the palace, and Athaliah went forth, with a few attendants, to inquire the reason of it. Following the sound, she came to the temple, and entered it, when she saw what was going on, and cried out, "Treason! treason!" By Jehoiada's order the guards seized her, conducted her out of the temple, and slew her (vers. 13—16).

Ver. 4.—**And the seventh year**—literally, *and in the seventh year;* i.e. in the course of it —Jehoiada sent and fetched the rulers over hundreds, with the captains and the guard; rather, *the captains over hundreds* (or, centurions) *of the Carites and the guard* (see the Revised Version). The "Carites," here first named, are generally regarded as identical with the Cherethites of earlier times (2 Sam. viii. 18; 1 Kings i. 38; 1 Chron. xviii. 17). They were undoubtedly a particular portion of the royal guard, and may, perhaps, as many suppose, have been "Carian" mercenaries, though we have no other evidence that the Carians had adopted the mercenary life so early as the time of Athaliah. Still, as their devotion to it had passed into a proverb when Archilochus wrote (B.C. 700—660), it is quite possible that they had begun the practice a century or two earlier. When Jehoiada is said to have "sent and fetched" the centurions, we must understand that he secretly invited them, and that they consented to come. He could not possibly have any authority over them, so as to require their attendance. The names of the five centurions, together with their fathers' names, were put on record by the writer of Chronicles (2 Chron. xxiii. 1), whose account of the revolution is in many respects fuller than that in Kings. **And brought them to him into the house of the Lord**—as the safest place for an interview which had to be kept secret from the queen—**and made a covenant with them, and took an oath of them in the house of the Lord.** We can easily understand that the soldiers, who had been willing to serve Athaliah under the notion that the house of David was extinct, might waver in their allegiance so soon as they heard that a scion of the old royal stock survived, and could be produced at a moment's notice. Their traditions would attach them to David

and his seed, not to the house of Ahab. **And showed them the king's son.** Having bound the centurions by a solemn covenant to the cause of the young king, Jehoiada introduced them into his presence. He had, no doubt, previously sworn them to secrecy.

Ver. 5.—**And he commanded them, saying, This is the thing that ye shall do.** It is evident, from 2 Chronicles and from Josephus, that a considerable interval of time separates the events of ver. 5 from those of ver. 4. The *immediate* arrangement made between Jehoiada and the centurions was that they should "go throughout the whole land" (Josephus, 'Ant. Jud.,' ix. 7. § 2), visit "all the cities of Judah" (2 Chron. xxiii. 2), and gather out of them a strong force of Levites and priests (Josephus), together with a certain number of other representative Israelites, which force they should bring with them to Jerusalem, and place at his disposal. To accomplish this must have taken some weeks. When the force had arrived, Jehoiada summoned it to meet him in the courts of the temple, and swore it to a similar covenant to that which he had made with the centurions. He then bided his time, completed his arrangements, utilized the store of arms laid up in the temple armoury (ver. 10), and finally gave two charges—one to the centurions, which is given here (vers. 5—8), and the other to the force collected from the cities of Judah, which is given in Chronicles (2 Chron. xxiii. 4—7). The orders given to the two forces were very similar, but not identical. **A third part of you that enter in on the sabbath.** The royal body-guard consisted of five divisions, each probably of a hundred men, and each commanded by its own captain (2 Chron. xxiii. 1). It was usual on the sabbath for three divisions out of the five to mount guard at the royal palace, while two were engaged outside, keeping order in the city, and especially at the temple. We do not know the ordinary disposition of the guard, either inside or outside the palace. On this occasion Jehoiada commanded that the palace-guard should be disposed as follows: one division at the palace proper, in the courts and halls and antechambers; a second at one of the issues from the palace, known as "the gate of Sur;" and a third at an issue called "the gate of the guard," which was certainly towards the east, where the palace fronted the temple. The object was to secure the palace, but not to prevent the queen from leaving it. **Shall even be keepers of the watch of the king's house;** *i.e.* of the royal palace.

Ver. 6.—**And a third part shall be at the gate of Sur.** The "gate of Sur" is not elsewhere mentioned. It seems to be called in Chronicles (2 Chron: xxiii. 5) "the gate of the foundation" (שַׁעַר יְסוֹד) instead of " the gate of Sur" (שַׁעַר סוּר), as here—the one reading having evidently arisen out of the other by a corruption. We must understand one of the *palace* gates, but which of them is uncertain. And a third part at the gate behind the guard; called in ver. 19 "the gate of the guard," and shown there to have been on the *east* side of the palace, where it faced the temple, and abutted on the Tyropœon. So shall ye keep the watch of the house—*i.e.* of the "*king's* house," or palace, which is contrasted with the "house of the Lord" of the next verse—that it be not broken down. This rendering is scarcely accepted at the present time by any writers. Ewald renders, "according to custom;" Keil, " for defence;" Fürst, "alternately;" our Revisers, "and be a barrier." The Hebrew word used occurs nowhere else, and it seems impossible to determine its sense. The LXX. simply omit it.

Ver. 7.—And two parts of all you that go forth on the sabbath. Three-fifths of the guard having been disposed of about the palace, there remained only two-fifths, or two "companies" (margin of Authorized Version). These Jehoiada commanded to enter the temple and protect the young king. Even they shall keep the watch of the house of the Lord about the king. According to Chronicles (2 Chron. xxiii. 7), the great body of the Levites gathered from the cities of Judah was also to be in the temple, and to assist in the protection of the monarch.

Ver. 8.—And ye shall compass the king round about; every man with his weapons in his hand. The guard was to take up a position, partly in front of the king, and partly behind him; interposing themselves between his person and any danger, and at the same time extending themselves across the entire court of the temple (ver. 11) from one wall to the other. They were, of course, to have their weapons in their hands, ready for use. And he that cometh within the ranges, let him be slain; rather, *within the ranks*. The order was that if any one entered the temple, and attempted to break through the ranks of the guard, either in front of the king or behind him, he should instantly be put to death. No attempt of the kind was made; and so the order remained a dead letter. And be ye with the king as he goeth out and as he cometh in; accompany him, *i e* in all his movements — let him never for a moment stray outside your ranks—continue to surround him whithersoever he goes. Boys are restless, and curiosity would lead the young prince to move from place to place in order to see what was going on.

Ver. 9.—And the captains over the hun-

dreds—*i.e.* the five centurions of the guard, Azariah the son of Jeroham, Azariah the son of Obed, Ishmael, Maaseiah, and Elishaphat—did according to all things that Jehoiada the priest commanded. The secular arm placed itself entirely at the disposal of the spirituality, and was content for once to be subordinate. And they took every man his men that were to come in on the sabbath, with them that should go out on the sabbath, and came to Jehoiada the priest. The position of Jehoiada as high priest ("*the* priest" always means "*high* priest") had not been previously mentioned, probably because it was presumed to be known. The Chronicler, writing much later, gives Jehoiada the title on the first occasion that he mentions him (2 Chron. xxii. 11). When it is said that "*all* the captains took their men and came to Jehoiada," the intention is to mark their exact obedience to the orders given them. Strictly speaking, only two out of the five actually appeared before Jehoiada on the day of the execution of his project, two divisions only having been summoned to come to the temple (ver. 7). The other three took up the positions assigned them in and about the royal palace.

Ver. 10.—And to the captains over hundreds did the priest give King David's spears and shields, that were in the temple of the Lord. We hear of David carrying with him to Jerusalem the "shields of gold," *i.e.* shields ornamented with gold, which he took from the servants of Hadadezer (2 Sam. viii. 7); but otherwise we are not told of his establishing an armoury. Solomon made six hundred shields of solid gold, and laid them up in the house of the forest of Lebanon (1 Kings x. 17); but these were carried off by Sheshonk, when he invaded Judæa in the reign of Rehoboam (1 Kings xiv. 26). Rehoboam, in their place, made three hundred brazen shields (1 Kings xiv. 27), which, however, were deposited in the guard-chamber of the royal palace. Of spears collected by David, and laid up in the temple, we know nothing beyond the present passage. There can be little doubt that the weapons were brought forth from their receptacle with the view (as Ewald says) of "consecrating the work of the restoration of the Davidic house with the sacred arms of the great founder himself" (see 'History of Israel,' vol. iv. p. 136)—not, however, with arms that he had worn, but with some which he had collected and laid up.

Ver. 11.—And the guard stood, every man with his weapons in his hand, round about the king, from the right corner of the temple to the left corner of the temple. "Corner" is a wrong word used in this connection. The Hebrew כָּתֵף is literally, "shoulder," and must mean here, not "corner," but "side" (so our Revisers). The guard was drawn up right across the temple court from wall to wall, probably in several ranks, both before and behind the king (see ver. 8). Along by the altar. The "altar" intended is, of course, the altar of burnt offering, which stood in the great court, a little way from the porch, right in front of it; not the altar of incense, which was inside the sanctuary. No one, it must be remembered, was ever allowed to enter inside the sanctuary but the priests and officiating Levites (see 2 Chron. xxiii. 6). And the temple. "The temple" is here the sanctuary, as in the passage of Chronicles just quoted. The guard occupied a position at the upper end of the court, immediately in front of the altar and the temple porch.

Ver. 12.—And he—i.e. Jehoiada—brought forth the king's son—produced him, i.e., from the chamber or chambers where he had been concealed hitherto. (On the temple chambers, see Neh. xiii. 4—9.) And put the crown upon him. That the Israelite kings actually wore crowns appears from 2 Sam. i. 10 and 1 Chron. xx. 2. The crown was probably a band of gold, either plain or set with jewels (Zech. ix. 16), fastened behind with a riband. It receives here the same name that is given to the high priest's diadem in Exod. xxix. 6 and xxxix. 30. And gave him the testimony. The words "gave him" are not in the original, and are superfluous. What is meant plainly is that the high priest laid on the young king's head a copy of the Law, or of some essential portion of it, perhaps the Decalogue, which is often called "the testimony" (Exod. xvi. 34; xxv. 16, 21, etc.). The object apparently was to show that the king was to rule by law, not arbitrarily—that he was to be, as Dean Stanley says, "not above, but beneath, the law of his country" ('Jewish Church,' vol. ii. p. 397). The ceremony seems to have been a new one, and is indicative of the gradual curtailment of the regal power under the later monarchy. And they made him king, and anointed him. A change is made from the singular to the plural, because, as we learn from 2 Chron. xxiii. 11, "Jehoiada and his sons anointed him." We have had no mention of the anointing of a new monarch in Judah since the time of Solomon (1 Kings i. 39). It may, however, have been the usual practice. And they—i.e. the people—all who were present—clapped their hands—an ordinary sign of joy (see Ps. xlvii. 1; xcviii. 8; Isa. lv. 12; Nah. iii. 19, etc.)—and said, God save the king! literally, long live the king! (comp. 1 Sam. x. 24; 2 Sam. xvi. 16; 1 Kings i. 25, 39).

Ver. 13.—And when Athaliah heard the noise of the guard (comp. 1 Kings i. 41—45, where the noise accompanying the coronation of Solomon was heard to an equal distance) and of the people. The "and," which is omitted in the present Hebrew text, may be supplied by a very slight alteration. We have only to read הָרָצִין הָעָם וְהָעָם for הָרָצִין הָעָם—an emendation rendered almost certain by the fact that the plural in ין- does not belong to the date of the writer of Kings. She came to the people into the temple of the Lord. It was not her habit to enter the temple on the sabbath, or on any other day; but, hearing the noise, she hurried across from the palace to learn its cause. It would seem that she was still unsuspicious of danger, and brought no guards with her, nor any large body of attendants.

Ver. 14.—And when she looked, behold, the king stood by a pillar; rather, on the pillar, or on the raised platform. The king's proper place in the temple seems to have been a raised standing-place (הָעַמּוּד, from עָמֹד, to stand) in front of the entrance to the sanctuary, which made him very conspicuous (comp. ch. xxiii. 3; 2 Chron. xxiii. 13, and xxxiv. 31). As the manner was—i.e. as was the usual practice when kings visited the temple—and the princes—i.e. the centurions or captains of the guard—and the trumpeters by the king—the officials whose business it was to blow the trumpet at a coronation (see 2 Sam. xv. 10; 1 Kings i. 39; ix. 13)—and all the people of the land rejoiced, and blew with trumpets; i.e. the people who had been admitted into the great court to witness the coronation. Some rumour of what was about to occur had got abroad, and many of the people had provided themselves with trumpets. As Dean Stanley puts it, "The temple court was crowded with spectators, and they too took part in the celebration, and themselves prolonged the trumpet-blast, blended with the musical instruments of the temple service." And Athaliah rent her clothes. Athaliah took in all with a single glance. She "saw that the fatal hour was come" (Stanley). With a strong hand she rent her royal robes, partly in horror, partly in despair; for the single glance which she had cast around was sufficient to show her that all was lost. And cried, Treason! Treason! or, conspiracy! conspiracy! The cry was scarcely an appeal for help, as Josephus makes it ('Ant. Jud.,' ix. 7. § 3), but rather an instinctive utterance, without distinct aim or object, wrung from her under the circumstances. It fell dead on the assembly.

Ver. 15.—But Jehoiada the priest commanded the captains—literally, princes—of the hundreds, the officers of the host—the commanders, i.e., of the small "army" assembled in the temple court—**and said unto them, Have her forth without the ranges;** rather, *have her forth*, or *conduct her out between your ranks.* The object was probably to preserve her from suffering violence at the hands of any of the people within the temple precincts, which Jehoiada desired to preserve free from pollution. **And him that followeth her kill with the sword;** *i.e.* if any come after her out of the temple, to attempt a rescue, slay them with the sword. The order, given aloud, was sufficient to deter persons from making the attempt. **For the priest had said, Let her not be slain in the house of the Lord.** Jehoiada had previously given an order that her execution should take place outside the temple.

Ver. 16.—**And they laid hands on her.** So the LXX. (ἐπέθηκαν αὐτῇ χεῖρας), the Vulgate, Luther, and others; but most moderns understand that they formed in two lines, one on either side of her, and so let her pass out of the temple and proceed towards the palace *untouched*—the divinity that hedged a queen preventing them from molesting her until the time came for her execution (see the Revised Version). **And she went by the way by the which the horses came into the king's house.** Josephus makes Athaliah pass out of the temple by the east gate, and descend into the Kedron valley. He says she was put to death "at the gate of the king's mules," but does not mark the locality. The gate intended can scarcely be the "horse gate" of Neh. iii. 28, which was in the eastern wall, and north of the temple. It was probably a gate on the western side of the Tyropœon valley, giving entrance to the stables of the palace (comp. 2 Chron. xxiii. 15, and see below, ver. 20). **And there was she slain;** "with the sword" (ver. 20). A single blow from one of the guardsmen probably sufficed.

Vers. 17—21.—*Further doings of Jehoiada.* The king being at present a mere puppet in his hands, Jehoiada had to determine the next steps which were necessary to be taken. These, in his judgment, were three. 1. A solemn covenant must be made between the king and the people; and another between the king, the people, and God—the latter pledging the king and people to maintain the worship of Jehovah, and never again to apostatize; the former pledging the king to govern according to law, and the people to remain faithful to him. 2. The temple of Baal, erected in Jerusalem at the instance of Athaliah, must be destroyed. 3. The king must be removed from the temple and installed in the palace

of his ancestors. A brief account of these proceedings concludes the present chapter.

Ver. 17.—**And Jehoiada made a covenant between the Lord and the king and the people.** In the original it is "made *the* covenant;" and the meaning is that the high priest renewed the old covenant understood to exist between king and people on the one hand and God on the other, that they would be faithful to God and God to them—that they would maintain his worship, and that he would continue his protection (see Exod. xix. 5—8; xxiv. 3—8; xxxiv. 10—28). The apostasy of Jehoram, Ahaziah, and Athaliah was regarded as having put an end to the old covenant, and therefore it was solemnly remade or renewed. **That they should be the Lord's people** (comp. Exod. xix. 5; Deut. iv. 20; ix. 29; xxxii. 9, etc.); **between the king also and the people.** The terms of this covenant are nowhere distinctly stated, but we can only suppose them to have expressed in words the intention of that novel act, the imposition of "the testimony" upon the head of the king at the time of his coronation (see the comment upon ver. 12).

Ver. 18.—**And all the people of the land**—*i.e.* all those who had come up to Jerusalem from the various cities of Judah to help Jehoiada (see 2 Chron. xxiii. 2)—**went into the house of Baal.** According to Josephus, "the house of Baal" here mentioned was built by Jehoram and Athaliah in the reign of the former ('Ant. Jud.,' ix. 7. § 4). But, if this was the case, it is rather strange that the writer of Chronicles, who enumerates so many of the evil acts of Jehoram (2 Chron. xxi. 4, 6, 11), does not mention it. The present narrative shows that the temple was in, or very near, Jerusalem; but there is nothing to fix the site of it. **And brake it down**—Josephus says they "razed it to the ground" (κατέσκαψαν)—**his altars and his images brake they in pieces thoroughly.** It was common among the heathen to have several altars in one temple, and not uncommon to have several images even of the same god, especially if he was a god worshipped under different forms, as Baal was (whence the word "Baalim"). The Baalim of this temple are mentioned by the writer of Chronicles (see 2 Chron. xxiv. 7). **And slew Mattan the priest of Baal before the altars.** The name "Mattan" recalls that of the last King of Judah, which was originally Mattan-iah, equivalent to "gift of Jehovah" (ch. xxiv. 17). Mattan would be simply "gift." We may presume that, though only called "priest," he was the high priest. **And the priest**—*i.e.* Jehoiada—**appointed officers over the house of the Lord.** The parallel passage of Chronicles

(2 Chron. xxiii. 18, 19) explains this statement. We are there told that "Jehoiada appointed the offices of the house of the Lord by the hand of the priests the Levites, . . . to offer the burnt offerings of the Lord, as it is written in the Law of Moses, with rejoicing and with singing, as it was ordained by David. And he set the porters at the gates of the house of the Lord, that none which was unclean in anything should enter in." During Athaliah's reign the temple service had ceased; breaches had been broken in the outer walls; and neither the priests nor the porters had served in their regular order; there had been no morning or evening sacrifice, and no antiphonal psalm-singing. Jehoiada re-established the regular courses and the worship.

Ver. 19.—**And he took the rulers**—literally, *princes*—**over hundreds**—*i.e.* the five centurions of 2 Chron. xxiii. 2—**and the captains**—rather, *and the Carites* (see the comment on ver. 4)—**and the guard**—*i.e.* the "runners," the other division of the guard—**and all the people of the land**—those who had flocked to his standard either originally (2 Chron. xxiii. 2) or since—**and they brought down the king from the house of the Lord.** They escorted Joash from the temple to the palace, first bringing him *down* into the valley of the Tyropœon, and then conducting him up the opposite, or western hill, on which the palace stood. **And came by the way of the gate of the guard to the king's house.** The "gate of the guard" is probably that called in ver. 6 "the gate behind the guard." We may presume that it was the main entrance to the palace on the eastern side. **And he sat on the throne of the kings.** Not till he had

placed Joash on the royal throne of his ancestors, in the great throne-room of the palace, was Jehoiada content with the work of the day.

Ver. 20.—**And all the people of the land rejoiced.** "All the people of the land" has here, perhaps, a wider signification than in vers. 18 and 19. The *whole land* was content with the revolution that had taken place. No opposition showed itself. Ewald has no ground for his statement that the heathenizing party was strong in Jerusalem, and that the worshippers of Jehovah "had for a long time to keep watch in the temple, to prevent surprise by the heathenizing party" ('History of Israel,' vol. iv. p. 136, note 3). He has mistaken the intention of the last clause of ver. 18. If anything is clear from the entire narrative of the early reign of Joash (ch. xi. 3—21; xii. 1—16; 2 Chron. xxiii. 1—21; xxiv. 1—14), it is that there was no heathenizing party in Jerusalem, or none that dared to show itself, until after the death of the high priest Jehoiada, which was later than the twenty-third year of Joash. **And the city**—*i.e.* Jerusalem—**was in quiet: and they slew**—it might be translated, *when they had slain* —**Athaliah with the sword** beside **the king's house.** The intention of the writer is to connect the period of tranquillity with the removal of Athaliah, and therefore to point her out as the cause of disturbance previously.

Ver. 21.—**Seven years old was Jehoash**—or, *Joash*—**when he began to reign** (comp. vers. 3 and 4 and 2 Chron. xxiv. 1). The clause would be better placed at the beginning of the next chapter

HOMILETICS.

Vers. 1—3 and 14—16.—*Athaliah and Jezebel, the wicked daughter and the wicked mother.* It has often been noted that, while women are, as a general rule, better than men, in the cases where they enter upon evil courses their wickedness exceeds that of their male associates. The character of Lady Macbeth is true to nature. Wicked women are more thorough-going than wicked men, more bloody, more daring, more unscrupulous. In Athaliah we have a sort of repetition of Jezebel—a second picture on the same lines—the picture of a fierce, ambitious, utterly unscrupulous woman, occupying much the same station as her mother, equally powerful, equally unsparing, and equally remorseless. Both women are represented as—

I. DEVOTEES OF THE SAME SENSUOUS AND IMMORAL CULT. Jezebel introduces the Baal and Ashtoreth worship into Israel; Athaliah into Judah. Each defiles the capital of her adopted country with a temple to Baal—a temple where images of Baal are set up, altars erected to him, and sacrifices offered to him. Each brings with her into her new home the Baal priesthood, and instals it in power.

II. OPEN ANTAGONISTS OF JEHOVAH. Jezebel persecutes the Jehovistic prophets, slaying as many as she can, and threatening the life even of Elijah (1 Kings xviii. 4; xix. 2). Athaliah stops the temple-worship at Jerusalem, has breaches made in the temple walls, and gives to Baal the offerings which properly belong to Jehovah (2 Chron. xxiv. 7).

III. MURDERESSES. Jezebel, of Naboth (1 Kings xxi. 8—14) and of the Jehovistic prophets (1 Kings xviii. 4); Athaliah, of "all the seed royal of the house of Judah" (2 Chron. xxii. 10).

IV. EAGER TO GRASP AND WIELD SOVEREIGN POWER. Jezebel governs Ahab (1 Kings xxi. 25), uses his signet (1 Kings xxi. 8), orders executions (1 Kings xviii. 4; xxi. 10), and the like. Athaliah governs Jehoram (ch. viii. 18) and Ahaziah (2 Chron. xxii. 3), and then seizes the royal power, and actually rules Judæa (ch. xi. 3).

Athaliah is, on the whole, the bolder of the two, and the more unscrupulous; since to destroy the entire seed royal, including several of her own grandchildren, was a more atrocious and unnatural deed than any committed by Jezebel; and the actual assumption of the royal name and power, in spite of her sex, was a more audacious proceeding than any on which her mother ventured. But her audacity verged on rashness, which cannot be said of Jezebel. She brought her fate upon herself; Jezebel succumbed to an inevitable stroke of adverse fortune. There was weakness in Athaliah's half-measures after she became queen, in her suffering Jehoiada to retain so much liberty and so much power, and still greater weakness in her unsuspiciousness. We cannot imagine Jezebel, if she had ever been actual queen, allowing herself to be put down in the way that Athaliah was. She would at least have made a fight for her life, instead of walking straight into a trap, which was what Athaliah did. *Quem Deus vult perdere prius dementat* is an old saying. Athaliah's folly at the last can only be accounted for by an infatuation, which may have been a Divine judgment on her.

Vers. 4—19.—*Jehoiada an example of a faithful and wise high priest under trying circumstances.* The history of the Jewish kingdom from the time of Saul to the Captivity furnishes but few examples of remarkable high priests. Zadok and Abiathar were personages of some importance in the time of David, and left behind them a name for zeal and fidelity; but otherwise no man of eminence had arisen among the high priests until Jehoiada. This may be partly accounted for by the fact that the high priesthood was hereditary, not elective; but still more by the nature of the office, which was not such as to bring its holder into historical prominence in quiet times. Jehoiada's opportunity for distinction arose from the difficult circumstances in which he was placed. Holding the office of high priest when the throne was usurped and religion outraged by Athaliah, it devolved on him to rescue Church and state alike from peril, and to counter-work the wicked schemes of an enemy alike bold and unscrupulous. He could not prevent the destruction of the royal stock by Athaliah, which was a crime so unnatural that none could have anticipated it; but he did what he could. At the peril of his life he saved one prince, concealed him from prying eyes, protected him, bred him up secretly, and did not allow his existence to be even suspected. In faith and patience he waited till the infant had become a boy of an age to interest people, and till Athaliah had lost the affections of all classes of her subjects. He then organized a counter-revolution to the one effected by Athaliah, with the greatest prudence, caution, and sagacity. It would have been easy to gather partisans and raise a revolt; but Jehoiada shrank from the horrors of a civil war, and from the risk of losing his precious charge by a stray shot or a chance sword-thrust. He therefore set to work to detach Athaliah's supporters from her cause by the peaceful method of persuasion. First he gained over the captains of her guard, then through them the rank-and-file, finally the "chief fathers" of Israel in the various cities (2 Chron. xxiii. 2). Doubting the sufficiency of this force, he further summoned to his aid a large body of Levites. And all this he did so secretly as to create no alarm, to arouse no suspicion. When the time for action came, he made his arrangements with the most consummate skill. He could not, indeed, have foreseen that Athaliah would so play into his hand, as she did, by coming within the temple walls with few or no attendants; but he had taken his measures in such a way as to make failure impossible, and to reduce to a minimum the probability of tumult or armed resistance. It was an indication of extraordinary prudence and political wisdom to be able to effect a complete revolution, both in Church and state, at the cost of two lives, both of them clearly forfeit by the Law of Moses. Up to this time, Jehoiada's wisdom had been chiefly conspicuous. Henceforth it is his fidelity that draws our admiration. Aiming at nothing for himself, his first thought is for the honour of God, and therefore he renews the Mosaic covenant; his next for the welfare of his country, and therefore he makes king and people mutually swear to each other; his third for the honour of true religion, and therefore he destroys the temple of Baal, and inaugurates afresh the Jehovistic service. As Bähr says, "If ever a man stood pure and blameless in the midst of such a bold, difficult, and far-reaching enterprise, then Jehoiada, *the ideal Israelitish priest*, did so here." The after-life of Jehoiada is less remarkable (ch. xii. 2—16; 2 Chron. xxiv. 2—14), but not unworthy of his earlier reputation.

Vers. 15—17.—*God's judgments not unfrequently fall in this life, though sometimes they are deferred to the life beyond the grave.* The Athaliahs and Mattans of history seldom come to a good end. Though the wicked man be often seen in prosperity, though he "flourishes as a green bay tree," yet it is not often that he continues flourishing to the close of his days, or dies in comfort, peace, and happiness. The psalmist was satisfied when he saw "the end" of the man whose long-continued prosperity had vexed and grieved him (Ps. lxxiii. 2—22). Heathen wisdom bade men "never to pronounce any one happy before his death," since in human life changes were of continual occurrence, and the higher a man's exaltation above his fellows at a given time, the lower was likely to be his depression and degradation at another. The *rationale* of the matter seems to be—

I. God has attached penalties to vice in the way of natural consequence, which take effect if time be allowed. Tyrants lay up for themselves a constantly increasing amount of hatred and resentment, which naturally bursts forth and sweeps them away after a while; *e.g.* Hipparchus, Tarquin, Dionysius, Caligula, Nero. Drunkards, gluttons, and profligate persons destroy their health. Reckless spendthrifts reduce themselves to poverty and want. Unfaithfulness strips men of their friends, and leaves them weak and defenceless against their adversaries. The prosperity of the wicked is naturally but for a time—give them the full term of human life, and, before they die, their sin will, to a certainty, find them out, and they will cease to prosper.

II. God does, on occasion, visit high-placed, prosperous sinners with sudden, signal punishments dealt by his own hand. Scripture gives us a certain number of examples, as those of the Pharaoh of the Exodus, Saul, Jezebel, Sennacherib, Nebuchadnezzar, Herod Agrippa, and the like, whose afflictions are distinctly declared to have been sent upon them by God himself in the way of punishment. While, no doubt, great caution is necessary in applying the principle thus indicated to other persons in history, and especially to living persons, we need not shrink from *some* application of it. God speaks to us in history, not only in his Word. When selfish usurpers, who have deluged whole continents in blood, and sacrificed tens or hundreds of thousands of lives to gratify their ambition, are cast down from their thrones, and die in exile or banishment, it is almost impossible not to see his hand in the occurrences, executing judgment. When an Arius, bent on the disruption of the Church, and seemingly at the point of triumph, expires silently in the night, or a Galerius, the most cruel of persecutors, perishes in most horrible agonies, there is no want of charity or of reverence in once more recognizing his finger interposed to save his Church or to avenge his martyred ones. "Some men's sins are open beforehand, going before to judgment" (1 Tim. v. 24); and, when the judgment falls, it would be wilful blindness on our part not to recognize it. We must be cautious, and remember that those on whom the tower in Siloam fell, and slew them, were not sinners above the other dwellers in Jerusalem (Luke xiii. 4); but, if it was God's vengeance that destroyed the cities of the plain, and that visited Nadab and Abihu, Korah, Dathan, and Abiram, Sihon and Og, Balaam, Adonizedek and his brother kings, Eglon, Sisera, Zebah, Zalmunna, Abimelech, Agag, Doeg, Shimei, Jezebel, Haman, Ananias, Sapphira, Herod Agrippa, Elymas, so we may be sure that it has fallen on hundreds of others whose names do not occur in Scripture, coming suddenly upon them, and cutting them off in their iniquities, generally when neither they nor others were in the least expecting it. God is still, as he has ever been, "the great, the mighty God, the Lord of hosts, great in counsel and mighty in work; his eyes are open upon all the ways of the sons of men, to give every one according to his ways and according to the fruit of his doings" (Jer. xxxii. 18, 19). Either in this life or in the life to come he will execute vengeance upon evil-doers. Well for them if it is in this life, and if they so escape the dreadful lot of those " to whom is reserved the blackness of darkness for ever " (Jude 13).

HOMILIES BY VARIOUS AUTHORS.

Vers. 1—16.—*The preservation and coronation of Joash.* This is a touching story of human wickedness and of God's overruling and preserving power. Three principal personages come before us here, from each of whom something may be learned.

I. ATHALIAH AND HER WORK. *Athaliah's life-work was a work of destruction.* She did much harm. She did no good. A daughter of Ahab and Jezebel (sometimes called a daughter of Omri, whose granddaughter she was), she had inherited all the evil propensities of her parents. *She destroyed her own husband,* Jehoram King of Judah. We read of him that " he walked in the way of the kings of Israel, like as did the house of Ahab : *for he had the daughter of Ahab to wife* : and he wrought that which was evil in the eyes of the Lord " (2 Chron. xxi. 6). *She destroyed also her son Ahaziah.* We read of him that " he also walked in the ways of the house of Ahab : *for his mother was his counsellor to do wickedly.* Wherefore he did evil in the sight of the Lord like the house of Ahab ; for they were his counsellors after the death of his father *to his destruction"* (2 Chron. xxi. 3, 4). And now she completes her destructive career by *putting to death her grandchildren,* the seed royal of the kingdom. There are many women like Athaliah, whose life-work is a work of destruction. What harm one wicked woman can do ! Some corrupt the morals of others. Some, by their evil-speaking and slander, do what they can to destroy the reputation and good name of their neighbours. The Jezebels and Athaliahs of Scripture story have their parallels in the Queen Marys, the Pompadours, the Medicis, and the Maintenons of more modern times.

II. JEHOSHEBA AND HER WORK. *Jehosheba's work was a work of preservation.* She too was a king's daughter. But she had not been corrupted by the wickedness of the court. She was the wife of Jehoiada the priest—a good wife of a good man. She rescued Joash from Athaliah's massacre, and kept him hid in the priests' apartments in the temple. There he was hid for six years, until the time that, as a boy-king, he was called to the throne. If there are Athaliahs in the world still, there are also Jehoshebas. If there are women of cruelty, there are also women of sympathetic and compassionate spirit. If there are women who are corrupters of others, how many there are who by their own pure life and conduct have been the preservers of public purity and morality ! If one wicked woman can do much harm, one pure-minded Christian woman can do a vast amount of good. What an amount of quiet beneficence is being carried on by Christian women throughout the world at the present day ! What a vast number of ladies who visit and minister to the poor ! What a vast number of ladies who, in hospitals and in private houses, devote themselves to the noble work of nursing the sick ! How many are engaged in instructing the young in our Sunday schools ! How many have gone forth as missionaries to heathen lands ! Woman's work in the Christian Church, and in the cause of charity and philanthropy, seems to be increasing every year.

III. JEHOIADA AND HIS WORK. Jehoiada's work was of a twofold nature. *His work was both destroying and preserving.* He destroyed idolatry. He put an end to Athaliah's reign and life. He did not believe in the policy of non-resistance. He believed in doing his utmost to overthrow even the power of the reigning queen, when that power was wickedly obtained, and exercised in an evil way, dishonouring to God and injurious to the interests of the nation. Like many another reformer, he incurred the charge of disloyalty and treason. But there are many things that need to be destroyed. And who can overestimate the harm done by a wicked ruler ? But Jehoiada was no mere revolutionist. He did not rebel against Athaliah for revolution's sake. He did not put an end to her reign because of his antipathy to governments. He would have agreed with St. Paul that " the powers that be are ordained of God." He set up another king in her place, and, in place of the idolatry which she had sanctioned, he set up the worship of the true God. We see in the whole narrative *the overruling providence of God.* Athaliah thought she would make her power secure by her holocaust of young princes. But man proposes, and God disposes. We see also *the use of human instrumentality.* God works by means. He used Jehosheba to preserve the young life which in the end was the means, in Jehoiada's hand, of overthrowing the wicked power of Athaliah.—C. H. I.

Vers. 17—21.—*The covenant and its results.* Jehoiada was faithful to God. All that he had hitherto done was but the work of a pioneer, preparing the way for the restoration of God's worship and God's Law in the land. We have here—

I. THE COVENANT MADE. Very early in the history of God's people we find them entering into covenants with him. When Jacob had that comforting vision at Bethel, he entered into a covenant. "If God will be with me, and will keep me in this way that I go, . . . so that I come again to my father's house in peace; then shall the Lord be my God; and this stone, which I have set for a pillar, shall be God's house: and of all that thou shalt give me I will surely give the tenth unto thee." The pillar he set up was the witness of the covenant. When God gave the ten commandments to the children of Israel, they entered into a covenant that they would keep them and do them. That covenant they publicly renewed and ratified many times in their subsequent history. They renewed it shortly before the death of Moses. They renewed it shortly before the death of Joshua, and on that occasion Joshua set up a great stone to be a witness of what they had done. On the occasion before us they renew it under the influence of Jehoiada. "And Jehoiada made a covenant between the Lord and the king and the people, that they should be the Lord's people; between the king also and the people." They renewed it also in the reign of Josiah, and under Ezra and Nehemiah after the return from the Captivity. In all these cases we find three important features, common to them all. In each case the duty of making the covenant was enjoined upon the people by eminent men of God—prophets, priests, and kings. In each case it was a public covenant, entered into by all the people. And in each case, when the covenant was renewed, it was accompanied by moral and spiritual revival and reformation. Have we not in the New Testament the same duty pointed out and practised, though not indeed under the same name? It was a public covenant with the Lord when on the Day of Pentecost the three thousand souls were baptized. When Paul praises the Churches of Macedonia for that "they first gave their own selves to the Lord;" when he calls his readers to present themselves a living sacrifice unto God; to remember that they are not their own, but are bought with a price; to come out from among the godless and be separate;—all these are just different ways of reminding them that as Christians they have entered into a covenant with God. Passing over the dark ages which came upon the Christian Church, we find that when the Bible truths began to shed their light once more in the surrounding darkness, the early Reformers found it necessary to band themselves together in a solemn covenant with God and with one another. By this means they kept before them their great purpose. By this means they stimulated and strengthened and encouraged one another. By this means they lifted up a testimony against surrounding error. Such a covenant was publicly agreed to by the Protestant princes and states of Germany, and also by the Huguenots of France. But the best-known and most memorable covenants are those of Scotland. John Knox laid the foundation of the Reformation in Scotland, but the covenants built it up and strengthened it. The first of these was called the National Covenant, first drawn up in the year 1580. It was signed by the king, nobles, and persons of all ranks—the king being James VI. of Scotland, afterwards James I. of England. By this memorable document the whole people of Scotland pledged themselves to renounce and resist all the errors of popery, and to maintain the truth as it is in Jesus. It was this covenant which was afterwards renewed in the Greyfriar's Churchyard at Edinburgh, when, among the immense multitude who signed it, many opened their veins and wrote their names with their own blood. The other was the Solemn League and Covenant, entered into between the two parliaments of England and Scotland, also for resistance to popery, and the maintenance of pure religion throughout the land. These things suggest to us that, in times of prevailing wickedness or of prevailing error, it is the duty of God's people to make public avowal of their faith in Christ and allegiance to him. It is a duty pointed out both in the Old Testament and in the New, and confirmed by the experience of God's Church both in Scripture times and in more recent days. If ever there was a time when it was the duty of Christ's people publicly and unitedly to confess him, that time is the present. Wickedness abounds. Tho lovo of many waxes cold. Many of Christ's professing people seem utterly indifferent to the claims of their Master and his cause. False doctrines are taught; and under the show of religion there is a growing conformity to the world. A faithful, strong, united testimony for Christ is urgently needed. *How, then, are we to carry out this duty of making a public covenant with God?* There is one way which is available to us all, and that is the Lord's Supper. It is an act of commemoration, communion, and *consecration*. In partaking of the Lord's Supper we enter into a covenant with God. It is a public covenant. The eyes of the world are upon us. They see us make a profession to be Christ's. Do they see that our practice corresponds with our profession? Each communion ought to be a personal covenant with God on the part of each individual believer. It ought to be a public covenant with God on the part of families. It ought to be a public covenant with God on the part of congregations.

II. THE COVENANT KEPT. Jehoiada and the people had entered into a covenant or engagement that they would be the Lord's. And they kept their promise. The first way in which they showed it was by breaking in pieces the idols and their altars, which were so abundant in the land. So, if we take Christ's vows upon us at his table, let us show that we mean what we profess. Let us show that we are on the Lord's side. "Better not to vow, than to vow and not pay." Let us begin with our own hearts. Are there no idols there that need to be thrown down, no besetting sins that need to be put away, no evil passions that need to be crucified? "If ye do return unto the Lord with all your hearts, then put away the strange gods and Ashtaroth from among you, and prepare your hearts unto the Lord, and serve him only" (1 Sam. vii. 3).

III. THE BLESSINGS OF THE COVENANT. "And all the people of the land rejoiced, and the city was in quiet." God kept them in perfect peace, because their minds were stayed on him. They kept their part of the covenant. God kept his. We find in Scripture that God promises special blessings to those who enter into a covenant with him. Before he gave the Law on Mount Sinai, he said to the children of Israel, "Now therefore, if ye will obey my voice indeed, and keep my covenant, then ye shall be a peculiar treasure unto me above all people: for all the earth is mine." Then again God says, "Come ye out from among them, and be ye separate, and touch not the unclean thing; and I will receive you, and will be a Father unto you, and ye shall be my sons and daughters, saith the Lord God Almighty." We also find that more than once these promises were fulfilled. In the days of Asa, when the people of Judah made a covenant with God, we read that "it was a time of great rejoicing, for they had sought the Lord with all their heart, and he was found of them; and the Lord gave them rest round about." So in the days of Josiah, when they made the covenant and put away the strange gods, we read, "Surely there was not holden such a Passover from the days of the judges that judged Israel, nor in all the days of the kings of Israel, nor of the kings of Judah." It was the same in more recent times. The covenanters, whose motto was "For Christ's crown and covenant," and who shed their blood in defence of Christ's authority, were a great means of preserving pure and undefiled religion in Scotland. Let us all, then, faithfully witness for him by our lives. "Come, and let us join ourselves to the Lord in a perpetual covenant that shall not be forgotten" (Jer. l. 5).—C. H. I.

Vers. 1—21.—*The history of Athaliah.* "And when Athaliah the mother of Ahaziah saw that her son was dead," etc. Among the blackest names in the long roll of the world's infamy are those of kings and queens, and amongst them Athaliah is not the least abhorrent and revolting. She was the daughter of Ahab King of Israel, and of Jezebel, his notorious wife. She married Joram (or Jehoram) King of Judah. She was the mother of Ahaziah, and advised him in his wickedness. After Jehu had slain him, she resolved to put an end to all the children of her husband by his former wives, and then mount the throne of Judah herself. But the half-sister of Ahaziah, Jehosheba, secured Joash, one of the children and heir to the throne, and secreted him with his nurse for six long years. In the seventh year the young prince was brought forth and placed on the throne. Crowds of people assembled to witness the ceremony, and Athaliah, hearing the shouts of the crowd, hastened to the temple, utterly unsuspicious even of the existence of the young king. When, however, she caught a sight of the young king and heard the hurrahs of the crowd, she felt that her atrocious plans had been frustrated, and in her savage humiliation rent her clothes and cried, "Treason! Treason!" But her hour was over; she was too late to rally a party in favour of her own interest, and by the command of the priest she was instantly removed and violently destroyed. In this woman's life, as here sketched, we have *hereditary depravity, outwitted wickedness*, and *just retribution*.

I. HEREDITARY DEPRAVITY. We find in this woman, Athaliah, the infernal tendencies of her father and her mother, Ahab and Jezebel. Though they had been swept as monsters from the earth, and were now lying in the grave, their hellish spirit lived and worked in this their daughter. It is, alas! often so. We have an immortality in *others*, as well as in ourselves. The men of long-forgotten generations still live in the present. Even the moral pulse of Adam throbs in all. By this fact we are reminded: 1. *That the moral qualities of parents may become physical tendencies in their children.* The man who voluntarily (and all moral qualities are voluntary productions) contracts habits of falsehood, dishonesty, profanity, incontinence, drunkenness, and general intemperance, transmits these to his children as physical tendencies. This is marvellous, but patent to every observer of society and student of history. Who cannot refer to both men and women who have received an unappeasable craving for strong drinks by the drunken habits contracted by their parents? 2. That the evil moral qualities of parents, reappearing in their children in the form of physical tendencies, is *no complete justification for the children's wickedness.* This is clear: (1) From the fact that God has endowed all with *sufficient force to control* all physical tendencies. Most men have sufficient mental faculties to quench the strongest physical passion. (2) From the *personal consciousness of every sinner.* When the conscience is quickened, the greatest liar, debauchee, drunkard, thief, becomes filled with compunctions for the crimes committed. Every sigh of remorse on account of sin is a testimony to the power of the human mind to control the passions. (3) From the *Divine Word as found in the Scriptures.* "Whatsoever good thing any man doeth, the same shall he receive of the Lord, whether he be bond or free." "He that doeth wrong shall receive for the wrong which he hath done: and there is no respect of persons." 3. *That the way to raise the human race is to improve their moral qualities.* Indoctrinate men's souls with truth, benevolence, piety, chastity, purity, etc., and you help on the race to its millennium. And in no other way. The gospel is the instrument for this.

II. OUTWITTED WICKEDNESS. No doubt this woman, who thought she had destroyed all the "seed royal," considered she had made her way to the throne clear and secure. For six long years she had no conception that one had escaped her bloody purpose. Now it was revealed to her, and her disappointment maddens her with vengeance, and excites the desperate cry, "Treason! Treason!" It is ever so. "He disappointeth the devices of the crafty." History abounds with the examples of the bafflement of wrong. The conduct of Joseph's brethren, Ahithophel, Sanballat, Haman, and the Jewish Sanhedrin in relation to Christ, are instances. Satan, the arch-enemy of the universe, will exemplify this through all the crises of his accursed future. A piece of conduct, wrought by the highest human skill and earnest industry, if not in accord with the immutable principles of right and truth, can no more succeed in its purpose than a house can stand, which is built regardless of the resistless laws of gravitation. The architecture may look well, the materials be most precious, and the production be most costly, yet down it must come, and confound the builder. Craftiness uses lies as concealment and defence, but the eternal law of Providence makes them snares. One lie leads to another, and so on, until they become so numerous that the author involves himself in contradictions, and he falls and flounders like a wild beast in a snare.

III. JUST RETRIBUTION. "Jehoiada the priest commanded the captains of the hundreds, the officers of the host, and said unto them, Have her forth without the ranges: and him that followeth her kill with the sword. . . . And they laid hands on her; and she went by the way by the which the horses came into the king's house: and there was she slain. . . . And all the people of the land rejoiced, and the city was in quiet: and they slew Athaliah with the sword beside the king's house." Thus *Sæpe intereunt aliis meditantes necem.* Those who plot the destruction of others often fall themselves. Here is: 1. A *terrible* retribution. 2. A *prompt* retribution. It came on her here before she passed into the other world. Retribution is going on now and here.   3. A retribution *administered by human hands.*   Truly "the triumphing of the wicked is short, and the joy of the hypocrite but for a moment.   Though his excellency mount up to the heavens, and his head reach unto the clouds; yet he shall perish for ever. . . . Yea, he shall be chased away as a vision of the night."   An Oriental poet thus vividly describes the retribution that must follow wickedness—

> " All vice to which man yields in greed to do it,
>   Or soon or late, be sure, he'll sorely rue it;
>   Experience deep, howe'er false seeming blind him,
>   Surcharged with retribution, out will find him.
>   It locks upon his soul a fatal fetter,
>   Explodes throughout his face in horrid tetter,
>   Over his shameless eyeballs brings a blurring,
>   Keeps in his heart a deadly fear-load stirring;
>   At all pure joys with fiendish talon snatches,
>   The noblest traits from out his being catches;
>   Each beam and hope and vision darkens,
>   His conscience stuns whene'er towards heaven he hearkens;
>   On goading thorns his sleepless longing tosses,
>   With soul remorse-foam pleasure's waves embosses.
>   Sometimes from phantom-fears impels him flying,
>   Sometimes in frantic horrors shrouds his dying;
>   Now turns his dearest friends to cease to love him,
>   Now spreads avenging Siva's form above him;
>   Makes this world black with prison walls and gibbets,
>   And in the next escape from hell prohibits.
>   The whole creation's strange and endless dealing,
>   In spite of shields and veils and arts concealing,
>   Proclaims that whosoe'er is long a sinner
>   Can only be by it of woe a winner."

                                                                    D. T.

Vers. 1—3.—*Athaliah's usurpation.*   Athaliah was the evil genius of Judah, as Jezebel was of Israel.   The mother was slain, but, unwarned by her fall, the daughter snatched at the reins of power, and held the throne for six years.   The track of both was marked by violence, bloodshed, and political convulsion.

I. THE WICKEDNESS OF ATHALIAH.   Ahaziah's death gave Athaliah her opportunity. Nothing could more clearly reveal the wicked disposition of the woman than the means by which she raised herself to the throne.   When she "saw that her son was dead, she arose and destroyed all the seed royal."   1. She was a *woman*, yet, to pave her way to power, she did not hesitate to crush every feminine instinct in her breast, and to imbrue her hands in innocent blood.   2. She was a *mother*, yet she remorselessly put to death her own grandchildren.   The youngest was a babe, but her savage temper made no distinctions.   Her son's offspring were only rivals, to be got out of the way by murder. In this tigress-like nature of the queen-mother all womanhood is effaced.   Truly " the tender mercies of the wicked are cruel" (Prov. xii. 10).

II. THE PRESERVATION OF JOASH.   After all, Athaliah's end was not gained. Unknown to this savage woman, one of Ahaziah's sons, the youngest, was saved from the general massacre by his aunt Jehosheba, and, after a temporary concealment in the store-chamber of the palace, was conveyed to the temple, and there secretly brought up.   We have in this deliverance of the young Joash: 1. *An example of faith and courage.*   It was "by faith" that the pious Jehosheba did this daring act, even as it was by faith that the parents of Moses hid their goodly child (Heb. xi. 23).   And faith, in this instance as in the other, had its reward.   2. *A proof of God's faithfulness to his promise.*   It had been promised to David that he should never want a man to sit on his throne (1 Kings viii. 25).   That promise seemed now frustrated, when to outward appearance every descendant of David was destroyed.   But "the counsel of the Lord standeth for ever" (Ps. xxxiii. 11).   No device of man can prevail against that.   3. *An illustration of how God can defeat the designs of the wicked.*   Skilfully as the wicked lay their plots, there is generally something overlooked, forgotten, which brings them to nought.   Some witness of their crimes is left undetected.   They seem to have closed up every chink and cranny through which defeat could enter, yet it is found that some loophole has been left. A good and true cause may be safely left in the hands of God. He will not suffer it to fall.—J. O.

Vers. 4—21.—*The coronation of Joash.* For six years Athaliah was dominant in Israel. Jehoiada meanwhile kept his secret well. Least of all did the usurping queen suspect that a legitimate heir to the throne was in hiding in the temple almost at her own palace door. Her reign must have grown well-nigh unendurable to the people, when they were so willing as the event proved to throw it off. At the six years' end Jehoiada prepared for his *coup d'état*.

I. JEHOIADA'S PREPARATIONS. 1. *Joash produced.* The good priest found it necessary to proceed with caution. His measures were taken with skill and secrecy. He first took into his confidence the five centurions of the life-guards, made them swear an oath of fidelity, then produced the king, and showed him to them. The soldiers entered into his plan at once. The risks were enormous, but God's shield was around this one remaining "lamp" of David's house, and did not allow its tremulous light to be extinguished. The boy-king was the feeble ark that bore the fortunes of David's house and of Messianic promise. Had he perished, God's Word would have fallen to the ground. The Chronicler tells how the captains of hundreds went forth and secretly spread among the Levites and chief of the fathers of Israel the tidings that there was still a living heir of David's line, and how these came to Jerusalem, and saw the young king too (2 Chron. xxiii. 2, 3). It is remarkable that a fact known to so many persons did not in some way leak out. But the people were of one heart and one soul, and Athaliah was left in her false security without a single friend to warn her of her danger. 2. *The eventful sabbath.* The day chosen for the public production of the king was probably a feast-day. Otherwise the large concourse of people from all parts of the land could hardly have failed to attract attention. It was a sabbath and an high day—"the better the day, the better the deed." What was contemplated was indeed a revolution, and might involve bloodshed; but it was also a reviving of the fallen theocracy, a replanting of the rod of Jesse, and therefore fit work for the sabbath. Nothing that favourably affects the fortunes of the kingdom of God is out of place on the sabbath day. Jehoiada made careful strategic preparations, combining apparently the Levites who went on and off duty in the temple with the life-guards under the captains, and assigning to different companies their respective posts. 3. *The palace and temple guarded.* Guards were told off both for the "king's house" and for the temple. (1) Those who entered on duty on the sabbath were divided into three parts, and posted round the palace. One third was posted at the principal entrance; a second third at "the gate Sur"—perhaps a side gate—and the remaining third was placed at a gate which communicated with the temple (ver. 19), where the guards or "runners" were usually stationed. (2) Those, again, who went off duty on the sabbath were placed within the court of the temple, stretching across from side to side, to guard the person of the king. To these weapons were given from David's spears and shields, which were in the temple of the Lord. While trusting in God, Jehoiada thus took every human precaution. Faith and works co-operate in God's service. Our dependence should be as entirely in God as if human means were unavailing, yet our use of means should be as diligent as if everything depended on their employment.

II. THE KING CROWNED. 1. *The safety of the king's person.* When the young king Joash was brought forth, and placed on a raised stand in the temple court, his guard stood firmly around him, each man clutching his weapon. The instructions were that any person attempting to break through the ranks should at once be slain. The person of David's son was too precious to be left without an effectual guard. Yet more effectual is the guard which God places round *his* sons (Ps. xxxiv. 6, 7). 2. *The ceremony of coronation.* The act of coronation of the child-king was then proceeded with. Jehoiada presided at the ceremony. (1) The crown—visible symbol of royal office—was placed upon his head. God's priest could well preside at the coronation of God's king. As son of David, Joash was the legitimate heir of the throne. Royal authority is from God, and investiture at the hands of God's ministers is our acknowledgment of this. Only those who rule by Divine favour can look for a blessing on their crown. (2) He had put upon his head "the testimony," *i.e.* the Law of Moses, by which kings of

Judah and Israel were to be guided (Deut. xvii. 18—20). "Finely are both the crown and the book presented to the king, that he might be not only mighty, but also wise, or, as we may say, know God's Word and right. Thus, even now, we make kings with a sword and book" (Luther). The highest in the land are not above the authority of God's Word. He by whom "kings reign" is mightier than the mightiest, and requires from the monarch the same allegiance as from the humblest of his subjects. A nation is happy, prosperous, and blessed only when God's Law is made the rule of its policy and the foundation of its government (Deut. iv. 6—8). (3) He was anointed with oil. For where God gives office he gives also qualification for that office. Oil is the symbol of the Holy Spirit. The Word without the Spirit to interpret it, and to give strength for obedience to it, is useless. Kings need the grace of God for the discharge of their duties as much as, even more than, ordinary people. Jesus is God's King, "anointed with the oil of gladness above his fellows" (Heb. i. 9). (4) He was acknowledged as king by popular acclamation. "They clapped their hands and said, God save the king!" The Divine choice was ratified by the free election of the people. While kingly, like all other authority, is derived from God, a throne is only strong when it rests on the loyal affection of the body of the people.

III. The death of Athaliah. 1. *The shout of a king.* Athaliah, though queen of Judah, was not a worshipper of the God of Judah. While the scenes above described were being transacted, she was either in her own "house of Baal," or in the palace. But now the ringing shouts of the people apprised her that something was wrong. The sight of the guards posted round her palace would add to her alarms. She hastened to the temple, and there beheld a spectacle which told her that her hour was come. The young Joash was standing on his platform, the crown on his head, the captains and trumpeters around him, while the air rang with the joyful huzzas of the people, with the notes of the silver trumpets, and with cries of "Let the king live!" Only in part could Athaliah read the meaning of the scene, for she did not know who this crowned boy was. But she saw enough to tell her that the loyalty of the people had found a new centre, and that her power was gone. The rejoicings of the people would be gall and wormwood to her heart, for they told her, not only that it was all over with her authority, but that the people were glad it was so. How swiftly, as by a bolt from a clear sky, does retribution often fall upon the wicked! An hour before Athaliah had no suspicion of any calamity. She had but to speak, and guards and servants were ready to yield her all obedience; now her authority has departed like a pricked bubble, and she stands helpless among a multitude—none so poor as to do her reverence. The passage is an illustration of the proverb, "When the righteous are in authority, the people rejoice; but when the wicked beareth rule, the people mourn" (Prov. xxix. 2). 2. *Treason to a traitress.* When Athaliah saw what was being done, heard the shouts, and witnessed the rejoicings, she rent her garments, and cried, "Treason! treason!" Treason is an act or series of acts designed to compass the overthrow of a constituted government, and is generally held to be punishable by death. It is wicked and illegitimate governments which make most of the crime of treason, and most severely enforce the penalties against it. Yet it is plain that these penalties are justified only on the supposition that the government against which the treason is directed is a legitimate one. A government which is itself born and bred of treason has no moral justification for punishing treason in others. Athaliah was queen, not by God's will, but in defiance of all right and morality. She had usurped the throne, and killed (or thought she had killed) the rightful heirs to it. Treason against such a government, itself the offspring of the blackest treachery, was not a crime, but might be the highest duty. Still, as if some horrid iniquity was being practised, the traitress rends her clothes, and cries, "Treason!" Her own treason is unthought of; she sees only the treason of her enemies. Is not this state of mind too common? Men are loud in denouncing transgressions which they themselves are flagrantly guilty of. They point to the mote in another's eye, without reflecting on the beam in their own. Callous as to their own falsehood, selfishness, and dishonesty, they detect in an instant, and loudly denounce, the same vices in their neighbours, especially when practised towards themselves. It is this which renders them inexcusable. For the power to detect sin in others implies a knowledge of the law which condemns the person judging if he does the same things (Rom. ii. 1). 3. *Just retribution.* The order of Jehoiada was that if any one ventured to follow Athaliah, he was to be killed with the sword. But no one seems to have shown any pity for the fallen queen. The downfall of her power was thus complete. A new government having been constituted, her own attempt to excite rebellion now fell under the category of treason, and was punishable. Jehoiada gives orders for her being taken beyond the temple bounds, and there slain. We see hands laid upon her, and she is led away, or goes, " by the way by the which the horses come into the king's house," and in that place of stables meets her death. An inglorious end! But what glory can we look for to crown a career of sin? In Athaliah, the last member of Ahab's cursed house met a deserved doom. Judgment against the sinner may not always be executed speedily, but the stroke will surely fall at last (Eccles. viii. 11).

IV. A COVENANT WITH JEHOVAH. 1. *The covenant with God renewed.* The people had received, as if from heaven, a new king of the line of David, and the moment was auspicious for a new covenant being entered into, and formally ratified, with God. It is good when special mercies are made an occasion of renewal of vows. The covenant promoted by Jehoiada was twofold. (1) It was a covenant between the king and people and Jehovah. In this transaction they solemnly pledged themselves to be the Lord's people. National covenanting is only appropriate when it springs from the spontaneous impulse of the masses of the people. Among the Hebrews, who, by the very form of their national existence, were a people in covenant with Jehovah, such renewal of religious vows was specially suitable. The idea of a " people of the Lord " is now embodied, not in a national form, but in the Church of Christ. Great is the honour of forming part of this "chosen generation," this "royal priesthood," this "holy nation," this "peculiar people" (1 Pet. ii. 9), and we should often recall the fact to ourselves, and make it the basis of new consecration. (2) It was a covenant between the king and the people. He, on his part, would pledge himself to maintain the government according to the Law of God; and they, on theirs, would promise him loyalty and obedience. Happy is it, when rulers and people stand in this bond of mutual confidence! 2. *Zeal in religious reform.* The earnest spirit awakened by this solemn act of covenant immediately showed itself in zealous efforts for the removal of abuses. We read that, not one or two, but "all the people of the land," set themselves to reforming work. (1) They went into the house of Baal, and brake it down. A house of Baal in Jerusalem, and possibly on the temple hill, was a deliberate insult to Jehovah. No respect for the beauty or costliness of the building was allowed to save it from destruction. When higher interests are involved, artistic and sentimental considerations must go to the wall. (2) They brake in pieces " thoroughly " Baal's altars and images. Idolatry was to be thoroughly rooted out in accordance with the word of the testimony (Deut. xii. 1—3). (3) They slew Mattan, the high priest of Baal. By the Law of Israel his life was forfeited through the practice of idolatry. (4) They restored the worship of the temple. This is implied in the statement, " The priest appointed officers over the house of the Lord." It is evident from the next chapter that the temple service had been allowed to become greatly disorganized. The zeal of these reformers had, therefore, its positive side. They sought to build up as well as cast down. The false worship of God was replaced by the true. Court fashion goes a long way in determining preferences in religion. When Athaliah worshipped Baal, it was fashionable to neglect Jehovah; now that Joash restored the worship of Jehovah, people flocked back to the temple. Those in high stations have great responsibilities, and not least for the examples they set in religion. 3. *The joy of the people.* Joash was now escorted in grand procession to the palace of his fathers. Athaliah was dead, and he sat on the throne of the kings. Joy filled the people's hearts, and quiet reigned in the city. When godliness is victorious, it diffuses peace and gladness through all minds.—J. O.

EXPOSITION.

CHAPTER XII.

Vers. 1—21.—THE REIGN OF JOASH. THE REPAIR OF THE TEMPLE. WAR OF JOASH WITH HAZAEL, AND HIS DEATH BY A CONSPIRACY.

Vers. 1—3.—The writer of Kings is extremely brief and incomplete in his account of the reign of Joash. He seems to have had a great tenderness for him, and to have determined that he would put on record nothing to his discredit. We have to go to Chronicles (2 Chron. xxiv.) for a complete account, and for an estimate of the real character of the king and of his reign. Both writers appear to have drawn from the same original document, but the writer of Kings made large omissions from it. In a few points only is his narrative fuller than Chronicles.

Ver. 1.—**In the seventh year of Jehu.** Athaliah began to reign very soon after the accession of Jehu (ch. xi. 1), and reigned six full years (ver. 3). The first year of Joash was thus parallel with Jehu's seventh. Jehoash—or *Joash,* as he is called sometimes in Kings (ch. xi. 2; xiii. 1, 10), and always in Chronicles—**began to reign; and forty years reigned he in Jerusalem**—the writer of Chronicles (2 Chron. xxiv. 1) and Josephus ('Ant. Jud.,' ix. 8. § 4) agree—and his mother's name was **Zibiah of Beersheba.** Josephus calls her " Sabia."

Ver. 2.—**And Jehoash did** that which was **right in the sight of the Lord all his days wherein Jehoiada the priest instructed him.** So the Septuagint, the Vulgate, Luther, De Wette, Keil, Bähr, and our Revisers. Only Ewald and Thenius attempt to make the passage contradict Chronicles by translating, " Jehoash did that which was right in the sight of the Lord all his days, because Jehoiada the priest had instructed him." But this translation is very forced and unnatural. The writer evidently intended to add a qualifying clause to his statement that Joash reigned well " all his days," but did not wish to draw too much attention to it.

Ver. 3.—**But the high places were not taken away.** So it had been with the best of the previous kings of Judah, as Asa (1 Kings xv. 14) and Jehoshaphat (1 Kings xxii. 43); and so it was with the other " good " kings (ch. xiv. 4; xv. 4, 35) until the reign of Hezekiah, by whom the high places were removed (see below, ch. xviii. 4). We must remember that it was Jehovah who was worshipped in the " high places," not Baal, or Moloch, or Ashtoreth (see the comment on 1 Kings xv. 14). **The people still sacrificed and burnt incense in the high places.** The *people,* not the king, in the earlier portion of his reign; but in the later portion, probably the king also (see 2 Chron. xxiv. 17, 18).

Vers. 4—16.—*The repair of the temple.* It is rather surprising that the temple had not been thoroughly repaired by Jehoiada during the long minority of Joash, when he must practically have had the sole management of affairs. Probably he did repair the worst of the damage done by Athaliah's orders (2 Chron. xxiv. 7), which may have been very considerable, but neglected the restoration of such portions of the edifice as appeared to him of secondary importance, as the walls of the courts and the outbuildings. Joash, however, when his minority came to an end, and he succeeded to the administration of the state, took a different view. To him the completion of the repairs seemed a pressing business. Probably he thought the honour of God required the entire obliteration of Athaliah's wicked proceedings, and the renewal of the temple's old glories. His six years' residence within the temple precincts may have also inspired him with a love of the building as a building.

Ver. 4.—**And Jehoash said to the priests.** The initiative of Joash is strongly marked, alike in Kings and Chronicles (2 Chron. xxiv. 4). The general weakness of his character, and want of vigour and decision, make it the more surprising that he should in this particular matter have shown himself capable of taking his own line and adhering to it (ver. 7). He has scarcely received from historians the credit that is due to him for his persistent and successful efforts to accomplish an object which was for the honour of religion, and which was yet not pressed forward by the priesthood. Certainly he was no mere puppet of the priestly order. **All the money of the dedicated things that is brought into the house of the Lord;** rather, *all the money of the holy gifts that is brought into the house of the Lord;* i.e. all that ye receive from the people in the way of money. This money accrued from three sources, which the king proceeded to enumerate. First, even **the money of every one that passeth** the account; *i.e.* the census money—the aggregate of the half-shekels received from the males of above twenty years old, whenever a census was taken (Exod. xxx. 12—16). The rendering, " current money," preferred by Thenius, Bähr, and our Revisers, is shown by Keil to be untenable. Secondly, **the money that every man is set at;** *i.e.* the redemption money, derived in part from the payments made for redeeming the firstborn (Numb. xviii. 15, 16); in part from the sums which the priests exacted from such as had vowed themselves (Lev. xxvii. 2—8), or those belonging to them, to God.

And [thirdly] **all the money that cometh into any man's heart to bring into the house of the Lord**; *i.e.* all the free-will offerings that should be made in money by any of the Israelites.

Ver. 5.—**Let the priests take it to them, every man of his acquaintance.** The money was to be gathered of " all Israel," out of all " the cities of Judah" (2 Chron. xxiv. 5). The priests of each locality were to be the collectors, and would therefore gather " of their acquaintance." As we cannot suppose that very much would accrue from either the first or second source, since a census was rarely taken, and personal vows were not very common, we must regard the command of Joash as, in the main, the authorization of a general collection throughout the kingdom of voluntary contributions towards the temple repairs, and so as analogous to the " letters " which our own sovereigns, or archbishops, issue from time to time for collections in churches for special objects. **And let them repair the breaches of the house, wheresoever any breach shall be found.** The " breaches," or dilapidations, may have been caused, partly by the neglect of necessary repairs during the reigns of Jehoram, Ahaziah, and Athaliah; but they were mainly the result of the wilful violence of Athaliah (2 Chron. xxiv. 7). Apparently, the damage done must have been very great.

Ver. 6.—**But it was so, that in the three and twentieth year of King Jehoash the priests had not repaired the breaches of the house.** No charge is made against the priests of malversation or embezzlement. They had simply been negligent. Probably very little money had come in; and they had not been very active in their endeavours to obtain larger contributions. It must be remembered that what went to the fabric fund would, for the most part, be a deduction from the ordinary revenue of the temple, which was not, perhaps, much in excess of the ordinary demands upon it. We can, therefore, quite understand that the king's policy would not be popular with the priests (see 2 Chron. xxiv. 5). Still, it is to be observed that they are not said to have executed no repairs, but only not to have " made haste" and completed their task by the time that the king looked for its completion.

Ver. 7.—**Then King Jehoash called for Jehoiada the priest.** So, too, the writer of Chronicles (2 Chron. xxiv. 6). The king did not take the matter into his own hands, but consulted with the head of the priestly order on the best steps to take in order to expedite the repairs. He made no " charge," delivered no " rebuke." He did not " remove the administration of the funds from the hands of the delinquent order " (Stanley). On the contrary, he left it in their hands (vers. 9—11). Two changes only were made: 1. A public chest was set up conspicuously in the temple court, near the great altar, and the people were invited to bring their contributions to the temple, and hand them to the priests,who should straightway deposit them in the chest in the sight of the congregation. 2. The chest was opened from time to time, and the money counted, in the presence of the high priest *and of a royal secretary*. It was then delivered over to " the overseers of the house "—persons, probably, of the priestly order—appointed by Jehoiada (ch. xi. 18), who disbursed it to the carpenters and masons (ch. xii. 11, 12). The chest was a sort of tangible evidence to the people of the purpose to which their contributions would be applied, and naturally stimulated their giving. The presence of the king's officer at the counting of the money, was equivalent, not really to an " audit " (Stanley), but to a publication of the accounts, and would prevent any suspension of the work, so long as it was clear that the money found in the chest had not been expended. Thus a new impetus was given to the movement. The measures taken completely answered. Contributions flowed in rapidly, and in a few years the whole work was accomplished (see 2 Chron. xxiv. 13, 14). **And the** other **priests, and said unto them, Why repair ye not the breaches of the house?** This shows that no repairs were going on in the twenty-third year of Joash, but not that none had been done previously. **Now therefore receive no** more **money of your acquaintance.** This was a revocation of the order given in ver. 5, and necessarily put an end to the local collections, which that order required. **But deliver it for the breaches of the house.** If the priests were not to " receive " the money, they could not " deliver " it. Obscurity is introduced by the desire for extreme brevity. In point of fact, they were to " receive " (ver. 9), but in a new way.

Ver. 8.—**And the priests consented to receive no** more **money of the people**—*i.e.* to put an end to the local collections ordered in ver. 5—**neither to repair the breaches of the house;** *i.e.* neither to be responsible severally for laying out the money which they collected in repairs.

Ver. 9.—**But Jehoiada the priest took a chest.** The writer of Chronicles says, " At the king's commandment, they made a chest " (2 Chron. xxiv. 8). The suggestion was probably the king's, but the ecclesiastical and civil authorities worked harmoniously in the business. **And bored a hole in the lid of it**—as hundreds of thousands have done since his time—**and set it beside** the altar, on the right side as one cometh into the house of the Lord. The altar intended is, of course, the altar of burnt offering, which was in the court of the temple, directly opposite the porch. The chest was placed outside the sanctuary (2 Chron. xxiv. 8), and, indeed, outside the porch, on the right hand as one entered into the court by the north door. It was thus very conspicuous. And the priests that kept the door— *i.e.* the door of the court—put therein all the money that was brought into the house of the Lord. The priests received the money from those who offered, at the gate of the court, and, proceeding to the chest, dropped it in through the aperture. A man could not see that all which he had given was put in, but he reckoned on the good faith of the priest, and was satisfied.

Ver. 10.—**And it was so, when they saw that there was much money in the chest.** "When they saw" means "when they perceived." They would not *see* that the chest was becoming full, but would know by the weight, and perhaps by the sound which the money made when it was dropped in. **That the king's scribe.** "Royal secretaries" were common in ancient Persia, and often acted as the king's commissioners (Herod., iii. 128; Xen., 'Cyrop.,' viii. 6. § 16; 'Œconom.,' iv. 8). Such persons are seen on the Assyrian sculptured slabs, with a roll of paper or parchment in one hand, and a pen in the other, taking account for the king of the spoil brought in from foreign countries (see 'Ancient Monarchies,' vol. ii. p. 86). **And the high priest.** Since the time of Joshua, the high priest had been called simply "the priest." The restoration of the full title (*hac-cohen hag-gâdol*) marks the increasing power of the priests and the diminishing power of the kings under the later monarchy. **Came up, and they put up in bags, and told, the money that was found in the house of the Lord.** Money was ordinarily put up in bags, containing a certain definite amount, the mouth of the bag being then tied round with a string (see ch. v. 23; and comp. Prov. vii. 20; Isa. xlvi. 6; Hag. i. 6). Hence putting money up in bags was sometimes called, as in this place, "binding it." No doubt they "told," or counted, the money first, and put it in the bags afterwards; but ὕστερον πρότερον is a very common figure of speech.

Ver. 11.—**And they gave the money, being told**—rather, *after weighing it* into the hands of them that did the work, that had the oversight of the house of the Lord. It must be remembered that no coins existed as yet; and the lumps of silver which passed as shekels and half-shekels, were of very uncertain weight. To know the value of the money in each bag, it was necessary, not only to count the pieces, but to weigh each bag separately. The bags, when weighed, were handed over by the high priest and the royal secretary to the officers whom Jehoiada had appointed (ch. xi. 18) to have the general superintendence of the "house." **And they laid it out to the carpenters and builders, that wrought upon the house of the Lord.** The "*paid* it out" of our Revisers is better than "laid it out." The overseers of the temple paid over to the carpenters and the builders, from time to time, such money as was needed for the work done or doing.

Ver. 12.—**And to masons;** rather, *to the masons.* The "masons" (*goderim*) are the actual artisans who worked under instructions from the "builders." **And hewers of stone**—or, *stone-cutters*—rather, those who sawed up the stones on the spot, than those who hewed them in the quarries—and to **buy timber and hewed stone to repair the breaches of the house of the Lord.** The writer of Chronicles mentions "workers in iron and brass" (bronze) also (2 Chron. xxiv. 12). Probably, when once the work was taken thoroughly in hand, it was found that repairs of all sorts and kinds were needed. The temple had stood for a hundred and thirty-six years, and up to this time it had, so far as we know, undergone no repairs at all. Certainly none are mentioned. **And for all that was laid out for the house to repair it.** This general clause shows how wide were the powers of the overseers. The suspicions and jealousies which modern writers have imagined contrast remarkably with the general confidence and trust which seem to have prevailed among all those concerned in the repairs.

Ver. 13.—**Howbeit there was not made for the house of the Lord bowls of silver, snuffers, basins, trumpets, any vessels of gold, or vessels of silver, of the money that was brought into the house of the Lord;** *i.e.* while the repairs were incomplete, while the work was still going on, no portion of the money taken from the chest was expended in the purchase of new sacred vessels, whether of gold or silver, whether bowls, or snuffers, or basins, or trumpets—the whole was rigidly applied to the renovation of the temple building. There is no contradiction between this statement and that of the writer of Chronicles (2 Chron. xxiv. 14), who tells us that, *after the entire repairs were completed,* the surplus money was expended in this way, on the purchase of "vessels to minister and to offer, spoons, and vessels of gold and silver." We can well understand that, after the spoiling of the temple by successive kings to buy off enemies—by Rehoboam to content Shishak (1 Kings xiv. 26), by Asa to gratify Benhadad (1 Kings xv. 18), and by Joash himself (ver. 18) to procure the retreat of Hazael from the siege of Jerusalem, the vessels of the temple must have required renovating almost as much as the fabric itself; and when it was found that there remained a surplus over and above all that was needed for building purposes, we cannot wonder that it was applied to the renewal of the vessels, absolutely essential as they were for the service of the sanctuary.

Ver. 14.—**But they gave that**—*i.e.* the whole money contributed—**to the workmen** —equivalent to "the carpenters, builders, masons, hewers of stone, etc., mentioned in vers. 11, 12—**and repaired therewith the house of the Lord;** *i.e.* expended the money on the repairs.

Ver. 15.—**Moreover they reckoned not with the men, into whose hand they delivered the money to be bestowed on workmen.** Society rests upon faith and trust. In all business transactions confidence must be reposed in some one, whose character is the guarantee of his honesty. In the case before us, the overseers of the temple were the persons trusted to expend the money aright (see ver. 11). The overseers (ch. xi. 18) had been appointed by the high priest. **For they dealt faithfully;** *i.e.* honestly.

Ver. 16.—**The trespass money.** When a man had injured another, he was bound by the Law to make compensation to the injured party at the valuation of the priest, with the addition of one-fifth more than the value (Lev. vi. 2—6; Numb. v. 6—8). The compensation was, primarily, to be made to the man himself; secondarily, if he were dead, to his nearest kinsman; finally, if he had left no kinsman, to the priest. **And sin money.** According to the Law, the priest was entitled to no money with a sin offering; but it seems to have become customary to make the priest who offered it a voluntary gift, to compensate him for his trouble. Such free gifts the priest was by the Law (Numb. v. 10) entitled to receive. **Was not brought into the house of the Lord**—*i.e.* it was not deposited in the chest, or applied to the repairs, but—**it was the priests'.**

Vers. 17, 18.—*The war of Joash with Hazael.* A considerable gap occurs between vers. 16 and 17. We learn from Chronicles some particulars of the interval. Not long after the completion of the repairs, Jehoiada, who had lived to a good old age in complete harmony with the monarch, expired. His piety, and his good services, as preserver of the house of David, as restorer of the temple-worship, and joint-repairer with Joash of the temple itself, were regarded as entitling him to extraordinary funeral honours; and by general consent he was interred within the city of Jerusalem, in the sepulchres of the kings (2 Chron. xxiv. 16). His removal led to a fresh religious revolution. "The Jewish aristocracy, who perhaps had never been free from the licentious and idolatrous taint introduced by Rehoboam and confirmed by Athaliah, and who may well have been galled by the new rise of the priestly order, presented themselves before Joash, and offered him the same obsequious homage that had been paid by the young nobles to Rehoboam. He, ... feeling himself released from personal obligations by the death of his adopted father, threw himself into their hands. Athaliah was avenged almost upon the spot where she had been first seized by her enemies" (Stanley, 'Jewish Church,' vol. ii. p. 345). Joash began by allowing the reintroduction of idolatry and grove-worship (2 Chron. xxiv. 18), and then, when remonstrated with by Zechariah, the son of Jehoiada, who had succeeded his father in the office of high priest, had the remonstrant set upon by the people and slain. The writer of Chronicles closely connects this murderous deed with the Syrian war, which followed it within a year (2 Chron. xxiv. 23), and was generally regarded as a Divine judgment.

Ver. 17.—**Then Hazael King of Syria went up, and fought against Gath.** Hitherto Judah had been safe from any attack on the part of Syria, since Israel had been interposed between the two powers. Now, however, that Hazael had conquered from Jehu the entire trans-Jordanic territory (ch. x. 33), the case was wholly altered—Judah and Syria had become conterminous along the line of the lower Jordan, and Syria could invade Judæa at any moment. It is surprising that Gath should have been the special object of attack, since Gath (*Abu-Gheith*) lay remote from the Syrian frontier, in the south-western part of Judæa, and could only be reached from Syria by an enemy who was not afraid of leaving Jerusalem behind him. Gath, when last mentioned, was a Judæan city, and was fortified by Rehoboam (2 Chron. xi. 8); but it was originally Philistine (1 Sam. v. 17), and the Philistines had recovered it before the time of Uzziah (2 Chron. xxvi. 6). To which power it belonged when Hazael made war upon it is uncertain. **And took it**—probably took it by storm, and plundered it, but did not attempt an occupation—and Hazael set his face to go up to Jerusalem. If Gath be *Abu-Gheith*, as appears probable, it would be distant from Jerusalem not less than forty miles in a direct line. If Hazael, however, was returning to the trans-Jordanic country taken from Israel, it would lie in his way, and might naturally tempt him to make a dash at it, more especially as he was flushed with victory.

Ver. 18.—**And Jehoash King of Judah took all the hallowed things.** The writer of Chronicles tells us that, first of all, there was a battle. "The army of the Syrians came with a small company of men, and the Lord delivered a very great host into their hand" (2 Chron. xxiv. 24). The loss was especially heavy among the nobles, who officered the Jewish army. Much plunder was taken by the visitors (2 Chron. xxiv. 23). Then, probably, the siege of the city was commenced, and Joash, like Rehoboam and Asa before him (1 Kings xiv. 26; xv. 18), and Hezekiah subsequently (ch. xviii. 15, 16), had recourse to the temple treasures, and with them bought off the invader. It is noticeable that Athaliah had not deprived the temple of them previously. **That Jehoshaphat, and Jehoram, and Ahaziah, his fathers, kings of Judah, had dedicated.** Though Jehoram and Ahaziah apostatized so far as to maintain the Baal-worship in Jerusalem, and even to force attendance on it (2 Chron. xxi. 11), yet they did not relinquish altogether the worship of Jehovah. That Jehoram called his son, Ahaziah, "possession of Jehovah," and Ahaziah one of his sons, Joash, "whom Jehovah supports," is indicative of this syncretism, which was common in ancient times, but against which pure Judaism made the strongest possible protest. **And his own hallowed things**—*i.e.* the gifts which he had himself made to the temple—**and all the gold that was found in the treasures of the house of the Lord.** This was probably not much; but some "vessels of gold" had been made (2 Chron. xxiv. 14) out of the residue of the money subscribed for the repairs. **And in the king's house.** The royal palace had been plundered by the Arabs and Philistines combined in the reign of Jehoram (2 Chron. xxi. 16, 17); but in the thirty years that had since elapsed there had been time for fresh accumulations. **And sent it to Hazael King of Syria: and he went away from Jerusalem.** The personal presence of Hazael at the siege seems to be here implied, while 2 Chron. xxiv. 23 rather implies his absence. Perhaps he was absent at first, but joined the besiegers after a while.

Vers. 19—21.—*The close of the reign of Joash—his murder by his servants.* Again

the narrative of Kings is to be supplemented by that of Chronicles. From Chronicles we learn that, before the withdrawal of the Syrians, Joash had fallen into a severe illness, which confined him to his apartment (2 Chron. xxiv. 25). This gave opportunity for conspiracy. Among the courtiers were two, perhaps more, whom the fate of Zechariah had grieved, and who were probably opposed to the entire series of later changes in religion which had been sanctioned by Joash (2 Chron. xxiv. 17, 18). These persons "made a conspiracy," which was successful, and "slew Joash on his bed" (2 Chron. xxiv. 25). They then buried him in Jerusalem, but "not in the sepulchres of the kings."

Ver. 19.—**And the rest of the acts of Joash, and all that he did, are they not written in the chronicles of the kings of Judah?** This formal phrase, with which he concludes his account of almost every Jewish king (1 Kings xiv. 29; xv. 7, 23; xxii. 45; ch. viii. 23; xiv. 18; xv. 6, etc.), cannot be regarded as an acknowledgment by the author of any special or designed reticence with respect to the reign of Joash. We must suppose him unconscious of any such design. He had to omit much in every case; in the present he happened to omit all the darker shades; and the result was an over-favourable portraiture of the monarch. But, in the providence of God, complete historical justice was secured by the labours and researches of a second inspired writer.

Ver. 20.—**And his servants arose, and made a conspiracy.** By "his servants" officers of his household are probably intended, attendants whose position would give them ready access to his person. **And slew Joash in the house of Millo.** Joash had probably transferred his residence to "the house of Millo," —the great fortress built by David (2 Sam. v. 9) and Solomon (1 Kings ix. 15, 24) in Jerusalem—for greater security during the siege; and, being there prostrated by sickness, could not remove from it when the siege was over. **Which goeth down to Silla.** No commentator has succeeded in explaining this passage. There is no other mention of Silla; and it is difficult to understand how a fortress could be said to "go down" to any place. Our Revisers' conjecture—"*on the way that goeth down* to Silla"—may be accepted as a possible explanation; but it implies that a word (בְּדֶרֶךְ) has dropped out of the text.

Ver. 21.—**For Jozachar the son of Shimeath;** called in Chronicles "Zabad," probably through a corruption of the text. His mother, Shimeath, was, according to Chronicles (2 Chron. xxiv. 26), an Ammonitess. **And Jehozabad the son of Shomer.** For "Shomer" we have in Chronicles "Shimrith," which is the feminine form of "Shomer," and we are told that she was a Moabitess. The Jews were at all times fond of taking wives from Moab and Ammon (Ruth i. 4; 1 Kings xi. 1; Ezra ix. 1, 2; Neh. xiii. 23), despite the prohibition of mixed marriages in the Law (see Deut. vii. 3). **His servants, smote him, and he died** (for their motives, see the introductory paragraph), **and they buried him with his fathers in the**

city of David. Some critics (as Thenius and Dean Stanley) see a contradiction between this statement and that of 2 Chron. xxiv. 25, that he was "not buried in the sepulchres of the kings;" but, as Bertheau, Keil, and Bähr observe, "the two statements are not irreconcilable," since he may have been regarded as "buried with his fathers," if his grave was anywhere in Jerusalem, even though he was excluded from the royal burying-place. **And Amaziah his son reigned in his stead.** (For the reign of Amaziah, see ch. xiv. 1—20.)

HOMILETICS.

Ver. 2.—*Weakness in a monarch almost as bad as wickedness.* The most prominent trait in the character of Joash was his lack of independence and moral weakness. He had no strength of will, no stamina; in the expressive, if inelegant, language of our times, "no backbone." He must always lean upon some one. Let us look at Joash—

I. IN HIS YOUTH. At this time he was so fortunate as to have a natural prop and support in Jehoiada, his uncle by marriage, and his guardian during the years of his minority. Jehoiada's was a strong character, and the life of Joash, while Jehoiada guided his steps, if not marked by any strikingly great actions, was correct, exemplary, worthy of praise. There was piety and right feeling in the pains which he took to promote the restoration of the temple, and prudence in the measures whereby he succeeded in effecting his purpose. The measures may have been—probably were—suggested by Jehoiada; but the king deserves some credit for adopting them.

> Οὗτος μὲν πανάριστος, ὃς αὐτὸς πάντα νοεῖται,
> Φρασσόμενος τά τ' ἔπειτα καὶ ἐς τέλος ἐστὶν ἀμείνω.
> Ἐσθλὸς δ' αὖ κἀκεῖνος, ὃς εὖ εἰπόντι πίθηται.

As the writer of Kings says, "Joash did that which was right in the sight of the Lord *all his days wherein Jehoiada the priest instructed him*" (ver. 2). But Jehoiada could not live for ever. He reached a very advanced age; but at last he "waxed old and died" (2 Chron. xxiv. 15), and Joash was left to manage as he might without him. Let us look at him now—

II. IN HIS MIDDLE AGE, AFTER THE DEATH OF JEHOIADA. Apparently his weakness is known, and it is at once assumed that he must put himself under directors. The "princes of Judah" go to him, pay him court, flatter him probably, at any rate offer him unusual honours. And at once he succumbs, and places himself under their influence. We cannot suppose him not to have been aware of what he was doing. He must have known the leanings of the "princes," and have understood that, in adopting them as his advisers, he was giving up all the traditions of his earlier life, and taking a new departure. Such lightness would not have been surprising in a mere youth; but Joash was now at least thirty years of age, probably more, and might have been expected to have formed and settled his principles and his character. Still, experience shows that even thirty years of a pious life, if it has been passed "under tutors and governors," does not fix a man's future in the same line—nay, often leads him to an almost irrepressible desire for revolt, and for departing widely from his antecedents. The desire is a temptation of the devil, and, if yielded to, has devilish results; but it is very often yielded to. Nero's outbreak after he had got rid of Seneca is the most palpable historical example; but the experience of most persons must have shown them scores of instances of men, trained and brought up in good courses till middle life, and then suddenly set free to take their own line, who have plunged into dissipation, impiety, and wickedness of all kinds. The case of Joash is extraordinary, not in its general features, but in the lengths to which he went. Under the influence of the "princes," he allowed the Baal-worship to be reintroduced, and gave it free tolerance.

When prophets remonstrated, and Zechariah denounced God's vengeance on those who had forsaken him (2 Chron. xxiv. 19, 20), then Joash, unaccustomed to opposition, was so exasperated that he went the length of murder—murder of a high priest, within the precincts of the temple, by the cruel death of stoning, and murder of one for whom he ought to have had a special kindness, in remembrance of the vast benefits which he had received from his father (2 Chron. xxix. 22). It is quite possible—nay, probable—that Joash (like Henry II. in the case of Becket) did not deliberately determine on the murder—that hasty words, uttered in extreme exasperation, were seized upon (Stanley) by his too-officious servants, and carried out in act before he could retract them. But this only emphasizes his weakness. A well-intentioned prince, yielding to evil influences, sanctions the most atrocious crime that the temple ever witnessed (Matt. xxiii. 35) and through his weakness involves the nation in guilt greater than any that had been incurred by the doings of the most wicked of preceding monarchs.

Vers. 4—8.—*Inconvenience of setting priests and ministers to "serve tables."* However convinced we may be of the honesty of the priests and Levites concerned in collecting money at this time for the repairs of the temple, it is undeniable that their proceedings in the matter created distrust and dissatisfaction. We know too little of the monetary arrangements previously in use among the Jews to see with any real clearness what exactly the complaint of the laity was, or how far the priests and Levites had a satisfactory answer to it. Probably the rules given were not sufficiently definite; and it may also well have been that the priests and Levites were not sufficiently versed in business transactions to understand completely what the rules laid down expressed. We must remember that, in the early Church, when the apostles had to occupy themselves with money matters, it was not long before complaints arose (Acts vi. 1), and the apostles refused any longer to " serve tables." The very foundation of society is a division of labour. In an organization like that of the Church, whether Jewish or Christian, it is of extreme importance to disconnect the performance of high spiritual functions from the duty of receiving, apportioning, and disbursing large sums of money. This is so—

I. BECAUSE, AS A GENERAL RULE, THE MOST SPIRITUALLY MINDED OF MEN ARE THE MOST INAPT FOR THE DETAILS OF BUSINESS. Different qualities of mind, qualities offering a strong contrast, and very rarely united in the same person, are requisite for success in business and for winning souls to God; also intimate acquaintance with an entirely different set of facts is in each case necessary. Spiritually minded men are in many instances woefully deficient in worldly knowledge, know nothing of book-keeping by double entry, and even find a difficulty in remembering the multiplication table. Their faculties are suited for something higher than " serving tables," and to employ them in such service is to waste valuable material in work for which it is wholly unsuited.

II. BECAUSE, IF BUSINESS TRANSACTIONS ARE ILL MANAGED, SUSPICIONS ARISE, AND GOD'S MINISTERS SHOULD BE ABOVE SUSPICION. A minister's usefulness is gone if once he is suspected in money matters. It is seriously impaired, even if nothing is proved against him beyond incapacity and blundering. Many a clergyman has got into most serious trouble by undertaking work of a worldly kind, which he never ought to have undertaken, and failing in the proper management of it, though his honesty was quite unimpeachable.

III. BECAUSE THE TIME GIVEN BY MINISTERS TO BUSINESS MATTERS MIGHT BE BETTER SPENT IN THE PROPER WORK OF THE MINISTRY. This was what the apostles felt (Acts vi. 2—4); they wished to give themselves wholly to " the ministry of the Word and to prayer." Modern clergymen have, in addition, parochial visiting and reading to employ them, both making large demands upon their time, and impossible to be shifted upon others. A congregation will, in ninety-nine cases out of a hundred, derive far more benefit from their minister having an additional hour a day, or two hours a day, for reading, than from his spending the time in slaving at accounts, collecting the children's pence, looking after clubs, and bargaining for coals or blankets. The study of the Bible, with all the new light which is thrown upon it by recent scholarship and research, is imperative; and it is also essential that a clergyman should have such a knowledge of the current and tendencies of modern thought as is only to be maintained by very diligent reading of the popular literature, periodical and other, of the day.

IV. Because it promotes harmony and union if the laity are employed in the business matters of the district, or Church, or parish. In almost every parish or congregation there will be among the laity persons quite fit to undertake the functions whereof we have been speaking. And such persons will in most cases be gratified by being asked to undertake them. They will be glad to be associated with the clergyman in parochial matters, and to relieve him of a portion of his burdens. It will be a satisfaction to them to be doing some work for Christ and his Church, to feel that they are a part of the organization, and that by their gratuitous service they are furthering the cause of their Lord and Master. And the greater intercourse which will thus take place between them and their spiritual guides will foster good feeling and mutual regard and respect.

Vers. 4—15.—*Church restoration a good work, acceptable to God.* David's desire to build God a house is often mentioned to his honour (2 Sam. vii. 2; 1 Chron. xvii. 1, 2; 2 Chron. vi. 7; Acts vii. 46). Solomon's reputation for piety and zeal rests mainly upon the pains which he took to erect for God's worship a noble and suitable edifice (Wisd. ix. 8; Ecclus. xlvii. 13; Acts vii. 47). The " repairing of the house of God " (2 Chron. xxiv. 27) by Joash obtained him his place among the good kings (ch. xii. 2). Josiah's restoration (ch. xxii. 3—7) helped to put him in the higher category of those who were in no way defective (Ecclus. xlix. 4). Zerubbabel and Jeshua were long held in honour, because they "builded the house, and set up an holy temple to the Lord" (Ecclus. xlix. 12). It was the great glory of Judas Maccabæus that he cleansed and "renewed the sanctuary" (1 Macc. v. 1). If God is to have any outward worship at all, if nations are to honour him openly, if men are to join in *common* prayer for mutual encouragement and edification, there must be buildings for the purpose; and natural reverence requires that they shall be kept solely for the purpose. He who provides such buildings does a good work; he who repairs them when they need it, or restores them when they have gone to decay, shows the same spirit as the original builder, and deserves scarcely less praise. Of course, we assume that both builders and repairers and restorers do their work in a proper frame of mind, and from proper motives; otherwise church-building, like almsgiving or any other good work, may cease to be pleasing to God, or may even become an "offence" to him. Church-builders and church-restorers should see—

I. That they do not their work out of ostentation or for their own glory. This their conscience will readily tell them if they honestly consult it.

II. That they do it not in a spirit of mere æstheticism, out of a love of art. Considering the personal character of those who built St. Peter's at Rome, and the dominant spirit of the age, it is difficult to suppose that the main motive at work among the promoters was not the æsthetic one. And there may be a danger of the same kind at the present day, when art is in such high estimation.

III. That they do it not out of strife, or jealousy, or emulation, but, if possible, with a single eye to God's honour, or, at any rate, with God's honour as their main object. As some preached the gospel out of strife (Phil. i. 15) in the apostles' time, so it may be that occasionally nowadays the desire of surpassing a neighbour, or outshining a rival, may be at the root of men's munificence in church-building and chapel-building. As "dead flies cause the ointment of the apothecary to stink" (Eccles. x. 1), so a wrong motive takes away all its sweet savour from a good action.

HOMILIES BY VARIOUS AUTHORS.

Vers. 1—3.—*The influence of a wise counsellor.* "Joash did that which was right in the sight of the Lord all his days wherein Jehoiada the priest instructed him."

I. Much depends upon the character of the sovereign. Compare England under the Stuarts with England under Cromwell or Queen Victoria. An impure and licentious court demoralizes a whole nation. A pure court is a standing rebuke to iniquity in high places. We have much need to pray "for kings, and for all that are in authority." We have much need to be thankful for the character and life of our present sovereign.

II. THE NATIONAL LIFE LARGELY DEPENDS UPON THE CHARACTER OF THE NATION'S COUNSELLORS. In our limited monarchy the "ministers of the Crown" are virtually the rulers of the nation. How important that a Christian nation should have Christian rulers, Christian legislators! The time has surely come when the voice of the Christian people of the British empire should be much more heard in Parliament. It is not so much the politics of party we need, as the politics of Christianity. We want rulers who will remember that "righteousness exalteth a nation." We want our laws to be based upon the eternal law of God. We want legislators who have the fear of God before their eyes. Christian people need to be aroused to their duty in this matter. They should see to it that, so far as they can secure it, Christian men are chosen to represent them in the legislature of the nation.—C. H. I.

Vers. 4—16.—*The repairing of the temple under Joash: a missionary sermon.* I. THIS WORK HAD ITS ORIGIN IN THE KING'S COMMAND. Kings get a great many hard knocks nowadays. But kings have not been all bad. Considering the fierce light which beats upon a throne, and the special temptations to which they are exposed, perhaps the character of kings will bear investigation as well as the character of many of their critics. If in Jewish history we find a Jeroboam and an Ahab, we also find a Solomon and a Hezekiah. If in Roman history we find a Nero staining with cruelty and bloodshed the imperial purple, we find others like Trajan and Marcus Aurelius, the patrons of literature, philosophy, and the arts. If in our British nation some of our sovereigns were not all they should have been, we can point to the influence for good which many of our rulers have exercised. So, although Joash ended badly, he began well. The first work of Joash and Jehoiada was to pull down the temple of Baal, and destroy his images. *Their next work was to repair the temple of the Lord.* Not merely had the house of the Lord been neglected for the worship of Baal, but, as we read in 2 Chronicles, "the sons of Athaliah, that wicked woman, had broken up the house of God; and also all the dedicated things of the house of the Lord did they bestow upon Baalim." Joash was grieved that the house of God should be in this shameful condition. He gave command that the temple should be repaired. He instructed the priests and Levites that they were to make collections for this purpose, not only in the temple, but throughout the land, every man from his acquaintance. 1. *We have got the command of a King in reference to his Church.* The Lord Jesus Christ expects that all who are his people will take an interest in building up that Church. We are first of all to build up the Church of Christ in our own land and in our own district. The professing Christian who enjoys the privileges of a Church, but contributes nothing to its support, is not obeying the teaching of God's Word. Then, also, we are to pray and give and labour for the extension of Christ's kingdom throughout the world. "Let him that heareth say, Come." "Go ye into all the world, and preach the gospel to every creature." "The harvest truly is plenteous, but the labourers are few; pray ye therefore the Lord of the harvest, that he will send forth labourers into his harvest." Here are three commands of Christ. How are we seeking to fulfil them? 2. *The cause of Christian missions rests upon the command of our King.* Some may think little of Christian missions. They may make light of their necessity, or undervalue the work they have done—though testimonies to the value of missionary work are becoming more frequent every year from explorers, from scientific men, from statesmen, even from heathen who have not become Christians. But it is enough for the true Christian that Christ has commanded the evangelization of the world. "That command," said the Duke of Wellington, "is the marching orders of the Christian Church."

II. THIS WORK WAS DELAYED BY NEGLECTFUL PRIESTS. Notwithstanding the command of King Joash, which would seem to have been given early in his reign, for a long time nothing was done. The time passed by till the twenty-third year of his reign, and still the priests had not repaired the breaches of the house of the Lord. Joash called the priests and the Levites together, and asked them why they had not carried out the work entrusted to them. Then he took it out of their hands in a certain measure. They who should have been the foremost in their zeal for the house of God had been tardy in this important work. How often it has unhappily been so in the history of the Christian Church! It was through the priesthood of the Western

Church in the Middle Ages that the greatest corruptions crept in. Forgetting their spiritual profession, they mixed themselves up with the political strife of their day. The popes aspired to be lords over God's heritage—a claim which Christ forbade his apostles to exercise. They thirsted for temporal power, and put the power of the Church into competition with the governments of the nations, just as the present pope is seeking to do in our own time. They thirsted for wealth and splendour, and thus began the traffic in indulgences against which Luther raised his mighty voice. All this time they were unfaithful to the high commission they professed to hold. They were forgetful of the plain statement of Christ, "My kingdom is not of this world." But this unfaithfulness of the teachers of religion is not confined to the Church of Rome. All Churches have suffered from it at one time or another. How much of the delay in the great work of Christian missions has been due to the neglect and unfaithfulness of religious teachers! For centuries scarcely anything was done to carry the gospel into heathen lands. Protestant missions can scarcely be said to have existed before the nineteenth century. The blight of moderatism, which was over all Christian communities in the last century, was fatal to all missionary effort for the time. *But God's work does not depend upon men, or on any class of men.* If those who are stewards of God are unfaithful to their trust, God will commit it to other hands. If men enter the sacred office of the ministry for the sake of earning a livelihood, God can deprive them even of that. How important for ministers of Christ to remember that they are watchmen upon the walls of Zion, and that if they neglect to warn the sinner, the blood of lost souls will be required at their hands! They are to be teachers and examples of the flock, leaders in every good work. Well it is for the Christian minister when he can say with the Apostle Paul, "I take you to record this day, that I am pure from the blood of all men, for I have not shunned to declare unto you all the counsel of God."

III. This work was supported by generous people. We may learn much from this chapter about *the place of money in the Church of God.* First of all, we see that *the people were regularly rated or assessed for the support of religious ordinances.* It is to this that Joash refers (ver. 4) when he speaks of the money of every one that passeth the account—the money that every man is set at. And in the account which is given in 2 Chronicles it is said that they made a proclamation throughout Judah and Jerusalem to bring in to the Lord the collection that Moses the servant of the Lord laid upon Israel in the wilderness. When we look into the thirtieth chapter of Exodus, the last chapter of Leviticus, and other passages, we find the clear instructions of God himself on this matter. When the numbering or census of the people was made, each one was assessed at so much for an atonement offering. This money was devoted to maintain the services of the sanctuary. Then again, if any one entered into a special vow to be the Lord's, he incurred *special* pecuniary obligations, and was rated accordingly. All these offerings Joash ordered to be set apart on this occasion for the repairs of the temple, with the exception of the sin and trespass offerings, which were secured to the priests, and which could not be touched for any other purpose. From these and other details we learn that God expected the Israelites to contribute regularly a fixed sum, in proportion to their income, for the support of religious ordinances. He expected of those who took special vows upon them that they should consecrate more of their money to his service. So God expects of his people still, and particularly of those who make the full profession of Christianity involved in attendance at the Lord's table. Some preacher stated lately that it is no "charity" when we give to the support of the Church with which we are connected. It is merely the payment of a debt—the fulfilment of obligations which every one incurs when he becomes a member of a Christian Church, and obligations which can no more be rightly shirked than any other just and lawful debt. Over and above that, he said, there is, of course, a large margin for the exercise of Christian charity and benevolence. This was the case when Joash appealed to the people to contribute, not only the fixed sum at which they were rated, but also "all the money that cometh into any man's heart to bring into the house of the Lord." He was not ashamed to appeal to them for money, for it was for a good cause. It was for God's cause, for God's house. He put the chest in a prominent place, where it could be seen (ver. 9). And his faithful, earnest appeal was not without effect. We read in 2 Chronicles (xxiv. 10) that "all the princes and all the people *rejoiced*, and brought in, and cast into the chest, until they had made an end." No doubt they experienced the blessing which is implied in the words, "*God loveth a cheerful giver*." We need to study God's Word more on this subject of Christian giving. We have seen what the Old Testament rules were. Here is one from the New Testament: "On the first day of the week let every one of you lay by him in store, as God hath prospered him." If we were to give *systematically*, as these words exhort, if we were to measure our weekly offerings by our prosperity, how much larger our offertories would be! what an overflowing offering of silver and gold would be given to carry the gospel to the heathen!

IV. THIS WORK WAS CARRIED OUT BY FAITHFUL WORKERS. Those are very remarkable words, "Moreover they reckoned not with the men, into whose hand they delivered the money to be bestowed on workmen: *for they dealt faithfully*" (ver. 15). There were faithful workmen, and faithful overseers of the work. And what was the explanation of this unusual confidence on the part of the contributors, and unusual faithfulness on the part of the workers? Ah! there had been a reformation of religion! Wherever true religion flourishes, *there* there will be honest and upright dealing between man and man. When the great revival of religion took place in Ulster in 1859, the change was soon manifest in the conduct of the whole community. Scenes of strife and turbulence became scenes of kindness and peace. The officers of justice had easy work in maintaining law and order, and at many of the sessions there was absolutely no criminal business. When men are influenced by the fear of God it will not be hard to procure obedience for the law of man. When the love of Christ is in men's hearts there will be love for our fellow-creatures also. May we not say the same of the great work of missions to the heathen, that it *is being carried on by faithful workers?* Where shall we find such a record of faithfulness, of patience, of devotedness, of perseverance, of heroic courage, as in the life and work of many a humble missionary to heathen lands? When we remember how many of those who have gone forth as missionaries, in connection with the Church and with the great missionary societies, have sacrificed high literary, or commercial, or professional prospects at home, it is but reasonable that the Christian Church should express its sympathy with such self-denial and devotedness by contributing liberally to the work of foreign missions (*vide infra*, on ch. xiii. 14—19).—C. H. I.

Vers. 17—21.—*The last days of Joash. He began well, but ended badly.* The close of the reign of Joash is a melancholy contrast to its beginning. In a most remarkable way preserved, by the providence of God and the kindness of a God-fearing woman, from the massacre of his brothers; then kept safe in the house of the Lord for six years of his helpless childhood;—one would think he would never have forgotten how much he owed to the watchful care and goodness of God. He had been surrounded with good influences. Jehoiada had watched over him like a father. When he came to the throne, Jehoiada had caused him to enter into a covenant with God. He began his reign with a great religious reformation. He ended it with a shameful forsaking of God. There were three causes of his fall. 1. *He retained the high places.* His reformation was not complete. The germs of future evil were there. How careful we should be of the beginnings of evil! It seemed a small matter to retain the high places. But that small act of negligence or want of courage prepared the way for national idolatry, and for the ultimate downfall of Joash. It accustomed the people to heathen modes of worship (cf. *infra*, on ch. xiv. 1—4). 2. *He listened to evil counsellors.* It was an evil day for Joash when Jehoiada passed away. "Now after the death of Jehoiada came the princes of Judah, and made obeisance to the king. *Then the king hearkened unto them.* And they left the house of the Lord God of their fathers, and served groves and idols: and wrath came upon Judah and Jerusalem for this their trespass" (2 Chron. xxiv. 17, 18). Ah! how true it is that "evil communications corrupt good manners"! 3. *He disregarded the warnings of God.* The Lord "sent prophets to them, to bring them again unto the Lord; . . . but they would not give ear" (2 Chron. xxiv. 19). Zechariah the son of Jehoiada came with a special warning. But here again we see the hardening effect of sin. Not only did Joash pay no attention to his warnings, but with the basest ingratitude, forgetful of all he owed to Jehoiada, Zechariah's father, he put Zechariah to death. The messenger of God may suffer for his faithfulness in rebuking sin, as John the Baptist was imprisoned by Herod, but no royal power can stay the judgments of God. Joash, who had slain God's prophet, was himself slain by his own servants. The nation had forsaken God, and God forsook them in their time of need. Such a career as that of Joash shows the necessity for constant watchfulness against sin. Many, like him, begin well, but end badly. They make a fair profession at first, but by-and-by, when troubles or persecutions arise, they are offended. They go back and walk no more with Christ. Or they become worldly minded, and, being engrossed in the present, forget the concerns of eternity. Many might utter the melancholy cry, " Our lamps are gone out." To every one of us the message may well be sent, " Let him that thinketh he standeth take heed lest he fall."—C. H. I.

Vers. 1—21.—*The history of Joash.* "In the seventh year," etc. The whole story of Joash is soon told. He was a son of Ahaziah, and the only one of his children who escaped the murderous policy of Athaliah. " It would seem that this child, whom the pity and affection of a pious aunt (Jehosheba) had preserved, was the only surviving male representative of the line of Solomon. Jehoram, his grandfather, who married Athaliah, in order to strengthen his position on the throne, slew all his brethren, and all his own sons were slain in an incursion by the Arabians, except Ahaziah, the youngest, who succeeded him; while on the death of Ahaziah, his wicked mother, Athaliah, 'arose and destroyed all the seed royal of the house of Judah,' except the little child Joash, who was rescued from her grasp. So that the unholy alliances formed by the descendants of Solomon, and the manifold disorders then accruing, had reduced everything to the verge of ruin. Measures were concerted by Jehoiada, the high priest, for getting rid of Athaliah, and placing Joash on the throne, after he had attained to the age of seven; and having in his youth the wise and the faithful round his throne, the earlier part of the reign of Joash was in accordance with the great principles of the theocracy. The Lord's house was repaired and set in order, while the temple and idols of Baal were thrown down. But after Jehoiada's death, persons of a different stamp got about him, and, notwithstanding the great and laudable zeal which he had shown for the proper restoration of God's house and worship, a return was made to idolatry to such an extent as to draw forth severe denunciations from Zechariah, the son of Jehoiada. Even this was not the worst, for the faithfulness of Zechariah was repaid with violence; he was even stoned to death, and this, it is said, at the express command of the king. The martyred priest exclaimed as he expired, ' The Lord look upon it, and require;' and it was required as in a whirlwind of wrath. For a Syrian host, under Hazael, made an incursion into Judæa, and both carried off much treasure and executed summary judgment on many in Jerusalem, not excepting Joash himself, whom they left in an enfeebled state, and who was shortly afterwards fallen upon and slain by his servants. Such was the unhappy termination of a career which began in much promise of good, and the cloud under which he died even followed him to the tomb, for while he was buried in the city of David, it was not in the sepulchres of the kings of Judah. He reigned forty years—from B.C. 878 to 838." The narrative, whether we regard it as inspired or not, reminds us of five things worth considering— the dilapidating influence of time upon the best material productions of mankind; the incongruity of worldly rulers busying themselves in religious institutions; the value of the co-operative principle in the enterprises of mankind; the potency of the religious element in the nature of even depraved people; and the power of money to subdue enemies.

I. THE DILAPIDATING INFLUENCE OF TIME UPON THE BEST MATERIAL PRODUCTIONS OF MANKIND. Joash here called upon the priests and the people " to repair the breaches of the house," *i.e.* the temple. The temple, therefore, though it had not been built more than about a hundred and sixty years, had got into a state of dilapidation, there were breaches in it; where the breaches were we are not told, whether in the roof, the floor, the walls, or in the ceiling. The crumbling hand of time had touched it. No human superstructure, perhaps, ever appeared on the earth built of better materials, or in a better way, than the temple of Solomon. It was the wonder of ages. Notwithstanding this, it was subject to the invincible law of decay. The law of dilapidation seems universal throughout organic nature; the trees of the forest, the flowers of the field, and the countless tribes of sentient life that crowd the ocean, earth, and air, all fall into decay; and so also with the material productions of feeble man. Throughout the civilized world we see mansions, churches, cathedrals, palaces, villages, towns, and cities, in ruins. All compound bodies tend to dissolution; there is nothing enduring but primitive elements or substances. This being so, how astoundingly preposterous is man's effort to perpetuate his memory in material monuments! The only productions of men that defy the touch of time, and that are enduring, are true thoughts, pure sympathies, and noble deeds. He who builds up the temple of a true moral character produces a superstructure that will last through the sweep of ages, the wreck of thrones, and the crash of doom.

II. THE INCONGRUITY OF WORLDLY RULERS BUSYING THEMSELVES IN RELIGIOUS INSTITUTIONS. Joash was no saint, the root of the matter was not in him; he had no vital and ruling sympathy with the Supreme Being, yet he seemed zealous in the work of repairing the temple. "Then King Joash called for Jehoiada the priest, and the other priests, and said unto them, Why repair ye not the breaches of the house? now therefore receive no more money of your acquaintance, but deliver it for the breaches of the house." Though the conduct of corrupt men in busying themselves with things pertaining to religion is incongruous, alas! it is not uncommon. Such conduct generally springs from one of two things, or from both—*policy* or *superstition*. The religion that is popular, whether it be true or false, rulers recognize and sanction. They use the religious element in the community as a means by which to strengthen their thrones and augment their fame. Not only, indeed, are kings actuated thus, but even the corrupt tradesman, lawyer, doctor, etc., must show some interest in the popular religion in order to succeed in his secular pursuits. But *superstition* as well as policy often prompts corrupt men to busy themselves in matters of religion. Do not many build and beautify churches and subscribe to religious institutions, hoping thereby to escape perdition and to ensure the favour of Heaven? Alas! some of the corruptest men are often most busy in religious affairs. The man that betrayed the Son of God at the last Passover was most busy on that awful night; "his hand was on the table."

III. THE VALUE OF THE CO-OPERATIVE PRINCIPLE IN THE ENTERPRISES OF MANKIND. It would seem that the work of repairing the temple was so great that no one man could have accomplished it. Hence the king called earnestly for the co-operation of all. "And Jehoash said to the priests, All the money of the dedicated things that is brought into the house of the Lord, even the money of every one that passeth the account, the money that every man is set at, and all the money that cometh into any man's heart to bring into the house of the Lord, let the priests take it to them, every man of his acquaintance: and let them repair the breaches of the house." They obeyed his voice. The people gave the money, and all set to work; the "priest that kept the door," the "high priest," the "carpenters," the "masons," the "builders," the "hewers of stone," etc. By this unity of action "they repaired the house of the Lord." Two remarks may be made concerning the principle of co-operation. 1. It is a principle that *should govern* all men in the undertakings of life. It was never the purpose of the Almighty that man should act alone for himself, should pursue alone his own individual interests. Men may, and often do, make large fortunes by it, but they destroy their own peace of mind, degrade their natures, and outrage the Divine laws of society. Men are all members of one great body; and was ever a member made to work alone? No; but for the good of the whole, the common weal. 2. It is a principle that has *done and is doing wonders* in the undertakings of life. Our colleges, hospitals, railways, etc., are all the products of co-operation. The more men get intellectually enlightened and morally improved, the more this principle will be put into operation. This principle, however, has its limits. In spiritual matters it must not infringe the realm of individual responsibility. There is no partnership in moral responsibility. Each man must think, repent, and believe for himself. "Every man must bear his own burden."

IV. THE POTENCY OF THE RELIGIOUS ELEMENT EVEN IN DEPRAVITY. At this time Israel was morally almost as corrupt as the heathen nations. From the beginning Israel was the Church of God in little more than a *metaphorical* sense. Never in the history of the world has there been a member of the true Church whose sympathies with Jehovah were not supreme. But how many of the Jews had this supreme sympathy?

Notwithstanding this, the religious sentiment was in them, as in all men, a constituent part of their natures; and this sentiment is here appealed to, and roused into excitement; and, being excited, men poured forth their treasures and employed their energies for the repairing of the temple. This element in man often sleeps under the influence of depravity, but mountains of depravity cannot crush it; it lies in human nature as the mightiest latent force. Peter the Hermit, Savanorola the priest, Wesley the Methodist, and others in every age, have roused it into mighty action, even amongst the most ignorant and depraved of the race. Cunning priests and crafty kings have appealed to it as the strongest force that can bear them on to the realization of their miserable ends. The truly good and godly must appeal to it if they would accomplish any great work for mankind. By its right action only can men rise; by its dormancy or wrong development men must inevitably fall.

V. The power of money to subdue enemies. "Hazael King of Syria . . . set his face to go up to Jerusalem. And Joash King of Judah took all the hallowed things that . . . his fathers . . . had dedicated, . . . and all the gold that was found in the treasures of the house of the Lord, . . . and sent it to Hazael King of Syria : and he went away from Jerusalem." Here is a man, a proud, daring monarch, who was determined to invade Judæa, and to take possession of Jerusalem, relinquishing his designs. What was the force that broke his purpose? *Money.* It is said that Joash sent gold to Hazael, "and he went away from Jerusalem." Truly money answereth for all things. Money can arrest the march of armies and terminate the fiercest campaigns. After contending armies have destroyed their thousands, it is money alone that brings the battle to a close. Money is the soul of all pacifying treaties. What fools the rulers of the people are not to employ money to prevent war and turn it away from their country! Enemies can be conquered by gifts. Evil can only be overcome by good. "If thine enemy hunger, offer him bread to eat; and if he be thirsty, give him water to drink: for in so doing thou shalt heap coals of fire upon his head."—D. T.

Vers. 1—3.—*A mixed character.* The reign of Joash began with bright hopes, showed for a while excellent promise, yet ended ingloriously. To explain this we may consider—

I. Joash's advantages. 1. *He had a pious education.* As a child he was brought up by his aunt Jehosheba, who, with her husband the high priest, would instil into his mind the principles of true godliness. In his strict seclusion he was kept free from sights of vice. Like Timothy, he would be taught from a child to know the things that make wise unto salvation (2 Tim. iii. 15). To have an early training of this kind is an inestimable advantage. 2. *He had a good counsellor.* The early education of our own Queen Victoria was carefully conducted with a view to the royal office she was afterwards to fill. It would not be otherwise with young Joash. Jehoiada would carefully impress upon his mind the principles of good government, and, after his coronation, this holy man continued to be his guide and counsellor. So it is said, "Jehoash did that which was right in the sight of the Lord all his days wherein Jehoiada the priest instructed him." It is a happy thing when a king is willing to receive counsel from older and wiser heads than his own (cf. 1 Kings xii. 6—11). 3. *He had an excellent opportunity.* Joash started with every advantage for reigning well. The people were animated with hatred of idolatry from the experience they had had of it in Athaliah's reign; they were enthusiastic in their return to the worship of Jehovah; they had inaugurated the restoration of the line of David by a new covenant with God, and by zealous acts of reform. The tide was with Joash, if he had shown strength of character sufficient to avail himself of it.

II. Joash's weakness. Circumstances test men, and it was to be proved that, with all his advantages, Joash was a weak king. 1. *He lacked independence of judgment.* Whether the early seclusion of his life had anything to do with this, we cannot tell; but it seems plain that he was not a king accustomed to think and act for himself, but one who was easily influenced and led by others. His nature was passive clay, on which the judgment of others stamped itself. While Jehoiada lived, he allowed himself to be led by him; and when this good priest and counsellor died, he allowed himself as readily to be turned into evil courses by the wicked nobility (2 Chron. xxiv. 17,18). 2. *He lacked firmness of will.* This defect flowed from the feebleness of judgment now indicated. Joash knew the right, but he had not the courage or persistence to do it when pressure was brought to bear on him in an opposite direction. His life thus proved at last a wretched failure. Notwithstanding Jehoiada's kindness to him, he was betrayed at length into shedding the blood of Zechariah, his benefactor's son (2 Chron. xxiv. 20—22). 3. *He lacked true surrender of heart to God.* This was the prime defect in his character. His goodness, such as it was—and for a time it seemed perfectly genuine—was the result of natural amiableness, of early training, of external influences; it did not spring from a root of true conviction. Therefore, when the sun was up, it was scorched, and withered away (Matt. xiii. 6). It was goodness like the morning cloud, and the early dew—unenduring (Hos. vi. 3). The lesson we learn is the need of a radical change of heart as the foundation of true and enduring piety.

III. JOASH'S IMPERFECT REFORMS. The one point noticed about him at this stage is that, while reforming the worship of the temple, the high places were not taken away as commanded by the Law. This was a reform, it is to be allowed, not easily achieved, but had Joash been a man of more character he might have accomplished it, as Hezekiah did after him (ch. xviii. 4). The fact that he did not attempt it, though popular feeling was so strongly on his side, is an evidence of that weak line in his character which came more clearly to light when Jehoiada was removed.—J. O.

Vers. 4—6.—*The temple repairs—a good purpose frustrated.* At an early period of his reign, Joash, instigated no doubt by the good Jehoiada, took steps to have the temple put in a proper state of repair.

I. THE REPAIR OF THE TEMPLE PROJECTED. 1. *The need of repair.* What is stated in Chronicles of the condition of the temple shows how terrible had been the blight which had fallen on true religion in Judah during the reign of Athaliah. "That wicked woman," we are told, "had broken up the house of God"—probably carried away its stones to build or adorn her own house of Baal; or, perhaps, had broken down part of the courts to make room for her temple on the same hill. Moreover, she had taken away all the dedicated things to bestow upon the house of Baal (2 Chron. xxiv. 7). There was thus much work to be done in repairing the temple, as the numbers of workmen afterwards employed show. Many are the inroads of the world upon the Church—God's spiritual temple; and any breaches found in *its* walls should give rise to earnest desires and efforts to see them mended. 2. *The resolve to repair.* Joash gave orders that the repairing of the temple should be proceeded with. He had, perhaps, by this time attained his majority. But it is a singular thing that, with such a wave of reforming zeal as passed over the nation at the time of his accession, the people themselves should have been content to let the temple lie out of repair so long. Care for God's house is one of the ways of showing honour to God himself. Yet how slow men are to move, or make sacrifices, that God's worship may be suitably provided for! They are content to dwell in ceiled houses, while God's house lies waste (Hag. i. 4).

II. THE REPAIR OF THE TEMPLE PROVIDED FOR. 1: *By sacred dues.* In ordaining that the temple should be repaired, Joash showed also how the funds for the work were to be obtained. The Chronicler gives prominence to the half-shekel tax, which in the days of Moses was levied for the benefit of the sanctuary (2 Chron. xxiv. 6, 9), and there were the other moneys to be paid on occasion of the fulfilment of vows (Lev. xxvii. 2—8). It is well when religion is not left to be supported by haphazard contributions, but when there is some definite principle of giving—some portion of income which is regularly set apart for the Lord's use. This creates a fund which can be readily drawn upon when any good work requires aid. 2. *By free-will offerings.* The stated dues were not to be the only source of revenue. There is named also "all the money that cometh into any man's heart to bring into the house of the Lord." It is expected that religion will touch the heart of a man, and make him willing to part with a portion of his substance for the service of God. If it does not, it is not of much value. On the other hand, it is the heart which is the source of true religious giving. The gifts which come from the hand, not from the heart, do not count for much in Heaven's reckoning. "God loveth a *cheerful* giver" (2 Cor. ix. 7).

III. THE REPAIR OF THE TEMPLE STILL UNEXECUTED. Years passed on. Joash had now been twenty-three years upon the throne, yet the repairs of the temple had not so much as begun. It seems unaccountable that in so holy a work such apathy should have prevailed. The fact may be attributed: 1. *To the inertia of the priesthood.* Everything seems at first to have been left to the priests and Levites. They were to go through the land, make proclamation of the king's purpose, and collect the money for the work. In this duty they appear to have been slack. "The Levites," the Chronicler says, "hastened it not" (2 Chron. xxiv. 5). Large bodies of men are slow to move. Some of the priests and Levites were probably men of no great religious enthusiasm. One can sympathize with them in their shrinking from the task of collecting money. There are few tasks more thankless. 2. *To the distrust of the people.* The people appear not to have had the requisite confidence in the priests to entrust them with large sums of money. At least the money seems to have come in more freely after Jehoiada made his chest with the hole in the lid of it, than it did before. The distrust of the people was natural, for the priests were in no hurry to lay out the revenues they collected. 3. *To the self-interest of a privileged class.* The priestly dues would suffer serious diminution during the reign of such a queen as Athaliah. Irregularities would creep in, and the priests and Levites, deprived of their proper income, would feel justified in appropriating primarily to their own support whatever moneys came to hand. Joash's decree had the effect of cutting off these perquisites, and of restoring them to their original use in keeping up the sanctuary. It could not be expected that the classes who were to suffer would be very eager in carrying out this decree. It is never safe to trust a privileged class to carry out measures which tell against its own interests. Average human nature is not so disinterested as to act enthusiastically for the promotion of reforms which injure itself.—J. O.

Vers. 7—16.—*The temple repairs—a good purpose accomplished.* When so many years had elapsed without anything being done, Joash called the priests to account, and ordered them to take no more of the money of the people for themselves, but to repair the breaches of the house. A new start was made, and this time success was attained. We may ascribe the success to—

I. PRUDENT ARRANGEMENTS. Wise, business-like arrangements have much to do with the success of any undertaking. Those now entered into were under the superintendence of Jehoiada, and afforded: 1. *Security against misappropriation.* Jehoiada obtained a chest, and bored a hole in the lid of it. It was placed beside the altar, on the right side, and all the money that was brought was put therein. There could thus be no suspicion of any mal-appropriation of the funds. Every worshipper had the certainty that what he gave would go for the purpose for which it was given. 2. *A removal of temptation.* The arrangement of the chest was an advantage to the priests as well as to the people. It no longer afforded any temptation to needy individuals among them to retain funds that were passing through their hands. It put the order, as a whole, above suspicion and reproach. It is well not to put needless temptations in any one's way. 3. *A convenience for giving.* The chest, as it stood there beside the altar, was a permanent depository to which the contributions of the faithful could be brought. The people had not to seek out persons to receive their gifts. They knew, without asking, where to take them. Sound arrangements of this sort, inspiring confidence, minimizing temptations to negligence or dishonesty, and consulting the convenience of the offerers, were admirably adapted to promote the ends aimed at. The example may be attended to with profit in the financial management of churches, charities, missionary societies, etc.

II. WILLING GIVERS. The fact that the work was taken partially out of the hands of the priests, and that the people had now security for their gifts being properly applied, had an immediate effect on the flow of contributions. We find: 1. *Liberal gifts brought.* It was not long, as we are told, before there was "much money" in the chest. People are seldom as willing to give for religion as they should be, but if a good cause is put before them, if they have the case properly presented, and if they feel secure as to the disposal of their gifts, it is wonderful often how freely liberality flows forth. We must not blame people for illiberality when their backwardness in giving arises from removable, and perhaps justifiable, causes. 2. *A strict account kept.* This is another feature in the business-like management of the funds which was now introduced, showing what great pains were taken to impress the minds of the people with confidence in the disposal of their money. When the chest was full, the king's scribe and the high priest came up, opened the box, put the money in bags, and made a strict account of the sums. Strictness in pecuniary details may seem a minor matter, but it is really not so. The man who is honest in his pecuniary affairs is likely to be honest all through. Nothing shakes confidence so much as the suspicion of small unfaithfulnesses in money transactions. Instinctively we apply the principle, "He that is faithful in that which is least is faithful also in much : and he that is unjust in the least is unjust also in much. If therefore ye have not been faithful in the unrighteous mammon, who will commit to your trust the true riches ? " (Luke xvi. 10, 11).

III. DILIGENT WORKERS. The money contributed by the people was applied to hire the services of workers to execute the needed repairs. 1. *The workers were many.* There were carpenters and builders, stonemasons and hewers, and part of the money was expended also on the purchase of materials. As in this temple-building so in the Christian Church, there is need not only for givers but for workers, and every variety of gift proves to be of service. Some can give who cannot work ; others can work who cannot give ; others can both give and work. There are needed those with mission talent—the quarrymen and excavators ; there are needed those who can educate, or hew and polish the stones when obtained ; there are needed the organizers and builders—those whose function it is to put the stones in their places, and build up the holy temple to the Lord. 2. *The workers were diligent.* They were set on as soon as funds were forthcoming to employ them, and they wrought with good heart till the work was finished. Labour in the kingdom of God should be diligent. The many workers did not work separately, but together, all of them helping one another; and similar combination and co-operation are necessary to overtake the work of Christ.

IV. FAITHFUL OVERSEERS. Another step in the right direction, following up the previous precautions to inspire confidence, was the appointment of men to superintend the work who could be implicitly trusted. It is a noble testimony borne concerning these men who did the part of overseers in the work of the temple, that they did not need to be reckoned with, "for they dealt faithfully." 1. *They were faithful in their oversight.* They were men of probity and honour, who conscientiously looked after the men set under them, seeing that the work committed to their care was properly done. It is difficult to estimate the value, even in an economical respect, of the higher moral qualities of character. How much loss, suffering, disease, death, not to speak of minor annoyance, is inflicted on mankind through badly inspected, ill-done work ? There is a sphere for faithfulness in the discharge of every kind of duty. Carlyle says of Louis XV, "His wide France, look at it from the fixed stars (themselves not yet infinitude), is no wider than thy narrow brickfield, where thou, too, didst faithfully, or didst unfaithfully. . . . It is not thy works, which are all mortal, infinitely little, and the greatest no greater than the least, but only the spirit thou workest in that can have worth or continuance." 2. *They were faithful in their money dealings.* So perfectly faithful that it was not felt necessary to keep a strict reckoning with them as to their expenditure upon the workmen. No better tribute could be paid to their incorruptible integrity than the trust thus reposed in them. It was only a very high degree of integrity which would warrant it. As a rule, it is wise to keep account even with those whose integrity we do not dispute.

V. RESPECT FOR RIGHTS. It is added that the revenues which properly belonged to the priests, the trespass money and sin money, were not touched for the purpose of the repairs. Neither was the money given for the restoration of the building applied, until the repairs were completed, to purchase new vessels for the sanctuary—bowls of silver, snuffers, trumpets, etc. Probably in connection with the above arrangements for collecting the people's money other steps were taken to put the priests' legitimate income, the tithe dues, etc., on a more satisfactory footing. A regard for justice is thus observable throughout the whole of these dealings. Right is the proper basis to take one's stand on in works of reformation.—J. O.

Vers. 17—21.—*Dark days for Judah.* The reign of Joash began with bright promise, but ended in gloom and tribulation. It furnishes another instance of the evil consequences of forsaking God.

I. JOASH'S APOSTASY. Of this a fuller account is given in the Book of Chronicles than here, though the statement in ver. 2, "Joash did right all his days wherein

Jehoiada the priest instructed him," already hints at a falling away after Jehoiada's death. From Chronicles we learn the nature of his apostasy. 1. *He yielded to bad counsel.* His good adviser having died at the extreme age of a hundred and thirty, he listened to the flatteries and seductions of the princes of Judah, whose bent was all towards evil (2 Chron. xxiv. 17). 2. *He revived idolatry.* If he did not actually participate in the renewed setting up of idols, he permitted it. Baal-worship, from which in infancy he had suffered so much, again lifted up its head in Jerusalem. For this trespass it is said, "wrath came upon Judah and Jerusalem" (2 Chron. xxiv. 18). 3. *He shed innocent blood.* This declension of Joash was not allowed to go unrebuked. God sent prophets to him to testify to him and warn him, especially Zechariah, the son, or perhaps grandson, of the priest Jehoiada. But so far had the infatuation of Joash gone that he actually permitted this son of his former friend and benefactor to be stoned with stones between the temple and the altar in the court of the Lord's house (2 Chron. xxiv. 20—22; cf. Matt. xxiii. 35). This ineffaceable crime completed his ruin. As Zechariah died he had said, "The Lord look upon it, and require it" (2 Chron. xxiv. 22); and God did require it. The Jews had a tradition that, at the capture of Jerusalem, this blood of Zechariah bubbled up from the floor of the temple court, and could not be pacified. Nebuzaradan brought rabbis, and slew them on it, still it was not quiet; he brought children, and slew them on it, still it was not quiet; he slew ninety-four thousand on it, yet it was not quiet. The fable illustrates at least the heinousness of the deed.

II. HAZAEL'S INVASION. The instrument employed to chastise Joash and the people for their sins was the redoubtable Hazael. He invaded the land by the way of Philistia, and reduced it to great distress. We note regarding the invasion: 1. *Its resistless character.* It was but a very small company of men that came with Hazael, but they seem to have swept the "very great host" of Judah before them with ease, destroying the princes of the people, who had been ringleaders in wickedness, and sending the spoil on to Damascus (cf. 2 Chron. xxiv. 24). It is a fatal thing to break faith with God, to apostatize from solemn covenants with him, to provoke him to anger by open wickedness and deeds of blood. The strength of a nation stands not in its mighty men, but in the favour of God, and where that is withdrawn, a handful of armed men will chase a thousand (cf. Deut. iv. 25—27; xxviii. 27—48). 2. *The ignominious tribute.* What, in so deplorable a case, could Joash do? His princes, so bold in counselling him in courses of sin, were cowards in the field; and Hazael seemed bent on utterly overthrowing him. He had no alternative but to make the best terms he could, and buy the invader off. To furnish the requisite tribute he had to strip both the temple and his own house of all their goodly treasures. He took the hallowed things of his forefathers out of the temple, and the gold that was found in its treasuries; he took also his own gold, and sent everything to Hazael. He, the restorer of the temple, is forced to become the spoiler of the temple. To such depths of ignominy and misery are men led by forsaking the ways of God. Yet nothing seems to avail sinners for warning! They go on as madly in ways of wickedness as if no one had ever tried these paths before them, and found them the ways of death.

III. THE FATAL CONSPIRACY. We have, finally, the account of how Joash met his end by a conspiracy of two of his servants. 1. *The origin of the conspiracy.* We cannot err in supposing that it had its origin in the seething discontent of the people. They saw the kingdom going to pieces in the hands of an unfaithful king; they saw righteous blood shed; they had suffered severely from the barbarities of invasion. The conspirators do not seem to have plotted any dynastic change. Their act only expressed the bitter hatred with which the person of the king had come to be regarded. How different from the day when the multitude shouted, "God save the king!" And that change had come about solely through Joash's departure from the right ways of God. 2. *Its fatal result.* The servants, whose names are given in the text, smote him in "the house of Millo" so that he died. Thus Joash fell by the stroke of an assassin, unpitied, unlamented by his people. When the bonds of godliness are loosed, the bonds of fidelity between man and man are loosed too (Hos. iv. 1, 2). 3. *The dishonour to his body.* The crowning ignominy put upon Joash was the refusal of the people to allow him to be buried in the sepulchre of the kings, as Jehoiada had been (2 Chron. xxiv. 25). This confirms what is said above of the odium in which he was held by his people.—J. O.

EXPOSITION.

CHAPTER XIII.

Vers. 1—25.—REIGNS OF JEHOAHAZ, SON OF JEHU, AND JOASH, SON OF JEHOAHAZ, OVER ISRAEL. NOTICES OF ELISHA. WAR OF ISRAEL WITH SYRIA.

Vers. 1—9.—THE REIGN OF JEHOAHAZ. The writer returns in this chapter to the history of the Israelite kingdom, taking it up from the death of Jehu, which was recorded in the closing verses of ch. x. He sketches briefly the reign of Jehu's son and successor, Jehoahaz, in the present section, after which he passes to that of Jehu's grandson, Jehoash or Joash. The Syrian oppression was the great event of Jehoahaz's reign.

Ver. 1.—In the three and twentieth year of Joash; rather, as in Josephus ('Ant. Jud.,' ix. 8. § 5), *in the one and twentieth year.* This is a correction required by ver. 10 and also by ch. xii. 1. The proof is given at somewhat tedious length by Keil ('Biblical Commentary,' pp. 373, 374) and Bähr ('Books of the Kings,' pp. 139, 140). It seems unnecessary to enter into a lengthy discussion of the point, since *all* the synchronisms of the later kings of Israel and Judah are in confusion, and appear to be the work of a later hand. The son of Ahaziah (comp. ch. xi. 2; 2 Chron. xxii. 11) King of Judah, Jehoahaz the son of Jehu began to reign over Israel; literally, *reigned over Israel.* The "later hand," which inserted the synchronism, neglected to bring the two portions of the verse into agreement. Our translators have sought to cover up his omission by translating *málak* "began to reign," and then supplying "and reigned" in the next clause. And reigned seventeen years (so also Josephus, *l. s. c.*).

Ver. 2.—And he did that which was evil in the sight of the Lord. There is no reason to believe that Jehoahaz re-introduced the Baal-worship, or sinned in any other flagrant way than by maintaining the calf-worship at Dan and Bethel. Jehu had done the same (ch. x. 29), as had all previous kings of Israel from the time of Jeroboam. The honour of God, however, required that idolatry of whatever kind should be punished, and the Samaritan kingdom could not otherwise be saved from destruction than by "casting away *all* the works of darkness" and returning to the *pure* worship of Jehovah. Hence Jehu himself, notwithstanding the good service that he had done in crushing the Baal-worship, was chastised by God (ch. x. 32, 33) on account of his continuance in the "sin of Jeroboam;" and now Jehoahaz was even more signally punished. As Keil remarks, "The longer and the more obstinately the sin was continued, the more severe did the punishment become." And followed the sins of Jeroboam the son of Nebat (comp. ch. x. 29, where the exegetical clause is added, "To wit, the golden calves that were in Bethel and in Dan") which made Israel to sin (comp. 1 Kings xv. 26; xvi. 19, 26; xxii. 52, etc.); he departed not therefrom. This is emphatic. Jehoahaz kept up the worship to the full, and in no way suffered it to decline.

Ver. 3.—And the anger of the Lord was kindled against Israel. We know so much less of the nature of the calf-worship and of the rites which accompanied it, that we cannot to the same extent justify the Divine severity in connection with it as in connection with the Baal and Astarte cult. Still, we must remember the coarse, lewd dancing which accompanied the first calf-worship (Exod. xxxii. 19), for which death was not thought too heavy a penalty (Exod. xxxii. 27), and the almost universal combination of unchastity with idolatrous ceremonies, which raises a suspicion that those who frequented the shrines at Dan and Bethel were not wholly innocent of impurity. And he delivered them into the hand of Hazael King of Syria. The national sins of Israel were mostly punished in this way, by the sword of some foreign foe. Hazael had been already made an instrument for the chastisement of Jehu (ch. x. 32, 33). Now he was to chastise Jehoahaz still more severely. And into the hand of Benhadad the son of Hazael, all their days; literally, *all the days.* Not certainly all the days of the two kings Hazael and Benhadad, for Benhadad was entirely worsted in his war with Joash (vers. 24, 25), but either all the days of Jehoahaz, or all the days that God had appointed for the duration of the calamity. It is perhaps against the former interpretation that Hazael appears to have outlived Jehoahaz (vers. 22—24); but Benhadad may have warred against him as his father's general (ver. 25) during his father's lifetime.

Ver. 4.—And Jehoahaz besought the Lord; literally, *besought the face of the Lord* (comp. 1 Kings xiii. 6, and the comment *ad loc.*). Jehoahaz, as Josephus says, "betook himself to prayer and supplication of God, entreating that he would deliver him out of the hands of Hazael, and not suffer him to continue subject" ('Ant. Jud.,' ix. 8. § 5). He did not turn from his sin of idolatry, perhaps did not suspect that it was this sin which had provoked God's anger; but in a general way he repented, humbled himself, and besought God's mercy and assistance. **And the Lord hearkened unto him.** God accepted his repentance, all imperfect as it was, so far as to save the people from the entire destruction with which it was threatened by the severe measures of Hazael (ver. 7), to continue the national existence (ver. 23), and ultimately to restore the national prosperity (ver. 25 and ch. xiv. 25—27). But he did not remove the oppression, as Josephus imagines, in Jehoahaz's time. Ver. 22 makes this fact absolutely certain. **For he saw the oppression of Israel, because the King of Syria oppressed them.** Oppression is always hateful to God, even when he is using it as his instrument for chastising or punishing a guilty people. He "sees" it, notes it, lays it up in his remembrance for future retribution (comp. Exod. iii. 7; Isa. x. 5—12, etc.). (On the nature and extent of the oppression of this period, see ver. 7, and the comment ad loc.)

Ver. 5.—**And the Lord gave Israel a saviour, so that they went out from under the hand of the Syrians.** A "saviour" means a deliverer from the hand of the Syrians (comp. Judg. iii. 9, 15; Neh. ix. 27, where in the Hebrew the word used is the same). The special "deliverer" was probably in the mind of the writer, Jeroboam II., by whom he says, in ch. xiv. 27, that God "saved" Israel; but Joash, who began the deliverance (ver. 25), may also be glanced at. **And the children of Israel dwelt in their tents.** Here, as so often elsewhere (1 Kings viii. 66; xii. 16; ch. xiv. 12; Zech. xii. 7), the word "tents" is a mere archaïsm for "abodes, houses." Israel had dwelt in tents until the going down into Egypt, and again from the time of quitting Egypt to the entrance into Canaan; and thus the word ohel had acquired a secondary meaning of "abode," "dwelling-place." In the time which followed on the deliverance from the Syrian yoke, the Israelites of the ten tribes were no longer engaged in marches and countermarches, in battles, skirmishes, or sieges, but quietly abode in their several houses. **As beforetime;** i.e. as in the peaceful time before the attacks of Hazael began.

Ver. 6.—**Nevertheless they departed not from the sins of the house of Jeroboam, who made Israel sin.** "The house of Jeroboam" is an unusual expression in this connection, and is scarcely appropriate, since every "house" had acted in the same way. Some

manuscripts omit the word, and it is wanting in the Chaldee, Syriac, and Arabic versions. Thenius would cancel it. But **walked therein;** literally, he walked. But here again a corruption may be suspected. Instead of הָלַךְ we should read חֵלְכוּ, which lost its final letter in consequence of the vau that immediately followed it. **And there remained the grove also in Samaria.** "The grove in Samaria" was that idolatrous emblem which Ahab had set up at Jezebel's suggestion (1 Kings xvi. 33), the nature of which has been much disputed. Some think that it was "an image of Astarte" (see 'Homiletic Commentary' on 1 Kings, p. 374); but more probably it was a mere emblem, analogous to the Assyrian "sacred tree." Its material may sometimes have been wood, but was perhaps more usually metal. The mistranslation "grove" originated with the Septuagint translators, who uniformly rendered אֲשֵׁרָה by ἄλσος. It is surprising that Jehu did not destroy the asherah together with the other idolatrous erections of Ahab in Samaria (ch. x. 26—28); but, for some reason or other, it seems to have been spared, and to have been still standing. So long as it stood, even if it did not attract the religious regards of any, it would be a standing dishonour to God, and would so increase the sin of the nation. Hence its mention in this passage.

Ver. 7.—**Neither did he leave of the people to Jehoahaz but fifty horsemen, and ten chariots, and ten thousand footmen.** This verse seems to be an exegetical note on ver. 4, which perhaps it once followed immediately, the parenthetic section (vers. 5 and 6) having been added later, as an afterthought, either by the original writer, or perhaps by a later hand. The meaning seems to be that Hazael limited the standing army of Jehoahaz to fifty horsemen, ten chariots, and ten thousand footmen, not that he slew the entire military population except this small remnant. The policy of limiting the forces to be maintained by a subjectking was one known to the Romans, and has often been adopted in the East. It is still a part of our own policy in the government of India. The limitation left the country at the mercy of all its neighbours (see ver. 20). **For the King of Syria had destroyed them, and had made them like the dust by threshing.** Possibly this means no more than an utter destruction—a trampling in the dust, as we phrase it (see Jer. li. 33; Micah iv. 12, 13; and perhaps Isa. xxi. 10). But it may be an allusion to that destruction of prisoners by means of a threshing instrument, which was certainly sometimes practised (2 Sam. xii. 31; Prov. xx. 26), and which is made a special charge against

Damascus (Amos i. 3. See Pusey's 'Minor Prophets,' p. 158).

Ver. 8.—**Now the rest of the acts of Jehoahaz, and all that he did, and his might**; rather, *his prowess*, or *his valour*. Though defeated and reduced to subjection by the Syrians, yet Jehoahaz had distinguished himself, and shown his own personal courage, in the course of the war. **Are they not written in the book of the chronicles of the kings of Israel?** (comp. ch. i. 18). The regular use of the phrase is one of the indications that the two Books of the Kings are by one author, and form one book.

Ver. 9.—**And Jehoahaz slept with his fathers; and they buried him in Samaria** (comp. 1 Kings xvi. 28; ch. x. 35; xiii. 13, etc.). The kings of Israel from the time of Omri were buried in the capital, Samaria, as those of Judah were in Jerusalem. It is uncertain whether they had one common mausoleum, like the kings of Judah (2 Chron. xxviii. 27), but it is most probable that they had. To rest with their fathers in the same royal sepulchre was to be duly honoured at their death; to be excluded from it was a disgrace. **And Joash his son reigned in his stead.**

Vers. 10—25.—THE REIGN OF JOASH. The writer passes from the reign of Jehoahaz, Jehu's son, to that of Joash, Jehu's grandson, which he seems to have intended at first to despatch in the short space of four verses (vers. 10—13). He afterwards, however, saw reason to add to his narrative, first, an account of an interview between Joash and Elisha, shortly before the death of the latter (vers. 14—19); secondly, an account of a miracle wrought soon afterwards by means of Elisha's corpse (vers. 20, 21); and thirdly, a brief notice of Joash's Syrian war (vers. 22—25).

Ver. 10.—**In the thirty and seventh year of Joash King of Judah.** Three years before his death, since he reigned forty years (ch. xii. 1). The two Joashes were thus contemporary monarchs for the space of three years. **Began Jehoash the son of Jehoahaz to reign over Israel in Samaria, and reigned sixteen years.** The construction is the same as that of ver. 1, and is equally ungrammatical. Our translators again amend the faulty phrase by introducing the words "and reigned." The "sixteen years" of the reign of Joash are confirmed by Josephus ('Ant. Jud.,' ix. 8. § 6), but still present some difficulty (see the comment on ch. xiv. 23).

Ver. 11.—**And he did that** which was evil in the sight of the Lord; he departed not from all the sins of Jeroboam the son of Nebat, who made Israel sin; but he walked therein. Josephus says that Joash was a good king, and quite unlike his father in disposition ('Ant. Jud.,' *l. s. c.*); but he is not likely to have had any independent data for judging of his character. Our author seems to include both son and father in the same category (comp. ver. 2). The narrative contained in ver. 14 is probably the foundation of the historian's favourable judgment.

Ver. 12.—**And the rest of the acts of Joash, and all that he did, and his might wherewith he fought against Amaziah King of Judah** (see ch. xiv. 11—14), **are they not written in the book of the chronicles of the kings of Israel?** Either this and the next verses have been displaced from their rightful position by some accident, or the author at one time intended to terminate his account of Joash at this point. The formula used is one which regularly closes the reign of each king. The proper place for it would have been after ver. 25.

Ver. 13.—**And Joash slept with his fathers; and Jeroboam sat upon his throne.** That Joash should call his eldest son Jeroboam, after the founder of the kingdom, indicated a thorough approval of that founder's policy and conduct, and perhaps a hope that he would be to the apparently decaying kingdom a sort of second founder. The name means, "he whose people is many," and was thus anticipative of that great enlargement of the Israelite kingdom, which took place under him (see ch. xiv. 25—28). **And Joash was buried in Samaria with the kings of Israel** (see the comment on ver. 9).

Ver. 14.—**Now Elisha was fallen sick of his sickness whereof he died.** Elisha, who was grown to manhood before the death of Ahab (1 Kings xix. 19), must have been at least eighty years old at the accession of Joash: His illness was therefore probably the result of mere natural decay. **And Joash the King of Israel came down unto him.** The visit of a king to a prophet, in the way of sympathy and compliment, would be a very unusual occurrence at any period of the world's history. In the East, and at the period of which the historian is treating, it was probably unprecedented. Prophets waited upon kings, not kings upon prophets: If a king came to a prophet's house, it was likely to be on an errand of vengeance (ch. vi. 32), not on one of kindness and sympathy: The act of Joash certainly implies a degree of tenderness and consideration on his part very uncommon at the time, and is a fact to which much weight should be attached in any estimate that we form of his character. He was, at any rate, a prince of an amiable disposition. **And wept over his face**—*i.e.* leant over the sick man as he lay on his bed, and shed tears, some of which fell *on* him—**and said, O my father, my father, the chariot of Israel, and the horsemen thereof.** As Elisha had addressed Elijah, when he was quitting the earth (ch. ii. 12), so Joash now addressed the dying Elisha, using exactly the same words, not (certainly) by a mere coincidence. Joash must have known the circumstances of Elijah's departure, which had probably been entered before this in the 'Book of the Kings,' and intended pointedly to allude to them. "O my father, my father," he meant to say, "when Elijah was taken from the earth, thou didst exclaim that the defence of Israel was gone" (see the comment on ch. ii. 12): "how much more must it be true that it is gone now, when thou art on the point of departure! He left thee as his successor; thou leavest no one!"

Ver. 15.—**And Elisha said unto him, Take bow and arrows.** The prophet was moved, no doubt, by a sudden inspiration. He was bidden to assure the weeping king of victory—speedy victory—over Syria. The defence of Israel would not fail because he —a mere weak instrument by whom God had been pleased to work—was taken from the earth. God would bless the king's own efforts. "Take bow and arrows," he exclaims under the prophetic afflatus. "Take them at once into thine hands, and do my bidding." Words would not have been enough; greater assurance and conviction was produced when prophecy took the shape of a symbolical action (comp. 1 Sam. xv. 27; 1 Kings xi. 30; Isa. xx. 3; Jer. xiii. 1—11; xviii. 3, 4, etc.). So the Spirit of the Lord moved the prophet to the performance of a symbolical act, or set of acts, which the historian now proceeds to describe. **And he took unto him bow and arrows.** Joash would take these from the hands of his attendants, who might be carrying his own special weapons after him, as was the practice in Persia ('Ancient Monarchies,' vol. iv. p. 161), or who would at any rate have arms of their own, since they would wait upon him not merely as attendants, but as guards.

Ver. 16.—**And he said to the King of Israel, Put thine hand upon the bow**—literally, *let thine hand ride upon the bow;* i.e. "Take it into active use—place thine hands as thou dost commonly for shooting"—**and he put his hand upon it**—he did as Elisha commanded—**and Elisha put his hands upon the king's hands.** Elisha, it would seem, rose from his bed, and took the attitude of an archer, covering the king's two hands with his own hands, and making as if he too was pulling the bow, so that the shooting

should be, or at least appear to be, the joint act of himself and the king. The intention was, no doubt, as Keil says, "to show that the power which was to be given to the bow-shot" was not the king's own power, but "came from the Lord through the mediation of his prophet."

Ver. 17.—**And he said, Open the window.** Though glass was unknown, or at any rate not applied to windows, yet the windows of sitting-rooms, and still more of bedrooms, had latticed shutters, which partially excluded the light and the air, and could be opened and closed at pleasure (see the comment on ch. i. 2). The prophet ordered the shutter to be opened, that the king might shoot from the window. He addressed, not the king, whose hands were both engaged, but his own servant, or one of the royal attendants. **Eastward.** Not so much in the direction of Syria, which was north-east of the Israelite territory, as in the direction of Gilead and Bashan, which had been the scene of Hazael's victories (ch. x. 33), and was now to be the scene of his reverses. Aphek lay almost due east of Shunem, where it is probable that Elisha was. **And he opened it;** or, *and one opened it,* or *they opened it.* The Hebrew idiom allows of this *indefinite* use of the third person singular. **Then Elisha said, Shoot. And he shot. And he**—*i.e.* Elisha—**said, The arrow of the Lord's deliverance, and the arrow of deliverance from Syria;** rather, *an arrow.* "This is," the prophet meant to say, "an arrow symbolical of deliverance about to come from Jehovah, of deliverance from the cruel oppression of the Syrians"—and not merely of deliverance, but of victory. **For thou shalt smite the Syrians in Aphek.** The Aphek intended is probably that which lay east of the Sea of Galilee, at the distance of about three miles, in lat. 32° 49' nearly. This place was on the direct route between Samaria and Damascus, and had already been the scene of one great victory gained by Israel over Syria (1 Kings xx. 26—30). The site is marked by the modern village of *Fik.* **Till thou have consumed** them; literally, *till consuming*—i.e. till the army which thou shalt defeat at that place is destroyed utterly. We have no account of the fulfilment of this prophecy, but may regard the defeat as one of those touched on in ver. 25.

Ver. 18.—**And he said, Take the arrows. And he took** them. Elisha bade the king take into his hand the remainder of the arrows which the quiver contained. This the king did, and held them in a bunch, as archers do when they have no quiver. **And he said unto the King of Israel, Smite upon the ground.** It is disputed what this means The LXX. translate Πάταξον εἰς τὴν γῆν

"Strike upon the ground;" and so Ewald, De Wette, and Thenius, who regard the order as one to strike with the arrows against the ground (*i.e.* the floor) or in the direction of the ground. Keil and Bähr, on the contrary, think that the order was to shoot the arrows down from the window and hit the earth with them. But some contrast seems to be intended between the "shoot" (יְרֵה) of ver. 19 and the "strike" (הַךְ) of the present passage. Ewald's explanation is thus to be preferred. **And he smote thrice, and stayed.** Joash struck with the arrows against the floor three times, and then paused, thinking he had done enough. He did not enter into the spirit of the symbolical act, which represented the smiting and slaying of enemies. Perhaps he had not much faith in the virtue of the symbolism, which he may even, with the arrogance of a proud and worldly minded man, have thought childish.

Ver. 19.—**And the man of God** (comp. ch. iv. 7, 25; vi. 6, 9; viii. 4, etc.) **was wroth with him.** Elisha was angered at the lukewarmness of Joash, and his lack of faith and zeal. He himself, from his higher standpoint, saw the greatness of the opportunity, the abundance of favour which God was ready to grant, and the way in which God's favour was stinted and narrowed by Joash's want of receptiveness. Had the king been equal to the occasion, a full end might at once have been made of Syria, and Israel might have been enabled to brace herself for the still more perilous struggle with Assyria, in which she ultimately succumbed. **And said, Thou shouldest have smitten five or six times; then hadst thou smitten Syria till thou hadst consumed it.** It has been suggested that Joash associated the number three with the notion of completeness, and "thought that what was done thrice was done perfectly" (Bahr); but in this case the prophet would scarcely have been angered. It is far more consonant with the entire narrative to suppose that he stopped from mere weariness, and want of strong faith and zeal. If he had been earnestly desirous of victory, and had had faith in the symbolical action as divinely directed, he would have kept on smiting till the prophet told him it was enough, or at any rate would have smitten the ground five or six times instead of three. The idea that he abstained from modesty or from prudence, "lest too extravagant demands might deprive him of all" (Von Gerlach), finds no support in the text of the narrative. He abstained (as Keil says) because "he was wanting in the proper zeal for obtaining the full promises of God." Had it been otherwise, the complete success obtained by Jeroboam II. (ch. iv. 25—

28) might have been anticipated by the space of fifteen or twenty years. Whereas now thou shalt smite Syria but thrice (comp. ver. 25, which declares that this prophecy was exactly accomplished).

Ver. 20.—**And Elisha died, and they buried him.** There had been no burial of Elijah, who "went up by a whirlwind into heaven" (ch. ii. 11). All the more anxious, therefore, would the Israelites be to bury their second great prophet with due honour. They prepared him, no doubt, one of those excavated sepulchres which were usual at the time and in the country—a squared or vaulted chamber cut in the native rock. St. Jerome says that the place of his sepulture was near Samaria ('Epitaph. Paulæ'), and this is sufficiently probable; but in the Middle Ages his grave was shown at Ruma, in Galilee (Ewald, 'Hist. of Israel,' vol. iv. p. 122, note 3). According to Josephus ('Ant. Jud.,' ix. 8. § 6), his funeral was magnificent. **And the bands of the Moabites invaded the land at the coming in of the year.** It seems to be implied that this was a usual occurrence. Just as the Syrians in the days of Naaman made marauding raids into the land from time to time (ch. v. 2), so now the Moabites each spring made an incursion. The weakness of Israel is strongly marked by this fact, and still more by the penetration of the Moabites so deep into their country. Amos (ii. 1) perhaps glances at these incursions of Moab.

Ver. 21.—**And it came to pass, as they were burying a man, that.** "They" is used indefinitely of some unnamed Israelites, like the French *on*. Certain persons, it does not matter who, were burying a man, *i.e.* about to bury him, and were carrying the corpse to the grave, when an interruption occurred. **Behold, they spied a band of men**—rather, *the band,* i.e. *the* band of that year—**and they cast the man into the sepulchre of Elisha.** There was no time for ceremony. Hastily, and somewhat roughly, it may be, the bearers of the body thrust it into Elisha's tomb, which happened to be at hand, and from the mouth of which they were able to remove the closing stone. They did not "throw" the body in, but pushed it in. **And when the man was let down.** The man was not "let down." Our translators seem to have been unacquainted with the Jewish mode of burial. They imagine that Elisha's tomb is a pit dug in the ground from the surface downwards, like a modern grave, and the man has therefore to be "let *down*," or to "go *down*" (marginal translation) into it. The Revised Version avoids the mistranslation, but weakens the force of the original. Translate, *and when the man came,* etc. **And touched the bones of Elisha, he revived.** The violent push given to the corpse imparted to it a movement which brought it in contact with the bones, *i.e.* the body (1 Kings xiii. 31) of Elisha, as it lay, wound in its grave-clothes, but uncoffined, on the floor of the sepulchral chamber. At the moment of contact the dead man came to life —"revived." **And stood up on his feet.** In many Jewish tombs the sepulchral chamber would allow of this.

Ver. 22.—**But Hazael King of Syria oppressed Israel all the days of Jehoahaz;** rather, *now Hazael King of Syria had oppressed Israel,* etc. The author, having parenthetically related the extraordinary miracle wrought by the instrumentality of Elisha's corpse, returns to the subject of the Syrian oppression. He had, in vers. 14—19, dwelt upon the promises of victory given by the prophet to Joash. He is now bent on relating their fulfilment. But before doing so he recapitulates. Ver. 22 refers back to ver. 3, and ver. 23 to vers. 4 and 5.

Ver. 23.—**And the Lord was gracious unto them, and had compassion on them.** Even in his wrath God "thinketh upon mercy." While he was still punishing Israel by the sword of Hazael, he was yet careful not to make a full end, not to allow the affliction to proceed too far. He still preserved the nation, and kept it in being. **And had respect unto them**—*i.e.* "considered them— kept them in his mind—did not permit them to slip out of his recollection"—**because of his covenant with Abraham, Isaac, and Jacob.** God's covenant with Abraham, Isaac, and Jacob was a covenant of mercy. By it he had pledged himself to multiply their seed, to be their God, and the God of their seed after them, and to give to their seed the whole land of Canaan for an *everlasting* possession (Gen. xvii. 4—8, etc.). This covenant bound him to extend his protection over the people of Israel so long as they had not utterly and entirely cast off their allegiance (comp. ch. xvii. 7—18). **And would not destroy them.** They were "persecuted, but not forsaken; cast down, but

not destroyed" (2 Cor. iv. 9). The national life might seem to hang by a thread, but the thread had not snapped. **Neither cast he them from his presence as yet.** The writer has it in his mind that ultimately they *were* cast away, rejected, removed out of God's sight (ch. xvii. 18, 20, 23); but it was not "as yet"—there was still an interval of a century, or a little more, before the blow fell, and the nation of the ten tribes ceased to exist.

Ver. 24.—**So Hazael King of Syria died;** rather, *and Hazael . . . died.* His death is a new fact, not involved in anything that has been previously stated. It appears by ver. 22 that he outlived Jehoahaz. **And Benhadad his son reigned in his stead.** Hazael, the usurper, gave his eldest son the name of the monarch whom he had murdered. It was an old royal name in Syria (1 Kings xv. 18), having been borne by at least two of Hazael's predecessors. The meaning which has been assigned to it ("Son of the sun") is doubtful.

Ver. 25.—**And Jehoash the son of Jehoahaz took again out of the hand of Benhadad the son of Hazael the cities, which he had taken out of the hand of Jehoahaz his father by war.** The capture of these cities by Benhadad had not been previously mentioned. It appears by the present passage, compared with ver. 22, that, during the lifetime of his father, Benhadad had led expeditions into the land of Israel, acting as his father's representative and general, and had made himself master of several Israelite towns. These were now recovered by Jehoash. They lay probably in the Cis-Jordanic territory. **Three times did Joash beat him, and recovered the cities of Israel** (comp. ver. 19). Thrice defeated, Hazael was forced to abandon his conquests in Western Samaria. He retained, however, the trans-Jordanic territory, which was not recovered by the Israelites till the reign of Jeroboam II. (see ch. xiv. 25).

HOMILETICS.

Vers. 1—7.—*God's severity and God's goodness alike shown in the history of Israel under Jehoahaz.* I. GOD'S SEVERITY. Two sins only are noted as existing among the people at this time—the calf-worship, and the maintenance of the "grove," or asherah (ver. 6). One of these, the worship of the calves, was ancestral. It had been an established usage for a hundred and twenty years, and had been upheld by every king from the date of its institution. Even the prophets, with one exception (1 Kings xiii. 2, 3), had not denounced it. The people at this time accepted it without question, and were probably quite unconscious that it was a sin at all. The other sin, the maintenance of the asherah, was negative rather than positive—the emblem still stood erect; it had not been removed—but it is not said that it was worshipped. Yet God, in his severity, visited the people for these two sins heavily, terribly (vers. 4 and 7). He did not accept thoughtlessness, unconsciousness, absence of any evil intention, as an excuse.

His honour was impugned by both practices, and he is very jealous of his honour. To leave the asherah standing, not to break it down, was to show a want of zeal for the purity of religion, for the honour of God, for the true faith, for virtue, for decency. To be indifferent to the calf-worship, to tolerate it, to continue it, was to live in constant violation of the second commandment. God could not, would not, tolerate this. If the conscience of the nation had gone to sleep, he must rouse it. By sharp pains, by severe afflictions, by actual agonies, if necessary, he must stir them from their self-satisfaction, awake them to self-examination and keen searchings of heart, and so bring them to a sense of their sinfulness, if not to a distinct recognition of their special sins.

II. God's goodness. As soon as any relenting is shown, as soon as the king acknowledges God's hand in his punishment, and turns to him and entreats his aid, even although he does not put a stop to the practices by which God's anger has been provoked (ver. 6), yet the Divine compassion is stirred. "The Lord hearkened unto him" (ver. 4). A saviour is given, in the Divine counsels, if not at once in fact. The nation's fall is arrested, its life prolonged. "O faithful Christian, if God heard Jehoahaz, how much more will he hear thee, if thou callest upon him! The Lord gave Israel a deliverer, but Jehoahaz did not live to see him. God hears the cry of those who earnestly call upon him, and helps them; but the time, and place, and manner of his aid are retained in his own discretion. Do not despair if thy prayer does not seem to be heard, and the Lord delays his assistance. He knows that fitting season as well as he knows what is useful to us" (Starke).

Ver. 6.—*The persistency of evil.* "There remained the grove." One would have thought that, in such a reformation as that of Jehu (ch. x. 15—28), there would have been a clean sweep, or, at any rate, that Ahab's pet idolatries (1 Kings xvi. 33) would have gone. But no! evil is terribly persistent. "The evil that men do lives after them," and not in men's recollections only, but in fact. No reformation ever sweeps away at once all that it was intended to sweep away. "The grove remains." How many heathen superstitions survived the supersession of heathenism by Christianity! How many iniquitous laws continue in all countries after every attempt that is made to reform the laws! How many abuses remain after each removal of abuses! The result is partly through the fault of the reformers, who are careless about doing their work thoroughly, and cease their efforts while much still remains to be done; but it is also caused in part by the tenacity of life which the things that need to be swept away possess in themselves. And, as evil is thus persistent in communities, so is it also in the character of individuals. *Naturam expellas furca, tamen usque recurret.* A man makes a great effort at self-reformation, changes his rules of conduct, his habits, the whole method of his life, as he thinks; but in some corner there still lurks a remnant of the old leaven, which shortly reasserts itself, and too often leavens the whole mass with its corrupting influence. The lesson to be learnt is watchfulness and perseverance. By care, by consideration, and by constant effort, the persistency of evil may be met and counteracted. God's Holy Spirit is always ready to assist our endeavours; and, whether in a community or in an individual, continued effort, divinely aided, will prevail at last.

Vers. 14—19.—*The closing scene of Elisha's life.* The time had come to Elisha which comes to all the sons of men, however great, however holy, at the last. He had exceeded man's ordinary term of three score years and ten—nay, he had exceeded the extended term of those who are exceptionally "strong" men, four score years (Ps. xc. 10)—but now at length he was overtaken by sickness, he was manifestly drawing near to death. What lessons does his departure teach us? It may teach us—

I. A lesson of consolation. It is a good thing so to have lived that our departure is felt as a loss, not merely to our family or to our own narrow circle of friends, but to our king and country. Not many persons can do the sort of service which Elisha did for Israel; but all may do some service. All may seek their country's good, labour for it, strive for it, pray for it. All may use the powers and talents committed to them by God in such a way that not themselves alone, but their country also, may derive advantage from them. Honest endeavours of this kind will at any rate bring to us "the answer of a good conscience" at the last—they may bring to us something more, viż. praise and acknowledgment on the part of those who represent the nation and have a right to speak on its behalf. Due acknowledgment is seldom grudged, when the end has come or approaches; and, though man's judgment is a "small thing" compared with God's, it is not altogether to be despised—we may feel in such acknowledgment a legitimate satisfaction.

II. A LESSON OF FORTITUDE. Elisha makes no moan, expresses no complaint. It is extraordinary how many men, even men who profess to believe in a future life of infinitely greater happiness than the present one, are discontented, and murmur, or even passionately cry out, when a mortal disease attacks them. And this although they have lived the full term of average human life in this world. Very few quit the scene gracefully, placidly, bravely. Almost all seem to regard the summons to set their house in order as untimely, and themselves as hardly used by the call being made upon them. There is always something for which they think they might as well have been allowed to wait—

"Half the cows to calve, and Barnaby Holmes to plough."

III. A LESSON OF PERSEVERANCE AND EFFORT TO THE VERY END. Elisha, though stricken with a mortal disease, does not give himself up to inaction, or cease to take an interest in the affairs of this life. On the contrary, he has his country's welfare most deeply at heart, and initiates and carries through a scene, in which his physical powers must have been severely tasked, for encouraging king and people in their death-struggle with Syria, and assuring them of final victory. The confidence inspired may have been a serious factor in the result. Elisha, at his age, might have been excused, had he remained wholly passive, and received the king's visit as the compliment which it was intended to be; but he could not be content without utilizing the visit to the utmost. He rouses the king from his despair (ver. 14); inspires in him hope, courage, energy; promises him success, actively participates in the symbolic drama, which at once indicates and helps forward the result aimed at. We may learn from this that, while we live, we have active duties to perform; we are not *exauctorati* till the last summons comes; on our sick-bed, on our death-bed, we may still be agents for good—we may advise, exhort, incite, rebuke evil (ver. 19), and be active ministers of good, impressing men more than we ever did before, when we speak from the verge of the grave, and having our "strength made perfect in weakness."

Vers. 20, 21.—*Life in death.* The miracle wrought by the instrumentality of Elisha's bones would seem to have been designed for three main ends or purposes.

I. FOR THE HONOUR OF THE PROPHET; that so he might have in his death (as Elijah had had in the method of his departure) a testimony from God that he was approved by him, and that he would have him respected and honoured by his countrymen. Worship of relics was not a Jewish superstition; and thus there was no danger of those ill results which followed on the alleged miracles wrought by the bodies of Christian martyrs. Those who witnessed or heard of the miracle in Elisha's tomb were led to venerate the memory of the prophet, to whom so great a testimony had been given; and might thence be moved to pay greater attention and stricter obedience to what they knew of his teaching.

II. FOR THE ENCOURAGEMENT OF THE NATION. The death of Elisha was no doubt felt as a national calamity. Many, besides the king, must have seen in it the loss to the nation of one who was more to it than "chariots and horsemen" (ver. 14). Despondency, we may be sure, weighed down the spirits of numbers who might think that God, in withdrawing his prophet, had forsaken his people. It was a great thing to such persons that they should have a clear manifestation that, though the prophet was gone, God still continued present with his people, was still among them, ready to help, potent to save. The more spiritually minded might view the miracle as symbolical, and interpret it to mean that, as the dead man had sprung to life again on contact with Elisha's bones, so the dead nation should, as it were, rise out of his tomb and recover itself, once more standing on its feet, in full possession of all its energies.

III. FOR THE HONOUR OF GOD, AND THE SHOWING FORTH OF HIS TRANSCENDENT POWER. To give life is among the highest of the Divine attributes. It is God's special privilege, one that he cannot communicate to a creature. Even modern scientists bow their heads before the mysterious, inconceivable act, and confess that they find it impossible to present it distinctly to their consciousness. But to give life to that which is held by death, in which decay is begun, which is under the law of dissolution and corruption, is a still more incomprehensible thing, stranger, more astonishing. And to crown all by bringing the new life out of death, making a dead corpse the source out of which vitality shall leap forth to fresh energy, is to surpass all that the most lively fancy could imagine of wonderful, and almost to reconcile contradictions. God willed at this time to show that he could effect even this marvellous thing—make death give life to that which was recently dead—educe from one dead in him the vital power that should resuscitate and reanimate another also dead, and make a tomb— the place of death—the scene of the transformation! " O Lord, thou art my God ; I will exalt thee, I will praise thy Name ; for thou hast done wonderful things " (Isa. xxv. 1); truly " wonderful art thou in thy doing towards the children of men " (Ps. lxvi. 4).

The miracle of Elisha's bones is no argument for relic-worship. Relic-worship implies a belief that a virtue exists in the remnants of a deceased saint's body, which enables them of themselves to exercise a miraculous power. Elisha's bones were never thought to possess any such property. They were not exhumed, placed in cases, or exhibited to the faithful to be touched with the hand or kissed by the lips. It was understood that God had been pleased to work one miracle by them ; it was never supposed that they might be expected to work any more. They were therefore suffered to remain in the tomb wherein they had been from the first deposited. It was not till the time of Julian that any importance was attached to them ; though then we must conclude that they had become objects of reverential regard, since the Apostate took the trouble to burn them.

HOMILIES BY VARIOUS AUTHORS.

Vers. 1—13, with 22—25.—*The reigns of Jehoahaz and Joash, kings of Israel.* Observe here—

I. The perpetuity of evil. How sad it is to read of one king after another, " He did that which was evil in the sight of the Lord " ! And then the statement is usually made, " He departed not from the sins of Jeroboam the son of Nebat, who made Israel to sin." A bad man does harm to others besides himself. " None of us liveth to himself." Not merely while we live, but after we are gone, our lives and words and deeds will influence others. We may think ourselves very obscure and insignificant, so insignificant that we may argue it does not matter to others how we live. But who can measure the circle of his influence? In ways that we know not, influence may reach other hearts and other lives. Oh! how dangerous is one evil influence in a community! It takes a long time to do away with its effects.

> " The evil that men do lives after them ;
> The good is oft interrèd with their bones."

Let us be careful how we are influencing others. For good or for evil we are exercising some influence, however unconsciously, on those around us. If we would influence men for good, we ourselves must live near to God.

II. The mercy of God. God punished Jehoahaz and his people for their sins. " He delivered them into the hand of Hazael King of Syria, and into the hand of Benhadad the son of Hazael, all their days." When suffering or troubles come, let us see whether the cause of them is not within our own hearts and lives. *But he mingled mercy with judgment.* God is ever on the watch for signs of the prodigal's return. His ear is ever open for the cry of penitence, for the faintest prayer for forgiveness and help. " Jehoahaz besought the Lord, and the Lord hearkened unto him ; for he saw the oppression of Israel, because the King of Syria oppressed them " (ver. 4 ; see also ver. 23).

> " Come, let us to the Lord our God
> With contrite hearts return ;
> Our God is gracious, nor will leave
> The desolate to mourn.

> " His voice commands the tempest forth,
>   And stills the stormy wave;
> And, though his arm be strong to smite,
>   'Tis also strong to save."

III. HUMAN INGRATITUDE. Though God delivered them from their difficulty and distress, and gave them peace from their enemies, yet, when the difficulty was over, they forgot all about God's mercy. They went back to their old sins. " Nevertheless they departed not from the sins of the house of Jeroboam the son of Nebat, . . . but walked therein " (ver. 6). How prone the human heart is to forsake God! The Books of Judges and Kings are full of illustrations of this painful fact. By forsaking God the Israelites brought themselves into misery and bondage. Time after time God raised up judges and kings and prophets to be the means of their deliverance. But when these were dead, or when the immediate danger had passed away, once again the people forsook God. It is the same in the history of the individual. How ungrateful we are for God's unceasing and unfailing goodness! How forgetful of his commandments and his promises! " The way of man is not in himself; and it is not in man that walketh to direct his steps." We need all the influence of Divine grace to keep us in the way that is right.

IV. A HUMBLED NATION. To what a low level sin reduces a nation! How shamefully Israel was humiliated before Syria! The King of Syria only left to Jehoahaz fifty horsemen, ten chariots, and ten thousand footmen; " for the King of Syria had destroyed them, and had made them like the dust by threshing." The fate of Israel, the fate of other mighty nations of the past, are a great national lesson to be remembered so long as the world shall last. Ought we not earnestly to pray that this great British empire, which has been built up by God-fearing men, and which God has blessed and honoured so highly, may not forsake God for secularism or gross corruption, and thus fall into the fate of the fallen nations of the past? Knowing how great are the forces of evil, it becomes every true Christian to be more valiant for the truth, to be more active in everything that will extend the kingdom of Christ in this and other lands.—C. H. I.

Vers. 14—19.—*A royal visit to a dying prophet.* What a peaceful death-bed Elisha's was! He had long since made his choice. He had lived not for time, but for eternity; not under the fear of man, but under the fear of God; not for the favour of kings or their rewards, but so as to win the approval of his conscience and his Creator. And now, when death came, it brought him no terrors. Not only so, but he was able to give encouragement to others. When King Joash sees the prophet on his death-bed, he feels how great is the loss which Israel is about to sustain. Good men are a nation's strength. And so Joash, bending in tears over the dying prophet's couch, exclaims, " O my father, my father, the chariot of Israel, and the horsemen thereof!" But Elisha wants to keep up his heart. He wants to teach him that, though the prophet dies, the prophet's God remains. The workmen pass away, but the work of God goes on. So the true Christian will ever look beyond his own death to the glory that awaits him, beyond the present hour of darkness or difficulty or delay to the ultimate triumph of the Church of Christ. It was in this spirit that the martyrs died. What a vision of the future lit up their suffering faces! What a prophetic instinct in such words as those which Bishop Latimer spoke to his fellow-reformer Ridley, as they stood side by side, waiting for the faggots to be kindled : " Be of good cheer, brother Ridley, and play the man; we shall this day light such a candle in England, as by God's grace shall never be put out." And here Elisha on his death-bed gives utterance to prophetic words. He told Joash that the arrow which, in obedience to his directions, he had shot forth from the open window, signified the arrow of the Lord's deliverance. But Joash was slow to learn the double lesson of God's unlimited power and the necessity for human effort which this simple illustration taught. Elisha had already told him that he should smite the Syrians till they were consumed, and then, *to teach him furthermore the necessity for perseverance and patience,* he commands him to smite upon the ground. Joash, seeing that the prophet had already revealed to him so much and encouraged him so greatly, might have continued until he was requested to cease. But instead of that, he only smote three times, and then gave up. Thus he illustrated his own want of faith in God's almighty power, his own want of patience and perseverance, and therefore how little he deserved God's interference on his behalf. The old proverb truly says, "God helps those that help themselves." The chief lesson of this incident is—*Want of faith a hindrance to success in Christian work.*

I. CHRISTIANS SHOW WANT OF FAITH, ALTHOUGH THEY HAVE DIVINE PROMISES. It was so here in the case of Joash. He had stood beside the bedside of Elisha in a state of utter dismay. It had seemed to him as if he already saw the downfall of his kingdom, as if all other resources were useless if the man of God, who had so often guided kings and people to victory, was taken away. But look at the encouragement which Elisha had given him. He had taken his thoughts away from human wisdom and human strength, and turned them upward to the almighty, unlimited power of God. "*The arrow of the Lord's deliverance.*" What suggestions of power, of help, of victory, were in those simple words! *The Lord's deliverance!* That almighty power which delivered Israel out of the hand of Pharaoh; that almighty power which turned back the waves of the Red Sea, and brought the people over safely on dry land; that almighty power which, only a few years since, filled the dry valley with water and thus gave victory to Israel, and which, by smiting the Syrians with blindness, delivered Israel out of the hands of their enemies;—that almighty power, O Joash, will be with *you, will deliver you.* Oh, what a thrill of determination, of resolute, energetic purpose, should have been awakened in his mind! Might he not reasonably have felt, "Yes, the Lord is on my side. Victory is sure. I shall redouble my efforts against the enemies of Israel, against the workers of evil. Out of gratitude to God I shall serve the Lord only"? But Joash failed when put to the test. When Elisha gave him an opportunity of showing his faith by his own efforts, he only showed how little faith he had in the promises of God. If we believe that God's Word is true, that his promises are true, it is but reasonable that he should expect us to act on them. To every unsaved soul God says, "Believe on the Lord Jesus Christ, and thou shalt be saved." The promise is salvation. But there is a duty, a condition, a necessity, coupled with it. That duty is faith in Christ—taking him as our Saviour, serving him as our King. How many act like Joash! They would like to get to heaven, but they are not willing to tread the narrow path. They would like to obtain salvation, but they are not willing to take God's way of obtaining it. They say, "If I'm to be saved, I shall be saved." To any one who has been thinking about eternity and the judgment to come, whose heart has been softened by sickness or bereavement, who has been impressed by any message from God's Word, but has not yet accepted Christ, we would say, "Stay not thine hand. Let not the good impressions pass away." "Then shall we know, if we follow on to know the Lord." Arise to-day, and in the strength of God smite your unbelief, smite the tempter to the ground. Strive to enter in at the narrow door. Then shall that good impression, then shall that warning voice, prove to be to you *the arrow of the Lord's deliverance.* Take the step, fulfil the condition, if you would obtain the blessing. The same applies to *Christian work.* How many call themselves God's servants, how many expect the reward of the faithful servant, who are doing absolutely nothing for the Lord! Jesus has given one very precious promise to his people: "Lo, I am with you alway, even unto the end of the world;" but it is to those who in some way are seeking to fulfil that command, "Go ye therefore, and preach the gospel to every creature." The truth is, the promise depends upon the work, and the work depends upon the promise. We cannot expect God's blessings if we are not doing his work. And we cannot do his work if we do not meditate much on his promises.

II. CHRISTIANS SHOW WANT OF FAITH, ALTHOUGH THEY HAVE PROOFS OF DIVINE POWER. In the history of his nation, even in the history of Elisha's life alone, Joash had many proofs of Divine power, yet still he showed a want of faith in God. In the whole history of God's kingdom in the world, in the whole history of the Christian Church, *we* have proofs of God's power, yet where is our faith at all proportionate to the strength of evidence on which it rests? There is no stronger testimony to the power of the gospel than *the history of modern missions.* It is just seventy years since the first missionaries landed in Madagascar; it is not thirty years since the terrible persecutions ceased there, by which the missionaries were driven out of the island, and the little companies of Christians who survived the massacre met for worship in secret, in dens and caves of the mountains, and were in constant danger of their lives.   Yet in that large island to-day there is a Christian population of nearly three hundred thousand, the idols have been publicly burned, and the Christian religion is publicly recognized by the state.   What hath God wrought!   Think of the work which Dr. Moffat accomplished among the degraded tribes of South Africa, not so many years ago.   The conversion of Africaner, the Hottentot chief, under his ministry, is well known.   Every one warned Moffat against him as a man who was a terror to the whole neighbourhood. But Moffat thought he was just the man to go to with the gospel.   He went, and was the means of leading the savage chief to Christ, and "Africaner's changed life convinced many, who had never believed in them before, of the efficacy of Christian missions."   Think of the progress of Christianity in Japan, in India, in China.   The following testimony was recently borne to mission work in China in his report to the Foreign Office by the late British Consul at Newchwang.   He says, "The labours of the missionaries indirectly benefit our merchants, manufacturers, and artisans.   I further believe that, partly owing to the Christian principles disseminated by the missionaries, the tone of morality among the Chinese people has during the last twenty years perceptibly attained a higher platform."   The Rev. William Swanson, a veteran missionary, and lately moderator of the English Presbyterian Church, states that when he went to China twenty-six years ago there were only five small churches at the treaty ports.   Now, in going from Canton to Shanghai, and travelling twenty or twenty-five miles a day, he could sleep every night, with one or two exceptions, in a village having a Christian church.   The first time Charles Darwin visited the island of Tierra del Fuego, he said that the people there were irreclaimable.   He saw four Christian Fuegians at a meeting in England, and was so impressed by what he heard of the work of the missionaries that he became an annual subscriber to the funds of the Missionary Society, and said he should feel proud if the committee would think fit to elect him one of its honorary members.   When we think of these things, of the wonderful work done in the South Sea Islands, and of the many nations where heathenism has yielded to the preaching of the cross, surely we may well say, "What hath God wrought!" To-day, just as in St. Paul's day, the gospel is "the power of God unto salvation to every one that believeth."   If we doubt the power of the gospel, our doubts are in the face of overwhelming and irresistible facts.

III. The evil results of this want of faith.   This want of faith has ill results on life and practice and Christian work.   Many who went part of the way with Christ turned back and walked no more with him because of their want of faith.   It is so still.   *Want of faith leads to low expectations and feeble efforts.*   True faith in God's presence and power, instead of making us inactive and careless, is the greatest stimulus to activity.   It rouses us to put forth all our energies.   It makes us patient under difficulties.   It causes us to persevere even when we see no immediate result. How many a good work has been begun, but given up, because of want of faith!   *This was nearly being the case at one time with what has since proved one of the most successful missions to the heathen.*   After twelve years' labour in the island of Tahiti, in the Pacific, the mission seemed to be an utter failure.   All but one of the missionaries left the South Sea Islands.   At home the directors of the London Missionary Society seriously discussed the abandoning of the mission.   But two members of the committee, men of strong faith in God and the gospel, strenuously opposed this, and proposed a season of special prayer for a blessing on its work.   This was agreed to; letters of encouragement were written to the missionaries; and while the ship that bore these letters was on her way to Tahiti, *another ship was bearing to England the rejected idols of the people.*   How had this happened?   Some of the missionaries who had left the island were led in some way to return.   One morning one of them went out into the fields for meditation, when he heard, with a thrill of joy, the voice of a native raised in prayer to God—the first token that their teaching had been blessed in Tahiti.   Soon they heard of others. A Christian Church was formed.   The priests publicly burned their idols; and thus, after a night of toil of sixteen years, the dawn at last broke (see 'Outlines of Protestant Missions,' by Rev. John Robson, D.D.).   What a rebuke to the weak faith of the directors who had proposed to abandon the mission!   What a lesson to every minister and missionary, to every Sunday-school teacher, to every Christian worker, *not to stay their hand, even when they see no results of their labour!* "He that goeth forth and weepeth, bearing precious seed, shall doubtless come again with rejoicing, bringing his sheaves with him." Work done for God never dies. *Stay not your hand in the matter of your own spiritual life.* Persevere in the conflict with your besetting sins. Persevere in the cultivation of Christian graces. Use the arrow of the Lord's deliverance. Put on the whole armour of God. *Persevere also in prayer for others.* Never give up as hopeless a single soul. Stay not thine hand. *You* can't do much for them, perhaps, but God can. Lay the case of erring child or godless friend before God in prayer. Ask him to open their eyes. Ask the Lord Jesus to lay his hand upon them—to speak the word only, and they shall be made whole. *Persevere also in Christian work.* "Be not weary in well-doing." Leave no work unfinished for which God gives you the strength and the means. Perhaps we have been shooting too few arrows, making too little effort in God's cause. Seek the guidance of God's hand and the power which God's presence gives, and then go forth to win victories for him.—C. H. I.

Vers. 20, 21.—*A resurrection and its lessons.* This miracle was wrought, in a time of prevailing unbelief, to teach a lesson to a faithless age. Strange sight indeed—for those who were engrossed with the sensual pleasures of the present world, thus unexpectedly to be brought face to face with the power of the Unseen!

I. GOD'S POWER TO RAISE THE DEAD. Here was something which their heathen gods could never do. Heathenism, agnosticism,—these systems bring no comfort to the bereaved and sorrowing spirit. Christ alone has brought life and immortality to light through the gospel. None but he has ever dared to say, "I am the Resurrection and the Life."

II. THE UNDYING INFLUENCE OF GOOD MEN. "Non omnis moriar" was the saying of the old heathen poet. But the humblest Christian who is faithful to God may have confidence that his influence for good will continue long after he has passed away from earth. 1. *Elisha's words were to continue.* The prophet was dead, but his words still lived. His words were the words of God. "Heaven and earth shall pass away, but my words shall not pass away." We see in the twenty-fifth verse how Elisha's prediction to Joash was literally fulfilled. Three times Joash defeated the Syrians and recovered the cities of Israel. Elisha's words still remain, to be our consolation and comfort. 2. *Elisha's work remained.* The memory of his faithfulness to God, of the wonders he was able to do by God's presence with him, remained to be a help and stimulus to many faithful servants of God when Israel was growing worse and worse. A good man's influence—who can tell how long it may last, or what unexpected places and persons it may reach?—C. H. I.

Vers. 1—21.—*The death of Elisha.* "In the three and twentieth," etc. The Book of Kings is, to a large extent, a record of crime, and of crime of the most heinous and aggravated character. The terrible monstrosities recorded are, for the most part, ascribable, directly or indirectly, to kings. In this very chapter we have a sketch of two of those monarchs who have been among the greatest curses of their race. Jehoahaz, son and successor of Jehu King of Israel, whose reign was disastrous to the kingdom to such a degree that his army was all but utterly destroyed, and had become like the dust on the "threshing-floor;" and Jehoash, who for three years was associated with his father in the government, and who, when his father was swept away, was a curse to the world for sixteen years. The only portion of this chapter which requires notice is from ver. 14 to ver. 21. These verses present to us four subjects of thought—a great man dying; a good man leaving the world interested in posterity; a wicked man regretting the event; and a dead man exerting a wonderful influence.

I. A GREAT MAN DYING. "Now Elisha was fallen sick of his sickness whereof he died." The whole history of Elisha is not only the history of the marvellous, but the history of loyalty to Heaven and of devotion to the interests of the Israelite race. But here we find this great and good man dying. Elijah, his master, had escaped death and had been borne to heaven in a chariot of fire, but Elisha had to die in the ordinary way of mankind, through sickness. It is true he was an old man; threescore years had passed since he commenced his prophetic ministry. For a great many years we are told nothing about him, but no doubt he had been actively and usefully engaged.

Even the most useful public men, and the most popular too, cease to attract great public attention as they pass into years. Often they become as "dead men out of sight," albeit they are useful. Though all men have to die, death is not the same to all men. It has a widely different significance to different men. To the good man it is life breaking through exuviæ and taking wing to revel in a sunny universe. It is the "mortal putting on immortality."

II. A WICKED MAN REGRETTING THE EVENT. "And Joash the King of Israel came down unto him, and wept over his face, and said, O my father, my father!" Why did he weep? Not because he had any sympathy with the character of the departing man. His moral sympathies were in antagonism to those of the prophet. Not because he felt that the prophet himself would suffer loss. He was not thinking of the prophet's gaining or losing by death. Not because he knew that the event would be a loss to the living in general. He cared nothing for his race, not he; but because he knew that the prophet was the "chariot of Israel, and the horsemen thereof." His chariots and horsemen were gone, and Elisha was his only hope.

III. A GOOD MAN LEAVING THE WORLD INTERESTED IN POSTERITY. Elisha, though dying, still took an interest in the future of his country. "Elisha said unto him, Take bow and arrows. And he took unto him bow and arrows," etc. (vers. 15—19). Elisha seems to have been touched by the king's tears; and he held out the hope that he would yet become victorious over the Syrians. The symbolic action which the prophet recommended, putting his hand upon the bow, opening the window, shooting the arrow, smiting the ground, does not, I think, necessarily mean that the prophet approved of the future wars of the king, but merely indicated the fact. He foretold his success; for, in three campaigns against the Syrians, he recovered the cities which they had taken from his father. He was also successful in the war with Amaziah King of Judah. But the point worth notice is the interest felt in the future by the prophet in his dying hours. Had he not done with life? Would he not soon be in his grave? What would the world be to him in the future? An interest in posterity seems to be an instinct in humanity. There is a nerve in humanity that runs through all races and all generations, linking men together. "No man liveth to himself;" all men are in one. The more moral goodness a man has in him the more sensitive this nerve becomes. Hence the best men in all ages have been the men who made provision for posterity.

IV. A DEAD MAN EXERTING A WONDERFUL INFLUENCE. "It came to pass, as they were burying a man, that, behold, they spied a band of men; and they cast the man into the sepulchre of Elisha: and when the man was let down, and touched the bones of Elisha, he revived, and stood up on his feet." The incident which takes place in his grave is as strange as it is significant and suggestive. The bearers of a dead man, struck with terror at the approach of enemies, instead of carrying the remains to their appointed resting-place, pushed them into the sepulchre where slept the bones of the illustrious Elisha. No sooner did the corpse touch the sacred relics of the great seer than it quivered with life, and the dead man, to the astonishment of all, revived, and stood on his feet. This miraculous incident was designed and calculated to make a wholesome moral impression on the mind of the age. It had a tendency to demonstrate to all the Divinity of the prophet's mission, to show the honour with which the Eternal treats the holy dead, to prove the existence of a Power superior to death, and to foreshadow a future state. Whilst I would at all times studiously endeavour to avoid the mistake of what is called spiritualizing God's Word, I feel that it is lawful to use an incident like this as an illustration of spiritual realities. The incident which occurred in the grave of Elisha on this occasion, viz. the deriving of life by contact with the holy dead, is, in the material department of things to which it belongs, sublimely singular. Such an event as this, perhaps, will never occur again; but a thing analogous to this in the spiritual domain is, thank God, of frequent occurrence. The dead minds of earth are constantly deriving life from contact with the spiritual remains of the dead.—D. T.

Vers. 1—7.—*Israel's humiliation under Jehoahaz.* The story of the reign of Jehoahaz, Jehu's son, is a story of unmitigated misfortune. We note—

I. JEHOAHAZ'S EVIL REIGN. 1. *The downward movement in Israel.* With the extinction of Ahab's house, the rooting out of Baal, and the establishment of Jehu's dynasty, Israel obtained a new chance of doing well. But Jehu's reforming zeal soon died out, and he fell back into godless ways. His son followed the worse, and not the better, traditions of his father's reign. Thus the downward movement again began. Of Jehoahaz also the old monotonous refrain has to be spoken, "He did that which was evil in the sight of the Lord." This is the burden of the song regarding every king of Israel. In the whole line, from first to last, there is not one of whom a different report can be given. 2. *The cardinal sin.* The foremost sin of all these monarchs—that which fatally entangled them in other sins—was the perpetuation of the worship of the calves. Religion affects the springs of morality, and this idolatrous *cultus* sent poisonous streams through the whole life of the nation. It was the grand transgression which, amidst all temporary reforms, was never abandoned.

II. THE SYRIAN OPPRESSION. 1. *Divine anger.* "The anger of the Lord was kindled against Israel." God had done so much for the people, had granted them so favourable an opportunity for repentance, had counselled and warned them so long by great prophets like Elijah and Elisha, that he was justly wroth with them for their continued transgressions. God is jealous of his honour, and presumptuous transgressors must expect to find his hand laid heavily upon them. When God's anger is kindled against a people, things cannot go well. Troubles break out on every side, and calamities fall thick and fast. 2. *Weighty chastisements.* God delivered the people of Israel into the hands of the kings of Syria—Hazael and Benhadad. This time it was no passing invasion. The completeness of the conquest, and the severity of the oppression, recall the days of the judges, or the Philistine oppression of the reign of Saul (Judg. v. 6, 7; 1 Sam. xiii. 19—22). Out of the hosts of Israel there was left to Jehoahaz but fifty horsemen, and ten chariots, and ten thousand footmen. Elisha's foresight of the evils which Hazael would inflict on the nation was thus terribly verified. Again is the reflection forced on us—How bitter is the fruit of sin! The Bible is little else than a repeated enforcement of the truth, "Say ye to the righteous, that it shall be well with him. . . . Woe unto the wicked! it shall be ill with him: for the reward of his hands shall be given him" (Isa. iii. 10, 11).

III. JEHOAHAZ'S PRAYER, AND ITS ANSWER. 1. *The king's prayer.* The very existence of the kingdom seemed threatened. Happily, the desperate straits to which he was reduced led Jehoahaz to humble himself before God. He felt himself in the hands of a living God, and, rightly tracing the calamities which had befallen him to Jehovah's anger, he turned to Jehovah for his help. The chastisements with which God visits men for their sins are designed to break their pride and stubbornness, and lead them to repentance. They often have the effect of producing a temporary submission, though they cannot of themselves change the heart. We have examples in Pharaoh (Exod. viii. 28) and in Ahab (1 Kings xxi. 27). 2. *God's answer to the prayer.* A prayer wrung from the king, not by the sense of his sin, but by the intolerable pressure of affliction, might have been thought undeserving of an answer. But the Lord is very pitiful, and welcomes the faintest approach of the sinner unto him. He does not thrust the suppliant away, but seeks, by giving him tokens of his grace, to ripen his imperfect desires into real repentance. Accordingly, the approaches of Jehoahaz to the throne of grace met with a gracious response. God promised a saviour to the land, and ultimately raised one up in the person of Joash, who, but for his want of perseverance, would have completely delivered the nation from the Syrians. The work which he left undone was finished by his son, Jeroboam II. Thus God shows himself ready to hear the cries even of the worst of men. None need despair in calling on Heaven when Jehoahaz was listened to in such dire straits. Happy they who are led to call, though it be from the depths, to God (Ps. cxxx. 1). He will not turn any away. His promise is, "Call upon me in the day of trouble: I will deliver thee" (Ps. l. 15). 3. *Imperfect repentance.* The imperfection of Jehoahaz's repentance is seen in the fact that the worship of the calves was still maintained; also there remained the symbol of Astarte in Samaria. God's promise having been given, was not revoked, and there were other reasons why he was willing to help the people (ver. 23). But these sins in high places wrought ruin afterwards.—J. O.

Vers. 8—19.—*Joash and Elisha.* Jehoahaz reigned for seventeen years, and was succeeded by his son Jehoash, or Joash. In this reign, after a long interval, Elisha again appears.

I. ACCESSION OF JOASH. The change of rulers was in some respects a gain for Israel. Joash was a man of better disposition than his father, and under his reign the kingdom, which had been so sorely broken down, was again partially built up. But he still adhered to the cardinal sin of the nation—the calf-worship—so that of him also the formula has to be employed, " He did that which was evil in the sight of the Lord." That is, notwithstanding military successes, and some signs of respect for and attention to Elisha's monitions, things still remained on a fundamentally false basis in the kingdom. So Herod feared John the Baptist, and observed him, and, when he heard him, did many things, and heard him gladly, yet remained a bad man (Mark vi. 20). God's judgment on men is not according to superficial characteristics, but according to the fundamental bent of their minds.

II. ELISHA ON HIS DEATH-BED. 1. *Elisha's sickness.* Elisha by this time was a very old man. He was Elijah's attendant in the reign of Ahab; he was a prominent figure in the reigns of Ahaziah and Jehoram; he gave the commission to Jehu to overthrow the incurably corrupt dynasty of Ahab, and lived through the twenty-eight years of that king's reign; he witnessed the troubles of the reign of Jehoahaz, and was per-haps the means of that monarch being led to humble himself before God; now, in Joash's reign, he is still alive. From the time of Jehu's accession he seems to have taken little part in the political life of the nation; at least, no accounts of his activity remain to us. When the curtain again lifts he is lying on his death-bed. It was not to be with him as with Elijah. He must pay the common debt to nature, experience the infirmities of age, be smitten with sickness, and succumb to death. The longest and most useful life thus comes to its close. It is well when, on a death-bed, one can look back on a life which has been spent in the service of God. 2. *The visit of Joash.* To the bedside of the dying Elisha came the King of Israel, apparently drawn thereto by sincere reverence and respect for the aged prophet. He came to him, it is said, and wept, saying, " O my father, my father, the chariot of Israel, and the horsemen thereof!" This language speaks to former relations of intimacy and friendship between the king and prophet. Probably Elisha had been the counsellor of his youth, and had guided and encouraged him in his duties as king. It is to be remembered also that the promised deliverance from the Syrians was not yet begun. The kingdom was still in humiliation and distress, and Joash may have felt as if, with the death of Elisha, the last spark of hope for the nation would be extinguished. We see how, in the hour of extremity, good men are felt, even by the ungodly, to be a tower of strength to the state. Their presence and prayers are its truest bulwark. The full extent of the loss sustained by their removal is only realized when they are taken away. We see also how possible it is to have great respect for God's servants, to appreciate their worth to the community, and to weep over and deeply regret their loss, and yet not do the things that they say. Joash shows fairly well in this narrative, but his conduct as a whole is stamped as "evil in the sight of the Lord."

III. THE ARROW OF DELIVERANCE. Once again had mighty deliverances for Israel been announced through Elisha. The last was to be the greatest of all. 1. *The pledge of deliverance.* Raising himself up on his bed, prophetic fire gleaming in his eye, Elisha bade the young and stalwart king take his bow and arrows. Joash did as the prophet required, not yet understanding his meaning, but no doubt forecasting some encouraging message. Elisha then bade him put his hand upon his bow, and placing his own hands on the king's, told him further to open the window eastward, and shoot. This was done. Then the symbolic action was explained. That arrow he had shot into the air was the arrow of the Lord's deliverance, an arrow pledging deliver-ance from the yoke of Syria. It was shot eastwards, because the Syrian ravages were com-monly from that quarter (ch. x. 32, 33). The action declares: (1) That deliverance in trouble is from God only. As he alone can give it, so he is the true Source from which to seek it. (2) God employs human agency in his deliverances. The bow and arrows were the symbols of the human instrumentality. Joash had to put his hands upon the bow. It was he who shot the arrow. It was he who was to smite the Syrians. Man has his part given him in all God's works of deliverance on earth. (3) The human agent could only succeed as God strengthened him. Elisha put his hands upon Joash's, signifying that the power to gain the predicted victories came from God. His hands were to be "made strong by the hands of the mighty God of Jacob" (Gen. xlix. 24). It is on God's power we must always rely for victory. "Not unto us, O Lord, not unto us," etc. (Ps. cxv. 1). 2. *The victories in detail.* The symbol was not yet complete. Joash's quiver was yet full, minus that one arrow, and the prophet bade him shoot other arrows, this time to the ground, as if smiting something down to it. Joash took his arrows and began to smite. He shot once, and twice, and thrice, then stayed. The prophet was wroth at this, and told him he should have gone on smiting, then would the Syrians have been wholly consumed, whereas now he would only gain three victories over them. These successive smitings, therefore, represented the victories in detail which Joash would gain over the Syrians. One is at a loss at first to see why the prophet should have dealt so severely with the king for what may have been a perfectly natural mistake. But the stopping with the third arrow no doubt brought to light a certain weak line in Joash's character—a want of perseverance, a tendency to be satisfied with partial results, to stop short of the ultimate goal of effort. And one can see how *that* may have hindered his complete success over the Syrians. We learn : (1) Very trivial actions often reveal a great deal of character. (2) We often have not from God because we ask not. These shootings of the arrows were at once prayers for victories from God, and pledges of victories. Joash, as it were, asked for only three victories, and he only got three. Had he asked for more, he would have got more. Had Abraham not ceased pleading for Sodom when he did, he might have got a yet further extension of grace for that doomed city (Gen. xviii. 32, 33). It is never in God we are straitened in our prayers; it is only in ourselves. (3) It displeases God that we do not ask more from him. His controversy with us is not that we ask too much, but that we do not ask enough. Joash missed the full blessing by stopping in his asking.—J. O.

Vers. 20, 21.—*Power in dead bones.* These verses contain a circumstantial notice of a singular miracle that was wrought at Elisha's sepulchre by contact with his bones. Bands of Moabites were ravaging the country, and one of these bands came upon the scene during a funeral. The mourners were terrified, and hastily thrust the corpse into Elisha's sepulchre, which was hard by ; whereupon the dead man, having touched the bones of Elisha, revived and stood upon his feet. We notice—

I. THE GOOD MAN LAID IN HIS GRAVE. Elisha's sickness had proved to be indeed unto death, and his mortal remains had been reverently conveyed to a sepulchre. He who had been the means of restoring life to others, whose very bones were made the instrument of reviving the dead, was not able to protect himself from the universal law. He left the world by the same gate as ordinary mortals. It is pathetic to reflect that, however long and useful a life may be, this is always the end of it. The certainty of removal by death from the scene of their labours should animate those who are still in the vigour of their powers to work while it is to-day (John ix. 4), and should lead those who enjoy the presence and services of good men to prize and honour these servants of God while they are here. From the side of the saint himself death is not a calamity, but a gain. "He rests from his labours, and his works follow him" (Rev. xiv. 13).

II. POWER ISSUING FROM THE GOOD MAN'S GRAVE. Though Elisha was not taken to heaven as Elijah was without tasting of death, he had yet great honour put upon him in his death. God set the seal on his prophetic work by making life-giving power to issue even from his grave. The miracle suggests to us the fact that from every good man's grave there issues in an important sense a life-giving power. The influence of men does not die with them. On the contrary, it is often greater after their deaths than during their lives. 1. *Sometimes in a literal sense the grave is a source of new life to men.* In the act of committing dust to dust, and ashes to ashes, holy impressions steal over men, new resolves take possession of their hearts. Many a man, *e.g.*, has been brought to his senses at the graveside of a father or mother, whose counsels, perhaps, he disregarded in life. 2. *Sometimes in a figurative sense souls are quickened by the bones of the dead.* A man's actions, for instance, are things of the past when he is dead. But they may be written in a book, and become a source of life to countless generations who read them afterwards. It is but a few facts of any man's life which can be thus rescued from oblivion—the mere bones of his history; but what a power is in them! So of a man's words. The fragments of a man's speech that can be preserved in any collection of his sayings are comparatively few. They are the mere bones of his speech. But they quicken souls through the ages. The words of David, of St. Paul, of the prophets, touch and work on souls to the present hour. The world is the living thing it is because of the influence of these dead men in it. They are

> "The dead but sceptred sov'rans,
> Who rule our spirits from their urns."

3. *The highest life has come out of death.* Jesus said, "Except a corn of wheat fall into the ground and die, it abideth alone," etc. (John xii. 24). Elisha communicated resurrection-power without himself rising from the dead; Christ has himself risen, and is now the Principle of resurrection-life to others.—J. O.

Vers. 22—25.—*Joash's victories.* We have in the closing verses a record of the fulfilment of the promise given through Elisha. Notice—

I. THE GROUND OF THESE VICTORIES. While God had respect to the prayer of Jehoahaz, there was a deeper ground for his interposition to save Israel. He was gracious to them, and had compassion on them, and had respect to them, we are told, because of his covenant with Abraham and Isaac and Jacob. More specifically, we have as grounds: 1. *Love to the fathers.* God remembered Abraham and Isaac and Jacob, and would not hastily cast off their posterity (cf. Deut. iv. 37; Rom. xi. 28). Many of the blessings which sinners enjoy, the forbearance God shows them, etc., are due to the prayers of godly ancestors. 2. *Regard for his own promise.* God had made a covenant with the patriarchs, and had promised to be a God to them, and to their seed after them. That covenant was the main fact in the history of Israel. It underlies and governs all God's dealings with them, past, present, and prospective. It was the remembrance of this covenant which led to the deliverance from Egypt (Exod. ii. 24, 25); to the settlement in Canaan (Deut. ix. 3); and to God's patient dealings with the nation amidst their various rebellions, and under their constant provocations. God saved them, not for their righteousness' sake, but for his own Name's sake. He is the God of unchanging faithfulness. 3. *Unwillingness to destroy the people.* God casts off none hastily, for he has "no pleasure in the death of him that dieth" (Ezek. xviii. 32). He bears long with men, if haply they will repent. Wherefore it is said, "He would not destroy them, neither cast he them from his presence as yet." There is a limit, however, to Divine forbearance. The time came when, still remaining impenitent, they were cast away, though even then not for ever.

II. THE EXTENT OF THESE VICTORIES. They amounted, as Elisha had predicted, only to three. Three times Joash beat the King of Syria, and recovered the cities of Israel from his hand. This was a great gain, but it might so easily have been greater, had Joash only fulfilled aright the conditions of success. How much blessing we often deprive ourselves of by our own unfaithfulness and shortcoming! It is reason for rejoicing that God does so much for us; but the joy must eternally be shaded by regret when we reflect that it is by our own doings that far more is not done.—J. O.

EXPOSITION.

CHAPTER XIV.

Vers. 1—29.—REIGNS OF AMAZIAH, SON OF JOASH KING OF JUDAH, OVER JUDAH, AND OF JEROBOAM, SON OF JOASH KING OF ISRAEL, OVER ISRAEL.

Vers. 1—20.—THE REIGN OF AMAZIAH OVER JUDAH. This chapter takes up the history of the kingdom of Judah from the end of ch. xii., with which it is closely con-

nected. The writer, after a few such general remarks as those with which he commonly opens the history of each reign (vers. 1—4), proceeds to relate (1) the punishment by Amaziah of the murderers of his father (vers. 5, 6); (2) the war of Amaziah with Edom (ver. 7); (3) the challenge which he sent to Joash King of Israel, that king's reply, and the war which followed (vers. 8—16); and (4) the circumstances of Amaziah's death (vers. 17—20). Between vers. 14 and 16 there is interposed a summary of the reign of King Joash of Judah, which is little more than a repetition of ch. xiii. 12, 13, and is thought by many to be an interpolation.

Ver. 1.—In the second year of Joash son of Jehoahaz King of Israel reigned Amaziah the son of Joash King of Judah. Again the chronology is defective. If Joash of Israel ascended the throne in the thirty-seventh year of Joash of Judah (ch. xiii. 10), and the latter reigned forty years (ch. xii. 1), Amaziah cannot have become king till the fourth or fifth year of the Israelitish Joash, instead of the second. The ordinary explanation of commentators is a double accession; but this is unsatisfactory. It is best to allow that the chronology of the later half of the Israelite kingdom is in confusion.

Ver. 2.—He was twenty and five years old when he began to reign, and reigned twenty and nine years in Jerusalem. Josephus ('Ant. Jud.,' ix.' 9. § 3) and the author of Chronicles (2 Chron. xxv. 1) confirm these numbers. And his mother's name was Jehoaddan of Jerusalem. Josephus (l. s. c.) calls her Jodade, but the LXX. have, more correctly, Joadim.

Ver. 3.—And he did that which was right in the sight of the Lord, yet not like David his father. Only one King of Judah hitherto, viz. Asa, had obtained the praise that he "did that which was right in the eyes of the Lord, as did David his father" (1 Kings xv. 11). All the others had fallen short more or less; and Amaziah fell short in many respects. He was wanting in "a perfect heart" (2 Chron. xxv. 2), i.e. a fixed intention to do God's will; he was proud and boastful (ver. 10); he gave way to idolatry in his later years (2 Chron. xxv. 14), and he despised the reproof of the prophet who was sent to rebuke his sin (2 Chron. xxv. 16). Though placed among the "good kings" by the authors of both Kings and Chronicles, it is, as it were, under protest, with a distinct intimation that, although better than most of his predecessors, he did not reach a high standard. He did according to all things as Joash his father did. There is something of Oriental hyperbole in this statement, which must be understood in the spirit, not in the letter. The two kings were differently circumstanced, and history did not "repeat itself" in their reigns. The position of Joash with respect to Jehoiada finds no parallel in the circumstances of the life of Amaziah. Still, the lives are parallel to some extent. Both kings began better than they ended. Both were zealous for Jehovah at first, but turned to idolatry at last. Both

opposed themselves to prophets, and treated their rebukes with scorn. Both roused conspiracy against them by their misconduct, and were murdered by the malcontents. Further, both were unsuccessful in war, had to withstand a siege of their capital, and bought off their enemy by the surrender of the greater part of its wealth, including the treasures of the temple (comp. ch. xii. 18 with ch. xiv. 14).

Ver. 4.—Howbeit the high places were not taken away. No king ventured to touch the "high places" until the time of Hezekiah, by whom they were put down (ch. xviii. 4). Even Asa did not remove them (1 Kings xv. 14). They were remnants of an old ancestral worship which went back to the time of the judges, and which had been connived at by judges and kings and prophets. Local feeling was everywhere in their favour, since they provided for local needs, and enabled men to dispense with the long] and tedious journey to the distant Jerusalem. As yet the people did sacrifice and burnt incense on the high places; literally, were sacrificing and burning incense; i.e. continued the practice, which had come down to them from their ancestors. (On the morality and legality of the practice, see the comment on 1 Kings iii. 2.)

Ver. 5.—And it came to pass, as soon as the kingdom was confirmed in his hand. Joash had been murdered in Jerusalem by conspirators (ch. xii. 20). A time of trouble had, no doubt, supervened. The conspirators would not wish to see Amaziah placed upon the throne, and may have opposed and delayed his appointment. But their efforts proved fruitless. After a time, the young king was confirmed (literally, "strengthened"), i.e. settled and established in his kingdom, all opposition being overcome or dying away. This seems to be what the writer means. He cannot intend a confirmation by a foreign suzerain, which the phrase used might import (ch. xv. 19), when he has given no hint of any subjection of the kingdom to any foreign power, or indeed of any serious attack on its independence. That he slew his servants. Jozachar and Jehozabad were "servants" of Joash, apparently domestic servants employed in his palace, and are therefore reckoned "servants" also of his successor. Which had slain the king his father. In the "house of Millo," where he lay sick. They "slew him on his bed" (see 2 Chron. xxiv. 25).

Ver. 6.—But the children of the murderers he slew not. It was the ordinary usage in the East for the sons of traitors to share the fate of their fathers. A Greek poet went so far as to say that a man was a fool who put to death the father, and allowed the son to live. The practice had a double ground.

Sons, it might be assumed, would be cognizant of their father's intention, and would so be accessories before the fact. And the law of *daim*, or " blood-feud," would make it dangerous to spare them, since they would be bound to avenge their father's death on his destroyer. That the practice prevailed among the Israelites appears from Josh. vii. 24, where we find the children of Achan involved in his fate, and again from 2 Kings ix. 26, where we are told that Naboth's sons suffered with their father. But it was contrary to an express command of the Law, as the writer goes on to show. **According unto that which is written in the book of the Law of Moses.** "The book of the Law of Moses" (מֵפֶר תּוֹרַת־מֹשֶׁה) may be either the Pentateuch regarded as one book, or Deuteronomy, the particular " book " of the Pentateuch in which the passage occurs. In either case the passage is fatal to the theory of the late composition of Deuteronomy, which is here found to have ruled the conduct of a Jewish king a hundred and fifty years before Manasseh, two hundred before Josiah, and two hundred and eighty before the return from the Captivity—the dates assigned to Deuteronomy by recent " advanced " critics. **Wherein the Lord commanded, saying, The fathers shall not be put to death for the children, nor the children be put to death for the fathers; but every man shall be put to death for his own sin.** As usual, when one sacred writer quotes another, the quotation is not exact. " But " (כִּי אִם) is inserted at the beginning of the final clause, and the form of the verb in the same clause is modified. It seems to be intended that we should be made to feel that it is the sentiment or meaning conveyed, and not the phraseology in which it is wrapped up, that is of importance.

Ver. 7.—**He slew of Edom in the valley of salt ten thousand.** Edom had revolted from Judah and recovered complete independence in the reign of Jehoram, about fifty years previously (ch. viii. 20). Since that time the two countries had remained at peace. Now, however, Amaziah resolved upon a great effort to resubjugate them. According to Josephus ('Ant. Jud.,' ix. 9. § 1) and Chronicles (2 Chron. xxv. 5), he levied an army of 400,000 men—300,000 Jews, and 100,000 hired Israelites—with which he marched against the three nations of the Amalekites, the Idumæans, and the Gabalites. Rebuked by a prophet for want of faith in calling to his aid all the wicked Israelites, he consented to dismiss them, and made the invasion at the head of his own troops only. These were carefully organized (2 Chron. xxv. 5), and met with a great success. Ten thousand of his enemies fell in battle, and an equal number were made prisoners. These last

were barbarously put to death by being precipitated from the top of a rock (2 Chron. xxv. 12). " The valley of salt," the scene of the battle, is probably identified with the sunken plain, now called *Es Sabkah*, at the southern extremity of the Dead Sea. This is " a large flat of at least six miles by ten, occasionally flooded " (Tristram), but dry in the summer-time. It is full of salt springs, and is bounded on the west and north-west by a long ridge of pure salt, known as the *Khasm Usdum*, so that the name " valley of salt " would be very appropriate. **And took Selah by war.** Selah with the article (*has-Selah*) can only be the Idumæan capital, which the Greeks called Petra (Πέτρα or ἡ Πέτρα), and which is one of the most remarkable sites in the world. In the rocky mountains which form the eastern boundary of the Arabah or sandy slope reaching from the edge of the Sabkah to the Red Sea, amid cliffs of gorgeous colours, pink and crimson and purple, and ravines as deep and narrow as that of Pfeffers, partly excavated in the rock, partly emplaced upon it, stood the Edomite town, difficult to approach, still more difficult to capture, more like the home of a colony of sea-gulls than that of a number of men. Petra is graphically described by Dean Stanley (' Sinai and Palestine,' pp. 88—92), and has also received notice from Robinson (' Researches,' vol. ii. pp. 518—538), Highton (' Dictionary of the Bible,' vol. iii. p. 1191), and others. **And called the name of it Joktheel;** *i.e.* " subdued by God." The name took no permanent hold. Selah is still " Sela " in Isaiah (xvi. 1), Obadiah (ver. 3), and Jeremiah (xlix. 16). It is known only as " Petra " to the Greeks and Romans. **Unto this day;** *i.e.* to the time of the writer who composed the account of Amaziah's reign for the ' Book of the Kings,' and whose words the author of Kings transcribes here as so often elsewhere.

Ver. 8.—**Then Amaziah sent messengers to Jehoash, the son of Jehoahaz son of Jehu, King of Israel, saying.** Amaziah had a cause of complaint against Jehoash, or at any rate against his subjects, which does not appear in the narrative of Kings. The author of Chronicles tells us that, when Amaziah dismissed his Israelite mercenaries, they were offended, and vented their anger by an inroad into his territories (2 Chron. xxv. 13), where they killed three thousand men and " took much spoil." This was a clear *casus belli*, if Amaziah chose to consider it such. **Come, let us look one another in the face.** A rude message, if it was actually couched in these terms. But perhaps the writer substitutes the gist of the message for the language in which it was wrapped up. Josephus says that Amaziah wrote a letter to Joash, and required him to submit himself and people to the authority of the Jewish state, and thus restore the state of things which had existed under David and Solomon. Otherwise the sword must decide between them (' Ant. Jud.,' ix. 9. § 2). Whatever its terms, pride and self-confidence, the result of his success against Edom, were at the root of the challenge.

Ver. 9.—**And Jehoash the King of Israel sent to Amaziah King of Judah, saying.** According to Josephus, the reply to the challenge was given in a formal letter, of which he presents us with a copy—

"King Joash to King Amaziah [sends greeting]:

"Once upon a time there was in Mount Lebanon a very tall cypress, and also there was a thistle. And the thistle sent to the cypress, saying, 'Contract thy daughter in marriage to my son.' And while this was transacting, a wild beast passed by and trod down the thistle. Let this be a warning to thee not to cherish immoderate desires, and not, because thou hast had success against Amalek, to pride thyself thereupon, and so draw down dangers both upon thee and upon thy kingdom."

The force of the original message is much weakened in this paraphrase. **The thistle that was in Lebanon.** "Thistle" is a better translation than "thorn-bush" (Keil), first, as a meaner. growth, and secondly, as more likely to be trodden down by a wild beast. The monarch intends to say that the meanest thing in the vegetable world sent to the grandest, claiming equality. **Sent to the cedar**—certainly "the cedar," and not "the cypress," as translated by Josephus—**that was in Lebanon, saying, Give thy daughter to my son to wife.** *Nube pari* was a Roman maxim; and the rule was one generally established throughout the ancient world. To ask a man's daughter in marriage for one's self or for one's son was to claim to be his equal. **And there passed by a wild beast**—literally, *a beast of the field*—**that was in Lebanon** (on Lebanon as the haunt of wild beasts, see Cant. iv. 8), and **trode down the thistle.** So levelling with the dust the pride of the impertinent one. We must not seek an exact application of all the details either of a fable or of a parable. It is not required that metaphors should "run on all fours."

Ver. 10.—**Thou hast indeed smitten Edom** (see ver. 7, and the comment), **and thine heart hath lifted thee up**—*i.e.* made thee proud, exalted thee above measure—**glory of this, and tarry at home**—*i.e.* rest content with the glory which thou hast gained in thy Edomite war; make thy boast thereof, but do not affront fresh dangers—**for why**

shouldest thou meddle to thy hurt—literally, *why wilt thou meddle with misfortune?*—**that thou shouldest fall, even thou, and Judah with thee?** Joash was as confident of success, if it came to war, as Amaziah. His three victories over Syria (ch. xiii. 25) were, he thought, at least as good evidence of military strength as Amaziah's one victory over Edom.

Ver. 11.—**But Amaziah would not hear.** The message of Joash was not conciliatory, but provocative. On hearing it, Amaziah (as Josephus says, 'Ant. Jud.,' ix. 9. § 3) was the more spurred on to make his expedition. **Therefore Jehoash King of Israel went up.** "Joash," as Bähr says, "did not wait for the attack of Amaziah, but anticipated his movements, and carried the war into the enemy's country." Defensive warfare often requires such an offensive movement. **And he and Amaziah King of Judah looked one another in the face**—*i.e.* came to an engagement (comp. ver. 8)—**at Beth-shemesh, which belongeth to Judah.** Beth-shemesh was assigned to Judah by Joshua (xix. 38), and lay on its western frontier line. Its position is marked by the modern *Ain-Shems*, which lies nearly due west of Jerusalem, on the road from Hebron to Jaffa. Ain-Shems itself is an Arab village, but "just to the west of it are the manifest traces of an ancient site" (Robinson, 'Researches,' vol. iii. p. 17). The position commands the approach from the Philistine plain; and we may suspect that Joash, avoiding the direct line of approach, led his troops to the attack through Philistia, as was so often done by the Syrians in their attacks on the Maccabees (see 1 Macc. iii. 40; xiii. 12, 13; xv. 40; xvi. 4—8, etc.).

Ver. 12.—**And Judah was put to the worse before Israel; and they fled every man to their tents;** *i.e.* "to their *homes*" (see the comment on ch. xiii. 5). This was the first trial of strength between the two nations of which we have any distinct account. It resulted in the complete discomfiture of Israel. There was another great struggle in the time of Pekah and Ahaz, wherein Judah suffered even more severely (see 2 Chron. xxviii. 6—8).

Ver. 13.—**And Jehoash King of Israel took Amaziah King of Judah, the son of Jehoash the son of Ahaziah, at Beth-shemesh**—Josephus says (*l. s. c.*) that Amaziah was deserted by his troops, who were seized with a sudden panic and fled from the field—**and came to Jerusalem, and brake down the wall of Jerusalem.** According to Josephus, Joash threatened his prisoner with death unless the gates of Jerusalem were opened to him, and his army admitted into the town; and it was upon Amaziah's representations that the surrender was made as soon as the Israelite army appeared before the place. The breach in the wall was therefore not the result of siege operations, but the act of a conqueror, who desired to leave his enemy as defenceless as possible. From the gate of Ephraim; *i.e.* the main gate in the northern wall of the city—that by which travellers ordinarily proceeded into the territory of the tribe of Ephraim. In later times it seems to have been called indifferently "the gate of Ephraim" (Neh. viii. 16; xii. 39) and "the gate of Benjamin" (Jer. xxxvii. 13; Zech. xiv. 10). The great north road, which passed through it, led across the Benjamite into the Ephraimite territory. Unto the corner gate. The "corner gate" is generally thought to have been that at the north-*western* angle of the city wall, where it turned southward, but this is perhaps doubtful. The exact line of the city wall in the time of Amaziah is exceedingly uncertain. Four hundred cubits; six hundred feet, or two hundred yards. This seems to have been the entire distance between the two gates. As there were at least thirteen gates in the circuit of the walls (Neh. iii. 1—31; xii. 31—39; Zech. xiv. 10), which were probably not more extensive than those of the present town (3960 yards), the distance of two hundred yards between one gate and another would not be improbable, the *average* distance being about three hundred yards.

Ver. 14.—And he took all the gold and silver, and all the vessels that were found in the house of the Lord. As Joash of Judah had, fifteen or twenty years previously, stript the temple of its treasures to buy off the hostility of Hazael (ch. xii. 18), there could not have been at this time very much for Joash of Israel to lay his hands on. Still, whatever there was passed into the possession of the Israelite king. And in the treasures of the king's house. Neither can this have amounted to much, unless the booty taken from Hazael after his defeats (ch. xiv. 25) was very considerable. And hostages. This is a new feature in the warfare of the time; but hostages were given and taken from an early date by the Persians (Xen., 'Cyrop.,' iv. 2. § 7; Herod., vi. 99), the Greeks, and the Romans.

Vers. 15, 16.—Now the rest of the acts of Jehoash which he did, and his might, and how he fought with Amaziah King of Judah, are they not written in the book of the chronicles of the kings of Israel? And Jehoash slept with his fathers, and was buried in Samaria with the kings of Israel; and Jeroboam his son reigned in his stead. These verses are repeated with very slight alterations from ch. xiii. 11, 12. Curiously, on both occasions they are out of place. It is scarcely worth while to consider how

they came into the text at this point, since no explanation could be more than a conjecture. In point of fact, they are redundant.

Ver. 17.—And Amaziah the son of Joash King of Judah lived after the death of Jehoash son of Jehoahaz King of Israel fifteen years. This note of time is based on ver. 2, which makes Amaziah begin to reign in the *second* year of Joash of Israel, and hold the throne for twenty-nine years. If he really began to reign in the *fourth* year of Joash, he would have survived him only thirteen years (see the comment on ver. 2).

Ver. 18.—And the rest of the acts of Amaziah—especially the circumstances of his war with Edom, as related in 2 Chron. xxv. 5—13, his idolatry (2 Chron. xxv. 14), and the rebuke which he received from one of God's prophets (2 Chron. xxv. 15, 16) in consequence—are they not written in the book of the chronicles of the kings of Judah?

Ver. 19.—Now they made a conspiracy against him in Jerusalem. The author of Chronicles connects this conspiracy with the idolatry of which Amaziah was guilty (2 Chron. xxv. 27); but, though his subjects may have been offended by his religious changes, and have become alienated from him in consequence, the actual conspiracy can scarcely have been prompted by an act which was fifteen, or at any rate thirteen, years old. It is more likely to have sprung out of dissatisfaction with Amaziah's military inaction from and after his defeat by Joash. While Jeroboam II. was carrying all before him in the north, recovering his border, pushing it as far as Hamath, and even exercising a suzerainty over Damascus (vers. 25, 28), Amaziah remained passive, cowed by his one defeat, and took no advantage of the state of weakness to which he had reduced Edom, but sat with folded hands, doing nothing. The conspirators who removed Amaziah, and placed his son Azariah, or Uzziah, upon the throne, may be credited with the wish and intention to bring the period of inaction to an end, and to effect in the south what Jeroboam was effecting in the north. It is true that Azariah was but sixteen years of age (ver. 21; comp. 2 Chron. xxvi. 1), but he may have given indications of his ambition and capacity. Sixteen, moreover, is the time of manhood in the East, and the conspirators had probably waited until Azariah was sixteen in order that his competency to reign should not be disputed. As soon as he was on the throne he initiated the warlike policy which they desired (see ver. 22). And he fled to Lachish. Lachish, one of the south-western Judæan towns (Josh. xv. 39), was at all times a fortress of importance. It resisted Joshua (x. 3, 31), and was taken by storm. It was fortified by Jeroboam against the Egyptians (2 Chron. xi. 9). It was besieged and taken by Sennacherib (ch. xviii. 14 ; Layard, 'Nineveh and Babylon,' pp. 149—152). The position is marked by the modern *Um-Lakis*, on "a low round swell or knoll," between Gaza and Beit-Jibrin, about thirteen miles from Gaza and nearly thirty-five from Jerusalem. **But they sent after him to Lachish, and slew him there.** So the author of Chronicles (2 Chron. xxv. 27) and Josephus ('Ant. Jud.,' ix. 9. § 3); but details are wanting.

Ver. 20.—**And they brought him on horses**; literally, *on the horses*, which must mean "on *his* horses." Probably Amaziah had fled to Lachish in the royal chariot, and his body was now brought back in it to Jerusalem. The conspirators were evidently minded to treat the royal corpse with all respect. **And he was buried at Jerusalem with his fathers in the city of David**; *i.e.* the city on the eastern hill, which David took from the Jebusites (see the comment on 1 Kings ii. 10).

Vers. 21, 22.—SUCCESSION OF AZARIAH AND RESUMPTION OF THE WAR WITH EDOM. Though reserving his account of the reign of Azariah to the next chapter (vers. 1—7), the writer is led by the circumstances of Amaziah's death to mention *at once* the fact of his son Azariah's succession, and the first important act of his reign, the resumption of war with Edom. He then breaks off suddenly, in order to interpose an account of the reign of Jeroboam II., who was contemporary with Amaziah during fourteen years of his reign.

Ver. 21.—**And all the people of Judah took Azariah.** This is a new expression, and implies a new, perhaps a tumultuary, proceeding. The *people*, uncertain probably of the intentions of the conspirators, and fearful that they might set up a king not of the house of David, took the initiative, went to the royal palace, and finding there a son of Amaziah—whether his eldest son or not, we cannot say—proclaimed him king and placed him upon the throne. The author of Chronicles (2 Chron. xvi. 1) agrees. Josephus is silent. **Which was sixteen years old.** Young certainly, considering that his father was fifty-four (see ver. 2), but not necessarily "a younger son," since Amaziah's earlier children may have been daughters, or he may have married late in life. It is not doubted that Manasseh was Hezekiah's eldest son, yet he was only twelve when Hezekiah died at the same age as Amaziah, viz. fifty-four. **And made**

him king instead of his father Amaziah. There are two forms of the king's name, Azariah and Uzziah. The difference between them is not so great in the Hebrew, where they both begin with the same letter; but still it is considerable. One name is not a mere contraction of the other. Some suppose that the king changed one name for the other upon his accession; others, that he was called indifferently by either, since they were very similar in meaning. "Azariah" is "he whose help is Jehovah;" "Uzziah," "he whose strength is Jehovah." "Uzziah" is the predominant form, occurring four times in 2 Kings, twelve times in 2 Chronicles, three times in Isaiah, once in Hosea, once in Amos, and once in Zechariah; while "Azariah" occurs only in 2 Kings (eight times) and in 1 Chron. iii. 12 (once). Josephus uses the form "Ozias" (equivalent to "Uzziah)," and so does St. Matthew (i. 8, 9).

Ver. 22.—**He built Elath, and restored it to Judah.** On the position of Elath, or Eloth, and its importance, see the comment on 1 Kings ix. 26. It had been the headquarters of Solomon's fleet (1 Kings ix. 26), and again of Jehoshaphat's (1 Kings xxii. 48; 2 Chron. xx. 36); but had been, of course, recovered by the Edomites when they revolted (ch. viii. 22). Azariah's re-occupation seems to imply an intention on his part of renewing the old Red Sea trade. By "built" in this passage we must understand "rebuilt," or (as in 2 Chron. xi. 6) "fortified." **After that the king slept with his fathers.** Keil is probably right in understanding this to mean "*immediately* after he had ascended the throne," or "as soon as ever his father was dead" (see the comment on ver. 19). His further military successes will be considered in the comment on his reign, as sketched in the next chapter.

Vers. 23—29.—REIGN OF JEROBOAM THE SON OF JOASH OVER ISRAEL. This reign, the most important of those belonging to the kingdom of Israel since that of Ahab, is treated with great brevity by the writer, whose interest is far more in Judah than in Israel. Seven verses only are devoted to him. The result of his wars is given without any account of the wars themselves. And the great fact of his ruling over Damascus only comes in by a sort of after-thought (ver. 28). The usual formulas are followed in introducing his reign and dismissing it.

Ver. 23.—**In the fifteenth year of Amaziah the son of Joash King of Judah**—this note of time agrees with those in ch. xiii. 10 and ch. xiv. 1, 17, but not with that in ch. xv. 1 (see the comment on that passage)—Jeroboam the son of Joash King of Israel began to reign in Samaria, and reigned forty and one years. Josephus says "forty years." Many moderns (Thenius, Bähr, and others) extend the term to fifty-one years. Some suppose that Jeroboam was joint-king with his father in Amaziah's third year, sole king from his fifteenth. But it is better to acknowledge the general confusion of the chronology, and to regard it as uncertain, unless where a synchronism is distinctly made out. Such assured synchronisms are the following: (1) The synchronism of Ahab with Jehoshaphat; (2) the synchronism of Jehoram, Ahab's son, with the same; (3) the synchronism of Jehu's first year with the first year of Athaliah; (4) the synchronism of Amaziah with Joash of Israel; (5) the synchronism of Pekah with Ahaz; (6) the synchronism of Hoshea's last year with Hezekiah's sixth; (7) the synchronism of Amaziah's fourteenth year with Jeroboam II.'s first, being twice asserted in two distinct forms (vers. 17 and 23), is, at any rate, highly probable. Numbers which occur once only in ancient writers can seldom be implicitly trusted, since the liability of numbers to corruption is excessive.

Ver. 24.—**And he did** that which was evil in the sight of the Lord: he departed not from all the sins of Jeroboam the son of Nebat, who made Israel to sin (comp. ch. x. 29 and xiii. 2, 11, where the same is said of his father, grandfather, and great-grandfather). The judgments which had fallen upon Jehu and Jehoahaz on account of these sins did not teach any lesson to Joash or Jeroboam II. The fatal taint, which was congenital with the Israelite monarchy, could never be purged out, but clung to it to the end.

Ver. 25.—**He restored the coast of Israel from the entering in of Hamath.** By "the entering in of Hamath" is to be understood the opening into the Cœle-Syrian valley a little north of Baalbec, where the ground begins to slope northwards, and the streams to flow in the same direction to form the Orontes. Hamath itself was between eighty and ninety miles further to the north, on the middle Orontes, about N. lat. 35° 22'. The "entering in of Hamath" was always reckoned the northern boundary of the Holy Land (see Numb. xxxiv. 8; Josh. xiii. 5; Judg. iii. 3; 1 Kings viii. 65). It corresponded with the watershed between the Orontes and the Litany. **Unto the sea of the plain.** The "sea of the plain" is undoubtedly the Dead Sea, "the plain" (*ha-Arabah*) being used as a sort of proper

name for the lower Jordan valley, like *El-Ghor* at the present day (see Deut. iii. 17; Josh. iii. 16; xii. 3, etc.). The territory recovered no doubt included all the trans-Jordanic region as far south as the river Arnon; but the recovery of dominion over Moab, and even over Ammon, which some have seen in this passage (Ewald, 'History of Israel,' vol. iv. p. 124), is scarcely contained in it. **According to the word of the Lord God of Israel, which he spake by the hand of his servant Jonah, the son of Amittai** (comp. Jonah i. 1). Jonah's date is determined by this passage. He was contemporary with Hosea and Amos, and earlier than Micah. His prophecy concerning Jeroboam is probably assigned to the early part of that king's reign. **The prophet, which was of Gath-hepher.** Gath-hepher is mentioned in Joshua, under the name of Gittah-hepher, as a city of Zebulon (ch. xix. 13), not far from Mount Tabor. It is conjecturally identified with *El-Meshhed* north of Nazareth, where the tomb of Jonah is shown.

Ver. 26.—**For the Lord saw the affliction of Israel, that it was very bitter** (comp. ch. xiii. 4, 23). The repetition is perhaps to be accounted for by the desire of the writer to explain how it came to pass that so great a deliverance was granted to Israel under a king who maintained the worship of the calves. He views it as the consequence of God's infinite compassion, and of the extreme bitterness of Israel's sufferings under the Syrians (comp. ch. xiii. 7 and Amos i. 3). **For there was not any shut up, nor any left** (see the comment on 1 Kings xiv. 10), **nor any helper for Israel.** Apart from Jehovah, Israel had no one to come to her aid. Judah would not help her, for Judah had just suffered at her hands (vers. 11—14); still less would Philistia, or Moab, or Ammon, who were her constant enemies. Her isolation rendered her all the more an object for the Divine compassion.

Ver. 27.—**And the Lord said not that he would blot out the name of Israel from under heaven.** God's decision under the circumstances was not, as it well might have been, considering Israel's ill desert, to blot out forthwith the very name of Israel from the earth. On the contrary, he gave the nation a breathing-space, a gleam of light, a second summer before the winter set in—a further opportunity of repenting and turning to him with all their hearts if they would only have taken advantage of it, a chance of redeeming the past and re-establishing themselves in his favour. He might well have destroyed them at this time if he had looked only to considerations of justice, if in his wrath he had not thought upon mercy. **But he saved them;** *i.e.* he gave them the deliverance promised first by Elisha (ch. xiii. 17), and then by Jonah the son of Amittai (ver. 25)—deliverance from Syria, recovery of their borders, and triumph over their enemies. He gave them all this by the hand of Jeroboam the son of Joash. Joash began the salvation, but it was reserved for Jeroboam to complete it. He was the true "saviour" (ch. xiii. 5), the true accomplisher of the work, for which his father only paved the way. Thus one Jeroboam founded the kingdom; another refounded it, restored its ancient glories, and gave it its old dimensions.

Ver. 28.—**Now the rest of the acts of Jeroboam, and all that he did, and his might, how he warred, and how he recovered Damascus and Hamath.** It has been suggested that these words mean no more than that Jeroboam took territory from Damascus and Hamath—from Damascus the trans-Jordanic territory which Hazael had conquered from Jehu (ch. x. 33); from Hamath some small portion of the Cœle-Syrian valley, about the head-streams of the Orontes and Litany (so Keil and Bähr). But there does not seem to be any sufficient reason for giving the words used this narrow signification. Damascus was conquered and annexed by David (2 Sam. viii. 6), and held for a time even by Solomon (1 Kings xi. 24), of whose kingdom Hamath also seems to have formed a part (1 Kings iv. 21—24; 2 Chron. viii. 4; ix. 26). The word "recovered" is, therefore, a suitable one. The prophecy of Amos, no doubt, represents Damascus as independent (Amos i. 3, 4); but this may have been written before Jeroboam conquered it. Hamath's subjection seems to be implied in Amos vi. 2, 14. We may, therefore, well understand, with Ewald ('History of Israel,' vol. iv. p. 124) and Dr. Pusey ('Minor Prophets,' pp. 157, 209), that Jeroboam "subdued Damascus and even Hamath," and added them to his kingdom. How long the subjection continued is a different ques-

tion. Probably, in the troubles that followed the death of Zachariah (ch. xv. 10—14), the yoke was thrown off. In the Assyrian Inscriptions, Damascus appears under its own king about B.C. 786 (G. Smith, 'Eponym Canon,' p. 115), and it was certainly independent in B.C. 743. At the latter date Hamath also appears as the capital of an independent kingdom (ibid., pp. 118, 120) under its own monarch. Which belonged **to Judah.** Keil and Bähr render, "Hamath of Judah," regarding ‏לִיהוּדָה‎ as a genitive. Ewald proposes to read ‏חֲמָת לְצוֹבָה‎, "Hamath of Zobah" (comp. 2 Chron. viii. 3), or else to cut out ‏לִיהוּדה‎ altogether. The passage is one of great difficulty. For Israel. It is questionable whether this meaning can be obtained from the present text, which is ‏בְּיִשְׂרָאֵל‎. Bähr thinks that it can; but Ewald regards the change into ‏לְיִשְׂרָאֵל‎ as one "of necessity." Might we not avoid all these alterations by translating simply—"how he recovered Damascus and Hamath *to* Judah *through* Israel"? Attaching them to Israel was a sort of recovering of them to Judah, to which (*i.e.* the Judah of David and Solomon) they had once belonged. Are they not written in the book of the chronicles of the kings of Israel?

Ver. 29.—**And Jeroboam slept with his fathers, even with the kings of Israel**—his father, grandfather, and great-grandfather had been actually among the kings of Israel; but *all* the kings, his predecessors, were probably reckoned among his ancestors—**and Zachariah his son reigned in his stead** (see the comment on ch. xv. 8). By Zachariah's accession the promise given to Jehu (ch. x. 30), that his "children to the fourth generation should sit on the throne of Israel," was literally fulfilled. No other royal house occupied the Israelitish throne for more than three generations.

HOMILETICS.

Vers. 3, 4.—*A father's evil example no justification for a son's misconduct.* Amaziah "did according to all things as Joash his father did." Like his father, he was half-hearted. In his earlier years he kept to the worship of Jehovah, and "did that which was right in the sight of the Lord," yet not with any zeal or energy. Afterwards he fell away, introduced idolatry (2 Chron. xxv. 14), and when a prophet rebuked him for his evil courses, answered him with scoffs and threatenings (2 Chron. xxv. 15, 16). His father Joash had done even worse after the death of Jehoiada. He had not only sanctioned idolatries (2 Chron. xxiv. 17, 18), but had had the servant of God who rebuked them put to death (2 Chron. xxiv. 21). This, however, is not held by the sacred writer to be any justification or excuse for Amaziah. The reasons are manifest.

I. No MAN IS TO BE CALLED MASTER, NOT EVEN A FATHER. God gives men in his Law and in their conscience a standard of right, which they are to follow. He nowhere bids them take any man but the "God-Man" for pattern. He warns them that men are, all of them, more or less imperfect. He requires that parents shall be "honoured," not imitated.

II. THE EVIL EXAMPLE OF A FATHER IS A WARNING TO SONS, WHICH SHOULD LEAD TO AVOIDANCE, NOT IMITATION. The sight of a drunken father should disgust sons with drunkenness. Blasphemous and violent words should so shock them as to suggest an exactly opposite behaviour. Looseness of morals should breed in them a determination never to offend in a way so absolutely revolting. Given that simplicity which is natural to youth, and every fault of a father should so keenly wound and vex their souls as to bend them in the exactly contrary direction. Sin is so ugly, so offensive, so coarse, that in another it naturally disgusts us; and the more plainly it is revealed, the closer it is brought to us, the more are we naturally provoked and angered by it.

III. THE PUNISHMENT WHICH SIN DRAWS AFTER IT SHOULD COME ESPECIALLY HOME TO THOSE WHOSE HOMES ARE CURSED WITH IT, AND ACT AS A DETERRENT. Disease, decay, the loss of others' respect, the severing of friendships, general dislike and aversion, in some cases contempt, dog the footsteps of sin, and mark it as a thing to be avoided. Sons are naturally sensitive with regard to their fathers' honour, and keen to mark whether they are held in respect or no. There can be no natural deterrent from evil courses stronger than the perception that one with whom we are bound up is deteriorating from day to day, not merely in character, but in reputation, falling in men's esteem, becoming a mark for their scorn. The father's fall should thus not produce the son's, but rather stimulate the son to rise to greater and greater heights of virtue.

Vers. 5, 6.—*A father's sins not to be visited by the civil magistrate on his children.* Human legislators have differed greatly in their judgments upon this point. In the East, and in early times, the idea was generally accepted that the guilt of the father attached to all his descendants, and was justly visited on them. "Lege cantum erat," says Q. Curtius ('Vit. Alex.,' vi. 11), " ut propinqui eorum, qui regi insidiati essent, cum ipsis necarentur." The family was regarded as the unit of society, and the crime of one member tainted the whole of it. What the Egyptian practice was is uncertain; but we find the Israelites, shortly after the Exodus, putting to death the whole family of Achan on account of their father's sin (Josh. vii. 24, 25), and the usage seems to have continued long afterwards (ch. ix. 26). The Greeks and Romans adopted a different line of action. Recognizing the separateness of the individual, they never executed a family *en masse*, but only the guilty member or members of it. Yet, in secondary punishments, the contrary idea to some extent prevailed. At Athens, when the sentence on a man was degradation from his rights of citizenship (ἀτιμία), the penalty was shared by his children. A similar disability attached to the children of those who were executed. So, even by our own law, attainder and forfeiture, which mainly affect the children, are attached to the crime of treason, and the property of felons escheats to the Crown. It is very remarkable that the Law of Moses should have anticipated the ultimate judgment of the human conscience upon the point, and have laid down so clearly and strongly the humane principle that the criminal *alone* should be punished for his own crime. To us at the present day the principle may appear axiomatic; but at the time when Moses enunciated it, the contrary idea was prevalent; and it is doubtful whether the broad assertion, "Every man shall be put to death for his own sins," had ever been heard previously. Even now, though in the letter the principle is universally accepted, infractions of its spirit are common enough—

I. BY NATIONS. Nations infringe it when they cashier a royal family for the fault, or even the crime, of the reigning sovereign. In an hereditary monarchy the son has a right to succeed, though his father may by unconstitutional acts have justly forfeited the crown. Still more unjust is the perpetual exile of all those whose ancestors have ever reigned over a country. Such persons are punished, not so much for the sins as for the merits—the wisdom, prowess, high renown—of their forefathers, since it is for their merits, ordinarily, that persons are first placed upon thrones. Confiscation of the property of exiled princes is still more indefensible, since it is at once unjust and mean. It may be added that forfeiture and attainder, as they exist in our own law, seem to be contrary to the spirit of the rule, which is that no one should be punished for anything but his own acts.

II. BY INDIVIDUALS. Individuals infringe this rule when they maintain a family feud, transferring to the children of those by whom they consider themselves to have been injured the animosity which they have long entertained towards their parents. Or when they treat a man with coldness or incivility because his father has done something disgraceful. Or, generally, when they attach blame or discredit to any one, not for anything that he has done, but for something that somebody connected with him has done. Strict justice requires that each man should "bear his own burden," and stand or fall by his own acts. If we allow anything but his own acts to affect our estimate of a man—still more, if we allow it to affect our demeanour towards him— we act unjustly, we infringe the principle of the law, "Every man shall be put to death [*i.e.* shall suffer] for *his own* sin."

Vers. 8—14.—*"Pride goes before a fall."* Amaziah's challenge and its result furnish a remarkable illustration of this maxim. The following points should be dwelt upon.

I. THE WEAK GROUND OF THE PRIDE. This was military success, which is just as often the result of good fortune, or one's enemies' mistakes, as of any merits of one's own. Amaziah's after-life showed that he did not possess any great military capacity, and so had nothing on which he ought to have prided himself. Men constantly over-estimate their own merits.

II. THE WRONGFUL WAY IN WHICH THE PRIDE VENTED ITSELF. In quarrel, cause-less quarrel with a neighbour. Amaziah had no grievance which he felt it necessary to redress, no need to quarrel with Joash. Having gained one success, he was simply greedy for more. And to gratify his self-esteem he was careless how many lives he sacrificed or what injuries he inflicted (1) on his adversaries; (2) on his own subjects. He forgot that the Israelites were of kindred blood (1 Kings xii. 24), of the same religion, a portion of God's people. He plunged into an unnecessary war—in itself always a sin—with a nation towards which he ought to have felt friendly, without obtaining or seeking any Divine sanction, in sole reliance on himself. What wonder that God punished such combined folly and wickedness!

III. THE OBSTINACY WITH WHICH THE WRONGFUL COURSE WAS PERSISTED IN. Proud men dislike above all things admitting that they are in the wrong. Amaziah had ample time to retract his challenge and give up his enterprise. Joash was not at all eager for the encounter; on the contrary, he was quite willing to have remained at peace if Amaziah would have let him. But to retract, still more to apologize, would have been unpleasant. The pride which had given birth to the challenge absolutely forbade its withdrawal.

IV. THE COMPLETENESS AND EXTREME IGNOMINY OF THE FALL. Amaziah had, no doubt, counted on an easy victory; he went to war "with a light heart." He would do with Israel as he had done with Edom—smite and slay, and make prisoners, and perhaps punish his prisoners with death (ver. 7). The result is, not a victory, not even a drawn battle, not a long war with alternations of success and defeat, but one crushing blow, from which there is no recovery even for an instant. His army is defeated, dispersed; he himself is a prisoner in the hands of his enemy, his capital is taken, its walls broken down, its treasures carried off. He is disgraced in the eyes of all his subjects, as well as of the neighbouring nations, and thenceforth remains absolutely quiescent, attempts nothing, but, humbled and confounded, "sits in the dust."

HOMILIES BY VARIOUS AUTHORS.

Vers. 1—4 with 7—20.—*Compromise and its consequences.* We read here of Amaziah that "he did that which was right in the sight of the Lord, yet not like David his father: he did according to all things as Joash his father did. *Howbeit the high places were not taken away;* as yet the people did sacrifice and burnt incense on the high places." And we read of him in 2 Chronicles that "he did that which was right in the sight of the Lord, but not with a perfect heart." To understand the meaning of the statement which we meet with so often, that "the high places were not taken away," we must go back to the period before the children of Israel entered the promised land. At that time the inhabitants of Canaan were heathen—pagans and idolaters. One of the peculiarities of their heathen worship was to have groves of trees, generally of oaks, planted on the summit of the hills. In these groves there was usually placed a shrine with an image of their deity, just as we see, when travelling on the continent, shrines of the blessed Virgin, or shrines with a crucifix, by the roadside and on the hill-tops. The custom of having groves of oaks for religious purposes was shared by the early inhabitants of Britain, and the Druids derived their name from this very practice. In these groves the heathen priests sacrificed and burnt incense to their gods. It was to such groves that the name of "high places" was given. When the Israelites were about to enter Canaan, God foresaw the temptation to which they would be exposed from the idolatry of the heathen inhabitants and of the neighbouring nations. He therefore charged them not only to drive out the heathen nations from Canaan, but also *to utterly destroy their high places*, to overthrow their altars, and break their graven images, and burn their groves with fire (Deut. xii. 2, 3). This command was repeated over and over again. But, notwithstanding this, the high places were never utterly abolished. Time after time during the period of the judges, the people set up a worship in the high places, which, though nominally that of Jehovah, was tinged with idolatrous practices. It was much the same under the kings. Now and then some courageous, God-fearing, whole-hearted king made a clean sweep of the high places. But the old habit was continually revived, and so in one reign after another we read *the policy of compromise*, " The high places were not taken away." *And when- ever that was the case, we find it had evil results.* It was so in the time of Solomon himself. It was so in the time of the two kings who succeeded him over the divided kingdom—Rehoboam and Jeroboam. It was so in the case of Amaziah now before us.

I. AMAZIAH'S COMPROMISE PREPARED THE WAY FOR POSITIVE SIN. The high places in themselves were not necessarily places of idolatry. There is no doubt that sincere worship to the true God was often offered up in them. Thus we find Solomon sacri- ficing to the Lord in Gibeon, which was the great high place. But the associations of these places were entirely idolatrous. From time immemorial they had been associated with the worship of the heathen gods. It was for this reason that God forbade the use of them. It was necessary to make the wall of separation between his people and the heathen as wide as possible—to teach them that they could not serve God and Baal, that there could be no compromise between right and wrong without danger to the right. The results showed the wisdom and necessity of God's strict command. The natural tendency of the human heart is to worship what is seen, to look at the outward symbol rather than at the thing signified. This was just what happened in Amaziah's case. He did not see that there was any harm in preserving the high places. Might not God be worshipped there as well as in Jerusalem? And so he made the com- promise : " The high places were not taken away." *But look at the result.* " Now it came to pass, after that Amaziah was come from the slaughter of the Edomites, that he brought the gods of the children of Seir, *and set them up to be his gods*, and bowed down himself before them, and burned incense unto them " (2 Chron. xxv. 14). What a falling off was there! This is that Amaziah who began his career by doing right in the sight of the Lord, now stupidly bowing down before the lifeless idols of the heathen! He conquered the heathen in one sense, but the heathen conquered him in another and more dangerous sense. Has it not been the same in the history of the Christian Church? The early Christian Church was simple in its worship and its government; its members were simple in their habits and pure in their lives. But when it became powerful at Rome, and in a sense captured pagan Rome, its very power was its danger. There was a sense in which the paganism of Rome captured the simplicity of the gospel. As Mourant Brock has so fully shown in that interesting book of his on 'Rome: Pagan and Papal,' and as Gibbon and other historians have pointed out, Christianity, in Rome at least, made a compromise with paganism. And the compromise was anything but an advantage to the Christian religion. The ill effects of it remain to this day in the images and pilgrimages, and the many other superstitions which deface the Roman branch of the Christian Church. Such facts of history carry with them a memorable lesson. The Christian Church ought ever to keep in mind the spiritual objects for which it exists. It ought, therefore, to guard most scrupulously the spirituality and scripturality of its wor- ship. "God is a Spirit, and they that worship him must worship him in spirit and in truth." It ought to guard also the spirituality and scripturality of its doctrine, and teach men to trust, not to penances or indulgences for their acceptance with God, but to the work and merits of Jesus Christ, the only Mediator between God and man. The countries of the Reformation are marked out among the nations of Europe for their prosperity and industry. The more thorough the work of religious reformation, the stronger has been the national character, the more vigorous the national life. And on the other hand, as we look at the general decay of the Roman Catholic nations, and the corruption that has marked their history, may we not trace the secret of their downfall in the words of the fourth verse, "The high places were not taken away"?

II. AMAZIAH'S COMPROMISE LED TO TEMPORAL DISASTER. Amaziah had elements of strength mingled with the elements of weakness in his character. He was capable of acting upon certain occasions with decision and firmness. What a pity he had not carried that spirit of decision into the most important duty for every human being—obedience to the Law of God! Once, indeed, he had done so. And the success which followed his obedience to God's command on that occasion should have encouraged him in a similar decision always. He was going forth to battle against the Edomites. He had raised out of his own kingdom of Judah alone an army of three hundred thousand men. In addition to these, he hired out of the kingdom of Israel a hundred thousand men for a hundred talents of silver, that is to say at a cost of about £50,000. But there came to him a man of God, saying, "O king, let not the army of Israel go with thee; for the Lord is not with Israel" (2 Chron. xxv. 7). Amaziah had not yet hardened his heart against God's message. He was not yet blinded to the evil results of forsaking God. So he considered seriously this difficulty, and saw that it would be folly to go forth in defiance of God's warning. But the question arose about the payment of these hired soldiers, and he said, "What shall we do for the hundred talents which I have given to the army of Israel?" And the man of God answered, "The Lord is able to give thee much more than this." Amaziah hesitated no longer. He sent away these hired troops, though he incurred their anger and vengeance in consequence; but when he went forth against the Edomites, his army gained a most decisive and overwhelming victory. Would that Amaziah had acted in a similar spirit of decision all through his life! Would that he had showed in other matters a similar spirit of dependence on God and obedience to him! Would that he had always remembered the prophet's words, "The Lord is able to give thee much more than this"! Oh that we would all remember this when tempted to make compromise with the world—when, for the sake of worldly gain, or popular applause, or the favour of men, or earthly rank, we are tempted to disregard the voice of conscience and of God! God's commands are clear. His promises are equally clear. *We never gain anything by making compromise with sin.* From the moment that Amaziah forsook God, success began to forsake his banners. He and his army were defeated by the army of Israel, and eventually he himself was slain by a conspiracy of his own servants. Let us learn that we should never, for the sake of any temporal advantage, make a compromise with sin, or disobey the command of God. *We may be the losers for the time, but the Lord is able to give us much more than this.* In an interesting book lately published, which gives an account of the mission to the fishermen in the North Sea, we are told that some of the owners of the fishing-vessels refused to allow their vessels to be used for a prayer-meeting or other religious service; but expected the men to work on the Lord's day as on others. There was a small fleet, all the skippers of which were anxious to have no fishing on Sunday, and accordingly sent home a "round robin" to the owners, praying for this concession. They waited anxiously for the return of the cutter with the owners' reply, and when at length it reached them, their hopes were utterly dashed, for the employers, while saying they would not forbid the skippers to keep their fishing-gear on board, gave them clearly to understand that any skipper doing so would run the risk of losing his berth at the end of the voyage. The matter was quietly and prayerfully discussed, and eventually all but one agreed, "We ought to obey God rather than man;" and so sabbath after sabbath this solitary dissentient laboured with his gear, while all the other vessels were lying-to. As each skipper's voyage expired, he ran home for the bi-monthly refit, yet not a word was said about discharging him, and as this happened to every skipper in turn, they made up their minds that the threat was an empty one. However, at Christmas the secret came out; for the owner, according to custom, read aloud to his assembled crews the list of the different vessels' earnings during the year. At last he stopped, and put down the paper. "Oh, but, sir," exclaimed several skippers, "you haven't read what So-and-so made," referring to the skipper who had fished seven days a week. "Why, what is that to *you?* I've read what *you've* made: doesn't that satisfy you?" "Why, no, sir, because, don't you see, he's fished every Sunday, while we've kept our trawls on board." "Well, well," muttered the owner, "I suppose it's sure to come out, so I may as well tell you. *He's at the bottom of the list.*" The man who related this story added reverently, "Them that honour me I will honour, but they that despise me shall be lightly esteemed." Those men showed true faithfulness. They would have no compromise. Cost what it might, they would obey the command of God, "Remember the sabbath day, to keep it holy." And he who gave the command honoured and rewarded them for their observance of it. He prospered their industry on the six days of the week more than the industry of the man who laboured on every day of the seven. Even in temporal blessings the policy of compromise is a policy of disaster. Much more when we look at the eternal consequences, "What shall it profit a man, if he shall gain the whole world, and lose his own soul?" We find that Amaziah's spirit of compromise infected his whole character. *Unfaithful himself, he did not like faithfulness in others.* When he began to worship the heathen idols, God sent a prophet to remonstrate with him. The prophet said to Amaziah, "Why hast thou sought after the gods of the people, which could not deliver their own people out of thine hand?" (2 Chron. xxv. 15). A very reasonable question, one would say. But the king was beyond rebuke. He commanded the prophet to cease, and threatened to punish him if he continued. It is a sign that something is wrong when men and women begin to dislike faithful preaching. Those whose own conscience is clear need feel no hurt when sin is rebuked. Beware of the policy of compromise. Let there be no compromise with the world, with godlessness, with sin; no compromise with godlessness in your family; no compromise with wrong in your business; no compromise with evil customs or companionships in your social life; no calling of evil good, and of good evil. Nail your colours to the mast. Let there be no compromise with your own besetting sins. Many a man has begun well, like Amaziah, but has ended badly, because he made a compromise with sin. He retained some old habit. He did not put away the high places of his pride, or his ambition, or his covetousness, or his passion—and in the long run his sin became too strong for him.—C. H. I.

Vers. 5, 6.—*Personal responsibility.* Amaziah visits with just execution the servants who had conspired against his father Joash. But he did not put to death the children of the murderers. He acted on the principle laid down by God through Moses (Deut. xxiv. 16), that "the fathers shall not be put to death for the children, nor the children for the fathers; every man shall be put to death for his own sin."

I. EVERY ONE OF US IS RESPONSIBLE FOR HIS OWN LIFE. "For we must all appear before the judgment-seat of Christ; that every one may receive the things done in his body, according to that he hath done, whether it be good or bad."

II. EVERY ONE OF US IS RESPONSIBLE FOR THE RIGHT DISCHARGE OF HIS OWN DUTIES. We cannot excuse ourselves by the unfaithfulness of others. Responsibility is something which we can never transfer to any one else. Men may deny their responsibility. They may refuse to fulfil it. They may neglect it. But there it is. They cannot get rid of it. Our responsibility to God for the life and opportunities which he has given is a truth we should do well to keep constantly before us.—C. H. I.

Vers. 1—29.—*Significant facts in God's government.* "In the second year of Joash," etc. In this chapter we have a sketch of a succession of kings both of Judah and Israel. Here are two kings of Judah—Amaziah and Azariah; and Joash, Jeroboam, and his son Zachariah, kings of Israel. The whole chapter suggests certain significant facts in God's government of mankind.

I. THE ENORMOUS FREEDOM OF ACTION WHICH HE ALLOWS WICKED MEN. Here we learn: 1. That God allows wicked men to *form wrong conceptions of himself.* All these kings, although descendants of Abraham, who was a monotheist, became idolaters. "The high places were not taken away: as yet the people did sacrifice and burnt incense on the high places." Golden calves, symbols of Egyptian worship, still stood in Dan and Bethel, at the extremities of the dominions. Terribly strange it seems to us that the Almighty Author of the human mind should permit it to think of him as some material object in nature, or as some production of the human hand. What human father, had he the power, would permit his children to form not only wrong but wicked impressions of himself? For what reason this is permitted I know not. Albeit it shows God's practical respect for that freedom of action with which he has endowed us. 2. That God allows wicked men to *obtain despotic dominion over others.* All these kings were wicked—Amaziah, Azariah, Joash, Jeroboam, and Zachariah, and yet they enjoyed an almost autocratic dominion over the rights, possessions, and lives of millions. Here we read of Amaziah slaying ten thousand men, capturing ten thousand prisoners, and taking Selah, the capital of the Edomites, and of Joash King of Israel using harshly the rights of the conqueror. "He came to Jerusalem, and brake down the wall of Jerusalem from the gate of Ephraim unto the corner gate." It is said of Jeroboam, who reigned forty-one years, that he "did evil in the sight of the Lord, and departed not from the sins of his father." Antecedently one might have concluded that, if a wicked man was allowed to live amongst his fellows, he would be doomed to obscurity and to social and political impotence; but it is not so. Why? Who shall answer?

II. GOD PUNISHES WICKED MEN BY THEIR OWN WICKEDNESS. 1. A wicked man is punished by *his own wickedness.* Amaziah's conduct is an example. Elated with his triumph over the Edomites, he sought occasion of war with the King of Israel. "He sent messengers to Joash, the son of Jehoahaz son of Jehu, King of Israel, saying, Come, let us look one another in the face," etc. About fifteen years after his defeat he fled from Jerusalem to Lachish to escape assassination, but the assassin pursued him, and struck him dead. It is ever so. Wickedness is its own punishment. The wicked passions of a corrupt man are his tormenting devils. Sin is suicidal. 2. A wicked man is punished by the *wickedness of others.* The thousands whom these despotic kings reduced to anguish, destitution, and death, were idolaters and rebels against Heaven, and by the hand of wicked men they were punished. Thus it ever is. Devils are their own tormentors. Sin converts a community of men into tormenting fiends; man becomes the avenging fate of man.

CONCLUSION. Learn: 1. *Humanity in this world is obviously in a morally abnormal condition.* It can never be that he whose power is immeasurable, whose wisdom and goodness are infinite and radiant everywhere above us and below us, could create such a state of things as we have here. He originates the good alone, permits the evil, and will ultimately overrule it for good. 2. *Faith in a future that shall rectify the evils of the present seems essential to true religion.* Genuine religion is a supreme love for the Supreme Existence. But who could love a Supreme Existence which could permit for ever such a state of existence as we have here? There must come a day of rectification: "When the Son of man shall come in his glory, and all the holy angels with him," etc. (Matt. xxv. 31—46).—D. T.

Vers. 1—7.—*Amaziah doing right.* The murder of Joash King of Judah, and the accession of his son Amaziah, took place a little after the accession of Joash the son of Jehoahaz in Israel, therefore just before the turn of the tide in the fortunes of the latter kingdom.

I. EARLY RIGHT-DOING. 1. *A promising beginning.* Amaziah was not, any more than his father, a man of strong character. He proved to be vain, boastful, and foolish. But he began well, giving heed to the counsels of God's prophets (cf. 2 Chron. xxv. 7—10), and therefore it is said of him, "He did right in the sight of the Lord." It is not, however, the beginning, but the end, which tests character (Col. i. 23; Heb. iii. 14). 2. *Significant shortcoming.* To the record of his right-doing it is added, "Yet not like David his father," or, as elsewhere, "not with a perfect heart." His conduct is likened to that of Joash his father, whose history very much resembled his own. Amaziah, like Joash, began well, afterwards lapsed into idolatry and cruelty, and died by conspiracy of his servants under a cloud of ignominy and contempt. Those who are like in sin need not wonder that they are like in doom. 3. *The high places unremoved.* This was one of the points in which Amaziah showed a want of thoroughness in right-doing. The sin was one of shortcoming rather than of positive transgression, like the keeping up of the worship of the calves in Israel. It is not, therefore, reckoned so hideous as the Baal-worship; but the after-effects show that no portion of God's Law can be neglected with impunity. The worship on high places was a temptation and snare to Judah. The neglect to remove them reacted seriously on the life of the nation.

II. JUST JUDGMENT. The treatment by Amaziah of his father's murderers gives further evidence of his early disposition to do well. We observe: 1. *The execution of justice.* The murderers were put to death. This was right. The existence of even real *grievances* does not justify resort to crime. David's treatment of Saul shows the right course to be pursued in such cases (1 Sam. xxiv. 4—12). And a nation is only secure when real crime is punished within its borders. 2. *Discrimination of innocent and guilty.* It is specially noted about Amaziah that, in taking this vengeance on the men who slew his father, he did not, as was a frequent custom in those times, slay the children of the murderers. He acted, therefore, on principle in his judgment, not in blind fury. His object was to vindicate justice, not to take revenge. He drew the line where it ought to be drawn—between the actually guilty and the innocent. There is a strong tendency, where anger is strongly kindled against a person or persons, to allow rage to overflow on those not directly implicated in their offence. The odium that attaches to them is extended also to their families, and pleasure is taken in inflicting insult and pain on their children and relatives. This ought not to be. 3. *Regard for God's Law.* The reason for Amaziah acting as he did was that it was so commanded in the Law of Moses (Deut. xxiv. 16). On the seeming contradiction between this passage and those which speak of the iniquity of the fathers being visited on the children, or which illustrate the actual punishment of children for their parents' sins—as in the case of Achan (Josh. vii. 24—26)—it may suffice to remark that the rule here laid down is one for *human* jurisprudence. There is a wider treatment of human beings, constantly finding illustration in providence, in which the principles of organic union and corporate responsibility have full play; but God does not entrust the enforcement of these to any human magistracy. What specially concerns us here is the fact that, finding such a rule laid down in the Word of God, Amaziah faithfully adhered to it. His conduct shows an advance in the moral conceptions of the time—a better appreciation of the fact of individuality.

III. EARLY VICTORY. In connection with this earlier and more promising part of Amaziah's reign, we are told of a great victory which he gained over the Edomites. The Edomites had revolted in Jehoram's reign (ch. viii. 20); but Amaziah now felt himself strong enough to attempt their resubjugation. In setting out on this war—the origin of which we do not precisely know—he had the countenance of God's prophets, and acted by their directions (2 Chron. xxv. 6—10). He had, as men always have when God is with them and they are content to be guided by his will, great success. He slew of Edom ten thousand, took Selah, or Petra, and changed its name. But the flush of his victory proved also the beginning of his ruin. 1. His conquest was not unmarked by great cruelty (cf. 2 Chron. xxv. 12). 2. He fell into idolatry, actually setting up the gods of the Edomites which he had brought home, and burning incense to them—those gods which, as a prophet reminded him, could not deliver their own people out of his hand (2 Chron. xxv. 15). From this point dates his declension. He acted precisely as his father had done in forcibly silencing the prophets; and God, in return, gave him up to a reprobate mind for his destruction. Prosperity tests a man's nature. There are few who can carry the full cup without becoming haughty and God-forgetful.—J. O.

Vers. 8—14.—*The boastful challenge, and its results.* It is in the light of the facts narrated in the Book of Chronicles, but not alluded to here, that we are to read the story of Amaziah's folly in his boastful challenge to Joash of Israel (cf. 2 Chron. xxv. 20).

I. THE BOASTFUL CHALLENGE. 1. *Its motives.* It is not difficult to conceive the kind of influences which led Amaziah to give this challenge to Joash. (1) Naturally vain-glorious, he was greatly elated by his successes over Edom, and was ambitious to pose as a great military conqueror. How many wars have had their origin in no higher source! To gratify the vanity and ambition of individuals, or the lust of glory in nations, torrents of blood have been shed. (2) Israel was at this time in a very humbled state, but showed signs of reviving. Amaziah probably thought it was a good time to bring back the revolted tribes to the sceptre of Judah. (3) The Israelites had given some provocation in attacks upon the cities of Judah (2 Chron. xxv. 13). This at least would furnish a pretext. 2. *Its nature.* The challenge took the form of a message to Joash, "Come, let us look one another in the face." In giving such a challenge, Amaziah did not count the cost (cf. Luke xiv. 31). He was puffed up with conceit, and did not reflect on the superior military abilities of Joash, already beginning to be displayed in his wars with the Syrians, or on his larger forces. Rather, Joash's rising reputation roused in him the ambition to measure himself against Joash. When men are left to themselves there are no limits to the extent to which their folly will lead them. 3. *Its lack of sanction from God.* This time God was not with Amaziah in his undertaking. No prophet's voice commanded, sanctioned, or promised blessings on the war. Amaziah was acting on his own motion, and in reliance solely on his own strength. God had left him, as he left Saul. In such condition a man but plunges on to his ruin.

II. The HAUGHTY REPLY. Joash perfectly took the measure of his challenger, and answered him according to his folly. 1. *His insulting parable.* First, he replied by a parable. He told how the briar (or thistle) of Lebanon sent to the cedar of Lebanon, demanding that the daughter of the cedar should be given in wife to his son. But a wild beast of the forest passed by, and trode down the briar. The idea of the parable is, of course, to ridicule the presumption of Amaziah in venturing to put himself on an equality with Joash. It was meant to sting and insult the Jewish king by intimating to him that in Joash's eyes he was no more than a contemptible briar in comparison with the majestic cedars. On it we remark (1) that Joash also cannot be acquitted of overweening arrogance. It is a scornful, haughty spirit which breathes in his parable. From the Israelitish point of view the ten tribes were *the* kingdom of Israel; Judah was the isolated tribe. But the state of Israel at this time, and in the recent past, did not warrant these boastful metaphors. The cedar, as well as the briar, had been pretty well trodden down by the wild beast of the forest. This arrogant spirit, moreover, is apt to lead its possessor into the error of despising things simply because they are outwardly weak. In this case the King of Israel very justly took the boastful Amaziah's measure. But it does not always follow that the cedar has the right to lord it over the briar. It is no uncommon thing for the weak things of the world to overcome the mighty (1 Cor. i. 27, 28). David was a feeble stripling in Goliath's sight, but Goliath fell before him (1 Sam. xvi. 43—51). The numbers may be few, but if they have a good cause, are inspired by faith, and go forward at God's call, one will chase a thousand (Deut. xxxii. 30; Josh. xxiii. 10). (2) Nevertheless, the parable was just in so far as Amaziah was matching himself against one who, as the event showed, was greatly his superior. Joash was by far the abler soldier, and had larger forces. Amaziah wished to show himself his equal, but lacked the power of taking a just estimate of his own capabilities. This is one of the first conditions of a man's strength—to know himself. "How many men may you meet in middle life whose career has been marked by bitter disappointments, and whose hearts have been soured by these! They began with vaulting hopes which have never been realized; and so they blame what they call their adverse fate. But you see the effect of one great blunder which has pursued them all their lives—you see that they have never sought to know themselves. They began in a fool's paradise, and they have never made their escape from it. A more exact and modest estimate of their own powers, a clear and honest apprehension of their own capacity, a readiness to do the work within their limits, the work they were meant to do, and they had been spared many bitter hours." 2. *His contemptuous advice.* Following up his parable, Joash gave the King of Judah a piece of advice, scornfully and contemptuously expressed, but such advice as, on the whole, Amaziah would have done well to take. (1) He touched truly enough the motive of his foolish challenge. "Thou hast indeed smitten Edom, and thine heart is lifted up." A measure of success turns the heads of some people, inflates their ideas of themselves, and incapacitates them for sober calculation of the future. (2) He bids him content himself with what he has achieved, and tarry at home. The tone is most insulting, implying the most perfect contempt for Amaziah's threatened attack; but the advice was wise. Amaziah was a fool to provoke a needless war, and run himself and his kingdom into danger from a mere motive of vain-glory. (3) He predicts to him what will happen if he persists in his foolish course. "Why shouldest thou meddle to thy hurt, that thou shouldest fall, even thou, and Judah with thee?" It perhaps was not to be expected that Amaziah should take advice so unpalatable, so tauntingly conveyed, so wounding to his pride and royal honour. But the result showed that Joash had not overstated his case. Amaziah meddled truly to his hurt, and he fell, even he, and Judah with him. It is the fatality of a foolish mind that it is impregnable to considerations which would show it its folly.

III. THE CRUSHING DEFEAT. Amaziah, as was to be expected, would not hear. No obstinate man does. He went on his foolish, headstrong way, and brought down upon himself an avalanche of trouble. 1. *The army was defeated.* He and Joash met in battle, and his army was utterly routed. It is characteristic that the fight took place at Beth-shemesh, in the territory of Judah. This shows that Joash was the first to move when he saw that war was inevitable. While Amaziah was dallying and mustering his men, Joash was already on the march, and took the offensive. For victory of any kind, much depends on promptitude, alertness, and activity on the part of the assailant. 2. *The king was taken prisoner.* Joash "took Amaziah." How long the king remained a captive is not said. He was probably delivered up after "hostages" had been given. But the humiliation was great and bitter. The people of Judah never forgot or forgave it. 3. *Jerusalem was captured and plundered.* The royal city shared the fate of its king. It had no alternative but to open its gates to the conqueror. Joash did not spare it. To mark the completeness of his conquest he, (1) brake down four hundred cubits of the city wall on the side towards Ephraim; (2) plundered the house of the Lord and the palace of the king of their treasures. The treasuries had been emptied in the preceding reign for Hazael (ch. xii. 18); now a second time their contents are taken away. Miserable people, and miserable king! No wonder burning indignation existed against Amaziah, who had led the kingdom into this trouble. We may see some parallel to it in the feelings of the French towards their emperor after the Franco-Prussian War. The lesson had been taught in the preceding reign, but Amaziah had not profited by his father's misfortunes; and, having followed his footsteps in sin, was now reaping the consequences in even severer chastisement.—J. O.

Vers. 15—22.—*Changes in two thrones.* The next events recorded are the accession of Jeroboam II. after the death of Joash, in Israel; and the conspiracy against Amaziah fifteen years later and the accession of Azariah, in Judah.

I. THE ACCESSION OF JEROBOAM. More is not told us, than we have already heard, of the "might" of Joash. Jeroboam, who succeeded him, proved the able son of an able father. But the stock of Jehu was godless as ever. The new king also, as we are to see, "did evil in the sight of the Lord," and kept up the "sin" of his namesake, Jeroboam I., in the worship of the calves. Great natural ability is often associated with godlessness of heart.

II. THE ACCESSION OF AZARIAH. 1. *Azariah made king.* The notice of the conspiracy against Amaziah precedes in the narrative the notice of Azariah's accession; but there is some reason from the chronology to think that the son was made king along with his father shortly after Amaziah's disastrous defeat. (1) It is stated in ch. xv. 8 that the son of Jeroboam II., Zachariah, began to *reign* in the thirty-eighth year of Azariah, and as there is no sign in the narrative of the interregnum of eleven years which chronologers usually introduce, it would follow that Azariah really began to reign about eleven years before his father's death. (2) This is in itself not unlikely when we remember the odium which must have fallen on Amaziah after his defeat and captivity, and the capture of Jerusalem. The proof he had given of incapacity for government would make it desirable, to secure the popularity of the throne, that his son should be associated with him in the kingdom. (3) There are indications in the narrative which point in this direction, *e.g.* the age of Amaziah, only sixteen years; the statement that Amaziah "lived" fifteen years after the death of Joash, where we might have expected the word "reigned;" lastly, the statement that Amaziah "built Elath, and restored it to Judah, after that the king slept with his fathers." 2. *Amaziah's ignominious end.* In any case, it seems certain that Amaziah's popularity never revived after the unhappy encounter with Joash. Fifteen years rolled on, and at length, from causes to us unknown, a plot was formed against him in Jerusalem.

He fled to Lachish, but was pursued and killed. The slain king was brought back on horses, and buried in Jerusalem in the royal sepulchre. Thus the sun of another descendant of David, who had forsaken the God of his fathers, went down in blood and shame.—J. O.

Vers. 23—29.—*The reign of Jeroboam II.* After the usual statement that Jeroboam " did evil in the sight of the Lord, and departed not from the sins of Jeroboam the son of Nebat, who made Israel to sin," we have some brief notices of his reign. Note—

I. THE REVIVED FORTUNES OF ISRAEL. 1. *Jeroboam's successes in war.* This able monarch continued the work of Joash. In fulfilment of the promise that God would give Israel a saviour, Jeroboam was enabled to complete the recovery of the cities and territories of Israel from the Syrians. "He restored the coast of Israel from the entering in of Hamath unto the sea of the plain," that is, he extended the boundaries of the kingdom as widely as they had ever reached in the days of its greatest prosperity. 2. *The cause of this—God's pity for Israel.* This remarkable turn in the fortunes of Israel was strange when it is remembered that Jeroboam was not a man who had the fear of God before him. The explanation is that already given (ch. xiii. 23), the pity which God had for Israel, his desire to give it one more chance before blotting out its name, his respect for the covenant with the fathers, and, subordinately, his regard to the prayer of Jehoahaz (ch. xiii. 4, 5). If, as the result of this revival of the nation's fortunes, piety did not also revive, destruction would come all the more speedily. In raising up this powerful king to save Israel, we see God's faithfulness to his promise.

II. PROPHETIC ACTIVITY. We have allusion in the text to the prophetic activity of Jonah, the son of Amittai, the same who was sent to Nineveh, and we know that in this reign other prophets, notably Hosea and Amos, exercised their ministry. The writings of the latter prophets show us how, amidst the sunshine of revived prosperity, the condition of the people did not improve, but grew more and more corrupt. But God's faithfulness and care and love for his people are shown in sending such prophets to warn them (cf. ch. xvii. 13). What could exceed the tender pathos of a ministry like Hosea's, or the fidelity and earnestness of a testimony like that of Amos, who bearded the highest in the land to bear witness against them (Amos vii. 10)? Yet the people would not hear, but attributed their prosperity to their idols, and worshipped them more than ever, while immorality, violence, and the loosening of all bonds between man and man abounded more and more (Hos. iv. 1).

III. THE EVE OF COLLAPSE. Jeroboam died, and was succeeded by his son Zachariah. This was the fourth generation of the house of Jehu, and it will be seen that he reigned only six months. From this time Israel went rapidly to its ruin. The height of prosperity reached in the reign of Jeroboam was but the last flicker of the light before final extinction. A little over thirty years after Jeroboam's death—forty at most—the words of the prophets were fulfilled, and the kingdom of Israel was destroyed, and its people carried away by the Assyrian.—J. O.

EXPOSITION.

CHAPTER XV.

Vers. 1—38.—REIGNS OF AZARIAH AND JOTHAM OVER JUDAH; AND OF ZACHARIAH, SHALLUM, MENAHEM, PEKAHIAH, AND PEKAH OVER ISRAEL.

Vers. 1—7.—THE REIGN OF AZARIAH OVER JUDAH. The writer now more and more compresses his narrative. Into a single chapter he crowds the events of seven reigns, covering the space of nearly seventy years. He is consequently compelled to omit several most important historical events, which are however, fortunately supplied by the writer of Chronicles. Azariah's reign, which here occupies only seven verses, in Chronicles fills an entire chapter (twenty-three verses). (See 2 Chron. xxvi. 1—23.)

Ver. 1.—In the twenty and seventh year of Jeroboam King of Israel began Azariah son of Amaziah King of Judah to reign. In ch. xiv. 23 it is distinctly stated that Jeroboam's reign of forty-one years commenced in the fifteenth of Amaziah, who from that time lived only fifteen years (ch. xiv. 17). Either, therefore, Azariah must have begun to reign in the fifteenth year of Jeroboam, or there must have been an interregnum of twelve years between the death of Amaziah and the accession of Azariah. As this last hypothesis is precluded by the narrative of 2 Chron. xxvi. 1 and ch. xiv. 20, 21, we must correct the "twenty-seventh year" of this verse into the "fifteenth." If we do this, corresponding changes will have to be made in vers. 8, 13, 23, and 27.

Ver. 2.—**Sixteen years old was he when he began to reign, and he reigned two and fifty years in Jerusalem.** These numbers are confirmed by Chronicles (2 Chron. xxvi. 1—3) and by Josephus (' Ant. Jud.,' ix. 10. § 4), who says that he reigned fifty-two years, and died at the age of sixty-eight. **And his mother's name was Jecholiah of Jerusalem.** Josephus ('Ant. Jud.,' ix. 10. § 3) calls her "Achiala."

Ver. 3.—**And he did that which was right in the sight of the Lord, according to all that his father Amaziah had done** (comp. ch. xiv. 3 and 2 Chron. xxvi. 4). Josephus uses still stronger expressions. "Azariah was," he says (*l. s. c.*), "a good king, naturally just and high-minded, and indefatigable in his administration of affairs." According to the author of Chronicles (2 Chron. xxvi. 5), he " sought God in the days of Zechariah."

Ver. 4.—**Save that the high places were not removed: the people sacrificed and burnt incense still on the high places** (comp. ch. xiv. 4, and the comment *ad loc.*).

Ver. 5.—**And the Lord smote the king.** This comes in somewhat strangely, following close upon a statement that the king " did that which was *right* in the sight of the Lord." We have to go to Chronicles for an explanation. By Chronicles it appears that, in the earlier portion of his reign, Azariah was a good and pious prince, and that God blessed him in all his undertakings. Not only did he recover Eloth (2 Chron. xxvi. 2), but he carried on a successful war with the Philistines—took Gath, Jabneh (Jamnia), and Ashdod, and dismantled them (2 Chron. xxvi. 6), defeated the Arabians of Gur-Baal, and the Mehunim or Maonites (2 Chron. xxvi. 7), forced the Ammonites to pay him a tribute, and caused his power to be known and feared far and wide (2 Chron. xxvi. 8). The standing army which he maintained numbered 307,500 men, under 2600 officers, well armed and equipped with shields, spears, helmets, breast-plates, bows, and slings (2 Chron. xxvi. 12—14). "His name spread far abroad, for he was wonderfully helped" (2 Chron. xxvi. 15). This marvellous prosperity developed in him a pride equal to that of his father, but one which vented itself differently. Azariah, deeming himself superior to all other men, and

exempt from ordinary rules, boldly invaded the priestly office, took a censer, and entered into the temple, and proceeded to burn incense upon the golden altar that was before the veil (2 Chron. xxvi. 16—18). It was then that "the Lord smote the king." As, in defiance of the high priest and his attendant train, who sought to prevent the lawless act, Azariah persisted in his endeavours, God struck him with leprosy, his forehead grew white with the unmistakable scaly scab, and in a moment his indomitable pride was quelled. The priests closed in upon him and began to thrust him out, but no violence was necessary. Aware of what had happened, "he himself also hasted to go out, because the Lord had smitten him" (2 Chron. xxvi. 20). It is not very clear why the writer of Kings passes over these facts; but certainly they are not discredited by his silence. At any rate, those who accept the entire series of conquests, whereof the writer of Kings says nothing, on the sole authority of Chronicles, are logically precluded from rejecting the circumstances accompanying the leprosy, which is acknowledged by the writer of Kings, and viewed as a judgment from God. **So that he was a leper unto the day of his death, and dwelt in a several house** (comp. 2 Chron. xxvi. 21). Lepers had to be separated from the congregation—to "dwell alone"—"without the camp" (Lev. xiii. 46). Ahaziah's "several house" is regarded by some as an "infirmary," or "hospital for lepers" (Ewald, Gesenius, Winer); but there is no reason to believe that hospitals of any kind existed among the Israelites. The lepers mentioned in ch. vii. 3 are houseless. בֵּית הַחָפְשִׁית is best translated "house of separation," and understood of a house standing by itself in the open country, separate from others. "Probably the house in which the leprous king lived was," as Bähr says, "especially built for him." **And Jotham the king's son** was **over the house**—not over the "several house," but over the royal palace—**judging the people of the land**; *i.e.* executing the royal functions, whereof "judging" was one of the highest. Azariah's infirmity made a regency necessary, and naturally his eldest son held the office.

Ver. 6.—**And the rest of the acts of Azariah, and all that he did, are they not written in the book of the chronicles of the kings of Judah?** For Azariah's principal acts, see the commentary on the first clause of ver. 5.

Ver. 7.—**So Azariah slept with his fathers; and they buried him with his fathers in the city of David.** Here again the writer of Chronicles is more exact. Azariah, he tells us (2 Chron. xxvi. 23), was not buried in the rock-sepulchre which contained the bodies of the other kings, but in another part of the field wherein the sepulchre was situated. This was quite consonant with Jewish feeling with respect to the uncleanness of the leper. **And Jotham his son reigned in his stead.** Jotham, already for some years prince regent, became king as a matter of course on his father's demise.

Vers. 8—12.—Reign of Zachariah over Israel. Fulfilment of the Promise made to Jehu. The writer has nothing to record of Zachariah but his murder by Shallum after a reign of six months. Vers. 8, 9, and 11 contain the usual formula. Ver. 10 gives the only event that needed record. Ver. 12 recalls to the reader's attention a previous passage, in which a prophecy had been mentioned, whereof Zachariah's reign was the fulfilment.

Ver. 8.—**In the thirty and eighth year of Azariah King of Judah did Zachariah the son of Jeroboam reign over Israel in Samaria.** If Azariah began to reign in the twenty-seventh year of Jeroboam (ver. 1), and Jeroboam died in his forty-first or forty-second year (ch. xiv. 23), Zachariah must have ascended the throne in the fifteenth or sixteenth year of Azariah. Even if Azariah became king in the fifteenth of Jeroboam, as has been shown to be probable (see the comment on ver. 1), Zachariah's accession cannot have been earlier than Azariah's twenty-sixth year. An interregnum between the death of Jeroboam and the accession of Zachariah is not to be thought of. **Six months.** So also Josephus (see 'Ant. Jud.,' ix. 11. § 1).

Ver. 9.—**And he did that which was evil in the sight of the Lord, as his fathers had done: he departed not from the sins of Jeroboam the son of Nebat, who made Israel to sin.** The customary formula, with nothing to emphasize it. In the short space of barely six months, Zachariah could not do either much good or much evil.

Ver. 10.—**And Shallum the son of Jabesh conspired against him.** Josephus calls Shallum Zachariah's "friend," but otherwise adds nothing to the present narrative. **And smote him before the people.** The phrase employed is very unusual, and has justly excited suspicion. It was not understood by the LXX., who translate ἐπάταξαν αὐτὸν Κεβλαάμ, which gives no sense. Ewald sought to solve the difficulty by inventing a king, "Zobolam," but other critics have found this expedient too bold. The rendering of our translators is generally accepted, though *qobal*, "before," only occurs here and in Daniel. If we accept this rendering,

we must suppose that the act of violence was done openly, like Jehu's murder of Jehoram. **And slew him, and reigned in his stead** (comp. ver. 13).

Ver. 11.—**And the rest of the acts of Zachariah, behold, they are written in the book of the chronicles of the kings of Israel.**

Ver. 12.—**This was the word of the Lord which he spake unto Jehu** (comp. ch. x. 30), saying, **Thy sons shall sit on the throne of Israel unto the fourth** generation. The direct promise was, "Thy house shall hold the throne so long;" the implied prophecy, "They shall not hold it longer." There had not been wanting other indications of the coming troubles. Hosea had declared that God would avenge the blood of Jezreel upon the house of Jehu (Hos. i. 4). Amos had gone further, and had openly proclaimed that God would "rise against the house of Jeroboam *with the sword*" (Amos vii. 9). The threat had been understood as a threat against Jeroboam himself (Amos vii. 11), but this was a misinterpretation. The words plainly pointed to a revolution in the time of his son. **And so it came to pass.** The house of Jehu ceased to reign in the fourth generation of the descendants of its founder. No considerations of prudence or of gratitude could keep the nation faithful to any dynasty for a longer time than this. In breaking off from the divinely chosen house of David, and choosing to themselves a king, the Israelites had sown the seeds of instability in their state, and put themselves at the mercy of any ambitious pretender. Five dynasties had already borne rule in the two hundred years that the kingdom had lasted; four more were about to hold the throne in the remaining fifty years of its existence. "Unstable as water, thou shalt not excel," though said of Reuben only (Gen. xlix. 4), fairly expressed the character of the entire kingdom, with which Reuben cast in its lot at the time of the separation.

Vers. 13—15.—Short and Unimportant Reign of Shallum. Three verses suffice for the reign of Shallum, the son of Jabesh, who held the throne for only thirty days. Hearing of his conspiracy, Menahem, the son of Gadi—"the general," as Josephus calls him ('Ant. Jud.,' x. 11. § 1)—marched from Tirzah to Samaria, got Shallum into his power, and put him to death (ver. 14). The writer concludes with the usual formula (ver. 15).

Ver. 13.—**Shallum the son of Jabesh began to reign in the nine and thirtieth year of Uzziah King of Judah.** This date follows from that of ver. 8, and must stand or fall with it. The true accession-year of Shallum was probably the twenty-seventh of Uzziah. **And he reigned a full month in Samaria** ; literally, *a month of days*—" thirty days " according to Josephus.

Ver. 14.—**For Menahem the son of Gadi went up from Tirzah.** Ewald supposes Tirzah to have been the " native city " of Menahem; but this is not stated. According to Josephus (*l. s. c.*), he was commander-in-chief, and happened to be in Tirzeh at the time. (On the probable site of Tirzeh, see the comment on 1 Kings xiv. 17.) It was the royal city of the kingdom of the ten tribes from the later part of Jeroboam's reign to the building of Samaria by Omri (see 1 Kings xiv. 17; xvi. 6, 8, 15, 23). **And came to Samaria, and smote Shallum the son of Jabesh in Samaria**—Josephus says that there was a battle, in which Shallum was slain—**and slew him, and reigned in his stead.**

Ver. 15.—**And the rest of the acts of Shallum, and his conspiracy which he made** (see ver. 10), **behold, they are written in the book of the chronicles of the kings of Israel.**

Vers. 16—22.— REIGN OF MENAHEM, AND EXPEDITION OF PUL AGAINST SAMARIA. Two events only of Menahem's reign receive notice from the writer. (1) His capture of Tiphsah, and severe treatment of the inhabitants (ver. 16). (2) The invasion of his land by an Assyrian monarch, called " Pul " or " Phul," and his submission to that monarch's authority. Pul's retirement was bought by a large sum of money, which Menahem collected from his subjects (vers. 19, 20).

Ver. 16.—**Then Menahem smote Tiphsah.** The only town of this name known to history or geography is the famous city on the Euphrates (1 Kings iv. 24), called by the Greeks Thapsacus. It has been thought that Menahem could not have pushed his conquests so far, and a second Tiphsah has been invented in the Israelite highland, between Tirzah and Samaria, of which there is no other notice anywhere. But " Tiphsah," which means " passage" or " fordway," is an unsuitable name for a city in such a situation. The view of Keil is clearly tenable—that Zachariah had intended to carry on his father's warlike policy, and had collected an army for a great Eastern expedition, which had its head-quarters at the royal city of Tirzah, and was under the command of Menahem. As the expedition was about to start, the news came that

Shallum had murdered Zachariah and usurped the throne. Menahem upon this proceeded from Tirzah to Samaria, crushed Shallum, and, returning to his army, carried out without further delay the expedition already resolved upon. The Assyrian records show that, at the probable date of the expedition, Assyria was exceptionally weak, and in no condition to resist an attack, though a little later, under Tiglath-pileser, she recovered herself. **And all that were therein, and the coasts thereof, from Tirzah.** " From Tirzah " means " starting from Tirzah," as in ver. 14. It is to be connected with " smote," not with " coasts." **Because they opened not** to him, **therefore he smote** it. Determined resistance on the part of a city summoned to surrender has always been regarded as justifying an extreme severity of treatment. It is not clear that Menahem transgressed the ordinary usages of war in what he did, however much he transgressed the laws of humanity. And **all the women therein that were with child** he ripped up (comp. ch. viii. 12, with the comment; and see also Isa. xiii. 18; Hos. x. 14 ; xiii. 16; Amos i. 13).

Ver. 17.—**In the nine and thirtieth year of Azariah King of Judah began Menahem the son of Gadi to reign over Israel** (comp. ver. 13, and the comment), **and reigned ten years in Samaria.** So Josephus ('Ant. Jud.,' ix. 11. § 1).

Ver. 18.—**And he did** that which was **evil in the sight of the Lord : he departed not all his days from the sins of Jeroboam the son of Nebat, who made Israel to sin.** The writer does not seem to regard Menahem as either better or worse than his predecessors. The usual formula suffices to describe the moral and religious aspect of his reign.

Ver. 19.—And **Pul the King of Assyria came against the land.** There is no connective in the Hebrew text, and it has been proposed to supply one; but there can be little doubt that the best emendation is that suggested by Thenius, who changes the כָּל-יָמֵי of ver. 18 into בְיָמָיו, and attaches that word to ver. 19. Ver. 19 will then read thus: " In his days Pul the King of Assyria came against the land "—and no connective will be wanted. The greatest doubt has been entertained with regard to the identity of Pul, whose name does not appear in the Assyrian Eponym Canon, or in any other purely Assyrian document. But recently discovered Babylonian documents seem to prove that Pul (Pulu) was the Babylonian name for Tiglath-pileser, who reigned under that name in Babylon during his last two years, and appears in the Canon of Ptolemy as " Porus." Tiglath-pileser, the great founder of the later Assyrian empire, made himself king in

B.C. 745, and proceeded to consolidate the Assyrian power on every side, after a period of great weakness and disorganization. He made several expeditions against Babylonia, and several into Syria and Palestine. The expedition in which he came into contact with Menahem is thought to have been that of his eighth year, B.C. 738 (see G. Smith, 'Eponym Canon,' pp. 117—120; and, for the identity of Tiglath-pileser with Pul, see the 'Transactions of the Society of Biblical Archæology' for 1884, p. 198). **And Menahem gave Pul a thousand talents of silver.** A vast sum certainly, equal to above a quarter of a million of our money, perhaps to some extent a punishment for the siege and sack of Tiphsah. But not a sum that it would have been impossible to pay. A King of Damascus, about fifty years previously, had bought off an Assyrian attack by the payment of two thousand three hundred talents of silver and twenty talents of gold (see 'Eponym Canon,' p. 115). **That his hand might be with him to confirm the kingdom in his hand;** i.e. that Pul might take him under his protection, accept him as one of his subject-princes, and (by implication) support him against possible rivals.

Ver. 20.—**And Menahem exacted the money of Israel.** Either he was not possessed of any accumulated treasure, such as the kings of Judah could commonly draw upon (1 Kings xv. 18; ch. xii. 18; xvi. 8; xviii. 15, 16), or he thought it more prudent to keep his stores untouched, and obtain the money from his subjects. **Even of all the mighty men of wealth.** The context shows this to be the meaning; and the rendering is justified by Ruth ii. 1; 1 Sam. ix. 1. "Mighty men of *valour*" cannot possibly be intended. **Of each man fifty shekels of silver, to give to the King of Assyria.** Fifty shekels was a heavy tax, not less than £5 or £6 of our money. To produce a thousand talents, this tax had to be levied on some sixty thousand persons. Tiglath-pileser mentions his receipt of tribute from "Minikhimmi of Tsammirin" (Menahem of Someron or Samaria), but does not tell us the amount (see 'Eponym Canon,' p. 120, line 29). **So the King of Assyria turned back, and stayed not there in the land.** Kings of Assyria usually returned home at the end of each campaign, and wintered in their own territory.

Ver. 21.—**And the rest of the acts of Menahem, and all that he did, are they not written in the book of the chronicles of the kings of Israel?** Nothing more is known of Menahem the son of Gadi, since he certainly cannot be identical with the prince of the same name who is mentioned as

"Menahem of Samaria" in the inscriptions of Sennacherib ('Eponym Canon,' p. 132, line 17). This second Menahem is probably a descendant of the first, who was allowed a sort of titular sovereignty over the conquered town.

Ver. 22.—**And Menahem slept with his fathers**—i.e. died—**and Pekahiah his son reigned in his stead.** So Josephus ('Ant. Jud.,' ix. 11. § 1), who calls him "Phakeias."

Vers. 23—26.—SHORT REIGN OF PEKAHIAH. The short reign of Pekahiah was wholly undistinguished. He held the throne for two years only, or perhaps for parts of two years, and performed no action that any historian has thought worthy of record. Our author has nothing to relate of him but the circumstances of his death (ver. 25), wherewith he combines the usual formulæ (vers. 23, 24, 26).

Ver. 23.—**In the fiftieth year of Azariah King of Judah;** really in the thirty-seventh year (see the comment on vers. 1, 8, and 27). Azariah is mentioned by Tiglath-pileser as contending with him in the year in which he took tribute from Menahem ('Eponym Canon,' pp. 117—120), which is thought to have been B.C. 738. Apparently, he too was forced to pay tribute (ibid., pp. 117, 118, lines 2, 3) to the Assyrian monarch. **Pekahiah the son of Menahem began to reign over Israel in Samaria, and reigned two years.** So Josephus (l. s. c.).

Ver. 24.—**And he did that which was evil in the sight of the Lord: he departed not from the sins of Jeroboam the son of Nebat, who made Israel to sin.** Josephus adds that he reigned with the same cruelty as his father (τῇ τοῦ πατρὸς κατακολουθήσας ὠμότητι), but we cannot be sure that this is more than a conjecture, founded on the shortness of his reign.

Ver. 25.—**But Pekah the son of Remaliah.** Remaliah was probably a man of some importance, since Pekah seems to have been almost better known by his patronymic, Ben-Remaliah, "son of Remaliah," than by his own proper name (see Isa. vii. 4, 5, 9; viii. 6). **A captain of his**—"captain of a thousand," according to Josephus (l. s. c.)—conspired against him, and smote him in Samaria, in the palace of the king's house; literally, *in the tower* (or *keep*) *of the king's house,* the loftiest part (אַרְמוֹן is from רוּם, to be high)—certainly not the harem (Ewald), if Pekahiah was feasting there with his friends (δολοφονηθεὶς ἐν συμποσίῳ μετὰ φίλων ἀπέθανε), as Josephus says. **With Argob and Arieh.** These seem to be the "friends" of Josephus, who were *with the king* and shared his fate, not fellow-conspirators with Pekah. The names are uncommon ones. **And with him**—*i.e.* Pekah—**fifty men of the Gileadites**; fifty men of "the Four Hundred," according to the LXX. "The Four Hundred" were probably the royal body-guard, which at this time may have consisted of Gileadites. **And he killed him, and reigned in his room.** It does not appear that Pekah had any grievance. His crime seems to have been simply prompted by ambition.

Ver. 26.—**And the rest of the acts of Pekahiah, and all that he did, behold, they** are written in the book of the chronicles of the kings of Israel.

Vers. 27—31.—REIGN OF PEKAH. The writer is again exceedingly brief. Pekah's reign was a remarkable one, and might have furnished much material to the historian. In conjunction with Rezin of Damascus, he made war upon Judæa, defeated Ahaz with great loss (2 Chron. xxviii. 6), and laid siege to Jerusalem (Isa. vii. 1). Ahaz called in the aid of Assyria, and Tiglath-pileser made two expeditions into Palestine—the one mentioned in ver. 29, and another some years afterwards. In the latter he seems to have had the assistance of Hoshea, who, with his sanction, slew Pekah, and became king. The scanty notices of our author must be supplemented from 2 Chron. xxviii.; Isa. vii. 1—9; viii. 1—8; and the Assyrian inscriptions.

Ver. 27.—**In the two and fiftieth year of Azariah King of Judah;** rather, *in the thirty-ninth* or *thirty-eighth year* (see the comment on ver. 23). Pekahiah's "two years" may not have been complete. **Pekah the son of Remaliah began to reign over Israel in Samaria, and reigned twenty years.** The Assyrian records make this number impossible. Tiglath-pileser's entire reign lasted only *eighteen* years, yet it more than covered the entire reign of Pekah. When he first invaded the kingdom of Samaria, Menahem was upon the throne ('Eponym Canon,' p. 120, line 29); when he last attacked it, probably in B.C. 730—two years before his death in B.C. 728—he set up Hoshea, or, at any rate, sanctioned his usurpation (ibid., pp. 123, 124, lines 15—18). Pekah's entire reign must have come in the interval, which is certainly not more than one of fifteen, probably not more than one of ten years.

Ver. 28.—**And he did that which was evil in the sight of the Lord: he departed not from the sins of Jeroboam the son of** Nebat, who made Israel to sin. Josephus ('Ant. Jud.,' ix. 11. § 1) says that Pekah was an irreligious king, and a transgressor of the Law (ἀσεβής τε καὶ παράνομος). Isaiah shows how he intrigued with foreigners against his brethren of the sister kingdom (Isa. vii. 2—6). The writer of Chronicles tells of his fierce anger against the Jews (2 Chron. xxviii. 9), and of the dreadful carnage which he sanctioned after the great battle.

Ver. 29.—**In the days of Pekah King of Israel came Tiglath-pileser King of Assyria.** Tiglath-pileser's records are not in the shape of annals, and are, moreover, in a very mutilated condition. He does not date events, like most Assyrian kings, by his regnal years. His first expedition into Syria is thought, however, to have been in his third year, B.C. 743, but there is no evidence that, on this occasion, he proceeded further south than Damascus, where he took tribute from Rezin. Some years after this—B.C. 738, according to Mr. G. Smith—he penetrated to Palestine, where his chief enemy was Azariah King of Judah, who had united under his sway most of the tribes as far as Hamath. After chastising Azariah, he extended his dominion over most of the neighbouring states and kingdoms; and it was at this time that (as related in ver. 19) he took tribute from Menahem. Subsequently (about B.C. 734) he made an expedition for the purpose of conquest, which receives very scant notice, in one inscription only. This is probably the expedition of the present passage. **And took Ijon, and Abel-beth-maachah.** These were places in the extreme north of the Israelite territory, in the vicinity of the Lake Merom, such as would naturally be among the first to fall before an Assyrian invader (on their exact position, see the comment on 1 Kings xv. 20). **And Janoah.** Janoah is now generally regarded as identical with the modern *Hunîn*, a village close by "an ancient fortress of great strength" (Robinson, 'Later Researches,' p. 371), in the hill country north-west of Merom. It is in a direct line between Abel-beth-maachah (*Abil*) and Kedesh (*Cades*), as we should expect from the present passage. **And Kedesh, and Hazor.** Kedesh is beyond all doubt the "Kedes," or "Cades," of to-day—an important site in the same mountain district, rather more than six miles south of Hunîn, and four from the "waters of Merom" (see Robinson, 'Later Researches,' pp. 366, 367). Hazor was in the near neighbourhood of Kedesh, towards the south probably. The exact position is disputed. Robinson's arguments in favour of El-Khureibeh are weighty; but the engineers employed by the Palestine Exploration Fund regard Khurbat-Harrah, between Kedesh and the Lake Merom, as a still more probable situation. **And Gilead.** "Gilead," in this connection, can scarcely be "the whole of the land to the east of the Jordan" (Keil, Bähr)—the territory of Gad, Reuben, and Manasseh, not of Naphtali. It is more likely to be a *small* district near Merom, perhaps the eastern coast of the lake (Gesenius), which was afterwards a part of Gaulonitis. The LXX., instead of Γαλαάδ, have Γαλαάν. **And Galilee;** Hebrew הַגָּלִילָה (see the comment on 1 Kings ix. 11, p. 190). The inscription of Tiglath-pileser, which appears to allude to this expedition, mentions "Galhi," and "Abel" (probably Abel-beth-maachah) as conquered at this time, and "added to Assyria." The places were, it says, on the border of the land of Beth-Omri (Samaria) (see the 'Eponym Canon,' p. 123, lines 6, 7). **And carried them captive to Assyria.** Deportation of captives was largely practised by Tiglath-pileser, as appears from the 'Eponym Canon,' pp. 118—120, and 122.

Ver. 30.—**And Hoshea the son of Elah made a conspiracy against Pekah the son of Remaliah, and smote him, and slew him, and reigned in his stead.** By a mutilated notice in the records of Tiglath-pileser, it appears that the revolution here related was the result of another invasion of the Israelite territory by that monarch. "The land of Beth-Omri," he says, ". . . the tribe . . . the goods of its people and their furniture I sent to Assyria. Pekah their king [I caused to be put to death?] and Hoshea I appointed to the kingdom over them; their tribute I received, and [their treasures?] to Assyria I sent" ('Eponym Canon,' pp. 123, 124, lines 15—19). It is probably this invasion of which the writer of Chronicles speaks (1 Chron. v. 26) as resulting in the deportation of the Reubenites, the Gadites, and the half-tribe of Manasseh. **In the twentieth year of Jotham the son of Uzziah.** This date stands in contradiction with ver. 33, where Jotham's entire reign is reckoned at sixteen years, and apparently must be a corrupt reading.

Ver. 31.—**And the rest of the acts of Pekah, and all that he did** (see the comment on vers. 27—31), **behold, they are written in the book of the chronicles of the kings of Israel.**

Vers. 32—38.—REIGN OF JOTHAM. Once more the writer turns from Israel to Judah, and proceeds to give an account of the reign of Jotham the son of Azariah, or Uzziah, who was appointed regent in his father's place, when Uzziah was struck with leprosy (ver. 5). The account given of the reign is somewhat scanty, and requires to be supplemented from Chronicles (2 Chron. xxvii.).

Ver. 32.—**In the second year of Pekah the son of Remaliah King of Israel began Jotham the son of Uzziah King of Judah to reign.** In the second year of Pekah, Azariah died, and Jotham became actual king; but his joint reign with his father commenced very much earlier. His sole reign was probably a short one.

Ver. 33.—**Five and twenty years old was he when he began to reign, and he reigned sixteen years in Jerusalem** — *i.e.* sixteen years from his appointment to be regent, as appears plainly from 2 Chron. xxvi. 23 and xxvii. 1 (comp. Josephus, 'Ant. Jud.,' ix. 10. § 4; 12. § 1)—and his mother's name was Jerusha, the daughter of Zadok. So the author of Chronicles (2 Chron. xxvii. 1); Josephus ('Ant. Jud.,' ix. 11. § 2) calls his mother "Jerasa."

Ver. 34.—**And he did that which was right in the sight of the Lord: he did according to all that his father Uzziah had done.** The author of Chronicles says the same, but adds, very pertinently, "Howbeit he entered not into the temple of the Lord"—*i.e.* he did not repeat his father's act of impiety. Josephus is still warmer in his praises. "This king," he says (*l. s. c.*), "was deficient in no manner of virtue; but was at once pious in things pertaining to God, and just in those pertaining to men. He was careful and watchful over the city; whatever needed reparation or adornment, he laboured to supply strenuously, as the porticoes in the temple and the gates thereof; and where any part of the wall had gone to ruin, he raised it up again, and built towers of vast size and difficult to capture. And in all other matters pertaining to the kingdom, where there had been neglect, he applied great care and attention."

Ver. 35.—**Howbeit the high places were not removed: the people sacrificed and burned incense . still in the high places. He built the higher gate of the house of the Lord.** The "higher gate" is thought to be that towards the north, and its fortification implied a fear of attack from that quarter. It must have become amply evident to the kings of Judah, at any rate from the time of the attack on Menahem (ver. 19), that the independence of both kingdoms was menaced by Assyria, and that it was of great importance that their principal fortresses should be placed in a state of efficient defence. Azariah had paid great attention to the fortifying and arming of Jerusalem (2 Chron. xxvi. 9, 15), and his son now followed in his footsteps. From 2 Chron. xxvii. 3 we learn that he not only built the high gate of the temple, but also "on the wall of Ophel built much."

Nor was he content with fortifying the capital. He also "built cities in the mountains of Judah, and in the forests he built castles and towers." Tiglath-pileser had made war on his father ('Eponym Canon,' pp. 117, 118). He felt that any day his own turn might come.

Ver. 36.—**Now the rest of the acts of Jotham, and all that he did.** The principal event of Jotham's reign was his war with Ammon. The writer of Chronicles says, "He fought also with the king of the Ammonites, and prevailed against them. And the children of Ammon gave him the same year an hundred talents of silver, and ten thousand measures of wheat, and ten thousand of barley. So much did the children of Ammon pay unto him, both the second year, and the third" (2 Chron. xxvii. 5). Josephus ('Ant. Jud.,' ix. 11. § 2) gives nearly the same account, but regards the payment as an annual tribute, intended to be permanent. **Are they not written in the book of the chronicles of the kings of Judah?**

Ver. 37.—**In those days the Lord began to send against Judah Rezin the King of Syria.** Rezin's name occurs in the Assyrian inscriptions early in the reign of Tiglath-pi-

leser, probably in the year B.C. 743. At that time he pays to the Assyrians a heavy tribute, consisting of eighteen talents of gold, three hundred talents of silver, two hundred talents of copper, and twenty talents of spices. Subsequently, about the year B.C. 734, he is found in revolt. His alliance with Pekah, here implied, is directly stated by Isaiah (vii. 2). Begun in Jotham's reign, it continued, and came to a head, in the reign of Ahaz (see ch. xvi. 5 and Isa. vii. 1—9; viii. 6). **And Pekah the son of Remaliah.** Pekah and Rezin intended to establish on the Jewish throne a certain Ben-Tabeal (Isa. vii. 6), a creature of their own, with whose aid they thought to offer an effectual resistance to Assyria.

Ver. 38.—**And Jotham slept with his fathers, and was buried with his fathers in the city of David his father: and Ahaz his son reigned in his stead.** It may be suspected that the full name of this king was Jeho-ahaz. Ahaz, "possession," is a name never assigned to any other Israelite, and it is one not likely to have been given by a religious father like Jotham. In the Assyrian inscriptions the Jewish king contemporary with Rezin and Pekah is called "Yahu-khazi."

HOMILETICS.

Vers. 1—7.—*The leper-king a pattern and a warning.* I. IN HIS EARLIER YEARS AZARIAH WAS A PATTERN KING. He "did that which was right in the sight of the Lord" (ver. 3); he "sought God" (2 Chron. xxvi. 5); he consorted with "Zechariah, who had understanding in the visions of God;" and the result was that "God made him to prosper." "God helped him against the Philistines and the Arabians and the Mehunim" (2 Chron. xxvi. 7), and he "was marvellously helped" (2 Chron. xxvi. 15). So far, he is a pattern to us, the model of a good king, of one who is at once religiously minded and full of practical zeal and energy, who serves God without ceasing to serve man, "not slothful in business, fervent in spirit, serving the Lord" (Rom. xii. 11). But there is a reverse to the picture.

II. IN HIS LATER YEARS AZARIAH WAS A WARNING TO KINGS AND GREAT MEN GENERALLY. Azariah, like his father (ch. xiv. 10), became "lifted up" (2 Chron. xxvi. 16). He was not content with his kingly power and greatness, his secular dignity and majesty; he would be first everywhere, and invaded the priestly office (2 Chron. xxvi. 16—19). It had pleased God, in the theocratic polity which he had set up, to draw the sharpest possible line between the sacerdotal order and the rest of the community. None were allowed to sacrifice, or to burn incense, or even to enter into the sanctuary, but "the priests the sons of Aaron"—the lineal descendants of the first and greatest of the high priests. Kings had their functions—great and high and (in a certain sense) sacred functions—to rule, to judge, to determine on peace or war; to lead armies, if it so pleased them; to direct the whole policy of the nation. But one thing they might not do, and that was to assume the duties which had been assigned to the priests and Levites, who had been appointed God's special ministers, to minister to him in the congregation. The exclusive right of the priests to their functions had been vindicated in a most terrible and awful way, when, soon after the institution of the Levitical priesthood, its honours were coveted by great men who did not belong to the privileged body. Korah, Dathan, and Abiram, with their company, were swallowed up, and "went down quick into hell," because they claimed to be as "holy" as the priests (Numb. xvi. 3), and to offer incense before the door of the tabernacle of the congregation, each from his own censer. The lesson taught by the miracle had been taken deeply to heart; and even such mighty monarchs as David and Solomon had carefully abstained from setting aside the privileges of the priests, or infringing upon them in any way. But Azariah despised the teaching of the past, and the example set him by his predecessors. See him as Josephus depicts him! On a great festival day, when the people had all come together in crowds to keep the feast, he robed himself in priestly garments, and entering into the sacred enclosure declared his intention of going within the temple building, and himself offering incense on the golden altar that was before the veil. In vain did the eighty priests in attendance, headed by the high priest, resist him, and exhort him to lay aside his design and retire; Azariah, hot with passion, refused, and threatened them with death if they made more ado. Then, Josephus declares, the ground suddenly rocked with an earthquake (comp. Amos i. 1; Zech. xiv. 5), and the roof of the temple gaped, and a sunbeam entering smote upon the head of the king, and at once leprosy spread over his face, and, overwhelmed with grief and shame, he departed ('Ant. Jud.,' ix. 10. § 4). Here Azariah is a warning to kings (1) that they attempt not to minister the Word and sacraments; and (2) that they in no way trench upon the rights of the priests or other ministers; and further, he is a warning to great men, or such as think themselves great, in less exalted positions, that they rest content with the performance of their own proper duties and do not invade the office of others; either (1) by dictating to ministers what doctrine they shall preach; or (2) by undue interference with schools, teachers, etc.; or (3) by any other form of arrogant and overbearing conduct. Punishment will assuredly fall upon those who so act. They will lose men's respect and God's approval. Failure will overtake them at the moment when they look to have their efforts crowned with complete success. Well for them if it be simply failure, and not an utter downfall. It often happens that he who covets more than he has any right or claim to have, loses that which was lawfully in his possession.

Vers. 8—31.—*Worldly prosperity not unfrequently the ruin of kingdoms.* I. EXAMPLE OF SAMARIA. Scarcely ever was there a more prosperous reign than that of Jeroboam II.—a reign of forty-one years of continual success, uncheckered by a misfortune—Syria defeated, the old border everywhere recovered, Hamath occupied, Damascus brought into a subject condition. As usual, where there is military success, wealth flowed in, and with wealth, luxury. "Great houses" were built (Amos iii. 15), "ivory houses," *i.e.* houses inlaid or panelled with ivory; distinct mansions were inhabited during the summer and during the winter time (Amos iii. 15). The children of Israel passed their lives in Samaria, lying "in the corner of a bed," and in Damascus lounging "upon a couch" (Amos iii. 12). "Flagons of wine" were "loved" (Hos. iii. 1); "whoredom and wine and new wine took away their heart" (Hos. iv. 11). And with this softness was blended, on the one hand, the seductive influence of a licentious religionism, on the other, the coarser and ruder vices to which luxury and self-indulgence inevitably lead. Patriotism disappeared, and self-seeking took its place. "Politically all was anarchy or misrule; kings made their way to the throne through the murder of their predecessors, and made way for their successors through their own. Shallum slew Zechariah (ch. xv. 10); Menahem slew Shallum (ver. 14); Pekah slew the son of Menahem (ver. 25); Hoshea slew Pekah (ver. 30). The whole kingdom of Israel was a military despotism, and, as in the Roman empire, those in command came to the throne" (Pusey's 'Minor Prophets,' p. 2). Society was corrupt to the core. The idolatries of the calves, of Baal, and of Moloch worked out their natural results, and bore their bitter fruit. "Creature-worship, as St. Paul points out (Rom. i. 23—32), was the parent of every sort of abomination; and religion having become creature-worship, what God gave as the check to sin became its incentive. Every commandment of God was broken, and that habitually. All was falsehood (Hos. iv. 1), adultery (Hos. iv. 11; Amos ii. 7), bloodshedding (Hos. v. 2; vi. 8); deceit of God (Hos. iv. 2) producing faithlessness to man; excess and luxury were supplied by secret or open robbery (Hos. vii. 1), oppression (Hos. xii. 7), false dealing (Amos viii. 5; Hos. xii. 7), perversion of justice (Hos. x. 4; Amos ii. 6), grinding of the poor (Hos. xii. 7). Blood was shed like water, until one stream met another (Hos. iv. 2), and overspread the land with one defiling deluge. Adultery was consecrated as an act of religion (Hos. iv.

14). Those who were first in rank were first in excess. People and king vied in debauchery (Hos. vii. 5); and the sottish king joined and encouraged the free-thinkers and blasphemers of his court (Hos. vii. 3). The idolatrous priests loved and shared in the sins of the people (Hos. iv. 8, 9); nay, they seem to have set themselves to intercept those on either side of Jordan, who would go to worship at Jerusalem, laying wait to murder them (Hos. v. 1; vi. 9). Corruption had spread through the whole land, even the places once sacred through God's revelations or other mercies to their forefathers—Bethel, Gilgal, Gilead, Mizpah, Shechem—were especial scenes of corruption or of sin (Hos. iv. 15; v. 1; vi. 8, 9, etc.). Every holy memory was effaced by present corruption. Could things be worse? There was one aggravation more. Remonstrance was useless (Hos. iv. 4); the knowledge of God was wilfully rejected (Hos. iv. 6); the people hated rebuke (Amos v. 10); the more they were called, the more they refused (Hos. xi. 2, 7); they forbade their prophets to prophesy (Amos ii. 12); and their false prophets hated God greatly (Hos. ix. 7, 9). All attempts to heal all this disease only showed its incurableness" (ibid., p. 3).

II. EXAMPLE OF TYRE. The prosperity of Tyre in the seventh and eighth centuries before our era was extraordinary. She was mistress of her sister cities, Sidon and Gebal and Arvad; she ruled over a hundred colonies; on her island-rock she was safe from Assyria; the trade of the world was in her hands. "Situate at the entry of the sea, a merchant of the people for many isles" (Ezek. xxvii. 3); full of wordly wisdom, the wisdom that gets increase of riches (Ezek. xxviii. 3—5); rich beyond all conception in precious metals, and in gems (Ezek. xxviii. 13), and in spices, and in broidered work (Ezek. xxvii. 22, 24), and in ivory and ebony (Ezek. xxvii. 15), and in all manner of merchandise; approved, respected, called "the renowned city, strong in the sea" (Ezek. xxvi. 17);—she had reached the acme of her glory, of her wealth, of her greatness. But with what results to her moral tone and temper? Her heart was "lifted up" (Ezek. xxviii. 5); her pride became excessive; she said in her heart, "I am of perfect beauty" (Ezek. xxvii. 3)—"I am a god; I sit in the seat of God" (Ezek. xxviii. 2). "Iniquity" of every kind was found in her (Ezek. xxviii. 15)—envp (Ezek. xxvi. 2), and "violence" (ver. 16), and corrupt wisdom (ver. 17), and profanation of sanctuaries (ver. 18), and even dishonesty in her traffic (ver. 18). And with iniquity, as usual, came ruin. Because of her pride, and her envy, and her violence, and her other iniquities, God brought a fire into her midst, which devoured her and reduced her to ashes (Ezek. xxvi. 18). The Babylonians were made God's instrument to chastise her, and carry off her wealth, and break down her walls, and destroy her pleasant houses, and slay her people with the sword (Ezek. xxvi. 11, 12), and make her a byword among the nations (Ezek. xxvii. 32)—a desolation, a hissing, and a terror (ver. 36).

III. EXAMPLE OF ROME. The ruin of Rome was undoubtedly wrought by that long career of unexampled military success which began with the closing years of the Second Punic War, and continued till she was the world's mistress. The wealth of Carthage, Macedonia, and Asia flowing into her coffers, destroyed the antique simplicity and severity of manners, stimulated ambition, provoked inordinate desire, and led to those terrific civil wars, in which the blood of the noblest and the bravest was shed like water, and "Rome fell ruined by her own strength" (Horace). It was not the influx of the barbarians that destroyed Rome; she fell from internal decay. The decline of Roman civilization dates from before the fall of the republic. It was then that population began to diminish, and the pure Roman blood to be mingled with the refuse of every nation. Slaves, freedmen, clients, glided into the tribes and gentes, and were followed by absolute foreigners, Greeks and Egyptians and Syrians, effete races in a state both of physical and moral degradation. "The Orontes flowed into the Tiber." The very names of those in the highest position became grotesque and strange, such as Cicero and Cato would have pronounced manifestly barbarous. A decay of moral principles followed this admixture. Slavery prevailed, and slavery in ancient as in modern times was "a hotbed of vice and selfish indulgence, enervating the spirit and vital forces of mankind, discouraging legitimate marriage, and enticing to promiscuous and barren concubinage. The fruit of such hateful unions, if fruit there were, engaged little regard from their selfish fathers, and both law and usage continued to sanction the exposure of infants, from which the female sex undoubtedly suffered most. The losses of Italy from this horrid practice were probably the greatest; but the provinces also lost proportionably, the imitation of Roman habits was rife on the remotest frontiers; the conquests of the empire were consolidated by the attractions of Roman indulgence and sensuality; slavery threw discredit on all manual labour, and engendered a false sentiment of honour, which constrained the poorer classes of freemen to dependence and celibacy; vice and idleness went hand-in-hand, and combined to stunt the moral and physical growth of the Roman citizen, leaving his weak and morbid frame exposed in an unequal contest to the fatal influences of his climate" (Merivale, 'Roman Empire,' vol. viii. pp. 353, 354). It was a race which had thus lost its stamina, and become effete and worn out, that succumbed to barbarian inroads which, a few centuries earlier, it would have repulsed without any difficulty.

HOMILIES BY VARIOUS AUTHORS.

Vers. 1—7.—*Prosperity and its dangers.* The contrast between the opening and the close of Uzziah's reign—here so sharply set before us—has few parallels in history. There is, indeed, no lack of monarchs who have risen to proud positions of authority and power, and then suddenly have fallen ignominiously from their pinnacle of pride. Memory at once recalls such names as Nebuchadnezzar, one day surveying with pride great Babylon that he had made, and the next dwelling among the beasts of the field, his body wet with the dew of heaven; or Napoleon, one day with all Europe at his feet, and but a few days after, like a caged lion, a baffled, helpless prisoner on the lonely island of St. Helena. But Uzziah's early career was different from that of most monarchs who have fallen. To all appearance he promised well. He did right in the sight of the Lord. He did indeed continue *that dangerous compromise* of which Amaziah, his father, had been guilty, of permitting the high places to remain. But still he worshipped the true God. He sought God's help and guidance. He honoured God's prophet. Moreover, he used his power well, not as a tyrant, but for the good of his people and for the prosperity and strengthening of the nation. And God prospered him in his efforts, as he will prosper all those who seek his help and blessing (2 Chron. xxvi. 5—15). But in an evil hour Uzziah (he is also called Azariah in this chapter) forgot that, though he was a king, he owed allegiance to a greater King. His prosperity turned his head. He forgot how much he owed to God. There was an old command of God, given after the rebellion of Korah and his sons, that none but the sons of Aaron—the priestly family—were to offer incense before the Lord. The obvious lesson was that special fitness, special holiness, was required of those who would stand as representatives of the people before God. But Uzziah disregards both the letter and the spirit of the command. He—poor weak mortal!—dares to defy the living God, and enters into the sanctuary to burn incense. It is another case of *compromise and its consequences.* He had been so accustomed to the violation of God's command in the matter of the high places, that now he thinks very little of this flagrant act of high-handed defiance. The priests remonstrated, but in vain. The proud king seizes the censer, and thrusts the priests aside with gestures of impatience and anger. But stay! What means that growing whiteness in his forehead? Ah! the symptoms are too well known. The hand of God is upon him. He is a leper. The censer falls from his hand. He can resist no longer. The priests thrust him forth from the holy place, and beyond the very precincts of the temple. Henceforth he is a king and yet an outcast, separated and secluded from the haunts and enjoyments of men (see 2 Chron. xxvi. 16—21).

I. PROSPERITY AND ITS UPWARD PATH. For a long time the career of Uzziah was an upward path. His motto would seem to have been, as the motto of every young person, of every one of us, ought to be, "Excelsior!" There were three elements in his progress, three sources of his prosperity, three steps in his upward path. Along these three steps every one of us may fairly and with advantage follow Uzziah. 1. First of all, *there was the fear of God.* As a young man, unquestionably he had the fear of God before his eyes. We read of him in 2 Chronicles that "*he sought the Lord.*" This implies that he honoured God's worship. He honoured God's house. He honoured God's Word, and sought guidance from the Divine Law. And what was the consequence? Just what the consequence of a God-fearing life will always be. "As long as he sought the Lord, God made him to prosper." It is so still. God keeps his word. He has never yet broken that promise, "Them that honour me I will honour." This was the starting-point in Uzziah's prosperity, and, so long as he prospered, the secret of it was that he sought the Lord. Godliness is the best foundation of all true and lasting prosperity. Men like the late Samuel Morley, or the late Sir William McArthur, were not less successful because they were God-fearing men, and their business did not suffer because of the large amount of time and attention and money they devoted to religious work. To seek God's guidance in everything, God's blessing on every undertaking and every event of life,—that is the secret of true prosperity and success. 2. The second step in Uzziah's prosperity was *a good man's influence.* We read in 2 Chronicles that "he sought the Lord in the days of Zechariah, who had understanding in the visions of God." While the Word of God and our own conscience are to be our chief guides, there are many details and plans of daily life in which we shall be greatly the better for the experience and advice of others. To what kind of men do you go for your advice or guidance? Go by all means to those who have best experience of the business or subject in question. But if you are to choose between the advice of a practical Christian man and that of a practical worldly man, surely for a Christian the Christian man's advice will carry most weight. Some one has well said, "You can never rise above the level of your companionship." *Cultivate the society, seek the advice, look for the sympathy, of good men and good women.* 3. The third step in Uzziah's prosperity was *his diligence in business.* Uzziah was no idler. He realized the responsibility of life. He realized the responsibilities of his high position. So we find him improving the defences of Jerusalem and building towers; improving also the condition of the country and digging wells, so useful to the traveller and the husband-man in the East; and, as it was a time of warfare, providing suitable equipments for his soldiers, and encouraging new inventions of military engines and weapons. No success is won without hard work. Whatsoever our hand findeth to do, we should do it with our might. By these three methods, then, Uzziah attained to great prosperity. "He was marvellously helped, till he was strong," are the words of the writer in 2 Chronicles. His name and fame became well known. If you want to attain to prosperity and success in your business—and it is a desirable thing to see wealth, honourably earned and wisely spent, in the hands of Christian men—then, with the strong arm of a vigorous resolution, cut these three steps in your upward path, and plant your feet firmly in them—*the fear of God, the influence of good men,* and *diligence in business.* This is prosperity and its upward path. But we have reached the summit of Uzziah's career. Hitherto all has been progress upward. Hitherto all has been bright as the path of the just. But the scene changes. The shadows gather. The footsteps that pointed upwards now are turned downwards. We must look now at the other side of the picture, at—

II. PROSPERITY AND ITS DOWNWARD PATH. We may gain prosperity by rightful means, but sometimes the difficulty is to keep our prosperity and our religion at the same time. Riches bring with them their own temptations and dangers. We see in Uzziah's case *the way* to prosperity, which we should follow; we also see the *dangers* of prosperity, which we should avoid. 1. *Prosperity leads to pride.* We read of Uzziah in 2 Chronicles: "But when he was strong, his heart was lifted up to his destruction." He became filled up with ideas of his own importance, and, instead of giving God the glory, reflected with complacency on all the great deeds that he had done, and all the benefits he had conferred upon the nation. When he was younger, and in the beginning of his career, he was humbler. He was very glad then to seek God's guidance, to have the help and influence of Zechariah. But now he has got beyond all that. His whole character is completely changed.

> " For lowliness is young ambition's ladder,
>   Whereto the climber upward turns his face;
>   But, when he once have gained the topmost round,
>   He then unto the ladder turns his back,
>   Looks in the clouds, scorning the base degrees
>   By which he did ascend."

Pride of riches, pride of rank, how vain, how foolish they are! Riches may bring with them bodily comforts and enjoyments. But, if health goes or troubles come, what comfort can they bring us? Can they give us any satisfaction or peace of mind? Can they banish care or sickness? Can they arrest the skinny hand of Death? Yet this is a common danger to those who are prosperous in worldly things—to be puffed up with this empty and unreasonable pride. How much we all need, in any time of prosperity, to pray for humility! If our business prospers, let us ask God to keep us humble. If our Church prospers, let our sincere utterance ever be "Not unto us, O Lord, not unto us, but unto thy Name be all the praise." 2. *Prosperity leads to presumption.* It is a step further than pride. Uzziah's pride was bad enough, but when it led him to trample on the Law of God and to violate the sacredness of God's holy place, his presumption was a bad example to others. Yet how many there are whose prosperity or whose wealth leads them to violate the laws of God! They think anything becomes them. They have become inflated with success, and the Law of God is a very small matter indeed in their eyes. Look at Claverhouse, inflated with his triumphs over the Scottish Covenanters, as with his dragoons he surrounded the cottage of John Brown of Priesthill. Touched by the prayers of John Brown, and the sight of his wife and helpless children gathered round him, the dragoons, with moistened eyes, refused to do their deadly work. Snatching a pistol from his belt, Claverhouse himself shot the good man through the head. Turning to the wife whom he had widowed, he said, "What do you think of your husband now?" "I always thought much of him, sir," replied the brave woman; "but never so much as I do this day. *But how are you to answer for this morning's work?*" "To men," he replied, "I can be answerable, and as for God, I will take him in my own hands." Four years afterwards, in the Pass of Killiecrankie, Claverhouse died by an unknown hand. How many think as Claverhouse did! Because they have rank, or wealth, or power, therefore they imagine they can trample on God's laws, or trample on morality. Napoleon the Great thought that when he divorced his innocent and faithful wife; and he afterwards testified that that false and guilty step was the beginning of his downfall and disgrace. Because, by their wealth or their position, men think they can defy public opinion, therefore they imagine they can also disregard the commands of God. But it is a great mistake. No prosperity, no riches, no position in life, can ever lift us above the Law of God.

> " In the corrupted currents of this world,
>   Offences' gilded hand may shove by justice,
>   And oft 'tis seen the wicked prize itself
>   Buys out the law. But 'tis not so above.
>   *There* is no shuffling; there the action lies
>   In his true nature; and we ourselves compelled,
>   Even to the teeth and forehead of our faults,
>   To give in evidence."

Ah! yes; that is the one message for rich and poor alike. "For we must all appear before the judgment-seat of Christ; that every one may receive the things done in his body, according to that he hath done, whether it be good or bad." Such, then, are the dangers which prosperity brings with it. There is a strong temptation to presumption and to pride. If we have much prosperity, then we need to be much in prayer. If riches increase, the responsibility to use them well increases also. If we look at worldly prosperity in relation to eternity, on the one hand it will seem *very poor and insignificant.* What are all the riches of this world compared with the "inheritance incorruptible and undefiled, that fadeth not away"? What are all the honours and privileges that worldly rank and prosperity bring with them, compared to the privilege of *being one of God's children?* What is all the society of earth in comparison with the fellowship of Jesus? If you are making worldly prosperity the be-all and end-all of your existence, sacrificing for it, as many do, health and conscience and your spiritual life, *pause and think! Is it worth it?* Put the two worlds in the balance. *To an unsaved soul, with a dark and hopeless eternity, earthly prosperity is only a mockery.* But, on the other hand, worldly prosperity, won by Christian efforts, guided by a Christian heart, and used by a Christian hand, *what a blessing it may become!* Let

Jesus be in your heart first. Let him abide there—his love your motive power, his Word your guide—and then there will be no danger in prosperity.—C. H. I.

Vers. 1—38.—*Some lessons from the history of kings.* "In the twenty and seventh year of Jeroboam," etc. The mighty Governor of the universe is represented as saying to the Jewish nation, "I gave thee a king in mine anger" (Hos. xiii. 2). And truly, with a certain number of exceptions here and there through the ages, kings have proved malific scourges of the race. In this chapter there are mentioned no less than seven of those men who are called kings, but who, instead of having one grain of moral royalty in their souls, were contemptible serfs to the last degree, slaves to their passions of sensuality and greed. How many conventional kings in all ages are moral paupers and vassals of Satan! Glance for a moment at each of the kings before us. Here is *Azariah*, elsewhere called Uzziah, who was the son and successor of Amaziah. Here is *Zachariah*, the son and successor of Jeroboam II. King of Israel, who reigned only six months, and then fell by the hand of Shallum. Here is *Shallum*, the fifteenth King of Israel, and the murderer of Zachariah, and who in his turn was murdered. Here is *Menahem*, the son of Gadi, who, having slain Shallum, reigned in his stead ten years—a reign characterized by ruthless cruelty and tyrannic oppression. Here is *Pekahiah*, the son and successor of Menahem, who reigned two years over Israel, and then was assassinated by Pekah. Here is *Pekah*, who was a general of the Israelitish army, and assassinated King Pekahiah in his palace, and usurped the govenment, reigning, according to the existing text, twenty years. Here is *Jotham*, the son and successor of Uzziah, the eleventh King of Judah, who reigned for sixteen years. He, perhaps, was the least wicked of all these princes. The whole chapter reminds us of several things worth note.

I. THE EXISTENCE OF RETRIBUTION IN THIS LIFE. Here we discover retribution in the leprosy of Azariah, and in the fate of the other kings. Of Azariah it is said, "The Lord smote the king, so that he was a leper unto the day of his death, and dwelt in a several house." Of all physical afflictions, perhaps that of leprosy is the most painful and revolting. It eats out the life of a man and dooms him to solitude. Disease strikes princes as well as paupers. Then see how the other wicked doers fared. The murderer is murdered, the slayer is slain; Shallum strikes down Zachariah; Menahem strikes down Shallum; and Pul, the King of Assyria, strikes Menahem with a terrible blow of humiliation and oppression; Pekah smites Pekahiah, and reigns twenty years when he is himself struck down by the blow of an assassin. Truly, even in this life, "with what measure ye mete it shall be measured to you again." Though retribution here may not be complete and adequate, still it is at work everywhere in human society. It comes as a pledge and a prophecy of that realm beyond the grave, where every man shall be dealt with according to his works.

II. THE MIGHTINESS OF RELIGIOUS ERROR. In this chapter there is the record of long periods and of great changes. Battles are fought, revolutions are effected, monarch succeeds monarch, and the years come and go; but one thing remains, that is, idolatry— "The high places were not removed: the people sacrificed and burnt incense still on the high places" (vers. 4 and 34). Among the many evil tendencies of man there is none so mighty and influential as the *pseudo-religious*. Two facts will account for this. 1. *The strength of the religious element in man.* Burke and others of the wisest of the race have designated man as a religious animal. Religion with man is not a faculty, but the substratum in which all the faculties inhere; it is the core and the root of his nature. Hence, wherever man is found, if he has no home, he has a shrine; if he has no friend, he has a god. 2. *The might of selfishness in man.* What man needs most presents the greatest motives to human avarice and ambition. Hence the creation of bodies of priests to bolster up false religions, and derive position and wealth from them. *Corruptio optimi pessima.* It is most sad when men seek to "make a gain of godliness."

III. THE CRAVEN-HEARTEDNESS OF ENSLAVED PEOPLES. Had the peoples of Judah and Israel been really men worthy of their humanity, would they have tolerated for a day such monsters as we have in this chapter? The existence of tyrants is the fault of the people.—D. T.

Vers. 1—7.—*Another king beginning well, ending ill.* It is remarkable that three kings of Judah in succession exhibited this characteristic. They begin well, serve God for a time and prosper, yet stumble and fail at last. We have seen the fates of Joash and Amaziah; and Azariah furnishes a third example.

I. AZARIAH'S REIGN. 1. *His righteous rule.* Azariah began to reign when only sixteen years of age; he reigned long—fifty-two years, and during the greater part of his reign he signalized himself as a king that did right. Save that the high places were unremoved, the praise given to him is unqualified. He was an able, energetic ruler, much more so than either his father or grandfather. The virtue of his reign is traced in Chronicles to the influence of a good man, Zechariah, " who had understanding in the visions of God " (2 Chron. xxvi. 5)—another example of the power for good exercised by prophets in the political history of Judah (cf. 2 Chron. xxiv. 2, 17; xxv. 7). 2. *His prosperity.* On this the Book of Chronicles dilates. So long as Azariah (or Uzziah) sought the Lord, God made him to prosper. Everything he touched went well with him. It was long since Judah had so enlightened, so enterprising, and so able a king. He subjugated the Philistines, the Arabians of Gur-baal, and the Ammonites; he greatly strengthened the defences of Jerusalem; he developed the resources of the country, and fostered agriculture; he brought the organization and equipment of the army to a high pitch of perfection. As it is stated, " His name spread far abroad; for he was marvellously helped, till he was strong " (2 Chron. xxvi. 15). It was as if God wished, by the abundance of his blessings, to teach Azariah and his people that assuredly their true advantage lay in his service. The previous reigns had given examples of this; but here was a new proof, still more undeniable than the preceding. Yet it was ineffectual to restrain from sin.

II. AZARIAH'S LEPROSY. 1. *The worm at the root.* Azariah had scarcely reached the acme of his power, when, as in the case of his predecessors, declension began. Unwarned by the past, he allowed his heart to grow proud and haughty. He was head of the state; why should he not also be head of the Church? His prophetic adviser was by this time removed, and he was left to the bent of his own will. In his arrogance, he insisted on going into the holy place of the temple to burn incense to the Lord. It was there his doom fell upon him. We are again reminded of the subtle temptations that lie in prosperity. When men wax fat, they kick; and their hearts are apt to be lifted up to their destruction (Deut. viii. 11—14; xxxii. 15). Once let pride enter the heart, and deterioration is rapid. Its beginnings may be unseen, but it by-and-by reveals itself in overt acts. 2. *The stroke from heaven.* It was Heaven's laws that Azariah was defying, and it was from heaven the blow came which struck his pride low. While yet he stood at God's altar, offering unhallowed incense, the leprous spot began to burn in his forehead, and in presence of the priests, whose protestations he despised, he felt himself a leper. The priests, in horror, thrust him out from the holy place. But it needed not their violence: " Yea, himself hasted also to go out, because the Lord had smitten him " (2 Chron. xxvi. 20). How quickly God can bring the haughtiness of men low! He is a jealous God, and what touches the honour of his sanctuary and worship is of special concern to him. We are warned against will-worship in God's service (Col. ii. 23; cf. Numb. x. 1, 2). The leprosy was but the outward token of the invisible sin of pride; yet how little shame the reality of sin occasions, as compared with that caused by an outward symbol of it like this! We may believe that in the end inward character will somehow stamp itself upon the outward appearance, and then men will see sin in its real loathsomeness. 3. *Jotham as vicegerent.* We are told that from this time Azariah took no more part in public business. He dwelt apart " in a several house "—a living evidence of the weakness of man in contending with God, of the dishonour which is the Nemesis of presumptuous sin, of the isolation which they bring upon themselves who refuse the bounds which God's Law prescribes. During this period, Jotham, the king's son, acted as his deputy. It would appear, from comparison with the Israelitish reigns, and with Assyrian chronology, that Jotham's sixteen regnal years include this period when " he was over the house, judging the people of the land." Sin is a living death. Azariah was king in name, but morally, physically, legally, he was dead; for leprosy in the body is simply a process of decay and death. When, in fact, he did die, he was buried in Jerusalem, but in a " several " tomb, as during life he had dwelt in a " several " house (2 Chron. xxvi. 23).—J. O.

Vers. 8—22.—*Anarchy in Israel.* With rapid descent the kingdom of Israel, which had risen to great external prosperity under Jeroboam II., hastened to its fall. The prophets give us vivid pictures of the corruption of the times. The bonds of social life were loosened, oppression was rampant, the fear of God seemed to have died out of the land; there was no confidence, peace, or good will among any classes in the nation. As a consequence, the throne was a prey to any adventurer who had power to seize it.

I. THE FALL OF JEHU'S HOUSE. 1. *The shadow of doom.* With the accession of Zachariah, Jeroboam's son, the fourth generation of Jehu's dynasty ascended the throne The shadow of doom may thus be said to have rested on this ill-fated king. A prophet had spoken it to the founder of the house, " Thy sons shall sit on the throne of Israel unto the fourth generation." That word had its bright side of reward, but it had also its dark side of penalty, and it is this which becomes prominent as the predicted term nears its close. Yet, as we can now also see, there is no fate in the matter. The reason why Jehu's sons were *only* to sit on the throne till the fourth generation lay in their own character and actions. God's decrees do not work against, but in harmony with, the existing nature of things, and the established connection of causes and effects. Jehu's house was about to fall (1) because Jehu's sons had been ungodly. None of them had sought God's glory or taken any pains to promote godliness in the nation. On the contrary, they had continued sowing the wind of disobedience to God's will, and the nation was now to reap the whirlwind. (2) Under the rule of these kings, irreligion and immorality had spread fast, and struck their roots deep and wide in the kingdom. This will undermine any dynasty, will overthrow any empire. Rulers make a great mistake when they fix attention solely on external prosperity. If the foundations are rotten, the structure will sooner or later inevitably come down. (3) Zachariah himself was a feeble king. This is implied even in the brief notice we have of him. It may be he who is referred to by Hosea, " In the day of our king the princes have made him sick with bottles of wine," etc. (Hos. vii. 5). In any case, we know that he was not only weak, but wicked—" He did evil in the sight of the Lord." 2. *The prophetic word fulfilled.* A brief six months of the throne was all that was allowed to Zachariah. He seems to have been held in contempt by the people. His feeble character would appear the more feeble in contrast with that of his energetic and victorious father. We have a similar contrast in English history between Richard Cromwell and his father, Oliver. But Zachariah was more than feeble, he was worthless. Therefore, when the conspirator Shallum smote the king in the light of public day, " before the people," no hand seems to have been raised in his defence. He perished, and the house of Jehu was extinguished with him. Sinners do not live out half their days (Ps. lv. 23). In due time the words of God are all fulfilled.

II. THE REIGN OF MENAHEM. We may pass by the brief reign of Shallum, which lasted only a month, and of which no events are recorded. He was slain by Menahem, the son of Gadi, illustrating the truth of which this chapter affords other exemplifications, that they who take the sword shall perish by the sword (Matt. xxvi. 52). In respect of Menahem, we notice: 1. *His violent usurpation.* He too possessed himself of the throne by violent means. He smote Shallum in Samaria, as Shallum had, a few weeks before, smitten Zachariah. The effect of these revolutions on the morals of the people and the administration of law may be imagined. What respect could be felt for royalty established by such methods? Shallum, indeed, was a murderer, but Menahem was no better. Neither by sanction of God nor by election of the people, but solely by brute force, did he set himself upon the throne. His rule was thus, in its inception and essence, a tyranny. To this had Israel come by rejecting their true Ruler—God. " They have set up kings," said God, " but not by me " (Hos. viii. 4). He who rejects God as his Sovereign must bear a heavier yoke. 2. *His sickening cruelties.* The fact that Menahem kept the throne for ten years shows him to have been a man of no small natural ability. But his disposition was savagely cruel. Not only did he smite Shallum—a deed which might be pardoned—but in his war with Tiphsah he was guilty of brutal atrocities on those who refused to submit to him (cf. ver. 16). In this he showed himself a man of a fierce and unscrupulous character. The people had become fierce, godless, and violent; and God gave them a king after their own image. 3. *His league with Assyria.* This is not the first contact of Israel with Assyria, but it is the first mention of that contact in the sacred history.

The King of Assyria, here named Pul, came against the land, evidently with hostile intent, but Menahem, by the payment of a huge tribute, bought him off, and secured his sanction to his occupancy of the throne. (On the identification of Pul, see the Exposition.) Israel now came under a foreign yoke, and "sorrowed," as Hosea says, "for the burden of the King of princes" (Hos. viii. 10). Sin, which is an effort after emancipation from the Law and authority of God, ends in the sinner being reduced to miserable bondage (Luke xv. 15, 16; John viii. 34). 4. *His oppression of the people.* To raise the money for Pul, Menahem was under the necessity of exacting large sums from the men of wealth in the land. From each, we are told, he took fifty shekels of silver. Much of this money had been wrung from the poor, and now it was taken from the rich. In the end, it was probably upon the poor that the burden would come back. Thus the land groaned under tyranny, foreign oppression, robbery, and grinding of class by class. The end was not quite yet, but it was fast approaching. We need not doubt that Menahem's oppressive reign was hateful to the people. He escaped, however, the penalty of his misdeeds in his own person, and "slept with his fathers." It was his son Pekahiah who reaped the harvest he had sown.

III. THE REIGN OF PEKAH. Pekahiah's reign of two years, like that of Shallum, may be passed over. A stronger hand was needed to hold together the warring elements in this distracted kingdom, and such a hand was that of Pekah, the son of Remaliah. 1. *Overthrow of the house of Menahem.* Menahem had succeeded in handing down the throne to his son, but the latter could not keep it. The bold and ambitious Pekah, one of Pekahiah's captains, having secured the co-operation of fifty Gileadites, smote the king in his palace, and his attendants with him. Thus another violent revolution took place in Israel. It is stated that Pekah kept the throne for twenty years, but there is great difficulty at this point in adjusting the chronology. It seems impossible, on the side of Judah, to shorten the reign of Ahaz, having regard to his own age, and that of his son Hezekiah, at their respective accessions. To bring the Jewish and Assyrian chronologies into accord, we must apparently either (1) shorten the reign of Pekah by about ten years, and bring down the reign of Ahaz to a date considerably below that usually given, which involves also the abandonment of the biblical date for the commencement of the reign of Hezekiah (ch. xviii. 1), and of the synchronisms of this period generally; or (2) suppose some break or hiatus of twenty years or so in the Assyrian lists at the epoch of the accession of Tiglath-pileser, *i.e.* the commencement of the new Assyrian empire. This view has its difficulties, but is not impossible. Pekah's reign was as evil as that of his predecessors. 2. *Invasions of Tiglath-pileser.* During this reign began those invasions of the Assyrians, and deportations of the population, which culminated in the fall of Samaria and carrying captive of the whole people, some years later. This expedition, of which mention is made in the Assyrian inscriptions, took place towards the end of Pekah's period of rule, and was a sequel to the events related in ch. xvi. 5—9. Pekah, in alliance with Rezin of Damascus, had made a plot to depose Ahaz of Judah, and to set a creature of his own upon the throne (Isa. vii. 1—6). To this proposed attack we owe Isaiah's magnificent prophecy of the Child Immanuel. 3. *Pekah's death.* This intriguing monarch also, as he had climbed to the throne by assassination, fell a victim to assassination. He was slain by Hoshea, the son of Elah, who succeeded him as the last King of Israel.—J. O.

Vers. 32—38.—*A good reign.* In welcome contrast with the character of the reigns we have been considering, stands this of Jotham, who walked in the footsteps of his father in all that was right.

I. JUDAH WELL GOVERNED. 1. *Rule in the fear of God.* Jotham proved an excellent ruler. He took warning from his father's example, and "prepared his ways before the Lord his God" (2 Chron. xxvii. 6). His reign, indeed, was a brief one compared with his father's, and, had time been given, he might have backslidden as had his predecessors. But, so far as it went, his conduct was blameless, except that the high places were still unremoved. If we assume that Jotham's years of rule are reckoned from the time when he took his father's place in the public administration, he cannot have reigned alone for more than five or six years. 2. *Religion honoured.* It is told of him, negatively, that he did not, like his father, enter into the temple of the Lord (2 Chron. xxvii. 2), and positively, that "he built the higher gate of the house of the Lord." Whereas a wicked ruler like Athaliah broke down the temple, this good king set himself to adorn and strengthen it. In this he showed a laudable zeal for God's honour. 3. *The kingdom strengthened.* Jotham strengthened the kingdom of Judah in many other ways—by just administration, by extensive works of building, by subjugation of enemies, etc. (2 Chron. xxvii. 3—6). If the annals of this reign, "written in the book of the chronicles of the kings of Judah," could be recovered, they would show Jotham to be one of the best kings Judah ever had—a worthy son of a very able father. Such rulers are a blessing to a country. Their loss is to be deplored, for there is no guarantee that their successors will be like them. From Jotham to Ahaz the descent is great.

II. JUDAH THREATENED. 1. *A discordant note.* It is said in Chronicles that, notwithstanding Jotham's enlightened and righteous government, "the people did yet corruptly" (2 Chron. xxvii. 2). It is not easy to purge out evil leaven when once it has got into a community; and the worship of the high places gave opportunity for evil practices to develop themselves away from the centre, which was more under the king's eye. The pictures Isaiah now begins to draw for us show that the corruption was not slight. 2. *Threatened invasion.* To this inward corruption of the people may be attributed the chastisements which God now saw fit to send on Judah. In Jotham's reign they but begin, but in the reign of Ahaz they develop to considerable proportions. In the text we are simply told, "In those days the Lord began to send against Judah Rezin the King of Syria, and Pekah the son of Remaliah." These two kings, as we shall subsequently see, had designs upon the throne of Judah. Chastisement is the more deserved when great privileges are given and fail to be improved.—J. O.

EXPOSITION.

CHAPTER XVI.

Vers. 1—20.—REIGN OF AHAZ OVER JUDAH. WAR OF AHAZ WITH PEKAH AND REZIN. EXPEDITION OF TIGLATH-PILESER AGAINST THEM. RELIGIOUS CHANGES MADE BY AHAZ. HIS DEATH.

Vers. 1—4.—*General character of the reign of Ahaz.* Ahaz was the most wicked king that had as yet reigned in Judah. The author, therefore, prefaces his account of the reign by a brief summary of some of the king's chief iniquities. (1) He departed from the way of David (ver. 2); (2) he made his son pass through the fire to Moloch (ver. 3); and (3) he took an active part in the worship at the high places and in the groves, at which most previous kings had winked, but which they had not countenanced.

Ver. 1.—**In the seventeenth year of Pekah the son of Remaliah Ahaz the son of Jotham King of Judah began to reign.** (For the chronological difficulties connected with this statement, see the comment on ch. xv. 27.)

Ver. 2.—**Twenty years old was Ahaz when he began to reign.** As sixteen years afterwards his son Hezekiah was twenty-five (ch. xviii. 2), it is scarcely possible that

Ahaz can have been no more than twenty at his accession, since in that case he must have married at ten years of age, and have had a son at eleven! The reading of "twenty-five" instead of "twenty," found in some Hebrew codices, in the Vatican manuscript of the Septuagint, and elsewhere, is therefore to be preferred. **And reigned sixteen years in Jerusalem.** So the author of Chronicles (2 Chron. xxviii. 1) and Josephus (' Ant. Jud.,' ix. 12. § 3). The reign of Ahaz probably lasted from B.C. 742 to B.C. 727. **And did not that which was right in the sight of the Lord his God, like David his father.** Compare what is said of Abijah (1 Kings xv. 3), but the form of speech here used is stronger. Manasseh (ch. xxi. 2) and Amon (ch. xxi. 20—22) alone, of all the kings of Judah, receive greater condemnation.

Ver. 3.—**But he walked in the way of the kings of Israel.** Not, of course, by establishing a worship of calves, but by following the worst practices of the worst Israelite kings, *e.g.* Ahab and Ahaziah, and reintroducing into Judah the Phœnician idolatry, which Joash and the high priest Jehoiada had cast out (ch. xi. 17, 18). As the writer of Chronicles says (2 Chron. xxviii. 2), "He walked in the ways of the kings of Israel, *and made also molten images for Baalim.*" *Baalim* is either a plural of dignity, or a word denoting the different forms under which Baal was worshipped, as Melkarth, Adonis, Rimmon, etc. Yea, and made his son to pass through the fire. In Chronicles (2 Chron. xxviii. 3) we are told that "he burnt incense in the valley of Hinnom, and burnt his *children* in the fire," as if he had sacrificed more than one son. The practice of offering children in sacrifice was not a feature of the Assyro-Babylonian religion, as some suppose, but an intrinsic part of the worship of the Phœnicians, common to them with the Moabites, Ammonites, and others. It was based upon the principle of a man's offering to God that which was dearest and most precious to himself, whence the crowning sacrifice of the kind was a man's offering of his firstborn son (see ch. iii. 27; Micah vi. 7). Some have supposed that the rite was a mere dedication or lustration, the children passing between two fires, and being thenceforward employed only in God's service. But the expressions used by the sacred writer and others, and still more the descriptions that have come down to us from heathen and patristic authors, make it absolutely certain that the "passing through the fire" was no such innocent ceremony as this, but involved the death of the children. The author of Chronicles says, "Ahaz *burnt* his children in the fire;" Jeremiah (xix. 5), "They have built also the high places of Baal, *to burn their sons with fire for burnt offerings* unto Baal;" Ezekiel (xvi. 21), "Thou hast *slain* my children, and delivered them to cause them to pass through the fire." Josephus declares of Ahaz that he "made his own son a whole burnt offering (ἴδιον ὡλοκαύτωσε παῖδα)." Diodorus Siculus describes the ceremony as it took place at Carthage, the Phœnician colony. There was in the great temple there, he says, an image of Saturn (Moloch), which was a human figure with a bull's head and outstretched arms. This image of metal was made glowing hot by a fire kindled within it; and the children, laid in its arms, rolled from thence into the fiery lap below. If the children cried, the parents stopped their noise by fondling and kissing them; for the victim ought not to weep, and the sound of complaint was drowned in the din of flutes and kettle-drums (Diod. Sic., xx. 14). "Mothers," says Plutarch ('De Superstitione,' § 13), "stood by without tears or sobs; if they wept or sobbed, they lost the honour of the act, and the children were sacrificed notwithstanding." The only doubtful point is whether the children were placed alive in the glowing arms of the image, or whether they were first killed and afterwards burnt in sacrifice; but the description of Diodorus seems to imply the more cruel of the two proceedings. According to the abominations of the heathen, whom the Lord cast out from before the children of Israel. (On the practice of this terrible rite by the Canaanitish nations at the time of the Israelite invasion, see Lev. xviii. 21; Deut. xii. 31; xviii. 9, 10; Ps. cvi. 37, 38.)

Ver. 4.—**And he sacrificed and burnt incense in the high places.** The special sin of Ahaz here noted is that he not only allowed the high-place and grove worship, as so many other kings of Judah had done, *e.g.* Solomon (1 Kings iii. 2), Rehoboam (1 Kings xiv. 23), Asa (1 Kings xv. 14), Jehoshaphat (1 Kings xxii. 43), Joash (ch. xii. 3), Amaziah (ch. xiv. 4), Azariah (ch. xv. 4), and Jotham (ch. xv. 35), but himself countenanced and took part in it, which no other king appears to have done. It was probably the stimulus that his example gave to the cult which induced Hezekiah to abolish it (see ch. xviii. 4). **And on the hills, and under every green tree** (comp. 1 Kings xiv. 23, with the comment).

Vers. 5, 6.—*War of Ahaz with Pekah and Rezin.*

Ver. 5.—**Then Rezin King of Syria and Pekah son of Remaliah King of Israel came up to Jerusalem to war.** The alliance between Rezin and Pekah has been already glanced at (ch. xvi. 37). It began, apparently, in the reign of Jotham. The policy which brought it about was one that was entirely new. Since Syria developed an aggressive tendency under the first Ben-hadad (1 Kings xx. 1), there had till now been no alliance made with her by either of the two Israelite kingdoms. She had been reckoned as their common enemy; and while they had on two occasions been allied together against her (1 Kings xxii. 4—36; ch. viii. 28), never as yet had either asked her help against the other. Now, however, Ephraim became confederate with Syria against Judah. The new policy must be ascribed to the new condition of things consequent upon the attitude assumed by Assyria under Tiglath-pileser. Assyria had been under a cloud for forty years. The nations of the western coast of Asia had ceased to fear her, and had felt at liberty to pursue their own quarrels. Her recovery of vigour altered the whole situation. It was at once evident to the statesmen who directed the policy of the small western states that, unless they combined, they were lost. Hence the alliance between Pekah and Rezin. Probably they would have been glad to have drawn Ahaz into the confederacy; but it would seem that he did not share their fears, and would not join them. Hereupon the design was formed to dethrone him, and set up in his place a new ruler, a certain Ben-Tabeal (Isa. vii. 6), on whose assistance they could rely. The two confederate princes then began the campaign. Pekah invaded Judæa, and gained a great victory over Ahaz, which is perhaps exaggerated in 2 Chron. xxviii. 6—15; Rezin carried his arms further south, took Elath, and re-established the Edomites in power (see the comment on ver. 6). Then the allies joined forces and proceeded to besiege Jerusalem. **And they besieged Ahaz, but could not overcome** him. The siege is mentioned by Isaiah (vii. 1), who was commissioned by God to comfort Ahaz, and assure him that the city would not fall (Isa. vii. 7). The fortifications of Uzziah (2 Chron. xxvi. 9) and Jotham (2 Chron. xxvii. 3) had, no doubt, greatly strengthened the city since the time when (as related in ch. xiv. 13) it was captured so easily by Joash.

Ver. 6.—**At that time Rezin King of Syria recovered Elath to Syria.** The Syrians had certainly never previously been masters of Elath, which had always hitherto been either Jewish or Edomite (see 1 Kings ix. 26; xxii. 48; ch. xiv. 22). Hence it seems to be necessary that we should either translate the Hebrew verb הֵשִׁיב by "gained," "conquered," instead of "recovered;" or else change אֲרָם, "Syria," into אֱדֹם, "Edom." The Syrians could "recover" Elath for Edom; they could only "gain" it for themselves. **And drave the Jews from Elath**—i.e. expelled the Jewish garrison which had been maintained in Elath from the time of its conquest by Uzziah (ch. xiv. 22)—**and the Syrians came to Elath;** rather, *the Edomites*—אֲדוֹמִים for אֲרוֹמִים. Rezin could not have thought of holding a place so remote from Damascus as Elath; and, had he done so, the danger of his kingdom in the next year would have necessitated the relinquishment of so distant a possession. **And dwelt there unto this day.** It is quite certain that Elath belonged to Edom, and not to Syria, at the time when the Books of Kings were written.

Vers. 7—9.—*Expedition of Tiglath-pileser against Pekah and Rezin.* In the extremity of his danger, when the confederacy had declared itself, or perhaps later, when he had suffered terrible defeats, and was about to be besieged in his capital (2 Chron. xxviii. 5, 6), Ahaz invoked the aid of Tiglath-pileser, sent him all the treasure on which he could lay his hands (ver. 8), offered to place himself and his kingdom under the Assyrian monarch's suzerainty, and entreated him to come and "save him out of the hands" of his enemies (ver. 7). Humanly speaking, he might be justified.

He had not called in one foreign power until Pekah had called in another. There was no other prospect (again humanly speaking) of escape. But, had he accepted the offers of Isaiah (vii. 4—16), and relied wholly on Jehovah, his position would have been far better. However, he was unable to see this; he made his application; and Tiglath-pileser "came up," and utterly crushed the Syro-Israelite confederacy (ver. 9).

Ver. 7.—**So Ahaz sent messengers to Tiglath-pileser King of Assyria, saying.** This appeal to man rather than to God, this trust in "an arm of flesh," was exactly what Isaiah had been endeavouring to prevent, what he viewed as unfaithfulness, and as inevitably drawing down God's wrath both upon king and kingdom. Ahaz was young, was weak, and had no doubt a large body of advisers, who considered the prophet to be a fanatic, who had no belief in supernatural aid, and who thought that in any emergency recourse was to be had to the measures which human prudence and human policy dictated. The aid of Tiglath-pileser seemed to them, under the circumstances, the only thing that could save them; and they persuaded the weak prince to adopt their views. **I am thy servant and thy son.** The offer of submission was unmistakable. "Servant," in the language of the time, meant "slave." Complete subjection, enrolment among Assyria's feudatories, the entire loss of independence, was well understood to be the price that had to be paid for Assyria's protection. Ahaz and his worldly advisers were prepared to pay it. They surrendered themselves, body and soul, into the hands of the great world-power of the period. **Come up, and save me out of the hand of the King of Syria, and out of the hand of the King of Israel, which rise up against me.** Syria is put forward as at once the more formidable of the two foes, and the one most open to Assyrian attack. Already Damascus had been more than once menaced by Assyrian armies ('Eponym Canon,' pp. 113, 115, 116), while the kingdom of Samaria had only suffered at her extremities (ch. xv. 29). Samaria could not well be approached excepting through Syria, and after Syria's downfall.

Ver. 8.—**And Ahaz took the silver and gold that was found in the house of the Lord, and in the treasures of the king's house.** Hitherto the temple treasures had been diverted from their proper use, and secularized for the sole purpose (except in one instance) of buying off the hostility of a foreign foe, who threatened the city and the temple itself with destruction (see 1 Kings xiv. 26; ch. xii. 18; xiv. 14). Now, as on *one* former occasion (1 Kings xv. 18), they were utilized to purchase an alliance. **And sent it for a present to the King of Assyria.** So Gyges King of Syria sent presents to Asshur-bani-pal to purchase his aid against the Cimmerians ('Records of the Past,' vol. i. p. 68), and Susub of Babylon sent his temple treasures to Umman-Minan of Elam (ibid., pp. 46, 47), to purchase his assistance against Sennacherib.

Ver. 9.—**And the King of Assyria hearkened unto him.** Overtures of the kind were almost certain to be accepted. The great conquering monarchs of the East were always glad to receive small states into their alliance for a time, and even to allow them a shadow of independence, while they made use of their services against their near neighbours. Tiglath-pileser was already bent on conquering Samaria and Damascus, and could not fail to perceive that their subjugation would be greatly facilitated by his having the support of Judæa. **For the King of Assyria** —rather, *and the King of Assyria*—went up **against Damascus.** Damascus was naturally attacked first, as nearer to Assyria than Samaria, and also as more wealthy and more important. Tiglath-pileser's records contain an account of the campaign, but it is unfortunately much mutilated. We may gather from it, however, that Rezin began by meeting his assailant in the field, and engaging him in a battle which was stoutly contested. Eventually the Assyrians were victorious, and Rezin, having fled hastily to Damascus, shut himself up within its walls. Tiglath-pileser pursued him, laid siege to the city, and eventually took it, though not perhaps till it had resisted for above a year ('Eponym Canon,' p. 65). The Assyrian monarch thus describes the siege (ibid., p. 121): "Damascus, his city, I besieged, and like a caged bird I enclosed him. His forests, the trees of which were without number, I cut down; I did not leave a tree standing. [I burnt] Hadara, the house of the father of Rezin, King of Syria." **And took it.** The ancient Damascene kingdom, which had lasted from the time of Solomon (1 Kings xi. 24), was thus brought to an end. Damascus gave the Assyrians no further trouble; and within little more than thirty years it had been so absolutely absorbed into the empire that its governor was one of the Assyrian oponyms ('Eponym Canon,' p. 68). The capture of the city, foretold by Amos (i. 4, 5), was followed by the destruction of its walls and palaces. **And carried** the people of it **captive.** The system of transplanting large masses of the population from one part of the empire to another seems to have begun with Tiglath-

pileser. In his very imperfect and fragmentary annals we find the removal of above thirty thousand captives recorded, of whom more than half are women. His example was followed by his successors on a still larger scale. **To Kir.** The situation of "Kir" (קִיר) is wholly uncertain. It has been identified with Kis (Elam or Kissia); with the country watered by the Kur; with Kourêna or Koura, on the river Mardus; with Kariné, the modern Kirrind; with Kirkhi near Diartekr; and with Kiransi in the Urumiyeh country. But the similarity of sound is the sole basis for each and all of these identifications. It is best to confess our ignorance. **And slew Rezin.** This is perhaps implied, but it is not distinctly stated, in the extant annals of Tiglath-pileser.

Vers. 10—18.—*Religious changes introduced into Judæa by Ahaz.* The new position into which Ahaz had brought himself with respect to Assyria was followed by certain religious changes, which were probably, in part at any rate, its consequence, though some of them may have been the result of his own religious (or irreligious) convictions. He had a new altar made and introduced into the temple, which at first he used for his own private sacrifices (vers. 10—13); then, that his new altar might occupy the post of honour, he removed from its place the old brazen altar of Solomon, and put it in an inferior position (ver. 14). After this, he required all sacrifices to be offered on the new altar (ver. 15). Finally, he proceeded to interfere with several other of Solomon's arrangements, with what particular object is not very apparent (vers. 17, 18). In carrying out all these changes, he had the high priest of the time for his obsequious servant.

Ver. 10.—**And King Ahaz went to Damascus to meet Tiglath-pileser King of Assyria.** It was a practice of the Assyrian monarchs to hold *durbars*, or courts, at central places in the provinces, in the course of their military expeditions, whereat to receive the subject princes of the neighbourhood, who were expected to do homage, and bring with them presents, or their fixed tribute. Tiglath-pileser held one such court in the earlier part of his reign at Arpad, a Syrian town, at which were present the kings of Commagene, Syria, Tyre, Carchemish, Gaugama, and others. He seems to have held another at some unknown place, about B.C. 732 (it may have been at Damascus), which was attended by the kings of Commagene, Car-chemish, Gebal, Hamath, Gaugama, Tubal, Arvad, Ammon, Moab, Askelon, Gaza, Edom, and Judah, the last-mentioned being Yahu-khazi (Jehoahaz), by which is probably meant Ahaz. It is with reason conjectured that this was the occasion mentioned in the text, when "King Ahaz went to Damascus to meet Tiglath-pileser." **And saw an altar that was at Damascus.** It is almost certain that this was an Assyrian altar. Ahaz may at one time have turned for help to the gods of Syria (2 Chron. xxviii. 23), and asked their aid against his enemies; but the glory of Syria was now gone, her gods were dis-credited, and the place of power was occupied by Assyria, which had asserted its supre-macy. When Ahaz visited Tiglath-pileser at Damascus, and "saw an altar," it was, in all probability, Tiglath-pileser's altar. The Assyrian kings were accustomed to carry altars about with them, and to have them set up in their fortified camps, or in other convenient places. They also, not unfre-quently, set up altars to the great gods in the countries which they conquered, and required the inhabitants to pay them rever-ence. Ahaz may either have been required by Tiglath-pileser to set up an Assyrian altar in the temple, or he may have volun-teered the act as one which was likely to please his suzerain. **And King Ahaz sent to Urijah the priest**—*i.e.* the high priest—**the fashion of the altar and the pattern of it.** Assyrian altars were quite different from Jewish ones. Generally they were of small size, either square with a battlemented edge, or round at the top and supported on a triangular base ('Dict. of the Bible,' *ad voc.* "Altar," vol. i. p. 55, woodcuts Nos. 3 and 5). It is scarcely likely that Ahaz was par-ticularly pleased with the pattern (Keil), and therefore wished to have one like it. He probably merely wished to satisfy his suzerain that he had conformed to some of his religious usages. **According to all the workmanship thereof.** Though not very elaborate, the Assyrian altars have an ornamentation which is peculiar and un-mistakable. Careful instructions would be needed for workmen who had never seen the sort of object which they were required to produce.

Ver. 11.—**And Urijah the priest.** No doubt the Uriah of Isaiah (viii. 2), who might be a "faithful witness" to the record of a fact, though a bad man, over-complaisant in carrying out the will of the king. **Built an altar according to all that King Ahaz had sent from Damascus:**—rather, *built the altar,* i.e. the altar commanded by the monarch—**so Urijah the priest made it against King Ahaz came from Damascus.** A bold high priest like Azariah (2 Chron. xxvi. 17)

would have refused to work the king's will in such a matter, which was certainly a desecration of the temple, and to some extent a compromise with idolatry. But Urijah was a man of a weaker fibre, and does not seem to have thought even of remonstrance, much less of resistance.

Ver. 12.—**And when the king was come from Damascus, the king saw the altar: and the king approached to the altar, and offered thereon.** It is not necessarily implied in these words that Ahaz, like Uzziah, usurped the priestly functions, though conceivably he may have done so, and Urijah may have stood tamely by. What the writer has it in his mind to record is that the king, on his return from Damascus, at once made use of the new altar for his private sacrifices. If he had meant to tax Ahaz with so great a sin as that which brought the curse of leprosy upon Uzziah, he would almost certainly have made his meaning clearer.

Ver. 13.—**And he burnt his burnt offering and his meat offering, and poured his drink offering, and sprinkled the blood of his peace offerings, upon the altar.** (On the different kinds of offerings, see Lev. i.—vii.)

Ver. 14.—**And he brought also the brazen altar, which** was **before the Lord.** One sin leads on to another. Having introduced his self-invented *quasi*-idolatrous altar into the temple, and so inserted "the thin end of the wedge," Ahaz was not satisfied, but proceeded to another innovation. Urijah, having had no express order from the king with respect to the position of the new altar, had placed it in front of the old one, between it and the eastern gate of the court. Thus the old altar, which was directly in front of the temple porch, seemed to cut the new altar off from the temple. Ahaz would not have this continue, and resolved on removing the altar of Solomon from its place, and putting it elsewhere. **From the forefront of the house** (comp. 1 Kings viii. 54), **from between the altar**—*i.e.* the new altar—**and the house of the Lord**—*i.e.* the temple building—**and put it on the north side of the altar.** The removal of Solomon's altar from its place of honour to a side position left the space clear between the temple and the new altar, which thus, without exactly occupying the same site, took practically the place of Solomon's altar. Solomon's altar, shifted to one side, was put, as it were, in the background; the eye rested on the new altar, right in front of the porch and temple, which so became "the main altar" (הַמִּזְבֵּחַ הַגָּדוֹל), as it is called in the next verse.

Ver. 15.—**And King Ahaz commanded Urijah the priest, saying.** Here the king, no doubt, stepped out of the sphere of his duties, not to usurp exactly the priestly office, but to give directions in matters which belonged, not to the *regale*, but to the *pontificale*. Urijah ought to have refused obedience. **Upon the great altar.** Certainly not so called because of its size (Keil), for it was probably much smaller than the old altar, but because of its position (see the comment on ver. 14). **Burn the morning burnt offering, and the evening meat offering**—*i.e.* offer the daily sacrifice both morning and evening—**and the king's burnt sacrifice, and his meat offering**—*i.e.* the customary royal sacrifices (see 1 Kings viii. 62)—**with the burnt offering of all the people of the land, and their meat offering, and their drink offerings**—*i.e.* all the private offerings of the people for themselves—**and sprinkle upon it all the blood of the burnt offering, and all the blood of the sacrifice** (comp. Exod. xxix. 16, 20; Lev. i. 5, 11; iii. 2, 8, 13; vii. 2; xvii. 6; Numb. xviii. 17, etc.) **and the brazen altar shall be for me to inquire** by; rather, *and as for the brazen altar, it will be for me to inquire concerning it;* i.e. I shall hereafter determine what use, if any, it shall be put to. As, by the king's directions, all the regular and all the occasional sacrifices were to be offered upon his new altar, the other would practically be superfluous. It would have been only logical to remove it, or break it up; but this the king was probably afraid of doing. He therefore said that he would take time to consider what he should do.

Ver. 16.—**Thus did Urijah the priest, according to all that King Ahaz commanded.** An emphatic condemnation of the high priest, whose subserviency evidently provokes the writer's indignation.

Ver. 17.—**And King Ahaz cut off the borders of the bases.** By "the bases" are probably meant the stands of the ten brazen lavers, which Hiram the Tyrian artificer made for Solomon, and which Solomon placed outside the temple, five on either side of the entrance (1 Kings vii. 39). The "borders of the bases" seem to have consisted of ornamental panels, on which were carved, in relief, figures of lions, oxen, and cherubim (1 Kings vii. 29). The object of Ahaz in these mutilations may have been merely destructive, as we find Egyptian kings, after a change of religion, mutilating the tablets, and erasing the inscriptions put up in honour of those gods who had ceased to be in favour with them. Or, possibly, he may, as Keil supposes, have wished to transfer the ornamental carvings to some other edifice, e.g. an idolatrous temple or a palace. **And removed the laver from off them**—removed, i.e., from each base "the laver" which stood upon it—**and took down the sea from off the brazen oxen that were under it.** (On Solomon's "molten sea," or

great laver, and the twelve oxen which supported it, comp. 1 Kings vii. 23—26, and Jer. lii. 20.) The "sea" was probably removed from off the backs of the oxen, in order that they might be made use of, as ornaments, elsewhere. **And put it upon a pavement of stones;** rather, *upon a pedestal of stone* (ἐπὶ βάσιν λιθίνην, LXX.).

Ver. 18.—**And the covert for the sabbath that they had built in the house.** The "covert for the sabbath" was probably (as Keil notes) "a covered place or stand in the court of the temple, to be used by the king whenever he visited the temple with his retinue on the sabbath, or on feast-days." It may have been elaborately ornamented. **And the king's entry without.** This may have been "the ascent into the house of the Lord," which Solomon constructed for his own use (1 Kings x. 5), and which was among those marvels of art that made the spirit of the Queen of Sheba faint within her. **Turned he from the house of the Lord for the King of Assyria.** It is not clear what meaning our translators intended to express, and it is still less clear what was the sense intended by the original writer. Ahaz did something to the royal stand inside the temple, and to the "ascent" which led to it, and what he did was done, not "*for* the King of Assyria," but "*for fear* of the King of Assyria;" but what exactly his action was, we cannot say. No satisfactory meaning has been assigned to הֵסֵב בֵּית יְהוָה by any commentator.

Vers. 19, 20.—*The death of Ahaz.* The writer terminates his account of the reign of Ahaz with his usual formulæ, which in this instance are wholly colourless. Ahaz's acts were written in the book of the chronicles of the kings; he died, and was buried with his fathers; Hezekiah, his son, reigned in his stead. This is all that he thinks it needful to say.

Ver. 19.—**Now the rest of the acts of Ahaz which he did, are they not written in the book of the chronicles of the kings of Judah?** The writer of Chronicles adds some important facts not found in the narrative of Kings. Among them are the following: (1) The complete defeat of Ahaz by Pekah, who "smote him with a great slaughter" (2 Chron. xxviii. 5), killing a hundred and twenty thousand of his soldiers, and carrying off two hundred thousand captives, men, women, and children (2 Chron. xxviii. 8); these captives were, however, afterwards restored (ver. 15). (2) His defeat by the Syrians (ver. 5). This is, perhaps, implied in ch. xvi. 6; but it is not expressly stated. (3) His defeat by the Edomites, who invaded his land, and made a large number of prisoners (2 Chron. xxviii. 17). (4) The conquest in his reign of a considerable portion of Southern Judæa by the Philistines (ver. 18). (5) The fact that Ahaz at one time in his life adopted the Syrian worship, and "sacrificed to the gods of Damascus which smote him" (ver. 23). (6) The fact that in his latter' years he shut up the temple (ver. 24), closing the doors of the porch (2 Chron. xxix. 7), extinguishing the lamps (2 Chron. xxix. 7), and putting an end to the burning of incense and the offering of sacrifice. (7) The fact that, not content with the previously existing high places, he set up a number of new ones, so that there should be a "high place"

in every several city. (2 Chron. xxviii. 25). The religious condition of Judæa can scarcely have been worse in the worst time of Manasseh or Amon.

Ver. 20.—**And Ahaz slept with his fathers, and was buried with his fathers in the city of David.** This must be taken in the same sense, and with the same limitations, as the same phrase in ch. xii. 21. The writer of Chronicles (2 Chron. xxviii. 27) says, " And Ahaz slept with his fathers, and they buried him in the city, even in Jerusalem : *but they brought him not into the sepulchres of the kings.*" Like Uzziah, he was not thought worthy of sepulture in the royal catacomb (see the comment on ch. xii. 21).

HOMILETICS.

Vers. 1—4.—*The godliness of parents does not secure the perseverance of their children in well-doing, but increases the children's guilt if they take to evil courses.* Ahaz, the worst of all the kings of Judah, is the son of one of whom it is said that " he did right in the sight of the Lord " (ch. xv. 34). Manasseh, perhaps the next worst, is the child of the one king for whom the sacred writers have no word of blame. Wicked Abimelech is the son of the pious Gideon (Judg. ix. 1). We naturally expect the contrary of this to happen. We suppose that education does everything, and we look to see the children of godly parents grow up godly, and are apt, without any inquiry into the circumstances, to suppose that every ill-conducted young man must have been badly brought up. The dictum of the wise man, " Train up a child in the way he should go: and when he is old, he will not depart from it" (Prov. xxii. 6), may be quoted in justification of such views, and is often so quoted, as if it were a rule without any exception. But no proverb is of this character. All are *general* rules, which admit of exceptions; and the exceptional character of this particular proverb is continually allowed in the Scriptures (Prov. xvii. 21, 25; xix. 13; Ezek. xviii. 10, etc.). The points to be urged practically are—

I. THAT PARENTS SHOULD MAKE EVERY POSSIBLE EFFORT, JUST AS IF THEIR CHILDREN'S CHARACTERS DEPENDED ENTIRELY UPON THEM. " Instruction," education, training, though sometimes of no avail, have, in the majority of cases, very great weight. Even when they seem to have failed, it often happens that their results remain deep buried in the soul, and in the end show themselves, and are of sufficient force to snatch many a brand from the burning. The parent must not despair because he does not see much fruit of his labours at once. He has to do his best, to " liberate his own soul," to see that, if his child be lost, it is not owing to his neglect. He has to " hope against hope," to persevere with his efforts, to be unwearied in his prayers, to do the utmost that lies in his power to lead his children into the right path. A parent ought never to despair. While there is life there is hope. The way of repentance is open to all ; and, historically, there have been repentances from such a depth of depravity that no case should seem quite hopeless. " Where sin abounded, grace did much more abound " (Rom. v. 20). The mercy of God is unsearchable, unfathomable. There is no saying what sinner may not turn from his sin, put away the iniquity of his doings, and become a true servant of the Most High.

II. THAT PARENTS SHOULD NOT BE OVER-SORROWFUL, OR DEPRESSED BEYOND MEASURE, BECAUSE THEIR EFFORTS TO KEEP THEIR CHILDREN IN THE RIGHT PATH HAVE IN SOME CASES FAILED. If, indeed, they have had many children, and their efforts have failed with *all*, they may reasonably suspect some defect in themselves or in their system. But if the results are varied, if a portion of their children have been all that they could wish, while others—despite all that they could do—have preferred to " walk in the way of sinners," and even to "sit in the seat of the scornful," then they have no need to sorrow overmuch, or to regard themselves as culpable. The influences which go to form each man's character are countless, and with hundreds of them a parent has nothing to do. Again, there is "the personal equation." There do seem to be some who, "*as soon as they are born*, go astray and speak lies." It is among the mysteries of man's existence here on earth that natural dispositions should so greatly vary. No parent of many children but knows, by certain experience, that this is so. One child gives no trouble, and scarcely requires any guidance. Another is wilful, perverse, headstrong, almost devoid of good impulses, and full of inclination to evil. Parents are answerable for neglect, for unwisdom, above all for bad example; but they need not fear, if they earnestly endeavour to do their duty by their children, that in God's just judgment the iniquity of their children will be imputed to them. "The son shall not bear the iniquity of the father, *neither shall the father bear the iniquity of the son*" (Ezek. xviii. 20); "The soul that sinneth, it shall die" (Ezek. xviii. 4).

III. THAT CHILDREN WHO HAVE BEEN RELIGIOUSLY BROUGHT UP, IF THEY TURN TO EVIL COURSES, INCUR A FEARFUL RESPONSIBILITY. "It had been better for them not to have known the way of righteousness, than, after they have known it, to turn from the holy commandment delivered unto them" (2 Pet. ii. 21). If children, notwithstanding a godly training, take to an evil life, what must we suppose that they would have done had they been born, as so many are, amidst adverse influences, and from infancy exposed to contact with indecency, drunkenness, blasphemy? Alas! every blessing abused becomes a curse; and to have a pattern of goodness before our eyes, to have virtue instilled into us, and then to reject it—to choose the evil and refuse the good—is to provoke God's heavy displeasure, and bring down his severe judgments upon us. What excuse can such persons offer for their misconduct? They know that by sin they displease God, grieve their parents, injure themselves, ruin their worldly prospects, imperil their salvation; yet for a little present pleasure they shut their eyes to all future consequences, and rush to their destruction. Their conduct is folly, madness, idiocy; but not the sort of madness which shuts out responsibility. They are answerable for it, and will have to answer at God's judgment-seat. Oh! that they would pause ere it is too late, recognize the folly of their evil courses, and "put away their iniquity"! God is still willing to pardon all whom he suffers to live. Let them "arise, and go to their Father," and say unto him, "We have sinned;" and he will go out to meet them, and receive them, and "there will be joy in the presence of the angels of God over each such sinner that repenteth, more than over ninety and nine just persons, which need no repentance" (Luke xv. 7, 10).

Vers. 5—7.—*God's punishments of a nation's sins are often long delayed, but, when they come, it is not by degrees, but suddenly, violently, and at once.* This subject may best be treated, as the last, under three heads, viz. (1) *the sins of Judah, which had provoked God;* (2) *the long delay in their punishment;* and (3) *the suddenness and overwhelming force with which the punishment came at last.*

I. THE SINS OF JUDAH. Though, on the whole, less guilty than her sister, Ephraim, still Judah had, from the division of the kingdom of Solomon, been more or less unfaithful to Jehovah in several respects. 1. An unauthorized and illegitimate high-place worship, tinged with superstition and perhaps even idolatry, had maintained its place by the side of the authorized Jehovah-cult, throughout the whole period of the divided monarchy, from the accession of Rehoboam to the death of Ahaz (1 Kings xiv. 23; xv. 14; xxii. 43; ch. xii. 3; xiv. 4; xv. 4, 35; xvi. 4). 2. The worship of Baal had been introduced from the sister kingdom by the influence of Athaliah, and had prevailed during the reigns of her husband, Jehoram, her son, Ahaziah, and her own (ch. viii. 18, 27; xi. 18). 3. Luxury and effeminacy had crept in, especially during the prosperous reigns of Uzziah and Jotham, and had led on to debauchery and licentiousness (Isa. i. 4; ii. 6—8; iii. 16—24; v. 11, 12; Joel i. 5; Amos vi. 1—6, etc.). 4. Injustice and oppression had become rife. The rich men sought to "join house to house, and field to field" (Isa. v. 8); they stripped the poor of their small properties by legal chicanery (Isa. iii. 14), oppressed them, and "ground their faces" (Isa. iii. 15). The judges in the courts accepted bribes (Isa. i. 23) and gave wrong judgments (Isa. v. 23). Widows and orphans were the special objects of attack, on account of their weakness and defencelessness (Isa. i. 17, 23; x. 2). 5. The forms of religion were kept up, but the spirit had evaporated. Men thronged God's courts, brought abundant offerings, made many prayers, kept the new moons and the sabbaths and the appointed feasts, but without any real care for the honour of God or any thought of seeking to serve and obey him. Hence their worship was "an offence;" their ceremonies were mockeries, their oblations "vain," their solemn meetings "iniquity." God was "weary to bear them" (Isa. i. 11—15).

II. THE LONG DELAY IN THEIR PUNISHMENT. More than two centuries had elapsed since Judah began to "do evil in the sight of the Lord, and to provoke him to jealousy with their sins which they had committed, above all that their fathers had done" (1 Kings xiv. 22). Above a century had passed since the apostasy of Jehoram and Ahaziah. During all this time Judah had maintained her independence, had received no severe blow, fallen under no crushing affliction. Latterly, she had even prospered. Under Uzziah she had recovered Elath (ch. xiv. 22), conquered a part of Philistia (2 Chron. xxvi. 6), defeated the Arabians and Mehunim (2 Chron. xxvi. 7), and made the Ammonites her tributaries (2 Chron. xxvi. 8); under Jotham she had maintained these conquests, and when Ammon revolted had reduced her to subjection (2 Chron. xxvii. 5) without any difficulty. God, in his long-suffering mercy, bore with his people. He would win them by kindness, draw them to him by cords of love, at any rate give them ample time for repentance. But it was in vain. The longer he left them unpunished, the further they wandered from the right way, and the more they hardened their hearts. The time came when the prophet could only say of them, "Ah sinful nation, a people laden with iniquity, a seed of evil-doers, children that are corrupters: they have forsaken the Lord, they have provoked the Holy One of Israel unto anger, they are gone away backward. . . . The whole head is sick, and the whole heart faint. From the sole of the foot even unto the head there is no soundness in it; but wounds, and bruises, and putrefying sores" (Isa. i. 4—6).

III. THE SUDDENNESS AND OVERWHELMING FORCE WITH WHICH THE PUNISHMENT DESCENDED WHEN IT CAME. Bishop Butler remarks how, in the punishment which God brings upon vicious individuals in this world, there is often a long respite. "After the chief bad consequences, temporal consequences, of their follies have been delayed for a great while; at length they break in irresistibly, like an armed force; repentance is too late to relieve, and can only serve to aggravate their distress; the case is become desperate, and poverty and sickness, remorse and anguish, infamy and death, the effects of their own doings, overwhelm them, beyond possibility of remedy or escape" ('Analogy of Religion, Natural and Revealed,' pt. i. ch. ii. p. 52). And so it is often with nations; so it was now with the nation of the Jews. As soon as the punishment began, blow was dealt upon blow. First, Rezin "smote them, and carried away a great multitude of them captives, and brought them to Damascus" (2 Chron. xxviii. 5). Then they were delivered into the hand of Pekah, who "smote them with a great slaughter, slaying a hundred and twenty thousand in one day, which were all valiant men" (2 Chron. xxviii. 5, 6). Next, Edom had her fling at the sick lion, and "came and smote Judah, and carried away captives" (2 Chron. xxviii. 17). Then Philistia attacked the cities of the low country, and of the south of Judah, and took a number of them, "and dwelt there" (2 Chron. xxviii. 18). Presently, Pekah and Rezin, joining their forces, advanced together to the siege of Jerusalem. All was lost, except only honour; and then honour was thrown into the gulf; Judah went down on her knees to Assyria, and implored aid, gave tribute, accepted a suzerain, made the inglorious confession, "I am thy servant and thy son" (ch. xvi. 7). Having incurred defeat, disgrace, the loss of military honour, the loss of the flower of her troops, she crowns all by giving up her national independence, inviting a master, and herself placing a foreign yoke upon her own shoulders. But for the wonderful efforts made by Hezekiah when he ascended the throne (ch. xviii. 3—8), Judæa's ruin would have been completed under Ahaz; and the punishment so long delayed, when it came, would have been final, "without escape or remedy."

Vers. 10—17.—*A wicked king allowed to have his way by a weak priest.* The double *régime*, civil and ecclesiastical, which it pleased God to establish in his first Church, the Jewish, and to continue, with certain modifications, in his second Church, the Christian, seems to have been designed for the mutual advantage of both parties.

Authority, in whatever hands it is placed, is always liable to be abused, to over-assert itself, to grow arbitrary, autocratic, tyrannical. Hence the necessity of checks, of a balance of forces, of counterpoise, of an arrangement by which the undue preponderance of any single authority shall be prevented. It is sometimes needful that the civil authority shall interpose to keep the spiritual within due bounds, and disallow the establishment of sacerdotal tyranny. It is quite as often requisite for the spiritualty to assert itself, and check the endeavours of kings and nobles to establish an unlimited autocracy. From time to time the two independent authorities, the civil and ecclesiastical, the *regale* and the *pontificale,* are sure to come into collision. Our own history presents instances in the struggles of Anselm against Rufus, of Becket against Henry II., and of the seven bishops against the last of the Stuart kings. Under such circumstances weakness on either side constitutes a serious peril to the community. A weak king, priest-ridden, makes dangerous concessions to the ecclesiastical order, and imperils the peace and prosperity of his kingdom by so doing. A weak priest, timid and time-serving, allows the rights of his order to be trampled on, and lays up no less an amount of trouble in the future for the nation to which he belongs. If Ahaz had been succeeded by another worldly minded and ambitious king, instead of the pious Hezekiah, there is no saying how low the ecclesiastical authority might not have sunk, or how soon the kingly office might not have freed itself from all checks, and have become absolute, and in a short time tyrannical. Urijah did his best to destroy the constitution of his country, and to turn the Judæan limited monarchy into a pure despotism. He was weak rather than wicked; but his weakness might have had the worst results. It was only the accident of Ahaz being succeeded by a truly religious prince that prevented the precedent, which he had set, from entailing ruinous consequences.

HOMILIES BY VARIOUS AUTHORS.

Vers. 1—20.—*Steps in a downward path: the reign of Ahaz.* In the opening chapters of Isaiah we have an account of the condition of the kingdom of Judah at the time that Ahaz succeeded to the throne. The prosperity which the country had enjoyed under Uzziah had been continued and increased under the righteous reign of his son Jotham. And now the grandson, Ahaz, a young man of twenty, finds the country abounding in wealth, full of silver and gold. Isaiah says there was no end of their treasure; their land also was full of horses, neither was there any end of their chariots. Their commerce, too, was in a thriving condition. "The ships of Tarshish, sailing from Elath, could boast their gilded prows and stems, and purple sails, and brought home rich cargoes from the distant East" (Geikie, 'Hours with the Bible: Rehoboam to Hezekiah,' p. 292). But before Ahaz died, all this was changed. Enemy after enemy invaded his country. The land became desolate. The king was reduced to great extremities to obtain money. Instead of the sunshine of prosperity, there was on every side the dark shadow of desolation and decay. We have the explanation of it all in the third and fourth verses. Ahaz began badly, and every fresh movement in his life was a step from bad to worse. His history is a further illustration of how one sin leads to another. It was a continuously downward path.

I. THE FIRST STEP IN THE DOWNWARD CAREER OF AHAZ WAS HIS IDOLATRY. (Vers. 3, 4.) He forsook the worship of the true and living God, and worshipped the gods of the heathen. Even that step he would seem to have taken gradually. At first he began with the high places, which had never been taken away. Then graven images and other heathen customs were used in the worship of God; and finally the idols of the false gods themselves were set up. The policy of compromise had now reached its fitting conclusion. When the right makes compromise with the wrong, the wrong is sure to gain the victory. So it was in this case. The people had got accustomed to the high places. They saw no harm in *them*. And now they see no harm in the idols. Isaiah describes the universal corruption when he says, "Their land also is full of idols; they worship the work of their own hands, that which their own fingers have made." And what a worship it was to substitute for the worship of the only true and living and almighty God! A *useless* worship, as Isaiah indicates, to worship the work of their own hands. It brought them no help in their hour of distress. But it was worse than useless. It was a *foul and degrading* worship. It is best described in the words of the third verse, " the abominations of the heathen." We can have but a faint conception of the loathsome practices associated with the worship of the pagan deities. The passage before us speaks of one act of worship—by no means the worst, though sufficiently cruel and revolting. This was the worship of Moloch. In the valley of Hinnom, afterwards called Gehenna or Tophet, an image of Moloch was erected. Dr. Thomson, in 'The Land and the Book,' refers to the passage in Jeremiah (xix.) where the valley of Hinnom is spoken of, and thinks, because it is said there that the image of Baal was there, that Moloch and Baal were one and the same. At any rate, part of the worship of Moloch consisted in making children pass through the fire before his image, or in actually burning them in it. The cries of the children were drowned by the sound of musical instruments and the shouts of the frenzied worshippers. It is to this that Milton refers when he says—

> " First, Moloch, horrid king, besmear'd with blood
> Of human sacrifice, and parents' tears ;
> Though for the noise of drums and timbrels loud
> Their children's cries unheard, that passed through fire
> To his grim idol."

Such was the worship which Ahaz, in his infatuation and desire to be like the nations round about him, substituted for the spiritual, elevating worship of the great Father of us all. After all, was he much worse than many in modern times who profess to be so enlightened that they regard the Christian religion as a superstition? And what do they give us in place of it? A worship of dead matter, of blind force ; of a mere supposition of their own minds. If Christianity be a superstition, what are some of the fancies of our philosophers? Before we give up our Christian religion, *let us know what we are to have in place of it.* Let us compare the results of Christianity with the results of any rival system, and how immeasurably superior to them all it stands, in the purity of its teaching, in the power it exercises to elevate and ennoble human life, and in the blessings it has brought to the nations! How it alone lights up the darkness of the grave, and breathes into the bereaved heart the inspiration and comfort of the heavenly hope! This was the first downward step in the career of Ahaz—*forsaking the worship of God.* So many a man has begun the downward path. The empty seat in the house of God indicates often the beginning of a useless and wasted life. Or if he comes to the house of God, he worships God in form only. His thoughts are far away. Self and the world, money and pleasure,—how often are these the idols men worship with the thoughts of their hearts and with all the efforts of their lives!

II. The next step in the downward path of Ahaz was the alliance he entered into. (Vers. 5—7.) The Syrians made war on him along with the King of Israel. Ahaz, in his difficulty, sought the help of the King of Assyria. How humiliating is his entreaty! "I am thy servant and thy son," was the message he sent : "come up and save me out of the hand of the King of Syria, and out of the hand of the King of Israel, which rise up against me." There was nothing wrong in itself in seeking the help of friendly kings. On this occasion, however, God absolutely warned Ahaz against seeking their help. But, to begin with, *there was something wanting.* Ahaz did not seek God's guidance in the matter. He did not seek God's help. He who had rejected the service of the living God, makes himself the cringing slave of the King of Assyria, and humbles himself to a heathen for help. What a mistake when a nation trusts to its resources or its strong alliances, and forgets to look to that Divine power from whom all blessings flow! There may be nothing wrong in all our efforts to improve our worldly position, but there may be *something wanting.* There may be nothing wrong in your life, but there may be *something wanting.* You may be anxious to be useful in the world ; but are you setting about it in the right way? One thing is needful, one thing is essential to all true happiness, to all true usefulness. That is the presence and help of God. Is the Lord Jesus dwelling in your heart? Whatever else may disappoint you, he will never fail.

> " When other helpers fail, and comforts flee,
> Help of the helpless, oh, abide with me ! "

III. The next downward step which Ahaz took was his plundering the house of God. (Vers. 8, 9, 17, 18.) Ahaz paid dear for his alliance with the King of Assyria. He had already disobeyed and dishonoured God by his idolatry. He had already dishonoured God by refusing to heed the warnings which Isaiah gave him. But now he commits a still more flagrant act of defiance and desecration. In order to reward the Assyrian king for his help, and to retain his friendship, he actually takes the silver and gold that was found in the house of the Lord, and sends it for a present to the King of Assyria. *The world's friendships are often dearly bought.* We pay for them, in peace of mind, in peace of conscience, in loss of money, in loss of time, a greater price than they are worth. Sooner or later the crisis must come in every man's life when he must choose between the friendship of God and the friendship of the world. What choice are *you* making? What choice would you make if you were put to the test now? Perhaps you are being put to the test in your daily life. Perhaps you are being tempted, for the sake of worldly friendship, for the sake of your business, for the sake of popularity, to sacrifice some principle, to trample on some command of God, to neglect some plain duty which conscience and the Word of God alike point out. Business! The great business of your life, of every man's life, is to fear God and keep his commandments. "Man's chief end is to glorify God, and enjoy him for ever." *Oh what a fearful thing it is to take from God that which rightfully belongs to him!* It is a crime against law, against morality, to take from our fellow-creatures, without their permission, that which belongs to them. But how much more guilty is he who would take from God that which is his! We condemn Ahaz for his impiety and sacrilege in taking from the temple those things which had been consecrated to God. *But let us look into our own hearts and lives.* Are we giving God that which is his due? Are we keeping back nothing from him? Has he no greater claim on our daily thoughts than a hurried prayer at morning or evening, or none at all? Has he no greater claim on our money than the few shillings, or, it may be, few pounds we give to him every year? Let us measure our service of God much less by what others do and give, and much more by our own responsibilities, by our own overflowing cup of mercies, by the relation of our own soul to God.

IV. The next downward step of Ahaz was to set up a heathen altar in the house of the Lord. (Vers. 10—17.) Ahaz had gone to Damascus to meet the King of Assyria. While there he saw an altar used in the worship of the heathen gods. Its workmanship may perhaps have pleased him. He sent to Urijah the priest a description, perhaps a drawing of it, and Urijah, influenced more by the fear of the king than by the fear of God, caused a similar altar to be erected in the temple at Jerusalem. When Ahaz returned, he substituted this altar for the altar of the Lord, although God himself had given the pattern of that altar to Moses and to David. *But all the idols and sacrifices of Ahaz did not benefit him much.* He thought the gods of the heathen would help him; but, says the writer in 2 Chronicles, "They were the ruin of him and of Israel." So in everyday experience many a man finds, when he forsakes the gospel of Christ, and turns his back upon the Law of God, to follow worldly gain or pleasure, or society, or dissipation, that these things are the ruin of him. "There is a way which seemeth right unto a man, but the end thereof are the ways of death."—C. H. I.

Vers. 1—20.—*A people's king and priest; or, kinghood and priesthood.* "In the seventeenth year of Pekah," etc. Throughout all lands, almost throughout all times, *two functionaries* have been at the head of the peoples, too often treading them down by oppression, and fattening on them by their greed. One of these functionaries was not, among the Jews, of Divine ordination; for the Almighty is represented as saying, "They have set up kings, but not by me: they have made princes, and I knew it not." Let us notice each functionary as presented in this chapter—the king and the priest—the one named *Ahaz*, the other *Urijah*.

I. The kinghood. It is said, "In the seventeenth year of Pekah the son of Remaliah Ahaz the son of Jotham King of Judah began to reign. Twenty years old was Ahaz when he began to reign, and reigned sixteen years in Jerusalem, and did not that which was right in the sight of the Lord his God, like David his father." Here we learn that Ahaz, who was the son of Jotham, began to reign over Judah in his twentieth year, and that his reign continued for sixteen years. Elsewhere we are told that

Hezekiah, his son, succeeded him at the age of twenty-five (see ch. xviii. 17). According to this he became a father when he was only eleven years of age. This is not, necessarily, a mistake of the historian, since among the Jews in Tiberias there are mothers of eleven years of age and fathers of thirteen. And in Abyssinia boys of ten years and twelve years enter into the marriage relationship (see Keil). The account given of Ahaz in this chapter furnishes us with an illustration of several enormous evils. 1. *The dehumanizing force of false religion.* Ahaz was an idolater. "He walked in the way of the kings of Israel," we are told. Instead of worshipping the one true and living God, he bowed down before the idols of the heathen. This false religion of his made him so *inhuman* that he "made his son to pass through the fire, according to the abominations of the heathen, whom the Lord cast out from before the children of Israel; and he sacrificed and burnt incense in the high places, and on the hills, and under every green tree." Moloch was this idol-god of fire, and the rabbins tell us "that it was made of brass, and placed on a brazen throne, and that the head was that of a calf, with a crown upon it. The throne and image were made hollow, and a furious fire was kindled within it. The flames penetrated into the body and limbs of the idol, and, when the arms were red hot, the victim was thrown into them, and was almost immediately burnt to death." The revolting cruelty of Moloch-worship is thus described by Milton—

> "In Argob and in Basan, to the stream
> Of utmost Arnon. Nor content with such
> Audacious neighbourhood, the wisest heart
> Of Solomon he led by fraud to build
> His temple right against the temple of God
> On that opprobrious hill; and made his grove
> The pleasant valley of Hinnom, Tophet thence
> And black Gehenna call'd, the type of hell."

Thus the idolatrous religion of this Ahaz dehumanized him, by destroying within him all parental affection and transforming him into a fiend. This is true, more or less, of all false religions. Idolatry is not the only religion that makes men cruel. A corrupt Judaism and a corrupt Christianity generate in their votaries the same dehumanizing results. False religion kindled in Paul the savage ferocity of a wild beast. "He breathed out slaughter." Ecclesiastical history abounds with illustrations. 2. *The national curse of a corrupt kinghood.* Then "Rezin King of Syria and Pekah son of Remaliah King of Israel came up to Jerusalem to war: and they besieged Ahaz, but could not overcome him. At that time Rezin King of Syria recovered Elath to Syria, and drave the Jews from Elath: and the Syrians came to Elath, and dwelt there unto this day." These two kings, Rezin of Syria and Pekah of Israel, had their eyes upon this Ahaz, saw, perhaps, how his wickedness had injured his people, had taken away their heart and exhausted their resources, until they felt that this was the time for striking at Jerusalem, taking possession of the metropolis, and subjugating the country. And they made the attempt. Although they could not "overcome" Ahaz, and failed to strike him down personally, yet they "recovered Elath to Syria [or, 'Edom'], and drave the Jews from Elath." So it has ever been; corrupt kings expose their country to danger, they invite the invader and make way for him.

> "Proudly up the regal heights they sit in pampered power,
> While fires smoulder underground that strengthen every hour."

3. *The mischievous issues of a temporary expediency.* Ahaz, in order to extricate himself from the difficulties and trials which Rezin and Pekah had brought on his country, applies to the King of Assyria. "So Ahaz sent messengers to Tiglath-pileser King of Assyria, saying, I am thy servant and thy son: come up, and save me out of the hand of the King of Syria, and out of the hand of the King of Israel, which rise up against me. And Ahaz took the silver and gold that was found in the house of the Lord, and in the treasures of the king's house, and sent it for a present to the King of Assyria. And the King of Assyria hearkened unto him: for the King of Assyria went up against Damascus, and took it, and carried the people of it captive to Kir, and slew Rezin." What else could he do? To whom could he have looked for help in his emergency? The *right* thing to have done would have been the utter renuncia-

tion of his idolatry, submission to the Divine will, and invocation of the Almighty's help; but he followed what appeared to him the expedient, not the right, and hence two evils ensued. (1) *He degraded himself.* He sold himself as a slave to the king whose help he invoked. " I am thy servant and thy son: come up, and save me out of the hand of the King of Syria." What more dishonourable thing can a man do than to renounce his independence and become the slave of another? He loses his self-respect, which is the very essence of true manhood. (2) *He impoverished his people.* " And Ahaz took the silver and gold that was found in the house of the Lord, and in the treasures of the king's house, and sent it for a present to the King of Assyria." This silver and gold belonged to the nation. It was public property. What right had he to dispose of a fraction? No right whatever. Alas! it is not uncommon for kings to rob their people, consume what they have never produced, live on the property of others, and thus impoverish their subjects! What happened with Ahaz must happen with all, in the long-run, who pursue the expedient rather than the right. The right alone is truly expedient.

II. THE PRIESTHOOD. Urijah is the priest. There seems to have been more priests than one of this name, and little is known of this Urijah more than what is recorded in the present chapter. He was the priest, who at this time presided in the temple of Jerusalem. He seems to have been influential in the state, and, although a professed monotheist, was in far too close connection with Ahaz the idolatrous king. Two things are worthy of note concerning him, which too frequently characterize wicked priests in all times. 1. *An obsequious obedience to the royal will.* The Assyrian king, having taken Damascus, is visited by Ahaz in the city, the object of his visit being, no doubt, to congratulate him on his triumphs. While at Damascus, Ahaz is struck with the beauty of an altar. He seems to have been so charmed with it that he commands Urijah, the priest, to make one exactly like it. " And King Ahaz sent to Urijah the priest the fashion of the altar, and the pattern of it, according to all the workman-ship thereof." Knowing the king's wishes, with shameful obsequiousness he sets to the work. " And Urijah the priest built an altar according to all that King Ahaz had sent from Damascus: so Urijah the priest made it against King Ahaz came from Damascus. And when the king was come from Damascus, the king saw the altar: and the king approached to the altar, and offered thereon." This obsequious priest not only did this, but, without one word of protest or reproof, he witnessed the sacri-fices of the king at the altar, and allowed the position of the brazen altar in the temple to be altered; further, he actually engaged, according to the king's command, in the services. " And King Ahaz commanded Urijah the priest, saying, Upon the great altar burn the morning burnt offering, and the evening meat offering, and the king's burnt sacrifice, and his meat offering, with the burnt offerings of all the people of the land, and their meat offering, and their drink offerings; and sprinkle upon it all the blood of the burnt offering, and all the blood of the sacrifice; and the brazen altar shall be for me to inquire by. Thus did Urijah the priest, according to all that King Ahaz commanded." Thus wicked priests have too often acted. 2. *An obsequious silence to the royal profanation.* See what the king did, no doubt in the presence of the priest. " And King Ahaz cut off the borders of the bases, and removed the laver from off them; and took down the sea from off the brazen oxen that were under it, and put it upon a pavement of stones. And the covert for the sabbath that they had built in the house, and the king's entry without, turned he from the house of the Lord for the King of Assyria." This fawning, sacerdotal traitor not only " did according to all King Ahaz commanded," but he stood by silently and witnessed without a word of protest this spoliation of the holy temple. Had he acted according to his profession as a minister of the most high God, he would have risen up in all the sternness of honesty and manhood against the first intimation of Ahaz concerning the construction of an unauthorized altar. He would have said, " We have a divinely sanctioned altar already; we do not need another." And when the command came to him to make such an altar, he would have felt it an insult to his conscience, an outrage on his loyalty to Heaven, and have broken into thunders of reproof. When he saw the king's hand employed in disturbing and altering the furniture of the temple, he would have resisted him, as Azariah resisted Uzziah when he wished to offer incense. But instead of this, he, like some of his class in almost every age, seems to have been transported with the honour of seeing the royal presence, hearing the royal voice, and doing the royal bidding. A true priest should, by inflexible loyalty to Heaven, mould kings to be lords paramount in all mundane affairs, and in none other; and should lead them to be very kings of men, governing, not by craft and force, fraud and violence, but by royal thoughts, actions, and aims.—D. T.

Vers. 1—4.—*The wickedness of Ahaz.* The history has passed rapidly over the later kings of Israel. That kingdom was lost beyond recovery. "The victim having once got his stroke-of-grace, the catastrophe can be considered as almost come. There is small interest now in watching his long low moans; notable only are his sharper agonies, what convulsive struggles he may make to cast the torture off from him; and then, finally, the last departure of life itself" (Carlyle). In Judah the crisis too is approaching, but it is not yet reached. Prophets and good kings are yet to do their utmost for the nation. But a reign like that of Ahaz is a sensible step in the advance to the catastrophe.

I. THE CHARACTER OF THE KING. Though the son of the vigorous Jotham, and already twenty or twenty-five years old when he ascended the throne, Ahaz proved one of the weakest and most incapable of rulers. One sees in him the reflection of the luxurious and effeminate age described by Isaiah (iii. 12—26). Feeble, petulant, arbitrary, in his ways of acting; without strength of mind or strength of will; busying interests of his kingdom were at stake; craven in war; above all, full of religiosity and himself in *dilettante* fashion with novelties, with altars and sun-dials, while the greatest superstition without the faintest spark of true religion—"this is that King Ahaz" (2 Chron. xxviii. 22). Possibly his father Jotham was too much occupied with state and public affairs to give the necessary attention to his son's education—a fatal mistake not unfrequently committed by parents.

II. HIS ABOUNDING IDOLATRIES. Ahaz displays great zeal of his own kind in religion, but it is zeal of the most perverse and suicidal description. We observe: 1. *His imitation of the kings of Israel.* He took for his pattern, not his ancestor David, the type of the true theocratic king, but the wicked kings of the northern kingdom, whose idolatries were bringing their own realm to ruin. He made, like them, molten images to Baal, and sacrificed to them (2 Chron. xxviii. 2). Wicked men seem absolutely impervious to warning. The northern kingdom was an object-lesson, to those who had eyes to see, of the folly and fatal effects of this very course on which Ahaz was now entering. Yet he would not be deterred. 2. *His reversion to Canaanitish practices.* Not content with importing the licentious Baal-worship patronized in Israel, Ahaz revived the worst abominations of the old Canaanitish religions. He even went so far as to sacrifice his own son to Moloch in the valley of Hinnom—a deed indicating a degree of fanaticism, a blunting of the moral sense, and a depth of superstition which could hardly have been believed possible in a King of Judah. It was, moreover, a daring defiance of the direct letter of God's Law (Deut. xii. 31). Well might such a deed bring down wrath on Judah! 3. *His extravagance in worship.* It is further narrated that Ahaz sacrificed and burnt incense in the high places, and on the hills, and under every green tree. Worship in this reign seemed to have run riot; yet there was no true religion in it. All this depraved religiosity was but a manifestation of self-will, of subjective caprice; it had its origin in superstition and an impure craving for excitement, not in the fear of God. Yet Ahaz, in his *dilettante* way of looking at things, may have thought that he was introducing improvements into Jewish religion. He may have flattered himself that he was robbing it of its narrowness, and giving it the philosophic breadth suitable to persons of taste and culture. He might argue that there was something good in all religions; that all were but diverse expressions, equally acceptable to God, of the fundamental instinct of worship; and that none, therefore, ought to be despised. We hear such arguments nowadays, and they may very well have been used then. Ahaz was but going in for a species of Jewish Broad-Churchism. But the Bible brands this so-called breadth of view as treason against the God who has definitely revealed his will to men, and taught them how they are, and how they are not, to worship him. The true lessons to be learned from this conduct of Ahaz is that religiosity—delight in sensuous and impure religious services—is far different from religion; that altars may be multiplied, yet multiplied only to sin (Hos. viii. 11) ; that the religious instinct, itself the noblest part of man, is capable of the most perverted developments; that only worship according to his own commandment is acceptable to God.

III. NOT ALONE IN SINNING. The lengths to which Ahaz could go, apparently without awakening any public opposition, show that the heart of the nation also had widely departed from God. This is borne out by the descriptions in Isaiah (cf. ii. 6—8; iii. 16—26; v. 8—25). The king's innovations were acceptable to a people wearied of the severer worship of Jehovah. They were glad to have the services adapted to their corrupt and dissolute tastes. "The carnal mind is enmity against God" (Rom. viii. 7).—J. O.

Vers. 5—9.—*The Syro-Israelitish war.* Again was the truth to be verified that national sins bring in their train national calamities. God is not mocked. He vindicates the reality of his moral government by visiting the transgressor with manifest strokes of his displeasure. In addition to the invasion of Pekah and Rezin spoken of below, we read of assaults of the Edomites and of the Philistines, by which Judah was brought very low (2 Chron. xxviii. 17—19). The kingdom also was brought into a state of servitude to Assyria.

I. THE ATTACK OF PEKAH AND REZIN. 1. *The Syro-Israelite conspiracy.* Israel and Syria had been hereditary enemies. Now they make common cause, on the one side against Assyria, and on the other against Judah. Their object in invading Judah was probably not the simple one of plunder, but the political one of still further strengthening themselves against the King of Assyria. Pekah was a mere military adventurer, and would be restrained from attacking Judah by no scruples of brotherhood. He and Rezin had begun their attacks while Jotham was still alive, but now that Ahaz was on the throne, their plans took bolder shape. They conceived the project of removing Ahaz, and putting a certain "son of Tabeal" in his place (Isa. vii. 6). The news of their expedition terrified Ahaz and his people. Instead of putting their trust in God, their hearts were moved "as the trees of the wood are moved by the wind" (Isa. vii. 2). They had cause to fear, for they showed no desire to forsake their sins, and when a people forsake God, they have no reason to hope that God will protect them. 2. *The assault on Jerusalem, and its discomfiture.* The earlier part of the joint expedition was crowned with great success. We read in Chronicles of terrible battles that were fought, and severe defeats that were sustained by the army of Judah. Large numbers of captives, with their spoil, were taken to Samaria, and were only restored by the intercession of the Prophet Oded (2 Chron. xxviii. 6—13). God permitted Judah to be thus far humbled. But when, elated with victory, the conquerors pressed on, and invested Jerusalem, he interposed to prevent their further progress. Not for the sake of Ahaz, but for his own Name's sake, he saved Jerusalem, and hindered the invaders from accomplishing their purpose of overthrowing the house of David. Isaiah had predicted this deliverance (vii. 7), and, but for the unbelief of Ahaz, and his sinful recourse to the King of Assyria, it is unlikely that the adversaries would have been permitted to go so far even as they did. Wicked men often receive mercies of which they are wholly undeserving. God spares them, not because they have any claim upon his favour, but for the sake of some oath or promise of his own, or from regard to the righteous who remain, or in order to give the sinners yet another opportunity of repentance. Because God had sworn to David that his seed should sit upon the throne (2 Sam. vii.), he did not allow even the wicked Ahaz to be removed. In the case of Pekah and Rezin, we see how entirely human movements are under the Divine control. It appeared as if these bold men would sweep all before them, but God had said, "Hitherto shalt thou come, but no further" (Job xxxviii. 11), and there their proud waves were stayed. 3. *The loss of Elath.* The war was not wholly without gain to the Syrians. They possessed themselves of the port of Elath, at the head of the Red Sea, and thus stripped Judah of another important dependency.

II. THE APPEAL TO ASSYRIA. In the distress to which the repeated attacks on his territory reduced him, Ahaz, instead of casting himself on Divine protection, foolishly betook himself to the King of Assyria. 1. *Short-sighted policy.* Israel had set the example of resort to the Assyrian, but the prophets had always denounced such insensate conduct (Hos. v. 13; viii. 9, 10; x. 6). Even from the point of view of worldly policy, the action was foolish. As well might the lamb invoke the help of the lion against the wolf, as any lesser power invoke the help of the King of Assyria against an enemy. The conqueror, pleased with any pretext for interfering in another nation's affairs, would not refuse his help, but only that the weaker power which had solicited the help might in the end be despoiled and devoured. Thus Ahaz found it. The King of Assyria was glad enough of the occasion to march against Israel and Damascus, but when once the conquest was effected, Ahaz found that he had derived no benefit, but only exchanged one oppressor for another. 2. *Expensive help.* To purchase the aid of Tiglath-pileser, Ahaz had (1) to become a vassal of the King of Assyria; and (2) to send him a large present of gold and silver. This he could only obtain by emptying once more the often-ransacked treasuries of the temple and the palace. The accumulations of years of prosperity under Uzziah and Jotham were again dispersed, and the freedom of the country was sold to boot. God's people passed formally under the yoke of a Gentile conqueror. To such straits was the kingdom brought by Ahaz's godless policy. 3. *The Assyrian a broken reed.* The King of Assyria marched against Pekah and Rezin, and soon reduced them to his power. Damascus was severely dealt with. Its king was slain, and the people carried captive. Pekah was also chastised; his territory was ravaged, and considerable parts of the population were removed (ch. xv. 29). The instruments employed in punishing Ahaz were thus themselves punished. The fact that men are used as instruments in God's providence does not exonerate them from guilt. Ahaz, however, as we learn from the parallel narrative, reaped no benefit, for "Tiglath-pileser King of Assyria came unto him, and distressed him, but strengthened him not" (2 Chron. xxviii. 20). It was his own ends, not those of his foolish vassal, that the King of Assyria was serving. Ahaz leaned on a bruised reed, and only got his hand pierced. Thus it usually is with those who put their trust in the help of man. They reap from their assiduous sowing but the gall and wormwood of chagrin and disappointment.—J. O.

Vers. 10—20.—*Religious innovations.* The remaining events of the reign of Ahaz recorded in this chapter shed a strong light on the king's frivolous and arbitrary character.

I. THE DAMASCUS ALTAR. 1. *Ahaz at Damascus.* We are now introduced to Tiglath-pileser holding court in Damascus, and Ahaz is there as one of the vassals and tributaries of the Assyrian king. He does not seem to feel the humiliation of his position, but is probably pleased to figure as part of so brilliant an assemblage. Thus the sinner, renouncing true freedom in God's service, for a time positively hugs the chains which sin binds upon him. He counts them no dishonour, but delights to wear them. Yet in the end they shall eat into his very flesh. 2. *The new altar.* So lightly does his vassalage sit on Ahaz, that his mind is free to lose itself in admiration of the pattern and workmanship of an altar he chanced to behold in that city. It was, no doubt, an altar to some heathen deity, but that did not matter. He was charmed with its appearance, and nothing would serve him but to have the like of it set up in Jerusalem. What a measure of this man's soul—frittering away his interest upon the shape and decorations of an altar, while his kingdom is sold into servitude; toying with trifles, while doing obeisance to a conqueror! Yet is the conduct of Ahaz any more strange than that of multitudes whose sole concern is for the vanities of time, while the realities of eternity stand unheeded? When men who are at variance with God, and bondslaves of sin, are found eagerly amusing themselves with worldly trifles, what are they doing but repeating the error of this frivolous monarch? There is the same lack of the sense of proportion in things; the same sacrifice of substance to shadow; the same indifference to supreme interests. 3. *The pliant priest.* Having obtained a pattern of the coveted altar—its fashion and workmanship—Ahaz sent the same to Urijah the priest, to get a similar one made for the temple at Jerusalem. This priest was of a different mould from that Azariah, who, with four score other priests, resisted King Uzziah in his presumptuous attempt to usurp sacerdotal functions (2 Chron. xxvi. 17, 18). Urijah was a courtier first, and a priest of the Lord afterwards, and he at once set about executing the orders he had received from the king. Facile priests of Urijah's stamp have not been rare in history. The tendency of high dignitaries in many countries to follow court fashion, and put a king's pleasure in room of every higher law, is notorious. Ecclesiastics cannot plead exemption, though in them the sin is greatest. When even ministers of the Lord cease to testify against evil, and willingly yield themselves as tools to the working out of a wicked king's purposes, religion is in bad case. But here most probably the proverb held true, "Like people, like priest" (Hos. iv. 9)—the general decay of religion reacted on the sacerdotal orders.

II. REVISED ORDINANCES. · Like a child with a new toy, Ahaz, on his return home, pleased himself to the top of his bent with his new altar. 1. *He offered his own sacrifices upon it.* The event was made the occasion of a great display. Ahaz is thought by some to have mounted the altar, and himself performed the sacrifices; none of the priests, apparently, daring to remonstrate with him. He offered his burnt offering and his meat offering, and poured out his drink offering, and sprinkled the blood of his peace offerings upon the altar. An artistic altar, however, does not make acceptable sacrifices. This pompous ritual was but an empty form, ministering, not to God's glory, but to a king's vanity. The motive was wrong; the method was unauthorized; the multitude of sacrifices but added to the magnitude of the hypocrisy. It is such ritual observances the prophet denounces : "To what purpose is the multitude of your sacrifices unto me? saith the Lord; I am full of the burnt offerings of rams," etc. (Isa. i. 11). The sacrifices of the wicked are an abomination to the Lord. The only acceptable worship is that which comes from the heart. 2. *He changed the position of the altar.* The altar which Solomon made for burnt offering—the brazen altar—was not good enough for King Ahaz. It must be shifted aside, and his brand-new altar take its place. This was to arrogate a right of altering the arrangements of the temple which no king had yet assumed. Ahaz was governed by a love of novelty, and perhaps by a desire to introduce the artistic into worship. Art has its legitimate place in the worship of God, but it is not to be the governing consideration. When a service degenerates into a mere artistic performance, intended to gratify the tastes of those who have no relish for spiritual worship, it is hateful in God's sight. The perfection of the art may conceal the utter absence of life. Most of all when central doctrines are removed—such doctrines as the atonement—to give place to rites and ceremonies which appeal to the carnal sense, is God mocked by the pretence of worship. 3. *He improvised new sacrificial arrangements.* The interference of Ahaz with the temple order did not yet cease. He altered the whole sacrificial usage, transferring the regular and occasional sacrifices to his new altar—now termed by him "the great altar"—and relegating the brazen altar, which still stood in the court, to a secondary condition. This usurpation by the king of the right to dictate the order of the temple services was tamely submitted to by Urijah, who did faithfully all that he was told. One is reminded of Wolsey's words, "Had I but served my God with half the zeal I served my king," etc. Happy for the nation had Urijah been as faithful in serving God as he was in carrying out the behests of Ahaz.

III. MINOR CHANGES. The history tells of other alterations effected by Ahaz in the temple. He cut off the borders of the bases of the lavers, and took down the sea from off the bronze oxen on which it had rested, substituting for the latter a pedestal of stone ; he changed also the position of some other erections in the sacred courts. These changes are said to have been wrought "before," or for fear of, "the King of Assyria"—perhaps to hide any evidences of wealth. Other novelties introduced by Ahaz, such as "the altars which were on the top of the upper chamber of Ahaz" (ch. xxiii. 12), had for their motive *imitation* of Assyrian or Damascene idolatries. What a contemptible picture of the king is thus presented! On the one hand, cringing before the King of Assyria, and dismantling the temple to avoid exciting his cupidity; on the other, slavishly imitating the religion of the foreigners—if indeed this also was not an attempt to court Assyrian favour. How total the loss of self-respect and of the spirit of independence! Other instances of the folly and sin of Ahaz are given in Chronicles ; e.g., his worship of the gods of Damascus for the reason, "Because the gods of the kings of Syria help them, therefore will I sacrifice to them, that they may help me" (2 Chron. xxviii. 23). One does not wonder after this to hear that Ahaz "shut up the doors of the house of the Lord," while he "made him altars in every corner of Jerusalem" (2 Chron. xxviii. 24). At length his sixteen years' reign ended, and the people, by this time sick of his doings, marked their sense of his unworthiness by refusing him a sepulchre in the tombs of the kings (2 Chron. xxviii. 27).—J. O.

EXPOSITION.

CHAPTER XVII.

Vers. 1—41.—The Reign of Hoshea over Israel. Destruction of the Israelite Kingdom, and the Grounds of it. Re-peopling of the Kingdom by Assyrian Colonists.

Vers. 1—6.—Reign of Hoshea. Hoshea, the last King of Israel, had a short reign of nine years only, during two of which he was besieged in his capital by the Assyrians. The writer notes that he was a bad king, but not so bad as most of his predecessors (ver. 2); that he submitted to Shalmaneser, and then rebelled against him (vers. 3, 4); that he called in the aid of So, King of Egypt (ver. 4); that he was besieged by Shalmaneser in Samaria (ver. 5); and that after three years, or in the third year of the siege, he was taken, and with his people carried off into captivity (ver. 6).

Ver. 1.—In the twelfth year of Ahaz King of Judah began Hoshea the son of Elah to reign in Samaria. In ch. xv. 30 Hoshea was said to have smitten Pekah and slain him, and become king in his stead, "*in the twentieth year of Jotham.*" This has been supposed to mean "in the twentieth year from the accession of Jotham," or, in other words, in the fourth year of Ahaz, since Jotham reigned only sixteen years (ch. xv. 33). But now the beginning of his reign is placed eight years later. An interregnum of this duration has been placed by some between Pekah and Hoshea; but this is contradicted by ch. xv. 30, and also by an inscription of Tiglath-pileser ('Eponym Canon,' pp. 123, 124, lines 17, 18). If Ahaz reigned sixteen years, the present statement would seem to be correct, and the former one wrong. Hoshea's accession may be confidently dated as in B.C. 730. **Nine years** (comp. ch. xviii. 10). It is certain that Hoshea's reign came to an end in the first year of Sargon, B.C. 722, from which to B.C. 730 would be eight complete, or nine incomplete, years.

Ver. 2.—And he did that which was evil in the sight of the Lord, but not as the kings of Israel that were before him. Hoshea's general attitude towards Jehovah was much the same as that of former kings of Israel. He maintained the calf-worship, leant upon "arms of flesh," and turned a deaf ear to the teaching of the prophets, e.g. Hoshea and Micah, who addressed their warnings to him. But he was not guilty

of any special wickedness—he set up no new idolatry; he seems to have allowed his subjects, if they pleased, to attend the festival worship at Jerusalem (2 Chron. xxx. 11, 18). The rabbis add that when the golden calf of Bethel had been carried off by the Assyrians in one of their incursions, he did not replace it ('Seder Olam,' ch. xxii.); but it is not at all clear that the image was carried away until Hoshea's reign was over (see Dr. Pusey's comment on Hos. x. 6 in his 'Minor Prophets,' p. 64).

Ver. 3.—Against him came up Shalmaneser King of Assyria. Shalmaneser's succession to Tiglath-pileser on the throne of Assyria, once doubted, is now rendered certain by the Eponym Canon, which makes him ascend the throne in B.C. 727, and cease to reign in B.C. 722. It is uncertain whether he was Tiglath-pileser's son or a usurper. The name, Shalmaneser (*Sali-manu-uzur*) was an old royal name in Assyria, and signified "Shalman protects" (compare the names Nabu-kudur-uzur, Nergal-asar-uzur, Nabu-pal-uzur, etc.). **And Hoshea became his servant.** Hoshea had been placed on the throne by Tiglath-pileser ('Eponym Canon,' pp. 123, 124, lines 17, 18), and had paid him tribute (ibid., lines 18, 19). We must suppose that on Tiglath-pileser's death, in B.C. 727, he had revolted, and resumed his independence. Shalmaneser, having become king, probably came up against Hoshea in the same year, and forced him to resume his position of Assyrian tributary. This may have been the time when "Shalman spoiled Beth-Arbel in the day of battle" (Hos. x. 14), defeating Hoshea near that place (Arbela, now *Irbid*, in Galilee), and taking it. **And gave him presents;** or, *rendered him tribute*, as in the margin of the Authorized Version.

Ver. 4.—And the King of Assyria found conspiracy in Hoshea: for he had sent messengers to So, King of Egypt. We learn from the Prophet Hosea that the expediency of calling in Egypt as a counterpoise to Assyria had long been in the thoughts of those who directed the policy of the Israelite state (see Hos. vii. 11; xii. 1, etc.). Now at last the plunge was taken. An Ethiopian dynasty of some strength and vigour had possession of Egypt, and held its court during some part of the year at Memphis (Hos. ix. 6). The king who occupied the throne was called Shabak or Shebek—a name which the Greeks represented by Sabakos or Sevechus, and the Hebrews by סוֹא. (The original vocalization of this word was probably סֶוֶה, *Seveh*; but in later times this vocalization was lost, and the Masorites pointed the word as סוֹא, *Soh* or *So*). The Assyrians knew the king as Sibakhi, and contended with him under Sargon. Hoshea now sent an embassy to this monarch's court, requesting his alliance and his support against the great Asiatic power by which the existence of all the petty states of Western Asia was threatened. Shalmaneser was at the time endeavouring to capture Tyre, and Hoshea might reasonably fear that, when Tyre was taken, his own turn would come. It is not clear how Shabak received Hoshea's overtures; but we may, perhaps, assume that it was with favour, since otherwise Hoshea would scarcely have ventured to withhold his tribute, as he seems to have done. It must have been in reliance on "the strength of Egypt" that he ventured to brave the anger of Assyria. And brought no present—or, *sent no tribute*—to the King of Assyria, as he had done year by year: therefore the King of Assyria shut him up, and bound him in prison. The ultimate result is mentioned at once, before the steps by which it was accomplished are related. Shalmaneser did not "summon Hoshea before his presence to listen to his explanations," and then, "as soon as he came, take him prisoner, put him in chains, and imprison him" (as Ewald thinks), but simply declared war, invaded Hoshea's country, besieged him in his capital, and ultimately, when he surrendered, consigned him to a prison, as Nebuchadnezzar afterwards did Jehoiachin (ch. xxiv. 15; xxv. 27). Otherwise Hoshea's reign would have come to an end in his sixth or seventh, and not in his ninth year.

Ver. 5.—Then the King of Assyria—rather, *and the King of Assyria*—came up throughout all the land—*i.e.* with an army that spread itself at once over the whole land, that came to conquer, not merely to strike a blow, and obtain submission, as on the former occasion (see ver. 3, and the comment)—and went up to Samaria, and besieged it three years. From some time in Hoshea's seventh year (ch. xviii. 9) to some time in his ninth (ch. xviii. 10). According to the Hebrew mode of reckoning, parts of years are counted as years; and thus the siege need not have lasted much over a year, though it may have been extended to nearly three years. In either case, there was ample time for Shabak to have brought up his forces, had he been so minded; and his failure to do so, or in any way to succour his ally, showed how little reliance was to be placed on Egyptian promises (comp. ch. xviii. 21).

Ver. 6.—In the ninth year of Hoshea the King of Assyria took Samaria. In B.C. 722, the ninth year of Hoshea, there seems to have been a revolution at Nineveh. The reign of Shalmaneser came to an end, and Sargon seated himself upon the throne. There have been commentators on Kings (Keil, Bähr) who have supposed that Shalmaneser and Sargon were the same person, and have even claimed that the Assyrian inscriptions support their view. But the fact is otherwise. Nothing is more certain than that, according to them, Sargon succeeded Shalmaneser IV. in B.C. 722 by a revolution, and was the head of a new dynasty. He claims in his annals, among his earliest acts, the siege and capture of Samaria ('Eponym Canon,' p. 125). It is remarkable that Scripture, while in no way connecting him with the capture, never distinctly assigns it to Shalmaneser. Here we are only told that "the King of Assyria" took it. In ch. xviii. 9, 10, where we are distinctly told that Shalmaneser "came up against Samaria, and besieged it," the capture is expressed by the phrase, "*they* took it," not "he took it." Perhaps neither king was present in person at the siege, or, at any rate, at its termination. The city may have been taken by an Assyrian general, while Shalmaneser and Sargon were contending for the crown. In that case, the capture might be assigned to either. Sargon certainly claims it; Shalmaneser's annals have been so mutilated by his successors that we cannot tell whether he claimed it or not. The city fell in B.C. 722; and the deportation of its inhabitants at once took place. And carried Israel away into Assyria. The inscription of Sargon above referred to mentions only the deportation, from the city of Samaria itself, of 27,290 persons. No doubt a vast number of others were carried off from the smaller towns and from the country districts. Still, the country was not left uninhabited, and Sargon assessed its tribute at the old rate ('Eponym Canon,' *l. s. c.*). Nor was the city of Samaria destroyed, since we hear of it subsequently more than once in the Assyrian annals. And placed them in Halah. "Halah" (חֲלַח) has been supposed by some to be the old Assyrian city (Gen. x. 11) of Calah (כֶּלַח), which was, down to the time of Tiglath-pileser, the main capital; but the difference of spelling is an objection, and the Assyrians do not seem to have ever transported subject-populations to their capitals. It is moreover reasonable to suppose that Halah, Habor, Gozan, and Hara (1 Chron. v. 26) were in the same neighbourhood. This last consideration points to the "Chalcitis" of Ptolemy (v. 18) as the true "Halah," since it was in the immediate vicinity of the Khabour, of Gauzanitis, and of Haran. And in Habor by the river of Gozan. This is a mistranslation. The Hebrew runs, "And on Habor (Khabor), the river of Gozan" (so also in ch. xviii. 11). "Habor, the river of Gozan," is undoubtedly one of the Khabours. Those who find Halah in Calah, or in Calacine (Calachene), generally prefer the eastern river which runs into the Tigris from Kurdistan a little below Jezireh. But there is no evidence that this river bore the name in antiquity. The Western Khabour, on the other hand, was well known to the Assyrians under that appellation, and is the Aborrhas of Strabo and Procopius, the Chaboras of Pliny and Ptolemy, the Aburas of Isadore of Charax, and the Abora of Zosimus. It adjoins a district called Chalcitis, and it drains the country of Gauzanitis or Mygdonia. The Western Khabour is a river of Upper Mesopotamia, and runs into the Euphrates from the north-east near the site of the ancient Circesion. The tract which it drains is called Mygdonia by Strabo, Gauzanitis by Ptolemy. **And in the cities of the Medes.** Media had been repeatedly invaded and ravaged by the Assyrians from the time of Vul-nirari IV. (about B.C. 810); but the first king to conquer any portion of it, and people its cities with settlers from other parts of his dominions, was Sargon (Oppert, 'Inscriptions des Sargonides,' pp. 25, 37). We learn from the present passage that a certain number of these settlers were Israelites (comp. ch. xviii. 11 and Tobit i. 14).

Vers. 7—23.—*The provocations which induced God to destroy the Israelite kingdom.* Here, for once, the writer ceases to be the mere historian, and becomes the religious teacher and prophet, drawing out the lessons of history, and justifying the ways of God to man. As Bähr says, he "does not carry on the narrative as taken from the original authorities, but himself here begins a review of the history and fate of Israel, which ends with ver. 23, and forms an independent section by itself." The section divides itself into four portions: (1) From ver. 7 to ver. 12, a general statement of Israel's wickedness; (2) from ver. 13 to ver. 15, a special aggravation of their guilt, viz. their rejection of prophets; (3) vers. 16 and 17 contain a specification of their chief acts of sin; and (4) from ver. 18 to ver. 23, a general summary, including some words of warning to Judah.

Ver. 7.—**For so it was, that the children of Israel had sinned against the Lord their God**; rather, *And it came to pass, when*, etc.

The clauses from the present to the end of ver. 17 depend on the "when" of this verse; the apodosis does not come till ver. 18, "When the children of Israel had done all that is stated in vers. 7—17, then the result was that the Lord was very angry with Israel, and removed them out of his sight." **Which had brought them up out of the land of Egypt.** So commencing his long series of mercies to the nation, and indicating his gracious favour towards it. "The deliverance from Egypt," as Bähr well says, "was not only the beginning, but the symbol, of all Divine grace towards Israel, and the pledge of its Divine guidance." Hence the stress laid upon it, both here and by the Prophet Hosea (comp. Hos. xi. 1; xii. 9, 13; xiii. 4). **From under the hand** —*i.e.* the oppression—**of Pharaoh King of Egypt, and had feared other gods;** *i.e.* reverenced and worshipped them.

Ver. 8.—**And walked in the statutes of the heathen.** The "statutes of the heathen" are their customs and observances, especially in matters of religion. The Israelites had been repeatedly warned not to follow these (see Lev. xviii. 3, 30; Deut. xii. 29—31; xviii. 9—14, etc.). **Whom the Lord cast out from before the children of Israel**—*i.e.* the Canaanitish nations, whose idolatries and other "abominations" were particularly hateful to God (see Lev. xviii. 26—29; Deut. xx. 18; xxix. 17; xxxii. 16, etc.)—**and of the kings of Israel.** The sins and idolatries of Israel had a double origin. The great majority were derived from the heathen nations with whom they were brought into contact, and were adopted voluntarily by the people themselves. Of this kind were the worship at "high places" (ver. 9), the "images" and "groves" (ver. 10), the causing of their children to "pass through the fire" (ver. 17), the employment of divination and enchantments (ver. 17), and perhaps the "worship of the host of heaven" (ver. 16). A certain number, however, came in from a different source, being imposed upon the people by their kings. To this class belong the desertion of the temple-worship, enforced by Jeroboam (ver. 21), the setting up of the calves at Dan and Bethel (ver. 16) by the same, and the Baal and Astarte worship (ver. 16), introduced by Ahab. This last and worst idolatry was not established without a good deal of persecution, as we learn from 1 Kings xviii. 4. **Which they had made.**

Ver. 9.—**And the children of Israel did secretly those things that were not right against the Lord their God.** Most of the evil practices of the Israelites were open and flagrant, but some sought the veil of secrecy, as the use of divination and enchantments (ver. 17). It is doubtful, however, whether the Hebrew words have the signification assigned to them in the Authorized Version. They may mean no more than that the Israelites made their evil deeds a barrier between themselves and God. **And they built them high places in all their cities** (comp. 1 Kings xiv. 23). "In *all* their cities" is probably rhetorical; but the gist of the charge is that, instead of keeping to the *one* temple and *one* altar commanded by God for the conservation of their belief in his unity, the Israelites "erected places of worship all over the country, after the fashion of the heathen" (Bähr), and so at once depraved their own faith, and ceased to be a perpetual protest to the surrounding nations. **From the tower of the watchmen to the fenced city;** *i.e.* from the smallest and most solitary place of human abode to the largest and most populous (comp. ch. xviii. 8). The expression was no doubt proverbial, and (as used here) is a strong hyperbole.

Ver. 10.—**And they set them up images;** rather, *pillars* (comp. Gen. xxviii. 18, 22; xxxi. 13, 45, 51, 52; xxxv. 14, 20; Exod. xxiv. 4; Deut. xii. 3; 2 Sam. xviii. 18, where the same word is so rendered). The *matsévôth* were stone pillars, anciently connected with the worship of Baal, but in Judah perhaps used in a debased and debasing worship of Jehovah with self-invented rites, instead of those which had the express sanction of God, being commanded in the Law (see the 'Speaker's Commentary,' vol. i. p. 417). **And groves** (compare the comment on 1 Kings xiv. 14 and 23, and see also that on ch. xiii. 6) **in every high hill** —rather, *on every high hill*—**and under every green tree.** Note that the "groves" (*asherim*) were "set up under green trees," and must therefore have been artificial structures of some kind, such as could stand beneath their boughs.

Ver. 11.—**And there they burnt incense in all the high places** (comp. 1 Kings iii. 3; xxii. 43; ch. xii. 3; xiv. 4; xv. 4, 35; xvi. 4). Incense symbolized prayer (Ps. cxli. 2), and ought to have been burnt only on the golden altar of incense within the veil. **As did the heathen whom the Lord carried away before them.** The offering of incense to their gods by the Canaanitish nations had not been previously mentioned; but the use of incense in religious worship was so widely spread in the ancient world, that their employment of it might have been assumed as almost certain. The Egyptians used incense largely in the worship of Ammon ('Records of the Past,' vol. x. p. 19). The Babylonians burnt a thousand talents' weight of it every year at the great festival of Bel-Merodach (Herod., i. 183). The Greeks and Romans offered it with every sacrifice. **And**

wrought wicked things to provoke the Lord to anger (see below, vers. 15—17).

Ver. 12.—**For they served idols;** rather, *and they served idols.* The sense flows on from ver. 7, each verse being joined to the preceding one by the *vau* connective. *Gillulim,* the term translated "idols," is a word rarely used, except by Ezekiel, with whom it is common. "It contains," as Bähr says, "a subordinate contemptuous and abusive signification;" the primary meaning of *gâlal* being "dung," "ordure." **Whereof the Lord had said unto them, Ye shall not do this thing** (see Exod. xx. 4, 5, 23; Deut. iv. 16—18, etc.).

Ver. 13.—**Yet the Lord testified**—rather, *and the Lord testified*—**against Israel, and against Judah, by all the prophets, and by all the seers.** A "seer" is, properly, one who *sees* visions; a "prophet," one inspired to pour forth utterances. But the words were used as synonyms (see 1 Sam. ix. 9). Ever since the revolt of Jeroboam, there had been a succession of prophets in both countries whose office it had been to rebuke sin and to enforce the precepts of the Law. In Judah there had been Shemaiah, contemporary with Rehoboam (2 Chron. xi. 2; xii. 5); Iddo, contemporary with Abijah (2 Chron. xiii. 22); Azariah, with Asa (2 Chron. xv. 1); Hanani, with the same (2 Chron. xvi. 7); Jehu, the son of Hanani, with Jehoshaphat (2 Chron. xix. 2); Jahaziel, the son of Zechariah, with the same (2 Chron. xx. 14); Eliezer, the son of Dodavah, also contemporary with the same (2 Chron. xx. 37); Zechariah, the son of Jehoiada, contemporary with Joash (2 Chron. xxiv. 20); another Zechariah, contemporary with Uzziah (2 Chron. xxvi. 5); Joel, Micah, and Isaiah, besides several whose names are unknown. In Israel, the succession had included Ahijah the Shilonite, contemporary with Jeroboam (1 Kings xiv. 2); Jehu, the son of Hanani, with Baasha (1 Kings xvi. 1); Elijah, and Micaiah the son of Imlah, with Ahab (1 Kings xxii. 8) and Ahaziah (ch. i. 3); Elisha, with Jehoram, Jehu, Jehoahaz, and Joash (ch. iii. 11—xiii. 14); Jonah, with Jeroboam II. (ch. xiv. 25); Hosea and Amos, with the same (Hos. i. 1; Amos i. 1); and Oded (2 Chron. xxviii. 9), contemporary with Pekah. God had never left himself without living witness. Besides the written testimony of the Law, he had sent them a continuous series of prophets, who "repeated and enforced the teaching of the Law by word of mouth, breathing into the old words a new life, applying them to the facts of their own times, urging them on the consciences of their hearers, and authoritatively declaring to them that the terrible threatenings of the Law were directed against the very sins which they habitually practised."

The prophets continually addressed them in the Name of God, saying, Turn ye from your evil ways, and keep my commandments and my statutes, according to all the Law which I commanded your fathers, and which I sent to you by my servants the prophets. This was the general burden of the prophetical teaching, both in Israel and in Judah, both before the captivity of Israel and afterwards (see Hos. xii. 6; xiv. 2; Joel ii. 12, 13; Amos v. 4—15; Isa. i. 16—20; xxxi. 6; Jer. iii. 7, 14; Ezek. xiv. 6; xviii. 30, etc.).

Ver. 14.—Notwithstanding they would not hear; rather, *and they would not hear.* The construction still runs on without any change (see the comment on vers. 7 and 12). But hardened their necks. (On the origin of the phrase, see 'Homiletic Commentary' on Exod. xxxii. 9.) The obstinate perversity of the Israelites, which the phrase expresses, is noted through the entire history (see Exod. xxxiii. 3, 5; xxxiv. 9; Deut. ix. 6, 13; Ps. lxxv. 5; 2 Chron. xxx. 8; xxxvi. 13; Neh. ix. 16, 17, 29; Jer. vii. 26; xvii. 23; Acts vii. 51, etc.). Like to the neck of their fathers, that did not believe in the Lord their God. The reference is especially to the many passages in the Pentateuch where the Israelites are called "a stiff-necked people" (see, besides those already quoted, Deut. xxxi. 27).

Ver. 15.—And they rejected his statutes, and his covenant that he made with their fathers. The covenant made at Sinai, first by the people generally (Exod. xix. 5—8), and then by their formal representatives (Exod. xxiv. 3—8), was, on their part, a solemn promise that "all which the Lord commanded them they would do." Rejecting the "statutes" of God was thus rejecting the "covenant." And his testimonies which he testified against them. The "testimonies" of God are* his commandments, considered as witnessing of him and setting forth his nature. The use of the term is common in Deuteronomy and in the Psalms, but otherwise rare. And they followed vanity, and became vain. False gods are "vanity;" false religions are "vanity;" there is nothing firm or substantial about them; they belong to the realm of futility and nothingness. And the followers of such religions derive weakness from them—they "become vain"—*i.e.* weak, futile, impotent. Their energies are wasted; they effect nothing of that which they wish to effect; they are completely powerless for good, at any rate; and they are not really powerful for evil. Their plans, for the most part, miscarry; and "their end is destruction." And went after the heathen that were round about them. Upon a neglect to keep God's commandments follows active revolt from him, and the doing of

that which he has forbidden. When they rejected God's statutes, the Israelites adopted "the statutes of the heathen" (ver. 8), and "walked in them." Concerning whom the Lord had charged them, that they should not do like them (see above, ver. 12, and compare the comment on ver. 8).

Vers. 16, 17.—The main sins of Israel are now specified, that they themselves may stand self-convicted, and that others may be warned against doing the like. First, generally.

Ver. 16.—They left all the commandments of the Lord their God; *i.e.* neglected them, rendered them no obedience, offered none of the stated sacrifices, attended none of the appointed feasts, broke the moral law (Hos. iv. 1, 2, 11; vii. 1, etc.) by swearing, and lying, and stealing, and committing adultery, by drunkenness, and lewdness, and bloodshed. And made them molten images, even two calves. These at least were undeniable—there they were at Dan and Bethel, until the Captivity came (Hos. viii. 5; x. 5, 6; xiii. 2; Amos viii. 14), worshipped, sworn by (Amos viii. 14), viewed as living gods (Amos viii. 14), offered to, trusted in. Every king had upheld them, so that Bethel was regarded as "the king's court," and "the king's chapel" (Amos vii. 13); all the people were devoted to them, and "brought their sacrifices to Bethel every morning" (Amos iv. 4), "and their tithes after three years." And made a grove. The "grove" (*ashêrah*) which Ahab set up at Samaria (1 Kings xvi. 38), and which remained there certainly to the time of Jehoahaz (see the comment on ch. xiii. 6). And worshipped all the host of heaven. This worship had not been mentioned before; and it is nowhere else ascribed to the Israelites of the northern kingdom. Manasseh seems to have introduced it into Judah (ch. xxi. 3; xxiii. 5, 11). Such knowledge as we have of the Western Asiatic religions seems to indicate that *astral* worship, strictly so called, was a peculiarity of the Assyro-Babylonian and Arabian systems only, and did not belong to the Syrian, or the Phoenician, or the Canaanite. It may be suspected that the present passage is somewhat rhetorical, and assigns to the Israelites the "worship of the host of heaven," simply because an astral character attached to Baal and Ashtoreth, who were associated in the religion of the Phoenicians with the sun and moon. On the other hand, it is just possible that the Assyro-Babylonian star-worship had been introduced into Israel under Menahem, Pekah, or Hoshea. And served Baal. The Baal-worship, introduced by Ahab (1 Kings xvi. 31), was not finally abolished by Jehu (ch. x. 28). Like other popular religions, it had a revival. Hosea, writing under the later kings from Jeroboam II. to Hoshea, alludes to the Baal-worship (Hos. II. 8, 17) as continuing.

Ver. 17.—**And they caused their sons and their daughters to pass through the fire.** (On this phrase, see the comment upon ch. xvi. 3.) The sin of child-murder had not been previously laid to the charge of Israel; but, as it had infected Judah (ch. xvi. 3), there is no reason why it should not have invaded also the sister kingdom. Perhaps it is alluded to by Hosea in iv. 2; v. 2; and vi. 8. It was an old sin of the Canaanitish nations (Lev. xviii. 21, etc.), and continued to be practised by the Moabites (ch. iii. 27; Amos ii. 1) and Ammonites, neighbours of Israel. **And used divination and enchantments.** The "witchcrafts" of Jezebel have been already mentioned (ch. ix. 22). Magical practices always accompanied idolatry, and were of many kinds. Sometimes divination was by means of staves or rods (rhabdomancy), which were manipulated in various ways (Herod., iv. 67; Schol. ad Nicandr., 'Theriac.,' 613; Tacit., 'German.,' § 10; Amm. Marc., xxxi. 2; Hos. iv. 12). Sometimes it was by arrows (Ezek. xxi. 21). Very often, especially in Greece and Rome, it was by inspecting the entrails of victims. Where faith in God wanes, a trust in magical practices, astrology, chiromancy, "sortes Virgilianæ," horoscopes, spirit-rapping, and the like, almost always supervenes. **And sold themselves to do evil in the sight of the Lord, to provoke him to anger.** (On the expression, "sold themselves to do evil," see the comment upon 1 Kings xxi. 20.)

Ver. 18.—**Therefore the Lord was very angry with Israel;** rather, *that then the Lord was very angry,* etc. We have here the apodosis of the long sentence beginning with ver. 7 and continuing to the end of ver 17. When all that is enumerated in these verses had taken place, then the Lord was moved to anger against Israel, then matters had reached a crisis, the cup of their iniquity was full, and God's wrath, long restrained, descended on them. **And removed them out of his sight.** Removal out of God's sight is loss of his favour and of his care. "The eyes of the Lord are over the righteous" (Ps. xxxiv. 15)—he "knoweth their way," "watcheth over them" (Jer. xxxi. 28), "careth for them" (Ps. cxlvi. 8); but "the countenance of the Lord is against them [averted from them] who do evil" (Ps. xxxiv. 16). He will not look upon them nor hear them. **There was none left but the tribe of Judah only.** The "tribe of Judah" stands for the kingdom of the two tribes of Judah and Benjamin (see 1 Kings xi. 31—36; xii. 23; 2 Chron. xvii. 14—18), into which the greater

part of Dan and Simeon had also been absorbed. This became now, exclusively, God's "peculiar people," the object of his love and of his care. The writer, it must be remembered, belongs to the period of the Captivity, and is not speaking of the restored Israel.

Ver. 19.—**Also Judah kept not the commandments of the Lord their God.** The sharp contrast which the writer has drawn between Israel and Judah in ver. 18 reminds him that the difference was only for a time. Judah followed in Israel's sins, and ultimately shared in her punishment. This verse and the next are parenthetic. **But walked in the statutes of Israel which they made;** *i.e.* followed Israel in all her evil courses, first in her Baal-worship, under Jehoram, Ahaziah, and Athaliah; then in her other malpractices under Ahaz (ch. xvi. 3, 4), Manasseh (ch. xxi. 2—9), and Amon (ch. xxi. 20—22). Of course, the calf-worship is excepted, Judah having no temptation to follow Israel in that.

Ver. 20.—**And the Lord rejected all the seed of Israel.** God is no respecter of persons. As he had rejected the ten tribes on account of certain transgressions, which have been enumerated (vers. 8—17), so, when Judah committed the self-same sins, and transgressed equally, Judah had equally to be rejected. "All the seed of Israel" is the entire nation—Israel in the widest sense, made up of Judah and of Israel in the narrow sense. So Keil, rightly. **And afflicted them**—by the hands of Sargon, and Sennacherib, and Esarhaddon (2 Chron. xxxiii. 11), and Pharaoh-Nechoh, and others **—and delivered them into the hands of spoilers.** The "spoilers" intended are probably, first, the "bands of the Chaldees, and of the Syrians, and of the Moabites, and of the children of Ammon," who were let loose upon Judæa by Nebuchadnezzar when Jehoiakim rebelled against him (ch. xxiv. 2), and secondly Nebuchadnezzar himself and Nebuzar-adan, who completed the spoliation of the country, and plundered Jerusalem itself, to punish the revolts of Jehoiachin and Zedekiah (ch. xxiv. 13—16 and xxv. 8—21), when all the treasures of the temple were carried off. **Until he had cast them out of his sight;** *i.e.* until he had punished Judah *as* he had previously punished Israel (ver. 18), which was what justice required.

Ver. 21.—**For he rent;** rather, *for he had rent.* The nexus of the verse is with ver. 18. The difference between the fates of Israel and Judah—the survival of Judah for a hundred and thirty-four years—is traced back to the separation under Rehoboam, and to the wicked policy which Jeroboam then pursued, and left as a legacy to his successors. Israel could suffer alone, while Judah was spared, because the kingdom of David and Solomon had been rent in twain, and the two states had thenceforth continued separate. **Israel from the house of David; and they made Jeroboam the son of Nebat king: and Jeroboam drave Israel from following the Lord.** The separation alone might not have had any ill result; but it was followed by the appointment of Jeroboam as king, and Jeroboam introduced the fatal taint of idolatry, from which all the other evils flowed, including the earlier destruction of the northern kingdom. Jeroboam not only introduced the worship of the calves, but he "drave Israel from following the Lord"—*i.e.* compelled the people to discontinue the practice of going up to worship at Jerusalem (2 Chron. xi. 13—16), and required them to take part in the calf-worship. **And [thus] made them sin a great sin.**

Ver. 22.—**For the children of Israel walked in all the sins of Jeroboam which he did.** The nation, having been once persuaded to adopt Jeroboam's innovations, continued to "walk" in them—followed Jeroboam's example in "*all* his sins"—gave up the temple-worship altogether; accepted the ministrations of priests not of the seed of Aaron (1 Kings xiii. 33; 2 Chron. xiii. 9); brought their tithes to these idol-priests; sacrificed to the calves at Dan and Bethel (Amos iv. 4); and put their trust in the "similitude of a calf that eateth hay." **They departed not from them** (comp. 1 Kings xv. 26, 34; xvi. 2, 19, 26, 31; ch. iii. 3; x. 29; xiii. 6, 11; xiv. 24; xv. 9, 18, 28).

Ver. 23.—**Until the Lord removed Israel out of his sight** (see the comment on ver. 18) **as he had said by all his servants the prophets.** The destruction of the kingdom of Israel had been distinctly prophesied by Ahijah the Shilonite (1 Kings xiv. 15, 16), Hosea (i. 4; ix. 3, 17), and Amos (vii. 17). General warnings and denunciations had been given by Moses (Lev. xxvi. 33; Deut. iv. 26, 27; xxviii. 36, etc.), by Isaiah (vii. 8; xxviii. 1—4), and probably by the entire series of prophets enumerated in the comment on ver. 13. **So was Israel carried away out of their own land to Assyria unto this day;** *i.e.* up to the time that the Second Book of Kings was written, about B.C. 580—560, the Israelites remained within the limits of the country to which they were carried by the conqueror. Not long after this time, about B.C. 538, a considerable number returned with Zerubbabel to Palestine, and others with Ezra (see Ezra ii. 70; iii. 1; vi. 16, 17; vii. 13; viii. 35; 1 Chron. ix. 2, 3; Zech. viii. 13). What became of the rest has been a fertile subject of speculation. Probably the more religious

united with the Jewish communities, which were gradually formed in almost all the cities of the East; while the irreligious laid aside their peculiar customs, and became blended indistinguishably with the heathen. There is no ground for expecting to find the "ten tribes" anywhere at the present day.

Vers. 24—41.—*Repeopling of the kingdom of Israel by Assyrian colonists, and formation of a mixed religion.* The writer, before dismissing the subject of the Israelite kingdom, proceeds to inform us of certain results of the conquest. Having removed the bulk of the native inhabitants, the Assyrians did not allow the country to lie waste, but proceeded to replace the population which they had carried off by settlers from other localities (ver. 24). These settlers were, after a short time, incommoded by lions, which increased upon them, and diminished their numbers (ver. 25). The idea arose that the visitation was supernatural, and might be traced to the fact that the newcomers, not knowing "the manner of the God of the land," displeased him by the neglect of his rites or by the introduction of alien worship (ver. 26). A remedy for this was sought in the sending to them from Assyria one of the priests who had been carried off, from whom it was thought they might learn how "the God of the land" was to be propitiated. This was the origin of the "mixed religion" which grew up in the country. While the nations who had replaced the Israelites brought in their own superstitions, and severally worshipped their own gods (vers. 30, 31), there was a general acknowledgment of Jehovah by all of them, and a continuance of Jehovistic worship in the various high places. The nations both "feared the Lord, and served their graven images," down to the time when the writer of Kings composed his work (vers. 33—41).

Ver. 24.—**And the King of Assyria brought men from Babylon.** It has been supposed, in connection with Ezra iv. 2, that no colonists were introduced into the country till the time of Esarhaddon, who began to reign in B.C. 681. But this, which would be intrinsically most improbable (for when did a king forego his tribute from a fertile country for forty-one years?), is contradicted by a statement of Sargon, that he placed colonists there in B.C. 715 ('Ancient

Monarchies,' vol. ii. p. 415). These were not necessarily the first; and, on the whole, it is probable that the repeopling of the country began earlier. Hamath was reduced by Sargon in B.C. 720, and punished severely. Its inhabitants were carried off, and replaced by Assyrians ('Eponym Canon,' p. 127). Probably some of them were at once settled in Samaria. The conquest of Babylon by Sargon was not till later. It occurred in B.C. 709, and was probably followed by the immediate deportation of some of its inhabitants to the same quarter. **And from Cuthah.** "Cuthah," or "Cutha," was an important Babylonian city, often mentioned in the Assyrian inscriptions ('Records of the Past,' vol. i. pp. 74, 75; vol. iii. p. 35; vol. v. pp. 93, 94, 102). Its ruins exist at the site now called Ibrahim, about fifteen miles north-east of Babylon. Sargon must have become master of it when he put down Merodach-Baladan and assumed the sovereignty of Babylonia, in B.C. 709. Why the later Jews called the Samaritans "Cuthæans," rather than Sepharvites, or Avites, or Hamathites, it is impossible to determine. Possibly the Cuthæan settlers preponderated in numbers over the others. **And from Ava.** "Ava" (עוא) is probably the same as the Ivah (עוה) of ch. xviii. 31 and xix. 13, and perhaps identical with the Ahava (אהוא) of Ezra (viii. 15, 21). The city intended is thought to be the "Is" of Herodotus (i. 179), and the modern Hit. Hit lies upon the Euphrates, about a hundred and thirty miles above Babylon, in lat. 33° 45′ nearly. It is famous for its bitumen springs. **And from Hamath** (see the comment on ch. xiv. 25). Hamath on the Orontes was conquered by Sargon in B.C. 720, two years after his capture of Samaria ('Eponym Canon,' pp. 126—129). Its rude inhabitants were carried off, and Assyrians were placed there. **And from Sepharvaim.** It is generally allowed that "Sepharvaim" is "Sippara," the dual form being accounted for by the fact that Sippara was a double town, partly on the right and partly on the left bank of a stream derived from the Euphrates. Hence Pliny speaks of it as "oppida Hipparenorum" ('Hist. Nat.,' vi. 30). The exact site, at Abu-Habba, sixteen miles south-west of Baghdad, has only recently been discovered (see the 'Transactions of the Society of Biblical Archæology' for 1885, vol. viii. pp. 172—176). **And placed them in the cities of Samaria instead of the children of Israel: and they possessed Samaria, and dwelt in the cities thereof.** Transplantation of nations, commenced by Tiglath-pileser, was practised on a still larger scale by Sargon. The following summary will illustrate this point: "In all his wars Sargon largely employed the system of wholesale

deportation. The Israelites were removed from Samaria, and planted partly in Gozan or Mygdonia, and partly in the cities recently taken from the Medes. Hamath and Damascus were peopled with captives from Armenia and other regions of the north. A portion of the Tibareni were carried captive to Assyria, and Assyrians were established in the Tiberenian country. Vast numbers of the inhabitants of the Zagros range were also transported to Assyria; Babylonians, Cuthæans, Sepharvites, Arabians, and others were placed in Samaria; men from the extreme east (perhaps Media) in Ashdod. The Comukha were removed from the extreme north to Susiana, and Chaldæans were brought from the extreme south to supply their places. Everywhere Sargon 'changed the abodes' of his subjects, his aim being, as it would seem, to weaken the stronger races by dispersion, and to destroy the spirit of the weaker ones by severing at a blow all the links which unite a patriotic people to the country it has long inhabited. The practice had not been unknown to previous monarchs; but it had never been employed by any of them so generally or on so grand a scale as it was by this king" (see 'Ancient Monarchies,' vol. ii. p. 423).

Ver. 25.—**And so it was at the beginning of their dwelling there, that they feared not the Lord.** They were ignorant, i.e., of Jehovah, and paid him no religious regard. They brought with them their own forms of heathenism (see vers. 30, 31). **Therefore the Lord sent lions among them.** Lions are not now found in Palestine, nor indeed in any part of Syria, though they are numerous in Mesopotamia; but anciently they appear to have been tolerably common in all parts of the Holy Land (see the comment on 1 Kings xiii. 24). We may gather from what is said here that, though new settlers had been brought into the country by the Assyrians, yet still there had been a considerable decrease in the population, which had been favourable to the lions multiplying. The new settlers, it is to be noted, were placed in the towns (ver. 24); and it is probable that many of the country districts lay waste and desolate. Still, the writer views the *great* increase in the number of the lions as a Divine judgment, which it may have been, though based upon a natural circumstance. **Which slew some of them.** (For the great boldness of the Palestinian lion, see 1 Kings xiii. 24; xx. 36; Prov. xxii. 13; Isa. xxxi. 4; xxxviii. 13; Jer. v. 6, etc.)

Ver. 26.—**Wherefore they spake to the King of Assyria, saying.** The meaning seems to be, not that the colonists made direct complaint to the king, but that some of the persons about the court, having heard of the matter, reported it to him as one requiring consideration and remedy. Hence the use of the third person instead of the first. **The nations which thou hast removed, and placed in the cities of Samaria** (see ver. 24), **know not the manner of the God of the land.** It was the general belief of the heathen nations of antiquity that each country and nation had its own god or gods, who presided over its destinies, protected it, went out at the head of its armies, and fought for it against its enemies. Each god had his own "manner," or ritual and method of worship, which was, in some respects at any rate, different from that of all other gods. Unless this ritual and method were known, new-comers into any land were almost sure to displease the local deity, who did not allow of any departure from traditional usage in his worship. **Therefore he hath sent lions among them, and, behold, they slay them, because they know not the manner of the God of the land.**

Ver. 27.—**Then the King of Assyria commanded, saying, Carry thither one of the priests whom ye brought from thence.** It does not appear that this was a suggestion of the colonists. Either it was the king's own idea, or that of one of his advisers. The priests, who ministered at the two national sanctuaries—those of Dan and Bethel—had, as important personages, been all carried off. Though a "remnant" of Israel was left in the land (2 Chron. xxxiv. 9), they were probably of the baser sort (comp. ch. xxv. 12), or at any rate could not be trusted to know the details and intricacies of the Samaritan ritual. Thus it was necessary to send back a priest. **And let them go and dwell there.** We should have expected, "Let him go;" but the writer assumes that the priest would have an *entourage*, assistant - ministers and servants, and so says, "Let *them* go;" but immediately afterwards, **And let him teach**—since he alone would be competent—**them the manner of the God of the land.**

Ver. 28.—**Then one of the priests whom they had carried away from Samaria**—the country, not the city, as in vers. 24 and 25—**came and dwelt in Bethel.** Bethel from a very early time greatly eclipsed Dan. While the allusions to Bethel, commonly called "Bethaven" ("House of nothingness" for "House of God"), are frequent in the Israelitish prophets (Hos. iv. 15; v. 8; x. 5, 8, 15; Amos iii. 14; iv. 4; v. 5, 6; vii. 10—13), there is but a single distinct allusion to Dan (Amos viii. 14). Bethel was "the king's chapel" and "the king's court" (Amos vii. 13). The priest selected by Sargon's advisers was a Bethelite priest, and, returning thither, took up the worship fami-

liar to him. **And taught them**—*i.e.* the new settlers—**how they should fear the Lord.** This worship could only be that of the calf-priests instituted by Jeroboam, which was, however, most certainly a worship of Jehovah, and an imitation or travesty of the temple - worship at Jerusalem. Whether the returned priest set up a new calf-idol, to replace the one which had been carried off to Assyria (Hos. x. 5), is doubtful.

Ver. 29.—**Howbeit every nation made gods of their own, and put them in the houses of the high places which the Samaritans had made, every nation in their cities wherein they dwelt.** The several bands of settlers found in the cities assigned to them "houses of the high places," or high-place temples (ver. 9), which had been left standing when the inhabitants were carried off. These "houses" they converted to their own use, setting up in them their several idolatries.

Ver. 30.—**And the men of Babylon made Succoth-benoth.** There is no deity of this name in the Assyrian or Babylonian lists. The explanation of the word as "tents" or "huts of daughters," which satisfied Selden, Calmet, Gesenius, Winer, Keil, and others, is rendered absolutely impossible by the context, which requires that the word, whatever its meaning, should be the name of a deity. The Septuagint interpreters, while as much puzzled as others by the word itself, at least saw this, and rendered the expression by τὴν Σουκχὼθ Βενίθ, showing that they regarded it as the name of a goddess. The Babylonian goddess who corresponds most nearly to the word, and is most likely to be intended, would seem to be Zirat-banit, the wife of Merodach ('Transactions of the Society of Biblical Archæology,' vol. iv. pp. 136—147). *Zirat-banit* means "the creating lady;" but the Hebrew interpreter seems to have mistaken the first element, which he confounded with *Zarat*, the Babylonian for "tents," and so translated by "Succoth." The goddess Zirat-banit was certainly one of the principal deities of Babylon, and would be more likely to be selected than any other goddess. Probably she was worshipped in combination with her husband, Merodach. **And the men of Cuth**—*i.e.* "Cuthah"—**made Nergal.** Nergal was the special deity of Cutha. He was the Babylonian war-god, and had a high position in the Assyrian pantheon also. His name appears as an element in the "Nergal-sharezer" of Jeremiah (xxxix. 3, 13) and the Neriglissar of Ptolemy and Berosus. **And the men of Hamath made Ashima.** Thenius conjectures that "Ashima" represents the Phœnician Eshmoun, one of the Cabiri, or eight "Great Ones." But the etymological resemblance of the two words is not close, and it is not at all certain that the Hamathites at any time acknowledged the Phœnician deities The Hamathite inscriptions are in the character now known as "Hittite;" and there is reason to believe that the people were non-Semitic. This identification, therefore, must be regarded as very doubtful. Perhaps "Ashima" represents Simi, the daughter of Hadad (see Melito, 'Apologia').

Ver. 31.—**And the Avites made Nibhaz and Tartak.** "Nibhaz" and "Tartak" are very obscure. The Sabians are said to have acknowledged an evil demon, whom they called Nib'az or Nabaz (Norberg, 'Onomasticon,' p. 100); and Tartak has been derived by Gesenius from the Pehlevi *Tar-thak,* "hero of darkness;" but these guesses cannot be regarded as entitled to much attention. We do not know what the religion of the Avites was, and need not be surprised that the names of their gods are new to us. The polytheism of the East was prolific of deities, and still more of divine names. Nibhaz and Tartak may have been purely local gods, or they may have been local names for gods worshipped under other appellations in the general pantheon of Babylonia. **And the Sepharvites burnt their children in fire to Adrammelech and Anammelech, the gods of Sepharvaim.** The god principally worshipped at Sippara was Shamas, "the sun." It is probable that "Adrammelech" (equivalent to *adir-melek,* "the glorious king," or *edir-malek,* "the arranging king") was one of his titles. Shamas, in the Babylonian mythology, was always closely connected with Anunit, a sun-goddess; and it is probably this name which is represented by Anammelech, which we may regard as an intentional corruption, derisive and contemptuous.

Ver. 32.—**So they feared the Lord**—rather, *and they (also) honoured Jehovah;* i.e. with their idolatrous worship they combined also the worship of Jehovah (comp. ver. 28)—**and made unto themselves of the lowest of them priests of the high places**—i.e. followed the example of Jeroboam in taking for priests persons of all ranks, even the lowest (see the comment on 1 Kings xii. 31)—**which sacrificed for them in the houses of the high places** (comp. ver. 29).

Ver. 33.—**They feared the Lord, and served their own gods.** This syncretism, this mixed religion, is so surprising to the writer, and so abhorrent to his religious sentiments, that he cannot but dwell upon it, not shrinking from repeating himself (see vers. 32, 33, 41), in order to arrest the reader's attention, and point out to him the folly and absurdity of such conduct. The practice was still going on in his own day (vers. 34, 41), and may have had attractions for the descendants of the small Israelite population which had

been left in the land. **After the manner of the nations whom they carried away from thence;** rather, *after the manner of the nations from whom they* (i.e. the authorities) *carried them away;* i.e. after the manner of their countrymen at home. The translation of the Revised Version gives the sense, while changing the construction—"after the manner of the nations from among whom they had been carried away."

Ver. 34.—**Unto this day**—i.e. the time at which Kings was written (about B.C. 580—560)—**they do after the former manners**—that is, they maintain the mixed religion, which they set up on the coming of the Samaritan priest from Assyria a hundred and fifty or sixty years previously—**they fear not the Lord.** This statement seems directly opposed to the thrice-repeated one (vers. 32, 33, 41), "They feared the Lord;" but the apparent contradiction is easily reconciled. The new immigrants "feared Jehovah" in a certain sense, i.e. externally. They admitted him into their pantheon, and had ritual observances in his honour. But they did not really fear him in their hearts. Had they done so, they would have inquired what were his laws, statutes, and ordinances, and would have set themselves to obey them. This they did not think of doing. **Neither do they after their statutes, or after their ordinances**—either the "statutes" and "ordinances" are regarded as having become *de jure* "theirs" by their occupation of the Holy Land, or "their" refers by anticipation to "the children of Jacob" towards the close of the verse—**or after the Law**—rather, *and after the Law*—and commandment which the Lord commanded the children of Jacob, whom he named Israel (see Gen. xxxii. 28).

Ver. 35.—**With whom the Lord had made a covenant, and charged them, saying, Ye shall not fear other gods, nor bow yourselves to them, nor serve them, nor sacrifice to them** (see Exod. xx. 3; Deut. v. 7; vi. 14; xi. 28. For the "covenant," see Exod. xix. 5—8; xxiv. 3—8).

Ver. 36.—**But the Lord, who brought you up out of the land of Egypt with great power and a stretched-out arm** (comp. Exod. vi. 6; Deut. iv. 34; v. 15; vii. 19; ix. 29; Ps. cxxxvi. 12, etc.), **him shall ye fear, and him shall ye worship, and to him shall ye do sacrifice** (see Deut. vi. 13; x. 20; xiii. 4; Josh. xxiv. 14, etc.).

Ver. 37.—**And the statutes, and the ordinances, and the Law, and the commandment, which he wrote for you**—i.e. which, by his Providence, were given you in a written form (comp. Exod. xxiv. 4; Deut. xxxi. 9; Josh. viii. 34)—**ye shall observe to do for evermore** (comp. Lev. xviii. 4, 5; xix. 37; Deut. iv. 6; v. 1; vi. 24, 25, etc.); **and ye** shall not fear other gods (see the comment on ver. 35).

Ver. 38.—And the covenant that I have made with you ye shall not forget. The "covenant" intended is not the covenant of circumcision, which God made with Abraham (Gen. xvii. 9—14), but the covenant of protection and obedience made at Sinai between God and the entire people (Exod. xix. 5—8), and most solemnly ratified by sprinkling with blood and by a covenant feast, as related in Exod. xxiv. 3—11. This was the covenant which Israel had been warned so frequently not to "forget" (Deut. iv. 23; viii. 11; xxvi. 13; Prov. ii. 17), yet which they had "forgotten," or, at any rate, "forsaken," as already declared in ver. 15. Neither shall ye fear other gods. The writer has probably a practical object in his re-iteration. He expects his words to reach the ears of the mixed race inhabiting Samaria in his day, and would fain warn them against their idolatrous practices, and point them to the pure worship of Jehovah. It is pleasing to remember that ultimately the mixed race was won to the true faith, and that the Samaritans of our Lord's time were as true worshippers of Jehovah, and as zealous followers of the Law, as the Jews themselves. The interesting community at Nablous still maintains Samaritan forms, and reads the Samaritan Pentateuch.

Ver. 39.—But the Lord your God ye shall fear (comp. ver. 36); and he shall deliver you out of the hand of all your enemies. This promise had been made repeatedly (see Exod. xxiii. 27; Lev. xxvi. 7, 8; Deut. vi. 18, 19; xx. 4; xxiii. 14; xxviii. 7, etc.). The writer of Chronicles aims at showing in detail that the promise was literally fulfilled in the history, victory in every case declaring itself in favour of God's people, when they were faithful and obedient, while reverses always befell them in the contrary

case (see 1 Chron. v. 20—22; x. 13; xiv. 10—16; 2 Chron. xii. 1—12; xiii. 4—18; xiv. 9—12; xx. 5—30, etc.).

Ver. 40.—Howbeit they did not hearken. The mixed race, with their mixed religion, though professing to be worshippers of Jehovah, paid no attention to the warnings and threatenings of the Law (ver. 34), which were to them a dead letter. But they did after their former manner; i.e. they continued to maintain the syncretism described in vers. 28—33.

Ver. 41.—So these nations—i.e. the Babylonians, Cuthæans, Hamathites, Avites, and Sepharvites settled in Samaria—feared the Lord, and served their graven images. The rabbinical writers tell us that Nergal was worshipped under the form of a cock, Ashima under the form of a goat, Nibhaz under the form of a dog, Tartak under that of an ass, while Adrammelech and Anammelech were represented by a mule and a horse respectively. Not much confidence can be placed in these representations. The Babylonian gods were ordinarily figured in human forms. Animal ones—as those of the bull and the lion, generally winged and human-headed, were in a few cases, but only in a few, used to represent the gods symbolically. Other emblems employed were the winged circle for Asshur; the disc plain or four-rayed for the male sun, six or eight-rayed for the female sun; the crescent for the moon-god Sin; the thunderbolt for the god of the atmosphere, Vul or Rimmon; the wedge or arrow-head, the fundamental element of writing, for Nebo. Images, however, were made of all the gods, and were no doubt set up by the several "nations" in their respective "cities." Both their children, and their children's children—i.e. their descendants to the time of the writer of Kings—as did their fathers, so do they unto this day.

HOMILETICS.

Vers. 1—4.—*The unwisdom of worldly craft and policy.* Hoshea came to the throne at a time of great danger and difficulty. The Assyrian system of gradual expansion and annexation was settled and almost declared. The petty states upon her borders were first invaded and ravaged; then they were taken under her protection; finally they were absorbed. The process had been going on from the days of Tiglath-pileser I. (about B.C. 1130), and was still in operation. Damascus was a recent example of it. Under these circumstances, Hoshea could not but feel his throne precarious, and the independence of his country more than threatened. How would he act most wisely for his own security and that of his country? There were three courses open to him.

I. HE MIGHT LOOK SOLELY TO THE ASSYRIAN KING. Absolute submission, fidelity, watchful regard for the suzerain's interests, punctual payment of the fixed tribute, liberal donations to the court officials and the monarch beyond the sum appointed, generally secured to the protected state the continuance of its suzerain's favour, and a prolongation of its protected existence. Hoshea might have adopted this policy. He might have bent all his efforts to the propitiation of the Assyrian monarch, and the obtaining of his favourable regard. In this way he would probably have secured to himself a long and quiet reign; and his country would have been spared for many a year the horrors of war, and his people the misery of being carried into captivity.

II. HE MIGHT LOOK FOR A HUMAN PROTECTOR AGAINST ASSYRIA. Human helps, negotiations, treaties, alliances, are the natural and ordinary resort of weak states when menaced by a stronger. Cannot a counterpoise be raised up against the monster community which threatens the existence of all its neighbours? Cannot a "balance of power" be established? Hoshea was particularly tempted at the time by the rise to greatness of a new dynasty in Egypt, which seemed to have greater strength and greater resources than had been possessed by its predecessors. It was probably regarded by his advisers as a wonderfully clever stroke of policy when they suggested that alliance with Shebek, the new King of Egypt, might be the salvation of Samaria under the circumstances. So Ætolia called in the aid of Rome against Macedon; and so recently, with better results, Sardinia called in the aid of France against Austria. Hoshea caught at the suggestion. Though pledged to Assyria, though actually owing his throne to an Assyrian monarch ('Eponym Canon,' pp. 123, 124), he accepted the advice, made alliance with Shebek, and broke with Shalmaneser, to his own destruction and that of his country.

III. HE MIGHT DISCARD "ARMS OF FLESH," AND LOOK WHOLLY TO JEHOVAH. The prophets were calling Israel to repentance. They were denouncing the calf-worship and the other idolatries. They were condemning reliance on either Egypt or Assyria (Hos. vii. 11; xii. 1). They were threatening the destruction of the kingdom unless Israel truly repented and turned to the Lord. They were pointing to a possible restoration to God's favour if these conditions were fulfilled (Hos. ii. 14—23; vii. 1—3; xiv. 1—9; Amos v. 4—9, and 14, 15), and urging compliance before it was too late. They taught that God could save by his own power, and "not by bow, nor by sword, nor by battle, by horses, nor by horsemen" (Hos. i. 7). True wisdom would have taught Hoshea and his advisers to look for salvation to this quarter; but they were so infatuated with their trust in the strength of Egypt that they seem not even to have given the alternative course a thought. The result showed that their (supposed) worldly wisdom was the extremest unwisdom, their perfection of policy the worst policy that could possibly have been adopted.

Vers. 7—23.—*The lessons to be learnt from the destruction of the kingdom of Samaria.* The first and main lesson is, of course, the great fact—

I. THAT NATIONS ARE TREATED BY GOD AS RESPONSIBLE UNITS, AND ARE PUNISHED, EVEN DESTROYED, FOR THEIR SINS. It was their "evil ways," their transgression against the commandments of God, that lay at the root of Israel's rejection. The prophets Hosea and Amos paint an awful picture of the condition of Samaria under its later kings. Luxury, oppression, lewdness, drunkenness, idolatry, prevailed. The service of God was a lip-service, which "his soul hated." There was no truth, no mercy, no real "knowledge of God," in the land (Hos. iv. 1). "By swearing, and lying, and killing, and stealing . . . they broke out, and blood touched blood" (Hos. iv. 2). "Whoredom and wine and new wine had taken away their heart" (Hos. iv. 11). "A man and his father would go in unto the same maid" (Amos ii. 7). False balances were employed (Amos viii. 5). "Companies of priests murdered in the way by consent" (Hos. vi. 9). *Therefore* was the doom pronounced against the nation—they should "go into captivity beyond Damascus" (Amos v. 27). "The Lord swore by his holiness . . . that he would take them away with hooks, and their posterity with fish-hooks" (Amos iv. 2). "The end came upon them; they could not be passed by any more" (Amos viii. 2). Minor lessons are—

II. THAT SINS ARE GREATLY AGGRAVATED IN GOD'S SIGHT WHEN THEY ARE INFRACTIONS OF A COVENANT MADE WITH HIM. Israel was under covenant with God —had been made God's "peculiar people" on the express condition of keeping his statutes, testimonies, commandments, and judgments (Exod. xix. 5—8). This they had bound themselves to do; but they had done the exact opposite. Hence the reproaches in vers. 15 and 35—40. It is the breach of the covenant by the northern kingdom that, in the view of the writer of Kings, is the main and special cause of its fall. All else might have been forgiven, but not that. A covenant is a holy thing, even when it is only between man and man (Gal. iii. 15); but a covenant between man and God—how can anything be more holy? Must not the infraction of such a covenant entail fearful consequences?

III. THAT IT IS A FURTHER GREAT AGGRAVATION OF THE GUILT OF SIN TO COMMIT IT AGAINST FREQUENT WARNINGS. "Yet the Lord testified against Israel, and against Judah, by all the prophets, and by all the seers, saying, Turn ye from your evil ways" (ver. 13). Comp. 2 Chron. xxxvi. 15, 16, "And the Lord God of their fathers sent to them by his messengers, rising up betimes, and sending; because he had compassion on his people, and on his dwelling-place: but they mocked the messengers of God, and despised his words, and misused his prophets, until the wrath of the Lord arose against his people, till there was no remedy." The sin of Israel would have been far less, would not perhaps have been quite "without remedy," had they not for so long a time turned a deaf ear to the warnings and exhortations of the prophets, refusing to "hear the voice of the charmers, charmed they never so wisely," and persisting in their disobedience, their wickedness, their greed, their cruelty, their besotted idolatry, despite the scathing denunciations, the tender pleadings, the wise counsels, almost uninterruptedly addressed to them. "Stiffnecked and uncircumcised in heart and ears" (Acts vii. 51), they "resisted the Holy Ghost;" and their doom had to be pronounced. Congregations in this country and at the present day may be reminded (1) that England is not without her national sins; (2) that the sins of Christians are, all of them, infractions of the covenant made in baptism between themselves and God; and (3) that the sins of Christians are committed against the constant warnings of God's appointed ministers, who stand to them as the prophets stood to the Israelites.

Vers. 24—41.—*The absurdity and uselessness of a mixed religion.* Syncretism has been at all times a form which religion is apt to assume in mixed communities. Theoretically, religions are antithetic, exclusive, mutually repulsive. Practically, where they coexist, they tend to give and take, to approximate one to the other, to drop differences, to blend together into an apparent, if not a real, union. Christianity had at first those who would sit in an idol-temple, and partake of idol-sacrifices (1 Cor. viii. 10). Judaism under the Seleucidæ, but for the rude impatience of Antiochus Epiphanes, was on the point of making terms with Hellenism. In Samaria, after the events related in vers. 24—28, a mixed religion—a "mingle-mangle," to use Reformation language—took its place as the religion of the mixed people. "They feared the Lord, and served their own gods." Jehovah was everywhere acknowledged, honoured, worshipped with sacrifice. But at the same time, heathen gods—partial, local, half-material, sacred, but not holy—were objects of a far more real and intense worship. Such a religion is (1) absurd, (2) useless.

I. SYNCRETISM IS ABSURD, since it is self-contradictory. "What concord has Christ with Belial?" (2 Cor. vi. 15). Religions which are really different have contradictory first principles; and agreement can only be effected by a dropping, on one side or the other, or both, of what is vital and essential. In the particular case before us, absolute monotheism was the very core and essence of the Jehovah-worship; actual polytheism was the root and groundwork of the other. The two were logically inconsistent, incompatible. Practically, the contradiction may not always have been perceived, for man, though a rational, is not a logical animal; but the *general* result, no doubt, was that the monotheistic idea had to give way: Jehovah, the one only God of the whole earth, had to sink into a "god of the land," and to receive an occasional and grudging acknowledgment from those whose hearts were with their own gods, Nergal and Ashima and Adrammelech. But, in this case, the worship of Jehovah was superfluous. God does not thank men for dragging him into a pantheon, and setting him side by side with beings who are no gods, but the fantastic inventions of imaginations depraved and corrupted by sin.

II. SYNCRETISM IS USELESS. Contrary systems of religion will not amalgamate, let men do what they may. Either each neutralizes the other, and the result is no religion at all; or one gets the upper hand, and the other element might as well be absent. There is no serving "God *and* mammon," "Christ *and* Belial." The mind cannot really, at one and the same time, accept contradictories. The lips may do so, but religion is an affair of the heart. Syncretism is an apparent, not a real, union. Theories mutually destructive cannot coalesce. Thus, practically, syncretism is useless. It is either a mere nominal union or a mode of eliminating religion from human life. In the case before us it seems to have left the Samaritans just as much polytheists, just as much idolaters, as it found them. Zerubbabel did well to allow them no part in the building of the second temple, and to give them the curt answer, "Ye have nothing to do with us to build a house unto our God" (Ezra iv. 3). Had he done otherwise, he would have merged Judaism in a polytheistic and idolatrous pseudo-religion.

HOMILIES BY VARIOUS AUTHORS.

Vers. 1—5.—*The reign of Hoshea.* I. A FOOLISH SERVICE. The life of every man is a service of some sort. We cannot, even if we would, be absolutely our own masters. Some men are the servants of self. Some are the servants of others. Some are the servants of good. Some are the servants of evil. Some are the servants of money, or of pleasure, or of their passions. What higher epitaph could be written over any man's tomb than the simple words, "A servant of God"? What higher choice could any man make than this, "As for me and my house, we will serve the Lord"? But that was not the choice which Hoshea made. He thought the service of God was slavery. He chose the service of the King of Assyria. What fools men are sometimes! How blind to their own best interests! The prodigal son in his father's house had every comfort, consideration, and care. But he thought there was too much restriction. He would like to have more of his own way. And so he went away from his father's house. But he was glad enough to return. He did not find the service of the world and of sin quite so pleasant as he expected. So many discover, when it is too late, "The wages of sin is death; but the gift of God is eternal life, through Jesus Christ our Lord."

II. A FAITHLESS SERVANT. Hoshea was unfaithful to God. And the man who is unfaithful to the claims of God—the highest of all claims—is generally unfaithful to his fellow-men. So it was in this case. "The King of Assyria found conspiracy in Hoshea." Hoshea had entered into engagements which he did not fulfil. *The best security for right dealing between man and man is obedience to the Law of God.* The history of nations and individuals teaches us that. The nation where God is honoured, where the Word of God is read, is generally superior to others in the industry, content-ment, and prosperity of its inhabitants. The man who fears God is the man who can be depended on. "He backbiteth not with his tongue, nor doeth evil to his neighbour, nor taketh up a reproach against his neighbour."—C. H. I.

Vers. 6—23.—*Captivity and its cause.* Here is the beginning of the dispersion of Israel. Soon that favoured nation will be "a people scattered and peeled." These verses give us the explanation of Israel's exile. It is a solemn warning against the neglect of opportunities.

I. COMMANDS DISOBEYED. "They rejected his statutes" (ver. 15); "They left all the commandments of the Lord their God" (ver. 16); "They served idols, whereof the Lord had said unto them, Ye shall not do this thing" (ver. 12). Consider: 1. *Whose commands they disobeyed.* The commands of the Lord their God. It was he who had brought them out of Egypt. It was he who had brought them into the promised land. It was he who had made of them—a race of humble shepherds—a great nation. When God gave the ten commandments, he prefaced them by reminding Israel of his claim upon them. "I am the Lord thy God, which have brought thee out of the land of Egypt, out of the house of bondage." This was a strong reason for obedience. "The preface to the ten commandments teaches us that because God is the Lord, and our God and Redeemer, therefore we are bound to keep all his commandments." God has a similar claim: (1) *Upon every human being.* This is the claim of creation and preser-vation and providence. "In him we live, and move, and have our being." Whether men like it or not, they cannot get rid of God's claim upon them. (2) *Upon every Christian.* He has brought us out of the house of bondage. "In whom we have redemption through his blood, even the forgiveness of sins." "According as he hath chosen us in him before the foundation of the world, that we should be holy and without blame before him in love." 2. *What commands they disobeyed.* All God's commandments were for their own good. They were rational and wise commandments. To forbid idolatry was to forbid a sin which in itself was ungrateful and dishonouring to the true God, and which was degrading and demoralizing in its consequences. Oh that men were wise, that they would consider the consequences of sin for time and for eternity! "The fear of the Lord is the beginning of wisdom, and to depart from evil is understanding."

II. WARNINGS DISREGARDED. Note: 1. *God's forbearance and mercy.* God did not cut them off at once for their sin. Time after time he forgave them. He sent them his prophets to invite them to return to him, to give them promises of pardon and blessing, to point out to them what must be the inevitable consequence of perseverance in sin. *His anxiety to save them was very great.* The phrase used in Jeremiah is a remarkable one. "They have not hearkened to my words, saith the Lord, which I sent unto them by my servants the prophets, *rising up early* and sending them." What a wonderful and touching description of God's desire to save!—"Rising up early." As if he wanted to be before men. As if he wanted to anticipate their temptations by his messages of warning and of guidance. If we make God's Word our morning study, what a help we shall find it in the difficulties and temptations and duties of each day! 2. *Man's folly and blindness.* "Notwithstanding they would not hear, but hardened their necks, like to the neck of their fathers, that did not believe in the Lord their God" (ver. 14). All the warnings were in vain. "They sold themselves to do evil in the sight of the Lord" (ver. 17). Is it not a true description of the life of the sinner? He imagines that sin is freedom, and he finds it to be the most grinding and oppressive slavery. He is "led captive by the devil at his will." *The sinner serves a hard master.* "They caused their sons and their daughters to pass through the fire" (ver. 17). How cruel is heathenism! How it crushes out the tender feelings of humanity and kindness! Look upon the picture of it as presented in its Molochs, in its Juggernauts, in its suttees. See how the aged and the sick are left alone to die. Contrast with all this the spirit and work of Christianity, its care for the sick and the poor, its sympathy for the oppressed. Heathenism makes slaves; Christianity emancipates them. This is true alike of the slavery of the body and the slavery of the mind. 3. *Sin's bitter fruit.* "And the Lord rejected all the seed of Israel, and afflicted them, and delivered them into the hand of spoilers, until he had cast them out of his sight." Calamity is never causeless. If we are afflicted, let us see whether the cause may not be in our own hearts, in our own lives. *What a warning is here to Churches!* What a warning against unfaithfulness, against setting up human ordinances in the worship of God! "Remember, therefore from whence thou art fallen, and repent, and do the first works; or else I will come unto thee quickly, and will remove thy candlestick out of his place, except thou repent." *What a warning is here against neglect of opportunities!* If we fail to use our opportunities and privileges, they will be certainly taken from us. Let us give an attentive ear to the warnings of God's Word, to the everyday warnings of God's providence. "Because I have called, and ye refused; I have stretched out my hand, and no man regarded; but ye have set at nought all my counsel, and would none of my reproof: I also will laugh at your calamity; I will mock when your fear cometh. . . . They would none of my counsel, they despised all my reproof. Therefore shall they eat of *the fruit of their own way,* and be filled with their own devices."—C. H. I.

Vers. 24—41.—*Samaria and its religion.* I. ITS EARLY GODLESSNESS. The land of Samaria was now deprived of its Israelitish inhabitants. The King of Assyria colonized it with heathen immigrants. "At the beginning of their dwelling there, they feared not the Lord." What a mistake to go anywhere without taking God's presence with us! How many journeys are undertaken, how many a business is entered on, without ever a word of prayer being offered to God! How many a home life is commenced without a family altar! As the young Scotch lad said of a house where he stayed for some time, and where there was no family prayer, "There is no roof on that house." "Except the Lord build the house, they labour in vain that build it."

II. ITS SUBSEQUENT JUDGMENTS. "Therefore the Lord sent lions among them, which slew some of them. Wherefore they spake to the King of Assyria, saying,

The nations which thou hast removed, and placed in the cities of Samaria, know not the manner of the God of the land: therefore he hath sent lions among them, and, behold, they slay them, because they know not the manner of the God of the land" (vers. 25, 26). It was judgment that first made them think of God. It is often so in the history of human life. Men live without God, prayerless, godless lives, so long as all appears to be going well with them. But when sickness comes, or troubles overtake them, or death is drawing near, they cry to the Lord then. There is something mean about this. It is better to call upon God and to come to him in trouble than not to call on him at all; but how much better it is to serve him in health as well as in sickness, in prosperity as well as in trouble!

III. Its MIXED RELIGION. Samaria tried the experiment of serving the true God and the gods of the heathen at the same time. It tried the impossible task of serving two masters. "They feared the Lord, and served their own gods, after the manner of the nations whom they carried away from thence" (ver. 33). In their case, as in every case, it proved to be an impossible task. "Unto this day they do after the former manners: they fear not the Lord, neither do they after their statutes, or after their ordinances, or after the Law and commandment which the Lord commanded the children of Jacob" (ver. 34); "So these nations feared the Lord, and served their graven images, both their children, and their children's children: as did their fathers, so do they unto this day" (ver. 41). They "feared the Lord:" that was profession. "They served their graven images:" that was practice. Yet there are many who are trying the same impossible task. They have a certain amount of *fear* of God. They are afraid to die, afraid of the judgment to come. So they think it desirable to be "religious." They go to church. They read the Bible occasionally, perhaps. They bear the name of good Christians. But it is a name only. Their life cannot be called a Christian life. They serve God on the Sunday in a kind of way, and the world or sin the rest of the week. They try, perhaps, to serve God and mammon. They try to serve God and the world. They are liberal-minded Christians. But this kind of *mixed religion is no religion* in the sight of God. He cannot have a divided service. This is emphatically brought out in the first chapter of Isaiah. There the inconsistency and uselessness of a religious profession combined with a godless life is clearly shown. "To what purpose is the multitude of your sacrifices unto me?" "Bring no more vain oblations;" "Wash you, make you clean; *put away the evil of your doings from before mine eyes*; cease to do evil; learn to do well; seek judgment, relieve the oppressed, judge the fatherless, plead for the widow." Here it is plainly taught that a religious profession is worthless without a religious life. If we regard iniquity in our heart, the Lord will not hear us. It is interesting to remember that even this degraded people of Samaria, with their mixed and corrupt religion, were permitted twice at least to receive the gospel message. They were looked down upon with contempt and aversion by the Jews. But there is mercy even for the most degraded. A city of Samaria received Christ himself, and many of its people believed on him, for the saying of the woman who testified, "He told me all things that ever I did." It was even in the apostate city of Samaria that, when Philip went down and preached Christ unto them, "the people with one accord gave heed unto the things which Philip spake," and many of them believed and were baptized. And we read that "there was great joy in that city." Even to these Samaritans, aliens from the ancient Jewish faith, a people despised and hated by the Jews, the gospel of Christ brought great joy. Surely there is here an encouragement for the greatest sinner. Surely there is here a reason for us to hope and work for the salvation even of the most degraded. Surely an encouragement for Christian missions to the heathen.—C. H. I.

Vers. 1—8.—*Aspects of a corrupt nation.* "In the twelfth year of Ahaz King of Judah began Hoshea the son of Elah to reign in Samaria over Israel nine years," etc. Hoshea, the king here mentioned, was the nineteenth and last King of Israel. He lived about seven hundred and twenty years or more before Christ. After a reign of nine years his subjects were carried away captive to Assyria, and the kingdom of Israel came to an end. The selection we have made from this chapter presents to us—*Aspects of a corrupt nation.* A nation appears here as an unfortunate inheritor of wrong; as a guilty worker of wrong; and as a terrible victim of wrong.

I. As AN UNFORTUNATE INHERITOR OF WRONG. Upon Hoshea and his age there came down the corrupting influence of no less than eighteen princes, all of whom were steeped in wickedness and fanatical idolatry. The whole nation had become completely immoral and idolatrous. This king—the last of the Israelitish—it is said, "did that which was evil in the sight of the Lord, but not as the kings of Israel that were before him." If one shade better than his predecessors, he was, notwithstanding, a man whose character seems unredeemed by one single virtue. It is one of not only the commonest, but the most perplexing, facts in history that one generation comes to *inherit*, to a great extent, the character of its predecessor. The thoughts, the principles, and the spirit that animated the men of the past, come down and take possession of the minds of the men of the present. Though the bodies of our predecessors are mouldering in the dust, they are still here in their thoughts and influences. This is an undoubted fact. It serves to explain three things. 1. *The vital connection between all the members of the race.* Though men are countless in number, and ever multiplying, *humanity is one.* All are branches of the same root, members of the same body, links in one chain. None can be affected without affecting others; the motion of one link propagates an influence to the end of the chain. None of us liveth unto himself. Solemn thought! Our very breathings may produce ripples upon the mighty lake of existence, which will spread in ever-widening circles to the very shores of eternity. There are mystic springs connecting us with the universe. Can we move without touching them? Can we give a touch that will not send its vibrations along the arches of the boundless future? The effects of a man's influence, either for good or evil, will be determined by his moral character. A bad man is a moral curse; the influence that streams from him will be moral poison. A good man, under God, is a blessing; his influence, like the living waters, will irrigate and beautify the mental districts through which it flows. 2. *The immense difficulty of improving the moral condition of the race.* There have been men in every age and land who have "striven even unto blood" to improve the race. Poets have depicted the charms of virtue, moralists have reasoned against wrong, martyrs have died for the right; and during the last eighteen centuries, throughout Christendom, the best men throughout all communions have struggled hard to bring the world's mind under the supreme reign of the true, the beautiful, and the good. But how miserable has been the result! Evil is everywhere the dominant force—dominant not merely in markets and governments, but even in Churches. Those of us who have lived longest in the world, looked deepest into its moral heart, and laboured most zealously and persistently for its improvement, feel, like Sisyphus in ancient fable, struggling to roll a large stone to the top of a mountain, which, as soon as we think some progress has been made, rolls back to its old position, and that with greater impetuosity. Scripture everywhere recognizes this difficulty, and speaks of the work as a "race," a "battle," a "crucifixion." I question whether the world is morally much better than it has ever been. 3. *The absolute need of super-human agency spiritually to redeem the race.* Philosophy shows that a bad world cannot improve itself, cannot make itself good. Bad men can neither help themselves morally nor help others. If the world is to be improved, thoughts and influences from superhuman regions must be transfused into its heart. Moral goodness must come in a new form, and ply new agencies. Herein is the gospel: "When we were without strength, in due time Christ died for the ungodly."

II. As A GUILTY WORKER OF WRONG. Hoshea and his people were not only the *inheritors* of the corruptions of past generations, but they themselves became agents in propagating and perpetuating the wickedness. See what is said of Hoshea here. "The King of Assyria found conspiracy in Hoshea." This is only one specimen or development of this man's wickedness. See what is said of his people. "The children of Israel had sinned against the Lord their God, which had brought them up out of the land of Egypt, from under the hand of Pharaoh King of Egypt, and had feared other gods." So that while they were the inheritors of a corrupt past, they were at the same time *guilty* agents in a wicked present. Strong as is the influence of the past upon us, it is not strong enough to *coerce* us into wrong. Gracious Heaven has endowed every man with the power of thought and resolve sufficient, if he uses it, to rise above the influence of the past, and to mount into a new moral orbit of life. He has the power to stand on the firm rock of his own individuality, and to say to the swelling sea of depravity, as its waves are approaching him, "So far shalt thou come, and no further." Because the father has been bad, there is no *just* reason why the child should be bad also. Because all the generations that have gone have been bad, there is no reason why this generation should be wicked. We are not like logs of wood on the surging seas of past wickedness, but rather like those snowy birds that can at pleasure mount from the billows, and quit them for the wide fields of air.

III. As A TERRIBLE VICTIM OF WRONG. What was the *judicial* outcome of all this wickedness? Retribution stern, rigorous, and crushing. "Then the King of Assyria came up throughout all the land, and went up to Samaria, and besieged it three years." "This was the third and final expedition of Shalmaneser against the whole of Syria, and it seems to have been after the lapse of a year or two from his second expedition. What new offence had excited his wrath has not been recorded; but as a determined resistance was made by his refractory vassal, Shalmaneser prepared for a regular siege of Samaria, which, through the stubborn valour of the Israelites themselves, or with the aid of Egyptian troops, lasted for nearly three years. At length the city capitulated; or, if Josephus is correct, was taken by storm. But the glory of this conquest was not enjoyed by Shalmaneser, who had been suddenly recalled by the outbreak of a domestic revolution occasioned, or at least encouraged, by his protracted absences from his capital. He was dethroned by the insurrection of an ambitious subject, and he seems to have died also before the fall of Samaria" (Dr. Jameson). Thus the whole of the inhabitants, one and all, were carried away by tyrannic force. "From inscriptions in the palace at Khorasbad," says a modern expositor, "which record the number of Israelitish captives, it appears that 27,280 were transported into Assyria from Samaria and other parts of the kingdom of Israel. The removal of entire populations from vanquished countries to some other portion of the conqueror's dominions had not been adopted, so far as reliable history testifies, as the policy of any ancient sovereigns in the East until it was introduced and acted upon by the later Assyrian kings. Soldiers when taken captive in battle, women and children belonging to the conquered enemy, it had, indeed, for ages been the custom to carry into the land of the victor. And even numerous tribes of foreigners, resident within the territory, and reduced to a state of bondage, like the Israelites in Egypt, had frequently, by the arbitrary will of ancient kings, been dragged to different quarters of their kingdom to labour on the public works." Here is the *temporal* retribution, at any rate, of two hundred years of idolatry and wickedness. During this period Israel had sinned away its liberty, its property, its country. The ten tribes sinned themselves into slavery, destitution, and everlasting obscurity. For where are they? Two thousand years have rolled away since this terrible catastrophe, and none can tell us who they are or where they are. "Be sure your sins will find you out." Retribution may move silently and slowly, but ever with a resistless step. It follows the sins of a *nation* as well as of an individual. It was the crimes of the Israelites that ruined the kingdom, and made them the victims of this terrible catastrophe. So it ever is; the great dynasties and kingdoms of the past have met with the same fate by the same inexorable law of retribution. There are sins in our England that are working towards its ruin. The sins of a nation work, like the subterranean fires, underground. The nation may have arts lovely as the landscape, institutions apparently grand and firm as the old mountains. But whilst the people revel in their exuberance of resources, their natural beauties, and in the grandeur of their institutions, and that for ages, sin, like an ocean of fire underground, will one day break out in flames, that will destroy the whole, as in the case of the ten tribes.—D. T.

Vers. 9—23.—*A great privilege, wickedness, and ruin.* "For so it was," etc. We have used the first verses of this chapter, in our last sketch, to set forth the *aspects of a corrupt nation.* The Israelitish people appear in that fragment of their history as an unfortunate inheritor of wrong, a guilty worker of wrong, and a terrible victim of wrong. These fifteen verses now under our notice present to us three subjects of thought—a great national privilege; a great national wickedness; and a great national ruin.

I. A GREAT NATIONAL PRIVILEGE. We learn herefrom that the Infinite Governor of the world had given them at least three great advantages—political freedom, right to the land, and the highest spiritual teaching. He had given them: 1. *Political freedom.* For ages they had been in political bondage, the mere slaves of despots; but here we are told that God had " brought them out of the land of Egypt, from under the hand of Pharaoh King of Egypt" (ver. 7). When they crossed the Red Sea, entered the desert, and stepped into Palestine, they were civilly free; the chains that had bound them so long were then completely broken, and each had the common right of liberty. Political freedom is the inalienable right of all men, is one of the greatest blessings of a people, but one which in every age has been outraged by despots. The millions are groaning in many a land still under political disabilities. 2. *A right to the land.* Canaan was the common right of all; true, it was divided amongst the ten tribes, but this was not for the private interests of any, but for the good of all. What we call "landlordism" scarcely existed, and perhaps it would have been as well had it never existed; it bars the common rights of mankind. When one thinks that all the land in Scotland, Ireland, Wales, and England is in the hands of eight thousand men, a number which could be crowded into Spurgeon's tabernacle, and that thirty millions have no portion in the land, it is impossible not to feel that the condition of things is anomalous. Archdeacon Paley, no mean authority, with his characteristic clearness and common sense, has the following remarkable words: " If you should see a flock of pigeons in a field of corn, and if (instead of each one picking where and what it liked, taking just as much as it wanted and no more) you should see ninety-nine of them gathering all they got in a heap, reserving nothing for themselves but the chaff and the refuse, keeping this heap for one, and that for the weakest, perhaps the worst pigeon of the flock, sitting round and looking on all the winter, whilst the one was devouring, throwing about, and wasting it; and if a pigeon more hardy or hungry than the rest touched a grain of the hoard, all the others instantly flying upon it and tearing it to pieces;—if you should see this, you would see nothing more than what is every day practised and established amongst men. Among men you see the ninety and nine toiling and scraping together a heap of superfluities for one (and this one too oftentimes the feeblest and worst of the whole set—a child, a woman, a madman, or a fool), getting nothing for themselves all the while but a little of the coarsest of the provision which their own industry produces, looking quietly on while they see the fruits of all the labour spent or spoiled, and if one of the number take or touch a particle of the hoard, the others joining against him and hanging him for the theft." What boots collecting and publishing facts concerning the sufferings of people, and entitling the tract the ' Bitter Cry of Outcast London,' unless something is done to put a greater share of the land into the hands of the people, not by violence or spoliation, but by a calm and just legislation? Alas! even good men, through a weakness of judgment and the workings of a traditional faith, seem to dream that by multiplying churches and chapels they will hush the " bitter cry." How absurd! 3. *The highest spiritual teaching.* "The Lord testified against Israel, and against Judah, by all the prophets, and by all the seers, saying, Turn ye from your evil ways, and keep my commandments and my statutes, according to all the Law which I commanded your fathers, and which I sent to you by my servants the prophets" (ver. 13). One of the fundamental needs of mankind is true *ethical* teaching; not the teaching of abstruse dogmas and vain ceremonies, but the teaching of immutable law—the "statutes of God." These statutes are not only written on paper, but on every page of Nature's magnificent volume, and on the tablets of human reason and conscience. "Do unto others as ye would have others do unto you." Genuine disciples of such teaching will evermore act rightly towards themselves, towards their fellow-men, and towards their God.

II. A GREAT NATIONAL WICKEDNESS. Possessing all these privileges, how acted these people—not merely the people of Israel, but the people of Judah as well? Was the sentiment of worship and justice regnant within them? Were they loyal to all that is beautiful, true, and good? Nay. 1. They *rejected God.* " They would not hear, but hardened their necks, like to the neck of their fathers, that did not believe in the Lord their God," etc. (vers. 14, 15). They declined the study of his statutes, and renounced his claim on their devotion. 2. They *adopted idols.* Mark: (1) The *earnestness* of their idolatry. With what unremitting zeal they promoted the cause of idolatry! " The children of Israel did secretly those things that were not right against the Lord their God, and they built them high places in all their cities" (ver. 9). It is also stated, "They made them molten images, even two calves, and made a grove, and worshipped all the host of heaven, and served Baal" (ver. 16). Error on this earth is more active than truth, wrong is more industrious than right, the spirit of evil knows no rest, it goes to and fro on the face of the earth. Here, then, is national wickedness. Are we, as a country, less wicked than the nation of Israel? I trow not. True, we are all, for the most part, theoretical theists, but how many practical atheists? For England to a large extent ignores the Almighty. It might be said of most of us, "God is not in all our thoughts."

> "With lips they own him Master, in life oppose his Word;
> They every day deny him, and yet they call him 'Lord;'
> No more is their religion like his in life and deed
> Than painted grain on canvas is like the living seed."

(2) The *cruelty* of their idolatry. "And they caused their sons and daughters to pass through the fire, and used divination and enchantments, and sold themselves to do evil in the sight of the Lord" (ver. 17).

III. GREAT NATIONAL RUIN. "Therefore the Lord was very angry with Israel, and removed them out of his sight" (ver. 18); "The Lord rejected all the seed of Israel, and afflicted them, and delivered them into the hand of spoilers, until he had cast them out of his sight" (ver. 20). 1. Their ruin involved the entire loss of *their country*. "So was Israel carried away out of their own land to Assyria unto this day" (ver. 23). Expatriation is an enormous trial. 2. Their ruin involved the loss of their *national existence*. "The Lord removed them out of his sight" (ver. 18). The ten tribes are gone, and it may be doubted whether they were ever worth looking after, for they were a miserable type of humanity. "The kingdom of the ten tribes," says Dr. Blackie, "was never restored, nor did the dispersed of Israel ever attempt to return in a body to their land." More than two hundred years of idolatry and wickedness have been followed by more than two thousand years of dispersion and alienation. Having said in their hearts to God, 'Depart from us!' God said to them, 'Depart from me!' The divorce was completed, and till a reconciliation shall take place, its sad, dark fruits must remain. 3. Their ruin involved the *retributive agency of Heaven*. The Assyrians were only the instruments. It is God's plan to punish the wicked by the wicked. No wonder that amid so gross a perversion of the worship of the true God, and the national propensity to do reverence to idols, the Divine patience was exhausted, and that the God whom they had forsaken by violating covenant, an adherence to which formed their title to the occupation of Canaan, permitted them to go into captivity, that they might learn the difference between his service and that of their despotic conquerors.—D. T.

Vers. 24—41.—*Subjects worth thinking about.* "And the King of Assyria brought men from Babylon," etc. This fragment of Israelitish history brings under our notice four subjects which run through all human history, and which find their illustration in the events of modern as well as ancient life.

I. THE TYRANNY OF MAN. Here we find the Assyrians committing two great enormities on the men of Israel—driving them out of their own land into Assyria, and taking possession of their own country and home. "And the King of Assyria brought men from Babylon, and from Cuthah, and from Ava, and from Hamath, and from Sepharvaim, and placed them in the cities of Samaria instead of the children of Israel: and they possessed Samaria, and dwelt in the cities thereof." Who that King of Assyria was at this time who carried away the last remnant of the ten tribes into a foreign land, and brought from various parts of his own country men to occupy their property and their homes, whether Shalmaneser or Esarhaddon, is a question not worth debating. He was a tyrant. The places from which he selected the men whom he placed in the cities of Samaria are mentioned. Cuthah, a city about fifteen miles north-east from Babylon; Ava, situated on the Euphrates, to the north of Babylon; Hamath, the chief city of Upper Syria; and Sepharvaim, supposed to be on a branch stream from the Euphrates, lying about sixteen miles from Babylon. Now, there was tyranny in both cases. There was tyranny in taking the Assyrians from their own countries and placing them in the cities of Samaria; as well as tyranny in taking away the ten tribes from

Samaria into foreign regions. Had the exchange taken place with the mutual consent of both parties, there would have been no outrage on the rights of man, but it might, indeed, have conduced to the interests of both parties concerned. Men are constantly changing their countries, especially in this age, when facilities for travelling are increasing every day, when the old countries are becoming over-populated, their resources rapidly decreasing, and new and fertile regions opening up in every part of the globe. All this is right enough, as well as often necessary and truly expedient. But to be forced away from home, this is tyranny, and such tyranny is not extinct even in our England. The tens of thousands that leave our shores every year for strange and distant lands, for the most part do it by a terrible coercion. Not only is he a tyrant who inflicts positive injustice on another, but also he who withholds from another his due. Tyranny is not confined to the throne of despots, but it sits in every heart where there is not a practical regard for the rights of others. It is in Belgravian mansions and ducal castles, where the groans of starving millions around are disregarded, as well as in the palace of the Czar of Russia, where the rights of millions are trodden underfoot.

> " Thinkest thou there is no tyranny but that
> Of blood and chains? The despotism of vice,
> The weakness and the wickedness of luxury,
> The negligence, the apathy, the evils
> Of sensual sloth—produce ten thousand tyrants,
> Whose delegated cruelty surpasses
> The worst acts of one energetic master,
> However harsh and hard in his own bearing."
> (Byron.)

II. THE RETRIBUTIONS OF LIFE. "And so it was at the beginning of their dwelling there, that they feared not the Lord : therefore the Lord sent lions among them, which slew some of them. Wherefore they spake to the King of Assyria, saying, The nations which thou hast removed, and placed in the cities of Samaria, know not the manner of the God of the land: therefore he hath sent lions among them, and, behold, they slay them, because they know not the manner of the God of the land." Probably the lions had been in the land of Samaria before the settlement of the Assyrian colonists, but after their settlement these furious beasts of prey seem to have 'been multiplied. Perhaps the colonists were too few in number to keep them down and to check their increase. Still, whatever the natural cause or causes of their increase, it was regarded by the new population as a retributive visitation. The statement of the courtiers to the king was, " The nations which thou hast removed, and placed in the cities of Samaria, know not the manner of the God of the land : therefore he hath sent lions among them," etc. The law of retribution is ever at work in human history, not only in the lives of nations, but in the lives of individuals. No man can do a wrong thing without suffering for it in some form or other. Nemesis surely, though silently, treads on the heels of wrong. " Whatsoever a man soweth, that shall he also reap." The lions of retribution track our steps as sinners stealthily, and are ready to spring on us at any moment. We are far enough from saying that retribution here is adequate and complete ; hence there is within all a "fearful looking for" of some future judgment. We do not fully discharge the debt ; as we go on it accumulates, and there is a balance to be settled in the great hereafter. Albeit the retribution here is a foretaste and pledge of a judgment to come.

> " Nature has her laws,
> That will not brook infringement; in all time,
> All circumstances, all state, in every clime
> She holds aloft the same avenging sword,
> And, sitting on her boundless throne sublime,
> The vials of her wrath, with Justice stored,
> Shall in her own good hour on all that's ill be poured."
> (Percival.)

III. THE PROSTITUTION OF RELIGION. The Assyrian king, it would seem, in answer to the alarm which was felt concerning the colonists whom he had settled in the cities of Samaria, conceived the plan of adopting religion as the remedy. " Then the King of

Assyria commanded, saying, Carry thither one of the priests whom ye brought from thence; and let them go and dwell there, and let him teach them the manner of the God of the land." The priest whom the king sent to them seems to have been one of the exiled priests who had formerly had his head-quarters at Bethel. It is not said this priest took a copy of the Pentateuch with him; perhaps he trusted to his religious intelligence and to his oral abilities. The fact of his being one of the exiled priests, and being settled in Bethel, would imply that he was not a Levite, but rather one of the calf-worshipping priests; his instructions, therefore, would most likely not be very sound or useful. Now, the question is, why did this Assyrian king introduce this religion? Not because he or his people *had any faith in it*. "Howbeit every nation made gods of their own, and put them in the houses of the high places which the Samaritans had made, every nation in their cities wherein they dwelt," etc. (vers. 29—31). Several of the gods of these people are here mentioned. "*Succoth-benoth*." The meaning of this word, which is thought to be "tents or booths of daughters," might seem to point to the places where the Babylonians celebrated impure rites; but here it represents one of the deities. "*Nergal*" is said to have been worshipped under the form of a cock; and from Layard, in his work on Nineveh and Babylon, we find that a cock was sometimes associated with a priest on the Assyrian monuments. "*Ashima*," according to some, was worshipped under the form of a he-goat, bald to the very skin. "*Nibhaz*." This deity was represented in the figure of a dog. "*Tartak*." According to the rabbis, this deity was represented in the form of an ass. "*Adrammelech*." This means the "fire-king," who was worshipped as a sun-god. "*Anammelech*," a deity worshipped, some say in the form of a hare, and some say in the form of a goat.[1] These were the gods in which the king and the colonists seem to have had faith, and not in the one true and living God. Why, then, did the king send this priest from Bethel to impart to them a knowledge of the God of Israel? Simply as a matter of *selfish policy*. The attention that they paid to any representation that the priest made of the true God was partial, insincere, and selfish. "So they feared the Lord, and made unto themselves of the lowest of them priests of the high places, which sacrificed for them in the houses of the high places. They feared the Lord, and served their own gods, after the manner of the nations whom they carried away from thence. Unto this day they do after the former manners," etc. Here you have one of the million examples of that *religion of policy* that has abounded in all lands and times. In every page in history, nay, in every scene of life, we find religion taken up as a means to an end, rather than as the grand end of being. Some use it as a means for secular advantage, others as a means for personal salvation—what is called the salvation of the soul. Rulers employ it as a means to govern the people, and priests employ it as a means to coerce men into ecclesiastical order or conventional morality. In such cases their own personal interests are by no means ignored. This is a prostitution of religion. True religion should ever be pursued as the supreme end of man. In it alone his highest obligations are fulfilled, his full powers employed, his true destiny realized. But, alas! everywhere we find it regarded as a subsidiary and partial element in man's calculations, experience, and life. What is here said applies to millions even in Christendom. "They feared the Lord, and served their own gods." The religion of policy will never rescue man from the rapacious jaws of the lions of retribution.

IV. THE THEISTIC HUNGER OF SOULS. All these men, both the colonists and the Israelites, would have their gods; a god seemed to them as necessary almost as their life. "So these nations feared the Lord, and served their graven images, both their children, and their children's children: as did their fathers, so do they unto this day." The same hunger for worship which the generations that preceded them possessed and developed had been transmitted to these their children as an innate force in their spiritual constitution. The religious element in man is not a passing sentiment, not a traditional belief, not something superadded to his nature. It is the very core of his being, the substratum in which all his higher faculties inhere. He who has this element in him (and who has not?) needs no argument to prove the existence of a God. If it be alive within him, all such arguments are an impertinence. The existence of a Supreme Being is independent of all proof. It is written on the consciousness of human

---

[1] See Layard on Nineveh and Babylon; and Rawlinson's 'Ancient Monarchies.'

nature. Like the fact of our own being, it is too near, too evident, too much a matter of living self, for outward argument to have any force. Faith in God springs from within. It is based on those immutable sentiments of the soul that outlive all theories and defy all scepticism. To deny the existence of God is to offer violence to all that is great and sacred in human nature.—D. T.

Vers. 1—6.—*The end of the kingdom of Israel.* We learn from the inscriptions that Hoshea, the murderer of Pekah, only secured his throne by acknowledging the supremacy of the King of Assyria. It was not long, however, before he conspired to achieve his independence. This led to the final overthrow of the kingdom.

I. A LAST FLICKER. 1. *Hoshea's better character.* It is said of this last King of Israel that he did evil in the sight of the Lord, "but not as the kings of Israel that were before him." The testimony rather points to the great wickedness of the earlier kings than implies any exceptional virtue in Hoshea, who came to the throne by blood, and showed no more reliance on God than the others. His character, however, must have had some redeeming qualities. Possibly he tried to check some of the excesses of wickedness in the land, and to discountenance at least foreign idolatries. The unfavourable judgment we are sometimes compelled to pass on men's characters as a whole need not blind us to what is praiseworthy in them. 2. *A hopeless task.* It is both curious and pathetic to see this last flicker of a better disposition in the kings of Israel just before the end. But even had Hoshea been a better ruler than he was, it was probably now too late to do the nation any good. Every attempt to bring the people back to God had proved in vain, and corruption had reached a height which made a crisis inevitable. The carcase was there, and the vultures were preparing to descend upon it. We have a modern example in the state of the French nation prior to the great Revolution. A nation, like an individual, has its day of grace, and if that is sinned away there remains only " a fearful looking for of judgment " (Heb. x. 27).

II. BROKEN ENGAGEMENTS. 1. *A policy of double-dealing.* Hoshea's desire from the first was to free his land from the yoke of Assyria. Some attempt of this kind, probably at the death of Tiglath-pileser, brought down upon him the new king, Shalmaneser, who compelled his submission, and exacted tribute. But Hoshea was not faithful to his engagements. While still pretending loyalty to Shalmaneser, he was carrying on a system of intrigue with So, King of Egypt (Sabaco). They "made a covenant with the Assyrians," and at the same time "oil was carried into Egypt" (Hos. xii. 1). It was not God Hoshea trusted in, but an alliance with Egypt. He relied on treachery, on double-dealing, on clever intrigue, to get him out of his difficulties. This kind of policy never permanently succeeds. 2. *Open revolt.* When Hoshea thought himself strong enough, he threw off his allegiance to Shalmaneser. He brought him no present, as he had done year by year. He was playing a desperate game, but he seems to have thought himself secure. A people is justified in rebellion against foreign authority when it is strong enough to make success probable ; but God's blessing could hardly be looked for on an attempt which was cradled in duplicity, and in which God himself was totally ignored. 3. *A bruised reed.* As might have been anticipated, So failed Hoshea in his hour of need. His "oil" and other presents had been sent in vain. The King of Assyria came against him; but there was no movement on the part of Egypt for his help. He had trusted in the staff of a bruised reed (ch. xviii. 21). How manifold are the disappointments of those who rely on "the help of man" (Ps. lx. 11), and put their "trust in princes" (Ps. cxlvi. 3) ! Hoshea himself was captured, and shut up in prison. His ultimate fate we do not know.

III. FINAL RUIN. 1. *The siege of Samaria.* The King of Assyria now marched against Samaria, which bravely held out for three years. Had details been given us, it would no doubt have been found that this was one of the great sieges of history—great in its horrors, as well as in its after-results. We may picture the extremities of the famine of ch. vi. repeated with additional horrors of anarchy and bloodshed ; or, with perhaps more truth, we may draw our ideas of this siege from the descriptions of the siege of Jerusalem by Nebuchadnezzar (cf. ch. xxiv., xxv.). That was the concluding act in the history of the southern kingdom, as this was the concluding act in the history of the northern. Both were long-delayed, and in the end terrible judgments of God. The cup of iniquity was full, and another cup—the cup of God's wrath—

was now put into the nation's hand (cf. Ps. lxxv. 8). The city at length fell, and the final blow descended. 2. *The captivity of the tribes.* We read on the monuments that, after the fall of Samaria, the King of Egypt, alarmed probably for his own safety, approached, and was defeated by Sargon, Shalmaneser's successor. In any case, help was now unavailing for the unhappy Israelites. The children of Israel were removed from their cities, and carried away captive into Assyria, being scattered up and down in the places named. 27,280, according to Sargon, were taken from Samaria alone. What sorrow was here! Torn from their land, exiles from house and home, forced to eat unclean things in Assyria (Hos. ix. 3, 4), their national existence extinguished, ruled by the heathen,—all because, when they knew God, they would not glorify him as God, but gave his glory to dumb idols, and defiled his land with their abominations, and misused the gifts he had so richly bestowed on them (cf. Hos. ii.).—J. O.

Vers. 7—23.—*Review of the history of Israel.* The Bible does not simply relate, but draws aside the veil and shows us the innermost springs of God's providence, and how they work. It teaches us to understand the deepest causes of the rise and fall of nations. The causes it insists on are not economical, or political, or intellectual, but religious, and its lessons are for all time. We may say of this survey of Israel's history—these things "are written for our admonition, upon whom the ends of the world are come" (1 Cor. x. 11). We have here—

I. MANIFOLD PROVOCATIONS. 1. *Ingratitude to God.* This is put in the foreground. It was the Lord " their God " Israel had sinned against—the God who had brought them up from Egypt, who had delivered them from bondage, who had made a nation of them, who had given them a land to dwell in, who had bound them to himself by solemn covenant. What people were ever under stronger obligations to obedience! Yet they apostatized, and "feared other gods." Sin appears more heinous against a background of mercies received. It is worse for a nation that has known God, that has possessed pure ordinances, and has been graciously dealt with by him, to backslide, than for another that has been less favoured. Our own nation has been blessed in these respects as few have been or are. Correspondingly great are our responsibilities. The individual may reflect that the fact of spiritual redemption—salvation through Christ—places him under greater obligations than could spring from any temporal deliverance. 2. *Heathenish ways.* The positive wickedness of the people is next detailed. The heart of man cannot exist without an object to fill and occupy it; and if God is neglected, something else must be found to take his place. The Israelites rejected Jehovah, but they took to following idols. They would have none of his statutes, but they walked in the statutes of the heathen, and of the kings of Israel. It is to be remembered that the heathen worships here referred to were saturated through and through with lust and vileness. It was because of the nameless abominations connected with them that the Lord, after long forbearance, cast out the former inhabitants from Canaan (Lev. xviii. 24—32; xx. 1—6). Yet these were the ways into which Israel turned back in the land which God had given them. May we not fear as we think of the vices, the impurities, the filthy abominations, which abound in our own nation? 3. *Zeal in the service of idols.* Israel had no heart for the service of God, but they showed unbounded zeal in the service of their idols. Publicly, and in secret also, in every city, on every hill, and under every green tree, wherever even there was a watchman's solitary tower, there they set up their high places, burnt incense, and " wrought wicked things to provoke the Lord to anger." The children of light may well learn a lesson from the children of this world in respect of zeal. If only one tithe of the earnestness with which men serve the devil were put into the service of God, how rapid would be the spread of true religion! The wicked throw the whole energy of their souls into their follies, their pursuit of pleasure, their service of the world, the devil, and the flesh. But how slack-handed and half-hearted oftentimes are Christians! What wonder God's cause suffers!

II. REJECTION OF PROPHETS. 1. *God's prophets sent.* God did not leave Israel to sin without trying every means to turn the people from their evil ways. Prophets were sent, and these not one or two, but "all the prophets" and "all the seers." They were sent both to Israel and to Judah. They spoke in God's Name to the people, testified against their sins, and exhorted them to return to the ways of right. They warned them also of the consequences of disobedience (ver. 23). Thus it was shown that God has no pleasure in the death of him that dieth (Ezek. xviii. 32). The fact of warning being given is a great aggravation of guilt if sin is persisted in. It leaves the transgressor without excuse. In our own land warnings abound. The Bible is widely circulated, the gospel is faithfully preached; there is no lack of voices proclaiming the need and duty of repentance. If men perish, it is not in ignorance. They sin against light, and their blood is on their own heads. 2. *Their testimony rejected.* The efforts of the prophets to bring the people back to God proved unavailing. No heed was paid to their warnings; rather the people grew bolder and more daring in sin. If faithful counsel does not soften, it hardens. Judged by outward results, no class of preachers ever had less success than the Hebrew prophets. Their exhortations seemed as water spilt upon the ground. Yet through them was preserved and kept alive in the nation a remnant according to grace (Rom. xi. 5), and to it belonged the great future of God's promises. The stubbornness of the Jewish character was proverbial—they were, and had ever been, a stiff-necked people. The root of their evil was they "did not believe in the Lord their God." When they did believe, the same basis of character discovers itself in their unyielding tenacity and perseverance in serving God and obeying the dictates of their conscience (cf. Dan. iii.). 3. *Aggravated wickedness.* The people latterly threw off all restraint in the practice of their evil. It was no longer "secretly," but openly, that they rejected the statutes of the Lord their God and his covenant, and the testimonies which he testified against them. It but aggravated the evil that in name they still claimed him as their God, and professed to do him honour, while in reality they had "left all his commandments," and had changed the whole substance of his religion. The form is nothing if the heart is wanting (Matt. xv. 7—9); but the Israelites changed even the form. They went after vanity, and became vain, imitating the heathen who were round about them, and unblushingly introducing the worst heathen abominations into their own worship. (1) They changed the fundamental law of Israel in making molten images—intended to represent Jehovah, no doubt, but still idols—Baalim. (2) They imported the Phœnician Baal-worship, with its pillars and asheras, and its licentious rites—another direct violation of fundamental laws. (3) They went further afield, and imported from Babylonia or Assyria the worship of "the host of heaven"—another thing directly forbidden on pain of death (Deut. xvii. 2—7). (4) Still unsatisfied, they abandoned themselves to the horrid rites of Moloch, and to the practice of every kind of divination and enchantment—the last and lowest stage in a people's religious degradation. This also was most emphatically forbidden to the Israelites under the most severe penalties (Lev. xx. 1—6). Thus they literally "sold" themselves to do evil, throwing off all shame or pretence of regard for God's authority, and became confirmed and wedded to their evil ways. In heart and outward conduct they had absolutely and utterly apostatized from God, and seemed bent only on provoking him to anger. Instead of marvelling at their final rejection, one wonders how a holy God should have borne with them so long. But is not God's patience with sinners and peoples still just as wonderful? Their iniquities literally go up to heaven before he cuts them off.

III. JUSTICE NO LONGER TARRYING. If the Lord's justice tarries, it does not sleep. And when the blow does fall, it is all the more severe that it has been so long delayed. 1. *Israel rejected.* This people had rejected God, and God now rejected them, as he had from the first threatened he would do (Lev. xxvi. 14—29). He did not cast them off without the warning afforded by many premonitory judgments. But when neither judgment nor mercy was regarded, and the cup of their transgression was brimming over, he gave them up, and "cast them out of his sight." They were carried away out of their own land to Assyria, and never, as a nation, returned. 2. *Judah not taking warning.* The sad thing was that Judah also, which had begun to walk in the same paths, did not take warning by the fall of the sister kingdom. "The princes of Judah were like them that remove the bound" (Hos. v. 10), and many warnings directed to Judah mingle with the prophetic denunciations of Israel. Yet, notwithstanding partial reformations, the people did not repent. The sight is not unparalleled. If wicked men could be deterred from sin, or led to repentance, by warnings, these are never wanting. History and experience bear uniform testimony that it is well with the righteous, ill with the wicked; men have daily examples of the ruinous effects of vice before their eyes; yet they go on heedless and blinded. It is not a question of reason, but of evil inclination, and wrong bent of will. Sin is truly named folly—it is the absolute unwisdom. 3. *The origin of the mischief.* Again, the source of all these evils which came on Israel is traced to Jeroboam's fatal step in setting up the two calves. It was he who "drave Israel from following the Lord, and made them sin a great sin." One step in the wrong direction carries many others in its train. That act of Jeroboam had in the heart of it a principle which logically meant the overthrow of the theocracy. It was not only a violation of the fundamental law of the second commandment; but it was an act of self-will in religion; the assertion of the right to set human will above God's ordinances, and change and alter them at pleasure. Once a principle of that kind is introduced and acted on, it cannot be prevented from logically working itself out. The consequences of a wrong step stretch far beyond the results immediately seen or intended.—J. O.

Vers. 24—41.—*Heathen occupants of the land.* The narrative of the fall of the northern kingdom concludes with an account of the arrangements made by the King of Assyria for resettling the land of Israel.

I. THE NEW SETTLERS. 1. *Their foreign origin.* The policy of removing rebellious populations to distant parts—at this time a favourite one with the Assyrians—led not only to the Israelites being carried away to Assyria, but to foreign settlers being brought and put down in their place. The nationalities of the new inhabitants are mentioned. They were men from Babylon, and Cuthah, and Ava, and Hamath, and Sepharvaim. These took possession of the cities of Samaria, and dwelt in them. Behold now God's holy land in the possession of aliens, men without one glimmer of knowledge of the true God and his ways! The Israelites had become heathen in heart, and were removed, and now real heathen were put in their place. In the sight of God the latter were less objectionable than the former. They had never known anything better than heathenism; while the Israelites had sinned against the clearest light and the strongest love. In the judgment-day, the heathen will rise up to condemn those who have abused the light of revelation (Matt. xii. 41). 2. *The visitation of lions.* Thick darkness had now settled on the land. Even the outward worship of Jehovah had ceased, and the only gods known were those of the heathen colonists. Yet the land was Jehovah's, and however he might "wink" at the ignorance of a rude, uninstructed people, it was not meet that something should not be done to arouse them to inquiry. The removal of the former inhabitants seems to have led to the multiplication of lions, and these now began to attack the people in a way which convinced them that the God of the land was displeased with them. It is not only the colonists who took this view of the matter. The sacred writer gives the same interpretation. God has his own ways of speaking to the consciences of men, and this was the one now adopted. The people were right in seeing in the visitation a reminder of their neglect of "the manner of the God of the land;" they were wrong in thinking that all that was necessary to remedy this neglect was the performance of certain external rites. It was moral conduct, based on a right knowledge of himself, which "the God of the land" required. But their error was only part of their dark heathen superstition. 3. *Their request for instruction.* The people were much concerned about the visitation which had befallen them, and their case was reported at once to the King of Assyria, who sent them one of the priests who had been carried away captive, to teach them "how they should fear the Lord." Alas! how shall the blind lead the blind! This priest was himself one who had no right knowledge of Jehovah. He was doubtless one of the priests of Bethel, who had been mixed up with the calf-worship and all the other sins for which Israel had been carried away. It is evident from the results that he gave the people no right instruction. He probably set up again at the Bethel sanctuary the disused rites of the former idolatry, and taught the people some external observances connected with the Name of Jehovah. A religion so deeply corrupted was hardly better than those they already practised. Jehovah remained to them a local deity, of whose real character they knew nothing, and whom they served from motives of fear.

II. MIXED RELIGIONS. 1. *Extraordinary syncretism.* An extraordinary scene was now witnessed. The new-comers, once settled in their cities, lost no time in organizing their religions—in this, at all events, setting an example to more enlightened peoples.

The high places formerly used by the Israelites stood temptingly ready to receive the new idols. Whatever may have been the character of the priest's instructions, they had no influence in checking the multiplication of strange gods. In the mixture of peoples, each nationality adhered to its own deity. The Babylonians made Succoth-benoth, the Cuthites made Nergal, the men of Hamath made Ashima, etc. The result was a chaotic confusion of religions, such as perhaps has never before or since been equalled. The new worships needed priests, and these were made from the lowest of the people. The whole is a sad but instructive picture of heathenism in its want of internal unity, its Babel-like confusion, its destitution of moral character, and its degrading and cruel practices, e.g. the burning of the children in the fire to Adrammelech, etc. Only monotheism can give true unity to life, religion, and worship. 2. *Jehovah and strange gods.* Meanwhile Jehovah was not overlooked, but had his place given him among the rest. The people "feared the Lord, and served their own gods." This showed, of course, that the first principles of the religion of Jehovah were not understood by them. But is it so uncommon a thing for men—not heathen, but professedly Christian—thus to attempt to combine incompatibilities? Is there not such a thing as attempting to combine the service of the Lord with the friendship of the world, which yet is declared to be "enmity with God" (Jas. iv. 4)? Is there no such thing as professing to serve God, yet giving the chief place in the heart to money, pleasure, fashion, or some other spiritual idol, which is duly worshipped upon its own high place? The less glaring idolatries are not always the least sinful. Ere condemning the irrational practices of these heathen, let us sit strictly in judgment on ourselves. 3. *The absence of true religion.* The cause of all this religious confusion was that the true God was not rightly known. Men may possess theoretically correct notions of God, and not act upon them; but it is impossible to base a right moral or religious life on conceptions of God which are fundamentally erroneous. These colonists did not know Jehovah's real character; they had not been properly instructed in his statutes; therefore they thought they were serving him when they were doing him the highest dishonour.

III. A PAST MEMORY. 1. *God's ancient covenant.* The sight of this indescribable chaos recalls to the historian the memory of that original covenant of God with Israel, by the terms of which the people were pledged not to serve strange gods, but to adhere to Jehovah, their Redeemer from Egypt, and to keep his holy statutes. Had they been faithful to that covenant, how different would have been the result! Instead of being in exile, the nation would have been safe, happy, and prosperous under Jehovah's care. 2. *The melancholy contrast.* As it was, the people had been driven from their land, and this motley crowd of heathen held possession of it. Their obedience was not better than that of the rejected Israelites, and, so far as experience had gone, they showed no sign of improvement. It is due, however, to the Samaritans to say that, when better instructed, they did improve, and, in Christ's time, they were as strict monotheists as the Jews, and more willing to receive the gospel.—J. O.

EXPOSITION.

Ch. xviii.—xxv.—THE HISTORY OF THE KINGDOM OF JUDAH AFTER THE FALL OF SAMARIA.

CHAPTER XVIII.

Ver. 1—ch. xix. 37.—THE ACCESSION OF HEZEKIAH. HIS SUCCESSES. HIS WAR WITH SENNACHERIB.

Vers. 1—8.—THE EARLY YEARS OF HEZE-KIAH. From his narrative of the destruction of the kingdom of Samaria, the writer turns, with evident relief, to the accession of the good king Hezekiah in Judah, and to a brief account of (1) his religious reformation

(vers. 3—6); (2) his revolt from Assyria (ver. 7); and (3) his war with the Philistines (ver. 8). The narrative is still exceedingly brief, and has to be filled out from the Second Book of Chronicles, where the religious reformation of Hezekiah is treated with great fulness (ch. xxix.—xxxi.).

Ver. 1.—**Now it came to pass in the third year of Hoshea son of Elah King of Israel, that Hezekiah the son of Ahaz King of Judah began to reign.** There can scarcely be any doubt of this synchronism, which is in close accordance with the dates in vers. 9, 10 of this chapter, and agrees well with the Assyrian inscriptions. Hezekiah's accession may be placed almost certainly in B.C. 727.

Ver. 2.—**Twenty and five years old was he when he began to reign** (on the difficulties connected with this statement, and the best mode of meeting them, see the comment upon ch. xvi. 1); **and he reigned twenty and nine years in Jerusalem.** So Josephus ('Ant. Jud.,' x. 3. § 1), and the author of Chronicles (2 Chron. xxix. 1).. He reigned fourteen years before his severe illness, and fifteen afterwards. **His mother's name also was Abi.** *Abi,* "my father," is scarcely a possible name. We must, therefore, correct Kings by Chronicles, and regard her true name as Abijah, which means "Jehovah is my father" (compare "Abiel"). **The daughter of Zachariah.** Perhaps the Zechariah of Isa. viii. 2.

Ver. 3.—**And he did that which was right in the sight of the Lord, according to all that David his father did.** Such unqualified praise is only assigned to two other kings of Judah—Asa (1 Kings xv. 11) and Josiah (ch. xxii. 2). It is curious that all three were the sons of wicked fathers. Hezekiah was probably, at an early age, brought under the influence of Isaiah, who was on familiar terms with his father Ahaz (Isa. vii. 3—16), and would be likely to do all that lay in his power to turn Hezekiah from his father's evil ways, and to foster all the germs of good in his character.

Ver. 4.—**He removed the high places.** This was a comparatively late step in Hezekiah's religious reformation. He began, as we learn from Chronicles (2 Chron. xxix. 3, 17), "in the first year of his reign, the first month, and the first day," by reopening the temple, which Ahaz had shut up, removing from it all the "filthiness" which Ahaz had allowed to accumulate (2 Chron. xxix. 5), gathering together the priests and Levites and exhorting them (2 Chron. xxix. 4—11), restoring and renewing the vessels which Ahaz had cut in pieces (2 Chron. xxix. 19), and then re-establishing the temple-worship with all due solemnity (2 Chron. xxix. 20—35). He next resolved on holding a grand Passover-festival, in the second month, as it had not been possible to keep it in the first (2 Chron. xxx. 2, 3), and invited thereto, not only his own subjects, but the Israelites of the neighbouring kingdom who were not yet carried off, but were still under the rule of Hoshea (2 Chron. xxx. 10, 11, 18). It was not until this festival was over that the removal of the high places was taken in hand. Then, in a fit of zeal, which no doubt the king encouraged, a multitude of those who had kept the feast went forth

from Jerusalem, first into the cities of Judah and Benjamin, and then into several of the cities of Israel, and "brake the images in pieces, and cut down the groves, and threw down the high places and the altars, . . . and utterly destroyed them all" (see 2 Chron. xxxi. 1). **And brake the images, and cut down the groves;** literally, *the grove,* according to the present text; but, as all the versions have the plural, Thenius thinks אֲשֵׁרִים should be changed into אֲשֵׁרִים. Keil and Bähr, on the contrary, would retain the singular, but understand it "collectively." That idolatry was practised at some of the high places seems clear from this place, as well as from 1 Kings xiv. 23. **And brake in pieces the brazen serpent that Moses had made** (see Numb. xxi. 9). Difficulties are raised with respect to this statement. Some argue that the serpent, having served its purpose, would have been left hanging at the place where it was set up in the wilderness; others, that Moses would have destroyed it, lest the Israelites should make it an idol; others, again, that it was not likely to have lasted seven hundred years from the Exodus, even if it was brought into Palestine and taken care of. It is supposed, therefore, that an imitation of the original serpent had been made by the Jews in the reign of Ahaz, had been called "the serpent of Moses," and was now destroyed. But there is no sufficient reason for any of these suppositions. Considering what the serpent typified (John iii. 14), it is not surprising that Moses should have been instructed to preserve it with the furniture of the tabernacle, or that, when once attached to that structure, it should have been preserved as a religious relic for seven hundred years. Many Egyptian figures in bronze now exist which are from three thousand to four thousand years old. The statement of the writer of Kings, that Hezekiah did now destroy "the serpent *that Moses had made,*" is of more weight than a thousand speculations concerning what is likely, or not likely, to have happened. **For unto those days the children of Israel did burn incense to it.** Not, certainly, "from Moses' time to Hezekiah's," but from a date left vague and undetermined to the time when Hezekiah took his religious reformation in hand. Hezekiah found the practice continuing; the writer is not concerned to say—perhaps does not know—when it began. He implies, however, that it was of long standing. Serpent-worship was widely spread in the East, and there was more excuse for directing religious regard toward this serpent than toward any other. **And he called it Nehushtan;** rather, *and it was called Nehushtan.* יִקְרָא is a singular with indefinite subject ("one called"), equivalent to "they called," or "it was called" (comp. Gen. xxv. 26; xxxviii. 29, 30). Nehushtan is not from נחש "serpent," but from נחשת, "brass," and means "the little brass thing," ן being a diminutive, expression of tenderness.

Ver. 5.—**He trusted in the Lord God of Israel.** Unlike Hoshea (see homiletics on ch. xvii. 1—4), unlike Ahaz (ch. xvi. 7—10), Hezekiah discarded trust in man, and—it may be after some hesitation—put his trust wholly in God. This was exactly what God required as the condition on which he would give his aid (Isa. xxx. 1—7), and what no previous king since the Assyrian troubles began could bring himself to do. **So that after him was none like him among all the kings of Judah, nor any that were before him.** It has been concluded from this statement that, "when the merits of the kings were summed up after the fall of the monarchy, Hezekiah was, by a deliberate judgment, put at the very top" (Stanley 'Lectures on the Jewish Church,' vol. ii. p. 397); but, as exactly the same words are used of Josiah in ch. xxiii. 25, the true conclusion would seem to be rather that Hezekiah and Josiah were selected from the rest, and placed upon a par, above all the others. At first sight there may seem to be contradiction between the two passages, since absolute pre-eminence over *all* the other kings is ascribed to Hezekiah in one of them, to Josiah in the other; but the context shows that the pre-eminence is not the same in the two cases. To Hezekiah is ascribed pre-eminence in *trust*; to Josiah, pre-eminence in an exact observance of the Law: one excels in faith, the other in works; Josiah's whole life is one of activity, Hezekiah's great merit lies in his being content, in the crisis of his fate, to "stand still, and see the salvation of God."

Ver. 6.—**For he clave to the Lord**—rather, *and he clave to the Lord;* i.e. he persevered through the whole of his life; he did not fall into sins at the last, like Asa and Azariah (see 2 Chron. xvi. 7—12; xxvi. 16—21)—and **departed not from following him.** The writer probably considers "the princes of Judah" answerable for the embassy to Egypt mentioned in Isa. xxx. 4, and excuses Hezekiah's ostentatious display of his treasures to the ambassadors of Merodach-Baladan (ch. xx. 13) as a weakness, not an actual breach of obedience. **But kept his commandments, which the Lord commanded Moses.**

Ver. 7.—**And the Lord was with him.** Of no other King of Judah or Israel is this said, except only of David (2 Sam. v. 10). It was the promise made to Moses (Exod. iii. 12), repeated to Joshua (Josh. i. 5, 7), and by implication given in them to all those who would rule his people faithfully (comp. 2

Chron. xv. 2). **And he prospered whithersoever he went forth;** rather, *in all his goings—in cunctis ad quæ procedebat* (Vulgate). Hezekiah's prosperity is enlarged upon by the writer of Chronicles, who says (2 Chron. xxxii. 27—30), "And Hezekiah had exceeding much riches and honour: and he made himself treasuries for silver, and for gold, and for precious stones, and for spices, and for shields, and for all manner of pleasant jewels; storehouses also for the increase of corn, and wine, and oil; and stalls for all manner of beasts, and cotes for flocks. Moreover he provided him cities, and possessions of flocks and herds in abundance: for God had given him substance very much. . . . And Hezekiah prospered in all his works." Many brought presents to him to Jerusalem, and he was magnified in the sight of all the surrounding nations (see 2 Chron. xxxii. 23). **And he rebelled against the King of Assyria, and served him not.** Hezekiah's "rebellion" probably took place at the very commencement of his reign, B.C. 727, in the year that Shalmaneser ascended the throne. Most likely it consisted simply in his withholding his tribute, and neither going in person nor sending representatives to Nineveh, to congratulate the new monarch on his accession. This would be understood as an assertion of independence. That it was not at once resented must be ascribed to Shalmaneser's difficulties with Samaria and with Tyre, which were more pressing, as they lay nearer to Assyria. Before these were over, Sargon usurped the crown. There is reason to believe that he made at least one expedition against Hezekiah; but the date of it is uncertain. Rebellion met him on all sides, and had to be crushed near home before he could venture to deal with it on the remote outskirts of his empire. Meanwhile Hezekiah strengthened himself and built up a considerable power.

Ver. 8.—**He smote the Philistines.** Hezekiah's Philistine war seems to have followed on an attempt which Sargon made to bring the whole country under the Assyrian dominion. Sargon attacked Philistia in B.C. 720, made Gaza and the other towns subject, and committed the custody of them to tributary kings, in whom he had confidence. But opposition soon manifested itself. Sargon's creatures were expelled—Akhimiti from Ashdod, Padi from Ekron. Hezekiah assisted in this war of independence, attacked Sargon's viceroys, and helped the cities to free themselves. About the year B.C. 711 Sargon speaks of a league against Assyria, to which the parties were Philistia, Judæa, Edom, and Moab (' Eponym Canon,' p. 130). The Philistines, whom Hezekiah "smote," must be regarded as Assyrian partisans, whom he chastised in the interests of the national party. He did not seek conquests in Philistia for himself. **Even unto Gaza.** Gaza seems to have remained faithful to Assyria from its capture in B.C. 720. **And the borders thereof, from the tower of the watchmen unto the fenced city.** (On this expression, see the comment upon ch. xvii. 9.)

Vers. 9—12.—THE PUNISHMENT OF SAMARIA FOR DISOBEDIENCE. In contrast with Hezekiah's piety and consequent prosperity, the author places the disobedience (ver. 12) and consequent extinction of the sister kingdom (vers. 9—11), which belonged to Hezekiah's earlier years, and was an event of the greatest importance to him, since it made his dominions conterminous with those of Assyria, and exposed his northern frontier to attack at any moment from the Assyrian forces. According to all probable human calculation, the fall of Samaria should have been followed *at once* by an attack on Judæa; and but for the change of dynasty, and troubles on all sides which ensued thereupon, this would naturally have taken place. As it was, Judæa was allowed a breathing-space, during which she strengthened her power in Philistia (see the comment on the preceding verse), and otherwise prepared herself to resist attack (see 2 Chron. xxxiii. 3—6; Isa. xxii. 8—11).

Ver. 9.—**And it came to pass in the fourth year of King Hezekiah, which was the seventh year of Hoshea son of Elah King of Israel.** Hezekiah began to reign before Hoshea had completed his third year (ver. 1). His first year thus ran parallel with part of Hoshea's third and part of his fourth; his fourth with part of Hoshea's sixth and part of his seventh; his sixth with part of Hoshea's eighth and part of his ninth. **That Shalmaneser King of Assyria came up against Samaria, and besieged it** (see the comment on ch. xvii. 4, 5).

Ver. 10.—**And at the end of three years they took it.** The expression, "at the *end* of three years," does not show that the three years were complete. On the contrary, as the siege began in Hezekiah's fourth year, probably in the spring, and was over in his sixth, say, by the autumn, the entire duration was not more than two years and a half. The plural verb, וַיִּלְכְּדֻהָ, "they took it," is remarkable, since it would have seemed more natural to write וַיִּלְכְּדָהּ, "he took it"—and so the LXX., the Vulgate, and the Syriac—but the writer seems to have known that Shalmaneser did not take it,

but died during the siege, the capture falling into the first year of Sargon (see the 'Eponym Canon,' pp. 65, 66). Even in the sixth year of Hezekiah, that is the ninth year of Hoshea King of Israel (see the comment on ver. 9), **Samaria was taken** (comp. ch. xvii. 6).

Ver. 11.—**And the King of Assyria**—*i.e.* Sargon—**did carry away Israel unto Assyria** —the empire, not the country—**and put them in Halah and in Habor by the river of Gozan, and in the cities of the Medes** (see the comment on ch. xvii. 6).

Ver. 12.—**Because they obeyed not the voice of the Lord their God, but transgressed his covenant, and all that Moses the servant of the Lord commanded, and would not hear them, nor do them** (compare the expanded version of this statement in ch. xvii. 7—23). The sin of Samaria may be summed up under three heads: (1) disobedience; (2) breach of the covenant; and (3) disregard of Moses, and the other "servants of the Lord."

Vers. 13—16.—FIRST EXPEDITION OF SENNACHERIB AGAINST HEZEKIAH. The writer now, as is his manner, omitting as comparatively unimportant all Hezekiah's dealings with Sargon, which were without positive result, proceeds to give a brief account of Sennacherib's first expedition against him, and of its unfortunate, if not disgraceful, issue: (1) the capture of all the important cities except Jerusalem; (2) the submission of Hezekiah to any terms which Sennacherib chose to impose; and (3) the purchase of peace by the payment of three hundred talents of silver and thirty talents of gold out of the treasures of the temple and of the royal palace. The narrative obtains copious illustration from the inscriptions of Sennacherib.

Ver. 13.—**Now in the fourteenth year of King Hezekiah did Sennacherib King of Assyria come up.** It is impossible to accept this note of time as genuine without rejecting altogether the authority of the Assyrian inscriptions. Sargon took Samaria in his first year, B.C. 722, and then had a reign of between seventeen and eighteen years, for fifteen of which we have his annals. He certainly did not associate Sennacherib with him on the throne, nor did the latter exercise any authority at all until B.C. 705, when, "on the 12th of Ab (July), he the throne ascended" ('Eponym Canon,' p. 67). Sennacherib places his first expedition against Hezekiah in his fourth year, B.C. 701. Thus, according to the Assyrian records, which are very ample, and of which we have the actual originals, twenty years intervened between the capture of Samaria and the attack of Sennacherib on Hezekiah; according to the present passage, compared with vers. 9, 10, eight years only intervened. No contradiction can be more absolute. It has been proposed to alter the date from "the fourteenth year" to "the twenty-sixth year;" but it seems most probable that the original writer inserted no date, but simply said, "And Sennacherib, King of Assyria, came up," etc., just as he had said, without a date, "Pul the King of Assyria came up against the land" (ch. xv. 19); and "against him (Hoshea) came up Shalmaneser" (ch. xvii. 3); and, with a very vague date, if it may be called a date, "In the days of Pekah King of Israel came Tiglath-pileser King of Assyria" (ch. xv. 29. Comp. also ch. xxiv. 1, 11). Later on, a redactor—perhaps the same who inserted the whole series of synchronisms—introduced the words, "In the fourteenth year of King Hezekiah," having obtained the number from ch. xx. 6, which he assumed to belong to the time of Sennacherib's attack. **Against all the fenced cities of Judah, and took them.** Sennacherib himself says, "And of Hezekiah of Judah, who did not submit to my yoke, *forty-six* strong cities, fortresses, and smaller cities round about them without number, by the march of my troops, . . . by the force of battering-rams, mining, and missiles, I besieged, I captured" ('Eponym Canon,' p. 134, lines 6—12. Comp. also 2 Chron. xxxii. 1 and Isa. xxxvi. 1).

Ver. 14.—**And Hezekiah King of Judah sent to the King of Assyria to Lachish, saying.** (On the position of Lachish, see the comment upon ch. xiv. 19.) A bas-relief in the British Museum is thought to represent Sennacherib at the siege of Lachish. He is seated on a highly ornamented throne, and is engaged in receiving prisoners. The city is represented as strongly fortified, and as attacked with scaling-ladders and battering-rams. The surrender is taking place, and the captives of importance are being conducted from one of the tower-gates to the presence of the conqueror. An accompanying inscription is to the following effect: "Sennacherib, the great king, the King of Assyria, sitting on the throne of judgment before the city of Lakhisha (Lachish). I give permission for its destruction." It would seem that, while Sennacherib was personally engaged in this siege, a portion of his army had invested Jerusalem, and were pressing the siege (see Isa. xxii. 1—7). **I have offended; return from me.** The tone of the submission is abject. In vain had Isaiah counselled resistance, and

promised deliverance if trust were placed in God (Isa. viii. 9—15; x. 24—26; xiv. 24, 25). When the siege commenced, all was dismay within the walls—it was "a day of trouble, and of treading down, and of perplexity" (Isa. xxii. 5). Some of the rulers fled (Isa. xxii. 3); others gave themselves up for lost, and resolved on "a short life and a merry one" (Isa. xxii. 13). Hezekiah found no encouragement to resist in any of his counsellors except Isaiah, and was therefore driven to despair—acknowledged himself in the wrong for rebelling, and besought Sennacherib to "return from him"—*i.e.* to retire and withdraw his troops. **That which thou puttest on me will I bear.** Whatever burden Sennacherib chooses to put upon him, Hezekiah says he will bear, be it tribute, be it cession of territory, be it indignity of any sort or kind. He makes no reservation; but of course he assumes that the terms about to be offered him will be such as, according to the usages of war at the time, would be regarded as reasonable. **And the King of Assyria appointed unto Hezekiah King of Judah three hundred talents of silver and thirty talents of gold.** Sennacherib says that the payment made him by Hezekiah was thirty talents of gold and *eight* hundred talents of silver ('Records of the Past,' vol. i. p. 39, line 34). He has, perhaps, exaggerated, or he may have counted in all the silver that he carried off from the whole of Judæa; or, possibly, the payment to purchase peace was eight hundred talents, the fixed tribute three hundred. We learn from Sennacherib's inscription that, besides making this money payment, Hezekiah had to consent to (1) a cession of territory towards the south-west, which was apportioned between Gaza, Ekron, and Ashdod; (2) the surrender of an Assyrian vassal king, detained in Jerusalem; and (3) the contribution to the harem at Nineveh of two if not more of his daughters.

Ver. 15.—**And Hezekiah gave him all the silver that was found in the house of the Lord, and in the treasures of the king's house.** Ahaz had exhausted both these stores of wealth about thirty years previously (ch. xvi. 8), and there could not have been very much accumulation since. Hence the stripping of the metal-plating from off the temple doors (see the next verse).

Ver. 16.—**At that time did Hezekiah cut off** the gold from the doors of the temple of **the Lord, and from the pillars which Hezekiah King of Judah had overlaid, and gave it to the King of Assyria.** In the time of his great wealth and prosperity, Hezekiah, while engaged in restoring the temple (2 Chron. xxix. 17—19), had adorned the pillars and doors of the sanctuary with a metal covering, which was probably gold, like Solomon's (1 Kings vi. 20—22, 28, 30, 32). To make up the "thirty talents of gold" he was now obliged to undo his own work, and strip the doors and pillars bare. Sennacherib tells us that, besides the two large sums of gold and silver, Hezekiah sent him at this time "woven cloth, scarlet, embroidered; precious stones of large size; couches of ivory; movable thrones of ivory; skins of buffaloes; horns of buffaloes; and two kinds of woods" ('Records of the Past,' vol. i. p. 39, lines 34—37). It was customary to accompany the fixed tribute with the more precious products of each country.

Vers. 17—37.—SECOND EXPEDITION OF SENNACHERIB. This section and ch. xix. form one continuous narrative, which can only have been divided on account of its great length (fifty-eight verses). The subject is one throughout, viz. Sennacherib's second expedition against Hezekiah. The narrative flows on without a break. It consists of (1) an account of the embassy of Rabshakeh (ch. xviii. 17—37; xix. 1—8); (2) an account of an insulting letter written by Sennacherib to Hezekiah, and of Hezekiah's "spreading it before the Lord" (ch. xix. 9—14); (3) the prayer of Hezekiah, and God's answer to it by the mouth of Isaiah (ch. xix. 15—34); (4) the destruction of Sennacherib's host, his flight to Nineveh, and his murder by two of his sons. The Assyrian inscriptions are absolutely silent with respect to this expedition and its result—it being a fixed rule with the historiographers of Assyria to pass over without notice all defeats and disasters.

Ver. 17.—And the King of Assyria sent Tartan and Rabsaris and Rabshakeh from Lachish to King Hezekiah with a great host against Jerusalem. Sennacherib appears, by his great inscription, to have returned to Nineveh, with his Judæan captives (more than two hundred thousand in number) and his rich booty, towards the close of the year B.C. 701. In the following year he was called into Babylonia, where troubles had broken out, and Hezekiah, left to himself, seems to have made up his mind to revolt, and to have called in the assistance of Egypt (Isa. xxx. 4; ch. xviii. 21). Sabatok was probably the nominal sovereign, but Tirhakah, who held his court at Meroë, was lord paramount. An alliance was made; and hopes held out that, if Sennacherib again marched into Judæa, Hezekiah would receive effectual aid, especially in chariots and horsemen (ver. 24). Under these cir-

cumstances, Sennacherib made his second expedition, probably in B.C. 600. Regarding Egypt as his main enemy, and Judæa as of small account, he led his army by the ordinary route into the Philistian plain, pressing southward, while he detached a moderate force to hold Jerusalem in check, to threaten it, and, if an opportunity offered, to seize it. At the head of this force were three commanders, who seem to have borne, all of them, official titles; viz. the Tartan, or "commander-in-chief;" the Rabsaris, or "chief eunuch;" and the Rabshakeh, or "chief cupbearer." The Tartan was the highest of all the officials of the empire, and ranked next to the king. Sennacherib detached this force from Lachish, which seems to have revolted, and to have been undergoing a second siege. And when they were come up, they came and stood by the conduit of the upper pool. It was, perhaps, this army which Isaiah saw in vision, advancing on Jerusalem from the pass of Michmash (x. 28—32), and "shaking its hand" at the city from the northern plateau outside the walls—the traditional "camp of the Assyrians." At any rate, the "upper pool" and the "fuller's field" were in this direction (see the comment on Isa. vii. 3). Which is in the highway of the fuller's field.

Ver. 18.—And when they had called to the king—i.e. when they had announced that they had a message to deliver to the king—there came out to them; by Hezekiah's order, doubtless. Learning that they were three of Sennacherib's highest officials, he sent out to them three of the chief officers of his own court. Eliakim the son of Hilkiah, which was over the household. Recently promoted to that high position, instead of Shebna, according to the prophecy (Isa. xxii. 19—22), and perhaps by the influence of Isaiah. And Shebna the scribe; or, secretary—the official employed to draw up documents, such as treaties, protocols, despatches, and the like. He had been removed to this inferior position, to make room for Eliakim, but had not yet suffered the banishment with which Isaiah (xxii. 18) had threatened him. And Joah the son of Asaph the recorder; or, remembrancer—the person whose chief duty it probably was to chronicle events as they occurred, and finally to draw up the memoir of each reign at its close. (For another view, see the comment on 1 Kings iv. 3.)

Ver. 19.—And Rabshakeh said unto them. Although the third in order of dignity, Rabshakeh took the word, probably because he was familiar with the Hebrew language, and could speak it fluently (see ver. 26). His being spokesman made him appear to be the chief ambassador, and made Isaiah, in the parallel passage (xxxvi.), pass over in silence the other two. **Speak ye now to Hezekiah.** It was a rude, almost an insulting commencement, to give Hezekiah no title—neither " the king," nor " King of Judah," nor even " your master," but to call him merely "Hezekiah." The same rudeness is persisted in throughout (vers. 22, 29, 30, 31, 32), and it is emphasized by the employment of some title or other, generally a lofty title, when Sennacherib is spoken of. Sennacherib himself is less rude in his inscriptions (see the 'Eponym Canon,' pp. 133, line 45; 134, line 6; 136, lines 21, 15). **Thus saith the great king, the King of Assyria.** The "great king "—*sarru rabu*—was the ordinary title assumed by Assyrian monarchs. It passed from them to the Babylonians and the Persians. Sennacherib calls himself, on Bellino's cylinder, " the great king, the powerful king, the King of Assyria, the king unrivalled, the pious monarch, the worshipper of the great gods, the protector of the just, the lover of the righteous, the noble warrior, the valiant hero, the first of all kings, the great punisher of unbelievers" (see ' Records of the Past,' vol. i. p. 25). **What confidence is this wherein thou trustest?** We may assume that Hezekiah had, at the beginning of the year, withheld his tribute. He had certainly not gone out to meet the "great king" as he approached his territories, to do homage, and place the forces of Judah at his disposal. On the contrary, he had taken up an attitude of hostility. He had fortified his capital (2 Chron. xxxii. 2—5); he had collected arms and soldiers, and had shut himself up in Jerusalem, having made every preparation for a siege. Sennacherib inquires why he has dared to do all this—on what strength does he rely? What is the ground of his confidence?

Ver. 20.—**Thou sayest (but they are but vain words)**; literally, *words of lips;* i.e. words which the lips speak, without the heart having any conviction of their truth. We must suppose that Sennacherib has either heard from his spies that Hezekiah is speaking to the people as he represents him to be speaking, or conjectures what he is likely to say. According to the writer of Chronicles (2 Chron. xxxii. 7, 8), what he did say was very different. He neither boasted of " counsel" nor of material "strength;" but simply said, " There be more with us than with him: with him is an arm of flesh; but with us is the Lord our God to help us and to fight our battles." I have counsel and strength for the war. Sennacherib imagines that Hezekiah's real trust is in the "fleshly arm" of Egypt, and in the counsellors who have advised and brought about the alliance. And perhaps he is not far wrong. Hezekiah, it would

seem, "halted between two opinions." He hoped for aid from Egypt; but, if it failed, then he hoped for the Divine help promised by Isaiah. **Now on whom dost thou trust, that thou rebellest against me?**

Ver. 21.—**Now, behold, thou trustest upon the staff of this bruised reed, even upon Egypt.** Sennacherib had good information. Hezekiah's embassy to Egypt (Isa. xxx. 2—7) was known to him; and he rightly judged that Hezekiah was expecting aid from this quarter. This expectation he ridicules. What is Egypt but a " bruised reed"? The Nile bulrush (רצץ) has a goodly show; it rears itself aloft, and looks strong and stately; but use it as a staff, lean upon it, and it snaps at once. Such is Pharaoh—nay, he is worse; he is a *bruised* reed, which can give no support at all, even for a moment. The Assyrian monarch was justified in his contempt. Egypt had never yet given any effectual support to the states attacked by Assyria. Shebek gave no manner of aid to Hoshea, but allowed Samaria to be conquered in B.C. 722 without making the slightest effort on her behalf. In B.C. 720 he came to the aid of Gaza ('Eponym Canon,' p. 126), but Gaza was captured notwithstanding. In B.C. 711 either he or Sabatok undertook the protection of Ashdod, but with the same lack of success (ibid., pp. 130, 131). " Kings of Egypt" assisted the Ascalonites against Sennacherib himself in B.C. 701, and were again completely defeated (ibid., pp. 133, 134). Sargon calls the King of Egypt, whose aid was invited by the Ashdodites (ibid., p. 130, line 37), " a monarch who could not save them." **On which if a man lean, it will go into his hand, and pierce it;** *i.e.* trust in Egypt will not only bring a country no advantage, but it will bring positive injury. The sharp silicious casing of a reed might run into the hand and give an ugly wound. **So is Pharaoh King of Egypt unto all that trust on him.** Sargon in one place (ibid., p. 130, line 36) speaks of a King of Egypt under the title of " Pharaoh."

Ver. 22.—**But if ye say unto me, We trust in the Lord our God.** Sennacherib had also heard of this second ground of trust, which Hezekiah had certainly put forward with great openness (2 Chron. xxxii. 8). No doubt he thought it purely fantastical and illusory. But he was not unaware that it might inspire a determined resistance. He therefore condescended to argue against reliance on it. **Is not that he, whose high places and whose altars Hezekiah hath taken away?** His counsellors have suggested to Sennacherib a specious argument— How can Hezekiah confidently rely on the protection of the God of the land, Jehovah, when he has been employing himself for years in the destruction of this very God's high places and altars? Surely the God will not favour one who has been pulling down his places of worship! Putting out of sight the special requirements of the Jewish Law, the argument might well seem unanswerable. At any rate, it was calculated to have a certain effect on the minds of those who were attached to the high-place worship, and desired its continuance. **And hath said to Judah and Jerusalem, Ye shall worship before this altar in Jerusalem.** A weak argument, if addressed to Jews of Jerusalem only, but likely to have weight with the country Jews, if, as is probable, they had crowded into the city when the invasion began.

Ver. 23.—**Now therefore, I pray thee, give pledges to my lord the King of Assyria, and I will deliver thee two thousand horses, if thou be able on thy part to set riders upon them.** "Pledge thyself," *i.e.* "to find the men, and I will pledge myself to find the horses." It is a strong expression of contempt for the military power of the Jews. They have not only no trained cavalry, but, were any one to furnish them with two thousand horses, they could not find the men to ride them. The Jewish army does, in fact, appear to have consisted of infantry and chariots only.

Ver. 24.—**How then wilt thou turn away the face of**—*i.e.* "repulse, "cause to retreat" —**one captain of the least of my master's servants**; literally, *one governor*—the word used is that which in modern times takes the form of "pasha," or "pacha." It properly applies to the rulers of provinces; but as these were expected to collect and command, upon occasions, the troops of their province, it has a secondary sense of "commander" or "captain." **And put thy trust**; rather, *and thou puttest thy trust*—in this extremity of weakness, so far as thine own forces are concerned, thou art so foolish as to put thy trust in Egypt, and to expect that her strength will make up for thine own impotence. Vain hope! (see ver. 21). **On Egypt for chariots and for horsemen?** or, *chariots and chariot-men.*

Ver. 25.—**Am I now come up without the Lord against this place to destroy it? The Lord said to me, Go up against this land, and destroy it.** The Assyrian monarchs constantly state that Asshur, their "great god," directs them to make war against this or that nation ('Records of the Past,' vol. i. pp. 48, 60, 70, 71, 82, etc.), but not that the god of the country to be attacked does so. It is difficult to account for Sennacherib's very exceptional boast, "Jehovah said to me, Go up against this land." Perhaps he identifies "Jehovah" with "Asshur." Perhaps he has heard of prophecies, uttered

in the name of Jehovah, by Jewish prophets, which threatened the land with desolation at the hand of the Assyrians (*e.g.* Isa. vii. 17—24; x. 5—12; Joel ii. 1—11, etc.). Or he may have made the statement in mere bravado, as one that might frighten some, and at any rate could not be contradicted.

Ver. 26.—**Then said Eliakim the son of Hilkiah, and Shebna, and Joah, unto Rabshakeh, Speak, I pray thee, to thy servants in the Syrian language;** literally, *in the Aramaic language.* Hebrew, Aramaic, and Assyrian were three cognate languages, closely allied, and very similar both in their grammatical forms and in their vocabularies, but still sufficiently different to be distinct languages, which were only intelligible to those who had learnt them. Rabshakeh had addressed the Jewish officials in Hebrew, probably as the language which they would best understand, if it were not even the only one that they would understand; not with the express "object of influencing the common people," as Bähr supposes. But the Jewish officials feared that the words uttered were influencing them. They proposed, therefore, that the further negotiations should be conducted in Aramaic, a tongue which they understood, and one which they supposed that Rabshakeh, as he knew Hebrew, would also know. Aramaic was spoken in most of the tract that lay between Assyria and Palestine, in Syria and Damascus certainly, in Upper Mesopotamia, along the line of the Euphrates, and perhaps as far as the Khabour river. **For we understand it.** It is not likely that the Jews of this time generally understood Aramaic; but high officials of the court, who might have to deal with embassies and negotiate treaties, found it necessary to understand it, just as such persons in our own country have to know French. **And talk not with us in the Jews' language in the ears of the people that are on the wall.** Besides the sentinels and other soldiers, there would probably be many idlers upon the wall, attracted by the unwonted spectacle of an ambassadorial *cortége,* and anxious to pick up intelligence. The loud voices of Orientals would be heard to a considerable distance.

Ver. 27.—**But Rabshakeh said unto them, Hath my master sent me to thy master, and to thee, to speak these words?** hath he not sent me to the men which sit on the wall? An intolerable speech on the part of an envoy, and one which might have justified an order to send an arrow through his head. Ambassadors are accredited by governments to governments, and the safe conduct granted to them is on the understanding that they will conduct themselves according to established usage. In no state of society can it have been allowable for envoys to intervene between the governors and the governed, and endeavour to stir up discontent among the latter. Yet this is what Rabshakeh did, and boasted of doing. Well might Isaiah say of such an arrogant and lawless aggressor, "He hath broken the covenant, he hath despised the cities, he regardeth no man" (see Isa. xxxiii. 8). **That they may eat their own dung, and drink their own piss with you?** Rabshakeh means to say that the effect of the men "sitting on the wall," and continuing the defence of the town, will be to bring them to the last extremity of hunger and thirst, when they will be forced even to consume their own excrement (comp. ch. vi. 25—29).

Ver. 28.—**Then Rabshakeh stood and cried with a loud voice in the Jews' language, and spake, saying.** Rabshakeh had probably been sitting before. He now stood up to attract attention, and raised his voice to be the better heard. Still speaking Hebrew, and not Aramaic, he addressed himself directly to the people on the wall, soldiers and others, doing the very opposite to what he had been requested to do, and outraging all propriety. History scarcely presents any other instance of such coarse and barefaced effrontery, unless the affronts put upon a Danubian principality by the envoy of a "great Power" may be regarded as constituting a parallel. **Hear the word of the great king, the King of Assyria.** It is scarcely likely that Sennacherib had anticipated his envoy's action, much less directed it, and told him exactly what he was to say. But Rabshakeh thinks his words will have more effect if he represents them as those of his master.

Ver. 29.—**Thus saith the king, Let not Hezekiah deceive you.** Rabshakeh and his master, no doubt, both of them thought Hezekiah's grounds of confidence would prove fallacious, and that all who should trust in them would find themselves "deceived." There were but two grounds that Hezekiah could possibly put forward: (1) deliverance by human means—by his own armed strength and that of his allies; (2) deliverance by supernatural means—by some great manifestation of miraculous power on the part of Jehovah. Rabshakeh thinks both equally impossible. The first, however, is too absurd for argument, and he therefore takes no further notice of it; but the second he proceeds to combat, in vers. 33—35. **For he shall not be able to deliver you out of his hand.** Correct grammar requires "out of *my* hand;" but Rabshakeh forgets that he is professing to report the words of Sennacherib.

Ver. 30.—**Neither let Hezekiah make you trust in the Lord.** Rabshakeh seems to be aware that this is the argument which Hezekiah is, in point of fact, mainly urging.

If at one time he had trusted in Egypt, that trust was now quite or well-nigh gone. The tone of his exhortations was that recorded in Chronicles (2 Chron. xxxii. 6—8), "He set captains of war over the people, and gathered them together to him in the street of the gate of the city, and spake comfortably to them, saying, Be strong and courageous, be not afraid nor dismayed for the King of Assyria, nor for all the multitude that is with him: for there be more with us than with him [see ch. vi. 16]; with him is an arm of flesh; but with us is the Lord our God to help us, and to fight our battles. And the people rested themselves upon the words of Hezekiah King of Judah." **Saying, The Lord will surely deliver us, and this city shall not be delivered into the hand of the King of Assyria.** Hezekiah's was, in part, a general conviction that God would not forsake his people, who had recently turned to him, if not with absolute sincerity, yet at any rate with public confession of sin, and public acknowledgment of his mercies, and public profession of an intention to serve him; in part, probably, a special reliance on some definite prophecies of Isaiah, that the city should not be taken (see Isa. xxxi. 4—6; xxxiiii. 20—22).

Ver. 31.—**Hearken not to Hezekiah: for thus saith the King of Assyria.** Rabshakeh, before concluding, tries the effect of blandishments. The King of Assyria is no harsh lord, as he has been represented to them. He will be a kinder master than Hezekiah. Hezekiah condemns them to all the hardships of a siege; and then, if they survive it, to a wasted land, ruined homes, broken cisterns. Sennacherib, if they will but yield to him, promises them peace and prosperity, a time of quiet enjoyment in their own land, and then removal to another equally good, where they will "live and not die," be happy and not miserable. It will be observed that none but material inducements are held out to them. They are expected to barter freedom, independence, religious privileges, country, home, for the sake of creature comforts—for ease, quiet, and security. Setting aside the question whether they could count on the performance of the promises made them, it will be felt that they did well not to be tempted. Better vigorous national life, with any amount of hardship, struggle, and suffering, than the gilded chains of the most peaceful servitude. **Make an agreement with me by a present**—rather, *make peace with me*, or "make *terms* with me" (Knobel, Thenius, Keil, Bähr); in other words, give in your submission—**and come out to me;** *i.e.* quit the town, surrender it (see 1 Sam. xi. 3; Jer. xxi. 9; xxxviii. 17), place yourselves at my mercy, "and then" see what great things I will do for you." The tone, as Bähr says, is one of "wheedling" and cajolement. **And** then **eat ye every man of his own vine, and every one of his fig tree.** Proverbial expressions for a peaceful, happy time (see 1 Kings iv. 25 ; Micah iv. 4 ; Zech. iii. 10), when there are no inroads, no ravages, no disturbances. Rabshakeh promises, in the name of Sennacherib, that they shall rest in their own land for a term—an indefinite term—in a blissful state of peace and quietness before any new resolution is taken about them. **And drink ye every one the waters of his cistern** ; rather, *of his well* (בר). Every man who had a field or a vineyard was sure to have a well in it. Cisterns for the storage of rain-water were comparatively uncommon.

Ver. 32.—**Until I come and take you away to a land like your own land.** Rabshakeh did not dissemble the fact that they must look for a transplantation. Probably he felt that, if he did, he would not be believed. The transplantations had been too numerous and too recent, the examples of Samaria, Damascus, Hamath, Ashdod, etc., were too notorious, for it to be worth his while to pretend that Judæa would have any other fate. He therefore set himself the task of persuading the Jews that transplantation had nothing about it displeasing or even disagreeable—that, in fact, they were to be envied rather than pitied for being about to experience it. The King of Assyria, in the goodness of his paternal breast, would select for them a land as nearly as possible " like their own land "—a land teeming with corn and wine and oil, full of rich arable tracts, of vineyards and of olive-grounds, which would yield them those fruits of the earth to which they were accustomed, in abundance. What security they had that these promises would be fulfilled, he did not attempt to show them ; much less did he explain to them why, if they were to gain rather than lose, it was worth while transplanting them at all ; how that transplanted nations lost all spirit and patriotism, sank into apathy, and gave no trouble to their masters. **A land of corn and wine, a land of bread and vineyards, a land of oil olive and of honey** (comp. Deut. viii. 8, 9, which has, no doubt, affected the language of the reporter, who gives the general tenor of Rabshakeh's speech, but could not have taken down or have remembered his exact words) **that ye may live, and** [**not die— as you will if you follow Hezekiah's advice —and** [therefore] **hearken not unto Hezekiah, when he persuadeth—***i.e.* seeketh to persuade **— you, saying, The Lord will deliver us** (see the comment on ver. 30).

Ver. 33.—**Hath any of the gods of the nations delivered at all his land out of the hand of the King of Assyria?** To Rab-

shakeh, and the Assyrians generally, this seemed a crushing and convincing, absolutely unanswerable, argument. It had all the force of what appeared to them a complete induction. As far back as they could remember, they had always been contending with different tribes and nations, each and all of whom had had gods in whom they trusted, and the result had been uniform— the gods had been unequal to the task of protecting their votaries against Assyria : how could it be imagined that Jehovah would prove an exception? If he was not exactly, as Knobel calls him, "the insignificant god of an insignificant people," yet how was he better or stronger than the others—than Chemosh, or Moloch, or Rimmon, or Baal, or Ashima, or Khaldi, or Bel, or Merodach? What had he done for the Jews hitherto? Nothing remarkable, so far as the Assyrians knew ; for their memories did not reach back so far as the time of Asa and the deliverance from Zerah, much less to the conquest of Canaan or the Exodus. He had not 'saved the trans-Jordanic tribes from Tiglath-pileser, or Samaria from his successors. Was it not madness to suppose that he would save Judæa from Sennacherib? A heathen reasoner could not see, could not be expected to see, the momentous difference ; that the gods of the other countries were "no gods" (ch. xix. 18), while Jehovah was "the Lord of the whole earth."

Ver. 34.—**Where** are **the gods of Hamath, and of Arpad?** Hamath and Arpad had been recently conquered (about B.C. 720) by Sargon (see the 'Eponym Canon,' pp. 126— 128). Of the latter city but little is known, not even its site. We find it generally connected with Damascus (Jer. xlix. 23 ; 'Eponym Canon,' pp. 68, 126) and Hamath (ch. xix. 13 ; Isa. x. 9 ; xxxvi. 19 ; xxxvii. 13 ; Jer. xlix. 23 ; 'Eponym Canon,' p. 126), and may conjecture that it lay between them, either in Cœle-Syria or in the Anti-Libanus. (On Hamath, see the commentary upon ch. xiv. 25 ; and for its special god, Ashima, see that on ch. xvii. 30.) **Where are the gods of Sepharvaim, Hena, and Ivah?** (On the cities and gods of Sepharvaim and Ivah (or Ava), see the comment on ch. xvii. 24 and 31.) "Hena," mentioned always with Sepharvaim and Ivah (ch. xix. 13 ; Isa. xxxviii. 13), is probably Anah on the Euphrates, about seventy miles above Hit (Ivah). Nothing is known of its gods. Probably Sepharvaim, Hena, and Ivah had rebelled in conjunction, and been reconquered at no distant date. Sargon mentions in his annals that he besieged and took Sepharvaim (Sippara) in his twelfth year (B.C. 710). **Have they delivered Samaria out of mine hand?** There is probably some compression of the original narrative here. The meaning is, "Have they delivered their several cities, or has the god of Samaria delivered his city out of my hand?" No god had hitherto delivered any city which the Assyrians had attacked.

Ver. 35.—**Who are they among all the gods of the countries**—*i.e.* the countries with which Assyria had been at war—**that have delivered their country out of mine hand, that the Lord should deliver Jerusalem out of mine hand?** "Produce an example of deliverance," Rabshakeh means to say, "before you speak of deliverance as probable, or even possible. If you cannot, relinquish the hope, and submit yourselves." Rabshakeh cannot conceive the idea that Jehovah is anything but a local god, on a par with all the other gods of the countries.

Ver. 36.—**But the people held their peace, and answered him not a word.** All Rabshakeh's efforts to produce open disaffection failed. Whatever impression his arguments may have made, no indication was given that they had produced any. If, then, he had hoped to bring about a mutiny, or even to create a disturbance, he was disappointed. **For the king's commandment was, saying, Answer him not.** Hezekiah had either anticipated Rabshakeh's tactics, and given an order beforehand that no word should be uttered, or he had promptly met them by sending such an order, on learning Rabshakeh's proceedings, The latter is more

probable, since such an outrageous course as that which Rabshakeh had pursued can scarcely have been expected.

Ver. 37.—**Then came Eliakim the son of Hilkiah, which was over the household, and Shebna the scribe, and Joah the son of Asaph the recorder, to Hezekiah with their clothes rent.** They had rent their clothes, not so much in grief or in alarm, as in horror at Rabshakeh's blasphemies. They were blasphemies, no doubt, arising from "invincible ignorance," and not intended as insults to the one Almighty Being who rules the earth, of whose existence Rabshakeh had probably no conception; but they struck on Jewish ears as insults to Jehovah, and therefore as dreadful and horrible (comp. Gen. xxxvii. 29; 1 Sam. iv. 12; 2 Sam. i. 2; Ezra ix. 3, etc.). **And told him the words of Rabshakeh;** reported to him, *i.e.* as nearly as they could, all that Rabshakeh had said. The three envoys would supplement, and perhaps correct, one another; and Hezekiah would have conveyed to him a full and, on the whole, exact account of the message sent to him through Rabshakeh by the Assyrian king, and of Rabshakeh's method of enforcing it. The crisis of Hezekiah's life was reached. As he acted under it would be fixed his own fate, his character in the judgment of all future time, and the fate of his own country.

HOMILETICS.

Ver. 4.—*Iconoclasm right or wrong, judicious or injudicious, according to circumstances.* The destruction of the brazen serpent of Moses by Hezekiah has always been a favourite argument with extreme iconoclasts for their extreme views. In the time of Henry VIII., and still more in that of Cromwell, statuary was destroyed or mutilated, precious pictures were burnt, priceless stained-glass windows were shivered to atoms, by those with whom a main justification of their conduct was the example of Hezekiah. Let that example, then, be considered, both in respect of what Hezekiah did, and of what he did not do.

I. WHAT HEZEKIAH DID. 1. He removed the high places, which were distinctly contrary to the Law, since the Law allowed sacrifice in one place only—before the ark of the covenant, in the tabernacle, or at Jerusalem. 2. He brake down the "images," or idolatrous emblems of Baal—mere *pillars* probably, which were the objects of an actual worship. 3. He cut down the groves, or idolatrous emblems of Ashtoreth—"sacred trees," also the objects of worship. 4. He brake in pieces the brazen serpent, to which the Israelites had for some time been in the habit of offering incense.

II. WHAT HEZEKIAH DID NOT DO. Hezekiah did not understand the second commandment in any other sense than Solomon. He allowed the ministry of art to religion. He left untouched the carved figures of cherubim and palm-trees and open flowers upon the walls of the temple (1 Kings vi. 29). He left untouched the brazen lavers, on the borders of which were lions, oxen, and cherubim (1 Kings vii. 29). He probably restored to their place, he certainly did not destroy, the twelve oxen (Jer. lii. 20) which Solomon had made to support his "brazen sea" (1 Kings vii. 25), and which Ahaz had removed from the temple (ch. xvi. 17). He himself added to the gold ornamentation of the doors and pillars (ch. xviii. 16). It is evident, therefore, that Hezekiah's iconoclasm was limited to those objects which were being actually abused to idolatrous uses at the time when he destroyed them. He did not spy around him, scenting *peril* of idolatry in every image or other representation of natural forms that had come down to him from former ages, even when they were employed in the service of religion. He was on the side of a rich and gorgeous and artistic ceremonial, of a musical service (2 Chron. xxix. 25—27), a highly ornamented sanctuary, a " house" as "magnifical" as art could make it (1 Chron. xxii. 5). He recognized that the preservation of artistic objects devoted to religion was the rule, destruction of them the rare exception, only justified (1) where idolatrous abuse had actually crept in; and (2) where such idolatrous abuse still continued. An observance of these wise limitations would have saved much that is now irrevocably lost in the past, and may be required to save what remains to us of religious art in the future.

Vers. 5—7.—*God's service not really a hard service.* God's service is not the *hard* service that some suppose it to be. No doubt it involves a certain amount of pain and suffering. For, first, there is no true service of God without self-denial; and self-denial is painful. Secondly, it involves chastening at the hand of God; for "whom the Lord loveth he chasteneth, and scourgeth every son whom he receiveth" (Heb. xii. 6); and chastening is "not joyous, but grievous" (Heb. xii. 11). But there are to be set against these pains so many and so great compensations as leave a vast preponderance of advantage, and even enjoyment, to the godly over the ungodly.

I. THE SATISFACTION OF A GOOD CONSCIENCE. Just as there is nothing so painful, so depressing, so burdensome, as an evil conscience, the continually abiding sense of guiltiness and ill desert, so there is nothing which is a greater comfort to a man, more calculated to sustain him and maintain within him a perpetual quiet cheerfulness, than "the answer of a good conscience towards God" (1 Pet. iii. 21), the knowledge that one has striven and is striving to do God's will, and that by God's grace one has been kept from falling away from him. Notwithstanding their self-depreciation and self-distrust, good men have, on the whole, a self-approving conscience (Rom. ii. 15), which is a source of inward satisfaction and enjoyment.

II. THE ESTEEM AND APPROVAL OF GOOD MEN. There is implanted in man a love of approbation, the gratification of which is the source of a very positive pleasure. Godly men, good men, whatever amount of dislike they may arouse among those whose designs they thwart, or to whom their lives are a continual reproach, elicit from the better sort a much greater amount of very warm and cordial approval. This cannot but be a satisfaction to them. The praise of men is not what they seek; but when it comes to them unsought, as it will almost certainly come at last, it cannot fail to be grateful and acceptable.

III. TEMPORAL PROSPERITY ARISING FROM MAN'S RESPECT AND ESTEEM. The approval of our fellow-men naturally leads on to temporal advantages. Men place those whom they esteem in situations of trust, which are also, generally or frequently, situations of emolument. They make them presents or leave them legacies. They give them their custom, and recommend their friends to do the same. The worldly maxim, "Honesty is the best policy," witnesses to the worldly advantage which accrues, by mere natural causation, to the upright, honest man. "*All things* work together for good to them that love God;" and, generally speaking, even this world's goods seem to gather round them, and to cling to them, in spite of their slight esteem for earthly dross, and their proneness to scatter their riches on those around them.

IV. TEMPORAL PROSPERITY ARISING FROM THE DIRECT ACTION OF DIVINE PROVIDENCE. Of this we have in Hezekiah a notable example. He "clave to the Lord, and departed not from following him, but kept his commandments, . . . and the Lord was with him; and *he prospered whithersoever he went forth.*" The Divine blessing rested on all that he did; God "prospered him in all his works." When he seemed at the point of death, he miraculously recovered from his sickness, and God added to his life fifteen years (ch. xx. 6). When he provoked a judgment by indiscreet ostentation, the boon was granted him that the judgment should not fall in his days (ch. xx. 19). When an overwhelming calamity seemed about to fall upon him, and to crush both him and his nation, the catastrophe was averted by a stupendous miracle—the Assyrian host was destroyed, and the peril escaped (ch. xix. 35). "Riches and honour exceeding much " were given him (2 Chron. xxxii. 27), and he was "magnified in the sight of all the nations" (2 Chron. xxxii. 23). It may be said that all this was abnormal, and belonged to "the age of miracles;" but the principles of God's action do not change, and if we examine human life at the present day dispassionately, we shall find that still, *as a general rule*, if men cleave to the Lord, and keep his commandments, and depart not from following him, he will be with them, and will, more or less, prosper them.

Vers. 13—17.—*The danger of trusting to a purchased peace.* I. IN THE HISTORY OF NATIONS a purchased peace is seldom more enduring or more trustworthy than this peace which Hezekiah bought of Sennacherib. Once successful in extorting money by threats, why should an enemy refrain from repeating the process? Why should he stop till he has squeezed the sponge dry, and there is no more to be got from his victim? Even then, why should he not step in and execute his original threat of destruction and ruin? So Samaria found when she gave her thousand talents to the Assyrians (ch. xv. 19). So Rome found when she bribed Attila and Alaric. So will all nations ever find who seek to prolong their lives a little bit by paying for being let alone. And so also—

II. IN THE HISTORY OF INDIVIDUALS. Persons frequently get themselves into some trouble or other, which they do not wish to be known, and their secret is discovered by some unscrupulous individual, who proceeds to trade upon it. What will they give him to remain silent? If they once consent to purchase a peace of their enemy, all peace in life is gone from them. A man's appetite is only whetted by the first bribe, and still more by the second. "Increase of appetite doth grow by what it feeds on." Demand follows demand, threat follows threat. The blood-sucker is insatiate. True wisdom consists in not yielding to the first threat, in declining to purchase peace, and defying the enemy. He may as well do his worst at once as at last. It will generally be found that his worst is not so very bad. Even if it is, it is the just penalty which has to be paid for our past transgression, and which must be paid in some way or other, and at some time, here or hereafter. It is best for us that it should be paid soon; for the penalty of sin, if not so paid, is apt to be demanded at last with a heavy accumulation of interest.

Vers. 20, 21.—*Bruised reeds.* It is astonishing what trust is still placed, by generation after generation of mankind, in "bruised reeds." Whatever may be the case with individuals, mankind, the human race, learns nothing from experience. Men still trust implicitly in such "bruised reeds" as these—

I. BIG BATTALIONS. They think they are safe if they have sufficient "strength for the war." They go on increasing their military establishments, adding regiment to regiment, and battery to battery, and *corps d'armée* to *corps d'armée*. They count the armies of their neighbours; they reckon up man against man, and gun against gun, and ship against ship; and calculate, and plan, and act, as if the "multitude of an host"—the number of troops capable of being brought at once into the field—was everything. They forget that "it is nothing to the Lord to help, whether with many or with them that have no power" (2 Chron. xiv. 11). They forget, or misread, history, and fail to note how often "the race has not been to the swift, nor the battle to the strong" (Eccles. ix. 11).

II. POWERFUL ALLIES. Weak powers have always some "Egypt" to which they look for succour. Strong powers count on "triple" or "quadruple" alliances to augment their strength, and render them irresistible. They forget how easily alliances are broken up, how sure they are to arouse discontents and jealousies, how little dependence can be placed on the promises of statesmen, or the persistence of a particular mood in a nation, or the view which a state may take of its interests. They forget that the friend of to-day may be the enemy of to-morrow, and may fail them at the moment of greatest need.

III. SAGACIOUS STATESMEN AND GENERALS. It is forgotten, or at any rate not borne steadily in mind, how intellect decays, how mental power lessens, as men grow old; how often under a prolonged strain the strongest intellect suddenly snaps and is no longer of any account. Nor is it generally felt and recognized how limited and imperfect even the greatest intellect always is—how incompetent to forecast all possibilities, or to deal with all emergencies. "The weakness of God is stronger than man, and the foolishness of God is wiser than man" (1 Cor. i. 25). Man's wisdom is at best a poor purblind wisdom, apt to err, apt to fail when most needed—a very "bruised reed" to trust in.

IV. GOOD LUCK OR A FORTUNATE STAR. The trust of the first Napoleon in his "star" is well known. It is not so well known, but it is sufficiently attested, that the third Napoleon had nearly as implicit a trust. Thousands of persons deem themselves "lucky," and trust in their "good luck," as if it were an actual tangible possession. Otherwise there would be far less gambling than there is. The poor peasants of Italy and Germany would waste less money in lotteries, and the simpletons of England less in bets upon horses. Persons' "luck" is, on the whole, probably about equal, and if a man has been "lucky" hitherto, he should expect to be "unlucky" in the future.

V. SOMETHING TURNING UP. The phrase is a vulgar one, but it would need a long periphrasis to express the idea otherwise, and even then we might not make our meaning clear. Men who do not think themselves particularly lucky are still constantly waiting for "something to turn up," looking for it, trusting in it. The trust is made an excuse for idleness, for inaction, for waste of the best years of life, even for dissipated courses—for gambling, drinking, frequenting evil company. This "bruised reed" is more rotten even than most of the others. For the idler, the waster of his time, the haunter of smoking saloons, billiard-rooms, and race-courses, nothing ever does "turn up." He offers no temptation to steady business-like men to employ him. He does not seek work, and work is not very likely to seek him. He is an idler, and will remain an idler to the end of the chapter. There is no help for him, unless he gives up his silly trust, and betakes himself to a better one.

HOMILIES BY VARIOUS AUTHORS.

Vers. 1—8.—*The secret of a successful life; or, trust in God, and its results.* What a refreshing contrast to some of the lives we have been considering, is this description of the life of Hezekiah! How pleasant it is to read of such a life as his, after we have read of so many kings of Judah and Israel, that "they did evil in the sight of the Lord, and walked in the ways of Jeroboam the son of Nebat, who made Israel to sin"! It is a pleasant contrast even to the life of Hezekiah's own father Ahaz. It is a somewhat strange thing that, brought up amid such evil surroundings, Hezekiah should have turned out so well. The chances were all against him. His father's example was anything but favourable to the development of religion in his son. How careful parents should be as to the example they set their children! The best help parents can give their children to begin life with is godly training and a Christian example. I read lately, "that of the anarchists at Chicago, who were executed for their crimes some time ago, almost all had either been deprived of their parents when young, or had never received any home training; they had never been to a Sunday school; the influences surrounding them had been utterly godless." What a responsibility rests on parents to train their children well! Much of their future happiness depends upon the home life of childhood and youth. Perhaps Hezekiah had a good mother. Perhaps he had been entrusted to the care of some one of the priests who remained faithful to God amid the prevailing unfaithfulness, idolatry, and sin. Perhaps he was early brought under the influence of Isaiah. At any rate, we read of him that he did right in the sight of the Lord. He is singled out for special praise. It is said of him that "*he trusted in the Lord God of Israel*; so that after him was none like him among the kings of Judah, nor any that were before him" (ver. 5). What was the consequence? Just what the consequence will be to all who put their trust in the Lord and walk in his ways: "*The Lord was with him; and he prospered whithersoever he went forth.*"

1. TRUST IN GOD LEADS TO PERSONAL RELIGION. Hezekiah's faith in God was not a mere idle profession. It did not consist in the mere belief of certain historical facts. It did not consist in the mere assent to certain doctrinal truths. It did not consist in the mere observance of certain outward forms and ceremonies. It was a real faith. It extended to his whole life. "He did that which was right in the sight of the Lord, according to all that David his father did" (ver. 3). "He clave unto the Lord, and departed not from following him, but kept his commandments, which the

Lord commanded Moses" (ver. 6). *Such is true religion.* Religion is the dedication of the heart and life to God. A man may differ from me in creed, and in the way he worships the same God; but if he loves the Lord Jesus Christ, and serves God in sincerity, he is a truly religious man. "In every nation he that feareth God, and worketh righteousness, is accepted with him." How expressive and instructive are some of these quaint old phrases! "*He clave unto the Lord.*" Hezekiah set before him one great aim at the commencement of his life, and that was to please God. Whatever it might cost, he made up his mind to keep close to God. It is a grand resolution for the young to make. It is a grand aim to keep before them in life. But Hezekiah had not merely a goal at which he aimed. *He had certain well-defined lines* along which he reached that goal. He knew that, to please God, he must keep his commandments. He did not set up his own will in opposition to the will of God, king though he was. He did not dispute the wisdom of God's commands. He felt that God knew much better than he did the path of wisdom and of duty. This is one of the best evidences of true faith—of real trust in God. We may not see the reason for a command of God, but let us obey it. A parent will give his child many commands, for which it is quite unnecessary, perhaps undesirable, that the child should know the reason. Obedience based on faith is one of the first principles of life. Here, then, was the beginning of Hezekiah's success in life. It began with the state of his own heart. He trusted in God. That trust in God moulded his whole character, and character is the foundation of all that is permanent in life.

II. TRUST IN GOD LEADS TO PRACTICAL EFFORT. Hezekiah very soon showed by his conduct that he was determined to serve God. He did not leave the people long in doubt as to which side he was on. In the very first year of his reign, and in the first month of it, he opened the doors of the temple of the Lord, which his father had closed, and repaired them (2 Chron. xxix. 3). As soon as the temple was set in proper order, he caused the priests and the Levites to commence at once the public service of God. Then, in the second month, he issued a proclamation throughout all the land of Israel and Judah, inviting the people to come to Jerusalem to keep the Passover in the house of the Lord. What a festival and time of rejoicing that was! For seven days they kept the Feast of Unleavened Bread with great gladness, and the Levites and the priests praised the Lord day by day, singing with loud instruments unto the Lord. Peace offerings were offered; confession of sin was made, not to the priests, but to the Lord God of their fathers; and the presence of the Lord was so manifested among the large congregation, that when the seven days of the Passover were ended, the whole assembly unanimously agreed to keep seven days more. "So there was great joy in Jerusalem: for since the time of Solomon the son of David King of Israel there was not the like in Jerusalem." The effect of the service was electrical. When the Passover was finished, the people went out to all the cities of Judah, and brake the images in pieces, and cut down the groves, and threw down the high places and the altars until they had utterly destroyed them all. In all this work of destroying the symbols of idolatry, *Hezekiah the king took a leading part.* Even *the brazen serpent* which Moses had made did not escape the destroying hand. It was an interesting relic of Israel's journeying in the wilderness, and of their wonderful deliverance by God. But it had become a snare to the people. It had become an object of worship to some, as relics and images become to many professing Christians. They worshipped it and burnt incense to it. Hezekiah was not the man to destroy anything that was a help to true devotion. He encouraged the Levites to use the trumpets, the harp, and the psaltery, to stir up and stimulate the singing of the congregation, and to render to God a hearty and glorious service of praise. But he saw that the brazen serpent had become an idol in itself, and was leading the thoughts of the people away from the true Object of worship. So he broke it in pieces. All honour to the determined reformer, who destroyed everything that had become dishonouring to God! All honour to those stern reformers who from time to time have broken in pieces the symbols of idolatry in the Church of Christ! Would that in the Church of Rome to-day some such reformer would arise, who would denounce and overthrow its image-worship and Mariolatry! Such was the work of reformation which Hezekiah accomplished among his people. *It shows how God honours those who are determined to serve him,* and *how he blesses immediate and decided action.* Hezekiah might well have hesitated in this work. The whole country was given over to idolatry. He might have dreaded a rebellion. In some parts of the country he got little sympathy in his efforts to restore the ancient religion. When the messengers inviting the people to the Passover passed through the country of Ephraim and Manasseh and Zebulon, the people there laughed them to scorn and mocked them. Such manifestations of popular feeling might have caused Hezekiah to falter in his decision. He might have thought that he would introduce his reforms gradually. But no! the idolatry was wrong, and it must be put down at once. The worship of the true God was right, and it must at once be resumed. *Hezekiah was right.* Had he waited, had he begun his reign by tolerating idolatry for a while, he would have found it much harder to overthrow afterwards. Is there not here a lesson for us all? *If you see the right path clearly pointed out to you, resolve to walk in it, though all men should be against you.* Remember the brave words of Athanasius. He was mocked at for his zeal for the truth. Some one said to him, "Athanasius, all the world is against you;" then said he, "Athanasius is against the world." Follow the light of conscience and of duty. What matter though you may incur danger or worldly loss by so doing?

> "And because right is right, to follow right
> Were reason in the scorn of consequence."

Furthermore, whatever work you see needs to be done, *do it at once.* Promptness and decision are two essential elements of success in life. Do you see that you need to believe on the Lord Jesus Christ if you are to be saved? *Then come to him to-day.* A more convenient season may never arrive. We know not what a day may bring forth. Do you hear God calling you by his Word to perform some act of kindness or forgiveness? *Then do it at once.* Do you hear God calling you to some work of usefulness in his Church? Begin at once to undertake it. If our trust in God is a real trust, it will lead us, not only to personal religion, *but also to practical effort.* We can trust him to take care of us when we are doing his work. "Therefore be ye steadfast, unmovable, always abounding in the work of the Lord, forasmuch as ye know that your labour is not in vain in the Lord."

III. Trust in God leads to success in life. "And the Lord was with him; and he prospered whithersoever he went forth" (ver. 7). He was victorious over his enemies. *He threw off the yoke of the King of Assyria, and drove back the Philistines,* who had made great inroads during the previous reign. *When the people honoured God, their God honoured them and gave them victories over their enemies.* As a reward of Hezekiah's faith and faithfulness, God gave him much riches and honour. Hezekiah had trusted God at the *beginning* of his reign. He had done God's will, though he did not know what it might cost him, and before he was established on the throne. And God did not disappoint his trust, but made him greater and more honoured than all the kings of Judah before or after his time. Even in a temporal point of view, no one ever loses by trusting God and doing what is right. Christ promises that every one who is willing to give up every earthly possession for his sake will receive an hundred-fold more in this life, and in the world to come life everlasting. We saw, above, the dangers of prosperity. Hezekiah's career shows us what is *the safeguard of prosperity.* "The Lord was with him." Where that can be said, there is no danger in prosperity. In the godless man, prosperity is often a curse. It hardens his heart. He thinks that he is rich and increased in goods and has need of nothing. But the prosperity of the Christian may be a great blessing to himself and others. Take with you into your business, into your social relations, into every plan you make and every work you undertake, the *presence of God*, the *fear of God*, the *commandments of God*; and then there will be no fear of your success. Trust in the Lord. Put your eternal interests into the hands of Jesus. He is worthy of your trust. They that trust themselves to him shall never perish. Trust in the Lord, that it may lead you to *personal religion*, to *practical effort*, to *success in life.*

> "Set thou thy trust upon the Lord.
> And be thou doing good,
> And so thou in the land shalt dwell,
> And verily have food."

C. H. I.

Vers. 9—12.—*Captivity and its cause.*   (See homily on preceding chapter, vers. 6—23.)—C. H. I.

Vers. 13—16.—*Hezekiah's weakness.* Hezekiah had now been for some time on the throne. God had been with him hitherto, and had prospered him. Perhaps Hezekiah began to trust too much to his own strength. In the seventh verse we are told that he rebelled against the King of Assyria, and served him not. It does not appear that Hezekiah sought God's guidance before taking this bold step. Perhaps it would have been wiser if he had waited a little longer. At any rate, now, when he begins to feel the consequences of his action, he is disposed to shrink from them. The King of Assyria "came up against all the fenced cities of Judah, and took them." Hezekiah was panic-stricken. He trembled for his throne. He sent a submissive message, saying, "I have offended; return from me; that which thou puttest on me will I bear." We learn here—

I. How WEAK EVEN A GOOD MAN IS WITHOUT THE HELP OF GOD. Hezekiah was a good man. He was a wise man. Yet when left to himself how weak he was! how foolishly he acted! "Let him that thinketh he standeth take heed lest he fall." It becometh us all to walk humbly with our God. "God forbid that I should glory, save in the cross of our Lord Jesus Christ."

II. THE EVIL RESULTS OF WANT OF FAITH. Hezekiah's faith in God failed him. When that went, he was helpless. Sennacherib, seeing his craven spirit, appointed him a tribute of "three hundred talents of silver and thirty talents of gold" (ver. 14). Hezekiah was in a difficulty. He had no money to meet this demand. So he followed the very dangerous example set him by his father, and stripped the gold from the doors and pillars of the house of God, and sent it to the King of Assyria. *Want of faith often leads men to use questionable methods.* Men are in need of money, and they cannot trust God to provide for them in the way of honest industry, so they have recourse to speculation and fraud. If we are doing God's will, we may trust him to take care of us.

"It may not be *my* way;
It may not be *thy* way;
But yet in his own way the Lord will provide."

C. H. I.

Vers. 17—37.—*The tempter and his methods: Rabshakeh's address to the leaders and people of Jerusalem.* Hezekiah's gift to the King of Assyria had not saved him. The weakness he showed was rather an encouragement to Sennacherib to continue his attacks upon Judæa. And now a detachment of Sennacherib's army, headed by three officers of rank, comes up to Jerusalem. Their first effort is to induce the people of Jerusalem to surrender. Rabshakeh is the spokesman. His speech is like the speech of a Mephistopheles. It may fairly be taken as an illustration of how the wily tempter himself proceeds in his desire to allure to sin and destruction the souls of men.

I. HE PRETENDS TO BE DOING GOD'S WORK. 1. *He ridicules their confidence in Egypt.* Isaiah himself could hardly have warned them more strongly against the vanity of alliance with other nations. "Thou trustest upon the staff of this bruised reed, even upon Egypt" (ver. 21). 2. *He censures Hezekiah for disrespect toward God.* "If ye say unto me, We trust in the Lord God: is not this he whose high places and whose altars Hezekiah hath taken away?" (ver. 22). So Satan sometimes appears as an angel of light. Men of sin and worldliness sometimes show a remarkable interest in the Church of God. 3. *He represents himself as having a commission from God.* "Am I now come up without the Lord against this place to destroy it? The Lord said to me, Go up against this land, and destroy it" (ver. 25). It is thus that sin constantly presents itself to men and women. It masks its real features. It presents itself in a religious garb. A debased theatre professes to be the teacher of morality. But for one whose life it has changed for the better, there are thousands whom it has changed for the worse. Perhaps we should be justified in going the length of Pollok, in his 'Course of Time,' and in saying, "It might do good, but never did." How many questionable practices defend themselves on the ground that they are sanctioned and encouraged by "religious" people!

II. HE MAKES LIGHT OF TRUST IN GOD. But soon the cloven foot appears. The tempter soon begins to wean the soul from that religion of whose interests he professes to be so jealous. See here the inconsistency of Rabshakeh's speech. He first of all made it appear that he was commissioned by God, and that therefore all their efforts to resist him would be futile. But now he proceeds to ridicule the idea of trusting to God's power. "Neither let Hezekiah make you trust in the Lord, saying, The Lord will surely deliver us" (ver. 30). "Hath any of the gods of the nations delivered at all his land out of the hand of the King of Assyria?" (vers. 33—35). So it is in the progress of sin. He who is led away by the allurements of the world and pleasure, first begins with pleasures which lie on the border-land between the bad and the good. These are the pleasures or pursuits about which men say, "Oh! there is *no harm* in *that.*" "No harm" is a very dangerous phrase. When we hear it, we may generally doubt its truth. It usually refers to pursuits or pleasures which are the stepping-stones to worse sins. Many a man crosses the bridge of "no harm," and enters for ever the land of "no good." Let us never be induced to waver in our trust in God and obedience to him. His way is the way of safety and peace. There are many whose work seems to be like that of Rabshakeh—to weaken the trust of others in God, to diminish the respect of others for the Law of God. "Whosoever therefore shall break one of these least commandments, and shall teach men so, he shall be called the least in the kingdom of heaven." Where God and conscience say to us, "You ought not," let not the tempter ever persuade us by saying, "You may."

III. HE MAKES FALSE PROMISES. How fair-spoken is Rabshakeh! How very alluring his promises! If the people of Jerusalem would only make an agreement with the King of Assyria by a present, then they would eat every man of his own vine and fig tree, until he would afterwards take them away to a land like their own land, "a land of corn and wine, a land of bread and vineyards, a land of oil olive and of honey, that ye may live and not die." In this specious way he held before them an attractive prospect. But it was as empty as the bubble in the summer breeze. It was the pleasant euphemism by which he sought to gloss over the prospect of conquest and captivity. So with the pleasures of sin. How bright and how attractive, to outward appearance, are the haunts of wickedness and vice! The bright lights of the gin-palace—how they allure its unhappy victims, often by the contrast with the dreariness and misery of their homes! What a pleasant prospect sin in various forms presents! But how terrible is the reality! How grim is the skeleton at the feast! "My son, if sinners entice thee, consent thou not." *Such are the tempter's methods still.* The thirty-sixth verse contains a very good suggestion as to the way of meeting temptation. "But the people held their peace, and answered him not a word; for the king's commandment was, saying, Answer him not." *It is a wise rule not to parley with the tempter.* If we pray, "Lead us not into temptation," then we ought to be careful not to put ourselves in temptation's way.—C. H. I.

Vers. 1—37.—*A striking reformation, a ruthless despotism, and an unprincipled diplomacy.* "Now it came to pass," etc. Amongst the incidents recorded and the characters mentioned in this chapter, there stand out in great prominence three subjects for practical contemplation: (1) *a striking reformation;* (2) *a ruthless despotism;* and (3) *an unprincipled diplomacy.* The many strange and somewhat revolting historic events that make up the bulk of this chapter will come out in the discussion of these three subjects.

I. A STRIKING REFORMATION. Hezekiah, who was now King of Judah, and continued such for about twenty-nine years, was a man of great excellence. The unknown historian here says that "he did that which was right in the sight of the Lord, according to all that David his father did," etc. (vers. 3—8). This is high testimony, and his history shows that on the whole it was well deserved. Compared with most of his predecessors and contemporaries, he appears to have been an extraordinarily good man. He lived in a period of great national trial and moral corruption. Israel, Judah's sister-kingdom, was in its death-throes, and his own people had fallen into idolatry of the grossest kind. In the very dawn of his reign he sets himself to the work of reformation. We find in 2 Chron. xxix. 2—36 a description of the desire for a thorough reformation which displayed itself. But the point of his reformative work, on which we would now fasten our attention, is that mentioned in ver. 4, "He removed the high places, and brake the images, and cut down the groves, and brake in pieces the brazen serpent that Moses had made: for unto those days the children of Israel did burn incense to it: and he called it Nehushtan." His method for extirpating idolatry from his country is detailed with minuteness in 2 Chron. xxix. 3; xxx. 1—9. In this destruction of the brazen serpent we are struck with two things. 1. *The perverting tendency of sin.* The brazen serpent (we learn from Numb. xxi. 9) was a beneficent ordinance of God to heal those in the wilderness who had been bitten by the fiery serpents. But this Divine ordinance, designed for a good purpose, and which had accomplished good, was now, through the forces of human depravity, become a great evil. The Jews turned what was a special display of Divine goodness into a great evil. I am disposed to honour them for preserving it for upwards of seven hundred years, and thus handing it down from sire to son as a *memorial* of heavenly mercy; but their conduct in establishing it as an object for worship must be denounced without hesitancy or qualification. But is not this the great law of depravity? Has it not always perverted the good things of God, and thus converted blessings into curses? It has ever done so. It is doing so now. See how this perverting power acts in relation to such Divine blessings as (1) health; (2) riches; (3) genius; (4) knowledge; (5) governments; and (6) religious institutions.[1] 2. *The true attributes of a reformer.* Here we observe: (1) spiritual insight. Hezekiah (if our translation is correct) saw in this serpent, which appeared like a god to the people, nothing but a piece of brass—"Nehustan." What is grand to the vulgar is contemptible to the spiritually thoughtful. The true reformer peers into the heart of things, and finds that the gods of the people are but of common brass. (2) Invincible honesty. He not only saw that it was brass, but said so—declared it in the ears of the people. How many there are who have eyes to see the vile and contemptible in the objects which popular feeling admires and adores, but who lack the honesty to express their convictions! A true man not only sees the wrong, but exposes it. (3) Practical courage. This reformer not only had the insight to see, and the honesty to expose the worthlessness of the people's gods, but he had the courage to strike them from their pedestal. "He brake in pieces the brazen serpent." I have no hope of any man doing any real spiritual good who has not these *three* instincts. He must not only have an eye to penetrate the seeming and to descry the real, nor merely be honest enough to speak out his views, but he must have also the manly hand to "break in pieces" the false, in order to do the Divine work of *reform*. The man that has the three combined is the reformer. Almighty Love! multiply amongst us men of this threefold instinct—men which the age, the world demands![2] 3. *The true soul of a reformer.* What is that which gave him the true insight and attributes of a reformer—which in truth was the soul of the whole? (1) Entire consecration to the right. "He trusted in the Lord God of Israel; so that after him was none like him among all the kings of Judah, nor any that were before him. For he clave to the Lord, and departed not from following him, but kept his commandments, which the Lord commanded Moses. He trusted in and clave to the One true and living God, and kept his commandments. And this is right, and there is no right but this. (2) Invincible antagonism to the wrong. "And he rebelled against the King of Assyria, and served him not." "The yearly tribute his father had stipulated to pay, he withheld. Pursuing the policy of a truly theocratic sovereign, he was, through the Divine blessing which rested on his government, raised to a position of great public and national strength. Shalmaneser was dead; and assuming, consequently, that full independent sovereignty which God had settled on the house of David, he both shook off the Assyrian yoke, and, by an energetic movement against the Philistines, recovered the credit which his father Ahaz had lost in his war with that people (2 Chron. xxviii. 18)."

II. A RUTHLESS DESPOTISM. There are two despots mentioned in this chapter—Shalmaneser and Sennacherib, both kings of Assyria. A brief description of the former we have in vers. 9, 10, 12. What is stated in these verses is but a repetition of what we have in the preceding chapter, and the remarks made on it in our last homily preclude the necessity of any observations here. This Shalmaneser was a tyrant of the

---

[1] See *Homilist*, vol. ii. p. 193.

[2] See a full discourse of this subject in 'Septem in Uno,' p. 96.

worst kind. He invaded and ravaged the land of Israel, threw Hoshea into prison, laid siege to Samaria, carried the Israelites into Assyria, and located in their homes strangers from various parts of the Assyrian dominions. Thus he utterly destroyed the kingdom of Israel. The other despot is Sennacherib (vers. 13—16). Shalmaneser is gone, and this Sennacherib takes his place. The ruthlessness of this man's despotism appears in the following facts, recorded in the present chapter. 1. *He had already invaded a country in which he had no right.* "Now in the fourteenth year of King Hezekiah did Sennacherib King of Assyria come up against all the fenced cities of Judah, and took them." "The names of the principal of these cities are perhaps enumerated by Micah (i. 11—16), viz. *Saphir,* lying between Ashdod and Eleutheropolis (Eusebius and Jerome, 'Onomast.,' Saphir; cf. Robinson, 'Bibl. Researches,' ii. p. 370); *Zaanan* or *Zenan* (Josh. xv. 37), (Septuagint Σευναὰρ); *Beth-Ezel* or *Azel* (Zech. xiv. 5), near Saphir and Zaanan; *Maroth* or *Maarath* (Josh. xv. 59), between these towns and Jerusalem; *Lachish* (*Um Lâkis*); *Moresheth-Gath,* situated in the direction of Gath; *Achzib,* between Keilah and Mareshah (Josh. xv. 44); *Mareshah,* situated in the low country of Judah (Josh. xv. 44); *Adullam,* near Mareshah (cf. Isa. xxiv. 1—12). Overrunning Palestine, Sennacherib laid siege to the fortress of Lachish, which lay seven Roman miles from Eleutheropolis, and, therefore, south-west of Jerusalem on the way to Egypt. Amongst the interesting illustrations of sacred history, furnished by the recent Assyrian excavations, is a series of bas-reliefs representing the siege of a town—a fenced town—among the uttermost cities of Judah (Josh. xv. 39; Robinson's 'Biblical Researches')." Now mark, he now determines on another invasion, although: 2. *He had received from the king most humble submission and large contributions to leave his country alone.* Mark his humiliating appeal, "And Hezekiah King of Judah sent to the King of Assyria to Lachish, saying, I have offended; return from me: that which thou puttest on me will I bear." Alas! herein is a yielding of this great man's courage. Why did he apologize, pay the tribute which his ancestor had immorally pledged? Up to this point he had been bold in withholding it. But here, in crouching fear, he makes an apology. And more than this, he unrighteously promises a large contribution in answer to the despot's demands. "And the King of Assyria appointed unto Hezekiah King of Judah three hundred talents of silver and thirty talents of gold." The sum that he promised was extravagant, amounting to three hundred and fifty thousand pounds; but what was worse, this sum was abstracted from the public funds, to which he had no right, and was also rifled from the temple, which was a desecration. "And Hezekiah gave him all the silver that was found in the house of the Lord, and in the treasures of the king's house. At that time did Hezekiah cut off the gold from the doors of the temple of the Lord, and from the pillars which Hezekiah King of Judah had overlaid, and gave it to the King of Assyria." The conduct of Hezekiah in this matter cannot be justified. Inasmuch as Sennacherib accepted the offering, he was in honour bound to abandon all idea of another invasion. Albeit, contrary to every principle of justice and kindness, not to say honour, he despatches his army again into Judæa. "And the King of Assyria sent Tartan," etc. (ver. 17). What monsters are such despots! and yet they are not rare. Is there a nation existing on the face of the earth to-day, whatever its form of government, that has not at one time or another played this part?

III. AN UNPRINCIPLED DIPLOMACY. On behalf of Hezekiah, "Eliakim the son of Hilkiah, which was over the household, and Shebna the scribe, and Joah the son of Asaph the recorder," appeared before the invading soldiers, and they are thus addressed by Rabshakeh, one of the leaders of the invading host: "And Rabshakeh said unto them, Speak ye now to Hezekiah, Thus saith the great king, the King of Assyria, What confidence is this wherein thou trustest?" etc. He appears as the diplomatist of the Assyrian war-king, and what does he do? By an impassioned harangue, fraught with insolence, falsehood, and blasphemy, he urges Hezekiah and his country to surrender. In doing this: 1. *He represents his master, the King of Assyria, to be far greater than he is.* "Thus saith the great king, the King of Assyria." Great, indeed! A flashing meteor and a gorgeous bubble, nothing more! A diplomatist is ever tempted to make his own country fabulously great in the presence of the one with whom he seeks to negotiate. 2. *He seeks to terrify them with a sense of their utter inability to resist the invading army.* "What confidence is this wherein thou trustest?"—D. T.

Vers. 1—8.—*Hezekiah the good.* It is with a sense of relief that we emerge from the dark and oppressive atmosphere of the time of Ahaz into the "clear shining" (2 Sam. xxiii. 4) of a reign like that of Hezekiah. Once more Divine mercy gave Judah a king in whom the best traditions of the theocracy were revived.

I. RIGHT CONDUCT. 1. *An evil upbringing belied.* As if to set laws of heredity at defiance, the worst King of Judah hitherto is succeeded by one of the best—*the* best after David. It is difficult on human principles to account for such a phenomenon. Hezekiah had every disadvantage in inherited tendency, in evil example, and in adverse surrounding influences. But Divine grace triumphed over all, and made out of him "a chosen vessel" (Acts ix. 15). Doubtless some human agency unknown to us was employed in moulding the young prince's character. It may have been his mother, "Abi, the daughter of Zachariah;" or perhaps the Prophet Isaiah, who had afterwards so much to do with him. 2. *A good example followed.* Hezekiah took as his model, not his own father, but David, the founder of his line, of whom God had said, "I have found David the son of Jesse a man after mine own heart, which shall fulfil all my will" (Acts xiii. 22). Hezekiah is the new David. Of no other since the times of Asa is it affirmed that he did "according to all that David his father did;" and even of Asa the testimony is less emphatic than here (1 Kings xv. 11). Hezekiah mounted to the original model. David was the model for the kings of Judah; we have a yet higher one—Christ. It is well in ordering our lives to go back to this ultimate standard, judging ourselves, not by the degree of likeness or unlikeness to our neighbours, but by the measure of conformity to him.

II. REFORMING ZEAL. Hezekiah evidenced the reality of his piety by his works. In carrying out his reforms Hezekiah would no doubt be strengthened and assisted by the prophets; and the people were perhaps prepared to acquiesce in them by their disgust at the extravagant idolatries of Ahaz (cf. 2 Chron. xxviii. 27). 1. *Temptation removed.* Hezekiah early took the step which had hitherto been neglected by even the best kings—he "removed the high places." This centralized the worship at Jerusalem, and did away with the temptations to idolatry which the local altars afforded. It was further important as an evidence of his thorough-going determination to carry out the provisions of God's Law. We may wonder how Hezekiah could venture on such a step without awakening widespread resistance and disaffection; but the Book of Chronicles shows that it happened while the wave of enthusiasm created by the great Passover was yet at its height—a sufficient explanation (2 Chron. xxxi. 1). 2. *Destruction of monuments of idolatry.* Hezekiah next proceeded to clear the land of those idols of which Isaiah, at an earlier period, had said that it was full (Isa. ii. 8). He brake the images, and cut down the asherah. These vigorous measures were indispensable if true religion was to be re-established. It is not otherwise with the individual heart. True repentance is a stripping the soul of its idols—love of money, fashion, gaiety, dress, etc. "Ye cannot serve God and mammon" (Matt. vi. 24). "Covetousness, which is idolatry" (Col. iii. 5).

> "The dearest idol I have known,
>   Whate'er that idol be,
> Help me to tear it from thy throne,
>   And worship only thee."

3. *Breaking of the brazen serpent.* Another noteworthy act of Hezekiah was his breaking in pieces the brazen serpent that Moses had made. This is the first and last glimpse we get of this venerable relic since the time when it was set up in the wilderness. Its preservation was natural; it had done a wonderful work in its day; it was the symbol of a great deliverance; it had clustered around it the associations of miracle; it was the type even of the salvation of Messiah. We cannot marvel that it was reverenced as a sacred object. Yet now it had become a snare to the people, who burnt incense to it, and Hezekiah ruthlessly destroyed it, calling it (or it was called) contemptuously Nehushtan—"a piece of brass." We see from this how things originally sacred may become a snare and a temptation. Superstition is a fungus of rank growth,

and fastens on nothing more readily than on the objects which call forth a natural reverence. Cf. the story of Gideon's ephod (Judg. viii. 24—27). Thus from the veneration of martyrs in the Christian Church there grew the worship of relics. So with all other aids to devotion, conceptions that fitly invest religious feelings, which, as Carlyle says ('On Heroes') are *eidola*, things seen, symbols of the invisible. When the sense and spiritual meaning goes out of these, and they become objects of superstitious reverence in themselves, it is time for them to be broken up. Even an object so sacred as the serpent which Moses made sinks to the level of a mere "piece of brass." We are reminded of Knox's reply when a prisoner in the galleys, and the image of the Virgin was presented to him to kiss. "Mother? Mother of God?" he said. "This is no mother of God; this is *a painted bradd*"—a piece of painted wood—and flung the thing into the river.

III. PRE-EMINENT GODLINESS. 1. *Hezekiah the best of his line.* Additional emphasis is given to the commendation of Hezekiah by the statement, "After him was none like him among all the kings of Judah, nor any that were before him." It is good to be pre-eminent, but most of all to be pre-eminent for godliness. When we remember that among the kings with whom Hezekiah is here compared are such as Asa, Jehoshaphat, and Uzziah before him, and Josiah after him, we see that the praise is very great. 2. *The praise particularized.* The general statement is expanded into its particulars. Hezekiah trusted in the Lord; he clave to the Lord; he departed not from following him; he kept his commandments, as given to Moses. Trust, fidelity, obedience, and perseverance, in all these were his distinctive characteristics. Some kings had trusted, but not with so entire a heart; some had been obedient, but not so fully; some had been faithful for a time, but had failed to persevere. Hezekiah had the better record. God puts special honour on whole-hearted service. We are to see, however, that, exceptional as his goodness was, Hezekiah was not perfect. He had his flaws, his sins, his failures too. The intention of the text is not to represent him as sinless, but only as pre-eminently great and good. "There is not a just man on earth that doeth good, and sinneth not" (Eccles. vii. 20).

IV. DIVINE REWARD. Hezekiah's piety won for him Divine favour, protection, and success. 1. *Freedom from servitude.* "He rebelled against the King of Assyria, and served him not." He thus rescued the kingdom from the humiliating dependence into which it had been brought by Ahaz. 2. *Victory over enemies.* Hezekiah had also important victories over the Philistines, and was prospered "whithersoever" he went forth. Spiritually, God gives to those who fear him deliverance from the power of sin within, and victory over the world, the devil, and the flesh.—J. O.

Vers. 13—17.—*Sennacherib's first assault.* We enter in this passage on the consideration of one of the most memorable crises Judah ever passed through. The Assyrian, the rod of God's anger (Isa. x. 4), hung over Jerusalem, showing how near destruction it was if God did not interpose. A mighty deliverance was vouchsafed, showing how inviolable was its security if only fleshly confidence was renounced, and the people put their trust in the living God.

I. SENNACHERIB'S EARLY SUCCESSES. 1. *Connection with the moral state of the people.* Despite the efforts of Hezekiah and Isaiah, the moral state of the people continued at bottom unchanged. The enthusiasm enkindled by Hezekiah's great Passover (2 Chron. xxx.) passed away, and things reverted very much to their former state. The idols which Hezekiah had destroyed were brought back (cf. Isa. x. 10, 11). The nation is pointedly described as "an hypocritical nation," and pictures of the saddest kind are drawn of its wickedness (Isa. x. 6; cf. ch. i., xxii.; Micah iii.). At one point, indeed, the Prophet Micah was sent with a direct announcement of judgment, and the fulfilment was only postponed by the earnest repentance of the king (Jer. xxvi. 18, 19; cf. Micah iii. 12). Hezekiah was not faultless, but had himself transgressed through pride on the occasion of the visit of the messengers from Babylon, which falls before this period (ch. xx. 12—19; 2 Chron. xxxii. 31). He had besides been seeking to strengthen himself by political alliance with Egypt (Isa. xxx.). What wonder that chastisement should be allowed to descend on a "sinful nation, a people laden with iniquity, a seed of evil-doers" (Isa. i. 4)! As we forget God, and abuse his favours, God withdraws from us. 2. *Extent of his successes.* (1) Sennacherib took all the fenced cities of Judah. His own annals mention forty-six strong cities, and lesser cities without number. He claims to have taken also 200,150 prisoners. This was a fearful blow to the prosperity and resources of the kingdom. (2) At this stage, moreover, Sennacherib invested Jerusalem. The text speaks only of Hezekiah paying tribute, and entreating Sennacherib to depart from him; but it is morally certain that at this time Jerusalem endured a severe siege, and was saved only by the submission referred to. (a) In 2 Chron. xxxii. 1—8 we have an account of Hezekiah's vigorous preparations for the siege. (b) Sennacherib, in his own annals, describes the siege. (c) The prophecy in Isa. xxii., which belongs to this period, depicts the state of Jerusalem during the siege, and a fearful picture of demoralization it is. The theory that this prophecy refers to an earlier siege under Sargon seems to us to have little probability. The hand of God was thus lying heavily on the people. Only by leading men to feel their own weakness does God train them to rely upon his help. When Hezekiah's trust in man was shattered, and he was led to look to God alone, Sennacherib's campaign came to an ignominious end.

II. HEZEKIAH'S SUBMISSION. 1. *The failure of the arm of flesh.* Hezekiah had been seeking alliances with Egypt and Ethiopia, but no help reached him in his hour of extremity. Isaiah had warned him of this (Isa. xxx.). The act of seeking such an alliance implied a distrust of God. Astute politicians no doubt thought an alliance with Egypt a much more tangible affair than an alliance with the invisible Jehovah. So long, however, as Hezekiah looked in this quarter for aid he was doomed to disappointment. Neither the King of Egypt nor strongly fortified walls availed to save him. He had to learn the lesson : " In returning and rest shall ye be saved ; in quietness and in confidence shall be your strength" (Isa. xxx. 15). 2. *The humiliating tribute.* Despairing of help from his ally, and faltering in his faith in God, Hezekiah made an unworthy submission. It may be gathered from Isa. xxii. that affairs in the city had reached an awful height of wickedness. Pestilence was sweeping off the people in crowds ; and Hezekiah may have felt that he could stand it no longer. The King of Assyria accepted his submission, and appointed him three hundred talents of silver and thirty talents of gold as tribute. To obtain this large sum he had not only to empty once more the often-ransacked treasuries of the temple and the king's house, but had to cut off the gold from the very doors and pillars of the temple. It was himself who had overlaid these pillars with the precious metal, but now they had to be stripped of their adornment, and all given to the rapacious Assyrian. Truly it was " a day of trouble, and of treading down, and of perplexity " (Isa. xxii. 5). What humiliations men are willing to endure rather than submit themselves heartily to the sway of the living God ! After all, "willing" is not the word, for they would fain escape these humiliations, but find they cannot. Yet they do not return. 3. *His submission no advantage.* Sennacherib withdrew to Lachish, and Hezekiah was left to hope that by this great sacrifice he had got rid of him. He was soon to be undeceived. What happened we do not know ; possibly some rumours reached the King of Assyria of the march of Tirhakah alluded to in ch. xix. 9, and he may have suspected further treachery on the part of Hezekiah. In any case, a new host was despatched against Jerusalem, and fresh demands were made for surrender (ver. 17). Hezekiah's distress must have been unspeakable. He had paid his tribute, and was no better than before. Waters of a full cup were wrung out to him (Ps. lxxiii. 10). It is thus evermore till men turn from the help of man to the help of God.—J. O.

Vers. 17—37.—*Rabshakeh's boastings.* From Lachish Sennacherib sent an army to Jerusalem, and with it some of his highest officers, the Tartan, Rabsaris, and Rabshakeh. Taking their stand by "the conduit of the upper pool," where they could be heard from the walls, they called for the king to come to them. Hezekiah did not come, but sent three envoys, Eliakim, Shebna, and Joah, to whom Rabshakeh, the orator of the party, addressed himself. His speech is a very skilful one from his own point of view, and falls into two parts. It is pervaded by the utmost arrogancy and contempt of the God of the Jews.

I. HIS ADDRESS TO THE ENVOYS. The question Rabshakeh had been sent by his master to ask of Hezekiah was—"What confidence is this wherein thou trustest?" He proceeds to demolish one by one Hezekiah's supposed confidences, and to show how vain it was for him to hope to carry on the war. 1. *Hezekiah's confidence in Egypt.* Rabshakeh answers his own question by declaring, first, that Hezekiah's confidence was placed in Egypt. This was true; and it was also true that, as the speaker next went on to say, this confidence was in a "bruised reed." The policy of relying on Egypt, instead of seeking help from God, was Hezekiah's great mistake. Rabshakeh did not denounce the worthlessness of this ground of confidence too scornfully. Pharaoh King of Egypt was indeed a bruised reed, on which, if a man leant, it would go into his hand, and pierce it. Isaiah's language had been not less strong (Isa. xxx.). The metaphor may be applied to any reliance on mere human wisdom, human power, or human help. Often it has proved so in individual experience and the history of nations. Through some overlooked factor in the calculations, some unexpected turn in providence, some treachery, self-interest, or delay on the part of allies, the best-laid schemes break down, the strongest combinations dissolve like smoke. 2. *Hezekiah's confidence in Jehovah.* Rabshakeh next deals with Hezekiah's trust in the Lord. He does not at this point urge the plea afterwards put forth, viz. that no gods can stand before the King of Assyria. Indeed, he claims (ver. 25) to be commissioned by Jehovah— either an idle boast or an allusion to what he had heard of Isaiah's prophecies (cf. Isa. vii. 17—25; x. 5—19). But he skilfully makes use of Hezekiah's action in destroying the high places and altars. "Is not this he whose high places and whose altars Hezekiah hath taken away, and hath said to Judah and Jerusalem, Ye shall worship before this altar in Jerusalem?" This sweeping away of the high places is represented as an outrage on the religion of Jehovah, which that Deity might be expected to avenge. How, then, could Hezekiah expect any help from him? The argument was a skilful one as directed to the body of the people. The high places were of long-standing sanctity, and they at least were disposed to regard them with superstitious reverence. What if, after all, Hezekiah had displeased Jehovah by suppressing them? Calamity upon calamity was falling on the nation: was there not a cause? A reformer must ever lay his account with charges of this kind. Any political, social, or religious change is apt to be blamed for troubles that arise on the back of it. *Post hoc, ergo propter hoc.* The early Christians were blamed for the calamities of the Roman empire; the Reformation was blamed for the civil convulsions that followed it; when drought or trouble falls on tribes which have been persuaded to abandon idolatry, they are apt to think the idols are angry, and to go back to their old worship. In this argument, however, Rabshakeh was as wrong as he was right in his first one. The fault was that the people did not trust God enough, and what he thought was a provocation of Jehovah was an act done in his honour, and in obedience to his will. 3. *Hezekiah's confidence in his resources.* Lastly, Rabshakeh ridicules the idea that Hezekiah can resist his master by force. Where are his chariots and horsemen? Or, if he had horses, where are the riders to put on them? He undertakes to give two thousand horses, if Hezekiah will furnish the men; and he knows he cannot. How, then, can he hope to put to flight even the least of Sennacherib's captains? Rabshakeh again was right in assuming that Hezekiah had not material forces wherewith to contend with Sennacherib, and Hezekiah himself was too well aware of the fact. He had not confidence in his forces, and therein the orator was wrong. But Rabshakeh's whole speech shows that he was himself committing the error he denounced in Hezekiah. If the question were retorted, "What confidence is this wherein *thou* trustest?" the answer could only be—In chariots and horses, in the proved might of the Assyrian arms. His speech breathes throughout the spirit of the man who has unbounded trust in armaments, provided only they are gigantic enough. Because Sennacherib has such immense armies, valiant soldiers, and such numbers of them, therefore he is invincible in war, and can defy God and man. The arm of flesh—"big battalions"—is every-thing here. Herein lay *his* profound mistake; and it was soon to be demonstrated. The might of the *Invisible* was to be declared against the power of the *visible.* Philistinism was to receive another overthrow—this time without even the sling and stones (1 Sam. xvi. 40—51).

II. ADDRESS TO THE JEWS. At this point Hezekiah's officers interposed, and requested Rabshakeh to speak, not in the Hebrew, but in the Syrian tongue, that his language might not be understood by the people on the wall. Rabshakeh had come on a mission of diplomacy, and it was proper that in the first instance only the king's representatives should be consulted with. The envoy, however, insolently broke through all customary bounds, and declared that it was the common people he wished to address. Taking up, therefore, a yet better position, he now spoke directly, and in louder tones, to the people, who by this time may be supposed to have crowded the battlements. Again declaring that he bears a message from "the great king, the King of Assyria," he bids them not let Hezekiah deceive them, and urges: 1. *The advantages of submission.* As it was, they were in evil case. But if they surrendered to Sennacherib, they had nothing to fear. Here Rabshakeh touches on delicate ground. He cannot deny that they will lose their liberty, and be transported as captives to Assyria. All he can do is to attempt to gild the pill. He tells them, first, that in the mean time they will be allowed the utmost freedom—to eat every man of his own vine and of his own fig tree, and to drink every man the waters of his own cistern. When the time does come that they must be removed—and he tries to represent this as a privilege—it will be to a land like their own, a land of corn and wine, of bread and vineyards, of oil and olives and honey; a land where they shall live, and not die. The promises were alluring only by contrast with the worse fate that awaited them if they did not submit to the Assyrian; but more than this, they were deceitful. They were promises which, if the people had trusted to them, would never have been fulfilled. Sennacherib was not in the habit of treating his captives tenderly. His good faith had just been tested by his perfidy towards Hezekiah. Is it not always so with the promises of the tempter? When a soul capitulates, and yields to sin, what becomes of the bright prospects that are opened up beforehand? Are they ever realized? There is a brief period of excitement, of giddy delight, then satiety, loathing, the sense of degradation, the dying out of all real joy. What, if by yielding to sin, some present evil be avoided, some immediate good gained? Is the good ever what was anticipated? or can it compensate for the exile from God and holiness which is its price? At all hazards the wise course is to adhere to God and duty. The visions of corn and wine, of bread and vineyards, of oil and olives, by which the soul is tempted from its allegiance, are illusions—as unsubstantial as the desert mirage. 2. *The futility of resistance.* To enforce his argument for submission, Rabshakeh returns to what is undeniably his strongest point, viz. the futility of resistance. Can they hope to be delivered? He had argued this before from the side of Hezekiah's weakness, showing the baselessness of his grounds of confidence; he now argues it from the side of Sennacherib's strength. Here undoubtedly he has a plausible case. (1) From the military point of view. "Let not Hezekiah deceive you: for he shall not be able to deliver you out of his hand." Since the days of Tiglath-pileser the Assyrian arms had swept on in a tide of almost uninterrupted conquest. Not only Hamath and Arpad and Sepharvaim, but Babylon, Damascus, Israel, Philistia, and Egypt, had felt the force of their resistless might. Judah had already severely suffered. What hope had Hezekiah, with his little handful of men, caged like a bird in Jerusalem, of rolling back this tide of conquest! The thing, on natural grounds, seemed an impossibility. (2) From a religious point of view. "Neither let Hezekiah make you trust in the Lord, saying, The Lord will surely deliver us." Here the position of the Assyrian conqueror seemed—from the heathen standpoint, but of course only from that—equally strong. In heathen view, the contest was not only a contest of man with man, but of Asshur and the other Assyrian gods, with the gods of other nations. And how had that contest gone? The gods of Assyria had in every case proved the stronger in the battle. Where were the gods of the conquered nations? What had they been able to do for their worshippers? What had even Jehovah been able to do for Samaria? Who among them all had delivered their country out of the hand of Sennacherib? What hope was there that Jerusalem would fare any better than Samaria had done? The validity of this conclusion depends entirely upon the soundness of the premises. If the gods of these nations had a real existence, and Jehovah was but one more local deity among the rest, it would be difficult to resist the inference that the chances were strongly in favour of Asshur. But the case was altered if these idol-gods were nullities, and Jehovah was the one Ruler of heaven and earth, in whose providence the movements even of Sennacherib and his all-conquering armies were embraced. And this, of course, was the faith of Isaiah and Hezekiah and the godly part of Judah. That it was the right one was shown by the result. We see from this example how a false view-point compels a false and mistaken reading of the whole facts of history and of human life. The view which history presents to one who denies the postulates of revelation will differ entirely from the view which it presents to a Christian believer. Belief in God is the right centre for understanding everything.

III. THE ANSWER OF SILENCE. To these harangues of Rabshakeh the people "answered not a word." Hezekiah had given this instruction to his officers, and they, when the people gathered, doubtless spread among them the knowledge of the king's wish. Accordingly they "held their peace." There were many reasons why this answer of silence was a wise one. 1. *Rabshakeh's words did not deserve an answer.* His address to the people on the wall was a breach of all diplomatic courtesy; it had for its object to sow the seeds of mutiny, and set the people against their king; it was obviously insincere in its tone and promises, scrupling at nothing which would induce the people to surrender their liberties; in relation to Jehovah, it was profane and blasphemous. Speeches of that kind are best left unanswered. A tempter is fittingly met with silence. A man who makes insincere proposals does not deserve to be reasoned with. Profanity and blasphemy should be left without reply (Matt. vii. 6). 2. *From Rabshakeh's point of view no reply was possible.* This has freely to be conceded. What would it have availed to point out to him that the gods of these other nations were no gods, and that Jehovah was the one living and true God? Such statements would have but provoked a new burst of mockery. It was better, therefore, to say nothing. In all reasoning with an opponent there must be a basis of common ground. When we reach a fundamental divergence of first principles, it is time to stop. At least, if argument is to proceed, it must go back on these first principles, and try to find a deeper unity. Failing in that, it must cease. Between the Christian and unchristian views of the world, *e.g.*, there is no middle term. 3. *Even from the Jewish point of view no reply was ready.* God was to be trusted, but would he indeed save? What if the iniquities of the people had provoked him to deliver them up, as he had delivered up Samaria? Deliverance was conditional on repentance: did the state of morals in the city show much sign of repentance? Or, if God meant to deliver them, how would he do it? They seemed fast in the lion's jaws. The way of escape from their present predicament was not obvious, yea, no way seemed possible. What, then, should they answer? At most, their belief in Jehovah's interposition was an act of faith, for which no justification could be given in outward appearances. In such crises, when all rests on faith, nothing on sight, the best attitude of the soul, at least in presence of the worldly, is silence. "Be still, and know that I am God," is the counsel given in the psalm supposed to commemorate this deliverance (Ps. xlvi. 10).—J. O.

EXPOSITION.

CHAPTER XIX.

Vers. 1—37.—SECOND EXPEDITION OF SENNACHERIB AGAINST HEZEKIAH (*continued*). The chapter falls into four portions: (1) The sequel to the embassy of Rabshakeh (vers. 1—8); (2) the insulting letter of Sennacherib (vers. 9—14); (3) Hezekiah's prayer, and God's answer to it by the mouth of Isaiah (vers. 15—34); and (4) the destruction of Sennacherib's host, his hurried flight, and his murder at Nineveh by his sons (vers. 35—37). The narrative runs parallel with that in Isa. xxxvii., with which it corresponds almost word for word.

Ver. 1.—And it came to pass, when King Hezekiah heard it, that he rent his clothes—following the example of his chief officers, who came into his presence "with their clothes rent" (see ch. xviii. 37)—and covered himself with sackcloth. A sign of grief and self-humiliation (comp. Gen. xxxvii. 34; 2 Sam. iii. 31; xxi. 10; 1 Kings xx. 31; xxi. 27; ch. vi. 30, etc.). It was natural that the king should be even more strongly affected than his ministers. And went into the house of the Lord; to open his griefs, ask counsel, and beg for aid.

Ver. 2.—And he sent Eliakim, which was over the household, and Shebna the scribe, and the elders of the priests. "The elders of the priests" are aged men holding the priestly office, not necessarily the high priest, or the most notable or most dignified of the priests. The king felt that his best hope, so far as man was concerned, lay in the prophetical order. Isaiah, Hosea, Joel, Micah, and perhaps Obadiah, were the prophets of the time; but it is not clear that any of them were accessible except Isaiah. He had been Ahaz's counsellor (Isa. vii. 4—16), and was now certainly among the regular counsellors of Hezekiah. Moreover, he was in Jerusalem, and could readily be consulted. Hezekiah, therefore, sends to him in his distress, and sends a most honourable and dignified embassy. It is his intention to treat the prophet with the utmost respect and courtesy. No doubt, at this period the prophetical order stood higher than the priestly one in general estimation; and not unworthily. If any living man could give the king sound advice under the circumstances, it was the son of Amoz. **Covered with sackcloth.** Probably by the king's command. Hezekiah wished to emphasize his own horror and grief in the eyes of the prophet, and could only do so by making his messengers assume the garb which he had judged suitable for himself on the occasion. **To Isaiah the prophet the son of Amoz.** Nothing more is known of Amoz beyond his being Isaiah's father. He is not to be confounded with the Prophet Amos, whose name is spelt quite differently: עָמוֹץ, not אָמוֹץ.

Ver. 3.—**And they said unto him, Thus saith Hezekiah, This day is a day of trouble, and of rebuke, and of blasphemy.** Of "trouble," or "distress," manifestly—a day on which the whole nation is troubled, grieved, alarmed, distressed, made miserable. It is also a day of "rebuke," or rather of "chastisement"—a day on which God's hand lies heavy upon us and chastises us for our sins. And it is a day, not of "blasphemy," but of "abhorrence" or of "contumely"—a day on which God contumeliously rejects his people, and allows them to be insulted by their enemies (see the comments of Keil and Bähr). **For the children are come to the birth, and there is not strength to bring forth.** A proverbial expression, probably meaning that a dangerous crisis approaches, and that the nation has no strength to carry it through the peril.

Ver. 4.—**It may be the Lord thy God**—still "thy God," at any rate, if he will not condescend to be called ours, since we have so grievously offended him by our many sins and backslidings—**will hear all the words of Rabshakeh.** "The words of Rabshakeh" (Isa. xxxvii. 4); but the expression here used is more emphatic. Hezekiah hoped that God would "hear" Rabshakeh's words, would note them, and punish them. **Whom the King of Assyria his master hath sent to reproach the living God.** (For the "reproaches" intended, see ch. xviii. 30—35. For the expression, "the living God," אֱלֹהִים חַי, see Deut. v. 26; Josh. iii. 10; 1 Sam. xvii. 26; Ps. xlii. 2; lxxxiv. 2; Hos. i. 10, etc.) A contrast is intended

between the "living" God, and the dead idols whom Rabshakeh has placed on a par with him. **And will reprove the words which the Lord thy God hath heard.** The "words of Rabshakeh," his contemptuous words concerning Jehovah (ch. xviii. 33—35) and his lying words (ch. xviii. 25), constituted the new feature in the situation, and, while a ground for "distress," were also a ground for hope: would not God in some signal way vindicate his own honour, and "reprove" them? **Wherefore lift up thy prayer for the remnant that are left.** Sennacherib, in his former expedition, wherein he took forty-six of the Judæan cities, besides killing vast numbers, had, as he himself tells us ('Eponym Canon,' p. 134), carried off into captivity 200,150 persons. He had also curtailed Hezekiah's dominions, detaching from them various cities with their territories, and attaching them to Ashdod, Gaza, and Ekron (ibid., p. 135). Thus it was only a "remnant" of the Jewish people that was left in the land (comp. Isa. i. 7—9).

Ver. 5.—**So the servants of King Hezekiah came to Isaiah.** Superfluous, according to modern notions, but rounding off the paragraph commenced with ver. 2.

Ver. 6.—**And Isaiah said unto them, Thus shall ye say to your master.** Isaiah seems to have been ready with a reply. The news of the words spoken by Rabshakeh had probably flown through the city, and reached him, and he had already laid the matter before God, and received God's instructions concerning it. He was therefore able to return an answer at once. **Thus saith the Lord, Be not afraid of the words which thou hast heard, with which the servants** —rather, lackeys; the term used is not the common one for "servants," viz. עֲבָדֵי, but a contemptuous one, נַעֲרֵי, "foot-boys," or "lackeys"—**of the King of Assyria have blasphemed me.**

Ver. 7.—**Behold, I will send a blast upon him.** The meaning is doubtful. Most modern critics translate, with the LXX., "I will put a spirit within him," and understand "a spirit of cowardice," or "a despondent mood" (Thenius), or "an extraordinary impulse of Divine inspiration, which is to hurry him blindly on" (Drechsler). But the idea of our translators, that the blast (רוּחַ) is external, and sent upon him, not put in him—that, in fact, the destruction of his army is referred to, seems defensible by such passages as Exod. xv. 8 and Isa. xxv. 4. The prophecy was, no doubt, intentionally vague—enough for its immediate purpose, which was to comfort and strengthen Hezekiah—but not intended to gratify man's curiosity by revealing the exact mode in which God would work. **And** he shall hear a rumour; literally, *he shall hear a hearsay;* i.e. he shall be told something, which shall determine him on a hasty retreat. It is best, I think, to understand, not news of Tirhakah's advance (Knobel, Keil, Bähr), much less news of an insurrection in some other part of the empire (Cheyne), but information of the disaster to his army. It is no objection to this that Sennacherib was "with his army." No doubt he was. But he would learn the catastrophe from the mouth of some one who came into his tent and told him—he would "hear a hearsay." **And shall return to his own land** (see ver. 36), **and I will cause him to fall by the sword in his own land.** (On Sennacherib's murder, see the comment upon ver. 37.)

Ver. 8.—**So Rabshakeh returned.** Rabshakeh's embassy came to an end with the retirement of Hezekiah's officers from their conference with the three envoys of Sennacherib. No further communication was held with him. He had outraged all propriety by his appeal to the "men upon the wall" (ch. xviii. 27—35); and it seems to have been thought most dignified to give him no answer at all. He had offered no terms—he had simply delivered a summons to surrender, and the closed gates and guarded walls were a sufficient reply. So he felt, and returned to his master, *re infecta.* **And found the King of Assyria warring against Libnah.** The position of Libnah relatively to Lachish is uncertain. The site of Lachish may be regarded as fixed to *Um-Lakis;* but that of Libnah rests wholly on conjecture. It has been placed at *Tel es-Safieh,* twelve miles north-east of *Um-Lakis;* at *Arak-el-Menshiyeh,* about five miles nearly due east of the same; and near *Ummel-Bikar,* four miles south-east of *Um-Lakis.* A removal from Um-Lakis to Tel-el-Safieh would mean a retreat. A march from Um-Lakis to either of the other sites would be quite compatible with an intention to push on to Egypt. **For he had heard that he was departed from Lachish.** Whether Lachish had been taken or not cannot be determined from these words. But we can scarcely suppose that a place of such slight strength can have defied the Assyrian arms successfully. It is best therefore to suppose, with Keil and Thenius, that Lachish had been taken.

Vers. 9—14.—*Sennacherib's letter to Hezekiah.* Sennacherib seems to have been induced to write to Hezekiah by the fact that he could not march against him at once. A forward movement on the part of Tirhakah was reported to him (ver. 9), and he thought it necessary to meet, or at least watch it. But he must vent his anger on the rebel Judæan monarch in some way. He sends a letter, therefore, as more weighty and impressive than a mere message. He warns Hezekiah against being himself deceived by Jehovah (ver. 10); and he expands his inductive argument in proof of the irresistible might of Assyria, by an enumeration of four more recent conquests (ver. 12). Otherwise, he does little but repeat what Rabshakeh had already urged.

Ver. 9.—**And when he heard say of Tirhakah King of Ethiopia.** Tirhakah was one of the most distinguished of the later Egyptian monarchs. An Ethiopian by birth, and originally ruling from Napata over the Upper Nile valley from the First Cataract to (perhaps) Khartoum, he extended his dominion over Egypt probably about B.C. 700, maintaining, however, Shabatok, as a sort of puppet-king, upon the throne. About B.C. 693 he succeeded Shabatok, and held the throne till B.C. 667, being engaged in many wars with the Assyrians. The native form of his name is "Tahrak" or "Tahark," the Assyrian "Tarku" or "Tarqu," the Greek "Taracos" or "Tearchon." He has left numerous memorials in Egypt and Ethiopia, and was regarded by the Greeks as a great conqueror. At the time of Sennacherib's second attack on Hezekiah (about B.C. 699) he was, as appears in the text, not yet King of Egypt, but only of Ethiopia. Still, he regarded Egypt as practically under his suzerainty, and when it was threatened by Sennacherib's approach, he marched to the rescue. **Behold, he is come out to fight against thee.** He may have regarded himself as bound in honour to come to the relief of Hezekiah, or he may have been simply bent on defending his own territory. **He sent messengers again unto Hezekiah, saying,**

Ver. 10.—**Thus shall ye speak to Hezekiah King of Judah, saying.** The messengers brought a "letter" (סְפָרִים), as we see from ver. 14; but still they were to "speak to Hezekiah"—*i.e.* they were first to read the contents to him, and then to hand him the copy. **Let not thy God in whom thou trustest deceive thee, saying, Jerusalem shall not be delivered into the hand of the King of Assyria.** Sennacherib drops the fiction that he himself is sent by Jehovah to attack Judæa and destroy it (ch. xviii. 25), and contents himself with suggesting that any announcements which Hezekiah may have received from his God are untrustworthy. Probably he spoke his convictions. He did not think it possible that Jerusalem could resist or escape him (comp. Isa. x. 8—11 and 13, 14).

Ver. 11.—Behold, thou hast heard what the kings of Assyria have done to all lands, by destroying them utterly (see the comment on ch. xviii. 33). The fact was indisputable (see ver. 17). The question remained—Would this triumphant career of success necessarily continue? And shalt thou be delivered? A perfect induction is impossible in practical matters. Anything short of a perfect induction is short of a proof.

Ver. 12.—Have the gods of the nations delivered them which my fathers have destroyed? The Assyrian kings always speak of all their predecessors as their ancestors. In point of fact, Sennacherib had had only one "father" among the previous kings, viz. Sargon. As Gozan (see the comment on ch. xvii. 6). It is uncertain at what time Gozan was finally conquered and absorbed. It was frequently overrun by the Assyrians from the reign of Tiglath-pileser I. (about B.C. 1100); but it was probably not absorbed until about B.C. 809. The Prefect of Gozan first appears in the list of Assyrian Eponyms in B.C. 794. And Haran. "Haran" is generally admitted to be the city of Terah (Gen. xi. 32), and indeed there is no rival claimant of the name. Its position was in the western part of the Gauzanitis region, on the Belik, about lat. 36° 50' N. It was probably conquered by Assyria about the same time as Gozan. And Rezeph. A town called "Razappa," probably "Rezeph," appears in the Assyrian inscriptions from an early date. It is thought to have been in the near vicinity of Haran, but had been conquered and absorbed as early as B.C. 818. Whether it is identical with the Resapha of Ptolemy ('Geograph.,' v. 15) is doubtful. And the children of Eden. Probably the inhabitants of a city called "Bit-Adinì" in the Assyrian inscriptions, which was on the Middle Euphrates, not far from Carchemish, on the left bank ('Records of the Past,' vol. iii. pp. 69, 71, etc.). This place was conquered by Asshur-nazir-pal, about B.C. 877. Which were in Thelasar. "Thelasar" is probably the Hebrew equivalent of "Tel-Asshur," "the hill or fort of Asshur," which may have been the Assyrian name of Bit-Adini, or of a city dependent on it. Asshur-nazir-pal gave Assyrian names to several cities on the Middle Euphrates (see 'Records of the Past,' vol. iii. p. 55, line 48; p. 69, line 50).

Ver. 13.—Where is the King of Hamath. Ilu-bid, King of Hamath, raised a rebellion against Sargon in B.C. 720, and was taken prisoner the same year and carried to Assyria (see the 'Eponym Canon,' p. 127). And the King of Arpad. Arpad revolted in conjunction with Hamath, and was reduced about the same time ('Eponym Canon,' p. 126). Its "king" is not mentioned, but he probably shared the fate of Ilu-bid. And the King of the city of Sepharvaim, of Hena, and Ivah? It is probably not meant that these three cities were all of them under the dominion of one and the same king. "King" is to be taken distributively. (On the sites of the cities, see the comment upon ch. xviii. 34.)

Ver. 14.—And Hezekiah received the letter. It had not been previously stated that Sennacherib had written a letter. But the author forgets this, and so speaks of "the letter." Kings generally communicated by letters, and not merely by messages (see ch. v. 5; xx. 12; 2 Chron. ii. 11; Neh. i. 9, etc.). Of the hand of the messengers, and read it. Probably Sennacherib had caused it to be written in Hebrew. And Hezekiah went up into the house of the Lord, and spread it before the Lord. Not as if God would not otherwise know the contents of the letter, but to emphasize his detestation of the letter, and to make it silently plead for him with God. Ewald rightly compares what Judas Maccabæus did with the disfigured copies of the Law at Maspha (1 Macc. iii. 48), but incorrectly calls it ('History of Israel,' vol. iv. p. 183, note 1, Eng. trans.) "a laying down of the object in the sanctuary." Maspha was "over against" the temple, at the distance of a mile or more.

Ver. 15.—And Hezekiah prayed before the Lord, and said, O Lord God of Israel. In the parallel passage of Isaiah (xxxvii. 16) we find, "O Lord of hosts, God of Israel." Our author probably abbreviates. Which dwellest between the cherubims; or, on the cherubim—"which hast thy seat," i.e., "behind the veil in the awful holy of holies, consecrated to thee, and where thou dost manifest thyself." Hezekiah, as Keil observes, calls into prominence "the covenant relation into which Jehovah, the Almighty Creator and Ruler of the whole world, had entered towards Israel. As the covenant God, who was enthroned above the cherubim, the Lord was bound to help his people, if they turned to him with faith in the time of their distress and entreated his assistance." Thou art the God, even thou alone, of all the kingdoms of the earth. Thou art not, i.e., as Sennacherib supposes, a mere local god, presiding over Judæa, and protecting it; but thou art the God of all the earth and of all its kingdoms, including his own, equally. Moreover, thou alone art the God of the kingdoms. Their supposed gods are no gods, have no existence, are the mere fictions of an idle and excited imagination, are mere "breath" and "nothingness." Thou hast made heaven and earth. Whereas they have done nothing, have given no proof of their existence (see Isa. xli. 23, 24).

Ver. 16.—Lord, bow down thine ear, and

hear. "Bow down thine ear" is a Hebrew idiom for "give ear," "attend " (see Ps. xxxi. 2; lxxi. 2; lxxxvi. 1; Prov. xxii. 17, etc.). It is based upon the fact that, when men wish to catch exactly what another says to them, they bend themselves towards him, and bring *one ear* as near to him as they can. **Open, Lord, thine eyes, and see.** Take cognizance both with eye and ear; *i.e.* take *full* cognizance—let nothing escape thee. **And hear the words of Sennacherib, which hath sent him to reproach the living God;** rather, *which he has sent to reproach.* The suffix translated "him" in our version really means "it"—*i.e.* the speech or letter of Sennacherib, which Hezekiah has "spread before the Lord."

Ver. 17.—**Of a truth, Lord, the kings of Assyria**—*i.e.* Sennacherib, and his predecessors—the long line of monarchs who have sat on the Assyrian throne for many past ages—**have destroyed the nations and their lands**; rather, *have laid waste*, as in the parallel passage of Isaiah (xxxvii. 18). "Destroyed" is too strong a word. Hezekiah fully admits the boast of the Assyrian monarch, that he and his predecessors have had a wonderful career of success (comp. Isa. x. 5—14); but he refuses to regard this past success as ensuring success in the future. All is in the hand of God, and will be determined as God pleases. It is not an iron necessity that rules the world, but a personal will, and this will may be affected by prayer, to which (ver. 19) he therefore has recourse.

Ver. 18.—**And have cast their gods into the fire.** The images worshipped by the various nations are regarded as "their *gods*," which they were, at any rate in the minds of the common people. The ordinary practice of the Assyrians was to carry off the images taken from a conquered people, and to set them up in their own country as trophies of victory (see Isa. xlvi. 1, 2, where a similar practice is ascribed by anticipation to the Persians). But there are places in the inscriptions where the gods are said to have been "destroyed" or "burnt." It is reasonable to suppose that the images destroyed were those of wood, stone, and bronze, which had little or no intrinsic value, while the gold and silver idols were carried off to the land of the conqueror. No doubt idols of the former far outnumbered those of the latter kind, and, at each sack of a city the "gods" which it contained were mostly burnt. **For they were no gods, but the work of men's hands, wood and stone** (comp. Isa. xlii. 17; xliv. 9—20; xlvi. 6, 7). Wooden images (the Greek ξόανα) were probably the earliest that were made, and, on account of their antiquity, were often especially reverenced. They were "carved, but rude, with undivided feet, and eyes

indicated by a line, the face coloured red, or white, or gilt. It was only later that ivory and gold plates were commonly laid over the wood, vested and decked out with ornaments" (Dollinger, 'Jew and Gentile,' vol. i. p. 240). Stone idols were at first shapeless masses, then pillars or cones, finally imitations of the human form, varying from the rudest representations to the priceless statues of Phidias. In Assyrian times, neither the wooden nor the stone idols were possessed of any artistic beauty. Therefore they have destroyed them. "Gods" of this kind could not help themselves, much less save their devotees or the cities supposed to be under their protection. It was not to be wondered at that the Assyrians had triumphed over such gods.

Ver. 19.—**Now therefore, O Lord our God.** Hezekiah draws the strongest possible contrast between Jehovah and the idols. Sennacherib had placed them upon a par (ch. xviii. 33—35; xix. 10—13). Hezekiah insists that the idols are "no gods," are "nothing"—at any rate are mere blocks of wood and stone, shaped by human hands. But Jehovah is "the God of all the kingdoms of the earth" (ver. 15), the Maker of heaven and earth (ver. 15), the one and only God (ver. 19)—answering to his name, self-existing, all-sufficient, the groundwork of all other existence. And he is "*our* God"—the special God of Israel, bound by covenant to protect *them* against all enemies. **I beseech thee, save thou us out of his hand;** *i.e.* "do that which this proud blasphemer thinks that thou canst not do" (ch. xviii. 35), show him that thou art far mightier than he supposes, wholly unlike those "no-gods," over whom he has hitherto triumphed—a "very present Help in trouble" potent to save. **That all the kingdoms of the earth may know that thou art the Lord God.** The glory of God is the end of creation; and God's true saints always bear the fact in mind, and desire nothing so much as that his glory should be shown forth everywhere and always. Moses, in his prayers for rebellious Israel in the wilderness, constantly urges upon God that it will not be for his glory to destroy or desert them (Exod. xxxii. 12; Numb. xiv. 13—16; Deut. ix. 26—29). David, in his great strait, asks the destruction of his enemies, "*that men may know* that thou, whose name alone is Jehovah, art the Most High over all the earth" (Ps. lxxxiii. 18), and again (Ps. lix. 13), "Consume them in wrath, consume them, that they may not be; and *let them know* that God ruleth in Jacob unto the ends of the earth." Hezekiah prays for a signal vengeance on Sennacherib, not for his own sake, not even for his people's sake, so much as for the vindication of God's honour among the nations of the earth—that it may be known far and wide that Jehovah is a God who can help, the real Ruler of the world, against whom earthly kings and earthly might avail nothing. Even thou only. It would not satisfy Hezekiah that Jehovah should be acknowledged as *a* mighty god, one of many. He asks for such a demonstration as shall convince men that he is unique, that he stands alone, that he is the *only* mighty God in all the earth.

Ver. 20.—**Then Isaiah the son of Amoz sent to Hezekiah, saying.** As Hezekiah prays, Isaiah is by Divine revelation made cognizant of his prayer, and commissioned to answer it favourably. That he *sends* his answer, instead of taking it, is indicative of the high status of the prophets at this period, which made it not unseemly that, in spiritual matters, they should claim at least equality with the monarch. **Thus saith the Lord God of Israel, That which thou hast prayed to me against Sennacherib King of Assyria I have heard.** First of all, Hezekiah is assured that his prayer has been "heard." God has "bowed down his ear" to it (ver. 16)—has taken it into his consideration, and has sent a reply. Then the reply follows, in fourteen verses arranged in four strophes or stanzas. The first (vers. 21—24) and second (vers. 25—28) are addressed to Sennacherib, and breathe a tone of scorn and contempt. The third (vers. 29—31), is addressed to Hezekiah, and is encouraging and consolatory. The fourth (vers. 32—34) is an assurance to all whom it may concern, that Jerusalem is safe, that Sennacherib will not take it, that he will not even commence its siege.

Ver. 21.—**This is the word that the Lord hath spoken concerning him.** "Him" is, of course, Sennacherib. It adds great liveliness and force to the opening portion of the oracle, that it should be addressed directly by Jehovah to Sennacherib, as an answer to his bold challenge. The only address at all similar in Scripture is that to Nebuchadnezzar (Dan. iv. 31, 32), spoken by "a voice from heaven." But the present passage is one of far greater force and beauty. **The virgin the daughter of Zion;** rather, *the virgin daughter of Zion,* or *the virgin daughter, Zion.* Cities were commonly personified by the sacred writers, and represented as "daughters" (see Isa. xxiii. 10, 12; xlvii. 1, 5, etc.). "Virgin daughter" here may perhaps represent "the consciousness of impregnability" (Drechsler); but the phrase seems to have been used rhetorically or poetically, to heighten the beauty or pathos of the picture (Isa. xxiii. 12; xlvii. 1; Jer. xlvi. 11; Lam. ii. 13), without any reference to the question whether the particular city had or had not been previously taken. Jerusalem certainly had been taken by

Shishak (1 Kings xiv. 26), and by Joash (ch. xiv. 13); but Zion, if it be taken as the name of the eastern city (Bishop Patrick, *ad loc.*), may have been still a "virgin fortress." **Hath despised thee, and laughed thee to scorn;** or, *despises thee and laughs thee to scorn.* The Hebrew preterite has often a present sense. Whatever was the case a little while ago (see Isa. xxii. 1—14), the city now laughs at thy threats. **The daughter of Jerusalem hath shaken her head at thee;** or, *wags her head at thee*—in scorn and ridicule (comp. Ps. xxii. 7).

Ver. 22.—**Whom hast thou reproached and blasphemed?** *i.e.* "Against whom hast thou been mad enough to measure thyself? Whom hast thou dared to insult and defy?" Not an earthly king—not a mere angelic being—but the Omnipotent, the Lord of earth and heaven. What utter folly is this! What mere absurdity? **And against whom hast thou exalted thy voice?** *i.e.* "spoken proudly"—in the tone in which a superior speaks of an inferior—**and lifted up thine eyes on high?**—*i.e.* "looked down upon"—treated with contempt, as not worth consideration—even **against the Holy One of Israel.** Isaiah's favourite phrase—used by him twenty-seven times, and only five times in the rest of Scripture—marks this entire prophecy as his genuine utterance, not the composition of the writer of Kings, but a burst of sudden inspiration from the Coryphæus of the prophetic band. The oracle bears all the marks of Isaiah's elevated, fervid, and highly poetic style.

Ver. 23.—**By thy messengers**—literally, *by the hand of thy messengers*—Rabshakeh and others (see ch. xviii. 30, 35; xix. 10—13)—**thou hast reproached the Lord, and hast said.** Sennacherib had not *said* what is here attributed to him, any more than Sargon had *said* the words ascribed to him in Isa. x. 13, 14. But he had *thought* it; and God accounts men's deliberate thoughts as their utterances. Isaiah's "oracle" brings out and places in a striking light the pride, self-confidence, and self-sufficiency which underlay Sennacherib's messages and letters. **With the multitude of my chariots;** or, *with chariots upon chariots.* The chariot-force was the main arm of the Assyrian military service—that on which most dependence was placed, and to which victory was commonly attributed. The number of chariots that could be brought into the field by the Assyrians is nowhere stated; but we find nearly four thousand hostile chariots collected to oppose an ordinary Assyrian invasion, and defeated (see 'Ancient Monarchies,' vol. ii. p. 362, note 8). The estimates of Cterias—eleven thousand for Ninus, and a hundred thousand for Semiramis (Diod. Sic., ii. 5. § 4)—are, of course, unhistorical.

I am come up to the height of the mountains. "The height of the mountains" is here the high ground which an army would have to traverse in passing from the Cœle-Syrian valley into Palestine. It is not exactly Lebanon, which runs parallel with the coast, and certainly does not "guard Palestine to the north," as Keil supposes; but it may be viewed as a "side" or "flank" of Lebanon. In point of fact, Lebanon and Hermon unite their roots to form a barrier between the Cœle-Syrian plain (El Buka'a) and the valley of the Jordan, and an invader from the north must cross this barrier. It is not so difficult or rugged but that the Assyrians could bring their chariots over it. They were accustomed to traverse far more difficult regions in Zagros and Niphates and Taurus, and to carry their chariots with them, dismounting when necessary, and having the vehicles lifted over obstacles by human hands (see 'Ancient Monarchies,' vol. ii. p. 74). To the sides of Lebanon. An army which invades Palestine by the Cœle-Syrian valley—quite the easiest and most usual line of invasion—necessarily passes along the entire eastern "side," or "flank," of Lebanon, which is the proper meaning of יַרְכָּה, and not "loftiest height" (Keil), or "innermost recess" (Revised Version). The plural, יַרְכְּתֵי, is natural when a mountain range, like Lebanon, is spoken of. And will cut down the tall cedar trees thereof, and the choice fir trees thereof. The felling of timber in the Syrian mountain-chains was a common practice of the Assyrian invaders, and had two quite distinct objects. Sometimes it was mere cruel devastation, done to injure and impoverish the inhabitants; but more often it was done for the sake of the timber, which the conqueror carried off into his own country. "The mountains of Amanus I ascended," says Asshur-nazir-pal; "wood for bridges, pines, box, cypress, I cut down . . . cedar-wood from Amanus I destined for Bit-Hira and my pleasure-house called Azmaku, and for the temple of the moon and sun, the exalted gods. I proceeded to the land of Iz-mehri, and took possession of it throughout: I cut down beams for bridges, and carried them to Nineveh" ('Records of the Past,' vol. iii. p. 74). The cedar (erez) and the pine, or juniper (bĕrôsh), were in special request. And I will enter into the lodgings of his borders—rather, the lodge of its border—perhaps a palace or hunting-lodge on the outskirt of the Lebanon forest region (comp. Cant. vii. 4)—and into the forest of his Carmel; rather, the forest of its orchard; i.e. the choicest part of the Lebanon forest region—the part which is rather park or orchard than mere forest.

Ver. 24.—I have digged and drunk strange waters; rather, perhaps, I dig, and drink . . . and dry up—the preterite having again a present sense. Sennacherib means that this is what he is wont to do. As mountains do not stop him (ver. 23), so deserts do not stop him—he digs wells in them, and drinks water "strange" to the soil—never before seen there. And with the sole of my feet have I dried up all the rivers of besieged places; rather, will I dry up all the rivers of Egypt (compare the Revised Version. "Mazor" is used for "Egypt" in Isa. xix. 6 and Micah vii. 12). It is the old singular from which was formed the dual Mizraim. Whether it meant "land of strength" (Pusey), or "land of distress" (Ewald), may be doubted, since we have no right to assume a Hebrew derivation. There was probably a native word, from which the Hebrew Mazor, the Assyrian Muzr, and the Arabic Misr were taken. Sennacherib's boast is that, as he makes deserts traversable by digging wells, so, if rivers try to stop him, he will find a way of drying them up. Compare the boasts of Alaric in Claudian ('Bell. Get.,' pp. 525–532), who had probably this passage of Kings in his thoughts—

"Te patior suadente fugam, cum cesserit omnis
Obsequiis natura meis? Subsidere nostris
Sub pedibus montes, arescere vidimus amnes.
Fregi Alpes, galeisque Padum victricibus hausi."

Ver. 25.—Hast thou not heard long ago how I have done it? The strain suddenly changes—the person of the speaker is altered. It is no longer Sennacherib who reveals the thoughts of his own heart, but Jehovah who addresses the proud monarch. "Hast thou not heard, how from long ago I have acted thus? Hast thou never been taught that revolutions, conquests, the rise and fall of nations, are God's doing, decreed by him long, long ago—ay, from the creation of the world? Art thou not aware that this is so, either from tradition, or by listening to the voice of reason within thine own heart?" It is implied that such knowledge ought to be in the possession of every man. And of ancient times that I have formed it? A rhetorical repetition of the previous question, needful for the balance of clauses, in which Hebrew poetry delights, but adding nothing to the sense. Now have I brought it to pass, that thou shouldest be to lay waste fenced cities into ruinous heaps. The idea was very familiar to Isaiah and his contemporaries. Years before, when Assyria first became threatening, Isaiah, speaking in the person of Jehovah, had exclaimed, "O Assyrian, the rod of mine anger, and the staff in their hand is mine indignation. I will send him against an hypocritical nation, and against the people of my wrath will I give him a charge, to take the spoil, and to take the prey, and to tread them down like the mire of the streets" (Isa. x. 5, 6). But the heathen kings whom God made his instruments to chasten sinful nations imagined that they conquered and destroyed and laid waste by their own strength (see Isa. x. 7—14).

Ver. 26.—**Therefore their inhabitants were of small power**; literally, *were short of hand* —unable, *i.e.*, to make an effectual resistance. When God has decreed a change in the distribution of power among the nations, his providence works doubly. It infuses confidence and strength into the aggressive people, and spreads dismay and terror among those who are attacked. Unaccountable panics seize them—they seem paralyzed; instead of making every possible preparation for resistance, they fold their hands and do nothing. They are like fascinated birds before the stealthy advance of the serpent. **They were dismayed and confounded.** Historically, the prophet declares, this was the cause of the general collapse of the nations whom the Assyrians attacked. God put a craven fear into their hearts. **They were as the grass of the field, and as the green herb, as the grass on the house-tops.** The "grass of the field" is one of the most frequent similes for weakness. "All flesh is grass" (Isa. xl. 6); "They shall soon be cut down like the grass" (Ps. xxxvii. 2); "The grass withereth, the flower fadeth" (Isa. xl. 8); "I am withered like grass" (Ps. cii. 11). In the hot sun of an Eastern sky nothing faded more quickly. But this weakness was intensified in the "grass of the house-tops." It "withered before it grew up" (Ps. cxxix. 6). The depth of earth was so slight, the exposure so great, the heat so scorching, that it sank in death almost as soon as it had sprung to life. Such has been the weakness of the nations given over as a prey to the Assyrians. **And as corn blasted before it be grown up.** Corn blasted before it shoots into a stalk is as frail as grass, or frailer. It dwindles and disappears without even asserting itself.

Ver. 27.—**But I know thy abode, and thy going out, and thy coming in.** "Resting in peace, going out, and coming in, cover all the activity of a man" (Bähr), or rather, cover his whole life, active and passive. Jehovah claims an absolute knowledge of all that Sennacherib does or thinks, both when he is in action and when he is at rest. Nothing is hid from him (comp. Ps. cxxxix. 1—16). Human pride should stand abashed before such absolute knowledge. **And thy rage against me.** Opposition to their will

fills violent men with fury and rage. Sennacherib's anger was primarily against Hezekiah, but when once he was convinced that Hezekiah really trusted in Jehovah (ver. 10), his fury would turn against God himself (comp. Ps. ii. 1—3, where the Lord's anointed is primarily David).

Ver. 28.—**Because thy rage against me, and thy tumult**—rather, *thy arrogancy* (see the Revised Version); שַׁאֲנַן is rather the quiet security of extreme pride and self-confidence than "tumult"—**is come up into mine ears**— *i.e.* has attracted my notice—**therefore I will put my hook in thy nose, and my bridle in thy lips.** The imagery is most striking. Captive kings were actually so treated by the Assyrians themselves. A hook or split-ring was thrust through the cartilage of the nose, or the fleshy part of the under lip, with a rope or thong attached to it, and in this guise they were led into the monarch's presence, to receive their final sentence at his hands. In the sculptures of Sargon at Khorsabad we see three prisoners brought before him in this fashion, one of whom he seems to be about to kill with a spear ('Ancient Monarchies,' vol. i. p. 367). In another sculpture set up by a Babylonian king, his vizier brings before him two captives similarly treated, but with the ring, apparently, passed through the cartilage of their noses (ibid., vol. iii. p. 436). Manasseh seems to have received the same treatment at the hands of the "captains" (2 Chron. xxxiii. 11) who brought him a prisoner to Esarhaddon at Babylon. Other allusions to the practice in Scripture will be found in Isa. xxx. 28; Ezek. xxix. 4; xxxviii. 4. The threat in the present passage was, of course, not intended to be understood literally, but only as a declaration that God would bring down the pride of Sennacherib, humiliate him, and reduce him to a state of abject weakness and abasement. **And I will turn thee back by the way by which thou camest** (comp. ver. 33). The meaning is clear. Sennacherib would not be allowed to come near Jerusalem. He would hurry back by the low coast route (ch. xviii. 17), by which he had made his invasion.

Ver. 29.—**And this shall be a sign unto thee.** Another sudden change in the address. The prophet turns from Sennacherib to Hezekiah, and proceeds to give him a sign, and otherwise speak to him encouragingly. Signs were at the time freely offered and given by God both to the faithful and the unfaithful (see ch. xx. 4; Isa. vii. 11, 14). They generally consisted in the prediction of some near event, whose occurrence was to serve as a pledge, or evidence, of the probable fulfilment of another prediction of an event more distant. Such signs are not necessarily miraculous. **Ye shall eat this year such** things as grow of themselves. The Assyrian invasion, coming early in the spring, as was usual, had prevented the Israelites from sowing their lands. But they would soon be gone, and then the Israelites could gather in such self-sown corn as they might find in the corn-lands. The next year, probably a sabbatical year, they were authorized to do the same, notwithstanding the general prohibition (Lev. xxv. 5); the third year they would return to their normal condition. The sign was not given with reference to Sennacherib's departure, which belonged to the first year, and must take place before the ingathering of the self-sown corn could begin, but with reference to the promise that Jerusalem should be free from any further attack on his part. Sennacherib reigned seventeen years longer, but led no further expedition into Palestine. **And in the second year that which springeth of the same; and in the third year sow ye, and reap, and plant vineyards, and eat the fruits thereof.**

Ver. 30.—**And the remnant that is escaped of the house of Judah.** Sennacherib, who in his first expedition had carried away out of Judæa 200,150 prisoners ('Eponym Canon,' p. 134, line 12), had in his second probably done considerable damage to the towns in the south-west of Palestine—Lachish, for instance, which was a city of Judah (Josh. xv. 39; ch. xiv. 19). The open country had been wasted, great numbers killed, and many probably carried off by famine and pestilence. Thus both Hezekiah (ver. 4) and Isaiah regard the population still in the land as a mere "remnant." **Shall yet again take root downward**—*i.e.* be firmly fixed and established in the land, like a vigorous tree that strikes its roots into the soil deeply—**and bear fruit upward;** *i.e.* exhibit all the outward signs of prosperity. The reign of Josiah, when the Jewish dominion embraced the whole of Palestine (ch. xxiii. 15—20), was the special fulfilment of this prophecy.

Ver. 31.—**For out of Jerusalem shall go forth a remnant.** The march of Sennacherib and the raid of Rabshakeh had driven the mass of the escaped population of Judæa to take refuge within the walls of Jerusalem, from which, on the retirement of the invaders, they would gladly "go forth," to recultivate their lands (ver. 29) and restore their ruined homes. **And they that escape**—rather, *that shall escape*—**out of Mount Zion**—"Mount Zion" is a variant for Jerusalem, as in ver. 21, and in Isaiah and the Psalms so continually—**the zeal of the Lord** of hosts shall do this. So in Isa. ix. 7 and xxxvii. 32. Here most manuscripts have "the zeal of the Lord,"

omitting "of hosts;" and this is probably the right reading. The meaning is that God's zealous love and care for his people will effect their complete restoration to prosperity and glory, difficult as it was at the time to imagine such a restoration.

Ver. 32.—**Therefore thus saith the Lord concerning the King of Assyria.** The oracle concludes with a general announcement, addressed to all whom it may concern, not to any one individually, concerning the existing distress. First, it is laid down what shall not be the issue. **He**—*i.e.* Sennacherib—**shall not come into**—rather, *unto*—**this city**—*i.e.* Jerusalem—**nor shoot an arrow there**—*i.e.* he shall not begin the attack, as was usually done, with discharges of arrows, to clear the walls of their defenders, and make it safe for the sappers and miners and the siege artillery to draw near—**nor come before it with shield**—*i.e.* advance close, to raise the scaling-ladders, or mine the walls, or fire the gates, under the protection of huge shields—**nor cast a bank against it.** Much less shall he proceed to the last extremity of raising mounds against the walls, and planting upon them his *balistæ* and his battering-rams, with the object of effecting a breach. Each of the successive stages of a siege is touched, and negatived. None of these things shall be done. There shall be no siege. (For representations of the Assyrian sieges, banks, and engines, see Layard, 'Monuments of Nineveh,' second series, plates 21, 31, 39, 43, etc.; and Rawlinson, 'Ancient Monarchies,' vol. i. p. 303; vol. ii. p. 81.)

Ver. 33.—**By the way that he came, by the same shall he return** (see ver. 28). Not merely, "he shall fail of his object" (Bähr, Keil), "he shall return disappointed;" but, literally, *he shall retrace his steps,* he shall quit Palestine by the same route by which he entered it—the coast route along the maritime plain, which left Jerusalem on the right at a distance of forty miles. **And shall not come into**—rather, *unto*—**this city, saith the Lord.** An emphatic ending (comp. Isa. xxii. 14; xlv. 13; liv. 17; lv. 8; lix. 20; lxv. 25; lxvi. 21, 23).

Ver. 34.—**For I will defend this city, to save it**—not merely with a view of saving it, but in such sort as effectually to save it—**for mine own sake**—*i.e.* because my own honour is concerned in its preservation, especially after the taunts of Sennacherib (ch. xviii. 32—35; xix. 10—13)—**and for my servant David's sake.** Not so much on account of the promises made to David, as on account of the love which God bore towards him for his faithfulness and earnest devotion.

Vers. 35—37.—DESTRUCTION OF SENNA-
CHERIB'S HOST, AND HIS OWN VIOLENT DEATH
AT NINEVEH. The sequel is told in a few
words. That night destruction came down
on the host of Sennacherib, as it lay encamped at some distance from Jerusalem,
silently and swiftly. Without noise, without disturbance, the sleeping men slept the
sleep of death, and in the morning, when
the survivors awoke, it was found that a
hundred and eighty-five thousand were
slain. Upon this, with the remnant of his
army, Sennacherib hastily returned to
Nineveh. There, some time after—about
seventeen years according to our reckoning
—a conspiracy was formed against him by
two of his sons, who murdered him as he
was worshipping in a temple, and fled into
Armenia. Another son, Esarhaddon, succeeded.

Ver. 35.—And it came to pass that night.
The important expression, "that night," is
omitted from the narrative of Isaiah
(xxxvii. 36), but is undoubtedly an original
portion of the present history. It can have
no other meaning—as Keil and Bähr have
seen—than "the night following the day
on which Isaiah had foretold to Hezekiah
the deliverance of Jerusalem." God's word
"runneth very swiftly." No sooner was the
promise given than the destroying angel
received his orders, and "that night" the
terrible stroke fell. That the angel of the
Lord went out; or, an angel (ἄγγελος Κυρίου,
LXX.). We cannot say, with Bähr, that it
was "the same one who smote the firstborn
in Egypt, and inflicted the pestilence after
the census under David." Revelation does
not tell us that there is definitely one
destroying angel. "The angel of death"
is a rabbinical invention. It accords
rather with the analogy of God's dealings
that he should use at one time the services
of one minister, at another time those of
another. And smote. Imagination has been
over-busy in conjecturing the exact manner
of the smiting. Some critics have suggested
pestilence, or more definitely "the plague"
(Gesenius, Dathe, Maurer, Ewald, Winer,
Thenius, Keil, etc.); others a terrible storm
(Vitringa, Stanley); others the simoom
(Prideaux, Milman); others a nocturnal
attack by Tirhakah (Ussher, Preiss, Michaelis). Some of these the text altogether
precludes, as the attack of Tirhakah, which
must have aroused the whole host, and not
left the disaster to be discovered by those
who "awoke early in the morning." Others
are improbable, as the simoom, or a terrible

storm with thunder and lightning, which
have never been known to accomplish such
a destruction. Pestilence is no doubt
possible, but a pestilence of a strange and
miraculous character, to which men succumbed without awaking or disturbing
others. But the narrative rather points to
sudden and silent death during sleep, such
as often happens to men in the course of
nature singly, and here on this occasion
was made to happen in one night to a
hundred and eighty-five thousand men by
the Divine omnipotence acting abnormally.
In the camp of the Assyrians. The destruction was not only at one time, but in
one place. "The camp of the Assyrians"
cannot mean half a dozen camps situated in
half a dozen different places, as Keil supposes. Sennacherib was somewhere with
his main army, encamped for the night, and
there, wherever it was, the blow fell. But
the exact locality is uncertain. All that
the narrative makes clear is that it was not
in the immediate vicinity of Jerusalem.
Herodotus places the catastrophe at Pelu-
sium (ii. 141). Bähr thinks it was probably
before Libnah. I should incline to place it
between Libnah and the Egyptian frontier,
Sennacherib, when he heard that Tirhakah
was coming against him (ver. 9), having
naturally marched forward to meet and
engage his army. An hundred four score
and five thousand. These figures do not
pretend to exactness, and can scarcely have
been more than a rough estimate. They
are probably the Assyrians' own estimate
of their loss, which the Jews would learn
from such of the fugitives as fell into
their hands. And when they—i.e. the
survivors—arose early in the morning, they
—i.e. the hundred and eighty-five thousand
—were all dead corpses—absolutely dead,
that is; not merely sick or dying. The fact
makes against the theory of a pestilence.

Ver. 36.—So Sennacherib King of Assyria
departed, and went and returned. The
original is more lively, and more expressive
of haste. Sennacherib, it is said, "de-
camped, and departed, and returned"—the
heaping up of the verbs expressing the
hurry of the march home (Keil); comp.
1 Kings xix. 3. And dwelt at Nineveh.
Nineveh was Sennacherib's favourite residence. He had built himself a palace
there, marked by the modern mound of
Koyunjik. Sargon, his father, had dwelt
mainly at Dur-Sargina or Khorsabad,
Tiglath-pileser and Shalmaneser at Calah
or Nimrud. Sennacherib's palace and his
other buildings at Nineveh are described
in his annals at some length (see 'Records
of the Past,' vol. i. pp. 50—52). The
expression, "dwelt at Nineveh," does not
mean that he never quitted it, but merely

implies that he dwelt there for some considerable time after his return, as he appears to have done by his annals. The Eponym Canon makes his last year B.C. 682.

Ver. 37.—**And it came to pass**—seventeen or eighteen years afterwards; not "fifty-five days" after, as the author of Tobit (i. 21) says—**as he was worshipping in the house of Nisroch his god.** The word "Nisroch" offers considerable difficulty. It has been connected with *nesher* (נֶשֶׁר), "eagle," and explained as a reference to the eagle-headed genius sometimes seen in the Assyrian sculptures ('Ancient Monarchies,' vol. ii. p. 265). But there is no evidence that the genii were ever worshipped in Assyria, much less that they had temples of their own, nor is any name resembling "Nisroch" attached to any of them. The word itself is somewhat doubtful, and different manuscripts of the Septuagint, here and in Isa. xxxvii. 38, have the variants of *Nasarach*, *Esorach*, *Meserach*, and *Asaruch*, while Josephus has *Araskas*. Asarach might conceivably be a strengthened form of Asshur; but the substitution of *samech* for *shin* is against this explanation. Still, Asshur was certainly Sennacherib's favourite god, the deity whom he principally worshipped. Josephus regards the name as belonging, not to the god, but to the temple (ἐν τῷ ἰδίῳ ναῷ 'Αράσκῃ λεγομένῳ), which is perhaps the true solution of the difficulty. Translate—"as he was worshipping his god in the house Nisroch." **That Adram-**

mclech and Sharezer his sons. Adrammelech is called "Adrammeles" by Abydenus, "Ardamazanes" by Polyhistor. Neither form resembles any known Assyrian name, but *Adrammelech* has a good Semitic derivation (see the comment on ch. xviii. 31). "Sharezer" is probably a shortened form of Nergal-shar-ozer (comp. "Shalman," Hos. x. 14), which was a name in use at the time ('Eponym Canon,' p. 68). Abydenus seems to have called him Nergilus. **Smote him with the sword.** So Josephus ('Ant. Jud.,' x. 1. § 5) and Mos. Chor. ('Hist. Armen.,' i. 22). A mutilated inscription of Esarhaddon's seems to have described his war with his brothers ('Records of the Past,' vol. iii. p. 103) at the commencement of his reign, but the earlier part is wanting. **And they escaped into the land of Armenia**; literally, *of Ararat*. The Hebrew "Ararat" is the Assyrian "Urarda"—the ordinary name for the country about Lakes Van and Urumiyeh. The name "Armenia" is not found earlier than the inscriptions of Darius Hystaspis. **And Esarhaddon his son reigned in his stead.** Esarhaddon (the *Sarchedon* of Tobit i. 21, and the Asshur-akh-iddin of the Assyrian inscriptions) succeeded his father in B.C. 681, and was engaged for some time in a war with his brothers on the Upper Euphrates, after which he made himself master of Nineveh. He reigned from B.C. 681 to B.C. 669, when he was succeeded by his son, Asshur-bani-pal. Assyria reached the acme of her prosperity in his time.

HOMILETICS.

Vers. 1—35.—*The wisdom of trust in God, and the foolishness of trust in self.* The contrast between the devout, God-fearing, God-trusting Hezekiah, and the proud, self-trusting, self-asserting Sennacherib is one of the most striking and instructive in Scripture. The two are set one over against the other in the most graphic way.

I. THE PICTURE OF HEZEKIAH shows him: 1. *Jealous of God's honour.* Sennacherib's words against God strike him with horror, appear to him such shocking blasphemy, that he rends his clothes and covers himself with sackcloth (ver. 1), as if he would wipe out the insult offered to God by one of his creatures' arrogancy, by causing to be presented before him the profoundest self-abasement and self-humiliation on the part of another. 2. *Sensible of his own weakness.* The day is "a day of trouble, of rebuke, and of contumely." Israel is despised, insulted, disgraced, and yet can do nothing. The time of her utmost trial has come, and she has "no strength" to carry her through the crisis. 3. *Trustful in God's power to save.* If God will, Hezekiah does not doubt he can "reprove" Sennacherib's words—disperse them, scatter them, show them to be vain words, words of nought. 4. *Reliant on the power of prayer.* "Wherefore lift up thy prayer for the remnant that are left." Prayer is the only key that can unlock a door of escape. He himself resorts to prayer (ver. 15), and he exhorts Isaiah to do the same. If he himself is sinful, Isaiah is a righteous man, God's prophet, and "the effectual fervent prayer of a righteous man availeth much" (Jas. v. 16).

II. THE PICTURE OF SENNACHERIB shows him: 1. *A hater and reviler of God.*

"Let not thy God . . . deceive thee" (ver. 10). As though God ever deceived, as though he were not the Truth itself. Sennacherib represents him as either a poor braggart who could not do what he had promised, or a malevolent being intentionally beguiling men to their ruin. "Jehovah," he says, "has sent *him* against Jerusalem," has bidden *him* "go up and destroy it" (ch. xviii. 25), while at the same time he was deluding Hezekiah with promises of deliverance. 2. *Absolutely confident in his own strength.* Who can stand against the Assyrians? Who has ever been able to resist them? "Hath any of the gods of the nations delivered at all his land out of the hand of the King of Assyria?" (ver. 33). And if not, "shalt thou be delivered?" He sets his own strength against Hezekiah's weakness (vers. 23, 24), and regards himself as irresistible. His will is law. What can hinder it? Not armies—least of all Egyptian armies—not mountains, not rivers, not deserts. Intoxicated with success, he thinks there is no power equal to him either in earth or heaven. The gods of the nations have all failed. Hezekiah's God will fail equally. 3. *Secure of the future, and without any thought of suing for Divine aid.* Why should Sennacherib sue? Success had always attended him in the past; surely "to-morrow would be as to-day," only "yet more abundant." He does not appear to give even his own gods a thought. Conventional ascription of his victories to Asshur may be found in his inscriptions; but, as Isaiah lays bare to us the workings of his innermost soul (ver. 23, 24), there is no leaning on any higher power, no recognition of anything behind his own greatness and material strength, no suspicion even of the possibility of a reverse. He is a god to himself; he commands the future; everything must necessarily go well with him.

The event shows the wisdom of Hezekiah's trust and the utter folly of Sennacherib's. "Out of the depths" Hezekiah "cries unto the Lord," and "the Lord hears his voice." "With the Lord there is mercy, and with him is plenteous redemption." Hezekiah may in the past have wavered, have listened to evil counsellors, have paid his court to Pharaoh, and put his trust in the broken reed Egypt; but now, at any rate, he has repented of such evil courses, he has put them away from him, and thrown himself wholly upon God. His words (vers. 15—19) have the unmistakable ring of sincerity and truth. To God he looks, and to him only. His strength is become perfected in his weakness; with the result that God hears his prayer (ver. 20), and grants the unparalleled deliverance related in ver. 35. Sennacherib, on the other hand, finds in a moment the whole ground of his self-confidence fail. It was as the master of many legions that he had thought to bend all things to his will. Bereft of his legions, he is nothing. To-day a mighty conqueror carrying everything before him, unfeignedly astonished that any one should dare to disobey his commands; on the morrow he is a wretched fugitive, hurrying homewards as fast as his chariot-steeds will bear him, only anxious to escape from the foes whom he so lately despised, and to bury his shame and his disgrace within the walls of his distant palace. In his pride and his self-trust he had thrown out a challenge to God. God took up the challenge, and struck him down to the earth. The circumstances of the catastrophe are unique in the world's history; but the lesson is one that the events of history have taught again and again. At the height of his pride and arrogancy and self-trust, the ungodly conqueror is stricken with failure, humiliated, beaten down to the ground, shown that, after all, he is a mere man, and that the fates of nations are not in his power, but in the hand of One whose name is "the Most High," and who ruleth in all the kingdoms of the earth.

HOMILIES BY VARIOUS AUTHORS.

Vers. 1—7.—*A good man's prayers sought.* Hezekiah is in deep distress of spirit at the haughty, defiant, confident tone of Rabshakeh. He wants help in his trouble. He sends not to his men of war, not to his statesmen, for advice, but to the man of God.

I. CHARACTER GIVES CONFIDENCE. Isaiah was known to live near to God. Therefore Hezekiah had confidence in him. *Here is a good test of the character of your companions and associates.* Would you go to them in time of trouble? Would you expect them to give you any comfort? Would you tell them the inner secrets of your heart? If not, is it not because you have no confidence in them? Their character does not command your respect.   Choose the company, seek the counsel, of good men.

11. CHARACTER GIVES POWER IN PRAYER.   "The effectual fervent prayer of a righteous man availeth much."   The man who expects an answer to his prayers is the man who habitually lives near to God.   Mary Queen of Scots said she feared the prayers of John Knox more than an army of ten thousand men.   Therefore : 1. *Live near to God if you would influence others.*   Power for service comes from fellowship with God.   Men like Isaiah have that quiet power that enables them to inspire others with confidence.   " Be not afraid of the words which thou hast heard " (ver. 6).   So with St. Paul on his perilous voyage to Rome.   "I exhort you to be of good cheer : for there shall be no loss of any man's life among you, but of the ship.   For there stood by me this night the angel of God, whose I am, and whom I serve, saying, Fear not, Paul. . . . Wherefore, sirs, *be of good cheer : for I believe God, that it shall be even as it was told me.*"   2. *Live near to God if you would have power in prayer.*   The man who prays most is the man who knows the power of prayer.

> " Thrice blest whose lives are faithful prayers,
>   Whose loves in higher love endure ;
>   What souls possess themselves so pure,
> Or is there blessedness like theirs? "

C. H. I.

Vers. 8—37.—*Our difficulties, and how to deal with them.*   We have seen that Hezekiah was a man distinguished by his trust in God.   We have seen how his trust in God led him to act in times of peace.   His trust in God led to *personal religion*, to *practical effort*, and to *prosperity in life.*   We see here how he acted when *troubles* came.   Depend upon it, the man who makes his peace with God when all is going well with him—he will have peace within his spirit when *the time of trouble comes.*   The man who does not allow the flowing tide of worldly prosperity or worldly pleasure to draw him away from God, he will find that God is near *to him* in the hour of danger and of need.   It was certainly an hour of danger and anxiety with Hezekiah.   With a vast army, Sennacherib, the King of Assyria, was threatening Jerusalem.   The very name of Assyria was at that time a terror to the nations, just as for a long time the name of Napoleon was a terror to Europe.   One by one, nation after nation had gone down before the triumphal progress of the Assyrian arms.   Sennacherib, conscious of his past successes, conscious of the mighty host that accompanies him, looks down with contempt upon Hezekiah and his attempt at resistance.   He sends him a letter, in which he points out how futile his efforts at resistance must prove.   The gods of the other nations had not been able to deliver *them,* and let him not think that his God whom he served would deliver him.   This letter and Hezekiah's action regarding it suggest to us some instructive lessons.

I. SENNACHERIB'S LETTER, AND THE TEMPTATION IT BROUGHT.   (Vers. 9—13.)   The drift of Sennacherib's letter was entirely to lead Hezekiah *to distrust God.*   Sennacherib was confident of victory; but he wanted Hezekiah to surrender to him, so that he might obtain as much tribute as he could, and at the same time incur no loss of life in his own army.   So he turns into ridicule Hezekiah's faith in his God.   "Let not thy God in whom thou trustest deceive thee, saying, Jerusalem shall not be delivered into the hand of the King of Assyria.   *Behold, thou hast heard what the kings of Assyria have done to all lands, by destroying them utterly : and shalt thou be delivered ?*   Have the gods of the nations delivered them which my fathers have destroyed ? . . .   Where is the King of Hamath, and the King of Arpad, and the King of the city of Sepharvaim, of Hena, and Ivah ? "   In a similar way Rabshakeh, one of Sennacherib's generals, had already spoken to the people of Jerusalem.   He had sought to influence their fears.   He had sought to tempt them by bribes.   He had said, "Let not Hezekiah deceive you : . . . neither let Hezekiah make you trust in the Lord. . . . Hearken not to Hezekiah : for thus saith the King of Assyria, Make an agreement with me by a present, and come ye out to me, and then eat ye every man of his own vine, and every one of his fig tree, and drink ye every one the waters of his cistern : until I come and take you away into a land like your own land, a land of corn and wine, a land of bread and vineyards, a land of oil olive and of honey, that ye may live, and not die : and hearken not unto Hezekiah, when he persuadeth you, saying, The Lord will deliver us." It is easy to imagine the effect of such statements upon a people few in number compared with the Assyrian's mighty host. The horrors of a protracted siege were in prospect. The longer they continued their resistance, the more desolation and devastation would be committed by the Assyrian army in their fields and homesteads. Many of them doubtless were already murmuring at Hezekiah, and some of them perhaps ready to make an agreement with the enemy. It was a trying position for Hezekiah. Both the letter of Sennacherib, and the circumstances in which he was placed, were a strong temptation to him to distrust God. *He might have said,* "Is this the reward which my service of God has brought me? I have been faithful to God's commands. I have restored the temple; I have restored the service of God. I have thrown down the altars and high places, and broken the images in pieces. Even the brazen serpent, which the people valued so highly as a relic of the past, I have ground to powder, because their idolatry of it was dishonouring to God. And now is it thus that God rewards me?" This is just the temptation that our difficulties and troubles constantly bring to us. They tempt us to distrust God. 1. It is so in the *growth of our own spiritual life.* How often the young beginner in the Christian life is discouraged by the difficulties which arise, and which he did not calculate on! He finds that there is still an old nature within him which has to be grappled with and conquered. He meets, perhaps, with opposition and discouragements from the world without, and perhaps even from those from whom he expected sympathy and help. These difficulties tempt many a one to distrust God. Many there are still who, like the disciples when difficulties arose, "go back, and walk no more with" God. One of the common difficulties which tempts us to distrust God is *the prosperity of the wicked.* Everything seems to prosper with men who have no respect for the Law of God. The temptation is for us, in distrust of God's promises, to imitate their godless practices. We begin to say, "There is no use in our being too scrupulous." Ah! what a mistake that is! Supposing we had all their prosperity, would it compensate us for the loss of a quiet conscience? Prosperity is dearly bought, business is dearly bought, for which we have to sacrifice one commandment of God, or silence the still small voice of conscience that speaks within. "What shall it profit a man if he shall gain the whole world, and lose his own soul?" Whenever this difficulty of the prosperity of godless men troubles you, and success which seems to be reached by questionable and unscrupulous means, remember the grand words of the thirty-seventh psalm, "Fret not thyself because of evil-doers, neither be thou envious against the workers of iniquity. For they shall soon be cut down like the grass, and wither as the green herb. *Commit thy way unto the Lord:* trust also in him; and he will bring it to pass." 2. In the same way there are *difficulties in Christian work.* How common a thing it is for Christians, who make much profession of their faith in God, to be dismayed and discouraged by difficulties that arise! Very often they are hindered from engaging in Christian work at all just by the difficulties that exist. I do not mean to say every person will suit every kind of work. There may be many kinds of work in which a man should not engage, because he has no fitness for them. But every Christian ought to be engaged in *some* work. If you *are doing nothing for the Master,* may we ask you why? What is your reason? What difficulty is in your way? *No difficulty is an excuse for idleness.* You may think yourself too young, or too inexperienced, or too humble; you may find others hard to work with; you may meet with discouragement and opposition; but *no one of these things is any excuse for idleness.* If difficulties were a reason for doing nothing, no Christian work would ever have been done—no churches built, no missionaries sent forth, no schools erected—for there never was a Christian work yet that had not its difficulties. Let us learn to take as our motto in Christian work, "I can do all things through Christ which strengtheneth me." Each one of you, no doubt, has his or her own difficulties to contend with—difficulties in your daily employment, difficulties from those you come in contact with, troubles and anxieties of spirit, cares and worries of various kinds. My message to you is this. Be not unduly cast down by your difficulties. Don't make too much of them. Just do with them as Hezekiah did, and you will see how soon they will disappear altogether, or at any rate they will be very considerably diminished.

II. HEZEKIAH'S PRAYER. (Vers. 14—19.) Hezekiah had learned by experience. As he grew older he became wiser.   A short time before, when Sennacherib was capturing his cities, and had advanced upon Jerusalem, Hezekiah sent a message to him, saying, "I have offended; return from me: that which thou puttest on me will I bear."   Sennacherib appointed him the exorbitant tribute of three hundred talents of silver and thirty talents of gold.   Hezekiah was in great straits for means to meet this demand.   In his difficulty he imitated the foolish action of his own father Ahaz, and took the silver that was found in the house of the Lord, besides cutting off the gold from the doors and pillars of the temple, and then sent this as a peace offering to Sennacherib.   But notwithstanding all this, *Sennacherib did not give up his warlike intentions.*   He once more threatened Jerusalem.   This time Hezekiah acts differently.   *He had learned now the mistake of rashly yielding to difficulties.*   It is *a lesson we all need to learn.*   If we *yield to our difficulties,* they will return again, and with renewed force.   One difficulty yielded to makes the next one harder to resist.   One difficulty resisted makes the next one far easier to overcome.   1. Hezekiah's first act, after he had read Sennacherib's letter, *was to go up into the house of the Lord.*   There he showed his wisdom.   If we want advice in sickness, advice as to our bodily health, we go to the house of our physician.   If we want to purchase food or clothing, we go where these necessaries of life are to be obtained.   Hezekiah was now in a difficulty where human help could be of little or no use to him.   So he goes to the one place where alone he might expect help—to the house of the Lord.   *The very act of going to the house of the Lord* is a wise one.   It reminds us that there is another world than that which is seen—the world of spirits, the world of the invisible.   It reminds us that there is One in whose hand every human life is, One to whom in all ages human hearts have turned, in every time of sorrow, of difficulty, and 'of helplessness, and One whose power and whose goodness men have acknowledged by raising temples for his honour and for their own and others' good.   Every true Christian must testify what a blessing the house of the Lord has been to him.   How should we have fared without its precious privileges?   How often have we felt, when the Sunday morning came round, and we joined in the song of praise, and approached the mercy-seat in company with other anxious, sinful, troubled, human hearts like our own; as we listened to the words of everlasting life; as we heard of him who is the "Man of sorrows and acquainted with grief," as we heard him saying to us, "Come unto me, all ye that labour and are heavy laden, and I will give you rest;"—how often have we felt that the difficulties of the week vanished; the burdens of the week were lightened; the cloud of sorrow that hung over us seemed suddenly to lift; we went forth again with new hope in our hearts, and with new strength in our lives; and upon our lips, perhaps, were such words as these—

> "Goodness and mercy all my life
> Shall surely follow me,
> And in God's house for evermore
> My dwelling-place shall be"!

Hezekiah, then, did a wise thing in going to the place where blessing was to be found.   But he did more than that.   2. *He spread the letter before the Lord.*   What a *faith* in God's presence that showed!—a real presence, indeed, not of body, but of that ever-present Spirit, in whom we live and move and have our being!   What a confidence it showed in God's interest in the affairs of all his people!   What a lesson it is for us all!   *The best thing we can do with our difficulties is to spread them out before God.*   Perhaps when we begin to spread them out before him, some of them will seem hardly worth talking about, hardly worth spreading, and the very act of doing so will bring us relief.   But whatever it may be that gives us trouble, even though it be a small matter—something unkind that has been said about us, an unpleasant letter that we have received, an unexpected loss in business, *let us spread it out before God.*   Your Sunday morning, before you go into God's house, would be well spent in thinking over the mercies you have to thank God for, the sins you have to confess, and the difficulties which trouble you, and then you would go into God's house asking just for what you need.   I know a servant of God who told me that he always made it a rule to be in his place in church at least five minutes before the service began.   That gave him time, he said, to calm his mind, and to look into his own heart.   The good seed then fell on prepared ground, and he said that whenever he did not do so, he did not get at all so much benefit from the service.

> " What a Friend we have in Jesus,
>   All our sins and griefs to bear!
> What a privilege to carry
>   Everything to God in prayer!
> Oh, what peace we often forfeit,
>   Oh, what needless pain we bear,
> All because we do not carry
>   Everything to God in prayer!"

Hezekiah's confidence in God had two results. (1) *It encouraged others.* He gathered the captains of war together in the street, and said to them, " Be strong and courageous, be not afraid nor dismayed for the King of Assyria, nor for all the multitude that is with him: *for there be more with us than with him :* with him is an arm of flesh; but with us is *the Lord our God* to help us, and to fight our battles" (2 Chron. xxxii. 7, 8). And so great was the confidence which the words of the king inspired, that we are told that all the people *rested themselves* upon the words of Hezekiah King of Judah. What a power the quiet influence of one believing man can exercise! What a power it gives us to live near to God! (2) Their *confidence was not misplaced.* God's people never trust in him in vain. *Hezekiah's prayer was answered.* That very night the angel of the Lord went out and smote in the camp of the Assyrians a hundred and eighty-five thousand men.

> " Like the leaves of the forest when summer is green,
> That host with their banners at sunset were seen :
> Like the leaves of the forest when autumn hath blown,
> That host on the morrow lay wither'd and strown.

> " For the Angel of Death spread his wings on the blast,
> And breathed in the face of the foe as he pass'd ;
> And the eyes of the sleepers wax'd deadly and chill,
> And their hearts but once heaved, and for ever were still!

> " And the widows of Asshur are loud in their wail,
> And the idols are broke in the temple of Baal;
> And the might of the Gentile, unsmote by the sword,
> Hath melted like snow in the glance of the Lord!"

Let us learn from this lesson that there is nothing too hard for God. Let us ask his help and guidance in every undertaking and event of life. Let us abide in his presence continually. Let us cling closer to the Rock of Ages. And then, come weal or come woe, come sickness or come health, come adversity or come success, we shall always be resigned to our Father's will, and shall possess within our hearts the peace which passeth all understanding.—C. H. I.

Vers. 1—37.—*A nation's calamities, counsellor, and God.* " And it came to pass, when King Hezekiah heard it, that he rent his clothes," etc. Our purpose in our sketches on this book has not allowed us to inquire into all the minute particulars of the characters or events recorded, or into the authorship of the book, or into the right of the prophet or prophets so frequently to say, " Thus saith the Lord," but simply in the briefest way to develop for practical purposes the truths either expressed or suggested. In this chapter we have three momentous events recorded—the terrible calamity to which Jerusalem was exposed; the utter destruction of the Assyrian army; and the death of Sennacherib the Assyrian despot. The whole should be read in connection with Isa. xxxvii. We have here for notice four subjects of thought—the exposure of a nation to an overwhelming calamity; the blessing to a nation of a ruler who looks to Heaven for help; the advantage to a nation of a truly wise counsellor; and the strength of a nation that has the true God on its side.

I. THE EXPOSURE OF A NATION TO AN OVERWHELMING CALAMITY. 1. The *nature* of the threatened calamity. It was the invasion of the King of Assyria. This was announced in startling terms and in a haughty and ruthless spirit by the messengers of Sennacherib. "Thus shall ye speak to Hezekiah King of Judah, saying, Let not thy God in whom thou trustest deceive thee, saying, Jerusalem shall not be delivered into the hand of the King of Assyria. Behold, thou hast heard what the kings of Assyria have done to all lands, by destroying them utterly: and shalt thou be delivered? Have the gods of the nations delivered them which my fathers have destroyed?" (vers. 10—13). The danger was near at hand. Sennacherib was on his way with his hundred and four score and five thousand men. The tramplings of the war-horses and the rattling of the armour would soon be heard in Jerusalem. The utter destruction of the city was contemplated, and seemed rapidly approaching. In a far worse position was the kingdom of Judah at this moment than was England when the Spanish Armada was approaching our shores. 2. *The influence of the threatened calamity.* (1) It struck the kingdom with a crushing terror. "And it came to pass, when King Hezekiah heard it, that he rent his clothes, and covered himself with sackcloth, and went into the house of the Lord. And he sent Eliakim, which was over the household, and Shebna the scribe, and the elders of the priests, covered with sackcloth, to Isaiah the prophet the son of Amoz. And they said unto him, Thus saith Hezekiah, This day is a day of trouble" (vers. 1—3). The rending of the "clothes" and the arraying in "sackcloth" were symbols to express the horror of the heart. (2) It struck the kingdom with a helpless feebleness. "This day is a day of trouble, and of rebuke, and blasphemy: for the children are come to the birth, and there is not strength to bring forth" (ver. 3). "The image is that of a parturient woman whose strength is exhausted, whose powers are paralyzed, at the moment when she required to put forth a vigorous effort. The expression in which the message was conveyed to the prophet described, by a strong figure, the desperate condition of the kingdom, together with the utter inability of the people to help themselves; and it intimated also a hope that the blasphemous defiance of Jehovah's power by the impious Assyrian might lead to some direct interposition for the vindication of his honour and supremacy to all heathen gods." Here is utter national helplessness in a terrible national calamity.

II. The blessing to a nation of a ruler who looks to Heaven for help. What, in the wretched condition of his country, does King Hezekiah do? He invokes the merciful interposition of Heaven. When the messengers came to Hezekiah with a threatening letter from the King of Assyria (see vers. 10—13), what did the monarch do? He took it into the house of the Lord, and there prayed. "And Hezekiah received the letter of the hand of the messengers, and read it: and Hezekiah went up into the house of the Lord, and spread it before the Lord. And Hezekiah prayed before the Lord, and said, O Lord God of Israel," etc. (vers. 14—19). In this wonderful prayer: 1. *He adores the God whom Sennacherib had blasphemed.* He addresses him as the "God of all the kingdoms of the earth," the Maker of "heaven and earth," the one and only Lord. 2. *He implores the Almighty for his own sake to deliver the country.* "Now therefore, O Lord our God, I beseech thee, save thou us out of his hand, that all the kingdoms of the earth may know that thou art the Lord God, even thou only." "The best pleas in prayer," says 'an old author, "are those that are taken from God's own honour; therefore the Lord's prayer begins with 'Hallowed be thy Name,' and concludes, 'Thine be the glory.'" Who is the greatest human king? Not the man who relies on his own power and skill to protect his nation from danger, and seeks to secure it in the possession and enjoyment of all its rights; nor the king who looks to his armies and navies in time of need; but he who practically realizes his dependence upon the "Lord" that made heaven and earth. Reverence for the Infinite is the soul of true royalty.

III. The advantage to a nation of a truly wise counsellor. Apart from his inspiration, Isaiah may be fairly taken in this case as the representative of a wise counsellor, and that for two reasons. 1. *He looked to heaven rather than to earth for his wisdom.* "Then Isaiah the son of Amoz sent to Hezekiah, saying, Thus saith the Lord God of Israel, That which thou hast prayed to me against Sennacherib King of Assyria I have heard. This is the word that the Lord hath spoken concerning him" (vers. 20, 21). The counsel which he had to give he here declares to have come from the Lord God of Israel. How the wisdom was conveyed to him, whether by an outward voice or an inner vision, does not appear; he had it from heaven. He only is the true counsellor of men who gets his wisdom from above. Whence do the advisers of sovereigns get their instructions? From hoary precedents or the fallible conclusions of their own feeble minds; and not directly from above. Hence the incessant blunders of cabinets, and the scandal in these days of one political party denouncing the blunders and professing to correct the mistakes of the other. 2. *What he received from heaven he communicated to men.* In the communication: (1) "Sennacherib is apostrophized in a highly poetic strain admirably descriptive of the turgid vanity, haughty pretensions, and heartless impiety of this despot. 'The virgin the daughter of Zion hath despised thee, and laughed thee to scorn; the daughter of Jerusalem hath shaken her head at thee,' etc. (vers. 21—28). (2) Hezekiah himself is personally addressed, and a sign given him of coming deliverance. He is told that for two years the presence of the enemy would interrupt the peaceful pursuits of husbandry, but in the third year the people would be in circumstances to till the earth, plant the vineyards, and reap the fruits, as formerly. 'And this shall be a sign unto thee, Ye shall eat this year such things as grow of themselves, and in the second year that which springeth of the same; and in the third year sow ye, and reap, and plant vineyards, and eat the fruits thereof,' etc. (vers. 29—31). (3) The issue of Sennacherib's invasion is announced. 'Thus saith the Lord concerning the King of Assyria, He shall not come into this city, nor shoot an arrow there, nor come before it with shield, nor cast a bank against it. By the way that he came, by the same shall he return,' etc. (vers. 32—34)" (Dr. Jamieson). Such was the communication which, in language passionate, poetic, and powerful, Isaiah made to this perplexed and terrified nation. It involves two things: (*a*) the deliverance of his country; (*b*) the ruin of the despot.

IV. THE STRENGTH OF A NATION THAT HAS GOD ON ITS SIDE. Who delivered the imperilled nation? Who overwhelmed the despot? "The zeal of the Lord of hosts." "And it came to pass that night, that the angel of the Lord went out, and smote in the camp of the Assyrians an hundred four score and five thousand: and when they arose early in the morning, behold, they were all dead corpses," etc. (vers. 35—37). Who was the "angel of the Lord"? Was it some transcendent personality, or some tremendous force in nature, such as a pestiferous blast, or an electric bolt? It matters not; the "angel" was but the instrument in the hand of God. 1. *How swiftly was the deliverance effected!* "That night." What a night was that!—one of the most memorable nights of the world. Perhaps the whole was effected even in one single hour, or even in one instant of that night. 2. *How terrible the ruin which that deliverance effected!* "An hundred four score and five thousand men" destroyed. At night, a glittering array; in the morning, "dead corpses."

> "Like the leaves of the forest when summer is green,
> That host with their banners at sunset were seen:
> Like the leaves of the forest when autumn hath blown,
> That host on the morrow lay wither'd and strown."

How rapidly God can do his work! he can annihilate a universe in the twinkling of an eye. Behold a mystery! Why should these hundred and eighty-five thousand be thus destroyed on account of the conduct of one man—Sennacherib?

> "God is his own Interpreter,
> And he will make it plain."

The forty-sixth psalm is supposed to be the triumphant outburst of the delivered people. "God is our Refuge and Strength, a very present Help in trouble. . . . The heathen raged, the kingdoms were moved: he uttered his voice, the earth melted." This Sennacherib, this ruthless despot, does not seem to have fallen with the others. His body was not found amongst the dead corpses. Albeit, he did not escape. "So Sennacherib King of Assyria departed, and went and returned, and dwelt at Nineveh. And it came to pass, as he was worshipping in the house of Nisroch his God, that Adrammelech and Sharezer his sons smote him with the sword: and they escaped into the land of Armenia. And Esarhaddon his son reigned in his stead" (vers. 36, 37). What greater calamity could befall a man than to be murdered by his own sons?—D. T.

Vers. 1—7.—*Hezekiah and Isaiah.* The messengers whom Hezekiah had sent having returned and reported to him the words of Rabshakeh (ch. xviii. 37), the king was plunged in unspeakable distress. We have now to observe his behaviour in his trouble.

I. HEZEKIAH'S GRIEF. 1. *He assumed the signs of deepest mourning.* The messengers had come to him with their clothes rent. Hezekiah now rent his clothes, and covered himself with sackcloth. His humiliation was sincere. The words he had heard had knocked from under him his last hope of help from man. He felt that God's "chastisement" (ver. 3) was upon him, and that God alone could deliver. This moment of the realization of his helplessness was also the moment of the return of God's favour to him. To this point it had been God's aim to bring him, and now that he threw himself in his utter weakness on God's strength, deliverance was assured. 2. *He sought God in his sanctuary.* He "went into the house of the Lord." Thither also Asaph had gone in his hour of trouble, and there his difficulties were removed (Ps. lxxiii. 17). Hezekiah no doubt sought the sanctuary for purposes of prayer. We see him do the same thing on receipt of Sennacherib's letter (ver. 14). We have every encouragement to come to God with our troubles (Ps. xci. 15), and nothing soothes the heart like pouring out all our sorrows before him (Phil. iv. 6, 7). Prayer is the soul's best resort in times of extremity.

II. THE DEPUTATION TO ISAIAH. In addition to praying himself to God, Hezekiah sent an honourable deputation to Isaiah, to request his intercession for the city. 1. *He sends to God's prophet.* Possibly for some time Hezekiah and Isaiah had not seen much of each other. The prophet's counsels had proved distasteful. His denunciations of the alliance with Egypt cannot have been received with favour (Isa. xxx.). His advice certainly had not been taken; nor can it have been with his approval that Hezekiah made his ill-fated submission to Sennacherib. Now, in the hour of trouble, Hezekiah sends once more to him. He sends his highest officers—the same who had conferred with Rabshakeh—and the elders of the priests. All went covered with sackcloth, in token of their grief, penitence, and humiliation of heart. This is what often happens. God's servants are not appreciated till the hour of real need comes; then men are glad to get their counsels and their prayers. It would be well if, in the conduct of state affairs, respect were paid to the counsels of religion earlier. It would save many a bitter hour afterwards. 2. *He makes full confession of his sad estate.* A crisis had come in which there was no ray of human hope. From Hezekiah's side it was a day of "trouble"—of deep distress and mortification; from God's side it was a day of "chastisement" (Hos. v. 2, "I am a Rebuker of them all"); from the side of the Assyrian, it was a day of "blasphemy"—of impious vaunting against Jehovah. And like a woman in pains of childbirth, without strength for delivery, they had no means of bringing themselves out of their perilous position. "The metaphor expresses in the most affecting manner, the ideas of extreme pain, imminent danger, critical emergency, utter weakness, and entire dependence on the aid of others" (Alexander). The spirit of self-trust is now utterly slain. In making this confession, Hezekiah owned that Isaiah was right, and he had all along been wrong. 3. *He entreats the prophet's prayers.* Hezekiah's one hope now was that, for his own glory's sake, Jehovah would "reprove" the blasphemous words which Rabshakeh had uttered, and he besought Isaiah to lift up his prayer for the remnant of Jews still left. It is a true instinct of the soul which leads us to seek the intercession on our behalf of those who stand nearer to God than ourselves. "The effectual fervent prayer of a righteous man availeth much" (Jas. v. 16). Thus Pharaoh besought Moses to intercede for him (Exod. viii. 8, 28; x. 16); Moses on various occasions intercded for the people (Exod. xxxii. 30—33; Deut. ix. 12—20); Elijah interceded for the land of Israel (1 Kings xviii. 11—45); the high priest interceded for the tribes; and Christ now intercedes for us (Rom. viii. 34; 1 John ii. 1). We cannot lay too much stress on the power of prayer, nor be too anxious to get an interest in the prayers of the holy. Hezekiah did well in joining with his own prayers this request for the intercession of Isaiah.

III. THE PROPHET'S REPLY. We have already and frequently seen how ready God is to respond to the faintest movements of the soul towards him. The prophet did not send those who now sought him away without comfort. He gave them: 1. *A word of encouragement.* "Be not afraid," etc. In his own heroic trust Isaiah had never faltered. Such trust is contagious. The words which Isaiah spoke would send a new thrill of hope to the hearts of the messengers. How marvellous a thing is faith in God! How it supports a man's own soul, lifts him above ordinary, and even extraordinary, discouragements, and makes him firm as a rock when others are trembling and despairing around (cf. Ps. xlvi.)! 2. *An assurance of deliverance.* In the name of God, Isaiah was able to give them, further, an assurance that Sennacherib would do them no hurt. God would put a spirit in him, and would cause him to hear tidings which would make him depart into his own land, and there he would perish with the sword. Nothing is said as yet of the destruction of the army, unless, indeed, it is the tidings of that which Sennacherib was to hear. Another boasting message of Sennacherib and another prayer of Hezekiah come in between this promise and the final and fuller one.—J. O.

Vers. 8—19.—*Sennacherib's letter.* While the foregoing events were taking place, Rabshakeh had returned to his royal master. The siege of Lachish had been concluded—adding another to the score of victories—and Sennacherib was now at Libnah. Here the news came that Tirhakah was on his march against him, and naturally Sennacherib wished to secure the capitulation of Jerusalem before the Ethiopian could arrive. To this end he sent another message to Hezekiah—this time in the form of a letter—renewing the attempt to frighten the Jewish king into surrender.

I. SENNACHERIB'S PROUD BOASTINGS. The letter is an echo of the speech of Rabshakeh, and is couched in the same boastful spirit. 1. *He makes light of the power of Jehovah.* "Let not thy God in whom thou trustest deceive thee," etc. Sennacherib assumes that Hezekiah may have received true oracles from his God, but he warns him not to trust them. In his arrogance, he defies all gods as well as men. To him Jehovah was but one god among many—the god of one small nation—not for a moment to be compared with the powerful Asshur. His idea of the morality of the gods is seen in the supposition that they practised deceit upon their worshippers. 2. *He extols his own prowess.* He again recounts the victories which he and previous kings of Assyria had gained. Their conquests had extended to all lands; gods and kings had everywhere gone down before them: how should Hezekiah escape? As an induction, Sennacherib's argument seems very complete. The countries he names *had* been conquered; their gods had not availed to save them; their kings had been overthrown. Logic seemed on his side. Only faith could furnish a sufficient answer. 3. *He is certain beforehand of victory.* In his assurance that he would overcome Hezekiah, Sennacherib is the type of many boasters. Often has the voice of the adversary been raised in exultation at his prospective victory over the people of God. Paganism, Mohammedanism, and infidelity have each boasted that they would extinguish Christianity. Voltaire predicted that in a century from his time the Bible would be found only in antiquarian libraries. The same scoffer said that it took twelve men to found Christianity, but he would show that one man was sufficient to overthrow it. Modern unbelieving science sometimes speaks in the same strain. The argument *per enumerationem* is often employed, as it was by Sennacherib. All other religions show a tendency to collapse; their miracles are exploded, belief in witchcraft, etc., disappears before the march of enlightenment; therefore Christianity cannot hope to stand. But arrogance is a bad prophet. "Before honour is humility;" but "pride goeth before destruction, and a haughty spirit before a fall" (Prov. xvi. 18; xviii. 12). It was so with Sennacherib, and it will be found to be so by his modern imitators.

II. HEZEKIAH'S PRAYER. When Hezekiah received this insulting epistle, he went as before to the temple, and spread it out before the Lord. He did as we should all do with our troubles, carried it straight to the presence-chamber. God in truth knows all we have need of before we ask him; but that is no reason why we should not present our petitions. God knew all that was in this boastful letter; but that was no reason why Hezekiah should not place it before him, and make its contents the basis of his prayer. The prayer he offered contained: 1. *An acknowledgment of God's supremacy.* To Sennacherib's false idea of Jehovah, Hezekiah opposes the true one, The Lord God of Israel was no local deity, but the God of the whole earth. (1) He is the God of revelation. "O Lord God of Israel, which sittest upon the cherubim." It was because

God had revealed himself to Israel, and dwelt in glory above the mercy-seat whereon stood the cherubim, that Hezekiah had come to the temple to offer up this supplication. Communion with God rests on God's revelation of himself to man.   Only as God has revealed his Being to us, and dwells among us in mercy, are we able to approach him. An unknown or unknowable God can call forth no trust.   (2) He is the God of providence.   "Thou art the God, even thou alone, of all the kingdoms of the earth."   This is involved in the name Jehovah, which denotes God as the Being who is, and remains one with himself in all that he thinks, purposes, and does.   His rule is unlimited; all events, great and small, are under his control; his counsel is the one stable factor in history.   This conception of the supremacy of God in providence is involved in the knowledge he has given us of himself in grace.   (3) He is the God of nature.   "Thou hast made heaven and earth."   This again is involved in the truth of God's unlimited rule in providence, for only the Maker of the world can be its absolute Ruler.   Reversing the order of thought—only because God is the Almighty Maker of heaven and earth, is he the Lord in providence; and because he is Lord in nature and providence, he can do all things for us in grace (Ps. cxxi. 1, 2; cxxxv. 5, 6).   2. *An exposure of Sennacherib's fallacy.*   Hezekiah does not dispute the facts recited by Sennacherib, nor does he attempt to belittle them in any way.   "Of a truth, Lord," he says, "the kings of Assyria have destroyed the nations and their lands."   No good can come of refusing to look facts in the face.   It has often happened in apologetics that the attempt has been made to deny, explain away, or minimize the force of facts which were supposed to conflict with religious truth—facts of geology, *e.g.*, or facts of history or human nature which did not square with religious doctrine.   This procedure is unwise, and invariably recoils to the injury of religion.   We are entitled to ask for proof of alleged facts, and to suspend our judgment till such proof is given; but when the facts are established, they should be frankly admitted, and our theories widened to find room for them.   Truth in one department can never conflict with truth in another, and religion, resting on its own strong foundations, can afford to deal fairly with every class of evidence.   Hezekiah did not dispute Sennacherib's facts; but he put his finger at once upon the fallacy of Sennacherib's argument.   The Assyrians had indeed conquered these many nations, and cast their gods into the fire; but why?   Because they were no gods, but the work of men's hands, wood and stone.   Therefore they had destroyed them. It was different when they had to deal with the true God, the Maker of heaven and earth.   The error of modern unbelief is distinguishable from, yet kindred with, the error of Sennacherib.   Sennacherib attributed a reality to his gods; unbelief allows none.   Yet it agrees with Sennacherib in denying to Jehovah his true character as the one living God of nature, providence, and grace.   Faith, coming to God, believes "that he is, and that he is the Rewarder of them that diligently seek him" (Heb. xi. 6). Denying this truth, unbelief scoffs at religion, at the Bible revelation, at prayer, providence, miracles, redemption.   It treats the confidence of Christians in their God as illusory, anticipates the downfall of their system, and mocks at their hopes of immortality.   Its arguments, often cogent enough if there is no living God, lose all force the moment faith in God reasserts itself.   3. *An argument for God's interposition.*   Having shown his grounds for the belief that God *can* interpose, Hezekiah urges two reasons why he *should* interpose.   (1) The first is the honour of his own Name.   The fact that Sennacherib had in his pride and ignorance thus "reproached the living God" was a reason why God should reveal himself in his true character for Sennacherib's discomfiture.   The blasphemous pride of the creature exalting itself against the Creator should be brought low.   (2) A second reason was that, by saving his people from Sennacherib, Jehovah would give a grand lesson of his sole Deity to all the nations of the earth: "That all the kingdoms of the earth may know that thou art the Lord God, even thou only."   It is God's glory which Hezekiah puts in the foreground.   He had no plea of merit to urge, either his own or the nation's; therefore he can but ask God to be merciful to them for his own Name's sake.—J. O.

Vers. 20—34.—*Isaiah's oracle.*   God is the Hearer of prayer.   As in the case of Daniel (Dan. ix. 20), while Hezekiah was still speaking, an answer was sent to him through Isaiah the prophet (cf. ch. xx. 4).   Thus also answers to prayer were sent in the cases of Paul (Acts ix. 10—18) and Cornelius (Acts x. 1—8).   Isaiah was the one person whose faith had remained unshaken through all this crisis. But it is not merely Isaiah's confidence which speaks in this composition. He brought to the king a direct "word of God." His oracle is one of surpassing beauty, grand and sustained in style, and expressing the greatest truths.

I. ZION'S DERISION OF THE INVADER. The introductory picture is very striking. The city Jerusalem is represented as a maiden, standing on a height, derision imprinted on every feature, shaking her head, and sending out bursts of mocking laughter after the retreating Sennacherib. Is she insane? So to the world it might have seemed. Insane at least it might appear to draw such a picture at a time when the condition of the city seemed past salvation. But faith's manifestations often seem like madness to the worldly (Acts xxvi. 24; 2 Cor. v. 13). Faith triumphs beforehand over all the power of the enemy (Luke x. 19, 20). It does not need to wait to see their overthrow; it is assured of it as if it had already happened. The strength of faith is seen in the degree in which it enables its possessor to rise above adverse circumstances. In its higher reaches it can not only hope and wait, but exults and treats the threats of the enemy with ridicule and scorn (cf. Ps. ii. 4).

II. SENNACHERIB AS GLASSED IN HIS OWN EYES. Jehovah next asserts himself as "the Holy One of Israel," and takes Sennacherib to task for his blasphemies against him. He puts language into Sennacherib's lips poetically expressive of that monarch's lofty ideas of his own power. Alluding both to what he has done and to what he intends to do, Sennacherib boasts, "With the multitude of my chariots I am come up to the height of the mountains. . . . I have digged and drunk strange waters; and with the sole of my feet will I dry up all the rivers of Egypt." The meaning is that no obstacles of nature can prevent the accomplishment of his designs. Mountains like Lebanon cannot stop his march; he will find water even in the desert; Egypt's rivers will be trodden disdainfully underfoot. His chariots pass over all heights; cedar trees and fir trees fall before him; he penetrates to the farthest lodging-place and most fruitful region of the country. It is "I," Sennacherib says, "who do all this." Such boasting is: 1. *Extravagant.* In his inflated self-consciousness, Sennacherib sets no bounds to what he can accomplish. His language is exaggerated and hyperbolical. It is a man puffing himself up to the dimensions of a god (cf. Isa. x. 13, 14; xiv. 13, 14; Dan. iv. 30). Napoleon was accustomed to use similar language to impress the minds of his ignorant enemies (Bähr's 'Commentary on 2 Kings,' p. 226). Only in part is this extravagant self-assertion delusion. Those who give vent to it know very well that much of it is theatrical and unreal—mere froth and foam. But it gratifies their pride to indulge in it. 2. *Irrational.* This on two grounds: (1) Even granting that these boastings rested on real exploits, such self-exaltation is unbecoming in any mortal. The mightiest conqueror has only to reflect how soon he will become weak as other men (Isa. xiv. 10—17), to see how foolish is his self-glorying. (2) The past is an unsafe ground for boasting as to the future. Because his arms had hitherto been so uniformly successful, Sennacherib imagined that it was impossible any reverse could now befall him. He had got into his head the idea of his own invincibility. Napoleon had the same confidence in the invincibility of his arms. Experience shows the baselessness of such confidence. A long run of victories, intoxicating the conqueror with his own success, is generally followed by a disastrous calamity. The castle gets built up too high, and in the end topples over. Napoleon learnt this at Moscow and Waterloo. Excess of pride usually ends in an overthrow. 3. *Impious.* Sennacherib's boastings, finally, were impious. It was the creature arrogating to himself the power of God. Any reference to Asshur Sennacherib may have made in his inscriptions was but a thin veil to cover his self-glorying. His particular blasphemies against the God of Israel arose from ignorance of Jehovah's true character. He thought he was contending against the petty god of a small tribe, whereas he had to deal with "the Holy One" who made heaven and earth. Men's mistakes as to God do not alter the realities of their relation to him. Because God is "the Holy One," he cannot overlook men's impieties. Holiness is the principle which guards the Divine honour. It "guards the eternal distinction between Creator and creature, between God and man, in the union effected between them; it preserves the Divine dignity and majesty from being infringed upon" (Martensen).

III. SENNACHERIB AS BEHELD BY GOD. Vastly different from Sennacherib's view of himself was the view taken of him by God his Maker. 1. *Sennacherib a mere instrument in God's hands for the execution of his purposes.* "Hast thou not heard how I have done it long ago, and formed it of ancient times? Now have I brought it to pass that thou shouldest be to lay waste," etc. Sennacherib was defying Jehovah, but it was this God who from everlasting had decreed the events that were taking place, and had assigned to Sennacherib the part he was to bear in them. Here was a strange reversal of Sennacherib's ideas! It was the axe boasting itself against him that heweth herewith, and the saw magnifying itself against him that shaketh it, and the rod shaking itself against them that lift it up (Isa. x. 16). This is the truth which ungodly men constantly ignore. They exalt themselves against God, forgetful that, without God, they could not think a thought or move a finger; that it is he who gave them their being, and continually sustains them; that his providence girds them round, and uses them as executors of its purposes; and that they have only as much power as he chooses to give them. 2. *His successes due to God.* "Therefore their inhabitants were of small power," etc. Sennacherib ascribed all his victories to his own prowess, and founded on them an argument for despising Jehovah, whereas it was because Jehovah had prospered him that he had gained these victories. It is God who brings low, and lifts up (1 Sam. ii. 7). When he is against a people, their strength is small, they are dismayed and confounded, they are like grass that withers, and blasted grain. Sennacherib did not understand this, and took all the glory to himself. 3. *God prescribes the limits of his power.* As the Assyrian was thus an instrument in God's hand, it was for God to say how far he would be permitted to go. The limit was reached when he began to rage and blaspheme against the power which controlled him. God had heard his words and seen his doings. "I know thy abode, and thy going out, and thy coming in, and thy rage against me." He had done enough. The curb was now to be applied. Drawing a metaphor from Sennacherib's own treatment of his captives, the oracle declared, "I will put my hook in thy nose, and my bridle in thy lips, and I will turn thee back by the way by which thou camest." The prediction was soon to be fulfilled. No comfort can be greater, in times of "trouble, and rebuke, and blasphemy," than to know that the hostile powers are under absolute Divine control, and that they cannot take one step beyond what God allows. "Surely the wrath of man shall praise thee: the remainder of wrath shalt thou restrain" (Ps. lxxvi. 10). When men turn against God in open blasphemy, their power is nearly at an end.

IV. A SIGN TO THE PEOPLE. 1. *A pledge of God's favour.* The immediate sign of the truth of this oracle would be the destruction of the invading army, which was to take place that very night. But as a further pledge of complete deliverance from the Assyrian—a token that he would not return—it was foretold that within three years the whole land would be again under cultivation. In the interval the people would be provided for by that which grew of itself. Material blessings are withdrawn when God frowns; restored when he smiles. 2. *The remnant would take root and increase.* The land had been deplorably thinned by invasion and captivity. Had the process gone on much longer, Judah would have disappeared, as Israel had done. A remnant, however, would be saved, and this, taking root downward, and bearing fruit upward, would by God's blessing so multiply and strengthen as speedily to renew the population. 3. *God's zeal engaged for the fulfilment of his promises.* They were great things which God had promised, but the "zeal" of the Lord of hosts—his jealousy for his own honour, and for his people and his land—would perform it. When God's "zeal" is engaged in any undertaking, can we doubt that it will prosper? "If God be for us, who can be against us?" (Rom. viii. 39). God's zeal *is* engaged in giving effect to all efforts for the extension of his gospel, the salvation of men, and the triumph of righteousness in the world.

V. THE SAFETY OF THE CITY. Finally, a definite assurance is given that, let Sennacherib rage as he may, the city would not be harmed. He should neither come into it, nor shoot an arrow into it, nor come before it with shield, nor cast a bank against it, as once before he had done. Instead, he would return by the way he came. This God would do (1) for his own sake, *i.e.* for the vindication of his own honour from the reproaches of Sennacherib; and (2) for his servant David's sake. Succeeding generations little know how much they owe to God's regard for his holy servants in days past. As was Jerusalem, so is the Church safe under God's protection (Matt. xvi. 18). For the higher David's sake, he will not let it perish. But for God's care and shielding power, it would long ere this have been destroyed.—J. O.

Vers. 35—37.—*The mighty deliverance.* God's word was not long in being fulfilled. That very night the angel of the Lord smote a hundred and eighty-five thousand of the host of the Assyrians. In few words—for the end is as good as reached with Isaiah's oracle—the sacred narrator sums up the facts of the catastrophe.

I. THE DESTRUCTION OF SENNACHERIB'S ARMY. 1. *Its historic truth.* On all hands, though Sennacherib's own annals pass over the event in silence, this seems to be admitted. "Thus," says Wellhausen, "it proved in the issue. By a still unexplained catastrophe, the main army of Sennacherib was annihilated on the frontier between Egypt and Palestine, and Jerusalem thereby freed from all danger. The Assyrian king had to save himself by a hurried retreat to Nineveh; Isaiah was triumphant." 2. *Its miraculous character.* Granting that the event happened, it seems impossible, in view of Isaiah's distinct prediction, to deny its supernatural character. God's hand is almost seen visibly stretched out for the deliverance of his city, and the bringing low of Sennacherib's pride. Allow that the sweeping off of this great army was in any way connected with Isaiah's faith, hope, and prayers, and a supernatural government of the world is established. 3. *Its spiritual lessons.* (1) We see the end which commonly overtakes worldly boasters. Greek story delights to dwell on the Nemesis which overtakes inordinate pride. Napoleon, the modern Sennacherib, met with a discomfiture not dissimilar to that here recorded. (2) We learn not to be afraid of spiritual boasters. The nations may rage, and the people imagine a vain thing; the kings of the earth may set themselves, and the rulers take counsel together, against the Lord and his anointed. But "he that sits in the heavens will laugh; the Lord will have them in derision" (Ps. ii. 4). Scientific and philosophic boasters have not prevailed against the Church yet, and are not likely to do so. (3) We learn the advantage of entire reliance on God. While Hezekiah leaned on the help of man, he could accomplish nothing. When he cast himself on God's help, he was saved. God has all power in heaven and earth at his command, and is able to do all things for us.

II. THE END OF SENNACHERIB. 1. *The great king's retreat.* At this point "the great king," the King of Assyria, his boasting effectually silenced, disappears for ever from Jewish history. He "departed, and went and returned, and dwelt in Nineveh." No more is heard of his exploits in these pages. 2. *His miserable end.* His end was a fitting satire on his boasts. Two of his own sons, Adrammelech and Sharezer, conspired against him, and slew him while he was worshipping in the house of his god. This is the god to whose power, it may be presumed, he attributed all his conquests. Poor god! that could not save his own worshipper. *Sic transit gloria mundi.* The sons who slew him could not keep the throne, which was taken by Esarhaddon.—J. O.

EXPOSITION.

CHAPTER XX.

Vers. 1—21.—ILLNESS OF HEZEKIAH AND EMBASSY OF MERODACH-BALADAN. HEZEKIAH'S DEATH. The writer proceeds to relate an illness and a recovery of Hezekiah, which happened about the middle of his reign, probably in B.C. 713, and which was accompanied by strange, if not miraculous, circumstances (vers. 1—11). Hezekiah's recovery was followed by an embassy of congratulation from Merodach-Baladan, King of Babylon, which led Hezekiah into an act of folly, and brought upon him the rebuke of Isaiah (vers. 12—19). The narrative terminates with a notice of some of Hezekiah's great works, and of his decease (vers. 20, 21).

Vers. 1—11.—*The illness and recovery of Hezekiah.*

Ver. 1.—**In those days.** This is a very vague note of time, and cannot be regarded as determining the position of the events here related with respect to the preceding narrative. Ver. 6, however, shows that a time anterior to Sennacherib's discomfiture is intended; and the same verse also fixes the date to Hezekiah's fourteenth year, which was B.C. 713. If the date in ch. xviii. 13 be regarded as genuine, we must consider that the illness happened in the year of Sennacherib's first expedition against Palestine; but if we regard that date as interpolated, and accept the Assyrian inscriptions as our chronological authorities, we must place the events of the present chapter twelve years earlier than that expedition, in the reign of Sargon over Assyria, and in the first reign of Merodach-Baladan over Babylon. It belongs, at any rate, to the middle part of Hezekiah's reign, while his treasures were intact (vers. 13—17), and had not been carried off to Nineveh. **Was Hezekiah sick unto death**; stricken, *i.e.*, by a malady which, in the ordinary course of nature, would have been fatal. **And the Prophet Isaiah the son of Amoz came to him.** The designation of Isaiah as "the prophet," and "the son of Amoz," as if previously unknown to the reader, indicates the original independency of the narrative, which the writer of Kings probably obtained from a separate source. **And said unto him, Thus saith the Lord, Set thine house in order; for thou shalt die, and not live.** The statement was a warning, not a prophecy. It is parallel to that of Jonah to the Ninevites, "Yet forty days, and Nineveh shall be overthrown."

Ver. 2.—**Then he turned his face to the wall**—*i.e.* away from those who were standing beside his bed, and might have distracted his attention, to pray with more concentration and earnestness—**and prayed unto the Lord, saying** (comp. ch. xix. 15). It was natural to Hezekiah, in every kind of affliction and distress, to take his trouble direct to God.

Ver. 3.—**I beseech thee, O Lord, remember now how I have walked before thee in truth and with a perfect heart.** There is no Pharisaical self-righteousness here. Hezekiah is conscious that he has honestly endeavoured to serve God, and to do his will—that, whatever may have been his shortcomings, his heart has been right towards God. He ventures, therefore, on something like expostulation. Why is he to be cut off in the midst of his days, at the age of thirty-nine, when such a wicked king as Uzziah has lived to be sixty-eight (ch. xv. 2), and Rehoboam to be fifty-eight (1 Kings xiv. 21)? It is to be remembered that, under the old covenant, length of days was expressly promised to the righteous (Prov. iii. 2; ix. 11; x. 27, etc.), and that a shortened life was the proclaimed penalty of wicked-doing (Job xv. 32, 33; xxii. 16; Ps. lv. 23; Prov. x. 27). Hezekiah's self-assertion is thus a sort of laying hold of God's promises. **And have done that which is good in thy sight**; comp. ch. xviii. 3—6; and note the similar pleadings of David, "*With my whole heart have I sought thee*" (Ps. cxix. 10); "I have remembered thy Name, O Lord, and have *kept thy Law*. This I had because I kept thy commandments" (Ps. cxix. 55, 56), and the like. **And Hezekiah wept sore.** Human nature shrinks from death instinctively, and it requires a very vivid imagination for even the Christian

in middle life to feel, with St. Paul, that "it is better for him to depart and to be with Christ." The Hebrew of Hezekiah's time had far more reason to regard death as an evil. His hopes of a life beyond the grave were feeble—his conceptions of the life, if life there were, faint and unattractive. *Sheôl*, like Hades, was a vague, awful, terrible thing. If we consider Hezekiah's words, "The grave cannot praise thee, death cannot celebrate thee: they that go down into the pit cannot hope for thy truth. The living, the living, he shall praise thee" (Isa. xxxviii. 18, 19), we may understand how the Hebrew shrank from the fearful change. And in Hezekiah's case there was a yet further reason for grief. Hezekiah had as yet no male offspring (Josephus, 'Ant. Jud.,' x. 2. § 1). Manasseh was as yet unborn (comp. ver. 6 with ch. xxi. 1). If he died now, his house would be cut off, he would be without posterity—a sore grief to every Hebrew. Ewald's references to Isa. xxxviii. 19 and xxxix. 7, as indicative of Hezekiah having sons at the time, are absolutely without value.

Ver. 4.—**And it came to pass, afore Isaiah was gone out into the middle court.** The narrative in Isaiah (xxxviii. 4) does not contain this touch, which is very graphic, and indicative of the eye-witness. "The middle court" is probably the second or intermediate court of the royal palace. Isaiah had not gone further than this, when he was arrested in his course by a Divine communication. **That the word of the Lord came to him, saying.** How the word of the Lord came to the prophets is an inscrutable mystery. Sometimes, no doubt, it came in vision, which to a certain extent we can understand. But how, when the prophet was secularly engaged, as in this instance, walking across a court, he knew that the thought which occurred to him was a Divine message, it is almost impossible to conceive. Still, we cannot doubt that if God determines to communicate his will to man, he must be able, with the message, to impart an absolute certainty of its source, an assured conviction that it is his word, which precludes all question, hesitation, or dubiety. Isaiah, in the middle of his walk, finds his steps arrested, a new injunction laid upon him, with a necessity of immediately obeying it.

Ver. 5.—**Turn again**—or, *turn back*—"retrace thy steps, and enter once more into the bedchamber of the king" **and tell Hezekiah the captain of my people.** An unusual title for the Jewish monarch, but one applied in 1 Sam. ix. 16 and x. 1 to Saul, and in 1 Sam. xiii. 14 and 2 Sam. v. 2 to David. The proper meaning of נָגִיד is "leader"—"one who goes in front." **Thus saith the Lord, the God of David thy** father—Hezekiah obtains mercy, both as David's son and as David's imitator (see ch. xviii. 3)—**I have heard thy prayer, I have seen thy tears** (comp. Exod. ii. 24; iii. 7; Ps. lvi. 8). There is not a cry, not a groan, not a tear, not a sigh of his faithful ones, to which the heart of God is not open, which does not touch him, move him, draw forth his sympathy. If he does not always grant our prayers, it is because we "ask amiss"—without faith, or without fervour, or things not good for us. Hezekiah's earnest, faithful, and not unwise prayer was, as all such prayers always are, effectual. **Behold, I will heal thee: on the third day thou shalt go up unto the house of the Lord;** i.e. thou shalt be so completely recovered as to be able to quit thy palace and pay thy vows in the courts of the Lord's house. God knows that to do this will be Hezekiah's first wish, as soon as his sickness is past (comp. Isa. xxxviii. 20).

Ver. 6.—**And I will add unto thy days fifteen years.** God "does exceeding abundantly more than we either ask or think" (Eph. iii. 20). Hezekiah had asked for nothing more than immediate escape from death. God grants him fifteen additional years of life, i.e. more than doubles the length of his reign. **And I will deliver thee and this city out of the hand of the King of Assyria.** If Hezekiah's illness took place in B.C. 713, and Jerusalem was then in danger of being attacked by the Assyrians, the king who threatened the attack must have been Sargon. Sargon made an expedition into Palestine in B.C. 720, another in B.C. 713, and a third in B.C. 711. In none of them does he seem to have invaded Judæa; but in the third he counts the Jews among his enemies ('Eponym Canon,' p. 130, line 32). Hezekiah, who had revolted from him (ch. xviii. 7), may well have felt alarm both in B.C. 713 and 711. **And I will defend this city for mine own sake, and for my servant David's sake** (comp. ch. xix. 34). The promise given in B.C. 713 in respect of Sargon was repeated in B.C. 699 (?) with respect to Sennacherib in almost the same words.

Ver. 7.—**And Isaiah said, Take a lump of figs.** Figs were the usual remedy for boils. Dioscorides says of the fig, διαφορεῖ σκληρίας; Pliny, "Ulcera aperit;" while Jerome, in his commentary on Isaiah, has the following: "Juxta artem medicorum omnis sanies siccioribus ficis atque contusis in cutis superficiem provocatur." The remedy is said to be still in use among Easterns. It can scarcely be supposed to have cured a malignant boil by its intrinsic force; but under the Divine blessing it was made effectual, and the cure followed. **And they took and laid it on the boil.** The

royal attendants obtained a lump of figs, and applied it to the inflamed boil or car-buncle, as Isaiah had suggested. It is impossible to say what exactly was the nature of the "boil," since diseases change their characters, and every age has its own special disorders; but modern medical science knows of more than one kind of pustular swelling, which, as soon as it is detected, is regarded as fatal. **And he recovered.** Not suddenly, but by degrees; after the manner of natural remedies. It was three days before he was well enough to quit the palace, and offer thanks in the temple for his miraculous cure (see ver. 5).

Ver. 8.—**And Hezekiah said unto Isaiah, What** shall be **the sign that the Lord will heal me?** Having regard to the weakness of human faith, God, under the old covenant, often gave, or offered, near "signs" of promised blessings that were more remote, in order to sustain and encourage the doubtful and the wavering (comp. Exod. iii. 12; ch. xix. 29; Isa. vii. 11, 14, etc.). Hezekiah assumes that a near "sign" will now be granted to him, and simply asks what the sign is to be. **And that I shall go up into the house of the Lord the third day?** Three days would be a long and weary time to wait. It was not unnatural that Hezekiah should crave some more immediate assurance that his prayer was indeed heard. Neither God nor the prophet was angry at his request.

Ver. 9.—**And Isaiah said, This sign shalt thou have of the Lord, that the Lord will do the thing that he hath spoken.** Hezekiah is no more reproved for asking for a sign than was Gideon (Judg. vi. 37, 39). Ahaz, his father, had been reproved for *not* asking (Isa. vii. 13). It would be faithless now for Christians to demand signs; but in an age of miracles, when there were prophets upon the earth empowered to give signs, faithful men might request them without incurring God's displeasure. **Shall the shadow go forward ten degrees?** The Hebrew text will scarcely bear this translation, which, however, seems to be required by Hezekiah's answer. Perhaps for הָלַךְ we should read הֲיֵלֵךְ. **Or go back ten degrees?** literally, in both clauses, *ten steps.* There are abundant reasons for believing that the early dials consisted of a gnomon set up on the top of a flight of steps, and that time was measured by the number of steps on which the shadow of the gnomon fell (see a paper by Mr. Bosanquet, in the 'Transactions of the Society of Biblical Archæology' for 1874, pp. 1—82).

Ver. 10.—**And Hezekiah answered, It is a light thing for the shadow to go down ten degrees.** Hezekiah views it as a comparatively easy thing for the shadow, which is already descending the steps, to accelerate its pace and rapidly descend fifteen degrees instead of slowly traversing them; and therefore accepts Isaiah's other offer. **Nay, but let the shadow return backward ten degrees.** Let it, *i.e.*, change its direction, and having descended a certain distance, suddenly return and ascend again. This will be no "light thing," but a great marvel, which will thoroughly convince him. The thought was natural, though perhaps not strictly logical.

Ver. 11.—And Isaiah the prophet cried unto the Lord. Though the sign had been promised, Isaiah regarded his own intercessional prayer as not out of place, and "cried unto the Lord," *i.e.* prayed with energy, that the king's wish might be accomplished. So, though we have God's promise to care for us, and keep us from want (Matt. vi. 25—30), yet we must daily beseech him to "give us this day our daily bread." **And he brought the shadow ten degrees backward.** How this was done, we are not told, and can therefore only conjecture. The earlier commentators imagined that the revolution of the earth upon its axis was actually reversed for a time; but this idea is now generally rejected. It is clear from 2 Chron. xxxii. 31 that the phenomenon, whatever may have been its cause, was local, "done in the land" of Judah, and not visible elsewhere. Some moderns have suggested an earthquake affecting the gnomon; some a trick on the part of Isaiah; others, and the generality, a very abnormal refraction of the sun's rays. An observed instance of something similar, which took place at Metz, in Lotheringia, in the year 1703, is on record. Two scientists, Professor Seyffarth and Mr. J. W. Bosanquet, think that the phenomenon was due to an eclipse, in which the upper limb of the sun was obscured temporarily. In such a case a slight recession of the shadow would certainly take place; but it would scarcely be such as to attract attention from any one but a scientific observer (Stanley, 'Lectures on the Jewish Church,' vol. ii. p. 537). On the whole, the most probable cause would seem to be refraction, which is accepted by Keil, Bähr, and Kay. **By which it had gone down in the dial of Ahaz;** literally, *on the steps of Ahaz.* Sun-dials were invented by the Babylonians (Herod., ii. 109), and were no doubt in use at Babylon long before the time of Hezekiah. They were of various kinds, and in some of them the gnomon was made to cast its shadow upon steps. There are still two dials in India—one at Benares, known as the Mânmandir, and the other at Delhi—where this is the case (see Mr. Bosanquet's paper, already quoted, plate opp. p. 35).

Vers. 12—19.—*The embassy of Merodach-Baladan.* Soon after his recovery, Hezekiah received an embassy from a new quarter. Hitherto Babylon and Judæa had been isolated from one another, and had perhaps scarcely known of each other's existence. Assyria had stood between them, and Babylonia had been for the most part an Assyrian dependency. But recently Babylonia had asserted herself. In B.C. 722, on the death of Shalmaneser, a native Chaldean named Merodach-Baladan had made himself king of the country, and maintained his independence against all the efforts of Sargon to reduce him. His position, however, was precarious, and it was probably in the hope of concluding an alliance with Hezekiah—also an enemy of Sargon's (see the comment on ver. 6)—that he sent his embassy. He had two excuses for it. A neighbouring king might well congratulate his brother monarch on his recovery; and a Chaldean prince might well inquire into an astronomical marvel (2 Chron. xxxiii. 31). The date of the embassy appears to have been B.C. 712, the year following on Hezekiah's illness.

Ver. 12.—At that time Berodach-Baladan. Isaiah gives the name more correctly as "Merodach-Baladan" (Isa. xxxix. 1). The native form is Marduk-pal-iddin, *i.e.* "Merodach a son has given." This king makes his first appearance in an inscription of Tiglath-pileser's, where he is one of many chieftains among whom Babylonia is divided. Subsequently he is mentioned as revolting from Sargon in the latter's first year, B.C. 722 ('Records of the Past,' vol. vii. p. 29), and holding the throne of Babylon for twelve years (ibid., p. 41), when Sargon conquered him, deposed him, and took the kingdom (ibid., p. 48). This twelve-years' reign is acknowledged by Ptolemy in his Canon, but the name of the king is given as Mardoc-Empadus. On the death of Sargon, in B.C. 705, Merodach-Baladan again revolted, and reigned for six months, when he was driven out of the country by Sennacherib, B.C. 704. He continued, however, to give trouble even after this ('Records of the Past,' vol. vii. p. 63); and his sons and grandsons were pretenders to the Babylonian throne in the reigns of Esarhaddon and his successor, Asshur-bani-pal (see 'Ancient Monarchies,' vol. ii. pp. 469 and 490). **The son of Baladan.** In the Assyrian inscriptions Merodach-Baladan is always called "the son of Yakin" ('Records of the Past,' vol. vii. p. 40; vol. ix. p. 13, etc.). Yakin, however, may have been his grandfather, as Nimshi was the grandfather of Jehu, and Baladan (Beldaan?) his father. **King of Babylon, sent letters and a present unto Hezekiah.** Thus opening diplomatic communication. It has been almost universally felt that the object of the embassy must have been to conclude, or at any rate to pave the way for, an alliance. So Josephus ('Ant. Jud.,' x. 2. § 2), Ewald, Von Gerlach, Thenius, Keil, Bähr, and others. Assyria menaced both countries, and the common danger produced naturally a mutual attraction. But it was prudent to disguise this motive. **For he had heard that Hezekiah had been sick.** Assyria could not take umbrage at an embassy of congratulation, nor at one for scientific purposes (2 Chron. xxxiii. 31). So these two objects were paraded.

Ver. 13.—**And Hezekiah hearkened unto them.** Hezekiah was dazzled by the prospect that opened upon him. It was a grand thing that his fame should have reached so far as Babylon, a still grander thing to be offered such an alliance. It must be remembered that he and his counsellors were inclined from the first to meet Assyrian menace by calling in foreign aid (ch. xviii. 21—24; Isa. xx. 6; xxx. 2—7; xxxvi. 6). He had not yet accepted the view of Isaiah, that human aid was vain, and that the only reasonable ground of hope or confidence was in Jehovah. **And showed them all the house of his precious things;** *i.e.* his treasury. Hezekiah did not do this in mere ostentation, though he may have had a certain pride in exhibiting his wealth. His main wish, no doubt, was to make known his resources, and show that he was a valuable ally. So Orœtes acted towards Polycrates (Herod., iii. 123), and Hannibal towards the Gortynians (Corn. Nep., ' Vit. Hannib.,' § 9). It is to be borne in mind that Hezekiah's treasures were, in B.C. 712, still intact, and included all that ample store which he sacrificed to save Jerusalem at the time of the first expedition of Sennacherib (see ch. xviii. 14—16, and comp. 'Eponym Canon,' p. 135, where we find enumerated among the treasures given up, besides gold and silver, "precious carbuncles, couches of ivory, elevated thrones of ivory, skins of buffaloes, horns of buffaloes, and weapons"). **The silver, and the gold, and the spices.** Compare the description of the wealth of Solomon (1 Kings x. 25). "Spices" always form an important portion of the treasure of Oriental kings (comp. Herod., iii. 97, *sub fin.*). **And the precious ointment;** rather, *the precious oil*—שֶׁמֶן, not לֶקַח (compare the Septuagint, τὸ ἔλαιον τὸ ἀγαθόν). It is thought (Keil, Bähr) that

the valuable balsam oil, which was obtained from the royal gardens, is intended. **And all the house of his armour;** or, *of his vessels;* but arms and armour are probably intended. It would be almost as important to show that he had abundant arms in store, as that he had abundant riches. **And all that was found in his treasures**—a clause implying that there was much more which had not been specified, as precious stones, ivory, ebony, and the like—**there was nothing in his house, nor in all his dominion, that Hezekiah showed them not.** This is a manifest hyperbole; but it can scarcely mean less than that he gave orders for them to be shown the collections of arms and stores which existed in his other strongholds besides Jerusalem. Hezekiah, no doubt, had many " store cities," as Solomon (2 Chron. viii. 6) and Rehoboam (2 Chron. xi. 5—12) had.

Ver. 14.—**Then came Isaiah the prophet unto King Hezekiah, and said unto him.** When a prophet came, unsummoned, into a king's presence, it was usually to rebuke him (comp. 2 Sam. xii. 1; xxiv. 11—13; 1 Kings xiii. 1, 2; xviii. 15—18; xxi. 18—22; ch. i. 15, 16; 2 Chron. xii. 5; xvi. 7; xx. 37; xxv. 7, 15, etc.). **What said these men? and from whence came they unto thee?** Isaiah does not ask because he does not know, but to obtain a confession, on which he may base the message that he has to deliver. **And Hezekiah said, They are come from a far country, even from Babylon.** Note first, that Hezekiah does not give any answer to the prophet's first question, " What said these men?" being unwilling probably to make known the overtures that he had received from them, since he knows that Isaiah is opposed to any reliance on an "arm of flesh;" and secondly, that he answers the second question, not with shame, but with complacency, " They are come to me from a very far country, whither my fame has reached—even from Babylon are they come, 'the glory of kingdoms, the beauty of the Chaldees' excellency' (Isa. xiii. 19)." Self-satisfaction shows itself in the answer. He thinks it redounds to his honour that he has been sought out from so great a distance, and by so great a city.

Ver. 15.—**And he said, What have they seen in thine house?** *i.e.* What hast thou showed them? Hast thou treated them like ordinary ambassadors, or hast thou gone out of thy way to court an alliance with their master? **And Hezekiah answered, All the things that are in mine house have they seen: there is nothing among my treasures that I have not showed them.** The reply is open and straightforward. Hezekiah is not ashamed of what he has done, or at any rate, will not, to escape blame, take refuge in lies or concealment. He readily acknowledges that he has shown the ambassadors *everything*.

Ver. 16.—**And Isaiah said unto Hezekiah, Hear the word of the Lord.** This is a phrase of warning very common in the mouth of the prophets, when they are about to deliver a rebuke or solemn condemnation (comp. 1 Kings xxii. 19; 2 Chron. xviii. 18; Isa. i. 10; xxviii. 14; Jer. vii. 2; ix. 20; x. 1; xix. 3, etc.; Ezek. xv. 35; xxxiv. 9; Hos. iv. 1; Amos iii. 1, etc.).

Ver. 17.—**Behold, the days come, that all that is in thine house, and that which thy fathers have laid up in store unto this day, shall be carried into Babylon.** These treasures of thy royal house, whereof thou art so proud, and which thou hast of thine own accord made known to the Babylonians, to obtain their alliance, will in fact excite their cupidity, and the time will come when they, or what remains of them and represents them, will be carried off as plunder to Babylon by a conquering monarch, who will strip thy palace of its valuables, and drag thy descendants into captivity, and degrade them to the condition of slaves or servants, and make them discharge menial offices about his court. The revelation was now, it would seem, for the first time made that Babylon, and not Assyria, was the true enemy which Judæa had to fear, the destined foe who would accomplish all the threats of the prophets from Moses downwards, who would destroy the holy city and the glorious temple of Solomon, and carry away the ark of the covenant, and tear the people from their homes, and bring the kingdom of David to an end, and give Jerusalem over as a prey to desolation for seventy years. Henceforth it was Babylon and not Assyria which was feared, Babylon and not Assyria whereto the prophetic gaze of Isaiah himself was directed, and which became in his later prophecies (xl.—lxvi.) the main object of his denunciations. Considering the circumstances of the time, the prophecy is a most extraordinary one. Babylonia was at the time merely one of several kingdoms bordering on Assyria which the Assyrians threatened with destruction. From the time of Tiglath-pileser she had been continually diminishing, while Assyria had been continually increasing, in power. Tiglath-pileser had overrun the country and established himself as king there. Shalmaneser's authority had been uncontested. If just at present a native prince held the throne, it was by a very uncertain tenure, and a few years later Assyria regained complete mastery. No *human* foresight could possibly have anticipated such a complete reversal of the relative positions of the two countries as was involved in Isaiah's prophecy—a reversal

which was only accomplished by the appearance on the scene of a new power, Media, which hitherto had been regarded as of the very slightest account. Nothing shall be left, saith the Lord (comp. ch. xxv. 13—17 and Jer. lii. 12—23).

Ver. 18.—**And of thy sons that shall issue from thee, which thou shalt beget.** Under "sons" are included by the Hebrew idiom all descendants, however remote (Pusey's 'Lectures on Daniel,' pp. 406—409). The princes carried off from Jerusalem by Nebuchadnezzar were Hezekiah's descendants, either in the fourth or the fifth generation. **Shall they take away.** Among the descendants of Hezekiah taken to Babylon by Nebuchadnezzar were Jehoiachin (ch. xxiv. 15), Zedekiah (ch. xxv. 7), Daniel (Dan. i. 3), and others. **And they shall be eunuchs in the palace of the King of Babylon.** Keil and Bähr translate סָרִיסִים in this place by "chamberlains" or "footmen;" but there is no reason why the word should not have its ordinary sense of "eunuchs" (see the Septuagint ἔσονται εὐνοῦχοι, and for the fulfilment, comp. Dan. i. 3—18).

Ver. 19.—**Then said Hezekiah unto Isaiah, Good is the word of the Lord which thou hast spoken.** Hezekiah accepts the rebuke, thereby acknowledging himself to have been in the wrong, and submits without remonstrance to his punishment. "Good is the word of the Lord"—who "in his wrath has thought upon mercy." The king feels that God might, in justice, have visited him, in his own person, with some immediate affliction or calamity. It is a relief to hear that the blow will not fall during his lifetime. There may be a tinge of selfishness in his acquiescence, but it is not very pronounced, and does not call for any severe animadversion. The Old Testament saints were not faultless, and are not set before us as perfect patterns. There is one only "Ensample" given us whose steps we are to follow in all things. **And he said**—apparently after a pause, perhaps turning to his courtiers, whose looks may have expressed astonishment at the words which he had just spoken—**Is it not good, if peace and truth be in my days?** *i.e.* Am I not right to acquiesce in the sentence and pronounce it "good," if it promises me "peace and truth," or "tranquillity and steadfastness"? Ought I not to accept with thankfulness the immediate boon, instead of troubling myself about a remote future? The sentiment is not far removed from that of the well-known lines—

"I do not ask to see
The distant scene; one step enough for me."

Vers. 20, 21.—*The great works of Hezekiah, and his decease.* Hezekiah was known, not only as a pious king, and the king in whose reign the pride of the Assyrians was dashed to the ground, but also as one who, by works of great importance, conferred permanent benefit on Jerusalem (see 2 Chron. xxxii. 3—5 and 30; Ecclus. xlviii. 17). The writer feels that he cannot conclude his notice of Hezekiah's reign without some mention of these works. He enters, however, into no description, but, having referred the reader for details to the "book of the chronicles," notes in the briefest possible way the decease of Hezekiah, and the accession of his son and successor.

Ver. 20.—**And the rest of the acts of Hezekiah, and all his might.** Hezekiah's "might" was chiefly shown in the earlier portion of his reign, when he "smote the Philistines, even unto Gaza, and the borders thereof" (ch. xviii. 8). Against Assyria he was unsuccessful, and must have succumbed, but for the miraculous destruction of Sennacherib's host. **And how he made a pool;** rather, *the pool,* or *the reservoir.* The writer of Kings either knows of one pool only in the neighbourhood of Jerusalem, or regards one as so superior that it deserves to be called κατ᾽ ἐξοχήν, "*the* pool." Recent discoveries make it highly probable that the "pool" intended is that of Siloam, or, if not the present Siloam reservoir, a larger one, a little below it, now known as *Birket el Hamra* (see the 'Quarterly Statement' of the Palestine Exploration Fund for April, 1886, p. 88). That there was at least one other pool in Hezekiah's time is evident from Isa. xxii. 9, 11. **And a conduit;** rather, *the conduit.* If "the pool" is Siloam, "the conduit" must almost certainly be that which was excavated under Ophel for the purpose of conveying the water from the Well of the Virgin in the Kedron valley to the Siloam reservoir on the western side of the spur. This conduit, which is curiously twisted, has a length of 1708 feet, with a height varying from two feet to four or five, and a width of about two feet. The roof is flat, the sides perpendicular, and the floor hollowed into a groove for the more rapid passage of the water. About nineteen feet from the southern extremity, where the

channel opens upon the Siloam pool, a niche has been cut in the right-hand wall in the shape of a square tablet, and smoothed to receive an inscription of six lines, the greater part of which has been recovered. The letters are of the old Hebrew or Phœnician type, and by their forms indicate a date "between the eighth and the sixth centuries" (Sayce). The inscription, so far as it is legible, appears to have run as follows: "Behold the tunnel! Now, this is the history of the tunnel. As the excavators were lifting up the pick, each towards the other, and while there were yet three cubits to be broken through . . . the voice of the one called to his neighbour, for there was an excess (?) of the rock on the right. Then they rose up . . . they struck on the west of the excavators; the excavators struck, each to meet the other, pick to pick. And the waters flowed from their outlet to the pool for a distance of a thousand cubits; and three-fourths (?) of a cubit was the height of the rock over the head of the excavation here." We learn from it that the workmen began at either end, and tunnelled through the rock until they met in the middle—a result which their previous divergences from the straight line force us to attribute more to good fortune than to engineering science. **And brought water into the city.** The Well of the Virgin was without, the Pool of Siloam within, the city—the wall of the town being carried across the Tyropœon valley from the extreme point of Ophel to the opposite hill (see Neh. iii. 15). **Are they not written in the book of the chronicles of the kings of Judah?** Hezekiah's fame rested very much upon these works, as we see by what is said of him by the son of Sirach (see the comment on vers. 20, 21).

Ver. 21.—**And Hezekiah slept with his fathers.** The writer of Chronicles adds, "And they buried him in the chiefest," or rather, in the topmost, "of the sepulchres of the sons of David" (2 Chron. xxxii. 33). The catacomb of David being now full, Hezekiah and his descendants (ch. xxi. 18, 26; xxiii. 30) had to be buried elsewhere. The tomb of Hezekiah was either over the catacomb of David, or on the ascent which led to it. **And Manasseh his son reigned in his stead.** So 2 Chron., *l. s. c.;* and Josephus, 'Ant. Jud.,' x. 3. § 1.

HOMILETICS.

Vers. 1—3.—*Aspects of death.* We may look on death from three points of view—that of the natural man, unenlightened by Divine revelation; that of the Israelite under the Law; and that of the Christian. The contemplation will be wholesome, for we are all too apt to turn our thoughts away from any consideration of the grim enemy, who will certainly have to be met and encountered one day.

I. DEATH FROM THE POINT OF VIEW OF THE NATURAL MAN. By nature man has an absolute horror of death. Self-preservation is the first law of his being. He will suffer anything, he will do anything, to avoid death. Death is in his eyes a fierce monster, cruel, relentless, detestable. To live may be hard, grievous, wretched, scarcely tolerable; but to die is wholly intolerable. It is to exchange the bright pure light of day for absolute darkness, or at best for a dim, dull, murky region in which souls wander without aim or hope. It is to be cut off from all that is known, customary, intelligible, and to be thrown into a world unknown, unfamiliar, full of terrors. It is to lose all energy, all vigour, all robustness, all sense of power. In the "happy hunting-fields," the shade of the living man may still pursue the unsubstantial forms of elk, or deer, or antelope; but the sport is a poor and colourless *replica* of that pursued on earth, and is anticipated with but little satisfaction. Better, in the eyes of the natural man, to live on earth, even as slave or hireling, the hardest of all possible earthly lives, than to hold the kingship of the world below and rule over the entire realm of shadows (Hom., ' Od.,' 489—491). In the vigour of his youth and early manhood the natural man forgets death, views it as so distant that the fear of it scarcely affects him sensibly; but let the shadow be suddenly cast across his path, and he starts from it with a cry of terror. He can, indeed, meet it without blenching in the battle-field, when his blood is hot, and to the last he does not know whether he will slay his foe, or his foe him ; but if he has to die, he accepts his death as a miserable necessity. It is hateful to him to die ; it is still more hateful to be cut off in his prime, while he is still strong, vigorous, lusty. It is not till old age comes on, and his arm grows weak, and his eye dim, that he can look on death without loathing. Then, perhaps, he may accept the necessity without protest, feeling that actual death can be little worse than the death-in-life whereto he has come.

II. DEATH FROM THE POINT OF VIEW OF THE ISRAELITE. The Israelite had not very much advantage over the natural man in respect of the contemplation of death. But little was revealed to him concerning the life beyond the grave. He *knew*, indeed, that his life did not end everything, that he would certainly go down to Sheol when he died, and there have a continued existence; but Sheol presented itself to him in as dismal colours as Hades did to the Greek. " The living, the living shall praise thee ; Sheol cannot praise thee, death cannot celebrate thee," cried Hezekiah from his bed of sickness (Isa. xxxviii. 18, 19). Thus the Israelite too shrank from death, not merely instinctively, but as a sad and poor condition compared with life. And untimely death was even more hateful to him than to the natural man, since under the Mosaic dispensation it was declared to be a mark of the displeasure of God. "The fear of the Lord prolongeth days ; but the years of the wicked shall be shortened," said Solomon (Prov. x. 27). " Bloodthirsty and deceitful men shall not live out half their days," sang David (Ps. lv. 23). " Long life " was a gift repeatedly promised to the righteous (Prov. iii. 2, 16 ; ix. 10, 11 ; Ps. xci. 16, etc.) ; and when a man found himself struck down by a dangerous disease in his middle age, it seemed to him, and to those about him, that he must have sinned grievously, and so brought down upon himself God's anger. Still more bitter was the feeling of one who was cut off in mid life, if he was childless. Then the man's name was " clean put out ; " his memorial perished with him ; he had no more part or lot in Israel, no more inheritance among his brethren. Thus death remained a terror and a calamity, even to the most religious Jew, until, about the time of Daniel, the doctrine of the resurrection began to be preached (Dan. xii. 1—3), and the life beyond the grave to take a more cheerful aspect.

III. DEATH FROM THE POINT OF VIEW OF THE CHRISTIAN. The whole relation of death to life and of life to death became changed by the revelation made to man in Christ. Then for the first time were " life and immortality " fully " brought to light." Then first it appeared that earth was a mere sojourning-place for those who were here as " strangers and pilgrims " upon it, having " no continuing city." Then first were the joys of heaven painted in glowing hues, and men told that " eye had not seen, nor ear heard, neither had it entered into the heart of man [to conceive], the things which God had prepared for those that love him " (1 Cor. ii. 9). No sensuous Paradise of earthly joys was depicted, no " Castle of Indolence," no mere haven of rest, but man's true home, the place and state for which he was created, where is his citizenship, where he will be reunited to those whom in life he loved, where his nature will be perfected, and where, above all, he will " be with Christ " (Phil. i. 23), will " see God " (1 John

iii. 2), and "know even as he is known" (1 Cor. xiii. 12). The prospect of death thus, to the true Christian, lost all its terrors. "I am in a strait betwixt two," says St. Paul, "*having a desire to depart*, and be with Christ, *which is far better*" (Phil. i. 23); and again, "I am willing rather to be absent from the body, and to be present with the Lord" (2 Cor. v. 8). Natural shrinking there may be, for "the flesh is weak;" but thousands have triumphed over it, have sought martyrdom, have gone gladly to their deaths, and preferred to die. Even when there is no such exaltation of feeling, death is contemplated with calmness, as a passage to a better world—a world where there is no sorrow nor sighing (Isa. xxxv. 10), where there is no sin, "where the wicked cease from troubling, and the weary are at rest" (Job iii. 17). Untimely death from natural disease or accident is to the Christian no sign of God's displeasure, but rather an indication of the contrary. God takes to himself those whom he recognizes as fit to die, of whom it may be said that τελειωθέντες ἐν ὀλίγῳ ἐπλήρωσαν χρόνους μακρούς. He takes them in love, not in wrath, to join the company of "the spirits of just men made perfect" (Heb. xii. 23), to be among his "jewels" (Isa. lxi. 10; Mal. iii. 17).

Vers. 12—18.—*The sunshine of prosperity a greater danger than the storms of adversity.* When Sennacherib threatens, when his messengers blaspheme, when the huge battalions of the most powerful kingdom in the world have entered his territory and are about to march upon his capital, the Jewish monarch remains firm; his faith is unshaken; he casts his care upon God, looks to him and him only; believes in him, trusts in him, regards prayer as the only door of safety. Similarly, when disease prostrates him, when a painful and dangerous malady confines him to his bed, and the prophet, instead of bringing him words of comfort, is commissioned to bid him "set his house in order; for he shall die, and not live" (ver. 1), his faith fails not, in God is still his refuge, to God alone he betakes himself, and prays and weeps sore (vers. 2, 3). The blasts of calamity cannot tear away from him the cloak of faith; he clutches it the tighter the more the storm rages; nothing will induce him to let it go. But the danger past, health restored, the admiration of foreign kings attracted, his ear besieged by congratulations and flatteries, his court visited by envoys from "a far country," and at once his grasp relaxes, the thought of God fades from his heart, his faith slips from him, and he is a mere worldling, bent on winning to himself a great alliance, and obtaining the aid of an "arm of flesh" against his enemies. And so it is and will ever be with most of us. We can bear the world's frowns, the buffets of fortune, the cruelty of oppressors, the open attacks of rivals and enemies; we can resist them, defy them, and still maintain our integrity; but let the world smile, let fortune favour us, let riches increase, let friends spring up on all sides, and how few of us can stand the sunshine! How few of us can remain as close to God as we were before! How few of us but drop the habits of prayer, of communing with God, of constant reliance upon him, which were familiar to us in the darker time, and substitute a mere occasional and perfunctory acknowledgment of his goodness! Alas, how few! Oh! may *our* cry, the cry of our heart, ever be, "In all time of our tribulation, *in all time of our wealth*, . . . good Lord, deliver us!"

HOMILIES BY VARIOUS AUTHORS.

Vers. 1—11.—*Hezekiah's sickness.* Every changing scene of life is depicted for us in the Bible. Whatever our circumstances may be, we can get some guidance, help, or comfort from that treasure-house of wisdom and experience. We have here—

I. A SOLEMN MESSAGE. "Set thine house in order; for thou shalt die, and not live." 1. *It was a solemn message for Hezekiah.* His kingdom seemed now to be securely established. God had helped him against the Philistines, and had overthrown them. He was doubtless looking forward to many years of rest and quietness, when he might enjoy for himself the benefits of peace, and develop the resources of the nation, so long desolated by invading armies. How startling, then, the announcement of his approaching death! 2. *It is a solemn message for every one.* It is a solemn thing for a human soul to pass from time into eternity, to enter into the immediate presence of the Eternal,

to stand before God.   3. *It is a message which may be truly spoken to every one.*
"Thou shalt die, and not live."   There is an hour of death in store for every one of us.
Somewhere in the unknown future there waits for us—

<blockquote>"The shadow feared of man."</blockquote>

We know not what a day may bring forth.   "In such an hour as ye think not the
Son of man cometh."   4. *The certainty of death suggests the necessity for immediate
preparation.*   "Set thine house in order."   Can you say that you are prepared to meet
your God?   Is your heart right with God?   Have you set your house in order?   *The
time for preparation is "now."*   Scripture is very clear on that point.   It is nowhere
said, "See that you make ready when death comes."   It is nowhere said, "Look forward
to being prepared for death."   No; that would only be deceiving us, because death
might come before we were prepared, though we might intend to be prepared if we
knew that death was near.   No; but it is said, "*Be* ready."   It is said, "Prepare to
meet thy God."   "*Now* is the accepted time, *now* is the day of salvation."

II. A SORROWFUL KING.   "Hezekiah wept sore."   1. *He was not sorrowful because
of a guilty conscience.*   He had endeavoured to serve God faithfully.   No doubt he
had made mistakes.   But his heart was right with God.   "I beseech thee, O Lord,
remember now how I have walked before thee in truth and with a perfect heart, and
have done that which is good in thy sight."   It is well to have a good conscience when
the hour of death draws nigh.   It is well when we can say with St. Paul, "Herein do
I exercise myself, to have always a conscience void of offence toward God and toward
men."   Such a man is always "ready to depart."   2. *He was sorrowful only because
of the shortening of his life.*   How little we know what is best for us!   It was after
this that Hezekiah was led astray, as we shall see, by the pride of his heart.   Though
God lengthened Hezekiah's life in answer to his piteous request, perhaps it would have
been better for him if he had been content to go when God first sent for him.   There is
often a great mystery to us when good men seem prematurely taken away.   But God
knows the reason why, and he doeth all things well.   Let us leave the time of our own
departure, and the departure of our friends, contentedly in God's hands.

III. A SPARED LIFE.   The life was spared in answer to prayer; and yet this case gives
no encouragement to what is commonly known as "healing by faith."   Isaiah directed
the attendants to take a lump of figs and lay it for a plaster on the boil, and Hezekiah
recovered (ver. 7; Isa. xxxviii. 21).   We believe in the power of faith and prayer to
heal the sick, and yet we believe in using the means.   We use food to preserve and
sustain our life from day to day.   There is no lack of faith in that.   And it shows no
lack of faith if we use means to restore our life, asking all the time that God's blessing
may accompany the means we use.   How many of our lives has God spared?   How
many of us has he brought back again from the gates of death?   Let the goodness
of God lead us to repentance.   Let the lives that he has spared be dedicated to
him.—C. H. I.

Vers. 12—21.—*Hezekiah and the ambassadors.*   Friendly greetings are always
welcome.   They are especially so after a time of sickness.   Hezekiah's illness, no doubt,
called forth many expressions of sympathy, and, among the rest, a message and present
from Merodach-Baladan King of Babylon.   The ambassadors who bore the message
and the present were very courteously received by Hezekiah.   Unfortunately, he allowed
himself to be unduly elated by the honour done to him by the heathen king.   He
showed the messengers all the house of his precious things, and all his treasures of gold
and silver and armour; "there was nothing in his house, nor in all his dominion, that
Hezekiah showed them not."   We see here—

I. FOOLISH PRIDE.   Hezekiah's prosperity for once led him astray.   1. *He gave not
glory to God.*   It was God who had prospered him, and crowned all his labours with
success.   But there is no word of this to the ambassadors.   He takes all the honour
and glory to himself.   He might have, perhaps, excused himself, as many do, by saying
that there is no use in obtruding our religion upon strangers.   But why should he have
been ashamed to acknowledge God's bountiful hand, if he was not ashamed to take
his bounties?   Why should any of us be ashamed to confess Christ?   To be ashamed
of Christ is not only weak and cowardly; it is unreasonable.   2. We see also how

foolish Hezekiah's pride was, when we remember *his recent sickness*. It was not so long since Hezekiah, now so vain and boastful, turned his face to the wall, and wept sore. The memory of that should have humbled him. Not only so, but when he was recovered of his sickness, he made special promises of praise to God and humility of spirit. "The living, the living, he shall praise thee, as I do this day." Where was Hezekiah's praise of God's goodness when these Babylonish ambassadors came to him? "I shall go softly all my years in the bitterness of my soul" (Isa. xxxviii. 15). Where now is Hezekiah's humility? On the contrary, as it is said in 2 Chron. xxxii. 25, "Hezekiah rendered not again according to the benefit done unto him; for his heart was lifted up." 3. We see here *how watchful we need to be over our own hearts*. We read in 2 Chron. xxxii. 31, "Howbeit in the business of the ambassadors of the princes of Babylon, who sent unto him to inquire of the wonder that was done in the land, *God left him, to try him, that he might know all that was in his heart*." We cannot tell how we may act until the temptation comes. Such a crisis as this may come to each of us. Let us watch and pray, that we enter not into temptation. "Above all treasure guard thy heart, for out of it are the fountains of life."

II. A FAITHFUL PROPHET. Isaiah did not delay in the path of duty. Hezekiah had humbled himself and his nation, and he had dishonoured God, before these heathen ambassadors. Isaiah at once proceeds to the king's presence, and rebukes him for his folly and pride (vers. 14—18). Not only so, but he foretells that Babylon, whose avarice had thus been aroused, would one day take advantage of this act of weakness, and take possession of the treasures of Jerusalem. Hezekiah's answer was wise and humble. He was a God-fearing, if mistaken, man. "Good is the word of the Lord which thou hast spoken." So let us receive God's judgments, in humility, submission, and patience, and not in rebellion and defiance. What a blessing to a king to have a faithful and wise counsellor! What a blessing to a nation and to a Church to have faithful ministers! They who fear God need not fear the face of man.—C. H. I.

Vers. 1—21.—*Death*. "In those days was Hezekiah sick unto death," etc. A thoughtful man might raise many questions on this chapter—indeed, on all the chapters in this book. He might ask—Who was the writer of this chapter, ay, and of the entire Books of Kings? A question this which has not been settled, and, perhaps, never will be. He might ask on what authority certain men, called prophets, such as Isaiah, speak as from heaven, and say, "Thus saith the Lord." Priests and leaders of all sects profess to speak in the name of the Lord, and say, "Thus saith the Lord." Such questions might open up discussions of critical and speculative interest, but would be of no practical benefit whatever. Anyhow, I forego them. My purpose all along has been to turn whatever I find in this or any other book of the Old Testament to some practical use. Some years before the overwhelming destruction of Sennacherib and his army, as recorded in the preceding chapter, Hezekiah was seized with some severe disease which threatened the extinction of his life: death was before him. The account leads us to consider death in three aspects: as (1) *consciously approaching*; as (2) *temporarily arrested*; and as (3) *ultimately triumphant*.

I. As CONSCIOUSLY APPROACHING. "In those days was Hezekiah sick unto death. And the Prophet Isaiah the son of Amoz came to him, and said unto him, Thus saith the Lord, Set thine house in order; for thou shalt die, and not live." Mark here three things. 1. *When* he became conscious of its approach. "In those days." "By this expression," says Dr. Keil, "the illness of Hezekiah is merely assigned in a general manner to the same time as the events previously described. That it did not occur after the departure of the Assyrians, . . . is evident from the sixth verse, both from the fact that, in answer to his prayer, fifteen years more of life were promised him, and that he, nevertheless, reigned only twenty-nine years (ch. xviii. 2); and also from the fact that God promised to deliver him out of the hand of the Assyrians, and to defend Jerusalem." 2. *How* he became conscious of its approach. "Thus saith the Lord, Set thine house in order; for thou shalt die, and not live." It needs no Isaiah, or any other prophet, to deliver this message to man. It comes to him from all history, from every graveyard, from every funeral procession, as well as from the inexorable law of decay working ever in his constitution. Yes; and not merely the announcement, but the duty: "Set thine house in order." (1) Men have much to do in this life. The "house" is out of order. (2) Unless the work is done *here*, it will not be done *yonder*. "Whatsoever thy hand findeth to do, do it with thy might," etc. 3. How he *felt* in the consciousness of its approach. "Then he turned his face to the wall." (1) He seems to have] been overwhelmingly distressed. "He wept sore." He turned away from the world, with all its multiplex concerns, from all his regal pomp, and peered into the invisible and the infinite. (2) He cried earnestly to heaven. "He prayed unto the Lord, saying, I beseech thee, O Lord, remember now how I have walked before thee in truth and with a perfect heart, and have done that which is good in thy sight." In his prayer we note the cry of nature. All men, even those who are atheistic in theory, are urged by the law of their spiritual nature to cry to heaven in great and conscious danger. In his prayer we also note something of self-righteousness. "Remember now how I have walked before thee in truth and with a perfect heart, and have done that which is good in thy sight." Though he had been free from most sins, and had displayed some virtues, he had not done this. Perhaps no man that ever appeared on this earth, save the "Son of man," could say, "I have walked before thee in truth and with a perfect heart." Moral self-deception is one of the most prevalent sins of the human heart. Like the Pharisee in the temple, we exult in virtues we have not. Now, death is approaching all men, whether we are *conscious* of the fact or not. The decree has gone forth, "Thou shalt die, and not live." Death is ever coming with stealthy steps, yet with resistless force. He is coming always, whether we are at home or abroad, on ocean or on land, in society or in solitude; asleep or awake, he, the king of terrors, is coming.

II. As TEMPORARILY ARRESTED. Five things are to be observed here. 1. The *primary Author* of its arrest. "And it came to pass, afore Isaiah was gone out into the middle court, that the word of the Lord came to him, saying, Turn again, and tell Hezekiah the captain of my people, Thus saith the Lord, the God of David thy father, I have heard thy prayer, I have seen thy tears: behold, I will heal thee." How came Isaiah into possession of this knowledge, this "word of the Lord," concerning Hezekiah's restoration? Was it by a dream, or through some other supernatural communication? On this point I confess my utter ignorance. The grand practical idea is that God can arrest death, and he only. Our times are in his hands. His constant visitation preserveth us. He is the absolute Master of death. At his bidding the most fragile creature may live for ever, the most robust expire. 2. The *secondary means* of its arrest. "Isaiah said, Take a lump of figs. And they took and laid it on the boil, and he recovered." It would seem that the ancients, in the case of boils, abscesses, and such like, frequently applied figs to the affected parts, and no doubt there was remedial virtue in the figs. For aught we know, there may be an antidote sleeping in plants and minerals for all our physical complaints. The man who lives by the medical art is untrue to his mission, and unfaithful to his patient, unless he, with an independent mind and a devoted heart, searches Nature for those remedial elements with which she is charged. 3. The *extraordinary sign* of its arrest. "And Hezekiah said unto Isaiah, What shall be the sign that the Lord will heal me, and that I shall go up into the house of the Lord the third day? And Isaiah said, This sign shalt thou have of the Lord, that the Lord will do the thing that he hath spoken: shall the shadow go forward ten degrees, or go back ten degrees? And Hezekiah answered, It is a light thing for the shadow to go down ten degrees: nay, but let the shadow return backward ten degrees. And Isaiah the prophet cried unto the Lord: and he brought the shadow ten degrees backward, by which it had gone down in the dial of Ahaz." Perhaps it was natural for a man, who when he felt himself on the brink of eternity was told he would recover, to desire some assurance of the fact so unexpected and yet so acceptable. Hezekiah desired a sign, and he had it. But what was the sign? We are told that the shadow on the dial-plate "returned ten degrees backwards." How was this? Did the sun recede, or, in other words, was the rotation of the earth reversed? I know not; neither does it matter. It is sufficient to know that, whether it was an illusion, or a natural eclipse of the sun, which some astronomers say did actually take place at this time (B.C. 689), or a physical miracle, it seems to have satisfied the king. It seems to be a law of mind, that phenomena which it earnestly expects often occur. "Be it to thee according to thy faith." 4. The *exact extension* of its arrest. "I will add unto thy days fifteen years." The addition

of fifteen years to man's brief existence in this life is a considerable item, and the more
so when that fifteen years is added at a period when the man has fully reached middle
life, and passed through the chief training experiences. He who can add fifteen years
to a man's life can add eternity. "Our times are in his hands." 5. The *mental ineffi-
ciency* of its arrest. What spiritual good did these additional fifteen years accomplish
for the king? They might have done much; they ought to have done much. But
did they make him a *morally better man,* or an intellectually wiser man? Not the
former, I trow, for mark his vanity. The letters which the King of Babylon, Merodach-Baladan, despatched to him, together with a present, so excited his egotism that
he "hearkened [or, as Isaiah puts it, 'was glad'] unto them," that is, the Babylonian
deputies; and "showed them all the house of his precious things, the silver, and the
gold, and the precious ointment, and all the house of his armour, and all that was
found in his treasures: there was nothing in his house, nor in all his dominion, that
Hezekiah showed them not." At this time he had enormous possessions. We find
from 2 Chron. xxxii. 23 that presents were brought to Hezekiah from various quarters.
"He had," says the Chronicler, "exceeding much riches and honour: and he made
himself treasuries for silver, and for gold, and for precious stones, and for spices, and
for shields, and for all manner of pleasant jewels; storehouses also for the increase of
corn, and wine, and oil; and stalls for all manner of beasts, and cotes for flocks"
(2 Chron. xxxii. 27, 28). All this, with an elated vanity, he exposed to the Babylonian
magnates. Vanity, for many reasons, is one of the worst of all the bad elements of
depravity; it is a species of moral evil, hideous to all beholders, and damnable to its
possessor. Did these fifteen years added to his life make Hezekiah an *intellectually
wiser man?* No; his judgment was not improved. In sooth, he seems to have lost
that penetration, that insight into things and men, which he had previously possessed.
How blind was he not to see that, by exposing his treasures, he was exciting the avarice
of the Babylonians, tempting them to make an invasion of his country! This Isaiah
told him: "Behold, the days come, that all that is in thine house, and that which thy
fathers have laid up in store unto this day, shall be carried into Babylon: nothing
shall be left, saith the Lord." Affliction does not always improve men, either morally
or intellectually. Ah me! how many have I known who, when they have "turned
their face to the wall," writhing in agony, with grim death before them, have solemnly
vowed improvement should they ever recover? They have recovered, and become
worse in every respect than before. What boots a term of fifteen years, or even a
thousand years, added to our existence, if our souls are not improved thereby?

III. As ULTIMATELY TRIUMPHANT. "And Hezekiah slept with his fathers." The
end of the fifteen years came, and he meets with the common destiny of all. The
unconquered conqueror is not to be defrauded of his prey, however long delayed. Since
death cannot be escaped by any, whether young or old, it has been asked, is there any
advantage in longevity? Rather, would it not be better to die in the first dawn of
infancy, than in any subsequent period? "Whom the gods love die young," was said
of yore. We may go a step further, and say, "Why live at all?"—D. T.

Vers. 1—11.—*Hezekiah's sickness.* In order of time, this recovery of King Hezekiah
from sickness stands before the destruction of Sennacherib, though in order of narration
it comes after it. So with the Babylonian embassy (see on ch. xviii. 1—13).
I. WARNING OF DEATH. 1. *Unexplained sickness.* "In those days was Hezekiah
sick unto death." His disease was some ulcerous growth, called in the narrative "a
boil." We have been accustomed in this history to see troubles of body, and calamities
in the state, connected with sin, as part of its temporal punishment. But there is no
reason to believe that Hezekiah was guilty of any special transgression which led to his
being visited with this sickness. His own conscience was clear, and there is no
indication of blame in the narrative. Affliction is sent for other reasons than the
punishment of sin, and we grievously err, and do great injustice to the sufferers, if we
insist on always interpreting it in this light. Job's friends committed this error (Job
xlii. 7, 8; cf. Luke xiii. 1—5; John ix. 1—3). In Hezekiah's case affliction was no
doubt sent as a purificatory and strengthening discipline, intended to try his faith, and
lead him to new experience of the grace of God. 2. *The announcement of death.* It
was while Hezekiah's mind was troubled about his sickness that the Prophet Isaiah

came to him, and brought the message, "Thus saith the Lord, . . . thou shalt die, and not live." In its natural course the sickness would have had a fatal issue. The fact of our mortality is one we should often have before us. Every ache, pain, and trouble of body, reminds us that we are here but for a time—that this is not our rest. They are prophetic of the end. A time, however, comes when the near approach of the end is unmistakable, if not to the individual himself, yet to others. If a man is dying, it is the truest kindness to let him know it. Isaiah might have withheld this information from Hezekiah on the ground that it would agitate him, might hasten his death, could do no good, etc.,—the usual pleas for keeping back from a patient the news of his hopeless condition. We have only to put the matter to ourselves: would we like to be within a few weeks or days of our death, and not be made aware of the fact? Would we in such circumstances like to be buoyed up by false hopes? Then why buoy up others? By acquainting a patient with his real state, we give him opportunity for setting his house in order; for prayer to God that might, as in Hezekiah's case, lead to his recovery; in any case, for suitably preparing his mind in view of departure. 3. *The duty of preparation.* "Set thine house in order," said Isaiah; "for thou shalt die." It is a duty incumbent on us, even in health, to have our worldly affairs so arranged that, if we should be unexpectedly removed, they would be found in order. The neglect of this simple duty—the putting it off under the idea that there is still plenty of time—leads in numberless cases to confusion, heartburning, strife, and loss. If the putting the house in order has not been attended to, the approach of death is a solemn call to do it. In any case, there will be final arrangements, last words, loving directions which belong peculiarly to the dying hour. If it is important to set our worldly affairs in order in view of death, how much more to have every *spiritual* preparation made!

II. PRAYER FOR LIFE. 1. *Hezekiah's distress.* The announcement that he was soon to die filled Hezekiah with deep grief. He turned his face to the wall, prayed earnestly to God, and wept sore. The grounds of his distress may be inferred from the hymn composed by him after his recovery (Isa. xxxviii. 9—20). (1) The natural love of life. This is implanted in every one. It has its root in a true instinct, for death in the case of the human being is unnatural. It was not a part of the primal order. Man as made by God was destined for immortality, not immortality of the soul only, but immortality of the whole person. Death is the violent wrenching asunder of two parts of his personality which were meant to be inseparable. It is the fruit of sin, and abnormal (Rom. v. 12). (2) The want of a clear hope of immortality. The experience of the Old Testament saints teaches us to distinguish between a mere idea of future existence, and such a hope of immortality as is now possessed by Christians. The Hebrew believed in the after-existence of the soul. But this of itself brought no comfort to them. Sheol was uniformly pictured as a region of gloom, silence, and inaction. Its shadowy life was no compensation for the loss of the rich, substantial joys of earthly existence. In hours of depression this was the view of Sheol that prevailed. Only in moments of strong faith did the believer rise to the confidence that God would be with him even in Sheol, and would deliver his soul out of these gloomy abodes. The Hebrew hope of immortality was really a hope of resurrection (Ps. xvi. 10; xlix. 14, 15). It is Jesus Christ who, in the full sense of the words, has brought life and immortality to light (2 Tim. i. 10). (3) The thought that death would cut him off from the comforts of God's presence, and the privilege of waiting on God and serving him. This is implied in his view of Sheol, and is expressed in his song (Isa. xxxviii. 11). It was, therefore, no unmanly fear of death which Hezekiah showed, but one resting on good and substantial reasons. 2. *Hezekiah's prayer.* Cut off from earthly help, Hezekiah betook himself in earnest prayer to God. The fact that he did pray, and that his prayer was answered, is an encouragement to us to pray for recovery from sickness. The New Testament also holds out this encouragement (Jas. v. 13—16). In his pleadings with God, Hezekiah adopted a tone which may seem to us to savour too much of self-righteousness. "I beseech thee, O Lord, remember now how I have walked before thee in truth and with a perfect heart," etc. It was not, however, in a spirit of self-righteousness that he urged this plea. He was conscious of many sins (cf. Isa. xxxviii. 17). His meaning was that he had endeavoured to serve God faithfully, and with an undivided heart, and had the claim which God's own promises gave him of life and blessing to those who acted thus. A good conscience is a great encouragement in prayer to God, though, with the deeper views of sin which the gospel gives, there is rightly a greater shrinking from pleading anything that might seem like one's own merit (see Perowne's ' Introduction to the Book of Psalms,' ch. iii. sect. 3, " Assertions of innocence in the Psalms ").

III. RECOVERY FROM SICKNESS. 1. *The promptitude of God's answer.* Scarcely had the prayer left Hezekiah's lips than the answer was communicated to Isaiah. The prophet had not yet left the palace, but was still within its precincts, " in the middle court," when word came to him to return to Hezekiah, and assure him of recovery. God in this case, as always, was " waiting to be gracious" (Isa. xxx. 18). The answer was given (1) out of regard to Hezekiah himself, " Tell Hezekiah the captain of my people ; " (2) in answer to his supplication, " I have heard thy prayer ; " (3) for the sake of David, " The Lord, the God of David thy father " (and cf. ver. 6). This recovery was one of " the sure mercies of David" (Isa. lv. 3). For similar examples of prompt answer to prayer, see on ch. xix. 20. 2. *The promise of lengthened life.* The message which Isaiah was to carry to Hezekiah contained three parts : (1) a promise that he would be healed, and able to go up to the house of the Lord on the third day. "A striking instance of the conditionalness of prophecy" (Cheyne). Hezekiah's first use of his recovered health is assumed to be a visit to God's house. (2) A promise of fifteen years more added to his life. God thus exceeds his servants' askings. The king sought only healing ; God assures him of a prolonged term of life (cf. Eph. iii. 20). (3) A promise that the city would be defended against the Assyrians. This was another word to Hezekiah through which God caused him to hope (Ps. cxix. 49). Yet he nearly forfeited it by his subsequent worldly policy (see previous chapters). 3. *The king's recovery.* Isaiah's word was fulfilled, and the king recovered. Whether " the lump of figs " was a simple remedy or a mere sign need not be discussed. In our case the duty of using means in connection with prayer is plain.

IV. THE SIGN OF THE SUN-DIAL. 1. *The request for a sign.* When Isaiah communicated his message to Hezekiah, the king said, " What shall be the sign that the Lord will heal me," etc. ? One wonders that to so good a man the prophet's word should not have been sufficient, and that he should have asked for this additional confirmation. But (1) It was an age of signs (Isa. vii. 10—12 ; viii. 18 ; ch. xix. 29). (2) The thing promised was very wonderful and hard to believe, especially after the announcement, " Thou shalt die, and not live," made a few minutes before. There is no doubt a greater blessing on those that have not seen, and yet have believed (John xx. 29) ; but weak faith too has its rights, and God shows his condescension in stooping to give it the needed supports. 2. *The sign given.* Isaiah had offered Ahaz a sign, either "in the depth, or in the height above " (Isa. vii. 11). Hezekiah had now proposed to him a sign in the height. The shadow on the steps of Ahaz's sun-dial would be made either to go forward ten degrees or go back ten degrees, according as Hezekiah should desire. As the more wonderful phenomenon of the two, Hezekiah asked that it might go back ten degrees, and at Isaiah's prayer it was done. We inquire in vain as to how the wonder was produced. The fact that it seems to have been a local sign, though widely noised abroad, suggests a miracle connected with the laws of refraction.—J. O.

Vers. 12—19.—*The Babylonian embassy.* Berodach-Baladan, or as he is more correctly termed in Isaiah, Merodach-Baladan (Isa. xxxix. 1), at this time held possession of the throne of Babylon, and was everywhere casting about for alliances to strengthen him against Assyria. We have here the account of his embassy to Hezekiah.

I. RECEPTION OF THE BABYLONIAN MESSENGERS. 1. *Hezekiah's visitors.* In the streets of Jerusalem were seen strange men, in princely robes, with servants bearing costly presents. They were the envoys of the King of Babylon, ostensibly come to congratulate Hezekiah on his recovery from sickness, and to inquire into the wonder that had been done in the land (2 Chron. xxxii. 31). This, however, was, it is probable, only a pretext to cover their real object, which was to establish an offensive and defensive alliance with Hezekiah against Assyria. Professions of friendship veiled the designs of a merely selfish policy. Does not much of what is called diplomacy consist of deceit, insincere profession, intrigue, subtle designs, covered by fair appearances ? 2. *Hezekiah's vanity.* Hezekiah seems to have been completely imposed on by the fair words of his visitors. He felt flattered at being singled out for notice by this king of "a far country," and spared no pains to impress the ambassadors with ideas of his own greatness. He showed them all his treasures, all the resources of his kingdom, his silver, his gold, his precious things, everything he had. This love of display, this vain desire to stand well in the estimation of a foreign potentate, this boasting of mere worldly wealth as the distinction of his kingdom, shows a weakness we should not have expected in this good king. No man is perfect. The best character has its side of weakness, and men are singularly apt to be led astray when skilful appeals are made to their vanity. 3. *Hezekiah's sin.* It was not a mere weakness of human nature that Hezekiah was guilty of when he "hearkened" unto the ambassadors, and showed them all his precious things. It was not for a mere yielding to vanity that Isaiah afterwards so severely rebuked him. His offence was of a graver kind. The ambassadors had come with proposals for an alliance, and in hearkening to them on this subject Hezekiah had really been unfaithful to his position as a theocratic king. He was departing from the example set him by David. As king of the holy nation, it was his duty to keep himself free from entangling worldly alliances, to make God his boast, to rely on him for defence and help, and to resist solicitations to worldly pride and vanity. From this ideal he had fallen. Flattered by the attention of his visitors, deceived by their specious proposals, and led away with the idea of figuring as an important political personage, he consented, or was disposed to consent, to the alliance sought. In displaying his treasures, he was practically placing them before God, as the glory and defence of his kingdom. In reciprocating the friendship of the foreigners, accepting their gifts, and encouraging their advances, he was taking a first step in that direction of forming worldly alliances, which afterwards brought such trouble on the state. It was this policy, indeed, which ultimately led to the Captivity, as already a similar policy had wrought the ruin of Israel. The lessons for the Christian are obvious. "The friendship of the world is enmity with God" (Jas. iv. 4). It is his duty to avoid worldly display, to guard against being ruled by worldly motives and ambitions, and to avoid ensnaring worldly alliances. He who gives way to these things is laying the foundations of his own spiritual overthrow.

II. PREDICTION OF THE BABYLONIAN CAPTIVITY. 1. *The prophet confronts the king.* In the theocracy the prophet stood beside the king, to be his friend, guide, and counsellor if he did right, and his accusing conscience if he did wrong. Thus Nathan confronted David (2 Sam. xii. 1—14), Elijah confronted Ahab (1 Kings xviii. 17; xxi. 17—24), Zechariah confronted Joash (2 Chron. xxiv. 20). Here Isaiah confronts Hezekiah, and calls him to account for his transgression. The king did not seem aware of his wrong-doing, for he answered the prophet's questions with the utmost frankness. (1) The questions Isaiah asked were searching ones. He made Hezekiah tell out of his own mouth who the men were that had come to him, whence they came, and how he had received them. The object of these interrogations was to make Hezekiah aware of his sin. Many a thing is done, of which we do not at first perceive the criminality, but the sin of which is obvious enough when we have had the deed set objectively before us. (2) Hezekiah's answers revealed the folly he had committed. In the very stating of what he had done, Hezekiah must have perceived the magnitude of his error. It is God's design in his questioning of us to bring us to conviction. He would have us judge ourselves. It does not follow, that because we are unconscious of sin, therefore we have no sin. The object of Divine discipline is to make us conscious. Every sinner will at the last be convicted out of his own mouth. 2. *The prophet predicts the Captivity.* If doubt remained in Hezekiah's mind as to his wrong-doing, it was speedily dispelled by Isaiah's stern answer to him. The prophet, without further parley, announced God's punishment for the sin committed. The penalty answered, as so many of God's penalties do, to the nature of the transgression. The messengers had come from Babylon; into Babylon should Hezekiah's sons (descendants) be carried away. He had displayed his treasures; these treasures would be carried to Babylon. He desired union with Babylon; he should have it in a way he did not look for. A prophecy of this nature implied a collapse of the kingdom of Judah as complete as that which had overtaken Israel. Such a collapse was, of course, the product of many causes, most of them already in operation. But not the least potent was the species of worldly policy of which Hezekiah's action was a typical example. As an outstanding and contributory cause, God fixes on it as the point of connection for the prophecy. We must take our share of the responsibility of every event which our actions have contributed to produce. 3. *The king's reply.* Hezekiah was no doubt shocked and startled by Isaiah's message. The only ray of consolation he derived was in the thought that the predicted evil was not to fall in his days, but in that of his descendants. His language on this point, " Is it not good, if peace and truth shall be in my days?" may seem selfish and even cynical. It is doubtful, however, if there is much room for blame. Hezekiah gathered that a period of respite was granted, and that the fulfilment of the threatening was somewhat remote. He rightly took this as an act of mercy to himself. There are probably few who would not feel relieved to know that, though calamities were to fall upon their land in future days, there would be peace and truth in their own lifetime. With lapse of time, too, opportunity was given for repentance; and who knew but that the sentence of doom might be reversed?—J. O.

Vers. 20, 21 sum up briefly the good deeds of Hezekiah for the city, and narrate his end (see 2 Chron. xxxii. 1—5).—J. O.

EXPOSITION.

CHAPTER XXI.

Vers. 1—26.—THE REIGNS OF MANASSEH AND AMON.

Vers. 1—18.—THE REIGN OF MANASSEH. Hezekiah's good and glorious reign was followed by one of exactly the opposite character. His son and successor, Manasseh, reversed Hezekiah's entire religious policy, and returned to the wicked practices of his grandfather Ahaz. In vers. 3—9 and ver. 16 his various abominations are enumerated, while in vers. 10—15 God's sentence is pronounced upon them. The account of his reign terminates with a brief summary (vers. 17, 18).

Ver. 1.—**Manasseh was twelve years old.** Manasseh was thus not born till three years after Hezekiah's dangerous illness, or till the year B.C. 710. Hezekiah may have given him the name in the spirit in which Joseph gave it to his firstborn (Gen. xli. 51), because God, in at last blessing him with a son, had "made him forget" his dangerous illness, with the griefs and regrets that accompanied it. "Manasseh" means "Forgetting." **When he began to reign**— in B.C. 698 or 697, the seventh or eighth year of Sennacherib—**and reigned fifty and five years in Jerusalem.** So the author of Chronicles (2 Chron. xxxiii. 1) and Josephus ('Ant. Jud.,' x. 3. § 2). The reign exceeds in length that of any other King of Judah or Israel. **And his mother's name was Hephzibah.** "Hephzibah" means "My delight is in her." Isaiah gives it as a name of honour to the restored Jerusalem

(Isa. lxii. 4). It has been conjectured that, as queen-mother, Hephzibah was regent during her son's minority. But there is no trace of her regency either in Kings or Chronicles.

Ver. 2.—**And he did** that which was **evil in the sight of the Lord.** Manasseh was too young at the death of his father for his character to have been then definitively formed. He probably fell under the influence of the " princes of Judah," who, supported by many of the priests, had maintained themselves as a party antagonistic to Isaiah during the whole of Hezekiah's reign. Hezekiah's reformation had been carried out against their wishes. They had always leant towards foreign alliances (Isa. xx. 5; xxx. 1—7) and foreign rites (Isa. ii. 6—9; lxv. 3). The accession of a boy-king would be joyfully hailed by them, and they would make every effort to draw him to their side. It would seem that they were successful. **After the abominations of the heathen**—the details which follow in vers. 3—9 sufficiently explain this strong expression— **whom the Lord cast out before the children of Israel.** It was solely because of their abominations that they were cast out (see Gen. xv. 16; Lev. xviii. 25; xx. 23; Deut. ix. 5; xviii. 12, etc.).

Ver. 3.—**For he built up again the high places which Hezekiah his father had destroyed** (comp. ch. xviii. 4, 22). On the high-place worship, see the comment upon 1 Kings xiv. 23. It is quite clear that the people were deeply attached to it, and gladly saw it restored. **And he reared up altars for Baal;** *i.e.* he reintroduced the Phœnician Baal-worship, the special abomination of the house of Ahab (1 Kings xvi.

31; xxii. 53; ch. viii. 18, 27, etc.), which Athaliah had been the first to introduce into Judah (ch. xi. 18), which Joash had put away (ch. xi. 18), but which Ahaz (2 Chron. xxviii. 2) had recalled. **And made a grove ;** literally, *an Asherah,* or emblem of Astarte (compare the comment on 1 Kings xiv. 23) **—as did Ahab King of Israel** (see 1 Kings xvi. 33) **and worshipped all the host of heaven, and served them.** The worship of the host of heaven, or the entire multitude of the heavenly bodies, commonly known as Sabæanism or Ssabianism, was an ancient Babylonian, Arabian, and Syrian practice. It had, perhaps, been introduced among the Jews by Ahaz (ch. xxiii. 12). At any rate, it was from the time of Manasseh one of the favourite idolatries of the Jewish people. The stars were believed to guide the destiny of men, and astrology was cultivated as a main part, or even as the essence, of religion. Astrological tracts form an important element in the literature of the Babylonians (see ' Records of the Past,' vol. i. pp. 153—163). The chief objects of adoration in this worship were the sun and moon, the five planets, and the signs of the zodiac.

Ver. 4.—**And he built altars in the house of the Lord.** He created, *i.e.,* altars to other gods in the very temple of Jehovah (see ver. 5). This was a pollution beyond any that either Athaliah or Ahaz had ventured on. **Of which the Lord had said, In Jerusalem will I put my Name** (see 1 Kings viii. 29; ix. 3; xiv. 21). Where Jehovah "put his Name," making the place his, and condescending, in a certain sense, to dwell there, it might at least have been expected that he would not find himself confronted with rivals.

Ver. 5.—**And he built altars for all the host of heaven in the two courts of the house of the Lord.** The temple of Solomon had two courts only, an inner and an outer. The outer court was for the people, the inner for the priests and Levites. Manasseh desecrated the temple to the extent of setting up in each of these two courts an idolatrous altar, dedicated to the worship of the host of heaven. In the inner court his altar was a rival to the great brazen altar of Solomon (1 Kings ix. 64 ; 2 Chron. iv. 1), which Ahaz had for a time removed from its place in front of the porch (ch. xvi. 14), but which Hezekiah had most certainly reinstated.

Ver. 6.— **And he made his son pass through the fire.** The author of Chronicles says, " his sons " (2 Chron. xxxiii. 6); but this is, perhaps, rhetorical. It was usually the eldest son, who, as the most precious possible offering, was sacrificed to Moloch (see ch. iii. 27; xvi. 3; and, for the true nature of the sacrifice, see the comment on this latter passage). **And observed times.** If this translation is right, the reference would be to a superstitious regard for lucky and unlucky days, such as we note in the accounts left of themselves by the Babylonian kings, who begin their buildings "in a happy month, on an auspicious day " (see the author's 'Herodotus,' vol. ii. p. 487). But probably the true meaning is, "he exercised βασκανία," or, " had regard to the evil eye," a common superstition in the East. **And used enchantments.** A use of spells is perhaps intended, such as those by which serpents (נְחָשִׁים) were charmed (see the comment on Isa. xlvii. 9). **And dealt with familiar spirits and wizards** — rather, *he placed in office necromancers* (literally, *a necromancer) and wizards;* i.e. he gave such persons official positions at his court, instead of putting them to death, as the Law (Lev. xx. 27) required—**he wrought much wickedness in the sight of the Lord, to provoke** him **to anger;** literally, *he multiplied to work wickedness;* i.e. he sought out every possible way ; he not only restored all the different kinds of heathen sacrifices and idolatrous customs which had been in use under Ahaz, but carried his opposition to Jehovah a great deal further. As Ewald says (' History of Israel,' vol. iv. p. 208), "He endeavoured to become acquainted with all the heathen religions he could find and introduce them into Judah. For this purpose he sent into the most distant lands where there was any famous cultus, and grudged no pains for his one object."

Ver. 7.—**And he set a graven image of the grove that he had made in the house.** He introduced into the temple, and set up there for adoration, an elaborately wrought Asherah, or " sacred tree," probably copied from the elaborate sacred trees of the Assyrians ('Ancient Monarchies,' vol. ii. p. 236). These had, in the centre, the essential *stelé,* or pillar, ornamented with rams' horns, symbols of fecundity, and crowned with a representation of a palm tree, the whole being encircled by a framework of metal, twined about it, and throwing out from the circumference, at intervals, either palms or blossoms, or in some instances pomegranates or fir-cones. All the parts represented either animal or vegetable productiveness. **Of which the Lord said to David, and to Solomon his son, In this house, and in Jerusalem, which I have chosen out of all the tribes of Israel, will I put my Name for ever.** It was the extremest aggravation of Manasseh's wickedness that he was not content to introduce his new religions into the land in other places, but brought them to God's special city which he had chosen, namely, Jerusalem, and there established them, not on the opposite hills, as Solomon had done (1 Kings xi. 7), or in a rival temple within the walls, as had been done by Athaliah (ch. xi. 18), but within God's holy temple itself. In each of the two courts he placed an idolatrous altar, whereon the people were invited to deposit their offerings; and probably in the temple building itself, perhaps in the very holy of holies, he placed that lust-exciting emblem of Astarte, which was the most horrible profanation of all true religion, turning the truth and grace of God into lasciviousness (Jude 4). What practical consequences followed on this profanation, we are not distinctly told; but we may readily surmise, especially in the light of ch. xxiii. 7.

Ver. 8.—**Neither will I make the feet of Israel move any more out of the land which I gave their fathers.** The writer's argument is that Manasseh, by these impieties, annulled God's promises, brought about the destruction of the temple and of Jerusalem, and caused the entire people to be carried off into captivity. The promises of permanence to the city and temple, and of the continued possession of the land by the people, were, he notes, conditional; and Manasseh, by breaking through the conditions, forfeited them (comp. ch. xxiv. 3). **Only if they will observe to do according to all that I have commanded them, and according to all that my servant Moses commanded them.** The words are not taken from any single passage, but express the general sense of numerous passages, as for example of Deut. iv. 25—27; xxx. 15—19; Ps. lxxxix. 28—32; 1 Kings ix. 4—9, etc.

Ver. 9.—**But they hearkened not.** The people, and not Manasseh alone, were disobedient. Had they remained faithful, Manasseh's sin would not have affected their future. **And Manasseh seduced them.** The influence of a young and gay king, always great, is in the East immense. When such a king succeeds one of strict and rigid principles, he easily carries away the multitude with him, and leads them on to any excess of profligacy and irreligion. The beginnings of sin are delightful, and the votaries of pleasure, readily beguiled into evil courses, know not where to stop. Manasseh seduced them, we are told, **to do more evil than did the nations whom the Lord destroyed before the children of Israel**; that is, than the Hivites, Hittites, Amorites, Canaanites, Perizzites, Gergashites, and Jebusites (Deut. vii. 1, etc.). The sin of Israel exceeded that of the Canaanitish nations, not so much in any outward and tangible features, as in the fact that it was committed against light, in spite of the Law, and against all the warnings and denunciations of the prophets (comp. ch. xvii. 13, 14).

Ver. 10.—**And the Lord spake by his servants the prophets, saying.** It is uncertain who were the prophets of Manasseh's time. Probably Isaiah was one of them (see 'Introduction to Isaiah,' p. iii.). Habakkuk is thought to have been another (Keil). Nahum and Zephaniah seem also to belong, in part, to his reign.

Ver. 11.—**Because Manasseh King of Judah hath done these abominations** (comp. ver. 2), **and hath done wickedly above all that the Amorites did, which** were before him (comp. ver. 9). The "Amorites" are put here (as in Gen. xv. 16; 1 Kings xxi. 26; and Amos ii. 9, 10) for the Canaanitish nations generally. Next to the Hittites, they were the most important of the seven nations. **And hath made Judah also to sin with his idols** (see the comment on ver. 9).

Ver. 12.—**Therefore thus saith the Lord God of Israel, Behold, I am bringing such evil upon Jerusalem and Judah, that whosoever heareth of it, both his ears shall tingle.** "As a sharp discordant note," says Bähr, "pains one's ears, so the news of this harsh punishment shall give pain to all who hear of it." The phrase is one never uttered by any other lips than those of Jehovah (1 Sam. iii. 11; Jer. xix. 3). "It denotes" (Keil) "such a judgment as has never been heard of before, and excites alarm and horror." Not the Jews only, but the other neighbouring nations, when they heard of the sufferings endured in the siege (ch. xxv. 3), and the severities exercised upon the king (ver. 7) and the city (vers. 9, 10) and the inhabitants (ver. 11), would have a thrill of pain go through them at the hearing, partly unselfish, partly perhaps selfish, since the treatment that was dealt out to others might also be reserved for them.

Ver. 13.—**And I will stretch over Jerusalem the line of Samaria;** i.e. "I will do to Jerusalem as I have done to Samaria; I will execute upon it a similar judgment." God applies his measuring-line, a perfectly uniform standard, to all nations, as to all individuals, and metes out to them an equal measure of justice. Jerusalem will be presently treated as Samaria has been recently treated; and a similar destruction will overtake it. The metaphor is not to be pressed, as if cities were destroyed with as much care as they are built, by constant use of the measuring-line and the plummet. **And the plummet of the house of Ahab.** The justice meted out to the house of Ahab shall be meted out also to the house of David. The ways of God are equal (Ezek. xviii. 25), and he is no "respecter of persons." He has one law for all; and, as the house of David has sinned in the same way, and to the same extent, as the house of Ahab had sinned, one and the same punishment will fall upon both of them. **And I will wipe Jerusalem as** a man **wipeth a dish, wiping it, and turning** it upside down. Jerusalem will be emptied, as a man empties his dish of the refuse scraps remaining on it, and will be then put away, as done with. The metaphor expresses contempt as well as condemnation.

Ver. 14.—**And I will forsake the remnant of mine inheritance.** "The remnant" here is not the remnant left of Judah after the deportation of two hundred thousand souls by Sennacherib (as in ch. xix. 4), but the remnant that is left of the whole people of Israel—the two tribes as distinct from the ten. The ten tribes were forsaken when the Assyrians took and destroyed Samaria (ch. xvii. 18, 23); the two remained. Now the two also would be forsaken, and the last remnant of God's inheritance cast out. **And deliver them into the hand of their enemies.** Not the Chaldeans only, who were not yet "their enemies," but their persistent and inveterate enemies, the Syrians, Moabites, Ammonites (see ch. xxiv. 2), and Edomites (Ezek. xxv. 12; Joel iii. 19), who all joined with Nebuchadnezzar at the last, and (as Ewald says, 'History of Israel,' vol. iv. p. 270) "indulged their ancient hatred by taking a very active part in the final war." **And they shall become a prey and a spoil to all their enemies** (comp. Jer. xli. 2—10; xlviii. 27; Obad. 10—14; Zeph. ii. 8, etc.). The years which immediately followed the Captivity were years of terrible suffering to the remnant whom Nebuchadnezzar left in the land (ch. xxv. 12). Every petty power in the neighbourhood felt itself at liberty to make incursions with Judæa at its pleasure, to plunder and ravage, and drive off captives, or massacre them in cold blood, or commit any other atrocity. Some critics regard the description of Isaiah in ch. xlii. 22—24 as prophetic of these sufferings.

Ver. 15.—**Because they have done that** which was **evil in my sight.** The chief sins of the people were the following: Altars for the worship of the host of heaven were erected upon almost every roof (Jer. xix. 13; Zeph. i. 5); offerings of cakes were made in the very streets to Astarte (Jer. vii. 18); the fire of Tophet—a huge furnace in the valley of Hinnom—was kept constantly burning, and the sacrifice of innocent children to the bloody sun-god, Moloch, was perpetual (Jer. vii. 31; Ezek. xxiii. 37); it was as common to swear by the name of Moloch as by that of Jehovah (Zeph. i. 5). Lascivious rites were practised. Close by the temple the unchaste priestesses of Venus had their habitations, and their wretched male attendants, the Galli of the classical writers, plied their trade (ch. xxiii. 7). Cruelty and oppression increased among the

upper classes (Zeph. iii. 1—3); the prophets were "light and treacherous persons;" the priests "polluted the sanctuary, and did violence to the Law" (Zeph. ii. 1—3). "Spoiling and violence," "strife and contention;" were rife throughout the city (Hab. i. 3). Ewald sums up the state of things as follows: "The atmosphere of the age was poisoned from above; and the leaders of the people of every class, whose moral decline had already become a subject of lament in the preceding century, sank into an almost incredible degeneracy. The prophets, who ought to have been ever the most loyal guardians of the truth, were for the most part like dumb and greedy dogs; many of the priests allowed themselves to be seduced into offering heathen sacrifices; the judges and nobles paid little heed to the eternal right. Equivocation and hypocrisy spread among those who ought to have been ministered most austerely to public truthfulness of life; while those who were engaged in commerce and trade sank into the harshest indifference to every higher aim, and thought only of the acquisition and enjoyment of wealth. So terrible was the demoralization which set in under Manasseh, that those who remained faithful to the ancient religion were either scoffed at as fools, or allowed to perish in cold contempt without any effort being made to save them, and were even derided after their death." **And have provoked me to anger, since the day their fathers came forth out of Egypt, even unto this day.** The moral and spiritual depravity of Judah, though it only came to a head in the time of Manasseh, had its roots in a long-distant past. As St. Stephen pointed out to the Sanhedrin (Acts vii. 39–43), it began in the wilderness with the worship of the golden calf, and went on to the worship of the host of heaven, of Moloch, and of Remphan; it was shown markedly in the terrible sin of Peor (Numb. xxv. 1—3); it stinted God's hand when the nations had to be driven out from Canaan (Judg. ii. 1–5); it provoked God's anger greatly during the whole period of the Judges (Judg. ii. 11—19); checked under David and Solomon, it broke out afresh on the accession of Rehoboam (1 Kings xiv. 22–24), and showed itself, more or less, under every subsequent king, culminating at last in that fearful condition of things which has been described above (see the comment on the first clause of this verse).

Ver. 16.—**Moreover Manasseh shed innocent blood very much.** We must not understand this of his own offerings to Moloch, for these have been already put on record against him (ver. 6), and this is something additional (note the strong expression, וְגַם), nor even of the multitudinous sacrifices of the same kind which were the result of his influence on the people. Some culminating horror is required, something not touched upon before, and something specially attaching to the monarch himself. These conditions are answered by supposing a bloody persecution of the faithful to be intended. Josephus declares positively that Manasseh "cruelly put to death all the righteous among the Hebrews, and did not even spare the prophets" ('Ant. Jud.,' x. 3. § 1). A tradition, very widely received, declared Isaiah to have been one of the victims ('Gemara Jebam.,' iv. 13; 'Sanhedr.,' f. 103; Tertullian, 'De Patientia,' § 14; Augustine, 'De Civ. Dei,' xviii. 24, etc.). Stanley says, "A reign of terror commenced against all who ventured to resist the reaction. Day by day a fresh batch of the prophetic order were ordered for execution. It seemed as if a devouring lion were let loose against them. From end to end of Jerusalem were to be seen traces of their blood. The nobles who took their part were thrown headlong from the rocky cliffs of Jerusalem" ('Lectures on the Jewish Church,' pt. ii. p. 492). The persecution has been compared to that of Anglicans under Mary Tudor. **Till he had filled Jerusalem from one end to another** —*i.e.* "till he had filled it with blood and slaughter" (comp. ch. xxiv. 4)—**beside his sin wherewith he made Judah to sin, in doing** that which was **evil in the sight of the Lord** (see ver. 9).

Ver. 17.—**Now the rest of the acts of Manasseh.** Important additions to the history of Manasseh are made by the writer of Chronicles. From him we learn that, after prophetical warnings had been in vain addressed to him and to his people (2 Chron. xxxiii. 10), he was visited with a Divine judgment, an Assyrian army under "captains" being sent against him, who took him prisoner, and carried him to Babylon— the city where Esarhaddon, the successor of Sennacherib, and contemporary of Manasseh, ordinarily held his court. Here he remained for some considerable time "in affliction" (ver. 12), and, becoming convinced of sin and deeply penitent for his manifold transgressions, he turned to God in sincerity and truth, and being restored by the Assyrians to his kingdom, he put away the idolatrous practices and emblems which he had previously introduced, "repaired the altar of the Lord" which had gone to decay, and re-established, so far as he could, the worship of Jehovah (ver. 16). A special prophet, Hosai, seems to have chronicled his sins and his repentance in a work which survived the Captivity, and is twice quoted by the compiler of the Books of Chronicles (2 Chron. xxxiii. 18, 19). The submission of Manasseh to Esarhaddon is noted in the latter's annals,

about the year B.C. 680 (see 'Eponym Canon,' p. 139, line 13). Other "acts" of Manasseh were the fortification of Jerusalem "on the west side of Gihon in the valley," the strengthening of the defences of Ophel, and the occupation with strong garrisons of the various fortresses within his dominions. He thus played his part of tributary ally to Assyria with zeal, placing the south-eastern frontier in an excellent condition to resist the assaults of Egypt. Manasseh outlived Esarhaddon, and was for many years contemporary with Asshur-bani-pal, his son, whose inscriptions, however, contain no mention of him. Most likely his name occurred on Cylinder C, line 3, which is now illegible (see G. Smith's 'History of Asshur-bani-pal,' p. 31, line c). **And all that he did, and his sin that he sinned, are they not written in the book of the chronicles of the kings of Judah?** The "sin which he sinned" is probably his persecution, which was viewed as his worst sin (see ver. 16; and comp. ch. xxiv. 4).

Ver. 18.—**And Manasseh slept with his fathers, and was buried in the garden of his own house.** We have already seen reason for believing that the catacomb of David was full, and that Hezekiah was buried outside it, though in the neighbourhood, on this account (see the comment on ch. xx. 21). Manasseh seems to have made a new family tomb in a garden belonging to his house (see ver. 26; and comp. ch. xxiii. 30). It is quite impossible to fix its site. **In the garden of Uzza.** Probably an addition to the old palace garden; perhaps a purchase made by Manasseh with the object of converting it into a burial-ground. "Uzza," or "Uzzah," was a common name among the Jews (2 Sam. vi. 8; Ezra ii. 49; Neh. vii. 51; 1 Chron. vi. 29; viii. 7; xiii. 7—11), and does not point to any definite individual. **And Amon his son reigned in his stead.** "Amon" in Hebrew means "Nursling," or "Darling," and it is quite possible that Manasseh gave his son the name in this sense. But it is also the ordinary Hebrew form of the term ("Amen," or "Amun") by which the Egyptians designated the great god of Thebes, whom the Greeks and Romans called "Ammon." It has therefore been thought by many that it was given by Manasseh to his son "in an idolatrous spirit." So Bishop Cotton in Smith's 'Dictionary of the Bible,' vol. i. p. 61, and others.

Vers. 19—26.—REIGN OF AMON. The short reign of Amon, the son and successor of Manasseh, was distinguished by only two events: (1) his restoration of all the idolatrous and wicked practices which his father had upheld during the earlier portion of his reign; and (2) his untimely death, in consequence of a conspiracy which was formed against him among the officers of his court. The writer of Kings is therefore able to despatch his history in eight verses.

Ver. 19.—**Amon was twenty and two years old when he began to reign.** So Josephus ('Ant. Jud.,' x. 4. § 1), and the author of Chronicles (2 Chron. xxxiii. 21). He must have been born in B.C. 664, early in the reign of Asshur-bani-pal, probably in the year of that monarch's expedition against Tyre. **And he reigned two years in Jerusalem.** The "twelve years" assigned to Amon by the Duke of Manchester ('Times of Daniel') are wholly devoid of foundation, and would throw the entire chronology into confusion. As it is, there is a very exact accordance in this part of the history between the profane and the scriptural dates. **And his mother's name was Meshullemeth, the daughter of Haruz of Jotbah.** Jotbah is probably the same city as the "Jotbath" of Deut. x. 7, and the "Jotbathah" of Numb. xxxiii. 33, which was in the neighbourhood of Ezion-geber, and therefore probably in the Arabah. Josephus, however, says that Jotbah was "a city of Judah."

Ver. 20.—**And he did that which was evil in the sight of the Lord, as his father Manasseh did** (comp. 2 Chron. xxxiii. 22, and Josephus, 'Ant. Jud.,' x. 4. § 1).

Ver. 21.—**And he walked in all the way that his father walked in.** There was not a single one among the early wickednesses of Manasseh which Amon did not imitate. The details of Josiah's reformation (ch. xxiii. 4—24) show that under Amon (1) the Asherah or "grove" maintained its place in the temple building; (2) the two idolatrous altars stood in the two courts; (3) the temple was the scene of the worship of Baal, Ashtoreth, and the host of heaven; (4) the unchaste priestesses of the Syrian goddess, with the male partners in their guilt, were lodged in houses close by the house of the Lord; (5) chariots and horses dedicated to the sun were maintained at one of the temple gates; (6) the fire of Tophet burnt continually in the valley of Hinnom, and children were there "passed through the fire to Moloch;" (7) an idolatrous worship held possession of all the high places all over Judæa and Samaria, and idolatrous priests, deriving their appointment from the king, burnt incense in the high places to Baal, to the sun, the moon, the planets, and all the host of heaven; and (8) magic and necromancy were practised openly under royal sanction throughout the length and breadth

of the land. **And served the idols that his father served**—as Baal, Ashtoreth, Moloch, the Asherah, and others—**and worshipped them.**

Ver. 22.—**And he forsook the Lord God of his fathers.** Other kings, as Ahaz, had made a sort of compromise between the worship of Jehovah and idolatry (ch. xvi. 10—15). Manasseh and Amon forsook the worship of Jehovah altogether. **And walked not in the way of the Lord;** i.e. did not even maintain an outward observance of the Law of Moses, but set it wholly aside.

Ver. 23.—**And the servants of Amon**—i.e. his attendants, the officers of his court—**conspired against him, and slew the king in his own house.** Conspiracies in the palace, frequent in Israel (see 1 Kings xvi. 9; ch. ix. 32—37; xi. 10, 25, 30), were not unknown in Judah (see ch. xii. 21). They naturally arose from various causes, as insults, injuries, hopes of advantage, ambition, etc. Where, as in the present case, no clue is given, it is idle to conjecture the motives by which the conspirators were actuated. Religious motives can scarcely have come into play.

Ver. 24.—**And the people of the land slew all them that had conspired against King Amon.** We certainly, therefore, cannot attribute Amon's murder to a popular reaction against his idolatries. Everything unites to prove that the foreign worships were in favour with the people at this period, and that the kings who patronized them were more generally popular than those who pursued the opposite course. **And the people of the land made Josiah his son king in his stead.** The prestige of the house of David was still strong. The conspirators may have intended a change of dynasty; but the mass of the people could not contemplate with equanimity the occupation of the throne by a stranger—one not of David's house. They there, in a tumultuary manner, having punished the conspirators with death, sought out the true heir, and, having found him, though he was a boy of but eight years of age, placed him upon his father's throne (comp. 2 Chron. xxxiii. 25).

Ver. 25.—**Now the rest of the acts of Amon which he did, are they not written in the book of the chronicles of the kings of Judah?** No other acts of Amon have come down to us. He was probably, during his short reign of two years, a submissive tributary of Asshur-bani-pal.

Ver. 26.—**And he was buried in his sepulchre in the garden of Uzza**—i.e. in the same place as his father (see ver. 18)—**and Josiah his son reigned in his stead.** So the writer of Chronicles (2 Chron. xxxiii. 25), and Josephus (l. s. c.).

HOMILETICS.

Vers. 1—18.—*The lesson of Manasseh's life, that it is far easier to do than to undo evil.* Manasseh, carried away by the impetuosity of youth, and under the advice of evil counsellors, threw himself into a movement the direct opposite of that instituted by his father, and in a short time completely changed in all respects the whole religion of the kingdom. His idea, so far as we can trace it, seems to have been a welcoming of heathen and idolatrous creeds and rites of all kinds and from all quarters, together with a stern repression of the religion of Jehovah. The bloody rites of Moloch, the licentious orgies of the Syrian goddess, the Phœnician Baal-worship, the Arabian astrology, the magic and necromancy of Babylon, were all regarded as equally worthy of his patronage, all given a home in his capital; one single cult was disallowed, and its exercise punished with death—the worship of "the Holy One of Israel." In all these respects Manasseh found it easy enough to work his will; no one resisted him; the awful child-sacrifices suited well with one side of the national temperament, the wild sensualism of Syrian and Phœnician orgies harmonized with another. Manasseh easily "seduced" the mass of the people to do as he would have them; and, when he met with recalcitrants, had a "short and easy method" with them—the method of instant execution. All went smoothly and satisfactorily with him, probably for near thirty years of his reign, when by some act—we know not what—he displeased his Assyrian suzerain, was carried captive to Babylon, and there, in the bitterness of confinement, brought to see the error of his ways. Restored to his throne, he thought to undo his evil-work as easily and completely as he had done it. Again, outwardly no one resisted his will. The external changes were made. "The strange gods" were "put away" (2 Chron. xxxiii. 15); the idols cleared out of the house of the Lord; the idolatrous altars banished; the formal worship of Jehovah reintroduced; the brazen altar of Solomon "repaired" (2 Chron. xxxiii. 16) and used for sacrifice; Judah commanded to serve Jehovah, the God of Israel. But the spirit of true and pure religion could not be brought back. Thirty years of idolatry had debauched the heart of the nation. Jehovah's faithful followers had been martyred. The rest of the people could only give to Jehovah a lip-service. And thus no sooner was Manasseh dead than everything reverted into its former condition. The idols were restored—the altars to the host of heaven replaced in the temple courts—the flames of Tophet relighted—the filthy rites of the Dea Syria re-established. When Josiah came to the throne, the state of things was as bad as it had ever been, even in the worst years of Manasseh. Baal was the god chiefly worshipped in Jerusalem (Zeph. i. 4); altars to the host of heaven covered the housetops; men commonly swore by Moloch; the whole nation had "turned back from Jehovah" (Zeph. i. 6), and the city was filled with "violence and deceit" (Zeph. i. 9). Not even could all Josiah's efforts remedy the evil which Manasseh had brought about. The corruption was too deep-seated; and it was Manasseh's evil-doing, which he could not undo, that caused the final destruction of the kingdom (ch. xxiii. 26, 27; xxiv. 3, 4).

HOMILIES BY VARIOUS AUTHORS.

Vers. 1—16.—*Manasseh's wicked reign.* Two thoughts are brought before us by the reign of Manasseh. They are a striking contrast to one another.

I. THE POWER OF SIN. 1. We see *how sin perpetuates itself.* The deeds of Manasseh were just a repetition of the worst deeds of his predecessors. "He did that which was evil in the sight of the Lord, after the abominations of the heathen." He built up again the high places. He made altars for Baal. He worshipped all the host of heaven. He made his son pass through the fire to Moloch. (What we have already said on these sins applies here.) 2. We see also *the progressive power of sin.* There is a progress in sin from bad to worse. Manasseh imitated the sins of his predecessors. But he went further than any of them. "He built altars for all the host of heaven in the two courts of the house of the Lord" (ver. 5). Worse than all, he set up a carved image, the idol that he had made, in the very temple of the living God. It is also stated that he shed innocent blood very much, till he had filled Jerusalem with blood from one end to the other (ver. 16). Let us beware of the beginnings of evil. 3. We see also *the power of sin to harden men's hearts*. We read in 2 Chronicles that "God spake to Manasseh and his people; but they would not hearken." How often God still speaks to men by his Word, by his providences, and yet sin has so hardened their hearts, that they pay no attention to his warnings, remonstrances, and appeals!

II. THE POWER OF PRAYER. There is no reference in this account of Manasseh to any prayer of his. And yet, strange though it may seem, prayer played an important part in Manasseh's history. When we turn to the summary of his life which is given in 2 Chron. xxxiii., we read (vers. 18, 19), "Now the rest of the acts of Manasseh, *and his prayer unto his God*, and the words of the seers that spake unto him in the name of the Lord God of Israel, behold, they are written in the book of the kings of Israel. *His prayer also, and how God was entreated of him*, and all his sins, and his trespass . . . before he was humbled : behold, they are written among the sayings of the seers." Now, what was this prayer of Manasseh? It was simply a prayer for pardon. *Observe how Manasseh learned to pray.* For all his wickedness the Lord brought judgments upon him (vers. 10—15). He brought upon him and his people "the captains of the host of the King of Assyria, which took Manasseh prisoner, and bound him with fetters, and carried him to Babylon." It was then, in his extremity and calamity, that Manasseh learned to pray. "And when he was in affliction, he besought the Lord his God, and humbled himself greatly before the God of his fathers, *and prayed unto him* : and he was entreated of him, and heard his supplication, and brought him again to Jerusalem into his kingdom. Then Manasseh knew that the Lord he was God" (2 Chron. xxxiii. 12, 13). Often it is affliction and trial that first teach men to pray, to turn to God. *We see here the power of penitent prayer.* We see here that no one is too great a sinner to pray to God for mercy. Your past life may have been given up to sin. So was Manasseh's. You may have dishonoured and disobeyed God. So did Manasseh. Yet he obtained mercy. The greatest, guiltiest sinner may get pardon at the cross. "Though your sins be as scarlet, they shall be as white as snow; though they be red like crimson, they shall be as wool."—C. H. I.

Vers. 19—24.—*Amon's wicked reign.* We have here more than one instructive lesson.

I. THE POWER OF EVIL OFTEN COUNTERACTS THE GOOD. Manasseh had humbled himself before God. He obtained pardon. But he could not undo the guilty past. He could not undo the effects of his evil example and influence. We see how his sins were imitated and continued by his son Amon. How careful we should be what influence we exercise, what an example we leave behind us! Many a penitent sinner would give worlds if he could undo the consequences to others of his own past sins.

II. THE LAW OF RETRIBUTION ONCE MORE. "With what measure ye mete, it shall be measured to you again." Every case of disobedience against God on the part of Israel and her kings brought its corresponding penalty. Amon was very defiant in his sin. "He humbled not himself before the Lord, . . . but trespassed more and more" (2 Chron. xxxiii. 23). He cast off the authority of God. The day came when his own servants rose in rebellion against his authority, and conspired against him, and slew him. The conspirators also met with their punishment. "The people of the land slew all them that had conspired against King Amon" (ver. 24). Amid all its corruptions, the nation had not yet utterly lost the sense of justice. "Whatsoever a man soweth, that shall he also reap."—C. H. I.

Vers. 1—18.—*Manasseh ; or, the material and moral in human life.* "Manasseh was twelve years old when he began to reign, and reigned fifty and five years in Jerusalem. And his mother's name was Hephzibah. And he did that which was evil in the sight of the Lord," etc. "Manasseh," says Keil, "having begun to reign at an early age, did not choose his father's ways, but set up the idolatry of his grandfather Ahaz again, since the godless party in the nation, all whose chief priests, and (false) prophets stood, and who would not hearken to the Law of the Lord, and in the time of Hezekiah had sought help against Assyria, not from Jehovah, but from the Egyptians, had obtained control of the young and inexperienced king. He built again 'the high places which Hezekiah had destroyed, erected altars for Baal, and Asherah, like Ahab of Israel.'" There are two great mistakes prevalent amongst men—one is an over-estimation of the secular; the other, a depreciation of the spiritual. Many theoretically hold, and more practically indicate, that man should attend mainly, if not entirely, to his secular interests, as a citizen of time; that the present, the palpable, and the certain should engage a far greater portion of his attention than the future, the unseen, and the probable. It is bad to hold these ideas, but it is worse to practise them. More respect, perhaps, is due to the mistaken men who theoretically adopt them, than to those who denounce in no very measured terms their votaries and yet practically carry them out in their daily life. And yet such characters abound in Christian England, abound in our congregations, and in our clergy too. The religionist who gives more of his thought, energy, and time to the secular than the spiritual, is carrying out in his everyday conduct the principles of those secular and infidel teachers against whom he is ever ready to thunder his condemnation. Far more distressed am I at the practical secularism of the Christian than at the theoretical secularism of the sceptic. The other mistake is overrating the spiritual at the expense of the secular. It is not very uncommon for religious teachers to profess to despise secular interests, and so to enforce the claims of piety as if they required the sacrifice of our corporeal and secular happiness. I have no faith in such representations of moral duty. Man is one, and all his duties and interests are concurrent and harmonious; the end of Christianity is to make man happy, body and soul, here and hereafter. These remarks are suggested by the history of Manasseh. He was the son of Hezekiah; was born upwards of seven hundred years before Christ; began to reign when he was twelve years of age; continued his rulership for fifty-five years, died at the age of sixty-eight, and was buried in a sepulchre which he had prepared for himself in his own garden (see 2 Chron. xxxiii. 1—20). His inner life or character will appear as we proceed in the illustration of our subject. In his biography we have three instructive views of the *secular* and *spiritual*. We have here—

I. THE ELEVATION OF THE SECULAR AND THE DEGRADATION OF THE SPIRITUAL. " He built up again the high places which Hezekiah his father had destroyed; and he reared up altars for Baal, and made a grove, as did Ahab King of Israel; and worshipped all the host of heaven, and served them," etc. Here is a man at the height of the secular elevation. He is raised to a throne, called to bear sway over a people the most enlightened, and in a country as fertile and lovely as any on the face of the earth. In the person of this Manasseh you have secular greatness in its highest altitude and most attractive position. But in connection with this you have spiritual degradation. Penetrate the gaudy trappings of his royalty, look within, and what see you? A low, wretched, infamous spirit, a spirit debased almost to the lowest point in morals. Few names in the history of our sinful world stand out with more prominent features of depravity and vice than this of Manasseh. Look at him: 1. *Socially.* How acted he as a son? His father, Hezekiah, was a man of undoubted piety—a monarch of distinguished worth. Many earnest prayers he offered, no doubt, for his son, and many tender counsels on religious subjects had he addressed to him. Yet what was the return for all this? His sire was scarcely cold in his grave before the son commenced undoing in the kingdom all that his pious father had for years endeavoured to accomplish. His insane fanaticism in the cause of debased religion was not surpassed even by the king in modern times who most resembled him, Philip II. of Spain. How did he act as a *parent?* Was he anxious for the virtue and happiness of his children? *No;* "he caused his children to pass through the fire of the son of Hinnom." History represents the god Moloch, to which this Manasseh presented his children, as a brazen statue, which was ever kept burning hot, with its arms outstretched. Into these outstretched arms the idolatrous parent threw his children, which soon fell down into the raging furnace beneath. 2. *Religiously.* A dupe of the most stupid imposture. "He observed times, and used enchantments [and used witchcraft], and dealt with familiar spirits and wizards." He was the maddened votary of the most cruel and monstrous superstition. 3. *Politically.* Ruining his own country, provoking the indignation of Heaven. "So Manasseh made Judah and the inhabitants of Jerusalem to err, and to do worse than the heathen, whom the Lord had destroyed before the children of Israel." The elevation of the secular and the degradation of the spiritual, so manifest, alas! in all times and lands, is not destitute of many grave and startling suggestions. 1. It shows the *moral disorganization of the human world.* This state of things can never be according to the original plan of the creation. Can it be accordant with the original purpose of the Creator that wickedness should sit on thrones and hold the sceptres of the world in its grasp? Can it be that Infinite Purity intended to endow depravity with such worldly wealth and power? Impossible. A terrible convulsion has happened to the human world, a convulsion that has thrown every part into disorder. "All the foundations of the earth are out of course." The social world is in a moral chaos. The Bible traces the cause and propounds the remedy of this terrible disorganization. 2. It shows the *perverting capability of the soul.* The greater the amount of worldly good a man possesses, the stronger is the appeal of the Creator for his gratitude and devotion. These earthly mercies urge self-consecration. Moreover, the larger the amount of worldly wealth and power, the greater the facilities as well as the obligations to a life of spiritual intelligence, holiness, and piety. But here, in the case of this monarch, you have, what indeed you find in different degrees everywhere in human life past and present, the soul turning these advantages to the most fiendish iniquity. The perverting capability of the soul within us may well fill us with amazement and alarm. We can darken the light of truth, make the tree of life drop poison, and cause the very breath of God to be pestilential. 3. It shows the *high probability of a judgment.* Under the government of a righteous monarch, will vice always have its banquets, its purple, and its crown? Will the *great Mechanician* always allow the human engine thus to ply its wondrous energies in confusion? Will the great Lord allow his stewards to misappropriate his substance, and never call them to account? It cannot be! There must come a day for balancing long-standing accounts; a day for making all that has been irregular in human history chime harmoniously with the original law of the universe.

II. The degradation of the secular and the elevation of the spiritual. The judgment of God, which must ever follow sin, at length overtook the wicked monarch. The Assyrian army, under the direction of Esarhaddon, invaded the country, and carried all before it. The miserable monarch can make no effectual resistance. He is seized, bound in chains, transported to Babylon, and then cast into prison. Here is secular degradation. Here, away in exile, chains, and prison, like the prodigal, he began to think. His guilty conduct passed under sad review—memory brought past crimes and abused mercies in awful and startling forms before him, and his heart is smitten with contrition. He prays; his prayer is heard; and here, bereft of every vestige of secular greatness, he begins to rise spiritually, to become an intellectual and moral man (2 Chron. xxxiii. 12). We may learn from this: 1. That *man's circumstances are no necessary hindrance to conversion.* If the question were asked—What circumstances are the most inimical to the cultivation of piety? I should unhesitatingly answer—*Adversity.* I am well aware, indeed, that adversity, as in the case before us, often succeeds in inducing religious thoughtfulness and penitence, when prosperity has failed; that afflictions have often broken the moral slumber of the soul, and led the careless to consider his ways. But, notwithstanding this, I cannot regard adversity itself as the most suited to the cultivation of the religious character. Sufferings are inimical to that grateful feeling and spiritual effort which religious culture requires. It is when the system bounds with health, when Providence smiles on the path, when the mind is not necessarily pressed with anxieties about the means of worldly subsistence, when leisure and facilities for religious reflection and effort are at command, that men are in the best position to discipline themselves into a godly life. But here we find a man in the most unfavourable position, away from religious institutions and friends and books, an imprisoned exile in a pagan land, beginning to think of his ways, and directing his feet into the paths of holiness. Such a case as this meets all the excuses which men offer for their want of religion. It is often said, "Were we in such and such circumstances we would be religious." The rich man says, "Were I in humble life, more free from the anxieties, cares, responsibilities, and associations of my position, I would live a godly life." Whilst the poor, on the other hand says, with far more reason, "Were my spirit not pressed down by the crushing forces of poverty; had I sufficient of worldly goods to remove me from all necessary anxiety, I would give my mind to religion, and serve my God." The man in the midst of the excitement and bustle of commercial life says, "Were I in a more retired situation, in some rural region away from the eternal din of business—away in quiet fields and under clear skies, amidst the music of birds and brooks, I would serve my Maker." Whilst on the contrary, and with greater reason, the tenant of these quiet scenes says, "Were I distant from this eternal monotony, amidst scenes of mental stimulus and social excitement, I should be roused from the apathy, which oppresses me, and I would be a religious man." The fact, after all, is that circumstances are no necessary hindrances or helps to a religious life. 2. That *Heaven's mercy is greater than man's iniquities.* When conscience-stricken with the enormity of his wickedness, this one of the chief of human sinners betakes himself to his knees in humble prayer "before the God of his fathers," how is he treated? Is he scathed with a flash of retributive displeasure? Who would have wondered if he had been so? But no. Is he upbraided for his past wickedness? Who would have been surprised if he had been stunned with thunders of reproof? But no. Is he received with cold indifference? No. "He was entreated of him, and heard his supplication, and brought him again to Jerusalem into his kingdom." What a confirmation is here of that promise, "Let the wicked forsake his way, and the unrighteous man his thoughts: and let him return unto the Lord, and he will have mercy on him; and to our God, for he will abundantly pardon"! "Abundantly!" This is a glorious word, a word that, like the boundless heavens of God, towers and expands over a universe of sin.

III. THE CONCURRENT ELEVATION BOTH OF THE SPIRITUAL AND THE SECULAR. The Almighty hears his prayer. He is emancipated from bondage, brought back to his own country, and restored to the throne of Israel. There he is now with a true heart, in a noble position—a real great man occupying a great office. This is a rare scene; and yet the only scene in accordance with the real constitution of things and the will of God. It seems to me that if man had remained in innocence, his outward position would always have been the product and type of his inner soul; that he who got a throne would do so because of the moral nobility of his nature, and that in all cases secular circumstances, whether elevated, affluent, or otherwise, would ever be the effects and exponents of spiritual character. Manasseh's restoration to the throne, and the work of reformation to which he sets himself, suggest two subjects of thought. 1. The *tendency of godliness to promote man's secular elevation.* The monarch comes back in spirit to God, and God brings him back to his throne. As the material condition of men depends upon their moral condition, improve the latter, and you improve the former. As the world gets spiritually holier, it will get secularly happier. Godliness is material as well as moral "gain." The system that best promotes godliness is the system that best promotes man's temporal well-being. And that system is the gospel. Hence, let philanthropists adopt this as their grand instrument. When Christianity shall have won its triumph over all souls, men's bodies will be restored to their lost inheritance of health, elasticity, force, and plenty, as Manasseh was now restored to his lost throne. There is a physical millennium for the world as well as a spiritual; the former will grow out of and reveal the latter, as trees and flowers their hidden life. 2. The *tendency of penitence to make retribution.* Concerning Manasseh, it is thus written: "Now after this he built a wall without the city of David, on the west side of Gihon, in the valley, even to the entering in at the fish gate, and compassed about Ophel, and raised it up a very great height, and put captains of war in all the fenced cities of Judah. And he took away the strange gods," etc. Here is restitution, and an earnest endeavour to undo the mischief which he had wrought. Thus Zacchæus acted, and thus all true penitents have ever acted and will ever act. True penitence has a restitutionary instinct. But how little, alas! of the mischief done can ever be undone! What can we do? We cannot destroy the fact of wrong. That fact will never be erased from the moral annals of the universe; it is chronicled with unfading ink on an imperishable substance. What can we do? We cannot destroy the influence of our wrong. The wrong that is gone out from us will roll its pestilential streams down through the ages. What can we do? We can "cease to do evil;" and, thank God! we can do more—we can make some compensation for the injury we have done the creation. We can, by Heaven's grace, open up within us a fountain for the washing away of sin and uncleanness—a fountain whose streams will bless with life and beauty many generations yet to come.—D. T.

Vers. 19—26.—*Amon.* "Amon was twenty and two years old when he began to reign, and he reigned two years in Jerusalem." This is a short account of the brief and wicked reign of Amon the son of Manasseh.

I. HIS REIGN WAS VERY SHORT. "He reigned two years," etc. The wonder is that such a man should have been permitted to breathe the breath of life. The sooner a bad king dies the better. 1. The better *for his own sake.* It restrains his own responsibilities and the aggravation of his guilt. 2. The better *for his race.* A fountain of moral poison has been dried up for him; the social air is less poisonous.

II. HIS REIGN WAS VERY WICKED. "And he walked in all the way that his father walked in, and served the idols that his father served, and worshipped them." Of the wickedness of kings we have had abundant examples in these sketches. It is, indeed, a fire that burns athwart the ages.

III. THE REIGN WAS VERY TRAGICAL. "And the servants of Amon conspired against him, and slew the king in his own house." How tragic the end of this man! His "servants," who should have guarded him, murdered him. "His own house," that should have been his castle of defence, was the place of his execution. In this verse the people : 1. *Did justice to the traitors who murdered their king.* 2. *Did kindness to themselves in preparing the way for Josiah.*—D. T.

Vers. 1—9, 16.—*The reaction under Manasseh.* Light and dark alternate strangely in the later history of Judah. Overlooking the brief reign of Amon, Hezekiah alternates with Ahaz, and Josiah with Manasseh. The good kings are very good, the bad kings very bad. The climax of wickedness is reached in Manasseh. He had a good father, as Hezekiah had a wicked one, yet he outstripped in daring ungodliness all the kings before and after him.

I. HIS PRECOCITY IN EVIL. 1. *His tendencies were evil.* Manasseh's tender years when he became king do not wholly explain the strong bent he showed towards evil. He became king, it is true, when he was but twelve, a mere boy, with character unformed, and open to the seductions of wicked courtiers; but Josiah, his grandson, was only eight when he ascended the throne, and he showed a disposition the very opposite. Nor does environment explain everything. Josiah had far fewer advantages than Manasseh. Evil influences were round the young prince, but there were good ones also. Hezekiah his father would give him the best of training; his mother, Hephzibah, if it was she that suggested the prophet's allusion in Isa. lxii. 5, seems to have left a fragrant memory behind her; Isaiah was still living to be his instructor, if he had been willing to be guided as Josiah was (ch. xii. 2); there were also the remarkable mercies God had shown to his father and to the nation but a few years before. Contrast Josiah's position, with Amon for a father, and the country in the state to which it was reduced after half a century of heathenism. There is no accounting for these differences through heredity, environment, or in any other way which ignores personality. While as a rule the children of the good turn out well, and the children of the wicked badly, there are startling exceptions on either side. Some from their childhood seem to be the subjects of an innate, virulent depravity, which only needs opportunity to break out into violent forms of evil. 2. *His environment was evil.* At the same time, it is to be admitted that the circumstances in which he was placed only afforded too much encouragement to the development of Manasseh's ungodly tendencies. It was undeniably a disadvantage to be so early deprived of a father's guidance, and saddled with the responsibilities of a throne. The courtly aristocratic party had never been in real sympathy with Hezekiah's reforms, and they doubtless eagerly embraced the opportunity afforded by the accession of a young king of influencing him to a different line of conduct. Throughout the country also Hezekiah's reformation had been largely external, and people were tired of the restraints which it imposed. The reaction which ensued has been compared to that of Queen Mary's reign after the death of Edward VI., or of the Restoration after the Puritan strictness of the Commonwealth. The upper and aristocratic classes of a country have seldom been marked by their fondness for earnest religion. The way of the world and fashion are far more ruling influences with them, and as at this time "Nineveh was to Western Asia what the Paris of Louis XIV. was to Europe," it can easily be understood that "not to imitate it was to be provincial and vulgar" (Geikie). The moment the heathen spirit got the upper hand, and secured the countenance of the king, it was sure to prevail. The earnest followers of Jehovah shrank down into an inconsiderable minority.

II. HIS EXCESSES IN IDOLATRY. The account given of Manasseh's doings shows to what lengths he went in undoing the arrangements of his father. He seems, in fact, to have aimed at nothing less than a complete suppression of the worship of Jehovah, and the reorganization of the religious cult of the nation upon foreign models. 1. *He rebuilt the high places.* These Hezekiah had pulled down—a point of attainment to conformity with God's Law not reached by any previous king. Manasseh now reversed that action of his father, and rebuilt the shrines. The centralization of worship in Jerusalem may have been felt to be irksome; perhaps, too, the bad character of many of the priests added to its unpopularity. Manasseh may have claimed to be going back to old custom, with the end of making religion more free, popular, and joyous in its character. In this he had the mass of the people, and most of the official classes with him, as " in England the bulk of the nation and of the clergy returned at once to Romanism, when restored by Mary, after the death of Edward VI." It is a sad thing to see a nation going back from any high point of attainment—Reformation or other—as, again, it is a sad thing to see one individual building again the things which he destroyed (Gal. ii. 18). 2. *His wholesale importation of idolatries.* (1) Foreign idolatries. Manasseh exceeded even Ahaz in the zeal with which he imported idolatries of every kind from foreign nations. Baal and Astarte worship, of course, was introduced after the pattern of Ahab, and the Asherah symbol again reared itself in public view in Jerusalem. The taste of Ahaz for new altars was more than surpassed under the auspices of his successor. There was imported also, in grander style than ever, the worship of the sun and moon and heavenly bodies—the white horses and chariots of the sun being now one of the institutions of the temple (ch. xxiii. 10, 11). " Hath a nation changed their gods, which are yet no gods ? " asks a prophet (Jer. ii. 11); but Judah had changed her God for senseless idols. A policy of this kind is bound to end in the dissolution of a nation. The deepest bond of nationality is religion, and when a people renounces its traditional faith, and becomes a mere receptacle for a chaos of foreign religious ideas, it is sure, ere long, to fall to pieces. The Roman Empire was in this condition before its fall. (2) The worst idolatries. It was not merely foreign idolatries which Manasseh introduced, but the worst, the vilest, and the most cruel of these idolatries. In particular, licence was given to the practice of the worst and vilest rites of the Astarte-worship, and that close by the very house of the Lord (ch. xxiii. 6, 7); while the fearful worship of Moloch, with its human sacrifices, was revived, and the king himself gave sanction to it by devoting at least one of his sons to the fire. These were the abominations for which God had cast out the original inhabitants of the land, and now they were reintroduced in full force. (3) The attendant superstitions of idolatry. Idolatry here, as elsewhere, brought in its train a host of other baleful superstitions. Those who forsake God have ever been prone to fall a prey to the most childish delusions and impostures. The worship of the heavenly bodies brought with it the practice of astrology; the craving for communion with the unseen world led to necromancy, witchcraft, and enchantments; boasting a false freedom, the mind fell into an abject slavery to demonism (cf. the development of spiritualism in our own day). The movers in this new introduction of idolatry would no doubt claim the praise due to minds enlightened and emancipated from the narrow ideas in which the people of Judah hitherto had been bound. They were bringing in a new era of toleration, culture, breadth of view and sentiment, and the result was to be a great improvement in the state of the nation. In reality they were loosening all religious and social bonds, and opening the floodgates to corruption. 3. *His desecration of the temple.* The tale of Manasseh's iniquities is not yet ended. Not content with bringing new idolatries into vogue, Manasseh set to work systematically to overthrow the worship of Jehovah, and put his foreign gods in the place devoted to Jehovah's honour. Neither Athaliah nor Ahaz had ventured to introduce idolatry into the temple, but Manasseh took this step beyond either of them. He set up his numerous altars in the house of the Lord. Specially he erected altars for the worship of the host of heaven in the two courts of the temple. Then, to cap all, he introduced into the very building itself an image of the Asherah he had made, replete as that was with vile associations. Insult to Jehovah could go no further. In that very place of which Jehovah had said, "In Jerusalem will I put my Name there;" "In this house, and in Jerusalem, which I have chosen out of all tribes of Israel, will I put my Name for ever;"—even there, in the very dwelling-place of the holy God among men, this impure symbol was erected. The Asherah-image in the temple was, as it were, the summing-up in symbol of the whole apostasy of the people, the formal token of their breach of the covenant, on fidelity to which depended their possession of the land, and as such, the desecration is frequently alluded to (Jer. vii. 30; xix. 3—5). 4. *His shedding of innocent blood.* This is the final and culminating charge against Manasseh, "He shed innocent blood very much, till he had filled Jerusalem from one end to another." The words speak to a deliberate and organized persecution of Jehovah's servants—perhaps a massacre such as that of St. Bartholomew in France, a determined attempt to crush out in blood all dissent from and opposition to the king's measures. This is the persecution in which it is said that Isaiah perished. It is the shedding of innocent blood which, we are told further, "the Lord would not pardon" (ch. xxiv. 4). "Precious in the sight of the Lord is the death of his saints" (Ps. cxvi. 15). We see from this example what the spirit of false toleration, of spurious culture, of the breadth of view which confounds truth and error, leads to; what real intolerance and hatred of God underlie it. Rights of conscience will meet with scant recognition under any system which denies the true God.

III. His LATE REPENTANCE. It is a valuable appendix to this history which we find in the Book of Chronicles. There we are told what we should not have suspected from the narrative before us, that Manasseh late in life repented of his sin, and obtained mercy from God (2 Chron. xxxiii. 11—17). We have had instances of kings reigning well through the greater parts of their lives and failing at the close; this is the first and only case of a Jewish king reigning ill and finally repenting. We are taught by the story of Manasseh's repentance: 1. *The seeds of early instruction may blossom after many days.* Who can doubt but that it was the impressions received in early days which at last revived, and brought Manasseh back to Jehovah. 2. *There is hope for the worst sinners.* After Manasseh, surely any one. Nor did his conversion take place till his course was nearly run. We should despair of none. Miracles of grace as great as this have perhaps rarely been witnessed, but they have been witnessed. 3. *God subdues men to himself by affliction.* It was while a prisoner in Babylon—taken there by the captains of the King of Assyria—that Manasseh found the Lord. 4. *Repentance does not always secure the reversal of the temporal effects of sin.* The wickedness of Manasseh through a long reign wrought out its effects independently of him. His conversion came too late to undo them. The blood he had shed "the Lord would not pardon." The nation was inculpated as well as he, and though he repented, it did not. It is an awful thought that no after-repentance can obliterate the effects of words spoken and deeds done while sin still had dominion over us. Nor can the effects of sin on our own health, characters, usefulness, etc., ever be completely recalled.—J. O.

Vers. 10—18.—*Prophetic denunciations.* In all that he had done, Manasseh had not only sinned himself, but had "seduced" others to sin (ver. 9). Persons in high positions have this great influence. They are the natural social leaders, and their example tells powerfully for good or evil. The prophets, however, though as it proved at the risk of their lives, did not fail to warn him. It was no doubt their faithful denunciations, and the terrible evils they predicted, which brought down upon them the king's wrath, and led to the great persecution.

I. MANASSEH MORE WICKED THAN THE CANAANITES. He had "done wickedly above all that the Amorites did." His deeds may have been the same, but his guilt was greater than theirs, inasmuch as: 1. *His light was greater than theirs.* The Canaanites had the light of nature, and that, indeed, sufficed to render them inexcusable (Rom. i. 18—32; ii. 14, 15). But Manasseh had the light of revelation. He was king of a nation to which God had made fully known the truth of his Being, character, and attributes; which had laws and statutes given to it such as no other nation possessed (Deut. iv. 6—8); and which enjoyed the living ministry of holy prophets. He had also had the advantage of a pious father's example and training. For such a one to go back to the sins of the Amorites was a heinous offence. It made his wickedness greater than theirs. We shall be judged by the light we possess (Luke xii. 47, 48), and if our light is not improved it will be more tolerable for heathen nations than for us (Matt. xi. 21—24; xii. 41, 42). 2. *He was guilty of apostasy; they were not.* If the Amorities did these abominations, and served these idols, it could at least be said that they had never lived under any other system. God had suffered them to walk in their own way (Acts xiv. 16; xvii. 30). But in his evil Manasseh was guilty of a direct act of apostasy. He was going back from past attainments. He was violating a covenant made at Sinai, and repeatedly renewed. It is a different thing for a heathen to commit the vile acts in which he has been brought up, and for a Christian to renounce Christian training and baptismal engagements, and do the same acts. 3. *The corruption of the best is the worst.* This is another principle which explains why Manasseh's abominations are represented as worse than those of the Amorites. A nation, being once enlightened, cannot sin as the semi-ignorant heathen do. It develops worse and more virulent evils. As a brute cannot sin in the same way as a man, or a child in the same way as an adult, so a nation enlightened by revelation can no longer sin as a nation does which has not this light. The higher consciousness reacts upon the sin and modifies it. There are evils possible under a Christian civilization which surpass anything known in heathenism. If our great cities show higher heights of virtue, they could also reveal lower depths of vice than Nineveh, Rome, Pekin, or Calcutta.

II. THE SEVERITY OF JERUSALEM'S PUNISHMENT. 1. *The grounds of the punishment.* These are twofold: (1) Manasseh's sins as above described. "Because Manasseh King of Judah hath done these abominations," etc. (ver. 11). In this sin of the king, however, the people shared. He "made Judah also to sin with his idols." King and people, therefore, must suffer together. There is a corporate responsibility, which involves a community in common guilt, whether the sin proceeds from the head or the members. (2) The entail of past transgression. "Because they have done evil in my sight . . . since the day their fathers came forth from Egypt, unto this day" (ver. 15). That entail would have been cut off by timely repentance, but, in default of repentance, the guilt continues to be handed down. This is another phase of corporate responsibility. The life of the nation is continuous, and one generation has to accept its responsibilities from another. We see the same principle, *e.g.*, in the handing down of national doubt. Christ views the Jewish nation of his day as chargeable with all the righteous blood that had been shed from the days of Abel downwards (Matt. xxiii. 35). 2. *The character of the punishment.* It would be: (1) Startling. "Such evil upon Jerusalem and Judah, that whosoever heareth of it, both his ears shall tingle." Wars, sieges of cities, and captivities, with the horrors attendant on them, were common enough in those days, but this vengeance of God on Jerusalem would be so awful as to shock and amaze even those familiarized with such scenes. The very report of it would produce a stinging sound in their ears. The fulfilment of the threat was partly under Nebuchadnezzar, but completely under the Romans (Matt. xxiv. 21). (2) Measured. "I will stretch over Jerusalem the line of Samaria, and the plummet of the house of Ahab." The idea is that God would take strict account of Judah's sin, as already he had done of that of Samaria. The measuring-line and plummet are introduced for purposes of precision. God would measure exactly the transgression of the people; would note precisely the degree of their deviation from righteousness (cf. Amos vii. 7—9); and to this measured guilt the punishment would be proportioned. The reason of measurement was that judgment was no more to be qualified by mercy. The nation was to bear the full load of its iniquity. It is a terrible thing when God thus "marks iniquity" (Ps. cxxx. 3); for then the case of the sinner is hopeless. (3) Complete. "I will wipe Jerusalem as a man wipeth a dish," etc. "I will forsake the remnant of my inheritance," etc. The figure of cleansing out a dish till it is as clean as wiping can make it is a very graphic one for the utter emptying and desolation that was to overtake Jerusalem. The city would not simply be humbled, as on many previous occasions, but would be completely destroyed, and the people led away by their enemies as a prey and a spoil. The predictions, as we know, were fulfilled to the letter. Manasseh might kill the men who uttered them, but he could not hinder their words from coming true; nay, his violence put a new seal on the certainty of their fulfilment. In the temporal calamities that were to overtake Jerusalem, we find a proof that verily there "is a God that judgeth in the earth" (Ps. lviii. 11), and we are warned lest we provoke his "wrath to the uttermost" (1 Thess. ii. 16) by our own impenitence.

III. MANASSEH'S DEATH. The reign of more than half a century came at length to a close, and, though the last years of it were marked by repentance, it left indelible traces of evil on the condition of the people. That by which Manasseh was specially remembered was "his sin that he sinned." He was buried in "the garden of his own house, the garden of Uzza." Amon also was buried in this garden (ver. 26). There was another garden which had a sepulchre in it (John xix. 41); but how different the sleepers!—J. O.

Vers. 19—26.—*The reign of Amon.* In this king we have—

I. A PALER COPY OF HIS FATHER. The only noteworthy facts about Amon, during his brief two years' reign, are: 1. *His imitation of Manasseh's wickedness.* His father, during the greater part of his reign, had set an evil example, but towards its close he had repented. Amon did not imitate the repentance, but imitated the sin. He walked in all the ways his father had walked in, apparently setting up again the idols which his father had latterly removed (2 Chron. xxxiii. 15). 2. *He was the father of a good son,* viz. Josiah, his successor. This is another of the surprising alternations of character already alluded to. How Josiah came out of such a home with the character he did must remain inexplicable, unless we are to attribute it to his grandfather's influence after his return from Babylon.

II. ANOTHER VICTIM OF COURT CONSPIRACY. Joash and Amaziah among the kings of Judah had met their death by conspiracy (ch. xii. 20, 21; xiv. 19), and many of the kings of Israel had thus perished. But no king of Judah came to this end till he had first fallen away from God. Amon had a like miserable death. His servants conspired against him, and slew him in his own house. The fact that they dared to do so may indicate a tendency to reaction in the public mind against the excesses of idolatry in which the king indulged. The people, however, had no intention of allowing conspirators to seize the throne, so they slew the murderers, and set up Josiah as king. This, again, for a time led to a great reaction for the better.—J. O.

EXPOSITION.

CHAPTER XXII.

Vers. 1–20.—ACCESSION OF JOSIAH. REPAIR OF THE TEMPLE. RECOVERY OF THE BOOK OF THE LAW.

Vers. 1—7.—GENERAL CHARACTER OF JOSIAH'S REIGN. *His repair of the temple.* The writer begins his account of Josiah's reign with the usual brief summary, giving his age at his accession, the length of his reign, his mother's name and birthplace (ver. 1), and the general character of his rule (ver. 2). He then proceeds to mention some circumstances connected with the repair of the temple, which Josiah had taken in hand (vers. 3—7).

Ver. 1.—Josiah was **eight years old when he began to reign.** So the writer of Chronicles (2 Chron. xxxiv. 1) and Josephus ('Ant. Jud.,' x. 4. § 1). He must have been born, therefore, when his father was no more than sixteen years of age, and Amon must have married when he was

only fifteen. **And he reigned thirty and one years in Jerusalem.** Probably from B.C. 640 to B.C. 609—a most important period of the world's history, including, as it does, (1) the great Scythic invasion; (2) the fall of Assyria; (3) the formation of the Median empire; and the foundation of the Babylonian empire by Nabopolasar. **And his mother's name was Jedidah**—*i.e.* "Darling"—**the daughter of Adaiah of Boscath.** Boscath is mentioned as among the cities of Judah (Josh. xv. 39). It lay in the Shefelah (Josh. xv. 33), not far from Lachish and Eglon. The recent explorers of Palestine identify it with the modern *Um-el-Bikar*, two miles and a half southeast of Ajlun (Eglon). (See the 'Map of Western Palestine,' published by Mr. Trelawny Saunders.)

Ver. 2.—**And he did that which was right in the sight of the Lord, and walked in all the way of David his father.** This is a stronger expression than any which has been used of any previous king of Judah except Hezekiah, and indicates a very high degree of approval. The son of Sirach says of Josiah, "The remembrance of Josias is like the composition of the perfume that is made by the art of the apothecary : it is sweet as honey in all mouths, and as music at a banquet of wine. He behaved himself uprightly in the conversion of the people, and took away the abominations of iniquity. He directed his heart unto the Lord, and in the time of the ungodly he established the worship of God. *All, except David and Ezekias and Josias, were defective:* for they forsook the Law of the Most High, even the kings of Judah failed" (see Ecclus. xlix. 1—4). **And turned not aside to the right hand or to the left;** *i.e.* he never deviated from the right path (comp. Deut. v. 32; xvii. 11, 20; xxviii. 14; Josh. i. 7; xxiii. 6).

Ver. 3.—**And it came to pass in the eighteenth year of King Josiah** (comp. 2 Chron. xxxiv. 8). The writer of Kings, bent on abbreviating as much as possible, omits the early reforms of Josiah, which are related in 2 Chron. xxxiv. 3—7, with perhaps some anticipation of what happened later. The young king gave marked indications of personal piety and attachment to true religion as early as the eighth year of his reign, when he was sixteen, and had just attained his majority (Ewald, 'History of Israel,' vol. iv. p. 232, note). Later, in his twelfth year, he began the purging of the temple and of Jerusalem, at the same time probably commencing the repairs spoken of in ver. 9. Jeremiah's prophesying, begun in the same or in the next year (Jer. i. 2), must have been a powerful assistance to his reformation. That **the king sent Shaphan the son of Azaliah, the son of Meshullam, the scribe, to the house of the Lord, saying.** Shaphan held the office which Shebna had held in the later part of Hezekiah's reign (ch. xviii. 18), an office of much importance and dignity. According to the author of Chronicles (2 Chron. xxxiv. 8), there were associated with him on this occasion two other personages of importance, viz. Maaseiah, the governor of the city (comp. 1 Kings xxii. 26), and Joah the son of Joahaz, the "recorder," or "remembrancer."

Ver. 4.—**Go up to Hilkiah the high priest.** Hilkiah is mentioned again in the genealogy of Ezra (Ezra vii. 1). He is there called "the son of Shallum." **That he may sum the silver which is brought into the house of the Lord.** A collection must have been progressing for some time. As in the reign of Joash, after the impieties and idolatry of Athaliah, it was found necessary to collect money for the repair of the temple (ch. xii. 4—14), so now, after the wicked doings of Manasseh and Amon, a renovation of the sacred building was required, and the money needed was being raised by a collection. Great care was taken in all

such cases that an exact account should be kept and rendered. **Which the keepers of the door**—literally, *of the threshold*—**have gathered of the people.** The money had, apparently, been allowed to accumulate in a box or boxes (see ch. xii. 9), from the time when the collection was first authorized, probably six years previously. The high priest was now required to count it, to take the sum of it, and undertake the distribution.

Ver. 5.—**And let them deliver it into the hand of the doers of the work, that have the oversight of the house of the Lord.** The "doers that have the oversight" are not the actual workmen, but the superintendents or overseers of the workmen, who hired them, looked after them, and paid them. **And let them give it to the doers of the work which** is in the house of the Lord—let the overseers, *i.e.*, give out the money to the actual workmen, the carpenters, etc., of the next verse—**to repair the breaches of the house;** rather, *the dilapidation of the house.* It is not implied that any violence had been used, such as is required to make a "breach." The "house" had simply been allowed to fall into disrepair.

Ver. 6.—**Unto carpenters, and builders, and masons, and to buy timber, and hewn stone to repair the house** (comp. 2 Chron. xxxiv. 11). The money had to be expended, partly in labour, partly in materials. The materials consisted of both wood and stone, since it was of these that Solomon's temple had been built (see 1 Kings v. 18; vi. 7, 9, 10, 15, 36).

Ver. 7.—**Howbeit there was no reckoning made with them of the money that was delivered into their hand, because they dealt faithfully** (comp. ch. xii. 15). The superintendents or overseers were persons of position, in whom full confidence was placed. Their names are given in 2 Chron. xxxiv. 12. They were, all of them, Levites.

Vers. 8—14.—*Discovery of the book of the Law.* When Shaphan had transacted with Hilkiah the business entrusted to him by the king, Hilkiah took the opportunity of sending word by him to the king with respect to a discovery that he had recently made, during the investigations connected with the repairs. He had found a book, which he called without any doubt or hesitation, "the book of the Law"—סֵפֶר הַתּוֹרָה —and this book he put into the hands of Shaphan, who "read it," *i.e.* some of it, and found it of such importance that he took it back with him to the palace, and read a portion to the king. Hereupon the king "rent his clothes," and required that special inquiry should be made of the Lord concerning the words of the book, and particularly concerning the threatenings contained in it. The persons entrusted with this task thought it best to lay the matter before Huldah, a prophetess, who lived in Jerusalem at the time, and proceeded to confer with her at her residence.

Ver. 8.—And Hilkiah the high priest said unto Shaphan the scribe, I have found the book of the Law in the house of the Lord. There has been great difference of opinion as to what it was which Hilkiah had found. Ewald believes it to have been the Book of Deuteronomy, which had, he thinks, been composed some thirty or forty years before in Egypt by a Jewish exile, and had found its way, *by a sort of chance*, into Palestine, where "*some priest*" had placed a copy of it in the temple ('History of Israel,' vol. iv. pp. 233—235). Thenius suggests "a collection of the laws and ordinances of Moses, which was afterwards worked up into the Pentateuch;" Bertheau, "the three middle books of the Pentateuch, Exodus, Leviticus, and Numbers;" Gramberg, "Exodus by itself." But there seem to be no sufficient grounds for questioning the ancient opinion—that of Josephus, and of the Jews generally—that it was a copy of the entire Pentateuch. (So De Wette, 'Einleitung in das Alt. Test.,' § 162 *a*; Keil, 'Commentary on Kings,' pp. 477, 478; Bahr, 'Commentary,' vol. vi. p. 257; and others). The words, סֵפֶר הַתּוֹרָה, "*the* book of the Law," are really sufficient to decide the point; since, as Keil says, they "cannot mean anything else, either grammatically or historically, than the Mosaic book of the Law (the Pentateuch), which is so designated, as is generally admitted, in the Chronicles and the Books of Ezra and Nehemiah." The same conclusion follows from the expression, "the book of the covenant" (סֵפֶר הַבְּרִית), in ch. xxiii. 2, and also from ch. xxiii. 24, 25, and 2¦ Chron. xxxiv. 14. Whether or no the copy was the actual original deposited in the ark of the covenant by Moses (Deut. xxxi. 26), as Keil believes, is doubtful. As Egyptian manuscripts which are from three to four thousand years old still exist in good condition, there can be no reason why a manuscript of Moses' time should not have been found and have been legible in Josiah's. But, if not the actual handwriting of Moses, it was probably its lineal descendant—the copy made for the temple service, and kept ordinarily "in the side of the ark"—which may well have been lost in the time of Manasseh or Amon, and which was now happily "found." And Hilkiah gave the book to Shaphan, and he read it. We need not suppose that Shaphan read the whole. But he read enough to show him how important the work was, and how necessary it was to make it known to the king.

Ver. 9.—And Shaphan the scribe came to the king, and brought the king word again, and said, Thy servants have gathered the money that was in the house (see above, vers. 4—6), and have delivered it into the hand of them that do the work, that have the oversight of the house of the Lord; *i.e.* "We have carried out the king's orders exactly, in every particular."

Ver. 10.—And Shaphan the scribe showed the king, saying, Hilkiah the priest hath delivered me a book. Shaphan does not venture to characterize the book, as Hilkiah has done. He is not officially learned in the Law. And he has only read a few passages of it. To him, therefore, it is only "a book," the authorship and value of which he leaves it to others to determine. And Shaphan read it before the king. It is most natural to understand here, as in ver. 8, that Shaphan read portions of the book. Where the author intends to say that the whole book was read, he expresses himself differently (see ch. xxiii. 2, "The king read in their ears *all the words* of the book of the covenant").

Ver. 11.—And it came to pass, when the king had heard the words of the book of the Law, that he rent his clothes. To Josiah the book was evidently, as to Hilkiah, in some sort a discovery. It was not, however, a wholly new thing; rather, he accepted it as the recovery of a thing that was known to have been lost, and was now happily found. And in accepting it he regarded it as authoritative. It was not to him "*a* book of Law" (Ewald), but "*the* book of *the* Law." We can well imagine that, although the book may have been lost early in Manasseh's reign, yet echoes of it had lingered on (1) in the liturgies of the Jehovistic worship; (2) in the teachings of the prophets; (3) in the traditional teaching of religious families; so that the pious ear recognized its phrases as familiar. It is also probable that there were external tokens about the book indicative of its character, which caused its ready acceptance.

Ver. 12.—And the king commanded Hilkiah the priest, and Ahikam the son of Shaphan. "Ahikam the son of Shaphan" is almost certainly Jeremiah's protector at the court of Jehoiakim (Jer. xxvi. 24), the father of the Gedaliah who was made governor of Judæa on Nebuchadnezzar's final conquest (Jer. xxxix. 14; xl. 7). "Shaphan," his father, is no doubt "Shaphan the scribe." **And Achbor the son of Michaiah.** The parallel passage of Chronicles (2 Chron. xxxiv. 20)'has "Abdon the son of Micah," which is probably a corrupt reading. Achbor was the father of El-nathan, one of the "princes of Judah" (Jer. xxxvi. 12) in Jehoiakim's reign. **And Shaphan the scribe, and Asahiah a servant of the king's**—or *Asaiah*, as the name is given in Chronicles, *l. s. c.*—**saying,**

Ver. 13.—**Go ye, inquire of the Lord for me.** Inquiry of the Lord, which from the time of Moses to that of David was ordinarily " by Urim and Thummim," was after David's time always made by the consultation of a prophet (see 1 Kings xxii. 5—8; ch. iii. 11; viii. 8; Jer. xxi. 2; xxxvii. 7; Ezek. xiv. 7; xx. 1, etc.). The officers, therefore, understood the king to mean that they were to seek out a prophet (see ver. 14), and so make the inquiry. **And for the people, and for all Judah**—the threats read in the king's ears were probably those of Deut. xxviii. 15—68 or Lev. xxvi. 16—39, which extended to the whole people—**concerning the words of this book that is found.** Not "whether they are authentic, whether they are really the words of Moses" (Duncker), for of that Josiah appears to have had no doubt; but whether they are words that are to have an immediate fulfilment, "whether," as Von Gerlach says, "the measure of sin is already full, or whether there is yet hope of grace?" (compare Huldah's answer in vers. 16—20, which shows what she understood the king's inquiry to be). **For great is the wrath of the Lord that is kindled against us.** Josiah recognized that Judah had done, and was still doing, exactly those things against which the threatenings of the Law were directed—had forsaken Jehovah, and gone after other gods, and made to themselves high places, and set up images, and done after the customs of the nations whom the Lord had cast out before them. He could not, therefore, doubt but that the wrath of the Lord "was kindled;" but would it blaze forth at once? **Because our fathers have not hearkened unto the words of this book, to do according unto all that which is written concerning us.** Josiah assumes that their fathers have had the book, and might have known its words, either because he conceives that it had not been very long lost, or because he regards them as having possessed other copies.

Ver. 14.—**So Hilkiah the priest, and Ahikam, and Achbor, and Shaphan, and Asahiah, went unto Huldah the prophetess, the wife of Shallum the son of Tikvah.** The principal prophets at or very near the time

were Jeremiah, whose mission had commenced in Josiah's thirteenth year (Jer. i. 2) and Zephaniah, the son of Cushi, whose prophecy appears by internal evidence to have belonged to the earliest part of Josiah's reign (Pusey, 'Minor Prophets,' p. 438). It might have been expected that the matter would have been laid before one of these two persons. Possibly, however, neither of them was at Jerusalem. Jeremiah's early home was Anathoth, and Zephaniah may have finished his course before Josiah's eighteenth year (see Pusey, *l. s. c.*). Huldah may thus have been the only possessor of the prophetic gift who was accessible. **The son of Harhas, keeper of the wardrobe;** literally, *keeper of the garments* (comp. ch. x. 22). In Chronicles the name of the keeper is given as "Hasrah." **Now she dwelt at Jerusalem in the college**—rather, *in the lower city* (comp. Zeph. i. 10 and Neh. xi. 9; literally, in each place, " the *second* city ")—**and they communed with her;** literally, *spoke with her;* ἐλάλησαν πρὸς αὐτήν, LXX.

Vers. 15—20.—*The prophecy of Huldah.* The word of the Lord comes to Huldah with the arrival of the messengers, or perhaps previous to it, and she is at once ready with her reply. It divides itself into two parts. In vers. 15—17 the inquiry made is answered—answered affirmatively, "Yes, the fiat is gone forth; it is too late to avert the sentence; the anger of the Lord is kindled, and *shall not be quenched.*" After this, in vers. 18—20, a special message is sent to the king, granting him an arrest of judgment, on account of his self-humiliation and abasement. "Because his heart was tender, and he had humbled himself before Jehovah, the evil should not happen in his day."

Ver. 15.—**And she said unto them, Thus saith the Lord God of Israel.** Huldah is the only example of a prophetess in Israel, who seems to rank on the same footing with the prophets. Miriam (Exod. xv. 20), Deborah (Judg. iv. 4), Isaiah's wife (Isa. viii. 2), and Anna (Luke ii. 36) are called "prophetesses," but in a secondary sense, as holy women, having a certain gift of song or prediction from God. Huldah has the full prophetic afflatus, and deliver's God's oracles, just as Isaiah and Jeremiah do. The case is a remarkable exception to the general rule that women should "keep silence in the Churches." **Tell the man that sent you to me.** The contrast between this unceremonious phrase and that used in ver. 18 is best explained by Thenius, who says, "In the first part Huldah has only the subject-matter in mind, while in ver. 18, in the quieter flow of her words, she takes notice of the state of mind of the particular person who sent to make the inquiry."

Ver. 16.—**Thus saith the Lord, Behold, I will bring evil upon this place**—*i.e.* Jerusalem—**and upon the inhabitants thereof,** even all the words of the book which the King of Judah hath read. In the parallel passage of Chronicles (2 Chron. xxxiv. 24) the expression used is stronger, viz. "Behold, I will bring evil upon this place, and upon the inhabitants thereof, even *all the curses* that are written in the book which they have read before the King of Judah." The passage which most strongly affected Josiah was probably that, already mentioned, in Deut. xxviii., which began with a series of curses.

Ver. 17.—**Because they have forsaken me.** This was the gist of their offence, the thing that was unpardonable. Against this were all the chief warnings in the Law (Deut. xii. 19; xxix. 25—28; xxxi. 16, 17; xxxii. 15, etc.) and the prophets (Judg. x. 13; 1 Sam. viii. 8; xii. 9; 1 Kings ix. 9; xi. 33; xviii. 18; Isa. i. 4; lxv. 11; Jer. i. 16; ii. 13, etc.). It was not merely that they broke the commandments, but they turned from God altogether, and "cast him behind their back." **And have burned incense unto other gods** (comp. ch. xxiii. 5; and see also Jer. i. 18; vii. 9; xi. 13; xliv. 19, etc.), **that they might provoke me to anger with all the works of their hands;** *i.e.* "with the idols that they have made for themselves" (Keil) (comp. 1 Kings xvi. 7). **Therefore my wrath shall be kindled against this place** —*i.e.* against Jerusalem—**and shall not be quenched.** Here lies the whole point of the answer. God's threatenings against nations are for the most part conditional, and may be escaped, or at least their fulfilment may be deferred indefinitely, by repentance, as we learn from the example of Nineveh (Jonah iii. 1—10). But if a nation persists long in evil-doing, there comes a time when the sentence can be no longer averted. A real repentance has become impossible, and a mock one does but provoke God the more. For such a state of things there is "no remedy" (2 Chron. xxxvi. 16), and this was the state of things reached by the Jews. God's anger against them could not be quenched.

Ver. 18.—**But to the King of Judah which sent you to inquire of the Lord, thus shall ye say to him** (see the comment on ver. 15), **Thus saith the Lord God of Israel, As** touching the words which thou hast heard; *i.e.* the words that were read to thee by Shaphan (ver. 10)—the awful threats which caused thee to rend thy clothes and to make inquiry of me.

Ver. 19.—**Because thine heart was tender** —or, *faint, timid* (comp. Deut. xx. 3; Isa. vii. 1) **and thou hast humbled thyself before the Lord.** Rending the garments (ver. 11) was an outward act of humiliation. Josiah had accompanied it by inward repentance and self-abasement. He had even been moved to tears (see the last clause but one of this verse). **When thou heardest what I spake against this place.** The book was, therefore, a record of what God had really spoken, not a fraud imposed on the king by the high priest, or on the high priest (Ewald, 'History of Israel,' vol. iv. p. 235) by an unknown Egyptian exile. **And against the inhabitants thereof, that they should become a desolation and a curse.** This is not a direct quotation from the Law, but a summary, in pregnant language, of the general effect of such passages as Lev. xxvi. 31—35 and Deut. xxviii. 15—20. The language is like that of Jeremiah in xxvi. 6; xli. 18; xliv. 22. **And hast rent thy clothes** (see ver. 11), **and wept before me.** This had not been previously stated, but might have been gathered from Josiah's evident sincerity, and from the ordinary habits of Orientals (comp. ch. viii. 11; xiii. 14; xx. 3). **I also have heard thee, saith the Lord.** The general sense of vers. 18, 19 is, as Bähr notes, "Because thou hast heard me and taken heed to my threats, I also have heard thee, and will delay their fulfilment."

Ver. 20.—**Behold therefore, I will gather thee unto thy fathers, and thou shalt be gathered into thy grave in peace.** There is a seeming contradiction between these words and the fact of Josiah's violent death in battle against Pharaoh-Nechoh (ch. xxiii. 29). But the contradiction is not a real one. Huldah was commissioned to assure Josiah that, though the destruction of his kingdom and the desolation of Judæa and Jerusalem, threatened in the Law, were at hand, yet they would not come in his day. He would not see the evil time. Before it came he would be "gathered to his fathers"— buried, *i.e.*, in Jerusalem, as his predecessors had been (ch. xxiii. 30), and not hurried off into captivity, to die in a foreign land, or given "the burial of an ass, drawn and cast forth before the gates of Jerusalem" (Jer. xxii. 19). The promise given him was fulfilled. He died in battle; but he was buried in peace (2 Chron. xxxv. 24, 25); and the fated enemy who was to destroy Jerusalem, and carry the Jewish nation into captivity, did not make any attack upon the land until three years later, when he was departed to his rest, and the throne was occupied by Jehoiakim (see ch. xxiv. 1). **And thine eyes shall not see all the evil which I will bring upon this place;** *i.e.* the three sieges of Nebuchadnezzar, the destruction of the temple and city by Nebuzar-adan (ch. xxv. 9, 10), the deportation of the bulk of the inhabitants (ch. xxv. 11), and the calamities which happened to the remnant left (ch. xxv. 22—26). Josiah did not witness any of this. He was " taken away from the

evil to come." **And they brought the king word again;** *i.e.* Hilkiah, Shaphan, and their companions (ver. 14) reported to Josiah the message which Huldah had sent by them.

HOMILETICS.

Vers. 1—13.—*A righteous branch from a wicked root.* Josiah is the most astonishing instance that is contained in Scripture of goodness springing up, and attaining high perfection under the most extraordinarily unfavourable circumstances. Josiah was—

I. THE SON OF AN EXTRAORDINARILY WICKED FATHER. Amon, Josiah's father, did evil in the sight of the Lord to an extent scarcely equalled even by any of the Israelite monarchs. "He forsook the Lord God of his fathers " (ch. xxi. 22), and gave himself wholly up to idolatry. And he did this notwithstanding the example of his father's fall, punishment, and repentance. As the writer of Chronicles says (2 Chron. xxxiii. 23), "he trespassed more and more." Every idolatry of every neighbouring country was adopted by him and reintroduced into Judah; the temple was defiled afresh; the fires of Tophet were relighted; sodomites polluted the temple precincts (ch. xxiii. 7). Wickedness of every kind was encouraged, not only idolatry and debauchery, but "violence and deceit" (Zeph. i. 9), profane swearing (Zeph. i. 5), luxury in apparel (Zeph. i. 8), covetousness (Zeph. i. 18), oppression (Zeph. iii. 1), injustice (Zeph. iii. 2), treachery (Zeph. iii. 3), and utter shamelessness (Zeph. iii. 5).

II. THE GRANDSON OF A STILL MORE WICKED GRANDFATHER. Manasseh was worse than Amon in that he set at nought all the restraints of his bringing up, the example of his saintly father, and the instruction of Isaiah, whom he is said to have executed. He was worse, again, as the original introducer of many most corrupting idolatries which, but for his example, Amon might never have thought of. And he was worse as enforcing his false and impure religion on those who were reluctant to adopt it by means of persecution, and so "filling Jerusalem with innocent blood from one end to another " (ch. xxi. 16)—a sin which is never laid to the charge of Amon. If heredity be indeed the strong predisposing cause which modern biologists assert it to be, what depths of depravity might not a prince have been expected to sound, who had such a father as Amon, such a grandfather as Manasseh!

III. BROUGHT UP IN A CORRUPT COURT. Manasseh's court, even after his repentance, was probably but half-purified. Amon's must have been a sink of corruption. Childish innocence is soon lost in an atmosphere of profligacy ; and Josiah, ere he was eight years of age, had probably been made to witness many of the worst forms of human depravity. "Nil dictu fœdum facture hæc limina tangat intra quæ puer est " was a maxim not likely to obtain much observance in a palace where the rites of the Syrian goddess were approved and practised.

IV. WITHOUT, SO FAR AS WE KNOW, ANY RELIGIOUS INSTRUCTOR. Isaiah had been martyred in the earlier portion of Manasseh's reign. Micah had gone to his rest even earlier. Jeremiah did not receive his call until Josiah's thirteenth year (Jer. i. 2). Habakkuk and Zephaniah lived, perhaps, under Amon, but are not likely to have been allowed access to his court, much less opportunity for influencing the heir to the throne. Josiah's official tutors and instructors under Amon must undoubtedly have been persons devoted to the court religion, which was the syncretic idolatry conceived by Manasseh and maintained by his successor. It is not quite easy to see how the young prince would come into contact with any of the professors of true religion, or obtain any knowledge of the Jehovistic worship.

Such, however, was the natural purity and strength of character by God's grace implanted in the young prince from the first, that to none of the evil influences within him or without him did he succumb. It is declared of him in the infallible Word, that "he did that which was right in the sight of the Lord, and walked in *all* the way of David his father, and turned not aside to the right hand or to the left " (ver. 2). As soon as he had any power to show what his inclinations were, as soon (that is) as he was free from the trammels which confined a Jewish prince during his minority, he courageously set himself to undo the ill that his father and grandfather had done, to abolish the strange rites, to drive out the foul idolatries, and to restore the worship of Jehovah. And he earned the praise that "Like unto him was there no king before him, that turned to the Lord with all his heart, and with all his soul, and with all his might, according to all the Law of Moses; neither after him arose there any like him" (ch. xxiii. 25). We may learn from this history not to assign too much weight to a man's surroundings, but to hold firm to the belief that there is in each man a sufficient force of personality and will to enable him, if his heart be set on well-doing, to resist any amount of external circumstances, and to mould his life and character for himself, even in the exact opposite shape to that whereto all the external circumstances pointed, and which they might have seemed to have rendered necessary.

Vers. 8—13.—*A strange loss, and a strange recovery.* The loss by a nation of its sacred book is a strange and extraordinary occurrence. Books deemed sacred are naturally so highly valued and so deeply reverenced that the utmost care is taken of them. Generally, copies are multiplied and are in so many hands that the loss of all, while the nation itself survives, is practically impossible. It is practically impossible, nowadays, that the Christians should lose their Bible, or the Mohammedans their Korán, or the Hindoos their Vedas, or the Parsees their Zendavesta, or the Chinese their Shu-King or their Taou-tih-King. To understand what had taken place in Palestine shortly before Josiah came to the throne, we must consider the peculiar circumstances of the Jewish religion, and the place which "the book of Law" occupied in it. The following points are especially worthy of note.

I. THE ORIGINAL BOOK OF THE LAW WAS DEPOSITED BESIDE THE ARK, AND KEPT THERE. "It came to pass," we are told, "when Moses had made an end of writing the words of this Law in a book, until they were finished, that Moses commanded the Levites, which bare the ark of the covenant of the Lord, saying, Take this book of the Law, and put it in the side of the ark of the covenant of the Lord your God, that it may be there for a witness against them" (Deut. xxxi. 24—26).

II. THERE WAS NO PROVISION FOR MAKING COPIES OF IT UNTIL SUCH TIME AS ISRAEL SHOULD HAVE KINGS. Then indeed each king was to "write him a copy of the Law in a book out of that which was before the priests the Levites" (Deut. xvii. 18). But, except on such occasions, the book, it would seem, remained in the ark, and was not lent about to be copied.

III. THE DESIGN WAS TO MAKE THE LAW KNOWN TO THE PEOPLE BY READING IT TO THEM PUBLICLY. Such reading was prescribed once in each seven years, in the sabbatical year, at the Feast of Tabernacles (Deut. xxxi. 10—13). Under Nehemiah certainly (Neh. viii. 2—5), perhaps at other times, the precept was acted on.

IV. MULTIPLICATION OF COPIES WAS NOT NEEDED FOR SYNAGOGUES, WHICH DID NOT AS YET EXIST. The result was that probably, besides the temple copy, very few copies of the Law had at any time existed. Irreligious kings, as Rehoboam, Abijah, Jehoram, Ahaziah, Ahaz, Manasseh, and Amon, would, as a matter of course, disobey the precept to make a copy; and it is not even certain that all religious kings would carry out the precept. David, whose delight was in the Law (Ps. cxix. 77), Asa, Jehoshaphat, Joash, Hezekiah, would almost certainly have made copies; but Solomon may not have done so, nor Amaziah, nor Uzziah, nor Jotham. If the prophets seem to show such a familiarity with the Law as implies constant study, it may well be that the "schools of the prophets" were in possession of some of the royal autograph copies, or the prophets may have been allowed access as often as they required it to the temple copy. Passages of the Law, as the Decalogue and other precepts regarding conduct, or, again, the promises made to the patriarchs, and to the nation at large through Moses, may have been widely known, being fixed in the memory of the people, and passed on from father to son by word of mouth. And these well-known passages may also have sometimes taken a written shape. But entire copies of the Law must, even in the time of the later kings, have been exceedingly scarce. Thus when an irreligious king like Manasseh set aside the Jehovistic worship, and thrust, it may be, into lumber-rooms, the old furniture of the temple, so that the book of the Law, *i.e.* the temple copy, became mislaid or lost, there was no very ready way of replacing it. Nor, perhaps, did there seem to be any absolute necessity of so doing. Except once in seven years, the reading of the Law does not appear to have formed a part of any temple service. The precepts of the Law were inculcated orally by priests and Levites, who had received them from their predecessors. Hilkiah and the priests generally were probably content to carry on the traditional teaching, and did not feel the need of seeking the water of life from the fountain-head. But suddenly a discovery was made. There had been no wanton or malignant destruction of the book of the Law. It had merely been thrust out of sight, and then forgotten. As the repair and restoration of the temple proceeded, and even lumber-rooms and closets were searched, that the whole building might be brought into proper order, those employed in the work came upon the lost volume. It was, probably, very easily recognized. As Bähr says, it may have been "distinguished by its external appearance, size, material, beauty of the writing," etc., as the Samaritan copy of the Pentateuch at Nablous is distinguished. Or it may have had for its title, "The Book of the Law of the Lord *by the hand of Moses*" (2 Chron. xxxiv. 14). There may even have been priests living who had seen the book before it was lost, and knew it as the volume with which, fifty years before, they had been familiar. At any rate, priests, king, and people unanimously, though with much grief and fear, accepted it. The prophetess, who was God's mouthpiece at the time, confirmed their view; and it remained for nineteenth-century critics to throw a doubt upon the conclusion thus come to, and to brand the work as a forgery of Hilkiah's, or as a *chance* production of a *chance* author, who had amused himself by composing a code of laws for a Utopia.

HOMILIES BY VARIOUS AUTHORS.

Ver. 1—ch. xxiii. 30.—*The reign of King Josiah.* The last days of Judah as an independent kingdom are fast hastening to a close. The people, in spite of all God's merciful dealings with them, in spite of all the judgments and warnings which he had sent to their fathers, in spite of the influence and example of good kings and holy prophets whom he had raised up, were becoming worse and worse. More than a hundred years before, God had already abolished the kingdom of Israel, when the ten tribes were led away into captivity. And now for their great idolatries the destruction of the kingdom of Judah also is close at hand. In the midst of this period of decline and decay Josiah came to the throne to redeem for a time the history of his nation, and for a time to save it from its impending doom.

I. JOSIAH'S EARLY DEVOTION. We read that in the eighth year of his reign, while he was yet young, he began to seek after the God of David his father. He was then sixteen years of age. 1. He began to seek after God *in a time of almost universal godlessness and corruption.* It is almost impossible for us to conceive the depth of degradation to which the nation had sunk. Two wicked kings in succession had undone all the reforms of good King Hezekiah. The first of these was Hezekiah's own son, Manasseh, the second was Manasseh's son, Amon. Manasseh worshipped all the host of heaven, and built altars for all the host of heaven in the two courts of the house of the Lord. He set up the worship of Moloch, which is almost too terrible to describe (see above on ch. xvi. 1—20). He made his own son to pass through the fire to Moloch. He introduced not only the horrid *cruelty* of heathenism, but also its most filthy *lusts.* The reign of Amon was no better, but worse. He revived and continued all the idolatries and all the corruption of his father's reign. It was at such a time as this that, when Amon died, his son Josiah, then only eight years old, came to the throne. At such a time as this he began to seek after the Lord his God. 2. *Moreover, he was the son of a godless and wicked father.* All the influences which surrounded him seem to have been unfavourable to the growth of true religion and the fear of God. But Josiah determined that, as for him, he would not bow down to idols, that he would serve the Lord only. And God gave him strength to serve him, and crowned his subsequent efforts with blessing and success. Learn here *the folly of excusing yourself from serving God by the circumstances in which you are placed.* You are responsible to God for your *own* life, and for your own conduct, no matter how others may act. It may cost us many a hard struggle to resist the temptations that surround us on every side; but it always succeeds in the end. You may be children of ungodly parents; you may be at service in ungodly households;

you may be thrown by your business among ungodly companions and surroundings;—no matter! God expects you to be faithful unto him. Young men, Josiah's early devotion is a bright example for you to follow. Never suffer yourselves to be led astray by the notion that religion is an unmanly thing. The truly religious man is the noblest and most perfect man. He is great in all that constitutes true manhood. And if you want to find the greatest heroes in the world's history, you will find them, not among the followers of the world's fashion and the world's pleasure, but among the prophets, apostles, martyrs, and humble Christians in the Church of God. It is the highest aim any young man can set before him to be a humble and devoted follower of Jesus Christ. Never mind what circumstances or companions surround you, except to try and make them better. Joseph was faithful to God in Egypt. His faithfulness sent him to a prison for a time; but afterwards it raised him to be the greatest man in Egypt after the king. Daniel was faithful to God in Babylon, though he knew well it was at the risk of his life. His faithfulness brought him for a little while to the lions' den; but it afterwards made him ruler over the whole province of Babylon. It is true heroism to be ready to suffer—to suffer bodily pain, to suffer the loss of worldly goods, yes, to suffer even the loss of reputation itself, for the sake of truth and purity and right. Like Josiah, the sooner you begin to serve God the better. You will never regret it. "Remember now thy Creator in the days of thy youth."

II. JOSIAH'S WORK OF REFORMATION. (Ver. 3—ch. xxiii. 25.) Here also he began *very early* to do what he believed to be right. It was in the *twelfth year* of his reign —when he was only *twenty years old*—that he began to purge Judah and Jerusalem from the high places and the idols. Then in the eighteenth year of his reign—when he was *twenty-six years old*—he began to repair the house of the Lord, which had been long disused and neglected. God so prospered him in this work, that the people brought large sums of money for the repairing of the temple. It was when this was being done that *Hilkiah the priest found in the temple the book of the Law.* There it lay, probably all covered with dust, like the unused Bible in many a home, a silent reproof to those who should have known what was right but did not do it. When the book of the Law was read to the king, he rent his clothes, in sorrow and in shame, when he thought of how the Law of God had been broken and neglected. It was determined that it should be so no longer, and, having gathered all the people together, he read in their ears all the words of the Law. Then, standing on a pillar, he made a covenant that they would serve the Lord and keep his commandments, and all the people agreed to it. After this was done, he appointed a solemn Passover to be kept by all the people. And it is said, "Surely there was not holden such a Passover from the days of the judges that judged Israel, nor in all the days of the kings of Israel, nor of the kings of Judah; but in the eighteenth year of King Josiah, wherein this Passover was holden to the Lord in Jerusalem" (ch. xxiii. 22, 23). It was a marvellous work for a young king to have accomplished in the twenty-sixth year of his age. He found the land full of idolatry and corruption. But he had already pulled down the altars, and burned the idols, and swept away the dens of vice. He found the temple closed, neglected, and in decay. He had already repaired it and restored the worship of the true God. He found the Law of God forgotten, forsaken, and unknown—the temple copy of it hidden away out of sight. He had already restored it to its proper place as the ruling principle of his government and of the nation's life. Truly a marvellous work for a young king of twenty-six. We see here, as we have seen in the life of Hezekiah, the *power of decision for what is right.* Josiah was not content merely to know God and serve him by himself. He was determined that, so far as he had any influence, others should know and serve God too. He might have said, in the spirit of many lukewarm Christians of modern times, "What matters it? They have their religion, and I have mine." He might have said that, as a ruler, he had nothing to do with his people's religion, but only with their conduct as members of the state. Not so. *He knew* that it is religion, or the want of it, which makes or mars the happiness and prosperity of the nation. *He knew* that, as a servant of God, he was bound to bear his testimony and to use every influence in his power against sin and in favour of what was right. *And so he acted*, not with half-measures, not with half-hearted hesitation, but with firmness, fearlessness, promptness, and determination, as becomes one who is doing the work of God. And so, also, *God stood by him*, and gave him success in all his work. Such an example is full of instruction for our modern life. Never be a consenting party, even by your silence, to what your conscience tells you is wrong. Never consent, even by your silence, to anything dishonouring to God or not in accordance with his will. Never be a consenting party to anything that you would be ashamed of in the sight of God and men—to acts of injustice to others, to dishonesty or unfairness of any kind, to profanity, to neglect of Sunday observance, or any other form of prevailing wickedness. "O my soul, come not thou into their secret; with their assembly, mine honour, be not thou united." Like Josiah, we can never begin too soon, not only to serve God ourselves, but also *to bring others to him.* Like Josiah, let every servant of God show the reality of his and her religion by deeds of usefulness, by bearing testimony against sin, and by unwavering firmness in the cause of Christ and duty.

III. JOSIAH'S EARLY DEATH. Josiah died at an early age. *He was mourned for with great lamentation.* Some think that it is of him that Jeremiah, in his Book of Lamentations, speaks when he says, "The breath of our nostrils, the anointed of Jehovah, was taken in their pits, of whom we said, Under his shadow we shall live among the heathen." The passage perhaps indicates how great was the influence for good which Josiah exercised, and how much the people depended upon him as their leader and defender. His early death, before he had completed his fortieth year, must have caused many to wonder at God's mysterious providence. But his work was done. He had really done the work of many lives in one. And so when servants of God are taken away in the prime of life—or prematurely, as we say—let us remember that God's ways are not our ways. In *his* sight their work is done. They have finished the work which he gave them to do. Let us so use the precious time which God has given us, that in our dying hour we shall not have to look back upon a wasted life. But let us live, as Josiah lived, a life of holiness, of usefulness, "redeeming the time." And then when we are drawing near to the gates of death, we shall feel that for us they are the gates of heaven. We shall be able humbly and thankfully to say, "I have fought the good fight, I have finished my course, I have kept the faith : henceforth there is laid up for me a crown of righteousness, which the Lord, the righteous Judge, shall give me at that day."—C. H. I.

Vers. 1—20.—*A monarch of rare virtue, and a God of retributive justice.* "Josiah was eight years old," etc. There are two subjects in this chapter that arrest our attention, and which are fertile with suggestions.

I. A MONARCH OF RARE VIRTUE. "Josiah was eight years old when he began to reign, and he reigned thirty and one years in Jerusalem," etc. In this monarch we discover four distinguished merits. 1. *Religiousness of action.* "He did that which was right in the sight of the Lord." This is the testimony of the historian, whoever he may be, and we are further told, "Josiah walked in all the way of David his father." Elsewhere we have given the biblical account of David's life.[1] From that account it might, perhaps, be questioned whether to "walk in the way of David" was a morally creditable life. But undoubtedly in the opinion of this writer, Josiah was a man whose activity was inspired by true religious feeling. Here we find him providing for the repairs of the temple. "And it came to pass in the eighteenth year of King Josiah, that the king sent Shaphan the son of Azaliah, the son of Meshullam, the scribe, to the house of the Lord, saying, Go up to Hilkiah the high priest, that he may sum the silver which is brought into the house of the Lord, which the keepers of the door have gathered of the people : and let them deliver it into the hand of the doers of the work, that have the oversight of the house of the Lord : and let them give it to the doers of the work which is in the house of the Lord, to repair the breaches of the house." The king who provides for the religious *instruction* and *worship* of his people proves thereby that he is under the influence of the religious sentiment. In repairing the temple, Josiah honours his people, not only by allowing, but by encouraging them to co-operate with him in the noble work. He coerces none; all were left free, and they did their work honestly and honourably. "Howbeit there was no reckoning made with them of the money that was delivered into their hand, because they dealt faithfully." 2. *Docility of mind.* "And Hilkiah the high priest said unto Shaphan the scribe, I have found the book of the Law in the house of the Lord. And Hilkiah gave the book to Shaphan, and he read it. And

[1] See 'Commentary: Book of Psalms,' vol. iii.

Shaphan the scribe came to the king, and brought the king word again. . . . And Shaphan the scribe showed the king, saying, Hilkiah the priest hath delivered me a book. And Shaphan read it before the king. And it came to pass, when the king had heard the words of the book of the Law, that he rent his clothes." What book was this? Old time buries the choicest books; volumes that once moved the intellects and fired the hearts of men are sunk in the black waves of oblivion. In all probability the book here was the Pentateuch, the five books of Moses. A copy of this, it seems, having been laid beside the ark in the most holy place (Deut. xxxi. 25, 26), had been lost, and now, during the repairing of the temple, it was discovered. Was this a Divine book? If so, why should its Author have suffered it to have been lost, perhaps for generations? A human author, had he the power to prevent it, would not suffer his productions to meet with such a fate. But the thoughts of God are independent of books; they are not only written on the pages of nature, but in imperishable characters on the souls of men. But how did Josiah act towards this discovered book? Did he reject it, or was he indifferent to it? No. "It came to pass, when the king had heard the words of the book of the Law, that he rent his clothes." Herein how unlike is this man, not only to ordinary mortals, but also to ordinary kings! How many kings have been ready to receive new light? Are they not for the most part so mailed in traditions and prejudices as to render the admission of a new truth well-nigh impossible? If the modern occupants of thrones would but universally open their eyes to those old truths of eternal right which come flashing from their graves, all oppressions would cease, and kingdoms would march on to freedom and light. "Be wise now therefore, O ye kings: be instructed, ye judges of the earth." 3. *Tenderness of heart.* See how the character of the book affected him. "He rent his clothes." It is also said, in ver. 19, "Thine heart was tender." Sensibility of heart gives life, worth, and power to intellect. Where sensibility and intellect are not in their due proportion, the character is defective. Where the sensibility is stronger than the intellect, the man is likely to become a morbid pietist or a reckless fanatic. Where the intellect is stronger in proportion to the sensibility, the man is likely to become a cold theorist, living in the frigid abstractions of his own brain. But where both are properly combined, you have a man fit for great things. A man who, if he be a friend, will give counsels that will tell alike on your understanding and heart. Sensibility feathers the arrows of argument, gives poetry and power to thought. 4. *Actualization of conviction.* When this discovered document came under Josiah's attention, and its import was realized, he was seized with a conviction that he, his fathers, and his people, had disregarded, and even outraged, the written precepts of Heaven. He exclaims, "Great is the wrath of the Lord that is kindled against us, because our fathers have not hearkened unto the words of this book, to do according unto all that which is written concerning us." With this new conviction burning within him, what does he do? Does he strive to quench it? or does he allow it to burn itself out without any effort on his part? No; he at once commands his servants to make an effort on behalf of himself and his people. "Go ye, inquire of the Lord for me, and for the people, and for all Judah, concerning the words of this book that is found." The new emotions that rushed into his tender heart prompted him to seek immediate counsel how to avert the curses under which his kingdom lay. They obeyed his behests. "So Hilkiah the priest, and Ahikam, and Achbor, and Shaphan, and Asahiah, went unto Huldah the prophetess, the wife of Shallum the son of Tikvah, the son of Harhas, keeper of the wardrobe (now she dwelt in Jerusalem in the college); and they communed with her. And she said unto them, Thus saith the Lord God of Israel, Tell the man that sent you to me, Thus saith the Lord, Behold, I will bring evil upon this place, and upon the inhabitants thereof, even all the words of the book which the King of Judah hath read: because they have forsaken me," etc. (vers. 14—18). Here the prophetess spoke the universal sentiment of mankind, viz. that where wrong is, suffering must follow. All experience, all history, attests the truth of the sentiment. But the noteworthy point here is that this tender-hearted man *translated his emotions into actions.* He did not allow his new feelings to pass away as the morning cloud, nor did he expend them in sentimental sighs and groans. Well would it be for all men if they acted thus; for this, in truth, is the only method of spiritual progress. It is only as men embody true thoughts and feelings in actions that they rise to true manhood.

II. A GOD OF RETRIBUTIVE JUSTICE. Such a God the prophetess here reveals.

"Thus saith the Lord God of Israel, Tell the man that sent you to me, Thus saith the Lord, Behold, I will bring evil upon this place, and upon the inhabitants thereof, even all the words of the book which the King of Judah hath read." The government over us, and to which we are bound with chains stronger than adamant, is retributive; it never allows evil to go unpunished. It links in indissoluble bonds sufferings to sin. Sorrows follow sin by a law as immutable and resistless as the waves follow the moon. " Whatsoever a man soweth, that shall he also reap." In this retribution (1) the wicked are treated with severity, and (2) the good are treated with favour. In the name of God this prophetess declares concerning Josiah, " As touching the words which thou hast heard; because thine heart was tender, and thou|hast humbled thyself before the Lord, when thou heardest what I spake against this place, and against the inhabitants thereof, that they should become a desolation and a curse, and hast rent thy clothes, and wept before me; I also have heard thee, saith the Lord. Behold therefore, I will gather thee unto thy fathers, and thou shalt be gathered into thy grave in peace; and thine eyes shall not see all the evil which I will bring upon this place." Though righteous judgments were soon to descend upon his country on account of its manifold and heinous sins, he, Josiah, who had proved faithful amongst the faithless, would be spared the terrible storm. He should neither feel it nor see it; his body would be sleeping in the quiet grave, and his spirit be gathered to his " fathers," with all the true men of past times. We are prone to think of death as an evil; it is an event that often appals us with the ghastly aspects that it assumes before our imagination. There are circumstances that make it appear especially sad. For example: when a man like Josiah, of immense influence for good, dies in the zenith of life, and in the midst of usefulness, we deem it an occasion of special sadness. But it is not so, either to the man himself or to his generation. He is taken away from the evil that is coming, and the circumstance of his death, and the loss caused by his departure, tend to rouse his contemporaries to serious and salutary thought. Death is no respecter of persons. The Divine government of the world is like a stream that rolls under us; men are only as bubbles that rise to its surface; some are brighter and larger, and sparkle longer in the sun than others: but all must break, whilst the mighty current rolls on in its wonted majesty. We are shadows, and following shadows. There is nothing real but God.—D. T.

Vers. 1—7.—*Josiah: the temple again repaired.* The reign of Josiah affords another example of the law of action and reaction in national life. Dr. R. Payne Smith says, " The nation itself had gradually swung round, as nations now do, and had begun to be as dissatisfied with Baal and Moloch as their fathers had been with Jehovah" ('Introduction to Jeremiah'); and Dean Stanley remarks, " The popular election which placed Josiah on the throne, of itself marks some strong change of public feeling " (Jewish Church,' vol. ii. p. 435). It is safer, however, to infer this change in public feeling from the support afterwards given to Josiah in his measures of reform, than from the mere fact of his accession; for as yet his disposition was quite uncertain. The craving for a *change* of some kind, with a secret weariness of the policy and extreme doings of the pagan party, had perhaps more to do with the young king's popularity than any real desire to serve Jehovah.

I. THREE BEGINNINGS. 1. *The beginning of a reign.* Josiah was but a boy of eight years old when he was placed upon the throne. At this age he was in danger, like his grandfather Manasseh, of being a mere puppet in the hands of the godless aristocracy. But God's providence seems to have watched over Josiah, and to have caused some care to be taken to guide the young king right. The queen-mother, Jedidah (" the beloved of God"), daughter of Adaiah (" the honoured of God"), " may perhaps have deserved her lofty name, and given her boy the priceless benefit of a godly mother's example and counsels" (Geikie). She may even have acted as regent during his minority, and in that capacity have gathered around her the worthy persons who afterwards figure in the narrative, Shaphan the scribe, etc. 2. *The beginning of grace.* Josiah from the first must have shown good dispositions, and a willingness to be guided and taught by godly counsellors. But it is to the eighth year of his reign, that is, his sixteenth year, that the Book of Chronicles attributes the first decided evidence of his determination to seek Jehovah. "For in the eighth year of his reign, while he was still young, he began to seek after the God of David his father" (2 Chron. xxxiv. 3). From this period his career seems to have been a singularly straightforward and consistent one: "He walked in all the way of David his father, and turned not aside to the right hand or to the left." What led to this decision in his eighth year we cannot tell. The age at which he had now arrived marks the time about which independent thought commonly begins; possibly some increase of responsibility led him to deeper reflection; it may well be that his mind had long been secretly brooding on religion, and he now took some public step which showed decidedly which side he was on. Nothing seems so beautiful as early piety. A character like Josiah's appearing after reigns like those of Manasseh and Amon is as a snowdrop at the close of winter. It is the piety which begins early that lasts longest, and shows the most blameless record. Beautiful in all, early grace is specially beautiful in those who occupy high positions, and are destined to exercise a wide influence. With many young men the sixteenth year of life is a turning-point in a different direction. Josiah then "began" to seek the Lord. Too often it is the period when the restraints of home religion are thrown off, and young men "begin" to think and act for themselves in forbidden ways. 3. *The beginning of reforms.* The chronicler gives us another date, viz. the twelfth year of Josiah's reign, as that in which he began to effect a religious reformation in the land. "In the twelfth year he began to purge Judah and Jerusalem from the high places, and the Asherim, and the graven images, and the molten images," etc. He was then twenty years of age, and the reforms mentioned, though begun in that year, extended on till after his eighteenth year. He had probably to begin cautiously, dealing with the more obvious abuses, and gradually feeling his way to bolder changes. A strong party, no doubt, were opposed to his reforms, and it is difficult to say how far they had advanced before the repair of the temple and the finding of the Law-book. The narratives of neither Chronicles nor Kings adhere strictly to chronological order, but we may suppose that before the projected repairs on the temple building were undertaken, both "the land and the house" had been purged of their worst abominations (2 Chron. xxxiv. 8). The Baal-altars, idols, and Asherim would be removed; idolatrous worship on the high places stopped, though the people may still have sacrificed on them, as in the latter days of Manasseh, "yet unto the Lord their God only" (2 Chron. xxxiii. 17); the sacrifices to Moloch in the valley of Hinnom put an end to. If this was so, it is certain that the temple, in which the worship of Jehovah, with a priest like Hilkiah at its head, had been restored, would not be left uncleared of its Baal-images, its horses of the sun, its prostitutes, etc. (ch. xxiii. 6, 7, 11). Things, in short, would be brought back to the state in which they had been left at Manasseh's death (2 Chron. xxxiii. 15—18). This Josiah might safely attempt, though passages in the prophets show that much idolatry still remained. Earnest religion invariably brings forth its appropriate fruits in zeal for the honour of God, the purification of his worship, and the purging away of evils and abuses.

II. THE EIGHTEENTH YEAR. Hitherto, whatever Josiah had done had been more or less the result of his individual action. The conscience of the nation had not been touched, nor had any enthusiasm been awakened in favour of the new reforms. On the contrary, these had probably aroused not a little bitterness and sullen hostility. At the head of this narrative in Kings, therefore, is placed the date of "the eighteenth year of King Josiah," when the movement enters on an altogether new phase, and swells to national dimensions. The immediate occasion of this change was the finding of the Law-book in the temple, and this again was owing to the repairs which the king had ordered to be executed on the sacred edifice. Glancing at present only at the narrative of these repairs on the temple, we find that they were: 1. *Much needed.* There is no record of repairs on the temple since the days of King Hezekiah (2 Chron. xxix. 3). In the interval the building had frequently suffered from total neglect, and idolatrous kings had made changes in its structure to suit their own purposes. There were "breaches" to repair (ver. 5), roofs to fit with "beams" (2 Chron. xxxiv. 11), and much carpentry and mason work to do with timber and hewn stone throughout the house. It is strange how indifferent those who dwell in their own "cieled houses" can often be to the state of the house wherein God is worshipped (Hag. i. 4). It is the sign of a true zeal for God when there is a proper desire shown to maintain even the outer fabric of ecclesiastical buildings in a decent condition of repair. 2. *Already collected for.* The means for executing the repairs on the Lord's house had been obtained by voluntary collections at the door of the temple. It is by the king's order, sent through Shaphan the scribe to Hilkiah the high priest, to sum up the money which had been thus gathered, that the matter first comes before us in the narrative. These collections from the people, which must have been going on for some time, show that the worship of Jehovah was now regularly conducted. They also afford us a lesson as to the mode of meeting the expense connected with church building and repairs. (1) The money was raised before the repairs were commenced. This was a sound principle, and, if more frequently acted upon, would save a good deal of trouble with Church debt. The temple was sorely in need of repair, and it might have been pleaded that the case was too urgent to admit of delay till the money was collected. It was resolved, however, to collect the money before a single workman was put upon the building. (2) It was raised by voluntary subscription. The people were not taxed, or forced in any way, to give this money. It was their own free-will offering. Yet apparently the sums required were raised without difficulty. The modern Church expedients of bazaars, etc., are surely inferior to this Old Testament plan. If the appeal to voluntary liberality sometimes does not yield all that we could wish, it is, on the whole, the surest source of income to rely on, and reacts, as no other does, on the heart of the giver. 3. *After a good precedent.* Alike in the collecting of the money, the distribution to the workmen, and the reliance placed in the fidelity of the overseers, those in charge of this business seem to have followed closely the precedents of the reign of Joash. It is good to learn from those who have gone before us.—J. O.

Vers. 8—20.—*The finding of the Law-book.* The finding of the book of the Law by Hilkiah in the temple marks a distinct turning-point in Josiah's reformation. It is admitted generally that this Law-book included, if it did not exclusively consist of, the Book of Deuteronomy. As it is further allowed that some of the main narrative documents of our present Pentateuch, and the book of the covenant (Exod. xxi.—xxiii.), if not also collections of priestly laws, were then in existence, and had long been, we see no reason to doubt that the "book of the Law" discovered by Hilkiah included the bulk of the writings which make up "the five books of Moses." Several legitimate inferences may be drawn from the narrative. 1. A "book of the Law" was known to have been once in existence. Hilkiah speaks of it as "*the* book of the Law"—a book long lost, now found, and at once recognized. 2. The copy found was the complete, standard, authoritative copy. It was this which gave it its peculiar value. 3. It would seem as if no other copies of the book were then known to exist, at any rate none were in possession of the parties named in this chapter. If they had been, we can hardly doubt that the contents would have been in some way communicated to the king. This last inference, however, must not be pushed too far. Complete copies of the Law would at all times be rare, and amidst the troubles and persecutions of Manasseh's long reign may well have been lost, especially as there do not seem to have been in Judah organized prophetic guilds such as existed in Israel, or at least the prophets we know, Jeremiah, Zephaniah, Huldah, etc., did not belong to them (cf. the state of matters before the Reformation in Europe, and the finding of the Latin Bible by Luther in the convent at Erfurt). But it does not follow that in prophetic circles no parts or fragments of the Law were in existence. The narrative parts of the Law would be more frequently copied than the legislative, and abstracts or summaries of the book of the covenant, or of the laws in Deuteronomy, perhaps selected passages from these books, may have been in circulation. There was even an order of "scribes" whom Jeremiah accuses of using their false pens to falsify the Law. "How do ye say, We are wise, and the Law of the Lord is with us? But, behold, the false pen of the scribes hath wrought falsely" (Jer. viii. 8). The scribes may have falsified the Law itself, altering its text, expunging its denunciations against idolatry, or making unauthorized additions to it; or they may have falsified it by their comments and interpretations of its meaning. The only thing certain is that the portions of the Law which so affected the conscience of the king were not in any current summaries or copies.

I. FINDING GOD'S WORD. "And Hilkiah the high priest said unto Shaphan the scribe, I have found the book of the Law in the house of the Lord." This Law-book—

"the book of the Law of Moses" (ch. xiv. 6)—had undergone strange vicissitudes. We see it: 1. *Sinfully lost.* What treasure, one would think, so precious as the words which God had spoken to this nation through their great law-giver Moses—the statutes and judgments and commandments he had ordered them to keep, and which constituted their great glory as a people (Deut. iv. 5—8)? "What advantage then hath the Jew? . . . Much every way: chiefly, because that unto them were committed the oracles of God" (Rom. iii. 1, 2). Yet this Law of God had been so sinfully neglected that the very knowledge of it had well-nigh perished out of the land, and the book which contained it, from which this knowledge might be revived, had disappeared. The king had neglected it, he who should have been its chief defender; the official classes of the court had neglected it; the priests who had charge of God's house had neglected it, and allowed it to remain unused till it had got into some corner or room where it was covered up with rubbish and lost sight of; the scribes used what knowledge they retained of it only to falsify it. What sin! It was as if there were a deliberate conspiracy to hunt this first Bible out of existence. If to-day there is not the same danger of the knowledge of the Bible being lost as at some past periods of history, it is not because among many classes there is not as strong a hatred of it or as great neglect. With how many is the Bible an unopened book from one week's end to the other! Multitudes are as ignorant of its contents as the far-off heathen; multitudes more have lost whatever knowledge they once had of it through neglect and misuse; in the case of yet greater multitudes its truths are as inoperative as if the book were indeed lost. 2. *Providentially found.* God's providence is seen in nothing more remarkably than in the care he has exercised over the written Word. He has wonderfully protected it through all ages alike from the neglect and the fury of men. If for a time the knowledge of it seemed lost, it was again revived at the most favourable juncture for the execution of his purposes. Thus at the Reformation we see a preparation for the new movement in the revival of learning, the invention of printing, the emergence into light of important manuscripts of the New Testament, etc. That was practically a finding of the Law-book of the Church, as marvellous and as providential as this discovery in the reign of Josiah. It was Josiah's zeal in the repairing of the temple which prepared the way for the discovery here; and the book was found just in time to give a new impetus to the reforming movement. In Divine providence, all things fit together in time and place. 3. *Reverently examined.* Hilkiah knew the book when he saw it, and he gave it to Shaphan the scribe, and he read it. It would be with trembling, eager hand that Shaphan turned over the pages, and, with his scribe's professional instinct, satisfied himself that this was the veritable lost copy of the Law. Taking it with him, he read it more leisurely, not completely, of course, but parts of it, those parts especially which were new to him. This was the right way to treat God's Word. Our chief anxiety, if we possess the sacred volume, should be to know what God the Lord will speak to us (Ps. lxxxv. 8). Cf. Edward Irving's lectures on "The Word of God"—(1) the preparation for consulting the Word of God; (2) the manner of consulting the Word of God; (3 and 4) the obeying of the Word of God ('Lectures,' vol. i.).

II. TREMBLING AT GOD'S WORD. 1. *Shaphan's announcement.* Having ascertained the contents of the book for himself, Shaphan lost no time in bringing it under the notice of the king. He seems to have felt the need of care in his manner of doing this. The book contained strong denunciations and terrible threatenings (cf. Deut. xxviii.), and he was not sure how the king would receive the ancient message. He resolved, therefore, not to prejudice its reception by any statements of his own, but simply to make the announcement of the discovery, and leave the book to speak for itself. He begins, accordingly, by stating the fulfilment of his commission in regard to the monies of the temple. Then he showed the book to the king, saying merely, "Hilkiah the priest hath delivered me a book." Critics have detected subtle meanings in the studiously simple way in which this announcement is made; but the above, probably, is the true explanation of it. 2. *The book read.* The king, whose interest was at once awakened, naturally asked to have part of the book read to him. Shaphan began to read, selecting apparently parts towards the close of the roll—Deut. xxviii., xxix., and the like. How much he read we are not informed, but the effect produced was instantaneous and profound. Our aim in reading the Scriptures should be to ascertain from it the whole counsel of God. We must not dwell on the promise to the exclusion of the threatening, or think that any part is without its use "for doctrine, for reproof, for correction," etc. (2 Tim iii. 16). 3. *Conviction by the Word.* "The Spirit of God," say the Westminster Divines, "maketh the reading, but especially the preaching of the Word, an effectual means of convincing and converting sinners." Remarkable revivals of religion have often been produced by the reading of the Word alone. It was so in the case of Josiah. The book of the Law was the only preacher, but, as Shaphan read it aloud, its words went like sharp swords to the heart of the king. He knew previously that the nation had committed great sins, with which God was displeased, and he had done what he could to institute reforms. Now for the first time he learned what direful woes were predicted on those who should commit such sins, and he saw the enormity of the nation's evil as he had never before realized it. In deepest emotion he rent his clothes, and sent at once an honourable deputation "to inquire of the Lord concerning the words of the book" of the Prophetess Huldah. We see: (1) The power of the Word to convince men of sin. This power belongs to the words of Scripture as to those of no other book. "The Law of the Lord is perfect, converting the soul," etc. (Ps. xix. 7). "The Word of God is quick and powerful, and sharper than any two-edged sword," etc. (Heb. iv. 12). The fact that it is so is an evidence of the divineness of Scripture. The power of the Bible is derived from the nature of the truths it declares, from the inspired grandeur of its utterances, from the "thus saith the Lord" which stands behind them and drives them home with authority, and from the inward attestation which its words find in the conscience (2 Cor. iv. 2). Great reformations have always been accompanied with an extended circulation of the Bible (Wickliffe, Tyndale, Luther, etc.). (2) An example of the right reception of the Word. Josiah did not act like the profane Jehoiakim, who, when God's threatenings were read to him, took his penknife and cut the prophet's roll to pieces, casting it into the fire (Jer. xxxvi. 20—24). He trembled at God's Word (Isa. lxvi. 2). He was, like Noah, "moved with fear," when he heard of the dreadful evils God would bring upon the nation. He did not dispute the justice of God's threatenings, but acknowledged that he was righteous, and the people wicked. He included himself in the general condemnation: "Great is the wrath of the Lord that is kindled against *us*, because our fathers have not hearkened," etc. This is how God's Word ought always to be received—with humility, with faith, with trembling of heart at his threatenings, if also with joy and hope at his promises.

III. Light sought on God's Word. 1. *A holy woman.* The king, as above stated, sent "to inquire of the Lord" at the hands of an accredited prophet, with the view of ascertaining what means should be adopted to reverse, if possible, the curse which the sins of long generations had brought upon the nation. The persons sent were five—Hilkiah the priest, Shaphan the scribe, and his son Ahikam, Achbor the son of Michaiah, and Asahiah a servant of the king's,—an honourable deputation. The person to whom they went was a prophetess named Huldah, who dwelt in Jerusalem. This holy woman was no recluse, but the wife of Shallum, the keeper of the royal (or priestly) wardrobe. In the distribution of God's gifts, woman is not less honoured than man. We learn from Huldah that religion and the duties of common life do not stand apart. 2. *The Word confirmed.* On the general question the prophetess had little to give them in the way of comfort. Probably she had already learned the tenor of the threatenings in the sacred book, or its words were now read to her; but she could only speak to give the threatenings emphatic confirmation. "Tell the man that sent you, Thus saith the Lord, Behold, I will bring evil upon this place," etc. The words of the Law would be fulfilled, because the people had committed the sins which the Law denounced: "They have forsaken me, and have burned incense unto other gods," etc. This is not contrary to Jeremiah's word, "If that nation, against whom I have pronounced, turn from their evil, I will repent of the evil that I thought to do unto them" (Jer. xviii. 8; cf. ch. xxvi. 3). It was the knowledge and foresight that Judah would not truly repent which gave the absoluteness to the prophecy. Jeremiah, while exhorting to repentance, also gives expression to the other side of the truth, that the nation's condition is hopeless (Jer. vii. 16; xv. 1, etc.). 3. *Mercy to the king.* To the "man" Huldah had no message of comfort; but to "the King of Judah" she had a word of mercy to send. Because Josiah's heart was tender, and he had humbled himself when he had heard of the desolation and the curse that would come upon the land, therefore God had heard him, and would spare him the experience of the evil that was to come. He would be taken away "from the evil to come" (Isa. lvii. 1). Had the nation as a whole repented in like manner, we cannot doubt that it would have been similarly spared. God never rejects the humble and contrite heart (Isa. lxvi. 2). It is noteworthy that this prediction was fulfilled in a way which externally was a great calamity to the nation, viz. Josiah's defeat and death at Megiddo, in battle with Pharaoh-Nechoh (ch. xxiii. 29, 30). God's mercy veils itself under strange disguises.—J. O.

EXPOSITION.

CHAPTER XXIII.

Vers. 1—37.—JOSIAH'S RENEWAL OF THE COVENANT. HIS REFORMS AND DEATH. REIGN OF JEHOAHAZ. ACCESSION OF JEHOIAKIM.

Vers. 1—3.—*Josiah's renewal of the covenant.* The first care of Josiah, on receiving Huldah's message, which stamped the book found as the true "book of the covenant," was to call together a great assembly of the nation, which should be sufficiently representative of it, and renew the covenant between God and his people made originally at Horeb (Exod. xix. 5—8; xxiv. 3—8), which it was apparent, by the words of the book, that he and his people had broken. His proceedings may be fitly compared with those of Jehoiada, the high priest after the reign of the idolatrous Athaliah, recorded in ch. xi. 17; but they were still more formal and solemn, inasmuch as the recent alienation of the people from Jehovah had been so much more prolonged, and so much more complete, than the alienation under Athaliah.

Ver. 1.—And the king sent, and they gathered unto him all the elders of Judah and of Jerusalem; *i.e.* all the elders of Jerusalem and of the rest of Judah. (On the important position held by "the elders" in the undivided kingdom, see 1 Kings viii. 1, and the comment *ad loc.*; and on their position in the divided kingdoms of Israel and Judah, see 1 Kings xx. 7, 8; xxi. 8, 11; ch. x. 1, etc.)

Ver. 2.—And the king went up into the house of the Lord. No place could be so suitable for the renewal of the covenant between God and his people as the house of God, where God was in a peculiar way present, and the ground was, like the ground at Horeb, holy. Josiah "went up" to the temple from the royal palace, which was on a lower level (comp. 1 Kings x. 5). And all the men of Judah and all the inhabitants of Jerusalem with him. Not only the "elders," who had been summoned, but of the people, as many as chose to attend, besides. The gathering was no doubt great; but the expressions used are (as with the Orientals generally) hyperbolical. And the priests, and the prophets. The representation would have been incomplete without these two classes—the priests, the ordinary and regular readers (Deut. xxxi. 11) and teachers (Deut. xxxiii. 10) of the Law; and the prophets, the extraordinary and occasional teachers, inspired from time to time, and commissioned to enforce the Law, and further to declare God's will to the people. And all the people, both small and great; *i.e.* without distinction of classes—all ranks of the people, high and low, rich and poor, noble and base-born. All were concerned, nay, concerned equally, in a matter which touched the national life and the prospects of each individual. And he read in their ears. There is no reason for translating, with Keil, "he caused to be read in their ears," as though either the Jewish kings could not read, or would be usurping the functions of the priests in publicly reading the Law to the people. If a king might, like Solomon (1 Kings viii. 22—61), lead the prayers of the congregation of Israel in the temple, much more might he read the Law to them. The readers in the Jewish synagogues are ordinarily lay people. All the words of the book of the covenant. Perhaps there is here some exaggeration, as in the phrases, "*all* the men of Judah," and "*all* the inhabitants of Jerusalem." The entire Pentateuch could scarcely be read through in less than ten hours. Possibly, the Book of Deuteronomy was alone read. Which was found in the house of the Lord (see above, ch. xxii. 8).

Ver. 3.—And the king stood by a pillar— הָעַמּוּד עַל is not "by the pillar," but (as in ch. xi. 14) "on the platform" (see the comment on that place)—and made a covenant before the Lord; literally, *made the covenant* (as in ch. xi. 17); *i.e.* made, or renewed, the old covenant with God (Exod. xxiv. 5—8), which had been broken by the complete neglect of the Law, and the manifold idolatries of Manasseh and Amon. He renewed this covenant " before the Lord," *i.e.* from his platform in the court, directly opposite the entrance to the temple, through which he could, perhaps, see the veil hanging in front of the holy of holies—at any rate being, and feeling himself to be, in the immediate presence of God. **To walk after the Lord**—*i.e.* to be his true follower and servant—**and to keep his commandments and his testimonies and his statutes.** (On the multiplication of such terms, see the comment upon 1 Kings ii. 3.) They are intended to express " the totality of the Law," all its requirements without exception. **With all their heart and all their soul**—obedience was worthless, unless paid from the heart and soul (see Deut. iv. 29 ; xxx. 2 ; Joel ii. 12, 13)—**to perform the words of this covenant that were written in this book. And all the people stood to the covenant.** The representatives of the people, one and all, were parties to the promise made on their behalf by the king, and signified their consent, probably as they had done in Horeb, when " Moses took the book of the covenant, and read in the audience of the people ; and they said, All that the Lord has said will we do, and be obedient " (see Deut. xxiv. 7).

Vers. 4—27.—*Josiah's reformation of religion.* The reformation of religion by Josiah next engages the writer's attention, and is treated, not chronologically, but rather geographically, under the three heads of (1) reforms in Jerusalem ; (2) reforms outside Jerusalem, but in the kingdom of Judah ; and (3) reforms in the territory which had belonged to the kingdom of Samaria (vers. 4—20). The celebration of the Passover is then briefly noticed (vers. 21—23) ; and the section concludes with a eulogy of Josiah (vers. 24, 25), who, however, it is noticed could not, with all his piety, obtain a revocation of the sentence passed on Judah in consequence of the sins of Manasseh. The fate of Judah was fixed (vers. 26, 27).

Ver. 4.—**And the king commanded Hilkiah the high priest, and the priests of the second order.** Not the " deputy-high priests," of whom there seems to have been only one at this period of the history (ch. xxv. 18); nor the " heads of the courses," who were not recognized as a distinct class of priests till much later ; but merely the common priests, as distinguished from the high priest. (So Keil, Bähr, and others.) **And the keepers of the door** ; literally, *the keepers of the threshold ;* i.e. the Levites, whose duty it was to keep watch and ward at the outer temple

gates (see 1 Chron. xxvi. 13—18). Their importance at this time appears again in ch. xxv. 18. **To bring forth out of the temple of the Lord all the vessels that were made for Baal.** The reformation naturally began with the purging of the temple. So the reformation under Jehoiada (ch. xi. 18) and that of Manasseh (2 Chron. xxxiii. 15). Under " the vessels " (הַכֵּלִים) would be included the entire paraphernalia of worship, even the two altars which had been set up in honour of Baal in the outer and the inner courts (comp. ch. xxi. 5). **And for the grove** (see ch. xxi. 3), **and for all the host of heaven.** The three worships are here united, because there was a close connection between them. Baal was, in one of his aspects, the sun ; and Astarte, the goddess of the " grove "-worship, was, in one of her aspects, the moon. The cult of " the host of heaven," though, perhaps, derived from a different source, naturally became associated with the cults of the sun and moon. **And he burned them without Jerusalem in the fields of Kidron.** The Law required that idols should be burnt with fire (Deut. vii. 25), and likewise " groves " (Deut. xii. 3). It was enough to " overthrow " altars (Deut. xii. 3) and to " break " pillars. But Josiah seems to have thought it best to destroy by fire, *i.e.* in the completest possible way, all the objects, of whatever kind, which had been connected with the idol-worship (see vers. 6, 12, 15, 16). The burning took place in " the fields of Kidron," *i.e.* in the upper part of the Kidron valley, to the north-east of Jerusalem, in order that not even the smoke should pollute the town (comp. 1 Kings xv. 13). **And carried the ashes of them unto Bethel.** This was a very unusual precaution, and shows Josiah's extreme scrupulousness. He would not have even the ashes of the wooden objects, or the calcined powder of the metal ones, remain even in the vicinity of the holy city, but transported them to a distance. In selecting Bethel as the place to convey them to, he was no doubt actuated by the circumstance that that village was in some sense the fount and origin of all the religious impurities which had overflowed the land. That which had proceeded from Bethel might well be taken back thither.

Ver. 5.—**And he put down the idolatrous priests** ; literally, *the chemarim.* The same word is used of idolatrous priests in Hos. x. 5 and Zeph. i. 4. It is best connected with the Arabic root *chamar, colere deum,* and with the Syriac *cumro,* " priest " or " sacrificer." The Syrian priests were probably so called at the time, and the Hebrews took the word, and applied it to all false priests or idolatrous priests, reserving their own *cohanim* (כֹּהֲנִים) for true Jehovistic priests only. **Whom the kings of Judah** had ordained to burn incense in the high places in the cities of Judah, and in the places round about Jerusalem. This practice had not been mentioned previously, and can scarcely have belonged to the earlier kingdom of Judah, when "the *people*" (as we are told so often) "worshipped and burnt incense in the high places." But it is quite in harmony with the other doings of Manasseh and Amon, that, when they re-established the high places (ch. xxi. 3, 21), they should have followed the custom of the Israelite monarchs at Dan and Bethel (1 Kings xii. 28—32), and have "ordained priests" to conduct the worship at them. **Them also that burned incense unto Baal, to the sun, and to the moon** (on the Baal-worship of Manasseh and Amon, see ch. xxi. 3; on the sun-worship, compare below, ver. 11; the moon-worship was probably a form of the worship of Astarte), **and to the planets;** rather, *to the twelve signs*. The constellations or signs of the zodiac are, no doubt, intended (comp. Job xxxviii. 32, where the term מַזָּרוֹת may be regarded as a mere variant form of the מַזָּלוֹת of this passage). The proper meaning of the term is "mansions," or "houses," the zodiacal signs being regarded as the "mansions of the sun" by the Babylonians (see 'Ancient Monarchies,' vol. iii. p. 419). **And to all the host of heaven** (see the comment on ch. xxi. 3).

Ver. 6.—**And he brought out the grove from the house of the Lord.** The Asherah set up by Manasseh (ch. xxi. 3 and 7), and if removed (2 Chron. xxxiii. 15), then replaced by Amon (2 Chron. xxxiii. 22), is intended. (On its probable form, see the comment upon ch. xxi. 7.) **Without Jerusalem, unto the brook Kidron** (see the comment on ver. 4), **and burned it at the brook Kidron.** After the example of Asa, who had treated in the same way the idol of the queen-mother Maachah (1 Kings xv. 13). Asa followed the example of Moses (Exod. xxxii. 20), when he destroyed the golden calf. **And stamped it small to powder.** Metals may be calcined by intense heat, and reduced into a state in which a very small application of force will crush them into a fine powder. It is clear from the present passage, that Manasseh's Asherah was made of metal, at any rate in part. **And cast the powder thereof upon the graves of the children of the people;** *i.e.* "upon the graves of the common people" (comp. Jer. xxvi. 23, where the expression used in the Hebrew is the same). The common people were not buried, like the better sort, in rock-hewn sepulchres, but in graves of the ordinary description. Burial-places were regarded as unclean, and were thus fit receptacles for any kind of impurity. Ver. 7.—**And he brake down the houses of the sodomites;** literally, *of the con-*

secrated ones. (See the comment on 1 Kings xiv. 24; and note that the male prostitutes, or Galli, who consecrated themselves to the Dea Syra, formed an essential element in the Astarte-worship, and accompanied it wherever it was introduced.) Döllinger says ('Jew and Gentile,' vol. i. pp. 430, 431) of these wretched persons, "To the exciting din of drums, flutes, and inspired songs, the Galli cut themselves on the arms; and the effect of this act, and of the music accompanying it, was so strong upon mere spectators, that all their bodily and mental powers were thrown into a tumult of excitement, and they too, seized by the desire to lacerate themselves, deprived themselves of their manhood by means of potsherds lying ready for the purpose. Thereupon they ran with the mutilated part through the city, and received from the houses which they threw them into, a woman's gear. Not chastity, but barrenness, was intended by the mutilation. In this the Galli only desired to be like their goddess. The relation of foul lust, which they thenceforward occupied towards women, was regarded as a holy thing, and was tolerated by husbands in their wives." **That were by the house of the Lord.** The near vicinity is an indication that the Galli took part in the foreign rites introduced into the temple by Manasseh and Amon. The awful profanation of the house of God by such orgies is too terrible to dwell on. **Where the women wove hangings for the grove.** "The women" are no doubt the priestesses of the Dea Syra, who are constantly mentioned with the Galli, and, indeed, lived with them. They employed themselves, among other occupations, in weaving "hangings" (literally, "houses," *i.e.* "coverings") for the Asherah. It may be gathered from Ezek. xvi. 16 that these "coverings" were dainty fabrics of many colours.

Ver. 8.—**And he brought all the priests out of the cities of Judah.** Here the writer diverges from his proper subject—the reforms in and near Jerusalem—to speak of changes which were made in other parts of Judæa. The Levitical priests, who in various cities of Judah had conducted the worship at the high places, were summoned to Jerusalem by Josiah, and forced to remain there, that the unauthorized worship which they had conducted might be brought to an end. **And defiled the high places where the priests had burned incense.** Hezekiah had "removed the high places, and broken the images, and cut down the groves" throughout his dominions (ch. xviii. 4), but he had not in any way "defiled the high places;" and therefore no sooner did a king take a different view of his duties than the worship was at once restored (ch. xxi. 3), and flourished as before. Josiah conceived the idea that, if the high places were "defiled," it would be impossible to renew the worship at them. **From Geba to Beersheba.** Geba takes here the place of Bethel as the northern limit of Judah. It was situated at a very short distance from Bethel, and was made to supersede it on account of the idolatries by which Bethel had been disgraced. The exact site is probably the modern *Jeba*, on the southern edge of the Wady Suweinit. **And brake down the high places of the gates.** The high-place worship had, it would seem, invaded Jerusalem itself. In some of the gates of the city, which were "large open buildings for public meetings and intercourse" (Bähr), altars, or more elaborate places of worship, had been established, and an unauthorized ritual of the high-place type had been set up. **That were** —rather, *that which was*—**in the entering in of the gate of Joshua the governor of the city.** This and the succeeding clauses are limitations of the general statement concerning the "high places of the gates," and indicate that two gates only had been polluted by high-place worship, viz. "the gate of Joshua," and the gate known κατ' ἐξοχὴν as "the city gate." Neither of these can be determinately fixed, since they are only mentioned in the present passage. **Which** were **on a man's left hand at the gate of the city**; rather, *and also that which was on the left-hand side in the gate of the city.* (So Thenius, Keil, and Bähr.)

Ver. 9.—**Nevertheless the priests of the high places came not up to the altar of the Lord in Jerusalem.** Though Josiah recalled to Jerusalem the Levitical priests who had recently been attached to the various high places, yet he did not attach them to the temple, or assign them any part in its services. Their participation in a semi-idolatrous service had disqualified them for the temple ministrations. **But they did eat of the unleavened bread among their brethren.** They were allowed, *i.e.*, their maintenance out of the priestly revenues, as were priests disqualified by a personal blemish (Lev. xxi. 21, 22). Practically they lived on the altar gifts intended for the priests (Lev. vi. 9, 10, 22), in which it was unlawful to mix leaven.

Ver. 10.—**And he defiled Topheth.** "Topheth" or "Tophet" was the name given to the place in the valley of Hinnom where the sacrifices were offered to Moloch. The root of the word is thought by some to be *taph* (קֹף), "a drum," because the cries of the children burnt there were drowned by the beating of drums. Others suggest as the root, *tuph* (קוּף), "to spit," because the place was "spat at" by the orthodox. But Gesenius and Böttcher derive it from an

Aryan root, *taph*, or *tap*, "to burn," whence Greek θάπτειν, τέφρα, Latin *tepidus*, Mod. Persian *tâftan*, Sanskrit *tap*, etc., and regard the meaning as simply "the place of burning" (see the comment on Isa. xxx. 33). **Which is in the valley of the children of Hinnom.** The valley of Hinnom, or of the sons of Hinnom, is generally allowed to be that which sweeps round the more western of the two hills whereon Jerusalem was built, in a direction at first south and then east, uniting itself with the Kidron valley a little to the south of Ophel. The origin of the name is uncertain; but it is most likely that the Beni-Hinnom were a tribe of Canaanites, settled on this side of Jerusalem in the time of Joshua (Josh. xv. 8). The "valley" is a ravine, deep and narrow, with steep, rocky sides. When the Moloch-worship first began in it we cannot say; but it was probably before the time of Solomon, who built a high place for Moloch (1 Kings xi. 11), on one of the heights by which the valley is enclosed. (On the horrible profanations of the Moloch-worship, see Jer. vii. 31, 32; xix. 4—13; xxxii. 35.) After the Captivity, the valley of Hinnom—Ge-Hinnom—was reckoned an accursed and abominable place, a sort of earthly counterpart of the place of final punishment, which, thence derived its name of "Gehenna" (Γέεννα); (see Matt. v. 22, 29, etc.). **That no man might make his son or his daughter to pass through the fire to Moloch** (see the comment on ch. xvi. 3).

Ver. 11.—**And he took away the horses that the kings of Judah had given to the sun.** The custom of dedicating horses to the sun was practised by many ancient nations; but it is only in Persia that we find horses *and chariots* so dedicated (Xen., 'Cyrop.,' viii. 3. § 12). The idea of the sun-god as a charioteer, who drove his horses daily across the sky, is one common to several of the Aryan nations, as the Greeks, the Romans, the Hindoos, and others; but we do not find it either in Egypt or among the Semitic peoples. The sacrifice of the horse to the sun was more general (Herod., i. 216; Xen., 'Cyrop.,' viii. 3. § 24; 'Anab.,' iv. 5. § 35; Rig Veda, vol. ii. pp. 112, *et seqq.*, etc.), but does not seem to have been adopted by the Hebrews. It is not at all clear whence the "kings of Judah"—*i.e.* Ahaz, Manasseh, and Amon—derived the idea of maintaining sacred chariots and horses to be used in their sun-worship. They certainly could not have received it, as Keil thinks, "through the Assyrians." **At the entering in of the house of the Lord**—the horses, *i.e.*, were kept near one of the entrances to the temple, to be ready for use in sacred processions —**by the chamber of Nathan-melech the**

chamberlain, **which was in the suburbs.**
There were many "chambers" attached to
the temple, which were sometimes used as
store-rooms for different materials (1 Chron.
ix. 26; 2 Chron. xxxi. 11, 12; Neh. x. 38;
xiii. 5), sometimes as residences (Neh. xiii.
7). In Josiah's time, "Nathan-melech the
chamberlain," or rather "the *eunuch*," occupied one of these. It was situated בַּפַּרְוָרִים
—"in the outskirts" or "purlieus" of the
temple. **And burned the chariots of the
sun with fire** (comp. vers. 4, 6, 15, etc.).
Josiah burnt all the material objects that
had been desecrated by the idolatries; the
persons and animals so desecrated he "removed," or deprived of their functions.

Ver. 12.—**And the altars that were on the
top of the upper chamber of Ahaz.** It would
seem that "the upper chamber of Ahaz"
was within the temple precincts, since the
pollutions spoken of, both before and after,
are pollutions belonging to the temple. It
may have been erected on the flat roof of
one of the gates, or on the top of a store-
chamber. Altars upon roofs were a new
form of idolatry, apparently connected with
the worship of the "host of heaven" (see
Jer. xix. 13; Zeph. i. 5). **Which the kings
of Judah**—*i.e.* Manasseh and Amon, perhaps
also Ahaz—**had made, and the altars which
Manasseh had made in the two courts of the
house of the Lord** (see above, ch. xxi. 4, 5).
As Manasseh, on his repentance, merely
"cast these altars out of the city" (2 Chron.
xxxiii. 15), it was easy for Amon to replace
them. They belonged to the worship of
the "host of heaven." **Did the king beat
down, and brake them down from thence,
and cast the dust of them into the brook
Kidron** (comp. ver. 6, and the comment
ad loc.).

Ver. 13.—**And the high places that were
before Jerusalem.** The high places which
Solomon established in the neighbourhood
of Jerusalem for the use of his wives, and
in the worship at which he became himself
entangled in his old age, appear to have
been situated on the ridge of the mountain
which lies over against Jerusalem to the
east, a part of which is Olivet. The southern
summit, the traditional *mons offensionis*,
was probably the high place of Moloch
(Milcom), while the most northern summit
(now called *Karem-es-Seyad*) has some
claim to be regarded as the high place of
Chemosh. (So Brocardus in A.D. 1280.)
The site of the high place of Ashtoreth is
doubtful. **Which were on the right hand
of the mount of corruption.** The name
"mount of corruption" seems to have been
given after Solomon's time to the entire
ridge of hills which lies over against
Jerusalem to the east, on account of the
rites which he had allowed to be estab-

lished on it. The "right hand" of the
mountain would, according to Jewish notions, be the more southern part. **Which
Solomon the King of Israel**—rather, *King
of Israel*, since there is no article—**had
builded for Ashtoreth the abomination of
the Zidonians** (see 1 Kings xi. 7). Though
Ashtoreth, or Astarte, or Ishtar, or the Dea
Syra, was worshipped generally throughout
Phœnicia, and perhaps even more widely,
yet she was in a peculiar way "the abomination of the Zidonians," being the deity
to whom the city of Sidon was especially
dedicated (see the inscription on the tomb
of Eshmunazar, published in the 'Records
of the Past,' vol. ix. pp. 113, 114). **And for
Chemosh the abomination of the Moabites.**
Chemosh appears as the special god of the
Moabites on the famous Moabite Stone
in eleven places. The stone itself was
dedicated to Chemosh (line 3). The Moabites
are spoken of as "the people of Chemosh"
(lines 5, 6). Success in war comes from
him, and defeat is the result of his anger.
One of his designations is "Ashtar-Chemosh"
(line 17), or "Chemosh, who is also Ashtar,"
Ashtar being the male principle corresponding to the female Astarte or Ashtoreth.
And for Milcom. Moloch was called by the
Jews "Milcom," or "Malcam" "their
king"—*i.e.* the king of the Ammonite
people, since he was the sole god whom
they acknowledged (see 1 Kings xi. 5;
Jer. xlix. 3 compared with Jer. xlviii. 7;
Amos i. 15; Zeph. i. 5). **The abomination
of the children of Ammon** (see 1 Kings
xi. 5, 7; and compare the comment on
1 Kings in the 'Pulpit Commentary,' p.
222). **Did the king defile.** The manner of
the defilement is stated in the next verse.

Ver. 14.—**And he brake in pieces the
images** — or, *pillars* (see the comment on
1 Kings xiv. 23)—**and cut down the groves—**
i.e. the *asherim*, or "sacred trees"—**and filled
their places with the bones of men.** Whatever spoke of death and dissolution was a
special defilement to shrines where the gods
worshipped were deities of productivity and
generation. Bones of men had also the
actual taint of corruption about them. The
"uncleanness" of dead bodies arose first out
of man's natural shrinking from death, and
was then further confirmed by the horrors
accompanying decay. The notion was probably coeval with death itself. It received
a sanction from the Law, which made it a
legal defilement to touch a corpse (Numb.
xix. 11, 16), and placed under a sentence of
uncleanness all that was in the tent where
a man died (Numb. xix. 14, 15).

Ver. 15.—**Moreover the altar that was at
Bethel, and the high place**; rather, *the altar
that was at Bethel, the high place*, without any
"and." הַבָּמָה is in apposition with הַמִּזְבֵּחַ.

By setting up an altar at Bethel, Jeroboam constituted Bethel a "high place." **Which Jeroboam the son of Nebat, who made Israel to sin, had made** (comp. 1 Kings xii. 33; xiii. 2), **both that altar and the high place he brake down.** "The high place" is *here* equivalent to the "house of high places" in 1 Kings xii. 31, and designates "the buildings of this sanctuary" (Keil). At such a national centre as Bethel a temple would, of course, accompany the altar. Whether the temple and altar were in use or not at the time when Josiah destroyed them, is uncertain. The mixed race which had superseded the Israelites in the country (ch. xvii. 24—41) may have continued the worship, or may have set it aside. **And burned the high place, and stamped** it **small to powder.** It is not clear that this latter clause applies to the high place. Perhaps we should translate—*And stamped small to powder,* **and burned, the grove.** It is for the most part only comparatively small objects that are "stamped small to powder" (see vers. 6, 12, and comp. 2 Chron. xv. 21).

Ver. 16.—**And as Josiah turned himself, he spied the sepulchres that were there in the mount.** The Israelite sepulchres, excavated in the rocky sides of hills, are everywhere conspicuous. Those of Bethel may have been in the low hill on which the town stands, or in the sides of the Wady Suweinit, a little further to the south. His *accidentally* "spying the sepulchres" gave Josiah the thought of completing his desecration of Bethel by having bones brought from them and burnt upon the altar—whereby he exactly accomplished the old prophecy (1 Kings xiii. 2), which was not at all in his mind. **And sent, and took the bones out of the sepulchres, and burned** them upon the altar, **and polluted it** (see the comment on ver. 14), **according to the word of the Lord which the man of God proclaimed, who proclaimed these words ;** rather, *who prophesied these things.* The reference is to 1 Kings xiii. 2, and the meaning is, not that Josiah acted as he did in order to fulfil the prophecy, but that in thus acting he unconsciously fulfilled it.

Ver. 17.—**Then he said, What title is that that I see ?** rather, *What pillar is that that I see?* Josiah's eye caught sight of a "pillar" or obelisk (צִיּוּן) among the tombs, or in their neighbourhood, and he had the curiosity to ask what it was. **And the men of the city told him, It is the sepulchre of the man of God, which came from Judah** (see 1 Kings xiii. 1). The "pillar" could not have been the actual "sepulchre," but was no doubt a monument connected with it. Many of the Phœnician excavated tombs are accompanied by monuments above

ground, which are very conspicuous (see Renan's 'Mission de Phénicie,' pls. xi., *et seqq.*). **And proclaimed these things that thou hast done against the altar of Bethel** (see 1 Kings xiii. 2). According to the present text of Kings, Josiah was prophesied of *by name,* as the king who would defile the altar; but it is possible that the words, "Josiah by name" (יֹאשִׁיָּהוּ שְׁמוֹ), have crept in from the margin.

Ver. 18.—**And he said, Let him alone ; let no man move his bones.** Josiah remembered the circumstances when they were recalled to him, and, in order to show honour to the "man of God" (1 Kings xiii., *passim*), commanded that his tomb should be undisturbed. **So they let his bones alone, with the bones of the prophet that came out of Samaria ;** *i.e.* with the bones of the Israelite prophet, who had taken care to be buried with him. The reference is to 1 Kings xiii. 31.

Ver. 19.—**And all the houses also of the high places that were in the cities of Samaria.** The writer of Chronicles enters into more detail. Josiah, he says, carried out his destruction of the high places, the groves, and the images "in the cities of Manasseh, and Ephraim, and Simeon, even unto Naphtali" (2 Chron. xxxiv. 6)—*i.e.* to the northern limit of the Holy Land, which was occupied by Naphtali and Asher. By what right Josiah exercised sovereign authority in the old kingdom of Samaria, which the Assyrians had conquered and attached to their empire, can only be conjectured. Some have supposed that the Assyrians had enlarged his sovereignty, and placed Samaria under his rule; others regard him as having transferred his allegiance to Nabopolassar, and having been made by him viceroy over Palestine. But it is, perhaps, most probable that he merely took advantage of the political commotions of the time to extend his dominion so far as it seemed safe to do so. Asshur-bani-pal, the last energetic King of Assyria, appears to have ceased to reign in Josiah's fourteenth year, when he was succeeded by a weak monarch, Asshur-ebil-ili. Great troubles now broke out. The Scythians ravaged Western Asia far and wide. Assyria was attacked by the Medes and Babylonians in combination. Under these circumstances, Josiah found himself practically independent, and began to entertain ambitious projects. He "extended his dominion from Jerusalem over Samaria" (Ewald). Assyria was too much occupied to take any notice. Babylonia was in the thick of the struggle. Josiah found himself able to reunite under his own headship all the scattered portions of the old Israelite kingdom, except, perhaps, the trans-Jordanic district. He levied taxes in Samaria as freely as in Judæa (2 Chron. xxxiii. 9). He reformed on the same model the religions of both countries. When finally he had to fight for his throne, he marched his army into the northern portion of Samaria, and there fought the battle which cost him his life. **Which the kings of Israel had made to provoke the Lord to anger.** The earlier kings of Israel had simply allowed the "high places" to continue, without actively increasing or multiplying them; but Manasseh had re-established them after their destruction by Hezekiah (ch. xxi. 3), and Amon had probably done the same after Manasseh's tardy reformation. **Josiah took away, and did to them according to all the acts that he had done in Bethel** (see above, ver. 15).

Ver. 20.—**And he slew all the priests of the high places that were there upon the altars.** It is not directly said that he had done this at Bethel, though it had been prophesied that he would do so (1 Kings xiii. 2). Possibly there were no priests at Bethel at the time, since the "calf" set up by Jeroboam had been carried off (Hos. x. 6) by the Assyrians. The difference between the treatment of the high-place priests in Israel and in Judah (ver. 9) clearly implies that the former were attached to the worship of false gods, while the latter were priests of Jehovah who worshipped him with superstitious and unauthorized rites and ceremonies. **And burned men's bones upon them** (comp. ver. 16), **and returned to Jerusalem.**

Ver. 21.—**And the king commanded all the people, saying, Keep the Passover.** The account given of Josiah's Passover is much more full in Chronicles than in Kings. In Chronicles it occupies nineteen verses of 2 Chron. xxxv. We learn from Chronicles that all the rites prescribed by the Law, whether in Exodus, Leviticus, or Deuteronomy, were duly observed, and that the festival was attended, not only by the Judæans, but by many Israelites from among the ten tribes, who still remained intermixed with the Assyrian colonists in the Samaritan country (see 2 Chron. xxxv. 17, 18). **Unto the Lord your God, as it is written in the book of this covenant.** The ordinances for the due observance of the Passover feast are contained chiefly in Exodus (xii. 3—20; xiii. 5—10). They are repeated, but with much less fulness, in Deut. xvi. 1—8. The "book of the covenant" found by Hilkiah must, therefore, certainly have contained Exodus (see below, ver. 25).

Ver. 22.—**Surely there was not holden such a Passover from the days of the judges that judged Israel, nor in all the days of the kings of Israel, nor of the kings of** Judah. *Such* a Passover, one so numerously attended (2 Chron. xxxv. 18), and so exactly kept according to every ordinance of the Law of Moses (2 Chron. xxxv. 6), had not been celebrated during all the period of the judges, from Joshua to Samuel, nor under the kings of all Israel, Saul, David, and Solomon, nor under those of the separated kingdom of Judah, from Rehoboam to this year (the eighteenth) of Josiah. It is an extraordinary perversity which concludes (as do De Wette and Thenius), from this comparison of the present with former Passovers under the judges and the kings, that there had been no such former Passovers at all! Two, at any rate, are recorded (Josh. v. 10, 11; 2 Chron. xxx. 13—26). Ewald has the good sense to express his dissent from this view, and to declare the meaning of the writer to be simply that "since the time of the judges there had never been such a celebration of the Passover, in such strict accordance, that is, with the prescriptions of a sacred book as that which now took place" (see his ' History of Israel,' vol. iv. p. 239, Eng. trans.).

Ver. 23.—**But in the eighteenth year of King Josiah,** wherein this Passover was **holden to the Lord in Jerusalem** (compare, on the date, ch. xxii. 3 and 2 Chron. xxxv. 19). The eighteenth year of Josiah corresponded probably, in part to B.C. 622, in part to B.C. 621.

Ver. 24.—**Moreover the workers with familiar spirits, and the wizards.** Persons of these classes had been encouraged by Manasseh, in his earlier reign (ch. xxi. 6), and probably by Amon (ch. xxi. 21). As Josiah designed a thorough reformation, it was necessary for him to put them down. **And the images;** literally, *the teraphim,* which are thought to have been small images kept as household gods in many Israelite families from a very ancient date (see Gen. xxxi. 19—35). The superstition was exceedingly persistent. We find it under the judges (Judg. xviii. 14), under Saul (1 Sam. xix. 13), here under the later kings, and it is still mentioned after the return from the Captivity (Zech. x. 2). The superstition was, apparently, Babylonian (Ezek. xxi. 21), and brought from Ur of the Chaldees by the family of Abraham. Besides being regarded as household gods, the teraphim were used in divination. **And the idols, and all the abominations that were spied.** The "idols," *gillulim,* are probably, like the teraphim, of a private nature, figures used as amulets or talismans. Excepting in Ezekiel, the word is an uncommon one. By the "abominations that were spied" are meant secret defilements and superstitious practices in households, which needed to be searched out. (So Thenius and Bähr.)

In the land of Judah and in Jerusalem. Not, apparently, in the cities of Samaria, where such a rigid inquisition would perhaps have provoked a stubborn resistance. Did Josiah put away, that he might perform the words of the Law ; rather, *that he might establish the words of the Law.* Laws against such practices as Josiah now put down will be found in Exod. xxii. 18; Lev. xix. 31; xx. 27; Deut. xviii. 10—12. Which were written in the book that Hilkiah the priest found in the house of the Lord (see ch. xxii. 8).

Ver. 25.—And like unto him was there no king before him (see the comment on ch. xviii. 5). The writer of Kings cannot be said to place Josiah above Hezekiah, or Hezekiah above Josiah. He accords them the same degree of praise, but, in Hezekiah's case, dwells upon his trust in God; in Josiah's, upon his exact obedience to the Law. On the whole, his judgment accords very closely with that of the son of Sirach (Ecclus. xlix. 4). " All, except David and Ezekias and Josias, were defective: for they forsook the Law of the Most High." That turned to the Lord with all his heart, and with all his soul, and with all his might. This triple enumeration is intended to include the whole moral and mental nature of man, all the energies of his understanding, his will, and his physical vitality (see the comment on Deut. vi. 5—a passage which is in the writer's mind). According to all the Law of Moses. This is an indication that, in the writer's view, the *whole* Law was contained in the book found by Hilkiah. Neither after him arose there any like him. This is but moderate praise, since the four kings who reigned after him—Jehoahaz, Jehoiakim, Jehoiachin, and Zedekiah — were, one and all, wicked princes.

Ver. 26. — Notwithstanding the Lord turned not from the fierceness of his great wrath. It was too late, not for God to forgive upon repentance, but for the nation to repent sincerely and heartily. Sin had become engrained in the national character. Vain were the warnings of Jeremiah, vain were his exhortations to repentance (iii. 12 —14, 22; iv. 1—8; vii. 3—7, etc.), vain his promises that, if they would turn to God, they would be forgiven and spared. Thirty years of irreligion and idolatry under Manasseh had sapped the national vigour, and made true repentance an impossibility. How weak and half-hearted must have been the return to God towards the close of Manasseh's reign, that it should have had no strength to resist Amon, a youth of twenty-two, but should have disappeared wholly on his accession ! And how far from sincere must have been the present conformity to the wishes of Josiah, the professed renewal

of the covenant (ver. 3), and revival of disused ceremonies (vers. 21—23)! Jeremiah searched in vain through the streets of Jerusalem to find a man that executed judgment, or sought the truth (Jer. v. 1). The people had " a revolting and rebellious heart; they were revolted and gone " (Jer. v. 23). Not only idolatry, but profligacy (Jer. v. 8) and injustice and oppression everywhere prevailed (Jer. v. 25—28). " From the least to the greatest of them, every one was given to covetousness " (Jer. vi. 13); even the prophets and the priests " dealt falsely " (Jer. vi. 13). The state of things was one which necessarily brought down the Divine judgment, and all that Josiah's efforts could do was a little to delay it. Wherewith his anger was kindled against Judah, because of all the provocations that Manasseh had provoked him withal. Manasseh's provocations lived in their consequences. God's judgment upon Israel was not mere vengeance for the sins that Manasseh had committed, or even for the multitudinous iniquities into which he had led the nation (ch. xxi. 9). It was punishment rendered necessary by the actual condition of the nation—the condition whereto it had been reduced by Manasseh's evil doings.

Ver. 27.—And the Lord said—God said in his secret counsels, came to the determination, and pronounced the sentence in his thoughts—I will remove Judah also out of my sight, as I have removed Israel (comp. ch. xvii. 18, "Therefore the Lord was very angry with Israel, and *removed them out of his sight*"). The sins of Judah were now as great as those of Israel had been ; therefore her punishment must be the same, as God is no respecter of persons. And I will cast off this city Jerusalem which I have chosen (comp. 1 Kings viii. 44, 48; xi. 13, 32, 36, etc.). God "chose " Jerusalem when he put it into the heart of David to bring up the ark thither (2 Sam. vi. 1—17). And the house of which I said, My Name shall be there (see Deut. xii. 11; 1 Kings viii. 29, etc.). A visible confirmation was given to all that David and Solomon had done in establishing the temple at Jerusalem as the head-quarters of the national religion, when " fire came down from heaven, and consumed the burnt offering and the sacrifices " made there, and " the glory of the Lord filled the house " (2 Chron. vii. 1; comp. 2 Chron. v. 13, 14).

Vers. 28—30.—The events of Josiah's reign from his eighteenth to his thirty-first year are left a blank, both here and in Chronicles. Politically, the time was a stirring one. The great invasion of Western Asia by the Scythic hordes (Herod., i. 103

—106), which is alluded to by Jeremiah (vi. 1—5), Ezekiel (xxxviii., xxxix.), and perhaps by Zephaniah (ii. 6), probably belongs to it; as also the attack of Psamatik I. upon Philistia (Herod., ii. 105), the fall of the Assyrian empire (circ. B.C. 617), and the destruction of Nineveh; the establishment of the independence of Babylon, and her rise to greatness; together with the transfer of power in the central part of Western Asia, from the Assyrians to the Medes. Amid the dangers which beset him, Josiah appears to have conducted himself prudently, gradually extending his power over Samaria and Galilee, without coming into hostile collision with any of the neighbouring nations, until about the year B.C. 609 or 608, when his land was invaded by Pharaoh-Nechoh, the Neku of the Egyptian monuments. Josiah felt himself called upon to resist this invasion, and, in doing so, met his death (vers. 29, 30).

Ver. 28.—**Now the rest of the acts of Josiah, and all that he did.** Josiah was reckoned a good rather than a great king. No mention is made of his "might." The writer of Chronicles (2 Chron. xxxv. 26) commemorates his "kindnesses" or "his good deeds." The son of Sirach speaks of his "upright" behaviour (Ecclus. xlix. 2). Josephus ('Ant. Jud.,' x. 4. § 1) praises his "justice" and his "piety," and says (ibid., x. 4. § 5) his later years were passed "in peace and opulence." Are **they not written in the book of the chronicles of the kings of Judah?** (see 2 Chron. xxxv. 27).

Ver. 29.—**In his days Pharaoh-Nechoh King of Egypt went up against the King of Assyria.** Neku, the "Pharaoh-Nechoh" of this passage, and the Necôs of Herodotus (ii. 158, 159), was the son of Psamatik I., and succeeded his father on the throne of Egypt, probably in B.C. 610. He was one of the most enterprising of the later Egyptian kings, and appears to have made this expedition in his second or third year. The unsettled condition of Western Asia after the Scythic invasion, and the fall of the Assyrian empire, seemed to give an opportunity for Egypt to reclaim her old dominion over Syria and Mesopotamia. The "King of Assyria," against whom Pharaoh-Nechoh "went up," was probably Nabopolassar, the father of Nebuchadnezzar. His proper title was "King of Babylon," which is what Nebuchadnezzar always calls him ('Records of the Past,' vol. v. p. 113, line 22; vol. vii. p. 71, line 6; p. 75, line 9); but the Jews not unnaturally regarded him as the inheritor of the Assyrian empire, as indeed they regarded the Persian monarchs also (Ezra vi. 22), and therefore gave him the title of "King of Assyria." **To the river Euphrates.** The author of Chronicles says that "Necho King of Egypt came up to fight against Carchemish" (or "at Carchemish") "by Euphrates," which shows that his design was to penetrate into Northern Syria, where Carchemish (now *Jerabus*) was situated, with a view probably of crossing the Euphrates by the ford at Bir, or by that at Balis, into Mesopotamia. **And King Josiah went against him.** It is possible that Josiah had accepted the position of Babylonian tributary after the fall of the Assyrian kingdom, and thought himself bound to resist an attack upon his suzerain. Or he may simply have resented the violation of his territory, without his permission, by a foreign army. Certainly, if he had allowed the free passage of the Egyptian troops, backwards and forwards, through his country, he would in a short time have lost even the shadow of independence. Nechoh's assurance that his expedition was not against him (Josiah), but against the Assyrians (2 Chron. xxxv. 21), was not a thing to be relied upon, any more than his declaration that God had commanded his expedition. **And he slew him at Megiddo, when he had seen him.** Megiddo is, beyond all doubt, the present *El-Ledjun* on the northern outskirt of the range of hills which separates the Plain of Esdraelon from that of Sharon. It is certainly surprising to find that Josiah had taken up a position so far to the north, leaving Jerusalem, and, indeed, all Judæa, unprotected. But he may have thought the advantages of the position such as to compensate for any risk to the Judæan cities, in which he would, of course, have left garrisons. Or, possibly, as Keil and Bähr suppose, Nechoh may have conveyed his troops to the Syrian coast by sea, and have landed in the Bay of Acre, close to the Plain of Esdraelon. In this case Josiah would have no choice, but, if he opposed the Egyptian monarch at all, must have met him where he did, in the Esdraelon plain, as he entered it from the Plain of Acre.

Ver. 30.—**And his servants carried him in a chariot**—his "second chariot," according to the writer of Chronicles (2 Chron. xxxv. 24), which was probably one kept in reserve in case flight should be necessary, of lighter construction, and drawn by fleeter horses, than his war-chariot—**dead from Megiddo.** Wounded to death, that is. From Chronicles we gather that his wound, which was from an arrow, was not immediately fatal (2 Chron. xxxv. 23, 24); but that he died of it on his way to Jerusalem, or directly after his arrival. **And brought him to Jerusalem, and buried him in his own sepulchre** (comp. ch. xxi. 18 and 26). The writer of Chronicles says, "in the sepulchre of his fathers," apparently meaning the burial-place in which were interred the bodies of Manasseh and Amon. We learn from Chronicles that a great lamentation was made for Josiah, the only King of Judah slain in battle, the last good king of David's line, the pious prince whose piety had not sufficed to avert the anger of Jehovah. Jeremiah "lamented for him" (2 Chron. xxxv. 25), perhaps in a set composition (Josephus, 'Ant. Jud.,' x. 5. § 1); though that composition is certainly not either the Book of Lamentations or the fourth chapter of that book. He was further mourned by "all the singing men and the singing women" (2 Chron., l. s. c.), who "spake of him in their lamentations," and "made them an ordinance in Israel," and entered these "lamentations," apparently in a book, which was called 'The Book of Lamentations,' or 'of Dirges.' **And the people of the land took Jehoahaz the son of Josiah.** Jehoahaz was otherwise named "Shallum" (1 Chron. iii. 15; Jer. xxii. 11). On what grounds the people preferred him to his elder brother, Eliakim, we do not know. Perhaps Eliakim had accompanied his father to Megiddo, and been made prisoner by Nechoh in the battle. **And anointed him** (see the comment on 1 Kings i. 34, and *supra*, ch. xi. 12), **and made him king in his father's stead.**

Vers. 31—33.—SHORT REIGN OF JEHOAHAZ. Pharaoh-Nechoh, having defeated Josiah, left Jerusalem and Judæa behind him, while he pressed forward on his original enterprise (see ver. 29) into Northern Syria and the district about Carchemish, or the tract north-east of Aleppo. It was three months before he had completed his conquests in these quarters, and, having arranged matters to his satisfaction, set out on his return to Egypt. During these three months Jehoahaz bore rule at Jerusalem (ver. 31), and "did evil in the sight of the Lord" (ver. 32). Ezekiel compares him to "a young lion," which "learned to catch the prey, and devoured men" (xix. 3). It may be suspected that he re-established the idolatries which Josiah had put down; but this is uncertain. Pharaoh-Nechoh, on his return from Carchemish, learning what the Jews had done, sent envoys to Jerusalem, and summoned Jehoahaz to his presence at Riblah, in the territory of Hamath (ver. 33;

comp. Josephus, 'Ant. Jud.,' x. 5. § 2). Jehoahaz obeyed the summons; and Nechoh, having obtained possession of his person, "put him in bands," and carried him off to Egypt, where he died (ver. 34; comp. Jer. xxii. 10—12; Josephus, l. s. c.).

Ver. 31.—**Jehoahaz was twenty and three years old when he began to reign.** He was, therefore, younger than his brother Eliakim, who, three months later, was "twenty-five years old" (ver. 36). His original name seems to have been "Shallum," as above noticed (see the comment on ver. 30). Probably he changed it to "Jehoahaz" ("Possession of Jehovah") on his accession. **And he reigned three months in Jerusalem**—three months *and ten days*, according to Josephus — **and his mother's name was Hamutal, the daughter of Jeremiah of Libnah.** The father of Hamutal was not, therefore, Jeremiah the prophet, who was a native of Anathoth (see Jer. i. 1).

Ver. 32.—**And he did that which was evil in the sight of the Lord** (see the comment on vers. 31—33). Josephus says that he was ἀσεβὴς καὶ μιαρὸς τὸν τρόπον (l. s. c.)— "irreligious and of impure habits." Ezekiel (xix. 3) seems to call him a persecutor. **According to all that his fathers had done.** As idolatry was the chief sin of his "fathers," Jehoahaz must have been an idolater.

Ver. 33.—**And Pharaoh-Nechoh put him in bands at Riblah.** "Riblah," which retains its name, was situated in the Cœle-Syrian plain, on the right bank of the Orontes, in lat. 34° 23' N. nearly. It commanded a ford over the river (Conder, 'Heth and Moab,' p. 17), and is in the midst of a rich, corn-producing country. Hamath, to which it was regarded as belonging, is situated more than fifty miles further down the river. Riblah was well placed as a centre for communication with the neighbouring countries. As Dr. Robinson says ('Researches,' vol. iii. p. 545), "From this point the roads were open by Aleppo and the Euphrates to Nineveh, or by Palmyra (Tadmor) to Babylon, by the end of Lebanon and the coast to Palestine (Philistia) and Egypt, or through the Buka'a and the Jordan valley to the centre of the Holy Land." Nebuchadnezzar followed the example of Nechoh in making Riblah his head-quarters during his sieges of Tyre and Jerusalem (see ch. xxv. 21; Jer. xxxix. 5; lii. 9, 10, 26, 27). **In the land of Hamath.** The "land of Hamath" was the upper part of the Cœle-Syrian valley from about lat. 34° to lat. 35° 30' N. **That he might not reign in Jerusalem.** Nechoh might naturally distrust the people's choice. He might also regard the setting up of *any* king at Jerusalem without his sanction as an act of contumacy on the part of a nation which had been practically conquered by the complete defeat of Josiah at Megiddo. Whether his conduct in seizing Jehoahaz after inviting him to a conference was justifiable or not may be questioned; but, in point of fact, he did but use the right of the conqueror somewhat harshly. **And put the land to a tribute of an hundred talents of silver, and a talent of gold.** (So Josephus, *l. s. c.*) The tribute was a very moderate one. A century earlier Sennacherib had enacted a tribute of *three* hundred talents of silver, and *thirty* of gold (see above, ch. xviii. 14). We may conjecture that Nechoh wished to conciliate the Jews, regarding them as capable of rendering him good service in the struggle, on which he had entered, with Babylon.

Vers. 34—37.—ACCESSION AND EARLY YEARS OF JEHOIAKIM. Pharaoh-Nechoh, when he deposed Jehoahaz, at once supplied his place by another king. He had no intention of altering the governmental system of Palestine, or of ruling his conquests in any other way than through dependent monarchs. His choice fell on Josiah's eldest surviving son (1 Chron. iii. 15), Eliakim, who was the natural successor of his father. Eliakim, on ascending the throne, changed his name, as Jehoahaz appears to have done (see the comment on ver. 31), and reigned as Jehoiakim. For three years (B.C. 608—605) he continued a submissive vassal of the Egyptian monarch, and remitted him his tribute regularly (ver. 36). But his rule was in all respects an evil one. He "did that which was evil in the sight of the Lord" (ver. 37). He leant towards idolatry (2 Chron. xxxvi. 8); he was oppressive and irreligious (Josephus, 'Ant. Jud.,' x. 5. § 2); he "shed innocent blood" (Jer. xxii. 17); he was luxurious (Jer. xxii. 14, 15), covetous (Jer. xxii. 17), and tyrannical (Ezek. xix. 6).

Ver. 34.—**And Pharaoh-Nechoh made Eliakim the son of Josiah king in the room of Josiah his father.** (On the general inclination of Oriental monarchs to support the hereditary principle, and to establish sons in their fathers' governments, even when the father's had been rebels or enemies, see Herod., iii. 15.) **And turned his name to Jehoiakim.** We may understand that Nechoh required him to take a new name, as a mark

of subjection (comp. Gen. xli. 45; Ezra v. 14; Dan. i. 7; and also ch. xxiv. 17), but left the choice of the name to himself. He made the change as slight as possible, merely substituting "Jehovah" for "El" as the initial element. The sense of the name remained the same, "God will set up." The idea that Nechoh was pleased with the new name on account of its apparent connection with the Egyptian moon-god, Aah (Menzel), is very fanciful. **And took Jehoahaz away** —*i.e.* carried him captive to Egypt (see Jer. xxii. 10, 11; Ezek. xix. 4), a very common practice of Egyptian conquerors, and one often accompanied by extreme severities—**and he came to Egypt, and died there** (see Jer. xxii. 12, where this is prophesied).

Ver. 35.—**And Jehoiakim gave the silver and the gold to Pharaoh.** Jehoiakim, *i.e.*, paid the tribute, which Nechoh had fixed (ver. 33), regularly. He did not, however, pay it out of the state treasury, which was exhausted. **But he taxed the land to give the money according to the commandment of Pharaoh: he exacted the silver and the gold of the people of the land, of every one according to his taxation, to give it unto Pharaoh-Nechoh;** rather, *he had the land valued* (comp. Lev. xxvii. 8), and "exacted the silver and the gold of the people of the land, of every one according to his *valuation*."

Ver. 36.—**Jehoiakim was twenty and five years old when he began to reign**—he was therefore two years older than his brother Jehoahaz (see the comment on ver. 31)—**and he reigned eleven years in Jerusalem** —probably from B.C. 608 to B.C. 597—and his mother's name was Zebudah—he was, therefore, only *half*-brother to Jehoahaz and Zedekiah, whose mother was "Hamutal" (see ver. 31 and ch. xxiv. 18)—**the daughter of Pedaiah of Rumah.** "Rumah" is probably the same city as the "Arumah" of Judg. ix. 41, which was in the vicinity of Shechem.

Ver. 37.—**And he did that which was evil in the sight of the Lord, according to all that his fathers had done.** Jeremiah says of Jehoiakim, "Woe unto him that buildeth his house by unrighteousness, and his chambers by wrong; that useth his neighbour's service without wages, and giveth him not for his work; that saith, I will build me a large house and wide chambers, and cutteth him out windows; and it is ceiled with cedar, and painted with vermilion. Shalt thou reign, because thou closest thyself in cedar? did not thy father eat and drink, and do judgment and justice, and then it was well with him? He judged the cause of the poor and needy; then it was well with him: was not this to know me? saith the Lord. But thine eyes and thine heart are not but for thy covetousness, and for to shed innocent blood, and for oppression, and for violence, to do it" (Jer. xxii. 13—17). Josephus calls him "an unjust man and an evil-doer, neither pious in his relations towards God, nor equitable in his dealings with his fellowmen" ('Ant. Jud.,' x. 5. § 2). His execution of Urijah, the son of Shemaiah, for prophesying the destruction of Jerusalem (Jer. xxvi. 20—23), was an act at once of cruelty and impiety. It is suspected (Ewald, 'History of Israel,' vol. iv. p. 252) that, besides reintroducing into Judah all the foreign rites extirpated by his father, he added Egyptian rites to their number. The tyranny which he practised was likewise of an Egyptian cast, including, as it did, the exaction of forced labour from his subjects (Jer. xxii. 13), an old custom of the Pharaohs, and it is quite possible that his "passion for building splendid and costly houses" (Ewald) was awakened by his knowledge of the magnificence which characterized the monarchs of the Saitic dynasty, who revived in Egypt the architectural glories of the Ramessides (see Herod., ii. 153, 175, 176).

HOMILETICS.

Vers. 1—3.—*Standing to the covenant.* With a heart stirred up to intense zeal for God by the words which he had heard read out of the newly found book—the precious "book of the Law," thrust into temporary oblivion by his wicked grandfather and father—Josiah felt that a great act of national repentance and national profession of faith was called for; and summoning "the men of Judah" by their representatives, and all the whole mass of the people of Jerusalem, he proceeded to call upon them to "stand to the covenant." The idea was well conceived and well carried out. After a national apostasy—an open, evident, and flagrant turning away from God, and adoption of idolatrous worships most abominable in his sight—it was only fitting, only decent, that there should be a sort of public reparation of the wrong done—a turning to God as open, evident, and manifest as the turning away had been. Accordingly, this was what Josiah determined on; and the public act of reparation resolved itself into three parts.

I. A PUBLIC RECITATION OF THE COVENANT. As the Law had been put out of sight, neglected, forgotten, during the space of two reigns, or the greater part of them, so now it was solemnly and publicly recited, proclaimed, declared to be the basis of the national life, the law of the community. The utmost possible honour was done to it by the king reading it himself in the ears of the people—reading it from first to last, "all the words of it," while the priests and the prophets and "all the people" stood attent, listening to the words so long unheard, so long forgotten, so long treated with contempt.

II. A DECLARATION OF ASSENT AND CONSENT TO THE WORDS OF THE COVENANT BY THE KING. The king was the federal head of the nation, and, in pledging himself to the keeping of the covenant, performed not a mere personal, but a representative and federal act. He pledged the nation as a whole to the acceptance and performance of the covenant, undertaking for them that they should "walk after the Lord, and keep his commandments and his testimonies and his statutes with all their heart and all their soul."

III. A DECLARATION OF ASSENT AND CONSENT TO THE WORDS OF THE COVENANT BY THE PEOPLE THEMSELVES INDIVIDUALLY. Nations cannot be saved *in the lump.* It is necessary that each individual come into personal relations with his Maker and Redeemer and Saviour. So "all the people," each of them severally, with one accord and one acclaim, "stood to the covenant"—pledged themselves to keep all the words of it henceforth with all their heart and with all their soul. A great wave of religious feeling seems to have passed over the people, and with a sincerity that was for the moment quite real and unfeigned, they declared their willing acceptance of the whole covenant, of its terrible threats as well as of its gracious promises, of its stern commands no less than of its comforting assurances. They bound themselves individually to observe all the words that were written in the book; so renewing their federal relation with God, and again becoming—what they had well-nigh ceased to be—his people. But something more was wanting. It is in no case enough to make a resolution unless we keep to it. Performance must follow upon promise. The people were bound, not merely to "stand to the covenant," in the way of profession, just once in their lives, but to stand to it, in the way of action, thenceforward perpetually. It was here that they failed; and it is here that men most commonly fail. To resolve is easy; to stick to our resolutions, difficult. The writings of Jeremiah prove to us that, within a very few years of their acceptance of the covenant in the eighteenth year of Josiah, the people of Judah cast it behind them, became a backsliding people, returned to their idolatries and abominations, forsook God, and sware by them that were no gods, committed adultery, assembled themselves by troops in the harlots' houses—were "as fed horses in the morning, every one neighing after his neighbour's wife" (Jer. v. 7, 8). A righteous God could not but "visit for these things"—could not but "be avenged upon such a nation as this" (Jer. v. 29).

Vers. 4—27.—*The inability of the best intentions and the strongest will to convert a nation that is corrupt to the core.* Josiah's reformation was the most energetic and the most thorough-going that was ever carried out by any Jewish king. It far transcended, not only the efforts made by Jehoiada in the time of Joash (ch. xi. 17— 21; xii. 1—16), and the feeble attempts of Manasseh on his return from Babylon (2 Chron. xxxiii. 15—19), but even the earnest endeavours of Hezekiah at the beginning of his reign (ch. xvii. 3—6). "It extended not only to the kingdom of Judah, but also to the former kingdom of Israel; not only to the public, but also to the private, life of the people. The evil was everywhere to be torn out, roots and all. Nothing which could perpetuate the memory of heathen or of illegitimate Jehovah-worship remained standing. All the places of worship, all the images, all the utensils, were not only destroyed, but also defiled; even the ashes were thrown into the river (?) at an unclean place, that they might be borne away for ever. The idol-priests themselves were slain, and the bones of those who were already dead were taken out of the graves and burnt. The priests of Jehovah, who had performed their functions upon the heights, were deposed from their office and dignity, and were not allowed to sacrifice any more at the altar of Jehovah" (Bähr). It may be added to this account that private superstitions, the use of *teraphim* and *gillulim*, together with the practice of witchcraft and magic arts, were put a stop to, and the rightful ordinances of the Mosaic religion restored and re-established with the utmost strictness and exactitude (vers. 24, 25). Josiah did all that a godly king could do to check the downward course of his nation and recall it to piety and virtue. And for his efforts the sacred writers give him the highest praise (ch. xxii. 2; xxiii. 25; 2 Chron. xxxiv. 2; xxxv. 26; Ecclus. xlix. 1—3). It has been reserved for modern criticism to discover that he defeated his own ends by the violence of his methods, and injured the cause of true religion by making a book—"especially such an imperfect law-book and history as the Pentateuch" —the fundamental law of the nation (Ewald, Eisenlohr). It has not, however, been as yet shown that Josiah's methods were any more violent than the Law required (Exod. xxii. 20; Deut. xiii. 5, 9, 15), much less that injury is done to the cause of true religion by the adoption of a sacred book as the standard of religious truth and morality. The real reason for the failure of his reformation was "the irreformability of the people." When they professed to turn to God, they did not do it "with their whole heart, but feignedly" (Jer. iii. 10)—at any rate, with but half their heart, moved by a gust of sentiment, not by any deep strong tide of religious feeling. And so they soon relapsed into their old ways. The severe religion, the stern morality, which Josiah sought to impose, had no attraction for them. They shrank from Mosaism as cold, hard, austere. They preferred the religions of the nations, with their lax morality, their gay rites, their consecration of voluptuousness. So they "slid back by a perpetual backsliding" (Jer. viii. 5); they reintroduced all the old abominations; they sinned in secret when they were unable to sin in public; they "proceeded from evil to evil" (Jer. ix. 4). It has been argued (Ewald, 'History of Israel,' vol. iv. pp. 242, 243) that if Josiah's life had not been cut short within thirteen years of his undertaking the great national reform, if he had been permitted to carry on for some years longer in the same spirit the work which he had initiated, there might have been a complete removal of all the ancient and deep-rooted evils, and a lasting impression might have been made upon the character of the whole people. But this seems too favourable a forecast. The nation was rotten to the core; the "whole head was sick, and the whole heart faint;" "from the sole of the foot even unto the head there was no soundness in it; but wounds, and bruises, and putrefying sores." When such is the case, no human efforts can avail anything—not the strongest will, not the wisest measures, not the purest and best intentions; the time for repentance and return to God is gone by, and nothing remains but "a certain fearful looking for of judgment and fiery indignation, which shall destroy God's adversaries" (Heb. x. 27).

HOMILIES BY VARIOUS AUTHORS.

Ver. 31—ch. xxiv. 7.—*Two royal brothers: the reigns of Jehoahaz and Jehoiakim.* I. THEY WERE BROTHERS IN WICKEDNESS. Of each of them it is said, "He did evil in the sight of the Lord." What the particular sins of Jehoahaz were we are not told. But the sins of Jehoiakim are fully and fearlessly stated and denounced by Jeremiah. "Woe unto him that buildeth his house by unrighteousness, and his chambers by wrong; that useth his neighbour's service without wages, and giveth him not for his work; that saith, I will build me a wide house and large chambers, and cutteth him out windows; and it is ceiled with cedar, and painted with vermilion. . . . Thine eyes and thine heart are not but for thy covetousness, and for to shed innocent blood, and for oppression, and for violence, to do it" (Jer. xxii. 13—17). Injustice, fraudulence, selfishness, covetousness, oppression, violence, murder,—such were the main characteristics of him who should have been an example of the people. Selfishness and covetousness were at the bottom of all the rest. And are they not common sins? In the rich they lead to injustice and oppression; in the poor they lead to discontent and envy and violence. The spirit of the gospel, by promoting unselfishness, would lead to fair and upright dealing between man and man.

II. THEY WERE BOTH WICKED, THOUGH THE SONS OF A GOOD FATHER. Even a good man may have bad sons. Perhaps the home training they received was defective. Josiah may have been so much engrossed with the cares of his kingdom, and the reformation of his people, that he neglected the state of his own household. But nevertheless, they had a good example, which they neglected to follow. Jeremiah reminds Jehoiakim of this. "Did not thy father eat and drink, and do judgment and justice, and then it was well with him? He judged the cause of the poor and needy; then it was well with him: was not this to know me? saith the Lord" (Jer. xxii. 15, 16). The privileges and the example they had received increased their guilt. "To whom much is given, of him shall much be required." If we have great privileges, we have also great responsibilities. Those who have been brought up in a Christian land or in a godly home will be expected to know better than those who have been brought up in a heathen country or amid careless and godless surroundings.

III. THEY WERE BOTH WICKED, THOUGH THE ONE HAD THE OTHER'S FATE AS A WARNING. Jehoahaz was sent into exile for his sins. Yet Jehoiakim, who succeeded him, did not profit by the warning. None of us are without many warnings against sin. We have the plain warnings of God's Word. We have the terrible warnings of his providence. How fearful, even in this life, are the consequences of many sins! We have warnings against putting off the offer of salvation to a more convenient season. "See that ye refuse not him that speaketh."

IV. THEY BOTH HAD A MISERABLE END. *Jehoahaz died in exile.* Pharaoh-Nechoh put him in prison at Riblah, and he died in captivity. Speaking of him, Jeremiah says, "Weep ye not for the dead, neither bemoan him: but weep sore for him that goeth away: for he shall return no more, nor see his native country" (Jer. xxii. 10). What a pathetic strain! The love of the Jews for their native land was most intense. "How shall we sing the Lord's song in a strange land?" "Yea, we wept, when we remembered Zion." But, after all, what a profitless kind of patriotism theirs was! They loved their native land, but they were blind to its best interests. They did not remember the secret of true prosperity and well-being. They did not remember that "righteousness exalteth a nation, but sin is a reproach to any people." They forsook him who was their nation's best Defender and unfailing Friend. A patriotism without righteousness will not benefit a nation much. *Jehoiakim died at Jerusalem. But what an ignominious fate was his!* Jeremiah had foretold it when he said, "They shall not lament for him, saying, Ah my brother! or, Ah sister! . . . He shall be buried with the burial of an ass, drawn and cast forth beyond the gates of Jerusalem" (Jer. xxii. 18, 19). It was Jehoiakim who cut with his penknife the roll on which were written the words of the Lord, and cast the leaves into the fire (Jer. xxxvi.). For this God said, regarding Jehoiakim, that he should have none to sit upon the throne of David; "and his dead body should be cast out in the day to the heat, and in the night to the frost." Jehoiakim perished, but the Word of God, which he sought to destroy, was fulfilled. God's Word cannot be destroyed. Roman emperors sought to destroy it. The Church of Rome, for the exaltation of the priesthood, kept it from the people. "But the Word of God is not bound." Contrast the fate of Jehoiakim, who despised and dishonoured the Word of God, with the universal lamentation that followed the death of his father Josiah, who honoured God's Word and obeyed its teachings.—C. H. I.

Vers. 1—25.—*Good aims and bad methods.* "And the king sent," etc. Did the world ever contain a people more morally corrupt than that of the Jews? When we mark them journeying in the wilderness forty years, a more murmuring, disorderly, rebellious set of men where else could we discover? When settled in Palestine, a "land flowing with milk and honey," we find them committing every crime of which humanity is capable—adulteries, suicides, murders, ruthless wars, gross idolatries, their priests impostors, their kings bloody tyrants. Even David, who is praised the most, was guilty of debauchery, falsehood, and blood. They were a nation steeped in depravity. They were "stiff-necked and uncircumcised in heart and ears;" they did "always resist the Holy Ghost" (see Acts vii. 51). No doubt there was always a true "Church of God" within the nation (1 Kings xix. 18); but to call the whole nation "the Jewish Church" is a misnomer, and far from a harmless one. It has encouraged Christian nations to fashion their communities after the Jewish model instead of after the Christian one. The verses I have selected record and illustrate *good aims* and *bad methods.*

I. Good AIMS. Josiah's aims, as here presented, were confessedly high, noble, and good. I offer two remarks concerning his purposes as presented in these verses. 1. *To reduce his people to a loyal obedience to Heaven.* His aim was to sweep every vestige of religious error and moral crime from his dominion. Truly, what more laudable purpose could any man have than this, to crush all evil within his domain, to crush it not only in its form but in its essence? This was indeed the great end of Christ's mission to the world. He came "to put away sin by the sacrifice of himself." 2. *Generated within him by the discovery of the Divine will.* Somehow or other, as was seen in the last chapter, the book of the Law which was to regulate the lives of the Jewish people had been lost in the temple, lost probably for many years, but Hilkiah the high priest had just discovered it, and Josiah becomes acquainted with its contents. What is the result? He is seized with the burning conviction that the whole nation is gone wrong, and forthwith he seeks to flash the same conviction into the souls of his people. "And the king sent, and they gathered unto him all the elders of Judah and of Jerusalem. And the king went up into the house of the Lord, and all the men of Judah and all the inhabitants of Jerusalem with him, and the priests, and the prophets, and all the people, both small and great: and he read in their ears all the words of the book of the covenant which was found in the house of the Lord. And the king stood by a pillar, and made a covenant before the Lord, to walk after the Lord, and to keep his commandments and his testimonies and his statutes with all their heart and all their soul, to perform the words of this covenant that were written in this book. And all the people stood to the covenant." Thus sprang his noble purpose. It was not a capricious whim or the outcome of a sudden and fitful impulse; it was rooted in an enlightened conviction. A noble purpose must be righteously founded.

II. BAD METHODS. Real good work requires not only a good purpose, but a good method also. Saul sought to honour the God of his fathers, and this was good; but his method, viz. that of persecuting the Christians, was *bad.* How did Josiah now seek to realize his purpose to sweep idolatry from the face of his country? Not by argument, suasion, and moral influence, but by brute *force* and *violence* (vers. 4—28). "All the vessels that were made for Baal, and for the grove" (ver. 4), that is, all the apparatus for idol-worship, these he ordered to be burnt outside Jerusalem, "in the fields of Kidron." He "stamped it small to powder, and cast the powder thereof upon the graves of the children of the people. And he brake down the houses of the sodomites" (vers. 6, 7). He also "brake in pieces the images, and cut down the groves, and filled their places with the bones of men" (ver. 14). Moreover, "he slew all the priests of the high places that were there upon the altars, and burned men's bones upon them" (ver. 20). In this way, the way of force and violence, he essayed to work out his grand purpose. I offer two remarks concerning his method. 1. *It was unphilosophic.* Moral evils cannot be put down by force; coercion cannot travel to a man's soul. The fiercest wind, the most vivid lightnings, cannot reach the moral Elijah in his cave. The "still small voice" alone can touch him, and bring him out to light and truth. After all this, were the people less idolatrous? Before Josiah was cold in his grave idolatry was as rife as ever. You may destroy to-day all heathen temples and priests on the face of the earth, but in doing this you have done nothing towards quenching the spirit of idolatry—that will remain as rampant as ever; phœnix-like, it will rise with new vitality and vigour from the ashes into which material fires have consumed its temples, its books, and its feasts. Ay, and you might destroy all the monastic orders and theological tomes of the Roman Catholic Church, and leave the spirit of popery as strong, nay, stronger than ever. Truth alone can conquer error, love alone can conquer wrath, right alone can conquer wrong. 2. *It was mischievous.* The evil was not extinguished; it burnt with fiercer flame. Persecution has always propagated the opinions it has sought to crush. The crucified Malefactor became the moral Conqueror and Commander of the people. Violence begets violence, anger begets anger, war begets war. "He that taketh the sword shall perish by the sword."—D. T.

Vers. 26—37.—*Lamentable unskilfulness and incorrigibility.* "Notwithstanding the Lord," etc. This short fragment of Jewish history reflects great disgrace on human nature, and may well humble us in the dust. It brings into prominence at least two subjects suggestive of solemn and practical thought.

I. THE WORTHLESSNESS OF UNWISELY DIRECTED EFFORTS TO BENEFIT MEN, HOWEVER WELL INTENDED. Josiah, it seems from the narrative, was one of the best of Israel's kings. "Like unto him was there no king before him." Most strenuous were his efforts to improve his country, to raise it from the worship of idols to the worship of the true God. He sacrifices his very life to his endeavours; and what was his success? *Nil.* "Notwithstanding the Lord turned not from the fierceness of his great wrath, wherewith his anger was kindled against Judah, because of all the provocations that Manasseh had provoked him withal. And the Lord said, I will remove Judah also out of my sight, as I have removed Israel, and will cast off this city Jerusalem which I have chosen, and the house of which I said, My Name shall be there. Now the rest of the acts of Josiah, and all that he did, are they not written in the book of the chronicles of the kings of Judah?" All the efforts of this noble king seemed to be abortive. But why? Because, as shown in our preceding homily, while his motive was good, his methods were bad. Instead of depending upon argument and suasion, moral influence, and the embodiment of moral goodness, he uses force. "He slew all the priests of the high places that were there upon the altars, and burned men's bones upon them," etc. Here is a principle in the Divine government of man. No man, however good, can accomplish a good thing unless he employs wise means. The Church of Rome is an example. Its aim, the bringing of the world into the one fold, is sublimely good, but the means it has employed not only neutralize the purpose, but drive large masses of the population away into the wilderness of infidelity and careless living. It is not enough for a Church to have good aims; it must have wise methods: not enough for preachers to desire the salvation of their people; they must use means in harmony with the laws of thought and feeling. Hence fanatical Churches and preachers have always done more harm than good. "If the iron be blunt, and he do not whet the edge, then must he put to more strength: but wisdom is profitable to direct." Indeed, this man's unwise efforts not only failed to benefit his country, they brought ruin on himself. He lost his life. "In his days Pharaoh-Nechoh King of Egypt went up against the King of Assyria to the river Euphrates: and King Josiah went against him; and he slew him at Megiddo, when he had seen him.   And his servants carried him in a chariot dead from Megiddo." No doubt Josiah was inspired with patriotic and religious purposes in going forth against Pharaoh-Nechoh, and in seeking to prevent the march of a bloody tyrant and a hostile force through his territory in order to attack the King of Assyria. But where was his wisdom? What chance had he to hurl back such a formidable invasion? None whatever. Single-handed, of course, he could do nothing. And what help could he obtain from his subjects, most of whom had fallen into that moral degradation which robs the soul of all true courage and skill?

II. THE AMAZING INCORRIGIBILITY OF THE JEWISH PEOPLE. Do we find that the men of Israel were improved by the efforts of such kings as Hezekiah and Josiah? Nay. They seemed to grow worse. Scarcely was Josiah in his grave before his son Jehoahaz, who was twenty-three years old, ascended the throne, and during the three months of his reign he "did that which was evil in the sight of the Lord;" and when he is struck down another son of Josiah, Eliakim, who was afterwards named Jehoiakim, received the throne, and, after a reign of twenty-five years, the record is, "He did that which is evil in the sight of the Lord." Here, then, is moral incorrigibility! In all history, ancient or modern, I know no people whose doings were of a baser type. With all the lofty advantages which they had, and with the interpositions of Heaven vouchsafed to them, they seemed to grow worse from age to age. The little springs of depravity that broke forth from their great ancestors, Abraham, Isaac, and Jacob, seemed to deepen, swell in volume, and widen as time rolled on. It was at last a kind of Stygian stream. You can scarcely point to one pellucid wave rising on its surface. It was foul from top to bottom. How sadly have many professed disciples of Christ misinterpreted Jewish history! So much so that they have Judaized the very gospel, and made Judaism a model after which they have shaped communities professedly Christian.

CONCLUSION. 1. A word *to those who desire to be useful.* Unless you practically recognize the truly scientific adaptation of means to ends, and understand the eternal principles by which the human mind can be rightly influenced, you will " labour in vain, and spend your strength for nought." There is no way by which coercion can travel to a man's soul, no way by which cruelties and persecutions can enlighten, strengthen, and ennoble souls. 2. A word, next, *to those who desire to be benefited.* You may have seers from heaven working among you, endeavouring to improve you and elevate you. But unless you yield to the influences and attend to the counsels, you will grow worse and worse. Pharaoh's heart grew harder under the ministry of Moses on the banks of the Nile; the Jewish people became worse and worse under the forty years' ministry in the wilderness, and the contemporaries of Christ filled up their measure of iniquity under his benign and enlightening ministrations. The things that belong to your peace may become the elements of your ruin.—D. T.

Vers. 1—14.—*Josiah's great reformation.* The narrative of Josiah's reforms contained in this chapter incorporates several particulars which, if the Book of Chronicles is to be regarded as giving the true chronology, belong to an earlier period. It is next to incredible that, after Jehovah's worship had been regularly established, such scandals as the prostitution alluded to in ver. 7, and the horses and chariots of the sun in ver. 11, should have been allowed to continue. The narrative in Kings seems specially designed to bring all Josiah's reforms into one view. We have—

I. SOLEMN COVENANTING. After the example of Jehoiada in the reign of Joash (2 Chron. xxiii. 16), and the still more ancient example of Moses (Deut. xxix.), Josiah convened the people together to renew the covenant made with them by God at Sinai (Exod. xxiv. 1—8). The covenanting took place appropriately in the house of the Lord—another evidence that the worst abominations had by this time been removed from the temple. All classes were assembled, high and low, priests, prophets, and people. In proposing to them to enter on this solemn engagement, in which he set them the example: 1. *The king asked them to do a right thing.* It was Israel's distinction among the peoples of the earth that they stood in covenant with God. God had chosen them as a people for himself, that they should serve him alone in the land he had given them. If they had failed to do this, and now repented of their disobedience, it was meet that they should acknowledge their transgressions, and anew pledge themselves to be the Lord's. This was what Josiah desired Judah and Jerusalem—" the remnant of God's inheritance"—to do. Standing on a raised platform, he set them the example of covenant. It is a good thing when nations have leaders who are themselves conspicuous examples of godliness, and who point the way in what is right to their people. The propriety of national covenants is a question to be settled by the circumstances of each particular age. The individual Christian, at least, is called to frequent renewal of his vows to God, and such an exercise is peculiarly suitable after seasons of backsliding. 2. *He did it on a right basis.* The covenant was based on the declarations of " the book of the covenant," the words of which were first read in the hearing of all the people. Then the people, following the example of their monarch, pledged themselves to walk after the Lord, to keep his commandments and his testimonies and his statutes with all their heart and soul, and to perform the words that were written in the book. Their covenant thus rested on the right foundation, viz. God's Word. It is God who, in his Word, draws near to us, declares to us his will, holds out his promises, invites us to engagement with himself, and lays down the rule of our obedience. A covenant means nothing save as it springs from faith in, acceptance of, and submission to the revealed Word of God. Our covenanting is to be (1) intelligent—based on the study of God's Word, and understanding of its requirements; (2) cordial—with all the heart and soul; and (3) dutiful—in the spirit of obedience, " to perform the words of this covenant that were written in this book." 3. *Yet the engagement was not sincere.* It was so in the case of Josiah, but not in the case of the people generally, though it is written, " All the people stood to the covenant." In lip they honoured God, but in heart they were far from him (Isa. xxix. 13). This is evident from the descriptions in the prophets. The movement was not a spontaneous one originating in the hearts of the people themselves, but came down to them from above through the king's command. The formal ceremonies of covenanting were gone through, and some temporary, and perhaps genuine, enthusiasm was awakened. But there was no real heart-change of the people. Their goodness was like the morning cloud and the early dew (Hos. vi. 4). This is too often the fate of movements originating with kings, princes, and those in high positions, and not springing from the people's own initiative. They are popular and fashionable, and draw many after them who have no real sympathy with their aims. But the effects do not endure. Rank, fashion, royalty, the adhesion of the great and mighty and noble of this world (1 Cor. i. 26), do not of themselves make a movement religious, though they may secure for it *éclat.* The Lord looketh on the heart (1 Sam. xvi. 7), and if the essence of religion is wanting, imposing external forms count for little.

II. THE TEMPLE CLEANSED. In the covenant they had just made, the people bound themselves in the most solemn manner to rid the land of all visible traces of idolatry (Exod. xxiii. 24; Deut. xii. 1—3). Josiah took this work in hand more systematically than any king who had gone before him (ver. 25). He began with the temple, the thorough purification of which had probably been left over till the repairs above referred to (ch. xxii.) could be overtaken. Similar zeal for the destruction of idols was manifested at the conclusion of the previous covenant under Joash (2 Chron. xxiii. 17). 1. *A cleansing away of the traces of Baal-worship.* In the first place, a careful clearing out was made of all the vessels and utensils that had been used in the service of Baal, or of the Asherah, or of the host of heaven. These were burned in the valley of Kidron, and the ashes of them carried to Bethel, as the appropriate source of this idolatry. The sacred tree itself—the Asherah—was then cut down, burned in the same valley, and its ashes sprinkled on the graves of the people, many of whom had shared in the guilt of its worship. Afterwards the altars erected to Baal in the temple courts were broken down, and the dust of them cast also into the valley of Kidron (ver. 12). Possibly the Asherah and these altars had been removed, and treated as described, at an earlier date. 2. *A cleansing away of the traces of Venus-worship.* The Asherah was devoted to the licentious Astarte, and rites the most shameless and abominable had been conducted in the temple courts in honour of this goddess. Houses, even, had been reared close to the sacred enclosure for the bands of depraved men and women who took part in these orgies. Doubtless the worship ere this had been stopped, and the filthy actors driven out, but the houses which remained as a reminder of its existence were now broken down. 3. *A cleansing away of the traces of sun-worship.* To the worship of the sun and of the host of heaven belonged the sacred horses and chariots (ver. 11), probably ere this removed, and the chariots burned; and the altars on the top of the upper chamber of Ahaz, which successive kings had set up. These, like the altars of Manasseh, were broken down, and their dust scattered in the adjoining valley. Every vestige of idolatry was thus cleansed out of the house of which the Lord had said, "In Jerusalem will I put my Name" (ch. xxi. 4).

III. IDOLATRY PUT AWAY. Judgment began at the house of God (1 Pet. iv. 17), but it spread thence throughout the whole land. 1. *Degradation of the priests.* The land apparently had been already "purged" of the idols, Asherahs, and sun-images, which were worshipped at the high places (2 Chron. xxxiv. 3, 4). Measures were now taken to degrade the priests who had ministered at these forbidden altars, and through whom, perhaps, the worship was still in many places carried on. These priests were of different kinds. (1) Some were "idolatrous priests"—chemarim—after the fashion of the priests of the northern kingdom. They do not appear to have been of Levitical descent at all, but were "ordained" of the kings of Judah to burn incense in the high places, and may have been drawn, like Jeroboam's chemarim, from "the lowest of the people" (1 Kings xii. 31). Some of them were ostensibly priests of Jehovah, serving him, probably, with idolatrous symbols; others served Baal, and the sun, moon, and planets. The whole of this illegitimate class of priests Josiah put sternly down— suppressing their order as contrary to the Law of Moses. (2) The second class of priests were true Levites, but they ministered at the high places. These were brought from their several cities to Jerusalem, and there provided for out of the temple revenues. They were not, however, permitted to minister at the altar of Jehovah, though, like the other priests, they received their support from the temple offerings. These stringent regulations effectually broke the power of this class throughout the country. God must be served by a pure ministry. 2. *Defilement of the high places.* The next part of Josiah's policy was to destroy and defile the high places themselves. One way in which this was done was by covering them with dead men's bones, or burning dead bones upon them. The high places were thus rendered unclean, and became hateful to the people. Two special acts of defilement are mentioned in addition to that of "the mount of corruption" next referred to, viz. (1) the defilement of the high places at the entrance of the gate of Joshua; and (2) the defilement of Topheth in the valley of Hinnom. The real defilement was in the idolatrous and murderous rites with which these places were associated, but Josiah put a special brand of pollution on them, and stamped them as spots to be held in abhorrence for their vileness. 3. *The defilement of "the mount of corruption."* Such was the appropriate name given to the hill on which Solomon, long before, had reared altars to the heathen gods worshipped by his wives—Ashtoreth, Chemosh, Moloch, etc. The high places of that mount, which directly overlooked Jerusalem, did Josiah now defile. Idolatry is none the less pernicious that it has the sanction of a great name, and flaunts itself under the guise of a spurious toleration. Any spot where God is not worshipped, but idols are set up in his place, soon becomes a mount of corruption. Heathenism is a mount of corruption. Godless civilization will become a mount of corruption. Our very hearts will turn to mounts of corruption if we allow God to be dethroned in them.

IV. LESSONS OF THE REFORMATION. 1. *From what it did accomplish.* Josiah's was a true "zeal for the Lord." He was actuated by a right motive, guided himself strictly by God's Word, and directed his efforts unswervingly to execute God's will. He wrought earnestly to purify his state from the evils that afflicted it, and to restore the influence of pure and undefiled religion. He deserves our highest admiration for the (1) determination, (2) energy, (3) method, and (4) thoroughness with which he did God's work. Externally, his work was a success. He cleansed the land from idolatry. We, too, have a call to labour for the purification of society, the dethronement of idols, and the spread of true religion. The age of idolatry is not past. Church, state, literature, science, art, have all their idols. There is self-idolatry, nature-idolatry, wealth-idolatry, art-idolatry, the idolatry of genius, and many more worships besides. Our own hearts are abodes of idols. We do well to imitate Josiah in the energy and thoroughness with which he laboured to uproot these false gods. We should be unsparing in our judgment of whatever vice, error, evil lusts, or passions, or inclinations, or tendencies, we discover in ourselves. Let high thoughts be mercilessly brought low, and proud imaginations abased (2 Cor. x. 5). Wherever sin is detected, let it be judged. Thus it was with the Corinthians, "For behold this selfsame thing, that ye sorrowed after a godly sort, what carefulness it wrought in you, yea, what clearing of yourselves, yea, what indignation, yea, what fear, yea, what vehement desire, yea, what zeal, yea, what revenge!" 2. *From what it did not accomplish.* This reformation of Josiah wrought, after all, only on the exterior of the nation's life. It lacked power to reach the heart. Therefore it failed to regenerate or save the nation. We are thus pointed to the need of a better covenant, that which Jeremiah predicts in ch. xxxi. 31—34 of his prophecies, "Behold, the days come, saith the Lord, that I will make a new covenant with the house of Israel, and with the house of Judah. . . . I will put my Law in their inward parts, and write it in their hearts," etc.—J. O.

Vers. 15—20.—*The altar at Bethel.* From Judah Josiah passed on to Israel, continuing his work of idol-demolition. Everywhere he went he proved himself a veritable "hammer of God"—levelling, defacing, dishonouring, destroying.

I. AN ANCIENT PROPHECY FULFILLED. 1. *Iconoclasm at Bethel.* Bethel had been the chief scene of Israel's idolatry—the head and front of its offending (cf. Hos. iv. 15; x. 4—9, etc.). On it Josiah's zeal first expended itself. Hosea had prophesied its desolation, the destruction of its high places, the carrying away of its calf, the cessation of its mirth and feasts, its abandonment to thorns and nettles (Hos. ii. 11; ix. 6; x. 8, etc.). But an older voice had foretold the end from the beginning. Scarcely had the schismatic altar, with its calf, been set up, when a prophet out of Judah denounced Jeroboam's sin to his face, and proclaimed that a future king would stain the altar-stones with the blood of the priests, and defile it by burning dead men's bones upon it. A sign had been given in confirmation of the truth of the prediction (1 Kings xiii. 1—10). That oracle stood at the head of the way of transgression, warning men away from it; but its voice had been unheeded. Now, centuries after, the prediction was fulfilled. Idolatry in some form still held its ground on the ancient spot, but Josiah put an end to it. The altar and high place he broke down, and burned the high place, and reduced it to powder, and burned the Asherah. The idolatry at Bethel had wrought out its effects in the ruin of the state. That evil was irremediable, but Josiah could show at least his detestation of the sin, and his determination that no more evil should be wrought, by totally demolishing the sanctuary. Special regard should be paid to the removal of centres of wickedness. It is useless to capture outworks, if strongholds are left standing. We should not rest content till the very name and memory of sin has perished in places that were conspicuous for it. 2. *The sepulchre invaded.* Josiah would have no half-measures. It was part of his settled policy, not simply to break down the high places, but to defile them, and unfit them for future use. In looking round him at Bethel for means to accomplish this end, he spied the sepulchres that were in the mount, and sent and took bones out of the sepulchres, and polluted the altar by burning them upon it. His immediate design was to defile the altar, but in taking the bones to burn, he dishonoured also the ashes of the dead. In his consuming zeal against idolatry he felt that no respect was due to the bones of those who, by their sins, had brought death upon the nation. It is easy to blame the act, and to compare it with the ruthless violations of the sanctity of the grave of which persecutors have often been guilty. It seems a paltry and vindictive proceeding to wreak one's vengeance on the dead. To Josiah, however, no sanctity attached to these graves, but only a curse. His very object was to do deeds which would make men feel, as they had never felt before, the hateful nature of idolatry, and the certainty of a Nemesis attending it. In having their bones dragged out and burned upon the altar, the dead idolaters were, in a sense, making atonement to God's insulted majesty (cf. Jer. viii. 1—3). The feeling, nevertheless, is one which might easily go too far, and be mixed up with mean and purely spiteful motives. However it might be under Jewish law, it can hardly be right now. None the less is it the case that a curse rests upon the very bones of the wicked dead. Death to them is the penal stroke of God's displeasure, and, when they rise, it is to the resurrection of damnation (John v. 29).

II. THE BONES OF THE PROPHET RESPECTED. 1. *A monument in a wicked place to a good man.* Among the tombs which Josiah beheld was one with a monument before it. He asked whose it was, and was told it was the monument of the man of God who prophesied of these things which had been done to the altar. That monument had, perhaps, been built by the hands of the very men whose sins the prophet had denounced, so great oftentimes is human inconsistency (cf. Matt. xxiii. 28—30). In any case, it stood there for centuries a silent witness against the iniquities that were perpetrated in its presence. Monuments to prophets, martyrs, saints, still crowd our burial and public places; we pay external honour to their memories; but what God will ask of us is—Do we imitate their spirit? As great men recede into the distance, it becomes easy to pay them reverence. These idolatrous Israelites no doubt magnified their descent from Abraham, and boasted of their great lawgiver Moses, at the very time that they were breaking his commandments. When the prophets were among them, they sought to kill them; then they built monuments in their honour. 2. *A solitary witness for truth justified by the event.* This prophet in his day stood alone. Even among the dead he lay alone. The multitudes around him were not those who believed, but those who had disregarded his word. If ever man was in a minority, he was. Century after century rolled by, and still the word he had spoken remained unfulfilled. Did it not seem as if the oracle were about to fail? But Wisdom in the end is justified of her children (Matt. xi. 19). The prophet's word came true at last, and it was seen and acknowledged of all that he was right. Thus is it with all God's true servants. We should not concern ourselves too much with man's gainsaying. We have but to bear our testimony and leave the issues with God. He will at length vindicate us. 3. *Discrimination between good and bad.* When Josiah learned whose the sepulchre was, he gave command that his bones should not be touched, nor yet the bones of the old prophet who was buried along with him (1 Kings xiii. 31). The righteous was discriminated from the sinners. So shall it be at the last day. No confusion will be made in the resurrection between good and bad. While the wicked come forth to the resurrection of judgment, the good shall come forth to the resurrection of life (John v. 29). A gracious Saviour watches over their dust.

III. THE SLAUGHTER OF THE PRIESTS. 1. *General demolition.* The wave of destruction spread from Bethel over all the other high places in the cities of Samaria. Josiah's procession through the land was the signal for the overthrow of every species of idolatry. " So did he," we are told, " in the cities of Manasseh, and Ephraim, and Simeon, even unto Naphtali, in their ruins round about " (2 Chron. xxxiv. 6). 2. *Priests of the high places slain.* In connection with this progress of Josiah through Israel is mentioned the fact that " he slew all the priests of the high places that were there upon the altars." If this stern policy had been confined to Israel, it would have been difficult to exculpate Josiah from partiality in his carrying out of the provisions of the Law; but the words in Chronicles imply that the like was, at least in some places, done in Judah also (2 Chron. xxxiv. 5). In what he did he was no doubt strictly within the letter of the Law, which he and the people had sworn to obey, for that undeniably denounced death against idolaters (Deut. xiii., etc.). To equal his act, therefore, with Manasseh's shedding of innocent blood is to miss the essential fact of the situation. This was not innocent blood by the fundamental law of the constitution. It is probably with reference to this, as to other parts of his conduct, that Josiah gets special praise for the fidelity of his obedience to the Law of Moses (ver. 25). It does not follow that his conduct is such as Christians, living under a milder and better dispensation, should now imitate. It does not even follow that every individual act which Josiah did was beyond blame. His human judgment may have erred at times on the side of severity. The holiest movements are not free from occasional excesses; but we should judge the movement by the soul which actuates it, and not by its superficial excrescences. —J. O.

Vers. 21—23.—*The reformation completed, yet Israel's sin not pardoned.* We have in these verses—

I. THE GREAT PASSOVER. 1. *A seal of the covenant.* This great year of reformation began with a covenant, and ended with a Passover. The ceremonies of the occasion are fully described in 2 Chron. xxxv. The Passover in the Old Testament was in some respects very much what the Lord's Supper is in the New. It took the people back to the origin of their history, revived vivid memories of the deliverance from Egypt, and ratified their engagement to be the Lord's. It reminded of the past, set a seal upon the present, and gave a pledge for the future. The Christian sacrament seals God's promises to the believer, and, at the same time, seals the believer's covenant with God. It establishes, nourishes, and strengthens the life received in the new birth. 2. *An historic celebration.* " Surely there was not holden such a Passover from the days of the judges that judged Israel," etc. A true religious awakening shows itself (1) in increased interest in God's ordinances; (2) in stricter fidelity in observing them; and (3) in joyful alacrity in taking advantage of them.

II. FIDELITY TO MOSES. 1. *Cleansing away the concomitants of idolatry.* Together with the idols, Josiah cleansed out of the land the tribes of wizards, necromancers, soothsayers, etc., who found their profit in the ignorance and superstition of the people. Where Bible religion returns, sanity returns. The hideous spectres begotten of fear and superstition vanish. Josiah further carefully eradicated any remaining traces of idol-worship that could be "spied." 2. *Pre-eminent fidelity.* In these deeds, and by his whole course as a reformer, Josiah earned for himself the distinction of being the most faithful king that had yet reigned. He and Hezekiah stand out pre-eminent the one for trust in God (ch. xviii. 5), the other for fidelity to the Law of Moses. "Like unto him was there no king before him," etc. Like gems, each of which has its special beauty and excels in its own kind, these two kings shine above all the rest. Only *one* character exhibits all spiritual excellences in perfection.

III. ISRAEL'S SIN YET UNPARDONED. 1. *God's unappeased anger.* "Notwithstanding the Lord turned not from the fierceness of his great wrath," etc. The sole reason of this was that, notwithstanding the zealous Josiah's reforms, the people had not in heart turned from their great sins. The spirit of Manasseh still lived in them. They were unchanged in heart, and, with favouring circumstances, were as ready to break out into idolatry as ever. The outward face of things was improved as regards religion, but social injustice and private morals were as bad as ever. Hence the Lord could not, and would not, turn from his wrath. It is real, not lip, repentance that God requires to turn away his anger from us. We see : (1) The posthumous influence of evil. " One sinner destroyeth much good " (Eccles. ix. 18). Manasseh's deeds lived after him. His repentance could not recall the mischief they had done to the nation. They went working on after his decease, propagating and multiplying their influence, till the nation was destroyed. (2) The righteousness of individuals cannot save an unrighteous people. Not even though these righteous persons are high in rank, are deeply concerned for the revival of religion, and labour with all their hearts to stem the tide of corruption. Their piety and prayers may *delay* judgment, but if impenitence is persisted in, they cannot finally avert it (cf. Jer. xv. 1, " Though Moses and Samuel stood before me, yet my mind could not be toward this people "). 2. *God's unshaken purpose.* " I will remove Judah also out of my sight," etc. Terrible is the severity of God when his forbearance is exhausted. Moral laws are inexorable. If the spiritual conditions, by which only a change could be effected, are wanting, they work on till the sinner is utterly destroyed.—J. O.

Vers. 29—37.—*Pharaoh-Nechoh and the Jewish kings.* A new power had risen in Egypt which was to play a temporary, but influential, part in the evolution of God's purposes towards Judah. Assyria was at this time in its death-agonies. The sceptre of empire was soon to pass to Babylon. But it was Pharaoh-Nechoh who, following the designs of his own ambition, was to set in motion a train of events which had the effect of bringing Judah within the power of the King of Babylon.

I. THE DEATH OF JOSIAH. 1. *Circumstances of his death.* Taking advantage of the troubles in the East, Pharaoh-Nechoh was bent on securing his own supremacy over Syria and extending it as far as the river Euphrates. He disclaimed all intention of interfering with Josiah (2 Chron. xxxv. 21), but that monarch thought it his duty to oppose him. It was a perilous venture, and Josiah seems to have entered upon it somewhat rashly. He certainly had not prophetic sanction for the enterprise. The issue was as might have been anticipated. He encountered Pharaoh-Nechoh at Megiddo, and was disastrously defeated. Wounded by the archers, he bade his servants carry him away, and, placing him in another chariot, they drove him off. It is to be inferred from Zech,

xii. 11 that he died at "Hadadrimmon in the valley of Megiddo," and that his dead body was afterwards brought to Jerusalem. By this defeat Judah was brought into subjection to Pharaoh-Nechoh, and the way prepared for its subjection to Nebuchadnezzar, when he, in turn, became master of the situation. It is wise not unduly to meddle with the quarrels of other nations. 2. *Mourning for his death.* The untimely death of Josiah was a cause of unexampled mourning throughout the whole land. The affection with which his people regarded him, and the confidence they placed in him, are strikingly shown by the sorrow felt at his loss. The mourning at Hadadrimmon is used by the prophet to illustrate the mourning which will take place at the national repentance of Israel in the times of the Messiah (Zech. xii. 9—14). It was as the mourning for a firstborn. Jeremiah composed an elegy for the good king departed, and the singing-men and singing-women kept up the practice of lamenting for him even unto the Captivity (2 Chron. xxxv. 24, 25). Well might Judah mourn. Josiah was the last great and good king they would see. But infinitely better would it have been if their sorrow had been the "godly sorrow" which "worketh repentance" (2 Cor. vii. 10). This unfortunately it was not, as the result showed. It is because it was not that, the mourning of Hadadrimmon will have to be done over again (Zech. xii. 10), next time in a very different spirit. We see that it is possible to lament good men, yet not profit by their example. The best tribute we can pay the just is to live like them. 3. *Providential aspects of his death.* (1) An irreparable loss to the nation, Josiah's death was yet great gain to himself. It was God's way of taking him away from the evil to come, and so of fulfilling the promise given by Huldah (ch. xxii. 20). Josiah, perhaps, erred in taking the step he did, but while God punished him for his error, he providentially overruled the event for his good. Death is sometimes a blessing. It may hide things from our eyes we had rather not see; as, in the case of the good, it translates to scenes of bliss beyond human conception. The "dark things" of God's providence are those in which we may ultimately recognize the greatest mercy. "Judge not the Lord by feeble sense," etc. (2) In regard to the nation, the providential aspects of this death were widely different. It took from them a gift which they had failed to prize, or at least to profit by. It was, moreover, a step in Providence towards the fulfilment of the threatenings of captivity. Pharaoh-Nechoh's conquest was the gate through which Nebuchadnezzar entered.

II. The deposition of Jehoahaz. 1. *A brief reign.* In virtue of the defeat of Josiah, Judah became *ipso facto* a dependency of Pharaoh-Nechoh. The people, however, were in no mood to acknowledge this subjection, and immediately set about making a king for themselves. They passed by Eliakim, Josiah's eldest son, and raised the next son, Shallum (Jer. xxii. 11), to the throne under the name of Jehoahaz. The younger son was probably the more spirited and warlike of the two. Ezekiel compares him to a young lion (xix. 3). Under him the nation cast off the restraints of the reign of Josiah, and reverted to its former sinful ways. It does not suffice to make a good king that he has (1) a good father—"the son of Josiah;" (2) a good name—Jehoahaz, "he whom the Lord sustains;" or (3) a solemn anointing—they "anointed him." The people probably thought otherwise, for it was they, apparently, who gave him this name, and took the step of formally consecrating him with the anointing oil. Anointing oil, without the grace which it symbolizes, is of little use. Jehoahaz was permitted to possess his throne only for three brief months. 2. *A hard captivity.* By the end of the period named, Pharaoh-Nechoh was sufficiently free to attend to the proceedings at Jerusalem. The city had flouted his supremacy, and he did not let it escape. His own camp was at Riblah, but he sent to Jerusalem, required Jehoahaz to attend his court at Riblah, there put him in chains, and carried him with him into Egypt (Ezek. xix. 4). This was a worse fate than Josiah's. "Weep ye not for the dead," said Jeremiah, "neither bemoan him: but weep sore for him that goeth away: for he shall return no more, nor see his native country" (xxii. 10). This captivity of Jehoahaz was a prelude to the captivity of the nation—the first drop of the shower soon about to fall. Yet the people would not hearken. 3. *A heavy tribute.* In addition to removing the king, Pharaoh-Nechoh put the land under a tribute. He exacted a hundred talents of silver and a talent of gold. Again we see how sin works out bondage, misery, and disgrace. An oft-read lesson, but how impossible, apparently, for this people to learn!

III. JEHOIAKIM'S VASSALAGE. 1. *Egypt dictates a king.* Once again, as in the earliest period of their history, Israel was in bondage to Egypt. Pharaoh-Nechoh used his power unsparingly. The eldest son of Josiah, who seems not to have been a favourite with the people, was willing to accept the throne as a vassal, and him, accordingly, Nechoh made king, changing his name, in token of subjection, from Eliakim to Jehoiakim. How bitter the satire—Jehoiakim, " he whom Jehovah has set up"! 2. *Jehoiakim becomes Egypt's tool.* Jehoiakim had, perhaps, no alternative but to give " the silver and the gold to Pharaoh," but in his manner of exacting it he showed himself the willing tool of the oppressor. To obtain the money, he put heavy taxation on the people. His rule was a bitter, ignominious, and oppressive one for Judah. Jeremiah says of him, " But thine eyes and thine heart are not but for thy covetousness, and for to shed innocent blood, and for oppression, and for violence, to do it " (xxii. 17). But such are the kings men must submit to when they reject God for their Sovereign. In a moral respect Jehoiakim's reign was " evil," and in a temporal respect it was the stumbling on from one misfortune to another.—J. O.

EXPOSITION.

CHAPTER XXIV.

Vers. 1—20.—REIGNS OF JEHOIAKIM, JEHOIACHIN, AND ZEDEKIAH.

Vers. 1—7.—REST OF THE REIGN OF JEHOIAKIM. Troubles now fell thick and fast upon Judæa. Within three years of the invasion of the country by Pharaoh-Nechoh, another hostile army burst in from the north. In B.C. 605, the last year of Nabopolassar, he sent his eldest son, Nebuchadnezzar, into Syria, to assert the dominion of Babylon over the countries lying between the Euphrates and the frontier of Egypt. Nechoh sought to defend his conquests, but was completely defeated at Carchemish in a great battle (Jer. xlvi. 2—12). Syria and Palestine then lay open to the new invader, and, resistance being regarded as hopeless, Jehoiakim made his submission to Nebuchadnezzar (ver. 1). But, three years later (B.C. 602), sustained by what hope we know not, he ventured on an act of rebellion, and declared himself independent. Nebuchadnezzar did not at once march against him, but caused him to be attacked, as it would seem, by his neighbours (ver. 2). A war without important result continued for four years. Then Nebuchadnezzar came up against him in person for a second time (2 Chron. xxxvi. 6), took Jerusalem, and made Jehoiakim prisoner. He designed at first to carry him to Babylon; but seems to have afterwards determined to have him executed, and to have treated his corpse with indignities (Jer. xxii. 30; xxxvi. 30). The writer of

Kings throws a veil over these transactions, closing his narrative with the customary phrase—Jehoiakim " slept with his fathers" (ver. 6).

Ver. 1.—**In his days Nebuchadnezzar King of Babylon came up.** The Hebrew נְבֻכַדְרֶאצַּר (*Nebuchadnezzar*) or נְבֻכַדְרֶאצַּר (*Nebuchadrezzar*, Jeremiah, Ezekiel) represents the Babylonian *Nabu-kudur-uzur* (" Nebo is the protector of landmarks"), a name very common in the Babylonian and Assyrian inscriptions. It was borne by three distinct kings of Babylon, the most important of whom was Nebuchadnezzar III., the son of Nabopolassar, the monarch of the present passage. According to Berosus, he was not at the time of this expedition the actual sovereign of Babylonia, but only the crown prince, placed by the actual king, Nabopolassar, at the head of his army. It is possible that his father may have associated him in the kingdom, for association was not unknown at Babylon; or the Jews may have mistaken his position; or the historian may call him king by *prolepsis*, as a modern might say, " The Emperor Napoleon invaded Italy and defeated the Austrians at Marengo " (see Pusey's 'Daniel,' p. 400). His father had grown too old and infirm to conduct a military expedition, and consequently sent his son in his place, with the object of chastising Nechoh, and recovering the territory whereof Nechoh had made himself master three years before (see ch. xxiii. 29—33, and compare below, ver. 7). **And Jehoiakim became his servant**—*i.e.* submitted to him, and became a tributary king—**three years** (from B.C. 605 to B.C. 602): **then he turned and rebelled against him.** How Jehoiakim came to venture on this step we are not told, and can only conjecture. It is, perhaps, most probable that (as Josephus says, 'Ant. Jud.,' x. 6, § 2) he was incited to take this course by the Egyptians, who were still under the rule of the brave and enterprising Nechoh, and who may have hoped to wipe out by fresh victories the disaster experienced at Carchemish. There is, perhaps, an allusion to Jehoiakim's expectation of Egyptian succours in the statement of ver. 7, that "the King of Egypt came not again any more out of his land."

Ver. 2.—**And the Lord sent against him bands of the Chaldees.** That Nebuchadnezzar did not promptly march against Jehoiakim to suppress his rebellion, but contented himself with sending against him a few "bands" (גְּדוּדֵי) of Chaldeans, and exciting the neighbouring Syrians, Ammonites, and Moabites to invade and ravage his territory, can scarcely be otherwise accounted for than by supposing that he was detained in Middle Asia by wars or rebellions nearer home. It may have been a knowledge of these embarrassments that induced Jehoiakim to lend an ear to the persuasions of Nechoh. **And bands of the Syrians, and bands of the Moabites, and bands of the children of Ammon** (comp. Ezek. xix. 8, "Then the nations set against him on every side from the provinces, and spread their net over him: he was taken in their pit"), **and sent them against Judah to destroy it**—i.e. to begin that waste and ruin which should terminate ultimately in the complete destruction and obliteration of the Judæan kingdom—**according to the word of the Lord, which he spake by his servants the prophets.** As Isaiah, Micah, Habakkuk, Jeremiah, Zephaniah, and Huldah (see ch. xxii. 16—20).

Ver. 3.—**Surely at the commandment of the Lord came** this **upon Judah**; literally, *only at the mouth of the Lord did this come upon Judah;* i.e. there was no other cause for it but the simple "mouth" or "word" of the Lord. The LXX., who translate πλὴν θυμὸς Κυρίου ἦν ἐπὶ τὸν Ἰούδαν, seem to have had אַף instead of פִּי in their copies. **To remove** them **out of his sight** (comp. ch. xxiii. 27; and see also the comment on ch. xvii. 18) **for the sins of Manasseh, according to all that he did.** The meaning is not that the nation was punished for the personal sins and crimes of the wicked Manasseh forty or fifty years previously, but that the class of sins introduced by Manasseh, being persisted in by the people, brought the stern judgments of God upon them. As W. G. Sumner well observes, "The sins of Manasseh had become a designation for a certain class of offences, and a particular form of public and social depravity, which was introduced by Ma-

nasseh, but of which generation after generation continued to be guilty." The special sins were (1) idolatry, accompanied by licentious rites; (2) child-murder, or sacrifice to Moloch; (3) sodomy (ch. xxiii. 7); and (4) the use of enchantments and the practice of magical arts (ch. xxi. 6).

Ver. 4.—**And also for the innocent blood that he shed** (comp. ch. xxi. 16, and the comment *ad loc.*). Like the other "sins of Manasseh," the shedding of innocent blood continued, both in the Moloch offerings (Jer. vii. 31) and in the persecution of the righteous (Jer. vii. 6, 9, etc.). Urijah was actually put to death by Jehoiakim (Jer. xxvi. 23); Jeremiah narrowly escaped. **For he filled Jerusalem with innocent blood; which the Lord would not pardon.** Blood "cries to God from the ground" on which it falls (Gen. iv. 11), and is "required" at the hands of the bloodshedder (Gen. ix. 5) unfailingly. Especially is the blood of saints slain for their religion avenged and exacted by the Most High (see Rev. vi. 10; xi. 18; xvi. 6; xix. 2, etc.).

Ver. 5.—**Now the rest of the acts of Jehoiakim, and all that he did, are they not written in the book of the chronicles of the kings of Judah?** Among the acts of Jehoiakim recorded elsewhere in the Old Testament, the most remarkable are the following: (1) His execution of Urijah the son of Shemaiah (Jer. xxvi. 23); (2) his destruction of the first collection of the early prophecies made by Jeremiah, in a fit of anger at hearing its contents (Jer. xxxvi. 20—23); (3) his order that Jeremiah and Baruch should be arrested (Jer. xxxvi. 26); (4) his capture by some of the "nations" which Nebuchadnezzar had stirred up against him, and delivery into the hands of that monarch (Ezek. xix. 9), probably at Jerusalem. How Nebuchadnezzar treated him is uncertain. Josephus says ('Ant. Jud.,' x. 6. § 3) that he put him to death, and cast him out unburied beyond the walls of the city. But from the biblical notices we can only gather that he died prematurely after a reign of no more than eleven years (B.C. 608 to B.C. 597), and was unlamented, "buried with the burial of an ass, drawn and cast forth beyond the gates of Jerusalem" (Jer. xxii. 18, 19). Conjecture has filled up the blanks of this history in several ways, the most purely imaginative being, perhaps, that of Ewald, who says ('History of Israel,' vol. iv. p. 262), "When the Chaldean armies presented themselves at the gates of the capital, Jehoiakim seems to have been betrayed into the same error as his brother (Jehoahaz), eleven years before. He gave ear to a crafty invitation of the enemy to repair for negotiations to their camp, where, in sight of his own city, he was made prisoner. He offered a frantic resistance, and was dragged away in a scuffle, and miserably cut down; while even an honourable burial for his corpse, which his family certainly solicited, was refused."

Ver. 6.—**So Jehoiakim slept with his fathers.** It is not certain that the writer means anything more by this than that "Jehoiakim died." His body may, however, possibly have been found by the Jews after the Babylonians had withdrawn from before Jerusalem, and have been entombed with those of Manasseh, Amon, and Josiah. **And Jehoiachin his son reigned in his stead.** Josephus says (*l. s. c.*) that Nebuchadnezzar placed him upon the throne, which is likely enough, since he would certainly not have quitted Jerusalem without setting up some king or other. Jehoiachin has in Scripture the two other names of Jeconiah (1 Chron. iii. 16, 17; Jer. xxvii. 20; xxviii. 4; xxix. 2) and Coniah (Jer. xxii. 24, 28; xxxvii. 1). Jehoiachin and Jeconiah differ only, as Jehoahaz and Ahaziah, by a reversal of the order of the two elements. Both mean "Jehovah will establish (him)." "Coniah" cuts off from "Jeconiah" the sign of futurity, and means "Jehovah establishes." It is used only by Jeremiah, and seems used by him to signify that though "Jehovah establishes," Jeconiah he would *not* establish.

Ver. 7.—**And the King of Egypt came not again any more out of his land.** Nechoh's two expeditions were enough for him. In the first he was completely successful, defeated Josiah (ch. xxiii. 29), overran Syria as far as Carchemish, and made Phœnicia, Judæa, and probably the adjacent countries tributary to him. In the second (Jer. xlvi. 2—12) he suffered a calamitous reverse, was himself defeated with great slaughter, forced to fly hastily, and to relinquish all his conquests. After this, he "came not any more out of his land." Whatever hopes he held out to Judæa or to Tyre, he was not bold enough to challenge the Babylonians to a third trial of strength, but remained peaceably within his own borders. **For the King of Babylon had taken from the river of Egypt.** The נַחַל מִצְרַיִם is not the Nile, but the Wady el Arish, the generally dry watercourse, which was the ordinarily accepted boundary between Egypt and Syria (see 1 Kings viii. 65; Isa. xxvii. 12). The Nile is the נְהַר מִצְרַיִם. **Unto the river Euphrates all that pertained to the King of Egypt;** *i.e.* all that he had conquered and made his own in his first expedition in the year B.C. 608.

Vers. 8—16.—REIGN OF JEHOIACHIN. The short reign of Jehoiachin is now described. It lasted but three months. For some reason which is unrecorded, Nebuchadnezzar, who had placed him on the throne, took offence at his conduct, and sent an army against him to effect his deposition. Jehoiachin offered scarcely any resistance. He "went out" of the city (ver. 12), with the queen-mother, the officers of the court, and the princes, and submitted himself to the will of the great king. But he gained nothing by his pusillanimity. The Babylonians entered Jerusalem, plundered the temple and the royal palace, made prisoners of the king, his mother, the princes and nobles, the armed garrison, and all the more skilled artisans, to the number altogether of ten thousand souls (Josephus says 10,832, 'Ant. Jud.,' x. 7. § 1), and carried them captive to Babylon. Zedekiah, the king's uncle, was made monarch in his room.

Ver. 8.—**Jehoiachin was eighteen years old when he began to reign.** In 2 Chron. xxxvi. 9 he is said to have been only eight years old, but this is probably an accidental corruption, the *yod*, which is the Hebrew sign for ten, easily slipping out. As he had "wives" (ver. 15) and "seed" (Jer. xxii. 28), he could not well be less than eighteen. **And he reigned in Jerusalem three months.** "Three months *and ten days*," according to 2 Chron. (*l. s. c.*) and Josephus ('Ant. Jud.,' *l. s. c.*). **And his mother's name was Nehushta, the daughter of Elnathan of Jerusalem.** Elnathan was one of the chief of the Jerusalem princes under Jehoiakim (Jer. xxvi. 22; xxxvi. 12, 25). His daughter, Nehushta—the Nosté of Josephus ('Ant. Jud.,' x. 6. § 3)—was probably the ruling spirit of the time during her son's short reign. We find mention of her in Jer. xxii. 26; xxix. 2; and in Josephus, 'Ant. Jud.,' x. 6. § 3, and x. 7. § 1. Ewald suggests that she "energetically supported" her son in the policy whereby he offended Nebuchadnezzar.

Ver. 9.—**And he did that which was evil in the sight of the Lord, according to all that his father had done** (see ch. xxiii. 37; and comp. 2 Chron. xxxvi. 9). Josephus says that Jehoiachin was φύσει χρηστὸς καὶ δίκαιος ('Ant. Jud.,' x. 7. § 1); but Jeremiah calls him "a despised broken idol," and "a vessel wherein is no pleasure" (Jer. xxii. 28). The present passage probably does not mean more than that he made no attempt at a religious reformation, but allowed the idolatries and superstitions which had prevailed under Jehoahaz and

Jehoiakim to continue. It is in his favour that he did not actively persecute Jeremiah.

Ver. 10.—**At that time the servants of Nebuchadnezzar King of Babylon came up against Jerusalem.** This siege fell probably into the year B.C. 597, which was " the eighth year of Nebuchadnezzar " (ver. 12). Nebuchadnezzar himself was, at the time, engaged in the siege of Tyre, which had revolted in B.C. 598 (see 'Ancient Monarchies,' vol. iii. p. 51), and therefore sent his "servants"—*i.e.* generals—against Jerusalem. **And the city was besieged.** Probably for only a short time. Jeconiah may at first have had some hope of support from Egypt, still under the rule of Nechoh; but when no movement was made in this quarter (see the comment on ver. 7), he determined not to provoke his powerful enemy by an obstinate resistance, but to propitiate him, if possible, by a prompt surrender.

Ver. 11.—**And Nebuchadnezzar King of Babylon came against the city, and his servants did besiege it;** rather, *his servants were besieging it.* While the siege conducted by his generals was still going on, Nebuchadnezzar made his appearance in person before the walls, probably bringing with him an additional force, which made a successful resistance hopeless. A council of war was no doubt held under the new circumstances, and a surrender was decided on.

Ver. 12.—**And Jehoiachin the King of Judah went out to the King of Babylon** (for the use of the expression, " went out to," in this sense of making a surrender, see 1 Sam. xi. 3; Jer. xxi. 0; xxxviii.] 17, etc.), **he, and his mother** (see the comment on ver. 8), **and his servants, and his princes, and his officers**—rather, *his eunuchs* (see the comment on ch. xx. 18)—**and the King of Babylon took him in the eighth year of his reign.** Nebuchadnezzar succeeded his father, Nabopolassar, in B.C. 605; but his first year was not complete till late in B.C. 604. His " eighth year " was thus B.C. 597.

Ver. 13.—**And he carried out thence all the treasures of the house of the Lord.** "Thence" means " from Jerusalem," which he entered and plundered, notwithstanding Jehoiachin's submission, so that not much was gained by the voluntary surrender. A beginning had been made of the carrying off the sacred vessels of the temple in Jehoiakim's third (fourth?) year (Dan. i. 1), which was the first of Nebuchadnezzar. The plundering was now carried a step further; while the final complete sweep of all that remained came eleven years later, at the end of the reign of Zedekiah (see ch. xxv. 13—17). **And the treasures of the king's house** (comp. ch. xx. 13). If the treasures which Hezekiah showed to the

envoys of Merodach-Baladan were carried off by Sennacherib (ch. xviii. 15), still there had probably been fresh accumulations made during their long reigns by Manasseh and Josiah. **And cut in pieces all the vessels of gold which Solomon King of Israel had made in the temple of the Lord.** (For an account of these vessels, see 1 Kings vii. 48—50.) They consisted in part of articles of furniture, like the altar of incense and the table of shrewbread, which were thickly covered with plates of gold; in part of vessels, etc., made wholly of the precious metal, as candlesticks, or rather candelabra, snuffers, tongs, basins, spoons, censers, and the like. **As the Lord had said** (comp. ch. xx. 17; Isa. xxxix. 6; Jer. xv. 13; xvii. 3; xx. 5, etc.).

Ver. 14.—**And he carried away all Jerusalem.** The expression has to be limited by what follows. " All Jerusalem " means all that was important in the population of Jerusalem—all the upper classes, the "princes" and " nobles," all the men trained to the use of arms, and all the skilled craftsmen and artisans of the city. The poor and weak and unskilled were left. The number deported, according to our author, was either ten or eleven thousand. The whole population of the ancient city has been calculated from its area at fifteen thousand. The largest estimate of the population of the modern city is seventeen thousand. **And all the princes.** The *sarim,* or " princes," are not males of the blood royal, but the nobles, or upper classes of Jerusalem (comp. Jer. xxv. 18; xxvi. 10—16, etc.). **And all the mighty men of valour**—*i.e.* "all the trained troops" (Ewald); not "all the men of wealth," as Bähr renders—even ten thousand captives. As the soldiers are reckoned below (ver. 16) at seven thousand, and the craftsmen at one thousand, the upper-class captives would seem to have been two thousand; unless, indeed, the " craftsmen " are additional to the ten thousand, in which case the upper-class captives would have numbered three thousand, and the prisoners have amounted altogether to eleven thousand. **And all the craftsmen and smiths.** Ewald understands "the *military* workmen and siege engineers" to be intended ('History of Israel,' vol. iv. p. 263, note 9); but the term חָרָשׁ in Hebrew includes all workers in stone, metal, or wood (Gen. iv. 22; Isa. xliv. 12; 1 Kings vii. 14), and there is nothing to limit it here to *military* craftsmen. It was an Oriental practice to weaken a state by the deportation of all the stronger elements of its population. **None remained, save the poorest sort of the people of the land.** These words must be taken with some latitude. There are still "princes" in Jerusalem under Zedekiah (Jer. xxxviii.

4, 25, 27), and courtiers of rank (Jer. xxxviii. 7), and "captains of forces" (Jer. xl. 7), and "men of war" (Jer. lii. 7). But the bulk of the inhabitants now left behind in Jerusalem were poor and of small account.

Ver. 15.—**And he carried away Jehoiachin to Babylon** (comp. 2 Chron. xxxvi. 10; Jer. xxii. 26; xxiv. 1; lii. 31; Josephus, 'Ant. Jud.,' x. 7. § 1). Jehoiachin continued a captive in Babylon during the remainder of Nebuchadnezzar's reign—a space of thirty-seven years (see the comment on ch. xxv. 27). **And the king's mother** (see above, ver. 12), **and the king's wives**—this is important, as helping to determine Jehoiachin's age (see the comment on ver. 8)—**and his officers** —rather, *his eunuchs* (comp. Jer. xxxviii. 7; xxxix. 16)—**and the mighty of the land.** Not only the "princes" and the trained soldiers and the skilled artisans (ver. 14), but all who were of much account, as the bulk of the priests and the prophets (see Jer. xxix. 1—24). Those **carried he into captivity from Jerusalem to Babylon.** "Babylon" (בָּבֶל) is tho city, not the country (as Thenius imagines). It was the practice for the conquering kings to carry their captives with them to their capital, for ostentation's sake, before determining on their destination. The Jewish prisoners were, no doubt, *ultimately* settled in various parts of Babylonia. Hence they are called (Ezra ii. 1; Neh. vii. 6) "the children of the *province.*"

Ver. 16.—**And all the men of might**—*i.e.* "the mighty men of valour" (or, "trained soldiers") of ver. 14—even **seven thousand, and craftsmen and smiths a thousand,** all that were **strong** and **apt for war**—the craftsmen and smiths would be pressed into the military service in the event of a siege —**even them the King of Babylon brought captive to Babylon;** *i.e.* he brought to Babylon, not only the royal personages, the officials of the court, and the captives who belonged to the upper classes (ver. 15), but also the entire military force which he had deported, and the thousand skilled artificers. All, without exception, were conducted to the capital.

Vers. 17—20.— EARLIER PORTION OF ZEDEKIAH'S REIGN. Nebuchadnezzar found a son of Josiah, named Mattaniah, still surviving at Jerusalem. At his father's death he must have been a boy of ten, but he was now, eleven years later, of the age of twenty-one. This youth, only three years older than his nephew Jehoiachin, he appointed king, at the same time requiring him to change his name, which he did from "Mattaniah" to "Zedekiah" (ver. 17). Zede-kiah pursued nearly the same course of action as the other recent kings. He showed no religious zeal, instituted no reform, but allowed the idolatrous practices, to which the people were so addicted, to continue (ver. 19). Though less irreligious and less inclined to persecute than Jehoiakim, he could not bring himself to turn to God. He was weak and vacillating, inclined to follow the counsels of Jeremiah, but afraid of the "princes," and ultimately took their advice, which was to ally himself with Egypt, and openly rebel against Nebuchadnezzar. This course of conduct brought about the destruction of the nation (ver. 20).

Ver. 17.—**And the King of Babylon made Mattaniah his father's brother king in his stead.** Josiah had four sons (1 Chron. iii. 15)—Johanan, the eldest, who probably died before his father; Jehoiakim, or Eliakim, the second, who was twenty-five years old at his father's death (ch. xxiii. 36); Jehoahaz, the third, otherwise called Shallum (1 Chron., *l. s. c.*; Jer. xxii. 11), who, when his father died, was aged twenty-three (ch. xxiii. 31); and Mattaniah, the youngest, who must have been then aged ten or nine. It was this fourth son, now grown to manhood, whom Nebuchadnezzar appointed king in Jehoiachin's room. **And changed his name to Zedekiah.** (On the practice of changing a king's name on his accession, see the comment upon ch. xxiii. 31, 34.) Mattaniah means "Gift of Jehovah;" Zedekiah, "Righteousness of Jehovah." Josiah had called his son the first of these names in humble acknowledgment of God's mercy in granting him a fourth son. So other pious Jews called their sons "Nathaniel," and Greeks "Theodotus" or "Theodorus," and Romans "Deodatua." Mattaniah, in taking the second of the names, may have had in his mind the prophecy of Jeremiah (xxiii. 5—8), where blessings are promised to the reign of a king whose name should be "*Jehovah-tsidkenu,*" i.e. "The Lord our Righteousness." Or he may simply have intended to declare that "the righteousness of Jehovah" was what he aimed at establishing. In this case it can only be said that it would have been happy for his country, had his professions been corroborated by his acts.

Ver. 18.—**Zedekiah was twenty and one years old when he began to reign, and he reigned eleven years in Jerusalem;** Probably from B.C. 597 to B.C. 586. He was thus contemporary with Nebuchadnezzar in Babylon, with Cyaxares and Astyages in Media, and with Psamatik II. and Ua-ap-ra

(Pharaoh - Hophra) in Egypt. **And his mother's name** was **Hamutal, the daughter of Jeremiah of Libnah.** He was thus full brother of Jehoahaz (ch. xxiii. 31), but only half-brother to Jehoiakim (ch. xxiii. 36). His father-in-law, "Jeremiah of Libnah," is not the prophet, who was of Anathoth.

Ver. 19.—**And he did that which was evil in the sight of the Lord, according to all that Jehoiakim had done.** Keil says, " His attitude towards the Lord exactly resembled that of his brother Jehoiakim, except that Zedekiah does not appear to have possessed so much energy for that which was evil." He allowed the people to continue their " pollutions" and " abominations" (2 Chron. xxxvi. 14). He let the " princes" have their way, and do whatever they pleased (Jer. xxxviii. 5), contenting himself with sometimes outwitting them, and counteracting their proceedings (Jer. xxxviii. 14—28). He fell into the old error of " putting trust in Egypt" (Jer. xxxvii. 5—7), and made an alliance with Apries (Pharaoh-Hophra), which was an act of rebellion, at once against God and against his Babylonian suzerain. He was, upon the whole, rather weak than wicked; but his weakness was as ruinous to his country as active wickedness would have been.

Ver. 20.—**For through the anger of the Lord it came to pass in Jerusalem and Judah.** It was " through the anger of the Lord" at the persistent impenitence of the people, that *that* came to pass which actually came to pass—the rejection of the nation by God and the casting of it out of his presence. In his anger he suffered the appointment of another perverse and faithless monarch, who made no attempt at a reformation of religion, and allowed him to run his evil course unchecked, and to embroil himself with his suzerain, and to bring destruction upon his nation. God's anger, long provoked (ch. xxi. 10—15; xxiii. 26, 27; xxiv. 3, 4), lay at the root of the whole series of events, not causing men's sins, but allowing them to go on until the cup of their iniquities was full, and the time had arrived for vengeance. **Until he had cast them out from his presence** (comp. ch. xvii. 18, 20; xxiii. 27; xxiv. 3). To be " cast out of God's presence" is to lose his protecting care, to be separated off from him, to be left defenceless against our enemies. When Israel was once finally cast off, its fate was sealed; there was no further hope for it; the end was come. **That Zedekiah rebelled against the King of Babylon;** rather, *And Zedekiah rebelled,* etc. The sentence is a detached one, and would, perhaps, better commence ch. xxv. than terminate, as it does, ch. xxiv. Zedekiah, when he received his investiture at the hands of Nebuchadnezzar (ver. 17), took a solemn oath of allegiance and fidelity (2 Chron. xxxvi. 13; Ezek. xvii. 13) to him and to his successors; but almost immediately afterwards he began to intrigue with Egypt, sent a contingent of troops to help Psamatik II. in his wars (Wiedemann, ' Geschichte Ægyptens,' p. 159), and thus sought to pave the way for an Egyptian alliance, on the strength of which he might venture upon a revolt. It was probably owing to the suspicions which these acts aroused that, in the fourth year of his reign, B.C. 594, he had to visit Babylon (Jer. li. 59), where, no doubt, he renewed his engagements and assured the Babylonian monarch of his fidelity. But these proceedings were nothing but a blind. On the accession of Hophra (Apries) to the throne of Egypt in B.C. 591, Zedekiah renewed his application to the Egyptian court, openly sending ambassadors (Ezek. xvii. 15), with a request for infantry and cavalry. Thus was his rebellion complete, his "oath despised," and his " covenant broken" (Ezek. xvii. 15, 16). The war with Babylon, and the siege of Jerusalem, were the natural consequences.

HOMILETICS.

Vers. 1—4.—*Conquering kings and nations instruments in God's hands to work out his purposes.* The sudden disappearance of Assyria from the scene, and the sudden appearance of Babylon upon it at this point of the history, are very remarkable. Without a word upon the circumstances that had brought it about, the writer of Kings shows us that a great crisis in the world's history has come and gone; that the mighty state which had dominated Western Asia for centuries is no more, and has been superseded by a new, and hitherto scarce heard of, power. " In his ⌈Jehoiakim's⌉ days Nebuchadnezzar King of Babylon came up." We have thus presented to us, by implication—

I. Assyria's fall. For nearly a thousand years Assyria had been " the rod of God's anger" (Isa. x. 5). She had been sent against nation after nation, to execute God's wrath, with " a charge, to take the spoil, and to take the prey, and to tread them down like the mire of the streets" (Isa. x. 6). As Hezekiah confessed in his prayer (ch. xix. 17, 18), their success had been continual: " Of a truth, Lord, the kings of Assyria *have* destroyed the nations and their lands, and have cast their gods into the fire," etc. But why and whence was this? Because God had used Assyria as his instrument. God had brought it to pass that Assyria should exist "to lay waste fenced cities into ruinous heaps. Therefore their inhabitants were of small power, they were dismayed and confounded; they were as the grass of the field, and as the green herb, as the grass on the house-tops, and as corn blasted before it be grown up" (ch. xix. 25, 26). But this time was now gone. Assyria had offended God by her pride and self-trust. She had said, "By the strength of my hand I have done this, and by my wisdom; for I am prudent: and I have removed the bounds of the people, and have robbed their treasures, and I have put down the inhabitants like a valiant man" (Isa. x. 13). The axe had "boasted itself against him that hewed therewith; and the saw had magnified itself against him that moved it to and fro" (Isa. x. 15). Therefore God thought it time to vindicate his own honour, and Assyria fell. Two other nations were raised up to break in pieces the proud and haughty conqueror; and, after a short struggle, Assyria sank, to rise no more (Nah. iii. 19).

II. BABYLON'S RISE TO GREATNESS. Babylon had in remote days (Gen. x. 8—10) been a powerful state, and had even possessed an empire; but for the last seven hundred years or more she had been content to play a very secondary part in Western Asia, and had generally been either an Assyrian feudatory or an integral part of the Assyrian monarchy. But in the counsels of God it had been long decreed that she, and not Assyria, should be God's instrument for the chastisement of his people (ch. xx. 16—19). Therefore, as the appointed time for Assyria's fall approached, Babylon was made to increase in power and greatness. A wave of invasion (Herod., i. 104, 105), which passed over the rest of Western Asia, left her untouched. A great monarch was given her in the person of Nabopolassar, who read aright the signs of the times, saw in Media a desirable ally, and, having secured Median co-operation, revolted against the long-established sovereign power. A short, sharp struggle followed, ending in the utter collapse of the great Assyrian empire, and the siege and fall of Nineveh. The two conquering states partitioned between them the Assyrian dominions—Media taking the countries which lay to the north-west and north, Babylon those towards the south-west and south. Thus, so far as the Jews were concerned, Babylon, between B.C. 625 and B.C. 608, had stepped into Assyria's place. She had become "the hammer of the whole earth" (Jer. l. 23); God's battle-axe and weapons of war (Jer. li. 20), wherewith he brake in pieces nations and kingdoms, man and woman, old and young, captains and rulers (Jer. li. 20—23). The prophecy of Isaiah to Hezekiah (ch. xx. 16—19), which seemed so unlikely of fulfilment at the time that it was uttered, found a natural and easy accomplishment, the course of events in the latter part of the seventh century B.C. having transferred to Babylonia, under Divine direction and arrangement, that grand position and dignity which had previously been Assyria's. When she had served God's purpose, Babylon's turn came; and she sank as suddenly as she had risen, because she too had been "proud against the Lord" (Jer. l. 29), and had provoked his indignation.

Vers. 1—6.—*The beginning of the end.* It has been already observed (see the homiletics to ch. xvi.) that God's punishment of a nation, though often long-deferred, when it comes at last comes suddenly, violently, and at once. Nineteen years only intervened—a brief space in the life of a nation—between the first intimation which the Jews received of danger impending from a new enemy, and the entire destruction, by that enemy, of temple, city, and nation. Peril first showed itself in B.C. 605; Jerusalem was destroyed and the Jews carried into captivity in B.C. 586. From first to last they were scarcely given a breathing-space. Blow was struck upon blow; calamity followed close upon calamity. "The beginning of the end" is to be dated from Nebuchadnezzar's first invasion—when "Nebuchadnezzar King of Babylon came up" against Jehoiakim, "and Jehoiakim became his servant three years" (ver. 1). When an iron vessel and an earthen one come into contact and collision, it is not difficult to foresee the result. Nebuchadnezzar's first campaign proved his absolute superiority over all the forces that could be brought against him by the nations of the west. Could the Jews have accepted, honestly and loyally, the position which Jehoiakim professedly took up—that of a faithful vassal and feudatory, who would keep watch over the interests of his suzerain, and aid him to the best of his power—a prolonged though inglorious existence would have been possible for the people. But the nation was too proud to submit itself. Neither king nor people had any intention of putting up with the loss of independence or becoming loyal Babylonian subjects, however strongly the duty might be pressed upon them by Jeremiah and the other Jehovistic prophets. A profound antagonism was developed from the first. Nebuchadnezzar probably carried off the captives " of the king's seed, and of the princes " (Dan. i. 3), from Jerusalem by way of hostages. Jehoiakim meditated revolt from the moment of his submission; and within three years threw off the mask, and rebelled openly. Five years of struggle followed. Prompted by Nebuchadnezzar, " the nations set upon him on every side from the provinces, and spread their net over him " (Ezek. xix. 8; comp. ch. xxiv. 2), ravaged his territory far and wide, " destroyed " multitudes of the people, and, at last, " took the king in their snare " (Ezek. xix. 8), and " brought him to the King of Babylon" (Ezek. xix. 9). Nebuchadnezzar punished him with death, cast out his body unburied, and took as hostages to Babylon three thousand more of the upper classes of the citizens (Josephus, ' Ant. Jud.,' x. 6. § 3). Distrust and suspicion on the one side, hatred and sense of cruel wrong on the other, must, under these circumstances, have grown and increased; the antagonism, instead of dying away with the lapse of time, must have become accentuated. " The end " already approached, though it " was not yet." The weaker party could not but go to the wall; and events were evidently hastening to a *dénouement*. With the death of Jehoiakim the first scene of the last act had terminated.

Vers. 8—16.—*Blow upon blow.* A mild and conciliatory policy might, perhaps, have won the Jews to acquiescence in their subjection. But Nebuchadnezzar's policy was the reverse, and could only tend to their exasperation. With what exact intention or expectation he made Jehoiachin king after executing his father, it is difficult to con-jecture. Perhaps he thought he had nothing to fear from a youth of eighteen. Perhaps he trusted to the known mildness of the youth's disposition (Josephus, ' Ant. Jud.,' x. 7. § 1). In either case, the experiment failed. Jehoiachin, within a few weeks, gave him cause of offence, or, at any rate, furnished him with some pretext for reopening the quarrel. Then blow was struck upon blow. An army was sent to besiege the city (ver. 10); soon the great king came up against it in person (ver. 11). In vain did Jehoiachin make submission. He was seized and carried off to Babylon, and there shut up in prison. The temple and the royal palace were plundered, and at least ten thousand of the inhabitants—the noblest, wealthiest, bravest, and most skilled—torn from their homes and led into captivity (vers. 12—16). A remnant only, consisting chiefly of " the poorest of the people of the land " (ver. 14), were left behind. Jeru-salem, denuded of more than half her population, can scarcely have known herself. She " sat solitary " (Lam. i. 1) and " wept sore in the night " (Lam. i. 2), and felt that her total destruction was nigh at hand. So ended the second scene of the last act.

HOMILIES BY VARIOUS AUTHORS.

Ver. 1—ch. xxv. 17.—*Wickedness, retribution, and Divine control, as revealed in Nebuchadnezzar's invasion of Judah.* " In his days Nebuchadnezzar," etc. In glancing through these chapters there are two objects that press on our attention. 1. *A national crisis.* The peace, the dignity, the wealth, the religious privileges of Judah are con-verging to a close. Israel has already been carried away by a despot to a foreign land, and now Judah is meeting the same fate. All nations have their crises—they have their rise, their fall, their dissolution. 2. *A terrible despot.* The name of Nebuchadnezzar comes for the first time under our attention. Who is he? He is a prominent figure in the histories and the prophecies of the old Scriptures. He was the son and successor of Nabopolassar, who, having revolted from Assyria and helped to destroy Nineveh, brought Babylon at once into pre-eminence. The victories of Nebuchadnezzar were stupendous and many. Egypt, Syria, Phœnicia, Palestine, all bowed to his triumphant arms. He made Babylon, his capital, one of the most wonderful cities of the world. The walls with which he fortified it contained, we are told, no less than five hundred million tons of masonry. He was at once the master and the terror of the age he lived in, which was six hundred years before Christ. There is no character in all history more pregnant with practical suggestions than his—a mighty fiend in human form. We have in these two chapters a view of (1) *the wickedness of man*; (2) *the retribution of Heaven*; (3) and *the supremacy of God*. Here we have—

I. THE WICKEDNESS OF MAN. The wickedness here displayed is marked: 1. *By inveteracy.* It is here said of Jehoiachin, "He did that which was evil in the sight of the Lord, according to all that his father had done." In ver. 19 the same is also said of Zedekiah: "He did that which was evil in the sight of the Lord, according to all that Jehoiakim had done." This has, indeed, been said of many kings of Judah, as of all the kings of Israel. What a hold, then, had wickedness taken on the Jewish people! It had so deeply struck its roots into their very being that neither the mercies nor the judgments of Heaven could uproot it. It was a cancer transmitted from sire to son, poisoning their blood and eating up their nature. Thus, then, from generation to generation the wickedness of the Jewish people seemed to be a disease hereditary, ineradicable, and incurable. 2. *By tyranny.* "At that time the servants of Nebuchadnezzar King of Babylon came up against Jerusalem, and the city was besieged. And Nebuchadnezzar King of Babylon came against the city, and his servants did besiege it." This is seen in the conduct of Nebuchadnezzar. What right had Nebuchadnezzar to leave his own country, invade Judah, plunder it of its wealth, and bear away by violence its population? None whatever. It was tyranny of the worst kind, an outrage on every principle of humanity and justice. Sin is evermore tyrannic. We see it everywhere. On all hands do we see men and women endeavouring to bring others into subjection—masters their servants, employers their *employés*, rulers their subjects. Tyranny everywhere is the evidence, the effect, and the instrument of wickedness. 3. *By inhumanity.* "And the King of Babylon . . . carried out thence all the treasures of the house of the Lord, and the treasures of the king's house, and cut in pieces all the vessels of gold which Solomon King of Israel had made in the temple of the Lord, as the Lord had said. And he carried away all Jerusalem, and all the princes, and all the mighty men of valour, even ten thousand captives, and all the craftsmen and smiths: none remained, save the poorest sort of the people of the land. And he carried away Jehoiachin to Babylon, and the king's mother, and the king's wives, and his officers, and the mighty of the land, those carried he into captivity from Jerusalem to Babylon. And all the men of might, even seven thousand, and craftsmen and smiths a thousand, and all that were strong and apt for war, even them the King of Babylon brought captive to Babylon." He rifled the country of its people and its property, and inflicted untold misery on thousands. Thus wickedness transforms man into a fiend, and turns society into a pandemonium. 4. *By profanity.* We read here that Nebuchadnezzar carried away all the treasures of the house of the Lord, and cut in pieces all the vessels of gold which Solomon had made in the temple thereof. We also read here that "he burnt the house of the Lord. . . . And the pillars of brass that were in the house of the Lord, and the bases, and the brazen sea that was in the house of the Lord, did the Chaldees break in pieces, and carried the brass of them to Babylon. And the pots, and the shovels, and the snuffers, and the spoons, and all the vessels of brass wherewith they ministered, took they away. . . . The two pillars, one sea, and the bases which Solomon had made for the house of the Lord; the brass of all these vessels was without weight." Thus this ruthless despot, becoming a scourge in God's hands, desecrated the most holy things in the city of Jerusalem and in the memory of millions. He reduced the magnificent pile of buildings to ashes, and rifled it of its sacred and priceless treasures. Wickedness is essentially profane. It has no reverence; it crushes every sentiment of sanctity in the soul. O sin, what hast thou done? Thou hast quenched the divinest instincts in human nature, and poisoned the fountain of religious and social sympathies, substituted cruelty for love, tyranny for justice, blind superstition and blasphemous profanity for devotion.

II. THE RETRIBUTION OF HEAVEN.

III. THE SUPREMACY OF GOD.—D. T.

Vers. 1—9.—*The advent of Nebuchadnezzar.* It had been predicted that the final blow on Judah would be delivered, not by the Assyrians, but by the Chaldeans. "The days come, that all that is in thine house . . . shall be carried into Babylon: nothing shall be left" (ch. xx. 17; cf. Micah iv. 10). That prediction now hasted to its accomplishment. Babylon had emerged as the successor to Assyria in the undisputed possession of imperial power. Its second king was Nebuchadnezzar, God's chosen instrument for the chastisement of Judah and surrounding nations (Jer. xxvii.).

I. JEHOIAKIM'S SUBMISSION. 1. *The defeat of Nechoh.* It was through Pharaoh-Nechoh, as previously stated, that Nebuchadnezzar was brought into relations with Judah, which did not end till the final ruin of the latter state. Nechoh had advanced to Carchemish on the Euphrates, when Nebuchadnezzar, finding his hands free, met him in battle, and completely defeated him (B.C. 605). All the country between Egypt and the Euphrates, which Nechoh had conquered, thus fell under the power of Babylon (ver. 7). Egypt might intrigue, but was thereafter powerless to help. Wonderful are the combinations of circumstances by which, in providence, God works out his ends. 2. *Nebuchadnezzar's advance on Jerusalem.* It was now the fourth year of Jehoiakim (Jer. xxv. 1), and, as Nechoh's vassal, he had probably contributed his contingent to the defeated Egyptian army. Nebuchadnezzar speedily came against him. We learn from other passages (2 Chron. xxxvi. 6, 7; Dan. i. 1, 2) that Jerusalem actually was besieged, and Jehoiakim bound in fetters, with the intention of being sent to Babylon. The king saved himself by submission; but the temple was plundered of its sacred vessels, and certain princes, among them Daniel, were taken away captive. This is the beginning of the seventy years' captivity (Jer. xxv. 11). 3. *The three years' servitude.* For three years Jehoiakim bore the heavy yoke of the King of Babylon, as before he had borne that of Nechoh. During that period his character underwent no improvement. He still proved himself the tyrant and oppressor of his people, was obstinate and headlong in his courses, and sought the life of God's prophets. He built magnificent palaces by forced labour (Jer. xxii. 13—17). When Jeremiah's roll was read to him, he cut it up with his penknife, and threw it in the fire (Jer. xxxvi. 20—23). He slew Urijah the prophet, and would have put Jeremiah also to death if he had dared (Jer. xxvi. 12—24). Under his reign heathenism underwent a great revival, and the moral condition of the people rapidly deteriorated. Judah, like Israel of former days, had become a hopelessly corrupt carcase, and nothing remained but to remove it from the face of the earth.

II. JEHOIAKIM'S REBELLION. 1. *Its motives.* Three years Jehoiakim served the King of Babylon, then "he turned and rebelled against him." Not much light is thrown on the motives of this rebellion beyond the fact that Nebuchadnezzar was at this time at a distance, and Jehoiakim may have thought he might assert his independence with impunity. Pharaoh-Nechoh was still intriguing to stir up disaffection; plots were always hatching to get the subject-nations to combine against their common oppressor (cf. Jer. xxvii. 3: on this occasion, however, Moab and Ammon were on the side of Nebuchadnezzar, ver. 2); and false prophets were never wanting to predict success (cf. Jer. xxviii.). Jeremiah gave a steady voice to the contrary, but it was unheeded. The proverb was again to be fulfilled—whom the gods wish to destroy, they first madden. Jehoiakim was given up to the delusions of his own vain and foolish notions, and the people cherished extravagant hopes based on their possession of the temple and the Law (Jer. vii. 4; viii. 8). But neither temple nor Law will avail those who refuse to "thoroughly amend" their "ways" and their "doings" (Jer. vii. 5). 2. *Human instruments of punishment.* "And the Lord sent against him bands of the Chaldees, and bands of the Syrians," etc. Nebuchadnezzar could not at the time attend to Jehoiakim in person; but he could lay his commands on neighbouring peoples, and these were ordered to keep up a galling and harassing attack on Judah by means of marauding bands. Detachments of his own Chaldeans were assisted by Syrians, Moabites, and Ammonites, and gave Jehoiakim no peace. God's heritage is compared by Jeremiah to "a speckled bird, the birds round about are against her" (Jer. xii. 9). Troubles rise on every side against those who forsake God. 3. *God over all.* It was the "Lord" who sent these hostile bands "against Judah to destroy it"—"surely at the commandment of the Lord came this upon Judah, to remove them out of his sight." In sacred history everything is looked at from the standpoint of Divine providence. From second causes it mounts invariably to the supreme cause. Nebuchadnezzar is God's "servant—his instrument for the chastisement of the nations" (Jer. xxvii. 4—7); and what, from the purely historical point of view, seems a lawless play of forces, is, from the Divine point of view, a scene full of meaning, interest, and purpose. The rejection of Judah is again in these verses connected with the sin of Manasseh, only, however, as before shown, because people and rulers made these sins their own, and would not depart from them. Heathenism was again rampant (cf. Ezek. viii.), and Jehoiakim, like Manasseh, was shedding "innocent blood" (Jer. xxii. 17). Scripture knows no fatalism beyond that which springs from the incorrigibleness of a people wedded to their sins. Neither is there any sin which, if sincerely repented of, God will not pardon, though its temporal effects may still have to be endured. But there is the awful possibility of getting beyond pardon through our own obduracy. Both sides of the truth are seen in Jeremiah—on the one hand exhortations to repentance, with assurances of forgiveness (Jer. xviii. 7—10; xxvi. 1—3; xxxv. 15); and on the other declarations that the time for pardon was past (Jer. vii. 13—16, 27, 28; xi. 11—14; xv. 1; xviii. 11, 12; xxxvi. 16, 17, etc.). It was not because the fathers had eaten sour grapes that the children's teeth were set on edge (Ezek. xviii. 2); but the children had walked in the fathers' ways.

III. JEHOIAKIM'S SON. 1. *Jehoiakim's end.* Like so many other wicked kings, Jehoiakim came to a miserable end, for there is no reason to doubt that Jeremiah's prophecy was fulfilled regarding him, "He shall be buried with the burial of an ass, drawn and cast forth beyond the gates of Jerusalem" (Jer. xxii. 18, 19). The circumstances are unknown. 2. *Jehoiachin's character.* Jehoiachin succeeded to the throne of his father, but, like Jehoahaz, he only held it for three months. Of him, too, the record is borne that he "did evil." He is, perhaps, the "young lion" of Ezek. xix. 5—9, whom the nations took in their net, and brought to the King of Babylon. There seem to have been some elements of nobleness in his nature, and, after a long captivity, he became the friend and companion of the Babylonian king who succeeded Nebuchadnezzar (ch. xxv. 27—30).—J. O.

Vers. 10—20.—*The first general captivity.* Some captives had been taken to Babylon on occasion of Nebuchadnezzar's first advance against Jerusalem (Dan. i. 1, 2). The full storm of predicted judgment was now, however, to descend. What prophets had so long foretold amidst the scoffing and incredulity of their godless contemporaries was now at length to be accomplished. The final tragedy falls into two parts, of which the first is before us.

I. JEHOIACHIN MAKES SURRENDER. 1. *The city besieged.* The attacks of the Chaldeans, Syrians, Moabites, etc., mentioned in ver. 2, had served an immediate purpose in weakening the strength and exhausting the resources of Judah. The great king, whose fame was already equalling that of a Sargon or a Sennacherib, was now able to send his main army against the city, and soon after appeared upon the scene in person. Again, as in the days of Hezekiah, the city was closely invested; but this time there was no Isaiah to hurl back scorn for scorn, and assure the trembling king of the complete discomfiture of the enemy. Neither was there a king of Hezekiah's stamp to lay the blasphemous messages of the invader before the Lord, and entreat his interposition (ch. xix. 14—19). It was another kind of message Jeremiah the prophet had to bear to king and people. The day for mercy was past; and in default of a general repentance, which was not to be expected, there remained nothing but "a certain fearful looking for of judgment and fiery indignation" (Heb. x. 27). The day of final reckoning surely comes for every sinner. It had come for Israel a hundred and twenty years before; it was now come for Israel's sister Judah. 2. *Jehoiachin's voluntary surrender.* Seeing resistance to be hopeless, Jehoiachin did what, on the most favourable interpretation of his conduct, was a noble thing. The city could not hold out; but if he and the other members of the royal house went and made voluntary surrender of themselves to Nebuchadnezzar, the worst horrors might be spared. This, indeed, was what Jeremiah always counselled. Jehoiachin accordingly went forth, with Nehushta his mother, and his servants, princes, and officers, and delivered themselves up to the Babylonian king. He might feel, with the lepers of Samaria, "If they save us alive, we shall live; and if they kill us, we shall but die" (ch. vii. 4). Or he may have been actuated by the nobler impulse to save the people, and may have thought, "It is expedient for us, that one man should die for the people, and that the whole nation perish not" (John xi. 50). His submission did avert the worst from the nation. His own life was spared, though he was led away a prisoner; the city was not sacked and burned, as afterwards; and no massacre of the inhabitants took place. A tender tone pervades Jeremiah's references to this unfortunate king (Jer. xxii. 24—30). Ezekiel likens him to "the highest branch of the cedar," which the "great eagle, with great wings, long-winged, full of feathers, which had divers colours," crops off (Ezek. xvii. 3, 4); and again (according to some) to "a young lion," who had "learned to catch the prey, and devoured men," but "the nations set against him on every side," and "he was taken in their pit," and put in chains, and brought to the King of Babylon (Ezek. xix. 5—9). We may share with Jeremiah in his sympathy for the unhappy young king in his exile (Jer. xxii. 28). Had his circumstances been more favourable, better things might have been hoped of him. The nobility of self-sacrifice redeems a character from many faults.

II. THE CITY DESPOILED. If Jehoiachin's surrender saved the people from slaughter, it could not save the city from plunder, nor its inhabitants from captivity. Nebuchadnezzar was no kid-gloved conqueror; where his mailed hand fell, he let it be felt. This city had rebelled against him, and he would effectually cripple its power to rebel again by impoverishing, degrading, and weakening it to the utmost. Nebuchadnezzar was intent only on his own ends, yet unconsciously he was carrying out to the letter the predictions which God's prophets had been dinning into the people's ears with so little result during all the years of their backsliding. The city was despoiled: 1. *Of its wealth and sacred vessels.* " He carried out thence all the treasures of the house of the Lord, and the treasures of the king's house, and cut in pieces all the vessels of gold which Solomon . . . had made," etc. Jehoiakim had saved his treasures at the expense of exactions from the people, and his "covetousness" had doubtless filled them still more (Jer. xxii. 17). These ill-gotten gains were now carried away, and with them such of the temple vessels as were made of, or plated with, gold, the "cutting to pieces" being probably confined to the latter, with such large articles as the golden candlestick, etc. Of the smaller articles some few were spared (ch. xxv. 15), and the rest were preserved in Babylon, and restored on the return (Ezra i. 7—11). Judgment thus again began at the house of God. As, with the wealth of the city, the wealth-producers were also taken (ver. 14), it is easy to see to what poverty it was reduced. 2. *Of its royal family and nobles.* "And he carried away Jehoiachin to Babylon, and the king's mother, and the king's wives," etc. The land was thus deflowered of its king and aristocracy. The nobles, indeed, had proved no source of strength to the nation, but had set an example of luxury, oppression, corruption, and idolatry. Still, they were the representatives of its old hereditary families; they had high social position and great influence; and they ought to have been, if they were not, patrons and examples of everything good and great. Those who have rank, fortune, and leisure may be of the highest service to a state, if only they devote their powers to its true welfare. They contribute elements of refinement, culture, and wealth to it, which cannot be lost without impoverishment. If, however, they abuse their opportunities, and grow luxurious, idle, and wicked, they have generally to suffer severely in the end. 3. *Of its artisans and warriors.* "And all the men of might, even seven thousand, and craftsmen and smiths a thousand, all that were strong and apt for war," etc. Besides removing from the city the wealth that enriched it, and the nobles who adorned it, Nebuchadnezzar took away the skilful hands that did its work, and the strong arms that fought for it. He left none "save the poorest sort of the people of the land." This was to drain the city dry of every element of its prosperity. The middle classes of a nation—its wealth-producers and skilled labourers—even more than its aristocracy— are the source of its strength. By them is created the capital of the country; through them that capital undergoes constant renewal and increase; they supply the wants of every other class; without them the nobles would be helpless, and on them "the poorest sort of people"—too often the unfortunate, the shiftless, the inefficient classes —depend for casual employment and support. Nebuchadnezzar looked well to his own interests when he deported these classes, and not the poor, the less able, less thrifty, to Babylon. But their departure was ruinous to Jerusalem, and this also Nebuchadnezzar intended. It was, indeed, an irretrievable, crushing blow which had fallen on the nation, none the less ruinous and terrible that it had been so long predicted, and was so richly deserved. Piety tends to the enrichment and strengthening of a nation, as of an individual, even temporally; but a course of ungodliness ends in the loss of temporal and spiritual possessions together.

III. ZEDEKIAH MADE KING. 1. *Accession of Zedekiah.* Jehoiachin was a man of spirited character, and Nebuchadnezzar seems to have thought that he would be better served by putting a weaker man upon the throne. The person chosen was an uncle of the young king's, a brother of Jehoiakim, whose name, Mattaniah, Nebuchadnezzar changed to Zedekiah—"the Righteousness of Jehovah." There was little honour now in being King of Judah; but at least the city and temple still stood; the priesthood had not been carried away; there were a few nobles left to grace the court; and by degrees new artisans and soldiers might have been got in, and the state again built up. It was the last chance, and was given only to show clearly how hopeless the moral condition of the people was. For if anything could have sobered them, and convinced them of the truth of the words of the prophets, it was such a catastrophe as had descended upon them. Deaf to all warnings, however, whether of mercy or judgment, the people only went on from bad to worse. 2. *His weak character.* The outstanding feature in Zedekiah's character was weakness—lack of courage and strength of will. He was not without good impulses. He showed a friendly disposition to Jeremiah; on various occasions he sought his advice and intercession (Jer. xxi. 1, 2; xxxvii. 3; xxxviii. 14—17); at Jeremiah's instigation he made a covenant with the people of Jerusalem, pledging them to give liberty to their bondmen (Jer. xxxiv, 8, 11), and once at least he refrained from entering into a proposed league against Nebuchadnezzar (Jer. xxvii. 3). But his timid, faithless, unstable nature reveals itself at every turn. He was like Herod, who did many things at the bidding of John the Baptist, and heard him gladly, yet at last beheaded him to please a wicked woman (Mark vi. 20). Zedekiah knew what was right, but did not do it (Jer. xxxvii. 2); he weakly allowed himself to be overruled by his nobles—when they broke through his covenant he had no power to resist (Jer. xxxiv. 11); when they urged him to put Jeremiah to death, he consented, saying, "Behold, he is in your hand: for the king is not he that can do anything against you" (Jer. xxxviii. 4, 5); then, when Ebed-Melech pleaded for the prophet, he gave orders for his deliverance (ver. 10); he disobeyed Jeremiah in throwing off his allegiance to Nebuchadnezzar, and in seeking an alliance with Egypt; and when Nebuchadnezzar again came up against him, he sought Jeremiah's counsel, but did not take it when it was given (Jer. xxxviii. 14—28), etc. Meanwhile idolatry had firmly established itself in the holy city, and within the very precincts of the temple (Ezek. viii.). Fitly, therefore, is the reign of this last king described, like the rest, as "evil." His weakness and vacillation, his unfaithfulness to his own best convictions, his sinful yielding to others in what he knew to be wrong, were his ruin. He was in a hard and difficult position, and he had no strength of mind to cope with it. 3. *His rebellion.* At length, yielding to the solicitations of his nobles, and hopeful of help from Egypt (Ezek. xvii. 15), he broke his oath of allegiance to Nebuchadnezzar, an act which Ezekiel strongly condemns (Ezek. xvii. 16—19). The cup was full, and the Lord left him thus far to himself, that the nation might be destroyed. Men who will not follow light, lose light. A blindness, as from heaven, falls upon them. They are left to the bent of their own hearts, and their own counsel is their ruin. Sin is the supreme folly, as righteousness is the supreme wisdom.—J. O.

EXPOSITION.

CHAPTER XXV.

Vers. 1—30.—THE LAST SIEGE OF JERUSALEM. THE JEWS LED INTO CAPTIVITY. HISTORY OF THE REMNANT LEFT BEHIND. RELEASE FROM PRISON OF JEHOIACHIN.

Vers. 1—10.—LAST SIEGE AND CAPTURE OF JERUSALEM. The open rebellion of Zedekiah was followed almost immediately by

the advance into Judæa of a Babylonian army under Nebuchadnezzar in person, and the strict investment of the capital. We learn the circumstances of the siege from Jeremiah, in the prophecy which bears his name, and in the Book of Lamentations. It lasted one year and seven months, and was accompanied by a blockade so strict that the defenders were reduced to the last extremity, and, as in Samaria under Jehoram (ch. vi. 29), and again in Jerusalem during the siege by Titus (Josephus, 'Bell. Jud.,' vi. 3. § 4), mothers ate their children (see Lam. ii. 20; iv. 10). When resistance was no longer possible, Zedekiah, with his men-at-arms, attempted to escape by night, and fled eastward, but were overtaken and captured in the plain of Jericho (Jer. xxxix. 4, 5). Meanwhile the city fell into the enemy's hands, and was treated with all the rigours of war. The temple, the royal palace, and the great houses of the rich men were first plundered and then delivered to the flames (ver. 9). The walls of the city were broken down (ver. 10), and the gates laid even with the ground (Lam. ii. 9). A great massacre of the population took place in the streets (Lam. ii. 3, 4).

Ver. 1.—**And it came to pass in the ninth year of his**—*i.e.* Zedekiah's—**reign, in the tenth month, in the tenth day of the month.** Extreme exactness with respect to a date indicates the extreme importance of the event dated. In the whole range of the history contained in the two Books of the Kings, there is no instance of the year, month, and day being all given excepting in the present chapter, where we find this extreme exactness three times (vers. 1, 4, and 8). The date in ver. 1 is confirmed by Jer. lii. 10 and Ezek. xxiv. 1. That **Nebuchadnezzar King of Babylon came, he, and all his host, against Jerusalem.** According to the description of the eye-witness, Jeremiah, the army was one of unusual magnitude. Nebuchadnezzar brought against Jerusalem at this time "*all his army*, and *all the kingdoms of the earth of his dominion*, and *all the people*" (Jer. xxxiv. 1). The march of the army was not direct upon Jerusalem; it at first spread itself over Judæa, wasting the country and capturing the smaller fortified towns (Josephus, 'Ant. Jud.,' x. 7. § 3) —among them Lachish, so famous in the war against Sennacherib (ch. xviii. 14, 17; xix. 8), and Azekah (Jer. xxxiv. 7). The capture of these two places was important as intercepting Zedekiah's line of communication with Egypt. Having made himself master of them, Nebuchadnezzar proceeded to invest the capital. **And pitched against it**—*i.e.* encamped, and commenced a regular siege—**and they built forts against it round about.** It has been argued that דָּיֵק does not mean a "fort" or "tower," but a "line of circumvallation" (Michaëlis, Hitzig, Thenius, Bähr). Jerusalem, however, can scarcely be surrounded by lines of circum-

vallation, which, moreover, were not employed in their sieges by the Orientals. *Dâyek* (דָּיֵק) seems to be properly a "watch tower," from דּוּק, *speculari*, whence it passed into the meaning of a "tower" generally. The towers used in sieges by the Assyrians and Babylonians were movable ones, made of planks, which were pushed up to the walls, so that the assailants might attack their adversaries, on a level, with greater advantage. Sometimes they contained battering-rams (see Layard, 'Monuments of Nineveh,' first series, pl. 19; and comp. Jer. lii. 4; Ezek. iv. 2; xvii. 17; xxvi. 8; Josephus, 'Ant. Jud.,' x. 8. § 1).

Ver. 2.—**And the city was besieged unto the eleventh year of King Zedekiah.** The writer omits all the details of the siege, and hastens to the final catastrophe. From Jeremiah and Ezekiel we learn that, after the siege had continued a certain time, the Egyptian monarch, Hophra or Apries, made an effort to carry out the terms of his agreement with Zedekiah, and marched an army into Southern Judæa, with the view of raising the siege (Jer. xxxvii. 5; Ezek. xvii. 17). Nebuchadnezzar hastened to meet him. With the whole or the greater part of his host he marched southward and offered battle to the Egyptians. Whether an engagement took place or not is uncertain. Josephus affirms it, and says that Apries was "defeated and driven out of Syria" ('Ant. Jud.,' x. 7. § 3). The silence of Jeremiah is thought to throw doubt on his assertion. At any rate, the Egyptians retired (Jer. xxxvii. 7) and took no further part in the struggle. The Babylonians returned, and the siege recommenced. A complete blockade was established, and the defenders of the city soon began to suffer from famine (Jer. xxi. 7, 9; Lam. ii. 12, 20). Ere long, as so often happens in sieges, famine was followed by pestilence (Jer. xxi. 6, 7; Josephus, 'Ant. Jud.,' *l. s. c.*), and after a time the place was reduced to the last extremity (Lam. iv. 3—9). Bread was no longer to be had, and mothers devoured their children (Lam. iv. 10). At length a breach was effected in the defences; the enemy poured in; and the city fell (see the comment on ver. 4).

Ver. 3.—**And on the ninth** day **of the fourth month.** The text of Kings is here incomplete, and has to be restored from Jer. lii. 6. Our translators have supplied the missing words. The famine prevailed in the city (see the comment on ver. 2). As I have elsewhere observed, "The intensity of the suffering endured may be gathered from Lamentations, Ezekiel, and Josephus. The complexions of the men grew black with famine (Lam. iv. 8; v. 10); their skin was shrunk and parched (Lam. iv. 8); the rich and noble women searched the dunghills for scraps of offal (Lam. iv. 5); the children perished for want, or were even devoured by their parents (Lam. ii. 20; iv. 3, 4, 10; Ezek. v. 10); water was scarce, as well as food, and was sold at a price (Lam. v. 4); a third part of the inhabitants died of the famine, and the plague which grew out of it (Ezek. v. 12)" (see the 'Speaker's Commentary,' vol. ii. p. 147). **And there was no bread for the people of the land.** Bread commonly fails comparatively early in a siege. It was some time before the fall of the city that Ebed-Melech expressed his fear that Jeremiah would starve, since there was no more bread in the place (see Jer. xxxviii. 9).

Ver. 4.—**And the city was broken up;** rather, *broken into;* i.e. a breach was made in the walls. Probably the breach was on the north side of the city, where the ground is nearly level (see Ezek. ix. 2). According to Josephus ('Ant. Jud.,' x. 8. § 2), the enemy entered through the breach about midnight. **And all the men of war**—*i.e.* all the soldiers who formed the garrison—**fled by night by the way of the gate between two walls**; rather, *between the two walls,* as in Jer. lii. 7. As the enemy broke in on the north, the king and garrison quitted the city on the south by a gate which opened into the Tyropœon valley, between the two walls that guarded the town on either side of it. **Which is by the king's garden.** The royal gardens were situated near the Pool of Siloam, at the mouth of the Tyropœon, and near the junction of the Hinnom with the Kidron valley (see Josephus, 'Ant. Jud.,' vii. 11). **(Now the Chaldees were against the city round about.)** The town, *i.e.,* was guarded on all sides by Chaldean troops, so that Zedekiah and his soldiers must either have attacked the line of guard, and broken through it, or have slipped between two of the blockading posts under cover of the darkness. As no collision is mentioned, either here or in Jeremiah, the latter seems the more probable supposition. **And the king went the way toward the plain;** literally, *and he went.* The writer supposes that his readers will understand that the king left the city with his troops; and so regards "*he* went" as sufficiently intelligible. Jeremiah (lii. 7) has "*they* went." By "the plain" (literally, "the Arabah") the valley of the Jordan is intended, and by "the way" to it the ordinary road from Jerusalem to Jericho.

Ver. 5.—**And the army of the Chaldees pursued after the king.** When the escape of Zedekiah and the soldiers of the garrison was discovered, hot pursuit was made, since the honour of the great king required that his enemies should be brought captive to his presence. The commanders at Jerusalem would feel this the more sensibly, since Nebuchadnezzar had for some time retired from the siege, and left its conduct to them, while he himself exercised a general superintendence over military affairs from Riblah (see ver. 6). They were liable to be held responsible for the escape. **And overtook him in the plains of Jericho.** The "plains of Jericho" (עַרְבוֹת יְרֵחוֹ) is the fertile tract on the right bank of the Jordan near its embouchure, which was excellently watered, and cultivated in gardens, orchards, and palm-groves. It is probable, though not certain, that Zedekiah intended to cross the Jordan, and seek a refuge in Moab. **And all his army were scattered from him** (comp. Ezek. xii. 14). This seems to be mentioned in order to account for there being no engagement. Perhaps, thinking themselves in security, and imagining that they were not followed, the troops had dispersed themselves among the farmhouses and homesteads, to obtain a much-needed refreshment.

Ver. 6.—**So they took the king [Zedekiah], and brought him up to the King of Babylon.** The presentation of rebel kings, when captured, to their suzerain, seated on his throne, is one of the most common subjects of Assyrian and Babylonian sculptures (see 'Ancient Monarchies,' vol. i. p. 292; vol. iii. p. 7; Layard, 'Monuments of Nineveh,' second series, pls. 23, 36, etc.). The Egyptian and Persian artists also represent it. **To Riblah.** (For the situation of Riblah, see the comment on ch. xxiii. 33.) As Nebuchadnezzar was engaged at one and the same time in directing the sieges both of Tyre and of Jerusalem, it was a most convenient position for him to occupy. **And they gave judgment upon him.** As a rebel, who had broken his covenant and his oath (Ezek. xvii. 16, 18), Zedekiah was brought to trial before Nebuchadnezzar and his great lords. The facts could not be denied, and sentence was therefore passed upon him, nominally by the court, practically by Nebuchadnezzar (Jer. lii. 9). By an unusual act of clemency, his life was spared; but the judgment was still sufficiently severe (see the next verse).

Ver. 7.—**And they slew the sons of Zedekiah before his eyes** (comp. Herod., iii. 14, and 2 Macc. vii., for similar aggravations of condemned persons' sufferings). As Zedekiah was no more than thirty-two years of age (ch. xxiv. 18), his sons must have been minors, who could not justly be held responsible for their father's doings. It was usual, however, in the East, and even among the Jews, to punish children for the sins of their fathers (see Josh. vii. 24, 25;

ch. ix. 26; xiv. 6; Dan. vi. 24). **And put out the eyes of Zedekiah.** This, too, was a common Oriental practice. The Philistines blinded Samson (Judg. xvi. 21). Sargon, in one of his sculptures, seems to be blinding a prisoner with a spear (Botta, 'Monumens de Ninive,' pl. 18). The ancient Persians often blinded criminals (Xen., 'Anab.,' i. 9. § 13; Ammian. Marc., xxvii. 12; Procop., 'De Bell. Pers.,' i. 11. p. 30). In modern Persia, it was, until very lately, usual for a king, on his accession, to blind all his brothers, in order that they might be disqualified from reigning. The operation was commonly performed in Persia by means of a red-hot iron rod (see Herod., vii. 18). Zedekiah's loss of eyesight reconciled the two apparently conflicting prophecies—that he would be carried captive to Babylon (Jer. xxii. 5, etc.), and that he would never see it (Ezek. xii. 13)—in a remarkable manner. **And bound him with fetters of brass;** literally, *with a pair of brazen fetters.* Assyrian fetters consisted of two thick rings of iron, joined together by a single long link (Botta, *l. s. c.*); Babylonian were probably similar. Captives of importance are usually represented as fettered in the sculptures. **And carried him to Babylon.** Jeremiah adds (lii. 11) that Nebuchadnezzar "put him in prison till the day of his death;" and so Josephus ('Ant. Jud.,' x. 8. § 7). The latter writer further tells us that, at his death, the Babylonian monarch gave him a royal funeral (comp. Jer. xxxiv. 5).

Ver. 8.—**And in the fifth month, on the seventh day of the month.** Jeremiah says (lii. 12) that it was on the *tenth* day of the month; and so Josephus ('Bell. Jud.,' vi. 4. § 8). The mistake probably arose from a copyist mistaking '(ten) for ז (seven). According to Josephus, it was on the same day of the same month that the final destruction of the temple by the soldiers of Titus was accomplished. **Which is the nineteenth year of King Nebuchadnezzar King of Babylon.** Nebuchadnezzar ascended the throne in B.C. 605, which was the fourth year of Jehoiakim, who began to reign in B.C. 608. The seven remaining years of Jehoiakim, added to the eleven of Zedekiah, and the three months of Jehoiachin, produce the result of the text—that the last year of Zedekiah was the nineteenth of Nebuchadnezzar. **Came Nebuzar-adan.** Nebuchadnezzar had apparently hesitated as to how he should treat Jerusalem, since nearly a month elapsed between the capture of the city and the commencement of the work of destruction. He was probably led to destroy the city by the length of the resistance, and the natural strength of the

position. The name, Nebuzar-adan, is probably a Hebraized form of the Babylonian Nebu-sar-iddina, "Nebo has given (us) a king." **Captain of the guard;** literally, *chief of the executioners;* but as the king's guard were employed to execute his commissions, and especially his death-sentences, the paraphrase is quite allowable. **A servant of the King of Babylon**—*i.e.* a subject—**unto Jerusalem.** He came doubtless with instructions, which he proceeded to carry out.

Ver. 9.—**And he burnt the house of the Lord.** After it had stood, according to Josephus ('Ant. Jud.,' x. 8. § 5), four hundred and seventy years six months and ten days. This calculation, however, seems to exceed the truth. Neither the Assyrians nor the Babylonians had any regard for the gods of other nations. They everywhere burnt the temples, plundered the shrines, and carried off the images as trophies of victory. In the temple of Jerusalem they would find no images except those of the two cherubim (1 Kings vi. 23—28), which they probably took away with them. **And the king's house** (see 1 Kings vii. 1, 8—12; ch. xi. 16). The royal palace was, perhaps, almost as magnificent as the temple; and its destruction was almost as great a loss to art. It doubtless contained Solomon's throne of ivory (1 Kings x. 18), to which there was an ascent by six steps, with two sculptured lions on each step. **And all the houses of Jerusalem.** This statement is qualified by the words of the following clause, which show that only the houses of the princes and great men were purposely set on fire. Many of the remaining habitations may have perished in the conflagration, but some probably escaped, and were inhabited by "the poor of the land." **And every great man's house burnt he with fire** (comp. 2 Chron. xxxvi. 19, where the Chaldeans are said to have burnt "all the palaces.").

Ver. 10.—**And all the army of the Chaldees, that were with the captain of the guard, brake down the walls of Jerusalem round about.** A complete demolition is not intended. When the exiles returned, and even in the time of Nehemiah (ii. 13, 15), much of the wall was still standing, and the circuit was easily traced. Probably the Babylonians did not do more than break one or two large breaches in the wall, as Joash had done (ch. xiv. 13) when he took Jerusalem in the reign of Amaziah.

Vers. 11—21.—*Fate of the inhabitants of Judah, and of the contents of the temple.* Having burnt the temple, the royal palace, and the grand residences of the principal citizens, Nebuzar-adan proceeded to divide the inhabitants of the city and country into two bodies—those whom he would leave in the land, and those whom he would carry off. The line of demarcation was, in a general way, a social one. The rich and well-to-do he would take with him; the poor and insignificant he would leave behind (vers. 11, 12). Among the former were included the high priest, the "second priest," three of the temple Levites, the commandant of the city, a certain number of the royal councillors, the "principal scribe of the host," and sixty of the "princes" (vers. 18, 19). The latter were chiefly persons of the agricultural class, who were left to be "vinedressers and husbandmen." From the temple, which had been already plundered twice (2 Chron. xxxvi. 7, 10), he carried off such vessels in gold and silver and bronze as were still remaining there, together with the bronze of the two pillars Jachin and Boaz, of the great laver, or "molten sea," and of the stands for the smaller lavers, all of which he broke up (ver. 13). Having reached Riblah, where Nebuchadnezzar still was, he delivered up to him both the booty and the prisoners. Rather more than seventy of the latter Nebuchadnezzar punished with death (ver. 21). The rest were taken to Babylon.

Ver. 11.—**Now the rest of the people** that were **left in the city**—*i.e.* that remained behind when the king and the garrison fled—**and the fugitives that fell away to the King of Babylon, with the remnant of the multitude**; rather, *both the fugitives that had fallen away to the King of Babylon, and the remnant of the multitude.* The writer means to divide "the rest of the people" into two classes: (1) those who during the siege, or before it, had deserted to the Babylonians, as no doubt many did, and as Jeremiah was accused of doing (Jer. xxxvii. 13); (2) those who were found inside the city when it was taken. **Did Nebuzar-adan the captain of the guard carry away.**

Ver. 12.—**But the captain of the guard left of the poor of the land.** It was inconvenient to deport persons who had little or nothing. In the Assyrian sculptures we see the captives, who are carried off, generally accompanied by their own baggage-animals, and taking with them a certain amount of their own household stuff. Pauper immigrants would not have been of any advan-

tage to a country. To be **vinedressers and husbandmen.** Jeremiah adds that Nebuzar-adan "gave" these persons "vineyards and fields at the same time" (Jer. xxxix. 10). The Babylonians did not wish Judæa to lie waste, since it could then have paid no tribute. On the contrary, they designed its continued cultivation; and Gedaliah, the governor of their appointment, made great efforts to have cultivation resumed and extended (see Jer. xl. 10, 12).

Ver. 13.—**And the pillars of brass that were in the house of the Lord.** The two columns, Jachin and Boaz, cast by Hiram under the directions of Solomon (1 Kings vii. 15—22), are intended. They were works of art of an elaborate character, but being too bulky to be carried off entire, they were "broken in pieces." **And the bases.** "The bases" were the stands for the lavers, also made by Hiram for Solomon (1 Kings vii. 27—37), and very elaborate, having "borders" ornamented with lions, oxen, and cherubim. **And the brazen sea that** was **in the house of the Lord.** This was the great laver, fifteen feet in diameter, emplaced originally on the backs of twelve oxen, three facing each way (1 Kings vii. 23—26), which King Ahaz had taken down from off the oxen (ch. xvi. 17) and "put upon a pavement of stones," but which Hezekiah had probably restored. The oxen are mentioned by Jeremiah (lii. 20) among the objects which Nebuzar-adan carried off. **Did the Chaldees break in pieces**—thus destroying the workmanship, in which their value mainly consisted—**and carried the brass of them to Babylon.** Brass, or rather bronze, was used by the Babylonians for vessels, arms, armour, and implements generally.

Ver. 14.—**And the pots.** The word used, מִירוֹת, is translated by "caldrons" in Jer. lii. 18, and "ash-pans" in Exod. xxvii. 3. The latter is probably right. **And the shovels**—appurtenances of the altar of burnt sacrifice — **and the snuffers** — rather, *the knives*—**and the spoons**—or, *incense-cups*—**and all the vessels of brass wherewith they ministered.** It appears that after the two previous spoliations of the temple by Nebuchadnezzar, in B.C. 605 and in B.C. 597, wherein so many of the more costly vessels had been carried off (Dan. i. 2; ch. xxiv. 13), the ministrations had to be performed mainly with vessels of bronze. **Took they away.** Soldiers are often represented in the Assyrian sculptures as carrying off vessels from temples, apparently on their own account (see 'Ancient Monarchies,' vol. i. p. 475, 2nd edit.).

Ver. 15.—**And the firepans, and the bowls;** rather, *the snuff-dishes* (Exod. xxv. 38; 1 Kings vii. 50) *and the bowls*, or *basins* (Exod.

xii. 22 ; 1 Kings vii. 50 ; 2 Chron. iv. 8). Of these Solomon made one hundred, all in gold. And such things as were of gold, in gold. The "and" supplied by our translators would be better omitted. The writer means that of the articles enumerated some were in gold and some in silver, though probably the greater part were in bronze. And of silver, in silver, the captain of the guard took away (comp. Jer. lii. 19).

Ver. 16.—The two pillars (see the comment on ver. 13), one sea—rather, *the one sea*—and the bases which Solomon had made for the house of the Lord; the brass of all these vessels was without weight; *i.e.* the quantity of the brass was so large that it was not thought to be worth while to weigh it. When gold and silver vessels were carried off, their weight was carefully taken by the royal scribes or secretaries (' Ancient Monarchies,' vol. i. p. 476), who placed it on record as a check upon embezzlement or peculation.

Ver. 17.—The height of the one pillar was eighteen cubits (comp. 1 Kings vii. 15 and Jer. lii. 21, in which latter place an even more elaborate account of the pillars is given), and the chapiter upon it was brass; rather, *and there was a chapiter* (or *capital*) *upon it of brass*—and the height of the chapiter three cubits. The measure given, both in 1 Kings vii. 16 and Jer. lii. 22, is "*five* cubits," which is generally regarded as correct ; but the proportion of 3 to 18, or one-sixth, is far more suitable for a capital than that of 5 to 18, or between a third and a fourth. And the wreathen work—rather, *and there was wreathen work*, or *network*—and pomegranates upon the chapiter round about, all of brass (comp. 1 Kings vii. 18, 19): and like unto these had the second pillar with wreathen work. The ornamentation of the second pillar was the same as that of the first (see Jer. lii. 22).

Ver. 18.—And the captain of the guard took Seraiah the chief priest. The "chief priest" is a new expression; but it can only mean the "high priest." Seraiah seems to have been the grandson of Hilkiah (1 Chron. vi. 13, 14), and an ancestor (grandfather or great-grandfather) of Ezra (Ezra vii. 1). He had stayed at his post till the city was taken, and was now seized by Nebuzar-adan as one of the most important personages whom he found in the city. And Zephaniah the second priest. Keil and Bähr translate "a priest of the second order," *i.e.* a mere ordinary priest; but something more than this must be intended by Jeremiah, who calls him (lii. 34), כֹּהֵן הַמִּשְׁנֶה, *i.e.* distinctly "*the* second priest." It is conjectured that he was the high priest's substitute, empowered to act for him on occasions. Possibly he was the Zephaniah, son of

Maaseiah, of whom we hear a good deal in Jeremiah (see Jer. xxi. 1 ; xxix. 25—29 ; xxxvii. 3). And the three keepers of the door; rather, *and three keepers of the threshold*. There were twenty-five "gatekeepers" of the temple (1 Chron. xxvi. 17, 18), all of them Levites. On what principle Nebuzar-adan selected three out of the twenty-four is uncertain, since we have no evidence that the temple had, as Bähr says it had, "three main entrances." Jer. xxxviii. 14 certainly does not prove this.

Ver. 19.—And out of the city he took an officer—literally, *a eunuch*—that was set over the men of war—eunuchs were often employed in the East as commanders of soldiers. Bagoas, general of the Persian monarch, Ochus, is a noted example—and five men of them that were in the king's presence—literally, *of them that saw the king's face;* i.e. that were habitually about the court; Jeremiah says (lii. 25) "seven men" instead of five—which were found in the city—the majority of the courtiers had, no doubt, dispersed, and were not to be found when Nebuzar-adan searched for them—and the principal scribe of the host; rather, as in the margin, *the scribe of the captain of the host* (τὸν γραμματέα τοῦ ἄρχοντος τῆς δυνάμεως, LXX.). "Scribes" or "secretaries" always accompanied the march of Assyrian armies, to count and record the number of the slain, to catalogue the spoil, perhaps to write despatches and the like. We may gather that Jewish commandants were similarly attended. Which mustered the people of the land—i.e. enrolled them, or entered them upon the army list, another of the "scribe's" duties—and threescore men of the people of the land that were found in the city. Probably notables of one kind or another, persons regarded as especially responsible for the revolt.

Ver. 20.—And Nebuzar-adan captain of the guard took these, and brought them to the King of Babylon to Riblah (see the comment on ver. 6). Two batches of prisoners seem to have been brought before Nebuchadnezzar at Riblah—first, the most important of all the captives, Zedekiah and his sons (vers. 6, 7); then, a month later, Seraiah the high priest, and the other persons enumerated in vers. 18 and 19. The remaining prisoners were no doubt brought also by Nebuzar-adan to Riblah, but were not conducted into the presence of the king.

Ver. 21.—And the King of Babylon smote them, and slew them at Riblah in the land of Hamath. Severities of this kind characterized all ancient warfare. The Assyrian sculptures show us prisoners of war impaled on crosses, beheaded, beaten on the head with maces, and sometimes extended on the ground and flayed. The inscriptions speak of hundreds as thus executed, and mention others as burnt in furnaces, or thrown to wild beasts, or cruelly mutilated. Herodotus says (iii. 159) that Darius Hystaspis crucified three thousand prisoners round about Babylon after one of its revolts. That monarch himself, in the Behistun inscription, speaks of many cases where, after capturing rebel chiefs in the field or behind walls, he executed them and their principal adherents (see Col. ii. Par. 13; Col. iii. Par. 8, 11). If Nebuchadnezzar contented himself with the execution of between seventy and eighty of the rebel inhabitants of Jerusalem, he cannot be charged with cruelty, or extreme severity, according to the notions of the time. **So Judah was carried away out of their land.** Jeremiah adds an estimate of the number carried off. These were, he says (lii. 28—30), in the captivity of the seventh (query, seventeenth?) year, 3023; in the captivity of the eighteenth year, 832; and in that of the twenty-third, five years later, 745, making a total of 4600. If we suppose these persons to be men, and multiply by four for the women and children, the entire number will still be no more than 18,400.

Vers. 22—26.—*History of the remnant left in the land by Nebuzar-adan.* Nebuchadnezzar, when he carried off Zedekiah to Babylon, appointed, as governor of Judæa, a certain Gedaliah, a Jew of good position, but not of the royal family. Gedaliah made Mizpah, near Jerusalem, his residence; and here he was shortly joined by a number of Jews of importance, who had escaped from Jerusalem and hidden themselves until the Babylonians were gone. Of these the most eminent were Johanan the son of Kareah, and Ishmael, a member of the royal house of David. Gedaliah urged the refugees to be good subjects of the King of Babylon, and to settle themselves to agricultural pursuits. His advice was accepted and at first followed; but presently a warning was given to Gedaliah by Johanan that Ishmael designed his destruction; and soon afterwards, as Gedaliah took no precautions, the murder was actually carried out. Other atrocities followed; but after a time Johanan and the other leading refugees took up arms, forced Ishmael to fly to the Ammonites, and then, fearing that Nebuchadnezzar would hold them responsible for Ishmael's act, against Jeremiah's remonstrances, fled, with the great mass of the Jews that had been left in the land, from Judæa into Egypt. Here

our writer leaves them (ver. 26), without touching on the calamities which befell them there, according to the prophetic announcements of Jeremiah (xliv. 2—28).

Ver. 22.—**And as for the people that remained in the land of Judah.** These consisted of Gedaliah and his court, which included Jeremiah, Baruch, and some princesses of the royal house (Jer. xliii. 6); the poor of the land, whom Nebuzar-adan had intentionally left behind; and a considerable number of Jewish refugees of a better class, who came in from the neighbouring nations, and from places in Judæa where they had been hiding themselves (Jer. xl. 7—12). For about two months all went well with this "remnant," who applied themselves to agricultural pursuits, in which they prospered greatly. **Whom Nebuchadnezzar King of Babylon had left** (see ver. 12), **even over them he made Gedaliah the son of Ahikam.** Ahikam had protected Jeremiah in his earlier days (Jer. xxvi. 24); Gedaliah protected him in the latter part of the siege (Jer. xxxix. 14). Nebuchadnezzar's choice of Gedaliah for governor was probably made from some knowledge of his having sided with Jeremiah, whose persistent endeavours to make the Jews submit to the Babylonian yoke seem to have been well known, not only to the Jews, but to the Babylonians; most likely by reason of the letter he sent to his countrymen already in captivity (Jer. xxix.). **The son of Shaphan, ruler.** Probably not "Shaphan the scribe" (ch. xxii. 3, 12), but an unknown person of the same name.

Ver. 23.—**And when all the captains of the armies;** rather, *the captains of the forces* (Revised Version); *i.e.* the officers in command of the troops which had defended Jerusalem, and, having escaped from the city, were dispersed and scattered in various directions, partly in Judæa, partly in foreign countries. **They and their men**—apparently, each of them had kept with him a certain number of the men under his command—**heard that the King of Babylon had made Gedaliah governor.** The news was gratifying to them. It was something to have a Jewish ruler set over them, and not a Babylonian; it was, perhaps, even more to have a man noted for his justice and moderation (Josephus, 'Ant. Jud.,' x. 9. § 12), who had no selfish aims, but desired simply the prosperity and good government of the country. **There came to Gedaliah to Mizpah, even Ishmael the son of Nethaniah, and Johanan the son of Careah**—Jeremiah (xl. 8) has "Johanan and Jonathan, the sons of Kareah"—**and Seraiah the son of Tanhumeth the Netophathite.** In Jer. xl. 8 we read, "And Seraiah the son of Tanhumeth, *and* the sons of Ephai the Netophathite," by which it would seem that some words have fallen out here. By "Netophathite" is to be understood "native of Netophah," now Antubah, near Bethlehem (see Ezra ii. 22; Neh. vii. 26). **And Jaazaniah the son of a Maachathite.** Called *Jezaniah* by Jeremiah, and said by him (xlii. 1) to have been the son of a certain Hoshaiah. Hoshaiah was a native of the Syrian kingdom, or district, known as Maachah, or Maachathi (Deut. iii. 14; 1 Chron. xix. 6, 7), which adjoined Bashan towards the north. **They and their men.** The persons mentioned, that is, with the soldiers under them, came to Gedaliah at Mizpah, and placed themselves under him as his subjects.

Ver. 24.—**And Gedaliah sware to them, and to their men.** As rebels, their lives were forfeit; but Gedaliah granted them an amnesty, and for their greater assurance swore to them that, so long as they remained peaceful subjects of the King of Babylon, they should suffer no harm. Jeremiah adds (xl. 10) that he urged them to apply themselves diligently to agricultural pursuits. **And said unto them, Fear not to be the servants of the Chaldees: dwell in the land, and serve the King of Babylon; and it shall be well with you;** rather, *and said unto them, Fear not because of the servants of the Chaldeans,* etc. "Do not be afraid," *i.e.,* "of the Chaldean officials and guards (Jer. xlii. 3) that are about my court. Be assured that they shall do you no hurt."

Ver. 25.—**And it came to pass in the seventh month** — two months only after Gedaliah received his appointment as governor, which was in the fifth month— **that Ishmael the son of Nethaniah, the son of Elishama**—"Nethaniah" is otherwise unknown; "Elishama" may be the "scribe" or secretary of Jehoiakim mentioned in Jer. xxxvi. 12, 20—of the seed royal. So Josephus ('Ant. Jud.,' x. 9. § 2) and Jeremiah (xli. 1). Josephus adds that he was a wicked and most crafty man, who, during the siege of Jerusalem, had made his escape from the place, and fled for shelter to Baalim (Baalis, Jer. xl. 14), King of Ammon, with whom he remained till the siege was over. **Came, and ten men with him**—as his retinue—**and smote Gedaliah, that he died.** Gedaliah had been warned by Johanan and the other captains (Jer. xl. 13—15) of Ishmael's probable intentions, but had treated the accusation as a calumny, and refused to believe that his life was in any danger. When Ishmael and his ten companions arrived, he still suspected nothing, but received them hospitably (Jer. xli. 1), entertained them at a grand banquet, according to Josephus ('Ant. Jud.,' x. 9. § 4), and being overtaken with drunkenness,

was attacked and killed without difficulty. **And the Jews and the Chaldees that were with him at Mizpah** (comp. Jer. xli. 3, "Ishmael also slew all the Jews that were with him, even with Gedaliah, at Mizpah, and the Chaldeans that were found there, and the men of war"). It is evident from this that Gedaliah had a Chaldean guard.

Ver. 26.—**And all the people, both small and great, and the captains of the armies** (see above, ver. 23). The leader of the movement was Johanan, the son of Careah. Having first attacked Ishmael, and forced him to fly to the Ammonites (Jer. xli. 15), he almost immediately afterwards conceived a fear of Nebuchadnezzar, who would, he thought, resent the murder of Gedaliah, and even avenge it upon those who had done all they could to prevent it. He therefore gathered together the people, and made a preliminary retreat to Chimham, near Bethlehem (Jer. xli. 17), on the road to Egypt, whence he subsequently, against the earnest remonstrances and prophetic warnings of Jeremiah (xlii. 9—22), carried them on into Egypt itself (Jer. xliii. 1—7). The first settlement was made at Tahpanhes, or Daphnæ. **Arose, and came into Egypt: for they were afraid of the Chaldees** (see Jer. xli. 18; xliii. 3). There does not appear to have been any real reason for this fear. Nebuchadnezzar might have been trusted to distinguish between the act of an individual and conspiracy on the part of the nation.

Vers. 27—30.—*Fate of Jehoiachin.* The writer of Kings, whose general narrative, since the time of Hezekiah, has been gloomy and dispiriting, seems to have desired to terminate his history in a more cheerful strain. He therefore mentions, as his last incident, the fate of Jehoiachin, who, after thirty-six years of a cruel and seemingly hopeless imprisonment, experienced a happy change of circumstances. The king who succeeded Nebuchadnezzar, his son, Evil-Merodach, in the first year of his sovereignty had compassion upon the miserable captive, and releasing him from prison, changed his garments (ver. 29), and gave him a place at his table, among other dethroned monarchs, even exalting him above the rest (ver. 28), and making him an allowance for his support (ver. 30). This alleviation of their king's condition could not but be felt by the captive Jews as a happy omen—a portent of the time when *their* lot too would be alleviated, and the Almighty Disposer of events, having punished them sufficiently for their sins, would relent at last, and put an end to their banishment, and give them rest and peace in their native country.

Ver. 27.—**And it came to pass in the seven and thirtieth year of the captivity of Jehoiachin King of Judah.** According to Berosus and the Canon of Ptolemy, Nebuchadnezzar reigned forty-four years. He carried off Jehoiachin to Babylon in his eighth year (ch. xxiv. 12), and thus the year of his death would exactly coincide with the thirty-seventh year of the captivity of the Jewish prince. **In the twelfth month, on the seven and twentieth day of the month.** The *five* and twentieth day, according to Jeremiah (lii. 31). (On the rarity of such exact dates in the historical Scriptures, see the comment on ver. 1.) That Evil - Merodach King of Babylon. The native name, which is thus expressed, seems to have been "Avil-Marduk." The meaning of *avil* is uncertain; but the name probably placed the prince under the protection of Merodach, who was Nebuchadnezzar's favourite god. Avil-Marduk ascended the Babylonian throne in B.C. 561, and reigned two years only, when he was murdered by Nériglissar, or Nergal-sar-uzur, his brother-in-law. **In the year that he began to reign**—the year B.C. 561—did lift up the head of Jehoiachin King of Judah out of prison. (For the phrase used, see Gen. xl. 13, 19, 20.) The act was probably part of a larger measure of pardon and amnesty, intended to in-augurate favourably the new reign.

Ver. 28.—**And he spake kindly to him;** literally, *he spake good things with him;* but the meaning is well expressed by our ren-dering. Evil-Merodach compassionated the sufferings of the unfortunate monarch, who had grown old in prison, and strove by kind speech to make up to him for them in a certain measure. **And set his throne above the throne of the kings that were with him in Babylon.** Evil-Merodach had at his court other captured kings besides Jehoiachin, whose presence was considered to enhance his dignity and grandeur (comp. Judg. i. 7). An honourable position and probably a seat of honour was assigned to each; but the highest position among them was now con-ferred on Jehoiachin. Whether he had actually a more elevated seat, is (as Bähr observes) a matter of no importance.

Ver. 29.—**And changed his prison gar-ments.** The subject to "changed" may be either "Jehoiachin" or "Evil-Merodach." Our translators preferred the latter, our Revisers the former. In either case the general meaning is the same. Evil-Mero-dach supplied suitable garments to the released monarch instead of his "prison garments," and Jehoiachin arrayed himself in the comely apparel before taking his seat among his equals. Dresses of honour are among the most common gifts which an Oriental monarch makes to his subjects (see Gen. xli. 42; Esth. vi. 8, 11; viii. 15; Dan. v. 29; Xen., 'Cyrop.,' v. 1. § 1). **And he**—*i.e.* Jehoiachin—**did eat bread continu-ally before him.** Besides giving occasional great feasts (see Esth. i. 3—9), Oriental monarchs usually entertain at their table daily a large number of guests, some of whom are specially invited, while others have the privilege of daily attendance (see 'Ancient Monarchies,' vol. iii. pp. 214, 215). It was to this latter class that Jehoiachin was admitted. Comp. 2 Sam. ix. 7—13, which shows that the custom was one not unknown at the Jewish court. **All the days of his**—*i.e.* Jehoiachin's—**life.** Jehoiachin enjoyed this privilege till his death. Whether this fell in the lifetime of Evil-Merodach or not, is scarcely in the writer's thoughts. He merely means to tell us that the comparative comfort and dignity which Jehoiachin enjoyed after the accession of Evil-Merodach to the throne was not sub-sequently clouded over or disturbed. He continued a privileged person at the Baby-lonian court so long as he lived.

Ver. 30.—**And his allowance was a con-tinual allowance.** Keil supposes that this "allowance" was a daily "ration of food," intended for the maintenance of a certain number of servants or retainers. But it is quite as likely to have been a money pay-ment. The word translated by "allowance" —אֲרֻחָה—does not point necessarily to food. It is a "portion" of any kind. **Given him of the king**—*i.e.* out of the privy purse, by the king's command—**a daily rate for every day**—or, *a certain amount day by day*—**all the days of his life** (see the comment on the preceding verse). Both the privileges ac-corded to Jehoiachin, his sustenance at the king's table, and his allowance, whether in money or in kind, continued to the day of his death. Neither of them was ever revoked or forfeited. Thus this last representative of the Davidic monarchy, after thirty-six years of chastisement, experienced a happy change of circumstances, and died in peace and comfort. Probably, as Keil says, "this event was intended as a comforting sign to the whole of the captive people, that the Lord would one day put an end to their banishment, if they would acknowledge that it was a well-merited punishment for their sins that they had been driven away from before his face, and would turn again to the Lord their God with all their heart."

HOMILETICS.

Vers. 1—10.— *The fall of Judah and Jerusalem a warning for all time to all nations.* Jerusalem had defied Zerah with his host of a million men (2 Chron. xiv. 9—15), and had triumphed over Sennacherib at the head of all the armed force of Assyria (ch. xix. 35, 36) : why did she succumb to Nebuchadnezzar? It is quite certain that Babylon was not a stronger power than either Egypt or Assyria when in their prime. There is no reason to believe that Nebuchadnezzar was a better general than Sennacherib, or even than Zerah. The ground of the difference in the result of Judah's struggle with Babylon, and her earlier struggles with Egypt and Assyria, is certainly not to be sought in the greater strength of her assailant, but in her own increased weakness. What, then, were the causes of this weakness?

I. IT WAS NOT THE RESULT OF ANY DECLINE IN MILITARY STRENGTH, AS ORDINARILY ESTIMATED. The population of Judæa may have diminished, but under Josiah her dominion had increased (ch. xxiii. 15—20), and it is probable that she could still put into the field as many men as at any former period. Even if there were a diminution in the number of her troops, the fact would not have been one of much importance, since her military successes had never been dependent upon the numerical proportion between her own forces and those of her adversaries, but had been most signal and striking where the disproportion had been the greatest (see Numb. xxxi. 3—47; Judg. vii. 7—22; viii. 4—12; xv. 15; 1 Sam. xiv. 11—16; 2 Chron. xiv. 8—12; xx. 15—24, etc.).

II. IT WAS NOT PRODUCED BY INTERNAL QUARREL OR DISSENSION. Ewald attributes the fall of Judah and Jerusalem mainly to the antagonism between the monarchy and the prophetical order, and to the violence employed by each against the other. "The kingdom of Judah was torn," he says, "with less and less hope of remedy, by the most irreconcilable internal divisions; and the sharpest dissensions at length made their way into the sanctity of every house." Violence on the part of the kings was met by violence on the part of the prophets; and "the sacred land went to ruin under the development of the element of force" ('History of Israel,' vol. iv. p. 289). It is difficult to discover any sufficient support for this view in the sacred narrative, which shows us Hezekiah on the most friendly terms with Isaiah, Josiah on the same terms with Huldah, and Zedekiah certainly not on unfriendly terms with Jeremiah. In the closing scene the antagonism is not between prophetism and monarchy, but between prophetism and an aristocratical clique. Nor is it at all clear that the final result was seriously affected by the antagonism in question. It may have somewhat relaxed the defence; but we cannot possibly imagine that, if there had been no difference of view, no sharp dissension, a successful resistance could have been made. The resistance might, perhaps, have been prolonged had all Israelites been of one mind; but still Babylon would have prevailed in the end.

III. IT WAS NOT FROM ANY TREACHERY OR DESERTION ON THE PART OF ALLIES. Allies had never done Judæa much good; and dependence on them was regarded as an indication of want of faith in Jehovah. But, so far as the matter of alliances went, Judah was in a superior, rather than in an inferior, position now than formerly. Her natural allies in any struggle with the dominant power of Western Asia were Phœnicia and Egypt; and at this time both Phœnicia and Egypt rendered her aid. Tyre was in revolt against Babylon from B.C. 598 to B.C. 585, and gave occupation to a considerable portion of the Babylonian forces while Jerusalem was being besieged. Egypt, under the enterprising Hophra (Apries), took the field soon after the siege began, and for a time succeeded in raising it. Babylon had to contend with the three allies, Tyre, Egypt, and Judæa, at one and the same time, but proved equal to the strain, and overcame all three antagonists.

Judæa's weakness lay in this—that she had offended God. From the time of Moses to that of Zedekiah, it was not her own inherent strength, or vigour, or energy, that had protected and sustained her, but the supporting hand of the Almighty. God had ever "gone forth with her armies" (Ps. lx. 10). God had given her "help from trouble." Through God she had "done valiantly." He it was who had "trodden down her enemies" (Ps. lx. 11, 12). Many of their deliverances had been through actual miracle; others were the result of a divinely infused courage pervading their own ranks, or a panic falling upon their adversaries. It was only as God's "peculiar people," enjoying his covenanted protection, that they could possibly hold their place among the nations of the earth, so soon as great empires were formed and mighty monarchs devised schemes of extensive conquests. God's arm had saved them from Egypt and from Assyria; he could as easily have saved them from Babylon. "It is nothing with God to help, whether with many, or with them that have no power" (2 Chron. xiv. 11). He could have bridled Nebuchadnezzar as easily as Zerah or Sennacherib, and have saved the Jews under Zedekiah as readily as under Asa or Hezekiah. But Judah's sins came between him and them. The persistent transgressions of the people from the time of Manasseh, their idolatries, immoralities, cruelties, and wickedness of all kinds, shortened God's arm, that he could not interpose to save them. As the author of Chronicles puts it, "there was no remedy" (2 Chron. xxxvi. 16). "They had transgressed very much after all the abominations of the heathen; and polluted the house of the Lord which he had hallowed in Jerusalem; . . . they had mocked the messengers of God, and despised his words, and misused his prophets" (2 Chron. xxxvi. 14—16); and so "filled up the measure of their iniquities." Under such circumstances, God could not spare even his own children (Isa. i. 4; lxiii. 16)— his own people. Can, then, any sinful nation hope to escape? Ought not each to feel the fate of Judah a warning to itself? a warning to repent of its evil ways, and turn from them, and walk in the paths of righteousness, according to the exhortation of Isaiah?—"Wash you, make you clean; put away the evil of your doings from before mine eyes; cease to do evil; learn to do well; seek judgment, relieve the oppressed, judge the fatherless, plead for the widow. Come now, and let us reason together, saith the Lord: though your sins be as scarlet, they shall be as white as snow; though they be red like crimson, they shall be as wool. If ye be willing and obedient, ye shall eat the good of the land: but if ye refuse and rebel, ye shall be devoured with the sword: for the mouth of the Lord hath spoken it" (Isa. i. 16—20).

Vers. 27—30.—"*The loving-kindness of the Lord.*" God, "in his wrath, thinketh upon mercy." The captive king, and the captive nation, each of them suffered a long and severe punishment. Each of them must have been inclined to sink into a state of hopelessness and apathy. Each may have thought that God had forgotten them altogether, or at any rate had forgotten, and would forget, to be gracious. Thirty-six years—how long a space is this in the life of a man! Jehoiachin had grown from a youth into a man of full age, and from a man of full age almost into an old man, for he was in his fifty-fifth year, and Jewish monarchs rarely reached the age of sixty. Yet he had not really been forgotten. God had had his eye upon him all the while, and had kept in reserve for him a happy change of circumstances. The Disposer of events brought Evil-Merodach to the throne, and put it into the heart of that monarch to have compassion upon the aged captive. Jehoiachin passed from a dungeon to a chair of state (ver. 28), from prison food and prison dress to royal banquets and apparel fitting his rank, from the extreme of misery to happiness, dignity, and honour. This was the doing of the Almighty Father, using men as his instruments; and it was a strong evidence of his loving-kindness. Would not the nation likewise experience his mercy? The penal sentence passed upon it was well deserved, and might, in strict justice, have been final. But would God exact the uttermost farthing? No. By the release and restoration to honour of Jehoiachin, he sufficiently indicated to his people that for them too there was a place of repentance, a day of grace, a restoration to his favour. A ray of light thus broke in upon the long darkness of the Captivity. God's gracious intent was indicated. The nation felt a stir of hope, and woke up to the expectation of a new life; Isaiah's later prophecies (xl.—lxvi.), which had seemed a dead letter, became living words, speaking to the heart of the people; and the later years of the Captivity were cheered by the prospect—ever becoming brighter and clearer—of a reinstatement in God's favour, a return to the Holy Land, and a restoration of the sanctuary (Dan. ix. 2—19).

HOMILIES BY VARIOUS AUTHORS.

Vers. 1—21.—*The last days of Jerusalem.* The shameful story of Judah's disobedience and sin is now drawing to a close. Here we have an account of the capture of Jerusalem and its king by Nebuchadnezzar King of Babylon. Zedekiah, the king, was taken prisoner. His sons were first put to death before his eyes. Then his own eyes were put out. He was bound in fetters of brass, and carried away to Babylon. Jerusalem itself, the city of David and Solomon, was a scene of desolation. Nebuzaradan, captain of the Babylonian guard, burnt with fire the house of the Lord and the king's house and all the principal houses of the city. The men of war had deserted their posts and fled from the city. All who remained there were taken captive. The poor of the land only were left to be vinedressers and husbandmen. What were the causes of this sad downfall?

I. THE WICKEDNESS OF ITS RULERS. One after the other, the kings of Judah had done evil in the sight of the Lord. 1. *They disobeyed God's commands.* They imitated the idolatry and the vices of the heathen. 2. *They ill-treated God's prophets.* When men begin to despise and ill-treat God's messengers, those who are trying to lead them to what is right, they are blind to their own true interests. The treatment which the Prophet Jeremiah in particular received showed how low in degradation the kingdom of Judah had sunk. After the prophet's fearless denunciations of national sin (Jer. xiii.—xix.), Pashur, who was chief governor of the temple, smote Jeremiah, and put him in the stocks, or pillory, that was in the high gate of Benjamin, near the temple, where all men might see him and mock at his disgrace. We have seen how Jehoiakim cut the roll of Jeremiah's prophecies with his penknife, and burned its leaves. Jeremiah's last years at Jerusalem were years of increased suffering and persecution. Zedekiah actually put him in prison. The princes cast him to perish in a hideous pit in the prison-house, where he sank in the mire, but at the intercession of an Ethiopian officer, Ebed-Melech, the king rescued him. *Wickedness in high places soon proves to be a nation's ruin.*

II. THE CORRUPTION OF ITS PEOPLE. Unhappily, the people were just as corrupt and as godless as their rulers. A nation is responsible for its national sins. The sins of Judah cried aloud to Heaven for vengeance. And in the days of the Captivity they were taught to feel that there is a God that reigneth in the earth. We learn from the fate of Judah and Jerusalem : 1. *The danger of forsaking God.* They forsook God in the day of their prosperity. And when the hour of their need came, the gods whom they served were not able to deliver them. 2. *The danger of disregarding God's Word.* How often, in these later years'of Judah's history, was the Law of God utterly neglected and forgotten! No life can be truly happy which is not based on the Word of God. No home can be truly happy where the Bible is not read. No nation can expect prosperity which disregards the Word of God. 3. *The danger of despising God's warnings.* Every message God sends us is for our good. If it is worth his while to speak to us, it is worth our while to listen. Neglected warnings—what guilt they involve! what danger they threaten! "Because I have called, and ye refused; I have stretched out my hand, and no man regarded; . . . I also will laugh at your calamity; I will mock when your fear cometh."—C. H. I.

Vers. 18—21.—*Space for repentance.* "And the captain of the guard took Seraiah the chief priest, and Zephaniah the second priest, and the three keepers of the door," etc. This piece of history may be usefully employed to illustrate that space which Heaven allows to be given men for improvement in this life. Notice here—

I. SPACE FOR IMPROVEMENT. "And the captain of the guard," etc. Though we have reason to think that the army of Chaldeans were much enraged against the city for holding out with so much stubbornness, yet they did not therefore put all to fire and sword as soon as they had taken the city (which is too commonly done in such cases), but three months after Nebuzar-adan was sent with orders to complete the destruction of Jerusalem. This space God gave them to repent after all the foregoing days of his patience; but in vain. Their hearts were still hardened. Thus wicked men constantly ignore "things that belong to their peace."

II. SPACE FOR IMPROVEMENT NEGLECTED. "And out of the city he took an officer that was set over the men of war," etc. These men, to whom time had been given to do the work required, day after day neglected it. No effort was put forth to avoid the threatened calamity. It is ever thus. Men are waiting for a more "convenient season." The cry, "Unless ye repent ye shall all likewise perish," was neglected.

III. NEGLECTED SPACE FOR IMPROVEMENT AVENGED. "And Nebuzar-adan captain of the guard took these, and brought them to the King of Babylon to Riblah." "Be sure your sins will find you out." "Rejoice, O, young man, in thy youth; . . . but know thou, that for all these things God will bring thee into judgment."

IV. THE AVENGEMENT OF THIS NEGLECT WAS TERRIBLE IN THE EXTREME. "And the King of Babylon smote them, and slew them at Riblah in the land of Hamath. So Judah was carried away out of their land." The city and the temple were burnt. The walls were never repaired until Nehemiah's time; and Judah was carried out of their land, etc. The history of this calamity is too well known to record here. "Because sentence against an evil work is not executed speedily, therefore the heart of the sons of men is fully set in them to do evil."—D. T.

Vers. 22—26.—*Rulers and their enemies.* "And as for the people that remained in the land of Judah, whom Nebuchadnezzar King of Babylon had left," etc. By this fragment of Jewish history two observations are suggested.

I. MEN ARE SOMETIMES ELEVATED INTO RESPONSIBLE POSITIONS. *Gedaliah*, a friend of Jeremiah's, and acting under the prophet's counsel, took the government of Judæa, and fixed his court at Mizpah. He seemed on the whole qualified for the office he assumed. The people committed to his charge were those who were left in the country after Judah had been carried away into Babylonian captivity. They were, perhaps, considered too insignificant to be removed. However, being peasantry, who could till the land and dress the vineyards, he counselled them to submit to his rule, promising them that they should retain their possessions and enjoy the produce of the land. Such was the responsible position to which this Gedaliah was elevated. In every age and land there are some men thus distinguished—men that rise to eminence and obtain distinction and power. Sometimes it may be by the force of their own genius and character, and sometimes by the force and patronage of others. Hence in Church and state, literature, commerce, and art, we have rulers ecclesiastical, political, scholastic, and mercantile. This arrangement in our social life has many signal advantages, although often exposed to many terrible evils.

II. MALIGNANT ENMITY SOMETIMES FRUSTRATES THE PURPOSE OF SUCH MEN. "But it came to pass in the seventh month, that Ishmael the son of Nathaniah, the son of Elishama, of the seed royal, came, and ten men with him, and smote Gedaliah, that he died, and the Jews and the Chaldees that were with him at Mizpah." Thus envy is always excited by superiority, and one of the most cruel of human passions terminated the life of Gedaliah and the purpose of his mission a few brief months after his elevation to office. Envy murdered Gedaliah, and drove back those poor scattered Jews to Egypt, which they loathed. Thus envy is ever at work, blasting the reputations and degrading the positions of distinguished men. "Envy is the daughter of Pride, the author of murder and revenge, the beginner of secret sedition, and the perpetual tormentor of virtue. Envy is the filthy slime of the soul; a worm, a poison or quicksilver which consumeth the flesh, and drieth up the marrow of the bones" (Socrates).—D. T.'

Vers. 27—30.—*Jehoiachin as a victim of tyrannic despotism, and as an object of delivering mercy.* "And it came to pass in the seven and thirtieth year," etc. The life of this man has been already sketched. The incident here recorded presents him—

I. AS A VICTIM OF TYRANNIC DESPOTISM. He had been in prison for thirty-seven years, and was fifty-five years of age. It was Nebuchadnezzar, the tyrannic King of Babylon, that stripped this man of liberty and freedom, and shut him up in a dungeon for this long period of time. Such despotism has prevailed in all ages and lands.

II. AS AN OBJECT OF DELIVERING MERCY. We are told that as soon as *Evil-Merodach* came to the throne on the death of his father Nebuchadnezzar, mercy stirred his heart and relieved this poor victim of tyranny. Corrupt as this world is, the element of mercy is not entirely extinct. This mercy gave honour and liberty to the man who had been so long in confinement and disgrace. Let not the victims of tyranny—and they abound everywhere—despair. Mercy will ere long sound the trump of jubilee over all the land. "The Spirit of the Lord," said the great Redeemer of the race, "is upon me, because he hath anointed me to preach the gospel to the poor; he hath sent me to heal the broken-hearted, to preach deliverance to the captives, and recovering of sight to the blind, to set at liberty them that are bruised."—D. T.

Vers. 1—10.—*The fall and destruction of Jerusalem.* With this account of the siege of Jerusalem by Nebuchadnezzar should be compared the narrative of its later destruction by Titus (A.D. 70). History does not always repeat itself; but in this instance it does so with marvellous fidelity. The close investment of the city, the desperate resistance, the horrors of famine within, the incidents of the capture, the burning of the temple, the demolition of the walls, and the captivity of the people, present striking parallels in the two cases. By one of those rare coincidences that sometimes occur, it was on the very same month and day of the month on which the temple was burned by Nebuchadnezzar, that the sanctuary was fired by the soldiers of Titus. The earlier destruction fulfilled the predictions of the prophets; the later the predictions of our Lord (Matt. xxiv.).

I. THE LAST SIEGE. 1. *Fatal dates.* The days which mark the different stages of this terrible siege of Nebuchadnezzar are minutely recorded and carefully remembered. "The ninth year" of Zedekiah, "in the tenth month, in the tenth day of the month," Nebuchadnezzar came, he and his host, against Jerusalem (ver. 1); in the eleventh year of Zedekiah "on the ninth day of the fourth month the famine prevailed in the city" (ver. 3), and a breach was effected; "in the fifth month, on the seventh day of the month, which is the nineteenth year of King Nebuchadnezzar," the temple and other buildings were burned by Nebuzar-adan (ver. 8). We have the same careful dating in Jer. xxxix. 1, 2; lii. 4, 12 (in the latter passage "tenth" for "seventh" as above). These were dates which burned themselves into the very memories of the wretched people crowded in the city, and could never be forgotten. Indirectly they testify to the intensity of misery which was endured, which made them so well remembered. They were observed afterwards as regular days of fasting (Zech. vii. 3, 5; viii. 19). 2. *The enemy without.* Nebuchadnezzar's army came up against the city, and closely invested it, building forts against it round about. Ezek. xxi. is a vivid prophecy of what was about to happen. The prophet announces the impending capture of the holy city. A sword was furbished which would work terrible destruction. Ezekiel is directed to mark off two ways along which this sword was to travel—the one leading to Jerusalem, and the other to Rabbath of Ammon. The scene changes, and we see the King of Babylon standing at the head of the ways, deliberating which one he shall choose. He shakes the arrows, consults images, looks for omens in the liver of dead beasts. The decision given is for advancing first against Jerusalem. Now he is at its gates, and has appointed captains "to open the mouth in the slaughter, to lift up the voice with shouting, to appoint battering-rams against the gates, to cast a mount, and to build a fort" (Ezek. xxi. 21, 22). 3. *The famine within.* For a year and five months the weary siege dragged itself on, the people within well knowing that, when once it was captured, they could expect no mercy. The writings of Jeremiah give us a vivid picture of the city during this period. From the first the prophet held out no hope. When Zedekiah, at the beginning of the siege entreated him, "Inquire, I pray thee, of the Lord for us," Jeremiah plainly told him that the city was delivered to the Chaldeans, and that Nebuchadnezzar would not spare them, "neither have pity, nor have mercy" (Jer. xxi. 1—7). Life was promised, however, to those who should surrender themselves to the enemy (vers. 8—10). This strain was kept up throughout, in spite of imprisonment, threats, and the contrary testimony of false prophets (cf. Jer. xxxii. 1—5; xxxiv. 1—7; xxxvii. 6—21; xxxviii., etc.). At one point an Egyptian army came forth against the Chaldeans, and great hopes were raised, but Jeremiah bade the people not deceive themselves, for the Chaldeans would prevail, as indeed they did, in spite of a temporary raising of the siege (Jer. xxxvii. 5—11). By-and-by, as in the previous long siege of Samaria by the Syrians (ch. vi. 24—33), the misery of the people became extreme. The bread was "spent" in the city (Jer. xxxvii. 21). The Book of Lamentations gives vivid glimpses of the horrors—the young children fainting for hunger at the top of every street (Lam. ii. 11, 19); crying to their mothers, Where is corn and wine? (Lam. ii. 12); and asking bread, and no man breaking it to them (Lam. iv. 4); the delicately nurtured lying on dunghills (Lam. iv. 5); women eating their own offspring (Lam. ii. 20), etc.

II. THE FATE OF ZEDEKIAH. As the vigour of the defence slackened, the besiegers redoubled their energies, till, on the ninth day of the fourth month, a breach was made in the walls, and Nebuchadnezzar's princes penetrated as far as the middle gate (Jer. xxix. 1—3). The stages that follow are, as respects Zedekiah, those of: 1. *Flight.* The besiegers had entered by the north side of the city, and the king, with his men of war, feeling that all was lost, made their escape by night through a gate of the city on the south—"the gate between the two walls, which is by the king's garden "—and, evading the Chaldeans in the darkness, fled towards the Jordan. By a symbolic action Ezekiel had foretold this flight, and the actual manner of the escape, down to its minutest details—a singular instance of the unerring prescience of these inspired prophets (Ezek. xii. 1—16). What the king's thoughts were as he fled that night with beating heart and covered face, who can tell? Jeremiah had been vindicated, and the prophets who had buoyed the people up with so many false hopes were now shown to be miserable deceivers. 2. *Capture.* The flight of the king was soon discovered, and a contingent of Chaldeans was despatched in pursuit. It was not long ere they overtook the fleeing monarch, no doubt faint with hunger, unnerved by fear, and exhausted with the miles he had already traversed, unable therefore to make any defence. If his followers made any stand, they were speedily scattered, and the king was taken on the plains of Jericho. His hopes, his plans, his intrigues with Egypt, all had come to nothing. He stood there, a prisoner of the Chaldeans, as Jeremiah declared he would be. It is God's Word that always comes true. Would that Zedekiah had believed it in time! 3. *Punishment.* The fate which awaited Zedekiah was not long deferred. With his sons, and the nobles who were with him (Jer. xxxix. 6; lii. 10), he was taken to Riblah, to have judgment passed on him by Nebuchadnezzar. Little mercy had he to look for from the haughty, infuriate king, who had given him his throne, and whose covenant he had broken, entailing on him the trouble and delay of a sixteen months' siege. Tortures, perhaps, and death in protracted agonies. The wonder is that Zedekiah escaped as mercifully as he did. But his punishment was, nevertheless, heart-breaking in its severity. (1) He saw his own sons slain before his eyes. It was the last spectacle he ever beheld; for (2) his own eyes were next put out. Then (3) he was bound with fetters of brass, and carried to Babylon, where he remained a prisoner all the rest of his life (Jer. lii. 11; cf. xxxiv. 5—8). The nobles of Judah were at the same time slain (Jer. xxxix. 6; lii. 10). Life thus ended for Zedekiah when he was yet a young man of little over thirty years of age. His sons must have been mere boys, and their pitiable death would be a pang in his heart greater even than the pain of the iron which pierced his eyes. The joy of life was lost to him, like the darkness which had now fallen for ever on the outer world. The dreary living death of the prison was all that was left to him. Miserable man, how bitterly he had to expiate his sin, and mourn over past errors and self-willed courses! Will it be otherwise with those who stand at the last before the judgment-seat of God, if their lives are spent in disobedience? If it was hard to face Nebuchadnezzar when he was "full of fury, and the form of his visage was changed" (Dan. iii. 19), how shall men endure "the wrath of the Lamb" (Rev. vi. 16)?

III. JERUSALEM DESTROYED. A month elapsed before the destruction of the now captured city was carried out. It was probably during this interval that Jeremiah composed his passionate and pathetic Lamentations. When at length the work was taken in hand by Nebuzar-adan, an officer deputed for the purpose, it was done with characteristic thoroughness, amidst the glee of Judah's hereditary enemies, whose shouts, "Rase it, rase it, even to the foundations thereof!" (Ps. cxxxvii. 7), stimulated the work of demolition. We see: 1. *The temple burned.* "He burnt the house of the Lord," etc. Thus came to an end the great and beautiful house of God, built by Solomon, consecrated by so many ceremonies and prayers (1 Kings viii.), and whose courts had so often resounded with the psalms and shouts of the multitude that kept holy day (Ps. xlii. 5). But idolatry and hypocrisy had made "the house of prayer" into "a den of robbers" (Isa. lvi. 7; Jer. vii. 11; Matt. xxi. 13), and God's glory had been seen by the prophet on the banks of the Chebar departing from it (Ezek. xi. 22, 23). The temple had been the special boast of the godless people. They had trusted in lying words, saying, "The temple of the Lord, The temple of the Lord, The temple of the Lord, are these" (Jer. vii. 4). This was to make the temple a fetish, and, as Hezekiah had broken the brazen serpent in pieces when it began to be worshipped (ch. xviii. 4), it had become necessary to destroy the temple also. 2. *The buildings burned.* "The king's house, and all the houses of Jerusalem, and every great man's house burnt he with fire." When the central glory of the city had perished, secular palaces and houses could not expect to escape. They also were set on fire, and the ruddy blaze, spreading from street to street, would consume most of the humbler houses as well. How faithfully had all this been foretold, yet none would believe it! Literally had Jerusalem now become heaps (Micah iii. 12). 3. *The walls broken down.* "All the army of the Chaldeans . . . brake down the walls of Jerusalem round about." This completed the catastrophe, made the holy city a heap of ruins, and rendered it impossible for inhabitants any longer to dwell in it. Gedaliah made his headquarters at Mizpah (ver. 23). The centre of Judah's nationality was destroyed. Jerusalem had been emptied, "as a man wipeth a dish, wiping it, and turning it upside down" (ch. xxi. 13). One stands appalled at so complete a wreck of a city which God had once honoured by making it the place of his abode, and for which he had done such great things in the past. But the lesson we are to learn from it is that nothing can reverse the action of moral laws. God is terrible in his justice. Though a person or place is as "the signet upon his right hand," yet will he pluck it thence, if it abandons itself to wickedness (Jer. xxii. 24, 28).—J. O.

Vers. 11—21.—*The final deportation.* An end having been made of the city, the next step was to complete the conquest by deporting to Babylon the remnant of the population, and carrying away the spoil. To this task Nebuzar-adan now addressed himself.

I. THE PEOPLE CARRIED AWAY. 1. *The gleanings taken.* Ten or eleven thousand persons had been carried away in the earlier captivity (ch. xxiv. 14), including amongst them the best part of the population (cf. Jer. xxiv. 3—10). The remnant had since been thinned by famine, pestilence, and war (Jer. xxi. 7; xxiv. 10). On the most probable view of Jer. lii. 28 ("seventeenth" for "seventh"), a further large deportation of captives—over three thousand—took place a year before the conclusion of the siege. Now there were only the gleanings to take away, and these amounted to but eight hundred and thirty-two persons (Jer. lii. 29). They were but a small handful compared with those who had perished, but they would comprise all the people of any position and influence. They consisted of those who were in the city, of those who had previously deserted to the Chaldeans, and of the pickings of the multitude outside. The mourning and lamentation occasioned by these captivities is poetically represented by Jeremiah in the well-known description of Rachel weeping for her children, and refusing to be comforted, as she sees the long trains defile away (Jer. xxxi. 15). 2. *The poor left.* As before, it was only the poorest of the land, those "which had nothing" (Jer. xxxix. 10) who were left behind, to till the fields and care for the vineyards. With the exception of these, the country was depopulated. The best even of this poorer class had been removed in the last sifting of the population, so that the residue must have been poor indeed. They formed but a scant remnant; but even they, as we shall see, were unable to hold together, and were soon to be expatriated, leaving the land utterly desolate.

II. THE BRAZEN VESSELS CARRIED AWAY. *The temple plunder.* The more valuable of the temple vessels had been carried away in the first captivity (ch. xxiv. 13), but there remained a large number of articles and utensils of brass, together with some of the precious metals (ver. 15), either formerly overlooked or subsequently replaced. All these had been gathered out before the temple was burnt, and were now carried away as spoil. They consisted of (1) the two brazen pillars, Jachin and Boaz, which stood in the porch of the temple, and by their symbolical names, "He shall establish," "In it is strength," witnessed to the fact that God's dwelling-place was now established in the midst of his people, and that its stability was secured by his presence.   (2) The bases, with their lavers, for washing the sacrifices; and the molten sea for the use of the priests.   (3) The common utensils connected with the service of the altar and sanctuary—pots, shovels, etc.   These brazen pillars, vessels, and utensils were the work of Hiram of Tyre, and were wrought with the utmost artistic skill (1 Kings vii. 13—51). The pillars were masterpieces of strength and ornamental beauty; the sea and bases were also exquisitely carved and adorned with figures of cherubim, palms, and flowers. They were the pride and glory of the temple, and as mere works of art stood in the highest place.   2. *Treatment of the vessels.*   The more grievous, for the above reasons, was the treatment to which these beautiful objects were now subjected.   Not only were they torn from their places and uses in the temple, but they were ruthlessly broken to pieces, that they might be the more easily carried away.   Hiram's masterpieces had sunk to the level of common brass, and were treated only as such.   The lesser vessels were, of course, taken away whole.   What could more significantly tell of the departure of God from his house, the rejection of its worship, and the reversal of the promises of stability, etc., he had given in connection with it, than this ignominious treatment of its sacred vessels?   They had, indeed, when his presence was withdrawn, become mere "pieces of brass," as did the brazen serpent of Moses, when men turned it into an occasion for sin (ch. xviii. 4).   Their house was left unto them desolate (Matt. xxiii. 38).

III. The slaughter of the chief men.   A final act of vengeance was yet to be perpetrated.   Singling out a number of the chief men, Nebuzar-adan brought them to Nebuchadnezzar at Riblah, and there " the King of Babylon smote them, and slew them."   The victims were contributed by: 1. *The temple.*   "Seraiah the chief priest, and Zephaniah the second priest, and three keepers of the door."   2. *The army and court.*   "An officer that was set over the men of war, and five men of them that were in the king's presence . . . and the principal scribe of the host."   3. *The citizens.* " Three score men of the people of the land that were found in the city."   All classes were thus represented, and bore their share in the expiation of the common guilt.   The slaughter was no doubt partly intended to inspire terror in those who were left.—J. O.

Vers. 22—26.—*Gedaliah and the remnant.*   Nothing could more effectually show the hopeless condition of the people, and their unfitness for self-government, than this brief narrative of events which followed the destruction of Jerusalem.   The detailed history is given in Jer. xl.—xliii.

I. Gedaliah made governor.   It was necessary to appoint a governor over the land, and for this purpose Nebuchadnezzar chose " Gedaliah the son of Ahikam, the son of Shaphan."   The country was desolate, and had been robbed of its chief elements of strength; but, had the people chosen to hold together, they might still have subsisted with a reasonable degree of comfort, and gradually again built up a prosperous community.   1. *They had a good governor.*   Gedaliah was one of themselves, a man of an honourable and godly stock, a sincere patriot, and of a kindly and generous nature.   Under his rule they had nothing to fear, and were assured of every help and encouragement.   2. *They had a good company.*   In numbers the population was probably still not inconsiderable, and it was soon reinforced by many Jews, " who returned out of all places whither they were driven, and came to the land of Judah, to Gedaliah, unto Mizpah " (Jer. xl. 12).   They came from Moab, from Ammon, from Edom, and " all the countries," attracted by the prospect of the fields and vineyards which were to be had for the asking (Jer. xxxix. 10; xl. 11).   A number of captains with their men also, who had been hiding in the fields, came to Gedaliah, and took possession of the cities (cf. Jer. xl. 10).   Their names are given—Ishmael, Johanan, Seraiah, Jaazaniah, etc.   There were here the elements of a community which, with proper cohesion, might soon have come to something.   3. *They had good promises.*   To those who came to him Gedaliah gave ready welcome and reassuring promises.   He swore to the captains that they need fear no harm.   Let them dwell in the land, and serve the King of Babylon, and it would be well with them.   Let them gather wine, and summer fruits, and oil, and dwell in the cities they had occupied (Jer. xl. 10).   It may, indeed, be affirmed that the bulk of the people now left in the land were better off materially than they had been for some time.   Formerly they were poor and starving, ground down by oppression, and many of them bondmen; now they had liberty, land, the choice of fields and vineyards, and the advantage of keeping to themselves the fruits of their labour.

II. GEDALIAH'S MURDER, AND THE FLIGHT UNTO EGYPT. What the people might have come to under Gedaliah's benevolent rule, time was not given to show. It soon became fatally evident that the people were incapable of making the best of their situation, and of working heartily and loyally together for the general good. Among the leaders there was a want of faith, of patriotism, of principle; among the people the sense of nationality was utterly broken. This hopeless want of cohesion and absence of higher sentiment was shown: 1. *In the murder of Gedaliah.* Turbulent spirits were among the captains, who had no concern but for their own advantage, and were utterly unscrupulous as to the means they took to gain it. Intrigue, treachery, and violence were more congenial to them than the restraints of settled government. One of these captains, Ishmael the son of Nethaniah, was of the seed royal, and naturally resented the elevation of a commoner like Gedaliah to the position of governor. Instigated by Baalis King of the Ammonites, he formed a plot for Gedaliah's assassination, and with the help of ten men he secretly carried it out, slaying not only the unsuspicious governor, but all the Jews and Chaldeans and men of war that were with him at Mizpah (cf. Jer. xl. 13—16; xli. 1—3). Ishmael gained nothing by his treachery, for he was immediately afterwards pursued, and his captives taken from him (Jer. xli. 11—18). What a picture of the wickedness of the human heart is given in his dastardly deed, and in the manner of its accomplishment! Ishmael's moving principle was envy, the source of so much crime. To gratify a base grudge against one whom he regarded as his rival, he was willing to become the tool of an enemy of his people, to break sacred pledges, to repay kindness with murder, and to plunge the affairs of a community that needed nothing so much as peace into irretrievable confusion. "From whence come wars and fightings among you?" etc. (Jas. iv. 1, 2). 2. *The flight into Egypt.* The narrative here only tells that, for fear of the vengeance of the Chaldeans, "all the people, both small and great, and the captains of the armies, arose, and came to Egypt." From Jeremiah, however, we learn, that first the leaders consulted the prophet as to what they should do, promising faithfully to abide by his directions; that he counselled them from the Lord to abide where they were, and not go down to Egypt; and that then they turned against him—"all the proud men"— and said, "Thou speakest falsely: the Lord our God hath not sent thee to say, Go not into Egypt to sojourn there" (Jer. xlii.; xliii. 1—7). They then took their own way, and compelled Jeremiah and all the people to go with them. Here the same unchastened, wayward, stubborn spirit reveals itself which had been the cause of all their troubles. Had they obeyed Jeremiah, they were assured that it would be well with them; while, if they went down to Egypt, it was foretold that the sword and famine, which they feared, would overtake them (Jer. xlii. 16), as from the recently disinterred ruins at Tahpanhes we know it actually did. But through this self-willed action of their own, God's Word was fulfilled, and the land of Judah swept clean of its remaining inhabitants.—J. O.

Vers. 27—30.—*Jehoiachin's restoration.* We have here—

I. A LONG CAPTIVITY. "In the thirty-seventh year of the reign of Jehoiachin King of Judah." 1. *Weary years.* Thirty-seven years was a long time to spend in prison. The king was but eighteen years of age when he was taken away, so that now he would be fifty-five. Existence must have seemed hopeless, yet he went on enduring. He was suffering even more for his fathers' sins, and for the nation's sins, than for his own. Life is sweet, and hard to part with, and the love of it is nowhere more strongly seen than when men go on clinging to it under conditions which might, if anything could, suggest the question, "Is life worth living?" Jehoiachin must have had a stout heart to endure so long. 2. *A change of rulers.* Nebuchadnezzar at length died, and his son Evil-Merodach ascended the throne. Possibly this prince may have formed a friendship with Jehoiachin in prison, and this may have contributed to sustain the captive king's hopes. A change of government usually brings many other changes in its train.

II. A GLIMPSE OF SUNSHINE AT THE CLOSE. 1. *At the close of Jehoiachin's life.*

The new ruler treated Jehoiachin as a human being, a friend, and a king.   (1) He took him out of prison, changing the policy of harshness for one of kindness.   (2) He set his throne above the throne of the kings that were with him in Babylon.   It was a shadowy honour; but is any earthly throne more than a shadow?   Evil-Merodach himself kept his for only two years, and was then murdered.   (3) He gave him suitable provision.   The ignominy of prison garments was changed for honourable clothing; the scarcity and hard fare of the dungeon was altered for the royal bounty of the king's own table.   Jehoiachin, in short, had now everything but freedom.   But how much does that mean!   He was still an exile.   All he enjoyed was but an alleviation of captivity.   2. *At the close of the book.*   It is not without purpose that the Book of Kings closes with this glimpse of brightness.   The story it has had to tell has been a sad one—a story of disappointment, failure, rejection, exile.   But there is unshaken faith, even amidst the gloom, that God's counsel will stand, and that he hath not cast off his people whom he foreknew (Rom. xi. 2).   Jeremiah had predicted the exile, but he had also predicted restoration after seventy years (Jer. xxv. 11, 12 ; xxix. 10).   That period had but half elapsed, but this kindness shown to Jehoiachin seemed prophetic of the end, and is inserted to sustain faith and hope in the minds of the exiles.   The history of the world, like the history in this book, will close in peace and brightness under Christ's reign.—J. O.

HOMILETICAL INDEX

TO

THE SECOND BOOK OF THE KINGS